FEDERAL SECURITIES LAWS

SELECTED STATUTES, RULES AND FORMS

Compiled
By
JOHN C. COFFEE, JR.
Adolf A. Berle Professor of Law
Columbia University School of Law

and

JOEL SELIGMAN
President
University of Rochester

2005 EDITION

FOUNDATION PRESS
New York, New York
2005

THOMSON
WEST

ISBN 1–58778–829–2

ISSN 1061–7078

PREFACE

The 2005 Edition of Federal Statutes, Rules and Forms follows the format of earlier years.

Over 200 changes occurred in this year's Federal Securities Laws, Regulations and Forms, all of which were regulatory.

New Rules 139a, 167, 190, 191, and 426 were added to the Securities Act of 1933. Amendments were made to Securities Act Rules 146, 166, 411, and 434. Securities Act Forms S-1, S-2, and S-3 were also amended. A new Regulation AB was adopted to address asset-backed securities.

New Rules 3a12-12, 3b-19, 13a-17, 13a-18, 13k-1, 15d-17, 15d-18, 15d-22, 15d-23, 17i-1 to 17i-8, 17Ad-20, and Regulation SHO were added to the Securities Exchange Act. Amendments were made to Rules 10a-1, 10A-3, 11Aa3-2, 12b-2, 12b-15, 12b-25, 13a-10, 13a-11, 13a-13, 13a-14, 13a-15, 13a-16, 15c2-8, 15c3-1, 15d-10, 15d-14, 15d-15, 15d-16, 17a-4, 17a-5, 17a-11, 17a-12, 17h-1T, 17h-2T, 19b-4, and 31. Securities Exchange Act Forms 10-Q, 10-QSB, 10-K, 10-KSB, 6-K, and 8-K were also amended.

The Investment Company Act was amended with the addition of new Rule 8b-33 and amendments to Rules O-1, 8b-1, 10f-3, 12b-1, 15a-4, 17a-7, 17a-8, 17d-1, 17d-3, 17g-1, 17j-1, 18f-3, 23c-3, 30a-2, and 31a-2.

The Investment Advisers Act of 1940 was amended by the addition of new Rules 202(a)(11)T, 203(b)(3)-2 and 204A-1. Rules 203(b)(3)-1, 203A-3, 204-2, 206(3)-1, 206(4)-2, and 222-2 were amended.

Amendments were also made to Regulation S-B Items 10, 308, 401, 406, and 601. Similarly, amendments were made to Regulation S-K Items 10, 202, 308, 406, 501, 503, 512, 601, and 701.

Regulation S-T was amended with the addition of new Items 312, 401, and 402 as well as amendments to Items 10, 11, 101, 104, 201, 202, 301, 305, and 311.

The SEC Rules of Practice were amended by the Adjustment of Civil Monetary Penalties - 2005. An amendment was also made to Regulation S-P §248.30.

We express our gratitude to Leanne Lustgarden, Class of 2002 Washington University School of Law, for providing invaluable research assistance.

This edition has a cutoff date of March 15, 2005.

JOHN C. COFFEE, JR.
New York, New York

JOEL SELIGMAN
Rochester, New York

*

TABLE OF CONTENTS

FEDERAL SECURITIES LAWS

SELECTED STATUTES, RULES AND FORMS

*

I. FEDERAL SECURITIES LAWS AND REGULATIONS

A. SECURITIES ACT OF 1933

15 U.S.C. § 77a et seq.

SECURITIES ACT OF 1933

TITLE I

Short Title

Section 1. This subchapter may be cited as the Securities Act of 1933.

Definitions

Sec. 2(a) Definitions. When used in this subchapter, unless the context otherwise requires—

(1) The term "security" means any note, stock, treasury stock, security future, bond, debenture, evidence of indebtedness, certificate of interest or participation in any profit-sharing agreement, collateral-trust certificate, preorganization certificate or subscription, transferable share, investment contract, voting-trust certificate, certificate of deposit for a security, fractional undivided interest in oil, gas, or other mineral rights, any put, call, straddle, option, or privilege on any security, certificate of deposit, or group or index of securities (including any interest therein or based on the value thereof), or any put, call, straddle, option, or privilege entered into on a national securities exchange relating to foreign currency, or, in general, any interest or instrument commonly known as a "security," or any certificate of interest or participation in, temporary or interim certificate for, receipt for, guarantee of, or warrant or right to subscribe to or purchase, any of the foregoing.

(2) The term "person" means an individual, a corporation, a partnership, an association, a joint-stock company, a trust, any unincorporated organization, or a government or political subdivision thereof. As used in this paragraph the term "trust" shall include only a trust where the interest or interests of the beneficiary or beneficiaries are evidenced by a security.

(3) The term "sale" or "sell" shall include every contract of sale or disposition of a security or interest in a security, for value. The term "offer to sell", "offer for sale", or "offer" shall include every attempt or offer to dispose of, or solicitation of an offer to buy, a security or interest in a security, for value. The terms defined in this paragraph and the term "offer to buy" as used in subsection (c) of section 5 shall not include preliminary negotiations or agreements between an issuer (or any person directly or indirectly controlling or controlled by an issuer, or under direct or indirect common control with an issuer) and any underwriter or among underwriters who are or are to be in privity of contract with an issuer (or any person directly or indirectly controlling or controlled by an issuer, or under direct or indirect common control with an issuer). Any security given or delivered with, or as a bonus on account of, any purchase of securities or any other thing, shall be conclusively presumed to constitute a part of the subject of such purchase and to have been offered and sold for value. The issue or transfer of a right or privilege, when originally issued or transferred with a security, giving the holder of such security the right to convert such security into another security of the same issuer or of another person, or giving a right to subscribe to another security of the same issuer or of another person, which right cannot be exercised until some future date, shall not be deemed to be an offer or sale of such other security; but the issue or transfer of such other security upon the exercise of such right of conversion or subscription shall be deemed a sale of such other security. Any offer or sale of a security

futures product by or on behalf of the issuer of the securities underlying the security futures product, an affiliate of the issuer, or an underwriter, shall constitute a contract for sale of, sale of, or offer to sell the underlying securities.

(4) The term "issuer" means every person who issues or proposes to issue any security; except that with respect to certificates of deposit, voting-trust certificates, or collateral-trust certificates, or with respect to certificates of interest or shares in an unincorporated investment trust not having a board of directors (or persons performing similar functions) or of the fixed, restricted management, or unit type, the term "issuer" means the person or persons performing the acts and assuming the duties of depositor or manager pursuant to the provisions of the trust or other agreement or instrument under which such securities are issued; except that in the case of an unincorporated association which provides by its articles for limited liability of any or all of its members, or in the case of a trust, committee, or other legal entity, the trustees or members thereof shall not be individually liable as issuers of any security issued by the association, trust, committee, or other legal entity; except that with respect to equipment-trust certificates or like securities, the term "issuer" means the person by whom the equipment or property is or is to be used; and except that with respect to fractional undivided interests in oil, gas, or other mineral rights, the term "issuer" means the owner of any such right or of any interest in such right (whether whole or fractional) who creates fractional interests therein for the purpose of public offering.

(5) The term "Commission" means the Securities and Exchange Commission.

(6) The term "Territory" means Puerto Rico, the Virgin Islands, and the insular possessions of the United States.

(7) The term "interstate commerce" means trade or commerce in securities or any transportation or communication relating thereto among the several States or between the District of Columbia or any Territory of the United States and any State or other Territory, or between any foreign country and any State, Territory, or the District of Columbia, or within the District of Columbia.

(8) The term "registration statement" means the statement provided for in section 6, and includes any amendment thereto and any report, document, or memorandum filed as part of such statement or incorporated therein by reference.

(9) The term "write" or "written" shall include printed, lithographed, or any means of graphic communication.

(10) The term "prospectus" means any prospectus, notice, circular, advertisement, letter, or communication, written or by radio or television, which offers any security for sale or confirms the sale of any security; except that (a) a communication sent or given after the effective date of the registration statement (other than a prospectus permitted under subsection (b) of section 10) shall not be deemed a prospectus if it is proved that prior to or at the same time with such communication a written prospectus meeting the requirements of subsection (a) of section 10 at the time of such communication was sent or given to the person to whom the communication was made, and (b) a notice, circular, advertisement, letter, or communication in respect of a security shall not be deemed to be a prospectus if it states from whom a written prospectus meeting the requirements of section 10 may be obtained and, in addition, does no more than identify the security, state the price thereof, state by whom orders will be executed, and contain such other information as the Commission, by rules or regulations deemed necessary or appropriate in the public interest and for the protection of investors, and subject to such terms and conditions as may be prescribed therein, may permit.

(11) The term "underwriter" means any person who has purchased from an issuer with a view to, or offers or sells for an issuer in connection with, the distribution of any security, or participates or has a direct or indirect participation in any such undertaking, or participates or has a participation in the direct or indirect underwriting of any such undertaking; but such term shall not include a person whose interest is limited to a commission from an underwriter or dealer not in excess of the usual and customary distributors' or sellers' commission. As used in this paragraph the term "issuer" shall include, in addition to an issuer, any person directly or indirectly controlling or controlled by the issuer, or any person under direct or indirect common control with the issuer.

(12) The term "dealer" means any person who engages either for all or part of his time, directly or indirectly, as agent, broker, or principal, in the business of offering, buying, selling, or otherwise dealing or trading in securities issued by another person.

(13) The term "insurance company" means a company which is organized as an insurance company, whose primary and predominant business activity is the writing of insurance or the re-insuring of risks underwritten by insurance companies, and which is subject to supervision by the insurance commissioner, or a similar official or agency of a State or territory or the District of Columbia; or any receiver or similar official or any liquidating agent for such company, in his capacity as such.

(14) The term "separate account" means an account established and maintained by an insurance company pursuant to the laws of any State or territory of the United States, the District of Columbia, or of Canada or any province thereof, under which income, gains and losses, whether or not realized, from assets allocated to such account, are, in accordance with the applicable contract, credited to or charged against such account without regard to other income, gains or losses of the insurance company.

(15) The term "accredited investor" shall mean—

(i) a bank as defined in section 3(a)(2) whether acting in its individual or fiduciary capacity; an insurance company as defined in paragraph (13) of this subsection; an investment company registered under the Investment Company Act of 1940 or a business development company as defined in section 2(a)(48) of that Act; a Small Business Investment Company licensed by the Small Business Administration; or an employee benefit plan, including an individual retirement account, which is subject to the provisions of the Employee Retirement Income Security Act of 1974, if the investment decision is made by a plan fiduciary, as defined in section 3(21) of such Act, which is either a bank, insurance company, or registered investment adviser; or

(ii) any person who, on the basis of such factors as financial sophistication, net worth, knowledge, and experience in financial matters, or amount of assets under management qualifies as an accredited investor under rules and regulations which the Commission shall prescribe.

(16) The terms "security future", "narrow-based security index", and "security futures product" have the same meaning as provided in section 3(a)(55) of the Securities Exchange Act of 1934.

(b) *Consideration of promotion of efficiency, competition, and capital formation.*—Whenever pursuant to this title the Commission is engaged in rulemaking and is required to consider or determine whether an action is necessary or appropriate in the public interest, the Commission shall also consider, in addition to the protection of investors, whether the action will promote efficiency, competition, and capital formation.

Swap Agreements

Sec. 2A. (a) *Non–Security–Based Swap Agreements.*—The definition of "security" in section 2(a)(1) of this title does not include any non-security-based swap agreement (as defined in section 206C of the Gramm–Leach–Bliley Act).

(b) *Security–Based Swap Agreements.*—

(1) The definition of "security" in section 2(a)(1) of this title does not include any security-based swap agreement (as defined in section 206B of the Gramm–Leach–Bliley Act).

(2) The Commission is prohibited from registering, or requiring, recommending, or suggesting, the registration under this title of any security-based swap agreement (as defined in section 206B of the Gramm–Leach–Bliley Act). If the Commission becomes aware that a registrant has filed a registration statement with respect to such a swap agreement, the Commission shall promptly so notify the registrant. Any such registration statement with respect to such a swap agreement shall be void and of no force or effect.

(3) The Commission is prohibited from—

(A) promulgating, interpreting, or enforcing rules; or

(B) issuing orders of general applicability; under this title in a manner that imposes or specifies reporting or recordkeeping requirements, procedures, or standards as prophylactic measures against fraud, manipulation, or insider trading with respect to any security-based swap agreement (as defined in section 206B of the Gramm–Leach–Bliley Act).

(4) References in this title to the "purchase" or "sale" of a security-based swap agreement shall be deemed to mean the execution, termination (prior to its scheduled maturity date), assignment, exchange, or similar transfer or conveyance of, or extinguishing of rights or obligations under, a security-based swap agreement (as defined in section 206B of the Gramm–Leach–Bliley Act), as the context may require.

Exempted Securities

Sec. 3. (a) Except as hereinafter expressly provided, the provisions of this title shall not apply to any of the following classes of securities:

(1) Reserved.

(2) Any security issued or guaranteed by the United States or any Territory thereof, or by the District of Columbia, or by any State of the United States, or by any political subdivision of a State or Territory or by any public instrumentality of one or more States or Territories, or by any person controlled or supervised by and acting as an instrumentality of the Government of the United States pursuant to authority granted by the Congress of the United States; or any certificate of deposit for any of the foregoing; or any security issued or guaranteed by any bank; or any security issued by or representing an interest in or a direct obligation of a Federal Reserve bank; or any interest or participation in any common trust fund or similar fund that is excluded from the definition of the term "investment company" under section 3(c)(3) of the Investment Company Act of 1940; or any security which is an industrial development bond (as defined in section 103(c)(2) of the Internal Revenue Code of 1954) the interest on which is excludable from gross income under section 103(a)(1) of such Code if, by reason of the application of paragraph (4) or (6) of section 103(c) of such Code (determined as if paragraphs (4)(A), (5), and (7) were not included in such section 103(c)), paragraph (1) of such section 103(c) does not apply to such security; or any interest or participation in a single trust fund, or in a collective trust fund maintained by a bank, or any security arising out of a contract issued by an insurance company, which interest, participation, or security is issued in

connection with (A) a stock bonus, pension, or profit-sharing plan which meets the requirements for qualification under section 401 of the Internal Revenue Code of 1954, (B) an annuity plan which meets the requirements for the deduction of the employer's contributions under section 404(a)(2) of such Code, or (C) a governmental plan as defined in section 414(d) of such Code which has been established by an employer for the exclusive benefit of its employees or their beneficiaries for the purpose of distributing to such employees or their beneficiaries the corpus and income of the funds accumulated under such plan, if under such plan it is impossible, prior to the satisfaction of all liabilities with respect to such employees and their beneficiaries, for any part of the corpus or income to be used for, or diverted to, purposes other than the exclusive benefit of such employees or their beneficiaries, other than any plan described in clause (A), (B), or (C) of this paragraph (i) the contributions under which are held in a single trust fund or in a separate account maintained by an insurance company for a single employer and under which an amount in excess of the employer's contribution is allocated to the purchase of securities (other than interests or participations in the trust or separate account itself) issued by the employer or any company directly or indirectly controlling, controlled by, or under common control with the employer, (ii) which covers employees some or all of whom are employees within the meaning of section 401(c)(1) of such Code, or (iii) which is a plan funded by an annuity contract described in section 403(b) of such Code. The Commission, by rules and regulations or order, shall exempt from the provisions of section 5 of this title any interest or participation issued in connection with a stock bonus, pension, profit-sharing, or annuity plan which covers employees some or all of whom are employees within the meaning of section 401(c)(1) of the Internal Revenue Code of 1954, if and to the extent that the Commission determines this to be necessary or appropriate in the public interest and consistent with the protection of investors and the purposes fairly intended by the policy and provisions of this title. For purposes of this paragraph, a security issued or guaranteed by a bank shall not include any interest or participation in any collective trust fund maintained by a bank; and the term "bank" means any national bank, or any banking institution organized under the laws of any State, Territory, or the District of Columbia, the business of which is substantially confined to banking and is supervised by the State or territorial banking commission or similar official; except that in the case of a common trust fund or similar fund, or a collective trust fund, the term "bank" has the same meaning as in the Investment Company Act of 1940.

(3) Any note, draft, bill of exchange, or banker's acceptance which arises out of a current transaction or the proceeds of which have been or are to be used for current transactions, and which has a maturity at the time of issuance of not exceeding nine months, exclusive of days of grace, or any renewal thereof the maturity of which is likewise limited;

(4) Any security issued by a person organized and operated exclusively for religious, educational, benevolent, fraternal, charitable, or reformatory purposes and not for pecuniary profit, and no part of the net earnings of which inures to the benefit of any person, private stockholder, individual, or any security of a fund that is excluded from the definition of an investment company under section 3(c)(10)(B) of the Investment Company Act of 1940;

(5) Any security issued (A) by a savings and loan association, building and loan association, cooperative bank, homestead association, or similar institution, which is supervised and examined by State or Federal authority having supervision over any such institution; or (B) by (i) a farmer's cooperative organization exempt from tax under section 521 of the Internal Revenue Code of

1954, (ii) a corporation described in section 501(c)(16) of such Code and exempt from tax under section 501(a) of such Code, or (iii) a corporation described in section 501(c)(2) of such Code which is exempt from tax under section 501(a) of such Code and is organized for the exclusive purpose of holding title to property, collecting income therefrom, and turning over the entire amount thereof, less expenses, to an organization or corporation described in clause (i) or (ii);

(6) Any interest in a railroad equipment trust. For purposes of this paragraph "interest in a railroad equipment trust" means any interest in an equipment trust, lease, conditional sales contract or other similar arrangement entered into, issued, assumed, guaranteed by, or for the benefit of a common carrier to finance the acquisition of rolling stock including motive power.

(7) Certificates issued by a receiver or by a trustee or debtor in possession in a case under Title 11 of the United States Code, with the approval of the court;

(8) Any insurance or endowment policy or annuity contract or optional annuity contract, issued by a corporation subject to the supervision of the insurance commissioner, bank commissioner, or any agency or officer performing like functions, of any State or Territory of the United States or the District of Columbia;

(9) Except with respect to a security exchanged in a case under Title 11 of the United States Code, any security exchanged by the issuer with its existing security holders exclusively where no commission or other remuneration is paid or given directly or indirectly for soliciting such exchange;

(10) Except with respect to a security exchanged in a case under Title 11 of the United States Code, any security which is issued in exchange for one or more bona fide outstanding securities, claims or property interests, or partly in such exchange and partly for cash, where the terms and conditions of such issuance and exchange are approved, after a hearing upon the fairness of such terms and conditions at which all persons to whom it is proposed to issue securities in such exchange shall have the right to appear, by any court, or by any official or agency of the United States, or by any State or Territorial banking or insurance commission or other governmental authority expressly authorized by law to grant such approval;

(11) Any security which is a part of an issue offered and sold only to persons resident within a single State or Territory, where the issuer of such security is a person resident and doing business within, or, if a corporation, incorporated by and doing business within, such State or Territory.

(12) Any equity security issued in connection with the acquisition by a holding company of a bank under section 3(a) of the Bank Holding Company Act of 1956 or a savings association under section 10(e) of the Home Owners' Loan Act, if—

(A) the acquisition occurs solely as part of a reorganization in which security holders exchange their shares of a bank or savings association for shares of a newly formed holding company with no significant assets other than securities of the bank or savings association and the existing subsidiaries of the bank or savings association;

(B) the security holders receive, after that reorganization, substantially the same proportional share interests in the holding company as they held in the bank or savings association, except for nominal changes in shareholders' interests resulting from lawful elimination of fractional interests and the exercise of dissenting shareholders' rights under State or Federal law;

(C) the rights and interests of security holders in the holding company are substantially the same as those in the bank or savings association prior to the transaction, other than as may be required by law; and

(D) the holding company has substantially the same assets and liabilities, on a consolidated basis, as the bank or savings association had prior to the transaction. For purposes of this paragraph, the term "savings association" means a savings association (as defined in section 3(b) of the Federal Deposit Insurance Act) the deposits of which are insured by the Federal Deposit Insurance Corporation.

(13) Any security issued by or any interest or participation in any church plan, company or account that is excluded from the definition of an investment company under section 3(c)(14) of the Investment Company Act of 1940.

(14) Any security futures product that is—

(A) cleared by a clearing agency registered under section 17A of the Securities Exchange Act of 1934 or exempt from registration under subsection (b)(7) of such section 17A; and

(B) traded on a national securities exchange or a national securities association registered pursuant to section 15A(a) of the Securities Exchange Act of 1934.

(b) The Commission may from time to time by its rules and regulations, and subject to such terms and conditions as may be prescribed therein, add any class of securities to the securities exempted as provided in this section, if it finds that the enforcement of this title with respect to such securities is not necessary in the public interest and for the protection of investors by reason of the small amount involved or the limited character of the public offering; but no issue of securities shall be exempted under this subsection where the aggregate amount at which such issue is offered to the public exceeds $5,000,000.

(c) The Commission may from time to time by its rules and regulations and subject to such terms and conditions as may be prescribed therein, add to the securities exempted as provided in this section any class of securities issued by a small business investment company under the Small Business Investment Act of 1958 if it finds, having regard to the purposes of that Act, that the enforcement of this Act with respect to such securities is not necessary in the public interest and for the protection of investors.

Exempted Transactions

Sec. 4. The provisions of section 5 shall not apply to—

(1) transactions by any person other than an issuer, underwriter, or dealer.

(2) transactions by an issuer not involving any public offering.

(3) transactions by a dealer (including an underwriter no longer acting as an underwriter in respect of the security involved in such transaction), except—

(A) transactions taking place prior to the expiration of forty days after the first date upon which the security was bona fide offered to the public by the issuer or by or through an underwriter,

(B) transactions in a security as to which a registration statement has been filed taking place prior to the expiration of forty days after the effective date of such registration statement or prior to the expiration of forty days after the first date upon which the security was bona fide offered to the public by the issuer or by or through an underwriter after such effective date, whichever is later (excluding in the computation of such forty days any time during which a stop order issued under section 8 is in effect as to the security), or such shorter period as the Commission may specify by rules and regulations or order, and

(C) transactions as to securities constituting the whole or a part of an unsold allotment to or subscription by such dealer as a participant in the distribution of such securities by the issuer or by or through an underwriter.

With respect to transactions referred to in clause (B), if securities of the issuer have not previously been sold pursuant to an earlier effective registration statement the applicable period, instead of forty days, shall be ninety days, or such shorter period as the Commission may specify by rules and regulations or order.

(4) brokers' transactions executed upon customers' orders on any exchange or in the over-the-counter market but not the solicitation of such orders.

(5)(A) Transactions involving offers or sales of one or more promissory notes directly secured by a first lien on a single parcel of real estate upon which is located a dwelling or other residential or commercial structure, and participation interests in such notes—

(i) where such securities are originated by a savings and loan association, savings bank, commercial bank, or similar banking institution which is supervised and examined by a Federal or State authority, and are offered and sold subject to the following conditions:

(a) the minimum aggregate sales price per purchaser shall not be less than $250,000;

(b) the purchaser shall pay cash either at the time of the sale or within sixty days thereof; and

(c) each purchaser shall buy for his own account only; or

(ii) where such securities are originated by a mortgagee approved by the Secretary of Housing and Urban Development pursuant to sections 203 and 211 of the National Housing Act, and are offered or sold subject to the three conditions specified in subparagraph (A)(i) to any institution described in such subparagraph or to any insurance company subject to the supervision of the insurance commissioner, or any agency or officer performing like function, of any State or territory of the United States or the District of Columbia, or the Federal Home Loan Mortgage Corporation, the Federal National Mortgage Association, or the Government National Mortgage Association.

(B) Transactions between any of the entities described in subparagraph (A)(i) or (A)(ii) hereof involving non-assignable contracts to buy or sell the foregoing securities which are to be completed within two years, where the seller of the foregoing securities pursuant to any such contract is one of the parties described in subparagraph (A)(i) or (A)(ii) who may originate such securities and the purchaser of such securities pursuant to any such contract is any institution described in subparagraph (A)(i) or any insurance company described in subparagraph (A)(ii), the Federal Home Loan Mortgage Corporation, Federal National Mortgage Association, or the Government National Mortgage Association and where the foregoing securities are subject to the three conditions for sale set forth in subparagraphs (A)(i)(a) through (c).

(C) The exemption provided by subparagraphs (A) and (B) hereof shall not apply to resales of the securities acquired pursuant thereto, unless each of the conditions for sale contained in subparagraphs (A)(i)(a) through (c) are satisfied.

(6) transactions involving offers or sales by an issuer solely to one or more accredited investors, if the aggregate offering price of an issue of securities offered in reliance on this paragraph does not exceed the amount allowed under section 3(b) of this title, if there is no advertising or public solicitation in connection with the transaction by the issuer or anyone acting on the issuer's behalf, and if the issuer files such notice with the Commission as the Commission shall prescribe.

Prohibitions Relating to Interstate Commerce and the Mails

Sec. 5. (a) Unless a registration statement is in effect as to a security, it shall be unlawful for any person, directly or indirectly—

(1) to make use of any means or instruments of transportation or communication in interstate commerce or of the mails to sell such security through the use or medium of any prospectus or otherwise; or

(2) to carry or cause to be carried through the mails or in interstate commerce, by any means or instruments of transportation, any such security for the purpose of sale or for delivery after sale.

(b) It shall be unlawful for any person, directly or indirectly—

(1) to make use of any means or instruments of transportation or communication in interstate commerce or of the mails to carry or transmit any prospectus relating to any security with respect to which a registration statement has been filed under this title, unless such prospectus meets the requirements of section 10; or

(2) to carry or cause to be carried through the mails or in interstate commerce any such security for the purpose of sale or for delivery after sale, unless accompanied or preceded by a prospectus that meets the requirements of subsection (a) of section 10.

(c) It shall be unlawful for any person, directly or indirectly, to make use of any means or instruments of transportation or communication in interstate commerce or of the mails to offer to sell or offer to buy through the use or medium of any prospectus or otherwise any security, unless a registration statement has been filed as to such security, or while the registration statement is the subject of a refusal order or stop order or (prior to the effective date of the registration statement) any public proceeding or examination under section 8.

Registration of Securities and Signing of Registration Statement

Sec. 6. (a) Any security may be registered with the Commission under the terms and conditions hereinafter provided, by filing a registration statement in triplicate, at least one of which shall be signed by each issuer, its principal executive officer or officers, its principal financial officer, its comptroller or principal accounting officer, and the majority of its board of directors or persons performing similar functions (or, if there is no board of directors or persons performing similar functions, by the majority of the persons or board having the power of management of the issuer), and in case the issuer is a foreign or Territorial person by its duly authorized representative in the United States; except that when such registration statement relates to a security issued by a foreign government, or political subdivision thereof, it need be signed only by the underwriter of such security. Signatures of all such persons when written on the said registration statements shall be presumed to have been so written by authority of the person whose signature is so affixed and the burden of proof, in the event such authority shall be denied, shall be upon the party denying the same. The affixing of any signature without the authority of the purported signer shall constitute a violation of this title. A registration statement shall be deemed effective only as to the securities specified therein as proposed to be offered.

(b) *Registration fee.*—

(1) *Recovery of cost of services.*—The Commission shall, in accordance with this subsection, collect registration fees that are designed to recover the costs to the government of the securities registration process, and costs related to such process, including enforcement activities, policy and rulemaking activities, administration, legal services, and international regulatory activities.

(2) Fee payment required.—At the time of filing a registration statement, the applicant shall pay to the Commission a fee at a rate

that shall be equal to $92 per $1,000,000* of the maximum aggregate price at which such securities are proposed to be offered, except that during fiscal year 2003 and any succeeding fiscal year such fee shall be adjusted pursuant to paragraph (5) or (6).

(3) Offsetting collections.—Fees collected pursuant to this subsection for any fiscal year—

(A) shall be deposited and credited as offsetting collections to the account providing appropriations to the Commission; and

(B) except as provided in paragraph (9), shall not be collected for any fiscal year except to the extent provided in advance in appropriation Acts.

(4) General revenues prohibited.—No fees collected pursuant to this subsection for fiscal year 2002 or any succeeding fiscal year shall be deposited and credited as general revenue of the Treasury.

(5) Annual adjustment.—For each of the fiscal years 2003 through 2011, the Commission shall by order adjust the rate required by paragraph (2) for such fiscal year to a rate that, when applied to the baseline estimate of the aggregate maximum offering prices for such fiscal year, is reasonably likely to produce aggregate fee collections under this subsection that are equal to the target offsetting collection amount for such fiscal year.

(6) Final rate adjustment.—For fiscal year 2012 and all of the succeeding fiscal years, the Commission shall by order adjust the rate required by paragraph (2) for all of such fiscal years to a rate that, when applied to the baseline estimate of the aggregate maximum offering prices for fiscal year 2012, is reasonably likely to produce aggregate fee collections under this subsection in fiscal year 2012 equal to the target offsetting collection amount for fiscal year 2011.

(7) Pro rata application.—The rates per $1,000,000 required by this subsection shall be applied pro rata to amounts and balances of less than $1,000,000.

(8) Review and effective date.—In exercising its authority under this subsection, the Commission shall not be required to comply with the provisions of section 553 of title 5, United States Code. An adjusted rate prescribed under paragraph (5) or (6) and published under paragraph (10) shall not be subject to judicial review. Subject to paragraphs (3)(B) and (9)—

(A) an adjusted rate prescribed under paragraph (5) shall take effect on the later of—

(i) the first day of the fiscal year to which such rate applies; or

(ii) five days after the date on which a regular appropriation to the Commission for such fiscal year is enacted; and

(B) an adjusted rate prescribed under paragraph (6) shall take effect on the later of—

(i) the first day of fiscal year 2012; or

(ii) five days after the date on which a regular appropriation to the Commission for fiscal year 2012 is enacted.

(9) Lapse of appropriation.—If on the first day of a fiscal year a regular appropriation to the Commission has not been enacted, the Commission shall continue to collect fees (as offsetting collections) under this subsection at the rate in effect during the preceding fiscal year, until 5 days after the date such a regular appropriation is enacted.

(10) Publication.—The Commission shall publish in the Federal Register notices of the rate applicable under this subsection and under sections 13(e) and 14(g) for each fiscal year not later than April 30 of the fiscal year preceding the fiscal year to which such rate applies, together with any esti-

* The Consolidated Appropriations Act of 2004, P.L. 108–199, 118 Stat. 3, increased the rate applicable to Section 6(b) to $126.70 per million effective January 28, 2004.

mates or projections on which such rate is based.

(11) Definitions.—For purposes of this subsection:

(A) Target offsetting collection amount.—The target offsetting collection amount for each of the fiscal years 2002 through 2011 is determined according to the following table:

Fiscal year:	Target offsetting collection amount
2002	$ 377,000,000
2003	$ 435,000,000
2004	$ 467,000,000
2005	$ 570,000,000
2006	$ 689,000,000
2007	$ 214,000,000
2008	$ 234,000,000
2009	$ 284,000,000
2010	$ 334,000,000
2011	$ 394,000,000

(B) Baseline estimate of the aggregate maximum offering prices.—The baseline estimate of the aggregate maximum offering prices for any fiscal year is the baseline estimate of the aggregate maximum offering price at which securities are proposed to be offered pursuant to registration statements filed with the Commission during such fiscal year as determined by the Commission, after consultation with the Congressional Budget Office and the Office of Management and Budget, using the methodology required for projections pursuant to section 257 of the Balanced Budget and Emergency Deficit Control Act of 1985.

(c) The filing with the Commission of a registration statement, or of an amendment to a registration statement, shall be deemed to have taken place upon the receipt thereof, but the filing of a registration statement shall not be deemed to have taken place unless it is accompanied by a United States postal money order or a certified bank check or cash for the amount of the fee required under subsection (b).

(d) The information contained in or filed with any registration statement shall be made available to the public under such regulations as the Commission may prescribe, and copies thereof, photostatic or otherwise, shall be furnished to every applicant at such reasonable charge as the Commission may prescribe.

Information Required in Registration Statement

Sec. 7. (a) The registration statement, when relating to a security other than a security issued by a foreign government, or political subdivision thereof, shall contain the information, and be accompanied by the documents specified in Schedule A, and when relating to a security issued by a foreign government, or political subdivision thereof, shall contain the information, and be accompanied by the documents, specified in Schedule B; except that the Commission may by rules or regulations provide that any such information or document need not be included in respect of any class of issuers or securities if it finds that the requirement of such information or document is inapplicable to such class and that disclosure fully adequate for the protection of investors is otherwise required to be included within the registration statement. If any accountant, engineer, or appraiser, or any person whose profession gives authority to a statement made by him, is named as having prepared or certified any part of the registration statement, or is named as having prepared or certified a report or valuation for use in connection with the registration statement, the written consent of such person shall be filed with the registration statement. If any such person is named as having prepared or certified a report or valuation (other than a public official document or statement) which is used in connection with the registration statement, but is not named as having prepared or certified such report or valuation for use in connection with the registration statement, the written consent of such person shall be filed with the registration statement unless the Commission dispenses with such filing as impracticable or as involving undue hardship on the person filing the registration statement. Any such registration statement shall contain such other information, and be accompanied by such other documents, as the Commission may by rules or regulations require as being necessary or appropriate in the public interest or for the protection of investors.

(b)(1) The Commission shall prescribe special rules with respect to registration statements filed by any issuer that is a blank check company. Such rules may, as the Commission determines necessary or appropriate in the public interest or for the protection of investors—

(A) require such issuers to provide timely disclosure, prior to or after such statement becomes effective under section 8, of (i) information regarding the company to be acquired and the specific application of the proceeds of the offering, or (ii) additional information necessary to prevent such statement from being misleading;

(B) place limitations on the use of such proceeds and the distribution of securities by such issuer until the disclosures required under subparagraph (A) have been made; and

(C) provide a right of rescission to shareholders of such securities.

(2) The Commission may, as it determines consistent with the public interest and the protection of investors, by rule or order exempt any issuer or class of issuers from the rules prescribed under paragraph (1).

(3) For purposes of paragraph (1) of this subsection, the term "blank check company" means any development stage company that is issuing a penny stock (within the meaning of section 3(a)(51) of the Securities Exchange Act of 1934) and that—

(A) has no specific business plan or purpose; or

(B) has indicated that its business plan is to merge with an unidentified company or companies.

Taking Effect of Registration Statements and Amendments Thereto

Sec. 8. (a) Except as hereinafter provided, the effective date of a registration statement shall be the twentieth day after the filing thereof or such earlier date as the Commission may determine, having due regard to the adequacy of the information respecting the issuer theretofore available to the public, to the facility with which the nature of the securities to be registered, their relationship to the capital structure of the issuer and the rights of holders thereof can be understood, and to the public interest and the protection of investors. If any amendment to any such statement is filed prior to the effective date of such statement, the registration statement shall be deemed to have been filed when such amendment was filed; except that an amendment filed with the consent of the Commission, prior to the effective date of the registration statement, or filed pursuant to an order of the Commission, shall be treated as a part of the registration statement.

(b) If it appears to the Commission that a registration statement is on its face incomplete or inaccurate in any material respect, the Commission may, after notice by personal service or the sending of confirmed telegraphic notice not later than ten days after the filing of the registration statement, and opportunity for hearing (at a time fixed by the Commission) within ten days after such notice by personal service or the sending of such telegraphic notice, issue an order prior to the effective date of registration refusing to permit such statement to become effective until it has been amended in accordance with such order. When such statement has been amended in accordance with such order the Commission shall so declare and the registration shall become effective at the time provided in subsection (a) or upon the date of such declaration, whichever date is the later.

(c) An amendment filed after the effective date of the registration statement, if such amendment, upon its face, appears to the Commission not to be incomplete or inaccurate in any material respect, shall become effective on such date as the Commission may determine, having due regard to the public interest and the protection of investors.

(d) If it appears to the Commission at any time that the registration statement includes any untrue statement of a material fact or omits to state any material fact required to be stated therein or necessary to make the statements therein not misleading, the Commission may, after notice by personal service or the sending of confirmed telegraphic notice, and opportunity for hearing (at a time fixed by the Commission) within fifteen days after such notice by personal service or the sending of such telegraphic notice, issue a stop order suspending the effectiveness of the registration statement. When such statement has been amended in accordance with such stop order the Commission shall so declare and thereupon the stop order shall cease to be effective.

(e) The Commission is hereby empowered to make an examination in any case in order to determine whether a stop order should issue under subsection (d). In making such examination the Commission or any officer or officers designated by it shall have access to and may demand the production of any books and papers of, and may administer oaths and affirmations to and examine, the issuer, underwriter, or any other person, in respect of any matter relevant to the examination, and may, in its discretion, require the production of a balance sheet exhibiting the assets and liabilities of the issuer, or its income statement, or both, to be certified to by a public or certified accountant approved by the Commission. If the issuer or underwriter shall fail to cooperate, or shall obstruct or refuse to permit the making of an examination, such conduct shall be proper ground for the issuance of a stop order.

(f) Any notice required under this section shall be sent to or served on the issuer, or, in case of a foreign government or political subdivision thereof, to or on the underwriter, or, in the case of a foreign or Territorial person, to or on its duly authorized representative in the United States named in the registration statement, properly directed in each case of telegraphic notice to the address given in such statement.

Cease-and-Desist Proceedings

Sec. 8A. (a) *Authority of the Commission.*—If the Commission finds, after notice and opportunity for hearing, that any person is violating, has violated, or is about to violate any provision of this title, or any rule or regulation thereunder, the Commission may publish its findings and enter an order requiring such person, and any other person that is, was, or would be a cause of the violation, due to an act or omission the person knew or should have known would contribute to such violation, to cease and desist from committing or causing such violation and any future violation of the same provision, rule or regulation. Such order may, in addition to requiring a person to cease and desist from committing or causing a violation, require such person to comply, or to take steps to effect compliance, with such provision, rule, or regulation, upon such terms and conditions and within such time as the Commission may specify in such order. Any such order may, as the Commission deems appropriate, require future compliance or steps to effect future compliance, either permanently or for such period of time as the Commission may specify, with such provision, rule, or regulation with respect to any security, any issuer, or any other person.

(b) *Hearing*.—The notice instituting proceedings pursuant to subsection (a) shall fix a hearing date not earlier than 30 days nor later than 60 days after service of the notice unless an earlier or a later date is set by the Commission with the consent of any respondent so served.

(c) *Temporary Order*.—

(1) *In General*.—Whenever the Commission determines that the alleged violation or threatened violation specified in the notice instituting proceedings pursuant to subsection (a), or the continuation thereof, is likely to result in significant dissipation or conversion of assets, significant harm to investors, or substantial harm to the public interest, including, but not limited to, losses to the Securities Investor Protection Corporation, prior to the completion of the proceedings, the Commission may enter a temporary order requiring the respondent to cease and desist from the violation or threatened violation and to take such action to prevent the violation or threatened violation and to prevent dissipation or conversion of assets, significant harm to investors, or substantial harm to the public interest as the Commission deems appropriate pending completion of such proceeding. Such an order shall be entered only after notice and opportunity for a hearing, unless the Commission determines that notice and hearing prior to entry would be impracticable or contrary to the public interest. A temporary order shall become effective upon service upon the respondent and, unless set aside, limited, or suspended by the Commission or a court of competent jurisdiction, shall remain effective and enforceable pending the completion of the proceedings.

(2) *Applicability*.—This subsection shall apply only to a respondent that acts, or, at the time of the alleged misconduct acted, as a broker, dealer, investment adviser, investment company, municipal securities dealer, government securities broker, government securities dealer, or transfer agent, or is, or was at the time of the alleged misconduct, an associated person of, or a person seeking to become associated with, any of the foregoing.

(d) *Review of Temporary Orders*.—

(1) *Commission Review*.—At any time after the respondent has been served with a temporary cease-and-desist order pursuant to subsection (c), the respondent may apply to the Commission to have the order set aside, limited, or suspended. If the respondent has been served with a temporary cease-and-desist order entered without a prior Commission hearing, the respondent may, within 10 days after the date on which the order was served, request a hearing on such application and the Commission shall hold a hearing and render a decision on such application at the earliest possible time.

(2) *Judicial Review*.—Within—

(A) 10 days after the date the respondent was served with a temporary cease-and-desist order entered with a prior Commission hearing, or

(B) 10 days after the Commission renders a decision on an application and hearing under paragraph (1), with respect to any temporary cease-and-desist order entered without a prior Commission hearing,

the respondent may apply to the United States district court for the district in which the respondent resides or has its principal place of business, or for the District of Columbia, for an order setting aside, limiting, or suspending the effectiveness or enforcement of the order, and the court shall have jurisdiction to enter such an order. A respondent served with a temporary cease-and-desist order entered without a prior Commission hearing may not apply to the court except after hearing and decision by the Commission on the respondent's application under paragraph (1) of this subsection.

(3) *No Automatic Stay of Temporary Order.*—The commencement of proceedings under paragraph (2) of this subsection shall not, unless specifically ordered by the court, operate as a stay of the Commission's order.

(4) *Exclusive Review.*—Section 9(a) of this title shall not apply to a temporary order entered pursuant to this section.

(e) *Authority to Enter an Order Requiring an Accounting and Disgorgement.*—In any cease-and-desist proceeding under subsection (a), the Commission may enter an order requiring accounting and disgorgement, including reasonable interest. The Commission is authorized to adopt rules, regulations, and orders concerning payments to investors, rates of interest, periods of accrual, and such other matters as it deems appropriate to implement this subsection.

(f) *Authority of the Commission to Prohibit Persons From Serving as Officers or Directors.*—In any cease-and-desist proceeding under subsection (a), the Commission may issue an order to prohibit, conditionally or unconditionally, and permanently or for such period of time as it shall determine, any person who has violated section 17(a)(1) or the rules or regulations thereunder, from acting as an officer or director of any issuer that has a class of securities registered pursuant to section 12 of the Securities Exchange Act of 1934, or that is required to file reports pursuant to section 15(d) of that Act, if the conduct of that person demonstrates unfitness to serve as an officer or director of any such issuer.

Court Review of Orders

Sec. 9. (a) Any person aggrieved by an order of the Commission may obtain a review of such order in the court of appeals of the United States, within any circuit wherein such person resides or has his principal place of business, or in the United States Court of Appeals for the District of Columbia, by filing in such Court, within sixty days after the entry of such order, a written petition praying that the order of the Commission be modified or be set aside in whole or in part. A copy of such petition shall be forthwith transmitted by the clerk of the court to the Commission, and thereupon the Commission shall file in the court the record upon which the order complained of was entered, as provided in section 2112 of title 28, United States Code. No objection to the order of the Commission shall be considered by the court unless such objection shall have been urged before the Commission. The finding of the Commission as to the facts, if supported by evidence, shall be conclusive. If either party shall apply to the court for leave to adduce additional evidence, and shall show to the satisfaction of the court that such additional evidence is material and that there were reasonable grounds for failure to adduce such evidence in the hearing before the Commission, the court may order such additional evidence to be taken before the Commission and to be adduced upon the hearing in such manner and upon such terms and conditions as to the court may seem proper. The Commission may modify its findings as to the facts by reason of the additional evidence so taken, and it shall file such modified or new findings, which, if supported by evidence, shall be conclusive, and its recommendation, if any, for the modification or setting aside of the original order. The jurisdiction of the court shall be exclusive and its judgment and decree, affirming, modifying, or setting aside, in whole or in part, any order of the Commission, shall be final, subject to review by the Supreme Court of the United States upon certiorari or certification as provided in section 1254 of title 28, United States Code.

(b) The commencement of proceedings under subsection (a) shall not, unless specifically ordered by the court, operate as a stay of the Commission's order.

Information Required in Prospectus

Sec. 10. (a) Except to the extent otherwise permitted or required pursuant to this subsection or subsections (c), (d), or (e)—

(1) a prospectus relating to a security other than a security issued by a foreign government or political subdivision thereof, shall contain the information contained in the registration statement, but it need not include the documents referred to in paragraphs (28) to (32), inclusive, of Schedule A;

(2) a prospectus relating to a security issued by a foreign government or political subdivision thereof shall contain the information contained in the registration statement, but it need not include the documents referred to in paragraphs (13) and (14) of Schedule B;

(3) notwithstanding the provisions of paragraphs (1) and (2) of this subsection (a) when a prospectus is used more than nine months after the effective date of the registration statement, the information contained therein shall be as of a date not more than sixteen months prior to such use, so far as such information is known to the user of such prospectus or can be furnished by such user without unreasonable effort or expense;

(4) there may be omitted from any prospectus any of the information required under this subsection (a) which the Commission may by rules or regulations designate as not being necessary or appropriate in the public interest or for the protection of investors.

(b) In addition to the prospectus permitted or required in subsection (a), the Commission shall by rules or regulations deemed necessary or appropriate in the public interest or for the protection of investors permit the use of a prospectus for the purposes of subsection (b)(1) of section 5 which omits in part or summarizes information in the prospectus specified in subsection (a). A prospectus permitted under this subsection shall, except to the extent the Commission by rules or regulations deemed necessary or appropriate in the public interest or for the protection of investors otherwise provides, be filed as part of the registration statement but shall not be deemed a part of such registration statement for the purposes of section 11. The Commission may at any time issue an order preventing or suspending the use of a prospectus permitted under this subsection (b), if it has reason to believe that such prospectus has not been filed (if required to be filed as part of the registration statement) or includes any untrue statement of a material fact or omits to state any material fact required to be stated therein or necessary to make the statements therein, in the light of the circumstances under which such prospectus is or is to be used, not misleading. Upon issuance of an order under this subsection, the Commission shall give notice of the issuance of such order and opportunity for hearing by personal service or the sending of confirmed telegraphic notice. The Commission shall vacate or modify the order at any time for good cause or if such prospectus has been filed or amended in accordance with such order.

(c) Any prospectus shall contain such other information as the Commission may by rules or regulations require as being necessary or appropriate in the public interest or for the protection of investors.

(d) In the exercise of its powers under subsections (a), (b), or (c), the Commission shall have authority to classify prospectuses according to the nature and circumstances of their use or the nature of the security, issue, issuer, or otherwise, and, by rules and regulations and subject to such terms and conditions as it shall specify therein, to prescribe as to each class the form and contents which it may find appropriate and consistent with the public interest and the protection of investors.

(e) The statements or information required to be included in a prospectus by or under authority of subsections (a), (b), (c), or (d), when written, shall be placed in a conspicuous part of the prospectus and, except as otherwise permitted by rules or regulations, in type as large as that used generally in the body of the prospectus.

(f) In any case where a prospectus consists of a radio or television broadcast, copies thereof shall be filed with the Commission under such rules and regulations as it shall prescribe. The Commission may by rules and regulations require the filing with it of forms and prospectuses used in connection with the offer or sale of securities registered under this title.

Civil Liabilities on Account of False Registration Statement

Sec. 11. (a) In case any part of the registration statement, when such part became effective, contained an untrue statement of a material fact or omitted to state a material fact required to be stated therein or necessary to make the statements therein not misleading, any person acquiring such security (unless it is proved that at the time of such acquisition he knew of such untruth or omission) may, either at law or in equity, in any court of competent jurisdiction, sue—

(1) every person who signed the registration statement;

(2) every person who was a director of (or person performing similar functions) or partner in, the issuer at the time of the filing of the part of the registration statement with respect to which his liability is asserted;

(3) every person who, with his consent, is named in the registration statement as being or about to become a director, person performing similar functions, or partner;

(4) every accountant, engineer, or appraiser, or any person whose profession gives authority to a statement made by him, who has with his consent been named as having prepared or certified any part of the registration statement, or as having prepared or certified any report or valuation which is used in connection with the registration statement, with respect to the statement in such registration statement, report, or valuation, which purports to have been prepared or certified by him;

(5) every underwriter with respect to such security.

If such person acquired the security after the issuer has made generally available to its security holders an earning statement covering a period of at least twelve months beginning after the effective date of the registration statement, then the right of recovery under this subsection shall be conditioned on proof that such person acquired the security relying upon such untrue statement in the registration statement or relying upon the registration statement and not knowing of such omission, but such reliance may be established without proof of the reading of the registration statement by such person.

(b) Notwithstanding the provisions of subsection (a) no person, other than the issuer, shall be liable as provided therein who shall sustain the burden of proof—

(1) that before the effective date of the part of the registration statement with respect to which his liability is asserted (A) he had resigned from or had taken such steps as are permitted by law to resign from, or ceased or refused to act in, every office, capacity, or relationship in which he was described in the registration statement as acting or agreeing to act, and (B) he had advised the Commission and the issuer in writing that he had taken such action and that he would not be responsible for such part of the registration statement; or

(2) that if such part of the registration statement became effective without his knowledge, upon becoming aware of such fact he forthwith acted and advised the Commission, in accordance with paragraph (1), and, in addition, gave reasonable public notice that such part of the registration statement had become effective without his knowledge; or

(3) that (A) as regards any part of the registration statement not purporting to be made on the authority of an expert, and not purporting to be a copy of or extract from a report or valuation of an expert, and not purporting to be made on the authority of a public official document or statement, he

had, after reasonable investigation, reasonable ground to believe and did believe, at the time such part of the registration statement became effective, that the statements therein were true and that there was no omission to state a material fact required to be stated therein or necessary to make the statements therein not misleading; and (B) as regards any part of the registration statement purporting to be made upon his authority as an expert or purporting to be a copy of or extract from a report or valuation of himself as an expert, (i) he had, after reasonable investigation, reasonable ground to believe and did believe, at the time such part of the registration statement became effective, that the statements therein were true and that there was no omission to state a material fact required to be stated therein or necessary to make the statements therein not misleading, or (ii) such part of the registration statement did not fairly represent his statement as an expert or was not a fair copy of or extract from his report or valuation as an expert; and (C) as regards any part of the registration statement purporting to be made on the authority of an expert (other than himself) or purporting to be a copy of or extract from a report or valuation of an expert (other than himself), he had no reasonable ground to believe and did not believe, at the time such part of the registration statement became effective, that the statements therein were untrue or that there was an omission to state a material fact required to be stated therein or necessary to make the statements therein not misleading, or that such part of the registration statement did not fairly represent the statement of the expert or was not a fair copy of or extract from the report or valuation of the expert; and (D) as regards any part of the registration statement purporting to be a statement made by an official person or purporting to be a copy of or extract from a public official document, he had no reasonable ground to believe and did not believe, at the time such part of the registration statement became effective, that the statements therein were untrue, or that there was an omission to state a material fact required to be stated therein or necessary to make the statements therein not misleading, or that such part of the registration statement did not fairly represent the statement made by the official person or was not a fair copy of or extract from the public official document.

(c) In determining, for the purpose of paragraph (3) of subsection (b) of this section, what constitutes reasonable investigation and reasonable ground for belief, the standard of reasonableness shall be that required of a prudent man in the management of his own property.

(d) If any person becomes an underwriter with respect to the security after the part of the registration statement with respect to which his liability is asserted has become effective, then for the purposes of paragraph (3) of subsection (b) of this section such part of the registration statement shall be considered as having become effective with respect to such person as of the time when he became an underwriter.

(e) The suit authorized under subsection (a) of this section may be to recover such damages as shall represent the difference between the amount paid for the security (not exceeding the price at which the security was offered to the public) and (1) the value thereof as of the time such suit was brought, or (2) the price at which such security shall have been disposed of in the market before suit, or (3) the price at which such security shall have been disposed of after suit but before judgment if such damages shall be less than the damages representing the difference between the amount paid for the security (not exceeding the price at which the security was offered to the public) and the value thereof as of the time such suit was brought: *Provided, that* if the defendant proves that any portion or all of such damages represents other than the depreciation in value of such security resulting from such part of the registration statement, with respect to which his liability is asserted, not being true or omitting to state a material fact required to be stated therein or necessary to make the statements therein not misleading, such portion of or all such damages shall not be recoverable. In no event shall any underwriter (unless such underwriter shall have knowingly received from the issuer for acting as an underwriter some benefit, directly or indirectly, in which all other underwriters similarly situated did not share in proportion to their respective interests in the underwriting) be liable in any suit or as a consequence of suits authorized under subsection (a) of this section for damages in excess of the total price at which the securities underwritten by him and distributed to the public were offered to the public. In any suit under this or any other section of this subchapter the court may, in its discretion, require an undertaking for the payment of the costs of such suit, including reasonable attorney's fees, and if judgment shall be rendered against a party litigant, upon the motion of the other party litigant, such costs may be assessed in favor of such party litigant (whether or not such undertaking has been required) if the court believes the suit or the defense to have been without merit, in an amount sufficient to reimburse him for the reasonable expenses incurred by him, in connection with such suit, such costs to be taxed in the manner usually provided for taxing of costs in the court in which the suit was heard.

(f)(1) Except as provided in paragraph (2), all, or any one or more of the persons specified in subsection (a) shall be jointly and severally liable, and every person who becomes liable to make any payment under this section may recover contribution as in cases of contract from any person who, if sued separately, would have been liable to make the same payment, unless the person who has become liable was, and the other was not, guilty of fraudulent misrepresentation.

(2)(A) The liability of an outside director under subsection (e) shall be determined in accordance with section 210(f) of the Securities Exchange Act of 1934.

(B) For purposes of this paragraph, the term "outside director" shall have the meaning given such term by rule or regulation of the Commission.

(g) In no case shall the amount recoverable under this section exceed the price at which the security was offered to the public.

Civil Liabilities Arising in Connection With Prospectuses and Communications

Sec. 12. (a) *In General.*—Any person who—

(1) offers or sells a security in violation of section 5, or

(2) offers or sells a security (whether or not exempted by the provisions of section 3, other than paragraphs (2) and (14) of subsection (a) thereof), by the use of any means or instruments of transportation or communication in interstate commerce or of the mails, by means of a prospectus or oral communication, which includes an untrue statement of a material fact or omits to state a material fact necessary in order to make the statements, in the light of the circumstances under which they were made, not misleading (the purchaser not knowing of such untruth or omission), and who shall not sustain the burden of proof that he did not know, and in the exercise of reasonable care could not have known, of such untruth or omission, shall be liable, subject to subsection (b) to the person purchasing such security from him, who may sue either at law or in equity in any court of competent jurisdiction, to recover the consideration paid for such security with interest thereon, less the amount of any income received thereon, upon the tender of such security, or for damages if he no longer owns the security.

(b) *Loss Causation.*—In an action described in subsection (a)(2), if the person who offered or sold such security proves that any portion or all of the amount recoverable under subsection (a)(2) represents other than the depreciation in value of the subject security resulting from such part of the prospectus or oral communication, with respect to which the liability of that person is asserted, not being true or omitting to state a material fact required to be stated therein or necessary to make the statement not misleading, then such portion or amount, as the case may be, shall not be recoverable.

Limitation of Actions

Sec. 13. No action shall be maintained to enforce any liability created under section 11 or section 12(a)(2) unless brought within one year after the discovery of the untrue statement or the omission, or after such discovery should have been made by the exercise of reasonable diligence, or, if the action is to enforce a liability created under section 12(a)(1), unless brought within one year after the violation upon which it is based. In no event shall any such action be brought to enforce a liability created under section 11 or section 12(a)(1) more than three years after the security was bona fide offered to the public, or under section 12(a)(2) more than three years after the sale.

Contrary Stipulations Void

Sec. 14. Any condition, stipulation, or provision binding any person acquiring any security to waive compliance with any provision of this title or of the rules and regulations of the Commission shall be void.

Liability of Controlling Persons

Sec. 15. Every person who, by or through stock ownership, agency, or otherwise, or who, pursuant to or in connection with an agreement or understanding with one or more other persons by or through stock ownership, agency, or otherwise, controls any person liable under section 11 or 12, shall also be liable jointly and severally with and to the same extent as such controlled person to any person to whom such controlled person is liable, unless the controlling person had no knowledge of or reasonable grounds to believe in the existence of the facts by reason of which the liability of the controlled person is alleged to exist.

Additional Remedies

Sec. 16. (a) *Remedies Additional.*—Except as provided in subsection (b), the rights and remedies provided by this title shall be in addition to any and all other rights and remedies that may exist at law or in equity.

(b) *Class Action Limitations.*—No covered class action based upon the statutory or common law of any State or subdivision thereof may be maintained in any State or Federal court by any private party alleging—

(1) an untrue statement or omission of a material fact in connection with the purchase or sale of a covered security; or

(2) that the defendant used or employed any manipulative or deceptive device or contrivance in connection with the purchase or sale of a covered security.

(c) *Removal of Covered Class Actions.*—Any covered class action brought in any State court involving a covered security, as set forth in subsection (b), shall be removable to the Federal district court for the district in which the action is pending, and shall be subject to subsection (b).

(d) *Preservation of Certain Actions.*—

(1) Actions under state law of state of incorporation.—

(A) Actions preserved.—Notwithstanding subsection (b) or (c), a covered class action described in subparagraph (B) of this paragraph that is based upon the statutory or common law of the State in which the issuer is incorporated (in the case of a corporation) or organized (in the case of any other entity) may be maintained in a State or Federal court by a private party.

(B) Permissible actions.—A covered class action is described in this subparagraph if it involves—

(i) the purchase or sale of securities by the issuer or an affiliate of the issuer exclusively from or to holders of equity securities of the issuer; or

(ii) any recommendation, position, or other communication with respect to the sale of securities of the issuer that—

(I) is made by or on behalf of the issuer or an affiliate of the issuer to holders of equity securities of the issuer; and

(II) concerns decisions of those equity holders with respect to voting their securities, acting in response to a tender or exchange offer, or exercising dissenters' or appraisal rights.

(2) State actions.—

(A) In general.—Notwithstanding any other provision of this section, nothing in this section may be construed to preclude a State or political subdivision thereof or a State pension plan from bringing an action involving a covered security on its own behalf, or as a member of a class comprised solely of other States, political subdivisions, or State pension plans that are named plaintiffs, and that have authorized participation, in such action.

(B) State pension plan defined.—For purposes of this paragraph, the term "State pension plan" means a pension plan established and maintained for its employees by the government of the State or political subdivision thereof, or by any agency or instrumentality thereof.

(3) Actions under contractual agreements between issuers and indenture trustees.—Notwithstanding subsection (b) or (c), a covered class action that seeks to enforce a contractual agreement between an issuer and an indenture trustee may be maintained in a State or Federal court by a party to the agreement or a successor to such party.

(4) Remand of removed actions.—In an action that has been removed from a State court pursuant to subsection (c), if the Federal court determines that the action may be maintained in State court pursuant to this subsection, the Federal court shall remand such action to such State court.

(e) *Preservation of State Jurisdiction.*—The securities commission (or any agency or office performing like functions) of any State shall retain jurisdiction under the laws of such State to investigate and bring enforcement actions.

(f) *Definitions.*—For purposes of this section, the following definitions shall apply:

(1) Affiliate of the issuer.—The term "affiliate of the issuer" means a person that directly or indirectly, through one or more intermediaries, controls or is controlled by or is under common control with, the issuer.

(2) Covered class action.—

(A) In general.—The term "covered class action" means—

(i) any single lawsuit in which—

(I) damages are sought on behalf of more than 50 persons or prospective class members, and questions of law or fact common to those persons or members of the prospective class, without reference to issues of individualized reliance on an alleged misstatement or omission, predominate over any questions affecting only individual persons or members; or

(II) one or more named parties seek to recover damages on a representative basis on behalf of themselves and other unnamed parties similarly situated, and questions of law or fact common to those persons or members of the prospective class predominate over any questions affecting only individual persons or members; or

(ii) any group of lawsuits filed in or pending in the same court and involving common questions of law or fact, in which—

(I) damages are sought on behalf of more than 50 persons; and

(II) the lawsuits are joined, consolidated, or otherwise proceed as a single action for any purpose.

(B) Exception for derivative actions.—Notwithstanding subparagraph (A), the term "covered class action" does not include an exclusively derivative action brought by one or more shareholders on behalf of a corporation.

(C) Counting of certain class members.—For purposes of this paragraph, a corporation, investment company, pension plan, partnership, or other entity, shall be treated as one person or prospective class member, but only if the entity is not established for the purpose of participating in the action.

(D) Rule of construction.—Nothing in this paragraph shall be construed to affect the discretion of a State court in determining whether actions filed in such court should be joined, consolidated, or otherwise allowed to proceed as a single action.

(3) Covered security.—The term "covered security" means a security that satisfies the standards for a covered security specified in paragraph (1) or (2) of section 18(b) at the time during which it is alleged that the misrepresentation, omission, or manipulative or deceptive conduct occurred, except that such term shall not include any debt security that is exempt from registration under this title pursuant to rules issued by the Commission under section 4(2).

Fraudulent, Interstate Transactions

Sec. 17. (a) It shall be unlawful for any person in the offer or sale of any securities or any security-based swap agreement (as defined in section 206B of the Gramm–Leach–Bliley Act) by the use of any means or instruments of transportation or communication in interstate commerce or by use of the mails, directly or indirectly—

(1) to employ any device, scheme, or artifice to defraud, or

(2) to obtain money or property by means of any untrue statement of a material fact or any omission to state a material fact necessary in order to make the statements made, in light of the circumstances under which they were made, not misleading; or

(3) to engage in any transaction, practice, or course of business which operates or would operate as a fraud or deceit upon the purchaser.

(b) It shall be unlawful for any person, by the use of any means or instruments of transportation or communication in interstate commerce or by the use of the mails, to publish, give publicity to, or circulate any notice, circular, advertisement, newspaper, article, letter, investment service, or communication which, though not purporting to offer a security for sale, describes such security for a consideration received or to be received, directly or indirectly, from an issuer, underwriter, or dealer, without fully disclosing the receipt, whether past or prospective, of such consideration and the amount thereof.

(c) The exemptions provided in section 3 shall not apply to the provisions of this section.

(d) The authority of the Commission under this section with respect to security-based swap agreements (as defined in section 206B of the Gramm–Leach–Bliley Act) shall be subject to the restrictions and limitations of section 2A(b) of this title.

Exemption From State Regulation of Securities Offerings

Sec. 18. (a) *Scope of exemption.*—Except as otherwise provided in this section, no law, rule, regulation, or order, or other administrative action of any State or any political subdivision thereof—

(1) requiring, or with respect to, registration or qualification of securities, or registration or qualification of securities transac-

tions, shall directly or indirectly apply to a security that—

(A) is a covered security; or

(B) will be a covered security upon completion of the transaction;

(2) shall directly or indirectly prohibit, limit, or impose any conditions upon the use of—

(A) with respect to a covered security described in subsection (b), any offering document that is prepared by or on behalf of the issuer; or

(B) any proxy statement, report to shareholders, or other disclosure document relating to a covered security or the issuer thereof that is required to be and is filed with the Commission or any national securities organization registered under section 15A of the Securities Exchange Act of 1934, except that this subparagraph does not apply to the laws, rules, regulations, or orders, or other administrative actions of the State of incorporation of the issuer; or

(3) shall directly or indirectly prohibit, limit, or impose conditions, based on the merits of such offering or issuer, upon the offer or sale of any security described in paragraph (1).

(b) *Covered securities.*—For purposes of this section, the following are covered securities:

(1) *Exclusive federal registration of nationally traded securities.*—A security is a covered security if such security is—

(A) listed, or authorized for listing, on the New York Stock Exchange or the American Stock Exchange, or listed or authorized for listing on the National Market System of the Nasdaq Stock Market (or any successor to such entities);

(B) listed, or authorized for listing, on a national securities exchange (or tier or segment thereof) that has listing standards that the Commission determines by rule (on its own initiative or on the basis of a petition) are substantially similar to the listing standards applicable to securities described in subparagraph (A); or

(C) is a security of the same issuer that is equal in seniority or that is a senior security to a security described in subparagraph (A) or (B).

(2) *Exclusive federal registration of investment companies.*—A security is a covered security if such security is a security issued by an investment company that is registered, or that has filed a registration statement, under the Investment Company Act of 1940.

(3) *Sales to qualified purchasers.*—A security is a covered security with respect to the offer or sale of the security to qualified purchasers, as defined by the Commission by rule. In prescribing such rule, the Commission may define the term "qualified purchaser" differently with respect to different categories of securities, consistent with the public interest and the protection of investors.

(4) *Exemption in connection with certain exempt offerings.*—A security is a covered security with respect to a transaction that is exempt from registration under this title pursuant to—

(A) paragraph (1) or (3) of section 4, and the issuer of such security files reports with the Commission pursuant to section 13 or 15(d) of the Securities Exchange Act of 1934;

(B) section 4(4);

(C) section 3(a), other than the offer or sale of a security that is exempt from such registration pursuant to paragraph (4), (10) or (11) of such section, except that a municipal security that is exempt from such registration pursuant to paragraph (2) of such section is not a covered security with respect to the offer or sale of such security in the State in which the issuer of such security is located; or

(D) Commission rules or regulations issued under section 4(2), except that this subparagraph does not prohibit a State from imposing notice filing requirements that are substantially similar to those required by rule or regulation under section 4(2) that are in effect on September 1, 1996.

(c) *Preservation of authority.*—

(1) *Fraud authority.*—Consistent with this section, the securities commission (or any agency or office performing like functions) of any State shall retain jurisdiction under the laws of such State to investigate and bring enforcement actions with respect to fraud or deceit, or unlawful conduct by a broker or dealer, in connection with securities or securities transactions.

(2) *Preservation of filing requirements.*—

(A) *Notice filings permitted.*—Nothing in this section prohibits the securities commission (or any agency or office performing like functions) of any State from requiring the filing of any document filed with the Commission pursuant to this title, together with annual or periodic reports of the value of securities sold or offered to be sold to persons located in the State (if such sales data is not included in documents filed with the Commission), solely for notice purposes and the assessment of any fee, together with a consent to service of process and any required fee.

(B) *Preservation of fees.*—

(i) *In general.*—Until otherwise provided by law, rule, regulation, or order, or other administrative action of any State, or any political subdivision thereof, adopted after the date of enactment of the National Securities Markets Improvement Act of 1996, filing or registration fees with respect to securities or securities transactions shall continue to be collected in amounts determined pursuant to State law as in effect on the day before such date.

(ii) *Schedule.*—The fees required by this subparagraph shall be paid, and all necessary supporting data on sales or offers for sales required under subparagraph (A), shall be reported on the same schedule as would have been applicable had the issuer not relied on the exemption provided in subsection (a).

(C) *Availability of preemption contingent on payment of fees.*—

(i) *In general.*—During the period beginning on the date of enactment of the National Securities Markets Improvement Act of 1996 and ending 3 years after that date of enactment, the securities commission (or any agency or office performing like functions) of any State may require the registration of securities issued by any issuer who refuses to pay the fees required by subparagraph (B).

(ii) *Delays.*—For purposes of this subparagraph, delays in payment of fees or underpayments of fees that are promptly remedied shall not constitute a refusal to pay fees.

(D) *Fees not permitted on listed securities.*—Notwithstanding subparagraphs (A), (B), and (C), no filing or fee may be required with respect to any security that is a covered security upon completion of the transaction, or is a security of the same issuer that is equal in seniority or that is a senior security to a security that is a covered security pursuant to subsection (b)(1).

(3) *Enforcement of requirements.*—Nothing in this section shall prohibit the securities commission (or any agency or office performing like functions) of any State from suspending the offer or sale of securities within such State as a result of the failure to submit any filing or fee required under law and permitted under this section.

(d) *Definitions.*—For purposes of this section, the following definitions shall apply:

(1) *Offering document.*—The term "offering document"—

(A) has the meaning given the term "prospectus" in section 2(a)(10), but without regard to the provisions of subparagraphs (a) and (b) of that section; and

(B) includes a communication that is not deemed to offer a security pursuant to a rule of the Commission.

(2) *Prepared by or on behalf of the issuer.*—Not later than 6 months after the date of enactment of the National Securities Markets Improvement Act of 1996, the Commission shall, by rule, define the term "prepared by or on behalf of the issuer" for purposes of this section.

(3) *State.*—The term "State" has the same meaning as in section 3 of the Securities Exchange Act of 1934.

(4) *Senior security.*—The term "senior security" means any bond, debenture, note, or similar obligation or instrument constituting a security and evidencing indebtedness, and any stock of a class having priority over any other class as to distribution of assets or payment of dividends.

Special Powers of Commission

Sec. 19. (a) The Commission shall have authority from time to time to make, amend, and rescind such rules and regulations as may be necessary to carry out the provisions of this title, including rules and regulations governing registration statements and prospectuses for various classes of securities and issuers, and defining accounting, technical, and trade terms used in this title. Among other things, the Commission shall have authority, for the purposes of this title, to prescribe the form or forms in which required information shall be set forth, the items or details to be shown in the balance sheet and earning statement, and the methods to be followed in the preparation of accounts, in the appraisal or valuation of assets and liabilities, in the determination of depreciation and depletion, in the differentiation of recurring and nonrecurring income, in the differentiation of investment and operating income, and in the preparation, where the Commission deems it necessary or desirable, of consolidated balance sheets or income accounts of any person directly or indirectly controlling or controlled by the issuer, or any person under direct or indirect common control with the issuer.

The rules and regulations of the Commission shall be effective upon publication in the manner which the Commission shall prescribe. No provision of this title imposing any liability shall apply to any act done or omitted in good faith in conformity with any rule or regulation of the Commission, notwithstanding that such rule or regulation may, after such act or omission, be amended or rescinded or be determined by judicial or other authority to be invalid for any reason.

(b) *Recognition of Accounting Standards.*—

(1) *In general.*—In carrying out its authority under subsection (a) and under section 13(b) of the Securities Exchange Act of 1934, the Commission may recognize, as "generally accepted" for purposes of the securities laws, any accounting principles established by a standard setting body—

(A) that—

(i) is organized as a private entity;

(ii) has, for administrative and operational purposes, a board of trustees (or equivalent body) serving in the public interest, the majority of whom are not, concurrent with their service on such board, and have not been during the 2-year period preceding such service, associated persons of any registered public accounting firm;

(iii) is funded as provided in section 109 of the Sarbanes–Oxley Act of 2002;

(iv) has adopted procedures to ensure prompt consideration, by majority vote of its members, of changes to accounting principles necessary to reflect emerging accounting issues and changing business practices; and

(v) considers, in adopting accounting principles, the need to keep standards current in order to reflect changes in the business environment, the extent to which international convergence on high quality accounting standards is necessary or appropriate in the public interest and for the protection of its investors; and

(B) that the Commission determines has the capacity to assist the Commission in fulfilling the requirements of subsection (a) and section 13(b) of the Securities Exchange Act of 1934, because, at a minimum, the standard setting body is capable of improving the accuracy and effectiveness of financial reporting and the protection of investors under the securities laws.

(2) *Annual report.*—A standard setting body described in paragraph (a) shall submit an annual report to the Commission and the public, containing audited financial statements of that standard setting body.

(c) For the purpose of all investigations which, in the opinion of the Commission, are necessary and proper for the enforcement of this title, any member of the Commission or any officer or officers designated by it are empowered to administer oaths and affirmations, subpena witnesses, take evidence, and require the production of any books, papers, or other documents which the Commission deems relevant or material to the inquiry. Such attendance of witnesses and the production of such documentary evidence may be required from any place in the United States or any Territory at any designated place of hearing.

(d)(1) The Commission is authorized to cooperate with any association composed of duly constituted representatives of State governments whose primary assignment is the regulation of the securities business within those States, and which, in the judgment of the Commission, could assist in effectuating greater uniformity in Federal-State securities matters. The Commission shall, at its discretion, cooperate, coordinate, and share information with such an association for the purposes of carrying out the policies and projects set forth in paragraphs (2) and (3).

(2) It is the declared policy of this subsection that there should be greater Federal and State cooperation in securities matters, including—

(A) maximum effectiveness of regulation,

(B) maximum uniformity in Federal and State regulatory standards,

(C) minimum interference with the business of capital formation, and

(D) a substantial reduction in costs and paperwork to diminish the burdens of raising investment capital (particularly by small business) and to diminish the costs of the administration of the Government programs involved.

(3) The purpose of this subsection is to engender cooperation between the Commission, any such association of State securities officials, and other duly constituted securities associations in the following areas:

(A) the sharing of information regarding the registration or exemption of securities issues applied for in the various States;

(B) the development and maintenance of uniform securities forms and procedures; and

(C) the development of a uniform exemption from registration for small issuers which can be agreed upon among several States or between the States and the Federal Government. The Commission shall have the authority to adopt such an exemption as agreed upon for Federal purposes. Nothing in this Act shall be construed as authorizing preemption of State law.

(4) In order to carry out these policies and purposes, the Commission shall conduct an annual conference as well as such other meetings as are deemed necessary, to which representatives from such securities associations,

securities self-regulatory organizations, agencies, and private organizations involved in capital formation shall be invited to participate.

(5) For fiscal year 1982, and for each of the three succeeding fiscal years, there are authorized to be appropriated such amounts as may be necessary and appropriate to carry out the policies, provisions, and purposes of this subsection. Any sums so appropriated shall remain available until expended.

(6) Notwithstanding any other provision of law, neither the Commission nor any other person shall be required to establish any procedures not specifically required by the securities laws, as that term is defined in section 3(a)(47) of the Securities Exchange Act of 1934, or by chapter 5 of title 5, United States Code, in connection with cooperation, coordination, or consultations with—

(A) any association referred to in paragraph (1) or (3) or any conference or meeting referred to in paragraph (4), while such association, conference, or meeting is carrying out activities in furtherance of the provisions of this subsection; or

(B) any forum, agency, or organization, or group referred to in section 503 of the Small Business Investment Incentive Act of 1980, while such forum, agency, organization, or group is carrying out activities in furtherance of the provisions of such section 503.

As used in this paragraph, the terms "association", "conference", "meeting", "forum", "agency", "organization", and "group" include any committee, subgroup, or representative of such entities.

Injunctions and Prosecution of Offenses

Sec. 20. (a) Whenever it shall appear to the Commission, either upon complaint or otherwise, that the provisions of this title, or of any rule or regulation prescribed under authority thereof, have been or are about to be violated, it may, in its discretion, either require or permit such person to file with it a statement in writing, under oath, or otherwise, as to all the facts and circumstances concerning the subject matter which it believes to be in the public interest to investigate, and may investigate such facts.

(b) Whenever it shall appear to the Commission that any person is engaged or about to engage in any acts or practices which constitute or will constitute a violation of the provisions of this title, or of any rule or regulation prescribed under authority thereof, the Commission may in its discretion, bring an action in any district court of the United States, or United States court of any Territory, to enjoin such acts or practices, and upon a proper showing, a permanent or temporary injunction or restraining order shall be granted without bond. The Commission may transmit such evidence as may be available concerning such acts or practices to the Attorney General who may, in his discretion, institute the necessary criminal proceedings under this title. Any such criminal proceeding may be brought either in the district wherein the transmittal of the prospectus or security complained of begins, or in the district wherein such prospectus or security is received.

(c) Upon application of the Commission, the district courts of the United States and the United States courts of any Territory shall have jurisdiction to issue writs of mandamus commanding any person to comply with the provisions of this title or any order of the Commission made in pursuance thereof.

(d) *Money Penalties in Civil Actions.*—

(1) *Authority of Commission.*—Whenever it shall appear to the Commission that any person has violated any provision of this subchapter, the rules or regulations thereunder, or a cease-and-desist order entered by the Commission pursuant to section 8A of this subchapter, other than by committing a violation subject to a penalty pursuant to section 21A of the Securities Exchange Act of 1934, the Commission may bring an action in a United States district court to seek, and the court shall have jurisdiction to impose, upon a proper showing, a

civil penalty to be paid by the person who committed such violation.

(2) *Amount of Penalty.*—

(A) *First tier.*—The amount of the penalty shall be determined by the court in light of the facts and circumstances. For each violation, the amount of the penalty shall not exceed the greater of (i) $5,000 for a natural person or $50,000 for any other person, or (ii) the gross amount of pecuniary gain to such defendant as a result of the violation.

(B) *Second tier.*—Notwithstanding subparagraph (A), the amount of penalty for each such violation shall not exceed the greater of (i) $50,000 for a natural person or $250,000 for any other person, or (ii) the gross amount of pecuniary gain to such defendant as a result of the violation, if the violation described in paragraph (1) involved fraud, deceit, manipulation, or deliberate or reckless disregard of a regulatory requirement.

(C) *Third tier.*—Notwithstanding subparagraphs (A) and (B), the amount of penalty for each such violation shall not exceed the greater of (i) $100,000 for a natural person or $500,000 for any other person, or (ii) the gross amount of pecuniary gain to such defendant as a result of the violation, if—

(I) the violation described in paragraph (1) involved fraud, deceit, manipulation, or deliberate or reckless disregard of a regulatory requirement; and

(II) such violation directly or indirectly resulted in substantial losses or created a significant risk of substantial losses to other persons.

(3) *Procedures for collection.*—

(A) *Payment of penalty to treasury.*—A penalty imposed under this section shall be payable into the Treasury of the United States, except as otherwise provided in section 308 of the Sarbanes–Oxley Act of 2002.

(B) *Collection of penalties.*—If a person upon whom such a penalty is imposed shall fail to pay such penalty within the time prescribed in the court's order, the Commission may refer the matter to the Attorney General who shall recover such penalty by action in the appropriate United States district court.

(C) *Remedy not exclusive.*—The actions authorized by this subsection may be brought in addition to any other action that the Commission or the Attorney General is entitled to bring.

(D) *Jurisdiction and venue.*—For purposes of section 22 of this subchapter, actions under this section shall be actions to enforce a liability or a duty created by this subchapter.

(4) *Special provisions relating to a violation of a cease-and-desist order.*—In an action to enforce a cease-and-desist order entered by the Commission pursuant to section 8A, each separate violation of such order shall be a separate offense, except that in the case of a violation through a continuing failure to comply with such an order, each day of the failure to comply with the order shall be deemed a separate offense.

(e) *Authority of a Court to Prohibit Persons From Serving as Officers and Directors.*—In any proceeding under subsection (b), the court may prohibit, conditionally or unconditionally, and permanently or for such period of time as it shall determine, any person who violated section 17(a)(1) of this title from acting as an officer or director of any issuer that has a class of securities registered pursuant to section 12 of the Securities Exchange Act of 1934 or that is required to file reports pursuant to section 15(d) of such Act if the person's conduct demonstrates unfitness to serve as an officer or director of any such issuer.

(f) *Prohibition of Attorneys' Fees Paid From Commission Disgorgement Funds.*—Except as otherwise ordered by the court upon motion by the Commission, or, in the case of an administrative action, as otherwise ordered by the Commission, funds disgorged as the result of an action brought by the Commission in Federal court, or as a result of any Commission administrative action, shall not be distributed as payment for attorneys' fees or expenses incurred by private parties seeking distribution of the disgorged funds.

(g) *Authority of a Court To Prohibit Persons From Participating in an Offering of Penny Stock.*—

(1) *In general.*—In any proceeding under subsection (a) against any person participating in, or, at the time of the alleged misconduct, who was participating in, any offering of penny stock, the court may prohibit that person from participating in an offering of penny stock, conditionally or unconditionally, and permanently or for such period of time as the court shall determine.

(2) *Definition.*—For purposes of this subsection, the term "person participating in an offering of penny stock" includes any person engaging in activities with a broker, dealer, or issuer for purposes of issuing, trading, or inducing or attempting to induce the purchase or sale of, any penny stock. The Commission may, by rule or regulation, define such term to include other activities, and may, by rule, regulation, or order, exempt any person or class of persons, in whole or in part, conditionally or unconditionally, from inclusion in such term.

Hearings by Commission

Sec. 21. All hearings shall be public and may be held before the Commission or an officer or officers of the Commission designated by it, and appropriate records thereof shall be kept.

Jurisdiction of Offenses and Suits

Sec. 22. (a) The district courts of the United States and the United States courts of any Territory shall have jurisdiction of offenses and violations under this title and under the rules and regulations promulgated by the Commission in respect thereto, and, concurrent with State and Territorial courts except as provided in section 16 with respect to covered class actions, of all suits in equity and actions at law brought to enforce any liability or duty created by this title. Any such suit or action may be brought in the district wherein the defendant is found or is an inhabitant or transacts business, or in the district where the offer or sale took place, if the defendant participated therein, and process in such cases may be served in any other district of which the defendant is an inhabitant or wherever the defendant may be found. Judgments and decrees so rendered shall be subject to review as provided in sections 1254, 1291, 1292, and 1294 of title 28, United States Code. Except as provided in section 16(c), no case arising under this title and brought in any State court of competent jurisdiction shall be removed to any court of the United States. No costs shall be assessed for or against the Commission in any proceeding under this title brought by or against it in the Supreme Court or such other courts.

(b) In case of contumacy or refusal to obey a subpena issued to any person, any of the said United States courts, within the jurisdiction of which said person guilty of contumacy or refusal to obey is found or resides, upon application by the Commission may issue to such person an order requiring such person to appear before the Commission, or one of its examiners designated by it, there to produce documentary evidence if so ordered, or there to give evidence touching the matter in question; and any failure to obey such order of the court may be punished by said court as a contempt thereof.

Unlawful Representations

Sec. 23. Neither the fact that the registration statement for a security has been filed or is in effect nor the fact that a stop order is not in effect with respect thereto shall be deemed a finding by the Commission that the registration statement is true and accurate on its face or that it does not contain an untrue statement of fact or omit to state a material fact, or be held to mean that the commission has in any way passed upon the merits of, or given approval to, such security. It shall be unlawful to make, or cause to be made, to any prospective purchaser any representation contrary to the foregoing provisions of this section.

Penalties

Sec. 24. Any person who willfully violates any of the provisions of this title, or the rules and regulations promulgated by the Commission under authority thereof, or any person who willfully, in a registration statement filed under this title, makes any untrue statement of a material fact or omits to state any material fact required to be stated therein or necessary to make the statements therein not misleading, shall upon conviction be fined not more than $10,000 or imprisoned not more than five years, or both.

Jurisdiction of Other Government Agencies Over Securities

Sec. 25. Nothing in this title shall relieve any person from submitting to the respective supervisory units of the Government of the United States information, reports, or other documents that are now or may hereafter be required by any provision of law.

Separability of Provisions

Sec. 26. If any provision of this Act, or the application of such provision to any person or circumstance, shall be held invalid, the remainder of this Act, or the application of such provision to persons or circumstances other than those as to which it is held invalid, shall not be affected thereby.

Private Securities Litigation

Sec. 27. (a) *Private Class Actions.—*

(1) *In General.*—The provisions of this subsection shall apply to each private action arising under this title that is brought as a plaintiff class action pursuant to the Federal Rules of Civil Procedure.

(2) *Certification Filed With Complaint.—*

(A) *In General.*—Each plaintiff seeking to serve as a representative party on behalf of a class shall provide a sworn certification, which shall be personally signed by such plaintiff and filed with the complaint, that—

(i) states that the plaintiff has reviewed the complaint and authorized its filing;

(ii) states that the plaintiff did not purchase the security that is the subject of the complaint at the direction of plaintiff's counsel or in order to participate in any private action arising under this title;

(iii) states that the plaintiff is willing to serve as a representative party on behalf of a class, including providing testimony at deposition and trial, if necessary;

(iv) sets forth all of the transactions of the plaintiff in the security that is the subject of the complaint during the class period specified in the complaint;

(v) identifies any other action under this title, filed during the 3–year period preceding the date on which the certification is signed by the plaintiff, in which the plaintiff has sought to serve, or served, as a representative party on behalf of a class; and

(vi) states that the plaintiff will not accept any payment for serving as a representative party on behalf of a class beyond the plaintiff's pro rata share of any recovery, except as ordered or approved by the court in accordance with paragraph (4).

(B) *Nonwaiver of Attorney–Client Privilege.*—The certification filed pursuant to subparagraph (A) shall not be construed to be a waiver of the attorney-client privilege.

(3) *Appointment of Lead Plaintiff.—*

(A) *Early Notice to Class Members.*—

(i) *In General.*—Not later than 20 days after the date on which the complaint is filed, the plaintiff or plaintiffs shall cause to be published, in a widely circulated national business-oriented publication or wire service, a notice advising members of the purported plaintiff class—

(I) of the pendency of the action, the claims asserted therein, and the purported class period; and

(II) that, not later than 60 days after the date on which the notice is published, any member of the purported class may move the court to serve as lead plaintiff of the purported class.

(ii) *Multiple Actions.*—If more than one action on behalf of a class asserting substantially the same claim or claims arising under this title is filed, only the plaintiff or plaintiffs in the first filed action shall be required to cause notice to be published in accordance with clause (i).

(iii) *Additional Notices May Be Required Under Federal Rules.*—Notice required under clause (i) shall be in addition to any notice required pursuant to the Federal Rules of Civil Procedure.

(B) *Appointment of Lead Plaintiff.*—

(i) *In General.*—Not later than 90 days after the date on which a notice is published under subparagraph (A)(i), the court shall consider any motion made by a purported class member in response to the notice, including any motion by a class member who is not individually named as a plaintiff in the complaint or complaints, and shall appoint as lead plaintiff the member or members of the purported plaintiff class that the court determines to be most capable of adequately representing the interests of class members (hereafter in this paragraph referred to as the "most adequate plaintiff") in accordance with this subparagraph.

(ii) *Consolidated Actions.*—If more than one action on behalf of a class asserting substantially the same claim or claims arising under this title has been filed, and any party has sought to consolidate those actions for pretrial purposes or for trial, the court shall not make the determination required by clause (i) until after the decision on the motion to consolidate is rendered. As soon as practicable after such decision is rendered, the court shall appoint the most adequate plaintiff as lead plaintiff for the consolidated actions in accordance with this subparagraph.

(iii) *Rebuttable Presumption.*—

(I) *In General.*—Subject to subclause (II), for purposes of clause (i), the court shall adopt a presumption that the most adequate plaintiff in any private action arising under this title is the person or group of persons that—

(aa) has either filed the complaint or made a motion in response to a notice under subparagraph (A)(i);

(bb) in the determination of the court, has the largest financial interest in the relief sought by the class; and

(cc) otherwise satisfies the requirements of Rule 23 of the Federal Rules of Civil Procedure.

(II) *Rebuttal Evidence.*—The presumption described in subclause (I) may be rebutted only upon proof by a member of the purported plaintiff class that the presumptively most adequate plaintiff—

(aa) will not fairly and adequately protect the interests of the class; or (bb) is subject to unique defenses that render such plaintiff incapable of adequately representing the class.

(iv) *Discovery.*—For purposes of this subparagraph, discovery relating to whether a member or members of the purported plaintiff class is the most adequate plaintiff may be conducted by a plaintiff only if the plaintiff first demonstrates a reasonable basis for a finding that the presumptively most adequate plaintiff is incapable of adequately representing the class.

(v) *Selection of Lead Counsel.*—The most adequate plaintiff shall, subject to the approval of the court, select and retain counsel to represent the class.

(vi) *Restrictions on Professional Plaintiffs.*—Except as the court may otherwise permit, consistent with the purposes of this section, a person may be a lead plaintiff, or an officer, director, or fiduciary of a lead plaintiff, in no more than 5 securities class actions brought as plaintiff class actions pursuant to the Federal Rules of Civil Procedure during any 3–year period.

(4) *Recovery by Plaintiffs.*—The share of any final judgment or of any settlement that is awarded to a representative party serving on behalf of a class shall be equal, on a per share basis, to the portion of the final judgment or settlement awarded to all other members of the class. Nothing in this paragraph shall be construed to limit the award of reasonable costs and expenses (including lost wages) directly relating to the representation of the class to any representative party serving on behalf of the class.

(5) *Restrictions on Settlements Under Seal.*—The terms and provisions of any settlement agreement of a class action shall not be filed under seal, except that on motion of any party to the settlement, the court may order filing under seal for those portions of a settlement agreement as to which good cause is shown for such filing under seal. For purposes of this paragraph, good cause shall exist only if publication of a term or provision of a settlement agreement would cause direct and substantial harm to any party.

(6) *Restrictions on Payment of Attorneys' Fees and Expenses.*—Total attorneys' fees and expenses awarded by the court to counsel for the plaintiff class shall not exceed a reasonable percentage of the amount of any damages and prejudgment interest actually paid to the class.

(7) *Disclosure of Settlement Terms to Class Members.*—Any proposed or final settlement agreement that is published or otherwise disseminated to the class shall include each of the following statements, along with a cover page summarizing the information contained in such statements:

(A) *Statement of Plaintiff Recovery.*—The amount of the settlement proposed to be distributed to the parties to the action, determined in the aggregate and on an average per share basis.

(B) *Statement of Potential Outcome of Case.*—

(i) *Agreement on Amount of Damages.*—If the settling parties agree on the average amount of damages per share that would be recoverable if the plaintiff prevailed on each claim alleged under this title, a statement concerning the average amount of such potential damages per share.

(ii) *Disagreement on Amount of Damages.*—If the parties do not agree on the average amount of damages per share that would be recoverable if the plaintiff prevailed on each claim alleged under this title, a statement from each settling party concerning the issue or issues on which the parties disagree.

(iii) *Inadmissibility for Certain Purposes.*—A statement made in accordance with clause (i) or (ii) concerning the amount of damages shall not be admissible in any Federal or State judicial action or administrative proceeding, other than an action or proceeding arising out of such statement.

(C) *Statement of Attorneys' Fees or Costs Sought.*—If any of the settling parties or their counsel intend to apply to the court for an award of attorneys' fees or costs from any fund established as part of the settlement, a statement indicating which parties or counsel intend to make such an application, the amount of fees and costs that will be sought (including the amount of such fees and costs determined on an average per share basis), and a brief explanation supporting the fees and costs sought.

(D) *Identification of Lawyers' Representatives.*—The name, telephone number, and address of one or more representatives of counsel for the plaintiff class who will be reasonably available to answer questions from class members concerning any matter contained in any notice of settlement published or otherwise disseminated to the class.

(E) *Reasons for Settlement.*—A brief statement explaining the reasons why the parties are proposing the settlement.

(F) *Other Information.*—Such other information as may be required by the court.

(8) *Attorney Conflict of Interest.*—If a plaintiff class is represented by an attorney who directly owns or otherwise has a beneficial interest in the securities that are the subject of the litigation, the court shall make a determination of whether such ownership or other interest constitutes a conflict of interest sufficient to disqualify the attorney from representing the plaintiff class.

(b) *Stay of Discovery; Preservation of Evidence.*—

(1) *In General.*—In any private action arising under this title, all discovery and other proceedings shall be stayed during the pendency of any motion to dismiss, unless the court finds, upon the motion of any party, that particularized discovery is necessary to preserve evidence or to prevent undue prejudice to that party.

(2) *Preservation of Evidence.*—During the pendency of any stay of discovery pursuant to this subsection, unless otherwise ordered by the court, any party to the action with actual notice of the allegations contained in the complaint shall treat all documents, data compilations (including electronically recorded or stored data), and tangible objects that are in the custody or control of such person and that are relevant to the allegations, as if they were the subject of a continuing request for production of documents from an opposing party under the Federal Rules of Civil Procedure.

(3) *Sanction for Willful Violation.*—A party aggrieved by the willful failure of an opposing party to comply with paragraph (2) may apply to the court for an order awarding appropriate sanctions.

(4) *Circumvention of Stay of Discovery.*—Upon a proper showing, a court may stay discovery proceedings in any private action in a State court as necessary in aid of its jurisdiction, or to protect or effectuate its judgments, in an action subject to a stay of discovery pursuant to this subsection.

(c) *Sanctions for Abusive Litigation.*—

(1) *Mandatory Review by Court.*—In any private action arising under this title, upon final adjudication of the action, the court shall include in the record specific findings regarding compliance by each party and each attorney representing any party with each requirement of Rule 11(b) of the Federal Rules of Civil Procedure as to any complaint, responsive pleading, or dispositive motion.

(2) *Mandatory Sanctions.*—If the court makes a finding under paragraph (1) that a party or attorney violated any requirement

of Rule 11(b) of the Federal Rules of Civil Procedure as to any complaint, responsive pleading, or dispositive motion, the court shall impose sanctions on such party or attorney in accordance with Rule 11 of the Federal Rules of Civil Procedure. Prior to making a finding that any party or attorney has violated Rule 11 of the Federal Rules of Civil Procedure, the court shall give such party or attorney notice and an opportunity to respond.

(3) *Presumption in Favor of Attorneys' Fees and Costs.*—

(A) *In General.*—Subject to subparagraphs (B) and (C), for purposes of paragraph (2), the court shall adopt a presumption that the appropriate sanction—

(i) for failure of any responsive pleading or dispositive motion to comply with any requirement of Rule 11(b) of the Federal Rules of Civil Procedure is an award to the opposing party of the reasonable attorneys' fees and other expenses incurred as a direct result of the violation; and

(ii) for substantial failure of any complaint to comply with any requirement of Rule 11(b) of the Federal Rules of Civil Procedure is an award to the opposing party of the reasonable attorneys' fees and other expenses incurred in the action.

(B) *Rebuttal Evidence.*—The presumption described in subparagraph (A) may be rebutted only upon proof by the party or attorney against whom sanctions are to be imposed that—

(i) the award of attorneys' fees and other expenses will impose an unreasonable burden on that party or attorney and would be unjust, and the failure to make such an award would not impose a greater burden on the party in whose favor sanctions are to be imposed; or

(ii) the violation of Rule 11(b) of the Federal Rules of Civil Procedure was de minimis.

(C) *Sanctions.*—If the party or attorney against whom sanctions are to be imposed meets its burden under subparagraph (B), the court shall award the sanctions that the court deems appropriate pursuant to Rule 11 of the Federal Rules of Civil Procedure.

(d) *Defendant's Right to Written Interrogatories.*—In any private action arising under this title in which the plaintiff may recover money damages only on proof that a defendant acted with a particular state of mind, the court shall, when requested by a defendant, submit to the jury a written interrogatory on the issue of each such defendant's state of mind at the time the alleged violation occurred.

Application of Safe Harbor for Forward-Looking Statements

Sec. 27A. (a) *Applicability.*—This section shall apply only to a forward-looking statement made by—

(1) an issuer that, at the time that the statement is made, is subject to the reporting requirements of section 13(a) or section 15(d) of the Securities Exchange Act of 1934;

(2) a person acting on behalf of such issuer;

(3) an outside reviewer retained by such issuer making a statement on behalf of such issuer; or

(4) an underwriter, with respect to information provided by such issuer or information derived from information provided by the issuer.

(b) *Exclusions.*—Except to the extent otherwise specifically provided by rule, regulation, or order of the Commission, this section shall not apply to a forward-looking statement—

(1) that is made with respect to the business or operations of the issuer, if the issuer—

(A) during the 3–year period preceding the date on which the statement was first made—

(i) was convicted of any felony or misdemeanor described in clauses (i) through (iv) of section 15(b)(4)(B) of the Securities Exchange Act of 1934; or

(ii) has been made the subject of a judicial or administrative decree or order arising out of a governmental action that—

(I) prohibits future violations of the antifraud provisions of the securities laws;

(II) requires that the issuer cease and desist from violating the antifraud provisions of the securities laws; or

(III) determines that the issuer violated the antifraud provisions of the securities laws;

(B) makes the forward-looking statement in connection with an offering of securities by a blank check company;

(C) issues penny stock;

(D) makes the forward-looking statement in connection with a rollup transaction; or

(E) makes the forward-looking statement in connection with a going private transaction; or

(2) that is—

(A) included in a financial statement prepared in accordance with generally accepted accounting principles;

(B) contained in a registration statement of, or otherwise issued by, an investment company;

(C) made in connection with a tender offer;

(D) made in connection with an initial public offering;

(E) made in connection with an offering by, or relating to the operations of, a partnership, limited liability company, or a direct participation investment program; or

(F) made in a disclosure of beneficial ownership in a report required to be filed with the Commission pursuant to section 13(d) of the Securities Exchange Act of 1934.

(c) *Safe Harbor.*—

(1) *In General.*—Except as provided in subsection (b), in any private action arising under this title that is based on an untrue statement of a material fact or omission of a material fact necessary to make the statement not misleading, a person referred to in subsection (a) shall not be liable with respect to any forward-looking statement, whether written or oral, if and to the extent that—

(A) the forward-looking statement is—

(i) identified as a forward-looking statement, and is accompanied by meaningful cautionary statements identifying important factors that could cause actual results to differ materially from those in the forward looking statement; or

(ii) immaterial; or

(B) the plaintiff fails to prove that the forward-looking statement—

(i) if made by a natural person, was made with actual knowledge by that person that the statement was false or misleading; or

(ii) if made by a business entity; was—

(I) made by or with the approval of an executive officer of that entity, and

(II) made or approved by such officer with actual knowledge by that officer that the statement was false or misleading.

(2) *Oral Forward-Looking Statements.*—In the case of an oral forward-looking statement made by an issuer that is subject to the reporting requirements of section 13(a) or section 15(d) of the Securities Exchange Act of 1934, or by a person acting on behalf of such issuer, the requirement set forth in paragraph (1)(A) shall be deemed to be satisfied—

(A) if the oral forward-looking statement is accompanied by a cautionary statement—

(i) that the particular oral statement is a forward-looking statement; and

(ii) that the actual results could differ materially from those projected in the forward-looking statement; and

(B) if—

(i) the oral forward-looking statement is accompanied by an oral statement that additional information concerning factors that could cause actual results to differ materially from those in the forward-looking statement is contained in a readily available written document, or portion thereof;

(ii) the accompanying oral statement referred to in clause (i) identifies the document, or portion thereof, that contains the additional information about those factors relating to the forward-looking statement; and

(iii) the information contained in that written document is a cautionary statement that satisfies the standard established in paragraph (1)(A).

(3) *Availability.*—Any document filed with the Commission or generally disseminated shall be deemed to be readily available for purposes of paragraph (2).

(4) *Effect on Other Safe Harbors.*—The exemption provided for in paragraph (1) shall be in addition to any exemption that the Commission may establish by rule or regulation under subsection (g).

(d) *Duty to Update.*—Nothing in this section shall impose upon any person a duty to update a forward-looking statement.

(e) *Dispositive Motion.*—On any motion to dismiss based upon subsection (c)(1), the court shall consider any statement cited in the complaint and cautionary statement accompanying the forward-looking statement, which are not subject to material dispute, cited by the defendant.

(f) *Stay Pending Decision on Motion.*—In any private action arising under this title, the court shall stay discovery (other than discovery that is specifically directed to the applicability of the exemption provided for in this section) during the pendency of any motion by a defendant for summary judgment that is based on the grounds that—

(1) the statement or omission upon which the complaint is based is a forward-looking statement within the meaning of this section; and

(2) the exemption provided for in this section precludes a claim for relief.

(g) *Exemption Authority.*—In addition to the exemptions provided for in this section, the Commission may, by rule or regulation, provide exemptions from or under any provision of this title, including with respect to liability that is based on a statement or that is based on projections or other forward-looking information, if and to the extent that any such exemption is consistent with the public interest and the protection of investors, as determined by the Commission.

(h) *Effect on Other Authority of Commission.*—Nothing in this section limits, either expressly or by implication, the authority of the Commission to exercise similar authority or to adopt similar rules and regulations with respect to forward-looking statements under any other statute under which the Commission exercises rulemaking authority.

(i) *Definitions.*—For purposes of this section, the following definitions shall apply:

(1) *Forward–Looking Statement.*—The term "forward-looking statement" means—

(A) a statement containing a projection of revenues, income (including income loss), earnings (including earnings loss) per share, capital expenditures, dividends, capital structure, or other financial items;

(B) a statement of the plans and objectives of management for future operations, including plans or objectives relating to the products or services of the issuer;

(C) a statement of future economic performance, including any such statement contained in a discussion and analysis of financial condition by the management or in the results of operations included pursuant to the rules and regulations of the Commission;

(D) any statement of the assumptions underlying or relating to any statement described in subparagraph (A), (B), or (C);

(E) any report issued by an outside reviewer retained by an issuer, to the extent that the report assesses a forward-looking statement made by the issuer; or

(F) a statement containing a projection or estimate of such other items as may be specified by rule or regulation of the Commission.

(2) *Investment Company.*—The term "investment company" has the same meaning as in section 3(a) of the Investment Company Act of 1940.

(3) *Penny Stock.*—The term "penny stock" has the same meaning as in section 3(a)(51) of the Securities Exchange Act of 1934, and the rules and regulations, or orders issued pursuant to that section.

(4) *Going Private Transaction.*—The term "going private transaction" has the meaning given that term under the rules or regulations of the Commission issued pursuant to section 13(e) of the Securities Exchange Act of 1934.

(5) *Securities Laws.*—The term "securities laws" has the same meaning as in section 3 of the Securities Exchange Act of 1934.

(6) *Person Acting on Behalf of an Issuer.*—The term "person acting on behalf of an issuer" means an officer, director, or employee of the issuer.

(7) *Other Terms.*—The terms "blank check company", "roll-up transaction", "partnership", "limited liability company", "executive officer of an entity" and "direct participation investment program", have the meanings given those terms by rule or regulation of the Commission.

General Exemptive Authority

Sec. 28. The Commission, by rule or regulation, may conditionally or unconditionally exempt any person, security, or transaction, or any class or classes of persons, securities, or transactions, from any provision or provisions of this title or of any rule or regulation issued under this title, to the extent that such exemption is necessary or appropriate in the public interest, and is consistent with the protection of investors.

Schedule A

(1) The name under which the issuer is doing or intends to do business;

(2) the name of the State or other sovereign power under which the issuer is organized;

(3) the location of the issuer's principal business office, and if the issuer is a foreign or territorial person, the name and address of its agent in the United States authorized to receive notice;

(4) the names and addresses of the directors or persons performing similar functions, and the chief executive, financial and accounting officers, chosen or to be chosen if the issuer be a corporation, association, trust, or other entity; of all partners, if the issuer be a partnership; and of the issuer, if the issuer be an individual; and of the promoters in the case of

a business to be formed, or formed within two years prior to the filing of the registration statement;

(5) the names and addresses of the underwriters;

(6) the names and addresses of all persons, if any, owning of record or beneficially, if known, more than 10 per centum of any class of stock of the issuer, or more than 10 per centum in the aggregate of the outstanding stock of the issuer as of a date within twenty days prior to the filing of the registration statement;

(7) the amount of securities of the issuer held by any person specified in paragraphs (4), (5), and (6) of this schedule, as of a date within twenty days prior to the filing of the registration statement, and, if possible, as of one year prior thereto, and the amount of the securities, for which the registration statement is filed, to which such persons have indicated their intention to subscribe;

(8) the general character of the business actually transacted or to be transacted by the issuer;

(9) a statement of the capitalization of the issuer, including the authorized and outstanding amounts of its capital stock and the proportion thereof paid up, the number and classes of shares in which such capital stock is divided, par value thereof, or if it has no par value, the stated or assigned value thereof, a description of the respective voting rights, preferences, conversion and exchange rights, rights to dividends, profits, or capital of each class, with respect to each other class, including the retirement and liquidation rights or values thereof;

(10) a statement of the securities, if any, covered by options outstanding or to be created in connection with the security to be offered, together with the names and addresses of all persons, if any, to be allotted more than 10 per centum in the aggregate of such options;

(11) the amount of capital stock of each class issued or included in the shares of stock to be offered;

(12) the amount of the funded debt outstanding and to be created by the security to be offered, with a brief description of the date, maturity, and character of such debt, rate of interest, character of amortization provisions, and the security, if any, therefor. If substitution of any security is permissible, a summarized statement of the conditions under which such substitution is permitted. If substitution is permissible without notice, a specific statement to that effect;

(13) the specific purposes in detail and the approximate amounts to be devoted to such purposes, so far as determinable, for which the security to be offered is to supply funds, and if the funds are to be raised in part from other sources, the amounts thereof and the sources thereof, shall be stated;

(14) the remuneration, paid or estimated to be paid, by the issuer or its predecessor, directly or indirectly, during the past year and ensuing year, to (a) the directors or persons performing similar functions, and (b) its officers and other persons, naming them wherever such remuneration exceeded $25,000 during any such year;

(15) the estimated net proceeds to be derived from the security to be offered;

(16) the price at which it is proposed that the security shall be offered to the public or the method by which such price is computed and any variation therefrom at which any portion of such security is proposed to be offered to any persons or classes of persons, other than the underwriters, naming them or specifying the class. A variation in price may be proposed prior to the date of the public offering of the security, but the Commission shall immediately be notified of such variation;

(17) all commissions or discounts paid or to be paid, directly or indirectly, by the issuer to the underwriters in respect of the sale of the security to be offered. Commissions shall include all cash, securities, contracts, or any-

thing else of value, paid, to be set aside, disposed of, or understandings with or for the benefit of any other persons in which any underwriter is interested, made, in connection with the sale of such security. A commission paid or to be paid in connection with the sale of such security by a person in which the issuer has an interest or which is controlled or directed by, or under common control with, the issuer shall be deemed to have been paid by the issuer. Where any such commission is paid the amount of such commission paid to each underwriter shall be stated;

(18) the amount or estimated amounts, itemized in reasonable detail, of expenses, other than commissions specified in paragraph (17) of this schedule, incurred or borne by or for the account of the issuer in connection with the sale of the security to be offered or properly chargeable thereto, including legal, engineering, certification, authentication, and other charges;

(19) the net proceeds derived from any security sold by the issuer during the two years preceding the filing of the registration statement, the price at which such security was offered to the public, and the names of the principal underwriters of such security;

(20) any amount paid within two years preceding the filing of the registration statement or intended to be paid to any promoter and the consideration for any such payment;

(21) the names and addresses of the vendors and the purchase price of any property, or goodwill, acquired or to be acquired, not in the ordinary course of business, which is to be defrayed in whole or in part from the proceeds of the security to be offered, the amount of any commission payable to any person in connection with such acquisition, and the name or names of such person or persons, together with any expense incurred or to be incurred in connection with such acquisition, including the cost of borrowing money to finance such acquisition;

(22) full particulars of the nature and extent of the interest, if any, of every director, principal executive officer, and of every stockholder holding more than 10 per centum of any class of stock or more than 10 per centum in the aggregate of the stock of the issuer, in any property acquired, not in the ordinary course of business of the issuer, within two years preceding the filing of the registration statement or proposed to be acquired at such date;

(23) the names and addresses of counsel who have passed on the legality of the issue;

(24) dates of and parties to, and the general effect concisely stated of every material contract made, not in the ordinary course of business, which contract is to be executed in whole or in part at or after the filing of the registration statement or which contract has been made not more than two years before such filing. Any management contract or contract providing for special bonuses or profit-sharing arrangements, and every material patent or contract for a material patent right, and every contract by or with a public utility company or an affiliate thereof, providing for the giving or receiving of technical or financial advice or service (if such contract may involve a charge to any party thereto at a rate in excess of $2,500 per year in cash or securities or anything else of value), shall be deemed a material contract;

(25) a balance sheet as of a date not more than ninety days prior to the date of the filing of the registration statement showing all of the assets of the issuer, the nature and cost thereof, whenever determinable, in such detail and in such form as the Commission shall prescribe (with intangible items segregated), including any loan in excess of $20,000 to any officer, director, stockholder or person directly or indirectly controlling or controlled by the issuer, or person under direct or indirect common control with the issuer. All the liabilities of the issuer in such detail and such form as the Commission shall prescribe, including surplus of the issuer showing how and from what sources such surplus was created, all as of a date not more than ninety days prior to the

filing of the registration statement. If such statement be not certified by an independent public or certified accountant, in addition to the balance sheet required to be submitted under this schedule, a similar detailed balance sheet of the assets and liabilities of the issuer, certified by an independent public or certified accountant, of a date not more than one year prior to the filing of the registration statement, shall be submitted;

(26) a profit and loss statement of the issuer showing earnings and income, the nature and source thereof, and the expenses and fixed charges in such detail and such form as the Commission shall prescribe for the latest fiscal year for which such statement is available and for the two preceding fiscal years, year by year, or, if such issuer has been in actual business for less than three years, then for such time as the issuer has been in actual business, year by year. If the date of the filing of the registration statement is more than six months after the close of the last fiscal year, a statement from such closing date to the latest practicable date. Such statement shall show what the practice of the issuer has been during the three years or lesser period as to the character of the charges, dividends or other distributions made against its various surplus accounts, and as to depreciation, depletion, and maintenance charges, in such detail and form as the Commission shall prescribe, and if stock dividends or avails from the sale of rights have been credited to income, they shall be shown separately with a statement of the basis upon which the credit is computed. Such statement shall also differentiate between any recurring and nonrecurring income and between any investment and operating income. Such statement shall be certified by an independent public or certified accountant;

(27) if the proceeds, or any part of the proceeds, of the security to be issued is to be applied directly or indirectly to the purchase of any business, a profit and loss statement of such business certified by an independent public or certified accountant, meeting the requirements of paragraph (26) of this schedule, for the three preceding fiscal years, together with a balance sheet, similarly certified, of such business, meeting the requirements of paragraph (25) of this schedule of a date not more than ninety days prior to the filing of the registration statement or at the date such business was acquired by the issuer if the business was acquired by the issuer more than ninety days prior to the filing of the registration statement;

(28) a copy of any agreement or agreements (or, if identical agreements are used, the forms thereof) made with any underwriter, including all contracts and agreements referred to in paragraph (17) of this schedule;

(29) a copy of the opinion or opinions of counsel in respect to the legality of the issue, with a translation of such opinion, when necessary, into the English language;

(30) a copy of all material contracts referred to in paragraph (24) of this schedule, but no disclosure shall be required of any portion of any such contract if the Commission determines that disclosure of such portion would impair the value of the contract and would not be necessary for the protection of the investors;

(31) unless previously filed and registered under the provisions of this title, and brought up to date, (a) a copy of its articles of incorporation, with all amendments thereof and of its existing bylaws or instruments corresponding thereto, whatever the name, if the issuer be a corporation; (b) copy of all instruments by which the trust is created or declared, if the issuer is a trust; (c) a copy of its articles of partnership or association and all other papers pertaining to its organization, if the issuer is a partnership, unincorporated association, joint-stock company, or any other form of organization; and

(32) a copy of the underlying agreements or indentures affecting any stock, bonds, or debentures offered or to be offered.

In case of certificates of deposit, voting trust certificates, collateral trust certificates, certificates of interest or shares in unincorporated investment trusts, equipment trust certificates, interim or other receipts for certificates, and like securities, the Commission shall establish rules and regulations requiring the submission of information of a like character applicable to such cases, together with such other information as it may deem appropriate and necessary regarding the character, financial or otherwise, of the actual issuer of the securities and/or the person performing the acts and assuming the duties of depositor or manager.

Schedule B

(1) Name of borrowing government or subdivision thereof;

(2) specific purposes in detail and the approximate amounts to be devoted to such purposes, so far as determinable, for which the security to be offered is to supply funds, and if the funds are to be raised in part from other sources, the amounts thereof and the sources thereof, shall be stated;

(3) the amount of the funded debt and the estimated amount of the floating debt outstanding and to be created by the security to be offered, excluding intergovernmental debt, and a brief description of the date, maturity, character of such debt, rate of interest, character of amortization provisions, and the security, if any, therefor. If substitution of any security is permissible, a statement of the conditions under which such substitution is permitted. If substitution is permissible without notice, a specific statement to that effect;

(4) whether or not the issuer or its predecessor has, within a period of twenty years prior to the filing of the registration statement, defaulted on the principal or interest of any external security, excluding intergovernmental debt, and, if so, the date, amount, and circumstances of such default, and the terms of the succeeding arrangement, if any;

(5) the receipts, classified by source, and the expenditures, classified by purpose, in such detail and form as the Commission shall prescribe for the latest fiscal year for which such information is available and the two preceding fiscal years, year by year;

(6) the names and addresses of the underwriters;

(7) the name and address of its authorized agent, if any, in the United States;

(8) the estimated net proceeds to be derived from the sale in the United States of the security to be offered;

(9) the price at which it is proposed that the security shall be offered in the United States to the public or the method by which such price is computed. A variation in price may be proposed prior to the date of the public offering of the security, but the Commission shall immediately be notified of such variation;

(10) all commissions paid or to be paid, directly or indirectly, by the issuer to the underwriters in respect of the sale of the security to be offered. Commissions shall include all cash, securities, contracts, or anything else of value, paid, to be set aside, disposed of, or understandings with or for the benefit of any other persons in which the underwriter is interested, made, in connection with the sale of such security. Where any such commission is paid, the amount of such commission paid to each underwriter shall be stated;

(11) the amount or estimated amounts, itemized in reasonable detail, of expenses, other than the commissions specified in paragraph (10) of this schedule, incurred or borne by or for the account of the issuer in connection with the sale of the security to be offered or properly chargeable thereto, including legal, engineering, certification, and other charges;

(12) the names and addresses of counsel who have passed upon the legality of the issue;

(13) a copy of any agreement or agreements made with any underwriter governing the sale of the security within the United States; and

(14) an agreement of the issuer to furnish a copy of the opinion or opinions of counsel in respect to the legality of the issue, with a

translation, where necessary, into the English language. Such opinion shall set out in full all laws, decrees, ordinances, or other acts of Government under which the issue of such security has been authorized.

SECURITIES ACT OF 1933

GENERAL RULES AND REGULATIONS

(Cite as 17 CFR 230.__)

GENERAL

Rule

SPECIAL EXEMPTIONS

REGULATION A—CONDITIONAL SMALL ISSUES EXEMPTION

Rule

REGULATION B—EXEMPTIONS RELATING TO FRACTIONAL UNDIVIDED INTERESTS IN OIL AND GAS RIGHTS [OMITTED]

REGULATION C—REGISTRATION

GENERAL REQUIREMENTS

FORM AND CONTENTS OF PROSPECTUSES

WRITTEN CONSENTS

FILINGS; FEES; EFFECTIVE DATE

Item
310. Financial Statements
401. Directors, Executive Officers, Promoters and Control Persons
402. Executive Compensation
403. Security Ownership of Certain Beneficial Owners and Management
404. Certain Relationships and Related Transactions
405. Compliance With Section 16(a) of the Exchange Act
406. Code of Ethics
501. Front of Registration Statement and Outside Front Cover of Prospectus
502. Inside Front and Outside Back Cover Pages of Prospectus
503. Summary Information and Risk Factors
504. Use of Proceeds
505. Determination of Offering Price
506. Dilution
507. Selling Security Holders
508. Plan of Distribution
509. Interest of Named Experts and Counsel
510. Disclosure of Commission Position on Indemnification for Securities Act Liabilities
511. Other Expenses of Issuance and Distribution
512. Undertakings
601. Exhibits
701. Recent Sales of Unregistered Securities; Use of Proceeds from Registered Securities
702. Indemnification of Directors and Officers
703. Purchases of Equity Securities by the Small Business Issuer and Affiliated Purchasers

REGULATION S–K—STANDARD INSTRUCTIONS FOR FILING FORMS UNDER SECURITIES ACT OF 1933, SECURITIES EXCHANGE ACT OF 1934 AND ENERGY POLICY AND CONSERVATION ACT OF 1975

(Cite as 17 CFR 229.___)

Item
10. General
101. Description of Business
102. Description of Property
103. Legal Proceedings
201. Market Price of and Dividends on the Registrant's Common Equity and Related Stockholder Matters
202. Description of Registrant's Securities
303. Management's Discussion and Analysis of Financial Conditions and Results of Operations
304. Changes in and Disagreements With Accountants on Accounting and Financial Disclosure
305. Quantitative and Qualitative Disclosures About Market Risk
306. Audit Committee Report
307. Disclosure Controls and Procedures
308. Internal Control Over Financial Reporting
401. Directors, Executive Officers, Promoters and Control Persons
402. Executive Compensation
403. Security Ownership of Certain Beneficial Owners and Management
404. Certain Relationships and Related Transactions
405. Compliance With Section 16(a) of the Exchange Act
406. Code of Ethics
501. Forepart of Registration Statement and Outside Front Cover Page of Prospectus
502. Inside Front and Outside Back Cover Pages of Prospectus
503. Prospectus Summary, Risk Factors, and Ratio of Earnings to Fixed Charges
504. Use of Proceeds
505. Determination of Offering Price
506. Dilution
507. Selling Security Holders
508. Plan of Distribution
509. Interests of Named Experts and Counsel

REGULATION M–A—MERGERS AND ACQUISITIONS

REGULATION S–T—GENERAL RULES AND REGULATIONS FOR ELECTRONIC FILINGS

FORMS UNDER THE SECURITIES ACT OF 1933

SECURITIES ACT OF 1933

GENERAL RULES AND REGULATIONS

GENERAL

ATTENTION ELECTRONIC FILERS

THIS REGULATION SHOULD BE READ IN CONJUNCTION WITH REGULATION S–T (PART 232 OF THIS CHAPTER), WHICH GOVERNS THE PREPARATION AND SUBMISSION OF DOCUMENTS IN ELECTRONIC FORMAT. MANY PROVISIONS RELATING TO THE PREPARATION AND SUBMISSION OF DOCUMENTS IN PAPER FORMAT CONTAINED IN THIS REGULATION ARE SUPERSEDED BY THE PROVISIONS OF REGULATION S–T FOR DOCUMENTS REQUIRED TO BE FILED IN ELECTRONIC FORMAT

Rule 100. Definitions of Terms Used in the Rules and Regulations

(a) As used in the rules and regulations prescribed by the Securities and Exchange Commission pursuant to the Securities Act of 1933, unless the context otherwise requires—

(1) The term "Commission" means the Securities and Exchange Commission.

(2) The term "Act" means the Securities Act of 1933.

(3) The term "rules and regulations" refers to all rules and regulations adopted by the Commission pursuant to the Act, including the forms and accompanying instructions thereto.

(4) The term "registrant" means the issuer of securities for which a registration statement is filed.

(5) The term "agent for service" means the person authorized in the registration statement to receive notices and communications from the Commission.

(6) The term "electronic filer" means a person or an entity that submits filings electronically pursuant to Rules 101, 901, 902 or 903 of Regulation S–T (§§ 232.101, 232.901, 232.902 or 232.903 of this chapter, respectively).

(7) The term "electronic filing" means a document under the federal securities laws that is transmitted or delivered to the Commission in electronic format.

(b) Unless otherwise specifically provided, the terms used in the rules and regulations shall have the meanings defined in the Act.

(c) A rule in the General Rules and Regulations which defines a term without express reference to the Act or to the rules and regulations or to a portion thereof defines such terms for all purposes as used both in the Act and in the rules and regulations, unless the context otherwise requires.

Rule 110. Business Hours of the Commission

(a) *General.* The principal office of the Commission, at 450 Fifth Street, N.W., Washington, D.C. 20549, is open each day, except Saturdays, Sundays and Federal Holidays, from 9:00 a.m. to 5:30 p.m., Eastern Standard Time or Eastern Daylight Saving Time, whichever is currently in effect *provided that* hours for the filing of documents pursuant to the Act or the rules and regulations thereunder are as set forth in paragraphs (b), (c) and (d) of this rule.

(b) *Submissions made in paper.* Paper documents filed with or otherwise furnished to the Commission may be submitted each day, except Saturdays, Sundays and federal holidays from 8 a.m. to 5:30 p.m., Eastern Standard Time or Eastern Daylight Saving Time, whichever is currently in effect.

(c) *Filings by direct transmission.* Filings made by direct transmission may be submitted to the Commission each day, except Saturdays, Sundays and federal holidays, from 8 a.m. to 10 p.m., Eastern Standard Time or Eastern Daylight Saving Time, whichever is currently in effect.

(d) *Filings by facsimile.* Registration statements and post-effective amendments thereto filed by facsimile transmission pursuant to Rule 462(b) (§ 230.462(b)) and Rule 455 (§ 230.455) may be filed with the Commission each day, except Saturdays, Sundays and federal holidays, from 5:30 p.m. to 10 p.m., Eastern Standard Time or Eastern Daylight Savings Time, whichever is currently in effect.

Rule 111. Payment of Fees

(a) All payments of fees for registration statements under the Act shall be made in cash or by U.S. postal money order, certified check, bank cashier's check, or bank money order payable to the Securities and Exchange Commission, omitting the name or title of any official of the Commission. In addition, all other filing fees may be paid by personal check. There will be no refunds.

(b) Notwithstanding paragraph (a) of this section, for registration statements filed pursuant to Rule 462(b) (§ 230.462(b)) and Rule 110(d) (§ 230.110(d)), payment of filing fees for the purposes of this section may be made by:

(1) The registrant or its agent instructing its bank or a wire transfer service to transmit to the Commission the applicable filing fee by a wire transfer of such amount from the issuer's account or its agent's account to the Commission's account at Mellon Bank as soon as practicable but no later than the close of the next business day following the filing of the registration statement; and

(2) The registrant submitting with the registration statement at the time of filing a certification that:

(i) The registrant or its agent has so instructed its bank or a wire transfer service;

(ii) The registrant or its agent will not revoke such instructions; and

(iii) The registrant or its agent has sufficient funds in such account to cover the amount of such filing fee.

Note to paragraph (b): Such instructions may be sent on the date of filing the registration statement after the close of business of such bank or wire transfer service, provided that the registrant undertakes in the certification sent to the Commission with the registration statement that it will confirm receipt of such instructions by the bank or wire transfer service during regular business hours on the following business day.

Rule 120. Inspection of Registration Statements

Except for material contracts or portions thereof accorded confidential treatment pursuant to § 230.406, all registration statements are available for public inspection, during business hours, at the principal office of the Commission in Washington, D.C. Electronic registration statements made through the Electronic Data Gathering, Analysis, and Retrieval system are publicly available through the Commission's Web site (http://www.sec.gov).

Rule 122. Nondisclosure of Information Obtained in the Course of Examinations and Investigations

Information or documents obtained by officers or employees of the Commission in the course of any examination or investigation pursuant to section 8(e) or 20(a) shall, unless made a matter of public record, be deemed confidential. Except as provided by 17 CFR 203.2, officers and employees are hereby prohibited from making such confidential information or documents or any other non-public records of the Commission available to anyone other than a member, officer, or employee of the Commission, unless the Commission or the General Counsel, pursuant to delegated authority, authorizes the disclosure of such information or the production of such documents as not being contrary to the public interest. Any officer or employee who is served with a subpoena requiring the disclosure of such information or the production of such documents shall appear in court and, unless the authorization described in the preceding sentence shall have been given, shall respectfully decline to disclose the information or produce the documents called for, basing his or her refusal upon this rule. Any officer or employee who is served with such subpoena shall promptly advise the General Counsel of the service of such subpoena, the nature of the information or documents sought, and any circumstances which may bear upon the desirability of making available such information or documents.

Rule 130. Definition of "Rules and Regulations" as Used in Certain Sections of the Act

The term "rules and regulations" as used in sections 7, 10(a), (c) and (d) and 19(a) of the Act, shall include the forms for registration of securities under the Act and the related instructions thereto.

Rule 131. Definition of Security Issued Under Governmental Obligations

(a) Any part of an obligation evidenced by any bond, note, debenture, or other evidence of indebtedness issued by any governmental unit specified in section 3(a)(2) of the Act which is payable from payments to be made in respect of property or money which is or will be used, under a lease, sale, or loan arrangement, by or for industrial or commercial enterprise, shall be deemed to be a separate "security" within the meaning of section 2(1) of the Act, issued by the lessee or obligor under the lease, sale or loan arrangement.

(b) An obligation shall not be deemed a separate "security" as defined in paragraph (a) hereof if, (1) the obligation is payable from the general revenues of a governmental unit, specified in section 3(a)(2) of the Act, having other resources which may be used for the payment of the obligation, or (2) the obligation relates to a public project or facility owned and operated by or on behalf of and under the control of a governmental unit specified in such section, or (3) the obligation relates to a facility which is leased to and under the control of an industrial or commercial enterprise but is a part of a public project which, as a whole, is owned by and under the general control of a governmental unit specified in such section, or an instrumentality thereof.

(c) This rule shall apply to transactions of the character described in paragraph (a) only with respect to bonds, notes, debentures or other evidences of indebtedness sold after December 31, 1968.

Rule 132. Definition of "Common Trust Fund" as Used in Section 3(a)(2) of the Act

The term "common trust fund" as used in section 3(a)(2) of the Act shall include a common trust fund which is maintained by a bank which is a member of an affiliated group, as defined in section 1504(a) of the Internal Revenue Code of 1954, and which is maintained exclusively for the collective investment and reinvestment of monies contributed thereto by one or more bank members of such affiliated group in the capacity of trustee, executor, administrator, or guardian, provided that:

(a) the common trust fund is operated in compliance with the same state and federal regulatory requirements as would apply if the bank maintaining such fund and any other contributing banks were the same entity; and

(b) the rights of persons for whose benefit a contributing bank acts as trustee, executor, administrator, or guardian would not be diminished by reason of the maintenance of such common trust fund by another bank member of the affiliated group.

Rule 134. Communications Not Deemed a Prospectus

The term "prospectus" as defined in section 2(10) of the Act shall not include a notice, circular, advertisement, letter, or other communication published or transmitted to any person after a registration statement has been filed if it contains only the statements required or permitted to be included therein by the following provisions of this rule:

(a) Such communication may include any one or more of the following items of information, which need not follow the numerical sequence of this paragraph:

(1) The name of the issuer of the security;

(2) The full title of the security and the amount being offered;

(3) A brief indication of the general type of business of the issuer, limited to the following:

(i) In the case of a manufacturing company, the general type of manufacturing and the principal products or classes of the products manufactured;

(ii) In the case of a public utility company the general type of services rendered and a brief indication of the area served;

(iii) In the case of any other type of company, a corresponding statement;

(4) The price of the security, or if the price is not known, the method of its determination or the probable price range as specified by the issuer or the managing underwriter;

(5) In the case of a debt security with a fixed (noncontingent) interest provision, the yield or, if the yield is not known, the probable yield range, as specified by the issuer or the managing underwriter;

(6) The name and address of the sender of the communication and the fact that he is participating, or expects to participate, in the distribution of the security;

(7) The names of the managing underwriters;

(8) The approximate date upon which it is anticipated the proposed sale to the public will commence;

(9) Whether, in the opinion of counsel, the security is a legal investment for savings banks, fiduciaries, insurance companies, or similar investors under the laws of any State or Territory or the District of Columbia;

(10) Whether, in the opinion of counsel, the security is exempt from specified taxes, or the extent to which the issuer has agreed to pay any tax with respect to the security or measured by the income therefrom;

(11) Whether the security is being offered through rights issued to security holders, and, if so, the class of securities the holders of which will be entitled to subscribe, the subscription ratio, the actual or proposed record date, the date upon which the rights were issued or are expected to be issued, the actual or anticipated date upon which they will expire, and approximate subscription price, or any of the foregoing;

(12) Any statement or legend required by any State law or administrative authority.

(13)(i) With respect to any class of debt securities, any class of convertible debt securities or any class of preferred stock, the security rating or ratings assigned to the class of securities by any nationally recognized statistical rating organization and the name or names of the nationally recognized statistical rating organization(s) which assigned such rating(s), and with respect to any class of debt securities, any class of convertible debt securities or any class of preferred stock registered on Form F–9 (§ 239.39 of this chapter), the security rating or ratings assigned to the class of securities by any other rating organization specified in the Instruction to paragraph (a)(2) of General Instruction I of Form F–9 and the name or names of the rating organization or organizations which assigned such rating(s).

(ii) For the purpose of paragraph (a)(13)(i) of this section, the term "nationally recognized statistical rating organization" shall have the same meaning as used in Rule 15c3–1(c)(2)(vi)(F) under the Securities Exchange Act of 1934.

(b) Except as provided in paragraph (c), every communication used pursuant to this rule shall contain the following:

(1) If the registration statement has not yet become effective, the following statement:

> A registration statement relating to these securities has been filed with the Securities and Exchange Commission but has not yet become effective. These securities may not be sold nor may offers to buy be accepted prior to the time the registration statement becomes effective. This (communication) shall not constitute an offer to sell or the solicitation of an offer to buy nor shall there be any sale of these securities in any State in which such offer, solicitation or sale would be unlawful prior to registration or qualification under the securities laws of any such State.

(2) A statement whether the security is being offered in connection with a distribution by the issuer or by a security holder, or both, and whether the issue represents new financing or refunding or both; and

(3) The name and address of a person or persons from whom a written prospectus meeting the requirements of section 10 of the Act may be obtained.

(c) Any of the statements or information specified in paragraph (b) may, but need not, be contained in a communication: (i) which does no more than state from whom a written prospectus meeting the requirements of section 10 of the Act may be obtained, identify the security, state the price thereof and state by whom orders will be executed; or (ii) which is accompanied or preceded by a prospectus or a summary prospectus which meets the requirements of section 10 of the Act at the date of such preliminary communication.

(d) A communication sent or delivered to any person pursuant to this rule which is accompanied or preceded by a prospectus which meets the requirements of section 10 of the Act at the date of such communication, may solicit from the recipient of the communication an offer to buy the security or request the recipient to indicate, upon an enclosed or attached coupon or card, or in some other manner, whether he might be interested in the security, if the communication contains substantially the following statement:

> No offer to buy the securities can be accepted and no part of the purchase price can be received until the registration statement has become effective, and any such offer may be withdrawn or revoked, without obligation or commitment of any kind, at any time prior to notice of its acceptance given after the effective date. An indication of interest in response to this advertisement will involve no obligation or commitment of any kind.

Provided, That such such statement need not be included in such a communication to a dealer if the communication refers to a prior communication to the dealer, with respect to the same security, in which the statement was included.

(e) This § 230.134 does not apply to a notice, circular, advertisement, letter, or other communication relating to an investment company registered under the Investment Company Act of 1940 (15 U.S.C. 80a–1 *et seq.*) or a business development company as defined in section 2(a)(48) of the Investment Company Act (15 U.S.C. 80a–2(a)(48)).

Rule 134a. Options Material Not Deemed a Prospectus

Written materials, including advertisements, relating to standardized options, as that term is defined in Rule 9b–1 under the Securities Exchange Act of 1934, shall not be deemed to be a prospectus for the purposes of Section 2(10) of the Securities Act of 1933: *Provided,* That such materials are limited to explanatory information describing the general nature of the standardized options markets or one or more strategies: *And, Provided further,* That:

(a) The potential risks related to options trading generally and to each strategy addressed are explained;

(b) No past or projected performance figures, including annualized rates of return are used;

(c) No recommendation to purchase or sell any option contract is made;

(d) No specific security is identified other than:

(1) An option or other security exempt from registration under the Act, or

(2) An index option, including the component securities of the index; and

(e) If there is a definitive options disclosure document, as defined in Rule 9b–1 under the Securities Exchange Act of 1934, the materials shall contain the name and address of a person or persons from whom a copy of such document may be obtained.

Rule 134b. Statements of Additional Information

For the purpose only of Section 5(b) of the Act (15 U.S.C. 77e(b)), the term "prospectus" as defined in Section 2(a)(10) of the Act (15 U.S.C. 77b(a)(10)) does not include a Statement of Additional Information filed as part of a registration statement on Form N–1A (§ 239.15A and § 274.11A of this chapter), Form N–2 (§ 239.14 and § 274.11a–1 of this chapter), Form N–3 (§ 239.17a and § 274.11b of this chapter), Form N–4 (§ 239.17b and 274.11c of this chapter), or Form N–6 (§ 239.17c and § 274.11d of this chapter) transmitted prior to the effective date of the registration statement if it is accompanied or preceded by a preliminary prospectus meeting the requirements of § 230.430.

Rule 135. Notice of Proposed Registered Offerings

(a) *When notice is not an offer.* For purposes of section 5 of the Act (15 U.S.C. 77e) only, an issuer or a selling security holder (and any person acting on behalf of either of them) that publishes through any medium a notice of a proposed offering to be registered under the Act will not be deemed to offer its securities for sale through that notice if:

(1) *Legend.* The notice includes a statement to the effect that it does not constitute an offer of any securities for sale; and

(2) *Limited notice content.* The notice otherwise includes no more than the following information:

(i) The name of the issuer;

(ii) The title, amount and basic terms of the securities offered;

(iii) The amount of the offering, if any, to be made by selling security holders;

(iv) The anticipated timing of the offering;

(v) A brief statement of the manner and the purpose of the offering, without naming the underwriters;

(vi) Whether the issuer is directing its offering to only a particular class of purchasers;

(vii) Any statements or legends required by the laws of any state or foreign country or administrative authority; and

(viii) In the following offerings, the notice may contain additional information, as follows:

(A) *Rights offering.* In a rights offering to existing security holders:

(1) The class of security holders eligible to subscribe;

(2) The subscription ratio and expected subscription price;

(3) The proposed record date;

(4) The anticipated issuance date of the rights; and

(5) The subscription period or expiration date of the rights offering.

(B) *Offering to employees*. In an offering to employees of the issuer or an affiliated company:

(1) The name of the employer;

(2) The class of employees being offered the securities;

(3) The offering price; and

(4) The duration of the offering period.

(C) *Exchange offer*. In an exchange offer:

(1) The basic terms of the exchange offer;

(2) The name of the subject company;

(3) The subject class of securities sought in the exchange offer.

(D) *Rule 145(a) offering*. In a § 230.145(a) offering:

(1) The name of the person whose assets are to be sold in exchange for the securities to be offered;

(2) The names of any other parties to the transaction;

(3) A brief description of the business of the parties to the transaction;

(4) The date, time and place of the meeting of security holders to vote on or consent to the transaction; and

(5) A brief description of the transaction and the basic terms of the transaction.

(b) *Corrections of misstatements about the offering*. A person that publishes a notice in reliance on this section may issue a notice that contains no more information than is necessary to correct inaccuracies published about the proposed offering.

NOTE to § 230.135: Communications under this section relating to business combination transactions must be filed as required by § 230.425(b).

Rule 135a. Generic Advertising

(a) For the purposes only of section 5 of the Act, a notice, circular, advertisement, letter, sign, or other communication, published or transmitted to any person which does not specifically refer by name to the securities of a particular investment company, to the investment company itself, or to any other securities not exempt under section 3(a) of the Act, will not be deemed to offer any security for sale, provided:

(1) Such communication is limited to any one or more of the following:

(i) Explanatory information relating to securities of investment companies generally or to the nature of investment companies, or to services offered in connection with the ownership of such securities,

(ii) The mention or explanation of investment companies of different generic types or having various investment objectives, such as "balanced funds," "growth funds," "income funds," "leveraged funds," "specialty funds," "variable annuities," "bond funds," and "no-load funds,"

(iii) Offers, descriptions, and explanations of various products and services not constituting a security subject to registration under the Act: *Provided,* That such offers, descriptions, and explanations do not relate directly to the desirability of owning or purchasing a security issued by a registered investment company,

(iv) Invitation to inquire for further information, and

(2) Such communication contains the name and address of a registered broker or

dealer or other person sponsoring the communication.

(b) If such communication contains a solicitation of inquiries and prospectuses for investment company securities are to be sent or delivered in response to such inquiries, the number of such investment companies and, if applicable, the fact that the sponsor of the communication is the principal underwriter or investment adviser in respect to such investment companies shall be stated.

(c) With respect to any communication describing any type of security, service, or product, the broker, dealer, or other person sponsoring such communication must offer for sale a security, service, or product of the type described in such communication.

Rule 135b. Materials Not Deemed an Offer to Sell or Offer to Buy

Materials meeting the requirements of § 240.9b–1 of this chapter shall not be deemed an offer to sell or offer to buy a security for purposes solely of Section 5 (15 U.S.C. 77e) of the Act, nor shall such materials be deemed a prospectus for purposes of Sections 2(a)(10) and 12(a)(2) (15 U.S.C. 77b(a)(10) and 77l(a)(2)) of the Act, even if such materials are referred to in, deemed to be incorporated by reference into, or otherwise in any manner deemed to be a part of a Form S–20 prospectus.

Rule 135c. Notice of Certain Proposed Unregistered Offerings

(a) For the purposes only of section 5 of the Act, a notice given by an issuer required to file reports pursuant to section 13 or 15(d) of the Securities Exchange Act of 1934 or a foreign issuer that is exempt from registration under the Securities Exchange Act of 1934 pursuant to § 240.12g3–2(b) of this chapter that it proposes to make, is making or has made an offering of securities not registered or required to be registered under the Act shall not be deemed to offer any securities for sale if:

(1) Such notice is not used for the purpose of conditioning the market in the United States for any of the securities offered;

(2) Such notice states that the securities offered will not be or have not been registered under the Act and may not be offered or sold in the United States absent registration or an applicable exemption from registration requirements; and

(3) Such notice contains no more than the following additional information:

(i) The name of the issuer;

(ii) The title, amount and basic terms of the securities offered, the amount of the offering, if any, made by selling security holders, the time of the offering and a brief statement of the manner and purpose of the offering without naming the underwriters;

(iii) In the case of a rights offering to security holders of the issuer, the class of securities the holders of which will be or were entitled to subscribe to the securities offered, the subscription ratio, the record date, the date upon which the rights are proposed to be or were issued, the term or expiration date of the rights and the subscription price, or any of the foregoing;

(iv) In the case of an offering of securities in exchange for other securities of the issuer or of another issuer, the name of the issuer and the title of the securities to be surrendered in exchange for the securities offered, the basis upon which the exchange may be made, or any of the foregoing;

(v) In the case of an offering to employees of the issuer or to employees of any affiliate of the issuer, the name of the employer and class or classes of employees to whom the securities are offered, the offering price or basis of the offering and the period during which the offering is to be or was made or any of the foregoing; and

(vi) Any statement or legend required by State or foreign law or administrative authority.

(b) Any notice contemplated by this section may take the form of a news release or a written communication directed to security holders or employees, as the case may be, or other published statements.

(c) Notwithstanding the provisions of paragraphs (a) and (b) of this section, in the case of a rights offering of a security listed or subject to unlisted trading privileges on a national securities exchange or quoted on the NASDAQ inter-dealer quotation system information with respect to the interest rate, conversion ratio and subscription price may be disseminated through the facilities of the exchange, the consolidated transaction reporting system, the NASDAQ system or the Dow Jones broad tape, provided such information is already disclosed in a Form 8–K (§ 249.308 of this chapter) on file with the Commission, in a Form 6–K (§ 249.306 of this chapter) furnished to the Commission or, in the case of an issuer relying on § 240.12g3–2(b) of this chapter, in a submission made pursuant to that Section to the Commission.

(d) The issuer shall file any notice contemplated by this section with the Commission under cover of Form 8–K (§ 249.308 of this chapter) or furnish such notice under Form 6–K (§ 249.306 of this chapter), as applicable, and, if relying on § 240.12g3–2(b) of this chapter, shall furnish such notice to the Commission in accordance with the provisions of that exemptive Section.

Rule 135e. Offshore Press Conferences, Meetings with Issuer Representatives Conducted Offshore, and Press-Related Materials Released Offshore

(a) For the purposes only of Section 5 of the Act [15 U.S.C. 77e], an issuer that is a foreign private issuer (as defined in § 230.405) or a foreign government issuer, a selling security holder of the securities of such issuers, or their representatives will not be deemed to offer any security for sale by virtue of providing any journalist with access to its press conferences held outside of the United States, to meetings with issuer or selling security holder representatives conducted outside of the United States, or to written press-related materials released outside the United States, at or in which a present or proposed offering of securities is discussed, if:

(1) The present or proposed offering is not being, or to be, conducted solely in the United States;

NOTE to Paragraph (a)(1): An offering will be considered not to be made solely in the United States under this paragraph (a)(1) only if there is an intent to make a bona fide offering offshore.

(2) Access is provided to both U.S. and foreign journalists; and

(3) Any written press-related materials pertaining to transactions in which any of the securities will be or are being offered in the United States satisfy the requirements of paragraph (b) of this section.

(b) Any written press-related materials specified in paragraph (a)(3) of this section must:

(1) State that the written press-related materials are not an offer of securities for sale in the United States, that securities may not be offered or sold in the United States absent registration or an exemption from registration, that any public offering of securities to be made in the United States will be made by means of a prospectus that may be obtained from the issuer or the selling security holder and that will contain detailed information about the company and management, as well as financial statements;

(2) If the issuer or selling security holder intends to register any part of the present or proposed offering in the United States, include a statement regarding this intention; and

(3) Not include any purchase order, or coupon that could be returned indicating interest in the offering, as part of, or at-

tached to, the written press-related materials.

(c) For the purposes of this section, "United States" means the United States of America, its territories and possessions, any State of the United States, and the District of Columbia.

Rule 136. Definition of Certain Terms in Relation to Assessable Stock

(a) An "offer," "offer to sell" or "offer for sale" of securities shall be deemed to be made to the holders of assessable stock of a corporation when such corporation shall give notice of an assessment to the holders of such assessable stock. A "sale" shall be deemed to occur when a stockholder shall pay or agree to pay all or any part of such an assessment.

(b) The term "transactions by any person other than an issuer, underwriter or dealer" in section 4(1) of the Act shall not be deemed to include the offering or sale of assessable stock, at public auction or otherwise, upon the failure of the holder of such stock to pay an assessment levied thereon by the issuer, where the offer or sale is made for the purpose of realizing the amount of the assessment and any of the proceeds of such sale are to be received by the issuer. However, any person whose functions are limited to acting as auctioneer at such an auction sale shall not be deemed to be an underwriter of the securities offered or sold at the auction sale. Any person who acquires assessable stock at any such public auction or other sale with a view to the distribution thereof shall be deemed to be an underwriter of such assessable stock.

(c) The term "assessable stock" means stock which is subject to resale by the issuer pursuant to statute or otherwise in the event of a failure of the holder of such stock to pay any assessment levied thereon.

Rule 137. Definition of "Offers", "Participates", or "Participation" in Section 2(11) in Relation to Certain Publications by Persons Independent of Participants in a Distribution

The terms "offers," "participates," or "participation" in section 2(11) of the Act shall not be deemed to apply to the publication or distribution of information, opinions or recommendations with respect to the securities of a registrant which is required to file reports pursuant to section 13 or 15(d) of the Securities Exchange Act of 1934 and proposes to file, has filed or has an effective registration statement under the Securities Act of 1933 if—

(a) Such information, opinions, and recommendations are published and distributed in the regular course of its business by a broker or dealer which is not and does not propose to be a participant in the distribution of the security to which the registration statement relates; and

(b) Such broker or dealer receives no consideration, directly or indirectly, in connection with the publication and distribution of such information, opinions or recommendations from the registrant, a selling security holder or any participant in the distribution or any other person interested in the securities to which the registration statement relates, and such information, opinions or recommendations are not published or distributed pursuant to any arrangement or understanding, direct or indirect, with such registrant, underwriter, dealer, or selling security holder; *Provided, however,* That nothing herein shall forbid payment of the regular subscription or purchase price of the document or other written communication in which such information, opinions or recommendations appear.

Rule 138. Definition of "Offer for Sale" and "Offer to Sell" in Sections 2(10) and 5(c) in Relation to Certain Publications

(a) Where a registrant which meets the requirements of paragraph (c)(1), (c)(2) or (c)(3) of this section proposes to file, has filed or has an effective registration statement under the Act relating solely to a nonconvertible debt security or to a nonconvertible, nonparticipating preferred stock, publication or distribution in the regular course of its business by a broker or dealer of information, opinions or recommendations relating solely to common stock or to debt or preferred stock convertible into common stock of such registrant shall not be deemed to constitute an offer for sale or offer to sell the security to which such registration statement relates for purposes of sections 2(10) and 5(c) of the Act (15 U.S.C. 77a *et seq.*) even though such broker or dealer is or will be a participant in the distribution of the security to which such registration statement relates.

(b) Where a registrant which meets the requirements of paragraph (c)(1), (c)(2) or (c)(3) of this section proposes to file, has filed or has an effective registration statement under the Act relating solely to common stock or to debt or preferred stock convertible into common stock, the publication or distribution in the regular course of its business by a broker or dealer of information, opinions or recommendations relating solely to a nonconvertible debt security, or to a nonconvertible nonparticipating preferred stock shall not be deemed to constitute an offer for sale or offer to sell the security to which such registration statement relates for purposes of sections 2(10) and 5(c) of the Act (15 U.S.C. 77a *et seq.*), even though such broker or dealer is or will be a participant in the distribution of the security to which such registration statement relates.

(c)(1) The registrant meets all of the conditions for the use of Form S–2 [§ 239.12 of this chapter] or Form F–2 [§ 239.32 of this chapter];

(2) The registrant meets the registrant requirements of Form S–3 [§ 239.13 of this chapter] or Form F–3 [§ 239.33 of this chapter]; or

(3) The registrant is a foreign private issuer which meets all the registrant requirements of Form F–3 [§ 239.33 of this chapter], other than the reporting history provisions of paragraph A.1. and A.2.(a) of General Instruction I of such form, and meets the minimum float or investment grade securities provisions of either paragraph B.1. or B.2. of General Instruction I. of such form and the registrant's securities have been traded for a period of at least 12 months on a designated offshore securities market, as defined in § 230.902(a).

Instruction to Rule 138.

When a registration statement relates to securities which are being registered for an offering to be made on a continuous or delayed basis pursuant to Rule 415(a)(1)(x) under the Act (§ 230.415(a)(1)(x)) and the securities which are being registered include classes of securities which are specified in both paragraphs (a) and (b) of this section on either an allocated or unallocated basis, a broker or dealer may nonetheless rely on:

1. Paragraph (a) of this section when the offering in which such broker or dealer is or will be a participant relates solely to classes of securities specified in paragraph (a) of this section, and

2. Paragraph (b) of this section when the offering in which such broker or dealer is or will be a participant relates solely to classes of securities specified in paragraph (b) of this section.

Rule 139. Definition of "Offer for Sale" and "Offer to Sell" in Sections 2(10) and 5(c) in Relation to Certain Publications

Where a registrant which is required to file reports pursuant to section 13 or 15(d) of the Securities Exchange Act of 1934 (15 U.S.C. 78a *et seq.*) or which is a foreign private issuer meeting the conditions of paragraph (a)(2) of this section proposes to file, has filed or has an effective registration statement under the Securities Act of 1933 (15 U.S.C. 77a *et seq.*) relating to its securities, the publication or distribution by a broker or dealer of information, an opinion or a recommendation with respect to the registrant or any class of its securities shall not be deemed to constitute an offer for sale or offer to sell the securities registered or proposed to be registered for purposes of sections 2(10) and 5(c) of the Act (15 U.S.C. 77a *et seq.*), even though such broker or dealer is or will be a participant in the distribution of such securities, if the conditions of paragraph (a) or (b) of this section have been met:

(a)(1) The registrant meets the registrant requirements of Form S–3 or Form F–3 and the minimum float or investment grade securities provisions of either paragraph (B)(1) or (2) of General Instruction I of the respective form and such information, opinion or recommendation is contained in a publication which is distributed with reasonable regularity in the normal course of business; or

(2) The registrant is a foreign private issuer that meets all the registrant requirements of Form F–3 (§ 239.33 of this chapter), other than the reporting history provisions of paragraphs A.1. and A.2.(a) of General Instruction I of such form, and meets the minimum float or investment grade securities provisions of either paragraph B.1. or B.2. of General Instruction I of such form, and the registrant's securities have been traded for a period of at least 12 months on a designated offshore securities market, as defined in § 230.902(a), and such information, opinion or recommendation is contained in a publication which is distributed with reasonable regularity in the normal course of business.

(b)(1) Such information, opinion or recommendation is contained in a publication which:

(i) Is distributed with reasonable regularity in the normal course of business and

(ii) Includes similar information, opinions or recommendations with respect to a substantial number of companies in the registrant's industry or sub-industry, or contains a comprehensive list of securities currently recommended by such broker or dealer;

(2) Such information, opinion or recommendation is given no materially greater space or prominence in such publication than that given to other securities or registrants; and

(3) An opinion or recommendation as favorable or more favorable as to the registrant or any class of its securities was published by the broker or dealer in the last publication of such broker or dealer addressing the registrant or its securities prior to the commencement of participation in the distribution.

Instructions to Rule 139.

1. For purposes of paragraph (a), a research report has not been distributed with "reasonable regularity" if it contains information, an opinion, or a recommendation concerning a company with respect to which a broker or dealer currently is not publishing research.

2. Where projections of a registrants sales or earnings are included, the publication must comply with the following in order to meet paragraphs (b)(1) and (b)(3).

A. The projections must have been published previously on a regular basis in order for the publication to meet paragraph (b)(1)(i);

B. The projections must be included with respect to either a substantial number of companies in the registrant's industry or sub-industry or all companies in a comprehensive list which is contained in the publication, and must cover the same periods with respect to such companies as with respect to the registrant, in order to meet the requirements of paragraph (b)(1)(ii); and

C. Because projections constitute opinions within the meaning of the Rule, they must come within paragraph (b)(3).

Rule 139a. Publications by Brokers or Dealers Distributing Asset-Backed Securities.

The publication or distribution by a broker or dealer of information, an opinion or a recommendation with respect to asset-backed securities meeting the criteria of General Instruction I.B.5. of Form S–3 (§ 239.13 of this chapter) ("S–3 ABS") shall not be deemed to constitute an offer for sale or offer to sell S–3 ABS registered or proposed to be registered for purposes of sections 2(a)(10) and 5(c) of the Act (15 U.S.C. 77b(a)(10) and 77e(c)) (the "registered securities"), even if such broker or dealer is or will be a participant in the distribution of the registered securities, if the following conditions are met:

(a) The broker or dealer shall have previously published or distributed with reasonable regularity information, opinions or recommendations relating to S–3 ABS backed directly (or, with respect to securitizations of other securities, indirectly) by substantially similar collateral as that directly or indirectly backing S–3 ABS that is the subject of the information,opinion or recommendation that is proposed to be published to be published or distributed.

(b) If the registered securities are proposed to be offered, offered or part of an unsold allotment or subscription, the information, opinion or recommendation shall not:

(1) Identify the registered securities;

(2) Give greater prominence to specific structural or collateral-related attributes of the registered securities than it gives to the same attributes of other asset-backed securities that it mentions; or

(3) Contain and *ABS informational and computational material* (as defined in § 229.1101 of this chapter) relating to the registered securities.

(c) If the material published by the broker or dealer identifies a specific asset-backed security of a specific issuer and specifically recommends that such asset-backed security by purchased, sold or held by persons receiving such material, then a recommendation as favorable or more favorable as to such asset-backed security shall have been published by the broker or dealer in the last publication of such broker or dealer addressing such asset-backed security prior to the commencement of its participation in the distribution of the registered securities.

(d) Sufficient information is available from one or more public sources to provide a reasonable basis for the view expressed by the broker or dealer with respect to the asset-backed securities that are the subject of the information, opinion or recommendation.

(e) If the material published by the broker or dealer identifies asset-backed securities backed directly or indirectly by substantially similar collateral as that directly or indirectly backing the registered securities and specifically recommends that such asset-backed securities by preferred over other asset-backed securities backed by different types of collateral, then the material shall explain in reasonable detail the reasons for such preference.

Rule 140. Definition of "Distribution" in Section 2(11), for Certain Transactions

A person, the chief part of whose business consists of the purchase of the securities of one issuer, or of two or more affiliated issuers, and the sale of its own securities, including the levying of assessments on its assessable stock and the resale of such stock upon the failure of the holder thereof to pay any assessment levied thereon, to furnish the proceeds with which to acquire the securities of such issuer or affiliated issuers, is to be regarded as engaged in the distribution of the securities of such issuer or affiliated issuers within the meaning of section 2(11) of the Act.

Rule 141. Definition of "Commission From an Underwriter or Dealer Not in Excess of the Usual and Customary Distributors' or Sellers' Commissions" in Section 2(11), for Certain Transactions

(a) The term "commission" in section 2(11) shall include such remuneration, commonly known as a spread, as may be received by a distributor or dealer as a consequence of reselling securities bought from an underwriter or dealer at a price below the offering price of such securities, where such resales afford the distributor or dealer a margin of profit not in excess of what is usual and customary in such transactions.

(b) The term "commission from an underwriter or dealer" in section 2(11) shall include commissions paid by an underwriter or dealer directly or indirectly controlling or controlled by, or under direct or indirect common control with the issuer.

(c) The term "usual and customary distributors' or sellers' commission" in section 2(11) shall mean a commission or remuneration, commonly known as a spread, paid to or received by any person selling securities either for his own account or for the account of others, which is not in excess of the amount usual and customary in the distribution and sale of issues of similar type and size, and not in excess of the amount allowed to other persons, if any, for comparable service in the distribution of the particular issue; but such term shall not include amounts paid to any person whose function is the management of the distribution of all or a substantial part of the particular issue, or who performs the functions normally performed by an underwriter or underwriting syndicate.

Rule 142. Definition of "Participates" and "Participation," as Used in Section 2(11), in Relation to Certain Transactions

(a) The terms "participates" and "participation" in section 2(11) shall not include the interest of a person (1) who is not in privity of contract with the issuer nor directly or indirectly controlling, controlled by, or under common control with, the issuer, and (2) who has no association with any principal underwriter of the securities being distributed, and (3) whose function in the distribution is confined to an undertaking to purchase all or some specified proportion of the securities remaining unsold after the lapse of some specified period of time, and (4) who purchases such securities for investment and not with a view to distribution.

(b) As used in this rule—

(1) The term "issuer" shall have the meaning defined in section 2(4) and in the last sentence of section 2(11).

(2) The term "association" shall include a relationship between two persons under which one—

(A) Is directly or indirectly controlling, controlled by, or under common control with, the other, or

(B) Has, in common with the other, one or more partners, officers, directors, trustees, branch managers, or other persons occupying a similar status or performing similar functions, or

(C) Has a participation, direct or indirect, in the profits of the other, or has a financial stake, by debtor-creditor relationship, stock ownership, contract or otherwise, in the income or business of the other.

(3) The term "principal underwriter" shall have the meaning defined in Rule 405.

Rule 143. Definition of "Has Purchased," "Sells for," "Participates," and "Participation," as Used in Section 2(11), in Relation to Certain Transactions of Foreign Governments for War Purposes

The terms "has purchased," "sells for," "participates," and "participation," in section 2(11), shall not be deemed to apply to any action of a foreign government in acquiring, for war purposes and by or in anticipation of the exercise of war powers, from any person subject to its jurisdiction securities of a person organized under the laws of the United States or any State or Territory, or in disposing of such securities with a view to their distribution by underwriters in the United States, notwithstanding the fact that the price to be paid to such foreign government upon the disposition of such securities by it may be measured by or may be in direct or indirect relation to such price as may be realized by the underwriters.

Rule 144. Persons Deemed Not to Be Engaged in a Distribution and Therefore Not Underwriters

Preliminary Note to Rule 144

Rule 144 is designed to implement the fundamental purposes of the Act, as expressed in its preamble, "To provide full and fair disclosure of the character of the securities sold in interstate commerce and through the mails, and to prevent fraud in the sale thereof . . ." The rule is designed to prohibit the creation of public markets in securities of issuers concerning which adequate current information is not available to the public. At the same time, where adequate current information concerning the issuer is available to the public, the rule permits the public sale in ordinary trading transactions of limited amounts of securities owned by persons controlling, controlled by or under common control with the issuer and by persons who have acquired restricted securities of the issuer.

Certain basic principles are essential to an understanding of the requirement of registration in the Act:

1. If any person utilizes the jurisdictional means to sell any non-exempt security to any other person, the security must be registered unless a statutory exemption can be found for the transaction.

2. In addition to the exemptions found in Section 3, four exemptions applicable to transactions in securities are contained in Section 4. Three of these Section 4 exemptions are clearly not available to anyone acting as an "underwriter" of securities. (The fourth, found in Section 4(4), is available only to those who act as brokers under certain limited circumstances.) An understanding of the term "underwriter" is therefore important to anyone who wishes to determine whether or not an exemption from registration is available for his sale of securities.

The term underwriter is broadly defined in Section 2(11) of the Act to mean any person who has purchased from an issuer with a view to, or offers or sells for an issuer in connection with, the distribution of any security, or participates or has a direct or indirect participation in any such undertaking, or participates or has a participation in the direct or indirect underwriting of any such undertaking. The interpretation of this definition has traditionally focused on the words "with a view to" in the phrase "purchased from an issuer with a view to . . . distribution." Thus, an investment banking firm which arranges with an issuer for the public sale of its securities is clearly an "underwriter" under that Section. Individual investors who are not professionals in the securities business may also be "underwriters" within the meaning of that term as used in the Act if they act as links in a chain of transactions through which securities move from an issuer to the public. Since it is difficult to ascertain the mental state of the purchaser at the time of his acquisition, subsequent acts and circumstances have been considered to determine whether such person took with a view to distribution at the time of his acquisition. Emphasis has been placed on factors such as the length of time the person has held the securities and whether there has been an unforeseeable change in circumstances of the holder. Experience has shown, however, that reliance upon such factors as the above has not assured adequate protection of investors through the maintenance of informed trading markets and has led to uncertainty in the application of the registration provisions of the Act.

It should be noted that the statutory language of Section 2(11) is in the disjunctive. Thus, it is insufficient to conclude that a person is not an underwriter solely because he did not purchase securities from an issuer with a view to their distribution. It must also be established that the person is not offering or selling for an issuer in connection with the distribution of the securities, does not participate or have a direct or indirect participation in any such undertaking, and does not participate or have a participation in the direct or indirect underwriting of such an undertaking.

In determining when a person is deemed not to be engaged in a distribution several factors must be considered.

First, the purpose and underlying policy of the Act to protect investors requires that there be adequate current information concerning the issuer, whether the resales of securities by persons result in a distribution or are effected in trading transactions. Accordingly, the availability of the rule is conditioned on the existence of adequate current public information.

Secondly, a holding period prior to resale is essential, among other reasons, to assure that those persons who buy under a claim of a Section 4(2) exemption have assumed the economic risks of investment, and therefore are not acting as conduits for sale to the public of unregistered securities, directly or indirectly, on behalf of an issuer. It should be noted that there is nothing in Section 2(11) which places a time limit on a person's status as an underwriter. The public has the same need for protection afforded by registration whether the securities are distributed shortly after their purchase or after a considerable length of time.

A third factor, which must be considered in determining what is deemed not to constitute a "distribution", is the impact of the particular transaction or transactions on the trading markets. Section 4(1) was intended to exempt only routine trading transactions between individual investors with respect to securities already issued and not to exempt distributions by issuers or acts of other individuals who engage in steps necessary to such distributions. Therefore, a person reselling securities under Section 4(1) of the Act must sell the securities in such limited quantities and in such a manner as not to disrupt the trading markets. The larger the amount of securities involved, the more likely it is that such resales may involve methods of offering and amounts of compensation usually associated with a distribution rather than routine trading transactions. Thus, solicitation of buy orders or the payment of extra compensation are not permitted by the rule.

In summary, if the sale in question is made in accordance with all of the provisions of the rule, as set forth below, any person who sells restricted securities shall be deemed not to be engaged in a distribution of such securities and therefore not an underwriter thereof. The rule also provides that any person who sells restricted or other securities on behalf of a person in a control relationship with the issuer shall be deemed not to be engaged in a distribution of such securities and therefore not to be an underwriter thereof, if the sale is made in accordance with *all* the conditions of the rule.

(a) *Definitions.* The following definitions shall apply for the purposes of this rule.

(1) An "affiliate" of an issuer is a person that directly, or indirectly through one or more intermediaries, controls, or is controlled by, or is under common control with, such issuer.

(2) The term "person" when used with reference to a person for whose account securities are to be sold in reliance upon this rule includes, in addition to such person, all of the following persons:

(i) Any relative or spouse of such person, or any relative of such spouse, any one of whom has the same home as such person;

(ii) Any trust or estate in which such person or any of the persons specified in (a)(2)(i) collectively own ten percent or more of the total beneficial interest or of which any of such persons serve as trustee, executor or in any similar capacity; and

(iii) Any corporation or other organization (other than the issuer) in which such person or any of the persons specified in paragraph (a)(2)(i) of this rule are the beneficial owners collectively of ten percent or more of any class of equity securities or ten percent or more of the equity interest.

(3) The term "restricted securities" means:

(i) Securities acquired directly or indirectly from the issuer, or from an affiliate of the issuer, in a transaction or chain of transactions not involving any public offering;

(ii) Securities acquired from the issuer that are subject to the resale limitations of § 230.502(d) under Regulation D or § 230.701(c);

(iii) Securities acquired in a transaction or chain of transactions meeting the requirements of § 230.144A;

(iv) Securities acquired from the issuer in a transaction subject to the conditions of Regulation CE (§ 230.1001);

(v) Equity securities of domestic issuers acquired in a transaction or chain of transactions subject to the conditions of § 230.901 or § 230.903 under Regulation S (§ 230.901 through § 230.905, and Preliminary Notes);

(vi) Securities acquired in a transaction made under § 230.801 to the same extent and proportion that the securities held by the security holder of the class with respect to which the rights offering was made were as of the record date for the rights offering "restricted securities" within the meaning of this paragraph (a)(3); and

(vii) Securities acquired in a transaction made under § 230.802 to the same extent and proportion that the securities that were tendered or exchanged in the exchange offer or business combination were "restricted securities" within the meaning of this paragraph (a)(3).

(b) *Conditions to Be Met.* Any affiliate or other person who sells restricted securities of an issuer for his own account, or any person who sells restricted or any other securities for the account of an affiliate of the issuer of such securities, shall be deemed not to be engaged in a distribution of such securities and therefore not to be an underwriter thereof within the meaning of Section 2(11) of the Act if all of the conditions of this rule are met.

(c) *Current Public Information.* There shall be available adequate current public information with respect to the issuer of the securities. Such information shall be deemed to be available only if either of the following conditions is met:

(1) *Filing of Reports.* The issuer has securities registered pursuant to section 12 of the Securities Exchange Act of 1934, has been subject to the reporting requirements of section 13 of that Act for a period of at least 90 days immediately preceding the sale of the securities and has filed all the reports required to be filed thereunder during the 12 months preceding such sale (or for such shorter period that the issuer was required to file such reports); other than Form 8–K reports (§ 249.308 of this chapter); or has securities registered pursuant to the Securities Act of 1933, has been subject to the reporting requirements of section 15(d) of the Securities Exchange Act of 1934 for a period of at least 90 days immediately preceding the sale of the securities and has filed all the reports required to be filed thereunder during the 12 months preceding such sale (or for such shorter period that the issuer was required to file such reports), other than Form 8–K reports (§ 249.308 of this chapter). The person for whose account the securities are to be sold shall be entitled to rely upon a statement in whichever is the most recent report, quarterly or annual, required to be filed and filed by the issuer that such issuer has filed all reports required to be filed by section 13 or 15(d) of

the Securities Exchange Act of 1934 during the preceding 12 months (or for such shorter period that the issuer was required to file such reports), other than Form 8–K reports (§ 249.308 of this chapter), and has been subject to such filing requirements for the past 90 days, unless he knows or has reason to believe that the issuer has not complied with such requirements. Such person shall also be entitled to rely upon a written statement from the issuer that it has complied with such reporting requirements unless he knows or has reason to believe that the issuer has not complied with such requirements.

(2) *Other public information.* If the issuer is not subject to section 13 or 15(d) of the Securities Exchange Act of 1934, there is publicly available the information concerning the issuer specified in paragraphs (a)(5)(i) to (xiv), inclusive, and paragraph (a)(5)(xvi) of Rule 15c2–11 under that Act or, if the issuer is an insurance company, the information specified in section 12(g)(2)(G)(i) of that Act.

(d) *Holding Period for Restricted Securities.* If the securities sold are restricted securities, the following provisions apply:

(1) *General rule.* A minimum of one year must elapse between the later of the date of the acquisition of the securities from the issuer or from an affiliate of the issuer, and any resale of such securities in reliance on this section for the account of either the acquiror or any subsequent holder of those securities. If the acquiror takes the securities by purchase, the one-year period shall not begin until the full purchase price or other consideration is paid or given by the person acquiring the securities from the issuer or from an affiliate of the issuer.

(2) *Promissory Notes, Other Obligations or Installment Contracts.* Giving the seller from whom the securities were purchased a promissory note or other obligation to pay the purchase price, or entering into an installment purchase contract with such seller, shall not be deemed full payment of the purchase price unless the promissory note, obligation or contract:

(i) provides for full recourse against the purchaser of the securities;

(ii) is secured by collateral, other than the securities purchased, having a fair market value at least equal to the purchase price of the securities purchased; and

(iii) shall have been discharged by payment in full prior to the sale of the securities.

(3) *Determination of Holding Period.* The following provisions shall apply for the purpose of determining the period securities have been held:

(i) *Stock Dividends, Splits and Recapitalizations.* Securities acquired from the issuer as a dividend or pursuant to a stock split, reverse split or recapitalization shall be deemed to have been acquired at the same time as the securities on which the dividend or, if more than one, the initial dividend was paid, the securities involved in the split or reverse split, or the securities surrendered in connection with the recapitalization;

(ii) *Conversions.* If the securities sold were acquired from the issuer for a consideration consisting solely of other securities of the same issuer surrendered for conversion, the securities so acquired shall be deemed to have been acquired at the same time as the securities surrendered for conversion;

(iii) *Contingent Issuance of Securities.* Securities acquired as a contingent payment of the purchase price of an equity interest in a business, or the assets of a business, sold to the issuer or an affiliate of the issuer shall be deemed to have been acquired at the time of such sale if the issuer or affiliate was then committed to issue the securities subject only to conditions other than the payment of further consideration for such securities. An agreement entered into in connection with any such purchase to remain in the employment of, or not to compete with, the issuer or affiliate or the rendering of services pursuant to such agreement shall not be deemed to be the payment of further consideration for such securities.

(iv) *Pledged Securities.* Securities which are bona fide pledged by an affiliate of the issuer when sold by the pledgee, or by a purchaser, after a default in the obligation secured by the pledge, shall be deemed to have been acquired when they were acquired by the pledgor, except that if the securities were pledged without recourse they shall be deemed to have been acquired by the pledgee at the time of the pledge or by the purchaser at the time of purchase.

(v) *Gifts of Securities.* Securities acquired from an affiliate of the issuer, by gift shall be deemed to have been acquired by the donee when they were acquired by the donor;

(vi) *Trusts.* Where a trust settlor is an affiliate of the issuer, securities acquired from the settlor by the trust, or acquired from the trust by the beneficiaries thereof, shall be deemed to have been acquired when they were acquired by the settlor;

(vii) *Estates.* Where a deceased person was an affiliate of the issuer, securities held by the estate of such person or acquired from such estate by the beneficiaries thereof shall be deemed to have been acquired when they were acquired by the deceased person, except that no holding period is required if the estate is not an affiliate of the issuer or if the securities are sold by a beneficiary of the estate who is not such an affiliate.

NOTE: While there is no holding period or amount limitation for estates and beneficiaries thereof which are not affiliates of the issuer, paragraphs (c), (h), and (i) of the rule apply to securities sold by such persons in reliance upon the rule.

(viii) *Rule 145(a) transactions.* The holding period for securities acquired in a transaction specified in Rule 145(a) shall be deemed to commence on the date the securities were acquired by the purchaser in such transaction. This provision shall not apply, however, to a transaction effected solely for the purpose of forming a holding company.

(e) *Limitation on Amount of Securities Sold.* Except as hereinafter provided, the amount of securities which may be sold in reliance upon this rule shall be determined as follows:

(1) *Sales by Affiliates.* If restricted or other securities are sold for the account of an affiliate of the issuer, the amount of securities sold, together with all sales of restricted and other securities of the same class for the account of such person within the preceding three months, shall not exceed the greater of (i) one percent of the shares or other units of the class outstanding as shown by the most recent report or statement published by the issuer, or (ii) the average weekly reported volume of trading in such securities on all national securities exchanges and/or reported through the automated quotation system of a registered securities association during the four calendar weeks preceding the filing of notice required by paragraph (h), or if no such notice is required the date of receipt of the order to execute the transaction by the broker or the date of execution of the transaction directly with a market maker, or (iii) the average weekly volume of trading in such securities reported through the consolidated transaction reporting system contemplated by Rule 11Aa3–1 under the Securities Exchange Act of 1934 during the four-week period specified in subdivision (ii) of this paragraph.

(2) *Sales by Persons Other Than Affiliates.* The amount of restricted securities sold for the account of any person other than an affiliate of the issuer, together with

all other sales of restricted securities of the same class for the account of such person within the preceding three months, shall not exceed the amount specified in paragraphs (e)(1)(i), (1)(ii), or (1)(iii) of this rule, whichever is applicable unless the conditions in paragraph (k) of this rule are satisfied.

(3) *Determination of Amount.* For the purpose of determining the amount of securities specified in paragraphs (e)(1) and (2) of this rule, the following provisions shall apply:

(i) Where both convertible securities and securities of the class into which they are convertible are sold, the amount of convertible securities sold shall be deemed to be the amount of securities of the class into which they are convertible for the purpose of determining the aggregate amount of securities of both classes sold;

(ii) The amount of securities sold for the account of a pledgee thereof, or for the account of a purchaser of the pledged securities, during any period of three months within one year after a default in the obligation secured by the pledge, and the amount of securities sold during the same three-month period for the account of the pledgor shall not exceed, in the aggregate, the amount specified in paragraph (e)(1) or (2) of this section, whichever is applicable;

(iii) The amount of securities sold for the account of a donee thereof during any period of three months within one year after the donation, and the amount of securities sold during the same three-month period for the account of the donor, shall not exceed, in the aggregate, the amount specified in paragraph (e)(1) or (2) of this section, whichever is applicable;

(iv) Where securities were acquired by a trust from the settlor of the trust, the amount of such securities sold for the account of the trust during any period of three months within one year after the acquisition of the securities by the trust, and the amount of securities sold during the same three-month period for the account of the settlor, shall not exceed, in the aggregate, the amount specified in paragraph (e)(1) or (2) of this section, whichever is applicable;

(v) The amount of securities sold for the account of the estate of a deceased person, or for the account of a beneficiary of such estate, during any period of three months and the amount of securities sold during the same period for the account of the deceased person prior to his death shall not exceed, in the aggregate, the amount specified in paragraph (e)(1) or (2) of this rule, whichever is applicable; *Provided,* that no limitation on amount shall apply if the estate or beneficiary thereof is not an affiliate of the issuer;

(vi) When two or more affiliates or other persons agree to act in concert for the purpose of selling securities of an issuer, all securities of the same class sold for the account of all such persons during any period of three months shall be aggregated for the purpose of determining the limitation on the amount of securities sold; and

(vii) The following sales of securities need not be included in determining the amount of securities sold in reliance upon this section: securities sold pursuant to an effective registration statement under the Act; securities sold pursuant to an exemption provided by Regulation A (§ 230.251 through § 230.263) under the Act; securities sold in a transaction exempt pursuant to Section 4 of the Act (15 U.S.C. 77d) and not involving any public offering; and securities sold offshore pursuant to Regulation S (§ 230.901 through § 230.905, and Preliminary Notes) under the Act.

(f) *Manner of Sale.* The securities shall be sold in "brokers' transactions" within the meaning of Section 4(4) of the Act or in transactions directly with a "market maker," as that term is defined in Section 3(a)(38) of the

Securities Exchange Act of 1934, and the person selling the securities shall not (1) solicit or arrange for the solicitation of orders to buy the securities in anticipation of or in connection with such transactions, or (2) make any payment in connection with the offer or sale of the securities to any person other than the broker who executes the order to sell the securities. The requirements of this paragraph, however, shall not apply to securities sold for the account of the estate of a deceased person or for the account of a beneficiary of such estate, provided the estate or beneficiary thereof is not an affiliate of the issuer; nor shall they apply to securities sold for the account of any person other than an affiliate of the issuer, provided the conditions of paragraph (k) of this rule are satisfied.

(g) *Brokers' Transactions.* The term "brokers' transactions" in Section 4(4) of the Act shall for the purposes of this rule be deemed to include transactions by a broker in which such broker—

(1) does no more than execute the order or orders to sell the securities as agent for the person for whose account the securities are sold; and receives no more than the usual and customary broker's commission;

(2) neither solicits nor arranges for the solicitation of customers' orders to buy the securities in anticipation of or in connection with the transaction; provided, that the foregoing shall not preclude (i) inquiries by the broker of other brokers or dealers who have indicated an interest in the securities within the preceding 60 days, (ii) inquiries by the broker of his customers who have indicated an unsolicited bona fide interest in the securities within the preceding 10 business days; or (iii) the publication by the broker of bid and ask quotations for the security in an inter-dealer quotation system provided that such quotations are incident to the maintenance of a bona fide inter-dealer market for the security for the broker's own account and that the broker has published bona fide bid and ask quotations for the security in an inter-dealer quotation system on each of at least twelve days within the preceding thirty calendar days with no more than four business days in succession without such two-way quotations;

NOTE to Subparagraph (g)(2)(ii): The broker should obtain and retain in his files written evidence of indications of bona fide unsolicited interest by his customers in the securities at the time such indications are received.

(3) after reasonable inquiry is not aware of circumstances indicating that the person for whose account the securities are sold is an underwriter with respect to the securities or that the transaction is a part of a distribution of securities of the issuer. Without limiting the foregoing, the broker shall be deemed to be aware of any facts or statements contained in the notice required by paragraph (h) below.

NOTES: (i) The broker, for his own protection, should obtain and retain in his files a copy of the notice required by paragraph (h).

(ii) The reasonable inquiry required by paragraph (g)(3) of this rule should include, but not necessarily be limited to, inquiry as to the following matters:

(a) The length of time the securities have been held by the person for whose account they are to be sold. If practicable, the inquiry should include physical inspection of the securities;

(b) The nature of the transaction in which the securities were acquired by such person;

(c) The amount of securities of the same class sold during the past three months by all persons whose sales are required to be taken into consideration pursuant to paragraph (e) of this section;

(d) Whether such person intends to sell additional securities of the same class through any other means;

(e) Whether such person has solicited or made any arrangement for the solicitation of buy orders in connection with the proposed sale of securities;

(f) Whether such person has made any payment to any other person in connection with the proposed sale of the securities; and

(g) The number of shares or other units of the class outstanding, or the relevant trading volume.

(h) *Notice of Proposed Sale.* If the amount of securities to be sold in reliance upon the rule during any period of three months exceeds 500 shares or other units or has an aggregate sale price in excess of $10,000, three copies of a notice on Form 144 shall be filed with the Commission at its principal office in Washington, D.C.; and if such securities are admitted to trading on any national securities exchange, one copy of such notice shall also be transmitted to the principal exchange on which such securities are so admitted. The Form 144 shall be signed by the person for whose account the securities are to be sold and shall be transmitted for filing concurrently with either the placing with a broker of an order to execute a sale of securities in reliance upon this rule or the execution directly with a market maker of such a sale. Neither the filing of such notice nor the failure of the Commission to comment thereon shall be deemed to preclude the Commission from taking any action it deems necessary or appropriate with respect to the sale of the securities referred to in such notice. The requirements of this paragraph, however, shall not apply to securities sold for the account of any person other than an affiliate of the issuer, provided the conditions of paragraph (k) of this rule are satisfied.

(i) *Bona Fide Intention to Sell.* The person filing the notice required by paragraph (h) shall have a bona fide intention to sell the securities referred to therein within a reasonable time after the filing of such notice.

(j) *Non-exclusive Rule.* Although this rule provides a means for reselling restricted securities and securities held by affiliates without registration, it is not the exclusive means for reselling such securities in that manner. Therefore, it does not eliminate or otherwise affect the availability of any exemption for resales under the Securities Act that a person or entity may be able to rely upon.

(k) *Termination of Certain Restrictions on Sales of Restricted Securities by Persons Other Than Affiliates.* The requirements of paragraphs (c), (e), (f) and (h) of this section shall not apply to restricted securities sold for the account of a person who is not an affiliate of the issuer at the time of the sale and has not been an affiliate during the preceding three months, provided a period of at least two years has elapsed since the later of the date the securities were acquired from the issuer or from an affiliate of the issuer. The two-year period shall be calculated as described in paragraph (d) of this section.

Rule 144A. Private Resales of Securities to Institutions

Preliminary Notes

1. This rule relates solely to the application of section 5 of the Act and not to antifraud or other provisions of the federal securities laws.

2. Attempted compliance with this rule does not act as an exclusive election; any seller hereunder may also claim the availability of any other applicable exemption from the registration requirements of the Act.

3. In view of the objective of this rule and the policies underlying the Act, this rule is not available with respect to any transaction or series of transactions that, although in technical compliance with this rule, is part of a plan or scheme to evade the registration provisions of the Act. In such cases, registration under the Act is required.

4. Nothing in this rule obviates the need for any issuer or any other person to comply with the securities registration or broker-dealer registration requirements of the Securities

Exchange Act of 1934 (the "Exchange Act"), whenever such requirements are applicable.

5. Nothing in this rule obviates the need for any person to comply with any applicable state law relating to the offer or sale of securities.

6. Securities acquired in a transaction made pursuant to the provisions of this rule are deemed to be "restricted securities" within the meaning of Rule 144(a)(3).

7. The fact that purchasers of securities from the issuer thereof may purchase such securities with a view to reselling such securities pursuant to this rule will not affect the availability to such issuer of an exemption under section 4(2) of the Act, or Regulation D under the Act, from the registration requirements of the Act.

(a) *Definitions.* (1) For purposes of this rule, "qualified institutional buyer" shall mean:

(i) Any of the following entities, acting for its own account or the accounts of other qualified institutional buyers, that in the aggregate owns and invests on a discretionary basis at least $100 million in securities of issuers that are not affiliated with the entity:

(A) Any *insurance company* as defined in section 2(13) of the Act;

Note: A purchase by an insurance company for one or more of its separate accounts, as defined by section 2(a)(37) of the Investment Company Act of 1940 (the "Investment Company Act"), which are neither registered under section 8 of the Investment Company Act nor required to be so registered, shall be deemed to be a purchase for the account of such insurance company.

(B) Any *investment company* registered under the Investment Company Act or any *business development company* as defined in section 2(a)(48) of that Act;

(C) Any *Small Business Investment Company* licensed by the U.S. Small Business Administration under section 301(c) or (d) of the Small Business Investment Act of 1958;

(D) Any *plan* established and maintained by a state, its political subdivisions, or any agency or instrumentality of a state or its political subdivisions, for the benefit of its employees;

(E) Any *employee benefit plan* within the meaning of title I of the Employee Retirement Income Security Act of 1974;

(F) Any trust fund whose trustee is a bank or trust company and whose participants are exclusively plans of the types identified in paragraph (a)(1)(i)(D) or (E) of this rule, except trust funds that include as participants individual retirement accounts or H.R. 10 plans.

(G) Any *business development company* as defined in section 202(a)(22) of the Investment Advisers Act of 1940;

(H) Any organization described in section 501(c)(3) of the Internal Revenue Code, corporation (other than a bank as defined in section 3(a)(2) of the Act or a savings and loan association or other institution referenced in section 3(a)(5)(A) of the Act or a foreign bank or savings and loan association or equivalent institution), partnership, or Massachusetts or similar business trust; and

(I) Any *investment adviser* registered under the Investment Advisers Act.

(ii) Any *dealer* registered pursuant to section 15 of the Exchange Act, acting for its own account or the accounts of other qualified institutional buyers, that in the aggregate owns and invests on a discretionary basis at least $10 million of securities of issuers that are not affiliated with the dealer, *Provided,* That securities constituting the whole or a part of an unsold allotment to or subscription by a dealer as a participant in a public offering shall not be deemed to be owned by such dealer;

(iii) Any *dealer* registered pursuant to section 15 of the Exchange Act acting in a riskless principal transaction on behalf of a qualified institutional buyer.

NOTE: A registered dealer may act as agent, on a non-discretionary basis, in a transaction with a qualified institutional buyer without itself having to be a qualified institutional buyer.

(iv) Any investment company registered under the Investment Company Act, acting for its own account or for the accounts of other qualified institutional buyers, that is part of a family of investment companies which own in the aggregate at least $100 million in securities of issuers, other than issuers that are affiliated with the investment company or are part of such family of investment companies. "Family of investment companies" means any two or more investment companies registered under the Investment Company Act, except for a unit investment trust whose assets consist solely of shares of one or more registered investment companies, that have the same investment adviser (or, in the case of unit investment trusts, the same depositor), *Provided,* That, for purposes of this section:

(A) Each series of a series company (as defined in Rule 18f–2 under the Investment Company Act shall be deemed to be a separate investment company); and

(B) Investment companies shall be deemed to have the same adviser (or depositor) if their advisers (or depositors) are majority-owned subsidiaries of the same parent, or if one investment company's adviser (or depositor) is a majority-owned subsidiary of the other investment company's adviser (or depositor);

(v) Any entity, all of the equity owners of which are qualified institutional buyers, acting for its own account or the accounts of other qualified institutional buyers; and

(vi) Any *bank* as defined in section 3(a)(2) of the Act, any savings and loan association or other institution as referenced in section 3(a)(5)(A) of the Act, or any foreign bank or savings and loan association or equivalent institution, acting for its own account or the accounts of other qualified institutional buyers, that in the aggregate owns and invests on a discretionary basis at least $100 million in securities of issuers that are not affiliated with it and that has an audited net worth of at least $25 million as demonstrated in its latest annual financial statements, as of a date not more than 16 months preceding the date of sale under the Rule in the case of a U.S. bank or savings and loan association, and not more than 18 months preceding such date of sale for a foreign bank or savings and loan association or equivalent institution.

(2) In determining the aggregate amount of securities owned and invested on a discretionary basis by an entity, the following instruments and interests shall be excluded: bank deposit notes and certificates of deposit; loan participations; repurchase agreements; securities owned but subject to a repurchase agreement, and currency, interest rate and commodity swaps.

(3) The aggregate value of securities owned and invested on a discretionary basis by an entity shall be the cost of such securities, except where the entity reports its securities holdings in its financial statements on the basis of their market value, and no current information with respect to the cost of those securities has been published. In the

latter event, the securities may be valued at market for purposes of this rule.

(4) In determining the aggregate amount of securities owned by an entity and invested on a discretionary basis, securities owned by subsidiaries of the entity that are consolidated with the entity in its financial statements prepared in accordance with generally accepted accounting principles may be included if the investments of such subsidiaries are managed under the direction of the entity, except that, unless the entity is a reporting company under section 13 or 15(d) of the Exchange Act, securities owned by such subsidiaries may not be included if the entity itself is a majority-owned subsidiary that would be included in the consolidated financial statements of another enterprise.

(5) For purposes of this rule, "riskless principle transaction" means a transaction in which a dealer buys a security from any person and makes a simultaneous offsetting sale of such security to a qualified institutional buyer, including another dealer acting as riskless principal for a qualified institutional buyer.

(6) For purposes of this rule, "effective conversion premium" means the amount, expressed as a percentage of the security's conversion value, by which the price at issuance of a convertible security exceeds its conversion value.

(7) For purposes of this rule, "effective exercise premium" means the amount, expressed as a percentage of the warrant's exercise value, by which the sum of the price at issuance and the exercise price of a warrant exceeds its exercise value.

(b) *Sales by persons other than issuers or dealers.* Any person, other than the issuer or a dealer, who offers or sells securities in compliance with the conditions set forth in paragraph (d) of this rule shall be deemed not to be engaged in a distribution of such securities and therefore not to be an underwriter of such securities within the meaning of sections 2(11) and 4(1) of the Act.

(c) *Sales by Dealers.* Any dealer who offers or sells securities in compliance with the conditions set forth in paragraph (d) of this rule shall be deemed not to be a participant in a distribution of such securities within the meaning of section 4(3)(C) of the Act and not to be an underwriter of such securities within the meaning of section 2(11) of the Act, and such securities shall be deemed not to have been offered to the public within the meaning of section 4(3)(A) of the Act.

(d) *Conditions to be met.* To qualify for exemption under this rule, an offer or sale must meet the following conditions:

(1) The securities are offered or sold only to a qualified institutional buyer or to an offeree or purchaser that the seller and any person acting on behalf of the seller reasonably believe is a qualified institutional buyer. In determining whether a prospective purchaser is a qualified institutional buyer, the seller and any person acting on its behalf shall be entitled to rely upon the following non-exclusive methods of establishing the prospective purchaser's ownership and discretionary investments of securities:

(i) The prospective purchaser's most recent publicly available financial statements, *Provided*, That such statements present the information as of a date within 16 months preceding the date of sale of securities under this rule in the case of a U.S. purchaser and within 18 months preceding such date of sale for a foreign purchaser;

(ii) The most recent publicly available information appearing in documents filed by the prospective purchaser with the Commission or another United States federal, state, or local governmental agency or self-regulatory organization, or with a foreign governmental agency or self-regulatory organization, *Provided* That any such information is as of a date within 16 months preceding the date of sale of securities under this rule in the case of a U.S. purchaser and within 18 months preceding such date of sale for a foreign purchaser;

(iii) The most recent publicly available information appearing in a recognized securities manual, *Provided* That such information is as of a date within 16 months preceding the date of sale of securities under this rule in the case of a U.S. purchaser and within 18 months preceding such date of sale for a foreign purchaser; or

(iv) A certification by the chief financial officer, a person fulfilling an equivalent function, or other executive officer of the purchaser, specifying the amount of securities owned and invested on a discretionary basis by the purchaser as of a specific date on or since the close of the purchaser's most recent fiscal year, or, in the case of a purchaser that is a member of a family of investment companies, a certification by an executive officer of the investment adviser specifying the amount of securities owned by the family of investment companies as of a specific date on or since the close of the purchaser's most recent fiscal year;

(2) The seller and any person acting on its behalf takes reasonable steps to ensure that the purchaser is aware that the seller may rely on the exemption from the provisions of section 5 of the Act provided by this rule;

(3) The securities offered or sold:

(i) Were not, when issued, of the same class as securities listed on a national securities exchange registered under section 6 of the Exchange Act or quoted in a U.S. automated inter-dealer quotation system; *Provided,* That securities that are convertible or exchangeable into securities so listed or quoted at the time of issuance and that had an effective conversion premium of less than 10 percent, shall be treated as securities of the class into which they are convertible or exchangeable; and that warrants that may be exercised for securities so listed or quoted at the time of issuance, for a period of less than 3 years from the date of issuance, or that had an effective exercise premium of less than 10 percent, shall be treated as securities of the class to be issued upon exercise; and *Provided further,* That the Commission may from time to time, taking into account then-existing market practices, designate additional securities and classes of securities that will not be deemed of the same class as securities listed on a national securities exchange or quoted in a U.S. automated inter-dealer quotation system; and

(ii) Are not securities of an open-end investment company, unit investment trust or face-amount certificate company that is or is required to be registered under section 8 of the Investment Company Act; and

(4)(i) In the case of securities of an issuer that is neither subject to section 13 or 15(d) of the Exchange Act, nor exempt from reporting pursuant to Rule 12g3–2(b) under the Exchange Act, nor a foreign government as defined in Rule 405 eligible to register securities under Schedule B of the Act, the holder and a prospective purchaser designated by the holder have the right to obtain from the issuer, upon request of the holder, and the prospective purchaser has received from the issuer, the seller, or a person acting on either of their behalf, at or prior to the time of sale, upon such prospective purchaser's request to the holder or the issuer, the following information (which shall be reasonably current in relation to the date of resale under this section); a very brief statement of the nature of the business of the issuer and the products and services it offers; and the issuer's most recent balance sheet and profit and loss and retained earnings statements, and similar financial statements for such part of the two preceding fiscal years as the issuer has been in operation (the financial statements should be audited to the extent reasonably available).

(ii) The requirement that the information be "reasonably current" will be presumed to be satisfied if:

(A) The balance sheet is as of a date less than 16 months before the date of resale, the statements of profit and loss and retained earnings are for the 12 months preceding the date of such balance sheet, and if such balance sheet is not as of a date less than 6 months before the date of resale, it shall be accompanied by additional statements of profit and loss and retained earnings for the period from the date of such balance sheet to a date less than 6 months before the date of resale; and

(B) The statement of the nature of the issuer's business and its products and services offered is as of a date within 12 months prior to the date of resale; or

(C) With regard to foreign private issuers, the required information meets the timing requirements of the issuer's home country or principal trading markets.

(e) Offers and sales of securities pursuant to this rule shall be deemed not to affect the availability of any exemption or safe harbor relating to any previous or subsequent offer or sale of such securities by the issuer or any prior or subsequent holder thereof.

Rule 145. Reclassifications of Securities, Mergers, Consolidations and Acquisitions of Assets

Preliminary Note

Rule 145 (§ 230.145 of this chapter) is designed to make available the protection provided by registration under the Securities Act of 1933, as amended (Act), to persons who are offered securities in a business combination of the type described in paragraphs (a)(1), (2) and (3) of the rule. The thrust of the rule is that an "offer," "offer to sell," "offer for sale," or "sale" occurs when there is submitted to security holders a plan or agreement pursuant to which such holders are required to elect, on the basis of what is in substance a new investment decision, whether to accept a new or different security in exchange for their existing security. Rule 145 embodies the Commission's determination that such transactions are subject to the registration requirements of the Act, and that the previously existing "no-sale" theory of Rule 133 is no longer consistent with the statutory purposes of the Act. See Release No. 33–5316 (October 6, 1972) [37 FR 23631]. Securities issued in transactions described in paragraph (a) of Rule 145 may be registered on Form S–4 or F–4 (§ 239.25 or § 239.34 of this chapter) or Form N–14 (§ 239.23 of this chapter) under the Act.

Transactions for which statutory exemptions under the Act, including those contained in sections 3(a)(9), (10), (11) and 4(2), are otherwise available are not affected by Rule 145.

Note 1: Reference is made to Rule 153a (§ 230.153a of this chapter) describing the prospectus delivery required in a transaction of the type referred to in Rule 145.

Note 2: A reclassification of securities covered by Rule 145 would be exempt from registration pursuant to section 3(a)(9) or (11) of the Act if the conditions of either of these sections are satisfied.

(a) Transactions within this section. An offer, offer to sell, offer for sale, or sale shall be deemed to be involved, within the meaning of section 2(3) of the Act, so far as the security holders of a corporation or other person are concerned where, pursuant to statutory provisions of the jurisdiction under which such corporation or other person is organized, or pursuant to provisions contained in its certificate of incorporation or similar controlling instruments, or otherwise, there is submitted for the vote or consent of such security holders a plan or agreement for—

(1) Reclassifications. A reclassification of securities of such corporation or other person, other than a stock split, reverse stock split, or change in par value, which involves the substitution of a security for another security;

(2) Mergers or Consolidations. A statutory merger or consolidation or similar plan or acquisition in which securities of such corporation or other person held by such security holders will become or be exchanged for securities of any person, unless the sole purpose of the transaction is to change an issuer's domicile solely within the United States; or

(3) Transfers of assets. A transfer of assets of such corporation or other person, to another person in consideration of the issuance of securities of such other person or any of its affiliates, if:

(i) Such plan or agreement provides for dissolution of the corporation or other person whose security holders are voting or consenting; or

(ii) Such plan or agreement provides for a pro rata or similar distribution of such securities to the security holders voting or consenting; or

(iii) The board of directors or similar representatives of such corporation or other person, adopts resolutions relative to paragraph (a)(3)(i) or (ii) of this section within 1 year after the taking of such vote or consent; or

(iv) The transfer of assets is a part of a preexisting plan for distribution of such securities, notwithstanding paragraph (a)(3)(i), (ii), or (iii) of this section.

(b) Communications before a Registration Statement is filed. Communications made in connection with or relating to a transaction described in paragraph (a) of this section that will be registered under the Act may be made under § 230.135, § 230.165 or § 230.166.

(c) Persons and parties deemed to be underwriters. For purposes of this section, any party to any transaction specified in paragraph (a) of this section, other than the issuer, or any person who is an affiliate of such party at the time any such transaction is submitted for vote or consent, who publicly offers or sells securities of the issuer acquired in connection with any such transaction, shall be deemed to be engaged in a distribution and therefore to be an underwriter thereof within the meaning of section 2(11) of the Act. The term "party" as used in this paragraph (c) shall mean the corporations, business entities, or other persons, other than the issuer, whose assets or capital structure are affected by the transactions specified in paragraph (a) of this section.

(d) Resale provisions for persons and parties deemed underwriters. Notwithstanding the provisions of paragraph (c), a person or party specified therein shall not be deemed to be engaged in a distribution and therefore not to be an underwriter of registered securities acquired in a transaction specified in paragraph (a) of this section if:

(1) Such securities are sold by such person or party in accordance with the provisions of paragraphs (c), (e), (f) and (g) of § 230.144;

(2) Such person or party is not an affiliate of the issuer, and a period of at least one year, as determined in accordance with paragraph (d) of § 230.144, has elapsed since the date the securities were acquired from the issuer in such transaction, and the issuer meets the requirements of paragraph (c) of § 230.144; or

(3) Such person or party is not, and has not been for at least three months, an affiliate of the issuer, and a period of at least two years, as determined in accordance with paragraph (d) of § 230.144, has elapsed since the date the securities were acquired from the issuer in such transaction.

(e) Definition of person. The term person as used in paragraphs (c) and (d) of this section, when used with reference to a person for whose account securities are to be sold, shall have the same meaning as the definition of that term in paragraph (a)(2) of § 230.144.

Rule 146. Rules Under Section 18 of the Act

(a) *Prepared by or on behalf of the issuer.* An offering document (as defined in Section 18(d)(1) of the Act [15 U.S.C. 77r(d)(1)]) is "prepared by or on behalf of the issuer" for purposes of Section 18 of the Act, if the issuer or an agent or representative:

(1) Authorizes the document's production; and

(2) Approves the document before its use.

(b) *Covered securities for purposes of Section 18.* (1) For purposes of Section 18(b) of the Act (15 U.S.C. 77r), the Commission finds that the following national securities exchanges, or segments or tiers thereof, have listing standards that are substantially similar to those of the New York Stock Exchange ("NYSE"), the American Stock Exchange ("Amex"), or the National Market System of the Nasdaq Stock Market ("Nasdaq/NMS"), and that securities listed on such exchanges shall be deemed covered securities:

(i) Tier I of the Pacific Exchange, Incorporated;

(ii) Tier I of the Philadelphia Stock Exchange, Incorporated;

(iii) The Chicago Board Options Exchange, Incorporated; and

(iv) Options listed on the International Securities Exchange, Incorporated.

(2) The designation of securities in paragraphs (b)(1)(i) through (iv) of this section as covered securities is conditioned on such exchanges' listing standards (or segments or tiers thereof) continuing to be substantially similar to those of the NYSE, Amex, or Nasdaq/NMS.

Rule 147. "Part of an Issue," "Person Resident," and "Doing Business Within" for Purposes of Section 3(a)(11)

Preliminary Notes

1. This rule shall not raise any presumption that the exemption provided by Section 3(a)(11) of the Act is not available for transactions by an issuer which do not satisfy all of the provisions of the rule.

2. Nothing in this rule obviates the need for compliance with any state law relating to the offer and sale of the securities.

3. Section 5 of the Act requires that all securities offered by the use of the mails or by any means or instruments of transportation or communication in interstate commerce be registered with the Commission. Congress, however, provided certain exemptions in the Act from such registration provisions where there was no practical need for registration or where the benefits of registration were too remote. Among those exemptions is that provided by Section 3(a)(11) of the Act for transactions in "any security which is a part of an issue offered and sold only to persons resident within a single State or Territory, where the issuer of such security is a person resident and doing business within ... such State or Territory." The legislative history of that Section suggests that the exemption was intended to apply only to issues genuinely local in character, which in reality represent local financing by local industries, carried out through local investment. Rule 147 is intended to provide more objective standards upon which responsible local businessmen intending to raise capital from local sources may rely in claiming the Section 3(a)(11) exemption.

All of the terms and conditions of the rule must be satisfied in order for the rule to be available. These are: (i) that the issuer be a resident of and doing business within the state or territory in which all offers and sales are made; and (ii) that no part of the issue be offered or sold to non-residents within the period of time specified in the rule. For purposes of the rule the definition of "issuer" in Section 2(4) of the Act shall apply.

All offers, offers to sell, offers for sale, and sales which are part of the same issue must meet all of the conditions of Rule 147 for the rule to be available. The determination whether offers, offers to sell, offers for sale and sales of securities are part of the same issue (i.e., are deemed to be "integrated") will continue to be a question of fact and will depend on the particular circumstances. See Securities Act of 1933 Release No. 4434 (December 6, 1961). Release 33–4434 indicates that in determining whether offers and sales should be regarded as part of the same issue and thus should be integrated any one or more of the following factors may be determinative:

(i) are the offerings part of a single plan of financing;

(ii) do the offerings involve issuance of the same class of securities;

(iii) are the offerings made at or about the same time;

(iv) is the same type of consideration to be received; and

(v) are the offerings made for the same general purpose.

Subparagraph (b)(2) of the rule, however, is designed to provide certainty to the extent feasible by identifying certain types of offers and sales of securities which will be deemed not part of an issue, for purposes of the rule *only*.

Persons claiming the availability of the rule have the burden of proving that they have satisfied all of its provisions. However, the rule does not establish exclusive standards for complying with the Section 3(a)(11) exemption. The exemption would also be available if the issuer satisfied the standards set forth in relevant administrative and judicial interpretations at the time of the offering but the issuer would have the burden of proving the availability of the exemption. Rule 147 relates to transactions exempted from the registration requirements of Section 5 of the Act by Section 3(a)(11). Neither the rule nor Section 3(a)(11) provides an exemption from the registration requirements of Section 12(g) of the Securities Exchange Act of 1934, the anti-fraud provisions of the federal securities laws, the civil liability provisions of Section 12(2) of the Act or other provisions of the federal securities laws.

Finally, in view of the objectives of the rule and the purposes and policies underlying the Act, the rule shall not be available to any person with respect to any offering which, although in technical compliance with the rule, is part of a plan or scheme by such person to make interstate offers or sales of securities. In such cases registration pursuant to the Act is required.

4. The rule provides an exemption for offers and sales by the issuer *only*. It is not available for offers or sales of securities by other persons. Section 3(a)(11) of the Act has been interpreted to permit offers and sales by persons controlling the issuer, if the exemption provided by that Section would have been available to the issuer at the time of the offering. See Securities Act Release No. 4434 (December 6, 1961). Controlling persons who want to offer or sell securities pursuant to Section 3(a)(11) may continue to do so in accordance with applicable judicial and administrative interpretations.

(a) *Transactions Covered.* Offers, offers to sell, offers for sale and sales by an issuer of its securities made in accordance with all of the terms and conditions of this rule shall be deemed to be part of an issue offered and sold only to persons resident within a single state or territory where the issuer is a person resident and doing business within such state or territory, within the meaning of Section 3(a)(11) of the Act.

(b) *Part of an Issue.*

(1) For purposes of this rule, all securities of the issuer which are part of an issue shall be offered, offered for sale or sold in accordance with all of the terms and conditions of this rule.

(2) For purposes of this rule only, an issue shall be deemed not to include offers, offers to sell, offers for sale or sales of securities of the issuer pursuant to the exemptions provided by Section 3 or Section 4(2) of the Act or pursuant to a registration statement filed under the Act, that take place prior to the six month period immediately preceding or after the six month period immediately following any offers, offers for sale or sales pursuant to this rule, *provided that,* there are during either of said six month periods no offers, offers for sale or sales of securities by or for the issuer of the same or similar class as those offered, offered for sale or sold pursuant to the rule.

NOTE: In the event that securities of the same or similar class as those offered pursuant to the rule are offered, offered for sale or sold less than six months prior to or subsequent to any offer, offer for sale or sale pursuant to this rule, see Preliminary Note 3, hereof as to which offers, offers to sell, offers for sale, or sales are part of an issue.

(c) *Nature of the Issuer.* The issuer of the securities shall at the time of any offers and the sales be a person resident and doing business within the state or territory in which all of the offers, offers to sell, offers for sale and sales are made.

(1) The issuer shall be deemed to be a resident of the state or territory in which:

(i) it is incorporated or organized, if a corporation, limited partnership, trust or other form of business organization that is organized under state or territorial law;

(ii) its principal office is located, if a general partnership or other form of business organization that is not organized under any state or territorial law;

(iii) his principal residence is located, if an individual.

(2) The issuer shall be deemed to be doing business within a state or territory if:

(i) the issuer derived at least 80% of its gross revenues and those of its subsidiaries on a consolidated basis

(A) for its most recent fiscal year, if the first offer of any part of the issue is made during the first six months of the issuer's current fiscal year; or

(B) for the first six months of its current fiscal year or during the twelve month fiscal period ending with such six month period, if the first offer of any part of the issue is made during the last six months of the issuer's current fiscal year

from the operation of a business or of real property located in or from the rendering of services within such state or territory; provided, however, that this provision does not apply to any issuer which has not had gross revenues in excess of $5,000 from the sale of products or services or other conduct of its business for its most recent twelve month fiscal period;

(ii) the issuer had at the end of its most recent semiannual fiscal period prior to the first offer of any part of the issue, at least 80% of its assets and those of its subsidiaries on a consolidated basis located within such state or territory;

(iii) the issuer intends to use and uses at least 80% of the net proceeds to the issuer from sales made pursuant to this rule in connection with the operation of a business or of real property, the purchase of real property located in, or the rendering of services within such state or territory; and

(iv) the principal office of the issuer is located within such state or territory.

(d) *Offerees and Purchasers: Person Resident.* Offers, offers to sell, offers for sale and sales of securities that are part of an issue shall be made only to persons resident within the state or territory of which the issuer is a resident. For purposes of determining the residence of offerees and purchasers:

(1) A corporation, partnership, trust or other form of business organization shall be deemed to be a resident of a state or territory if, at the time of the offer and sale to it, it has its principal office within such state or territory.

(2) An individual shall be deemed to be a resident of a state or territory if such individual has, at the time of the offer and sale to him, his principal residence in the state or territory.

(3) A corporation, partnership, trust or other form of business organization which is organized for the specific purpose of acquiring part of an issue offered pursuant to this rule shall be deemed not to be a resident of a state or territory unless all of the beneficial owners of such organization are residents of such state or territory.

(e) *Limitation of Resales.* During the period in which securities that are part of an issue are being offered and sold by the issuer, and for a period of nine months from the date of the last sale by the issuer of such securities, all resales of any part of the issue, by any person, shall be made only to persons resident within such state or territory.

NOTES: 1. In the case of convertible securities resales of either the convertible security, or if it is converted, the underlying security, could be made during the period described in paragraph (e) only to persons resident within such state or territory. For purposes of this rule a conversion in reliance on Section 3(a)(9) of the Act does not begin a new period.

2. Dealers must satisfy the requirements of Rule 15c2–11 under the Securities Exchange Act of 1934 prior to publishing any quotation for a security, or submitting any quotation for publication, in any quotation medium.

(f) *Precautions Against Interstate Offers and Sales.*

(1) The issuer shall, in connection with any securities sold by it pursuant to this rule:

(i) place a legend on the certificate or other document evidencing the security stating that the securities have not been registered under the Act and setting forth the limitations on resale contained in paragraph (e);

(ii) issue stop transfer instructions to the issuer's transfer agent, if any, with respect to the securities, or, if the issuer transfers its own securities, make a notation in the appropriate records of the issuer; and

(iii) obtain a written representation from each purchaser as to his residence.

(2) The issuer shall, in connection with the issuance of new certificates for any of the securities that are part of the same issue that are presented for transfer during the time period specified in paragraph (e), take the steps required by subsections (f)(1)(i) and (ii).

(3) The issuer shall, in connection with any offers, offers to sell, offers for sale or sales by it pursuant to this rule, disclose, in writing, the limitations on resale contained in paragraph (e) and the provisions of subsections (f)(1)(i) and (ii) and subparagraph (f)(2).

Rule 149. Definition of "Exchanged" in Section 3(a)(9), for Certain Transactions

The term "exchanged" in section 3(a)(9) shall be deemed to include the issuance of a security in consideration of the surrender, by the existing security holders of the issuer, of outstanding securities of the issuer, notwithstanding the fact that the surrender of the outstanding securities may be required by the terms of the plan of exchange to be accompanied by such payment in cash by the security holder as may be necessary to effect an equitable adjustment, in respect of dividends or interest paid or payable on the securities involved in the exchange, as between such security holder and other security holders of the same class accepting the offer of exchange.

Rule 150. Definition of "Commission or Other Remuneration" in Section 3(a)(9), for Certain Transactions

The term "commission or other remuneration" in section 3(a)(9) shall not include payments made by the issuer, directly or indirectly, to its security holders in connection with an exchange of securities for outstanding securities, when such payments are part of the terms of the offer of exchange.

Rule 151. Safe Harbor Definition of Certain "Annuity Contracts or Optional Annuity Contracts" Within the Meaning of Section 3(a)(8)

(a) Any annuity contract or optional annuity contract (a "contract") shall be deemed to be within the provisions of section 3(a)(8) of the Securities Act of 1933, *Provided,* That

(1) The annuity or optional annuity contract is issued by a corporation (the "insurer") subject to the supervision of the insurance commissioner, bank commissioner, or any agency or officer performing like functions, of any State or Territory of the United States or the District of Columbia;

(2) The insurer assumes the investment risk under the contract as prescribed in paragraph (b) of this section; and

(3) The contract is not marketed primarily as an investment.

(b) The insurer shall be deemed to assume the investment risk under the contract if:

(1) The value of the contract does not vary according to the investment experience of a separate account;

(2) The insurer for the life of the contract

(i) Guarantees the principal amount of purchase payments and interest credited thereto, less any deduction (without regard to its timing) for sales, administrative or other expenses or charges; and

(ii) Credits a specified rate of interest (as defined in paragraph (c) of this section) to net purchase payments and interest credited thereto; and

(3) The insurer guarantees that the rate of any interest to be credited in excess of that described in paragraph (b)(2)(ii) of this section will not be modified more frequently than once per year.

(c) The term "specified rate of interest," as used in paragraph (b)(2)(ii) of this section, means a rate of interest under the contract that is at least equal to the minimum rate required to be credited by the relevant nonforfeiture law in the jurisdiction in which the contract is issued. If that jurisdiction does not have any applicable nonforfeiture law at the time the contract is issued (or if the minimum rate applicable to an existing contract is no longer mandated in that jurisdiction), the specified rate under the contract must at least be equal to the minimum rate then required for individual annuity contracts by the NAIC Standard Nonforfeiture Law.

Rule 152. Definition of "Transactions by an Issuer Not Involving Any Public Offering" in Section 4(2), for Certain Transactions

The phrase "transactions by an issuer not involving any public offering" in section 4(2) shall be deemed to apply to transactions not involving any public offering at the time of said transactions although subsequently thereto the issuer decides to make a public offering and/or files a registration statement.

Rule 152a. Offer or Sale of Certain Fractional Interests

Any offer or sale of a security, evidenced by a scrip certificate, order form or similar document which represents a fractional interest in a share of stock or similar security shall be deemed a transaction by a person other than an issuer, underwriter or dealer, within the meaning of section 4(1) of the Act, if the fractional interest (i) resulted from a stock dividend, stock split, reverse stock split, conversion, merger or similar transaction, and (ii) is offered or sold pursuant to arrangements for the purchase and sale of fractional interests among the person entitled to such fractional interests for the purpose of combining such interests into whole shares, and for the sale of such number of whole shares as may be necessary to compensate security holders for any remaining fractional interests not so combined, notwithstanding that the issuer or an affiliate of the issuer may act on behalf of or as agent for the security holders in effecting such transactions.

Rule 153. Definition of "Preceded by a Prospectus," as Used in Section 5(b)(2), in Relation to Certain Transactions

(a) The term "preceded by a prospectus," as used in section 5(b)(2) of the Securities Act of 1933, as amended, in respect of any requirement of delivery of a prospectus to a member of a national securities exchange, on account of a transaction in a security effected on such exchange, shall mean delivery, prior to such transaction, of copies of a prospectus descriptive of such security and meeting the requirements of section 10(a), to such exchange by the issuer or any underwriter, for the purpose of redelivery to members of such exchange upon their request: *Provided,* That as to any transaction occurring prior to the expiration of 40 days after the effective date of the registration statement or the expiration of 40 days after the first date upon which the security was *bona fide* offered to the public by the issuer or by or through an underwriter after such effective date, whichever is later (exclusive of the time during which a stop order issued under section 8 is in effect as to such security)—

(1) Such exchange shall theretofore have requested of the issuer or, if such request shall not have been complied with, of a "principal underwriter" (as that term is defined in Rule 405), from time to time, such number of copies of such prospectus as may have appeared reasonably necessary to comply with the requests of its members, and shall have delivered from its supply on hand a copy to any member theretofore making a written request therefor; and

(2) The issuer or any underwriter shall theretofore have furnished such exchange with such reasonable number of copies of such prospectus as may have been requested by the exchange for the purpose stated above.

(b) The term "national securities exchange," as used herein, shall mean a securities exchange registered as a national securities exchange under the Securities Exchange Act of 1934, as amended.

Rule 153a. Definition of "Preceded by a Prospectus" as Used in Section 5(b)(2) of the Act, in Relation to Certain Transactions Requiring Approval of Security Holders

The term "preceded by a prospectus," as used in section 5(b)(2) of the Act with respect to any requirement for the delivery of a prospectus to security holders of a corporation or other person, in connection with transactions of the character specified in paragraph (a) of Rule 145, shall mean the delivery of a prospectus:

(a) Prior to the vote of security holders on such transactions; or,

(b) With respect to actions taken by consent, prior to the earliest date on which the corporate action may be taken;

to all security holders of record of such corporation or other person, entitled to vote on or consent to the proposed transaction, at their address of record on the transfer records of the corporation or other person.

Rule 153b. Definition of "Preceded by a Prospectus", as Used in Section 5(b)(2), in Connection With Certain Transactions in Standardized Options

The term "preceded by a prospectus", as used in Section 5(b)(2) of the Act with respect to any requirement for the delivery of a prospectus relating to standardized options registered on Form S–20, shall mean the delivery, prior to any transactions, of copies of such prospectus to each options market upon which the options are traded, for the purpose of redelivery to options customers upon their request, *Provided* That:

(a) Such options market shall thereto have requested of the issuer, from time to time, such number of copies of such prospectus as may have appeared reasonably necessary to comply with the requests of options customers, and shall have delivered promptly from its supply on hand a copy to any options customer making a request thereof; and

(b) The issuer shall have furnished such options market with such reasonable number of copies of such prospectus as may have been requested by the options market for the purpose stated above.

Rule 154. Delivery of Prospectuses to Investors at the Same Address

(a) *Delivery of a single prospectus.* If you must deliver a prospectus under the federal securities laws, for purposes of sections 5(b) and 2(a)(10) of the Act (15 U.S.C. 77e(b) and 77b(a)(10)) or § 240.15c2–8(b) of this chapter, you will be considered to have delivered a prospectus to investors who share an address if:

(1) You deliver a prospectus to the shared address;

(2) You address the prospectus to the investors as a group (for example, "ABC Fund [or Corporation] Shareholders," "Jane Doe and Household," "The Smith Family") or to each of the investors individually (for example, "John Doe and Richard Jones"); and

(3) The investors consent in writing to delivery of one prospectus.

(b) *Implied consent.* You do not need to obtain written consent from an investor under paragraph (a)(3) of this section if all of the following conditions are met:

(1) The investor has the same last name as the other investors, or you reasonably believe that the investors are members of the same family;

(2) You have sent the investor a notice at least 60 days before you begin to rely on this section concerning delivery of prospectuses to that investor. The notice must be a separate written statement and:

(i) State that only one prospectus will be delivered to the shared address unless you receive contrary instructions;

(ii) Include a toll-free telephone number or be accompanied by a reply form that is pre-addressed with postage provided, that the investor can use to notify you that he or she wishes to receive a separate prospectus;

(iii) State the duration of the consent;

(iv) Explain how an investor can revoke consent;

(v) State that you will begin sending individual copies to an investor within 30 days after you receive revocation of the investor's consent; and

(vi) Contain the following prominent statement, or similar clear and understandable statement, in bold-face type: "Important Notice Regarding Delivery of

Shareholder Documents." This statement also must appear on the envelope in which the notice is delivered. Alternatively, if the notice is delivered separately from other communications to investors, this statement may appear either on the notice or on the envelope in which the notice is delivered;

Note to paragraph (b)(2): The notice should be written in plain English. See § 230.421(d)(2) of this chapter for a discussion of plain English principles.

(3) You have not received the reply form or other notification indicating that the investor wishes to continue to receive an individual copy of the prospectus, within 60 days after you sent the notice; and

(4) You deliver the prospectus to a post office box or to a residential street address. You can assume a street address is a residence unless you have information that indicates it is a business.

(c) *Revocation of consent*. If an investor, orally or in writing, revokes consent to delivery of one prospectus to a shared address (provided under paragraphs (a)(3) or (b) of this section), you must begin sending individual copies to that investor within 30 days after you receive the revocation. If the individual's consent concerns delivery of the prospectus of a registered open-end management investment company, at least once a year you must explain to investors who have consented how they can revoke their consent. The explanation must be reasonably designed to reach these investors.

(d) *Definition of address*. For purposes of this section, address means a street address, a post office box number, an electronic mail address, a facsimile telephone number, or other similar destination to which paper or electronic documents are delivered, unless otherwise provided in this section. If you have reason to believe that an address is the street address of a multi-unit building, the address must include the unit number.

Rule 155. Integration of Abandoned Offerings

Preliminary Note: Compliance with paragraph (b) or (c) of this section provides a nonexclusive safe harbor from integration of private and registered offerings. Because of the objectives of Rule 155 and the policies underlying the Act, Rule 155 is not available to any issuer for any transaction or series of transactions that, although in technical compliance with the rule, is part of a plan or scheme to evade the registration requirements of the Act.

(a) *Definition of terms.* For the purposes of this section only, a *private offering* means an unregistered offering of securities that is exempt from registration under Section 4(2) or 4(6) of the Act (15 U.S.C. 77d(2) and 77d(6)) or Rule 506 of Regulation D (§ 230.506).

(b) *Abandoned private offering followed by a registered offering.* A private offering of securities will not be considered part of an offering for which the issuer later files a registration statement if:

(1) No securities were sold in the private offering;

(2) The issuer and any person(s) acting on its behalf terminate all offering activity in the private offering before the issuer files the registration statement;

(3) The Section 10(a) final prospectus and any Section 10 preliminary prospectus used in the registered offering disclose information about the abandoned private offering, including:

(i) The size and nature of the private offering;

(ii) The date on which the issuer abandoned the private offering;

(iii) That any offers to buy or indications of interest given in the private offering were rejected or otherwise not accepted; and

(iv) That the prospectus delivered in the registered offering supersedes any offering materials used in the private offering; and

(4) The issuer does not file the registration statement until at least 30 calendar days after termination of all offering activity in the private offering, unless the issuer and any person acting on its behalf offered securities in the private offering only to persons who were (or who the issuer reasonably believes were):

(i) Accredited investors (as that term is defined in § 230.501(a)); or

(ii) Persons who satisfy the knowledge and experience standard of § 230.506(b)(2)(ii).

(c) *Abandoned registered offering followed by a private offering.* An offering for which the issuer filed a registration statement will not be considered part of a later commenced private offering if:

(1) No securities were sold in the registered offering;

(2) The issuer withdraws the registration statement under § 230.477;

(3) Neither the issuer nor any person acting on the issuer's behalf commences the private offering earlier than 30 calendar days after the effective date of withdrawal of the registration statement under § 230.477;

(4) The issuer notifies each offeree in the private offering that:

(i) The offering is not registered under the Act;

(ii) The securities will be "restricted securities" (as that term is defined in § 230.144(a)(3)) and may not be resold unless they are registered under the Act or an exemption from registration is available;

(iii) Purchasers in the private offering do not have the protection of Section 11 of the Act (15 U.S.C. 77k); and

(iv) A registration statement for the abandoned offering was filed and withdrawn, specifying the effective date of the withdrawal; and

(5) Any disclosure document used in the private offering discloses any changes in the issuer's business or financial condition that occurred after the issuer filed the registration statement that are material to the investment decision in the private offering.

Rule 156. Investment Company Sales Literature

(a) Under the federal securities laws, including section 17(a) of the Securities Act of 1933 and section 10(b) of the Securities Exchange Act of 1934 and Rule 10b–5 thereunder, it is unlawful for any person, directly or indirectly, by the use of any means or instrumentality of interstate commerce of the mails, to use sales literature which is materially misleading in connection with the offer or sale of securities issued by an investment company. Under these provisions, sales literature is materially misleading if it (1) contains an untrue statement of a material fact or (2) omits to state a material fact necessary in order to make a statement made, in the light of the circumstances of its use, not misleading.

(b) Whether or not a particular description, representation, illustration, or other statement involving a material fact is misleading depends on evaluation of the context in which it is made. In considering whether a particular statement involving a material fact is or might be misleading, weight should be given to all pertinent factors, including, but not limited to, those listed below.

(1) A statement could be misleading because of:

(i) Other statements being made in connection with the offer of sale or sale of the securities in question;

(ii) The absence of explanations, qualifications, limitations or other statements necessary or appropriate to make such statement not misleading; or

(iii) General economic or financial conditions or circumstances.

(2) Representations about past or future investment performance could be misleading because of statements or omissions made involving a material fact, including situations where:

(i) Portrayals of past income, gain, or growth of assets convey an impression of the net investment results achieved by an actual or hypothetical investment which would not be justified under the circumstances, including portrayals that omit explanations, qualifications, limitations, or other statements necessary or appropriate to make the portrayals not misleading; and

(ii) Representations, whether express or implied, about future investment performance, including: (A) representations, as to security of capital, possible future gains or income, or expenses associated with an investment; (B) representations implying that future gain or income may be inferred from or predicted based on past investment performance; or (C) portrayals of past performance, made in a manner which would imply that gains or income realized in the past would be repeated in the future.

(3) A statement involving a material fact about the characteristics or attributes of an investment company could be misleading because of:

(i) Statements about possible benefits connected with or resulting from services to be provided or methods of operation which do not give equal prominence to discussion of any risks or limitations associated therewith;

(ii) Exaggerated or unsubstantiated claims about management skill or techniques, characteristics of the investment company or an investment in securities issued by such company, services, security of investment or funds, effects of government supervision, or other attributes; and

(iii) Unwarranted or incompletely explained comparisons to other investment vehicles or to indexes.

(c) For purposes of this section, the term "sales literature" shall be deemed to include any communication (whether in writing, by radio, or by television) used by any person to offer to sell or induce the sale of securities of any investment company. Communications between issuers, underwriters and dealers are included in this definition of sales literature if such communications, or the information contained therein, can be reasonably expected to be communicated to prospective investors in the offer or sale of securities or are designed to be employed in either written or oral form in the offer or sale of securities.

Rule 157. Small Entities Under the Securities Act for Purposes of the Regulatory Flexibility Act

For purposes of Commission rulemaking in accordance with the provisions of Chapter Six of the Administrative Procedure Act, and unless otherwise defined for purposes of a particular rulemaking proceeding, the term "small business" or "small organization" shall—

(a) When used with reference to an issuer, other than an investment company, for purposes of the Securities Act of 1933, mean an issuer whose total assets on the last day of its most recent fiscal year were $5,000,000 or less and that is engaged or proposing to engage in small business financing. An issuer is considered to be engaged or proposing to engage in small business financing under this section if it is conducting or proposes to conduct an offering of securities which does not exceed the dollar limitation prescribed by section 3(b) of the Securities Act.

(b) When used with reference to an investment company that is an issuer for purposes of the Act, have the meaning ascribed to those terms by § 270.0–10 of this chapter.

Rule 158. Definitions of Certain Terms in the Last Paragraph of Section 11(a)

(a) An "earning statement" made generally available to security holders of the registrant pursuant to the last paragraph of section 11(a) of the Act shall be sufficient for the purposes of such paragraph if (1) there is included the information required for statements of income contained either (i) in Item 8 of Form 10–K and Form 10–KSB, Part I, Item 1 of Form 10–Q and Form 10–QSB, or Rule 14a–3(b) under the Securities Exchange Act of 1934; (ii) in Item 17 of Form 20–F, if appropriate; or (iii) in Form 40–F; and (2) the information specified in the last paragraph of section 11(a) is contained in one report or any combination of reports either (i) on Form 10–K and Form 10–KSB, Form 10–Q and Form 10–QSB, Form 8–K, or in the annual report to security holders pursuant to Rule 14a–3 under the Securities Exchange Act of 1934, or (ii) on Form 20–F, Form 40–F or Form 6–K. A subsidiary issuing debt securities guaranteed by its parent will be deemed to have met the requirements of this paragraph if the parent's income statements satisfy the criteria of this paragraph and information respecting the subsidiary is included to the same extent as was presented in the registration statement. An "earning statement" not meeting the requirements of this paragraph may otherwise be sufficient for purposes of the last paragraph of section 11(a).

(b) For purposes of the last paragraph of section 11(a) only, the "earning statement" contemplated by paragraph (a) of this Rule shall be deemed to be "made generally available to its security holders" if the registrant (1) is required to file reports pursuant to section 13 or 15(d) of the Securities Exchange Act of 1934 and (2) has filed its report or reports on Form 10–K and Form 10–KSB, Form 10–Q and Form 10–QSB, Form 8–K, Form 20–F, Form 40–F or Form 6–K, or has supplied to the Commission copies of the annual report sent to security holders pursuant to Rule 14a–3(c), containing such information. A registrant may use other methods to make an earning statement "generally available to its security holders" for purposes of the last paragraph of section 11(a).

(c) For purposes of the last paragraph of section 11(a) only, the "effective date of the registration statement" is deemed to be the date of the latest to occur of (1) the effective date of the registration statement; (2) the effective date of the last post-effective amendment to the registration statement, next preceding a particular sale by the registrant of registered securities to the public filed for purposes of (i) including any prospectus required by section 10(a)(3) of the Act, (ii) reflecting in the prospectus any facts or events arising after the effective date of the registration statement (or the most recent post-effective amendment thereof) which, individually or in the aggregate, represent a fundamental change in the information set forth in the registration statement, or (iii) including any material information with respect to the plan of distribution not previously disclosed in this registration statement or any material change to such information in the registration statement, or (3) the date of filing of the last report of the registrant incorporated by reference into the prospectus, and relied upon in lieu of filing a post-effective amendment for purposes of paragraphs (c)(2)(i) and (ii) of this rule, next preceding a particular sale by the registrant of registered securities to the public.

(d) If an earnings statement was made available by "other methods" than those specified in paragraphs (a) and (b) of this rule, the earnings statement must be filed as exhibit 99 to the next periodic report required by section 13 or 15(d) of the Exchange Act covering the period in which the earnings statement was released.

Rule 160. Registered Investment Company Exemption from Section 101(c)(1) of the Electronic Signatures in Global and National Commerce Act

A prospectus for an investment company registered under the Investment Company Act of 1940 (15 U.S.C. 80a–1 *et seq.*) that is sent or given for the sole purpose of permitting a communication not to be deemed a prospectus under section 2(a)(10)(a) of the Act (15 U.S.C. 77b(a)(10)(a)) shall be exempt from the requirements of section 101(c)(1) of the Electronic Signatures in Global and National Commerce Act.

Rule 161. Amendments to Rules and Regulations Governing Exemptions

The rules and regulations governing the exemption of securities under section 3(b) of the Act, as in effect at the time the securities are first bona fide offered to the public in conformity therewith, shall continue to govern the exemption of such securities notwithstanding the subsequent amendment of such rules and regulations. This rule shall not apply, however, to any new offering of such securities by an issuer or underwriter after the effective date of any such amendment, nor shall it apply to any offering after January 1, 1959, of securities by an issuer or underwriter pursuant to Regulation D or pursuant to Regulation A as in effect at any time prior to July 23, 1956.

Rule 162. Submission of Tenders in Registered Exchange Offers

(a) Notwithstanding section 5(a) of the Act (15 U.S.C. 77e(a)), offerors may solicit tenders of securities in an exchange offer subject to § 240.13e–4(e) or § 240.14d–4(b) of this chapter before a registration statement is effective as to the security offered, so long as no securities are purchased until the registration statement is effective and the tender offer has expired in accordance with the tender offer rules.

(b) Notwithstanding section 5(b)(2) of the Act (15 U.S.C. 77e(b)(2)), a prospectus that meets the requirements of section 10(a) of the Act (15 U.S.C. 77j(a)) need not be delivered to security holders in an exchange offer subject to § 240.13e–4(e) or § 240.14d–4(b) of this chapter, so long as a preliminary prospectus, prospectus supplements and revised prospectuses are delivered to security holders in accordance with § 240.13e–4(e)(2) or § 240.14d–4(b) of this chapter, as applicable.

Rule 165. Offers Made in Connection With a Business Combination Transaction

Preliminary Note: This section is available only to communications relating to business combinations. The exemption does not apply to communications that may be in technical compliance with this section, but have the primary purpose or effect of conditioning the market for another transaction, such as a capital-raising or resale transaction.

(a) *Communications before a registration statement is filed.* Notwithstanding section 5(c) of the Act (15 U.S.C. 77e(c)), the offeror of securities in a business combination transaction to be registered under the Act may make an offer to sell or solicit an offer to buy those securities from and including the first public announcement until the filing of a registration statement related to the transaction, so long as any written communication (other than non-public communications among participants) made in connection with or relating to the transaction (i.e., prospectus) is filed in accordance with § 230.425 and the conditions in paragraph (c) of this section are satisfied.

(b) *Communications after a registration statement is filed.* Notwithstanding section 5(b)(1) of the Act (15 U.S.C. 77e(b)(1)), any written communication (other than non–public communications among participants) made in connection with or relating to a business combination transaction (i.e., prospectus) after the filing of a registration statement related to the transaction need not satisfy the requirements of section 10 (15 U.S.C. 77j) of the Act, so long as the prospectus is filed in accordance with § 230.424 or § 230.425 and the conditions in paragraph (c) of this section are satisfied.

(c) *Conditions.* To rely on paragraphs (a) and (b) of this section:

(1) Each prospectus must contain a prominent legend that urges investors to read the relevant documents filed or to be filed with

the Commission because they contain important information. The legend also must explain to investors that they can get the documents for free at the Commission's web site and describe which documents are available free from the offeror; and

(2) In an exchange offer, the offer must be made in accordance with the applicable tender offer rules (§§ 240.14d–1 through 240.14e–8 of this chapter); and, in a transaction involving the vote of security holders, the offer must be made in accordance with the applicable proxy or information statement rules (§§ 240.14a–1 through 240.14a–101 and §§ 240.14c–1 through 240.14c–101 of this chapter).

(d) *Applicability*. This section is applicable not only to the offeror of securities in a business combination transaction, but also to any other participant that may need to rely on and complies with this section in communicating about the transaction.

(e) *Failure to file or delay in filing*. An immaterial or unintentional failure to file or delay in filing a prospectus described in this section will not result in a violation of section 5(b)(1) or (c) of the Act (15 U.S.C. 77e(b)(1) and (c)), so long as:

(1) A good faith and reasonable effort was made to comply with the filing requirement; and

(2) The prospectus is filed as soon as practicable after discovery of the failure to file.

(f) *Definitions*.

(1) A business combination transaction means any transaction specified in § 230.145(a) or exchange offer;

(2) A participant is any person or entity that is a party to the business combination transaction and any persons authorized to act on their behalf; and

(3) Public announcement is any oral or written communication by a participant that is reasonably designed to, or has the effect of, informing the public or security holders in general about the business combination transaction.

Rule 166. Exemption From Section 5(c) for Certain Communications in Connection With Business Combination Transactions

Preliminary Note: This section is available only to communications relating to business combinations. The exemption does not apply to communications that may be in technical compliance with this section, but have the primary purpose or effect of conditioning the market for another transaction, such as a capital-raising or resale transaction.

(a) *Communications*. In a registered offering involving a business combination transaction, any communication made in connection with or relating to the transaction before the first public announcement of the offering will not constitute an offer to sell or a solicitation of an offer to buy the securities offered for purposes of section 5(c) of the Act (15 U.S.C. 77e(c)), so long as the participants take all reasonable steps within their control to prevent further distribution or publication of the communication until either the first public announcement is made or the registration statement related to the transaction is filed.

(b) *Definitions*. The terms business combination transaction, participant and public announcement have the same meaning as set forth in § 230.165(f).

Rule 167. Communications in Connection with Certain Registered Offerings of Asset-Backed Securities

Preliminary Note: This section is available only to communications in connection with certain offerings of asset-backed securities. The exemption does not apply to communications that may be in technical compliance with this section, but have the primary purpose or effect of conditioning the market for another transaction or are part of a plan or scheme to evade the requirements of section 5 of the Act (15 U.S.C. 77e).

(a) In an offering of asset-backed securities meeting the requirements of General Instruction I.B.5 of Form S–3 (§ 239.13 of this chapter) and registered under the Act on Form S–3 pursuant to § 230.415, *ABS informational and computational material* regarding such securities used after the effective date of the registration statement and before the sending or giving to investors of a final prospectus that meets the requirements of section 10(a) of the Act (15 U.S.C. 77j(a)) regarding such offering is exempt from section 5(b)(1) of the Act (15 U.S.C. 77e(b)(1)), if the conditions in paragraph (b) of this section are met.

(b) *Conditions*. To rely on paragraph (a) of this section:

(1) The communications shall be filed to the extent required pursuant to § 230.426.

(2) Every communication used pursuant to this section shall include prominently on the cover page or otherwise at the beginning of such communication:

(i) The issuing entity's name and the depositor's name, if applicable;

(ii) The Commission file number for the related registration statement;

(iii) A statement that such communication is *ABS informational and computational material* used in reliance on Securities Act Rule 167 (§ 230.167); and

(iv) A legend that urges investors to read the relevant documents filed or to be filed with the Commission because they contain important information. The legend also shall explain to investors that they can get the documents for free at the Commission's Web site and describe which documents are available free from the issuer or an underwriter.

(c) This section is applicable not only to the offeror of the asset-backed securities, but also to any other participant that may need to rely on and complies with this section in communicating about the transaction. A participant for purposes of this section is any person or entity that is a party to the asset-backed securities transaction and any persons authorized to act on their behalf.

(d) Failure by a particular underwriter to cause the filing of a prospectus described in this section will not affect the ability of any other underwriter who has complied with the procedures to rely on the exemption.

(e) An immaterial or unintentional failure to file or delay in filing a prospectus described in this section will not result in a violation of section 5(b)(1) of the Act (15 U.S.C. 77e(b)(1)), so long as:

(1) A good faith and reasonable effort was made to comply with the filing requirement; and

(2) The prospectus is filed as soon as practicable after discovery of the failure to file.

(f) Terms used in this section have the same meaning as in Item 1101 of Regulation AB (§ 229.1101 of this chapter).

Rule 170. Prohibition of Use of Certain Financial Statements

Financial statements which purport to give effect to the receipt and application of any part of the proceeds from the sale of securities for cash shall not be used unless such securities are to be offered through underwriters and the underwriting arrangements are such that the underwriters are or will be committed to take and pay for all of the securities, if any are taken, prior to or within a reasonable time after the commencement of the public offering, or if the securities are not so taken to refund to all subscribers the full amount of all subscription payments made for the securities. The caption of any such financial statement shall clearly set forth the assumptions upon which such statement is based. The caption shall be in type at least as large as that used generally in the body of the statement.

Rule 171. Disclosure Detrimental to the National Defense or Foreign Policy

(a) Any requirement to the contrary notwithstanding, no registration statement, prospectus, or other document filed with the Commission or used in connection with the offering or sale of any securities shall contain any document or information which, pursuant to Executive order, has been classified by an appropriate department or agency of the United States for protection in the interests of national defense or foreign policy.

(b) Where a document or information is omitted pursuant to paragraph (a) hereof, there shall be filed, in lieu of such document or information, a statement from an appropriate department or agency of the United States to the effect that such document or information has been classified or that the status thereof is awaiting determination. Where a document is omitted pursuant to paragraph (a) hereof, but information relating to the subject-matter of such document is nevertheless included in material filed with the Commission pursuant to a determination of an appropriate department or agency of the United States that disclosure of such information would not be contrary to the interests of national defense or foreign policy, a statement from such department or agency to that effect shall be submitted for the information of the Commission. A registrant may rely upon any such statement in filing or omitting any document or information to which the statement relates.

(c) The Commission may protect any information in its possession which may require classification in the interests of national defense or foreign policy pending determination by an appropriate department or agency as to whether such information should be classified.

(d) It shall be the duty of the registrant to submit the documents or information referred to in paragraph (a) to the appropriate department or agency of the United States prior to filing them with the Commission and to obtain and submit to the Commission, at the time of filing such documents or information, or in lieu thereof, as the case may be, the statements from such department or agency required by paragraph (b). All such statements shall be in writing.

Rule 174. Delivery of Prospectus by Dealers; Exemptions Under Section 4(3) of the Act

The obligations of a dealer (including an underwriter no longer acting as an underwriter in respect of the security involved in such transactions) to deliver a prospectus in transactions in a security as to which a registration statement has been filed taking place prior to the expiration of the 40 or 90 day period specified in section 4(3) of the Act after the effective date of such registration statement or prior to the expiration of such period after the first date upon which the security was bona fide offered to the public by the issuer or by or through an underwriter after such effective date, whichever is later, shall be subject to the following provisions:

(a) No prospectus need be delivered if the registration statement is on Form F–6.

(b) No prospectus need be delivered if the issuer is subject, immediately prior to the time of filing the registration statement, to the reporting requirements of Section 13 or 15(d) of the Securities Exchange Act of 1934.

(c) Where a registration statement relates to offerings to be made from time to time no prospectus need be delivered after the expiration of the initial prospectus delivery period specified in section 4(3) of the Act following the first bona fide offering of securities under such registration statement.

(d) If (1) the registration statement relates to the security of an issuer that is not subject, immediately prior to the time of filing the registration statement, to the reporting requirements of Section 13 or 15(d) of the Securities Exchange Act of 1934, and (2) as of the offering date, the security is listed on a registered national securities exchange or authorized for inclusion in an electronic inter-dealer quotation system sponsored and governed by the rules of a registered securities association, no prospectus need be delivered after the expiration of twenty-five calendar days after the offering date. For purposes of this provision, the term "offering date" refers to the later of the effective date of the registration statement or the first date on which the security was bona fide offered to the public.

(e) Notwithstanding the foregoing, the period during which a prospectus must be delivered by a dealer shall be:

(1) As specified in section 4(3) of the Act if the registration statement was the subject of a stop order issued under section 8 of the Act; or

(2) As the Commission may provide upon application or on its own motion in a particular case.

(f) Nothing in this section shall affect the obligation to deliver a prospectus pursuant to the provisions of section 5 of the Act by a dealer who is acting as an underwriter with respect to the securities involved or who is engaged in a transaction as to securities constituting the whole or part of an unsold allotment to or subscription by such dealer as a participant in the distribution of such securities by the issuer or by or through an underwriter.

(g) If the registration statement relates to an offering of securities of a "blank check company," as defined in Rule 419 under the Act the statutory period for prospectus delivery specified in section 4(3) of the Act shall not terminate until 90 days after the date funds and securities are released from the escrow or trust account pursuant to Rule 419 under the Act.

Rule 175. Liability for Certain Statements by Issuers

(a) A statement within the coverage of paragraph (b) of this rule which is made by or on behalf of an issuer or by an outside reviewer retained by the issuer shall be deemed not to be a fraudulent statement (as defined in paragraph (d) of this rule), unless it is shown that such statement was made or reaffirmed without a reasonable basis or was disclosed other than in good faith.

(b) This rule applies to the following statements:

(1) A forward-looking statement (as defined in paragraph (c) of this rule) made in a document filed with the Commission, in Part I of a quarterly report on Form 10–Q and Form 10–QSB, or in an annual report to shareholders meeting the requirements of Rules 14a–3(b) and (c) or 14c–3(a) and (b) under the Securities Exchange Act of 1934, a statement reaffirming such forward-looking statement subsequent to the date the document was filed or the annual report was made publicly available, or a forward-looking statement made prior to the date the document was filed or the date the annual report was publicly available if such statement is reaffirmed in a filed document, in Part I of a quarterly report on Form 10–Q and Form 10–QSB, or in an annual report made publicly available within a reasonable time after the making of such forward-looking statement;

Provided, That

(i) At the time such statements are made or reaffirmed, either the issuer is subject to the reporting requirements of section 13(a) or 15(d) of the Securities Exchange Act of 1934 and has complied with the requirements of Rule 13a–1 or 15d–1 thereunder, if applicable, to file its most recent annual report on Form 10–K and Form KSB, Form 20–F, or 40–F; or if the issuer is not subject to the reporting requirements of section 13(a) or 15(d) of the Securities Exchange Act of 1934, the statements are made in a registration statement filed under the Securities Act of 1933, offering statement or solicitation of interest written document or broadcast script under Regulation A or pursuant to section 12(b) or (g) of the Securities Exchange Act of 1934, and

(ii) The statements are not made by or on behalf of an issuer that is an investment company registered under the Investment Company Act of 1940; and

(2) Information which is disclosed in a document filed with the Commission, in Part I of a quarterly report on Form 10–Q and Form 10–QSB or in an annual report to shareholders meeting the requirements of Rules 14a–3(b) and (c) or 14c–3(a) and (b) under the Securities Exchange Act of 1934 and which relates to (i) the effects of changing prices on the business enterprise, presented voluntarily or pursuant to Item 303 of Regulation S–K or Regulation S–B Management's Discussion and Analysis of Financial Condition and Results of Operations, or Item 5 of Form 20–F, Operating and Financial Review and Prospects, (§ 249.220f of this chapter); Item 302 of Regulation S–K, "Supplementary financial information," or Rule 3–20(c) of Regulation S–X, or (ii) the value of proved oil and gas reserves (such as a standardized measure of discounted future net cash flows relating to proved oil and gas reserves as set forth in paragraphs 30–34 of Statement of Financial Accounting Standards No. 69) presented voluntarily or pursuant to Item 302 of Regulation S–K.

(c) For the purpose of this rule the term "forward-looking statement" shall mean and shall be limited to:

(1) A statement containing a projection of revenues, income (loss), earnings (loss) per share, capital expenditures, dividends, capital structure or other financial items;

(2) A statement of management's plans and objectives for future operations;

(3) A statement of future economic performance contained in management's discussion and analysis of financial condition and results of operations included pursuant to Item 303 of Regulation S–K or Item 5 of Form 20–F; or

(4) Disclosed statements of the assumptions underlying or relating to any of the statements described in paragraphs (c)(1), (2) or (3) above.

(d) For the purpose of this rule the term "fraudulent statement" shall mean a statement which is an untrue statement of a material fact, a statement false or misleading with respect to any material fact, an omission to state a material fact necessary to make a statement not misleading, or which constitutes the employment of a manipulative, deceptive, or fraudulent device, contrivance, scheme, transaction, act, practice, course of business, or an artifice to defraud, as those terms are used in the Securities Act of 1933 or the rules or regulations promulgated thereunder.

Rule 176. Circumstances Affecting the Determination of What Constitutes Reasonable Investigation and Reasonable Grounds for Belief Under Section 11 of the Securities Act

In determining whether or not the conduct of a person constitutes a reasonable investigation or a reasonable ground for belief meeting the standard set forth in section 11(c), relevant circumstances include, with respect to a person other than the issuer:

(a) The type of issuer;

(b) The type of security;

(c) The type of person;

(d) The office held when the person is an officer;

(e) The presence or absence of another relationship to the issuer when the person is a director or proposed director;

(f) Reasonable reliance on officers, employees, and others whose duties should have given them knowledge of the particular facts (in the light of the functions and responsibilities of the particular person with respect to the issuer and the filing);

(g) When the person is an underwriter, the type of underwriting arrangement, the role of the particular person as an underwriter and the availability of information with respect to the registrant; and

(h) Whether, with respect to a fact or document incorporated by reference, the particular person had any responsibility for the fact or document at the time of the filing from which it was incorporated.

Rule 180. Exemption From Registration of Interests and Participations Issued in Connection With Certain H.R. 10 Plans

(a) Any interest or participation in a single trust fund or in a collective trust fund maintained by a bank, or any security arising out of a contract issued by an insurance company, issued to an employee benefit plan shall be exempt from the provisions of section 5 of the Act if the following terms and conditions are met:

(1) The plan covers employees, some or all of whom are employees within the meaning of section 401(c)(1) of the Internal Revenue Code of 1954, and is either: (i) a pension or profit-sharing plan which meets the requirements for qualification under section 401 of such Code, or (ii) an annuity plan which meets the requirements for the deduction of the employer's contribution under section 404(a)(2) of such Code;

(2) The plan covers only employees of a single employer or employees of interrelated partnerships; and

(3) The issuer of such interest, participation or security shall have reasonable grounds to believe and, after making reasonable inquiry, shall believe immediately prior to any issuance that:

(i) The employer is a law firm, accounting firm, investment banking firm, pension consulting firm or investment advisory firm that is engaged in furnishing services of a type that involve such knowledge and experience in financial and business matters that the employer is able to represent adequately its interests and those of its employees; or

(ii) In connection with the plan, the employer prior to adopting the plan obtains the advice of a person or entity that (A) is not a financial institution providing any funding vehicle for the plan, and is neither an affiliated person as defined in section 2(a)(3) of the Investment Company Act of 1940 of, nor a person who has a material business relationship with, a financial institution providing a funding vehicle for the plan; and (B) is, by virtue of knowledge and experience in financial and business matters, able to represent adequately the interests of the employer and its employees.

(b) Any interest or participation issued to a participant in either a pension or profit-sharing plan which meets the requirements for qualification under section 401 of the Internal Revenue Code of 1954 or an annuity plan which meets the requirements for the deduction of the employer's contribution under section 404(a)(2) of such Code, and which covers employees, some or all of whom are employees within the meaning of section 401(c)(1) of such Code, shall be exempt from the provisions of section 5 of the Act.

Rule 190. Registration of Underlying Securities in Asset-Backed Securities Transactions

(a) In an offering of asset-backed securities where the asset pool includes securities of another issuer ("underlying securities"), unless the underlying securities are themselves exempt from registration under section 3 of the Act (15 U.S.C. 77c), the offering of the relevant underlying securities itself must be registered as a primary offering of such securities in accordance with paragraph (b) of this section unless all of the following are true. Terms used in this section have the same meaning as in Item 1101 of Regulation AB (§ 229.1101 of this chapter)

(1) Neither the issuer of the underlying securities nor any of its affiliates has a direct or indirect agreement, arrangement, relationship or understanding, written or otherwise, relating to the underlying securities and the asset-backed securities transaction;

(2) Neither the issuer of the underlying securities nor any of its affiliates is an affili-

ate of the sponsor, depositor, issuing entity or underwriter of the asset-backed securities transaction; and

(3) The depositor would be free to publicly resell the underlying securities without registration under the Act. For example:

(i) If the underlying securities are restricted securities, as defined in § 230.144(a)(3), the underlying securities must meet the conditions set forth in § 230.144(k) for the sale of restricted securities; and

(ii) The offering of the asset-backed security does not constitute part of a distribution of the underlying securities. An offering of asset-backed securities with an asset pool containing underlying securities that at the time of the purchase for the asset pool are part of a subscription or unsold allotment would be a distribution of the underlying securities. For purposes of this section, in an offering of asset-backed securities involving a sponsor, depositor or underwriter that was an underwriter or an affiliate of an underwriter in a registered offering of the underlying securities, the distribution of the asset-backed securities will not constitute part of a distribution of the underlying securities if the underlying securities were purchased at arm's length in the secondary market at least three months after the last sale of any unsold allotment or subscription by the affiliated underwriter that participated in the registered offering of the underlying securities.

(b) If all of the conditions in paragraph (a) of this section are not met, the offering of the relevant underlying securities itself must be registered as a primary offering of such securities in accordance with the following:

(1) If the offering of asset-backed securities is registered on Form S-3 (§ 239.13 of this chapter), the offering of the underlying securities itself must be eligible to be registered under Form S–3 or F–3 (§ 239.33 of this chapter) as a primary offering of such securities;

(2) The plan of distribution in the registration statement for the offering of the underlying securities contemplates this type of distribution at the time of the commencement of the offering of the asset-backed securities;

(3) The prospectus for the asset-backed securities offering describes the plan of distribution for both the underlying securities and the asset-backed securities;

(4) The prospectus relating to the offering of the underlying securities is delivered simultaneously with the delivery of the prospectus relating to the offering of the asset-backed securities, and the prospectus for the asset-backed securities includes disclosure that the prospectus for the offering of the underlying securities will be delivered along with, or is combined with, the prospectus for the offering of the asset-backed securities;

(5) The prospectus for the asset-backed securities offering identifies the issuing entity, depositor, sponsor and each underwriter for the offering of the asset-backed securities as an underwriter for the offering of the underlying securities;

(6) Neither prospectus disclaims or limits responsibility by the issuing entity, sponsor, depositor, trustee or any underwriter for information regarding the underlying securities; and

(7) If the offering of the asset-backed securities and the underlying securities is not made on a firm commitment basis, the issuing entity or the underwriters for the offering of the asset-backed securities must distribute a preliminary prospectus for both the underlying securities offering and the asset-backed securities offering that identifies the issuer of the underlying securities and the expected amount of the issuer's underlying securities that is to be included in the asset pool to any person who is expected to receive a confirmation of sale of

the asset-backed securities at least 48 hours prior to sending such confirmation.

(c) Notwithstanding paragraphs (a) and (b) of this section, if the asset pool for the asset-backed securities includes a pool asset representing an interest in or the right to the payments or cash flows of another asset pool, then that pool asset is not considered an "underlying security" for purposes of this section (although its distribution in connection with the asset-backed securities transaction may need to be separately registered) if the following conditions are met:

(1) Both the issuing entity for the asset-backed securities and the entity issuing the pool asset were established under the direction of the same sponsor and depositor;

(2) The pool asset is created solely to satisfy legal requirements or otherwise facilitate the structuring of the asset-backed securities transaction;

(3) The pool asset is not part of a scheme to avoid registration or the requirements of this section; and

(4) The pool asset is held by the issuing entity and is a part of the asset pool for the asset-backed securities.

Rule 191. Definition of "Issuer" in Section 2(a)(4) of the Act in Relation to Asset-Backed Securities

The following applies with respect to asset-backed securities under the Act. Terms used in this section have the same meaning as in Item 1101 of Regulation AB (§ 229.1101 of this chapter).

(a) The depositor for the asset-backed securities acting solely in its capacity as depositor to the issuing entity is the "issuer" for purposes of the asset-backed securities of that issuing entity.

(b) The person acting in the capacity as the depositor specified in paragraph (a) of this section is a different "issuer" from that same person acting as a depositor for another issuing entity or for purposes of that person's own securities.

SPECIAL EXEMPTIONS

Rule 215. Accredited Investor

The term "accredited investor" as used in section 2(15)(ii) of the Securities Act of 1933 shall include the following persons:

(a) Any savings and loan association or other institution specified in section 3(a)(5)(A) of the Act whether acting in its individual or fiduciary capacity; any broker or dealer registered pursuant to section 15 of the Securities and Exchange Act of 1934; any plan established and maintained by a state, its political subdivisions, or any agency or instrumentality of a state or its political subdivisions, for the benefit of its employees, if such plan has total assets in excess of $5,000,000; any employee benefit plan within the meaning of Title I of the Employee Retirement Income Security Act of 1974, if the investment decision is made by a plan fiduciary, as defined in section 3(21) of such Act, which is a savings and loan association, or if the employee benefit plan has total assets in excess of $5,000,000 or, if a self-directed plan, with investment decisions made solely by persons that are accredited investors;

(b) Any private business development company as defined in section 202(a)(22) of the Investment Advisers Act of 1940;

(c) Any organization described in section 501(c)(3) of the Internal Revenue Code, corporation, Massachusetts or similar business trust, or partnership, not formed for the specific purpose of acquiring the securities offered, with total assets in excess of $5,000,000;

(d) Any director, executive officer, or general partner of the issuer of the securities being offered or sold, or any director, executive officer, or general partner of a general partner of that issuer;

(e) Any natural person whose individual net worth, or joint net worth with that person's spouse, at the time of his purchase exceeds $1,000,000;

(f) Any natural person who had an individual income in excess of $200,000 in each of the two most recent years or joint income with that person's spouse in excess of $300,000 in each of those years and has a reasonable expectation of reaching the same income level in the current year;

(g) Any trust, with total assets in excess of $5,000,000, not formed for the specific purpose of acquiring the securities offered, whose purchase is directed by a sophisticated person as described in Rule 506(b)(2)(ii); and

(h) Any entity in which all of the equity owners are accredited investors.

Rule 236. Exemption of Shares Offered in Connection With Certain Transactions

Shares of stock or similar security offered to provide funds to be distributed to shareholders of the issuer of such securities in lieu of issuing fractional shares, scrip certificates or order forms, in connection with a stock dividend, stock split, reverse stock split, conversion, merger or similar transaction, shall be exempt from registration under the Act if the following conditions are met:

(a) The issuer of such shares is required to file and has filed reports with the Commission pursuant to section 13 or 15(d) of the Securities Exchange Act of 1934.

(b) The aggregate gross proceeds from the sale of all shares offered in connection with the transaction for the purpose of providing such funds does not exceed $300,000.

(c) At least ten days prior to the offering of the shares, the issuer shall furnish to the Commission in writing the following information: (1) that it proposes to offer shares in reliance upon the exemption provided by this rule; (2) the estimated number of shares to be so offered; (3) the aggregate market value of such shares as of the latest practicable date; and (4) a brief description of the transaction in connection with which the shares are to be offered.

Rule 237. Exemption for Offers and Sales to Certain Canadian Tax–Deferred Retirement Savings Accounts

(a) *Definitions.* As used in this section:

(1) *Canadian law* means the federal laws of Canada, the laws of any province or territory of Canada, and the rules or regulations of any federal, provincial, or territorial regulatory authority, or any self-regulatory authority, of Canada.

(2) *Canadian Retirement Account* means a trust or other arrangement, including, but not limited to, a "Registered Retirement Savings Plan" or "Registered Retirement Income Fund" administered under Canadian law, that is managed by the Participant and:

(i) Operated to provide retirement benefits to a Participant; and

(ii) Established in Canada, administered under Canadian law, and qualified for tax-deferred treatment under Canadian law.

(3) *Eligible Security* means a security issued by a Qualified Company that:

(i) Is offered to a Participant, or sold to his or her Canadian Retirement Account, in reliance on this section; and

(ii) May also be purchased by Canadians other than Participants.

(4) *Foreign Government* means the government of any foreign country or of any political subdivision of a foreign country.

(5) *Foreign Issuer* means any issuer that is a Foreign Government, a national of any foreign country or a corporation or other organization incorporated or organized under the laws of any foreign country, except an issuer meeting the following conditions:

(i) More than 50 percent of the outstanding voting securities of the issuer are held of record either directly or through voting trust certificates or depositary receipts by residents of the United States; and

(ii) Any of the following:

(A) The majority of the executive officers or directors are United States citizens or residents;

(B) More than 50 percent of the assets of the issuer are located in the United States; or

(C) The business of the issuer is administered principally in the United States.

(iii) For purposes of this definition, the term *resident,* as applied to security holders, means any person whose address appears on the records of the issuer, the voting trustee, or the depositary as being located in the United States.

(6) *Participant* means a natural person who is a resident of the United States, or is temporarily present in the United States, and who contributes to, or is or will be entitled to receive the income and assets from, a Canadian Retirement Account.

(7) *Qualified Company* means a Foreign Issuer whose securities are qualified for investment on a tax-deferred basis by a Canadian Retirement Account under Canadian law.

(8) *United States* means the United States of America, its territories and possessions, any State of the United States, and the District of Columbia.

(b) *Exemption.* The offer to a Participant, or the sale to his or her Canadian Retirement Account, of Eligible Securities by any person is exempt from Section 5 of the Act (15 U.S.C. 77e) if the person:

(1) Includes in any written offering materials delivered to a Participant, or to his or her Canadian Retirement Account, a prominent statement that the Eligible Security is not registered with the U.S. Securities and Exchange Commission and the Eligible Security is being offered or sold in the United States under an exemption from registration.

(2) Has not asserted that Canadian law, or the jurisdiction of the courts of Canada, does not apply in a proceeding involving an Eligible Security.

Rule 238. Exemption for Standardized Options

(a) *Exemption.* Except as expressly provided in paragraphs (b) and (c) of this section, the Act does not apply to any standardized option, as that term is defined by section 240.9b–1(a)(4) of this chapter, that is:

(1) Issued by a clearing agency registered under section 17A of the Securities Exchange Act of 1934 (15 U.S.C. 78q–1); and

(2) Traded on a national securities exchange registered pursuant to section 6(a) of the Securities Exchange Act of 1934 (15 U.S.C. 78f(a)) or on a national securities association registered pursuant to section 15A(a) of the Securities Exchange Act of 1934 (15 U.S.C. 78o–3(a)).

(b) *Limitation.* The exemption provided in paragraph (a) of this section does not apply to the provisions of section 17 of the Act (15 U.S.C. 77q).

(c) *Offers and sales.* Any offer or sale of a standardized option by or on behalf of the issuer of the securities underlying the standardized option, an affiliate of the issuer, or an underwriter, will constitute a contract for sale of, sale of, offer for sale, or offer to sell the underlying securities as defined in section 2(a)(3) of the Act (15 U.S.C. 77b(a)(3)).

REGULATION A—CONDITIONAL SMALL ISSUES EXEMPTION

Rule 251. Scope of Exemption

A public offer or sale of securities that meets the following terms and conditions shall be exempt under section 3(b) from the registration requirements of the Securities Act of 1933 (the "Securities Act"):

(a) *Issuer.* The issuer of the securities:

(1) is an entity organized under the laws of the United States or Canada, or any State, Province, Territory or possession thereof, or the District of Columbia, with its principal place of business in the United States or Canada;

(2) is not subject to section 13 or 15(d) of the Securities Exchange Act of 1934 immediately before the offering;

(3) is not a development stage company that either has no specific business plan or purpose, or has indicated that its business plan is to merge with an unidentified company or companies;

(4) is not an investment company registered or required to be registered under the Investment Company Act of 1940;

(5) is not issuing fractional undivided interests in oil or gas rights as defined in Rule 300, or a similar interest in other mineral rights; and

(6) is not disqualified because of Rule 262.

(b) *Aggregate Offering Price.* The sum of all cash and other consideration to be received for the securities ("aggregate offering price") shall not exceed $5,000,000, including no more than $1,500,000 offered by all selling security holders, less the aggregate offering price for all securities sold within the twelve months before the start of and during the offering of securities in reliance upon Regulation A. No affiliate resales are permitted if the issuer has not had net income from continuing operations in at least one of its last two fiscal years.

Note: Where a mixture of cash and non-cash consideration is to be received, the aggregate offering price shall be based on the price at which the securities are offered for cash. Any portion of the aggregate offering price attributable to cash received in a foreign currency shall be translated into United States currency at a currency exchange rate in effect on or at a reasonable time prior to the date of the sale of the securities. If securities are not offered for cash, the aggregate offering price shall be based on the value of the consideration as established by bona fide sales of that consideration made within a reasonable time, or, in the absence of sales, on the fair value as determined by an accepted standard. Valuations of non-cash consideration must be reasonable at the time made.

(c) *Integration with Other Offerings.* Offers and sales made in reliance on this Regulation A will not be integrated with:

(1) prior offers or sales of securities; or

(2) subsequent offers or sales of securities that are:

(i) registered under the Securities Act, except as provided in Rule 254(d);

(ii) made in reliance on Rule 701;

(iii) made pursuant to an employee benefit plan;

(iv) made in reliance on Regulation S; or

(v) made more than six months after the completion of the Regulation A offering.

Note: If the issuer offers or sells securities for which the safe harbor rules are unavailable, such offers and sales still may not be integrated with the Regulation A offering, depending on the particular facts and circumstances. See Securities Act Release No. 4552 (November 6, 1962) [27 FR 11316].

(d) *Offering Conditions.*

(1) *Offers.*

(i) Except as allowed by Rule 254, no offer of securities shall be made unless a Form 1–A offering statement has been filed with the Commission.

(ii) After the Form 1–A offering statement has been filed:

(A) oral offers may be made;

(B) written offers under Rule 255 may be made;

(C) printed advertisements may be published or radio or television broadcasts made, if they state from whom a Preliminary Offering Circular or Final Offering Circular may be obtained, and contain no more than the following information:

(*1*) the name of the issuer of the security;

(*2*) the title of the security, the amount being offered and the per unit offering price to the public;

(*3*) the general type of the issuer's business; and

(*4*) a brief statement as to the general character and location of its property.

(iii) After the Form 1–A offering statement has been qualified, other written offers may be made, but only if accompanied with or preceded by a Final Offering Circular.

(2) *Sales.*

(i) No sale of securities shall be made until:

(A) The Form 1–A offering statement has been qualified;

(B) A Preliminary Offering Circular or Final Offering Circular is furnished to the prospective purchaser at least 48 hours prior to the mailing of the confirmation of sale to that person; and

(C) A Final Offering Circular is delivered to the purchaser with the confirmation of sale, unless it has been delivered to that person at an earlier time.

(ii) Sales by a dealer (including an underwriter no longer acting in that capacity for the security involved in such transaction) that take place within 90 days after the qualification of the Regulation A offering statement may be made only if the dealer delivers a copy of the current offering circular to the purchaser before or with the confirmation of sale. The issuer or underwriter of the offering shall provide requesting dealers with reasonable quantities of the offering circular for this purpose.

(3) *Continuous or delayed offerings.* Continuous or delayed offerings may be made under this Regulation A if permitted by Rule 415.

Rule 252. Offering Statement

(a) *Documents to be included.* The offering statement consists of the facing sheet of Form 1–A, the contents required by the form and any other material information necessary to make the required statements, in the light of the circumstances under which they are made, not misleading.

(b) *Paper, printing, language and pagination.* The requirements for offering statements are the same as those specified in Rule 403 for registration statements under the Act.

(c) *Confidential treatment.* A request for confidential treatment may be made under Rule 406 for information required to be filed, and § 200.83 of this chapter for information not required to be filed.

(d) *Signatures.* The issuer, its Chief Executive Officer, Chief Financial Officer, a majority of the members of its board of directors or other governing body, and each selling security holder shall sign the offering statement. If a signature is by a person on behalf of any other person, evidence of authority to sign shall be filed, except where an executive officer signs for the issuer. If the issuer is Canadian, its authorized representative in the United States shall sign. If the issuer is a limited partnership, a majority of the board of directors of any corporate general partner also shall sign.

(e) *Number of copies and where to file.* Seven copies of the offering statement, at least one of which is manually signed, shall be filed with the Commission's main office in Washington, D.C.

(g) *Qualification.* (1) If there is no delaying notation as permitted by paragraph (g)(2) of this rule or suspension proceeding under Rule 258, an offering statement is qualified without Commission action on the 20th calendar day after its filing.

(2) An offering statement containing the following notation can be qualified only by order of the Commission, unless such notation is removed prior to Commission action as described in paragraph (g)(3) of this rule:

> This offering statement shall only be qualified upon order of the Commission, unless a subsequent amendment is filed indicating the intention to become qualified by operation of the terms of Regulation A.

(3) The delaying notation specified in paragraph (g)(2) of this rule can be removed only by an amendment to the offering statement that contains the following language:

> This offering statement shall become qualified on the 20th calendar day following the filing of this amendment.

(h) *Amendments.*

(1) If any information in the offering statement is amended, an amendment, signed in the same manner as the initial filing, shall be filed. Seven copies of every amendment shall be filed with the Commission's main office in Washington, D.C.

(2) An amendment to include a delaying notation pursuant to paragraph (g)(2) or to remove one pursuant to paragraph (g)(3) of this section after the initial filing of an offering statement may be made by telegram, letter or facsimile transmission. Each such telegraphic amendment shall be confirmed in writing within a reasonable time by filing a signed copy. Such confirmation shall not be deemed an amendment.

Rule 253. Offering Circular

(a) *Contents.* An offering circular shall include the narrative and financial information required by Form 1–A.

(b) *Presentation of information.* (1) Information in the offering circular shall be presented in a clear, concise and understandable manner and in a type size that is easily readable. Repetition of information should be avoided; cross-referencing of information within the document is permitted.

(2) Where an offering circular is distributed through an electronic medium, issuers may satisfy legibility requirements applicable to printed documents by presenting all required information in a format readily communicated to investors.

(c) *Date.* An offering circular shall be dated approximately as of the date of the qualification of the offering statement of which it is a part.

(d) *Cover page legend.* The cover page of every offering circular shall display the following statement in capital letters printed in boldfaced type at least as large as that used generally in the body of such offering circular:

THE UNITED STATES SECURITIES AND EXCHANGE COMMISSION DOES NOT PASS UPON THE MERITS OF OR GIVE ITS APPROVAL TO ANY SECURITIES OFFERED OR THE TERMS OF THE OFFERING, NOR DOES IT PASS UPON THE ACCURACY OR COMPLETENESS OF ANY OFFERING CIRCULAR OR OTHER SELLING LITERATURE. THESE SECURITIES ARE OFFERED PURSUANT TO AN EXEMPTION FROM REGISTRATION WITH THE COMMISSION; HOWEVER, THE COMMISSION HAS NOT MADE AN INDEPENDENT DETERMINATION THAT THE

SECURITIES OFFERED HEREUNDER ARE EXEMPT FROM REGISTRATION.

(e) *Revisions.* (1) An offering circular shall be revised during the course of an offering whenever the information it contains has become false or misleading in light of existing circumstances, material developments have occurred, or there has been a fundamental change in the information initially presented.

(2) An offering circular for a continuous offering shall be updated to include, among other things, updated financial statements, 12 months after the date the offering statement was qualified.

(3) Every revised or updated offering circular shall be filed as an amendment to the offering statement and requalified in accordance with Rule 252.

Rule 254. Solicitation of Interest Document for Use Prior to an Offering Statement

(a) An issuer may publish or deliver to prospective purchasers a written document or make scripted radio or television broadcasts to determine whether there is any interest in a contemplated securities offering. Following submission of the written document or script of the broadcast to the Commission, as required by paragraph (b) of this rule, oral communications with prospective investors and other broadcasts are permitted. The written documents, broadcasts and oral communications are each subject to the antifraud provisions of the federal securities laws. No solicitation or acceptance of money or other consideration, nor of any commitment, binding or otherwise, from any prospective investor is permitted. No sale may be made until qualification of the offering statement.

(b) While not a condition to any exemption pursuant to this rule:

(1) On or before the date of its first use, the issuer shall submit a copy of any written document or the script of any broadcast with the Commission's main office in Washington, D.C. (Attention: Office of Small Business Review). The document or broadcast script shall either contain or be accompanied by the name and telephone number of a person able to answer questions about the document or the broadcast.

Note: Only solicitation of interest material that contains substantive changes from or additions to previously submitted material needs to be submitted.

(2) The written document or script of the broadcast shall:

(i) state that no money or other consideration is being solicited, and if sent in response, will not be accepted;

(ii) state that no sales of the securities will be made or commitment to purchase accepted until delivery of an offering circular that includes complete information about the issuer and the offering;

(iii) state that an indication of interest made by a prospective investor involves no obligation or commitment of any kind; and

(iv) identify the chief executive officer of the issuer and briefly and in general its business and products.

(3) Solicitations of interest pursuant to this provision may not be made after the filing of an offering statement.

(4) Sales may not be made until 20 calendar days after the last publication or delivery of the document or radio or television broadcast.

(c) Any written document under this rule may include a coupon, returnable to the issuer indicating interest in a potential offering, revealing the name, address and telephone number of the prospective investor.

(d) Where an issuer has a bona fide change of intention and decides to register an offering after using the process permitted by this rule without having filed the offering statement prescribed by Rule 252, the Regulation A exemption for offers made in reliance upon this rule will not be subject to integration with the registered offering, if at least 30 calendar days have elapsed between the last solicitation of interest and the filing of the registration statement with the Commission, and all solicitation of interest documents have been submitted to the Commission. With respect to integration with other offerings, see Rule 251(c).

(e) Written solicitation of interest materials submitted to the Commission and otherwise in compliance with this rule shall not be deemed to be a prospectus as defined in section 2(10) of the Securities Act.

Rule 255. Preliminary Offering Circulars

(a) Prior to qualification of the required offering statement, but after its filing, a written offer of securities may be made if it meets the following requirements:

(1) The outside front cover page of the material bears the caption "Preliminary Offering Circular," the date of issuance, and the following statement, which shall run along the left hand margin of the page and be printed perpendicular to the text, in boldfaced type at least as large as that used generally in the body of such offering circular:

> An offering statement pursuant to Regulation A relating to these securities has been filed with the Securities and Exchange Commission.
>
> Information contained in this Preliminary Offering Circular is subject to completion or amendment. These securities may not be sold nor may offers to buy be accepted prior to the time an offering circular which is not designated as a Preliminary Offering Circular is delivered and the offering statement filed with the Commission becomes qualified. This Preliminary Offering Circular shall not constitute an offer to sell or the solicitation of an offer to buy nor shall there be any sales of these securities in any state in which such offer, solicitation or sale would be unlawful prior to registration or qualification under the laws of any such state.

(2) The Preliminary Offering Circular contains substantially the information required in an offering circular by Form 1–A, except that information with respect to offering price, underwriting discounts or commissions, discounts or commissions to dealers, amount of proceeds, conversion rates, call prices, or other matters dependent upon the offering price may be omitted. The outside front cover page of the Preliminary Offering Circular shall include a bona fide estimate of the range of the maximum offering price and maximum number of shares or other units of securities to be offered or a bona fide estimate of the principal amount of debt securities to be offered.

(3) The material is filed as a part of the offering statement.

(b) If a Preliminary Offering Circular is inaccurate or inadequate in any material respect, a revised Preliminary Offering Circular or a complete Offering Circular shall be furnished to all persons to whom securities are to be sold at least 48 hours prior to the mailing of any confirmation of sale to such persons, or shall be sent to such persons under such circumstances that it would normally be received by them 48 hours prior to receipt of confirmation of the sale.

Rule 256. Filing of Sales Material

While not a condition to an exemption pursuant to this provision, seven copies of any advertisement or written communication, or the script of any radio or television broadcast, shall be filed with the main office of the Commission in Washington, D.C.

Note: Only sales material that contains substantive changes from or additions from previously filed material needs to be filed.

Rule 257. Reports of Sales and Use of Proceeds

While not a condition to an exemption pursuant to this provision, the issuer and/or each selling security holder shall file seven copies of a report concerning sales and use of proceeds on Form 2–A (§ 239.91 of this chapter), or other prescribed form with the main office of the Commission in Washington, D.C. This report shall be filed at the following times:

(a) Every six months after the qualification of the offering statement or any amendment until substantially all the proceeds have been applied; and

(b) within 30 calendar days after the termination, completion or final sale of securities in the offering, or the application of the proceeds from the offering, whichever is the latest event. This report should be labelled the final report. For purposes of this rule, the temporary investment of proceeds pending final application shall not constitute application of the proceeds.

Rule 258. Suspension of the Exemption

(a) The Commission may at any time enter an order temporarily suspending a Regulation A exemption if it has reason to believe that:

(1) no exemption is available or any of the terms, conditions or requirements of the Regulation have not been complied with, including failures to provide the Commission a copy of the document or broadcast script under Rule 254, to file any sales material as required by Rule 256 or report as required by Rule 257;

(2) the offering statement, any sales or solicitation of interest material contains any untrue statement of a material fact or omits to state a material fact necessary in order to make the statements made, in light of the circumstances under which they are made, not misleading;

(3) the offering is being made or would be made in violation of section 17 of the Securities Act;

(4) an event has occurred after the filing of the offering statement which would have rendered the exemption hereunder unavailable if it had occurred prior to such filing;

(5) any person specified in paragraph (a) of Rule 262 has been indicted for any crime or offense of the character specified in paragraph (a)(3) of Rule 262, or any proceeding has been initiated for the purpose of enjoining any such person from engaging in or continuing any conduct or practice of the character specified in paragraph (a)(4) of Rule 262;

(6) any person specified in paragraph (b) of Rule 262 has been indicted for any crime or offense of the character specified in paragraph (b)(1) of Rule 262, or any proceeding has been initiated for the purpose of enjoining any such person from engaging in or continuing any conduct or practice of the character specified in paragraph (b)(2) of Rule 262; or

(7) the issuer or any promoter, officer, director or underwriter has failed to cooperate, or has obstructed or refused to permit the making of an investigation by the Commission in connection with any offering made or proposed to be made in reliance on Regulation A.

(b) Upon the entry of an order under paragraph (a) of this rule, the Commission will promptly give notice to the issuer, any underwriter and any selling security holder:

(1) that such order has been entered, together with a brief statement of the reasons for the entry of the order; and

(2) that the Commission, upon receipt of a written request within 30 calendar days after the entry of the order, will within 20 calendar days after receiving the request, order a hearing at a place to be designated by the Commission.

(c) If no hearing is requested and none is ordered by the Commission, an order entered under paragraph (a) of this rule shall become permanent on the 30th calendar day after its entry and shall remain in effect unless or until it is modified or vacated by the Commission. Where a hearing is requested or is ordered by the Commission, the Commission will, after notice of and opportunity for such hearing, either vacate the order or enter an order permanently suspending the exemption.

(d) The Commission may, at any time after notice of and opportunity for hearing, enter an order permanently suspending the exemption for any reason upon which it could have entered a temporary suspension order under paragraph (a) of this rule. Any such order shall remain in effect until vacated by the Commission.

(e) All notices required by this rule shall be given by personal service, registered or certified mail to the addresses given by the issuer, any underwriter and any selling security holder in the offering statement.

Rule 259. Withdrawal or Abandonment of Offering Statements

(a) If none of the securities which are the subject of an offering statement have been sold and such offering statement is not the subject of a proceeding under Rule 258, the offering statement may be withdrawn with the Commission's consent. The application for withdrawal shall state the reason the offering statement is to be withdrawn, shall be signed by an authorized representative of the issuer and shall be provided to the main office of the Commission in Washington, D.C.

(b) When an offering statement has been on file with the Commission for nine months without amendment and has not become qualified, the Commission may, in its discretion, proceed in the following manner to determine whether such offering statement has been abandoned by the issuer. If the offering statement has been amended, the 9–month period shall be computed from the date of the latest amendment.

(1) Notice will be sent to the issuer, and to any counsel for the issuer named in the offering statement, by registered or certified mail, return receipt requested, addressed to the most recent addresses for the issuer and issuer's counsel as reflected in the offering statement. Such notice will inform the issuer and issuer's counsel that the offering statement or amendments thereto is out of date and must be either amended to comply with applicable requirements of Regulation A or be withdrawn within 30 calendar days after the notice.

(2) If the issuer or issuer's counsel fail to respond to such notice by filing a substantive amendment or withdrawing the offering statement or does not furnish a satisfactory explanation as to why the issuer has not done so within 30 calendar days, the Commission may declare the offering statement abandoned.

Rule 260. Insignificant Deviations From a Term, Condition or Requirement of Regulation A

(a) A failure to comply with a term, condition or requirement of Regulation A will not result in the loss of the exemption from the requirements of section 5 of the Securities Act for any offer or sale to a particular individual or entity, if the person relying on the exemption establishes:

(1) the failure to comply did not pertain to a term, condition or requirement directly intended to protect that particular individual or entity;

(2) the failure to comply was insignificant with respect to the offering as a whole, provided that any failure to comply with paragraphs (a), (b), (d)(1) and (3) of Rule 251 shall be deemed to be significant to the offering as a whole; and

(3) a good faith and reasonable attempt was made to comply with all applicable terms, conditions and requirements of Regulation A.

(b) A transaction made in reliance upon Regulation A shall comply with all applicable terms, conditions and requirements of the regulation. Where an exemption is established only through reliance upon paragraph (a) of this rule, the failure to comply shall nonetheless be actionable by the Commission under section 20 of the Act.

(c) This provision provides no relief or protection from a proceeding under Rule 258.

Rule 261. Definitions

As used in this Regulation A, all terms have the same meanings as in Rule 405, except that all references to "registrant" in those definitions shall refer to the issuer of the securities to be offered and sold under Regulation A. In addition, these terms have the following meanings:

(a) *Final Offering Circular*—The current offering circular contained in a qualified offering statement;

(b) *Preliminary Offering Circular*—The offering circular described in Rule 255(a).

Rule 262. Disqualification Provisions

Unless, upon a showing of good cause and without prejudice to any other action by the Commission, the Commission determines that it is not necessary under the circumstances that the exemption provided by this Regulation A be denied, the exemption shall not be available for the offer or sale of securities, if:

(a) the issuer, any of its predecessors or any affiliated issuer:

(1) has filed a registration statement which is the subject of any pending proceeding or examination under section 8 of the Act, or has been the subject of any refusal order or stop order thereunder within 5 years prior to the filing of the offering statement required by Rule 252;

(2) is subject to any pending proceeding under Rule 258 or any similar section adopted under section 3(b) of the Securities Act, or to an order entered thereunder within 5 years prior to the filing of such offering statement;

(3) has been convicted within 5 years prior to the filing of such offering statement of any felony or misdemeanor in connection with the purchase or sale of any security or involving the making of any false filing with the Commission;

(4) is subject to any order, judgment, or decree of any court of competent jurisdiction temporarily or preliminarily restraining or enjoining, or is subject to any order, judgment or decree of any court of competent jurisdiction, entered within 5 years prior to the filing of such offering statement, permanently restraining or enjoining, such person from engaging in or continuing any conduct or practice in connection with the purchase or sale of any security or involving the making of any false filing with the Commission; or

(5) is subject to a United States Postal Service false representation order entered under 39 U.S.C. § 3005 within 5 years prior to the filing of the offering statement, or is subject to a temporary restraining order or preliminary injunction entered under 39 U.S.C. § 3007 with respect to conduct alleged to have violated 39 U.S.C. § 3005. The entry of an order, judgment or decree against any affiliated entity before the affiliation with the issuer arose, if the affiliated entity is not in control of the issuer and if the affiliated entity and the issuer are not under the common control of a third party who was in control of the affiliated entity at the time of such entry does not come within the purview of this paragraph (a) of this rule.

(b) any director, officer or general partner of the issuer, beneficial owner of 10 percent or more of any class of its equity securities, any promoter of the issuer presently connected with it in any capacity, any underwriter of the securities to be offered, or any partner, director or officer of any such underwriter:

(1) has been convicted within 10 years prior to the filing of the offering statement required by Rule 252 of any felony or misdemeanor in connection with the purchase or sale of any security, involving

the making of a false filing with the Commission, or arising out of the conduct of the business of an underwriter, broker, dealer, municipal securities dealer, or investment adviser;

(2) is subject to any order, judgment, or decree of any court of competent jurisdiction temporarily or preliminarily enjoining or restraining, or is subject to any order, judgment, or decree of any court of competent jurisdiction, entered within 5 years prior to the filing of such offering statement, permanently enjoining or restraining such person from engaging in or continuing any conduct or practice in connection with the purchase or sale of any security, involving the making of a false filing with the Commission, or arising out of the conduct of the business of an underwriter, broker, dealer, municipal securities dealer, or investment adviser;

(3) is subject to an order of the Commission entered pursuant to section 15(b), 15B(a), or 15B(c) of the Exchange Act, or section 203(e) or (f) of the Investment Advisers Act of 1940;

(4) is suspended or expelled from membership in, or suspended or barred from association with a member of, a national securities exchange registered under section 6 of the Exchange Act or a national securities association registered under section 15A of the Exchange Act for any act or omission to act constituting conduct inconsistent with just and equitable principles of trade; or

(5) is subject to a United States Postal Service false representation order entered under 39 U.S.C. § 3005 within 5 years prior to the filing of the offering statement required by Rule 252, or is subject to a restraining order or preliminary injunction entered under 39 U.S.C. § 3007 with respect to conduct alleged to have violated 39 U.S.C. § 3005.

(c) any underwriter of such securities was an underwriter or was named as an underwriter of any securities:

(1) covered by any registration statement which is the subject of any pending proceeding or examination under section 8 of the Act, or is the subject of any refusal order or stop order entered thereunder within 5 years prior to the filing of the offering statement required by Rule 252; or

(2) covered by any filing which is subject to any pending proceeding under Rule 258 or any similar rule adopted under section 3(b) of the Securities Act, or to an order entered thereunder within 5 years prior to the filing of such offering statement.

Rule 263. Consent to Service of Process

(a) If the issuer is not organized under the laws of any of the states of or the United States of America, it shall at the time of filing the offering statement required by Rule 252, furnish to the Commission a written irrevocable consent and power of attorney on Form F–X [§ 239.42 of this chapter].

(b) Any change to the name or address of the agent for service of the issuer shall be communicated promptly to the Commission through amendment of the requisite form and referencing the file number of the relevant offering statement.

REGULATION C—REGISTRATION

ATTENTION ELECTRONIC FILERS

THIS REGULATION SHOULD BE READ IN CONJUNCTION WITH REGULATION S–T (PART 232 OF THIS CHAPTER), WHICH GOVERNS THE PREPARATION AND SUBMISSION OF DOCUMENTS IN ELECTRONIC FORMAT. MANY PROVISIONS RELATING TO THE PREPARATION AND SUBMISSION OF DOCUMENTS IN PAPER FORMAT CONTAINED IN THIS REGULATION ARE SUPERSEDED BY THE PROVISIONS OF REGULATION S–T FOR DOCUMENTS REQUIRED TO BE FILED IN ELECTRONIC FORMAT.

Rule 400. Application of §§ 230.400 to 230.494, inclusive

Rules 400 to 494 shall govern every registration of securities under the Act, except that any provision in a form, or an item of Regulation S–K referred to in such form, covering the same subject matter as any such rule shall be controlling unless otherwise specifically provided in Rules 400 to 494.

GENERAL REQUIREMENTS

Rule 401. Requirements as to Proper Form

(a) The form and contents of a registration statement and prospectus shall conform to the applicable rules and forms as in effect on the initial filing date of such registration statement and prospectus.

(b) If an amendment to a registration statement and prospectus is filed for the purpose of meeting the requirements of section 10(a)(3) of the Act or pursuant to the provisions of section 24(e) or 24(f) of the Investment Company Act of 1940, the form and contents of such an amendment shall conform to the applicable rules and forms as in effect on the filing date of such amendment.

(c) An amendment to a registration statement and prospectus, other than an amendment described in paragraph (b) of this section, may be filed on any shorter Securities Act registration form for which it is eligible on the filing date of the amendment. At the issuer's option, the amendment also may be filed on the same Securities Act registration form used for the most recent amendment described in paragraph (b) of this section or, if no such amendment has been filed, the initial registration statement and prospectus.

(d) The form and contents of a prospectus forming part of a registration statement which is the subject of a stop order entered under section 8(d) of the Act, if used after the date such stop order ceases to be effective, shall conform to the applicable rules and forms as in effect on the date such stop order ceases to be effective.

(e) A prospectus filed as part of an amendment to an effective registration statement, or other amendment to such registration statement, on any form may be prepared in accordance with the requirements of any other form which would then be appropriate for the registration of securities to which the prospectus or other amendment relates, provided that all of the other requirements of such other form and applicable rules (including any required undertakings) are met.

(f) Notwithstanding the provisions of this section, a registrant (1) shall comply with the rules and forms as in effect at a date different from those specified in paragraphs (a), (b), (c) and (d) of this section if the rules or forms or amendments thereto specifically so provide; and (2) may comply voluntarily with the rules and forms as in effect at dates subsequent to those specified in paragraphs (a), (b), (c) and (d) of this section, provided that all of the requirements of the particular rules and forms in effect at such dates (including any required undertakings) are met.

(g) Except for registration statements and post-effective amendments that become effective automatically pursuant to §§ 230.462 and 230.464, a registration statement or any amendment thereto is deemed filed on the proper form unless the Commission objects to the form before the effective date.

Rule 402. Number of Copies; Binding; Signatures

(a) Three copies of the complete registration statement, including exhibits and all other papers and documents filed as a part of the statement, shall be filed with the Commission. Each copy shall be bound, in one or more parts, without stiff covers. The binding shall be made on the side or stitching margin in such manner as to leave the reading matter legible. At least one such copy of every registration shall be signed by the persons specified in section 6(a) of the Act. Unsigned copies shall be conformed.

(b) Ten additional copies of the registration statement, similarly bound, shall be furnished for use in the examination of the registration statement, public inspection, copying and other purposes. Where a registration statement incorporates into the prospectus documents which are required to be delivered with the prospectus in lieu of prospectus presentation, the ten additional copies of the registration statement shall be accompanied by ten copies of such documents. No other exhibits are required to accompany such additional copies.

(c) Notwithstanding any other provision of this rule, if a registration statement is filed on Form–8, three copies of the complete registration statement, including exhibits and all other papers and documents filed as a part of the statement, shall be filed with the Commission. Each copy shall be bound, in one or more parts, without stiff covers. The binding shall be made on the side or stitching margin in such manner as to leave the reading matter legible. At least one such copy shall be signed by the persons specified in Section 6(a) of the Act. Unsigned copies shall be conformed. Three additional copies of the registration statement, similarly bound, also shall be furnished to the Commission for use in the examination of the registration statement, public inspection, copying and other purposes. No exhibits are required to accompany the additional copies of registration statements filed on Form S–8.

(d) Notwithstanding any other provision of this section, if a registration statement is filed pursuant to Rule 462(b) (§ 230.462(b)) and Rule 110(d) (§ 230.110(d)), one copy of the complete registration statement, including exhibits and all other papers and documents filed as a part thereof shall be filed with the Commission. Such copy should not be bound and may contain facsimile versions of manual signatures in accordance with paragraph (e) of this section.

(e) *Signatures.* Where the Act or the rules thereunder, including paragraphs (a) and (c) of this section, require a document filed with or furnished to the Commission to be signed, such document shall be manually signed, or signed using either typed signatures or duplicated or facsimile versions of manual signatures. Where typed, duplicated or facsimile signatures are used, each signatory to the filing shall manually sign a signature page or other document authenticating, acknowledging or otherwise adopting his or her signature that appears in the filing. Such document shall be executed before or at the time the filing is made and shall be retained by the registrant for a period of five years. Upon request, the registrant shall furnish to the Commission or its staff a copy of any or all documents retained pursuant to this section.

Rule 403. Requirements as to Paper, Printing, Language and Pagination

(a) Registration statements, applications and reports shall be filed on good quality, unglazed, white paper no larger than 8½ × 11 inches in size, insofar as practicable. To the extent that the reduction of larger documents would render them illegible, such documents may be filed on paper larger than 8½ × 11 inches in size.

(b) The registration statement and, insofar as practicable, all papers and documents filed as a part thereof shall be printed, lithographed, mimeographed or typewritten. However, the statement or any portion thereof may be prepared by any similar process which, in the opinion of the Commission, produces copies suitable for a permanent record. Irrespective of the process used, all copies of any such material shall be clear, easily readable and suitable for repeated photocopying. Debits in credit categories and credits in debit categories shall be designated so as to be clearly distinguishable as such on photocopies.

(c)(1) All Securities Act filings and submissions must be in the English language, except as otherwise provided by this section. If a registration statement or other filing requires the inclusion of a document that is in a foreign language, the filer must submit instead a fair and accurate English translation of the entire foreign language document, except as provided by paragraph (c)(3) of this section.

(2) If a registration statement or other filing or submission subject to review by the Division of Corporation Finance requires the inclusion of a foreign language document as an exhibit or attachment, the filer must submit a fair and accurate English translation of the foreign language document if consisting of any of the following, or an amendment of any of the following:

(i) Articles of incorporation, memoranda of association, bylaws, and other comparable documents, whether original or restated;

(ii) Instruments defining the rights of security holders, including indentures qualified or to be qualified under the Trust Indenture Act of 1939;

(iii) Voting agreements, including voting trust agreements;

(iv) Contracts to which directors, officers, promoters, voting trustees or security holders named in a registration statement are parties;

(v) Contracts upon which a filer's business is substantially dependent;

(vi) Audited annual and interim consolidated financial information; and

(vii) Any document that is or will be the subject of a confidential treatment request under § 230.406 or § 240.24b–2 of this chapter.

(3)(i) A filer may submit an English summary instead of an English translation of a foreign language document as an exhibit or attachment to a filing subject to review by the Division of Corporation Finance as long as:

(A) The foreign language document does not consist of any of the subject matter enumerated in paragraph (c)(2) of this section; or

(B) The applicable form permits the use of an English summary.

(ii) Any English summary submitted under paragraph (c)(3) of this section must:

(A) Fairly and accurately summarize the terms of each material provision of the foreign language document; and

(B) Fairly and accurately describe the terms that have been omitted or abridged.

(4) When submitting an English summary or English translation of a foreign language document under this section, a filer must identify the submission as either an English summary or English translation. A filer may submit a copy of the unabridged foreign language document when including an English summary or English translation of a foreign language document in a filing. A filer must provide a copy of any foreign language document upon the request of Commission staff.

(5) A Canadian issuer may file an exhibit or other part of a registration statement on Form F–7, F–8, F–9, F–10, or F–80 (§§ 239.37, 239.38, 239.39, 239.40, or 239.41 of this chapter), that contains text in both French and English if the issuer included the French text to comply with the requirements of the Canadian securities administrator or other Canadian authority and, for

an electronic filing, if the filing is an HTML document, as defined in Regulation S–T Rule 11(§ 232.11).

(d) The manually signed original (or in the case of duplicate originals, one duplicate original) of all registrations, applications, statements, reports or other documents filed under the Act shall be numbered sequentially (in addition to any internal numbering which otherwise may be present) by handwritten, typed, printed or other legible form of notation from the first page of the document through the last page of that document and any exhibits or attachments thereto. Further, the total number of pages contained in a numbered original shall be set forth on the first page of the document.

Rule 404. Preparation of Registration Statement

(a) A registration statement shall consist of the facing sheet of the applicable form; a prospectus containing the information called for by Part I of such form; the information, list of exhibits, undertakings and signatures required to be set forth in Part II of such form; financial statements and schedules; exhibits; any other information or documents filed as part of the registration statement; and all documents or information incorporated by reference in the foregoing (whether or not required to be filed).

(b) All general instructions, instructions to items of the form, and instructions as to financial statements, exhibits, or prospectuses are to be omitted from the registration statement in all cases.

(c) The prospectus shall contain the information called for by all of the items of Part I of the applicable form, except that unless otherwise specified, no reference need be made to inapplicable items, and negative answers to any item in Part I may be omitted. A copy of the prospectus may be filed as a part of the registration statement in lieu of furnishing the information in item-and-answer form. Wherever a copy of the prospectus is filed in lieu of information in item-and-answer form, the text of the items of the form is to be omitted from the registration statement, as well as from the prospectus, except to the extent provided in paragraph (d) of this rule.

(d) Where any items of a form call for information not required to be included in the prospectus, generally Part II of such form, the text of such items, including the numbers and captions thereof, together with the answers thereto shall be filed with the prospectus under cover of the facing sheet of the form as a part of the registration statement. However, the text of such items may be omitted provided the answers are so prepared as to indicate the coverage of the item without the necessity of reference to the text of the item. If any such item is inapplicable, or the answer thereto is in the negative, a statement to that effect shall be made. Any financial statements not required to be included in the prospectus shall also be filed as a part of the registration statement proper, unless incorporated by reference pursuant to Rule 411.

Rule 405. Definitions of Terms

Unless the context otherwise requires, all terms used in Rules 400 to 494, inclusive, or in the forms for registration have the same meanings as in the Act and in the general rules and regulations. In addition, the following definitions apply, unless the context otherwise requires:

Affiliate. An "affiliate" of, or person "affiliated" with, a specified person, is a person that directly, or indirectly through one or more intermediaries, controls or is controlled by, or is under common control with, the person specified.

Amount. The term "amount," when used in regard to securities, means the principal amount if relating to evidences of indebtedness, the number of shares if relating to shares, and the number of units if relating to any other kind of security.

Associate. The term "associate," when used to indicate a relationship with any person, means (1) a corporation or organization (other than the registrant or a majority-owned subsidiary of the registrant) of which such person is an officer or partner or is, directly or indirectly, the beneficial owner of 10 percent or more of any class of equity securities, (2) any trust or other estate in which such person has a substantial beneficial interest or as to which such person serves as trustee or in a similar capacity, and (3) any relative or spouse of such person, or any relative of such spouse, who has the same home as such person or who is a director or officer of the registrant or any of its parents or subsidiaries.

Business development company. The term "business development company" refers to a company which has elected to be regulated as a business development under sections 55 through 65 of the Investment Company Act of 1940.

Certified. The term "certified," when used in regard to financial statements, means examined and reported upon with an opinion expressed by an independent public or certified public accountant.

Charter. The term "charter" includes articles of incorporation, declarations of trust, articles of association or partnership, or any similar instrument, as amended, affecting (either with or without filing with any governmental agency) the organization or creation of an incorporated or unincorporated person.

Commission. The term "Commission" means the Securities and Exchange Commission.

Common equity. The term "common equity" means any class of common stock or an equivalent interest, including but not limited to a unit of beneficial interest in a trust or a limited partnership interest.

Control. The term "control" (including the terms "controlling," "controlled by" and "under common control with") means the possession, direct or indirect, of the power to direct or cause the direction of the management and policies of a person, whether through the ownership of voting securities, by contract, or otherwise.

Depositary share. The term "depositary share" means a security, evidenced by an American Depositary Receipt, that represents a foreign security or a multiple of or fraction thereof deposited with a depositary.

Director. The term "director" means any director of a corporation or any person performing similar functions with respect to any organization whether incorporated or unincorporated.

Dividend or interest reinvestment plan. The term "dividend or interest reinvestment plan" means a plan which is offered solely to the existing security holders of the registrant, which allows such persons to reinvest dividends or interest paid to them on securities issued by the registrant, and also may allow additional cash amounts to be contributed by the participants in the plan, provided the securities to be registered are newly issued, or are purchased for the account of plan participants, at prices not in excess of current market prices at the time of purchase, or at prices not in excess of an amount determined in accordance with a pricing formula specified in the plan and based upon average or current market prices at the time of purchase.

Electronic filer. The term electronic filer means a person or an entity that submits filings electronically pursuant to Rules 100 and 101 of Regulation S–T (§§ 232.100 and 232.101 of this chapter, respectively).

Electronic filing. The term *electronic filing* means a document under the federal securities laws that is transmitted or delivered to the Commission in electronic format.

Employee. The term "employee" does not include a director, trustee, or officer.

Employee benefit plan. The term *employee benefit plan* means any written purchase, savings, option, bonus, appreciation, profit sharing, thrift, incentive, pension or similar plan or written compensation contract solely for employees, directors, general partners, trustees (where the registrant is a business trust), officers, or consultants or advisors. However, consultants or advisors may participate in an employee benefit plan only if:

(1) They are natural persons;

(2) They provide *bona fide* services to the registrant; and

(3) The services are not in connection with the offer or sale of securities in a capital-raising transaction, and do not directly or indirectly promote or maintain a market for the registrant's securities.

Equity security. The term *equity security* means any stock or similar security, certificate of interest or participation in any profit sharing agreement, preorganization certificate or subscription, transferable share, voting trust certificate or certificate of deposit for an equity security, limited partnership interest, interest in a joint venture, or certificate of interest in a business trust; any security future on any such security; or any security convertible, with or without consideration into such a security, or carrying any warrant or right to subscribe to or purchase such a security; or any such warrant or right; or any put, call, straddle, or other option or privilege of buying such a security from or selling such a security to another without being bound to do so.

Executive officer. The term "executive officer," when used with reference to a registrant, means its president, any vice president of the registrant in charge of a principal business unit, division or function (such as sales, administration or finance), any other officer who performs a policy making function or any other person who performs similar policy making functions for the registrant. Executive officers of subsidiaries may be deemed executive officers of the registrant if they perform such policy making functions for the registrant.

Fiscal year. The term "fiscal year" means the annual accounting period or, if no closing date has been adopted, the calendar year ending on December 31.

Foreign government. The term "foreign government" means the government of any foreign country or of any political subdivision of a foreign country.

Foreign issuer. The term "foreign issuer" means any issuer which is a foreign government, a national of any foreign country or a corporation or other organization incorporated or organized under the laws of any foreign country.

Foreign private issuer. The term foreign private issuer means any foreign issuer other than a foreign government except an issuer meeting the following conditions:

(1) More than 50 percent of the outstanding voting securities of such issuer are directly or indirectly owned of record by residents of the United States; and

(2) Any of the following:

(i) The majority of the executive officers or directors are United States citizens or residents;

(ii) More than 50 percent of the assets of the issuer are located in the United States; or

(iii) The business of the issuer is administered principally in the United States.

Instructions to paragraph (1) of this definition: To determine the percentage of outstanding voting securities held by U.S. residents:

A. Use the method of calculating record ownership in Rule 12g3–2(a) under the Exchange Act (§ 240.12g3–2(a) of this chapter), except that your inquiry as to the amount of shares represented by accounts of customers resident in the United States may be limited to brokers, dealers, banks and other nominees located in:

(1) The United States,

(2) Your jurisdiction of incorporation, and

(3) The jurisdiction that is the primary trading market for your voting securities, if different than your jurisdiction of incorporation.

B. If, after reasonable inquiry, you are unable to obtain information about the amount of shares represented by accounts of customers resident in the United States, you may assume, for purposes of this definition, that the customers are residents of the jurisdiction in which the nominee has its principal place of business.

C. Count shares of voting securities beneficially owned by residents of the United States as reported on reports of beneficial ownership that are provided to you or publicly filed and based on information otherwise provided to you.

Graphic communication. The term *graphic communication,* which appears in the definition of "write, written" in Section 2(9) of the Securities Act, shall include magnetic impulses or other forms of computer data compilation.

Majority-owned subsidiary. The term "majority-owned subsidiary" means a subsidiary more than 50 percent of whose outstanding securities representing the right, other than as affected by events of default, to vote for the election of directors, is owned by the subsidiary's parent and/or one or more of the parent's other majority-owned subsidiaries.

Material. The term "material," when used to qualify a requirement for the furnishing of information as to any subject, limits the information required to those matters to which there is a substantial likelihood that a reasonable investor would attach importance in determining whether to purchase the security registered.

Officer. The term "officer" means a president, vice president, secretary, treasurer or principal financial officer, comptroller or principal accounting officer, and any person routinely performing corresponding functions with respect to any organization whether incorporated or unincorporated.

Parent. A "parent" of a specified person is an affiliate controlling such person directly, or indirectly through one or more intermediaries.

Predecessor. The term "predecessor" means a person the major portion of the business and assets of which another person acquired in a single succession, or in a series of related successions in each of which the acquiring person acquired the major portion of the business and assets of the acquired person.

Principal underwriter. The term "principal underwriter" means an underwriter in privity of contract with the issuer of the securities as to which he is underwriter, the term "issuer" having the meaning given in sections 2(4) and 2(11) of the Act.

Promoter. (1) The term "promoter" includes—

(i) Any person who, acting alone or in conjunction with one or more other persons, directly or indirectly takes initiative in founding and organizing the business or enterprise of an issuer; or

(ii) Any person who, in connection with the founding and organizing of the business or enterprise of an issuer, directly or indirectly receives in consideration of services or property, or both services and property, 10 percent or more of any class of securities of the issuer or 10 percent or more of the proceeds from the sale of any class of such securities. However, a person who receives such securities or proceeds either solely as underwriting commissions or solely in consideration of property shall not be deemed a promoter within the meaning of this paragraph if such person does not otherwise take part in founding and organizing the enterprise.

(2) All persons coming within the definition of "promoter" in paragraph (1) of this definition may be referred to as "founders" or "organizers" or by another term provided that such term is reasonably descriptive of those persons' activities with respect to the issuer.

Prospectus. Unless otherwise specified or the context otherwise requires, the term "prospectus" means a prospectus meeting the requirements of section 10(a) of the Act.

Registrant. The term "registrant" means the issuer of the securities for which the registration statement is filed.

Share. The term "share" means a share of stock in a corporation or unit of interest in an unincorporated person.

Significant subsidiary. The term "significant subsidiary" means a subsidiary, including its subsidiaries, which meets any of the following conditions:

(1) The registrant's and its other subsidiaries' investments in and advances to the subsidiary exceed 10 percent of the total assets of the registrant and its subsidiaries consolidated as of the end of the most recently completed fiscal year (for a proposed business combination to be accounted for as a pooling of interests, this condition is also met when the number of common shares exchanged or to be exchanged by the registrant exceeds 10 percent of its total common shares outstanding at the date the combination is initiated); or

(2) The registrant's and its other subsidiaries' proportionate share of the total assets (after intercompany eliminations) of the subsidiary exceeds 10 percent of the total assets of the registrants and its subsidiaries consolidated as of the end of the most recently completed fiscal year; or

(3) The registrant's and its other equity in the income from continuing operations before income taxes, extraordinary items and cumulative effect of a change in accounting principle of the subsidiary exceeds 10 percent of such income of the registrant and its subsidiaries consolidated for the most recently completed year.

Computational Note: For purposes of making the prescribed income test the following guidance should be applied:

1. When a loss has been incurred by either the parent and its subsidiaries consolidated or the tested subsidiary, but not both, the equity in the income or loss of the tested subsidiary should be excluded from the income of the registrant and its subsidiaries consolidated for purposes of the computation.

2. If income of the registrant and its subsidiaries consolidated for the most recent fiscal year is at least 10 percent lower than the average of the income for the last five fiscal years, such average income should be substituted for purposes of the computation. Any loss years should be omitted for purposes of computing average income.

Small business issuer. The term "small business issuer" means an entity that meets the following criteria:

(1) has revenues of less than $25,000,000;

(2) is a U.S. or Canadian issuer;

(3) is not an investment company; and

(4) if a majority owned subsidiary, the parent corporation is also a small business issuer.

Provided however, that an entity is not a small business issuer if it has a public float (the aggregate market value of the outstanding voting and non-voting common equity held by non affiliates) of $25,000,000 or more.

NOTE: The public float of a reporting company shall be computed by use of the price at which the stock was last sold, or the average of the bid and asked prices of such stock, on a date within 60 days prior to the end of its most recent fiscal year. The public float of a company filing an initial registration statement under the Exchange Act shall be determined as of a date within 60 days of the date the registration statement is filed. In the case of an initial public offering of securities, public float shall be computed on the basis of the number of shares outstanding prior to the offering and the estimated public offering price of the securities.

Subsidiary. A "subsidiary" of a specified person is an affiliate controlled by such person directly, or indirectly through one or more intermediaries. (See also "majority owned subsidiary," "significant subsidiary," "totally held subsidiary," and "wholly owned subsidiary.")

Succession. The term "succession" means the direct acquisition of the assets comprising a going business, whether by merger, consolidation, purchase, or other direct transfer. The term does not include the acquisition of control of a business unless followed by the direct acquisition of its assets. The terms "succeed" and "successor" have meanings correlative to the foregoing.

Totally held subsidiary. The term "totally held subsidiary" means a subsidiary (1) substantially all of whose outstanding securities are owned by its parent and/or the parent's other totally held subsidiaries, and (2) which is not indebted to any person other than its parent and/or the parent's other totally held subsidiaries in an amount which is material in relation to the particular subsidiary, excepting indebtedness incurred in the ordinary course of business which is not overdue and which matures within one year from the date of its creation, whether evidenced by securities or not.

Voting securities. The term "voting securities" means securities the holders of which are presently entitled to vote for the election of directors.

Wholly owned subsidiary. The term "wholly owned subsidiary" means a subsidiary substantially all of whose outstanding voting securities are owned by its parent and/or the parent's other wholly owned subsidiaries.

Rule 406. Confidential Treatment of Information Filed With the Commission

Preliminary Notes: (1) Confidential treatment of supplemental information or other information not required to be filed under the Act should be requested under 17 CFR § 200.83 and not under this rule.

(2) All confidential treatment requests shall be submitted in paper format only, whether or not the filer is an electronic filer. *See* Rule 101(c)(1)(i) of Regulation S–T (§ 232.101(c)(1)(i) of this chapter).

(a) Any person submitting any information in a document required to be filed under the Act may make written objection to its public disclosure by following the procedure in paragraph (b) of this rule, which shall be the exclusive means of requesting confidential treatment of information included in any document (hereinafter referred to as the "material filed") required to be filed under the Act, *except* that if the material filed is a registration statement on Form S–8 (§ 239.16b of this chapter) or on Form S–3, F–2, F–3 (§ 239.13, 32 or 33 of this chapter) relating to a dividend or interest reinvestment plan, or on Form S–4 complying with General Instruction G of that Form, or if the material filed is a registration statement that does not contain a delaying amendment pursuant to Rule 473, the person shall comply with the procedure in paragraph (b) *prior* to the filing of a registration statement.

(b) The person shall omit from the material filed the portion thereof which it desires to keep undisclosed (hereinafter called the "confidential portion"). In lieu thereof, the person shall indicate at the appropriate place in the material filed that the confidential portion has been so omitted and filed separately with the Commission. The person shall file with the material filed:

(1) One copy of the confidential portion, marked "Confidential Treatment," of the material filed with the Commission. The copy shall contain an appropriate identification of the item or other requirement involved and, notwithstanding that the confidential portion does not constitute the whole of the answer or required disclosure, the entire answer or required disclosure, except that in the case where the confidential portion is part of a financial statement or schedule, only the particular financial statement or schedule need be included. The copy of the confidential portion shall be in the same form as the remainder of the material filed;

(2) An application making objection to the disclosure of the confidential portion. Such application shall be on a sheet or sheets separate from the confidential portion, and shall contain (i) an identification of the portion; (ii) a statement of the grounds of the objection referring to and analyzing the applicable exemption(s) from disclosure under § 200.80 of this chapter, the Commission's rule adopted under the Freedom of Information Act (5 U.S.C. 552), and a justification of the period of time for which confidential treatment is sought; (iii) a detailed explanation of why, based on the facts and circumstances of the particular case, disclosure of the information is unnecessary for the protection of investors; (iv) a written consent to the furnishing of the confidential portion to other government agencies, offices or bodies and to the Congress; and (v) the name, address and telephone number of the person to whom all notices and orders issued under this rule at any time should be directed;

(3) The copy of the confidential portion and the application filed in accordance with this paragraph (b) shall be enclosed in a separate envelope marked "Confidential Treatment" and addressed to The Secretary, Securities and Exchange Commission, Washington, DC 20549.

(c) Pending a determination as to the objection, the material for which confidential treatment has been applied will not be made available to the public.

(d) If it is determined by the Division, acting pursuant to delegated authority, that the application should be granted, an order to that effect will be entered, and a notation to that effect will be made at the appropriate place in the material filed. Such a determination will not preclude reconsideration whenever appropriate, such as upon receipt of any subsequent request under the Freedom of Information Act and, if appropriate, revocation of the confidential status of all or a portion of the information in question.

(e) If the Commission denies the application, or the Division, acting pursuant to delegated authority, denies the application and Commission review is not sought pursuant to § 201.431 of this chapter, confirmed telegraphic notice of the order of denial will be sent to the person named in the application pursuant to paragraph (b)(2)(v) of this rule. In such case, if the material filed may be withdrawn pursuant to an applicable statute, rule, or regulation, the registrant shall have the right to withdraw the material filed in accordance with the terms of the applicable statute, rule, or regulation, but without the necessity of stating any grounds for the withdrawal or of obtaining the further assent of the Commission. In the event of such withdrawal, the confidential portion will be returned to the registrant. If the material filed may not be so withdrawn, the confidential portion will be made available for public inspection in the same manner as if confidential treatment had been revoked under paragraph (h) of this section.

(f) If a right of withdrawal pursuant to paragraph (e) of this section is not exercised, the confidential portion will be made available for public inspection as part of the material filed, and the registrant shall amend the material filed to include all information required to be set forth in regard to such confidential portion.

(g) In any case where a prior grant of confidential treatment has been revoked, the person named in the application pursuant to paragraph (b)(2)(v) of this rule will be so informed by registered or certified mail. Pursuant to § 201.431 of this chapter, persons making objections to disclosure may petition the Commission for review of a determination by the Division revoking confidential treatment.

(h) Upon revocation of confidential treatment, the confidential portion shall be made available to the public at the time and according to the conditions specified in paragraphs (h)(1)–(2):

(1) Upon the lapse of five days after the dispatch of notice by registered or certified mail of a determination disallowing an objection, if prior to the lapse of such five days the person shall not have communicated to the Secretary of the Commission his intention to seek review by the Commission under § 201.431 of this chapter of the determination made by the Division; or

(2) If such a petition for review shall have been filed under § 201.431 of this chapter, upon final disposition adverse to the petitioner.

(i) If the confidential portion is made available to the public, one copy thereof shall be attached to each copy of the material filed with the Commission.

Rule 408. Additional Information

In addition to the information expressly required to be included in a registration statement, there shall be added such further material information, if any, as may be necessary to make the required statements, in the light of the circumstances under which they are made, not misleading.

Rule 409. Information Unknown or Not Reasonably Available

Information required need be given only insofar as it is known or reasonably available to the registrant. If any required information is unknown and not reasonably available to the registrant, either because the obtaining thereof would involve unreasonable effort or expense, or because it rests peculiarly within the knowledge of another person not affiliated with the registrant, the information may be omitted, subject to the following conditions:

(a) The registrant shall give such information on the subject as it possesses or can acquire without unreasonable effort or expense, together with the sources thereof.

(b) The registrant shall include a statement either showing that unreasonable effort or expense would be involved or indicating the absence of any affiliation with the person within whose knowledge the information rests and stating the result of a request made to such persons for the information.

Rule 410. Disclaimer of Control

If the existence of control is open to reasonable doubt in any instance, the registrant may disclaim the existence of control and any admission thereof; in such case, however, the registrant shall state the material facts pertinent to the possible existence of control.

Rule 411. Incorporation by Reference

(a) *Prospectus.* Except as provided by this section, Item 1100(c) of Regulation AB (§ 229.1100(c) of this chapter) for registered offerings of asset-backed securities, or unless otherwise provided in the appropriate form, information shall not be incorporated by reference in a prospectus. Where a summary or outline of the provisions of any document is required in the prospectus, the summary or outline may incorporate by reference particular items, sections or paragraphs of any exhibit and may be qualified in its entirety by such reference.

(b) *Information Not Required in a Prospectus.* Except for exhibits covered by Paragraph (c) of this section, information may be incorporated by reference in answer, or partial answer, to any item that calls for information not required to be included in a prospectus subject to the following provisions:

(1) Non-financial information may be incorporated by reference to any document;

(2) Financial information may be incorporated by reference to any document, provided any financial statement so incorporated meets the requirements of the forms on which the statement is filed. Financial statements or other financial data required to be given in comparative form for two or more fiscal years or periods shall not be incorporated by reference unless the information incorporated by reference includes the entire period for which the comparative data is given;

(3) Information contained in any part of the registration statement, including the prospectus, may be incorporated by reference in answer, or partial answer, to any item that calls for information not required to be included in the prospectus; and

(4) Unless the information is incorporated by reference to a document which complies with the time limitations of § 228.10(f) and § 229.10(d) of this chapter, then the document, or part thereof, containing the incorporated information is required to be filed as an exhibit.

(c) *Exhibits.* Any document or part thereof filed with the Commission pursuant to any Act administered by the Commission may, subject to the limitations of § 228.10(f) and § 229.10(d) of this chapter, be incorporated by reference as an exhibit to any registration statement. If any modification has occurred in the text of any document incorporated by reference since the filing thereof, the registrant shall file with the reference a statement containing the text of such modification and the date thereof.

(d) *General.* Any incorporation by reference of information pursuant to this section shall be subject to the provisions of Rule 24 of the Commission's Rules of Practice restricting incorporation by reference of documents which incorporate by reference other information. Information incorporated by reference shall be clearly identified in the reference by page, paragraph, caption or otherwise. If the information is incorporated by reference to a previously filed document, the file number of such document shall be included. Where only certain pages of a document are incorporated by reference and filed with the statement, the document from which the information is taken shall be clearly identified in the reference. An express statement that the specified matter is incorporated by reference shall be made at the particular place in the registration statement where the information is required. Information shall not be incorporated by reference in any case where such incorporation would render the statement incomplete, unclear or confusing.

Rule 412. Modified or Superseded Documents

(a) Any statement contained in a document incorporated or deemed to be incorporated by reference shall be deemed to be modified or superseded for purposes of the registration statement or the prospectus to the extent that a statement contained in the prospectus or in any other subsequently filed document which also is or is deemed to be incorporated by reference modifies or replaces such statement.

(b) The modifying or superseding statement may, but need not, state that it has modified or superseded a prior statement or include any other information set forth in the document which is not so modified or superseded. The making of a modifying or superseding statement shall not be deemed an admission that the modified or superseded statement, when made, constituted an untrue statement of a material fact, an omission to state a material fact necessary to make a statement not misleading, or the employment of a manipulative, deceptive, or fraudulent device, contrivance, scheme, transaction, act, practice, course of business or artifice to defraud, as those terms are used in the Act, the Securities Exchange Act of 1934, the Public Utility Holding Company Act of 1935, the Investment Company Act of 1940, or the rules and regulations thereunder.

(c) Any statement so modified shall not be deemed in its unmodified form to constitute part of the registration statement or prospectus for purpose of the Act. Any statement so superseded shall not be deemed to constitute a part of the registration statement or the prospectus for purposes of the Act.

Rule 413. Registration of Additional Securities

Except as provided in sections 24(e)(1) and 24(f) of the Investment Company Act of 1940, the registration of additional securities of the same class as other securities for which a registration statement is already in effect shall be effected through a separate registration statement relating to the additional securities.

Rule 414. Registration by Certain Successor Issuers

If any issuer, except a foreign issuer exempted by Rule 3a12–3, incorporated under the laws of any State or foreign government and having securities registered under the Act has been succeeded by an issuer incorporated under the laws of another State or foreign government for the purpose of changing the State or country of incorporation of the enterprises, or if any issuer has been succeeded by an issuer for the purpose of changing its form of organization, the registration statement of the predecessor issuer shall be deemed the registration statement of the successor issuer for the purpose of continuing the offering provided—

(a) Immediately prior to the succession the successor issuer had no assets or liabilities other than nominal assets or liabilities;

(b) The succession was effected by a merger or similar succession pursuant to statutory provisions or the terms of the organic instruments under which the successor issuer acquired all of the assets and assumed all of the liabilities and obligations of the predecessor issuer;

(c) The succession was approved by security holders of the predecessor issuer at a meeting for which proxies were solicited pursuant to section 14(a) of the Securities Exchange Act of 1934 or section 20(a) of the Investment Company Act of 1940 or information was furnished to security holders pursuant to section 14(c) of the Securities Exchange Act of 1934; and

(d) The successor issuer has filed an amendment to the registration statement of the predecessor issuer expressly adopting such statements as its own registration statement for all purposes of the Act and the Securities Exchange Act of 1934 and setting forth any additional information necessary to reflect any material changes made in connection with or resulting from the succession, or necessary to keep the registration statement from being misleading in any material respect, and such amendment has become effective.

Rule 415. Delayed or Continuous Offering and Sale of Securities

(a) Securities may be registered for an offering to be made on a continuous or delayed basis in the future. *Provided,* That—

(1) The registration statement pertains only to:

(i) Securities which are to be offered or sold solely by or on behalf of a person or persons other than the registrant, a subsidiary of the registrant or a person of which the registrant is a subsidiary;

(ii) Securities which are to be offered and sold pursuant to a dividend or interest reinvestment plan or an employee benefit plan of the registrant;

(iii) Securities which are to be issued upon the exercise of outstanding options, warrants or rights;

(iv) Securities which are to be issued upon conversion of other outstanding securities;

(v) Securities which are pledged as collateral;

(vi) Securities which are registered on Form F–6;

(vii) Mortgage related securities, including such securities as mortgage backed debt and mortgage participation or pass through certificates;

(viii) Securities which are to be issued in connection with business combination transactions;

(ix) Securities the offering of which will be commenced promptly, will be made on a continuous basis and may continue for a period in excess of 30 days from the date of initial effectiveness;

(x) Securities registered (or qualified to be registered) on Form S-3 or Form F-3 (§ 239.13 or 239.33 of this chapter) which are to be offered and sold on a continuous or delayed basis by or on behalf of the registrant, a subsidiary of the registrant or a person of which the registrant is a subsidiary; or

(xi) Shares of common stock which are to be offered and sold on a delayed or continuous basis by or on behalf of a registered closed-end management investment company or business development company that makes periodic repurchase offers pursuant to § 270.23c-3 of this chapter.

(2) Securities in paragraphs (a)(1)(viii) through (x) may only be registered in an amount which, at the time the registration statement becomes effective, is reasonably expected to be offered and sold within two years from the initial effective date of the registration.

(3) The registrant furnishes the undertakings required by Item 512(a) of Regulation S-K.

(4) In the case of a registration statement pertaining to an at the market offering of equity securities by or on behalf of the registrant:

(i) The offering comes within paragraph (a)(1)(x); (ii) where voting stock is registered, the amount of securities registered for such purposes must not exceed 10% of the aggregate market value of the registrant's outstanding voting stock held by non-affiliates of the registrant (calculated as of a date within 60 days prior to the date of filing); (iii) the securities must be sold through an underwriter or underwriters, acting as principal(s) or as agent(s) for the registrant; and (iv) the underwriter or underwriters must be named in the prospectus which is part of the registration statement. As used in this paragraph, the term "at the market offering" means an offering of securities into an existing trading market for outstanding shares of the same class at other than a fixed price on or through the facilities of a national securities exchange or to or through a market maker otherwise than on an exchange.

(b) This section shall not apply to any registration statement pertaining to securities issued by a face-amount certificate company or redeemable securities issued by an open-end management company or unit investment trust under the Investment Company Act of 1940 or any registration statement filed by any foreign government or political subdivision thereof.

Rule 416. Securities to Be Issued as a Result of Stock Splits, Stock Dividends, and Anti-dilution Provisions and Interests to Be Issued Pursuant to Certain Employee Benefit Plans

(a) If a registration statement purports to register securities to be offered pursuant to terms which provide for a change in the amount of securities being offered or issued to prevent dilution resulting from stock splits, stock dividends or similar transactions, such registration statement shall, unless otherwise expressly provided, be deemed to cover the additional securities to be offered or issued in connection with any such provision.

(b) If prior to completion of the distribution of the securities covered by a registration statement, additional securities of the same class are issued or issuable as a result of a stock split or stock divided, the registration statement shall, unless otherwise expressly provided therein, be deemed to cover such additional securities resulting from the split of, or the stock dividend on, the registered securities. If prior to completion of the distribution of the securities covered by a registration statement, all the securities of a class which includes the registered securities are combined by a reverse split into a lesser amount of securities of the same class, the amount of undistributed securities of such class deemed to be covered by the registration statement shall be proportionately reduced. If paragraph (a) of this rule is not applicable, the registration statement shall be amended prior to the offering of such additional or lesser amount of securities to reflect the change in the amount of securities registered.

(c) Where a registration statement on Form S–8 relates to securities to be offered pursuant to an employee benefit plan, including interests in such plan that constitute separate securities required to be registered under the Act, such registration statement shall be deemed to register an indeterminate amount of such plan interests.

Rule 417. Date of Financial Statements

Whenever financial statements of any person are required to be furnished as of a date within a specified period prior to the date of filing the registration statement and the last day of such period falls on a Saturday, Sunday or holiday, such registration statement may be filed on the first business day following the last day of the specified period.

Rule 418. Supplemental Information

(a) The Commission or its staff may, where it is deemed appropriate, request supplemental information concerning the registrant, the registration statement, the distribution of the securities, market activities and underwriters' activities. Such information includes, but is not limited to, the following items which the registrant should be prepared to furnish promptly upon request:

(1)(i) Any reports or memoranda which have been prepared for external use by the registrant or a principal underwriter, as defined in Rule 405, in connection with the proposed offering;

(ii) A statement as to the actual or proposed use and distribution of the reports or memoranda specified in paragraph (a)(1)(i) of this rule, identifying each class of persons who have received or will receive such reports or memoranda and the number of copies distributed to each such class;

(2) In the case of a registration statement relating to a business combination as defined in Rule 145(a), exchange offer, tender offer or similar transaction, any feasibility studies, management analyses, fairness opinions or similar reports prepared by or for any of the parties to the subject transaction in connection with such transaction;

(3) Except in the case of a registrant eligible to use Form S–2 or Form S–3, any engineering, management or similar reports or memoranda relating to broad aspects of the business, operations or products of the registrant, which have been prepared within the past twelve months for or by the registrant, any affiliate of the registrant or any principal underwriter, as defined in Rule 405, of the securities being registered except for:

(i) Reports solely comprised of recommendations to buy, sell or hold the securities of the registrant, unless such recommendations have changed within the past six months; and

(ii) Any information contained in documents already filed with the Commission.

(4) Where there is a registration of an at the market offering, as defined in § 242.100 of this Chapter, of more than 10 percent of the securities outstanding, where the offering includes securities owned by officers, directors or affiliates of the registrant and where there is no underwriting agreement, information (i) concerning contractual arrangements between selling security holders of a limited group or of several groups of related shareholders to comply with the anti-manipulation rules until the offering by all members of the group is completed and to inform the exchange, brokers and selling security holders when the distribution by the members of the group is over, or (ii) concerning the registrant's efforts to notify members of a large group of unrelated sellers of the applicable Commission rules and regulations;

(5) Where the registrant recently has introduced a new product or has begun to do business in a new industry segment or has made public its intentions to introduce a new product or to do business in a new industry segment, and this action requires the investment of a material amount of the assets of the registrant or otherwise is material, copies of any studies prepared for the registrant by outside persons or any internal studies, documents, reports or memoranda the contents of which were material to the decision to develop the product or to do business in the new segment including, but not limited to, documents relating to financial requirements and engineering, competitive, environmental and other considerations, but excluding technical documents;

(6) Where reserve estimates are referred to in a document, a copy of the full report of the engineer or other expert who estimated the reserves; and

(7) With respect to the extent of the distribution of a preliminary prospectus, information concerning:

(i) The date of the preliminary prospectus distributed;

(ii) The dates or approximate dates of distribution;

(iii) The number of prospective underwriters and dealers to whom the preliminary prospectus was furnished;

(iv) The number of prospectuses so distributed;

(v) The number of prospectuses distributed to others, identifying them in general terms; and

(vi) The steps taken by such underwriters and dealers to comply with the provisions of Rule 15c2–8 under the Securities Exchange Act of 1934.

(b) Supplemental information described in paragraph (a) of this section shall not be required to be filed with or deemed part of the registration statement. The information shall be returned to the registrant upon request, provided that:

(1) Such request is made at the time such information is furnished to the staff;

(2) The return of such information is consistent with the protection of investors;

(3) The return of such information is consistent with the provisions of the Freedom of Information Act; and

(4) The information was not filed in electronic format.

Rule 419. Offerings by Blank Check Companies

(a) *Scope of the rule and definitions.* (1) The provisions of this rule shall apply to every registration statement filed under the Act relating to an offering by a blank check company.

(2) For purposes of this rule, the term "blank check company" shall mean a company that:

(i) Is a development stage company that has no specific business plan or purpose or has indicated that its business plan is to engage in a merger or acquisition with an unidentified company or companies, or other entity or person; and

(ii) Is issuing "penny stock," as defined in Rule 3a51–1 under the Securities Exchange Act of 1934 ("Exchange Act").

(3) For purposes of this rule the term "purchaser" shall mean any person acquiring securities directly or indirectly in the offering, for cash or otherwise, including promoters or others receiving securities as compensation in connection with the offering.

(b) *Deposit of securities and proceeds in escrow or trust account*—(1) General. (i) Except as otherwise provided in this rule or prohibited by other applicable law, all securities issued in connection with an offering by a blank check company and the gross proceeds from the offering shall be deposited promptly into:

(A) An escrow account maintained by an "insured depository institution," as that term is defined in section 3(c)(2) of the Federal Deposit Insurance Act (12 U.S.C. 1813(C)(2)); or

(B) A separate bank account established by a broker or dealer registered under the Exchange Act maintaining net capital equal to or exceeding $25,000 (as calculated pursuant to Exchange Act Rule 15c3–1), in which the broker or dealer acts as trustee for persons having the beneficial interests in the account.

(ii) If funds and securities are deposited into an escrow account maintained by an insured depository institution, the deposit account records of the insured depository institution must provide that funds in the escrow account are held for the benefit of the purchasers named and identified in accordance with 12 CFR 330.1 of the regulations of the Federal Deposit Insurance Corporation, and the records of the escrow agent, maintained in good faith and in the regular course of business, must show the name and interest of each party to the account. If funds and securities are deposited in a separate bank account established by a broker or dealer acting as a trustee, the books and records of the broker-dealer must indicate the name, address, and interest of each person for whom the account is held.

(2) Deposit and investment of proceeds. (i) All offering proceeds, after deduction of cash paid for underwriting commissions, underwriting expenses and dealer allowances, and amounts permitted to be released to the registrant pursuant to paragraph (b)(2)(vi) of this rule shall be deposited promptly into the escrow or trust account; *provided, however,* that no deduction may be made for underwriting commissions, underwriting expenses or dealer allowances payable to an affiliate of the registrant.

(ii) Deposited proceeds shall be in the form of checks, drafts, or money orders payable to the order of the escrow agent or trustee.

(iii) Deposited proceeds and interest or dividends thereon, if any, shall be held for the sole benefit of the purchasers of the securities.

(iv) Deposited proceeds shall be invested in one of the following:

(A) An obligation that constitutes a "deposit," as that term is defined in section 3(*l*) of the Federal Deposit Insurance Act (12 U.S.C. 1813(*l*));

(B) Securities of any open-end investment company registered under the Investment Company Act of 1940 that holds itself out as a money market fund meeting the conditions of paragraphs (c)(2), (c)(3), and (c)(4) of Rule 2a–7 under the Investment Company Act; or

(C) Securities that are direct obligations of, or obligations guaranteed as to principal or interest by, the United States.

Note to Rule 419(b)(2)(iv): Issuers are cautioned that investments in government securities are inappropriate unless such securities can be readily sold or otherwise disposed of for cash at the time required without any dissipation of offering proceeds invested.

(v) Interest or dividends earned on the funds, if any, shall be held in the escrow or trust account until the funds are released in accordance with the provisions of this rule. If funds held in the escrow or trust account are released to a purchaser of the securities, the purchasers shall receive interest or dividends earned, if any, on such funds up to the date of release. If funds held in the escrow or trust account are released to the registrant, interest or dividends earned on such funds up to the date of release may be released to the registrant.

(vi) The registrant may receive up to 10 percent of the proceeds remaining after payment of underwriting commissions, underwriting expenses and dealer allowances permitted by paragraph (b)(2)(i) of this rule, exclusive of interest or dividends, as those proceeds are deposited into the escrow or trust account.

(3) Deposit of securities. (i) All securities issued in connection with the offering, whether or not for cash consideration, and any other securities issued with respect to such securities, including securities issued with respect to stock splits, stock dividends, or similar rights, shall be deposited directly into the escrow or trust account promptly upon issuance. The identity of the purchaser of the securities shall be included on the stock certificates or other documents evidencing such securities. See also Rule 15g–8 regarding restrictions on sales of, or offers to sell, securities deposited in the escrow or trust account.

(ii) Securities held in the escrow or trust account are to remain as issued and deposited and shall be held for the sole benefit of the purchasers, who shall have voting rights, if any, with respect to securities held in their names, as provided by applicable state law. No transfer or other disposition of securities held in the escrow or trust account or any interest related to such securities shall be permitted other than by will or the laws of descent and distribution, or pursuant to a qualified domestic relations order as defined by the Internal Revenue Code of 1986 as amended (26 U.S.C. 1 *et seq.*) or Title 1 of the Employee Retirement Income Security Act (29 U.S.C. 1001 *et seq.*), or the rules thereunder.

(iii) Warrants, convertible securities or other derivative securities relating to securities held in the escrow or trust account may be exercised or converted in accordance with their terms; *provided, however,* that securities received upon exercise or conversion, together with any cash or other consideration paid in connection with the exercise or conversion, are promptly deposited into the escrow or trust account.

(4) Escrow or trust agreement. A copy of the executed escrow or trust agreement shall be filed as an exhibit to the registration statement and shall contain the provisions of paragraphs (b)(2), (b)(3), and (e)(3) of this rule.

(5) Request for supplemental information. Upon request by the Commission or the staff, the registrant shall furnish as supplemental information the names and addresses of persons for whom securities are held in the escrow or trust account.

Note to Rule 419(b): With respect to a blank check offering subject to both Rule 419 and Exchange Act Rule 15c2–4, the requirements of Rule 15c2–4 are applicable only until the conditions of the offering governed by that Rule are met (*e.g.*, reaching the minimum in a "part-or-none" offering). When those conditions are satisfied, Rule 419 continues to govern the use of offering proceeds.

(c) *Disclosure of offering terms.* The initial registration statement shall disclose the specific terms of the offering, including, but not limited to:

(1) The terms and provisions of the escrow or trust agreement and the effect thereof upon the registrant's right to receive funds and the effect of the escrow or trust agreement upon the purchaser's funds and securities required to be deposited into the escrow or trust account, including, if applicable, any material risk of non-insurance of purchasers' funds resulting from deposits in excess of the insured amounts; and

(2) The obligation of the registrant to provide, and the right of the purchaser to receive, information regarding an acquisition, including the requirement that pursuant to this rule, purchasers confirm in writing their investment in the registrant's securities as specified in paragraph (e) of this rule.

(d) *Probable acquisition post-effective amendment requirement.* If, during any period in which offers or sales are being made, a significant acquisition becomes probable, the registrant shall file promptly a post-effective amendment disclosing the information specified by the applicable registration statement form and Industry Guides, including financial statements of the registrant and the company to be acquired as well as pro forma financial information required by the form and applicable rules and regulations. Where warrants, rights or other derivative securities issued in the initial offering are exercisable, there is a continuous offering of the underlying security.

(e) *Release of deposited and funds securities*—(1) Post-effective amendment for acquisition agreement. Upon execution of an agreement(s) for the acquisition(s) of a business(es) or assets that will constitute the business (or a line of business) of the registrant and for which the fair value of the business(es) or net assets to be acquired represents at least 80 percent of the maximum offering proceeds, including proceeds received or to be received upon the exercise or conversion of any securities offered, but excluding amounts payable to non-affiliates for underwriting commissions, underwriting expenses, and dealer allowances, the registrant shall file a post-effective amendment that:

(i) Discloses the information specified by the applicable registration statement form and Industry Guides, including financial statements of the registrant and the company acquired or to be acquired and pro forma financial information required by the form and applicable rules and regulations;

(ii) Discloses the results of the initial offering, including but not limited to:

(A) The gross offering proceeds received to date, specifying the amounts paid for underwriter commissions, underwriting expenses and dealer allowances, amounts disbursed to the registrant, and amounts remaining in the escrow or trust account; and

(B) The specific amount, use and application of funds disbursed to the registrant to date, including, but not limited to, the amounts paid to officers, directors, promoters, controlling shareholders or affiliates, either directly or indirectly, specifying the amounts and purposes of such payments; and

(iii) Discloses the terms of the offering as described pursuant to paragraph (e)(2) of this rule.

(2) Terms of the offering. The terms of the offering must provide, and the registrant must satisfy, the following conditions:

(i) Within five business days after the effective date of the post-effective amendment(s), the registrant shall send by first class mail or other equally prompt means, to each purchaser of securities held in escrow or trust, a copy of the prospectus contained in the post-effective amendment and any amendment or supplement thereto;

(ii) Each purchaser shall have no fewer than 20 business days and no more than 45 business days from the effective date of the post-effective amendment to notify the registrant in writing that the purchaser elects to remain an investor. If the registrant has not received such written notification by the 45th business day following the effective date of the post-effective amendment, funds and interest or dividends, if any, held in the escrow or trust account shall be sent by first class mail or other equally prompt means to the purchaser within five business days;

(iii) The acquisition(s) meeting the criteria set forth in paragraph (e)(1) of this rule will be consummated if a sufficient number of purchasers confirm their investments; and

(iv) If a consummated acquisition(s) meeting the requirements of this rule has not occurred by a date 18 months after the effective date of the initial registration statement, funds held in the escrow or trust account shall be returned by first class mail or equally prompt means to the purchaser within five business days following that date.

(3) Conditions for release of deposited securities and funds. Funds held in the escrow or trust account may be released to the registrant and securities may be delivered to the purchaser or other registered holder identified on the deposited securities only at the same time as or after:

(i) The escrow agent or trustee has received a signed representation from the registrant, together with other evidence acceptable to the escrow agent or trustee, that the requirements of paragraphs (e)(1) and (e)(2) of this rule have been met; and

(ii) Consummation of an acquisition(s) meeting the requirements of paragraph (e)(2)(iii) of this rule.

(4) Prospectus supplement. If funds and securities are released from the escrow or trust account to the registrant pursuant to this paragraph, the prospectus shall be supplemented to indicate the amount of funds and securities released and the date of release.

Notes to Rule 419(e)

Note 1. With respect to a blank check offering subject to both Rule 419 and Exchange Act Rule 10b–9 the requirements of Rule 10b–9 are applicable only until the conditions of the offering governed by that Rule are met (*e.g.,* reaching the minimum in a "part-or-none" offering). When those conditions are satisfied, Rule 419 continues to govern the use of offering proceeds.

Note 2. If the business(es) or assets are acquired for cash, the fair value shall be presumed to be equal to the cash paid. If all or part of the consideration paid consists of securities or other non-cash consideration, the fair value shall be determined by an accepted standard, such as bona fide sales of the assets or similar assets made within a reasonable time, forecasts of expected cash flows, independent appraisals, etc. Such valuation must be reasonable at the time made.

(f) *Financial statements.* The registrant shall:

(1) Furnish to security holders audited financial statements for the first full fiscal year of operations following consummation of an acquisition pursuant to paragraph (e) of this rule, together with the information required by Item 303(a) of Regulation S–K (229.303(a)), no later than 90 days after the end of such fiscal year; and

(2) File the financial statements and additional information with the Commission under cover of Form 8–K (249.308); *provided, however,* that such financial statements and related information need not be filed separately if the registrant is filing reports pursuant to Section 13(a) or 15(d) of the Exchange Act.

FORM AND CONTENTS OF PROSPECTUSES

Rule 420. Legibility of Prospectuses

(a) The body of all printed prospectuses and all notes to financial statements and other tabular data included therein shall be in roman type at least as large and as legible as 10-point modern type. However, (1) to the extent necessary for convenient presentation, financial statements and other tabular data, including tabular data in notes, and (2) prospectuses deemed to be omitting prospectuses under rule 482 may be in roman type at least as large and as legible as 8-point modern type. All such type shall be leaded at least 2-points.

(b) Where a prospectus is distributed through an electronic medium, issuers may satisfy legibility requirements applicable to printed documents, such as paper size, type size and font, boldface type, italics and red ink, by presenting all required information in a format readily communicated to investors, and where indicated, in a manner reasonably calculated to draw investor attention to specific information.

Rule 421. Presentation of Information in Prospectuses

(a) The information required in a prospectus need not follow the order of the items or other requirements in the form. Such information shall not, however, be set forth in such fashion as to obscure any of the required information or any information necessary to keep the required information from being incomplete or misleading. Where an item requires information to be given in a prospectus in tabular form it shall be given in substantially the tabular form specified in the item.

(b) You must present the information in a prospectus in a clear, concise and understandable manner. You must prepare the prospectus using the following standards:

(1) Present information in clear, concise sections, paragraphs, and sentences. Whenever possible, use short, explanatory sentences and bullet lists;

(2) Use descriptive headings and subheadings;

(3) Avoid frequent reliance on glossaries or defined terms as the primary means of explaining information in the prospectus. Define terms in a glossary or other section of the document only if the meaning is unclear from the context. Use a glossary only if it facilitates understanding of the disclosure; and

(4) Avoid legal and highly technical business terminology.

Note to § 230.421(b):

In drafting the disclosure to comply with this section, you should avoid the following:

1. Legalistic or overly complex presentations that make the substance of the disclosure difficult to understand;

2. Vague "boilerplate" explanations that are imprecise and readily subject to different interpretations;

3. Complex information copied directly from legal documents without any clear and concise explanation of the provision(s); and

4. Disclosure repeated in different sections of the document that increases the size of the document but does not enhance the quality of the information.

(c) All information required to be included in a prospectus shall be clearly understandable without the necessity of referring to the particular form or to the general rules and regulations. Except as to financial statements and information required in a tabular form, the information set forth in a prospectus may be expressed in condensed or summarized form. In lieu of repeating information in the form of notes to financial statements, references may be made to other parts of the prospectus where such information is set forth.

(d)(1) To enhance the readability of the prospectus, you must use plain English principles in the organization, language, and design of the front and back cover pages, the summary, and the risk factors section.

(2) You must draft the language in these sections so that at a minimum it substantially complies with each of the following plain English writing principles:

(i) Short sentences;

(ii) Definite, concrete, everyday words;

(iii) Active voice;

(iv) Tabular presentation or bullet lists for complex material, whenever possible;

(v) No legal jargon or highly technical business terms; and

(vi) No multiple negatives.

(3) In designing these sections or other sections of the prospectus, you may include pictures, logos, charts, graphs, or other design elements so long as the design is not misleading and the required information is clear. You are encouraged to use tables, schedules, charts and graphic illustrations of the results of operations, balance sheet, or other financial data that present the data in an understandable manner. Any presentation must be consistent with the financial statements and non-financial information in the prospectus. You must draw the graphs and charts to scale. Any information you provide must not be misleading.

Instruction to § 230.421

You should read Securities Act Release No. 33–7497 (January 28, 1998) for information on plain English principles.

Rule 423. Date of Prospectuses

Except for a form of prospectus used after the effective date of the registration statement and before the determination of the offering price as permitted by Rule 430A(c) under the Securities Act or before the opening of bids as permitted by Rule 445(c) under the Securities Act, each prospectus used after the effective date of the registration statement shall be dated approximately as of such effective date; provided, however, that a revised or amended prospectus used thereafter need only bear the approximate date of its issuance. Each supplement to a prospectus shall be dated separately the approximate date of its issuance.

Rule 424. Filing of Prospectuses, Number of Copies

(a) Except as provided in paragraph (f) of this section, five copies of every form of prospectus sent or given to any person prior to the effective date of the registration statement which varies from the form or forms of prospectus included in the registration statement as filed pursuant to Rule 402(a) of this chapter shall be filed as a part of the registration statement not later than the date such form of prospectus is first sent or given to any person: *Provided, however,* that only a form of prospectus that contains substantive changes from or additions to a prospectus previously filed with the Commission as part of a registration statement need be filed pursuant to this paragraph (a).

(b) Ten copies of each form of prospectus purporting to comply with section 10 of the Securities Act, except for documents constituting a prospectus pursuant to Rule 428(a), shall be filed with the Commission in the form in which it is used after the effectiveness of the registration statement and identified as required by paragraph (e); *Provided, however,* that only a form of prospectus that contains substantive changes from or additions to a previously filed prospectus is required to be filed; *Provided, further,* that this paragraph (b) shall not apply in respect of a form of prospectus contained in a registration statement and relating solely to securities offered at competitive bidding, which prospectus is intended for use prior to the opening of bids. The ten copies shall be filed or transmitted for filing as follows:

(1) A form of prospectus that discloses information previously omitted from the prospectus filed as part of an effective registration statement in reliance upon Rule 430A under the Securities Act shall be filed with the commission no later than the second business day following the earlier of the date of determination of the offering price or the date it is first used after effectiveness in connection with a public offering or sales, or transmitted by a means reasonably calculated to result in filing with the Commission by that date.

(2) A form of prospectus used in connection with a primary offering of securities on a delayed basis pursuant to Rule 415(a)(1)(vii), (viii) or (x) under the Securities Act, that discloses the public offering price, description of securities, specific method of distribution or similar matters shall be filed with the Commission no later than the second business day following the earlier of the date of the determination of the offering price or the date it is first used after effectiveness in connection with a public offering or sales, or transmitted by a means reasonably calculated to result in filing with the Commission by that date.

(3) A form of prospectus that reflects facts or events other than those covered in paragraphs (b)(1), (2) and (6) of this rule that constitute a substantive change from or addition to the information set forth in the last form of prospectus filed with the Commission under this rule or as part of a registration statement under the Securities Act shall be filed with the Commission no later than the fifth business day after the date it is first used after effectiveness in connection with a public offering or sales, or transmitted by a means reasonably calculated to result in filing with the Commission by that date.

(4) A form of prospectus that discloses information, facts or events covered in both

paragraphs (b)(1) and (3) shall be filed with the Commission no later than the second business day following the earlier of the date of the determination of the offering price or the date it is first used after effectiveness in connection with a public offering or sales, or transmitted by a means reasonably calculated to result in filing with the Commission by that date.

(5) A form of prospectus that discloses information, facts or events covered in both paragraphs (b)(2) and (3) shall be filed with the Commission no later than the second business day following the earlier of the date of the determination of the offering price or the date it is first used after effectiveness in connection with a public offering or sales, or transmitted by a means reasonably calculated to result in filing with the Commission by that date.

(6) A form of prospectus used in connection with an offering of securities under Canada's National Policy Statement No. 45 pursuant to Rule 415 under the Securities Act that is not made in the United States shall be filed with the Commission no later than the date it is first used in Canada, or transmitted by a means reasonably calculated to result in filing with the Commission by that date.

(7) Ten copies of a term sheet or abbreviated term sheet sent or given in reliance upon Rule 434 under the Act (§ 230.434) shall be filed with the Commission pursuant to this paragraph no later than the second business day following the earlier of the date of determination of the offering price, or the date it is first used after effectiveness in connection with a public offering or sales, or transmitted by a means reasonably calculated to result in filing with the Commission by that date. In addition to the information required by paragraph (e) of this section, each copy of such term sheet or abbreviated term sheet shall include the information required by Rule 434(e) (§ 230.434(e)).

Instruction 1: Notwithstanding Rule 424(b)(2) and (b)(5) above, a form of prospectus or prospectus supplement relating to an offering of mortgage-related securities on a delayed basis under Rule 415(a)(1)(vii) or asset-backed securities on a delayed basis under Rule 415(a)(1)(x) that is required to be filed pursuant to paragraph (b) of this rule shall be filed with the Commission no later than the second business day following the date it is first used after effectiveness in connection with a public offering or sales, or transmitted by a means reasonably calculated to result in filing with the Commission by that date.

Instruction 2: Notwithstanding paragraphs (b)(1), (b)(2), (b)(4) and (b)(5) of this section, a form of prospectus sent or given in reliance on Rule 434(c) (§ 230.434(c)) with respect to securities registered on Form S–3 or Form F–3 (§ 239.13 or § 239.33 of this chapter), other than an abbreviated term sheet filed pursuant to paragraph (b)(7) of this section, shall be filed with the Commission on or prior to the date on which a confirmation is sent or given.

(c) If a form of prospectus, other than one filed pursuant to paragraph (b)(1) or (b)(4) of this rule, consists of a prospectus supplement attached to a form of prospectus that (1) previously has been filed or (2) was not required to be filed pursuant to paragraph (b) because it did not contain substantive changes from a prospectus that previously was filed, only the prospectus supplement need be filed under paragraph (b) of this rule, provided that the first page of each prospectus supplement includes a cross references to the date(s) of the related prospectus and any prospectus supplements thereto that together constitute the prospectus required to be delivered by Section 5(b) of the Securities Act with respect to the securities currently being offered or sold. The cross reference may be set forth in longhand, provided it is legible.

Note:—Any prospectus supplement being filed separately that is smaller than a prospectus page should be attached to an 8½″ X 11″ sheet of paper.

(d) Every prospectus consisting of a radio or television broadcast shall be reduced to writing. Five copies of every such prospectus shall be filed with the Commission in accordance with the requirements of this section.

(e) Each copy of a form of prospectus filed under this rule shall contain in the upper right corner of the cover page the paragraph of this rule, including the subparagraph if applicable, under which the filing is made, and the file number of the registration statement to which the prospectus relates. The information required by this paragraph may be set forth in longhand, provided it is legible.

(f) This rule shall not apply with respect to prospectuses of an investment company registered under the Investment Company Act of 1940 or a business development company.

Rule 425. Filing of Certain Prospectuses and Communications under § 230.135 in Connection With Business Combination Transactions

(a) All written communications made in reliance on § 230.165 are prospectuses that must be filed with the Commission under this section on the date of first use.

(b) All written communications that contain no more information than that specified in § 230.135 must be filed with the Commission on or before the date of first use except as provided in paragraph (d)(1) of this section. A communication limited to the information specified in § 230.135 will not be deemed an offer in accordance with § 230.135 even though it is filed under this section.

(c) Each prospectus or § 230.135 communication filed under this section must identify the filer, the company that is the subject of the offering and the Commission file number for the related registration statement or, if that file number is unknown, the subject company's Exchange Act or Investment Company Act file number, in the upper right corner of the cover page.

(d) Notwithstanding paragraph (a) of this section, the following need not be filed under this section:

(1) Any written communication that is limited to the information specified in § 230.135 and does not contain new or different information from that which was previously publicly disclosed and filed under this section.

(2) Any research report used in reliance on § 230.137, § 230.138 and § 230.139;

(3) Any confirmation described in § 240.10b–10 of this chapter; and

(4) Any prospectus filed under § 230.424.

Notes to § 230.425: 1. File five copies of the prospectus or § 230.135 communication if paper filing is permitted.

2. No filing is required under § 240.13e–4(c), § 240.14a–12(b), § 240.14d–2(b), or § 240.14d–9(a), if the communication is filed under this section. Communications filed under this section also are deemed filed under the other applicable sections.

Rule 426. Filing of Certain Prospectuses Under § 230.167 in Connection with Certain Offerings of Asset-Backed Securities

(a) All written communications made in reliance on § 230.167 are prospectuses that must be filed with the Commission in accordance with paragraphs (b) and (c) of this section on Form 8-K (§ 249.308 of this chapter) and incorporated by reference to the related registration statement for the offering of asset- backed securities. Each prospectus filed under this section must identify the Commission file number of the related registration statement on the cover page of the related Form 8-K in addition to any other information required by that form. The information contained in any such prospectus shall be deemed to be a part of the registration statement as of the earlier of the time of filing of such information or the time of the filing of the final prospectus that meets the requirements of section 10(a) of the

Act (15 U.S.C. 77j(a)) relating to such offering pursuant to § 230.424(b).

(b) Except as specified in paragraph (c) of this section, ABS *informational and computational material* made in reliance on § 230.167 that meet the conditions in paragraph (b)(1) of this section must be filed within the time frame specified in paragraph (b)(2) of this section.

(1) *Conditions for which materials must be filed*. The materials are provided to prospective investors under the following conditions:

(i) If a prospective investor has indicated to the issuer or an underwriter that it will purchase all or a portion of the class of asset-backed securities to which such materials relate, all materials relating to such class that are or have been provided to such prospective investor; and

(ii) For any other prospective investor, all materials provided to such prospective investor after the final terms have been established for all classes of the offering.

(2) *Time frame to file the materials*. The materials must be filed by the later of:

(i) The due date for filing the final prospectus relating to such offering that meets the requirements of section 10(a) of the Act (15 U.S.C. 77j(a)) pursuant to § 230.424(b); or

(ii) Two business days after first use.

(c) Notwithstanding paragraphs (a) and (b) of this section, the following need not be filed under this section:

(1) *ABS informational and computational material* that relate to abandoned structures or that are furnished to a prospective investor prior to the time the final terms have been established for all classes of the offering where such prospective investor has not indicated to the issuer or an underwriter its intention to purchase the asset-backed securities.

(2) Any *ABS informational and computational material* if a prospectus that meets the requirements of section 10(a) of the Act (15 U.S.C. 77j(a)) relating to the offering of such asset-backed securities accompanies or precedes the use of such material.

(3) Any *ABS informational and computational material* that does not contain new or different information from that which was previously disclosed and filed under this section.

(4) Any written communication that is limited to the information specified in § 230.134, 230.135 or 230.135c.

(5) Any research report used in reliance on § 230.137, 230.138, 230.139 or 230.139a.

(6) Any confirmation described in § 240.10b–10 of this chapter.

(7) Any prospectus filed under § 230.424.

(d) Terms used in this section have the same meaning as in Item 1101 of Regulation AB (§ 229.1101 of this chapter).

Instruction to § 230.426.

The issuer may aggregate data presented in *ABS informational and computational material* that are to be filed and file such data in consolidated form. Any such aggregation, however, must not result in either the omission of any information contained in such material otherwise to be filed, or a presentation that makes the information misleading.

Rule 427. Contents of Prospectus Used After Nine Months

There may be omitted from any prospectus used more than 9 months after the effective date of the registration statement any information previously required to be contained in the prospectus insofar as later information covering the same subjects, including the latest available certified financial statement, as of a date not more than 16 months prior to the use of the prospectus is contained therein.

Rule 428. Documents Constituting a Section 10(a) Prospectus for Form S–8 Registration Statement; Requirements Relating to Offerings of Securities Registered on Form S–8

(a)(1) Where securities are to be offered pursuant to a registration statement on Form S–8, the following, taken together, shall constitute a prospectus that meets the requirements of section 10(a) of the Act: (i) The document(s), or portions thereof as permitted by paragraph (b)(1)(ii) of this rule, containing the employee benefit plan information required by Item 1 of the Form; (ii) the statement of availability of registrant information, employee benefit plan annual reports and other information required by Item 2; and (iii) the documents containing registrant information and employee benefit plan annual reports that are incorporated by reference in the registration statement pursuant to Item 3.

(2) The registrant shall maintain a file of the documents that, pursuant to paragraph (a) of this rule, at any time are part of the section 10(a) prospectus, except for documents required to be incorporated by reference in the registration statement pursuant to Item 3 of Form S–8. Each such document shall be included in the file until five years after it is last used as part of the Section 10(a) prospectus to offer or sell securities pursuant to the plan. With respect to documents containing specifically designated portions that constitute part of the section 10(a) prospectus pursuant to paragraph (b)(1)(ii) of this rule, the entire document shall be maintained in the file. Upon request, the registrant shall furnish to the Commission or its staff a copy of any or all of the documents included in the file.

(b) Where securities are offered pursuant to a registration statement on Form S–8:

(1)(i) The registrant shall deliver or cause to be delivered, to each employee who is eligible to participate (or selected by the registrant to participate, in the case of a stock option or other plan with selective participation) in an employee benefit plan to which the registration statement relates, the information required by Part I of Form S–8. The information shall be in written form and shall be updated in writing in a timely manner to reflect any material changes during any period in which offers or sales are being made. When updating information is furnished, documents previously furnished need not be redelivered, but the registrant shall furnish promptly without charge to each employee, upon written or oral request, a copy of all documents containing the plan information required by Part I that then constitute part of the section 10(a) prospectus.

(ii) The registrant may designate an entire document or only portions of a document as constituting part of the section 10(a) prospectus. If the registrant designates only portions of a document as constituting part of the prospectus, rather than the entire document, a statement clearly identifying such portions, for example, by reference to section headings, section numbers, paragraphs or page numbers within the document must be included in a conspicuous place in the forepart of the document, or such portions must be specifically designated throughout the text of the document. Registrants shall not designate only words or sentences within a paragraph as part of a prospectus. Unless the portions of a document constituting part of the section 10(a) prospectus are clearly identified, the entire document shall constitute part of the prospectus.

(iii) The registrant shall date any document constituting part of the section 10(a) prospectus or containing portions constituting part of the prospectus and shall include the following printed, stamped or typed legend in a conspicuous place in the forepart of the document, substituting the bracketed language as appropriate: "This document [Specifically designated portions of this document] constitutes [constitute] part of a prospectus covering securities that have been registered under the Securities Act of 1933."

(iv) The registrant shall revise the document(s) containing the plan information sent or given to newly eligible participants pursuant to paragraph (b)(1)(i) of this rule, if documents containing updating information would obscure the readability of the plan information.

(2) The registrant shall deliver or cause to be delivered with the document(s) containing the information required by Part I of Form S–8, to each employee to whom such information is sent or given, a copy of any one of the following:

(i) The registrant's annual report to security holders containing the information required by Rule 14a–3(b) (§ 240.14a–3(b) of this chapter) under the Securities Exchange Act of 1934 (Exchange Act) for its latest fiscal year;

(ii) The registrant's annual report on Form 10–K and Form 10–KSB (§ 249.310 of this chapter), U5S (§ 259.5s of this chapter), 20–F (§ 249.220f of this chapter) or, in the case of registrants described in General Instruction A.(2) of Form 40–F, 40–F (§ 249.240f of this chapter) for its latest fiscal year;

(iii) The latest prospectus filed pursuant to Rule 424(b) (§ 230.424(b) of this chapter) under the Act that contains audited financial statements for the registrant's latest fiscal year, Provided that the financial statements are not incorporated by reference from another filing, and Provided further that such prospectus contains substantially the information required by Rule 14a–3(b) or the registration statement was on Form SB–2 (§ 239.28 of this chapter) or F–1 (§ 239.31 of this chapter); or

(iv) The registrant's effective Exchange Act registration statement on Form 10 and Form 10–SB (§ 249.210 of this chapter), 20–F or, in the case of registrants described in General Instruction A.(2) of Form 40–F, 40–F containing audited financial statements for the registrant's latest fiscal year.

Instructions. 1. If a registrant has previously sent or given an employee a copy of any document specified in clauses (i)–(iv) of paragraph (b)(2) for the latest fiscal year, it need not be re-delivered, but the registrant shall furnish promptly, without charge, a copy of such document upon written or oral request of the employee.

2. If the latest fiscal year of the registrant has ended within 120 days (or 190 days with respect to foreign private issuers) prior to the delivery of the documents containing the information specified by Part I of Form S–8, the registrant may deliver a document containing financial statements for the fiscal year preceding the latest fiscal year, *provided that* within the 120 or 190 day period a document containing financial statements for the latest fiscal year is furnished to each employee.

(3) The registrant shall deliver or cause to be delivered promptly, without charge, to each employee to whom information is required to be delivered, upon written or oral request, a copy of the information that has been incorporated by reference pursuant to Item 3 of Form S–8 (not including exhibits to the information that is incorporated by reference unless such exhibits are specifically incorporated by reference into the information that the registration statement incorporates).

(4) Where interests in a plan are registered, the registrant shall deliver or cause to be delivered promptly, without charge, to each employee to whom information is required to be delivered, upon written or oral request, a copy of the then latest annual report of the plan filed pursuant to Section 15(d) of the Exchange Act, whether on Form 11–K or included as part of the registrant's annual report on Form 10–K and Form 10–KSB.

(5) The registrant shall deliver or cause to be delivered to all employees participating in a stock option plan or plan fund that invests in registrant securities (and other plan participants who request such information oral-

ly or in writing) who do not otherwise receive such material, copies of all reports, proxy statements and other communications distributed to its security holders generally, provided that such material is sent or delivered no later than the time it is sent to security holders.

(c) As used in this Rule, the term "employee benefit plan" is defined in Rule 405 of Regulation C and the term "employee" is defined in General Instruction A.1 of Form S–8.

Rule 429. Prospectus Relating to Several Registration Statements

(a) Where a registrant has filed two or more registration statements, it may file a single prospectus in the latest registration statement in order to satisfy the requirements of the Act and the rules and regulations thereunder for that offering and any other offering(s) registered on the earlier registration statement(s). The combined prospectus in the latest registration statement must include all of the information that currently would be required in a prospectus relating to all offering(s) that it covers. The combined prospectus may be filed as part of the initial filing of the latest registration statement, in a pre-effective amendment to it or in a post-effective amendment to it.

(b) Where a registrant relies on paragraph (a) of this section, the registration statement containing the combined prospectus shall act, upon effectiveness, as a post-effective amendment to any earlier registration statement whose prospectus has been combined in the latest registration statement. The registrant must identify any earlier registration statement to which the combined prospectus relates by setting forth the Commission file number at the bottom of the facing page of the latest registration statement.

Rule 430. Prospectus for Use Prior to Effective Date

(a) A form of prospectus filed as a part of the registration statement shall be deemed to meet the requirements of section 10 of the Act for the purpose of section 5(b)(1) thereof prior to the effective date of the registration statement, provided such form of prospectus contains substantially the information required by the Act and the rules and regulations thereunder to be included in a prospectus meeting the requirements of section 10(a) of the Act for the securities being registered, or contains substantially that information except for the omission of information with respect to the offering price, underwriting discounts or commissions, discounts or commissions to dealers, amount of proceeds, conversion rates, call prices, or other matters dependent upon the offering price. Every such form of prospectus shall be deemed to have been filed as a part of the registration statement for the purpose of section 7 of the Act.

(b) A form of prospectus filed as part of a registration statement on Form N–1A (§239.15A and § 274.11A of this chapter), Form N–2 (§ 239.14 and § 274.11a–1 of this chapter), Form N–3 (§ 239.17a and § 274.11b of this chapter), Form N–4 (§ 239.17b and § 274.11c of this chapter), or Form N–6 (§ 239.17c and § 274.11d of this chapter) shall be deemed to meet the requirements of Section 10 of the Act (15 U.S.C. 77j) for the purpose of Section 5(b)(1) thereof (15 U.S.C. 77e(b)(1)) prior to the effective date of the registration statement, provided that:

(1) Such form of prospectus meets the requirements of paragraph (a) of this rule; and

(2) Such registration statement contains a form of Statement of Additional Information that is made available to persons receiving such prospectus upon written or oral request, and without charge, unless the form of prospectus contains the information otherwise required to be disclosed in the form of Statement of Additional Information. Every such form of prospectus shall be deemed to have been filed as part of the registration statement for the purpose of section 7 of the Act.

Rule 430A. Prospectus in a Registration Statement at the Time of Effectiveness

(a) The form of prospectus filed as part of a registration statement that is declared effective may omit information with respect to the public offering price, underwriting syndicate (including any material relationships between the registrant and underwriters not named therein), underwriting discounts or commissions, discounts or commissions to dealers, amount of proceeds, conversion rates, call prices and other items dependent upon the offering price, delivery dates, and terms of the securities dependent upon the offering date; and such form of prospectus need not contain such information in order for the registration statement to meet the requirements of Section 7 of the Securities Act for the purposes of Section 5 thereof, *Provided that*:

(1) The securities to be registered are offered for cash;

(2) The registrant furnishes the undertakings required by Item 512(i) of Regulation S-K; and

(3) The information omitted in reliance upon paragraph (a) from the form of prospectus filed as part of a registration statement that is declared effective is contained in a form of prospectus filed with the Commission pursuant to Rule 424(b) or Rule 497(h) under the Securities Act; except that if such form of prospectus is not so filed by the later of fifteen business days after the effective date of the registration statement or fifteen business days after the effectiveness of a post-effective amendment thereto that contains a form of prospectus, or transmitted by a means reasonably calculated to result in filing with the Commission by that date, the information omitted in reliance upon paragraph (a) must be contained in an effective post-effective amendment to the registration statement.

Instruction to paragraph (a): A decrease in the volume of securities offered or change in the bona fide estimate of the maximum offering price range from that indicated in the form of prospectus filed as part of a registration statement that is declared effective may be disclosed in the form of prospectus filed with the Commission pursuant to Rule 424(b) or Rule 497(h) under the Securities Act so long as the decrease in the volume or change in the price range would not materially change the disclosure contained in the registration statement at effectiveness. Notwithstanding the foregoing, any increase or decrease in volume (if the total dollar value of securities offered would not exceed that which was registered) and any deviation from the low or high end of the range may be reflected in the form of prospectus filed with the Commission pursuant to Rule 424(b)(1) (§ 230.424(b)(1)) or Rule 497(h) (§ 230.497(h)) if, in the aggregate, the changes in volume and price represent no more than a 20% change in the maximum aggregate offering price set forth in the "Calculation of Registration Fee" table in the effective registration statement.

(b) The information omitted in reliance upon paragraph (a) from the form of prospectus filed as part of an effective registration statement, and contained in the form of prospectus filed with the Commission pursuant to Rule 424(b) or Rule 497(h) under the Securities Act, shall be deemed to be a part of the registration statement as of the time it was declared effective.

(c) When used prior to determination of the offering price of the securities, a form of prospectus relating to the securities offered pursuant to a registration statement that is declared effective with information omitted from the form of prospectus filed as part of such effective registration statement in reliance upon this Rule 430A need not contain information omitted pursuant to paragraph (a), in order to meet the requirements of Section 10 of the Securities Act for the purpose of Section 5(b)(1) thereof. This provision shall not limit the information required to be contained in a form of prospectus meeting the requirements of Section 10(a) of the Act for the purposes of

Section 5(b)(2) thereof or exception (a) of Section 2(10) thereof.

(d) This rule shall not apply to registration statements for securities to be offered by competitive bidding.

(e) In the case of a registration statement filed on Form N–1A (§ 239.15A and § 274.11A of this chapter), Form N–2 (§ 239.14 and § 274.11a–1 of this chapter), Form N–3 (§ 239.17a and § 274.11b of this chapter), Form N–4 (§ 239.17b and § 274.11c of this chapter), or Form N–6 (§ 239.17c and § 274.11d of this chapter), the references to "form of prospectus" in paragraphs (a) and (b) of this section and the accompanying Note shall be deemed also to refer to the form of Statement of Additional Information filed as part of such a registration statement.

Note: If information is omitted in reliance upon paragraph (a) from the form of prospectus filed as part of an effective registration statement, or effective post-effective amendment thereto, the registrant must ascertain promptly whether a form of prospectus transmitted for filing under Rule 424(b) or Rule 497(h) under the Securities Act actually was received for filing by the Commission and, in the event that it was not, promptly file such prospectus.

Rule 431. Summary Prospectuses

(a) A summary prospectus prepared and filed (except a summary prospectus filed by an open-end management investment company registered under the Investment Company Act of 1940) as part of a registration statement in accordance with this section shall be deemed to be a prospectus permitted under section 10(b) of the Act (15 U.S.C. 77j(b)) for the purposes of section 5(b)(1) of the Act (15 U.S.C. 77e(b)(1)) if the form used for registration of the securities to be offered provides for the use of a summary prospectus and the following conditions are met:

(1)(i) The registrant is organized under the laws of the United States or any State or Territory or the District of Columbia and has its principal business operations in the United States or its territories; or

(ii) The registrant is a foreign private issuer eligible to use Form F–2;

(2) The registrant has a class of securities registered pursuant to section 12(b) of the Securities Exchange Act of 1934 or has a class of equity securities registered pursuant to section 12(g) of that Act or is required to file reports pursuant to section 15(d) of that Act;

(3) The registrant: (i) Has been subject to the requirements of section 12 or 15(d) of the Securities Exchange Act of 1934 and has filed all the material required to be filed pursuant to sections 13, 14 or 15(d) of that Act for a period of at least thirty-six calendar months immediately preceding the filing of the registration statement; and (ii) has filed in a timely manner all reports required to be filed during the twelve calendar months and any portion of a month immediately preceding the filing of the registration statement and, if the registrant has used (during the twelve calendar months and any portion of a month immediately preceding the filing of the registration statement) Rule 12b–25(b) under the Securities Exchange Act of 1934 with respect to a report or portion of a report, that report or portion thereof has actually been filed within the time period prescribed by that Rule; and

(4) Neither the registrant nor any of its consolidated or unconsolidated subsidiaries has, since the end of its last fiscal year for which certified financial statements of the registrant and its consolidated subsidiaries were included in a report filed pursuant to section 13(a) or 15(d) of the Securities Exchange Act of 1934: (i) failed to pay any dividend or sinking fund installment on preferred stock; or (ii) defaulted on any installment or installments on indebtedness for borrowed money, or on any rental on one or more long term leases, which defaults in the aggregate are material to the financial position of the registrant and its consolidated

and unconsolidated subsidiaries, taken as a whole.

(b) A summary prospectus shall contain the information specified in the instructions as to summary prospectuses in the form used for registration of the securities to be offered. Such prospectus may include any other information the substance of which is contained in the registration statement except as otherwise specifically provided in the instructions as to summary prospectuses in the form used for registration. It shall not include any information the substance of which is not contained in the registration statement except that a summary prospectus may contain any information specified in Rule 134(a). No reference need be made to inapplicable terms and negative answers to any item of the form may be omitted.

(c) All information included in a summary prospectus, other than the statement required by paragraph (e) of this section, may be expressed in such condensed or summarized form as may be appropriate in the light of the circumstances under which the prospectus is to be used. The information need not follow the numerical sequence of the items of the form used for registration. Every summary prospectus shall be dated approximately as of the date of its first use.

(d) When used prior to the effective date of the registration statement, a summary prospectus shall be captioned a "Preliminary Summary Prospectus" and shall comply with the applicable requirements relating to a preliminary prospectus.

(e) A statement to the following effect shall be prominently set forth in conspicuous print at the beginning or at the end of every summary prospectus:

"Copies of a more complete prospectus may be obtained from" (Insert name(s), address(es) and telephone number(s)).

Copies of a summary prospectus filed with the Commission pursuant to paragraph (g) of this section may omit the names of persons from whom the complete prospectus may be obtained.

(f) Any summary prospectus published in a newspaper, magazine or other periodical need only be set in type at least as large as 7 point modern type. Nothing in this rule shall prevent the use of reprints of a summary prospectus published in a newspaper, magazine, or other periodical, if such reprints are clearly legible.

(g) Eight copies of every proposed summary prospectus shall be filed as a part of the registration statement, or as an amendment thereto, at least 5 days (exclusive of Saturdays, Sundays and holidays) prior to the use thereof, or prior to the release for publication by any newspaper, magazine or other person, whichever is earlier. The Commission may, however, in its discretion, authorize such use or publication prior to the expiration of the 5-day period upon a written request for such authorization. Within 7 days after the first use or publication thereof, 5 additional copies shall be filed in the exact form in which it was used or published.

Rule 432. Additional Information Required to Be Included in Prospectuses Relating to Tender Offers

Notwithstanding the provisions of any form for the registration of securities under the Act, any prospectus relating to securities to be offered in connection with a tender offer for, or a request or invitation for tenders of, securities subject to either § 240.13e–4 or section 14(d) of the Securities Exchange Act of 1934 (15 U.S.C. 78n(d)) must include the information required by § 240.13e–4(d)(1) or § 240.14d–6(d)(1) of this chapter, as applicable, in all tender offers, requests or invitations that are published, sent or given to the security holders.

Rule 434. Prospectus Delivery Requirements in Firm Commitment Underwritten Offerings of Securities for Cash

(a) Where securities are offered for cash in a firm commitment underwritten offering or investment grade debt securities are offered for cash on an agency basis under a medium term note program, and such securities are neither asset-backed securities nor structured securities, and the conditions described in paragraph (b) or paragraph (c) of this section are satisfied, then:

(1) The prospectus subject to completion and the term sheet described in paragraph (b) of this section, taken together, and the prospectus subject to completion and the abbreviated term sheet described in paragraph (c) of this section, taken together, shall constitute prospectuses that meet the requirements of section 10(a) of the Act (15 U.S.C. 77j(a)) for purposes of section 5(b)(2) of the Act (15 U.S.C. 77e(b)(2)) and section 2(10)(a) of the Act (15 U.S.C. 77b(10)(a)); and

(2) The section 10(a) prospectus described in paragraph (a)(1) of this section shall have:

(i) Been sent or given prior to or at the same time that a confirmation is sent or given for purposes of section 2(10)(a) of the Act; and

(ii) Accompanied or preceded the transmission of the securities for purpose of sale or for delivery after sale for purposes of Section 5(b)(2) of the Act.

(b) With respect to offerings of securities that are registered on a form other than Form S–3 or Form F–3 (§ 239.13 or § 239.33 of this chapter), and with respect to offerings of securities by only those investment companies registered under the Investment Company Act of 1940 (15 U.S.C. 80a–1 *et seq.*) that register their securities on Form N–2 (§ 274.11a–1 of this chapter) or Form S–6 (§ 239.16 of this chapter), the following conditions are satisfied:

(1) A prospectus subject to completion and any term sheet described in paragraph (b)(3) of this section, together or separately, are sent or given prior to or at the same time with the confirmation:

(2) Such prospectus subject to completion and term sheet, together, are not materially different from the prospectus in the registration statement at the time of its effectiveness or an effective post-effective amendment thereto (including, in both instances, information deemed to be a part of the registration statement at the time of effectiveness pursuant to Rule 430A(b) (§ 230.430A(b))); and

(3) A term sheet under this paragraph (b) shall set forth all information material to investors with respect to the offering that is not disclosed in the prospectus subject to completion or the confirmation.

(c) With respect to offerings of securities registered on Form S–3 or Form F–3 (§ 239.13 or § 239.33 of this chapter), the following conditions are satisfied.

(1) A prospectus subject to completion and the abbreviated term sheet described in paragraph (c)(3) of this section, together or separately, are sent or given prior to or at the same time with the confirmation:

(2) A form of prospectus that:

(i) Discloses information previously omitted from the prospectus filed as part of an effective registration statement in reliance upon Rule 430A (§ 230.430A), to the extent not set forth in the abbreviated term sheet (as described in paragraph (c)(3) of this section), shall be filed pursuant to Rule 424(b) (§ 230.424(b)) on or prior to the date on which a confirmation is sent or given; or

(ii) Discloses the public offering price, description of securities, to the extent not set forth in the abbreviated term sheet (as described in paragraph (c)(3) of this section), and specific method of distribution or similar matters shall be filed pursuant to Rule 424(b) (§ 230.424(b)) on or prior to the date on which a conformation is sent or given; and

(3) The abbreviated term sheet under this paragraph (c) shall set forth, if not previously disclosed in the prospectus subject to completion or the registrant's Exchange Act

filings incorporated by reference into the prospectus:

(i) The description of securities required by Item 202 of Regulation S–K (§ 229.202 of this chapter) or by Items 9, 10 and 12 of Form 20–F (§ 249.220f of this chapter) as applicable, or a fair and accurate summary thereof; and

(ii) All material changes to the registrant's affairs required to be disclosed pursuant to Item 11 of Form S–3 or Item 5 of Form F–3 (§ 239.13 or § 239.33 of this chapter), as applicable.

(d) Except in the case of offerings pursuant to Rule 415(a)(1)(x), (§ 230.415(a)(1)(x)), the information contained in any term sheet or abbreviated term sheet described under this section shall be deemed to be a part of the registration statement as of the time such registration statement was declared effective. In the case of offerings pursuant to Rule 415(a)(1)(x) (§ 230.415(a)(1)(x)), the information contained in any term sheet or abbreviated term sheet described under this section shall be deemed to be a part of the registration statement as of the time such information is filed with the Commission.

Instruction: With respect to the obligation to file any form of prospectus, term sheet, or abbreviated term sheet used in reliance on this section, see Rule 424(b) (§ 230.424(b)) or Rule 497(h) (§ 230.497(h)).

(e) Any term sheet or abbreviated term sheet described under this section shall, in the top center of the cover page thereof, state that such document is a supplement to a prospectus and identify that prospectus by issuer name and date; clearly identify that such document is a term sheet or abbreviated term sheet used in reliance on Rule 434; set forth the approximate date of first use of such document; and clearly identify the documents that, when taken together, constitute the Section 10(a) prospectus.

(f) For purposes of this section, *asset-backed securities* shall mean asset-backed securities as defined in § 229.1101 of this chapter.

(g) For purposes of this section, *prospectus subject to completion* shall mean any prospectus that is either a preliminary prospectus used in reliance on Rule 430 (§ 230.430), a prospectus omitting information in reliance upon Rule 430A (§ 230.430A), or a prospectus omitting information that is not yet known concerning a delayed offering pursuant to Rule 415(a)(i)(x) (§ 230.415(a)(1)(x)) that is contained in a registration statement at the time of effectiveness or as subsequently revised.

(h) For purposes of this section, *structured securities* shall mean securities whose cash flow characteristics depend upon one or more indices or that have embedded forwards or options or securities where an investor's investment return and the issuer's payment obligations are contingent on, or highly sensitive to, changes in the value of underlying assets, indices, interest rates or cash flows.

(i) For purposes of this section, *investment grade securities* shall mean investment grade securities as defined in General Instruction I.B.2. of Form S–3 or Form F–3 (§ 239.13 or § 239.33 of this chapter).

(j) For the purposes of this section, a firm commitment underwritten offering shall include a firm commitment underwritten offering of securities by a closed-end company or by a unit investment trust registered under the Investment Company Act of 1940.

WRITTEN CONSENTS

Rule 436. Consents Required in Special Cases

(a) If any portion of the report or opinion of an expert or counsel is quoted or summarized as such in the registration statement or in a prospectus, the written consent of the expert or counsel shall be filed as an exhibit to the registration statement and shall expressly state that the expert or counsel consents to such quotation or summarization.

(b) If it is stated that any information contained in the registration statement has been reviewed or passed upon by any persons and that such information is set forth in the registration statement upon the authority of or in reliance upon such persons as experts, the written consents of such persons shall be filed as exhibits to the registration statement.

(c) Notwithstanding the provisions of paragraph (b) of this section, a report on unaudited interim financial information (as defined in paragraph (d) of this section) by an independent accountant who has conducted a review of such interim financial information shall not be considered a part of a registration statement prepared or certified by an accountant or a report prepared or certified by an accountant within the meaning of sections 7 and 11 of the Act.

(d) The term "report on unaudited interim financial information" shall mean a report which consists of the following: (1) a statement that the review of interim financial information was made in accordance with established professional standards for such reviews; (2) an identification of the interim financial information reviewed; (3) a description of the procedures for a review of interim financial information; (4) a statement that a review of interim financial information is substantially less in scope than an examination in accordance with generally accepted auditing standards, the objective of which is an expression of opinion regarding the financial statements taken as a whole, and, accordingly, no such opinion is expressed; and (5) a statement about whether the accountant is aware of any material modifications that should be made to the accompanying financial information so that it conforms with generally accepted accounting principles.

(e) Where a counsel is named as having acted for the underwriters or selling security holders, no consent will be required by reason of his being named as having acted in such capacity.

(f) Where the opinion of one counsel relies upon the opinion of another counsel, the consent of the counsel whose prepared opinion is relied upon need not be furnished.

(g)(1) Notwithstanding the provisions of paragraphs (a) and (b) of this section, the security rating assigned to a class of debt securities, a class of convertible debt securities, or a class of preferred stock by a nationally recognized statistical rating organization, or with respect to registration statements on Form F–9 (§ 239.39 of this chapter) by any other rating organization specified in the Instruction to paragraph (a)(2) of General Instruction I of Form F–9, shall not be considered a part of the registration statement prepared or certified by a person within the meaning of sections 7 and 11 of the Act.

(2) For the purpose of paragraph (g)(1) of this section, the term "nationally recognized statistical rating organization" shall have the same meaning as used in Rule 15c3–1(c)(2)(vi)(F).

Rule 437. Application to Dispense With Consent

An application to the Commission to dispense with any written consent of an expert pursuant to section 7 of the Act shall be made by the registrant and shall be supported by an affidavit or affidavits establishing that the obtaining of such consent is impracticable or involves undue hardships on the registrant. Such application shall be filed and the consent of the Commission shall be obtained prior to the effective date of the registration statement.

Rule 438. Consents of Persons About to Become Directors

If any person who has not signed the registration statement is named therein as about to become a director, the written consent of such person shall be filed with the registration statement. Any such consent, however, may be omitted if there is filed with the registration statement a statement by the registrant, supported by an affidavit or affidavits, setting forth the reasons for such omission and establishing that the obtaining of such consent is impracticable or involves undue hardship on the registrant.

Rule 439. Consent to Use of Material Incorporated by Reference

(a) If the Act or the rules and regulations of the Commission require the filing of a written consent to the use of any material in connection with the registration statement, such consent shall be filed as an exhibit to the registration statement even though the material is incorporated therein by reference. Where the filing of a written consent is required with respect to material incorporated in the registration statement by reference, which is to be filed subsequent to the effective date of the registration statement, such consent shall be filed as an amendment to the registration statement no later than the date on which such material is filed with the Commission, unless express consent to incorporation by reference is contained in the material to be incorporated by reference.

(b) Notwithstanding paragraph (a) of this section, any required consent may be incorporated by reference into a registration statement filed pursuant to Rule 462(b) under the Act (§ 230.462(b)) from a previously filed registration statement relating to that offering, provided that, the consent contained in the previously filed registration statement expressly provides for such incorporation.

FILINGS; FEES; EFFECTIVE DATE

Rule 455. Place of Filing

All registration statements and other papers filed with the Commission shall be filed at its principal office, except for statements of Form SB–1 (§ 239.9 of this chapter) and Form SB–2 (§ 239.10 of this chapter). Registration statements on Form SB–1 or SB–2 may be filed with the Commission either at its principal office or at the Commission's regional or district offices as specified in General Instruction A to each of those forms, except that registration statements and post-effective amendments thereto on such forms that are filed pursuant to Rule 462(b) (§ 230.462(b)) and Rule 110(d) (§ 230.110(d)) shall be filed at the Commission's principal office. Such material may be filed by delivery to the Commission through the mails or otherwise; provided, however, that only registration statements and post-effective amendments thereto filed pursuant to Rule 462(b) (§ 230.462(b)) and Rule 110(d) (§ 230.110(d)) may be filed by means of facsimile transmission.

Rule 456. Date of Filing

The date on which any papers are actually received by the Commission shall be the date of filing thereof, if all the requirements of the Act and the rules with respect to such filing have been complied with and the required fee paid. The failure to pay an insignificant amount of the required fee at the time of filing, as the result of a *bona fide* error, shall not be deemed to affect the date of filing.

Rule 457. Computation of Fee

(a) If a filing fee based on a bona fide estimate of the maximum offering price, computed in accordance with this rule where applicable, has been paid, no additional filing fee shall be required as a result of changes in the proposed offering price. If the number of shares or other units of securities, or the principal amount of debt securities to be offered is increased by an amendment filed prior to the effective date of the registration statement, an additional filing fee, computed on the basis of the offering price of the additional securities, shall be paid. There will be no refund once the statement is filed.

(b) A required fee shall be reduced in an amount equal to any fee paid with respect to such transaction pursuant to sections 13(e) and 14(g) of the Securities Exchange Act of 1934 or any applicable provision of this section; the fee requirements under sections 13(e) and 14(g) shall be reduced in an amount equal to the fee paid the Commission with respect to a transaction under this section. No part of a filing fee is refundable.

(c) Where securities are to be offered at prices computed upon the basis of fluctuating market prices, the registration fee is to be calculated upon the basis of the price of securities of the same class, as follows: either the average of the high and low prices reported in the consolidated reporting system (for exchange traded securities and last sale reported over-the-counter securities) or the average of the bid and asked price (for other over-the-counter securities) as of a specified date within 5 business days prior to the date of filing the registration statement.

(d) Where securities are to be offered at varying prices based upon fluctuating values of underlying assets, the registration fee is to be calculated upon the basis of the market value of such assets as of a specified date within fifteen days prior to the date of filing, in accordance with the method to be used in calculating the daily offering price.

(e) Where securities are to be offered to existing security holders and the portion, if any, not taken by such security holders is to be reoffered to the general public, the registration fee is to be calculated upon the basis of the proposed offering price to such security holders or the proposed reoffering price to the general public, whichever is higher.

(f) Where securities are to be offered in exchange for other securities (except where such exchange results from the exercise of a conversion privilege) or in a reclassification or recapitalization which involves the substitution of a security for another security, a merger, a consolidation, or a similar plan of acquisition, the registration fee is to be calculated as follows:

(1) Upon the basis of the market value of the securities to be received by the registrant or cancelled in the exchange or transaction as established by the price of securities of the same class, as determined in accordance with paragraph (c) of this section.

(2) If there is no market for the securities to be received by the registrant or cancelled in the exchange or transaction, the book value of such securities computed as of the latest practicable date prior to the date of filing the registration statement shall be used, unless the issuer of such securities is in bankruptcy or receivership or has an accumulated capital deficit, in which case one-third of the principal amount, par value or stated value of such securities shall be used.

(3) If any cash is to be received by the registrant in connection with the exchange or transaction, the amount thereof shall be added to the value of the securities to be received by the registrant or cancelled as computed in accordance with (f)(1) or (2) of this section. If any cash is to be paid by the registrant in connection with the exchange or transaction, the amount thereof shall be deducted from the value of the securities to be received by the registrant in exchange as computed in accordance with (e)(1) or (2) of this section.

(4) Securities to be offered directly or indirectly for certificates of deposit shall be deemed to be offered for the securities represented by the certificates of deposit.

(5) If a filing fee is paid under this paragraph for the registration of an offering and the registration statement also covers the resale of such securities, no additional filing fee is required to be paid for the resale transaction.

(g) Where securities are to be offered pursuant to warrants or other rights to purchase such securities and the holders of such warrants or rights may be deemed to be underwriters, as defined in section 2(11) of the Act, with respect to the warrants or rights or the securities subject thereto, the registration fee is to be calculated upon the basis of the price at which the warrants or rights or securities subject thereto are to be offered to the public. If such offering price cannot be determined at the time of filing the registration statement, the registration fee is to be calculated upon the basis of the highest of the following: (1) the price at which the warrants or rights may be exercised, if known at the time of filing the registration statement; (2) the offering price of securities of the same class included in the registration statement; or (3) the price of securities of the same class, as determined in accordance with paragraph (c) of this section. If the fee is to be calculated upon the basis of the price at which the warrants or rights may be exercised and they are exercisable over a period of time at progressively higher prices, the fee shall be calculated on the basis of the highest price at which they may be exercised. If the warrants or rights are to be registered for distribution in the same registration statement as the securities to be offered pursuant thereto, no separate registration fee shall be required.

(h)(1) Where securities are to be offered pursuant to an employee benefit plan, the aggregate offering price and the amount of the registration fee shall be computed with respect to the maximum number of the registrant's securities issuable under the plan that are covered by the registration statement. If the offering price is not known, the fee shall be computed upon the basis of the price of securities of the same class, as determined in accordance with paragraph (c) of this rule. In the case of an employee stock option plan, the aggregate offering price and the fee shall be computed upon the basis of the price at which the options may be exercised, or, if such price is not known, upon the basis of the price of securities of the same class, as determined in accordance with paragraph (c) of this rule. If there is no market for the securities to be offered, the book value of such securities computed as of the latest practicable date prior to the date of filing the registration statement shall be used.

(2) If the registration statement registers securities of the registrant and also registers interests in the plan constituting separate securities, no separate fee is required with respect to the plan interests.

(3) Where a registration statement includes securities to be offered pursuant to an employee benefit plan and covers the resale of the same securities, no additional filing fee shall be paid with respect to the securities to be offered for resale. A filing fee determined in accordance with paragraph (c) of this rule shall be paid with respect to any additional securities to be offered for resale.

(i) Where convertible securities and the securities into which conversion is offered are registered at the same time, the registration fee is to be calculated on the basis of the proposed offering price of the convertible securities alone, except that if any additional consideration is to be received in connection with the exercise of the conversion privilege the maximum amount which may be received shall be added to the proposed offering price of the convertible securities.

(j) Where securities are sold prior to the registration thereof and are subsequently registered for the purpose of making an offer of rescission of such sale or sales, the registration fee is to be calculated on the basis of the amount at which such securities were sold, except that where securities repurchased pursuant to such offer of rescission are to be reoffered to the general public at a price in excess of such amount the registration fee is to be calculated on the basis of the proposed reoffering price.

(k) Notwithstanding the other provisions of this rule, the proposed maximum aggregate offering price of Depositary Shares evidenced by American Depositary Receipts shall, only for the purpose of calculating the registration fee, be computed upon the basis of the maximum aggregate fees or charges to be imposed in connection with the issuance of such receipts.

(*l*) Notwithstanding the other provisions of this rule, the proposed maximum aggregate offering price of any put or call option which is traded on an exchange and registered by such exchange or a facility thereof which is traded over the counter shall, for the purpose of calculating the registration fee, be computed upon the basis of the maximum aggregate fees or charges to be imposed by such registrant in connection with the issuance of such option.

(m) Notwithstanding the other provisions of this rule, where the securities to be registered include (1) any note, draft, bill of exchange, or bankers' acceptance which meets all the conditions of section 3(a)(3) hereof, and (2) any note, draft, bill of exchange or bankers' acceptance which has a maturity at the time of issuance of not exceeding nine months exclusive of days of grace, or any renewal thereof the maturity date of which is likewise limited, but which otherwise does not meet the conditions of section (a)(3), the registration fee shall be calculated by taking one-fiftieth of 1 per centum of the maximum principal amount of only those securities not meeting the conditions of section 3(a)(3).

(n) Where the securities to be offered are guarantees of other securities which are being registered concurrently, no separate fee for the guarantees shall be payable.

(*o*) Where an issuer registers an offering of securities, the registration fee may be calculated on the basis of the maximum aggregate offering price of all the securities listed in the "Calculation of Registration Fee" table. The number of shares or units of securities need not be included in the "Calculation of Registration Fee" Table. If the maximum aggregate offering price increases prior to the effective date of the registration statement, a pre-effective amendment must be filed to increase the maximum dollar value being registered and the additional filing fee shall be paid.

(p) Where all or a portion of the securities offered under a registration statement remain unsold after the offering's completion or termination, or withdrawal of the registration statement, the aggregate total dollar amount of the filing fee associated with those unsold securities (whether computed under § 230.457(a) or (*o*)) may be offset against the total filing fee due for a subsequent registration statement or registration statements. The subsequent registration statement(s) must be filed within five years of the initial filing date of the earlier registration statement, and must be filed by the same registrant (including a successor within the meaning of § 230.405), a majority-owned subsidiary of that registrant, or a parent that owns more than 50 percent of the registrant's outstanding voting securities. A note should be added to the "Calculation of Registration Fee" table in the subsequent registration statement(s) stating the dollar amount of the filing fee previously paid that is offset against the currently due filing fee, the file number of the earlier registration statement from which the filing fee is offset, and the name of the registrant and the initial filing date of that earlier registration statement.

(q) Notwithstanding any other provisions of this section, no filing fee is required for the registration of an indeterminate amount of securities to be offered solely for market-making purposes by an affiliate of the registrant.

Rule 459. Calculation of Effective Date

Saturdays, Sundays, and holidays shall be counted in computing the effective date of registration statements under section 8(a) of the Act. In the case of statements which become effective on the 20th day after filing, the 20th day shall be deemed to begin at the expiration of 19 periods of 24 hours each from 5:30 p.m. Eastern Standard Time or Eastern Daylight-Saving Time, whichever is in effect at the principal office of the Commission on the date of filing.

Rule 460. Distribution of Preliminary Prospectus

(a) Pursuant to the statutory requirement that the Commission in ruling upon requests for acceleration of the effective date of a registration statement shall have due regard to the adequacy of the information respecting the issuer theretofore available to the public, the Commission may consider whether the persons making the offering have taken reasonable steps to make the information contained in the registration statement conveniently available to underwriters and dealers who it is reasonably anticipated will be invited to participate in the distribution of the security to be offered or sold.

(b)(1) As a minimum, reasonable steps to make the information conveniently available would involve the distribution, to each underwriter and dealer who it is reasonably anticipated will be invited to participate in the distribution of the security, a reasonable time in advance of the anticipated effective date of the registration statement, of as many copies of the proposed form of preliminary prospectus permitted by Rule 430 as appears to be reasonable to secure adequate distribution of the preliminary prospectus.

(2) In the case of a registration statement filed by a closed-end investment company on Form N–2, reasonable steps to make information conveniently available would involve distribution of a sufficient number of copies of the Statement of Additional Information required by Rule 430(b) as it appears to be reasonable to secure their adequate distribution either to each underwriter or dealer who it is reasonably anticipated will be invited to participate in the distribution of the security, or to the underwriter, dealer or other source named on the cover page of the preliminary prospectus as being the person investors should contact in order to obtain the Statement of Additional Information.

(c) The granting of acceleration will not be conditioned upon

(1) The distribution of a preliminary prospectus in any state where such distribution would be illegal; or

(2) The distribution of a preliminary prospectus

(i) in the case of a registration statement relating solely to securities to be offered at competitive bidding, provided the undertaking in Item 512(d)(1) of Regulation S–K (§ 229.512(d)(2) of this chapter) is included in the registration statement and distribution of prospectuses pursuant to such undertaking is made prior to the publication or distribution of the invitation for bids, or

(ii) In the case of a registration statement relating to a security issued by a face-amount certificate company or a redeemable security issued by an open- end management company or unit investment trust if any other security of the same class is currently being offered or sold, pursuant to an effective registration statement by the issuer or by or through an underwriter, or

(iii) In the case of an offering of subscription rights unless it is contemplated that the distribution will be made through dealers and the underwriters intend to make the offering during the stockholders' subscription period, in which case copies of the preliminary prospectus must be distributed to dealers prior to the effective date of the registration statement in the same fashion as is required in the case of other offerings through underwriters, or

(iv) In the case of a registration statement pertaining to a security to be offered pursuant to an exchange offer or transaction described in Rule 145(§ 230.145).

Rule 461. Acceleration of Effective Date

(a) Requests for acceleration of the effective date of a registration statement shall be made by the registrant and the managing underwriters of the proposed issue, or, if there are no managing underwriters, by the principal underwriters of the proposed issue, and shall state the date upon which it is desired that the registration statement shall become effective. Such requests may be made in writing or orally, provided that, if an oral request is to be made, a letter indicating that fact and stating that the registrant and the managing or principal underwriters are aware of their obligations under the Act must accompany the registration statement for a pre-effective amendment thereto at the time of filing with the Commission. Written requests may be sent to the Commission by facsimile transmission. If, by reason of the expected arrangement in connection with the offering, it is to be requested that the registration statement shall become effective at a particular hour of the day, the Commission must be advised to that effect not later than the second business day before the day which it is desired that the registration statement shall become effective. A person's request for acceleration will be considered confirmation of such person's awareness of the person's obligations under the Act. Not later than the time of filing the last amendment prior to the effective date of the registration statement, the registrant shall inform the Commission as to whether or not the amount of compensation to be allowed or paid to the underwriters and any other arrangements among the registrant, the underwriters and other broker dealers participating in the distribution, as described in the registration statement, have been reviewed to the extent required by the National Association of Securities Dealers, Inc. and such Association has issued a statement expressing no objections to the compensation and other arrangements.

(b) Having due regard to the adequacy of information respecting the registrant theretofore available to the public, to the facility with which the nature of the securities to be registered, their relationship to the capital structure of the registrant issuer and the rights of holders thereof can be understood, and to the public interest and the protection of investors, as provided in section 8(a) of the Act, it is the general policy of the Commission, upon request, as provided in paragraph (a) of this section, to permit acceleration of the effective date of the registration statement as soon as possible after the filing of appropriate amendments, if any. In determining the date on which a registration statement shall become effective, the following are included in the situations in which the Commission considers that the statutory standards of section 8(a) may not be met and may refuse to accelerate the effective date:

(1) Where there has not been a bona fide effort to make the prospectus reasonably concise, readable, and in compliance with the plain English requirements of Rule 421(d) of Regulation C (17 CFR 230, 421(d)) in order to facilitate an understanding of the information in the prospectus.

(2) Where the form of preliminary prospectus, which has been distributed by the issuer or underwriter, is found to be inaccurate or inadequate in any material respect, until the Commission has received satisfactory assurance that appropriate correcting material has been sent to all underwriters and dealers who received such preliminary prospectus or prospectuses in quantity sufficient for their information and the information of others to whom the inaccurate or inadequate material was sent.

(3) Where the Commission is currently making an investigation of the issuer, a person controlling the issuer, or one of the underwriters, if any, of the securities to be offered, pursuant to any of the Acts administered by the Commission.

(4) Where one or more of the underwriters, although firmly committed to purchase securities covered by the registration statement, is subject to and does not meet the financial responsibility requirements of Rule 15c3–1 under the Securities Exchange Act of 1934. For the purposes of this paragraph underwriters will be deemed to be firmly committed even though the obligation to purchase is subject to the usual conditions as to receipt of opinions of counsel, accountants, etc., the accuracy of warranties or representations, the happening of calamities or the occurrence of other events the determination of which is not expressed to be in the sole or absolute discretion of the underwriters.

(5) Where there have been transactions in securities of the registrant by persons connected with or proposed to be connected with the offering which may have artificially affected or may artificially affect the market price of the security being offered.

(6) Where the amount of compensation to be allowed or paid to the underwriters and any other arrangements among the regis-

trant, the underwriters and other broker dealers participating in the distribution, as described in the registration statement, if required to be reviewed by the National Association of Securities Dealers, Inc. (NASD), have been reviewed by the NASD and the NASD has not issued a statement expressing no objections to the compensation and other arrangements.

(7) Where, in the case of a significant secondary offering at the market, the registrant, selling security holders and underwriters have not taken sufficient measures to insure compliance with Regulation M.

(c) Insurance against liabilities arising under the Act, whether the cost of insurance is borne by the registrant, the insured or some other person, will not be considered a bar to acceleration, unless the registrant is a registered investment company or a business development company and the cost of such insurance is borne by other than an insured officer or director of the registrant. In the case of such a registrant, the Commission may refuse to accelerate the effective date of the registration statement when the registrant is organized or administered pursuant to any instrument (including a contract for insurance against liabilities arising under the Act) that protects or purports to protect any director or officer of the company against any liability to the company or its security holders to which he or she would otherwise be subject by reason of willful misfeasance, bad faith, gross negligence or reckless disregard of the duties involved in the conduct of his or her office.

Rule 462. Immediate Effectiveness of Certain Registration Statements and Post-Effective Amendments

(a) A registration statement on Form S-8 (§ 239.16b of this chapter) and a registration statement on Form S-3 (§ 239.13 of this chapter) or on Form F-3 (§ 239.33 of this chapter) for a dividend or interest reinvestment plan shall become effective upon filing with the Commission.

(b) A registration statement and any post-effective amendment thereto shall become effective upon filing with the Commission if:

(1) The registration statement is for registering additional securities of the same class(es) as were included in an earlier registration statement for the same offering and declared effective by the Commission;

(2) The new registration statement is filed prior to the time confirmations are sent or given; and

(3) The new registration statement registers additional securities in an amount and at a price that together represent no more than 20% of the maximum aggregate offering price set forth for each class of securities in the "Calculation of Registration Fee" table contained in such earlier registration statement.

(c) If the prospectus contained in a post-effective amendment filed prior to the time confirmations are sent or given contains no substantive changes from or additions to the prospectus previously filed as part of the effective registration statement, other than price-related information omitted from the registration statement in reliance on Rule 430A of the Act (§ 230.430A), such post-effective amendment shall become effective upon filing with the Commission.

(d) A post-effective amendment filed solely to add exhibits to a registration statement shall become effective upon filing with the Commission.

Rule 463. Report of Offering of Securities and Use of Proceeds Therefrom

(a) Except as provided in this section, following the effective date of the first registration statement filed under the Act by an issuer, the issuer or successor issuer shall report the use of proceeds pursuant to Item 701 of Regulation S-B or S-K or Item 14(e) of Form 20-F, as applicable, on its first periodic report filed pursuant to Sections 13(a) and 15(d) (15 U.S.C. 78m(a) and 78o(d)) of the Securities Exchange Act of 1934 after effectiveness, and thereafter on each of its subsequent periodic reports filed pursuant to Sections 13(a) and 15(d) of the Securities Exchange Act of 1934 through the later of disclosure of the application of all the offering proceeds or disclosure of the termination of the offering.

(b) A successor issuer shall comply with paragraph (a) of this section only if a report of the use of proceeds is required with respect to the first effective registration statement of the predecessor issuer.

(c) For purposes of this section:

(1) The term "offering proceeds" shall not include any amount(s) received for the account(s) of any selling security holder(s).

(2) The term "application" shall not include the temporary investment of proceeds by the issuer pending final application.

(d) This section shall not apply to any effective registration statement for securities to be issued:

(1) In a business combination described in Rule 145(a);

(2) By an issuer which pursuant to a business combination described in Rule 145(a) has succeeded to another issuer that prior to such business combination had a registration statement become effective under the Act and on the date of such business combination was not subject to paragraph (a) of this section;

(3) Pursuant to an employee benefit plan;

(4) Pursuant to a dividend or interest reinvestment plan;

(5) As American depository receipts for foreign securities;

(6) By any investment company registered under the Investment Company Act of 1940 and any issuer that has elected to be regulated as a business development company under sections 54 through 65 of the Investment Company Act of 1940;

(7) By any public utility company or public utility holding company required to file reports with any State or Federal authority;

(8) In a merger in which a vote or consent of the security holders of the company being acquired is not required pursuant to applicable state law; or

(9) In an exchange offer for the securities of the issuer or another entity.

Rule 464. Effective Date of Post-Effective Amendments to Registration Statements Filed on Form S-8 and on Certain Forms S-3, S-4, F-2 and F-3

Provided, That, at the time of filing of each post-effective amendment with the Commission, the issuer continues to meet the requirements of filing on Form S-8; or on Form S-3, F-2 or F-3 for a registration statement relating to a dividend or interest reinvestment plan; or in the case of a registration statement on Form S-4 that there is continued compliance with General Instruction G of that Form:

(a) The post-effective amendment shall become effective upon filing with the Commission; and

(b) With respect to securities sold on or after the filing date pursuant to a prospectus which forms a part of a Form S-8 registration statement; or a Form S-3, F-2, or F-3 registration statement relating to a dividend or interest reinvestment plan; or a Form S-4 registration statement complying with General Instruction G of that Form and which has been amended to include or incorporate new full year financial statements or to comply with the provisions of section 10(a)(3) of the Act, the effective date of the registration statement shall be deemed to be the filing date of the post-effective amendment.

Rule 466. Effective Date of Certain Registration Statements on Form F-6

(a) A depositary that previously has filed a registration statement on Form F-6 (§ 239.36 of this chapter) may designate a date and time for a registration statement (including post-effective amendments) on Form F-6 to become effective and such registration statement shall become effective in accordance with such designation if the following conditions are met:

(1) The depositary previously has filed a registration statement on Form F–6 (§ 239.36 of this chapter), which the Commission has declared effective, with identical terms of deposit, except for the number of foreign securities a Depositary Share represents, and the depositary so certifies; and

(2) The designation of the effective date and time is set forth on the facing-page of the registration statement, or in any pre-effective amendment thereto. A pre-effective amendment containing such a designation properly made shall be deemed to have been filed with the consent of the Commission.

(b)(1) The Commission may, in the manner and under the circumstances set forth in paragraph (b)(2) of this section, suspend the ability of a depositary to designate the date and time of effectiveness of a registration statement, and such suspension shall remain in effect until the Commission furnishes written notice to the depositary that the suspension has been terminated. Any suspension, so long as it is in effect, shall apply to any registration statement that has been filed but has not, at the time of such suspension, become effective and to any registration statement the depositary files after such suspension. Any such suspension applies only to the ability to designate the date and time of effectiveness under paragraph (a) of this section and does not otherwise affect the registration statement.

(2) Any suspension under paragraph (b)(1) of this section becomes effective when the Commission furnishes written notice thereof to the depositary. The Commission may issue a suspension if it appears to the Commission: (i) that any registration statement containing a designation under this section is incomplete or inaccurate in any material respect, whether or not such registration has become effective, or (ii) that the depositary has not complied with any of the conditions of this section. The depositary may petition the Commission to review the suspension. The Commission will order a hearing on the matter if a request for such a hearing is included in the petition.

Rule 467. Effectiveness of Registration Statements and Post-Effective Amendments Thereto Made on Forms F–7, F–8, F–9, F–10 and F–80

(a) A registration statement on Form F–7, Form F–8 or Form F–80 and any amendment thereto, shall become effective upon filing with the Commission. A registration statement on Form F–9 or Form F–10, and any amendment thereto, relating to an offering being made contemporaneously in the United States and Canada shall become effective upon filing with the Commission, unless designated as preliminary material on the Form.

(b) Where no contemporaneous offering is being made in Canada, a registrant filing on Form F–9 or Form F–10 may designate on the facing page of the registration statement, or any amendment thereto, a date and time for such filing to become effective that is not earlier than seven calendar days after the date of filing with the Commission, and such registration statement or amendment shall become effective in accordance with such designation; *provided, however,* that such registration statement or amendment may become effective prior to seven calendar days after the date of filing with the Commission if the securities regulatory authority in the review jurisdiction issues a receipt or notification of clearance with respect thereto before such time elapses, in which case the registration statement or amendment shall become effective by order of the Commission as soon as practicable after receipt of written notification by the Commission from the registrant or the applicable Canadian securities regulatory authority of the issuance of such receipt or notification of clearance.

AMENDMENTS; WITHDRAWALS

Rule 470. Formal Requirements for Amendments

Except for telegraphic amendments filed pursuant to Rule 473, amendments to a registration statement shall be filed under cover of an appropriate facing sheet, shall be numbered consecutively in the order in which filed, and shall indicate on the facing sheet the applicable registration form on which the amendment is prepared and the file number of the registration statement.

Rule 471. Signatures to Amendments

(a) Except as provided in Rule 447 and in Rule 478, every amendment to a registration statement shall be signed by the persons specified in section 6(a) of the Act. At least one copy of every amendment filed with the Commission shall be signed. Unsigned copies shall be conformed.

(b) Where the Act or the rules thereunder require a document filed with or furnished to the Commission to be signed, such document shall be manually signed, or signed using either typed signatures or duplicated or facsimile versions of manual signatures. Where typed, duplicated or facsimile signatures are used, each signatory to the filing shall manually sign a signature page or other document authenticating, acknowledging or otherwise adopting his or her signature that appears in the filing. Such document shall be executed before or at the time the filing is made and shall be retained by the registrant for a period of five years. Upon request, the registrant shall furnish to the Commission or its staff a copy of any or all documents retained pursuant to this section.

Rule 472. Filing of Amendments; Number of Copies

(a) Except for telegraphic amendments filed pursuant to Rule 473, there shall be filed with the Commission three complete, unmarked copies of every amendment, including exhibits and all other papers and documents filed as part of the amendment, and eight additional copies of such amendment at least five of which shall be marked to indicate clearly and precisely, by underlining or in some other appropriate manner, the changes effected in the registration statement by the amendment. Where the amendment to the registration statement incorporates into the prospectus documents which are required to be delivered with the prospectus in lieu of prospectus presentation, the eight additional copies shall be accompanied by eight copies of such documents. No other exhibits are required to accompany such additional copies.

(b) Every amendment which relates to a prospectus shall include copies of the prospectus as amended. Each such copy of the amended prospectus shall be accompanied by a copy of the cross reference sheet required by Rule 481(a) (§ 230.481(a)) where applicable, if the amendment of the prospectus resulted in any change in the accuracy of the cross reference sheet previously filed. Notwithstanding the foregoing provisions of this paragraph, only copies of the changed pages of the prospectus, and the cross reference sheet if amended, need be included in an amendment filed pursuant to an undertaking referred to in Item 512(d) of Regulation S–K.

(c) Every amendment of a financial statement which is not included in the prospectus shall include copies of the financial statement as amended. Every amendment relating to a certified financial statement shall include the consent of the certifying accountant to the use of his certificate in connection with the amended financial statement in the registration statement or prospectus and to being named as having certified such financial statement.

(d) Notwithstanding any other provision of this rule, if a registration statement filed on Form S–8 is amended, there shall be filed with the Commission three complete, unmarked copies of every amendment, including exhibits and all other papers and documents filed as part of the amendment. Three additional, unmarked copies of such amendments shall be furnished to the Commission. No exhibits are required to accompany the additional copies of amendments to registration statements filed on Form S–8.

(e) Notwithstanding any other provision of this section, if a post-effective amendment is filed pursuant to Rule 462(b) (§ 230.462(b)) and Rule 110(d) (§ 230.110(d)), one copy of the complete post-effective amendment, including exhibits and all other papers and documents filed as a part thereof shall be filed with the Commission. Such copy should not be bound and may contain facsimile versions of manual signatures in accordance with Rule 402(e) (§ 230.402(e)).

Rule 473. Delaying Amendments

(a) An amendment in the following form filed with a registration statement, or as an amendment to a registration statement which has not become effective, shall be deemed, for the purpose of section 8(a) of the Act, to be filed on such date or dates as may be necessary to delay the effective date of such registration statement (1) until the registrant shall file a further amendment which specifically states as provided in paragraph (b) of this rule that such registration statement shall thereafter become effective in accordance with section 8(a) of the Act, or (2) until the registration statement shall become effective on such date as the Commission, acting pursuant to section 8(a), may determine:

> The registrant hereby amends this registration statement on such date or dates as may be necessary to delay its effective date until the registrant shall file a further amendment which specifically states that this registration statement shall thereafter become effective in accordance with section 8(a) of the Securities Act of 1933 or until the registration statement shall become effective on such date as the Commission acting pursuant to said section 8(a), may determine.

(b) An amendment which for the purpose of paragraph (a)(1) of this rule specifically states that a registration statement shall thereafter become effective in accordance with section 8(a) of the Act, shall be in the following form:

> This registration statement shall hereafter become effective in accordance with the provisions of section 8(a) of the Securities Act of 1933.

(c) An amendment pursuant to paragraph (a) of this rule which is filed with a registration statement shall be set forth on the facing page thereof following the calculation of the registration fee. Any such amendment filed after the filing of the registration statement, any amendment altering the proposed date of public sale of the securities being registered, or any amendment filed pursuant to paragraph (b) of this section may be made by telegram, letter, or facsimile transmission. Each such telegraphic amendment shall be confirmed in writing within a reasonable time by the filing of a signed copy of the amendment. Such confirmation shall not be deemed an amendment.

(d) No amendments pursuant to paragraph (a) of this rule may be filed with a registration statement on Form F–7, F–8 or F–80; on Form F–9 or F–10 relating to an offering being made contemporaneously in the United States and the registrant's home jurisdiction; on Form S–8; on Form S–3, F–2 or F–3 relating to a dividend or interest reinvestment plan; or on Form S–4 complying with General Instruction G of that Form.

Rule 474. Date of Filing of Amendments

The date on which amendments are actually received by the Commission shall be the date of filing thereof, if all the requirements of the Act and the rules with respect to such filing have been complied with.

Rule 475. Amendment Filed With Consent of Commission

An application for the Commission's consent to the filing of an amendment with the effect provided in section 8(a) of the Act may be filed before or after or concurrently with the filing of the amendment. The application shall be signed and shall state fully the grounds upon which it is made. The Commission's consent shall be deemed to have been given and the amendment shall be treated as a part of the registration statement only when the Commission shall after the filing of such amendment enter an order to that effect.

Rule 475a. Certain Pre-Effective Amendments Deemed Filed With the Consent of Commission

Amendments to a registration statement on Form F–2 (§ 239.32 of this chapter) relating to a dividend or interest reinvestment plan, or on Form S–4 (§ 239.25 of this chapter) complying with General Instruction G of that Form, filed prior to the effectiveness of such registration statement shall be deemed to have been filed with a consent of the Commission and shall accordingly be treated as part of the registration statement.

Rule 476. Amendment Filed Pursuant to Order of Commission

An amendment filed prior to the effective date of a registration statement shall be deemed to have been filed pursuant to an order of the Commission within the meaning of section 8(a) of the Act so as to be treated as a part of the registration statement only when the Commission shall after the filing of such amendment enter an order declaring that it has been filed pursuant to the Commission's previous order.

Rule 477. Withdrawal of Registration Statement or Amendment

(a) Except as provided in paragraph (b) of this section, any registration statement or any amendment or exhibit thereto may be withdrawn upon application if the Commission, finding such withdrawal consistent with the public interest and the protection of investors, consents thereto.

(b) Any application for withdrawal of a registration statement filed on Form F–2 (§ 239.32 of this chapter) relating to a dividend or interest reinvestment plan, or on Form S–4 (§ 239.25 of this chapter) complying with General Instruction G of that Form, and/or any pre-effective amendment thereto, will be deemed granted upon filing if such filing is made prior to the effective date. Any other application for withdrawal of an entire registration statement made before the effective date of the registration statement will be deemed granted at the time the application is filed with the Commission unless, within 15 calendar days after the registrant files the application, the Commission notifies the registrant that the application for withdrawal will not be granted.

(c) The registrant must sign any application for withdrawal and must state fully in it the grounds on which the registrant makes the application. The fee paid upon the filing of the registration statement will not be refunded to the registrant. The registrant must state in the application that no securities were sold in connection with the offering. If the registrant applies for withdrawal in anticipation of reliance on § 230.155(c), the registrant must, without discussing any terms of the private offering, state in the application that the registrant may undertake a subsequent private offering in reliance on § 230.155(c).

(d) Any withdrawn document will remain in the Commission's public files, as well as the related request for withdrawal.

Rule 478. Powers to Amend or Withdraw Registration Statement

All persons signing a registration statement shall be deemed, in the absence of a statement to the contrary, to confer upon the registrant, and upon the agent for service named in the registration statement, the following powers:

(a) A power to amend the registration statement (1) by the filing of an amendment as provided in Rule 473; (2) by filing any written consent; (3) by correcting typographical errors; or (4) by reducing the amount of securities registered, pursuant to an undertaking contained in the registration statement.

(b) A power to make application pursuant to Rule 475 for the Commission's consent to the filing of an amendment.

(c) A power to withdraw the registration statement or any amendment or exhibit thereto.

(d) A power to consent to the entry of an order under section 8(b) of the Act, waiving notice and hearing, such order being entered without prejudice to the right of the registrant thereafter to have the order vacated upon a showing to the Commission that the registration statement as amended is no longer incomplete or inaccurate on its face in any material respect.

Rule 479. Procedure With Respect to Abandoned Registration Statements and Post–Effective Amendments

When a registration statement, or a post-effective amendment to such a statement, has been on file with the Commission for a period of nine months and has not become effective the Commission may, in its discretion, proceed in the following manner to determine whether such registration statement or amendment has been abandoned by the registrant. If the registration statement has been amended, otherwise than for the purpose of delaying the effective date thereof, or if the post-effective amendment has been amended, the nine-month period shall be computed from the date of the latest such amendment.

(a) A notice will be sent to the registrant, and to the agent for service named in the registration statement, by registered or certified mail, return receipt requested, addressed to the most recent addresses for the registrant and the agent for service reflected in the registration statement. Such notice will inform the registrant and the agent for service that the registration statement or amendment is out of date and must be either amended to comply with the applicable requirements of the Act and the rules and regulations thereunder or be withdrawn within 30 days after the date of such notice.

(b) If the registrant or the agent for service fails to respond to such notice by filing a substantive amendment or withdrawing the registration statement and does not furnish a satisfactory explanation as to why it has not done so within such 30 days, the Commission may, where consistent with the public interest and the protection of investors, enter an order declaring the registration statement or amendment abandoned.

(c) When such an order is entered by the Commission the papers comprising the registration statement or amendment will not be removed from the files of the Commission but an order shall be included in the file for the registration statement in the following manner: "Declared abandoned by order dated ______."

INVESTMENT COMPANIES; BUSINESS DEVELOPMENT COMPANIES

NOTE: The rules which comprise this section of Regulation C (Rules 480 to 489) are applicable only to investment companies and business development companies, except Rule 489, which applies to certain entities excepted from the definition of investment company by rules under the Investment Company Act of 1940. The rules comprising the rest of Regulation C (Rules 400 to 479 and Rules 490 to 494) are, unless the context specifically indicates otherwise, also applicable to investment companies and business development companies. See Rule 400.

Rule 480. Title of Securities

If a registration statement is prepared on a form available solely to investment companies registered under the Investment Company Act of 1940, or a business development company which is selling or proposing to sell its securities pursuant to a registration statement which has been filed under the Act, wherever the title of securities is required to be stated there shall be given such information as will indicate the type and general character of the securities, including the following:

(a) In the case of shares, the par or stated value, if any; the rate of dividends, if fixed, and whether cumulative or non-cumulative; a brief indication of the preference, if any;

and, if convertible, a statement to that effect.

(b) In the case of funded debt, the rate of interest; the date of maturity, or, if the issue matures serially, a brief indication of the serial maturities such as "maturing serially from 1950 to 1960"; if the payment of principal or interest is contingent, an appropriate indication of such contingency; a brief indication of the priority of the issue; and, if convertible, a statement to that effect.

(c) In the case of any other kind of security, appropriate information of comparable character.

Rule 481. Information Required in Prospectus

Disclose the following in registration statements prepared on a form available solely to investment companies registered under the Investment Company Act of 1940 or in registration statements filed under the Act for a company that has elected to be regulated as a business development company under Sections 55 through 65 of the Investment Company Act (15 U.S.C. 80a–54–80a–64):

(a) *Facing page.* Indicate the approximate date of the proposed sale of the securities to the public.

(b) *Outside front cover page.* If applicable, include the following in plain English as required by § 230.421(d):

(1) Commission legend. Provide a legend that indicates that the Securities and Exchange Commission has not approved or disapproved of the securities or passed upon the accuracy or adequacy of the disclosure in the prospectus and that any contrary representation is a criminal offense. The legend may be in one of the following or other clear and concise language:

Example A: The Securities and Exchange Commission has not approved or disapproved these securities or passed upon the adequacy of this prospectus. Any representation to the contrary is a criminal offense.

Example B: The Securities and Exchange Commission has not approved or disapproved these securities or determined if this prospectus is truthful or complete. Any representation to the contrary is a criminal offense.

(2) "Subject to Completion" legend.

(i) If a prospectus or Statement of Additional Information will be used before the effective date of the registration statement, include on the outside front cover page of the prospectus or Statement of Additional Information, a prominent statement that:

(A) The information in the prospectus or Statement of Additional Information will be amended or completed;

(B) A registration statement relating to these securities has been filed with the Securities and Exchange Commission;

(C) The securities may not be sold until the registration statement becomes effective; and

(D) In a prospectus, that the prospectus is not an offer to sell the securities and it is not soliciting an offer to buy the securities in any state where offers or sales are not permitted, or in a Statement of Additional Information, that the Statement of Additional Information is not a prospectus.

(ii) The legend may be in the following language or other clear and understandable language:

The information in this prospectus (or Statement of Additional Information) is not complete and may be changed. We may not sell these securities until the registration statement filed with the Securities and Exchange Commission is effective. This prospectus (or Statement of Additional Information) is not an offer to sell these securities and is not soliciting an offer to buy these securities in any state where the offer or sale is not permitted.

(iii) In the case of a prospectus that omits pricing information under § 230.430A, provide the information and legend in paragraph (b)(2) of this section if the prospectus or Statement of Additional Information is used before the initial public offering price is determined.

(c) *Table of contents.* Include on either the outside front, inside front, or outside back cover page of the prospectus, a reasonably detailed table of contents. It must show the page number of the various sections or subdivisions of the prospectus. Include this table of contents immediately following the cover page in any prospectus delivered electronically.

(d) *Stabilization and Other Transactions.* (1) Indicate on the front cover page of the prospectus if the underwriter has any arrangement with the issuer, such as an over-allotment option, under which the underwriter may purchase additional shares in connection with the offering, and state the amount of additional shares the underwriter may purchase under the arrangement. Provide disclosure in the prospectus that briefly describes any transaction that the underwriter intends to conduct during the offering that stabilizes, maintains, or otherwise affects the market price of the offered securities. Include information on stabilizing transactions, syndicate short covering transactions, penalty bids, or any other transactions that affect the offered security's price. Describe the nature of the transactions clearly and explain how the transactions affect the offered security's price. Identify the exchange or other market on which these transactions may occur. If true, disclose that the underwriter may discontinue these transactions at any time;

(2) If the stabilizing began before the effective date of the registration statement, disclose in the prospectus the amount of securities bought, the prices at which they were bought and the period within which they were bought. In the event that § 230.430A of this chapter is used, the prospectus filed under § 230.497(h) or included in a post-effective amendment must contain information on the stabilizing transactions that took place before the determination of the public offering price shown in the prospectus; and

(3) If you are making a warrant or rights offering of securities to existing security holders and the securities not purchased by existing security holders are to be reoffered to the public, disclose in the prospectus used in connection with the reoffering:

(i) The amount of securities bought in stabilization activities during the offering period and the price or range of prices at which the securities were bought;

(ii) The amount of the offered securities subscribed for during the offering period;

(iii) The amount of the offered securities subscribed for by the underwriters during the offering period;

(iv) The amount of the offered securities sold during the offering period by the underwriters and the price or range of prices at which the securities were sold; and

(v) The amount of the offered securities to be reoffered to the public and the public offering price.

(e) *Dealer prospectus delivery obligations.* On the outside back cover page of the prospectus, advise dealers of their prospectus delivery obligation, including the expiration date specified by Section 4(3) of the Act (15 U.S.C. 77d(3)) and § 230.174. If the expiration date is not known on the effective date of the registration statement, include the expiration date in the copy of the prospectus filed under § 230.497. This information need not be included if dealers are not required to deliver a prospectus under § 230.174 or Section 24(d) of the Investment Company Act of 1940 (15 U.S.C. 80a–24). Use the following or other clear, plain language:

Dealer Prospectus Delivery Obligation

Until (insert date), all dealers that effect transactions in these securities, whether or not participating in this offering, may be required to deliver a prospectus. This is in addition to the dealers' obligation to deliver a prospectus when acting as underwriters and with respect to their unsold allotments or subscriptions.

(f) *Electronic distribution.* Where a prospectus is distributed through an electronic medium, issuers may satisfy legibility requirements applicable to printed documents, such as paper size, type size and font, bold-face type, italics and red ink, by presenting all required information in a format readily communicated to investors, and where indicated, in a manner reasonably calculated to draw investor attention to specific information.

Rule 482. Advertising by an Investment Company as Satisfying Requirements of Section 10

(a) *Scope of rule.* This section applies to an advertisement or other sales material (*advertisement*) with respect to securities of an investment company registered under the Investment Company Act of 1940 (15 U.S.C. 80a–1 *et seq.*)(*1940 Act*), or a business development company, that is selling or proposing to sell its securities pursuant to a registration statement that has been filed under the Act. This section does not apply to an advertisement that is excepted from the definition of prospectus by section 2(a)(10) of the Act (15 U.S.C. 77b(a)(10)), or a Profile under § 230.498. An advertisement that complies with this section, which may include information the substance of which is not included in the prospectus specified in section 10(a) of the Act (15 U.S.C. 77j(a)), will be deemed to be a prospectus under section 10(b) of the Act (15 U.S.C. 77j(b)) for the purpose of section 5(b)(1) of the Act (15 U.S.C. 77e(b)(1)).

Note to paragraph (a): The fact that an advertisement complies with this section does not relieve the investment company, underwriter, or dealer of any obligations with respect to the advertisement under the antifraud provisions of the federal securities laws. For guidance about factors to be weighed in determining whether statements, representations, illustrations, and descriptions contained in investment company advertisements are misleading, see § 230.156. In addition, an advertisement that complies with this section is subject to the legibility requirements of § 230.420.

(b) *Required disclosure.* This paragraph describes information that is required to be included in an advertisement in order to comply with this section.

(1) *Availability of additional information.* An advertisement must include a statement that:

(i) Advises an investor to consider the investment objectives, risks, and charges and expenses of the investment company carefully before investing; explains that the prospectus contains this and other information about the investment company; identifies a source from which an investor may obtain a prospectus; and states that the prospectus should be read carefully before investing; or

(ii) If used with a Profile, advises an investor to consider the investment objectives, risks, and charges and expenses of the investment company carefully before investing; explains that the accompanying Profile contains this and other information about the investment company; describes the procedures for investing in the investment company; and indicates the availability of the investment company's prospectus.

(2) *Advertisements used prior to effectiveness of registration statement.* An advertisement that is used prior to effectiveness of the investment company's registration statement or the determination of the public offering price (in the case of a registration statement that becomes effective omitting information from the prospectus contained in the registration statement in reliance upon § 230.430A) must include the "Subject to Completion" legend required by § 230.481(b)(2).

(3) *Advertisements including performance data.* An advertisement that includes performance data of an open-end management investment company or a separate account registered under the 1940 Act as a unit investment trust offering variable annuity contracts (*trust account*) must include the following:

(i) A legend disclosing that the performance data quoted represents past performance; that past performance does not guarantee future results; that the investment return and principal value of an investment will fluctuate so that an investor's shares, when redeemed, may be worth more or less than their original cost; and that current performance may be lower or higher than the performance data quoted. The legend should also identify either a toll-free (or collect) telephone number or a website where an investor may obtain performance data current to the most recent month-end unless the advertisement includes total return quotations current to the most recent month ended seven business days prior to the date of use. An advertisement for a money market fund may omit the disclosure about principal value fluctuation; and

Note to paragraph (b)(3)(i): The date of use refers to the date or dates when an advertisement is used by investors, not the date on which an advertisement is published or submitted for publication. The date of use refers to the entire period of use by investors and not simply the first date on which an advertisement is used.

(ii) If a sales load or any other nonrecurring fee is charged, the maximum amount of the load or fee, and if the sales load or fee is not reflected, a statement that the performance data does not reflect the deduction of the sales load or fee, and that, if reflected, the load or fee would reduce the performance quoted.

(4) *Money market funds.* An advertisement for an investment company that holds itself out to be a money market fund must include the following statement:

> An investment in the Fund is not insured or guaranteed by the Federal Deposit Insurance Corporation or any other government agency. Although the Fund seeks to preserve the value of your investment at $1.00 per share, it is possible to lose money by investing in the Fund.

A money market fund that does not hold itself out as maintaining a stable net asset value may omit the second sentence of this statement.

(5) *Presentation.* In a print advertisement, the statements required by paragraphs (b)(1) through (b)(4) of this section must be presented in a type size at least as large as and of a style different from, but at least as prominent as, that used in the major portion of the advertisement, provided that when performance data is presented in a type size smaller than that of the major portion of the advertisement, the statements required by paragraph (b)(3) of this section may appear in a type size no smaller than that of the performance data. If an advertisement is delivered through an electronic medium, the legibility requirements for the statements required by paragraphs (b)(1) through (b)(4) of this section relating to type size and style may be satisfied by presenting the statements in any manner reasonably calculated to draw investor attention to them. In a radio or television advertisement, the statements required by paragraphs (b)(1) through (b)(4) of this section must be given emphasis equal to that used in the major portion of the advertisement. The statements required by paragraph (b)(3) of this section must be presented in close proximity to the performance data, and, in a print advertisement, must be presented in the body of the advertisement and not in a footnote.

(6) *Commission legend.* An advertisement that complies with this section need not

contain the Commission legend required by § 230.481(b)(1).

(c) *Use of applications.* An advertisement that complies with this section may not contain or be accompanied by any application by which a prospective investor may invest in the investment company, except that:

(1) *Variable annuity and variable life insurance contracts.* A prospectus meeting the requirements of section 10(a) of the Act (15 U.S.C. 77j(a)) by which a unit investment trust offers variable annuity or variable life insurance contracts may contain a contract application although the prospectus includes, or is accompanied by, information about an investment company in which the unit investment trust invests that, pursuant to this section, is deemed a prospectus under section 10(b) of the Act (15 U.S.C. 77j(b)); and

(2) *Profile.* An advertisement that complies with this section may be used with a Profile that includes, or is accompanied by, an application to purchase shares of the investment company as permitted under § 230.498.

(d) *Performance data for non-money market funds.* In the case of an open-end management investment company or a trust account (other than a money market fund referred to in paragraph (e) of this section), any quotation of the company's performance contained in an advertisement shall be limited to quotations of:

(1) *Current yield.* A current yield that:

(i) Is based on the methods of computation prescribed in Form N–1A (§§ 239.15A and 274.11A of this chapter), N–3 (§§ 239.17a and 274.11b of this chapter), or N–4 (§§ 239.17b and 274.11c of this chapter);

(ii) Is accompanied by quotations of total return as provided for in paragraph (d)(3) of this section;

(iii) Is set out in no greater prominence than the required quotations of total return; and

(iv) Adjacent to the quotation and with no less prominence than the quotation, identifies the length of and the date of the last day in the base period used in computing the quotation.

(2) *Tax-equivalent yield.* A tax-equivalent yield that:

(i) Is based on the methods of computation prescribed in Form N–1A (§§ 239.15A and 274.11A of this chapter), N–3 (§§ 239.17a and 274.11b of this chapter), or N–4 (§§ 239.17b and 274.11c of this chapter);

(ii) Is accompanied by quotations of yield as provided for in paragraph (d)(1) of this section and total return as provided for in paragraph (d)(3) of this section;

(iii) Is set out in no greater prominence than the required quotations of yield and total return;

(iv) Relates to the same base period as the required quotation of yield; and

(v) Adjacent to the quotation and with no less prominence than the quotation, identifies the length of and the date of the last day in the base period used in computing the quotation.

(3) *Average annual total return.* Average annual total return for one, five, and ten year periods, except that if the company's registration statement under the Act (15 U.S.C. 77a *et seq.*) has been in effect for less than one, five, or ten years, the time period during which the registration statement was in effect is substituted for the period(s) otherwise prescribed. The quotations must:

(i) Be based on the methods of computation prescribed in Form N–1A (§§ 239.15A and 274.11A of this chapter), N–3 (§§ 239.17a and 274.11b of this chapter), or N–4 (§§ 239.17b and 274.11c of this chapter);

(ii) Be current to the most recent calendar quarter ended prior to the submission of the advertisement for publication;

(iii) Be set out with equal prominence; and

(iv) Adjacent to the quotation and with no less prominence than the quotation, identify the length of and the last day of the one, five, and ten year periods.

(4) *After-tax return.* For an open-end management investment company, average annual total return (after taxes on distributions) and average annual total return (after taxes on distributions and redemption) for one, five, and ten year periods, except that if the company's registration statement under the Act (15 U.S.C. 77a *et seq.*) has been in effect for less than one, five, or ten years, the time period during which the registration statement was in effect is substituted for the period(s) otherwise prescribed. The quotations must:

(i) Be based on the methods of computation prescribed in Form N–1A (§§ 239.15A and 274.11A of this chapter);

(ii) Be current to the most recent calendar quarter ended prior to the submission of the advertisement for publication;

(iii) Be accompanied by quotations of total return as provided for in paragraph (d)(3) of this section;

(iv) Include both average annual total return (after taxes on distributions) and average annual total return (after taxes on distributions and redemption);

(v) Be set out with equal prominence and be set out in no greater prominence than the required quotations of total return; and

(vi) Adjacent to the quotations and with no less prominence than the quotations, identify the length of and the last day of the one, five, and ten year periods.

(5) *Other performance measures.* Any other historical measure of company performance (not subject to any prescribed method of computation) if such measurement:

(i) Reflects all elements of return;

(ii) Is accompanied by quotations of total return as provided for in paragraph (d)(3) of this section;

(iii) In the case of any measure of performance adjusted to reflect the effect of taxes, is accompanied by quotations of total return as provided for in paragraph (d)(4) of this section;

(iv) Is set out in no greater prominence than the required quotations of total return; and

(v) Adjacent to the measurement and with no less prominence than the measurement, identifies the length of and the last day of the period for which performance is measured.

(e) *Performance data for money market funds.* In the case of a money market fund:

(1) *Yield.* Any quotation of the money market fund's yield in an advertisement shall be based on the methods of computation prescribed in Form N–1A (§§ 239.15A and 274.11A of this chapter), N–3 (§§ 239.17a and 274.11b of this chapter), or N–4 (§§ 239.17b and 274.11c of this chapter) and may include:

(i) A quotation of current yield that, adjacent to the quotation and with no less prominence than the quotation, identifies the length of and the date of the last day in the base period used in computing that quotation;

(ii) A quotation of effective yield if it appears in the same advertisement as a quotation of current yield and each quotation relates to an identical base period and is presented with equal prominence; or

(iii) A quotation or quotations of tax-equivalent yield or tax-equivalent effective yield if it appears in the same advertisement as a quotation of current yield and each quotation relates to the same base period as the quotation of current yield, is presented with equal prominence, and states the income tax rate used in the calculation.

(2) *Total return.* Accompany any quotation of the money market fund's total return in an advertisement with a quotation of the money market fund's current yield under paragraph (e)(1)(i) of this section. Place the quotations of total return and current yield next to each other, in the same size print, and if there is a material difference between the quoted total return and the quoted current yield, include a statement that the yield quotation more closely reflects the current earnings of the money market fund than the total return quotation.

(f) *Advertisements that make tax representations.* An advertisement for an open-end management investment company (other than a company that is permitted under § 270.35d–1(a)(4) of this chapter to use a name suggesting that the company's 1distributions are exempt from federal income tax or from both federal and state income tax) that represents or implies that the company is managed to limit or control the effect of taxes on company performance must accompany any quotation of the company's performance permitted by paragraph (d) of this section with quotations of total return as provided for in paragraph (d)(4) of this section.

(g) *Timeliness of performance data.* All performance data contained in any advertisement must be as of the most recent practicable date considering the type of investment company and the media through which the data will be conveyed, except that any advertisement containing total return quotations will be considered to have complied with this paragraph provided that:

(1)(i) The total return quotations are current to the most recent calendar quarter ended prior to the submission of the advertisement for publication; and

(ii) Total return quotations current to the most recent month ended seven business days prior to the date of use are provided at the toll-free (or collect) telephone number or website identified pursuant to paragraph (b)(3)(i) of this section; or

(2) The total return quotations are current to the most recent month ended seven business days prior to the date of use of the advertisement.

Note to paragraph (g): The date of use refers to the date or dates when an advertisement is used by investors, not the date on which an advertisement is published or submitted for publication. The date of use refers to the entire period of use by investors and not simply the first date on which an advertisement is used.

(h) *Filing.* An advertisement that complies with this section need not be filed as part of the registration statement filed under the Act.

Note to paragraph (h): These advertisements, unless filed with NASD Regulation, Inc., are required to be filed in accordance with the requirements of § 230.497.

Rule 483. Exhibits for Certain Registration Statements

If a registration statement is prepared on a form available solely to investment companies registered under the Investment Company Act of 1940, or a business development company which is selling or proposing to sell its securities pursuant to a registration statement which has been filed under the Act, the following provisions apply:

(a) Such registration statement shall contain an exhibit index, which should immediately precede the exhibits filed with such registration statement. The exhibit index shall indicate by handwritten, typed, printed or other legible form of notation in the manually signed original registration statement the page number in the sequential numbering system where such exhibit can be found. Where exhibits are incorporated by reference, this fact shall be noted in the exhibit index referred to in the preceding sentence. Further, the first page of the manually signed registration statement shall list the page in the filing where the exhibit index is located.

(b) If any name is signed to the registration statement pursuant to a power of attorney, copies of such powers of attorney shall be filed as an exhibit to the registration statement. In addition, if the name of any officer signing on behalf of the registrant, or attesting the registrant's seal, is signed pursuant to a power of attorney, certified copies of a resolution of the registrant's board of directors authorizing such signature shall also be filed as an exhibit to the registration statement. A power of attorney that is filed with the Commission shall relate to a specific filing, an amendment thereto, or a related registration statement that is to be effective upon filing pursuant to Rule 462(b) (§ 230.462(b)) under the Act.

(c) (1) All written consents are required to be filed as an exhibit to the registration statement, together with a list thereof. Such consents shall be dated and manually signed. Where the consent of an expert or counsel is contained in his report or opinion, a reference shall be made in the list to the report or opinion containing the consent.

(2) In a registration statement filed pursuant to Rule 462(b) (§ 230.462(b)) by a closed-end company, any required consent may be incorporated by reference into the registration statement from a previously filed registration statement related to the offering, provided that the consent contained in the previously filed registration statement expressly provides for such incorporation. Any consent filed in a Rule 462(b) (§ 230.462(b)) registration statement may contain duplicated or facsimile versions of required signatures, and such signatures shall be considered manually filed for the purposes of the Act and the rules thereunder.

(d) The registrant—

(1) May file such exhibits as it may desire in addition to those required by the appropriate form. Such exhibits shall be so marked as to indicate clearly the subject matters to which they refer;

(2) In any case where two or more indentures, contracts, franchises, or other documents required to be filed as exhibits are substantially identical in all material respects except as to the parties thereto, the dates of execution, or other details, need file a copy of only one of such documents, with a schedule identifying the other documents omitted and setting forth the material details in which such documents differ from the document of which a copy is filed. The Commission may at any time in its discretion require filing of copies of any documents so omitted; and

(3) If an exhibit to a registration statement (other than an opinion or consent), filed in preliminary form, has been changed only (i) to insert information as to interest, dividend or conversion rates, redemption or conversion prices, purchase or offering prices, underwriters' or dealers' commission, names, addresses or participation of underwriters or similar matters, which information appears elsewhere in an amendment to the registration statement, or (ii) to correct typographical errors, insert signatures or make other similar immaterial changes, then, notwithstanding any contrary requirement of any rule or form, need not refile such exhibit as so amended; provided the registrant states in the amendment to the registration statement the basis provided by this rule for not refiling such exhibit. Any such incomplete exhibit may not, however, be incorporated by reference in any subsequent filing under any Act administered by the Commission.

Rule 484. Undertaking Required in Certain Registration Statements

If a registration statement is prepared on a form available solely to investment companies registered under the Investment Company Act of 1940, or a business development company which is selling or proposing to sell its securities pursuant to a registration statement which has been filed under the Act, if

(a) Any acceleration is requested of the effective date of the registration statement pursuant to Rule 461 (§ 230.461), and

(b)(1) Any provision or arrangement exists whereby the registrant may indemnify a director, officer or controlling person of the registrant against liabilities arising under the Act, or

(2) The underwriting agreement contains provisions by which indemnification against such liabilities is given by the registrant to the underwriter or controlling persons of the underwriter and the director, officer or controlling person of the registrant is such an underwriter or controlling person thereof or a member of any firm which is an underwriter, and

(3) The benefits of such indemnification are not waived by such persons; the registration statement shall include a brief description of the indemnification provisions and an undertaking in substantially the following form:

> Insofar as indemnification for liability arising under the Securities Act of 1933 may be permitted to directors, officers and controlling persons of the registrant pursuant to the foregoing provisions, or otherwise, the registrant has been advised that in the opinion of the Securities and Exchange Commission such indemnification is against public policy as expressed in the Act and is, therefore, unenforceable. In the event that a claim for indemnification against such liabilities (other than the payment by the registrant of expenses incurred or paid by a director, officer or controlling person of the registrant in the successful defense of any action, suit or proceeding) is asserted by such director, officer or controlling person in connection with the securities being registered, the registrant will, unless in the opinion of its counsel the matter has been settled by controlling precedent, submit to a court of appropriate jurisdiction the question whether such indemnification by it is against public policy as expressed in the Act and will be governed by the final adjudication of such issue.

Rule 485. Effective Date of Post-Effective Amendments Filed by Certain Registered Investment Companies

(a) *Automatic Effectiveness.* (1) Except as otherwise provided in this section, a post-effective amendment to a registration statement filed by a registered open-end management investment company, unit investment trust or separate account as defined in section 2(a)(37) of the Investment Company Act of 1940 [15 U.S.C. 80a–2(a)(37)] shall become effective on the sixtieth day after the filing thereof, or a later date designated by the registrant on the facing sheet of the amendment, which date shall be no later than eighty days after the date on which the amendment is filed.

(2) A post-effective amendment filed by a registered open-end management investment company for the purpose of adding a series shall become effective on the seventy-fifth day after the filing thereof or a later date designated by the registrant on the facing sheet of the amendment, which date shall be no later than ninety-five days after the date on which the amendment is filed.

(3) The Commission, having due regard to the public interest and the protection of investors, may declare an amendment filed under this paragraph (a) effective on an earlier date.

(b) *Immediate Effectiveness.* Except as otherwise provided in this section, a post-effective amendment to a registration statement filed by a registered open-end management investment company, unit investment trust or separate account as defined in section 2(a)(37) of the Investment Company Act of 1940 [15 U.S.C. 80a–2(a)(37)] shall become effective on the date upon which it is filed with the Commission, or a later date designated by the registrant on the facing sheet of the amendment, which date shall be not later than thirty days after the date on which the amendment is filed, except that a post-effective amendment including a designation of a new effective date pursuant to paragraph (b)(1)(v) of this section shall become effective on the new effective date designated therein, *Provided,* that the following conditions are met:

(1) It is filed for no purpose other than one or more of the following:

(i) Bringing the financial statements up to date under section 10(a)(3) of the Securities Act of 1933 [15 U.S.C. 77j(a)(3)] or Rules 3–12 or 3–18 of Regulation S–X [17 CFR 210.3–12 and 210.3–18];

(ii) Complying with an undertaking to file an amendment containing financial statements, which may be unaudited, within four to six months after the effective date of the registrant's registration statement under the Securities Act of 1933 [15 U.S.C. 77a *et seq.*];

(iii) Designating a new effective date for a previously filed post-effective amendment pursuant to paragraph (a) of this section, which has not yet become effective, *Provided,* that the new effective date shall be no earlier than the effective date designated in the previously filed amendment under paragraph (a) of this section and no later than thirty days after that date;

(iv) Disclosing or updating the information required by Items 5(c) or 5A of Form N–1A [17 CFR 239.15A and 274.11A];

(v) Making any non-material changes which the registrant deems appropriate;

(vi) In the case of a separate account registered as a unit investment trust, to make changes in the disclosure in the unit investment trust's registration statement to reflect changes to disclosure in the registration statement of the investment company in which the unit investment trust invests all of its assets; and

(vii) Any other purpose which the Commission shall approve.

(2) The registrant represents that the amendment is filed solely for one or more of the purposes specified in paragraph (b)(1) of this section and that no material event requiring disclosure in the prospectus, other than one listed in paragraph (b)(1) of this section or one for which the Commission has approved a filing under paragraph (b)(1)(vii) of this section, has occurred since the latest of the following three dates:

(i) the effective date of the registrant's registration statement;

(ii) the effective date of its most recent post-effective amendment to its registration statement which included a prospectus; or

(iii) the filing date of a post-effective amendment filed under paragraph (a) of this section which has not become effective.

(3) The amendment recites on its facing sheet that the registrant proposes that the amendment will become effective under paragraph (b) of this section.

(4) The representations of the registrant referred to in paragraph (b)(2) of this section shall be made by certification on the signature page of the post-effective amendment that the amendment meets all the requirements for effectiveness under paragraph (b) of this section. If counsel prepared or reviewed the post-effective amendment filed under paragraph (b) of this section, counsel shall furnish to the Commission at the time the amendment is filed a written representation that the amendment does not contain disclosures that would render it ineligible to become effective under paragraph (b) of this section.

(c) *Incomplete or Inaccurate Amendments; Suspension of Use of Paragraph (b) of this section.* (1) No amendment shall become effective under paragraph (a) of this section if, prior to the effective date of the amendment, it should appear to the Commission that the amendment may be incomplete or inaccurate in any material respect, and the Commission furnishes to the registrant written notice that the effective date of the amendment is to be suspended. Following such action by the Commission, the registrant may file with the Commission at any time a petition for review of the suspension. The Commission will order a hearing on the matter if a request for such a hearing is included in the petition. If the Commission has suspended the effective date of an amendment, the amendment shall become effective on such date as the Commission may determine, having due regard to the public interest and the protection of investors.

(2) The Commission may, in the manner and under the circumstances set forth in this paragraph (c)(2), suspend the ability of registrant to file a post-effective amendment under paragraph (b) of this section. The notice of such suspension shall be in writing and shall specify the period for which such suspension shall remain in effect. The Commission may issue a suspension if it appears to the Commission that a registrant which files a post-effective amendment under paragraph (b) of this section has not complied with the conditions of that paragraph. Any suspension under this paragraph (c)(2) shall become effective at such time as the Commission furnishes written notice thereof to the registrant. Any such suspension, so long as it is in effect, shall apply to any post-effective amendment that has been filed but has not, at the time of such suspension, become effective, and to any post-effective amendment that may be filed after the suspension. Any suspension shall apply only to the ability to file a post-effective amendment pursuant to paragraph (b) of this section and shall not otherwise affect any post-effective amendment. Following this action by the Commission the registrant may file with the Commission at any time a petition for review of the suspension. The Commission will order a hearing on the matter if a request for a hearing is included in the petition.

(d) *Subsequent Amendments.* (1) Except as provided in paragraph (d)(2) of this section, a post-effective amendment that includes a prospectus shall not become effective under paragraph (a) of this section if a subsequent post-effective amendment relating to the prospectus is filed before such amendment becomes effective.

(2) A post-effective amendment that includes a prospectus shall become effective under paragraph (a) of this section notwithstanding the filing of a subsequent post-effective amendment relating to the prospectus, *Provided*, that the following conditions are met:

(i) the subsequent amendment is filed under paragraph (b) of this section; and

(ii) the subsequent amendment designates as its effective date either:

(A) the date on which the prior post-effective amendment was to become effective under paragraph (a) of this section; or

(B) a new effective date designated under paragraph (b)(1)(iii) of this section; in this case the prior post-effective amendment filed under paragraph (a) of this section and any prior post-effective amendment filed under paragraph (b) of this section shall also become effective on the new effective date designated under paragraph (b)(1)(iii) of this section.

(3) Notwithstanding paragraphs (d)(1) and (d)(2) of this section, if another post-effective amendment relating to the same prospectus is filed under paragraph (a) of this section before the prior amendments filed pursuant to paragraphs (a) and (b) of this section have become effective, none of such prior amendments shall become effective under this section.

(e) *Certain Separate Accounts.* For purposes of this section, a post-effective amendment to a registration statement for an offering of securities by a registered open-end management investment company or unit investment trust as those terms are used in paragraphs (a), (b), and (e) of this section and as such amendments are referred to in paragraphs (c) and (d) of this section, shall include a post-effective amendment to an offering of securities by an insurance company funded through a separate account, as defined in section 2(a)(37) of the Investment Company Act of 1940 [15 U.S.C. 80a–2(a)(37)], where the separate account need not register under the Investment Company Act of 1940 under section 3(c)(11) thereof [15 U.S.C. 80a–3(c)(11)].

(f) *Electronic Filers.* When ascertaining the date of filing, electronic filers should not presume a registration statement has been accepted until notice of acceptance has been received from the Commission.

Note: To determine the date of automatic effectiveness, the day following the filing date is the first day of the time period. For example, a post-effective amendment filed under paragraph (a) of this section on November 1 would become effective on December 31.

Rule 486. Effective Date of Post–Effective Amendments and Registration Statements Filed by Certain Closed–End Management Investment Companies

(a) *Automatic Effectiveness.* Except as otherwise provided in this section, a post-effective amendment to a registration statement, or a registration statement filed for the purpose of registering additional shares of common stock for which a registration statement filed on Form N–2 (§§ 239.14 and 274.11a–1 of this chapter) is effective, filed by a registered closed-end management investment company or business development company which makes periodic repurchase offers under § 270.23c–3 of this chapter, shall become effective on the sixtieth day after the filing thereof, or a later date designated by the registrant on the facing sheet of the amendment or registration statement, which date shall not be later than eighty days after the date on which the amendment or registration statement is filed, *Provided,* that the Commission, having due regard to the public interest and the protection of investors, may declare an amendment or registration statement filed under this paragraph (a) effective on an earlier date.

(b) *Immediate Effectiveness.* Except as otherwise provided in this section, a post-effective amendment to a registration statement, or a registration statement for additional shares of common stock, filed by a registered closed-end management investment company or business development company which makes periodic repurchase offers under § 270.23c–3 of this chapter, shall become effective on the date on which it is filed with the Commission, or a later date designated by the registrant on the facing sheet of the amendment or registration statement, which date shall be not later than thirty days after the date on which the amendment or registration statement is filed, except that a post-effective amendment including a designation of a new effective date under paragraph (b)(1)(iii) of this section shall become effective on the new effective date designated therein, *Provided,* that the following conditions are met:

(1) It is filed for no purpose other than one or more of the following:

(i) Registering additional shares of common stock for which a registration statement filed on Form N–2 (§§ 239.14 and 274.11a–1 of this chapter) is effective;

(ii) Bringing the financial statements up to date under section 10(a)(3) of the Act [15 U.S.C. 77j(a)(3)] or rule 3–18 of Regulation S–X [17 CFR 210.3–18];

(iii) Designating a new effective date for a previously filed post-effective amendment or registration statement for additional shares under paragraph (a) of this section, which has not yet become effective, *Provided,* that the new effective date shall be no earlier than the effective date designated in the previously filed amendment or registration statement under paragraph (a) of this section and no later than thirty days after that date;

(iv) Disclosing or updating the information required by Item 9c of Form N–2 [17 CFR 239.14 and 274.11a–1];

(v) Making any non-material changes which the registrant deems appropriate; and

(vi) Any other purpose which the Commission shall approve.

(2) The registrant represents that the amendment is filed solely for one or more of the purposes specified in paragraph (b)(1) of this section and that no material event requiring disclosure in the prospectus, other than one listed in paragraph (b)(1) or one for which the Commission has approved a filing under paragraph (b)(1)(vi) of this section, has occurred since the latest of the following three dates:

(i) the effective date of the registrant's registration statement;

(ii) the effective date of its most recent post-effective amendment to its registration statement which included a prospectus; or

(iii) the filing date of a post-effective amendment or registration statement filed under paragraph (a) of this section which has not become effective; and

(3) The amendment or registration statement recites on the facing sheet thereof that the registrant proposes that the amendment or registration statement will become effective under paragraph (b) of this section.

(4) The representations of the registrant referred to in paragraph (b)(2) of this section shall be made by certification on the signature page of the post-effective amendment or registration statement that the amendment or registration statement meets all of the requirements for effectiveness under paragraph (b) of this section. If counsel prepared or reviewed the post-effective amendment or registration statement filed under paragraph (b) of this section, counsel shall furnish to the Commission at the time the amendment or registration statement is filed a written representation that the amendment or registration statement does not contain disclosure which would render it ineligible to become effective under paragraph (b) of this section.

(c) *Incomplete or Inaccurate Amendments; Suspension of Use of Paragraph (b) of this section.* (1) No amendment or registration statement shall become effective under paragraph (a) of this section if, prior to the effective date of the amendment or registration statement, it should appear to the Commission that the amendment or registration statement may be incomplete or inaccurate in any material respect, and the Commission furnishes to the registrant written notice that the effective date of the amendment or registration statement is to be suspended. Following such action by the Commission, the registrant may file with the Commission at any time a petition for review of the suspension. The Commission will order a hearing on the matter if a request for such a hearing is included in the petition. If the Commission has suspended the effective date of an amendment or registration statement, the amendment or registration statement shall become effective on such date as the Commission may determine, having due regard to the public interest and the protection of investors.

(2) The Commission may, in the manner and under the circumstances set forth in this paragraph (c)(2), suspend the ability of a registrant to file a post-effective amendment or registration statement under paragraph (b) of this section. The notice of such suspension shall be in writing and shall specify the period for which such suspension shall remain in effect. The Commission may issue a suspension if it appears to the Commission that a registrant which files a post-effective amendment under paragraph (b) of this section has not complied with the conditions of that paragraph. Any suspension under this paragraph shall become effective at such time as the Commission furnishes written notice thereof to the company. Any such suspension, so long as it is in effect, shall apply to any post-effective amendment or registration statement that has been filed but has not, at the time of such suspension, become effective, and to any

post-effective amendment or registration statement that may be filed after the suspension. Any suspension shall apply only to the ability to file a post-effective amendment or registration statement under paragraph (b) of this section and shall not otherwise affect any post-effective amendment or registration statement. Following this action by the Commission, the registrant may file with the Commission at any time a petition for review of the suspension. The Commission will order a hearing on the matter if a request for a hearing is included in the petition.

(d) *Subsequent Amendments.* (1) Except as provided in paragraph (d)(2) of this section, a post-effective amendment or registration statement which includes a prospectus shall not become effective under paragraph (a) of this section if a subsequent post-effective amendment or registration statement relating to the prospectus is filed before such amendment or registration statement becomes effective.

(2) A post-effective amendment or registration statement which includes a prospectus shall become effective under paragraph (a) of this section notwithstanding the filing of a subsequent post-effective amendment or registration statement relating to the prospectus, *Provided,* that the following conditions are met:

(i) the subsequent amendment or registration statement is filed under paragraph (b) of this section; and

(ii) the subsequent amendment or registration statement designates as its effective date either:

(A) the date on which the prior post-effective amendment or registration statement was to become effective under paragraph (a) of this section or

(B) a new effective date designated under paragraph (b)(1)(iii) of this section.

In this case the prior post-effective amendment or registration statement filed under paragraph (a) of this section and any prior post-effective amendment or registration statement filed under paragraph (b) of this section shall also become effective on the new effective date designated under paragraph (b)(1)(iii) of this section.

(3) Notwithstanding paragraphs (d)(1) and (d)(2) of this section, if another post-effective amendment or registration statement relating to the same prospectus is filed under paragraph (a) of this section before the prior amendments or registration statements filed under paragraphs (a) and (b) of this section have become effective, none of such prior amendments or registration statements shall become effective under this section.

(e) *Condition to Use of Paragraphs (a) or (b).* A post-effective amendment or new registration statement shall not become effective under paragraph (a) or (b) of this section unless within two years prior to the filing thereof a post-effective amendment or registration statement relating to the common stock of the registrant has become effective.

(f) *Electronic Filers.* When ascertaining the date of filing, electronic filers should not presume a registration statement has been accepted until notice of acceptance has been received from the Commission.

Note: To determine the date of automatic effectiveness, the day following the filing date is the first day of the time period. For example, a post-effective amendment filed under paragraph (a) of this section on November 1 would become effective on December 31.

REGISTRATION BY FOREIGN GOVERNMENTS OF POLITICAL SUBDIVISIONS THEREOF

Rule 489. Filing of Form by Foreign Banks and Insurance Companies and Certain of Their Holding Companies and Finance Subsidiaries

(a) The following foreign issuers shall file Form F–N under the Act appointing an agent for service of process when filing a registration statement under the Act:

(1) A foreign issuer that is a foreign bank or foreign insurance company excepted from the definition of investment company by Rule 3a–6 under the Investment Company Act of 1940 (the "1940 Act");

(2) A foreign issuer that is a finance subsidiary of a foreign bank or foreign insurance company, as those terms are defined in rule 3a–6 under the 1940 Act, if the finance subsidiary is excepted from the definition of investment company by rule 3a–5 under the 1940 Act; or

(3) A foreign issuer that is excepted from the definition of investment company by rule 3a–1 under the 1940 Act because some or all of its majority-owned subsidiaries are foreign banks or insurance companies excepted from the definition of investment company by rule 3a–6 under the 1940 Act.

(b) The requirements of paragraph (a) of this rule shall not apply to:

(1) A foreign issuer that has filed Form F–X under the Securities Act of 1933 with respect to the securities being offered; and

(2) A foreign issuer filing a registration statement relating to debt securities or non-voting preferred stock that has on file with the Commission a currently accurate Form N–6C9 under the 1940 Act.

(c) Six copies of Form F–N, one of which shall be manually signed, shall be filed with the Commission at its principal office.

OFFERINGS BY FOREIGN GOVERNMENTS

Rule 490. Information to be Furnished Under Paragraph (3) of Schedule B

Any issuer filing a registration statement pursuant to Schedule B of the Act need not furnish the detailed information specified in paragraph (3) as to issues of outstanding funded debt the aggregate amount of which outstanding is less than 5 percent of the total funded debt outstanding and to be created by the security to be offered, provided the amount thereof is included in the statement of the total amount of funded debt outstanding and a statement is made as to the title, amount outstanding, rate of interest, and date of maturity of each such issue.

Rule 491. Information to be Furnished Under Paragraph (6) of Schedule B

Any foreign government filing a registration statement pursuant to Schedule B of the Act need state, in furnishing the information required by paragraph (6), the names and addresses only of principal underwriters, namely, underwriters in privity of contract with the registrant, provided they are designated as principal underwriters and a brief statement is made as to the discounts and commissions to be received by subunderwriters or dealers.

Rule 492. Omissions From Prospectuses

In the case of a security for which a registration statement conforming to Schedule B is in effect, the following information, contained in the registration statement, may be omitted from any prospectus: Information in answer to paragraph (3) of the Schedule with respect to the amortization and retirement provisions for debt not being registered, and with respect to the provisions for the substitution of security for such debt; *the addresses of underwriters in answer to paragraph (b);* information in answer to paragraph (11); *the addresses of counsel in answer to paragraph (12);* the copy of any agreement or agreements required by paragraph (13); the agreement required by paragraph (14); *and* all information, whether contained in the registration statement itself or in any exhibit thereto, not required by Schedule B.

Rule 493. Additional Schedule B Disclosure and Filing Requirements

(a) The copy of the opinion or opinions of counsel required by paragraph (14) of Schedule B shall be filed either as a part of the registration statement as originally filed, or as an amendment to the registration statement.

(b) A foreign government or political subdivision of a foreign government must file a registration statement submitted under Schedule B of the Act on the Commission's Electronic Data Gathering and Retrieval System (EDGAR) unless it has obtained a hardship exemption under § 232.201 or § 232.202 of this chapter (Regulation S–T).

(c) A foreign government or political subdivision must disclose in its Schedule B registration statement:

(1) That the Commission maintains an Internet site that contains reports and other information regarding issuers that file electronically with the Commission; and

(2) The address for the Commission Internet site (http://www.sec.gov). A foreign government or political subdivision filing on EDGAR is further encouraged to give its Internet address, if available.

Rule 494. Newspaper Prospectuses

(a) This rule shall apply only to newspaper prospectuses relating to securities, as to which a registration statement has become effective, issued by a foreign national government with which the United States maintains diplomatic relations. The term "newspaper prospectus" means an advertisement of securities in newspapers, magazines or other periodicals which are admitted to the mails as second-class matter and which are not distributed by the advertiser. The term does not include reprints, reproductions or detached copies of such advertisements. A newspaper prospectus shall not be deemed a prospectus meeting the requirements of Section 10 for the purpose of Section 2(10)(a) or 5(b)(2) or the Act.

(b) All information included in a newspaper prospectus may be expressed in such condensed or summarized form as may be necessary in the light of the circumstances under which newspaper prospectuses are authorized to be used. The information need not follow the order in which the information is set forth in the registration statement or in the full prospectus. No information need be set forth in tabular form.

(c) The following statement shall be set forth at the head of every newspaper prospectus in conspicuous print:

"These securities, though registered, have not been approved or disapproved by the Securities and Exchange Commission, which does not pass on the merits of any registered securities."

Rule 495. Preparation of Registration Statement

(a) A registration statement on Form N–1A (§ 239.15A and § 274.11A of this chapter), Form N–2 (§ 239.14 and § 274.11a–1 of this chapter), Form N–3 (§ 239.17a and § 274.11b of this chapter), Form N–4 (§ 239.17b and § 274.11c of this chapter), or Form N–6 (§ 239.17c and § 274.11d of this chapter), shall consist of the facing sheet of the applicable form; a prospectus containing the information called for by such form; the information, list of exhibits, undertakings and signatures required to be set forth in such form; financial statements and schedules; exhibits; and other information or documents filed as part of the registration statement; and all documents or information incorporated by reference in the foregoing (whether or not required to be filed).

(b) All general instructions, instructions to items of the form, and instructions as to financial statements, exhibits, or prospectuses are to be omitted from the registration statement in all cases.

(c) In the case of a registration statement filed on Form N–1A (§ 239.15A and § 274.11A of this chapter), Form N–2 (§ 239.14 and § 274.11a–1 of this chapter), Form N–3 (§ 239.17a and § 274.11b of this chapter), Form N–4 (§ 239.17b and § 274.11c of this chapter), or Form N–6 (§ 239.17c and § 274.11d of this chapter), Parts A and B shall contain the information called for by each of the items of the applicable Part, except that unless otherwise specified, no reference need be made to inapplicable items, and negative answers to any item may be omitted. Copies of Parts A and B may be filed as part of the registration statement in lieu of furnishing the information in item-and-answer form. Wherever such copies are filed in lieu of information in item-and-answer form, the text of the items of the form is to be omitted from the registration statement, as well as from Parts A and B, except to the extent provided in paragraph (d) of the section.

(d) In the case of a registration statement filed on Form N–1A (§ 239.15A and § 274.11A of this chapter), Form N–2 (§ 239.14 and § 274.11a–1 of this chapter), Form N–3 (§ 239.17a and § 274.11b of this chapter), Form N–4 (§ 239.17b and § 274.11c of this chapter), or Form N–6 (§ 239.17c and § 274.11d of this chapter), where any item of those forms calls for information not required to be included in Parts A and B (generally Part C of such form), the text of such items, including the numbers and captions thereof, together with the answers thereto, shall be filed with Parts A or B under cover of the facing sheet of the form as part of the registration statement. However, the text of such items may be omitted, provided the answers are so prepared as to indicate the coverage of the item without the necessity of reference to the text of the item. If any such item is inapplicable, or the answer thereto is in the negative, a statement to that effect shall be made. Any financial statements not required to be included in Parts A and B shall also be filed as part of the registration statement proper, unless incorporated by reference pursuant to § 230.411.

Rule 496. Contents of Prospectus and Statement of Additional Information Used After Nine Months

In the case of a registration statement filed on Form N–1A (§ 239.15A and § 274.11A of this chapter), Form N–2 (§ 239.14 and § 274.11a–1 of this chapter), Form N–3 (§ 239.17a and § 274.11b of this chapter), Form N–4 (§ 239.17b and § 274.11c of this chapter), or Form N–6 (§ 239.17c and § 274.11d of this chapter), there may be omitted from any prospectus or Statement of Additional Information used more than 9 months after the effective date of the registration statement any information previously required to be contained in the prospectus or the Statement of Additional Information insofar as later information covering the same subjects, including the latest available certified financial statements, as of a date not more than 16 months prior to the use of the prospectus or the Statement of Additional Information is contained therein.

Rule 497. Filing of Investment Company Prospectuses—Number of Copies

(a) Five copies of every form of prospectus sent or given to any person prior to the effective date of the registration statement that varies from the form or forms of prospectus included in the registration statement filed pursuant to § 230.402(a) shall be filed as part of the registration statement not later than the date that form of prospectus is first sent or given to any person, except that:

(1) An investment company advertisement under § 230.482 shall be filed under this paragraph (a) (but not as part of the registration statement) unless filed under paragraph (i) of this section; and

(2) A profile under § 230.498 shall be filed in accordance with paragraph (k) of this section and not as part of the registration statement.

(b) Within 5 days after the effective date of a registration statement or the commencement of a public offering after the effective date of a registration statement, whichever occurs later, 10 copies of each form of prospectus used after the effective date in connection with such offering shall be filed with the Commission in the exact form in which it was used.

(c) For investment companies filing on Form N–1A (§ 239.15A and § 274.11A of this chapter), Form N–2 (§ 239.14 and § 274.11a–1 of this chapter), Form N–3 (§ 239.17a and § 274.11b of this chapter), Form N–4

(§ 239.17b and § 274.11c of this chapter), or form N–6 (§ 239.17c and § 274.11d of this chapter), within five days after the effective date of a registration statement or the commencement of a public offering after the effective date of a registration statement, whichever occurs later, ten copies of each form of prospectus and form of Statement of Additional Information used after the effective date in connection with such offering shall be filed with the Commission in the exact form in which it was used.

(d) After the effective date of a registration statement no prospectus which purports to comply with section 10 of the Act and which varies from any form of prospectus filed pursuant to paragraph (b) or (c) of this rule shall be used until 10 copies thereof have been filed with, or mailed for filing to, the Commission, together with 5 copies of a cross reference sheet similar to that previously filed, if changed.

(e) For investment companies filing on Form N–1A (§ 239.15A and § 274.11A of this chapter), Form N–2 (§ 239.14 and § 274.11a–1 of this chapter), Form N–3 (§ 239.17a and § 274.11b of this chapter), Form N–4 (§ 239.17b and § 274.11c of this chapter), or Form N–6 (§ 239.17c and § 274.11d of this chapter), after the effective date of a registration statement, no prospectus that purports to comply with Section 10 of the Act (15 U.S.C. 77j) or Statement of Additional Information that varies from any form of prospectus or form of Statement of Additional Information filed pursuant to paragraph (c) of this section shall be used until five copies thereof have been filed with, or mailed for filing to the Commission.

(f) Every prospectus consisting of a radio or television broadcast shall be reduced in writing. Five copies of every such prospectus shall be filed with the Commission in accordance with the requirements of this section.

(g) Each copy of a prospectus under this rule shall contain in the upper right corner of the cover page the paragraph of this rule under which the filing is made and the file number of the registration statement to which the prospectus relates. In addition, each investment company advertisement deemed to be a Section 10(b) prospectus pursuant to Rule 482 of this chapter shall contain in the upper right hand corner of the cover page the legend "Rule 482 ad." The information required by this paragraph may be set forth in longhand, provided it is legible.

(h)(1) No later than the second business day following the earlier of the date of the determination of the offering price or the date it is first used after effectiveness in connection with a public offering or sales, ten copies of every form of prospectus and Statement of Additional Information, where applicable, that discloses the information previously omitted from the prospectus filed as part of an effective registration statement in reliance upon Rule 430A under the Securities Act shall be filed with the Commission in the exact form in which it is used, or transmitted by a means reasonably calculated to result in filing with the Commission by that date.

(2) Ten copies of each term sheet or abbreviated term sheet sent or given in reliance upon Rule 434 (§ 230.434) shall be filed with the Commission no later than the second business day following the earlier of the date of determination of the offering price, or the date it is first used after effectiveness in connection with a public offering or sales, or transmitted by a means reasonably calculated to result in filing with the Commission by that date.

(i) An investment company advertisement deemed to be a Section 10(b) prospectus pursuant to Rule 482 of this chapter shall be considered to be filed with the Commission upon filing with a national securities association registered under Section 15A of the Securities Exchange Act of 1934 that has adopted rules providing standards for the investment company advertising practices of its members and has established and implemented procedures to review that advertising.

(j) In lieu of filing under paragraph (b) or (c) of this rule, a registrant may file a certification that:

(1) the form of prospectus and Statement of Additional Information that would have been filed under paragraph (b) or (c) of this rule would not have differed from that contained in the most recent registration statement or amendment, and

(2) the text of the most recent registration statement or amendment has been filed electronically.

(k)(1) Profile filing requirements. A form of profile under § 230.498 shall not be used unless:

(i) The form of profile that has not been previously filed with the Commission is filed at least 30 days before the date that it is first sent or given to any person.

(A) No additional filing is required during the 30–day period for changes (material or otherwise) to a form of profile filed under this paragraph if the changes are included in the definitive profile that is filed with the Commission under paragraph (k)(2)(ii) of this section.

(B) The form of profile filed under this paragraph (k)(1)(i) can be used on the later of 30 days after the date of filing or, if the profile is filed in connection with an initial registration statement or a post-effective amendment that adds a series of an investment company to a registration statement, or reflects changes to a prospectus included in a post-effective amendment filed to update a registration statement under § 230.485, the date that the registration statement or post-effective amendment becomes effective.

(ii) A definitive form of a profile filed under paragraph (k)(1)(i) of this section is filed with the Commission no later than the fifth business day after the date that it is used.

(iii) A form of profile that differs from any definitive form of profile that was filed under this paragraph (k) is filed with the Commission in definitive form no later than the fifth business day after the date that it is first used. This filing shall be made under one of the following according to the character of the change contained in the form of profile:

(A) A form of profile that contains a material change to the information disclosed under § 230.498 (c)(2)(i)–(iii); and

(B) A form of profile that does not contain a material change to the information under § 230.498(c)(2)(i)–(iii).

(2) Filing procedures. (i) Designate, at the top of the first page of any form of profile that is filed under this paragraph (k), the paragraph and sub-paragraph under which the profile is filed.

(ii) Send two additional copies of the first definitive form of profile filed electronically under paragraph (k)(1)(ii) of this section to the Commission, in the primary form intended to be used for distribution to investors (e.g., paper, electronic media), by mail or other means reasonable calculated to result in receipt by the Commission, no later than the fifth business day after the date the profile is first sent or given to any person. Send copies to the following address: Office of Disclosure and Review, Division of Investment Management, U.S. Securities and Exchange Commission, 450 Fifth St., N.W., Mail Stop 5–6, Washington, D.C. 20549–6009. Note prominently that the submission is made in accordance with § 230.497(k)(2) of Regulation C under the Securities Act. If the profile is distributed primarily on the Internet, supply, in lieu of copies, the electronic address ("URL") of the profile page(s) in an exhibit to the electronic filing under this paragraph (k). Filers may fulfill the requirements of this paragraph by submitting with their definitive form of profile filed electronically under paragraph (k)(1)(ii) of this section an unofficial PDF copy of the profile in accordance with § 232.104 of this chapter. This additional requirement will expire on June 1, 2000.

Rule 498. Profiles for Certain Open-End Management Investment Companies

(a) *Definitions.* (1) A Fund means an open-end management investment company, or any series of such a company, that has, or is included in, an effective registration statement on Form N–1A (§§ 274.11A and 239.15A of this chapter) and that has a current prospectus under section 10(a) of the Act (15 U.S.C. 77j(a)).

(2) A Profile means a summary prospectus that is authorized under section 10(b) of the Act (15 U.S.C. 77j(b)) and section 24(g) of the Investment Company Act (15 U.S.C. 80a–24(g)) for the purpose of section 5(b)(1) of the Act (15 U.S.C. 77e(b)(1)).

(b) *General requirements.* A Fund may provide a Profile to investors, which may include, or be accompanied by, an application that investors may use to purchase the Fund's shares, if the Profile contains the information required or not precluded by paragraph (c) of this section and does not incorporate any information by reference to another document.

Instructions to paragraph (b)

1. The Profile is intended to be a standardized summary of key information in the Fund's prospectus under section 10(b) of the Act. Additional information is available in the Fund's prospectus under section 10(a) of the Act, in the Fund's Statement of Additional Information under Form N–1A, and in the Fund's annual and semi-annual shareholder reports prepared in accordance with § 270.30d–1. Funds may not use cross-references in the Profile to other Fund disclosure documents unless required or permitted by this rule. Funds should minimize cross-references and the use of footnotes within the Profile; cross-references and footnotes should generally be used only to promote a better understanding of the information about the Fund contained in the Profile.

2. Provide clear and concise information in the Profile in a format designed to communicate the information effectively. Avoid excessive detail, technical or legal terms, and long sentences and paragraphs. Provide the information in the Profile using the plain English writing principles in § 230.421(d).

3. A Fund may use document design techniques intended to promote effective communication of the information in the Profile unless inconsistent with the requirements of this section.

4. A Profile may describe more than one Fund or class of a Fund. A Profile that offers the securities of more than one Fund or class of a Fund does not need to repeat information that is the same for each Fund or class of Fund described in the Profile.

5. File the Profile with the Commission as required by § 230.497(k).

(c) *Specific requirements.* (1) Include on the cover page of the Profile or at the beginning of the Profile:

(i) The Fund's name and, at the Fund's option, the Fund's investment objective or the type of fund or class offered, or both;

(ii) A statement identifying the document as a "Profile," without using the term "prospectus";

(iii) The approximate date of the Profile's first use;

(iv) The following legend:

This Profile summarizes key information about the Fund that is included in the Fund's prospectus. The Fund's prospectus includes additional information about the Fund, including a more detailed description of the risks associated with investing in the Fund that you may want to consider before you invest. You may obtain the prospectus and other information about the Fund at no cost by calling ———.

(v) Provide a toll-free (or collect) telephone number that investors can use to obtain the prospectus and other information. The Fund may indicate, as applicable, that the prospectus and other information is available on the Fund's Internet site or by E-mail request. The Fund also may indicate, if applicable, that the prospectus and other information is available from a financial intermediary (such as a broker-dealer or bank) through which shares of the Fund may be purchased or sold.

Instruction to Paragraph (c)(1)(v). When the Fund (or financial intermediary through which shares of the Fund may be purchased or sold) receives a request for the Fund's prospectus, the Fund's Statement of Additional Information, or the Fund's annual or semi-annual report, the Fund (or financial intermediary) must send the requested document within three business days of receipt of the request, by first-class mail or other means designed to ensure equally prompt delivery. Funds are encouraged to send other information requested by shareholders within the same period.

(2) Provide the information required by paragraphs (c)(2)(i) through (ix) of this section in the order indicated:

(i) Fund objectives/goals. Provide the information about the Fund's investment objectives or goals required by Item 2(a) of Form N–1A.

(ii) Principal investment strategies of the Fund. Provide the information about the Fund's principal investment strategies required by Item 2(b) of Form N–1A. In addition, a Fund (other than a Fund that has not yet been required to deliver a semi-annual or annual report under § 270.30d–1 of this chapter) must provide disclosure to the following effect:

> Additional information about the Fund's investments is available in the Fund's annual and semi-annual reports to shareholders. In the Fund's annual report you will find a discussion of the market conditions and investment strategies that significantly affected the Fund's performance during the last fiscal year. You may obtain either or both of these reports at no cost by calling ______.

(iii) Principal risks of investing in the Fund. Provide the narrative disclosure, bar chart, and table required by Item 2(c) of Form N–1A. Provide in the table the Fund's average annual total returns and, if applicable, yield as of the end of the most recent calendar quarter prior to the Profile's first use. Update the return information as of the end of each succeeding calendar quarter as soon as practicable after the completion of the quarter. Disclose the date of the return information adjacent to the table.

Instruction to Paragraph (c)(2)(iii). A Fund may reflect the updated performance information in this section of the profile by affixing a label or sticker, or by other reasonable means.

(iv) Fees and expenses of the Fund. Include the fee table required by Item 3 of Form N–1A.

(v) Investment adviser, sub-adviser(s) and portfolio manager(s) of the Fund.

(A) Identify the Fund's investment adviser.

(B) Identify the Fund's sub-adviser(s) (if any) except that:

(*1*) A Fund need not identify a sub-adviser(s) whose sole responsibility for the Fund is limited to day-to-day management of the Fund's holdings of cash and cash equivalent instruments, unless the Fund is a money market fund or other Fund with a principal investment strategy of regularly holding cash and cash equivalent instruments.

(*2*) A Fund having three or more sub-advisers, each of which manages a portion of the Fund's portfolio, need not identify each such sub-adviser, except that the Fund must identify any sub-adviser that is (or is reasonably expected to be) responsible for the management of a significant portion of the Fund's net assets. For purposes of this paragraph (c)(2)(v)(B)(*2*), a significant portion of a Fund's net assets generally will be deemed to be 30% or more of the fund's net assets.

(C) State the name and length of service of the person or persons employed by or associated with the Fund's investment adviser (or the Fund) who are primarily responsible for the day-to-day management of the Fund's portfolio and summarize each person's business experience for the last five years in accordance with the Instructions to Item 6(a)(2) of Form N–1A. A Fund with three or more such persons, each of whom is (or is reasonably expected to be) responsible for the management of a portion of the Fund's portfolio, need not identify each person, except that a Fund must identify and summarize the business experience for the last five years of each person who is (or is reasonably expected to be) responsible for the management of a significant portion of the Fund's net assets. For purposes of this paragraph (c)(2)(v)(C), a significant portion of a Fund's net assets generally will be deemed to be 30% or more of the Fund's net assets.

(vi) Purchase of Fund shares. Disclose the Fund's minimum initial or subsequent investment requirements, the initial sales load (or other loads) to which the Fund's shares are subject, and, if applicable, the initial sales load breakpoints or waivers.

(vii) Sale of Fund shares. Disclose that the Fund's shares are redeemable, identify the procedures for redeeming shares (e.g., on any business day by written request, telephone, or wire transfer), and identify any charges or sales loads that may be assessed upon redemption (including, if applicable, the existence of waivers of these charges).

(viii) Fund distributions and tax information. Describe how frequently the Fund intends to make distributions and what options for reinvestment of distributions (if any) are available to investors. State, as applicable, that the Fund intends to make distributions that may be taxed as ordinary income or capital gains (which may be taxable at different rates depending on the length of time that the Fund holds its assets) or that the Fund intends to distribute tax-exempt income. If a Fund expects that its distributions, as a result of its investment objectives or strategies, primarily will consist of ordinary income or capital gains, provide disclosure to that effect. For a Fund that holds itself out as investing in securities generating tax-exempt income, provide, as applicable, a general statement to the effect that a portion of the Fund's distributions may be subject to federal income tax.

(ix) Other services are available from the Fund. Provide a brief summary of services available to the Fund's shareholders (e.g., any exchange privileges or automated information services), unless otherwise disclosed in response to paragraphs (c)(2)(vi) through (viii) of this section.

Instruction to Paragraph (c)(2)(ix). A Fund should disclose only those services that generally are available to typical investors in the Fund.

(3) The Profile may include an application that a prospective investor can use to purchase the Fund's shares as long as the application explains with equal prominence that an investor has the option of purchasing shares of the Fund after reviewing the information in the Profile or after requesting and reviewing the Fund's prospectus (and other information) before making a decision about investing in the Fund.

Instruction to Paragraph (c)(3). A Fund may include the application in a Profile or otherwise provide an application together with a Profile in any manner reasonably designed to alert investors that the application is to be considered along with the information about the Fund disclosed in the Profile.

(d) Modified Profile for certain funds. (1) A Fund may modify or omit the information required by paragraphs (c)(2)(vi) through (ix) of this section for a Profile to be used for a Fund that is offered as an investment option for:

(i) A defined contribution plan that meets the requirements for qualification under section 401(k) of the Internal Revenue Code (26 U.S.C. 401(k));

(ii) A tax-deferred arrangement under section 403(b) or 457 of the Internal Revenue Code (26 U.S.C. 403(b) and 457); and

(iii) Variable contracts as defined in section 817(d) of the Internal Revenue Code (26 U.S.C. 817(d)).

(2) A Fund that uses a Profile permitted under paragraph (d)(1) of this section may:

(i) Alter the legend required by paragraph (c)(1)(iv) of this section to include a statement to the effect that the Profile is intended for use in connection with a defined contribution plan, another tax-deferred arrangement, or a variable contract, as applicable, and is not intended for use by other investors; and

(ii) Modify other disclosure in a Profile consistent with offering the Fund as a specific investment option for a defined contribution plan, tax-deferred arrangement, or variable contract.

(3) A Profile used under paragraph (d)(1)(i) or (ii), but not paragraph (d)(1)(iii), of this section may include, or be accompanied by, an enrollment form for the plan or arrangement. The enrollment form does not need to be filed with the Profile under § 230.497.

REGULATION D—RULES GOVERNING THE LIMITED OFFER AND SALE OF SECURITIES WITHOUT REGISTRATION UNDER THE SECURITIES ACT OF 1933

Preliminary Notes

1. The following rules relate to transactions exempted from the registration requirements of section 5 of the Securities Act of 1933 (the "Act"). Such transactions are not exempt from the antifraud, civil liability, or other provisions of the federal securities laws. Issuers are reminded of their obligation to provide such further material information, if any, as may be necessary to make the information required under this regulation, in light of the circumstances under which it is furnished, not misleading.

2. Nothing in these rules obviates the need to comply with any applicable state law relating to the offer and sale of securities. Regulation D is intended to be a basic element in a uniform system of federal-state limited offering exemptions consistent with the provisions of sections 18 and 19(c) of the Act. In those states that have adopted Regulation D, or any version of Regulation D, special attention should be directed to the applicable state laws and regulations, including those relating to registration of persons who receive remuneration in connection with the offer and sale of securities, to disqualification of issuers and other persons associated with offerings based on state administrative orders or judgments, and to requirements for filings of notices of sales.

3. Attempted compliance with any rule in Regulation D does not act as an exclusive election; the issuer can also claim the availability of any other applicable exemption. For instance, an issuer's failure to satisfy all the terms and conditions of Rule 506 shall not raise any presumption that the exemption provided by section 4(2) of the Act is not available.

4. These rules are available only to the issuer of the securities and not to any affiliate of that issuer or to any other person for resales of the issuer's securities. The rules provide an exemption only for the transactions in which the securities are offered or sold by the issuer, not for the securities themselves.

5. These rules may be used for business combinations that involve sales by virtue of Rule 145(a) or otherwise.

6. In view of the objectives of these rules and the policies underlying the Act, Regulation D is not available to any issuer for any transaction or chain of transactions that, although in technical compliance with these rules, is part of a plan or scheme to evade the registration provisions of the Act. In such cases, registration under the Act is required.

7. Securities offered and sold outside the United States in accordance with Regulation S need not be registered under the Act. See Release No. 33–6863. Regulation S may be relied upon for such offers and sales even if coincident offers and sales are made in accordance with Regulation D inside the United States. Thus, for example, persons who are offered and sold securities in accordance with Regulation S would not be counted in the calculation of the number of purchasers under Regulation D. Similarly, proceeds from such sales would not be included in the aggregate offering price. The provisions of this note, however, do not apply if the issuer elects to rely solely on Regulation D for offers or sales to persons made outside the United States.

Rule 501. Definitions and Terms Used in Regulation D

As used in Regulation D, the following terms shall have the meaning indicated:

(a) *Accredited Investor*. "Accredited investor" shall mean any person who comes within any of the following categories, or who the issuer reasonably believes comes within any of the following categories, at the time of the sale of the securities to that person:

(1) Any bank as defined in section 3(a)(2) of the Act, or any savings and loan association or other institution as defined in section 3(a)(5)(A) of the Act whether acting in its individual or fiduciary capacity; any broker or dealer registered pursuant to section 15 of the Securities Exchange Act of 1934; any insurance company as defined in section 2(13) of the Act; any investment company registered under the Investment Company Act of 1940 or a business development company as defined in section 2(a)(48) of that Act; any Small Business Investment Company licensed by the U.S. Small Business Administration under section 301(c) or (d) of the Small Business Investment Act of 1958; any plan established and maintained by a state, its political subdivisions, or any agency or instrumentality of a state or its political subdivisions, for the benefit of its employees, if such plan has total assets in excess of $5,000,000; any employee benefit plan within the meaning of the Employee Retirement Income Security Act of 1974, if the investment decision is made by a plan fiduciary, as defined in section 3(21) of such act, which is either a bank, savings and loan association, insurance company, or registered investment adviser, or if the employee benefit plan has total assets in excess of $5,000,000 or, if a self-directed plan, with investment decisions made solely by persons that are accredited investors;

(2) Any private business development company as defined in section 202(a)(22) of the Investment Advisers Act of 1940;

(3) Any organization described in section 501(c)(3) of the Internal Revenue Code, corporation, Massachusetts or similar business trust, or partnership, not formed for the specific purpose of acquiring the securities offered, with total assets in excess of $5,000,000;

(4) Any director, executive officer, or general partner of the issuer of the securities being offered or sold, or any director, executive officer, or general partner of a general partner of that issuer;

(5) Any natural person whose individual net worth, or joint net worth with that person's spouse, at the time of his purchase exceeds $1,000,000;

(6) Any natural person who had an individual income in excess of $200,000 in each of the two most recent years or joint income with that person's spouse in excess of $300,000 in each of those years and has a reasonable expectation of reaching the same income level in the current year;

(7) Any trust, with total assets in excess of $5,000,000, not formed for the specific purpose of acquiring the securities offered, whose purchase is directed by a sophisticated person as described in Rule 506(b)(2)(ii); and

(8) Any entity in which all of the equity owners are accredited investors.

(b) *Affiliate.* An "affiliate" of, or person "affiliated" with, a specified person shall mean a person that directly, or indirectly through one or more intermediaries, controls or is controlled by, or is under common control with, the person specified.

(c) *Aggregate Offering Price.* "Aggregate offering price" shall mean the sum of all cash, services, property, notes, cancellation of debt, or other consideration to be received by an issuer for issuance of its securities. Where securities are being offered for both cash and non-cash consideration, the aggregate offering price shall be based on the price at which the securities are offered for cash. Any portion of the aggregate offering price attributable to cash received in a foreign currency shall be translated into United States currency at the currency exchange rate in effect at a reasonable time prior to or on the date of the sale of the securities. If securities are not offered for cash, the aggregate offering price shall be based on the value of the consideration as established by bona fide sales of that consideration made within a reasonable time, or, in the absence of sales, on the fair value as determined by an accepted standard. Such valuations of non-cash consideration must be reasonable at the time made.

(d) *Business Combination.* "Business combination" shall mean any transaction of the type specified in paragraph (a) of Rule 145 under the Act and any transaction involving the acquisition by one issuer, in exchange for all or a part of its own or its parent's stock, of stock of another issuer if, immediately after the acquisition, the acquiring issuer has control of the other issuer (whether or not it had control before the acquisition).

(e) *Calculation of Number of Purchasers.* For purposes of calculating the number of purchasers under Rules 505(b) and 506(b) only, the following shall apply:

(1) The following purchasers shall be excluded:

(i) Any relative, spouse or relative of the spouse of a purchaser who has the same principal residence as the purchaser;

(ii) Any trust or estate in which a purchaser and any of the persons related to him as specified in paragraph (e)(1)(i) or (e)(1)(iii) of this Rule 501 collectively have more than 50 percent of the beneficial interest (excluding contingent interests);

(iii) Any corporation or other organization of which a purchaser and any of the persons related to him as specified in paragraph (e)(1)(i) or (e)(1)(ii) of this Rule 501 collectively are beneficial owners of more than 50 percent of the equity securities (excluding directors' qualifying shares) or equity interests; and

(iv) Any accredited investor.

(2) A corporation, partnership or other entity shall be counted as one purchaser. If, however, that entity is organized for the specific purpose of acquiring the securities offered and is not an accredited investor under paragraph (a)(8) of this Rule 501, then each beneficial owner of equity securities or equity interests in the entity shall count as a separate purchaser for all provisions of Regulation D, except to the extent provided in paragraph (e)(1) of this Rule.

(3) A non-contributory employee benefit plan within the meaning of Title I of the Employee Retirement Income Security Act of 1974 shall be counted as one purchaser where the trustee makes all investment decisions for the plan.

(f) *Executive Officer.* "Executive officer" shall mean the president, any vice president in charge of a principal business unit, division or function (such as sales, administration or finance), any other officer who performs a policy making function, or any other person who performs similar policy making functions for the issuer. Executive officers of subsidiaries may be deemed executive officers of the issuer if they perform such policy making functions for the issuer.

(g) *Issuer.* The definition of the term "issuer" in section 2(4) of the Act shall apply, except that in the case of a proceeding under the Federal Bankruptcy Code, the trustee or debtor in possession shall be considered the issuer in an offering under a plan or reorganization, if the securities are to be issued under the plan.

(h) *Purchaser Representative.* "Purchaser representative" shall mean any person who satisfies all of the following conditions or who the issuer reasonably believes satisfies all of the following conditions:

(1) Is not an affiliate, director, officer or other employee of the issuer, or beneficial owner of 10 percent or more of any class of the equity securities or 10 percent or more of the equity interest in the issuer, except where the purchaser is:

(i) A relative of the purchaser representative by blood, marriage or adoption and not more remote than a first cousin;

(ii) A trust or estate in which the purchaser representative and any persons related to him as specified in paragraph (h)(1)(i) or (h)(1)(iii) of this Rule 501 collectively have more than 50 percent of the beneficial interest (excluding contingent interest) or of which the purchaser representative serves as trustee, executor, or in any similar capacity; or

(iii) A corporation or other organization of which the purchaser representative and any persons related to him as specified in paragraph (h)(1)(i) or (h)(1)(ii) of this Rule 501 collectively are the beneficial owners of more than 50 percent of the equity securities (excluding directors' qualifying shares) or equity interests;

(2) Has such knowledge and experience in financial and business matters that he is capable of evaluating, alone, or together with other purchaser representatives of the purchaser, or together with the purchaser, the merits and risks of the prospective investment;

(3) Is acknowledged by the purchaser in writing, during the course of the transaction, to be his purchaser representative in connection with evaluating the merits and risks of the prospective investment; and

(4) Discloses to the purchaser in writing a reasonable time prior to the sale of securities to that purchaser any material relationship between himself or his affiliates and the issuer or its affiliates that then exists, that is mutually understood to be contemplated, or that has existed at any time during the previous two years, and any compensation received or to be received as a result of such relationship.

NOTE 1: A person acting as a purchaser representative should consider the applicability of the registration and antifraud provisions relating to brokers and dealers under the Securities Exchange Act of 1934 ("Exchange Act") and relating to investment advisers under the Investment Advisers Act of 1940.

NOTE 2: The acknowledgment required by paragraph (h)(3) and the disclosure required by paragraph (h)(4) of this Rule 501 must be made with specific reference to each prospective investment. Advance blanket acknowledgment, such as for "all securities transactions" or "all private placements," is not sufficient.

NOTE 3: Disclosure of any material relationships between the purchaser representative or his affiliates and the issuer or its affiliates does not relieve the purchaser representative of his obligation to act in the interest of the purchaser.

Rule 502. General Conditions to Be Met

The following conditions shall be applicable to offers and sales made under Regulation D:

(a) *Integration.* All sales that are part of the same Regulation D offering must meet all of the terms and conditions of Regulation D. Offers and sales that are made more than six months before the start of a Regulation D offering or are made more than six months after completion of a Regulation D offering will not be considered part of that Regulation D offering, so long as during those six month periods there are no offers or sales of securities by or for the issuer that are of the same or a similar class as those offered or sold under Regulation D, other than those offers or sales of securities under an employee benefit plan as defined in Rule 405 under the Act.

NOTE: The term "offering" is not defined in the Act or in Regulation D. If the issuer offers or sells securities for which the safe harbor rule in paragraph (a) of this Rule 502 is unavailable, the determination as to whether separate sales of securities are part of the same offering (i.e. are considered "integrated") depends on the particular facts and circumstances. Generally, transactions otherwise meeting the requirements of an exemption will not be integrated with simultaneous offerings being made outside the United States in compliance with Regulation S. See Release No. 33–6863.

The following factors should be considered in determining whether offers and sales should be integrated for purposes of the exemptions under Regulation D:

(a) Whether the sales are part of a single plan of financing;

(b) Whether the sales involve issuance of the same class of securities;

(c) Whether the sales have been made at or about the same time;

(d) Whether the same type of consideration is received; and

(e) Whether the sales are made for the same general purpose. See Release No. 33–4552 (November 6, 1962).

(b) *Information Requirements.*

(1) *When Information Must Be Furnished.*

If the issuer sells securities under Rules 505 or 506 to any purchaser that is not an accredited investor, the issuer shall furnish the information specified in paragraph (b)(2) of this Rule 502 to such purchaser a reasonable time prior to sale. The issuer is not required to furnish the specified information to purchasers when it sells securities under Rule 504, or to any accredited investor.

Note: When an issuer provides information to investors pursuant to paragraph (b)(1), it should consider providing such information to accredited investors as well, in view of the anti-fraud provisions of the federal securities laws.

(2) *Type of Information to Be Furnished.*

(i) If the issuer is not subject to the reporting requirements of section 13 or 15(d) of the Exchange Act, at a reasonable time prior to the sale of securities the issuer shall furnish to the purchaser, to the extent material to an understanding of the issuer, its business, and the securities being offered:

(A) *Non-financial statement information.* If the issuer is eligible to use Regulation A, the same kind of information as would be required in Part II of Form 1–A. If the issuer is not eligible to use Regulation A, the same kind of information as required in Part I of a registration statement filed under the Securities Act on the form that the issuer would be entitled to use.

(B) *Financial statement information.—(1) Offerings up to $2,000,000.* The information required in Item 310 of Regulation S–B, except that only the issuer's balance sheet, which shall be dated within 120 days of the start of the offering, must be audited.

(2) *Offerings up to $7,500,000.* The financial statement information required in Form SB–2. If an issuer, other than a limited partnership, cannot obtain audited financial statements without unreasonable effort or expense, then only the issuer's balance sheet, which shall be dated within 120 days of the start of the offering, must be audited. If the issuer is a limited partnership and cannot obtain the required financial statements without unreasonable effort or expense, it may furnish financial statements that have been prepared on the basis of federal income tax requirements and examined and reported on in accordance with generally accepted auditing standards by an independent public or certified accountant.

(3) *Offerings Over $7,500,000.* The financial statement as would be re-

quired in a registration statement filed under the Act on the form that the issuer would be entitled to use. If an issuer, other than a limited partnership, cannot obtain audited financial statements without unreasonable effort or expense, then only the issuer's balance sheet, which shall be dated within 120 days of the start of the offering, must be audited. If the issuer is a limited partnership and cannot obtain the required financial statements without unreasonable effort or expense, it may furnish financial statements that have been prepared on the basis of federal income tax requirements and examined and reported on in accordance with generally accepted auditing standards by an independent public or certified accountant.

(C) If the issuer is a foreign private issuer eligible to use Form 20–F, the issuer shall disclose the same kind of information required to be included in a registration statement filed under the Act on the form that the issuer would be entitled to use. The financial statements need be certified only to the extent required by paragraph (b)(2)(i)(B)(1), (2) or (3) of this rule, as appropriate.

(ii) If the issuer is subject to the reporting requirements of section 13 or 15(d) of the Exchange Act, at a reasonable time prior to the sale of securities the issuer shall furnish to the purchaser the information specified in paragraph (b)(2)(ii)(A) or (B) of this rule and in either event the information specified in paragraph (b)(2)(ii)(C) of this Rule 502:

(A) The issuer's annual report to shareholders for the most recent fiscal year, if such annual report meets the requirements of Rule 14a–3 or 14c–3 under the Exchange Act, the definitive proxy statement filed in connection with that annual report, and, if requested by the purchaser in writing, a copy of the issuer's most recent Form 10–K and Form KSB under the Exchange Act.

(B) The information contained in an annual report on Form 10–K or 10–KSB under the Exchange Act or in a registration statement on Form S–1, SB–1, SB–2 or Form S–11, or Form SB–2 under the Act or on Form 10 and Form 10–SB under the Exchange Act, whichever filing is the most recent required to be filed.

(C) The information contained in any reports or documents required to be filed by the issuer under sections 13(a), 14(a), 14(c), and 15(d) of the Exchange Act since the distribution or filing of the report or registration statement specified in paragraph (A) or (B), and a brief description of the securities being offered, the use of the proceeds from the offering, and any material changes in the issuer's affairs that are not disclosed in the documents furnished.

(D) If the issuer is a foreign private issuer, the issuer may provide in lieu of the information specified in paragraphs (b)(2)(ii)(A) or (B) of this rule, the information contained in its most recent filing on Form 20–F or Form F–1.

(iii) Exhibits required to be filed with the Commission as part of a registration statement or report, other than an annual report to shareholders or parts of that report incorporated by reference in a Form 10–K and Form 10–KSB report, need not be furnished to each purchaser that is not an accredited investor if the contents of material exhibits are identified and such exhibits are made available to a purchaser, upon his written request, a reasonable time prior to his purchase.

(iv) At a reasonable time prior to the sale of securities to any purchaser that is not an accredited investor in a transaction under Rule 505 or 506, the issuer shall furnish to the purchaser a brief description in writing of any material written information concerning the offering that has been provided by the issuer to any accredited investor but not previously delivered to such unaccredited purchaser. The issuer shall furnish any portion or all of this information to the purchaser, upon his written request a reasonable time prior to his purchase.

(v) The issuer shall also make available to each purchaser at a reasonable time prior to his purchase of securities in a transaction under Rule 505 or 506 the opportunity to ask questions and receive answers concerning the terms and conditions of the offering and to obtain any additional information which the issuer possesses or can acquire without unreasonable effort or expense that is necessary to verify the accuracy of information furnished under paragraph (b)(2)(i) or (ii) of this Rule 502.

(vi) For business combinations or exchange offers, in addition to information required by Form S–4 the issuer shall provide to each purchaser at the time the plan is submitted to security holders, or, with an exchange, during the course of the transaction and prior to sale, written information about any terms or arrangements of the proposed transactions that are materially different from those for all other security holders. For purposes of this subsection, an issuer which is not subject to the reporting requirements of section 13 or 15(d) of the Exchange Act may satisfy the requirements of Part I.B. or C. of Form S–4 by compliance with paragraph (b)(2)(i) of this Rule 502.

(vii) At a reasonable time prior to the sale of securities to any purchaser that is not an accredited investor in a transaction under Rules 505 or 506, the issuer shall advise the purchaser of the limitations on resale in the manner contained in paragraph (d)(2) of this Rule. Such disclosure may be contained in other materials required to be provided by this paragraph.

(c) *Limitation on Manner of Offering.* Except as provided in Rule 504(b)(1), neither the issuer nor any person acting on its behalf shall offer or sell the securities by any form of general solicitation or general advertising, including, but not limited to, the following:

(1) Any advertisement, article, notice or other communication published in any newspaper, magazine, or similar media or broadcast over television or radio; and

(2) Any seminar or meeting whose attendees have been invited by any general solicitation or general advertising;

Provided, however, that publication by an issuer of a notice in accordance with Rule 135c shall not be deemed to constitute general solicitation or general advertising for purposes of this section; *Provided further,* that, if the requirements of § 230.135e are satisfied, providing any journalist with access to press conferences held outside of the United States, to meetings with issuer or selling security holder representatives conducted outside of the United States, or to written press-related materials released outside the United States, at or in which a present or proposed offering of securities is discussed, will not be deemed to constitute general solicitation or general advertising for purposes of this section.

(d) *Limitations on Resale.* Except as provided in Rule 504(b)(1), securities acquired in a transaction under Regulation D shall have the status of securities acquired in a transaction under Section 4(2) of the Act and cannot be resold without registration under the Act or an exemption therefrom. The issuer shall exercise reasonable care to assure that the purchasers of the securities are not underwriters within the meaning of section 2(11) of the Act, which reasonable care may be demonstrated by the following:

(1) Reasonable inquiry to determine if the purchaser is acquiring the securities for himself or for other persons;

(2) Written disclosure to each purchaser prior to sale that the securities have not been registered under the Act and, therefore, cannot be resold unless they are registered under the Act or unless an exemption from registration is available; and

(3) Placement of a legend on the certificate or other document that evidences the securities stating that the securities have not been registered under the Act and setting forth or referring to the restrictions on transferability and sale of the securities.

While taking these actions will establish the requisite reasonable care, it is not the exclusive method to demonstrate such care. Other actions by the issuer may satisfy this provision. In addition, Rule 502(b)(2)(vii) requires the delivery of written disclosure of the limitations on resale to investors in certain instances.

Rule 503. Filing of Notice of Sales

(a) An issuer offering or selling securities in reliance of Rules 504, 505 or 506 shall file with the Commission five copies of a notice on Form D no later than 15 days after the first sale of securities.

(b) One copy of every notice on Form D shall be manually signed by a person duly authorized by the issuer.

(c) If sales are made under Rule 505, the notice shall contain an undertaking by the issuer to furnish to the Commission, upon the written request of its staff, the information furnished by the issuer under Rule 502(b)(2) to any purchaser that is not an accredited investor.

(d) Amendments to notices filed under paragraph (a) of this Rule 503 need only report the issuer's name and the information required by Part C and any material change in the facts from those set forth in Parts A and B.

(e) A notice on Form D shall be considered filed with the Commission under paragraph (a) of this Rule 503.

(1) As of the date on which it is received at the Commission's principal office in Washington, DC; or

(2) As of the date on which the notice is mailed by means of United States registered or certified mail to the Commission's principal office in Washington, DC, if the notice is delivered to such office after the date on which it is required to be filed.

Rule 504. Exemption for Limited Offerings and Sales of Securities Not Exceeding $1,000,000

(a) *Exemption.* Offers and sales of securities that satisfy the conditions in paragraph (b) of this Rule 504 by an issuer that is not:

(1) subject to the reporting requirements of section 13 or 15(d) of the Exchange Act;

(2) an investment company; or

(3) a development stage company that either has no specific business plan or purpose or has indicated that its business plan is to engage in a merger or acquisition with an unidentified company or companies, or other entity or person, shall be exempt from the provision of section 5 of the Act under section 3(b) of the Act.

(b) *Conditions to be met.* (1) *General conditions.* To qualify for exemption under this § 230.504, offers and sales must satisfy the terms and conditions of §§ 230.501 and 230.502(a), (c) and (d), except that the provisions of § 230.502 (c) and (d) will not apply to offers and sales of securities under this § 230.504 that are made:

(i) Exclusively in one or more states that provide for the registration of the securities, and require the public filing and delivery to investors of a substantive disclosure document before sale, and are made in accordance with those state provisions;

(ii) In one or more states that have no provision for the registration of the securities or the public filing or delivery of a disclosure document before sale, if the securities have been registered in at least one state that provides for such registration, public filing and delivery before sale, offers and sales are made in that state in accordance with such provisions, and the disclosure document is delivered before sale to all purchasers (including those in the states that have no such procedure); or

(iii) Exclusively according to state law exemptions from registration that permit general solicitation and general advertising so long as sales are made only to "accredited investors" as defined in § 230.501(a).

(2) The aggregate offering price for an offering of securities under this Rule 504, as defined in Rule 501(c), shall not exceed $1,000,000, less the aggregate offering price for all securities sold within the twelve months before the start of and during the offering of securities under this Rule 504, in reliance on any exemption under section 3(b), or in violation of section 5(a) of the Securities Act.

NOTE 1: The calculation of the aggregate offering price is illustrated as follows:

If an issuer sold $900,000 on June 1, 1987 under this Rule 504 and an additional $4,100,000 on December 1, 1987 under Rule 505, the issuer could not sell any of its securities under this Rule 504 until December 1, 1988. Until then the issuer must count the December 1, 1987 sale towards the $1,000,000 limit within the preceding twelve months.

NOTE 2: If a transaction under Rule 504 fails to meet the limitation on the aggregate offering price, it does not affect the availability of this Rule 504 for the other transactions considered in applying such limitation. For example, if an issuer sold $1,000,000 worth of its securities on January 1, 1988 under this Rule 504 and an additional $500,000 worth on July 1, 1988, this Rule 504 would not be available for the later sale, but would still be applicable to the January 1, 1988 sale.

Rule 505. Exemption for Limited Offers and Sales of Securities Not Exceeding $5,000,000

(a) *Exemption.* Offers and sales of securities that satisfy the conditions in paragraph (b) of this Rule 505 by an issuer that is not an investment company shall be exempt from the provisions of section 5 of the Act under section 3(b) of the Act.

(b) *Conditions to Be Met.*

(1) *General Conditions.* To qualify for exemption under this Rule 505, offers and sales must satisfy the terms and conditions of Rules 501 and 502.

(2) *Specific Conditions.*

(i) *Limitation on Aggregate Offering Price.* The aggregate offering price for an offering of securities under this Rule 505, as defined in Rule 501(c), shall not exceed $5,000,000, less the aggregate offering price for all securities sold within the twelve months before the start of and during the offering of securities under this Rule 505 in reliance on any exemption under section 3(b) of the Act or in violation of section 5(a) of the Act.

NOTE: The calculation of the aggregate offering price is illustrated as follows:

Example 1. If an issuer sold $2,000,000 of its securities on June 1, 1982 under this Rule 505 and an additional $1,000,000 on September 1, 1982, the issuer would be permitted to sell only $2,000,000 more under this Rule 505 until June 1, 1983. Until that date the issuer must count both prior sales towards the $5,000,000 limit. However, if the issuer made its third sale on June 1, 1983, the issuer could then sell $4,000,000 of its securities because the

June 1, 1982 sale would not be within the preceding twelve months.

Example 2. If an issuer sold $500,000 of its securities on June 1, 1982 under Rule 504 and an additional $4,500,000 on December 1, 1982 under this Rule 505, then the issuer could not sell any of its securities under this Rule 505 until June 1, 1983. At that time it could sell an additional $500,000 of its securities.

(ii) *Limitation on Number of Purchasers.* There are no more than or the issuer reasonably believes that there are no more than 35 purchasers of securities from the issuer in any offering under this Rule 505.

NOTE: See Rule 501(e) for the calculation of the number of purchasers and Rule 502(a) for what may or may not constitute an offering under this rule.

(iii) *Disqualifications.* No exemption under this Rule 505 shall be available for the securities of any issuer described in Rule 262 of Regulation A, except that for purposes of this Rule 505 only:

(A) The term "filing of the offering statement required by Rule 252" as used in Rule 262(a), (b) and (c) shall mean the first sale of securities under this Rule 505;

(B) The term "underwriter" as used in Rule 262(b) and (c) shall mean a person that has been or will be paid directly or indirectly remuneration for solicitation of purchasers in connection with sales of securities under this Rule 505; and

(C) paragraph (b)(2)(iii) of this Rule 505 shall not apply to any issuer if the Commission determines, upon a showing of good cause, that it is not necessary under the circumstances that the exemption be denied. Any such determination shall be without prejudice to any other action by the Commission in any other proceeding or matter with respect to the issuer or any other person.

Rule 506. Exemption for Limited Offers and Sales Without Regard to Dollar Amount of Offering

(a) *Exemption.* Offers and sales of securities by an issuer that satisfy the conditions in paragraph (b) of this Rule 506 shall be deemed to be transactions not involving any public offering within the meaning of section 4(2) of the Act.

(b) *Conditions to Be Met.*

(1) *General Conditions.* To qualify for exemption under this Rule 506, offers and sales must satisfy all the terms and conditions of Rules 501 and 502.

(2) *Specific Conditions.*

(i) *Limitation on Number of Purchasers.* There are no more than or the issuer reasonably believes that there are no more than 35 purchasers of securities from the issuer in any offering under this Rule 506.

NOTE: See Rule 501(e) for the calculation of the number of purchasers and Rule 502(a) for what may or may not constitute an offering under this Rule 506.

(ii) *Nature of Purchasers.* Each purchaser who is not an accredited investor either alone or with his purchaser representative(s) has such knowledge and experience in financial and business matters that he is capable of evaluating the merits and risks of the prospective investment, or the issuer reasonably believes immediately prior to making any sale that such purchaser comes within this description.

Rule 507. Disqualifying Provision Relating to Exemptions Under Rules 504, 505 and 506

(a) No exemption under Rules 504, 505 or 506 shall be available for an issuer if such issuer, any of its predecessors or affiliates have been subject to any order, judgment, or decree of any court of competent jurisdiction temporarily, preliminary or permanently enjoining such person for failure to comply with Rule 503.

(b) Paragraph (a) of this rule shall not apply if the Commission determines, upon a showing of good cause, that it is not necessary under the circumstances that the exemption be denied.

Rule 508. Insignificant Deviations From a Term, Condition or Requirement of Regulation D

(a) A failure to comply with a term, condition or requirement of Rules 504, 505 or 506 will not result in the loss of the exemption from the requirements of section 5 of the Act for any offer or sale to a particular individual or entity, if the person relying on the exemption shows:

(1) The failure to comply did not pertain to a term, condition or requirement directly intended to protect that particular individual or entity; and

(2) The failure to comply was insignificant with respect to the offering as a whole, provided that any failure to comply with paragraph (c) of Rule 502, paragraph (b)(2) of Rule 504, paragraphs (b)(2)(i) and (ii) of Rule 505 and paragraph (b)(2)(i) of Rule 506 shall be deemed to be significant to the offering as a whole; and

(3) A good faith and reasonable attempt was made to comply with all applicable terms, conditions and requirements of Rules 504, 505 or 506.

(b) A transaction made in reliance on Rules 504, 505 or 506 shall comply with all applicable terms, conditions and requirements of Regulation D. Where an exemption is established only through reliance upon paragraph (a) of this rule, the failure to comply shall nonetheless be actionable by the Commission under section 20 of the Act.

C.F.R. § 239.500 Form D, Notice of Sales of Securities Under Regulation D and Section 4(6) of the Securities Act of 1933

(a) Five copies of a notice on this form shall be filed with the Commission no later than 15 days after the first sale of securities in an offering under Regulation D or under section 4(6) of the Securities Act of 1933.

(b) One copy of every notice on Form D shall be manually signed by a person duly authorized by the issuer.

(c) When sales are made under Rule 505, the notice shall contain an undertaking by the issuer to furnish to the Commission, upon the written request of its staff, the information furnished to non-accredited investors.

(d) Amendments to notices filed under paragraph (a) need only report the issuer's name and the information required by Part C and any material change in the facts from those set forth in Parts A and B.

(e) A notice on Form D shall be considered filed with the Commission under paragraph (a) of this section:

(1) As of the date on which it is received at the Commission's principal office in Washington DC; or

(2) As of the date on which the notice is mailed by means of United States registered or certified mail to the Commission's principal office in Washington, DC, if the notice is delivered to such office after the date on which it is required to be filed.

EXEMPTION FOR CERTAIN COMPENSATORY BENEFIT PLANS

Rule 701. Exemption for Offers and Sales of Securities Pursuant to Certain Compensatory Benefit Plans and Contracts Relating to Compensation

Preliminary Notes

(1) This section relates to transactions exempted from the registration requirements of section 5 of the Act (15 U.S.C. 77e). These transactions are not exempt from the antifraud, civil liability, or other provisions of the

federal securities laws. Issuers and persons acting on their behalf have an obligation to provide investors with disclosure adequate to satisfy the antifraud provisions of the federal securities laws.

(2) In addition to complying with this section, the issuer also must comply with any applicable state law relating to the offer and sale of securities.

(3) An issuer that attempts to comply with this section, but fails to do so, may claim any other exemption that is available.

(4) This section is available only to the issuer of the securities. Affiliates of the issuer may not use this section to offer or sell securities. This section also does not cover resales of securities by any person. This section provides an exemption only for the transactions in which the securities are offered or sold by the issuer, not for the securities themselves.

(5) The purpose of this section is to provide an exemption from the registration requirements of the Act for securities issued in compensatory circumstances. This section is not available for plans or schemes to circumvent this purpose, such as to raise capital. This section also is not available to exempt any transaction that is in technical compliance with this section but is part of a plan or scheme to evade the registration provisions of the Act. In any of these cases, registration under the Act is required unless another exemption is available.

(a) *Exemption.* Offers and sales made in compliance with all of the conditions of this section are exempt from section 5 of the Act (15 U.S.C. 77e).

(b) *Issuers eligible to use this section.* (1) *General.* This section is available to any issuer that is not subject to the reporting requirements of section 13 or 15(d) of the Securities Exchange Act of 1934 (the "Exchange Act") (15 U.S.C. 78m or 78o(d)) and is not an investment company registered or required to be registered under the Investment Company Act of 1940 (15 U.S.C. 80a–1 *et seq.*).

(2) *Issuers that become subject to reporting.* If an issuer becomes subject to the reporting requirements of section 13 or 15(d) of the Exchange Act (15 U.S.C. 78m or 78o(d)) after it has made offers complying with this section, the issuer may nevertheless rely on this section to sell the securities previously offered to the persons to whom those offers were made.

(3) *Guarantees by reporting companies.* An issuer subject to the reporting requirements of section 13 or 15(d) of the Exchange Act (15 U.S.C. 78m, 78o(d)) may rely on this section if it is merely guaranteeing the payment of a subsidiary's securities that are sold under this section.

(c) *Transactions exempted by this section.* This section exempts offers and sales of securities (including plan interests and guarantees pursuant to paragraph (d)(2)(ii) of this section) under a written compensatory benefit plan (or written compensation contract) established by the issuer, its parents, its majority-owned subsidiaries or majority-owned subsidiaries of the issuer's parent, for the participation of their employees, directors, general partners, trustees (where the issuer is a business trust), officers, or consultants and advisors, and their family members who acquire such securities from such persons through gifts or domestic relations orders. This section exempts offers and sales to former employees, directors, general partners, trustees, officers, consultants and advisors only if such persons were employed by or providing services to the issuer at the time the securities were offered. In addition, the term "employee" includes insurance agents who are exclusive agents of the issuer, its subsidiaries or parents, or derive more than 50% of their annual income from those entities.

(1) *Special requirements for consultants and advisors.* This section is available to consultants and advisors only if:

(i) They are natural persons;

(ii) They provide *bona fide* services to the issuer, its parents, its majority-owned subsidiaries or majority-owned subsidiaries of the issuer's parent; and

(iii) The services are not in connection with the offer or sale of securities in a capital-raising transaction, and do not directly or indirectly promote or maintain a market for the issuer's securities.

(2) *Definition of "Compensatory Benefit Plan."* For purposes of this section, a *compensatory benefit plan* is any purchase, savings, option, bonus, stock appreciation, profit sharing, thrift, incentive, deferred compensation, pension or similar plan.

(3) *Definition of "Family Member."* For purposes of this section, *family member* includes any child, stepchild, grandchild, parent, stepparent, grandparent, spouse, former spouse, sibling, niece, nephew, mother-in-law, father-in-law, son-in-law, daughter-in-law, brother-in-law, or sister-in-law, including adoptive relationships, any person sharing the employee's household (other than a tenant or employee), a trust in which these persons have more than fifty percent of the beneficial interest, a foundation in which these persons (or the employee) control the management of assets, and any other entity in which these persons (or the employee) own more than fifty percent of the voting interests.

(d) *Amounts that may be sold.* (1) *Offers.* Any amount of securities may be offered in reliance on this section. However, for purposes of this section, sales of securities underlying options must be counted as sales on the date of the option grant.

(2) *Sales.* The aggregate sales price or amount of securities sold in reliance on this section during any consecutive 12-month period must not exceed the greatest of the following:

(i) $1,000,000;

(ii) 15% of the total assets of the issuer (or of the issuer's parent if the issuer is a wholly-owned subsidiary and the securities represent obligations that the parent fully and unconditionally guarantees), measured at the issuer's most recent balance sheet date (if no older than its last fiscal year end); or

(iii) 15% of the outstanding amount of the class of securities being offered and sold in reliance on this section, measured at the issuer's most recent balance sheet date (if no older than its last fiscal year end).

(3) *Rules for calculating prices and amounts.* (i) *Aggregate sales price.* The term *aggregate sales price* means the sum of all cash, property, notes, cancellation of debt or other consideration received or to be received by the issuer for the sale of the securities. Non-cash consideration must be valued by reference to *bona fide* sales of that consideration made within a reasonable time or, in the absence of such sales, on the fair value as determined by an accepted standard. The value of services exchanged for securities issued must be measured by reference to the value of the securities issued. Options must be valued based on the exercise price of the option.

(ii) *Time of the calculation.* With respect to options to purchase securities, the aggregate sales price is determined when an option grant is made (without regard to when the option becomes exercisable). With respect to other securities, the calculation is made on the date of sale. With respect to deferred compensation or similar plans, the calculation is made when the irrevocable election to defer is made.

(iii) *Derivative securities.* In calculating outstanding securities for purposes of paragraph (d)(2)(iii) of this section, treat the securities underlying all currently exercisable or convertible options, warrants, rights or other securities, other than those issued under this exemption, as outstanding. In calculating the amount of securities sold for other purposes of paragraph (d)(2) of this section, count the amount of securities that would be acquired upon exercise or conversion in connection with sales of options, warrants, rights or other exercisable or convertible securities, including those to be issued under this exemption.

(iv) *Other exemptions.* Amounts of securities sold in reliance on this section do not affect "aggregate offering prices" in other exemptions, and amounts of securities sold in reliance on other exemptions do not affect the amount that may be sold in reliance on this section.

(e) *Disclosure that must be provided.* The issuer must deliver to investors a copy of the compensatory benefit plan or the contract, as applicable. In addition, if the aggregate sales price or amount of securities sold during any consecutive 12-month period exceeds $5 million, the issuer must deliver the following disclosure to investors a reasonable period of time before the date of sale:

(1) If the plan is subject to the Employee Retirement Income Security Act of 1974 ("ERISA") (29 U.S.C. 1104–1107), a copy of the summary plan description required by ERISA;

(2) If the plan is not subject to ERISA, a summary of the material terms of the plan;

(3) Information about the risks associated with investment in the securities sold pursuant to the compensatory benefit plan or compensation contract; and

(4) Financial statements required to be furnished by Part F/S of Form 1–A (Regulation A Offering Statement) (§ 239.90 of this chapter) under Regulation A (§§ 230.251 through 230.263). Foreign private issuers as defined in § 230.405 must provide a reconciliation to generally accepted accounting principles in the United States (U.S. GAAP) if their financial statements are not prepared in accordance with U.S. GAAP (Item 17 of Form 20–F (§ 249.220f of this chapter)). The financial statements required by this section must be as of a date no more than 180 days before the sale of securities in reliance on this exemption.

(5) If the issuer is relying on paragraph (d)(2)(ii) of this section to use its parent's total assets to determine the amount of securities that may be sold, the parent's financial statements must be delivered. If the parent is subject to the reporting requirements of section 13 or 15(d) of the Exchange Act (15 U.S.C. 78m or 78o(d)), the financial statements of the parent required by Rule 10–01 of Regulation S-X (§ 210.10–01 of this chapter) and Item 310 of Regulation S-B (§ 228.310 of this chapter), as applicable, must be delivered.

(6) If the sale involves a stock option or other derivative security, the issuer must deliver disclosure a reasonable period of time before the date of exercise or conversion. For deferred compensation or similar plans, the issuer must deliver disclosure to investors a reasonable period of time before the date the irrevocable election to defer is made.

(f) *No integration with other offerings.* Offers and sales exempt under this section are deemed to be a part of a single, discrete offering and are not subject to integration with any other offers or sales, whether registered under the Act or otherwise exempt from the registration requirements of the Act.

(g) *Resale limitations.* (1) Securities issued under this section are deemed to be "restricted securities" as defined in § 230.144.

(2) Resales of securities issued pursuant to this section must be in compliance with the registration requirements of the Act or an exemption from those requirements.

(3) Ninety days after the issuer becomes subject to the reporting requirements of section 13 or 15(d) of the Exchange Act (15 U.S.C. 78m or 78o(d)), securities issued under this section may be resold by persons who are not affiliates (as defined in § 230.144) in reliance on § 230.144, without compliance with paragraphs (c), (d), (e) and (h) of § 230.144, and by affiliates without compliance with paragraph (d) of § 230.144.

EXEMPTIONS FOR CROSS-BORDER RIGHTS OFFERINGS, EXCHANGE OFFERS AND BUSINESS COMBINATIONS

General Notes to Rules 800, 801 and 802

1. Sections 230.801 and 230.802 relate only to the applicability of the registration provisions of the Act (15 U.S.C. 77e) and not to the applicability of the anti-fraud, civil liability or other provisions of the federal securities laws.

2. The exemptions provided by § 230.801 and § 230.802 are not available for any securities transaction or series of transactions that technically complies with § 230.801 and § 230.802 but are part of a plan or scheme to evade the registration provisions of the Act.

3. An issuer who relies on § 230.801 or an offeror who relies on § 230.802 must still comply with the securities registration or broker-dealer registration requirements of the Securities Exchange Act of 1934 (15 U.S.C. 78a et seq.) and any other applicable provisions of the federal securities laws.

4. An issuer who relies on § 230.801 or an offeror who relies on § 230.802 must still comply with any applicable state laws relating to the offer and sale of securities.

5. Attempted compliance with § 230.801 or § 230.802 does not act as an exclusive election; an issuer making an offer or sale of securities in reliance on § 230.801 or § 230.802 may also rely on any other applicable exemption from the registration requirements of the Act.

6. Section 230.801 and § 230.802 provide exemptions only for the issuer of the securities and not for any affiliate of that issuer or for any other person for resales of the issuer's securities. These sections provide exemptions only for the transaction in which the issuer or other person offers or sells the securities, not for the securities themselves. Securities acquired in a § 230.801 or § 230.802 transaction may be resold in the United States only if they are registered under the Act or an exemption from registration is available.

7. Unregistered offers and sales made outside the United States will not affect contemporaneous offers and sales made in compliance with § 230.801 or § 230.802. A transaction that complies with § 230.801 or § 230.802 will not be integrated with offerings exempt under other provisions of the Act, even if both transactions occur at the same time.

8. Securities acquired in a rights offering under § 230.801 are "restricted securities" within the meaning of § 230.144(a)(3) to the same extent and proportion that the securities held by the security holder as of the record date for the rights offering were restricted securities. Likewise, securities acquired in an exchange offer or business combination subject to § 230.802 are "restricted securities" within the meaning of § 230.144(a)(3) to the same extent and proportion that the securities tendered or exchanged by the security holder in that transaction were restricted securities.

9. Section 230.801 does not apply to a rights offering by an investment company registered or required to be registered under the Investment Company Act of 1940 (15 U.S.C. 80a–1 et seq.), other than a registered closed-end investment company. Section 230.802 does not apply to exchange offers or business combinations by an investment company registered or required to be registered under the Investment Company Act of 1940 (15 U.S.C. 80a–1 et seq.), other than a registered closed-end investment company.

Rule 800. Definitions for Rules 800, 801, and 802

The following definitions apply in §§ 230.800, 230.801 and 230.802.

(a) *Business combination. Business combination* means a statutory amalgamation, merger, arrangement or other reorganization requiring the vote of security holders of one or more of the participating companies. It also includes a statutory short form merger that does not require a vote of security holders.

(b) *Equity security. Equity security* means the same as in § 240.3a11–1 of this chapter, but for purposes of this section only does not include:

(1) Any debt security that is convertible into an equity security, with or without consideration;

(2) Any debt security that includes a warrant or right to subscribe to or purchase an equity security;

(3) Any such warrant or right; or

(4) Any put, call, straddle, or other option or privilege that gives the holder the option of buying or selling a security but does not require the holder to do so.

(c) *Exchange offer. Exchange offer* means a tender offer in which securities are issued as consideration.

(d) *Foreign private issuer. Foreign private issuer* means the same as in § 230.405 of Regulation C.

(e) *Foreign subject company. Foreign subject company* means any foreign private issuer whose securities are the subject of the exchange offer or business combination.

(f) *Home jurisdiction. Home jurisdiction* means both the jurisdiction of the foreign subject company's (or in the case of a rights offering, the foreign private issuer's) incorporation, organization or chartering and the principal foreign market where the foreign subject company's (or in the case of a rights offering, the issuer's) securities are listed or quoted.

(g) *Rights offering. Rights offering* means offers and sales for cash of equity securities where:

(1) The issuer grants the existing security holders of a particular class of equity securities (including holders of depositary receipts evidencing those securities) the right to purchase or subscribe for additional securities of that class; and

(2) The number of additional shares an existing security holder may purchase initially is in proportion to the number of securities he or she holds of record on the record date for the rights offering. If an existing security holder holds depositary receipts, the proportion must be calculated as if the underlying securities were held directly.

(h) *U.S. holder. U.S. holder* means any security holder resident in the United States. To determine the percentage of outstanding securities held by U.S. holders:

(1) Calculate percentage of outstanding securities held by U.S. holders as of the record date for a rights offering, or 30 days before the commencement of an exchange offer or the solicitation for a business combination.

(2) Include securities underlying American Depositary Shares convertible or exchangeable into the securities that are the subject of the tender offer when calculating the number of subject securities outstanding, as well as the number held by U.S. holders. Exclude from the calculations other types of securities that are convertible or exchangeable into the securities that are the subject of the exchange offer, business combination or rights offering, such as warrants, options and convertible securities. Exclude from those calculations securities held by persons who hold more than 10 percent of the subject securities in an exchange offer, business combination or rights offering, or that are held by the offeror in an exchange offer or business combination;

(3) Use the method of calculating record ownership in Rule 12g3–2(a) under the Exchange Act (§ 240.12g3–2(a) of this chapter), except that your inquiry as to the amount of securities represented by accounts of customers resident in the United States may be limited to brokers, dealers, banks and other nominees located in the United States, the subject company's jurisdiction of incorporation or that of each participant in a business combination, and the jurisdiction that is the primary trading market for the subject securities, if different from the subject company's jurisdiction of incorporation;

(4) If, after reasonable inquiry, you are unable to obtain information about the amount of securities represented by accounts of customers resident in the United States, you may assume, for purposes of this provision, that the customers are residents of the jurisdiction in which the nominee has its principal place of business.

(5) Count securities as owned by U.S. holders when publicly filed reports of beneficial ownership or information that is otherwise provided to you indicates that the securities are held by U.S. residents.

(i) *United States. United States* means the United States of America, its territories and possessions, any State of the United States, and the District of Columbia.

Rule 801. Exemption in Connection With a Rights Offering

A rights offering is exempt from the provisions of Section 5 of the Act (15 U.S.C. 77e), so long as the following conditions are satisfied:

(a) *Conditions.*—

(1) *Eligibility of issuer.* The issuer is a foreign private issuer on the date the securities are first offered to U.S. holders.

(2) *Limitation on U.S. ownership.* U.S. holders hold no more than 10 percent of the outstanding class of securities that is the subject of the rights offering (as determined under the definition of "U.S. holder" in § 230.800(h)).

(3) *Equal treatment.* The issuer permits U.S. holders to participate in the rights offering on terms at least as favorable as those offered the other holders of the securities that are the subject of the offer. The issuer need not, however, extend the rights offering to security holders in those states or jurisdictions that require registration or qualification.

(4) *Informational documents.*

(i) If the issuer publishes or otherwise disseminates an informational document to the holders of the securities in connection with the rights offering, the issuer must furnish that informational document, including any amendments thereto, in English, to the Commission on Form CB (§ 239.800 of this chapter) by the first business day after publication or dissemination. If the issuer is a foreign company, it must also file a Form F–X (§ 239.42 of this chapter) with the Commission at the same time as the submission of Form CB to appoint an agent for service in the United States.

(ii) The issuer must disseminate any informational document to U.S. holders, including any amendments thereto, in English, on a comparable basis to that provided to security holders in the home jurisdiction.

(iii) If the issuer disseminates by publication in its home jurisdiction, the issuer must publish the information in the United States in a manner reasonably calculated to inform U.S. holders of the offer.

(5) *Eligibility of securities.* The securities offered in the rights offering are equity securities of the same class as the securities held by the offerees in the United States directly or through American Depositary Receipts.

(6) *Limitation on transferability of rights.* The terms of the rights prohibit transfers of the rights by U.S. holders except in accordance with Regulation S (§ 230.901 through § 230.905).

(b) *Legends.* The following legend or an equivalent statement in clear, plain language, to the extent applicable, appears on the cover page or other prominent portion of any informational document the issuer disseminates to U.S. holders:

This rights offering is made for the securities of a foreign company. The offer is subject to the disclosure requirements of a foreign country that are different from those of the United States. Financial statements included in the document, if any, have been prepared in accordance with foreign accounting standards that may not be comparable to the financial statements of United States companies.

It may be difficult for you to enforce your rights and any claim you may have arising under the federal securities laws, since the issuer is located in a foreign country, and some or all of its officers and directors may be residents of a foreign country. You may not be able to sue the foreign company or its officers or directors in a foreign court for violations of the U.S. securities laws. It may be difficult to compel a foreign company and its affiliates to subject themselves to a U.S. court's judgment.

Rule 802. Exemption for Offerings in Connection With an Exchange Offer or Business Combination for the Securities of Foreign Private Issuers

Offers and sales in any exchange offer for a class of securities of a foreign private issuer, or in any exchange of securities for the securities of a foreign private issuer in any business combination, are exempt from the provisions of section 5 of the Act (15 U.S.C. 77e), if they satisfy the following conditions:

(a) *Conditions to be met.*—

(1) *Limitation on U.S. ownership.* Except in the case of an exchange offer or business combination that is commenced during the pendency of a prior exchange offer or business combination made in reliance on this paragraph, U.S. holders of the foreign subject company must hold no more than 10 percent of the securities that are the subject of the exchange offer or business combination (as determined under the definition of "U.S. holder" in § 230.800(h)). In the case of a business combination in which the securities are to be issued by a successor registrant, U.S. holders may hold no more than 10 percent of the class of securities of the successor registrant, as if measured immediately after completion of the business combination.

(2) *Equal treatment.* The issuer must permit U.S. holders to participate in the exchange offer or business combination on terms at least as favorable as those offered any other holder of the subject securities. The issuer, however, need not extend the offer to security holders in those states or jurisdictions that require registration or qualification, except that the issuer must offer the same cash alternative to security holders in any such state that it has offered to security holders in any other state or jurisdiction.

(3) *Informational documents.*

(i) If the issuer publishes or otherwise disseminates an informational document to the holders of the subject securities in connection with the exchange offer or business combination, the issuer must furnish that informational document, including any amendments thereto, in English, to the Commission on Form CB (§ 239.800 of this chapter) by the first business day after publication or dissemination. If the bidder is a foreign company, it must also file a Form F–X (§ 239.42 of this chapter) with the Commission at the same time as the submission of Form CB to appoint an agent for service in the United States.

(ii) The issuer must disseminate any informational document to U.S. holders, including any amendments thereto, in English, on a comparable basis to that provided to security holders in the foreign subject company's home jurisdiction.

(iii) If the issuer disseminates by publication in its home jurisdiction, the issuer must publish the information in the United States in a manner reasonably calculated to inform U.S. holders of the offer.

(b) *Legends.* The following legend or an equivalent statement in clear, plain language, to the extent applicable, must be included on the cover page or other prominent portion of any informational document the offeror publishes or disseminates to U.S. holders:

This exchange offer or business combination is made for the securities of a foreign company. The offer is subject to disclosure requirements of a foreign country that are different from those of the United States. Financial statements included in the document, if any, have been prepared in accordance with foreign accounting standards that may not be comparable to the financial statements of United States companies.

It may be difficult for you to enforce your rights and any claim you may have arising under the federal securities laws, since the issuer is located in a foreign country, and some or all of its officers and directors may be residents of a foreign country. You may not be able to sue a foreign company or its officers or directors in a foreign court for violations of the U.S. securities laws. It may be difficult to compel a foreign company and its affiliates to subject themselves to a U.S. court's judgment.

You should be aware that the issuer may purchase securities otherwise than under the exchange offer, such as in open market or privately negotiated purchases.

(c) *Presumption for certain offers*. For exchange offers conducted by persons other than the issuer of the subject securities or its affiliates, the issuer of the subject securities will be presumed to be a foreign private issuer and U.S. holders will be presumed to hold 10 percent or less of the outstanding subject securities, unless:

(1) The exchange offer is made pursuant to an agreement with the issuer of the subject securities;

(2) The aggregate trading volume of the subject class of securities on all national securities exchanges in the United States, on the Nasdaq market or on the OTC market, as reported to the NASD, over the 12–calendar-month period ending 30 days before commencement of the offer, exceeds 10 percent of the worldwide aggregate trading volume of that class of securities over the same period;

(3) The most recent annual report or annual information filed or submitted by the issuer with securities regulators of the home jurisdiction or with the Commission indicates that U.S. holders hold more than 10 percent of the outstanding subject class of securities; or

(4) The offeror knows, or has reason to know, that U.S. ownership exceeds 10 percent of the subject securities.

PART 244—REGULATION G

§ 244.100. General Rules Regarding Disclosure of Non–GAAP Financial Measures

(a) Whenever a registrant, or person acting on its behalf, publicly discloses material information that includes a non-GAAP financial measure, the registrant must accompany that non-GAAP financial measure with:

(1) A presentation of the most directly comparable financial measure calculated and presented in accordance with Generally Accepted Accounting Principles (GAAP); and

(2) A reconciliation (by schedule or other clearly understandable method), which shall be quantitative for historical non-GAAP measures presented, and quantitative, to the extent available without unreasonable efforts, for forward-looking information, of the differences between the non-GAAP financial measure disclosed or released with the most comparable financial measure or measures calculated and presented in accordance with GAAP identified in paragraph (a)(1) of this section.

(b) A registrant, or a person acting on its behalf, shall not make public a non-GAAP financial measure that, taken together with the information accompanying that measure and any other accompanying discussion of that measure, contains an untrue statement of a material fact or omits to state a material fact necessary in order to make the presentation of the non-GAAP financial measure, in light of the circumstances under which it is presented, not misleading.

(c) This section shall not apply to a disclosure of a non-GAAP financial measure that is made by or on behalf of a registrant that is a foreign private issuer if the following conditions are satisfied:

(1) The securities of the registrant are listed or quoted on a securities exchange or inter-dealer quotation system outside the United States;

(2) The non-GAAP financial measure is not derived from or based on a measure calculated and presented in accordance with generally accepted accounting principles in the United States; and

(3) The disclosure is made by or on behalf of the registrant outside the United States, or is included in a written communication that is released by or on behalf of the registrant outside the United States.

(d) This section shall not apply to a non-GAAP financial measure included in disclosure relating to a proposed business combination, the entity resulting therefrom or an entity that is a party thereto, if the disclosure is contained in a communication that is subject to § 230.425 of this chapter, § 240.14a–12 or § 240.14d–2(b)(2) of this chapter or § 229.1015 of this chapter.

Notes to § 244.100: 1.If a non-GAAP financial measure is made public orally, telephonically, by Web cast, by broadcast, or by similar means, the requirements of paragraphs (a)(1)(i) and (a)(1)(ii) of this section will be satisfied if:

(i) The required information in those paragraphs is provided on the registrant's Web site at the time the non-GAAP financial measure is made public; and

(ii) The location of the web site is made public in the same presentation in which the non-GAAP financial measure is made public.

2. The provisions of paragraph (c) of this section shall apply notwithstanding the existence of one or more of the following circumstances:

(i) A written communication is released in the United States as well as outside the United States, so long as the communication is released in the United States contemporaneously with or after the release outside the United States and is not otherwise targeted at persons located in the United States;

(ii) Foreign journalists, U.S. journalists or other third parties have access to the information;

(iii) The information appears on one or more web sites maintained by the registrant, so long as the web sites, taken together, are not available exclusively to, or targeted at, persons located in the United States; or

(iv) Following the disclosure or release of the information outside the United States, the information is included in a submission by the registrant to the Commission made under cover of a Form 6–K.

§ 244.101. Definitions

This section defines certain terms as used in Regulation G (§§ 244.100 through 244.102).

(a)(1) *Non-GAAP financial measure.* A non-GAAP financial measure is a numerical measure of a registrant's historical or future financial performance, financial position or cash flows that:

(i) Excludes amounts, or is subject to adjustments that have the effect of excluding amounts, that are included in the most directly comparable measure calculated and presented in accordance with GAAP in the statement of income, balance sheet or statement of cash flows (or equivalent statements) of the issuer; or

(ii) Includes amounts, or is subject to adjustments that have the effect of including amounts, that are excluded from the most directly comparable measure so calculated and presented.

(2) A non-GAAP financial measure does not include operating and other financial measures and ratios or statistical measures calculated using exclusively one or both of:

(i) Financial measures calculated in accordance with GAAP; and

(ii) Operating measures or other measures that are not non-GAAP financial measures.

(3) A non-GAAP financial measure does not include financial measures required to be disclosed by GAAP, Commission rules, or a system of regulation of a government or governmental authority or self-regulatory organization that is applicable to the registrant.

(b) *GAAP.* GAAP refers to generally accepted accounting principles in the United States, except that:

(1) In the case of foreign private issuers whose primary financial statements are prepared in accordance with non-U.S. generally accepted accounting principles, GAAP refers to the principles under which those primary financial statements are prepared; and

(2) In the case of foreign private issuers that include a non-GAAP financial measure derived from a measure calculated in accordance with U.S. generally accepted accounting principles, GAAP refers to U.S. generally accepted accounting principles for purposes of the application of the requirements of Regulation G to the disclosure of that measure.

(c) *Registrant.* A registrant subject to this regulation is one that has a class of securities registered under Section 12 of the Securities Exchange Act of 1934 (15 U.S.C. 78*l*), or is required to file reports under Section 15(d) of the Securities Exchange Act of 1934 (15 U.S.C. 78o(d)), excluding any investment company registered under Section 8 of the Investment Company Act of 1940 (15 U.S.C. 80a–8).

(d) *United States.* United States means the United States of America, its territories and possessions, any State of the United States, and the District of Columbia.

§ 244.102. No Effect on Antifraud Liability

Neither the requirements of this Regulation G (17 CFR 244.100 through 244.102) nor a person's compliance or non-compliance with the requirements of this Regulation shall in itself affect any person's liability under Section 10(b) (15 U.S.C. 78j(b)) of the Securities Exchange Act of 1934 or § 240.10b–5 of this chapter.

REGULATION S—RULES GOVERNING OFFERS AND SALES MADE OUTSIDE THE UNITED STATES WITHOUT REGISTRATION UNDER THE SECURITIES ACT OF 1933

PRELIMINARY NOTES

1. The following rules relate solely to the application of Section 5 of the Securities Act of 1933 (the "Act") and not to antifraud or other provisions of the federal securities laws.

2. In view of the objective of these rules and the policies underlying the Act, Regulation S is not available with respect to any transaction or series of transactions that, although in technical compliance with these rules, is part of a plan or scheme to evade the registration provisions of the Act. In such cases, registration under the Act is required.

3. Nothing in these rules obviates the need for any issuer or any other person to comply with the securities registration or broker-dealer registration requirements of the Securities Exchange Act (the "Exchange Act"), whenever such requirements are applicable.

4. Nothing in these rules obviates the need to comply with any applicable state law relating to the offer and sale of securities.

5. Attempted compliance with any rule in Regulation S does not act as an exclusive election; a person making an offer or sale of securities may also claim the availability of any applicable exemption from the registration requirements of the Act. The availability of the Regulation S safe harbor to offers and sales that occur outside of the United States will not be affected by the subsequent offer and sale of these securities into the United States or to U.S. persons during the distribution compliance period, as long as the subsequent offer and sale are made pursuant to registration or an exemption therefrom under the Act.

6. Regulation S is available only for offers and sales of securities outside the United States. Securities acquired overseas, whether or not pursuant to Regulation S, may be resold in the United States only if they are registered under the Act or an exemption from registration is available.

7. Nothing in these rules precludes access by journalists for publications with a general circulation in the United States to offshore press conferences, press releases and meetings with company press spokespersons in which an offshore offering or tender offer is discussed, provided that the information is made available to the foreign and United States press generally and is not intended to induce purchases of securities by persons in the United States or tenders of securities by United States holders in the case of exchange offers. Where applicable, issuers and bidders may also look to § 230.135e and § 240.14d–1(c) of this chapter.

8. The provisions of this Regulation S shall not apply to offers and sales of securities issued by open-end investment companies or unit investment trusts registered or required to be registered or closed-end investment companies required to be registered, but not registered, under the Investment Company Act of 1940 (the "1940 Act").

Rule 901. General Statement

For the purposes only of Section 5 of the Act, the terms "offer," "offer to sell," "sell," "sale," and "offer to buy" shall be deemed to include offers and sales that occur within the United States and shall be deemed not to include offers and sales that occur outside the United States.

Rule 902. Definitions

As used in Regulation S, the following terms shall have the meanings indicated.

(a) *Debt securities.* "Debt securities" of an issuer is defined to mean any security other than an equity security as defined in § 230.405, as well as the following:

(1) Non-participatory preferred stock, which is defined as non-convertible capital stock, the holders of which are entitled to a preference in payment of dividends and in distribution of assets on liquidation, dissolu-

tion, or winding up of the issuer, but are not entitled to participate in residual earnings or assets of the issuer; and

(2) Asset-backed securities, which are securities of a type that either:

(i) Represent an ownership interest in a pool of discrete assets, or certificates of interest or participation in such assets (including any rights designed to assure servicing, or the receipt or timeliness of receipt by holders of such assets, or certificates of interest or participation in such assets, of amounts payable thereunder), provided that the assets are not generated or originated between the issuer of the security and its affiliates; or

(ii) Are secured by one or more assets or certificates of interest or participation in such assets, and the securities, by their terms, provide for payments of principal and interest (if any) in relation to payments or reasonable projections of payments on assets meeting the requirements of paragraph (a)(2)(i) of this section, or certificates of interest or participations in assets meeting such requirements.

(iii) For purposes of paragraph (a)(2) of this section, the term "assets" means securities, installment sales, accounts receivable, notes, leases or other contracts, or other assets that by their terms convert into cash over a finite period of time.

(b) *Designated offshore securities market.* "Designated offshore securities market" means:

(1) The Eurobond market, as regulated by the International Securities Market Association; the Alberta Stock Exchange; the Amsterdam Stock Exchange; the Australian Stock Exchange Limited; the Bermuda Stock Exchange; the Bourse de Bruxelles; the Copenhagen Stock Exchange; the European Association of Securities Dealers Automated Quotation; the Frankfurt Stock Exchange; the Helsinki Stock Exchange; The Stock Exchange of Hong Kong Limited; the Irish Stock Exchange; the Istanbul Stock Exchange; the Johannesburg Stock Exchange; the London Stock Exchange; the Bourse de Luxembourg; the Mexico Stock Exchange; the Borsa Valori di Milan; the Montreal Stock Exchange; the Oslo Stock Exchange; the Bourse de Paris; the Stock Exchange of Singapore Ltd.; the Stockholm Stock Exchange; the Tokyo Stock Exchange; the Toronto Stock Exchange; the Vancouver Stock Exchange; the Warsaw Stock Exchange and the Zurich Stock Exchange; and

(2) Any foreign securities exchange or non-exchange market designated by the Commission. Attributes to be considered in determining whether to designate an offshore securities market among others, include:

(i) Organization under foreign law;

(ii) Association with a generally recognized community of brokers, dealers, banks, or other professional intermediaries with an established operating history;

(iii) Oversight by a governmental or self-regulatory body;

(iv) Oversight standards set by an existing body of law;

(v) Reporting of securities transactions on a regular basis to a governmental or self-regulatory body;

(vi) A system for exchange of price quotations through common communications media; and

(vii) An organized clearance and settlement system.

(c) *Directed selling efforts.* (1) "Directed selling efforts" means any activity undertaken for the purpose of, or that could reasonably be expected to have the effect of, conditioning the market in the United States for any of the securities being offered in reliance on this Regulation S (§ 230.901 through § 230.905, and Preliminary Notes). Such activity includes placing an advertisement in a publication with a general circulation in the United States that refers to the offering of securities being made in reliance upon this Regulation S.

(2) Publication "with a general circulation in the United States":

(i) Is defined as any publication that is printed primarily for distribution in the United States, or has had, during the preceding twelve months, an average circulation in the United States of 15,000 or more copies per issue; and

(ii) Will encompass only the U.S. edition of any publication printing a separate U.S. edition if the publication, without considering its U.S. edition would not constitute a publication with a general circulation in the United States.

(3) The following are not "directed selling efforts":

(i) Placing an advertisement required to be published under U.S. or foreign law, or under rules or regulations of a U.S. or foreign regulatory or self-regulatory authority, provided the advertisement contains no more information than legally required and includes a statement to the effect that the securities have not been registered under the Act and may not be offered or sold in the United States (or to a U.S. person, if the advertisement relates to an offering under Category 2 or 3 (paragraph (b)(2) or (b)(3)) in § 230.903) absent registration or an applicable exemption from the registration requirements;

(ii) Contact with persons excluded from the definition of "U.S. person" pursuant to paragraph (k)(2)(vi) of this section or persons holding accounts excluded from the definition of "U.S. person" pursuant to paragraph (k)(2)(i) of this section, solely in their capacities as holders of such accounts;

(iii) A tombstone advertisement in any publication with a general circulation in the United States, provided:

(A) The publication has less than 20% of its circulation, calculated by aggregating the circulation of its U.S. and comparable non-U.S. editions, in the United States;

(B) Such advertisement contains a legend to the effect that the securities have not been registered under the Act and may not be offered or sold in the United States (or to a U.S. person, if the advertisement relates to an offering under Category 2 or 3 (paragraph (b)(2) or (b)(3)) in § 230.903) absent registration or an applicable exemption from the registration requirements; and

(C) Such advertisement contains no more information than:

(1) The issuer's name;

(2) The amount and title of the securities being sold;

(3) A brief indication of the issuer's general type of business;

(4) The price of the securities;

(5) The yield of the securities, if debt securities with a fixed (non-contingent) interest provision;

(6) The name and address of the person placing the advertisement, and whether such person is participating in the distribution;

(7) The names of the managing underwriters;

(8) The dates, if any, upon which the sales commenced and concluded;

(9) Whether the securities are offered or were offered by rights issued to security holders and, if so, the class of securities that are entitled or were entitled to subscribe, the subscription ratio, the record date, the dates (if any) upon which the rights were issued and expired, and the subscription price; and

(10) Any legend required by law or any foreign or U.S. regulatory or self-regulatory authority.

(iv) Bona fide visits to real estate, plants or other facilities located in the United States and tours thereof conducted for a prospective investor by an issuer, a distributor, any of their respective affiliates or a person acting on behalf of any of the foregoing;

(v) Distribution in the United States of a foreign broker-dealer's quotations by a third-party system that distributes such quotations primarily in foreign countries if:

(A) Securities transactions cannot be executed between foreign broker-dealers and persons in the United States through the system; and

(B) The issuer, distributors, their respective affiliates, persons acting on behalf of any of the foregoing, foreign broker-dealers and other participants in the system do not initiate contacts with U.S. persons or persons within the United States, beyond those contacts exempted under § 240.15a–6 of this chapter; and

(vi) Publication by an issuer of a notice in accordance with § 230.135 or § 230.135c.

(vii) Providing any journalist with access to press conferences held outside of the United States, to meetings with the issuer or selling security holder representatives conducted outside the United States, or to written press-related materials released outside the United States, at or in which a present or proposed offering of securities is discussed, if the requirements of § 230.135e are satisfied.

(d) *Distributor:* "Distributor" means any underwriter, dealer, or other person who participates, pursuant to a contractual arrangement, in the distribution of the securities offered or sold in reliance on this Regulation S (§ 230.901 through § 230.905, and Preliminary Notes).

(e) *Domestic issuer/Foreign issuer.* "Domestic issuer" means any issuer other than a "foreign government" or "foreign private issuer" (both as defined in § 230.405). "Foreign issuer" means any issuer other than a "domestic issuer."

(f) *Distribution compliance period.* "Distribution compliance period" means a period that begins when the securities were first offered to persons other than distributors in reliance upon this Regulation S (§ 230.901 through § 230.905, and Preliminary Notes) or the date of closing of the offering, whichever is later, and continues until the end of the period of time specified in the relevant provision of § 230.903, except that:

(1) All offers and sales by a distributor of an unsold allotment or subscription shall be deemed to be made during the distribution compliance period;

(2) In a continuous offering, the distribution compliance period shall commence upon completion of the distribution, as determined and certified by the managing underwriter or person performing similar functions;

(3) In a continuous offering of non-convertible debt securities offered and sold in identifiable tranches, the distribution compliance period for securities in a tranche shall commence upon completion of the distribution of such tranche, as determined and certified by the managing underwriter or person performing similar functions; and

(4) That in a continuous offering of securities to be acquired upon the exercise of warrants, the distribution compliance period shall commence upon completion of the distribution of the warrants, as determined and certified by the managing underwriter or person performing similar functions, if requirements of § 230.903(b)(5) are satisfied.

(g) *Offering restrictions.* "Offering restrictions" means:

(1) Each distributor agrees in writing:

(i) That all offers and sales of the securities prior to the expiration of the distribution compliance period specified in Category 2 or 3 (paragraph (b)(2) or (b)(3)) in § 230.903, as applicable, shall be made only in accordance with the provisions of § 230.903 or § 230.904; pursuant to registration of the securities under the Act; or pursuant to an available exemption from the registration requirements of the Act; and

(ii) For offers and sales of equity securities of domestic issuers, not to engage in hedging transactions with regard to such securities prior to the expiration of the distribution compliance period specified in Category 2 or 3 (paragraph (b)(2) or (b)(3)) in § 230.903, as applicable, unless in compliance with the Act; and

(2) All offering materials and documents (other than press releases) used in connection with offers and sales of the securities prior to the expiration of the distribution compliance period specified in Category 2 or 3 (paragraph (b)(2) or (b)(3)) in § 230.903, as applicable, shall include statements to the effect that the securities have not been registered under the Act and may not be offered or sold in the United States or to U.S. persons (other than distributors) unless the securities are registered under the Act, or an exemption from the registration requirements of the Act is available. For offers and sales of equity securities of domestic issuers, such offering materials and documents also must state that hedging transactions involving those securities may not be conducted unless in compliance with the Act. Such statements shall appear:

(i) On the cover or inside cover page of any prospectus or offering circular used in connection with the offer or sale of the securities;

(ii) In the underwriting section of any prospectus or offering circular used in connection with the offer or sale of the securities; and

(iii) In any advertisement made or issued by the issuer, any distributor, any of their respective affiliates, or any person acting on behalf of any of the foregoing. Such statements may appear in summary form on prospectus cover pages and in advertisements.

(h) *Offshore transaction.* (1) An offer or sale of securities is made in an "offshore transaction" if:

(i) The offer is not made to a person in the United States; and

(ii) Either:

(A) At the time the buy order is originated, the buyer is outside the United States, or the seller and any person acting on its behalf reasonably believe that the buyer is outside the United States; or

(B) For purposes of:

(*1*) Section 230.903, the transaction is executed in, on or through a physical trading floor of an established foreign securities exchange that is located outside the United States; or

(*2*) Section 230.904, the transaction is executed in, on or through the facilities of a designated offshore securities market described in paragraph (b) of this section, and neither the seller nor any person acting on its behalf knows that the transaction has been pre-arranged with a buyer in the United States.

(2) Notwithstanding paragraph (h)(1) of this section, offers and sales of securities specifically targeted at identifiable groups of U.S. citizens abroad, such as members of the U.S. armed forces serving overseas, shall not be deemed to be made in "offshore transactions."

(3) Notwithstanding paragraph (h)(1) of this section, offers and sales of securities to persons excluded from the definition of "U.S. person" pursuant to paragraph (k)(2)(vi) of this section or persons holding accounts excluded from

the definition of "U.S. person" pursuant to paragraph (k)(2)(i) of this section solely in their capacities as holders of such accounts, shall be deemed to be made in "offshore transactions."

(i) *Reporting issuer.* "Reporting issuer" means an issuer other than an investment company registered or required to register under the 1940 Act that:

(1) Has a class of securities registered pursuant to Section 12(b) or 12(g) of the Exchange Act (15 U.S.C. 78l(b) or 78l(g)) or is required to file reports pursuant to Section 15(d) of the Exchange Act (15 U.S.C. 78o(d)); and

(2) Has filed all the material required to be filed pursuant to Section 13(a) or 15(d) of the Exchange Act (15 U.S.C. 78m(a) or 78o(d)) for a period of at least twelve months immediately preceding the offer or sale of securities made in reliance upon this Regulation S (§ 230.901 through § 230.905, and Preliminary Notes) (or for such shorter period that the issuer was required to file such material).

(j) *Substantial U.S. market interest.* (1) "Substantial U.S. market interest" with respect to a class of an issuer's equity securities means:

(i) The securities exchanges and inter-dealer quotation systems in the United States in the aggregate constituted the single largest market for such class of securities in the shorter of the issuer's prior fiscal year or the period since the issuer's incorporation; or

(ii) 20 percent or more of all trading in such class of securities took place in, on or through the facilities of securities exchanges and inter-dealer quotation systems in the United States and less than 55 percent of such trading took place in, on or through the facilities of securities markets of a single foreign country in the shorter of the issuer's prior fiscal year or the period since the issuer's incorporation.

(2) "Substantial U.S. market interest" with respect to an issuer's debt securities means:

(i) Its debt securities, in the aggregate, are held of record (as that term is defined in § 240.12g5–1 of this chapter and used for purposes of paragraph (j)(2) of this section) by 300 or more U.S. persons;

(ii) $1 billion or more of The principal amount outstanding of its debt securities, the greater of liquidation preference or par value of its securities described in § 230.902(a)(1), and the principal amount or principal balance of its securities described in § 230.902(a)(2), in the aggregate is held of record by U.S. persons; and

(iii) 20 percent or more of The principal amount outstanding of its debt securities, the greater of liquidation preference or par value of its securities described in § 230.902(a)(1), and the principal amount or principal balance of its securities described in § 230.902(a)(2), in the aggregate, is held of record by U.S. persons.

(3) Notwithstanding paragraph (j)(2) of this section, substantial U.S. market interest with respect to an issuer's debt securities is calculated without reference to securities that qualify for the exemption provided by Section 3(a)(3) of the Act (15 U.S.C. 77c(a)(3)).

(k) *U.S. person.* (1) "U.S. person" means:

(i) Any natural person resident in the United States;

(ii) Any partnership or corporation organized or incorporated under the laws of the United States;

(iii) Any estate of which any executor or administrator is a U.S. person;

(iv) Any trust of which any trustee is a U.S. person;

(v) Any agency or branch of a foreign entity located in the United States;

(vi) Any non-discretionary account or similar account (other than an estate or trust) held by a dealer or other fiduciary for the benefit or account of a U.S. person;

(vii) Any discretionary account or similar account (other than an estate or trust) held by a dealer or other fiduciary organized, incorporated, or (if an individual) resident in the United States; and

(viii) Any partnership or corporation if:

(A) Organized or incorporated under the laws of any foreign jurisdiction; and

(B) Formed by a U.S. person principally for the purpose of investing in securities not registered under the Act, unless it is organized or incorporated, and owned, by accredited investors (as defined in § 230.501(a)) who are not natural persons, estates or trusts.

(2) The following are not "U.S. persons":

(i) Any discretionary account or similar account (other than an estate or trust) held for the benefit or account of a non-U.S. person by a dealer or other professional fiduciary organized, incorporated, or (if an individual) resident in the United States;

(ii) Any estate of which any professional fiduciary acting as executor or administrator is a U.S. person if:

(A) An executor or administrator of the estate who is not a U.S. person has sole or shared investment discretion with respect to the assets of the estate; and

(B) The estate is governed by foreign law;

(iii) Any trust of which any professional fiduciary acting as trustee is a U.S. person, if a trustee who is not a U.S. person has sole or shared investment discretion with respect to the trust assets, and no beneficiary of the trust (and no settlor if the trust is revocable) is a U.S. person;

(iv) An employee benefit plan established and administered in accordance with the law of a country other than the United States and customary practices and documentation of such country;

(v) Any agency or branch of a U.S. person located outside the United States if:

(A) The agency or branch operates for valid business reasons; and

(B) The agency or branch is engaged in the business of insurance or banking and is subject to substantive insurance or banking regulation, respectively, in the jurisdiction where located; and

(vi) The International Monetary Fund, the International Bank for Reconstruction and Development, the Inter–American Development Bank, the Asian Development Bank, the African Development Bank, the United Nations, and their agencies, affiliates and pension plans, and any other similar international organizations, their agencies, affiliates and pension plans.

(*l*) United States. "United States" means the United States of America, its territories and possessions, any State of the United States, and the District of Columbia.

Rule 903. Offers or Sales of Securities by the Issuer, a Distributor, Any of Their Respective Affiliates, or Any Person Acting on Behalf of Any of the Foregoing; Conditions Relating to Specific Securities

(a) An offer or sale of securities by the issuer, a distributor, any of their respective affiliates, or any person acting on behalf of any of the foregoing, shall be deemed to occur outside the United States within the meaning of § 230.901 if:

(1) The offer or sale is made in an offshore transaction;

(2) No directed selling efforts are made in the United States by the issuer, a distribu-

tor, any of their respective affiliates, or any person acting on behalf of any of the foregoing; and

(3) The conditions of paragraph (b) of this section, as applicable, are satisfied.

(b) *Additional Conditions.* (1) Category 1. No conditions other than those set forth in § 230.903(a) apply to securities in this category. Securities are eligible for this category if:

(i) The securities are issued by a foreign issuer that reasonably believes at the commencement of the offering that:

(A) There is no substantial U.S. market interest in the class of securities to be offered or sold (if equity securities are offered or sold);

(B) There is no substantial U.S. market interest in its debt securities (if debt securities are offered or sold);

(C) There is no substantial U.S. market interest in the securities to be purchased upon exercise (if warrants are offered or sold); and

(D) There is no substantial U.S. market interest in either the convertible securities or the underlying securities (if convertible securities are offered or sold);

(ii) The securities are offered and sold in an overseas directed offering, which means:

(A) An offering of securities of a foreign issuer that is directed into a single country other than the United States to the residents thereof and that is made in accordance with the local laws and customary practices and documentation of such country; or

(B) An offering of non-convertible debt securities of a domestic issuer that is directed into a single country other than the United States to the residents thereof and that is made in accordance with the local laws and customary practices and documentation of such country, provided that the principal and interest of the securities (or par value, as applicable) are denominated in a currency other than U.S. dollars and such securities are neither convertible into U.S. dollar-denominated securities nor linked to U.S. dollars (other than through related currency or interest rate swap transactions that are commercial in nature) in a manner that in effect converts the securities to U.S. dollar-denominated securities.

(iii) The securities are backed by the full faith and credit of a foreign government; or

(iv) The securities are offered and sold to employees of the issuer or its affiliates pursuant to an employee benefit plan established and administered in accordance with the law of a country other than the United States, and customary practices and documentation of such country, provided that:

(A) The securities are issued in compensatory circumstances for bona fide services rendered to the issuer or its affiliates in connection with their businesses and such services are not rendered in connection with the offer or sale of securities in a capital-raising transaction;

(B) Any interests in the plan are not transferable other than by will or the laws of descent or distribution;

(C) The issuer takes reasonable steps to preclude the offer and sale of interests in the plan or securities under the plan to U.S. residents other than employees on temporary assignment in the United States; and

(D) Documentation used in connection with any offer pursuant to the plan contains a statement that the securities have not been registered under the Act and may not be offered or sold in the United States unless registered or an exemption from registration is available.

(2) Category 2. The following conditions apply to securities that are not eligible for Category 1 (paragraph (b)(1)) of this section and that are equity securities of a reporting foreign issuer, or debt securities of a report-

ing issuer or of a non-reporting foreign issuer.

(i) Offering restrictions are implemented;

(ii) The offer or sale, if made prior to the expiration of a 40–day distribution compliance period, is not made to a U.S. person or for the account or benefit of a U.S. person (other than a distributor); and

(iii) Each distributor selling securities to a distributor, a dealer, as defined in section 2(a)(12) of the Act (15 U.S.C. 77b(a)(12)), or a person receiving a selling concession, fee or other remuneration in respect of the securities sold, prior to the expiration of a 40–day distribution compliance period, sends a confirmation or other notice to the purchaser stating that the purchaser is subject to the same restrictions on offers and sales that apply to a distributor.

(3) Category 3. The following conditions apply to securities that are not eligible for Category 1 or 2 (paragraph (b)(1) or (b)(2) of this section):

(i) Offering restrictions are implemented:

(ii) In the case of debt securities:

(A) The offer or sale, if made prior to the expiration of a 40–day distribution compliance period, is not made to a U.S. person or for the account or benefit of a U.S. person (other than a distributor); and

(B) The securities are represented upon issuance by a temporary global security which is not exchangeable for definitive securities until the expiration of the 40–day distribution compliance period and, for persons other than distributors, until certification of beneficial ownership of the securities by a non-U.S. person or a U.S. person who purchased securities in a transaction that did not require registration under the Act;

(iii) In the case of equity securities:

(A) The offer or sale, if made prior to the expiration of a one-year distribution compliance period, is not made to a U.S. person or for the account or benefit of a U.S. person (other than a distributor); and

(B) The offer or sale, if made prior to the expiration of a one-year distribution compliance period, is made pursuant to the following conditions:

(1) The purchaser of the securities (other than a distributor) certifies that it is not a U.S. person and is not acquiring the securities for the account or benefit of any U.S. person or is a U.S. person who purchased securities in a transaction that did not require registration under the Act;

(2) The purchaser of the securities agrees to resell such securities only in accordance with the provisions of this Regulation S (§ 230.901 through § 230.905, and Preliminary Notes), pursuant to registration under the Act, or pursuant to an available exemption from registration; and agrees not to engage in hedging transactions with regard to such securities unless in compliance with the Act;

(3) The securities of a domestic issuer contain a legend to the effect that transfer is prohibited except in accordance with the provisions of this Regulation S (§ 230.901 through § 230.905, and Preliminary Notes), pursuant to registration under the Act, or pursuant to an available exemption from registration; and that hedging transactions involving those securities may not be conducted unless in compliance with the Act;

(4) The issuer is required, either by contract or a provision in its bylaws, articles, charter or comparable docu-

ment, to refuse to register any transfer of the securities not made in accordance with the provisions of this Regulation S (§ 230.901 through § 230.905, and Preliminary Notes), pursuant to registration under the Act, or pursuant to an available exemption from registration; provided, however, that if the securities are in bearer form or foreign law prevents the issuer of the securities from refusing to register securities transfers, other reasonable procedures (such as a legend described in paragraph (b)(3)(iii)(B)(3) of this section) are implemented to prevent any transfer of the securities not made in accordance with the provisions of this Regulation S; and

(iv) Each distributor selling securities to a distributor, a dealer (as defined in section 2(a)(12) of the Act (15 U.S.C. 77b(a)(12))), or a person receiving a selling concession, fee or other remuneration, prior to the expiration of a 40–day distribution compliance period in the case of debt securities, or a one-year distribution compliance period in the case of equity securities, sends a confirmation or other notice to the purchaser stating that the purchaser is subject to the same restrictions on offers and sales that apply to a distributor.

(4) Guaranteed securities. Notwithstanding paragraphs (b)(1) through (b)(3) of this section, in offerings of debt securities fully and unconditionally guaranteed as to principal and interest by the parent of the issuer of the debt securities, only the requirements of paragraph (b) of this section that are applicable to the offer and sale of the guarantee must be satisfied with respect to the offer and sale of the guaranteed debt securities.

(5) Warrants. An offer or sale of warrants under Category 2 or 3 (paragraph (b)(2) or (b)(3)) of this section also must comply with the following requirements:

(i) Each warrant must bear a legend stating that the warrant and the securities to be issued upon its exercise have not been registered under the Act and that the warrant may not be exercised by or on behalf of any U.S. person unless registered under the Act or an exemption from such registration is available;

(ii) Each person exercising a warrant is required to give:

(A) Written certification that it is not a U.S. person and the warrant is not being exercised on behalf of a U.S. person; or

(B) A written opinion of counsel to the effect that the warrant and the securities delivered upon exercise thereof have been registered under the Act or are exempt from registration thereunder; and

(iii) Procedures are implemented to ensure that the warrant may not be exercised within the United States, and that the securities may not be delivered within the United States upon exercise, other than in offerings deemed to meet the definition of "offshore transaction" pursuant to § 230.902(h), unless registered under the Act or an exemption from such registration is available.

Rule 904. Offshore Resales

(a) An offer or sale of securities by any person other than the issuer, a distributor, any of their respective affiliates (except any officer or director who is an affiliate solely by virtue of holding such position), or any person acting on behalf of any of the foregoing, shall be deemed to occur outside the United States within the meaning of § 230.901 if:

(1) The offer or sale are made in an offshore transaction;

(2) No directed selling efforts are made in the United States by the seller, an affiliate, or any person acting on their behalf; and

(3) The conditions of paragraph (b) of this section, if applicable, are satisfied.

(b) *Additional conditions.* (1) Resales by dealers and persons receiving selling concessions. In the case of an offer or sale of securities prior to the expiration of the distribution compliance period specified in Category 2 or 3 (paragraph (b)(2) or (b)(3)) of § 230.903, as applicable, by a dealer, as defined in Section 2(a)(12) or a person receiving a selling concession, fee or other remuneration in respect of the securities offered or sold:

(i) Neither the seller nor any person acting on its behalf knows that the offeree or buyer of the securities is a U.S. person; and

(ii) If the seller or any person acting on the seller's behalf knows that the purchaser is a dealer, as defined in Section 2(a)(12) of the Act (15 U.S.C. 77b(a)(12)), or is a person receiving a selling concession, fee or other remuneration in respect of the securities sold, the seller or a person acting on the seller's behalf sends to the purchaser a confirmation or other notice stating that the securities may be offered and sold during the distribution compliance period only in accordance with the provisions of this Regulation S (§ 230.901 through § 230.905, and Preliminary Notes); pursuant to registration of the securities under the Act; or pursuant to an available exemption from the registration requirements of the Act.

(2) Resales by certain affiliates. In the case of an offer or sale of securities by an officer or director of the issuer or a distributor, who is an affiliate of the issuer or distributor solely by virtue of holding such position, no selling concession, fee or other remuneration is paid in connection with such offer or sale other than the usual and customary broker's commission that would be received by a person executing such transaction as agent.

Rule 905. Resale Limitations

Equity securities of domestic issuers acquired from the issuer, a distributor, or any of their respective affiliates in a transaction subject to the conditions of § 230.901 or § 230.903 are deemed to be "restricted securities" as defined in § 230.144. Resales of any of such restricted securities by the offshore purchaser must be made in accordance with this Regulation S (§ 230.901 through § 230.905, and Preliminary Notes), the registration requirements of the Act or an exemption therefrom. Any "restricted securities," as defined in § 230.144, that are equity securities of a domestic issuer will continue to be deemed to be restricted securities, notwithstanding that they were acquired in a resale transaction made pursuant to § 230.901 or § 230.904.

REGULATION CE—COORDINATED EXEMPTIONS FOR CERTAIN ISSUES OF SECURITIES EXEMPT UNDER STATE LAW

Rule 1001. Exemption for Transactions Exempt From Qualification Under § 25102(n) of the California Corporations Code

Preliminary Notes: (1) Nothing in this section is intended to be or should be construed as in any way relieving issuers or persons acting on behalf of issuers from providing disclosure to prospective investors necessary to satisfy the antifraud provisions of the federal securities laws. This section only provides an exemption from the registration requirements of the Securities Act of 1933 ("the Act") [15 U.S.C. 77a *et seq.*].

(2) Nothing in this section obviates the need to comply with any applicable state law relating to the offer and sales of securities.

(3) Attempted compliance with this section does not act as an exclusive election; the issuer also can claim the availability of any other applicable exemption.

(4) This exemption is not available to any issuer for any transaction which, while in technical compliance with the provision of this section, is part of a plan or scheme to evade the registration provisions of the Act. In such cases, registration under the Act is required.

(a) *Exemption.* Offers and sales of securities that satisfy the conditions of paragraph (n) of § 25102 of the California Corporations Code, and paragraph (b) of this section, shall be exempt from the provisions of Section 5 of the Securities Act of 1933 by virtue of Section 3(b) of that Act.

(b) *Limitation on and computation of offering price.* The sum of all cash and other consideration to be received for the securities shall not exceed $5,000,000, less the aggregate offering price for all other securities sold in the same offering of securities, whether pursuant to this or another exemption.

(c) *Resale limitations.* Securities issued pursuant to this § 230.1001 are deemed to be "restricted securities" as defined in Securities Act, Rule 144 [§ 230.144]. Resales of such securities must be made in compliance with the registration requirements of the Act or an exemption therefrom.

REGULATION S–B—PART 228—INTEGRATED DISCLOSURE SYSTEM FOR SMALL ISSUERS

(Cite as 17 CFR 228.___)

SUBPART A—REGULATION S–B

Subpart A—Regulation S–B

ATTENTION ELECTRONIC FILERS

THIS REGULATION SHOULD BE READ IN CONJUNCTION WITH REGULATION S–T (PART 232 OF THIS CHAPTER), WHICH GOVERNS THE PREPARATION AND SUBMISSION OF DOCUMENTS IN ELECTRONIC FORMAT. MANY PROVISIONS RELATING TO THE PREPARATION AND SUBMISSION OF DOCUMENTS IN PAPER FORMAT CONTAINED IN THIS REGULATION ARE SUPERSEDED BY THE PROVISIONS OF REGULATION S–T FOR DOCUMENTS REQUIRED TO BE FILED IN ELECTRONIC FORMAT.

Item 10. General

(a) *Application of Regulation S–B.* Regulation S–B is the source of disclosure requirements for "small business issuer" filings under the Securities Act of 1933 (the "Securities Act") and the Securities Exchange Act of 1934 (the "Exchange Act").

(1) *Definition of small business issuer.* A small business issuer is defined as a company that meets all of the following criteria:

(i) has revenues of less than $25,000,000;

(ii) is a U.S. or Canadian issuer;

(iii) Is not an investment company and is not an asset-backed issuer (as defined in § 229.1101 of this chapter); and

(iv) if a majority owned subsidiary, the parent corporation is also a small business issuer.

Provided however, that an entity is not a small business issuer if it has a public float (the aggregate market value of the issuer's outstanding voting and non-voting common equity held by non-affiliates) of $25,000,000 or more.

Note: The public float of a reporting company shall be computed by use of the price at which the stock was last sold, or the average of the bid and asked prices of such stock, on a date within 60 days prior to the end of its most recent fiscal year. The public float of a company filing an initial registration statement under the Exchange Act shall be determined as of a date within 60 days of the date the registration statement is filed. In the case of an initial public offering of securities, public float shall be computed on the basis of the number of shares outstanding prior to the offering and the estimated public offering price of the securities.

(2) *Entering and Exiting the Small Business Disclosure System.* (i) A company that meets the definition of small business issuer may use Form SB–2 for registration of its securities under the Securities Act; Form 10–SB for registration of its securities under the Exchange Act; and Forms 10–KSB and 10–QSB for its annual and quarterly reports.

(ii) For a non-reporting company entering the disclosure system for the first time either by filing a registration statement under the Securities Act on Form SB–2 or a registration statement under the Exchange Act on Form 10–SB, the determination as to whether a company is a small business issuer is made with reference to its revenues during its last fiscal year and public float as of a date within 60 days of the date the registration statement is filed. *See* Note to paragraph (a) of this Item.

(iii) Once a small business issuer becomes a reporting company it will remain a small business issuer until it exceeds the revenue limit or the public float limit at the end of two consecutive years. For example, if a company exceeds the revenue limit for two consecutive years, it will no longer be considered a small business. However, if it exceeds the revenue limit in one year and the next year exceeds the public float limit, but not the revenue limit, it will still be considered a small business. *See* Note to paragraph (a) of this Item.

(iv) A reporting company that is not a small business company must meet the definition of a small business issuer at the end of two consecutive fiscal years before it will be considered a small business issuer for purposes of using Form SB–2, Form 10–SB, Form 10–KSB and Form 10–QSB. *See* Note to paragraph (a) of this Item.

(v) The determination as to the reporting category (small business issuer or other issuer) made for a non-reporting company at the time it enters the disclosure system governs all reports relating to the remainder of the fiscal year. The determination made for a reporting company at the end of its fiscal year governs all reports relating to the next fiscal year. An issuer may not change from one category to another with respect to its reports under the Exchange Act for a single fiscal year. A company may, however, choose not to use a Form SB–2 for a registration under the Securities Act.

(b) *Definitions of terms.*

(1) *Common Equity.* means the small business issuer's common stock. If the small business issuer is a limited partnership, the term refers to the equity interests in the partnership.

(2) *Public market.* no public market shall be deemed to exist unless, within the past 60 business days, both bid and asked quotations at fixed prices (excluding "bid wanted" or "offer wanted" quotations) have appeared regularly in any established quotation system on at least half of such business days. Transactions arranged without the participation of a broker or dealer functioning as such are not indicative of a "public market."

(3) *Reporting company.* means a company that is obligated to file periodic reports with the Securities and Exchange Commission under section 15(d) or 13(a) of the Exchange Act.

(4) *Small business issuer.* refers to the issuer and all of its consolidated subsidiaries.

(c) *Preparing the disclosure document.* (1) The purpose of a disclosure document is to inform investors. Hence, information should be presented in a clear, concise and understandable fashion. Avoid unnecessary details, repetition or the use of technical language. The responses to the items of this Regulation should be brief and to the point.

(2) Small business issuers should consult the General Rules and Regulations under the Securities Act and Exchange Act for requirements concerning the preparation and filing of documents. Small business issuers should be aware that there are special rules concerning such matters as the kind and size of paper that is allowed and how filings should be bound. These special rules are located in Regulation C of the Securities Act (Rule 400 *et seq.*) and in Regulation 12B of the Exchange Act (Rule 12b–1 *et seq.*).

(d) *Commission policy on projections.* The Commission encourages the use of management's projections of future economic performance that have a reasonable basis and are presented in an appropriate format. The guidelines below set forth the Commission's views on important factors to be considered in preparing and disclosing such projections. (*See also* Rule 175 and Rule 3b–6).

(1) *Basis for projections.* Management has the option to present in Commission filings its good faith assessment of a small business issuer's future performance. Management, however, must have a reasonable basis for such an assessment. An outside review of management's projections may furnish additional support in this regard. If management decides to include a report of such a review in a Commission filing, it should also disclose the qualifications of the reviewer, the extent of the review, the relationship between the reviewer and the registrant, and other material factors concerning the process by which any outside review was sought or obtained. Moreover, in the case of a registration statement under the Securities Act, the reviewer would be deemed an expert and an appropriate consent must be filed with the registration statement.

(2) *Format for projections.* Traditionally, projections have been given for three financial items generally considered to be of primary importance to investors (revenues, net income (loss) and earnings (loss) per share), projection information need not necessarily be limited to these three items. However, management should take care to assure that the choice of items projected is not susceptible to misleading inferences through selective projection of only favorable items. It generally would be misleading to present sales or revenue projections without one of the foregoing measures of income. The period that appropriately may be covered by a projection depends to a large extent on the particular circumstances of the company involved. For certain companies in certain industries, a projection covering a two or three year period may be entirely reasonable. Other companies may not have a rea-

sonable basis for projections beyond the current year.

(3) *Investor understanding.* Disclosures accompanying the projections should facilitate investor understanding of the basis for and limitations of projections. The Commission believes that investor understanding would be enhanced by disclosure of the assumptions which in management's opinion are most significant to the projections or are the key factors upon which the financial results of the enterprise depend and encourages disclosure of assumptions in a manner that will provide a frame-work for analysis of the projection. Management also should consider whether disclosure of the accuracy or inaccuracy of previous projections would provide investors with important insights into the limitations of projections.

(e) *Commission policy on security ratings.* In view of the importance of security ratings ("ratings") to investors and the marketplace, the Commission permits small business issuers to disclose ratings assigned by rating organizations to classes of debt securities, convertible debt securities and preferred stock in registration statements and periodic reports. In addition, the Commission permits, disclosure of ratings assigned by any nationally recognized statistical rating organizations ("NRSROs") in certain communications deemed not to be a prospectus ("tombstone advertisements"). Below are the Commission's views on important matters to be considered in disclosing security ratings.

(1)(i) If a small business issuer includes in a filing any rating(s) assigned to a class of securities, it should consider including any other rating assigned by a different NRSRO that is materially different. A statement that a security rating is not a recommendation to buy, sell or hold securities and that it may be subject to revision or withdrawal at any time by the assigning rating organization should also be included.

(ii)(A) If the rating is included in a filing under the Securities Act, the written consent of any rating organization that is not a NRSRO whose rating is included should be filed. The consent of any NRSRO is not required. (See Rule 436(g) under the Securities Act.)

(B) If a change in a rating already included is available before effectiveness of the registration statement, the small business issuer should consider including such rating change in the prospectus. If the rating change is material, consideration should be given to recirculating the preliminary prospectus.

(C) If a materially different additional NRSRO rating or a material change in a rating already included becomes available during any period in which offers or sales are being made, the small business issuer should consider disclosing this information in a sticker to the prospectus.

(iii) If there is a material change in the rating(s) assigned by any NRSRO(s) to any outstanding class(es) of securities of a reporting company, the registrant should consider filing a report on Form 8–K or other appropriate report under the Exchange Act disclosing such rating change.

(f) *Incorporation by reference.* Where rules, regulations, or instructions to forms of the Commission permit incorporation by reference, a document may be so incorporated by reference to the specific document and to the prior filing or submission in which such document was physically filed or submitted. Except where a registrant or issuer is expressly required to incorporate a document or documents by reference, reference may not be made to any document which incorporates another document by reference if the pertinent portion of the document containing the information or financial statements to be incorporated by reference includes an incorporation by reference to another document. No document on file with the Commission for more than five years may be incorporated by reference except:

(1) Documents contained in registration statements, which may be incorporated by reference as long as the registrant has a reporting requirement with the Commission; or

(2) Documents that the registrant specifically identifies by physical location by SEC file number reference, provided such materials have not been disposed of by the Commission pursuant to its Records Control Schedule (17 CFR 200.80f).

(g) *Quantitative and qualitative disclosures about market risk.* The safe harbor provision included in paragraph (d) of Item 305 of Regulation S–K (§ 229.305(d) of this chapter) shall apply to information required by Item 305 of Regulation S–K (§ 229.305 of this chapter) that is voluntarily provided by or on behalf of a small business issuer as defined in Rule 12b–2 of the Exchange Act.

Note to paragraph (g): Such small business issuers are not required to provide the information required by Item 305 of Regulation S–K.

(h) *Use of non-GAAP financial measures in Commission filings.* (1) Whenever one or more non-GAAP financial measures are included in a filing with the Commission:

(i) The registrant must include the following in the filing:

(A) A presentation, with equal or greater prominence, of the most directly comparable financial measure or measures calculated and presented in accordance with Generally Accepted Accounting Principles (GAAP);

(B) A reconciliation (by schedule or other clearly understandable method), which shall be quantitative for historical non-GAAP measures presented, and quantitative, to the extent available without unreasonable efforts, for forward-looking information, of the differences between the non-GAAP financial measure disclosed or released with the most directly comparable financial measure or measures calculated and presented in accordance with GAAP identified in paragraph (h)(1)(i)(A) of this section;

(C) A statement disclosing the reasons why the registrant's management believes that presentation of the non-GAAP financial measure provides useful information to investors regarding the registrant's financial condition and results of operations; and

(D) To the extent material, a statement disclosing the additional purposes, if any, for which the registrant's management uses the non-GAAP financial measure that are not disclosed pursuant to paragraph (h)(1)(i)(C) of this section; and

(ii) A registrant must not:

(A) Exclude charges or liabilities that required, or will require, cash settlement, or would have required cash settlement absent an ability to settle in another manner, from non-GAAP liquidity measures, other than the measures earnings before interest and taxes (EBIT) and earnings before interest, taxes, depreciation, and amortization (EBITDA);

(B) Adjust a non-GAAP performance measure to eliminate or smooth items identified as non-recurring, infrequent or unusual, when the nature of the charge or gain is such that it is reasonably likely to recur within two years or there was a similar charge or gain within the prior two years;

(C) Present non-GAAP financial measures on the face of the registrant's financial statements prepared in accordance with GAAP or in the accompanying notes;

(D) Present non-GAAP financial measures on the face of any pro forma financial information required to be disclosed by Article 11 of Regulation S–X (17 CFR 210.11–01 through 210.11–03); or

(E) Use titles or descriptions of non-GAAP financial measures that are the same as, or confusingly similar to, titles or descriptions used for GAAP measures; and

(iii) If the filing is not an annual report on Form 10–KSB (17 CFR 249.310b), a registrant need not include the information required by paragraphs (h)(1)(i)(C) and (h)(1)(i)(D) of this section if that information was included in its most recent annual report on Form 10–KSB or a more recent filing, provided that the required information is updated to the extent necessary to meet the requirements of paragraphs (h)(1)(i)(C) and (h)(1)(i)(D) of this section at the time of the registrant's current filing.

(2) For purposes of this paragraph (h), a non-GAAP financial measure is a numerical measure of a registrant's historical or future financial performance, financial position or cash flow that:

(i) Excludes amounts, or is subject to adjustments that have the effect of excluding amounts, that are included in the most directly comparable measure calculated and presented in accordance with GAAP in the statement of income, balance sheet or statement of cash flows (or equivalent statements) of the issuer; or

(ii) Includes amounts, or is subject to adjustments that have the effect of including amounts, that are excluded from the most directly comparable measure so calculated and presented.

(3) For purposes of this paragraph (h), GAAP refers to generally accepted accounting principles in the United States.

(4) For purposes of this paragraph (h), non-GAAP financial measures exclude:

(i) Operating and other statistical measures; and

(ii) Ratios or statistical measures calculated using exclusively one or both of:

(A) Financial measures calculated in accordance with GAAP; and

(B) Operating measures or other measures that are not non-GAAP financial measures.

(5) For purposes of this paragraph (h), non-GAAP financial measures exclude financial measures required to be disclosed by GAAP, Commission rules, or a system of regulation of a government or governmental authority or self-regulatory organization that is applicable to the registrant. However, the financial measure should be presented outside of the financial statements unless the financial measure is required or expressly permitted by the standard setter that is responsible for establishing the GAAP used in such financial statements.

(6) The requirements of paragraph (h) of this section shall not apply to a non-GAAP financial measure included in disclosure relating to a proposed business combination, the entity resulting therefrom or an entity that is a party thereto, if the disclosure is contained in a communication that is subject to § 230.425 of this chapter, § 240.14a–12 or § 240.14d–2(b)(2) of this chapter or § 229.1015 of this chapter.

Item 101. Description of Business

(a) *Business Development.* Describe the development of the small business issuer during the last three years. If the small business issuer has not been in business for three years, give the same information for predecessor(s) of the small business issuer if there are any. This business development description should include:

(1) Form and year of organization;

(2) Any bankruptcy, receivership or similar proceeding; and

(3) Any material reclassification, merger, consolidation, or purchase or sale of a significant amount of assets not in the ordinary course of business.

(b) *Business of Issuer.* Briefly describe the business and include, to the extent material to an understanding of the issuer:

(1) Principal products or services and their markets;

(2) Distribution methods of the products or services;

(3) Status of any publicly announced new product or service;

(4) Competitive business conditions and the small business issuer's competitive position in the industry and methods of competition;

(5) Sources and availability of raw materials and the names of principal suppliers;

(6) Dependence on one or a few major customers;

(7) Patents, trademarks, licenses, franchises, concessions, royalty agreements or labor contracts, including duration;

(8) Need for any government approval of principal products or services. If government approval is necessary and the small business issuer has not yet received that approval, discuss the status of the approval within the government approval process;

(9) Effect of existing or probable governmental regulations on the business;

(10) Estimate of the amount spent during each of the last two fiscal years on research and development activities, and if applicable the extent to which the cost of such activities are borne directly by customers;

(11) Costs and effects of compliance with environmental laws (federal, state and local); and

(12) Number of total employees and number of full time employees.

(c) *Reports to security holders.* Disclose the following in any registration statement you file under the Securities Act of 1933:

(1) If you are not required to deliver an annual report to security holders, whether you will voluntarily send an annual report and whether the report will include audited financial statements;

(2) Whether you file reports with the Securities and Exchange Commission. If you are a reporting company, identify the reports and other information you file with the SEC; and

(3) That the public may read and copy any materials you file with the SEC at the SEC's Public Reference Room at 450 Fifth Street, N.W., Washington, D.C. 20549. State that the public may obtain information on the operation of the Public Reference Room by calling the SEC at 1–800–SEC–0330. If you are an electronic filer, state that the SEC maintains an Internet site that contains reports, proxy and information statements, and other information regarding issuers that file electronically with the SEC and state the address of that site (http://www.sec.gov). You are encouraged to give your Internet address, if available;

(d) *Canadian Issuers.* Provide the information required by Items 101(f)(2) and 101(g) of Regulation S–K (§ 229.101(f)(2) and (g)).

Item 102. Description of Property

(a) Give the location of the principal plants and other property of the small business issuer and describe the condition of the property. If the small business issuer does not have complete ownership of the property, for example, others also own the property or there is a mortgage or lien on the property, describe the limitations on the ownership.

Instructions to Item 102(a). 1. Small business issuers engaged in significant mining operations also should provide the information in Guide 7 (§ 229.801(g) and § 229.802(g) of this chapter).

2. Small business issuers engaged in oil and gas producing activities also should provide the information in Guide 2 (§ 229.801(b) and § 229.802(b) of this chapter).

3. Small business issuers engaged in real estate activities should, in addition to Guide 5 (§ 229.801(e) of this chapter) provide responses to the following Items:

(b) *Investment Policies.* Describe the policy of the small business issuer with respect to each of the following types of investments. State whether there are any limitations on the percentage of assets which may be invested in any one investment, or type of investment, and indicate whether such policy may be changed without a vote of security holders. State whether it is the small business issuer's policy to acquire assets primarily for possible capital gain or primarily for income.

(1) *Investments in real estate or interests in real estate.* Indicate the types of real estate in which the small business issuer may invest, for example, office or apartment buildings, shopping centers, industrial or commercial properties, special purpose buildings and undeveloped acreage, and the geographic area(s) of these properties. Briefly describe the method, or proposed method, of operating and financing these properties. Indicate any limitations on the number or amount of mortgages which may be placed on any one piece of property.

(2) *Investments in real estate mortgages.* Indicate the types of mortgages, for example, first or second mortgages, and the types of properties subject to mortgages in which the small business issuer intends to invest, for example, single family dwellings, apartment buildings, office buildings, unimproved land, and the nature of any guarantees or insurance. Describe each type of mortgage activity in which the small business issuer intends to engage such as originating, servicing and warehousing, and the portfolio turnover policy.

(3) *Securities of or interests in persons primarily engaged in real estate activities.* Indicate the types of securities in which the small business issuer may invest, for example, common stock, interest in real estate investment trusts, partnership interests. Indicate the primary activities of persons in which the small business issuer will invest, such as mortgage sales, investments in developed or undeveloped properties and state the investment policies of such persons.

(c) *Description of Real Estate and Operating Data.* This information shall be furnished separately for each property the book value of which amounts to ten percent or more of the total assets of the small business issuer and its consolidated subsidiaries for the last fiscal year. With respect to other properties, the information shall be given by such classes or groups and in such detail as will reasonably convey the information required.

(1) Describe the general character and location of all materially important properties held or intended to be acquired by or leased to the small business issuer and describe the present or proposed use of such properties and their suitability and adequacy for such use. Properties not yet acquired shall be identified as such.

(2) State the nature of the small business issuer's title to, or other interest in such properties and the nature and amount of all material mortgages, liens or encumbrances against such properties. Disclose the current principal amount of each material encumbrance, interest and amortization provisions, prepayment provisions, maturity date and the balance due at maturity assuming no prepayments.

(3) Outline briefly the principal terms of any lease of any of such properties or any option or contract to purchase or sell any of such properties.

(4) Outline briefly any proposed program for the renovation, improvement or development of such properties, including the estimated cost thereof and the method of financing to be used. If there are no present plans for the improvement or development of any unimproved or undeveloped property, so state and indicate the purpose for which the property is to be held or acquired.

(5) Describe the general competitive conditions to which the properties are or may be subject.

(6) Include a statement as to whether, in the opinion of the management of the small business issuer, the properties are adequately covered by insurance.

(7) With respect to each improved property which is separately described, provide the following in addition to the above:

(i) Occupancy rate;

(ii) Number of tenants occupying ten percent or more of the rentable square footage and principal nature of business of each such tenant and the principal provisions of each of their leases;

(iii) Principal business, occupations and professions carried on in, or from the building;

(iv) The average effective annual rental per square foot or unit;

(v) Schedule of the lease expirations for each of the ten years starting with the year in which the registration statement is filed, stating:

(A) the number of tenants whose leases will expire,

(B) the total area in square feet covered by such leases,

(C) the annual rental represented by such leases, and

(D) the percentage of gross annual rental represented by such leases;

(vi) Each of the properties and components thereof upon which depreciation is taken, setting forth the:

(A) federal tax basis,

(B) rate,

(C) method, and

(D) life claimed with respect to such property or component thereof for purposes of depreciation;

(vii) The realty tax rate, annual realty taxes and estimated taxes on any proposed improvements.

Instruction: If the small business issuer has a number of properties, the information may be given in tabular form.

Item 103. Legal Proceedings

(a) If a small business issuer is a party to any pending legal proceeding (or its property is the subject of a pending legal proceeding), give the following information (no information is necessary as to routine litigation that is incidental to the business):

(1) name of court or agency where proceeding is pending;

(2) date proceeding began;

(3) principal parties;

(4) description of facts underlying the proceedings; and

(5) relief sought.

(b) Include the information called for by paragraphs (a)(1) through (5) of this Item for any proceeding that a governmental authority is contemplating (if the small business issuer is aware of the proceeding).

Instructions to Item 103. 1. A proceeding that primarily involves a claim for damages does not need to be described if the amount involved, exclusive of interest and costs, does not exceed 10% of the current assets of the small business issuer. If any proceeding presents the same legal and factual issues as other proceedings pending or known to be contemplated, the amount involved in such other proceedings shall be included in computing such percentage.

2. The following types of proceedings with respect to the registrant are not "routine litigation incidental to the business" and, notwithstanding instruction 1 of this Item, must be described: bankruptcy, receivership, or similar proceeding.

3. Any proceeding that involves federal, state or local environmental laws must be described if it is material; involves a damages claim for more than 10% of the current assets of the issuer; or potentially involves more

than $100,000 in sanctions and a governmental authority is a party.

4. Disclose any material proceeding to which any director, officer or affiliate of the issuer, any owner of record or beneficially of more than 5% of any class of voting securities of the small business issuer, or security holder is a party adverse to the small business issuer or has a material interest adverse to the small business issuer.

Item 201. Market for Common Equity and Related Stockholder Matters

(a) *Market information.* (1) Identify the principal market or markets where the small business issuer's common equity is traded. If there is no public trading market, so state.

(i) If the principal market for the small business issuer's common equity is an exchange, give the high and low sales prices for each quarter within the last two fiscal years and any subsequent interim period for which financial statements are required by Item 310(b).

(ii) If the principal market is not an exchange, give the range of high and low bid information for the small business issuer's common equity for each quarter within the last two fiscal years and any subsequent interim period for which financial statements are required by Item 310(b). Show the source of the high and low bid information. If over-the-counter market quotations are provided, also state that the quotations reflect inter-dealer prices, without retail mark-up, mark-down or commission and may not represent actual transactions.

(2) If the information called for by paragraph (a) of this Item is being presented in a registration statement relating to a class of common equity for which at the time of filing there is no established public trading market, indicate the amount(s) of common equity:

(i) that is subject to outstanding options or warrants to purchase, or securities convertible into, common equity of the registrant;

(ii) that could be sold pursuant to Rule 144 under the Securities Act or that the registrant has agreed to register under the Securities Act for sale by security holders; or

(iii) that is being or has been proposed to be, publicly offered by the registrant unless such common equity is being offered pursuant to an employee benefit plan (or dividend reinvestment plan), the offering of which could have a material effect on the market price of the registrant's common equity.

(b) *Holders.* Give the approximate number of holders of record of each class of common equity.

(c) *Dividends.* (1) Discuss any cash dividends declared on each class of common equity for the last two fiscal years and in any subsequent period for which financial information is required.

(2) Describe any restrictions that limit the ability to pay dividends on common equity or that are likely to do so in the future.

(d) *Securities authorized for issuance under equity compensation plans.* (1) In the following tabular format, provide the information specified in paragraph (d)(2) of this Item as of the end of the most recently completed fiscal year with respect to compensation plans (including individual compensation arrangements) under which equity securities of the small business issuer are authorized for issuance, aggregated as follows:

(i) All compensation plans previously approved by security holders; and

(ii) All compensation plans not previously approved by security holders.

EQUITY COMPENSATION PLAN INFORMATION

Plan category	Number of securities to be issued upon exercise of outstanding options, warrants and rights	Weighted-average exercise price of outstanding options, warrants and rights	Number of securities remaining available for future issuance under equity compensation plans (excluding securities reflected in column (a))
	(a)	(b)	(c)
Equity compensation plans approved by security holders			
Equity compensation plans not approved by security holders			
Total			

(2) The table shall include the following information as of the end of the most recently completed fiscal year for each category of equity compensation plan described in paragraph (d)(1) of this Item:

(i) The number of securities to be issued upon the exercise of outstanding options, warrants and rights (column (a));

(ii) The weighted-average exercise price of the outstanding options, warrants and rights disclosed pursuant to paragraph (d)(2)(i) of this Item (column (b)); and

(iii) Other than securities to be issued upon the exercise of the outstanding options, warrants and rights disclosed in paragraph (d)(2)(i) of this Item, the number of securities remaining available for future issuance under the plan (column (c)).

(3) For each compensation plan under which equity securities of the small business issuer are authorized for issuance that was adopted without the approval of security holders, describe briefly, in narrative form, the material features of the plan.

Instructions to Paragraph (d).

1. Disclosure shall be provided with respect to any compensation plan and individual compensation arrangement of the small business issuer (or parent, subsidiary or affiliate of the small business issuer) under which equity securities of the small business issuer are authorized for issuance to employees or non-employees (such as directors, consultants, advisors, vendors, customers, suppliers or lenders) in exchange for consideration in the form of goods or services as described in Statement of Financial Accounting Standards No. 123, *Accounting for Stock–Based Compensation*, or any successor standard. No disclosure is required with respect to:

a. Any plan, contract or arrangement for the issuance of warrants or rights to all security holders of the small business issuer as such on a pro rata basis (such as a stock rights offering) or

b. Any employee benefit plan that is intended to meet the qualification requirements of Section 401(a) of the Internal Revenue Code (26 U.S.C. 401(a)).

2. For purposes of this paragraph, an "individual compensation arrangement" includes, but is not limited to, the following: a written compensation contract within the meaning of "employee benefit plan" under § 230.405 of this chapter and a plan (whether or not set forth in any formal document) applicable to one person as provided under Item 402(a)(7)(ii) of Regulation S–B (§ 228.402(a)(7)(ii)).

3. If more than one class of equity security is issued under its equity compensation plans, a small business issuer should aggregate plan information for each class of security.

4. A small business issuer may aggregate information regarding individual compensation arrangements with the plan information required under paragraph (d)(1)(i) and (ii) of this item, as applicable.

5. A small business issuer may aggregate information regarding a compensation plan assumed in connection with a merger, consolidation or other acquisition transaction pursuant to which the small business issuer may make subsequent grants or awards of its equity securities with the plan information required under paragraph (d)(1)(i) and (ii) of this Item, as applicable. A small business issuer shall disclose on an aggregated basis in a footnote to the table the information required under paragraph (d)(2)(i) and (ii) of this Item with respect to any individual options, warrants or rights assumed in connection with a merger, consolidation or other acquisition transaction.

6. To the extent that the number of securities remaining available for future issuance disclosed in column (c) includes securities available for future issuance under any compensation plan or individual compensation arrangement other than upon the exercise of an option, warrant or right, disclose the number of securities and type of plan separately for each such plan in a footnote to the table.

7. If the description of an equity compensation plan set forth in a small business issuer's financial statements contains the disclosure required by paragraph (d)(3) of this Item, a cross-reference to such description will satisfy the requirements of paragraph (d)(3) of this Item.

8. If an equity compensation plan contains a formula for calculating the number of securities available for issuance under the plan, including, without limitation, a formula that automatically increases the number of securities available for issuance by a percentage of the number of outstanding securities of the small business issuer, a description of this formula shall be disclosed in a footnote to the table.

9. Except where it is part of a document that is incorporated by reference into a prospectus, the information required by this paragraph need not be provided in any registration statement filed under the Securities Act.

Instruction: Canadian issuers should, in addition to the information called for by this Item, provide the information in Item 201(a)(1)(iv) of Regulation S–K and Instruction 4 thereto.

Item 202. Description of Securities

(a) *Common or Preferred Stock.* (1) If the small business issuer is offering common equity, describe any dividend, voting and preemption rights.

(2) If the small business issuer is offering preferred stock, describe the dividend, voting, conversion and liquidation rights as well as redemption or sinking fund provisions.

(3) Describe any other material rights of common or preferred stockholders.

(4) Describe any provision in the charter or by-laws that would delay, defer or prevent a change in control of the small business issuer.

(b) *Debt Securities.* (1) If the small business issuer is offering debt securities, describe the maturity date, interest rate, conversion or redemption features and sinking fund requirements.

(2) Describe all other material provisions giving or limiting the rights of debtholders. For example, describe subordination provisions, limitations on the declaration of dividends, restrictions on the issuance of additional debt, maintenance of asset ratios, etc.

(3) Give the name of any trustee(s) designated by the indenture and describe the circumstances under which the trustee must act on behalf of the debtholders.

(4) Discuss the tax effects of any securities offered at an "original issue discount."

(c) *Other Securities To Be Registered.* If the small business issuer is registering other securities, provide similar information concerning the material provisions of those securities.

Item 303. Management's Discussion and Analysis or Plan of Operation

Small business issuers that have not had revenues from operations in each of the last two fiscal years, or the last fiscal year and any interim period in the current fiscal year for which financial statements are furnished in the disclosure document, shall provide the information in paragraphs (a) and (c) of this Item. All other issuers shall provide the information in paragraphs (b) and (c) of this Item.

(a) *Plan of Operation.* (1) Describe the small business issuer's plan of operation for the next twelve months. This description should include such matters as:

(i) a discussion of how long the small business issuer can satisfy its cash requirements and whether it will have to raise additional funds in the next twelve months;

(ii) a summary of any product research and development that the small business issuer will perform for the term of the plan;

(iii) any expected purchase or sale of plant and significant equipment; and

(iv) any expected significant changes in the number of employees.

(b) *Management's Discussion and Analysis of Financial Condition and Results of Operations.*

(1) *Full fiscal years.* Discuss the small business issuer's financial condition, changes in financial condition and results of operations for each of the last two fiscal years. This discussion should address the past and future financial condition and results of operation of the small business issuer, with particular emphasis on the prospects for the future. The discussion should also address those key variable and other qualitative and quantitative factors which are necessary to an understanding and evaluation of the small business issuer. If material, the small business issuer should disclose the following:

(i) Any known trends, events or uncertainties that have or are reasonably likely to have a material impact on the small business issuer's short-term or long-term liquidity;

(ii) Internal and external sources of liquidity;

(iii) Any material commitments for capital expenditures and the expected sources of funds for such expenditures;

(iv) Any known trends, events or uncertainties that have had or that are reasonably expected to have a material impact on the net sales or revenues or income from continuing operations;

(v) Any significant elements of income or loss that do not arise from the small business issuer's continuing operations;

(vi) The causes for any material changes from period to period in one or more line items of the small business issuer's financial statements; and

(vii) Any seasonal aspects that had a material effect on the financial condition or results of operation.

(2) *Interim Periods.* If the small business issuer must include interim financial statements in the registration statement or report, provide a comparable discussion that will enable the reader to assess material changes in financial condition and results of operations since the end of the last fiscal year and for the comparable interim period in the preceding year.

Instructions to Item 303. 1. The discussion and analysis shall focus specifically on material events and uncertainties known to management that would cause reported financial information not to be necessarily indicative of future operating results or of future financial condition.

2. Small business issuers are encouraged, but not required, to supply forward looking information. This is distinguished from presently known data which will impact upon future operating results, such as known future

increases in costs of labor or materials. This latter data may be required to be disclosed.

(c) *Off-balance sheet arrangements.* (1) In a separately-captioned section, discuss the small business issuer's off-balance sheet arrangements that have or are reasonably likely to have a current or future effect on the small business issuer's financial condition, changes in financial condition, revenues or expenses, results of operations, liquidity, capital expenditures or capital resources that is material to investors. The disclosure shall include the items specified in paragraphs (c)(1)(i), (ii), (iii) and (iv) of this Item to the extent necessary to an understanding of such arrangements and effect and shall also include such other information that the small business issuer believes is necessary for such an understanding.

(i) The nature and business purpose to the small business issuer of such off-balance sheet arrangements;

(ii) The importance to the small business issuer of such off-balance sheet arrangements in respect of its liquidity, capital resources, market risk support, credit risk support or other benefits; (iii) The amounts of revenues, expenses and cash flows of the small business issuer arising from such arrangements; the nature and amounts of any interests retained, securities issued and other indebtedness incurred by the small business issuer in connection with such arrangements; and the nature and amounts of any other obligations or liabilities (including contingent obligations or liabilities) of the small business issuer arising from such arrangements that are or are reasonably likely to become material and the triggering events or circumstances that could cause them to arise; and

(iv) Any known event, demand, commitment, trend or uncertainty that will result in or is reasonably likely to result in the termination, or material reduction in availability to the small business issuer, of its off-balance sheet arrangements that provide material benefits to it, and the course of action that the small business issuer has taken or proposes to take in response to any such circumstances.

(2) As used in paragraph (c) of this Item, the term *off-balance sheet arrangement* means any transaction, agreement or other contractual arrangement to which an entity unconsolidated with the small business issuer is a party, under which the small business issuer has:

(i) Any obligation under a guarantee contract that has any of the characteristics identified in paragraph 3 of FASB Interpretation No. 45, *Guarantor's Accounting and Disclosure Requirements for Guarantees, Including Indirect Guarantees of Indebtedness of Others* (November 2002) ("FIN 45"), as may be modified or supplemented, and that is not excluded from the initial recognition and measurement provisions of FIN 45 pursuant to paragraphs 6 or 7 of that Interpretation;

(ii) A retained or contingent interest in assets transferred to an unconsolidated entity or similar arrangement that serves as credit, liquidity or market risk support to such entity for such assets;

(iii) Any obligation, including a contingent obligation, under a contract that would be accounted for as a derivative instrument, except that it is both indexed to the small business issuer's own stock and classified in stockholders' equity in the small business issuer's statement of financial position, and therefore excluded from the scope of FASB Statement of Financial Accounting Standards No. 133, *Accounting for Derivative Instruments and Hedging Activities* (June 1998), pursuant to paragraph 11(a) of that Statement, as may be modified or supplemented; or

(iv) Any obligation, including a contingent obligation, arising out of a variable interest (as referenced in FASB Interpretation No. 46, *Consolidation of Variable Interest Entities* (January 2003), as may be modified or supplemented) in an unconsolidated entity that is held by, and material to, the small business issuer, where such entity provides financing, liquidity, market risk or credit risk support to, or engages in leasing, hedging or research and development services with, the small business issuer.

Instructions to paragraph (c) of Item 303. 1. No obligation to make disclosure under paragraph (c) of this Item shall arise in respect of an off-balance sheet arrangement until a definitive agreement that is unconditionally binding or subject only to customary closing conditions exists or, if there is no such agreement, when settlement of the transaction occurs.

2. Small business issuers should aggregate off-balance sheet arrangements in groups or categories that provide material information in an efficient and understandable manner and should avoid repetition and disclosure of immaterial information. Effects that are common or similar with respect to a number of off-balance sheet arrangements must be analyzed in the aggregate to the extent the aggregation increases understanding. Distinctions in arrangements and their effects must be discussed to the extent the information is material, but the discussion should avoid repetition and disclosure of immaterial information.

3. For purposes of paragraph (c) of this Item only, contingent liabilities arising out of litigation, arbitration or regulatory actions are not considered to be off-balance sheet arrangements.

4. Generally, the disclosure required by paragraph (c) of this Item shall cover the most recent fiscal year. However, the discussion should address changes from the previous year where such discussion is necessary to an understanding of the disclosure.

5. In satisfying the requirements of paragraph (c) of this Item, the discussion of off-balance sheet arrangements need not repeat information provided in the footnotes to the financial statements, provided that such discussion clearly cross-references to specific information in the relevant footnotes and integrates the substance of the footnotes into such discussion in a manner designed to inform readers of the significance of the information that is not included within the body of such discussion.

(d) *Safe harbor.* (1) The safe harbor provided in section 27A of the Securities Act of 1933 (15 U.S.C. 77z–2) and section 21E of the Securities Exchange Act of 1934 (15 U.S.C. 78u–5) ("statutory safe harbors") shall apply to forward-looking information provided pursuant to paragraph (c) of this Item, provided that the disclosure is made by: an issuer; a person acting on behalf of the issuer; an outside reviewer retained by the issuer making a statement on behalf of the issuer; or an underwriter, with respect to information provided by the issuer or information derived from information provided by the issuer.

(2) For purposes of paragraph (d) of this Item only:

(i) All information required by paragraph (c) of this Item is deemed to be a "forward looking statement" as that term is defined in the statutory safe harbors, except for historical facts.

(ii) With respect to paragraph (c) of this Item, the meaningful cautionary statements element of the statutory safe harbors will be satisfied if a small business issuer satisfies all requirements of that same paragraph (c) of this Item.

Item 304. Changes in and Disagreements With Accountants on Accounting and Financial Disclosure

(a)(1) If, during the small business issuer's two most recent fiscal years or any later interim period, the principal independent accountant or a significant subsidiary's independent accountant on whom the principal accountant expressed reliance in its report, resigned (or declined to stand for re-election) or was dismissed, then the small business issuer shall state:

(i) Whether the former accountant resigned, declined to stand for re-election or was dismissed and the date;

(ii) Whether the principal accountant's report on the financial statements for either of the past two years contained an adverse opinion or disclaimer of opinion, or was modified as to uncertainty, audit scope, or accounting principles, and also describe the nature of each such adverse opinion, disclaimer of opinion or modification;

(iii) Whether the decision to change accountants was recommended or approved by the board of directors or an audit or similar committee of the board of directors; and

(iv)(A) Whether there were any disagreements with the former accountant, whether or not resolved, on any matter of accounting principles or practices, financial statement disclosure, or auditing scope or procedure, which, if not resolved to the former accountant's satisfaction, would have caused it to make reference to the subject matter of the disagreement(s) in connection with its report; or

(B) The following information only if applicable. Indicate whether the former accountant advised the small business issuer that:

(*1*) internal controls necessary to develop reliable financial statements did not exist; or

(*2*) information has come to the attention of the former accountant which made the accountant unwilling to rely on management's representations, or unwilling to be associated with the financial statements prepared by management; or

(*3*) the scope of the audit should be expanded significantly, or information has come to the accountant's attention that the accountant has concluded will, or if further investigated might, materially impact the fairness or reliability of a previously issued audit report or the underlying financial statements, or the financial statements issued or to be issued covering the fiscal period(s) subsequent to the date of the most recent audited financial statements (including information that might preclude the issuance of an unqualified audit report), and the issue was not resolved to the accountant's satisfaction prior to its resignation or dismissal; and

(C) The subject matter of each such disagreement or event identified in response to paragraph (a)(1)(iv) of this Item;

(D) Whether any committee of the board of directors, or the board of directors, discussed the subject matter of the disagreement with the former accountant; and

(E) Whether the small business issuer has authorized the former accountant to respond fully to the inquiries of the successor accountant concerning the subject matter of each of such disagreements or events and, if not, describe the nature of and reason for any limitation.

(2) If during the period specified in paragraph (a)(1) of this Item, a new accountant has been engaged as either the principal accountant to audit the issuer's financial statements or as the auditor of a significant subsidiary and on whom the principal accountant is expected to express reliance in its report, identify the new accountant and the engagement date. Additionally, if the issuer (or someone on its behalf) consulted the new accountant regarding:

(i) The application of accounting principles to a specific completed or contemplated transaction, or the type of audit opinion that might be rendered on the small business issuer's financial statements and either written or oral advice was provided that was an important factor considered by the small business issuer in reaching a decision as to the accounting, auditing or financial reporting issue; or

(ii) Any matter that was the subject of a disagreement or event identified in response to paragraph (a)(1)(iv) of this Item, then the small business issuer shall:

(A) Identify the issues that were the subjects of those consultations;

(B) Briefly describe the views of the new accountant given to the small business issuer and, if written views were received by the small business issuer, file them as an exhibit to the report or registration statement;

(C) State whether the former accountant was consulted by the small business issuer regarding any such issues, and if so, describe the former accountant's views; and

(D) Request the new accountant to review the disclosure required by this Item before it is filed with the Commission and provide the new accountant the opportunity to furnish the small business issuer with a letter addressed to the Commission containing any new information, clarification of the small business issuer's expression of its views, or the respects in which it does not agree with the statements made in response to this Item. Any such letter shall be filed as an exhibit to the report or registration statement containing the disclosure required by this Item.

(3) The small business issuer shall provide the former accountant with a copy of the disclosures it is making in response to this Item no later than the day that the disclosures are filed with the Commission. The small business issuer shall request the former accountant to furnish a letter addressed to the Commission stating whether it agrees with the statements made by the issuer and, if not, stating the respects in which it does not agree. The small business issuer shall file the letter as an exhibit to the report or registration statement containing this disclosure. If the letter is unavailable at the time of filing, the small business issuer shall request the former accountant to provide the letter so that it can be filed with the Commission within ten business days after the filing of the report or registration statement. Notwithstanding the ten business day period, the letter shall be filed within two business days of receipt. The former accountant may provide an interim letter highlighting specific areas of concern and indicating that a more detailed letter will be forthcoming within the ten business day period noted above. The interim letter, if any, shall be filed with the report or registration statement or by amendment within two business days of receipt.

(b) If the conditions in paragraphs (b)(1) through (b)(3) of this Item exist, the small business issuer shall describe the nature of the disagreement or event and the effect on the financial statements if the method had been followed which the former accountants apparently would have concluded was required (unless that method ceases to be generally accepted because of authoritative standards or interpretations issued after the disagreement or event):

(1) In connection with a change in accountants subject to paragraph (a) of this Item, there was any disagreement or event as described in paragraph (a)(1)(iv) of this Item;

(2) During the fiscal year in which the change in accountants took place or during the later fiscal year, there have been any transactions or events similar to those involved in such disagreement or event; and

(3) Such transactions or events were material and were accounted for or disclosed in a manner different from that which the former accountants apparently would have concluded was required.

Instructions to Item 304. 1. The disclosure called for by paragraph (a) of this Item need not be provided if it has been previously reported as that term is defined in Rule 12b–2 under the Exchange Act; the disclosure called for by paragraph (a) of this Item must be provided, however, notwithstanding prior disclosure, if required pursuant to Item 9 of Schedule 14A. The disclosure called for by paragraph (b) of this Item must be furnished, where required, notwithstanding any prior disclosure about accountant changes or disagreements.

2. When disclosure is required by paragraph (a) of this Item in an annual report to security holders pursuant to Rule 14a–3 or Rule 14c–3, or in a proxy or information statement filed pursuant to the requirements of Schedule 14A or 14C in lieu of a letter pursuant to paragraph (a)(2)(ii)(D) or (a)(3) of this Item, before filing such materials with or furnishing such materials to the Commission, the small business issuer shall furnish the disclosure required by paragraph (a) of this Item to each accountant who was engaged during the period set forth in paragraph (a) of this Item. If any such accountant believes that the statements made in response to paragraph (a) of this Item are incorrect or incomplete, it may present its views in a brief statement, ordinarily expected not to exceed 200 words, to be included in the annual report or proxy or information statement. This statement shall be submitted to the small business issuer within ten business days of the date the accountant receives the small business issuer's disclosure. Further, unless the written views of the newly engaged accountant required to be filed as an exhibit by paragraph (a)(2)(ii)(D) of this Item have been previously filed with the Commission, the small business issuer shall file a Form 8–K along with the annual report or proxy or information statement for the purpose of filing the written views as exhibits.

3. The information required by this Item need not be provided for a company being acquired by the small business issuer if such acquiree has not been subject to the filing requirements of either section 13(a) or 15(d) of the Exchange Act, or, because of section 12(i) of the Exchange Act, has not furnished an annual report to security holders pursuant to Rule 14a–3 or Rule 14c–3 for its latest fiscal year.

4. In determining whether any disagreement or reportable event has occurred, an oral communication from the engagement partner or another person responsible for rendering the accounting firm's opinion (or their designee) will generally suffice as the accountant advising the small business issuer of a reportable event or as a statement of a disagreement at the "decision-making level" within the accounting firm and require disclosure under this Item.

Item 306. Audit Committee Report

(a) The audit committee must state whether:

(1) The audit committee has reviewed and discussed the audited financial statements with management;

(2) The audit committee has discussed with the independent auditors the matters required to be discussed by SAS 61, as may be modified or supplemented;

(3) The audit committee has received the written disclosures and the letter from the independent accountants required by Independence Standards Board Standard No. 1 (Independence Standards Board Standard No. 1, Independence Discussions with Audit Committees), as may be modified or supplemented, and has discussed with the independent accountant the independent accountant's independence; and

(4) Based on the review and discussions referred to in paragraphs (a)(1) through (a)(3) of this Item, the audit committee recommended to the Board of Directors that the audited financial statements be included in the company's Annual Report on Form 10–KSB (17 CFR 249.310b) for the last fiscal year for filing with the Commission.

(b) The name of each member of the company's audit committee (or, in the absence of an audit committee, the board committee performing equivalent functions or the entire board of directors) must appear below the disclosure required by this Item.

(c) The information required by paragraphs (a) and (b) of this Item shall not be deemed to be "soliciting material," or to be "filed" with the Commission or subject to Regulation 14A or 14C (17 CFR 240.14a–1 et seq. or 240.14c–1 et seq.), other than as provided in this Item, or to the liabilities of section 18 of the Exchange Act (15 U.S.C. 78r), except to the extent that the company specifically requests that the information be treated as soliciting material or specifically incorporates it by reference into a document filed under the Securities Act or the Exchange Act.

(d) The information required by paragraphs (a) and (b) of this Item need not be provided in any filings other than a registrant proxy or information statement relating to an annual meeting of security holders at which directors are to be elected (or special meeting or written consents in lieu of such meeting). Such information will not be deemed to be incorporated by reference into any filing under the Securities Act or the Exchange Act, except to the extent that the registrant specifically incorporates it by reference.

Item 307. Disclosure Controls and Procedures

Disclose the conclusions of the small business issuer's principal executive and principal financial officers, or persons performing similar functions, regarding the effectiveness of the small business issuer's disclosure controls and procedures (as defined in § 240.13a–15(e) or § 240.15d–15(e) of this chapter) as of the end of the period covered by the report, based on the evaluation of these controls and procedures required by paragraph (b) of § 240.13a–15 or § 240.15d–15 of this chapter.

Item 308. Internal Control Over Financial Reporting

(a) *Management's annual report on internal control over financial reporting.* Provide a report of management on the small business issuer's internal control over financial reporting (as defined in § 240.13a–15(f) or 240.15d–15(f) of this chapter) that contains:

(1) A statement of management's responsibility for establishing and maintaining adequate internal control over financial reporting for the small business issuer;

(2) A statement identifying the framework used by management to evaluate the effectiveness of the small business issuer's internal control over financial reporting as required by paragraph (c) of § 240.13a–15 or 240.15d–15 of this chapter;

(3) Management's assessment of the effectiveness of the small business issuer's internal control over financial reporting as of the end of the small business issuer's most recent fiscal year, including a statement as to whether or not internal control over financial reporting is effective. This discussion must include disclosure of any material weakness in the small business issuer's internal control over financial reporting identified by management. Management is not permitted to conclude that the small business issuer's internal control over financial reporting is effective if there are one or more material weaknesses in the small business issuer's internal control over financial reporting; and

(4) A statement that the registered public accounting firm that audited the financial statements included in the annual report containing the disclosure required by this Item has issued an attestation report on management's assessment of the small business issuer's internal control over financial reporting.

(b) *Attestation report of the registered public accounting firm.* Provide the registered public accounting firm's attestation report on management's assessment of the small business issuer's internal control over financial reporting in the small business issuer's annual report containing the disclosure required by this Item.

(c) *Changes in internal control over financial reporting.* Disclose any change in the small business issuer's internal control over financial reporting identified in connection with the evaluation required by paragraph (d) of § 240.13a–15 or 240.15d–15 of this chapter that occurred during the small business issuer's last fiscal quarter (the small business issuer's fourth fiscal quarter in the case of an annual report) that has materially affected, or is reasonably likely to materially affect, the small business issuer's internal control over financial reporting.

Instructions to Item 308 The small business issuer must maintain evidential matter, including documentation, to provide reasonable support for management's assessment of the effectiveness of the small business issuer's internal control over financial reporting.

Item 310. Financial Statements

Notes: 1. Financial statements of a small business issuer, its predecessors or any businesses to which the small business issuer is a successor shall be prepared in accordance with generally accepted accounting principles in the United States.

2. Regulation S–X (17 CFR 210.1 through 210.12) Form and Content of and Requirements for Financial Statements shall not apply to the preparation of such financial statements, except that the report and qualifications of the independent accountant shall comply with the requirements of Article 2 of Regulation S–X (17 CFR 210.2), Item 8A of Form 20–F (17 CFR 249.220f) and Article 3–20 of Regulation S–X (17 CFR 210.3–20) shall apply to financial statements of foreign private issuers, the description of accounting policies shall comply with Article 4–08(n) of Regulation S–X (17 CFR 210.4–08(n)), and small business issuers engaged in oil and gas producing activities shall follow the financial accounting and reporting standards specified in Article 4–10 of Regulation S–X (17 CFR 210.4–10) with respect to such activities. To the extent that Article 11–01 [17 CFR 210.11–01] (Pro Forma Presentation Requirements) offers enhanced guidelines for the preparation, presentation and disclosure of pro forma financial information, small business issuers may wish to consider these items. Financial statements of foreign private issuers shall be prepared and presented in accordance with the requirements of Item 18 of Form 20–F except that Item 17 may be followed for financial statements included in filings other than registration statements for offerings of securities unless the only securities being offered are: (a) upon the exercise of outstanding rights granted by the issuer of the securities to be offered, if such rights are granted by the issuer of the securities to be offered, if such rights are granted on a pro rata basis to all existing securities holders of the class of securities to which the rights attach and there is no standby underwriting in the United States or similar arrangement; or (b) pursuant to a dividend or interest reinvestment plan; or (c) upon the conversion of outstanding convertible securities or upon the exercise of outstanding transferrable warrants issued by the issuer of the securities being offered, or by an affiliate of such issuer.

3. Financial statements for a subsidiary of a small business issuer that issues securities guaranteed by the small business issuer or guarantees securities issued by the small business issuer must be presented as required by Rule 3–10 of Regulation S–X (17 CFR 210.3–10), except that the periods presented are those required by paragraph (a) of this item.

4. Financial statements for a small business issuer's affiliates whose securities constitute a substantial portion of the collateral for any class of securities registered or being registered must be presented as required by Rule 3–16 of Regulation S–X (17 CFR 210.3–16), except that the periods presented are those required by paragraph (a) of this item.

5. The Commission, where consistent with the protection of investors, may permit the omission of one or more of the financial statements or the substitution of appropriate statements of comparable character. The Commission by informal written notice may require the filing of other financial statements where necessary or appropriate.

(a) *Annual Financial Statements.* Small business issuers shall file an audited balance sheet as of the end of the most recent fiscal year, or as of a date within 135 days if the issuers existed for a period less than one fiscal year, and audited statements of income, cash flows and changes in stockholders' equity for each of the two fiscal years preceding the date of such audited balance sheet (or such shorter period as the registrant has been in business).

(b) *Interim Financial Statements.* Interim financial statements may be unaudited; however, prior to filing, interim financial statements included in quarterly reports on Form 10–QSB (17 CFR 249.308b) must be reviewed by an independent public accountant using professional standards and procedures for conducting such reviews, as established by generally accepted auditing standards, as may be modified or supplemented by the Commission. If, in any filing, the issuer states that interim financial statements have been reviewed by an independent public accountant, a report of the accountant on the review must be filed with the interim financial statements. Interim financial statements shall include a balance sheet as of the end of the issuer's most recent fiscal quarter and income statements and statements of cash flows for the interim period up to the date of such balance sheet and the comparable period of the preceding fiscal year.

Instructions to Item 310(b). 1. Where Item 310 is applicable to a Form 10–QSB (§ 249.308b) and the interim period is more than one quarter, income statements must also be provided for the most recent interim quarter and the comparable quarter of the preceding fiscal year.

2. Interim financial statements must include all adjustments which in the opinion of management are necessary in order to make the financial statements not misleading. An affirmative statement that the financial statements have been so adjusted must be included with the interim financial statements.

(1) *Condensed Format.* Interim financial statements may be condensed as follows:

(i) Balance sheets should include separate captions for each balance sheet component presented in the annual financial statements which represents 10% or more of total assets. Cash and retained earnings should be presented regardless of relative significance to total assets. Registrants which present a classified balance sheet in their annual financial statements should present totals for current assets and current liabilities.

(ii) Income statements should include net sales or gross revenue, each cost and expense category presented in the annual financial statements which exceeds 20% of sales or gross revenues, provision for income taxes, discontinued operations, extraordinary items and cumulative effects of changes in accounting principles or practices. (Financial institutions should substitute net interest income for sales for purposes of determining items to be disclosed.) Dividends per share should be presented.

(iii) Cash flow statements should include cash flows from operating, investing and financing activities as well as cash at the beginning and end of each period and the increase or decrease in such balance.

(iv) Additional line items may be presented to facilitate the usefulness of the interim financial statements including their comparability with annual financial statements.

(2) *Disclosure required and additional instructions as to Content.* (i) *Footnotes.* Footnote and other disclosures should be provided as needed for fair presentation and to ensure that the financial statements are not misleading.

(ii) *Material Subsequent Events and Contingencies.* Disclosure must be provided of material subsequent events and material contingencies notwithstanding disclosure in the annual financial statements.

(iii) *Significant Equity Investees.* Sales, gross profit, net income (loss) from continuing operations and net income must be disclosed for equity investees which constitute 20% or more of a registrant's consolidated assets, equity or income from continuing operations.

(iv) *Significant Dispositions and Purchase Business Combinations.* If a significant disposition or purchase business combination has occurred during the most recent interim period and the transaction required the filing of a Form 8–K pro forma data must be presented which reflects revenue, income from continuing operations, net income and income per share for the current interim period and the corresponding interim period of the preceding fiscal year as though the transaction occurred at the beginning of the periods.

(v) *Material Accounting Changes.* Disclosure must be provided of the date and reasons for any material accounting change. The registrant's independent accountant must provide a letter in the first Form 10–QSB (§ 249.308b of this chapter) filed subsequent to the change indicating whether or not the change is to a preferable method. Disclosure must be provided of any retroactive change to prior period financial statements, including the effect of any such change on income and income per share.

(vi) *Development Stage Companies.* A registrant in the development stage must provide cumulative from inception financial information.

(c) *Financial Statements of Businesses Acquired or to be Acquired.* (1) If a business combination accounted for as a "purchase" has occurred or is probable, or if a business combination accounted for as a "pooling of interest" is probable, financial statements of the business acquired or to be acquired shall be furnished for the periods specified in paragraph (c)(3) of this Item.

(i) The term "purchase" encompasses the purchase of an interest in a business accounted for by the equity method.

(ii) Acquisitions of a group of related businesses that are probable or that have occurred subsequent to the latest fiscal year-end for which audited financial statements of the issuer have been filed shall be treated as if they are a single business combination for purposes of this section. The required financial statements of related businesses may be presented on a combined basis for any periods they are under common control or management. A group of businesses are deemed to be related if:

(A) They are under common control or management;

(B) The acquisition of one business is conditional on the acquisition of each other business; or

(C) Each acquisition is conditioned on a single common event.

(iii) Annual financial statements required by this paragraph (c) shall be audited. The form and content of the financial statements shall be in accordance with paragraphs (a) and (b) of this Item.

(2) The periods for which financial statements are to be presented are determined by comparison of the most recent annual financial statements of the business acquired or to be acquired and the small business issuer's most recent annual financial statements filed at or prior to the date of acquisition to evaluate each of the following conditions:

(i) Compare the small business issuer's investments in and advances to the acquiree to the total consolidated assets of the small business issuer as of the end of the most recently completed fiscal year. For a proposed business combination to be accounted for as a pooling of interests, also compare the number of common shares exchanged or to be exchanged by the small business issuer to its total common shares outstanding at the date the combination is initiated.

(ii) Compare the small business issuer's proportionate share of the total assets (after intercompany eliminations) of the acquiree to the total consolidated assets of the small business issuer as of the end of the most recently completed fiscal year.

(iii) Compare the small business issuer's equity in the income from continuing operations before income taxes, extraordinary items and cumulative effect of a change in accounting principles of the acquiree to such consolidated income of the small business issuer for the most recently completed fiscal year.

Computational note to paragraph (c)(2): For purposes of making the prescribed income test the following guidance should be applied: If income of the small business issuer and its subsidiaries consolidated for the most recent fiscal year is at least 10 percent lower than the average of the income for the last five fiscal years, such average income should be substituted for purposes of the computation. Any loss years should be omitted for purposes of computing average income.

(3)(i) If none of the conditions specified in paragraph (c)(2) of this Item exceeds 20%, financial statements are not required. If any of the conditions exceed 20%, but none exceeds 40%, financial statements shall be furnished for the most recent fiscal year and any interim periods specified in paragraph (b) of this item. If any of the conditions exceed 40%, financial statements shall be furnished for the two most recent fiscal years and any interim periods specified in paragraph (b) of this item.

(ii) The separate audited balance sheet of the acquired business is not required when the small business issuer's most recent audited balance sheet filed is for a date after the acquisition was consummated.

(iii) If the aggregate impact of individually insignificant businesses acquired since the date of the most recent audited balance sheet filed for the registrant exceeds 50%, financial statements covering at least the substantial majority of the businesses acquired shall be furnished. Such financial statements shall be for the most recent fiscal year and any interim periods specified in paragraph (b) of this Item.

(iv) Registration statements not subject to the provisions of § 230.419 of this chapter (Regulation C) and proxy statements need not include separate financial statements of the acquired or to be acquired business if it does not meet or exceed any of the conditions specified in paragraph (c)(2) of this Item at the 50 percent level, and either:

(A) The consummation of the acquisition has not yet occurred; or

(B) The effective date of the registration statement, or mailing date in the case of a proxy statement, is no more than 74 days after consummation of the business combination, and the financial statements have not been filed previously by the registrant.

(v) An issuer that omits from its initial registration statement financial statements of a recently consummated business combination pursuant to paragraph (c)(3)(iv) of this section shall furnish those financial statements and any pro forma information specified by paragraph (d) of this Item under cover of Form 8–K (§ 249.308 of this chapter) no later than 75 days after consummation of the acquisition.

(4) If the small business issuer made a significant business acquisition subsequent to the latest fiscal year end and filed a report on Form 8–K which included audited financial statements of such acquired business for the periods required by paragraph (c)(3) of this Item and the pro forma financial information required by paragraph (d) of this Item, the determination of significance may be made by using pro forma amounts for the latest fiscal year in the report on Form 8–K rather than by using the historical amounts of the registrant. The tests may not be made by "annualizing" data.

(d) *Pro Forma Financial Information.* (1) Pro forma information showing the effects of the acquisition shall be furnished if financial statements of a business acquired or to be acquired are presented.

(2) Pro forma statements should be condensed, in columnar form showing pro forma adjustments and results and should include the following:

(i) If the transaction was consummated during the most recent fiscal year or subsequent interim period, pro forma statements of income reflecting the combined operations of the entities for the latest fiscal year and interim period, if any, or;

(ii) If consummation of the transaction has occurred or is probable after the date of the most recent balance sheet required by paragraph (a) or (b) of this Item, a pro forma balance sheet giving effect to the combination as of the date of the most recent balance sheet. For a purchase, pro forma statements of income reflecting the combined operations of the entities for the latest fiscal year and interim period, if any, and for a pooling of interests, pro forma statements of income for all periods for which income statements of the small business issuer are required.

(e) *Real Estate Operations Acquired or to be Acquired.* If, during the period for which income statements are required, the small business issuer has acquired one or more properties which in the aggregate are significant, or since the date of the latest balance sheet required by paragraph (a) or (b) of this Item, has acquired or proposes to acquire one or more properties which in the aggregate are significant, the following shall be furnished with respect to such properties:

(1) Audited income statements (not including earnings per unit) for the two most recent years, which shall exclude items not comparable to the proposed future operations of the property such as mortgage interest, leasehold rental, depreciation, corporate expenses and federal and state income taxes; *Provided, however,* That such audited statements need be presented for only the most recent fiscal year if:

(i) the property is not acquired from a related party;

(ii) material factors considered by the small business issuer in assessing the property are described with specificity in the registration statement with regard to the property, including source of revenue (including, but not limited to, competition in the rental market, comparative rents, occupancy rates) and expenses (including but not limited to, utilities, *ad valorem* tax rates, maintenance expenses, capital improvements anticipated); and

(iii) the small business issuer indicates that, after reasonable inquiry, it is not aware of any material factors relating to the specific property other than those discussed in response to paragraph (e)(1)(ii) of this Item that would cause the reported financial information not to be necessarily indicative of future operating results.

(2) If the property will be operated by the small business issuer, a statement shall be furnished showing the estimated taxable operating results of the small business issuer based on the most recent twelve-month period including such adjustments as can be factually supported. If the property will be acquired subject to a net lease, the estimated taxable operating results shall be based on the rent to be paid for the first year of the lease. In either case, the estimated amount of cash to be made available by operations shall be shown. Disclosure must be provided of the principal assumptions which have been made in preparing the statements of estimated taxable operating results and cash to be made available by operations.

(3) If appropriate under the circumstances, a table should be provided which shows, for a limited number of years, the estimated cash distribution per unit indicating the portion reportable as taxable income and the portion representing a return of capital with an explanation of annual variations, if any. If taxable net income per unit

will be greater than the cash available for distribution per unit, that fact and approximate year of occurrence shall be stated, if significant.

(f) *Limited Partnerships.* (1) Small business issuers which are limited partnerships must provide the balance sheets of the general partners as described in paragraphs (f)(2) through (f)(4) of this Item.

(2) Where a general partner is a corporation, the audited balance sheet of the corporation as of the end of its most recently completed fiscal year must be filed. Receivables, other than trade receivables, from affiliates of the general partner should be deducted from shareholders' equity of the general partner. Where an affiliate has committed itself to increase or maintain the general partner's capital, the audited balance sheet of such affiliate must also be presented.

(3) Where a general partner is a partnership, there shall be filed an audited balance sheet of such partnership as of the end of its most recently completed fiscal year.

(4) Where the general partner is a natural person, there shall be filed, as supplemental information, a balance sheet of such natural person as of a recent date. Such balance sheet need not be audited. The assets and liabilities should be carried at estimated fair market value, with provisions for estimated income taxes on unrealized gains. The net worth of such general partner(s), based on such balance sheet(s), singly or in the aggregate, shall be disclosed in the registration statement.

(g) *Age of Financial Statements.* At the date of filing, financial statements included in filings other than filings on Form 10–KSB must be not less current than financial statements which would be required in Forms 10–KSB and 10–QSB if such reports were required to be filed. If required financial statements are as of a date 135 days or more prior to the date a registration statement becomes effective or proxy material is expected to be mailed, the financial statements shall be updated to include financial statements for an interim period ending within 135 days of the effective or expected mailing date. Interim financial statements should be prepared and presented in accordance with paragraph (b) of this Item:

(1) When the anticipated effective or mailing date falls within 45 days after the end of the fiscal year, the filing may include financial statements only as current as the end of the third fiscal quarter; *Provided, however,* That if the audited financial statements for the recently completed fiscal year are available or become available prior to effectiveness or mailing, they must be included in the filing;

(2) If the effective date or anticipated mailing date falls after 45 days but within 90 days of the end of the small business issuer's fiscal year, the small business issuer is not required to provide the audited financial statements for such year end provided that the following conditions are met:

(i) If the small business issuer is a reporting company, all reports due must have been filed;

(ii) For the most recent fiscal year for which audited financial statements are not yet available, the small business issuer reasonably and in good faith expects to report income from continuing operations before taxes; and

(iii) For at least one of the two fiscal years immediately preceding the most recent fiscal year the small business issuer reported income from continuing operations before taxes.

Item 401. Directors, Executive Officers, Promoters and Control Persons

(a) *Identify directors and executive officers.* (1) List the names and ages of all directors and executive officers and all persons nominated or chosen to become such;

(2) List the positions and offices that each such person held with the small business issuer;

(3) Give the person's term of office as a director and the period during which the person has served;

(4) Briefly describe the person's business experience during the past five years; and

(5) If a director, identify other directorships held in reporting companies naming each company.

(b) *Identify Significant Employees.* Give the information specified in paragraph (a) of this Item for each person who is not an executive officer but who is expected by the small business issuer to make a significant contribution to the business.

(c) *Family relationships.* Describe any family relationships among directors, executive officers, or persons nominated or chosen by the small business issuer to become directors or executive officers.

(d) *Involvement in certain legal proceedings.* Describe any of the following events that occurred during the past five years that are material to an evaluation of the ability or integrity of any director, person nominated to become a director, executive officer, promoter or control person of the small business issuer:

(1) Any bankruptcy petition filed by or against any business of which such person was a general partner or executive officer either at the time of the bankruptcy or within two years prior to that time;

(2) Any conviction in a criminal proceeding or being subject to a pending criminal proceeding (excluding traffic violations and other minor offenses);

(3) Being subject to any order, judgment, or decree, not subsequently reversed, suspended or vacated, of any court of competent jurisdiction, permanently or temporarily enjoining, barring, suspending or otherwise limiting his involvement in any type of business, securities or banking activities; and

(4) Being found by a court of competent jurisdiction (in a civil action), the Commission or the Commodity Futures Trading Commission to have violated a federal or state securities or commodities law, and the judgment has not been reversed, suspended, or vacated.

(e) *Audit committee financial expert.* (1)(i) Disclose that the small business issuer's board of directors has determined that the small business issuer either:

(A) Has at least one audit committee financial expert serving on its audit committee; or

(B) Does not have an audit committee financial expert serving on its audit committee.

(ii) If the small business issuer provides the disclosure required by paragraph (e)(1)(i)(A) of this Item, it must disclose the name of the audit committee financial expert and whether that person is *independent*, as that term is used in Item 7(d)(3)(iv) of Schedule 14A (240.14a–101 of this chapter) under the Exchange Act.

(iii) If the small business issuer provides the disclosure required by paragraph (e)(1)(i)(B) of this Item, it must explain why it does not have an audit committee financial expert.

Instruction to paragraph (e)(1) of Item 401. If the small business issuer's board of directors has determined that the small business issuer has more than one audit committee financial expert serving on its audit committee, the small business issuer may, but is not required to, disclose the names of those additional persons. A small business issuer choosing to identify such persons must indicate whether they are independent pursuant to Item 401(e)(1)(ii).

(2) For purposes of this Item, an *audit committee financial expert* means a person who has the following attributes:

(i) An understanding of generally accepted accounting principles and financial statements;

(ii) The ability to assess the general application of such principles in connection with the accounting for estimates, accruals and reserves;

(iii) Experience preparing, auditing, analyzing or evaluating financial statements that present a breadth and level of complexity of accounting issues that are generally comparable to the breadth and complexity of issues that can reasonably be expected to be raised by the small business issuer's financial statements, or experience actively supervising one or more persons engaged in such activities;

(iv) An understanding of internal control over financial reporting; and

(v) An understanding of audit committee functions.

(3) A person shall have acquired such attributes through:

(i) Education and experience as a principal financial officer, principal accounting officer, controller, public accountant or auditor or experience in one or more positions that involve the performance of similar functions;

(ii) Experience actively supervising a principal financial officer, principal accounting officer, controller, public accountant, auditor or person performing similar functions;

(iii) Experience overseeing or assessing the performance of companies or public accountants with respect to the preparation, auditing or evaluation of financial statements; or

(iv) Other relevant experience.

(4) *Safe Harbor.* (i) A person who is determined to be an audit committee financial expert will not be deemed an *expert* for any purpose, including without limitation for purposes of section 11 of the Securities Act of 1933 (15 U.S.C. 77k), as a result of being designated or identified as an audit committee financial expert pursuant to this Item 401.

(ii) The designation or identification of a person as an audit committee financial expert pursuant to this Item 401 does not impose on such person any duties, obligations or liability that are greater than the duties, obligations and liability imposed on such person as a member of the audit committee and board of directors in the absence of such designation or identification.

(iii) The designation or identification of a person as an audit committee financial expert pursuant to this Item 401 does not affect the duties, obligations or liability of any other *member of the audit committee or board* of directors.

Instructions to Item 401(e). 1. The disclosure under Item 401(e) is required only in a small business issuer's annual report. The small business issuer need not provide the disclosure required by this Item 401(e) in a proxy or information statement unless that small business issuer is electing to incorporate this information by reference from the proxy or information statement into its annual report pursuant to general instruction E(3) to Form 10–KSB.

2. If a person qualifies as an audit committee financial expert by means of having held a position described in paragraph (e)(3)(iv) of this Item, the small business issuer shall provide a brief listing of that person's relevant experience. Such disclosure may be made by reference to disclosures required under paragraph (a)(4) of this Item 401 (§ 229.401(a)(4) or this chapter).

3. In the case of a foreign private issuer with a two-tier board of directors, for purposes of this Item 401(e), the term *board of directors* means the supervisory or non-management board. Also, in the case of a foreign private issuer, the term *generally accepted accounting principles* in paragraph (e)(2)(i) of this Item means the body of generally accepted accounting principles used by that issuer in its primary financial statements filed with the Commission.

4. Following the effective date of the first registration statement filed under the Securities Act (15 U.S.C. 77a *et seq.*) or Securities Exchange Act (15 U.S.C. 78a *et seq.*) by a small business issuer, the small business issuer or successor issuer need not make the disclosures required by this Item in its first annual report filed pursuant to Section 13(a) or 15(d) (15 U.S.C. 78m(a) or 78o(d)) of the Exchange Act after effectiveness.

(f) *Identification of the audit committee.*

(1) If you meet the following requirements, provide the disclosure in paragraph (f)(2) of this section:

(i) You are a listed issuer, as defined in § 240.10A–3 of this chapter;

(ii) You are filing either an annual report on Form 10–KSB (17 CFR 249.310b), or a proxy statement or information statement pursuant to the Exchange Act (15 U.S.C. 78a *et seq.*) if action is to be taken with respect to the election of directors; and

(iii) You are neither:

(A) A subsidiary of another listed issuer that is relying on the exemption in § 240.10A–3(c)(2) of this chapter; nor

(B) Relying on any of the exemptions in § 240.10A–3(c)(4) through (c)(7) of this chapter.

(2)(i) State whether or not the small business issuer has a separately-designated standing audit committee established in accordance with section 3(a)(58)(A) of the Exchange Act (15 U.S.C. 78c(a)(58)(A)), or a committee performing similar functions. If the small business issuer has such a committee, however designated, identify each committee member. If the entire board of directors is acting as the small business issuer's audit committee as specified in section 3(a)(58)(B) of the Exchange Act (15 U.S.C. 78c(a)(58)(B)), so state.

(ii) If applicable, provide the disclosure required by § 240.10A–3(d) of this chapter regarding an exemption from the listing standards for audit committees.

(g) Describe any material changes to the procedures by which security holders may recommend nominees to the registrant's board of directors, where those changes were implemented after the registrant last provided disclosure in response to the requirements of Item 7(d)(2)(ii)(G) of Schedule 14A (§ 240.14a–101), or this Item.

Instructions to paragraph (g) of Item 401:

1. The disclosure required in paragraph (g) need only be provided in a registrant's quarterly or annual reports.

2. For purposes of paragraph (g), adoption of procedures by which security holders may recommend nominees to the registrant's board of directors, where the registrant's most recent disclosure in response to the requirements of Item 7(d)(2)(ii)(G) of Schedule 14A (§ 240.14a–101), or this Item, indicated that the registrant did not have in place such procedures, will constitute a material change.

Item 402. Executive Compensation

(a) *General.* (1) *All compensation covered.* This item requires clear, concise and understandable disclosure of all plan and non-plan compensation awarded to, earned by, or paid to the named executive officers designated under paragraph (a)(2) of this item, and directors covered by paragraph (f) of this item by any person for all services rendered in all capacities to the registrant and its subsidiaries, unless otherwise specified in this item. Except as provided by paragraph (a)(4) of this item, all such compensation shall be reported pursuant to this item even if also called for by another requirement, including transactions between the registrant and a third party where the primary purpose of the transaction is to furnish compensation to any such named executive officer or director. No item reported as compensation for one fiscal year need be reported as compensation for a subsequent fiscal year.

(2) *Persons covered.* Disclosure shall be provided pursuant to this item for each of the following (the "named executive officers"):

(i) All individuals serving as the registrant's chief executive officer or acting in a similar capacity during the last completed fiscal year ("CEO"), regardless of compensation level;

(ii) The registrant's four most highly compensated executive officers other than the CEO who were serving as executive officers at the end of the last completed fiscal year; and

(iii) Up to two additional individuals for whom disclosure would have been provided pursuant to paragraph (a)(2)(ii) of this item but for the fact that the individual was not serving as an executive officer of the registrant at the end of the last completed fiscal year.

Instructions to Item 402(a)(2).

1. *Determination of Most Highly Compensated Executive Officers.* The determination as to which executive officers are most highly compensated shall be made by reference to total annual salary and bonus for the last completed fiscal year (as required to be disclosed pursuant to paragraph (b)(2)(iii)(A) and (B) of this item), but including the dollar value of salary or bonus amounts forgone pursuant to Instruction 3 to paragraph (b)(2)(iii)(A) and (B) of this item, *provided, however,* that no disclosure need be provided for any executive officer, other than the CEO, whose total annual salary and bonus, as so determined, does not exceed $100,000.

2. *Inclusion of Executive Officer of Subsidiary.* It may be appropriate in certain circumstances for a registrant to include an executive officer of a subsidiary in the disclosure required by this item. See Rule 3b–7 under the Exchange Act.

3. *Exclusion of Executive Officer due to Unusual or Overseas Compensation.* It may be appropriate in limited circumstances for a registrant not to include in the disclosure required by this item an individual, other than its CEO, who is one of the registrant's most highly compensated executive officers. Among the factors that should be considered in determining not to name an individual are: (a) the distribution or accrual of an unusually large amount of cash compensation (such as a bonus or commission) that is not part of a recurring arrangement and is unlikely to continue; and (b) the payment of amounts of cash compensation relating to overseas assignments that may be attributed predominantly to such assignments.

(3) *Information for full fiscal year.* If the CEO served in that capacity during any part of a fiscal year with respect to which information is required, information should be provided as to all of his or her compensation for the full fiscal year. If a named executive officer (other than the CEO) served as an executive officer of the registrant (whether or not in the same position) during any part of a fiscal year with respect to which information is required, information shall be provided as to all compensation of that individual for the full fiscal year.

(4) *Transactions with third parties reported under item 404.* This item includes transactions between the registrant and a third party where the primary purpose of the transaction is to furnish compensation to a named executive officer. No information need be given in response to any paragraph of this item as to any such third-party transaction if the transaction has been reported in response to Item 404 of Regulation S–B (§ 228.404).

(5) *Omission of table or column.* A table or column may be omitted, if there has been no compensation awarded to, earned by or paid to any of the named executives required to be reported in that table or column in any fiscal year covered by that table.

(6) *Definitions.* For purposes of this item:

(i) The term *stock appreciation rights (SARs)* refers to SARs payable in cash or stock, including SARs payable in cash or stock at the election of the registrant or a named executive officer.

(ii) The term *plan* includes, but is not limited to, the following: any plan, contract, authorization or arrangement, whether or not set forth in any formal documents, pursuant to which the following may be received: cash, stock, restricted stock or restricted stock units, phantom stock, stock options, SARs, stock options in tandem with SARs, warrants, convertible securities, performance units and performance shares, and similar instruments. A plan may be applicable to one person. Registrants may omit information regarding group life, health, hospitalization, medical reimbursement or relocation plans that do not discriminate in scope, terms or operation, in favor of executive officers or directors of the registrant and that are available generally to all salaried employees.

(iii) The term *long-term incentive plan* means any plan providing compensation intended to serve as incentive for performance to occur over a period longer than one fiscal year, whether such performance is measured by reference to financial performance of the registrant or an affiliate, the registrant's stock price, or any other measure, but excluding restricted stock, stock option and SAR plans.

(7) *Location of specified information.* The information required by paragraph (h) of this item need not be provided in any filings other than a registrant proxy or information statement relating to an annual meeting of security holders at which directors are to be elected (or special meeting or written consents in lieu of such meeting). Such information will not be deemed to be incorporated by reference into any filing under the Securities Act or the Exchange Act, except to the extent that the registrant specifically incorporates it by reference.

(b) *Summary compensation table* —(1) *General.* The information specified in paragraph (b)(2) of this item, concerning the compensation of the named executive officers for each of the registrant's last three completed fiscal years, shall be provided in a Summary Compensation Table, in the tabular format specified below.

SUMMARY COMPENSATION TABLE

		Annual compensation			Long term compensation			
					Awards		Payouts	
Name and principal position	Year	Salary ($)	Bonus ($)	Other annual compensation ($)	Restricted stock award(s) ($)	Securities underlying options/SARs (#)	LTIP payouts ($)	All other compensation ($)
(a)	(b)	(c)	(d)	(e)	(f)	(g)	(h)	(i)
CEO								
A								
B								
C								
D								

(2) The Table shall include: (i) The name and principal position of the executive officer (column (a));

(ii) Fiscal year covered (column (b));

(iii) Annual compensation (columns (c), (d) and (e)), including:

(A) The dollar value of base salary (cash and non-cash) earned by the named executive officer during the fiscal year covered (column (c));

(B) The dollar value of bonus (cash and non-cash) earned by the named executive officer during the fiscal year covered (column (d)); and

Instructions to Item 402(b)(2)(iii)(A) and (B). 1. Amounts deferred at the election of a named executive officer, whether pursuant to a plan established under section 401(k) of the Internal Revenue Code, or otherwise, shall be included in the salary column (column (c)) or bonus column (column (d)), as appropriate, for the fiscal year in which earned. If the amount of salary or bonus earned in a given fiscal year is not calculable through the latest practicable date, that fact must be disclosed in a footnote and such amount must be disclosed in the subsequent fiscal year in the appropriate column for the fiscal year in which earned.

2. For stock or any other form of non-cash compensation, disclose the fair market value at the time the compensation is awarded, earned or paid.

3. Registrants need not include in the salary column (column (c)) or bonus column (column (d)) any amount of salary or bonus forgone at the election of a named executive officer pursuant to a registrant program under which stock, stock-based or other forms of non-cash compensation may be received by a named executive in lieu of a portion of annual compensation earned in a covered fiscal year. However, the receipt of any such form of non-cash compensation in lieu of salary or bonus earned for a covered fiscal year must be disclosed in the appropriate column of the Table corresponding to that fiscal year (i.e., restricted stock awards (column (f))); options or SARs (column (g)); all other compensation (column (i)), or, if made pursuant to a long-term incentive plan and therefore not reportable at grant in the Summary Compensation Table, a footnote must be added to the salary or bonus column so disclosing and referring to the Long-Term Incentive Plan Table (required by paragraph (e) of this item) where the award is reported.

(C) The dollar value of other annual compensation not properly categorized as salary or bonus, as follows (column (e)):

(*1*) Perquisites and other personal benefits, securities or property, unless the aggregate amount of such compensation is the lesser of either $50,000 or 10% of the total of annual salary and bonus reported for the named executive officer in columns (c) and (d);

(*2*) Above-market or preferential earnings on restricted stock, options, SARs or deferred compensation paid during the fiscal year or payable during that period but deferred at the election of the named executive officer;

(*3*) Earnings on long-term incentive plan compensation paid during the fiscal year or payable during that period but deferred at the election of the named executive officer;

(*4*) Amounts reimbursed during the fiscal year for the payment of taxes; and

(*5*) The dollar value of the difference between the price paid by a named executive officer for any security of the registrant or its subsidiaries purchased from the registrant or its subsidiaries (through deferral of salary or bonus, or otherwise), and the fair market value of such security at the date of purchase, unless that discount is available generally, either to all security holders or to all salaried employees of the registrant.

Instructions to Item 402(b)(2)(iii)(C). 1. Each perquisite or other personal benefit exceeding 25% of the total perquisites and other personal benefits reported for a named executive officer must be identified by type and amount in a footnote or accompanying narrative discussion to column (e).

2. Perquisites and other personal benefits shall be valued on the basis of the aggregate incremental cost to the registrant and its subsidiaries.

3. Interest on deferred or long-term compensation is above-market only if the rate of interest exceeds 120% of the applicable federal long-term rate, with compounding (as prescribed under section 1274(d) of the Internal Revenue Code), at the rate that corresponds most closely to the rate under the registrant's plan at the time the interest rate or formula is set. In the event of a discretionary reset of the interest rate, the requisite calculation must be made on the basis of the interest rate at the time of such reset, rather than when originally established. Only the above-market portion of the interest must be included. If the applicable interest rates vary depending upon conditions such as a minimum period of continued service, the reported amount should be calculated assuming satisfaction of all conditions to receiving interest at the highest rate.

4. Dividends (and dividend equivalents) on restricted stock, options, SARs or deferred compensation denominated in stock ("deferred stock") are preferential only if earned at a rate higher than dividends on the registrant's common stock. Only the preferential portion of the dividends or equivalents must be included.

(iv) Long-term compensation (columns (f), (g) and (h)), including:

(A) The dollar value (net of any consideration paid by the named executive officer) of any award of restricted stock, including share units (calculated by multiplying the closing market price of the registrant's unrestricted stock on the date of grant by the number of shares awarded) (column (f));

(B) The sum of the number of securities underlying stock options granted (including options that subsequently have been transferred), with or without tandem SARs, and the number of freestanding SARs (column (g)); and

(C) The dollar value of all payouts pursuant to long-term incentive plans ("LTIPs") as defined in paragraph (a)(6)(iii) of this item (column (h)).

Instructions to Item 402(b)(2)(iv). 1. Awards of restricted stock that are subject to performance-based conditions to vesting, in addition to lapse of time and/or continued service with the registrant or a subsidiary, may be reported as LTIP awards pursuant to paragraph (e) of this item instead of in column (f). If this approach is selected, once the restricted stock vests, it must be reported as an LTIP payout in column (h).

2. The registrant shall, in a footnote to the Summary Compensation Table (appended to column (f), if included), disclose:

a. The number and value of the aggregate restricted stock holdings at the end of the last completed fiscal year. The value shall be calculated in the manner specified in paragraph (b)(2)(iv)(A) of this item using the value of the registrant's shares at the end of the last completed fiscal year;

b. For any restricted stock award reported in the Summary Compensation Table that will vest, in whole or in part, in under three years from the date of grant, the total number of shares awarded and the vesting schedule; and

c. Whether dividends will be paid on the restricted stock reported in column (f).

3. If at any time during the last completed fiscal year, the registrant has adjusted or amended the exercise price of stock options or freestanding SARs previously awarded to a named executive officer, whether through amendment, cancellation or replacement grants, or any other means ("repriced"), the registrant shall include the number of options or freestanding SARs so repriced as Stock Options/SARs granted and required to be reported in column (g).

4. If any specified performance target, goal or condition to payout was waived with respect to any amount included in LTIP payouts re-

ported in column (h), the registrant shall so state in a footnote to column (h).

(v) All other compensation for the covered fiscal year that the registrant could not properly report in any other column of the Summary Compensation Table (column (i)). Any compensation reported in this column for the last completed fiscal year shall be identified and quantified in a footnote. Such compensation shall include, but not be limited to:

(A) The amount paid, payable or accrued to any named executive officer pursuant to a plan or arrangement in connection with:

(*1*) The resignation, retirement or any other termination of such executive officer's employment with the registrant and its subsidiaries; or

(*2*) A change in control of the registrant or a change in the executive officer's responsibilities following such a change in control.

(B) The dollar value of above-market or preferential amounts earned on restricted stock, options, SARs or deferred compensation during the fiscal year, or calculated with respect to that period, except that if such amounts are paid during the period, or payable during the period but deferred at the election of a named executive officer, this information shall be reported as Other Annual Compensation in column (e). See Instructions 3 and 4 to paragraph 402(b)(2)(iii)(C) of this item;

(C) The dollar value of amounts earned on long-term incentive plan compensation during the fiscal year, or calculated with respect to that period, except that if such amounts are paid during that period, or payable during that period at the election of the named executive officer, this information shall be reported as Other Annual Compensation in column (e);

(D) Annual registrant contributions or other allocations to vested and unvested defined contribution plans; and

(E) The dollar value of any insurance premiums paid by, or on behalf of, the registrant during the covered fiscal year with respect to term life insurance for the benefit of a named executive officer, and, if there is any arrangement or understanding, whether formal or informal, that such executive officer has or will receive or be allocated an interest in any cash surrender value under the insurance policy, either:

(*1*) The full dollar value of the remainder of the premiums paid by, or on behalf of, the registrant; or

(*2*) If the premiums will be refunded to the registrant on termination of the policy, the dollar value of the benefit to the executive officer of the remainder of the premium paid by, or on behalf of, the registrant during the fiscal year. The benefit shall be determined for the period, projected on an actuarial basis, between payment of the premium and the refund.

Instructions to Item 402(b)(2)(v). 1. LTIP awards and amounts received on exercise of options and SARs need not be reported as All Other Compensation in column (i).

2. Information relating to defined benefit and actuarial plans need not be reported.

3. Where alternative methods of reporting are available under paragraph (b)(2)(v)(E) of this item, the same method should be used for each of the named executive officers. If the registrant chooses to change methods from one year to the next, that fact, and the reason therefor, should be disclosed in a footnote to column (i).

Instruction to Item 402(b). Information with respect to fiscal years prior to the last completed fiscal year will not be required if the registrant was not a reporting company pursuant to Section 13(a) or 15(d) of the Exchange

Act at any time during that year, except that the registrant will be required to provide information for any such year if that information previously was required to be provided in response to a Commission filing requirement.

(c) *Option/SAR grants table.* (1) The information specified in paragraph (c)(2) of this item, concerning individual grants of stock options (whether or not in tandem with SARs) and freestanding SARs (including options and SARs that subsequently have been transferred) made during the last completed fiscal year to each of the named executive officers shall be provided in the tabular format specified as follows:

OPTION/SAR GRANTS IN LAST FISCAL YEAR
[Individual Grants]

Name (a)	Number of securities underlying options/SARs granted (#) (b)	Percent of total options/ SARs granted to employees in fiscal year (c)	Exercise or base price ($/ Sh) (d)	Expiration date (e)
CEO				
A				
B				
C				
D				

(2) The Table shall include, with respect to each grant:

(i) The name of the executive officer (column (a));

(ii) The number of securities underlying SARs granted (column (b));

(iii) The percent the grant represents of total options and SARs granted to employees during the fiscal year (column (c));

(iv) The per-share exercise or base price of the options or SARs granted (column (d)). If such exercise or base price is less than the market price of the underlying security on the date of grant, a separate, adjoining column shall be added showing market price on the date of grant; and

(v) The expiration date of the options or SARs (column (e)).

Instructions to Item 402(c). 1. If more than one grant of options and/or freestanding SARs was made to a named executive officer during the last completed fiscal year, a separate line should be used to provide disclosure of each such grant. However, multiple grants during a single fiscal year may be aggregated where each grant was made at the same exercise and/or base price and has the same expiration date, and the same performance vesting thresholds, if any. A single grant consisting of options and/or freestanding SARs shall be reported as separate grants with respect to each tranche with a different exercise and/or base price, performance vesting threshold, or expiration date.

2. Options or freestanding SARs granted in connection with an option repricing transaction shall be reported in this table. See Instruction 3 to paragraph (b)(2)(iv) of this item.

3. Any material term of the grant, including but not limited to the date of exercisability, the number of SARs, performance units or other instruments granted in tandem with options, a performance-based condition to exercisability, a reload feature, or a tax-reimbursement feature, shall be footnoted.

4. If the exercise or base price is adjustable over the term of any option or freestanding SAR in accordance with any prescribed stan-

dard or formula, including but not limited to an index or premium price provision, describe the following, either by footnote to column (c) or in narrative accompanying the Table:

(a) The standard or formula; and

(b) Any constant assumption made by the registrant regarding any adjustment to the exercise price in calculating the potential option or SAR value.

5. If any provision of a grant (other than an antidilution provision) could cause the exercise price to be lowered, registrants must clearly and fully disclose these provisions and their potential consequences either by a footnote or accompanying textual narrative.

6. In determining the grant-date market or base price of the security underlying options or freestanding SARs, the registrant may use either the closing market price per share of the security, or any other formula prescribed for the security.

(d) *Aggregated option/SAR exercises and fiscal year-end option/SAR Value Table.* (1) The information specified in paragraph (d)(2) of this item, concerning each exercise of stock options (or tandem SARs) and freestanding SARs during the last completed fiscal year by each of the named executive officers and the fiscal year-end value of unexercised options and SARs, shall be provided on an aggregated basis in the tabular format specified below:

AGGREGATED OPTION/SAR EXERCISES IN LAST FISCAL YEAR AND FY–END OPTION/SAR VALUES

Name (a)	Shares acquired on exercise (#) (b)	Value realized ($) (c)	Number of securities underlying unexercised options/SARs at FY-end (#) exercisable/ unexercisable (d)	Value of unexercised in-the-money options/SARs at FY-end ($) exercisable/ unexercisable (e)
CEO				
A				
B				
C				
D				

(2) The table shall include:

(i) The name of the executive officer (column (a));

(ii) The number of shares received upon exercise, or, if no shares were received, the number of securities with respect to which the options or SARs were exercised (column (b));

(iii) The aggregate dollar value realized upon exercise (column (c));

(iv) The total number of securities underlying unexercised options and SARs held at the end of the last completed fiscal year, separately identifying the exercisable and unexercisable options and SARs (column (d)); and

(v) The aggregate dollar value of in-the-money, unexercised options and SARs held at the end of the fiscal year, separately identifying the exercisable and unexercisable options and SARs (column (e)).

Instructions to Item 402(d)(2). 1. Options or freestanding SARs are in-the-money if the fair market value of the underlying securities exceeds the exercise or base price of the option or SAR. The dollar values in columns (c) and (e) are calculated by determining the difference between the fair market value of the securities underlying the options or SARs and the exercise or base price of the options or SARs at exercise or fiscal year-end, respectively.

2. In calculating the dollar value realized upon exercise (column (c)), the value of any related payment or other consideration provided (or to be provided) by the registrant to or on behalf of a named executive officer, whether in payment of the exercise price or related taxes, shall not be included. Payments by the registrant in reimbursement of tax obligations incurred by a named executive officer are required to be disclosed in accordance with paragraph (b)(2)(iii)(C)(*4*) of this item.

(e) *Long-Term Incentive Plan ("LTIP") awards table.* (1) The information specified in paragraph (e)(2) of this item, regarding each award made to a named executive officer in the last completed fiscal year under any LTIP, shall be provided in the tabular format specified below:

LONG-TERM INCENTIVE PLANS—AWARDS IN LAST FISCAL YEAR

			Estimated Future Payouts under Non-Stock Price-Based Plans		
(a) Name	(b) Number of shares, units or other rights (#)	(c) Performance or other period until maturation or payout	(d) Threshold ($ or #)	(e) Target ($ or #)	(f) Maximum ($ or #)
CEO..........................					
A............................					
B............................					
C............................					
D............................					

(2) The Table shall include: (i) The name of the executive officer (column (a));

(ii) The number of shares, units or other rights awarded under any LTIP, and, if applicable, the number of shares underlying any such unit or right (column (b));

(iii) The performance or other time period until payout or maturation of the award (column (c)); and

(iv) For plans not based on stock price, the dollar value of the estimated payout, the number of shares to be awarded as the payout or a range of estimated payouts denominated in dollars or number of shares under the award (threshold, target and maximum amount) (columns (d) through (f)).

Instructions to Item 402(e). 1. For purposes of this paragraph, the term "long-term incentive plan" or "LTIP" shall be defined in accordance with paragraph (a)(6)(iii) of this item.

2. Describe in a footnote or in narrative text accompanying this table the material terms of any award, including a general description of the formula or criteria to be applied in determining the amounts payable. Registrants are not required to disclose any factor, criterion or performance-related or other condition to payout or maturation of a particular award that involves confidential commercial or business information, disclosure of which would adversely affect the registrant's competitive position.

3. Separate disclosure shall be provided in the Table for each award made to a named executive officer, accompanied by the information specified in Instruction 2 to this paragraph. If awards are made to a named executive officer during the fiscal year under more

than one plan, identify the particular plan under which each such award was made.

4. For column (d), "threshold" refers to the minimum amount payable for a certain level of performance under the plan. For column (e), "target" refers to the amount payable if the specified performance target(s) are reached. For column (f), "maximum" refers to the maximum payout possible under the plan.

5. In column (e), registrants must provide a representative amount based on the previous fiscal year's performance if the target award is not determinable.

6. A tandem grant of two instruments, only one of which is pursuant to a LTIP, need be reported only in the table applicable to the other instrument. For example, an option granted in tandem with a performance share would be reported only as an option grant, with the tandem feature noted.

(f) *Compensation of directors.* (1) *Standard arrangements.* Describe any standard arrangements, stating amounts, pursuant to which directors of the registrant are compensated for any services provided as a director, including any additional amounts payable for committee participation or special assignments.

(2) *Other arrangements.* Describe any other arrangements pursuant to which any director of the registrant was compensated during the registrant's last completed fiscal year for any service provided as a director, stating the amount paid and the name of the director.

Instruction to Item 402(f)(2). The information required by paragraph (f)(2) of this item shall include any arrangement, including consulting contracts, entered into in consideration of the director's service on the board. The material terms of any such arrangement shall be included.

(g) *Employment contracts and termination of employment and change-in-control arrangements.* Describe the terms and conditions of each of the following contracts or arrangements:

(1) Any employment contract between the registrant and a named executive officer; and

(2) Any compensatory plan or arrangement, including payments to be received from the registrant, with respect to a named executive officer, if such plan or arrangement results or will result from the resignation, retirement or any other termination of such executive officer's employment with the registrant and its subsidiaries or from a change-in-control of the registrant or a change in the named executive officer's responsibilities following a change-in-control and the amount involved, including all periodic payments or installments, exceeds $100,000.

(h) *Report on repricing of options/SARs.* (1) If at any time during the last completed fiscal year, the registrant, while a reporting company pursuant to section 13(a) or 15(d) of the Exchange Act, has adjusted or amended the exercise price of stock options or SARs previously awarded to any of the named executive officers, whether through amendment, cancellation or replacement grants, or any other means ("repriced"), the registrant shall provide the information specified in paragraph (h)(2) of this item.

(2) The compensation committee (or other board committee performing equivalent functions or, in the absence of any such committee, the entire board of directors) shall explain in reasonable detail any such repricing of options and/or SARs held by a named executive officer in the last completed fiscal year, as well as the basis for each such repricing.

Instructions to Item 402(h). 1. A replacement grant is any grant of options or SARs reasonably related to any prior or potential option or SAR cancellation, whether by an exchange of existing options or SARs for options or SARs with new terms; the grant of new options or SARs in tandem with previously granted options or SARs that will operate to cancel the previously granted options or SARs upon exercise; repricing of previously granted options or SARs; or otherwise. If a corresponding original grant was canceled in a prior year, information about such grant nevertheless must be disclosed pursuant to this paragraph.

2. If the replacement grant is not made at the current market price, describe the terms of the grant in a footnote or accompanying textual narrative.

3. This paragraph shall not apply to any repricing occurring through the operation of:

a. A plan formula or mechanism that results in the periodic adjustment of the option or SAR exercise or base price;

b. A plan antidilution provision; or

c. A recapitalization or similar transaction equally affecting all holders of the class of securities underlying the options or SARs.

Item 403. Security Ownership of Certain Beneficial Owners and Management

(a) *Security ownership of certain beneficial owners.* Complete the table below for any person (including any "group") who is known to the small business issuer to be the beneficial owner of more than five percent of any class of the small business issuer's voting securities.

(1) Title of class	(2) Name and address of beneficial owner	(3) Amount and nature of beneficial owner	(4) Percent of class

(b) *Security ownership of management.* Furnish the following information, as of the most recent practicable date, in substantially the tabular form indicated, as to each class of equity securities of the registrant or any of its parents or subsidiaries other than directors' qualifying shares, beneficially owned by all directors and nominees, naming them, each of the named executive officers as defined in Item 402(a)(2) (§ 228.402(a)(2)), and directors and executive officers of the registrant as a group, without naming them. Show in column (3) the total number of shares beneficially owned and in column (4) the percent of class so owned. Of the number of shares shown in column (3), indicate, by footnote or otherwise, the amount of shares with respect to which such persons have the right to acquire beneficial ownership as specified in § 240.13d–3(d)(1) of this chapter.

(1) Title of class	(2) Name and address of beneficial owner	(3) Amount and nature of beneficial owner	(4) Percent of class

(c) *Changes in control.* Describe any arrangements which may result in a change in control of the small business issuer.

Instructions to Item 403. 1. Of the number of shares shown in column (3) of paragraphs (a) and (b) of this Item, state in a footnote the amount which the listed beneficial owner has the right to acquire within sixty days, from options, warrants, rights, conversion privilege or similar obligations.

2. Where persons hold more than 5% of a class under a voting trust or similar agreement, provide the following:

(a) the title of such securities;

(b) the amount that they hold under the trust or agreement (if not clear from the table);

(c) the duration of the agreement;

(d) the names and addresses of the voting trustees; and

(e) a brief outline of the voting rights and other powers of the voting trustees under the trust or agreement.

3. Calculate the percentages on the basis of the amount of outstanding securities plus, for each person or group, any securities that person or group has the right to acquire within 60 days pursuant to options, warrants, conversion privileges or other rights.

4. In this Item, a *beneficial owner* of a security means:

(a) Any person who, directly or indirectly, through any contract, arrangement, understanding, relationship or otherwise has or shares:

(1) Voting power, which includes the power to vote, or to direct the voting of, such security; or

(2) Investment power, which includes the power to dispose, or to direct the disposition of, such security.

(b) Any person who, directly or indirectly, creates or uses a trust, proxy, power of attorney, pooling arrangement or any other contract, arrangement or device with the purpose or effect of divesting such person of beneficial ownership of a security or preventing the vesting of such beneficial ownership.

5. All securities of the same class beneficially owned by a person, regardless of the form that such beneficial ownership takes, shall be totaled in calculating the number of shares beneficially owned by such person.

6. The small business issuer is responsible for knowing the contents of any statements filed with the Commission under section 13(d) or 13(g) of the Exchange Act concerning the beneficial ownership of securities and may rely upon the information in such statements unless it knows or has reason to believe that the information is not complete or accurate.

7. The term "group" means two or more persons acting as a partnership, syndicate, or other group for the purpose of acquiring, holding or disposing of securities of an issuer.

8. Where the small business issuer lists more than one beneficial owner for the same securities, adequate disclosure should be included to avoid confusion.

Item 404. Certain Relationships and Related Transactions

(a) Describe any transaction during the last two years, or proposed transactions, to which the small business issuer was or is to be a party, in which any of the following persons had or is to have a direct or indirect material interest. Give the name of the person, the relationship to the issuer, nature of the person's interest in the transaction and the amount of such interest:

(1) Any director or executive officer of the small business issuer;

(2) Any nominee for election as a director;

(3) Any security holder named in response to Item 403 (§ 228.403); and

(4) Any member of the immediate family (including spouse, parents, children, siblings, and in-laws) of any of the persons in paragraphs (a)(1), (2) or (3) of this Item.

(b) No information need be included for any transaction where:

(1) Competitive bids determine the rates or charges involved in the transaction;

(2) The transaction involves services at rates or charges fixed by law or governmental authority;

(3) The transaction involves services as a bank depositary of funds, transfer agent, registrar, trustee under a trust indenture, or similar services;

(4) The amount involved in the transaction or a series of similar transactions does not exceed $60,000; or

(5) The interest of the person arises solely from the ownership of securities of the small business issuer and the person receives no extra or special benefit that was not shared equally (pro rata) by all holders of securities of the class.

(c) List all parents of the small business issuer showing the basis of control and as to each parent, the percentage of voting securities owned or other basis of control by its immediate parent if any.

(d) *Transactions with promoters.* Issuers organized within the past five years shall:

(1) State the names of the promoters, the nature and amount of anything of value (including money, property, contracts, options or rights of any kind) received or to be received by each promoter, directly or indirectly, from the issuer and the nature and amount of any assets, services or other consideration therefor received or to be received by the registrant; and

(2) As to any assets acquired or to be acquired from a promoter, state the amount at which the assets were acquired or are to be acquired and the principle followed or to be followed in determining such amount and identify the persons making the determination and their relationship, if any, with the registrant or any promoter. If the assets were acquired by the promoter within two years prior to their transfer to the issuer, also state the cost thereof to the promoter.

Instructions to Item 404. 1. A person does not have a material indirect interest in a transaction within the meaning of this Item where:

(a) The interest arises only:

(1) from such person's position as a director of another corporation or organization (other than a partnership) which is a party to the transaction and/or

(2) from the total ownership (direct or indirect) by all specified persons of less than a 10% equity interest in another person (other than a partnership) which is a party to the transaction;

(b) The interest arises only from such person's position as a limited partner in a partnership in which he and all other specified persons had an interest of less than 10 percent; or

(c) The interest of such person arises solely from holding an equity interest (but not a general partnership interest) or a creditor interest in another person that is a party to the transaction and the transaction is not material to such other person.

2. Include information for any material underwriting discounts and commissions upon the sale of securities by the small business issuer where any of the specified persons was or is to be a principal underwriter or is a controlling person or member of a firm that was or is to be a principal underwriter.

3. As to any transaction involving the purchase or sale of assets by or to the small business issuer otherwise than in the ordinary course of business, state the cost of the assets to the purchase and if acquired by the seller within two years before the transaction, the cost thereof to the seller.

Item 405. Compliance With Section 16(a) of the Exchange Act

Every small business issuer that has a class of equity securities registered pursuant to Section 12 of the Exchange Act shall:

(a) Based solely upon a review of Forms 3 and 4 (17 CFR 249.103 and 249.104 of this chapter) and amendments thereto furnished to the registrant under Rule 16a–3(e) during its most recent fiscal year and Form 5 and amendments thereto (§ 249.105 of this chapter) furnished to the registrant with respect to its most recent fiscal year, and any written representation referred to in paragraph (b)(2)(i) of this Item:

(1) Under the caption "Section 16(a) Beneficial Ownership Reporting Compliance," identify each person who, at any time during the fiscal year, was a director, officer, or beneficial owner of more than ten percent of any class of equity securities of the registrant registered pursuant to section 12 ("reporting person"), that failed to file on a timely basis, as disclosed in the above Forms, reports required by section 16(a) of the Exchange Act during the most recent fiscal year or prior fiscal years.

(2) For each such person, set forth the number of late reports, the number of transactions that were not reported on a timely basis, and any known failure to file a required Form. A known failure to file would

include, but not be limited to, a failure to file a Form 3, which is required of all reporting persons, and a failure to file a Form 5 in the absence of the written representation referred to in paragraph (b)(2)(i) of this section, unless the registrant otherwise knows that no Form 5 is required.

Note: The disclosure requirement is based on a review of the forms submitted to the registrant during and with respect to its most recent fiscal year, as specified above. Accordingly, a failure to file timely need only be disclosed once. For example, if in the most recently concluded fiscal year a reporting person filed a Form 4 disclosing a transaction that took place in the prior fiscal year, and should have been reported in that year, the registrant should disclose that late filing and transaction pursuant to this Item for the most recent fiscal year, but not in material filed with respect to subsequent years.

(b) With respect to the disclosure required by paragraph (a) of this Item:

(1) A form received by the registrant within three calendar days of the required filing date may be presumed to have been filed with the Commission by the required filing date.

(2) If the registrant:

(i) receives a written representation from the reporting person that no Form 5 is required; and

(ii) maintains the representation for two years, making a copy available to the Commission or its staff upon request, the registrant need not identify such reporting person pursuant to paragraph (a) of this Item as having failed to file a Form 5 with respect to that fiscal year.

Item 406. Code of Ethics

(a) Disclose whether the small business issuer has adopted a code of ethics that applies to the small business issuer's principal executive officer, principal financial officer, principal accounting officer or controller, or persons performing similar functions. If the small business issuer has not adopted such a code of ethics, explain why it has not done so.

(b) For purposes of this Item 406, the term *code of ethics* means written standards that are reasonably designed to deter wrongdoing and to promote:

(1) Honest and ethical conduct, including the ethical handling of actual or apparent conflicts of interest between personal and professional relationships;

(2) Full, fair, accurate, timely, and understandable disclosure in reports and documents that a small business issuer files with, or submits to, the Commission and in other public communications made by the small business issuer;

(3) Compliance with applicable governmental laws, rules and regulations;

(4) The prompt internal reporting of violations of the code to an appropriate person or persons identified in the code; and

(5) Accountability for adherence to the code.

(c) The small business issuer must:

(1) File with the Commission a copy of its code of ethics that applies to the small business issuer's principal executive officer, principal financial officer, principal accounting officer or controller, or persons performing similar functions, as an exhibit to its annual report;

(2) Post the text of such code of ethics on its Internet website and disclose, in its annual report, its Internet address and the fact that it has posted such code of ethics on its Internet website; or

(3) Undertake in its annual report filed with the Commission to provide to any person without charge, upon request, a copy of such code of ethics and explain the manner in which such request may be made.

(d) If the small business issuer intends to satisfy the disclosure requirement under Item 10 of Form 8–K regarding an amendment to, or a waiver from, a provision of its code of ethics that applies to the small business issuer's principal executive officer, principal financial officer, principal accounting officer or controller, or persons performing similar functions and that relates to any element of the code of ethics definition enumerated in paragraph (b) of this Item by posting such information on its Internet website, disclose the small business issuer's Internet address and such intention.

Instructions to Item 406. 1. A small business issuer may have separate codes of ethics for different types of officers. Furthermore, a *code of ethics* within the meaning of paragraph (b) of this Item may be a portion of a broader document that addresses additional topics or that applies to more persons than those specified in paragraph (a). In satisfying the requirements of paragraph (c), a small business issuer need only file, post or provide the portions of a broader document that constitutes a *code of ethics* as defined in paragraph (b) and that apply to the persons specified in paragraph (a).

2. If a small business issuer elects to satisfy paragraph (c) of this Item by posting its code of ethics on its website pursuant to paragraph (c)(2), the code of ethics must remain accessible on its website for as long as the small business issuer remains subject to the requirements of this Item and chooses to comply with this Item by posting its code on its Web site pursuant to paragraph (c)(2).

Item 501. Front of Registration Statement and Outside Front Cover of Prospectus

The small business issuer must furnish the following information in plain English. See § 230.421(d) of Regulation C of this chapter.

(a) Limit the outside front cover page of the prospectus to one page and include the following information:

(1) The registrant's name. A foreign registrant also must give the English translation of its name;

(2) The title, amount, and description of securities offered. If the underwriter has any arrangement with the issuer, such as an over-allotment option, under which the underwriter may purchase additional shares in connection with the offering, indicate that this arrangement exists and state the amount of additional shares that the underwriter may purchase under the arrangement;

(3) If there are selling security holders, a statement to that effect;

(4) Whether any national securities exchange or the Nasdaq Stock Market lists the securities offered, naming the particular market(s), and identifying the trading symbol(s) for those securities;

(5) A cross-reference to the risk factors section, including the page number where it appears in the prospectus. Highlight this cross-reference by prominent type or in another manner;

(6) Any legend or statement required by the law of any state in which the securities are offered;

(7) A legend that indicates that neither the Securities and Exchange Commission nor any state securities commission has approved or disapproved of the securities or passed on the adequacy or accuracy of the disclosures in the prospectus. Also make clear that any representation to the contrary is a criminal offense. You may use one of the following or other clear, plain language:

Example A: Neither the Securities and Exchange Commission nor any state securities commission has approved or disapproved of these securities or passed upon the adequacy or accuracy of the prospectus. Any representation to the contrary is a criminal offense.

Example B: Neither the Securities and Exchange Commission nor any state securities commission has approved or disapproved of these securities or determined if this prospectus is truthful or complete. Any representation to the contrary is a criminal offense.

(8) If you are not a reporting company and the preliminary prospectus will be circulated, as applicable:

(i) A bona fide estimate of the range of the maximum offering price and maximum number of shares or units offered; or

(ii) A bona fide estimate of the principal amount of debt securities offered;

(9)(i) Name(s) of the lead or managing underwriter(s) and an identification of the nature of the underwriting arrangements;

(ii) If the offering is not made on a firm commitment basis, a brief description of the underwriting arrangements;

(iii) If you offer the securities on a best efforts or best efforts minimum/maximum basis, the date the offering will end, any minimum purchase requirements, and whether or not there are any arrangements to place the funds in an escrow, trust, or similar account; and

(iv) If you offer the securities for cash, the price to the public for the securities, the underwriting discounts and commissions, and proceeds to the registrant or other persons. Show the information on both a per share or unit basis and for the total amount of the offering. If you make the offering on a minimum/maximum basis, show this information based on the total minimum and total maximum amount of the offering. You may present the information in a table, term sheet format, or other clear presentation. You may present the information in any format that fits the design of the cover page so long as the information can be easily read and is not misleading;

(10) If the prospectus will be used before the effective date of the registration statement, a prominent statement that:

(i) The information in the prospectus will be amended or completed;

(ii) A registration statement relating to these securities has been filed with the Securities and Exchange Commission;

(iii) The securities may not be sold until the registration statement becomes effective; and

(iv) The prospectus is not an offer to sell the securities and it is not soliciting an offer to buy the securities in any state where offers or sales are not permitted. You may use the following or other clear, plain language:

> The information in this prospectus is not complete and may be changed. We may not sell these securities until the registration statement filed with the Securities and Exchange Commission is effective. This prospectus is not an offer to sell these securities and it is not soliciting an offer to buy these securities in any state where the offer or sale is not permitted.

(11) If you use § 230.430A of this chapter to omit pricing information and the prospectus is used before you determine the public offering price, the information in paragraph (a)(10) of this section; and

(12) The date of the prospectus.

Item 502. Inside Front and Outside Back Cover Pages of Prospectus

The small business issuer must furnish the following information in plain English. See § 230.421(d) of Regulation C of this chapter.

(a) *Table of contents.* On either the inside front or outside back cover page of the prospectus, provide a reasonably detailed table of contents. It must show the page number of the various sections or subdivisions of the prospectus. Include a specific listing of the risk factors section required by Item 503 of this Regulation S–B (17 CFR 228.503). You must include the table of contents immediately following the cover page in any prospectus you deliver electronically;

(b) *Dealer prospectus delivery obligation.* If applicable to your offering, on the outside back cover page of the prospectus, advise dealers of their prospectus delivery obligation, including the expiration date specified by Section 4(3) of the Securities Act (15 U.S.C. 77d(3)) and § 230.174 of this chapter. You may use the following or other clear, plain language:

Dealer Prospectus Delivery Obligation.

Until (insert date), all dealers that effect transactions in these securities, whether or not participating in this offering, may be required to deliver a prospectus. This is in addition to the dealers' obligation to deliver a prospectus when acting as underwriters and with respect to their unsold allotments or subscriptions.

Item 503. Summary Information and Risk Factors

The small business issuer must furnish the following information in plain English. See § 230.421(d) of Regulation C of this chapter.

(a) *Summary.* Provide a summary of the information in the prospectus where the length or complexity of the prospectus makes a summary useful. The summary should be brief. The summary should not contain, and is not required to contain, all of the detailed information in the prospectus. If you provide summary business or financial information, even if you do not caption it as a summary, you still must provide that information in plain English.

Instruction to paragraph 503(a)

The summary should not merely repeat the text of the prospectus but should provide a brief overview of the key aspects of the offering. Carefully consider and identify those aspects of the offering that are the most significant and determine how best to highlight those points in clear, plain language.

(b) *Address and phone number.* Include, either on the cover page or in the summary section of the prospectus, the complete mailing address and telephone number of your principal executive offices.

(c) *Risk factors:* (1) Discuss in a section captioned "Risk Factors" any factors that make the offering speculative or risky. The factors may include, among other things, the following:

(i) Your lack of an operating history;

(ii) Your lack of recent profits from operations;

(iii) Your poor financial position;

(iv) Your business or proposed business; or

(v) The lack of a market for your common equity securities.

(2) The risk factor discussion must immediately follow the summary section. If you do not include a summary section, the risk factor discussion must immediately follow the cover page or the pricing information that immediately follows the cover page. Pricing information means price and price-related information that you may omit from the prospectus in an effective registration statement based on § 230.430A(a) of this chapter.

Item 504. Use of Proceeds

State how the net proceeds of the offering will be used, indicating the amount to be used for each purpose and the priority of each purpose, if all of the securities are not sold. If all or a substantial part of the proceeds are not allocated for a specific purpose, so state and discuss the principal reasons for the offering.

Instructions to Item 504. 1. If a material amount of proceeds will discharge debt, state the interest rate and maturity. If that debt was incurred within one year, describe the use of the proceeds of that debt other than short-term borrowings used for working capital.

2. If any material amount of the proceeds is to be used to acquire assets or finance the acquisitions of other businesses, describe the assets or businesses and identify the persons

from whom they will be bought. State the cost of the assets and, where such assets are to be acquired from affiliates of the small business issuer or their associates, give the names of the persons from whom they are to be acquired and set forth the principle followed in determining the cost to the small business issuer.

Item 505. Determination of Offering Price

(a) If there is no established public market for the common equity being registered or if there is a significant difference between the offering price and the market price of the stock, give the factors that were considered in determining the offering price.

(b) If warrants, rights and convertible securities are being registered and there is no public market for the underlying securities, describe the factors considered in determining the exercise or conversion price.

Item 506. Dilution

(a) If the small business issuer is not a reporting company and is selling common equity at a price significantly more than the price paid by officers, directors, promoters and affiliated persons for common equity purchased by them during the past five years (or which they have rights to purchase), compare these prices.

(b) If paragraph (a) of this Item applies and the issuer had losses in each of its last three fiscal years, or since its inception, whichever period is shorter, and there is a material dilution of the purchasers' equity interest, disclose the following:

(1) The net tangible book value per share before and after the distribution;

(2) The amount of the increase in such net tangible book value per share attributable to the cash payments made by purchasers of the shares being offered; and

(3) The amount of the immediate dilution from the public offering price which will be absorbed by such purchasers.

Item 507. Selling Security Holders

If security holders of a small business issuer are offering securities, name each selling security holder, state any position, office, or other material relationship which the selling security holder has had within the past three years with the small business issuer or any of its predecessors or affiliates, and state the amount of securities of the class owned by such security holder before the offering, the amount to be offered for the security holder's account, the amount and (if one percent or more) the percentage of the class to be owned by such security holder after the offering is complete.

Instruction. Responses to this item may be combined with disclosure in response to Item 403.

Item 508. Plan of Distribution

(a) *Underwriters and underwriting obligations.* If the securities are to be offered through underwriters, name the principal underwriters, and state the respective amounts underwritten. Identify each such underwriter having a material relationship with the small business issuer and state the nature of the relationship. State the nature of the obligation of the underwriter(s) to take the securities, *i.e.,* firm commitment, best efforts. The small business issuer must disclose the offering expenses specified in Item 511 of this Regulation S–B (17 CFR 228.511). If there is an arrangement under which the underwriter may purchase additional shares in connection with the offering, such as an over-allotment option, describe that arrangement and disclose information on the total offering price, underwriting discounts and commissions, and total proceeds assuming the underwriter purchases all of the shares subject to that arrangement.

(b) *New underwriters.* Describe the business experience of managing or principal underwriters that have been in business less than three years, state their principal business function and identify any material relationships between the promoters of the issuer and the underwriter(s). This information need not be given if:

(1) the issuer is a reporting company; and

(2) an offering has no material risks.

(c) *Other distributions.* Outline briefly the plan of distribution of any securities to be registered that are to be offered otherwise than through underwriters.

(d) *Underwriter's representative on the board of directors.* Describe any arrangement whereby the underwriter has the right to designate or nominate a member or members of the board of directors of the small business issuer. Identify any director so designated or nominated and indicate any relationship with the small business issuer.

(e) *Indemnification of underwriters.* If the underwriting agreement provides for indemnification by the small business issuer of the underwriters or their controlling persons against any liability arising under the Securities Act, furnish a brief description of such indemnification provisions.

(f) *Dealers' compensation.* State briefly the discounts and commissions to be allowed or paid to dealers, including all cash, securities, contracts or other considerations to be received by any dealer in connection with the sale of the securities.

(g) *Finders.* Identify any finder and describe the nature of any material relationship between such finder and the small business issuer or associates or affiliates of the small business issuer.

(h) *Discretionary accounts.* If the small business issuer is not a reporting company, identify any principal underwriter that intends to sell to any discretionary accounts and include an estimate of the amount of securities so intended to be sold. The response to this paragraph shall be contained in a pre-effective amendment which shall be circulated if the information is not available when the registration statement is filed.

(i) *Passive market making.* If the underwriters or any selling group members intend to engage in passive market making transactions as permitted by Rule 103 of Regulation M, indicate such intention and briefly describe passive market making.

(j) *Stabilization and other transactions.* (1) Briefly describe any transaction that the underwriter intends to conduct during the offering that stabilizes, maintains, or otherwise affects the market price of the offered securities. Include information on stabilizing transactions, syndicate short covering transactions, penalty bids, or any other transaction that affects the offered security's price. Describe the nature of the transactions clearly and explain how the transactions affect the offered security's price. Identify the exchange or other market on which these transactions may occur. If true, disclose that the underwriter may discontinue these transactions at any time;

(2) If the stabilizing began before the effective date of the registration statement, disclose the amount of securities bought, the prices at which they were bought, and the period within which they were bought. If you use § 230.430A of this chapter, the final prospectus must contain information on the stabilizing transactions that took place before the public offering price was set; and

(3) If you are making a warrant or rights offering of securities to existing security holders and the securities not purchased by existing security holders are to be reoffered to the public, disclose the following information in the reoffer prospectus:

(i) The amount of securities bought in stabilization activities during the offering period and the price or range of prices at which the securities were bought;

(ii) The amount of the offered securities subscribed for during the offering period;

(iii) The amount of the offered securities purchased by the underwriter during the offering period;

(iv) The amount of the offered securities sold by the underwriter during the offering period and the price or range of prices at which the securities were sold; and

(v) The amount of the offered securities that will be reoffered to the public and the offering price.

Item 509. Interest of Named Experts and Counsel

If an "expert" or "counsel" was hired on a contingent basis, will receive a direct or indirect interest in the small business issuer or was a promoter, underwriter, voting trustee, director, officer, or employee of the small business issuer, describe the contingent basis, interest, or connection.

(a) *Expert.* is a person who is named as preparing or certifying all or part of the small business issuer's registration statement or a report or valuation for use in connection with the registration statement.

(b) *Counsel.* is counsel named in the prospectus as having given an opinion on the validity of the securities being registered or upon other legal matters concerning the registration or offering of the securities.

Instruction to Item 509. 1. The small business issuer does not need to disclose the interest of an expert (other than an accountant) or counsel if their interest (including the fair market value of all securities of the small business issuer received and to be received, or subject to options, warrants or rights received or to be received) does not exceed $50,000.

Item 510. Disclosure of Commission Position on Indemnification for Securities Act Liabilities

Describe the indemnification provisions for directors, officers and controlling persons of the small business issuer against liability under the Securities Act. This includes any provision in the underwriting agreement which indemnifies the underwriter or its controlling persons against such liabilities where a director, officer or controlling person of the small business issuer is such an underwriter or controlling person or a member of any firm which is such an underwriter. In addition, provide the undertaking in the first sentence of Item 512(e).

Item 511. Other Expenses of Issuance and Distribution

(a) Give an itemized statement of all expenses of the offering, other than underwriting discounts and commissions. If any of the securities are registered for sale by security holders, state how much of the expenses the security holders will pay.

(1) The itemized list should generally include registration fees, federal taxes, state taxes and fees, trustees' and transfer agents' fees, costs of printing and engraving, legal, accounting, and engineering fees and any listing fees.

(2) Include as a separate item any premium paid by the small business issuer or any selling security holder on any policy to insure or indemnify directors or officers against any liabilities they may incur in the registration, offering, or sale of these securities.

(b) [Reserved.]

Instruction to Item 511. 1. If the amounts of any items are not known, give estimates but identify them as such.

Item 512. Undertakings

Include each of the following undertakings that apply to the offering.

(a) *Rule 415 Offering.* If the small business issuer is registering securities under Rule 415 of the Securities Act, that the small business issuer will:

(1) File, during any period in which it offers or sells securities, a post-effective amendment to this registration statement to:

(i) Include any prospectus required by section 10(a)(3) of the Securities Act;

(ii) Reflect in the prospectus any facts or events which, individually or together, represent a fundamental change in the information in the registration statement.

Notwithstanding the foregoing, any increase or decrease in volume of securities offered (if the total dollar value of securities offered would not exceed that which was registered) and any deviation from the low or high end of the estimated maximum offering range may be reflected in the form of prospectus filed with the Commission pursuant to Rule 424(b) (§ 230.424(b) of this chapter) if, in the aggregate, the changes in volume and price represent no more than a 20% change in the maximum aggregate offering price set forth in the "Calculation of Registration Fee" table in the effective registration statement.

(iii) Include any additional or changed material information on the plan of distribution.

Note: Small business issuers do not need to give the statements in paragraphs (a)(1)(i) and (a)(1)(ii) of this Item if the registration statement is on Form S–3 or S–8 (§§ 239.13 or 239.16b of this chapter), and the information required in a post-effective amendment is incorporated by reference from periodic reports filed by the small business issuer under the Exchange Act.

(2) For determining liability under the Securities Act, treat each post-effective amendment as a new registration statement of the securities offered, and the offering of the securities at that time to be the initial bona fide offering.

(3) File a post-effective amendment to remove from registration any of the securities that remain unsold at the end of the offering.

(b) *Warrants and rights offerings.* If the small business issuer will offer the securities to existing security holders under warrants or rights and the small business issuer will reoffer to the public any securities not taken by security holders, with any modifications that suit the particular case—The small business issuer will supplement the prospectus, after the end of the subscription period, to include the results of the subscription offer, the transactions by the underwriters during the subscription period, the amount of unsubscribed securities that the underwriters will purchase and the terms of any later reoffering. If the underwriters make any public offering of the securities on terms different from those on the cover page of the prospectus, the small business issuer will file a post-effective amendment to state the terms of such offering.

(c) *Competitive bids.* If the small business issuer is offering securities at competitive bidding, with modifications to suit the particular case, the small business issuer will:

(1) use its best efforts to distribute before the opening of bids, to prospective bidders, underwriters, and dealers, a reasonable number of copies of a prospectus that meet the requirements of section 10(a) of the Securities Act, and relating to the securities offered at competitive bidding, as contained in the registration statement, together with any supplements; and

(2) file an amendment to the registration statement reflecting the results of bidding, the terms of the reoffering and related matters where required by the applicable form, not later than the first use, authorized by the issuer after the opening of bids, of a prospectus relating to the securities offered at competitive bidding, unless the issuer proposes no further public offering of such securities by the issuer or by the purchasers.

(d) *Equity offerings of nonreporting small business issuers.* If a small business issuer that before the offering had no duty to file reports with the Commission under section 13(a) or 15(d) of the Exchange Act is registering equity securities for sale in an underwritten offering—The small business issuer will provide to the underwriter at the closing specified in the underwriting agreement certificates in such denominations and registered in such names as required by the underwriter to permit prompt delivery to each purchaser.

(e) *Request for acceleration of effective date.* If the small business issuer will request acceleration of the effective date of the registration statement under Rule 461 under the Securities Act, include the following:

> Insofar as indemnification for liabilities arising under the Securities Act of 1933 (the "Act") may be permitted to directors, officers and controlling persons of the small business issuer pursuant to the foregoing provisions, or otherwise, the small business issuer has been advised that in the opinion of the Securities and Exchange Commission such indemnification is against public policy as expressed in the Act and is, therefore, unenforceable.

In the event that a claim for indemnification against such liabilities (other than the payment by the small business issuer of expenses incurred or paid by a director, officer or controlling person of the small business issuer in the successful defense of any action, suit or proceeding) is asserted by such director, officer or controlling person in connection with the securities being registered, the small business issuer will, unless in the opinion of its counsel the matter has been settled by controlling precedent, submit to a court of appropriate jurisdiction the question whether such indemnification by it is against public policy as expressed in the Securities Act and will be governed by the final adjudication of such issue.

(f) If the issuer relies on Rule 430A under the Securities Act, that the small business issuer will:

(1) For determining any liability under the Securities Act, treat the information omitted from the form of prospectus filed as part of this registration statement in reliance upon Rule 430A and contained in a form of prospectus filed by the small business issuer under Rule 424(b)(1), or (4) or 497(h) under the Securities Act as part of this registration statement as of the time the Commission declared it effective.

(2) For determining any liability under the Securities Act, treat each post-effective amendment that contains a form of prospectus as a new registration statement for the securities offered in the registration statement, and that offering of the securities at that time as the initial bona fide offering of those securities.

Item 601. Exhibits

(a) *Exhibits and index of exhibits.* (1) The exhibits required by the exhibit table generally must be filed or incorporated by reference.

(2) Each filing must have an index of exhibits. The exhibit index must list exhibits in the same order as the exhibit table. If the exhibits are incorporated by reference, this fact should be noted in the exhibit index. In the manually signed registration statement or report, the exhibit index should give the page number of each exhibit.

(3) If a material contract or plan of acquisition, reorganization, arrangement, liquidation or succession is executed or becomes effective during the reporting period covered by a Form 10–QSB or Form 10–KSB, it must be filed as an exhibit to the Form 10–QSB or Form 10–KSB filed for the same period. Whenever an electronic confirming copy of an exhibit is filed pursuant to a hardship exemption (§ 232.201 or § 232.202(d) of this chapter), the exhibit index should specify where the confirming electronic copy can be located; in addition, the designation "CE" (confirming electronic) should be placed next to the listed exhibit in the exhibit index. The amendment or modification does not need to be filed if the previously filed exhibit would not be currently required.

Instructions to Item 601(a). 1. If an exhibit (other than an opinion or consent) is filed in preliminary form and is later changed to include only interest, dividend or conversion rates, redemption or conversion prices, purchase or offering prices, underwriters' or dealers' commissions, names, addresses or participation of underwriters or similar matters and the information appears elsewhere in the registration statement or a prospectus, no amendment need be filed.

2. Small business issuers may file copies of each exhibit, rather than originals, except as otherwise specifically noted.

3. *Electronic filings.* Whenever an exhibit is filed in paper pursuant to a hardship exemption (§§ 232.201 and 232.202 of this chapter), the letter "P" (paper) should be placed next to the exhibit in the list of exhibits required by Item 601(a)(2) of this Rule. Whenever an electronic confirming copy of an exhibit is filed pursuant to a temporary hardship exemption (§ 232.201 of this chapter), the exhibit index should specify where the confirming electronic copy can be located; in addition, the designation "CE" (confirming electronic) should be placed next to the listed exhibit in the exhibit index.

EXHIBIT TABLE

	Securities Act Forms					Exchange Act Forms			
	SB–1	S–2	S–3	S–4[3]	S–8	10–SB[5]	8–K	10–QSB	10–KSB
(1) Underwriting agreement	X	X	X	X			X		
(2) Plan of purchase, sale, reorganization, arrangement, liquidation, or succession	X	X	X	X		X	X	X	X
(3) (i) Articles of incorporation	X			X		X	X	X	X
(ii) Bylaws	X			X		X	X	X	X
(4) Instruments defining the rights of security holders, including identures	X	X	X	X	X	X	X	X	X
(5) Opinion on legality	X	X	X	X	X				
(6) No exhibit required	N/A	N/A	N/A	N/A	N/A	N/A	N/A	N/A	N/A
(7) Correspondence from an independent accountant regarding non-reliance on a previously issued audit report or completed interim review							X		
(8) Opinion on tax matters	X	X	X	X					
(9) Voting trust agreement and amendments	X			X		X			X
(10) Material contracts	X	X		X		X		X	X
(11) Statement re: computation of per share earnings	X	X		X		X		X	X
(12) No exhibit required	N/A	N/A	N/A	N/A	N/A	N/A	N/A	N/A	N/A
(13) Annual report to security holders, Form 10–Q and Form 10–SB, or quarterly report to security holders[1]	X	X		X					X
(14) Code of Ethics							X		X
(15) Letter on unaudited interim financial information	X	X	X	X	X			X	
(16) Letter on change in certifying accountant[4]	X	X		X		X	X		X
(17) Letter on director resignation							X		
(18) Letter on change in accounting principles								X	X
(19) Report furnished to security holders								X	
(20) Other documents or statements to security holders or any document incorporated by reference								X	X

	Securities Act Forms					Exchange Act Forms			
	SB–1	S–2	S–3	S–4[3]	S–8	10–SB[5]	8–K	10–QSB	10–KSB
(21) Subsidiaries of the small business issuer	X			X		X			X
(22) Published report regarding matters submitted to vote of security holders...........								X	X
(23) Consents of experts and counsel	X	X	X	X	X		X[2]	X[2]	X[2]
(24) Power of attorney	X	X	X	X	X	X	X	X	X
(25) Statement of eligibility of trustee	X	X	X	X					
(26) Invitations for competitive bids		X	X	X	X				
(27) through (30) [Reserved]									
(31) Rule 13a–14(a)/15d–14(a) Certifications								X	X
(32) Section 1350 Certifications..								X	X
(33) through (98) [Reserved]									
(99) Additional Exhibits	X	X	X	X	X	X	X	X	X
(100) XBRL–Related Documents						X	X	X	X

1. Only if incorporated by reference into a prospectus and delivered to holders along with the prospectus as permitted by the registration statement; or in the case of a Form 10–KSB, where the annual report is incorporated by reference into the text of the Form 10–KSB.

2. Where the opinion of the expert or counsel has been incorporated by reference into a previously filed Securities Act registration statement.

3. An issuer need not provide an exhibit if: (1) an election was made under Form S–4 to provide S–2 or S–3 disclosure; and (2) the form selected (S–2 or S–3) would not require the company to provide the exhibit.

4. If required under Item 304 of Regulation S–B.

5. A Form 8–K exhibit is required only if relevant to the subject matter reported on the Form 8–K report. For example, if the Form 8–K pertains to the departure of a director, only the exhibit described in paragraph (b)(17) of this section need be filed. A required exhibit may be incorporated by reference from a previous filing.

(b) *Description of exhibits.* Below is a description of each document listed in the exhibit table.

(1) *Underwriting agreement.* Each agreement with a principal underwriter for the distribution of the securities. If the terms have been determined and the securities are to be registered on Form S–3 (§ 239.13), the agreement may be filed on Form 8–K (§ 249.308) after the effectiveness of the registration statement.

(2) *Plan of purchase, sale, reorganization, arrangement, liquidation or succession.* Any such plan described in the filing. Schedules or attachments may be omitted if they are listed in the index and provided to the Commission upon request.

(3) *Articles of incorporation and bylaws.*

(i) A complete copy of the articles of incorporation. Whenever the small business issuer files an amendment to its articles of incorporation, it must file a complete copy of the articles as amended. However, if such amendment is being reported on Form 8–K (§ 249.308 of this chapter), the small business issuer is required to file only the text of the amendment as a Form 8–K exhibit. In such cases, a complete copy of the articles of incorporation as amended must be filed as an exhibit to the next Securities Act registration statement or periodic report filed by the small business issuer to which this exhibit requirement applies.

(i) A complete copy of the bylaws. Whenever the small business issuer files an amendment to its bylaws, it must file a complete copy of the bylaws as amended. However, if such amendment is being reported on Form 8–K (§ 249.308 of this chapter), the small business issuer is required to file only the text of the amendment as a Form 8–K exhibit. In such cases, a complete copy of the bylaws as amended must be filed as an exhibit to the next Securities Act registration statement or periodic report filed by the small business issuer to which this exhibit requirement applies.

(4) *Instruments defining the rights of security holders, including indentures.* (i) All instruments that define the rights of holders of the equity or debt securities that the issuer is registering, including the pages from the articles of incorporation or by-laws that define those rights.

(ii) All instruments defining the rights of holders of long term debt unless the total amount of debt covered by the instrument does not exceed 10% of the total assets of the small business issuer.

(iii) Copies of indentures to be qualified under the Trust Indenture Act of 1939 shall include an itemized table of contents and a cross reference sheet showing the location of the provisions inserted in accordance with Sections 310 through 318(a) of that Act.

Instruction to Item 601(b)(4)(iii) for electronic filings. If the instrument defining the rights of security holders is in the form of a certificate, the text appearing on the certificate shall be reproduced in an electronic filing together with a description of any other graphic and image material appearing on the certificate, as provided in Rule 304 of Regulation S–T (§ 232.304 of this chapter).

(5) *Opinion on legality.* (i) An opinion of counsel on the legality of the securities being registered stating whether they will, when sold, be legally issued, fully paid and non-assessable, and, if debt securities, whether they will be binding obligations of the small business issuer.

(ii) If the securities being registered are issued under a plan that is subject to the requirements of ERISA furnish either:

(A) An opinion of counsel which confirms compliance with ERISA; or

(B) A copy of the Internal Revenue Service determination letter that the plan is qualified under section 401 of the Internal Revenue Code.

If the plan is later amended, the small business issuer must have the opinion of counsel and the IRS determination letter updated to confirm compliance and qualification.

(6) No Exhibit Required.

(7) *Correspondence from an independent accountant regarding non-reliance on a previously issued audit report or completed interim review.* Any written notice from the small business issuer's current or previously engaged independent accountant that the independent accountant is withdrawing a previously issued audit report or that a previously issued audit report or completed interim review, covering one or more years or interim periods for which the small business issuer is required to provide financial statements under this Regulation S–B, should no longer be relied upon. In addition, any letter, pursuant to Item 4.02(c) of Form 8–K (§ 249.308 of this chapter), from the independent accountant to the Commission stating whether the independent accountant agrees with the statements made by the small business issuer describing the events giving rise to the notice.

(8) *Opinion on tax matters.* If tax consequences of the transaction are material to an investor, an opinion of counsel, an independent public or certified public accountant or, a revenue ruling from the Internal Revenue Service, supporting the tax matters and consequences to the shareholders. The exhibit is required for filings to which Securities Act Industry Guide 5 applies.

(9) *Voting trust agreement and amendments.*

(10) *Material contracts.* (i) Every material contract, not made in the ordinary course

of business, that will be performed after the filing of the registration statement or report or was entered into not more than two years before such filing. Also include the following contracts:

(A) Any contract to which directors, officers, promoters, voting trustees, security holders named in the registration statement or report, or underwriters are parties other than contracts involving only the purchase or sale of current assets having a determinable market price, at such market price;

(B) Any contract upon which the small business issuer's business is substantially dependent, such as contracts with principal customers, principal suppliers, franchise agreements, etc.;

(C) Any contract for the purchase or sale of any property, plant or equipment for a consideration exceeding 15 percent of such assets of the small business issuer; or

(D) Any material lease under which a part of the property described in the registration statement or report is held by the small business issuer.

(ii)(A) Any management contract or any compensatory plan, contract or arrangement, including but not limited to plans relating to options, warrants or rights, pension, retirement or deferred compensation or bonus, incentive or profit sharing (or if not set forth in any formal document, a written description thereof) in which any director or any of the named executive officers of the registrant as defined by Item 402(a)(2) participates shall be deemed material and shall be filed; and any other management contract or any other compensatory plan, contract, or arrangement in which any other executive officer of the registrant participates shall be filed unless immaterial in amount or significance.

(B) Any compensatory plan, contract or arrangement adopted without the approval of security holders pursuant to which equity may be awarded, including, but not limited to, options, warrants or rights (or if not set forth in any formal document, a written description thereof), in which any employee (whether or not an executive officer of the small business issuer) participates shall be filed unless immaterial in amount or significance. A compensation plan assumed by a small business issuer in connection with a merger, consolidation or other acquisition transaction pursuant to which the small business issuer may make further grants or awards of its equity securities shall be considered a compensation plan of the small business issuer for purposes of the preceding sentence.

(C) The following management contracts or compensatory plans need not be filed:

(*1*) Ordinary purchase and sales agency agreements;

(*2*) Agreements with managers of stores in a chain organization or similar organization;

(*3*) Contracts providing for labor or salesmen's bonuses or payments to a class of security holders, as such;

(*4*) Any compensatory plan which is available to employees, officers or directors generally and provides for the same method of allocation of benefits between management and nonmanagement participants; and

(*5*) Any compensatory plan if the issuer is a wholly owned subsidiary of a reporting company and is filing a report on Form 10–KSB (§ 249.310b), or registering debt or non-voting preferred stock on Form S–2 (§ 239.12).

Instruction 1 to Item 601(b)(10). Only copies of the various remunerative plans need be filed. Each individual director's or executive officer's personal agreement under the plans need not be filed, unless they contain material provisions.

Instruction 2 to Item 601(b)(10). If a material contract is executed or becomes effective during the reporting period reflected by a Form 10–QSB or Form 10–KSB, it shall be filed as an exhibit to the Form 10–QSB or Form 10–KSB filed for the corresponding period. *See* paragraph (a)(3) of this Item. With respect to quarterly reports on Form 10–QSB, only those contracts executed or becoming effective during the most recent period reflected in the report shall be filed.

(11) *Statement re: computation of per share earnings.* An explanation of the computation of per share earnings on both a primary and fully diluted basis unless the computation can be clearly determined from the registration statement or report.

(12) No exhibit required.

(13)(i) Annual report to security holders for the last fiscal year, Form 10–Q or 10–QSB or quarterly report to security holders, if incorporated by reference in the filing. Such reports, except for the parts which are expressly incorporated by reference in the filing are not deemed "filed" as part of the filing. If the financial statements in the report have been incorporated by reference in the filing, the accountant's certificate shall be manually signed in one copy. See Rule 411(b) (§ 230.411(b) of this chapter).

(ii) Statement re computation of per share earnings. An explanation of the computation of per share earnings on both a primary and fully diluted basis unless the computation can be clearly determined from the registration statement or report.

(14) *Code of ethics.* Any code of ethics, or amendment thereto, that is the subject of the disclosure required by Item 406 of Regulation S–B (§ 228.406) or Item 10 of Form 8–K (§ 249.308 of this chapter), to the extent that the small business issuer intends to satisfy the Item 406 or Item 10 requirements through filing of an exhibit.

(15) *Letter on unaudited interim financial information.* A letter, where applicable, from the independent accountant which acknowledges awareness of the use in a registration statement of a report on unaudited interim financial information. The letter is not considered a part of a registration statement prepared or certified by an accountant or a report prepared or certified by an accountant within the meaning of sections 7 and 11 of the Securities Act. Such letter may be filed with the registration statement, an amendment thereto, or a report on Form 10–QSB (§ 249.308b) which is incorporated by reference into the registration statement.

(16) *Letter on change in certifying accountant.* File the letter required by Item 304(a)(3).

(17) *Correspondence on departure of director.* Any written correspondence from a former director concerning the circumstances surrounding the former director's retirement, resignation, refusal to stand for re-election or removal, including any letter from the former director to the small business issuer stating whether the former director agrees with statements made by the small business issuer describing the former director's departure.

(18) *Letter on change in accounting principles.* Unless previously filed, a letter from the issuer's accountant stating whether any change in accounting principles or practices followed by the issuer, or any change in the method of applying any such accounting principles or practices, which affected the financial statements being filed with the Commission in the report or which is expected to affect the financial statements of future fiscal years is to an alternative principle which in his judgment is preferable under the circumstances. No such letter need be filed when such change is made in response to a standard adopted by the Financial Accounting Standards Board that creates a new accounting principle, that expresses a preference for an accounting principle, or that rejects a specific accounting principle.

(19) *Report furnished to security holders.* If the issuer makes available to its stockholders or otherwise publishes, within the period prescribed for filing the report, a document or statement containing information meeting some or all of the requirements of Part I of Form 10–Q or 10–QSB, the information called for may be incorporated by reference to such published document or statement provided copies thereof are included as an exhibit to the registration statement or to Part I of the Form 10–Q or 10–QSB report.

(20) Other documents or statements to security holders or any document incorporated by reference.

(21) *Subsidiaries of the small business issuer.* A list of all subsidiaries, the state or other jurisdiction of incorporation or organization of each, and the names under which such subsidiaries do business.

(22) *Published report regarding matters submitted to vote of security holders.* Published reports containing all of the information called for by Item 4 of Part II of Form 10–Q (or 10–QSB) or Item 4 of Part I of Form 10–K or 10–KSB which is referred to therein in lieu of providing disclosure in Form 10–Q (10–QSB) or 10–K (10–KSB), which are required to be filed as exhibits by Rule 12b–23(a)(3) under the Exchange Act.

(23) *Consents of experts and counsel.* (i) Securities Act filingsDated and manually signed written consents or a reference in the index to the location of the consent.

(ii) Exchange Act reports. If required to file a consent for material incorporated by reference in a previously filed registration statement under the Securities Act, the dated and manually signed consent to the material incorporated by reference. The consents shall be dated and manually signed.

(24) *Power of attorney.* A power of attorney that is filed with the Commission must relate to a specific filing or an amendment, provided, however, that a power of attorney relating to a registration statement under the Securities Act or an amendment thereto also may relate to any registration statement for the same offering that is to be effective upon filing pursuant to Rule 462(b) under the Securities Act (§ 230.462(b)) of this chapter.

(25) *Statement of eligibility of trustee.* (i) Form T–1 (§ 269.1 of this chapter) if an indenture is being qualified under the Trust Indenture Act, bound separately from the other exhibits.

(ii) The requirement to bind separately the statement of eligibility and qualification does not apply to statements submitted in electronic format. Rather, such statements must be submitted as exhibits in the same electronic submission as the registration statement to which they relate, or in an amendment thereto, except that electronic filers that rely on Trust Indenture Act Section 305(b)(2) for determining the eligibility of the trustee under indentures for securities to be issued, offered or sold on a delayed basis by or on behalf of the registrant shall file such statements separately in the manner prescribed by § 260.5b–1 through § 260.5b–3 of this chapter and by the EDGAR Filer Manual.

(26) *Invitations for competitive bids.* If the registration statement covers securities that the small business issuer is offering at competitive bidding, any invitation for competitive bid that the small business issuer will send or give to any person shall be filed.

(27) through (30) [Reserved].

(31) *Rule 13a–14(a)/15d–14(a) Certifications.* The certifications required by Rule 13a–14(a) (17 CFR 240.13a–14(a)) or Rule 15d–14(a) (17 CFR 240.15d–14(a)) exactly as set forth below:

Certifications *

I, [identify the certifying individual], certify that:

1. I have reviewed this [specify report] of [identify small business issuer];

2. Based on my knowledge, this report does not contain any untrue statement of a material fact or omit to state a material fact necessary to make the statements made, in light of the circumstances under which such statements were made, not misleading with respect to the period covered by this report;

3. Based on my knowledge, the financial statements, and other financial information included in this report, fairly present in all material respects the financial condition, results of operations and cash flows of the small business issuer as of, and for, the periods presented in this report;

4. The small business issuer's other certifying officer(s) and I are responsible for establishing and maintaining disclosure controls and procedures (as defined in Exchange Act Rules 13a–15(e) and 15d–15(e)) and internal control over financial reporting (as defined in Exchange Act Rules 13a–15(f) and 15d–15(f)) for the small business issuer and have:

(a) Designed such disclosure controls and procedures, or caused such disclosure controls and procedures to be designed under our supervision, to ensure that material information relating to the small business issuer, including its consolidated subsidiaries, is made known to us by others within those entities, particularly during the period in which this report is being prepared;

(b) Designed such internal control over financial reporting, or caused such internal control over financial reporting to be designed under our supervision, to provide reasonable assurance regarding the reliability of financial reporting and the preparation of financial statements for external purposes in accordance with generally accepted accounting principles;

(c) Evaluated the effectiveness of the small business issuer's disclosure controls and procedures and presented in this report our conclusions about the effectiveness of the disclosure controls and procedures, as of the end of the period covered by this report based on such evaluation; and

(d) Disclosed in this report any change in the small business issuer's internal control over financial reporting that occurred during the small business issuer's most recent fiscal quarter (the small business issuer's fourth fiscal quarter in the case of an annual report) that has materially affected, or is reasonably likely to materially affect, the small business issuer's internal control over financial reporting; and

5. The small business issuer's other certifying officer(s) and I have disclosed, based on our most recent evaluation of internal control over financial reporting, to the small business issuer's auditors and the audit committee of the small business issuer's board of directors (or persons performing the equivalent functions):

(a) All significant deficiencies and material weaknesses in the design or operation of internal control over financial reporting which are reasonably likely to adversely affect the small business issuer's ability to record, process, summarize and report financial information; and

(b) Any fraud, whether or not material, that involves management or other employees who have a significant role in the small business issuer's internal control over financial reporting.

Date:

____

____

[Signature]
[Title]

* Provide a separate certification for each principal executive officer and principal financial officer of the small business issuer. See Rules 13a–14(a) and 15d–14(a).

(32) *Section 1350 Certifications.*

(i) The certifications required by Rule 13a–14(b) (17 CFR 240.13a–14(b)) or Rule 15d–14(b) (17 CFR 240.15d–14(b)) and Section 1350 of Chapter 63 of Title 18 of the United States Code (18 U.S.C. 1350).

(ii) A certification furnished pursuant to this Item will not be deemed "filed" for purposes of section 18 of the Exchange Act, or otherwise subject to the liability of that section. Such certification will not be deemed to be incorporated by reference into any filing under the Securities Act or the Exchange Act, except to the extent that the small business issuer specifically incorporates it by reference.

(33) through (98) [Reserved].

(99) *Additional exhibits.* (i) Any additional exhibits if listed and described in the exhibit index.

(ii) If pursuant to Section 11(a) of the Securities Act (15 U.S.C. 77k(a)) an issuer makes generally available to its security holders an earnings statement covering a period of at least 12 months beginning after the effective date of the registration statement, and if such earnings statement is made available by "other methods" than those specified in paragraphs (a) or (b) of § 230.158 of this chapter, it must be filed as an exhibit to the Form 10–QSB or the Form 10–KSB, as appropriate, covering the period in which the earnings statement was released.

(100) *XBRL-Related Documents*. An electronic filer that participates in the voluntary XBRL (eXtensible Business Reporting Language) program may submit XBRL-Related Documents (§ 232.11 of this chapter) in electronic format as an exhibit to: the filing to which they relate; an amendment to such filing; or a Form 8–K (§ 249.308 of this chapter) that references such filing, if the Form 8–K is submitted no earlier than the date of that filing.

Item 701. Recent Sales of Unregistered Securities; Use of Proceeds from Registered Securities

Give the following information for all securities that the small business issuer sold within the past three years without registering the securities under the Securities Act.

(a) The date, title and amount of securities sold.

(b) Give the names of the principal underwriters, if any. If the small business issuer did not publicly offer any securities, identify the persons or class of persons to whom the small business issuer sold the securities.

(c) For securities sold for cash, the total offering price and the total underwriting discounts or commissions. For securities sold other than for cash, describe the transaction and the type and amount of consideration received by the small business issuer.

(d) The section of the Securities Act or the rule of the Commission under which the small business issuer claimed exemption from registration and the facts relied upon to make the exemption available.

(e) If the information called for by this paragraph (e) is being presented on Form 8–K, Form 10–QSB, Form 10–Q, Form 10–KSB or Form 10–K (§§ 249.308, 249.308b, 249.308a, 249.310b or 249.310) under the Exchange Act, and where the securities sold by the registrant are convertible or exchangeable into equity securities, or are warrants or options representing equity securities, disclose the terms of conversion or exercise of the securities.

(f) As required by § 230.463 of this chapter, following the effective date of the first registration statement filed under the Securities Act by an issuer, the issuer or successor issuer shall report the use of proceeds on its first periodic report filed pursuant to sections 13(a) and 15(d) of the Exchange Act (15 U.S.C. 78m(a) and 78o(d)) after effectiveness of its Securities Act registration statement, and thereafter on each of its subsequent periodic reports filed pursuant to sections 13(a) and 15(d) of the Exchange Act through the later of disclosure of the application of all the offering proceeds, or disclosure of the termination of the offering. If a report of the use of proceeds is required with respect to the first effective registration statement of the predecessor issuer, the successor issuer shall provide such a report. The information provided pursuant to paragraphs (f)(2) through (f)(4) of this Item need only be provided with respect to the first periodic report filed pursuant to sections 13(a) and 15(d) of the Exchange Act after effectiveness of the registration statement filed under the Securities Act. Subsequent periodic reports filed pursuant to sections 13(a) and 15(d) of the Exchange Act need only provide the information required in paragraphs (f)(2) through (f)(4) of this Item if any of such required information has changed since the last periodic report filed. In disclosing the use of proceeds in the first periodic report filed pursuant to the Exchange Act, the issuer or successor issuer should include the following information:

(1) The effective date of the Securities Act registration statement for which the use of proceeds information is being disclosed and the Commission file number assigned to the registration statement;

(2) If the offering has commenced, the offering date, and if the offering has not commenced, an explanation why it has not;

(3) If the offering terminated before any securities were sold, an explanation for such termination; and

(4) If the offering did not terminate before any securities were sold, disclose:

(i) Whether the offering has terminated and, if so, whether it terminated before the sale of all securities registered;

(ii) The name(s) of the managing underwriter(s), if any;

(iii) The title of each class of securities registered and, where a class of convertible securities is being registered, the title of any class of securities into which such securities may be converted;

(iv) For each class of securities (other than a class of securities into which a class of convertible securities registered may be converted without additional payment to the issuer) the following information, provided for both the account of the issuer and the account(s) of any selling security holder(s): the amount registered, the aggregate price of the offering amount registered, the amount sold and the aggregate offering price of the amount sold to date;

(v) From the effective date of the Securities Act registration statement to the ending date of the reporting period, the amount of expenses incurred for the issuer's account in connection with the issuance and distribution of the securities registered for underwriting discounts and commissions, finders' fees, expenses paid to or for underwriters, other expenses and total expenses. Indicate if a reasonable estimate for the amount of expenses incurred is provided instead of the actual amount of expenses. Indicate whether such payments were:

(A) Direct or indirect payments to directors, officers, general partners of the issuer or their associates; to persons owning ten (10) percent or more of any class of equity securities of the issuer, and to affiliates of the issuer; or

(B) Direct or indirect payments to others;

(vi) The net offering proceeds to the issuer after deducting the total expenses described in paragraph (f)(4)(v) of this Item:

(vii) From the effective date of the Securities Act registration statement to the ending date of the reporting period, the amount of net offering proceeds to the issuer used for construction of plant, building and facilities; purchase and installation of machinery and equipment; purchases of real estate; acquisition of other business(es); repayment of indebtedness; working capital; temporary investments (which should be specified); and any other purposes for which at least five (5) percent of the issuer's total offering proceeds or $100,000 (whichever is less) has been used (which should be specified). Indicate if a reasonable estimate for the amount of net offering proceeds applied is provided instead of the actual amount of net offering proceeds used. Indicate whether such payments were:

(A) Direct or indirect payments to directors, officers, general partners of the issuer or their associates; to persons owning ten (10) percent or more of any class of equity securities of the issuer, and to affiliates of the issuer; or

(B) Direct or indirect payments to others; and

(viii) If the use of proceeds in paragraph (f)(4)(vii) of this Item represents a material change in the use of proceeds described in the prospectus, the issuer should describe briefly the material change.

Item 702. Indemnification of Directors and Officers

State whether any statute, charter provisions, by-laws, contract or other arrangements that insures or indemnifies a controlling person, director or officer of the small business issuer affects his or her liability in that capacity.

Item 703. Purchases of Equity Securities by the Small Business Issuer and Affiliated Purchasers

(a) In the following tabular format, provide the information specified in paragraph (b) of this Item with respect to any purchase made by or on behalf of the small business issuer or any "affiliated purchaser," as defined in Rule 10b–18(a)(3) of this chapter, of shares or other units of any class of the small business issuer's equity securities that is registered by the small business issuer pursuant to section 12 of the Exchange Act. (15 U.S.C.A. 78*l*).

SMALL BUSINESS ISSUER PURCHASES OF EQUITY SECURITIES

Period	(a) Total Number of Shares (or Units) Purchased	(b) Average Price Paid per Share (or Unit)	(c) Total Number of Shares (or Units) Purchased as Part of Publicly Announced Plans or Programs	(d) Maximum Number (or Approximate Dollar Value) of Shares (or Units) that May Yet Be Purchased Under the Plans or Programs
Month #1 (identify beginning and ending dates)				
Month #2 (identify beginning and ending dates)				
Month #3 (identify beginning and ending dates)				
Total				

(b) The table shall include the following information for each class or series of securities for each month included in the period covered by the report:

(1) The total number of shares (or units) purchased (column (a));

Instruction to paragraph (b)(1) of Item 703

Include in this column all small business issuer repurchases, including those made pursuant to publicly announced plans or programs and those not made pursuant to publicly announced plans or programs. Briefly disclose, by footnote to the table, the number of shares purchased other than through a publicly announced plan or program and the nature of the transaction (e.g., whether the purchases were made in open-market transactions, tender offers, in satisfaction of the company's obligations upon exercise of outstanding put options issued by the company, or other transactions).

(2) The average price paid per share (or unit) (column (b));

(3) The total number of shares (or units) purchased as part of publicly announced repurchase plans or programs (column (c)); and

(4) The maximum number (or approximate dollar value) of shares (or units) that may yet be purchased under the plans or programs (column (d)).

Instructions to paragraphs (b)(3) and (b)(4) of Item 703

1. In the table, disclose this information in the aggregate for all plans or programs publicly announced.

2. By footnote to the table, indicate:

a. The date each plan or program was announced;

b. The dollar amount (or share or unit amount) approved;

c. The expiration date (if any) of each plan or program;

d. Each plan or program that has expired during the period covered by the table; and

e. Each plan or program the small business issuer has determined to terminate prior to expiration, or under which the small business issuer does not intend to make further purchases.

Instruction to Item 703

Disclose all purchases covered by this Item, including purchases that do not satisfy the conditions of the safe harbor of Rule 10b–18 of this chapter.

REGULATION S–K—STANDARD INSTRUCTIONS FOR FILING FORMS UNDER SECURITIES ACT OF 1933, SECURITIES EXCHANGE ACT OF 1934 AND ENERGY POLICY AND CONSERVATION ACT OF 1975

(Cite as 17 CFR 229.__)

Subpart 1—General

ATTENTION ELECTRONIC FILERS

THIS REGULATION SHOULD BE READ IN CONJUNCTION WITH REGULATION S–T (PART 232 OF THIS CHAPTER), WHICH GOVERNS THE PREPARATION AND SUBMISSION OF DOCUMENTS IN ELECTRONIC FORMAT. MANY PROVISIONS RELATING TO THE PREPARATION AND SUBMISSION OF DOCUMENTS IN PAPER FORMAT CONTAINED IN THIS REGULATION ARE SUPERSEDED BY THE PROVISIONS OF REGULATION S–T FOR DOCUMENTS REQUIRED TO BE FILED IN ELECTRONIC FORMAT.

Item 10. General

(a) *Application of Regulation S–K.* This part (together with the General Rules and Regulations under the Securities Act of 1933, as amended (''Securities Act''), and the Securities Exchange Act of 1934, as amended (''Exchange Act'') the Interpretative Releases under these Acts) and the forms under these Acts states the requirements applicable to the content of the non-financial statement portions of:

(1) Registration statements under the Securities Act to the extent provided in the forms to be used for registration under such Act; and

(2) Registration statements under section 12 (subpart C of part 249 of this chapter), annual or other reports under sections 13 and 15(d) (subparts D and E of part 249 of this chapter), going-private transaction statements under section 13 (part 240 of this chapter), tender offer statements under sections 13 and 14 (part 240 of this chapter), annual reports to security holders and proxy and information statements under section 14 (part 240 of this chapter), and any other

documents required to be filed under the Exchange Act, to the extent provided in the forms and rules under that Act.

(b) *Commission Policy on Projections.* The Commission encourages the use in documents specified in Rule 175 under the Securities Act and Rule 3b–6 under the Exchange Act of management's projections of future economic performance that have a reasonable basis and are presented in an appropriate format. The guidelines set forth herein represent the Commission's views on important factors to be considered in formulating and disclosing such projections.

(1) *Basis for Projections.* The Commission believes that management must have the option to present in Commission filings its good faith assessment of a registrant's future performance. Management, however, must have a reasonable basis for such an assessment. Although a history of operations or experience in projecting may be among the factors providing a basis for management's assessment, the Commission does not believe that a registrant always must have had such a history or experience in order to formulate projections with a reasonable basis. An outside review of management's projections may furnish additional support for having a reasonable basis for a projection. If management decides to include a report of such a review in a Commission filing, there also should be disclosure of the qualifications of the reviewer, the extent of the review, the relationship between the reviewer and the registrant, and other material factors concerning the process by which any outside review was sought or obtained. Moreover, in the case of a registration statement under the Securities Act, the reviewer would be deemed an expert and an appropriate consent must be filed with the registration statement.

(2) *Format for Projections.* In determining the appropriate format for projections included in Commission filings, consideration must be given to, among other things, the financial items to be projected, the period to be covered, and the manner of presentation to be used. Although traditionally projections have been given for three financial items generally considered to be of primary importance to investors (revenues, net income (loss) and earnings (loss) per share), projection information need not necessarily be limited to these three items. However, management should take care to assure that the choice of items projected is not susceptible of misleading inferences through selective projection of only favorable items. Revenues, net income (loss) and earnings (loss) per share usually are presented together in order to avoid any misleading inferences that may arise when the individual items reflect contradictory trends. There may be instances, however, when it is appropriate to present earnings (loss) from continuing operations, or income (loss) before extraordinary items in addition to or in lieu of net income (loss). It generally would be misleading to present sales or revenue projections without one of the foregoing measures of income. The period that appropriately may be covered by a projection depends to a large extent on the particular circumstances of the company involved. For certain companies in certain industries, a projection covering a two or three year period may be entirely reasonable. Other companies may not have a reasonable basis for projections beyond the current year. Accordingly, management should select the period most appropriate in the circumstances. In addition, management, in making a projection, should disclose what, in its opinion, is the most probable specific amount or the most reasonable range for each financial item projected based on the selected assumptions. Ranges, however, should not be so wide as to make the disclosures meaningless. Moreover, several projections based on varying assumptions may be judged by management to be more meaningful than a single number or range and would be permitted.

(3) *Investor Understanding.* (i) When management chooses to include its projec-

tions in a Commission filing, the disclosures accompanying the projections should facilitate investor understanding of the basis for and limitations of projections. In this regard investors should be cautioned against attributing undue certainty to management's assessment, and the Commission believes that investors would be aided by a statement indicating management's intention regarding the furnishing of updated projections. The Commission also believes that investor understanding would be enhanced by disclosure of the assumptions which in management's opinion are most significant to the projections or are the key factors upon which the financial results of the enterprise depend and encourages disclosure of assumptions in a manner that will provide a framework for analysis of the projection.

(ii) Management also should consider whether disclosure of the accuracy or inaccuracy of previous projections would provide investors with important insights into the limitations of projections. In this regard, consideration should be given to presenting the projections in a format that will facilitate subsequent analysis of the reasons for differences between actual and forecast results. An important benefit may arise from the systematic analysis of variances between projected and actual results on a continuing basis, since such disclosure may highlight for investors the most significant risk and profit-sensitive areas in a business operation.

(iii) With respect to previously issued projections, registrants are reminded of their responsibility to make full and prompt disclosure of material facts, both favorable and unfavorable, regarding their financial condition. This responsibility may extend to situations where management knows or has reason to know that its previously disclosed projects no longer have a reasonable basis.

(iv) Since a registrant's ability to make projections with relative confidence may vary with all the facts and circumstances, the responsibility for determining whether to discontinue or to resume making projections is best left to management. However, the Commission encourages registrants not to discontinue or to resume projections in Commission filings without a reasonable basis.

(c) *Commission Policy on Security Ratings.* In view of the importance of security ratings ("ratings") to investors and the marketplace, the Commission permits registrants to disclose, on a voluntary basis, ratings assigned by rating organizations to classes of debt securities, convertible debt securities and preferred stock in registration statements and periodic reports. In addition, the Commission permits, pursuant to Rule 134(a)(14) under the Securities Act, voluntary disclosure of ratings assigned by any nationally recognized statistical rating organizations ("NRSROs") in certain communications deemed not to be a prospectus ("tombstone advertisements"). Set forth herein are the Commission's views on important matters to be considered in disclosing security ratings.

(1) *Securities Act Filings.* (i) If a registrant includes in a registration statement filed under the Securities Act any rating(s) assigned to a class of securities, it should consider including: (A) Any other rating intended for public dissemination assigned to such class by a NRSRO ("additional NRSRO rating") that is available on the date of the initial filing of the document and that is materially different from any rating disclosed; and (B) the name of each rating organization whose rating is disclosed; each such rating organization's definition or description of the category in which it rated the class of securities; the relative rank of each rating within the assigning rating organization's overall classification system; and a statement informing investors that a security rating is not a recommendation to buy, sell or hold securities, that it may be subject to revision or withdrawal at any time by the assigning rating organization, and

that each rating should be evaluated independently of any other rating. The registrant also should include the written consent of any rating organization that is not a NRSRO whose rating is included. With respect to the written consent of any NRSRO whose rating is included, see Rule 436(g) under the Securities Act. When the registrant has filed a registration statement on Form F–9 (§ 239.39 of this chapter), see Rule 436(g) (§ 230.436(g) of this chapter) under the Securities Act with respect to the written consent of any rating organization specified in the Instruction to paragraph (a)(2) of General Instruction I of Form F–9.

(ii) If a change in a rating already included is available subsequent to the filing of the registration statement, but prior to its effectiveness, the registrant should consider including such rating change in the final prospectus. If the rating change is material or if a materially different rating from any disclosed becomes available during this period, the registrant should consider amending the registration statement to include the rating change or additional rating and recirculating the preliminary prospectus.

(iii) If a materially different additional NRSRO rating or a material change in a rating already included becomes available during any period in which offers or sales are being made, the registrant should consider disclosing such additional rating or rating change by means of post-effective amendment or sticker to the prospectus pursuant to Rule 424(b) under the Securities Act, unless, in the case of a registration statement on Form S–3, it has been disclosed in a document incorporated by reference into the registration statement subsequent to its effectiveness and prior to the termination of the offering.

(2) *Exchange Act Filings.* (i) If a registrant includes in a registration statement or periodic report filed under the Exchange Act any rating(s) assigned to a class of securities, it should consider including the information specified in paragraphs (c)(1)(i)(A) and (B) of this section.

(ii) If there is a material change in the rating(s) assigned by any NRSRO(s) to any outstanding class(es) of securities of a registrant subject to the reporting requirements of section 13(a) or 15(d) of the Exchange Act, the registrant should consider filing a report on Form 8–K or other appropriate report under the Exchange Act disclosing such rating change.

(d) *Incorporation by Reference.* Where rules, regulations, or instructions to forms of the Commission permit incorporation by reference, a document may be so incorporated by reference to the specific document and to the prior filing or submission in which such document was physically filed or submitted. Except where a registrant or issuer is expressly required to incorporate a document or documents by reference (or for purposes of Item 1100(c) of Regulation AB (§ 229.1100(c)) with respect to an asset-backed issuer, as that term is defined in Item 1101 of Regulation AB (§ 229.1101)), reference may not be made to any document which incorporates another document by reference if the pertinent portion of the document containing the information or financial statements to be incorporated by reference includes an incorporation by reference to another document. No document on file with the Commission for more than five years may be incorporated by reference except:

(1) Documents contained in registration statements, which may be incorporated by reference as long as the registrant has a reporting requirement with the Commission; or

(2) Documents that the registrant specifically identifies by physical location by SEC file number reference, provided such materials have not been disposed of by the Commission pursuant to its Records Control Schedule (17 CFR 200.80f).

(e) *Use of non-GAAP financial measures in Commission filings.* (1) Whenever one or more non-GAAP financial measures are included in a filing with the Commission:

(i) The registrant must include the following in the filing:

(A) A presentation, with equal or greater prominence, of the most directly comparable financial measure or measures calculated and presented in accordance with Generally Accepted Accounting Principles (GAAP);

(B) A reconciliation (by schedule or other clearly understandable method), which shall be quantitative for historical non-GAAP measures presented, and quantitative, to the extent available without unreasonable efforts, for forward-looking information, of the differences between the non-GAAP financial measure disclosed or released with the most directly comparable financial measure or measures calculated and presented in accordance with GAAP identified in paragraph (e)(1)(i)(A) of this section;

(C) A statement disclosing the reasons why the registrant's management believes that presentation of the non-GAAP financial measure provides useful information to investors regarding the registrant's financial condition and results of operations; and

(D) To the extent material, a statement disclosing the additional purposes, if any, for which the registrant's management uses the non-GAAP financial measure that are not disclosed pursuant to paragraph (e)(1)(i)(C) of this section; and

(ii) A registrant must not:

(A) Exclude charges or liabilities that required, or will require, cash settlement, or would have required cash settlement absent an ability to settle in another manner, from non-GAAP liquidity measures, other than the measures earnings before interest and taxes (EBIT) and earnings before interest, taxes, depreciation, and amortization (EBITDA);

(B) Adjust a non-GAAP performance measure to eliminate or smooth items identified as non-recurring, infrequent or unusual, when the nature of the charge or gain is such that it is reasonably likely to recur within two years or there was a similar charge or gain within the prior two years;

(C) Present non-GAAP financial measures on the face of the registrant's financial statements prepared in accordance with GAAP or in the accompanying notes;

(D) Present non-GAAP financial measures on the face of any *pro forma* financial information required to be disclosed by Article 11 of Regulation S–X (17 CFR 210.11–01 through 210.11–03); or

(E) Use titles or descriptions of non-GAAP financial measures that are the same as, or confusingly similar to, titles or descriptions used for GAAP financial measures; and

(iii) If the filing is not an annual report on Form 10–K or Form 20–F (17 CFR 249.220f), a registrant need not include the information required by paragraphs (e)(1)(i)(C) and (e)(1)(i)(D) of this section if that information was included in its most recent annual report on Form 10–K or Form 20–F or a more recent filing, provided that the required information is updated to the extent necessary to meet the requirements of paragraphs (e)(1)(i)(C) and (e)(1)(i)(D) of this section at the time of the registrant's current filing.

(2) For purposes of this paragraph (e), a non-GAAP financial measure is a numerical measure of a registrant's historical or future financial performance, financial position or cash flows that:

(i) Excludes amounts, or is subject to adjustments that have the effect of excluding amounts, that are included in the most directly comparable measure calculated and presented in accordance with GAAP in the statement of income, balance sheet or statement of cash flows (or equivalent statements) of the issuer; or

(ii) Includes amounts, or is subject to adjustments that have the effect of including amounts, that are excluded from the most directly comparable measure so calculated and presented.

(3) For purposes of this paragraph (e), GAAP refers to generally accepted accounting principles in the United States, except that:

(i) In the case of foreign private issuers whose primary financial statements are prepared in accordance with non-U.S. generally accepted accounting principles, GAAP refers to the principles under which those primary financial statements are prepared; and

(ii) In the case of foreign private issuers that include a non-GAAP financial measure derived from or based on a measure calculated in accordance with U.S. generally accepted accounting principles, GAAP refers to U.S. generally accepted accounting principles for purposes of the application of the requirements of this paragraph (e) to the disclosure of that measure.

(4) For purposes of this paragraph (e), non-GAAP financial measures exclude:

(i) Operating and other statistical measures; and

(ii) Ratios or statistical measures calculated using exclusively one or both of:

(A) Financial measures calculated in accordance with GAAP; and

(B) Operating measures or other measures that are not non-GAAP financial measures.

(5) For purposes of this paragraph (e), non-GAAP financial measures exclude financial measures required to be disclosed by GAAP, Commission rules, or a system of regulation of a government or governmental authority or self-regulatory organization that is applicable to the registrant. However, the financial measure should be presented outside of the financial statements unless the financial measure is required or expressly permitted by the standard-setter that is responsible for establishing the GAAP used in such financial statements.

(6) The requirements of paragraph (e) of this section shall not apply to a non-GAAP financial measure included in disclosure relating to a proposed business combination, the entity resulting therefrom or an entity that is a party thereto, if the disclosure is contained in a communication that is subject to § 230.425 of this chapter, § 240.14a–12 or § 240.14d–2(b)(2) of this chapter or § 229.1015 of this chapter.

(7) The requirements of paragraph (e) of this section shall not apply to investment companies registered under section 8 of the Investment Company Act of 1940 (15 U.S.C. 80a–8).

Note to paragraph (e). A non-GAAP financial measure that would otherwise be prohibited by paragraph (e)(1)(ii) of this section is permitted in a filing of a foreign private issuer if:

1. The non-GAAP financial measure relates to the GAAP used in the registrant's primary financial statements included in its filing with the Commission;

2. The non-GAAP financial measure is required or expressly permitted by the standard-setter that is responsible for establishing the GAAP used in such financial statements; and

3. The non-GAAP financial measure is included in the annual report prepared by the registrant for use in the jurisdiction in which it is domiciled, incorporated or organized or for distribution to its security holders.

Subpart 100—Business

Item 101. Description of Business

(a) *General Development of Business.* Describe the general development of the business of the registrant, its subsidiaries and any predecessor(s) during the past five years, or such shorter period as the registrant may have been engaged in business. Information shall be disclosed for earlier periods if material to an understanding of the general development of the business.

(1) In describing developments, information shall be given as to matters such as the following: the year in which the registrant was organized and its form of organization; the nature and results of any bankruptcy, receivership or similar proceedings with respect to the registrant or any of its significant subsidiaries; the nature and results of any other material reclassification, merger or consolidation of the registrant or any of its significant subsidiaries; the acquisition or disposition of any material amount of assets otherwise than in the ordinary course of business; and any material changes in the mode of conducting the business.

(2) Registrants, (i) filing a registration statement on Form S–1 under the Securities Act or on Form 10 under the Exchange Act, (ii) not subject to the reporting requirements of section 13(a) or 15(d) of the Exchange Act immediately prior to the filing of such registration statement, and (iii) that (including predecessors) have not received revenue from operations during each of the three fiscal years immediately prior to the filing of registration statement, shall provide the following information: (A) if the registration statement is filed prior to the end of the registrant's second fiscal quarter, a description of the registrant's plan of operation for the remainder of the fiscal year; or (B) if the registration statement is filed subsequent to the end of the registrant's second fiscal quarter, a description of the registrant's plan of operation for the remainder of the fiscal year and for the first six months of the next fiscal year. If such information is not available, the reasons for its not being available shall be stated. Disclosure relating to any plan shall include such matters as:

(1) In the case of a registration statement on Form S–1, a statement in narrative form indicating the registrant's opinion as to the period of time that the proceeds from the offering will satisfy cash requirements and whether in the next six months it will be necessary to raise additional funds to meet the expenditures required for operating the business of the registrant; the specific reasons for such opinion shall be set forth and categories of expenditures and sources of cash resources shall be identified; however, amounts of expenditures and cash resources need not be provided; in addition, if the narrative statement is based on a cash budget, such budget shall be furnished to the Commission as supplemental information, but not as part of the registration statement;

(2) An explanation of material product research and development to be performed during the period covered in the plan;

(3) Any anticipated material acquisition of plant and equipment and the capacity thereof;

(4) Any anticipated material changes in number of employees in the various departments such as research and development, production, sales or administration; and

(5) Other material areas which may be peculiar to the registrant's business.

(b) *Financial Information About Segments.* Report for each segment, as defined by generally accepted accounting principles, revenues from external customers, a measure of profit or loss and total assets. A registrant must report this information for each of the last three fiscal years or for as long as it has been in business, whichever period is shorter. If the information provided in response to this paragraph (b) conforms with generally accepted accounting principles, a registrant may include in its financial statements a cross reference to this data in lieu of presenting duplicative information in the financial statements; conversely, a registrant may cross reference to the financial statements.

(1) If a registrant changes the structure of its internal organization in a manner that causes the composition of its reportable segments to change, the registrant must restate the corresponding information for earlier periods, including interim periods, unless it is impracticable to do so. Following a change in the composition of its reportable segments, a registrant shall disclose whether it has restated the corresponding items of segment information for earlier periods. If it has not restated the items from earlier periods, the registrant shall disclose in the year in which the change occurs segment information for the current period under both the old basis and the new basis of segmentation, unless it is impracticable to do so.

(2) If the registrant includes, or is required by Article 3 of Regulation S–X to include, interim financial statements, discuss any facts relating to the performance of any of the segments during the period which, in the opinion of management, indicate that the three year segment financial data may not be indicative of current or future operations of the segment. Comparative financial information shall be included to the extent necessary to the discussion.

(c) *Narrative Description of Business.* (1) Describe the business done and intended to be done by the registrant and its subsidiaries, focusing upon the registrant's dominant segment or each reportable segment about which financial information is presented in the financial statements. To the extent material to an understanding of the registrant's business taken as a whole, the description of each such segment shall include the information specified in paragraphs (c)(1)(i) through (x) of this Item. The matters specified in paragraphs (c)(1)(xi) through (xiii) of this Item shall be discussed with respect to the registrant's business in general; where material, the segments to which these matters are significant shall be identified.

(i) The principal products produced and services rendered by the registrant in the segment and the principal markets for, and methods of distribution of, the segment's principal products and services. In addition, state for each of the last three fiscal years the amount or percentage of total revenue contributed by any class of similar products or services which accounted for 10 percent or more of consolidated revenue in any of the last three fiscal years or 15 percent or more of consolidated revenue, if total revenue did not exceed $50,000,000 during any of such fiscal years.

(ii) A description of the status of a product or segment (e.g. whether in the planning stage, whether prototypes exist, the degree to which product design has progressed or whether further engineering is necessary), if there has been a public announcement of, or if the registrant otherwise has made public information about, a new product or segment that would require the investment of a material amount of the assets of the registrant or that otherwise is material. This paragraph is not intended to require disclosure of otherwise nonpublic corporate information the disclosure of which would affect adversely the registrant's competitive position.

(iii) The sources and availability of raw materials.

(iv) The importance to the segment and the duration and effect of all patents, trademarks, licenses, franchises and concessions held.

(v) The extent to which the business of the segment is or may be seasonal.

(vi) The practices of the registrant and the industry (respective industries) relating to working capital items (e.g., where the registrant is required to carry significant amounts of inventory to meet rapid delivery requirements of customers or to assure itself of a continuous allotment of goods from suppliers; where the registrant provides rights to return merchandise; or where the registrant has provided extended payment terms to customers).

(vii) The dependence of the segment upon a single customer, or a few customers, the loss of any one or more of which would have a material adverse effect on the segment. The name of any customer and its relationship, if any, with the registrant or its subsidiaries shall be disclosed if sales to the customer by one or more segments are made in an aggregate amount equal to 10 percent or more of the registrant's consolidated revenues and the loss of such customer would have a material adverse effect on the registrant and its subsidiaries taken as a whole. The names of other customers may be included, unless in the particular case the effect of including the names would be misleading. For purposes of this paragraph, a group of customers under common control or customers that are affiliates of each other shall be regarded as a single customer.

(viii) The dollar amount of backlog orders believed to be firm, as of a recent date and as of a comparable date in the preceding fiscal year, together with an indication of the portion thereof not reasonably expected to be filled within the current fiscal year, and seasonal or other material aspects of the backlog. (There may be included as firm orders government orders that are firm but not yet funded and contracts awarded but not yet signed, provided an appropriate statement is added to explain the nature of such orders and the amount thereof. The portion of orders already included in sales or operating revenues on the basis of percentage of completion or program accounting shall be excluded.)

(ix) A description of any material portion of the business that may be subject to renegotiation of profits or termination of contracts or subcontracts at the election of the Government.

(x) Competitive conditions in the business involved including, where material, the identity of the particular markets in which the registrant competes, an estimate of the number of competitors and the registrant's competitive position, if known or reasonably available to the registrant. Separate consideration shall be given to the principal products or services or classes of products or services of the segment, if any. Generally, the names of competitors need not be disclosed. The registrant may include such names, unless in the particular case the effect of including the names would be misleading. Where, however, the registrant knows or has reason to know that one or a small number of competitors is dominant in the industry it shall be identified. The principal methods of competition (e.g., price, service, warranty or product performance) shall be identified, and positive and negative factors pertaining to the competitive position of the registrant, to the extent that they exist, shall be explained if known or reasonably available to the registrant.

(xi) If material, the estimated amount spent during each of the last three fiscal years on company-sponsored research and development activities determined in accordance with generally accepted accounting principles. In addition, state, if material, the estimated dollar amount spent during each of such years on customer-sponsored research activities relating to the development of new products, services or techniques or the improvement of existing products, services or techniques.

(xii) Appropriate disclosure also shall be made as to the material effects that compliance with Federal, State and local provisions which have been enacted or adopted regulating the discharge of materials into the environment, or otherwise relating to the protection of the environment, may have upon the capital expenditures, earnings and competitive position of the registrant and its subsidiaries. The registrant shall disclose any material estimated capital expenditures for environmental control facilities for the remainder of its current fiscal year and its succeeding fiscal year and for such further periods as the registrant may deem material.

(xiii) The number of persons employed by the registrant.

(d) *Financial Information About Geographic Areas.* (1) State for each of the registrant's last three fiscal years, or for each fiscal year the registrant has been engaged in business, whichever period is shorter:

(i) Revenues from external customers attributed to:

(A) The registrant's country of domicile;

(B) All foreign countries, in total, from which the registrant derives revenues; and

(C) Any individual foreign country, if material. Disclose the basis for attributing revenues from external customers to individual countries.

(ii) Long-lived assets, other than financial instruments, long-term customer relationships of a financial institution, mortgage and other servicing rights, deferred policy acquisition costs, and deferred tax assets, located in:

(A) The registrant's country of domicile;

(B) All foreign countries, in total, in which the registrant holds assets; and

(C) Any individual foreign country, if material.

(2) A registrant shall report the amounts based on the financial information that it uses to produce the general-purpose financial statements. If providing the geographic information is impracticable, the registrant shall disclose that fact. A registrant may wish to provide, in addition to the information required by paragraph (d)(1) of this section, subtotals of geographic information about groups of countries. To the extent that the disclosed information conforms with generally accepted accounting principles, the registrant may include in its financial statements a cross reference to this data in lieu of presenting duplicative data in its financial statements; conversely, a registrant may cross-reference to the financial statements.

(3) A registrant shall describe any risks attendant to the foreign operations and any dependence on one or more of the registrant's segments upon such foreign operations, unless it would be more appropriate to discuss this information in connection with the description of one or more of the registrant's segments under paragraph (c) of this item.

(4) If the registrant includes, or is required by Article 3 of Regulation S-X (17 CFR 210), to include, interim financial statements, discuss any facts relating to the information furnished under this paragraph (d) that, in the opinion of management, indicate that the three year financial data for geographic areas may not be indicative of current or future operations. To the extent necessary to the discussion, include comparative information.

(e) *Available information.* Disclose the information in paragraphs (e)(1), (e)(2) and (e)(3) of this section in any registration statement you file under the Securities Act (15 U.S.C. 77a *et seq.*), and disclose the information in paragraphs (e)(3) and (e)(4) of this section if you are an accelerated filer (as defined in § 240.12b–2 of this chapter) filing an annual report on Form 10–K (§ 249.310 of this chapter):

(1) Whether you file reports with the Securities and Exchange Commission. If you

are a reporting company, identify the reports and other information you file with the SEC.

(2) That the public may read and copy any materials you file with the SEC at the SEC's Public Reference Room at 450 Fifth Street, NW., Washington, DC 20549. State that the public may obtain information on the operation of the Public Reference Room by calling the SEC at 1–800–SEC–0330. If you are an electronic filer, state that the SEC maintains an Internet site that contains reports, proxy and information statements, and other information regarding issuers that file electronically with the SEC and state the address of that site (*http://www.sec.gov*).

(3) You are encouraged to give your Internet address, if available, except that if you are an accelerated filer filing your annual report on Form 10–K, you must disclose your Internet address, if you have one.

(4)(i) Whether you make available free of charge or through your Internet website, if you have one, your annual report on Form 10–K, quarterly reports on Form 10–Q (§ 249.308a of this chapter), current reports on Form 8–K (§ 249.308 of this chapter), and amendments to those reports filed or furnished pursuant to Section 13(a) or 15(d) of the Exchange Act (15 U.S.C. 78m(a) or 78o(d)) as soon as reasonably practicable after you electronically file such material with, or furnish it to, the SEC;

(ii) If you do not make your filings available in this manner, the reasons you do not do so (including, where applicable, that you do not have an Internet website); and

(iii) If you do not make your filings available in this manner, whether you voluntarily will provide electronic or paper copies of your filings free of charge upon request.

(f) *Reports to security holders.* Disclose the following information in any registration statement you file under the Securities Act:

(1) If the SEC's proxy rules or regulations, or stock exchange requirements, do not require you to send an annual report to security holders or to holders of American depository receipts, describe briefly the nature and frequency of reports that you will give to security holders. Specify whether the reports that you give will contain financial information that has been examined and reported on, with an opinion expressed "by" an independent public or certified public accountant.

(2) For a foreign private issuer, if the report will not contain financial information prepared in accordance with U.S. generally accepted accounting principles, you must state whether the report will include a reconciliation of this information with U.S. generally accepted accounting principles.

(g) *Enforceability of civil liabilities against foreign persons.* Disclose the following if you are a foreign private issuer filing a registration statement under the Securities Act:

(1) Whether or not investors may bring actions under the civil liability provisions of the U.S. federal securities laws against the foreign private issuer, any of its officers and directors who are residents of a foreign country, any underwriters or experts named in the registration statement that are residents of a foreign country, and whether investors may enforce these civil liability provisions when the assets of the issuer or these other persons are located outside of the United States. The disclosure must address the following matters:

(i) The investor's ability to effect service of process within the United States on the foreign private issuer or any person;

(ii) The investor's ability to enforce judgments obtained in U.S. courts against foreign persons based upon the civil liability provisions of the U.S. federal securities laws;

(iii) The investor's ability to enforce, in an appropriate foreign court, judgments of U.S. courts based upon the civil liability provisions of the U.S. federal securities laws; and

(iv) The investor's ability to bring an original action in an appropriate foreign court to enforce liabilities against the foreign private issuer or any person based upon the U.S. federal securities laws.

(2) If you provide this disclosure based on an opinion of counsel, name counsel in the prospectus and file as an exhibit to the registration statement a signed consent of counsel to the use of its name and opinion.

Instructions to Item 101. 1. In determining what information about the segments is material to an understanding of the registrant's business taken as a whole and therefore required to be disclosed, pursuant to paragraph (c) of this Item, the registrant should take into account both quantitative and qualitative factors such as the significance of the matter to the registrant (e.g., whether a matter with a relatively minor impact on the registrant's business is represented by management to be important to its future profitability), the pervasiveness of the matter (e.g., whether it affects or may affect numerous items in the segment information), and the impact of the matter (e.g., whether it distorts the trends reflected in the segment information). Situations may arise when information should be disclosed about a segment, although the information in quantitative terms may not appear significant to the registrant's business taken as a whole.

2. Base the determination of whether information about segments is required for a particular year upon an evaluation of interperiod comparability. For instance, interperiod comparability would require a registrant to report segment information in the current period even if not material under the criteria for reportability of SFAS No. 131 if a segment has been significant in the immediately preceding period and the registrant expects it to be significant in the future.

3. The Commission, upon written request of the registrant and where consistent with the protection of investors, may permit the omission of any of the information required by this Item or the furnishing in substitution thereof of appropriate information of comparable character.

Item 102. Description of Property

State briefly the location and general character of the principal plants, mines and other materially important physical properties of the registrant and its subsidiaries. In addition, identify the segment(s) that use the properties described. If any such property is not held in fee or is held subject to any major encumbrance, so state and describe briefly how held.

Instructions to Item 102. 1. What is required is such information as reasonably will inform investors as to the suitability, adequacy, productive capacity and extent of utilization of the facilities by the registrant. Detailed descriptions of the physical characteristics of individual properties or legal descriptions by metes and bounds are not required and shall not be given.

2. In determining whether properties should be described, the registrant should take into account both quantitative and qualitative factors. See Instruction 1 to Item 101 of Regulation S–K.

3. In the case of an extractive enterprise, material information shall be given as to production, reserves, locations, development and the nature of the registrant's interest. If individual properties are of major significance to an industry segment:

A. More detailed information concerning these matters shall be furnished; and

B. Appropriate maps shall be used to disclose location data of significant properties except in cases for which numerous maps would be required.

4. A. If reserve estimates are referred to in the document, the staff of the Office of Engineering, Division of Corporation Finance of the Commission, shall be consulted. That Office may request that a copy of the full report of the engineer or other expert who estimated the reserves be furnished as supplemental information and not as part of the filing. See Rule 418 of Regulation C and Rule 12b–4 of Regulation 12B with respect to the submission to, and return by, the Commission of supplemental information.

B. If the estimates of reserves, or any estimated valuation thereof, are represented as being based on estimates prepared or reviewed by independent consultants, those independent consultants shall be named in the document.

5. Estimates of oil or gas reserves other than proved or, in the case of other extractive reserves, estimates other than proved or probable reserves, and any estimated values of such reserves shall not be disclosed in any document publicly filed with the Commission, unless such information is required to be disclosed in the document by foreign or state law; provided, however, that where such estimates previously have been provided to a person (or any of its affiliates) that is offering to acquire, merge or consolidate with the registrant or otherwise to acquire the registrant's securities, such estimates may be included in documents relating to such acquisition.

6. The definitions in § 210.4–10(a) of Regulation S–X shall apply to this Item with respect to oil and gas operations.

Item 103. Legal Proceedings

Describe briefly any material pending legal proceedings, other than ordinary routine litigation incidental to the business, to which the registrant or any of its subsidiaries is a party or of which any of their property is the subject. Include the name of the court or agency in which the proceedings are pending, the date instituted, the principal parties thereto, a description of the factual basis alleged to underlie the proceeding and the relief sought. Include similar information as to any such proceedings known to be contemplated by governmental authorities.

Instructions to Item 103. 1. If the business ordinarily results in actions for negligence or other claims, no such action or claim need be described unless it departs from the normal kind of such actions.

2. No information need be given with respect to any proceeding that involves primarily a claim for damages if the amount involved, exclusive of interest and costs, does not exceed 10 percent of the current assets of the registrant and its subsidiaries on a consolidated basis. However, if any proceeding presents in large degree the same legal and factual issues as other proceedings pending or known to be contemplated, the amount involved in such other proceedings shall be included in computing such percentage.

3. Notwithstanding Instructions 1 and 2, any material bankruptcy, receivership, or similar proceeding with respect to the registrant or any of its significant subsidiaries shall be described.

4. Any material proceedings to which any director, officer or affiliate of the registrant, any owner of record or beneficially of more than five percent of any class of voting securities of the registrant, or any associate of any such director, officer, affiliate of the registrant, or security holder is a party adverse to the registrant or any of its subsidiaries or has a material interest adverse to the registrant or any of its subsidiaries also shall be described.

5. Notwithstanding the foregoing, an administrative or judicial proceeding (including, for purposes of A and B of this Instruction, proceedings which present in large degree the same issues) arising under any Federal, State or local provisions that have been enacted or adopted regulating the discharge of materials into the environment or primary for the purpose of protecting the environment shall not be deemed "ordinary routine litigation incidental to the business" and shall be described if:

A. Such proceeding is material to the business or financial condition of the registrant;

B. Such proceeding involves primarily a claim for damages, or involves potential monetary sanctions, capital expenditures, deferred charges or charges to income and the amount involved, exclusive of interest and costs, exceeds 10 percent of the current assets of the registrant and its subsidiaries on a consolidated basis; or

C. A governmental authority is a party to such proceeding and such proceeding involves potential monetary sanctions, unless the registrant reasonably believes that such proceeding will result in no monetary sanctions, or in monetary sanctions, exclusive of interest and costs, of less than $100,000; *Provided, however,* That such proceedings which are similar in nature may be grouped and described generically.

Subpart 200—Securities of the Registrant

Item 201. Market Price of and Dividends on the Registrant's Common Equity and Related Stockholder Matters

(a) *Market Information.* (1)(i) Identify the principal United States market or markets in which each class of the registrant's common equity is being traded. Where there is no established public trading market for a class of common equity, furnish a statement to that effect. For purposes of this Item the existence of limited or sporadic quotations should not of itself be deemed to constitute an "established public trading market." In the case of foreign registrants, also identify the principal established foreign public trading market, if any, for each class of the registrant's common equity.

(ii) If the principal United States market for such common equity is an exchange, state the high and low sales prices for the equity for each full quarterly period within the two most recent fiscal years and any subsequent interim period for which financial statements are included, or are required to be included by Article 3 of Regulation S–X, as reported in the consolidated transaction reporting system or, if not so reported, as reported on the principal exchange market for such equity.

(iii) If the principal United States market for such common equity is not an exchange, state the range of high and low bid information for the equity for each full quarterly period within the two most recent fiscal years and any subsequent interim period for which financial statements are included, or are required to be included by Article 3 of Regulation S–X, as regularly quoted in the automated quotation system of a registered securities association, or where the equity is not quoted in such a system, the range of reported high and low bid quotations, indicating the source of such quotations. Indicate, as applicable, that such over-the-counter market quotations reflect inter-dealer prices, without retail mark-up, mark-down or commission and may not necessarily represent actual transactions. Where there is an absence of an established public trading market, reference to quotations shall be qualified by appropriate explanation.

(iv) Where a foreign registrant has identified a principal established foreign trading market for its common equity pursuant to paragraph (a)(1) of this Item, also provide market price information comparable, to the extent practicable, to that required for the principal United States market, including the source of such information. Such prices shall be stated in the currency in which they are quoted. The registrant may translate such prices into United States currency at the currency exchange rate in effect on the date the price disclosed was reported on the foreign exchange. If the primary United States market for the registrant's common equity trades using American Depositary Receipts, the United States prices disclosed shall be on that basis.

(v) If the information called for by this Item is being presented in a registration statement filed pursuant to the Securities Act or a proxy or information statement filed pursuant to the Exchange Act, the document also shall include price information as of the latest practicable date, and, in the case of securities to be issued in connection with an acquisition, business combination or other reorganization, as of the date immediately prior to the public announcement of such transaction.

(2) If the information called for by this paragraph (a) is being presented in a registration statement on Form S–1 or Form SB–2 under the Securities Act or on Form 10 and Form 10–SB under the Exchange Act relating to a class of common equity for which at the time of filing there is no established United States public trading market, indicate the amount(s) of common equity (i) that is subject to outstanding options or warrants to purchase, or securities convertible into, common equity of the registrant; (ii) that could be sold pursuant to Rule 144 under the Securities Act or that the registrant has agreed to register under the Securities Act for sale by security holders; or (iii) that is being, or has been publicly proposed to be, publicly offered by the registrant (unless such common equity is being offered pursuant to an employee benefit plan or dividend reinvestment plan), the offering of which could have a material effect on the market price of the registrant's common equity.

(b) *Holders.* (1) Set forth the approximate number of holders of each class of common equity of the registrant as of the latest practicable date.

(2) If the information called for by this paragraph (b) is being presented in a registration statement filed pursuant to the Securities Act or a proxy statement or information statement filed pursuant to the Exchange Act that relates to an acquisition, business combination or other reorganization, indicate the effect of such transaction on the amount and percentage of present holdings of the registrant's common equity owned beneficially by (i) any person (including any group as that term is used in section 13(d)(3) of the Exchange Act) who is known to the registrant to be the beneficial owner of more than five percent of any class of the registrant's common equity and (ii) each director and nominee and (iii) all directors and officers as a group, and the registrant's present commitments to such persons with respect to the issuance of shares of any class of its common equity.

(c) *Dividends.* (1) State the frequency and amount of any cash dividends declared on each class of its common equity by the registrant for the two most recent fiscal years and any subsequent interim period for which financial statements are required to be presented by § 210.3 of Regulation S–X. Where there are restrictions (including, where appropriate, restrictions on the ability of registrant's subsidiaries to transfer funds to the registrant in the form of cash dividends, loans or advances) that currently materially limit the registrant's ability to pay such dividends or that the registrant reasonably believes are likely to limit materially the future payment of dividends on the common equity so state and either (i) describe briefly (where appropriate quantify) such restrictions, or (ii) cross reference to the specific discussion of such restrictions in the Management's Discussion and Analysis of financial condition and operating results prescribed by Item 303 of Regulation S–K and the description of such restrictions required by Regulation S–X in the registrant's financial statements.

(2) Where registrants have a record of paying no cash dividends although earnings indicate an ability to do so, they are encouraged to consider the question of their intention to pay cash dividends in the foreseeable future and, if no such intention exists, to make a statement of that fact in the filing. Registrants which have a history of paying cash dividends also are encouraged to indicate whether they currently expect that comparable cash dividends will continue to be paid in the future and, if not, the nature of the change in the amount or rate of cash dividend payments.

(d) *Securities authorized for issuance under equity compensation plans.* (1) In the following tabular format, provide the information specified in paragraph (d)(2) of this Item as of the end of the most recently completed fiscal year with respect to compensation plans (including individual compensation arrangements) under which equity securities of the registrant are authorized for issuance, aggregated as follows:

(i) All compensation plans previously approved by security holders; and

(ii) All compensation plans not previously approved by security holders.

EQUITY COMPENSATION PLAN INFORMATION

Plan category	Number of securities to be issued upon exercise of outstanding options, warrants and rights	Weighted-average exercise price of outstanding options, warrants and rights	Number of securities remaining available for future issuance under equity compensation plans (excluding securities reflected in column (a))
	(a)	(b)	(c)
Equity compensation plans approved by security holders			
Equity compensation plans not approved by security holders			
Total			

(2) The table shall include the following information as of the end of the most recently completed fiscal year for each category of equity compensation plan described in paragraph (d)(1) of this Item:

(i) The number of securities to be issued upon the exercise of outstanding options, warrants and rights (column (a));

(ii) The weighted-average exercise price of the outstanding options, warrants and rights disclosed pursuant to paragraph (d)(2)(i) of this Item (column (b)); and

(iii) Other than securities to be issued upon the exercise of the outstanding options, warrants and rights disclosed in paragraph (d)(2)(i) of this Item, the number of securities remaining available for future issuance under the plan (column (c)).

(3) For each compensation plan under which equity securities of the registrant are authorized for issuance that was adopted without the approval of security holders, describe briefly, in narrative form, the material features of the plan.

Instructions to Paragraph (d).

1. Disclosure shall be provided with respect to any compensation plan and individual compensation arrangement of the registrant (or parent, subsidiary or affiliate of the registrant) under which equity securities of the registrant are authorized for issuance to employees or non-employees (such as directors, consultants, advisors, vendors, customers, suppliers or lenders) in exchange for consideration in the form of goods or services as described in Statement of Financial Accounting Standards No. 123, *Accounting for Stock–Based Compensation,* or any successor standard. No disclosure is required with respect to:

a. Any plan, contract or arrangement for the issuance of warrants or rights to all security holders of the registrant as such on a pro rata basis (such as a stock rights offering) or

b. Any employee benefit plan that is intended to meet the qualification requirements of Section 401(a) of the Internal Revenue Code (26 U.S.C. 401(a)).

2. For purposes of this paragraph, an "individual compensation arrangement" includes, but is not limited to, the following: a written compensation contract within the meaning of "employee benefit plan" under § 230.405 of this chapter and a plan (whether or not set forth in any formal document) applicable to one person as provided under Item 402(a)(7)(ii) of Regulation S–K (§ 229.402(a)(7)(ii)).

3. If more than one class of equity security is issued under its equity compensation plans, a registrant should aggregate plan information for each class of security.

4. A registrant may aggregate information regarding individual compensation arrangements with the plan information required under paragraph (d)(1)(i) and (ii) of this Item, as applicable.

5. A registrant may aggregate information regarding a compensation plan assumed in connection with a merger, consolidation or other acquisition transaction pursuant to which the registrant may make subsequent grants or awards of its equity securities with the plan information required under paragraph (d)(1)(i) and (ii) of this Item, as applicable. A registrant shall disclose on an aggregated basis in a footnote to the table the information required under paragraph (d)(2)(i) and (ii) of this Item with respect to any individual options, warrants or rights assumed in connection with a merger, consolidation or other acquisition transaction.

6. To the extent that the number of securities remaining available for future issuance disclosed in column (c) includes securities available for future issuance under any compensation plan or individual compensation arrangement other than upon the exercise of an option, warrant or right, disclose the number of securities and type of plan separately for each such plan in a footnote to the table.

7. If the description of an equity compensation plan set forth in a registrant's financial statements contains the disclosure required by paragraph (d)(3) of this Item, a cross-reference to such description will satisfy the requirements of paragraph (d)(3) of this Item.

8. If an equity compensation plan contains a formula for calculating the number of securities available for issuance under the plan, including, without limitation, a formula that automatically increases the number of securities available for issuance by a percentage of the number of outstanding securities of the registrant, a description of this formula shall be disclosed in a footnote to the table.

9. Except where it is part of a document that is incorporated by reference into a prospectus, the information required by this paragraph need not be provided in any registration statement filed under the Securities Act.

Instructions to Item 201. 1. Registrants, the common equity of which is listed for trading on more than one securities exchange registered under the Exchange Act, are required to indicate each such exchange pursuant to paragraph (a)(1)(i) of this Item; such registrants, however, need only report one set of price quotations pursuant to paragraph (a)(1)(ii) of this Item; where available, these shall be the prices as reported in the consolidated transaction reporting system and, where the prices are not so reported, the prices on the most significant (in terms of volume) securities exchange for such shares.

2. Market prices and dividends reported pursuant to this Item shall be adjusted to give retroactive effect to material changes resulting from stock dividends, stock splits and reverse stock splits.

3. The computation of the approximate number of holders of registrant's common equity may be based upon the number of record holders or also may include individual participants in security position listings. See Rule 17Ad–8 under the Exchange Act. The method of computation that is chosen shall be indicated.

4. If the registrant is a foreign issuer, describe briefly:

A. Any governmental laws, decrees or regulations in the country in which the registrant is organized that restrict the export or import of capital, including, but not limited to, foreign exchange controls, or that affect the remittance of dividends or other payments to nonresident holders of the registrant's common equity; and

B. All taxes, including withholding provisions, to which United States common equity holders are subject under existing laws and regulations of the foreign country in which the registrant is organized. Include a brief description of pertinent provisions of any reciprocal tax treaty between such foreign country and the United States regarding withholding. If there is no such treaty, so state.

5. If the registrant is a foreign private issuer whose common equity of the class being registered is wholly or partially in bearer form, the response to this Item shall so indicate together with as much information as the registrant is able to provide with respect to security holdings in the United States. If the securities being registered trade in the United States in the form of American Depositary Receipts or similar certificates, the response to this Item shall so indicate together with the name of the depositary issuing such receipts and the number of shares or other units of the underlying security representing the trading units in such receipts.

Item 202. Description of Registrant's Securities

NOTE: If the securities being described have been accepted for listing on an exchange, the exchange may be identified. The document should not however, convey the impression that the registrant may apply successfully for listing of the securities on an exchange or that, in the case of an underwritten offering, the underwriters may request the registrant to apply for such listing, unless there is reasonable assurance that the securities to be offered will be acceptable to a securities exchange for listing.

(a) *Capital Stock.* If capital stock is to be registered, state the title of the class and describe such of the matters listed in paragraphs (a)(1) through (5) as are relevant. A complete legal description of the securities need not be given.

(1) Outline briefly: (i) dividend rights; (ii) terms of conversion; (iii) sinking fund provisions; (iv) redemption provisions; (v) voting rights, including any provisions specifying the vote required by security holders to take action; (vi) any classification of the Board of Directors, and the impact of such classification where cumulative voting is permitted or required; (vii) liquidation rights; (viii) preemption rights; and (ix) liability to further calls or to assessment by the registrant and for liabilities of the registrant imposed on its stockholders under state statutes (e.g., to laborers, servants or employees of the registrant), unless such disclosure would be immaterial because the financial resources of the registrant or other factors make it improbable that liability under such state statutes would be imposed; (x) any restriction on alienability of the securities to be registered; and (xi) any provision discriminating against any existing or prospective holder of such securities as a result of such security holder owning a substantial amount of securities.

(2) If the rights of holders of such stock may be modified otherwise than by a vote of a majority or more of the shares outstanding, voting as a class, so state and explain briefly.

(3) If preferred stock is to be registered, describe briefly any restriction on the repurchase or redemption of shares by the registrant while there is any arrearage in the payment of dividends or sinking fund installments. If there is no such restriction, so state.

(4) If the rights evidenced by, or amounts payable with respect to, the shares to be registered are, or may be, materially limited or qualified by the rights of any other authorized class of securities, include the information regarding such other securities as will enable investors to understand such limitations or qualifications. No information need be given, however, as to any class of securities all of which will be retired, provided appropriate steps to ensure such retirement will be completed prior to or upon delivery by the registrant of the shares.

(5) Describe briefly or cross-reference to a description in another part of the document, any provision of the registrant's charter or by-laws that would have an effect of delaying, deferring or preventing a change in control of the registrant and that would operate only with respect to an extraordinary corporate transaction involving the registrant (or any of its subsidiaries), such as a merger, reorganization, tender offer, sale or transfer of substantially all of its assets, or liquidation. Provisions and arrangements required by law or imposed by governmental or judicial authority need not be described or discussed pursuant to this paragraph (a)(5). Provisions or arrangements adopted by the registrant to effect, or further, compliance with laws or governmental or judicial mandate are not subject to the immediately preceding sentence where such compliance did not require the specific provisions or arrangements adopted.

(b) *Debt Securities.* If debt securities are to be registered, state the title of such securities, the principal amount being offered, and, if a series, the total amount authorized and the total amount outstanding as of the most recent practicable date; and describe such of the matter listed in paragraphs (b)(1) through (10) as are relevant. A complete legal description of the securities need not be given. For purposes solely of this Item, debt securities that differ from one another only as to the interest rate or maturity shall be regarded as securities of the same class. Outline briefly:

(1) Provisions with respect to maturity, interest, conversion, redemption, amortization, sinking fund, or retirement;

(2) Provisions with respect to the kind and priority of any lien securing the securities, together with a brief identification of the principal properties subject to such lien;

(3) Provisions with respect to the subordination of the rights of holders of the securities to other security holders or creditors of the registrant; where debt securities are designated as subordinated in accordance with Instruction 1 to this Item, set forth the aggregate amount of outstanding indebtedness as of the most recent practicable date that by the terms of such debt securities would be senior to such subordinated debt and describe briefly any limitation on the issuance of such additional senior indebtedness or state that there is no such limitation;

(4) Provisions restricting the declaration of dividends or requiring the maintenance of any asset ratio or the creation or maintenance of reserves;

(5) Provisions restricting the incurrence of additional debt or the issuance of additional securities; in the case of secured debt, whether the securities being registered are to be issued on the basis of unbonded bondable property, the deposit of cash or otherwise; as of the most recent practicable date, the approximate amount of unbonded bondable property available as a basis for the issuance of bonds; provisions permitting the withdrawal of cash deposited as a basis for the issuance of bonds; and provisions permitting the release or substitution of assets securing the issue; *Provided, however,* That provisions permitting the release of assets upon the deposit of equivalent funds or the pledge of equivalent property, the release of property no longer required in the business, obsolete property, or property taken by eminent domain or the application of insurance

moneys, and other similar provisions need not be described;

(6) The general type of event that constitutes a default and whether or not any periodic evidence is required to be furnished as to the absence of default or as to compliance with the terms of the indenture;

(7) Provisions relating to modification of the terms of the security or the rights of security holders;

(8) If the rights evidenced by the securities to be registered are, or may be, materially limited or qualified by the rights of any other authorized class of securities, the information regarding such other securities as will enable investors to understand the rights evidenced by the securities; to the extent not otherwise disclosed pursuant to this Item; no information need be given, however, as to any class of securities all of which will be retired, provided appropriate steps to ensure such retirement will be completed prior to or upon delivery by the registrant of the securities;

(9) If debt securities are to be offered at a price such that they will be deemed to be offered at an "original issue discount" as defined in section 1273 of the Internal Revenue Code, or if a debt security is sold in a package with another security and the allocation of the offering price between the two securities may have the effect of offering the debt security at such an original issue discount, the tax effects thereof pursuant to section 1271–1278; and

(10) The name of the trustee(s) and the nature of any material relationship with the registrant or with any of its affiliates; the percentage of securities of the class necessary to require the trustee to take action; and what indemnification the trustee may require before proceeding to enforce the lien.

(c) *Warrants and Rights.* If the securities described are to be offered pursuant to warrants or rights state:

(1) The amount of securities called for by such warrants or rights;

(2) The period during which and the price at which the warrants or rights are exercisable;

(3) The amount of warrants or rights outstanding;

(4) Provisions for changes to or adjustments in the exercise price; and

(5) Any other material terms of such rights on warrants.

(d) *Other Securities.* If securities other than capital stock, debt, warrants or rights are to be registered, include a brief description (comparable to that required in paragraphs (a), (b) and (c) of Item 202) of the rights evidenced thereby.

(e) *Market Information for Securities Other Than Common Equity.* If securities other than common equity are to be registered and there is an established public trading market for such securities (as that term is used in Item 201 of Regulation S–K) provide market information with respect to such securities comparable to that required by paragraph (a) of Item 201 of Regulation S–K.

(f) *American Depositary Receipts.* If Depositary Shares represented by American Depositary Receipts are being registered, furnish the following information:

(1) The name of the depositary and the address of its principal executive office.

(2) State the title of the American Depositary Receipts and identify the deposited security. Describe briefly the terms of deposit, including the provisions, if any, with respect to: (i) the amount of deposited securities represented by one unit of American Depositary Receipts; (ii) the procedure for voting, if any, the deposited securities; (iii) the collection and distribution of dividends; (iv) the transmission of notices, reports and proxy soliciting material; (v) the sale or exercise of rights; (vi) the deposit or sale of securities resulting from dividends, splits or plans of reorganization;

(vii) amendment, extension or termination of the deposit; (viii) rights of holders of receipts to inspect the transfer books of the depositary and the list of holders of receipts; (ix) restrictions upon the right to deposit or withdraw the underlying securities; (x) limitation upon the liability of the depositary.

(3) Describe all fees and charges which may be imposed directly or indirectly against the holder of the American Depositary Receipts, indicating the type of service, the amount of fee or charges and to whom paid.

Instructions to Item 202. 1. Wherever the title of securities is required to be stated, there shall be given such information as will indicate the type and general character of the securities, including the following:

A. In the case of shares, the par or stated value, if any; the rate of dividends, if fixed, and whether cumulative or non-cumulative; a brief indication of the preference, if any; and if convertible or redeemable, a statement to that effect;

B. In the case of debt, the rate of interest; the date of maturity or, if the issue matures serially, a brief indication of the serial maturities, such as "maturing serially from 1955 to 1960"; if the payment of principal or interest is contingent, an appropriate indication of such contingency; a brief indication of the priority of the issue; and, if convertible or callable, a statement to that effect; or

C. In the case of any other kind of security, appropriate information of comparable character.

2. If the registrant is a foreign registrant, include (to the extent not disclosed in the document pursuant to Item 201 of Regulation S–K or otherwise) in the description of the securities:

A. A brief description of any limitations on the right of nonresident or foreign owners to hold or vote such securities imposed by foreign law or by the charter or other constituent document of the registrant, or if no such limitations are applicable, so state;

B. A brief description of any governmental laws, decrees or regulations in the country in which the registrant is organized affecting the remittance of dividends, interest and other payments to nonresident holders of the securities being registered;

C. A brief outline of all taxes, including withholding provisions, to which United States security holders are subject under existing laws and regulations of the foreign country in which the registrant is organized; and

D. A brief description of pertinent provisions of any reciprocal tax treaty between such foreign country and the United States regarding withholding or, if there is no such treaty, so state.

3. Section 305(a)(2) of the Trust Indenture Act of 1939, as amended ("Trust Indenture Act"), shall not be deemed to require the inclusion in a registration statement or in a prospectus of any information not required by this Item.

4. Where convertible securities or stock purchase warrants are being registered that are subject to redemption or call, the description of the conversion terms of the securities or material terms of the warrants shall disclose:

A. Whether the right to convert or purchase the securities will be forfeited unless it is exercised before the date specified in a notice of the redemption or call;

B. The expiration or termination date of the warrants;

C. The kinds, frequency and timing of notice of the redemption or call, including the cities or newspapers in which notice will be published (where the securities provide for a class of newspapers or group of cities in which the publication may be made at the discretion of the registrant, the registrant should describe such provision); and

D. In the case of bearer securities, that investors are responsible for making arrangements to prevent loss of the right to convert or purchase in the event of redemption of call, for example, by reading the newspapers in which the notice of redemption or call may be published.

5. The response to paragraph (f) shall include information with respect to fees and charges in connection with (A) the deposit or substitution of the underlying securities; (B) receipt and distribution of dividends; (C) the sale or exercise of rights; (D) the withdrawal of the underlying security; and (E) the transferring, splitting or grouping of receipts. Information with respect to the right to collect the fees and charges against dividends received and deposited securities shall be included in response to this item.

6. For asset-backed securities, see also Item 1113 of Regulation AB (§ 229.1113).

Subpart 300—Financial Information

Item 301. Selected Financial Data

Furnish in comparative columnar form the selected financial data for the registrant referred to below, for

(a) Each of the last five fiscal years of the registrant (or for the life of the registrant and its predecessors, if less), and

(b) Any additional fiscal years necessary to keep the information from being misleading.

Instructions to Item 301. 1. The purpose of the selected financial data shall be to supply in a convenient and readable format selected financial data which highlight certain significant trends in the registrant's financial condition and results of operations.

2. Subject to appropriate variation to conform to the nature of the registrant's business, the following items shall be included in the table of financial data: net sales or operating revenues; income (loss) from continuing operations; income (loss) from continuing operations per common share; total assets; long-term obligations and redeemable preferred stock (including long-term debt, capital leases, and redeemable preferred stock as defined in § 210.5–02.28(a)) of Regulation S–X; and cash dividends declared per common share. Registrants may include additional items which they believe would enhance an understanding of and would highlight other trends in their financial condition and results of operations.

Briefly describe, or cross-reference to a discussion thereof, factors such as accounting changes, business combinations or dispositions of business operations, that materially affect the comparability of the information reflected in selected financial data. Discussion of, or reference to, any material uncertainties should also be included where such matters might cause the data reflected herein not to be indicative of the registrant's future financial condition or results of operations.

3. All references to the registrant in the table of selected financial data and in this Item shall mean the registrant and its subsidiaries consolidated.

4. If interim period financial statements are included, or are required to be included, by Article 3 of Regulation S–X, registrants should consider whether any or all of the selected financial data need to be updated for such interim periods to reflect a material change in the trends indicated; where such updating information is necessary, registrants shall provide the information on a comparative basis unless not necessary to an understanding of such updating information.

5. A foreign private issuer shall disclose also the following information in all filings containing financial statements:

A. In the forepart of the document and as of the latest practicable date, the exchange rate into U.S. currency of the foreign currency in which the financial statements are denominated;

B. A history of exchange rates for the five most recent years and any subsequent interim period for which financial statements are presented setting forth the rates for period end, the average rates, and the range of high and low rates for each year; and

C. If equity securities are being registered, a five year summary of dividends per share stated in both the currency in which the financial statements are denominated and United States currency based on the exchange rates at each respective payment date.

6. A foreign private issuer shall present the selected financial data in the same currency as its financial statements. The issuer may present the selected financial data on the basis of the accounting principles used in its primary financial statements but in such case shall present this data also on the basis of any reconciliations of such data to United States generally accepted accounting principles and Regulation S–X made pursuant to Rule 4–01 of Regulation S–X.

7. For purposes of this rule, the rate of exchange means the noon buying rate in New York City for cable transfers in foreign currencies as certified for customs purposes by the Federal Reserve Bank of New York. The average rate means the average of the exchange rates on the last day of each month during a year.

Item 302. Supplementary Financial Information

(a) *Selected Quarterly Financial Data.* Registrants specified in paragraph (a)(5) of this Item shall provide the information specified below.

(1) Disclosure shall be made of net sales, gross profit (net sales less costs and expenses associated directly with or allocated to products sold or services rendered), income (loss) before extraordinary items and cumulative effect of a change in accounting, per share data based upon such income (loss), and net income (loss), for each full quarter within the two most recent fiscal years and any subsequent interim period for which financial statements are included or are required to be included by Article 3 of Regulation S–X.

(2) When the data supplied pursuant to this paragraph (a) vary from the amounts previously reported on the Form 10–Q and Form 10–QSB filed for any quarter, such as would be the case when a pooling of interests occurs or where an error is corrected, reconcile the amounts given with those previously reported and describe the reason for the difference.

(3) Describe the effect of any disposals of segments of a business, and extraordinary, unusual or infrequently occurring items recognized in each full quarter within the two most recent fiscal years and any subsequent interim period for which financial statements are included or are required to be included by Article 3 of Regulation S–X, as well as the aggregate effect and the nature of year-end or other adjustments which are material to the results of that quarter.

(4) If the financial statements to which this information relates have been reported on by an accountant, appropriate professional standards and procedures, as enumerated in the Statements of Auditing Standards issued by the Auditing Standards Board of the American Institute of Certified Public Accountants, shall be followed by the reporting accountant with regard to the data required by this paragraph (a).

(5) This paragraph (a) applies to any registrant, except a foreign private issuer, that has securities registered pursuant to sections 12(b) (15 U.S.C. § 78*l*(b)) (other than mutual life insurance companies) or 12(g) of the Exchange Act (15 U.S.C. § 78*l*(g)).

(b) *Information About Oil and Gas Producing Activities.* Registrants engaged in oil and gas producing activities shall present information about oil and gas producing activities (as those activities are defined in Regulation S–X,

§ 210.4–10(a)) specified in paragraphs 9–34 of Statement of Financial Accounting Standards ("SFAS") No. 69, "Disclosures about Oil and Gas Producing Activities," if such oil and gas producing activities are regarded as significant under one or more of the tests set forth in paragraph 8 of SFAS No. 69.

Instructions to Paragraph (b). 1. (a) SFAS No. 69 disclosures that relate to annual periods shall be presented for each annual period for which an income statement is required, (b) SFAS No. 69 disclosures required as of the end of an annual period shall be presented as of the date of each audited balance sheet required, and (c) SFAS No. 69 disclosures required as of the beginning of an annual period shall be presented as of the beginning of each annual period for which an income statement is required.

2. This paragraph, together with § 210.4–10 of Regulation S–X, prescribes financial reporting standards for the preparation of accounts by persons engaged, in whole or in part, in the production of crude oil or natural gas in the United States, pursuant to Section 503 of the Energy Policy and Conservation Act of 1975 ("EPCA") and Section 11(c) of the Energy Supply and Environmental Coordination Act of 1974 ("ESECA") as amended by Section 505 of EPCA. The application of this paragraph to those oil and gas producing operations of companies regulated for ratemaking purposes on an individual-company-cost-of-service basis may, however, give appropriate recognition to differences arising because of the effect of the ratemaking process.

3. Any person exempted by the Department of Energy from any record-keeping or reporting requirements pursuant to Section 11(c) of ESECA, as amended, is similarly exempted from the related provisions of this paragraph in the preparation of accounts pursuant to EPCA. This exemption does not affect the applicability of this paragraph to filings pursuant to the federal securities laws.

Item 303. Management's Discussion and Analysis of Financial Condition and Results of Operations

(a) *Full Fiscal Years.* Discuss registrant's financial condition, changes in financial condition and results of operations. The discussion shall provide information as specified in paragraphs (a)(1) through (s) of this Item and also shall provide such other information that the registrant believes to be necessary to an understanding of its financial condition, changes in financial condition and results of operations. Discussions of liquidity and capital resources may be combined whenever the two topics are interrelated. Where in the registrant's judgment a discussion of segment information or of other subdivisions of the registrant's business would be appropriate to an understanding of such business, the discussion shall focus on each relevant, reportable segment or other subdivision of the business and on the registrant as a whole.

(1) *Liquidity.* Identify any known trends or any known demands, commitments, events or uncertainties that will result in or that are reasonably likely to result in the registrant's liquidity increasing or decreasing in any material way. If a material deficiency is identified, indicate the course of action that the registrant has taken or proposes to take to remedy the deficiency. Also identify and separately describe internal and external sources of liquidity, and briefly discuss any material unused sources of liquid assets.

(2) *Capital Resources.* (i) Describe the registrant's material commitments for capital expenditures as of the end of the latest fiscal period, and indicate the general purpose of such commitments and the anticipated source of funds needed to fulfill such commitments.

(ii) Describe any known material trends, favorable or unfavorable, in the registrant's capital resources. Indicate any expected material changes in the mix and relative cost of such resources. The discussion shall consider changes between equity, debt and any off-balance sheet financing arrangements.

(3) *Results of Operations.* (i) Describe any unusual or infrequent events or transactions or any significant economic changes that materially affected the amount of reported income from continuing operations and, in each case, indicate the extent to which income was so affected. In addition, describe any other significant components of revenues or expenses that, in the registrant's judgment, should be described in order to understand the registrant's results of operations.

(ii) Describe any known trends or uncertainties that have had or that the registrant reasonably expects will have a material favorable or unfavorable impact on net sales or revenues or income from continuing operations. If the registrant knows of events that will cause a material change in the relationship between costs and revenues (such as known future increases in costs of labor or materials or price increases or inventory adjustments), the change in the relationship shall be disclosed.

(iii) To the extent that the financial statements disclose material increases in net sales or revenues, provide a narrative discussion of the extent to which such increases are attributable to increases in prices or to increases in the volume or amount of goods or services being sold or to the introduction of new products or services.

(iv) For the three most recent fiscal years of the registrant, or for those fiscal years in which the registrant has been engaged in business, whichever period is shortest, discuss the impact of inflation and changing prices on the registrant's net sales and revenues and on income from continuing operations.

(4) *Off-balance sheet arrangements.* (i) In a separately-captioned section, discuss the registrant's off-balance sheet arrangements that have or are reasonably likely to have a current or future effect on the registrant's financial condition, changes in financial condition, revenues or expenses, results of operations, liquidity, capital expenditures or capital resources that is material to investors. The disclosure shall include the items specified in paragraphs (a)(4)(i)(A), (B), (C) and (D) of this Item to the extent necessary to an understanding of such arrangements and effect and shall also include such other information that the registrant believes is necessary for such an understanding.

(A) The nature and business purpose to the registrant of such off-balance sheet arrangements;

(B) The importance to the registrant of such off-balance sheet arrangements in respect of its liquidity, capital resources, market risk support, credit risk support or other benefits;

(C) The amounts of revenues, expenses and cash flows of the registrant arising from such arrangements; the nature and amounts of any interests retained, securities issued and other indebtedness incurred by the registrant in connection with such arrangements; and the nature and amounts of any other obligations or liabilities (including contingent obligations or liabilities) of the registrant arising from such arrangements that are or are reasonably likely to become material and the triggering events or circumstances that could cause them to arise; and

(D) Any known event, demand, commitment, trend or uncertainty that will result in or is reasonably likely to result in the termination, or material reduction in availability to the registrant, of its off-balance sheet arrangements that provide material benefits to it, and the course of action that the registrant has taken or proposes to take in response to any such circumstances.

(ii) As used in this paragraph (a)(4), the term *off-balance sheet arrangement* means any transaction, agreement or other contractual arrangement to which an entity unconsolidated with the registrant is a party, under which the registrant has:

(A) Any obligation under a guarantee contract that has any of the characteristics identified in paragraph 3 of FASB Interpretation No. 45, *Guarantor's Accounting and Disclosure Requirements for Guarantees, Including Indirect Guarantees of Indebtedness of Others* (November 2002) ("FIN 45"), as may be modified or supplemented, and that is not excluded from the initial recognition and measurement provisions of FIN 45 pursuant to paragraphs 6 or 7 of that Interpretation;

(B) A retained or contingent interest in assets transferred to an unconsolidated entity or similar arrangement that serves as credit, liquidity or market risk support to such entity for such assets;

(C) Any obligation, including a contingent obligation, under a contract that would be accounted for as a derivative instrument, except that it is both indexed to the registrant's own stock and classified in stockholders' equity in the registrant's statement of financial position, and therefore excluded from the scope of FASB Statement of Financial Accounting Standards No. 133, *Accounting for Derivative Instruments and Hedging Activities* (June 1998), pursuant to paragraph 11(a) of that Statement, as may be modified or supplemented; or

(D) Any obligation, including a contingent obligation, arising out of a variable interest (as referenced in FASB Interpretation No. 46, *Consolidation of Variable Interest Entities* (January 2003), as may be modified or supplemented) in an unconsolidated entity that is held by, and material to, the registrant, where such entity provides financing, liquidity, market risk or credit risk support to, or engages in leasing, hedging or research and development services with, the registrant.

Instructions to Paragraph 303(a)(4):

1. No obligation to make disclosure under paragraph (a)(4) of this Item shall arise in respect of an off-balance sheet arrangement until a definitive agreement that is unconditionally binding or subject only to customary closing conditions exists or, if there is no such agreement, when settlement of the transaction occurs.

2. Registrants should aggregate off-balance sheet arrangements in groups or categories that provide material information in an efficient and understandable manner and should avoid repetition and disclosure of immaterial information. Effects that are common or similar with respect to a number of off-balance sheet arrangements must be analyzed in the aggregate to the extent the aggregation increases understanding. Distinctions in arrangements and their effects must be discussed to the extent the information is material, but the discussion should avoid repetition and disclosure of immaterial information.

3. For purposes of paragraph (a)(4) of this Item only, contingent liabilities arising out of litigation, arbitration or regulatory actions are not considered to be off-balance sheet arrangements.

4. Generally, the disclosure required by paragraph (a)(4) shall cover the most recent fiscal year. However, the discussion should address changes from the previous year where such discussion is necessary to an understanding of the disclosure.

5. In satisfying the requirements of paragraph (a)(4) of this Item, the discussion of off-balance sheet arrangements need not repeat information provided in the footnotes to the financial statements, provided that such discussion clearly cross-references to specific information in the relevant footnotes and integrates the substance of the footnotes into such discussion in a manner designed to inform readers of the signifi-

cance of the information that is not included within the body of such discussion.

(5) *Tabular disclosure of contractual obligations.* (i) In a tabular format, provide the information specified in this paragraph (a)(5) as of the latest fiscal year end balance sheet date with respect to the registrant's known contractual obligations specified in the table that follows this paragraph (a)(5)(i). The registrant shall provide amounts, aggregated by type of contractual obligation. The registrant may disaggregate the specified categories of contractual obligations using other categories suitable to its business, but the presentation must include all of the obligations of the registrant that fall within the specified categories. A presentation covering at least the periods specified shall be included. The tabular presentation may be accompanied by footnotes to describe provisions that create, increase or accelerate obligations, or other pertinent data to the extent necessary for an understanding of the timing and amount of the registrant's specified contractual obligations.

Contractual obligations	Payments due by period				
	Total	Less than 1 year	1–3 years	3–5 years	More than 5 years
[Long-Term Debt Obligations]	....	....	....	....	....
[Capital Lease Obligations]	....	....	....	....	....
[Operating Lease Obligations]	....	....	....	....	....
[Purchase Obligations]	....	....	....	....	....
[Other Long-Term Liabilities Reflected on the Registrant's Balance Sheet under GAAP]	....	....	....	....	....
Total	....	....	....	....	....

(ii) *Definitions:* The following definitions apply to this paragraph (a)(5):

(A) *Long-Term Debt Obligation* means a payment obligation under long-term borrowings referenced in FASB Statement of Financial Accounting Standards No. 47 *Disclosure of Long-Term Obligations* (March 1981), as may be modified or supplemented.

(B) *Capital Lease Obligation* means a payment obligation under a lease classified as a capital lease pursuant to FASB Statement of Financial Accounting Standards No. 13 *Accounting for Leases* (November 1976), as may be modified or supplemented.

(C) *Operating Lease Obligation* means a payment obligation under a lease classified as an operating lease and disclosed pursuant to FASB Statement of Financial Accounting Standards No. 13 *Accounting for Leases* (November 1976), as may be modified or supplemented.

(D) *Purchase Obligation* means an agreement to purchase goods or services that is enforceable and legally binding on the registrant that specifies all significant terms, including: fixed or minimum quantities to be purchased; fixed, minimum or variable price provisions; and the approximate timing of the transaction.

Instructions to Paragraph 303(a). 1. The registrant's discussion and analysis shall be of the financial statements and of other statistical data that the registrant believes will enhance a reader's understanding of its financial condition, changes in financial condition and results of operations. Generally, the discussion shall cover the three year period covered by the financial statements and shall use year-to-year comparisons or any other formats that in the registrant's judgment enhance a reader's understanding. However, where trend information is relevant, reference to the five year selected financial data appearing pursuant to Item 301 of Regulation S–K may be necessary.

2. The purpose of the discussion and analysis shall be to provide to investors and other users information relevant to an assessment of the financial condition and results of operations of the registrant as determined by evaluating the amounts and certainty of cash flows from operations and from outside sources.

3. The discussion and analysis shall focus specifically on material events and uncertainties known to management that would cause reported financial information not to be necessarily indicative of future operating results or of future financial condition. This would include descriptions and amounts of (A) matters that would have an impact on future operations and have not had an impact in the past, and (B) matters that have had an impact on reported operations and are not expected to have an impact upon future operations.

4. Where the consolidated financial statements reveal material changes from year to year in one or more line items, the causes for the changes shall be described to the extent necessary to an understanding of the registrant's businesses as a whole; *Provided, however,* That if the causes for a change in one line item also relate to other line items, no repetition is required and a line-by-line analysis of the financial statements as a whole is not required or generally appropriate. Registrants need not recite the amounts of changes from year to year which are readily computable from the financial statements. The discussion shall not merely repeat numerical data contained in the consolidated financial statements.

5. The term "liquidity" as used in this Item refers to the ability of an enterprise to generate adequate amounts of cash to meet the enterprise's needs for cash. Except where it is otherwise clear from the discussion, the registrant shall indicate those balance sheet conditions or income or cash flow items which the registrant believes may be indicators of its liquidity condition. Liquidity generally shall be discussed on both a long-term and short-term basis. The issue of liquidity shall be discussed in the context of the registrant's own business or businesses. For example a discussion of working capital may be appropriate for certain manufacturing, industrial or related operations but might be inappropriate for a bank or public utility.

6. Where financial statements presented or incorporated by reference in the registration statement are required by § 210.4–08(e)(3) of Regulation S–X to include disclosure of restrictions on the ability of both consolidated and unconsolidated subsidiaries to transfer funds to the registrant in the form of cash dividends, loans or advances, the discussion of liquidity shall include a discussion of the nature and extent of such restrictions and the impact such restrictions have had and are expected to have on the ability of the parent company to meet its cash obligations.

7. Any forward-looking information supplied is expressly covered by the safe harbor rule for projections. See Rule 175 under the Securities Act, Rule 3b–6 under the Exchange Act and Securities Act Release No. 6084 (June 25, 1979).

8. Registrants are only required to discuss the effects of inflation and other changes in prices when considered material. This discussion may be made in whatever manner appears appropriate under the circumstances. All that is required is a brief textual presentation of management's views. No specific numerical financial data need be presented except as Rule 3–20(c) of Regulation S–X (§ 210.3–20(c) of this chapter) otherwise requires. However, registrants may elect to voluntarily disclose supplemental information on the effects of changing prices as provided for in Statement of Financial Accounting Standards No. 89, "Financial Reporting and Changing Prices" or through other supplemental disclosures. The Commission encourages experimentation with these disclosures in order to provide the most meaningful presentation of the impact of price changes on the registrant's financial statements.

9. Registrants that elect to disclose supplementary information on the effects of changing prices as specified by SFAS No. 89, "Financial Reporting and Changing Prices," may combine such explanations with the discussion and analysis required pursuant to this Item or may supply such information separately with appropriate cross reference.

10. All references to the registrant in the discussion and in this Item shall mean the registrant and its subsidiaries consolidated.

11. Foreign private registrants also shall discuss briefly any pertinent governmental economic, fiscal, monetary, or political policies or factors that have materially affected or could materially affect, directly or indirectly, their operations or investments by United States nationals.

12. If the registrant is a foreign private issuer, the discussion shall focus on the primary financial statements presented in the registration statement or report. There shall be a reference to the reconciliation to United States generally accepted accounting principles, and a discussion of any aspects of the difference between foreign and United States generally accepted accounting principles, not discussed in the reconciliation, that the registrant believes is necessary for an understanding of the financial statements as a whole.

(b) *Interim Periods.* If interim period financial statements are included or are required to be included by Article 3 of Regulation S–X, a management's discussion and analysis of the financial condition and results of operations shall be provided so as to enable the reader to assess material changes in financial condition and results of operations between the periods specified in paragraphs (b)(1) and (2) of this Item. The discussion and analysis shall include a discussion of material changes in those items specifically listed in paragraph (a) of this Item, except that the impact of inflation and changing prices on operations for interim periods need not be addressed.

(1) *Material Changes in Financial Condition.* Discuss any material changes in financial condition from the end of the preceding fiscal year to the date of the most recent interim balance sheet provided. If the interim financial statements include an interim balance sheet as of the corresponding interim date of the preceding fiscal year, any material changes in financial condition from that date to the date of the most recent interim balance sheet provided also shall be discussed. If discussions of changes from both the end and the corresponding interim date of the preceding fiscal year are required, the discussions may be combined at the discretion of the registrant.

(2) *Material Changes in Results of Operations.* Discuss any material changes in the registrant's results of operations with respect to the most recent fiscal year-to-date period for which an income statement is provided and the corresponding year-to-date period of the preceding fiscal year. If the registrant is required to or has elected to provide an income statement for the most recent fiscal quarter, such discussion also shall cover material changes with respect to that fiscal quarter and the corresponding fiscal quarter in the preceding fiscal year. In addition, if the registrant has elected to provide an income statement for the twelve-month period ended as of the date of the most recent interim balance sheet provided, the discussion also shall cover material changes with respect to that twelve-month period and the twelve-month period ended as of the corresponding interim balance sheet date of the preceding fiscal year. Notwithstanding the above, if for purposes of a registration statement a registrant subject to paragraph (b) of § 210.3–03 of Regulation S–X provides a statement of income for the twelve-month period ended as of the date of the most recent interim balance sheet provided in lieu of the interim income statements otherwise required, the discussion of material changes in that twelve-month period will be in respect to the preceding fiscal

year rather than the corresponding preceding period.

Instructions to Paragraph (b) of Item 303. 1. If interim financial statements are presented together with financial statements for full fiscal years, the discussion of the interim financial information shall be prepared pursuant to this paragraph (b) and the discussion of the full fiscal year's information shall be prepared pursuant to paragraph (a) of this Item. Such discussions may be combined.

2. In preparing the discussion and analysis required by this paragraph (b), the registrant may presume that users of the interim financial information have read or have access to the discussion and analysis required by paragraph (a) for the preceding fiscal year.

3. The discussion and analysis required by this paragraph (b) is required to focus only on material changes. Where the interim financial statements reveal material changes from period to period in one or more significant line items, the causes for the changes shall be described if they have not already been disclosed: *Provided, however,* That if the causes for a change in one line item also relate to other line items, no repetition is required. Registrants need not recite the amounts of changes from period to period which are readily computable from the financial statements. The discussion shall not merely repeat numerical data contained in the financial statements. The information provided shall include that which is available to the registrant without undue effort or expense and which does not clearly appear in the registrant's condensed interim financial statements.

4. The registrant's discussion of material changes in results of operations shall identify any significant elements of the registrant's income or loss from continuing operations which do not arise from or are not necessarily representative of the registrant's ongoing business.

5. The registrant shall discuss any seasonal aspects of its business which have had a material effect upon its financial condition or results of operation.

6. Any forward-looking information supplied is expressly covered by the safe harbor rule for projections. See Rule 175 under the Securities Act, Rule 3b–6 under the Exchange Act and Securities Act Release No. 6084 (June 25, 1979).

7. The registrant is not required to include the table required by paragraph (a)(5) of this Item for interim periods. Instead, the registrant should disclose material changes outside the ordinary course of the registrant's business in the specified contractual obligations during the interim period.

(c) *Safe harbor.* (1) The safe harbor provided in section 27A of the Securities Act of 1933 (15 U.S.C. 77z–2) and section 21E of the Securities Exchange Act of 1934 (15 U.S.C. 78u–5) ("statutory safe harbors") shall apply to forward-looking information provided pursuant to paragraphs (a)(4) and (5) of this Item, provided that the disclosure is made by: an issuer; a person acting on behalf of the issuer; or an underwriter, with respect to information provided by the issuer or information derived from information provided by the issuer.

(2) For purposes of paragraph (c) of this Item only:

(i) All information required by paragraphs (a)(4) and (5) of this Item is deemed to be a *forward looking statement* as that term is defined in the statutory safe harbors, except for historical facts.

(ii) With respect to paragraph (a)(4) of this Item, the meaningful cautionary statements element of the statutory safe harbors will be satisfied if a registrant satisfies all requirements of that same paragraph (a)(4) of this Item.

Item 304. Changes in and Disagreements With Accountants on Accounting and Financial Disclosure

(a)(1) If during the registrant's two most recent fiscal years or any subsequent interim period, an independent accountant who was previously engaged as the principal accountant to audit the registrant's financial statements, or an independent accountant who was previously engaged to audit a significant subsidiary and on whom the principal accountant expressed reliance in its report, has resigned (or indicated it has declined to stand for re-election after the completion of the current audit) or was dismissed, then the registrant shall

(i) State whether the former accountant resigned, declined to stand for re-election or was dismissed and the date thereof.

(ii) State whether the principal accountant's report on the financial statements for either of the past two years contained an adverse opinion or a disclaimer of opinion, or was qualified or modified as to uncertainty, audit scope, or accounting principles; and also describe the nature of each such adverse opinion, disclaimer of opinion, modification, or qualification.

(iii) State whether the decision to change accountants was recommended or approved by:

(A) any audit or similar committee of the board of directors, if the issuer has such a committee; or

(B) the board of directors, if the issuer has no such committee.

(iv) State whether during the registrant's two most recent fiscal years and any subsequent interim period preceding such resignation, declination or dismissal there were any disagreements with the former accountant on any matter of accounting principles or practices, financial statement disclosure, or auditing scope or procedure, which disagreement(s), if not resolved to the satisfaction of the former accountant, would have caused it to make reference to the subject matter of the disagreement(s) in connection with its report. Also, (A) describe each such disagreement; (B) state whether any audit or similar committee of the board of directors, or the board of directors, discussed the subject matter of each of such disagreements with the former accountant; and (C) state whether the registrant has authorized the former accountant to respond fully to the inquiries of the successor accountant concerning the subject matter of each of such disagreements and, if not, describe the nature of any limitation thereon and the reason therefor. The disagreements required to be reported in response to this Item include both those resolved to the former accountant's satisfaction and those not resolved to the former accountant's satisfaction. Disagreements contemplated by this Item are those that occur at the decision-making level; i.e., between personnel of the registrant responsible for presentation of its financial statements and personnel of the accounting firm responsible for rendering its report.

(v) Provide the information required by paragraph (a)(1)(iv) of this Item for each of the kinds of events (even though the registrant and the former accountant did not express a difference of opinion regarding the event) listed in paragraphs (a)(1)(v)(A) through (D) of this section, that occurred within the registrant's two most recent fiscal years and any subsequent interim period preceding the former accountant's resignation, declination to stand for re-election, or dismissal ("reportable events"). If the event led to a disagreement or difference of opinion, then the event should be reported as a disagreement under paragraph (a)(1)(iv) and need not be repeated under this paragraph.

(A) The accountant's having advised the registrant that the internal controls necessary for the registrant to develop reliable financial statements do not exist;

(B) the accountant's having advised the registrant that information has come to the accountant's attention that has led it to no longer be able to rely on management's representations, or that has made it unwilling to be associated with the financial statements prepared by management;

(C)(*1*) the accountant's having advised the registrant of the need to expand significantly the scope of its audit, or that information has come to the accountant's attention during the time period covered by Item 304(a)(1)(iv), that if further investigated may (*i*) materially impact the fairness or reliability of either: a previously issued audit report or the underlying financial statements, or the financial statements issued or to be issued covering the fiscal period(s) subsequent to the date of the most recent financial statements covered by an audit report (including information that may prevent it from rendering an unqualified audit report on those financial statements), or (*ii*) cause it to be unwilling to rely on management's representations or be associated with the registrant's financial statements, and (*2*) due to the accountant's resignation (due to audit scope limitations or otherwise) or dismissal, or for any other reason, the accountant did not so expand the scope of its audit or conduct such further investigation; or

(D)(*1*) the accountant's having advised the registrant that information has come to the accountant's attention that it has concluded materially impacts the fairness or reliability of either (*i*) a previously issued audit report or the underlying financial statements, or (*ii*) the financial statements issued or to be issued covering the fiscal period(s) subsequent to the date of the most recent financial statements covered by an audit report (including information that, unless resolved to the accountant's satisfaction, would prevent it from rendering an unqualified audit report on those financial statements), and (*2*) due to the accountant's resignation, dismissal or declination to stand for reelection, or for any other reason, the issue has not been resolved to the accountant's satisfaction prior to its resignation, dismissal or declination to stand for re-election.

(*2*) If during the registrant's two most recent fiscal years or any subsequent interim period, a new independent accountant has been engaged as either the principal accountant to audit the registrant's financial statements, or as an independent accountant to audit a significant subsidiary and on whom the principal accountant is expected to express reliance in its report, then the registrant shall identify the newly engaged accountant and indicate the date of such accountant's engagement. In addition, if during the registrant's two most recent fiscal years, and any subsequent interim period prior to engaging that accountant, the registrant (or someone on its behalf) consulted the newly engaged accountant regarding (*i*) either: the application of accounting principles to a specified transaction, either completed or proposed; or the type of audit opinion that might be rendered on the registrant's financial statements, and either a written report was provided to the registrant or oral advice was provided that the new accountant concluded was an important factor considered by the registrant in reaching a decision as to the accounting, auditing or financial reporting issue; or (*ii*) any matter that was either the subject of a disagreement (as defined in paragraph 304(a)(1)(iv) and the related instructions to this item) or a reportable event (as described in paragraph 304(a)(1)(v)), then the registrant shall:

(A) so state and identify the issues that were the subjects of those consultations;

(B) briefly describe the views of the newly engaged accountant as expressed orally or in writing to the registrant on each such issue and, if written views were received by the registrant, file them as an exhibit to the report or registration statement requiring compliance with this Item 304(a);

(C) state whether the former accountant was consulted by the registrant regarding any such issues, and if so, provide a summary of the former accountant's views; and

(D) request the newly engaged accountant to review the disclosure required by this Item 304(a) before it is filed with the Commission and provide the new accountant the opportunity to furnish the registrant with a letter addressed to the Commission containing any new information, clarification of the registrant's expression of its views, or the respects in which it does not agree with the statements made by the registrant in response to Item 304(a). The registrant shall file any such letter as an exhibit to the report or registration statement containing the disclosure required by this Item.

(3) The registrant shall provide the former accountant with a copy of the disclosures it is making in response to this Item 304(a) that the former accountant shall receive no later than the day that the disclosures are filed with the Commission. The registrant shall request the former accountant to furnish the registrant with a letter addressed to the Commission stating whether it agrees with the statements made by the registrant in response to this Item 304(a) and, if not, stating the respects in which it does not agree. The registrant shall file the former accountant's letter as an exhibit to the report or registration statement containing this disclosure. If the former accountant's letter is unavailable at the time of filing such report or registration statement, then the registrant shall request the former accountant to provide the letter as promptly as possible so that the registrant can file the letter with the Commission within ten business days after the filing of the report or registration statement. Notwithstanding the ten business day period, the registrant shall file the letter by amendment within two business days of receipt; if the letter is received on a Saturday, Sunday or holiday on which the Commission is not open for business, then the two business day period shall begin to run on and shall include the first business day thereafter. The former accountant may provide the registrant with an interim letter highlighting specific areas of concern and indicating a subsequent, more detailed letter will be forthcoming within the ten business day period noted above. If not filed with the report or registration statement containing the registrant's disclosure under this Item 304(a), then the interim letter, if any, shall be filed by the registrant by amendment within two calendar days of receipt.

(b) If, (1) in connection with a change in accountants subject to paragraph (a) of this Item 304, there was any disagreement of the type described in paragraph (a)(1)(iv) or any reportable event as described in paragraph (a)(1)(v) of this Item, (2) during the fiscal year in which the change in accountants took place or during the subsequent fiscal year, there have been any transactions or events similar to those which involved such disagreement or reportable event and (3) such transactions or events were material and were accounted for or disclosed in a manner different from that which the former accountants apparently would have concluded was required, the registrant shall state the existence and nature of the disagreement or reportable event and also state the effect on the financial statements if the method had been followed which the former accountants apparently would have concluded was required. These disclosures need not be made if the method asserted by the former accountants ceases to be generally accepted because of authoritative standards or interpretations subsequently issued.

Instructions to Item 304: 1. The disclosure called for by paragraph (a) of this Item need not be provided if it has been previously reported (as that term is defined in Rule 12b–2 under the Exchange Act); the disclosure called for by paragraph (a) must be provided, however, notwithstanding prior disclosure, if required pursuant to Item 9 of Schedule 14A. The disclosure called for by paragraph (b) of this section must be furnished, where required, notwithstanding any prior disclosure about accountant changes or disagreements.

2. When disclosure is required by paragraph (a) of this section in an annual report to security holders pursuant to Rule 14a–3 or Rule 14c–3, or in a proxy or information statement filed pursuant to the requirements of Schedule 14A or 14C, in lieu of a letter pursuant to paragraph (a)(2)(D) or (a)(3), prior to filing such materials with or furnishing such materials to the Commission, the registrant shall furnish the disclosure required by paragraph (a) of this section to any former accountant engaged by the registrant during the period set forth in paragraph (a) of this section and to the newly engaged accountant. If any such accountant believes that the statements made in response to paragraph (a) of this section are incorrect or incomplete, it may present its views in a brief statement, ordinarily expected not to exceed 200 words, to be included in the annual report or proxy or information statement. This statement shall be submitted to the registrant within ten business days of the date the accountant receives the registrant's disclosure. Further, unless the written views of the newly engaged accountant required to be filed as an exhibit by paragraph (a)(2)(B) of this Item 304 have been previously filed with the Commission the registrant shall file a Form 8–K concurrently with the annual report or proxy or information statement for the purpose of filing the written views as exhibits thereto.

3. The information required by Item 304(a) need not be provided for a company being acquired by the registrant that is not subject to the filing requirements of either section 13(a) or 15(d) of the Exchange Act, or, because of section 12(i) of the Exchange Act, has not furnished an annual report to security holders pursuant to Rule 14a–3 or Rule 14c–3 for its latest fiscal year.

4. The term "disagreements" as used in this Item shall be interpreted broadly, to include any difference of opinion concerning any matter of accounting principles or practices, financial statement disclosure, or auditing scope or procedure which (if not resolved to the satisfaction of the former accountant) would have caused it to make reference to the subject matter of the disagreement in connection with its report. It is not necessary for there to have been an argument to have had a disagreement, merely a difference of opinion. For purposes of this Item, however, the term disagreements does not include initial differences of opinion based on incomplete facts or preliminary information that were later resolved to the former accountant's satisfaction by, and providing the registrant and the accountant do not continue to have a difference of opinion upon, obtaining additional relevant facts or information.

5. In determining whether any disagreement or reportable event has occurred, an oral communication from the engagement partner or another person responsible for rendering the accounting firm's opinion (or their designee) will generally suffice as the accountant advising the registrant of a reportable event or as a statement of a disagreement at the "decision-making-level" within the accounting firm and require disclosure under this Item.

Item 305. Quantitative and Qualitative Disclosures about Market Risk

(a) *Quantitative information about market risk.* *(1)* Registrants shall provide, in their reporting currency, quantitative information about market risk as of the end of the latest fiscal year, in accordance with one of the following three disclosure alternatives. In preparing this quantitative information, registrants shall categorize market risk sensitive instruments into instruments entered into for trading purposes and instruments entered into for purposes other than trading purposes. Within both the trading and other than trading portfolios, separate quantitative information shall be presented, to the extent material, for each market risk exposure category (*i.e.*, interest rate risk, foreign currency exchange rate risk, commodity price risk, and other relevant market risks, such as equity price risk). A registrant may use one of the three alternatives set forth in this section for all of the required quantitative disclosures about market risk. A registrant also may choose, from among the three alternatives, one disclosure alternative for market risk sensitive instruments entered into for trading purposes and another disclosure alternative for market risk sensitive instruments entered into for other than trading purposes. Alternatively, a registrant may choose any disclosure alternative, from among the three alternatives, for each risk exposure category within the trading and other than trading portfolios. The three disclosure alternatives are:

(i)(A)*(1)* Tabular presentation of information related to market risk sensitive instruments; such information shall include fair values of the market risk sensitive instruments and contract terms sufficient to determine future cash flows from those instruments, categorized by expected maturity dates.

(2) Tabular information relating to contract terms shall allow readers of the table to determine expected cash flows from the market risk sensitive instruments for each of the next five years. Comparable tabular information for any remaining years shall be displayed as an aggregate amount.

(3) Within each risk exposure category, the market risk sensitive instruments shall be grouped based on common characteristics. Within the foreign currency exchange rate risk category, the market risk sensitive instruments shall be grouped by functional currency and within the commodity price risk category, the market risk sensitive instruments shall be grouped by type of commodity.

(4) See the Appendix to this Item for a suggested format for presentation of this information; and

(B) Registrants shall provide a description of the contents of the table and any related assumptions necessary to understand the disclosures required under paragraph (a)(1)(i)(A) of this Item 305; or

(ii)(A) Sensitivity analysis disclosures that express the potential loss in future earnings, fair values, or cash flows of market risk sensitive instruments resulting from one or more selected hypothetical changes in interest rates, foreign currency exchange rates, commodity prices, and other relevant market rates or prices over a selected period of time. The magnitude of selected hypothetical changes in rates or prices may differ among and within market risk exposure categories; and

(B) Registrants shall provide a description of the model, assumptions, and parameters, which are necessary to understand the disclosures required under paragraph (a)(1)(ii)(A) of this Item 305; or

(iii)(A) Value at risk disclosures that express the potential loss in future earnings, fair values, or cash flows of market risk sensitive instruments over a selected period of time, with a selected likelihood of occurrence, from changes in interest rates, foreign currency exchange rates, commodity prices, and other relevant market rates or prices;

(B)*(1)* For each category for which value at risk disclosures are required under paragraph (a)(1)(iii)(A) of this Item 305, provide either:

(i) The average, high and low amounts, or the distribution of the value at risk amounts for the reporting period; or

(ii) The average, high and low amounts, or the distribution of actual changes in fair values, earnings, or cash flows from the market risk sensitive instruments occurring during the reporting period; or

(iii) The percentage or number of times the actual changes in fair values, earnings, or cash flows from the market risk sensitive instruments exceeded the value at risk amounts during the reporting period;

(2) Information required under paragraph (a)(1)(iii)(B)*(1)* of this Item 305 is not required for the first fiscal year end in which a registrant must present Item 305 information; and

(C) Registrants shall provide a description of the model, assumptions, and parameters, which are necessary to understand the disclosures required under paragraphs (a)(1)(iii)(A) and (B) of this Item 305.

(2) Registrants shall discuss material limitations that cause the information required under paragraph (a)(1) of this Item 305 not to reflect fully the net market risk exposures of the entity. This discussion shall include summarized descriptions of instruments, positions, and transactions omitted from the quantitative market risk disclosure information or the features of instruments, positions, and transactions that are included, but not reflected fully in the quantitative market risk disclosure information.

(3) Registrants shall present summarized market risk information for the preceding fiscal year. In addition, registrants shall discuss the reasons for material quantitative changes in market risk exposures between the current and preceding fiscal years. Information required by this paragraph (a)(3), however, is not required if disclosure is not required under paragraph (a)(1) of this Item 305 for the current fiscal year. Information required by this paragraph (a)(3) is not required for the first fiscal year end in which a registrant must present Item 305 information.

(4) If registrants change disclosure alternatives or key model characteristics, assumptions, and parameters used in providing quantitative information about market risk (*e.g.*, changing from tabular presentation to value at risk, changing the scope of instruments included in the model, or changing the definition of loss from fair values to earnings), and if the effects of any such change is material, the registrant shall:

(i) Explain the reasons for the change; and

(ii) Either provide summarized comparable information, under the new disclosure method, for the year preceding the current year or, in addition to providing disclosure for the current year under the new method, provide disclosures for the current year and preceding fiscal year under the method used in the preceding year.

Instructions to Paragraph 305(a)

1. Under paragraph 305(a)(1):

A. For each market risk exposure category within the trading and other than trading portfolios, registrants may report the average, high, and low sensitivity analysis or value at risk amounts for the reporting period, as an alternative to reporting year-end amounts.

B. In determining the average, high, and low amounts for the fiscal year under instruction 1.A. of the Instructions to Paragraph 305(a), registrants should use sensitivity analysis or value at risk amounts relating to at least four equal time periods throughout the reporting period (*e.g.*, four quarter-end amounts, 12 month-end amounts, or 52 week-end amounts).

C. Functional currency means functional currency as defined by generally accepted accounting principles (see, *e.g.*, FASB, *Statement of Financial Accounting Standards No.*

52, *"Foreign Currency Translation"*, ("FAS 52") paragraph 20 (December 1981)).

D. Registrants using the sensitivity analysis and value at risk disclosure alternatives are encouraged, but not required, to provide quantitative amounts that reflect the aggregate market risk inherent in the trading and other than trading portfolios.

2. Under paragraph 305(a)(1)(i):

A. Examples of contract terms sufficient to determine future cash flows from market risk sensitive instruments include, but are not limited to:

i. Debt instruments—principal amounts and weighted average effective interest rates;

ii. Forwards and futures—contract amounts and weighted average settlement prices;

iii. Options—contract amounts and weighted average strike prices;

iv. Swaps—notional amounts, weighted average pay rates or prices, and weighted average receive rates or prices; and

v. Complex instruments—likely to be a combination of the contract terms presented in 2.A.i. through iv. of this Instruction;

B. When grouping based on common characteristics, instruments should be categorized, at a minimum, by the following characteristics, when material:

i. Fixed rate or variable rate assets or liabilities;

ii. Long or short forwards and futures;

iii. Written or purchased put or call options with similar strike prices;

iv. Receive fixed and pay variable swaps, receive variable and pay fixed swaps, and receive variable and pay variable swaps;

v. The currency in which the instruments' cash flows are denominated;

vi. Financial instruments for which foreign currency transaction gains and losses are reported in the same manner as translation adjustments under generally accepted accounting principles (see, *e.g.*, FAS 52 paragraph 20 (December 1981)); and

vii. Derivatives used to manage risks inherent in anticipated transactions;

C. Registrants may aggregate information regarding functional currencies that are economically related, managed together for internal risk management purposes, and have statistical correlations of greater than 75% over each of the past three years;

D. Market risk sensitive instruments that are exposed to rate or price changes in more than one market risk exposure category should be presented within the tabular information for each of the risk exposure categories to which those instruments are exposed;

E. If a currency swap (see, *e.g.*, FAS 52 Appendix E for a definition of currency swap) eliminates all foreign currency exposures in the cash flows of a foreign currency denominated debt instrument, neither the currency swap nor the foreign currency denominated debt instrument are required to be disclosed in the foreign currency risk exposure category. However, both the currency swap and the foreign currency denominated debt instrument should be disclosed in the interest rate risk exposure category; and

F. The contents of the table and related assumptions that should be described include, but are not limited to:

i. The different amounts reported in the table for various categories of the market risk sensitive instruments (*e.g.*, principal amounts for debt, notional amounts for swaps, and contract amounts for options and futures);

ii. The different types of reported market rates or prices (*e.g.*, contractual rates or prices, spot rates or prices, forward rates or prices); and

iii. Key prepayment or reinvestment assumptions relating to the timing of reported amounts.

3. Under paragraph 305(a)(1)(ii):

A. Registrants should select hypothetical changes in market rates or prices that are expected to reflect reasonably possible near-term changes in those rates and prices. In this regard, absent economic justification for the selection of a different amount, registrants should use changes that are not less than 10 percent of end of period market rates or prices;

B. For purposes of instruction 3.A. of the Instructions to Paragraph 305(a), the term *reasonably possible* has the same meaning as defined by generally accepted accounting principles (see, *e.g.*, FASB, *Statement of Financial Accounting Standards No. 5, "Accounting for Contingencies,"* ("FAS 5") paragraph 3 (March 1975));

C. For purposes of instruction 3.A. of the Instructions to Paragraph 305(a), the term *near term* means a period of time going forward up to one year from the date of the financial statements (see generally AICPA, Statement of Position 94–6, *"Disclosure of Certain Significant Risks and Uncertainties,"* ("SOP 94–6") at paragraph 7 (December 30, 1994));

D. Market risk sensitive instruments that are exposed to rate or price changes in more than one market risk exposure category should be included in the sensitivity analysis disclosures for each market risk category to which those instruments are exposed;

E. Registrants with multiple foreign currency exchange rate exposures should prepare foreign currency sensitivity analysis disclosures that measure the aggregate sensitivity to changes in all foreign currency exchange rate exposures, including the effects of changes in both transactional currency/functional currency exchange rate exposures and functional currency/reporting currency exchange rate exposures. For example, assume a French division of a registrant presenting its financial statements in U.S. dollars ($US) invests in a deutschmark (DM)-denominated debt security. In these circumstances, the $US is the reporting currency and the DM is the transactional currency. In addition, assume this division determines that the French franc (FF) is its functional currency according to FAS 52. In preparing the foreign currency sensitivity analysis disclosures, this registrant should report the aggregate potential loss from hypothetical changes in both the DM/FF exchange rate exposure and the FF/$US exchange rate exposure; and

F. Model, assumptions, and parameters that should be described include, but are not limited to, how *loss* is defined by the model (*e.g.*, loss in earnings, fair values, or cash flows), a general description of the modeling technique (*e.g.*, duration modeling, modeling that measures the change in net present values arising from selected hypothetical changes in market rates or prices, and a description as to how optionality is addressed by the model), the types of instruments covered by the model (*e.g.*, derivative financial instruments, other financial instruments, derivative commodity instruments, and whether other instruments are included voluntarily, such as certain commodity instruments and positions, cash flows from anticipated transactions, and certain financial instruments excluded under instruction 3.C.ii. of the General Instructions to Paragraphs 305(a) and 305(b)), and other relevant information about the model's assumptions and parameters, (*e.g.*, the magnitude and timing of selected hypothetical changes in market rates or prices used, the method by which discount rates are determined, and key prepayment or reinvestment assumptions).

4. Under paragraph 305(a)(1)(iii):

A. The confidence intervals selected should reflect reasonably possible near-term changes in market rates and prices. In this regard, absent economic justification for the selection of different confidence intervals, registrants should use intervals that are 95 percent or higher;

B. For purposes of instruction 4.A. of the Instructions to Paragraph 305(a), the term *reasonably possible* has the same meaning as defined by generally accepted accounting principles (see, *e.g.*, FAS 5, paragraph 3 (March 1975));

C. For purposes of instruction 4.A. of the Instructions to Paragraphs 305(a), the term *near term* means a period of time going forward up to one year from the date of the financial statements (see generally SOP 94–6, at paragraph 7 (December 30, 1994));

D. Registrants with multiple foreign currency exchange rate exposures should prepare foreign currency value at risk analysis disclosures that measure the aggregate sensitivity to changes in all foreign currency exchange rate exposures, including the aggregate effects of changes in both transactional currency/functional currency exchange rate exposures and functional currency/reporting currency exchange rate exposures. For example, assume a French division of a registrant presenting its financial statements in U.S. dollars ($US) invests in a deutschmark (DM)-denominated debt security. In these circumstances, the $US is the reporting currency and the DM is the transactional currency. In addition, assume this division determines that the French franc (FF) is its functional currency according to FAS 52. In preparing the foreign currency value at risk disclosures, this registrant should report the aggregate potential loss from hypothetical changes in both the DM/FF exchange rate exposure and the FF/$US exchange rate exposure; and

E. Model, assumptions, and parameters that should be described include, but are not limited to, how *loss* is defined by the model (*e.g.*, loss in earnings, fair values, or cash flows), the type of model used (*e.g.*, variance/covariance, historical simulation, or Monte Carlo simulation and a description as to how optionality is addressed by the model), the types of instruments covered by the model (*e.g.*, derivative financial instruments, other financial instruments, derivative commodity instruments, and whether other instruments are included voluntarily, such as certain commodity instruments and positions, cash flows from anticipated transactions, and certain financial instruments excluded under instruction 3.C.ii. of the General Instructions to Paragraphs 305(a) and 305(b)), and other relevant information about the model's assumptions and parameters, (*e.g.*, holding periods, confidence intervals, and, when appropriate, the methods used for aggregating value at risk amounts across market risk exposure categories, such as by assuming perfect positive correlation, independence, or actual observed correlation).

5. Under paragraph 305(a)(2), limitations that should be considered include, but are not limited to:

A. The exclusion of certain market risk sensitive instruments, positions, and transactions from the disclosures required under paragraph 305(a)(1) (*e.g.*, derivative commodity instruments not permitted by contract or business custom to be settled in cash or with another financial instrument, commodity positions, cash flows from anticipated transactions, and certain financial instruments excluded under instruction 3.C.ii. of the General Instructions to Paragraphs 305(a) and 305(b)). Failure to include such instruments, positions, and transactions in preparing the disclosures under paragraph 305(a)(1) may be a limitation because the resulting disclosures may not fully reflect the net market risk of a registrant; and

B. The ability of disclosures required under paragraph 305(a)(1) to reflect fully the market risk that may be inherent in instruments with leverage, option, or prepayment features (*e.g.*, options, including written options, structured notes, collateralized mortgage obligations, leveraged swaps, and options embedded in swaps).

(b) *Qualitative information about market risk.* (1) To the extent material, describe:

(i) The registrant's primary market risk exposures;

(ii) How those exposures are managed. Such descriptions shall include, but not be limited to, a discussion of the objectives, general strategies, and instruments, if any, used to manage those exposures; and

(iii) Changes in either the registrant's primary market risk exposures or how those exposures are managed, when compared to what was in effect during the most recently completed fiscal year and what is known or expected to be in effect in future reporting periods.

(2) Qualitative information about market risk shall be presented separately for market risk sensitive instruments entered into for trading purposes and those entered into for purposes other than trading.

Instructions to Paragraph 305(b)

1. For purposes of disclosure under paragraph 305(b), *primary market risk exposures* means:

A. The following categories of market risk: interest rate risk, foreign currency exchange rate risk, commodity price risk, and other relevant market rate or price risks (*e.g.*, equity price risk); and

B. Within each of these categories, the particular markets that present the primary risk of loss to the registrant. For example, if a registrant has a material exposure to foreign currency exchange rate risk and, within this category of market risk, is most vulnerable to changes in dollar/yen, dollar/pound, and dollar/peso exchange rates, the registrant should disclose those exposures. Similarly, if a registrant has a material exposure to interest rate risk and, within this category of market risk, is most vulnerable to changes in short-term U.S. prime interest rates, it should disclose the existence of that exposure.

2. For purposes of disclosure under paragraph 305(b), registrants should describe primary market risk exposures that exist as of the end of the latest fiscal year, and how those exposures are managed.

General Instructions to Paragraphs 305(a) and 305(b)

1. The disclosures called for by paragraphs 305(a) and 305(b) are intended to clarify the registrant's exposures to market risk associated with activities in derivative financial instruments, other financial instruments, and derivative commodity instruments.

2. In preparing the disclosures under paragraphs 305(a) and 305(b), registrants are required to include derivative financial instruments, other financial instruments, and derivative commodity instruments.

3. For purposes of paragraphs 305(a) and 305(b), derivative financial instruments, other financial instruments, and derivative commodity instruments (collectively referred to as "market risk sensitive instruments") are defined as follows:

A. *Derivative financial instruments* has the same meaning as defined by generally accepted accounting principles (see, *e.g.*, FASB, *Statement of Financial Accounting Standards No. 119, "Disclosure about Derivative Financial Instruments and Fair Value of Financial Instruments,"* ("FAS 119") paragraphs 5–7 (October 1994)), and includes futures, forwards, swaps, options, and other financial instruments with similar characteristics;

B. *Other financial instruments* means all financial instruments as defined by generally accepted accounting principles for which fair value disclosures are required (see, *e.g.*, FASB, *Statement of Financial Accounting Standards No. 107, "Disclosures about Fair Value of Financial Instruments,"* ("FAS 107") paragraphs 3 and 8 (December 1991)), except for derivative financial instruments, as defined above;

C. i. Other financial instruments include, but are not limited to, trade accounts receivable, investments, loans, structured notes, mortgage-backed securities, trade accounts payable, indexed debt instruments, interest-only and principal-only obligations, deposits, and other debt obligations;

ii. Other financial instruments exclude employers' and plans' obligations for pension and other post-retirement benefits, substantively extinguished debt, insurance contracts, lease contracts, warranty obligations and rights, unconditional purchase obligations, investments accounted for under the equity method, minority interests in consolidated enterprises, and equity instruments issued by the registrant and classified in stockholders' equity in the statement of financial position (*see e.g.*, FAS 107, paragraph 8 (December 1991)). For purposes of this item, trade accounts receivable and trade accounts payable need not be considered other financial instruments when their carrying amounts approximate fair value; and

D. *Derivative commodity instruments* include, to the extent such instruments are not derivative financial instruments, commodity futures, commodity forwards, commodity swaps, commodity options, and other commodity instruments with similar characteristics that are permitted by contract or business custom to be settled in cash or with another financial instrument. For purposes of this paragraph, settlement in cash includes settlement in cash of the net change in value of the derivative commodity instrument (*e.g.*, net cash settlement based on changes in the price of the underlying commodity).

4. A. In addition to providing required disclosures for the market risk sensitive instruments defined in instruction 2. of the General Instructions to Paragraphs 305(a) and 305(b), registrants are encouraged to include other market risk sensitive instruments, positions, and transactions within the disclosures required under paragraphs 305(a) and 305(b). Such instruments, positions, and transactions might include commodity positions, derivative commodity instruments that are not permitted by contract or business custom to be settled in cash or with another financial instrument, cash flows from anticipated transactions, and certain financial instruments excluded under instruction 3.C.ii. of the General Instructions to Paragraphs 305(a) and 305(b).

B. Registrants that voluntarily include other market risk sensitive instruments, positions and transactions within their quantitative disclosures about market risk under the sensitivity analysis or value at risk disclosure alternatives are not required to provide separate market risk disclosures for any voluntarily selected instruments, positions, or transactions. Instead, registrants selecting the sensitivity analysis and value at risk disclosure alternatives are permitted to present comprehensive market risk disclosures, which reflect the combined market risk exposures inherent in both the required and any voluntarily selected instruments, position, or transactions. Registrants that choose the tabular presentation disclosure alternative should present voluntarily selected instruments, positions, or transactions in a manner consistent with the requirements in Item 305(a) for market risk sensitive instruments.

C. If a registrant elects to include voluntarily a particular type of instrument, position, or transaction in their quantitative disclosures about market risk, that registrant should include all, rather than some, of those instruments, positions, or transactions within those disclosures. For example, if a registrant holds in inventory a particular type of commodity position and elects to include that commodity position within their market risk disclosures, the registrant should include the entire commodity position, rather than only a portion thereof, in their quantitative disclosures about market risk.

5. A. Under paragraphs 305(a) and 305(b), a materiality assessment should be made for each market risk exposure category within the trading and other than trading portfolios.

B. For purposes of making the materiality assessment under instruction 5.A. of the General Instructions to Paragraphs 305(a) and 305(b), registrants should evaluate both:

i. The materiality of the fair values of derivative financial instruments, other financial instruments, and derivative commodity instruments outstanding as of the end of the latest fiscal year; and

ii. The materiality of potential, near-term losses in future earnings, fair values, and/or cash flows from reasonably possible near-term changes in market rates or prices.

iii. If either paragraphs B.i. or B.ii. in this instruction of the General Instructions to Paragraphs 305(a) and 305(b) are material, the registrant should disclose quantitative and qualitative information about market risk, if such market risk for the particular market risk exposure category is material.

C. For purposes of instruction 5.B.i. of the General Instructions to Paragraphs 305(a) and 305(b), registrants generally should not net fair values, except to the extent allowed under generally accepted accounting principles (see, *e.g.*, FASB *Interpretation No. 39, "Offsetting of Amounts Related to Certain Contracts"* (March 1992)). For example, under this instruction, the fair value of assets generally should not be netted with the fair value of liabilities.

D. For purposes of instruction 5.B.ii. of the General Instructions to Paragraphs 305(a) and 305(b), registrants should consider, among other things, the magnitude of:

i. Past market movements;

ii. Reasonably possible, near-term market movements; and

iii. Potential losses that may arise from leverage, option, and multiplier features.

E. For purposes of instructions 5.B.ii and 5.D.ii of the General Instructions to Paragraphs 305(a) and 305(b), the term *near term* means a period of time going forward up to one year from the date of the financial statements (see generally SOP 94–6, at paragraph 7 (December 30, 1994)).

F. For the purpose of instructions 5.B.ii. and 5.D.ii. of the General Instructions to Paragraphs 305(a) and 305(b), the term *reasonably possible* has the same meaning as defined by generally accepted accounting principles (see, *e.g.*, FAS–5, paragraph 3 (March 1975)).

6. For purposes of paragraphs 305(a) and 305(b), registrants should present the information outside of, and not incorporate the information into, the financial statements (including the footnotes to the financial statements). In addition, registrants are encouraged to provide the required information in one location. However, alternative presentation, such as inclusion of all or part of the information in Management's Discussion and Analysis, may be used at the discretion of the registrant. If information is disclosed in more than one location, registrants should provide cross-references to the locations of the related disclosures.

7. For purposes of the instructions to paragraphs 305(a) and 305(b), *trading purposes* has the same meaning as defined by generally accepted accounting principles (see, *e.g.*, FAS 119, paragraph 9a (October 1994)). In addition, *anticipated transactions* means transactions (other than transactions involv-

ing existing assets or liabilities or transactions necessitated by existing firm commitments) an enterprise expects, but is not obligated, to carry out in the normal course of business (see, *e.g.*, FASB, *Statement of Financial Accounting Standards No. 80, "Accounting for Futures Contracts,"* paragraph 9 (August 1984)).

(c) *Interim periods.* If interim period financial statements are included or are required to be included by Article 3 of Regulation S–X (17 CFR 210), discussion and analysis shall be provided so as to enable the reader to assess the sources and effects of material changes in information that would be provided under Item 305 of Regulation S–K from the end of the preceding fiscal year to the date of the most recent interim balance sheet.

Instructions to Paragraph 305(c)

1. Information required under paragraph (c) of this Item 305 is not required until after the first fiscal year end in which this Item 305 is applicable.

(d) *Safe Harbor.* (1) The safe harbor provided in Section 27A of the Securities Act of 1933 (15 U.S.C. 77z–2) and Section 21E of the Securities Exchange Act of 1934 (15 U.S.C. 78u–5) ("statutory safe harbors") shall apply, with respect to all types of issuers and transactions, to information provided pursuant to paragraphs (a), (b), and (c) of this Item 305, provided that the disclosure is made by: an issuer; a person acting on behalf of the issuer; an outside reviewer retained by the issuer making a statement on behalf of the issuer; or an underwriter, with respect to information provided by the issuer or information derived from information provided by the issuer.

(2) For purposes of paragraph (d) of this Item 305 only:

(i) All information required by paragraphs (a), (b)(1)(i), (b)(1)(iii), and (c) of this Item 305 is considered *forward looking statements* for purposes of the statutory safe harbors, except for historical facts such as the terms of particular contracts and the number of market risk sensitive instruments held during or at the end of the reporting period; and

(ii) With respect to paragraph (a) of this Item 305, the *meaningful cautionary statements* prong of the statutory safe harbors will be satisfied if a registrant satisfies all requirements of that same paragraph (a) of this Item 305.

(e) *Small business issuers.* Small business issuers, as defined in § 230.405 of this chapter and § 230.12b–2 of this chapter, need not provide the information required by this Item 305, whether or not they file on forms specially designated as small business issuer forms.

General Instructions to Paragraphs 305(a), 305(b), 305(c), 305(d), and 305(e)

1. Bank registrants, thrift registrants, and non-bank and non-thrift registrants with market capitalizations on January 28, 1997 in excess of $2.5 billion should provide Item 305 disclosures in filings with the Commission that include annual financial statements for fiscal years ending after June 15, 1997. Non-bank and non-thrift registrants with market capitalizations on January 28, 1997 of $2.5 billion or less should provide Item 305 disclosures in filings with the Commission that include financial statements for fiscal years ending after June 15, 1998.

2. A. For purposes of instruction 1. of the General Instructions to Paragraphs 305(a), 305(b), 305(c), 305(d), and 305(e), *bank registrants and thrift registrants* include any registrant which has control over a depository institution.

B. For purposes of instruction 2.A. of the General Instructions to Paragraphs 305(a), 305(b), 305(c), 305(d), and 305(e), a registrant has control over a depository institution if:

i. The registrant directly or indirectly or acting through one or more other persons owns, controls, or has power to vote

25% or more of any class of voting securities of the depository institution;

ii. The registrant controls in any manner the election of a majority of the directors or trustees of the depository institution; or

iii. The Federal Reserve Board or Office of Thrift Supervision determines, after notice and opportunity for hearing, that the registrant directly or indirectly exercises a controlling influence over the management or policies of the depository institution.

C. For purposes of instruction 2.B. of the General Instructions to Paragraphs 305(a), 305(b), 305(c), 305(d), and 305(e), a depository institution means any of the following:

i. An insured depository institution as defined in section 3(c)(2) of the Federal Deposit Insurance Act (12 U.S.C.A. Sec. 1813(c));

ii. An institution organized under the laws of the United States, any State of the United States, the District of Columbia, any territory of the United States, Puerto Rico, Guam, American Somoa, or the Virgin Islands, which both accepts demand deposits or deposits that the depositor may withdraw by check or similar means for payment to third parties or others and is engaged in the business of making commercial loans.

D. For purposes of instruction 1. of the General Instructions to Paragraphs 305(a), 305(b), 305(c), 305(d) and 305(e), *market capitalization* is the aggregate market value of common equity as set forth in General Instruction I.B.1. of Form S–3; provided however, that common equity held by affiliates is included in the calculation of market capitalization; and provided further that instead of using the 60 day period prior to filing referenced in General Instruction I.B.1. of Form S–3, the measurement date is January 28, 1997.

Appendix to Item 305—Tabular Disclosures

The tables set forth below are illustrative of the format that might be used when a registrant elects to present the information required by paragraph (a)(1)(i)(A) of Item 305 regarding terms and information about derivative financial instruments, other financial instruments, and derivative commodity instruments. These examples are for illustrative purposes only. Registrants are not required to display the information in the specific format illustrated below. Alternative methods of display are permissible as long as the disclosure requirements of the section are satisfied. Furthermore, these examples were designed primarily to illustrate possible formats for presentation of the information required by the disclosure item and do not purport to illustrate the broad range of derivative financial instruments, other financial instruments, and derivative commodity instruments utilized by registrants.

Interest Rate Sensitivity

The table below provides information about the Company's derivative financial instruments and other financial instruments that are sensitive to changes in interest rates, including interest rate swaps and debt obligations. For debt obligations, the table presents principal cash flows and related weighted average interest rates by expected maturity dates. For interest rate swaps, the table presents notional amounts and weighted average interest rates by expected (contractual) maturity dates. Notional amounts are used to calculate the contractual payments to be exchanged under the contract. Weighted average variable rates are based on implied forward rates in the yield curve at the reporting date. The information is presented in U.S. dollar equivalents, which is the Company's reporting currency. The instrument's actual cash flows are denominated in both U.S. dollars ($US) and German deutschmarks (DM), as indicated in parentheses.

December 31, 19X1

	Expected maturity date							
	19X2	19X3	19X4	19X5	19X6	There-after	Total	Fair value
Liabilities	(US$ Equivalent in millions)							
Long-term Debt:								
Fixed Rate ($US)	$XXX	$XXX	$XXX	$XXX	$XXX	$XXX	$XXX	$XXX
Average interest rate	X.X%	X.X%	X.X%	X.X%	X.X%	X.X%	X.X%	
Fixed Rate (DM)	XXX	XXX	XXX	XXX	XXX	XXX	XXX	XXX
Average interest rate	X.X%	X.X%	X.X%	X.X%	X.X%	X.X%	X.X%	
Variable Rate ($US)	XXX	XXX	XXX	XXX	XXX	XXX	XXX	XXX
Average interest rate	X.X%	X.X%	X.X%	X.X%	X.X%	X.X%	X.X%	
Interest Rate Derivatives	(In millions)							
Interest Rate Swaps:								
Variable to Fixed ($US)	$XXX	$XXX	$XXX	$XXX	$XXX	$XXX	$XXX	$XXX
Average pay rate	X.X%	X.X%	X.X%	X.X%	X.X%	X.X%	X.X%	
Average receive rate	X.X%	X.X%	X.X%	X.X%	X.X%	X.X%	X.X%	
Fixed to Variable ($US)	XXX	XXX	XXX	XXX	XXX	XXX	XXX	XXX
Average pay rate	X.X%	X.X%	X.X%	X.X%	X.X%	X.X%	X.X%	
Average receive rate	X.X%	X.X%	X.X%	X.X%	X.X%	X.X%	X.X%	

Exchange Rate Sensitivity

The table below provides information about the Company's derivative financial instruments, other financial instruments, and firmly committed sales transactions by functional currency and presents such information in U.S. dollar equivalents.[1] The table summarizes information on instruments and transactions that are sensitive to foreign currency exchange rates, including foreign currency forward exchange agreements, deutschmark (DM)-denominated debt obligations, and firmly committed DM sales transactions. For debt obligations, the table presents principal cash flows and related weighted average interest rates by expected maturity dates. For firmly committed DM-sales transactions, sales amounts are presented by the expected transaction date, which are not expected to exceed two years. For foreign currency forward exchange agreements, the table presents the notional amounts and weighted average exchange rates by expected (contractual) maturity dates. These notional amounts generally are used to calculate the contractual payments to be exchanged under the contract.

December 31, 19X1

	Expected maturity date							
	19X2	19X3	19X4	19X5	19X6	There-after	Total	Fair value
On-Balance Sheet Financial Instruments	(US$ Equivalent in millions)							
$US Functional Currency [2]:								
Liabilities								
Long-Term Debt:								
Fixed Rate (DM)	$XXX	$XXX	$XXX	$XXX	$XXX	$XXX	$XXX	$XXX
Average interest rate	X.X	X.X	X.X	X.X	X.X	X.X	X.X	....
Anticipated Transactions and Related Derivatives [3]	Expected maturity or transaction date (US$ Equivalent in millions)							
$US Functional Currency:								

December 31, 19X1

	Expected maturity date							
	19X2	19X3	19X4	19X5	19X6	There-after	Total	Fair value
Firmly committed Sales Contracts (DM)	$XXX	$XXX	....	....	....	....	$XXX	$XXX
Forward Exchange Agreements (Receive $US/Pay DM):								
Contract Amount	XXX	XXX	....	....	....	....	XXX	XXX
Average Contractual Exchange Rate	X.X	X.X	....	....	....	....	X.X	....

Average Contractual Exchange Rate	X.X	X.X	....	....	....	X.X	....

[1] The information is presented in U.S. dollars because that is the registrant's reporting currency.

[2] Similar tabular information would be provided for other functional currencies.

[3] Pursuant to General Instruction 4. to Items 305(a) and 305(b) of Regulation S–K, registrants may include cash flows from anticipated transactions and operating cash flows resulting from non-financial and non-commodity instruments.

Commodity Price Sensitivity

The table below provides information about the Company's corn inventory and futures contracts that are sensitive to changes in commodity prices, specifically corn prices. For inventory, the table presents the carrying amount and fair value at December 31, 19X1. For the futures contracts the table presents the notional amounts in bushels, the weighted average contract prices, and the total dollar contract amount by expected maturity dates, the latest of which occurs one year from the reporting date. Contract amounts are used to calculate the contractual payments and quantity of corn to be exchanged under the futures contracts.

December 31, 19X1		
	Carrying amount	Fair value
	(In millions)	
On Balance Sheet Commodity Position and Related Derivatives		
Corn Inventory [4]	$XXX	$XXX
	Expected maturity 1992	Fair value
Related Derivatives		
Futures Contracts (Short):		
Contract Volumes (100,000 bushels)	XXX	....
Weighted Average Price (Per 100,000 bushels)	$X.XX	....
Contract Amount ($US in millions)	$XXX	$XXX

[4] Pursuant to General Instruction 4. to Items 305(a) and 305(b) of Regulation S–K, registrants may include information on commodity positions, such as corn inventory.

Item 306. Audit Committee Report

(a) The audit committee must state whether:

(1) The audit committee has reviewed and discussed the audited financial statements with management;

(2) The audit committee has discussed with the independent auditors the matters required to be discussed by SAS 61, as may be modified or supplemented;

(3) The audit committee has received the written disclosures and the letter from the independent accountants required by Independence Standards Board Standard No. 1 (Independence Standards Board Standard No. 1, Independence Discussions with Audit Committees), as may be modified or supplemented, and has discussed with the independent accountant the independent accountant's independence; and

(4) Based on the review and discussions referred to in paragraphs (a)(1) through (a)(3) of this Item, the audit committee recommended to the Board of Directors that the audited financial statements be included in the company's Annual Report on Form 10–K (17 CFR 249.310) (or, for closed-end investment companies registered under the Investment Company Act of 1940 (15 U.S.C. 80a–1 et seq.), the annual report to shareholders required by Section 30(e) of the Investment Company Act of 1940 (15 U.S.C. 80a–29(e)) and Rule 30d–1 (17 CFR 270.30d–1) thereunder) for the last fiscal year for filing with the Commission.

(b) The name of each member of the company's audit committee (or, in the absence of an audit committee, the board committee performing equivalent functions or the entire board of directors) must appear below the disclosure required by this Item.

(c) The information required by paragraphs (a) and (b) of this Item shall not be deemed to be "soliciting material," or to be "filed" with the Commission or subject to Regulation 14A or 14C (17 CFR 240.14a–1 et seq. or 240.14c–1 et seq.), other than as provided in this Item, or to the liabilities of section 18 of the Exchange Act (15 U.S.C. 78r), except to the extent that the company specifically requests that the information be treated as soliciting material or specifically incorporates it by reference into a document filed under the Securities Act or the Exchange Act.

(d) The information required by paragraphs (a) and (b) of this Item need not be provided in any filings other than a registrant proxy or information statement relating to an annual meeting of security holders at which directors are to be elected (or special meeting or written consents in lieu of such meeting). Such information will not be deemed to be incorporated by reference into any filing under the Securities Act or the Exchange Act, except to the extent that the registrant specifically incorporates it by reference.

Item 307. Disclosure Controls and Procedures

Disclose the conclusions of the registrant's principal executive and principal financial officers, or persons performing similar functions, regarding the effectiveness of the registrant's disclosure controls and procedures (as defined in § 240.13a–15(e) or 240.15d–15(e) of this chapter) as of the end of the period covered by the report, based on the evaluation of these controls and procedures required by paragraph (b) of § 240.13a–15 or 240.15d–15 of this chapter.

Item 308. Internal Control over Financial Reporting

(a) *Management's annual report on internal control over financial reporting.* Provide a report of management on the registrant's internal control over financial reporting (as defined in § 240.13a–15(f) or 240.15d–15(f) of this chapter) that contains:

(1) A statement of management's responsibility for establishing and maintaining adequate internal control over financial reporting for the registrant;

(2) A statement identifying the framework used by management to evaluate the effectiveness of the registrant's internal control over financial reporting as required by paragraph (c) of § 240.13a–15 or 240.15d–15 of this chapter;

(3) Management's assessment of the effectiveness of the registrant's internal control over financial reporting as of the end of the registrant's most recent fiscal year, including a statement as to whether or not internal control over financial reporting is effective. This discussion must include disclosure of any material weakness in the registrant's internal control over financial reporting identified by management. Management is not permitted to conclude that the registrant's internal control over financial reporting is effective if there are one or more material weaknesses in the registrant's internal control over financial reporting; and

(4) A statement that the registered public accounting firm that audited the financial statements included in the annual report containing the disclosure required by this Item has issued an attestation report on management's assessment of the registrant's internal control over financial reporting.

(b) *Attestation report of the registered public accounting firm.* Provide the registered public accounting firm's attestation report on management's assessment of the registrant's internal control over financial reporting in the registrant's annual report containing the disclosure required by this Item.

(c) *Changes in internal control over financial reporting.* Disclose any change in the registrant's internal control over financial reporting identified in connection with the evaluation required by paragraph (d) of § 240.13a–15 or 240.15d–15 of this chapter that occurred during the registrant's last fiscal quarter (the registrant's fourth fiscal quarter in the case of an annual report) that has materially affected, or is reasonably likely to materially affect, the registrant's internal control over financial reporting.

Instructions to Item 308. The registrant must maintain evidential matter, including documentation, to provide reasonable support for management's assessment of the effectiveness of the registrant's internal control over financial reporting.

2. A registrant that is an Asset-Backed Issuer (as defined in § 229.1101) is not required to disclose the information required by this Item.

Subpart 400—Management and Certain Security Holders

Item 401. Directors, Executive Officers, Promoters and Control Persons

(a) *Identification of Directors.* List the names and ages of all directors of the registrant and all persons nominated or chosen to become directors; indicate all positions and offices with the registrant held by each such person; state his term of office as director and any period(s) during which he has served as such; describe briefly any arrangement or understanding between him and any other person(s) (naming such person(s)) pursuant to which he was or is to be selected as a director or nominee.

Instructions to Paragraph (a) of Item 401. 1. Do not include arrangements or understandings with directors or officers of the registrant acting solely in their capacities as such.

2. No nominee or person chosen to become a director who has not consented to act as such shall be named in response to this Item. In this regard, with respect to proxy statements, see Rule 14a–4(d) under the Exchange Act.

3. If the information called for by this paragraph (a) is being presented in a proxy or information statement, no information need be given respecting any director whose term of office as a director will not continue after the meeting to which the statement relates.

4. With regard to proxy statements in connection with action to be taken concerning the election of directors, if fewer nominees are named than the number fixed by or pursuant to the governing instruments, state the reasons for this procedure and that the proxies cannot be voted for a greater number of persons than the number of nominees named.

5. With regard to proxy statements in connection with action to be taken concerning the election of directors, if the solicitation is made by persons other than management, information shall be given as to nominees of the persons making the solicitation. In all other instances, information shall be given as to directors and persons nominated for election or chosen by management to become directors.

(b) *Identification of Executive Officers.* List the names and ages of all executive officers of the registrant and all persons chosen to become executive officers; indicate all positions and offices with the registrant held by each such person; state his term of office as officer and the period during which he has served as such and describe briefly any arrangement or understanding between him and any other person(s) (naming such person) pursuant to which he was or is to be selected as an officer.

Instructions to Paragraph (b) of Item 401. 1. Do not include arrangements or understandings with directors or officers of the registrant acting solely in their capacities as such.

2. No person chosen to become an executive officer who has not consented to act as such shall be named in response to this Item.

3. The information regarding executive officers called for by this Item need not be furnished in proxy or information statements prepared in accordance with Schedule 14A under the Exchange Act (§ 240.14a–101 of this chapter) by those registrants relying on General Instruction G of Form 10–K and Form 10–

KSB under the Exchange Act, *Provided,* That such information is furnished in a separate item captioned "Executive officers of the registrant," and included in Part I of the registrant's annual report on Form 10–K and Form 10–KSB.

(c) *Identification of Certain Significant Employees.* Where the registrant employs persons such as production managers, sales managers, or research scientists who are not executive officers but who make or are expected to make significant contributions to the business of the registrant, such persons shall be identified and their background disclosed to the same extent as in the case of executive officers. Such disclosure need not be made if the registrant was subject to section 13(a) or 15(d) of the Exchange Act or was exempt from section 13(a) by section 12(g)(2)(G) of such Act immediately prior to the filing of the registration statement, report, or statement to which this Item is applicable.

(d) *Family Relationships.* State the nature of any family relationship between any director, executive officer, or person nominated or chosen by the registrant to become a director or executive officer.

Instruction to Paragraph 401(d). The term "family relationship" means any relationship by blood, marriage, or adoption, not more remote than first cousin.

(e) *Business Experience.* (1) *Background.* Briefly describe the business experience during the past five years of each director, executive officer, person nominated or chosen to become a director or executive officer, and each person named in answer to paragraph (c) of Item 401, including: each person's principal occupations and employment during the past five years; the name and principal business of any corporation or other organization in which such occupations and employment were carried on; and whether such corporation or organization is a parent, subsidiary or other affiliate of the registrant. When an executive officer or person named in response to paragraph (c) of Item 401 has been employed by the registrant or a subsidiary of the registrant for less than five years, a brief explanation shall be included as to the nature of the responsibility undertaken by the individual in prior positions to provide adequate disclosure of his prior business experience. What is required is information relating to the level of his professional competence, which may include, depending upon the circumstances, such specific information as the size of the operation supervised.

(2) *Directorships.* Indicate any other directorships held by each director or person nominated or chosen to become a director in any company with a class of securities registered pursuant to section 12 of the Exchange Act or subject to the requirements of section 15(d) of such Act or any company registered as an investment company under the Investment Company Act of 1940, 15 U.S.C. 80a–1, et seq., as amended, naming such company.

Instruction to Paragraph (e) of Item 401. For the purposes of paragraph (e)(2), where the other directorships of each director or person nominated or chosen to become a director include directorships of two or more registered investment companies that are part of a "fund complex" as that term is defined in Item 22(a) of Schedule 14A under the Exchange Act (§ 240.14a–101 of this chapter), the registrant may, rather than listing each such investment company, identify the fund complex and provide the number of investment company directorships held by the director or nominee in such fund complex.

(f) *Involvement in Certain Legal Proceedings.* Describe any of the following events that occurred during the past five years and that are material to an evaluation of the ability or integrity of any director, person nominated to become a director or executive officer of the registrant:

(1) A petition under the Federal bankruptcy laws or any state insolvency law was filed by or against, or a receiver, fiscal agent or similar officer was appointed by a court for the business or property of such person,

or any partnership in which he was a general partner at or within two years before the time of such filing, or any corporation or business association of which he was an executive officer at or within two years before the time of such filing;

(2) Such person was convicted in a criminal proceeding or is a named subject of a pending criminal proceeding (excluding traffic violations and other minor offenses);

(3) Such person was the subject of any order, judgment, or decree, not subsequently reversed, suspended or vacated, of any court of competent jurisdiction, permanently or temporarily enjoining him from, or otherwise limiting, the following activities:

(i) Acting as a futures commission merchant, introducing broker, commodity trading advisor, commodity pool operator, floor broker, leverage transaction merchant, any other person regulated by the Commodity Futures Trading Commission, or an associated person of any of the foregoing, or as an investment adviser, underwriter, broker or dealer in securities, or as an affiliated person, director or employee of any investment company, bank, savings and loan association or insurance company, or engaging in or continuing any conduct or practice in connection with such activity;

(ii) Engaging in any type of business practice; or

(iii) Engaging in any activity in connection with the purchase or sale of any security or commodity or in connection with any violation of Federal or State securities laws or Federal commodities laws;

(4) Such person was the subject of any order, judgment or decree, not subsequently reversed, suspended or vacated, of any Federal or State authority barring, suspending or otherwise limiting for more than 60 days the right of such person to engage in any activity described in paragraph (f)(3)(i) of this Item, or to be associated with persons engaged in any such activity; or

(5) Such person was found by a court of competent jurisdiction in a civil action or by the Commission to have violated any Federal or State securities law, and the judgment in such civil action or finding by the Commission has not been subsequently reversed, suspended, or vacated.

(6) Such person was found by a court of competent jurisdiction in a civil action or by the Commodities Futures Trading Commission to have violated any Federal commodities law, and the judgment in such civil action or finding by the Commodities Futures Trading Commission has not been subsequently reversed, suspended or vacated.

Instructions to Paragraph (f) of Item 401. 1. For purposes of computing the five year period referred to in this paragraph, the date of a reportable event shall be deemed the date on which the final order, judgment or decree was entered, or the date on which any rights of appeal from preliminary orders, judgments, or decrees have lapsed. With respect to bankruptcy petitions, the computation date shall be the date of filing for uncontested petitions or the date upon which approval of a contested petition became final.

2. If any event specified in this paragraph (f) has occurred and information in regard thereto is omitted on the grounds that it is not material, the registrant may furnish to the Commission, at time of filing (or at the time preliminary materials are filed, or ten days before definitive materials are filed if preliminary filing is not required, pursuant to Rule 14a–6 or 14c–5 under the Exchange Act), as supplemental information and not as part of the registration statement, report, or proxy or information statement, materials to which the omission relates, a description of the event and a statement of the reasons for the omission of information in regard thereto.

3. The registrant is permitted to explain any mitigating circumstances associated with events reported pursuant to this paragraph.

4. If the information called for by this paragraph (f) is being presented in a proxy or information statement, no information need be given respecting any director whose term of office as a director will not continue after the meeting to which the statement relates.

(g) *Promoters and control persons.*

(1) Registrants, which have not been subject to the reporting requirements of Section 13(a) or 15(d) of the Exchange Act for the twelve months immediately prior to the filing of the registration statement, report, or statement to which this Item is applicable, and which were organized within the last five years, shall describe with respect to any promoter, any of the events enumerated in paragraphs (f)(1) through (f)(6) of this section that occurred during the past five years and that are material to a voting or investment decision.

(2) Registrants, which have not been subject to the reporting requirements of Section 13(a) or 15(d) of the Exchange Act for the twelve months immediately prior to the filing of the registration statement, report, or statement to which this Item is applicable, shall describe with respect to any control person, any of the events enumerated in paragraphs (f)(1) through (f)(6) of this section that occurred during the past five years and that are material to a voting or investment decision.

Instructions to Paragraph (g) of Item 401. 1. Instructions 1. through 3. to paragraph (f) shall apply to this paragraph (g).

2. Paragraph (g) shall not apply to any subsidiary of a registrant which has been reporting pursuant to Section 13(a) or 15(d) of the Exchange Act for the twelve months immediately prior to the filing of the registration statement, report or statement.

(h) *Audit committee financial expert.* (1)(i) Disclose that the registrant's board of directors has determined that the registrant either:

(A) Has at least one audit committee financial expert serving on its audit committee; or

(B) Does not have an audit committee financial expert serving on its audit committee.

(ii) If the registrant provides the disclosure required by paragraph (h)(1)(i)(A) of this Item, it must disclose the name of the audit committee financial expert and whether that person is *independent,* as that term is used in Item 7(d)(3)(iv) of Schedule 14A (240.14a–101 of this chapter) under the Exchange Act.

(iii) If the registrant provides the disclosure required by paragraph (h)(1)(i)(B) of this Item, it must explain why it does not have an audit committee financial expert.

Instructions to Item 401(h)

1. The disclosure under Item 401(h) is required only in a registrant's annual report. The registrant need not provide the disclosure required by this Item 401(h) in a proxy or information statement unless that registrant is electing to incorporate this information by reference from the proxy or information statement into its annual report pursuant to general instruction G(3) to Form 10–K.

(2) For purposes of this Item, an *audit committee financial expert* means a person who has the following attributes:

(i) An understanding of generally accepted accounting principles and financial statements;

(ii) The ability to assess the general application of such principles in connection with the accounting for estimates, accruals and reserves;

(iii) Experience preparing, auditing, analyzing or evaluating financial statements that present a breadth and level of complexity of accounting issues that are generally comparable to the breadth and complexity of issues that can reasonably be expected to be raised by the registrant's financial statements, or experience actively supervising one or more persons engaged in such activities;

(iv) An understanding of internal control over financial reporting; and

(v) An understanding of audit committee functions.

(3) A person shall have acquired such attributes through:

(i) Education and experience as a principal financial officer, principal accounting officer, controller, public accountant or auditor or experience in one or more positions that involve the performance of similar functions;

(ii) Experience actively supervising a principal financial officer, principal accounting officer, controller, public accountant, auditor or person performing similar functions;

(iii) Experience overseeing or assessing the performance of companies or public accountants with respect to the preparation, auditing or evaluation of financial statements; or

(iv) Other relevant experience.

(4) *Safe Harbor.* (i) A person who is determined to be an audit committee financial expert will not be deemed an *expert* for any purpose, including without limitation for purposes of section 11 of the Securities Act of 1933 (15 U.S.C. 77k), as a result of being designated or identified as an audit committee financial expert pursuant to this Item 401.

(ii) The designation or identification of a person as an audit committee financial expert pursuant to this Item 401 does not impose on such person any duties, obligations or liability that are greater than the duties, obligations and liability imposed on such person as a member of the audit committee and board of directors in the absence of such designation or identification.

(iii) The designation or identification of a person as an audit committee financial expert pursuant to this Item 401 does not affect the duties, obligations or liability of any other member of the audit committee or board of directors.

Instructions to Item 401(h).

1. The disclosure under Item 401(h) is required only in a registrant's annual report. The registrant need not provide the disclosure required by this Item 401(h) in a proxy or information statement unless that registrant is electing to incorporate this information by reference from the proxy or information statement into its annual report pursuant to general instruction G(3) to Form 10–K.

2. If a person qualifies as an audit committee financial expert by means of having held a position described in paragraph (h)(3)(iv) of this Item, the registrant shall provide a brief listing of that person's relevant experience. Such disclosure may be made by reference to disclosures required under paragraph (e) of this Item 401 (§ 229.401(e) or this chapter).

3. In the case of a foreign private issuer with a two-tier board of directors, for purposes of this Item 401(h), the term *board of directors* means the supervisory or non-management board. In the case of a foreign private issuer meeting the requirements of § 240.10A–3(c)(3), for purposes of this Item 401(h), the term *board of directors* means the issuer's board of auditors (or similar body) or statutory auditors, as applicable. Also, in the case of a foreign private issuer, the term generally accepted accounting principles in paragraph (h)(2)(i) of this Item means the body of *generally accepted accounting principles* used by that issuer in its primary financial statements filed with the Commission.

4. A registrant that is an Asset–Backed Issuer (as defined in § 240.13a–14(g) and § 240.15d–14(g) of this chapter) is not required to disclose the information required by this Item 401(h).

(i) *Identification of the audit committee.* (1) If you meet the following requirements, provide the disclosure in paragraph (i)(2) of this section:

(i) You are a listed issuer, as defined in § 240.10A–3 of this chapter;

(ii) You are filing either an annual report on Form 10–K or 10–KSB (17 CFR 249.310 or 17 CFR 249.310b), or a proxy statement or information statement pursuant to the Exchange Act (15 U.S.C. 78a *et seq.*) if action is to be taken with respect to the election of directors; and

(iii) You are neither:

(A) A subsidiary of another listed issuer that is relying on the exemption in § 240.10A–3(c)(2) of this chapter; nor

(B) Relying on any of the exemptions in § 240.10A–3(c)(4) through (c)(7) of this chapter.

(2)(i) State whether or not the registrant has a separately-designated standing audit committee established in accordance with section 3(a)(58)(A) of the Exchange Act (15 U.S.C. 78c(a)(58)(A)), or a committee performing similar functions. If the registrant has such a committee, however designated, identify each committee member. If the entire board of directors is acting as the registrant's audit committee as specified in section 3(a)(58)(B) of the Exchange Act (15 U.S.C. 78c(a)(58)(B)), so state.

(ii) If applicable, provide the disclosure required by § 240.10A–3(d) under the Exchange Act regarding an exemption from the listing standards for audit committees.

(j) Describe any material changes to the procedures by which security holders may recommend nominees to the registrant's board of directors, where those changes were implemented after the registrant last provided disclosure in response to the requirements of Item 7(d)(2)(ii)(G) of Schedule 14A (§ 240.14a–101) or this Item.

Instructions to paragraph (j) of Item 401:

1. The disclosure required in paragraph (j) need only be provided in a registrant's quarterly or annual reports.

2. For purposes of paragraph (j), adoption of procedures by which security holders may recommend nominees to the registrant's board of directors, where the registrant's most recent disclosure in response to the requirements of Item 7(d)(2)(ii)(G) of Schedule 14A (§ 240.14a–101), or this Item, indicated that the registrant did not have in place such procedures, will constitute a material change.

Item 402. Executive Compensation

(a) *General.* (1) *Treatment of specific types of issuers.* (i) *Small business issuers.* A registrant that qualifies as "small business issuer," as defined by Item 10(a)(1) of Regulation S–B, will be deemed to comply with this item if it provides the information required by paragraph (b) (Summary Compensation Table), paragraphs (c)(1) and (c)(2)(i)–(v) (Option/SAR Grants Table), paragraph (d) (Aggregated Option/SAR Exercise and Fiscal Year–End Option/SAR Value Table), paragraph (e) (Long–Term Incentive Plan Awards Table), paragraph (g) (Compensation of Directors), paragraph (h) (Employment Contracts, Termination of Employment and Change in Control Arrangements) and paragraph (i)(1) and (2) (Report on Repricing of Options/SARs) of this item.

(ii) *Foreign private issuers.* A foreign private issuer will be deemed to comply with this item if it provides the information required by Items 6B and 6E2 of Form 20–F (17 CFR 249.220f), with more detailed information provided if otherwise made publicly available.

(2) *All compensation covered.* This item requires clear, concise and understandable disclosure of all plan and non-plan compensation awarded to, earned by, or paid to the named executive officers designated under paragraph (a)(3) of this item, and directors covered by paragraph (g) of this item by any person for all services rendered in all capacities to the registrant and its subsidiaries, unless otherwise specified in this item. Except as provided by paragraph (a)(5) of this item, all such compensation shall be reported pursuant to this item, even if also called for by another requirement,

including transactions between the registrant and a third party where the primary purpose of the transaction is to furnish compensation to any such named executive officer or director. No item reported as compensation for one fiscal year need be reported as compensation for a subsequent fiscal year.

(3) *Persons covered.* Disclosure shall be provided pursuant to this item for each of the following (the "named executive officers"):

(i) All individuals serving as the registrant's chief executive officer or acting in a similar capacity during the last completed fiscal year ("CEO"), regardless of compensation level;

(ii) The registrant's four most highly compensated executive officers other than the CEO who were serving as executive officers at the end of the last completed fiscal year; and

(iii) Up to two additional individuals for whom disclosure would have been provided pursuant to paragraph (a)(3)(ii) of this item but for the fact that the individual was not serving as an executive officer of the registrant at the end of the last completed fiscal year.

Instructions to Item 402(a)(3). 1. *Determination of Most Highly Compensated Executive Officers.* The determination as to which executive officers are most highly compensated shall be made by reference to total annual salary and bonus for the last completed fiscal year (as required to be disclosed pursuant to paragraph (b)(2)(iii)(A) and (B) of this item), but including the dollar value of salary or bonus amounts forgone pursuant to Instruction 3 to paragraph (b)(2)(iii)(A) and (B) of this item: *Provided, however,* That no disclosure need be provided for any executive officer, other than the CEO, whose total annual salary and bonus, as so determined, does not exceed $100,000.

2. *Inclusion of Executive Officer of Subsidiary.* It may be appropriate in certain circumstances for a registrant to include an executive officer of a subsidiary in the disclosure required by this item. *See* Rule 3b–7 under the Exchange Act.

3. *Exclusion of Executive Officer due to Unusual or Overseas Compensation.* It may be appropriate in limited circumstances for a registrant not to include in the disclosure required by this item an individual, other than its CEO, who is one of the registrant's most highly compensated executive officers. Among the factors that should be considered in determining not to name an individual are: (a) the distribution or accrual of an unusually large amount of cash compensation (such as a bonus or commission) that is not part of a recurring arrangement and is unlikely to continue; and (b) the payment of amounts of cash compensation relating to overseas assignments that may be attributed predominantly to such assignments.

(4) *Information for full fiscal year.* If the CEO served in that capacity during any part of a fiscal year with respect to which information is required, information should be provided as to all of his or her compensation for the full fiscal year. If a named executive officer (other than the CEO) served as an executive officer of the registrant (whether or not in the same position) during any part of a fiscal year with respect to which information is required, information shall be provided as to all compensation of that individual for the full fiscal year.

(5) *Transactions with third parties reported under item 404.* This item includes transactions between the registrant and a third party where the primary purpose of the transaction is to furnish compensation to a named executive officer. No information need be given in response to any paragraph of this item, other than paragraph (j), as to any such third-party transaction if the transaction has been reported in response to Item 404 of Regulation S–K.

(6) *Omission of table or column.* A table or column may be omitted, if there has been no compensation awarded to, earned by or paid to any of the named executives required to be

reported in that table or column in any fiscal year covered by that table.

(7) *Definitions.* For purposes of this item:

(i) The term *stock appreciation rights (SARs)* refers to SARs payable in cash or stock, including SARs payable in cash or stock at the election of the registrant or a named executive officer.

(ii) The term *plan* includes, but is not limited to, the following: Any plan, contract, authorization or arrangement, whether or not set forth in any formal documents, pursuant to which the following may be received: cash, stock, restricted stock or restricted stock units, phantom stock, stock options, SARs, stock options in tandem with SARs, warrants, convertible securities, performance units and performance shares, and similar instruments. A plan may be applicable to one person. Registrants may omit information regarding group life, health, hospitalization, medical reimbursement or relocation plans that do not discriminate in scope, terms or operation, in favor of executive officers or directors of the registrant and that are available generally to all salaried employees.

(iii) The term *long-term incentive plan* means any plan providing compensation intended to serve as incentive for performance to occur over a period longer than one fiscal year, whether such performance is measured by reference to financial performance of the registrant or an affiliate, the registrant's stock price, or any other measure, but excluding restricted stock, stock option and SAR plans.

(8) *Location of specified information.* The information required by paragraphs (i), (k) and (*l*) of this item need not be provided in any filings other than a registrant proxy or information statement relating to an annual meeting of security holders at which directors are to be elected (or special meeting or written consents in lieu of such meeting). Such information will not be deemed to be incorporated by reference into any filing under the Securities Act or the Exchange Act, except to the extent that the registrant specifically incorporates it by reference.

(9) *Liability for specified information.* The information required by paragraphs (k) and (*l*) of this item shall not be deemed to be "soliciting material" or to be "filed" with the Commission or subject to Regulations 14A or 14C, other than as provided in this item, or to the liabilities of section 18 of the Exchange Act, except to the extent that the registrant specifically requests that such information be treated as soliciting material or specifically incorporates it by reference into a filing under the Securities Act or the Exchange Act.

(b) *Summary Compensation Table.* (1) *General.* The information specified in paragraph (b)(2) of this item, concerning the compensation of the named executive officers for each of the registrant's last three completed fiscal years, shall be provided in a Summary Compensation Table, in the tabular format specified below.

SUMMARY COMPENSATION TABLE

		Annual compensation			Long term compensation			
					Awards		Payouts	
Name and principal position (a)	Year (b)	Salary ($) (c)	Bonus ($) (d)	Other annual compensation ($) (e)	Restricted stock award(s) ($) (f)	Securities underlying options/ SARs (#) (g)	LTIP payouts ($) (h)	All other compensation ($) (i)
CEO								
A								
B								
C								
D								

(2) The Table shall include:

(i) The name and principal position of the executive officer (column (a));

(ii) Fiscal year covered (column (b));

(iii) Annual compensation (columns (c), (d) and (e)), including:

(A) The dollar value of base salary (cash and non-cash) earned by the named executive officer during the fiscal year covered (column (c));

(B) The dollar value of bonus (cash and non-cash) earned by the named executive officer during the fiscal year covered (column (d)); and

Instructions to Item 402(b)(2)(iii)(A) and (B). 1. Amounts deferred at the election of a named executive officer, whether pursuant to a plan established under Section 401(k) of the Internal Revenue Code, or otherwise, shall be included in the salary column (column (c)) or bonus column (column (d)), as appropriate, for the fiscal year in which earned. If the amount of salary or bonus earned in a given fiscal year is not calculable through the latest practicable date, that fact must be disclosed in a footnote and such amount must be disclosed in the subsequent fiscal year in the appropriate column for the fiscal year in which earned.

2. For stock or any other form of non-cash compensation, disclose the fair market value at the time the compensation is awarded, earned or paid.

3. Registrants need not include in the salary column (column (c)) or bonus column (column (d)) any amount of salary or bonus forgone at the election of a named executive officer pursuant to a registrant program under which stock, stock-based or other forms of non-cash compensation may be received by a named executive in lieu of a portion of annual compensation earned in a covered fiscal year. However, the receipt of any such form of non-cash compensation in lieu of salary or bonus earned for a covered fiscal year must be disclosed in the appropriate column of the Table corresponding to that fiscal year (i.e., restricted stock awards (column (f)); options or SARs (column (g)); all other compensation (column (i)), or, if made pursuant to a long-term incentive plan and therefore not reportable at grant in the Summary Compensation Table), a footnote must be added to the salary or bonus column so disclosing and referring to the Long–Term Incentive Plan Table (required by paragraph (e) of this item) where the award is reported.

(C) The dollar value of other annual compensation not properly categorized as salary or bonus, as follows (column (e)):

(*1*) Perquisites and other personal benefits, securities or property, unless the aggregate amount of such compensation is the lesser of either $50,000 or 10% of the total of annual salary and bonus reported for the named executive officer in columns (c) and (d);

(*2*) Above-market or preferential earnings on restricted stock, options, SARs or deferred compensation paid during the fiscal year or payable during that period but deferred at the election of the named executive officer;

(*3*) Earnings on long-term incentive plan compensation paid during the fiscal year or payable during that period but deferred at the election of the named executive officer;

(*4*) Amounts reimbursed during the fiscal year for the payment of taxes; and

(*5*) The dollar value of the difference between the price paid by a named executive officer for any security of the registrant or its subsidiaries purchased from the registrant or its subsidiaries (through deferral of salary or bonus, or otherwise), and the fair market value of such security at the date of purchase, unless that discount is available generally, either to all security holders or to all salaried employees of the registrant.

Instructions to Item 402(b)(2)(iii)(C). 1. Each perquisite or other personal benefit exceeding 25% of the total perquisites and other personal benefits reported for a named executive officer must be identified by type and amount in a footnote or accompanying narrative discussion to column (e).

2. Perquisites and other personal benefits shall be valued on the basis of the aggregate incremental cost to the registrant and its subsidiaries.

3. Interest on deferred or long-term compensation is above-market only if the rate of interest exceeds 120% of the applicable federal long-term rate, with compounding (as prescribed under section 1274(d) of the Internal Revenue Code) at the rate that corresponds most closely to the rate under the registrant's plan at the time the interest rate or formula is set. In the event of a discretionary reset of the interest rate, the requisite calculation must be made on the basis of the interest rate at the time of such reset, rather than when originally established. Only the above-market portion of the interest must be included. If the applicable interest rates vary depending upon conditions such as a minimum period of continued service, the reported amount should be calculated assuming satisfaction of all conditions to receiving interest at the highest rate.

4. Dividends (and dividend equivalents) on restricted stock, options, SARs or deferred compensation denominated in stock ("deferred stock") are preferential only if earned at a rate higher than dividends on the registrant's common stock. Only the preferential portion of the dividends or equivalents must be included.

(iv) Long-term compensation (columns (f), (g) and (h)), including:

(A) The dollar value (net of any consideration paid by the named executive officer) of any award of restricted stock, including share units (calculated by multiplying the closing market price of the registrant's unrestricted stock on the date of grant by the number of shares awarded) (column (f));

(B) The sum of the number of securities underlying stock options granted (including options that subsequently have been transferred), with or without tandem SARs, and the number of freestanding SARs (column (g)); and

(C) The dollar value of all payouts pursuant to long-term incentive plans ("LTIPs") as defined in paragraph (a)(7)(iii) of this item (column (h)).

Instructions to Item 402(b)(2)(iv). 1. Awards of restricted stock that are subject to performance-based conditions on vesting, in addition to lapse of time and/or continued service with the registrant or a subsidiary, may be reported as LTIP awards pursuant to paragraph (e) of this item instead of in column (f). If this approach is selected, once the restricted stock vests, it must be reported as an LTIP payout in column (h).

2. The registrant shall, in a footnote to the Summary Compensation Table (appended to column (f), if included), disclose:

a. The number and value of the aggregate restricted stock holdings at the end of the last completed fiscal year. The value shall be calculated in the manner specified in paragraph (b)(2)(iv)(A) of this item using the value of the registrant's shares at the end of the last completed fiscal year;

b. For any restricted stock award reported in the Summary Compensation Table that will vest, in whole or in part, in under three years from the date of grant, the total number of shares awarded and the vesting schedule; and

c. Whether dividends will be paid on the restricted stock reported in column (f).

3. If at any time during the last completed fiscal year, the registrant has adjusted or amended the exercise price of stock options or freestanding SARs previously awarded to a named executive officer, whether through amendment, cancellation or replacement

grants, or any other means ("repriced"), the registrant shall include the number of options or freestanding SARs so repriced as Stock Options/SARs granted and required to be reported in column (g).

4. If any specified performance target, goal or condition to payout was waived with respect to any amount included in LTIP payouts reported in column (h), the registrant shall so state in a footnote to column (h).

(v) All other compensation for the covered fiscal year that the registrant could not properly report in any other column of the Summary Compensation Table (column (i)). Any compensation reported in this column for the last completed fiscal year shall be identified and quantified in a footnote. Such compensation shall include, but not be limited to:

(A) The amount paid, payable or accrued to any named executive officer pursuant to a plan or arrangement in connection with:

(*1*) The resignation, retirement or any other termination of such executive officer's employment with the registrant and its subsidiaries; or

(*2*) A change in control of the registrant or a change in the executive officer's responsibilities following such a change in control;

(B) The dollar value of above-market or preferential amounts earned on restricted stock, options, SARs or deferred compensation during the fiscal year, or calculated with respect to that period, except that if such amounts are paid during the period, or payable during the period but deferred at the election of a named executive officer, this information shall be reported as Other Annual Compensation in column (e). See Instructions 3 and 4 to paragraph 402(b)(2)(iii)(C) of this item;

(C) The dollar value of amounts earned on long-term incentive plan compensation during the fiscal year, or calculated with respect to that period, except that if such amounts are paid during that period, or payable during that period at the election of the named executive officer, this information shall be reported as Other Annual Compensation in column (e);

(D) Annual registrant contributions or other allocations to vested and unvested defined contribution plans; and

(E) The dollar value of any insurance premiums paid by, or on behalf of, the registrant during the covered fiscal year with respect to term life insurance for the benefit of a named executive officer, and, if there is any arrangement or understanding, whether formal or informal, that such executive officer has or will receive or be allocated an interest in any cash surrender value under the insurance policy, either:

(*1*) The full dollar value of the remainder of the premiums paid by, or on behalf of, the registrant; or

(*2*) If the premiums will be refunded to the registrant on termination of the policy, the dollar value of the benefit to the executive officer of the remainder of the premium paid by, or on behalf of, the registrant during the fiscal year. The benefit shall be determined for the period, projected on an actuarial basis, between payment of the premium and the refund.

Instructions to Item 402(b)(2)(v). 1. LTIP awards and amounts received on exercise of options and SARs need not be reported as All Other Compensation in column (i).

2. Information relating to defined benefit and actuarial plans should not be reported pursuant to paragraph (b) of this item, but instead should be reported pursuant to paragraph (f) of this item.

3. Where alternative methods of reporting are available under paragraph (b)(2)(v)(E) of this item, the same method should be used for each of the named executive officers. If the

registrant chooses to change methods from one year to the next, that fact, and the reason therefor, should be disclosed in a footnote to column (i).

Instruction to Item 402(b). Information with respect to fiscal years prior to the last completed fiscal year will not be required if the registrant was not a reporting company pursuant to Section 13(a) or 15(d) of the Exchange Act at any time during that year, except that the registrant will be required to provide information for any such year if that information previously was required to be provided in response to a Commission filing requirement.

(c) *Option/SAR Grants Table.* (1) The information specified in paragraph (c)(2) of this item, concerning individual grants of stock options (whether or not in tandem with SARs) and freestanding SARs (including options and SARs that subsequently have been transferred) made during the last completed fiscal year to each of the named executive officers shall be provided in the tabular format specified as follows:

OPTION/SAR GRANTS IN LAST FISCAL YEAR

Individual Grants					Potential realizable value at assumed annual rates of stock price appreciation for option term		Alternative to (f) and (g): Grant date value
Name (a)	Number of securities underlying options/ SARs Granted (#) (b)	Percent of total options/ SARs granted to employees in fiscal year (c)	Exercise or base price ($/Sh) (d)	Expiration date (e)	5% ($) (f)	10% ($) (g)	Grant date present value $ (f)
CEO							
A							
B							
C							
D							

(2) The Table shall include, with respect to each grant:

(i) The name of the executive officer (column (a));

(ii) The number of securities underlying options/SARs granted (column (b));

(iii) The percent the grant represents of total options and SARs granted to employees during the fiscal year (column (c));

(iv) The per-share exercise or base price of the options or SARs granted (column (d)). If such exercise or base price is less than the market price of the underlying security on the date of grant, a separate, adjoining column shall be added showing market price on the date of grant;

(v) The expiration date of the options or SARs (column (e)); and

(vi) Either (A) the potential realizable value of each grant of options or freestanding SARs or (B) the present value of each grant, as follows:

(A) The potential realizable value of each grant of options or freestanding SARs, assuming that the market price of the underlying security appreciates in value from the date of grant to the end of the option or SAR term, at the following annualized rates:

(*1*) 5% (column (f));

(*2*) 10% (column (g)); and

(*3*) If the exercise or base price was below the market price of the underlying security at the date of grant, provide an additional column labeled 0%, to show the value at grant-date market price; or

(B) The present value of the grant at the date of grant, under any option pricing model (alternative column (f)).

Instructions to Item 402(c). 1. If more than one grant of options and/or freestanding SARs was made to a named executive officer during the last completed fiscal year, a separate line should be used to provide disclosure of each such grant. However, multiple grants during a single fiscal year may be aggregated where each grant was made at the same exercise and/or base price and has the same expiration date, and the same performance vesting thresholds, if any. A single grant consisting of options and/or freestanding SARs shall be reported as separate grants with respect to each tranche with a different exercise and/or base price, performance vesting threshold, or expiration date.

2. Options or freestanding SARs granted in connection with an option repricing transaction shall be reported in this table. See Instruction 3 to paragraph (b)(2)(iv) of this item.

3. Any material term of the grant, including but not limited to the date of exercisability, the number of SARs, performance units or other instruments granted in tandem with options, a performance-based condition to exercisability, a reload feature, or a tax-reimbursement feature, shall be footnoted.

4. If the exercise or base price is adjustable over the term of any option or freestanding SAR in accordance with any prescribed standard or formula, including but not limited to an index or premium price provision, describe the following, either by footnote to column (c) or in narrative accompanying the Table: (a) the standard or formula; and (b) any constant assumption made by the registrant regarding any adjustment to the exercise price in calculating the potential option or SAR value.

5. If any provision of a grant (other than an antidilution provision) could cause the exercise price to be lowered, registrants must clearly and fully disclose these provisions and their potential consequences either by a footnote or accompanying textual narrative.

6. In determining the grant-date market or base price of the security underlying options or freestanding SARs, the registrant may use either the closing market price per share of the security, or any other formula prescribed for the security.

7. The potential realizable dollar value of a grant (columns (f) and (g)) shall be the product of:

(a) The difference between:

(i) The product of the per-share market price at the time of the grant and the sum of 1 plus the adjusted stock price appreciation rate (the assumed rate of appreciation compounded annually over the term of the option or SAR); and

(ii) The per-share exercise price of the option or SAR; and

(b) The number of securities underlying the grant at fiscal year-end.

8. Registrants may add one or more separate columns using the formula prescribed in Instruction 7 to paragraph (c) of this item, to reflect the following:

a. The registrant's historic rate of appreciation over a period equivalent to the term of such options and/or SARs;

b. 0% appreciation, where the exercise or base price was equal to or greater than the market price of the underlying securities on the date of grant; and

c. N% appreciation, the percentage appreciation by which the exercise or base price exceeded the market price at grant. Where the grant included multiple tranches with exercise or base prices exceeding the market price of the underlying security by varying degrees, include an additional column for each additional tranche.

9. Where the registrant chooses to use the grant-date valuation alternative specified in paragraph (c)(2)(vi)(B) of this item, the valuation shall be footnoted to describe the valuation method used. Where the registrant has used a variation of the Black–Scholes or binomial option pricing model, the description shall identify the use of such pricing model and describe the assumptions used relating to the expected volatility, risk-free rate of return, dividend yield and time of exercise. Any adjustments for nontransferability or risk of forfeiture also shall be disclosed. In the event another valuation method is used, the registrant is required to describe the methodology as well as any material assumptions.

(d) *Aggregated option/SAR exercises and fiscal year-end option/SAR value table.* (1) The information specified in paragraph (d)(2) of this item, concerning each exercise of stock options (or tandem SARs) and freestanding SARs during the last completed fiscal year by each of the named executive officers and the fiscal year-end value of unexercised options and SARs, shall be provided on an aggregated basis in the tabular format specified below:

AGGREGATED OPTION/SAR EXERCISES IN LAST FISCAL YEAR AND FY–END OPTION/SAR VALUES

Name (a)	Shares acquired on exercise (#) (b)	Value Realized ($) (c)	Number of securities underlying unexercised options/SARs at fiscal year-end (#) Exercisable/ Unexercisable (d)	Value of unexercised in-the-money options/SARs at fiscal year-end ($) Exercisable/ Unexercisable (e)
CEO	....	....	....	....
A	....	....	....	....
B	....	....	....	....
C	....	....	....	....
D	....	....	....	....

(2) The table shall include:

(i) The name of the executive officer (column (a));

(ii) The number of shares received upon exercise, or, if no shares were received, the number of securities with respect to which the options or SARs were exercised (column (b));

(iii) The aggregate dollar value realized upon exercise (column (c));

(iv) The total number of securities underlying unexercised options and SARs held at the end of the last completed fiscal year, separately identifying the exercisable and unexercisable options and SARs (column (d)); and

(v) The aggregate dollar value of in-the-money, unexercised options and SARs held at the end of the fiscal year, separately identifying the exercisable and unexercisable options and SARs (column (e)).

Instructions to Item 402(d)(2). 1. Options or freestanding SARs are in-the-money if the fair market value of the underlying securities exceeds the exercise or base price of the option or SAR. The dollar values in columns (c) and (e) are calculated by determining the difference between the fair market value of the securities underlying the options or SARs and the exercise or base price of the options or SARs at exercise or fiscal year-end, respectively.

2. In calculating the dollar value realized upon exercise (column (c)), the value of any related payment or other consideration provided (or to be provided) by the registrant to or

on behalf of a named executive officer, whether in payment of the exercise price or related taxes, shall not be included. Payments by the registrant in reimbursement of tax obligations incurred by a named executive officer are required to be disclosed in accordance with paragraph (b)(2)(iii)(C)(*4*) of this item.

(e) *Long–Term Incentive Plan ("LTIP") awards table.* (1) The information specified in paragraph (e)(2) of this item, regarding each award made to a named executive officer in the last completed fiscal year under any LTIP, shall be provided in the tabular format specified below:

LONG–TERM INCENTIVE PLANS—AWARDS IN LAST FISCAL YEAR

			Estimated future payouts under non-stock price-based plans		
Name (a)	Number of shares, units or other rights (#) (b)	Performance or other period until maturation or payout (c)	Threshold ($ or #) (d)	Target ($ or #) (e)	Maximum ($ or #) (f)
CEO					
A					
B					
C					
D					

(2) The Table shall include:

(i) The name of the executive officer (column (a));

(ii) The number of shares, units or other rights awarded under any LTIP, and, if applicable, the number of shares underlying any such unit or right (column (b));

(iii) The performance or other time period until payout or maturation of the award (column (c)); and

(iv) For plans not based on stock price, the dollar value of the estimated payout, the number of shares to be awarded as the payout or a range of estimated payouts denominated in dollars or number of shares under the award (threshold, target and maximum amount) (columns (d) through (f)).

Instructions to Item 402(e). 1. For purposes of this paragraph, the term "long-term incentive plan" or "LTIP" shall be defined in accordance with paragraph (a)(7)(iii) of this item.

2. Describe in a footnote or in narrative text accompanying this table the material terms of any award, including a general description of the formula or criteria to be applied in determining the amounts payable. Registrants are not required to disclose any factor, criterion or performance-related or other condition to payout or maturation of a particular award that involves confidential commercial or business information, disclosure of which would adversely affect the registrant's competitive position.

3. Separate disclosure shall be provided in the Table for each award made to a named executive officer, accompanied by the information specified in Instruction 2 to this paragraph. If awards are made to a named executive officer during the fiscal year under more than one plan, identify the particular plan under which each such award was made.

4. For column (d), "threshold" refers to the minimum amount payable for a certain level of performance under the plan. For column (e), "target" refers to the amount payable if the specified performance target(s) are reached. For column (f), "maximum" refers to the maximum payout possible under the plan.

5. In column (e), registrants must provide a representative amount based on the previous fiscal year's performance if the target award is not determinable.

6. A tandem grant of two instruments, only one of which is pursuant to a LTIP, need be reported only in the table applicable to the other instrument. For example, an option granted in tandem with a performance share would be reported only as an option grant, with the tandem feature noted.

(f) *Defined benefit or actuarial plan disclosure.* (1) *Pension plan table.* (i) For any defined benefit or actuarial plan under which benefits are determined primarily by final compensation (or average final compensation) and years of service, provide a separate Pension Plan Table showing estimated annual benefits payable upon retirement (including amounts attributable to any defined benefit supplementary or excess pension award plans) in specified compensation and years of service classifications in the format specified below.

PENSION PLAN TABLE

Remuneration	Years of service 15	20	25	30	35
125,000	....	....	....	....	....
150,000	....	....	....	....	....
175,000	....	....	....	....	....
200,000	....	....	....	....	....
225,000	....	....	....	....	....
250,000	....	....	....	....	....
300,000	....	....	....	....	....
400,000	....	....	....	....	....
450,000	....	....	....	....	....
500,000	....	....	....	....	....

(ii) Immediately following the Table, the registrant shall disclose:

(A) The compensation covered by the plan(s), including the relationship of such covered compensation to the annual compensation reported in the Summary Compensation Table required by paragraph (b)(2)(iii) of this item, and state the current compensation covered by the plan for any named executive officer whose covered compensation differs substantially (by more than 10%) from that set forth in the annual compensation columns of the Summary Compensation Table;

(B) The estimated credited years of service for each of the named executive officers; and

(C) A statement as to the basis upon which benefits are computed (e.g., straight-life annuity amounts), and whether or not the benefits listed in the Pension Plan Table are subject to any deduction for Social Security or other offset amounts.

(2) *Alternative pension plan disclosure.* For any defined benefit or actuarial plan under which benefits are not determined primarily by final compensation (or average final compensation) and years of service, the registrant shall state in narrative form:

(i) The formula by which benefits are determined; and

(ii) The estimated annual benefits payable upon retirement at normal retirement age for each of the named executive officers.

Instructions to Item 402(f). 1. *Pension Levels.* Compensation set forth in the Pension Plan Table pursuant to paragraph (f)(1)(i) of this item shall allow for reasonable increases in existing compensation levels; alternatively, registrants may present as the highest compensation level in the Pension Plan Table an amount equal to 120% of the amount of covered compensation of the most highly compensated individual named in the Summary Compensation Table required by paragraph (b)(2) of this item.

2. *Normal Retirement Age.* The term "normal retirement age" means normal retirement age as defined in a pension or similar plan or, if not defined therein, the earliest time at which a participant may retire without any benefit reduction due to age.

(g) *Compensation of Directors.* (1) *Standard arrangements.* Describe any standard arrangements, stating amounts, pursuant to which directors of the registrant are compensated for any services provided as a director, including any additional amounts payable for committee participation or special assignments.

(2) *Other arrangements.* Describe any other arrangements pursuant to which any director of the registrant was compensated during the registrant's last completed fiscal year for any service provided as a director, stating the amount paid and the name of the director.

Instruction to Item 402(g)(2). The information required by paragraph (g)(2) of this item shall include any arrangement, including consulting contracts, entered into in consideration of the director's service on the board. The material terms of any such arrangement shall be included.

(h) *Employment contracts and termination of employment and change-in-control arrangements.* Describe the terms and conditions of each of the following contracts or arrangements:

(1) Any employment contract between the registrant and a named executive officer; and

(2) Any compensatory plan or arrangement, including payments to be received from the registrant, with respect to a named executive officer, if such plan or arrangement results or will result from the resignation, retirement or any other termination of such executive officer's employment with the registrant and its subsidiaries or from a change-in-control of the registrant or a change in the named executive officer's responsibilities following a change-in-control and the amount involved, including all periodic payments or installments, exceeds $100,000.

(i) *Report on repricing of options/SARs.* (1) If at any time during the last completed fiscal year, the registrant, while a reporting company pursuant to section 13(a) or 15(d) of the Exchange Act, has adjusted or amended the exercise price of stock options or SARs previously awarded to any of the named executive officers, whether through amendment, cancellation or replacement grants, or any other means ("repriced"), the registrant shall provide the information specified in paragraphs (i)(2) and (i)(3) of this item.

(2) The compensation committee (or other board committee performing equivalent functions or, in the absence of any such committee, the entire board of directors) shall explain in reasonable detail any such repricing of options and/or SARs held by a named executive officer in the last completed fiscal year, as well as the basis for each such repricing.

(3)(i) The information specified in paragraph (i)(3)(*ii*) of this item, concerning all such repricings of options and SARs held by any executive officer during the last ten completed fiscal years, shall be provided in the tabular format specified below:

TEN–YEAR OPTION/SAR REPRICINGS

Name (a)	Date (b)	Number of securities underlying options/ SARs repriced or amended (#) (c)	Market price of stock at time of repricing or amendment ($) (d)	Exercise price at time of repricing or amendment ($) (e)	New exercise price ($) (f)	Length of original option term remaining at date of repricing or amendment (g)

(ii) The Table shall include, with respect to each repricing:

(A) The name and position of the executive officer (column (a));

(B) The date of each repricing (column (b));

(C) The number of securities underlying replacement or amended options or SARs (column (c));

(D) The per-share market price of the underlying security at the time of repricing (column (d));

(E) The original exercise price or base price of the cancelled or amended option or SAR (column (e));

(F) The per-share exercise price or base price of the replacement option or SAR (column (f)); and

(G) The amount of time remaining before the replaced or amended option or SAR would have expired (column (g)).

Instructions to Item 402(i). 1. The required report shall be made over the name of each member of the registrant's compensation committee, or other board committee performing equivalent functions or, in the absence of any such committee, the entire board of directors.

2. A replacement grant is any grant of options or SARs reasonably related to any prior or potential option or SAR cancellation, whether by an exchange of existing options or SARs for options or SARs with new terms; the grant of new options or SARs in tandem with previously granted options or SARs that will operate to cancel the previously granted options or SARs upon exercise; repricing of previously granted options or SARs; or otherwise. If a corresponding original grant was canceled in a prior year, information about such grant nevertheless must be disclosed pursuant to this paragraph.

3. If the replacement grant is not made at the current market price, describe the terms of the grant in a footnote or accompanying textual narrative.

4. This paragraph shall not apply to any repricing occurring through the operation of:

a. A plan formula or mechanism that results in the periodic adjustment of the option or SAR exercise or base price;

b. A plan antidilution provision; or

c. A recapitalization or similar transaction equally affecting all holders of the class of securities underlying the options or SARs.

5. Information required by paragraph (i)(3) of this item shall not be provided for any repricings effected before the registrant became a reporting company pursuant to section 13(a) or 15(d) of the Exchange Act.

(j) *Additional information with respect to Compensation Committee Interlocks and Insider Participation in compensation decisions.* Under the caption "Compensation Committee Interlocks and Insider Participation,"

(1) The registrant shall identify each person who served as a member of the compensation committee of the registrant's board of directors (or board committee performing equivalent functions) during the last completed fiscal year, indicating each committee member who:

(i) Was, during the fiscal year, an officer or employee of the registrant or any of its subsidiaries;

(ii) Was formerly an officer of the registrant or any of its subsidiaries; or

(iii) Had any relationship requiring disclosure by the registrant under any paragraph of Item 404 of Regulations S–K. In this event, the disclosure required by Item 404 shall accompany such identification.

(2) If the registrant has no compensation committee (or other board committee performing equivalent functions), the registrant shall identify each officer and employee of the registrant or any of its subsidiaries, and any former officer of the registrant or any of its subsidiaries, who, during the last com-

pleted fiscal year, participated in deliberations of the registrant's board of directors concerning executive officer compensation.

(3) The registrant shall describe any of the following relationships that existed during the last completed fiscal year:

(i) An executive officer of the registrant served as a member of the compensation committee (or other board committee performing equivalent functions or, in the absence of any such committee, the entire board of directors) of another entity, one of whose executive officers served on the compensation committee (or other board committee performing equivalent functions or, in the absence of any such committee, the entire board of directors) of the registrant;

(ii) An executive officer of the registrant served as a director of another entity, one of whose executive officers served on the compensation committee (or other board committee performing equivalent functions or, in the absence of any such committee, the entire board of directors) of the registrant; and

(iii) An executive officer of the registrant served as a member of the compensation committee (or other board committee performing equivalent functions or, in the absence of any such committee, the entire board of directors) of another entity, one of whose executive officers served as a director of the registrant.

(4) Disclosure required under paragraph (j)(3) of this item regarding any compensation committee member or other director of the registrant who also served as an executive officer of another entity shall be accompanied by the disclosure called for by Item 404 with respect to that person.

Instruction to Item 402(j). For purposes of this paragraph, the term "entity" shall not include an entity exempt from tax under section 501(c)(3) of the Internal Revenue Code.

(k) *Board compensation committee report on executive compensation.* (1) Disclosure of the compensation committee's compensation policies applicable to the registrant's executive officers (including the named executive officers), including the specific relationship of corporate performance to executive compensation, is required with respect to compensation reported for the last completed fiscal year.

(2) Discussion is required of the compensation committee's bases for the CEO's compensation reported for the last completed fiscal year, including the factors and criteria upon which the CEO's compensation was based. The committee shall include a specific discussion of the relationship of the registrant's performance to the CEO's compensation for the last completed fiscal year, describing each measure of the registrant's performance, whether qualitative or quantitative, on which the CEO's compensation was based.

(3) The required disclosure shall be made over the name of each member of the registrant's compensation committee (or other board committee performing equivalent functions or, in the absence of any such committee, entire board of directors). If the board of directors modified or rejected in any material way any action or recommendation by such committee with respect to such decisions in the last completed fiscal year, the disclosure must so indicate and explain the reasons for the board's actions, and be made over the names of all members of the board.

Instructions to Item 402(k). 1. Boilerplate language should be avoided in describing factors and criteria underlying awards or payments of executive compensation in the statement required.

2. Registrants are not required to disclose target levels with respect to specific quantitative or qualitative performance-related factors considered by the committee (or board), or any factors or criteria involving confidential commercial or business information, the disclosure of which would have an adverse effect on the registrant.

(*l*) *Performance graph.* (1) Provide a line graph comparing the yearly percentage change in the registrant's cumulative total shareholder return on a class of common stock registered under section 12 of the Exchange Act (as measured by dividing (i) the sum of (A) the cumulative amount of dividends for the measurement period, assuming dividend reinvestment, and (B) the difference between the registrant's share price at the end and the beginning of the measurement period; by (ii) the share price at the beginning of the measurement period) with

(i) The cumulative total return of a broad equity market index assuming reinvestment of dividends, that includes companies whose equity securities are traded on the same exchange or NASDAQ market or are of comparable market capitalization; *Provided, however,* That if the registrant is a company within the Standard & Poor's 500 Stock Index, the registrant must use that index; and

(ii) The cumulative total return, assuming reinvestment of dividends, of:

(A) A published industry or line-of-business index;

(B) Peer issuer(s) selected in good faith. If the registrant does not select its peer issuer(s) on an industry or line-of-business basis, the registrant shall disclose the basis for its selection; or

(C) Issuer(s) with similar market capitalization(s), but only if the registrant does not use a published industry or line-of-business index and does not believe it can reasonably identify a peer group. If the registrant uses this alternative, the graph shall be accompanied by a statement of the reasons for this selection.

(2) For purposes of paragraph (*l*)(1) of this item, the term "measurement period" shall be the period beginning at the "measurement point" established by the market close on the last trading day before the beginning of the registrant's fifth preceding fiscal year, through and including the end of the registrant's last completed fiscal year. If the class of securities has been registered under section 12 of the Exchange Act for a shorter period of time, the period covered by the comparison may correspond to that time period.

(3) For purposes of paragraph (*l*)(1)(ii)(A) of this item, the term "published industry or line-of-business index" means any index that is prepared by a party other than the registrant or an affiliate and is accessible to the registrant's security holders; *Provided, however,* That registrants may use an index prepared by the registrant or affiliate if such index is widely recognized and used.

(4) If the registrant selects a different index from an index used for the immediately preceding fiscal year, explain the reason(s) for this change and also compare the registrant's total return with that of both the newly selected index and the index used in the immediately preceding fiscal year.

Instructions to Item 402(l). 1. In preparing the required graphic comparisons, the registrant should:

a. Use, to the extent feasible, comparable methods of presentation and assumptions for the total return calculations required by paragraph (*l*)(1) of this item; *Provided, however,* That if the registrant constructs its own peer group index under paragraph (*l*)(1)(ii)(B), the same methodology must be used in calculating both the registrant's total return and that on the peer group index; and

b. Assume the reinvestment of dividends into additional shares of the same class of equity securities at the frequency with which dividends are paid on such securities during the applicable fiscal year.

2. In constructing the graph:

(a) The closing price at the measurement point must be converted into a fixed investment, stated in dollars, in the registrant's stock (or in the stocks represented by a given index), with cumulative returns for each subsequent fiscal year measured as a change from that investment; and

(b) Each fiscal year should be plotted with points showing the cumulative total return as of that point. The value of the investment as of each point plotted on a given return line is the number of shares held at that point multiplied by the then-prevailing share price.

3. The registrant is required to present information for the registrant's last five fiscal years, and may choose to graph a longer period; but the measurement point, however, shall remain the same.

4. Registrants may include comparisons using performance measures in addition to total return, such as return on average common shareholders' equity, so long as the registrant's compensation committee (or other board committee performing equivalent functions or in the absence of any such committee the entire board of directors) describes the link between that measure and the level of executive compensation in the statement required by paragraph (k) of this Item.

5. If the registrant uses a peer issuer(s) comparison or comparison with issuer(s) with similar market capitalizations, the identity of those issuers must be disclosed and the returns of each component issuer of the group must be weighted according to the respective issuer's stock market capitalization at the beginning of each period for which a return is indicated.

Item 403. Security Ownership of Certain Beneficial Owners and Management

(a) *Security Ownership of Certain Beneficial Owners.* Furnish the following information, as of the most recent practicable date, substantially in the tabular form indicated, with respect to any person (including any "group" as that term is used in section 13(d)(3) of the Exchange Act) who is known to the registrant to be the beneficial owner of more than five percent of any class of the registrant's voting securities. The address given in column (2) may be a business, mailing or residence address. Show in column (3) the total number of shares beneficially owned and in column (4) the percentage of class so owned. Of the number of shares shown in column (3), indicate by footnote or otherwise the amount known to be shares with respect to which such listed beneficial owner has the right to acquire beneficial ownership as specified in Rule 13d–3(d)(1) under the Exchange Act.

(1) Title of class	(2) Name and address of beneficial owner	(3) Amount and nature of beneficial ownership	(4) Percent of class

(b) *Security Ownership of Management.* Furnish the following information, as of the most recent practicable date, in substantially the tabular form indicated, as to each class of equity securities of the registrant or any of its parents or subsidiaries other than directors' qualifying shares, beneficially owned by all directors and nominees, naming them, each of the named executive officers as defined in Item 402(a)(3), and directors and executive officers of the registrant as a group, without naming them. Show in column (3) the total number of shares beneficially owned and in column (4) the percent of class so owned. Of the number of shares shown in column (3), indicate, by footnote or otherwise, the amount of shares with respect to which such persons have the right to acquire beneficial ownership as specified in Rule 13d–3(d)(1) under the Exchange Act.

(1) Title of class	(2) Name of beneficial owner	(3) Amount and nature of beneficial ownership	(4) Percent of class

(c) *Changes in Control.* Describe any arrangements, known to the registrant, including any pledge by any person of securities of the registrant or any of its parents, the operation of which may at a subsequent date result in a change in control of the registrant.

Instructions to Item 403. 1. The percentages are to be calculated on the basis of the amount of outstanding securities, excluding securities held by or for the account of the registrant or its subsidiaries, plus securities deemed outstanding pursuant to Rule 13d–3(d)(1) under the Exchange Act. For purposes of paragraph (b), if the percentage of shares beneficially owned by any director or nominee, or by all directors and officers of the registrant as a group, does not exceed one percent of the class so owned, the registrant may, in lieu of furnishing a precise percentage, indicate this fact by means of an asterisk and explanatory footnote or other similar means.

2. For the purposes of this Item, beneficial ownership shall be determined in accordance with Rule 13d–3 under the Exchange Act. Include such additional subcolumns or other appropriate explanation of column (3) necessary to reflect amounts as to which the beneficial owner has (A) sole voting power, (B) shared voting power, (C) sole investment power, or (D) shared investment power.

3. The registrant shall be deemed to know the contents of any statements filed with the Commission pursuant to section 13(d) or 13(g) of the Exchange Act. When applicable, a registrant may rely upon information set forth in such statements unless the registrant knows or has reason to believe that such information is not complete or accurate or that a statement or amendment should have been filed and was not.

4. For purposes of furnishing information pursuant to paragraph (a) of this Item, the registrant may indicate the source and date of such information.

5. Where more than one beneficial owner is known to be listed for the same securities, appropriate disclosure should be made to avoid confusion. For purposes of paragraph (b), in computing the aggregate number of shares owned by directors and officers of the registrant as a group, the same shares shall not be counted more than once.

6. Paragraph (c) of this Item does not require a description of ordinary default provisions contained in the charter, trust indentures or other governing instruments relating to securities of the registrant.

7. Where the holder(s) of voting securities reported pursuant to paragraph (a) hold more than five percent of any class of voting securities of the registrant pursuant to any voting trust or similar agreement, state the title of such securities, the amount held or to be held pursuant to the trust or agreement (if not clear from the table) and the duration of the agreement. Give the names and addresses of the voting trustees and outline briefly their voting rights and other powers under the trust or agreement.

Item 404. Certain Relationships and Related Transactions

(a) *Transactions With Management and Others.* Describe briefly any transaction, or series of similar transactions, since the beginning of the registrant's last fiscal year, or any currently proposed transaction, or series of similar transactions, to which the registrant or any of its subsidiaries was or is to be a party, in which the amount involved exceeds $60,000, and in which any of the following persons had, or will have, a direct or indirect material interest, naming such person and indicating the person's relationship to the registrant, the nature of such person's interest in the transaction(s), the amount of such transaction(s) and, where practicable, the amount of such person's interest in the transaction(s):

(1) Any director or executive officer of the registrant;

(2) Any nominee for election as a director;

(3) Any security holder who is known to the registrant to own of record or beneficially more than five percent of any class of the registrant's voting securities; and

(4) Any member of the immediate family of any of the foregoing persons.

Instructions to Paragraph (a) of Item 404. 1. The materiality of any interest is to be determined on the basis of the significance of the information to investors in light of all the circumstances of the particular case. The importance of the interest to the person having the interest, the relationship of the parties to the transaction with each other and the amount involved in the transactions are among the factors to be considered in determining the significance of the information to investors.

2. For purposes of paragraph (a), a person's immediate family shall include such person's spouse; parents; children; siblings; mothers and fathers-in-law; sons and daughters-in-law; and brothers and sisters-in-law.

3. In computing the amount involved in the transaction or series of similar transactions, include all periodic installments in the case of any lease or other agreement providing for periodic payments or installments.

4. The amount of the interest of any person specified in paragraphs (a)(1) through (4) shall be computed without regard to the amount of the profit or loss involved in the transaction(s).

5. In describing any transaction involving the purchase or sale of assets by or to the registrant or any of its subsidiaries, otherwise than in the ordinary course of business, state the cost of the assets to the purchaser and, if acquired by the seller within two years prior to the transaction, the cost thereof to the seller. Indicate the principle followed in determining the registrant's purchase or sale price and the name of the person making such determination.

6. Information shall be furnished in answer to paragraph (a) with respect to transactions that involve remuneration from the registrant or its subsidiaries, directly or indirectly, to any of the persons specified in paragraphs (a)(1) through (4) for services in any capacity unless the interest of such person arises solely from the ownership individually and in the aggregate of less than ten percent of any class of equity securities of another corporation furnishing the services to the registrant or its subsidiaries.

7. No information need be given in answer to paragraph (a) as to any transactions where:

A. The rates or charges involved in the transaction are determined by competitive bids, or the transaction involves the rendering of services as a common or contract carrier, or public utility, at rates or charges fixed in conformity with law or governmental authority;

B. The transaction involves services as a bank depositary of funds, transfer agent, registrar, trustee under a trust indenture, or similar services; or

C. The interest of the person specified in paragraphs (a)(1) through (4) arises solely from the ownership of securities of the registrant and such person receives no extra or special benefit not shared on a pro rata basis.

8. Paragraph (a) requires disclosure of indirect, as well as direct, material interests in transactions. A person who has a position or relationship with a firm, corporation, or other entity that engages in a transaction with the registrant or its subsidiaries may have an indirect interest in such transaction by reason of such position or relationship. Such an interest, however, shall not be deemed "material" within the meaning of paragraph (a) where:

A. The interest arises only (i) from such person's position as a director of another corporation or organization which is a party to the transaction; or (ii) from the direct or indirect ownership by such person and all other persons specified in paragraphs (a)(1) through (4), in the aggregate, of less than a ten percent equity interest in another person (other than a partnership) which is a party to the transaction; or (iii) from both such position and ownership;

B. The interest arises only from such person's position as a limited partner in a partnership in which the person and all other persons specified in paragraphs (a)(1) through (4) have an interest of less than ten percent; or

C. The interest of such person arises solely from the holding of an equity interest (including a limited partnership interest, but excluding a general partnership interest) or a creditor interest in another person that is a party to the transaction with the registrant or any of its subsidiaries, and the transaction is not material to such other person.

9. There may be situations where, although these instructions do not expressly authorize nondisclosure, the interest of a person specified in paragraphs (a)(1) through (4) in a particular transaction or series of transactions is not a direct or indirect material interest. In that case, information regarding such interest and transaction is not required to be disclosed in response to this paragraph.

(b) *Certain Business Relationships.* Describe any of the following relationships regarding directors or nominees for director that exist, or have existed during the registrant's last fiscal year, indicating the identity of the entity with which the registrant has such a relationship, the name of the nominee or director affiliated with such entity and the nature of such nominee's or director's affiliation, the relationship between such entity and the registrant and the amount of the business done between the registrant and the entity during the registrant's last full fiscal year or proposed to be done during the registrant's current fiscal year:

(1) If the nominee or director is, or during the last fiscal year has been, an executive officer of, or owns, or during the last fiscal year has owned, of record or beneficially in excess of ten percent equity interest in, any business or professional entity that has made during the registrant's last full fiscal year, or proposes to make during the registrant's current fiscal year, payments to the registrant or its subsidiaries for property or services in excess of five percent of (i) the registrant's consolidated gross revenues for its last full fiscal year, or (ii) the other entity's consolidated gross revenues for its last full fiscal year;

(2) If the nominee or director is, or during the last fiscal year has been, an executive officer of, or owns, or during the last fiscal year has owned, of record or beneficially in excess of ten percent equity interest in, any business or professional entity to which the registrant or its subsidiaries has made during the registrant's last full fiscal year, or proposes to make during the registrant's current fiscal year, payments for property or services in excess of five percent of (i) the registrant's consolidated gross revenues for its last full fiscal year, or (ii) the other entity's consolidated gross revenues for its last full fiscal year;

(3) If the nominee or director is, or during the last fiscal year has been, an executive officer of, or owns, or during the last fiscal year has owned, of record or beneficially in excess of ten percent equity interest in, any business or professional entity to which the registrant or its subsidiaries was indebted at the end of the registrant's last full fiscal year in an aggregate amount in excess of five percent of the registrant's total consolidated assets at the end of such fiscal year;

(4) If the nominee or director is, or during the last fiscal year has been, a member of, or of counsel to, a law firm that the issuer has retained during the last fiscal year or proposes to retain during the current fiscal year; *Provided, however,* that the dollar amount of fees paid to a law firm by the registrant need not be disclosed if such amount does not exceed five percent of the law firm's gross revenues for that firm's last full fiscal year;

(5) If the nominee or director is, or during the last fiscal year has been, a partner or executive officer of any investment banking firm that has performed services for the registrant, other than as a participating underwriter in a syndicate, during the last

fiscal year or that the registrant proposes to have perform services during the current year; *Provided, however*, that the dollar amount of compensation received by an investment banking firm need not be disclosed if such amount does not exceed five percent of the investment banking firm's consolidated gross revenues for that firm's last full fiscal year; or

(6) Any other relationships that the registrant is aware of between the nominee or director and the registrant that are substantially similar in nature and scope to those relationships listed in paragraphs (b)(1) through (5).

Instructions to Paragraph (b) of Item 404. 1. In order to determine whether payments or indebtedness exceed five percent of the consolidated gross revenues of any entity, other than the registrant, it is appropriate to rely on information provided by the nominee or director.

2. In calculating payments for property and services the following may be excluded:

A. Payments where the rates or charges involved in the transaction are determined by competitive bids, or the transaction involves the rendering of services as a common contract carrier, or public utility, at rates or charges fixed in conformity with law or governmental authority;

B. Payments that arise solely from the ownership of securities of the registrant and no extra or special benefit not shared on a pro rata basis by all holders of the class of securities is received; or

C. Payments made or received by subsidiaries other than significant subsidiaries as defined in Rule 1–02(w) of Regulation S–X, provided that all such subsidiaries making or receiving payments, when considered in the aggregate as a single subsidiary, would not constitute a significant subsidiary as defined in Rule 1–02(w).

3. In calculating indebtedness the following may be excluded:

A. Debt securities that have been publicly offered, admitted to trading on a national securities exchange, or quoted on the automated quotation system of a registered securities association;

B. Amounts due for purchases subject to the usual trade terms; or

C. Indebtedness incurred by subsidiaries other than significant subsidiaries as defined in Rule 1–02(w) of Regulation S–X, provided that all such subsidiaries incurring indebtedness, when considered in the aggregate as a single subsidiary, would not constitute a significant subsidiary as defined in Rule 1–02(w).

4. No information called for by paragraph (b) need be given respecting any director who is no longer a director at the time of filing the registration statement or report containing such disclosure. If such information is being presented in a proxy or information statement, no information need be given respecting any director whose term of office as a director will not continue after the meeting to which the statement relates.

(c) *Indebtedness of Management.* If any of the following persons has been indebted to the registrant or its subsidiaries at any time since the beginning of the registrant's last fiscal year in an amount in excess of $60,000, indicate the name of such person, the nature of the person's relationship by reason of which such person's indebtedness is required to be described, the largest aggregate amount of indebtedness outstanding at any time during such period, the nature of the indebtedness and of the transaction in which it was incurred, the amount thereof outstanding as of the latest practicable date and the rate of interest paid or charged thereon:

(1) Any director or executive officer of the registrant;

(2) Any nominee for election as a director;

(3) Any member of the immediate family of the persons specified in paragraph (c)(1) or (2);

(4) Any corporation or organization (other than the registrant or a majority-owned subsidiary of the registrant) of which any of the persons specified in paragraph (c)(1) or (2) is an executive officer or partner or is, directly or indirectly, the beneficial owner of ten percent or more of any class of equity securities; and

(5) Any trust or other estate in which any of the persons specified in paragraph (c)(1) or (2) has a substantial beneficial interest or as to which such person serves as a trustee or in a similar capacity.

Instructions to Paragraph (c) of Item 404. 1. For purposes of paragraph (c), the members of a person's immediate family are those persons specified in Instruction 2 to Item 404(a).

2. Exclude from the determination of the amount of indebtedness all amounts due from the particular person for purchases subject to usual trade terms, for ordinary travel and expense payments and for other transactions in the ordinary course of business.

3. If the lender is a bank, savings and loan association, or broker-dealer extending credit under Federal Reserve Regulation T (12 CFR Part 220) and the loans are not disclosed as nonaccrual, past due, restructured, or potential problems (see Item III.C.1. and 2. of Industry Guide 3, Statistical Disclosure by Bank Holding Companies), disclosure may consist of a statement, if such is the case, that the loans to such persons (A) were made in the ordinary course of business, (B) were made on substantially the same terms, including interest rates and collateral, as those prevailing at the time for comparable transactions with other persons, and (C) did not involve more than the normal risk of collectibility or present other unfavorable features.

4. If any indebtedness required to be described arose under Section 16(b) of the Exchange Act and has not been discharged by payment, state the amount of any profit realized, that such profit will inure to the benefit of the registrant or its subsidiaries and whether suit will be brought or other steps taken to recover such profit. If, in the opinion of counsel, a question reasonably exists as to the recoverability of such profit, it will suffice to state all facts necessary to describe the transactions, including the prices and number of shares involved.

(d) *Transaction With Promoters.* Registrants that have been organized within the past five years and that are filing a registration statement on Form S–1 under the Securities Act or on Form 10 and Form 10–SB under the Exchange Act shall:

(1) State the names of the promoters, the nature and amount of anything of value (including money, property, contracts, options or rights of any kind) received or to be received by each promoter, directly or indirectly, from the registrant and the nature and amount of any assets, services or other consideration therefor received or to be received by the registrant; and

(2) As to any assets acquired or to be acquired by the registrant from a promoter, state the amount at which the assets were acquired or are to be acquired and the principal followed or to be followed in determining such amount and identify the persons making the determination and their relationship, if any, with the registrant or any promoter. If the assets were acquired by the promoter within two years prior to their transfer to the registrant, also state the cost thereof to the promoter.

Instructions to Item 404. 1. No information need be given in response to any paragraph of Item 404 as to any compensation or other transaction reported in response to any other paragraph of Item 404 or to Item 402 of Regulation S–K or as to any compensation with respect to which information may be omitted pursuant to Item 402.

2. If the information called for by Item 404 is being presented in a registration statement filed pursuant to the Securities Act or the Exchange Act, information shall be given for the periods specified in this Item and, in addition, for the two fiscal years preceding the registrant's last fiscal year.

3. A foreign private issuer will be deemed to comply with Item 404 if it provides the information required by Item 7B of Form 20–F (17 CFR 249.220f).

Item 405. Compliance With Section 16(a) of the Exchange Act

Every registrant having a class of equity securities registered pursuant to Section 12 of the Exchange Act, every closed-end investment company registered under the Investment Company Act of 1940, and every holding company registered pursuant to the Public Utility Holding Company Act of 1935 shall:

(a) Based solely upon a review of Forms 3 and 4 and amendments thereto furnished to the registrant pursuant to rule 16a–3(e) during its most recent fiscal year and Forms 5 and amendments thereto furnished to the registrant with respect to its most recent fiscal year, and any written representation referred to in (b)(2)(i) below:

(1) Under the caption "Section 16(a) Beneficial Ownership Reporting Compliance," identify each person who, at any time during the fiscal year, was a director, officer, beneficial owner of more than ten percent of any class of equity securities of the registrant registered pursuant to section 12 of the Exchange Act, or any other person subject to section 16 of the Exchange Act with respect to the registrant because of the requirements of section 30 of the Investment Company Act or section 17 of the Public Utility Holding Company Act ("reporting person") that failed to file on a timely basis, as disclosed in the above Forms, reports required by section 16(a) of the Exchange Act during the most recent fiscal year or prior fiscal years.

(2) For each such person, set forth the number of late reports, the number of transactions that were not reported on a timely basis, and any known failure to file a required Form. A known failure to file would include, but not be limited to, a failure to file a Form 3, which is required of all reporting persons, and a failure to file a Form 5 in the absence of the written representation referred to in paragraph (b)(2)(i) of this section, unless the registrant otherwise knows that no Form 5 is required.

Note: The disclosure requirement is based on a review of the forms submitted to the registrant during and with respect to its most recent fiscal year, as specified above. Accordingly, a failure to file timely need only be disclosed once. For example, if in the most recently concluded fiscal year a reporting person filed a Form 4 disclosing a transaction that took place in the prior fiscal year, and should have been reported in that year, the registrant should disclose that late filing and transaction pursuant to this Item 405 with respect to the most recently concluded fiscal year, but not in material filed with respect to subsequent years.

(b) With respect to the disclosure required by paragraph (a) of this Item:

(1) A form received by the registrant within three calendar days of the required filing date may be presumed to have been filed with the Commission by the required filing date.

(2) If the registrant (i) receives a written representation from the reporting person that no Form 5 is required; and (ii) maintains the representation for two years, making a copy available to the Commission or its staff upon request, the registrant need not identify such reporting person pursuant to paragraph (a) as having failed to file a Form 5 with respect to that fiscal year.

Item 406. Code of Ethics

(a) Disclose whether the registrant has adopted a code of ethics that applies to the registrant's principal executive officer, principal financial officer, principal accounting officer or controller, or persons performing similar functions. If the registrant has not adopted such a code of ethics, explain why it has not done so.

(b) For purposes of this Item 406, the term *code of ethics* means written standards that are reasonably designed to deter wrongdoing and to promote:

(1) Honest and ethical conduct, including the ethical handling of actual or apparent conflicts of interest between personal and professional relationships;

(2) Full, fair, accurate, timely, and understandable disclosure in reports and documents that a registrant files with, or submits to, the Commission and in other public communications made by the registrant;

(3) Compliance with applicable governmental laws, rules and regulations;

(4) The prompt internal reporting of violations of the code to an appropriate person or persons identified in the code; and

(5) Accountability for adherence to the code.

(c) The registrant must:

(1) File with the Commission a copy of its code of ethics that applies to the registrant's principal executive officer, principal financial officer, principal accounting officer or controller, or persons performing similar functions, as an exhibit to its annual report;

(2) Post the text of such code of ethics on its Internet website and disclose, in its annual report, its Internet address and the fact that it has posted such code of ethics on its Internet Web site; or

(3) Undertake in its annual report filed with the Commission to provide to any person without charge, upon request, a copy of such code of ethics and explain the manner in which such request may be made.

(d) If the registrant intends to satisfy the disclosure requirement under Item 10 of Form 8–K regarding an amendment to, or a waiver from, a provision of its code of ethics that applies to the registrant's principal executive officer, principal financial officer, principal accounting officer or controller, or persons performing similar functions and that relates to any element of the code of ethics definition enumerated in paragraph (b) of this Item by posting such information on its Internet website, disclose the registrant's Internet address and such intention.

Instructions to Item 406. 1. A registrant may have separate codes of ethics for different types of officers. Furthermore, a *code of ethics* within the meaning of paragraph (b) of this Item may be a portion of a broader document that addresses additional topics or that applies to more persons than those specified in paragraph (a). In satisfying the requirements of paragraph (c), a registrant need only file, post or provide the portions of a broader document that constitutes a *code of ethics* as defined in paragraph (b) and that apply to the persons specified in paragraph (a).

2. If a registrant elects to satisfy paragraph (c) of this Item by posting its code of ethics on its website pursuant to paragraph (c)(2), the code of ethics must remain accessible on its Web site for as long as the registrant remains subject to the requirements of this Item and chooses to comply with this Item by posting its code on its Web site pursuant to paragraph (c)(2).

Subpart 500—Registration Statement and Prospectus Provisions

Item 501. Forepart of Registration Statement and Outside Front Cover Page of Prospectus

The registrant must furnish the following information in plain English. See § 230.421(d) of Regulation C of this chapter.

(a) *Front cover page of the registration statement.* Where appropriate, include the delaying amendment legend from § 230.473 of Regulation C of this chapter.

(b) *Outside front cover page of the prospectus.* Limit the outside cover page to one page. If the following information applies to your offering, disclose it on the outside cover page of the prospectus.

(1) Name. The registrant's name. A foreign registrant must give the English translation of its name.

Instruction to paragraph 501(b)(1).

If your name is the same as that of a company that is well known, include information to eliminate any possible confusion with the other company. If your name indicates a line of business in which you are not engaged or you are engaged only to a limited extent, include information to eliminate any misleading inference as to your business. In some circumstances, disclosure may not be sufficient and you may be required to change your name. You will not be required to change your name if you are an established company, the character of your business has changed, and the investing public is generally aware of the change and the character of your current business.

(2) Title and amount of securities. The title and amount of securities offered. Separately state the amount of securities offered by selling security holders, if any. If the underwriter has any arrangement with the issuer, such as an over-allotment option, under which the underwriter may purchase additional shares in connection with the offering, indicate that this arrangement exists and state the amount of additional shares that the underwriter may purchase under the arrangement. Give a brief description of the securities except where the information is clear from the title of the security. For example, you are not required to describe common stock that has full voting, dividend and liquidation rights usually associated with common stock.

(3) Offering price of the securities. Where you offer securities for cash, the price to the public of the securities, the underwriter's discounts and commissions, the net proceeds you receive, and any selling shareholder's net proceeds. Show this information on both a per share or unit basis and for the total amount of the offering. If you make the offering on a minimum/maximum basis, show this information based on the total minimum and total maximum amount of the offering. You may present the information in a table, term sheet format, or other clear presentation. You may present the information in any format that fits the design of the cover page so long as the information can be easily read and is not misleading:

Instructions to paragraph 501(b)(3)

1. If a preliminary prospectus is circulated and you are not subject to the reporting requirements of Section 13(a) or 15(d) of the Exchange Act, provide, as applicable:

(A) A bona fide estimate of the range of the maximum offering price and the maximum number of securities offered; or

(B) A bona fide estimate of the principal amount of the debt securities offered.

2. If it is impracticable to state the price to the public, explain the method by which the price is to be determined. If the securities are to be offered at the market price, or if the offering price is to be determined by a formula related to the market price, indicate the mar-

ket and market price of the securities as of the latest practicable date.

3. If you file a registration statement on Form S–8, you are not required to comply with this paragraph (b)(3).

(4) Market for the securities. Whether any national securities exchange or the Nasdaq Stock Market lists the securities offered, naming the particular market(s), and identifying the trading symbol(s) for those securities;

(5) Risk factors. A cross-reference to the risk factors section, including the page number where it appears in the prospectus. Highlight this cross-reference by prominent type or in another manner;

(6) State legend. Any legend or statement required by the law of any state in which the securities are to be offered. You may combine this with any legend required by the SEC, if appropriate;

(7) Commission legend. A legend that indicates that neither the Securities and Exchange Commission nor any state securities commission has approved or disapproved of the securities or passed upon the accuracy or adequacy of the disclosures in the prospectus and that any contrary representation is a criminal offense. You may use one of the following or other clear, plain language:

Example A: Neither the Securities and Exchange Commission nor any state securities commission has approved or disapproved of these securities or passed upon the adequacy or accuracy of this prospectus. Any representation to the contrary is a criminal offense.

Example B: Neither the Securities and Exchange Commission nor any state securities commission has approved or disapproved of these securities or determined if this prospectus is truthful or complete. Any representation to the contrary is a criminal offense.

(8) Underwriting. (i) Name(s) of the lead or managing underwriter(s) and an identification of the nature of the underwriting arrangements;

(ii) If the offering is not made on a firm commitment basis, a brief description of the underwriting arrangements. You may use any clear, concise, and accurate description of the underwriting arrangements. You may use the following descriptions of underwriting arrangements where appropriate:

Example A: Best efforts offering. The underwriters are not required to sell any specific number or dollar amount of securities but will use their best efforts to sell the securities offered.

Example B: Best efforts, minimum-maximum offering. The underwriters must sell the minimum number of securities offered (insert number) if any are sold. The underwriters are required to use only their best efforts to sell the maximum number of securities offered (insert number).

(iii) If you offer the securities on a best efforts or best efforts minimum/maximum basis, the date the offering will end, any minimum purchase requirements, and any arrangements to place the funds in an escrow, trust, or similar account. If you have not made any of these arrangements, state this fact and describe the effect on investors;

(9) Date of prospectus. The date of the prospectus;

(10) Prospectus "Subject to Completion" legend. If you use the prospectus before the effective date of the registration statement, a prominent statement that:

(i) The information in the prospectus will be amended or completed;

(ii) A registration statement relating to these securities has been filed with the Securities and Exchange Commission;

(iii) The securities may not be sold until the registration statement becomes effective; and

(iv) The prospectus is not an offer to sell the securities and it is not soliciting an offer to buy the securities in any state where offers or sales are not permitted. The legend may be in the following or other clear, plain language:

The information in this prospectus is not complete and may be changed. We may not sell these securities until the registration statement filed with the Securities and Exchange Commission is effective. This prospectus is not an offer to sell these securities and it is not soliciting an offer to buy these securities in any state where the offer or sale is not permitted.

(11) If you use § 230.430A of this chapter to omit pricing information and the prospectus is used before you determine the public offering price, the information and legend in paragraph (b)(10) of this section.

Instruction to Item 501. For asset-backed securities, see also Item 1102 of Regulation AB (§ 229.1102).

Item 502. Inside Front and Outside Back Cover Pages of Prospectus

The registrant must furnish this information in plain English. See § 230.421(d) of Regulation C of this chapter.

(a) *Table of contents.* On either the inside front or outside back cover page of the prospectus, provide a reasonably detailed table of contents. It must show the page number of the various sections or subdivisions of the prospectus. Include a specific listing of the risk factors section required by Item 503 of this Regulation S–K (17 CFR 229.503). You must include the table of contents immediately following the cover page in any prospectus you deliver electronically.

(b) *Dealer prospectus delivery obligation.* On the outside back cover page of the prospectus, advise dealers of their prospectus delivery obligation, including the expiration date specified by Section 4(3) of the Securities Act (15 U.S.C. 77d(3)) and § 230.174 of this chapter. If you do not know the expiration date on the effective date of the registration statement, include the expiration date in the copy of the prospectus you file under § 230.424(b) of this chapter. You do not have to include this information if dealers are not required to deliver a prospectus under § 230.174 of this chapter or Section 24(d) of the Investment Company Act (15 U.S.C. 30a–24). You may use the following or other clear, plain language:

Dealer Prospectus Delivery Obligation

Until (insert date), all dealers that effect transactions in these securities, whether or not participating in this offering, may be required to deliver a prospectus. This is in addition to the dealers' obligation to deliver a prospectus when acting as underwriters and with respect to their unsold allotments or subscriptions.

Item 503. Prospectus Summary, Risk Factors, and Ratio of Earnings to Fixed Charges

The registrant must furnish this information in plain English. See § 230.421(d) of Regulation C of this chapter.

(a) *Prospectus summary.* Provide a summary of the information in the prospectus where the length or complexity of the prospectus makes a summary useful. The summary should be brief. The summary should not contain, and is not required to contain, all of the detailed information in the prospectus. If you provide summary business or financial information, even if you do not caption it as a summary, you still must provide that information in plain English.

Instruction to paragraph 503(a).

The summary should not merely repeat the text of the prospectus but should provide a brief overview of the key aspects of the offering. Carefully consider and identify those aspects of the offering that are the most significant and determine how best to highlight those points in clear, plain language.

(b) *Address and telephone number.* Include, either on the cover page or in the summary section of the prospectus, the complete mailing address and telephone number of your principal executive offices.

(c) *Risk factors.* Where appropriate, provide under the caption "Risk Factors" a discussion of the most significant factors that make the offering speculative or risky. This discussion must be concise and organized logically. Do not present risks that could apply to any issuer or any offering. Explain how the risk affects the issuer or the securities being offered. Set forth each risk factor under a subcaption that adequately describes the risk. The risk factor discussion must immediately follow the summary section. If you do not include a summary section, the risk factor section must immediately follow the cover page of the prospectus or the pricing information section that immediately follows the cover page. Pricing information means price and price-related information that you may omit from the prospectus in an effective registration statement based on § 230.430A(a) of this chapter. The risk factors may include, among other things, the following:

(1) Your lack of an operating history;

(2) Your lack of profitable operations in recent periods;

(3) Your financial position;

(4) Your business or proposed business; or

(5) The lack of a market for your common equity securities or securities convertible into or exercisable for common equity securities.

(d) *Ratio of earnings to fixed charges.* If you register debt securities, show a ratio of earnings to fixed charges. If you register preference equity securities, show the ratio of combined fixed charges and preference dividends to earnings. Present the ratio for each of the last five fiscal years and the latest interim period for which financial statements are presented in the document. If you will use the proceeds from the sale of debt or preference securities to repay any of your outstanding debt or to retire other securities and the change in the ratio would be ten percent or greater, you must include a ratio showing the application of the proceeds, commonly referred to as the pro forma ratio.

Instructions to paragraph 503(d)

1. *Definitions.* In calculating the ratio of earnings to fixed charges, you must use the following definitions:

(A) Fixed charges. The term "fixed charges" means the sum of the following: (a) interest expensed and capitalized, (b) amortized premiums, discounts and capitalized expenses related to indebtedness, (c) an estimate of the interest within rental expense, and (d) preference security dividend requirements of consolidated subsidiaries.

(B) Preference security dividend. The term "preference security dividend" is the amount of pre-tax earnings that is required to pay the dividends on outstanding preference securities. The dividend requirement must be computed as the amount of the dividend divided by (1 minus the effective income tax rate applicable to continuing operations).

(C) Earnings. The term "earnings" is the amount resulting from adding and subtracting the following items. Add the following: (a) Pre-tax income from continuing operations before adjustment for minority interests in consolidated subsidiaries or income or loss from equity investees, (b) fixed charges, (c) amortization of capitalized interest, (d) distributed income of equity investees, and (e) your share of pre-tax losses of equity investees for which charges arising from guarantees are included in fixed charges. From the total of the added items, subtract the following: (a) interest capitalized, (b) preference security dividend requirements of consolidated subsidiaries, and (c) the minority interest in pre-tax income of subsidiaries that have not incurred fixed charges. Equity investees are investments that you account for using the equity method of accounting. Public utilities following SFAS 71 should not add amortization of capitalized interest in determining earnings, nor reduce fixed charges by any allowance for funds used during construction.

2. *Disclosure.* Disclose the following information when showing the ratio of earnings to fixed charges:

(A) Deficiency. If a ratio indicates less than one-to-one coverage, disclose the dollar amount of the deficiency.

(B) Pro forma ratio. You may show the pro forma ratio only for the most recent fiscal year and the latest interim period. Use the net change in interest or dividends from the refinancing to calculate the pro forma ratio.

(C) Foreign private issuers. A foreign private issuer must show the ratio based on the figures in the primary financial statement. A foreign private issuer must show the ratio based on the figures resulting from the reconciliation to U.S. generally accepted accounting principles if this ratio is materially different.

(D) Summary Section. If you provide a summary or similar section in the prospectus, show the ratios in that section.

3. *Exhibit.* File an exhibit to the registration statement to show the figures used to calculate the ratios. See paragraph (b)(12) of Item 601 of Regulation S–K (17 CFR 229.601(b)(12)).

Instruction to Item 503. For asset-backed securities, see also Item 1103 of Regulation AB (§ 229.1103).

Item 504. Use of Proceeds

State the principal purposes for which the net proceeds to the registrant from the securities to be offered are intended to be used and the approximate amount intended to be used for each such purpose. Where registrant has no current specific plan for the proceeds, or a significant portion thereof, the registrant shall so state and discuss the principal reasons for the offering.

Instructions to Item 504. 1. Where less than all the securities to be offered may be sold and more than one use is listed for the proceeds, indicate the order of priority of such purposes and discuss the registrant's plans if substantially less than the maximum proceeds are obtained. Such discussion need not be included if underwriting arrangements with respect to such securities are such that, if any securities are sold to the public, it reasonably can be expected that the actual proceeds will not be substantially less than the aggregate proceeds to the registrant shown pursuant to Item 501 of Regulation S–K (§ 229.501).

2. Details of proposed expenditures need not be given; for example, there need be furnished only a brief outline of any program of construction or addition of equipment. Consideration should be given as to the need to include a discussion of certain matters addressed in the discussion and analysis of registrant's financial condition and results of operations, such as liquidity and capital expenditures.

3. If any material amounts of other funds are necessary to accomplish the specified purposes for which the proceeds are to be obtained, state the amounts and sources of such other funds needed for each such specified purpose and the sources thereof.

4. If any material part of the proceeds is to be used to discharge indebtedness, set forth the interest rate and maturity of such indebtedness. If the indebtedness to be discharged was incurred within one year, describe the use of the proceeds of such indebtedness other than short-term borrowings used for working capital.

5. If any material amount of the proceeds is to be used to acquire assets, otherwise than in the ordinary course of business, describe briefly and state the cost of the assets and, where such assets are to be acquired from affiliates of the registrant or their associates, give the names of the persons from whom they are to be acquired and set forth the principle

followed in determining the cost to the registrant.

6. Where the registrant indicates that the proceeds may, or will, be used to finance acquisitions of other businesses, the identity of such businesses, if known, or, if not known, the nature of the businesses to be sought, the status of any negotiations with respect to the acquisition, and a brief description of such business shall be included. Where, however, pro forma financial statements reflecting such acquisition are not required by Regulation S–X to be included, in the registration statement, the possible terms of any transaction, the identification of the parties thereto or the nature of the business sought need not be disclosed, to the extent that the registrant reasonably determines that public disclosure of such information would jeopardize the acquisition. Where Regulation S–X would require financial statements of the business to be acquired to be included, the description of the business to be acquired shall be more detailed.

7. The registrant may reserve the right to change the use of proceeds, provided that such reservation is due to certain contingencies that are discussed specifically and the alternatives to such use in that event are indicated.

Item 505. Determination of Offering Price

(a) *Common Equity.* Where common equity is being registered for which there is no established public trading market for purposes of paragraph (a) of Item 201 of Regulation S–K or where there is a material disparity between the offering price of the common equity being registered and the market price of outstanding shares of the same class, describe the various factors considered in determining such offering price.

(b) *Warrants, Rights and Convertible Securities.* Where warrants, rights or convertible securities exercisable for common equity for which there is no established public trading market for purposes of paragraph (a) of Item 201 of Regulation S–K are being registered, describe the various factors considered in determining their exercise or conversion price.

Item 506. Dilution

Where common equity securities are being registered and there is substantial disparity between the public offering price and the effective cash cost to officers, directors, promoters and affiliated persons of common equity acquired by them in transactions during the past five years, or which they have the right to acquire, and the registrant is not subject to the reporting requirements of section 13(a) or 15(d) of the Exchange Act immediately prior to filing of the registration statement, there shall be included a comparison of the public contribution under the proposed public offering and the effective cash contribution of such persons. In such cases, and in other instances where common equity securities are being registered by a registrant that has had losses in each of its last three fiscal years and there is a material dilution of the purchasers' equity interest, the following shall be disclosed:

(a) The net tangible book value per share before and after the distribution;

(b) The amount of the increase in such net tangible book value per share attributable to the cash payments made by purchasers of the shares being offered; and

(c) the amount of the immediate dilution from the public offering price which will be absorbed by such purchasers.

Item 507. Selling Security Holders

If any of the securities to be registered are to be offered for the account of security holders, name each such security holder, indicate the nature of any position, office, or other material relationship which the selling security holder has had within the past three years with the registrant or any of its predecessors or affiliates, and state the amount of securities of the class owned by such security holder prior to the offering, the amount to be offered for the security holder's account, the amount and (if one percent or more) the percentage of the class to be owned by such security holder after completion of the offering.

Item 508. Plan of Distribution

(a) *Underwriters and Underwriting Obligation.* If the securities are to be offered through underwriters, name the principal underwriters, and state the respective amounts underwritten. Identify each such underwriter having a material relationship with the registrant and state the nature of the relationship. State briefly the nature of the obligation of the underwriter(s) to take the securities.

Instruction to Paragraph 508(a). All that is required as to the nature of the underwriters' obligation is whether the underwriters are or will be committed to take and to pay for all of the securities if any are taken, or whether it is merely an agency or the type of "best efforts" arrangement under which the underwriters are required to take and to pay for only such securities as they may sell to the public. Conditions precedent to the underwriters' taking the securities, including "market-outs," need not be described except in the case of an agency or "best efforts" arrangement.

(b) *New Underwriters.* Where securities being registered are those of a registrant that has not previously been required to file reports pursuant to section 13(a) or 15(d) of the Exchange Act, or where a prospectus is required to include reference on its cover page to material risks pursuant to Item 501 of Regulation S–K and any one or more of the managing underwriter(s) (or where there are no managing underwriters, a majority of the principal underwriters) has been organized, reactivated, or first registered as a broker-dealer within the past three years, these facts concerning such underwriter(s) shall be disclosed in the prospectus together with, where applicable, the disclosures that the principal business function of such underwriter(s) will be to sell the securities to be registered, or that the promoters of the registrant have a material relationship with such underwriter(s). Sufficient details shall be given to allow full appreciation of such underwriter(s) experience and its relationship with the registrant, promoters and their controlling persons.

(c) *Other Distributions.* Outline briefly the plan of distribution of any securities to be registered that are to be offered otherwise than through underwriters.

(1) If any securities are to be offered pursuant to a dividend or interest reinvestment plan the terms of which provide for the purchase of some securities on the market, state whether the registrant or the participant pays fees, commissions, and expenses incurred in connection with the plan. If the participant will pay such fees, commissions and expenses, state the anticipated cost to participants by transaction or other convenient reference.

(2) If the securities are to be offered through the selling efforts of brokers or dealers, describe the plan of distribution and the terms of any agreement, arrangement, or understanding entered into with broker(s) or dealer(s) prior to the effective date of the registration statement, including volume limitations on sales, parties to the agreement and the conditions under which the agreement may be terminated. If known, identify the broker(s) or dealer(s) which will participate in the offering and state the amount to be offered through each.

(3) If any of the securities being registered are to be offered otherwise than for cash, state briefly the general purposes of the distribution, the basis, upon which the securities are to be offered, the amount of compensation and other expenses of distribution, and by whom they are to be borne. If the distribution is to be made pursuant to a plan of acquisition, reorganization, readjustment or succession, describe briefly the general effect of the plan and state when it became or is to become operative. As to any material amount of assets to be acquired under the plan, furnish information corresponding to that required by Instruction 5 of Item 504 of Regulation S–K.

(d) *Offerings on Exchange.* If the securities are to be offered on an exchange, indicate the exchange. If the registered securities are to be offered in connection with the writing of exchange-traded call options, describe briefly such transactions.

(e) *Underwriter's compensation.* Provide a table that sets out the nature of the compensation and the amount of discounts and commissions to be paid to the underwriter for each security and in total. The table must show the separate amounts to be paid by the company and the selling shareholders. In addition, include in the table all other items considered by the National Association of Securities Dealers to be underwriting compensation for purposes of that Association's Rules of Fair Practice.

Instructions to paragraph 508(e)

1. The term "commissions" is defined in paragraph (17) of Schedule A of the Securities Act. Show separately in the table the cash commissions paid by the registrant and selling security holders. Also show in the table commissions paid by other persons. Disclose any finder's fee or similar payments in the table.

2. Disclose the offering expenses specified in Item 511 of Regulation S–K (17 CFR 229.511).

3. If the underwriter has any arrangement with the issuer, such as an over-allotment option, under which the underwriter may purchase additional shares in connection with the offering, indicate that this arrangement exists and state the amount of additional shares that the underwriter may purchase under the arrangement. Where the underwriter has such an arrangement, present maximum-minimum information in a separate column to the table, based on the purchase of all or none of the shares subject to the arrangement. Describe the key terms of the arrangement in the narrative.

(f) *Underwriter's Representative on Board of Directors.* Describe any arrangement whereby the underwriter has the right to designate or nominate a member or members of the board of directors of the registrant. The registrant shall disclose the identify of any director so designated or nominated, and indicate whether or not a person so designated or nominated, or allowed to be designated or nominated by the underwriter is or may be a director, officer, partner, employee or affiliate of the underwriter.

(g) *Indemnification of Underwriters.* If the underwriting agreement provides for indemnification by the registrant of the underwriters or their controlling persons against any liability arising under the Securities Act, furnish a brief description of such indemnification provisions.

(h) *Dealers' Compensation.* State briefly the discounts and commissions to be allowed or paid to dealers, including all cash, securities, contracts or other considerations to be received by any dealer in connection with the sale of the securities. If any dealers are to act in the capacity of subunderwriters and are to be allowed or paid any additional discounts or commissions for acting in such capacity, a general statement to that effect will suffice without giving the additional amounts to be sold.

(i) *Finders.* Identify any finder and, if applicable, describe the nature of any material relationship between such finder and the registrant, its officers, directors, principal stockholders, finders or promoters or the principal underwriter(s), or if there is a managing underwriter(s), the managing underwriter(s), (including, in each case, affiliates or associates thereof).

(j) *Discretionary Accounts.* If the registrant was not, immediately prior to the filing of the registration statement, subject to the requirements of section 13(a) or 15(d) of the Exchange Act, identify any principal underwriter that intends to sell to any accounts over which it exercises discretionary authority and include an estimate of the amount of securities so intended to be sold. The response to this paragraph shall be contained in a pre-effective amendment which shall be circulated if the information is not available when the registration statement is filed.

(k) *Passive market making.* If the underwriters or any selling group members intend to engage in passive market making transactions as permitted by Rule 103 of Regulation M, indicate such intention and briefly describe passive market making.

(*l*) Stabilization and other transactions. (1) Briefly describe any transaction that the underwriter intends to conduct during the offering that stabilizes, maintains, or otherwise affects the market price of the offered securities. Include information on stabilizing transactions, syndicate short covering transactions, penalty bids, or any other transaction that affects the offered security's price. Describe the nature of the transactions clearly and explain how the transactions affect the offered security's price. Identify the exchange or other market on which these transactions may occur. If true, disclose that the underwriter may discontinue these transactions at any time;

(2) If the stabilizing began before the effective date of the registration statement, disclose the amount of securities bought, the prices at which they were bought and the period within which they were bought. If you use § 230.430A of this chapter, the prospectus you file under § 230.424(b) of this chapter or include in a post-effective amendment must contain information on the stabilizing transactions that took place before the determination of the public offering price; and

(3) If you are making a warrants or rights offering of securities to existing security holders and any securities not purchased by existing security holders are to be reoffered to the public, disclose in a supplement to the prospectus or in the prospectus used in connection with the reoffering:

(i) The amount of securities bought in stabilization activities during the offering period and the price or range of prices at which the securities were bought;

(ii) The amount of the offered securities subscribed for during the offering period;

(iii) The amount of the offered securities subscribed for by the underwriter during the offering period;

(iv) The amount of the offered securities sold during the offering period by the underwriter and the price or price ranges at which the securities were sold; and

(v) The amount of the offered securities that will be reoffered to the public and the public offering price.

Item 509. Interests of Named Experts and Counsel

If (a) any expert named in the registration statement as having prepared or certified any part thereof (or is named as having prepared or certified a report or valuation for use in connection with the registration statement), or (b) counsel for the registrant, underwriters or selling security holders named in the prospectus as having given an opinion upon the validity of the securities being registered or upon other legal matters in connection with the registration or offering of such securities, was employed for such purpose on a contingent basis, or at the time of such preparation, certification or opinion or at any time thereafter, through the date of effectiveness of the registration statement or that part of the registration statement to which such preparation, certification or opinion relates, had, or is to receive in connection with the offering, a substantial interest, direct or indirect, in the registrant or any of its parents or subsidiaries or was connected with the registrant or any of its parents or subsidiaries as a promoter, managing underwriter (or any principal underwriter, if there are no managing underwriters) voting trustee, director, officer, or employee, furnish a brief statement of the nature of such contingent basis, interest, or connection.

Instructions to Item 509. 1. The interest of an expert (other than an accountant) or counsel will not be deemed substantial and need not be disclosed if the interest, including the fair market value of all securities of the registrant owned, received and to be received, or subject to options, warrants or rights received or to be received by the expert or counsel does not exceed $50,000. For the purpose of this Instruction, the term "expert" or counsel includes the firm, corporation, partnership or other entity, if any, by which such expert or counsel is employed or of which he is a member or of counsel to and all attorneys in the case of counsel, and all nonclerical personnel in the case of named experts, participating in such matter on behalf of such firm, corporation, partnership or entity.

2. Accountants, providing a report on the financial statements, presented or incorporated by reference in the registration statement, should note § 210.2–01 of Regulation S–X for the Commission's requirements regarding "Qualification of Accountants" which discusses disqualifying interests.

Item 510. Disclosure of Commission Position on Indemnification for Securities Act Liabilities

In addition to the disclosure prescribed by Item 702 of Regulation S–K, if the undertaking required by paragraph (h) of Item 512 of Regulation S–K is not required to be included in the registration statement because acceleration of the effective date of the registration statement is not being requested, and if waivers have not been obtained comparable to those specified in paragraph (h), a brief description of the indemnification provisions relating to directors, officers and controlling persons of the registrant against liability arising under the Securities Act (including any provision of the underwriting agreement which relates to indemnification of the underwriter or its controlling persons by the registrant against such liabilities where a director, officer or controlling person of the registrant is such an underwriter or controlling person thereof or a member of any firm which is such an underwriter) shall be included in the prospectus, together with a statement in substantially the following form:

Insofar as indemnification for liabilities arising under the Securities Act of 1933 may be permitted to directors, officers or persons controlling the registrant pursuant to the foregoing provisions, the registrant has been informed that in the opinion of the Securities and Exchange Commission such indemnification is against public policy as expressed in the Act and is therefore unenforceable.

Item 511. Other Expenses of Issuance and Distribution

Furnish a reasonably itemized statement of all expenses in connection with the issuance and distribution of the securities to be registered, other than underwriting discounts and commissions. If any of the securities to be registered are to be offered for the account of security holders, indicate the portion of such expenses to be borne by such security holder.

Instruction to Item 511. Insofar as practicable, registration fees, Federal taxes, States taxes and fees, trustees' and transfer agent's fees, costs of printing and engraving, and legal, accounting, and engineering fees shall be itemized separately. Include as a separate item any premium paid by the registrant or any selling security holder on any policy obtained in connection with the offering and sale of the securities being registered which insures or indemnifies directors or officers against any liabilities they may incur in connection with the registration, offering, or sale of such securities. The information may be given as subject to future contingencies. If the amounts of any items are not known, estimates, identified as such, shall be given.

Item 512. Undertakings

Include each of the following undertakings that is applicable to the offering being registered.

(a) *Rule 415 Offering*. Include the following if the securities are registered pursuant to Rule 415 under the Securities Act:

The undersigned registrant hereby undertakes:

(1) To file, during any period in which offers or sales are being made, a post-effective amendment to this registration statement:

(i) To include any prospectus required by section 10(a)(3) of the Securities Act of 1933;

(ii) To reflect in the prospectus any facts or events arising after the effective date of the registration statement (or the most recent post-effective amendment thereof) which, individually or in the aggregate, represent a fundamental change in the information set forth in the registration statement. Notwithstanding the foregoing, any increase or decrease in volume of securities offered (if the total dollar value of securities offered would not exceed that which was registered) and any deviation from the low or high end of the estimated maximum offering range may be reflected in the form of prospectus filed with the Commission pursuant to Rule 424(b) (§ 230.424(b) of this chapter) if, in the aggregate, the changes in volume and price represent no more than 20% change in the maximum aggregate offering price set forth in the "Calculation of Registration Fee" table in the effective registration statement.

(iii) To include any material information with respect to the plan of distribution not previously disclosed in the registration statement or any material change to such information in the registration statement.

Provided, however, That paragraphs (a)(1)(i) and (a)(1)(ii) of this section do not apply if the registration statement is on Form S–3 (§ 239.13 of this chapter), Form S–8 (§ 239.16b of this chapter) or Form F–3 (§ 239.33 of this chapter), and the information required to be included in a post-effective amendment by those paragraphs is contained in periodic reports filed with or furnished to the Commission by the registrant pursuant to section 13 or section 15(d) of the Securities Exchange Act of 1934 that are incorporated by reference in the registration statement.

Provided further, however, that paragraphs (a)(1)(i) and (a)(1)(ii) do not apply if the registration statement is for an offering of asset-backed securities on Form S–1 (§ 239.11 of this chapter) or Form S–3 (§ 239.13 of this chapter), and the information required to be included in a post-effective amendment is provided pursuant to Item 1100(c) of Regulation AB (§ 229.1100(c)).

(2) That, for the purpose of determining any liability under the Securities Act of 1933, each such post-effective amendment shall be deemed to be a new registration statement relating to the securities offered therein, and the offering of such securities at that time shall be deemed to be the initial bona fide offering thereof.

(3) To remove from registration by means of a post-effective amendment any of the securities being registered which remain unsold at the termination of the offering.

(4) If the registrant is a foreign private issuer, to file a post-effective amendment to the registration statement to include any financial statements required by Item 8A of Form 20–F (17 CFR 249.220f) at the start of any delayed offering or throughout a continuous offering. Financial statements and information otherwise required by Section 10(a)(3) of the Act need not be furnished, *provided* that the registrant includes in the prospectus, by means of a post-effective amendment, financial statements required pursuant to this paragraph (a)(4) and other information necessary to ensure that all other information in the prospectus is at least as current as the date of those financial statements. Notwithstanding the foregoing,

with respect to registration statements on Form F–3 (§ 239.33 of this chapter), a post-effective amendment need not be filed to include financial statements and information required by Section 10(a)(3) of the Act or § 210.3–19 of this chapter if such financial statements and information are contained in periodic reports filed with or furnished to the Commission by the registrant pursuant to section 13 or section 15(d) of the Securities Exchange Act of 1934 that are incorporated by reference in the Form F–3.

(b) *Filings Incorporating Subsequent Exchange Act Documents by Reference.* Include the following if the registration statement incorporates by reference any Exchange Act document filed subsequent to the effective date of the registration statement:

The undersigned registrant hereby undertakes that, for purposes of determining any liability under the Securities Act of 1933, each filing of the registrant's annual report pursuant to section 13(a) or section 15(d) of the Securities Exchange Act of 1934 (and, where applicable, each filing of an employee benefit plan's annual report pursuant to section 15(d) of the Securities Exchange Act of 1934) that is incorporated by reference in the registration statement shall be deemed to be a new registration statement relating to the securities offered therein, and the offering of such securities at that time shall be deemed to be the initial bona fide offering thereof.

(c) *Warrants and Rights Offerings.* Include the following, with appropriate modifications to suit the particular case, if the securities to be registered are to be offered to existing security holders pursuant to warrants or rights and any securities not taken by security holders are to be reoffered to the public:

The undersigned registrant hereby undertakes to supplement the prospectus, after the expiration of the subscription period, to set forth the results of the subscription offer, the transactions by the underwriters during the subscription period, the amount of unsubscribed securities to be purchased by the underwriters, and the terms of any subsequent reoffering thereof. If any public offering by the underwriters is to be made on terms differing from those set forth on the cover page of the prospectus, a post-effective amendment will be filed to set forth the terms of such offering.

(d) *Competitive Bids.* Include the following, with appropriate modifications to suit the particular case, if the securities to be registered are to be offered at competitive bidding:

The undersigned registrant hereby undertakes (1) to use its best efforts to distribute prior to the opening of bids, to prospective bidders, underwriters, and dealers, a reasonable number of copies of a prospectus which at that time meets the requirements of section 10(a) of the Act, and relating to the securities offered at competitive bidding, as contained in the registration statement, together with any supplements thereto and (2) to file an amendment to the registration statement reflecting the results of bidding, the terms of the reoffering and related matters to the extent required by the applicable form, not later than the first use, authorized by the issuer after the opening of bids, of a prospectus relating to the securities offered at competitive bidding, unless no further public offering of such securities by the issuer and no reoffering of such securities by the purchasers is proposed to be made.

(e) *Incorporated Annual and Quarterly Reports.* Include the following if the registration statement specifically incorporates by reference (other than by indirect incorporation by reference through a Form 10–K and Form 10–KSB report) in the prospectus all or any part of the annual report to security holders meeting the requirements of Rule 14a–3 or Rule 14c–3 under the Exchange Act:

The undersigned registrant hereby undertakes to deliver or cause to be delivered with the prospectus, to each person to whom the prospectus is sent or given, the latest annual report to security holders that is incorporated by reference in the prospectus and furnished pursuant to and meeting the requirements of Rule 14a–3 or Rule 14c–3 under the Securities Exchange Act of 1934; and, where interim financial information required to be presented by Article 3 of Regulation S–X are not set forth in the prospectus, to deliver, or cause to be delivered to each person to whom the prospectus is sent or given, the latest quarterly report that is specifically incorporated by reference in the prospectus to provide such interim financial information.

(f) *Equity Offerings of Nonreporting Registrants.* Include the following if equity securities of a registrant that prior to the offering had no obligation to file reports with the Commission pursuant to section 13(a) or 15(d) of the Exchange Act are being registered for sale in an underwritten offering:

The undersigned registrant hereby undertakes to provide to the underwriter at the closing specified in the underwriting agreements certificates in such denominations and registered in such names as required by the underwriter to permit prompt delivery to each purchaser.

(g) *Registration on Form S–4 or F–4 of Securities Offered for Resale.* Include the following if the securities are being registered on Form S–4 or F–4 in connection with a transaction specified in paragraph (a) of Rule 145.

(1) The undersigned registrant hereby undertakes as follows: that prior to any public reoffering of the securities registered hereunder through use of a prospectus which is a part of this registration statement, by any person or party who is deemed to be an underwriter within the meaning of Rule 145(c), the issuer undertakes that such reoffering prospectus will contain the information called for by the applicable registration form with respect to reofferings by persons who may be deemed underwriters, in addition to the information called for by the other Items of the applicable form.

(2) The registrant undertakes that every prospectus (i) that is filed pursuant to paragraph (1) immediately preceding, or (ii) that purports to meet the requirements of section 10(a)(3) of the Act and is used in connection with an offering of securities subject to Rule 415, will be filed as a part of an amendment to the registration statement and will not be used until such amendment is effective, and that, for purposes of determining any liability under the Securities Act of 1933, each such post-effective amendment shall be deemed to be a new registration statement relating to the securities offered therein, and the offering of such securities at that time shall be deemed to be the initial bona fide offering thereof.

(h) *Request for Acceleration of Effective Date or Filing of Registration Statement on Form S–8.* Include the following if any acceleration is requested of the effective date of the registration statement pursuant to Rule 461 under the Securities Act, or if the registration statement is filed on Form S–8, and

(1) any provision or arrangement exists whereby the registrant may indemnify a director, officer or controlling person of the registrant against liabilities arising under the Securities Act, or

(2) the underwriting agreement contains a provision whereby the registrant indemnifies the underwriter or controlling persons of the underwriter against such liabilities and a director, officer or control-

ling person of the registrant is such an underwriter or controlling person thereof or a member of any firm which is such an underwriter, and

(3) the benefits of such indemnification are not waived by such persons:

Insofar as indemnification for liabilities arising under the Securities Act of 1933 may be permitted to directors, officers and controlling persons of the registrant pursuant to the foregoing provisions, or otherwise, the registrant has been advised that in the opinion of the Securities and Exchange Commission such indemnification is against public policy as expressed in the Act and is, therefore, unenforceable. In the event that a claim for indemnification against such liabilities (other than the payment by the registrant of expenses incurred or paid by a director, officer or controlling person of the registrant in the successful defense of any action, suit or proceeding) is asserted by such director, officer or controlling person in connection with the securities being registered, the registrant will, unless in the opinion of its counsel the matter has been settled by controlling precedent, submit to a court of appropriate jurisdiction the question whether such indemnification by it is against public policy as expressed in the Act and will be governed by the final adjudication of such issue.

(i) Include the following in a registration statement permitted by Rule 430A under the Securities Act of 1933:

The undersigned registrant hereby undertakes that:

(1) For purposes of determining any liability under the Securities Act of 1933, the information omitted from the form of prospectus filed as part of a registration statement in reliance upon Rule 430A and contained in the form of prospectus filed by the registrant pursuant to Rule 424(b)(1) or (4) or 497(h) under the Securities Act shall be deemed to be part of the registration statement as of the time it was declared effective.

(2) For the purpose of determining any liability under the Securities Act of 1933, each post-effective amendment that contains a form of prospectus shall be deemed to be a new registration statement relating to the securities offered therein, and the offering of such securities at that time shall be deemed to be the initial bona fide offering thereof.

(j) *Qualification of Trust Indentures under the Trust Indenture Act of 1939 for delayed offerings.* Include the following if the registrant intends to rely on section 305(b)(2) of the Trust Indenture Act of 1939 for determining the eligibility of the trustee under indentures for securities to be used, offered, or sold on a delayed basis by or on behalf of the registrant:

"The undersigned registrant hereby undertakes to file an application for the purpose of determining the eligibility of the trustee to act under subsection (a) of section 310 of the Trust Indenture Act ('Act') in accordance with the rules and regulations prescribed by the Commission under section 305(b)(2) of the Act."

(k) Filings regarding asset-backed securities incorporating by reference subsequent Exchange Act documents by third parties. Include the following if the registration statement incorporates by reference any Exchange Act document filed subsequent to the effective date of the registration statement pursuant to Item 1100(c) of Regulation AB (§ 229.1100(c)):

The undersigned registrant hereby undertakes that, for purposes of determining any liability under the Securities Act of 1933, each filing of the annual report pursuant to section 13(a) or section 15(d) of the Securities Exchange Act of 1934 of a third party that is incorporated by reference in the registration statement in accordance with Item 1100(c)(1) of Regulation AB (17 CFR 229.1100(c)(1)) shall be deemed to be a new registration statement relating to the securities offered therein, and the offering of such securities at that time shall be deemed to be the initial bona fide offering thereof.

(*l*) Filings regarding asset-backed securities that provide certain information through an Internet Web site. Include the following if the registration statement is to provide information required by Item 1105 of Regulation AB (§ 229.1105) through an Internet Web site in accordance with Rule 312 of Regulation S–T (§ 232.312 of this chapter):

The undersigned registrant hereby undertakes that, except as otherwise provided by Item 1105 of Regulation AB (17 CFR 229.1105), information provided in response to that Item pursuant to Rule 312 of Regulation S–T (17 CFR 232.312) through the specified Internet address in the prospectus is deemed to be a part of the prospectus included in the registration statement. In addition, the undersigned registrant hereby undertakes to provide to any person without charge, upon request, a copy of the information provided in response to Item 1105 of Regulation AB pursuant to Rule 312 of Regulation S–T through the specified Internet address as of the date of the prospectus included in the registration statement if a subsequent update or change is made to the information.

Subpart 600—Exhibits

Item 601. Exhibits

(a) *Exhibits and Index Required.* (1) Subject to Rule 411(c) under the Securities Act and Rule 12b–32 under the Exchange Act regarding incorporation of exhibits by reference, the exhibits required by in the exhibit table shall be filed as indicated, as part of the registration statement or report. (2) Each registration statement or report shall contain an exhibit index, which shall precede immediately the exhibits filed with such registration statement. For convenient reference, each exhibit shall be listed in the exhibit index according to the number assigned to it in the exhibit table. The exhibit index shall indicate, by handwritten, typed, printed, or other legible form of notation in the manually signed original registration statement or report, the page number in the sequential numbering system where such exhibit can be found. Where exhibits are incorporated by reference, this fact shall be noted in the exhibit index referred to in the preceding sentence. Further, the first page of the manually signed registration statement shall list the page in the filing where the exhibit index is located. For a description of each of the exhibits included in the exhibit table, see paragraph (b) of this Item. (3) This Item applies only to the forms specified in the exhibit table. With regard to forms not listed in that table, reference shall be made to the appropriate form for the specific exhibit filing requirements applicable thereto. Notwithstanding the provisions of paragraphs (b)(27) and (c) of this Item, registered investment companies and business development companies filing on forms available solely to investment companies shall be subject to the provisions of Rule 483 under the Securities Act of 1933, and any provision or instruction therein shall be controlling with respect to registered investment companies and business development companies unless otherwise specifically provided in rules or instructions pertaining to the submission of a specific form. (4) If a material contract or plan of acquisition, reorganization, arrangement, liquidation or succession is executed or becomes effective during the reporting period reflected by a Form 10–Q and Form 10–QSB or Form 10–K and Form 10–KSB, it shall be filed as an exhibit to the Form 10–Q and Form 10–QSB or Form 10–K and Form 10–KSB filed for the corresponding period. Any amendment or modification to a previously filed exhibit to a Form 10 and Form 10–KSB, Form 10–K, or Form 10–Q document shall be filed as an exhibit to a Form 10–Q and

Form 10–QSB or Form 10–K and Form 10–KSB. Such amendment or modification need not be filed where such previously filed exhibit would not be currently required.

Instructions to Item 601. (1) If an exhibit to a registration statement (other than an opinion or consent), filed in preliminary form, has been changed only (A) to insert information as to interest, dividend or conversion rates, redemption or conversion prices, purchase or offering prices, underwriters' or dealers' commissions, names, addresses or participation of underwriters or similar matters, which information appears elsewhere in an amendment to the registration statement or a prospectus filed pursuant to Rule 424(b) under the Securities Act, or (B) to correct typographical errors, insert signatures or make other similar immaterial changes, then, notwithstanding any contrary requirement of any rule or form, the registrant need not refile such exhibit as so amended. Any such incomplete exhibit may not, however, be incorporated by reference in any subsequent filing under any Act administered by the Commission.

2. In any case where two or more indentures, contracts, franchises, or other documents required to be filed as exhibits are substantially identical in all material respects except as to the parties thereto, the dates of execution, or other details, the registrant need file a copy of only one of such documents, with a schedule identifying the other documents omitted and setting forth the material details in which such documents differ from the document a copy of which is filed. The Commission may at any time in its discretion require filing of copies of any documents so omitted.

3. Only copies, rather than originals, need be filed of each exhibit required except as otherwise specifically noted.

4. *Electronic filings.* Whenever an exhibit is filed in paper pursuant to a hardship exemption (§§ 232.201 and 232.202 of this chapter), the letter "P" (paper) shall be placed next to the exhibit in the list of exhibits required by Item 601(a)(2) of this Rule. Whenever an electronic confirming copy of an exhibit is filed pursuant to a grant of a temporary hardship exemption (§ 232.201 or § 232.202(d) of this chapter), the exhibit index shall specify where the confirming electronic copy can be located; in addition, the designation "CE" (confirming electronic) shall be placed next to the listed exhibit in the exhibit index.

EXHIBIT TABLE

	Securities Act Forms										Exchange Act Forms				
	S–1	S–2	S–3	S–4[3]	S–8	S–11	F–1	F–2	F–3	F–4[5]	10	8–K	10–D	10–Q	10–K
(1) Underwriting agreement	X	X	X	X		X	X	X	X	X		X			
(2) Plan of reorganization, arrangement, liquidation, or succession	X	X	X	X		X	X	X	X	X	X	X		X	X
(3) (i) Articles of incorporation	X			X		X	X			X	X	X	X	X	X
(ii) Bylaws	X			X		X	X			X	X	X	X	X	X
(4) Instruments defining the rights of security holders, including identures	X	X	X	X	X	X	X	X	X	X	X	X	X	X	X
(5) Opinion re legality	X	X	X	X	X	X	X	X	X	X					
(6) [Reserved]	N/A	N/A	N/A	N/A	N/A	N/A	N/A	N/A	N/A	N/A	N/A	N/A	N/A	N/A	N/A
(7) Correspondence from an independent accountant regarding non-reliance on a previously issued audit report or completed interim review												X			
(8) Opinion re tax matters	X	X	X	X		X	X	X	X	X					
(9) Voting trust, agreement	X			X		X	X			X	X				X
(10) Material contracts	X	X		X		X	X	X		X	X		X	X	X
(11) Statement re computation of per share earnings	X	X		X		X	X	X		X	X			X	X
(12) Statements re computation of ratios	X	X	X	X		X	X	X		X	X				X

	Securities Act Forms										Exchange Act Forms				
	S–1	S–2	S–3	S–4[3]	S–8	S–11	F–1	F–2	F–3	F–4[5]	10	8–K	10–D	10–Q	10–K
(13) Annual report to security holders, Form 10–Q and 10–QSB, or quarterly report to security holders[1]		X		X											X
(14) Code of Ethics												X			X
(15) Letter re unaudited interim financial information	X	X	X	X	X	X	X	X	X	X				X	
(16) Letter re change in certifying accountant[4]	X	X		X		X					X	X			X
(17) Correspondence on departure of director												X			
(18) Letter re change in accounting principles														X	X
(19) Report furnished to security holders														X	
(20) Other documents or statements to security holders												X			
(21) Subsidiaries of the registrant	X			X		X	X			X	X				X
(22) Published report regarding matters submitted to vote of security holders													X	X	X
(23) Consents of experts and counsel	X	X	X	X	X	X	X	X	X	X		X[2]	X[2]	X[2]	X[2]
(24) Power of attorney	X	X	X	X	X	X	X	X	X	X	X	X	X	X	X
(25) Statement of eligibility of trustee	X	X	X	X		X	X	X	X	X					
(26) Invitations for competitive bids	X	X	X	X			X	X	X	X					
(27) through (30) [Reserved]															
(31) (i) Rule 13a–14(a)/15d–14(a) Certifications														X	X
(ii) Rule 13a–14(d)/15d–14(d) Certifications[6]															X
(32) Section 1350 Certifications[6]														X	X
(33) Report on assessment of compliance with servicing criteria for asset-backed securities															X
(34) Attestation report on assessment of compliance with servicing criteria for asset-backed securities															X
(35) Servicer compliance statement	X	X	X	X		X	X	X	X	X		X			
(36) through (98) [Reserved]	N/A	N/A	N/A	N/A	N/A	N/A	N/A	N/A	N/A	N/A	N/A	N/A	N/A	N/A	N/A
(99) Additional exhibits	X	X	X	X	X	X	X	X	X	X	X	X	X	X	X
(100) XBRL-Related Documents											X	X		X	X

1. Where incorporated by reference into the text of the prospectus and delivered to security holders along with the prospectus as permitted by the registration statement; or, in the case of the Form 10–K, where the annual report to security holders is incorporated by reference into the text of the Form 10–K.

2. Where the opinion of the expert or counsel has been incorporated by reference into a previously filed Securities Act registration statement.

3. An exhibit need not be provided about a company if: (1) with respect to such company an election has been made under Form S–4 or F–4 to provide information about such company at a level prescribed by Form S–2, S–3, F–2 or F–3; and (2) the form, the level of which has been elected under Form S–4 or F–4, would not require such company to provide such exhibit if it were registering a primary offering.

4. If required pursuant to Item 304 of Regulation S–K.

5. A Form 8–K Exhibit is required only if relevant to the subject matter reported on the Form 8–K report. For example, if the Form 8–K pertains to the departure of a director, only the exhibit described in paragraph (b)(17) of this section need be filed. A required exhibit may be incorporated by reference from a previous filing.

6. Pursuant to §§ 240.13a–13(b)(3) and 240.15d–13(b)(3) of this chapter, asset-backed issuers are not required to file reports on Form 10–Q.

Instructions to the Exhibit Table. 1. The exhibit table indicates those documents that must be filed as exhibits to the respective forms listed.

2. The "X" designation indicates the documents which are required to be filed with each form even if filed previously with another document, *Provided, However,* that such previously filed documents may be incorporated by reference to satisfy the filing requirements.

3. The number used in the far left column of the table refers to the appropriate subsection in paragraph (b) where a description of the exhibit can be found. Whenever necessary, alphabetical or numerical subparts may be used.

(b) *Description of Exhibits.* Set forth below is a description of each document listed in the exhibit tables.

(1) *Underwriting Agreement.* Each underwriting contract or agreement with a principal underwriter pursuant to which the securities being registered are to be distributed; if the terms of such documents have not been determined, the proposed forms thereof. Such agreement may be filed as an exhibit to a report on Form 8–K which is incorporated by reference into a registration statement subsequent to its effectiveness.

(2) *Plan of Acquisition, Reorganization, Arrangement, Liquidation or Succession.* Any material plan of acquisition, disposition, reorganization, readjustment, succession, liquidation or arrangement and any amendments thereto described in the statement or report. Schedules (or similar attachments) to these exhibits shall not be filed unless such schedules contain information which is material to an investment decision and which is not otherwise disclosed in the agreement or the disclosure document. The plan filed shall contain a list briefly identifying the contents of all omitted schedules, together with an agreement to furnish supplementally a copy of any omitted schedule to the Commission upon request.

(3)(i) *Articles of Incorporation.* The articles of incorporation of the registrant or instruments corresponding thereto as currently in effect and any amendments thereto. Whenever the registrant files an amendment to its articles of incorporation, it must file a complete copy of the articles as amended. However, if such amendment is being reported on Form 8–K (§ 249.308 of this chapter), the registrant is required to file only the text of the amendment as a Form 8–K exhibit. In such case, a complete copy of the articles of incorporation as amended must be filed as an exhibit to the next Securities Act registration statement or periodic report filed by the registrant to which this exhibit requirement applies. Where it is impracticable for the registrant to file a charter amendment authorizing new securities with the appropriate state authority prior to the effective date of the registration statement registering such securities, the registrant may file as an exhibit to the registration statement the form of amendment to be filed with the state authority. In such a case, if material changes are made after the copy is filed, the registrant must also file the changed copy.

(ii) *Bylaws.* The bylaws of the registrant or instruments corresponding thereto as currently in effect and any amendments thereto. Whenever the registrant files an amendment to the bylaws, it must file a complete copy of the amended bylaws. However, if such amendment is being reported on Form 8–K (§ 249.308 of this chapter), the registrant is required to file only the text of the amendment as a Form 8–K exhibit. In such case, a complete copy of the bylaws as amended must be filed as an exhibit to the next Securities Act registration statement or periodic report filed by the registrant to which this exhibit requirement applies.

(4) *Instruments Defining the Rights of Security Holders, Including Indentures.* (i) All instruments defining the rights of holders of the equity or debt securities being registered including, where applicable, the relevant portion of the articles of incorporation or bylaws of the registrant.

(ii) Except as set forth in (iii) below, for filings on Forms S–1, S–4, S–11, S–14 and F–4 under the Securities Act and Forms 10 and 10–K under the Exchange Act all instruments defining the rights of holders of long-term debt of the registrant and its consolidated subsidiaries and for any of its unconsolidated subsidiaries for which financial statements are required to be filed.

(iii) Where the instrument defines the rights of holders of long-term debt of the registrant and its consolidated subsidiaries and for any of its unconsolidated subsidiaries for which financial statements are required to be filed, there need not be filed (A) any instrument with respect to long-term debt not being registered if the total amount of securities authorized thereunder does not exceed 10 percent of the total assets of the registrant and its subsidiaries on a consolidated basis and if there is filed an agreement to furnish a copy of such agreement to the Commission upon request; (B) any instrument with respect to any class of securities if appropriate steps to assure the redemption or retirement of such class will be taken prior to or upon delivery by the registrant of the securities being registered; or (C) copies of instruments evidencing scrip certificates for fractions of shares.

(iv) If any of the securities being registered are, or will be, issued under an indenture to be qualified under the Trust Indenture Act, the copy of such indenture which is filed as an exhibit shall include or be accompanied by (A) a reasonably itemized and informative table of contents; and (B) a cross-reference sheet showing the location in the indenture of the provisions inserted pursuant to sections 310 through 318(a) inclusive of the Trust Indenture Act of 1939.

(v) With respect to Forms 8–K and 10–Q under the Exchange Act which are filed and which disclose, in the text of the Form 10–Q and Form 10–QSB, the interim financial statements, or the footnotes thereto the creation of a new class of securities or indebtedness or the modification of existing rights of security holders, file all instruments defining the rights of holders of these securities or indebtedness. However, there need not be filed any instrument with respect to long-term debt not being registered which meets the exclusion set forth above in paragraph (iii)(A).

Instruction 1. There need not be filed any instrument which defines the rights of participants (not as security holders) pursuant to an employee benefit plan.

Instruction 2 to paragraph (b)(4) (for electronic filings). If the instrument defining the rights of security holders is in the form of a certificate, the text appearing on the certificate shall be reproduced in an electronic filing together with a description of any other graphic and image material appearing on the certificate, as provided in Rule 304 of Regulation S–T (§ 232.304 of this chapter).

(5) *Opinion re Legality.* (i) An opinion of counsel as to the legality of the securities being registered, indicating whether they will, when sold, be legally issued, fully paid and non-assessable, and, if debt securities, whether they will be binding obligations of the registrant.

(ii) If the securities being registered are issued under a plan and the plan is subject to the requirements of ERISA furnish either:

(A) An opinion of counsel which confirms compliance of the provisions of the written documents constituting the plan with the requirements of ERISA pertaining to such provisions; or

(B) A copy of the Internal Revenue Service determination letter that the plan is qualified under section 401 of the Internal Revenue Code; or

(iii) If the securities being registered are issued under a plan which is subject to the requirements of ERISA and the plan has been amended subsequent to the filing of (ii)(A) or (B) above, furnish either:

(A) An opinion of counsel which confirms compliance of the amended provisions of the plan with the requirements of ERISA pertaining to such provisions; or

(B) A copy of the Internal Revenue Service determination letter that the amended plan is qualified under section 401 of the Internal Revenue Code.

Note: Attention is directed to Item 8 of Form S–8 for exemptions to this exhibit requirement applicable to that Form.

(7) *Correspondence From an Independent Accountant Regarding Non-Reliance on a Previously Issued Audit Report or Completed Interim Review.* Any written notice from the registrant's current or previously engaged independent accountant that the independent accountant is withdrawing a previously issued audit report or that a previously issued audit report or completed interim review, covering one or more years or interim periods for which the small registrant is required to provide financial statements under Regulation S–X (part 210 of this chapter), should no longer be relied upon. In addition, any letter, pursuant to Item 4.02(c) of Form 8–K (§ 249.308 of this chapter), from the independent accountant to the Commission stating whether the independent accountant agrees with the statements made by the registrant describing the events giving rise to the notice.

(8) *Opinion re Tax Matters.* For filings on Form S–11 under the Securities Act (§ 239.18) or those to which Securities Act Industry Guide 5 applies, an opinion of counsel or of an independent public or certified public accountant or, in lieu thereof, a revenue ruling from the Internal Revenue Service, supporting the tax matters and consequences to the shareholder as described in the filing when such tax matters are material to the transaction for which the registration statement is being filed. This exhibit otherwise need only be filed with the other applicable registration forms where the tax consequences are material to an investor and a representation as to tax consequences is set forth in the filing. If a tax opinion is set forth in full in the filing, an indication that such is the case may be made in lieu of filing the otherwise required exhibit. Such tax opinions may be conditioned or may be qualified, so long as such conditions and qualifications are adequately described in the filing.

(9) *Voting Trust Agreement.* Any voting trust agreements and amendments thereto.

(10) *Material Contracts.* (i) Every contract not made in the ordinary course of business which is material to the registrant and is to be performed in whole or in part at or after the filing of the registration statement or report or was entered into not more than two years before such filing. Only contracts need be filed as to which the registrant or subsidiary of the registrant is a party or has succeeded to a party by assumption or assignment or in which the registrant or such subsidiary has a beneficial interest.

(ii) If the contract is such as ordinarily accompanies the kind of business conducted by the registrant and its subsidiaries, it will be deemed to have been made in the ordinary course of business and need not be filed unless it falls within one or more of the following categories, in which case it shall be filed except where immaterial in amount or significance:

(A) Any contract to which directors, officers, promoters, voting trustees, security holders named in the registration statement or report, or underwriters are parties other than contracts involving only the purchase or sale of current assets having a determinable market price, at such market price;

(B) Any contract upon which the registrant's business is substantially dependent, as in the case of continuing contracts to sell the major part of registrant's products or services or to purchase the major part of registrant's requirements of goods, services or raw materials or any franchise or license or other agreement to use a patent, formula, trade secret, process or trade name upon which registrant's business depends to a material extent;

(C) Any contract calling for the acquisition or sale of any property, plant or equipment for a consideration exceeding 15 percent of such fixed assets of the registrant on a consolidated basis; or

(D) Any material lease under which a part of the property described in the registration statement or report is held by the registrant.

(iii)(A) Any management contract or any compensatory plan, contract or arrangement, including but not limited to plans relating to options, warrants or rights, pension, retirement or deferred compensation or bonus, incentive or profit sharing (or if not set forth in any formal document, a written description thereof) in which any director or any of the named executive officers of the registrant, as defined by Item 402(a)(3), participates shall be deemed material and shall be filed; and any other management contract or any other compensatory plan, contract, or arrangement in which any other executive officer of the registrant participates shall be filed unless immaterial in amount or significance.

(B) Any compensatory plan, contract or arrangement adopted without the approval of security holders pursuant to which equity may be awarded, including, but not limited to, options, warrants or rights (or if not set forth in any formal document, a written description thereof), in which any employee (whether or not an executive officer of the registrant) participates shall be filed unless immaterial in amount or significance. A compensation plan assumed by a registrant in connection with a merger, consolidation or other acquisition transaction pursuant to which the registrant may make further grants or awards of its equity securities shall be considered a compensation plan of the registrant for purposes of the preceding sentence.

(C) Notwithstanding paragraph (iii)(A) above, the following management contracts or compensatory plans, contracts or arrangements need not be filed:

(*1*) Ordinary purchase and sales agency agreements.

(*2*) Agreements with managers of stores in a chain organization or similar organization.

(*3*) Contracts providing for labor or salesmen's bonuses or payments to a class of security holders, as such.

(*4*) Any compensatory plan, contract or arrangement which pursuant to its terms is available to employees, officers or directors generally and which in operation provides for the same method of allocation of benefits between management and non-management participants.

(*5*) Any compensatory plan, contract or arrangement if the registrant is a foreign private issuer that furnishes compensatory information on an aggregate basis as permitted by General Instruction 1 to Item 402 or by Item 6B of Form 20–F (§ 249.220f of this chapter).

(*6*) Any compensatory plan, contract, or arrangement if the registrant is a wholly owned subsidiary of a company that has a class of securities registered pursuant to section 12 or files reports pursuant to section 15(d) of the Exchange Act and is filing a report on Form 10–K and Form 10–KSB or registering debt instruments or preferred stock which are not voting securities on Form S–2.

Instruction 1 to paragraph (b)(10): With the exception of management contracts, in order to comply with paragraph (iii) above, registrants need only file copies of the various remunerative plans and need not file each individual director's or executive officer's personal agreement under the plans unless there are particular provisions in such personal agreements whose disclosure in an exhibit is necessary to an investor's understanding of that individual's remuneration under the plan.

Instruction 2 to paragraph (b)(10). If a material contract is executed or becomes effective during the reporting period reflected by a Form 10–Q or Form 10–K, it shall be filed as an exhibit to the Form 10–Q or Form 10–K filed for the corresponding period. *See* paragraph (a)(4) of this Item. With respect to quarterly reports on Form 10–Q, only those contracts executed or becoming effective during the most recent period reflected in the report shall be filed.

(11) *Statement re Computation of Per Share Earnings.* A statement setting forth in reasonable detail the computation of per share earnings, unless the computation can be clearly determined from the material contained in the registration statement or report. The information with respect to the computation of per share earnings on both primary and fully diluted bases, presented by exhibit or otherwise, must be furnished even though the amounts of per share earnings on the fully diluted basis are not required to be presented in the income statement under the provisions of Accounting Principles Board Opinion No. 15. That Opinion provides that any reduction of less than 3% need not be considered as dilution (see footnote to paragraph 14 of the Opinion) and that a computation on the fully diluted basis which results in improvement of earnings per share not be taken into account (see paragraph 40 of the Opinion).

(12) *Statements re Computation of Ratios.* A statement setting forth in reasonable detail the computation of any ratio of earnings to fixed charges, any ratio of earnings to combined fixed charges and preferred stock dividends or any other ratios which appear in the registration statement or report. See Item 503(d) of Regulation S–K.

(13) *Annual Report to Security Holders, Form 10–Q and Form 10–QSB, or Quarterly Report to Security Holders.* (i) The registrant's annual report to security holders for its last fiscal year, its Form 10–Q and Form 10–QSB (if specifically incorporated by reference in the prospectus) or its quarterly report to security holders, if all or a portion thereof is incorporated by reference in the filing. Such report, except for those portions thereof which are expressly incorporated by reference in the filing, is to be furnished for the information of the Commission and is not to be deemed "filed" as part of the filing. If the financial statements in the report have been incorporated by reference in the filing, the accountant's certificate shall be manually signed in one copy. See Rule 411(b).

(ii) *Electronic filings.* If all, or any portion, of the annual or quarterly report to security holders is incorporated by reference into any electronic filing, all, or such portion of the annual or quarterly report to security holders so incorporated, shall be filed in electronic format as an exhibit to the filing.

(14) *Code of ethics.* Any code of ethics, or amendment thereto, that is the subject of the disclosure required by Item 406 of Regulation S–K (§ 229.406) or Item 10 of Form 8–K (§ 249.308 of this chapter), to the extent that the registrant intends to satisfy the Item 406 or Item 10 requirements through filing of an exhibit.

(15) *Letter re Unaudited Interim Financial Information.* A letter, where applicable, from the independent accountant which acknowledges awareness of the use in a registration statement of a report on unaudited interim financial information which pursuant to Rule 436(c) under the Securities Act is not considered a part of a registration statement prepared or certified by an accountant or a report prepared or certified by an accountant within the meaning of sections 7 and 11 of that Act. Such letter may be filed with the registration statement, an

amendment thereto, or a report on Form 10–Q which is incorporated by reference into the registration statement.

(16) *Letter re Change in Certifying Accountant.* A letter from the registrant's former independent accountant regarding its concurrence or disagreement with the statements made by the registrant in the current report concerning the resignation or dismissal as the registrant's principal accountant.

(17) *Correspondence on Departure of Director.* Any written correspondence from a former director concerning the circumstances surrounding the former director's retirement, resignation, refusal to stand for re-election or removal, including any letter from the former director to the registrant stating whether the former director agrees with statements made by the registrant describing the former director's departure.

(18) *Letter re Change in Accounting Principles.* Unless previously filed, a letter from the registrant's independent accountant indicating whether any change in accounting principles or practices followed by the registrant, or any change in the method of applying any such accounting principles or practices, which affected the financial statements being filed with the Commission in the report or which is reasonably certain to affect the financial statements of future fiscal years is to an alternative principle which in his judgment is preferable under the circumstances. No such letter need be filed when such change is made in response to a standard adopted by the Financial Accounting Standards Board that creates a new accounting principle, that expresses a preference for an accounting principle, or that rejects a specific accounting principle.

(19) *Report Furnished to Security Holders.* If the registrant makes available to its stockholders or otherwise publishes, within the period prescribed for filing the report, a document or statement containing information meeting some or all of the requirements of Part I of Form 10–Q and Form 10–QSB, the information called for may be incorporated by reference to such published document or statement provided copies thereof are included as an exhibit to the registration statement or to Part I of the Form 10–Q and Form 10–QSB report.

(20) *Other Documents or Statements to Security Holders.* If the registrant makes available to its stockholders or otherwise publishes, within the period prescribed for filing the report, a document or statement containing information meeting some or all of the requirements of this form the information called for may be incorporated by reference to such published document or statement provided copies thereof are filed as an exhibit to the report on this form.

(21) *Subsidiaries of the Registrant.* (i) List all subsidiaries of the registrant, the state or other jurisdiction of incorporation or organization of each, and the names under which such subsidiaries do business. This list may be incorporated by reference from a document which includes a complete and accurate list.

(ii) The names of particular subsidiaries may be omitted if the unnamed subsidiaries, considered in the aggregate as a single subsidiary, would not constitute a significant subsidiary as of the end of the year covered by this report. (See the definition of "significant subsidiary" in Rule 1–02(w) of Regulation S–X.) The names of consolidated wholly-owned multiple subsidiaries carrying on the same line of business, such as chain stores or small loan companies, may be omitted, provided the name of the immediate parent, the line of business, the number of omitted subsidiaries operating in the United States and the number operating in foreign countries are given. This instruction shall not apply, however, to banks, insurance companies, savings and loan associations or to any subsidiary subject to regulation by another Federal agency.

(22) *Published Report Regarding Matters Submitted to Vote of Security Holders.* Published reports containing all of the information called for by Item 4 of Part II of Form 10–Q and Form 10–QSB or Item 4 of Part I of Form 10–K and Form 10–KSB which is referred to therein in lieu of providing disclosure in Form 10–Q and Form 10–QSB or 10–K, which are required to be filed as exhibits by Rule 12b–23(a)(3) under the Exchange Act.

(23) *Consents of Experts and Counsel.* (i) *Securities Act Filings.* All written consents required to be filed shall be dated and manually signed. Where the consent of an expert or counsel is contained in his report or opinion or elsewhere in the registration statement or document filed therewith, a reference shall be made in the index to the report, the part of the registration statement or document or opinion, containing the consent.

(ii) *Exchange Act Reports.* Where the filing of a written consent is required with respect to material incorporated by reference in a previously filed registration statement under the Securities Act, such consent may be filed as exhibit to the material incorporated by reference. Such consents shall be dated and manually signed.

(24) *Power of Attorney.* If any name is signed to the registration statement or report pursuant to a power of attorney, manually signed copies of such power of attorney shall be filed. Where the power of attorney is contained elsewhere in the registration statement or documents filed therewith a reference shall be made in the index to the part of the registration statement or document containing such power of attorney. In addition, if the name of any officer signing on behalf of the registrant is signed pursuant to a power of attorney, certified copies of a resolution of the registrant's board of directors authorizing such signature shall also be filed. A power of attorney that is filed with the Commission shall relate to a specific filing or an amendment thereto, provided, however, that a power of attorney relating to a registration statement under the Securities Act or an amendment thereto also may relate to any registration statement for the same offering that is to be effective upon filing pursuant to Rule 462(b) under the Securities Act (§ 230.462(b) of this chapter).

(25) *Statement of Eligibility of Trustee.* (i) A statement of eligibility and qualification of each person designated to act as trustee under an indenture to be qualified under the Trust Indenture Act of 1939. Such statement of eligibility shall be bound separately from the other exhibits.

(ii) *Electronic filings.* The requirement to bind separately the statement of eligibility and qualification of each person designated to act as a trustee under the Trust Indenture Act of 1939 from other exhibits shall not apply to statements submitted in electronic format. Rather, such statements must be submitted as exhibits in the same electronic submission as the registration statement to which they relate, or in an amendment thereto, except that electronic filers that rely on Trust Indenture Act Section 305(b)(2) for determining the eligibility of the trustee under indentures for securities to be issued, offered or sold on a delayed basis by or on behalf of the registrant shall file such statements separately in the manner prescribed by § 260.5b–1 through § 260.5b–3 of this chapter and by the EDGAR Filer Manual.

(26) *Invitations for Competitive Bids.* If the registration statement covers securities to be offered at competitive bidding, any form of communication which is an invitation for competitive bid which will be sent or given to any person shall be filed.

(27) through (30) [Reserved].

(31)(i) *Rule 13a–14(a)/15d–14(a) Certifications.* The certifications required by Rule 13a–14(a) (17 CFR 240.13a–14(a)) or Rule 15d–14(a) (17 CFR 240.15d–14(a)) exactly as set forth below:

(ii) *Rule 13a–14(d)/15d–14(d) Certifications.* If an asset-backed issuer (as defined in § 229.1101), the certifications required by Rule 13a–14(d)) exactly as set forth below:

Certifications[1]

I, [identify the certifying individual], certify that:

1. I have reviewed this report on Form 10–K and all reports on Form 10–D required to be filed in respect of the period covered by this report on Form 10–K of [identify the issuing entity] (the "Exchange Act periodic reports");

2. Based on my knowledge, the Exchange Act periodic reports, taking as a whole, do not contain any untrue statement of a material fact or omit to state a material fact necessary to make the statements made, in light of the circumstances under which such statements were made, not misleading with respect to the period covered by this report;

3. Based on my knowledge, all of the distribution, servicing and other information required to be provided under Form 10–D for the period covered by this report is included in the Exchange Act periodic reports;

4. [I am responsible for reviewing the activities performed by the servicer(s) and based on my knowledge and the compliance review(s) conducted in preparing the servicer compliance statement(s) required in this report under Item 1123 of Regulation AB, and except as disclosed in the Exchange Act periodic reports, the servicer(s) [has/have] fulfilled [its/their] obligations under the servicing agreements(s); and]

[Based on my knowledge and the servicer compliance statement(s) required in this report under Item 1123 of Regulation AB, and except as disclosed in the Exchange Act periodic reports, the servicer(s) [has/have] fulfilled [its/their] obligations under the servicing agreements(s); and][2]

5. All of the reports on assessment of compliance with servicing criteria for asset-backed securities and their related attestation reports on assessment of compliance with servicing criteria for asset-backed securities required to be included in this report in accordance with Item 1122 of Regulation AB and Exchange Act Rules 13a–18 and 15d–18 have been included as an exhibit to this report, except as otherwise disclosed in this report. Any material instances of noncompliance described in such report, except as otherwise disclosed in this report. Any material instances of noncompliance described in such reports have been disclosed in this report on Form 10–K.[3]

[In giving the certifications above, I have reasonably relied on information provided to me by the following unaffiliated parties [name of servicer, sub-servicer, co-servicer, depositor or trustee].][4]

1. With respect to asset-backed issuers, the certification must be signed by either: (1) The senior officer in charge of securitization of the depositor if the depositor is signing the report on Form 10–K; or (2) The senior officer in charge of the servicing function of the servicer if the servicer is signing the report on Form 10–K on behalf of the issuing entity. See Rules 13a–14(e) and 15d–14(e) (§§ 240.13a–14(e) and 240.15d–14(e)). If multiple servicers are involved in servicing the pool assets, the senior officer in charge of the servicing function of the master servicer (or entity performing the equivalent function) must sign if a representative of the servicer is to sign the certification. If there is a master servicer and one or more underlying servicers, the references in the certification relate to the master servicer. A natural person must sign the certification in his or her individual capacity, although the title of that person in the organization of which he or she is an officer may be included under the signature.

2. The first version of paragraph 4 is to be used when the servicer is signing the report on behalf of the issuing entity. The second version of paragraph 4 is to be used when the depositor is signing the report.

3. The certification refers to the reports prepared by parties participating in the servicing function that are required to be included as an exhibit to the Form 10–K. See Item 1122 of Regulation AB (§ 229.1122) and Rules 13a–18 and 15d–18 (§§ 240.13a–18 and 240.15d–18 of this chapter). If a report that is otherwise required to be included is not attached, disclosure that the report is not included and an associated explanation must be provided in the Form 10–K report.

4. Because the signer of the certification must rely in certain circumstances on information provided by unaffiliated parties outside of the signer's control, this paragraph must be included if the signer is reasonably relying on

Date:

____

____

[Signature]
[Title]

*Certifications**

I, [identify the certifying individual], certify that:

1. I have reviewed this [specify report] of [identify small business issuer];

2. Based on my knowledge, this report does not contain any untrue statement of a material fact or omit to state a material fact necessary to make the statements made, in light of the circumstances under which such statements were made, not misleading with respect to the period covered by this report;

3. Based on my knowledge, the financial statements, and other financial information included in this report, fairly present in all material respects the financial condition, results of operations and cash flows of the registrant as of, and for, the periods presented in this report;

4. The registrant's other certifying officer(s) and I are responsible for establishing and maintaining disclosure controls and procedures (as defined in Exchange Act Rules 13a–15(e) and 15d–15(e)) and internal control over financial reporting (as defined in Exchange Act Rules 13a–15(f) and 15d–15(f)) for the registrant and have:

(a) Designed such disclosure controls and procedures, or caused such disclosure controls and procedures to be designed under our supervision, to ensure that material information relating to the registrant, including its consolidated subsidiaries, is made known to us by others within those entities, particularly during the period in which this report is being prepared;

(b) Designed such internal control over financial reporting, or caused such internal control over financial reporting to be designed under our supervision, to provide reasonable assurance regarding the reliability of financial reporting and the preparation of financial statements for external purposes in accordance with generally accepted accounting principles;

(c) Evaluated the effectiveness of the registrant's disclosure controls and procedures and presented in this report our conclusions about the effectiveness of the disclosure controls and procedures, as of the end of the period covered by this report based on such evaluation; and

(d) Disclosed in this report any change in the registrant's internal control over financial reporting that occurred during the registrant's most recent fiscal quarter (the registrant's fourth fiscal quarter in the case of an annual report) that has materially affected, or is reasonably likely to materially affect, the registrant's internal control over financial reporting; and

5. The registrant's other certifying officer(s) and I have disclosed, based on our most recent evaluation of internal control over financial reporting, to the registrant's auditors and the audit committee of the registrant's board of directors (or persons performing the equivalent functions):

(a) All significant deficiencies and material weaknesses in the design or operation of internal control over financial reporting which are reasonably likely to adversely affect the registrant's ability to record, process, summarize and report financial information; and

(b) Any fraud, whether or not material, that involves management or other employees who have a significant role in the registrant's internal control over financial reporting.

Date:

____

____

information that unaffiliated trustees, depositors, servicers, sub-servicers or co-servicers have provided.

____

[Signature]

____

[Title]

*Provide a separate certification for each principal executive officer and principal financial officer of the registrant. See Rules 13a–14(a) and 15d–14(a).

(32) *Section 1350 Certifications.*

(i) The certifications required by Rule 13a–14(b) (17 CFR 240.13a–14(b)) or Rule 15d–14(b) (17 CFR 240.15d–14(b)) and Section 1350 of Chapter 63 of Title 18 of the United States Code (18 U.S.C. 1350).

(ii) A certification furnished pursuant to this item will not be deemed "filed" for purposes of Section 18 of the Exchange Act (15 U.S.C. 78r), or otherwise subject to the liability of that section. Such certification will not be deemed to be incorporated by reference into any filing under the Securities Act or the Exchange Act, except to the extent that the registrant specifically incorporates it by reference.

(33) *Report on assessment of compliance with servicing criteria for asset-backed securities.* Each report on assessment of compliance with servicing criteria required by § 229.1122(a).

(34) Attestation report on assessment of compliance with servicing criteria for asset-backed securities. Each attestation report on assessment of compliance with servicing criteria for asset-backed securities required by § 229.1122(b).

(35) Servicer compliance statement. Each servicer compliance statement required by § 229.1123.

(36) to (98) [Reserved]

(99) *Additional Exhibits.* (i) Any additional exhibits which the registrant may wish to file shall be so marked as to indicate clearly the subject matters to which they refer. (ii) Any document (except for an exhibit) or part thereof which is incorporated by reference in the filing and is not otherwise required to be filed by this Item or is not a Commission filed document incorporated by reference in a Securities Act registration statement. (iii) If pursuant to Section 11(a) of the Securities Act (15 U.S.C. 77k(a)) an issuer makes generally available to its security holders an earnings statement covering a period of at least 12 months beginning after the effective date of the registration statement, and if such earnings statement is made available by "other methods" than those specified in paragraphs (a) or (b) of § 230.158 of this chapter, it must be filed as an exhibit to the Form 10–Q or the Form 10–K, as appropriate, covering the period in which the earnings statement was released.

(100) XBRL-Related Documents. An electronic filer that participates in the voluntary XBRL (eXtensible Business Reporting Language) program may submit XBRL-Related Documents (§ 232.11 of this chapter) in electronic format as an exhibit to: the filing to which they relate; an amendment to such filing; or a Form 8–K (§ 249.308 of this chapter) that references such filing, if the Form 8–K is submitted no earlier than date of that filing.

Subpart 700—Miscellaneous

Item 701. Recent Sales of Unregistered Securities; Use of Proceeds from Registered Securities

Furnish the following information as to all securities of the registrant sold by the registrant within the past three years which were not registered under the Securities Act. Include sales of reacquired securities, as well as new issues, securities issued in exchange for property, services, or other securities, and new securities resulting from the modification of outstanding securities.

(a) *Securities Sold.* Give the date of sale and the title and amount of securities sold.

(b) *Underwriters and Other Purchasers.* Give the names of the principal underwriters, if any. As to any such securities not publicly offered, name the persons or identify the class of persons to whom the securities were sold.

(c) *Consideration.* As to securities sold for cash, state the aggregate offering price and the aggregate underwriting discounts or commissions. As to any securities sold otherwise than for cash, state the nature of the transaction and the nature and aggregate amount of consideration received by the registrant.

(d) *Exemption from Registration Claimed.* Indicate the section of the Securities Act or the rule of the Commission under which exemption from registration was claimed and state briefly the facts relied upon to make the exemption available.

(e) *Terms of conversion or exercise.* If the information called for by this paragraph (e) is being presented on Form 8–K, Form 10–QSB, Form 10–Q, Form 10–KSB, Form 10–K or Form 10–D (§ 249.308, 249.308b, 249.308a, 249.310b, 249.310 or 249.312) under the Exchange Act, and where the securities sold by the registrant are convertible or exchangeable into equity securities, or are warrants or options representing equity securities, disclose the terms of conversion or exercise of the securities.

(f) *Use of Proceeds.* As required by § 230.463 of this chapter, following the effective date of the first registration statement filed under the Securities Act by an issuer, the issuer or successor issuer shall report the use of proceeds on its first periodic report filed pursuant to sections 13(a) and 15(d) of the Exchange Act (15 U.S.C. 78m(a) and 78o(d)) after effectiveness of its Securities Act registration statement, and thereafter on each of its subsequent periodic reports filed pursuant to sections 13(a) and 15(d) of the Exchange Act through the later of disclosure of the application of all the offering proceeds or disclosure of the termination of the offering. If a report of the use of proceeds is required with respect to the first effective registration statement of the predecessor issuer, the successor issuer shall provide such a report. The information provided pursuant to paragraphs (f)(2) through (f)(4) of this Item need only be provided with respect to the first periodic report filed pursuant to sections 13(a) and 15(d) of the Exchange Act after effectiveness of the registration statement filed under the Securities Act. Subsequent periodic reports filed pursuant to sections 13(a) and 15(d) of the Exchange Act need only provide the information required in paragraphs (f)(2) through (f)(4) of this Item if any of such required information has changed since the last periodic report filed. In disclosing the use of proceeds in the first periodic report filed pursuant to the Exchange Act, the issuer or successor issuer should include the following information:

(1) The effective date of the Securities Act registration statement for which the use of proceeds information is being disclosed and the Commission file number assigned to the registration statement;

(2) If the offering has commenced, the offering date, and if the offering has not commenced, an explanation why it has not;

(3) If the offering terminated before any securities were sold, an explanation for such termination; and

(4) If the offering did not terminate before any securities were sold, disclose:

(i) Whether the offering has terminated and, if so, whether it terminated before the sale of all securities registered;

(ii) The name(s) of the managing underwriter(s), if any;

(iii) The title of each class of securities registered and, where a class of convertible securities is being registered, the title of any class of securities into which such securities may be converted;

(iv) For each class of securities (other than a class of securities into which a class of convertible securities registered may be converted without additional payment to the issuer) the following information, provided for both the account of the issuer and the account(s) of any selling security holder(s): the amount registered, the aggregate price of the offering amount registered, the amount sold and the aggregate offering price of the amount sold to date;

(v) From the effective date of the Securities Act registration statement to the ending date of the reporting period, the amount of expenses incurred for the issuer's account in connection with the issuance and distribution of the securities registered for underwriting discounts and commissions, finders' fees, expenses paid to or for underwriters, other expenses and total expenses. Indicate if a reasonable estimate for the amount of expenses incurred is provided instead of the actual amount of expense. Indicate whether such payments were:

(A) Direct or indirect payments to directors, officers, general partners of the issuer or their associates; to persons owning ten (10) percent or more of any class of equity securities of the issuer; and to affiliates of the issuer; or

(B) Direct or indirect payments to others;

(vi) The net offering proceeds to the issuer after deducting the total expenses described in paragraph (f)(4)(v) of this Item;

(vii) From the effective date of the Securities Act registration statement to the ending date of the reporting period, the amount of net offering proceeds to the issuer used for construction of plant, building and facilities; purchase and installation of machinery and equipment; purchases of real estate; acquisition of other business(es); repayment of indebtedness; working capital; temporary investments (which should be specified); and any other purposes for which at least five (5) percent of the issuer's total offering proceeds or $100,000 (whichever is less) has been used (which should be specified). Indicate if a reasonable estimate for the amount of net offering proceeds applied is provided instead of the actual amount of net offering proceeds used. Indicate whether such payments were:

(A) Direct or indirect payments to directors, officers, general partners of the issuer or their associates; to persons owning ten (10) percent or more of any class of equity securities of the issuer; and to affiliates of the issuer; or

(B) Direct or indirect payments to others; and

(viii) If the use of proceeds in paragraph (f)(4)(vii) of this Item represents a material change in the use of proceeds described in the prospectus, the issuer should describe briefly the material change.

Instructions. 1. Information required by this Item 701 need not be set forth as to notes, drafts, bills of exchange, or bankers' acceptances which mature not later than one year from the date of issuance.

2. If the sales were made in a series of transactions, the information may be given by such totals and periods as will reasonably convey the information required.

Item 702. Indemnification of Directors and Officers

State the general effect of any statute, charter provisions, by-laws, contract or other arrangements under which any controlling persons, director or officer of the registrant is insured or indemnified in any manner against liability which he may incur in his capacity as such.

Item 703. Purchases of Equity Securities by the Issuer and Affiliated Purchasers

(a) In the following tabular format, provide the information specified in paragraph (b) of this Item with respect to any purchase made by or on behalf of the small business issuer or any "affiliated purchaser," as defined in § 240.10b–18(a)(3) of this chapter, of shares or other units of any class of the issuer's equity securities that is registered by the issuer pursuant to section 12 of the Exchange Act (15 U.S.C. 78*l*).

ISSUER PURCHASES OF EQUITY SECURITIES

Period	(a) Total Number of Shares (or Units) Purchased	(b) Average Price Paid per Share (or Unit)	(c) Total Number of Shares (or Units) Purchased as Part of Publicly Announced Plans or Programs	(d) Maximum Number (or Approximate Dollar Value) of Shares (or Units) that May Yet Be Purchased Under the Plans or Programs
Month #1 (identify beginning and ending dates)				
Month #2 (identify beginning and ending dates)				
Month #3 (identify beginning and ending dates)				
Total				

(b) The table shall include the following information for each class or series of securities for each month included in the period covered by the report:

(1) The total number of shares (or units) purchased (column (a));

Instruction to paragraph (b)(1) of Item 703

Include in this column all issuer repurchases, including those made pursuant to publicly announced plans or programs and those not made pursuant to publicly announced plans or programs. Briefly disclose, by footnote to the table, the number of shares purchased other than through a publicly announced plan or program and the nature of the transaction (e.g., whether the purchases were made in open-market transactions, tender offers, in satisfaction of the company's obligations upon exercise of outstanding put options issued by the company, or other transactions).

(2) The average price paid per share (or unit) (column (b));

(3) The total number of shares (or units) purchased as part of publicly announced repurchase plans or programs (column (c)); and

(4) The maximum number (or approximate dollar value) of shares (or units) that may yet be purchased under the plans or programs (column (d)).

Instructions to paragraphs (b)(3) and (b)(4) of Item 703

1. In the table, disclose this information in the aggregate for all plans or programs publicly announced.

2. By footnote to the table, indicate:

a. The date each plan or program was announced;

b. The dollar amount (or share or unit amount) approved;

c. The expiration date (if any) of each plan or program;

d. Each plan or program that has expired during the period covered by the table; and

e. Each plan or program the issuer has determined to terminate prior to expiration, or under which the issuer does not intend to make further purchases.

Instruction to Item 703

Disclose all purchases covered by this Item, including purchases that do not satisfy the conditions of the safe harbor of § 240.10b–18 of this chapter.

Subpart 800—List of Industry Guides

Item 801. Securities Act Industry Guides

(b) *Guide 2.* Disclosure of oil and gas operations.

(c) *Guide 3.* Statistical disclosure by bank holding companies.

(d) *Guide 4.* Prospectuses relating to interests in oil and gas programs.

(e) *Guide 5.* Preparation of registration statements relating to interests in real estate limited partnerships.

(f) *Guide 6.* Disclosures concerning unpaid claims and claim adjustment expenses of property-casualty insurance underwriters.

(g) *Guide 7.* Description of Property by Issuers Engaged or to be Engaged in Significant Mining Operations.

Item 802. Exchange Act Industry Guides

(b) *Guide 2.* Disclosure of oil and gas operations.

(c) *Guide 3.* Statistical disclosure by bank holding companies.

(d) *Guide 4.* Disclosures concerning unpaid claims and claim adjustment expenses of property-casualty underwriters.

(g) *Guide 7.* Description of Property by Issuers Engaged or to be Engaged in Significant Mining Operations.

Subpart 900—Roll–Up Transactions

Item 901. Definitions

For the purposes of this subpart 900:

(a) *General partner* means the person or persons responsible under state law for managing or directing the management of the business and affairs of a partnership that is the subject of a roll-up transaction including, but not limited to, the general partner(s), board of directors, board of trustees, or other person(s) having a fiduciary duty to such partnership.

(b)(1) *Partnership* means any:

(i) Finite-life limited partnership; or

(ii) Other finite-life entity.

(2)(i) Except as provided in paragraph (b)(2)(ii) of this Item 901, a limited partnership or other entity is "finite-life" if:

(A) It operates as a conduit vehicle for investors to participate in the ownership of assets for a limited period of time; and

(B) It has a policy or purpose distributing to investors proceeds from the sale, financing or refinancing of assets or cash from operations, rather than reinvesting such proceeds or cash in the business (whether for the term of the entity or after an initial period of time following commencement of operations).

(ii) A real estate investment trust as defined in I.R.C. section 856 is not *finite-life* solely because of the distribution to investors of net income as provided by the I.R.C. if its policies or purposes do not include the distribution to investors of proceeds from the sale, financing or refinancing of assets, rather than the reinvestment of such proceeds in the business.

(3) *Partnership* does not include any entity registered under the Investment Company Act of 1940 or any Business Development Company as defined in section 2(a)(48) of that Act.

(c)(1) Except as provided in paragraph (c)(2) or (c)(3) of this Item, (§ 229.901(c)(2) or (c)(3)) *roll-up transaction* means a transaction involving the combination or reorganization of one or more partnerships, directly or indirectly, in which some or all of the investors in any of such partnerships will receive new securities, or securities in another entity.

(2) Notwithstanding paragraph (c)(1) of this Item, (§ 229.901(c)(1)) *roll-up transaction* shall not include:

(i) A transaction wherein the interests of all of the investors in each of the partnerships are repurchased, recalled, or exchanged in accordance with the terms of the preexisting partnership agreement for securities in an operating company specifically identified at the time of the formation of the original partnership;

(ii) A transaction in which the securities to be issued or exchanged are not required to be and are not registered under the Securities Act of 1933 (15 U.S.C. 77a *et seq.*);

(iii) A transaction that involves only issuers that are not required to register or report under Section 12 of the Securities Exchange Act of 1934 (15 U.S.C. 78*l*), both before and after the transaction;

(iv) A transaction that involves the combination or reorganization of one or more partnerships in which a non-affiliated party succeeds to the interests of a general partner or sponsor, if:

(A) Such action is approved by not less than 66⅔% of the outstanding units of each of the participating partnerships; and

(B) As a result of the transaction, the existing general partners will receive only compensation to which they are entitled as expressly provided for in the preexisting partnership agreements;

(v) A transaction in which the securities offered to investors are securities of another entity that are reported under a transaction reporting plan declared effective before December 17, 1993 by the Commission under Section 11A of the Securities Exchange Act of 1934 (15 U.S.C. 78k–1), if:

(A) Such other entity was formed, and such class of securities was reported and regularly traded, not less than 12 months before the date on which soliciting material is mailed to investors; and

(B) The securities of that entity issued to investors in the transaction do not exceed 20% of the total outstanding securities of the entity, exclusive of any securities of such class held by or for the account of the entity or a subsidiary of the entity; and

(C) For purposes of paragraph (c)(2)(v) of this Item (§ 229.901(c)(2)(v)), *regularly traded* security means any security with a minimum closing price of $2.00 or more for a majority of the business days during the preceding three-month period and a six-month minimum average daily trading volume of 1,000 shares;

(vi) A transaction in which all of the investors' partnership securities are reported under a transaction reporting plan declared effective before December 17, 1993 by the Commission under Section 11A of the Securities Exchange Act of

1934 (15 U.S.C. 78k–1) and such investors receive new securities or securities in another entity that are reported under a transaction reporting plan declared effective before December 17, 1993 by the Commission under Section 11A of the Securities Exchange Act of 1934 (15 U.S.C. 78k–1), except that, for purposes of this paragraph, securities that are reported under a transaction reporting plan declared effective before December 17, 1993 by the Commission under Section 11A of the Securities Exchange Act of 1934 shall not include securities listed on the American Stock Exchange's Emerging Company Marketplace;

(vii) A transaction in which the investors in any of the partnerships involved in the transaction are not subject to a significant adverse change with respect to voting rights, the terms of existence of the entity, management compensation or investment objectives; or

(viii) A transaction in which all investors are provided an option to receive or retain a security under substantially the same terms and conditions as the original issue.

(3) The Commission, upon written request or upon its own motion, may exempt by rule or order any security or class of securities, any transaction or class of transactions, or any person or class of persons, in whole or in part, conditionally or unconditionally, from the definition of roll-up transaction or the requirements imposed on roll-up transactions by Items 902–915 of Regulation S–K (§§ 229.902–229.915), if it finds such action to be consistent with the public interest and the protection of investors.

(d) *Sponsor* means the person proposing the roll-up transaction.

(e) *Successor* means the surviving entity after completion of the roll-up transaction or the entity whose securities are being offered or sold to, or acquired by, limited partners of the partnerships or the limited partnerships to be combined or reorganized.

Instruction to Item 901. If a transaction is a roll-up transaction as defined in Item 901(c) of this subpart, the requirements of this subpart apply to each entity proposed to be included in the roll-up transaction, whether or not the entity is a "partnership" as defined in Item 901(b) of this subpart.

Item 902. Individual Partnership Supplements

(a) If two or more entities are proposed to be included in the roll-up transaction, provide the information specified in this Item 902 in a separate supplement to the disclosure document for each entity.

(b) The separate supplement required by paragraph (a) of this Item 902 shall be filed as part of the registration statement, shall be delivered with the prospectus to investors in the partnership covered thereby, and shall include:

(1) A statement in the forepart of the supplement to the effect that:

(i) Supplements have been prepared for each partnership;

(ii) The effects of the roll-up transaction may be different for investors in the various partnerships; and

(iii) Upon receipt of a written request by an investor or his representative who has been so designated in writing, a copy of any supplement will be transmitted promptly, without charge, by the general partner or sponsor.

This statement must include the name and address of the person to whom investors should make their request.

(2) A brief description of each material risk and effect of the roll-up transaction, including, but not limited to, federal income tax consequences, for investors in the partnership, with appropriate cross references to the discussions of the risks, effects and tax consequences of the roll-up transaction re-

quired in the principal disclosure document pursuant to Items 904 and 915 of this subpart. Such discussion shall address the effect of the roll-up transaction on the partnership's financial condition and results of operations.

(3) A statement concerning whether the general partner reasonably believes that the roll-up transaction is fair or unfair to investors in the partnership, together with a brief discussion of the bases for such belief, with appropriate cross references to the discussion of the fairness of the roll-up transaction required in the principal disclosure document pursuant to Item 910 of this subpart. If there are material differences between the fairness analysis for the partnership and for the other partnerships, such differences shall be described briefly in the supplement.

(4) A brief, narrative description of the method of calculating the value of the partnership and allocating interests in the successor to the partnership, and a table showing such calculation and allocation. Such table shall include the following information (or other information of a comparable character necessary to a thorough understanding of the calculation and allocation):

(i) The appraised value of each separately appraised significant asset (as defined in Item 911(c)(5) of this subpart) held by the partnership, or, if appraisals have not been obtained for each significant asset, the value assigned for purposes of the valuation of the partnership to each significant asset for which an appraisal has not been obtained;

(ii) The dollar amount of any mortgages or other similar liabilities to which each of such assets is subject;

(iii) Cash and cash equivalent assets held by the partnership;

(iv) Other assets held by the partnership;

(v) Other liabilities of the partnership;

(vi) The value assigned to the partnership;

(vii) The value assigned to the partnership per interest held by investors in the partnership (on an equivalent interest basis, such as per $1,000 original investment);

(viii) The aggregate number of interests in the successor to be allocated to the partnership and the percentage of the total interests of the successor;

(ix) The number of interests in the successor to be allocated to investors in the partnership for each interest held by such investors (on an equivalent interest basis, such as per $1,000 original investment); and

(x) The value assigned to the general partner's interest in the partnership, and the number of interests in the successor or other consideration to be allocated in the roll-up transaction to the general partner for such general partnership interest or otherwise as compensation or reimbursement for claims against or interests in the partnership, such as foregone fees, unearned fees and for fees to be earned on the sale or refinancing of an asset.

(5) The amounts of compensation paid, and cash distributions made, to the general partner and its affiliates by the partnership for the last three fiscal years and the most recently completed interim period and the amounts that would have been paid if the compensation and distributions structure to be in effect after the roll-up transaction had been in effect during such period. If any proposed change(s) in the business or operations of the successor after the roll-up transaction would change materially the compensation and distributions that would have been paid by the successor (e.g., if properties will be sold or purchased after the roll-up transaction and no properties were sold or purchased during the period covered by the table), describe such changes and the effects

thereof on the compensation and distributions to be paid by the successor.

(6) Cash distributions made to investors during each of the last five fiscal years and most recently completed interim period, identifying any such distributions which represent a return of capital.

(7) An appropriate cross reference to selected financial information concerning the partnership and the pro forma financial statements included in the principal disclosure document in response to Item 914(b)(2) of this subpart.

Item 903. Summary

(a) Provide in the forepart of the disclosure document a clear, concise and comprehensible summary of the roll-up transaction.

(b) The summary required by paragraph (a) of this Item 903 shall include a summary description of each of the following items, as well as any other material terms or consequences of the roll-up transaction necessary to an understanding of such transaction:

(1) Each material risk and effect on investors, including, but not limited to:

(i) Changes in the business plan, voting rights, cash distribution policies, form of ownership interest or management compensation;

(ii) The general partner's conflicts of interest in connection with the roll-up transaction and in connection with the successor's future operations; and

(iii) The likelihood that securities received by investors in the roll-up transaction will trade at prices substantially below the value assigned to such securities in the roll-up transaction and/or the value of the successor's assets;

(2) The material terms of the roll-up transaction, including the valuation method used to allocate securities in the successor to investors in the partnerships;

(3) Whether the general partner reasonably believes that the roll-up transaction is fair or unfair to investors in each partnership, including a brief discussion of the bases for such belief;

(4) Any opinion from an outside party concerning the fairness of the roll-up transaction, including whether the opinion addresses the fairness of all possible combinations of partnerships or portions of partnerships, and contacts with any outside party concerning fairness opinions, valuations or reports in connection with the roll-up transaction required to be disclosed pursuant to Item 911(a)(5) of this subpart;

(5) The background of and reasons for the roll-up transaction, as well as alternatives to the roll-up transaction described in response to Item 908(b) of this subpart;

(6) Rights of investors to exercise dissenters' or appraisal rights or similar rights and to obtain a list of investors in the partnership in which the investor holds an interest; and

(7) If any affiliates of the general partner or the sponsor may participate in the business of the successor or receive compensation from the successor, an organizational chart showing the relationships between the general partner, the sponsor and their affiliates.

Instruction to Item 903. The description of the material risks and effects of the roll-up transaction required by paragraph (b)(1) of this Item 903 must be presented prominently in the forepart of the summary.

Item 904. Risk Factors and Other Considerations

(a) Immediately following the summary required by Item 903 of this subpart, describe in reasonable detail each material risk and effect of the roll-up transaction on investors in each partnership, including, but not limited to:

(1) The potential risks, adverse effects and benefits of the roll-up transaction for

investors and for the general partner, including those which result from each matter described in response to Item 905 of this subpart, with appropriate cross references to the comparative information required by Item 905;

(2) The material risks arising from an investment in the successor; and

(3) The likelihood that securities of the successor received by investors in the roll-up transaction will trade in the securities markets at a price substantially below the value assigned to such securities in the roll-up transaction and/or the value of the assets of the successor, and the effects on investors of such a trading market discount.

(b) Quantify each risk or effect to the extent practicable.

(c) State whether any of such risks or effects may be different for investors in any partnership and, if so, identify such partnership(s) and describe such difference(s).

Instruction to Item 904. The requirement to quantify the effects of the roll-up transaction shall include, but not be limited to:

(i) If cost savings resulting from combined administration of the partnerships is identified as a potential benefit of the roll-up transaction, the amount of cost savings and a comparison of such amount to the costs of the roll-up transaction; and

(ii) If there may be a material conflict of interest of the sponsor or general partner arising from its receipt of payments or other consideration as a result of the roll-up transaction, the amount of such payments and other consideration to be obtained in the roll-up transaction and a comparison of such amounts to the amounts to which the sponsor or general partner would be entitled without the roll-up transaction.

Item 905. Comparative Information

(a)(1) Describe the voting and other rights of investors in the successor under the successor's governing instruments and under applicable law. Compare such rights to the voting and other rights of investors in each partnership subject to the transaction under the partnerships' governing instruments and under applicable law. Describe the effects of the change(s) in such rights.

(2) Describe the duties owed by the general partner of the successor to investors in the successor under the successor's governing instruments and under applicable law. Compare such duties to the duties owed by the general partner of each partnership to investors in the partnership under the partnership's governing instruments and under applicable law. Describe the effects of the change(s) in such duties.

(b)(1) Describe each item of compensation (including reimbursement of expenses) payable by the successor after the roll-up transaction to the general partner and its affiliates or to any affiliate of the successor. Compare such compensation to the compensation currently payable to the general partner and its affiliates by each partnership. Describe the effects of the change(s) in compensation arrangements.

(2) Describe each instance in which cash or other distributions may be made by the successor to the general partner and its affiliates or to any affiliate of the successor. Compare such distributions to the distributions currently paid or payable to the general partner and its affiliates by each partnership. Describe the effects of the change(s) in distribution arrangements. If distributions similar to those currently paid or payable by any partnership to the general partner or its affiliates will not be made by the successor, state whether or not other compensation arrangements with the successor described in response to paragraph (b)(1) of this Item 905 (e.g., incentive fees payable upon sale of a property) will, in effect, replace such distributions.

(3) Provide a table demonstrating the changes in such compensation and distributions setting forth among other things:

(i) The actual amounts of compensation and distributions, separately identified, paid by the partnerships on a combined basis to the general partner and its affiliates for the partnerships' last three fiscal years and most recently ended interim periods; and

(ii) The amounts of compensation and distributions that would have been paid if the compensation and distributions structure to be in effect after the roll-up transaction had been in effect during such period.

(4) If any proposed change(s) in the business or operations of the successor after the roll-up transaction would change materially the compensation and distributions that would have been paid by the successor from that shown in the table provided in response to paragraph (b)(3)(ii) of this Item 905 (e.g., if properties will be sold or purchased after the roll-up transaction and no properties were sold or purchased during the period covered by the table), describe such changes and the effects thereof on the compensation and distributions to be paid by the successor.

(5) Describe the material conflicts that may arise between the interests of the sponsor or general partner and the interests of investors in the successor as a result of the compensation and distribution arrangements described in response to paragraphs (b)(1) and (2) of this Item 905 and describe any steps that will be taken to resolve any such conflicts.

(c) Describe any provisions in the governing instruments of the successor and any policies of the general partner of the successor relating to distributions to investors of cash from operations, proceeds from the sale, financing or refinancing of assets, and any other distributions. Compare such provisions and policies to those of each of the partnerships. Describe the effects of any change(s) in such provisions or policies.

(d)(1) Describe each material investment policy of the successor, including, without limitation, policies with respect to borrowings by the successor. Compare such investment policies to the investment policies of each of the partnerships. Describe the effects of any change(s) in such policies.

(2) Describe any plans of the general partner, sponsor or of any person who will be an affiliate of the successor with respect to:

(i) A sale of any material assets of the partnerships;

(ii) A purchase of any material assets; and

(iii) Borrowings.

(3)(i) State whether or not specific assets have been identified for sale, financing, refinancing or purchase following the roll-up transaction.

(ii) If specific assets have been so identified, describe the assets and the proposed transaction.

(e) Describe any other similar terms or policies of the successor that are material to an investment in the successor. Compare any such terms or policies to those of each of the partnerships. Describe the effects of any change(s) in any such terms or policies.

Instructions to Item 905. (1) The information provided in response to this Item 905 should be illustrated in tables or other readily understandable formats, which should be included together with the disclosures required by this Item.

(2) The information required by this Item 905 shall be set forth in appropriate separate sections of the principal disclosure document.

Item 906. Allocation of Roll–Up Consideration

(a) Describe in reasonable detail the method used to allocate interests in the successor to investors in the partnerships and the reasons why such method was used.

(b) Provide a table showing the calculation of the valuation of each partnership and the allocation of interests in the successor to investors. Such table shall include for each partnership the following information (or other information of a comparable character necessary to an understanding of the calculation and allocation):

(1) The value assigned to each significant category of assets of the partnership and the total value assigned to the partnership;

(2) The total value assigned to all partnerships;

(3) The aggregate amount of interests in the successor to be allocated to each partnership and the percentage of the total amount of all such interests represented thereby; and

(4) The amount of interests of the successor to be issued to investors per interest held in each partnership (on an equivalent interest basis, such as per $1,000 invested).

(c) If interests in the successor will be allocated to the general partner in exchange for its general partner interest or otherwise or if the general partner will receive other consideration in connection with the roll-up transaction:

(1) Describe in reasonable detail the method used to allocate interests in the successor to the general partner or to determine the amount of consideration payable to the general partner and the reasons such method(s) was used; and

(2) Identify the consideration paid by the general partner for interests in the partnerships that will be exchanged in the roll-up transaction.

Item 907. Background of the Roll–Up Transaction

(a)(1) Furnish a summary of the background of the transaction. Such summary shall include, but not be limited to, a description of any contacts, negotiations or transactions concerning any of the following matters:

(i) A merger, consolidation, or combination of any of the partnerships;

(ii) An acquisition of any of the partnerships or a material amount of any of their assets;

(iii) A tender offer for or other acquisition of securities of any class issued by any of the partnerships; or

(iv) A change in control of any of the partnerships.

(2) The summary required by paragraph (a)(1) of this Item shall:

(i) Cover the period beginning with each partnership's second full fiscal year preceding the date of the filing of the roll-up transaction;

(ii) Include contacts, negotiations or transactions between the general partner or its affiliates and any person who would have a direct interest in the matters listed in paragraph (a)(1)(i)–(iv) of this Item; and

(iii) Identify the person who initiated such contacts, negotiations or transactions.

(b) Briefly describe the background of each partnership, including, but not limited to:

(1) The amount of capital raised from investors, the extent to which net proceeds from the original offering of interests have been invested, the extent to which funds have been invested as planned and the amount not yet invested; and

(2) The partnership's investment objectives and the extent to which the partnership has achieved its investment objectives.

(c) Discuss whether the general partner (including any affiliated person materially dependent on the general partner's compensation arrangement with the partnership) or any partnership has experienced since the commencement of the most recently completed fiscal year or is likely to experience any material adverse financial developments. If so, describe such developments and the effect of the transaction on such matters.

Item 908. Reasons for and Alternatives to the Roll–Up Transaction

(a) Describe the reason(s) for the roll-up transaction.

(b)(1) If the general partner or sponsor considered alternatives to the roll-up transaction being proposed, describe such alternative(s) and state the reason(s) for their rejection.

(2) Whether or not described in response to paragraph (b)(1) of this Item 908, describe in reasonable detail the potential alternative of continuation of the partnerships in accordance with their existing business plans, including the effects of such continuation and the material risks and benefits that likely would arise in connection therewith, and, if applicable, the general partner's reasons for not considering such alternative.

(3) Whether or not described in response to paragraph (b)(1) of this Item 908, describe in reasonable detail the potential alternative of liquidation of the partnerships, the procedures required to accomplish liquidation, the effects of liquidation, the material risks and benefits that likely would arise in connection with liquidation, and, if applicable, the general partner's reasons for not considering such alternative.

(c) State the reasons for the structure of the roll-up transaction and for undertaking such transaction at this time.

(d) State whether the general partner initiated the roll-up transaction and, if not, whether the general partner participated in the structuring of the transaction.

(e) State whether the general partner recommends the roll-up transaction and briefly describe the reasons for such recommendation.

Item 909. Conflicts of Interest

(a) Briefly describe the general partner's fiduciary duties to each partnership subject to the roll-up transaction and each actual or potential material conflict of interest between the general partner and the investors relating to the roll-up transaction.

(b)(1) State whether or not the general partner has retained an unaffiliated representative to act on behalf of investors for purposes of negotiating the terms of the roll-up transaction. If no such representative has been retained, describe the reasons therefor and the risks arising from the absence of separate representation.

(2) If an unaffiliated representative has been retained to represent investors:

(i) Identify such unaffiliated representative;

(ii) Briefly describe the representative's qualifications, including a brief description of any other transaction similar to the roll-up transaction in which the representative has served in a similar capacity within the past five years;

(iii) Describe the method of selection of such representative, including a statement as to whether or not any investors were consulted in the selection of the representative and, if so, the names of such investors;

(iv) Describe the scope and terms of the engagement of the representative, including, but not limited to, what party will be responsible for paying the representative's fees and whether such fees are contingent upon the outcome of the roll-up transaction;

(v) Describe any material relationship between the representative or its affiliates and:

(A) The general partner, sponsor, any affiliate of the general partner or sponsor; or

(B) Any other person having a material interest in the roll-up transaction,

which existed during the past two years or is mutually understood to be contemplated and any compensation received or to be received as a result of such relationship;

(vi) Describe in reasonable detail the actions taken by the representative on behalf of investors; and

(vii) Describe the fiduciary duties or other legal obligations of the representative to investors in each of the partnerships.

Item 910. Fairness of the Transaction

(a) State whether the general partner reasonably believes that the roll-up transaction is fair or unfair to investors and the reasons for such belief. Such discussion must address the fairness of the roll-up transaction to investors in each of the partnerships and as a whole. If the roll-up transaction may be completed with a combination of partnerships consisting of less than all partnerships, or with portions of partnerships, the belief stated must address each possible combination.

(b) Discuss in reasonable detail the material factors upon which the belief stated in paragraph (a) of this Item 910 is based and, to the extent practicable, the weight assigned to each such factor. Such discussion should include an analysis of the extent, if any, to which such belief is based on the factors set forth in Instructions (2) and (3) to this Item 910, paragraph (b)(1) of Item 909 of this subpart and Item 911 of this subpart. This discussion also must:

(1) Compare the value of the consideration to be received in the roll-up transaction to the value of the consideration that would be received pursuant to each of the alternatives discussed in response to Item 908(b) of this subpart; and

(2) Describe any material differences among the partnerships (e.g., different types of assets or different investment objectives) relating to the fairness of the transaction.

(c) If any offer of the type described in Instruction (2)(viii) to this Item 910 has been received, describe such offer and state the reason(s) for its rejection.

(d) Describe any factors known to the general partner that may affect materially the value of the consideration to be received by investors in the roll-up transaction, the values assigned to the partnerships for purposes of the comparisons to alternatives required by paragraph (b) of this Item 910 and the fairness of the transaction to investors.

(e) State whether the general partner's statements in response to paragraphs (a) and (b) of this Item 910 are based, in whole or in part, on any report, opinion or appraisal described in response to Item 911 of this subpart. If so, describe any material uncertainties known to the general partner that relate to the conclusions in any such report, opinion or appraisal including, but not limited to, developments or trends that have affected or are reasonably likely to affect materially such conclusions.

Instructions to Item 910. (1) A statement that the general partner has no reasonable belief as to the fairness of the roll-up transaction to investors will not be considered sufficient disclosure in response to paragraph (a) of this Item 910(a).

(2) The factors which are important in determining the fairness of a roll-up transaction to investors and the weight, if any, which should be given to them in a particular context will vary. Normally such factors will include, among others, those referred to in paragraph (b)(1) of Item 909 and whether the consideration offered to investors constitutes fair value in relation to:

(i) Current market prices, if any;

(ii) Historic market prices, if any;

(iii) Net book value;

(iv) Going concern value;

(v) Liquidation value;

(vi) Purchases of limited partnership interests by the general partner or sponsor or their affiliates since the commencement of the partnership's second full fiscal year preceding the date of filing of the disclosure document for the roll-up transaction;

(vii) Any report, opinion, or appraisal described in Item 911 of this subpart; and

(viii) Offers of which the general partner or sponsor is aware made during the preceding eighteen months for a merger, consolidation, or combination of any of the partnerships; an acquisition of any of the partnerships or a material amount of their assets; a tender offer for or other acquisition of securities of any class issued by any of the partnerships; or a change in control of any of the partnerships.

(3) The discussion concerning fairness should specifically address material terms of the transaction including whether the consideration offered to investors constitutes fair value in relation to:

(i) The form and amount of consideration to be received by investors and the sponsor in the roll-up transaction;

(ii) The methods used to determine such consideration; and

(iii) The compensation to be paid to the sponsor in the future.

(4) Conclusory statements, such as "The roll-up transaction is fair to investors in relation to net book value, going concern value, liquidation value and future prospects of the partnership," will not be considered sufficient disclosure in response to paragraph (b) of this Item 910.

(5) Consideration should be given to presenting the comparative numerical data as to the value of the consideration being received by investors, liquidation value and other values in a tabular format. Financial and other information concerning the partnerships should be prepared based upon the most recent available information, such as, in the case of financial information, the periods covered by interim selected financial information included in the prospectus in accordance with Item 914 of this subpart.

Item 911. Reports, Opinions and Appraisals

(a)(1) *All material reports, opinions or appraisals.* State whether or not the general partner or sponsor has received any report, opinion (other than an opinion of counsel) or appraisal from an outside party which is materially related to the roll-up transaction including, but not limited to, any such report, opinion or appraisal relating to the consideration or the fairness of the consideration to be offered to investors in connection with the roll-up transaction or the fairness of such transaction to the general partner or investors.

(2) With respect to any report, opinion or appraisal described in paragraph (a)(1) of this Item 911;

(i) Identify such outside party;

(ii) Briefly describe the qualifications of such outside party;

(iii) Describe the method of selection of such outside party;

(iv) Describe any material relationship between:

(A) The outside party or its affiliates; and

(B) The general partner, sponsor, the successor or any of their affiliates, which existed during the past two years or is mutually understood to be contemplated and any compensation received or to be received as a result of such relationship;

(v) If such report, opinion or appraisal relates to the fairness of the consideration, state whether the general partner, sponsor or affiliate determined the amount of consideration to be paid or whether the outside party recommended the amount of consideration to be paid.

(vi) Furnish a summary concerning such report, opinion or appraisal which shall include, but not be limited to, the procedures followed; the findings and recommendations; the bases for and methods of arriving at such findings and recommendations; instructions received from the general partner, sponsor or its affiliates; and any limitation imposed by the general partner, sponsor or affiliate on the scope of the investigation. If any limitation was imposed by the general partner, sponsor or affiliate on the scope of the investigation, including, but not limited to, access to its personnel, premises, and relevant books and records, state the reasons therefor.

(vii) State whether any compensation paid to such outside party is contingent on the approval or completion of the roll-up transaction and, if so, the reasons for compensating such parties on a contingent basis.

(3) Furnish a statement to the effect that upon written request by an investor or his representative who has been so designated in writing, a copy of any such report, opinion or appraisal shall be transmitted promptly, without charge, by the general partner or sponsor. The statement also must include the name and address of the person to whom investors or their representatives should make their request.

(4) All reports, opinions or appraisals referred to in paragraph (a)(1) of this Item 911 shall be filed as exhibits to the registration statement.

(5)(i) Describe any contacts in connection with the roll-up transaction between the sponsor or the general partner and any outside party with respect to the preparation by such party of an opinion concerning the fairness of the roll-up transaction, a valuation of a partnership or its assets, or any other report with respect to the roll-up transaction. No description is required, however, of contacts with respect to reports, opinions or appraisals filed as exhibits pursuant to paragraph (a)(4) of this Item 911.

(ii) The description of contacts with any outside party required by paragraph (a)(5)(i) of this Item 911 shall include the following:

(A) The identity of each such party;

(B) The nature of the contact;

(C) The actions taken by such party;

(D) Any views, preliminary or final, expressed on the proposed subject matter of the report, opinion or appraisal; and

(E) Any reasons such party did not provide a report, opinion or appraisal.

(b) *Fairness opinions:* (1) If any report, opinion or appraisal relates to the fairness of the roll-up transaction to investors in the partnerships, state whether or not the report, opinion or appraisal addresses the fairness of:

(i) The roll-up transaction as a whole and to investors in each partnership; and

(ii) All possible combinations of partnerships in the roll-up transaction (including portions of partnerships if the transaction is structured to permit portions of partnerships to participate). If all possible combinations are not addressed:

(A) Identify the combinations that are addressed;

(B) Identify the person(s) that determined which combinations would be addressed and state the reasons for the selection of the combinations; and

(C) State that if the roll-up transaction is completed with a combination of partnerships not addressed, no report, opinion or appraisal concerning the fairness of the roll-up transaction will have been obtained.

(2) If the sponsor or the general partner has not obtained any opinion on the fairness of the proposed roll-up transaction to investors in each of the affected partnerships, state the sponsor's or general partner's reasons for concluding that such an opinion is not necessary in order to permit the limited partners or shareholders to make an informed decision on the proposed transaction.

(c) *Appraisals.* If the report, opinion or appraisal consists of an appraisal of the assets of the partnerships:

(1) Describe the purpose(s) for which the appraisals were obtained and their use in connection with the roll-up transaction;

(2) Describe which assets are covered by the appraisals and state the aggregate appraised value of the assets covered by the appraisals (including such value net of associated indebtedness). Provide a description of, and valuation of, any assets subject to any material qualifications by the appraiser and a summary of such qualifications;

(3) Identify the date as of which the appraisals were prepared. State whether and in what circumstances the appraisals will be updated. State whether any events have occurred or conditions have changed since the date of the appraisals that may have caused a material change in the value of the assets;

(4) Include as an appendix to the prospectus one or more tables setting forth the following information:

(i) The appraised value of any separately appraised asset that is significant to the partnership holding such asset;

(ii) If the appraiser considered different valuation approaches in preparing the appraisals of the assets identified in response to paragraph (c)(4)(i) of this Item 911, the value of each such asset under each valuation approach considered by the appraiser, identifying the valuation approach used by the appraiser in determining the appraised value and the reason such approach was chosen; and

(iii) All material assumptions used by the appraiser in appraising the assets identified in response to paragraph (c)(4)(i) of this Item 911, and, if the appraiser used different assumptions for any of such assets, the reasons the different assumptions were chosen.

(5) For purposes of this Item and Item 902 of this subpart, an asset is "significant" to a partnership if it represents more than 10% of the value of the partnership's assets as of the end of the most recently-completed fiscal year or recently-completed interim period or if 10% or more of the partnership's cash flow or net income for the most recently-completed fiscal year or most recently-completed subsequent interim period was derived from such asset.

Instructions to Item 911. (1) The reports, opinions and appraisals required to be identified in response to paragraph (a) of this Item 911 include any reports, opinions and appraisals which materially relate to the roll-up transaction whether or not relied upon, such as reports or opinions regarding alternatives to the roll-up transaction whether or not the alternatives were rejected.

(2) The information called for by paragraph (a)(2) of this Item 911 should be given with respect to the firm which provides the report, opinion or appraisal rather than the employees of such firm who prepared it.

(3) With respect to appraisals, a summary prepared by the appraisers should not be included in lieu of the description of the appraisals required by paragraph (c) of this Item 911. A clear and concise summary description of the appraisals is required.

Item 912. Source and Amount of Funds and Transactional Expenses

(a) State the source and total amount of funds or other consideration to be used in the roll-up transaction.

(b)(1) Furnish a reasonably itemized statement of all expenses incurred or estimated to be incurred in connection with the roll-up transaction including, but not limited to, filing fees, legal, financial advisory, accounting and appraisal fees, solicitation expenses and printing costs. Identify the persons responsible for paying any or all of such expenses.

(2) State whether or not any partnership subject to the roll-up transaction will be, directly or indirectly, responsible for any or all of the expenses of the transaction. If any partnership will be so responsible, state the amount to be provided by each partnership and the sources of capital to finance such amount.

(c) If all or any part of the consideration to be used by the sponsor or successor in the roll-up transaction is expected to be, directly or indirectly, provided by any partnership, state the amount to be provided by each partnership and the sources of capital to finance such amount.

(d) If all or any part of the funds or other consideration is, or is expected to be, directly or indirectly borrowed by the sponsor or successor for the purpose of the roll-up transaction:

(1) Provide a summary of each such loan agreement containing the identity of the parties, the term, the collateral, the stated and effective interest rates, and other material terms or conditions; and

(2) Briefly describe any plans or arrangements to finance or repay such borrowing, or, if no plans or arrangements have been made, make a statement to that effect.

(e) If the source of all or any part of the funds to be used in the roll-up transaction is a loan made in the ordinary course of business by a bank as defined by section 3(a)(6) of the Exchange Act and section 13(d) or 14(d) is applicable to such transaction, the name of such bank shall not be made available to the public if the person filing the statement so requests in writing and files such request, naming such bank, with the Secretary of the Commission.

Item 913. Other Provisions of the Transaction

(a) State whether or not appraisal rights are provided under applicable state law, under the partnership's governing instruments or will be voluntarily accorded by the successor, the general partner or the sponsor (or any of their affiliates) in connection with the roll-up transaction. If so, summarize such appraisal rights. If appraisal rights will not be available to investors who object to the transaction, briefly outline the rights which may be available to such investors under such law.

(b) If any provision has been made to allow investors to obtain access to the books and records of the partnership or to obtain counsel or appraisal services at the expense of the successor, the general partner, the partnership, the sponsor (or any of their affiliates), describe such provision.

(c) Discuss the investors' rights under federal and state law to obtain a partnership's list of investors.

Item 914. Pro Forma Financial Statements: Selected Financial Data

(a) In addition to the information required by Item 301 of Regulation S–K, Selected Financial Data, and Item 302 of Regulation S–K, Supplementary Financial Information, for each partnership proposed to be included in a roll-up transaction provide: Ratio of earnings to fixed charges, cash and cash equivalents, total assets at book value, total assets at the value assigned for purposes of the roll-up transaction (if applicable), total liabilities, general and limited partners' equity, net increase (decrease) in cash and cash equivalents, net cash provided by operating activities, distributions; and per unit data for net income (loss), book value, value assigned for purposes of the roll-up transaction (if applicable), and distributions (separately identifying distributions that represent a return of capital). This information should be provided for the same period(s) for which Selected Financial Data and Supplementary Financial Information are required to be provided. Additional or other information should be provided if material to an understanding of each partnership proposed to be included in a roll-up transaction.

(b) Provide pro forma financial information (including oil and gas reserves and cash flow disclosure, if appropriate), assuming:

(1) All partnerships participate in the roll-up transaction; and

(2) Participation in a roll-up transaction of those partnerships that on a combined basis have the lowest combined net cash provided by operating activities for the last fiscal year of such partnerships, *provided* participation by such partnerships satisfies all conditions to consummation of the roll-up transaction. If the combination of all partnerships proposed to be included in a roll-up transaction results in such lowest combined net cash provided by operating activities, this shall be noted and no separate pro forma financial statements are required.

(c) The pro forma financial statements required by paragraph (b) of this Item 914 shall disclose the effect of the roll-up transaction on the successor's:

(1) Balance sheet as of the later of the end of the most recent fiscal year or the latest interim period;

(2) Statement of income (with separate line items to reflect income (loss) excluding and including the roll-up expenses and payments), earnings per share amounts, and ratio of earnings to fixed charges for the most recent fiscal year and the latest interim period;

(3) Statement of cash flows for the most recent fiscal year and the latest interim period; and

(4) Book value per share as of the later of the end of the most recent fiscal year or the latest interim period.

Instructions to Item 914. (1) Notwithstanding the provisions of this Item 914, any or all of the information required by paragraphs (b) and (c) of this Item 914 that is not material for the exercise of prudent judgment in regard to the matter to be acted upon, may be omitted.

(2) If the roll-up transaction is structured to permit participation by portions of partnerships, consideration should be given to the effect of such participation in preparing the pro forma financial statements reflecting a partial roll-up.

Item 915. Federal Income Tax Consequences

(a) Provide a brief, clear and understandable summary of the material Federal income tax consequences of the roll-up transaction and an investment in the successor. Where a tax opinion has been provided, briefly summarize the substance of such opinion, including identification of the material consequences upon which counsel has not been asked, or is unable, to opine. If any of the material Federal income tax consequences are not expected to be the same for investors in all partnerships, the differences shall be described.

(b) State whether or not the opinion of counsel is included as an appendix to the prospectus. If filed as an exhibit to the registration statement and not included as an appendix to the prospectus, include a statement to the effect that, upon receipt of a written request by an investor or his representative who has been so designated in writing, a copy of the opinion of counsel will be transmitted promptly, without charge, by the general partner or sponsor. The statement should include the name and address of the person to whom investors should make their request.

REGULATION M–A—MERGERS AND ACQUISITIONS

Item 1000. Definitions

The following definitions apply to the terms used in Regulation M–A (§§ 229.1000 through 229.1016), unless specified otherwise:

(a) *Associate* has the same meaning as in § 240.12b–2 of this chapter;

(b) *Instruction C* means General Instruction C to Schedule 13E–3 (§ 240.13e–100 of this chapter) and General Instruction C to Schedule TO (§ 240.14d–100 of this chapter);

(c) *Issuer tender offer* has the same meaning as in § 240.13e–4(a)(2) of this chapter;

(d) *Offeror* means any person who makes a tender offer or on whose behalf a tender offer is made;

(e) *Rule 13e–3* transaction has the same meaning as in § 240.13e–3(a)(3) of this chapter;

(f) *Subject company* means the company or entity whose securities are sought to be acquired in the transaction (e.g., the target), or that is otherwise the subject of the transaction;

(g) *Subject securities* means the securities or class of securities that are sought to be acquired in the transaction or that are otherwise the subject of the transaction; and

(h) *Third-party tender offer* means a tender offer that is not an issuer tender offer.

Item 1001. Summary Term Sheet

Summary term sheet. Provide security holders with a summary term sheet that is written in plain English. The summary term sheet must briefly describe in bullet point format the most material terms of the proposed transaction. The summary term sheet must provide security holders with sufficient information to understand the essential features and significance of the proposed transaction. The bullet points must cross-reference a more detailed discussion contained in the disclosure document that is disseminated to security holders.

Instructions to Item 1001:

1. The summary term sheet must not recite all information contained in the disclosure document that will be provided to security holders. The summary term sheet is intended to serve as an overview of all material matters that are presented in the accompanying documents provided to security holders.

2. The summary term sheet must begin on the first or second page of the disclosure document provided to security holders.

3. Refer to Rule 421(b) and (d) of Regulation C of the Securities Act (§ 230.421 of this chapter) for a description of plain English disclosure.

Item 1002. Subject Company Information

(a) *Name and address*. State the name of the subject company (or the issuer in the case of an issuer tender offer), and the address and telephone number of its principal executive offices.

(b) *Securities*. State the exact title and number of shares outstanding of the subject class of equity securities as of the most recent practicable date. This may be based upon information in the most recently available filing with the Commission by the subject company unless the filing person has more current information.

(c) *Trading market and price*. Identify the principal market in which the subject securities are traded and state the high and low sales prices for the subject securities in the principal market (or, if there is no principal market, the range of high and low bid quotations and the source of the quotations) for each quarter during the past two years. If there is no established trading market for the securities (except for limited or sporadic quotations), so state.

(d) *Dividends*. State the frequency and amount of any dividends paid during the past two years with respect to the subject securities. Briefly describe any restriction on the subject company's current or future ability to pay dividends. If the filing person is not the subject company, furnish this information to the extent known after making reasonable inquiry.

(e) *Prior public offerings*. If the filing person has made an underwritten public offering of the subject securities for cash during the past three years that was registered under the Securities Act of 1933 or exempt from registration under Regulation A (§ 230.251 through § 230.263 of this chapter), state the date of the offering, the amount of securities offered, the offering price per share (adjusted for stock splits, stock dividends, etc. as appropriate) and the aggregate proceeds received by the filing person.

(f) *Prior stock purchases*. If the filing person purchased any subject securities during the past two years, state the amount of the securities purchased, the range of prices paid and the average purchase price for each quarter during that period. Affiliates need not give information for purchases made before becoming an affiliate.

Item 1003. Identity and Background of Filing Person

(a) *Name and address*. State the name, business address and business telephone number of each filing person. Also state the name and address of each person specified in Instruction C to the schedule (except for Schedule 14D–9 (§ 240.14d–101 of this chapter)). If the filing person is an affiliate of the subject company, state the nature of the affiliation. If the filing person is the subject company, so state.

(b) *Business and background of entities*. If any filing person (other than the subject company) or any person specified in Instruction C to the schedule is not a natural person, state the person's principal business, state or other place of organization, and the information required by paragraphs (c)(3) and (c)(4) of this section for each person.

(c) *Business and background of natural persons*. If any filing person or any person specified in Instruction C to the schedule is a natural person, provide the following information for each person:

(1) Current principal occupation or employment and the name, principal business and address of any corporation or other or-

ganization in which the employment or occupation is conducted;

(2) Material occupations, positions, offices or employment during the past five years, giving the starting and ending dates of each and the name, principal business and address of any corporation or other organization in which the occupation, position, office or employment was carried on;

(3) A statement whether or not the person was convicted in a criminal proceeding during the past five years (excluding traffic violations or similar misdemeanors). If the person was convicted, describe the criminal proceeding, including the dates, nature of conviction, name and location of court, and penalty imposed or other disposition of the case;

(4) A statement whether or not the person was a party to any judicial or administrative proceeding during the past five years (except for matters that were dismissed without sanction or settlement) that resulted in a judgment, decree or final order enjoining the person from future violations of, or prohibiting activities subject to, federal or state securities laws, or a finding of any violation of federal or state securities laws. Describe the proceeding, including a summary of the terms of the judgment, decree or final order; and

(5) Country of citizenship.

(d) *Tender offer*. Identify the tender offer and the class of securities to which the offer relates, the name of the offeror and its address (which may be based on the offeror's Schedule TO (§ 240.14d–100 of this chapter) filed with the Commission).

Instruction to Item 1003:

If the filing person is making information relating to the transaction available on the Internet, state the address where the information can be found.

Item 1004. Terms of the Transaction

(a) *Material terms*. State the material terms of the transaction.

(1) *Tender offers*. In the case of a tender offer, the information must include:

(i) The total number and class of securities sought in the offer;

(ii) The type and amount of consideration offered to security holders;

(iii) The scheduled expiration date;

(iv) Whether a subsequent offering period will be available, if the transaction is a third-party tender offer;

(v) Whether the offer may be extended, and if so, how it could be extended;

(vi) The dates before and after which security holders may withdraw securities tendered in the offer;

(vii) The procedures for tendering and withdrawing securities;

(viii) The manner in which securities will be accepted for payment;

(ix) If the offer is for less than all securities of a class, the periods for accepting securities on a pro rata basis and the offeror's present intentions in the event that the offer is oversubscribed;

(x) An explanation of any material differences in the rights of security holders as a result of the transaction, if material;

(xi) A brief statement as to the accounting treatment of the transaction, if material; and

(xii) The federal income tax consequences of the transaction, if material.

(2) *Mergers or similar transactions*. In the case of a merger or similar transaction, the information must include:

(i) A brief description of the transaction;

(ii) The consideration offered to security holders;

(iii) The reasons for engaging in the transaction;

(iv) The vote required for approval of the transaction;

(v) An explanation of any material differences in the rights of security holders as a result of the transaction, if material;

(vi) A brief statement as to the accounting treatment of the transaction, if material; and

(vii) The federal income tax consequences of the transaction, if material.

Instruction to Item 1004(a):

If the consideration offered includes securities exempt from registration under the Securities Act of 1933, provide a description of the securities that complies with Item 202 of Regulation S–K (§ 229.202). This description is not required if the issuer of the securities meets the requirements of General Instructions I.A, I.B.1 or I.B.2, as applicable, or I.C. of Form S–3 (§ 239.13 of this chapter) and elects to furnish information by incorporation by reference; only capital stock is to be issued; and securities of the same class are registered under section 12 of the Exchange Act and either are listed for trading or admitted to unlisted trading privileges on a national securities exchange; or are securities for which bid and offer quotations are reported in an automated quotations system operated by a national securities association.

(b) *Purchases*. State whether any securities are to be purchased from any officer, director or affiliate of the subject company and provide the details of each transaction.

(c) *Different terms*. Describe any term or arrangement in the Rule 13e–3 transaction that treats any subject security holders differently from other subject security holders.

(d) *Appraisal rights*. State whether or not dissenting security holders are entitled to any appraisal rights. If so, summarize the appraisal rights. If there are no appraisal rights available under state law for security holders who object to the transaction, briefly outline any other rights that may be available to security holders under the law.

(e) *Provisions for unaffiliated security holders*. Describe any provision made by the filing person in connection with the transaction to grant unaffiliated security holders access to the corporate files of the filing person or to obtain counsel or appraisal services at the expense of the filing person. If none, so state.

(f) *Eligibility for listing or trading*. If the transaction involves the offer of securities of the filing person in exchange for equity securities held by unaffiliated security holders of the subject company, describe whether or not the filing person will take steps to assure that the securities offered are or will be eligible for trading on an automated quotations system operated by a national securities association.

Item 1005. Past Contacts, Transactions, Negotiations and Agreements

(a) *Transactions*. Briefly state the nature and approximate dollar amount of any transaction, other than those described in paragraphs (b) or (c) of this section, that occurred during the past two years, between the filing person (including any person specified in Instruction C of the schedule) and;

(1) The subject company or any of its affiliates that are not natural persons if the aggregate value of the transactions is more than one percent of the subject company's consolidated revenues for:

(i) The fiscal year when the transaction occurred; or

(ii) The past portion of the current fiscal year, if the transaction occurred in the current year; and

Instruction to Item 1005(a)(1):

The information required by this Item may be based on information in the subject company's most recent filing with the Commission, unless the filing person has reason to believe the information is not accurate.

(2) Any executive officer, director or affiliate of the subject company that is a natural person if the aggregate value of the transaction or series of similar transactions with that person exceeds $60,000.

(b) *Significant corporate events.* Describe any negotiations, transactions or material contacts during the past two years between the filing person (including subsidiaries of the filing person and any person specified in Instruction C of the schedule) and the subject company or its affiliates concerning any:

(1) Merger;

(2) Consolidation;

(3) Acquisition;

(4) Tender offer for or other acquisition of any class of the subject company's securities;

(5) Election of the subject company's directors; or

(6) Sale or other transfer of a material amount of assets of the subject company.

(c) *Negotiations or contacts.* Describe any negotiations or material contacts concerning the matters referred to in paragraph (b) of this section during the past two years between:

(1) Any affiliates of the subject company; or

(2) The subject company or any of its affiliates and any person not affiliated with the subject company who would have a direct interest in such matters.

Instruction to paragraphs (b) and (c) of Item 1005:

Identify the person who initiated the contacts or negotiations.

(d) *Conflicts of interest.* If material, describe any agreement, arrangement or understanding and any actual or potential conflict of interest between the filing person or its affiliates and:

(1) The subject company, its executive officers, directors or affiliates; or

(2) The offeror, its executive officers, directors or affiliates.

Instruction to Item 1005(d):

If the filing person is the subject company, no disclosure called for by this paragraph is required in the document disseminated to security holders, so long as substantially the same information was filed with the Commission previously and disclosed in a proxy statement, report or other communication sent to security holders by the subject company in the past year. The document disseminated to security holders, however, must refer specifically to the discussion in the proxy statement, report or other communication that was sent to security holders previously. The information also must be filed as an exhibit to the schedule.

(e) *Agreements involving the subject company's securities.* Describe any agreement, arrangement, or understanding, whether or not legally enforceable, between the filing person (including any person specified in Instruction C of the schedule) and any other person with respect to any securities of the subject company. Name all persons that are a party to the agreements, arrangements, or understandings and describe all material provisions.

Instructions to Item 1005(e):

1. The information required by this Item includes: the transfer or voting of securities, joint ventures, loan or option arrangements, puts or calls, guarantees of loans, guarantees against loss, or the giving or withholding of proxies, consents or authorizations.

2. Include information for any securities that are pledged or otherwise subject to a contingency, the occurrence of which would give another person the power to direct the voting or disposition of the subject securities. No disclosure, however, is required about standard default and similar provisions contained in loan agreements.

Item 1006. Purposes of the Transaction and Plans or Proposals

(a) *Purposes.* State the purposes of the transaction.

(b) *Use of securities acquired.* Indicate whether the securities acquired in the transaction will be retained, retired, held in treasury, or otherwise disposed of.

(c) *Plans.* Describe any plans, proposals or negotiations that relate to or would result in:

(1) Any extraordinary transaction, such as a merger, reorganization or liquidation, involving the subject company or any of its subsidiaries;

(2) Any purchase, sale or transfer of a material amount of assets of the subject company or any of its subsidiaries;

(3) Any material change in the present dividend rate or policy, or indebtedness or capitalization of the subject company;

(4) Any change in the present board of directors or management of the subject company, including, but not limited to, any plans or proposals to change the number or the term of directors or to fill any existing vacancies on the board or to change any material term of the employment contract of any executive officer;

(5) Any other material change in the subject company's corporate structure or business, including, if the subject company is a registered closed-end investment company, any plans or proposals to make any changes in its investment policy for which a vote would be required by Section 13 of the Investment Company Act of 1940 (15 U.S.C. 80a–13);

(6) Any class of equity securities of the subject company to be delisted from a national securities exchange or cease to be authorized to be quoted in an automated quotations system operated by a national securities association;

(7) Any class of equity securities of the subject company becoming eligible for termination of registration under section 12(g)(4) of the Act (15 U.S.C. 78l);

(8) The suspension of the subject company's obligation to file reports under Section 15(d) of the Act (15 U.S.C. 78o);

(9) The acquisition by any person of additional securities of the subject company, or the disposition of securities of the subject company; or

(10) Any changes in the subject company's charter, bylaws or other governing instruments or other actions that could impede the acquisition of control of the subject company.

(d) *Subject company negotiations.* If the filing person is the subject company:

(1) State whether or not that person is undertaking or engaged in any negotiations in response to the tender offer that relate to:

(i) A tender offer or other acquisition of the subject company's securities by the filing person, any of its subsidiaries, or any other person; or

(ii) Any of the matters referred to in paragraphs (c)(1) through (c)(3) of this section; and

(2) Describe any transaction, board resolution, agreement in principle, or signed contract that is entered into in response to the tender offer that relates to one or more of the matters referred to in paragraph (d)(1) of this section.

Instruction to Item 1006(d)(1):

If an agreement in principle has not been reached at the time of filing, no disclosure under paragraph (d)(1) of this section is required of the possible terms of or the parties to the transaction if in the opinion of the board of directors of the subject company disclosure would jeopardize continuation of the negotiations. In that case, disclosure indicating that negotiations are being undertaken or are underway and are in the preliminary stages is sufficient.

Item 1007. Source and Amount of Funds or Other Consideration

(a) *Source of funds.* State the specific sources and total amount of funds or other consideration to be used in the transaction. If the transaction involves a tender offer, disclose the amount of funds or other consideration required to purchase the maximum amount of securities sought in the offer.

(b) *Conditions*. State any material conditions to the financing discussed in response to paragraph (a) of this section. Disclose any alternative financing arrangements or alternative financing plans in the event the primary financing plans fall through. If none, so state.

(c) *Expenses*. Furnish a reasonably itemized statement of all expenses incurred or estimated to be incurred in connection with the transaction including, but not limited to, filing, legal, accounting and appraisal fees, solicitation expenses and printing costs and state whether or not the subject company has paid or will be responsible for paying any or all expenses.

(d) *Borrowed funds*. If all or any part of the funds or other consideration required is, or is expected, to be borrowed, directly or indirectly, for the purpose of the transaction:

(1) Provide a summary of each loan agreement or arrangement containing the identity of the parties, the term, the collateral, the stated and effective interest rates, and any other material terms or conditions of the loan; and

(2) Briefly describe any plans or arrangements to finance or repay the loan, or, if no plans or arrangements have been made, so state.

Instruction to Item 1007(d):

If the transaction is a third-party tender offer and the source of all or any part of the funds used in the transaction is to come from a loan made in the ordinary course of business by a bank as defined by section 3(a)(6) of the Act (15 U.S.C. 78c), the name of the bank will not be made available to the public if the filing person so requests in writing and files the request, naming the bank, with the Secretary of the Commission.

Item 1008. Interest in Securities of the Subject Company

(a) *Securities ownership*. State the aggregate number and percentage of subject securities that are beneficially owned by each person named in response to Item 1003 of Regulation M–A (§ 229.1003) and by each associate and majority-owned subsidiary of those persons. Give the name and address of any associate or subsidiary.

Instructions to Item 1008(a):

1. For purposes of this section, beneficial ownership is determined in accordance with Rule 13d–3 (§ 240.13d–3 of this chapter) under the Exchange Act. Identify the shares that the person has a right to acquire.

2. The information required by this section may be based on the number of outstanding securities disclosed in the subject company's most recently available filing with the Commission, unless the filing person has more current information.

3. The information required by this section with respect to officers, directors and associates of the subject company must be given to the extent known after making reasonable inquiry.

(b) *Securities transactions*. Describe any transaction in the subject securities during the past 60 days. The description of transactions required must include, but not necessarily be limited to:

(1) The identity of the persons specified in the Instruction to this section who effected the transaction;

(2) The date of the transaction;

(3) The amount of securities involved;

(4) The price per share; and

(5) Where and how the transaction was effected.

Instructions to Item 1008(b):

1. Provide the required transaction information for the following persons:

(a) The filing person (for all schedules);

(b) Any person named in Instruction C of the schedule and any associate or majority-owned subsidiary of the issuer or filing person (for all schedules except Schedule 14D–9 (§ 240.14d–101 of this chapter));

(c) Any executive officer, director, affiliate or subsidiary of the filing person (for Schedule 14D–9 (§ 240.14d–101 of this chapter));

(d) The issuer and any executive officer or director of any subsidiary of the issuer or filing person (for an issuer tender offer on Schedule TO (§ 240.14d–100 of this chapter)); and

(e) The issuer and any pension, profit-sharing or similar plan of the issuer or affiliate filing the schedule (for a going-private transaction on Schedule 13E–3 (§ 240.13e–100 of this chapter)).

2. Provide the information required by this Item if it is available to the filing person at the time the statement is initially filed with the Commission. If the information is not initially available, it must be obtained and filed with the Commission promptly, but in no event later than three business days after the date of the initial filing, and if material, disclosed in a manner reasonably designed to inform security holders. The procedure specified by this instruction is provided to maintain the confidentiality of information in order to avoid possible misuse of inside information.

Item 1009. Persons/Assets, Retained, Employed, Compensated or Used

(a) *Solicitations or recommendations.* Identify all persons and classes of persons that are directly or indirectly employed, retained, or to be compensated to make solicitations or recommendations in connection with the transaction. Provide a summary of all material terms of employment, retainer or other arrangement for compensation.

(b) *Employees and corporate assets.* Identify any officer, class of employees or corporate assets of the subject company that has been or will be employed or used by the filing person in connection with the transaction. Describe the purpose for their employment or use.

Instruction to Item 1009(b):

Provide all information required by this Item except for the information required by paragraph (a) of this section and Item 1007 of Regulation M–A (§ 229.1007).

Item 1010. Financial Statements

(a) *Financial information.* Furnish the following financial information:

(1) Audited financial statements for the two fiscal years required to be filed with the company's most recent annual report under sections 13 and 15(d) of the Exchange Act (15 U.S.C. 78m; 15 U.S.C. 78o);

(2) Unaudited balance sheets, comparative year-to-date income statements and related earnings per share data, statements of cash flows, and comprehensive income required to be included in the company's most recent quarterly report filed under the Exchange Act;

(3) Ratio of earnings to fixed charges, computed in a manner consistent with Item 503(d) of Regulation S–K (§ 229.503(d)), for the two most recent fiscal years and the interim periods provided under paragraph (a)(2) of this section; and

(4) Book value per share as of the date of the most recent balance sheet presented.

(b) *Pro forma information.* If material, furnish pro forma information disclosing the effect of the transaction on:

(1) The company's balance sheet as of the date of the most recent balance sheet presented under paragraph (a) of this section;

(2) The company's statement of income, earnings per share, and ratio of earnings to fixed charges for the most recent fiscal year and the latest interim period provided under paragraph (a)(2) of this section; and

(3) The company's book value per share as of the date of the most recent balance

sheet presented under paragraph (a) of this section.

(c) *Summary information*. Furnish a fair and adequate summary of the information specified in paragraphs (a) and (b) of this section for the same periods specified. A fair and adequate summary includes:

(1) The summarized financial information specified in § 210.1–02(bb)(1) of this chapter;

(2) Income per common share from continuing operations (basic and diluted, if applicable);

(3) Net income per common share (basic and diluted, if applicable);

(4) Ratio of earnings to fixed charges, computed in a manner consistent with Item 503(d) of Regulation S–K (§ 229.503(d));

(5) Book value per share as of the date of the most recent balance sheet; and

(6) If material, pro forma data for the summarized financial information specified in paragraphs (c)(1) through (c)(5) of this section disclosing the effect of the transaction.

Item 1011. Additional Information

(a) *Agreements, regulatory requirements and legal proceedings*. If material to a security holder's decision whether to sell, tender or hold the securities sought in the tender offer, furnish the following information:

(1) Any present or proposed material agreement, arrangement, understanding or relationship between the offeror or any of its executive officers, directors, controlling persons or subsidiaries and the subject company or any of its executive officers, directors, controlling persons or subsidiaries (other than any agreement, arrangement or understanding disclosed under any other sections of Regulation M–A (§§ 229.1000 through 229.1016));

Instruction to paragraph (a)(1):

In an issuer tender offer disclose any material agreement, arrangement, understanding or relationship between the offeror and any of its executive officers, directors, controlling persons or subsidiaries.

(2) To the extent known by the offeror after reasonable investigation, the applicable regulatory requirements which must be complied with or approvals which must be obtained in connection with the tender offer;

(3) The applicability of any anti-trust laws;

(4) The applicability of margin requirements under section 7 of the Act (15 U.S.C. 78g) and the applicable regulations; and

(5) Any material pending legal proceedings relating to the tender offer, including the name and location of the court or agency in which the proceedings are pending, the date instituted, the principal parties, and a brief summary of the proceedings and the relief sought.

Instruction to Item 1011(a)(5):

A copy of any document relating to a major development (such as pleadings, an answer, complaint, temporary restraining order, injunction, opinion, judgment or order) in a material pending legal proceeding must be furnished promptly to the Commission staff on a supplemental basis.

(b) *Other material information*. Furnish such additional material information, if any, as may be necessary to make the required statements, in light of the circumstances under which they are made, not materially misleading.

Item 1012. The Solicitation or Recommendation

(a) *Solicitation or recommendation*. State the nature of the solicitation or the recommendation. If this statement relates to a recommendation, state whether the filing person is advising holders of the subject securities to accept or reject the tender offer or to take other action with respect to the tender offer and, if so, describe the other action recommended. If the filing person is the subject company and is not making a recommendation, state whether the subject company is expressing no opinion and is remaining neutral toward the tender offer or is unable to take a position with respect to the tender offer.

(b) *Reasons*. State the reasons for the position (including the inability to take a position) stated in paragraph (a) of this section. Conclusory statements such as "The tender offer is in the best interests of shareholders" are not considered sufficient disclosure.

(c) *Intent to tender*. To the extent known by the filing person after making reasonable inquiry, state whether the filing person or any executive officer, director, affiliate or subsidiary of the filing person currently intends to tender, sell or hold the subject securities that are held of record or beneficially owned by that person.

(d) *Intent to tender or vote in a going-private transaction*. To the extent known by the filing person after making reasonable inquiry, state whether or not any executive officer, director or affiliate of the issuer (or any person specified in Instruction C to the schedule) currently intends to tender or sell subject securities owned or held by that person and/or how each person currently intends to vote subject securities, including any securities the person has proxy authority for. State the reasons for the intended action.

Instruction to Item 1012(d):

Provide the information required by this section if it is available to the filing person at the time the statement is initially filed with the Commission. If the information is not available, it must be filed with the Commission promptly, but in no event later than three business days after the date of the initial filing, and if material, disclosed in a manner reasonably designed to inform security holders.

(e) *Recommendations of others*. To the extent known by the filing person after making reasonable inquiry, state whether or not any person specified in paragraph (d) of this section has made a recommendation either in support of or opposed to the transaction and the reasons for the recommendation.

Item 1013. Purposes, Alternatives, Reasons and Effects in a Going-Private Transaction

(a) *Purposes*. State the purposes for the Rule 13e–3 transaction.

(b) *Alternatives*. If the subject company or affiliate considered alternative means to accomplish the stated purposes, briefly describe the alternatives and state the reasons for their rejection.

(c) *Reasons*. State the reasons for the structure of the Rule 13e–3 transaction and for undertaking the transaction at this time.

(d) *Effects*. Describe the effects of the Rule 13e–3 transaction on the subject company, its affiliates and unaffiliated security holders, including the federal tax consequences of the transaction.

Instructions to Item 1013:

1. Conclusory statements will not be considered sufficient disclosure in response to this section.

2. The description required by paragraph (d) of this section must include a reasonably detailed discussion of both the benefits and detriments of the Rule 13e–3 transaction to the subject company, its affiliates and unaffiliated security holders. The benefits and detriments of the Rule 13e–3 transaction must be quantified to the extent practicable.

3. If this statement is filed by an affiliate of the subject company, the description required by paragraph (d) of this section must include, but not be limited to, the effect of the Rule 13e–3 transaction on the affiliate's interest in the net book value and net earnings of the subject company in terms of both dollar amounts and percentages.

Item 1014. Fairness of the Going-Private Transaction

(a) *Fairness*. State whether the subject company or affiliate filing the statement reasonably believes that the Rule 13e–3 transaction is fair or unfair to unaffiliated security holders. If any director dissented to or abstained from voting on the Rule 13e–3 transaction, identify the director, and indicate, if known, after making reasonable inquiry, the reasons for the dissent or abstention.

(b) *Factors considered in determining fairness*. Discuss in reasonable detail the material factors upon which the belief stated in paragraph (a) of this section is based and, to the extent practicable, the weight assigned to each factor. The discussion must include an analysis of the extent, if any, to which the filing person's beliefs are based on the factors described in Instruction 2 of this section, paragraphs (c), (d) and (e) of this section and Item 1015 of Regulation M–A (§ 229.1015).

(c) *Approval of security holders*. State whether or not the transaction is structured so that approval of at least a majority of unaffiliated security holders is required.

(d) *Unaffiliated representative*. State whether or not a majority of directors who are not employees of the subject company has retained an unaffiliated representative to act solely on behalf of unaffiliated security holders for purposes of negotiating the terms of the Rule 13e–3 transaction and/or preparing a report concerning the fairness of the transaction.

(e) *Approval of directors*. State whether or not the Rule 13e–3 transaction was approved by a majority of the directors of the subject company who are not employees of the subject company.

(f) *Other offers*. If any offer of the type described in paragraph (viii) of Instruction 2 to this section has been received, describe the offer and state the reasons for its rejection.

Instructions to Item 1014:

1. A statement that the issuer or affiliate has no reasonable belief as to the fairness of the Rule 13e–3 transaction to unaffiliated security holders will not be considered sufficient disclosure in response to paragraph (a) of this section.

2. The factors that are important in determining the fairness of a transaction to unaffiliated security holders and the weight, if any, that should be given to them in a particular context will vary. Normally such factors will include, among others, those referred to in paragraphs (c), (d) and (e) of this section and whether the consideration offered to unaffiliated security holders constitutes fair value in relation to:

(i) Current market prices;

(ii) Historical market prices;

(iii) Net book value;

(iv) Going concern value;

(v) Liquidation value;

(vi) Purchase prices paid in previous purchases disclosed in response to Item 1002(f) of Regulation M–A (§ 229.1002(f));

(vii) Any report, opinion, or appraisal described in Item 1015 of Regulation M–A (§ 229.1015); and

(viii) Firm offers of which the subject company or affiliate is aware made by any unaffiliated person, other than the filing persons, during the past two years for:

(A) The merger or consolidation of the subject company with or into another company, or vice versa;

(B) The sale or other transfer of all or any substantial part of the assets of the subject company; or

(C) A purchase of the subject company's securities that would enable the holder to exercise control of the subject company.

3. Conclusory statements, such as "The Rule 13e–3 transaction is fair to unaffiliated security holders in relation to net book value, going concern value and future prospects of the issuer" will not be considered sufficient

disclosure in response to paragraph (b) of this section.

Item 1015. Reports, Opinions, Appraisals and Negotiations

(a) *Report, opinion or appraisal.* State whether or not the subject company or affiliate has received any report, opinion (other than an opinion of counsel) or appraisal from an outside party that is materially related to the Rule 13e–3 transaction, including, but not limited to: Any report, opinion or appraisal relating to the consideration or the fairness of the consideration to be offered to security holders or the fairness of the transaction to the issuer or affiliate or to security holders who are not affiliates.

(b) *Preparer and summary of the report, opinion or appraisal.* For each report, opinion or appraisal described in response to paragraph (a) of this section or any negotiation or report described in response to Item 1014(d) of Regulation M–A (§ 229.1014) or Item 14(b)(6) of Schedule 14A (§ 240.14a–101 of this chapter) concerning the terms of the transaction:

(1) Identify the outside party and/or unaffiliated representative;

(2) Briefly describe the qualifications of the outside party and/or unaffiliated representative;

(3) Describe the method of selection of the outside party and/or unaffiliated representative;

(4) Describe any material relationship that existed during the past two years or is mutually understood to be contemplated and any compensation received or to be received as a result of the relationship between:

(i) The outside party, its affiliates, and/or unaffiliated representative; and

(ii) The subject company or its affiliates;

(5) If the report, opinion or appraisal relates to the fairness of the consideration, state whether the subject company or affiliate determined the amount of consideration to be paid or whether the outside party recommended the amount of consideration to be paid; and

(6) Furnish a summary concerning the negotiation, report, opinion or appraisal. The summary must include, but need not be limited to, the procedures followed; the findings and recommendations; the bases for and methods of arriving at such findings and recommendations; instructions received from the subject company or affiliate; and any limitation imposed by the subject company or affiliate on the scope of the investigation.

Instruction to Item 1015(b):

The information called for by paragraphs (b)(1), (2) and (3) of this section must be given with respect to the firm that provides the report, opinion or appraisal rather than the employees of the firm that prepared the report.

(c) *Availability of documents.* Furnish a statement to the effect that the report, opinion or appraisal will be made available for inspection and copying at the principal executive offices of the subject company or affiliate during its regular business hours by any interested equity security holder of the subject company or representative who has been so designated in writing. This statement also may provide that a copy of the report, opinion or appraisal will be transmitted by the subject company or affiliate to any interested equity security holder of the subject company or representative who has been so designated in writing upon written request and at the expense of the requesting security holder.

Item 1016. Exhibits

File as an exhibit to the schedule:

(a) Any disclosure materials furnished to security holders by or on behalf of the filing person, including:

(1) Tender offer materials (including transmittal letter);

(2) Solicitation or recommendation (including those referred to in Item 1012 of Regulation M–A (§ 229.1012));

(3) Going-private disclosure document;

(4) Prospectus used in connection with an exchange offer where securities are registered under the Securities Act of 1933; and

(5) Any other disclosure materials;

(b) Any loan agreement referred to in response to Item 1007(d) of Regulation M–A (§ 229.1007(d));

Instruction to Item 1016(b):

If the filing relates to a third-party tender offer and a request is made under Item 1007(d) of Regulation M–A (§ 229.1007(d)), the identity of the bank providing financing may be omitted from the loan agreement filed as an exhibit.

(c) Any report, opinion or appraisal referred to in response to Item 1014(d) or Item 1015 of Regulation M–A (§ 229.1014(d) or § 229.1015);

(d) Any document setting forth the terms of any agreement, arrangement, understanding or relationship referred to in response to Item 1005(e) or Item 1011(a)(1) of Regulation M–A (§ 229.1005(e) or § 229.1011(a)(1));

(e) Any agreement, arrangement or understanding referred to in response to § 229.1005(d), or the pertinent portions of any proxy statement, report or other communication containing the disclosure required by Item 1005(d) of Regulation M–A (§ 229.1005(d));

(f) A detailed statement describing security holders' appraisal rights and the procedures for exercising those appraisal rights referred to in response to Item 1004(d) of Regulation M–A (§ 229.1004(d));

(g) Any written instruction, form or other material that is furnished to persons making an oral solicitation or recommendation by or on behalf of the filing person for their use directly or indirectly in connection with the transaction; and

(h) Any written opinion prepared by legal counsel at the filing person's request and communicated to the filing person pertaining to the tax consequences of the transaction.

Subpart 229.1100—Asset-Backed Securities (Regulation AB)

Subpart 229.1100—Asset-Backed Securities (Regulation AB)

§ 229.1100 (Item 1100) General.

(a) *Application of Regulation AB*. Regulation AB (§§ 229.1100 through 229.1123) is the source of various disclosure items and requirements for "asset-backed securities" filings under the Securities Act of 1933 (15 U.S.C. 77a et seq.) (the "Securities Act") and the Securities Exchange Act of 1934 (the "Exchange Act") (15 U.S.C. 78a et seq.). Unless otherwise specified, definitions to be used in this Regulation AB, including the definition of "asset-backed security," are set forth in Item 1101.

(b) *Presentation of historical delinquency and loss information*. Several Items in Regulation AB call for the presentation of historical information and data on delinquencies and loss information. In providing such information:

(1) Present delinquency experience in 30 or 31 day increments, as applicable, beginning at least with assets that are 30 or 31 days delinquent, as applicable, through the point that assets are written off or charged off as uncollectable. At a minimum, present such information by number of accounts and dollar amount. Present statistical information in a tabular or graphical format, if such presentation will aid understanding.

(2) Disclose the total amount of delinquent assets as a percentage of the aggregate asset pool.

(3) Present loss and cumulative loss information, as applicable, regarding charge-offs, charge-off rate, gross losses, recoveries and net losses (with a description of how these terms are defined), the number and amount of assets experiencing a loss and the number and amount of assets with a recovery, the ratio of aggregate net losses to average portfolio balance and the average of net loss on all assets that have experienced a net loss.

(4) Categorize all delinquency and loss information by pool asset type.

(5) In a registration statement under the Securities Act or the Exchange Act or in a prospectus to be filed pursuant to § 230.424, describe how delinquencies, charge-offs and uncollectable accounts are defined or determined, addressing the effect of any grace period, re-aging, restructure, partial payments considered current or other practices on delinquency and loss experience.

(6) Describe any other material information regarding delinquencies and losses particular to the pool asset type(s), such as repossession information, foreclosure information and real estate owned (REO) or similar information.

(c) *Presentation of certain third party financial information*.

If financial information of a third party is required in a filing by Item 1112(b) of this Regulation AB (Information regarding significant obligors) or Items 1114(b)(2) or 1115(b) of this Regulation AB (Information regarding significant provider of enhancement or other support), such information, in lieu of including such information, may be provided as follows:

(1) *Incorporation by reference*. If the following conditions are met, you may incorporate by reference (by means of a statement to that effect) the reports filed by the third party (or the entity that consolidates the third party) pursuant to section 13(a) or 15(d) of the Exchange Act (15 U.S.C. 78m(a) or 78o(d)):

(i) Such third party or the entity that consolidates the third party is required to file reports with the Commission pursuant to section 13(a) or 15(d) of the Exchange Act.

(ii) Such third party or the entity that consolidates the third party has filed all reports and other materials required to be filed by such requirements during the preceding 12 months (or such shorter period that such party was required to file such reports and materials).

(iii) The reports filed by such third party, or entity that consolidates the third party, include (or properly incorporate by reference) the financial statements of such third party.

(iv) If incorporated by reference into a prospectus or registration statement, the prospectus also states that all documents subsequently filed by such third party, or the entity that consolidates the third party, pursuant to section 13(a) or 15(d) of the Exchange Act prior to the termination of the offering also shall be deemed to be incorporated by reference into the prospectus.

Instructions to Item 1100(c)(1).

1. In addition to the conditions in paragraph (c)(1) of this section, any information incorporated by reference must comply with all applicable Commission rules pertaining to incorporation by reference, such as Item 10(d) of Regulation S–K (§ 229.10(d)), Rule 303 of Regulation S–T (§ 232.303 of this chapter), Rule 411 of Regulation C (§ 230.411 of this chapter), and Rules 12b–23 and 12b–32 under the Exchange Act (§§ 240.12b–23 and 240.12b–32 of this chapter).

2. In addition, any applicable requirements under the Securities Act or the rules and regulations of the Commission regarding the filing of a written consent for the use of incorporated material apply to the material incorporated by reference. See, for example, § 230.439 of this chapter.

3. Any undertakings set forth in Item 512 of Regulation S–K (§ 229.512) apply to any material incorporated by reference in a registration statement or prospectus.

4. If neither the third party nor any of its affiliates has had a direct or indirect agreement, arrangement, relationship or understanding, written or otherwise, relating to the ABS transaction, and neither the third party nor any of its affiliates is an affiliate of the sponsor, depositor, issuing entity or underwriter of the ABS transaction, then paragraph (c)(1)(ii) of this section is qualified by the knowledge of the registrant.

5. If you are relying on paragraph (c)(1) of this section to provide information required by Item 1112 of this Regulation AB regarding a significant obligor that is an asset-backed issuer and the pool assets relating to such significant obligor are asset-backed securities, then for purposes of paragraph (c)(1)(iii) of this section, the term "financial statements" means the information required by Instruction 3 of Item 1112 of this Regulation AB. Such information required by Instruction 3.a. of Item 1112 of this Regulation AB may be incorporated by reference from a prospectus that contains such information and is included in an effective Securities Act registration statement or filed pursuant to § 230.424 of this chapter.

(2) *Reference information for significant obligors.* If the third party information relates to a significant obligor and the following conditions are met, you may include a reference to the third party's periodic reports (or the third party's parent with respect to paragraph (c)(2)(ii)(C) of this section) under section 13(a) or 15(d) of the Exchange Act (15 U.S.C. 78m(a) or 78o(d)) that are on file with the Commission (or otherwise publicly available with respect to paragraph (c)(2)(ii)(F) of this section), along with a statement of how those reports may be accessed, including the third party's name and Commission file number, if applicable (See, e.g., Item 1118 of this Regulation AB):

(i) Neither the third party nor any of its affiliates has had a direct or indirect agreement, arrangement, relationship or understanding, written or otherwise, relating to the asset-backed securities transaction, and neither the third party nor any of its affiliates is an affiliate of the sponsor, depositor, issuing entity or underwriter of the asset-backed securities transaction.

(ii) To the knowledge of the registrant, any of the following is true:

(A) The third party is eligible to use Form S–3 or F–3 (§ 239.13 or 239.33 of this chapter) for a primary offering of non-investment grade securities pursuant to General Instruction I.B.1 of such forms.

(B) The third party meets the requirements of General Instruction I.A. of Form S–3 or General Instructions 1.A.1, 2, 3, 4 and 6 of Form F–3 and the pool assets relating to such third party are non-convertible investment grade securities, as described in General Instruction 1.B.2 of Form S–3 or Form F–3.

(C) If the third party does not meet the conditions of paragraph (c)(2)(ii)(A) or (c)(2)(ii)(B) of this section and the pool assets relating to the third party are fully and unconditionally guaranteed by a direct or indirect parent of the third party, General Instruction I.C.3 of Form S–3 or General Instruction I.A.5(iii) of Form F–3 is met with respect to the pool assets relating to such third party and the requirements of Rule 3–10 of Regulation S–X (§ 210.3–10 of this chapter) are satisfied regarding the information in the reports to be referenced.

(D) If the pool assets relating to the third party are guaranteed by a wholly owned subsidiary of the third party and the subsidiary does not meet the conditions of paragraph (c)(2)(ii)(A) or (c)(2)(ii)(B) of this section, the criteria in either paragraph (c)(2)(ii)(A) or paragraph (c)(2)(ii)(B) of this section are met with respect to the third party and the requirements of Rule 3–10 of Regulation S–X (§ 210.3–10 of this chapter) are satisfied regarding the information in the reports to be referenced.

(E) The pool assets relating to such third party are asset-backed securities and the third party is filing reports pursuant to section 12 or 15(d) of the Exchange Act (15 U.S.C. 78l or 78o(d)) and has filed all the material that would be required to be filed pursuant to section 13, 14 or 15(d) of the Exchange Act (15 U.S.C. 78m, 78n or 78o(d)) for a period of at least twelve calendar months and any portion of a month immediately preceding the filing referencing the third party's reports (or such shorter period that such third party was required to file such materials).

(F) The third party is a U.S. government-sponsored enterprise, has outstanding securities held by non-affiliates with an aggregate market value of $75 million or more, and makes information publicly available on an annual and quarterly basis, including audited financial statements prepared in accordance with generally accepted accounting principles covering the same periods that would be required for audited financial statements under Regulation S–X (§§ 210.1–01 through 210.12–29 of this chapter) and non-financial information consistent with that required by Regulation S–K (§§ 229.10 through 229.1123).

Instruction to Item 1101(c)(2). If you are relying on paragraph (c)(2)(ii)(E) of this section because the pool assets relating to such third party are asset-backed securities, then for purposes of a registration statement under the Securities Act or the Exchange Act or a prospectus to be filed pursuant to § 230.424 for your securities, you also must include a reference (including Commission reporting number and filing date) to the prospectus for the third party asset-backed securities that: (a) Is either included in an effective Securities Act registration statement or filed pursuant to § 230.424 of this chapter; and (b) Contains the information required by Instruction 3.a. of Item 1112 of this Regulation AB.

(d) *Other participants to the transaction and pool assets representing interests in certain other asset pools.*

(1) If the asset-backed securities transaction involves additional or intermediate parties not specifically identified in this Regulation AB, the disclosure required by this Regulation AB includes information to the extent material regarding any such party and its role, function and experience in relation to the asset-backed securities and the asset pool. Describe the material terms of

any agreement with such party regarding the transaction, and file such agreement as an exhibit.

(2) If the asset pool backing the asset-backed securities includes one or more pool assets representing an interest in or the right to the payments or cash flows of another asset pool, then for purposes of this Regulation AB and §§ 240.13a–18 and 240.15d–18 of this chapter, references to the asset pool and the pool assets of the issuing entity also include the other asset pool and its pool assets if the following conditions are met:

(i) Both the issuing entity for the asset-backed securities and the entity issuing the pool asset to be included in the issuing entity's asset pool were established under the direction of the same sponsor or depositor.

(ii) The pool asset was created solely to satisfy legal requirements or otherwise facilitate the structuring of the asset-backed securities transaction.

Instruction to Item 1100(d)(2).

Reference to the underlying asset pool includes, without limitation, compliance with applicable servicing criteria referenced in §§ 240.13a–18 and 240.15d–18 of this chapter and the servicer compliance statement required by Item 1123 of this Regulation AB. In addition, provide clear and concise disclosure, including by flow chart or other illustration, of the transaction and the various parties involved.

(e) *Foreign asset-backed securities.* If the asset-backed securities are issued by a foreign issuer (as defined in § 230.405 of this chapter), backed by pool assets that are foreign assets, or affected by enhancement or support contemplated by Items 1114 or 1115 of this Regulation AB provided by a foreign entity, then in providing the disclosure required by this Regulation AB (including, but not limited to, Items 1104 and 1110 of this Regulation AB regarding origination and securitization practices, Item 1107 of this Regulation AB regarding the sale or transfer of the pool assets, bankruptcy remoteness and collateral protection, Item 1108 of this Regulation AB regarding servicing, Item 1109 of this Regulation AB regarding the rights, duties and responsibilities of the trustee, Item 1111 of this Regulation AB regarding the terms, nature and treatment of the pool assets and Items 1114 or 1115 of this Regulation AB, as applicable, regarding the enhancement provider), the filing must describe any pertinent governmental, legal or regulatory or administrative matters and any pertinent tax matters, exchange controls, currency restrictions or other economic, fiscal, monetary or potential factors in the applicable home jurisdiction that could materially affect payments on, the performance of, or other matters relating to, the assets contained in the pool or the asset-backed securities. See also Instruction 2 to Item 202 of Regulation S–K (§ 229.202). In addition, in a registration statement under the Securities Act, provide the information required by Item 101(g) of Regulation S–K (§ 229.101(g)). Disclosure also is required in Forms 10–D (§ 249.312 of this chapter) and 10–K (§ 249.310 of this chapter) with respect to the asset-backed securities regarding any material impact caused by foreign legal and regulatory developments during the period covered by the report which have not been previously described in a Form 10–D, 10–K or 8–K (§ 249.308 of this chapter) filed under the Exchange Act.

(f) *Filing of required exhibits.* Where agreements or other documents in this Regulation AB are specified to be filed as exhibits to a Securities Act registration statement, such final agreements or other documents, if applicable, may be incorporated by reference as an exhibit to the registration statement, such as by filing a Form 8–K in the case of offerings registered on Form S–3 (§ 239.13 of this chapter).

§ 229.1101 (Item 1101) Definitions.

The following definitions apply to the terms used in Regulation AB (§§ 229.1100 through 229.1123), unless specified otherwise:

(a) *ABS informational and computational material* means a written communication consisting solely of one or some combination of the following:

(1) Factual information regarding the asset-backed securities being offered and the structure and basic parameters of the securities, such as the number of classes, seniority, payment priorities, terms of payment, the tax, Employment Retirement Income Security Act of 1974, as amended, (29 U.S.C. 1001 et seq.) ("ERISA") or other legal conclusions of counsel, and descriptive information relating to each class (e.g., principal amount, coupon, minimum denomination, anticipated price, yield, weighted average life, credit enhancements, anticipated ratings, and other similar information relating to the proposed structure of the offering);

(2) Factual information regarding the pool assets underlying the asset-backed securities, including origination, acquisition and pool selection criteria, information regarding any prefunding or revolving period applicable to the offering, information regarding significant obligors, data regarding the contractual and related characteristics of the underlying pool assets (e.g., weighted average coupon, weighted average maturity, delinquency and loss information and geographic distribution) and other factual information concerning the parameters of the asset pool appropriate to the nature of the underlying assets, such as the type of assets comprising the pool and the programs under which the loans were originated;

(3) Identification of key parties to the transaction, such as servicers, trustees, depositors, sponsors, originators and providers of credit enhancement or other support, including a brief description of each such party's roles, responsibilities, background and experience;

(4) Static pool data, as referenced in Item 1105 of this Regulation AB, such as for the sponsor's and/or servicer's portfolio, prior transactions or the asset pool itself;

(5) Statistical information displaying for a particular class of asset-backed securities the yield, average life, expected maturity, interest rate sensitivity, cash flow characteristics, total rate of return, option adjusted spread or other financial or statistical information relating to the class or classes under specified prepayment, interest rate, loss or other hypothetical scenarios. Examples of such information under the definition include:

(i) Statistical results of interest rate sensitivity analyses regarding the impact on yield or other financial characteristics of a class of securities from changes in interest rates at one or more assumed prepayment speeds;

(ii) Statistical information showing the cash flows that would be associated with a particular class of asset-backed securities at a specified prepayment speed; and

(iii) Statistical information reflecting the financial impact of losses based on a variety of loss or default experience, prepayment, interest rate and related assumptions.

(6) The names of underwriters participating in the offering of the securities, and their additional roles, if any, within the underwriting syndicate;

(7) The anticipated schedule for the offering (including the approximate date upon which the proposed sale to the public will begin) and a description of marketing events (including the dates, times, locations, and procedures for attending or otherwise accessing them); and

(8) A description of the procedures by which the underwriters will conduct the offering and the procedures for transactions in connection with the offering with an underwriter or participating dealer (including procedures regarding account-opening and submitting indications of interest and conditional offers to buy).

(b) *Asset-backed issuer* means an issuer whose reporting obligation results from either the registration of an offering of asset-backed securities under the Securities Act, or the registration of a class of asset-backed securities under section 12 of the Exchange Act (15 U.S.C. 78l).

(c)(1) *Asset-backed security* means a security that is primarily serviced by the cash flows of a discrete pool of receivables or other financial assets, either fixed or revolving, that by their terms convert into cash within a finite time period, plus any rights or other assets designed to assure the servicing or timely distributions of proceeds to the security holders; provided that in the case of financial assets that are leases, those assets may convert to cash partially by the cash proceeds from the disposition of the physical property underlying such leases.

(2) The following additional conditions apply in order to be considered an *asset-backed security*:

(i) Neither the depositor nor the issuing entity is an investment company under the Investment Company Act of 1940 (15 U.S.C. 80a-1 et seq.) nor will become an investment company as a result of the asset-backed securities transaction.

(ii) The activities of the issuing entity for the asset-backed securities are limited to passively owning or holding the pool of assets, issuing the asset-backed securities supported or serviced by those assets, and other activities reasonably incidental thereto.

(iii) No non-performing assets are part of the asset pool as of the measurement date.

(iv) Delinquent assets do not constitute 50% or more, as measured by dollar volume, of the asset pool as of the measurement date.

(v) With respect to securities that are backed by leases, the portion of the securitized pool balance attributable to the residual value of the physical property underlying the leases, as determined in accordance with the transaction agreements for the securities, does not constitute:

(A) For motor vehicle leases, 65% or more, as measured by dollar volume, of the securitized pool balance as of the measurement date.

(B) For all other leases, 50% or more, as measured by dollar volume, of the securitized pool balance as of the measurement date.

(3) Notwithstanding the requirement in paragraph (c)(1) of this section that the asset pool be a discrete pool of assets, the following are considered to be a discrete pool of assets for purposes of being considered an asset-backed security:

(i) *Master trusts*. The offering related to the securities contemplates adding additional assets to the pool that backs such securities in connection with future issuances of asset-backed securities backed by such pool. The offering related to the securities also may contemplate additions to the asset pool, to the extent consistent with paragraphs (c)(3)(ii) and (c)(3)(iii) of this section, in connection with maintaining minimum pool balances in accordance with the transaction agreements for master trusts with revolving periods or receivables or other financial assets that arise under revolving accounts.

(ii) *Prefunding periods*. The offering related to the securities contemplates a prefunding account where a portion of the proceeds of that offering is to be used for the future acquisition of additional pool assets, if the duration of the prefunding period does not extend for more than one year from the date of issuance of the securities and the portion of the proceeds for such prefunding account does not involve in excess of:

(A) For master trusts, 50% of the aggregate principal balance of the total asset pool whose cash flows support the securities; and

(B) For other offerings, 50% of the proceeds of the offering.

(iii) *Revolving periods.* The offering related to the securities contemplates a revolving period where cash flows from the pool assets may be used to acquire additional pool assets, provided, that, for securities backed by receivables or other financial assets that do not arise under revolving accounts, the revolving period does not extend for more than three years from the date of issuance of the securities and the additional pool assets are of the same general character as the original pool assets.

Instructions to Item 1101(c).

1. For purposes of determining non-performing, delinquency and residual value thresholds, the "measurement date" means either:

a. The designated cut-off date for the transaction (i.e., the date on and after which collections on the pool assets accrue for the benefit of asset-backed security holders), if applicable; or

b. In the case of master trusts, the date as of which delinquency and loss information or securitized pool balance information, as applicable, is presented in the prospectus for the asset-backed securities to be filed pursuant to § 230.424(b) of this chapter.

2. Non-performing and delinquent assets that are not funded or purchased by proceeds from the securities and that are not considered in cash flow calculations for the securities need not be considered as part of the asset pool for purposes of determining non-performing and delinquency thresholds.

3. For purposes of determining non-performing, delinquency and residual value thresholds for master trusts, calculations are to be measured against the total asset pool whose cash flows support the securities.

4. For purposes of determining residual value thresholds, residual values need not be included in measuring against the thresholds to the extent a separate party is obligated for such amounts (e.g., through a residual value guarantee, residual value insurance or where the lessee is obligated to cover any residual losses).

(d) *Delinquent*, for purposes of determining if a pool asset is delinquent, means if a pool asset is more than 30 or 31 days or a single payment cycle, as applicable, past due from the contractual due date, as determined in accordance with any of the following:

(1) The transaction agreements for the asset-backed securities;

(2) The delinquency recognition policies of the sponsor, any affiliate of the sponsor that originated the pool asset or the servicer of the pool asset; or

(3) The delinquency recognition policies applicable to such pool asset established by the primary safety and soundness regulator of any entity listed in paragraph (d)(2) of this section or the program or regulatory entity that oversees the program under which the pool asset was originated.

(e) *Depositor* means the depositor who receives or purchases and transfers or sells the pool assets to the issuing entity. For asset-backed securities transactions where there is not an intermediate transfer of the assets from the sponsor to the issuing entity, the term depositor refers to the sponsor. For asset-backed securities transactions where the person transferring or selling the pool assets is itself a trust, the depositor of the issuing entity is the depositor of that trust.

(f) *Issuing entity* means the trust or other entity created at the direction of the sponsor or depositor that owns or holds the pool assets and in whose name the asset-backed securities supported or serviced by the pool assets are issued.

(g) *Non-performing*, for purposes of determining if a pool asset is non-performing, means a pool asset if any of the following is true:

(1) The pool asset would be treated as wholly or partially charged-off under the requirements in the transaction agreements for the asset-backed securities;

(2) The pool asset would be treated as wholly or partially charged-off under the charge-off policies of the sponsor, an affiliate of the sponsor that originates the pool asset or a servicer that services the pool asset; or

(3) The pool asset would be treated as wholly or partially charged-off under the charge-off policies applicable to such pool asset established by the primary safety and soundness regulator of any entity listed in paragraph (g)(2) of this section or the program or regulatory entity that oversees the program under which the pool asset was originated.

(h) *NRSRO* has the same meaning as the term "nationally recognized statistical rating organization" as used in § 240.15c3-1(c)(2)(vi)(F) of this chapter.

(i) *Obligor* means any person who is directly or indirectly committed by contract or other arrangement to make payments on all or part of the obligations on a pool asset.

(j) *Servicer* means any person responsible for the management or collection of the pool assets or making allocations or distributions to holders of the asset-backed securities. The term servicer does not include a trustee for the issuing entity or the asset-backed securities that makes allocations or distributions to holders of the asset-backed securities if the trustee receives such allocations or distributions from a servicer and the trustee does not otherwise perform the functions of a servicer.

(k) *Significant obligor* means any of the following:

(1) An obligor or a group of affiliated obligors on any pool asset or group of pool assets if such pool asset or group of pool assets represents 10% or more of the asset pool.

(2) A single property or group of related properties securing a pool asset or a group of pool assets if such pool asset or group of pool assets represents 10% or more of the asset pool.

(3) A lessee or group of affiliated lessees if the related lease or group of leases represents 10% or more of the asset pool.

Instructions to Item 1101(k).

1. Regarding paragraph (k)(3) of this section, the calculation must focus on the leases whose cash flow supports the asset-backed securities directly or indirectly (including the residual value of the physical property underlying the leases if a portion of the securitized pool balance is attributable to the residual value of such property), regardless of whether the asset pool contains the leases themselves, mortgages on properties that are the subject of the leases or other assets related to the leases.

2. If separate pool assets, or properties underlying pool assets, are cross-defaulted and/or cross-collateralized, such pool assets are to be aggregated and considered together in determining concentration levels.

3. If the pool asset is a mortgage or lease relating to real estate, the pool asset is nonrecourse to the obligor, and the obligor does not manage the property or does not own other assets and has no other operations, then the obligor need not be considered a separate significant obligor from the real estate. Otherwise, the obligor is a separate significant obligor.

4. The determination of significant obligors is to be made as of the designated cut-off date for the transaction (i.e., the date on and after which collections on the pool assets accrue for the benefit of asset-backed security holders), provided, that, in the case of master trusts, the determination is to be made as of the cut-off date (or issuance date if there is not a cut-off date) for each issuance of asset-backed securities backed by the same asset pool. In addition, if disclosure is required pursuant to either Item 6.05 of Form 8-K (17 CFR 249.308) or in a Form 10-D (17 CFR 249.312) pursuant to Item 1121(b) of this Regulation AB, the deter-

mination of significant obligors is to be made against the asset pool described in such report. However, if the percentage concentration regarding an obligor falls below 10% subsequent to the determination dates discussed in this Instruction, the obligor no longer need be considered a significant obligor.

(*l*) *Sponsor* means the person who organizes and initiates an asset-backed securities transaction by selling or transferring assets, either directly or indirectly, including through an affiliate, to the issuing entity.

§ 229.1102 (Item 1102) Forepart of registration statement and outside cover page of the prospectus.

In addition to the information required by Item 501 of Regulation S-K (§ 229.501), provide the following information on the outside front cover page of the prospectus. Present information regarding multiple classes in tables if doing so will aid understanding. If information regarding multiple classes cannot appear on the cover page due to space limitations, include the information in the summary or in an immediately preceding separate table.

(a) Identify the sponsor, the depositor and the issuing entity (if known).

(b) In identifying the title of the securities, include the series number, if applicable. If there is more than one class of securities offered, state the class designations of the securities offered.

(c) Identify the asset type(s) being securitized.

(d) Include a statement, if applicable and appropriately modified to the transaction, that the securities represent the obligations of the issuing entity only and do not represent the obligations of or interest in the sponsor, depositor or any of their affiliates.

(e) Identify the aggregate principal amount of all securities offered and the principal amount, if any, of each class of securities offered. If a class has no principal amount, disclose that fact, and, if applicable, state the notional amount, clearly identifying that the amount is a notional one. If the amounts are approximate, disclose that fact.

(f) Indicate the interest rate or specified rate of return of each class of security offered. If a class of securities does not bear interest or a specified return, disclose that fact. If the rate is based on a formula or is calculated in reference to a generally recognized interest rate index, such as a U.S. Treasury securities index, either provide the formula on the cover, or indicate that the rate is variable, indicate the index upon which the rate is based and indicate that further disclosure of how the rate is determined is included in the transaction summary.

(g) Identify the distribution frequency, by class or series where applicable, and the first expected distribution date for the asset-backed securities.

(h) Briefly describe any credit enhancement or other support for the transaction and identify any enhancement or support provider referenced in Items 1114(b) or 1115 of this Regulation AB.

Instruction to Item 1102. Also see Item 1113(f)(2) of this Regulation AB regarding the title of any class of securities with an optional redemption or termination feature that may be exercised when 25% or more of the original principal balance of the pool assets are still outstanding.

§ 229.1103 (Item 1103) Transaction summary and risk factors.

(a) Prospectus summary. In providing the information required by Item 503(a) of Regulation S-K (§ 229.503(a)), provide the following information in the prospectus summary, as applicable. Present information regarding multiple classes in tables if doing so will aid understanding. Consider using diagrams to illustrate the relationships among the parties, the structure of the securities offered (including, for example, the flow of funds or any subordination features) and any other material features of the transaction.

(1) Identify the participants in the transaction, including the sponsor, depositor, issuing entity, trustee and servicers contemplated by Item 1108(a)(2) of this Regulation AB, and their respective roles. Describe the roles briefly if they are not apparent from the title of the role. Identify any originator contemplated by Item 1110 of this Regulation AB and any significant obligor.

(2) Briefly identify the pool assets and summarize briefly the size and material characteristics of the asset pool. Identify the cut-off date or similar date for establishing the composition of the asset pool, if applicable.

(3) State briefly the basic terms of each class of securities offered. In particular:

(i) Identify the classes offered by the prospectus and any classes issued in the same transaction or residual or equity interests in the transaction that are not being offered by the prospectus.

(ii) State the interest rate or rate of return on each class of securities offered, to the extent that the rates on any class of securities were not disclosed in full on the prospectus cover page.

(iii) State the expected final and final scheduled maturity or principal distribution dates, if applicable, of each class of securities offered.

(iv) Identify the denominations in which the securities may be issued.

(v) Identify the distribution frequency on the securities.

(vi) Summarize the flow of funds, payment priorities and allocations among the classes of securities offered, the classes of securities that are not offered, and fees and expenses, to the extent necessary to understand the payment characteristics of the classes that are offered by the prospectus.

(vii) Identify any events in the transaction agreements that can trigger liquidation or amortization of the asset pool or other performance triggers that would alter the transaction structure or the flow of funds.

(viii) Identify any optional or mandatory redemption or termination features.

(ix) Identify any credit enhancement or other support for the transaction, as referenced in Items 1114(a) and 1115 of this Regulation AB, and briefly describe what protection or support is provided by the enhancement. Identify any enhancement provider referenced in Items 1114(b) and 1115 of this Regulation AB. Summarize how losses not covered by credit enhancement or support will be allocated to the securities.

(4) Identify any outstanding series or classes of securities that are backed by the same asset pool or otherwise have claims on the pool assets. In addition, state if additional series or classes of securities may be issued that are backed by the same asset pool and briefly identify the circumstances under which those additional securities may be issued. Specify if security holder approval is necessary for such issuances and if security holders will receive notice of such issuances.

(5) If the transaction will include prefunding or revolving periods, indicate:

(i) The term or duration of the prefunding or revolving period.

(ii) For prefunding periods, the amount of proceeds to be deposited in the prefunding account.

(iii) For revolving periods, the maximum amount of additional assets that may be acquired during the revolving period, if applicable.

(iv) The percentage of the asset pool and any class or series of the asset-backed securities represented by the prefunding account or the revolving period, if applicable.

(v) Any limitation on the ability to add pool assets.

(vi) The requirements for assets that may be added to the pool.

(6) If pool assets can otherwise be added, removed or substituted (for example, in the event of a breach in representations or warranties regarding pool assets), summarize briefly the circumstances under which such actions can occur.

(7) Summarize the amount or formula for calculating the fee that the servicer will receive for performing its duties, and identify from what source those fees will be paid and the distribution priority of those fees.

(8) Summarize the federal income tax issues material to investors of each class of securities offered.

(9) Indicate whether the issuance or sale of any class of offered securities is conditioned on the assignment of a rating by one or more rating agencies. If so, identify each rating agency and the minimum rating that must be assigned.

(b) Risk factors. In providing the information required by Item 503(c) of Regulation S-K (§ 229.503(c)), identify any risks that may be different for investors in any offered class of asset-backed securities, and if so, identify such classes and describe such difference(s).

§ 229.1104 (Item 1104) Sponsors.

Provide the following information about the sponsor:

(a) State the sponsor's name and describe the sponsor's form of organization.

(b) Describe the general character of the sponsor's business.

(c) Describe the sponsor's securitization program and state how long the sponsor has been engaged in the securitization of assets. The description must include, to the extent material, a general discussion of the sponsor's experience in securitizing assets of any type as well as a more detailed discussion of the sponsor's experience in and overall procedures for originating or acquiring and securitizing assets of the type included in the current transaction. Include to the extent material information regarding the size, composition and growth of the sponsor's portfolio of assets of the type to be securitized and information or factors related to the sponsor that may be material to an analysis of the origination or performance of the pool assets, such as whether any prior securitizations organized by the sponsor have defaulted or experienced an early amortization triggering event.

(d) Describe the sponsor's material roles and responsibilities in its securitization program, including whether the sponsor or an affiliate is responsible for originating, acquiring, pooling or servicing the pool assets, and the sponsor's participation in structuring the transaction.

§ 229.1105 (Item 1105) Static pool information.

(a) For amortizing asset pools, unless the registrant determines that such information is not material:

(1) Provide static pool information, to the extent material, regarding delinquencies, cumulative losses and prepayments for prior securitized pools of the sponsor for that asset type.

(2) If the sponsor has less than three years of experience securitizing assets of the type to be included in the offered asset pool, consider providing instead static pool information, to the extent material, regarding delinquencies, cumulative losses and prepayments by vintage origination years regarding originations or purchases by the sponsor, as applicable, for that asset type. A vintage origination year represents assets originated during the same year.

(3) In providing the information required by paragraphs (a)(1) and (a)(2) of this section:

(i) Provide the requested information for prior pools or vintage origination years, as applicable, relating to the following time period, to the extent material:

(A) Five years, or

(B) For so long as the sponsor has been either securitizing assets of the same asset type (in the case of paragraph (a)(1) of this section) or making originations or purchases of assets of the same asset type (in the case of paragraph (a)(2) of this section) if less than five years.

(ii) Present delinquency, cumulative loss and prepayment data for each prior securitized pool or vintage origination year, as applicable, in periodic increments (e.g., monthly or quarterly), to the extent material, over the life of the prior securitized pool or vintage origination year. The most recent periodic increment for the data must be as of a date no later than 135 days of the date of first use of the prospectus.

(iii) Provide summary information for the original characteristics of the prior securitized pools or vintage origination years, as applicable and material. While the material summary characteristics may vary, these characteristics may include, among other things, the following: number of pool assets; original pool balance; weighted average initial pool balance; weighted average interest or note rate; weighted average original term; weighted average remaining term; weighted average and minimum and maximum standardized credit score or other applicable measure of obligor credit quality; product type; loan purpose; loan-to-value information; distribution of assets by loan or note rate; and geographic distribution information.

(b) For revolving asset master trusts, unless the registrant determines that such information is not material, provide, to the extent material, data regarding delinquencies, cumulative losses, prepayments, payment rate, yield and standardized credit scores or other applicable measure of obligor credit quality in separate increments based on the date of origination of the pool assets. While the material increments may vary, consider presenting such data at a minimum in 12–month increments through the first five years of the account's life (e.g., 0–12 months, 13–24 months, 25–36 months, 37–48 months, 49–60 months and 61 months or more).

(c) If the information that would otherwise be required by paragraph (a)(1), (a)(2) or (b) of this section is not material, but alternative static pool information would provide material disclosure, provide such alternative information instead. Similarly, information contemplated by paragraph (a)(1), (a)(2) or (b) of this section regarding a party or parties other than the sponsor may be provided in addition to or in lieu of such information regarding the sponsor if appropriate to provide material disclosure. In addition, other explanatory disclosure, including disclosure explaining the absence of any static pool information, may be provided.

(d) The following information provided in response to this section shall not be deemed to be a prospectus or part of a prospectus for the asset-backed securities nor shall such information be deemed to be part of the registration statement for the asset-backed securities:

(1) With respect to information regarding prior securitized pools of the sponsor that do not include the currently offered pool, information regarding prior securitized pools that were established before January 1, 2006; and

(2) With respect to information regarding the currently offered pool, information about the pool for periods before January 1, 2006.(e) For prospectuses to be filed pursuant to § 230.424 of this chapter that include information specified in paragraph (d)(1) or (d)(2) of this section, the prospectus shall disclose that such information is not deemed to be part of that prospectus or the registration statement for the asset-backed securities.

(f) If any of the information identified in paragraph (d)(1) or (d)(2) of this section that is to be provided in response to this section is unknown and not available to the registrant without unreasonable effort or expense, such information may be omitted, provided the registrant provides the information on the subject it possesses or can acquire without unreasonable effort or expense, and the registrant includes a statement in the prospectus showing that unreasonable effort or expense would be involved in obtaining the omitted information.

§ 229.1106 (Item 1106) Depositors.

If the depositor is not the same entity as the sponsor, provide separately the information regarding the depositor called for by paragraphs (a) and (b) of Item 1104 of this Regulation AB, and, to the extent the information would be material and materially different from the sponsor, paragraphs (c) and (d) of Item 1104 of this Regulation AB. In addition, provide the following information:

(a) The ownership structure of the depositor.

(b) The general character of any activities the depositor is engaged in other than securitizing assets and the time period during which it has been so engaged.

(c) Any continuing duties of the depositor after issuance of the asset-backed securities being registered regarding the asset-backed securities or the pool assets.

§ 229.1107 (Item 1107) Issuing entities.

Provide the following information about the issuing entity:

(a) State the issuing entity's name and describe the issuing entity's form of organization, including the State or other jurisdiction under whose laws the issuing entity is organized. File the issuing entity's governing documents as an exhibit.

(b) Describe the permissible activities and restrictions on the activities of the issuing entity under its governing documents, including any restrictions on the ability to issue or invest in additional securities, to borrow money or to make loans to other persons. Describe any provisions in the issuing entity's governing documents allowing for modification of the issuing entity's governing documents, including its permissible activities.

(c) Describe any specific discretionary activities with regard to the administration of the asset pool or the asset-backed securities, and identify the person or persons authorized to exercise such discretion.

(d) Describe any assets owned or to be owned by the issuing entity, apart from the pool assets, as well as any liabilities of the issuing entity, apart from the asset-backed securities. Disclose the fiscal year end of the issuing entity.

(e) If the issuing entity has executive officers, a board of directors or persons performing similar functions, provide the information required by Items 401, 402, 403 and 404 of Regulation S-K (§§ 229.401, 229.402, 229.403 and 229.404) for the issuing entity.

(f) Describe the terms of any management or administration agreement regarding the issuing entity. File any such agreement as an exhibit.

(g) Describe the capitalization of the issuing entity and the amount or nature of any equity contribution to the issuing entity by the sponsor, depositor or other party.

(h) Describe the sale or transfer of the pool assets to the issuing entity as well as the creation (and perfection and priority status) of any security interest in favor of the issuing entity, the trustee, the asset-backed security holders or others, including the material terms of any agreement providing for such sale, transfer or creation of a security interest. File any such agreements as an exhibit. In addition to an appropriate narrative description, also provide this information graphically or in a flow chart if it will aid understanding.

(i) If the pool assets are securities, as defined under the Securities Act, state the market price of the securities and the basis on which the market price was determined.

(j) If expenses incurred in connection with the selection and acquisition of the pool assets are to be payable from offering proceeds, disclose the amount of such expenses. If such expenses are to be paid to the sponsor, servicer contemplated by Item 1108(a)(2) of this Regulation AB, depositor, issuing entity, originator contemplated by Item 1110 of this Regulation AB, underwriter, or any affiliate of the foregoing, separately identify the type and amount of expenses paid to each such party.

(k) Describe to the extent material any provisions or arrangements included to address any one or more of the following issues:

(1) Whether any security interests granted in connection with the transaction are perfected, maintained and enforced.

(2) Whether declaration of bankruptcy, receivership or similar proceeding with respect to the issuing entity can occur.

(3) Whether in the event of a bankruptcy, receivership or similar proceeding with respect to the sponsor, originator, depositor or other seller of the pool assets, the issuing entity's assets will become part of the bankruptcy estate or subject to the bankruptcy control of a third party.

(4) Whether in the event of a bankruptcy, receivership or similar proceeding with respect to the issuing entity, the issuing entity's assets will become subject to the bankruptcy control of a third party.

(*l*) If applicable law prohibits the issuing entity from holding the pool assets directly (for example, an "eligible lender" trustee must hold student loans originated under the Federal Family Education Loan Program of the Higher Education Act of 1965 (20 U.S.C. 1001 et seq.)), describe the arrangements instituted to hold the pool assets on behalf of the issuing entity. Include disclosure regarding the arrangements taken, as applicable, regarding the items in paragraph (k) of this section with respect to any such additional entity that holds such assets on behalf of the issuing entity.

§ 229.1108 (Item 1108) Servicers.

Provide the following information for the servicer.

(a) *Multiple servicers*. Where servicing of the pool assets utilizes multiple servicers (e.g., master servicers that oversee the actions of other servicers, primary servicers that have primary contact with the obligor, or special servicers for specific servicing functions):

(1) Provide a clear introductory description of the roles, responsibilities and oversight requirements of the entire servicing structure and the parties involved. In addition to an appropriate narrative discussion of the allocation of servicing responsibilities, also consider presenting the information graphically if doing so will aid understanding.(2) Identify:

(i) Each master servicer;

(ii) Each affiliated servicer;

(iii) Each unaffiliated servicer that services 10% or more of the pool assets; and

(iv) Any other material servicer responsible for calculating or making distributions to holders of the asset-backed securities, performing work-outs or foreclosures, or other aspect of the servicing of the pool assets or the asset-backed securities upon which the performance of the pool assets or the asset-backed securities is materially dependent.

(3) Provide the information in paragraphs (b), (c) and (d) of this section, as applicable depending on the servicer's role, for each servicer identified in paragraphs (a)(2)(i), (ii) and (iv) of this section and each unaffiliated servicer identified in paragraph (a)(2)(iii) of this section that services 20% or more of the pool assets

(b) *Identifying information and experience.*

(1) State the servicer's name and describe the servicer's form of organization.

(2) State how long the servicer has been servicing assets. Provide, to the extent material, a general discussion of the servicer's experience in servicing assets of any type as well as a more detailed discussion of the servicer's experience in, and procedures for

the servicing function it will perform in the current transaction for assets of the type included in the current transaction. Include to the extent material information regarding the size, composition and growth of the servicer's portfolio of serviced assets of the type included in the current transaction and information on factors related to the servicer that may be material to an analysis of the servicing of the assets or the asset-backed securities, as applicable.

(3) Describe any material changes to the servicer's policies or procedures in the servicing function it will perform in the current transaction for assets of the same type included in the current transaction during the past three years.

(4) Provide information regarding the servicer's financial condition to the extent that there is a material risk that the effect on one or more aspects of servicing resulting from such financial condition could have a material impact on pool performance or performance of the asset-backed securities.

(c) *Servicing agreements and servicing practices.*

(1) Describe the material terms of the servicing agreement and the servicer's duties regarding the asset-backed securities transaction. File the servicing agreement as an exhibit.

(2) Describe to the extent material the manner in which collections on the assets will be maintained, such as through a segregated collection account, and the extent of commingling of funds that occurs or may occur from the assets with other funds, serviced assets or other assets of the servicer.

(3) Describe to the extent material any special or unique factors involved in servicing the particular type of assets included in the current transaction, such as subprime assets, and the servicer's processes and procedures designed to address such factors.

(4) Describe to the extent material the terms of any arrangements whereby the servicer is required or permitted to provide advances of funds regarding collections, cash flows or distributions, including interest or other fees charged for such advances and terms of recovery by the servicer of such advances. To the extent material, provide statistical information regarding servicer advances on the pool assets and the servicer's overall servicing portfolio for the past three years.

(5) Describe to the extent material the servicer's process for handling delinquencies, losses, bankruptcies and recoveries, such as through liquidation of the underlying collateral, note sale by a special servicer or borrower negotiation or workouts.

(6) Describe to the extent material any ability of the servicer to waive or modify any terms, fees, penalties or payments on the assets and the effect of any such ability, if material, on the potential cash flows from the assets.

(7) If the servicer has custodial responsibility for the assets, describe material arrangements regarding the safekeeping and preservation of the assets, such as the physical promissory notes, and procedures to reflect the segregation of the assets from other serviced assets. If no servicer has custodial responsibility for the assets, disclose that fact, identify the party that has such responsibility and provide the information called for by this paragraph for such party.

(8) Describe any limitations on the servicer's liability under the transaction agreements regarding the asset-backed securities transaction.

(d) Back-up servicing. Describe the material terms regarding the servicer's removal, replacement, resignation or transfer, including:

(1) Provisions for selection of a successor servicer and financial or other requirements that must be met by a successor servicer.

(2) The process for transferring servicing to a successor servicer.

(3) Provisions for payment of expenses associated with a servicing transfer and any additional fees charged by a successor servicer. Specify the amount of any funds set aside for a servicing transfer.

(4) Arrangements, if any, regarding a back-up servicer for the assets and the identity of any such back-up servicer.

§ 229.1109 (Item 1109) Trustees.

Provide the following information for each trustee:

(a) State the trustee's name and describe the trustee's form of organization.

(b) Describe to what extent the trustee has had prior experience serving as a trustee for asset-backed securities transactions involving similar pool assets, if applicable.

(c) Describe the trustee's duties and responsibilities regarding the asset-backed securities under the governing documents and under applicable law. In addition, describe any actions required by the trustee, including whether notices are required to investors, rating agencies or other third parties, upon an event of default, potential event of default (and how defined) or other breach of a transaction covenant and any required percentage of a class or classes of asset-backed securities that is needed to require the trustee to take action.

(d) Describe any limitations on the trustee's liability under the transaction agreements regarding the asset-backed securities transaction.

(e) Describe any indemnification provisions that entitle the trustee to be indemnified from the cash flow that otherwise would be used to pay the asset-backed securities.

(f) Describe any contractual provisions or understandings regarding the trustee's removal, replacement or resignation, as well as how the expenses associated with changing from one trustee to another trustee will be paid.

Instruction to Item 1109. If multiple trustees are involved in the transaction, provide a description of the roles and responsibilities of each trustee.

§ 229.1110 (Item 1110) Originators.

(a) Identify any originator or group of affiliated originators, apart from the sponsor or its affiliates, that originated, or is expected to originate, 10% or more of the pool assets.

(b) Provide the following information for any originator or group of affiliated originators, apart from the sponsor or its affiliates, that originated, or is expected to originate, 20% or more of the pool assets:

(1) The originator's form of organization.

(2) To the extent material, a description of the originator's origination program and how long the originator has been engaged in originating assets. The description must include a discussion of the originator's experience in originating assets of the type included in the current transaction. In providing the description, include, if material, information regarding the size and composition of the originator's origination portfolio as well as information material to an analysis of the performance of the pool assets, such as the originator's credit-granting or underwriting criteria for the asset types being securitized.

§ 229.1111 (Item 1111) Pool assets.

Describe the pool assets, including the information required by this Item 1111. Present statistical information in tabular or graphical format, if such presentation will aid understanding. Present statistical information in appropriate distributional groups or incremental ranges in addition to presenting appropriate overall pool totals, averages and weighted averages, if such presentation will aid in the understanding of the data. In addition to presenting the number, amount and percentage of pool assets by distributional group or range, also provide statistical information for each group or range by variables, to the extent material, such as, average balance, weighted average coupon, average age and remaining term, average loan-to-value or similar ratio and weighted average standardized credit score or other applicable measure of obligor credit quality. These variables are just examples and should be tailored to the particular asset class backing the asset-backed securities. Consider providing minimums and maximums when presenting averages on an aggregate basis and within each group or range. In addition, provide historical data on the pool assets as appropriate (e.g., the lesser of three years or the time such assets have existed) to allow material evaluation of the pool data. In making any calculations regarding overall pool balances, disregard any funds set aside for a prefunding account.

(a) *General information regarding pool asset types and selection criteria.* Provide the following information:

(1) A brief description of the type or types of pool assets to be securitized.

(2) A general description of the material terms of the pool assets.

(3) A description of the solicitation, credit-granting or underwriting criteria used to originate or purchase the pool assets, including, to the extent known, any changes in such criteria and the extent to which such policies and criteria are or could be overridden.

(4) The method and criteria by which the pool assets were selected for the transaction.

(5) The cut-off date or similar date for establishing the composition of the asset pool, if applicable.

(6) If legal or regulatory provisions (such as bankruptcy, consumer protection, predatory lending, privacy, property rights or foreclosure laws or regulations) may materially affect pool asset performance or payments or expected payments on the asset-backed securities, briefly identify these provisions and their effects on such items.

Instruction to Item 1111(a)(6). Unless a material concentration of assets exists, it is not necessary to provide details of the laws in each jurisdiction. Even in that case, a legalistic description or recitation of the laws or regulations in a particular jurisdiction is not required.

(b) *Pool characteristics.* Describe the material characteristics of the asset pool. Provide appropriate introductory and explanatory information to introduce the characteristics, the methodology used in determining or calculating the characteristics and any terms or abbreviations used. While the material characteristics will vary depending on the nature of the pool assets, such characteristics may include, among other things:

(1) Number of each type of pool assets.

(2) Asset size, such as original balance and outstanding balance as of a designated cut-off date.

(3) Interest rate or rate of return, including type of interest rate if the pool includes different types, such as fixed and floating rates.

(4) Capitalized or uncapitalized accrued interest.

(5) Age, maturity, remaining term, average life (based on different prepayment assumptions), current payment/prepayment speeds and pool factors, as applicable.

(6) Servicer distribution, if different servicers service different pool assets.

(7) If a loan or similar receivable:

(i) Amortization period.

(ii) Loan purpose (*e.g.*, whether a purchase or refinance) and status, if applicable (*e.g.*, repayment or deferment).

(iii) Loan-to-value (LTV) ratios and debt service coverage ratios (DSCR), as applicable.

(iv) Type and/or use of underlying property, product or collateral (e.g., occupancy type for residential mortgages or industry sector for commercial mortgages).

(8) If a receivable or other financial asset that arises under a revolving account, such as a credit card receivable:

(i) Monthly payment rate.

(ii) Maximum credit lines.

(iii) Average account balance.

(iv) Yield percentages.

(v) Type of asset.

(vi) Finance charges, fees and other income earned.

(vii) Balance reductions granted for refunds, returns, fraudulent charges or other reasons.

(viii) Percentage of full-balance and minimum payments made.

(9) If the asset pool includes commercial mortgages, the following information, to the extent material:

(i) For all commercial mortgages:

(A) The location and present use of each mortgaged property.

(B) Net operating income and net cash flow information, as well as the components of net operating income and net cash flow, for each mortgaged property.

(C) Current occupancy rates for each mortgaged property.

(D) The identity, square feet occupied by and lease expiration dates for the three largest tenants at each mortgaged property.

(E) The nature and amount of all other material mortgages, liens or encumbrances against such properties and their priority.

(ii) For each commercial mortgage that represents, by dollar value, 10% or more of the asset pool, as measured as of the cut-off date:

(A) Any proposed program for the renovation, improvement or development of such properties, including the estimated cost thereof and the method of financing to be used.

(B) The general competitive conditions to which such properties are or may be subject.

(C) Management of such properties.

(D) Occupancy rate expressed as a percentage for each of the last five years.

(E) Principal business, occupations and professions carried on in, or from the properties.

(F) Number of tenants occupying 10% or more of the total rentable square footage of such properties and principal nature of business of such tenant, and the principal provisions of the leases with those tenants including, but not limited to: rental per annum, expiration date, and renewal options.

(G) The average effective annual rental per square foot or unit for each of the last three years prior to the date of filing.

(H) Schedule of the lease expirations for each of the ten years starting with the year in which the registration statement is filed (or the year in which the prospectus supplement is dated, as applicable), stating:

(1) The number of tenants whose leases will expire.

(2) The total area in square feet covered by such leases.

(3) The annual rental represented by such leases.

(4) The percentage of gross annual rental represented by such leases.

Instruction to Item 1111(b)(9). What is required is information material to an investor's understanding of the asset-backed securities. Detailed descriptions of the physical characteristics of individual properties or legal descriptions by metes and bounds are not required.

(10) Whether the pool asset is secured or unsecured, and if secured, the type(s) of collateral.

(11) Standardized credit scores of obligors and other information regarding obligor credit quality.

(12) Billing and payment procedures, including frequency of payment, payment op-

tions, fees, charges and origination or payment incentives.

(13) Information about the origination channel and origination process for the pool assets, such as originator information (and how acquired) and the level of origination documentation required, as applicable.

(14) Geographic distribution, such as by state or other material geographic region. If 10% or more of the pool assets are or will be located in any one state or other geographic region, describe any economic or other factors specific to such state or region that may materially impact the pool assets or pool asset cash flows.

Instruction to Item 1111(b)(14). For most assets, such as credit card accounts, motor vehicle leases, trade receivables and student loans, the location of the asset is the underlying obligor's billing address. For assets involving real estate, such as mortgages, the location of the asset is where the physical property underlying the asset is located.

(15) Other concentrations material to the asset type (*e.g.*, school type for student loans). If material, provide information required by paragraph (b)(14) of this section regarding such concentrations, as applicable.

(c) *Delinquency and loss information.* Provide delinquency and loss information for the asset pool, including statistical information regarding delinquencies and losses.

(d) *Sources of pool cash flow.* If the cash flows from the pool assets that are to be used to support the asset-backed securities are to come from more than one source (such as separate cash flows from lease payments and from the sale of the residual asset at the termination of the lease), provide the following information:(1) Disclose the specific sources of funds that will be used to make the payments and distributions on the asset-backed securities, and, if applicable, provide information on the relative amount and percentage of funds that are to be derived from each source, including a description of any assumptions, data, models and methodology used to derive such amounts. If payments on different classes or different categories of payments on or related to the asset-backed securities (e.g., principal, interest or expenses) are to come from different or segregated cash flows from the pool assets or other sources, disclose the source of funds that will be used for such payments.

(2) *Residual value information.* If the asset pool includes leases or other assets where a portion of the securitized pool balance is attributable to the residual value of the underlying physical property underlying the leases, disclose the following:

(i) How the residual values used to structure the transaction were estimated, including an explanation of any material discount rates, models or assumptions used and who selected such rates, models or assumptions.

(ii) Any material procedures or requirements incorporated to preserve residual values during the term of the lease, such as lessee responsibilities, prohibitions on subletting, indemnification or required insurance or guarantees.

(iii) The procedures by which the residual values will be realized and by whom those procedures will be carried out, including information on the experience of such party, any affiliations with a party described in Item 1119(a) of this Regulation AB and the compensation arrangements with such party.

(iv) Whether the pool assets are open-end leases (e.g., where the lessee is required to cover the shortfall between the residual value of the leased property and the sale proceeds) or closed-end leases (e.g., where the lessor is responsible for such shortfalls), and where both types of leases are included in the asset pool, the percentage of each.

(v) To the extent material, any lessor obligations that are required under the leases, and the effect or potential effect on the asset-backed securities from failure by the lessor to perform its obligations.

(vi) Statistical information regarding estimated residual values for the pool assets.

(vii) Summary historical statistics on turn-in rates, if applicable, and residual value realization rates by the party responsible for such process over the past three years, or such longer period as is material to an evaluation of the pool assets.

(viii) The effect on security holders if not enough cash flow is received from the realization of the residual values, whether there are any provisions to address this contingency, and how any cash flow greater than that necessary to pay security holders will be allocated.

(e) *Representations and warranties and repurchase obligations regarding pool assets.* Summarize any representations and warranties made concerning the pool assets by the sponsor, transferor, originator or other party to the transaction, and describe briefly the remedies available if those representations and warranties are breached, such as repurchase obligations.

(f) *Claims on pool assets.* Describe any material direct or contingent claim that parties other than the holders of the asset-backed securities have on any pool assets. Also, describe any material cross-collateralization or cross-default provisions relating to the pool assets.

(g) *Revolving periods, prefunding accounts and other changes to the asset pool.* If the transaction contemplates a prefunding or revolving period, provide the following information, as applicable. Provide similar information regarding any other circumstances where pool assets may be added, substituted or removed from the asset pool, such as in the event of additional issuances of asset-backed securities in a master trust or a breach of a pool asset representation or warranty:

(1) The term or duration of any prefunding or revolving period.

(2) For prefunding periods, the amount of proceeds to be deposited in the prefunding account.

(3) For revolving periods, the maximum amount of additional assets that may be acquired during the revolving period, if applicable.

(4) The percentage of the asset pool and any class or series of the asset-backed securities represented by the prefunding account or the revolving account, if applicable.

(5) Triggers or events that would trigger limits on or terminate the prefunding or revolving period and the effects of such triggers. In particular for a revolving period, describe the operation of the revolving period and the amortization period.

(6) When and how new pool assets may be acquired during the prefunding or revolving period, and if, when and how pool assets can be removed or substituted. Describe any limits on the amount, type or speed with which pool assets may be acquired, substituted or removed.

(7) The acquisition or underwriting criteria for additional pool assets to be acquired during the prefunding or revolving period, including a description of any differences from the criteria used to select the current asset pool.

(8) Which party has the authority to add, remove or substitute assets from the asset pool or determine if such pool assets meet the acquisition or underwriting criteria for additional pool assets. In addition, disclose whether or not there will be any independent verification of such person's exercise of authority or determinations.

(9) Any requirements to add or remove minimum amounts of pool assets and any effects of not meeting those requirements.

(10) If applicable, the procedures and standards for the temporary investment of funds in a prefunding or revolving account

pending use (including the disposition of gains and losses on pending funds) and a description of the financial products or instruments eligible for such accounts.

(11) The circumstances under which funds in a prefunding or revolving account will be returned to investors or otherwise disposed of.

(12) A statement of whether, and if so, how, investors will be notified of changes to the asset pool.

§ 229.1112 (Item 1112) Significant obligors of pool assets.

(a) *Descriptive information*. Provide the following information for each significant obligor:

(1) The name of the obligor.

(2) The organizational form and general character of the business of the obligor.

(3) The nature of the concentration of the pool assets with the obligor.

(4) The material terms of the pool assets and the agreements with the obligor involving the pool assets.

(b) *Financial information*. (1) If the pool assets relating to a significant obligor represent 10% or more, but less than 20%, of the asset pool, provide selected financial data required by Item 301 of Regulation S-K (§ 229.301) for the significant obligor, provided, however, that for a significant obligor under Item 1101(k)(2) of this Regulation AB, only net operating income for the most recent fiscal year and interim period is required.

(2) If pool assets relating to a significant obligor represent 20% or more of the asset pool, provide financial statements meeting the requirements of Regulation S-X (§§ 210.1–01 through 210.12–29 of this chapter), except § 210.3–05 of this chapter and Article 11 of Regulation S-X (§§ 210.11–01 through 210.11–03 of this chapter), of the significant obligor. Financial statements of such obligor and its subsidiaries consolidated (as required by § 240.14a–3(b) of this chapter) shall be filed under this item.

Instructions to Item 1112(b).

1. No information need be provided pursuant to paragraph (b) of this section if the obligations of the significant obligor as they relate to the pool assets are backed by the full faith and credit of the United States.

2. No information need be provided pursuant to paragraph (b) of this section if the obligations of the significant obligor as they relate to the pool assets are backed by the full faith and credit of a foreign government (as defined in § 240.3b-4(a) of this chapter) if the pool assets are investment grade securities as defined in Item I.B.2 of Form S-3 (§ 239.13 of this chapter). If the pool assets are not investment grade securities, information required by paragraph (5) of Schedule B of the Securities Act (15 U.S.C. 77aa) regarding the foreign government may be incorporated by reference from a Commission filing in lieu of providing the financial information required pursuant to paragraph (b) of this section.

3. If the significant obligor is an asset-backed issuer and the pool assets relating to the significant obligor are asset-backed securities, provide the following information in lieu of the information required by paragraph (b) of this section:

a. For a registration statement under the Securities Act or the Exchange Act or a prospectus to be filed pursuant to § 230.424 of this chapter, the information required by Items 1104 through 1115, 1117 and 1119 of this Regulation AB regarding such asset-backed securities; and

b. For an Exchange Act report on Form 10–K or Form 10–D (§ 249.310 or 249.312 of this chapter), the information required by General Instruction J. of Form 10–K regarding such asset-backed securities for the period for which the last Form 10–K of the asset-backed securities was due (or would have been due if such asset-backed securities are not required to file reports with the Commission pursuant to section 13(a) or 15(d) of the Exchange Act (15 U.S.C. 78m(a) or 78o(d)).

4. If the significant obligor is a foreign business (as defined § 210.1–02 of this chapter):

a. Paragraph (b)(1) of this section may be complied with by providing the information required by Item 3.A. of Form 20–F (§ 249.220f of this chapter). If a reconciliation to U.S. generally accepted accounting principles called for by Instruction 2. to Item 3.A. of Form 20–F is unavailable or not obtainable without unreasonable cost or expense, at a minimum provide a narrative description of all material variations in accounting principles, practices and methods used in preparing the non-U.S. GAAP financial statements used as a basis for the selected financial data from those accepted in the U.S.

b. Paragraph (b)(2) of this section may be complied with by providing financial statements meeting the requirements of Item 17 of Form 20–F for the periods specified by Item 8.A. of Form 20–F.

§ 229.1113 (Item 1113) Structure of the transaction.

(a) *Description of the securities and transaction structure.* In providing the information required by Item 202 of Regulation S-K (§ 229.202), address the following specific factors relating to the asset-backed securities, as applicable:(1) The types or categories of securities that may be offered, such as interest-weighted or principal-weighted classes (including IO (interest only) or PO (principal only) securities), planned amortization or companion classes or residual or subordinated interests.

(2) The flow of funds for the transaction, including the payment allocations, rights and distribution priorities among all classes of the issuing entity's securities, and within each class, with respect to cash flows, credit enhancement or other support and any other structural features designed to enhance credit, facilitate the timely payment of monies due on the pool assets or owing to security holders, adjust the rate of return on the asset-backed securities, or preserve monies that will or might be distributed to security holders. In addition to an appropriate narrative discussion of the allocation and priority structure of pool cash flows, present the flow of funds graphically if doing so will aid understanding. In the flow of funds discussion, provide information regarding any requirements directing cash flows from the pool assets (such as to reserve accounts, cash collateral accounts or expenses) and the purpose and operation of such requirements.

(3) In describing the interest rate or rate of return on the asset-backed securities and how such amounts are payable, explain how the rate is determined and how frequently it will be determined. If the rate to be paid can be a combination of two or more rates (such as the lesser of a variable rate or the actual weighted average net coupon on the pool assets), provide clear information regarding each rate and when each rate applies.

(4) How principal, if any, will be paid on the asset-backed securities, including maturity dates, amortization or principal distribution schedules, principal distribution dates, formulas for calculating principal distributions from the cash flows and other factors that will affect the timing or amount of principal payments for each class of securities.

(5) The denominations in which the asset-backed securities may be issued.

(6) Any specified changes to the transaction structure that would be triggered upon a default or event of default (such as a change in distribution priority among classes).

(7) Any liquidation, amortization, performance or similar triggers or events, and the rights of investors or changes to the transaction structure or flow of funds if such events were to occur.

(8) Whether the servicer or other party is required to provide periodic evidence of the absence of a default or of compliance with the terms of the transaction agreements.

(9) If applicable, the extent, expressed as a percentage, the transaction is overcollateralized or undercollateralized as measured by comparing the principal balance of the asset-backed securities to the asset pool.

(10) Any provisions contained in other securities that could result in a cross-default or cross-collateralization.

(11) Any minimum standards, restrictions or suitability requirements regarding potential investors in purchasing the securities or any restrictions on ownership or transfer of the securities.

(12) Security holder vote required to amend the transaction documents and allocation of voting rights among security holders.

(b) Distribution frequency and cash maintenance.

(1) Disclose the frequency of distribution dates for the asset-backed securities and the collection periods for the pool assets.

(2) Describe how cash held pending distribution or other uses is held and invested. Also describe the length of time cash will be held pending distributions to security holders. Identify the party or parties with access to cash balances and the authority to invest cash balances. Specify who determines any decisions regarding the deposit, transfer or disbursement of pool asset cash flows and whether there will be any independent verification of the transaction accounts or account activity.

(c) Fees and expenses. Provide in a separate table an itemized list of all fees and expenses to be paid or payable out of the cash flows from the pool assets. In itemizing the fees and expenses, also indicate their general purpose, the party receiving such fees or expenses, the source of funds for such fees or expenses (if different from other fees or expenses or if such fees or expenses are to be paid from a specified portion of the cash flows) and the distribution priority of such expenses. If the amount of such fees or expenses is not fixed, provide the formula used to determine such fees or expenses. The tabular presentation should be accompanied by footnotes or other accompanying narrative disclosure to the extent necessary for an understanding of the timing or amount of such fees or expenses, such as any restrictions or limits on fees or whether the estimate may change in certain instances, such as in an event of default (and how the fees would change in such an instance or the factors that would affect the change). In addition, through footnote or other accompanying narrative disclosure, describe if any, and if so how, such fees or expenses can be changed without notice to, or approval by, security holders and any restrictions on the ability to change a fee or expense amount, such as due to a change in transaction party.

(d) Excess cash flow.

(1) Describe the disposition of residual or excess cash flows. Identify who owns any residual or retained interests to the cash flows if such person is affiliated with the sponsor, depositor, issuing entity or any entity identified in Item 1119(a) of this Regulation AB or if such person has rights that may alter the transaction structure beyond receipt of residual or excess cash flows. Describe such rights, as material.

(2) Disclose any requirements in the transaction agreements to maintain a minimum amount of excess cash flow or spread from, or retained interest in, the transaction and any actions that would be required or changes to the transaction structure that would occur if such requirements were not met.

(3) To the extent material to an understanding of the asset-backed securities, disclose any features or arrangements to facilitate a securitization of the excess cash flow or retained interest from the transaction, including whether any material changes to

the transaction structure may be made without the consent of asset-backed security holders in connection with these securitizations.

(e) *Master trusts.* If one or more additional series or classes have been or may be issued that are backed by the same asset pool, provide information regarding the additional securities to the extent material to an understanding of their effect on the securities being offered, including the following:

(1) Relative priority of such additional securities to the securities being offered and rights to the underlying pool assets and their cash flows.

(2) Allocation of cash flow from the asset pool and any expenses or losses among the various series or classes.

(3) Terms under which such additional series or classes may be issued and pool assets increased or changed.

(4) The terms of any security holder approval or notification of such additional securities.

(5) Which party has the authority to determine whether such additional securities may be issued. In addition, if there are conditions to such additional issuance, disclose whether or not there will be an independent verification of such person's exercise of authority or determinations.

(f) *Optional or mandatory redemption or termination.*

(1) If any class of the asset-backed securities includes an optional or mandatory redemption or termination feature, provide the following information:(i) Terms for triggering the redemption or termination.

(ii) The identity of the party that holds the redemption or termination option or obligation, as well as whether such party is an affiliate of the sponsor, depositor, issuing entity or any entity identified in Item 1119(a) of this Regulation AB.

(iii) The amount of the redemption or repurchase price or formula for determining such amount.

(iv) The procedures for redemption or termination, including any notices to security holders.

(v) If the amount allocated to security holders is reduced by losses, the policy regarding any amounts recovered after redemption or termination.

(2) The title of any class of securities with an optional redemption or termination feature that may be exercised when 25% or more of the original principal balance of the pool assets is still outstanding must include the word "callable," *provided, however*, that in the case of a master trust, a title of a class of securities must include the word "callable" when an optional redemption or termination feature may be exercised when 25% or more of the original principal balance of the particular series in which the class was issued is still outstanding.

(g) *Prepayment, maturity and yield considerations.*

(1) Describe any models, including the related material assumptions and limitations, used as a means to identify cash flow patterns with respect to the pool assets.

(2) Describe to the extent material the degree to which each class of securities is sensitive to changes in the rate of payment on the pool assets (*e.g.*, prepayment or interest rate sensitivity), and describe the consequences of such changing rate of payment. Provide statistical information of such effects, such as the effect of prepayments on yield and weighted average life.

(3) Describe any special allocations of prepayment risks among the classes of securities, and whether any class protects other classes from the effects of the uncertain timing of cash flow.

§ 229.1114 (Item 1114) Credit enhancement and other support, except for certain derivatives instruments.

(a) *Descriptive information*. To the extent material, describe the following, including a clear discussion of the manner in which each potential item is designed to affect or ensure timely payment of the asset-backed securities:

(1) Any external credit enhancement designed to ensure that the asset-backed securities or pool assets will pay in accordance with their terms, such as bond insurance, letters of credit or guarantees.

(2) Any mechanisms to ensure that payments on the asset-backed securities are timely, such as liquidity facilities, lending facilities, guaranteed investment contracts and minimum principal payment agreements.

(3) Any derivatives whose primary purpose is to provide credit enhancement related to pool assets or the asset-backed securities.

(4) Any internal credit enhancement as a result of the structure of the transaction that increases the likelihood that payments will be made on one or more classes of the asset-backed securities in accordance with their terms, such as subordination provisions, overcollateralization, reserve accounts, cash collateral accounts or spread accounts.

Instructions to Item 1114(a).

1. Include a description of the material terms of any enhancement or support described, including any limits on the timing or amount of the enhancement or support or any conditions that must be met before the enhancement or support can be accessed. The enhancement or support agreement is to be filed as an exhibit. Also describe any provisions regarding the substitution of enhancement or support.

2. This Item should not be construed as allowing anything other than an asset-backed security whose payment is based primarily by reference to the performance of the receivables or other financial assets in the asset pool

(b) *Information regarding significant enhancement providers.*

(1) *Descriptive information*. If an entity or group of affiliated entities providing enhancement or other support described in paragraph (a) of this section is liable or contingently liable to provide payments representing 10% or more of the cash flow supporting any offered class of asset-backed securities, provide the following information:

(i) The name of such enhancement provider.

(ii) The organizational form of enhancement provider.

(iii) The general character of the business of such enhancement provider.

(2) *Financial information*. (i) If any entity or group of affiliated entities providing enhancement or other support described in paragraph (a) of this section is liable or contingently liable to provide payments representing 10% or more, but less than 20%, of the cash flow supporting any offered class of the asset-backed securities, provide financial data required by Item 301 of Regulation S-K (§ 229.301) for each such entity or group of affiliated entities.

(ii) If any entity or group of affiliated entities providing enhancement or other support described in paragraph (a) of this section is liable or contingently liable to provide payments representing 20% or more of the cash flow supporting any offered class of the asset-backed securities, provide financial statements meeting the requirements of Regulation S-X (§§ 210.1–01 through 210.12–29 of this chapter), except § 210.3–05 of this chapter and Article 11 of Regulation S-X (§§ 210.11–01 through 210.11–03 of this chapter), of such entity or group of affiliated entities. Financial statements of such enhancement provider and its subsidiaries consolidated (as required by § 240.14a-3(b) of this chapter) shall be filed under this item.

Instructions to Item 1114.

1. The requirements in paragraph (b) of this section apply to all providers of external credit enhancement or other support, other than those described in Item 1115 of this Regulation AB. Enhancement may support payment on the pool assets or payments on the asset-backed securities themselves.

2. No information need be provided pursuant to paragraph (b)(2) of this section if the obligations of the enhancement provider are backed by the full faith and credit of the United States.

3. No information need be provided pursuant to paragraph (b)(2) of this section if the obligations of the enhancement provider are backed by the full faith and credit of a foreign government (as defined in § 240.3b-4(a) of this chapter) if the enhancement provider has an investment grade credit rating, as the term investment grade is used in Item I.B.2 of Form S-3 (§ 239.13 of this chapter). If the enhancement provider does not have an investment grade credit rating, information required by paragraph (5) of Schedule B of the Securities Act (15 U.S.C. 77aa) regarding the foreign government may be incorporated by reference from a Commission filing in licu of providing the financial information required pursuant to paragraph (b)(2) of this section.

4. If the pool assets are student loans originated under the Federal Family Education Loan Program of the Higher Education Act of 1965 (20 U.S.C. 1001 et seq.) and the enhancement provider for the pool assets is a guarantee agency as defined under the Higher Education Act, then the following information may be provided in lieu of providing financial information required pursuant to paragraph (b)(2) of this section:

a. The number of pool assets and aggregate outstanding principal balance of pool assets guaranteed by the guarantee agency (both by number and percentage of the asset pool as of the cut-off date or other applicable date).

b. Disclosure of the following with respect to the guarantee agency, as applicable, including a brief description regarding the method of calculation, covering at least five federal fiscal years:

i. Aggregate principal amount of all student loans guaranteed.

ii. Reserve ratio.

iii. Recovery rate.

iv. Loss rate.

v. Claims rate.

5. If the enhancement provider is a foreign business (as defined § 210.1–02 of this chapter):

a. Paragraph (b)(2)(i) of this section may be complied with by providing the information required by Item 3.A. of Form 20–F (§ 249.220f of this chapter). If a reconciliation to U.S. generally accepted accounting principles called for by Instruction 2. to Item 3.A. of Form 20–F is unavailable or not obtainable without unreasonable cost or expense, at a minimum provide a narrative description of all material variations in accounting principles, practices and methods used in preparing the non-U.S. GAAP financial statements used as a basis for the selected financial data from those accepted in the U.S.

b. Paragraph (b)(2)(ii) of this section may be complied with by providing financial statements meeting the requirements of Item 17 of Form 20–F for the periods specified by Item 8.A. of Form 20–F.

§ 229.1115 (Item 1115) Certain derivatives instruments.

This item relates to derivative instruments, such as interest rate and currency swap agreements, that are used to alter the payment characteristics of the cashflows from the issuing entity and whose primary purpose is not to provide credit enhancement related to the pool assets or the asset-backed securities. For purposes of this section, the "significance estimate" of the derivative instrument is to be determined based on a reasonable good-faith estimate of maximum probable exposure, made in substantially the same manner as that used in the sponsor's internal risk management process in respect of similar instruments. The "significance percentage" is the percentage that the amount of the significance estimate represents of the aggregate principal balance of the pool assets, provided, that if the derivative instrument relates only to one or more classes of the asset-backed securities, the "significance percentage" is the percentage that the amount of the significance estimate represents of the aggregate principal balance of such classes.

(a) *Descriptive information.*

(1) Describe the following regarding the external counterparty:

(i) The name of the derivative counterparty.

(ii) The organizational form of the derivative counterparty.

(iii) The general character of the business of the derivative counterparty.

(2) Describe the operation and material terms of the derivative instrument, including any limits on the timing or amount of payments or any conditions to payments.

(3) Describe any material provisions regarding substitution of the derivative instrument.

(4) At a minimum, disclose whether the significance percentage, as calculated in accordance with this section, is less than 10%, at least 10% but less than 20%, or 20% or more.

(5) File the agreement relating to the derivative instrument as an exhibit.

(b) *Financial information.*

(1) If the aggregate significance percentage related to any entity or group of affiliated entities providing derivative instruments contemplated by this section is 10% or more, but less than 20%, provide financial data required by Item 301 of Regulation S-K (§ 229.301) for such entity or group of affiliated entities.

(2) If the aggregate significance percentage related to any entity or group of affiliated entities providing derivative instruments contemplated by this section is 20% or more, provide financial statements meeting the requirements of Regulation S-X (§§ 210.1-01 through 210.12–29 of this chapter), except § 210.3–05 of this chapter and Article 11 of Regulation S-X (§§ 210.11–01 through 210.11–03 of this chapter), of such entity or group of affiliated entities. Financial statements of such entity and its subsidiaries consolidated (as required by § 240.14a-3(b) of this chapter) shall be filed under this item.

Instructions to Item 1115.

1. Instructions 2, 3 and 5 to Item 1114 of this Regulation AB apply to the information contemplated by paragraph (b) of this item.

2. This Item should not be construed as allowing anything other than an asset-backed security whose payment is based primarily by reference to the performance of the receivables or other financial assets in the asset pool.

§ 229.1116 (Item 1116) Tax matters.

Provide a brief, clear and understandable summary of:

(a) The tax treatment of the asset-backed securities transaction under federal income tax laws.

(b) The material federal income tax consequences of purchasing, owning and selling the asset-backed securities. If any of the material federal income tax consequences are not expected to be the same for investors in all classes offered by the registration statement, describe the material differences.

(c) The substance of counsel's tax opinion, including identification of the material consequences upon which counsel has not been asked, or is unable, to opine.

§ 229.1117 (Item 1117) Legal proceedings.

Describe briefly any legal proceedings pending against the sponsor, depositor, trustee, issuing entity, servicer contemplated by Item 1108(a)(3) of this Regulation AB, originator contemplated by Item 1110(b) of this Regulation AB, or other party contemplated by Item 1100(d)(1) of this Regulation AB, or of which any property of the foregoing is the subject, that is material to security holders. Include similar information as to any such proceedings known to be contemplated by governmental authorities.

§ 229.1118 (Item 1118) Reports and additional information.

(a) Reports required under the transaction documents.Describe the reports or other documents provided to security holders required under the transaction agreements, including information included, schedule and manner of distribution or other availability, and the entity or entities that will prepare and provide the reports.

(b) Reports to be filed with the Commission.

(1) Specify the names, and if available, the Commission file numbers of the entity or entities under which reports about the asset-backed securities will be filed with the Securities and Exchange Commission. Identify the reports and other information filed with the Commission.

(2) State that the public may read and copy any materials filed with the Commission at the Commission's Public Reference Room at 450 Fifth Street, NW., Washington, DC 20549. State that the public may obtain information on the operation of the Public Reference Room by calling the Securities and Exchange Commission at 1–800–SEC-0330. State that the Commission maintains an Internet site that contains reports, proxy and information statements, and other information regarding issuers that file electronically with the Commission and state the address of that site (http://www.sec.gov).

(c) Web site access to reports.

(1) State whether the issuing entity's annual reports on Form 10–K (§ 249.310 of this chapter), distribution reports on Form 10–D (§ 249.312 of this chapter), current reports on Form 8–K (§ 249.308 of this chapter), and amendments to those reports filed or furnished pursuant to section 13(a) or 15(d) of the Exchange Act (15 U.S.C. 78m(a) or

78o(d)) will be made available on the Web site of a specified transaction party (e.g., the sponsor, depositor, servicer, issuing entity or trustee) as soon as reasonably practicable after such material is electronically filed with, or furnished to, the Commission.

(2) Disclose whether other reports to security holders or information about the asset-backed securities will be made available in this manner.

(3) If filings and other reports will be made available in this manner, disclose the Web site address where such filings may be found.

(4) If filings and other reports will not be made available in this manner, describe the reasons why they will not and whether an identified transaction party voluntarily will provide electronic or paper copies of those filings and other reports free of charge upon request.

§ 229.1119 (Item 1119) Affiliations and certain relationships and related transactions.

(a) Describe if so, and how, the sponsor, depositor or issuing entity is an affiliate (as defined in § 230.405 of this chapter) of any of the following parties as well as, to the extent known and material, if so, and how, any of the following parties are affiliates of any of the other following parties:

(1) Servicer contemplated by Item 1108(a)(3) of this Regulation AB.

(2) Trustee.

(3) Originator contemplated by Item 1110 of this Regulation AB.

(4) Significant obligor contemplated by Item 1112 of this Regulation AB.

(5) Enhancement or support provider contemplated by Items 1114 or 1115 of this Regulation AB.

(6) Any other material parties related to the asset-backed securities contemplated by Item 1100(d)(1) of this Regulation AB.

(b) Describe whether there is, and if so the general character of, any business relationship, agreement, arrangement, transaction or understanding that is entered into outside the ordinary course of business or is on terms other than would be obtained in an arm's length transaction with an unrelated third party, apart from the asset-backed securities transaction, between the sponsor, depositor or issuing entity and any of the parties in paragraphs (a)(1) through (a)(6) of this section, or any affiliates of such parties, that currently exists or that existed during the past two years and that is material to an investor's understanding of the asset-backed securities.

Instruction to Item 1119(b). What is required is information material to an investor's understanding of the asset-backed securities. A detailed description or itemized listing of all commercial relationships among the parties is not required. Instead, the disclosure should indicate whether any relationships outside of the asset-backed securities transaction do exist that are outside the normal course and the general character of those relationships.

(c) Notwithstanding paragraph (b) of this section, describe, to the extent material, any specific relationships involving or relating to the asset-backed securities transaction or the pool assets, including the material terms and approximate dollar amount involved, between the sponsor, depositor or issuing entity and any of the parties in paragraphs (a)(1) through (a)(6) of this section, or any affiliates of such parties, that currently exists or that existed during the past two years.

Instruction to Item 1119. With respect to disclosure in an annual report on Form 10–K, information required by this Item 1119 may be omitted to the extent that substantially the same information had been provided previously in an annual report on Form 10–K (§ 249.310) for the asset-backed securities or in an effective registration statement under the Securities Act or a prospectus timely filed pursuant to § 230.424 of this chapter under the same Central Index Key (CIK) code as the current annual report on Form 10–K.

§ 229.1120 (Item 1120) Ratings.

Disclose whether the issuance or sale of any class of offered securities is conditioned on the assignment of a rating by one or more rating agencies, whether or not NRSROs. If so, identify each rating agency and the minimum rating that must be assigned. Describe any arrangements to have such rating monitored while the asset-backed securities are outstanding.

§ 229.1121 (Item 1121) Distribution and pool performance information.

(a) Describe the distribution for the related distribution period and the performance of the asset pool during the distribution period. Provide appropriate introductory and explanatory information to introduce any material terms, parties or abbreviations used (or a cross-reference to a Commission filing where such information may be found). Present statistical information in tabular or graphical format, if such presentation will aid understanding. While the material information regarding the related distribution and pool performance will vary depending on the nature of the transaction, such information may include, among other things:

(1) Any applicable record dates, accrual dates, determination dates for calculating distributions and actual distribution dates for the distribution period.

(2) Cash flows received and the sources thereof for distributions, fees and expenses (including portfolio yield, if applicable).

(3) Calculated amounts and distribution of the flow of funds for the period itemized by type and priority of payment, including:(i) Fees or expenses accrued and paid, with an identification of the general purpose of such fees and the party receiving such fees or expenses.

(ii) Payments accrued or paid with respect to enhancement or other support identified in Item 1114 of this Regulation AB (such as insurance premiums or other enhancement maintenance fees), with an identification of the general purpose of such payments and the party receiving such payments.

(iii) Principal, interest and other distributions accrued and paid on the asset-backed securities by type and by class or series and any principal or interest shortfalls or carryovers.

(iv) The amount of excess cash flow or excess spread and the disposition of excess cash flow.

(4) Beginning and ending principal balances of the asset-backed securities.

(5) Interest rates applicable to the pool assets and the asset-backed securities, as applicable. Consider providing interest rate information for pool assets in appropriate distributional groups or incremental ranges.

(6) Beginning and ending balances of transaction accounts, such as reserve accounts, and material account activity during the period.

(7) Any amounts drawn on any credit enhancement or other support identified in Item 1114 of this Regulation AB, as applicable, and the amount of coverage remaining under any such enhancement, if known and applicable.

(8) Number and amount of pool assets at the beginning and ending of each period, and updated pool composition information, such as weighted average coupon, weighted average life, weighted average remaining term, pool factors and prepayment amounts. For asset-backed securities backed by leases where a portion of the securitized pool balance is attributable to residual values of the physical property underlying the leases, this information also would include turn-in rates and residual value realization rates.

(9) Delinquency and loss information for the period. In addition, describe any material changes to the information specified in Item 1100(b)(5) of this Regulation AB regarding the pool assets.

(10) Information on the amount, terms and general purpose of any advances made or reimbursed during the period, including the general use of funds advanced and the general source of funds for reimbursements.

(11) Any material modifications, extensions or waivers to pool asset terms, fees, penalties or payments during the distribution period or that have cumulatively become material over time.

(12) Material breaches of pool asset representations or warranties or transaction covenants.

(13) Information on ratio, coverage or other tests used for determining any early amortization, liquidation or other performance trigger and whether the trigger was met.

(14) Information regarding any new issuance of asset-backed securities backed by the same asset pool, any pool asset changes (other than in connection with a pool asset converting into cash in accordance with its terms), such as additions or removals in connection with a prefunding or revolving period and pool asset substitutions and repurchases (and purchase rates, if applicable), and cash flows available for future purchases, such as the balances of any prefunding or revolving accounts, if applicable. Disclose any material changes in the solicitation, credit-granting, underwriting, origi-

nation, acquisition or pool selection criteria or procedures, as applicable, used to originate, acquire or select the new pool assets.

(b) During a prefunding or revolving period, or if there has been a new issuance of asset-backed securities backed by the same pool under a master trust during the fiscal year of the issuing entity, provide the information required by Items 1110, 1111 and 1112 of this Regulation AB applied taking the revised pool composition into account in the Form 10–D report (§ 249.312 of this chapter) for the last required distribution of the fiscal year of the issuing entity. In addition, provide such updated information in the first Form 10–D report for the period in which the prefunding or revolving period ends (if applicable). However, no disclosure need be provided by this paragraph if the information has not materially changed from that previously provided in an Exchange Act report relating to the asset-backed securities or in an effective registration statement under the Securities Act or a prospectus timely filed pursuant to § 230.424 of this chapter under the same Central Index Key (CIK) code regarding a subsequent issuance of asset-backed securities backed by a pool of assets that includes the pool assets that are the subject of this paragraph.

§ 229.1122 (Item 1122) Compliance with applicable servicing criteria.

(a) *Reports on assessment of compliance with servicing criteria for asset-backed securities.* As required by paragraph (b) of § 240.13a-18 or 240.15d-18 of this chapter, provide as an exhibit from each party participating in the servicing function a report on an assessment of compliance with the servicing criteria set forth in paragraph (d) of this section that contains the following:

(1) A statement of the party's responsibility for assessing compliance with the servicing criteria applicable to it;

(2) A statement that the party used the criteria in paragraph (d) of this section to assess compliance with the applicable servicing criteria;

(3) The party's assessment of compliance with the applicable servicing criteria as of and for the period ending the end of the fiscal year covered by the Form 10–K report (§ 249.310 of this chapter). This discussion must include disclosure of any material instance of noncompliance identified by the party; and

(4) A statement that a registered public accounting firm has issued an attestation report on the party's assessment of compliance with the applicable servicing criteria as of and for the period ending the end of the fiscal year covered by the Form 10–K report.

(b) *Registered public accounting firm attestation reports.* Provide the registered public accounting firm's attestation report required by paragraph (c) of § 240.13a-18 or 240.15d-18 of this chapter on the party's assessment of compliance with the applicable servicing criteria as an exhibit.

(c) *Additional disclosure for the Form 10–K report.*

(1) If any party's report on assessment of compliance with servicing criteria required by paragraph (a) of this section, or related registered public accounting firm attestation report required by paragraph (b) of this section, identifies any material instance of noncompliance with the servicing criteria, identify the material instance of noncompliance in the report on Form 10–K.

(2) If any party's report on assessment of compliance with servicing criteria required by paragraph (a) of this section, or related registered public accounting firm attestation report required by paragraph (b) of this section, is not included as an exhibit to the Form 10–K report, disclosure that the report is not included and an associated explanation must be provided in the report on Form 10–K.

(d) *Servicing criteria.*

(1) *General servicing considerations.*

(i) Policies and procedures are instituted to monitor any performance or other triggers and events of default in accordance with the transaction agreements.(ii) If any material servicing activities are outsourced to third parties, policies and procedures are instituted to monitor the third party's performance and compliance with such servicing activities.

(iii) Any requirements in the transaction agreements to maintain a back-up servicer for the pool assets are maintained.

(iv) A fidelity bond and errors and omissions policy is in effect on the party participating in the servicing function throughout the reporting period in the amount of coverage required by and otherwise in accordance with the terms of the transaction agreements.

(2) *Cash collection and administration*.

(i) Payments on pool assets are deposited into the appropriate custodial bank accounts and related bank clearing accounts no more than two business days of receipt, or such other number of days specified in the transaction agreements.

(ii) Disbursements made via wire transfer on behalf of an obligor or to an investor are made only by authorized personnel.

(iii) Advances of funds or guarantees regarding collections, cash flows or distributions, and any interest or other fees charged for such advances, are made, reviewed and approved as specified in the transaction agreements.

(iv) The related accounts for the transaction, such as cash reserve accounts or accounts established as a form of overcollateralization, are separately maintained (e.g., with respect to commingling of cash) as set forth in the transaction agreements.

(v) Each custodial account is maintained at a federally insured depository institution as set forth in the transaction agreements. For purposes of this criterion, "federally insured depository institution" with respect to a foreign financial institution means a foreign financial institution that meets the requirements of § 240.13k-1(b)(1) of this chapter.

(vi) Unissued checks are safeguarded so as to prevent unauthorized access.

(vii) Reconciliations are prepared on a monthly basis for all asset-backed securities related bank accounts, including custodial accounts and related bank clearing accounts. These reconciliations:

(A) Are mathematically accurate;

(B) Are prepared within 30 calendar days after the bank statement cutoff date, or such other number of days specified in the transaction agreements;

(C) Are reviewed and approved by someone other than the person who prepared the reconciliation; and

(D) Contain explanations for reconciling items. These reconciling items are resolved within 90 calendar days of their original identification, or such other number of days specified in the transaction agreements.

(3) *Investor remittances and reporting*.

(i) Reports to investors, including those to be filed with the Commission, are maintained in accordance with the transaction agreements and applicable Commission requirements. Specifically, such reports:

(A) Are prepared in accordance with timeframes and other terms set forth in the transaction agreements;

(B) Provide information calculated in accordance with the terms specified in the transaction agreements;

(C) Are filed with the Commission as required by its rules and regulations; and

(D) Agree with investors' or the trustee's records as to the total unpaid principal balance and number of pool assets serviced by the servicer.

(ii) Amounts due to investors are allocated and remitted in accordance with timeframes, distribution priority and other terms set forth in the transaction agreements.(iii) Disbursements made to an investor are posted within two business days to the servicer's investor records, or such other number of days specified in the transaction agreements.

(iv) Amounts remitted to investors per the investor reports agree with cancelled checks, or other form of payment, or custodial bank statements.

(4) *Pool asset administration*.

(i) Collateral or security on pool assets is maintained as required by the transaction agreements or related pool asset documents.

(ii) Pool assets and related documents are safeguarded as required by the transaction agreements.

(iii) Any additions, removals or substitutions to the asset pool are made, reviewed and approved in accordance with any conditions or requirements in the transaction agreements.

(iv) Payments on pool assets, including any payoffs, made in accordance with the related pool asset documents are posted to the applicable servicer's obligor records maintained no more than two business days after receipt, or such other number of days specified in the transaction agreements, and allocated to principal, interest or other items (e.g., escrow) in accordance with the related pool asset documents.

(v) The servicer's records regarding the pool assets agree with the servicer's records with respect to an obligor's unpaid principal balance.

(vi) Changes with respect to the terms or status of an obligor's pool asset (e.g., loan modifications or re-agings) are made, reviewed and approved by authorized personnel in accordance with the transaction agreements and related pool asset documents.

(vii) Loss mitigation or recovery actions (e.g., forbearance plans, modifications and deeds in lieu of foreclosure, foreclosures and repossessions, as applicable) are initiated, conducted and concluded in accordance with the timeframes or other requirements established by the transaction agreements.

(viii) Records documenting collection efforts are maintained during the period a pool asset is delinquent in accordance with the transaction agreements. Such records are maintained on at least a monthly basis, or such other period specified in the transaction agreements, and describe the entity's activities in monitoring delinquent pool assets including, for example, phone calls, letters and payment rescheduling plans in cases where delinquency is deemed temporary (e.g., illness or unemployment).

(ix) Adjustments to interest rates or rates of return for pool assets with variable rates are computed based on the related pool asset documents.

(x) Regarding any funds held in trust for an obligor (such as escrow accounts):

(A) Such funds are analyzed, in accordance with the obligor's pool asset documents, on at least an annual basis, or such other period specified in the transaction agreements;

(B) Interest on such funds is paid, or credited, to obligors in accordance with applicable pool asset documents and state laws; and

(C) Such funds are returned to the obligor within 30 calendar days of full repayment of the related pool asset, or such other number of days specified in the transaction agreements.

(xi) Payments made on behalf of an obligor (such as tax or insurance payments) are made on or before the related penalty or expiration dates, as indicated on the appropriate bills or notices for such payments, provided that such support has been received by the servicer at least 30 calendar days prior to these dates, or such other number of days specified in the transaction agreements.

(xii) Any late payment penalties in connection with any payment to be made on behalf of an obligor are paid from the servicer's funds and not charged to the obligor, unless the late payment was due to the obligor's error or omission.

(xiii) Disbursements made on behalf of an obligor are posted within two business days to the obligor's records maintained by the servicer, or such other number of days specified in the transaction agreements.

(xiv) Delinquencies, charge-offs and uncollectable accounts are recognized and recorded in accordance with the transaction agreements.

(xv) Any external enhancement or other support, identified in Item 1114(a)(1) through (3) or Item 1115 of this Regulation AB, is maintained as set forth in the transaction agreements.

Instructions to Item 1122.

1. If certain servicing criteria are not applicable to the asserting party based on the activities it performs with respect to asset-backed securities transactions taken as a whole involving such party and that are backed by the same asset type backing the class of asset-backed securities, the inapplicability of the criteria must be disclosed in that asserting party's and the related registered public accounting firm's reports.

2. If multiple parties are participating in the servicing function, a separate assessment report and attestation report must be included for each party participating in the servicing function. A party participating in the servicing function means any entity (e.g., master servicer, primary servicers, trustees) that is performing activities that address the criteria in paragraph (d) of this section, unless such entity's activities relate only to 5% or less of the pool assets.

3. If the asset pool backing the asset-backed securities includes a pool asset representing an interest in or the right to the payments or cash flows of another asset pool and both the issuing entity for the asset-backed securities and the entity issuing the asset to be included in the issuing entity's asset pool were established under the direction of the same sponsor and depositor, see also Item 1100(d)(2) of this Regulation AB.

§ 229.1123 (Item 1123) Servicer compliance statement.

Provide as an exhibit a statement of compliance from the servicer, signed by an authorized officer of such servicer, to the effect that:

(a) A review of the servicer's activities during the reporting period and of its performance under the applicable servicing agreement has been made under such officer's supervision.

(b) To the best of such officer's knowledge, based on such review, the servicer has fulfilled all of its obligations under the agreement in all material respects throughout the reporting period or, if there has been a failure to fulfill any such obligation in any material respect, specifying each such failure known to such officer and the nature and status thereof.

Instruction to Item 1123. If multiple servicers are involved in servicing the pool assets, a separate servicer compliance statement is required from each servicer that meets the criteria in Item 1108(a)(2)(i) through (iii) of this Regulation AB.

REGULATION S–T—GENERAL RULES AND REGULATIONS FOR ELECTRONIC FILINGS

(Cite as 17 CFR 232.___)

GENERAL

GENERAL

§ 232.10 Application of Part 232

(a) This part, in conjunction with the EDGAR Filer Manual and the electronic filing provisions of applicable rules, regulations and forms, shall govern the electronic submission of documents filed or otherwise submitted to the Commission and shall be controlling for an electronic format document in the manner and respects provided in this part.

(b) Each registrant, third party filer, or agent to whom the Commission previously has not assigned a Central Index Key (CIK) code, must, before filing on EDGAR:

(1) File electronically a Form ID (§§ 239.63, 249.446, 259.602, 269.7 and 274.402 of this chapter), the uniform application for access codes to file on EDGAR, and

(2) File in paper by fax, within two business days before or after electronically filing the Form ID, a notarized document, manually signed by the applicant over the applicant's typed signature, that includes the information contained in the Form ID, confirms the authenticity of the Form ID and, if filed after electronically filing the Form ID, includes the accession number assigned to the electronically filed Form ID as a result of its filing.

§ 232.11 Definition of Terms Used in Part 232

Unless otherwise specifically provided, the terms used in Regulation S–T have the same meanings as in the federal securities laws and the rules, regulations and forms promulgated thereunder. In addition, the following definitions of terms apply specifically to electronic format documents and shall apply wherever they appear in laws, rules, regulations and forms governing such documents, unless the context otherwise specifies:

Animated graphics. The term *animated graphics* means text or images that do not remain static but that may move when viewed in a browser.

ASCII document. The term *ASCII document* means an electronic text document with contents limited to American Standard Code for Information Interchange (ASCII) characters and that is tagged with Standard Generalized Mark Up Language (SGML) tags in the format required for ASCII/SGML documents by the EDGAR Filer Manual.

Business development company. The term *business development company* has the meaning set forth in section 2(a)(48) of the Investment Company Act.

Direct transmission. The term *direct transmission* means the transmission of one or more electronic submissions via a telephonic communication session.

Disruptive code. The term *disruptive code* means any active content or other executable code, or any program or set of electronic computer instructions inserted into a computer, operating system, or program that replicates itself or that actually or potentially modifies or in any way alters, damages, destroys or disrupts the file content or the operation of any computer, computer file, computer database, computer system, computer network or software, and as otherwise set forth in the EDGAR Filer Manual.

EDGAR. The term EDGAR (Electronic Data Gathering, Analysis, and Retrieval) means the computer system for receipt, acceptance, review and dissemination of documents submitted in electronic format.

EDGAR Filer Manual. The term *EDGAR Filer Manual* means the current version of the manual prepared by the Commission setting out the technical format requirements for an electronic submission.

Note: See Rule 301 of Regulation S–T.

Electronic document. The term *electronic document* means the portion of an electronic submission separately tagged as an individual document in the format required by the EDGAR Filer Manual.

Electronic filer. The term *electronic filer* means a person or an entity that submits filings electronically pursuant to Rules 100 and 101 of Regulation S–T (§§ 232.100 and 232.101, respectively).

Electronic filing. The term *electronic filing* means one or more electronic documents filed under the federal securities laws that are transmitted or delivered to the Commission in electronic format.

Electronic format. The term *electronic format* means the computerized format of a document prepared in accordance with the EDGAR Filer Manual.

Electronic submission. The term *electronic submission* means any document, such as a filing, correspondence, or modular submission, or any discrete set of documents, transmitted or delivered to the Commission in electronic format.

Exchange Act. The term *Exchange Act* means the Securities Exchange Act of 1934.

Executable code. The term *executable code* means instructions to a computer to carry out operations that use features beyond the viewer's, reader's, or Internet browser's native ability to interpret and display HTML, PDF, and static graphic files. Such code may be in binary (machine language) or in script form. Executable code includes disruptive code.

HTML document. The term *HTML document* means an electronic text document tagged with HyperText Markup Language tags in the format required by the EDGAR Filer Manual.

Omitted.

Header information. The term *header information* means information designated by the EDGAR Filer Manual to precede the text of each electronic submission and document submitted therewith via EDGAR that identifies characteristics of the submission and documents in order to facilitate electronic processing by the EDGAR system.

Hypertext links or hyperlinks. The term *hypertext links* or *hyperlinks* means the representation of an Internet address in a form that an Internet browser application can recognize as an Internet address.

Investment Company Act. The term *Investment Company Act* means the Investment Company Act of 1940.

Modular submission. The term *modular submission* means an electronic submission that contains one or more documents, or portions of a document, submitted for storage in the non-public EDGAR data storage area for purposes of subsequent inclusion in one or more electronic filings pursuant to Rule 501(a) of Regulation S–T.

Official filing. The term *official filing* means any filing that is received and accepted by the Commission, regardless of filing medium and exclusive of header information, tags and any other technical information required in an electronic filing.

Original. The term *original,* when used or implied in the securities laws, rules, regulations or forms, includes the writing itself or any counterpart intended to have the same effect by a person executing or issuing it. If data are stored in a computer or similar device, any printout or other output readable by sight, shown to reflect the data accurately, is an original.

Paper format. The term *paper format* means a paper document.

Public Utility Act. The term *Public Utility Act* means the Public Utility Holding Company Act of 1935.

Registrant. The term *registrant* means an issuer of securities for which a Securities Act registration statement is required to be filed and/or an issuer of securities with respect to which an Exchange Act registration statement or report is required to be filed and/or an investment company required to file an Investment Company Act registration statement or report.

Securities Act. The term *Securities Act* means the Securities Act of 1933.

Segmented Filing. The term *segmented filing* means an electronic format document assembled from segments previously submitted to the non-public EDGAR data storage for one-time inclusion in an electronic filing pursuant to Rule 501(b) of Regulation S–T.

Tag. The term *tag* means an identifier that highlights specific information to EDGAR that is in the format required by the EDGAR Filer Manual.

Third party filer. The term *third party filer* means any person or entity that files documents with the Commission with respect to another entity.

Trust Indenture Act. The term *Trust Indenture Act* means the Trust Indenture Act of 1939.

Unofficial PDF copy. The term *unofficial PDF copy* means an optional copy of an electronic document that may be included in an EDGAR submission tagged as a Portable Document Format document in the format required by the EDGAR Filer Manual and submitted in accordance with Rule 104 of Regulation S–T (§ 232.104).

XBRL-Related Documents. The term *XBRL-Related Documents* means documents related to presenting information in eXtensible Business Reporting Language that are part of a voluntary submission in electronic format in accordance with § 232.401.

§ 232.12 Business Hours of the Commission

(a) *General.* The principal office of the Commission, at 450 Fifth Street, N.W., Washington, DC 20549, is open each day, except Saturdays, Sundays, and federal holidays, from 9 a.m. to 5:30 p.m., Eastern Standard Time or Eastern Daylight Saving Time, whichever is currently in effect, *provided that* hours for the filing of documents pursuant to the Acts or the rules and regulations thereunder are as set forth in paragraphs (b) and (c) of this section.

(b) *Submissions made in paper.* Filers may submit paper documents filed with or otherwise furnished to the Commission each day, except Saturdays, Sundays and federal holidays, from 8 a.m. to 5:30 p.m., Eastern Standard Time or Eastern Daylight Saving Time, whichever is currently in effect.

(c) *Submissions by direct transmission.* Electronic filings and other documents may be submitted by direct transmission, via dial-up modem or Internet, to the Commission each day, except Saturdays, Sundays and federal holidays, from 8 a.m. to 10 p.m., Eastern Standard Time or Eastern Daylight Saving Time, whichever is currently in effect.

§ 232.13 Date of Filing; Adjustment of Filing Date

(a) *General.* (1) Except as provided in paragraph (b) of this section the business day on which a filing is received by the Commission shall be the date of filing thereof, if:

(i) All requirements of the Acts and rules applicable to such filing have been complied with;

(ii) The filing conforms to the applicable technical standards regarding electronic format in the EDGAR Filer Manual; and

(iii) With respect to Securities Act filings, including filings under section 24(f) of the Investment Company Act (15 U.S.C. 80a–24(f)), the required fee payment has been confirmed, *provided that* the failure to pay an insignificant amount of the fee at the time of the filing, as a result of a *bona fide* error, shall not affect the date of filing.

(2) If the conditions of paragraph (a)(1) of this section are otherwise satisfied, all filings submitted by direct transmission commencing on or before 5:30 p.m. Eastern Standard Time or Eastern Daylight Saving Time, whichever is currently in effect, shall be deemed filed on the same business day, and all filings submitted by direct transmission commencing after 5:30 p.m. Eastern Standard Time or Eastern Daylight Saving Time, whichever is currently in effect, shall be deemed filed as of the next business day.

(3) Notwithstanding paragraph (a)(2) of this section, any registration statement or any post-effective amendment thereto filed pursuant to Rule 462(b) (§ 230.462(b) of this chapter) by direct transmission commencing on or before 10 p.m. Eastern Standard Time or East-

ern Daylight Savings Time, whichever is currently in effect, shall be deemed filed on the same business day.

(4) Notwithstanding paragraph (a)(2) of this section, a Form 3, 4 or 5 (§§ 249.103, 249.104 and 249.105 of this chapter) submitted by direct transmission on or before 10 p.m. Eastern Standard Time or Eastern Daylight Savings Time, whichever is currently in effect, shall be deemed filed on the same business day.

Note: Electronic filings that have an automatic or immediate effective date must be deemed filed, as provided in paragraph (a) of this section, before any waiting period for automatic effectiveness commences or before the filing becomes immediately effective, whichever applies.

(b) *Adjustment of the filing date.* If an electronic filer in good faith attempts to file a document with the Commission in a timely manner but the filing is delayed due to technical difficulties beyond the electronic filer's control, the electronic filer may request an adjustment of the filing date of such document. The Commission, or the staff acting pursuant to delegated authority, may grant the request if it appears that such adjustment is appropriate and consistent with the public interest and the protection of investors.

(c) *Payment of fees.* Fees required with respect to a filing that is submitted electronically shall be paid in accordance with the procedures set forth in Instructions for Filing Fees—Rule 3a of the Commission's Informal and Other Procedures (§ 202.3a of this chapter).

Note: All filing fees paid by electronic filers must be submitted to the lockbox depository, as provided in Rule 3a, including those pertaining to documents filed in paper pursuant to a hardship exemption.

(d) Where the Commission's rules, schedules and forms provide that a document must be filed on the same day it is published, furnished, sent or given to security holders or others, an electronic filer may file the document with the Commission electronically before or on the date the document is published, furnished, sent or given, or if such publication or distribution does not occur during the official business hours of the Commission, as soon as practicable on the next business day. Any associated time periods shall be calculated on the basis of the publication or distribution date (as applicable), and not on the basis of the date of filing.

§ 232.14 Paper Filings Not Accepted Without Exemption

The Commission will not accept in paper format any filing required to be submitted electronically under Rules 100 and 101 of Regulation S–T (§§ 232.100 and 232.101 respectively), unless the filing satisfies the requirements for a temporary or continuing hardship exemption under Rule 201 or 202 of Regulation S–T (§§ 232.201 or 232.202 respectively).

ELECTRONIC FILING REQUIREMENTS

§ 232.100 Persons and Entities Subject to Mandated Electronic Filing

The following persons or entities shall be subject to the electronic filing requirements of this part 232:

(a) Registrants whose filings are subject to review by the Division of Corporation Finance;

(b) Registrants whose filings are subject to review by the Division of Investment Management; and

(c) Any party (including natural persons) that files a document jointly with, or as a third party filer with respect to, a registrant that is subject to mandated electronic filing requirements.

§ 232.101 Mandated Electronic Submissions and Exceptions

(a) *Mandated electronic submissions.* (1) The following filings, including any related correspondence and supplemental information, except as otherwise provided, shall be submitted in electronic format:

(i) Registration statements and prospectuses filed pursuant to the Securities Act (15 U.S.C. 77a, *et seq.*) or registration statements filed pursuant to Sections 12(b) or 12(g) of the Exchange Act (15 U.S.C. 78*l* (b) or (g));

(ii) Statements and applications filed with the Commission pursuant to the Trust Indenture Act (15 U.S.C. 77aaa, et seq.), other than applications for exemptive relief filed pursuant to section 304 (15 U.S.C. 77ddd) and section 310 (15 U.S.C. 77jjj) of that Act;

(iii) Statements, reports and schedules filed with the Commission pursuant to sections 13, 14, 15(d) or 16(a) of the Exchange Act (15 U.S.C. 78m, 78n, 78o(d) and 78p(a)), and proxy materials required to be furnished for the information of the Commission in connection with annual reports on Form 10–K (§ 249.310 of this chapter) or Form 10–KSB (§ 249.310b of this chapter) filed pursuant to section 15(d) of the Exchange Act.

Note 1. Electronic filers filing Schedules 13D and 13G with respect to foreign private issuers should include in the submission header all zeroes (i.e., 00–0000000) for the IRS tax identification number because the EDGAR system requires an IRS number tag to be inserted for the subject company as a prerequisite to acceptance of the filing.

Note 2. Foreign private issuers must file or submit their Form 6–K reports (§ 249.306 of this chapter) in electronic format, except as otherwise permitted by paragraphs (b)(1) and (b)(7) of this section.

(iv) Documents filed with the Commission pursuant to sections 8, 17, 20, 23(c), 24(e), 24(f), and 30 of the Investment Company Act (15 U.S.C. 80a-8, 80a–17, 80a–20, 80a–23(c), 80a–24(e), 80a–24(f) and 80a–29); provided, however, that submissions under section 6(c), or 17(g) of that Act (15 U.S.C. 80a–6(c), or 80a–17(g)), or documents related to applications for exemptive relief under any section of that Act, shall not be made in electronic format;

(v) Documents filed with the Commission pursuant to the Public Utility Act;

(vi) Form CB (§§ 239.800 and 249.480 of this chapter) filed or submitted under § 230.801 or 230.802 of this chapter or § 240.13e–4(h)(8), 240.14d–1(c), or § 240.14e–2(d) of this chapter if the party filing or submitting the Form CB is subject to the reporting requirements of Section 13 or 15(d) of the Exchange Act (15 U.S.C. 78m or 78o(d));

(vii) Form F–X (§ 239.42 of this chapter) except as otherwise provided by § 232.101(b)(9);

(viii) Form F–N (§ 239.43 of this chapter) filed by foreign banks and insurance companies and certain of their holding companies and finance subsidiaries under § 230.489 of this chapter;

(ix) Form ID (§ 239.63, 249.446, 259.602, 269.7 and 274.402 of this chapter), except that the authenticating document required by Rule 10(b) of Regulation S–T (§ 232.10(b)) shall not be filed in electronic format, and related correspondence and supplemental information submitted after filing Form ID shall not be submitted in electronic format; and

(x) Form 19b–4 (§ 249.819 of this chapter).

(2) The following amendments to filings, including any related correspondence and supplemental information except as otherwise provided, shall be submitted as follows:

(i) Any amendment to a filing by or relating to a registrant required to file electronically, including any amendment to a paper filing, shall be submitted in electronic format;

(ii) The first electronic amendment to a paper format Schedule 13D (§ 240.13d–101 of this chapter) or Schedule 13G (§ 240.13d–102 of this chapter), shall restate the entire text of the Schedule 13D or 13G, but previously filed paper exhibits to such Schedules are not required to be restated electronically. See Rule 102 (§ 232.102) regarding amendments to exhibits previously filed in paper format. Notwithstanding the foregoing, if the sole purpose of filing the first electronic Schedule 13D or 13G amendment is to report a change in beneficial ownership that would terminate the filer's obligation to report, the amendment need not include a restatement of the entire text of the Schedule being amended.

(3) Supplemental information shall be submitted in electronic format except as provided in paragraph (c)(2) of this section. The information shall be stored in the non-public EDGAR data storage area as correspondence. Supplemental information that is submitted in electronic format shall not be returned.

Note: Failure to submit a required electronic filing pursuant to this paragraph (a), as well as any required confirming electronic copy of a paper filing made in reliance on a hardship exemption, as provided in Rules 201 and 202 of Regulation S–T, will result in ineligibility to use Forms S–2, S–3, S–8, F–2 and F–3, restrict incorporation by reference of the document submitted in paper (see Rule 303 of Regulations S–T), or toll certain time periods associated with tender offers (see Rule 13e–4(f)(12) and Rule 14e–1(e)).

(b) *Permitted electronic submissions.* The following documents may be submitted to the Commission in electronic format, at the option of the electronic filer:

(1) Annual reports to security holders furnished for the information of the Commission under § 240.14a–3(c) of this chapter or § 240.14c–(b) of this chapter, under the requirements of Form 10–K or Form 10–KSB (§§ 249.310 or 249.310b of this chapter) filed by registrants under Exchange Act Section 15(d) (15 U.S.C. 78o(d)), or by foreign private issuers filed on Form 6–K (§ 249.306 of this chapter) under § 240.13a–16 of this chapter or § 240.15d–16 of this chapter;

(2) Notices of exempt solicitation furnished for the information of the Commission pursuant to Rule 14a–6(g) (§ 240.14a–6(g) of this chapter) and notices of exempt preliminary roll-up communications furnished for the information of the Commission pursuant to Rule 14a–6(n) (§ 240.14a–6(n) of this chapter);

(3) Form 11–K (§ 249.311 of this chapter). Registrants who satisfy their Form 11–K filing obligations by filing amendments to Forms 10–K or 10–KSB, as provided by Rule 15d–21 (§ 240.15d–21 of this chapter), also may choose to file such amendments in paper or electronic format;

(4) Form 144 (§ 239.144 of this chapter), where the issuer of the securities is subject to the reporting requirements of Section 13 or 15(d) of the Exchange Act (15 U.S.C. 78m or 78o(d), respectively);

(5) Periodic reports and reports with respect to distributions of primary obligations filed by:

(i) The International Bank for Reconstruction and Development under Section 15(a) of the Bretton Woods Agreements Act (22 U.S.C. 286k–1(a)) and Part 285 of this chapter;

(ii) The Inter–American Development Bank under Section 11(a) of the Inter–American Development Bank Act (22 U.S.C. 283h(a)) and Part 286 of this chapter;

(iii) The Asian Development Bank under Section 11(a) of the Asian Development Bank Act (22 U.S.C. 285h(a)) and Part 287 of this chapter;

(iv) The African Development Bank under Section 9(a) of the African Development Bank Act (22 U.S.C. 290i–9(a)) and Part 288 of this chapter;

(v) The International Finance Corporation under Section 13(a) of the International Finance Corporation Act (22 U.S.C. 282k(a)) and Part 289 of this chapter; and

(vi) The European Bank for Reconstruction and Development under Section 9(a) of the European Bank for Reconstruction and Development Act (22 U.S.C. 290*l*–7(a)) and Part 290 of this chapter;

(6) A report or other document submitted by a foreign private issuer under cover of Form 6–K (§ 249.306 of this chapter) that the issuer must furnish and make public under the laws of the jurisdiction in which the issuer is incorporated, domiciled or legally organized (the foreign private issuer's "home country"), or under the rules of the home country exchange on which the is-

suer's securities are traded, as long as the report or other document is not a press release, is not required to be and has not been distributed to the issuer's security holders, and, if discussing a material event, has already been the subject of a Form 6–K or other Commission filing or submission on EDGAR;

(7) Form CB (§§ 239.800 and 249.480 of this chapter) if the party filing or submitting the Form CB is not subject to the reporting requirements of Section 13 or 15(d) of the Exchange Act (15 U.S.C. 78m or 78o(d));

(8) Form F–X (§ 239.42 of this chapter) if:

(i) The party filing or submitting a Form CB (§§ 239.800 and 249.480 of this chapter) is not subject to the reporting requirements of Section 13 or Section 15(d) of the Exchange Act (15 U.S.C. 78m or 15 U.S.C. 78o(d)); or

(ii) Filed by a Canadian issuer when qualifying an offering statement pursuant to the provisions of Regulation A (§§ 230.251–230.263 of this chapter); and

(9) Form 25 (§ 249.25 of this chapter).

(c) *Documents to be filed in paper only.* The following shall not be submitted in electronic format:

(1)(i) Confidential treatment requests and the information with respect to which confidential treatment is requested;

(ii) Preliminary proxy materials and information statements with respect to a matter specified in Item 14 of Schedule 14A for which confidential treatment has been requested in the manner prescribed by Rule 14a–6(e)(2) or Rule 14c–5(d)(2);

(2) Supplemental information, if the submitter requests that the information be protected from public disclosure under the Freedom of Information Act (5 U.S.C. 552) pursuant to a request for confidential treatment under Rule 83 (§ 200.83 of this chapter) or if the submitter requests that the information be returned after staff review and the information is of the type typically returned by the staff pursuant to Rule 418(b) of Regulation C (§ 230.418(b) of this chapter) or Rule 12b–4 of Regulation 12B (§ 240.12b–4 of this chapter);

(3) Shareholder proposals and all related correspondence submitted pursuant to Rule 14a–8 of the Exchange Act (§ 240.14a–8 of this chapter);

(4) No-action and interpretive letter requests (§ 200.81 of this chapter and 15 U.S.C. 78*l* (h));

(5) Applications for exemptive relief filed pursuant to Sections 304 and 310 of the Trust Indenture Act;

(6) Filings relating to offerings exempt from registration under the Securities Act, including filings made pursuant to Regulation A (§§ 230.251–230.263 of this chapter), Regulation D (§§ 230.501–230.506 of this chapter) and Regulation E (§§ 230.601–230.610a of this chapter), as well as filings on Form 144 (§ 239.144 of this chapter) where the issuer of the securities is not subject to the reporting requirements of section 13 or 15(d) of the Exchange Act (15 U.S.C. 78m or 78o(d), respectively);

(7) Promotional and Sales Material submitted pursuant to Securities Act Industry Guide 5 (§ 229.801(e) of this chapter) or otherwise supplementally furnished for review by the staff of the Division of Corporation Finance; and sales literature submitted under Rule 24b–2 of the Investment Company Act (§ 270.24b–2 of this chapter);

(8) Documents and symbols in a foreign language (see Rule 306 of Regulation S–T);

(9) Exchange Act filings submitted to the Division of Market Regulation, except for Form 19b–4 (§ 249.819 of this chapter);

(10) Documents relating to investigations and litigation submitted pursuant to Subpart D of Part 201 of this chapter;

(11) Submissions under Sections 6(c), 17(g), and 33 of the Investment Company

Act (15 U.S.C. 80a–6(c), 80a–17(g), and 80a–32) and documents related to applications for exemptive relief under any section of the Act;

(12) Annual Reports to Security Holders furnished by Public Utility Holding Companies under Exhibit A to Form U5S (§ 259.5s of this chapter) or under rule 29 (§ 250.29 of this chapter);

(13) Reports to State Commissions, if furnished by Public Utility Holding Companies under Exhibit E to Form U5S (§ 259.5s of this chapter); and

(14) Maps furnished by Public Utility Holding Companies under Exhibits E to Forms U5B and U–1 (§§ 259.5b and 259.101 of this chapter);

(15) Annual reports filed with the Commission by indenture trustees pursuant to Section 313 of the Trust Indenture Act (15 U.S.C. 77mmm); and

(16) Applications for an exemption from Exchange Act reporting obligations filed pursuant to Section 12(h) of the Exchange Act (15 U.S.C. 78*l*(h)).

§ 232.102 Exhibits

(a) Exhibits to an electronic filing that have not previously been filed with the Commission shall be filed in electronic format, absent a hardship exemption. Previously filed exhibits, whether in paper or electronic format, may be incorporated by reference into an electronic filing to the extent permitted by § 228.10(f) and § 229.10 of this chapter, Rule 411 under the Securities Act (§ 230.411 of this chapter), Rule 12b–23 or 12b–32 under the Exchange Act (§ 240.12b–23 or § 240.12b–32 of this chapter), Rule 22 under the Public Utility Holding Company Act (§ 250.22 of this chapter), Rules 0–4, 8b–23, and 8b–32 under the Investment Company Act (§ 270.0–4, § 270.8b–23 and § 270.8b–32 of this chapter) and Rule 303 of Regulation S–T (§ 232.303). An electronic filer may, at its option, restate in electronic format an exhibit incorporated by reference that originally was filed in paper format.

Note to paragraph a: Exhibits to a Commission schedule filed pursuant to Section 13 or 14(d) of the Exchange Act may be filed in paper under cover of Form SE where such exhibits previously were filed in paper (prior to a registrant's becoming subject to mandated electronic filing or pursuant to a hardship exemption) and are required to be refiled pursuant to the schedule's general instructions. *See* Rule 311(b) of Regulation S–T (17 CFR 232.311(b)).

(b) Amendments to all exhibits shall be filed in electronic format, absent a hardship exemption.

(c) Notwithstanding any other provision of this section, an electronic filer shall, upon amendment, restate in electronic format its articles of incorporation, by-laws or investment advisory agreement (in the case of a registered investment company or a business development company).

(d) Each electronic filing requiring exhibits shall contain an exhibit index, which should immediately precede the exhibits filed with the document. The index shall list each exhibit filed. Whenever an exhibit is filed in paper pursuant to a temporary or continuing hardship exemption, the letter "P" shall be placed next to the listed exhibit in the exhibit index to reflect that the exhibit was filed in paper pursuant to such exemption. Whenever an electronic confirming copy of an exhibit is filed pursuant to a hardship exemption (§ 232.201 or § 232.202(d)), the exhibit index should specify where the confirming electronic copy can be located; in addition, the designation "CE" (confirming electronic) should be placed next to the listed exhibit in the exhibit index.

(e) Notwithstanding the provisions of paragraphs (a) through (d) of this section, any incorporation by reference by a registered investment company or a business development company must relate only to documents that have been filed in electronic format, unless the document has been filed in paper under a hardship exemption (§ 232.201 or 232.202) and any required confirming copy has been submitted:

(1) The document has been filed in paper pursuant to a hardship exemption (§§ 232.201 and 232.202 of this chapter) and any required confirming copy has been submitted or

(2) The document is an exhibit, filed in paper in accordance with applicable rules, to Form N–SAR being incorporated by reference only into another Form N–SAR filing.

(f) Persons submitting filings electronically under the Public Utility Act shall not be subject to paragraph (c) of this section.

§ 232.103 Liability for Transmission Errors or Omissions in Documents Filed Via EDGAR

An electronic filer shall not be subject to the liability and anti-fraud provisions of the federal securities laws with respect to an error or omission in an electronic filing resulting solely from electronic transmission errors beyond the control of the filer, where the filer corrects the error or omission by the filing of an amendment in electronic format as soon as reasonably practicable after the electronic filer becomes aware of the error or omission.

§ 232.104 Unofficial PDF Copies Included in an Electronic Submission

(a) An electronic submission, other than a Form 3 (§ 249.103 of this chapter), a Form 4 (§ 249.104 of this chapter), a Form 5 (§ 249.105 of this chapter) or a Form ID (§§ 239.63, 249.446, 259.602, 269.7 and 274.402 of this chapter), may include one unofficial PDF copy of each electronic document contained within that submission, tagged in the format required by the EDGAR filer manual.

(b) Except as provided in paragraphs (c) and (f) of this section, each unofficial PDF copy must be substantively equivalent to its associated electronic document contained in the electronic submission. An unofficial PDF copy may contain graphic and image material (but not animated graphics, or audio or video material), notwithstanding the fact that its HTML or ASCII document counterpart may not contain such material but instead may contain a fair and accurate narrative description or tabular representation of any omitted graphic or image material.

(c) If a filer omits an unofficial PDF copy from, or submits one or more flawed unofficial PDF copies in, the electronic submission of an official filing, the filer may add or resubmit an unofficial PDF copy by electronically submitting an amendment to the filing to which it relates. The amendment must include an explanatory note that the purpose of the amendment is to add or to correct an unofficial PDF copy.

(1) If such an amendment is filed, the official amendment may consist solely of the cover page (or first page of the document), the explanatory note, and the signature page and exhibit index (where appropriate). The corresponding unofficial copy must include the complete text of the official filing document for which the amendment is being submitted.

(2) If the amendment is being filed to add or resubmit an unofficial PDF copy of one or more exhibits, the submission may consist of the following: the official filing—consisting of the cover page (or first page of the document), the explanatory note, the signature page (where appropriate), the exhibit index, and a separate electronic exhibit document for each exhibit for which an unofficial PDF copy is being submitted—and the corresponding unofficial PDF copy of each exhibit document. However, the text of the official exhibit document need not repeat the text of the exhibit; that document may contain only the following legend: RESUBMITTED TO ADD/REPLACE UNOFFICIAL PDF COPY OF EXHIBIT.

(d) An unofficial PDF copy is not filed for purposes of section 11 of the Securities Act (15 U.S.C. 77k), section 18 of the Exchange Act (15 U.S.C. 78r), section 16 of the Public Utility Act (15 U.S.C. 79p), section 323 of the Trust Indenture Act (15 U.S.C. 77www), or section

34(b) of the Investment Company Act (15 U.S.C. 80a–33(b)), or otherwise subject to the liabilities of such sections, and is not part of any registration statement to which it relates. An unofficial PDF copy is, however, subject to all other civil liability and anti-fraud provisions of the above Acts or other laws.

(e) Unofficial PDF copies that are prospectuses are subject to liability under Section 12 of the Securities Act (15 U.S.C. 77*l*).

(f) An unofficial PDF copy of a correspondence document contained in an electronic submission need not be substantively equivalent to that correspondence document.

§ 232.105 Limitation on Use of HTML Documents and Hypertext Links

(a) Electronic filers must submit the following documents in ASCII: Form N–SAR (§ 274.101 of this chapter) and Form 13F (§ 249.325 of this chapter). Notwithstanding the provisions of this section, electronic filers may submit exhibits to Form N–SAR in HTML.

(b) Electronic filers may not include in any HTML document hypertext links to sites, locations, or documents outside the HTML document, except to links to officially filed documents within the current submission and to documents previously filed electronically and located in the EDGAR database on the Commission's public web site (www.sec.gov). Electronic filers also may include within an HTML document hypertext links to different sections within that single HTML document.

(c) If a filer includes an external hypertext link within a filed document, the information contained in the linked, material will not be considered part of the document for determining compliance with reporting obligations, but the inclusion of the link will cause the filer to be subject to the civil liability and antifraud provisions of the federal securities laws with reference to the information contained in the linked material.

§ 232.106 Prohibition Against Electronic Submissions Containing Executable Code

(a) Electronic submissions must not contain executable code. Attempted submissions identified as containing executable code will be suspended, unless the executable code is contained only in one or more PDF documents, in which case the submission will be accepted but the PDF document(s) containing executable code will be deleted and not disseminated.

(b) If an electronic submission has been accepted, and the Commission staff later determines that the accepted submission contains executable code, the staff may delete from the EDGAR system the entire accepted electronic submission or any document contained in the accepted electronic submission. The Commission staff may direct the electronic filer to resubmit electronically replacement document(s) or a replacement submission in its entirety, in compliance with this provision and the EDGAR Filer Manual.

Note to § 232.106: A violation of this section or the relevant EDGAR Filer Manual section also may be a violation of the Computer Fraud and Abuse Act of 1986, as amended, and other statutes and laws.

HARDSHIP EXEMPTIONS

§ 232.201 Temporary Hardship Exemption

(a) If an electronic filer experiences unanticipated technical difficulties preventing the timely preparation and submission of an electronic filing, other than a Form 3 (§ 249.103 of this chapter), a Form 4 (§ 249.104 of this chapter), a Form 5 (§ 249.105 of this chapter) or a Form ID (§§ 239.63, 249.446, 259.602, 269.7 and 274.402 of this chapter), the electronic filer may file the subject filing, under cover of Form TH (§§ 239.65, 249.447, 259.604, 269.10 and 274.404 of this chapter), in paper format no later than one business day after the date on which the filing was to be made.

(1) A microfiche copy of the paper format document shall be the official filing of the registrant for purposes of the federal securities laws.

(2) The following legend shall be set forth in capital letters on the cover page of the paper format document:

IN ACCORDANCE WITH RULE 201 OF REGULATION S–T, THIS (SPECIFY DOCUMENT) IS BEING FILED IN PAPER PURSUANT TO A TEMPORARY HARDSHIP EXEMPTION

(3) Signatures to the paper format document may be in typed form rather than manual format. See Rule 302 of Regulation S–T. All other requirements relating to paper format filings shall be satisfied.

(4) If the exemption pertains to a document filed pursuant to section 13(a) or 15(d) of the Exchange Act or section 30 of the Investment Company Act and the paper format document is filed in the manner specified in paragraph (a) of this section, the filing shall be deemed to have been filed by its required due date.

Notes: 1. Where a temporary hardship exemption relates to an exhibit only, the paper format exhibit shall be filed under cover of Form SE (§§ 239.64, 249.444, 259.603, 269.8, and 274.403 of this chapter).

2. Filers unable to submit a report within a prescribed time period because of electronic difficulties shall comply with the provisions of this section and shall not use Form 12b–25 (§ 249.322 of this chapter) as a notification of late filing.

(b) An electronic format copy of the filed paper format document shall be submitted to the Commission within six business days of filing the paper format document. The electronic format version shall contain the following statement in capital letters at the top of the first page of the document:

THIS DOCUMENT IS A COPY OF THE (SPECIFY DOCUMENT) FILED ON (DATE) PURSUANT TO A RULE 201 TEMPORARY HARDSHIP EXEMPTION

Note 1: Failure to submit the confirming electronic copy of a paper filing made in reliance on the temporary hardship exemption, as required in paragraph (b) of this section, will result in ineligibility to use Forms S–2, S–3, S–8, F–2 and F–3 (*see* §§ 239.12, 239.13, 239.16b, 239.32 and 239.33 of this section, respectively), restrict incorporation by reference of the document submitted in paper (*see* Rule 303 of Regulation S–T (§ 232.303)), and toll certain time periods associated with tender offers (*see* Rule 13e–4(f)(12) and Rule 14e–1(e)).

Note 2: If the exemption relates to an exhibit only, the requirement to submit a confirming electronic copy shall be satisfied by refiling the exhibit in electronic format in an amendment to the filing to which it relates. The confirming copy tag should not be used. The amendment should note that the purpose of the amendment is to add an electronic copy of an exhibit previously filed in paper pursuant to a temporary hardship exemption.

§ 232.202 Continuing Hardship Exemption

(a) An electronic filer may apply in writing for a continuing hardship exemption if all or part of a filing or group of filings, other than a Form ID (§§ 239.63, 249.446, 259.602, 269.7 and 274.402 of this chapter), otherwise to be filed in electronic format cannot be so filed without undue burden or expense. Such written application shall be made at least ten business days prior to the required due date of the filing(s) or the proposed filing date, as appropriate, or within such shorter period as may be permitted. The written application shall contain the information set forth in paragraph (b) of this section.

(1) The application shall not be deemed granted until the applicant is notified by the Commission or the staff.

(2) If the Commission, or the staff acting pursuant to delegated authority, denies the application for a continuing hardship exemption, the electronic filer shall file the required document in electronic format on the required due date or the proposed filing date or such other date as may be permitted.

(3) If the Commission, or the staff acting pursuant to delegated authority, determines that the grant of the exemption is appropriate and consistent with the public interest and the protection of investors and so notifies the applicant, the electronic filer shall follow the procedures set forth in paragraph (c) of this section.

(b) The request for the continuing hardship exemption shall include, but not be limited to, the following:

(1) The reason(s) that the necessary hardware and software is not available without unreasonable burden and expense;

(2) The burden and expense involved to employ alternative means to make the electronic submission; and/or

(3) The reasons for not submitting electronically the document or group of documents, as well as justification for the requested time period.

(c) If the request is granted, the electronic filer shall submit the document or group of documents for which the continuing hardship exemption is granted in paper format on the required due date specified in the applicable form, rule or regulation, or the proposed filing date, as appropriate. The following legend shall be placed in capital letters at the top of the cover page of the paper format document(s):

IN ACCORDANCE WITH RULE 202 OF REGULATION S–T, THIS (SPECIFY DOCUMENT) IS BEING FILED IN PAPER PURSUANT TO A CONTINUING HARDSHIP EXEMPTION

(d) If a continuing hardship exemption is granted for a limited time period, the grant may be conditioned upon the filing of the document or group of documents that is the subject of the exemption in electronic format upon the expiration of the period for which the exemption is granted. The electronic format version shall contain the following statement in capital letters at the top of the first page of the document:

THIS DOCUMENT IS A COPY OF THE (SPECIFY DOCUMENT) FILED ON (DATE) PURSUANT TO A RULE 202(d) CONTINUING HARDSHIP EXEMPTION.

Note 1: Where a continuing hardship exemption is granted with respect to an exhibit only, the paper format exhibit shall be filed under cover of Form SE (§§ 239.64, 249.444, 259.603, 269.8 and 274.403 of this chapter).

Note 2: If the exemption relates to an exhibit only and a confirming electronic copy of the exhibit is required to be submitted, the exhibit should be refiled in electronic format in an amendment to the filing to which it relates. The confirming copy tag should not be used. The amendment should note that the purpose of the amendment is to add an electronic copy of an exhibit previously filed in paper pursuant to a continuing hardship exemption.

Note 3: Failure to submit a required confirming electronic copy of a paper filing made in reliance on a continuing hardship exemption granted pursuant to paragraph (d) of this section will result in ineligibility to use Forms S–2, S–3, S–8, F–2 and F–3 (see, §§ 239.12, 239.13, 239.16b, 239.32 and 239.33, respectively), restrict incorporation by reference of the document submitted in paper (see Rule 303 of Regulation S–T (§ 232.303)), and toll certain time periods associated with tender offers (see Rule 13e–4(f)(12) (§ 240.13e–4(f)(12)) and Rule 14e–1(e) (§ 240.14e–1(e))).

PREPARATION OF ELECTRONIC SUBMISSIONS

§ 232.301 EDGAR Filer Manual

Filers must prepare electronic filings in the manner prescribed by the EDGAR Filer Manual, promulgated by the Commission, which sets out the technical formatting requirements for electronic submissions. The requirements for filers using modernized EDGARLink are set forth in the EDGAR Release 8.10 EDGARLink Filer Manual Volume I, dated February 2005. Additional provisions applicable to Form N–SAR filers and Online Forms filers are set forth in the EDGAR Release 8.10 N–SAR Supplement Filer Manual Volume II, dated February 2005, and the EDGAR Release 8.10 OnlineForms Filer Manual Volume III, dated February 2005. All of these provisions have been incorporated by reference into the Code of Federal Regulations, which action was approved by the Director of the Federal Register in accordance with 5 U.S.C. 552(a) and 1 CFR Part 51. You must comply with these requirements in order for documents to be timely received and accepted. You can obtain paper copies of the EDGAR Filer Manual from the following address: Public Reference Room, U.S. Securities and Exchange Commission, 450 Fifth Street, NW., Washington, DC 20549–0102 or by calling Thomson Financial Inc at

(800) 638–8241. Electronic format copies are available on the Commission's Web site. The address for the Filer Manual is http://www.sec.gov/info/edgar.shtml. You can also photocopy the document at the National Archives and Records Administration (NARA). For information on the availability of this material at NARA, call 202–741–6030, or go to: http://www.archives.gov/federal_register/code_of_federal_regulations/ibr_locations.html.

§ 232.302 Signatures

(a) Required signatures to, or within, any electronic submission (including, without limitation, signatories within the certifications required by §§240.13a–14, 240.15d–14 and 270.30a–2 of this chapter) must be in typed form rather than manual format. Signatures in an HTML document that are not required may, but are not required to, be presented in an HTML graphic or image file within the electronic filing, in compliance with the formatting requirements of the EDGAR Filer Manual. When used in connection with an electronic filing the term "signature" means an electronic entry in the form of a magnetic impulse or other form of computer data compilation of any letters or series of letters or characters comprising a name, executed, adopted or authorized as a signature. Signatures are not required in unofficial PDF copies submitted in accordance with § 232.104.

(b) Each signatory to an electronic filing (including, without limitation, each signatory to the certifications required by §§240.13a–14, 240.15d–14 and 270.30a–2 of this chapter) shall manually sign a signature page or other document authenticating, acknowledging or otherwise adopting his or her signature that appears in typed form within the electronic filing. Such document shall be executed before or at the time the electronic filing is made and shall be retained by the filer for a period of five years. Upon request, an electronic filer shall furnish to the Commission or its staff a copy of any or all documents retained pursuant to this section.

(c) Where the Commission's rules require a registrant to furnish to a national securities exchange or national securities association paper copies of a document filed with the Commission in electronic format, signatures to such paper copies may be in typed form.

§ 232.303 Incorporation by Reference

(a) The following documents shall not be incorporated by reference into an electronic filing:

(1) Any document filed in paper in violation of mandated electronic filing requirements;

(2) Any document filed in paper pursuant to a hardship exemption for which a required confirming electronic copy has not been submitted.

(3) For a registered investment company or a business development company, documents that have not been filed in electronic format, unless the document has been filed in paper under a hardship exemption (§ 232.201 or 232.202 of this chapter) and any required confirming copy has been submitted.

(b) If a filer incorporates by reference into an electronic filing any portion of an annual or quarterly report to security holders, it must also file the portion of the annual or quarterly report to security holders in electronic format as an exhibit to the filing, as required by Regulation S–K Item 601(b)(13) (§ 229.601(b)(13) of this chapter) and Regulation S–B Item 601(b)(13) (§ 228.601(b)(13) of this chapter). If a foreign private issuer incorporates by reference into an electronic filing any portion of an annual or other report to security holders, or of a Form 6–K report (§ 249.306 of this chapter) filed or submitted in paper, it must also file the incorporated portion in electronic format as an exhibit to the filing. The requirements of this paragraph do not apply to incorporation by reference by an investment company from an annual or quarterly report to security holders.

§ 232.304 Graphic, Image, Audio and Video Material

(a) If a filer includes graphic, image, audio or video material in a document delivered to investors and others that is not reproduced in an electronic filing, the electronically filed version of that document must include a fair and accurate narrative description, tabular representation or transcript of the omitted material. Such descriptions, representations or transcripts may be included in the text of the electronic filing at the point where the graphic, image, audio or video material is presented in the delivered version, or they may be listed in an appendix to the electronic filing. Immaterial differences between the delivered and electronically filed versions, such as pagination, color, type size or style, or corporate logo need not be described.

Note to paragraph (a): If the omitted graphic, image, audio or video material includes data, filers must include a tabular representation or other appropriate representation of that data in the electronically filed version of the document.

(b)(1) The graphic, image, audio and video material in the version of a document delivered to investors and others is deemed part of the electronic filing and subject to the civil liability and anti-fraud provisions of the federal securities laws.

(2) Narrative descriptions, tabular representations or transcripts of graphic, image, audio and video material included in an electronic filing or appendix thereto also are deemed part of the filing. However, to the extent such descriptions, representations or transcripts represent a good faith effort to fairly and accurately describe omitted graphic, image, audio or video material, they are not subject to the civil liability and anti-fraud provisions of the federal securities laws.

(c) An electronic filer must retain for a period of five years a copy of each publicly distributed document, in the format used, that contains graphic, image, audio or video material where such material is not included in the version filed with the Commission. The five-year period shall commence as of the filing date, or the date that appears on the document, whichever is later. Upon request, an electronic filer shall furnish to the Commission or its staff a copy of any or all of the documents contained in the file.

(d) For electronically filed ASCII documents, the performance graph that is to appear in registrant proxy and information statements relating to annual meetings of security holders (or special meetings or written consents in lieu of such meetings) at which directors will be elected, as required by Item 402(*l*) of Regulation S–K (§ 229.402(*l*) of this chapter), and the line graph that is to appear in registrant annual reports to security holders or prospectuses, as required by paragraph (b) of Item 5 of Form N–1A (§ 274.11A of this chapter), must be furnished to the Commission by presenting the data in tabular or chart form within the electronic ASCII document, in compliance with paragraph (a) of this section and the formatting requirements of the EDGAR Filer Manual.

(e) Notwithstanding the provisions of paragraphs (a) through (d) of this section, electronically filed HTML documents must present the following information in an HTML graphic or image file within the electronic submission in compliance with the formatting requirements of the EDGAR Filer Manual: the performance graph that is to appear in registrant proxy and information statements relating to annual meetings of security holders (or special meetings or written consents in lieu of such meetings) at which directors will be elected, as required by Item 402(*l*) of Regulation S–K (§ 229.402(*l*) of this chapter); the line graph that is to appear in registrant annual reports to security holders or prospectuses, as required by paragraph (b) of Item 5 of Form N–1A (§ 274.11A of this chapter); and any other graphic material required by rule or form to be filed with the Commission. Filers may, but are not required to, submit any other graphic material in an HTML document by presenting the data in an HTML graphic or image file within the electronic filing, in compliance with the formatting requirements of the EDGAR

Filer Manual. However, filers may not present in a graphic or image file information such as text or tables that users must be able to search and/or download into spreadsheet form (*e.g.*, financial statements); filers must present such material as text in an ASCII document or as text or an HTML table in an HTML document.

(f) Electronic filers may not include animated graphics in any EDGAR document.

§ 232.305 Number of Characters Per Line; Tabular and Columnar Information

(a) The narrative portion of a document shall not exceed 80 characters per line, including blank spaces, and shall not be presented in multi-column newspaper format. Non-narrative information (*e.g.*, financial statements) may be presented in tabular or columnar format and may exceed 80 positions only if it is tagged as specified in the EDGAR Filer Manual. In no event shall information presented in tabular or columnar format exceed 132 positions wide.

(b) Paragraph (a) of this section does not apply to HTML documents or XBRL-Related Documents (§ 232.11).

§ 232.306 Foreign Language Documents and Symbols

(a) All electronic filings and submissions must be in the English language, except as otherwise provided by paragraph (d) of this section. If a filing or submission requires the inclusion of a document that is in a foreign language, a party must submit instead a fair and accurate English translation of the foreign language document in accordance with § 230.403(c) or § 240.12b–12(d) of this chapter, except as otherwise provided by paragraph (c) of this section. Alternatively, if the foreign language document is an exhibit or attachment to a filing or submission subject to review by the Division of Corporation Finance, a party may provide a fair and accurate English summary of the foreign language document if permitted by § 230.403(c)(3) or § 240.12b–12(d)(3) of this chapter.

(b) When including an English summary or English translation of a foreign language document in an electronic filing or submission, a party may also submit a copy of the unabridged foreign language document in paper under cover of Form SE (§§ 239.64, 249.444, 259.603, 269.8, and 274.403 of this chapter) in accordance with § 232.311 of this chapter. A filer must provide a copy of any foreign language document upon the request of Commission staff.

(c) A foreign government or its political subdivision must electronically file a fair and accurate English translation, if available, of its latest annual budget as presented to its legislative body, as Exhibit B to Form 18 (§ 249.218 of this chapter) or Exhibit (c) to Form 18–K (§ 249.318 of this chapter). If no English translation is available, a foreign government or political subdivision must submit a copy of the foreign language version of its latest annual budget in paper under cover of Form SE (§§ 239.64, 249.444, 259.603, 269.8, and 274.403 of this chapter).

(d) A Canadian issuer may file an HTML document, as defined in § 232.11 of this chapter, that contains text in both French and English if the issuer included the French text to comply with the requirements of the Canadian securities administrator or other Canadian authority, and the French text is in an exhibit to or part of:

(1) A registration statement on Form F–7, F–8, F–9, F–10, or F–80 (§§ 239.37, 239.38, 239.39, 239.40, and 239.41 of this chapter);

(2) A registration statement or annual report on Form 40–F (§ 249.240f of this chapter); or

(3) A Schedule 13E–4F (§ 240.13e–102 of this chapter), Schedule 14D–1F (§ 240.14d–102), or Schedule 14D–9F (§ 240.14d–103).

(e) Foreign currency denominations must be expressed in words or letters in the English language rather than representative symbols, except that HTML documents may include any representative foreign currency symbols that the EDGAR Filer Manual specifies. The limitations of this paragraph do not apply to unofficial PDF copies submitted in accordance with Rule 104 of Regulation S–T (§ 232.104).

§ 232.307 Bold Face Type

(a) Provisions requiring presentation of information in bold face type shall be satisfied in an electronic format document by presenting such information in capital letters.

(b) Paragraph (a) of this section does not apply to HTML documents.

§ 232.308 Type Size and Font; Legibility

Provisions relating to type size, font and other legibility requirements shall not apply to electronic format documents.

§ 232.309 Paper Size; Binding; Sequential Numbering; Number of Copies

(a) Requirements as to paper size, binding, and sequential page numbering shall not apply to electronic format documents.

(b) An electronic format document, submitted in the manner prescribed by the EDGAR Filer Manual, shall satisfy any requirement that more than one copy of such document be filed with or provided to the Commission.

§ 232.310 Marking Changed Material

Provisions requiring the marking of changed materials are satisfied in ASCII and HTML documents by inserting the tag <R> before and the tag </R> following a paragraph containing changed material. HTML documents may be marked to show changed materials within paragraphs. Financial statements and notes thereto need not be marked for changed material.

§ 232.311 Documents Submitted in Paper Under Cover of Form SE

Form SE (§§ 239.64, 249.444, 259.603, 269.8, and 274.403 of this chapter) shall be filed as a paper cover sheet to the following documents submitted to the Commission in paper:

(a) Exhibits filed in paper pursuant to a hardship exemption shall be filed under cover of Form SE. See Rules 201 and 202 of Regulation S–T.

(b) Exhibits to a Commission schedule filed pursuant to Section 13 or 14(d) of the Exchange Act may be filed in paper under cover of Form SE where such exhibits previously were filed in paper (prior to a registrant's becoming subject to mandated electronic filing or pursuant to a hardship exemption) and are required to be refiled pursuant to the schedule's general instructions.

(c) Annual Reports to Security Holders furnished by Public Utility Holding Companies as Exhibit A to Form U5S or under Rule 29 (§ 250.29 of this chapter) shall be filed in paper under cover of Form SE.

(d) Reports to State Commissions, if furnished by Public Utility Holding Companies as Exhibit E to Form U5S, shall be filed in paper under cover of Form SE.

(e) Maps furnished by Public Utility Holding Companies under Exhibits E to Forms U5B and U–1 (§§ 259.5b and 259.101 of this chapter) shall be filed in paper under cover of Form SE.

(f) A party may submit a copy of an unabridged foreign language document in paper under cover of Form SE if the electronic filing or submission includes an English summary or English translation of the foreign language document in accordance with § 232.306(b) or if permitted by the applicable form.

(g) A foreign government or political subdivision that is not filing in electronic format an English translation of its latest annual budget submitted as Exhibit B to Form 18 (§ 249.218 of this chapter) or Exhibit (c) to Form 18–K (§ 249.318 of this chapter) must file a copy of the foreign language version of its latest annual budget in paper under cover of Form SE in accordance with § 232.306(c) of this chapter.

(h) The Form SE shall be submitted in the following manner:

(1) If the subject of a temporary hardship exemption is an exhibit only, the exhibit shall be filed under cover of Form SE no later than one business day after the date the exhibit was to be filed electronically.

(2) An exhibit filed pursuant to a continuing hardship exemption, or any other document filed in paper under cover of Form SE (other than an exhibit filed pursuant to a temporary hardship exemption), as allowed by paragraphs (a) through (g) of this section, may be filed up to six business days prior to, or on the date of filing of, the electronic format document to which it relates but shall not be filed after such filing date. If a paper document is submitted in this manner, requirements that the document be filed with, provided with or accompany the electronic filing shall be satisfied.

(i) Any requirements as to delivery or furnishing the information to persons other than the Commission shall not be affected by this section.

§ 232.312 Accommodation for certain information in filings with respect to asset-backed securities

(a) For filings with respect to asset-backed securities filed on or before December 31, 2009, the information provided in response to Item 1105 of Regulation AB (§ 229.1105 of this chapter) may be provided under the following conditions on an Internet Web site for inclusion in the prospectus for the asset-backed securities, and will be deemed to be included in the prospectus included in the registration statement, in lieu of reproducing the information in the electronically filed version of that document. Terms used in this section have the same meaning as in Item 1101 of Regulation AB (§ 229.1101 of this chapter).

(1) The prospectus in the registration statement at the time of effectiveness shall disclose the intention to provide such information through a Web site and the prospectus to be filed pursuant to § 230.424 of this chapter shall provide the specific Internet address where the information is posted.

(2) Such information shall be provided through the Web site unrestricted as to access and free of charge.

(3) Such information shall remain available on the Web site for a period of not less than five years. If a subsequent update or change is made to the information, the date of such update or change shall be clearly indicated on the Web site.

(4) The registrant shall retain all versions of such information provided through the Web site for a period of not less than five years in a form that permits delivery to an investor or the Commission. Upon request, the registrant shall furnish to the Commission or its staff a copy of any or all information retained pursuant to this requirement.

(5) The registration statement shall contain the undertakings required by Item 512(*l*) of Regulation S-K (§ 229.512(*l*) of this chapter) that:

(i) Except as otherwise provided by this section, such information provided through the specified Internet address is deemed to be a part of the prospectus included in the registration statement for the asset-backed securities.

(ii) The registrant shall provide to any person without charge, upon request, a copy of such information provided through the specified Internet address as of the date of the prospectus included in the registration statement if a subsequent update or change is made to that information.

Note to paragraph (a). With respect to paragraphs (a)(3) and (a)(4) of this section, the five-year period shall commence from the filing date of the prospectus filed pursuant to § 230.424 of this chapter, or the date of first use of the prospectus, whichever is earlier.

(b) This section does not affect any obligation to provide any other information in the filing electronically on EDGAR.

§ 232.401 XBRL–Related Document submissions

(a) An electronic filer that participates in the voluntary XBRL (eXtensible Business Reporting Language) program may submit XBRL-Related Documents (§ 232.11) in electronic format as an exhibit to: the filing to which they relate; an amendment to such filing; or, if the electronic filer is eligible to file a Form 8–K (§ 249.308 of this chapter) or a Form 6–K (§ 249.306 of this chapter), a Form 8–K or a Form 6–K, as applicable, that references the filing to which the XBRL-Related Documents relate if such Form 8–K or Form 6–K is submitted no earlier than the date of that filing. The XBRL-Related Documents must comply with the content and format requirements of this section, be submitted as an exhibit to a form that contains the disclosure required by this section and be submitted in accordance with the EDGAR Filer Manual and, as applicable, one of Item 601(b)(100) of Regulation S–K (§ 229.601(b)(100) of this chapter), Item 601(b)(100) of Regulation S–B (§ 228.601(b)(100) of this chapter), Form 20–F (§ 249.220f of this chapter), Form 6–K or § 270.8b–33 of this chapter.

(b) XBRL-Related Documents must consist of mandatory content and may consist of optional content but only if the optional content accompanies the mandatory content in the same submission.

(1) Mandatory content consists of a complete set of information for all periods presented in the corresponding official EDGAR filing from one or more of the following categories (as filed in the corresponding official EDGAR filing):

(i) The complete set of financial statements (the only exceptions are that notes to the financial statements and schedules related to the financial statements may be omitted unless the electronic filer is a registered management investment company in which case it must include Schedule I—Investments in Securities of Unaffiliated Issuers (§ 210.12–12 of this chapter);

(ii) Earnings information set forth in Form 6–K or Items 2.02 or 8.01 of Form 8–K (whether contained in the body of the Form 6–K or Form 8–K or in an exhibit, and whether filed or furnished); or

(iii) Financial highlights or condensed financial information set forth in Item 8(a) of Form N–1A (§ 239.15A and § 274.11A of this chapter), Item 4.1 of Form N–2 (§ 239.14 and § 274.11a–1 of this chapter) or Item 4(a) of Form N–3 (§ 239.17a and § 274.11b of this chapter), as applicable.

(2) Optional content can consist only of a complete set of information that is:

(i) For all periods presented in the corresponding official EDGAR filing;

(ii) Related to financial information in the corresponding official EDGAR filing that is simultaneously submitted as mandatory content (as specified in paragraph (b)(1) of this section); and

(iii) From one or more of the following categories (as filed in the corresponding official EDGAR filing):

(A) Audit opinions (as specified by Rule 2–02 of Regulation S–X (§ 210.2–02 of this chapter));

(B) Interim review reports (as specified by Rule 10–01(d) of Regulation S–X (§ 210.10–01(d) of this chapter));

(C) Reports of management on the financial statements;

(D) Certifications;

(E) Management's discussion and analysis of financial condition and results of operations (as specified by Item 303 of Regulation S–K (§ 229.303 of this chapter));

(F) Management's discussion and analysis or plan of operation (as specified by Item 303 of Regulation S–B (§ 228.303 of this chapter));

(G) Operating and financial review and prospects (as specified by Item 5 of Form 20–F); or

(H) Management's discussion of fund performance (as specified by Item 22(b)(7) of Form N–1A).

(c) XBRL-Related Documents must appear in voluntary program format. XBRL-Related Documents appear in voluntary program format if:

(1) Each data element (i.e., all text and all line item names and associated values, dates and other labels) contained in the XBRL-Related Documents reflects the same information in the corresponding official EDGAR filing (i.e., the HTML or ASCII version);

(2) No data element contained in the corresponding official EDGAR filing is changed, deleted or summarized in the XBRL-Related Documents;

(3) The XBRL-Related Documents correlate to the appropriate version of a standard taxonomy, supplemented with extension taxonomies as specified in the EDGAR Filer Manual (§ 232.11);

(4) Each data element contained in the XBRL-Related Documents is matched with an appropriate tag in accordance with any applicable taxonomy; and

(5) The XBRL-Related Documents contain any additional mark-up related content (e.g., the XBRL tags themselves, identification of the core XML documents used and other technology related content) not found in the corresponding official EDGAR filing that are necessary to comply with the EDGAR Filer Manual requirements.

(d) The filing with which XBRL-Related Documents are submitted as an exhibit must contain the disclosures specified in paragraph (d)(1) of this section in the location specified in paragraph (d)(2) of this section.

(1) The filing must disclose:

(i) That the financial information contained in the XBRL-Related Documents is "unaudited" or "unreviewed," as applicable;

(ii) That the purpose of submitting the XBRL-Related Documents is to test the related format and technology and, as a result, investors should not rely on the XBRL-Related Documents in making investment decisions; and

(iii) The identity of the corresponding official EDGAR filing (but only if the filing is a Form 8–K or Form 6–K or an amendment to a Form 8–K or Form 6–K and a purpose of filing the form was to submit as an exhibit XBRL-Related Documents that present information related to financial information filed as part of a different form in the corresponding official EDGAR filing).

(2) The disclosures required by paragraph (d)(1) of this section must appear, as applicable, in:

(i) The exhibit index of a Form 10–K (§ 249.310 of this chapter), 10–Q (§ 249.308a of this chapter), 10 (§ 249.210 of this chapter), 10–SB (§ 249.210b of this chapter), 10–KSB (§ 249.310b of this chapter), 10–QSB (§ 249.308b of this chapter) or 20–F;

(ii) Item 2.02 or 8.01 of a Form 8–K; or

(iii) The body of a Form 6–K, N–CSR (§ 274.128 of this chapter) or N–Q (§ 274.130 of this chapter).

Note to § 232.401: Although XBRL-Related Documents are required by this section to comply with content and format requirements related to the corresponding official EDGAR filing, the purpose of submitting the XBRL-Related Documents is to test the related format and technology and, as a result, investors and others should continue to rely on the official version of the filing and not rely on the XBRL-Related Documents in making investment decisions.

§ 232.402 Liability for XBRL-Related Documents

(a) *Not deemed filed for liability purposes.* XBRL-Related Documents, regardless of whether they are exhibits to a document incorporated by reference into a filing:

(1) Are not deemed filed for purposes of section 18 of the Exchange Act (15 U.S.C. 78r) or section 34(b) of the Investment Company Act (15 U.S.C. 80a–33(b)) or otherwise subject to the liabilities of these sections;

(2) Are not deemed incorporated by reference;

(3) Are subject to all other liability and anti-fraud provisions of these Acts; and

(4) Are deemed filed for purposes of Item 103 of Regulation S–T (§ 232.103).

(b) *Accurate reflection of underlying documents.* An electronic filer is not liable under the Securities Act, Exchange Act, Public Utility Act, Trust Indenture Act or Investment Company Act for information in its XBRL-Related Documents that complies with the requirements of Item 401 of Regulation S–T (§ 232.401) to the extent that such information was not materially false or misleading in the corresponding official EDGAR filing. To the extent the information in an electronic filer's XBRL-Related Documents does not comply with the requirements of Item 401, the information in the XBRL-Related Documents will be deemed to comply with Item 401 for purposes of this paragraph if the electronic filer makes a good faith and reasonable attempt to comply with Item 401 and, as soon as reasonably practicable after the electronic filer becomes aware that the information in the XBRL-Related Documents does not comply with Item 401, the electronic filer amends the XBRL-Related Documents and, as a result, the information complies with Item 401.

EDGAR FUNCTIONS

§ 232.501 Modular Submissions and Segmented Filings

An electronic filer may use the following procedures to submit information to the EDGAR system for subsequent inclusion in an electronic filing:

(a) *Modular submissions.* (1) One or more electronic format documents may be submitted for storage in the non-public EDGAR data storage area as a modular submission for subsequent inclusion in one or more electronic submissions.

(2) An electronic filer shall be permitted a maximum of ten modular submissions in the non-public EDGAR data storage area at any time, not to exceed a total of one megabyte of digital information. If an electronic filer attempts to submit a modular filing which would cause either of these limits to be exceeded, EDGAR will suspend the modular submission and notify the electronic filer by electronic mail. After six business days, the modular submission held in suspense will be deleted from the system.

(3) A modular submission may be corrected or amended only by resubmitting the entire modular submission.

(b) *Segmented filings.* (1) Segments of a document intended to become an electronic filing may be submitted to the non-public EDGAR data storage area for assembly as a segmented filing.

(2) Segments shall be submitted no more than six business days in advance of the anticipated filing date and are not limited in number or size. They may be submitted from several geographic locations by more than one filing entity. Segments may be included in only one electronic filing. Once used, segments will be removed from the non-public EDGAR data storage area. The

assembly of segments into a segmented filing shall be effected pursuant to the applicable provisions of the EDGAR Filer Manual. If segments are not prepared in accordance with the EDGAR Filer Manual, the filing will not be constructed. The filing date of a segmented filing shall be the date upon which the filing is assembled and satisfies the requirements of Rule 13(a) of Regulation S–T (§ 232.13(a)).

(3) Segments may be corrected or amended only by resubmitting the entire segment.

(c) A modular submission or segment shall not:

(1) be publicly available;

(2) be deemed filed with the Commission for purposes of Securities Act section 11, Exchange Act section 18, Public Utility Act section 16, Trust Indenture Act section 323, or Investment Company Act section 34(b) prior to its inclusion in a filing; or

(3) be deemed to constitute an official filing prior to its inclusion in a filing under the federal securities laws. Once a modular submission or segment has been included in an electronic filing, the liability and anti-fraud provisions of the Securities Act, the Exchange Act, the Trust Indenture Act, the Public Utility Act and the Investment Company Act shall apply to the electronic filing.

FORMS UNDER THE SECURITIES ACT OF 1933

1. FORMS PURSUANT TO REGULATION A

FORM 1–A

REGULATION A OFFERING STATEMENT UNDER THE SECURITIES ACT OF 1933

(Exact name of issuer as specified in its charter)

(State or other jurisdiction of incorporation or organization)

(Address, including zip code, and telephone number, including area code of issuer's principal executive offices)

(Name, address, including zip code, and telephone number, including area code, of agent for service)

(Primary standard Industrial Classification Code Number) (I.R.S. Employer Identification Number)

The following delaying notation is optional, but see Rule 252(g) before omitting it:

This offering statement shall only be qualified upon order of the Commission, unless a subsequent amendment is filed indicating the intention to become qualified by operation of the terms of Regulation A.

GENERAL INSTRUCTIONS

I. Eligibility Requirements for Use of Form 1–A

This form is to be used for securities offerings made pursuant to Regulation A. Careful attention should be directed to the terms, conditions and requirements of the regulation, especially Rule 251, inasmuch as the exemption is not available to all issuers or to every type of securities transaction. Further, the aggregate offering amount of securities which may be sold in any 12 month period is strictly limited to $5 million.

II. Preparation and Filing of the Offering Statement

An offering statement shall be prepared by all persons seeking exemption pursuant to the provisions of Regulation A. Parts I, II and III shall be addressed by all issuers. Part II of the form which relates to the content of the required offering circular provides several alternate formats depending upon the nature and/or business of the issuer; only one format needs to be followed and provided in the offering statement. General information regarding the preparation, format, content of, and where to file the offering statement is contained in Rule 252. Requirements relating to the offering circular are contained in Rules 253 and 255. The offering statement may be printed, mimeographed, lithographed, or typewritten or prepared by any similar process which will result in clearly legible copies.

III. Supplemental Information

The following information shall be furnished to the Commission as supplemental information:

(1) A statement as to whether or not the amount of compensation to be allowed or paid

to the underwriter has been cleared with the NASD.

(2) Any engineering, management or similar report referenced in the offering circular.

(3) Such other information as requested by the staff in support of statements, representations and other assertions contained in the offering statement.

PART I—NOTIFICATION

The information requested shall be provided in the order which follows specifying each item number; the text of each item as presented in this form may be omitted. All items shall be addressed and negative responses should be included.

Item 1. Significant Parties

List the full names and business and residential addresses, as applicable, for the following persons:

(a) the issuer's directors;

(b) the issuer's officers;

(c) the issuer's general partners;

(d) record owners of 5 percent or more of any class of the issuer's equity securities;

(e) beneficial owners of 5 percent or more of any class of the issuer's equity securities;

(f) promoters of the issuer;

(g) affiliates of the issuer;

(h) counsel to the issuer with respect to the proposed offering;

(i) each underwriter with respect to the proposed offering;

(j) the underwriter's directors;

(k) the underwriter's officers;

(*l*) the underwriter's general partners; and

(m) counsel to the underwriter.

Item 2. Application of Rule 262

(a) State whether any of the persons identified in response to Item 1 are subject to any of the disqualification provisions set forth in Rule 262.

(b) If any such person is subject to these provisions, provide a full description including pertinent names, dates and other details, as well as whether or not an application has been made pursuant to Rule 262 for a waiver of such disqualification and whether or not such application has been granted or denied.

Item 3. Affiliate Sales

If any part of the proposed offering involves the resale of securities by affiliates of the issuer, confirm that the following description does not apply to the issuer.

The issuer has not had a net income from operations of the character in which the issuer intends to engage for at least one of its last two fiscal years.

Item 4. Jurisdictions in Which Securities Are to be Offered

(a) List the jurisdiction in which the securities are to be offered by underwriters, dealers or salespersons.

(b) List the jurisdictions in which the securities are to be offered other than by underwriters, dealers or salesmen and state the method by which such securities are to be offered.

Item 5. Unregistered Securities Issued or Sold Within One Year

(a) As to any unregistered securities issued by the issuer or any of its predecessors or affiliated issuers within one year prior to the filing of this Form 1–A, state:

(1) the name of such issuer;

(2) the title and amount of securities issued;

(3) the aggregate offering price or other consideration for which they were issued

and the basis for computing the amount thereof;

(4) the names and identities of the persons to whom the securities were issued.

(b) As to any unregistered securities of the issuer or any of its predecessors or affiliated issuers which were sold within one year prior to the filing of this Form 1–A by or for the account of any person who at the time was a director, officer, promoter or principal security holder of the issuer of such securities, or was an underwriter of any securities of such issuer, furnish the information specified in subsections (1) through (4) of paragraph (a).

(c) Indicate the section of the Securities Act or Commission rule or regulation relied upon for exemption from the registration requirements of such Act and state briefly the facts relied upon for such exemption.

Item 6. Other Present or Proposed Offerings

State whether or not the issuer or any of its affiliates is currently offering or contemplating the offering of any securities in addition to those covered by this Form 1–A. If so, describe fully the present or proposed offering.

Item 7. Marketing Arrangements

(a) Briefly describe any arrangement known to the issuer or to any person named in response to Item 1 above or to any selling securityholder in the offering covered by this Form 1–A for any of the following purposes:

(1) To limit or restrict the sale of other securities of the same class as those to be offered for the period of distribution;

(2) To stabilize the market for any of the securities to be offered;

(3) For withholding commissions, or otherwise to hold each underwriter or dealer responsible for the distribution of its participation.

(b) Identify any underwriter that intends to confirm sales to any accounts over which it exercises discretionary authority and include an estimate of the amount of securities so intended to be confirmed.

Item 8. Relationship with Issuer of Experts Named in Offering Statement

If any expert named in the offering statement as having prepared or certified any part thereof was employed for such purpose on a contingent basis or, at the time of such preparation or certification or at any time thereafter, had a material interest in the issuer or any of its parents or subsidiaries or was connected with the issuer or any of its subsidiaries as a promoter, underwriter, voting trustee, director, officer or employee furnish a brief statement of the nature of such contingent basis, interest or connection.

Item 9. Use of a Solicitation of Interest Document

Indicate whether or not a written document or broadcast script authorized by Rule 254 was used prior to the filing of this notification. If so, indicate the date(s) of such use.

PART II—OFFERING CIRCULAR

Financial Statement requirements, regardless of the applicable disclosure model, are specified in Part F/S of this Form 1–A.

The Commission encourages the use of management's projections of future economic performance that have a reasonable basis and are presented in an appropriate format. See 17 CFR 228.10(e), 17 CFR 229.10. The Commission's safe harbor provision relative to projections is contained in Rule 175.

The narrative disclosure contents of offering circulars are specified as follows:

A: For all corporate issuers—the information required by Model A of this Part II of Form 1–A.

B: For all other issuers and for any issuer that so chooses—the information required by either Part I of Form SB–2, except for the financial statements called for there, or Model B of this Part II of Form 1–A. Offering circulars prepared pursuant to this instruction need not follow the order of the items or other requirements of the disclosure form. Such information shall not, however, be set forth in such a fashion as to obscure any of the required information or any information necessary to keep the required information from being incomplete or misleading. Information requested to be presented in a specified tabular format shall be given in substantially the tabular form specified in the item.

OFFERING CIRCULAR MODEL A

GENERAL INSTRUCTIONS:

Each question in each paragraph of this part shall be responded to; and each question and any notes, but not any instructions thereto, shall be restated in its entirety. If the question or series of questions is inapplicable, so state. If the space provided in the format is insufficient, additional space should be created by cutting and pasting the format to add more lines.

Be very careful and precise in answering all questions. Give full and complete answers so that they are not misleading under the circumstances involved. Do not discuss any future performance or other anticipated event unless you have a reasonable basis to believe that it will actually occur within the foreseeable future. If any answer requiring significant information is materially inaccurate, incomplete or misleading, the Company, its management and principal shareholders may have liability to investors. The selling agents should exercise appropriate diligence to determine that no such inaccuracy or incompleteness has occurred, or they may be liable.

COVER PAGE

____
(Exact name of Company as set forth in Charter)

Type of securities offered: ________________

Maximum number of securities offered: _____

Minimum number of securities offered: _____

Price per security: $_______

Total proceeds: If maximum sold: $_______ If minimum sold: $_______

(See Questions 9 and 10)

Is a commissioned selling agent selling the securities in this offering?

[ ] Yes [ ] No

If yes, what percent is commission of price to public? _______%.

Is there other compensation to selling agent(s)?

[ ] Yes [ ] No

Is there a finder's fee or similar payment to any person?

[ ] Yes [ ] No (See Question No. 22)

Is there an escrow of proceeds until minimum is obtained?

[ ] Yes [ ] No (See Question No. 26)

Is this offering limited to members of a special group, such as employees of the Company or individuals?

[ ] Yes [ ] No (See Question No. 25)

Is transfer of the securities restricted?

[ ] Yes [ ] No (See Question No. 25)

INVESTMENT IN SMALL BUSINESSES INVOLVES A HIGH DEGREE OF RISK, AND INVESTORS SHOULD NOT INVEST ANY FUNDS IN THIS OFFERING UNLESS THEY CAN AFFORD TO LOSE THEIR ENTIRE INVESTMENT. SEE QUESTION NO. 2 FOR THE RISK FACTORS THAT MANAGEMENT BELIEVES PRESENT THE MOST SUBSTANTIAL RISKS TO AN INVESTOR IN THIS OFFERING.

IN MAKING AN INVESTMENT DECISION INVESTORS MUST RELY ON THEIR OWN EXAMINATION OF THE ISSUER AND THE TERMS OF THE OFFERING, INCLUDING THE MERITS AND RISKS INVOLVED. THESE SECURITIES HAVE NOT BEEN RECOMMENDED OR APPROVED BY ANY FEDERAL OR STATE SECURITIES COMMISSION OR REGULATORY AUTHORITY. FURTHERMORE, THESE AUTHORITIES HAVE NOT PASSED UPON THE ACCURACY OR ADEQUACY OF THIS DOCUMENT. ANY REPRESENTATION TO THE CONTRARY IS A CRIMINAL OFFENSE.

THE U.S. SECURITIES AND EXCHANGE COMMISSION DOES NOT PASS UPON THE MERITS OF ANY SECURITIES OFFERED OR THE TERMS OF THE OFFERING, NOR DOES IT PASS UPON THE ACCURACY OR COMPLETENESS OF ANY OFFERING CIRCULAR OR SELLING LITERATURE. THESE SECURITIES ARE OFFERED UNDER AN EXEMPTION FROM REGISTRATION; HOWEVER, THE COMMISSION HAS NOT MADE AN INDEPENDENT DETERMINATION THAT THESE SECURITIES ARE EXEMPT FROM REGISTRATION.

This Company:

[ ] Has never conducted operations.

[ ] Is in the development stage.

[ ] Is currently conducting operations.

[ ] Has shown a profit in the last fiscal year.

[ ] Other (Specify): ________________

(Check at least one, as appropriate)

This offering has been registered for offer and sale in the following states:

State	*State File No.*	*Effective Date*

INSTRUCTION: The Cover Page of the Offering Circular is a summary of certain essential information and should be kept on one page if at all possible. For purposes of characterizing the Company on the cover page, the term "development stage" has the same meaning as that set forth in Statement of Financial Accounting Standards No. 7 (June 1, 1975).

TABLE OF CONTENTS

THIS OFFERING CIRCULAR CONTAINS ALL OF THE REPRESENTATIONS BY THE COMPANY CONCERNING THIS OFFERING, AND NO PERSON SHALL MAKE DIFFERENT OR BROADER STATEMENTS THAN THOSE CONTAINED HEREIN. INVESTORS ARE CAUTIONED NOT TO RELY UPON ANY INFORMATION NOT EXPRESSLY SET FORTH IN THIS OFFERING CIRCULAR.

This Offering Circular, together with Financial Statements and other Attachments, consists of a total of ___ pages.

THE COMPANY

1. Exact corporate name: ________________
State and date of incorporation: ________________
Street address of principal office:
____
Company Telephone Number: (   ) ___
Fiscal year: ________________

(month) (day)

Person(s) to contact at Company with respect to offering:

____

Telephone Number (if different from above):
( ) __________

RISK FACTORS

2. List in the order of importance the factors which the Company considers to be the most substantial risks to an investor in this offering in view of all facts and circumstances or which otherwise make the offering one of high risk or speculative (i.e., those factors which constitute the greatest threat that the investment will be lost in whole or in part, or not provide an adequate return).

(1) ______________________________
(2) ______________________________
(3) ______________________________
(4) ______________________________
(5) ______________________________
(6) ______________________________
(7) ______________________________
(8) ______________________________
(9) ______________________________
(10) ______________________________
(11) ______________________________
(12) ______________________________
(13) ______________________________
(14) ______________________________
(15) ______________________________
(16) ______________________________

Note: In addition to the above risks, businesses are often subject to risks not foreseen or fully appreciated by management. In reviewing this Offering Circular potential investors should keep in mind other possible risks that could be important.

INSTRUCTION: The Company should avoid generalized statements and include only those factors which are unique to the Company. No specific number of risk factors is required to be identified. If more than 16 significant risk factors exist, add additional lines and number as appropriate. Risk factors may be due to such matters as cash flow and liquidity problems, inexperience of management in managing a business in the particular industry, dependence of the Company on an unproven product, absence of an existing market for the product (even though management may believe a need exists), absence of an operating history of the Company, absence of profitable operations in recent periods, an erratic financial history, the financial position of the Company, the nature of the business in which the Company is engaged or proposes to engage, conflicts of interest with management, arbitrary establishment of offering price, reliance on the efforts of a single individual, or absence of a trading market if a trading market is not expected to develop. Cross references should be made to the Questions where details of the risks are described.

BUSINESS AND PROPERTIES

3. With respect to the business of the Company and its properties:

(a) Describe in detail what business the Company does and proposes to do, including what products or goods are or will be produced or services that are or will be rendered.

(b) Describe how these products or services are to be produced or rendered and how and when the Company intends to carry out its activities. If the Company plans to offer a new product(s), state the present stage of development, including whether or not a working prototype(s) is in existence. Indicate if completion of development of the product would require a material amount of the resources of the Company, and the estimated amount. If the Company is or is expected to be dependent upon one or a limited number of suppliers for essential raw materials, energy or other items, describe. Describe any major existing supply contracts.

(c) Describe the industry in which the Company is selling or expects to sell its products or services and, where applicable, any recognized trends within that industry. Describe that part of the industry and the geographic area in which the business competes or will compete.

Indicate whether competition is or is expected to be by price, service, or other basis. Indicate (by attached table if appropriate) the current or anticipated prices or price ranges for the Company's products or services, or the formula for determining prices, and how these prices compare with those of competitors' products or services, including a description of any variations in product or service features. Name the principal competitors that the Company has or expects to have in its area of competition. Indicate the relative size and financial and market strengths of the Company's competitors in the area of competition in which the Company is or will be operating. State why the Company believes it can effectively compete with these and other companies in its area of competition.

Note: Because this Offering Circular focuses primarily on details concerning the Company rather than the industry in which the Company operates or will operate, potential investors may wish to conduct their own separate investigation of the Company's industry to obtain broader insight in assessing the Company's prospects.

(d) Describe specifically the marketing strategies the Company is employing or will employ in penetrating its market or in developing a new market. Set forth in response to Question 4 below the timing and size of the results of this effort which will be necessary in order for the Company to be profitable. Indicate how and by whom its products or services are or will be marketed (such as by advertising, personal contact by sales representatives, etc.), how its marketing structure operates or will operate and the basis of its marketing approach, including any market studies. Name any customers that account for, or based upon existing orders will account for a major portion (20% or more) of the Company's sales. Describe any major existing sales contracts.

(e) State the backlog of written firm orders for products and/or services as of a recent date (within the last 90 days) and compare it with the backlog of a year ago from that date.

As of: ____/____/____ $_______
(a recent date)

As of: ____/____/____ $_______
(one year earlier)

Explain the reason for significant variations between the two figures, if any. Indicate what types and amounts of orders are included in the backlog figures. State the size of typical orders, if the Company's sales are seasonal or cyclical, explain.

(f) State the number of the Company's present employees and the number of employees it anticipates it will have within the next 12 months. Also, indicate the number by type of employee (i.e., clerical, operations, administrative, etc.) the Company will use, whether or not any of them are subject to collective bargaining agreements, and the expiration date(s) of any collective bargaining agreement(s). If the Company's employees are on strike, or have been in the past three years, or are threatening to strike, describe the dispute. Indicate any supplemental benefits or incentive arrangements the Company has or will have with its employees.

(g) Describe generally the principal properties (such as real estate, plant and equipment, patents, etc.) that the Company owns, indicating also what properties it leases and a summary of the terms under those leases, including the amount of payments, expiration dates and the terms of any renewal options. Indicate what properties the Company intends to acquire in the immediate future, the cost of such acquisitions and the sources of financing it expects to use in obtaining these properties, whether by purchase, lease or otherwise.

(h) Indicate the extent to which the Company's operations depend or are expected to depend upon patents, copyrights, trade secrets, know-how or other proprietary information and the steps undertaken to secure and protect this intellectual property, including any use of confidentiality agreements, covenants-not-to-compete and the like. Summarize the principal terms and expiration dates of any significant license agreements. Indicate the amounts expended by the Company for research and development during the last fiscal year, the amount expected to be spent this year and what percentage of revenues research and development expenditures were for the last fiscal year.

(i) If the Company's business, products, or properties are subject to material regulation (including environmental regulation) by federal, state, or local governmental agencies, indicate the nature and extent of regulation and its effects or potential effects upon the Company.

(j) State the names of any subsidiaries of the Company, their business purposes and ownership, and indicate which are included in the Financial Statements attached hereto. If not included, or if included but not consolidated, please explain.

(k) Summarize the material events in the development of the Company (including any material mergers or acquisitions) during the past five years, or for whatever lesser period the Company has been in existence. Discuss any pending or anticipated mergers, acquisitions, spin-offs or recapitalizations. If the Company has recently undergone a stock split, stock dividend or recapitalization in anticipation of this offering, describe (and adjust historical per share figures elsewhere in this Offering Circular accordingly).

4. (a) If the Company was not profitable during its last fiscal year, list below in chronological order the events which in management's opinion must or should occur or the milestones which in management's opinion the Company must or should reach in order for the Company to become profitable, and indicate the expected manner of occurrence or the expected method by which the Company will achieve the milestones.

	Event or Milestone	Expected manner of occurrence or method of achievement	Date or number of months after receipt of proceeds when should be accomplished
(1)	______	______	______
(2)	______	______	______
(3)	______	______	______
(4)	______	______	______

Event or Milestone	Expected manner of occurrence or method of achievement	Date or number of months after receipt of proceeds when should be accomplished
______	______	
______	______	
(5) ______	______	______
______	______	
______	______	
______	______	
______	______	
______	______	

(b) State the probable consequences to the Company of delays in achieving each of the events or milestones within the above time schedule, and particularly the effect of any delays upon the Company's liquidity in view of the Company's then anticipated level of operating costs. (See Question Nos. 11 and 12)

Note: After reviewing the nature and timing of each event or milestone, potential investors should reflect upon whether achievement of each within the estimated time frame is realistic and should assess the consequences of delays or failure of achievement in making an investment decision.

INSTRUCTION: The inquiries under Business and Properties elicit information concerning the nature of the business of the Company and its properties. Make clear what aspects of the business are presently in operation and what aspects are planned to be in operation in the future. The description of principal properties should provide information which will reasonably inform investors as to the suitability, adequacy, productive capacity and extent of utilization of the facilities used in the enterprise. Detailed descriptions of the physical characteristics of the individual properties or legal descriptions by metes and bounds are not required and should not be given.

As to Question 4, if more than five events or milestones exist, add additional lines as necessary. A "milestone" is a significant point in the Company's development or an obstacle which the Company must overcome in order to become profitable.

OFFERING PRICE FACTORS

If the securities offered are common stock, or are exercisable for or convertible into common stock, the following factors may be relevant to the price at which the securities are being offered.

5. What were net, after-tax earnings for the last fiscal year?

Total $______ ($______ per share)

6. If the Company had profits, show offering price as a multiple of earnings. Adjust to reflect for any stock splits or recapitalizations, and use conversion or exercise price in lieu of offering price, if applicable.

$$\frac{\text{Offering Price Per Share}}{\text{Net After–Tax Earnings Last Year Per Share}} = \underline{\qquad\qquad} \text{ (price/earnings multiple)}$$

7. (a) what is the net tangible book value of the Company? (If deficit, show in parentheses.) For this purpose, net tangible book value means total assets (exclusive of copyrights, patents, goodwill, research and development costs and similar intangible items) minus total liabilities.

$______ ($______ per share)

If the net tangible book value per share is substantially less than this offering (or exercise or conversion) price per share, explain the reasons for the variation.

(b) State the dates on which the Company sold or otherwise issued securities during the last 12 months, the amount of such securities sold, the number of persons to whom they were sold, any relationship of such persons to the company at the time of sale, the price at which they were sold and, if not sold for cash, a concise description of the consideration. (Exclude bank debt.)

8. (a) What percentage of the outstanding shares of the Company will the investors in this offering have? Assume exercise of outstanding options, warrants or rights and conversion of convertible securities, if the respective exercise or conversion prices are at or less than the offering price. Also assume exercise of any options, warrants or rights and conversions of any convertible securities offered in this offering.

If the maximum is sold: ______%

If the minimum is sold: ______%

(b) What post-offering value is management implicitly attributing to the entire Company by establishing the price per security set forth on the cover page (or exercise or conversion price if common stock is not offered)? (Total outstanding shares after offering times offering price, or exercise or conversion price if common stock is not offered.)

If maximum is sold: $______*

If minimum is sold: $______*

(For above purposes, assume outstanding options are exercised in determining "shares" if the exercise prices are at or less than the offering price. All convertible securities, including outstanding convertible securities, shall be assumed converted and any options, warrants or rights in this offering shall be assumed exercised.)

* These values assume that the Company's capital structure would be changed to reflect any conversions of outstanding convertible securities and any use of outstanding securities as payment in the exercise of outstanding options, warrants or rights included in the calculation. The type and amount of convertible or other securities thus eliminated would be: ____________ These values also assume an increase in cash in the Company by the amount of any cash payments that would be made upon cash exercise of options, warrants or rights included in the calculations. The amount of such cash would be: $______

Note: After reviewing the above, potential investors should consider whether or not the offering price (or exercise or conversion price, if applicable) for the securities is appropriate at the present stage of the Company's development.

INSTRUCTION: Financial information in response to Questions 5, 6 and 7 should be consistent with the Financial Statements. Earnings per share for purposes of Question 5 should be calculated by dividing earnings for the last fiscal year by the weighted average of outstanding shares during that year. No calculations should be shown for periods of less than one year or if earnings are negative or nominal. For purposes of Question 8, the "offering price" of any options, warrants or rights or convertible securities in the offering is the respective exercise or conversion price.

USE OF PROCEEDS

9. (a) The following table sets forth the use of the proceeds from this offering:

	If Minimum Sold Amount %	If Maximum Sold Amount
Total Proceeds	$______	$______
	100%	100%
Less: Offering Expenses		
Commissions & Finders Fees	______	______
Legal & Accounting	______	______
Copying & Advertising	______	______
Other (Specify):	______	______
______	______	______
______	______	______
Net Proceeds from Offering	______	______
Use of Net Proceeds	______	______
	______	______

Total Proceeds	If Minimum Sold Amount %	If Maximum Sold Amount
	$	$
	$	$
Total Use of Net Proceeds		
	$	$
	100%	100%

(b) If there is no minimum amount of proceeds that must be raised before the Company may use the proceeds of the offering, describe the order of priority in which the proceeds set forth above in the column "If Maximum Sold" will be used.

Note: After reviewing the portion of the offering allocated to the payment of offering expenses, and to the immediate payment to management and promoters of any fees, reimbursements, past salaries or similar payments, a potential investor should consider whether the remaining portion of his investment, which would be that part available for future development of the Company's business and operations, would be adequate.

10. (a) If material amounts of funds from sources other than this offering are to be used in conjunction with the proceeds from this offering, state the amounts and sources of such other funds, and whether funds are firm or contingent. If contingent, explain.

(b) If any material part of the proceeds is to be used to discharge indebtedness, describe the terms of such indebtedness, including interest rates. If the indebtedness to be discharged was incurred within the current or previous fiscal year, describe the use of proceeds of such indebtedness.

(c) If any material amount of proceeds is to be used to acquire assets, other than in the ordinary course of business, briefly describe and state the cost of the assets and other material terms of the acquisitions. If the assets are to be acquired from officers, directors, employees or principal stockholders of the Company or their associates, give the names of the persons from whom the assets are to be acquired and set forth the cost to the Company, the method followed in determining the cost, and any profit to such persons.

(d) If any amount of the proceeds is to be used to reimburse any officer, director, employee or stockholder for services already rendered, assets previously transferred, or monies loaned or advanced, or otherwise, explain:

11. Indicate whether the Company is having or anticipates having within the next 12 months any cash flow or liquidity problems and whether or not it is in default or in breach of any note, loan, lease or other indebtedness or financing arrangement requiring the Company to make payments. Indicate if a significant amount of the Company's trade payables have not been paid within the stated trade term. State whether the Company is subject

to any unsatisfied judgments, liens or settlement obligations and the amounts thereof. Indicate the Company's plans to resolve any such problems.

12. Indicate whether proceeds from this offering will satisfy the Company's cash requirements for the next 12 months, and whether it will be necessary to raise additional funds. State the source of additional funds, if known.

INSTRUCTION: Use of net proceeds should be stated with a high degree of specificity. Suggested (but not mandatory) categories are: leases, rent, utilities, payroll (by position or type), purchase or lease of specific items of equipment or inventory, payment of notes, accounts payable, etc., marketing or advertising costs, taxes, consulting fees, permits, professional fees, insurance and supplies. Categories will vary depending on the Company's plans. Use of footnotes or other explanation is recommended where appropriate. Footnotes should be used to indicate those items of offering expenses that are estimates. Set forth in separate categories all payments which will be made immediately to the Company's executive officers, directors and promoters, indicating by footnote that these payments will be so made to such persons. If a substantial amount is allocated to working capital, set forth separate sub-categories for use of the funds in the Company's business.

If any substantial portion of the proceeds has not been allocated for particular purposes, a statement to that effect as one of the Use of Net Proceeds categories should be included together with a statement of the amount of proceeds not so allocated and a footnote explaining how the Company expects to employ such funds not so allocated.

CAPITALIZATION

13. Indicate the capitalization of the Company as of the most recent balance sheet date (adjusted to reflect any subsequent stock splits, stock dividends, recapitalizations or refinancings) and as adjusted to reflect the sale of the minimum and maximum amount of securities in this offering and the use of the net proceeds therefrom:

	Amount Outstanding As of: / / (date)	As Adjusted Minimum	As Adjusted Maximum
Debt:			
Short-term debt (average interest rate ____%)	$____	$____	$____
Long-term debt (average interest rate ____%)	$____	$____	$____
Total debt	$____	$____	$____
Stockholders equity (deficit):			
Preferred stock—par or stated value (by class of preferred in order of preferences)			
____	$____	$____	$____
____	$____	$____	$____
____	$____	$____	$____
Common stock—par or stated value	$____	$____	$____
Additional paid in capital	$____	$____	$____
Retained earnings (deficit)	$____	$____	$____
Total stockholders equity (deficit)	$____	$____	$____
Total Capitalization	$____	$____	$____

Number of preferred shares authorized to be outstanding:

Class of Preferred	Number of Shares Authorized	Par Value Per Share
______	______	$______
______	______	$______
______	______	$______

Number of common shares authorized: ______ shares. Par or stated value per share, if any: $______

Number of common shares reserved to meet conversion requirements or for the issuance upon exercise of options, warrants or rights: ______ shares.

INSTRUCTION: Capitalization should be shown as of a date no earlier than that of the most recent Financial Statements provided pursuant to Question 46. If the Company has mandatory redeemable preferred stock, include the amount thereof in "long term debt" and so indicate by footnote to that category in the capitalization table.

DESCRIPTION OF SECURITIES

14. The securities being offered hereby are:

[ ] Common Stock

[ ] Preferred or Preference Stock

[ ] Notes or Debentures

[ ] Units of two or more types of securities composed of: ______

[ ] Other: ______

15. These securities have:

Yes	No	
[ ]	[ ]	Cumulative voting rights
[ ]	[ ]	Other special voting rights
[ ]	[ ]	Preemptive rights to purchase in new issues of shares
[ ]	[ ]	Preference as to dividends or interest
[ ]	[ ]	Preference upon liquidation
[ ]	[ ]	Other special rights or preferences (specify):

Explain:

16. Are the securities convertible? [ ] Yes [ ] No

If so, state conversion price or formula. ___

Date when conversion becomes effective: ___/___/___

Date when conversion expires: ___/___

17. (a) If securities are notes or other types of debt securities:

(1) What is the interest rate? ______%

If interest rate is variable or multiple rates, describe: ______

(2) What is the maturity date? ___/___/___

If serial maturity dates, describe: ______

(3) Is there a mandatory sinking fund?

[ ] Yes [ ] No

Describe: ______

(4) Is there a trust indenture? [ ] Yes [ ] No

Name, address and telephone number of Trustee

(5) Are the securities callable or subject to redemption? [ ] Yes [ ] No

Describe, including redemption prices: ___

(6) Are the securities collateralized by real or personal property?

[ ] Yes [ ] No Describe: ______

(7) If these securities are subordinated in right of payment of interest or principal, explain the terms of such subordination.

How much currently outstanding indebtedness of the Company is senior to the securities in right of payment of interest or principal? $______

How much indebtedness shares in right of payment on an equivalent (pari passu) basis? $______

How much indebtedness is junior (subordinated) to the securities? $______

(b) If notes or other types of debt securities are being offered and the Company had earnings during its last fiscal year, show the ratio of earnings to fixed charges on an actual and pro forma basis for that fiscal year. "Earnings" means pretax income from continuing operations plus fixed charges and capitalized interest. "Fixed charges" means interest (including capitalized interest), amortization of debt discount, premium and expense, preferred stock dividend requirements of majority owned subsidiary, and such portion of rental expense as can be demonstrated to be representative of the interest factor in the particular case. The pro forma ratio of earnings to fixed charges should include incremental interest expense as a result of the offering of the notes or other debt securities.

	Last Fiscal Year Actual	Pro Forma Minimum	Pro Forma Maximum
"Earnings" / "Fixed Charges" =	______	______	______
If no earnings show "Fixed Charges" only	______	______	______

Note: Care should be exercised in interpreting the significance of the ratio of earnings to fixed charges as a measure of the "coverage" of debt service, as the existence of earnings does not necessarily mean that the Company's liquidity at any given time will permit payment of debt service requirements to be timely made. See Question Nos. 11 and 12. See also the Financial Statements and especially the Statement of Cash Flows.

18. If securities are Preference or Preferred stock:

Are unpaid dividends cumulative? [ ] Yes [ ] No

Are securities callable? [ ] Yes [ ] No

Explain:

Note: Attach to this Offering Circular copies or a summary of the charter, bylaw or contractual provision or document that gives rise to the rights of holders of Preferred or Preference Stock, notes or other securities being offered.

19. If securities are capital stock of any type, indicate restrictions on dividends under loan or other financing arrangements or otherwise:

20. Current amount of assets available for payment of dividends if deficit must be first made up, (show deficit in parenthesis): $______

PLAN OF DISTRIBUTION

21. The selling agents (that is, the persons selling the securities as agent for the Company for a commission or other compensation) in this offering are:

Name: ______	Name: ______
Address: ______	Address: ______
Telephone No. ( )	Telephone No. ( )

22. Describe any compensation to selling agents or finders, including cash, securities, contracts or other consideration, in addition to the cash commission set forth as a percent of the offering price on the cover page of this Offering Circular. Also indicate whether the Company will indemnify the selling agents or finders against liabilities under the securities laws. ("Finders" are persons who for compensation act as intermediaries in obtaining selling agents or otherwise making introductions in furtherance of this offering.)

23. Describe any material relationships between any of the selling agents or finders and the Company or its management.

Note: After reviewing the amount of compensation to the selling agents or finders for selling the securities, and the nature of any relationship between the selling agents or finders and the Company, a potential investor should assess the extent to which it may be inappropriate to rely upon any recommendation by the selling agents or finders to buy the securities.

24. If this offering is not being made through selling agents, the names of persons at the Company through which this offering is being made:

Name: ____________ Name: ____________
Address: __________ Address: __________
Telephone No. ( ) Telephone No. ( )

25. If this offering is limited to a special group, such as employees of the Company, or is limited to a certain number of individuals (as required to qualify under Subchapter S of the Internal Revenue Code) or is subject to any other limitations, describe the limitations and any restrictions on resale that apply:

Will the certificates bear a legend notifying holders of such restrictions?

[ ] Yes [ ] No

26. (a) Name, address and telephone number of independent bank or savings and loan association or other similar depository institution acting as escrow agent if proceeds are escrowed until minimum proceeds are raised:

(b) Date at which funds will be returned by escrow agent if minimum proceeds are not raised:

Will interest on proceeds during escrow period be paid to investors? [ ] Yes [ ] No

27. Explain the nature of any resale restrictions on presently outstanding shares, and when those restrictions will terminate, if this can be determined:

Note: Equity investors should be aware that unless the Company is able to complete a further public offering or the Company is able to be sold for cash or merged with a public company that their investment in the Company may be illiquid indefinitely.

DIVIDENDS, DISTRIBUTIONS AND REDEMPTIONS

28. If the Company has within the last five years paid dividends, made distributions upon its stock or redeemed any securities, explain how much and when:

OFFICERS AND KEY PERSONNEL OF THE COMPANY

29. Chief Executive Officer: Title: ________
Name: ____________ Age: ________
Office Street Address: Telephone No.:
____________________ ( ) –

Name of employers, titles and dates of positions held during past five years with an indication of job responsibilities.

Education (degrees, schools, and dates): ___
____

Also a Director of the Company [ ] Yes [ ] No

Indicate amount of time to be spent on Company matters if less than full time:

30. Chief Operating Officer: Title: ________
Name: ____________ Age: ________
Office Street Address: Telephone No.:
____________________ ( ) –

Names of employers, titles and dates of positions held during past five years with an indication of job responsibilities.

Education (degrees, schools, and dates): ___
____

Also a Director of the Company? [ ] Yes [ ] No

Indicate amount of time to be spent on Company matters if less than full time:

31. Chief Financial Officer: Title: ________
Name: ____________ Age: ________
Office Street Address: Telephone No.:
____________________ ( ) –

Names of employers, titles and dates of positions held during past five years with an indication of job responsibilities.

Education (degrees, schools, and dates): ____
____

Also a Director of the Company? [ ] Yes [ ] No

Indicate amount of time to be spent on Company matters if less than full time:

32. Other Key Personnel:

(A) Name: ____________ Age: ______
Title: ____________
Office Street Address: Telephone No.:
____________ ( ) –

Names of employers, titles and dates of positions held during past five years with an indication of job responsibilities.

Education (degrees, schools, and dates): ___
____

Also a Director of the Company? [ ] Yes [ ] No

Indicate amount of time to be spent on Company matters if less than full time:

(B) Name: ____________ Age: ______
Title: ____________
Office Street Address: Telephone No.:
____________ ( ) –

Names of employers, titles and dates of positions held during past five years with an indication of job responsibilities.

Education (degrees, schools, and dates): ___
____

Also a Director of the Company? [ ] Yes [ ] No

Indicate amount of time to be spent on Company matters if less than full time:

INSTRUCTION: The term "Chief Executive Officer" means the officer of the Company who has been delegated final authority by the board of directors to direct all aspects of the Company's affairs. The term "Chief Operating Officer" means the officer in charge of the actual day-to-day operations of the Company's business. The term "Chief Financial Officer" means the officer having accounting skills who is primarily in charge of assuring that the Company's financial books and records are properly kept and maintained and financial statements prepared.

The term "key personnel" means persons such as vice presidents, production managers, sales managers, or research scientists and similar persons, who are not included above, but who make or are expected to make significant contributions to the business of the Company, whether as employees, independent contractors, consultants or otherwise.

DIRECTORS OF THE COMPANY

33. Number of Directors: ______. If Directors are not elected annually, or are elected under a voting trust or other arrangement, explain:

34. Information concerning outside or other Directors (i.e. those not described above):

(A) Name: ____________ Age: ______
Office Street Address: Telephone No.:
____________ ( ) –

Names of employers, titles and dates of positions held during past five years with an indication of job responsibilities.

Education (degrees, schools, and dates): ___
____

(B) Name: ____________ Age: ______
Office Street Address: Telephone No.:
____________ ( ) –

Names of employers, titles and dates of positions held during past five years with an indication of job responsibilities.

Education (degrees, schools, and dates): ___
____

(C) Name: ____________ Age: ______
Office Street Address: Telephone No.:
____________ ( ) –

Names of employers, titles and dates of positions held during past five years with an indication of job responsibilities.

Education (degrees, schools, and dates): ___
____

35. (a) Have any of the Officers or Directors ever worked for or managed a company (including a separate subsidiary or division of a larger enterprise) in the same business as the Company?

[ ] Yes [ ] No

Explain:

(b) If any of the Officers, Directors or other key personnel have ever worked for or managed a company in the same business or industry as the Company or in a related business or industry, describe what precautions, if any, (including the obtaining of releases or consents from prior employers) have been taken to preclude claims by prior employers for conversion or theft of trade secrets, know-how or other proprietary information.

(c) If the Company has never conducted operations or is otherwise in the development stage, indicate whether any of the Officers or Directors has ever managed any other company in the start-up or development stage and describe the circumstances, including relevant dates.

(d) If any of the Company's key personnel are not employees but are consultants or other independent contractors, state the details of their engagement by the Company.

(e) If the Company has key man life insurance policies on any of its Officers, Directors or key personnel, explain, including the names of the persons insured, the amount of insurance, whether the insurance proceeds are payable to the Company and whether there are arrangements that require the proceeds to be used to redeem securities or pay benefits to the estate of the insured person or a surviving spouse.

36. If a petition under the Bankruptcy Act or any State insolvency law was filed by or against the Company or its Officers, Directors or other key personnel, or a receiver, fiscal agent or similar officer was appointed by a court for the business or property of any such persons, or any partnership in which any of such persons was a general partner at or within the past five years, or any corporation or business association of which any such person was an executive officer at or within the past five years, set forth below the name of such persons, and the nature and date of such actions.

Note: After reviewing the information concerning the background of the Company's Officers, Directors and other key personnel, potential investors should consider whether or not these persons have adequate background and experience to develop and operate this Company and to make it successful. In this regard, the experience and ability of management are often considered the most significant factors in the success of a business.

PRINCIPAL STOCKHOLDERS

37. Principal owners of the Company (those who beneficially own directly or indirectly 10% or more of the common and preferred stock presently outstanding) starting with the largest common stockholder. Include separately all common stock issuable upon conversion of convertible securities (identifying them by asterisk) and show average price per share as if conversion has occurred. Indicate by footnote if the price paid was for a consideration other than cash and the nature of any such consideration.

Class of Shares	Average Price Per Share	No. of Shares Now Held	% of Total	No. of Shares Held After Offering if All Securities Sold	% of Total
Name:					
______	______	______	______	______	______
______	______	______	______	______	______

Office Street Address:

______

______

______

Telephone No.

(___) ___–___

Principal occupation:

______

38. Number of shares beneficially owned by Officers and Directors as a group:

Before offering: _______ shares (_______% of total outstanding)

After offering:

a) Assuming minimum securities sold:

_______ shares (_______% of total outstanding)

b) Assuming maximum securities sold:

_______ shares (_______% of total outstanding)

(Assume all options exercised and all convertible securities converted.)

INSTRUCTION: If shares are held by family members, through corporations or partnerships, or otherwise in a manner that would allow a person to direct or control the voting of the shares (or share in such direction or control—as, for example, a co-trustee) they should be included as being "beneficially owned." An explanation of these circumstances should be set forth in a footnote to the "Number of Shares Now Held."

MANAGEMENT RELATIONSHIPS, TRANSACTIONS AND REMUNERATION

39. (a) If any of the Officers, key personnel or principal stockholders are related by blood or marriage, please describe.

(b) If the Company has made loans to or is doing business with any of its Officers, Directors, key personnel or 10% stockholders, or any of their relatives (or any entity controlled directly or indirectly by any such persons) within the last two years, or proposes to do so within the future, explain. (This includes sales or lease of goods, property or services to or from the Company, employment or stock purchase contracts, etc.) State the principal terms of any significant loans, agreements, leases, financing or other arrangements.

(c) If any of the Company's Officers, Directors, key personnel or 10% stockholders has guaranteed or co-signed any of the Company's bank debt or other obligations, including any indebtedness to be retired from the proceeds of this offering, explain and state the amounts involved.

40. (a) List all remuneration by the Company to Officers, Directors and key personnel for the last fiscal year:

	Cash	Other
Chief Executive Officer	$_____	$_____
Chief Operating Officer	_____	_____
Chief Accounting Officer	_____	_____
Key Personnel:		
_____________________	_____	_____
_____________________	_____	_____
_____________________	_____	_____
Others:		
_____________________	_____	_____
_____________________	_____	_____
_____________________	_____	_____
Total:	$_____	$_____
Directors as a group (number of persons ___)	$_____	$_____

(b) If remuneration is expected to change or has been unpaid in prior years, explain:

(c) If any employment agreements exist or are contemplated, describe:

41. (a) Number of shares subject to issuance under presently outstanding stock purchase agreements, stock options, warrants or rights: _______ shares (% of total shares to be outstanding after the completion of the offering if all securities sold, assuming exercise of options and conversion of convertible securities). Indicate which have been approved by shareholders. State the expiration dates, exercise prices and other basic terms for these securities:

(b) Number of common shares subject to issuance under existing stock purchase or option plans but not yet covered by outstanding purchase agreements, options or warrants: _______ shares.

(c) Describe the extent to which future stock purchase agreements, stock options, warrants or rights must be approved by shareholders.

42. If the business is highly dependent on the services of certain key personnel, describe any arrangement to assure that these persons will remain with the Company and not compete upon any termination:

Note: After reviewing the above, potential investors should consider whether or not the compensation to management and other key personnel directly or indirectly, is reasonable in view of the present stage of the Company's development.

INSTRUCTION: For purposes of Question 39(b), a person directly or indirectly controls an entity if he is part of the group that directs or is able to direct the entity's activities or affairs. A person is typically a member of a control group if he is an officer, director, general partner, trustee or beneficial owner of a 10% or greater interest in the entity. In Question 40, the term "Cash" should indicate salary, bonus, consulting fees, nonaccountable expense accounts and the like. The column captioned "Other" should include the value of any options or securities given, any annuity, pension or retirement benefits, bonus or profit-sharing plans, and personal benefits (club memberships, company cars, insurance benefits not generally available to employees, etc.). The nature of these benefits should be explained in a footnote to this column.

LITIGATION

43. Describe any past, pending or threatened litigation or administrative action which has held or may have a material effect upon the Company's business, financial condition, or operations, including any litigation or action involving the Company's Officers, Directors or other key personnel. State the names of the principal parties, the nature and current status of the matters, and amounts involved. Give an evaluation by management or counsel, to the extent feasible, of the merits of the proceedings or litigation and the potential impact on the Company's business, financial condition, or operations.

FEDERAL TAX ASPECTS

44. If the Company is an S corporation under the Internal Revenue Code of 1986, and it is anticipated that any significant tax benefits will be available to investors in the offering, indicate the nature and amount of such anticipated tax benefits and the material risks of their disallowance. Also, state the name, address and telephone number of any tax advisor that has passed upon these tax benefits. Attach any opinion or description of the tax consequences of an investment in the securities by the tax advisor.

Name of Tax Advisor: ______________

Address: ______________________

Telephone No. (   )   –

Note: Potential investors are encouraged to have their own personal tax consultant contact the tax advisor to review details of the tax benefits and the extent that the benefits would be available and advantageous to the particular investor.

MISCELLANEOUS FACTORS

45. Describe any other material factors, either adverse or favorable, that will or could affect the Company or its business (for example, discuss any defaults under major contracts, any breach of bylaw provisions, etc.) or which are necessary to make any other information in this Offering Circular not misleading or incomplete.

FINANCIAL STATEMENTS

46. Provide the financial statements required by Part F/S of this Offering Circular section of Form 1–A.

MANAGEMENT'S DISCUSSION AND ANALYSIS OF CERTAIN RELEVANT FACTORS

47. If the Company's financial statements show losses from operations, explain the causes underlying these losses and what steps the Company has taken or is taking to address these causes.

48. Describe any trends in the Company's historical operating results. Indicate any changes now occurring in the underlying economics of the industry or the Company's business which, in the opinion of Management, will have a significant impact (either favorable or adverse) upon the Company's results of operations within the next 12 months, and give a rough estimate of the probable extent of the impact, if possible.

49. If the Company sells a product or products and has had significant sales during its last fiscal year, state the existing gross margin (net sales less cost of such sales as presented in accordance with generally accepted accounting principles) as a percentage of sales for the last fiscal year: __%. What is the anticipated gross margin for the next year of operations? Approximately __%. If this is expected to change, explain. Also, if reasonably current gross margin figures are available for the industry, indicate these figures and the source or sources from which they are obtained.

50. Foreign sales as a percent of total sales for last fiscal year: __%. Domestic government sales as a percent of total domestic sales for last fiscal year: __%. Explain the nature of these sales, including any anticipated changes:

OFFERING CIRCULAR MODEL B.

Item 1. Cover Page

The cover page of the offering circular shall include the following information:

(a) Name of the issuer;

(b) The mailing address of the issuer's principal executive offices including the zip code and the issuer's telephone number;

(c) Date of the offering circular;

(d) Description and amount of securities offered (*Note:* this description should include, for example, appropriate disclosure of redemption and conversion features of debt securities);

(e) The statement required by Rule 253;

(f) The table(s) required by Item 2;

(g) The name of the underwriter or underwriters;

(h) Any materials required by the law of any state in which the securities are to be offered;

(i) If applicable, identify material risks in connection with the purchase of the securities; and

(j) Approximate date of commencement of proposed sale to the public.

Instruction: Where the name of the issuer is the same as the name of another well-known company or indicates a line of business in which the issuer is not engaged or is engaged to only a limited extent, a statement should be furnished to that effect. In some circumstances, however, disclosure may not be sufficient, and a change of name may be the only way to cure its misleading character.

Item 2. Distribution Spread

(a) The information called for by the following table shall be given, in substantially the tabular form indicated, on the outside front cover page of the offering circular as to all securities being offered (estimate, if necessary).

	Price to public	Underwriting discount and commissions	Proceeds to issuer or other persons
Per unit			
Total			

If the securities are to be offered on a best efforts basis, the cover page should set forth the termination date, if any, of the offering, any minimum required sale and any arrangements to place the funds received in an escrow, trust, or similar arrangement. The following tabular presentation of the total maximum and minimum securities to be offered should be combined with the table required above.

	Price to public	Underwriting discount and commissions	Proceeds to issuer or other persons
Total Minimum	______	______	______
Total Maximum	______	______	______

Instructions. 1. The term "commissions" shall include all cash, securities, contracts, or anything else of value, paid, to be set aside, disposed of, or understandings with or for the benefit of any other persons in which any underwriter is interested, made in connection with the sale of such security.

2. Only commissions paid by the issuer in cash are to be indicated in the table. Commissions paid by other persons or any form of non-cash compensation shall be briefly identified in a note to the table with a cross-reference to a more complete description elsewhere in the offering circular.

3. Prior to the commencement of sales pursuant to Regulation A, the issuer shall inform the Commission whether or not the amount of compensation to be allowed or paid to the underwriters, as described in the offering statement, has been cleared with the National Association of Securities Dealers, Inc.

4. If the securities are not to be offered for cash, state the basis upon which the offering is to be made.

5. If it is impracticable to state the price to the public, the method by which it is to be determined shall be explained.

(b) Any finder's fees or similar payments shall be disclosed on the cover page with a reference to a more complete discussion in the offering circular. Such disclosure should identify the finder, the nature of the services rendered and the nature of any relationship between the finder and the issuer, its officers, directors, promoters, principal stockholders and underwriters (including any affiliates thereof.)

(c) The amount of the expenses of the offering borne by the issuer, including underwriting expenses to be borne by the issuer, should be disclosed in a footnote to the table.

Item 3. Summary Information, Risk Factors and Dilution

(a) Where appropriate to a clear understanding by investors, there should be set forth in the forepart of the offering circular, under an appropriate caption, a carefully organized series of short, concise paragraphs, summarizing the principal factors which make the offering one of high risk or speculative.

Note: These factors may be due to such matters as an absence of an operating history of the issuer, an absence of profitable operations in recent periods, an erratic financial history, the financial position of the issuer, the nature of the business in which the issuer is engaged or proposed to engage, conflicts of interest with management, reliance on the efforts of a single individual, or the method of determining the market price where no market currently exists. Issuers should *avoid* generalized statements and include only those factors which are unique to the issuer.

(b) Where there is a material disparity between the public offering price and the effective cash cost to officers, directors, promoters and affiliated persons for shares acquired by them in a transaction during the past three years, or which they have a right to acquire, there should be included a comparison of the public contribution under the proposed public offering and the effective cash contribution of such persons. In such cases, and in other instances where the extent of the dilution makes is appropriate, the following shall be given: (1) the net tangible book value per share before and after the distribution; (2) the amount of the increase in such net tangible book value per share attributable to the cash payment made by purchasers of the shares being offered; and (3) the amount of the immediate dilution from the public offering price which will be absorbed by such purchasers.

Item 4. Plan of Distribution

(a) If the securities are to be offered through underwriters, give the names of the principal underwriters, and state the respective amounts underwritten. Identify each such underwriter having a material relationship to the issuer and state the nature of the relationship. State briefly the nature of the underwriters' obligation to take the securities.

(b) State briefly the discounts and commissions to be allowed or paid to dealers, including all cash, securities, contracts or other consideration to be received by any dealer in connection with the sale of the securities.

(c) Outline briefly the plan of distribution of any securities being issued which are to be offered through the selling efforts of brokers or dealers or otherwise than through underwriters.

(d) If any of the securities are to be offered for the account of security holders, indicate on the cover page the total amount to be offered for their account and include a cross-reference to a fuller discussion elsewhere in the offering circular. Such discussion should identify each selling security holder, state the amount owned by him, the amount offered for his account and the amount to be owned after the offering.

(e)(1) Describe any arrangements for the return of funds to subscribers if all of the securities to be offered are not sold; if there are no such arrangements, so state.

(2) If there will be a material delay in the payment of the proceeds of the offering by the underwriter to the issuer, the salient provisions in this regard and the effects on the issuer should be stated.

Instruction: Attention is directed to the provisions of Rules 10b–9 and 15c2–4 under the Securities Exchange Act of 1934. These rules outline, among other things, antifraud provisions concerning the return of funds to subscribers and the transmission of proceeds of an offering to a seller.

Item 5. Use of Proceeds to Issuer

State the principal purposes for which the net proceeds to the issuer from the securities to be offered are intended to be used, and the approximate amount intended to be used for each such purpose.

Instructions: 1. If any substantial portion of the proceeds has not been allocated for particular purposes, a statement to that effect shall be made together with a statement of the amount of proceeds not so allocated and how the registrant expects to employ such funds not so allocated.

2. Include a statement as to the use of the actual proceeds if they are not sufficient to accomplish the purpose set forth and the order of priority in which they will be applied. However, such statement need not be made if the underwriting arrangements are such that, if any securities are sold to the public, it can be reasonably expected that the actual proceeds of the issue will not be substantially less than the estimated aggregate proceeds to the issuer as shown under Item 2.

3. If any material amounts of other funds are to be used in conjunction with the proceeds, state the amounts and sources of such other funds.

4. If any material part of the proceeds is to be used to discharge indebtedness, describe the terms of such indebtedness. If the indebtedness to be discharged was incurred within one year, describe the use of the proceeds of such indebtedness.

5. If any material amount of the proceeds is to be used to acquire assets, otherwise than in the ordinary course of business, briefly describe and state the cost of the assets. If the assets are to be acquired from affiliates of the issuer or their associates, give the names of the persons from whom they are to be acquired and set forth the principle followed in determining the cost to the issuer.

6. The issuer may reserve the right to change the use of proceeds provided that such reservation is due to certain contingencies which are adequately disclosed.

Item 6. Description of Business

(a) Narrative description of business.

(1) Describe the business done and intended to be done by the issuer and its subsidiaries and the general development of the business during the past five years or such shorter period as the issuer may have been in business. Such description should include, but not be limited to, a discussion of the following factors if such factors are material to an understanding of the issuer's business:

(i) The principal products produced and services rendered and the principal markets for and method of distribution of such products and services.

(ii) The status of a product or service if the issuer has made public information about a new product or service which would require the investment of a material amount of the assets of the issuer or is otherwise material.

(iii) The estimated amount spent during each of the last two fiscal years on company-sponsored research and development activities determined in accordance with generally accepted accounting principles. In addition, state the estimated dollar amount spent during each of such years on material customer-sponsored research activities relating to the development of new products, services or techniques or the improvement of existing products, services or techniques.

(iv) The number of persons employed by the issuer, indicating the number employed full time.

(v) The material effects that compliance with Federal, State and Local provisions which have been enacted or adopted regulating the discharge of materials into the environment, may have upon the capital expenditures, earnings and competitive position of the issuer and its subsidiaries. The issuer shall disclose any material estimated capital expenditures for environmental control facilities for the remainder of its current fiscal year and for such further periods as the issuer may deem material.

(2) The issuer should also describe those distinctive or special characteristics of the issuer's operation or industry which may have a material impact upon the issuer's future financial performance. Examples of factors which might be discussed include dependence on one or a few major customers or suppliers (including suppliers of raw materials or financing), existing or probable governmental regulation, material terms of and/or expiration of material labor contracts or patents, trademarks, licenses, franchises, concessions or royalty agreements, unusual competitive conditions in the industry, cyclicality of the industry and anticipated raw material or energy shortages to the extent management may not be able to secure a continuing source of supply.

(3) The following requirement in subparagraph (i) applies only to issuers (including predecessors) which have not received revenue from operations during each of the three fiscal years immediately prior to the filing of the offering statement.

(i) Describe, if formulated, the issuer's plan of operation for the twelve months following the commencement of the proposed offering. If such information is not available, the reasons for its unavailability shall be stated. Disclosure relating to any plan should include, among other things, a statement indicating whether, in the issuer's opinion, the proceeds from the offering will satisfy its cash requirements and whether, in the next six months, it will be necessary to raise additional funds.

(ii) Any engineering, management or similar reports which have been prepared or provided for external use by the issuer or by a principal underwriter in connection with the proposed offering should be furnished to the Commission at the time of filing the offering statement or as soon as practicable thereafter. There should also be furnished at the same time a statement as to the actual or proposed use and distribution of such report or memorandum. Such statement should identify each class of persons who have received or will receive the report or memorandum, and state the number of copies distributed to each such class. If no such report or memorandum has been prepared, the Commission should be so informed in writing at the time the report or memorandum would otherwise have been submitted.

(b) Segment Data. If the issuer is required to include segment information in its financial statements, an appropriate cross-reference shall be included in the description of business.

Item 7. Description of Property

State briefly the location and general character of the principal plants, and other materially important physical properties of the issuer and its subsidiaries. If any such property is not held in fee or is held subject to any major encumbrance, so state and briefly describe how held.

Instruction: What is required is information essential to an investor's appraisal of the securities being offered. Such information should be furnished as will reasonably inform investors as to the suitability, adequacy, productive capacity and extent of utilization of the facilities used in the enterprise. Detailed descriptions of the physical characteristics of individual properties or legal descriptions by metes and bounds are not required and should not be given.

Item 8. Directors, Executive Officers and Significant Employees

(a) List the names and ages of each of the following persons stating his term of office and any periods during which he has served as such and briefly describe any arrangement or understanding between him and any other person(s) (naming such person(s)) pursuant to which he was or is to be selected to his office or position:

(1) directors;

(2) persons nominated to become directors;

(3) executive officers;

(4) persons chosen to become executive officers;

(5) significant employees.

Instructions: 1. No nominee or person chosen to become a director or person chosen to be an executive officer who has not consented to act as such should be named in response to this item.

2. The term "executive officer" means the president, secretary, treasurer, any vice-president in charge of a principal business function (such as sales, administration, or finance) and any other person who performs similar policy making functions for the issuer.

3. The term "significant employee" means persons such as production managers, sales managers, or research scientists, who are not executive officers, but who make or are expected to make significant contributions to the business of the issuer.

(b) Family relationships. State the nature of any family relationship between any director, executive officer, person nominated or chosen by the issuer to become a director or executive officer or any significant employee.

Instruction: The term "family relationship" means any relationship by blood, marriage, or adoption, not more remote than first cousin.

(c) Business experience. Give a brief account of the business experience during the past five years of each director, person nominated or chosen to become a director or executive officer, and each significant employee, including his principal occupations and employment during that period and the name and principal business of any corporation or other organization in which such occupations and employment were carried on. When an executive officer or significant employee has been employed by the issuer for less than five years, a brief explanation should be included as to the nature of the responsibilities undertaken by the individual in prior positions to provide adequate disclosure of this prior business experience. What is required is information relating to the level of his professional competence which may include, depending upon the circumstances, such specific information as the size of the operation supervised.

(d) Involvement in certain legal proceedings. Describe any of the following events which occurred during the past five years and which are material to an evaluation of the ability or integrity of any director, person nominated to become a director or executive officer of the issuer.

(1) A petition under the Bankruptcy Act or any State insolvency law was filed by or against, or a receiver, fiscal agent or similar officer was appointed by a court for the business or property of such person, or any partnership in which he was general partner at or within 2 years before the time of such filing, or any corporation or business association of which he was an executive officer at or within two years before the time of such filing;

(2) Such person was convicted in a criminal proceeding (excluding traffic violations and other minor offenses).

Item 9. Remuneration of Directors and Officers

(a) Furnish, in substantially the tabular form indicated, the aggregate annual remuneration of each of the three highest paid persons who are officers or directors as a group during the issuer's last fiscal year. State the number of persons in the group referred to above without naming them.

Name of individual or identity of group	Capacities in remuneration was received	Aggregate remuneration

Instructions: 1. In case of remuneration paid or to be paid otherwise than in cash, if it is impracticable to determine the cash value thereof, state in a note to the table the nature and amount thereof.

2. This item is to be answered on an accrual basis if practicable; if not so answered, state the basis used.

(b) Briefly describe all remuneration payments proposed to be made in the future pursuant to any ongoing plan or arrangement to the individuals and group specified in Item 9(a). The description should include a summary of how each plan operates, any performance formula or measure in effect (or the criteria used to determine payment amounts), the time periods over which the measurements of benefits will be determined, payment schedules, and any recent material amendments to the plan. Information need not be furnished with respect to any group life, health, hospitalization, or medical reimbursement plans which do not discriminate in scope, terms or operation in favor of officers or directors of the registrant and which are available generally to all salaried employees.

Item 10. Security Ownership of Management and Certain Securityholders

(a) Voting securities and principal holders thereof. Furnish the following information, in substantially the tabular form indicated, with respect to voting securities held of record by:

(1) each of the three highest paid persons who are officers and directors of the issuer; *Note* —In the event none of the issuer's officers or directors have received a salary in the past twelve months, this item should be responded to for every officer and director;

(2) all officers and directors as a group;

(3) each shareholder who owns more than 10% of any class of the issuer's securities, including those shares subject to outstanding options.

(1) Title of Class	(2) Name and address of owner	(3) Amount owned before the offering	(4) Amount owned after the offering	(5) Percent of Class

Instruction: Column (4) need not be responded to if the information would be the same as that appearing under column (3).

(b) If, to the knowledge of the issuer, any other person holds or shares the power to vote or direct the voting of securities described pursuant to subsection (a) above, appropriate disclosure should be made. In addition, if any person other than those named pursuant to subsection (a) holds or shares the power to vote 10% or more of the issuer's voting securities, the information required by the table should be provided with respect to such person.

(c) Non-voting securities and principal holders thereof. Furnish the same information as required in subsection (a) above with respect to securities that are not entitled to vote.

(d) Options, warrants, and rights. Furnish the information required by the table as to options, warrants or rights to purchase securities from the issuer or any of its subsidiaries held by each of the individuals and referred to in subsection (a) above:

Name of holder	Title and amount securities called for by options, warrants or rights	Exercise price	Date of Exercise

Instruction: Where the total market value of securities called for by all outstanding options, warrants or rights does not exceed $10,000 for any officer, director, or principal shareholder named in answer to this item, or $50,000 for all officers and directors as a group, this item need not be answered with respect to options, warrants or rights held by such person or group. If the issuer cannot ascertain the market value of its securities, the offering price may be used for purposes of this subsection. If, as is the case with offerings of debt securities, the offering price cannot be determined at the time of filing the offering statement, the issuer may utilize any reasonable method of valuation.

(e) List all parents of the issuer, showing the basis of control and as to each parent the percentage of voting securities owned or other basis of control by its immediate parent, if any.

Item 11. Interest of Management and Others in Certain Transactions

Describe briefly any transactions during the previous two years or any presently proposed transactions, to which the issuer or any of its subsidiaries was or is to be a party, in which any of the following persons had or is to have a direct or indirect material interest, naming such person and stating his relationship to the issuer, the nature of his interest in the transaction and, where practicable, the amount of such interest:

(1) Any director or officer of the issuer;

(2) Any nominee for election as a director;

(3) Any principal securityholder named in answer to Item 10(a);

(4) If the issuer was incorporated or organized within the past three years, any promoter of the issuer;

(5) Any relative or spouse of any of the foregoing persons, or any relative of such spouse, who has the same house as such person or who is a director or officer of any parent or subsidiary of the issuer.

Instructions: 1. No information need be given in answer to this item as to any transaction where:

(a) The rates of charges involved in the transaction are determined by competitive bids, or the transaction involves the rendering of services as a common or contract carrier fixed in conformity with law or governmental authority;

(b) The transaction involves services as a bank depositary of funds, transfer agent, registrar, trustee under a trust indenture, or similar services;

(c) The amount involved in the transaction or a series of similar transactions, including all periodic installments in the case of any lease or other agreement providing for periodic payments or installments does not exceed $50,000; or

(d) The interest of the specified person arises solely from the ownership of securities of the issuer and the specified person receives no extra or special benefit not shared on a pro-rata basis by all of the holders of securities of the class.

2. It should be noted that this Item calls for disclosure of indirect as well as direct material interests in transactions. A person who has a position or relationship with a firm, corporation, or other entity which engages in a transaction with the issuer or its subsidiaries may have an indirect interest in such transaction by reason of such position or relationship. However, a person shall be deemed not to have a material indirect interest in a transaction within the meaning of this Item where:

(a) the interest arises only (i) from such person's position as a director of another corporation or organization (other than a partnership) which is a party to the transaction, or (ii) from the direct or indirect ownership by such person and all other persons specified in subparagraphs (1) through (5) above, in the aggregate, of less than a 10 percent equity interest in another person (other than a partnership) which is a party to the transaction, or (iii) from both such position and ownership;

(b) the interest arises only from such person's position as a limited partner in a partnership in which he and all other persons specified in (1) through (5) above had an interest of less than 10 percent; or

(c) the interest of such person arises solely from the holding of an equity interest (including a limited partnership interest but excluding a general partnership interest) or a creditor interest in another person which is a party to the transaction with the issuer or any of its subsidiaries and the transaction is not material to such other person.

3. Include the name of each person whose interest in any transaction is described and the nature of the relationships by reason of which such interest is required to be described. The amount of the interest of any specified person shall be computed without regard to the amount of the profit or loss involved in the transaction. Where it is not practicable to state the approximate amount of the interest, the approximate amount involved in the transaction shall be disclosed.

4. Information should be included as to any material underwriting discounts and commissions upon the sale of securities by the issuer where any of the specified persons was or is to be a principal underwriter or is a controlling person, or member, of a firm which was or is to be a principal underwriter. Information need not be given concerning ordinary management fees paid by underwriters to a managing underwriter pursuant to an agreement among underwriters the parties to which do not include the issuer or its subsidiaries.

5. As to any transaction involving the purchase or sale of assets by or to any issuer or any subsidiary, otherwise than in the ordinary course of business, state the cost of the assets to the purchaser and if acquired by the seller within two years prior to the transaction, the cost thereof to the seller.

6. Information shall be furnished in answer to this Item with respect to transactions not excluded above which involve remuneration from the issuer or its subsidiaries, directly or indirectly, to any of the specified persons for services in any capacity unless the interest of

such persons arises solely from the ownership individually and in the aggregate of less than 10 percent of any class of equity securities of another corporation furnishing the services to the issuer or its subsidiaries.

Item 12. Securities Being Offered

(a) If capital stock is being offered, state the title of the class and furnish the following information:

(1) Outline briefly: (i) dividend rights; (ii) voting rights; (iii) liquidation rights; (iv) preemptive rights; (v) conversion rights; (vi) redemption provisions; (vii) sinking fund provisions; and (viii) liability to further calls or to assessment by the issuer.

(2) Briefly describe potential liabilities imposed on shareholders under state statutes or foreign law, e.g., to laborers, servants or employees of the registrant, unless such disclosure would be immaterial because the financial resources of the registrant are such as to make it unlikely that the liability will ever be imposed.

(b) If debt securities are being offered, outline briefly the following:

(1) Provisions with respect to interest, conversion, maturity, redemption, amortization, sinking fund or retirement.

(2) Provisions with respect to the kind and priority of any lien securing the issue, together with a brief identification of the principal properties subject to such lien.

(3) Provisions restricting the declaration of dividends or requiring the maintenance of any ratio of assets, the creation or maintenance of reserves or the maintenance of properties.

(4) Provisions permitting or restricting the issuance of additional securities, the withdrawal of cash deposited against such issuance, the incurring of additional debt, the release or substitution of assets securing the issue, the modification of the terms of the security, and similar provisions.

Instruction: In the case of secured debt there should be stated (i) the approximate amount of unbonded property available for use against the issuance of bonds, as of the most recent practicable date, and (ii) whether the securities being issued are to be issued against such property, against the deposit of cash, or otherwise.

(c) If securities described are to be offered pursuant to warrants, rights, or convertible securities, state briefly:

(1) the amount of securities called for by such warrants, convertible securities or rights;

(2) the period during which and the price at which the warrants, convertible securities or rights are exercisable;

(3) the amounts of warrants, convertible securities or rights outstanding; and

(4) any other material terms of such securities.

(d) In the case of any other kind of securities, appropriate information of a comparable character.

PART F/S

The following financial statements of the issuer, or the issuer and its predecessors or any businesses to which the issuer is a successor shall be filed as part of the offering statement and included in the offering circular which is distributed to investors.

Such financial statements shall be prepared in accordance with generally accepted accounting principles (GAAP) in the United States. If the issuer is a Canadian company, a reconciliation to GAAP in the United States shall be filed as part of the financial statements.

Issuers which have audited financial statements because they prepare them for other purposes, shall provide them.

The Commission's Regulation S–X, 17 CFR 210.1 et seq. relating to the form, content of and requirements for financial statements shall not apply to the financial statements required by this part, except that if audited financial statements are filed, the qualifications and reports of an independent auditor shall comply with the requirements of Article 2 of Regulation S–X.

Issuers which are limited partners are required to also file the balance sheets of general partners: (1) if such general partner is a corporation, the balance sheet shall be as of the end of its most recently completed fiscal year; receivables from a parent or affiliate of such general partner (including notes receivable, but excluding trade receivables) should be deductions from shareholders equity of the general partner; where a parent or affiliate has committed to increase or maintain the general partner's capital, there shall also be filed the balance sheet of such parent or affiliate as of the end of its most recently completed fiscal year; (2) if such general partner is a partnership, its balance sheet as of the end of its most recently completed fiscal year; (3) if such general partner is a natural person, the net worth of such general partner(s) based on the estimated fair market value of their assets and liabilities, singly or in the aggregate shall be disclosed in the offering circular, and balance sheets of each of the individual general partners supporting such net worth shall be provided as supplemental information.

(1) Balance Sheet—as of a date within 90 days prior to filing the offering statement or such longer time, not exceeding 6 months, as the Commission may permit at the written request of the issuer upon a showing of good cause; for filings made after 90 days subsequent to the issuer's most recent fiscal year, the balance sheet shall be dated as of the end of the most recent fiscal year.

(2) Statements of income, cash flows, and other stockholders equity—for each of the 2 fiscal years preceding the date of the most recent balance sheet being filed, and for any interim period between the end of the most recent of such fiscal years and the date of the most recent balance sheet being filed, or for the period of the issuer's existence if less than the period above.

Income statements shall be accompanied by a statement that in the opinion of management all adjustments necessary for a fair statement of results for the interim period have been included. If all such adjustments are of a normal recurring nature, a statement to that effect shall be made. If otherwise, there shall be furnished as supplemental information and not as part of the offering statement, a letter describing in detail the nature and amount of any adjustments other than normal recurring adjustments entering into the determination of results shown.

(3) Financial Statements of Businesses Acquired or to be Acquired.

(a) Financial statements for the periods specified in (c) below should be furnished if any of the following conditions exist:

(i) Consummation of a significant business combination accounted for as a purchase has occurred or is probable (for purposes of this rule, the term "purchase" encompasses the purchase of an interest in a business accounted for by the equity method); or

(ii) Consummation of a significant business combination to be accounted for as a pooling is probable.

(b) A business combination shall be considered significant if a comparison of the most recent annual financial statements of the business acquired or to be acquired and the registrant's most recent annual consolidated financial statements filed at or prior to the date of acquisition indicates that the business would be a significant subsidiary pursuant to the conditions specified in Rule 405 of Regulation C.

(c)(i) The financial statements shall be furnished for the periods up to the date of acquisition, for those periods for which the registrant is required to furnish financial statements.

(ii) These financial statements need not be audited.

(iii) The separate balance sheet of the acquired business is not required when the registrant's most recent balance sheet filed is for a date after the acquisition was consummated.

(iv) If none of the conditions in the definitions of significant subsidiary in Rule 405 exceeds 20%, income statements of the acquired business for only the most recent fiscal year and any interim period need be filed.

(d) If consummation of more than one transaction has occurred or is probable, the tests of significance shall be made using the aggregate impact of the businesses and the required financial statements may be presented on a combined basis, if appropriate.

(e) This paragraph (3) shall not apply to a business which is totally held by the registrant prior to consummation of the transaction.

(4) Pro Forma Financial Information.

(a) Pro forma information shall be furnished if any of the following conditions exist (for purposes of this rule, the term "purchase" encompasses the purchase of an interest in a business accounted for by the equity method);

(i) During the most recent fiscal year or subsequent interim period for which a balance sheet of the registrant is required, a significant business combination accounted for as a purchase has occurred;

(ii) After the date of the registrant's most recent balance sheet, consummation of a significant business combination to be accounted for by either the purchase method or pooling of interests method of accounting has occurred or is probable.

(b) The provisions of paragraph (3)(b), (d) and (e) apply to this paragraph (4).

(c) Pro forma statements shall ordinarily be in columnar form showing condensed historical statements, pro forma adjustments, and the pro forma results and should include the following:

(i) If the transaction was consummated during the most recent fiscal year or in the subsequent interim period, pro forma statements of income reflecting the combined operations of the entities for the latest fiscal year and interim period, if any, or

(ii) If consummation of the transaction has occurred or is probable after the date of the most recent balance sheet, a pro forma balance sheet giving effect to the combination as of the date of the most recent balance sheet required by paragraph (b). For a purchase, pro forma statements of income reflecting the combined operations of the entities for the latest fiscal year and interim period, if any, and for a pooling of interests, pro forma statements of income for all periods for which income statements of the registrant are required.

PART III—EXHIBITS

Item 1. Index to Exhibits

(a) An index to the exhibits filed should be presented immediately following the cover page to Part III.

(b) Each exhibit should be listed in the exhibit index according to the number assigned to it under Item 2 below.

(c) The index to exhibits should identify the location of the exhibit under the sequential page numbering system for this Form 1–A.

(d) Where exhibits are incorporated by reference, the reference shall be made in the index of exhibits.

Instructions: 1. Any document or part thereof filed with the Commission pursuant to any

Act administered by the Commission may, subject to the limitations of Rule 24 of the Commission's Rule of Practice, be incorporated by reference as an exhibit to any offering statement.

2. If any modification has occurred in the text of any document incorporated by reference since the filing thereof, the issuer shall file with the reference a statement containing the text of such modification and the date thereof.

3. Procedurally, the techniques specified in Rule 411(d) of Regulation C shall be followed.

Item 2. Description of Exhibits

As appropriate, the following documents should be filed as exhibits to the offering statement.

(1) *Underwriting Agreement.* Each underwriting contract or agreement with a principal underwriter or letter pursuant to which the securities are to be distributed; where the terms have yet to be finalized, proposed formats may be provided.

(2) *Charter and by-laws.* The charter and by-laws of the issuer or instruments corresponding thereto as presently in effect and any amendments thereto.

(3) *Instruments defining the rights of security holders.* (a) All instruments defining the rights of any holder of the issuer's securities, including but not limited to (i) holders of equity or debt securities being issued; (ii) holders of long-term debt of the issuer, and of all subsidiaries for which consolidated or unconsolidated financial statements are required to be filed.

(b) The following instruments need not be filed if the issuer agrees to provide them to the Commission upon request: (i) instruments defining the rights of holders of long-term debt of the issuer and all of its subsidiaries for which consolidated financial statements are required to be filed if such debt is not being issued pursuant to this Regulation A offering and the total amount of such authorized issuance does not exceed 5% of the total assets of the issuer and its subsidiaries on a consolidated basis; (ii) any instrument with respect to a class of securities which is to be retired or redeemed prior to the issuance or upon delivery of the securities being issued pursuant to this Regulation A offering and appropriate steps have been taken to assure such retirement or redemption; and (iii) copies of instruments evidencing scrip certificates or fractions of shares.

(4) *Subscription agreement.* The form of any subscription agreement to be used in connection with the purchase of securities in this offering.

(5) *Voting trust agreement.* Any voting trust agreements and amendments thereto.

(6) *Material contracts.* (a) Every contract not made in the ordinary course of business which is material to the issuer and is to be performed in whole or in part at or after the filing of the offering statement or was entered into not more than 2 years before such filing. Only contracts need be filed as to which the issuer or subsidiary of the issuer is a party or has succeeded to a party by assumption or assignment or in which the issuer or such subsidiary has a beneficial interest.

(b) If the contract is such as ordinarily accompanies the kind of business conducted by the issuer and its subsidiaries, it is made in the ordinary course of business and need not be filed unless it falls within one or more of the following categories, in which case it should be filed except where immaterial in amount or significance: (i) any contract to which directors, officers, promoters, voting trustees, security holders named in the offering statement, or underwriters are parties except where the contract merely involves the purchase or sale of current assets having a determinable market price, at such market price; (ii) any contract upon which the issuer's business is substantially dependent, as in the case of continuing contracts to sell the major part of the issuer's products or services or to purchase the major part of the issuer's requirements of goods, services or raw materials or any franchise or license or other agreement to use a patent, formula, trade secret, process or trade name upon which the issuer's business depends to a material extent; (iii) any contract calling for the acquisition or sale of any property, plant or equipment for a consideration exceeding 15% of such fixed assets of the issuer on a consolidated basis; or (iv) any material lease under which a part of the property described in the offering statement is held by the issuer.

(c) Any management contract or any compensatory plan, contract or arrangement including but not limited to plans relating to options, warrants or rights, pension, retirement or deferred compensation or bonus, incentive or profit sharing (or if not set forth in any formal document, a written description thereof) shall be deemed material and shall be filed except for the following: (i) ordinary purchase and sales agency agreements; (ii) agreements with managers of stores in a chain organization or similar organization; (iii) contracts providing for labor or salesmen's bonuses or payments to a class of security holders, as such; (iv) any compensatory plan, contract or arrangement which pursuant to its terms is available to employees generally and which in operation provides for the same method of allocation of benefits between management and non-management participants.

(7) *Material foreign patents.* Each material foreign patent for an invention not covered by a United States patent. If a substantial part of the securities to be offered or if the proceeds therefrom have been or are to be used for the particular purposes of acquiring, developing or exploiting one or more material foreign patents or patent rights, furnish a list showing the number and a brief identification of each such patent or patent right.

(8) *Plan of acquisition, reorganization, arrangement, liquidation, or succession.* Any material plan of acquisition, disposition, reorganization, readjustment, succession, liquidation or arrangement and any amendments thereto described in the offering statement. Schedules (or similar attachments) to these exhibits shall not be filed unless such schedules contain information which is material to an investment decision and which is not otherwise disclosed in the agreement or the offering statement. The plan filed shall contain a list briefly identifying the contents of all omitted schedules, together with an agreement to furnish supplementally a copy of any omitted schedule to the Commission upon request.

(9) *Escrow agreements.* Any escrow agreement or similar arrangement which has been executed in connection with the Regulation A offering.

(10) *Consents.* (a) Experts: The written consent of (i) any account, engineer, geologist, appraiser or any person whose profession gives authority to a statement made by them and who is named in the offering statement as having prepared or certified any part of the document or is named as having prepared or certified a report or evaluation whether or not for use in connection with the offering statement; (ii) the expert that authored any portion of a report quoted or summarized as such in the offering statement, expressly stating their consent to the use of such quotation or summary; (iii) any persons who are referenced as having reviewed or passed upon any information in the offering statement, and that such information is being included on the basis of their authority or in reliance upon their status as experts.

(b) Underwriters: A written consent and certification in the form which follows signed by each underwriter of the securities proposed to be offered. All underwriters may, with appropriate modifications, sign the same consent and certification or separate consents and certifications may be signed by any underwriter or group of underwriters.

CONSENT AND CERTIFICATION BY UNDERWRITER

1. The undersigned hereby consents to being named as underwriter in an offering statement filed with the Securities and Exchange Commission by [insert name of issuer] pursuant to Regulation A in connection with a proposed offering of [insert title of securities] to the public.

2. The undersigned hereby certifies that it furnished the statements and information set forth in the offering statement with respect to the undersigned, its directors and officers or partners, that such statements and information are accurate, complete and fully responsive to the requirements of Parts I, II and III of the Offering Statement thereto, and do not omit any information required to be stated therein with respect of any such persons, or necessary to make the statements and information therein with respect to any of them not misleading.

3. If Preliminary Offering Circulars are distributed, the undersigned hereby undertakes to keep an accurate and complete record of the name and address of each person furnished a Preliminary Offering Circular and, if such Preliminary Offering Circular is inaccurate or inadequate in any material respect, to furnish a revised Preliminary Offering Circular or a Final Offering Circular to all persons to whom the securities are to be sold at least 48 hours prior to the mailing of any confirmation of sale to such persons, or to send such a circular to such persons under circumstances that it would normally be received by them 48 hours prior to their receipt of confirmation of the sale.

____
(Underwriter)

By __________________________

Date / /

(c) All written consents shall be dated and manually signed.

(11) *Opinion re legality.* An opinion of counsel as to the legality of the securities covered by the Offering Statement, indicating whether they will, when sold, be legally issued, fully paid and nonassessable, and if debt securities, whether they will be binding obligations of the issuer.

(12) *Sales Material.* Any material required to be filed by virtue of Rule 256.

(13) *"Test the Water" Material.* Any written document or broadcast script used under the authorization of Rule 254.

(14) *Appointment of Agent for Service of Process.* A Canadian issuer shall provide Form F–X.

(15) *Additional exhibits.* Any additional exhibits which the issuer may wish to file, which shall be so marked to indicate clearly the subject matters to which they refer.

SIGNATURES

The issuer has duly caused this offering statement to be signed on its behalf by the undersigned, thereunto duly authorized, in the City of ______, State of ______, on ______, 19__

(Issuer) ____

By (Signature and Title) ______________________________

This offering statement has been signed by the following persons in the capacities and on the dates indicated.

(Signature) ____

(Title) ____

(Selling security holder) ____________________

(Date) ____________________

Instructions: 1. The offering statement shall be signed by the issuer, its Chief Executive Officer, Chief Financial Officer, a majority of the members of its board of directors or other governing instrumentality, and each person, other than the issuer, for whose account any of the securities are to be offered. If a signature is by a person on behalf of any other person, evidence of authority to sign shall be filed with the offering statement, except where an executive officer signs on behalf of the issuer. If the issuer is Canadian, its authorized representative in the United States also shall sign. Where the issuer is a limited partnership, the offering statement shall also be signed by a majority of the board of directors of any corporate general partner.

2. The name of each person signing the offering statement shall be typed or printed beneath the signature.

FORM 2–A

REPORT OF SALES AND USES OF PROCEEDS PURSUANT TO RULE 257 OF REGULATION A

File No. 24– —

For period ending / /—

Indicate whether the report is an initial report [ ]

amendment [ ]

or final report [ ]

If the report is an amendment, indicate the number of such amendment. ☐ ☐

If the offering has terminated, indicate the date of termination / /

General Instructions

The report shall be filed in accordance with the provisions of Rule 257 of Regulation A.

Answer each item in the box(es) or spaces provided. If additional space is required for any response, continue the response on an attached sheet.

If the issuer is required to file any report(s) on this form subsequent to its initial filing, each subsequent filing shall be deemed an amendment to the initial filing. Do not report in any amendment responses to Items 3–11 unless the information has changed.

No fee is required to accompany this filing.

Seven copies of the form shall be filed with the main office of the Commission in Washington, D.C. At least one copy of the form shall be manually signed; other copies may bear typed or printed signatures.

1. ____________________
Exact name of issuer as specified in its charter.

2. Date of qualification of the offering statement:
☐☐ ☐☐ ☐☐

3. Has the offering commenced? [ ] Yes [ ] No.
If yes, date of commencement: ☐☐ ☐☐ ☐☐
If no, explain briefly:
____

4. Did the offering terminate before any securities were sold? [ ] Yes [ ] No.
   If yes, explain briefly:
   ____
   If "yes", do not answer Items 5–11.
5. Did the offering terminate prior to the sale of all the securities qualified under Regulation A? [ ] Yes [ ] No.
   If yes, explain briefly:
   ____
6. Indicate the total number of shares or other units offered and sold to date:
   ______ (issuer's account) ______ (selling securityholders)
   Indicate the number of shares or other units still being offered:
   ______ (issuer's account) ______ (selling securityholders)
7. Total amount of dollars received from the public to date. $______
   Total amount allocable to selling securityholders: $______

Underwriting discount or commission allowed	$______
Underwriting expenses paid	$______
Finders' Fees	$______
Other expenses paid to date by or for issuer:	
Legal (including organization)	$______
Accounting	$______
Engineering	$______
Printing and Advertising	$______
Other (specify) ______	$______
______	$______
______	$______
______	$______
Total costs and expenses	$______
Total net proceeds remaining.	$______

8. Uses of net proceeds to date.
   Instructions:
   1. Do not include any amount in "working capital" to which a more specific category is applicable.
   2. Round all amounts to the nearest dollar.
   3. Specify under "other purposes" any purpose for which at least 5% of the issuer's proceeds or $50,000, whichever is less, has been used.

Salaries and fees	$______
Construction of plant, building and facilities	$______
Purchases and installation of machinery and equipment	$______
Purchase of real estate	$______
Acquisition of other business(es)	$______
Repayment of indebtedness	$______
Working capital	$______
Development expense (product development, research, patent costs, etc.)	$______
Temporary investment (specify) ______	$______
______	$______
______	$______
______	$______
Other purposes (specify)	
______	$______
______	$______
______	$______

______ $______
______ $______
______ $______
______ $______
______ $______

9. Do the use(s) of proceeds in Item 8 represent a material change in the use(s) of proceeds described in the offering circular? [ ] Yes [ ] No.
If yes, explain briefly:

______

10. State the number of shares held by each promoter, director, officer or controlling person of the issuer, if different from the amount stated in the offering circular.

______

11. List the names and addresses of all brokers and dealers who have, to the knowledge of the issuer or underwriters, participated in the distribution of the securities during the period covered by this report.

______

SIGNATURE

Pursuant to the requirements of Rule 257 and Regulation A, ______ has caused this report to be signed on its behalf by the undersigned thereunto duly authorized.

______
Issuer

______ By ______
Date Signature

Instruction: The report shall be signed by an executive officer, general partner or counsel of the issuer or by any other duly authorized person. The name and any title of the person who signs the report shall be typed or printed beneath the signature.

2. REGISTRATION AND OTHER FORMS UNDER THE 1933 ACT

FORM S–1

SECURITIES AND EXCHANGE COMMISSION

Washington, D.C. 20549

FORM S–1

REGISTRATION STATEMENT UNDER THE SECURITIES ACT OF 1933

______
(Exact name of registrant as specified in its charter)

______
(State or other jurisdiction of incorporation or organization)

______
(Primary Standard Industrial Classification Code Number)

______
(I.R.S. Employer Identification No.)

______
(Address, including zip code, and telephone number, including area code, of registrant's principal executive offices)

(Name, address, including zip code, and telephone number, including area code, of agent for service)

Approximate date of commencement of proposed sale to the public ____________

If any of the securities being registered on this Form are to be offered on a delayed or continuous basis pursuant to Rule 415 under the Securities Act, check the following box. ☐

If this Form is filed to register additional securities for an offering pursuant to Rule 462(b) under the Securities Act, please check the following box and list the Securities Act registration statement number of the earlier effective registration statement for the same offering. ☐

If this Form is a post-effective amendment filed pursuant to Rule 462(c) under the Securities Act, check the following box and list the Securities Act registration statement number of the earlier effective registration statement for the same offering. ☐

If this Form is a post-effective amendment filed pursuant to Rule 462(d) under the Securities Act, check the following box and list the Securities Act registration statement number of the earlier effective registration statement for the same offering. ☐

If delivery of the prospectus is expected to be made pursuant to rule 434, please check the following box. ☐

Calculation of Registration Fee

Title of each class of securities to be registered	Amount to be registered	Proposed maximum offering price per unit	Proposed maximum aggregate offering price	Amount of registration fee

Note: Specific details relating to the fee calculation shall be furnished in notes to the table, including references to provisions of Rule 457 relied upon, if the basis of the calculation is not otherwise evident from the information presented in the table.

GENERAL INSTRUCTIONS

I. Eligibility Requirements for Use of Form S–1

This Form shall be used for the registration under the Securities Act of 1933 ("Securities Act") of securities of all registrants for which no other form is authorized or prescribed, except that this Form shall not be used for securities of foreign governments or political subdivisions thereof.

II. Application of General Rules and Regulations

A. Attention is directed to the General Rules and Regulations under the Securities Act, particularly those comprising Regulation C thereunder. That Regulation contains general requirements regarding the preparation and filing of the registration statement.

B. Attention is directed to Regulation S–K for the requirements applicable to the content of the nonfinancial statement portions of registration statements under the Securities Act. Where this Form directs the registrant to furnish information required by Regulation S–K and the item of Regulation S–K so provides, information need only be furnished to the extent appropriate.

III. Exchange Offers

If any of the securities being registered are to be offered in exchange for securities of any other issuer the prospectus shall also include the information which would be required by Item 11 if the securities of such other issuer were registered on this Form. There shall also be included the information concerning such securities of such other issue which would be called for by Item 9 if such securities were being registered. In connection with this instruction, reference is made to Rule 409.

IV. Roll-up Transactions

If the securities to be registered on this Form will be issued in a roll-up transaction as defined in Item 901(c) of Regulation S–K (17 CFR 229.901(c)), attention is directed to the requirements of Form S–4 applicable to roll-up transactions, including, but not limited to, General Instruction I.

V. Registration of Additional Securities

With respect to the registration of additional securities for an offering pursuant to Rule 462(b) under the Securities Act, the registrant may file a registration statement consisting only of the following: The facing page; a statement that the contents of the earlier registration statement, identified by file number, are incorporated by reference; required opinions and consents; the signature page; and any price-related information omitted from the earlier registration statement in reliance on Rule 430A that the registrant chooses to include in the new registration statement. The information contained in such a Rule 462(b) registration statement shall be deemed to be a part of the earlier registration statement as of the date of effectiveness of the rule 462(b) registration statement. Any opinion or consent required in the Rule 462(b) registration statement may be incorporated by reference from the earlier registration statement with respect to the offering, if: (i) Such opinion or consent expressly provides for such incorporation; and (ii) such opinion relates to the securities registered pursuant to rule 462(b). See Rule 411(c) and rule 439(b) under the Securities Act.

VI. Offerings of Asset-Backed Securities

The following applies if a registration statements of this form S–1 is being used to register an offering of asset-backed securities. Terms used in this General Instruction VI. have the same meaning as in Item 1101 of Regulation AB (17 CFR 229.1101).

A. *Items that may be Omitted.*

Such registrants may omit the information called for by Item 11, Information with Respect to the Registrant.

B. *Substitute Information to be Included.*

In addition to the Items that are otherwise required by this Form, the registrant must furnish in the prospectus the information required by Items 1102 through 1120 of Regulation AB (17 CFR 229.1102 through 229.1120).

C. *Signatures.*

The registration statement must be signed by the depositor, the depositor's principal executive officer or officers, principal financial officer and controller or principal accounting officer, and by at least a majority of the depositor's board of directors or persons performing similar functions.

PART I—INFORMATION REQUIRED IN PROSPECTUS

Item 1. Forepart of the Registration Statement and Outside Front Cover Page of Prospectus

Set forth in the forepart of the registration statement and on the outside front cover page of the prospectus the information required by Item 501 of Regulation S–K.

Item 2. Inside Front and Outside Back Cover Pages of Prospectus

Set forth on the inside front cover page of the prospectus or, where permitted, on the outside back cover page, the information required by Item 502 of Regulation S–K.

Item 3. Summary Information, Risk Factors and Ratio of Earnings to Fixed Charges

Furnish the information required by Item 503 of Regulation S–K.

Item 4. Use of Proceeds

Furnish the information required by Item 504 of Regulation S–K.

Item 5. Determination of Offering Price

Furnish the information required by Item 505 of Regulation S–K.

Item 6. Dilution

Furnish the information required by Item 506 of Regulation S–K.

Item 7. Selling Security Holders

Furnish the information required by Item 507 of Regulation S–K.

Item 8. Plan of Distribution

Furnish the information required by Item 508 of Regulation S–K.

Item 9. Description of Securities to Be Registered

Furnish the information required by Item 202 of Regulation S–K.

Item 10. Interests of Named Experts and Counsel

Furnish the information required by Item 509 of Regulation S–K.

Item 11. Information with Respect to the Registrant

Furnish the following information with respect to the registrant:

(a) Information required by Item 101 of Regulation S–K, description of business;

(b) Information required by Item 102 of Regulation S–K, description of property;

(c) Information required by Item 103 of Regulation S–K, legal proceedings;

(d) Where common equity securities are being offered, information required by Item 201 of Regulation S–K, market price of and dividends on the registrant's common equity and related stockholder matters;

(e) Financial statements meeting the requirements of Regulation S–X (Schedules required under Regulation S–X shall be filed as "Financial Statement Schedules" pursuant to Item 15, Exhibits and Financial Statement Schedules, of this Form), as well as any Financial information required by Rule 3–05 and Article 11 of Regulation S–X;

(f) Information required by Item 301 of Regulation S–K, selected financial data;

(g) Information required by Item 302 of Regulation S–K, supplementary financial information;

(h) Information required by Item 303 of Regulation S–K, management's discussion and analysis of financial condition and results of operations;

(i) Information required by Item 304 of Regulation S–K, changes in and disagreements with accountants on accounting and financial disclosure;

(j) Information required by Item 305 of Regulation S–K (§ 229.305 of this chapter), quantitative and qualitative disclosures about market risk.

(k) Information required by Item 401 of Regulation S–K, directors and executive officers;

(*l*) Information required by Item 402 of Regulation S–K, executive compensation;

(m) Information required by Item 403 of Regulation S–K, security ownership of certain beneficial owners and management; and

(n) Information required by Item 404 of Regulation S–K, certain relationships and related transactions.

Item 12. Disclosure of Commission Position on Indemnification for Securities Act Liabilities

Furnish the information required by Item 510 of Regulation S–K.

PART II—INFORMATION NOT REQUIRED IN PROSPECTUS

Item 13. Other Expenses of Issuance and Distribution

Furnish the information required by Item 511 of Regulation S–K.

Item 14. Indemnification of Directors and Officers

Furnish the information required by Item 702 of Regulation S–K.

Item 15. Recent Sales of Unregistered Securities

Furnish the information required by Item 701 of Regulation S–K.

Item 16. Exhibits and Financial Statement Schedules

(a) Subject to the rules regarding incorporation by reference, furnish the exhibits as required by Item 601 of Regulation S–K.

(b) Furnish the financial statement schedules required by Regulation S–X and Item 11(e) of this Form. These schedules shall be lettered or numbered in the manner described for exhibits in paragraph (a).

Item 17. Undertakings

Furnish the undertakings required by Item 512 of Regulation S–K.

SIGNATURES

Pursuant to the requirements of the Securities Act of 1933, the registrant has duly caused this registration statement to be signed on its behalf by the undersigned, thereunto duly authorized, in the City of ______, State of ______, on ______, 19__.

(Registrant) ____________________

By (Signature and Title) ____________________

Pursuant to the requirements of the Securities Act of 1933, this registration statement has been signed by the following persons in the capacities and on the dates indicated.

(Signature) ____________________

(Title) ____________________

(Date) ____________________

Instructions. 1. The registration statement shall be signed by the registrant, its principal executive officer or officers, its principal financial officer, its controller or principal accounting officer and by at least a majority of the board of directors or persons performing similar functions. If the registrant is a foreign person, the registration statement shall also be signed by its authorized representative in the United States. Where the registrant is a limited partnership, the registration statement shall be signed by a majority of the board of directors of any corporate general partner signing the registration statement.

2. The name of each person who signs the registration statement shall be typed or printed beneath his signature. Any person who occupies more than one of the specified positions shall indicate each capacity in which he signs the registration statement. Attention is directed to Rule 402 concerning manual signatures and to Item 601 of Regulation S–K concerning signatures pursuant to powers of attorney.

INSTRUCTIONS AS TO SUMMARY PROSPECTUSES

1. A summary prospectus used pursuant to Rule 431 shall at the time of its use contain such of the information specified below as is then included in the registration statement. All other information and documents contained in the registration statement may be omitted.

(a) As to Item 1, the aggregate offering price to the public, the aggregate underwriting discounts and commissions and the offering price per unit to the public;

(b) As to Item 4, a brief statement of the principal purposes for which the proceeds are to be used;

(c) As to Item 7, a statement as to the amount of the offering, if any, to be made for the account of security holders;

(d) As to Item 8, the name of the managing underwriter or underwriters and a brief statement as to the nature of the underwriter's obligation to take the securities; if any securities to be registered are to be offered otherwise than through underwriters, a brief statement as to the manner of distribution; and, if securities are to be offered otherwise than for cash, a brief statement as to the general purposes of the distribution, the basis upon which the securities are to be offered, the amount of compensation and other expenses of distribution, and by whom they are to be borne;

(e) As to Item 9, a brief statement as to dividend rights, voting rights, conversion rights, interest, maturity;

(f) As to Item 11, a brief statement of the general character of the business done and intended to be done, the selected financial data (Item 301 of Regulation S–K) and a brief statement of the nature and present status of any material pending legal proceedings; and

(g) A tabular presentation of notes payable, long term debt, deferred credits, minority interests, if material, and the equity section of the latest balance sheet filed, as may be appropriate.

2. The summary prospectus shall not contain a summary or condensation of any other required financial information except as provided above.

3. Where securities being registered are to be offered in exchange for securities of any other issuer, the summary prospectus also shall contain that information as to Items 9 and 11 specified in paragraphs (e) and (f) above which would be required if the securities of such other issuer were registered on this Form.

4. The Commission may, upon the request of the registrant, and where consistent with the protection of investors, permit the omission of any of the information herein required or the furnishing in substitution therefor of appropriate information of comparable character. The Commission may also require the inclusion of other information in addition to, or in substitution for, the information herein required in any case where such information is necessary or appropriate for the protection of investors.

FORM S–2

SECURITIES AND EXCHANGE COMMISSION

Washington, D.C. 20549

FORM S–2

REGISTRATION STATEMENT UNDER THE SECURITIES ACT OF 1933

____

(Exact name of registrant as specified in its charter)

____

(State or other jurisdiction of incorporation or organization)

____

(I.R.S. Employer Identification No.)

____

(Address, including zip code, and telephone number, including area code, of registrant's principal executive offices)

____

(Name, address, including zip code, and telephone number, including area code, of agent for service)

Approximate date of commencement of proposed sale to the public ______________

If any of the securities being registered on this Form are to be offered on a delayed or continuous basis pursuant to Rule 415 under the Securities Act, check the following box. ☐

If the registrant elects to deliver its latest annual report to security holders, or a complete and legible facsimile thereof, pursuant to

Item 11(a)(1) of this Form, check the following box. ☐

If this Form is filed to register additional securities for an offering pursuant to Rule 462(b) under the Securities Act, check the following box and list the Securities Act registration statement number of the earlier effective registration statement for the same offering. ☐

If this Form is a post-effective amendment filed pursuant to Rule 462(c) under the Securities Act, check the following box and list the Securities Act registration statement number of the earlier effective registration statement for the same offering. ☐

If this Form is a post-effective amendment filed pursuant to Rule 462(d) under the Securities Act, check the following box and list the Securities Act registration statement number of the earlier effective registration statement for the same offering. ☐

If delivery of the prospectus is expected to be made pursuant to rule 434, check the following box. ☐

Calculation of Registration Fee

Title of each class of securities to be registered	Amount to be registered	Proposed maximum offering price per unit	Proposed maximum aggregate offering price	Amount of registration fee

Note: Specific details relating to the fee calculation shall be furnished in notes to the table, including references to provisions of Rule 457 relied upon, if the basis of the calculation is not otherwise evident from the information presented in the table.

GENERAL INSTRUCTIONS

I. Eligibility Requirements for Use of Form S–2

Any registrant which meets the following conditions may use this Form for registration of securities under the Securities Act of 1933 ("Securities Act") which are offered or to be offered in any transaction other than an exchange offer for securities of another person:

A. The registrant is organized under the laws of the United States or any State or Territory or the District of Columbia and has its principal business operations in the United States or its territories.

B. The registrant has a class of securities registered pursuant to Section 12(b) of the Securities Exchange Act of 1934 ("Exchange Act") or has a class of equity securities registered pursuant to Section 12(g) of the Exchange Act or is required to file reports pursuant to Section 15(d) of the Exchange Act.

C. The registrant:

(1) has been subject to the requirements of Section 12 or 15(d) of the Exchange Act and has filed all the material required to be filed pursuant to Section 13, 14 or 15(d) for a period of at least thirty-six calendar months immediately preceding the filing of the registration statement on this Form; and

(2) has filed in a timely manner all reports required to be filed during the twelve calendar months and any portion of a month immediately preceding the filing of the registration statement, other than a report that is required solely pursuant to Item 1.01, 1.02, 2.03, 2.04, 2.05, 2.06 or 4.02(a) of Form 8–K (§ 249.308 of this chapter). If the registrant has used (during the twelve calendar months and any portion of a month immediately preceding the filing of the registration statement) Rule 12b–25(b) (§ 240.12b–25(b) of this chapter) under the Exchange Act with respect to a report or a portion of a report, that report or portion thereof has actually been filed within the time period prescribed by that rule.

D. Neither the registrant nor any of its consolidated or unconsolidated subsidiaries have, since the end of their last fiscal year for which certified financial statements of the registrant and its consolidated subsidiaries were included in a report filed pursuant to Section 13(a) or 15(d) of the Exchange Act: (a) failed to pay any dividend or sinking fund installment on preferred stock; or (b) defaulted (i) on any installment or installments on indebtedness for borrowed money, or (ii) on any rental on one or more long term leases, which defaults in the aggregate are material to the financial position of the registrant and its consolidated and unconsolidated subsidiaries, taken as a whole.

E. A foreign private issuer, other than a foreign government, which satisfies all of the above provisions of these registrant eligibility requirements except the provisions in I.A. relating to organization and principal business shall be deemed to have met these registrant eligibility requirements provided that such foreign issuer files the same reports with the Commission under Section 13(a) or 15(d) of the Exchange Act as a domestic registrant pursuant to I.C. above.

F. If a registrant is a successor registrant it shall be deemed to have met conditions A., B., C., and D. above if: (1) its predecessor and it, taken together, do so, provided that the succession was primarily for the purpose of changing the state of incorporation of the predecessor or forming a holding company and that the assets and liabilities of the successor at the time of succession were substantially the same as those of the predecessor, or (2) all predecessors met the conditions at the time of succession and the registrant has continued to do so since the succession.

G. If a registrant is a majority-owned subsidiary which does not itself meet the conditions of these eligibility requirements, it shall nevertheless be deemed to have met such conditions if its parent meets the conditions and if the parent fully guarantees the securities being registered as to principal and interest. Note: In such an instance the parent-guarantor is the issuer of a separate security consisting of the guarantee which must be concurrently registered but may be registered on the same registration statement as are the guaranteed securities.

H. *Electronic filings.* In addition to satisfying the foregoing conditions, a registrant subject to the electronic filing requirements of Rule 101 of Regulation S–T (§ 232.101 of this chapter) shall have filed with the Commission:

All required electronic filings, including confirming electronic copies of documents submitted in paper pursuant to a hardship exemption as provided by Rule 201 or Rule 202(d) of Regulation S–T (§ 232.201 or § 232.202(d) of this chapter).

I. *Asset-backed securities.* This form shall not be used for an offering of asset-backed securities, as defined in § 229.1101 of this chapter.

II. Application of General Rules and Regulations

A. Attention is directed to the General Rules and Regulations under the Securities Act, particularly those comprising Regulation C thereunder. That Regulation contains general requirements regarding the preparation and filing of registration statements.

B. Attention is directed to Regulation S–K for the requirements applicable to the content of the non-financial statement portions of registration statements under the Securities Act. Where this Form directs the registrant to furnish information required by Regulation S–K and the item of Regulation S–K so provides, information need only be furnished to the extent appropriate.

C. A "small business issuer," defined in Rule 405, that is eligible to use Form S–2, shall refer to the disclosure items in Regulation S–B and not Regulation S–K. For example, while Item 1 of Form S–2 requires the information required by Item 501 of Regulation S–K, a small business issuer shall provide the information in Item 501 of Regulation S–B. Where Regulation S–B does not contain a comparable Item, for example there is no Item "301" in Regulation S–B, then a small business issuer may omit the Item. A small business issuer shall provide the financial information in Item 310 of Regulation S–B in lieu of the financial information called for by Item 11 of Form S–2.

III. Registration of Additional Securities

With respect to the registration of additional securities for an offering pursuant to Rule 462(b) under the Securities Act, the registrant may file a registration statement consisting only of the following: the facing page; a statement that the contents of the earlier registration statement, identified by file number, are incorporated by reference; required opinions and consents; the signature page; and any price-related information omitted from the earlier registration statement in reliance on Rule 430A that the registrant chooses to include in the new registration statement. The information contained in such a Rule 462(b) registration statement shall be deemed to be a part of the earlier registration statement as of the date of effectiveness of the Rule 462(b) registration statement. Any opinion or consent required in the Rule 462(b) registration statement may be incorporated by reference from the earlier registration statement with respect to the offering, if: (i) such opinion or consent expressly provides for such incorporation; and (ii) such opinion relates to the securities registered pursuant to Rule 462(b). See Rule 411(c) and Rule 439(b) under the Securities Act.

PART 1—INFORMATION REQUIRED IN PROSPECTUS

Item 1. Forepart of the Registration Statement and Outside Front Cover Page of Prospectus

Set forth in the forepart of the registration statement and on the outside front cover page of the prospectus the information required by Item 501 of Regulation S–K.

Item 2. Inside Front and Outside Back Cover Pages of Prospectus

Set forth on the inside front cover page of the prospectus or, where permitted, on the outside back cover page, the information required by Item 502 of Regulation S–K.

Item 3. Summary Information, Risk Factors and Ratio of Earnings to Fixed Charges

Furnish the information required by Item 503 of Regulation S–K.

Item 4. Use of Proceeds

Furnish the information required by Item 504 of Regulation S–K.

Item 5. Determination of Offering Price

Furnish the information required by Item 505 of Regulation S–K.

Item 6. Dilution

Furnish the information required by Item 506 of Regulation S–K.

Item 7. Selling Security Holders

Furnish the information required by Item 507 of Regulation S–K.

Item 8. Plan of Distribution

Furnish the information required by Item 508 of Regulation S-K.

Item 9. Description of Securities to Be Registered

Furnish the information required by Item 202 of Regulation S-K.

Item 10. Interests of Named Experts and Counsel

Furnish the information required by Item 509 of Regulation S-K.

Item 11. Information With Respect to the Registrant

Furnish the information required by either paragraph (a) or paragraph (b) of this Item. The information required by paragraph (b) shall be furnished if the registrant satisfies the conditions of paragraph (c) of this Item.

(a) If the registrant elects to deliver this prospectus together with a copy of either its latest Form 10–K or Form 10–KSB filed pursuant to Sections 13(a) or 15(d) of the Exchange Act or its latest annual report to security holders, which at the time of original preparation met the requirements of either Rule 14a–3 or Rule 14c–3:

(1) Indicate that the prospectus is accompanied by either a copy of the registrant's latest Form 10–K or Form 10–KSB or a copy of its latest annual report to security holders, whichever the registrant elects to deliver pursuant to paragraph (a) of this Item.

(2) Provide financial and other information with respect to the registrant in the form required by Part I of Form 10–Q or Form 10–QSB as of the end of the most recent fiscal quarter which ended after the end of the latest fiscal year for which certified financial statements were included in the latest Form 10–K or Form 10–KSB or the latest report to security holders (whichever the registrant elects to deliver pursuant to paragraph (a) of this Item), and more than forty-five days prior to the effective date of this registration statement (or as of a more recent date) by one of the following means:

(i) Including such information in the prospectus; or

(ii) Providing without charge to each person to whom a prospectus is delivered a copy of the registrant's latest Form 10–Q or Form 10–QSB; or

(iii) Providing without charge to each person to whom a prospectus is delivered a copy of the registrant's latest quarterly report which was delivered to its shareholders and which included the required financial information.

(3) If not reflected in the registrant's latest Form 10–K or Form 10–KSB or its latest annual report to security holders (whichever the registrant elects to deliver pursuant to paragraph (a) of this Item), provide information required by Rule 3–05 (§ 210.3–05 of this chapter) and Article 11 (§ 210.11–01 through § 210.11.03 of this chapter) of Regulation S–X.

(4) Describe any and all material changes in the registrant's affairs which have occurred since the end of the latest fiscal year for which certified financial statements were included in the latest Form 10–K or Form 10–KSB or the latest annual report to security holders (whichever the registrant elects to deliver pursuant to paragraph (a) of this Item) and which were not described in a Form 10–Q, Form 10–QSB or quarterly report delivered with the prospectus in accordance with paragraph (a)(2)(ii) or (iii) of this Item.

Instruction. Where the registrant elects to deliver the documents identified in paragraph (a) with a preliminary prospectus, such documents need not be redelivered with the final prospectus.

(b) If the registrant does not elect to deliver its latest Form 10–K or 10–KSB or its latest annual report to security holders:

(1) Furnish a brief description of the business done by the registrant and its subsidiaries during the most recent fiscal year as required by Rule 14a–3 to be included in annual reports to security holders. The description also should take into account changes in its business which have occurred between the end of the last fiscal year and the effective date of the registration statement.

(2) Include financial statements and information as required by Rule 14a–3(b)(1) to

be included in annual reports to security holders as well as: (i) the interim financial information required by Rule 10–01 of Regulation S–X for a filing on Form 10–Q and Form 10–QSB; (ii) any financial information required by Rule 3–05 and Article 11 of Regulation S–X; and (iii) any financial information required because of a material disposition of assets outside the normal course of business. The financial statements shall be restated if there has been a change in accounting principles or a correction of an error where such change or correction requires a material retroactive restatement of financial statements, or where one or more business combinations accounted for by the pooling of interest method of accounting have been consummated subsequent to the most recent fiscal year and the acquired businesses, considered in the aggregate, are significant pursuant to Rule 11–01(b).

(3) Furnish information relating to industry segments, classes or similar products or services, foreign and domestic operations, and export sales required by paragraphs (b), (c)(1)(i) and (d) of Item 101 of Regulation S–K (§ 229.101 of this chapter).

(4) Where common equity securities are being offered, furnish information required by Item 201 of Regulation S–K (§ 229.201 of this chapter), market price and dividends on the registrant's common stock and related stockholder matters.

(5) Furnish selected financial data required by Item 301 of Regulation S–K (§ 229.301 of this chapter).

(6) Furnish supplementary financial information required by Item 302 of Regulation S–K (§ 229.302 of this chapter).

(7) Furnish management's discussion and analysis of the registrant's financial condition and results of operations required by Item 303 of Regulation S–K (§ 229.303 of this chapter).

(8) Furnish information concerning changes in and disagreements with accountants on accounting and financial disclosure required by Item 304 of Regulation S–K (§ 229.304) of this chapter.

(9) Furnish quantitative and qualitative disclosures about market risk required by Item 305 of Regulation S–K (§ 229.305 of this chapter).

(c) The registrant shall furnish the information required by paragraph (b) of this Item if:

(1) the registrant was required to make a material retroactive restatement of financial statements because of:

(i) a change in accounting principles; or

(ii) a correction of an error; or

(iii) a consummation of one or more business combinations accounted for by the pooling of interest method of accounting was effected subsequent to the most recent fiscal year and the acquired businesses considered in the aggregate meet the test of a significant subsidiary;

OR

(2) the registrant engaged in a material disposition of assets outside the normal course of business; AND

(3) such restatement of financial statements or disposition of assets was not reflected in the registrant's latest annual report to security holders and/or its latest Form 10–K or Form 10–KSB filed pursuant to Sections 13(a) or 15(d) of the Exchange Act.

Item 12. Incorporation of Certain Information by Reference

(a) The documents listed in (1), (2), and, if applicable, the portions of the documents listed in (3) and (4) below, shall be specifically incorporated by reference into the prospectus, by means of a statement to that effect in the prospectus listing all such documents. In lieu of incorporating portions of the documents listed in (3) and (4) below, the registrant may incorporate by reference its entire annual or quarterly report to security holders.

(1) The registrant's latest Form 10–K filed pursuant to Section 13(a) or 15(d) of the Exchange Act which contains certified financial statements for the registrant's latest fiscal year for which a Form 10–K was required to have been filed.

(2) All other reports filed pursuant to Section 13(a) or 15(d) of the Exchange Act since the end of the fiscal year covered by the annual report referred to in (1) above.

(3) If the registrant elects to deliver its latest annual report to security holders, pursuant to Item 11(a)(1) of this Form:

(i) description of business furnished in accordance with the provisions of Rule 14a–3(b)(6) under the Exchange Act;

(ii) financial statements and information furnished in accordance with the provisions of Rule 14a–3(b)(1);

(iii) information relating to industry segments, classes of similar products or services, foreign and domestic operations, and export sales furnished as required by paragraphs (b), (c)(1)(i) and (d) of Item 101 of Regulation S-K;

(iv) where common equity securities are being offered, market price and dividends on the registrant's common equity and related stockholder matters furnished as required by Item 201 of Regulation S-K;

(v) selected financial data furnished as required by Item 301 of Regulation S-K;

(vi) supplementary financial information furnished as required by Item 302 of Regulation S-K;

(vii) management's discussion and analysis of financial condition and results of operations furnished as required by Item 303 of Regulation S-K;

(viii) information concerning disagreements with accountants on accounting and financial disclosure furnished as required by Item 304 of Regulation S-K; and

(ix) quantitative and qualitative disclosures about market risk as required by Item 305 of Regulation S–K (§ 229.305 of this chapter).

(4) If the registrant elects, pursuant to Item 11(a)(2)(iii) of this Form, to provide a copy of its latest quarterly report which was delivered to shareholders, the financial information equivalent to that required to be presented in Part I of Form 10–Q.

Instruction. Attention is directed to Rule 439 regarding consent to use of material incorporated by reference.

(b) The registrant may also state, if it so chooses, that specifically described portions of its annual or quarterly report to security holders, other than those portions required to be incorporated by reference pursuant to paragraphs (a)(3) and (4) above, are not a part of the registration statement. In such case, the description of portions which are not incorporated by reference or which are excluded shall be made with clarity and in reasonable detail.

(c) *Electronic filings.* Electronic filers electing to deliver and incorporate by reference all, or any portion, of the quarterly or annual report to security holders pursuant to this Item shall file as an exhibit such quarterly or annual report to security holders, or such portion thereof that is incorporated by reference, in electronic format.

(d)(1) You must state (i) that you will provide to each person, including any beneficial owner, to whom a prospectus is delivered, a copy of any or all of the information that has been incorporated by reference in the prospectus but not delivered with the prospectus;

(ii) that you will provide this information upon written or oral request;

(iii) that you will provide this information at no cost to the requester; and

(iv) the name, address, and telephone number to which the request for this information must be made.

Note to Item 12(d)(1)

If you send any of the information that is incorporated by reference in the prospectus to security holders, you also must send any exhibits that are specifically incorporated by reference in that information.

(2) You must (i) identify the reports and other information that you file with the SEC; and

(ii) state that the public may read and copy any materials you file with the SEC at the SEC's Public Reference Room at 450 Fifth Street, N.W., Washington, D.C. 20549. State that the public may obtain information on the operation of the Public Reference Room by calling the SEC at 1–800–SEC–0330. If you are an electronic filer, state that the SEC maintains an Internet site that contains reports, proxy and information statements, and other information regarding issuers that file electronically with the SEC and state the address of that site (http://www.sec.gov). You are encouraged to give your Internet address, if available.

Item 13. Disclosure of Commission Position on Indemnification for Securities Act Liabilities

Furnish the information required by Item 510 of Regulation S-K.

PART II—INFORMATION NOT REQUIRED IN PROSPECTUS

Item 14. Other Expenses of Issuance and Distribution

Furnish the information required by Item 511 of Regulation S-K.

Item 15. Indemnification of Directors and Officers

Furnish the information required by Item 702 of Regulation S-K.

Item 16. Exhibits

Subject to the rules regarding incorporation by reference, furnish the exhibits required by Item 601 of Regulation S-K.

Item 17. Undertakings

Furnish the undertakings required by Item 512 of Regulation S-K.

SIGNATURES

Pursuant to the requirements of the Securities Act of 1933, the registrant certifies that it has reasonable grounds to believe that it meets all of the requirements for filing on Form S–2 and has duly caused this registration statement to be signed on its behalf by the undersigned, thereunto duly authorized, in the City of ______, State of ______ on ______, 19__.

(Registrant) ____________________

By (Signature and Title) ____________

Pursuant to the requirements of the Securities Act of 1933, this registration statement has been signed by the following persons in the capacities and on the dates indicated.

(Signature) ____________________

(Title) ________________________

(Date) ________________________

Instructions. 1. The registration statement shall be signed by the registrant, its principal executive officer, or officers, its principal financial officer, its controller or principal accounting officer, and by at least a majority of the board of directors or persons performing similar functions. If the registrant is a foreign person, the registration statement shall also be signed by its authorized representative in the United States. Where the registrant is a limited partnership, the registration statement shall be signed by a majority of the board of directors of any corporate general partner signing the registration statement.

2. The name of each person who signs the registration statement shall be typed or printed beneath his signature. Any person who occupies more than one of the specified positions shall indicate each capacity in which he signs the registration statement. Attention is directed to Rule 402 concerning manual signatures and to Item 601 of Regulation S-K con-

cerning signatures pursuant to powers of attorney.

INSTRUCTIONS AS TO SUMMARY PROSPECTUSES

1. A summary prospectus used pursuant to Rule 431 shall at the time of its use contain such of the information specified below as is then included in the registration statement. All other information and documents contained in the registration statement may be omitted.

(a) As to Item 1, the aggregate offering price to the public, the aggregate underwriting discounts and commissions and the offering price per unit to the public;

(b) As to Item 4, a brief statement of the principal purposes for which the proceeds are to be used;

(c) As to Item 7, a statement as to the amount of the offering, if any, to be made for the account of security holders;

(d) As to Item 8, the name of the managing underwriter or underwriters and a brief statement as to the nature of the underwriter's obligation to take the securities, if any securities to be registered are to be offered otherwise than through underwriters, a brief statement as to the manner of distribution;

(e) As to Item 9 (a brief statement as to dividend rights, voting rights, conversion rights, interest, maturity);

(f) As to Item 11, a brief statement of the general character of the business done and intended to be done and the selected financial data Item 301 of Regulation S-K; and

(g) A tabular presentation of notes payable, long term debt, deferred credits, minority interests, if material and the equity section of the latest balance sheet filed, as may be appropriate.

2. The summary prospectus shall not contain a summary or condensation of any other required financial information except as provided above.

3. The Commission may, upon the request of the registrant, and where consistent with the protection of investors, permit the omission of any of the information herein required or the furnishing in substitution therefor of appropriate information of comparable character. The Commission may also require the inclusion of other information in addition to, or in substitution for, the information herein required in any case where such information is necessary or appropriate for the protection of investors.

FORM S-3

SECURITIES AND EXCHANGE COMMISSION

REGISTRATION STATEMENT UNDER THE SECURITIES ACT OF 1933

____
(Exact name of registrant as specified in its charter)

____
(State or other jurisdiction of incorporation or organization)

____
(I.R.S. Employer Identification No.)

____
(Address, including zip code, and telephone number, including area code, of registrant's principal executive offices)

____
(Name, address, including zip code, and telephone number, including area code, of agent for service)

Approximate date of commencement of proposed sale to the public ____________

If the only securities being registered on this Form are being offered pursuant to dividend or interest reinvestment plans, please check the following box. ☐

If any of the securities being registered on this Form are to be offered on a delayed or continuous basis pursuant to Rule 415 under the Securities Act of 1933, other than securities offered only in connection with dividend or interest reinvestment plans, check the following box. ☐

If this Form is filed to register additional securities for an offering pursuant to Rule 462(b) under the Securities Act, please check the following box and list the Securities Act registration statement number of the earlier effective registration statement for the same offering. ☐

If this Form is a post-effective amendment filed pursuant to Rule 462(c) under the Securities Act, check the following box and list the Securities Act registration statement number of the earlier effective registration statement for the same offering. ☐

If delivery of the prospectus is expected to be made pursuant to Rule 434, please check the following box. ☐

Calculation of Registration Fee

Title of each class of securities to be registered	Amount to be registered	Proposed maximum offering price per unit	Proposed maximum aggregate offering price	Amount of registration fee

Note: Specific details relating to the fee calculation shall be furnished in notes to the table, including references to provisions of Rule 457 relied upon, if the basis of the calculation is not otherwise evident from the information presented in the table.

GENERAL INSTRUCTIONS

I. Eligibility Requirements for Use of Form S-3

This instruction sets forth registrant requirements and transaction requirements for the use of Form S-3. Any registrant which meets the requirements of I. A. below ("Registrant Requirements") may use this Form for the registration of securities under the Securities Act of 1933 ("Securities Act") which are offered in any transaction specified in I. B. below ("Transaction Requirement") provided that the requirements applicable to the specified transaction are met. With respect to majority-owned subsidiaries, see Instruction I. C. below.

A. *Registrant Requirements.* Registrants must meet the following conditions in order to use this Form for registration under the Securities Act of securities offered in the transactions specified in I. B. below:

1. The registrant is organized under the laws of the United States or any State or Territory or the District of Columbia and has its principal business operations in the United States or its territories.

2. The registrant has a class of securities registered pursuant to Section 12(b) of the Securities Exchange Act of 1934 ("Exchange Act") or a class of equity securities registered pursuant to Section 12(g) of the Exchange Act or is required to file reports pursuant to Section 15(d) of the Exchange Act.

3. The registrant:

(a) has been subject to the requirements of Section 12 or 15(d) of the Exchange Act and has filed all the material required to be filed pursuant to Section 13, 14 or 15(d) for a period of at least twelve calendar months immediately preceding the filing of the registration statement on this Form; and

(b) has filed in a timely manner all reports required to be filed during the twelve calendar months and any portion of a month immediately preceding the filing of the registration statement, other than a report that is required solely pursuant to Item 1.01, 1.02, 2.03, 2.04, 2.05, 2.06 or 4.02(a), 6.01, 6.03, or 6.05 of Form 8–K (§ 249.308 of this chapter). If the registrant has used (during the twelve calendar months and any portion of a month immediately preceding the filing of the registration statement) Rule 12b–25(b) (§ 240.12b–25(b) of this chapter) under the Exchange Act with respect to a report or a portion of a report, that report or portion thereof has actually been filed within the time period prescribed by that rule.

4. The provisions in paragraphs A.2. and A.3.(a) above do not apply to any registered offerings of securities described in I.B.5 below. However, for such offerings of asset-backed securities, to the extent the depositor or any issuing entity previously established, directly or indirectly, by the depositor or any affiliate of the depositor (as defined in Item 1101 of Regulation AB (17 CFR 229.1101)) are or were at any time during the twelve calendar months and any portion of a month immediately preceding the filing of the registration statement on this Form subject to the requirements of section 12 or 15(d) of the Exchange Act (15 U.S.C. 78/ or 78o(d)) for such period (0r such shorter period that each such entity was required to file such materials). In addition, such material must have been filed in a timely manner, other than a report that is required solely pursuant to Item 1.01, 1.02, 2.03, 2.04, 2.05, 2.06, 4.02(a), 6.01, 6.03 or 6.05 of Form 8–K (17 CFR 249.308). If Rule 12b–25(b) (17 CFR 240.12b–25(b)) under the Exchange Act was used during such period with respect to a report or a portion of a report, that report or portion thereof has actually been filed within the time period prescribed by that rule. Regarding an affiliated depositor that became an affiliate as a result of a business combination transaction during such period, the filing of any material prior to the business combination transaction relating to asset-backed securities of an issuing entity previously established, directly or indirectly, by such affiliated depositor is excluded from this section, provided such business combination transaction was no part of a plan or scheme to evade the requirements of the Securities Act or the Exchange Act. See the definition of "affiliate" in Securities Act Rule 405 (17 CFR 230.405).

5. Neither the registrant nor any of its consolidated or unconsolidated subsidiaries have, since the end of the last fiscal year for which certified financial statements of the registrant and its consolidated subsidiaries were included in a report filed pursuant to Section 13(a) or 15(d) of the Exchange Act: (a) failed to pay any dividend or sinking fund installment on preferred stock; or (b) defaulted (i) on any installment or installments on indebtedness for borrowed money, or (ii) on any rental on one or more long term leases, which defaults in the aggregate are material to the financial position of the registrant and its consolidated and unconsolidated subsidiaries, taken as a whole.

6. A foreign issuer, other than a foreign government, which satisfies all of the above provisions of these registrant eligibility requirements except the provisions in I. A. 1. relating to organization and principal business shall be deemed to have met these registrant eligibility requirements provided that such foreign issuer files the same reports with the Commission under Section 13(a) or 15(d) of the Exchange Act as a domestic registrant pursuant to I. A. 3. above.

7. If the registrant is a successor registrant, it shall be deemed to have met conditions 1., 2., 3., and 5., above if: (a) its predecessor and it, taken together, do so, provided that the succession was primarily for the purpose of changing the state of incorporation of the predecessor or forming a holding company and that

the assets and liabilities of the successor at the time of succession were substantially the same as those of the predecessor, or (b) if all predecessors met the conditions at the time of succession and the registrant has continued to do so since the succession.

8. *Electronic filings:* In addition to satisfying the foregoing conditions, a registrant subject to the electronic filing requirements of Rule 101 of Regulation S–T shall have filed with the Commission:

All required electronic filings, including confirming electronic copies of documents submitted in paper pursuant to a hardship exemption as provided by Rule 201 or Rule 202(d) of Regulation S–T (§ 232.201 or § 232.202(d) of this chapter).

B. *Transaction Requirements.* Security offerings meeting any of the following conditions and made by registrant meeting the Registrant Requirements specified in I.A. above may be registered on this Form:

1. *Primary Offerings By Certain Registrants.* Securities to be offered for cash by or on behalf of a registrant, or outstanding securities to be offered for cash for the account of any person other than the registrant, including securities acquired by standby underwriters in connection with the call or redemption by the registrant of warrants or a class of convertible securities; *Provided* That the aggregate market value of the voting and non-voting common equity held by non-affiliates of the registrant is $75 million or more.

Instruction. For the purposes of this Form, "common equity" is as defined in Securities Act Rule 405 (§ 230.405 of this chapter). The aggregate market value of the registrant's outstanding voting and non-voting common equity shall be computed by use of the price at which the common equity was last sold, or the average of the bid and asked prices of such common equity, in the principal market for such common equity as of a date within 60 days prior to the date of filing. See the definition of "affiliate" in Securities Act Rule 405.

2. *Primary Offerings of Non-convertible Investment Grade Securities.* Non-convertible securities to be offered for cash by or on behalf of a registrant, provided such securities at the time of sale are "investment grade securities," as defined below. A non-convertible security is an "investment grade security" if, at the time of sale, at least one nationally recognized statistical rating organization (as that term is used in Rule 15c3–1(c)(2)(vi)(F) under the Securities Exchange Act of 1934) has rated the security in one of its generic rating categories which signifies investment grade; typically, the four highest rating categories (within which there may be sub-categories or gradations indicating relative standing) signify investment grade.

3. *Transactions Involving Secondary Offerings.* Outstanding securities to be offered for the account of any person other than the issuer, including securities acquired by standby underwriters in connection with the call or redemption by the issuer of warrants or a class of convertible securities, if securities of the same class are listed and registered on a national securities exchange or are quoted on the automated quotation system of a national securities association. (In addition, attention is directed to General Instruction C to Form S–8 for the registration of employee benefit plan securities for resale.)

4. *Rights Offerings, Dividend or Interest Reinvestment Plans, and Conversions, Warrants and Options.*

(a) Securities to be offered (1) upon the exercise of outstanding rights granted by the issuer of the securities to be offered, if such rights are granted on a *pro rata* basis to all existing security holders of the class of securities to which the rights attach, (2) under a dividend or interest reinvestment plan, or (3) upon the conversion of outstanding convertible securities or the exercise of outstanding warrants or options issued by the issuer of the securities to be offered, or an affiliate of that issuer.

(b) However, Form S–3 is available for registering these securities only if the issuer has sent, within the twelve calendar months immediately before the registration statement is filed, material containing the information required by Rule 14a–3(b) (§ 240.14a–3(b) of this chapter) under the Exchange Act to:

(1) All record holders of the rights,

(2) All participants in the plans, or

(3) All record holders of the convertible securities, warrants or options, respectively.

(c) The issuer also must have provided, within the twelve calendar months immediately before the Form S–3 registration statement is filed, the information required by Items 401, 402 and 403 of Regulation S-K (§§ 229.401–229.403 of this chapter) to:

(1) Holders of rights exercisable for common stock,

(2) Holders of securities convertible into common stock, and

(3) Participants in plans that may invest in common stock, securities convertible into common stock, or warrants or options exercisable for common stock, respectively.

5. *Offerings of Investment Grade Asset-Backed Securities.*

(a) Asset-backed securities (as defined in 17 CFR 229.1101) to be offered for cash, provided:

(i) The securities are "investment grade securities," as defined in I.B.2 above (Primary Offerings of Non-convertible Investment Grade Securities);

(ii) Delinquent assets do not constitute 20% or more, as measured by dollar volume, of the asset pool as of the measurement date; and

(iii) With respect to securities that are backed by leases other than motor vehicle leases, the portion of the securitized pool balance attributable to the residual value of the physical property underlying the leases, as determined in accordance with the transaction agreements for the securities, does not constitute 20% or more, as measured by dollar volume, of the securitized pool balance as of the measurement date.

Instruction. For purposes of making the determinations required by paragraphs (a)(ii) and (a)(iii) of this General Instruction I.B.5, refer to the Instructions to Item 1101(c) of Regulation AB (17 CFR 229.1101(c)).

(b) Securities relating to an offering of asset-backed securities registered in accordance with paragraph (a) of this General Instruction I.B.5 where those securities represent an interest in or the right to the payments of cash flows of another asset pool and meet the requirements of Securities Act Rule 190(c)(1) through (4) (17 CFR 240.190(c)(1) through (4)).

C. *Majority-owned Subsidiaries.* If a registrant is a majority-owned subsidiary, security offerings may be registered on this Form if:

1. the registrant-subsidiary itself meets the Registrant Requirements and the applicable Transaction Requirement;

2. the parent of the registrant-subsidiary meets the Registrant Requirements and the conditions of Transaction Requirement B.2. (Primary Offerings of Non-convertible Investment Grade Securities) are met; or

3. the parent of the registrant-subsidiary meets the Registrant Requirements and the applicable Transaction Requirement, and fully and unconditionally

guarantees the payment obligations on the securities being registered, and the securities being registered are non-convertible securities. Note: In such an instance, the parent-guarantor is the issuer of a separate security consisting if the guarantee which must be concurrently registered but may be registered on the same registration statement as are the guaranteed securities.

II. Application of General Rules and Regulations

A. Attention is directed to the General Rules and Regulations under the Securities Act, particularly Regulation C thereunder. That Regulations contains general requirements regarding the preparation and filing of registration statements.

B. Attention is directed to Regulation S-K for the requirements applicable to the content of the non-financial statement portions of registration statements under the Securities Act. Where this Form directs the registrant to furnish information required by Regulation S-K and the item of Regulation S-K so provides, information need only be furnished to the extent appropriate. Notwithstanding Item 501 and 502 of Regulation S-K, no table of contents is required to be included in the prospectus or registration statement prepared on this form. In addition to the information expressly required to be included in a registration statement on this Form S–3, registrants also may provide such other information as they may deem appropriate.

C. A "small business issuer," defined in Rule 405, that is eligible to use Form S–3 shall refer to the disclosure items in Regulation S–B and not Regulation S–K. For example, while Item 1 of Form S–3 requires the information required by Item 501 of Regulation S–K, small business issuers shall provide the information in Item 501 of Regulation S–B. Where Regulation S–B does not contain a comparable Item, for example there is no Item "301" in Regulation S–B, then small business issuers may omit the Item. Small business issuers shall provide the financial information called for by Item 310 of Regulation S–B in lieu of the financial information called for by Item 11.

D. Where two or more classes of securities being registered on this Form pursuant to General Instruction I.B.1. or I.B.2. are to be offered on a delayed or continuous basis pursuant to Rule 415(a)(1)(x), Rule 457(*o*) under the Securities Act permits the registration fee to be calculated on the basis of the maximum offering price of all the securities listed in the "Calculation of Registration Fee" Table ("Fee Table"). In this event, while the Fee Table would list each of the classes of securities being registered and the aggregate proceeds to be raised, the Fee Table need not specify by each class information as to the amount to be registered, proposed maximum offering price per unit, and proposed maximum aggregate offering price.

III. Dividend or Interest Reinvestment Plans: Filing and Effectiveness of Registration Statement; Requests for Confidential Treatment

A registration statement on this Form S–3 relating solely to securities offered pursuant to a dividend or interest reinvestment plan will become effective automatically (Rule 462) upon filing (Rule 456). Post-effective amendments of such a registration statement on this Form shall become effective upon filing (Rule 464).

Post-effective amendments to such a registration statement on this Form shall become effective upon the date of filing (Rule 464). Delaying amendments are not permitted in connection with either original filings or amendments on such a registration statement (Rule 473(d)), and any attempt to interpose a delaying amendment of any kind will be ineffective. All filings made on or in connection with this Form become public upon filing with the Commission. As a result, requests for confidential treatment made under Rule 406 must be processed with the Commission staff prior to the filing of such a registration statement. The number of copies of the registration statement and of each amendment required by rules 402 and 472 shall be filed with the Commission: *Provided, however,* That the number of additional copies referred to in Rule 402(b) may be reduced from ten to three and the number of additional copies referred to in Rule 472(a) may be reduced from eight to three, one of which shall be marked clearly and precisely to indicate changes.

IV. Registration of Additional Securities

With respect to the registration of additional securities for an offering pursuant to Rule 462(b) under the Securities Act, the registrant may file a registration statement consisting only of the following: The facing page; a statement that the contents of the earlier registration statement, identified by file number, are incorporated by reference; required opinions and consents; the signature page; and any price-related information omitted from the earlier registration statement in reliance on Rule 430A that the registrant chooses to include in the new registration statement. The information contained in such a Rule 462(b) registration statement shall be deemed to be a part of the earlier registration statement as of the date of effectiveness of the Rule 462(b) registration statement. Any opinion or consent required in the Rule 462(b) registration statement may be incorporated by reference from the earlier registration statement with respect to the offering, if: (i) Such opinion or consent expressly provides for such incorporation; and (ii) such opinion relates to the securities registered pursuant to Rule 462(b). See Rule 411(c) and Rule 439(b) under the Securities Act.

V. Offerings of Asset-Backed Securities

The following applies if a registration statement on this Form S–3 relating to an offering of asset-backed securities, in addition to the Items that are otherwise required by this Form, the registrant must furnish in the prospectus the information required by Items 1102 through 1120 of Regulation AB (17 CFR 229.1102 through 229.1120).

A. *Disclosure.*

1. For a registration statement on this Form S–3 relating to an offering of asset-backed securities, in addition to the Items that are otherwise required by this Form, the registrant must furnish in the prospectus the information required by Items 1102 through 1120 of Regulation AB (17 CFR 229.1102 through 229.1120).

2. For registered offerings pursuant to Securities Act Rule 415(a)(1)(x) (17 CFR 230.415(a)(1)(x)) that include a base prospectus and form of prospectus supplement, a separate base prospectus and form of prospectus supplement must be presented for each asset class that may be securitized in a discrete pool in a takedown of asset-backed securities under the registration statement. A separate base prospectus and form of prospectus supplement also must be presented for each country of origin or country of property securing pool assets that may be securitized in a discrete pool in a takedown of asset-backed securities under the registration statement. Fro both separate asset classes and jurisdictions of origin or property, a separate base prospectus and form of supplements is not required fortransactions that principally consist of a particular asset class or jurisdiction which also describe one or more potential additional asset classes or jurisdictions, so long as the pool assets for the additional classes or jurisdictions in the aggregate are below 10% of the pool, as measured by dollar volume, for any particular takedown. When a preliminary prospectus is required under this Form pursuant to Securities Act Rule 190(b)(7) (17 CFR 230.190(b)(7)), the information to be included in the base prospectus and prospectus supplement is to be substantially similar to that which would be included if the preliminary prospectus was required under Form S–1 (17 CFR 239.11) pursuant to such rules.

B. *Signatures.*

The registration statement must be signed by the depositor, the depositor's principal executive officer or officers, principal financial officer and controller or principal accounting officer, and by at least a majority of the depositor's board of directors of persons performing similar functions.

PART I—INFORMATION REQUIRED IN PROSPECTUS

Item 1. Forepart of the Registration Statement and Outside Front Cover Page of Prospectus

Set forth in the forepart of the registration statement and on the outside from cover page of the prospectus the information required by Item 501 of Regulation S–K.

Item 2. Inside Front and Outside Back Cover Pages of Prospectus

Set forth on the inside front cover page of the prospectus or, where permitted, on the outside back cover page, the information required by Item 502 of Regulation S-K.

Item 3. Summary Information, Risk Factors and Ratio of Earnings to Fixed Charges

Furnish the information required by Item 503 of Regulation S-K.

Item 4. Use of Proceeds

Furnish the information required by Item 504 of Regulation S-K.

Item 5. Determination of Offering Price

Furnish the information required by Item 505 of Regulation S-K.

Item 6. Dilution

Furnish the information required by Item 506 of Regulation S-K.

Item 7. Selling Security Holders

Furnish the information required by Item 507 of Regulation S-K.

Item 8. Plan of Distribution

Furnish the information required by Item 508 of Regulation S-K.

Item 9. Description of Securities to Be Registered

Furnish the information required by Item 202 of Regulation S-K, unless capital stock is to be registered and securities of the same class are registered pursuant to Section 12 of the Exchange Act.

Item 10. Interests of Named Experts and Counsel

Furnish the information required by Item 509 of Regulation S-K.

Item 11. Material Changes

(a) Describe any and all material changes in the registrant's affairs which have occurred since the end of the latest fiscal year for which certified financial statements were included in the latest annual report to security holders and which have not been described in a report on Form 10–Q or Form 8–K filed under the Exchange Act.

(b) Include in the prospectus, if not incorporated by reference therein from the reports filed under the Exchange Act specified in Item 12(a), a proxy or information statement filed pursuant to Section 14 of the Exchange Act, a prospectus previously filed pursuant to Rule 424(b) or (c) under the Securities Act or, where no prospectus was required to be filed pursuant to Rule 424(b), the prospectus included in the registration statement at effectiveness, or a Form 8–K filed during either of the two preceding years: (i) information required by Rule 3–05 and Article 11 of Regulation S-X; (ii) restated financial statements prepared in accordance with Regulation S-X if there has been a change in accounting principles or a correction in an error where such change or correction requires a material retroactive restatement of financial statements; (iii) restated financial statements prepared in accordance with Regulation S-X where one or more business combinations accounted for by the pooling of interest method of accounting have been consummated subsequent to the most recent fiscal year and the acquired businesses, considered in the aggregate, are significant pursuant to Rule 11–01(b), or (iv) any financial information required because of a material disposition of assets outside the normal course of business.

Item 12. Incorporation of Certain Information by Reference

(a) The documents listed in (1) and (2) below shall be specifically incorporated by reference into the prospectus, by means of a statement to that effect in the prospectus listing all such documents.

(1) the registrant's latest annual report on Form 10–K filed pursuant to Section 13(a) or 215(d) of the Exchange Act which contains financial statements for the registrant's latest fiscal year for which a Form 10–K was required to have been filed; and

(2) all other reports filed pursuant to Section 13(a) or 15(d) of the Exchange Act since the end of the fiscal year covered by the annual report referred to in (1) above; and

(3) if capital stock is to be registered and securities of the same class are registered under Section 12 of the Exchange Act, the description of such class of securities which is contained in a registration statement filed under the Exchange Act, including any amendment or reports filed for the purpose of updating such description.

(b) The prospectus shall also state that all documents subsequently filed by the registrant pursuant to Sections 13(a), 13(c), 14 or 15(d) of the Exchange Act, prior to the termination of the offering shall be deemed to be incorporated by reference into the prospectus.

(c)(1) You must state (i) that you will provide to each person, including any beneficial owner, to whom a prospectus is delivered, a copy of any or all of the information that has been incorporated by reference in the prospectus but not delivered with the prospectus:

(ii) that you will provide this information upon written or oral request;

(iii) that you will provide this information at no cost to the requester; and

(iv) the name, address, and telephone number to which the request for this information must be made.

Note to Item 12(c)(1)

If you send any of the information that is incorporated by reference in the prospectus to security holders, you also must send any exhibits that are specifically incorporated by reference in that information.

(2) You must (i) identify the reports and other information that you file with the SEC; and

(ii) state that the public may read and copy any materials you file with the SEC at the SEC's Public Reference Room at 450 Fifth Street, N.W., Washington, D.C. 20549. State that the public may obtain information on the operation of the Public Reference Room by calling the SEC at 1–800–SEC–0330. If you are an electronic filer, state that the SEC maintains an Internet site that contains reports, proxy and information statements, and other information regarding issuers that file electronically with the SEC and state the address of that site (http://www.sec.gov). You are encouraged to give your Internet address, if available.

Instruction. Attention is directed to Rule 439 regarding consent to use of material incorporated by reference.

Item 13. Disclosure of Commission Position on Indemnification for Securities Act Liabilities

Furnish the information required by Item 510 of Regulation S-K.

PART II—INFORMATION NOT REQUIRED IN PROSPECTUS

Item 14. Other Expenses of Issuance and Distribution

Furnish the information required by Item 511 of Regulation S-K.

Item 15. Indemnification of Directors and Officers

Furnish the information required by Item 702 of Regulation S-K.

Item 16. Exhibits

Subject to the rules regarding incorporation by reference, furnish the exhibits required by Item 601 of Regulation S-K.

Item 17. Undertakings

Furnish the undertakings required by Item 512 of Regulation S-K.

SIGNATURES

Pursuant to the requirements of the Securities Act of 1933, the registrant certifies that it has reasonable grounds to believe that it meets all of the requirements for filing on Form S–3 and has duly caused this registration statement to be signed on its behalf by the undersigned, thereunto duly authorized, in the City of ______, State of ______, on ______, 19__.

(Registrant) ______________________

By (Signature and Title) ______________________

Pursuant to the requirements of the Securities Act of 1933, this registration statement has been signed by the following persons in the capacities and on the dates indicated.

(Signature) ______________________

(Title) ______________________

(Date) ______________________

Instructions. 1. The registration statement shall be signed by the registrant, its principal executive officer or officers, its principal financial officer, its controller or principal accounting officer, and by at least a majority of the board of directors or persons performing similar functions. If the registrant is a foreign person, the registration statement shall also be signed by its authorized representative in the United States. Where the registrant is a limited partnership, the registration statement shall be signed by a majority of the board of directors of any corporate general partner signing the registration statement.

2. The name of each person who signs the registration statement shall be typed or printed beneath his signature. Any person who occupies more than one of the specified positions shall indicate each capacity in which he signs the registration statement. Attention is directed to Rule 402 concerning manual signatures and Item 601 of Regulation S-K concerning signatures pursuant to powers of attorney.

3. Where eligibility for use of the Form is based on the assignment of a security rating pursuant to Transaction Requirement B.2., or B.5., the registrant may sign the registration statement notwithstanding the fact that such security rating has not been assigned by the filing date, provided that the registrant reasonably believes, and so states, that the security rating requirement will be met by the time of sale.

FORM S–4

SECURITIES AND EXCHANGE COMMISSION

Washington, D.C. 20549

FORM S–4

REGISTRATION STATEMENT UNDER THE SECURITIES ACT OF 1933

____

(Exact name of registrant as specified in its charter)

____

(State or other jurisdiction of incorporation or organization)

____

(Primary Standard Industrial Classification Code Number)

(I.R.S. Employer Identification No.)

(Address, including zip code, and telephone number, including area code, of registrant's principal executive officers)

(Name, address, including zip code, and telephone number, including area code, of agent for service)

Approximate date of commencement of proposed sale of the securities to the public ______

If the securities being registered on this Form are being offered in connection with the formation of a holding company and there is compliance with General Instruction G, check the following box. ☐

If this Form is filed to register additional securities for an offering pursuant to Rule 462(b) under the Securities Act, check the following box and list the Securities Act registration statement number of the earlier effective registration statement for the same offering. ☐

If this Form is a post-effective amendment filed pursuant to Rule 462(d) under the Securities Act, check the following box and list the Securities Act registration statement number of the earlier effective registration statement for the same offering. ☐

Calculation of Registration Fee

Title of each class of securities to be registered	Amount to be registered	Proposed maximum offering price per unit	Proposed maximum aggregate offering price	Amount of registration fee

Note: Specific details relating to the fee calculation shall be furnished in notes to the table, including references to provisions of Rule 457 relied upon, if the basis of the calculation is not otherwise evident from the information presented in the table.

GENERAL INSTRUCTIONS

A. Rule as to Use of Form S–4.

1. This Form may be used for registration under the Securities Act of 1933 ("Securities Act") of securities to be issued (1) in a transaction of the type specified in paragraph (a) of Rule 145 (§ 230.145 of this chapter); (2) in a merger in which the applicable state law would not require the solicitation of the votes or consents of all of the security holders of the company being acquired; (3) in an exchange offer for securities of the issuer or another entity; (4) in a public reoffering or resale of any such securities acquired pursuant to this registration statement; or (5) in more than one of the kinds of transaction listed in (1) through (4) registered on one registration statement.

2. If the registrant meets the requirements of and elects to comply with the provisions in any item of this Form or Form F–4 that provides for incorporation by reference of information about the registrant or the company being acquired, the prospectus must be sent to the security holders no later than 20 business days prior to the date on which the meeting of such security holders is held or, if no meeting is held, at least 20 business days prior to either (1) the date the votes, consents or authorizations may be used to effect the corporate action or, (2) if votes, consents or authorizations are not used, the date the transaction is consummated. Attention is directed to Sections 13(e), 14(d) and 14(e) of the Securities Exchange Act of 1934 ("Exchange Act") the rules and regulations thereunder regarding other time periods in connection with exchange offers and going private transactions.

3. This Form shall not be used if the registrant is a registered investment company or a

business development company as defined in Section 2(a)(48) of the Investment Company Act of 1940.

B. Information With Respect to the Registrant.

1. Information with respect to the registrant shall be provided in accordance with the items referenced in one of the following subparagraphs:

a. Items 10 and 11 of this Form, if the registrant elects this alternative and meets the following requirements of Form S–3 (hereinafter, with respect to the registrant, "meets the requirements for use of Form S–3") for this offering of securities:

(i) the registrant meets the requirements of General Instruction I. A. of Form S–3; and

(ii) one of the following is met

A. The registrant meets the aggregate market value requirement of General Instruction I. B. 1. of Form S–3; or

B. Non-convertible debt or preferred securities are to be offered pursuant to this registration statement and are "investment grade securities" as defined in General Instruction I. B. 2. of Form S–3; or

C. The registrant is a majority-owned subsidiary and one of the conditions of General Instruction I. C. of Form S–3 is met.

b. Items 12 and 13 of this Form, if the registrant meets the requirements for use of Form S–2 or Form S–3 and elects this alternative; or

c. Item 14 of this Form, if the registrant does not meet the requirements for use of Form S–2 or S–3, or if it otherwise elects this alternative.

2. If the registrant is a real estate entity of the type described in General Instruction A to Form S–11, the information prescribed by Items 12, 13, 14, 15 and 16 of Form S–11 shall be furnished about the registrant in addition to the information provided pursuant to Items 10 through 14 of this Form. The information prescribed by such Items of Form S–11 may be incorporated by reference into the prospectus if (a) a registrant qualifies for and elects to provide information pursuant to alternative 1.a. or 1.b. of this instruction and (b) the documents incorporated by reference pursuant to such elected alternative contain such information.

C. Information With Respect to the Company Being Acquired.

1. Information with respect to the company whose securities are being acquired (hereinafter including, where securities of the registrant are being offered in exchange for securities of another company, such other company) shall be provided in accordance with the items referenced in one of the following subparagraphs:

a. Item 15 of this Form, if the company being acquired meets the requirements of General Instructions I. A. and I. B. 1. of Form S–3 (hereinafter, with respect to the company being acquired, "meets the requirements for use of Form S–3") of Form S–3 and this alternative is elected;

b. Item 16 of this Form, if the company being acquired meets the requirements for use of Form S–2 or S–3 and this alternative is elected; or

c. Item 17 of this Form, if the company being acquired does not meet the requirements for use of Form S–2 or S–3 or if this alternative is otherwise elected.

2. If the company being acquired is a real estate entity of the type described in General Instruction A to Form S–11, the information that would be required by Items 13, 14, 15 and 16(a) of Form S–11 if securities of such company were being registered shall be furnished about such company being acquired in addition to the information provided pursuant to this Form. The information prescribed by such Items of Form S–11 may be incorporated

by reference into the prospectus if (a) the company being acquired would qualify for use of the level of disclosure prescribed by alternative 1.a. or 1.b. of this instruction and such alternative is elected and (b) the documents incorporated by reference pursuant to such elected alternative contain such information.

D. Application of General Rules and Regulations.

1. Attention is directed to the General Rules and Regulations under the Securities Act, particularly those comprising Regulation C thereunder. That Regulation contains general requirements regarding the preparation and filing of registration statements.

2. Attention is directed to Regulation S–K for the requirements applicable to the content of non-financial statement portions of registration statements under the Securities Act. Where this Form directs the registrant to furnish information required by Regulation S–K and the item of Regulation S–K so provides, information need only be furnished to the extent appropriate.

3. *A small business issuer,* defined in Rule 405, shall refer to the disclosure items in Regulation S–B and not Regulation S–K except with respect to disclosure called for by subpart 900 of Regulation S–K. Small business issuers shall provide or incorporate by reference the information called for by Item 310 of Regulation S–B.

E. Compliance With Exchange Act Rules.

1. If a corporation or other person submits a proposal to its security holders entitled to vote on, or consent to, the transaction in which the securities being registered are to be issued, and such person's submission to its security holders is subject to Regulation 14A or 14C under the Exchange Act, then the provisions of such Regulations shall apply in all respects to such person's submission, except that (a) the prospectus may be in the form of a proxy or information statement and may contain the information required by this Form in lieu of that required by Schedule 14A or 14C of Regulation 14A or 14C under the Exchange Act; and (b) copies of the preliminary and definitive proxy or information statement, form of proxy or other material filed as a part of the registration statement shall be deemed filed pursuant to such person's obligations under such Regulations.

2. If the proxy or information material sent to security holders is not subject to Regulation 14A or 14C, all such material shall be filed as a part of the registration statement at the time the statement is filed or as an amendment thereto prior to the use of such material.

3. If the transaction in which the securities being registered are to be issued is subject to Section 13(e), 14(d) or 14(e) of the Exchange Act, the provisions of those sections and the rules and regulations thereunder shall apply to the transaction in addition to the provisions of this Form.

F. Transactions Involving Foreign Private Issuers.

If a U.S. registrant is acquiring a foreign private issuer, as defined by Rule 405, such registrant may use this Form and may present information about the foreign private issuer pursuant to Form F–4. If the registrant is a foreign private issuer, such registrant may use Form F–4 and (1) if the company being acquired is a foreign private issuer, may present information about such foreign company pursuant to Form F–4 or (2) if the company being acquired is a U.S. company, may present information about such company pursuant to this Form.

G. Filing and Effectiveness of Registration Statement Involving Formation of Holding-Companies; Requests for Confidential Treatment; Number of Copies.

Original registration statements on this Form S–4 will become effective automatically on the twentieth day after the date of filing, pursuant to the provisions of Section 8(a) of the Act provided:

1. The transaction in connection with which securities are being registered involves the organization of a bank or savings and loan holding company for the sole purpose of issuing common stock to acquire all of the common stock of the company that is organizing the holding company; and

2. The following conditions are met:

a. the financial institution furnishes its security holders with an annual report that includes financial statements prepared on the basis of generally accepted accounting principles;

b. there are no anticipated changes in the security holders' relative equity ownership interest in the underlying company's assets except for redemption of no more than a nominal number of shares of unaffiliated persons who dissent;

c. in the aggregate, only nominal borrowings are to be incurred for such purposes as organizing the holding company to pay non-affiliated persons who dissent, or to meet minimum capital requirements;

d. there are no new classes of stock authorized other than those corresponding to the stock of the company being acquired immediately prior to the reorganization;

e. there are no plans or arrangements to issue any additional shares to acquire any business other than the company being acquired; and

f. there has been no material adverse change in the financial condition of the company being acquired since the latest fiscal year end included in the annual report to security holders.

Pre-effective amendments with respect to such a registration statement may be filed prior to effectiveness, and such amendments will be deemed to have been filed with the consent of the Commission (Rule 475a). Accordingly, the filing of a pre-effective amendment to such a registration statement will not commence a new twenty-day period. Post-effective amendments to such a registration statement on this Form shall become effective upon the date of filing (Rule 464). Delaying amendments are not permitted in connection with either original filings or amendments on such a registration statement (Rule 473(d)), and any attempt to interpose a delaying amendment of any kind will be ineffective. All filings made on or in connection with this Form pursuant to this instruction become public upon filing with the Commission. As a result, requests for confidential treatment made under Rule 406 must be processed by the Commissions staff prior to the filing of such a registration statement. The number of copies of such a registration statement and of each amendment required by Rules 402 and 472 shall be filed with the Commission; *provided, however,* that the number of additional copies referred to in Rule 402(b) may be reduced from ten to three and the number of additional copies referred to in Rule 472(a) may be reduced from eight to three, one of which shall be marked to clearly and precisely indicate changes.

H. Registration Statements Subject to Rule 415(a)(1)(viii).

If the registration statement relates to offerings of securities pursuant to Rule 415(a)(1)(viii), required information about the type of contemplated transaction or the company to be acquired only need be furnished as of the date of initial effectiveness of the registration statement to the extent practicable. The required information about the specific transaction and the particular company being acquired, however, must be included in the prospectus by means of a post-effective amendment; *Provided, however,* that where the transaction in which the securities are being offered pursuant to a registration statement under the Securities Act of 1933 would itself qualify for an exemption from Section 5 of the Act, absent the existence of other similar (prior or subsequent) transactions, a prospectus supplement could be used to furnish the information necessary in connection with such transaction.

I. Roll-Up Transactions.

1. If securities to be registered on this Form will be issued in a roll-up transaction as defined in Item 901(c) of Regulation S-K, then the disclosure provisions of subpart 900 of Regulation S-K shall apply to the transaction in addition to the provisions of this Form. A "small business issuer," defined in § 230.405, that is engaged in a roll-up transaction shall refer to the disclosure items in subpart 900 of Regulation S-K. To the extent that the disclosure requirements of subpart 900 are inconsistent with the disclosure requirements of any other applicable forms or schedules, the requirements of subpart 900 are controlling.

2. If securities to be registered on this Form will be issued in a roll-up transaction as defined in Item 901(c) of Regulation S-K, the prospectus must be distributed to security holders no later than the lesser of 60 calendar days prior to the date on which action is to be taken or the maximum number of days permitted for giving notice under applicable state law.

3. Attention is directed to the proxy rules (17 CFR 240.14a-1-240.14a-104) and Rule 14e-7 of the tender offer rules (17 CFR 240.14e-7) if securities to be registered on this Form will be issued in a roll-up transaction. Such rules contain provisions specifically applicable to roll-up transactions, whether or not the entities involved have securities registered pursuant to Section 12 of the Exchange Act.

J. Where two or more classes of securities being registered on this Form pursuant to General Instruction H. are to be offered on a delayed or continuous basis pursuant to Rule 415(a)(1)(viii), Rule 457(*o*) under the Securities Act permits the registration fee to be calculated on the basis of the maximum offering price of all the securities listed in the "Calculation of Registration Fee" Table ("Fee Table"). In this event, while the Fee Table would list each of the classes of securities being registered and the aggregate proceeds to be raised, the Fee Table need not specify by each class information as to the amount to be registered, proposed maximum offering price per unit, and proposed maximum aggregate offering price.

K. Registration of Additional Securities

With respect to the registration of additional securities for an offering pursuant to Rule 462(b) under the Securities Act, the registrant may file a registration statement consisting only of the following: the facing page; a statement that the contents of the earlier registration statement, identified by file number, are incorporated by reference; required opinions and consents; the signature page; and any price-related information omitted from the earlier registration statement in reliance on Rule 430A that the registrant chooses to include in the new registration statement. The information contained in such a Rule 462(b) registration statement shall be deemed to be a part of the earlier registration statement as of the date of effectiveness of the Rule 462(b) registration statement. Any opinion or consent required in the Rule 462(b) registration statement may be incorporated by reference from the earlier registration statement with respect to the offering, if: (i) such opinion or consent expressly provides for such incorporation; and (ii) such opinion relates to the securities registered pursuant to Rule 462(b). See Rule 411(c) and Rule 439(b) under the Securities Act.

PART I—INFORMATION REQUIRED IN THE PROSPECTUS

A. INFORMATION ABOUT THE TRANSACTION

Item 1. Forepart of Registration Statement and Outside Front Cover Page of Prospectus

Set forth in the forepart of the registration statement and on the outside front cover page of the prospectus the information required by Item 501 of Regulation S-K.

Item 2. Inside Front and Outside Back Cover Pages of Prospectus

Provide the information required by Item 502 of Regulation S-K. In addition, on the inside front cover page, you must state (1) that the prospectus incorporates important business and financial information about the company that is not included in or delivered with the document; and

(2) that this information is available without charge to security holders upon written or oral request. Give the name, address, and telephone number to which security holders must make this request. In addition, you must state that to obtain timely delivery, security holders must request the information no later than five business days before the date they must make their investment decision. Specify the date by which security holders must request this information. You must highlight this statement by print type or otherwise.

Note to Item 2.

If you send any of the information that is incorporated by reference in the prospectus to security holders, you also must send any exhibits that are specifically incorporated by reference in that information.

Item 3. Risk Factors, Ratio of Earnings to Fixed Charges and Other Information

Provide in the forepart of the prospectus a summary containing the information required by Item 503 of Regulation S-K and the following:

(a) The name, complete mailing address (including the Zip Code), and telephone number (including the area code) of the principal executive offices of the registrant and the company being acquired;

(b) A brief description of the general nature of the business conducted by the registrant and by the company being acquired;

(c) A brief description of the transaction in which the securities being registered are to be offered;

(d) The information required by Item 301 of Regulation S-K (selected financial data) for the registrant and the company being acquired. To the extent the information is required to be presented in the prospectus pursuant to Items 12, 14, 16 or 17, it need not be repeated pursuant to this Item.

(e) If material, the information required by Item 301 of Regulation S-K for the registrant on a pro forma basis, giving effect to the transaction. To the extent the information is required to be presented in the prospectus pursuant to Items 12 or 14, it need not be repeated pursuant to this Item.

(f) In comparative columnar form, historical and pro forma per share data of the registrant and historical and equivalent pro forma per share data of the company being acquired for the following items:

(1) book value per share as of the date financial data presented pursuant to Item 301 of Regulation S-K (selected financial data);

(2) cash dividends declared per share for the periods for which financial data is presented pursuant to Item 301 of Regulation S-K (selected financial data);

(3) income (loss) per share from continuing operations for the periods for which financial data is presented pursuant to Item 301 of Regulation S-K (selected financial data).

Instruction to paragraphs (e) and (f). For a business combination accounted for as a purchase, the financial information required by paragraphs (e) and (f) shall be presented only for the most recent fiscal year and interim period. For a business combination accounted for as a pooling, the financial information required by paragraphs (e) and (f) (except for information with regard to book value) shall be presented for the most recent three fiscal years and interim period. For a business combination accounted for as a pooling, information with regard to book value shall be presented as of the end of the most recent fiscal year and interim period. Equivalent pro forma per share amounts shall be calculated by multiplying the pro forma income (loss) per share before non-recurring charges or credits directly attributable to the transaction, pro forma book value per share, and the pro forma dividends per share of the registrant by the exchange ratio so that the per share amounts are equated to the respective values for one share of the company being acquired.

(g) In comparative columnar form, the market value of securities of the company being acquired (on an historical and equivalent per share basis) and the market value of the securities of the registrant (on an historical basis) as of the date preceding public announcement of the proposed transaction, or, if no such public announcement was made, as of the day preceding the day the agreement with respect to the transaction was entered into;

(h) With respect to the registrant and the company being acquired, a brief statement comparing the percentage of outstanding shares entitled to vote held by directors, executive officers and their affiliates and the vote required for approval of the proposed transaction;

(i) A statement as to whether any federal or state regulatory requirements must be complied with or approval must be obtained in connection with the transaction, and if so, the status of such compliance or approval;

(j) A statement about whether or not dissenters' rights of appraisal exist, including a cross-reference to the information provided pursuant to Item 18 or 19 of this Form; and

(k) A brief statement about the tax consequences of the transaction, or if appropriate, consisting of a cross-reference to the information provided pursuant to Item 4 of this Form.

Item 4. Terms of the Transaction

(a) Furnish a summary of the material features of the proposed transaction. The summary shall include, where applicable:

(1) A brief summary of the terms of the acquisition agreement;

(2) The reasons of the registrant and of the company being acquired for engaging in the transaction;

(3) The information required by Item 202 of Regulation S–K, description of registrant's securities, unless: (i) the registrant would meet the requirements for use of Form S–3, and elects to furnish information pursuant to Item 10, (ii) capital stock is to be registered and (iii) securities of the same class are registered under Section 12 of the Exchange Act and (i) listed for trading or admitted to unlisted trading privileges on a national securities exchange; or (ii) are securities for which bid and offer quotations are reported in an automated quotations system operated by a national securities association;

(4) An explanation of any material differences between the rights of security holders of the company being acquired and the rights of holders of the securities being offered;

(5) A brief statement as to accounting treatment of the transaction; and

(6) The federal income tax consequences of the transaction.

(b) If a report, opinion or appraisal materially relating to the transaction has been received from an outside party, and such report, opinion or appraisal is referred to in the prospectus, furnish the same information as would be required by Item 9(b)(1) through (6) of Schedule 13E–3.

(c) Incorporate the acquisition agreement by reference into the prospectus by means of a statement to that effect.

Item 5. Pro Forma Financial Information

Furnish financial information required by Article 11 of Regulation S–X with respect to this transaction.

Instruction. 1. Any other Article 11 information that is presented (rather than incorporated by reference) pursuant to other Items of this Form shall be presented together with the information provided pursuant to Item 5, but the presentation shall clearly distinguish between this transaction and any other.

2. If pro forma financial information with respect to all other transactions is incorporated by reference pursuant to Item 11 or 15 of this Form only the pro forma results need be presented as part of the pro forma financial information required by this Item.

Item 6. Material Contacts With the Company Being Acquired

Describe any past, present or proposed material contracts, arrangements, understandings, relationships, negotiations or transactions during the periods for which financial statements are presented or incorporated by reference pursuant to Part I. B. or C. of this Form between the company being acquired or its affiliates and the registrant or its affiliates, such as those concerning: a merger, consolidation or acquisition; a tender offer or other acquisition of securities; an election of directors; or a sale or other transfer of a material amount of assets.

Item 7. Additional Information Required for Reoffering by Persons and Parties Deemed to Be Underwriters

If any of the securities are to be reoffered to the public by any person or party who is deemed to be an underwriter thereof, furnish the following information in the prospectus, at the time it is being used for the reoffer of the securities to the extent it is not already furnished therein:

(a) The information required by Item 507 of Regulation S–K, selling security holders; and

(b) Information with respect to the consummation of the transaction pursuant to which the securities were acquired and any material change in the registrant's affairs subsequent to the transaction.

Item 8. Interests of Named Experts and Counsel

Furnish the information required by Item 509 of Regulation S–K.

Item 9. Disclosure of Commission Position on Indemnification for Securities Act Liabilities

Furnish the information required by Item 510 of Regulation S–K.

B. INFORMATION ABOUT THE REGISTRANT

Item 10. Information With Respect to S–3 Registrants

If the registrant meets the requirements for use of Form S–3 and elects to furnish information in accordance with the provisions of this Item, furnish information as required below:

(a) Describe any and all material changes in the registrant's affairs that have occurred since the end of the latest fiscal year for which audited financial statements were included in the latest annual report to security holders and that have not been described in a report on Form 10–Q or Form 8–K filed under the Exchange Act.

(b) Include in the prospectus, if not incorporated by reference from the reports filed under the Exchange Act specified in Item 11 of this Form, a proxy or information statement filed pursuant to section 14 of the Exchange Act, a prospectus previously filed pursuant to Rule 424 under the Securities Act or, where no prospectus is required to be filed pursuant to Rule 424(b), the prospectus included in the registration statement at effectiveness, or a Form 8–K filed during either of the two preceding fiscal years:

(1) Financial information required by Rule 3–05 and Article 11 of Regulation S–X with respect to transactions other than that pursuant to which the securities being registered are to be issued;

(2) Restated financial statements prepared in accordance with Regulation S–X, if there has been a change in accounting principles or a correction of an error where such change or correction requires a material retroactive restatement of financial statements;

(3) Restated financial statements prepared in accordance with Regulation S–X where one or more business combinations accounted for by the pooling of interest method of accounting have been consummated subsequent to the most recent fiscal year and the acquired businesses, considered in the aggregate, are significant pursuant to Rule 11–01(b) of Regulation S–X; or

(4) Any financial information required because of a material disposition of assets outside the normal course of business.

Item 11. Incorporation of Certain Information by Reference

If the registrant meets the requirements of Form S–3 and elects to furnish information in accordance with the provisions of Item 10 of this Form:

(a) Incorporate by reference into the prospectus, by means of a statement to that effect listing all documents so incorporated, the documents listed in paragraphs (1), (2) and, if applicable, (3) below.

(1) The registrant's latest annual report on Form 10–K filed pursuant to Section 13(a) or 15(d) of the Exchange Act which contains financial statements for the registrant's latest fiscal year for which a Form 10–K was required to be filed;

(2) All other reports filed pursuant to Section 13(a) or 15(d) of the Exchange Act since the end of the fiscal year covered by the annual report referred to in Item 11(a)(1) of this Form; and

(3) If capital stock is to be registered and securities of the same class are registered under Section 12 of the Exchange Act and: (i) listed for trading or admitted to unlisted trading privileges on a national securities exchange; or (ii) are securities for which bid and offer quotations are reported in an automated quotations system operated by a national securities association, the description of such class of securities which is contained in a registration statement filed under the Exchange Act, including any amendment or reports filed for the purpose of updating such description.

(b) The prospectus also shall state that all documents subsequently filed by the registrant pursuant to Sections 13(a), 13(c), 14 or 15(d) of the Exchange Act, prior to one of the following dates, whichever is applicable, shall be deemed to be incorporated by reference into the prospectus:

(1) If a meeting of security holders is to be held, the date on which such meeting is held;

(2) If a meeting of security holders is not to be held, the date on which the transaction is consummated;

(3) If securities of the registrant are being offered in exchange for securities of any other issuer, the date the offering is terminated; or

(4) If securities are being offered in a reoffering or resale of securities acquired pursuant to this registration statement, the date the reoffering is terminated.

Instruction. Attention is directed to Rule 439 regarding consent to the use of material incorporated by reference.

(c) You must (1) identify the reports and other information that you file with the SEC; and

(2) state that the public may read and copy any materials you file with the SEC at the SEC's Public Reference Room at 450 Fifth Street, N.W., Washington, D.C. 20549. State that the public may obtain information on the operation of the Public Reference Room by calling the SEC at 1-800-SEC-0330. If you are an electronic filer, state that the SEC maintains an Internet site that contains reports, proxy and information statements, and other information regarding issuers that file electronically with the SEC and state the address of that site (http://www.sec.gov). You are encouraged to give your Internet address, if available.

Item 12. Information With Respect to S-2 or S-3 Registrants

If the registrant meets the requirements for use of Form S-2 or S-3 and elects to comply with this Item, furnish the information required by either paragraph (a) or paragraph (b) of this Item. The information required by paragraph (b) shall be furnished if the registrant satisfies the conditions of paragraph (c) of this Item.

(a) If the registrant elects to deliver this prospectus together with a copy of either its latest Form 10-K or Form 10-KSB filed pursuant to Sections 13(a) or 15(d) of the Exchange Act or its latest annual report to security holders, which at the time of original preparation met the requirements of either Rule 14a-3 or Rule 14c-3:

(1) Indicate that the prospectus is accompanied by either a copy of the registrant's latest Form 10-K or Form 10-KSB or a copy of its latest annual report to security holders, whichever the registrant elects to deliver pursuant to paragraph (a) of this Item.

(2) Provide financial and other information with respect to the registrant in the form required by Part I of Form 10-Q, or 10-QSB as of the end of the most recent fiscal quarter which ended after the end of the last fiscal year for which audited financial statements were included in the latest Form 10-K or Form 10-KSB or the latest report to security holders (whichever the registrant elects to deliver pursuant to paragraph (a) of this Item), and more than 45 days prior to the effective date of this registration statement (or as of a more recent date) by one of the following means:

(i) including such information in the prospectus;

(ii) providing without charge to each person to whom a prospectus is delivered a copy of the registrant's latest Form 10-Q or Form 10-QSB; or

(iii) providing without charge to each person to whom a prospectus is delivered a copy of the registrant's latest quarterly report that was delivered to its security holders and which included the required financial information.

(3) If not reflected in the registrant's latest Form 10-K or Form 10-KSB or its latest annual report to security holders, (whichever the registrant elects to deliver pursuant to paragraph (a) of this Item) provide information required by Rule 3-05 and Article 11 of Regulation S-X.

(4) Describe any and all material changes in the registrant's affairs that have occurred since the end of the latest fiscal year for which audited financial statements were included in the latest Form 10-K or 10-KSB or the latest annual report to security holders (whichever the registrant elects to deliver pursuant to paragraph (a) of this Item) and that were not described in a Form 10-Q, Form 10-QSB or quarterly report delivered with the prospectus in accordance with paragraphs (a)(2)(ii) or (iii) of this Item.

Instruction. Where the registrant elects to deliver the documents identified in paragraph

(a) with a preliminary prospectus, such documents need not be redelivered with the final prospectus.

(b) If the registrant does not elect to deliver its latest Form 10–K or Form 10–KSB or its latest annual report to security holders:

(1) Furnish a brief description of the business done by the registrant and its subsidiaries during the most recent fiscal year as required by Rule 14a–3 to be included in an annual report to security holders. The description also should taken into account changes in the registrant's business that have occurred between the end of the latest fiscal year and the effective date of the registration statement.

(2) Include financial statements and information as required by Rule 14a–3(b)(1) to be included in an annual report to security holders. In addition, provide:

(i) the interim financial information required by Rule 10–01 of Regulation S–X for a filing on Form 10–Q;

(ii) financial information required by Rule 3–05 and Article 11 of Regulation S–X with respect to transactions other than that pursuant to which the securities being registered are to be issued;

(iii) restated financial statements prepared in accordance with Regulation S–X if there has been a change in accounting principles or a correction of an error where such change or correction requires a material retroactive restatement of financial statements;

(iv) Restated financial statements prepared in accordance with Regulation S–X where one or more business combinations accounted for by the pooling of interest method of accounting have been consummated subsequent to the most recent fiscal year and the acquired businesses, considered in the aggregate, are significant pursuant to Rule 11–01(b) of Regulation S–X; and

(v) Any financial information required because of a material disposition of assets outside of the normal course of business.

(3) Furnish the information required by the following:

(i) Item 101(b), (c)(1)(i) and (d) of Regulation S–K, industry segments, classes of similar products or services, foreign and domestic operations and export sales;

(ii) where common equity securities are being offered, Item 201 of Regulation S–K, market price of and dividends on the registrant's common equity and related stockholder matters;

(iii) Item 301 of Regulation S–K, selected financial data;

(iv) Item 302 of Regulation S–K, supplementary financial information;

(v) Item 303 of Regulation S–K, management's discussion and analysis of financial condition and results of operations;

(vi) Item 304 of Regulation S–K, changes in and disagreements with accountants on accounting and financial disclosure; and

(vii) Item 305 of Regulation S–K (§ 229.305 of this chapter), quantitative and qualitative disclosures about market risk.

(c) The registrant shall furnish the information required by paragraph (b) of this Item if:

(1) The registrant was required to make a material retroactive restatement of financial statements because of

(i) A change in accounting principles; or

(ii) A correction of an error; or

(iii) A consummation of one or more business combinations accounted for by the pooling of interest method of accounting was effected subsequent to the most recent fiscal year and the acquired businesses considered in the aggregate meet the test of a significant subsidiary;

or

(2) The registrant engaged in a material disposition of assets outside the normal course of business;

and

(3) Such restatement of financial statements or disposition of assets was not reflected in the registrant's latest annual report to security holders and/or its latest Form 10–K or Form 10–KSB filed pursuant to Sections 13(a) or 15(d) of the Exchange Act.

Item 13. Incorporation of Certain Information by Reference

If the registrant meets the requirements of Form S–2 or S–3 and elects to furnish information in accordance with the provisions of Item 12 of this Form:

(a) Incorporate by reference into the prospectus, by means of a statement to that effect in the prospectus listing all documents so incorporated, the documents listed in paragraphs (1) and (2) of this Item and, if applicable, the portions of the documents listed in paragraphs (3) and (4) thereof.

(1) The registrant's latest annual report on Form 10–K filed pursuant to Section 13(a) or 15(d) of the Exchange Act which contains audited financial statements for the registrant's latest fiscal year for which a Form 10–K was required to be filed.

(2) All other reports filed pursuant to Section 13(a) or 15(d) of the Exchange Act since the end of the fiscal year covered by the annual report referred to in paragraph (a)(1) of this Item.

(3) If the registrant elects to deliver its latest annual report to security holders pursuant to Item 12 of this Form, the information furnished in accordance with the following:

(i) Item 101(b), (c)(1)(i) and (d) of Regulation S–K, segments, classes of similar products or services, foreign and domestic operations and export sales;

(ii) Where common equity securities are being issued, Item 201 of Regulation S–K, market price of and dividends on the registrant's common equity and related stockholder matters;

(iii) Item 301 of Regulation S–K, selected financial data;

(iv) Item 302 of Regulation S–K, supplementary financial information;

(v) Item 303 of Regulation S–K, management's discussion and analysis of financial condition and results of operations;

(vi) Item 304 of Regulation S–K, changes in and disagreements with accountants on accounting and financial disclosure; and

(vii) Item 305 of Regulation S–K (§ 229.305 of this chapter), quantitative and qualitative disclosures about market risk.

(4) If the registrant elects, pursuant to Item 12(a)(2)(iii) of this Form, to provide a copy of its latest quarterly report which was delivered to security holders, financial information equivalent to that required to be presented in Part I of Form 10–Q.

Instruction. Attention is directed to Rule 439 regarding consent to the use of material incorporated by reference.

(b) The registrant also may state, if it so chooses, that specifically described portions of its annual or quarterly report to security holders, other than those portions required to be incorporated by reference pursuant to paragraphs (a)(3) and (4) of this Item, are not part of the registration statement. In such case, the description of portions that are not incorporated by reference or that are excluded shall be made with clarity and in reasonable detail.

(c) *Electronic filings.* Electronic filers electing to deliver and incorporate by reference all, or any portion, of the quarterly or annual report to security holders pursuant to this Item shall file as an exhibit such quarterly or annual report to security holders, or such portion thereof that is incorporated by reference, in electronic format.

(d) You must (1) identify the reports and other information that you file with the SEC; and

(2) state that the public may read and copy any materials you file with the SEC at the SEC's Public Reference Room at 450 Fifth Street, N.W., Washington, D.C. 20549. State that the public may obtain information on the operation of the Public Reference Room by calling the SEC at 1–800–SEC–0330. If you are an electronic filer, state that the SEC maintains an Internet site that contains reports, proxy and information statements, and other information regarding issuers that file electronically with the SEC and state the address of that site (http://www.sec.gov). You are encouraged to give your Internet address, if available.

Item 14. Information With Respect to Registrants Other Than S–3 or S–2 Registrants

If the registrant does not meet the requirements for use of Form S–2 or S–3, or otherwise elects to comply with this Item in lieu of Item 10 or 12, furnish the information required by:

(a) Item 101 of Regulation S–K, description of business;

(b) Item 102 of Regulation S–K, description of property;

(c) Item 103 of Regulation S–K, legal proceedings;

(d) Where common equity securities are being issued, Item 201 of Regulation S–K, market price of and dividends on the registrant's common equity and related stockholder matters;

(e) Financial statements meeting the requirements of Regulation S–X, (schedules required by Regulation S–X shall be filed as "Financial Statement Schedules" pursuant to Item 21 of this Form), as well as financial information required by Rule 3–05 and Article 11 of Regulation S–X with respect to transactions other than that pursuant to which the securities being registered are to be issued;

(f) Item 301 of Regulation S–K, selected financial data;

(g) Item 302 of Regulation S–K, supplementary financial information;

(h) Item 303 of Regulation S–K, management's discussion and analysis of financial condition and results of operations;

(i) Item 304 of Regulation S–K, changes in and disagreements with accountants on accounting and financial disclosure; and

(j) Item 305 of Regulation S–K (§ 229.305 of this chapter), quantitative and qualitative disclosures about market risk.

C. INFORMATION ABOUT THE COMPANY BEING ACQUIRED

Item 15. Information With Respect to S–3 Companies

If the company being acquired meets the requirements for use of Form S–3 and compliance with this Item is elected, furnish the information that would be required by Items 10 and 11 of this Form if securities of such company were being registered.

Item 16. Information With Respect to S–2 or S–3 Companies

(a) If the company being acquired meets the requirements for use of Form S–2 or S–3 and compliance with this Item is elected, furnish the information that would be required by Items 12 and 13 of this Form if securities of such company were being registered.

(b) *Electronic filings.* In addition to satisfying the requirements of paragraph (a) of this Item, electronic filers that elect to deliver and incorporate by reference all, or any portion, of the quarterly or annual report to security holders of a company being acquired pursuant to this Item shall file as an exhibit such quarterly or annual report to security holders, or such portion thereof that is incorporated by reference, in electronic format.

Item 17. Information With Respect to Companies Other Than S–3 or S–2 Companies

If the company being acquired does not meet the requirements for use of Form S–2 or S–3, or compliance with this Item is otherwise elected in lieu of Item 15 or 16, furnish the information required by paragraph (a) or (b) of this Item, whichever is applicable.

(a) If the company being acquired is subject to the reporting requirements of Section 13(a) or 15(d) of the Exchange Act, or compliance with this subparagraph in lieu of subparagraph (b) of this Item is selected, furnish the information that would be required by Item 14 of this Form is the securities of such company were being registered; *however,* only those schedules required by Rules 12–15, 28 and 29 of Regulation S–X need be provided with respect to the company being acquired.

(b) If the company being acquired is not subject to the reporting requirements of either Section 13(a) or 15(d) of the Exchange Act; or, because of Section 12(i) of the Exchange Act, has not furnished an annual report to security holders pursuant to Rule 14a–3 or Rule 14c–3 for its latest fiscal year; furnish the information that would be required by the following if securities of such company were being registered:

(1) a brief description of the business done by the company which indicates the general nature and scope of the business;

(2) Item 201 of Regulation S–K, market price of and dividends on the registrant's common equity and related stockholder matters;

(3) Item 301 of Regulation S–K, selected financial data;

(4) Item 302 of Regulation S–K, supplementary financial information;

(5) Item 303 of Regulation S–K, management's discussion and analysis of financial condition and results of operations;

(6) Item 304(b) of Regulation S–K, changes in and disagreements with accountants on accounting and financial disclosure;

(7) Financial statements that would be required in an annual report sent to security holders under Rules 14a–3(b)(1) and (b)(2) (§ 240.14b–3 of this chapter), if an annual report was required. If the registrant's security holders are not voting, the transaction is not a roll-up transaction (as described by Item 901 of Regulation S–K (§ 229.901 of this chapter)), and:

(i) The company being acquired is significant to the registrant in excess of the 20% level as determined under § 210.3–05(b)(2), provide financial statements of the company being acquired for the latest fiscal year in conformity with GAAP. In addition, if the company being acquired has provided its security holders with financial statements prepared in conformity with GAAP for either or both of the two fiscal years before the latest fiscal year, provide the financial statements for those years; or

(ii) The company being acquired is significant to the registrant at or below the 20% level, no financial information (including pro forma and comparative per share information) for the company being acquired need be provided.

Instructions:

1. The financial statements required by this paragraph for the latest fiscal year need be audited only to the extent practicable. The financial statements for the fiscal years before the latest fiscal year need not be audited if they were not previously audited.

2. If the financial statements required by this paragraph are prepared on the basis of a comprehensive body of accounting principles other than U.S. GAAP, provide a reconciliation to U.S. GAAP in accordance with Item 17 of Form 20–F (§ 249.220f of this chapter) unless a reconciliation is unavailable or not obtainable without unreasonable cost or expense. At a minimum, provide a narrative description of all material variations in accounting principles, practices and methods used in preparing the non–U.S. GAAP financial statements from those accepted in the U.S. when the financial statements are prepared on a basis other than U.S. GAAP.

3. If this Form is used to register resales to the public by any person who is deemed an underwriter within the meaning of Rule 145(c) (§ 230.145(c) of this chapter) with respect to the securities being reoffered, the financial statements must be audited for the fiscal years required to be presented under paragraph (b)(2) of Rule 3–05 of Regulation S–X (17CFR 210.3–05(b)(2)).

4. In determining the significance of an acquisition for purposes of this paragraph, apply the tests prescribed in Rule 1–02(w) (§ 210.1–02(w) of this chapter).

(8) the quarterly financial and other information as would have been required had the company being acquired been required to file Part I of Form 10–Q for the most recent quarter for which such a report would have been on file at the time the registration statement becomes effective or for a period ending as of a more recent date;

(9) schedules required by Rules 12–15, 28 and 29 of Regulation S–X;

(10) Item 305 of Regulation S–K (§ 229.305 of this chapter), quantitative and qualitative disclosures about market risk.

D. VOTING AND MANAGEMENT INFORMATION

Item 18. Information if Proxies, Consents or Authorizations Are to Be Solicited

(a) If proxies, consents or authorizations are to be solicited, furnish the following information, except as provided by paragraph (b) of this Item:

(1) The information required by Item 1 of Schedule 14A, date, time and place information;

(2) The information required by Item 2 of Schedule 14A, revocability of proxy;

(3) The information required by Item 3 of Schedule 14A, dissenters' rights of appraisal;

(4) The information required by Item 4 of Schedule 14A, persons making the solicitation;

(5) With respect to both the registrant and the company being acquired, the information required by:

(i) Item 5 of Schedule 14A, interest of certain persons in matters to be acted upon; and

(ii) Item 6 of Schedule 14A, voting securities and principal holders thereof;

(6) The information required by Item 21 of Schedule 14A, vote required for approval; and

(7) With respect to each person who will serve as a director or an executive officer of the surviving or acquiring company, the information required by:

(i) Item 401 of Regulation S–K, directors and executive officers;

(ii) Item 402 of Regulation S–K, executive compensation; and

(iii) Item 404 of Regulation S–K, certain relationships and related transactions.

(b) If the registrant or the company being acquired meets the requirements for use of Form S–2 or S–3, any information required by paragraphs (a)(5)(ii) and (7) of this Item with respect to such company may be incorporated by reference from its latest annual report on Form 10–K.

Item 19. Information if Proxies, Consents or Authorizations Are not to Be Solicited or in an Exchange Offer

(a) If the transaction is an exchange offer or if proxies, consents or authorizations are not to be solicited, furnish the following information, except as provided by paragraph (c) of this Item:

(1) The information required by Item 2 of Schedule 14C, statement that proxies are not to be solicited;

(2) The date, time and place of the meeting of security holders, unless such information is otherwise disclosed in material furnished to security holders with the prospectus;

(3) The information required by Item 3 of Schedule 14A, dissenters' rights of appraisal;

(4) With respect to both the registrant and the company being acquired, a brief description of any material interest, direct or indirect, by security holdings or otherwise, of affiliates of the registrant and of the company being acquired, in the proposed transaction;

Instruction. This subparagraph shall not apply to any interest arising from the ownership of securities of the registrant where the security holder receives no extra or special benefit not shared on a pro rata basis by all other holders of the same class.

(5) With respect to both the registrant and the company being acquired, the information required by Item 6 of Schedule 14A, voting securities and principal holders thereof;

(6) The information required by Item 21 of Schedule 14A, vote required for approval; and

(7) With respect to each person who will serve as a director or an executive officer of the surviving or acquiring company, the information required by:

(i) Item 401 of Regulation S–K, directors and executive officers;

(ii) Item 402 of Regulation S–K, executive compensation; and

(iii) Item 404 of Regulation S–K, certain relationships and related transactions.

(b) If the transaction is an exchange offer, furnish the information required by paragraphs (a)(4), (a)(5), and (a)(7) of this Item, except as provided by paragraph (c) of this Item.

(c) If the registrant or the company being acquired meets the requirements for use of Form S–2 or S–3, any information required by paragraphs (a)(5) and (7) of this Item with respect to such company may be incorporated by reference from its latest annual report on Form 10–K.

PART II—INFORMATION NOT REQUIRED IN PROSPECTUS

Item 20. Indemnification of Directors and Officers

Furnish the information required by Item 702 of Regulation S–K.

Item 21. Exhibits and Financial Statement Schedules

(a) Subject to the rules regarding incorporation by reference, furnish the exhibits as required by Item 601 of Regulation S–K.

(b) Furnish the financial statement schedules required by Regulation S–X and Item 14(e), Item 17(a) or Item 17(b)(8) of this Form. These schedules should be lettered or numbered in the manner described for exhibits in paragraph (a) of this Item.

(c) If information is provided pursuant to Item 4(b) of this Form, furnish the report, opinion or appraisal as an exhibit hereto, unless it is furnished as part of the prospectus.

Item 22. Undertakings

(a) Furnish the undertakings required by Item 512 of Regulation S–K.

(b) Furnish the following undertaking:

The undersigned registrant hereby undertakes to respond to requests for information that is incorporated by reference into the prospectus pursuant to Items 4, 10(b), 11, or 13 of this Form, within one business day of receipt of such request, and to send the incorporated documents by first class mail or other equally prompt means. This includes information contained in documents filed subsequent to the effective date of the registration statement through the date of responding to the request.

(c) Furnish the following undertaking:

The undersigned registrant hereby undertakes to supply by means of a post-effective amendment all information concerning a transaction, and the company being acquired involved therein, that was not the subject of and included in the registration statement when it became effective.

SIGNATURES

Pursuant to the requirements of the Securities Act, the registrant has duly caused this registration statement to be signed on its behalf by the undersigned, thereunto duly authorized, in the City of ....,

State of ....,

on ....,

19....

(Registrant) ....

By (Signature and Title) ....

Pursuant to the requirements of the Securities Act of 1933, this registration statement has been signed by the following persons in the capacities and on the dates indicated.

(Signature) ....

(Title) ....

(Date) ....

Instructions. 1. The registration statement shall be signed by the registrant, its principal executive officer or officers, its principal financial officer, its controller or principal accounting officer, and by at least a majority of the board of directors or persons performing similar functions. If the registrant is a foreign person, the registration statement shall also be signed by its authorized representative in the United States. Where the registrant is a limited partnership, the registration statement shall be signed by a majority of the board of directors of any corporate general partner signing the registration statement.

2. The name of each person who signs the registration statement shall be typed or printed beneath his signature. Any person who occupies more than one of the specified positions shall indicate each capacity in which he signs the registration statement. Attention is directed to Rule 402 concerning manual signatures and Item 601 concerning signatures pursuant to powers of attorney.

3. If the securities to be offered are those of a corporation not yet in existence at the time the registration statement is filed which will be a party to a consolidation involving two or more existing corporations, then each such

existing corporation shall be deemed a registrant and shall be so designated on the cover page of this Form, and the registration statement shall be signed by each such existing corporation and by the officers and directors of each such existing corporation as if each such existing corporation were the registrant.

FORM S–8

REGISTRATION STATEMENT UNDER THE SECURITIES ACT OF 1933

(Exact name of registrant as specified in its charter)

(State or other jurisdiction of incorporation or organization) | (I.R.S. Employer Identification No.)

(Address of Principal Executive Offices) | (Zip Code)

(Full title of the plan)

(Name and address of agent for service)

(Telephone number, including area code, of agent for service)

Calculation of Registration Fee

Title of securities to be registered	Amount to be registered	Proposed maximum offering price per unit	Proposed maximum aggregate offering price	Amount of registration fee

Notes

1. If plan interests are being registered, include the following: In addition, pursuant to Rule 416(c) under the Securities Act of 1933, this registration statement also covers an indeterminate amount of interests to be offered or sold pursuant to the employee benefit plan(s) described herein.

2. Specific details relating to the fee calculation shall be furnished in notes to the table, including references to provisions of Rule 457 relied upon, if the basis of the calculation is not otherwise evident from the information presented in the table.

GENERAL INSTRUCTIONS

A. Rule as to Use of Form S–8.

1. Any registrant that, immediately prior to the time of filing a registration statement on this form, is subject to the requirement to file reports pursuant to Section 13 or 15(d) of the Securities Exchange Act of 1934 (“Exchange Act”), and has filed all reports and other materials required to be filed by such requirements during the preceding 12 months (or for such shorter period that the registrant was required to file such reports and materials), may use this form for registration under

the Securities Act of 1933 ("Act") of the following securities:

(a) Securities of the registrant to be offered under any employee benefit plan to its employees or employees of its subsidiaries or parents. For purposes of this form, the term "employee benefit plan" is defined in Rule 405 of Regulation C (¶ 230.405).

(1) For purposes of this form, the term "employee" is defined as any employee, director, general partner, trustee (where the registrant is a business trust), officer, or consultant or advisor. Form S–8 is available for the issuance of securities to consultants or advisors only if:

(i) They are natural persons;

(ii) They provide *bona fide* services to the registrant; and

(iii) The services are not in connection with the offer or sale of securities in a capital-raising transaction, and do not directly or indirectly promote or maintain a market for the registrant's securities.

(2) In addition, the term "employee" includes insurance agents who are exclusive agents of the registrant, its subsidiaries or parents, or derive more than 50% of their annual income from those entities.

(3) The term *employees* also includes former employees as well as executors, administrators or beneficiaries of the estates of deceased employees, guardians or members of a committee for incompetent former employees, or similar persons duly authorized by law to administer the estate or assets of former employees. The inclusion of all individuals described in the preceding sentence in the term "employee" is only to permit registration on Form S–8 of:

(i) The exercise of employee benefit plan stock options and the subsequent sale of the securities, if these exercises and sales are permitted under the terms of the plan; and

(ii) The acquisition of registrant securities pursuant to intra-plan transfers among plan funds, if these transfers are permitted under the terms of the plan.

(4) The term *registrant* as used in this Form means the company whose securities are to be offered pursuant to the plan, and also may mean the plan itself.

(5) The form also is available for the exercise of employee benefit plan options and the subsequent resale of the underlying securities by an employee's family member who has acquired the options from the employee through a gift or a domestic relations order. For purposes of this form, "family member" includes any child, stepchild, grandchild, parent, stepparent, grandparent, spouse, former spouse, sibling, niece, nephew, mother-in-law, father-in-law, son-in-law, daughter-in-law, brother-in-law, or sister-in-law, including adoptive relationships, any person sharing the employee's household (other than a tenant or employee), a trust in which these persons have more than fifty percent of the beneficial interest, a foundation in which these persons (or the employee) control the management of assets, and any other entity in which these persons (or the employee) own more than fifty percent of the voting interests. Form S–8 is not available for the exercise of options transferred for value. The following transactions are not prohibited transfers for value:

(i) A transfer under a domestic relations order in settlement of marital property rights; and

(ii) A transfer to an entity in which more than fifty percent of the voting interests are owned by family members (or the employee) in exchange for an interest in that entity.

(b) Interests in the above plans, if such interests constitute securities and are required to be registered under the Act. (See

Release No. 33–6188 (February 1, 1980) and Section 3(a)(2) of the Act.)

2. Where interests in a plan are being registered and the plan's latest annual report filed pursuant to Section 15(d) of the Exchange Act is to be incorporated by reference pursuant to the requirements of Form S–8, the plan shall either: (i) have been subject to the requirement to file reports pursuant to Section 15(d) and shall have filed all reports required to be filed by such requirements during the preceding 12 months (or for such shorter period that the plan was required to file such reports); or (ii) if the plan has not previously been subject to the reporting requirements of Section 15(d), concurrently with the filing of the registration statement on Form S–8, the plan shall file an annual report for its latest fiscal year (or if the plan has not yet completed its first fiscal year, then for a period ending not more than 90 days prior to the filing of this registration statement), provided that if the plan has not been in existence for at least 90 days prior to the filing date, the requirement to file an employee plan annual report concurrently with the Form S–8 registration statement shall not apply.

3. *Electronic filings.* In addition to satisfying the foregoing conditions, a registrant subject to the electronic filing requirements of Rule 101 of Regulation S–T shall have filed with the Commission:

All required electronic filings, including confirming electronic copies of documents submitted in paper pursuant to a hardship exemption as provided by Rule 201 or Rule 202(d) of Regulation S–T (§ 232.201 or § 232.202(d) of this chapter).

B. Application of General Rules and Regulations.

1. Attention is directed to the General Rules and Regulations under the Act, particularly those comprising Regulation C thereunder (17 CFR 230.400 to 230.499). That Regulation contains general requirements regarding the preparation and filing of registration statements. However, any provision in this form covering the same subject matter as any such requirement shall be controlling unless otherwise specifically provided in Regulation C (see § 230.400).

2. Attention is directed to Regulation S–K (17 CFR Part 229) for the requirements applicable to the content of the non-financial portions of registration statements under the Act. Where this form directs the registrant to furnish information required by any item of Regulation S–K, information need only be furnished to the extent appropriate.

3. A "small business issuer," defined in Rule 405, shall refer to the disclosure items in Regulation S–B and not Regulation S–K.

C. Reoffers and Resales.

1. *Securities.* Reoffers and resales of the following securities may be made on a continuous and delayed basis in the future, as provided by Rule 415, pursuant to a registration statement on this form by means of a separate prospectus ("reoffer prospectus"), which is prepared in accordance with the requirements of Part I of Form S–3 (or, if the registrant is a foreign private issuer, in accordance with Part I of Form F–3), filed with the registration statement on Form S–8 or, in the case of control securities, a post-effective amendment thereto:

(a) *Control securities,* which are defined for purposes of this General Instruction C as securities acquired under a Securities Act registration statement held by affiliates of the registrant as defined in Rule 405. Control securities may be included in a reoffer prospectus only if they have been or will be acquired by the selling security holder pursuant to an employee benefit plan; or

(b) *Restricted securities,* which are defined for purposes of this General Instruction C as securities issued under any employee benefit plan of the registrant meeting the definition of "restricted securities" in Rule 144(a)(3), whether or not held by affiliates of the registrant. Restricted securities may be included in a reoffer prospectus only if they have been acquired by the selling security holder prior to the filing of the registration statement.

2. *Limitations.* The reoffer prospectus may be used as follows:

(a) If the registrant, at the time of filing such prospectus, satisfies the registrant requirements for use of Form S–3 (or if the registrant is a foreign private issuer, the registrant requirements for use of Form F–3), then control and restricted securities may be registered for reoffer and resale without any limitations.

(b) If the registrant, at the time of filing such prospectus, does not satisfy the registrant requirements for use of Form S–3 or F–3, as appropriate, then the following limitation shall apply with respect to both control securities and restricted securities: the amount of securities to be reoffered or resold by means of the reoffer prospectus, by each person, and any other person with whom he or she is acting in concert for the purpose of selling securities of the registrant, may not exceed, during any three month period, the amount specified in Rule 144(e).

3. *Selling Security Holders.*

(a) *Control Securities.* If the names of the security holders who intend to resell are not known by the registrant at the time of filing the Form S–8 registration statement, the registrant may either: (1) refer to the selling security holders in a generic manner in the reoffer prospectus; later, as their names and the amounts of securities to be reoffered become known, the registrant must supplement the reoffer prospectus with that information; or (2) name in the reoffer prospectus all persons eligible to resell and the amounts of securities available to be resold, whether or not they have a present intent to do so; any additional persons must be added by prospectus supplement. Prospectus supplements must be filed with the Commission as required by Rule 424(b). The registrant may file a reoffer prospectus covering control securities as part of the initial registration statement or by means of a post-effective amendment to the Form S–8 registration statement.

(b) *Restricted Securities.*

(A) All persons (including non-affiliates) holding restricted securities registered for reoffer or resale pursuant to a reoffer prospectus are to be named as selling shareholders in the reoffer prospectus; *provided, however,* that any non-affiliate who holds less than the lesser of 1000 shares or 1% of the shares issuable under the plan to which the Form S–8 registration statement relates need not be named if the reoffer prospectus indicates that certain unnamed non-affiliates, each of whom may sell up to that amount, may use the reoffer prospectus for reoffers and resales. The reoffer prospectus covering restricted securities must be filed with the initial registration statement, not a post-effective amendment thereto.

Notes to General Instruction C

1. The term "person" as used in this General Instruction C shall be the same as set forth in Rule 144(a)(2).

2. If the conditions of this General Instruction C are not satisfied, registration of reoffers or resales must be made by means of a separate registration statement using whichever form is applicable.

D. Filing and Effectiveness of Registration Statement; Requests for Confidential Treatment; Number of Copies.

A registration statement on this Form S–8 will become effective automatically (Rule 462) upon filing (Rule 456). In addition, post-effective amendments on this form shall become effective upon filing (Rules 464, and 456). Delaying amendments are not permitted in connection with any registration statement on this form (Rule 473(d)), and any attempt to interpose a delaying amendment of any kind will be ineffective. All filings made on or in connection with this form become public upon filing with the Commission. As a result, requests for confidential treatment made under either Rule 406 or Exchange Act Rule 24b–2 in connection with documents incorporated by reference, must be acted upon, *i.e.*, granted or denied, by the Commission staff prior to the filing of the registration statement. The number of copies of the filing required by Rules 402(c) and 472(d) shall be filed with the Commission.

E. Registration of Additional Securities.

With respect to the registration of additional securities of the same class as other securities for which a registration statement filed on this form relating to the same employee benefit plan is effective, the registrant may file a registration statement consisting only of the following: the facing page; a statement that the contents of the earlier registration statement, identified by file number, are incorporated by reference; required opinions and consents; the signature page; and any information required in the new registration statement that is not in the earlier registration statement. If the new registration statement covers restricted securities being offered for resale, it shall include the required reoffer prospectus. If the earlier registration statement included a reoffer prospectus, the new registration statement shall be deemed to include that reoffer prospectus; *provided, however,* that a revised reoffer prospectus shall be filed, if the reoffer prospectus is substantively different from that filed in the earlier registration statement. The filing fee required by the Act and Rule 457 shall be paid with respect to the additional securities only.

F. Registration of Plan Interests.

Where a registration statement on this form relates to securities to be offered pursuant to an employee stock purchase, savings, or similar plan, the registration statement shall be deemed to register an indeterminate amount of interests in such plan that are separate securities and required to be registered under the Securities Act. (See Rule 416(c)).

G. Updating.

Updating of information constituting the Section 10(a) prospectus pursuant to Rule 428(a) during the offering of the securities shall be accomplished as follows:

(1) Plan information specified by Item 1 of Form S–8 required to be sent or given to employees shall be updated as specified in Rule 428(b)(1). Such information need not be filed with the Commission.

(2) Registrant information shall be updated by the filing of Exchange Act reports, which are incorporated by reference in the registration statement and the Section 10(a) prospectus. Any material changes in the registrant's affairs required to be disclosed in the registration statement but not required to be included in a specific Exchange Act report shall be reported on Form 8–K pursuant to Item 5 thereof (or, if the registrant is a foreign private issuer, on Form 6–K).

(3) An employee plan annual report incorporated by reference in the registration statement from Form 11–K (or Form 10–K and 10–KSB, as permitted by Rule 15d–21) shall be updated by the filing of a subsequent plan annual report on Form 11–K or 10–K and 10–KSB.

PART I—INFORMATION REQUIRED IN THE SECTION 10(a) PROSPECTUS

Note: The document(s) containing the information specified in this Part I will be sent or given to employees as specified by Rule 428(b)(1). Such documents need not be filed with the Commission either as part of this registration statement or as prospectuses or prospectus supplements pursuant to Rule 424. These documents and the documents incorporated by reference in the registration statement pursuant to Item 3 of Part II of this form, taken together, constitute a prospectus that meets the requirements of Section 10(a) of the Securities Act. See Rule 428(a)(1).

Item 1. Plan Information.

The registrant shall deliver or cause to be delivered to each participant material information regarding the plan and its operations that will enable participants to make an informed decision regarding investment in the plan. This information shall include, to the extent material to the particular plan being described, but not be limited to, the disclosure specified in (a) through (j) below. Any unusual risks associated with participation in the plan not described pursuant to a specified item shall be prominently disclosed, as, for example, when the plan imposes a substantial restriction on the ability of a participant to withdraw contributions, or when plan participation may obligate the participant's general credit in connection with purchases on a margin basis. The information may be in one or several documents, provided that it is presented in a clear, concise and understandable manner. See Rule 421.

(a) *General Plan Information*

(1) Give the title of the plan and the name of the registrant whose securities are to be offered pursuant to the plan.

(2) Briefly state the general nature and purpose of the plan, its duration, and any provisions for its modification, earlier termination or extension to the extent that they affect the participants.

(3) Indicate whether the plan is subject to any provisions of the Employee Retirement Income Security Act of 1974 ("ERISA"), and if so, the general nature of those provisions to which it is subject.

(4) Give an address and a telephone number, including area code, which participants may use to obtain additional information about the plan and its administrators. State the capacity in which the plan administrators act (*e.g.*, trustees or managers) and the functions that they perform. If any person other than a participating employee has discretion with respect to the investment of all or any part of the assets of the plan in one or more investment media, name such person and describe the policies followed and to be followed with respect to the type and proportion of securities or other property in which funds of the plan may be invested. If the plan is not subject to ERISA: (i) state the nature of any material relationship between the administrators and the employees, the registrant or its affiliates; and (ii) describe the manner in which the plan administrators are selected, their term of office, and the manner in which they may be removed from office.

(b) *Securities to be Offered*

(1) State the title and total amount of securities to be offered pursuant to the plan.

(2) Furnish the information required by Item 202 of Regulation S–K, except that if common stock registered under Section 12 of the Exchange Act is offered, such information is unnecessary. If plan interests are being registered, they need not be described pursuant to this item.

(c) *Employees Who May Participate in the Plan*

Indicate each class or group of employees that may participate in the plan and the basis upon which the eligibility of employees to participate therein is to be determined.

(d) *Purchase of Securities Pursuant to the Plan and Payment for Securities Offered*

(1) State the period of time within which employees may elect to participate in the plan, the price at which the securities may be purchased or the basis upon which such price is to be determined, and any terms regarding the amount of securities that an eligible employee can purchase.

(2) State when and the manner in which employees are to pay for the securities purchased pursuant to the plan. If payment is to be made by payroll deductions or other installment payments, state the percentage

of wages or salaries or other basis for computing such payments, and the time and manner in which an employee may alter the amount of such deduction or payment.

(3) State the amount each employee is required or permitted to contribute or, if not a fixed amount, the percentage of wages or salaries or other basis of computing contributions.

(4) If contributions are to be made under the plan by the registrant or any employer, state who is to make such contributions, when they are to be made and the nature and amount of each contribution. If such contributions are not a fixed amount, state the basis for computing contributions.

(5) State the nature and frequency of any reports to be made to participating employees as to the amount and status of their accounts.

(6) If the plan is not subject to ERISA, state whether securities are to be purchased in the open market or otherwise. If they are not to be purchased in the open market, then state from whom they are to be purchased and describe the fees, commissions or other charges paid. If the employer or any of its affiliates, or any person having a material relationship with the employer or any of its affiliates, directly or indirectly, receives any part of the aggregate purchase price (including fees, commissions or other charges), explain the basis for compensation.

Note: If the plan is one under which credit is extended to finance the acquisition of securities, consideration should be given to the applicability of Regulation G (12 CFR Part 207) or T (12 CFR Part 220).

(e) *Resale Restrictions*

Describe briefly any restriction on resale of the securities purchased under the plan which may be imposed upon the employee purchaser.

(f) *Tax Effects of Plan Participation*

Describe briefly the tax effects that may accrue to employees as a result of a plan participation as well as the tax effects, if any, upon the registrant and whether or not the plan is qualified under Section 401(a) of the Internal Revenue Code.

Note: If the plan is not qualified under Section 401 of the Internal Revenue Code of 1986, as amended, consideration should be given to the applicability of the Investment Company Act of 1940. *See* Securities Act Release No. 4790 (July 13, 1965).

(g) *Investment of Funds*

If participating employees may direct all or any part of the assets under the plan to two or more investment media, furnish a brief description of the provisions of the plan with respect to the alternative investment media; and provide a tabular or other meaningful presentation of financial data for each of the past three fiscal years (or such lesser period for which the data is available with respect to each investment medium) that, in the opinion of the registrant, will apprise employees of material trends and significant changes in the performance of alternative investment media and enable them to make informed investment decisions. Financial data shall be presented for any additional fiscal years necessary to keep the information from being misleading or that the registrant deems appropriate, but the total period presented need not exceed five years.

(h) *Withdrawal from the Plan; Assignment of Interest*

(1) Describe the terms and conditions under which a participating employee may (i) withdraw from the plan and terminate his or her interest therein; or (ii) withdraw funds or investments held for the employee's account without terminating his or her interest in the plan.

(2) State whether, and the terms and conditions upon which, the plan permits an employee to assign or hypothecate his or her interest in the plan.

(3) No information need be provided as to the effect of a qualified domestic relations

order as defined in ERISA Section 206(d) (29 U.S.C. 1056(d)).

(i) *Forfeitures and Penalties*

Describe briefly every event which could, under the plan, result in a forfeiture by, or a penalty to, a participant, and the consequences thereof.

(j) *Charges and Deductions and Liens Therefor*

(1) Describe all charges and deductions (other than deductions described in paragraph (d) and taxes) that may be made against employees participating in the plan or against funds, securities or other property held under the plan and indicate who will receive, directly or indirectly, any part thereof. Such description should include charges and deductions that may be made upon the termination of an employee's interest in the plan, or upon partial withdrawals from the employee's account thereunder.

(2) State whether or not under the plan, or pursuant to any contract in connection therewith, any person has or may create a lien on any funds, securities, or other property held under the plan. If so, describe fully the circumstances under which the lien was or may be created.

(3) No information need be provided as to the effect of a qualified domestic relations order as defined in ERISA Section 206(d) (29 U.S.C. 1056(d)).

Item 2. Registrant Information and Employee Plan Annual Information.

The registrant shall provide a written statement to participants advising them of the availability without charge, upon written or oral request, of the documents incorporated by reference in Item 3 of Part II of the registration statement, and stating that these documents are incorporated by reference into the Section 10(a) prospectus. The statement also shall indicate the availability without charge, upon written or oral request, of other documents required to be delivered to employees pursuant to Rule 428(b). The statement shall include the address (giving title or department) and telephone number to which the request is to be directed.

PART II—INFORMATION REQUIRED IN THE REGISTRATION STATEMENT

Item 3. Incorporation of Documents by Reference.

The registrant, and where interests in the plan are being registered, the plan, shall state that the documents listed in (a) through (c) below are incorporated by reference in the registration statement; and shall state that all documents subsequently filed by it pursuant to Sections 13(a), 13(c), 14 and 15(d) of the Securities Exchange Act of 1934, prior to the filing of a post-effective amendment which indicates that all securities offered have been sold or which deregisters all securities then remaining unsold, shall be deemed to be incorporated by reference in the registration statement and to be part thereof from the date of filing of such documents. Copies of these documents are not required to be filed with the registration statement.

(a) The registrant's latest annual report, and where interests in the plan are being registered, the plan's latest annual report, filed pursuant to Sections 13(a) or 15(d) of the Exchange Act, or in the case of the registrant either: (1) the latest prospectus filed pursuant to Rule 424(b) under the Act that contains audited financial statements for the registrant's latest fiscal year for which such statements have been filed, or (2) the registrant's effective registration statement on Form 10 and 10–SB, Form 20–F or, in the case of registrants described in General Instruction A.(2) of Form 40–F, on Form 40–F filed under the Exchange Act containing audited financial statements for the registrant's latest fiscal year.

(b) All other reports filed pursuant to Section 13(a) or 15(d) of the Exchange Act since the end of the fiscal year covered by the registrant document referred to in (a) above.

(c) If the class of securities to be offered is registered under Section 12 of the Exchange Act, the description of such class of securities contained in a registration statement filed under such Act, including any amendment or report filed for the purpose of updating such description.

Item 4. Description of Securities.

If the class of securities to be offered is not registered under Section 12 of the Exchange Act, set forth the information required by Item 202 of Regulation S–K. If plan interests are being registered, they need not be described pursuant to this item.

Item 5. Interests of Named Experts and Counsel.

Furnish the information required by Item 509 of Regulation S–K.

Item 6. Indemnification of Directors and Officers.

Furnish the information required by Item 702 of Regulation S–K.

Item 7. Exemption from Registration Claimed.

With respect to restricted securities to be reoffered or resold pursuant to this registration statement, the registrant shall indicate the section of the Act or Rule of the Commission under which exemption from registration was claimed and set forth briefly the facts relied upon to make the exemption available.

Item 8. Exhibits.

Furnish the exhibits required by Item 601 Regulation S–K (§ 229.601 of this chapter), except that, with respect to Item 601(b)(5):

(a) An opinion of counsel as to the legality of the securities being registered is required only with respect to original issuance securities.

(b) Neither an opinion of counsel concerning compliance with the requirements of ERISA nor an Internal Revenue Service determination letter that the plan is qualified under Section 401 of the Internal Revenue Code shall be required if, in lieu thereof, the response to this Item 8 includes an undertaking that the registrant will submit or has submitted the plan and any amendment thereto to the Internal Revenue Service ("IRS") in a timely manner and has made or will make all changes required by the IRS in order to qualify the plan.

Item 9. Undertakings.

Furnish the undertakings required by Item 512 (a), (b) and (h) of Regulation S–K (§ 229.512(a), (b) and (h) of this chapter), as well as any other applicable undertakings in Item 512.

Notes to Item 9: (1) The Regulation S–K Item 512(a) undertakings are usually required pursuant to this item since most registration statements on Form S–8 involve the continuous offering and sale of securities under Rule 415 (§ 230.415 of this chapter).

(2) With respect to registration statements filed on this form, foreign private issuers eligible to file on Form 20–F are not required to furnish the Item 512(a)(4) undertaking.

SIGNATURES

The Registrant. Pursuant to the requirements of the Securities Act of 1933, the registrant certifies that it has reasonable grounds to believe that it meets all of the requirements for filing on Form S–8 and has duly caused this registration statement to be signed on its behalf by the undersigned, thereunto duly authorized, in the City of ______, State of ______, on ______, 19__

(Registrant) ____________________

By (Signature and Title) ______________________________

Pursuant to the requirements of the Securities Act of 1933, this registration statement has been signed by the following persons in the capacities and on the date indicated.

(Signature) ______________________________

(Title) ______________________________

(Date) ______________________________

The Plan. Pursuant to the requirements of the Securities Act of 1933, the trustees (or other persons who administer the employee benefit plan) have duly caused this registration statement to be signed on its behalf by the undersigned, thereunto duly authorized, in the City of ______, State of ______, on ______, 19__

____

(Plan) ______________________________

By (Signature and Title) ______________________________

Instructions. 1. The registration statement shall be signed by the registrant, its principal executive officer or officers, its principal financial officer, its controller or principal accounting officer, and by at least a majority of the board of directors or persons performing similar functions. Where interests in the plan are being registered, the registration statement shall be signed by the plan. If the signing person is a foreign person, the registration statement shall also be signed by its authorized representative in the United States. Where the signing person is a limited partnership, the registration statement shall be signed by a majority of the board of directors of any corporate general partner signing the registration statement.

2. The name of each person who signs the registration statement shall be typed or printed beneath the signature. Any person who occupies more than one of the specified positions shall indicate each capacity in which he or she signs the registration statement. Attention is directed to Rule 402 concerning manual signatures and Item 601 (§ 229.601) of Regulation S–K concerning signatures pursuant to powers of attorney.

FORM SB–1

U.S. Securities and Exchange Commission
Washington, D.C. 20549

Form SB–1

REGISTRATION STATEMENT UNDER THE SECURITIES ACT OF 1933

(Amendment No. ___)

____
(Name of small business issuer in its charter)

____
(State or jurisdiction of incorporation or organization)

____
(Primary Standard Industrial Classification Code Number)

____
(I.R.S. Employer Identification No.)

____
(Address and telephone number of principal executive offices)

(Address of principal place of business or intended principal place of business)

(Name, address, and telephone number of agent for service)

Approximate date of commencement of proposed sale to the public ______

If this Form is filed to register additional securities for an offering pursuant to Rule 462(b) under the Securities Act, check the following box and list the Securities Act registration statement number of the earlier effective registration statement for the same offering. ☐ ______

If this Form is a post-effective amendment filed pursuant to Rule 462(c) under the Securities Act, check the following box and list the Securities Act registration statement number of the earlier effective registration statement for the same offering. ☐ ______

If this Form is a post-effective amendment filed pursuant to Rule 462(d) under the Securities Act, check the following box and list the Securities Act registration statement number of the earlier effective registration statement for the same offering. ☐ ______

If delivery of the prospectus is expected to be made pursuant to Rule 434, check the following box. ☐

CALCULATION OF REGISTRATION FEE

Title of each class of securities to be registered	Dollar amount to be registered	Proposed maximum offering price per unit	Proposed maximum aggregate offering price	Amount of registration fee

The following delaying amendment is optional, but see Rule 473 before omitting it: The registrant hereby amends this registration statement on such date or dates as may be necessary to delay its effective date until the registrant shall file a further amendment which specifically states that this registration statement shall thereafter become effective in accordance with Section 8(a) of the Securities Act of 1933 or until the registration statement shall become effective on such date as the Commission, acting pursuant to said Section 8(a), may determine.

Disclosure alternative used (check one): Alternative 1 ______; Alternative 2 ______

GENERAL INSTRUCTIONS

A. Use of Form and Place of Filing

1. (a) A "small business issuer," defined in Rule 405 of the Securities Act of 1933 (the "Securities Act") may use this form to register up to $10,000,000 of securities to be sold for cash, if they have not registered more than $10,000,000 in securities offerings in any continuous 12–month period, including the transaction being registered. In calculating the $10,000,000 ceiling, issuers should include all offerings which were registered under the Securities Act, other than any amounts registered on Form S–8.

(b) A small business issuer may use this form until it (1) registers more than $10 million under the Securities Act in any continuous 12–month period (other than securities registered on Form S–8), (2) elects to file on a non-transitional disclosure document (other than the proxy statement disclosure in Schedule 14A), or (3) no longer meets the definition of small business issuer. Non-transitional disclosure documents include: (1) Securities Act registration statement forms other than Forms SB–1, S–3 (if the issuer incorporates by reference transitional Exchange Act reports), S–8 and S–4 (if the issuer relies upon the transitional disclosure format in that form); (2) Exchange Act periodic reporting Forms 10–K and 10–Q; (3) Exchange Act registration statement Form 10; and (4) reports or registration statements on Forms 10–KSB, 10–QSB or 10–SB which do not use the transitional disclosure document format. A reporting company may not return to the transitional disclosure forms.

2. The small business issuer shall file the registration statement in the Washington, D.C. office.

3. If the small business issuer is a reporting company or a holding company of a bank (see the definition of "bank" in section 12(i) of the Securities Exchange Act of 1934), it should file the registration statement in the Commission's Washington, D.C. headquarters.

B. General Requirements

1. In preparing a registration statement on this Form, reference should be made to the General Rules and Regulations under the Securities Act, particularly Regulation C which sets forth requirements for the preparation and filing of a registration statement such as paper type and size.

2. Issuers registering securities for the first time should be aware of Form SR and Rule 463 under the Securities Act concerning sales of registered securities and the use of proceeds. First-time issuers also should be aware of Exchange Act Rule 15c2–8, which requires broker-dealers to deliver a prospectus 48 hours before a sale of securities can be confirmed.

3. Issuers engaged in real estate, oil and gas or mining activities should consult the Industry Guides in Item 801 of Regulation S-K. Real estate companies also should refer to Item 13 [Investment Policies of Registrant], Item 14 [Description of Real Estate], and Item 15 [Operating Data] of Form S–11.

C. Preparation and Filing of the Registration Statement

Part I of this form, which relates to the content of certain information about the issuer, provides several alternative disclosure formats. The registrant may elect any of these alternative formats.

D. Financial Statement Requirements

Regardless of the disclosure model used, all registrants shall provide the financial statements required by Part F/S of this Form SB–1.

E. Composition of Prospectus

The information required by Part I and Part F/S of this regulation statement shall comprise the prospectus.

F. Cover Page of Registration Statement

Issuers electing Alternative 1 should furnish the information required by Item 501 of Regulation S-B in lieu of the information required by Alternative 1 with respect to the cover page of the registration statement. Issuers electing Alternative 2 should furnish the information required by Item 501 of Regulation S-B in lieu of the information required by Item 1 of Alternative 2.

G. Canadian Issuer—Consent of Service

Canadian issuers eligible to use this Form should file as an exhibit to this registration statement a written irrevocable consent and power of attorney on Form F-X (§ 239.42 of this title).

H. Registration of Additional Securities

With respect to the registration of additional securities for an offering pursuant to Rule 462(b) under the Securities Act, the registrant may file a registration statement consisting only of the following: The facing page; a statement that the contents of the earlier registration statement, identified by file number, are incorporated by reference; required opinions and consents; the signature page; and any price-related information omitted from the earlier registration statement in reliance on Rule 430A that the registrant chooses to include in the new registration statement. The information contained in such a Rule 462(b) registration statement shall be deemed to be a part of the earlier registration statement as of the date of effectiveness of the Rule 462(b) registration statement. Any opinion or consent required in the Rule 462(b) registration statement may be incorporated by reference from the earlier registration statement with respect to the offering, if: (i) Such opinion or consent expressly provides for such incorporation; and (ii) such opinion relates the securities registered pursuant to Rule 462(b). See Rule 411(c) and Rule 439(b) under the Securities Act.

PART I—NARRATIVE INFORMATION REQUIRED IN PROSPECTUS

Alternative 1

Corporate issuers may elect to furnish the information required by Model A of Form 1–A, as well as the following information.

Item 1. Inside Front and Outside Back Cover Pages of Prospectus.

Furnish the information required by Item 502 of Regulation S-B.

Item 2. Significant Parties.

List the full names and business and residential addresses, as applicable, for the following persons:

(1) the issuer's directors;

(2) the issuer's officers;

(3) the issuer's general partners;

(4) record owners of 5 percent or more of any class of the issuer's equity securities;

(5) beneficial owners of 5 percent or more of any class of the issuer's equity securities;

(6) promoters of the issuer;

(7) affiliates of the issuer;

(8) counsel to the issuer with respect to the proposed offering;

(9) each underwriter with respect to the proposed offering;

(10) the underwriter's directors;

(11) the underwriter's officers;

(12) the underwriter's general partners; and

(13) counsel to the underwriter.

Item 3. Relationship with Issuer of Experts Named in Registration Statement.

Furnish the information required by Item 509 of Regulation S-B, if applicable.

Item 4. Selling Security Holders.

Furnish the information required by Item 507 of Regulation S-B, if applicable.

Item 5. Changes in and Disagreements with Accountants.

Furnish the information required by Item 304 of Regulation S-B, if applicable.

Item 6. Disclosure of Commission position on Indemnification for Securities Act Liabilities.

Furnish the information required by Item 510 of Regulation S-B.

Alternative 2

Any issuer may elect to furnish the information required by Model B of Part II of Form 1–A, as well as the following information.

Item 1. Inside Front and Outside Back Cover Pages of Prospectus.

Furnish the information required by Item 502 of Regulation S-B.

Item 2. Significant Parties.

List the full names and business and residential addresses, as applicable, for the following persons:

(1) the issuer's directors;

(2) the issuer's officers;

(3) the issuer's general partners;

(4) record owners of 5 percent or more of any class of the issuer's equity securities;

(5) beneficial owners of 5 percent or more of any class of the issuer's equity securities;

(6) promoters of the issuer;

(7) affiliates of the issuer;

(8) counsel to the issuer with respect to the proposed offering;

(9) each underwriter with respect to the proposed offering;

(10) the underwriter's directors;

(11) the underwriter's officers;

(12) the underwriter's general partners; and

(13) counsel to the underwriter.

Item 3. Relationship with Issuer of Experts Named in Registration Statement.

Furnish the information required by Item 509 of Regulation S-B, if applicable.

Item 4. Legal Proceedings.

Furnish the information required by Item 103 of Regulation S-B.

Item 5. Changes in and Disagreements with Accountants.

Furnish the information required by Item 304 of Regulation S-B, if applicable.

Item 6. Disclosure of Commission position on Indemnification for Securities Act Liabilities.

Furnish the information required by Item 510 of Regulation S-B.

Part F/S—Financial Information Required in Prospectus

Furnish the information required by Item 310 of Regulation S-B.

PART II—INFORMATION NOT REQUIRED IN PROSPECTUS

Item 1. Indemnification of Directors and Officers.

Furnish the information required by Item 702 of Regulation S-B.

Item 2. Other Expenses of Issuance and Distribution.

Furnish the information required by Item 511 of Regulation S-B.

Item 3. Undertakings.

Furnish the undertakings required by Item 512 of Regulation S-B.

Item 4. Unregistered Securities Issued or Sold Within One Year.

(a) As to any unregistered securities issued by the issuer or any of its predecessors or affiliated issuers within one year prior to the filing of this Form SB–1, state:

(1) the name of such issuer;

(2) the title and amount of securities issued;

(3) the aggregate offering price or other consideration for which they were issued and the basis for computing the amount thereof;

(4) the names and identities of the persons to whom the securities were issued.

(b) As to any unregistered securities of the issuer or any of its predecessors or affiliated issuers which were sold within one year prior to the filing of this Form SB–1 by or for the account of any person who at the time was a director, officer, promoter or principal security holder of the issuer of such securities, or was an underwriter of any securities of such issuer, furnish the information specified in subsections (1) through (4) of paragraph (a).

(c) Indicate the section of the Securities Act or Commission rule or regulation relied upon for exemption from the registration requirements of such Act and state briefly the facts relied upon for such exemption.

Item 5. Index to Exhibits.

(a) An index to the exhibits should be presented.

(b) Each exhibit should be listed in the exhibit index according to the number assigned to it in Part III of Form 1–A or Item 2, below.

(c) The index to exhibits should identify the location of the exhibit under the sequential page numbering system for this Form SB–1.

(d) Where exhibits are incorporated by reference, the reference shall be made in the index of exhibits.

Instructions:

1. Any document or part thereof filed with the Commission pursuant to any Act administered by the Commission may, subject to the limitations of Rule 24 of the Commission's Rules of Practice, be incorporated by reference as an exhibit to any registration statement.

2. If any modification has occurred in the text of any document incorporated by reference since the filing thereof, the issuer shall file with the reference a statement containing the text of such modification and the date thereof.

3. Procedurally, the techniques specified in Rule 411(d) of Regulation C shall be followed.

Item 6. Description of Exhibits.

As appropriate, the issuer should file as exhibits those documents required to be filed under Part III of Form 1–A. Part III of Form 1–A lists 10 exhibits. The registrant also shall file:

(11) *Opinion re legality*—An opinion of counsel as to the legality of the securities covered by the Registration Statement, indicating whether they will, when sold, be legally issued, fully paid and non-assessable, and if debt securities, whether they will be binding obligations of the issuer.

(12) *Additional exhibits*—Any additional exhibits which the issuer may wish to file, which shall be so marked as to indicate clearly the subject matters to which they refer.

(13) *Form F–X*—Canadian issuers shall file a written irrevocable consent and power of attorney on Form F–X.

SIGNATURES

In accordance with the requirements of the Securities Act of 1933, the registrant certifies that it has reasonable grounds to believe that it meets all of the requirements of filing on Form SB–1 and authorized this registration statement to be signed on its behalf by the undersigned, in the City of ______ State of ______, on ______, 19__

(Registrant) ______________________________

By (Signature and Title) ______________________________

In accordance with the requirements of the Securities Act of 1933, this registration statement was signed by the following persons in the capacities and on the dates stated.

(Signature) ______________________________

(Title) ______________________________

(Date) ______________________________

Instructions for signatures.

(1) Who must sign: the small business issuer, its principal executive officer or officers, its principal financial officer, its controller or principal accounting officer and at least the majority of the board of directors or persons

performing similar functions. If the issuer is a limited partnership then the general partner and a majority of its board of directors if a corporation.

(2) Beneath each signature, type or print the name of each signatory. Any person who occupies more than one of the specified positions shall indicate each capacity in which he or she signs the registration statement. See Rule 402 of Regulation C concerning manual signatures and Item 601 of Regulation S-B concerning signatures by powers of attorney.

FORM SB–2

U.S. Securities and Exchange Commission
Washington, D.C. 20549

Form SB–2

REGISTRATION STATEMENT UNDER THE SECURITIES ACT OF 1933

(Amendment No. ____.)

(Name of small business issuer in its charter)

(State or jurisdiction of incorporation or organization)

(Primary Standard Industrial Classification Code Number)

(I.R.S.Employer Identification No.)

(Address and telephone number of principal executive offices)

(Address of principal place of business or intended principal place of business)

(Name, address and telephone number of agent for service)

Approximate date of commencement of proposed sale to the public ______

If this Form is filed to register additional securities for an offering pursuant to Rule 462(b) under the Securities Act, check the following box and list the Securities Act registration statement number of the earlier effective registration statement for the same offering. ☐ ______

If this Form is a post-effective amendment filed pursuant to Rule 462(c) under the Securities Act, check the following box and list the Securities Act registration statement number of the earlier effective registration statement for the same offering. ☐ ______

If this Form is a post-effective amendment filed pursuant to Rule 462(d) under the Securities Act, check the following box and list the Securities Act registration statement number of the earlier effective registration statement for the same offering. ☐ ______

If delivery of the prospectus is expected to be made pursuant to Rule 434, check the following box. ☐

CALCULATION OF REGISTRATION FEE

Title of each class of securities to be registered	Dollar Amount to be registered	Proposed maximum offering price per unit	Proposed maximum aggregate offering price	Amount of registration fee

Note: Specific details relating to the fee

calculation shall be furnished in notes to the table, including references to provisions of Rule 457 relied upon, if the basis of the calculation is not otherwise evident from the information presented in the table.

The registrant hereby amends this registration statement on such date or dates as may be necessary to delay its effective date until the registrant shall file a further amendment which specifically states that this registration statement shall thereafter become effective in accordance with Section 8(a) of the Securities Act of 1933 or until the registration statement shall become effective on such date as the Commission, acting pursuant to said Section 8(a), may determine.

GENERAL INSTRUCTIONS

A. Use of Form and Place of Filing

1. A "small business issuer," defined in Rule 405 of the Securities Act of 1933 (the "Securities Act") may use this form to register securities to be sold for cash. See also Item 10(a) of Regulation S–B (17 CFR 228.10 et seq.)

2. Offerings on Form SB–2 shall be filed in the Washington, D.C. office.

3. If the small business issuer is a reporting company or a holding company of a bank (see the definition of "bank" in section 12(i) of the Exchange Act), it should file the registration statement in the Commission's Washington, D.C. headquarters.

B. General Requirements

1. Issuers registering securities for the first time should be aware of Form SR and Rule 463 under the Securities Act concerning sales of registered securities and the use of proceeds. First time issuers also should be aware of Exchange Act Rule 15c2–8 which requires broker dealers to deliver a prospectus 48 hours before a sale of securities can be confirmed.

2. Issuers engaged in real estate, oil and gas or mining activities should consult the Industry Guides in Item 801 of Regulation S–K. Real estate companies also should refer to Item 13 [Investment Policies of Registrant], Item 14 [Description of Real Estate], and Item 15 [Operating Data] of Form S–11 (17 CFR 239.18).

3. If the issuer is not organized under the laws of any of the states of or the United States of America, it shall at the time of filing this registration statement, file with the Commission a written irrevocable consent and power of attorney on Form F–X [§ 239.42]. Any change to the name or address of the agent for service of the issuer shall be communicated promptly to the Commission through amendment of the requisite form and referencing the file number of the registration statement.

C. Registration of Additional Securities

With respect to the registration of additional securities for an offering pursuant to Rule 462(b) under the Securities Act, the registrant may file a registration statement consisting only of the following: The facing page; a statement that the contents of the earlier registration statement, identified by file number, are incorporated by reference; required opinions and consents; the signature page; and any price-related information omitted from the earlier registration statement in reliance on Rule 430A that the registrant chooses to include the new registration statement. The information contained in such a Rule 462(b) registration statement shall be deemed to be a part of the earlier registration statement as of the date of effectiveness of the Rule 462(b) registration statement. Any opinion or consent required in the Rule 462(b) registration statement may be incorporated by reference from the earlier registration statement with respect to the offering, if: (i) Such opinion or consent expressly provides for such incorporation; and (ii) such opinion relates to the securities registered pursuant to Rule 462(b). See Rule 411(c) and Rule 439(b) under the Securities Act.

PART I—INFORMATION REQUIRED IN PROSPECTUS

Item 1. Front of Registration Statement and Outside Front Cover of Prospectus.

Furnish the information required by Item 501 of Regulation S–B.

Item 2. Inside Front and Outside Back Cover Pages of Prospectus.

Furnish the information required by Item 502 of Regulation S–B.

Item 3. Summary Information and Risk Factors.

Furnish the information required by Item 503 of Regulation S–B.

Item 4. Use of Proceeds.

Furnish the information required by Item 504 of Regulation S–B.

Item 5. Determination of Offering Price.

Furnish the information required by Item 505 of Regulation S–B.

Item 6. Dilution.

Furnish the information required by Item 506 of Regulation S–B.

Item 7. Selling Security Holders.

Furnish the information required by Item 507 of Regulation S–B.

Item 8. Plan of Distribution.

Furnish the information required by Item 508 of Regulation S–B.

Item 9. Legal Proceedings.

Furnish the information required by Item 103 of Regulation S–B.

Item 10. Directors, Executive Officers, Promoters and Control Persons.

Furnish the information required by Item 401 of Regulation S–B.

Item 11. Security Ownership of Certain Beneficial Owners and Management.

Furnish the information required by Item 403 of Regulation S–B.

Item 12. Description of Securities.

Furnish the information required by Item 202 of Regulation S–B.

Item 13. Interest of Named Experts and Counsel.

Furnish the information required by Item 509 of Regulation S–B.

Item 14. Disclosure of Commission Position on Indemnification for Securities Act Liabilities.

Furnish the information required by Item 510 of Regulation S–B.

Item 15. Organization Within Last Five Years.

Furnish the information required by Item 404 of Regulation S–B.

Item 16. Description of Business.

Furnish the information required by Item 101 of Regulation S–B.

Item 17. Management's Discussion and Analysis or Plan of Operation.

Furnish the information required by Item 303 of Regulation S–B.

Item 18. Description of Property.

Furnish the information required by Item 102 of Regulation S–B.

Item 19. Certain Relationships and Related Transactions.

Furnish the information required by Item 404 of Regulation S–B.

Item 20. Market for Common Equity and Related Stockholder Matters.

Furnish the information required by Item 201 of Regulation S–B.

Item 21. Executive Compensation.

Furnish the information required by Item 402 of Regulation S–B.

Item 22. Financial Statements.

Furnish the information required by Item 310 of Regulation S–B.

Item 23. Changes In and Disagreements With Accountants on Accounting and Financial Disclosure.

Furnish the information required by Item 304 of Regulation S–B.

PART II—INFORMATION NOT REQUIRED IN PROSPECTUS

Item 24. Indemnification of Directors and Officers.

Furnish the information required by Item 702 of Regulation S–B.

Item 25. Other Expenses of Issuance and Distribution.

Furnish the information required by Item 511 of Regulation S–B.

Item 26. Recent Sales of Unregistered Securities.

Furnish the information required by Item 701 of Regulation S–B.

Item 27. Exhibits.

Furnish the exhibits required by Item 601 of Regulation S–B.

Item 28. Undertakings.

Furnish the undertakings required by Item 512 of Regulation S–B.

SIGNATURES

In accordance with the requirements of the Securities Act of 1933, the registrant certifies that it has reasonable grounds to believe that it meets all of the requirements of filing on Form SB–2 and authorized this registration statement to be signed on its behalf by the undersigned, in the City of ______, State of ______ on ______, 19__

(Registrant) ______

By (Signature and Title) ______

In accordance with the requirements of the Securities Act of 1933, this registration statement was signed by the following persons in the capacities and on the dates stated.

(Signature) ______

(Title) ______

(Date) ______

Instructions for signatures: (1) Who must sign: the small business issuer, its principal executive officer or officers, its principal financial officer, its controller or principal accounting officer, and at least the majority of the board of directors or persons performing similar functions. If the issuer is a limited partnership then the general partner and a majority of its board of directors if a corporation.

(2) Beneath each signature, type or print the name of each signatory. Any person who oc-

cupies more than one of the specified positions shall indicate each capacity in which he or she signs the registration statement. *See* Rule 402 of Regulation C concerning manual signatures and Item 601 of Regulation S–B concerning signatures by powers of attorney.

OMB APPROVAL
OMB Number: 3235-0101
Expires: September 30, 1995
Estimated average burden hours per response 2.0

SEC USE ONLY
DOCUMENT SEQUENCE NO.
CUSIP NUMBER
WORK LOCATION

UNITED STATES
SECURITIES AND EXCHANGE COMMISSION
Washington, D.C. 20549

FORM 144

NOTICE OF PROPOSED SALE OF SECURITIES PURSUANT TO RULE 144 UNDER THE SECURITIES ACT OF 1933

ATTENTION: *Transmit for filing 3 copies of this form concurrently with either placing an order with a broker to execute sale or executing a sale directly with a market maker.*

1 (a) NAME OF ISSUER *(Please type or print)*			(b) IRS IDENT. NO.	(c) S.E.C. FILE NO.	
1 (d) ADDRESS OF ISSUER	STREET	CITY	STATE	ZIP CODE	(e) TELEPHONE NO. AREA CODE NUMBER
2 (a) NAME OF PERSON FOR WHOSE ACCOUNT THE SECURITIES ARE TO BE SOLD	(b) IRS IDENT. NO.	(c) RELATIONSHIP TO ISSUER	(d) ADDRESS STREET	CITY	STATE ZIP CODE

INSTRUCTION: The person filing this notice should contact the issuer to obtain the I.R.S. Identification Number and the S.E.C. File Number.

3 (a) Title of the Class of Securities To Be Sold	(b) Name and Address of Each Broker Through Whom the Securities are to be Offered or Each Market Maker who is Acquiring the Securities	SEC USE ONLY Broker-Dealer File Number	(c) Number of Shares or Other Units To Be Sold *(See instr. 3(c))*	(d) Aggregate Market Value *(See instr. 3(d))*	(e) Number of Shares or Other Units Outstanding *(See instr. 3(e))*	(f) Approximate Date of Sale *(See instr. 3(f))* (MO. DAY YR.)	(g) Name of Each Securities Exchange *(See instr. 3(g))*

INSTRUCTIONS:

1. (a) Name of issuer
   (b) Issuer's I.R.S. Identification Number
   (c) Issuer's S.E.C. file number if any
   (d) Issuer's address, including zip code
   (e) Issuer's telephone number, including area code

2. (a) Name of person for whose account the securities are to be sold
   (b) Such person's I.R.S. identification number, if such person is an entity
   (c) Such person's relationship to the issuer (e.g., officer, director, 10% stockholder, or member of immediate family of any of the foregoing)
   (d) Such person's address, including zip code

3. (a) Title of the class of securities to be sold
   (b) Name and address of each broker through whom the securities are intended to be sold
   (c) Number of shares or other units to be sold (if debt securities, give the aggregate face amount)
   (d) Aggregate market value of the securities to be sold as of a specified date within 10 days prior to the filing of this notice
   (e) Number of shares or other units of the class outstanding, or if debt securities the face amount thereof outstanding, as shown by the most recent report or statement published by the issuer
   (f) Approximate date on which the securities are to be sold
   (g) Name of each securities exchange, if any, on which the securities are intended to be sold

SEC 1147 (9-93)

TABLE I — SECURITIES TO BE SOLD

Furnish the following information with respect to the acquisition of the securities to be sold and with respect to the payment of all or any part of the purchase price or other consideration therefor:

Title of the Class	Date you Acquired	Nature of Acquisition Transaction	Name of Person from Whom Acquired (*If gift, also give date donor acquired*)	Amount of Securities Acquired	Date of Payment	Nature of Payment

INSTRUCTIONS: 1. If the securities were purchased and full payment therefor was not made in cash at the time of purchase, explain in the table or in a note thereto the nature of the consideration given. If the consideration consisted of any note or other obligation, or if payment was made in installments describe the arrangement and state when the note or other obligation was discharged in full or the last installment paid.

2. If within two years after the acquisition of the securities the person for whose account they are to be sold had any short positions, put or other option to dispose of securities referred to in paragraph (d)(3) of Rule 144, furnish full information with respect thereto.

TABLE II — SECURITIES SOLD DURING THE PAST 3 MONTHS

Furnish the following information as to all securities of the issuer sold during the past 3 months by the person for whose account the securities are to be sold.

Name and Address of Seller	Title of Securities Sold	Date of Sale	Amount of Securities Sold	Gross Proceeds

REMARKS:

INSTRUCTIONS:
See the definition of "person" in paragraph (a) of Rule 144. Information is to be given not only as to the person for whose account the securities are to be sold but also as to all other persons included in that definition. In addition, information shall be given as to sales by all personswhose sales are required by paragraph (e) of Rule 144 to be aggregated with sales for the account of the person filing this notice.

ATTENTION:
The person for whose account the securities to which this notice relates are to be sold hereby represents by signing this notice that he does not know any material adverse information in regard to the current and prospective operations of the Issuer of the securities to be sold which has not been publicly disclosed.

______________________ DATE OF NOTICE

______________________ (SIGNATURE)

The notice shall be signed by the person for whose account the securities are to be sold. At least one copy of the notice shall be manually signed. Any copies not manually signed shall bear typed or printed signatures.

ATTENTION: Intentional misstatements or omission of facts constitute Federal Criminal Violations (See 18 U.S.C. 1001)

SEC 1147 (9-93)

FORM D

OMB APPROVAL
OMB Number: 3235-0076
Expires: December 31, 1996
Estimated average burden hours per response. . . .16.00

UNITED STATES
SECURITIES AND EXCHANGE COMMISSION
Washington, D.C. 20549

FORM D

NOTICE OF SALE OF SECURITIES PURSUANT TO REGULATION D, SECTION 4(6), AND/OR UNIFORM LIMITED OFFERING EXEMPTION

SEC USE ONLY	
Prefix	Serial
DATE RECEIVED	

Name of Offering (☐ check if this is an amendment and name has changed, and indicate change.)

Filing Under (Check box(es) that apply): ☐ Rule 504 ☐ Rule 505 ☐ Rule 506 ☐ Section 4(6) ☐ ULOE

Type of Filing: ☐ New Filing ☐ Amendment

A. BASIC IDENTIFICATION DATA

1. Enter the information requested about the issuer

Name of Issuer (☐ check if this is an amendment and name has changed, and indicate change.)

Address of Executive Offices (Number and Street, City, State, Zip Code)	Telephone Number (Including Area Code)
Address of Principal Business Operations (Number and Street, City, State, Zip Code) (if different from Executive Offices)	Telephone Number (Including Area Code)

Brief Description of Business

Type of Business Organization
☐ corporation ☐ limited partnership, already formed ☐ other (please specify):
☐ business trust ☐ limited partnership, to be formed

Actual or Estimated Date of Incorporation or Organization: Month ☐☐ Year ☐☐ ☐ Actual ☐ Estimated

Jurisdiction of Incorporation or Organization: (Enter two-letter U.S. Postal Service abbreviation for State: CN for Canada; FN for other foreign jurisdiction) ☐☐

GENERAL INSTRUCTIONS

Federal:

Who Must File: All issuers making an offering of securities in reliance on an exemption under Regulation D or Section 4(6), 17 CFR 230.501 et seq. or 15 U.S.C. 77d(6).

When To File: A notice must be filed no later than 15 days after the first sale of securities in the offering. A notice is deemed filed with the U.S. Securities and Exchange Commission (SEC) on the earlier of the date it is received by the SEC at the address given below or, if received at that address after the date on which it is due, on the date it was mailed by United States registered or certified mail to that address.

Where to File: U.S. Securities and Exchange Commission, 450 Fifth Street, N.W., Washington, D.C. 20549.

Copies Required: Five (5) copies of this notice must be filed with the SEC, one of which must be manually signed. Any copies not manually signed must be photocopies of the manually signed copy or bear typed or printed signatures.

Information Required: A new filing must contain all information requested. Amendments need only report the name of the issuer and offering, any changes thereto, the information requested in Part C, and any material changes from the information previously supplied in Parts A and B. Part E and the Appendix need not be filed with the SEC.

Filing Fee: There is no federal filing fee.

State:

This notice shall be used to indicate reliance on the Uniform Limited Offering Exemption (ULOE) for sales of securities in those states that have adopted ULOE and that have adopted this form. Issuers relying on ULOE must file a separate notice with the Securities Administrator in each state where sales are to be, or have been made. If a state requires the payment of a fee as a precondition to the claim for the exemption, a fee in the proper amount shall accompany this form. This notice shall be filed in the appropriate states in accordance with state law. The Appendix to the notice constitutes a part of this notice and must be completed.

ATTENTION

Failure to file notice in the appropriate states will not result in a loss of the federal exemption. Conversely, failure to file the appropriate federal notice will not result in a loss of an available state exemption unless such exemption is predicated on the filing of a federal notice.

SEC 1972 (1/94) 1 of 8

A. BASIC IDENTIFICATION DATA

2. Enter the information requested for the following:
   - Each promoter of the issuer, if the issuer has been organized within the past five years;
   - Each beneficial owner having the power to vote or dispose, or direct the vote or disposition of, 10% or more of a class of equity securities of the issuer;
   - Each executive officer and director of corporate issuers and of corporate general and managing partners of partnership issuers; and
   - Each general and managing partner of partnership issuers.

Check Box(es) that Apply: ☐ Promoter ☐ Beneficial Owner ☐ Executive Officer ☐ Director ☐ General and/or Managing Partner

Full Name (Last name first, if individual)

Business or Residence Address (Number and Street, City, State, Zip Code)

Check Box(es) that Apply: ☐ Promoter ☐ Beneficial Owner ☐ Executive Officer ☐ Director ☐ General and/or Managing Partner

Full Name (Last name first, if individual)

Business or Residence Address (Number and Street, City, State, Zip Code)

Check Box(es) that Apply: ☐ Promoter ☐ Beneficial Owner ☐ Executive Officer ☐ Director ☐ General and/or Managing Partner

Full Name (Last name first, if individual)

Business or Residence Address (Number and Street, City, State, Zip Code)

Check Box(es) that Apply: ☐ Promoter ☐ Beneficial Owner ☐ Executive Officer ☐ Director ☐ General and/or Managing Partner

Full Name (Last name first, if individual)

Business or Residence Address (Number and Street, City, State, Zip Code)

Check Box(es) that Apply: ☐ Promoter ☐ Beneficial Owner ☐ Executive Officer ☐ Director ☐ General and/or Managing Partner

Full Name (Last name first, if individual)

Business or Residence Address (Number and Street, City, State, Zip Code)

Check Box(es) that Apply: ☐ Promoter ☐ Beneficial Owner ☐ Executive Officer ☐ Director ☐ General and/or Managing Partner

Full Name (Last name first, if individual)

Business or Residence Address (Number and Street, City, State, Zip Code)

Check Box(es) that Apply: ☐ Promoter ☐ Beneficial Owner ☐ Executive Officer ☐ Director ☐ General and/or Managing Partner

Full Name (Last name first, if individual)

Business or Residence Address (Number and Street, City, State, Zip Code)

(Use blank sheet, or copy and use additional copies of this sheet, as necessary.)

2 of 8 SEC 1972 (1/94)

B. INFORMATION ABOUT OFFERING

	Yes	No
1. Has the issuer sold, or does the issuer intend to sell, to non-accredited investors in this offering?	☐	☐

Answer also in Appendix, Column 2, if filing under ULOE.

2. What is the minimum investment that will be accepted from any individual? $____________

	Yes	No
3. Does the offering permit joint ownership of a single unit?	☐	☐

4. Enter the information requested for each person who has been or will be paid or given, directly or indirectly, any commission or similar remuneration for solicitation of purchasers in connection with sales of securities in the offering. If a person to be listed is an associated person or agent of a broker or dealer registered with the SEC and/or with a state or states, list the name of the broker or dealer. If more than five (5) persons to be listed are associated persons of such a broker or dealer, you may set forth the information for that broker or dealer only..

Full Name (Last name first, if individual)

Business or Residence Address (Number and Street, City, State, Zip Code)

Name of Associated Broker or Dealer

States in Which Person Listed Has Solicited or Intends to Solicit Purchasers

(Check "All States" or check individual States) ☐ All States

[AL]	[AK]	[AZ]	[AR]	[CA]	[CO]	[CT]	[DE]	[DC]	[FL]	[GA]	[HI]	[ID]
[IL]	[IN]	[IA]	[KS]	[KY]	[LA]	[ME]	[MD]	[MA]	[MI]	[MN]	[MS]	[MO]
[MT]	[NE]	[NV]	[NH]	[NJ]	[NM]	[NY]	[NC]	[ND]	[OH]	[OK]	[OR]	[PA]
[RI]	[SC]	[SD]	[TN]	[TX]	[UT]	[VT]	[VA]	[WA]	[WV]	[WI]	[WY]	[PR]

Full Name (Last name first, if individual)

Business or Residence Address (Number and Street, City, State, Zip Code)

Name of Associated Broker or Dealer

States in Which Person Listed Has Solicited or Intends to Solicit Purchasers

(Check "All States" or check individual States) ☐ All States

[AL]	[AK]	[AZ]	[AR]	[CA]	[CO]	[CT]	[DE]	[DC]	[FL]	[GA]	[HI]	[ID]
[IL]	[IN]	[IA]	[KS]	[KY]	[LA]	[ME]	[MD]	[MA]	[MI]	[MN]	[MS]	[MO]
[MT]	[NE]	[NV]	[NH]	[NJ]	[NM]	[NY]	[NC]	[ND]	[OH]	[OK]	[OR]	[PA]
[RI]	[SC]	[SD]	[TN]	[TX]	[UT]	[VT]	[VA]	[WA]	[WV]	[WI]	[WY]	[PR]

Full Name (Last name first, if individual)

Business or Residence Address (Number and Street, City, State, Zip Code)

Name of Associated Broker or Dealer

States in Which Person Listed Has Solicited or Intends to Solicit Purchasers

(Check "All States" or check individual States) ☐ All States

[AL]	[AK]	[AZ]	[AR]	[CA]	[CO]	[CT]	[DE]	[DC]	[FL]	[GA]	[HI]	[ID]
[IL]	[IN]	[IA]	[KS]	[KY]	[LA]	[ME]	[MD]	[MA]	[MI]	[MN]	[MS]	[MO]
[MT]	[NE]	[NV]	[NH]	[NJ]	[NM]	[NY]	[NC]	[ND]	[OH]	[OK]	[OR]	[PA]
[RI]	[SC]	[SD]	[TN]	[TX]	[UT]	[VT]	[VA]	[WA]	[WV]	[WI]	[WY]	[PR]

(Use blank sheet, or copy and use additional copies of this sheet, as necessary.)

3 of 8

SEC 1972 (1/94)

C. OFFERING PRICE, NUMBER OF INVESTORS, EXPENSES AND USE OF PROCEEDS

1. Enter the aggregate offering price of securities included in this offering and the total amount already sold. Enter "0" if answer is "none" or "zero." If the transaction is an exchange offering, check this box ☐ and indicate in the columns below the amounts of the securities offered for exchange and already exchanged.

Type of Security	Aggregate Offering Price	Amount Already Sold
Debt	$________	$________
Equity	$________	$________
☐ Common ☐ Preferred		
Convertible Securities (including warrants)	$________	$________
Partnership Interests	$________	$________
Other (Specify ________________)	$________	$________
Total	$________	$________

Answer also in Appendix, Column 3, if filing under ULOE.

2. Enter the number of accredited and non-accredited investors who have purchased securities in this offering and the aggregate dollar amounts of their purchases. For offerings under Rule 504, indicate the number of persons who have purchased securities and the aggregate dollar amount of their purchases on the total lines. Enter "0" if answer is "none" or "zero."

	Number Investors	Aggregate Dollar Amount of Purchases
Accredited Investors	________	$________
Non-accredited Investors	________	$________
Total (for filings under Rule 504 only)	________	$________

Answer also in Appendix, Column 4, if filing under ULOE.

3. If this filing is for an offering under Rule 504 or 505, enter the information requested for all securities sold by the issuer, to date, in offerings of the types indicated, in the twelve (12) months prior to the first sale of securities in this offering. Classify securities by type listed in Part C - Question 1.

Type of offering	Type of Security	Dollar Amount Sold
Rule 505	________	$________
Regulation A	________	$________
Rule 504	________	$________
Total	________	$________

4. a. Furnish a statement of all expenses in connection with the issuance and distribution of the securities in this offering. Exclude amounts relating solely to organization expenses of the issuer. The information may be given as subject to future contingencies. If the amount of an expenditure is not known, furnish an estimate and check the box to the left of the estimate.

Transfer Agent's Fees	☐	$________
Printing and Engraving Costs	☐	$________
Legal Fees	☐	$________
Accounting Fees	☐	$________
Engineering Fees	☐	$________
Sales Commissions (specify finders' fees separately)	☐	$________
Other Expenses (identify) ____________	☐	$________
Total	☐	$________

C. OFFERING PRICE, NUMBER OF INVESTORS, EXPENSES AND USE OF PROCEEDS

b. Enter the difference between the aggregate offering price given in response to Part C - Question 1 and total expenses furnished in response to Part C - Question 4.a. This difference is the "adjusted gross proceeds to the issuer." .... $______

5. Indicate below the amount of the adjusted gross proceeds to the issuer used or proposed to be used for each of the purposes shown. If the amount for any purpose is not known, furnish an estimate and check the box to the left of the estimate. The total of the payments listed must equal the adjusted gross proceeds to the issuer set forth in response to Part C - Question 4.b above.

	Payments to Officers, Directors, & Affiliates	Payments To Others
Salaries and fees	☐ $______	☐ $______
Purchase of real estate	☐ $______	☐ $______
Purchase, rental or leasing and installation of machinery and equipment	☐ $______	☐ $______
Construction or leasing of plant buildings and facilities	☐ $______	☐ $______
Acquisition of other businesses (including the value of securities involved in this offering that may be used in exchange for the assets or securities of another issuer pursuant to a merger)	☐ $______	☐ $______
Repayment of indebtedness	☐ $______	☐ $______
Working capital	☐ $______	☐ $______
Other (specify): ______	☐ $______	☐ $______
______	☐ $______	☐ $______
Column Totals	☐ $______	☐ $______
Total Payments Listed (column totals added)	☐ $______	

D. FEDERAL SIGNATURE

The issuer has duly caused this notice to be signed by the undersigned duly authorized person. If this notice is filed under Rule 505, the following signature constitutes an undertaking by the issuer to furnish to the U.S. Securities and Exchange Commission, upon written request of its staff, the information furnished by the issuer to any non-accredited investor pursuant to paragraph (b)(2) of Rule 502.

Issuer (Print or Type)	Signature	Date
Name of Signer (Print or Type)	Title of Signer (Print or Type)	

ATTENTION

Intentional misstatements or omissions of fact constitute federal criminal violations. (See 18 U.S.C. 1001.)

E. STATE SIGNATURE

1. Is any party described in 17 CFR 230.262 presently subject to any of the disqualification provisions of such rule? .... Yes ☐ No ☐

See Appendix, Column 5, for state response.

2. The undersigned issuer hereby undertakes to furnish to any state administrator of any state in which this notice is filed, a notice on Form D (17 CFR 239.500) at such times as required by state law.

3. The undersigned issuer hereby undertakes to furnish to the state administrators, upon written request, information furnished by the issuer to offerees.

4. The undersigned issuer represents that the issuer is familiar with the conditions that must be satisfied to be entitled to the Uniform limited Offering Exemption (ULOE) of the state in which this notice is filed and understands that the issuer claiming the availability of this exemption has the burden of establishing that these conditions have been satisfied.

The issuer has read this notification and knows the contents to be true and has duly caused this notice to be signed on its behalf by the undersigned duly authorized person.

Issuer (Print or Type)	Signature	Date
Name (Print or Type)	Title (Print or Type)	

Instruction:
Print the name and title of the signing representative under his signature for the state portion of this form. One copy of every notice on Form D must be manually signed. Any copies not manually signed must be photocopies of the manually signed copy or bear typed or printed signatures.

APPENDIX

1	2		3	4				5	
	Intend to sell to non-accredited investors in State (Part B-Item 1)		Type of security and aggregate offering price offered in state (Part C-Item1)	Type of investor and amount purchased in State (Part C-Item 2)				Disqualification under State ULOE (if yes, attach explanation of waiver granted) (Part E-Item1)	
State	**Yes**	**No**		**Number of Accredited Investors**	**Amount**	**Number of Non-Accredited Investors**	**Amount**	**Yes**	**No**
AL									
AK									
AZ									
AR									
CA									
CO									
CT									
DE									
DC									
FL									
GA									
HI									
ID									
IL									
IN									
IA									
KS									
KY									
LA									
ME									
MD									
MA									
MI									
MN									
MS									
MO									

7 of 8

SEC 1972 (1/94)

APPENDIX

1	2		3	4				5	
	Intend to sell to non-accredited investors in State (Part B-Item 1)		Type of security and aggregate offering price offered in state (Part C-Item1)	Type of investor and amount purchased in State (Part C-Item 2)				Disqualification under State ULOE (if yes, attach explanation of waiver granted) (Part E-Item1)	
State	**Yes**	**No**		**Number of Accredited Investors**	**Amount**	**Number of Non-Accredited Investors**	**Amount**	**Yes**	**No**
MT									
NE									
NV									
NH									
NJ									
NM									
NY									
NC									
ND									
OH									
OK									
OR									
PA									
RI									
SC									
SD									
TN									
TX									
UT									
VT									
VA									
WA									
WV									
WI									
WY									
PR									

B. SECURITIES EXCHANGE ACT OF 1934

15 U.S.C. § 78a et seq.

Act	15 U.S.C.	
1	78a	Short Title
2	78b	Necessity for Regulation
3	78c	Definitions and Application
3A	78c–1	Swap Agreements
4	78d	Securities and Exchange Commission
4A	78d–1	Delegation of Functions by Commission
4B	78d–2	Transfer of Functions With Respect to Assignment of Personnel to Chairman
4C	78d–3	Appearance and Practice Before the Commission
5	78e	Transactions on Unregistered Exchanges
6	78f	National Securities Exchanges
7	78g	Margin Requirements
8	78h	Restrictions on Borrowing and Lending by Members, Brokers, and Dealers
9	78i	Manipulation of Security Prices
10	78j	Regulation of the Use of Manipulative and Deceptive Devices
10A		Audit Requirements
11	78k	Trading by Members of Exchanges, Brokers, and Dealers
11A	78k–1	National Market System for Securities; Securities Information Processors
12	78*l*	Registration Requirements for Securities
13	78m	Periodical and Other Reports
14	78n	Proxies
15	78*o*	Registration and Regulation of Brokers and Dealers
15A	78*o*–3	Registered Securities Associations
15B	78*o*–4	Municipal Securities
15C	78*o*–5	Government Securities Brokers and Dealers
15D	78*o*–6	Securities Analysts and Research Reports
16	78p	Directors, Officers, and Principal Stockholders
17	78q	Records and Reports
17A	78q–1	National System for Clearance and Settlement of Securities Transactions
17B	78q–2	Automated Quotation Systems for Penny Stocks
18	78r	Liability for Misleading Statements
19	78s	Registration, Responsibilities, and Oversight of Self-Regulatory Organizations
20	78t	Liability of Controlling Persons and Persons Who Aid and Abet Violations
20A	78t–1	Liability to Contemporaneous Traders for Insider Trading
21	78u	Investigations and Actions
21A	78u–1	Civil Penalties for Insider Trading
21B	78u–2	Civil Remedies in Administrative Proceedings
21C	78u–3	Cease and Desist Proceedings
21D		Private Securities Litigation
21E		Application of Safe Harbor for Forward-Looking Statements
22	78v	Hearings by Commission
23	78w	Rules, Regulations, and Orders; Annual Reports
24	78x	Public Availability of Information
25	78y	Court Review of Orders and Rules
26	78z	Unlawful Representations
27	78aa	Jurisdiction of Offenses and Suits
27A	78aa–1	Special Provision Relating to Statute of Limitations on Private Causes of Action
28	78bb	Effect on Existing Law
29	78cc	Validity of Contracts
30	78dd	Foreign Securities Exchanges
30A	78dd–1	Prohibited Foreign Trade Practices by Issuers

SECURITIES EXCHANGE ACT OF 1934

Short Title

Section 1. This act may be cited as the "Securities Exchange Act of 1934."

Necessity for Regulation

Sec. 2. For the reasons hereinafter enumerated, transactions in securities as commonly conducted upon securities exchanges and over-the-counter markets are affected with a national public interest which makes it necessary to provide for regulation and control of such transactions and of practices and matters related thereto, including transactions by officers, directors, and principal security holders, to require appropriate reports, to remove impediments to and perfect the mechanisms of a national market system for securities and a national system for the clearance and settlement of securities transactions and the safeguarding of securities and funds related thereto, and to impose requirements necessary to make such regulation and control reasonably complete and effective, in order to protect interstate commerce, the national credit, the Federal taxing power, to protect and make more effective the national banking system and Federal Reserve System, and to insure the maintenance of fair and honest markets in such transactions:

(1) Such transactions (a) are carried on in large volume by the public generally and in large part originate outside the States in which the exchanges and over-the-counter markets are located and/or are effected by means of the mails and instrumentalities of interstate commerce; (b) constitute an important part of the current of interstate commerce; (c) involve in large part the securities of issuers engaged in interstate commerce; (d) involve the use of credit, directly affect the financing of trade, industry, and transportation in interstate commerce, and directly affect and influence the volume of interstate commerce; and affect the national credit.

(2) The prices established and offered in such transactions are generally disseminated and quoted throughout the United States and foreign countries and constitute a basis for determining and establishing the prices at which securities are bought and sold, the amount of certain taxes owing to the United States and to the several States by owners, buyers, and sellers of securities, and the value of collateral for bank loans.

(3) Frequently the prices of securities on such exchanges and markets are susceptible to manipulation and control, and the dissemination of such prices gives rise to excessive speculation, resulting in sudden and unreasonable fluctuations in the prices of securities which (a) cause alternately unreasonable expansion and unreasonable contraction of the volume of credit available for trade, transportation, and industry in interstate commerce, (b) hinder the proper appraisal of the value of securities and thus prevent a fair calculation of taxes owing to the United States and to the several States by owners, buyers, and sellers of securities, and (c) prevent the fair valuation of collateral for bank loans and/or obstruct the effective operation of the national banking system and Federal Reserve System.

(4) National emergencies, which produce widespread unemployment and the dislocation of trade, transportation, and industry, and which burden interstate commerce and adversely affect the general welfare, are precipitated, intensified, and prolonged by manipulation and sudden and unreasonable fluctuations of security prices and by excessive speculation on such exchanges and markets, and to meet such emergencies the Federal Government is put to such great expense as to burden the national credit.

Definitions and Application

Sec. 3. (a) When used in this title, unless the context otherwise requires—

(1) The term "exchange" means any organization, association, or group of persons, whether incorporated or unincorporated, which constitutes, maintains, or provides a market place or facilities for bringing together purchasers and sellers of securities or for otherwise performing with respect to securities the functions commonly performed by a stock exchange as that term is generally understood, and includes the market place and the market facilities maintained by such exchange.

(2) The term "facility" when used with respect to an exchange includes its premises, tangible or intangible property whether on the premises or not, any right to the use of such premises or property or any service thereof for the purpose of effecting or reporting a transaction on an exchange (including, among other things, any system of communication to or from the exchange, by ticket or otherwise, maintained by or with the consent of the exchange), and any right of the exchange to the use of any property or service.

(3)(A) The term "member" when used with respect to a national securities exchange means (i) any natural person permitted to effect transactions on the floor of the exchange without the services of another person acting as broker, (ii) any registered broker or dealer with which such a natural person is associated, (iii) any registered broker or dealer permitted to designate as a representative such a natural person, and (iv) any other registered broker or dealer which agrees to be regulated by such exchange and with respect to which the exchange undertakes to enforce compliance with the provisions of this title, the rules and regulations thereunder, and its own rules. For purposes of sections 6(b)(1), 6(b)(4), 6(b)(6), 6(b)(7), 6(d), 17(d), 19(d), 19(e), 19(g), 19(h), and 21 of this title, the term "member" when used with respect to a national securities exchange also means, to the extent of the rules of the exchange specified by the Commission, any person required by the Commission to comply with such rules pursuant to section 6(f) of this title.

(B) The term "member" when used with respect to a registered securities association means any broker or dealer who agrees to be regulated by such association and with respect to whom the association undertakes to enforce compliance with the provisions of this title, the rules and regulations thereunder, and its own rules.

(4) *Broker.*—

(A) *In General.*—The term "broker" means any person engaged in the business of effecting transactions in securities for the account of others.

(B) *Exception for Certain Bank Activities.*—A bank shall not be considered to be a broker because the bank engages in any one or more of the following activities under the conditions described:

(i) *Third Party Brokerage Arrangements.*—The bank enters into a contractual or other written arrangement with a broker or dealer registered under this chapter under which the broker or dealer offers brokerage services on or off the premises of the bank if—

(I) such broker or dealer is clearly identified as the person performing the brokerage services;

(II) the broker or dealer performs brokerage services in an area that is clearly marked and, to the extent practicable, physically separate from the routine deposit-taking activities of the bank;

(III) any materials used by the bank to advertise or promote generally the availability of brokerage services under the arrangement clearly indicate that the brokerage services are being provided by the broker or dealer and not by the bank;

(IV) any materials used by the bank to advertise or promote generally the availability of brokerage services under the arrangement are in compliance with the Federal securities laws before distribution;

(V) bank employees (other than associated persons of a broker or dealer who are qualified pursuant to the rules of a self-regulatory organization) perform only clerical or ministerial functions in connection with brokerage transactions including scheduling appointments with the associated persons of a broker or dealer, except that bank employees may forward customer funds or securities and may describe in general terms the types of investment vehicles available from the bank and the broker or dealer under the arrangement;

(VI) bank employees do not receive incentive compensation for any brokerage transaction unless such employees are associated persons of a broker or dealer and are qualified pursuant to the rules of a self-regulatory organization,except that the bank employees may receive compensation for the referral of any customer if the compensation is a nominal one-time cash fee of a fixed dollar amount and the payment of the fee is not contingent on whether the referral results in a transaction;

(VII) such services are provided by the broker or dealer on a basis in which all customers that receive any services are fully disclosed to the broker or dealer;

(VIII) the bank does not carry a securities account of the customer except as permitted under clause (ii) or (viii) of this subparagraph; and

(IX) the bank, broker, or dealer informs each customer that the brokerage services are provided by the broker or dealer and not by the bank and that the securities are not deposits or other obligations of the bank, are not guaranteed by the bank, and are not insured by the Federal Deposit Insurance Corporation.

(ii) *Trust Activities.*—The bank effects transactions in a trustee capacity, or effects transactions in a fiduciary capacity in its trust department or other department that is regularly examined by bank examiners for compliance with fiduciary principles and standards, and—

(I) is chiefly compensated for such transactions, consistent with fiduciary principles and standards, on the basis of an administration or annual fee (payable on a monthly, quarterly, or other basis), a percentage of assets under management, or a flat or capped per order processing fee equal to not more than the cost incurred by the bank in connection with executing securities transactions for trustee and fiduciary customers, or any combination of such fees; and

(II) does not publicly solicit brokerage business, other than by advertising that it effects transactions in securities in conjunction with advertising its other trust activities.

(iii) *Permissible Securities Transactions.*—The bank effects transactions in—

(I) commercial paper, bankers acceptances, or commercial bills;

(II) exempted securities;

(III) qualified Canadian government obligations as defined in section 24 of Title 12, in conformity with section 78o–5 of this title and the rules and regulations thereunder, or obligations of the North American Development Bank; or

(IV) any standardized, credit enhanced debt security issued by a foreign government pursuant to the March 1989 plan of then Secretary of the Treasury Brady, used by such foreign government to retire outstanding commercial bank loans.

(iv) *Certain Stock Purchase Plans.*—

(I) *Employee benefit plans.*—The bank effects transactions, as part of its transfer agency activities, in the securities of an issuer as part of any pension, retirement, profit-sharing, bonus, thrift, savings, incentive, or other similar benefit plan for the employees of that issuer or its affiliates (as defined in section 1841 of Title 12), if the bank does not solicit transactions or provide investment advice with respect to the purchase or sale of securities in connection with the plan.

(II) *Dividend reinvestment plans.*—The bank effects transactions, as part of its transfer agency activities, in the securities of an issuer as part of that issuer's dividend reinvestment plan, if—

(aa) the bank does not solicit transactions or provide investment advice with respect to the purchase or sale of securities in connection with the plan; and

(bb) the bank does not net shareholders' buy and sell orders, other than for programs for odd-lot holders or plans registered with the Commission.

(III) *Issuer Plans.*—The bank effects transactions, as part of its transfer agency activities, in the securities of an issuer as part of a plan or program for the purchase or sale of that issuer's shares, if—

(aa) the bank does not solicit transactions or provide investment advice with respect to the purchase or sale of securities in connection with the plan or program; and

(bb) the bank does not net shareholders' buy and sell orders, other than for programs for odd-lot holders or plans registered with the Commission.

(IV) *Permissible Delivery of Materials.*—The exception to being considered a broker for a bank engaged in activities described in subclauses (I), (II), and (III) will not be affected by delivery of written or electronic plan materials by a bank to employees of the issuer, shareholders of the issuer, or members of affinity groups of the issuer, so long as such materials are—

(aa) comparable in scope or nature to that permitted by the Commission as of November 12, 1999; or

(bb) otherwise permitted by the Commission.

(v) *Sweep Accounts.*—The bank effects transactions as part of a program for the investment or reinvestment of deposit funds into any no-load, open-end management investment company registered under the Investment Company Act of 1940 [15 U.S.C.A. § 80a–1 et seq.] that holds itself out as a money market fund.

(vi) *Affiliate Transactions.*—The bank effects transactions for the account of any affiliate of the bank (as defined in section 1841 of Title 12) other than—

(I) a registered broker or dealer; or

(II) an affiliate that is engaged in merchant banking, as described in section 1843(k)(4)(H) of Title 12.

(vii) *Private Securities Offerings.*—The bank—

(I) effects sales as part of a primary offering of securities not involving a public offering, pursuant to section 77c(b), 77d(2), or 77d(6) of this title or the rules and regulations issued thereunder;

(II) at any time after the date that is 1 year after November 12, 1999, is not affiliated with a broker or dealer that has been registered for more than 1 year in accordance with this chapter, and engages in dealing, market making, or underwriting activities, other than with respect to exempted securities; and

(III) if the bank is not affiliated with a broker or dealer, does not effect any primary offering described in subclause (I) the aggregate amount of which exceeds 25 percent of the capital of the bank, except that the limitation of this subclause shall not apply with respect to any sale of government securities or municipal securities.

(viii) *Safekeeping and Custody Activities.*—

(I) *In general.*—The bank, as part of customary banking activities—

(aa) provides safekeeping or custody services with respect to securities, including the exercise of warrants and other rights on behalf of customers;

(bb) facilitates the transfer of funds or securities, as a custodian or a clearing agency, in connection with the clearance and settlement of its customers' transactions in securities;

(cc) effects securities lending or borrowing transactions with or on behalf of customers as part of services provided to customers pursuant to division (aa) or (bb) or invests cash collateral pledged in connection with such transactions;

(dd) holds securities pledged by a customer to another person or securities subject to purchase or resale agreements involving a customer, or facilitates the pledging or transfer of such securities by book entry or as otherwise provided under applicable law, if the bank maintains records separately identifying the securities and the customer; or

(ee) serves as a custodian or provider of other related administrative services to any individual retirement account, pension, retirement, profit sharing, bonus, thrift savings, incentive, or other similar benefit plan.

(II) *Exception for Carrying Broker Activities.*—The exception to being considered a broker for a bank engaged in activities described in subclause (I) shall not apply if the bank, in connection with such activities, acts in the United States as a carrying broker (as such term, and different formulations thereof, are used in section 78o(c)(3) of this title and the rules and regulations thereunder) for any broker or dealer, unless such carrying broker activities are engaged in with respect to government securities (as defined in paragraph (42) of this subsection).

(ix) *Identified Banking Products.*—The bank effects transactions in identified banking products as defined in section 206 of the Gramm–Leach–Bliley Act [15 U.S.C.A. § 78c note].

(x) *Municipal Securities.*—The bank effects transactions in municipal securities.

(xi) *De Minimis Exception.*—The bank effects, other than in transactions referred to in clauses (i) through (x), not more than 500 transactions in securities in any calendar year, and such transactions are not effected by an employee of the bank who is also an employee of a broker or dealer.

(C) *Execution by Broker or Dealer.*—The exception to being considered a broker for a bank engaged in activities described in clauses (ii), (iv), and (viii) of subparagraph (B) shall not apply if the activities described in such provisions result in the trade in the United States of any security that is a publicly traded security in the United States, unless—

(i) the bank directs such trade to a registered broker or dealer for execution;

(ii) the trade is a cross trade or other substantially similar trade of a security that—

(I) is made by the bank or between the bank and an affiliated fiduciary; and

(II) is not in contravention of fiduciary principles established under applicable Federal or State law; or

(iii) the trade is conducted in some other manner permitted under rules, regulations, or orders as the Commission may prescribe or issue.

(D) *Fiduciary Capacity.*—For purposes of subparagraph (B)(ii), the term "fiduciary capacity" means—

(i) in the capacity as trustee, executor, administrator, registrar of stocks and bonds, transfer agent, guardian, assignee, receiver, or custodian under a uniform gift to minor act, or as an investment adviser if the bank receives a fee for its investment advice;

(ii) in any capacity in which the bank possesses investment discretion on behalf of another; or

(iii) in any other similar capacity.

(E) *Exception for Entities Subject to Section 78o(e) of this Title.*—The term "broker" does not include a bank that—

(i) was, on the day before November 12, 1999, subject to section 78o(e) of this title; and

(ii) is subject to such restrictions and requirements as the Commission considers appropriate.

(5) *Dealer.*—

(A) *In General.*—The term "dealer" means any person engaged in the business of buying and selling securities for such person's own account through a broker or otherwise.

(B) *Exception for Person not Engaged in the Business of Dealing.*—The term "dealer" does not include a person that buys or sells securities for such person's own account, either individually or in a fiduciary capacity, but not as a part of a regular business.

(C) *Exception for Certain Bank Activities.*—A bank shall not be considered to be a dealer because the bank engages in any of the following activities under the conditions described:

(i) *Permissible securities transactions.*—The bank buys or sells—

(I) commercial paper, bankers acceptances, or commercial bills;

(II) exempted securities;

(III) qualified Canadian government obligations as defined in section 24 of Title 12, in conformity with section 78o–5 of this title and the rules and regulations thereunder, or obligations of the North American Development Bank; or

(IV) any standardized, credit enhanced debt security issued by a foreign government pursuant to the March 1989 plan of then Secretary of the Treasury Brady, used by such foreign government to retire outstanding commercial bank loans.

(ii) *Investment, trustee, and fiduciary transactions.*—The bank buys or sells securities for investment purposes—

(I) for the bank; or

(II) for accounts for which the bank acts as a trustee or fiduciary.

(iii) *Asset-backed transactions.*—The bank engages in the issuance or sale to qualified investors, through a grantor trust or other separate entity, of securities backed by or representing an interest in notes, drafts, acceptances, loans, leases, receivables, other obligations (other than securities of which the bank is not the issuer), or pools of any such obligations predominantly originated by—

(I) the bank;

(II) an affiliate of any such bank other than a broker or dealer; or

(III) a syndicate of banks of which the bank is a member, if the obligations or pool of obligations consists of mortgage obligations or consumer-related receivables.

(iv) *Identified banking products.*—The bank buys or sells identified banking products, as defined in section 206 of the Gramm–Leach–Bliley Act.*

(6) The term "bank" means (A) a banking institution organized under the laws of the United States, (B) a member bank of the Federal Reserve System, (C) any other banking institution, whether incorporated or not, doing business under the laws of any State or of the United States, a substantial portion of the business of which consists of receiving deposits or exercising fiduciary powers similar to those permitted to national banks under the authority of the Comptroller of the Currency pursuant to the first section of Public Law 87–722 (12 U.S.C. 92a), and which is supervised and examined by State or Federal authority having supervision over banks, and which is not operated for the purpose of evading the provisions of this title, and (D) a receiver, conservator, or other liquidating agent of any institution or firm included in clauses (A), (B), or (C) of this paragraph.

(7) The term "director" means any director of a corporation or any person per-

* Section 206(a) of the Gramm–Leach–Bliley Act provides:

For purposes of paragraphs (4) and (5) of section 3(a) of the Securities Exchange Act of 1934 (15 U.S.C. 78c(a)(4), (5)), the term "identified banking product" means—

(1) a deposit account, savings account, certificate of deposit, or other deposit instrument issued by a bank;

(2) a banker's acceptance;

(3) a letter of credit issued or loan made by a bank;

(4) a debit account at a bank arising from a credit card or similar arrangement;

(5) a participation in a loan which the bank or an affiliate of the bank (other than a broker or dealer) funds, participates in, or owns that is sold—

(A) to qualified investors; or

(B) to other persons that—

(i) have the opportunity to review and assess any material information, including information regarding the borrower's credit worthiness; and

(ii) based on such factors as financial sophistication, net worth, and knowledge and experience in financial matters, have the capability to evaluate the information available, as determined under generally applicable banking standards or guidelines; or

(6) any swap agreement, including credit and equity swaps, except that an equity swap that is sold directly to any person other than a qualified investor (as defined in section 3(a)(54) of the Securities Act of 1934 [subsec. (a)(54) of this section]) shall not be treated as an identified banking product.

(b) *Definition of swap agreement.*—For purposes of subsection (a)(6), the term "swap agreement" means any individually negotiated contract, agreement, warrant, note, or option that is based, in whole or in part, on the value of, any interest in, or any quantitative measure or the occurrence of any event relating to, one or more commodities, securities, currencies, interest or other rates, indices, or other assets, but does not include any other identified banking product, as defined in paragraphs (1) through (5) of subsection (a).

(c) *Classification limited.*—Classification of a particular product as an identified banking product pursuant to this section shall not be construed as finding or implying that such product is or is not a security for any purpose under the securities laws, or is or is not an account, agreement, contract, or transaction for any purpose under the Commodity Exchange Act.

forming similar functions with respect to any organization, whether incorporated or unincorporated.

(8) The term "issuer" means any person who issues or proposes to issue any security; except that with respect to certificates of deposit for securities, voting-trust certificates, or collateral-trust certificates, or with respect to certificates of interest or shares in an unincorporated investment trust not having a board of directors or of the fixed, restricted management, or unit type, the term "issuer" means the person or persons performing the acts and assuming the duties of depositor or manager pursuant to the provisions of the trust or other agreement or instrument under which such securities are issued; and except that with respect to equipment-trust certificates or like securities, the term "issuer" means the person by whom the equipment or property is, or is to be, used.

(9) The term "person" means a natural person, company, government, or political subdivision, agency, or instrumentality of a government.

(10) The term "security" means any note, stock, treasury stock, security future, bond, debenture, certificate of interest or participation in any profit-sharing agreement or in any oil, gas, or other mineral royalty or lease, any collateral-trust certificate, preorganization certificate or subscription, transferable share, investment contract, voting-trust certificate, certificate of deposit for a security, any put, call, straddle, option, or privilege on any security, certificate of deposit, or group or index of securities (including any interest therein or based on the value thereof), or any put, call, straddle, option, or privilege entered into on a national securities exchange relating to foreign currency, or in general, any instrument commonly known as a "security"; or any certificate of interest or participation in, temporary or interim certificate for, receipt for, or warrant or right to subscribe to or purchase, any of the foregoing; but shall not include currency or any note, draft, bill of exchange, or banker's acceptance which has a maturity at the time of issuance of not exceeding nine months, exclusive of days of grace, or any renewal thereof the maturity of which is likewise limited.

(11) The term "equity security" means any stock or similar security; or any security future on any such security; or any security convertible, with or without consideration, into such a security, or carrying any warrant or right to subscribe to or purchase such a security; or any such warrant or right; or any other security which the Commission shall deem to be of similar nature and consider necessary or appropriate, by such rules and regulations as it may prescribe in the public interest or for the protection of investors, to treat as an equity security.

(12)(A) The term "exempted security" or "exempted securities" includes—

(i) government securities, as defined in paragraph (42) of this subsection;

(ii) municipal securities, as defined in paragraph (29) of this subsection;

(iii) any interest or participation in any common trust fund or similar fund that is excluded from the definition of the term "investment company" under section 3(c)(3) of the Investment Company Act of 1940;

(iv) any interest or participation in a single trust fund, or a collective trust fund maintained by a bank, or any security arising out of a contract issued by an insurance company, which interest, participation, or security is issued in connection with a qualified plan as defined in subparagraph (C) of this paragraph;

(v) any security issued by or any interest or participation in any pooled income fund, collective trust fund, collective investment fund, or similar fund that is excluded from the definition of an investment company under section 3(c)(10)(B) of the Investment Company Act of 1940;

(vi) solely for purposes of sections 12, 13, 14, and 16 of this title, any security issued by or any interest or participation in any church plan, company, or account that is excluded from the definition of an investment company under section 3(c)(14) of the Investment Company Act of 1940; and

(vii) such other securities (which may include, among others, unregistered securities, the market in which is predominantly intrastate) as the Commission may, by such rules and regulations as it deems consistent with the public interest and the protection of investors, either unconditionally or upon specified terms and conditions or for stated periods, exempt from the operation of any one or more provisions of this title which by their terms do not apply to an "exempted security" or to "exempted securities".

(B)(i) Notwithstanding subparagraph (A)(i) of this paragraph, government securities shall not be deemed to be "exempted securities" for the purposes of section 17A of this title.

(ii) Notwithstanding subparagraph (A)(ii) of this paragraph, municipal securities shall not be deemed to be "exempted securities" for the purposes of sections 15 and 17A of this title.

(C) For purposes of subparagraph (A)(iv) of this paragraph, the term "qualified plan" means (i) a stock bonus, pension, or profit-sharing plan which meets the requirements for qualification under section 401 of the Internal Revenue Code of 1954, (ii) an annuity plan which meets the requirements for the deduction of the employer's contribution under section 404(a)(2) of such Code, or (iii) a governmental plan as defined in section 414(d) of such Code which has been established by an employer for the exclusive benefit of its employees or their beneficiaries for the purpose of distributing to such employees or their beneficiaries the corpus and income of the funds accumulated under such plan, if under such plan it is impossible, prior to the satisfaction of all liabilities with respect to such employees and their beneficiaries, for any part of the corpus or income to be used for, or diverted to, purposes other than the exclusive benefit of such employees or their beneficiaries, other than any plan described in clause (i), (ii), or (iii) of this subparagraph which (I) covers employees some or all of whom are employees within the meaning of section 401(c) of such Code, or (II) is a plan funded by an annuity contract described in section 403(b) of such Code.

(13) The terms "buy" and "purchase" each include any contract to buy, purchase, or otherwise acquire. For security futures products, such term includes any contract, agreement, or transaction for future delivery.

(14) The terms "sale" and "sell" each include any contract to sell or otherwise dispose of. For security futures products, such term includes any contract, agreement, or transaction for future delivery.

(15) The term "Commission" means the Securities and Exchange Commission established by section 4 of this title.

(16) The term "State" means any State of the United States, the District of Columbia, Puerto Rico, the Virgin Islands, or any other possession of the United States.

(17) The term "interstate commerce" means trade, commerce, transportation, or communication among the several States, or between any foreign country and any State, or between any State and any place or ship outside thereof. The term also includes intrastate use of (A) any facility of a national securities exchange or of a telephone or other interstate means of communication, or (B) any other interstate instrumentality.

(18) The term "person associated with a broker or dealer" or "associated person of a broker or dealer" means any partner, officer, director, or branch manager of such broker or dealer (or any person occupying a similar status or performing similar func-

tions), any person directly or indirectly controlling, controlled by, or under common control with such broker or dealer, or any employee of such broker or dealer, except that any person associated with a broker or dealer whose functions are solely clerical or ministerial shall not be included in the meaning of such term for purposes of section 15(b) of this title (other than paragraph (6) thereof).

(19) The terms "investment company", "affiliated person", "insurance company", "separate account", and "company" have the same meanings as in the Investment Company Act of 1940.

(20) The terms "investment adviser" and "underwriter" have the same meanings as in the Investment Advisers Act of 1940.

(21) The term "person associated with a member" or "associated person of a member" when used with respect to a member of a national securities exchange or registered securities association means any partner, officer, director, or branch manager of such member (or any person occupying a similar status or performing similar functions), any person directly or indirectly controlling, controlled by, or under common control with such member, or any employee of such member.

(22)(A) The term "securities information processor" means any person engaged in the business of (i) collecting, processing, or preparing for distribution or publication, or assisting, participating in, or coordinating the distribution or publication of, information with respect to transactions in or quotations for any security (other than an exempted security) or (ii) distributing or publishing (whether by means of a ticker tape, a communications network, a terminal display device, or otherwise) on a current and continuing basis, information with respect to such transactions or quotations. The term "securities information processor" does not include any bona fide newspaper, news magazine, or business or financial publication of general and regular circulation, any self-regulatory organization, any bank, broker, dealer, building and loan, savings and loan, or homestead association, or cooperative bank, if such bank, broker, dealer, association, or cooperative bank would be deemed to be a securities information processor solely by reason of functions performed by such institutions as part of customary banking, brokerage, dealing, association, or cooperative bank activities, or any common carrier, as defined in section 3 of the Communications Act of 1934, subject to the jurisdiction of the Federal Communications Commission or a State commission, as defined in section 3 of that Act, unless the Commission determines that such carrier is engaged in the business of collecting, processing, or preparing for distribution or publication, information with respect to transactions in or quotations for any security.

(B) The term "exclusive processor" means any securities information processor or self-regulatory organization which, directly or indirectly, engages on an exclusive basis on behalf of any national securities exchange or registered securities association, or any national securities exchange or registered securities association which engages on an exclusive basis on its own behalf, in collecting, processing, or preparing for distribution or publication any information with respect to (i) transactions or quotations on or effected or made by means of any facility of such exchange or (ii) quotations distributed or published by means of any electronic system operated or controlled by such association.

(23)(A) The term "clearing agency" means any person who acts as an intermediary in making payments or deliveries or both in connection with transactions in securities or who provides facilities for comparison of data respecting the terms of settlement of securities transactions, to reduce the number of settlements of securities transactions, or for the allocation of securities settlement responsibilities. Such term also means any person, such as a securities depository, who (i) acts as a custodian of securities in connection with a system for the central handling of securities whereby all securities of a particular class or series of any issuer deposited within the system are treated as fungible and may be transferred, loaned, or pledged by bookkeeping entry without physical delivery of securities certificates, or (ii) otherwise permits or facilitates the settlement of securities transactions or the hypothecation or lending of securities without physical delivery of securities certificates.

(B) The term "clearing agency" does not include (i) any Federal Reserve bank, Federal home loan bank, or Federal land bank; (ii) any national securities exchange or registered securities association solely by reason of its providing facilities for comparison of data respecting the terms of settlement of securities transactions effected on such exchange or by means of any electronic system operated or controlled by such association; (iii) any bank, broker, dealer, building and loan, savings and loan, or homestead association, or cooperative bank if such bank, broker, dealer, association, or cooperative bank would be deemed to be a clearing agency solely by reason of functions performed by such institution as part of customary banking, brokerage, dealing, association, or cooperative banking activities, or solely by reason of acting on behalf of a clearing agency or a participant therein in connection with the furnishing by the clearing agency of services to its participants or the use of services of the clearing agency by its participants, unless the Commission, by rule, otherwise provides as necessary or appropriate to assure the prompt and accurate clearance and settlement of securities transactions or to prevent evasion of this title; (iv) any life insurance company, its registered separate accounts, or a subsidiary of such insurance company solely by reason of functions commonly performed by such entities in connection with variable annuity contracts or variable life policies issued by such insurance company or its separate accounts; (v) any registered open-end investment company or unit investment trust solely by reason of functions commonly performed by it in connection with shares in such registered open-end investment company or unit investment trust, or (vi) any person solely by reason of its performing functions described in paragraph 25(E) of this subsection.

(24) The term "participant" when used with respect to a clearing agency means any person who uses a clearing agency to clear or settle securities transactions or to transfer, pledge, lend, or hypothecate securities. Such term does not include a person whose only use of a clearing agency is (A) through another person who is a participant or (B) as a pledgee of securities.

(25) The term "transfer agent" means any person who engages on behalf of an issuer of securities or on behalf of itself as an issuer of securities in (A) countersigning such securities upon issuance; (B) monitoring the issuance of such securities with a view to preventing unauthorized issuance, a function commonly performed by a person called a registrar; (C) registering the transfer of such securities; (D) exchanging or converting such securities; or (E) transferring record ownership of securities by bookkeeping entry without physical issuance of securities certificates. The term "transfer agent" does not include any insurance company or separate account which performs such functions solely with respect to variable annuity contracts or variable life policies which it issues or any registered clearing agency which performs such functions solely with respect to options contracts which it issues.

(26) The term "self-regulatory organization" means any national securities exchange, registered securities association, or registered clearing agency, or (solely for purposes of sections 19(b), 19(c), and 23(b) of this title) the Municipal Securities Rulemak-

ing Board established by section 15B of this title.

(27) The term "rules of an exchange", "rules of an association", or "rules of a clearing agency" means the constitution, articles of incorporation, bylaws, and rules, or instruments corresponding to the foregoing, of an exchange, association of brokers and dealers, or clearing agency, respectively, and such of the stated policies, practices, and interpretations of such exchange, association, or clearing agency as the Commission, by rule, may determine to be necessary or appropriate in the public interest or for the protection of investors to be deemed to be rules of such exchange, association, or clearing agency.

(28) The term "rules of a self-regulatory organization" means the rules of an exchange which is a national securities exchange, the rules of an association of brokers and dealers which is a registered securities association, the rules of a clearing agency which is a registered clearing agency, or the rules of the Municipal Securities Rulemaking Board.

(29) The term "municipal securities" means securities which are direct obligations of, or obligations guaranteed as to principal or interest by, a State or any political subdivision thereof, or any agency or instrumentality of a State or any political subdivision thereof, or any municipal corporate instrumentality of one or more States, or any security which is an industrial development bond (as defined in section 103(c)(2) of the Internal Revenue Code of 1954) the interest on which is excludable from gross income under section 103(a)(1) of such Code if, by reason of the application of paragraph (4) or (6) of section 103(c) of such Code (determined as if paragraphs (4)(A), (5), and (7) were not included in such section 103(c)), paragraph (1) of such section 103(c) does not apply to such security.

(30) The term "municipal securities dealer" means any person (including a separately identifiable department or division of a bank) engaged in the business of buying and selling municipal securities for his own account, through a broker or otherwise, but does not include—

(A) any person insofar as he buys or sells such securities for his own account, either individually or in some fiduciary capacity, but not as a part of a regular business; or

(B) a bank, unless the bank is engaged in the business of buying and selling municipal securities for its own account other than in a fiduciary capacity, through a broker or otherwise: *Provided, however,* That if the bank is engaged in such business through a separately identifiable department or division (as defined by the Municipal Securities Rulemaking Board in accordance with section 15B(b)(2)(H) of this title), the department or division and not the bank itself shall be deemed to be the municipal securities dealer.

(31) The term "municipal securities broker" means a broker engaged in the business of effecting transactions in municipal securities for the account of others.

(32) The term "person associated with a municipal securities dealer" when used with respect to a municipal securities dealer which is a bank or a division or department of a bank means any person directly engaged in the management, direction, supervision, or performance of any of the municipal securities dealer's activities with respect to municipal securities, and any person directly or indirectly controlling such activities or controlled by the municipal securities dealer in connection with such activities.

(33) The term "municipal securities investment portfolio" means all municipal securities held for investment and not for sale as part of a regular business by a municipal securities dealer or by a person, directly or indirectly, controlling, controlled by, or under common control with a municipal securities dealer.

(34) The term "appropriate regulatory agency" means—

(A) When used with respect to a municipal securities dealer:

(i) the Comptroller of the Currency, in the case of a national bank or a bank operating under the Code of Law for the District of Columbia, or a subsidiary or a department or division of any such bank;

(ii) the Board of Governors of the Federal Reserve System, in the case of a State member bank of the Federal Reserve System, a subsidiary or a department or division thereof, a bank holding company, a subsidiary of a bank holding company which is a bank other than a bank specified in clause (i) or (iii) of this subparagraph, or a subsidiary or a department or division of such subsidiary;

(iii) the Federal Deposit Insurance Corporation, in the case of a bank insured by the Federal Deposit Insurance Corporation (other than a member of the Federal Reserve System), or a subsidiary or department or division thereof; and

(iv) the Commission in the case of all other municipal securities dealers.

(B) When used with respect to a clearing agency or transfer agent:

(i) the Comptroller of the Currency, in the case of a national bank or a bank operating under the Code of Law for the District of Columbia, or a subsidiary of any such bank;

(ii) the Board of Governors of the Federal Reserve System, in the case of a State member bank of the Federal Reserve System, a bank holding company, or a subsidiary of a bank holding company, or a subsidiary of a bank holding company which is a bank other than a bank specified in clause (i) or (iii) of this subparagraph when the appropriate regulatory agency for such clearing agency is not the Commission;

(iii) the Federal Deposit Insurance Corporation, in the case of a bank insured by the Federal Deposit Insurance Corporation (other than a member of the Federal Reserve System) when the appropriate regulatory agency for such clearing agency is not the Commission, and

(iv) the Commission in the case of all other clearing agencies and transfer agents.

(C) When used with respect to a participant or applicant to become a participant in a clearing agency or a person requesting or having access to services offered by a clearing agency;

(i) the Comptroller of the Currency, in the case of a national bank or a bank operating under the Code of Law for the District of Columbia when the appropriate regulatory agency for such clearing agency is not the Commission;

(ii) the Board of Governors of the Federal Reserve System in the case of a State member bank of the Federal Reserve System, a bank holding company, or a subsidiary of a bank holding company, or a subsidiary of a bank holding company which is a bank other than a bank specified in clause (i) or (iii) of this subparagraph when the appropriate regulatory agency for such clearing agency is not the Commission;

(iii) the Federal Deposit Insurance Corporation, in the case of a bank insured by the Federal Deposit Insurance Corporation (other than a member of the Federal Reserve System) when the appropriate regulatory agency for such clearing agency is not the Commission; and

(iv) the Commission in all other cases.

(D) When used with respect to an institutional investment manager which is a bank the deposits of which are insured in accordance with the Federal Deposit Insurance Act:

(i) the Comptroller of the Currency, in the case of a national bank or a bank operating under the Code of Law for the District of Columbia;

(ii) the Board of Governors of the Federal Reserve System, in the case of any other member bank of the Federal Reserve System; and

(iii) the Federal Deposit Insurance Corporation, in the case of any other insured bank.

(E) When used with respect to a national securities exchange or registered securities association, member thereof, person associated with a member thereof, applicant to become a member thereof or to become associated with a member thereof, or person requesting or having access to services offered by such exchange or association or member thereof, or the Municipal Securities Rulemaking Board, the Commission.

(F) When used with respect to a person exercising investment discretion with respect to an account:

(i) the Comptroller of the Currency, in the case of a national bank or a bank operating under the Code of Law for the District of Columbia;

(ii) the Board of Governors of the Federal Reserve System in the case of any other member bank of the Federal Reserve System;

(iii) the Federal Deposit Insurance Corporation, in the case of any other bank the deposits of which are insured in accordance with the Federal Deposit Insurance Act; and

(iv) the Commission in the case of all other such persons.

(G) When used with respect to a government securities broker or government securities dealer, or person associated with a government securities broker or government securities dealer:

(i) the Comptroller of the Currency, in the case of a national bank, a bank in the District of Columbia examined by the Comptroller of the Currency, or a Federal branch or Federal agency of a foreign bank (as such terms are used in the International Banking Act of 1978);

(ii) the Board of Governors of the Federal Reserve System, in the case of a State member bank of the Federal Reserve System, a foreign bank, an uninsured State branch or State agency of a foreign bank, a commercial lending company owned or controlled by a foreign bank (as such terms are used in the International Banking Act of 1978), or a corporation organized or having an agreement with the Board of Governors of the Federal Reserve System pursuant to section 25 or section 25A of the Federal Reserve Act;

(iii) the Federal Deposit Insurance Corporation, in the case of a bank insured by the Federal Deposit Insurance Corporation (other than a member of the Federal Reserve System or a Federal savings bank) or an insured State branch of a foreign bank (as such terms are used in the International Banking Act of 1978);

(iv) the Director of the Office of Thrift Supervision, in the case of a savings association (as defined in section 3(b) of the Federal Deposit Insurance Act) the deposits of which are insured by the Federal Deposit Insurance Corporation;

(v) the Commission, in the case of all other government securities brokers and government securities dealers.

(H) When used with respect to an institution described in subparagraph (D), (F), or (G) of section 1841(c)(2), or held under section 1843(f), of Title 12—

(i) the Comptroller of the Currency, in the case of a national bank or a bank in the District of Columbia examined by the Comptroller of the Currency;

(ii) the Board of Governors of the Federal Reserve System, in the case of a State member bank of the Federal Reserve System or any corporation chartered under section 25A of the Federal Reserve Act;

(iii) the Federal Deposit Insurance Corporation, in the case of any other bank the deposits of which are insured in accordance with the Federal Deposit Insurance Act; or

(iv) the Commission in the case of all other such institutions.

As used in this paragraph, the terms "bank holding company" and "subsidiary of a bank holding company" have the meanings given them in section 2 of the Bank Holding Company Act of 1956, and the term "District of Columbia savings and loan association" means any association subject to examination and supervision by the Office of Thrift Supervision under section 8 of the Home Owners' Loan Act of 1933.

(35) A person exercises "investment discretion" with respect to an account if, directly or indirectly, such person (A) is authorized to determine what securities or other property shall be purchased or sold by or for the account, (B) makes decisions as to what securities or other property shall be purchased or sold by or for the account even though some other person may have responsibility for such investment decisions, or (C) otherwise exercises such influence with respect to the purchase and sale of securities or other property by or for the account as the Commission, by rule, determines, in the public interest or for the protection of investors, should be subject to the operation of the provisions of this title and the rules and regulations thereunder.

(36) A class of persons or markets is subject to "equal regulation" if no member of the class has a competitive advantage over any other member thereof resulting from a disparity in their regulation under this title which the Commission determines is unfair and not necessary or appropriate in furtherance of the purposes of this title.

(37) The term "records" means accounts, correspondence, memorandums, tapes, discs, papers, books, and other documents or transcribed information of any type, whether expressed in ordinary or machine language.

(38) The term "market maker" means any specialist permitted to act as a dealer, any dealer acting in the capacity of block positioner, and any dealer who with respect to a security, holds himself out (by entering quotations in an inter-dealer communications system or otherwise) as being willing to buy and sell such security for his own account on a regular or continuous basis.

(39) A person is subject to a "statutory disqualification" with respect to membership or participation in, or association with a member of a self-regulatory organization, if such person—

(A) has been and is expelled or suspended from membership or participation in, or barred or suspended from being associated with a member of, any self-regulatory organization, foreign equivalent of a self-regulatory organization, foreign or international securities exchange, contract market designated pursuant to section 5 of the Commodity Exchange Act (7 U.S.C. 7), or any substantially equivalent foreign statute or regulation, or futures association registered under section 17 of such Act (7 U.S.C. 21), or has been and is denied trading privileges on any such contract market or foreign equivalent;

(B) is subject to—

(i) an order of the Commission, other appropriate regulatory agency, or foreign financial regulatory authority—

(I) denying, suspending for a period not exceeding 12 months, or revoking his registration as a broker, dealer, municipal securities dealer, government securities broker, or government securities dealer or limiting his activities as a foreign person performing a function substantially equivalent to any of the above; or

(II) barring or suspending for a period not exceeding 12 months his being associated with a broker, dealer, municipal securities dealer, government securities broker, government securities dealer, or foreign person performing a function substantially equivalent to any of the above;

(ii) an order of the Commodity Futures Trading Commission denying, suspending, or revoking his registration under the Commodity Exchange Act (7 U.S.C. 1 et seq.); or

(iii) an order by a foreign financial regulatory authority denying, suspending, or revoking the person's authority to engage in transactions in contracts of sale of a commodity for future delivery or other instruments traded on or subject to the rules of a contract market, board of trade, or foreign equivalent thereof,

(C) by his conduct while associated with a broker, dealer, municipal securities dealer, government securities broker, or government securities dealer, or while associated with an entity or person required to be registered under the Commodity Exchange Act, has been found to be a cause of any effective suspension, expulsion, or order of the character described in subparagraph (A) or (B) of this paragraph, and in entering such a suspension, expulsion, or order, the Commission, an appropriate regulatory agency, or any such self-regulatory organization shall have jurisdiction to find whether or not any person was a cause thereof;

(D) by his conduct while associated with any broker, dealer, municipal securities dealer, government securities broker, government securities dealer, or any other entity engaged in transactions in securities, or while associated with an entity engaged in transactions in contracts of sale of a commodity for future delivery or other instruments traded on or subject to the rules of a contract market, board of trade, or foreign equivalent thereof, has been found to be a cause of any effective suspension, expulsion, or order by a foreign or international securities exchange or foreign financial regulatory authority empowered by a foreign government to administer or enforce its laws relating to financial transactions as described in subparagraphs (A) or (B) of this paragraph,

(E) has associated with him any person who is known, or in the exercise of reasonable care should be known, to him to be a person described by subparagraph (A), (B), (C), or (D) of this paragraph; or

(F) has committed or omitted any act, or is subject to an order or finding, enumerated in subparagraph (D), (E), (H), or (G) of paragraph (4) of section 78*o*(b) of this title, has been convicted of any offense specified in subparagraph (B) of such paragraph (4) or any other felony within ten years of the date of the filing of an application for membership or participation in, or to become associated with a member of, such self-regulatory organization, is enjoined from any action, conduct, or practice specified in subparagraph (C) of such paragraph (4), has willfully made or caused to be made in any application for membership or participation in, or to become associated with a member of, a self-regulatory organization, report required to be filed with a self-regulatory organization, or proceeding before a self-regulatory organization, any statement which was at the time, and in light of the circumstances under which it was made, false or misleading with respect to any material fact, or has omitted to state in any such application, report, or proceeding any material fact which is required to be stated therein.

(40) The term "financial responsibility rules" means the rules and regulations of the Commission or the rules and regulations prescribed by any self-regulatory organization relating to financial responsibility and related practices which are designated by the Commission, by rule or regulation, to be financial responsibility rules.

(41) The term "mortgage related security" means a security that is rated in one of the two highest rating categories by at least one nationally recognized statistical rating organization, and either:

(A) represents ownership of one or more promissory notes or certificates of interest or participation in such notes (including any rights designed to assure servicing of, or the receipt or timeliness of receipt by the holders of such notes, certificates, or participations of amounts payable under, such notes, certificates, or participations), which notes:

(i) are directly secured by a first lien on a single parcel of real estate, including stock allocated to a dwelling unit in a residential cooperative housing corporation, upon which is located a dwelling or mixed residential and commercial structure, or on a residential manufactured home as defined in section 603(6) of the National Manufactured Housing Construction and Safety Standards Act of 1974, whether such manufactured home is considered real or personal property under the laws of the State in which it is to be located; and

(ii) were originated by a savings and loan association, savings bank, commercial bank, credit union, insurance company, or similar institution which is supervised and examined by a Federal or State authority, or by a mortgagee approved by the Secretary of Housing and Urban Development pursuant to sections 203 and 211 of the National Housing Act, or, where such notes involve a lien on the manufactured home, by any such institution or by any financial institution approved for insurance by the Secretary of Housing and Urban Development pursuant to section 2 of the National Housing Act; or

(B) is secured by one or more promissory notes or certificates of interest or participations in such notes (with or without recourse to the issuer thereof) and, by its terms, provides for payments of principal in relation to payments, or reasonable projections of payments, on notes meeting the requirements of subparagraphs (A)(i) and (ii) or certificates of interest or participations in promissory notes meeting such requirements.

For the purpose of this paragraph, the term "promissory note", when used in connection with a manufactured home, shall also include a loan, advance, or credit sale as evidence by a retail installment sales contract or other instrument.

(42) The term "government securities" means—

(A) securities which are direct obligations of, or obligations guaranteed as to principal or interest by, the United States;

(B) securities which are issued or guaranteed by corporations in which the United States has a direct or indirect interest and which are designated by the Secretary of the Treasury for exemption as necessary or appropriate in the public interest or for the protection of investors;

(C) securities issued or guaranteed as to principal or interest by any corporation the securities of which are designated, by statute specifically naming such corporation, to constitute exempt securities within the meaning of the laws administered by the Commission;

(D) for purposes of section 15C and 17A, any put, call, straddle, option, or privilege on a security described in subparagraph (A), (B), or (C) other than a put, call, straddle, option, or privilege—

(i) that is traded on one or more national securities exchanges; or

(ii) for which quotations are disseminated through an automated quotation system operated by a registered securities association; or

(E) for purposes of sections 15, 15C, and 17A as applied to a bank, a qualified Canadian government obligation as defined in section 5136 of the Revised Statutes of the United States.

(43) The term "government securities broker" means any person regularly engaged in the business of effecting transactions in government securities for the account of others, but does not include—

(A) any corporation the securities of which are government securities under subparagraph (B) or (C) of paragraph (42) of this subsection; or

(B) any person registered with the Commodity Futures Trading Commission, any contract market designated by the Commodity Futures Trading Commission, such contract market's affiliated clearing organization, or any floor trader on such contract market, solely because such person effects transactions in government securities that the Commission, after consultation with the Commodity Futures Trading Commission, has determined by rule or order to be incidental to such person's futures-related business.

(44) The term "government securities dealer" means any person engaged in the business of buying and selling government securities for his own account, through a broker or otherwise, but does not include—

(A) any person insofar as he buys or sells such securities for his own account, either individually or in some fiduciary capacity, but not as a part of a regular business;

(B) any corporation the securities of which are government securities under subparagraph (B) or (C) of paragraph (42) of this subsection;

(C) any bank, unless the bank is engaged in the business of buying and selling government securities for its own account other than in a fiduciary capacity, through a broker or otherwise; or

(D) any person registered with the Commodity Futures Trading Commission, any contract market designated by the Commodity Futures Trading Commission, such contract market's affiliated clearing organization, or any floor trader on such contract market, solely because such person effects transactions in government securities that the Commission, after consultation with the Commodity Futures Trading Commission, has determined by rule or order to be incidental to such person's futures-related business.

(45) The term "person associated with a government securities broker or government securities dealer" means any partner, officer, director, or branch manager of such government securities broker or government securities dealer (or any person occupying a similar status or performing similar functions), and any other employee of such government securities broker or government securities dealer who is engaged in the management, direction, supervision, or performance of any activities relating to government securities, and any person directly or indirectly controlling, controlled by, or under common control with such government securities broker or government securities dealer.

(46) The term "financial institution" means—

(A) a bank (as defined in paragraph (6) of this subsection);

(B) a foreign bank (as such term is used in the International Banking Act of 1978); and

(C) a savings association (as defined in section 3(b) of the Federal Deposit Insurance Act) the deposits of which are insured by the Federal Deposit Insurance Corporation.

(47) The term "securities laws" means the Securities Act of 1933 (15 U.S.C. 77a et seq.), the Securities Exchange Act of 1934 (15 U.S.C. 78a et seq.), the Sarbanes–Oxley Act of 2002, the Public Utility Holding Company Act of 1935 (15 U.S.C. 79a et seq.), the Trust Indenture Act of 1939 (15 U.S.C. 77aaa et seq.), the Investment Company Act of 1940 (15 U.S.C. 80a–1 et seq.), the Investment Advisers Act of 1940 (15 U.S.C. 80b et seq.), and the Securities Investor Protection Act of 1970 (15 U.S.C. 78aaa et seq.).

(48) The term "registered broker or dealer" means a broker or dealer registered or required to register pursuant to section 15 or 15B of this title, except that in paragraph (3) of this subsection and sections 6 and 15A the term means such a broker or dealer and a government securities broker or government securities dealer registered or required to register pursuant to section 15C(a)(1)(A) of this title.

(49) The term "person associated with a transfer agent" and "associated person of a transfer agent" mean any person (except an employee whose functions are solely clerical or ministerial) directly engaged in the management, direction, supervision, or performance of any of the transfer agent's activities with respect to transfer agent functions, and any person directly or indirectly controlling such activities or controlled by the transfer agent in connection with such activities.

(50) The term "foreign securities authority" means any foreign government, or any governmental body or regulatory organization empowered by a foreign government to administer or enforce its laws as they relate to securities matters.

(51)(A) The term "penny stock" means any equity security other than a security that is—

(i) registered or approved for registration and traded on a national securities exchange that meets such criteria as the Commission shall prescribe by rule or regulation for purposes of this paragraph;

(ii) authorized for quotation on an automated quotation system sponsored by a registered securities association, if such system (I) was established and in operation before January 1, 1990, and (II) meets such criteria as the Commission shall prescribe by rule or regulation for purposes of this paragraph;

(iii) issued by an investment company registered under the Investment Company Act of 1940;

(iv) excluded, on the basis of exceeding a minimum price, net tangible assets of the issuer, or other relevant criteria, from the definition of such term by rule or regulation which the Commission shall prescribe for purposes of this paragraph; or

(v) exempted, in whole or in part, conditionally or unconditionally, from the definition of such term by rule, regulation, or order prescribed by the Commission.

(B) The Commission may, by rule, regulation, or order, designate any equity security or class of equity securities described in clause (i) or (ii) of subparagraph (A) as within the meaning of the term "penny stock" if such security or class of securities is traded other than on a national securities exchange or through an automated quotation system described in clause (ii) of subparagraph (A).

(C) In exercising its authority under this paragraph to prescribe rules, regulations, and orders, the Commission shall determine that such rule, regulation, or order is consistent with the public interest and the protection of investors.

(52) The term "foreign financial regulatory authority" means any (A) foreign securities authority, (B) other governmental body or foreign equivalent of a self-regulatory organization empowered by a foreign government to administer or enforce its laws relating to the regulation of fiduciaries, trusts, commercial lending, insurance, trading in contracts of sale of a commodity for future delivery, or other instruments traded on or subject to the rules of a contract market, board of trade, or foreign equivalent, or other financial activities, or (C) membership organization a function of which is to regulate participation of its members in activities listed above.

(53)(A) The term "small business related security" means a security that is rated in 1 of the 4 highest rating categories by at least 1 nationally recognized statistical rating organization, and either—

(i) represents an interest in 1 or more promissory notes or leases of personal property evidencing the obligation of a small business concern and originated by an insured depository institution, insured credit union, insurance company, or similar institution which is supervised and examined by a Federal or State authority, or a finance company or leasing company; or

(ii) is secured by an interest in 1 or more promissory notes or leases of personal property (with or without recourse to the issuer or lessee) and provides for payments of principal in relation to payments, or reasonable projections of payments, on notes or leases described in clause (i).

(B) For purposes of this paragraph—

(i) an "interest in a promissory note or a lease of personal property" includes ownership rights, certificates of interest or participation in such notes or leases, and rights designed to assure servicing of such notes or leases, or the receipt or timely receipt of amounts payable under such notes or leases;

(ii) the term "small business concern" means a business that meets the criteria for a small business concern established by the Small Business Administration under section 3(a) of the Small Business Act;

(iii) the term "insured depository institution" has the same meaning as in section 3 of the Federal Deposit Insurance Act; and

(iv) the term "insured credit union" has the same meaning as in section 101 of the Federal Credit Union Act.

(54) *Qualified Investor.*—

(A) *Definition.*—Except as provided in subparagraph (B), for purposes of this chapter, the term "qualified investor" means—

(i) any investment company registered with the Commission under section 80a–8 of this title;

(ii) any issuer eligible for an exclusion from the definition of investment company pursuant to section 80a–3(c)(7) of this title;

(iii) any bank (as defined in paragraph (6) of this subsection), savings association (as defined in section 1813(b) of Title 12), broker, dealer, insurance company (as defined in section 77b(a)(13) of this title), or business development company (as defined in section 80a–2(a)(48) of this title);

(iv) any small business investment company licensed by the United States Small Business Administration under section 681(c) or (d) of this title;

(v) any State sponsored employee benefit plan, or any other employee benefit plan, within the meaning of the Employee Retirement Income Security Act of 1974, other than an individual retirement account, if the investment decisions are made by a plan fiduciary, as defined in section 1002(21) of Title 29, which is either a bank, savings and loan association, insurance company, or registered investment adviser;

(vi) any trust whose purchases of securities are directed by a person described in clauses (i) through (v) of this subparagraph;

(vii) any market intermediary exempt under section 80a–3(c)(2) of this title;

(viii) any associated person of a broker or dealer other than a natural person;

(ix) any foreign bank (as defined in section 3101(b)(7) of Title 12);

(x) the government of any foreign country;

(xi) any corporation, company, or partnership that owns and invests on a discretionary basis, not less than $25,000,000 in investments;

(xii) any natural person who owns and invests on a discretionary basis, not less than $25,000,000 in investments;

(xiii) any government or political subdivision, agency, or instrumentality of a government who owns and invests on a discretionary basis not less than $50,000,000 in investments; or

(xiv) any multinational or supranational entity or any agency or instrumentality thereof.

(B) *Altered Thresholds for Asset-Backed Securities and Loan Participations.*—For purposes of subsection (a)(5)(C)(iii) of this section and section 206(a)(5) of the Gramm–Leach–Bliley Act [15 U.S.C.A. § 78c note], the term "qualified investor" has the meaning given such term by subparagraph (A) of this paragraph except that clauses (xi) and (xii) shall be applied by substituting "$10,000,000" for "$25,000,000".

(C) *Additional Authority.*—The Commission may, by rule or order, define a "qualified investor" as any other person, taking into consideration such factors as the financial sophistication of the person, net worth, and knowledge and experience in financial matters.

(55)(A) The term "security future" means a contract of sale for future delivery of a single security or of a narrow-based security index, including any interest therein or based on the value thereof, except an exempted security under section 3(a)(12) of the Securities Exchange Act of 1934 as in effect on the date of the enactment of the Futures Trading Act of 1982 (other than any municipal security as defined in section 3(a)(29) as in effect on the date of the enactment of the Futures Trading Act of 1982). The term "security future" does not include any agreement, contract, or transaction excluded from the Commodity Exchange Act under section 2(c), 2(d), 2(f), or 2(g) of the Commodity Exchange Act (as in effect on the date of the enactment of the Commodity Futures Modernization Act of 2000) or title IV of the Commodity Futures Modernization Act of 2000.

(B) The term "narrow-based security index" means an index—

(i) that has 9 or fewer component securities;

(ii) in which a component security comprises more than 30 percent of the index's weighting;

(iii) in which the five highest weighted component securities in the aggregate comprise more than 60 percent of the index's weighting; or

(iv) in which the lowest weighted component securities comprising, in the aggregate, 25 percent of the index's weighting have an aggregate dollar value of average daily trading volume of less than $50,000,000 (or in the case of an index with 15 or more component securities, $30,000,000), except that if there are two or more securities with equal weighting that could be included in the calculation of the lowest weighted component securities comprising, in the aggregate, 25 percent of the index's weighting, such securities shall be ranked from lowest to highest dollar value of average daily trading volume and shall be included in the calculation based on their ranking starting with the lowest ranked security.

(C) Notwithstanding subparagraph (B), an index is not a narrow-based security index if—

(i)(I) it has at least nine component securities;

(II) no component security comprises more than 30 percent of the index's weighting; and

(III) each component security is—

(aa) registered pursuant to section 12 of the Securities Exchange Act of 1934;

(bb) one of 750 securities with the largest market capitalization; and

(cc) one of 675 securities with the largest dollar value of average daily trading volume;

(ii) a board of trade was designated as a contract market by the Commodity Futures Trading Commission with respect to a contract of sale for future delivery on the index, before the date of the enactment of the Commodity Futures Modernization Act of 2000;

(iii)(I) a contract of sale for future delivery on the index traded on a designated contract market or registered derivatives transaction execution facility for at least 30 days as a contract of sale for future delivery on an index that was not a narrow-based security index; and

(II) it has been a narrow-based security index for no more than 45 business days over 3 consecutive calendar months;

(iv) a contract of sale for future delivery on the index is traded on or subject to the rules of a foreign board of trade and meets such requirements as are jointly established by rule or regulation by the Commission and the Commodity Futures Trading Commission;

(v) no more than 18 months have passed since the date of the enactment of the Commodity Futures Modernization Act of 2000 and—

(I) it is traded on or subject to the rules of a foreign board of trade;

(II) the offer and sale in the United States of a contract of sale for future delivery on the index was authorized before the date of the enactment of the Commodity Futures Modernization Act of 2000; and

(III) the conditions of such authorization continue to be met; or

(vi) a contract of sale for future delivery on the index is traded on or subject to the rules of a board of trade and meets such requirements as are jointly established by rule, regulation, or order by the Commission and the Commodity Futures Trading Commission.

(D) Within 1 year after the enactment of the Commodity Futures Modernization Act of 2000, the Commission and the Commodity Futures Trading Commission jointly shall adopt rules or regulations that set forth the requirements under clause (iv) of subparagraph (C).

(E) An index that is a narrow-based security index solely because it was a narrow-based security index for more than 45 business days over 3 consecutive calendar months pursuant to clause (iii) of subparagraph (C) shall not be a narrow-based security index for the 3 following calendar months.

(F) For purposes of subparagraphs (B) and (C) of this paragraph—

(i) the dollar value of average daily trading volume and the market capitalization shall be calculated as of the preceding 6 full calendar months; and

(ii) the Commission and the Commodity Futures Trading Commission shall, by rule or regulation, jointly specify the method to be used to determine market capitalization and dollar value of average daily trading volume.

(56) The term "security futures product" means a security future or any put, call, straddle, option, or privilege on any security future.

(57)(A) The term "margin", when used with respect to a security futures product, means the amount, type, and form of collateral required to secure any extension or maintenance of credit, or the amount, type, and form of collateral required as a performance bond related to the purchase, sale, or carrying of a security futures product.

(B) The terms "margin level" and "level of margin", when used with respect to a security futures product, mean the amount of margin required to secure any extension or maintenance of credit, or the amount of margin required as a performance bond related to the purchase, sale, or carrying of a security futures product.

(C) The terms "higher margin level" and "higher level of margin", when used with respect to a security futures product, mean a margin level established by a national securities exchange registered pursuant to section 6(g) that is higher than the minimum amount established and in effect pursuant to section 7(c)(2)(B).

(58) *Audit committee.*—The term "audit committee" means—

(A) a committee (or equivalent body) established by and amongst the board of directors of an issuer for the purpose of overseeing the accounting and financial reporting processes of the issuer and audits of the financial statements of the issuer; and

(B) if no such committee exists with respect to an issuer, the entire board of directors of the issuer.

(59) *Registered public accounting firm.*—The term "registered public accounting firm" has the same meaning as in section 2 of the Sarbanes–Oxley Act of 2002.

(b) The Commission and the Board of Governors of the Federal Reserve System, as to matters within their respective jurisdictions, shall have power by rules and regulations to define technical, trade, accounting, and other terms used in this title, consistently with the provisions and purposes of this title.

(c) No provision of this title shall apply to, or be deemed to include, any executive department or independent establishment of the United States, or any leading agency which is wholly owned, directly or indirectly, by the United States, or any officer, agent, or employee of any such department, establishment, or agency, acting in the course of his official duty as such, unless such provision makes specific reference to such department, establishment, or agency.

(d) No issuer of municipal securities or officer or employee thereof acting in the course of his official duties as such shall be deemed to be a "broker", "dealer", or "municipal securities dealer" solely by reason of buying, selling, or effecting transactions in the issuer's securities.

(e) *Charitable Organizations.*—

(1) *Exemption.*—Notwithstanding any other provision of this title, but subject to paragraph (2) of this subsection, a charitable organization, as defined in section 3(c)(10)(D) of the Investment Company Act of 1940, or any trustee, director, officer, employee, or volunteer of such a charitable organization acting within the scope of such person's employment or duties with such organization, shall not be deemed to be a "broker", "dealer", "municipal securities

broker", "municipal securities dealer", "government securities broker", or "government securities dealer" for purposes of this title solely because such organization or person buys, holds, sells, or trades in securities for its own account in its capacity as trustee or administrator of, or otherwise on behalf of or for the account of—

(A) such a charitable organization;

(B) a fund that is excluded from the definition of an investment company under section 3(c)(10)(B) of the Investment Company Act of 1940; or

(C) a trust or other donative instrument described in section 3(c)(10)(B) of the Investment Company Act of 1940, or the settlors (or potential settlors) or beneficiaries of any such trust or other instrument.

(2) *Limitation on Compensation.*—The exemption provided under paragraph (I) shall not be available to any charitable organization, or any trustee, director, officer, employee, or volunteer of such a charitable organization, unless each person who, on or after 90 days after the date of enactment of this subsection, solicits donations on behalf of such charitable organization from any donor to a fund that is excluded from the definition of an investment company under section 3(c)(10)(B) of the Investment Company Act of 1940, is either a volunteer or is engaged in the overall fund raising activities of a charitable organization and receives no commission or other special compensation based on the number or the value of donations collected for the fund.

(f) *Consideration of Promotion of Efficiency, Competition, and Capital Formation.*—Whenever, pursuant to this title, the Commission is engaged in rulemaking, or in the review of a rule of a self-regulatory organization, and is required to consider or determine whether an action is necessary or appropriate in the public interest, the Commission shall also consider, in addition to the protection of investors, whether the action will promote efficiency, competition, and capital formation.

(g) *Church Plans.*—No church plan described in section 414(e) of the Internal Revenue Code of 1986, no person or entity eligible to establish and maintain such a plan under the Internal Revenue Code of 1986, no company or account that is excluded from the definition of an investment company under section 3(c)(14) of the Investment Company Act of 1940, and no trustee, director, officer or employee of or volunteer for such plan, company, account person, or entity, acting within the scope of that person's employment or activities with respect to such plan, shall be deemed to be a "broker", "dealer", "municipal securities broker", "municipal securities dealer", "government securities broker", "government securities dealer", "clearing agency", or "transfer agent" for purposes of this title—

(1) solely because such plan, company, person, or entity buys, holds, sells, trades in, or transfers securities or acts as an intermediary in making payments in connection with transactions in securities for its own account in its capacity as trustee or administrator of, or otherwise on behalf of, or for the account of, any church plan, company, or account that is excluded from the definition of an investment company under section 3(c)(14) of the Investment Company Act of 1940; and

(2) if no such person or entity receives a commission or other transaction-related sales compensation in connection with any activities conducted in reliance on the exemption provided by this subsection.

Swap Agreements

Sec. 3A. (a) *Non–Security–Based Swap Agreements.*—The definition of "security" in section 3(a)(10) of this title does not include any non-security-based swap agreement (as defined in section 206C of the Gramm–Leach–Bliley Act).

(b) *Security–Based Swap Agreements.*—

(1) The definition of "security" in section 3(a)(10) of this title does not include any security-based swap agreement (as defined in section 206B of the Gramm–Leach–Bliley Act).

(2) The Commission is prohibited from registering, or requiring, recommending, or suggesting, the registration under this title of any security-based swap agreement (as defined in section 206B of the Gramm–Leach–Bliley Act). If the Commission becomes aware that a registrant has filed a registration application with respect to such a swap agreement, the Commission shall promptly so notify the registrant. Any such registration with respect to such a swap agreement shall be void and of no force or effect.

(3) Except as provided in section 16(a) with respect to reporting requirements, the Commission is prohibited from—

(A) promulgating, interpreting, or enforcing rules; or

(B) issuing orders of general applicability;

under this title in a manner that imposes or specifies reporting or recordkeeping requirements, procedures, or standards as prophylactic measures against fraud, manipulation, or insider trading with respect to any security-based swap agreement (as defined in section 206B of the Gramm–Leach–Bliley Act).

(4) References in this title to the "purchase" or "sale" of a security-based swap agreement (as defined in section 206B of the Gramm–Leach–Bliley Act) shall be deemed to mean the execution, termination (prior to its scheduled maturity date), assignment, exchange, or similar transfer or conveyance of, or extinguishing of rights or obligations under, a security-based swap agreement, as the context may require.

Securities and Exchange Commission

Sec. 4. (a) There is hereby established a Securities and Exchange Commission (hereinafter referred to as the "Commission") to be composed of five commissioners to be appointed by the President by and with the advice and consent of the Senate. Not more than three of such commissioners shall be members of the same political party, and in making appointments members of different political parties shall be appointed alternately as nearly as may be practicable. No commissioner shall engage in any other business, vocation, or employment than that of serving as commissioner, nor shall any commissioner participate, directly or indirectly, in any stock-market operations or transactions of a character subject to regulation by the Commission pursuant to this title. Each Commissioner shall hold office for a term of five years and until his successor is appointed and has qualified, except that he shall not so continue to serve beyond the expiration of the next session of Congress subsequent to the expiration of said fixed term of office, and except (1) any Commissioner appointed to fill a vacancy occurring prior to the expiration of the term for which his predecessor was appointed shall be appointed for the remainder of such term, and (2) the terms of office of the Commissioners first taking office after the enactment of this title shall expire as designated by the President at the time of nomination, one at the end of one year, one at the end of two years, one at the end of three years, one at the end of four years, and one at the end of five years, after the date of the enactment of this title.

(b) *Appointment and Compensation of Staff and Leasing Authority.*—

(1) *Appointment and Compensation.* The Commission shall appoint and compensate officers, attorneys, economists, examiners, and other employees in accordance with section 4802 of title 5, United States Code.

(2) *Reporting of information.* In establishing and adjusting schedules of compensation and benefits for officers, attorneys, economists, examiners, and other employees of the Commission under applicable provisions of law, the Commission shall inform the heads of the agencies referred to under section 1206 of

the Financial Institutions Reform, Recovery, and Enforcement Act of 1989 (*12 U.S.C. 1833b*) and Congress of such compensation and benefits and shall seek to maintain comparability with such agencies regarding compensation and benefits.

(3) *Leasing Authority.*—Notwithstanding any other provision of law, the Commission is authorized to enter directly into leases for real property for office, meeting, storage, and such other space as is necessary to carry out its functions, and shall be exempt from any General Services Administration space management regulations or directives.

(c) Notwithstanding any other provision of law, in accordance with regulations which the Commission shall prescribe to prevent conflicts of interest, the Commission may accept payment and reimbursement, in cash or in kind, from non-Federal agencies, organizations, and individuals for travel, subsistence, and other necessary expenses incurred by Commission members and employees in attending meetings and conferences concerning the functions or activities of the Commission. Any payment or reimbursement accepted shall be credited to the appropriated funds of the Commission. The amount of travel, subsistence, and other necessary expenses for members and employees paid or reimbursed under this subsection may exceed per diem amounts established in official travel regulations, but the Commission may include in its regulations under this subsection a limitation on such amounts.

(d) Notwithstanding any other provision of law, former employers of participants in the Commission's professional fellows programs may pay such participants their actual expenses for relocation to Washington, District of Columbia, to facilitate their participation in such programs, and program participants may accept such payments.

(e) Notwithstanding any other provision of law, whenever any fee is required to be paid to the Commission pursuant to any provision of the securities laws or any other law, the Commission may provide by rule that such fee shall be paid in a manner other than in cash, and the Commission may also specify the time that such fee shall be determined and paid relative to the filing of any statement or document with the Commission.

(f) *Reimbursement of Expenses for Assisting Foreign Securities Authorities.*—Notwithstanding any other provision of law, the Commission may accept payment and reimbursement, in cash or in kind, from a foreign securities authority, or made on behalf of such authority, for necessary expenses incurred by the Commission, its members, and employees in carrying out any investigation pursuant to section 21(a)(2) of this title or in providing any other assistance to a foreign securities authority. Any payment or reimbursement accepted shall be considered a reimbursement to the appropriated funds of the Commission.

Delegation of Functions by Commission

Sec. 4A. (a) In addition to its existing authority, the Securities and Exchange Commission shall have the authority to delegate, by published order or rule, any of its functions to a division of the Commission, an individual Commissioner, an administrative law judge, or an employee or employee board, including functions with respect to hearing, determining, ordering, certifying, reporting, or otherwise acting as to any work, business, or matter. Nothing in this section shall be deemed to supersede the provisions of section 556(b) of title 5, or to authorize the delegation of the function of rule-making as defined in subchapter II of chapter 5 of title 5, United States Code, with reference to general rules as distinguished from rules of particular applicability, or of the making of any rule pursuant to section 19(c) of this title.

(b) With respect to the delegation of any of its functions, as provided in subsection (a) of this section, the Commission shall retain a discretionary right to review the action of any such division of the Commission, individual Commissioner, administrative law judge, employee, or employee board, upon its own initiative or upon petition of a party to or intervenor in such action, within such time and in such manner as the Commission by rule shall prescribe. The vote of one member of the Commission shall be sufficient to bring any such action before the Commission for review. A person or party shall be entitled to review by the Commission if he or it is adversely affected by action at a delegated level which (1) denies any request for action pursuant to section 8(a) or section 8(c) of the Securities Act of 1933 or the first sentence of section 12(d) of this title; (2) suspends trading in a security pursuant to section 12(k) of this title; or (3) is pursuant to any provision of this title in a case of adjudication, as defined in section 551 of title 5, United States Code, not required by this title to be determined on the record after notice and opportunity for hearing (except to the extent there is involved a matter described in section 554(a)(1) through (6) of such title 5).

(c) If the right to exercise such review is declined, or if no such review is sought within the time stated in the rules promulgated by the Commission, then the action of any such division of the Commission, individual Commissioner, administrative law judge, employee, or employee board, shall, for all purposes, including appeal or review thereof, be deemed the action of the Commission.

Transfer of Functions With Respect to Assignment of Personnel to Chairman

Sec. 4B. In addition to the functions transferred by the provisions of Reorganization Plan Numbered 10 of 1950 (64 Stat. 1265), there are hereby transferred from the Commission to the Chairman of the Commission the functions of the Commission with respect to the assignment of Commission personnel, including Commissioners, to perform such functions as may have been delegated by the Commission to the Commission personnel, including Commissioners, pursuant to section 4A of this title.

Appearance and Practice Before the Commission

Sec. 4C. (a) *Authority To Censure.*—The Commission may censure any person, or deny, temporarily or permanently, to any person the privilege of appearing or practicing before the Commission in any way, if that person is found by the Commission, after notice and opportunity for hearing in the matter—

(1) not to possess the requisite qualifications to represent others;

(2) to be lacking in character or integrity, or to have engaged in unethical or improper professional conduct; or

(3) to have willfully violated, or willfully aided and abetted the violation of, any provision of the securities laws or the rules and regulations issued thereunder.

(b) *Definition.*—With respect to any registered public accounting firm or associated person, for purposes of this section, the term "improper professional conduct" means—

(1) intentional or knowing conduct, including reckless conduct, that results in a violation of applicable professional standards; and

(2) negligent conduct in the form of—

(A) a single instance of highly unreasonable conduct that results in a violation of applicable professional standards in circumstances in which the registered public accounting firm or associated person knows, or should know, that heightened scrutiny is warranted; or

(B) repeated instances of unreasonable conduct, each resulting in a violation of applicable professional standards, that indicate a lack of competence to practice before the Commission.

Transactions on Unregistered Exchanges

Sec. 5. It shall be unlawful for any broker, dealer, or exchange, directly or indirectly, to make use of the mails or any means or instrumentality of interstate commerce for the purpose of using any facility of an exchange within or subject to the jurisdiction of the United States to effect any transaction in a security, or to report any such transaction, unless such exchange (1) is registered as a national securities exchange under section 6 of this title, or (2) is exempted from such registration upon application by the exchange because, in the opinion of the Commission, by reason of the limited volume of transactions effected on such exchange, it is not practicable and not necessary or appropriate in the public interest or for the protection of investors to require such registration.

National Securities Exchanges

Sec. 6. (a) An exchange may be registered as a national securities exchange under the terms and conditions hereinafter provided in this section and in accordance with the provisions of section 19(a) of this title, by filing with the Commission an application for registration in such form as the Commission, by rule, may prescribe containing the rules of the exchange and such other information and documents as the Commission, by rule, may prescribe as necessary or appropriate in the public interest or for the protection of investors.

(b) An exchange shall not be registered as a national securities exchange unless the Commission determines that—

(1) Such exchange is so organized and has the capacity to be able to carry out the purposes of this title and to comply, and (subject to any rule or order of the Commission pursuant to section 17(d) or 19(g)(2) of this title) to enforce compliance by its members and persons associated with its members, with the provisions of this title, the rules and regulations thereunder, and the rules of the exchange.

(2) Subject to the provisions of subsection (c) of this section, the rules of the exchange provide that any registered broker or dealer or natural person associated with a registered broker or dealer may become a member of such exchange and any person may become associated with a member thereof.

(3) The rules of the exchange assure a fair representation of its members in the selection of its directors and administration of its affairs and provide that one or more directors shall be representative of issuers and investors and not be associated with a member of the exchange, broker, or dealer.

(4) The rules of the exchange provide for the equitable allocation of reasonable dues, fees, and other charges among its members and issuers and other persons using its facilities.

(5) The rules of the exchange are designed to prevent fraudulent and manipulative acts and practices, to promote just and equitable principles of trade, to foster cooperation and coordination with persons engaged in regulating, clearing, settling, processing information with respect to, and facilitating transactions in securities, to remove impediments to and perfect the mechanism of a free and open market and a national market system, and, in general, to protect investors and the public interest; and are not designed to permit unfair discrimination between customers, issuers, brokers, or dealers, or to regulate by virtue of any authority conferred by this title matters not related to the purposes of this title or the administration of the exchange.

(6) The rules of the exchange provide that (subject to any rule or order of the Commission pursuant to section 17(d) or 19(g)(2) of this title) its members and persons associated with its members shall be appropriately disciplined for violation of the provisions of this title, the rules or regulations thereunder, or the rules of the exchange, by expulsion, suspension, limitation of activities, functions, and operations, fine, censure, being suspended or barred from being associated with a member, or any other fitting sanction.

(7) The rules of the exchange are in accordance with the provisions of subsection (d)

of this section, and in general, provide a fair procedure for the disciplining of members and persons associated with members, the denial of membership to any person seeking membership therein, the barring of any person from becoming associated with a member thereof, and the prohibition or limitation by the exchange of any person with respect to access to services offered by the exchange or a member thereof.

(8) The rules of the exchange do not impose any burden on competition not necessary or appropriate in furtherance of the purposes of this title.

(9) The rules of the exchange prohibit the listing of any security issued in a limited partnership rollup transaction (as such term is defined in paragraphs (4) and (5) of section 14(h)), unless such transaction was conducted in accordance with procedures designed to protect the rights of limited partners, including—

(A) the right of dissenting limited partners to one of the following:

(i) an appraisal and compensation;

(ii) retention of a security under substantially the same terms and conditions as the original issue;

(iii) approval of the limited partnership rollup transaction by not less than 75 percent of the outstanding securities of each of the participating limited partnerships;

(iv) the use of a committee of limited partners that is independent, as determined in accordance with rules prescribed by the exchange, of the general partner or sponsor, that has been approved by a majority of the outstanding units of each of the participating limited partnerships, and that has such authority as is necessary to protect the interest of limited partners, including the authority to hire independent advisors, to negotiate with the general partner or sponsor on behalf of the limited partners, and to make a recommendation to the limited partners with respect to the proposed transaction; or

(v) other comparable rights that are prescribed by rule by the exchange and that are designed to protect dissenting limited partners;

(B) the right not to have their voting power unfairly reduced or abridged;

(C) the right not to bear an unfair portion of the costs of a proposed limited partnership rollup transaction that is rejected; and

(D) restrictions on the conversion of contingent interests or fees into non-contingent interests or fees and restrictions on the receipt of a non-contingent equity interest in exchange for fees for services which have not yet been provided.

As used in this paragraph, the term "dissenting limited partner" means a person who, on the date on which soliciting material is mailed to investors, is a holder of a beneficial interest in a limited partnership that is the subject of a limited partnership rollup transaction, and who casts a vote against the transaction and complies with procedures established by the exchange, except that for purposes of an exchange or tender offer, such person shall file an objection in writing under the rules of the exchange during the period during which the offer is outstanding.

(c)(1) A national securities exchange shall deny membership to (A) any person, other than a natural person, which is not a registered broker or dealer or (B) any natural person who is not, or is not associated with, a registered broker or dealer.

(2) A national securities exchange may, and in cases in which the Commission, by order, directs as necessary or appropriate in the public interest or for the protection of investors shall, deny membership to any registered broker or dealer or natural person associated with a registered broker or deal-

er, and bar from becoming associated with a member any person, who is subject to a statutory disqualification. A national securities exchange shall file notice with the Commission not less than thirty days prior to admitting any person to membership or permitting any person to become associated with a member, if the exchange knew, or in the exercise of reasonable care should have known, that such person was subject to a statutory disqualification. The notice shall be in such form and contain such information as the Commission, by rule, may prescribe as necessary or appropriate in the public interest or for the protection of investors.

(3)(A) A national securities exchange may deny membership to, or condition the membership of, a registered broker or dealer if (i) such broker or dealer does not meet such standards of financial responsibility or operational capability or such broker or dealer or any natural persons associated with such broker or dealer does not meet such standards of training, experience, and competence as are prescribed by the rules of the exchange or (ii) such broker or dealer or person associated with such broker or dealer has engaged and there is a reasonable likelihood he will again engage in acts or practices inconsistent with just and equitable principles of trade. A national securities exchange may examine and verify the qualifications of an applicant to become a member and the natural persons associated with such an applicant in accordance with procedures established by the rules of the exchange.

(B) A national securities exchange may bar a natural person from becoming a member or associated with a member, or condition the membership of a natural person or association of a natural person with a member, if such natural person (i) does not meet such standards of training, experience, and competence as are prescribed by the rules of the exchange or (ii) has engaged and there is a reasonable likelihood he will again engage in acts or practices inconsistent with just and equitable principles of trade. A national securities exchange may examine and verify the qualifications of an applicant to become a person associated with a member in accordance with procedures established by the rules of the exchange and require any person associated with a member, or any class of such persons, to be registered with the exchange in accordance with procedures so established.

(C) A national securities exchange may bar any person from becoming associated with a member if such person does not agree (i) to supply the exchange with such information with respect to its relationship and dealings with the member as may be specified in the rules of the exchange and (ii) to permit the examination of its books and records to verify the accuracy of any information so supplied.

(4) A national securities exchange may limit (A) the number of members of the exchange and (B) the number of members and designated representatives of members permitted to effect transactions on the floor of the exchange without the services of another person acting as broker: *Provided, however,* That no national securities exchange shall have the authority to decrease the number of memberships in such exchange, or the number of members and designated representatives of members permitted to effect transactions on the floor of such exchange without the services of another person acting as broker, below such number in effect on May 1, 1975, or the date such exchange was registered with the Commission whichever is later: *And provided further,* That the Commission, in accordance with the provisions of section 19(c) of this title, may amend the rules of any national securities exchange to increase (but not to decrease) or to remove any limitation on the number of memberships in such exchange or the number of members or designated repre-

sentatives of members permitted to effect transactions on the floor of the exchange without the services of another person acting as broker, if the Commission finds that such limitation imposes a burden on competition not necessary or appropriate in furtherance of the purposes of this title.

(d)(1) In any proceeding by a national securities exchange to determine whether a member or person associated with a member should be disciplined (other than a summary proceeding pursuant to paragraph (3) of this subsection), the exchange shall bring specific charges, notify such member or person of, and give him an opportunity to defend against, such charges, and keep a record. A determination by the exchange to impose a disciplinary sanction shall be supported by a statement setting forth—

(A) any act or practice in which such member or person associated with a member has been found to have engaged, or which such member or person has been found to have omitted;

(B) the specific provision of this title, the rules or regulations thereunder, or the rules of the exchange which any such act or practice, or omission to act, is deemed to violate; and

(C) the sanction imposed and the reasons therefor.

(2) In any proceeding by a national securities exchange to determine whether a person shall be denied membership, barred from becoming associated with a member, or prohibited or limited with respect to access to services offered by the exchange or a member thereof (other than a summary proceeding pursuant to paragraph (3) of this subsection), the exchange shall notify such person of, and give him an opportunity to be heard upon, the specific grounds for denial, bar, or prohibition or limitation under consideration and keep a record. A determination by the exchange to deny membership, bar a person from becoming associated with a member, or prohibit or limit a person with respect to access to services offered by the exchange or a member thereof shall be supported by a statement setting forth the specific grounds on which the denial, bar, or prohibition or limitation is based.

(3) A national securities exchange may summarily (A) suspend a member or person associated with a member who has been and is expelled or suspended from any self-regulatory organization or barred or suspended from being associated with a member of any self-regulatory organization, (B) suspend a member who is in such financial or operating difficulty that the exchange determines and so notifies the Commission that the member cannot be permitted to continue to do business as a member with safety to investors, creditors, other members, or the exchange, or (C) limit or prohibit any person with respect to access to services offered by the exchange if subparagraph (A) or (B) of this paragraph is applicable to such person or, in the case of a person who is not a member, if the exchange determines that such person does not meet the qualification requirements or other prerequisites for such access and such person cannot be permitted to continue to have such access with safety to investors, creditors, members, or the exchange. Any person aggrieved by any such summary action shall be promptly afforded an opportunity for a hearing by the exchange in accordance with the provisions of paragraph (1) or (2) of this subsection. The Commission, by order, may stay any such summary action on its own motion or upon application by any person aggrieved thereby, if the Commission determines summarily or after notice and opportunity for hearing (which hearing may consist solely of the submission of affidavits or presentation of oral arguments) that such stay is consistent with the public interest and the protection of investors.

(e)(1) On and after the date of enactment of the Securities Acts Amendments of 1975, no national securities exchange may impose any schedule or fix rates of commissions, allowances, discounts, or other fees to be charged by its members: *Provided, however,* That until May 1, 1976, the preceding provisions of this paragraph shall not prohibit any such exchange from imposing or fixing any schedule of commissions, allowances, discounts, or other fees to be charged by its members for acting as broker on the floor of the exchange or as odd-lot dealer: *And provided further,* That the Commission, in accordance with the provisions of section 19(b) of this title as modified by the provisions of paragraph (3) of this subsection, may—

(A) permit a national securities exchange, by rule, to impose a reasonable schedule or fix reasonable rates of commissions, allowances, discounts, or other fees to be charged by its members for effecting transactions on such exchange prior to November 1, 1976, if the Commission finds that such schedule or fixed rates of commissions, allowances, discounts, or other fees are in the public interest; and

(B) permit a national securities exchange, by rule, to impose a schedule or fix rates of commissions, allowances, discounts, or other fees to be charged by its members for effecting transactions on such exchange after November 1, 1976, if the Commission finds that such schedule or fixed rates of commissions, allowances, discounts, or other fees (i) are reasonable in relation to the costs of providing the service for which such fees are charged (and the Commission publishes the standards employed in adjudging reasonableness) and (ii) do not impose any burden on competition not necessary or appropriate in furtherance of the purposes of this title, taking into consideration the competitive effects of permitting such schedule or fixed rates weighed against the competitive effects of other lawful actions which the Commission is authorized to take under this title.

(2) Notwithstanding the provisions of section 19(c) of this title, the Commission, by rule, may abrogate any exchange rule which imposes a schedule or fixes rates of commissions, allowances, discounts, or other fees, if the Commission determines that such schedule or fixed rates are no longer reasonable, in the public interest, or necessary to accomplish the purposes of this title.

(3)(A) Before approving or disapproving any proposed rule change submitted by a national securities exchange which would impose a schedule or fix rates of commissions, allowances, discounts, or other fees to be charged by its members for effecting transactions on such exchange, the Commission shall afford interested persons (i) an opportunity for oral presentation of data, views, and arguments and (ii) with respect to any such rule concerning transactions effected after November 1, 1976, if the Commission determines there are disputed issues of material fact, to present such rebuttal submissions and to conduct (or have conducted under subparagraph (B) of this paragraph) such cross-examination as the Commission determines to be appropriate and required for full disclosure and proper resolution of such disputed issues of material fact.

(B) The Commission shall prescribe rules and make rulings concerning any proceeding in accordance with subparagraph (A) of this paragraph designed to avoid unnecessary costs or delay. Such rules or rulings may (i) impose reasonable time limits on each interested person's oral presentations, and (ii) require any cross-examination to which a person may be entitled under subparagraph (A) of this paragraph to be conducted by the Commission on behalf of that person in such manner as the Commission determines to be appropriate and required for full disclosure and proper resolution of disputed issues of material fact.

(C)(i) If any class of persons, the members of which are entitled to conduct (or have conducted) cross-examination under subparagraphs (A) and (B) of this paragraph and which have, in the view of the Commission, the same or similar interests in the proceeding, cannot agree upon a single representative of such interest for purposes of cross-examination, the Commission may make rules and rulings specifying the manner in which such interests shall be represented and such cross-examination conducted.

(ii) No member of any class of persons with respect to which the Commission has specified the manner in which its interests shall be represented pursuant to clause (i) of this subparagraph shall be denied, pursuant to such clause (i), the opportunity to conduct (or have conducted) cross-examination as to issues affecting his particular interests if he satisfies the Commission that he has made a reasonable and good faith effort to reach agreement upon group representation and there are substantial and relevant issues which would not be presented adequately by group representation.

(D) A transcript shall be kept of any oral presentation and cross-examination.

(E) In addition to the bases specified in subsection 25(a), a reviewing Court may set aside an order of the Commission under section 19(b) approving an exchange rule imposing a schedule or fixing rates of commissions, allowances, discounts or other fees, if the Court finds

(1) a Commission determination under subparagraph (A) of this paragraph that an interested person is not entitled to conduct cross-examination or make rebuttal submissions, or

(2) a Commission rule or ruling under subparagraph (B) of this paragraph limiting the petitioner's cross-examination or rebuttal submissions,

has precluded full disclosure and proper resolution of disputed issues of material fact which were necessary for fair determination by the Commission.

(f) The Commission, by rule or order, as it deems necessary or appropriate in the public interest and for the protection of investors, to maintain fair and orderly markets, or to assure equal regulation, may require—

(1) any person not a member or a designated representative of a member of a national securities exchange effecting transactions on such exchange without the services of another person acting as a broker, or

(2) any broker or dealer not a member of a national securities exchange effecting transactions on such exchange on a regular basis.

to comply with such rules of such exchange as the Commission may specify.

(g) *Notice Registration of Security Futures Product Exchanges.*—

(1) *Registration Required.*—An exchange that lists or trades security futures products may register as a national securities exchange solely for the purposes of trading security futures products if—

(A) the exchange is a board of trade, as that term is defined by the Commodity Exchange Act (7 U.S.C. 1a(2)), that—

(i) has been designated a contract market by the Commodity Futures Trading Commission and such designation is not suspended by order of the Commodity Futures Trading Commission; or

(ii) is registered as a derivative transaction execution facility under section 5a of the Commodity Exchange Act and such registration is not suspended by the Commodity Futures Trading Commission; and

(B) such exchange does not serve as a market place for transactions in securities other than—

(i) security futures products; or

(ii) futures on exempted securities or groups or indexes of securities or options thereon that have been authorized under section 2(a)(1)(C) of the Commodity Exchange Act.

(2) *Registration by Notice Filing.*—

(A) *Form and Content.*—An exchange required to register only because such exchange lists or trades security futures products may register for purposes of this section by filing with the Commission a written notice in such form as the Commission, by rule, may prescribe containing the rules of the exchange and such other information and documents concerning such exchange, comparable to the information and documents required for national securities exchanges under section 6(a), as the Commission, by rule, may prescribe as necessary or appropriate in the public interest or for the protection of investors. If such exchange has filed documents with the Commodity Futures Trading Commission, to the extent that such documents contain information satisfying the Commission's informational requirements, copies of such documents may be filed with the Commission in lieu of the required written notice.

(B) *Immediate Effectiveness.*—Such registration shall be effective contemporaneously with the submission of notice, in written or electronic form, to the Commission, except that such registration shall not be effective if such registration would be subject to suspension or revocation.

(C) *Termination.*—Such registration shall be terminated immediately if any of the conditions for registration set forth in this subsection are no longer satisfied.

(3) *Public Availability.*—The Commission shall promptly publish in the Federal Register an acknowledgment of receipt of all notices the Commission receives under this subsection and shall make all such notices available to the public.

(4) *Exemption of Exchanges from Specified Provisions.*—

(A) *Transaction Exemptions.*—An exchange that is registered under paragraph (1) of this subsection shall be exempt from, and shall not be required to enforce compliance by its members with, and its members shall not, solely with respect to those transactions effected on such exchange in security futures products, be required to comply with, the following provisions of this title and the rules thereunder:

(i) Subsections (b)(2), (b)(3), (b)(4), (b)(7), (b)(9), (c), (d), and (e) of this section.

(ii) Section 8.

(iii) Section 11.

(iv) Subsections (d), (f), and (k) of section 17.

(v) Subsections (a), (f), and (h) of section 19.

(B) *Rule Change Exemptions.*—An exchange that registered under paragraph (1) of this subsection shall also be exempt from submitting proposed rule changes pursuant to section 19(b) of this title, except that—

(i) such exchange shall file proposed rule changes related to higher margin levels, fraud or manipulation, recordkeeping, reporting, listing standards, or decimal pricing for security futures products, sales practices for security futures products for persons who effect transactions in security futures products, or rules effectuating such exchange's obligation to enforce the securities laws pursuant to section 19(b)(7);

(ii) such exchange shall file pursuant to sections 19(b)(1) and 19(b)(2) proposed rule changes related to margin, except for changes resulting in higher margin levels; and

(iii) such exchange shall file pursuant to section 19(b)(1) proposed rule changes that have been abrogated by the Commission pursuant to section 19(b)(7)(C).

(5) *Trading in Security Futures Products.*—

(A) *In General.*—Subject to subparagraph (B), it shall be unlawful for any person to execute or trade a security futures product until the later of—

(i) 1 year after the date of the enactment of the Commodity Futures Modernization Act of 2000; or

(ii) such date that a futures association registered under section 17 of the Commodity Exchange Act has met the requirements set forth in section 15A(k)(2) of this title.

(B) *Principal-to-Principal Transactions.*—Notwithstanding subparagraph (A), a person may execute or trade a security futures product transaction if—

(i) the transaction is entered into—

(I) on a principal-to-principal basis between parties trading for their own accounts or as described in section 1a(12)(B)(ii) of the Commodity Exchange Act; and

(II) only between eligible contract participants (as defined in subparagraphs (A), (B)(ii), and (C) of such section 1a(12)) at the time at which the persons enter into the agreement, contract, or transaction; and

(ii) the transaction is entered into on or after the later of—

(I) 8 months after the date of the enactment of the Commodity Futures Modernization Act of 2000; or

(II) such date that a futures association registered under section 17 of the Commodity Exchange Act has met the requirements set forth in section 15A(k)(2) of this title.

(h) *Trading in Security Futures Products.*—

(1) *Trading on Exchange or Association Required.*—It shall be unlawful for any person to effect transactions in security futures products that are not listed on a national securities exchange or a national securities association registered pursuant to section 15A(a).

(2) *Listing Standards Required.*—Except as otherwise provided in paragraph (7), a national securities exchange or a national securities association registered pursuant to section 15A(a) may trade only security futures products that (A) conform with listing standards that such exchange or association files with the Commission under section 19(b) and (B) meet the criteria specified in section 2(a)(1)(D)(i) of the Commodity Exchange Act.

(3) *Requirements for Listing Standards and Conditions for Trading.*—Such listing standards shall—

(A) except as otherwise provided in a rule, regulation, or order issued pursuant to paragraph (4), require that any security underlying the security future, including each component security of a narrow-based security index, be registered pursuant to section 12 of this title;

(B) require that if the security futures product is not cash settled, the market on which the security futures product is traded have arrangements in place with a registered clearing agency for the payment and delivery of the securities underlying the security futures product;

(C) be no less restrictive than comparable listing standards for options traded on a national securities exchange or national securities association registered pursuant to section 15A(a) of this title;

(D) except as otherwise provided in a rule, regulation, or order issued pursuant to paragraph (4), require that the security future be based upon common stock and such other equity securities as the Commission and the Commodity Futures Trading Commission jointly determine appropriate;

(E) require that the security futures product is cleared by a clearing agency that has in place provisions for linked and coordinated clearing with other clearing agencies that clear security futures products, which permits the security futures product to be purchased on one market and offset on another market that trades such product;

(F) require that only a broker or dealer subject to suitability rules comparable to those of a national securities association registered pursuant to section 15A(a) effect transactions in the security futures product;

(G) require that the security futures product be subject to the prohibition against dual trading in section 4j of the Commodity Exchange Act (7 U.S.C. 6j) and the rules and regulations thereunder or the provisions of section 11(a) of this title and the rules and regulations thereunder, except to the extent otherwise permitted under this title and the rules and regulations thereunder;

(H) require that trading in the security futures product not be readily susceptible to manipulation of the price of such security futures product, nor to causing or being used in the manipulation of the price of any underlying security, option on such security, or option on a group or index including such securities;

(I) require that procedures be in place for coordinated surveillance among the market on which the security futures product is traded, any market on which any security underlying the security futures product is traded, and other markets on which any related security is traded to detect manipulation and insider trading;

(J) require that the market on which the security futures product is traded has in place audit trails necessary or appropriate to facilitate the coordinated surveillance required in subparagraph (I);

(K) require that the market on which the security futures product is traded has in place procedures to coordinate trading halts between such market and any market on which any security underlying the security futures product is traded and other markets on which any related security is traded; and

(L) require that the margin requirements for a security futures product comply with the regulations prescribed pursuant to section 7(c)(2)(B), except that nothing in this subparagraph shall be construed to prevent a national securities exchange or national securities association from requiring higher margin levels for a security futures product when it deems such action to be necessary or appropriate.

(4) *Authority to Modify Certain Listing Standard Requirements.—*

(A) *Authority to Modify.*—The Commission and the Commodity Futures Trading Commission, by rule, regulation, or order, may jointly modify the listing standard requirements specified in subparagraph (A) or (D) of paragraph (3) to the extent such modification fosters the development of fair and orderly markets in security futures products, is necessary or appropriate in the public interest, and is consistent with the protection of investors.

(B) *Authority to Grant Exemptions.*—The Commission and the Commodity Futures Trading Commission, by order, may jointly exempt any person from compliance with the listing standard requirement specified in subparagraph (E) of paragraph (3) to the extent such exemption fosters the development of fair and orderly markets in security futures products, is necessary or appropriate in the public interest, and is consistent with the protection of investors.

(5) *Requirements for Other Persons Trading Security Future Products.*—It shall be unlawful for any person (other than a national securities exchange or a national securities association registered pursuant to section 15A(a)) to constitute, maintain, or provide a marketplace or facilities for bringing together purchasers and sellers of security future products or to otherwise perform with respect to security future products the functions commonly performed by a stock exchange as that term is generally understood, unless a national securities association registered pursuant to section 15A(a) or a national securities exchange of which such person is a member—

(A) has in place procedures for coordinated surveillance among such person, the market trading the securities underlying the security future products, and other markets trading related securities to detect manipulation and insider trading;

(B) has rules to require audit trails necessary or appropriate to facilitate the coordinated surveillance required in subparagraph (A); and

(C) has rules to require such person to coordinate trading halts with markets trading the securities underlying the security future products and other markets trading related securities.

(6) *Deferral of Options on Security Futures Trading.*—No person shall offer to enter into, enter into, or confirm the execution of any put, call, straddle, option, or privilege on a security future, except that, after 3 years after the date of the enactment of this subsection, the Commission and the Commodity Futures Trading Commission may by order jointly determine to permit trading of puts, calls, straddles, options, or privileges on any security future authorized to be traded under the provisions of this Act and the Commodity Exchange Act.

(7) *Deferral of Linked and Coordinated Clearing.*—

(A) Notwithstanding paragraph (2), until the compliance date, a national securities exchange or national securities association registered pursuant to section 15A(a) may trade a security futures product that does not—

(i) conform with any listing standard promulgated to meet the requirement specified in subparagraph (E) of paragraph (3); or

(ii) meet the criterion specified in section 2(a)(1)(D)(i)(IV) of the Commodity Exchange Act.

(B) The Commission and the Commodity Futures Trading Commission shall jointly publish in the Federal Register a notice of the compliance date no later than 165 days before the compliance date.

(C) For purposes of this paragraph, the term "compliance date" means the later of—

(i) 180 days after the end of the first full calendar month period in which the average aggregate comparable share volume for all security futures products based on single equity securities traded on all national securities exchanges, any national securities associations registered pursuant to section 15A(a), and all other persons equals or exceeds 10 percent of the average aggregate comparable share volume of options on single equity securities traded on all national securities exchanges and any national securities associations registered pursuant to section 15A(a); or

(ii) 2 years after the date on which trading in any security futures product commences under this title.

(i) Consistent with this title, each national securities exchange registered pursuant to subsection (a) of this section shall issue such rules as are necessary to avoid duplicative or conflicting rules applicable to any broker or dealer registered with the Commission pursuant to section 15(b) (except paragraph (11) thereof), that is also registered with the Commodity Futures Trading Commission pursuant to section 4f(a) of the Commodity Exchange Act (except paragraph (2) thereof), with respect to the application of—

(1) rules of such national securities exchange of the type specified in section 15(c)(3)(B) involving security futures products; and

(2) similar rules of national securities exchanges registered pursuant to section 6(g) and national securities associations registered pursuant to section 15A(k) involving security futures products.

(j) *Procedures and Rules for Security Future Products.*—A national securities exchange registered pursuant to subsection (a) shall implement the procedures specified in section 6(h)(5)(A) of this title and adopt the rules specified in subparagraphs (B) and (C) of section 6(h)(5) of this title not later than 8 months after the date of receipt of a request from an alternative trading system for such implementation and rules.

(k)(1) To the extent necessary or appropriate in the public interest, to promote fair competition, and consistent with the promotion of market efficiency, innovation, and expansion of investment opportunities, the protection of investors, and the maintenance of fair and orderly markets, the Commission and the Commodity Futures Trading Commission shall jointly issue such rules, regulations, or orders as are necessary and appropriate to permit the offer and sale of a security futures product traded on or subject to the rules of a foreign board of trade to United States persons.

(2) The rules, regulations, or orders adopted under paragraph (1) shall take into account, as appropriate, the nature and size of the markets that the securities underlying the security futures product reflect.

Margin Requirements

Sec. 7. (a) For the purpose of preventing the excessive use of credit for the purchase or carrying of securities, the Board of Governors of the Federal Reserve System shall, prior to the effective date of this section and from time to time thereafter, prescribe rules and regulations with respect to the amount of credit that may be initially extended and subsequently maintained on any security (other than an exempted security or a security future product). For the initial extension of credit, such rules and regulations shall be based upon the following standard: An amount not greater than whichever is the higher of—

(1) 55 per centum of the current market price of the security, or

(2) 100 per centum of the lowest market price of the security during the preceding thirty-six calendar months, but not more than 75 per centum of the current market price.

Such rules and regulations may make appropriate provision with respect to the carrying of undermargined accounts for limited periods and under specified conditions; the withdrawal of funds or securities; the substitution or additional purchases of securities; the transfer of accounts from one lender to another; special or different margin requirements for delayed deliveries, short sales, arbitrage transactions, and securities to which paragraph (2) of this subsection does not apply; the bases and the methods to be used in calculating loans, and margins and market prices; and similar administrative adjustments and details. For the purposes of paragraph (2) of this subsection, until July 1, 1936, the lowest price at which a security has sold on or after July 1, 1933, shall be considered as the lowest price at which such security has sold during the preceding thirty-six calendar months.

(b) Notwithstanding the provisions of subsection (a) of this section, the Board of Governors of the Federal Reserve System may, from time to time, with respect to all or specified securities or transactions, or classes of securities, or classes of transactions, by such rules and regulations (1) prescribe such lower margin requirements for the initial extension or maintenance of credit as it deems necessary or appropriate for the accommodation of commerce and industry, having due regard to the general credit situation of the country, and (2) prescribe such higher margin requirements for the initial extension or maintenance of credit as it may deem necessary or appropriate to prevent the excessive use of credit to finance transactions in securities.

(c) *Unlawful Credit Extension to Customers.*—

(1) *Prohibition.*—It shall be unlawful for any member of a national securities exchange or any broker or dealer, directly or indirectly, to extend or maintain credit or arrange for the extension or maintenance of credit to or for any customer—

(A) on any security (other than an exempted security), except as provided in paragraph (2) in contravention of the rules and regulations which the Board of Governors of the Federal Reserve System (hereafter in this section referred to as the "Board") shall prescribe under subsections (a) and (b); and

(B) without collateral or on any collateral other than securities, except in accordance with such rules and regulations as the Board may prescribe—

(i) to permit under specified conditions and for a limited period any such member, broker, or dealer to maintain a credit initially extended in conformity with the rules and regulations of the Board; and

(ii) to permit the extension or maintenance of credit in cases where the extension or maintenance of credit is not for the purpose of purchasing or carrying securities or of evading or circumventing the provisions of subparagraph (A).

(2) *Margin Regulations.*—

(A) *Compliance with Margin Rules Required.*—It shall be unlawful for any broker, dealer, or member of a national securities exchange to, directly or indirectly, extend or maintain credit to or for, or collect margin from any customer on, any security futures product unless such activities comply with the regulations—

(i) which the Board shall prescribe pursuant to subparagraph (B); or

(ii) if the Board determines to delegate the authority to prescribe such regulations, which the Commission and the Commodity Futures Trading Commission shall jointly prescribe pursuant to subparagraph (B).

If the Board delegates the authority to prescribe such regulations under clause (ii) and the Commission and the Commodity Futures Trading Commission have not jointly prescribed such regulations within a reasonable period of time after the date of such delegation, the Board shall prescribe such regulations pursuant to subparagraph (B).

(B) *Criteria for Issuance of Rules.*—The Board shall prescribe, or, if the authority is delegated pursuant to subparagraph (A)(ii), the Commission and the Commodity Futures Trading Commission shall jointly prescribe, such regulations to establish margin requirements, including the establishment of levels of margin (initial and maintenance) for security futures products under such terms, and at such levels, as the Board deems appropriate, or as the Commission and the Commodity Futures Trading Commission jointly deem appropriate—

(i) to preserve the financial integrity of markets trading security futures products;

(ii) to prevent systemic risk;

(iii) to require that—

(I) the margin requirements for a security future product be consistent with the margin requirements for comparable option contracts traded on any exchange registered pursuant to section 6(a) of this title; and

(II) initial and maintenance margin levels for a security future product not be lower than the lowest level of margin, exclusive of premium, required for any comparable option contract traded on any exchange registered pursuant to section 6(a) of this title, other than an option on a security future;

except that nothing in this subparagraph shall be construed to prevent a national securities exchange or national securities association from requiring higher margin levels for a security future product when it deems such action to be necessary or appropriate; and

(iv) to ensure that the margin requirements (other than levels of margin), including the type, form, and use of collateral for security futures products, are and remain consistent with the requirements established by the Board, pursuant to subparagraphs (A) and (B) of paragraph (1).

(3) *Exception.*—This subsection and the rules and regulations issued under this subsection shall not apply to any credit extended, maintained, or arranged by a member of a national securities exchange or a broker or dealer to or for a member of a national securities exchange or a registered broker or dealer—

(A) a substantial portion of whose business consists of transactions with persons other than brokers or dealers; or

(B) to finance its activities as a market maker or an underwriter;

except that the Board may impose such rules and regulations, in whole or in part, on any credit otherwise exempted by this paragraph if the Board determines that such action is necessary or appropriate in the public interest or for the protection of investors.

(d) *Unlawful Credit Extension in Violation of Rules and Regulations; Exceptions to Application of Rules, Etc.*—

(1) *Prohibition.*—It shall be unlawful for any person not subject to subsection (c) to extend or maintain credit or to arrange for the extension or maintenance of credit for the purpose of purchasing or carrying any security, in contravention of such rules and regulations as the Board shall prescribe to prevent the excessive use of credit for the purchasing or carrying of or trading in securities in circumvention of the other provisions of this section. Such rules and regulations may impose upon all loans made for the purpose of purchasing or carrying securities limitations similar to those imposed upon members, brokers, or dealers by subsection (c) and the rules and regulations thereunder.

(2) *Exceptions.*—This subsection and the rules and regulations issued under this subsection shall not apply to any credit extended, maintained, or arranged—

(A) by a person not in the ordinary course of business;

(B) on an exempted security;

(C) to or for a member of a national securities exchange or a registered broker or dealer—

(i) a substantial portion of whose business consists of transactions with persons other than brokers or dealers; or

(ii) to finance its activities as a market maker or an underwriter;

(D) by a bank on a security other than an equity security; or

(E) as the Board shall, by such rules, regulations, or orders as it may deem necessary or appropriate in the public interest or for the protection of investors, exempt, either unconditionally or upon specified terms and conditions or for stated periods, from the operation of this subsection and the rules and regulations thereunder.

(3) *Board Authority.*—The Board may impose such rules and regulations, in whole or in part, on any credit otherwise exempted by subparagraph (C) if it determines that such action is necessary or appropriate in the public interest or for the protection of investors.

(e) The provisions of this section or the rules and regulations thereunder shall not apply on or before July 1, 1937, to any loan or extension of credit made prior to the enactment of this title or to the maintenance, renewal, or extension of any such loan or credit, except to the extent that the Board of Governors of the Federal Reserve System may by rules and regulations prescribe as necessary to prevent the circumvention of the provisions of this section or the rules and regulations thereunder by means of withdrawals of funds or securities, substitutions of securities, or additional purchases or by any other device.

(f)(1) It is unlawful for any United States person, or any foreign person controlled by a United States person or acting on behalf of or in conjunction with such person, to obtain, receive, or enjoy the beneficial use of a loan or other extension of credit from any lender (without regard to whether the lender's office or place of business is in a State or the transaction occurred in whole or in part within a State) for the purpose of (A) purchasing or carrying United States securities, or (B) purchasing or carrying within the United States of any other securities, if, under this section or rules and regulations prescribed thereunder, the loan or other credit transaction is prohibited or would be prohibited if it had been made or the transaction had otherwise occurred in a lender's office or other place of business in a State.

(2) For the purposes of this subsection—

(A) The term "United States person" includes a person which is organized or exists under the laws of any State or, in the case of a natural person, a citizen or resident of the United States; a domestic estate; or a trust in which one or more of the foregoing persons has a cumulative direct or indirect beneficial interest in excess of 50 per centum of the value of the trust.

(B) The term "United States security" means a security (other than an exempted security) issued by a person incorporated under the laws of any State, or whose principal place of business is within a State.

(C) The term "foreign person controlled by a United States person" includes any noncorporate entity in which United States persons directly or indirectly have more than a 50 per centum beneficial interest, and any corporation in which one or more United States persons, directly or indirectly, own stock possessing more than 50 per centum of the total combined voting power of all classes of stock entitled to vote, or more than 50per centum of the total value of shares of all classes of stock.

(3) The Board of Governors of the Federal Reserve System may, in its discretion and with due regard for the purposes of this section, by rule or regulation exempt any class of United States persons or foreign persons controlled by a United States person from the application of this subsection.

(g) Subject to such rules and regulations as the Board of Governors of the Federal Reserve System may adopt in the public interest and for the protection of investors, no member of a national securities exchange or broker or dealer shall be deemed to have extended or maintained credit or arranged for the extension or maintenance of credit for the purpose of purchasing a security within the meaning of this section, by reason of a bona fide agreement for delayed delivery of a mortgage related security or a small business related security against full payment of the purchase price thereof upon such delivery within one hundred and eighty days after the purchase, or within such shorter period as the Board of Governors of the Federal Reserve System may prescribe by rule or regulation.

Restrictions on Borrowing and Lending by Members, Brokers, and Dealers

Sec. 8. It shall be unlawful for any registered broker or dealer, member of a national securities exchange, or broker or dealer who transacts a business in securities through the medium of any member of a national securities exchange directly or indirectly—

(a) In contravention of such rules and regulations as the Commission shall prescribe for the protection of investors to hypothecate or arrange for the hypothecation of any securities carried for the account of any customer under circumstances (1) that will permit the commingling of his securities without his written consent with the securities of any other customer, (2) that will permit such securities to be commingled with the securities of any person other than a bona fide customer, or (3) that will permit such securities to be hypothecated, or subjected to any lien or claim of the pledgee, for a sum in excess of the aggregate indebtedness of such customers in respect of such securities.

(b) To lend or arrange for the lending of any securities carried for the account of any customer without the written consent of such customer or in contravention of such rules and regulations as the Commission shall prescribe for the protection of investors.

Manipulation of Security Prices

Sec. 9. (a) It shall be unlawful for any person, directly or indirectly, by the use of the mails or any means or instrumentality of interstate commerce, or of any facility of any national securities exchange, or for any member of a national securities exchange—

(1) For the purpose of creating a false or misleading appearance of active trading in any security registered on a national securities exchange, or a false or misleading appearance with respect to the market for any such security, (A) to effect any transaction in such security which involves no change in the beneficial ownership thereof, or (B) to enter an order or orders for the purchase of such security with the knowledge that an order or orders of substantially the same size, at substantially the same time and at substantially the same price, for the sale of any such security, has been or will be entered by or for the same or different parties, or (C) to enter any order or orders for the sale of any such security with the knowledge that an order or orders of substantially the same size, at substantially the same time, and at substantially the same price, for the purchase of such security, has been or will be entered by or for the same or different parties.

(2) To effect, alone or with one or more other persons, a series of transactions in any security registered on a national securities exchange or in connection with any security-based swap agreement (as defined in section 206B of the Gramm–Leach–Bliley Act) with respect to such security creating actual or apparent active trading in such security, or raising or depressing the price of such security, for the purpose of inducing the purchase or sale of such security by others.

(3) If a dealer or broker, or other person selling or offering for sale or purchasing or offering to purchase the security or a security-based swap agreement (as defined in section 206B of the Gramm–Leach–Bliley Act) with respect to such security, to induce the purchase or sale of any security registered on a national securities exchange or any security-based swap agreement (as defined in section 206B of the Gramm–Leach–Bliley Act) with respect to such security by the circulation or dissemination in the ordinary course of business of information to the effect that the price of any such security will or is likely to rise or fall because of market operations of any one or more persons conducted for the purpose of raising or depressing the price of such security.

(4) If a dealer or broker, or the person selling or offering for sale or purchasing or offering to purchase the security or a security-based swap agreement (as defined in section 206B of the Gramm–Leach–Bliley Act) with respect to such security, to make, regarding any security registered on a national securities exchange or any security-based swap agreement (as defined in section 206B of the Gramm–Leach–Bliley Act) with respect to such security, for the purpose of inducing the purchase or sale of such security or such security-based swap agreement, any statement which was at the time and in the light of the circumstances under which it was made, false or misleading with respect to any material fact, and which he knew or had reasonable ground to believe was so false or misleading.

(5) For a consideration, received directly or indirectly from a dealer or broker, or other person selling or offering for sale or purchasing or offering to purchase the security or a security-based swap agreement (as defined in section 206B of the Gramm–Leach–Bliley Act) with respect to such security, to induce the purchase of any security registered on a national securities exchange or any security-based swap agreement (as defined in section 206B of the Gramm–Leach–Bliley Act) with respect to such security by the circulation or dissemination of information to the effect that the price of any such security will or is likely to rise or fall because of the market operations of any one or more persons conducted for the purpose of raising or depressing the price of such security.

(6) To effect either alone or with one or more other persons any series of transactions for the purchase and/or sale of any security registered on a national securities exchange for the purpose of pegging, fixing, or stabilizing the price of such security in contravention of such rules and regulations as the Commission may prescribe as necessary or appropriate in the public interest or for the protection of investors.

(b) It shall be unlawful for any person to effect, by use of any facility of a national securities exchange, in contravention of such rules and regulations as the Commission may prescribe as necessary or appropriate in the public interest or for the protection of investors—

(1) any transaction in connection with any security whereby any party to such transaction acquires (A) any put, call, straddle, or other option or privilege of buying the security from or selling the security to another without being bound to do so or (B) any security futures product on the security; or

(2) any transaction in connection with any security with relation to which he has, directly or indirectly, any interest in any (A) such put, call, straddle, option, or privilege; or (B) such security futures product; or

(3) any transaction in any security for the account of any person who he has reason to believe has, and who actually has, directly or indirectly, any interest in any (A) such put, call, straddle, option, or privilege; or (B) such security futures product with relation to such security.

(c) It shall be unlawful for any member of a national securities exchange directly or indirectly to endorse or guarantee the performance of any put, call, straddle, option, or privilege in relation to any security registered on a national securities exchange, in contravention of such rules and regulations as the Commission may prescribe as necessary or appropriate in the public interest or for the protection of investors.

(d) The terms "put", "call", "straddle", "option", or "privilege" as used in this section shall not include any registered warrant, right, or convertible security.

(e) Any person who willfully participates in any act or transaction in violation of subsection (a), (b), or (c) of this section, shall be liable to any person who shall purchase or sell any security at a price which was affected by such act or transaction, and the person so injured may sue in law or in equity in any court of competent jurisdiction to recover the damages sustained as a result of any such act or transaction. In any such suit the court may, in its discretion, require an undertaking for the payment of the costs of such suit, and assess reasonable costs, including reasonable attorneys' fees, against either party litigant. Every person who becomes liable to make any payment under this subsection may recover contribution as in cases of contract from any person who, if joined in the original suit, would have been liable to make the same payment. No action shall be maintained to enforce any liability created under this section, unless brought within one year after the discovery of the facts constituting the violation and within three years after such violation.

(f) The provisions of subsection (a) shall not apply to an exempted security.

(g)(1) Notwithstanding any other provision of law, the Commission shall have the authority to regulate the trading of any put, call, straddle, option, or privilege on any security, certificate of deposit, or group or index of securities (including any interest therein or based on the value thereof), or any put, call, straddle, option, or privilege entered into on a national securities exchange relating to foreign currency (but not, with respect to any of the foregoing, an option on a contract for future delivery other than a security futures product).

(2) Notwithstanding the Commodity Exchange Act, the Commission shall have the authority to regulate the trading of any security futures product to the extent provided in the securities laws.

(h) *Limitations on Practices That Affect Market Volatility.*—It shall be unlawful for any person, by the use of the mails or any means or instrumentality of interstate commerce or of any facility of any national securities exchange, to use or employ any act or practice in connection with the purchase or sale of any equity security in contravention of such rules or regulations as the Commission may adopt, consistent with the public interest, the protection of investors, and the maintenance of fair and orderly markets—

(1) to prescribe means reasonably designed to prevent manipulation of price levels of the equity securities market or a substantial segment thereof; and

(2) to prohibit or constrain, during periods of extraordinary market volatility, any trading practice in connection with the purchase or sale of equity securities that the Commission determines (A) has previously contributed significantly to extraordinary levels of volatility that have threatened the maintenance of fair and orderly markets; and (B) is reasonably certain to engender such levels of volatility if not prohibited or constrained.

In adopting rules under paragraph (2), the Commission shall, consistent with the purposes of this subsection, minimize the impact on the normal operations of the market and a natural person's freedom to buy or sell any equity security.

(i) The authority of the Commission under this section with respect to security-based swap agreements (as defined in section 206B of the Gramm–Leach–Bliley Act) shall be subject to the restrictions and limitations of section 3A(b) of this title.

Regulation of the Use of Manipulative and Deceptive Devices

Sec. 10. It shall be unlawful for any person, directly or indirectly, by the use of any means or instrumentality of interstate commerce or of the mails, or of any facility of any national securities exchange—

(a)(1) To effect a short sale, or to use or employ any stop-loss order in connection with the purchase or sale, of any security registered on a national securities exchange, in contravention of such rules and regulations as the Commission may prescribe as necessary or appropriate in the public interest or for the protection of investors.

(2) Paragraph (1) of this subsection shall not apply to security futures products.

(b) To use or employ, in connection with the purchase or sale of any security registered on a national securities exchange or any security not so registered, or any securities-based swap agreement (as defined in section 206B of the Gramm–Leach–Bliley Act), any manipulative or deceptive device or contrivance in contravention of such rules and regulations as the Commission may prescribe as necessary or appropriate in the public interest or for the protection of investors.

Rules promulgated under subsection (b) that prohibit fraud, manipulation, or insider trading (but not rules imposing or specifying reporting or recordkeeping requirements, procedures, or standards as prophylactic measures against fraud, manipulation, or insider trading), and judicial precedents decided under subsection (b) and rules promulgated thereunder that prohibit fraud, manipulation, or insider trading, shall apply to security-based swap agreements (as defined in section 206B of the Gramm–Leach–Bliley Act) to the same extent as they apply to securities. Judicial precedents decided under section 17(a) of the Securities Act of 1933 and sections 9, 15, 16, 20, and 21A of this title, and judicial precedents decided under applicable rules promulgated under such sections, shall apply to security-based swap agreements (as defined in section 206B of the Gramm–Leach–Bliley Act) to the same extent as they apply to securities.

Sec. 10A. Audit Requirements.

(a) *In General.*—Each audit required pursuant to this title of the financial statements of an issuer by a registered public accounting firm shall include, in accordance with generally accepted auditing standards, as may be modified or supplemented from time to time by the Commission—

(1) procedures designed to provide reasonable assurance of detecting illegal acts that would have a direct and material effect on the determination of financial statement amounts;

(2) procedures designed to identify related party transactions that are material to the financial statements or otherwise require disclosure therein; and

(3) an evaluation of whether there is substantial doubt about the ability of the issuer to continue as a going concern during the ensuing fiscal year.

(b) *Required Response to Audit Discoveries.*—

(1) *Investigation and Report to Management.*—If, in the course of conducting an audit pursuant to this title to which subsection (a) applies, the registered public accounting firm detects or otherwise becomes aware of information indicating that an illegal act (whether or not perceived to have a material effect on the financial statements of the issuer) has or may have occurred, the firm shall, in accordance with generally accepted auditing standards, as may be modified or supplemented from time to time by the Commission—

(A)(i) determine whether it is likely that an illegal act has occurred; and

(ii) if so, determine and consider the possible effect of the illegal act on the financial statements of the issuer, including any contingent monetary effects, such as fines, penalties, and damages; and

(B) as soon as practicable, inform the appropriate level of the management of the issuer and assure that the audit committee of the issuer, or the board of directors of the issuer in the absence of such a committee, is adequately informed with respect to illegal acts that have been detected or have otherwise come to the attention of such firm in the course of the audit, unless the illegal act is clearly inconsequential.

(2) *Response to Failure to Take Remedial Action.*—If, after determining that the audit committee of the board of directors of the

issuer, or the board of directors of the issuer in the absence of an audit committee, is adequately informed with respect to illegal acts that have been detected or have otherwise come to the attention of the firm in the course of the audit of such firm, the registered public accounting firm concludes that—

(A) the illegal act has a material effect on the financial statements of the issuer;

(B) the senior management has not taken, and the board of directors has not caused senior management to take, timely and appropriate remedial actions with respect to the illegal act; and

(C) the failure to take remedial action is reasonably expected to warrant departure from a standard report of the auditor, when made, or warrant resignation from the audit engagement;

the registered public accounting firm shall, as soon as practicable, directly report its conclusions to the board of directors.

(3) *Notice to Commission; Response to Failure to Notify.*—An issuer whose board of directors receives a report under paragraph (2) shall inform the Commission by notice not later than 1 business day after the receipt of such report and shall furnish the registered public accounting firm making such report with a copy of the notice furnished to the Commission. If the registered public accounting firm fails to receive a copy of the notice before the expiration of the required 1–business–day period, the registered public accounting firm shall—

(A) resign from the engagement; or

(B) furnish to the Commission a copy of its report (or the documentation of any oral report given) not later than 1 business day following such failure to receive notice.

(4) *Report After Resignation.*—If a registered public accounting firm resigns from an engagement under paragraph (3)(A), the accountant shall, not later than 1 business day following the failure by the issuer to notify the Commission under paragraph (3), furnish to the Commission a copy of the report of the firm (or the documentation of any oral report given).

(c) *Auditor Liability Limitation.*—No registered public accounting firm shall be liable in a private action for any finding, conclusion, or statement expressed in a report made pursuant to paragraph (3) or (4) of subsection (b), including any rule promulgated pursuant thereto.

(d) *Civil Penalties in Cease–and–Desist Proceedings.*—If the Commission finds, after notice and opportunity for hearing in a proceeding instituted pursuant to section 21C, that an independent public accountant has willfully violated paragraph (3) or (4) of subsection (b), the Commission may, in addition to entering an order under section 21C, impose a civil penalty against the independent public accountant and any other person that the Commission finds was a cause of such violation. The determination to impose a civil penalty and the amount of the penalty shall be governed by the standards set forth in section 21B.

(e) *Preservation of Existing Authority.*—Except as provided in subsection (d), nothing in this section shall be held to limit or otherwise affect the authority of the Commission under this title.

(f) *"Illegal Act" Definitions.*—As used in this section, the term "illegal act" means an act or omission that violates any law, or any rule or regulation having the force of law.

As used in this section, the term "issuer" means an issuer (as defined in section 3), the securities of which are registered under section 12, or that is required to file reports pursuant to section 15(d), or that files or has filed a registration statement that has not yet become effective under the Securities Act of 1933 (15 U.S.C. 77a et seq.), and that it has not withdrawn.

(g) Prohibited Activities.—Except as provided in subsection (h), it shall be unlawful for a registered public accounting firm (and any associated person of that firm, to the extent determined appropriate by the Commission) that performs for any issuer any audit required by this title or the rules of the Commission under this title or, beginning 180 days after the date of commencement of the operations of the Public Company Accounting Oversight Board established under section 101 of the Sarbanes–Oxley Act of 2002 (in this section referred to as the "Board"), the rules of the Board, to provide to that issuer, contemporaneously with the audit, any non-audit service, including—

(1) bookkeeping or other services related to the accounting records or financial statements of the audit client;

(2) financial information systems design and implementation;

(3) appraisal or valuation services, fairness opinions, or contribution-in-kind reports;

(4) actuarial services;

(5) internal audit outsourcing services;

(6) management functions or human resources;

(7) broker or dealer, investment adviser, or investment banking services;

(8) legal services and expert services unrelated to the audit; and

(9) any other service that the Board determines, by regulation, is impermissible.

(h) Preapproval Required for Non-Audit Services.—A registered public accounting firm may engage in any non-audit service, including tax services, that is not described in any of paragraphs (1) through (9) of subsection (g) for an audit client, only if the activity is approved in advance by the audit committee of the issuer, in accordance with subsection (i).

(i) Preapproval Requirements.—

(1) In general.—

(A) Audit committee action.—All auditing services (which may entail providing comfort letters in connection with securities underwritings or statutory audits required for insurance companies for purposes of State law) and non-audit services, other than as provided in subparagraph (B), provided to an issuer by the auditor of the issuer shall be preapproved by the audit committee of the issuer.

(B) De minimus exception.—The preapproval requirement under subparagraph (A) is waived with respect to the provision of non-audit services for an issuer, if—

(i) the aggregate amount of all such non-audit services provided to the issuer constitutes not more than 5 percent of the total amount of revenues paid by the issuer to its auditor during the fiscal year in which the nonaudit services are provided;

(ii) such services were not recognized by the issuer at the time of the engagement to be non-audit services; and

(iii) such services are promptly brought to the attention of the audit committee of the issuer and approved prior to the completion of the audit by the audit committee or by 1 or more members of the audit committee who are members of the board of directors to whom authority to grant such approvals has been delegated by the audit committee.

(2) Disclosure to investors.—Approval by an audit committee of an issuer under this subsection of a non-audit service to be performed by the auditor of the issuer shall be disclosed to investors in periodic reports required by section 13(a).

(3) Delegation authority.—The audit committee of an issuer may delegate to 1 or more designated members of the audit committee who are independent directors of the board of directors, the authority to grant preapprovals required by this subsection. The decisions of any member to whom authority is delegated under this paragraph to preapprove an activity under this subsection shall be presented to the full audit committee at each of its scheduled meetings.

(4) Approval of audit services for other purposes.—In carrying out its duties under subsection (m)(2), if the audit committee of an issuer approves an audit service within the scope of the engagement of the auditor, such audit service shall be deemed to have been preapproved for purposes of this subsection.

(j) Audit Partner Rotation.—It shall be unlawful for a registered public accounting firm to provide audit services to an issuer if the lead (or coordinating) audit partner (having primary responsibility for the audit), or the audit partner responsible for reviewing the audit, has performed audit services for that issuer in each of the 5 previous fiscal years of that issuer.

(k) Reports to Audit Committees.—Each registered public accounting firm that performs for any issuer any audit required by this title shall timely report to the audit committee of the issuer—

(1) all critical accounting policies and practices to be used;

(2) all alternative treatments of financial information within generally accepted accounting principles that have been discussed with management officials of the issuer, ramifications of the use of such alternative disclosures and treatments, and the treatment preferred by the registered public accounting firm; and

(3) other material written communications between the registered public accounting firm and the management of the issuer, such as any management letter or schedule of unadjusted differences.

(*l*) Conflicts of Interest.—It shall be unlawful for a registered public accounting firm to perform for an issuer any audit service required by this title, if a chief executive officer, controller, chief financial officer, chief accounting officer, or any person serving in an equivalent position for the issuer, was employed by that registered independent public accounting firm and participated in any capacity in the audit of that issuer during the 1-year period preceding the date of the initiation of the audit.

(m) Standards Relating to Audit Committees.—

(1) Commission rules.—

(A) In general.—Effective not later than 270 days after the date of enactment of this subsection, the Commission shall, by rule, direct the national securities exchanges and national securities associations to prohibit the listing of any security of an issuer that is not in compliance with the requirements of any portion of paragraphs (2) through (6).

(B) Opportunity to cure defects.—The rules of the Commission under subparagraph (A) shall provide for appropriate procedures for an issuer to have an opportunity to cure any defects that would be the basis for a prohibition under subparagraph (A), before the imposition of such prohibition.

(2) Responsibilities relating to registered public accounting firms.—The audit committee of each issuer, in its capacity as a committee of the board of directors, shall be directly responsible for the appointment, compensation, and oversight of the work of any registered public accounting firm employed by that issuer (including resolution of disagreements between management and the auditor regarding financial reporting) for the purpose of preparing or issuing an audit report or related work, and each such registered public accounting firm shall report directly to the audit committee.

(3) Independence.—

(A) In general.—Each member of the audit committee of the issuer shall be a member of the board of directors of the issuer, and shall otherwise be independent.

(B) Criteria.—In order to be considered to be independent for purposes of this paragraph, a member of an audit committee of an issuer may not, other than in his or her capacity as a member of the audit committee, the board of directors, or any other board committee—

(i) accept any consulting, advisory, or other compensatory fee from the issuer; or

(ii) be an affiliated person of the issuer or any subsidiary thereof.

(C) Exemption authority.—The Commission may exempt from the requirements of subparagraph (B) a particular relationship with respect to audit committee members, as the Commission determines appropriate in light of the circumstances.

(4) Complaints.—Each audit committee shall establish procedures for—

(A) the receipt, retention, and treatment of complaints received by the issuer regarding accounting, internal accounting controls, or auditing matters; and

(B) the confidential, anonymous submission by employees of the issuer of concerns regarding questionable accounting or auditing matters.

(5) Authority to engage advisers.—Each audit committee shall have the authority to engage independent counsel and other advisers, as it determines necessary to carry out its duties.

(6) Funding.—Each issuer shall provide for appropriate funding, as determined by the audit committee, in its capacity as a committee of the board of directors, for payment of compensation—

(A) to the registered public accounting firm employed by the issuer for the purpose of rendering or issuing an audit report; and

(B) to any advisers employed by the audit committee under paragraph (5).

Trading by Members of Exchanges, Brokers, and Dealers

Sec. 11. (a)(1) It shall be unlawful for any member of a national securities exchange to effect any transaction on such exchange for its own account, the account of an associated person, or an account with respect to which it or an associated person thereof exercises investment discretion: *Provided, however,* That this paragraph shall not make unlawful—

(A) any transaction by a dealer acting in the capacity of market maker;

(B) any transaction for the account of an odd-lot dealer in a security in which he is so registered;

(C) any stabilizing transaction effected in compliance with rules under section 10(b) of this title to facilitate a distribution of a security in which the member effecting such transaction is participating;

(D) any bona fide arbitrage transaction, any bona fide hedge transaction involving a long or short position in an equity security and a long or short position in a security entitling the holder to acquire or sell such equity security, or any risk arbitrage transaction in connection with a merger, acquisition, tender offer, or similar transaction involving a recapitalization;

(E) any transaction for the account of a natural person, the estate of a natural person, or a trust created by a natural person for himself or another natural person;

(F) any transaction to offset a transaction made in error;

(G) any other transaction for a member's own account provided that (i) such member is primarily engaged in the business of underwriting and distributing securities issued by other persons, selling securities to customers, and acting as broker, or any one or more of such activities, and whose gross income normally is derived principally from such business and related activities and (ii) such transaction is effected in compliance with rules of the Commission which, at a minimum, assure that the transaction is not inconsistent with the maintenance of fair and orderly markets and yields priority, parity, and precedence in execution to orders for the account of persons who are not members or associated with members of the exchange;

(H) any transaction for an account with respect to which such member or an associated person thereof exercises investment discretion if such member—

(i) has obtained, from the person or persons authorized to transact business for the account, express authorization for such member or associated person to effect such transactions prior to engaging in the practice of effecting such transactions;

(ii) furnishes the person or persons authorized to transact business for the account with a statement at least annually disclosing the aggregate compensation received by the exchange member in effecting such transactions; and

(iii) complies with any rules the Commission has prescribed with respect to the requirements of clauses (i) and (ii); and

(I) any other transaction of a kind which the Commission, by rule, determines is consistent with the purposes of this paragraph, the protection of investors, and the maintenance of fair and orderly markets.

(2) The Commission, by rule, as it deems necessary or appropriate in the public interest and for the protection of investors, to maintain fair and orderly markets, or to assure equal regulation of exchange markets and markets occurring otherwise than on an exchange, may regulate or prohibit:

(A) transactions on a national securities exchange not unlawful under paragraph (1) of this subsection effected by any member thereof for its own account (unless such member is acting in the capacity of market maker or odd-lot dealer), the account of an associated person, or an account with respect to which such member or an associated person thereof exercises investment discretion;

(B) transactions otherwise than on a national securities exchange effected by use of the mails or any means or instrumentality of interstate commerce by any member of a national securities exchange, broker, or dealer for the account of such member, broker, or dealer (unless such member, broker, or dealer is acting in the capacity of a market maker) the account of an associated person, or an account with respect to which such member, broker, or dealer or associated person thereof exercises investment discretion; and

(C) transactions on a national securities exchange effected by any broker or dealer not a member thereof for the account of such broker or dealer (unless such broker or dealer is acting in the capacity of market maker), the account of an associated person, or an account with respect to which such broker or dealer or associated person thereof exercises investment discretion.

(3) The provisions of paragraph (1) of this subsection insofar as they apply to transactions on a national securities exchange effected by a member thereof who was a member on February 1, 1978 shall not become effective until February 1, 1979. Nothing in this paragraph shall be construed to impair or limit the authority of the Commission to regulate or prohibit such transactions prior to February 1, 1979, pursuant to paragraph (2) of this subsection.

(b) When not in contravention of such rules and regulations as the Commission may prescribe as necessary or appropriate in the public interest and for the protection of investors, to maintain fair and orderly markets, or to remove impediments to and perfect the mechanism of a national market system, the rules of a national securities exchange may permit (1) a member to be registered as an odd-lot dealer and as such to buy and sell for his own account so far as may be reasonably necessary to carry on such odd-lot transactions, and (2) a member to be registered as a specialist. Under the rules and regulations of the Commission a specialist may be permitted to act as a broker and dealer or limited to acting as a broker or dealer. It shall be unlawful for a specialist or an official of the exchange to disclose information in regard to orders placed with such specialist which is not available to all members of the exchange, to any person other than an official of the exchange, a representative of the Commission, or a specialist who may be acting for such specialist: *Provided, however,* That the Commission, by rule, may require disclosure to all members of the exchange of all orders placed with specialists, under such rules and regulations as the Commission may prescribe as necessary or appropriate in the public interest or for the protection of investors. It shall also be unlawful for a specialist permitted to act as a broker and dealer to effect on the exchange as broker any transaction except upon a market or limited price order.

(c) If because of the limited volume of transactions effected on an exchange, it is in the opinion of the Commission impracticable and not necessary or appropriate in the public interest or for the protection of investors to apply any of the foregoing provisions of this section or the rules and regulations thereunder, the Commission shall have power, upon application of the exchange and on a showing that the rules of such exchange are otherwise adequate for the protection of investors, to exempt such exchange and its members from any such provision or rules and regulations.

(d) It shall be unlawful for a member of a national securities exchange who is both a dealer and a broker, or for any person who both as a broker and a dealer transacts a business in securities through the medium of a member or otherwise, to effect through the use of any facility of a national securities exchange or of the mails or of any means or instrumentality of interstate commerce, or otherwise in the case of a member, (1) any transaction in connection with which, directly or indirectly, he extends or maintains or arranges for the extension or maintenance of credit to or for a customer on any security (other than an exempted security) which was a part of a new issue in the distribution of which he participated as a member of a selling syndicate or group within thirty days prior to such transaction: *Provided,* That credit shall not be deemed extended by reason of a bona fide delayed delivery of (i) any such security against full payment of the entire purchase price thereof upon such delivery within thirty-five days after such purchase or (ii) any mortgage related security or any small business related security against full payment of the entire purchase price thereof upon such delivery within one hundred and eighty days after such purchase, or within such shorter period as the Commission may prescribe by rule or regulation, or (2) any transaction with respect to any security (other than an exempted security) unless, if the transaction is with a customer, he discloses to such customer in writing at or before the completion of the transaction whether he is acting as a dealer for his own account, as a broker for such customer, or as a broker for some other person.

National Market System for Securities; Securities Information Processors

Sec. 11A. (a)(1) The Congress finds that—

(A) The securities markets are an important national asset which must be preserved and strengthened.

(B) New data processing and communications techniques create the opportunity for more efficient and effective market operations.

(C) It is in the public interest and appropriate for the protection of investors and the maintenance of fair and orderly markets to assure—

(i) economically efficient execution of securities transactions;

(ii) fair competition among brokers and dealers, among exchange markets, and between exchange markets and markets other than exchange markets;

(iii) the availability to brokers, dealers, and investors of information with respect to quotations for and transactions in securities;

(iv) the practicability of brokers executing investors' orders in the best market; and

(v) an opportunity, consistent with the provisions of clauses (i) and (iv) of this subparagraph, for investors' orders to be executed without the participation of a dealer.

(D) The linking of all markets for qualified securities through communication and data processing facilities will foster efficiency, enhance competition, increase the information available to brokers, dealers, and investors, facilitate the offsetting of investors' orders, and contribute to best execution of such orders.

(2) The Commission is directed, therefore, having due regard for the public interest, the protection of investors, and the maintenance of fair and orderly markets, to use its authority under this title to facilitate the establishment of a national market system for securities (which may include subsystems for particular types of securities with unique trading characteristics) in accordance with the findings and to carry out the objectives set forth in paragraph (1) of this subsection. The Commission, by rule, shall designate the securities or classes of securities qualified for trading in the national market system from among securities other than exempted securities. (Securities or classes of securities so designated hereinafter in this section referred to as "qualified securities".)

(3) The Commission is authorized in furtherance of the directive in paragraph (2) of this subsection—

(A) to create one or more advisory committees pursuant to the Federal Advisory Committee Act (which shall be in addition to the National Market Advisory Board established pursuant to subsection (d) of this section) and to employ one or more outside experts;

(B) by rule or order, to authorize or require self-regulatory organizations to act jointly with respect to matters as to which they share authority under this title in planning, developing, operating, or regulating a national market system (or a subsystem thereof) or one or more facilities thereof; and

(C) to conduct studies and make recommendations to the Congress from time to time as to the possible need for modifications of the scheme of self-regulation provided for in this title so as to adapt it to a national market system.

(b)(1) Except as otherwise provided in this section, it shall be unlawful for any securities information processor unless registered in accordance with this subsection, directly or indirectly, to make use of the mails or any means or instrumentality of interstate commerce to perform the functions of a securities information processor. The Commission, by rule or order, upon its own motion or upon application, may conditionally or unconditionally exempt any securities information processor or class of securities information processors or security or class of securities from any provision of this section or the rules or regulations thereunder, if the Commission finds that such exemption is consistent with the public interest, the protection of investors, and the purposes of this section, including the maintenance of fair and orderly markets in securities and the removal of impediments to and perfection of the mechanism of a national market system: *Provided*, however, That a securities information processor not acting as the exclusive processor of any information with respect to quotations for or transactions in securities is exempt from the requirement to register in accordance with this subsection unless the Commission, by rule or order, finds that the registration of such securities information processor is necessary or appropriate in the public interest, for the protection of investors, or for the achievement of the purposes of this section.

(2) A securities information processor may be registered by filing with the Commission an application for registration in such form as the Commission, by rule, may prescribe containing the address of its principal office, or offices, the names of the securities and markets for which it is then acting and for which it proposes to act as a securities information processor, and such other information and documents as the Commission, by rule, may prescribe with regard to performance capability, standards and procedures for the collection, processing, distribution, and publication of information with respect to quotations for and transactions in securities, personnel qualifications, financial condition, and such other matters as the Commission determines to be germane to the provisions of this title and the rules and regulations thereunder, or necessary or appropriate in furtherance of the purposes of this section.

(3) The Commission shall, upon the filing of an application for registration pursuant to paragraph (2) of this subsection, publish notice of the filing and afford interested persons an opportunity to submit written data, views, and arguments concerning such application. Within ninety days of the date of the publication of such notice (or within such longer period as to which the applicant consents) the Commission shall—

(A) by order grant such registration, or

(B) institute proceedings to determine whether registration should be denied. Such proceedings shall include notice of the grounds for denial under consideration and opportunity for hearing and shall be concluded within one hundred eighty days of the date of publication of notice of the filing of the application for registration. At the conclusion of such proceedings the Commission, by order, shall grant or deny such registration. The Commission may extend the time for the conclusion of such proceedings for up to sixty days if it finds good cause for such extension and publishes its reasons for so finding or for such longer periods as to which the applicant consents.

The Commission shall grant the registration of a securities information processor if the Commission finds that such securities information processor is so organized, and has the capacity, to be able to assure the prompt, accurate, and reliable performance of its functions as a securities information processor, comply with the provisions of this title and the rules and regulations thereunder, carry out its functions in a manner consistent with the purposes of this section, and, insofar as it is acting as an exclusive processor, operate fairly and efficiently. The Commission shall deny the registration of a securities information processor if the Commission does not make any such finding.

(4) A registered securities information processor may, upon such terms and conditions as the Commission deems necessary or appropriate in the public interest or for the protection of investors, withdraw from registration by filing a written notice of withdrawal with the Commission. If the Commission finds that any registered securities information processor is no longer in existence or has ceased to do business in the capacity specified in its application for registration, the Commission, by order, shall cancel the registration.

(5)(A) If any registered securities information processor prohibits or limits any person in respect of access to services offered, directly or indirectly, by such securities information processor, the registered securities information processor shall promptly file notice thereof with the Commission. The notice shall be in such form and contain such information as the Commission, by rule, may prescribe as necessary or appropriate in the public interest or for the protection of investors. Any prohibition or limitation on access to services with respect to which a registered securities information processor is required by this paragraph to file notice shall be subject to review by the Commission on its own motion, or upon application by any person aggrieved thereby filed within thirty days after such notice has been filed with the Commission and received by such aggrieved person, or within such longer period as the Commission may determine. Application to the Commission for review, or the institution of review by the Commission on its own motion, shall not operate as a stay of such prohibition or limitation, unless the Commission otherwise orders, summarily or after notice and opportunity for hearing on the question of a stay (which hearing may consist solely of the submission of affidavits or presentation of oral arguments). The Commission shall establish for appropriate cases an expedited procedure for consideration and determination of the question of a stay.

(B) In any proceeding to review the prohibition or limitation of any person in respect of access to services offered by a registered securities information processor, if the Commission finds, after notice and opportunity for hearing, that such prohibition or limitation is consistent with the provisions of this title and the rules and regulations thereunder and that such person has not been discriminated against unfairly, the Commission, by order, shall dismiss the proceeding. If the Commission does not make any such finding or if it finds, that such prohibition or limitation imposes any burden on competition not necessary or appropriate in furtherance of the purposes of this title, the Commission, by order, shall set aside the prohibition or limitation and require the registered securities information processor to permit such person access to services offered by the registered securities information processor.

(6) The Commission, by order, may censure or place limitations upon the activities, functions, or operations of any registered securities information processor or suspend for a period not exceeding twelve months or revoke the registration of any such processor, if the Commission finds, on the record after notice and opportunity for hearing, that such censure, placing of limitations, suspension, or revocation is in the public interest, necessary or appropriate for the protection of investors or to assure the prompt, accurate, or reliable performance of the functions of such securities information processor, and that such securities information processor has violated or is unable to comply with any provision of this title or the rules or regulations thereunder.

(c)(1) No self-regulatory organization, member thereof, securities information processor, broker, or dealer shall make use of the mails or any means or instrumentality of interstate commerce to collect, process, distribute, publish, or prepare for distribution or publication any information with respect to quotations for or transactions in any security other than an exempted security, to assist, participate in, or coordinate the distribution or publication of such information, or to effect any transaction in, or to induce or attempt to induce the purchase or sale of, any such security in contravention of such rules and regulations as the Commission shall prescribe as necessary or appropriate in the public interest, for the protection of investors, or otherwise in furtherance of the purposes of this title to—

(A) prevent the use, distribution, or publication of fraudulent, deceptive, or manipulative information with respect to quotations for and transactions in such securities;

(B) assure the prompt, accurate, reliable, and fair collection, processing, distribution, and publication of information with respect to quotations for and transactions in such securities and the fairness and usefulness of the form and content of such information;

(C) assure that all securities information processors may, for purposes of distribution and publication, obtain on fair and reasonable terms such information with respect to quotations for and transactions in such securities as is collected, processed, or prepared for distribution or publication by any exclusive processor of such information acting in such capacity;

(D) assure that all exchange members, brokers, dealers, securities information processors, and, subject to such limitations as the Commission, by rule, may impose as necessary or appropriate for the protection of investors or maintenance of fair and orderly markets, all other persons may obtain on terms which are not unreasonably discriminatory such information with respect to quotations for and transactions in such securities as is published or distributed by any self-regulatory organization or securities information processor;

(E) assure that all exchange members, brokers, and dealers transmit and direct orders for the purchase or sale of qualified securities in a manner consistent with the establishment and operation of a national market system; and

(F) assure equal regulation of all markets for qualified securities and all exchange members, brokers, and dealers effecting transactions in such securities.

(2) The Commission, by rule, as it deems necessary or appropriate in the public interest or for the protection of investors, may require any person who has effected the purchase or sale of any qualified security by use of the mails or any means or instrumentality of interstate commerce to report such purchase or sale to a registered securities information processor, national securities exchange, or registered securities association and require such processor, exchange, or association to make appropriate distribution and publication of information with respect to such purchase or sale.

(3)(A) The Commission, by rule, is authorized to prohibit brokers and dealers from effecting transactions in securities registered pursuant to section 12(b) otherwise than on a national securities exchange, if the Commission finds, on the record after notice and opportunity for hearing, that—

(i) as a result of transactions in such securities effected otherwise than on a national securities exchange the fairness or orderliness of the markets for such securities has been affected in a manner contrary to the public interest or the protection of investors;

(ii) no rule of any national securities exchange unreasonably impairs the ability of any dealer to solicit or effect transactions in such securities for his own account or unreasonably restricts competition among dealers in such securities or between dealers acting in the capacity of market makers who are specialists in such securities and such dealers who are not specialists in such securities, and

(iii) the maintenance or restoration of fair and orderly markets in such securities may not be assured through other lawful means under this title.

The Commission may conditionally or unconditionally exempt any security or transaction or any class of securities or transactions from any such prohibition if the Commission deems such exemption consistent with the public interest, the protection of investors, and the maintenance of fair and ordinary markets.

(B) For the purposes of subparagraph (A) of this paragraph, the ability of a dealer to solicit or effect transactions in securities for his own account shall not be deemed to be unreasonably impaired by any rule of an exchange fairly and reasonably prescribing the sequence in which orders brought to the exchange must be executed or which has been adopted to effect compliance with a rule of the Commission promulgated under this title.

(4) The Commission is directed to review any and all rules of national securities exchanges which limit or condition the ability of members to effect transactions in securities otherwise than on such exchanges.

(5) No national securities exchange or registered securities association may limit or condi-

tion the participation of any member in any registered clearing agency.

(d)(1) Not later than one hundred eighty days after the date of enactment of the Securities Acts Amendments of 1975, the Commission shall establish a National Market Advisory Board (hereinafter in this section referred to as the "Advisory Board") to be composed of fifteen members, not all of whom shall be from the same geographical area of the United States, appointed by the Commission for a term specified by the Commission of not less than two years or more than five years. The Advisory Board shall consist of persons associated with brokers and dealers (who shall be a majority) and persons not so associated who are representative of the public and, to the extent feasible, have knowledge of the securities markets of the United States.

(2) It shall be the responsibility of the Advisory Board to formulate and furnish to the Commission its views on significant regulatory proposals made by the Commission or any self-regulatory organization concerning the establishment, operation, and regulation of the markets for securities in the United States.

(3)(A) The Advisory Board shall study and make recommendations to the Commission as to the steps it finds appropriate to facilitate the establishment of a national market system. In so doing, the Advisory Board shall assume the responsibilities of any advisory committee appointed to advise the Commission with respect to the national market system which is in existence at the time of the establishment of the Advisory Board.

(B) The Advisory Board shall study the possible need for modifications of the scheme of self-regulation provided for in this title so as to adapt it to a national market system, including the need for the establishment of a new self-regulatory organization (hereinafter in this section referred to as a "National Market Regulatory Board" or "Regulatory Board") to administer the national market system. In the event the Advisory Board determines a National Market Regulatory Board should be established, it shall make recommendations as to:

(i) the point in time at which a Regulatory Board should be established;

(ii) the composition of a Regulatory Board;

(iii) the scope of the authority of a Regulatory Board;

(iv) the relationship of a Regulatory Board to the Commission and to existing self-regulatory organizations; and

(v) the manner in which a Regulatory Board should be funded.

The Advisory Board shall report to the Congress, on or before December 31, 1976, the results of such study and its recommendations, including such recommendations for legislation as it deems appropriate.

(C) In carrying out its responsibilities under this paragraph, the Advisory Board shall consult with self-regulatory organizations, brokers, dealers, securities information processors, issuers, investors, representatives of Government agencies, and other persons interested or likely to participate in the establishment, operation, or regulation of the national market system.

(e) *National Markets System for Security Futures Products.*—

(1) *Consultation and Cooperation Required.*—With respect to security futures products, the Commission and the Commodity Futures Trading Commission shall consult and cooperate so that, to the maximum extent practicable, their respective regulatory responsibilities may be fulfilled and the rules and regulations applicable to security futures products may foster a national market system for security futures products if the Commission and the Commodity Futures Trading Commission jointly determine that such a system would be consistent with the congressional findings in subsection (a)(1). In accordance with this objective, the Commission shall, at least 15 days prior

to the issuance for public comment of any proposed rule or regulation under this section concerning security futures products, consult and request the views of the Commodity Futures Trading Commission.

(2) *Application of Rules by Order of CFTC.*—No rule adopted pursuant to this section shall be applied to any person with respect to the trading of security futures products on an exchange that is registered under section 6(g) unless the Commodity Futures Trading Commission has issued an order directing that such rule is applicable to such persons.

Registration Requirements for Securities

Sec. 12. (a) It shall be unlawful for any member, broker, or dealer to effect any transaction in any security (other than an exempted security) on a national securities exchange unless a registration is effective as to such security for such exchange in accordance with the provisions of this title and the rules and regulations thereunder. The provisions of this subsection shall not apply in respect of a security futures product traded on a national securities exchange.

(b) A security may be registered on a national securities exchange by the issuer filing an application with the exchange (and filing with the Commission such duplicate originals thereof as the Commission may require), which application shall contain—

(1) Such information, in such detail, as to the issuer and any person directly or indirectly controlling or controlled by, or under direct or indirect common control with, the issuer, and any guarantor of the security as to principal or interest or both, as the Commission may by rules and regulations require, as necessary or appropriate in the public interest or for the protection of investors, in respect of the following:

(A) the organization, financial structure and nature of the business;

(B) the terms, position, rights, and privileges of the different classes of securities outstanding;

(C) the terms on which their securities are to be, and during the preceding three years have been, offered to the public or otherwise;

(D) the directors, officers, and underwriters, and each security holder of record holding more than 10 per centum of any class of any equity security of the issuer (other than an exempted security), their remuneration and their interests in the securities of, and their material contracts with, the issuer and any person directly or indirectly controlling or controlled by, or under direct or indirect common control with, the issuer;

(E) remuneration to others than directors and officers exceeding $20,000 per annum;

(F) bonus and profit-sharing arrangements;

(G) management and service contracts;

(H) options existing or to be created in respect of their securities;

(I) material contracts, not made in the ordinary course of business, which are to be executed in whole or in part at or after the filing of the application or which were made not more than 2 years before such filing, and every material patent or contract for a material patent right shall be deemed a material contract;

(J) balance sheets for not more than the three preceding fiscal years, certified if required by the rules and regulations of the Commission by a registered public accounting firm;

(K) profit and loss statements for not more than the three preceding fiscal years, certified if required by the rules and regulations of the Commission by a registered public accounting firm; and

(L) any further financial statements which the Commission may deem necessary or appropriate for the protection of investors.

(2) Such copies of articles of incorporation, by-laws, trust indentures, or corresponding documents by whatever name known, underwriting arrangements, and other similar documents of, and voting trust agreements with respect to, the issuer and any person directly or indirectly controlling or controlled by, or under direct or indirect common control with, the issuer as the Commission may require as necessary or appropriate for the proper protection of investors and to insure fair dealing in the security.

(3) Such copies of material contracts, referred to in paragraph (1)(I) above, as the Commission may require as necessary or appropriate for the proper protection of investors and to insure fair dealing in the security.

(c) If in the judgment of the Commission any information required under subsection (b) is inapplicable to any specified class or classes of issuers, the Commission shall require in lieu thereof the submission of such other information of comparable character as it may deem applicable to such class of issuers.

(d) If the exchange authorities certify to the Commission that the security has been approved by the exchange for listing and registration, the registration shall become effective thirty days after the receipt of such certification by the Commission or within such shorter period of time as the Commission may determine. A security registered with a national securities exchange may be withdrawn or stricken from listing and registration in accordance with the rules of the exchange and, upon such terms as the Commission may deem necessary to impose for the protection of investors, upon application by the issuer or the exchange to the Commission; whereupon the issuer shall be relieved from further compliance with the provisions of this section and section 13 of this title and any rules or regulations under such sections as to the securities so withdrawn or stricken. An unissued security may be registered only in accordance with such rules and regulations as the Commission may prescribe as necessary or appropriate in the public interest or for the protection of investors.

(e) Notwithstanding the foregoing provisions of this section, the Commission may by such rules and regulations as it deems necessary or appropriate in the public interest or for the protection of investors permit securities listed on any exchange at the time the registration of such exchange as a national securities exchange becomes effective, to be registered for a period ending not later than July 1, 1935, without complying with the provisions of this section.

(f)(1)(A) Notwithstanding the preceding subsections of this section, any national securities exchange, in accordance with the requirements of this subsection and the rules hereunder, may extend unlisted trading privileges to—

(i) any security that is listed and registered on a national securities exchange, subject to subparagraph (B); and

(ii) any security that is otherwise registered pursuant to this section, or that would be required to be so registered except for the exemption from registration provided in subparagraph (B) or (G) of subsection (g)(2), subject to subparagraph (E) of this paragraph.

(B) A national securities exchange may not extend unlisted trading privileges to a security described in subparagraph (A)(i) during such interval, if any, after the commencement of an initial public offering of such security, as is or may be required pursuant to subparagraph (C).

(C) Not later than 180 days after the date of enactment of the Unlisted Trading Privileges Act of 1994, the Commission shall prescribe, by rule or regulation, the duration of the interval referred to in subparagraph (B), if any, as the Commission determines to be necessary or appropriate for the maintenance of fair and orderly markets, the protection of investors and the public interest, or otherwise in furtherance of the purposes of this title. Until the earlier of the effective date of such rule or regulation or 240 days after such date of enactment, such interval shall begin at the opening of trading on the day on which such security commences trading on the national securities exchange with which such security is registered and end at the conclusion of the next day of trading.

(D) The Commission may prescribe, by rule or regulation such additional procedures or requirements for extending unlisted trading privileges to any security as the Commission deems necessary or appropriate for the maintenance of fair and orderly markets, the protection of investors and the public interest, or otherwise in furtherance of the purposes of this title.

(E) No extension of unlisted trading privileges to securities described in subparagraph (A)(ii) may occur except pursuant to a rule, regulation, or order of the Commission approving such extension or extensions. In promulgating such rule or regulation or in issuing such order, the Commission—

(i) shall find that such extension or extensions of unlisted trading privileges is consistent with the maintenance of fair and orderly markets, the protection of investors and the public interest, and otherwise in furtherance of the purposes of this title;

(ii) shall take account of the public trading activity in such securities, the character of such trading, the impact of such extension on the existing markets for such securities, and the desirability of removing impediments to and the progress that has been made toward the development of a national market system; and

(iii) shall not permit a national securities exchange to extend unlisted trading privileges to such securities if any rule of such national securities exchange would unreasonably impair the ability of a dealer to solicit or effect transactions in such securities for its own account, or would unreasonably restrict competition among dealers in such securities or between such dealers acting in the capacity of market makers who are specialists and such dealers who are not specialists.

(F) An exchange may continue to extend unlisted trading privileges in accordance with this paragraph only if the exchange and the subject security continue to satisfy the requirements for eligibility under this paragraph, including any rules and regulations issued by the Commission pursuant to this paragraph, except that unlisted trading privileges may continue with regard to securities which had been admitted on such exchange prior to July 1, 1964, notwithstanding the failure to satisfy such requirements. If unlisted trading privileges in a security are discontinued pursuant to this subparagraph, the exchange shall cease trading in that security, unless the exchange and the subject security thereafter satisfy the requirements of this paragraph and the rules issued hereunder.

(G) For purposes of this paragraph—

(i) a security is the subject of an initial public offering if—

(I) the offering of the subject security is registered under the Securities Act of 1933; and

(II) the issuer of the security, immediately prior to filing the registration statement with respect to the offering, was not subject to the reporting requirements of section 13 or 15(d) of this title; and

(ii) an initial public offering of such security commences at the opening of trading on the day on which such security commences trading on the national securities exchange with which such security is registered.

(2)(A) At any time within 60 days of commencement of trading on an exchange of a security pursuant to unlisted trading privileges, the Commission may summarily suspend such unlisted trading privileges on the exchange. Such suspension shall not be reviewable under section 25 of this title and shall not be deemed to be a final agency action for purposes of section 704 of title 5, United States Code. Upon such suspension—

(i) the exchange shall cease trading in the security by the close of business on the date of such suspension, or at such time as the Commission may prescribe by rule or order for the maintenance of fair and orderly markets, the protection of investors and the public interest, or otherwise in furtherance of the purposes of this title; and

(ii) if the exchange seeks to extend unlisted trading privileges to the security, the exchange shall file an application to reinstate its ability to do so with the Commission pursuant to such procedures as the Commission may prescribe by rule or order for the maintenance of fair and orderly markets, the protection of investors and the public interest, or otherwise in furtherance of the purposes of this title.

(B) A suspension under subparagraph (A) shall remain in effect until the Commission, by order, grants approval of an application to reinstate, as described in subparagraph (A)(ii).

(C) A suspension under subparagraph (A) shall not affect the validity or force of an extension of unlisted trading privileges in effect prior to such suspension.

(D) The Commission shall not approve an application by a national securities exchange to reinstate its ability to extend unlisted trading privileges to a security unless the Commission finds, after notice and opportunity for hearing, that the extension of unlisted trading privileges pursuant to such application is consistent with the maintenance of fair and orderly markets, the protection of investors and the public interest, and otherwise in furtherance of the purposes of this title. If the application is made to reinstate unlisted trading privileges to a security described in paragraph (1)(A)(ii), the Commission—

(i) shall take account of the public trading activity in such security, the character of such trading, the impact of such extension on the existing markets for such a security, and the desirability of removing impediments to and the progress that has been made toward the development of a national market system; and

(ii) shall not grant any such application if any rule of the national securities exchange making application under this subsection would unreasonably impair the ability of a dealer to solicit or effect transactions in such security for its own account, or would unreasonably restrict competition among dealers in such security or between such dealers acting in the capacity of marketmakers who are specialists and such dealers who are not specialists.

(3) Notwithstanding paragraph (2), the Commission shall by rules and regulations suspend unlisted trading privileges in whole or in part for any or all classes of securities for a period not exceeding twelve months, if it deems such suspension necessary or appropriate in the public interest or for the protection of investors or to prevent evasion of the purposes of this title.

(4) On the application of the issuer of any security for which unlisted trading privileges on any exchange have been continued or extended pursuant to this subsection, or of any broker or dealer who makes or creates a market for such security, or of any other person having a bona fide interest in the question of termination or suspension of such unlisted trading privileges, or on its own motion, the Commission shall by order terminate, or suspend for a period not exceeding twelve months, such unlisted trading privileges for such security if the Commission finds, after appropriate notice and opportunity for hearing, that such termination or suspension is necessary or appropriate in the public interest or for the protection of investors.

(5) In any proceeding under this subsection in which appropriate notice and opportunity

for hearing are required, notice of not less than ten days to the applicant in such proceeding, to the issuer of the security involved, to the exchange which is seeking to continue or extend or has continued or extended unlisted trading privileges for such security, and to the exchange, if any, on which such security is listed and registered, shall be deemed adequate notice, and any broker or dealer who makes or creates a market for such security, and any other person having a bona fide interest in such proceeding, shall upon application be entitled to be heard.

(6) Any security for which unlisted trading privileges are continued or extended pursuant to this subsection shall be deemed to be registered on a national securities exchange within the meaning of this title. The powers and duties of the Commission under this title shall be applicable to the rules of an exchange in respect of any such security. The Commission may, by such rules and regulations as it deems necessary or appropriate in the public interest or for the protection of investors, either unconditionally or upon specified terms and conditions, or for stated periods, exempt such securities from the operation of any provision of section 13, 14, or 16 of this title.

(g)(1) Every issuer which is engaged in interstate commerce, or in a business affecting interstate commerce, or whose securities are traded by use of the mails or any means or instrumentality of interstate commerce shall—

(A) within one hundred and twenty days after the last day of its first fiscal year ended after the effective date of this subsection on which the issuer has total assets exceeding $1,000,000 and a class of equity security (other than an exempted security) held of record by seven hundred and fifty or more persons; and

(B) within one hundred and twenty days after the last day of its first fiscal year ended after two years from the effective date of this subsection on which the issuer has total assets exceeding $1,000,000 and a class of equity security (other than an exempted security) held of record by five hundred or more but less than seven hundred and fifty persons,

register such security by filing with the Commission a registration statement (and such copies thereof as the Commission may require) with respect to such security containing such information and documents as the Commission may specify comparable to that which is required in an application to register a security pursuant to subsection (b) of this section. Each such registration statement shall become effective sixty days after filing with the Commission or within such shorter period as the Commission may direct. Until such registration statement becomes effective it shall not be deemed filed for the purposes of section 18 of this title. Any issuer may register any class of equity security not required to be registered by filing a registration statement pursuant to the provisions of this paragraph. The Commission is authorized to extend the date upon which any issuer or class of issuers is required to register a security pursuant to the provisions of this paragraph.

(2) The provisions of this subsection shall not apply in respect of—

(A) any security listed and registered on a national securities exchange.

(B) any security issued by an investment company registered pursuant to section 8 of the Investment Company Act of 1940.

(C) any security, other than permanent stock, guaranty stock, permanent reserve stock, or any similar certificate evidencing nonwithdrawable capital, issued by a savings and loan association, building and loan association, cooperative bank, homestead association, or similar institution, which is supervised and examined by State or Federal authority having supervision over any such institution.

(D) any security of an issuer organized and operated exclusively for religious, educational, benevolent, fraternal, charitable, or reformatory purposes and not for pecuniary profit, and no part of the net earnings of which inures to the benefit of any private shareholder or individual; or any security of a fund that is excluded from the definition of an investment company under section 3(c)(10)(B) of the Investment Company Act of 1940.

(E) any security of an issuer which is a "cooperative association" as defined in the Agricultural Marketing Act, approved June 15, 1929, as amended, or a federation of such cooperative associations, if such federation possesses no greater powers or purposes than cooperative associations so defined.

(F) any security issued by a mutual or cooperative organization which supplies a commodity or service primarily for the benefit of its members and operates not for pecuniary profit, but only if the security is part of a class issuable only to persons who purchase commodities or services from the issuer, the security is transferable only to a successor in interest or occupancy of premises serviced or to be served by the issuer, and no dividends are payable to the holder of the security.

(G) any security issued by an insurance company if all of the following conditions are met:

(i) Such insurance company is required to and does file an annual statement with the Commissioner of Insurance (or other officer or agency performing a similar function) of its domiciliary State, and such annual statement conforms to that prescribed by the National Association of Insurance Commissioners or in the determination of such State commissioner, officer or agency substantially conforms to that so prescribed.

(ii) Such insurance company is subject to regulation by its domiciliary State of proxies, consents, or authorizations in respect of securities issued by such company and such regulation conforms to that prescribed by the National Association of Insurance Commissioners.

(iii) After July 1, 1966, the purchase and sales of securities issued by such insurance company by beneficial owners, directors, or officers of such company are subject to regulation (including reporting) by its domiciliary State substantially in the manner provided in section 16 of this title.

(H) any interest or participation in any collective trust funds maintained by a bank or in a separate account maintained by an insurance company which interest or participation is issued in connection with (i) a stock-bonus, pension, or profit-sharing plan which meets the requirements for qualification under section 401 of the Internal Revenue Code of 1954, or (ii) an annuity plan which meets the requirements for deduction of the employer's contribution under section 404(a)(2) of such Code.

(3) The Commission may by rules or regulations or, on its own motion, after notice and opportunity for hearing, by order, exempt from this subsection any security of a foreign issuer, including any certificate of deposit for such a security, if the Commission finds that such exemption is in the public interest and is consistent with the protection of investors.

(4) Registration of any class of security pursuant to this subsection shall be terminated ninety days, or such shorter period as the Commission may determine, after the issuer files a certification with the Commission that the number of holders of record of such class of security is reduced to less than three hundred persons. The Commission shall after notice and opportunity for hearing deny termination of registration if it finds that the certification is untrue. Termination of registration shall be deferred pending final determination on the question of denial.

(5) For the purposes of this subsection the term "class" shall include all securities of an issuer which are of substantially similar character and the holders of which enjoy substantially similar rights and privileges. The Com-

mission may for the purpose of this subsection define by rules and regulations the terms "total assets" and "held of record" as it deems necessary or appropriate in the public interest or for the protection of investors in order to prevent circumvention of the provisions of this subsection. For purposes of this subsection, a security futures product shall not be considered a class of equity security of the issuer of the securities underlying the security futures product.

(h) The Commission may by rules and regulations, or upon application of an interested person, by order, after notice and opportunity for hearing, exempt in whole or in part any issuer or class of issuers from the provisions of subsection (g) of this section or from section 13, 14, or 15(d) or may exempt from section 16 any officer, director, or beneficial owner of securities of any issuer, any security of which is required to be registered pursuant to subsection (g) hereof, upon such terms and conditions and for such period as it deems necessary or appropriate, if the Commission finds, by reason of the number of public investors, amount of trading interest in the securities, the nature and extent of the activities of the issuer, income or assets of the issuer, or otherwise, that such action is not inconsistent with the public interest or the protection of investors. The Commission may, for the purposes of any of the above-mentioned sections or subsections of this title, classify issuers and prescribe requirements appropriate for each such class.

(i) In respect of any securities issued by banks and savings associations the deposits of which are insured in accordance with Federal Deposit Insurance Act, the powers, functions, and duties vested in the Commission to administer and enforce sections 10A(m), 12, 13, 14(a), 14(c), 14(d), 14(f), and 16 of this Act, and sections 302, 303, 304, 306, 401(b), 404, 406, and 407 of the Sarbanes–Oxley Act of 2002, (1) with respect to national banks and banks operating under the Code of Law for the District of Columbia are vested in the Comptroller of the Currency, (2) with respect to all other member banks of the Federal Reserve System are vested in the Board of Governors of the Federal Reserve System, (3) with respect to all other insured banks are vested in the Federal Deposit Insurance Corporation, and (4) with respect to savings associations the accounts of which are insured by the Federal Deposit Insurance Corporation are vested in the Office of Thrift Supervision. The Comptroller of the Currency, the Board of Governors of the Federal Reserve System, the Federal Deposit Insurance Corporation, and the Office of Thrift Supervision shall have the power to make such rules and regulations as may be necessary for the execution of the functions vested in them as provided in this subsection. In carrying out their responsibilities under this subsection, the agencies named in the first sentence of this subsection shall issue substantially similar regulations to regulations and rules issued by the Commission under sections 10A(m), 12, 13, 14(a), 14(c), 14(d), 14(f), and 16 of this Act, and sections 302, 303, 304, 306, 401(b), 404, 406, and 407 of the Sarbanes–Oxley Act of 2002, unless they find that implementation of substantially similar regulations with respect to insured banks and insured institutions are not necessary or appropriate in the public interest or for protection of investors, and publish such findings, and the detailed reasons therefor, in the Federal Register. Such regulations of the above-named agencies, or the reasons for failure to publish such substantially similar regulations to those of the Commission, shall be published in the Federal Register within 120 days of the date of enactment of this subsection, and, thereafter, within 60 days of any changes made by the Commission in its relevant regulations and rules.

(j) The Commission is authorized, by order, as it deems necessary or appropriate for the protection of investors to deny, to suspend the effective date of, to suspend for a period not exceeding twelve months, or to revoke the registration of a security, if the Commission finds, on the record after notice and opportunity for hearing, that the issuer of such security has failed to comply with any provision of this title or the rules and regulations thereunder. No member of a national securities exchange, broker, or dealer shall make use of the mails or any means or instrumentality of interstate commerce to effect any transaction in, or to induce the purchase or sale of, any security the registration of which has been and is suspended or revoked pursuant to the preceding sentence.

(k) *Trading Suspensions; Emergency Authority.*—

(1) *Trading Suspensions.*—If in its opinion the public interest and the protection of investors so require, the Commission is authorized by order—

(A) summarily to suspend trading in any security (other than an exempted security) for a period not exceeding 10 business days, and

(B) summarily to suspend all trading on any national securities exchange or otherwise, in securities other than exempted securities, for a period not exceeding 90 calendar days.

The action described in subparagraph (B) shall not take effect unless the Commission notifies the President of its decision and the President notifies the Commission that the President does not disapprove of such decision. If the actions described in subparagraph (A) or (B) involve a security futures product, the Commission shall consult with and consider the views of the Commodity Futures Trading Commission.

(2) *Emergency Orders.*—

(A) The Commission, in an emergency, may by order summarily take such action to alter, supplement, suspend, or impose requirements or restrictions with respect to any matter or action subject to regulation by the Commission or a self-regulatory organization under this title, as the Commission determines is necessary in the public interest and for the protection of investors—

(i) to maintain or restore fair and orderly securities markets (other than markets in exempted securities); or

(ii) to ensure prompt, accurate, and safe clearance and settlement of transactions in securities (other than exempted securities).

(B) An order of the Commission under this paragraph (2) shall continue in effect for the period specified by the Commission, and may be extended, except that in no event shall the Commission's action continue in effect for more than 10 business days, including extensions. If the actions described in subparagraph (A) involve a security futures product, the Commission shall consult with and consider the views of the Commodity Futures Trading Commission. In exercising its authority under this paragraph, the Commission shall not be required to comply with the provisions of section 553 of title 5, United States Code, or with the provisions of section 19(c) of this title.

(3) *Termination of Emergency Actions by President.*—The President may direct that action taken by the Commission under paragraph (1)(B) or paragraph (2) of this subsection shall not continue in effect.

(4) *Compliance With Orders.*—No member of a national securities exchange, broker, or dealer shall make use of the mails or any means or instrumentality of interstate commerce to effect any transaction in, or to induce the purchase or sale of, any security in contravention of an order of the Commission under this subsection unless such order has been stayed, modified, or set aside as provided in paragraph (5) of this subsection or has ceased to be effective upon direction of the President as provided in paragraph (3).

(5) *Limitations on Review of Orders.*—An order of the Commission pursuant to this subsection shall be subject to review only as provided in section 25(a) of this title. Review shall be based on an examination of all the information before the Commission at the time such order was issued. The reviewing court shall not enter a stay, writ of mandamus, or

similar relief unless the court finds, after notice and hearing before a panel of the court, that the Commission's action is arbitrary, capricious, an abuse of discretion, or otherwise not in accordance with law.

(6) *Definition of Emergency.*—For purposes of this subsection, the term "emergency" means a major market disturbance characterized by or constituting—

(A) sudden and excessive fluctuations of securities prices generally, or a substantial threat thereof, that threaten fair and orderly markets, or

(B) a substantial disruption of the safe or efficient operation of the national system for clearance and settlement of securities, or a substantial threat thereof.

(*l*) It shall be unlawful for an issuer, any class of whose securities is registered pursuant to this section or would be required to be so registered except for the exemption from registration provided by subsection (g)(2)(B) or (g)(2)(G) of this section, by the use of any means or instrumentality of interstate commerce, or of the mails, to issue, either originally or upon transfer, any of such securities in a form or with a format which contravenes such rules and regulations as the Commission may prescribe as necessary or appropriate for the prompt and accurate clearance and settlement of transactions in securities. The provisions of this subsection shall not apply to variable annuity contracts or variable life policies issued by an insurance company or its separate accounts.

Periodical and Other Reports

Sec. 13. (a) Every issuer of a security registered pursuant to section 12 of this title shall file with the Commission, in accordance with such rules and regulations as the Commission may prescribe as necessary or appropriate for the proper protection of investors and to insure fair dealing in the security—

(1) such information and documents (and such copies thereof) as the Commission shall require to keep reasonably current the information and documents required to be included in or filed with an application or registration statement filed pursuant to section 12, except that the Commission may not require the filing of any material contract wholly executed before July 1, 1962.

(2) such annual reports (and such copies thereof), certified if required by the rules and regulations of the Commission by independent public accountants, and such quarterly reports (and such copies thereof), as the Commission may prescribe.

Every issuer of a security registered on a national securities exchange shall also file a duplicate original of such information, documents, and reports with the exchange.

(b)(1) The Commission may prescribe, in regard to reports made pursuant to this title, the form or forms in which the required information shall be set forth, the items or details to be shown in the balance sheet and the earning statement, and the methods to be followed in the preparation of reports, in the appraisal or valuation of assets and liabilities, in the determination of depreciation and depletion, in the differentiation of recurring and nonrecurring income, in the differentiation of investment and operating income, and in the preparation, where the Commission deems it necessary or desirable, of separate and/or consolidated balance sheets or income accounts of any person directly or indirectly controlling or controlled by the issuer, or any person under direct or indirect common control with the issuer; but in the case of the reports of any person whose methods of accounting are prescribed under the provisions of any law of the United States, or any rule or regulation thereunder, the rules and regulations of the Commission with respect to reports shall not be inconsistent with the requirements imposed by such law or rule or regulation in respect of the same subject matter, (except that such rules and regulations of the Commission may be inconsistent with such requirements to the extent that the Commission determines that the public interest or the protection of investors so requires).

(2) Every issuer which has a class of securities registered pursuant to section 12 of this title and every issuer which is required to file reports pursuant to section 15(d) of this title shall—

(A) make and keep books, records, and accounts, which, in reasonable detail, accurately and fairly reflect the transactions and dispositions of the assets of the issuer;

(B) devise and maintain a system of internal accounting controls sufficient to provide reasonable assurances that—

(i) transactions are executed in accordance with management's general or specific authorization;

(ii) transactions are recorded as necessary (I) to permit preparation of financial statements in conformity with generally accepted accounting principles or any other criteria applicable to such statements, and (II) to maintain accountability for assets;

(iii) access to assets is permitted only in accordance with management's general or specific authorization; and

(iv) the recorded accountability for assets is compared with the existing assets at reasonable intervals and appropriate action is taken with respect to any differences; and

(C) notwithstanding any other provision of law, pay the allocable share of such issuer of a reasonable annual accounting support fee or fees, determined in accordance with section 109 of the Sarbanes–Oxley Act of 2002.

(3)(A) With respect to matters concerning the national security of the United States, no duty or liability under paragraph (2) of this subsection shall be imposed upon any person acting in cooperation with the head of any Federal department or agency responsible for such matters if such act in cooperation with such head of a department or agency was done upon the specific, written directive of the head of such department or agency pursuant to Presidential authority to issue such directives. Each directive issued under this paragraph shall set forth the specific facts and circumstances with respect to which the provisions of this paragraph are to be invoked. Each such directive shall, unless renewed in writing, expire one year after the date of issuance.

(B) Each head of a Federal department or agency of the United States who issues a directive pursuant to this paragraph shall maintain a complete file of all such directives and shall, on October 1 of each year, transmit a summary of matters covered by such directives in force at any time during the previous year to the Permanent Select Committee on Intelligence of the House of Representatives and the Select Committee on Intelligence of the Senate.

(4) No criminal liability shall be imposed for failing to comply with the requirements of paragraph (2) of this subsection except as provided in paragraph (5) of this subsection.

(5) No person shall knowingly circumvent or knowingly fail to implement a system of internal accounting controls or knowingly falsify any book, record, or account described in paragraph (2).

(6) Where an issuer which has a class of securities registered pursuant to section 12 of this title or an issuer which is required to file reports pursuant to section 15(d) of this title holds 50 per centum or less of the voting power with respect to a domestic or foreign firm, the provisions of paragraph (2) require only that the issuer proceed in good faith to use its influence, to the extent reasonable under the issuer's circumstances, to cause such domestic or foreign firm to devise and maintain a system of internal accounting controls consistent with paragraph (2). Such circumstances include the relative degree of the issuer's ownership of the domestic or foreign firm and the laws and practices governing the business operations of the country in which such firm is located. An issuer which demonstrates good faith efforts to use such influence

shall be conclusively presumed to have complied with the requirements of paragraph (2).

(7) For the purpose of paragraph (2) of this subsection, the terms "reasonable assurances" and "reasonable detail" mean such level of detail and degree of assurance as would satisfy prudent officials in the conduct of their own affairs.

(c) If in the judgment of the Commission any report required under subsection (a) is inapplicable to any specified class or classes of issuers, the Commission shall require in lieu thereof the submission of such reports of comparable character as it may deem applicable to such class or classes of issuers.

(d)(1) Any person who, after acquiring directly or indirectly the beneficial ownership of any equity security of a class which is registered pursuant to section 12 of this title, or any equity security of an insurance company which would have been required to be so registered except for the exemption contained in section 12(g)(2)(G) of this title, or any equity security issued by a closed-end investment company registered under the Investment Company Act of 1940 or any equity security issued by a Native Corporation pursuant to Section 37(d)(6) of the Alaska Native Claims Settlement Act, is directly or indirectly the beneficial owner of more than 5 per centum of such class shall, within ten days after such acquisition, send to the issuer of the security at its principal executive office, by registered or certified mail, send to each exchange where the security is traded, and file with the Commission, a statement containing such of the following information, and such additional information, as the Commission may by rules and regulations prescribe as necessary or appropriate in the public interest or for the protection of investors—

(A) the background, and identity, residence, and citizenship of, and the nature of such beneficial ownership by, such person and all other persons by whom or on whose behalf the purchases have been or are to be effected;

(B) the source and amount of the funds or other consideration used or to be used in making the purchases, and if any part of the purchase price or proposed purchase price is represented or is to be represented by funds or other consideration borrowed or otherwise obtained for the purpose of acquiring, holding, or trading such security, a description of the transaction and the names of the parties thereto, except that where a source of funds is a loan made in the ordinary course of business by a bank, as defined in section 3(a)(6) of this title, if the person filing such statement so requests, the name of the bank shall not be made available to the public;

(C) if the purpose of the purchases or prospective purchases is to acquire control of the business of the issuer of the securities, any plans or proposals which such persons may have to liquidate such issuer, to sell its assets to or merge it with any other persons, or to make any other major change in its business or corporate structure;

(D) the number of shares of such security which are beneficially owned, and the number of shares concerning which there is a right to acquire, directly or indirectly, by (i) such person, and (ii) by each associate of such person, giving the background, identity, residence, and citizenship of each such associate; and

(E) information as to any contracts, arrangements, or understandings with any person with respect to any securities of the issuer, including but not limited to transfer of any of the securities, joint ventures, loan or option arrangements, puts or calls, guaranties of loans, guaranties against loss or guaranties of profits, division of losses or profits, or the giving or withholding of proxies, naming the persons with whom such contracts, arrangements, or understandings have been entered into, and giving the details thereof.

(2) If any material change occurs in the facts set forth in the statements to the issuer

and the exchange, and in the statement filed with the Commission, an amendment shall be transmitted to the issuer and the exchange and shall be filed with the Commission, in accordance with such rules and regulations as the Commission may prescribe as necessary or appropriate in the public interest or for the protection of investors.

(3) When two or more persons act as a partnership, limited partnership, syndicate, or other group for the purpose of acquiring, holding, or disposing of securities of an issuer, such syndicate or group shall be deemed a "person" for the purposes of this subsection.

(4) In determining, for purposes of this subsection, any percentage of a class of any security, such class shall be deemed to consist of the amount of the outstanding securities of such class, exclusive of any securities of such class held by or for the account of the issuer or a subsidiary of the issuer.

(5) The Commission, by rule or regulation or by order, may permit any person to file in lieu of the statement required by paragraph (1) of this subsection or the rules and regulations thereunder, a notice stating the name of such person, the number of shares of any equity securities subject to paragraph (1) which are owned by him, the date of their acquisition and such other information as the Commission may specify, if it appears to the Commission that such securities were acquired by such person in the ordinary course of his business and were not acquired for the purpose of and do not have the effect of changing or influencing the control of the issuer nor in connection with or as a participant in any transaction having such purpose or effect.

(6) The provisions of this subsection shall not apply to—

(A) any acquisition or offer to acquire securities made or proposed to be made by means of a registration statement under the Securities Act of 1933;

(B) any acquisition of the beneficial ownership of a security which, together with all other acquisitions by the same person of securities of the same class during the preceding twelve months, does not exceed 2 per centum of that class;

(C) any acquisition of an equity security by the issuer of such security;

(D) any acquisition or proposed acquisition of a security which the Commission, by rules or regulations or by order, shall exempt from the provisions of this subsection as not entered into for the purpose of, and not having the effect of, changing or influencing the control of the issuer or otherwise as not comprehended within the purposes of this subsection.

(e)(1) It shall be unlawful for an issuer which has a class of equity securities registered pursuant to section 12 of this title, or which is a closed-end investment company registered under the Investment Company Act of 1940, to purchase any equity security issued by it if such purchase as in contravention of such rules and regulations as the Commission, in the public interest or for the protection of investors, may adopt (A) to define acts and practices which are fraudulent, deceptive, or manipulative, and (B) to prescribe means reasonably designed to prevent such acts and practices. Such rules and regulations may require such issuer to provide holders of equity securities of such class with such information relating to the reasons for such purchase, the source of funds, the number of shares to be purchased, the price to be paid for such securities, the method of purchase, and such additional information, as the Commission deems necessary or appropriate in the public interest or for the protection of investors, or which the Commission deems to be material to a determination whether such security should be sold.

(2) For the purpose of this subsection, a purchase by or for the issuer or any person controlling, controlled by, or under common control with the issuer, or a purchase subject to control of the issuer or any such person, shall be deemed to be a purchase by the issuer. The Commission shall have power to make

rules and regulations implementing this paragraph in the public interest and for the protection of investors, including exemptive rules and regulations covering situations in which the Commission deems it unnecessary or inappropriate that a purchase of the type described in this paragraph shall be deemed to be a purchase by the issuer for purposes of some or all of the provisions of paragraph (1) of this subsection.

(3) At the time of filing such statement as the Commission may require by rule pursuant to paragraph (1) of this subsection, the person making the filing shall pay to the Commission a fee at a rate that, subject to paragraphs (5) and (6), is equal to $92 per $1,000,000* of the value of securities proposed to be purchased. The fee shall be reduced with respect to securities in an amount equal to any fee paid with respect to any securities issued in connection with the proposed transaction under section 6(b) of the Securities Act of 1933, or the fee paid under that section shall be reduced in an amount equal to the fee paid to the Commission in connection with such transaction under this paragraph.

(4) Offsetting collections.—Fees collected pursuant to this subsection for any fiscal year shall be deposited and credited as offsetting collections to the account providing appropriations to the Commission, and, except as provided in paragraph (9), shall not be collected for any fiscal year except to the extent provided in advance in appropriation Acts. No fees collected pursuant to this subsection for fiscal year 2002 or any succeeding fiscal year shall be deposited and credited as general revenue of the Treasury.

(5) Annual adjustment.—For each of the fiscal years 2003 through 2011, the Commission shall by order adjust the rate required by paragraph (3) for such fiscal year to a rate that is equal to the rate (expressed in dollars per million) that is applicable under section 6(b) of the Securities Act of 1933 for such fiscal year.

(6) Final rate adjustment.—For fiscal year 2012 and all of the succeeding fiscal years, the Commission shall by order adjust the rate required by paragraph (3) for all of such fiscal years to a rate that is equal to the rate (expressed in dollars per million) that is applicable under section 6(b) of the Securities Act of 1933 for all of such fiscal years.

(7) Pro rata application.—The rates per $1,000,000 required by this subsection shall be applied pro rata to amounts and balances of less than $1,000,000.

(8) Review and effective date.—In exercising its authority under this subsection, the Commission shall not be required to comply with the provisions of section 553 of title 5, United States Code. An adjusted rate prescribed under paragraph (5) or (6) and published under paragraph (10) shall not be subject to judicial review. Subject to paragraphs (4) and (9)—

(A) an adjusted rate prescribed under paragraph (5) shall take effect on the later of—

(i) the first day of the fiscal year to which such rate applies; or

(ii) five days after the date on which a regular appropriation to the Commission for such fiscal year is enacted; and

(B) an adjusted rate prescribed under paragraph (6) shall take effect on the later of—

(i) the first day of fiscal year 2012; or

(ii) five days after the date on which a regular appropriation to the Commission for fiscal year 2012 is enacted.

(9) Lapse of appropriation.—If on the first day of a fiscal year a regular appropriation to the Commission has not been enacted, the Commission shall continue to collect fees (as offsetting collections) under this subsection at the rate in effect during the preceding fiscal year, until 5 days after the date such a regular appropriation is enacted.

* The Consolidated Appropriations Act of 2004, P.L. 108–199, 118 Stat. 3, increased the rate applicable to Section 13(e) to $126.70 per million effective January 28, 2004.

(10) Publication.—The rate applicable under this subsection for each fiscal year is published pursuant to section 6(b)(10) of the Securities Act of 1933.

(f)(1) Every institutional investment manager which uses the mails, or any means or instrumentality of interstate commerce in the course of its business as an institutional investment manager and which exercises investment discretion with respect to accounts holding equity securities of a class described in section 13(d)(1) of this title having an aggregate fair market value on the last trading day in any of the preceding twelve months of at least $100,000,000 or such lesser amount (but in no case less than $10,000,000) as the Commission, by rule, may determine, shall file reports with the Commission in such form, for such periods, and at such times after the end of such periods as the Commission, by rule, may prescribe, but in no event shall such reports be filed for periods longer than one year or shorter than one quarter. Such reports shall include for each such equity security held on the last day of the reporting period by accounts (in aggregate or by type as the Commission, by rule, may prescribe) with respect to which the institutional investment manager exercises investment discretion (other than securities held in amounts which the Commission, by rule, determines to be insignificant for purposes of this subsection), the name of the issuer and the title, class, CUSIP number, number of shares or principal amount, and aggregate fair market value of each such security. Such reports may also include for accounts (in aggregate or by type) with respect to which the institutional investment manager exercises investment discretion such of the following information as the Commission, by rule, prescribes—

(A) the name of the issuer and the title, class, CUSIP number, number of shares or principal amount, and aggregate fair market value or cost or amortized cost of each other security (other than an exempted security) held on the last day of the reporting period by such accounts;

(B) the aggregate fair market value or cost or amortized cost of exempted securities (in aggregate or by class) held on the last day of the reporting period by such accounts;

(C) the number of shares of each equity security of a class described in section 13(d)(1) of this title held on the last day of the reporting period by such accounts with respect to which the institutional investment manager possesses sole or shared authority to exercise the voting rights evidenced by such securities;

(D) the aggregate purchases and aggregate sales during the reporting period of each security (other than an exempted security) effected by or for such accounts; and

(E) with respect to any transaction or series of transactions having a market value of at least $500,000 or such other amount as the Commission, by rule, may determine, effected during the reporting period by or for such accounts in any equity security of a class described in section 13(d)(1) of this title—

(i) the name of the issuer and the title, class, and CUSIP number of the security;

(ii) the number of shares or principal amount of the security involved in the transaction;

(iii) whether the transaction was a purchase or sale;

(iv) the per share price or prices at which the transaction was effected;

(v) the date or dates of the transaction;

(vi) the date or dates of the settlement of the transaction;

(vii) the broker or dealer through whom the transaction was effected;

(viii) the market or markets in which the transaction was effected; and

(ix) such other related information as the Commission, by rule, may prescribe.

(2) The Commission, by rule or order, may exempt, conditionally or unconditionally, any institutional investment manager or security or any class of institutional investment managers or securities from any or all of the provisions of this subsection or the rules thereunder.

(3) The Commission shall make available to the public for a reasonable fee a list of all equity securities of a class described in section 13(d)(1) of this title, updated no less frequently than reports are required to be filed pursuant to paragraph (1) of this subsection. The Commission shall tabulate the information contained in any report filed pursuant to this subsection in a manner which will, in the view of the Commission, maximize the usefulness of the information to other Federal and State authorities and the public. Promptly after the filing of any such report, the Commission shall make the information contained therein conveniently available to the public for a reasonable fee in such form as the Commission, by rule, may prescribe, except that the Commission, as it determines to be necessary or appropriate in the public interest or for the protection of investors, may delay or prevent public disclosure of any such information in accordance with section 552 of title 5, United States Code. Notwithstanding the preceding sentence, any such information identifying the securities held by the account of a natural person or an estate or trust (other than a business trust or investment company) shall not be disclosed to the public.

(4) In exercising its authority under this subsection, the Commission shall determine (and so state) that its action is necessary or appropriate in the public interest and for the protection of investors or to maintain fair and orderly markets or, in granting an exemption, that its action is consistent with the protection of investors and the purposes of this subsection. In exercising such authority the Commission shall take such steps as are within its power, including consulting with the Comptroller General of the United States, the Director of the Office of Management and Budget, the appropriate regulatory agencies, Federal and State authorities which, directly or indirectly, require reports from institutional investment managers of information substantially similar to that called for by this subsection, national securities exchanges, and registered securities associations, (A) to achieve uniform, centralized reporting of information concerning the securities holdings of and transactions by or for accounts with respect to which institutional investment managers exercise investment discretion, and (B) consistently with the objective set forth in the preceding subparagraph, to avoid unnecessarily duplicative reporting by, and minimize the compliance burden on, institutional investment managers. Federal authorities which, directly or indirectly, require reports from institutional investment managers of information substantially similar to that called for by this subsection shall cooperate with the Commission in the performance of its responsibilities under the preceding sentence. An institutional investment manager which is a bank, the deposits of which are insured in accordance with the Federal Deposit Insurance Act, shall file with the appropriate regulatory agency a copy of every report filed with the Commission pursuant to this subsection.

(5)(A) For purposes of this subsection the term "institutional investment manager" includes any person, other than a natural person, investing in or buying and selling securities for its own account, and any person exercising investment discretion with respect to the account of any other person.

(B) The Commission shall adopt such rules as it deems necessary or appropriate to prevent duplicative reporting pursuant to this subsection by two or more institutional investment managers exercising investment discretion with respect to the same amount.

(g)(1) Any person who is directly or indirectly the beneficial owner of more than 5 per centum of any security of a class described in subsection (d)(1) of this section shall send to the issuer of the security and shall file with the Commission a statement setting forth, in such form and at such time as the Commission may, by rule, prescribe—

(A) such person's identity, residence, and citizenship; and

(B) the number and description of the shares in which such person has an interest and the nature of such interest.

(2) If any material change occurs in the facts set forth in the statement sent to the issuer and filed with the Commission, an amendment shall be transmitted to the issuer and shall be filed with the Commission, in accordance with such rules and regulations as the Commission may prescribe as necessary or appropriate in the public interest or for the protection of investors.

(3) When two or more persons act as a partnership, limited partnership, syndicate, or other group for the purpose of acquiring, holding, or disposing of securities of an issuer, such syndicate or group shall be deemed a "person" for the purposes of this subsection.

(4) In determining, for purposes of this subsection, any percentage of a class of any security, such class shall be deemed to consist of the amount of the outstanding securities of such class, exclusive of any securities of such class held by or for the account of the issuer or a subsidiary of the issuer.

(5) In exercising its authority under this subsection, the Commission shall take such steps as it deems necessary or appropriate in the public interest or for the protection of investors (A) to achieve centralized reporting of information regarding ownership, (B) to avoid unnecessarily duplicative reporting by and minimize the compliance burden on persons required to report, and (C) to tabulate and promptly make available the information contained in any report filed pursuant to this subsection in a manner which will, in the view of the Commission, maximize the usefulness of the information to other Federal and State agencies and the public.

(6) The Commission may, by rule or order, exempt, in whole or in part, any person or class of persons from any or all of the reporting requirements of this subsection as it deems necessary or appropriate in the public interest or for the protection of investors.

(h) *Large Trader Reporting.*—

(1) *Identification Requirements for Large Traders.*—For the purpose of monitoring the impact on the securities markets of securities transactions involving a substantial volume or a large fair market value or exercise value and for the purpose of otherwise assisting the Commission in the enforcement of this title, each large trader shall—

(A) provide such information to the Commission as the Commission may by rule or regulation prescribe as necessary or appropriate, identifying such large trader and all accounts in or through which such large trader effects such transactions; and

(B) identify, in accordance with such rules or regulations as the Commission may prescribe as necessary or appropriate, to any registered broker or dealer by or through whom such large trader directly or indirectly effects securities transactions, such large trader and all accounts directly or indirectly maintained with such broker or dealer by such large trader in or through which such transactions are effected.

(2) *Recordkeeping and Reporting Requirements for Brokers and Dealers.*—Every registered broker or dealer shall make and keep for prescribed periods such records as the Commission by rule or regulation prescribes as necessary or appropriate in the public interest, for the protection of investors, or otherwise in furtherance of the purposes of this title, with respect to securities transactions that equal or exceed the reporting activity level effected directly or indirectly by or through such registered broker or dealer of or for any person that such broker or dealer knows is a large trader, or any person that such broker or dealer has reason to know is a large trader on the basis of transactions in securities effected by or

through such broker or dealer. Such records shall be available for reporting to the Commission, or any self-regulatory organization that the Commission shall designate to receive such reports, on the morning of the day following the day the transactions were effected, and shall be reported to the Commission or a self-regulatory organization designated by the Commission immediately upon request by the Commission or such a self-regulatory organization. Such records and reports shall be in a format and transmitted in a manner prescribed by the Commission (including, but not limited to, machine readable form).

(3) *Aggregation Rules.*—The Commission may prescribe rules or regulations governing the manner in which transactions and accounts shall be aggregated for the purpose of this subsection, including aggregation on the basis of common ownership or control.

(4) *Examination of Broker and Dealer Records.*—All records required to be made and kept by registered brokers and dealers pursuant to this subsection with respect to transactions effected by large traders are subject at any time, or from time to time, to such reasonable periodic, special, or other examinations by representatives of the Commission as the Commission deems necessary or appropriate in the public interest, for the protection of investors, or otherwise in furtherance of the purposes of this title.

(5) *Factors to be Considered in Commission Actions.*—In exercising its authority under this subsection, the Commission shall take into account—

(A) existing reporting systems;

(B) the costs associated with maintaining information with respect to transactions effected by large traders and reporting such information to the Commission or self-regulatory organizations; and

(C) the relationship between the United States and international securities markets.

(6) *Exemptions.*—The Commission, by rule, regulation, or order, consistent with the purposes of this title, may exempt any person or class of persons or any transaction or class of transactions, either conditionally or upon specified terms and conditions or for stated periods, from the operation of this subsection, and the rules and regulations thereunder.

(7) *Authority of Commission to Limit Disclosure of Information.*—Notwithstanding any other provision of law, the Commission shall not be compelled to disclose any information required to be kept or reported under this subsection. Nothing in this subsection shall authorize the Commission to withhold information from Congress, or prevent the Commission from complying with a request for information from any other Federal department or agency requesting information for purposes within the scope of its jurisdiction, or complying with an order of a court of the United States in an action brought by the United States or the Commission. For purposes of section 552 of title 5, United States Code, this subsection shall be considered a statute described in subsection (b)(3)(B) of such section 552.

(8) *Definitions.*—For purposes of this subsection—(A) the term "large trader" means every person who, for his own account or an account for which he exercises investment discretion, effects transactions for the purchase or sale of any publicly traded security or securities by use of any means or instrumentality of interstate commerce or of the mails, or of any facility of a national securities exchange, directly or indirectly by or through a registered broker or dealer in an aggregate amount equal to or in excess of the identifying activity level;

(B) the term "publicly traded security" means any equity security (including an option on individual equity securities, and an option on a group or index of such securities) listed, or admitted to unlisted trading privileges, on a national securities exchange, or quoted in an automated interdealer quotation system;

(C) the term "identifying activity level" means transactions in publicly traded securities at or above a level of volume, fair market value, or exercise value as shall be fixed from time to time by the Commission by rule or regulation, specifying the time interval during which such transactions shall be aggregated;

(D) the term "reporting activity level" means transactions in publicly traded securities at or above a level of volume, fair market value, or exercise value as shall be fixed from time to time by the Commission by rule, regulation, or order, specifying the time interval during which such transactions shall be aggregated; and

(E) the term "person" has the meaning given in section 3(a)(9) of this title and also includes two or more persons acting as a partnership, limited partnership, syndicate, or other group, but does not include a foreign central bank.

(i) Accuracy of Financial Reports.—Each financial report that contains financial statements, and that is required to be prepared in accordance with (or reconciled to) generally accepted accounting principles under this title and filed with the Commission shall reflect all material correcting adjustments that have been identified by a registered public accounting firm in accordance with generally accepted accounting principles and the rules and regulations of the Commission.

(j) Off-Balance Sheet Transactions.— Not later than 180 days after the date of enactment of the Sarbanes–Oxley Act of 2002, the Commission shall issue final rules providing that each annual and quarterly financial report required to be filed with the Commission shall disclose all material off-balance sheet transactions, arrangements, obligations (including contingent obligations), and other relationships of the issuer with unconsolidated entities or other persons, that may have a material current or future effect on financial condition, changes in financial condition, results of operations, liquidity, capital expenditures, capital resources, or significant components of revenues or expenses.

(k) Prohibition on Personal Loans to Executives.—

(1) In general.—It shall be unlawful for any issuer (as defined in section 2 of the Sarbanes–Oxley Act of 2002), directly or indirectly, including through any subsidiary, to extend or maintain credit, to arrange for the extension of credit, or to renew an extension of credit, in the form of a personal loan to or for any director or executive officer (or equivalent thereof) of that issuer. An extension of credit maintained by the issuer on the date of enactment of this subsection shall not be subject to the provisions of this subsection, provided that there is no material modification to any term of any such extension of credit or any renewal of any such extension of credit on or after that date of enactment.

(2) Limitation.—Paragraph (1) does not preclude any home improvement and manufactured home loans (as that term is defined in section 5 of the Home Owners' Loan Act (12 U.S.C. 1464)), consumer credit (as defined in section 103 of the Truth in Lending Act (15 U.S.C. 1602)), or any extension of credit under an open end credit plan (as defined in section 103 of the Truth in Lending Act (15 U.S.C. 1602), or a charge card (as defined in section 127(c)(4)(e) of the Truth in Lending Act (15 U.S.C. 1637(c)(4)(e)), or any extension of credit by a broker or dealer registered under section 15 of this title to an employee of that broker or dealer to buy, trade, or carry securities, that is permitted under rules or regulations of the Board of Governors of the Federal Reserve System pursuant to section 7 of this title (other than an extension of credit that would be used to purchase the stock of that issuer), that is—

(A) made or provided in the ordinary course of the consumer credit business of such issuer;

(B) of a type that is generally made available by such issuer to the public; and

(C) made by such issuer on market terms, or terms that are no more favorable than those offered by the issuer to the general public for such extensions of credit.

(3) Rule of construction for certain loans.—Paragraph (1) does not apply to any loan made or maintained by an insured depository institution (as defined in section 3 of the Federal Deposit Insurance Act (12 U.S.C. 1813)), if the loan is subject to the insider lending restrictions of section 22(h) of the Federal Reserve Act (12 U.S.C. 375b).

(*l*) Real Time Issuer Disclosures.—Each issuer reporting under section 13(a) or 15(d) shall disclose to the public on a rapid and current basis such additional information concerning material changes in the financial condition or operations of the issuer, in plain English, which may include trend and qualitative information and graphic presentations, as the Commission determines, by rule, is necessary or useful for the protection of investors and in the public interest.

Proxies

Sec. 14. (a) It shall be unlawful for any person, by the use of the mails or by any means or instrumentality of interstate commerce or of any facility of a national securities exchange or otherwise, in contravention of such rules and regulations as the Commission may prescribe as necessary or appropriate in the public interest or for the protection of investors, to solicit or to permit the use of his name to solicit any proxy or consent or authorization in respect of any security (other than an exempted security) registered pursuant to section 12 of this title.

(b)(1) It shall be unlawful for any member of a national securities exchange, or any broker or dealer registered under this title, or any bank, association, or other entity that exercises fiduciary powers, in contravention of such rules and regulations as the Commission may prescribe as necessary or appropriate in the public interest or for the protection of investors, to give, or to refrain from giving a proxy, consent, authorization, or information statement in respect of any security registered pursuant to section 12 of this title, or any security issued by an investment company registered under the Investment Company Act of 1940, and carried for the account of a customer.

(2) With respect to banks, the rules and regulations prescribed by the Commission under paragraph (1) shall not require the disclosure of the names of beneficial owners of securities in an account held by the bank on the date of enactment of this paragraph unless the beneficial owner consents to the disclosure. The provisions of this paragraph shall not apply in the case of a bank which the Commission finds has not made a good faith effort to obtain such consent from such beneficial owners.

(c) Unless proxies, consents, or authorizations in respect of a security registered pursuant to section 12 of this title, or a security issued by an investment company registered under the Investment Company Act of 1940, are solicited by or on behalf of the management of the issuer from the holders of record of such security in accordance with the rules and regulations prescribed under subsection (a) of this section, prior to any annual or other meeting of the holders of such security, such issuer shall, in accordance with rules and regulations prescribed by the Commission, file with the Commission and transmit to all holders of record of such security information substantially equivalent to the information which would be required to be transmitted if a solicitation were made, but no information shall be required to be filed or transmitted pursuant to this subsection before July 1, 1964.

(d)(1) It shall be unlawful for any person, directly or indirectly, by use of the mails or by any means or instrumentality of interstate commerce or of any facility of a national securities exchange or otherwise, to make a tender offer for, or a request or invitation for tenders of, any class of any equity security which is registered pursuant to section 12 of this title, or any equity security of an insurance company which would have been required to be so registered except for the exemption contained in section 12(g)(2)(G) of this title, or any equity security issued by a closed-end investment company registered under the Investment Company Act of 1940, if, after consummation thereof, such person would, directly or indirectly, be the beneficial owner of more than 5 per centum of such class, unless at the time copies of the offer or request or invitation are first published or sent or given to security holders such person has filed with the Commission a statement containing such of the information specified in section 13(d) of this title, and such additional information as the Commission may by rules and regulations prescribed as necessary or appropriate in the public interest or for the protection of investors. All requests or invitations for tenders or advertisements making a tender offer or requesting or inviting tenders of such a security shall be filed as a part of such statement and shall contain such of the information contained in such statement as the Commission may by rules and regulations prescribe. Copies of any additional material soliciting or requesting such tender offers subsequent to the initial solicitation or request shall contain such information as the Commission may by rules and regulations prescribe as necessary or appropriate in the public interest or for the protection of investors, and shall be filed with the Commission not later than the time copies of such material are first published or sent or given to security holders. Copies of all statements, in the form in which such material is furnished to security holders and the Commission, shall be sent to the issuer not later than the date such material is first published or sent or given to any security holders.

(2) When two or more persons act as a partnership, limited partnership, syndicate, or other group for the purpose of acquiring, holding, or disposing of securities of an issuer, such syndicate or group shall be deemed a "person" for purposes of this subsection.

(3) In determining, for purposes of this subsection, any percentage of a class of any security, such class shall be deemed to consist of the amount of the outstanding securities of such class, exclusive of any securities of such class held by or for the account of the issuer or a subsidiary of the issuer.

(4) Any solicitation or recommendation to the holders of such a security to accept or reject a tender offer or request or invitation for tenders shall be made in accordance with such rules and regulations as the Commission may prescribe as necessary or appropriate in the public interest or for the protection of investors.

(5) Securities deposited pursuant to a tender offer or request or invitation for tenders may be withdrawn by or on behalf of the depositor at any time until the expiration of seven days after the time definitive copies of the offer or request or invitation are first published or sent or given to security holders, and at any time after sixty days from the date of the original tender offer or request or invitation, except as the Commission may otherwise prescribe by rules, regulations, or order as necessary or appropriate in the public interest or for the protection of investors.

(6) Where any person makes a tender offer, or request or invitation for tenders, for less than all the outstanding equity securities of a class, and where a greater number of securities is deposited pursuant thereto within ten days after copies of the offer or request or invitation are first published or sent or given to security holders than such person is bound or willing to take up and pay for the securities taken up shall be taken up as nearly as may be pro rata, disregarding fractions, according to the number of securities deposited by each depositor. The provisions of this subsection shall also apply to securities deposited within ten days after notice of an increase in the consideration offered to security holders, as described in paragraph (7), is first published or sent or given to security holders.

(7) Where any person varies the terms of a tender offer or request or invitation for tenders before the expiration thereof by increas-

ing the consideration offered to holders of such securities, such person shall pay the increased consideration to each security holder whose securities are taken up and paid for pursuant to the tender offer or request or invitation for tenders whether or not such securities have been taken up by such person before the variation of the tender offer or request or invitation.

(8) The provisions of this subsection shall not apply to any offer for, or request or invitation for tenders of, any security—

(A) if the acquisition of such security, together with all other acquisitions by the same person of securities of the same class during the preceding twelve months, would not exceed 2 per centum of that class;

(B) by the issuer of such security; or

(C) which the Commission, by rules or regulations or by order, shall exempt from the provisions of this subsection as not entered into for the purpose of, and not having the effect of, changing or influencing the control of the issuer or otherwise as not comprehended within the purposes of this subsection.

(e) It shall be unlawful for any person to make any untrue statement of a material fact or omit to state any material fact necessary in order to make the statements made, in the light of the circumstances under which they are made, not misleading, or to engage in any fraudulent, deceptive, or manipulative acts or practices, in connection with any tender offer or request or invitation for tenders, or any solicitation of security holders in opposition to or in favor of any such offer, request, or invitation. The Commission shall, for the purposes of this subsection, by rules and regulations define, and prescribe means reasonably designed to prevent, such acts and practices as are fraudulent, deceptive, or manipulative.

(f) If, pursuant to any arrangement or understanding with the person or persons acquiring securities in a transaction subject to subsection (d) of this section or subsection (d) of section 13 of this title, any persons are to be elected or designated as directors of the issuer, otherwise than at a meeting of security holders, and the persons so elected or designated will constitute a majority of the directors of the issuer, then, prior to the time any such person takes office as a director, and in accordance with rules and regulations prescribed by the Commission, the issuer shall file with the Commission, and transmit to all holders of record of securities of the issuer who would be entitled to vote at a meeting for election of directors, information substantially equivalent to the information which would be required by subsection (a) or (c) of this section to be transmitted if such person or persons were nominees for election as directors at a meeting of such security holders.

(g)(1)(A) At the time of filing such preliminary proxy solicitation material as the Commission may require by rule pursuant to subsection (a) of this section that concerns an acquisition, merger, consolidation, or proposed sale or other disposition of substantially all the assets of a company, the person making such filing, other than a company registered under the Investment Company Act of 1940, shall pay to the Commission the following fees:

(i) for preliminary proxy solicitation material involving an acquisition, merger, or consolidation, if there is a proposed payment of cash or transfer of securities or property to shareholders, a fee at a rate that, subject to paragraphs (5) and (6), is equal to $92 per $1,000,000* of such proposed payment, or of the value of such securities or other property proposed to be transferred; and

(ii) for preliminary proxy solicitation material involving a proposed sale or other disposition of substantially all of the assets of a company, a fee at a rate that, subject to paragraphs (5) and (6), is equal to $92 per $1,000,000* of the cash or of the value of

* The Consolidated Appropriations Act of 2004, P.L. 108–199, 118 Stat. 3, increased the rate applicable to Section 14(g) to $126.70 per million effective January 28, 2004.

any securities or other property proposed to be received upon such sale or disposition.

(B) The fee imposed under subparagraph (A) shall be reduced with respect to securities in an amount equal to any fee paid to the Commission with respect to such securities in connection with the proposed transaction under section 6(b) of the Securities Act of 1933 (15 U.S.C. 77f(b)), or the fee paid under that section shall be reduced in an amount equal to the fee paid to the Commission in connection with such transaction under this subsection. Where two or more companies involved in an acquisition, merger, consolidation, sale, or other disposition of substantially all the assets of a company must file such proxy material with the Commission, each shall pay a proportionate share of such fee.

(2) At the time of filing such preliminary information statement as the Commission may require by rule pursuant to subsection (c) of this section, the issuer shall pay to the Commission the same fee as required for preliminary proxy solicitation material under paragraph (1) of this subsection.

(3) At the time of filing such statement as the Commission may require by rule pursuant to subsection (d)(1) of this section, the person making the filing shall pay to the Commission a fee at a rate that, subject to paragraphs (5) and (6), is equal to $92 per $1,000,000* of the aggregate amount of cash or of the value of securities or other property proposed to be offered. The fee shall be reduced with respect to securities in an amount equal to any fee paid with respect to such securities in connection with the proposed transaction under section 6(b) of the Securities Act of 1933 (15 U.S.C. 77f(b)), or the fee paid under that section shall be reduced in an amount equal to the fee paid to the Commission in connection with such transaction under this subsection.

(4) Offsetting collections.—Fees collected pursuant to this subsection for any fiscal year shall be deposited and credited as offsetting collections to the account providing appropriations to the Commission, and, except as provided in paragraph (9), shall not be collected for any fiscal year except to the extent provided in advance in appropriation Acts. No fees collected pursuant to this subsection for fiscal year 2002 or any succeeding fiscal year shall be deposited and credited as general revenue of the Treasury.

(5) Annual adjustment.—For each of the fiscal years 2003 through 2011, the Commission shall by order adjust each of the rates required by paragraphs (1) and (3) for such fiscal year to a rate that is equal to the rate (expressed in dollars per million) that is applicable under section 6(b) of the Securities Act of 1933 for such fiscal year.

(6) Final rate adjustment.—For fiscal year 2012 and all of the succeeding fiscal years, the Commission shall by order adjust each of the rates required by paragraphs (1) and (3) for all of such fiscal years to a rate that is equal to the rate (expressed in dollars per million) that is applicable under section 6(b) of the Securities Act of 1933 for all of such fiscal years.

(7) Pro rata application.—The rates per $1,000,000 required by this subsection shall be applied pro rata to amounts and balances of less than $1,000,000.

(8) Review and effective date.—In exercising its authority under this subsection, the Commission shall not be required to comply with the provisions of section 553 of title 5, United States Code. An adjusted rate prescribed under paragraph (5) or (6) and published under paragraph (10) shall not be subject to judicial review. Subject to paragraphs (4) and (9)—

(A) an adjusted rate prescribed under paragraph (5) shall take effect on the later of—

(i) the first day of the fiscal year to which such rate applies; or

* The Consolidated Appropriations Act of 2004, P.L. 108–199, 118 Stat. 3, increased the rate applicable to Section 14(g) to $126.70 per million effective January 28, 2004.

(ii) five days after the date on which a regular appropriation to the Commission for such fiscal year is enacted; and

(B) an adjusted rate prescribed under paragraph (6) shall take effect on the later of—

(i) the first day of fiscal year 2012; or

(ii) five days after the date on which a regular appropriation to the Commission for fiscal year 2012 is enacted.

(9) Lapse of appropriation.—If on the first day of a fiscal year a regular appropriation to the Commission has not been enacted, the Commission shall continue to collect fees (as offsetting collections) under this subsection at the rate in effect during the preceding fiscal year, until 5 days after the date such a regular appropriation is enacted.

(10) Publication.—The rate applicable under this subsection for each fiscal year is published pursuant to section 6(b)(10) of the Securities Act of 1933.

(11) Notwithstanding any other provision of law, the Commission may impose fees, charges, or prices for matters not involving any acquisition, merger, consolidation, sale, or other disposition of assets described in this subsection, as authorized by section 9701 of title 31, United States Code, or otherwise.

(h) Proxy Solicitations and Tender Offers in Connection With Limited Partnership Rollup Transactions.—

(1) Proxy rules to contain special provisions.—It shall be unlawful for any person to solicit any proxy, consent, or authorization concerning a limited partnership rollup transaction, or to make any tender offer in furtherance of a limited partnership rollup transaction, unless such transaction is conducted in accordance with rules prescribed by the Commission under subsections (a) and (d) as required by this subsection. Such rules shall—

(A) permit any holder of a security that is the subject of the proposed limited partnership rollup transaction to engage in preliminary communications for the purpose of determining whether to solicit proxies, consents, or authorizations in opposition to the proposed limited partnership rollup transaction, without regard to whether any such communication would otherwise be considered a solicitation of proxies, and without being required to file soliciting material with the Commission prior to making that determination, except that—

(i) nothing in this subparagraph shall be construed to limit the application of any provision of this title prohibiting, or reasonably designed to prevent, fraudulent, deceptive, or manipulative acts or practices under this title; and

(ii) any holder of not less than 5 percent of the outstanding securities that are the subject of the proposed limited partnership rollup transaction who engages in the business of buying and selling limited partnership interests in the secondary market shall be required to disclose such ownership interests and any potential conflicts of interests in such preliminary communications;

(B) require the issuer to provide to holders of the securities that are the subject of the limited partnership rollup transaction such list of the holders of the issuer's securities as the Commission may determine in such form and subject to such terms and conditions as the Commission may specify;

(C) prohibit compensating any person soliciting proxies, consents, or authorizations directly from security holders concerning such a limited partnership rollup transaction—

(i) on the basis of whether the solicited proxy, consent, or authorization either approves or disapproves the proposed limited partnership rollup transaction; or

(ii) contingent on the approval, disapproval, or completion of the limited partnership rollup transaction;

(D) set forth disclosure requirements for soliciting material distributed in connection with a limited partnership rollup transaction, including requirements for clear, concise, and comprehensible disclosure with respect to—

(i) any changes in the business plan, voting rights, form of ownership interest, or the compensation of the general partner in the proposed limited partnership rollup transaction from each of the original limited partnerships;

(ii) the conflicts of interest, if any, of the general partner;

(iii) whether it is expected that there will be a significant difference between the exchange values of the limited partnerships and the trading price of the securities to be issued in the limited partnership rollup transaction;

(iv) the valuation of the limited partnerships and the method used to determine the value of the interests of the limited partners to be exchanged for the securities in the limited partnership rollup transaction;

(v) the differing risks and effects of the limited partnership rollup transaction for investors in different limited partnerships proposed to be included, and the risks and effects of completing the limited partnership rollup transaction with less than all limited partnerships;

(vi) the statement by the general partner required under subparagraph (E);

(vii) such other matters deemed necessary or appropriate by the Commission;

(E) require a statement by the general partner as to whether the proposed limited partnership rollup transaction is fair or unfair to investors in each limited partnership, a discussion of the basis for that conclusion, and an evaluation and a description by the general partner of alternatives to the limited partnership rollup transaction, such as liquidation;

(F) provide that, if the general partner or sponsor has obtained any opinion (other than an opinion of counsel), appraisal, or report that is prepared by an outside party and that is materially related to the limited partnership rollup transaction, such soliciting materials shall contain or be accompanied by clear, concise, and comprehensible disclosure with respect to—

(i) the analysis of the transaction, scope of review, preparation of the opinion, and basis for and methods of arriving at conclusions, and any representations and undertakings with respect thereto;

(ii) the identity and qualifications of the person who prepared the opinion, the method of selection of such person, and any material past, existing, or contemplated relationships between the person or any of its affiliates and the general partner, sponsor, successor, or any other affiliate;

(iii) any compensation of the preparer of such opinion, appraisal, or report that is contingent on the transaction's approval or completion; and

(iv) any limitations imposed by the issuer on the access afforded to such preparer to the issuer's personnel, premises, and relevant books and records;

(G) provide that, if the general partner or sponsor has obtained any opinion, appraisal, or report as described in subparagraph (F) from any person whose compensation is contingent on the transaction's approval or completion or who has not been given access by the issuer to its personnel and premises and relevant books and records, the general partner or sponsor shall state the reasons therefor;

(H) provide that, if the general partner or sponsor has not obtained any opinion on the fairness of the proposed limited partnership rollup transaction to investors in each of the affected partnerships, such soliciting materials shall contain or be accompanied by a statement of such partner's or sponsor's reasons for concluding that such an opinion is not necessary in order to permit the limited partners to make an informed decision on the proposed transaction;

(I) require that the soliciting material include a clear, concise, and comprehensible summary of the limited partnership rollup transaction (including a summary of the matters referred to in clauses (i) through (vii) of subparagraph (D) and a summary of the matter referred to in subparagraphs (F), (G), and (H)), with the risks of the limited partnership rollup transaction set forth prominently in the fore part thereof;

(J) provide that any solicitation or offering period with respect to any proxy solicitation, tender offer, or information statement in a limited partnership rollup transaction shall be for not less than the lesser of 60 calendar days or the maximum number of days permitted under applicable State law; and

(K) contain such other provisions as the Commission determines to be necessary or appropriate for the protection of investors in limited partnership rollup transactions.

(2) Exemptions.—The Commission may, consistent with the public interest, the protection of investors, and the purposes of this title, exempt by rule or order any security or class of securities, any transaction or class of transactions, or any person or class of persons, in whole or in part, conditionally or unconditionally, from the requirements imposed pursuant to paragraph (1) or from the definition contained in paragraph (4).

(3) Effect on Commission authority.—Nothing in this subsection limits the authority of the Commission under subsection (a) or (d) or any other provision of this title or precludes the Commission from imposing, under subsection (a) or (d) or any other provision of this title, a remedy or procedure required to be imposed under this subsection.

(4) Definition of limited partnership rollup transaction.—Except as provided in paragraph (5), as used in this subsection, the term "limited partnership rollup transaction" means a transaction involving the combination or reorganization of one or more limited partnerships, directly or indirectly, in which—

(A) some or all of the investors in any of such limited partnerships will receive new securities, or securities in another entity, that will be reported under a transaction reporting plan declared effective before the date of enactment of this subsection by the Commission under section 11A;

(B) any of the investors' limited partnership securities are not, as of the date of filing, reported under a transaction reporting plan declared effective before the date of enactment of this subsection by the Commission under section 11A;

(C) investors in any of the limited partnerships involved in the transaction are subject to a significant adverse change with respect to voting rights, the term of existence of the entity, management compensation, or investment objectives; and

(D) any of such investors are not provided an option to receive or retain a security under substantially the same terms and conditions as the original issue.

(5) Exclusions from definition.—Notwithstanding paragraph (4), the term "limited

partnership rollup transaction" does not include—

(A) a transaction that involves only a limited partnership or partnerships having an operating policy or practice of retaining cash available for distribution and reinvesting proceeds from the sale, financing, or refinancing of assets in accordance with such criteria as the Commission determines appropriate;

(B) a transaction involving only limited partnerships wherein the interests of the limited partners are repurchased, recalled, or exchanged in accordance with the terms of the preexisting limited partnership agreements for securities in an operating company specifically identified at the time of the formation of the original limited partnership;

(C) a transaction in which the securities to be issued or exchanged are not required to be and are not registered under the Securities Act of 1933;

(D) a transaction that involves only issuers that are not required to register or report under section 12, both before and after the transaction;

(E) a transaction, except as the Commission may otherwise provide by rule for the protection of investors, involving the combination or reorganization of one or more limited partnerships in which a non-affiliated party succeeds to the interests of a general partner or sponsor, if—

(i) such action is approved by not less than 66⅔ percent of the outstanding units of each of the participating limited partnerships; and

(ii) as a result of the transaction, the existing general partners will receive only compensation to which they are entitled as expressly provided for in the preexisting limited partnership agreements; or

(F) a transaction, except as the Commission may otherwise provide by rule for the protection of investors, in which the securities offered to investors are securities of another entity that are reported under a transaction reporting plan declared effective before the date of enactment of this subsection by the Commission under section 11A, if—

(i) such other entity was formed, and such class of securities was reported and regularly traded, not less than 12 months before the date on which soliciting material is mailed to investors; and

(ii) the securities of that entity issued to investors in the transaction do not exceed 20 percent of the total outstanding securities of the entity, exclusive of any securities of such class held by or for the account of the entity or a subsidiary of the entity.

Registration and Regulation of Brokers and Dealers

Sec. 15. (a)(1) It shall be unlawful for any broker or dealer which is either a person other than a natural person or a natural person not associated with a broker or dealer which is a person other than a natural person (other than such a broker or dealer whose business is exclusively intrastate and who does not make use of any facility of a national securities exchange) to make use of the mails or any means or instrumentality of interstate commerce to effect any transactions in, or to induce or attempt to induce the purchase or sale of, any security (other than an exempted security or commercial paper, bankers' acceptances, or commercial bills) unless such broker or dealer is registered in accordance with subsection (b) of this section.

(2) The Commission, by rule or order, as it deems consistent with the public interest and the protection of investors, may conditionally or unconditionally exempt from paragraph (1) of this subsection any broker or dealer or class of brokers or dealers specified in such rule or order.

(b)(1) A broker or dealer may be registered by filing with the Commission an application for registration in such form and containing such information and documents concerning such broker or dealer and any persons associated with such broker or dealer as the Commission, by rule, may prescribe as necessary or appropriate in the public interest or for the protection of investors. Within forty-five days of the date of the filing of such application (or within such longer period as to which the applicant consents), the Commission shall—

(A) by order grant registration, or

(B) institute proceedings to determine whether registration should be denied. Such proceedings shall include notice of the grounds for denial under consideration and opportunity for hearing and shall be concluded within one hundred twenty days of the date of the filing of the application for registration. At the conclusion of such proceedings, the Commission, by order, shall grant or deny such registration. The order granting registration shall not be effective until such broker or dealer has become a member of a registered securities association, or until such broker or dealer has become a member of a national securities exchange if such broker or dealer effects transactions solely on that exchange, unless the Commission has exempted such broker or dealer, by rule or order, from such membership. The Commission may extend the time for conclusion of such proceedings for up to ninety days if it finds good cause for such extension and publishes its reasons for so finding or for such longer period as to which the applicant consents.

The Commission shall grant such registration if the Commission finds that the requirements of this section are satisfied. The Commission shall deny such registration if it does not make such a finding or if it finds that if the applicant were so registered, its registration would be subject to suspension, or revocation under paragraph (4) of this subsection.

(2)(A) An application for registration of a broker or dealer to be formed or organized may be made by a broker or dealer to which the broker or dealer to be formed or organized is to be the successor. Such application, in such form as the Commission, by rule, may prescribe, shall contain such information and documents concerning the applicant, the successor, and any persons associated with the applicant or the successor, as the Commission, by rule, may prescribe as necessary or appropriate in the public interest or for the protection of investors. The grant or denial of registration to such an applicant shall be in accordance with the procedures set forth in paragraph (1) of this subsection. If the Commission grants such registration, the registration shall terminate on the forty-fifth day after the effective date thereof, unless prior thereto the successor shall, in accordance with such rules and regulations as the Commission may prescribe, adopt the application for registration as its own.

(B) Any person who is a broker or dealer solely by reason of acting as municipal securities dealer or municipal securities broker, who so acts through a separately identifiable department or division, and who so acted in such a manner on the date of enactment of the Securities Acts Amendments of 1975, may, in accordance with such terms and conditions as the Commission, by rule, prescribes as necessary and appropriate in the public interest and for the protection of investors, register such separately identifiable department or division in accordance with this subsection. If any such department or division is so registered, the department or division and not such person himself shall be the broker or dealer for purposes of this title.

(C) Within six months of the date of the granting of registration to a broker or dealer, the Commission, or upon the authorization and direction of the Commission, a registered securities association or national securities exchange of which such broker or dealer is a member, shall conduct an inspection of the broker or dealer to determine whether it is operating in conformity with the provisions of this title and the rules and regulations thereunder: *Provided, however,* That the Commission may delay such inspection of any class of brokers or dealers for a period not to exceed six months.

(3) Any provision of this title (other than section 5 and subsection (a) of this section) which prohibits any act, practice, or course of business if the mails or any means or instrumentality of interstate commerce is used in connection therewith shall also prohibit any such act, practice, or course of business by any registered broker or dealer or any person acting on behalf of such a broker or dealer, irrespective of any use of the mails or any means or instrumentality of interstate commerce in connection therewith.

(4) The Commission, by order, shall censure, place limitations on the activities, functions, or operations of, suspend for a period not exceeding twelve months, or revoke the registration of any broker or dealer if it finds, on the record after notice and opportunity for hearing, that such censure, placing of limitations, suspension, or revocation is in the public interest and that such broker or dealer, whether prior or subsequent to becoming such, or any person associated with such broker or dealer, whether prior or subsequent to becoming so associated—

(A) has willfully made or caused to be made in any application for registration or report required to be filed with the Commission or with any other appropriate regulatory agency under this title, or in any proceeding before the Commission with respect to registration, any statement which was at the time and in the light of the circumstances under which it was made false or misleading with respect to any material fact, or has omitted to state in any such application or report any material fact which is required to be stated therein.

(B) has been convicted within ten years preceding the filing of any application for registration or at any time thereafter of any felony or misdemeanor of a substantially equivalent crime by a foreign court of competent jurisdiction which the Commission finds—

(i) involves the purchase or sale of any security, the taking of a false oath, the making of a false report, bribery, perjury, burglary, any substantially equivalent activity however denominated by the laws of the relevant foreign government or conspiracy to commit any such offense;

(ii) arises out of the conduct of the business of a broker, dealer, municipal securities dealer, government securities broker, government securities dealer, investment adviser, bank, insurance company, fiduciary, transfer agent, foreign person performing a function substantially equivalent to any of the above or entity or person required to be registered under the Commodity Exchange Act (7 U.S.C. 1 et seq.) or any substantially equivalent foreign statute or regulation;

(iii) involves the larceny, theft, robbery, extortion, forgery, counterfeiting, fraudulent concealment, embezzlement, fraudulent conversion, or misappropriation of funds or securities, or substantially equivalent activity however denominated by the laws of the relevant foreign government, or

(iv) involves the violation of section 152, 1341, 1342, or 1343 or chapter 25 or 47 of title 18, United States Code or a violation of a substantially equivalent foreign statute.

(C) is permanently or temporarily enjoined by order, judgment, or decree of any court of competent jurisdiction from acting as an investment adviser, underwriter, broker, dealer, municipal securities dealer, government securities broker, government securities dealer, transfer agent, foreign person performing a function substantially equivalent to any of the above, or entity or person required to be registered under the Commodity Exchange Act, or any substantially equivalent foreign statute or regulation, or as an affiliated person or employee of any investment company, bank, insurance company, foreign entity substantially equivalent to any of the above, or entity or person required to be registered under the Commodity Exchange Act or any substantially equivalent foreign statute or regulation, or from engaging in or continuing any conduct or practice in connection with any such activity, or in connection with the purchase or sale of any security.

(D) has willfully violated any provision of the Securities Act of 1933, the Investment Advisers Act of 1940, the Investment Company Act of 1940, the Commodity Exchange Act, this title, the rules or regulations under any of such statutes, or the rules of the Municipal Securities Rulemaking Board, or is unable to comply with any such provision.

(E) has willfully aided, abetted, counseled, commanded, induced, or procured the violation by any person of any provision of the Securities Act of 1933, the Investment Advisers Act of 1940, the Investment Company Act of 1940, the Commodity Exchange Act, this title, the rules or regulations under any of such statutes, or the rules of the Municipal Securities Rulemaking Board, or has failed reasonably to supervise, with a view to preventing violations of the provisions of such statutes, rules, and regulations, another person who commits such a violation, if such other person is subject to his supervision. For the purposes of this subparagraph (E) no person shall be deemed to have failed reasonably to supervise any other person, if—

(i) there have been established procedures, and a system for applying such procedures, which would reasonably be expected to prevent and detect, insofar as practicable, any such violation by such other person, and

(ii) such person has reasonably discharged the duties and obligations incumbent upon him by reason of such procedures and system without reasonable cause to believe that such procedures and system were not being complied with.

(F) is subject to an order of the Commission barring or suspending the right of the person to be associated with a broker or dealer;

(G) has been found a foreign financial regulatory authority to have—

(i) made or caused to be made in any application for registration or report required to be filed with a foreign financial regulatory authority, or in any proceeding before a foreign financial regulatory authority with respect to registration, any statement that was at the time and in the light of the circumstances under which it was made false or misleading with respect to any material fact, or has omitted to state in any application or report to the foreign financial regulatory authority any material fact that is required to be stated therein;

(ii) violated any foreign statute or regulation regarding transactions in securities, or contracts of sale of a commodity for future delivery, traded on or subject to the rules of a contract market or any board of trade;

(iii) aided, abetted, counseled, commanded, induced, or procured the violation by any person of any provision of any statutory provisions enacted by a foreign government, or rules or regulations thereunder, empowering a foreign financial regulatory authority regarding transactions in securities, or contracts of sale of a commodity for future delivery, traded on or subject to the rules of a contract market or any board of trade, or has been found, by a foreign financial regulatory authority, to have failed reasonably to supervise, with a view to preventing violations of such statutory provisions, rules, and regulations, another person who commits such a violation, if such other person is subject to his supervision; or

(H) is subject to any final order of a State securities commission (or any agency or officer performing like functions), State authority that supervises or examines banks, savings associations, or credit unions, State insurance commission (or any agency or office performing like functions), an appropriate Federal banking agency (as defined in section 3 of the Federal Deposit Insurance Act (12 U.S.C. 1813(q))), or the National Credit Union Administration, that—

(i) bars such person from association with an entity regulated by such commission, authority, agency, or officer, or from engaging in the business of securities, insurance, banking, savings association activities, or credit union activities; or

(ii) constitutes a final order based on violations of any laws or regulations that prohibit fraudulent, manipulative, or deceptive conduct.

(5) Pending final determination whether any registration under this subsection shall be revoked, the Commission, by order, may suspend such registration, if such suspension appears to the Commission, after notice and opportunity for hearing, to be necessary or appropriate in the public interest or for the protection of investors. Any registered broker or dealer may, upon such terms and conditions as the Commission deems necessary or appropriate in the public interest or for the protection of investors, withdraw from registration by filing a written notice of withdrawal with the Commission. If the Commission finds that any registered broker or dealer is no longer in existence or has ceased to do business as a broker or dealer, the Commission, by order, shall cancel the registration of such broker or dealer.

(6)(A) With respect to any person who is associated, who is seeking to become associated, or, at the time of the alleged misconduct, who was associated or was seeking to become associated with a broker or dealer, or any person participating, or, at the time of the alleged misconduct, who was participating, in an offering of any penny stock, the Commission, by order, shall censure, place limitations on the activities or functions of such person, or suspend for a period not exceeding 12 months, or bar such person from being associated with a broker or dealer, or from participating in an offering of penny stock, if the Commission finds, on the record after notice and opportunity for a hearing, that such censure, placing of limitations, suspension, or bar is in the public interest and that such person—

(i) has committed or omitted any act or is subject to an order or finding enumerated in subparagraph (A), (D), (E), (H), or (G) of paragraph (4) of this subsection;

(ii) has been convicted of any offense specified in subparagraph (B) of such paragraph (4) within 10 years of the commencement of the proceedings under this paragraph; or

(iii) is enjoined from any action, conduct, or practice specified in subparagraph (C) of such paragraph (4).

(B) It shall be unlawful—

(i) for any person as to whom an order under subparagraph (A) is in effect, without the consent of the Commission, willfully to become, or to be, associated with a broker or dealer in contravention of such order, or to participate in an offering of penny stock in contravention of such order;

(ii) for any broker or dealer to permit such a person, without the consent of the Commission, to become or remain, a person associated with the broker or dealer in contravention of such order, if such broker or dealer knew, or in the exercise of reasonable care should have known, of such order; or

(iii) for any broker or dealer to permit such a person, without the consent of the Commission, to participate in an offering of penny stock in contravention of such order, if such broker or dealer knew, or in the exercise of reasonable care should have known, of such order and of such participation.

(C) For purposes of this paragraph, the term "person participating in an offering of penny stock" includes any person acting as any promoter, finder, consultant, agent, or other person who engages in activities with a broker, dealer, or issuer for purposes of the issuance or trading in any penny stock, or inducing or attempting to induce the purchase or sale of any penny stock. The Commission may, by rule or regulation, define such term to include other activities, and may, by rule, regulation, or order, exempt any person or class of persons, in whole or in part, conditionally or unconditionally, from such term.

(7) No registered broker or dealer or government securities broker or government securities dealer registered (or required to register) under section 15C(a)(1)(A) shall effect any transaction in, or induce the purchase or sale of, any security unless such broker or dealer meets such standards of operational capability and such broker or dealer and all natural persons associated with such broker or dealer meet such standards of training, experience, competence, and such other qualifications as the Commission finds necessary or appropriate in the public interest or for the protection of investors. The Commission shall establish such standards by rules and regulations, which may—

(A) specify that all or any portion of such standards shall be applicable to any class of brokers and dealers and persons associated with brokers and dealers;

(B) require persons in any such class to pass tests prescribed in accordance with such rules and regulations, which tests shall, with respect to any class of partners, officers, or supervisory employees (which latter term may be defined by the Commission's rules and regulations and as so defined shall include branch managers of brokers or dealers) engaged in the management of the broker or dealer, include questions relating to bookkeeping, accounting, internal control over cash and securities, supervision of employees, maintenance of records, and other appropriate matters; and

(C) provide that persons in any such class other than brokers and dealers and partners, officers, and supervisory employees of brokers or dealers, may be qualified solely on the basis of compliance with such standards of training and such other qualifications as the Commission finds appropriate.

The Commission, by rule, may prescribe reasonable fees and charges to defray its costs in carrying out this paragraph, including, but not limited to, fees for any test administered by it or under its direction. The Commission may cooperate with registered securities associations and national securities exchanges in devising and administering tests and may require registered brokers and dealers and persons associated with such brokers and dealers to pass tests administered by or on behalf of any such association or exchange and to pay such association or exchange reasonable fees or charges to defray the costs incurred by such association or exchange in administering such tests.

(8) It shall be unlawful for any registered broker or dealer to effect any transaction in, or induce or attempt to induce the purchase or sale of, any security (other than commercial paper, bankers' acceptances, or commercial bills), unless such broker or dealer is a member of a securities association registered pursuant to section 15A of this title or effects transactions in securities solely on a national securities exchange of which it is a member.

(9) The Commission by rule or order, as it deems consistent with the public interest and the protection of investors, may conditionally or unconditionally exempt from paragraph (8) of this subsection any broker or dealer or class of brokers or dealers specified in such rule or order.

(10) For the purposes of determining whether a person is subject to a statutory disqualification under section 6(c)(2), 15A(g)(2), or 17A(b)(4)(A) of this title, the term "Commission" in paragraph (4)(B) of this subsection shall mean "exchange", "association", or "clearing agency", respectively.

(11) *Broker/Dealer Registration With Respect to Transactions in Security Futures Products.*—

(A) *Notice Registration.*—

(i) *Contents of Notice.*—Notwithstanding paragraphs (1) and (2), a broker or dealer required to register only because it effects transactions in security futures products on an exchange registered pursuant to section 6(g) may register for purposes of this section by filing with the Commission a written notice in such form and containing such information concerning such broker or dealer and any persons associated with such broker or dealer as the Commission, by rule, may prescribe as necessary or appropriate in the public interest or for the protection of investors. A broker or dealer may not register under this paragraph unless that broker or dealer is a member of a national securities association registered under section 15A(k).

(ii) *Immediate Effectiveness.*—Such registration shall be effective contemporaneously with the submission of notice, in written or electronic form, to the Commission, except that such registration shall not be effective if the registration would be subject to suspension or revocation under paragraph (4).

(iii) *Suspension.*—Such registration shall be suspended immediately if a national securities association registered pursuant to section 15A(k) of this title suspends the membership of that broker or dealer.

(iv) *Termination.*—Such registration shall be terminated immediately if any of the above stated conditions for registration set forth in this paragraph are no longer satisfied.

(B) *Exemptions for Registered brokers and Dealers.*—A broker or dealer registered pursuant to the requirements of subparagraph (A) shall be exempt from the following provisions of this title and the rules thereunder with respect to transactions in security futures products:

(i) Section 8.

(ii) Section 11.

(iii) Subsections (c)(3) and (c)(5) of this section.

(iv) Section 15B.

(v) Section 15C.

(vi) Subsections (d), (e), (f), (g), (h), and (i) of section 17.

(12) *Exemption for Security Futures Product Exchange Members.*—

(A) *Registration Exemption.*—A natural person shall be exempt from the registration requirements of this section if such person—

(i) is a member of a designated contract market registered with the Commission as an exchange pursuant to section 6(g);

(ii) effects transactions only in securities on the exchange of which such person is a member; and

(iii) does not directly accept or solicit orders from public customers or provide advice to public customers in connection with the trading of security futures products.

(B) *Other Exemptions.*—A natural person exempt from registration pursuant to subparagraph (A) shall also be exempt from the following provisions of this title and the rules thereunder:

(i) Section 8.

(ii) Section 11.

(iii) Subsections (c)(3), (c)(5), and (e) of this section.

(iv) Section 15B.

(v) Section 15C.

(vi) Subsections (d), (e), (f), (g), (h), and (i) of section 17.

(c)(1)(A) No broker or dealer shall make use of the mails or any means or instrumentality of interstate commerce to effect any transaction in, or to induce or attempt to induce the purchase or sale of, any security (other than commercial paper, bankers' acceptances, or commercial bills) otherwise than on a national securities exchange of which it is a member, or any security-based swap agreement (as defined in section 206B of the Gramm–Leach–Bliley Act), by means of any manipulative, deceptive, or other fraudulent device or contrivance.

(B) No municipal securities dealer shall make use of the mails or any means or instrumentality of interstate commerce to effect any transaction in, or to induce or attempt to induce the purchase or sale of, any municipal security or any security-based swap agreement (as defined in section 206B of the Gramm–Leach–Bliley Act) involving a municipal security by means of any manipulative, deceptive, or other fraudulent device or contrivance.

(C) No government securities broker or government securities dealer shall make use of the mails or any means or instrumentality of interstate commerce to effect any transaction in, or to induce or to attempt to induce the purchase or sale of, any government security or any security-based swap agreement (as defined in section 206B of the Gramm–Leach–Bliley Act) involving a government security by means of any manipulative, deceptive, or other fraudulent device or contrivance.

(2)(A) No broker or dealer shall make use of the mails or any means or instrumentality of interstate commerce to effect any transaction in, or to induce or attempt to induce the purchase or sale of, any security (other than an exempted security or commercial paper, bankers' acceptances, or commercial bills) otherwise than on a national securities exchange of which it is a member, in connection with which such broker or dealer engages in any fraudulent, deceptive, or manipulative act or practice, or makes any fictitious quotation.

(B) No municipal securities dealer shall make use of the mails or any means or instrumentality of interstate commerce to effect any transaction in, or to induce or attempt to induce the purchase or sale of, any municipal security in connection with which such municipal securities dealer engages in any fraudulent, deceptive, or manipulative act or practice, or makes any fictitious quotation.

(C) No government securities broker or government securities dealer shall make use of the mails or any means or instrumentality of interstate commerce to effect any transaction in, or induce or attempt to induce the purchase or sale of, any government security in connection with which such government securities broker or government securities dealer engages in any fraudulent, deceptive, or manipulative act or practice, or makes any fictitious quotation.

(D) The Commission shall, for the purposes of this paragraph, by rules and regulations define, and prescribe means reasonably designed to prevent, such acts and practices as are fraudulent, deceptive, or manipulative and such quotations as are fictitious.

(E) The Commission shall, prior to adopting any rule or regulation under subparagraph (C), consult with and consider the views of the Secretary of the Treasury and each appropriate regulatory agency. If the Secretary of the Treasury or any appropriate regulatory agency comments in writing on a proposed rule or regulation of the Commission under such subparagraph (C) that has been published for comment, the Commission shall respond in writing to such written comment before adopting the proposed rule. If the Secretary of the Treasury determines, and notifies the Commission, that such rule or regulation, if implemented, would, or as applied does (i) adversely affect the liquidity or efficiency of the market for government securities; or (ii) impose any burden on competition not necessary or appropriate in furtherance of the purposes of this section, the Commission shall, prior to adopting the proposed rule or regulation, find that such rule or regulation is necessary and appropriate in furtherance of the purposes of this section notwithstanding the Secretary's determination.

(3)(A) No broker or dealer (other than a government securities broker or government securities dealer, except a registered broker or dealer) shall make use of the mails or any means or instrumentality of interstate commerce to effect any transaction in, or to induce or attempt to induce the purchase or sale of, any security (other than an exempted security (except a government security) or commercial paper, bankers' acceptances, or commercial bills) in contravention of such rules and regulations as the Commission shall prescribe as necessary or appropriate in the public interest or for the protection of investors to provide safeguards with respect to the financial responsibility and related practices of brokers and dealers including, but not limited to, the acceptance of custody and use of customers' securities and the carrying and use of customers' deposits or credit balances. Such rules and regulations shall (A) require the maintenance of reserves with respect to customers' deposits or credit balances, and (B) no later than September 1, 1975, establish minimum financial responsibility requirements for all brokers and dealers.

(B) Consistent with this title, the Commission, in consultation with the Commodity Futures Trading Commission, shall issue such rules, regulations, or orders as are necessary to avoid duplicative or conflicting regulations applicable to any broker or dealer registered with the Commission pursuant to section 15(b) (except paragraph (11) thereof), that is also registered with the Commodity Futures Trading Commission pursuant to section 4f(a) of the Commodity Exchange Act (except paragraph (2) thereof), with respect to the application of: (i) the provisions of section 8, section 15(c)(3), and section 17 of this title and the rules and regulations thereunder related to the treatment of customer funds, securities, or property, maintenance of books and records, financial reporting, or other financial responsibility rules, involving security futures products; and (ii) similar provisions of the Commodity Exchange Act and rules and regulations thereunder involving security futures products.

(4) If the Commission finds, after notice and opportunity for a hearing, that any person subject to the provisions of section 12, 13, 14, or subsection (d) of section 15 of this title or any rule or regulation thereunder has failed to comply with any such provision, rule or regulation in any material respect, the Commission may publish its findings and issue an order requiring such person, and any person who was a cause of the failure to comply due to an act or omission the person knew or should have known would contribute to the failure to comply, to comply, or to take steps to effect compliance, with such provision or such rule or regulation thereunder upon such terms and conditions and within such time as the Commission may specify in such order.

(5) No dealer (other than a specialist registered on a national securities exchange) acting in the capacity of market maker or otherwise shall make use of the mails or any means or instrumentality of interstate commerce to effect any transaction in, or to induce or attempt to induce the purchase or sale of, any security (other than an exempted security or a municipal security) in contravention of such specified and appropriate standards with respect to dealing as the Commission, by rule, shall prescribe as necessary or appropriate in the public interest and for the protection of investors, to maintain fair and orderly markets, or to remove impediments to and perfect the mechanism of a national market system. Under the rules of the Commission a dealer in a security may be prohibited from acting as a broker in that security.

(6) No broker or dealer shall make use of the mails or any means or instrumentality of interstate commerce to effect any transaction in, or to induce or attempt to induce the purchase or sale of, any security (other than an exempted security, municipal security, commercial paper, bankers' acceptances, or commercial bills) in contravention of such rules

and regulations as the Commission shall prescribe as necessary or appropriate in the public interest and for the protection of investors or to perfect or remove impediments to a national system for the prompt and accurate clearance and settlement of securities transactions, with respect to the time and method of, and the form and format of documents used in connection with, making settlements of and payments for transactions in securities, making transfers and deliveries of securities, and closing accounts. Nothing in this paragraph shall be construed (A) to affect the authority of the Board of Governors of the Federal Reserve System, pursuant to section 7 of this title, to prescribe rules and regulations for the purpose of preventing the excessive use of credit for the purchase or carrying of securities, or (B) to authorize the Commission to prescribe rules or regulations for such purpose.

(7) In connection with any bid for or purchase of a government security related to an offering of government securities by or on behalf of an issuer, no government securities broker, government securities dealer, or bidder for or purchaser of securities in such offering shall knowingly or willfully make any false or misleading written statement or omit any fact necessary to make any written statement made not misleading.

(8) *Prohibition of Referral Fees.*—No broker or dealer, or person associated with a broker or dealer, may solicit or accept, directly or indirectly, remuneration for assisting an attorney in obtaining the representation of any person in any private action arising under this title or under the Securities Act of 1933.

(d) Each issuer which has filed a registration statement containing an undertaking which is or becomes operative under this subsection as in effect prior to the date of enactment of the Securities Acts Amendments of 1964, and each issuer which shall after such date file a registration statement which has become effective pursuant to the Securities Act of 1933, as amended, shall file with the Commission, in accordance with such rules and regulations as the Commission may prescribe as necessary or appropriate in the public interest or for the protection of investors, such supplementary and periodic information, documents, and reports as may be required pursuant to section 13 of this title in respect of a security registered pursuant to section 12 of this title. The duty to file under this subsection shall be automatically suspended if and so long as any issue of securities of such issuer is registered pursuant to section 12 of this title. The duty to file under this subsection shall also be automatically suspended as to any fiscal year, other than the fiscal year within which such registration statement became effective, if, at the beginning of such fiscal year, the securities of each class to which the registration statement relates are held of record by less than three hundred persons. For the purposes of this subsection, the term "class" shall be construed to include all securities of an issuer which are of substantially similar character and the holders of which enjoy substantially similar rights and privileges. The Commission may, for the purpose of this subsection, define by rules and regulations the term "held of record" as it deems necessary or appropriate in the public interest or for the protection of investors in order to prevent circumvention of the provisions of this subsection. Nothing in this subsection shall apply to securities issued by a foreign government or political subdivision thereof.

(e) The Commission, by rule, as it deems necessary or appropriate in the public interest and for the protection of investors or to assure equal regulation, may require any member of a national securities exchange not required to register under section 15 of this title and any person associated with any such member to comply with any provision of this title (other than section 15(a)) or the rules or regulations thereunder which by its terms regulates or prohibits any act, practice, or course of business by a "broker or dealer" or "registered broker or dealer" or a "person associated with a broker or dealer," respectively.

(f) Every registered broker or dealer shall establish, maintain and enforce written policies and procedures reasonably designed, taking into consideration the nature of such broker's or dealer's business, to prevent the misuse in violation of this title, or the rules or regulations thereunder, of material, nonpublic information by such broker or dealer or any person associated with such broker or dealer. The Commission, as it deems necessary or appropriate in the public interest or for the protection of investors, shall adopt rules or regulations to require specific policies or procedures reasonably designed to prevent misuse in violation of this title (or the rules or regulations thereunder) of material, nonpublic information.

(g) *Requirements for Transactions in Penny Stocks.*—

(1) *In General.*—No broker or dealer shall make use of the mails or any means or instrumentality of interstate commerce to effect any transaction in, or to induce or attempt to induce the purchase or sale of, any penny stock by any customer except in accordance with the requirements of this subsection and the rules and regulations prescribed under this subsection.

(2) *Risk Disclosure With Respect to Penny Stocks.*—Prior to effecting any transaction in any penny stock, a broker or dealer shall give the customer a risk disclosure document that—

(A) contains a description of the nature and level of risk in the market for penny stocks in both public offerings and secondary trading;

(B) contains a description of the broker's or dealer's duties to the customer and of the rights and remedies available to the customer with respect to violations of such duties or other requirements of Federal securities laws;

(C) contains a brief, clear, narrative description of a dealer market, including "bid" and "ask" prices for penny stocks and the significance of the spread between the bid and ask prices;

(D) contains the toll free telephone number for inquiries on disciplinary actions established pursuant to section 15A(i) of this title;

(E) defines significant terms used in the disclosure document or in the conduct of trading in penny stocks; and

(F) contains such other information, and is in such form (including language, type size, and format), as the Commission shall require by rule or regulation.

(3) *Commission Rules Relating to Disclosure.*—The Commission shall adopt rules setting forth additional standards for the disclosure by brokers and dealers to customers of information concerning transactions in penny stocks. Such rules—

(A) shall require brokers and dealers to disclose to each customer, prior to effecting any transaction in, and at the time of confirming any transaction with respect to any penny stock, in accordance with such procedures and methods as the Commission may require consistent with the public interest and the protection of investors—

(i) the bid and ask prices for penny stock, or such other information as the Commission may, by rule, require to provide customers with more useful and reliable information relating to the price of such stock;

(ii) the number of shares to which such bid and ask prices apply, or other comparable information relating to the depth and liquidity of the market for such stock; and

(iii) the amount and a description of any compensation that the broker or dealer and the associated person thereof will receive or has received in connection with such transaction;

(B) shall require brokers and dealers to provide, to each customer whose account with the broker or dealer contains penny stocks, a monthly statement indicating the market value of the penny stocks in that account or indicating that the market value of such stock cannot be determined because of the unavailability of firm quotes; and

(C) may, as the Commission finds necessary or appropriate in the public interest or for the protection of investors, require brokers and dealers to disclose to customers additional information concerning transactions in penny stocks.

(4) *Exemptions.*—The Commission, as it determines consistent with the public interest and the protection of investors, may by rule, regulation, or order exempt in whole or in part, conditionally or unconditionally, any person or class of persons, or any transaction or class of transactions, from the requirements of this subsection. Such exemptions shall include an exemption for brokers and dealers based on the minimal percentage of the broker's or dealer's commissions, commission-equivalents, and markups received from transactions in penny stocks.

(5) *Regulations.*—It shall be unlawful for any person to violate such rules and regulations as the Commission shall prescribe in the public interest or for the protection of investors or to maintain fair and orderly markets—

(A) as necessary or appropriate to carry out this subsection; or

(B) as reasonably designed to prevent fraudulent, deceptive, or manipulative acts and practices with respect to penny stocks.

(h) *Limitations on State Law.*—

(1) *Capital, Margin, Books and Records, Bonding, and Reports.*—No law, rule, regulation, or order, or other administrative action of any State or political subdivision thereof shall establish capital, custody, margin, financial responsibility, making and keeping records, bonding, or financial or operational reporting requirements for brokers, dealers, municipal securities dealers, government securities brokers, or government securities dealers that differ from, or are in addition to, the requirements in those areas established under this title. The Commission shall consult periodically the securities commissions (or any agency or office performing like functions) of the States concerning the adequacy of such requirements as established under this title.

(2) *De Minimis Transactions by Associated Persons.*—No law, rule, regulation, or order, or other administrative action of any State or political subdivision thereof may prohibit an associated person of a broker or dealer from effecting a transaction described in paragraph (3) for a customer in such State if—

(A) such associated person is not ineligible to register with such State for any reason other than such a transaction;

(B) such associated person is registered with a registered securities association and at least one State; and

(C) the broker or dealer with which such person is associated is registered with such State.

(3) *Described Transactions.*—

(A) *In General.*—A transaction is described in this paragraph if—

(i) such transaction is effected—

(I) on behalf of a customer that, for 30 days prior to the day of the transaction, maintained an account with the broker or dealer; and

(II) by an associated person of the broker or dealer—

(aa) to which the customer was assigned for 14 days prior to the day of the transaction; and

(bb) who is registered with a State in which the customer was a resident or was present for at least 30 consecutive days during the 1–year period prior to the day of the transaction; or

(ii) the transaction is effected—

(I) on behalf of a customer that, for 30 days prior to the day of the transaction, maintained an account with the broker or dealer; and

(II) during the period beginning on the date on which such associated person files an application for registration with the State in which the transaction is effected and ending on the earlier of—

(aa) 60 days after the date on which the application is filed; or

(bb) the date on which such State notifies the associated person that it has denied the application for registration or has stayed the pendency of the application for cause.

(B) *Rules of Construction.*—For purposes of subparagraph (A)(i)(II)—

(i) each of up to 3 associated persons of a broker or dealer who are designated to effect transactions during the absence or unavailability of the principal associated person for a customer may be treated as an associated person to which such customer is assigned; and

(ii) if the customer is present in another State for 30 or more consecutive days or has permanently changed his or her residence to another State, a transaction is not described in this paragraph, unless the associated person of the broker or dealer files an application for registration with such State not later than 10 business days after the later of the date of the transaction, or the date of the discovery of the presence of the customer in the other State for 30 or more consecutive days or the change in the customer's residence.

(i) *Rulemaking to Extend Requirements to New Hybrid Products.*—

(1) *Consultation.*—Prior to commencing a rulemaking under this subsection, the Commission shall consult with and seek the concurrence of the Board concerning the imposition of broker or dealer registration requirements with respect to any new hybrid product. In developing and promulgating rules under this subsection, the Commission shall consider the views of the Board, including views with respect to the nature of the new hybrid product; the history, purpose, extent, and appropriateness of the regulation of the new product under the Federal banking laws; and the impact of the proposed rule on the banking industry.

(2) *Limitation.*—The Commission shall not—

(A) require a bank to register as a broker or dealer under this section because the bank engages in any transaction in, or buys or sells, a new hybrid product; or

(B) bring an action against a bank for a failure to comply with a requirement described in subparagraph (A), unless the Commission has imposed such requirement by rule or regulation issued in accordance with this section.

(3) *Criteria for Rulemaking.*—The Commission shall not impose a requirement under paragraph (2) of this subsection with respect to any new hybrid product unless the Commission determines that—

(A) the new hybrid product is a security; and

(B) imposing such requirement is necessary and appropriate in the public interest and for the protection of investors.

(4) *Considerations.*—In making a determination under paragraph (3), the Commission shall consider—

(A) the nature of the new hybrid product; and

(B) the history, purpose, extent, and appropriateness of the regulation of the new hybrid product under the Federal securities laws and under the Federal banking laws.

(5) *Objection to Commission Regulation.*—

(A) Filing of petition for review.—The Board may obtain review of any final regulation described in paragraph (2) in the United States Court of Appeals for the District of Columbia Circuit by filing in such court, not later than 60 days after the date of publication of the final regulation, a written petition requesting that the regulation be set aside. Any proceeding to challenge any such rule shall be expedited by the Court of Appeals.

(B) *Transmittal of Petition and Record.*—A copy of a petition described in subparagraph (A) shall be transmitted as soon as possible by the Clerk of the Court to an officer or employee of the Commission designated for that purpose. Upon receipt of the petition, the Commission shall file with the court the regulation under review and any documents referred to therein, and any other relevant materials prescribed by the court.

(C) *Exclusive Jurisdiction.*—On the date of the filing of the petition under subparagraph (A), the court has jurisdiction, which becomes exclusive on the filing of the materials set forth in subparagraph (B), to affirm and enforce or to set aside the regulation at issue.

(D) *Standard of Review.*—The court shall determine to affirm and enforce or set aside a regulation of the Commission under this subsection, based on the determination of the court as to whether—

(i) the subject product is a new hybrid product, as defined in this subsection;

(ii) the subject product is a security; and

(iii) imposing a requirement to register as a broker or dealer for banks engaging in transactions in such product is appropriate in light of the history, purpose, and extent of regulation under the Federal securities laws and under the Federal banking laws, giving deference neither to the views of the Commission nor the Board.

(E) *Judicial Stay.*—The filing of a petition by the Board pursuant to subparagraph (A) shall operate as a judicial stay, until the date on which the determination of the court is final (including any appeal of such determination).

(F) *Other Authority to Challenge.*—Any aggrieved party may seek judicial review of the Commission's rulemaking under this subsection pursuant to section 78y of this title.

(6) *Definitions.*—For purposes of this subsection:

(A) New hybrid product.—The term "new hybrid product" means a product that—

(i) was not subjected to regulation by the Commission as a security prior to November 12, 1999;

(ii) is not an identified banking product as such term is defined in section 206 of such Act; and

(iii) is not an equity swap within the meaning of section 206(a)(6) of such Act.

(B) *Board.*—The term "Board" means the Board of Governors of the Federal Reserve System.

(i) The authority of the Commission under this section with respect to security-based swap agreements (as defined in section 206B of the Gramm–Leach–Bliley Act) shall be subject to the restrictions and limitations of section 3A(b) of this title.*

Registered Securities Associations

Sec. 15A. (a) An association of brokers and dealers may be registered as a national securities association pursuant to subsection (b), or as an affiliated securities association pursuant to subsection (d), under the terms and conditions hereinafter provided in this

* There are currently two section 15(i)s.

section and in accordance with the provisions of section 19(a) of this title, by filing with the Commission an application for registration in such form as the Commission, by rule, may prescribe containing the rules of the association and such other information and documents as the Commission, by rule, may prescribe as necessary or appropriate in the public interest or for the protection of investors.

(b) An association of brokers and dealers shall not be registered as a national securities association unless the Commission determines that—

(1) By reason of the number and geographical distribution of its members and the scope of their transactions, such association will be able to carry out the purposes of this section.

(2) Such association is so organized and has the capacity to be able to carry out the purposes of this title and to comply, and (subject to any rule or order of the Commission pursuant to section 17(d) or 19(g)(2) of this title) to enforce compliance by its members and persons associated with its members, with the provisions of this title, the rules and regulations thereunder, the rules of the Municipal Securities Rulemaking Board, and the rules of the association.

(3) Subject to the provisions of subsection (g) of this section, the rules of the association provide that any registered broker or dealer may become a member of such association and any person may become associated with a member thereof.

(4) The rules of the association assure a fair representation of its members in the selection of its directors and administration of its affairs and provide that one or more directors shall be representative of issuers and investors and not be associated with a member of the association, broker, or dealer.

(5) The rules of the association provide for the equitable allocation of reasonable dues, fees, and other charges among members and issuers and other persons using any facility or system which the association operates or controls.

(6) The rules of the association are designed to prevent fraudulent and manipulative acts and practices, to promote just and equitable principles of trade, to foster cooperation and coordination with persons engaged in regulating, clearing, settling, processing information with respect to, and facilitating transactions in securities, to remove impediments to and perfect the mechanism of a free and open market and a national market system, and, in general, to protect investors and the public interest; and are not designed to permit unfair discrimination between customers, issuers, brokers, or dealers, to fix minimum profits, to impose any schedule or fix rates of commissions, allowances, discounts, or other fees to be charged by its members, or to regulate by virtue of any authority conferred by this title matters not related to the purposes of this title or the administration of the association.

(7) The rules of the association provide that (subject to any rule or order of the Commission pursuant to section 17(d) or 19(g)(2) of this title) its members and persons associated with its members shall be appropriately disciplined for violation of any provision of this title, the rules or regulations thereunder, the rules of the Municipal Securities Rulemaking Board, or the rules of the association, by expulsion, suspension, limitation of activities, functions, and operations, fine, censure, being suspended or barred from being associated with a member, or any other fitting sanction.

(8) The rules of the association are in accordance with the provisions of subsection (h) of this section, and, in general, provide a fair procedure for the disciplining of members and persons associated with members, the denial of membership to any person seeking membership therein, the barring of any person from becoming associated with a member thereof, and the prohibition or limitation by the association of any person with

respect to access to services offered by the association or a member thereof.

(9) The rules of the association do not impose any burden on competition not necessary or appropriate in furtherance of the purposes of this title.

(10) The requirements of subsection (c), insofar as these may be applicable, are satisfied.

(11) The rules of the association include provisions governing the form and content of quotations relating to securities sold otherwise than on a national securities exchange which may be distributed or published by any member or person associated with a member, and the persons to whom such quotations may be supplied. Such rules relating to quotations shall be designed to produce fair and informative quotations, to prevent fictitious or misleading quotations, and to promote orderly procedures for collecting, distributing, and publishing quotations.

(12) The rules of the association to promote just and equitable principles of trade, as required by paragraph (6), include rules to prevent members of the association from participating in any limited partnership rollup transaction (as such term is defined in paragraphs (4) and (5) of section 14(h)) unless such transaction was conducted in accordance with procedures designed to protect the rights of limited partners, including—

(A) the right of dissenting limited partners to one of the following:

(i) an appraisal and compensation;

(ii) retention of a security under substantially the same terms and conditions as the original issue;

(iii) approval of the limited partnership rollup transaction by not less than 75 percent of the outstanding securities of each of the participating limited partnerships;

(iv) the use of a committee that is independent, as determined in accordance with rules prescribed by the association, of the general partner or sponsor, that has been approved by a majority of the outstanding securities of each of the participating partnerships, and that has such authority as is necessary to protect the interest of limited partners, including the authority to hire independent advisors, to negotiate with the general partner or sponsor on behalf of the limited partners, and to make a recommendation to the limited partners with respect to the proposed transaction; or

(v) other comparable rights that are prescribed by rule by the association and that are designed to protect dissenting limited partners;

(B) the right not to have their voting power unfairly reduced or abridged;

(C) the right not to bear an unfair portion of the costs of a proposed limited partnership rollup transaction that is rejected; and

(D) restrictions on the conversion of contingent interests or fees into non-contingent interests or fees and restrictions on the receipt of a non-contingent equity interest in exchange for fees for services which have not yet been provided.

As used in this paragraph, the term "dissenting limited partner" means a person who, on the date on which soliciting material is mailed to investors, is a holder of a beneficial interest in a limited partnership that is the subject of a limited partnership rollup transaction, and who casts a vote against the transaction and complies with procedures established by the association, except that for purposes of an exchange or tender offer, such person shall file an objection in writing under the rules of the association during the period in which the offer is outstanding.

(13) The rules of the association prohibit the authorization for quotation on an automated interdealer quotation system sponsored by the association of any security designated by the Commission as a national market system security resulting from a limited partnership rollup transaction (as such term is defined in paragraphs (4) and (5) of section 14(h)), unless such transaction was conducted in accordance with procedures designed to protect the rights of limited partners, including—

(A) the right of dissenting limited partners to one of the following:

(i) an appraisal and compensation;

(ii) retention of a security under substantially the same terms and conditions as the original issue;

(iii) approval of the limited partnership rollup transaction by not less than 75 percent of the outstanding securities of each of the participating limited partnerships;

(iv) the use of a committee that is independent, as determined in accordance with rules prescribed by the association, of the general partner or sponsor, that has been approved by a majority of the outstanding securities of each of the participating partnerships, and that has such authority as is necessary to protect the interest of limited partners, including the authority to hire independent advisors, to negotiate with the general partner or sponsor on behalf of the limited partners, and to make a recommendation to the limited partners with respect to the proposed transaction; or

(v) other comparable rights that are prescribed by rule by the association and that are designed to protect dissenting limited partners;

(B) the right not to have their voting power unfairly reduced or abridged;

(C) the right not to bear an unfair portion of the costs of a proposed limited partnership rollup transaction that is rejected; and

(D) restrictions on the conversion of contingent interests or fees into non-contingent interests or fees and restrictions on the receipt of a non-contingent equity interest in exchange for fees for services which have not yet been provided.

As used in this paragraph, the term "dissenting limited partner" means a person who, on the date on which soliciting material is mailed to investors, is a holder of a beneficial interest in a limited partnership that is the subject of a limited partnership rollup transaction, and who casts a vote against the transaction and complies with procedures established by the association, except that for purposes of an exchange or tender offer, such person shall file an objection in writing under the rules of the association during the period during which the offer is outstanding.

(c) The Commission may permit or require the rules of an association applying for registration pursuant to subsection (b), to provide for the admission of an association registered as an affiliated securities association, pursuant to subsection (d), to participation in said applicant association as an affiliate thereof, under terms permitting such power and responsibilities to such affiliates, and under such other appropriate terms and conditions, as may be provided by the rules of said applicant association, if such rules appear to the Commission to be necessary or appropriate in the public interest or for the protection of investors and to carry out the purposes of this section. The duties and powers of the Commission with respect to any national securities association or any affiliated securities association shall in no way be limited by reason of any such affiliation.

(d) An applicant association shall not be registered as an affiliated securities association unless it appears to the Commission that—

(1) such association, notwithstanding that it does not satisfy the requirements set forth in paragraph (1) of subsection (b), will, forthwith upon the registration thereof, be admitted to affiliation with an association registered as a national securities association pursuant to said subsection (b), in the manner and under the terms and conditions provided by the rules of said national securities association in accordance with subsection (c); and

(2) such association and its rules satisfy the requirements set forth in paragraphs (2) to (10), inclusive, and paragraph (12), of subsection (b); except that in the case of any such association any restrictions upon membership therein of the type authorized by paragraph (3) of subsection (b) shall not be less stringent than in the case of the national securities association with which such association is to be affiliated.

(e)(1) The rules of a registered securities association may provide that no member thereof shall deal with any nonmember professional (as defined in paragraph (2) of this subsection) except at the same prices, for the same commissions or fees, and on the same terms and conditions as are by such member accorded to the general public.

(2) For the purposes of this subsection, the term "nonmember professional" shall include (A) with respect to transactions in securities other than municipal securities, any registered broker or dealer who is not a member of any registered securities association, except such a broker or dealer who deals exclusively in commercial paper, bankers' acceptances, and commercial bills, and (B) with respect to transactions in municipal securities, any municipal securities dealer (other than a bank or division or department of a bank) who is not a member of any registered securities association and any municipal securities broker who is not a member of any such association.

(3) Nothing in this subsection shall be so construed or applied as to prevent (A) any member of a registered securities association from granting to any other member of any registered securities association any dealer's discount, allowance, commission, or special terms, in connection with the purchase or sale of securities, or (B) any member of a registered securities association or any municipal securities dealer which is a bank or a division or department of a bank from granting to any member of any registered securities association or any such municipal securities dealer any dealer's discount, allowance, commission, or special terms in connection with the purchase or sale of municipal securities: *Provided, however,* That the granting of any such discount, allowance, commission, or special terms in connection with the purchase or sale of municipal securities shall be subject to rules of the Municipal Securities Rulemaking Board adopted pursuant to section 15B(b)(2)(K) of this title.

(f) Nothing in subsection (b)(6) or (b)(11) of this section shall be construed to permit a registered securities association to make rules concerning any transaction by a registered broker or dealer in a municipal security.

(g)(1) A registered securities association shall deny membership to any person who is not a registered broker or dealer.

(2) A registered securities association may, and in cases in which the Commission, by order, directs as necessary or appropriate in the public interest or for the protection of investors shall, deny membership to any registered broker or dealer, and bar from becoming associated with a member any person, who is subject to a statutory disqualification. A registered securities association shall file notice with the Commission not less than thirty days prior to admitting any registered broker or dealer to membership or permitting any person to become associated with a member, if the association knew, or in the exercise of reasonable care should have known, that such broker or dealer or person was subject to a statutory disqualification. The notice shall be in such form and contain such information as the Commission, by rule, may prescribe as neces-

sary or appropriate in the public interest or for the protection of investors.

(3)(A) A registered securities association may deny membership to, or condition the membership of, a registered broker or dealer if (i) such broker or dealer does not meet such standards of financial responsibility or operational capability or such broker or dealer or any natural person associated with such broker or dealer does not meet such standards of training, experience, and competence as are prescribed by the rules of the association or (ii) such broker or dealer or person associated with such broker or dealer has engaged and there is a reasonable likelihood he will again engage in acts or practices inconsistent with just and equitable principles of trade. A registered securities association may examine and verify the qualifications of an applicant to become a member and the natural persons associated with such an applicant in accordance with procedures established by the rules of the association.

(B) A registered securities association may bar a natural person from becoming associated with a member or condition the association of a natural person with a member if such natural person (i) does not meet such standards of training, experience, and competence as are prescribed by the rules of the association or (ii) has engaged and there is a reasonable likelihood he will again engage in acts or practices inconsistent with just and equitable principles of trade. A registered securities association may examine and verify the qualifications of an applicant to become a person associated with a member in accordance with procedures established by the rules of the association and require a natural person associated with a member, or any class of such natural persons, to be registered with the association in accordance with procedures so established.

(C) A registered securities association may bar any person from becoming associated with a member if such person does not agree (i) to supply the association with such information with respect to its relationship and dealings with the member as may be specified in the rules of the association and (ii) to permit examination of its books and records to verify the accuracy of any information so supplied.

(D) Nothing in subparagraph (A), (B), or (C) of this paragraph shall be construed to permit a registered securities association to deny membership to or condition the membership of, or bar any person from becoming associated with or condition the association of any person with, a broker or dealer that engages exclusively in transactions in municipal securities.

(4) A registered securities association may deny membership to a registered broker or dealer not engaged in a type of business in which the rules of the association require members to be engaged: Provided, however, That no registered securities association may deny membership to a registered broker or dealer by reason of the amount of such type of business done by such broker or dealer or the other types of business in which he is engaged.

(h)(1) In any proceeding by a registered securities association to determine whether a member or person associated with a member should be disciplined (other than a summary proceeding pursuant to paragraph (3) of this subsection) the association shall bring specific charges, notify such member or person of, and give him an opportunity to defend against, such charges, and keep a record. A determination by the association to impose a disciplinary sanction shall be supported by a statement setting forth—

(A) any act or practice in which such member or person associated with a member has been found to have engaged, or which such member or person has been found to have omitted;

(B) the specific provision of this title, the rules or regulations thereunder, the rules of the Municipal Securities Rulemaking Board, or the rules of the association which any such act or practice, or omission to act, is deemed to violate; and

(C) the sanction imposed and the reason therefor.

(2) In any proceeding by a registered securities association to determine whether a person shall be denied membership, barred from becoming associated with a member, or prohibited or limited with respect to access to services offered by the association or a member thereof (other than a summary proceeding pursuant to paragraph (3) of this subsection), the association shall notify such person of, and give him an opportunity to be heard upon, the specific grounds for denial, bar, or prohibition or limitation under consideration and keep a record. A determination by the association to deny membership, bar a person from becoming associated with a member, or prohibit or limit a person with respect to access to services offered by the association or a member thereof shall be supported by a statement setting forth the specific grounds on which the denial, bar, or prohibition or limitation is based.

(3) A registered securities association may summarily (A) suspend a member or person associated with a member who has been and is expelled or suspended from any self-regulatory organization or barred or suspended from being associated with a member of any self-regulatory organization, (B) suspend a member who is in such financial or operating difficulty that the association determines and so notifies the Commission that the member cannot be permitted to continue to do business as a member with safety to investors, creditors, other members, or the association, or (C) limit or prohibit any person with respect to access to services offered by the association if subparagraph (A) or (B) of this paragraph is applicable to such person or, in the case of a person who is not a member, if the association determines that such person does not meet the qualification requirements or other prerequisites for such access and such person cannot be permitted to continue to have such access with safety to investors, creditors, members, or the association. Any person aggrieved by any such summary action shall be promptly afforded an opportunity for a hearing by the association in accordance with the provisions of paragraph (1) or (2) of this subsection. The Commission, by order, may stay any such summary action on its own motion or upon application by any person aggrieved thereby, if the Commission determines summarily or after notice and opportunity for hearing (which hearing may consist solely of the submission of affidavits or presentation of oral arguments) that such stay is consistent with the public interest and the protection of investors.

(i) A registered securities association shall, within one year from the date of enactment of this section, (1) establish and maintain a toll-free telephone listing to receive inquiries regarding disciplinary actions involving its members and their associated persons, and (2) promptly respond to such inquiries in writing. Such association may charge persons, other than individual investors, reasonable fees for written responses to such inquiries. Such an association shall not have any liability to any person for any actions taken or omitted in good faith under this paragraph.

(j) *Registration for sales of private securities offerings.*—A registered securities association shall create a limited qualification category for any associated person of a member who effects sales as part of a primary offering of securities not involving a public offering, pursuant to section 3(b), 4(2), or 4(6) of the Securities Act of 1933 and the rules and regulations thereunder, and shall deem qualified in such limited qualification category, without testing, any bank employee who, in the six month period preceding the date of the enactment of the Gramm–Leach–Bliley Act, engaged in effecting such sales.

(k) *Limited Purpose National Securities Association.*—

(1) *Regulation of Members With Respect to Security Futures Products.*—A futures association registered under section 17 of the Commodity Exchange Act shall be a registered national securities association for the limited purpose of regulating the activities of members who are registered as brokers or dealers in security futures products pursuant to section 15(b)(11).

(2) *Requirements for Registration.*—Such a securities association shall—

(A) be so organized and have the capacity to carry out the purposes of the securities laws applicable to security futures products and to comply, and (subject to any rule or order of the Commission pursuant to section 19(g)(2)) to enforce compliance by its members and persons associated with its members, with the provisions of the securities laws applicable to security futures products, the rules and regulations thereunder, and its rules;

(B) have rules that—

(i) are designed to prevent fraudulent and manipulative acts and practices, to promote just and equitable principles of trade, and, in general, to protect investors and the public interest, including rules governing sales practices and the advertising of security futures products reasonably comparable to those of other national securities associations registered pursuant to subsection (a) that are applicable to security futures products; and

(ii) are not designed to regulate by virtue of any authority conferred by this title matters not related to the purposes of this title or the administration of the association;

(C) have rules that provide that (subject to any rule or order of the Commission pursuant to section 19(g)(2)) its members and persons associated with its members shall be appropriately disciplined for violation of any provision of the securities laws applicable to security futures products, the rules or regulations thereunder, or the rules of the association, by expulsion, suspension, limitation of activities, functions, and operations, fine, censure, being suspended or barred from being associated with a member, or any other fitting sanction; and

(D) have rules that ensure that members and natural persons associated with members meet such standards of training, experience, and competence necessary to effect transactions in security futures products and are tested for their knowledge of securities and security futures products.

(3) *Exemption From Rule Change Submission.*—Such a securities association shall be exempt from submitting proposed rule changes pursuant to section 19(b) of this title, except that—

(A) the association shall file proposed rule changes related to higher margin levels, fraud or manipulation, recordkeeping, reporting, listing standards, or decimal pricing for security futures products, sales practices for, advertising of, or standards of training, experience, competence, or other qualifications for security futures products for persons who effect transactions in security futures products, or rules effectuating the association's obligation to enforce the securities laws pursuant to section 19(b)(7);

(B) the association shall file pursuant to sections 19(b)(1) and 19(b)(2) proposed rule changes related to margin, except for changes resulting in higher margin levels; and

(C) the association shall file pursuant to section 19(b)(1) proposed rule changes that have been abrogated by the Commission pursuant to section 19(b)(7)(C).

(4) *Other Exemptions.*—Such a securities association shall be exempt from and shall not be required to enforce compliance by its members, and its members shall not, solely with respect to their transactions effected in security futures products, be required to comply, with the following provisions of this title and the rules thereunder:

(A) Section 8.

(B) Subsections (b)(1), (b)(3), (b)(4), (b)(5), (b)(8), (b)(10), (b)(11), (b)(12), (b)(13), (c), (d), (e), (f), (g), (h), and (i) of this section.

(C) Subsections (d), (f), and (k) of section 17.

(D) Subsections (a), (f), and (h) of section 19.

(*l*) Consistent with this title, each national securities association registered pursuant to subsection (a) of this section shall issue such rules as are necessary to avoid duplicative or conflicting rules applicable to any broker or dealer registered with the Commission pursuant to section 15(b) (except paragraph (11) thereof), that is also registered with the Commodity Futures Trading Commission pursuant to section 4f(a) of the Commodity Exchange Act (except paragraph (2) thereof), with respect to the application of—

(1) rules of such national securities association of the type specified in section 15(c)(3)(B) involving security futures products; and

(2) similar rules of national securities associations registered pursuant to subsection (k) of this section and national securities exchanges registered pursuant to section 6(g) involving security futures products.

(m) *Procedures and Rules for Security Future Products.*—A national securities association registered pursuant to subsection (a) shall, not later than 8 months after the date of the enactment of the Commodity Futures Modernization Act of 2000, implement the procedures specified in section 6(h)(5)(A) of this title and adopt the rules specified in subparagraphs (B) and (C) of section 6(h)(5) of this title.

Municipal Securities

Sec. 15B. (a)(1) It shall be unlawful for any municipal securities dealer (other than one registered as a broker or dealer under section 15 of this title) to make use of the mails or any means or instrumentality of interstate commerce to effect any transaction in, or to induce or attempt to induce the purchase or sale of, any municipal security unless such municipal securities dealer is registered in accordance with this subsection.

(2) A municipal securities dealer may be registered by filing with the Commission an application for registration in such form and containing such information and documents concerning such municipal securities dealer and any persons associated with such municipal securities dealer as the Commission, by rule, may prescribe as necessary or appropriate in the public interest or for the protection of investors. Within forty-five days of the date of the filing of such application (or within such longer period as to which the applicant consents), the Commission shall—

(A) by order grant registration, or

(B) institute proceedings to determine whether registration should be denied. Such proceedings shall include notice of the grounds for denial under consideration and opportunity for hearing and shall be concluded within one hundred twenty days of the date of the filing of the application for registration. At the conclusion of such proceedings the Commission, by order, shall grant or deny such registration. The Commission may extend the time for the conclusion of such proceedings for up to ninety days if it finds good cause for such extension and publishes its reasons for so finding or for such longer period as to which the applicant consents.

The Commission shall grant the registration of a municipal securities dealer if the Commission finds that the requirements of this section are satisfied. The Commission shall deny such registration if it does not make such a finding or if it finds that if the applicant were so registered, its registration would be subject to suspension or revocation under subsection (c) of this section.

(3) Any provision of this title (other than section 5 or paragraph (1) of this subsection) which prohibits any act, practice, or course of business if the mails or any means or instrumentality of interstate commerce is used in

connection therewith shall also prohibit any such act, practice, or course of business by any registered municipal securities dealer or any person acting on behalf of such municipal securities dealer, irrespective of any use of the mails or any means or instrumentality of interstate commerce in connection therewith.

(4) The Commission, by rule or order, upon its own motion or upon application, may conditionally or unconditionally exempt any broker, dealer, or municipal securities dealer or class of brokers, dealers, or municipal securities dealers from any provision of this section or the rules or regulations thereunder, if the Commission finds that such exemption is consistent with the public interest, the protection of investors, and the purposes of this section.

(b)(1) Not later than one hundred twenty days after the date of enactment of the Securities Acts amendments of 1975, the Commission shall establish a Municipal Securities Rulemaking Board (hereinafter in this section referred to as the "Board") to be composed initially of fifteen members appointed by the Commission, which shall perform the duties set forth in this section. The initial members of the Board shall serve as members for a term of two years, and shall consist of (A) five individuals who are not associated with any broker, dealer, or municipal securities dealer (other than by reason of being under common control with, or indirectly controlling, any broker or dealer which is not a municipal securities broker or municipal securities dealer), at least one of whom shall be representative of issuers of municipal securities (which members are hereinafter referred to as "public representatives"); (B) five individuals who are associated with and representative of municipal securities brokers and municipal securities dealers which are not banks or subsidiaries or departments or divisions of banks (which members are hereinafter referred to as "broker-dealer representatives"); and (C) five individuals who are associated with and representative of municipal securities dealers which are banks or subsidiaries or departments or divisions of banks (which members are hereinafter referred to as "bank representatives"). Prior to the expiration of the terms of office of the initial members of the Board, an election shall be held under rules adopted by the Board (pursuant to subsection (b)(2)(B) of this section) of the members to succeed such initial members.

(2) The Board shall propose and adopt rules to effect the purposes of this title with respect to transactions in municipal securities effected by brokers, dealers, and municipal securities dealers. (Such rules are hereinafter collectively referred to in this title as "rules of the Board".) The rules of the Board, as a minimum, shall:

(A) provide that no municipal securities broker or municipal securities dealer shall effect any transaction in, or induce or attempt to induce the purchase or sale of, any municipal security unless such municipal securities broker or municipal securities dealer meets such standards of operational capability and such municipal securities broker or municipal securities dealer and every natural person associated with such municipal securities broker or municipal securities dealer meets such standards of training, experience, competence, and such other qualifications as the Board finds necessary or appropriate in the public interest or for the protection of investors. In connection with the definition and application of such standards the Board may—

(i) appropriately classify municipal securities brokers and municipal securities dealers (taking into account relevant matters, including types of business done, nature of securities other than municipal securities sold, and character of business organization), and persons associated with municipal securities brokers and municipal securities dealers;

(ii) specify that all or any portion of such standards shall be applicable to any such class;

(iii) require persons in any such class to pass tests administered in accordance with subsection (c)(7) of this section; and

(iv) provide that persons in any such class other than municipal securities brokers and municipal securities dealers and partners, officers, and supervisory employees of municipal securities brokers or municipal securities dealers, may be qualified solely on the basis of compliance with such standards of training and such other qualifications as the Board finds appropriate.

(B) establish fair procedures for the nomination and election of members of the Board and assure fair representation in such nominations and elections of municipal securities brokers and municipal securities dealers. Such rules shall provide that the membership of the Board shall at all times be equally divided among public representatives, broker-dealer representatives, and bank representatives, and that the public representatives shall be subject to approval by the Commission to assure that no one of them is associated with any broker, dealer, or municipal securities dealer (other than by reason of being under common control with, or indirectly controlling, any broker or dealer which is not a municipal securities broker or municipal securities dealer) and that at least one is representative of investors in municipal securities and at least one is representative of issuers of municipal securities. Such rules shall also specify the term members shall serve and may increase the number of members which shall constitute the whole Board provided that such number is an odd number.

(C) be designed to prevent fraudulent and manipulative acts and practices, to promote just and equitable principles of trade, to foster cooperation and coordination with persons engaged in regulating, clearing, settling, processing information with respect to, and facilitating transactions in municipal securities, to remove impediments to and perfect the mechanism of a free and open market in municipal securities, and, in general, to protect investors and the public interest; and not be designed to permit unfair discrimination between customers, issuers, municipal securities brokers, or municipal securities dealers, to fix minimum profits, to impose any schedule or fix rates of commissions, allowances, discounts, or other fees to be charged by municipal securities brokers or municipal securities dealers, to regulate by virtue of any authority conferred by this title matters not related to the purposes of this title or the administration of the Board, or to impose any burden on competition not necessary or appropriate in furtherance of the purpose of this title.

(D) if the Board deems appropriate, provide for the arbitration of claims, disputes, and controversies relating to transactions in municipal securities: Provided, however, That no person other than a municipal securities broker, municipal securities dealer, or person associated with such a municipal securities broker or municipal securities dealer may be compelled to submit to such arbitration except at his instance and in accordance with section 29 of this title.

(E) provide for the periodic examination in accordance with subsection (c)(7) of this section of municipal securities brokers and municipal securities dealers to determine compliance with applicable provisions of this title, the rules and regulations thereunder, and the rules of the Board. Such rules shall specify the minimum scope and frequency of such examinations and shall be designed to avoid unnecessary regulatory duplication or undue regulatory burdens for any such municipal securities broker or municipal securities dealer.

(F) include provisions governing the form and content of quotations relating to municipal securities which may be distributed or published by any municipal securities broker, municipal securities dealer, or person associated with such a municipal securities broker or municipal securities dealer, and the persons to whom such quotations may be supplied. Such rules relating to quotations shall be designed to produce fair and informative quotations, to prevent fictitious or misleading quotations, and to promote orderly procedures for collecting, distributing, and publishing quotations.

(G) prescribe records to be made and kept by municipal securities brokers and municipal securities dealers and the periods for which such records shall be preserved.

(H) define the term "separately identifiable department or division", as that term is used in section 3(a)(30) of this title, in accordance with specified and appropriate standards to assure that a bank is not deemed to be engaged in the business of buying and selling municipal securities through a separately identifiable department or division unless such department or division is organized and administered so as to permit independent examination and enforcement of applicable provisions of this title, the rules and regulations thereunder and the rules of the Board. A separately identifiable department or division of a bank may be engaged in activities other than those relating to municipal securities.

(I) provide for the operation and administration of the Board, including the selection of a Chairman from among the members of the Board, the compensation of the members of the Board, and the appointment and compensation of such employees, attorneys, and consultants as may be necessary or appropriate to carry out the Board's functions under this section.

(J) provide that each municipal securities broker and each municipal securities dealer shall pay to the Board such reasonable fees and charges as may be necessary or appropriate to defray the costs and expenses of operating and administering the Board. Such rules shall specify the amount of such fees and charges.

(K) establish the terms and conditions under which any municipal securities dealer may sell, or prohibit any municipal securities dealer from selling, any part of a new issue of municipal securities to a municipal securities investment portfolio during the underwriting period.

(3) Nothing in this section shall be construed to impair or limit the power of the Commission under this title.

(c)(1) No broker, dealer, or municipal securities dealer shall make use of the mails or any means or instrumentality of interstate commerce to effect any transaction in, or to induce or attempt to induce the purchase or sale of, any municipal security in contravention of any rule of the Board.

(2) The Commission, by order, shall censure, place limitations on the activities, functions, or operations, suspend for a period not exceeding twelve months, or revoke the registration of any municipal securities dealer, if it finds, on the record after notice and opportunity for hearing, that such censure, placing of limitations, denial, suspension, or revocation, is in the public interest and that such municipal securities dealer has committed or omitted any act, or is subject to an order or finding, enumerated in subparagraph (A), (D), (E), (H), or (G) of paragraph (4) of section 15(b) of this title, has been convicted of any offense specified in subparagraph (B) of such paragraph (4) within ten years of the commencement of the proceedings under this paragraph, or is enjoined from any action, conduct, or practice specified in subparagraph (C) of such paragraph (4).

(3) Pending final determination whether any registration under this section shall be revoked, the Commission, by order, may suspend such registration, if such suspension appears to the Commission, after notice and opportunity for hearing, to be necessary or appropriate in the public interest or for the protection of investors. Any registered municipal securities dealer may, upon such terms and conditions as the Commission may deem necessary in the public interest or for the protection of investors, withdraw from

registration by filing a written notice of withdrawal with the Commission. If the Commission finds that any registered municipal securities dealer is no longer in existence or has ceased to do business as a municipal securities dealer, the Commission, by order, shall cancel the registration of such municipal securities dealer.

(4) The Commission, by order, shall censure or place limitations on the activities or functions of any person associated, seeking to become associated, or, at the time of the alleged misconduct, associated or seeking to become associated with a municipal securities dealer, or suspend for a period not exceeding twelve months or bar any such person from being associated with a municipal securities dealer, if the Commission finds, on the record after notice and opportunity for hearing, that such censure, placing of limitations, suspension, or bar is in the public interest and that such person has committed any act, or is subject to an order or finding, enumerated in subparagraph (A), (D), (E), (H), or (G) of paragraph (4) of section 15(b) of this title, has been convicted of any offense specified in subparagraph (B) of such paragraph (4) within 10 years of the commencement of the proceedings under this paragraph, or is enjoined from any action, conduct, or practice specified in subparagraph (C) of such paragraph (4). It shall be unlawful for any person as to whom an order entered pursuant to this paragraph or paragraph (5) of this subsection suspending or barring him from being associated with a municipal securities dealer is in effect willfully to become, or to be, associated with a municipal securities dealer without the consent of the Commission, and it shall be unlawful for any municipal securities dealer to permit such a person to become, or remain, a person associated with him without the consent of the Commission, if such municipal securities dealer knew, or, in the exercise of reasonable care should have known, of such order.

(5) With respect to any municipal securities dealer for which the Commission is not the appropriate regulatory agency, the appropriate regulatory agency for such municipal securities dealer may sanction any such municipal securities dealer in the manner and for the reasons specified in paragraph (2) of this subsection and any person associated with such municipal securities dealer in the manner and for the reasons specified in paragraph (4) of this subsection. In addition, such appropriate regulatory agency may, in accordance with section 8 of the Federal Deposit Insurance Act (12 U.S.C. 1818) enforce compliance by such municipal securities dealer or any person associated with such municipal securities dealer with the provisions of this section, section 17 of this title, the rules of the Board, and the rules of the Commission pertaining to municipal securities dealers, persons associated with municipal securities dealers, and transactions in municipal securities. For purposes of the preceding sentence, any violation of any such provision shall constitute adequate basis for the issuance of any order under section 8(b) or 8(c) of the Federal Deposit Insurance Act, and the customers of any such municipal securities dealer shall be deemed to be "depositors" as that term is used in section 8(c) of that Act. Nothing in this paragraph shall be construed to affect in any way the powers of such appropriate regulatory agency to proceed against such municipal securities dealer under any other provision of law.

(6)(A) The Commission, prior to the entry of an order of investigation, or commencement of any proceedings, against any municipal securities dealer, or person associated with any municipal securities dealer, for which the commission is not the appropriate regulatory agency, for violation of any provision of this section, section 15(c)(1) or 15(c)(2) of this title, any rule or regulation under any such section, or any rule of the Board, shall (i) give notice to the appropriate regulatory agency for such municipal securities dealer of the identity of such municipal securities dealer or person associated with such municipal securities dealer or person associated with such municipal securities dealer, the nature of and basis for such proposed action, and whether the Commission is seeking a monetary penalty against such municipal securities dealer or such associated person pursuant to section 21B of this title; and (ii) consult with such appropriate regulatory agency concerning the effect of such proposed action on sound banking practices and the feasibility and desirability of coordinating such action with any proceeding or proposed proceeding by such appropriate regulatory agency against such municipal securities dealer or associated person.

(B) The appropriate regulatory agency for a municipal securities dealer (if other than the Commission), prior to the entry of an order of investigation, or commencement of any proceedings, against such municipal securities dealer or person associated with such municipal securities dealer, for violation of any provision of this section, the rules of the Board, or the rules or regulations of the Commission pertaining to municipal securities dealers, persons associated with municipal securities dealers, or transactions in municipal securities shall (i) give notice to the Commission of the identity of such municipal securities dealer or person associated with such municipal securities dealer and the nature of and basis for such proposed action and (ii) consult with the Commission concerning the effect of such proposed action on the protection of investors and the feasibility and desirability of coordinating such action with any proceeding or proposed proceeding by the Commission against such municipal securities dealer or associated person.

(C) Nothing in this paragraph shall be construed to impair or limit (other than by the requirement of prior consultation) the power of the Commission or the appropriate regulatory agency for a municipal securities dealer to initiate any action of a class described in this paragraph or to affect in any way the power of the Commission or such appropriate regulatory agency to initiate any other action pursuant to this title or any other provision of law.

(7)(A) Tests required pursuant to subsection (b)(2)(A)(iii) of this section shall be administered by or on behalf of and periodic examinations pursuant to subsection (b)(2)(E) of this section shall be conducted by—

(i) a registered securities association, in the case of municipal securities brokers and municipal securities dealers who are members of such association; and

(ii) the appropriate regulatory agency for any municipal securities broker or municipal securities dealer, in the case of all other municipal securities brokers and municipal securities dealers.

(B) A registered securities association shall make a report of any examination conducted pursuant to subsection (b)(2)(E) of this section and promptly furnish the Commission a copy thereof and any data supplied to it in connection with such examination. Subject to such limitations as the Commission, by rule, determines to be necessary or appropriate in the public interest or for the protection of investors, the Commission shall, on request, make available to the Board a copy of any report of an examination of a municipal securities broker or municipal securities dealer made by or furnished to the Commission pursuant to this paragraph or section 17(c)(3) of this title.

(8) The Commission is authorized, by order, if in its opinion such action is necessary or appropriate in the public interest, for the protection of investors, or otherwise in furtherance of the purposes of this title, to remove from office or censure any member or employee of the Board, who, the Commission finds, on the record after notice and opportunity for hearing, has willfully (A) violated any provision of this title, the rules and regulations thereunder, or the rules of the Board or (B) abused his authority.

(d)(1) Neither the Commission nor the Board is authorized under this title, by rule or regulation, to require any issuer of municipal securities, directly or indirectly through a purchaser or prospective purchaser of securities from the issuer, to file with the Commission or the Board prior to the sale of such securities by the issuer any application, report, or document in connection with the issuance, sale, or distribution of such securities.

(2) The Board is not authorized under this title to require any issuer of municipal securities, directly or indirectly through a municipal securities broker or municipal securities dealer or otherwise, to furnish to the Board or to a purchaser or prospective purchaser of such securities any application, report, document, or information with respect to such issuer: *Provided, however,* That the Board may require municipal securities brokers and municipal securities dealers to furnish to the Board or purchasers or prospective purchasers of municipal securities applications, reports, documents, and information with respect to the issuer thereof which is generally available from a source other than such issuer. Nothing in this paragraph shall be construed to impair or limit the power of the Commission under any provision of this title.

Government Securities Brokers and Dealers

Sec. 15C. (a)(1)(A) It shall be unlawful for any government securities broker or government securities dealer (other than a registered broker or dealer or a financial institution) to make use of the mails or any means or instrumentality of interstate commerce to effect any transaction in, or to induce or attempt to induce the purchase or sale of, any government security unless such government securities broker or government securities dealer is registered in accordance with paragraph (2) of this subsection.

(B)(i) It shall be unlawful for any government securities broker or government securities dealer that is a registered broker or dealer or a financial institution to make use of the mails or any means or instrumentality of interstate commerce to effect any transaction in, or to induce or attempt to induce the purchase or sale of, any government security unless such government securities broker or government securities dealer has filed with the appropriate regulatory agency written notice that it is a government securities broker or government securities dealer. When such a government securities broker or government securities dealer ceases to act as such it shall file with the appropriate regulatory agency a written notice that it is no longer acting as a government securities broker or government securities dealer.

(ii) Such notices shall be in such form and contain such information concerning a government securities broker or government securities dealer that is a financial institution and any persons associated with such government securities broker or government securities dealer as the Board of Governors of the Federal Reserve System shall, by rule, after consultation with each appropriate regulatory agency (including the Commission), prescribe as necessary or appropriate in the public interest or for the protection of investors. Such notices shall be in such form and contain such information concerning a government securities broker or government securities dealer that is a registered broker or dealer and any persons associated with such government securities broker or government securities dealer as the Commission shall, by rule, prescribe as necessary or appropriate in the public interest or for the protection of investors.

(iii) Each appropriate regulatory agency (other than the Commission) shall make available to the Commission the notices which have been filed with it under this subparagraph, and the Commission shall maintain and make available to the public such notices and the notices it receives under this subparagraph.

(2) A government securities broker or a government securities dealer subject to the registration requirement of paragraph (1)(A) of this subsection may be registered by filing with the Commission an application for registration in such form and containing such information and documents concerning such government securities broker or government securities dealer and any persons associated with such government securities broker or government securities dealer as the Commission, by rule, may prescribe as necessary or appropriate in

the public interest or for the protection of investors. Within 45 days of the date of filing of such application (or within such longer period as to which the applicant consents), the Commission shall—

(i) by order grant registration, or

(ii) institute proceedings to determine whether registration should be denied. Such proceedings shall include notice of the grounds for denial under consideration and opportunity for hearing and shall be concluded within 120 days of the date of the filing of the application for registration. At the conclusion of such proceedings, the Commission, by order, shall grant or deny such registration. The order granting registration shall not be effective until such government securities broker or government securities dealer has become a member of a national securities exchange registered under section 6 of this title, or a securities association registered under section 15A of this title, unless the Commission has exempted such government securities broker or government securities dealer, by rule or order, from such membership. The Commission may extend the time for the conclusion of such proceedings for up to 90 days if it finds good cause for such extension and publishes its reasons for so finding or for such longer period as to which the applicant consents.

The Commission shall grant the registration of a government securities broker or a government securities dealer if the Commission finds that the requirements of this section are satisfied. The Commission shall deny such registration if it does not make such a finding or if it finds that if the applicant were so registered, its registration would be subject to suspension or revocation under subsection (c) of this section.

(3) Any provision of this title (other than section 5 or paragraph (1) of this subsection) which prohibits any act, practice, or course of business if the mails or any means or instrumentality of interstate commerce is used in connection therewith shall also prohibit any such act, practice, or course of business by any government securities broker or government securities dealer registered or having filed notice under paragraph (1) of this subsection or any person acting on behalf of such government securities broker or government securities dealer, irrespective of any use of the mails or any means or instrumentality of interstate commerce in connection therewith.

(4) No government securities broker or government securities dealer that is required to register under paragraph (1)(A) and that is not a member of the Securities Investor Protection Corporation shall effect any transaction in any security in contravention of such rules as the Commission shall prescribe pursuant to this subsection to assure that its customers receive complete, accurate, and timely disclosure of the inapplicability of Securities Investor Protection Corporation coverage to their accounts.

(5) The Secretary of the Treasury (hereinafter in this section referred to as the "Secretary"), by rule or order, upon the Secretary's own motion or upon application, may conditionally or unconditionally exempt any government securities broker or government securities dealer, or class of government securities brokers or government securities dealers, from any provision of subsection (a), (b), or (d) of this section, other than subsection (d)(3), or the rules thereunder, if the Secretary finds that such exemption is consistent with the public interest, the protection of investors, and the purposes of this title.

(b)(1) The Secretary shall propose and adopt rules to effect the purposes of this title with respect to transactions in government securities effected by government securities brokers and government securities dealers as follows:

(A) Such rules shall provide safeguards with respect to the financial responsibility and related practices of government securities brokers and government securities dealers including, but not limited to, capital adequacy standards, the acceptance of custody and use of customers' securities, the carrying and use of customers' deposits or credit balances, and the transfer and control of government securities subject to repurchase agreements and in similar transactions.

(B) Such rules shall require every government securities broker and government securities dealer to make reports to and furnish copies of records to the appropriate regulatory agency, and to file with the appropriate regulatory agency, annually or more frequently, a balance sheet and income statement certified by an independent public accountant, prepared on a calendar or fiscal year basis, and such other financial statements (which shall, as the Secretary specifies, be certified) and information concerning its financial condition as required by such rules.

(C) Such rules shall require records to be made and kept by government securities brokers and government securities dealers and shall specify the periods for which such records shall be preserved.

(2) *Risk Assessment for Holding Company Systems.—*

A. *Obligations to Obtain Maintain, and Report Information.*—Every person who is registered as a government securities broker or government securities dealer under this section shall obtain such information and make and keep such records as the Secretary by rule prescribes concerning the registered person's policies, procedures, or systems for monitoring and controlling financial and operational risks to it resulting from the activities of any of its associated persons, other than a natural person. Such records shall describe, in the aggregate, each of the financial and securities activities conducted by, and customary sources of capital and funding of, those of its associated persons whose business activities are reasonably likely to have a material impact on the financial or operational condition of such registered person, including its capital, its liquidity, or its ability to conduct or finance its operations. The Secretary, by rule, may require summary reports of such information to be filed with the registered person's appropriate regulatory agency no more frequently than quarterly.

(B) *Authority to Require Additional Information.*—If, as a result of adverse market conditions or based on reports provided pursuant to subparagraph (A) of this paragraph or other available information, the appropriate regulatory agency reasonably concludes that it has concerns regarding the financial or operational condition of any government securities broker or government securities dealer registered under this section, such agency may require the registered person to make reports concerning the financial and securities activities of any of such person's associated persons, other than a natural person, whose business activities are reasonably likely to have a material impact on the financial or operational condition of such registered person. The appropriate regulatory agency, in requiring reports pursuant to this subparagraph, shall specify the information required, the period for which it is required, the time and date on which the information must be furnished, and whether the information is to be furnished directly to the appropriate regulatory agency or to a self-regulatory organization with primary responsibility for examining the registered person's financial and operational condition.

(C) *Special Provisions With Respect to Associated Persons Subject to Federal Banking Regulation.—*

(i) *Cooperation in Implementation.*—In developing and implementing reporting requirements pursuant to subparagraph (A) of this paragraph with respect to associated persons subject to examination by or reporting requirements of a Federal banking agency, the Secretary shall consult with and consider the views of each such Federal banking agency. If a Federal banking agency comments in writing on a proposed rule of the Secretary under this paragraph that has been published for comment, the Secretary shall respond in writing to such written comment before adopting the proposed rule. The Secretary shall, at the request of a Federal banking agency, publish such comment and response in the Federal Register at the time of publishing the adopted rule.

(ii) *Use of Banking Agency Reports.*—A registered government securities broker or government securities dealer shall be in compliance with any recordkeeping or reporting requirement adopted pursuant to subparagraph (A) of this paragraph concerning an associated person that is subject to examination by or reporting requirements of a Federal banking agency if such government securities broker or government securities dealer utilizes for such recordkeeping or reporting requirement copies of reports filed by the associated person with the Federal banking agency pursuant to section 5211 of the Revised Statutes, section 9 of the Federal Reserve Act, section 7(a) of the Federal Deposit Insurance Act, section 10(b) of the Home Owners' Loan Act, or section 8 of the Bank Holding Company Act of 1956. The Secretary may, however, by rule adopted pursuant to subparagraph (A), require any registered government securities broker or government securities dealer filing such reports with the appropriate regulatory agency to obtain, maintain, or report supplemental information if the Secretary makes an explicit finding, based on information provided by the appropriate regulatory agency, that such supplemental information is necessary to inform the appropriate regulatory agency regarding potential risks to such government securities broker or government securities dealer. Prior to requiring any such supplemental information, the Secretary shall first request the Federal banking agency to expand its reporting requirements to include such information.

(iii) *Procedure for Requiring Additional Information.*—Prior to making a request pursuant to subparagraph (B) of this paragraph for information with respect to an associated person that is subject to examination by or reporting requirements of a Federal banking agency, the appropriate regulatory agency shall—

(I) notify such banking agency of the information required with respect to such associated person; and

(II) consult with such agency to determine whether the information required is available from such agency and for other purposes, unless the appropriate regulatory agency determines that any delay resulting from such consultation would be inconsistent with ensuring the financial and operational condition of the government securities broker or government securities dealer or the stability or integrity of the securities markets.

(iv) *Exclusion for Examination Reports.*—Nothing in this subparagraph shall be construed to permit the Secretary or an appropriate regulatory agency to require any registered government securities broker or government securities dealer to obtain, maintain, or furnish any examination report of any Federal banking agency or any supervisory recommendations or analysis contained therein.

(v) *Confidentiality of Information Provided.*—No information provided to or obtained by an appropriate regulatory agency from any Federal banking agency pursuant to a request under clause (iii) of this subparagraph regarding any associated person which is subject to examination by or reporting requirements of a Federal banking agency may be disclosed to any other person (other than a self-regulatory organization), without the prior written approval of the Federal banking agency. Nothing in this clause shall authorize the Secretary or any appropriate regulatory agency to withhold information from Congress, or prevent the Secretary or any appropriate regulatory agency from complying with a request for information from any other Federal department or agency requesting the information for purposes within the scope of its jurisdiction, or complying with an order of a court of the United States in an action brought by the United States or the Commission.

(vi) *Notice to Banking Agencies Concerning Financial and Operational Condition Concerns.*—The Secretary or appropriate regulatory agency shall notify the Federal banking agency of any concerns of the Secretary or the appropriate regulatory agency regarding significant financial or operational risks resulting from the activities of any government securities broker or government securities dealer to any associated person thereof which is subject to examination by or reporting requirements of the Federal banking agency.

(vii) *Definition.*—For purposes of this subparagraph, the term "Federal banking agency" shall have the same meaning as the term "appropriate Federal banking agency" in section 3(q) of the Federal Deposit Insurance Act (12 U.S.C. 1813(q)).

(D) *Exemptions.*—The Secretary by rule or order may exempt any person or class of persons, under such terms and conditions and for such periods as the Secretary shall provide in such rule or order, from the provisions of this paragraph, and the rules thereunder. In granting such exemptions, the Secretary shall consider, among other factors—

(i) whether information of the type required under this paragraph is available from a supervisory agency (as defined in section 1101(6) of the Right to Financial Privacy Act of 1978 (12 U.S.C. 3401(6))), a State insurance commission or similar State agency, the Commodity Futures Trading Commission, or a similar foreign regulator;

(ii) the primary business of any associated person;

(iii) the nature and extent of domestic or foreign regulation of the associated person's activities;

(iv) the nature and extent of the registered person's securities transactions; and

(v) with respect to the registered person and its associated persons, on a consolidated basis, the amount and proportion of assets devoted to, and revenues derived from, activities in the United States securities markets.

(E) *Conformity With Requirements Under Section 17(h).*—In exercising authority pursuant to subparagraph (A) of this paragraph concerning information with respect to associated persons of government securities brokers and government securities dealers who are also associated persons of registered brokers or dealers reporting to the Commission pursuant to section 17(h) of this title, the requirements relating to such associated persons shall conform, to the greatest extent practicable, to the requirements under section 17(h).

(F) *Authority to Limit Disclosure of Information.*—Notwithstanding any other provision of law, the Secretary and any appropriate regulatory agency shall not be compelled to disclose any information required to be reported under this paragraph, or any information supplied to the Secretary or any appropriate regulatory agency by any domestic or foreign regulatory agency that relates to the financial or operational condition of any associated person of a registered government securities broker or a government securities dealer. Nothing in this paragraph shall authorize the Secretary or any appropriate regulatory agency to withhold information from Congress, or prevent the Secretary or any appropriate regulatory agency from complying with a request for information from any other Federal department or agency requesting the information for purposes within the scope of its jurisdiction, or complying with an order of a court of the United States in an action brought by the United States or the Commission. For purposes of section 552 of title 5, United States Code, this paragraph shall be considered a statute described in subsection (b)(3)(B) of such section 552.

(3)(A) With respect to any financial institution that has filed notice as a government securities broker or government securities dealer or that is required to file notice under subsection (a)(1)(B), the appropriate regulatory agency for such government securities broker or government securities dealer may issue such rules and regulations with respect to transactions in government securities as may be necessary to prevent fraudulent and manipulative acts and practices and to promote just and equitable principles of trade. If the Secretary of the Treasury determines, and notifies the appropriate regulatory agency, that such rule or regulation, if implemented, would, or as applied does (i) adversely affect the liquidity or efficiency of the market for government securities; or (ii) impose any burden on competition not necessary or appropriate in furtherance of the purposes of this section, the appropriate regulatory agency shall, prior to adopting the proposed rule or regulation, find that such rule or regulation is necessary and appropriate in furtherance of the purposes of this section notwithstanding the Secretary's determination.

(B) The appropriate regulatory agency shall consult with and consider the views of the Secretary prior to approving or amending a rule or regulation under this paragraph, except where the appropriate regulatory agency determines that an emergency exists requiring expeditious and summary action and publishes its reasons therefor. If the Secretary comments in writing to the appropriate regulatory agency on a proposed rule or regulation that has been published for comment, the appropriate regulatory agency shall respond in writing to such written comment before approving the proposed rule or regulation.

(C) In promulgating rules under this section, the appropriate regulatory agency shall consider the sufficiency and appropriateness of then existing laws and rules applicable to government securities brokers, government securities dealers, and persons associated with government securities brokers and government securities dealers.

(4) Rules promulgated and orders issued under this section shall—

(A) be designed to prevent fraudulent and manipulative acts and practices and to protect the integrity, liquidity, and efficiency of the market for government securities, investors, and the public interest; and

(B) not be designed to permit unfair discrimination between customers, issuers, government securities brokers, or government securities dealers, or to impose any burden on competition not necessary or appropriate in furtherance of the purposes of this title.

(5) In promulgating rules and issuing orders under this section, the Secretary—

(A) may appropriately classify government securities brokers and government securities dealers (taking into account relevant matters, including types of business done, nature of securities other than government securities purchased or sold, and character of business organization) and persons associated with government securities brokers and government securities dealers;

(B) may determine, to the extent consistent with paragraph (2) of this subsection and with the public interest, the protection of investors, and the purposes of this title, not to apply, in whole or in part, certain rules under this section, or to apply greater, lesser, or different standards, to certain classes of government securities brokers, government securities dealers, or persons associated with government securities brokers or government securities dealers;

(C) shall consider the sufficiency and appropriateness of then existing laws and rules applicable to government securities brokers, government securities dealers, and persons associated with government securities brokers and government securities dealers; and

(D) shall consult with and consider the views of the Commission and the Board of Governors of the Federal Reserve System, except where the Secretary determines that an emergency exists requiring expeditious or summary action and publishes its reasons for such determination.

(6) If the Commission or the Board of Governors of the Federal Reserve System comments in writing on a proposed rule of the

Secretary that has been published for comment, the Secretary shall respond in writing to such written comment before approving the proposed rule.

(7) No government securities broker or government securities dealer shall make use of the mails or any means or instrumentality of interstate commerce to effect any transaction in, or to induce or attempt to induce the purchase or sale of, any government security in contravention of any rule under this section.

(c)(1) With respect to any government securities broker or government securities dealer registered or required to register under subsection (a)(1)(A) of this section—

(A) The Commission, by order, shall censure, place limitations on the activities, functions, or operations of, suspend for a period not exceeding 12 months, or revoke the registration of such government securities broker or government securities dealer, if it finds, on the record after notice and opportunity for hearing, that such censure, placing of limitations, suspension, or revocation is in the public interest and that such government securities broker or government securities dealer, or any person associated with such government securities broker or government securities dealer (whether prior or subsequent to becoming so associated), has committed or omitted any act, or is subject to an order or finding, enumerated in subparagraph (A), (D), (E), (H), or (G) of paragraph (4) of section 15(b) of this title, has been convicted of any offense specified in subparagraph (B) of such paragraph (4) within 10 years of the commencement of the proceedings under this paragraph, or is enjoined from any action, conduct, or practice specified in subparagraph (C) of such paragraph (4).

(B) Pending final determination whether registration of any government securities broker or government securities dealer shall be revoked, the Commission, by order, may suspend such registration, if such suspension appears to the Commission, after notice and opportunity for hearing, to be necessary or appropriate in the public interest or for the protection of investors. Any registered government securities broker or registered government securities dealer may, upon such terms and conditions as the Commission may deem necessary in the public interest or for the protection of investors, withdraw from registration by filing a written notice of withdrawal with the Commission. If the Commission finds that any registered government securities broker or registered government securities dealer is no longer in existence or has ceased to do business as a government securities broker or government securities dealer, the Commission, by order, shall cancel the registration of such government securities broker or government securities dealer.

(C) The Commission, by order, shall censure or place limitations on the activities or functions of any person associated, or seeking to become associated, with a government securities broker or government securities dealer registered or required to register under subsection (a)(1)(A) of this section or suspend for a period not exceeding 12 months or bar any such person from being associated with such a government securities broker or government securities dealer, if the Commission finds, on the record after notice and opportunity for hearing, that such censure, placing of limitations, suspension, or bar is in the public interest and that such person has committed or omitted any act, or is subject to an order or finding, enumerated in subparagraph (A), (D), (E), (H), or (G) of paragraph (4) of section 15(b) of this title, has been convicted of any offense specified in subparagraph (B) of such paragraph (4) within 10 years of the commencement of the proceedings under this paragraph, or is enjoined from any action, conduct, or practice specified in subparagraph (C) of such paragraph (4).

(2)(A) With respect to any government securities broker or government securities dealer which is not registered or required to register under subsection (a)(1)(A) of this section, the appropriate regulatory agency for such government securities broker or government securities dealer may, in the manner and for the reasons specified in paragraph (1)(A) of this subsection, censure, place limitations on the activities, functions, or operations of, suspend for a period not exceeding 12 months, or bar from acting as a government securities broker or government securities dealer any such government securities broker or government securities dealer, and may sanction any person associated with such government securities broker or government securities dealer in the manner and for the reasons specified in paragraph (1)(C) of this subsection.

(B) In addition, where applicable, such appropriate regulatory agency may, in accordance with section 8 of the Federal Deposit Insurance Act (12 U.S.C. 1818), section 5 of the Home Owners' Loan Act of 1933 (12 U.S.C. 1464), or section 407 of the National Housing Act (12 U.S.C. 1730), enforce compliance by such government securities broker or government securities dealer or any person associated with such government securities broker or government securities dealer with the provisions of this section and the rules thereunder.

(C) For purposes of subparagraph (B) of this paragraph, any violation of any such provision shall constitute adequate basis for the issuance of any order under section 8(b) or 8(c) of the Federal Deposit Insurance Act, section 5(d)(2) or 5(d)(3) of the Home Owners' Loan Act of 1933, or section 407(e) or 407(f) of the National Housing Act, and the customers of any such government securities broker or government securities dealer shall be deemed, respectively, "depositors" as that term is used in section 8(c) of the Federal Deposit Insurance Act, "savings account holders" as that term is used in section 5(d)(3) of the Home Owners' Loan Act of 1933, or "insured members" as that term is used in section 407(f) of the National Housing Act.

(D) Nothing in this paragraph shall be construed to affect in any way the powers of such appropriate regulatory agency to proceed against such government securities broker or government securities dealer under any other provision of law.

(E) Each appropriate regulatory agency (other than the Commission) shall promptly notify the Commission after it has imposed any sanction under this paragraph on a government securities broker or government securities dealer, or a person associated with a government securities broker or government securities dealer, and the Commission shall maintain, and make available to the public, a record of such sanctions and any sanctions imposed by it under this subsection.

(3) It shall be unlawful for any person as to whom an order entered pursuant to paragraph (1) or (2) of this subsection suspending or barring him from being associated with a government securities broker or government securities dealer is in effect willfully to become, or to be, associated with a government securities broker or government securities dealer without the consent of the appropriate regulatory agency, and it shall be unlawful for any government securities broker or government securities dealer to permit such a person to become, or remain, a person associated with it without the consent of the appropriate regulatory agency, if such government securities broker or government securities dealer knew, or, in the exercise of reasonable care should have known, of such order.

(d)(1) All records of a government securities broker or government securities dealer are subject at any time, or from time to time, to such reasonable periodic, special, or other examinations by representatives of the appropriate regulatory agency for such government securities broker or government securities dealer as such appropriate regulatory agency deems necessary or appropriate in the public interest, for the protection of investors, or otherwise in furtherance of the purposes of this title.

(2) Information received by an appropriate regulatory agency, the Secretary, or the Commission from or with respect to any government securities broker, government securities dealer, any person associated with a government securities broker or government securities dealer, or any other person subject to this section or rules promulgated thereunder, may be made available by the Secretary or the recipient agency to the Commission, the Secretary, the Department of Justice, the Commodity Futures Trading Commission, any appropriate regulatory agency, any self-regulatory organization, or any Federal Reserve Bank.

(3) Government Securities Trade Reconstruction.—

(A) Furnishing Records.—Every government securities broker and government securities dealer shall furnish to the Commission on request such records of government securities transactions, including records of the date and time of execution of trades, as the Commission may require to reconstruct trading in the course of a particular inquiry or investigation being conducted by the Commission for enforcement or surveillance purposes. In requiring information pursuant to this paragraph, the Commission shall specify the information required, the period for which it is required, the time and date on which the information must be furnished, and whether the information is to be furnished directly to the Commission, to the Federal Reserve Bank of New York, or to an appropriate regulatory agency or self-regulatory organization with responsibility for examining the government securities broker or government securities dealer. The Commission may require that such information be furnished in machine readable form notwithstanding any limitation in subparagraph (B). In utilizing its authority to require information in machine readable form, the Commission shall minimize the burden such requirement may place on small government securities brokers and dealers.

(B) Limitation; construction.—The Commission shall not utilize its authority under this paragraph to develop regular reporting requirements, except that the Commission may require information to be furnished under this paragraph as frequently as necessary for particular inquiries or investigations for enforcement or surveillance purposes. This paragraph shall not be construed as requiring, or as authorizing the Commission to require, any government securities broker or government securities dealer to obtain or maintain any information for purposes of this paragraph which is not otherwise maintained by such broker or dealer in accordance with any other provision of law or usual and customary business practice. The Commission shall, where feasible, avoid requiring any information to be furnished under this paragraph that the Commission may obtain from the Federal Reserve Bank of New York.

(C) Procedures for requiring information.—At the time the Commission requests any information pursuant to subparagraph (A) with respect to any government securities broker or government securities dealer for which the Commission is not the appropriate regulatory agency, the Commission shall notify the appropriate regulatory agency for such government securities broker or government securities dealer and, upon request, furnish to the appropriate regulatory agency any information supplied to the Commission.

(D) Consultation.—Within 90 days after the date of enactment of this paragraph, and annually thereafter, or upon the request of any other appropriate regulatory agency, the Commission shall consult with the other appropriate regulatory agencies to determine the availability of records that may be required to be furnished under this paragraph and, for those records available directly from the other appropriate regulatory agencies, to develop a procedure for furnishing such records expeditiously upon the Commission's request.

(E) Exclusion for examination reports.—Nothing in this paragraph shall be construed so as to permit the Commission to require any government securities broker or government securities dealer to obtain, maintain, or furnish any examination report of any appropriate regulatory agency other than the Commission or any supervisory recommendations or analysis contained in any such examination report.

(F) Authority to limit disclosure of information.—Notwithstanding any other provision of law, the Commission and the appropriate regulatory agencies shall not be compelled to disclose any information required or obtained under this paragraph. Nothing in this paragraph shall authorize the Commission or any appropriate regulatory agency to withhold information from Congress, or prevent the Commission or any appropriate regulatory agency from complying with a request for information from any other Federal department or agency requesting information for purposes within the scope of its jurisdiction, or from complying with an order of a court of the United States in an action brought by the United States, the Commission, or the appropriate regulatory agency. For purposes of section 552 of title 5, United States Code, this subparagraph shall be considered a statute described in subsection (b)(3)(B) of such section 552.

(e)(1) It shall be unlawful for any government securities broker or government securities dealer registered or required to register with the Commission under subsection (a)(1)(A) to effect any transaction in, or induce or attempt to induce the purchase or sale of, any government security, unless such government securities broker or government securities dealer is a member of a national securities exchange registered under section 6 of this title or a securities association registered under section 15A of this title.

(2) The Commission, after consultation with the Secretary, by rule or order, as it deems consistent with the public interest and the protection of investors, may conditionally or unconditionally exempt from paragraph (1) of this subsection any government securities broker or government securities dealer or class of government securities brokers or government securities dealers specified in such rule or order.

(f) Large Position Reporting.—

(1) Reporting requirements.—The Secretary may adopt rules to require specified persons holding, maintaining, or controlling large positions in to-be-issued or recently issued Treasury securities to file such reports regarding such positions as the Secretary determines to be necessary and appropriate for the purpose of monitoring the impact in the Treasury securities market of concentrations of positions in treasury securities and for the purpose of otherwise assisting the Commission in the enforcement of this title, taking into account any impact of such rules on the efficiency and liquidity of the Treasury securities market and the cost to taxpayers of funding the Federal debt. Unless otherwise specified by the Secretary, reports required under this subsection shall be filed with the Federal Reserve Bank of New York, acting as agent for the Secretary. Such reports shall, on a timely basis, be provided directly to the Commission by the person with whom they are filed.

(2) Recordkeeping requirements.—Rules under this subsection may require persons holding, maintaining, or controlling large positions in Treasury securities to make and keep for prescribed periods such records as the Secretary determines are necessary or appropriate to ensure that such persons can comply with reporting requirements under this subsection.

(3) Aggregation rules. Rules under this subsection—

(A) may prescribe the manner in which positions and accounts shall be aggregated for the purpose of this subsection, including aggregation on the basis of common ownership or control; and

(B) may define which persons (individually or as a group) hold, maintain, or control large positions.

(4) Definitional authority; determination of reporting threshold.—

(A) In prescribing rules under this subsection, the Secretary may, consistent with the purpose of this subsection, define terms used in this subsection that are not otherwise defined in section 3 of this title.

(B) Rules under this subsection shall specify—

(i) the minimum size of positions subject to reporting under this subsection, which shall be no less than the size that provides the potential for manipulation or control of the supply or price, or the cost of financing arrangements, of an issue or the portion thereof that is available for trading;

(ii) the types of positions (which may include financing arrangements) to be reported;

(iii) the securities to be covered; and

(iv) the form and manner in which reports shall be transmitted, which may include transmission in machine readable form.

(5) Exemptions.—Consistent with the public interest and the protection of investors, the Secretary by rule or order may exempt in whole or in part, conditionally or unconditionally, any person or class of persons, or any transaction or class of transactions, from the requirements of this subsection.

(6) Limitation on disclosure of information.—Notwithstanding any other provision of law, the Secretary and the Commission shall not be compelled to disclose any information required to be kept or reported under this subsection. Nothing in this subsection shall authorize the Secretary or the Commission to withhold information from Congress, or prevent the Secretary or the Commission from complying with a request for information from any other Federal department or agency requesting information for purposes within the scope of its jurisdiction, or from complying with an order of a court of the United States in an action brought by the United States, the Secretary, or the Commission. For purposes of section 552 of title 5, United States Code, this paragraph shall be considered a statute described in subsection (b)(3)(B) of such section 552.

(g)(1) Nothing in this section except paragraph (2) of this subsection shall be construed to impair or limit the authority under any other provision of law of the Commission, the Secretary of the Treasury, the Board of Governors of the Federal Reserve System, the Comptroller of the Currency, the Federal Deposit Insurance Corporation, the Director of the Office of Thrift Supervision, the Federal Savings and Loan Insurance Corporation, the Secretary of Housing and Urban Development, and the Government National Mortgage Association.

(2) Notwithstanding any other provision of this title, the Commission shall not have any authority to make investigations of, require the filing of a statement by, or take any other action under this title against a government securities broker or government securities dealer, or any person associated with a government securities broker or government securities dealer, for any violation or threatened violation of the provisions of this section, other than subsection (d)(3), or the rules or regulations thereunder, unless the Commission is the appropriate regulatory agency for such government securities broker or government securities dealer. Nothing in the preceding sentence shall be construed to limit the authority of the Commission with respect to violations or threatened violations of any provision of this title other than this section, (except subsection (d)(3)) or the rules or regulations under any such other provision.

Securities Analysts and Research Reports

Sec. 15D. (a) *Analyst Protections.*—The Commission, or upon the authorization and direction of the Commission, a registered securities association or national securities exchange, shall have adopted, not later than 1 year after the date of enactment of this section, rules reasonably designed to address conflicts of interest that can arise when securities analysts recommend equity securities in research reports and public appearances, in order to improve the objectivity of research and provide investors with more useful and reliable information, including rules designed—

(1) to foster greater public confidence in securities research, and to protect the objectivity and independence of securities analysts, by—

(A) restricting the prepublication clearance or approval of research reports by persons employed by the broker or dealer who are engaged in investment banking activities, or persons not directly responsible for investment research, other than legal or compliance staff;

(B) limiting the supervision and compensatory evaluation of securities analysts to officials employed by the broker or dealer who are not engaged in investment banking activities; and

(C) requiring that a broker or dealer and persons employed by a broker or dealer who are involved with investment banking activities may not, directly or indirectly, retaliate against or threaten to retaliate against any securities analyst employed by that broker or dealer or its affiliates as a result of an adverse, negative, or otherwise unfavorable research report that may adversely affect the present or prospective investment banking relationship of the broker or dealer with the issuer that is the subject of the research report, except that such rules may not limit the authority of a broker or dealer to discipline a securities analyst for causes other than such research report in accordance with the policies and procedures of the firm;

(2) to define periods during which brokers or dealers who have participated, or are to participate, in a public offering of securities as underwriters or dealers should not publish or otherwise distribute research reports relating to such securities or to the issuer of such securities;

(3) to establish structural and institutional safeguards within registered brokers or dealers to assure that securities analysts are separated by appropriate informational partitions within the firm from the review, pressure, or oversight of those whose involvement in investment banking activities might potentially bias their judgment or supervision; and

(4) to address such other issues as the Commission, or such association or exchange, determines appropriate.

(b) *Disclosure.*—The Commission, or upon the authorization and direction of the Commission, a registered securities association or national securities exchange, shall have adopted, not later than 1 year after the date of enactment of this section, rules reasonably designed to require each securities analyst to disclose in public appearances, and each registered broker or dealer to disclose in each research report, as applicable, conflicts of interest that are known or should have been known by the securities analyst or the broker or dealer, to exist at the time of the appearance or the date of distribution of the report, including—

(1) the extent to which the securities analyst has debt or equity investments in the issuer that is the subject of the appearance or research report;

(2) whether any compensation has been received by the registered broker or dealer, or any affiliate thereof, including the securities analyst, from the issuer that is the subject of the appearance or research report,

subject to such exemptions as the Commission may determine appropriate and necessary to prevent disclosure by virtue of this paragraph of material non-public information regarding specific potential future investment banking transactions of such issuer, as is appropriate in the public interest and consistent with the protection of investors;

(3) whether an issuer, the securities of which are recommended in the appearance or research report, currently is, or during the 1-year period preceding the date of the appearance or date of distribution of the report has been, a client of the registered broker or dealer, and if so, stating the types of services provided to the issuer;

(4) whether the securities analyst received compensation with respect to a research report, based upon (among any other factors) the investment banking revenues (either generally or specifically earned from the issuer being analyzed) of the registered broker or dealer; and

(5) such other disclosures of conflicts of interest that are material to investors, research analysts, or the broker or dealer as the Commission, or such association or exchange, determines appropriate.

(c) *Definitions.*—In this section—

(1) the term "securities analyst" means any associated person of a registered broker or dealer that is principally responsible for, and any associated person who reports directly or indirectly to a securities analyst in connection with, the preparation of the substance of a research report, whether or not any such person has the job title of "securities analyst"; and

(2) the term "research report" means a written or electronic communication that includes an analysis of equity securities of individual companies or industries, and that provides information reasonably sufficient upon which to base an investment decision.

(b) *Enforcement.*—Section 21B(a) of the Securities Exchange Act of 1934 (15 U.S.C. 78u–2(a)) is amended by inserting "15D," before "15B".

(c) *Commission Authority.*—The Commission may promulgate and amend its regulations, or direct a registered securities association or national securities exchange to promulgate and amend its rules, to carry out section 15D of the Securities Exchange Act of 1934, as added by this section, as is necessary for the protection of investors and in the public interest.

Directors, Officers, and Principal Stockholders

Sec. 16. (a) *Disclosure Required.*—

(1) *Directors, officers, and principal stockholders required to file.*—Every person who is directly or indirectly the beneficial owner of more than 10 percent of any class of any equity security (other than an exempted security) which is registered pursuant to section 12, or who is a director or an officer of the issuer of such security, shall file the statements required by this subsection with the Commission (and, if such security is registered on a national securities exchange, also with the exchange).

(2) *Time of filing.*—The statements required by this subsection shall be filed—

(A) at the time of the registration of such security on a national securities exchange or by the effective date of a registration statement filed pursuant to section 12(g);

(B) within 10 days after he or she becomes such beneficial owner, director, or officer;

(C) if there has been a change in such ownership, or if such person shall have purchased or sold a security-based swap agreement (as defined in section 206(b) of the Gramm–Leach–Bliley Act (15 U.S.C. 78c note)) involving such equity security, before the end of the second business day following the day on which the subject transaction has been executed, or at such other time as the Commission shall establish, by rule, in any case in which the Commission determines that such 2–day period is not feasible.

(3) *Contents of statements.*—A statement filed—

(A) under subparagraph (A) or (B) of paragraph (2) shall contain a statement of the amount of all equity securities of such issuer of which the filing person is the beneficial owner; and

(B) under subparagraph (C) of such paragraph shall indicate ownership by the filing person at the date of filing, any such changes in such ownership, and such purchases and sales of the security-based swap agreements as have occurred since the most recent such filing under such subparagraph.

(4) *Electronic filing and availability.*—

(A) a statement filed under subparagraph (C) of paragraph (2) shall be filed electronically;

(B) the Commission shall provide each such statement on a publicly accessible Internet site not later than the end of the business day following that filing; and

(C) the issuer (if the issuer maintains a corporate website) shall provide that statement on that corporate website, not later than the end of the business day following that filing.

(b) For the purpose of preventing the unfair use of information which may have been obtained by such beneficial owner, director, or officer by reason of his relationship to the issuer, any profit realized by him from any purchase and sale, or any sale and purchase, of any equity security of such issuer (other than an exempted security) or a security-based swap agreement (as defined in section 206B of the Gramm–Leach–Bliley Act) involving any such equity security within any period of less than six months, unless such security or security-based swap agreement was acquired in good faith in connection with a debt previously contracted, shall inure to and be recoverable by the issuer, irrespective of any intention on the part of such beneficial owner, director, or officer in entering into such transaction of holding the security or security-based swap agreement purchased or of not repurchasing the security or security-based swap agreement sold for a period exceeding six months. Suit to recover such profit may be instituted at law or in equity in any court of competent jurisdiction by the issuer, or by the owner of any security of the issuer in the name and in behalf of the issuer if the issuer shall fail or refuse to bring such suit within sixty days after request or shall fail diligently to prosecute the same thereafter; but no such suit shall be brought more than two years after the date such profit was realized. This subsection shall not be construed to cover any transaction where such beneficial owner was not such both at the time of the purchase and sale, or the sale and purchase, of the security or security-based swap agreement (as defined in section 206B of the Gramm–Leach–Bliley Act) involved, or any transaction or transactions which the Commission by rules and regulations may exempt as not comprehended within the purpose of this subsection.

(c) It shall be unlawful for any such beneficial owner, director, or officer, directly or indirectly, to sell any equity security of such issuer (other than an exempted security), if the person selling the security or his principal (1) does not own the security sold, or (2) if owning the security, does not deliver it against such sale within twenty days thereafter, or does not within five days after such sale deposit it in the mails or other usual channels of transportation; but no person shall be deemed to have violated this subsection if he proves that notwithstanding the exercise of good faith he was unable to make such delivery or deposit within such time, or that to do so would cause undue inconvenience or expense.

(d) The provisions of subsection (b) of this section shall not apply to any purchase and sale, or sale and purchase, and the provisions of subsection (c) of this section shall not apply to any sale, of an equity security not then or theretofore held by him in an investment account, by a dealer in the ordinary course of his business and incident to the establishment or maintenance by him of a primary or secondary market (otherwise than on a national securities exchange or an exchange exempted from registration under section 5 of this title) for such security. The Commission may, by such rules and regulations as it deems necessary or appropriate in the public interest, define and prescribe terms and conditions with respect to securities held in an investment account and transactions made in the ordinary course of business and incident to the establishment or maintenance of a primary or secondary market.

(e) The provisions of this section shall not apply to foreign or domestic arbitrage transactions unless made in contravention of such rules and regulations as the Commission may adopt in order to carry out the purposes of this section.

(f) *Treatment of Transactions in Security Futures Products.*—The provisions of this section shall apply to ownership of and transactions in security futures products.

(g) The authority of the Commission under this section with respect to security-based swap agreements (as defined in section 206B of the Gramm–Leach–Bliley Act) shall be subject to the restrictions and limitations of section 3A(b) of this title.

Records and Reports

Sec. 17. (a)(1) Every national securities exchange, member thereof, broker or dealer who transacts a business in securities through the medium of any such member, registered securities association, registered broker or dealer, registered municipal securities dealer, registered securities information processor, registered transfer agent, and registered clearing agency and the Municipal Securities Rulemaking Board shall make and keep for prescribed periods such records, furnish such copies thereof, and make and disseminate such reports as the Commission, by rule, prescribes as necessary or appropriate in the public interest, for the protection of investors, or otherwise in furtherance of the purposes of this title.

(2) Every registered clearing agency shall also make and keep for prescribed periods such records, furnish such copies thereof, and make and disseminate such reports, as the appropriate regulatory agency for such clearing agency, by rule, prescribes as necessary or appropriate for the safeguarding of securities and funds in the custody or control of such clearing agency or for which it is responsible.

(3) Every registered transfer agent shall also make and keep for prescribed periods such records, furnish such copies thereof, and make such reports as the appropriate regulatory agency for such transfer agent, by rule, prescribes as necessary or appropriate in furtherance of the purposes of section 17A of this title.

(b) *Records Subject to Examination.*—

(1) *Procedures for Cooperation with Other Agencies.*—All records of persons described in subsection (a) of this section are subject at any time, or from time to time, to such reasonable periodic, special, or other examinations by representatives of the Commission and the appropriate regulatory agency for such persons as the Commission or the appropriate regulatory agency for such persons deems necessary or appropriate in the public interest, for the protection of investors, or otherwise in furtherance of the purposes of this title: *Provided, however,* That the Commission shall, prior to conducting any such examination of a—

(A) registered clearing agency, registered transfer agent, or registered municipal securities dealer for which it is not the appropriate regulatory agency, give notice to the appropriate regulatory agency for such clearing agency, transfer agent, or municipal securities dealer of such proposed examination and consult with such appropriate regulatory agency concerning the feasibility and desirability of coordinating such examination with examinations conducted by such appropriate regulatory agency with a view to avoiding unnecessary regulatory duplication or undue regulatory burdens for such clearing agency, transfer agent, or municipal securities dealer; or

(B) broker or dealer registered pursuant to section 15(b)(11), exchange registered pursuant to section 6(g), or national securities association registered pursuant to section 15A(k) gives notice to the Commodity Futures Trading Commission of such proposed examination and consults with the Commodity Futures Trading Commission concerning the feasibility and desirability of coordinating such examination with examinations conducted by the Commodity Futures Trading Commission in order to avoid unnecessary regulatory duplication or undue regulatory burdens for such broker or dealer or exchange.

(2) *Furnishing Data and Reports to CFTC.*—The Commission shall notify the Commodity Futures Trading Commission of any examination conducted of any broker or dealer registered pursuant to section 15(b)(11), exchange registered pursuant to section 6(g), or national securities association registered pursuant to section 15A(k) and, upon request, furnish to the Commodity Futures Trading Commission any examination report and data supplied to, or prepared by, the Commission in connection with such examination.

(3) *Use of CFTC Reports.*—Prior to conducting an examination under paragraph (1), the Commission shall use the reports of examinations, if the information available therein is sufficient for the purposes of the examination, of—

(A) any broker or dealer registered pursuant to section 15(b)(11);

(B) exchange registered pursuant to section 6(g); or

(C) national securities association registered pursuant to section 15A(k);

that is made by the Commodity Futures Trading Commission, a national securities association registered pursuant to section 15A(k), or an exchange registered pursuant to section 6(g).

(4) *Rules of Construction.*—

(A) Notwithstanding any other provision of this subsection, the records of a broker or dealer registered pursuant to section 15(b)(11), an exchange registered pursuant to section 6(g), or a national securities association registered pursuant to section 15A(k) described in this subparagraph shall not be subject to routine periodic examinations by the Commission.

(B) Any recordkeeping rules adopted under this subsection for a broker or dealer registered pursuant to section 15(b)(11), an exchange registered pursuant to section 6(g), or a national securities association registered pursuant to section 15A(k) shall be limited to records with respect to persons, accounts, agreements, contracts, and transactions involving security futures products.

(C) Nothing in the proviso in paragraph (1) shall be construed to impair or limit (other than by the requirement of prior consultation) the power of the Commission under this subsection to examine any clearing agency, transfer agent, or municipal securities dealer or to affect in any way the power of the Commission under any other provision of this title or otherwise to inspect, examine, or investigate any such clearing agency, transfer agent, or municipal securities dealer.

(c)(1) Every clearing agency, transfer agent, and municipal securities dealer for which the Commission is not the appropriate regulatory agency shall (A) file with the appropriate regulatory agency for such clearing agency, transfer agent, or municipal securities dealer a copy of any application, notice, proposal, report, or document filed with the Commission by reason of its being a clearing agency, transfer agent, or municipal securities dealer and (B) file with the Commission a copy of any application, notice, proposal, report, or document filed with such appropriate regulatory agency by reason of its being a clearing agency, transfer agent, or municipal securities dealer. The Municipal Securities Rulemaking Board shall file with each agency enumerated in section 3(a)(34)(A) of this title copies of every proposed rule change filed with the Commission pursuant to section 19(b) of this title.

(2) The appropriate regulatory agency for a clearing agency, transfer agent, or municipal securities dealer for which the Commission is not the appropriate regulatory agency shall file with the Commission notice of the commencement of any proceeding and a copy of any order entered by such appropriate regulatory agency against such clearing agency, transfer agent, municipal securities dealer, or person associated with a transfer agent or municipal securities dealer, and the Commission shall file with such appropriate regulatory agency, if any, notice of the commencement of any proceeding and a copy of any order entered by the Commission against the clearing agency, transfer agent, or municipal securities dealer, or against any person associated with a transfer agent or municipal securities dealer for which the agency is the appropriate regulatory agency.

(3) The Commission and the appropriate regulatory agency for a clearing agency, transfer agent, or municipal securities dealer for which the Commission is not the appropriate regulatory agency shall each notify the other and make a report of any examination conducted by it of such clearing agency, transfer agent, or municipal securities dealer, and, upon request, furnish to the other a copy of such report and any data supplied to it in connection with such examination.

(4) The Commission or the appropriate regulatory agency may specify that documents required to be filed pursuant to this subsection with the Commission or such agency, respectively, may be retained by the originating clearing agency, transfer agent, or municipal securities dealer, or filed with another appropriate regulatory agency. The Commission or the appropriate regulatory agency (as the case may be) making such a specification shall continue to have access to the document on request.

(d)(1) The Commission, by rule or order, as it deems necessary or appropriate in the public interest and for the protection of investors, to foster cooperation and coordination among self-regulatory organizations, or to remove impediments to and foster the development of a national market system and national system for the clearance and settlement of securities transactions, may—

(A) with respect to any person who is a member of or participant in more than one self-regulatory organization, relieve any such self-regulatory organization of any responsibility under this title (i) to receive regulatory reports from such person, (ii) to examine such person for compliance, or to enforce compliance by such person, with specified provisions of this title, the rules and regulations thereunder, and its own rules, or (iii) to carry out other specified regulatory functions with respect to such person, and

(B) allocate among self-regulatory organizations the authority to adopt rules with respect to matters as to which, in the absence of such allocation, such self-regulatory organizations share authority under this title.

In making any such rule or entering any such order, the Commission shall take into consideration the regulatory capabilities and procedures of the self-regulatory organizations, availability of staff, convenience of location, unnecessary regulatory duplication, and such other factors as the Commission may consider germane to the protection of investors, cooperation and coordination among self-regulatory organizations, and the development of a national market system and a national system for the clearance and settlement of securities transactions. The Commission, by rule or order, as it deems necessary or appropriate in the public interest and for the protection of investors, may require any self-regulatory organization relieved of any responsibility pursuant to this paragraph, and any person with respect to whom such responsibility relates, to take such steps as are specified in any such rule or order to notify customers of, and persons doing business with, such person of the limited nature of such self-regulatory organization's responsibility for such person's acts, practices, and course of business.

(2) A self-regulatory organization shall furnish copies of any report of examination of any person who is a member of or a participant in such self-regulatory organization to any other self-regulatory organization of which such person is a member or in which such person is a participant upon the request of such person, such other self-regulatory organization, or the Commission.

(e)(1)(A) Every registered broker or dealer shall annually file with the Commission a balance sheet and income statement certified by a registered public accounting firm, prepared on a calendar or fiscal year basis, and such other financial statements (which shall, as the Commission specifies, be certified) and information concerning its financial condition as the Commission, by rule, may prescribe as necessary or appropriate in the public interest or for the protection of investors.

(B) Every registered broker and dealer shall annually send to its customers its certified balance sheet and such other financial statements and information concerning its financial condition as the Commission, by rule, may prescribe pursuant to subsection (a) of this section.

(C) The Commission, by rule or order, may conditionally or unconditionally exempt any registered broker or dealer, or class of such brokers or dealers, from any provision of this paragraph if the Commission determines that such exemption is consistent with the public interest and the protection of investors.

(2) The Commission, by rule, as it deems necessary or appropriate in the public interest or for the protection of investors, may prescribe the form and content of financial statements filed pursuant to this title and the accounting principles and accounting standards used in their preparation.

(f)(1) Every national securities exchange, member thereof, registered securities association, broker, dealer, municipal securities dealer, government securities broker, government securities dealer, registered transfer agent, registered clearing agency, participant therein, member of the Federal Reserve System, and bank whose deposits are insured by the Federal Deposit Insurance Corporation shall—

(A) report to the Commission or other person designated by the Commission and, in the case of securities issued pursuant to chapter 31 of title 31, United States Code, to the Secretary of the Treasury such information about missing, lost, counterfeit, or stolen securities, in such form and within such time as the Commission, by rule, determines is necessary or appropriate in the public interest or for the protection of investors; such information shall be available on request for a reasonable fee, to any such exchange, member, association, broker, dealer, municipal securities dealer, transfer agent, clearing agency, participant, member of the Federal Reserve System, or insured bank, and such other persons as the Commission, by rule, designates; and

(B) make such inquiry with respect to information reported pursuant to this subsection as the Commission, by rule, prescribes as necessary or appropriate in the public interest or for the protection of investors, to determine whether securities in their custody or control, for which they are responsible, or in which they are effecting, clearing, or settling a transaction have been reported as missing, lost, counterfeit, or stolen.

(2) Every member of a national securities exchange, broker, dealer, registered transfer agent, and registered clearing agency, shall require that each of its partners, directors, officers, and employees be fingerprinted and

shall submit such fingerprints, or cause the same to be submitted, to the Attorney General of the United States for identification and appropriate processing. The Commission, by rule, may exempt from the provisions of this paragraph upon specified terms, conditions, and periods, any class of partners, directors, officers, or employees of any such member, broker, dealer, transfer agent, or clearing agency, if the Commission finds that such action is not inconsistent with the public interest or the protection of investors. Notwithstanding any other provision of law, in providing identification and processing functions, the Attorney General shall provide the Commission and self-regulatory organizations designated by the Commission with access to all criminal history record information.

(3)(A) In order to carry out the authority under paragraph (1) above, the Commission or its designee may enter into agreement with the Attorney General to use the facilities of the National Crime Information Center ("NCIC") to receive, store, and disseminate information in regard to missing, lost, counterfeit, or stolen securities and to permit direct inquiry access to NCIC's file on such securities for the financial community.

(B) In order to carry out the authority under paragraph (1) of this subsection, the Commission or its designee and the Secretary of the Treasury shall enter into an agreement whereby the Commission or its designee will receive, store, and disseminate information in the possession, and which comes into the possession, of the Department of the Treasury in regard to missing, lost, counterfeit, or stolen securities.

(4) In regard to paragraphs (1), (2), and (3), above insofar as such paragraphs apply to any bank or member of the Federal Reserve System, the Commission may delegate its authority to:

(A) the Comptroller of the Currency as to national banks and banks operating under the Code of Law for the District of Columbia;

(B) the Federal Reserve Board in regard to any member of the Federal Reserve System which is not a national bank or a bank operating under the Code of Law for the District of Columbia; and

(C) the Federal Deposit Insurance Corporation for any State bank which is insured by the Federal Deposit Insurance Corporation but which is not a member of the Federal Reserve System.

(5) The Commission shall encourage the insurance industry to require their insured to report expeditiously instances of missing, lost, counterfeit, or stolen securities to the Commission or to such other person as the Commission may, by rule, designate to receive such information.

(g) Any broker, dealer or other person extending credit who is subject to the rules and regulations prescribed by the Board of Governors of the Federal Reserve System pursuant to this title shall make such reports to the Board as it may require as necessary or appropriate to enable it to perform the functions conferred upon it by this title. If any such broker, dealer, or other person shall fail to make any such report or fail to furnish full information therein, or, if in the judgment of the Board it is otherwise necessary, such broker, dealer, or other person shall permit such inspections to be made by the Board with respect to the business operations of such broker, dealer, or other person as the Board may deem necessary to enable it to obtain the required information.

(h) *Risk Assessment for Holding Company Systems.*—

(1) *Obligations to Obtain, Maintain, and Report Information.*—Every person who is (A) a registered broker or dealer, or (B) a registered municipal securities dealer for which the Commission is the appropriate regulatory agency, shall obtain such information and make and keep such records as the Commission by rule prescribes concerning the registered person's policies, proce-

dures, or systems for monitoring and controlling financial and operational risks to it resulting from the activities of any of its associated persons, other than a natural person. Such records shall describe, in the aggregate, each of the financial and securities activities conducted by, and the customary sources of capital and funding of, those of its associated persons whose business activities are reasonably likely to have a material impact on the financial or operational condition of such registered person, including its net capital, its liquidity, or its ability to conduct or finance its operations. The Commission, by rule, may require summary reports of such information to be filed with the Commission no more frequently than quarterly.

(2) *Authority to Require Additional Information.*—If, as a result of adverse market conditions or based on reports provided to the Commission pursuant to paragraph (1) of this subsection or other available information, the Commission reasonably concludes that it has concerns regarding the financial or operational condition of (A) any registered broker or dealer, or (B) any registered municipal securities dealer, government securities broker, or government securities dealer for which the Commission is the appropriate regulatory agency, the Commission may require the registered person to make reports concerning the financial and securities activities of any of such person's associated persons, other than a natural person, whose business activities are reasonably likely to have a material impact on the financial or operational condition of such registered person. The Commission, in requiring reports pursuant to this paragraph, shall specify the information required, the period for which it is required, the time and date on which the information must be furnished, and whether the information is to be furnished directly to the Commission or to a self-regulatory organization with primary responsibility for examining the registered person's financial and operational condition.

(3) *Special Provisions With Respect to Associated Persons Subject to Federal Banking Regulations.*—

(A) *Cooperation in Implementation.*—In developing and implementing reporting requirements pursuant to paragraph (1) of this subsection with respect to associated persons subject to examination by or reporting requirements of a Federal banking agency, the Commission shall consult with and consider the views of each such Federal banking agency. If a Federal banking agency comments in writing on a proposed rule of the Commission under this subsection that has been published for comment, the Commission shall respond in writing to such written comment before adopting the proposed rule. The Commission shall, at the request of the Federal banking agency, publish such comment and response in the Federal Register at the time of publishing the adopted rule.

(B) *Use of Banking Agency Reports.*—A registered broker, dealer, or municipal securities dealer shall be in compliance with any recordkeeping or reporting requirement adopted pursuant to paragraph (1) of this subsection concerning an associated person that is subject to examination by or reporting requirements of a Federal banking agency if such broker, dealer, or municipal securities dealer utilizes for such recordkeeping or reporting requirement copies of reports filed by the associated person with the Federal banking agency pursuant to section 5211 of the Revised Statutes, section 9 of the Federal Reserve Act, section 7(a) of the Federal Deposit Insurance Act, section 10(b) of the Home Owners' Loan Act, or section 8 of the Bank Holding Company Act of 1956. The Commission may, however, by rule adopted pursuant to paragraph (1), require any broker, dealer, or municipal securities dealer filing such reports with the Commission to obtain, maintain, or report supplemental information if the Commission makes an explicit finding that such supplemental information is necessary to inform the Commission regarding potential risks to such broker, dealer, or municipal securities dealer. Prior to requiring any such supplemental information, the Commission shall first request the Federal banking agency to expand its reporting requirements to include such information.

(C) *Procedure for Requiring Additional Information.*—Prior to making a request pursuant to paragraph (2) of this subsection for information with respect to an associated person that is subject to examination by or reporting requirements of a Federal banking agency, the Commission shall—

(i) notify such agency of the information required with respect to such associated person; and

(ii) consult with such agency to determine whether the information required is available from such agency and for other purposes, unless the Commission determines that any delay resulting from such consultation would be inconsistent with ensuring the financial and operational condition of the broker, dealer, municipal securities dealer, government securities broker, or government securities dealer or the stability or integrity of the securities markets.

(D) *Exclusion for Examination Reports.*—Nothing in this subsection shall be construed to permit the Commission to require any registered broker or dealer, or any registered municipal securities dealer, government securities broker, or government securities dealer for which the Commission is the appropriate regulatory agency, to obtain, maintain, or furnish any examination report of any Federal banking agency or any supervisory recommendations or analysis contained therein.

(E) *Confidentiality of Information Provided.*—No information provided to or obtained by the Commission from any Federal banking agency pursuant to a request by the Commission under subparagraph (C) of this paragraph regarding any associated person which is subject to examination by or reporting requirements of a Federal banking agency may be disclosed to any other person (other than a self-regulatory organization), without the prior written approval of the Federal banking agency. Nothing in this subsection shall authorize the Commission to withhold information from Congress, or prevent the Commission from complying with a request for information from any other Federal department or agency requesting the information for purposes within the scope of its jurisdiction, or complying with an order of a court of the United States in an action brought by the United States or the Commission.

(F) *Notice to Banking Agencies Concerning Financial and Operational Condition Concerns.*—The Commission shall notify the Federal banking agency of any concerns of the Commission regarding significant financial or operational risks resulting from the activities of any registered broker or dealer, or any registered municipal securities dealer, government securities broker, or government securities dealer for which the Commission is the appropriate regulatory agency, to any associated person thereof which is subject to examination by or reporting requirements of the Federal banking agency.

(G) *Definition.*—For purposes of this paragraph, the term "Federal banking agency" shall have the same meaning as the term "appropriate Federal bank agency" in section 3(q) of the Federal Deposit Insurance Act (12 U.S.C. 1813(q)).

(4) *Exemptions.*—The Commission by rule or order may exempt any person or class of persons, under such terms and conditions and for such periods as the Commission shall provide in such rule or order, from the provisions of this subsection, and the rules

thereunder. In granting such exemptions, the Commission shall consider, among other factors—

(A) whether information of the type required under this subsection is available from a supervisory agency (as defined in section 1101(6) of the Right to Financial Privacy Act of 1978 (12 U.S.C. 3401(6))), a State insurance commission or similar State agency, the Commodity Futures Trading Commission, or a similar foreign regulator;

(B) the primary business of any associated person;

(C) the nature and extent of domestic or foreign regulation of the associated person's activities;

(D) the nature and extent of the registered person's securities activities; and

(E) with respect to the registered person and its associated persons, on a consolidated basis, the amount and proportion of assets devoted to, and revenues derived from, activities in the United States securities markets.

(5) *Authority to Limit Disclosure of Information.*—Notwithstanding any other provision of law, the Commission shall not be compelled to disclose any information required to be reported under this subsection, or any information supplied to the Commission by any domestic or foreign regulatory agency that relates to the financial or operational condition of any associated person of a registered broker, dealer, government securities broker, government securities dealer, or municipal securities dealer. Nothing in this subsection shall authorize the Commission to withhold information from Congress, or prevent the Commission from complying with a request for information from any other Federal department or agency requesting the information for purposes within the scope of its jurisdiction, or complying with an order of a court of the United States in an action brought by the United States or the Commission. For purposes of section 552 of title 5, United States Code, this subsection shall be considered a statute described in subsection (b)(3)(B) of such section 552. In prescribing regulations to carry out the requirements of this subsection, the Commission shall designate information described in or obtained pursuant to subparagraph (B) or (C) of paragraph (3) of this subsection as confidential information for purposes of section 24(b)(2) of this title.

(i) *Investment Bank Holding Companies.*—

(1) *Elective Supervision of an Investment Bank Holding Company not Having a Bank or Savings Association Affiliate.*—

(A) *In General.*—An investment bank holding company that is not—

(i) an affiliate of an insured bank (other than an institution described in subparagraph (D), (F), or (G) of section 1841(c)(2) of Title 12, or held under section 1843(f) of Title 12), or a savings association;

(ii) a foreign bank, foreign company, or company that is described in section 3106(a) of Title 12; or

(iii) a foreign bank that controls, directly or indirectly, a corporation chartered under section 25A of the Federal Reserve Act,

may elect to become supervised by filing with the Commission a notice of intention to become supervised, pursuant to subparagraph (B) of this paragraph. Any investment bank holding company filing such a notice shall be supervised in accordance with this section and comply with the rules promulgated by the Commission applicable to supervised investment bank holding companies.

(B) *Notification of Status as a Supervised Investment Bank Holding Company.*—An investment bank holding company that elects under subparagraph (A) to become supervised by the Commission shall file with the Commission a written notice of intention to become supervised by the Commission in such form and containing such information and documents concerning such investment bank holding company as the Commission, by rule, may prescribe as necessary or appropriate in furtherance of the purposes of this section. Unless the Commission finds that such supervision is not necessary or appropriate in furtherance of the purposes of this section, such supervision shall become effective 45 days after the date of receipt of such written notice by the Commission or within such shorter time period as the Commission, by rule or order, may determine.

(2) *Election not to be Supervised by the Commission as an Investment Bank Holding Company.—*

(A) *Voluntary Withdrawal.—*A supervised investment bank holding company that is supervised pursuant to paragraph (1) may, upon such terms and conditions as the Commission deems necessary or appropriate, elect not to be supervised by the Commission by filing a written notice of withdrawal from Commission supervision. Such notice shall not become effective until 1 year after receipt by the Commission, or such shorter or longer period as the Commission deems necessary or appropriate to ensure effective supervision of the material risks to the supervised investment bank holding company and to the affiliated broker or dealer, or to prevent evasion of the purposes of this section.

(B) *Discontinuation of Commission Supervision.* If the Commission finds that any supervised investment bank holding company that is supervised pursuant to paragraph (1) is no longer in existence or has ceased to be an investment bank holding company, or if the Commission finds that continued supervision of such a supervised investment bank holding company is not consistent with the purposes of this section, the Commission may discontinue the supervision pursuant to a rule or order, if any, promulgated by the Commission under this section.

(3) *Supervision of Investment Bank Holding Companies.—*

(A) *Recordkeeping and Reporting.—*

(i) *In General.—*Every supervised investment bank holding company and each affiliate thereof shall make and keep for prescribed periods such records, furnish copies thereof, and make such reports, as the Commission may require by rule, in order to keep the Commission informed as to—

(I) the company's or affiliate's activities, financial condition, policies, systems for monitoring and controlling financial and operational risks, and transactions and relationships between any broker or dealer affiliate of the supervised investment bank holding company; and

(II) the extent to which the company or affiliate has complied with the provisions of this chapter and regulations prescribed and orders issued under this chapter.

(ii) *Form and Contents.—*Such records and reports shall be prepared in such form and according to such specifications (including certification by a registered public accounting firm), as the Commission may require and shall be provided promptly at any time upon request by the Commission. Such records and reports may include—

(I) a balance sheet and income statement;

(II) an assessment of the consolidated capital of the supervised investment bank holding company;

(III) an independent auditor's report attesting to the supervised investment bank holding company's compliance with its internal risk management and internal control objectives; and

(IV) reports concerning the extent to which the company or affiliate has complied with the provisions of this chapter and any regulations prescribed and orders issued under this chapter.

(B) *Use of Existing Reports.*—

(i) *In General.*—The Commission shall, to the fullest extent possible, accept reports in fulfillment of the requirements under this paragraph that the supervised investment bank holding company or its affiliates have been required to provide to another appropriate regulatory agency or self-regulatory organization.

(ii) *Availability.*—A supervised investment bank holding company or an affiliate of such company shall provide to the Commission, at the request of the Commission, any report referred to in clause (i).

(C) *Examination Authority.*—

(i) *Focus of Examination Authority.*—The Commission may make examinations of any supervised investment bank holding company and any affiliate of such company in order to—

(I) inform the Commission regarding—

(aa) the nature of the operations and financial condition of the supervised investment bank holding company and its affiliates;

(bb) the financial and operational risks within the supervised investment bank holding company that may affect any broker or dealer controlled by such supervised investment bank holding company; and

(cc) the systems of the supervised investment bank holding company and its affiliates for monitoring and controlling those risks; and

(II) monitor compliance with the provisions of this subsection, provisions governing transactions and relationships between any broker or dealer affiliated with the supervised investment bank holding company and any of the company's other affiliates, and applicable provisions of subchapter II of chapter 53, Title 31 [31 U.S.C.A. § 5311 et seq.] (commonly referred to as the "Bank Secrecy Act") and regulations thereunder.

(ii) *Restricted Focus of Examinations.*—The Commission shall limit the focus and scope of any examination of a supervised investment bank holding company to—

(I) the company; and

(II) any affiliate of the company that, because of its size, condition, or activities, the nature or size of the transactions between such affiliate and any affiliated broker or dealer, or the centralization of functions within the holding company system, could, in the discretion of the Commission, have a materially adverse effect on the operational or financial condition of the broker or dealer.

(iii) *Deference to Other Examinations.*—For purposes of this subparagraph, the Commission shall, to the fullest extent possible, use the reports of examination of an institution described in subparagraph (D), (F), or (G) of section 1841(c)(2) of Title 12, or held under section 1843(f) of Title 12, made by the appropriate regulatory agency, or of a licensed insurance company made by the appropriate State insurance regulator.

(4) *Functional Regulation of Banking and Insurance Activities of Supervised Investment Bank Holding Companies.*—The Commission shall defer to—

(A) the appropriate regulatory agency with regard to all interpretations of, and the enforcement of, applicable banking laws relating to the activities, conduct, ownership, and operations of banks, and institutions described in subparagraph (D), (F), and (G) of section 1841(c)(2) of Title 12, or held under section 1843(f) of Title 12; and

(B) the appropriate State insurance regulators with regard to all interpretations of, and the enforcement of, applicable State insurance laws relating to the activities, conduct, and operations of insurance companies and insurance agents.

(5) *Definitions.*—For purposes of this subsection:

(A) The term "investment bank holding company" means—

(i) any person other than a natural person that owns or controls one or more brokers or dealers; and

(ii) the associated persons of the investment bank holding company.

(B) The term "supervised investment bank holding company" means any investment bank holding company that is supervised by the Commission pursuant to this subsection.

(C) The terms "affiliate", "bank", "bank holding company", "company", "control", and "savings association" have the same meanings as given in section 2 of the Bank Holding Company Act of 1956 (12 U.S.C. 1841).

(D) The term "insured bank" has the same meaning as given in section 1813 of Title 12.

(E) The term "foreign bank" has the same meaning as given in section 3101(b)(7) of Title 12.

(F) The terms "person associated with an investment bank holding company" and "associated person of an investment bank holding company" mean any person directly or indirectly controlling, controlled by, or under common control with, an investment bank holding company.

(j) *Authority to Limit Disclosure of Information.*—Notwithstanding any other provision of law, the Commission shall not be compelled to disclose any information required to be reported under subsection (h) or (i) or any information supplied to the Commission by any domestic or foreign regulatory agency that relates to the financial or operational condition of any associated person of a broker or dealer, investment bank holding company, or any affiliate of an investment bank holding company. Nothing in this subsection shall authorize the Commission to withhold information from Congress, or prevent the Commission from complying with a request for information from any other Federal department or agency or any self-regulatory organization requesting the information for purposes within the scope of its jurisdiction, or complying with an order of a court of the United States in an action brought by the United States or the Commission. For purposes of section 552 of Title 5, this subsection shall be considered a statute described in subsection (b)(3)(B) of such section 552. In prescribing regulations to carry out the requirements of this subsection, the Commission shall designate information described in or obtained pursuant to subparagraphs (A), (B), and (C) of subsection (i)(5) as confidential information for purposes of section 78x(b)(2) of this title.

(k) *Coordination of Examining Authorities.*—

(1) *Elimination of Duplication.*—The Commission and the examining authorities, through cooperation and coordination of examination and oversight activities, shall eliminate any unnecessary and burdensome duplication in the examination process.

(2) *Coordination of Examinations.*—The Commission and the examining authorities shall share such information, including reports of examinations, customer complaint information, and other nonpublic regulatory

information, as appropriate to foster a coordinated approach to regulatory oversight of brokers and dealers that are subject to examination by more than one examining authority.

(3) *Examinations for Cause.*—At any time, any examining authority may conduct an examination for cause of any broker or dealer subject to its jurisdiction.

(4) *Confidentiality.*—

(A) *In general.*—Section 24 shall apply to the sharing of information in accordance with this subsection. The Commission shall take appropriate action under section 24(c) to ensure that such information is not inappropriately disclosed.

(B) *Appropriate disclosure not prohibited.*—Nothing in this paragraph authorizes the Commission or any examining authority to withhold information from the Congress, or prevent the Commission or any examining authority from complying with a request for information from any other Federal department or agency requesting the information for purposes within the scope of its jurisdiction, or complying with an order of a court of the United States in an action brought by the United States or the Commission.

(5) *Definition.*—For purposes of this subsection, the term "examining authority" means a self-regulatory organization registered with the Commission under this title (other than a registered clearing agency) with the authority to examine, inspect, and otherwise oversee the activities of a registered broker or dealer.

National System for Clearance and Settlement of Securities Transactions

Sec. 17A. (a)(1) The Congress finds that—

(A) The prompt and accurate clearance and settlement of securities transactions, including the transfer of record ownership and the safeguarding of securities and funds related thereto, are necessary for the protection of investors and persons facilitating transactions by and acting on behalf of investors.

(B) Inefficient procedures for clearance and settlement impose unnecessary costs on investors and persons facilitating transactions by and acting on behalf of investors.

(C) New data processing and communications techniques create the opportunity for more efficient, effective, and safe procedures for clearance and settlement.

(D) The linking of all clearance and settlement facilities and the development of uniform standards and procedures for clearance and settlement will reduce unnecessary costs and increase the protection of investors and persons facilitating transactions by and acting on behalf of investors.

(2)(A) The Commission is directed, therefore, having due regard for the public interest, the protection of investors, the safeguarding of securities and funds, and maintenance of fair competition among brokers and dealers, clearing agencies, and transfer agents, to use its authority under this title—

(i) to facilitate the establishment of a national system for the prompt and accurate clearance and settlement of transactions in securities (other than exempt securities); and

(ii) to facilitate the establishment of linked or coordinated facilities for clearance and settlement of transactions in securities, securities options, contracts of sale for future delivery and options thereon, and commodity options;

in accordance with the findings and to carry out the objectives set forth in paragraph (1) of this subsection.

(B) The Commission shall use its authority under this title to assure equal regulation under this title of registered clearing agencies and registered transfer agents. In carrying out its responsibilities set forth in subparagraph (A)(ii) of this paragraph, the Commission shall coordinate with the Commodity Futures Trading Commission and consult with the Board of Governors of the Federal Reserve System.

(b)(1) Except as otherwise provided in this section, it shall be unlawful for any clearing agency, unless registered in accordance with this subsection, directly or indirectly, to make use of the mails or any means or instrumentality of interstate commerce to perform the functions of a clearing agency with respect to any security (other than an exempted security). The Commission, by rule or order, upon its own motion or upon application, may conditionally or unconditionally exempt any clearing agency or security or any class of clearing agencies or securities from any provision of this section or the rules or regulations thereunder, if the Commission finds that such exemption is consistent with the public interest, the protection of investors, and the purposes of this section, including the prompt and accurate clearance and settlement of securities transactions and the safeguarding of securities and funds. A clearing agency or transfer agent shall not perform the functions of both a clearing agency and a transfer agent unless such clearing agency or transfer agent is registered in accordance with this subsection and subsection (c) of this section.

(2) A clearing agency may be registered under the terms and conditions hereinafter provided in this subsection and in accordance with the provisions of section 19(a) of this title, by filing with the Commission an application for registration in such form as the Commission, by rule, may prescribe containing the rules of the clearing agency and such other information and documents as the Commission, by rule, may prescribe as necessary or appropriate in the public interest or for the prompt and accurate clearance and settlement of securities transactions.

(3) A clearing agency shall not be registered unless the Commission determines that—

(A) Such clearing agency is so organized and has the capacity to be able to facilitate the prompt and accurate clearance and settlement of securities transactions and derivative agreements, contracts, and transactions for which it is responsible, to safeguard securities and funds in its custody or control or for which it is responsible, to comply with the provisions of this title and the rules and regulations thereunder, to enforce (subject to any rule or order of the Commission pursuant to section 17(d) or 19(g)(2) of this title) compliance by its participants with the rules of the clearing agency, and to carry out the purposes of this section.

(B) Subject to the provisions of paragraph (4) of this subsection, the rules of the clearing agency provide that any (i) registered broker or dealer, (ii) other registered clearing agency, (iii) registered investment company, (iv) bank, (v) insurance company, or (vi) other person or class of persons as the Commission, by rule, may from time to time designate as appropriate to the development of a national system for the prompt and accurate clearance and settlement of securities transactions may become a participant in such clearing agency.

(C) The rules of the clearing agency assure a fair representation of its shareholders (or members) and participants in the selection of its directors and administration of its affairs. (The Commission may determine that the representation of participants is fair if they are afforded a reasonable opportunity to acquire voting stock of the clearing agency, directly or indirectly, in reasonable proportion to their use of such clearing agency.)

(D) The rules of the clearing agency provide for the equitable allocation of reasonable dues, fees, and other charges among its participants.

(E) The rules of the clearing agency do not impose any schedule of prices, or fix rates or other fees, for services rendered by its participants.

(F) The rules of the clearing agency are designed to promote the prompt and accurate clearance and settlement of securities transactions and, to the extent applicable, derivative agreements, contracts, and transactions, to assure the safeguarding of securities and funds which are in the custody or control of the clearing agency or for which it is responsible, to foster cooperation and coordination with persons engaged in the clearance and settlement of securities transactions, to remove impediments to and perfect the mechanism of a national system for the prompt and accurate clearance and settlement of securities transactions, and, in general, to protect investors and the public interest; and are not designed to permit unfair discrimination in the admission of participants or among participants in the use of the clearing agency, or to regulate by virtue of any authority conferred by this title matters not related to the purposes of this section or the administration of the clearing agency.

(G) The rules of the clearing agency provide that (subject to any rule or order of the Commission pursuant to section 17(d) or 19(g)(2) of this title) its participants shall be appropriately disciplined for violation of any provision of the rules of the clearing agency by expulsion, suspension, limitation of activities, functions, and operations, fine, censure, or any other fitting sanction.

(H) The rules of the clearing agency are in accordance with the provisions of paragraph (5) of this subsection, and, in general, provide a fair procedure with respect to the disciplining of participants, the denial of participation to any person seeking participation therein, and the prohibition or limitation by the clearing agency of any person with respect to access to services offered by the clearing agency.

(I) The rules of the clearing agency do not impose any burden on competition not necessary or appropriate in furtherance of the purposes of this title.

(4)(A) A registered clearing agency may, and in cases in which the Commissioner, by order, directs as appropriate in the public interest shall, deny participation to any person subject to a statutory disqualification. A registered clearing agency shall file notice with the Commission not less than thirty days prior to admitting any person to participation, if the clearing agency knew, or in the exercise of reasonable care should have known, that such person was subject to a statutory disqualification. The notice shall be in such form and contain such information as the Commission, by rule, may prescribe as necessary or appropriate in the public interest or for the protection of investors.

(B) A registered clearing agency may deny participation to, or condition the participation of, any person if such person does not meet such standards of financial responsibility, operational capability, experience, and competence as are prescribed by the rules of the clearing agency. A registered clearing agency may examine and verify the qualifications of an applicant to be a participant in accordance with procedures established by the rules of the clearing agency.

(5)(A) In any proceeding by a registered clearing agency to determine whether a participant should be disciplined (other than a summary proceeding pursuant to subparagraph (C) of this paragraph), the clearing agency shall bring specific charges, notify such participant of, and give him an opportunity to defend against such charges, and keep a record. A determination by the clearing agency to impose a disciplinary sanction shall be supported by a statement setting forth—

(i) any act or practice in which such participant has been found to have engaged, or which such participant has been found to have omitted;

(ii) the specific provisions of the rules of the clearing agency which any such act or practice, or omission to act, is deemed to violate; and

(iii) the sanction imposed and the reasons therefor.

(B) In any proceeding by a registered clearing agency to determine whether a person shall be denied participation or prohibited or limited with respect to access to services offered by the clearing agency, the clearing agency shall notify such person of, and give him an opportunity to be heard upon, the specific grounds for denial or prohibition or limitation under consideration and keep a record. A determination by the clearing agency to deny participation or prohibit or limit a person with respect to access to services offered by the clearing agency shall be supported by a statement setting forth the specific grounds on which the denial or prohibition or limitation is based.

(C) A registered clearing agency may summarily suspend and close the accounts of a participant who (i) has been and is expelled or suspended from any self-regulatory organization, (ii) is in default of any delivery of funds or securities to the clearing agency, or (iii) is in such financial or operating difficulty that the clearing agency determines and so notifies the appropriate regulatory agency for such participant that such suspension and closing of accounts are necessary for the protection of the clearing agency, its participants, creditors, or investors. A participant so summarily suspended shall be promptly afforded an opportunity for a hearing by the clearing agency in accordance with the provisions of subparagraph (A) of this paragraph. The appropriate regulatory agency for such participant, by order, may stay any such summary suspension on its own motion or upon application by any person aggrieved thereby, if such appropriate regulatory agency determines summarily or after notice and opportunity for hearing (which hearing may consist solely of the submission of affidavits or presentation of oral arguments) that such stay is consistent with the public interest and protection of investors.

(6) No registered clearing agency shall prohibit or limit access by any person to services offered by any participant therein.

(7)(A) A clearing agency that is regulated directly or indirectly by the Commodity Futures Trading Commission through its association with a designated contract market for security futures products that is a national securities exchange registered pursuant to section 6(g), and that would be required to register pursuant to paragraph (1) of this subsection only because it performs the functions of a clearing agency with respect to security futures products effected pursuant to the rules of the designated contract market with which such agency is associated, is exempted from the provisions of this section and the rules and regulations thereunder, except that if such a clearing agency performs the functions of a clearing agency with respect to a security futures product that is not cash settled, it must have arrangements in place with a registered clearing agency to effect the payment and delivery of the securities underlying the security futures product.

(B) Any clearing agency that performs the functions of a clearing agency with respect to security futures products must coordinate with and develop fair and reasonable links with any and all other clearing agencies that perform the functions of a clearing agency with respect to security futures products, in order to permit, as of the compliance date (as defined in section 6(h)(6)(C)), security futures products to be purchased on one market and offset on another market that trades such products.

(8) A registered clearing agency shall be permitted to provide facilities for the clearance and settlement of any derivative agreements, contracts, or transactions that are excluded from the Commodity Exchange Act, subject to the requirements of this section and to such rules and regulations as the Commission may prescribe as necessary or appropriate in the public interest, for the protection of investors, or otherwise in furtherance of the purposes of this title.

(c)(1) Except as otherwise provided in this section, it shall be unlawful for any transfer agent, unless registered in accordance with this section, directly or indirectly, to make use of the mails or any means or instrumentality of interstate commerce to perform the function of a transfer agent with respect to any security registered under section 12 of this title or which would be required to be registered except for the exemption from registration provided by subsection (g)(2)(B) or (g)(2)(G) of that section. The appropriate regulatory agency, by rule or order, upon its own motion or upon application, may conditionally or unconditionally exempt any person or security or class of persons or securities from any provision of this section or any rule or regulation prescribed under this section, if the appropriate regulatory agency finds (A) that such exemption is in the public interest and consistent with the protection of investors and the purposes of this section, including the prompt and accurate clearance and settlement of securities transactions and the safeguarding of securities and funds, and (B) the Commission does not object to such exemption.

(2) A transfer agent may be registered by filing with the appropriate regulatory agency for such transfer agent an application for registration in such form and containing such information and documents concerning such transfer agent and any persons associated with the transfer agent as such appropriate regulatory agency may prescribe as necessary or appropriate in furtherance of the purposes of this section. Except as hereinafter provided, such registration shall become effective 45 days after receipt of such application by such appropriate regulatory agency or within such shorter period of time as such appropriate regulatory agency may determine.

(3) The appropriate regulatory agency for a transfer agent, by order, shall deny registration to, censure, place limitations on the activities, functions, or operations of, suspend for a period not exceeding 12 months, or revoke the registration of such transfer agent, if such appropriate regulatory agency finds, on the record after notice and opportunity for hearing, that such denial, censure, placing of limitations, suspension, or revocation is in the public interest and that such transfer agent, whether prior or subsequent to becoming such, or any person associated with such transfer agent, whether prior or subsequent to becoming so associated—

(A) has committed or omitted any act, or is subject to an order or finding, enumerated in subparagraph (A), (D), (E), (H), or (G) of paragraph (4) of section 15(b) of this title, has been convicted of any offense specified in subparagraph (B) of such paragraph (4) within ten years of the commencement of the proceedings under this paragraph, or is enjoined from any action, conduct, or practice specified in subparagraph (C) of such paragraph (4); or

(B) is subject to an order entered pursuant to subparagraph (C) of paragraph (4) of this subsection barring or suspending the right of such person to be associated with a transfer agent.

(4)(A) Pending final determination whether any registration by a transfer agent under this subsection shall be denied, the appropriate regulatory agency for such transfer agent, by order, may postpone the effective date of such registration for a period not to exceed fifteen days, but if, after notice and opportunity for hearing (which may consist solely of affidavits and oral arguments), it shall appear to such appropriate regulatory agency to be necessary or appropriate in the public interest or for the protection of investors to postpone the effective date of such registration until final determination, such appropriate regulatory agency shall so order. Pending final determination whether any registration under this subsection shall be revoked, such appropriate regulatory agency, by order, may suspend such registration, if such suspension appears to such appropriate regulatory agency, after notice and opportunity for hearing, to be necessary or appropriate in the public interest or for the protection of investors.

(B) A registered transfer agent may, upon such terms and conditions as the appropriate regulatory agency for such transfer agent deems necessary or appropriate in the public interest, for the protection of investors, or in furtherance of the purposes of this section, withdraw from registration by filing a written notice of withdrawal with such appropriate regulatory agency. If such appropriate regulatory agency finds that any transfer agent for which it is the appropriate regulatory agency, is no longer in existence or has ceased to do business as a transfer agent, such appropriate regulatory agency, by order, shall cancel or deny the registration.

(C) The appropriate regulatory agency for a transfer agent, by order, shall censure or place limitations on the activities or functions of any person associated, seeking to become associated, or, at the time of the alleged misconduct, associated or seeking to become associated with the transfer agent, or suspend for a period not exceeding twelve months or bar any such person from being associated with the transfer agent, if the appropriate regulatory agency finds, on the record after notice and opportunity for hearing, that such censure, placing of limitations, suspension, or bar is in the public interest and that such person has committed or omitted any act, or is subject to an order or finding, enumerated in subparagraph (A), (D), (E), (H), or (G) of paragraph (4) of section 15(b) of this title has been convicted of any offense specified in subparagraph (B) of such paragraph (4) within ten years of the commencement of the proceedings under this paragraph, or is enjoined from any action, conduct, or practice specified in subparagraph (C) of such paragraph (4). It shall be unlawful for any person as to whom such an order suspending or barring him from being associated with a transfer agent is in effect willfully to become, or to be, associated with a transfer agent without the consent of the appropriate regulatory agency that entered the order and the appropriate regulatory agency for that transfer agent. It shall be unlawful for any transfer agent to permit such a person to become, or remain, a person associated with it without the consent of such appropriate regulatory agencies, if the transfer agent knew, or in the exercise of reasonable care should have known, of such order. The Commission may establish, by rule, procedures by which a transfer agent reasonably can determine whether a person associated or seeking to become associated with it is subject to any such order, and may require, by rule, that any transfer agent comply with such procedures.

(d)(1) No registered clearing agency or registered transfer agent shall, directly or indirectly, engage in any activity as clearing agency or transfer agent in contravention of such rules and regulations (A) as the Commission may prescribe as necessary or appropriate in the public interest, for the protection of investors, or otherwise in furtherance of the purposes of this title, or (B) as the appropriate regulatory agency for such clearing agency or transfer agent may prescribe as necessary or appropriate for the safeguarding of securities and funds.

(2) With respect to any clearing agency or transfer agent for which the Commission is not the appropriate regulatory agency, the appropriate regulatory agency for such clearing agency or transfer agent may, in accordance with section 8 of the Federal Deposit Insurance Act (12 U.S.C. 1818), enforce compliance by such clearing agency or transfer agent with the provisions of this section, sections 17 and 19 of this title, and the rules and regulations thereunder. For purpose of the preceding sentence, any violation of any such provision shall constitute adequate basis for the issuance of an order under section 8(b) or 8(c) of the Federal Deposit Insurance Act, and the participants in any such clearing agency and the persons doing business with any such transfer agent shall be deemed to be "depositors" as that term is used in section 8(c) of that Act.

(3)(A) With respect to any clearing agency or transfer agent for which the Commission is not the appropriate regulatory agency, the Commission and the appropriate regulatory agency for such clearing agency or transfer agent shall consult and cooperate with each other, and, as may be appropriate, with State banking authorities having supervision over such clearing agency or transfer agent toward the end that, to the maximum extent practicable, their respective regulatory responsibilities may be fulfilled and the rules and regulations applicable to such clearing agency or transfer agent may be in accord with both sound banking practices and a national system for the prompt and accurate clearance and settlement of securities transactions. In accordance with this objective—

(i) the Commission and such appropriate regulatory agency shall, at least fifteen days prior to the issuance for public comment of any proposed rule or regulation or adoption of any rule or regulation concerning such clearing agency or transfer agent, consult and request the views of the other; and

(ii) such appropriate regulatory agency shall assume primary responsibility to examine and enforce compliance by such clearing agency or transfer agent with the provisions of this section and sections 17 and 19 of this title.

(B) Nothing in the preceding subparagraph or elsewhere in this title shall be construed to impair or limit (other than by the requirement of notification) the Commission's authority to make rules under any provision of this title or to enforce compliance pursuant to any provision of this title by any clearing agency, transfer agent, or person associated with a transfer agent with the provisions of this title and the rules and regulations thereunder.

(4) Nothing in this section shall be construed to impair the authority of any State banking authority or other State or Federal regulatory authority having jurisdiction over a person registered as a clearing agency, transfer agent, or person associated with a transfer agent, to make and enforce rules governing such person which are not inconsistent with this title and the rules and regulations thereunder.

(5) A registered transfer agent may not, directly or indirectly, engage in any activity in connection with the guarantee of a signature of an endorser of a security, including the acceptance or rejection of such guarantee, in contravention of such rules and regulations as the Commission may prescribe as necessary or appropriate in the public interest, for the protection of investors, to facilitate the equitable treatment of financial institutions which issue such guarantees, or otherwise in furtherance of the purposes of this title.

(e) The Commission shall use its authority under this title to end the physical movement of securities certificates in connection with the settlement among brokers and dealers of transactions in securities consummated by means of the mails or any means or instrumentalities of interstate commerce.

(f)(1) Notwithstanding any provision of State law, except as provided in paragraph (3), if the Commission makes each of the findings described in paragraph (2)(A), the Commission may adopt rules concerning—

(A) the transfer of certificated or uncertificated securities (other than government securities issued pursuant to chapter 31 of title 31, United States Code, or securities otherwise processed within a book-entry system operated by the Federal Reserve banks pursuant to a Federal book-entry regulation) or limited interests (including security interests) therein; and

(B) rights and obligations of purchasers, sellers, owners, lenders, borrowers, and financial intermediaries (including brokers, dealers, banks, and clearing agencies) involved in or affected by such transfers, and the rights of third parties whose interests in such securities devolve from such transfers.

(2)(A) The findings described in this paragraph are findings by the Commission that—

(i) such rule is necessary or appropriate for the protection of investors or in the public interest and is reasonably designed to promote the prompt, accurate, and safe clearance and settlement of securities transactions;

(ii) in the absence of a uniform rule, the safe and efficient operation of the national system for clearance and settlement of securities transactions will be, or is, substantially impeded; and

(iii) to the extent such rule will impair or diminish, directly or indirectly, rights of persons specified in paragraph (1)(B) under State law concerning transfers of securities (or limited interests therein), the benefits of such rule outweigh such impairment or diminution of rights.

(B) In making the findings described in subparagraph (A), the Commission shall give consideration to the recommendations of the Advisory Committee established under paragraph (4), and it shall consult with and consider the views of the Secretary of the Treasury and the Board of Governors of the Federal Reserve System. If the Secretary of the Treasury objects, in writing, to any proposed rule of the Commission on the basis of the Secretary's view on the issues described in clauses (i), (ii), and (iii) of subparagraph (A), the Commission shall consider all feasible alternatives to the proposed rule, and it shall not adopt any such rule unless the Commission makes an explicit finding that the rule is the most practicable method for achieving safe and efficient operation of the national clearance and settlement system.

(3) Any State may, prior to the expiration of 2 years after the Commission adopts a rule under this subsection, enact a statute that specifically refers to this subsection and the specific rule thereunder and establishes, prospectively from the date of enactment of the State statute, a provision that differs from that applicable under the Commission's rule.

(4)(A) Within 90 days after the date of enactment of this subsection, the Commission shall (and at such times thereafter as the Commission may determine, the Commission may), after consultation with the Secretary of the Treasury and the Board of Governors of the Federal Reserve System, establish an advisory committee under the Federal Advisory Committee Act (5 U.S.C.App.). The Advisory Committee shall be directed to consider and report to the Commission on such matters as the Commission, after consultation with the Secretary of the Treasury and the Board of Governors of the Federal Reserve System, determines, including the areas, if any, in which State commercial laws and related Federal laws concerning the transfer of certificated or uncertificated securities, limited interests (including security interests) in such securities, or the creation or perfection of security interests in such securities do not provide the necessary certainty, uniformity, and clarity for purchasers, sellers, owners, lenders, borrowers, and financial intermediaries concerning their respective rights and obligations.

(B) The Advisory Committee shall consist of 15 members, of which—

(i) 11 shall be designated by the Commission in accordance with the Federal Advisory Committee Act; and

(ii) 2 each shall be designated by the Board of Governors of the Federal Reserve System and the Secretary of the Treasury.

(C) The Advisory Committee shall conduct its activities in accordance with the Federal Advisory Committee Act. Within 6 months of its designation, or such longer time as the Commission may designate, the Advisory Committee shall issue a report to the Commission, and shall cause copies of that report to be delivered to the Secretary of the Treasury and the Chairman of the Board of Governors of the Federal Reserve System.

Automated Quotation Systems for Penny Stocks

Sec. 17B. (a) *Findings.*—The Congress finds that—

(1) the market for penny stocks suffers from a lack of reliable and accurate quotation and last sale information available to investors and regulators;

(2) it is in the public interest and appropriate for the protection of investors and the

maintenance of fair and orderly markets to improve significantly the information available to brokers, dealers, investors, and regulators with respect to quotations for and transactions in penny stocks; and

(3) a fully implemented automated quotation system for penny stocks would meet the information needs of investors and market participants and would add visibility and regulatory and surveillance data to that market.

(b) *Mandate to Facilitate the Establishment of Automated Quotation Systems.*—

(1) *In General.*—The Commission shall facilitate the wide-spread dissemination of reliable and accurate last sale and quotation information with respect to penny stocks in accordance with the findings set forth in subsection (a), with a view toward establishing, at the earliest feasible time, one or more automated quotation systems that will collect and disseminate information regarding all penny stocks.

(2) *Characteristics of Systems.*—Each such automated quotation system shall—

(A) be operated by a registered securities association or a national securities exchange in accordance with such rules as the Commission and these entities shall prescribe;

(B) collect and disseminate quotation and transaction information;

(C) except as provided in subsection (c), provide bid and ask quotations of participating brokers or dealers, or comparably accurate and reliable pricing information, which shall constitute firm bids or offers for at least such minimum numbers of shares or minimum dollar amounts as the Commission and the registered securities association or national securities exchange shall require; and

(D) provide for the reporting of the volume of penny stock transactions, including last sale reporting, when the volume reaches appropriate levels that the Commission shall specify by rule or order.

(c) *Exemptive Authority.*—The Commission may, by rule or order, grant such exemptions, in whole or in part, conditionally or unconditionally, to any penny stock or class of penny stocks from the requirements of subsection (b) as the Commission determines to be consistent with the public interest, the protection of investors, and the maintenance of fair and orderly markets.

(d) *Commission Reporting Requirements.*—The Commission shall, in each of the first 5 annual reports (under section 23(b)(1) of this title) submitted more than 12 months after the date of enactment of this section, include a description of the status of the penny stock automated quotation system or systems required by subsection (b). Such description shall include—

(1) a review of the development, implementation, and progress of the project, including achievement of significant milestones and current project schedule; and

(2) a review of the activities of registered securities associations and national securities exchanges in the development of the system.

Liability for Misleading Statements

Sec. 18. (a) Any person who shall make or cause to be made any statement in any application, report, or document filed pursuant to this title or any rule or regulation thereunder or any undertaking contained in a registration statement as provided in subsection (d) of section 15 of this title, which statement was at the time and in the light of the circumstances under which it was made false or misleading with respect to any material fact, shall be liable to any person (not knowing that such statement was false or misleading) who, in reliance upon such statement, shall have purchased or sold a security at a price which was affected by such statement, for damages caused by such reliance, unless the person sued shall prove that he acted in good faith and had no knowledge that such statement was false or misleading. A person seeking to enforce such liability may sue at law or in equity in any court of competent jurisdiction. In any such suit the court may, in its discretion, require an undertaking for the payment of the costs of such suit, and assess reasonable costs, including reasonable attorneys' fees, against either party litigant.

(b) Every person who becomes liable to make payment under this section may recover contribution as in cases of contact from any person who, if joined in the original suit, would have been liable to make the same payment.

(c) No action shall be maintained to enforce any liability created under this section unless brought within one year after the discovery of the facts constituting the cause of action and within three years after such cause of action accrued.

Registration, Responsibilities, and Oversight of Self-Regulatory Organizations

Sec. 19. (a)(1) The Commission shall, upon the filing of an application for registration as a national securities exchange, registered securities association, or registered clearing agency, pursuant to section 6, 15A, or 17A of this title, respectively, publish notice of such filing and afford interested persons an opportunity to submit written data, views, and arguments concerning such application. Within ninety days of the date of publication of such notice (or within such longer period as to which the applicant consents), the Commission shall—

(A) by order grant such registration, or

(B) institute proceedings to determine whether registration should be denied. Such proceedings shall include notice of the grounds for denial under consideration and opportunity for hearing and shall be concluded within one hundred eighty days of the date of publication of notice of the filing of the application for registration. At the conclusion of such proceedings the Commission, by order, shall grant or deny such registration. The Commission may extend the time for conclusion of such proceedings for up to ninety days if it finds good cause for such extension and publishes its reasons for so finding or for such longer period as to which the applicant consents.

The Commission shall grant such registration if it finds that the requirements of this title and the rules and regulations thereunder with respect to the applicant are satisfied. The Commission shall deny such registration if it does not make such finding.

(2) With respect to an application for registration filed by a clearing agency for which the Commission is not the appropriate regulatory agency—

(A) The Commission shall not grant registration prior to the sixtieth day after the date of publication of notice of the filing of such application unless the appropriate regulatory agency for such clearing agency has notified the Commission of such appropriate regulatory agency's determination that such clearing agency is so organized and has the capacity to be able to safeguard securities and funds in its custody or control or for which it is responsible and that the rules of such clearing agency are designed to assure the safeguarding of such securities and funds.

(B) The Commission shall institute proceedings in accordance with paragraph (1)(B) of this subsection to determine whether registration should be denied if the appropriate regulatory agency for such clearing agency notifies the Commission within sixty days of the date of publication of notice of the filing of such application of such appropriate regulatory agency's (i) determination that such clearing agency may not be so organized or have the capacity to be able to safeguard securities or funds in its custody or control or for which it is responsible or that the rules of such clearing agency may not be designed to assure the safeguarding of such securities and funds and (ii) reasons for such determination.

(C) The Commission shall deny registration if the appropriate regulatory agency for such clearing agency notifies the Commission prior to the conclusion of proceedings instituted in accordance with paragraph (1)(B) of this subsection of such appropriate regulatory agency's (i) determination that such clearing agency is not so organized or does not have the capacity to be able to safeguard securities or funds in its custody or control or for which it is responsible or that the rules of such clearing agency are not designed to assure the safeguarding of such securities or funds and (ii) reasons for such determination.

(3) A self-regulatory organization may, upon such terms and conditions as the Commission, by rule, deems necessary or appropriate in the public interest or for the protection of investors, withdraw from registration by filing a written notice of withdrawal with the Commission. If the Commission finds that any self-regulatory organization is no longer in existence or has ceased to do business in the capacity specified in its application for registration, the Commission, by order, shall cancel its registration. Upon the withdrawal of a national securities association from registration or the cancellation, suspension, or revocation of the registration of a national securities association, the registration of any association affiliated therewith shall automatically terminate.

(b)(1) Each self-regulatory organization shall file with the commission, in accordance with such rules as the Commission, may prescribe, copies of any proposed rule or any proposed change in, addition to, or deletion from the rules of such self-regulatory organization (hereinafter in this subsection collectively referred to as a "proposed rule change") accompanied by a concise general statement of the basis and purpose of such proposed rule change. The Commission shall, upon the filing of any proposed rule change, publish notice thereof together with the terms of substance of the proposed rule change or a description of the subjects and issues involved. The Commission shall give interested persons an opportunity to submit written data, views, and arguments concerning such proposed rule change. No proposed rule change shall take effect unless approved by the Commission or otherwise permitted in accordance with the provisions of this subsection.

(2) Within thirty-five days of the date of publication of notice of the filing of a proposed rule change in accordance with paragraph (1) of this subsection, or within such longer period as the Commission may designate up to ninety days of such date if it finds such longer period to be appropriate and publishes its reasons for so finding or as to which the self-regulatory organization consents, the Commission shall—

(A) by order approve such proposed rule change, or

(B) institute proceedings to determine whether the proposed rule change should be disapproved. Such proceedings shall include notice of the grounds for disapproval under consideration and opportunity for hearing and be concluded within one hundred eighty days of the date of publication of notice of the filing of the proposed rule change. At the conclusion of such proceedings the Commission, by order, shall approve or disapprove such proposed rule change. The Commission may extend the time for conclusion of such proceedings for up to sixty days if it finds good cause for such extension and publishes its reasons for so finding or for such longer period as to which the self-regulatory organization consents.

The Commission shall approve a proposed rule change of a self-regulatory organization if it finds that such proposed rule change is consistent with the requirements of this title and the rules and regulations thereunder applicable to such organization. The Commission shall disapprove a proposed rule change of a self-regulatory organization if it does not make such finding. The Commission shall not approve any proposed rule change prior to the thirtieth day after the date of publication of notice of the filing thereof, unless the Commission finds good cause for so doing and publishes its reasons for so finding.

(3)(A) Notwithstanding the provisions of paragraph (2) of this subsection, a proposed rule change may take effect upon filing with the Commission if designated by the self-regulatory organization as (i) constituting a stated policy, practice, or interpretation with respect to the meaning, administration, or enforcement of an existing rule of the self-regulatory organization, (ii) establishing or changing a due, fee, or other charge imposed by the self-regulatory organization, or (iii) concerned solely with the administration of the self-regulatory organization or other matters which the Commission, by rule, consistent with the public interest and the purposes of this subsection, may specify as without the provisions of such paragraph (2).

(B) Notwithstanding any other provision of this subsection, a proposed rule change may be put into effect summarily if it appears to the Commission that such action is necessary for the protection of investors, the maintenance of fair and orderly markets, or the safeguarding of securities or funds. Any proposed rule change so put into effect shall be filed promptly thereafter in accordance with the provisions of paragraph (1) of this subsection.

(C) Any proposed rule change of a self-regulatory organization which has taken effect pursuant to subparagraph (A) or (B) of this paragraph may be enforced by such organization to the extent it is not inconsistent with the provisions of this title, the rules and regulations thereunder, and applicable Federal and State law. At any time within sixty days of the date of filing of such a proposed rule change in accordance with the provisions of paragraph (1) of this subsection, the Commission summarily may abrogate the change in the rules of the self-regulatory organization made thereby and require that the proposed rule change be refiled in accordance with the provisions of paragraph (1) of this subsection and reviewed in accordance with the provisions of paragraph (2) of this subsection, if it appears to the Commission that such action is necessary or appropriate in the public interest, for the protection of investors, or otherwise in furtherance of the purposes of this title. Commission action pursuant to the preceding sentence shall not affect the validity or force of the rule change during the period it was in effect and shall not be reviewable under section 25 of this title nor deemed to be "final agency action" for purposes of section 704 of title 5, United States Code.

(4) With respect to a proposed rule change filed by a registered clearing agency for which the Commission is not the appropriate regulatory agency—

(A) The Commission shall not approve any such proposed rule change prior to the thirtieth day after the date of publication of notice of the filing thereof unless the appropriate regulatory agency for such clearing agency has notified the Commission of such appropriate regulatory agency's determination that the proposed rule change is consistent with the safeguarding of securities and funds in the custody or control of such clearing agency or for which it is responsible.

(B) The Commission shall institute proceedings in accordance with paragraph (2)(B) of this subsection to determine whether any such proposed rule change should be disapproved, if the appropriate regulatory agency for such clearing agency notifies the Commission within thirty days of the date of publication of notice of the filing of the proposed rule change of such appropriate regulatory agency's (i) determination that the proposed rule change may be inconsistent with the safeguarding of securities or funds in the custody or control of such clearing agency or for which it is responsible and (ii) reasons for such determination.

(C) The Commission shall disapprove any such proposed rule change if the appropriate regulatory agency for such clearing agency notifies the Commission prior to the conclusion of proceedings instituted in accordance with paragraph (2)(B) of this subsection of such appropriate regulatory agency's (i) determination that the proposed rule change is inconsistent with the safeguarding of securities or funds in the custody or control of such clearing agency or for which it is responsible and (ii) reasons for such determination.

(D) The Commission shall abrogate any change in the rules of such a clearing agency made by a proposed rule change which has taken effect pursuant to paragraph (3) of this subsection, require that the proposed rule change be refiled in accordance with the provisions of paragraph (1) of this subsection, and reviewed in accordance with the provisions of paragraph (2) of this subsection, if the appropriate regulatory agency for such clearing agency notifies the Commission within thirty days of the date of filing of such proposed rule change of such appropriate regulatory agency's (i) determination that the rules of such clearing agency as so changed may be inconsistent with the safeguarding of securities or funds in the custody or control of such clearing agency or for which it is responsible and (ii) reasons for such determination.

(5) The Commission shall consult with and consider the views of the Secretary of the Treasury prior to approving a proposed rule filed by a registered securities association that primarily concerns conduct related to transactions in government securities, except where the Commission determines that an emergency exists requiring expeditious or summary action and publishes its reasons therefor. If the Secretary of the Treasury comments in writing to the Commission on a proposed rule that has been published for comment, the Commission shall respond in writing to such written comment before approving the proposed rule. If the Secretary of the Treasury determines, and notifies the Commission, that such rule, if implemented, would, or as applied does (i) adversely affect the liquidity or efficiency of the market for government securities; or (ii) impose any burden on competition not necessary or appropriate in furtherance of the purposes of this section, the Commission shall, prior to adopting the proposed rule, find that such rule is necessary and appropriate in furtherance of the purposes of this section notwithstanding the Secretary's determination.

(6) In approving rules described in paragraph (5), the Commission shall consider the sufficiency and appropriateness of then existing laws and rules applicable to government securities brokers, government securities dealers, and persons associated with government securities brokers and government securities dealers.

(7) *Security Futures Product Rule Changes.—*

(A) *Filing Required.*—A self-regulatory organization that is an exchange registered with the Commission pursuant to section 6(g) of this title or that is a national securities association registered pursuant to section 15A(k) of this title shall file with the Commission, in accordance with such rules as the Commission may prescribe, copies of any proposed rule change or any proposed change in, addition to, or deletion from the rules of such self-regulatory organization (hereinafter in this paragraph collectively referred to as a "proposed rule change") that relates to higher margin levels, fraud or manipulation, recordkeeping, reporting, listing standards, or decimal pricing for security futures products, sales practices for security futures products for persons who effect transactions in security futures products, or rules effectuating such self-regulatory organization's obligation to enforce the securities laws. Such proposed rule change shall be accompanied by a concise general statement of the basis and purpose of such proposed rule change. The Commission shall, upon the filing of any proposed rule change, promptly publish notice thereof together with the terms of substance of the proposed rule change or a description of the subjects and issues involved. The Commission shall give interested persons an opportunity to submit data, views, and arguments concerning such proposed rule change.

(B) *Filing With CFTC.*—A proposed rule change filed with the Commission pursuant to subparagraph (A) shall be filed concurrently with the Commodity Futures Trading Commission. Such proposed rule change may take effect upon filing of a written certification with the Commodity Futures Trading Commission under section 5c(c) of the Commodity Exchange Act, upon a determination by the Commodity Futures Trading Commission that review of the proposed rule change is not necessary, or upon approval of the proposed rule change by the Commodity Futures Trading Commission.

(C) *Abrogation of Rule Changes.*—Any proposed rule change of a self-regulatory organization that has taken effect pursuant to subparagraph (B) may be enforced by such self-regulatory organization to the extent such rule is not inconsistent with the provisions of this title, the rules and regulations thereunder, and applicable Federal law. At any time within 60 days of the date of the filing of a written certification with the Commodity Futures Trading Commission under section 5c(c) of the Commodity Exchange Act, the date the Commodity Futures Trading Commission determines that review of such proposed rule change is not necessary, or the date the Commodity Futures Trading Commission approves such proposed rule change, the Commission, after consultation with the Commodity Futures Trading Commission, may summarily abrogate the proposed rule change and require that the proposed rule change be refiled in accordance with the provisions of paragraph (1), if it appears to the Commission that such proposed rule change unduly burdens competition or efficiency, conflicts with the securities laws, or is inconsistent with the public interest and the protection of investors. Commission action pursuant to the preceding sentence shall not affect the validity or force of the rule change during the period it was in effect and shall not be reviewable under section 25 of this title nor deemed to be a final agency action for purposes of section 704 of title 5, United States Code.

(D) *Review of Resubmitted Abrogated Rules.*—

(i) *Proceedings.*—Within 35 days of the date of publication of notice of the filing of a proposed rule change that is abrogated in accordance with subparagraph (C) and refiled in accordance with paragraph (1), or within such longer period as the Commission may designate up to 90 days after such date if the Commission finds such longer period to be appropriate and publishes its reasons for so finding or as to which the self-regulatory organization consents, the Commission shall—

(I) by order approve such proposed rule change; or

(II) after consultation with the Commodity Futures Trading Commission, institute proceedings to determine whether the proposed rule change should be disapproved. Proceedings under subclause (II) shall include notice of the grounds for disapproval under consideration and opportunity for hearing and be concluded within 180 days after the date of publication of notice of the filing of the proposed rule change. At the conclusion of such proceedings, the Commission, by order, shall approve or disapprove such proposed rule change. The Commission may extend the time for conclusion of such proceedings for up to 60 days if the Commission finds good cause for such extension and publishes its reasons for so finding or for such longer period as to which the self-regulatory organization consents.

(ii) *Grounds for Approval.*—The Commission shall approve a proposed rule change of a self-regulatory organization under this subparagraph if the Commission finds that such proposed rule change does not unduly burden competition or efficiency, does not conflict with the securities laws, and is not inconsistent with the public interest or the protection of investors. The Commission shall disapprove such a proposed rule change of a self-regulatory organization if it does not make such finding. The Commission shall not approve any proposed rule change prior to the 30th day after the date of publication of notice of the filing thereof, unless the Commission finds good cause for so doing and publishes its reasons for so finding.

(8) *Decimal Pricing.*—Not later than 9 months after the date on which trading in any security futures product commences under this title, all self-regulatory organizations listing or trading security futures products shall file proposed rule changes necessary to implement decimal pricing of security futures products. The Commission may not require such rules to contain equal minimum increments in such decimal pricing.

(9) *Consultation with CFTC.*—

(A) *Consultation Required.*—The Commission shall consult with and consider the views of the Commodity Futures Trading Commission prior to approving or disapproving a proposed rule change filed by a national securities association registered pursuant to section 15A(a) or a national securities exchange subject to the provisions of subsection (a) that primarily concerns conduct related to transactions in security futures products, except where the Commission determines that an emergency exists requiring expeditious or summary action and publishes its reasons therefor.

(B) *Responses to CFTC Comments and Findings.*—If the Commodity Futures Trading Commission comments in writing to the Commission on a proposed rule that has been published for comment, the Commission shall respond in writing to such written comment before approving or disapproving the proposed rule. If the Commodity Futures Trading Commission determines, and notifies the Commission, that such rule, if implemented or as applied, would—

(i) adversely affect the liquidity or efficiency of the market for security futures products; or

(ii) impose any burden on competition not necessary or appropriate in furtherance of the purposes of this section,

the Commission shall, prior to approving or disapproving the proposed rule, find that such rule is necessary and appropriate in furtherance of the purposes of this section notwithstanding the Commodity Futures Trading Commission's determination.

(c) The Commission, by rule, may abrogate, add to, and delete from (hereinafter in this subsection collectively referred to as "amend") the rules of a self-regulatory organization (other than a registered clearing agency) as the Commission deems necessary or appropriate to insure the fair administration of the self-regulatory organization, to conform its rules to requirements of this title and the rules and regulations thereunder applicable to such organization, or otherwise in furtherance of the purposes of this title, in the following manner:

(1) The Commission shall notify the self-regulatory organization and publish notice of the proposed rulemaking in the Federal Register. The notice shall include the text of the proposed amendment to the rules of the self-regulatory organization and a statement of the Commission's reasons, including any pertinent facts, for commencing such proposed rulemaking.

(2) The Commission shall give interested persons an opportunity for the oral presentation of data, views, and arguments, in addition to an opportunity to make written submissions, a transcript shall be kept of any oral presentation.

(3) A rule adopted pursuant to this subsection shall incorporate the text of the amendment to the rules of the self-regulatory organization and a statement of the Com-

mission's basis for and purpose in so amending such rules. This statement shall include an identification of any facts on which the Commission considers its determination so to amend the rules of the self-regulatory agency to be based, including the reasons for the Commission's conclusions as to any of such facts which were disputed in the rulemaking.

(4)(A) Except as provided in paragraphs (1) through (3) of this subsection, rulemaking under this subsection shall be in accordance with the procedures specified in section 553 of title 5, United States Code, for rulemaking not on the record.

(B) Nothing in this subsection shall be construed to impair or limit the Commission's power to make, or to modify or alter the procedures the Commission may follow in making rules and regulations pursuant to any other authority under this title.

(C) Any amendment to the rules of a self-regulatory organization made by the Commission pursuant to this subsection shall be considered for all purposes of this title to be part of the rules of such self-regulatory organization and shall not be considered to be a rule of the Commission.

(5) With respect to rules described in subsection (b)(5), the Commission shall consult with and consider the views of the Secretary of the Treasury before abrogating, adding to, and deleting from such rules, except where the Commission determines that an emergency exists requiring expeditious or summary action and publishes its reasons therefor.

(d)(1) If any self-regulatory organization imposes any final disciplinary sanction on any member thereof or participant therein, denies membership or participation to any applicant, or prohibits or limits any person in respect to access to services offered by such organization or member thereof or if any self-regulatory organization (other than a registered clearing agency) imposes any final disciplinary sanction on any person associated with a member or bars any person from becoming associated with a member, the self-regulatory organization shall promptly file notice thereof with the appropriate regulatory agency for the self-regulatory organization and (if other than the appropriate regulatory agency for the self-regulatory organization) the appropriate regulatory agency for such member, participant, applicant, or other person. The notice shall be in such form and contain such information as the appropriate regulatory agency for the self-regulatory organization, by rule, may prescribe as necessary or appropriate in furtherance of the purposes of this title.

(2) Any action with respect to which a self-regulatory organization is required by paragraph (1) of this subsection to file notice shall be subject to review by the appropriate regulatory agency for such member, participant, applicant, or other person, on its own motion, or upon application by any person aggrieved thereby filed within thirty days after the date such notice was filed with such appropriate regulatory agency and received by such aggrieved person, or within such longer period as such appropriate regulatory agency may determine. Application to such appropriate regulatory agency for review, or the institution of review by such appropriate regulatory agency on its own motion, shall not operate as a stay of such action unless such appropriate regulatory agency otherwise orders, summarily or after notice and opportunity for hearing on the question of a stay (which hearing may consist solely of submission of affidavits or presentation of oral arguments). Each appropriate regulatory agency shall establish for appropriate cases an expedited procedure for consideration and determination of the question of a stay.

(3) The provisions of this subsection shall apply to an exchange registered pursuant to section 6(g) of this title or a national securities association registered pursuant to section 15A(k) of this title only to the extent that such exchange or association imposes any final disciplinary sanction for—

(A) a violation of the Federal securities laws or the rules and regulations thereunder; or

(B) a violation of a rule of such exchange or association, as to which a proposed change would be required to be filed under section 19 of this title, except that, to the extent that the exchange or association rule violation relates to any account, agreement, contract, or transaction, this subsection shall apply only to the extent such violation involves a security futures product.

(e)(1) In any proceeding to review a final disciplinary sanction imposed by a self-regulatory organization on a member thereof or participant therein or a person associated with such a member, after notice and opportunity for hearing (which hearing may consist solely of consideration of the record before the self-regulatory organization and opportunity for the presentation of supporting reasons to affirm, modify, or set aside the sanction)—

(A) if the appropriate regulatory agency for such member, participant, or person associated with a member finds that such member, participant, or person associated with a member has engaged in such acts or practices, or has omitted such acts, as the self-regulatory organization has found him to have engaged in or omitted, that such acts or practices, or omissions to act, are in violation of such provisions of this title, the rules or regulations thereunder, the rules of the self-regulatory organization, or, in the case of a registered securities association, the rules of the Municipal Securities rulemaking Board as have been specified in the determination of the self-regulatory organization, and that such provisions are, and were applied in a manner, consistent with the purposes of this title, such appropriate regulatory agency, by order, shall so declare and, as appropriate, affirm the sanction imposed by the self-regulatory organization, modify the sanction in accordance with paragraph (2) of this subsection, or remand to the self-regulatory organization for further proceedings; or

(B) if such appropriate regulatory agency does not make any such finding it shall, by order, set aside the sanction imposed by the self-regulatory organization and, if appropriate, remand to the self-regulatory organization for further proceedings.

(2) If the appropriate regulatory agency for a member, participant, or person associated with a member, having due regard for the public interest and the protection of investors, finds after a proceeding in accordance with paragraph (1) of this subsection that a sanction imposed by a self-regulatory organization upon such member, participant, or person associated with a member imposes any burden on competition not necessary or appropriate in furtherance of the purposes of this title or is excessive or oppressive, the appropriate regulatory agency may cancel, reduce, or require the remission of such sanction.

(f) In any proceeding to review the denial of membership or participation in a self-regulatory organization to any applicant, the barring of any person from becoming associated with a member of a self-regulatory organization, or the prohibition or limitation by a self-regulatory organization of any person with respect to access to services offered by the self-regulatory organization or any member thereof, if the appropriate regulatory agency for such applicant or person, after notice and opportunity for hearing (which hearing may consist solely of consideration of the record before the self-regulatory organization and opportunity for the presentation of supporting reasons to dismiss the proceeding or set aside the action of the self-regulatory organization) finds that the specific grounds on which such denial, bar, or prohibition or limitation is based exist in fact, that such denial, bar, or prohibition or limitation is in accordance with the rules of the self-regulatory organization, and that such rules are, and were applied in a manner, consistent with the purposes of this title, such appropriate regulatory agency, by order, shall dismiss the proceeding. If such appropriate regulatory agency does not make any such finding or if it finds that such denial, bar, or prohibition or limitation imposes any burden on competition not necessary or appropriate in furtherance of the purposes of this title, such appropriate regulatory agency, by order, shall set aside the action of the self-regulatory organization and require it to admit such applicant to membership or participation, permit such person to become associated with a member, or grant such person access to services offered by the self-regulatory organization or member thereof.

(g)(1) Every self-regulatory organization shall comply with the provisions of this title, the rules and regulations thereunder, and its own rules, and (subject to the provisions of section 17(d) of this title, paragraph (2) of this subsection, and the rules thereunder) absent reasonable justification or excuse enforce compliance—

(A) in the case of a national securities exchange, with such provisions by its members and persons associated with its members;

(B) in the case of a registered securities association, with such provisions and the provisions of the rules of the Municipal Securities Rulemaking Board by its members and persons associated with its members; and

(C) in the case of a registered clearing agency, with its own rules by its participants.

(2) The Commission, by rule, consistent with the public interest, the protection of investors, and the other purposes of this title, may relieve any self-regulatory organization of any responsibility under this title to enforce compliance with any specified provision of this title or the rules or regulations thereunder by any member of such organization or person associated with such a member, or any class of such members or persons associated with a member.

(h)(1) The appropriate regulatory agency for a self-regulatory organization is authorized, by order, if in its opinion such action is necessary or appropriate in the public interest, for the protection of investors, or otherwise in furtherance of the purposes of this title, to suspend for a period not exceeding twelve months or revoke the registration of such self-regulatory organization, or to censure or impose limitations upon the activities, functions, and operations of such self-regulatory organization, if such appropriate regulatory agency finds, on the record after notice and opportunity for hearing, that such self-regulatory organization has violated or is unable to comply with any provision of this title, the rules or regulations thereunder, or its own rules or without reasonable justification or excuse has failed to enforce compliance—

(A) in the case of a national securities exchange, with any such provision by a member thereof or a person associated with a member thereof;

(B) in the case of a registered securities association, with any such provision or any provision of the rules of the Municipal Securities Rulemaking Board by a member thereof or a person associated with a member thereof; or

(C) in the case of a registered clearing agency, with any provision of its own rules by a participant therein.

(2) The appropriate regulatory agency for a self-regulatory organization is authorized, by order, if in its opinion such action is necessary or appropriate in the public interest, for the protection of investors, or otherwise in furtherance of the purposes of this title, to suspend for a period not exceeding twelve months or expel from such self-regulatory organization any member thereof or participant therein, if such member or participant is subject to an order of the Commission pursuant to section 15(b)(4) of this title or if such appropriate regulatory agency finds, on the record after notice and opportunity for hearing, that such member or participant has willfully violated or has effected any transaction for any other person who, such member or participant had rea-

son to believe, was violating with respect to such transaction—

(A) in the case of a national securities exchange, any provision of the Securities Act of 1933, the Investment Advisers Act of 1940, the Investment Company Act of 1940, this title, or the rules or regulations under any of such statutes;

(B) in the case of a registered securities association, any provision of the Securities Act of 1933, the Investment Advisers Act of 1940, the Investment Company Act of 1940, this title, the rules and regulations under any of such statutes, or the rules of the Municipal Securities Rulemaking Board; or

(C) in the case of a registered clearing agency, any provision of the rules of the clearing agency.

(3) The appropriate regulatory agency for a national securities exchange or registered securities association is authorized, by order, if in its opinion such action is necessary or appropriate in the public interest, for the protection of investors, or otherwise in furtherance of the purposes of this title, to suspend for a period not exceeding twelve months or to bar any person from being associated with a member of such national securities exchange or registered securities association, if such person is subject to an order of the Commission pursuant to section 15(b)(6) or if such appropriate regulatory agency finds, on the record after notice and opportunity for hearing, that such person has willfully violated or has effected any transaction for any other person who, such person associated with a member had reason to believe, was violating with respect to such transaction—

(A) in the case of a national securities exchange, any provision of the Securities Act of 1933, the Investment Advisers Act of 1940, the Investment Company Act of 1940, this title, or the rules or regulations under any of such statutes; or

(B) in the case of a registered securities association, any provision of the Securities Act of 1933, the Investment Advisers Act of 1940, the Investment Company Act of 1940, this title, the rules or regulations under any of the statutes, or the rules of the Municipal Securities Rulemaking Board.

(4) The appropriate regulatory agency for a self-regulatory organization is authorized, by order, if in its opinion such action is necessary or appropriate in the public interest, for the protection of investors, or otherwise in furtherance of the purposes of this title, to remove from office or censure any officer or director of such self-regulatory organization, if such appropriate regulatory agency finds, on the record after notice and opportunity for hearing, that such officer or director has willfully violated any provision of this title, the rules or regulations thereunder, or the rules of such self-regulatory organization, willfully abused his authority, or without reasonable justification or excuse has failed to enforce compliance—

(A) in the case of a national securities exchange, with any such provision by any member or person associated with a member;

(B) in the case of a registered securities association, with any such provision or any provision of the rules of the Municipal Securities Rulemaking Board by any member or person associated with a member; or

(C) in the case of a registered clearing agency, with any provision of the rules of the clearing agency by any participant.

(i) If a proceeding under subsection (h)(1) of this section results in the suspension or revocation of the registration of a clearing agency, the appropriate regulatory agency for such clearing agency may, upon notice to such clearing agency, apply to any court of competent jurisdiction specified in section 21(d) or 27 of this title for the appointment of a trustee. In the event of such an application, the court may, to the extent it deems necessary or appropriate, take exclusive jurisdiction of such clearing agency and the records and assets thereof, wherever located; and the court shall appoint the appropriate regulatory agency for such clearing agency or a person designated by such appropriate regulatory agency as trustee with power to take possession and continue to operate or terminate the operations of such clearing agency in an orderly manner for the protection of participants and investors, subject to such terms and conditions as the court may prescribe.

Liability of Controlling Persons and Persons Who Aid and Abet Violations

Sec. 20. (a) Every person who, directly or indirectly, controls any person liable under any provision of this title or of any rule or regulation thereunder shall also be liable jointly and severally with and to the same extent as such controlled person to any person to whom such controlled person is liable, unless the controlling person acted in good faith and did not directly or indirectly induce the act or acts constituting the violation or cause of action.

(b) It shall be unlawful for any person, directly or indirectly, to do any act or thing which it would be unlawful for such person to do under the provisions of this title or any rule or regulation thereunder through or by means of any other person.

(c) It shall be unlawful for any director or officer of, or any owner of any securities issued by, any issuer required to file any document, report, or information under this title or any rule or regulation thereunder without just cause to hinder, delay, or obstruct the making or filing of any such document, report, or information.

(d) Wherever communicating, or purchasing or selling a security while in possession of, material nonpublic information would violate, or result in liability to any purchaser or seller of the security under any provisions of this title, or any rule or regulation thereunder, such conduct in connection with a purchase or sale of a put, call, straddle, option, privilege or security-based swap agreement (as defined in section 206B of the Gramm–Leach–Bliley Act) with respect to such security or with respect to a group or index of securities including such security, shall also violate and result in comparable liability to any purchaser or seller of that security under such provision, rule, or regulation.

(e) *Prosecution of Persons Who Aid and Abet Violations.*—For purposes of any action brought by the Commission under paragraph (1) or (3) of section 21(d), any person that knowingly provides substantial assistance to another person in violation of a provision of this title, or of any rule or regulation issued under this title, shall be deemed to be in violation of such provision to the same extent as the person to whom such assistance is provided.

(f) The authority of the Commission under this section with respect to security-based swap agreements (as defined in section 206B of the Gramm–Leach–Bliley Act) shall be subject to the restrictions and limitations of section 3A(b) of this title.

Liability to Contemporaneous Traders for Insider Trading

Sec. 20A. (a) *Private Rights of Action Based on Contemporaneous Trading.*—Any person who violates any provision of this title or the rules or regulations thereunder by purchasing or selling a security while in possession of material, nonpublic information shall be liable in an action in any court of competent jurisdiction to any person who, contemporaneously with the purchase or sale of securities that is the subject of such violation, has purchased (where such violation is based on a sale of securities) or sold (where such violation is based on a purchase of securities) securities of the same class.

(b) *Limitations on Liability.*—

(1) *Contemporaneous trading actions limited to profit gained or loss avoided.*—The total amount of damages imposed under subsection (a) shall not exceed the profit gained or loss avoided in the transaction or

transactions that are the subject of the violation.

(2) *Offsetting disgorgements against liability.*—The total amount of damages imposed against any person under subsection (a) shall be diminished by the amounts, if any, that such person may be required to disgorge, pursuant to a court order obtained at the instance of the Commission, in a proceeding brought under section 21(d) of this title relating to the same transaction or transactions.

(3) *Controlling person liability.*—No person shall be liable under this section solely by reason of employing another person who is liable under this section, but the liability of a controlling person under this section shall be subject to section 20(a) of this title.

(4) *Statute of limitations.*—No action may be brought under this section more than 5 years after the date of the last transaction that is the subject of the violation.

(c) *Joint and Several Liability for Communicating.*—Any person who violates any provision of this title or the rules or regulations thereunder by communicating material, nonpublic information shall be jointly and severally liable under subsection (a) with, and to the same extent as, any person or persons liable under subsection (a) to whom the communication was directed.

(d) *Authority Not to Restrict Other Express or Implied Rights of Action.*—Nothing in this section shall be construed to limit or condition the right of any person to bring an action to enforce a requirement of this title or the availability of any cause of action implied from a provision of this title.

(e) *Provisions Not To Affect Public Prosecutions.*—This section shall not be construed to bar or limit in any manner any action by the Commission or the Attorney General under any other provision of this title, nor shall it bar or limit in any manner any action to recover penalties, or to seek any other order regarding penalties.

Investigations and Actions

Sec. 21. (a)(1) The Commission may, in its discretion, make such investigations as it deems necessary to determine whether any person has violated, is violating, or is about to violate any provision of this title, the rules or regulations thereunder, the rules of a national securities exchange or registered securities association of which such person is a member or a person associated with a member, the rules of a registered clearing agency in which such person is a participant, the rules of the Public Company Accounting Oversight Board, of which such person is a registered public accounting firm or a person associated with such a firm, or the rules of the Municipal Securities Rulemaking Board, and may require or permit any person to file with it a statement in writing, under oath or otherwise as the Commission shall determine, as to all the facts and circumstances concerning the matter to be investigated. The Commission is authorized in its discretion, to publish information concerning any such violations, and to investigate any facts, conditions, practices, or matters which it may deem necessary or proper to aid in the enforcement of such provisions, in the prescribing of rules and regulations under this title, or in securing information to serve as a basis for recommending further legislation concerning the matters to which this title relates.

(2) On request from a foreign securities authority, the Commission may provide assistance in accordance with this paragraph if the requesting authority states that the requesting authority is conducting an investigation which it deems necessary to determine whether any person has violated, is violating, or is about to violate any laws or rules relating to securities matters that the requesting authority administers or enforces. The Commission may, in its discretion, conduct such investigation as the Commission deems necessary to collect information and evidence pertinent to the request for assistance. Such assistance may be provided without regard to whether the facts stated

in the request would also constitute a violation of the laws of the United States. In deciding whether to provide such assistance, the Commission shall consider whether (A) the requesting authority has agreed to provide reciprocal assistance in securities matters to the Commission; and (B) compliance with the request would prejudice the public interest of the United States.

(b) For the purpose of any such investigation, or any other proceeding under this title, any member of the Commission or any officer designated by it is empowered to administer oaths and affirmations, subpena witnesses, compel their attendance, take evidence, and require the production of any books, papers, correspondence, memoranda, or other records which the Commission deems relevant or material to the inquiry. Such attendance of witnesses and the production of any such records may be required from any place in the United States or any State at any designated place of hearing.

(c) In case of contumacy by, or refusal to obey a subpena issued to, any person, the Commission may invoke the aid of any court of the United States within the jurisdiction of which such investigation or proceeding is carried on, or where such person resides or carries on business, in requiring the attendance and testimony of witnesses and the production of books, papers, correspondence, memoranda, and other records. And such court may issue an order requiring such person to appear before the Commission or member or officer designated by the Commission, there to produce records, if so ordered, or to give testimony touching the matter under investigation or in question; and any failure to obey such order of the court may be punished by such court as a contempt thereof. All process in any such case may be served in the judicial district whereof such person is an inhabitant or wherever he may be found. Any person who shall, without just cause, fail or refuse to attend and testify or to answer any lawful inquiry or to produce books, papers, correspondence, memoranda, and other records, if in his power so to do, in obedience to the subpena of the Commission, shall be guilty of a misdemeanor and, upon conviction, shall be subject to a fine of not more than $1,000 or to imprisonment for a term of not more than one year, or both.

(d)(1) Whenever it shall appear to the Commission that any person is engaged or is about to engage in acts or practices constituting a violation of any provision of this title, the rules or regulations thereunder, the rules of a national securities exchange or registered securities association of which such person is a member or a person associated with a member, the rules of a registered clearing agency in which such person is a participant, the rules of the Public Company Accounting Oversight Board, of which such person is a registered public accounting firm or a person associated with such a firm, or the rules of the Municipal Securities Rulemaking Board, it may in its discretion bring an action in the proper district court of the United States, the United States District Court for the District of Columbia, or the United States courts of any territory or other place subject to the jurisdiction of the United States, to enjoin such acts or practices, and upon a proper showing a permanent or temporary injunction or restraining order shall be granted without bond. The Commission may transmit such evidence as may be available concerning such acts or practices as may constitute a violation of any provision of this title or the rules or regulations thereunder to the Attorney General, who may, in his discretion, institute the necessary criminal proceedings under this title.

(2) *Authority of a Court to Prohibit Persons From Serving as Officers and Directors.*—In any proceeding under paragraph (1) of this subsection, the court may prohibit, conditionally or unconditionally, and permanently or for such period of time as it shall determine, any person who violated section 10(b) of this title or the rules or regulations thereunder from acting as an officer or director of any issuer that has a class of securities registered pursu-

ant to section 12 of this title or that is required to file reports pursuant to section 15(d) of this title if the person's conduct demonstrates unfitness to serve as an officer or director of any such issuer.

(3) *Money Penalties in Civil Actions.*—

(A) *Authority of Commission.*—Whenever it shall appear to the Commission that any person has violated any provision of this title, the rules or regulations thereunder, or a cease-and-desist order entered by the Commission pursuant to section 21C of this title, other than by committing a violation subject to a penalty pursuant to section 21A, the Commission may bring an action in a United States district court to seek, and the court shall have jurisdiction to impose, upon a proper showing, a civil penalty to be paid by the person who committed such violation.

(B) *Amount of Penalty.*—

(i) *First tier.*—The amount of the penalty shall be determined by the court in light of the facts and circumstances. For each violation, the amount of the penalty shall not exceed the greater of (I) $5,000 for a natural person or $50,000 for any other person, or (II) the gross amount of pecuniary gain to such defendant as a result of the violation.

(ii) *Second tier.*—Notwithstanding clause (i), the amount of penalty for each such violation shall not exceed the greater of (I) $50,000 for a natural person or $250,000 for any other person, or (II) the gross amount of pecuniary gain to such defendant as a result of the violation, if the violation described in subparagraph (A) involved fraud, deceit, manipulation, or deliberate or reckless disregard of a regulatory requirement.

(iii) *Third tier.*—Notwithstanding clauses (i) and (ii), the amount of penalty for each such violation shall not exceed the greater of (I) $100,000 for a natural person or $500,000 for any other person, or (II) the gross amount of pecuniary gain to such defendant as a result of the violation, if—

(aa) the violation described in subparagraph (A) involved fraud, deceit, manipulation, or deliberate or reckless disregard of a regulatory requirement; and

(bb) such violation directly or indirectly resulted in substantial losses or created a significant risk of substantial losses to other persons.

(C) *Procedures for Collection.*—

(i) *Payment of Penalty to Treasury.*—A penalty imposed under this section shall be payable into the Treasury of the United States, except as otherwise provided in section 308 of the Sarbanes–Oxley Act of 2002.

(ii) *Collection of Penalties.*—If a person upon whom such a penalty is imposed shall fail to pay such penalty within the time prescribed in the court's order, the Commission may refer the matter to the Attorney General who shall recover such penalty by action in the appropriate United States district court.

(iii) *Remedy Not Exclusive.*—The actions authorized by this paragraph may be brought in addition to any other action that the Commission or the Attorney General is entitled to bring.

(iv) *Jurisdiction and Venue.*—For purposes of section 27 of this title, action under this paragraph shall be actions to enforce a liability or a duty created by this title.

(D) *Special Provisions Relating to a Violation of a Cease-and-desist Order.*—In an action to enforce a cease-and-desist order entered by the Commission pursuant to section 21C, each separate violation of such order shall be a separate offense, except that in the case of a violation through a continuing failure to comply with the order, each day of the failure to comply shall be deemed a separate offense.

(4) *Prohibition of Attorneys' Fees Paid From Commission Disgorgement Funds.*—Except as otherwise ordered by the court upon motion by the Commission, or, in the case of an administrative action, as otherwise ordered by the Commission, funds disgorged as the result of an action brought by the Commission in Fed-

eral court, or as a result of any Commission administrative action, shall not be distributed as payment for attorneys' fees or expenses incurred by private parties seeking distribution of the disgorged funds.

(5) *Equitable Relief.*—In any action or proceeding brought or instituted by the Commission under any provision of the securities laws, the Commission may seek, and any Federal court may grant, any equitable relief that may be appropriate or necessary for the benefit of investors.

(6) *Authority of a Court to Prohibit Persons From Participating in an Offering of Penny Stock.*—

(A) *In general.*—In any proceeding under paragraph (1) against any person participating in, or, at the time of the alleged misconduct who was participating in, an offering of penny stock, the court may prohibit that person from participating in an offering of penny stock, conditionally or unconditionally, and permanently or for such period of time as the court shall determine.

(B) *Definition.*—For purposes of this paragraph, the term "person participating in an offering of penny stock" includes any person engaging in activities with a broker, dealer, or issuer for purposes of issuing, trading, or inducing or attempting to induce the purchase or sale of, any penny stock. The commission may, by rule or regulation, define such term to include other activities, and may, by rule, regulation, or order, exempt any person or class of persons, in whole or in part, conditionally or unconditionally, from inclusion in such term.

(e) Upon application of the Commission the district courts of the United States and the United States courts of any territory or other place subject to the jurisdiction or the United States shall have jurisdiction to issue writs of mandamus, injunctions, and orders commanding (1) any person to comply with the provisions of this title, the rules, regulations, and orders thereunder, the rules of a national securities exchange or registered securities association of which such person is a member or person associated with a member, the rules of a registered clearing agency in which such person is a participant, the rules of the Public Company Accounting Oversight Board, of which such person is a registered public accounting firm or a person associated with such a firm, the rules of the Municipal Securities Rulemaking Board, or any undertaking contained in a registration statement as provided in subsection (d) of section 15 of this title, (2), any national securities exchange or registered securities association to enforce compliance by its members and persons associated with its members with the provisions of this title, the rules, regulations, and orders thereunder, and the rules of such exchange or association, or (3) any registered clearing agency to enforce compliance by its participants with the provisions of the rules of such clearing agency.

(f) Notwithstanding any other provision of this title, the Commission shall not bring any action pursuant to subsection (d) or (e) of this section against any person for violation of, or to command compliance with, the rules of a self-regulatory organization or the Public Company Accounting Oversight Board unless it appears to the Commission that (1) such self-regulatory organization or the Public Company Accounting Oversight Board is unable or unwilling to take appropriate action against such person in the public interest and for the protection of investors, or (2) such action is otherwise necessary or appropriate in the public interest or for the protection of investors.

(g) Notwithstanding the provisions of section 1407(a) of title 28, United States Code, or any other provision of law, no action for equitable relief instituted by the Commission pursuant to the securities laws shall be consolidated or coordinated with other actions not brought by the Commission, even though such other actions may involve common questions of fact, unless such consolidation is consented to by the Commission.

(h)(1) The Right to Financial Privacy Act of 1978 shall apply with respect to the Commission, except as otherwise provided in this subsection.

(2) Notwithstanding section 1105 or 1107 of the Right to Financial Privacy Act of 1978, the Commission may have access to and obtain copies of, or the information contained in financial records of a customer from a financial institution without prior notice to the customer upon an ex parte showing to an appropriate United States district court that the Commission seeks such financial records pursuant to a subpena issued in conformity with the requirements of section 19(b) of the Securities Act of 1933, section 21(b) of the Securities Exchange Act of 1934, section 18(c) of the Public Utility Holding Company Act of 1935, section 42(b) of the Investment Company Act of 1940, or section 209(b) of the Investment Advisers Act of 1940, and that the Commission has reason to believe that—

(A) delay in obtaining access to such financial records, or the required notice, will result in—

(i) flight from prosecution;

(ii) destruction of or tampering with evidence;

(iii) transfer of assets or records outside the territorial limits of the United States;

(iv) improper conversion of investor assets; or

(v) impeding the ability of the Commission to identify or trace the source or disposition of funds involved in any securities transaction;

(B) such financial records are necessary to identify or trace the record or beneficial ownership interest in any security;

(C) the acts, practices or course of conduct under investigation involve—

(i) the dissemination of materially false or misleading information concerning any security, issuer, or market, or the failure to make disclosures required under the securities laws, which remain uncorrected; or

(ii) a financial loss to investors or other persons protected under the securities laws which remains substantially uncompensated; or

(D) the acts, practices or course of conduct under investigation—

(i) involve significant financial speculation in securities; or

(ii) endanger the stability of any financial or investment intermediary.

(3) Any application under paragraph (2) for a delay in notice shall be made with reasonable specificity.

(4)(A) Upon a showing described in paragraph (2), the presiding judge or magistrate shall enter an ex parte order granting the requested delay for a period not to exceed ninety days and an order prohibiting the financial institution involved from disclosing that records have been obtained or that a request for records has been made.

(B) Extensions of the period of delay of notice provided in subparagraph (A) of up to ninety days each may be granted by the court upon application, but only in accordance with this subsection or section 1109(a), (b)(1), or (b)(2) of the Right to Financial Privacy Act of 1978.

(C) Upon expiration of the period of delay of notification ordered under subparagraph (A) or (B), the customer shall be served with or mailed a copy of the subpena insofar as it applies to the customer together with the following notice which shall describe with reasonable specificity the nature of the investigation for which the Commission sought the financial records:

"Records or information concerning your transactions which are held by the financial institution named in the attached subpena were supplied to the Securities and Exchange Commission on (date). Notification was withheld pursuant to a determination by the (title of court so ordering) under section 21(h) of the Securities Exchange Act of 1934 that (state reason). The purpose of the investigation or official proceeding was (state purpose)."

(5) Upon application by the Commission, all proceedings pursuant to paragraphs (2) and (4) shall be held in camera and the records thereof sealed until expiration of the period of delay or such other date as the presiding judge or magistrate may permit.

(6) The Commission shall compile an annual tabulation of the occasions on which the Commission used each separate subparagraph or clause of paragraph (2) of this subsection or the provisions of the Right to Financial Privacy Act of 1978 to obtain access to financial records of a customer and include it in its annual report to the Congress. Section 1121(b) of the Right to Financial Privacy Act of 1978 shall not apply with respect to the Commission.

(7)(A) Following the expiration of the period of delay of notification ordered by the court pursuant to paragraph (4) of this subsection, the customer may, upon motion, reopen the proceeding in the district court which issued the order. If the presiding judge or magistrate finds that the movant is the customer to whom the records obtained by the Commission pertain, and that the Commission has obtained financial records or information contained therein in violation of this subsection, other than paragraph (1), it may order that the customer be granted civil penalties against the Commission in an amount equal to the sum of—

(i) $100 without regard to the volume of records involved;

(ii) any out-of-pocket damages sustained by the customer as a direct result of the disclosure; and

(iii) if the violation is found to have been willful, intentional, and without good faith, such punitive damages as the court may allow, together with the costs of the action and reasonable attorney's fees as determined by the court.

(B) Upon a finding that the Commission has obtained financial records or information contained therein in violation of this subsection, other than paragraph (1), the court, in its discretion, may also or in the alternative issue injunctive relief to require the Commission to comply with this subsection with respect to any subpena which the Commission issues in the future for financial records of such customer for purposes of the same investigation.

(C) Whenever the court determines that the Commission has failed to comply with this subsection, other than paragraph (1), and the court finds that the circumstances raise questions of whether an officer or employee of the Commission acted in a willful and intentional manner and without good faith with respect to the violation, the Office of Personnel Management shall promptly initiate a proceeding to determine whether disciplinary action is warranted against the agent or employee who was primarily responsible for the violation. After investigating and considering the evidence submitted, the Office of Personnel Management shall submit its findings and recommendations to the Commission and shall send copies of the findings and recommendations to the officer or employee or his representative. The Commission shall take the corrective action that the Office of Personnel Management recommends.

(8) The relief described in paragraphs (7) and (10) shall be the only remedies or sanctions available to a customer for a violation of this subsection, other than paragraph (1), and nothing herein or in the Right to Financial Privacy Act of 1978 shall be deemed to prohibit the use in any investigation or proceeding of financial records, or the information contained therein, obtained by a subpena issued by the Commission. In the case of an unsuccessful action under paragraph (7), the court shall award the costs of the action and attorney's fees to the Commission if the presiding judge or magistrate finds that the customer's claims were made in bad faith.

(9)(A) The Commission may transfer financial records or the information contained therein to any government authority if the Commission proceeds as a transferring agency in accordance with section 1112 of the Right to Financial Privacy Act of 1978, except that the customer notice required under section 1112(b) or (c) of such Act may be delayed upon a showing by the Commission, in accordance with the procedure set forth in paragraphs (4) and (5), that one or more of subparagraphs (A) through (D) of paragraph (2) apply.

(B) The Commission may, without notice to the customer pursuant to section 1112 of the Right to Financial Privacy Act of 1978, transfer financial records or the information contained therein to a State securities agency or to the Department of Justice. Financial records or information transferred by the Commission to the Department of Justice or to a State securities agency pursuant to the provisions of this subparagraph may be disclosed or used only in an administrative, civil, or criminal action or investigation by the Department of Justice or the State securities agency which arises out of or relates to the acts, practices, or courses of conduct investigated by the Commission, except that if the Department of Justice or the State securities agency determines that the information should be disclosed or used for any other purpose, it may do so if it notifies the customer, except as otherwise provided in the Right to Financial Privacy Act of 1978, within 30 days of its determination, or complies with the requirements of section 1109 of such Act regarding delay of notice.

(10) Any government authority violating paragraph (9) shall be subject to the procedures and penalties applicable to the Commission under paragraph (7)(A) with respect to a violation by the Commission in obtaining financial records.

(11) Notwithstanding the provisions of this subsection, the Commission may obtain financial records from a financial institution or transfer such records in accordance with provisions of the Right to Financial Privacy Act of 1978.

(12) Nothing in this subsection shall enlarge or restrict any rights of a financial institution to challenge requests for records made by the Commission under existing law. Nothing in this subsection shall entitle a customer to assert any rights of a financial institution.

(13) Unless the context otherwise requires, all terms defined in the Right to Financial Privacy Act of 1978 which are common to this subsection shall have the same meaning as in such Act.

(i) *Information to CFTC.*—The Commission shall provide the Commodity Futures Trading Commission with notice of the commencement of any proceeding and a copy of any order entered by the Commission against any broker or dealer registered pursuant to section 15(b)(11), any exchange registered pursuant to section 6(g), or any national securities association registered pursuant to section 15A(k).

Civil Penalties for Insider Trading

Sec. 21A. (a) *Authority To Impose Civil Penalties.*

(1) *Judicial actions by commission authorized.*—Whenever it shall appear to the Commission that any person has violated any provision of this title or the rules or regulations thereunder by purchasing or selling a security or security-based swap agreement (as defined in section 206B of the Gramm–Leach–Bliley Act) while in possession of material, nonpublic information in, or has violated any such provision by communicating such information in connection with, a transaction on or through the facilities of a national securities exchange or from or through a broker or dealer, and which is not part of a public offering by an issuer of securities other than standardized options or security futures products, the Commission—

(A) may bring an action in a United States district court to seek and the court shall have jurisdiction to impose, a civil penalty to be paid by the person who committed such violation; and

(B) may, subject to subsection (b)(1) bring an action in a United States district court to seek, and the court shall have jurisdiction to impose, a civil penalty to be paid by a person who, at the time of the violation directly or indirectly controlled the person who committed such violation.

(2) *Amount of penalty for person who committed violation.*—The amount of the penalty which may be imposed on the person who committed such violation shall be determined by the court in light of the fact and circumstances, but shall not exceed three times the profit gained or loss avoided as a result of such unlawful purchase, sale, or communication.

(3) *Amount of penalty for controlling person.*—The amount of the penalty which may be imposed on any person who, at the time of the violation, directly or indirectly controlled the person who committed such violation, shall be determined by the court in light of the facts and circumstances, but shall not exceed the greater of $1,000,000, or three times the amount of the profit gained or loss avoided as a result of such controlled person's violation. If such controlled person's violation was a violation by communication, the profit gained or loss avoided as a result of the violation shall, for purposes of this paragraph only, be deemed to be limited to the profit gained or loss avoided by the person or persons to whom the controlled person directed such communication.

(b) *Limitations on Liability.*—

(1) *Liability of controlling persons.*—No controlling person shall be subject to a penalty under subsection (a)(1)(B) unless the Commission establishes that—

(A) such controlling person knew or recklessly disregarded the fact that such controlled person was likely to engage in the act or acts constituting the violation and failed to take appropriate steps to prevent such act or acts before they occurred; or

(B) such controlling person knowingly or recklessly failed to establish, maintain, or enforce any policy or procedure required under section 15(f) of this title or section 204A of the Investment Advisers Act of 1940 and such failure substantially contributed to or permitted the occurrence of the act or acts constituting the violation.

(2) *Additional restrictions on liability.*—No person shall be subject to a penalty under subsection (a) solely by reason of employing another person who is subject to a penalty under such subsection, unless such employing person is liable as a controlling person under paragraph (1) of this subsection. Section 20(a) of this title shall not apply to actions under subsection (a) of this section.

(c) *Authority of Commission.*—The Commission, by such rules, regulations, and orders as it considers necessary or appropriate in the public interest or for the protection of investors, may exempt, in whole or in part, either unconditionally or upon specific terms and conditions, any person or transaction or class of persons or transactions from this section.

(d) *Procedures for Collection.*—

(1) *Payment of penalty to treasury.*—A penalty imposed under this section shall (subject to subsection (e)) be payable into the Treasury of the United States, except as otherwise provided in section 308 of the Sarbanes–Oxley Act of 2002.

(2) *Collection of penalties.*—If a person upon whom such a penalty is imposed shall fail to pay such penalty within the time prescribed in the court's order, the Commission may refer the matter to the Attorney General who shall recover such penalty by action in the appropriate United States district court.

(3) *Remedy not exclusive.*—The actions authorized by this section may be brought in addition to any other actions that the Commission or the Attorney General are entitled to bring.

(4) *Jurisdiction and venue.*—For purposes of section 27 of this title, actions under this section shall be actions to enforce a liability or a duty created by this title.

(5) *Statute of limitations.*—No action may be brought under this section more than 5 years after the date of the purchase or sale. This section shall not be construed to bar or limit in any manner any action by the Commission or the Attorney General under any other provision of this title, nor shall it bar or limit in any manner any action to recover penalties, or to seek any other order regarding penalties, imposed in an action commenced within 5 years of such transaction.

(e) *Authority to Award Bounties to Informants.*—Notwithstanding the provisions of subsection (d)(1), there shall be paid from amounts imposed as a penalty under this section and recovered by the Commission or the Attorney General, such sums, not to exceed 10 percent of such amounts, as the Commission deems appropriate, to the person or persons who provide information leading to the imposition of such penalty. Any determinations under this subsection, including whether, to whom, or in what amount to make payments, shall in the sole discretion of the Commission, except that no such payment shall be made to any member, officer, or employee of any appropriate regulatory agency, the Department of Justice, or a self-regulatory organization. Any such determination shall be final and not subject to judicial review.

(f) *Definition.*—For purposes of this section, "profit gained" or "loss avoided" is the difference between the purchase or sale price of the security and the value of that security as measured by the trading price of the security a reasonable period after public dissemination of the nonpublic information.

(g) The authority of the Commission under this section with respect to security-based swap agreements (as defined in section 206B of the Gramm–Leach–Bliley Act) shall be subject to the restrictions and limitations of section 3A(b) of this title.

Civil Remedies in Administrative Proceedings

Sec. 21B. (a) *Commission Authority to Assess Money Penalties.*—In any proceeding instituted pursuant to sections 15(b)(4), 15(b)(6), 15B, 15C, or 17A of this title against any person, the Commission or the appropriate regulatory agency may impose a civil penalty if it finds, on the record after notice and opportunity for hearing that such person—

(1) has willfully violated any provision of the Securities Act of 1933, the Investment Company Act of 1940, the Investment Advisers Act of 1940, or this title, or the rules or regulations thereunder, or the rules of the Municipal Securities Rulemaking Board;

(2) has willfully aided, abetted, counseled, commanded, induced, or procured such a violation by any other person;

(3) has willfully made or caused to be made in any application for registration or report required to be filed with the Commission or with any other appropriate regulatory agency under this title, or in any proceeding before the Commission with respect to registration, any statement which was, at the time and in the light of the circumstances under which it was made, false or misleading with respect to any material fact, or has omitted to state in any such application or report any material fact which is required to be stated therein; or

(4) has failed reasonably to supervise, within the meaning of section 15(b)(4)(E) of this title, with a view to preventing violations of the provisions of such statutes, rules and regulations, another person who commits such a violation, if such other person is subject to his supervision; and that such penalty is in the public interest.

(b) *Maximum Amount of Penalty.*—

(1) *First tier.*—The maximum amount of penalty for each act or omission described in subsection (a) shall be $5,000 for a natural person or $50,000 for any other person.

(2) *Second tier.*—Notwithstanding paragraph (1), the maximum amount of penalty for each such act or omission shall be $50,000 for a natural person or $250,000 for any other

person if the act or omission described in subsection (a) involved fraud, deceit, manipulation, or deliberate or reckless disregard of a regulatory requirement.

(3) *Third tier.*—Notwithstanding paragraphs (1) and (2), the maximum amount of penalty for each such act or omission shall be $100,000 for a natural person or $500,000 for any other person if—

(A) The act or omission described in subsection (a) involved fraud, deceit, manipulation, or deliberate or reckless disregard of a regulatory requirement; and

(B) such act or omission directly or indirectly resulted in substantial losses or created a significant risk of substantial losses to other persons or resulted in substantial pecuniary gain to the person who committed the act or omission.

(c) *Determination of Public Interest.*—In considering under this section whether a penalty is in the public interest, the Commission or the appropriate regulatory agency may consider—

(1) whether the act or omission for which such penalty is assessed involved fraud, deceit, manipulation, or deliberate or reckless disregard of a regulatory requirement;

(2) the harm to other persons resulting either directly or indirectly from such act or omission;

(3) the extent to which any person was unjustly enriched, taking into account any restitution made to persons injured by such behavior;

(4) whether such person previously has been found by the Commission, another appropriate regulatory agency, or a self-regulatory organization to have violated the Federal securities laws, State securities laws, or the rules of a self-regulatory organization, has been enjoined by a court of competent jurisdiction from violations of such laws or rules, or has been convicted by a court of competent jurisdiction of violations of such laws or any felony or misdemeanor described in section 15(b)(4)(B) of this title;

(5) the need to deter such person and other persons from committing such acts or omissions; and

(6) such other matters as justice may require.

(d) *Evidence Concerning Ability to Pay.*—In any proceeding in which the Commission or the appropriate regulatory agency may impose a penalty under this section, a respondent may present evidence of the respondent's ability to pay such penalty. The Commission or the appropriate regulatory agency may, in its discretion, consider such evidence in determining whether such penalty is in the public interest. Such evidence may relate to the extent of such person's ability to continue in business and the collectability of a penalty, taking into account any other claims of the United States or third parties upon such person's assets and the amount of such person's assets.

(e) *Authority to Enter an Order Requiring an Accounting and Disgorgement.*—In any proceeding in which the Commission or the appropriate regulatory agency may impose a penalty under this section, the Commission or the appropriate regulatory agency may enter an order requiring accounting and disgorgement, including reasonable interest. The Commission is authorized to adopt rules, regulations, and orders concerning payments to investors, rates of interest, periods of accrual, and such other matters as it deems appropriate to implement this subsection.

Cease and Desist Proceedings

Sec. 21C. (a) *Authority of the Commission.*—If the Commission finds, after notice and opportunity for hearing, that any person is violating, has violated, or is about to violate any provision of this title, or any rule or regulation thereunder, the Commission may publish its findings and enter an order requiring such person, and any other person that is, was, or would be a cause of the violation, due to an act or omission the person knew or should have known would contribute to such violation, to cease and desist from committing or causing such violation and any future violation of the same provision, rule, or regulation. Such order may, in addition to requiring a person to cease and desist from committing or causing a violation, require such person to comply, or to take steps to effect compliance, with such provision, rule, or regulation, upon such terms and conditions and within such time as the Commission may specify in such order. Any such order may, as the Commission deems appropriate, require future compliance or steps to effect future compliance, either permanently or for such period of time as the Commission may specify, with such provision, rule, or regulation with respect to any security, any issuer, or any other person.

(b) *Hearing.*—The notice instituting proceedings pursuant to subsection (a) shall fix a hearing date not earlier than 30 days nor later than 60 days after service of the notice unless an earlier or a later date is set by the Commission with the consent of any respondent so served.

(c) *Temporary Order.*—

(1) *In General.*—Whenever the Commission determines that the alleged violation or threatened violation specified in the notice instituting proceedings pursuant to subsection (a), or the continuation thereof, is likely to result in significant dissipation or conversion of assets, significant harm to investors, or substantial harm to the public interest, including, but not limited to, losses to the Securities Investor Protection Corporation, prior to the completion of the proceedings, the Commission may enter a temporary order requiring the respondent to cease and desist from the violation or threatened violation and to take such action to prevent the violation or threatened violation and to prevent dissipation or conversion of assets, significant harm to investors, or substantial harm to the public interest as the Commission deems appropriate pending completion of such proceedings. Such an order shall be entered only after notice and opportunity for a hearing, unless the Commission determines that notice and hearing prior to entry would be impracticable or contrary to the public interest. A temporary order shall become effective upon service upon the respondent and, unless set aside, limited, or suspended by the Commission or a court of competent jurisdiction, shall remain effective and enforceable pending the completion of the proceedings.

(2) *Applicability.*—Paragraph (1) shall apply only to a respondent that acts, or, at the time of the alleged misconduct acted, as a broker, dealer, investment adviser, investment company, municipal securities dealer, government securities broker, government securities dealer, registered public accounting firm (as defined in section 2 of the Sarbanes–Oxley Act of 2002), or transfer agent, or is, or was at the time of the alleged misconduct, an associated person of, or a person seeking to become associated with, any of the foregoing.

(3) *Temporary Freeze.*—

(A) *In general.*—

(i) *Issuance of temporary order.*—Whenever, during the course of a lawful investigation involving possible violations of the Federal securities laws by an issuer of publicly traded securities or any of its directors, officers, partners, controlling persons, agents, or employees, it shall appear to the Commission that it is likely that the issuer will make extraordinary payments (whether compensation or otherwise) to any of the foregoing persons, the Commission may petition a Federal district court for temporary order requiring the issuer to escrow, subject to court supervision, those payments in an interest-bearing account for 45 days.

(ii) *Standard.*—A temporary order shall be entered under clause (i), only after notice and opportunity for a hearing, unless the court determines that notice and hearing prior to entry of the order would be impracticable or contrary to the public interest.

(iii) *Effective period.*—A temporary order issued under clause (i) shall—

(I) become effective immediately;

(II) be served upon the parties subject to it; and

(III) unless set aside, limited or suspended by a court of competent jurisdiction, shall remain effective and enforceable for 45 days.

(iv) *Extensions authorized.*—The effective period of an order under this subparagraph may be extended by the court upon good cause shown for not longer than 45 additional days, provided that the combined period of the order shall not exceed 90 days.

(B) *Process on determination of violations.*—

(i) *Violations charged.*—If the issuer or other person described in subparagraph (A) is charged with any violation of the Federal securities laws before the expiration of the effective period of a temporary order under subparagraph (A) (including any applicable extension period), the order shall remain in effect, subject to court approval, until the conclusion of any legal proceedings related thereto, and the affected issuer or other person, shall have the right to petition the court for review of the order.

(ii) *Violations not charged.*—If the issuer or other person described in subparagraph (A) is not charged with any violation of the Federal securities laws before the expiration of the effective period of a temporary order under subparagraph (A) (including any applicable extension period), the escrow shall terminate at the expiration of the 45–day effective period (or the expiration of any extension period, as applicable), and the payments (with accrued interest) shall be returned to the issuer or other affected person.

(d) *Review of Temporary Orders.*—

(1) *Commission Review.*—At any time after the respondent has been served with a temporary cease-and-desist order pursuant to subsection (c), the respondent may apply to the Commission to have the order set aside, limited, or suspended. If the respondent has been served with a temporary cease-and-desist order entered without a prior Commission hearing, the respondent may, within 10 days after the date on which the order was served, request a hearing on such application and the Commission shall hold a hearing and render a decision on such application at the earliest possible time.

(2) *Judicial Review.* Within—

(A) 10 days after the date the respondent was served with a temporary cease-and-desist order entered with a prior Commission hearing, or

(B) 10 days after the Commission renders a decision on an application and hearing under paragraph (1), with respect to any temporary cease-and-desist order entered without a prior Commission hearing,

the respondent may apply to the United States district court for the district in which the respondent resides or has its principal place of business, or for the District of Columbia, for an order setting aside, limiting, or suspending the effectiveness or enforcement of the order, and the court shall have jurisdiction to enter such an order. A respondent served with a temporary cease-and-desist order entered without a prior Commission hearing may not apply to the court except after hearing and decision by the Commission on the respondent's application under paragraph (1) of this subsection.

(3) *No Automatic Stay of Temporary Order.*—The commencement of proceedings under paragraph (2) of this subsection shall not, unless specifically ordered by the court, operate as a stay of the Commission's order.

(4) *Exclusive Review.*—Section 25 of this title shall not apply to a temporary order entered pursuant to this section.

(e) *Authority to Enter an Order Requiring an Accounting and Disgorgement.*—In any cease-and-desist proceeding under subsection (a), the Commission may enter an order requiring accounting and disgorgement, including reasonable interest. The Commission is authorized to adopt rules, regulations, and orders concerning payments to investors, rates of interest, periods of accrual, and such other matters as it deems appropriate to implement this subsection.

(f) *Authority of the Commission to Prohibit Persons From Serving as Officers or Directors.*—In any cease-and-desist proceedings under subsection (a), the Commission may issue an order to prohibit, conditionally or unconditionally, and permanently or for such period of time as it shall determine, any person who has violated section 10(b) or the rules or regulations thereunder, from acting as an officer or director of any issuer that has a class of securities registered pursuant to section 12, or that is required to file reports pursuant to section 15(d), if the conduct of that person demonstrates unfitness to serve as an officer or director of any such issuer.

Sec. 21D. Private Securities Litigation.

(a) *Private Class Actions.*—

(1) In General.—The provisions of this subsection shall apply in each private action arising under this title that is brought as a plaintiff class action pursuant to the Federal Rules of Civil Procedure.

(2) *Certification Filed With Complaint.*—

(A) *In General.*—Each plaintiff seeking to serve as a representative party on behalf of a class shall provide a sworn certification, which shall be personally signed by such plaintiff and filed with the complaint, that—

(i) states that the plaintiff has reviewed the complaint and authorized its filing;

(ii) states that the plaintiff did not purchase the security that is the subject of the complaint at the direction of plaintiff's counsel or in order to participate in any private action arising under this title;

(iii) states that the plaintiff is willing to serve as a representative party on behalf of a class, including providing testimony at deposition and trial, if necessary;

(iv) sets forth all of the transactions of the plaintiff in the security that is the subject of the complaint during the class period specified in the complaint;

(v) identifies any other action under this title, filed during the 3–year period preceding the date on which the certification is signed by the plaintiff, in which the plaintiff has sought to serve as a representative party on behalf of a class; and

(vi) states that the plaintiff will not accept any payment for serving as a representative party on behalf of a class beyond the plaintiff's pro rata share of any recovery, except as ordered or approved by the court in accordance with paragraph (4).

(B) *Nonwaiver of Attorney–Client Privilege.*—The certification filed pursuant to subparagraph (A) shall not be construed to be a waiver of the attorney-client privilege.

(3) *Appointment of Lead Plaintiff.*—

(A) *Early Notice to Class Members.*—

(i) *In General.*—Not later than 20 days after the date on which the complaint is filed, the plaintiff or plaintiffs shall cause to be published, in a widely circulated national business-oriented publication or wire service, a notice advising members of the purported plaintiff class—

(I) of the pendency of the action, the claims asserted therein, and the purported class period; and

(II) that, not later than 60 days after the date on which the notice is published, any member of the purported class may move the court to serve as lead plaintiff of the purported class.

(ii) *Multiple Actions.*—If more than one action on behalf of a class asserting substantially the same claim or claims arising under this title is filed, only the plaintiff or plaintiffs in the first filed action shall be required to cause notice to be published in accordance with clause (i).

(iii) *Additional Notices May Be Required Under Federal Rules.*—Notice required under clause (i) shall be in addition to any notice required pursuant to the Federal Rules of Civil Procedure.

(B) *Appointment of Lead Plaintiff.*—

(i) *In General.*—Not later than 90 days after the date on which a notice is published under subparagraph (A)(i), the court shall consider any motion made by a purported class member in response to the notice, including any motion by a class member who is not individually named as a plaintiff in the complaint or complaints, and shall appoint as lead plaintiff the member or members of the purported plaintiff class that the court determines to be most capable of adequately representing the interests of class members (hereafter in this paragraph referred to as the "most adequate plaintiff") in accordance with this subparagraph.

(ii) *Consolidated Actions.*—If more than one action on behalf of a class asserting substantially the same claim or claims arising under this title has been filed, and any party has sought to consolidate those actions for pretrial purposes or for trial, the court shall not make the determination required by clause (i) until after the decision on the motion to consolidate is rendered. As soon as practicable after such decision is rendered, the court shall appoint the most adequate plaintiff as lead plaintiff for the consolidated actions in accordance with this paragraph.

(iii) *Rebuttable Presumption.*—

(I) *In General.*—Subject to subclause (II), for purposes of clause (i), the court shall adopt a presumption that the most adequate plaintiff in any private action arising under this title is the person or group of persons that—

(aa) has either filed the complaint or made a motion in response to a notice under subparagraph (A)(i);

(bb) in the determination of the court, has the largest financial interest in the relief sought by the class; and

(cc) otherwise satisfies the requirements of Rule 23 of the Federal Rules of Civil Procedure.

(II) *Rebuttal Evidence.*—The presumption described in subclause (1) may be rebutted only upon proof by a member of the purported plaintiff class that the presumptively most adequate plaintiff—

(aa) will not fairly and adequately protect the interests of the class; or

(bb) is subject to unique defenses that render such plaintiff incapable of adequately representing the class.

(iv) *Discovery.*—For purposes of this subparagraph, discovery relating to whether a member or members of the purported plaintiff class is the most adequate plaintiff may be conducted by a plaintiff only if the plaintiff first demonstrates a reasonable basis for a finding that the presumptively most adequate plaintiff is incapable of adequately representing the class.

(v) *Selection of Lead Counsel.*—The most adequate plaintiff shall, subject to the approval of the court, select and retain counsel to represent the class.

(vi) *Restrictions on Professional Plaintiffs.*—Except as the court may otherwise permit, consistent with the purposes of this section, a person may be a lead plaintiff, or an officer, director, or fiduciary of a lead plaintiff, in no more than 5 securities class actions brought as plaintiff class actions pursuant to the Federal Rules of Civil Procedure during any 3–year period.

(4) *Recovery by Plaintiffs.*—The share of any final judgment or of any settlement that is awarded to a representative party serving on behalf of a class shall be equal, on a per share basis, to the portion of the final judgment or settlement awarded to all other members of the class. Nothing in this paragraph shall be construed to limit the award of reasonable costs and expenses (including lost wages) directly relating to the representation of the class to any representative party serving on behalf of a class.

(5) *Restrictions on Settlements Under Seal.*—The terms and provisions of any settlement agreement of a class action shall not be filed under seal, except that on motion of any party to the settlement, the court may order filing under seal for those portions of a settlement agreement as to which good cause is shown for such filing under seal. For purposes of this paragraph, good cause shall exist only if publication of a term or provision of a settlement agreement would cause direct and substantial harm to any party.

(6) *Restrictions on Payment of Attorneys' Fees and Expenses.*—Total attorneys' fees and expenses awarded by the court to counsel for the plaintiff class shall not exceed a reasonable percentage of the amount of any damages and prejudgment interest actually paid to the class.

(7) *Disclosure of Settlement Terms to Class Members.*—Any proposed or final settlement agreement that is published or otherwise disseminated to the class shall include each of the following statements, along with a cover page summarizing the information contained in such statements:

(A) *Statement of Plaintiff Recovery.*—The amount of the settlement proposed to be distributed to the parties to the action, determined in the aggregate and on an average per share basis.

(B) *Statement of Potential Outcome of Case.*—

(i) *Agreement on Amount of Damages.*—If the settling parties agree on the average amount of damages per share that would be recoverable if the plaintiff prevailed on each claim alleged under this title, a statement concerning the average amount of such potential damages per share.

(ii) *Disagreement on Amount of Damages.*—If the parties do not agree on the average amount of damages per share that would be recoverable if the plaintiff prevailed on each claim alleged under this title, a statement from each settling party concerning the issue or issues on which the parties disagree.

(iii) *Inadmissibility for Certain Purposes.*—A statement made in accordance with clause (i) or (ii) concerning the amount of damages shall not be admissible in any Federal or State judicial action or administrative proceeding, other than an action or proceeding arising out of such statement.

(C) *Statement of Attorneys' Fees or Costs Sought.*—If any of the settling parties or their counsel intend to apply to the court for an award of attorneys' fees or costs from any fund established as part of the settlement, a statement indicating which parties or counsel intend to make such an application, the amount of fees and costs that will be sought (including the amount of such fees and costs determined on an average per share basis), and a brief explanation supporting the fees and costs sought. Such information shall be clearly summarized on the cover page of any notice to a party of any proposed or final settlement agreement.

(D) *Identification of Lawyers' Representatives.*—The name, telephone number, and address of one or more representatives of counsel for the plaintiff class who will be reasonably available to answer questions from class members concerning any matter contained in any notice of settlement published or otherwise disseminated to the class.

(E) *Reasons for Settlement.*—A brief statement explaining the reasons why the parties are proposing the settlement.

(F) *Other Information.*—Such other information as may be required by the court.

(8) *Security for Payment of Costs in Class Actions.*—In any private action arising under this title that is certified as a class action pursuant to the Federal Rules of Civil Procedure, the court may require an undertaking from the attorneys for the plaintiff class, the plaintiff class, or both, or from the attorneys for the defendant, the defendant, or both, in such proportions and at such times as the court determines are just and equitable, for the payment of fees and expenses that may be awarded under this subsection.

(9) *Attorney Conflict of Interest.*—If a plaintiff class is represented by an attorney who directly owns or otherwise has a beneficial interest in the securities that are the subject of the litigation, the court shall make a determination of whether such ownership or other interest constitutes a conflict of interest sufficient to disqualify the attorney from representing the plaintiff class.

(b) *Requirements for Securities Fraud Actions.*—

(1) *Misleading Statements and Omissions.*—In any private action arising under this title in which the plaintiff alleges that the defendant—

(A) made an untrue statement of a material fact; or

(B) omitted to state a material fact necessary in order to make the statements made, in the light of the circumstances in which they were made, not misleading;

the complaint shall specify each statement alleged to have been misleading, the reason or reasons why the statement is misleading, and, if an allegation regarding the statement or omission is made on information and belief, the complaint shall state with particularity all facts on which that belief is formed.

(2) *Required State of Mind.*—In any private action arising under this title in which the plaintiff may recover money damages only on proof that the defendant acted with a particular state of mind, the complaint shall, with respect to each act or omission alleged to violate this title, state with particularity facts giving rise to a strong inference that the defendant acted with the required state of mind.

(3) *Motion to Dismiss; Stay of Discovery.*—

(A) *Dismissal for Failure to Meet Pleading Requirements.*—In any private action arising under this title, the court shall, on the motion of any defendant, dismiss the complaint if the requirements of paragraphs (1) and (2) are not met.

(B) *Stay of Discovery.*—In any private action arising under this title, all discovery and other proceedings shall be stayed during the pendency of any motion to dismiss, unless the court finds upon the motion of any party that particularized discovery is necessary to preserve evidence or to prevent undue prejudice to that party.

(C) *Preservation of Evidence.—*

(i) *In General.*—During the pendency of any stay of discovery pursuant to this paragraph, unless otherwise ordered by the court, any party to the action with actual notice of the allegations contained in the complaint shall treat all documents, data compilations (including electronically recorded or stored data), and tangible objects that are in the custody or control of such person and that are relevant to the allegations, as if they were the subject of a continuing request for production of documents from an opposing party under the Federal Rules of Civil Procedure.

(ii) *Sanction for Willful Violation.*—A party aggrieved by the willful failure of an opposing party to comply with clause (i) may apply to the court for an order awarding appropriate sanctions.

(D) *Circumvention of Stay of Discovery.*—Upon a proper showing, a court may stay discovery proceedings in any private action in a State court, as necessary in aid of its jurisdiction, or to protect or effectuate its judgments, in an action subject to a stay of discovery pursuant to this paragraph.

(4) *Loss Causation.*—In any private action arising under this title, the plaintiff shall have the burden of proving that the act or omission of the defendant alleged to violate this title caused the loss for which the plaintiff seeks to recover damages.

(c) *Sanctions for Abusive Litigation.—*

(1) *Mandatory Review by Court.*—In any private action arising under this title, upon final adjudication of the action, the court shall include in the record specific findings regarding compliance by each party and each attorney representing any party with each requirement of Rule 11(b) of the Federal Rules of Civil Procedure as to any complaint, responsive pleading, or dispositive motion.

(2) *Mandatory Sanctions.*—If the court makes a finding under paragraph (1) that a party or attorney violated any requirement of Rule 11(b) of the Federal Rules of Civil Procedure as to any complaint, responsive pleading, or dispositive motion, the court shall impose sanctions on such party or attorney in accordance with Rule 11 of the Federal Rules of Civil Procedure. Prior to making a finding that any party or attorney has violated Rule 11 of the Federal Rules of Civil Procedure, the court shall give such party or attorney notice and an opportunity to respond.

(3) *Presumption in Favor of Attorneys' Fees and Costs.—*

(A) *In General.*—Subject to subparagraphs (B) and (C), for purposes of paragraph (2), the court shall adopt a presumption that the appropriate sanction—

(i) for failure of any responsive pleading or dispositive motion to comply with any requirement of Rule 11(b) of the Federal Rules of Civil Procedure is an award to the opposing party of the reasonable attorneys' fees and other expenses incurred as a direct result of the violation; and

(ii) for substantial failure of any complaint to comply with any requirement of Rule 11(b) of the Federal Rules of Civil Procedure is an award to the opposing party of the reasonable attorneys' fees and other expenses incurred in the action.

(B) *Rebuttal Evidence.* The presumption described in subparagraph (A) may be rebutted only upon proof by the party or attorney against whom sanctions are to be imposed that—

(i) the award of attorneys' fees and other expenses will impose an unreasonable burden on that party or attorney and would be unjust, and the failure to make such an award would not impose a greater burden on the party in whose favor sanctions are to be imposed; or

(ii) the violation of Rule 11(b) of the Federal Rules of Civil Procedure was de minimis.

(C) *Sanctions.*—If the party or attorney against whom sanctions are to be imposed meet its burden under subparagraph (B), the court shall award the sanctions that the court deems appropriate pursuant to Rule 11 of the Federal Rules of Civil Procedure.

(d) *Defendant's Right to Written Interrogatories.*—In any private action arising under this title in which the plaintiff may recover money damages, the court shall, when requested by a defendant, submit to the jury a written interrogatory on the issue of each such defendant's state of mind at the time the alleged violation occurred.

(e) *Limitation on Damages.*—

(1) *In General.*—Except as provided in paragraph (2), in any private action arising under this title in which the plaintiff seeks to establish damages by reference to the market price of a security, the award of damages to the plaintiff shall not exceed the difference between the purchase or sale price paid or received, as appropriate, by the plaintiff for the subject security and the mean trading price of that security during the 90–day period beginning on the date on which the information correcting the misstatement or omission that is the basis for the action is disseminated to the market.

(2) *Exception.*—In any private action arising under this title in which the plaintiff seeks to establish damages by reference to the market price of a security, if the plaintiff sells or repurchases the subject security prior to the expiration of the 90–day period described in paragraph (1), the plaintiff's damages shall not exceed the difference between the purchase or sale price paid or received, as appropriate, by the plaintiff for the security and the mean trading price of the security during the period beginning immediately after dissemination of information correcting the misstatement or omission and ending on the date on which the plaintiff sells or repurchases the security.

(3) *Definition.*—For purposes of this subsection, the "mean trading price" of a security shall be an average of the daily trading price of that security, determined as of the close of the market each day during the 90–day period referred to in paragraph (1).

(f) *Proportionate Liability.*—

(1) *Applicability.*—Nothing in this subsection shall be construed to create, affect, or in any manner modify, the standard for liability associated with any action arising under the securities laws.

(2) *Liability for Damages.*—

(A) *Joint and Several Liability.*—Any covered person against whom a final judgment is entered in a private action shall be liable for damages jointly and severally only if the trier of fact specifically determines that such covered person knowingly committed a violation of the securities laws.

(B) *Proportionate Liability.*—

(i) *In General.*—Except as provided in subparagraph (A), a covered person against whom a final judgment is entered in a private action shall be liable solely for the portion of the judgment that corresponds to the percentage of responsibility of that covered person, as determined under paragraph (3).

(ii) *Recovery by and Costs of Covered Person.*—In any case in which a contractual relationship permits, a covered person that prevails in any private action may recover the attorney's fees and costs of that covered person in connection with the action.

(3) *Determination of Responsibility.*—

(A) *In General.*—In any private action, the court shall instruct the jury to answer special interrogatories, or if there is no jury, shall make findings, with respect to each covered person and each of the other persons claimed by any of the parties to have caused or contributed to the loss incurred by the plaintiff, including persons who have entered into settlements with the plaintiff or plaintiffs, concerning—

(i) whether such person violated the securities laws;

(ii) the percentage of responsibility of such person, measured as a percentage of the total fault of all persons who caused or contributed to the loss incurred by the plaintiff; and

(iii) whether such person knowingly committed a violation of the securities laws.

(B) *Contents of Special Interrogatories or Findings.*—The responses to interrogatories, or findings, as appropriate, under subparagraph (A) shall specify the total amount of damages that the plaintiff is entitled to recover and the percentage of responsibility of each covered person found to have caused or contributed to the loss incurred by the plaintiff or plaintiffs.

(C) *Factors for Consideration.*—In determining the percentage of responsibility under this paragraph, the trier of fact shall consider—

(i) the nature of the conduct of each covered person found to have caused or contributed to the loss incurred by the plaintiff or plaintiffs; and

(ii) the nature and extent of the causal relationship between the conduct of each such person and the damages incurred by the plaintiff or plaintiffs.

(4) *Uncollectible Share.*—

(A) *In General.*—Notwithstanding paragraph (2)(B), upon motion made not later than 6 months after a final judgment is entered in any private action, the court determines that all or part of the share of the judgment of the covered person is not collectible against that covered person, and is also not collectible against a covered person described in paragraph (2)(A), each covered person described in paragraph (2)(B) shall be liable for the uncollectible share as follows:

(i) *Percentage of Net Worth.*—Each covered person shall be jointly and severally liable for the uncollectible share if the plaintiff establishes that—

(I) the plaintiff is an individual whose recoverable damages under the final judgment are equal to more than 10 percent of the net worth of the plaintiff; and

(II) the net worth of the plaintiff is equal to less than $200,000.

(ii) *Other Plaintiffs.*—With respect to any plaintiff not described in subclauses (I) and (II) of clause (i), each covered person shall be liable for the uncollectible share in proportion to the percentage of responsibility of that covered person, except that the total liability of a covered person under this clause may not exceed 50 percent of the proportionate share of that covered person, as determined under paragraph (3)(B).

(iii) *Net Worth.*—For purposes of this subparagraph, net worth shall be determined as of the date immediately preceding the date of the purchase or sale (as applicable) by the plaintiff of the security that is the subject of the action, and shall be equal to the fair market value of assets, minus liabilities, including the net value of the investments of the plaintiff in real and personal property (including personal residences).

(B) *Overall Limit.*—In no case shall the total payments required pursuant to subparagraph (A) exceed the amount of the uncollectible share.

(C) *Covered Persons Subject to Contribution.*—A covered person against whom judgment is not collectible shall be subject to contribution and to any continuing liability to the plaintiff on the judgment.

(5) *Right of Contribution.*—To the extent that a covered person is required to make an additional payment pursuant to paragraph (4), that covered person may recover contribution—

(A) from the covered person originally liable to make the payment;

(B) from any covered person liable jointly and severally pursuant to paragraph (2)(A);

(C) from any covered person held proportionately liable pursuant to this paragraph who is liable to make the same payment and has paid less than his or her proportionate share of that payment; or

(D) from any other person responsible for the conduct giving rise to the payment that would have been liable to make the same payment.

(6) *Nondisclosure to Jury.*—The standard for allocation of damages under paragraphs (2) and (3) and the procedure for reallocation of uncollectible shares under paragraph (4) shall not be disclosed to members of the jury.

(7) *Settlement Discharge.*—

(A) *In General.*—A covered person who settles any private action at any time before final verdict or judgment shall be discharged from all claims for contribution brought by other persons. Upon entry of the settlement by the court, the court shall enter a bar order constituting the final discharge of all obligations to the plaintiff of the settling covered person arising out of the action. The order shall bar all future claims for contribution arising out of the action—

(i) by any person against the settling covered person; and

(ii) by the settling covered person against any person, other than a person whose liability has been extinguished by the settlement of the settling covered person.

(B) *Reduction.*—If a covered person enters into a settlement with the plaintiff prior to final verdict or judgment, the verdict or judgment shall be reduced by the greater of—

(i) an amount that corresponds to the percentage of responsibility of that covered person; or

(ii) the amount paid to the plaintiff by that covered person.

(8) *Contribution.*—A covered person who becomes jointly and severally liable for damages in any private action may recover contribution from any other person who, if joined in the original action, would have been liable for the same damages. A claim for contribution shall be determined based on the percentage of responsibility of the claimant and of each person against whom a claim for contribution is made.

(9) *Statute of Limitations for Contribution.*—In any private action determining liability, an action for contribution shall be brought not later than 6 months after the entry of a final, nonappealable judgment in the action, except that an action for contribution brought by a covered person who was required to make an additional payment pursuant to paragraph (4) may be brought not later than 6 months after the date on which such payment was made.

(10) *Definitions.*—For purposes of this subsection—

(A) a covered person "knowingly commits a violation of the securities laws"—

(i) with respect to an action that is based on an untrue statement of material fact or omission of a material fact necessary to make the statement not misleading, if—

(I) that covered person makes an untrue statement of a material fact, with actual knowledge that the representation is false, or omits to state a fact necessary in order to make the statement made not misleading, with actual knowledge that, as a result of the omission, one of the material representations of the covered person is false; and

(II) persons are likely to reasonably rely on that misrepresentation or omission; and

(ii) with respect to an action that is based on any conduct that is not described in clause (i), if that covered person engages in that conduct with actual knowledge of the facts and circumstances that make the conduct of that covered person a violation of the securities laws;

(B) reckless conduct by a covered person shall not be construed to constitute a knowing commission of a violation of the securities laws by that covered person;

(C) the term "covered person" means—

(i) a defendant in any private action arising under this title; or

(ii) a defendant in any private action arising under section 11 of the Securities Act of 1933, who is an outside director of the issuer of the securities that are the subject of the action; and

(D) the term "outside director" shall have the meaning given such term by rule or regulation of the Commission.

Sec. 21E. Application of Safe Harbor for Forward–Looking Statements.

(a) *Applicability.*—This section shall apply only to a forward-looking statement made by—

(1) an issuer that, at the time that the statement is made, is subject to the reporting requirements of section 13(a) or section 15(d);

(2) a person acting on behalf of such issuer;

(3) an outside reviewer retained by such issuer making a statement on behalf of such issuer; or

(4) an underwriter, with respect to information provided by such issuer or information derived from information provided by such issuer.

(b) *Exclusions.*—Except to the extent otherwise specifically provided by rule, regulation, or order of the Commission, this section shall not apply to a forward-looking statement—

(1) that is made with respect to the business or operations of the issuer, if the issuer—

(A) during the 3–year period preceding the date on which the statement was first made—

(i) was convicted of any felony or misdemeanor described in clauses (i) through (iv) of section 15(b)(4)(B); or

(ii) has been made the subject of a judicial or administrative decree or order arising out of a governmental action that—

(I) prohibits future violations of the antifraud provisions of the securities laws;

(II) requires that the issuer cease and desist from violating the antifraud provisions of the securities laws; or

(III) determines that the issuer violated the antifraud provisions of the securities laws;

(B) makes the forward-looking statement in connection with an offering of securities by a blank check company;

(C) issues penny stock;

(D) makes the forward-looking statement in connection with a rollup transaction; or

(E) makes the forward-looking statement in connection with a going private transaction; or

(2) that is—

(A) included in a financial statement prepared in accordance with generally accepted accounting principles;

(B) contained in a registration statement of, or otherwise issued by, an investment company;

(C) made in connection with a tender offer;

(D) made in connection with an initial public offering;

(E) made in connection with an offering by, or relating to the operations of, a partnership, limited liability company, or a direct participation investment program; or

(F) made in a disclosure of beneficial ownership in a report required to be filed with the Commission pursuant to section 13(d).

(c) *Safe Harbor.*—

(1) *In General.*—Except as provided in subsection (b), in any private action arising under this title that is based on an untrue statement of a material fact or omission of a material fact necessary to make the statement not misleading, a person referred to in subsection (a) shall not be liable with respect to any forward-looking statement, whether written or oral, if and to the extent that—

(A) the forward-looking statement is—

(i) identified as a forward-looking statement, and is accompanied by meaningful cautionary statements identifying important factors that could cause actual results to differ materially from those in the forward-looking statement; or

(ii) immaterial; or

(B) the plaintiff fails to prove that the forward-looking statement—

(i) if made by a natural person, was made with actual knowledge by that person that the statement was false or misleading; or

(ii) if made by a business entity; was—

(I) made by or with the approval of an executive officer of that entity; and

(II) made or approved by such officer with actual knowledge by that officer that the statement was false or misleading.

(2) *Oral Forward–Looking Statements.*—In the case of an oral forward-looking statement made by an issuer that is subject to the reporting requirements of section 13(a) or section 15(d), or by a person acting on behalf of such issuer, the requirement set forth in paragraph (1)(A) shall be deemed to be satisfied—

(A) if the oral forward-looking statement is accompanied by a cautionary statement—

(i) that the particular oral statement is a forward-looking statement; and

(ii) that the actual results might differ materially from those projected in the forward-looking statement; and

(B) if—

(i) the oral forward-looking statement is accompanied by an oral statement that additional information concerning factors that could cause actual results to materially differ from those in the forward-looking statement is contained in a readily available written document, or portion thereof;

(ii) the accompanying oral statement referred to in clause (i) identifies the document, or portion thereof, that contains the additional information about those factors relating to the forward-looking statement; and

(iii) the information contained in that written document is a cautionary statement that satisfies the standard established in paragraph (1)(A).

(3) *Availability.*—Any document filed with the Commission or generally disseminated shall be deemed to be readily available for purposes of paragraph (2).

(4) *Effect on Other Safe Harbors.*—The exemption provided for in paragraph (1) shall be in addition to any exemption that the Commission may establish by rule or regulation under subsection (g).

(d) *Duty to Update.*—Nothing in this section shall impose upon any person a duty to update a forward-looking statement.

(e) *Dispositive Motion.*—On any motion to dismiss based upon subsection (c)(1), the court shall consider any statement cited in the complaint and any cautionary statement accompanying the forward-looking statement, which are not subject to material dispute, cited by the defendant.

(f) *Stay Pending Decision on Motion.*—In any private action arising under this title, the court shall stay discovery (other than discovery that is specifically directed to the applicability of the exemption provided for in this section) during the pendency of any motion by a defendant for summary judgment that is based on the grounds that—

(1) the statement or omission upon which the complaint is based is a forward-looking statement within the meaning of this section; and

(2) the exemption provided for in this section precludes a claim for relief.

(g) *Exemption Authority.*—In addition to the exemptions provided for in this section, the Commission may, by rule or regulation, provide exemptions from or under any provision of this title, including with respect to liability that is based on a statement or that is based on projections or other forward-looking information, if and to the extent that any such exemption is consistent with the public interest and the protection of investors, as determined by the Commission.

(h) *Effect on Other Authority of Commission.*—Nothing in this section limits, either expressly or by implication, the authority of the Commission to exercise similar authority or to adopt similar rules and regulations with respect to forward-looking statements under any other statute under which the Commission exercises rulemaking authority.

(i) *Definitions.*—For purposes of this section, the following definitions shall apply:

(1) *Forward–Looking Statement.*—The term ''forward-looking statement'' means—

(A) a statement containing a projection of revenues, income (including income loss), earnings (including earnings loss) per share, capital expenditures, dividends, capital structure, or other financial items;

(B) a statement of the plans and objectives of management for future operations, including plans or objectives relating to the products or services of the issuer;

(C) a statement of future economic performance, including any such statement contained in a discussion and analysis of financial condition by the management or in the results of operations included pursuant to the rules and regulations of the Commission;

(D) any statement of the assumptions underlying or relating to any statement described in subparagraph (A), (B), or (C);

(E) any report issued by an outside reviewer retained by an issuer, to the extent that the report assesses a forward-looking statement made by the issuer; or

(F) a statement containing a projection or estimate of such other items as may be specified by rule or regulation of the Commission.

(2) *Investment Company.*—The term ''investment company'' has the same meaning

as in section 3(a) of the Investment Company Act of 1940.

(3) *Going Private Transaction.*—The term "going private transaction" has the meaning given that term under the rules or regulations of the Commission issued pursuant to section 13(e).

(4) *Person Acting on Behalf of an Issuer.*—The term "person acting on behalf of an issuer" means any officer, director, or employee of such issuer.

(5) *Other Terms.*—The terms "blank check company", "roll-up transaction", "partnership", "limited liability company", "executive officer of an entity" and "direct participation investment program", have the meanings given those terms by rule or regulation of the Commission.

Hearings by Commission

Sec. 22. Hearings may be public and may be held before the Commission, any member or members thereof, or any officer or officers of the Commission designated by it, and appropriate records thereof shall be kept.

Rules, Regulations, and Orders; Annual Reports

Sec. 23. (a)(1) The Commission, the Board of Governors of the Federal Reserve System, and the other agencies enumerated in section 3(a)(34) of this title shall each have power to make such rules and regulations as may be necessary or appropriate to implement the provisions of this title for which they are responsible or for the execution of the functions vested in them by this title, and may for such purposes classify persons, securities, transactions, statements, applications, reports, and other matters within their respective jurisdictions, and prescribe greater, lesser, or different requirements for different classes thereof. No provision of this title imposing any liability shall apply to any act done or omitted in good faith in conformity with a rule, regulation, or order of the Commission, the Board of Governors of the Federal Reserve System, other agency enumerated in section 3(a)(34) of this title or any self-regulatory organization, notwithstanding that such rule, regulation, or order may thereafter be amended or rescinded or determined by judicial or other authority to be invalid for any reason.

(2) The Commission and the Secretary of the Treasury, in making rules and regulations pursuant to any provisions of this title, shall consider among other matters the impact any such rule or regulation would have on competition. The Commission and the Secretary of the Treasury shall not adopt any such rule or regulation which would impose a burden on competition not necessary or appropriate in furtherance of the purposes of this title. The Commission and the Secretary of the Treasury shall include in the statement of basis and purpose incorporated in any rule or regulation adopted under this title, the reasons for the Commission's or the Secretary's determination that any burden on competition imposed by such rule or regulation is necessary or appropriate in furtherance of the purposes of this title.

(3) The Commission and the Secretary in making rules and regulations pursuant to any provision of this title, considering any application for registration in accordance with section 19(a) of this title, or reviewing any proposed rule change of a self-regulatory organization in accordance with section 19(b) of this title, shall keep in a public file and make available for copying all written statements filed with the Commission and the Secretary and all written communications between the Commission and the Secretary and any person relating to the proposed rule, regulation, application, or proposed rule change; *Provided, however,* That the Commission and the Secretary shall not be required to keep in a public file or make available for copying and such statement or communication which it may withhold from the public in accordance with the provisions of section 552 of title 5, United States Code,

(b)(1) The Commission, the Board of Governors of the Federal Reserve System, and the other agencies enumerated in section 3(a)(34) of this title, shall each make an annual report to the Congress on its work for the preceding year, and shall include in each such report whatever information, data, and recommendations for further legislation it considers advisable with regard to matters within its respective jurisdiction under this title.

(2) The appropriate regulatory agency for a self-regulatory organization shall include in its annual report to the Congress for each fiscal year, a summary of its oversight activities under this title with respect to such self-regulatory organization, including a description of any examination conducted as part of such activities of any such organization, any material recommendation presented as part of such activities to such organization for changes in its organization or rules, and any action by such organization in response to any such recommendation.

(3) The appropriate regulatory agency for any class of municipal securities dealers shall include in its annual report to the Congress for each fiscal year a summary of its regulatory activities pursuant to this title with respect to such municipal securities dealers, including the nature of and reason for any sanction imposed pursuant to this title against any such municipal securities dealer.

(4) The Commission shall also include in its annual report to the Congress for each fiscal year—

(A) a summary of the Commission's oversight activities with respect to self-regulatory organizations for which it is not the appropriate regulatory agency, including a description of any examination of any such organization, any material recommendation presented to any such organization for changes in its organization or rules, and any action by any such organization in response to any such recommendation;

(B) a statement and analysis of the expenses and operations of each self-regulatory organization in connection with the performance of its responsibilities under this title, for which purpose data pertaining to such expenses and operations shall be made available by such organization to the Commission at its request;

(C) the steps the Commission has taken and the progress it has made toward ending the physical movement of the securities certificate in connection with the settlement of securities transactions, and its recommendations, if any, for legislation to eliminate the securities certificate;

(D) the number of requests for exemptions from provisions of this title received, the number granted, and the basis upon which any such exemption was granted;

(E) a summary of the Commission's regulatory activities with respect to municipal securities dealers for which it is not the appropriate regulatory agency, including the nature of, and reason for, any sanction imposed in proceedings against such municipal securities dealers;

(F) a statement of the time elapsed between the filing of reports pursuant to section 13(f) of this title and the public availability of the information contained therein, the costs involved in the Commission's processing of such reports and tabulating such information, the manner in which the Commission uses such information, and the steps the Commission has taken and the progress it has made toward requiring such reports to be filed and such information to be made available to the public in machine language;

(G) information concerning (i) the effects its rules and regulations are having on the viability of small brokers and dealers; (ii) its attempts to reduce any unnecessary reporting burden on such brokers and dealers; and (iii) its efforts to help to assure the continued participation of small brokers and dealers in the United States securities markets;

(H) a statement detailing its administration of the Freedom of Information Act, section 552 of title 5, United States Code, including a copy of the report filed pursuant to subsection (d) of such section; and

(I) the steps that have been taken and the progress that has been made in promoting the timely public dissemination and availability for analytical purposes (on a fair, reasonable, and nondiscriminatory basis) of information concerning government securities transactions and quotations, and its recommendations, if any, for legislation to assure timely dissemination of (i) information on transactions in regularly traded government securities sufficient to permit the determination of the prevailing market price for such securities, and (ii) reports of the highest published bids and lowest published offers for government securities (including the size at which persons are willing to trade with respect to such bids and offers).

(c) The Commission, by rule, shall prescribe the procedure applicable to every case pursuant to this title of adjudication (as defined in section 551 of title 5, United States Code) not required to be determined on the record after notice and opportunity for hearing. Such rules shall, as a minimum, provide that prompt notice shall be given of any adverse action or final disposition and that such notice and the entry of any order shall be accompanied by a statement of written reasons.

(d) *Cease-and-Desist Procedures.*—Within 1 year after the date of enactment of this subsection, the Commission shall establish regulations providing for the expeditious conduct of hearings and rendering of decisions under section 21C of this title, section 8A of the Securities Act of 1933, section 9(f) of the Investment Company Act of 1940, and section 203(k) of the Investment Advisers Act of 1940.

Public Availability of Information

Sec. 24. (a) For purposes of section 552 of title 5, United States Code, the term "records" includes all applications, statements, reports, contracts, correspondence, notices, and other documents filed with or otherwise obtained by the Commission pursuant to this title or otherwise.

(b) It shall be unlawful for any member, officer, or employee of the Commission to disclose to any person other than a member, officer, or employee of the Commission, or to use for personal benefit, any information contained in any application, statement, report, contract, correspondence, notice, or other document filed with or otherwise obtained by the Commission (1) in contravention of the rules and regulations of the Commission under section 552 of Title 5, United States Code, or (2) in circumstances where the Commission has determined pursuant to such rules to accord confidential treatment to such information.

(c) *Confidential Disclosures.*—The Commission may, in its discretion and a showing that such information is needed, provide all "records" (as defined in subsection (a)) and other information in its possession to such persons, both domestic and foreign, as the Commission by rule deems appropriate if the person receiving such records or information provides such assurances of confidentiality as the Commission deems appropriate.

(d) *Records Obtained From Foreign Securities Authorities.*—Except as provided in subsection (e), the Commission shall not be compelled to disclose records obtained from a foreign securities authority if (1) the foreign securities authority has in good faith determined and represented to the Commission that public disclosure of such records would violate the laws applicable to that foreign securities authority, and (2) the Commission obtains such records pursuant to (A) such procedure as the Commission may authorize for use in connection with the administration or enforcement of the securities laws, or (B) a memorandum of understanding. For purposes of section 552 of title 5, United States Code, this subsection shall be considered a statute described in subsection (b)(3)(B) of such section 552.

(e) *Savings Provisions.*—Nothing in this section shall—

(1) alter the Commission's responsibilities under the Right to Financial Privacy Act (12 U.S.C. 3401 et seq.), as limited by section 21(h) of this Act, with respect to transfers of records covered by such statutes, or

(2) authorize the Commission to withhold information from the Congress or prevent the Commission from complying with an order of a court of the United States in an action commenced by the United States or the Commission.

Court Review of Orders and Rules

Sec. 25. (a)(1) A person aggrieved by a final order of the Commission entered pursuant to this title may obtain review of the order in the United States Court of Appeals for the circuit in which he resides or has his principal place of business, or for the District of Columbia Circuit, by filing in such court, within sixty days after the entry of the order, a written petition requesting that the order be modified or set aside in whole or in part.

(2) A copy of the petition shall be transmitted forthwith by the clerk of the court to a member of the Commission or an officer designated by the Commission for that purpose. Thereupon the Commission shall file in the court the record on which the order complained of is entered, as provided in section 2112 of title 28, United States Code, and the Federal Rules of Appellate Procedure.

(3) On the filing of the petition, the court has jurisdiction, which becomes exclusive on the filing of the record, to affirm or modify and enforce or to set aside the order in whole or in part.

(4) The findings of the Commission as to the facts, if supported by substantial evidence, are conclusive.

(5) If either party applies to the court for leave to adduce additional evidence and shows to the satisfaction of the court that the additional evidence is material and that there was reasonable ground for failure to adduce it before the Commission, the court may remand the case to the Commission for further proceedings, in whatever manner and on whatever conditions the court considers appropriate. If the case is remanded to the Commission, it shall file in the court a supplemental record containing any new evidence, any further or modified findings, and any new order.

(b)(1) A person adversely affected by a rule of the Commission promulgated pursuant to section 6, 9(h)(2), 11, 11A, 15(c)(5) or (6), 15A, 17, 17A, or 19 of this title may obtain review of this rule in the United States Court of Appeals for the circuit in which he resides or has his principal place of business or for the District of Columbia Circuit, by filing in such court, within sixty days after the promulgation of the rule, a written petition requesting that the rule be set aside.

(2) A copy of the petition shall be transmitted forthwith by the clerk of the court to a member of the Commission or an officer designated for that purpose. Thereupon, the Commission shall file in the court the rule under review and any documents referred to therein, the Commission's notice of proposed rulemaking and any documents referred to therein, all written submissions and the transcript of any oral presentations in the rulemaking, factual information not included in the foregoing that was considered by the Commission in the promulgation of the rule or proffered by the Commission as pertinent to the rule, the report of any advisory committee received or considered by the Commission in the rulemaking, and any other materials prescribed by the court.

(3) On the filing of the petition, the court has jurisdiction, which becomes exclusive on the filing of the materials set forth in paragraph (2) of this subsection, to affirm and enforce or to set aside the rule.

(4) The findings of the Commission as to the facts identified by the Commission as the basis, in whole or in part, of the rule, if supported by substantial evidence, are conclusive. The court shall affirm and enforce the rule unless the Commission's action in promulgating the rule is found to be arbitrary, capricious, an abuse of discretion, or otherwise not

in accordance with law; contrary to constitutional right, power, privilege, or immunity; in excess of statutory jurisdiction, authority, or limitations, or short of statutory right; or without observance of procedure required by law.

(5) If proceedings have been instituted under this subsection in two or more courts of appeals with respect to the same rule, the Commission shall file the materials set forth in paragraph (2) of this subsection in that court in which a proceeding was first instituted. The other courts shall thereupon transfer all such proceedings to the court in which the materials have been filed. For the convenience of the parties in the interest of justice that court may thereafter transfer all the proceedings to any other court of appeals.

(c)(1) No objection to an order or rule of the Commission, for which review is sought under this section, may be considered by the court unless it was urged before the Commission or there was reasonable ground for failure to do so.

(2) The filing of a petition under this section does not operate as a stay of the Commission's order or rule. Until the court's jurisdiction becomes exclusive, the Commission may stay its order or rule pending judicial review if it finds that justice so requires. After the filing of a petition under this section, the court, on whatever conditions may be required and to the extent necessary to prevent irreparable injury, may issue all necessary and appropriate process to stay the order or rule or to preserve status or rights pending its review; but (notwithstanding section 705 of title 5, United States Code) no such process may be issued by the court before the filing of the record or the materials set forth in subsection (b)(2) of this section unless: (A) the Commission has denied a stay or failed to grant requested relief, (B) a reasonable period has expired since the filing of an application for a stay without a decision by the Commission, or (C) there was reasonable ground for failure to apply to the Commission.

(3) When the same order or rule is the subject of one or more petitions for review filed under this section and an action for enforcement filed in a district court of the United States under section 21(d) or (e) of this title, that court in which the petition or the action is first filed has jurisdiction with respect to the order or rule to the exclusion of any other court, and thereupon all such proceedings shall be transferred to that court; but, for the convenience of the parties in the interest of justice, that court may thereafter transfer all the proceedings to any other court of appeals or district court of the United States, whether or not a petition for review or an action for enforcement was originally filed in the transferee court. The scope of review by a district court under section 21(d) or (e) of this title is in all cases the same as by a court of appeals under this section.

(d)(1) For purposes of the preceding subsections of this section, the term "Commission" includes the agencies enumerated in section 3(a)(34) of this title insofar as such agencies are acting pursuant to this title and the Secretary of the Treasury insofar as he is acting pursuant to section 15C of this title.

(2) For purposes of subsection (a)(4) of this section and section 706 of title 5, United States Code, an order of the Commission pursuant to section 19(a) of this title denying registration to a clearing agency for which the Commission is not the appropriate regulatory agency or pursuant to section 19(b) of this title disapproving a proposed rule change by such a clearing agency shall be deemed to be an order of the appropriate regulatory agency for such clearing agency insofar as such order was entered by reason of a determination by such appropriate regulatory agency pursuant to section 19(a)(2)(C) or 19(b)(4)(C) of this title that such registration or proposed rule change would be inconsistent with the safeguarding of securities or funds.

Unlawful Representations

Sec. 26. No action or failure to act by the Commission or the Board of Governors of the

Federal Reserve System, in the administration of this title shall be construed to mean that the particular authority has in any way passed upon the merits of, or given approval to, any security or any transaction or transactions therein, nor shall such action or failure to act with regard to any statement or report filed with or examined by such authority pursuant to this title or rules and regulations thereunder, be deemed a finding by such authority that such statement or report is true and accurate on its face or that it is not false or misleading. It shall be unlawful to make, or cause to be made, to any prospective purchaser or seller of a security any representation that any such action or failure to act by any such authority is to be so construed or has such effect.

Jurisdiction of Offenses and Suits

Sec. 27. The district courts of the United States and the United States courts of any Territory or other place subject to the jurisdiction of the United States shall have exclusive jurisdiction of violations of this title or the rules and regulations thereunder, and of all suits in equity and actions at law brought to enforce any liability or duty created by this title or the rules and regulations thereunder. Any criminal proceeding may be brought in the district wherein any act or transaction constituting the violation occurred. Any suit or action to enforce any liability or duty created by this title or rules and regulations thereunder, or enjoin any violation of such title or rules and regulations, may be brought in any such district or in the district wherein the defendant is found or is an inhabitant or transacts business, and process in such cases may be served in any other district of which the defendant is an inhabitant or wherever the defendant may be found. Judgments and decrees so rendered shall be subject to review as provided in sections 1254, 1291, 1292, and 1294 of title 28, United States Code. No costs shall be assessed for or against the Commission in any proceeding under this title brought by or against it in the Supreme Court or such other courts.

Special Provision Relating to Statute of Limitations on Private Causes of Action

Sec. 27A. (a) *Effect on Pending Causes of Action.*—The limitation period for any private civil action implied under section 10(b) of this Act that was commenced on or before June 19, 1991, shall be the limitation period provided by the laws applicable in the jurisdiction, including principles of retroactivity, as such laws existed on June 19, 1991.

(b) *Effect on Dismissed Causes of Action.*—Any private civil action implied under section 10(b) of this Act that was commenced on or before June 19, 1991—

(1) which was dismissed as time barred subsequent to June 19, 1991, and

(2) which would have been timely filed under the limitation period provided by the laws applicable in the jurisdiction, including principles of retroactivity, as such laws existed on June 19, 1991,

shall be reinstated on motion by the plaintiff not later than 60 days after the date of enactment of this section.

Effect on Existing Law

Sec. 28. (a) Except as provided in subsection (f), the rights and remedies provided by this title shall be in addition to any and all other rights and remedies that may exist at law or in equity; but no person permitted to maintain a suit for damages under the provisions of this title shall recover, through satisfaction of judgment in one or more actions, a total amount in excess of his actual damages on account of the act complained of. Except as otherwise specifically provided in this title, nothing in this title shall affect the jurisdiction of the securities commission (or any agency or officer performing like functions) of any State over any security or any person insofar as it does not conflict with the provisions of this title or the rules and regulations thereunder.

No State law which prohibits or regulates the making or promoting of wagering or gaming contracts, or the operation of "bucket shops" or other similar or related activities, shall invalidate any put, call, straddle, option, privilege, or other security subject to this title or apply to any activity which is incidental or related to the offer, purchase, sale, exercise, settlement, or closeout of any such security. No provision of State law regarding the offer, sale, or distribution of securities shall apply to any transaction in a security futures product, except that this sentence shall not be construed as limiting any State antifraud law of general applicability.

(b) Nothing in this title shall be construed to modify existing law with regard to the binding effect (1) on any member of or participant in any self-regulatory organization of any action taken by the authorities of such organization to settle disputes between its members or participants, (2) on any municipal securities dealer or municipal securities broker of any action taken pursuant to a procedure established by the Municipal Securities Rulemaking Board to settle disputes between municipal securities dealers and municipal securities brokers, or (3) of any action described in paragraph (1) or (2) on any person who has agreed to be bound thereby.

(c) The stay, setting aside, or modification pursuant to section 19(e) of this title of any disciplinary sanction imposed by a self-regulatory organization on a member thereof, person associated with a member, or participant therein, shall not affect the validity or force of any action taken as a result of such sanction by the self-regulatory organization prior to such stay, setting aside, or modification: *Provided,* That such action is not inconsistent with the provisions of this title or the rules or regulations thereunder. The rights of any person acting in good faith which arise out of any such action shall not be affected in any way by such stay, setting aside, or modification.

(d) No State or political subdivision thereof shall impose any tax on any change in beneficial or record ownership of securities effected through the facilities of a registered clearing agency or registered transfer agent or any nominee thereof or custodian therefor or upon the delivery or transfer of securities to or through or receipt from such agency or agent or any nominee thereof or custodian therefor, unless such change in beneficial or record ownership or such transfer or delivery or receipt would otherwise be taxable by such State or political subdivision if the facilities of such registered clearing agency, registered transfer agent, or any nominee thereof or custodian therefor were not physically located in the taxing State or political subdivision. No State or political subdivision thereof shall impose any tax on securities which are deposited in or retained by a registered clearing agency, registered transfer agent, or any nominee thereof or custodian therefor, unless such securities would otherwise be taxable by such State or political subdivision if the facilities of such registered clearing agency, registered transfer agent, or any nominee thereof or custodian therefor were not physically located in the taxing State or political subdivision.

(e)(1) No person using the mails, or any means or instrumentality of interstate commerce, in the exercise of investment discretion with respect to an account shall be deemed to have acted unlawfully or to have breached a fiduciary duty under State or Federal law unless expressly provided to the contrary by a law enacted by the Congress or any State subsequent to the date of enactment of the Securities Acts Amendments of 1975 solely by reason of his having caused the account to pay a member of an exchange, broker, or dealer an amount of commission for effecting a securities transaction in excess of the amount of commission another member of an exchange, broker, or dealer would have charged for effecting that transaction, if such person determined in good faith that such amount of commission was reasonable in relation to the value of the brokerage and research services provided by such member, broker, or dealer, viewed in terms of either that particular transaction or his overall responsibilities with respect to the accounts as to which he exercises investment discretion. This subsection is exclusive and plenary insofar as conduct is covered by the foregoing, unless otherwise expressly provided by contract: Provided, however, That nothing in this subsection shall be construed to impair or limit the power of the Commission under any other provision of this title or otherwise.

(2) A person exercising investment discretion with respect to an account shall make such disclosure of his policies and practices with respect to commissions that will be paid for effecting securities transactions, at such times and in such manner, as the appropriate regulatory agency, by rule, may prescribe as necessary or appropriate in the public interest or for the protection of investors.

(3) For purposes of this subsection a person provides brokerage and research services insofar as he—

(A) furnishes advice, either directly or through publications or writings, as to the value of securities, the advisability of investing in purchasing or selling securities, and the availability of securities or purchasers or sellers of securities;

(B) furnishes analyses and reports concerning issuers, industries, securities, economic factors and trends, portfolio strategy, and the performance of accounts; or

(C) effects securities transactions and performs functions incidental thereto (such as clearance, settlement, and custody) or required in connection therewith by rules of the Commission or a self-regulatory organization of which such person is a member or person associated with a member or in which such person is a participant.

(4) The provisions of this subsection shall not apply with regard to securities that are security futures products.

(f) Limitations on Remedies.—

(1) Class action limitations.—No covered class action based upon the statutory or common law of any State or subdivision thereof may be maintained in any State or Federal court by any private party alleging—

(A) a misrepresentation or omission of a material fact in connection with the purchase or sale of a covered security; or

(B) that the defendant used or employed any manipulative or deceptive device or contrivance in connection with the purchase or sale of a covered security.

(2) Removal of covered class actions.—Any covered class action brought in any State court involving a covered security, as set forth in paragraph (1), shall be removable to the Federal district court for the district in which the action is pending, and shall be subject to paragraph (1).

(3) Preservation of certain actions.—

(A) Actions under state law of state of incorporation.—

(i) Actions preserved.—Notwithstanding paragraph (1) or (2), a covered class action described in clause (ii) of this subparagraph that is based upon the statutory or common law of the State in which the issuer is incorporated (in the case of a corporation) or organized (in the case of any other entity) may be maintained in a State or Federal court by a private party.

(ii) Permissible actions.—A covered class action is described in this clause if it involves—

(I) the purchase or sale of securities by the issuer or an affiliate of the issuer exclusively from or to holders of equity securities of the issuer; or

(II) any recommendation, position, or other communication with respect to the sale of securities of an issuer that—

(aa) is made by or on behalf of the issuer or an affiliate of the issuer to holders of equity securities of the issuer; and

(bb) concerns decisions of such equity holders with respect to voting their securities, acting in response to a tender or exchange offer, or exercising dissenters' or appraisal rights.

(B) State actions.—

(i) In general.—Notwithstanding any other provision of this subsection, nothing in this subsection may be construed to preclude a State or political subdivision thereof or a State pension plan from bringing an action involving a covered security on its own behalf, or as a member of a class comprised solely of other States, political subdivisions, or State pension plans that are named plaintiffs, and that have authorized participation, in such action.

(ii) State pension plan defined.—For purposes of this subparagraph, the term "State pension plan" means a pension plan established and maintained for its employees by the government of a State or political subdivision thereof, or by any agency or instrumentality thereof.

(C) Actions under contractual agreements between issuers and indenture trustees.—Notwithstanding paragraph (1) or (2), a covered class action that seeks to enforce a contractual agreement between an issuer and an indenture trustee may be maintained in a State or Federal court by a party to the agreement or a successor to such party.

(D) Remand of removed actions.—In an action that has been removed from a State court pursuant to paragraph (2), if the Federal court determines that the action may be maintained in State court pursuant to this subsection, the Federal court shall remand such action to such State court.

(4) Preservation of state jurisdiction.—The securities commission (or any agency or office performing like functions) of any State shall retain jurisdiction under the laws of such State to investigate and bring enforcement actions.

(5) Definitions.—For purposes of this subsection, the following definitions shall apply:

(A) Affiliate of the issuer.—The term "affiliate of the issuer" means a person that directly or indirectly, through one or more intermediaries, controls or is controlled by or is under common control with, the issuer.

(B) Covered class action.—The term "covered class action" means—

(i) any single lawsuit in which—

(I) damages are sought on behalf of more than 50 persons or prospective class members, and questions of law or fact common to those persons or members of the prospective class, without reference to issues of individualized reliance on an alleged misstatement or omission, predominate over any questions affecting only individual persons or members; or

(II) one or more named parties seek to recover damages on a representative basis on behalf of themselves and other unnamed parties similarly situated, and questions of law or fact common to those persons or members of the prospective class predominate over any questions affecting only individual persons or members; or

(ii) any group of lawsuits filed in or pending in the same court and involving common questions of law or fact, in which—

(I) damages are sought on behalf of more than 50 persons; and

(II) the lawsuits are joined, consolidated, or otherwise proceed as a single action for any purpose.

(C) Exception for derivative actions.—Notwithstanding subparagraph (B), the term "covered class action" does not include an exclusively derivative action brought by one or more shareholders on behalf of a corporation.

(D) Counting of certain class members.—For purposes of this paragraph, a corporation, investment company, pension plan, partnership, or other entity, shall be treated as one person or prospective class member, but only if the entity is not established for the purpose of participating in the action.

(E) Covered security.—The term "covered security" means a security that satisfies the standards for a covered security specified in paragraph (1) or (2) of section 18(b) of the Securities Act of 1933, at the time during which it is alleged that the misrepresentation, omission, or manipulative or deceptive conduct occurred, except that such term shall not include any debt security that is exempt from registration under the Securities Act of 1933 pursuant to rules issued by the Commission under section 4(2) of that Act.

(F) Rule of construction.—Nothing in this paragraph shall be construed to affect the discretion of a State court in determining whether actions filed in such court should be joined, consolidated, or otherwise allowed to proceed as a single action.

Validity of Contracts

Sec. 29. (a) Any condition, stipulation, or provision binding any person to waive compliance with any provision of this title or of any rule or regulation thereunder, or of any rule of an exchange required thereby shall be void.

(b) Every contract made in violation of any provision of this title or of any rule or regulation thereunder, and every contract (including any contract for listing a security on an exchange) heretofore or hereafter made the performance of which involves the violation of, or the continuance of any relationship or practice in violation of, any provision of this title or any rule or regulation thereunder, shall be void (1) as regards the rights of any person who, in violation of any such provision, rule, or regulation, shall have made or engaged in the performance of any such contract, and (2) as regards the rights of any person who, not being a party to such contract, shall have acquired any right thereunder with actual knowledge of the facts by reason of which the making or performance of such contract was in violation of any such provision, rule, or regulation: *Provided,* (A) That no contract shall be void by reason of this subsection because of any violation of any rule or regulation prescribed pursuant to paragraph (3) of subsection (c) of section 15 of this title, and (B) that no contract shall be deemed to be void by reason of this subsection in any action maintained in reliance upon this subsection, by any person to or for whom any broker or dealer sells, or from or for whom any broker or dealer purchases, a security in violation of any rule or regulation prescribed pursuant to paragraph (1) or (2) of subsection (c) of section 15 of this title, unless such action is brought within one year after the discovery that such sale or purchase involves such violation and within 3 years after such violation. The Commission may, in a rule or regulation prescribed pursuant to such paragraph (2), of such section 15(c), designate such rule or regulation, or portion thereof, as a rule or regulation, or portion thereof, a contract in violation of which shall not be void by reason of this subsection.

(c) Nothing in this title shall be construed (1) to affect the validity of any loan or extension of credit (or any extension or renewal thereof) made or of any lien created prior or subsequent to the enactment of this title, unless at the time of the making of such loan or extension of credit (or extension or renewal thereof) or the creating of such lien, the person making such loan or extension of credit (or extension or renewal thereof) or acquiring such lien shall have actual knowledge of facts by reason of which the making of such loan or extension of credit (or extension or renewal thereof) or the acquisition of such lien is a violation of the provisions of this title or any rule or regulation thereunder, or (2) to afford a defense to the collection of any debt or obligation or the enforcement of any lien by any person who shall have acquired such debt, obligation, or lien in good faith for value and without actual knowledge of the violation of any provision of this title or any rule or regulation thereunder affecting the legality of such debt, obligation, or lien.

Foreign Securities Exchanges

Sec. 30. (a) It shall be unlawful for any broker or dealer, directly or indirectly, to make use of the mails or of any means or instrumentality of interstate commerce for the purpose of effecting on an exchange not within or subject to the jurisdiction of the United States, any transaction in any security the issuer of which is a resident of, or is organized under the laws of, or has its principal place of business in, a place within or subject to the jurisdiction of the United States, in contravention of such rules and regulations as the Commission may prescribe as necessary or appropriate in the public interest or for the protection of investors or to prevent the evasion of this title.

(b) The provisions of this title or of any rule or regulation thereunder shall not apply to any person insofar as he transacts a business in securities without the jurisdiction of the United States, unless he transacts such business in contravention of such rules and regulations as the Commission may prescribe as necessary or appropriate to prevent the evasion of this title.

Prohibited Foreign Trade Practices by Issuers

Sec. 30A. (a) *Prohibition.*—It shall be unlawful for any issuer which has a class of securities registered pursuant to section 12 of this title or which is required to file reports under section 15(d) of this title, or for any officer, director, employee, or agent of such issuer or any stockholder thereof acting on behalf of such issuer, to make use of the mails or any means or instrumentality of interstate commerce corruptly in furtherance of an offer, payment promise to pay, or authorization of the payment of any money, or offer, gift, promise to give, or authorization of the giving of anything of value to—

(1) any foreign official for purposes of—

(A)(i) influencing any act or decision of such foreign official in his official capacity, (ii) inducing such foreign official to do or omit to do any act in violation of the lawful duty of such official, or (iii) securing any improper advantage; or

(B) inducing such foreign official to use his influence with a foreign government or instrumentality thereof to affect or influence any act or decision of such government or instrumentality,

in order to assist such issuer in obtaining or retaining business for or with, or directing business to, any person;

(2) any foreign political party or official thereof or any candidate for foreign political office for purposes of—

(A)(i) influencing any act or decision of such party, official, or candidate in its or his official capacity, (ii) inducing such party, official, or candidate to do or omit to do an act in violation of the lawful duty of such party, official, or candidate, or (iii) securing any improper advantage; or

(B) inducing such party, official, or candidate to use its or his influence with a foreign government or instrumentality thereof to affect or influence any act or decision of such government or instrumentality,

in order to assist such issuer in obtaining or retaining business for or with, or directing business to, any person; or

(3) any person, while knowing that all or a portion of such money or thing of value

will be offered, given, or promised, directly or indirectly, to any foreign official, to any foreign political party or official thereof, or to any candidate for foreign political office, for purposes of—

(A)(i) influencing any act or decision of such foreign official, political party, party official, or candidate in his or its official capacity, (ii) inducing such foreign official, political party, party official, or candidate to do or omit to do any act in violation of the lawful duty of such foreign official, political party, party official, or candidate, or (iii) securing any improper advantage;

(B) inducing such foreign official, political party, party official, or candidate to use his or its influence with a foreign government or instrumentality thereof to affect or influence any act or decision of such government or instrumentality,

in order to assist such issuer in obtaining or retaining business for or with, or directing business to, any person.

(b) *Exception for Routine Governmental Action.*—Subsection (a) and (g) shall not apply to any facilitating or expediting payment to a foreign official, political party, or party official the purpose of which is to expedite or to secure the performance of a routine governmental action by a foreign official, political party, or party official.

(c) *Affirmative Defenses.*—It shall be an affirmative defense to actions under subsection (a) and (g) that—

(1) the payment, gift, offer, or promise of anything of value that was made, was lawful under the written laws and regulations of the foreign official's, political party's, party official's, or candidate's country; or

(2) the payment, gift, offer, or promise of anything of value that was made, was a reasonable and bona fide expenditure, such as travel and lodging expenses, incurred by or on behalf of a foreign official, party, party official, or candidate and was directly related to—

(A) the promotion, demonstration, or explanation of products or services; or

(B) the execution or performance of a contract with a foreign government or agency thereof.

(d) *Guidelines by the Attorney General.*—Not later than one year after the date of the enactment of the Foreign Corrupt Practices Act Amendments of 1988, the Attorney General, after consultation with the Commission, the Secretary of Commerce, the United States Trade Representative, the Secretary of State, and the Secretary of the Treasury, and after obtaining the views of all interested persons through public notice and comment procedures, shall determine to what extent compliance with this section would be enhanced and the business community would be assisted by further clarification of the preceding provisions of this section and may, based on such determination and to the extent necessary and appropriate, issue—

(1) guidelines describing specific types of conduct, associated with common types of export sales arrangements and business contracts, which for purposes of the Department of Justice's present enforcement policy, the Attorney General determines would be in conformance with the preceding provisions of this section; and

(2) general precautionary procedures which issuers may use on a voluntary basis to conform their conduct to the Department of Justice's present enforcement policy regarding the preceding provisions of this section.

The Attorney General shall issue the guidelines and procedures referred to in the preceding sentence in accordance with the provisions of subchapter II of chapter 5 of title 5, United States Code, and those guidelines and procedures shall be subject to the provisions of chapter 7 of that title.

(e) *Opinions of the Attorney General.*—(1) The Attorney General, after consultation with appropriate departments and agencies of the

United States and after obtaining the views of all interested persons through public notice and comment procedures, shall establish a procedure to provide responses to specific inquiries by issuers concerning conformance of their conduct with the Department of Justice's present enforcement policy regarding the preceding provisions of this section. The Attorney General shall, within 30 days after receiving such a request, issue an opinion in response to that request. The opinion shall state whether or not certain specified prospective conduct would, for purposes of the Department of Justice's present enforcement policy, violate the preceding provisions of this section. Additional requests for opinions may be filed with the Attorney General regarding other specified prospective conduct that is beyond the scope of conduct specified in previous requests. In any action brought under the applicable provisions of this section, there shall be a rebuttable presumption that conduct, which is specified in a request by an issuer and for which the Attorney General has issued an opinion that such conduct is in conformity with the Department of Justice's present enforcement policy, is in compliance with the preceding provisions of this section. Such a presumption may be rebutted by a preponderance of the evidence. In considering the presumption for purposes of this paragraph, a court shall weigh all relevant factors, including but not limited to whether the information submitted to the Attorney General was accurate and complete and whether it was within the scope of the conduct specified in any request received by the Attorney General. The Attorney General shall establish the procedures required by this paragraph in accordance with the provisions of subchapter II of chapter 5 of title 5, United States Code, and that procedure shall be subject to the provisions of chapter 7 of that title.

(2) Any document or other material which is provided to, received by, or prepared in the Department of Justice or any other department or agency of the United States in connection with a request by an issuer under the procedure established under paragraph (1), shall be exempt from disclosure under section 552 of title 5, United States Code, and shall not, except with the consent of the issuer, be made publicly available, regardless of whether the Attorney General responds to such a request or the issuer withdraws such request before receiving a response.

(3) Any issuer who has made a request to the Attorney General under paragraph (1) may withdraw such request prior to the time the Attorney General issues an opinion in response to such request. Any request so withdrawn shall have no force or effect.

(4) The Attorney General shall, to the maximum extent practicable, provide timely guidance concerning the Department of Justice's present enforcement policy with respect to the preceding provisions of this section to potential exporters and small businesses that are unable to obtain specialized counsel on issues pertaining to such provisions. Such guidance shall be limited to responses to requests under paragraph (1) concerning conformity of specified prospective conduct with the Department of Justice's present enforcement policy regarding the preceding provisions of this section and general explanations of compliance responsibilities and of potential liabilities under the preceding provisions of this section.

(f) *Definitions.*—For purposes of this section:

(1)(A) The term "foreign official" means any officer or employee of a foreign government or any department, agency, or instrumentality thereof, or of a public international organization, or any person acting in an official capacity for or on behalf of any such government or department, agency, or instrumentality, or for or on behalf of any such public international organization.

(B) For purposes of subparagraph (A), the term "public international organization" means—

(i) an organization that is designated by Executive order pursuant to section 1 of the International Organizations Immunities Act (22 U.S.C. 288); or

(ii) any other international organization that is designated by the President by Executive order for the purposes of this section, effective as of the date of publication of such order in the Federal Register.

(2)(A) A person's state of mind is "knowing" with respect to conduct, a circumstance, or a result if—

(i) such person is aware that such person is engaging in such conduct, that such circumstance exists, or that such result is substantially certain to occur; or

(ii) such person has a firm belief that such circumstance exists or that such result is substantially certain to occur.

(B) When knowledge of the existence of a particular circumstance is required for an offense, such knowledge is established if a person is aware of a high probability of the existence of such circumstance, unless the person actually believes that such circumstance does not exist.

(3)(A) The term "routine governmental action" means only an action which is ordinarily and commonly performed by a foreign official in—

(i) obtaining permits, licenses, or other official documents to qualify a person to do business in a foreign country;

(ii) processing governmental papers, such as visas and work orders;

(iii) providing police protection, mail pick-up and delivery, or scheduling inspections associated with contract performance or inspections related to transit of goods across country;

(iv) providing phone service, power and water supply, loading and unloading cargo, or protecting perishable products or commodities from deterioration; or

(v) actions of a similar nature.

(B) The term "routine governmental action" does not include any decision by a foreign official whether, or on what terms, to award new business to or to continue business with a particular party, or any action taken by a foreign official involved in the decisionmaking process to encourage a decision to award new business to or continue business with a particular party.

(g) *Alternative Jurisdiction.*—

(1) It shall also be unlawful for any issuer organized under the laws of the United States, or a State, territory, possession, or commonwealth of the United States or a political subdivision thereof and which has a class of securities registered pursuant to section 12 of this title or which is required to file reports under section 15(d) of this title, or for any United States person that is an officer, director, employee, or agent of such issuer or a stockholder thereof acting on behalf of such issuer, to corruptly do any act outside the United States in furtherance of an offer, payment, promise to pay, or authorization of the payment of any money, or offer, gift, promise to give, or authorization of the giving of anything of value to any of the persons or entities set forth in paragraphs (1), (2), and (3) of subsection (a) of this section for the purposes set forth therein, irrespective of whether such issuer or such officer, director, employee, agent, or stockholder makes use of the mails or any means or instrumentality of interstate commerce in furtherance of such offer, gift, payment, promise, or authorization.

(2) As used in this subsection, the term "United States person" means a national of the United States (as defined in section 101 of the Immigration and Nationality Act (8 U.S.C. 1101)) or any corporation, partnership, association, joint-stock company, business trust, unincorporated organization, or sole proprietorship organized under the laws of the United States or any State, territory, possession, or commonwealth of the United States, or any political subdivision thereof.

Transaction Fees

Sec. 31.

(a) Recovery of cost of services. The Commission shall, in accordance with this section, collect transaction fees and assessments that are designed to recover the costs to the Government of the supervision and regulation of securities markets and securities professionals, and costs related to such supervision and regulation, including enforcement activities, policy and rulemaking activities, administration, legal services, and international regulatory activities.

(b) Exchange-traded securities. Subject to subsection (j), each national securities exchange shall pay to the Commission a fee at a rate equal to $15 per $1,000,000* of the aggregate dollar amount of sales of securities (other than bonds, debentures, other evidences of indebtedness, security futures products, and options on securities indexes (excluding a narrow-based security index)) transacted on such national securities exchange.

(c) Off-exchange trades of exchange registered and last-sale-reported securities. Subject to subsection (j), each national securities association shall pay to the Commission a fee at a rate equal to $15 per $1,000,000* of the aggregate dollar amount of sales transacted by or through any member of such association otherwise than on a national securities exchange of securities (other than bonds, debentures, other evidences of indebtedness, security futures products, and options on securities indexes (excluding a narrow-based security index)) registered on a national securities exchange or subject to prompt last sale reporting pursuant to the rules of the Commission or a registered national securities association.

(d) Assessments on security futures transactions. Each national securities exchange and national securities association shall pay to the Commission an assessment equal to $0.009 for each round turn transaction (treated as including one purchase and one sale of a contract of sale for future delivery) on a security future traded on such national securities exchange or by or through any member of such association otherwise than on a national securities exchange except that for fiscal year 2007 and each succeeding fiscal year such assessment shall be equal to $0.0042 for each such transaction.

(e) Dates for payment. The fees and assessments required by subsections (b), (c), and (d) of this section shall be paid—

(1) on or before March 15, with respect to transactions and sales occurring during the period beginning on the preceding September 1 and ending at the close of the preceding December 31; and

(2) on or before September 30, with respect to transactions and sales occurring during the period beginning on the preceding January 1 and ending at the close of the preceding August 31.

(f) Exemptions. The Commission, by rule, may exempt any sale of securities or any class of sales of securities from any fee or assessment imposed by this section, if the Commission finds that such exemption is consistent with the public interest, the equal regulation of markets and brokers and dealers, and the development of a national market system.

(g) Publication. The Commission shall publish in the Federal Register notices of the fee and assessment rates applicable under this section for each fiscal year not later than April 30 of the fiscal year preceding the fiscal year to which such rate applies, together with any estimates or projections on which such fees are based.

(h) Pro rata application. The rates per $1,000,000 required by this section shall be

* The Consolidated Appropriations Act of 2004, P.L. 108–199, 118 Stat. 3, changed the Section 31 fee rate applicable to securities transactions on registered exchanges and the Nasdaq to $39.00 per million.

* The Consolidated Appropriations Act of 2004, P.L. 108–199, 118 Stat. 3, changed the Section 31 fee rate applicable to securities transactions on registered exchanges and the Nasdaq to $39.00 per million.

applied pro rata to amounts and balances of less than $1,000,000.

(i) Deposit of fees.

(1) Offsetting collections. Fees collected pursuant to subsections (b), (c), and (d) for any fiscal year—

(A) shall be deposited and credited as offsetting collections to the account providing appropriations to the Commission; and

(B) except as provided in subsection (k), shall not be collected for any fiscal year except to the extent provided in advance in appropriation Acts.

(2) General revenues prohibited. No fees collected pursuant to subsections (b), (c), and (d) for fiscal year 2002 or any succeeding fiscal year shall be deposited and credited as general revenue of the Treasury.

(j) Recapture of projection windfalls for further rate reductions.

(1) Annual adjustment. For each of the fiscal years 2003 through 2011, the Commission shall by order adjust each of the rates applicable under subsections (b) and (c) for such fiscal year to a uniform adjusted rate that, when applied to the baseline estimate of the aggregate dollar amount of sales for such fiscal year, is reasonably likely to produce aggregate fee collections under this section (including assessments collected under subsection (d)) that are equal to the target offsetting collection amount for such fiscal year.

(2) Mid-year adjustment. For each of the fiscal years 2002 through 2011, the Commission shall determine, by March 1 of such fiscal year, whether, based on the actual aggregate dollar volume of sales during the first 5 months of such fiscal year, the baseline estimate of the aggregate dollar volume of sales used under paragraph (1) for such fiscal year (or $48,800,000,000,000 in the case of fiscal year 2002) is reasonably likely to be 10 percent (or more) greater or less than the actual aggregate dollar volume of sales for such fiscal year. If the Commission so determines, the Commission shall by order, no later than such March 1, adjust each of the rates applicable under subsections (b) and (c) for such fiscal year to a uniform adjusted rate that, when applied to the revised estimate of the aggregate dollar amount of sales for the remainder of such fiscal year, is reasonably likely to produce aggregate fee collections under this section (including fees collected during such 5–month period and assessments collected under subsection (d)) that are equal to the target offsetting collection amount for such fiscal year. In making such revised estimate, the Commission shall, after consultation with the Congressional Budget Office and the Office of Management and Budget, use the same methodology required by subsection (l)(2).

(3) Final rate adjustment. For fiscal year 2012 and all of the succeeding fiscal years, the Commission shall by order adjust each of the rates applicable under subsections (b) and (c) for all of such fiscal years to a uniform adjusted rate that, when applied to the baseline estimate of the aggregate dollar amount of sales for fiscal year 2012, is reasonably likely to produce aggregate fee collections under this section in fiscal year 2012 (including assessments collected under subsection (d)) equal to the target offsetting collection amount for fiscal year 2011.

(4) Review and effective date. In exercising its authority under this subsection, the Commission shall not be required to comply with the provisions of section 553 of title 5, United States Code. An adjusted rate prescribed under paragraph (1), (2), or (3) and published under subsection (g) shall not be subject to judicial review. Subject to subsections (i)(1)(B) and (k)—

(A) an adjusted rate prescribed under paragraph (1) shall take effect on the later of—

(i) the first day of the fiscal year to which such rate applies; or

(ii) thirty days after the date on which a regular appropriation to the Commission for such fiscal year is enacted;

(B) an adjusted rate prescribed under paragraph (2) shall take effect on April 1 of the fiscal year to which such rate applies; and

(C) an adjusted rate prescribed under paragraph (3) shall take effect on the later of—

(i) the first day of fiscal year 2012; or

(ii) thirty days after the date on which a regular appropriation to the Commission for fiscal year 2012 is enacted.

(k) Lapse of appropriation Caution: The authorities provided by this subsection shall not apply until October 1, 2002, as provided by § 11(c) of Act Jan. 16, 2002, P.L. 107–123, which appears as a note to this section. If on the first day of a fiscal year a regular appropriation to the Commission has not been enacted, the Commission shall continue to collect (as offsetting collections) the fees and assessments under subsections (b), (c), and (d) at the rate in effect during the preceding fiscal year, until 30 days after the date such a regular appropriation is enacted.

(*l*) Definitions. For purposes of this section:

(1) Target offsetting collection amount. The target offsetting collection amount for each of the fiscal years 2002 through 2011 is determined according to the following table:

Fiscal year:	Target offsetting Collection amount
2002	$ 732,000,000
2003	$ 849,000,000
2004	$ 1,028,000,000
2005	$ 1,220,000,000
2006	$ 1,435,000,000
2007	$ 881,000,000
2008	$ 892,000,000
2009	$ 1,023,000,000
2010	$ 1,161,000,000
2011	$ 1,321,000,000

(2) Baseline estimate of the aggregate dollar amount of sales. The baseline estimate of the aggregate dollar amount of sales for any fiscal year is the baseline estimate of the aggregate dollar amount of sales of securities (other than bonds, debentures, other evidences of indebtedness, security futures products, and options on securities indexes (excluding a narrow-based security index)) to be transacted on each national securities exchange and by or through any member of each national securities association (otherwise than on a national securities exchange) during such fiscal year as determined by the Commission, after consultation with the Congressional Budget Office and the Office of Management and Budget, using the methodology required for making projections pursuant to section 257 of the Balanced Budget and Emergency Deficit Control Act of 1985 *2 USCS § 907*.

Penalties

Sec. 32. (a) Any person who willfully violates any provision of this title (other than Section 30A) or any rule or regulation thereunder the violation of which is made unlawful or the observance of which is required under the terms of this title, or any person who willfully and knowingly makes, or causes to be made, any statement in any application, report, or document required to be filed under this title or any rule or regulation thereunder or any undertaking contained in a registration statement as provided in subsection (d) of section 15 of this title or by any self-regulatory organization in connection with an application for membership or participation therein or to become associated with a member thereof, which statement was false or misleading with respect to any material fact, shall upon conviction be fined not more than $5,000,000, or imprisoned not more than 20 years, or both, except that when such person is a person other than a natural person, a fine not exceeding $25,000,000 may be imposed; but no person shall be subject to imprisonment under this section for the violation of any rule or regulation if he proves that he had no knowledge of such rule or regulation.

(b) Any issuer which fails to file information, documents, or reports required to be filed under subsection (d) of section 15 of this title or any rule or regulation thereunder shall forfeit to the United States the sum of $100 for each and every day such failure to file shall continue. Such forfeiture, which shall be in lieu of any criminal penalty for such failure to file which might be deemed to arise under subsection (a) of this section, shall be payable into the Treasury of the United States and shall be recoverable in a civil suit in the name of the United States.

(c)(1)(A) Any issuer that violates subsection (a) or (g) of section 30A shall be fined not more than $2,000,000.

(B) Any issuer that violates subsection (a) or (g) of section 30A shall be subject to a civil penalty of not more than $10,000 imposed in an action brought by the Commission.

(2)(A) Any officer, director, employee, or agent of an issuer, or stockholder acting on behalf of such issuer, who willfully violates subsection (a) or (g) of section 30A of this title shall be fined not more than $100,000, or imprisoned not more than 5 years, or both.

(B) Any officer, director, employee, or agent of an issuer, or stockholder acting on behalf of such issuer, who violates subsection (a) or (g) of section 30A of this title shall be subject to a civil penalty of not more than $10,000 imposed in an action brought by the Commission.

(3) Whenever a fine is imposed under paragraph (2) upon any officer, director, employee, agent, or stockholder of an issuer, such fine may not be paid, directly or indirectly, by such issuer.

Separability of Provisions

Sec. 33. If any provision of this act, or the application of such provision to any person or circumstances, shall be held invalid, the remainder of the act, and the application of such provision to persons or circumstances other than those as to which it is held invalid, shall not be affected thereby.

Effective Date

Sec. 34. This act shall become effective on July 1, 1934, except that sections 6 and 12(b), (c), (d), and (e) shall become effective on September 1, 1934; and sections 5, 7, 8, 9(a)(6), 10, 11, 12(a), 13, 14, 15, 16, 17, 18, 19, and 30 shall become effective on October 1, 1934.

Authorization of Appropriations

Sec. 35. In addition to any other funds authorized to be appropriated to the Commission, there are authorized to be appropriated to carry out the functions, powers, and duties of the Commission, $776,000,000 for fiscal year 2003, of which—

(1) $102,700,000 shall be available to fund additional compensation, including salaries and benefits, as authorized in the Investor and capital Markets Fee Relief Act (Public Law 107–123; 115 Stat. 2390 et seq.);

(2) $108,400,000 shall be available for information technology, security enhancements, and recovery and mitigation activities in light of the terrorist attacks of September 11, 2001; and

(3) $98,000,000 shall be available to add not fewer than an additional 200 qualified professionals to provide enhanced oversight of auditors and audit services required by the Federal securities laws, and to improve

Commission investigative and disciplinary efforts with respect to such auditors and services, as well as for additional professional support staff necessary to strengthen the programs of the Commission involving Full Disclosure and Prevention and Suppression of Fraud, risk management, industry technology review, compliance, inspections, examinations, market regulation, and investment management.

Requirements for the EDGAR System

Sec. 35A. The Commission, by rule or regulation—

(1) shall provide that any information in the EDGAR system that is required to be disseminated by the contractor—

(A) may be sold or disseminated by the contractor only pursuant to a uniform schedule of fees prescribed by the Commission;

(B) may be obtained by a purchaser by direct interconnection with the EDGAR system;

(C) shall be equally available on equal terms to all persons; and

(D) may be used, resold, or redisseminated by any person who has lawfully obtained such information without restriction and without payment of additional fees or royalties; and

(2) shall require that persons, or classes of persons, required to make filings with the Commission submit such filings in a form and manner suitable for entry into the EDGAR system and shall specify the date that such requirement is effective with respect to that person or class; except that the Commission may exempt persons or classes of persons, or filings or classes of filings, from such rules or regulations in order to prevent hardships or to avoid imposing unreasonable burdens or as otherwise may be necessary or appropriate.

Sec. 36. General Exemptive Authority.

(a) *Authority.*—

(1) *In General.*—Except as provided in subsection (b), but notwithstanding any other provision of this title, the Commission, by rule, regulation, or order, may conditionally or unconditionally exempt any person, security, or transaction, or any class or classes of persons, securities, or transactions, from any provision or provisions of this title or of any rule or regulation thereunder, to the extent that such exemption is necessary or appropriate in the public interest, and is consistent with the protection of investors.

(2) *Procedures.*—The Commission shall, by rule or regulation, determine the procedures under which an exemptive order under this section shall be granted and may, in its sole discretion, decline to entertain any application for an order of exemption under this section.

(b) *Limitation.*—The Commission may not, under this section, exempt any person, security, or transaction, or any class or classes of persons, securities, or transactions from section 15C or the rules or regulations issued thereunder or (for purposes of section 15C and the rules and regulations issued thereunder) from any definition in paragraph (42), (43), (44), or (45) of section 3(a).

RULES AND REGULATIONS UNDER THE SECURITIES EXCHANGE ACT OF 1934

(Cite as 17 CFR 240.__)

RULES OF GENERAL APPLICATION

DEFINITION OF "EQUITY SECURITY" AS USED IN SECTIONS 12(g) AND 16

MISCELLANEOUS EXEMPTIONS

REGULATION 13A. REPORTS OF ISSUERS OF SECURITIES REGISTERED PURSUANT TO SECTION 12

ANNUAL REPORTS

REGULATION 13D–G

EXEMPTION OF CERTAIN SECURITIES FROM SECTION 15(a)

REGISTRATION OF BROKERS AND DEALERS

RULES RELATING TO OVER–THE–COUNTER MARKETS

REGULATION 15D. REPORTS OF REGISTRANTS UNDER THE SECURITIES ACT OF 1933

ANNUAL REPORTS

OTHER REPORTS

EXEMPTION OF CERTAIN ISSUERS FROM SECTION 15(d) OF THE ACT

PENNY STOCKS

NATIONAL AND AFFILIATED SECURITIES ASSOCIATIONS

REGISTRATION OF GOVERNMENT SECURITIES BROKERS AND GOVERNMENT SECURITIES DEALERS

REPORTS OF DIRECTORS, OFFICERS, AND PRINCIPAL SHAREHOLDERS

EXEMPTION OF CERTAIN TRANSACTIONS FROM SECTION 16(b)

EXEMPTION OF CERTAIN TRANSACTIONS FROM SECTION 16(c)

ARBITRAGE TRANSACTIONS

PRESERVATION OF RECORDS AND REPORTS OF CERTAIN STABILIZING ACTIVITIES

SUPERVISED INVESTMENT BANK HOLDING COMPANY RULES

17Ad–4. Applicability of Rules 17Ad–2, 17Ad–3 and 17Ad–6(a)(1) Through (7) and (11)
17Ad–5. Written Inquiries and Requests
17Ad–6. Recordkeeping
17Ad–7. Record Retention
17Ad–8. Securities Position Listings
17Ad–9. Definitions
17Ad–10. Prompt Posting of Certificate Detail to Master Securityholder Files, Maintenance of Accurate Securityholder Files, Communications Between Co-transfer Agents and Recordkeeping Transfer Agents, Maintenance of Current Control Book, Retention of Certificate Detail and "Buy-in" of Physical Over-Issuance
17Ad–11. Reports Regarding Aged Record Differences, Buy-ins and Failure to Post Certificate Detail to Master Securityholder and Subsidiary Files
17Ad–12. Safeguarding of Funds and Securities
17Ad–13. Annual Study and Evaluation of Internal Accounting Control
17Ad–14. Tender Agents
17Ad–15. Signature Guarantees
17Ad–16. Notice of Assumption or Termination of Transfer Agent Services
17Ad–17. Transfer Agents' Obligation to Search for Lost Securityholders
17Ad–18. Year 2000 Reports to Be Made by Certain Transfer Agents
17Ad–19. Requirements for Cancellation, Processing, Storage, Transportation, and Destruction or Other Disposition of Securities Certificates
17Ad–20. Issuer Restrictions or Prohibitions on Ownership by Securities Intermediaries
19b–4. Filings With Respect to Proposed Rule Changes by Self-Regulatory Organizations
19b–5. Temporary Exemption From the Filing Requirements of Section 19(b) of the Act
19b–7. Filings With Respect to Proposed Rule Changes Submitted Pursuant to Section 19(b)(7) of the Act
19c–1. Governing Certain Off-Board Agency Transactions by Members of National Securities Exchanges
19c–3. Governing Off-Board Trading by Members of National Securities Exchanges
19c–4. Governing Certain Listing or Authorization Determinations by National Securities Exchanges and Associations
19c–5. Governing the Multiple Listing of Options on National Securities Exchanges
19d–1. Notices by Self-Regulatory Organizations of Final Disciplinary Actions, Denials, Bars, or Limitations Respecting Membership, Association, Participation, or Access to Services, and Summary Suspensions
19d–2. Applications for Stays of Disciplinary Sanctions or Summary Suspensions by a Self-Regulatory Organization
19d–3. Applications for Review of Final Disciplinary Sanctions, Denials of Membership, Participation or Association, or Prohibitions or Limitations of Access to Services Imposed by Self-Regulatory Organizations
19d–4. Notice by the Public Company Accounting Oversight Board of Disapproval of Registration or of Disciplinary Action
19g2–1. Enforcement of Compliance by National Securities Exchanges and Registered Securities Associations With the Act and Rules and Regulations Thereunder
19h–1. Notice by a Self-Regulatory Organization of Proposed Admission to or Continuance in Membership or Participation or Association With a Member of Any Person Subject to a Statutory Disqualification, and Applications to the Commission for Relief Therefrom

INSPECTION AND PUBLICATION OF INFORMATION FILED UNDER THE ACT

24b–1. Documents to Be Kept Public by Exchanges
24b–2. Nondisclosure of Information Filed With the Commission and With Any Exchange
24b–3. Information Filed by Issuers and Others Under Sections 12, 13, 14, and 16
24c–1. Access to Nonpublic Information.
31. Transaction Fees
36a1–1. Exemption From Section 7 for OTC Derivatives Dealers
36a1–2. Exemption From SIPA for OTC Derivatives Dealers

REGULATION BTR—BLACKOUT TRADING RESTRICTION

Sec.

100. Definitions
101. Prohibition of Insider Trading During Pension Fund Blackout Periods
102. Exceptions to Definition of Blackout Period
103. Issuer Right of Recovery; Right of Action by Equity Security Owner
104. Notice.

REGULATION FD

Rule

100. General Rule Regarding Selective Disclosure
101. Definitions
102. No Effect on Antifraud Liability
103. No Effect on Exchange Act Reporting Status

REGULATIONS M, SHO, ATS, AND AC AND CUSTOMER MARGIN REQUIREMENTS FOR SECURITY FUTURES

REGULATION M

Rule

100. Preliminary Note; Definitions
101. Activities by Distribution Participants
102. Activities by Issuers and Selling Security Holders During a Distribution
103. NASDAQ Passive Market Making
104. Stabilizing and Other Activities in Connection With an Offering
105. Short Selling in Connection With a Public Offering

REGULATION SHO—REGULATION OF SHORT SALES

200. Definition of "Short Sale" and Marking Requirements
201. Price test [Reserved]
202T. Temporary Short Sale Rule Suspension
203. Borrowing and Delivery Requirements

REGULATION ATS—ALTERNATIVE TRADING SYSTEMS

Rule

300. Definitions
301. Requirements For Alternative Trading Systems
302. Recordkeeping Requirements For Alternative Trading Systems
303. Record Preservation Requirements For Alternative Trading Systems

CUSTOMER MARGIN REQUIREMENTS FOR SECURITY FUTURES

400. Customer Margin Requirements For Security Futures—Authority, Purpose, Interpretation, and Scope
401. Definitions
402. General Provisions
403. Required Margin
404. Type, Form and Use of Margin
405. Withdrawal of Margin
406. Undermargined Accounts

REGULATION AC—ANALYST CERTIFICATION

500. Definitions
501. Certifications In Connection With Research Reports
502. Certifications In Connection With Public Appearances

Rule

503. Certain Foreign Research Reports
504. Notification to Associated Persons
505. Exclusion for News Media

FORMS UNDER THE SECURITIES EXCHANGE ACT OF 1934

Form

3. Initial Statement of Beneficial Ownership of Securities
4. Statement of Changes in Beneficial Ownership of Securities
5. Annual Statement of Beneficial Ownership of Securities

8–A. For Registration of Certain Classes of Securities Pursuant to Section 12(b) or (g) of the Securities Exchange Act of 1934

10. General Form for Registration of Securities Pursuant to Section 12(b) or (g) of the Securities Exchange Act of 1934

10–SB. General Form for Registration of Securities of Small Business Issuers

10–Q. Quarterly Report Under Section 13 or 15(d) of the Exchange Act

10–QSB. Form for Quarterly or Transition Reports by Small Business Issuers Under Section 13 or 15(d) of the Exchange Act

10–K. Annual and Transition Reports Pursuant to Section 13 or 15(d) of the Securities Exchange Act of 1934

10–KSB. Form for Annual and Transitional Reports of Small Business Issuers Under Section 13 or 15(d) of the Exchange Act of 1934

6–K. Report of Foreign Issuer

8–K. Current Report Pursuant to Section 13 or 15(d) of the Exchange Act of 1934

RULES AND REGULATIONS UNDER THE SECURITIES EXCHANGE ACT OF 1934

(Cite as 17 CFR 240.__)

RULES OF GENERAL APPLICATION

ATTENTION ELECTRONIC FILERS

THIS REGULATION SHOULD BE READ IN CONJUNCTION WITH REGULATION S–T (PART 232 OF THIS CHAPTER), WHICH GOVERNS THE PREPARATION AND SUBMISSION OF DOCUMENTS IN ELECTRONIC FORMAT. MANY PROVISIONS RELATING TO THE PREPARATION AND SUBMISSION OF DOCUMENTS IN PAPER FORMAT CONTAINED IN THIS REGULATION ARE SUPERSEDED BY THE PROVISIONS OF REGULATION S–T FOR DOCUMENTS REQUIRED TO BE FILED IN ELECTRONIC FORMAT.

Rule 0–1. Definitions

(a) As used in the rules and regulations prescribed by the Commission pursuant to Title I of the Securities Exchange Act of 1934, unless the context otherwise specifically requires—

(1) The term ''Commission'' means the Securities and Exchange Commission.

(2) The term ''Act'' means Title I of the Securities Exchange Act of 1934.

(3) The term ''section'' refers to a section of the Securities Exchange Act of 1934.

(4) The term ''rules and regulations'' refers to all rules and regulations adopted by the Commission pursuant to the Act, including the forms for registration and reports and the accompanying instructions thereto.

(5) The term ''electronic filer'' means a person or an entity that submits filings electronically pursuant to Rules 100 and 101 of Regulation S–T (§§ 232.100 and 232.101 of this chapter, respectively).

(6) The term *electronic filing* means a document under the federal securities laws that is transmitted or delivered to the Commission in electronic format.

(b) Unless otherwise specifically stated, the terms used in the rules and regulations shall have the meaning defined in the Act.

(c) A rule or regulation which defines a term without express reference to the Act or to the rules and regulations, or to a portion thereof, defines such term for all purposes as used both in the Act and in the rules and regulations, unless the context otherwise specifically requires.

(d) Unless otherwise specified or the context otherwise requires, the term ''prospectus'' means a prospectus meeting the requirements of section 10(a) of the Securities Act of 1933 as amended.

Rule 0–2. Business Hours of the Commission

(a) The principal office of the Commission, at 450 Fifth Street, NW., Washington, DC 20549, is open each day, except Saturdays, Sundays, and federal holidays, from 9 a.m. to 5:30 p.m., Eastern Standard Time or Eastern Daylight Saving Time, whichever currently is in effect in Washington, DC, *provided that* hours for the filing of documents pursuant to the Act or the rules and regulations thereunder are as set forth in paragraphs (b) and (c) of this section.

(b) *Submissions made in paper.* Paper documents filed with or otherwise furnished to the Commission may be submitted to the Commission each day, except Saturdays, Sundays and federal holidays, from 8 a.m. to 5:30 p.m., Eastern Standard Time or Eastern Daylight Saving Time, whichever is currently in effect.

(c) *Electronic filings.* Filings made by direct transmission may be submitted to the Commission each day, except Saturdays, Sundays and federal holidays, from 8 a.m. to 10 p.m., Eastern Standard Time or Eastern Daylight Saving Time, whichever is currently in effect.

Rule 0–3. Filing of Material With the Commission

(a) All papers required to be filed with the Commission pursuant to the Act or the rules and regulations thereunder shall be filed at the principal office in Washington, D.C. Material may be filed by delivery to the Commission, through the mails or otherwise. The date on which papers are actually received by the Commission shall be the date of filing thereof if all of the requirements with respect to the filing have been complied with, except that if the last day on which papers can be accepted as timely filed falls on a Saturday, Sunday or holiday, such papers may be filed on the first business day following.

(b) The manually signed original (or in the case of duplicate originals, one duplicate original) of all registrations, applications, statements, reports, or other documents filed under the Securities Exchange Act of 1934, as amended, shall be numbered sequentially (in addition to any internal numbering which otherwise may be present) by handwritten, typed, printed or other legible form of notation from the facing page of the document through the last page of that document and any exhibits or attachments thereto. Further, the total number of pages contained in a numbered original shall be set forth on the first page of the document.

(c) Each document filed shall contain an exhibit index, which should immediately precede the exhibits filed with such document. The index shall list each exhibit filed and identify by handwritten, typed, printed, or other legible form of notation in the manually signed original, the page number in the sequential numbering system described in paragraph (b) of this section where such exhibit can be found or where it is stated that the exhibit is incorporated by reference. Further, the first page of the manually signed document shall list the page in the filing where the exhibit index is located.

Rule 0–4. Nondisclosure of Information Obtained in Examinations and Investigations

Information or documents obtained by officers or employees of the Commission in the course of any examination or investigation pursuant to section 17(a) or 21(a) shall, unless made a matter of public record, be deemed confidential. Except as provided by 17 CFR 203.2, officers and employees are hereby prohibited from making such confidential information or documents or any other nonpublic records of the Commission available to anyone other than a member, officer, or employee of the Commission, unless the Commission or the General Counsel, pursuant to delegated authority, authorizes the disclosure of such information or the production of such documents as not being contrary to the public interest. Any officer or employee who is served with a subpoena requiring the disclosure of such information or the production of such documents shall appear in court and, unless the authorization described in the preceding sentence shall have been given, shall respectfully decline to disclose the information or produce the documents called for, basing his refusal upon this rule. Any officer or employee who is served with such a subpoena shall promptly advise the General Counsel of the service of such subpoena, the nature of the information or document sought, and any circumstances which may bear upon the desirability of making available such information or documents.

Rule 0–5. Reference to Rule by Obsolete Designation

Wherever in any rule, form, or instruction book specific reference is made to a rule by number or other designation, which is now obsolete, such reference shall be deemed to be made to the corresponding rule or rules in these General Rules and Regulations.

Rule 0–6. Disclosure Detrimental to the National Defense or Foreign Policy

(a) Any requirement to the contrary notwithstanding, no registration statement, report, proxy statement or other document filed with the Commission or any securities exchange shall contain any document or information which, pursuant to Executive order, has been classified by an appropriate department or agency of the United States for protection in the interests of national defense or foreign policy.

(b) Where a document or information is omitted pursuant to paragraph (a) hereof, there shall be filed, in lieu of such document or information, a statement from an appropriate department or agency of the United States to the effect that such document or information has been classified or that the status thereof is awaiting determination. Where a document is omitted pursuant to paragraph (a) hereof, but information relating to the subject matter of such document is nevertheless included in material filed with the Commission pursuant to a determination of an appropriate department or agency of the United States that disclosure of such information would not be contrary to the interests of national defense or foreign policy, a statement from such department or agency to that effect shall be submitted for the information of the Commission. A registrant may rely upon any such statement in filing or omitting any document or information to which the statement relates.

(c) The Commission may protect any information in its possession which may require classification in the interests of national defense or foreign policy pending determination by an appropriate department or agency as to whether such information should be classified.

(d) It shall be the duty of the registrant to submit the documents or information referred to in paragraph (a) to the appropriate department or agency of the United States prior to filing them with the Commission and to obtain and submit to the Commission, at the time of filing such documents or information, or in lieu thereof, as the case may be, the statements from such department or agency required by paragraph (b). All such statements shall be in writing.

Rule 0–8. Application of Rules to Registered Broker-Dealers

Any provision of any rule or regulation under the Act which prohibits any act, practice, or course of business by any person if the mails or any means or instrumentality of interstate commerce are used in connection therewith, shall also prohibit any such act, practice, or course of business by any broker or dealer registered pursuant to section 15(b) of the Act, or any person acting on behalf of such a broker or dealer, irrespective of any use of the mails or any means or instrumentality of interstate commerce.

Rule 0–9. Payment of Fees

All payment of fees shall be made in cash, certified check or by United States postal money order, bank cashier's check or bank money order payable to the Securities and Exchange Commission, omitting the name or title of any official of the Commission. Payment of fees required by this section shall be made in accordance with the directions set forth in § 202.3a of this chapter.

Rule 0–10. Small Entities Under the Securities Exchange Act for Purposes of the Regulatory Flexibility Act

For purposes of Commission rulemaking in accordance with the provisions of Chapter Six of the Administrative Procedure Act, and unless otherwise defined for purposes of a particular rulemaking proceeding, the term "small business" or "small organization" shall—

(a) When used with reference to an "issuer" or a "person," other than an investment company, mean an "issuer" or "person" that, on the last day of its most recent fiscal year, had total assets of $5 million or less;

(b) When used with reference to an "issuer" or "person" that is an investment company, have the meaning ascribed to those terms by § 270.0–10 of this chapter;

(c) When used with reference to a broker or dealer, mean a broker or dealer that:

(1) Had total capital (net worth plus subordinated liabilities) of less than $500,000 on the date in the prior fiscal year as of which its audited financial statements were prepared pursuant to Rule 17a–5(d) or, if not required to file such statements, a broker or dealer that had total capital (net worth plus subordinated liabilities) of less than $500,000 on the last business day of the preceding fiscal year (or in the time that it has been in business, if shorter); and

(2) Is not affiliated with any person (other than a natural person) that is not a small business or small organization as defined in this section;

(d) When used with reference to a clearing agency, mean a clearing agency that:

(1) Compared, cleared and settled less than $500 million in securities transactions during the preceding fiscal year (or in the time that it has been in business, if shorter);

(2) Had less than $200 million of funds and securities in its custody or control at all times during the preceding fiscal year (or in the time that it has been in business, if shorter); and

(3) Is not affiliated with any person (other than a natural person) and is not a small business or small organization as defined in this section;

(e) When used with reference to an exchange, mean any exchange that:

(1) Has been exempted from the reporting requirements of § 240.11Aa3–1; and

(2) Is not affiliated with any person (other than a natural person) that is not a small business or small organization as defined in this section;

(f) When used with reference to a municipal securities dealer that is a bank (including any separately identifiable department or division of a bank), mean any such municipal securities dealer that:

(1) Had, or is a department of a bank that had, total assets of less than $10 million at all times during the preceding fiscal year (or in the time that it has been in business, if shorter);

(2) Had an average monthly volume of municipal securities transactions in the preceding fiscal year (or in the time it has been registered, if shorter) of less than $100,000; and

(3) Is not affiliated with any person (other than a natural person) that is not a small business or small organization as defined in this section;

(g) When used with reference to a securities information processor, mean a securities information processor that:

(1) Had gross revenues of less than $10 million during the preceding fiscal year (or in the time it has been in business, if shorter);

(2) Provided service to fewer than 100 interrogation devices or moving tickers at all times during the preceding fiscal year (or in the time that it has been in business, if shorter); and

(3) Is not affiliated with any person (other than a natural person) that is not a

small business or small organization under this section; and

(h) When used with reference to a transfer agent, mean a transfer agent that:

(1) Received less than 500 items for transfer and less than 500 items for processing during the preceding six months (or in the time that it has been in business, if shorter);

(2) Transferred items only of issuers that would be deemed "small businesses" or "small organizations" as defined in this section; and

(3) Maintained master shareholder files that in the aggregate contained less than 1,000 shareholder accounts or was the named transfer agent for less than 1,000 shareholder accounts at all times during the preceding fiscal year (or in the time that it has been in business, if shorter); and

(4) Is not affiliated with any person (other than a natural person) that is not a small business or small organization under this section.

(i) For purposes of paragraph (c) of this section, a broker or dealer is affiliated with another person if:

(1) Such broker or dealer controls, is controlled by, or is under common control with such other person; a person shall be deemed to control another person if that person has the right to vote 25 percent or more of the voting securities of such other person or is entitled to receive 25 percent or more of the net profits of such other person or is otherwise able to direct or cause the direction of the management or policies of such other person; or

(2) Such broker or dealer introduces transactions in securities, other than registered investment company securities or interests or participations in insurance company separate accounts, to such other person, or introduces accounts of customers or other brokers or dealers, other than accounts that hold only registered investment company securities or interests or participations in insurance company separate accounts, to such other person that carries such accounts on a fully disclosed basis.

(j) For purposes of paragraphs (d) through (h) of this section, a person is affiliated with another person if that person controls, is controlled by, or is under common control with such other person; a person shall be deemed to control another person if that person has the right to vote 25 percent or more of the voting securities of such other person or is entitled to receive 25 percent or more of the net profits of such other person or is otherwise able to direct or cause the direction of the management or policies of such other person.

(k) For purposes of paragraph (g) of this section, "interrogation device" shall refer to any device that may be used to read or receive securities information, including quotations, indications of interest, last sale data and transaction reports, and shall include proprietary terminals or personal computers that receive securities information via computer-to-computer interfaces or gateway access.

Rule 0–11. Filing Fees for Certain Acquisitions, Dispositions and Similar Transactions

(a) *General.* (1) At the time of filing a disclosure document described in paragraphs (b) through (d) of this section relating to certain acquisitions, dispositions, business combinations, consolidations or similar transactions, the person filing the specified document shall pay a fee payable to the Commission to be calculated as set forth in paragraph (b) through (d) of this section.

(2) Only one fee per transaction is required to be paid. A required fee shall be reduced in an amount equal to any fee paid with respect to such transaction pursuant to either Section 6(b) of the Securities Act of 1933 or any appli-

cable provision of this rule; the fee requirements under Section 6(b) shall be reduced in an amount equal to the fee paid the Commission with respect to a transaction under this regulation. No part of a filing fee is refundable.

(3) If at any time after the initial payment the aggregate consideration offered is increased, an additional filing fee based upon such increase shall be paid with the required amended filing.

(4) When the fee is based upon the market value of securities, such market value shall be established by either the average of the high and low prices reported in the consolidated reporting system (for exchange traded securities and last sale reported over-the-counter securities) or the average of the bid and asked price (for other over-the-counter securities) as of a specified date within 5 business days prior to the date of the filing. If there is no market for the securities, the value shall be based upon the book value of the securities computed as of the latest practicable date prior to the date of the filing, unless the issuer of the securities is in bankruptcy or receivership or has an accumulated capital deficit, in which case one-third of the principal amount, par value or stated value of the securities shall be used.

(5) The cover page of the filing shall set forth the calculation of the fee in tabular format, as well as the amount offset by a previous filing and the identification of such filing, if applicable.

(b) *Section 13(e)(1) Filings.* At the time of filing such statement as the Commission may require pursuant to section 13(e)(1) of the Exchange Act, a fee of one-fiftieth of one percent of the value of the securities proposed to be acquired by the acquiring person. The value of the securities proposed to be acquired shall be determined as follows:

(1) The value of the securities to be acquired solely for cash shall be the amount of cash to be paid for them;

(2) The value of the securities to be acquired with securities or other non-cash consideration, whether or not in combination with a cash payment for the same securities, shall be based upon the market value of the securities to be received by the acquiring person as established in accordance with paragraph (a)(4) of this section.

(c) *Proxy and information statement filings.* At the time of filing a preliminary proxy statement pursuant to Rule 14a–6(a) or preliminary information statement pursuant to Rule 14c–5(a) that concerns a merger, consolidation, acquisition of a company, or proposed sale or other disposition of substantially all the assets of the registrant (including a liquidation), the following fee:

(1) For preliminary material involving a vote upon a merger, consolidation or acquisition of a company, a fee of one-fiftieth of one percent of the proposed cash payment or of the value of the securities and other property to be transferred to security holders in the transaction. The fee is payable whether the registrant is acquiring another company or being acquired.

(i) The value of securities or other property to be transferred to security holders, whether or not in combination with a cash payment for the same securities, shall be based upon the market value of the securities to be received by the acquiring person as established in accordance with paragraph (a)(4) of this section.

(ii) Notwithstanding the above, where the acquisition, merger or consolidation is for the sole purpose of changing the registrant's domicile, no filing fee is required to be paid.

(2) For preliminary material involving a vote upon a proposed sale or other disposition of substantially all the assets of the registrant, a fee of one-fiftieth of one percent of the aggregate of the cash and the value of the securities (other than its own) and other property to be received by the registrant. In the case of a disposition in which the registrant will not receive any property, such as a liqui-

dation or spin-off, the fee shall be one-fiftieth of one percent of the aggregate of the cash and the value of the securities and other property to be distributed to security holders.

(i) The value of the securities to be received (or distributed in the case of a spin-off or liquidation) shall be based upon the market value of such securities as established in accordance with paragraph (a)(4) of this section.

(ii) The value of other property shall be a bona fide estimate of the fair market value of such property.

(3) Where two or more companies are involved in the transaction, each shall pay a proportionate share of such fee, determined by the persons involved.

(4) Notwithstanding the above, the fee required by this paragraph (c) shall not be payable for a proxy statement filed by a company registered under the Investment Company Act of 1940.

(d) *Schedule 14D–1 filings.* At the time of filing a Schedule 14D–1, a fee of one-fiftieth of one percent of the aggregate of the cash or of the value of the securities or other property offered by the bidder. Where the bidder is offering securities or other non-cash consideration for some or all of the securities to be acquired, whether or not in combination with a cash payment for the same securities, the value of the consideration to be offered for such securities shall be based upon the market value of the securities to be received by the bidder as established in accordance with paragraph (a)(4) of this section.

Rule 0–12. Commission Procedures for Filing Applications for Orders for Exemptive Relief Under Section 36 of the Exchange Act

(a) The application shall be in writing in the form of a letter, must include any supporting documents necessary to make the application complete, and otherwise must comply with § 240.0–3. All applications must be submitted to the Office of the Secretary of the Commission. Requestors may seek confidential treatment of their applications to the extent provided under § 200.81 of this chapter. If an application is incomplete, the Commission, through the Division handling the application, may request that the application be withdrawn unless the applicant can justify, based on all the facts and circumstances, why supporting materials have not been submitted and undertakes to submit the omitted materials promptly.

(b) An applicant may submit a request electronically in standard electronic mail text or ASCII format. The electronic mailbox to use for these applications is described on the Commission's website at www.sec.gov in the "Exchange Act Exemptive Applications" subsection located under the "Current SEC Rulemaking" section. In the event electronic mailboxes are revised in the future, applicants can find the appropriate mailbox by accessing the Commission's website directory of electronic mailboxes at http://www.sec.gov/asec/mailboxs.htm.

(c) An applicant also may submit a request in paper format. Five copies of every paper application and every amendment to such an application must be submitted to the Office of the Secretary at 450 Fifth Street, N.W., Washington, D.C. 20549. Applications must be on white paper no larger than 8½ by 11 inches in size. The left margin of applications must be at least 1½ inches wide, and if the application is bound, it must be bound on the left side. All typewritten or printed material must be on one side of the paper only and must be set forth in black ink so as to permit photocopying.

(d) Every application (electronic or paper) must contain the name, address and telephone number of each applicant and the name, address, and telephone number of a person to whom any questions regarding the application should be directed. The Commission will not consider hypothetical or anonymous requests for exemptive relief. Each applicant shall state the basis for the relief sought, and identify the anticipated benefits for investors and any conditions or limitations the applicant believes would be appropriate for the protection of investors. Applicants should also cite to and discuss applicable precedent.

(e) Amendments to the application should be prepared and submitted as set forth in these procedures and should be marked to show what changes have been made.

(f) After the filing is complete, the applicable Division will review the application. Once all questions and issues have been answered to the satisfaction of the Division, the staff will make an appropriate recommendation to the Commission. After consideration of the recommendation by the Commission, the Commission's Office of the Secretary will issue an appropriate response and will notify the applicant. If the application pertains to a section of the Exchange Act pursuant to which the Commission has delegated its authority to the appropriate Division, the Division Director or his or her designee will issue an appropriate response and notify the applicant.

(g) The Commission, in its sole discretion, may choose to publish in the Federal Register a notice that the application has been submitted. The notice would provide that any person may, within the period specified therein, submit to the Commission any information that relates to the Commission action requested in the application. The notice also would indicate the earliest date on which the Commission would take final action on the application, but in no event would such action be taken earlier than 25 days following publication of the notice in the Federal Register.

(h) The Commission may, in its sole discretion, schedule a hearing on the matter addressed by the application.

DEFINITION OF "EQUITY SECURITY" AS USED IN SECTIONS 12(g) AND 16

Rule 3a1–1. Exemption From the Definition of "Exchange" under Section 3(a)(1) of the Act

(a) An organization, association, or group of persons shall be exempt from the definition of the term "exchange" under section 3(a)(1) of the Act, (15 U.S.C. 78c(a)(1)), if such organization, association, or group of persons:

(1) Is operated by a national securities association;

(2) Is in compliance with Regulation ATS, 17 CFR 242.300 through 242.303; or

(3) Pursuant to paragraph (a) of § 242.301 of Regulation ATS, 17 CFR 242.301(a), is not required to comply with Regulation ATS, 17 CFR 242.300 through 242.303.

(b) Notwithstanding paragraph (a) of this section, an organization, association, or group of persons shall not be exempt under this section from the definition of "exchange," if:

(1) During three of the preceding four calendar quarters such organization, association, or group of persons had:

(i) Fifty percent or more of the average daily dollar trading volume in any security and five percent or more of the average daily dollar trading volume in any class of securities; or

(ii) Forty percent or more of the average daily dollar trading volume in any class of securities; and

(2) The Commission determines, after notice to the organization, association, or group of persons, and an opportunity for such organization, association, or group of persons to respond, that such an exemption would not be necessary or appropriate in the public interest or consistent with the protection of investors taking into account the requirements for exchange registration under section 6 of the Act, (15 U.S.C. 78f), and

the objectives of the national market system under section 11A of the Act, (15 U.S.C 78k–1).

(3) For purposes of paragraph (b) of this section, each of the following shall be considered a "class of securities":

(i) Equity securities, which shall have the same meaning as in § 240.3a11–1;

(ii) Listed options, which shall mean any options traded on a national securities exchange or automated facility of a national securities exchange;

(iii) Unlisted options, which shall mean any options other than those traded on a national securities exchange or automated facility of a national securities association;

(iv) Municipal securities, which shall have the same meaning as in section 3(a)(29) of the Act, (15 U.S.C. 78c(a)(29));

(v) Investment grade corporate debt securities, which shall mean any security that:

(A) Evidences a liability of the issuer of such security;

(B) Has a fixed maturity date that is at least one year following the date of issuance;

(C) Is rated in one of the four highest ratings categories by at least one Nationally Recognized Statistical Ratings Organization; and

(D) Is not an exempted security, as defined in section 3(a)(12) of the Act, (15 U.S.C. 78c(a)(12));

(vi) Non-investment grade corporate debt securities, which shall mean any security that:

(A) Evidences a liability of the issuer of such security;

(B) Has a fixed maturity date that is at least one year following the date of issuance;

(C) Is not rated in one of the four highest ratings categories by at least one Nationally Recognized Statistical Ratings Organization; and

(D) Is not an exempted security, as defined in section 3(a)(12) of the Act, (15 U.S.C. 78o);

(vii) Foreign corporate debt securities, which shall mean any security that:

(A) Evidences a liability of the issuer of such debt security;

(B) Is issued by a corporation or other organization incorporated or organized under the laws of any foreign country; and

(C) Has a fixed maturity date that is at least one year following the date of issuance; and

(viii) Foreign sovereign debt securities, which shall mean any security that:

(A) Evidences a liability of the issuer of such debt security;

(B) Is issued or guaranteed by the government of a foreign country, any political subdivision of a foreign country, or any supranational entity; and

(C) Does not have a maturity date of a year or less following the date of issuance.

Rule 3a4–1. Associated Persons of an Issuer Deemed Not to Be Brokers

(a) An associated person of an issuer of securities shall not be deemed to be a broker solely by reason of his participation in the sale of the securities of such issuer if the associated person:

(1) Is not subject to a statutory disqualification, as that term is defined in Section 3(a)(39) of the Act, at the time of his participation; and

(2) Is not compensated in connection with his participation by the payment of commissions or other remuneration based either directly or indirectly on transactions in securities; and

(3) Is not at the time of his participation an associated person of a broker or dealer; and

(4) Meets the conditions of any one of paragraphs (a)(4)(i), (ii), or (iii) of this section.

(i) The association person restricts his participation to transactions involving offers and sales of securities:

(A) To a registered broker or dealer; a registered investment company (or registered separate account); an insurance company; a bank; a savings and loan association; a trust company or similar institution supervised by a state or federal banking authority; or a trust for which a bank, a savings and loan association, a trust company, or a registered investment adviser either is the trustee or is authorized in writing to make investment decisions; or

(B) That are exempted by reason of Section 3(a)(7), 3(a)(9) or 3(a)(10) of the Securities Act of 1933 from the registration provisions of that Act; or

(C) That are made pursuant to a plan or agreement submitted for the vote or consent of the security holders who will receive securities of the issuer in connection with a reclassification of securities of the issuer, a merger or consolidation or a similar plan of acquisition involving an exchange of securities, or a transfer of assets of any other person to the issuer in exchange for securities of the issuer; or

(D) That are made pursuant to a bonus, profit-sharing, pension, retirement, thrift, savings, incentive, stock purchase, stock ownership, stock appreciation, stock option, dividend reinvestment or similar plan for employees of an issuer or a subsidiary of the issuer;

(ii) The associated person meets all of the following conditions:

(A) The associated person primarily performs, or is intended primarily to perform at the end of the offering, substantial duties for or on behalf of the issuer otherwise than in connection with transactions in securities; and

(B) The associated person was not a broker or dealer, or an associated person of a broker or dealer, within the preceding 12 months; and

(C) The associated person does not participate in selling an offering of securities for any issuer more than once every 12 months other than in reliance on paragraphs (a)(4)(i) or (a)(4)(iii) of this section, except that for securities issued pursuant to Rule 415 under the Securities Act of 1933, the 12 months shall begin with the last sale of any security included within one Rule 415 registration.

(iii) The associated person restricts his participation to any one or more of the following activities;

(A) Preparing any written communication or delivering such communication through the mails or other means that does not involve oral solicitation by the associated person of a potential purchaser; *provided, however,* that the content of such communication is approved by a partner, officer or director of the issuer;

(B) Responding to inquiries of a potential purchaser in a communication initiated by the potential purchaser; *provided, however,* that the content of such responses are limited to information contained in a registration statement filed under the Securities Act of 1933 or other offering document; or

(C) Performing ministerial and clerical work involved in effecting any transaction.

(b) No presumption shall arise that an associated person of an issuer has violated Section 15(a) of the Act solely by reason of his participation in the sale of securities of the issuer if he does not meet the conditions specified in paragraph (a) of this section.

(c) *Definitions.* When used in this section:

(1) The term "associated person of an issuer" means any natural person who is a partner, officer, director, or employee of:

(i) The issuer;

(ii) A corporate general partner of a limited partnership that is the issuer;

(iii) A company or partnership that controls, is controlled by, or is under common control with, the issuer; or

(iv) An investment adviser registered under the Investment Advisers Act of 1940 to an investment company registered under the Investment Company Act of 1940 which is the issuer.

(2) The term "associated person of a broker or dealer" means any partner, officer, director, or branch manager of such broker or dealer (or any person occupying a similar status or performing similar functions), any person directly or indirectly controlling, controlled by, or under common control with such broker or dealer, or any employee of such broker or dealer, except that any person associated with a broker or dealer whose functions are solely clerical or ministerial and any person who is required under the laws of any state to register as a broker or dealer in that state solely because such person is an issuer of securities or associated person of an issuer of securities shall not be included in the meaning of such term for purposes of this section.

Rule 3a4–2. Exemption From the Definition of "Broker" for Bank Calculating Compensation for Effecting Transactions in Fiduciary Accounts

(a) A bank that meets the conditions for exception from the definition of the term "broker" under Section 3(a)(4)(B)(ii) of the Act (15 U.S.C. 78c(a)(4)(B)(ii)), except for the "chiefly compensated" condition in Section 3(a)(4)(B)(ii)(I) of the Act (15 U.S.C. 78c(a)(4)(B)(ii)(I)), is exempt from the definition of the term "broker" under Section 3(a)(4) of the Act (15 U.S.C. 78c(a)(4)) solely for effecting transactions in securities pursuant to Section 3(a)(4)(B)(ii) of the Act (15 U.S.C. 78c(a)(4)(B)(ii)) if:

(1) The bank can demonstrate that sales compensation, as defined in § 240.3b–17(j), received during the immediately preceding year is less than 10% of the total amount of relationship compensation, as defined in § 240.3b–17(i), received during that year;

(2) The bank maintains procedures reasonably designed to ensure compliance with the "chiefly compensated" condition in Section 3(a)(4)(B)(ii)(I) of the Act (15 U.S.C. 78c(a)(4)(B)(ii)(I)) with respect to a trust or fiduciary account:

(i) When the account is opened;

(ii) When the compensation arrangement for the account is changed; and

(iii) When sales compensation, as defined in § 240.3b–17, received from the account is reviewed by the bank for purposes of determining an employee's compensation; and

(3) The bank complies with Section 3(a)(4)(C) of the Act (15 U.S.C. 78c(a)(4)(C)).

(b) For purposes of this section, the term *year* means either a calendar year or other fiscal year consistently used by the bank for recordkeeping and reporting purposes.

Rule 3a4–3. Exemption From the Definition of "Broker" for Bank Effecting Transactions as an Indenture Trustee in a No–Load Money Market Fund

A bank that meets the conditions for exception from the definition of the term "broker" under Section 3(a)(4)(B)(ii) of the Act (15 U.S.C. 78c(a)(4)(B)(ii)), except for the "chiefly compensated" condition in Section 3(a)(4)(B)(ii)(I) of the Act (15 U.S.C. 78c(a)(4)(B)(ii)(I)), is exempt from the definition of the term "broker" under Section 3(a)(4) of the Act (15 U.S.C. 78c(a)(4)) solely for effecting transactions as an indenture trustee in a no-load money market fund, as defined in § 240.3b–17(f) and § 240.3b–17(e), respectively.

Rule 3a4–4. Exemption From the Definition of "Broker" for Small Bank Effecting Transactions in Investment Company Securities in a Tax–Deferred Custody Account

(a) A small bank is exempt from the definition of the term "broker" under Section 3(a)(4) of the Act (15 U.S.C. 78c(a)(4)) solely for effecting transactions in securities of an open-end management investment company registered under the Investment Company Act of 1940 (15 U.S.C. 80a–1 *et seq.*) in a tax-deferred account for which the bank acts as custodian under Section 3(a)(4)(B)(viii) of the Act (15 U.S.C. 78c(a)(4)(B)(viii)) if:

(1) The bank is not associated with a broker or dealer and does not have an arrangement with a broker or dealer to effect transactions in securities for the bank's customers;

(2) Any bank employee effecting such transactions:

(i) Is not an associated person of a broker or dealer;

(ii) Primarily performs duties for the bank other than effecting transactions in securities for customers; and

(iii) Does not receive compensation for such transactions from the bank, the executing broker or dealer, or any other person related to:

(A) The size, value, or completion of any securities transaction;

(B) The amount of securities-related assets gathered; or

(C) The size or value of any customer's securities account;

(3) The bank complies with Section 3(a)(4)(C) of the Act (15 U.S.C. 78c(a)(4)(C));

(4) The bank makes available to the tax-deferred account the securities of investment companies that are not affiliated persons, as defined in Section 2(a)(3) of the Investment Company Act of 1940 (15 U.S.C. 80a–2(a)(3)), of the bank and that have similar characteristics to the securities of investment companies made available that are affiliated persons;

(5) The bank does not solicit securities transactions except through the following activities:

(i) Delivering advertising and sales literature for the security that is prepared by the registered broker-dealer that is the principal underwriter of an open-end management investment company registered under the Investment Company Act of 1940 (15 U.S.C. 80a–1 *et seq.*), or prepared by an open-end management investment company registered under the Investment Company Act of 1940 (15 U.S.C. 80a–1 *et seq.*) that is not an affiliated person, as defined in Section 2(a)(3) of the Investment Company Act of 1940 (15 U.S.C. 80a–2(a)(3)), of the bank;

(ii) Responding to inquiries of a potential purchaser in a communication initiated by the potential purchaser; provided, however, that the content of such responses is limited to information contained in a registration statement for the security of an investment company filed under the Securities Act of 1933 (15 U.S.C. 77a *et seq.*) or sales literature prepared by the investment company security's principal underwriter that is a registered broker-dealer;

(iii) Advertising of trust activities, if any, permitted under Section 3(a)(4)(B)(ii)(II) of the Act (15 U.S.C. 78c(a)(4)(B)(ii)(II)); or

(iv) Notifying its existing customers that it accepts orders for investment company securities in conjunction with solicitations related to its other activities concerning tax-deferred accounts; and

(6) The bank's annual compensation related to effecting transactions in securities pursuant to this exemption is less than 3% of its annual revenue.

(b) *Definitions.* For purposes of this section:

(1) The phrase *compensation related to effecting transactions in securities pursuant to this exemption* means the total annual compensation received for effecting transactions in securities pursuant to this exemption, including fees received from investment companies for distribution.

(2) The term *networking arrangement* means a contractual or other written arrangement with a broker or dealer to effect transactions in securities for the bank's customers.

(3) The term *principal underwriter* has the meaning given in Section 2(a)(29) of the Investment Company Act of 1940 (15 U.S.C. 80a–2(a)(29)).

(4) The term *revenue* means the total annual net interest income and noninterest income from the bank's most recent Consolidated Reports of Condition and Income (Call Reports) or any successor forms the bank is required to file by its appropriate Federal banking agency (as defined in Section 3 of the FDIA (12 U.S.C. 1813)).

(5) (i) The term *small bank* means a bank that:

(A) Had less than $100 million in assets as of December 31 of both of the prior two calendar years; and

(B) Is not, and since December 31 of the third prior calendar year has not been, an affiliate of a bank holding company or a financial holding company that as of December 31 of both of the prior two calendar years had consolidated assets of more than $1 billion.

(ii) For purposes of this paragraph (b)(5) the terms *affiliate, bank holding company,* and *financial holding company* have the same meanings as given in the Bank Holding Company Act of 1956 (12 U.S.C. 1841 *et seq.*).

(6) The term *tax-deferred account* means those accounts described in Sections 401(a), 403, 408, and 408A under Subchapter D and in Section 457 under Subchapter E of the Internal Revenue Code of 1986 (26 U.S.C. 1 *et seq.*).

Rule 3a4–5. Exemption From the Definition of "Broker" for Banks Effecting Transactions in Securities in a Custody Account

(a) A bank is exempt from the definition of the term "broker" under Section 3(a)(4) of the Act (15 U.S.C. 78c(a)(4)) solely for effecting transactions in securities in an account for which the bank acts as custodian under Section 3(a)(4)(B)(viii) of the Act (15 U.S.C. 78c(a)(4)(B)(viii)) if:

(1) The bank does not directly or indirectly receive any compensation for effecting such transactions;

(2) Any bank employee effecting such transactions:

(i) Is not an associated person of a broker or dealer;

(ii) Primarily performs duties for the bank other than effecting transactions in securities for customers;

(iii) Does not receive compensation for such transactions related to:

(A) The size, value, or completion of any securities transaction;

(B) The amount of securities-related assets gathered; or

(C) The size or value of any customer's securities account; and

(iv) Does not receive compensation for the referral of any customer to the broker or dealer;

(3) The bank complies with Section 3(a)(4)(C) of the Act (15 U.S.C. 78c(a)(4)(C));

(4) The bank makes available to the account the securities of investment companies with similar characteristics that are not affiliated persons, as defined in Section 2(a)(3) of the Investment Company Act of 1940 (15 U.S.C. 80a–2(a)(3)), of the bank, if

the bank makes available the securities of investment companies that are affiliated persons, as defined in Section 2(a)(3) of the Investment Company Act of 1940 (15 U.S.C. 80a–2(a)(3)); and

(5) The bank does not solicit securities transactions except through the following activities:

(i) Delivering advertising and sales literature for the security that is prepared by the registered broker-dealer that is the principal underwriter of an investment company, or prepared by an investment company that is not an affiliated person, as defined in Section 2(a)(3) of the Investment Company Act of 1940 (15 U.S.C. 80a–2(a)(3)), of the bank;

(ii) Responding to inquiries of a potential purchaser in a communication initiated by the potential purchaser of the security; provided, however, that the content of such responses is limited to information contained in a registration statement for the security filed under the Securities Act of 1933 (15 U.S.C. 77a *et seq.*) or sales literature prepared by the principal underwriter that is a registered broker-dealer;

(iii) Advertising of trust activities, if any, permitted under Section 3(a)(4)(B)(ii)(II) of the Act (15 U.S.C. 78c(a)(4)(B)(ii)(II)); and

(iv) Notifying its existing customers that it accepts orders for securities in conjunction with solicitations related to its other custody activities.

(b) For purposes of this section, the term *principal underwriter* has the meaning given in Section 2(a)(29) of the Investment Company Act of 1940 (15 U.S.C. 80a–2(a)(29)).

Rule 3a4–6. Exemption From the Definition of "Broker" for Banks that Execute Transactions in Investment Company Securities Through NSCC Mutual Fund Services

A bank that meets the conditions for an exception or exemption from the definition of the term "broker," except for the condition in Section 3(a)(4)(C)(i) of the Act (15 U.S.C. 78c(a)(4)(C)(i)), is exempt from such condition solely for transactions in investment company securities effected through the National Securities Clearing Corporation's Mutual Fund Services.

Rule 3a5–1. Exemption From the Definition of "Dealer" for a Bank Engaged in Riskless Principal Transactions

(a) A bank is exempt from the definition of the term "dealer" to the extent that it engages in or effects riskless principal transactions if the number of such riskless principal transactions during a calendar year combined with transactions in which the bank is acting as an agent for a customer pursuant to section 3(a)(4)(B)(xi) of the Act (15 U.S.C. 78c(a)(4)(B)(xi)) during that same year does not exceed 500.

(b) For purposes of this section, the term riskless principal transaction means a transaction in which, after having received an order to buy from a customer, the bank purchased the security from another person to offset a contemporaneous sale to such customer or, after having received an order to sell from a customer, the bank sold the security to another person to offset a contemporaneous purchase from such customer.

Rule 3a11–1. Definition of the Term "Equity Security"

The term *equity security* is hereby defined to include any stock or similar security, certificate of interest or participation in any profit sharing agreement, preorganization certificate or subscription, transferable share, voting trust certificate or certificate of deposit for an equity security, limited partnership interest, interest in a joint venture, or certificate of interest in a business trust; any security future on such security; or any security convertible, with or without consideration into such a security, or carrying any warrant or right to subscribe to or purchase such a security; or any such warrant or right; or any put, call, straddle, or other option or privilege of buying such a security from or selling such a security to another without being bound to do so.

MISCELLANEOUS EXEMPTIONS

Rule 3a12–1. Exemption of Certain Mortgages and Interests in Mortgages

Mortgages, as defined in section 302(d) of the Emergency Home Finance Act of 1970, which are or have been sold by the Federal Home Loan Mortgage Corporation are hereby exempted from the operation of such provisions of the Act as by their terms do not apply to an "exempted security" or to "exempted securities".

Rule 3a12–3. Exemption From Sections 14(a), 14(b), 14(c), 14(f) and 16 for Securities of Certain Foreign Issuers

(a) Securities for which the filing of registration statements on Form 18 are authorized shall be exempt from the operation of sections 14 and 16 of the Act.

(b) Securities registered by a foreign private issuer, as defined in Rule 3b–4, shall be exempt from sections 14(a), 14(b), 14(c), 14(f) and 16 of the Act.

Rule 3a12–4. Exemptions From Sections 15(a) and 15(c)(3) for Certain Mortgage Securities

(a) When used in this Rule the following terms shall have the meanings indicated:

(1) The term "whole loan mortgage" means an evidence of indebtedness secured by mortgage, deed of trust, or other lien upon real estate or upon leasehold interests therein where the entire mortgage, deed or other lien is transferred with the entire evidence of indebtedness.

(2) The term "aggregated whole loan mortgage" means two or more whole loan mortgages that are grouped together and sold to one person in one transaction.

(3) The term "participation interest" means an undivided interest representing one of only two such interests in a whole loan mortgage or in an aggregated whole loan mortgage, provided that the other interest is retained by the originator of such participation interest.

(4) The term "commitment" means a contract to purchase a whole loan mortgage, an aggregated whole loan mortgage or a participation interest which by its terms requires that the contract be fully executed within 2 years.

(5) The term "mortgage security" means a whole loan mortgage, an aggregated whole loan mortgage, a participation interest, or a commitment.

(b) A mortgage security shall be deemed an "exempted security" for purposes of subsections (a) and (c)(3) of section 15 of the Act provided that, in the case of and at the time of any sale of the mortgage security by a broker or dealer, such mortgage security is not in default and has an unpaid principal amount of at least $50,000.

Rule 3a12–5. Exemption of Certain Investment Contract Securities From Sections 7 and 11(d)(1)

(a) An investment contract security involving the direct ownership of specified residential real property shall be exempted from the provisions of Section 7(c) and 11(d)(1) of the Act with respect to any transaction by a broker or dealer who, directly or indirectly, arranges for the extension or maintenance of credit on the security to or from a customer, if the credit:

(1) is secured by a lien, mortgage, deed of trust, or any other similar security interest related only to real property; *Provided, however*, That this provision shall not pre-

vent a lender from requiring (i) a security interest in the common areas and recreational facilities or furniture and fixtures incidental to the investment contract if the purchase of such furniture and fixtures is required by, or subject to the approval of, the issuer, as a condition of purchase; or (ii) an assignment of future rentals in the event of default by the purchaser or a co-signer or guarantor on the debt obligation other than the issuer, its affiliates, or any broker or dealer offering such securities;

(2) is to be repaid by periodic payments of principal and interest pursuant to an amortization schedule established by the governing instruments; *Provided, however*, That this provision shall not prevent the extension of credit on terms which require the payment of interest only, if extended in compliance with the other provisions of this rule; and

(3) is extended by a lender which is not, directly or indirectly controlling, controlled by, or under common control with the broker or dealer or the issuer of the securities or affiliates thereof.

(b) For purposes of this rule:

(1) "residential real property" shall mean real property containing living accommodations, whether used on a permanent or transient basis, and may include furniture or fixtures if required as a condition of purchase of the investment contract or if subject to the approval of the issuer.

(2) "direct ownership" shall mean ownership of a fee or leasehold estate or a beneficial interest in a trust the purchase of which, under applicable local law, is financed and secured by a security interest therein similar to a mortgage or deed of trust, but it shall not include an interest in a real estate investment trust, an interest in a general or limited partnership, or similar indirect interest in the ownership of real property.

Rule 3a12–6. Definition of "Common Trust Fund" as Used in Section 3(a)(12) of the Act

The term "common trust fund" as used in section 3(a)(12) of the Act shall include a common trust fund which is maintained by a bank which is a member of an affiliated group, as defined in section 1504(a) of the Internal Revenue Code of 1954, and which is maintained exclusively for the collective investment and reinvestment of monies contributed thereto by one or more bank members of such affiliated group in the capacity of trustee, executor, administrator, or guardian, provided that:

(a) the common trust fund is operated in compliance with the same state and federal regulatory requirements as would apply if the bank maintaining such fund and any other contributing banks were the same entity; and

(b) the rights of persons for whose benefit a contributing bank acts as trustee, executor, administrator, or guardian would not be diminished by reason of the maintenance of such common trust fund by another bank member of the affiliated group.

Rule 3a12–7. Exemption for Certain Derivative Securities Traded Otherwise Than on a National Securities Exchange

Any put, straddle, option, or privilege traded exclusively otherwise than on a national securities exchange and for which quotations are not disseminated through an automated quotation system of a registered securities association, which relates to any securities which are direct obligations of, or obligations guaranteed as to principal or interest by, the United States, or securities issued or guaranteed by a corporation in which the United States has a direct or indirect interest as shall be designated for exemption by the Secretary of the Treasury pursuant to Section 3(a)(12) of the Act, shall be exempt from all provisions of the Act which by their terms do not apply to any "exempted security" or "exempted securities," provided that the securities underlying such put, call, straddle, option or privilege represent an obligation equal to or exceeding $250,000 principal amount.

Rule 3a12-8. Exemption for Designated Foreign Government Securities for Purposes of Futures Trading

(a) When used in this Rule, the following terms shall have the meaning indicated: (1) the term "designated foreign government security" shall mean a security not registered under the Securities Act of 1933 nor the subject of any American depositary receipt so registered, and representing a debt obligation of the government of

(i) the United Kingdom of Great Britain and Northern Ireland;

(ii) Canada;

(iii) Japan;

(iv) the Commonwealth of Australia;

(v) the Republic of France;

(vi) New Zealand;

(vii) the Republic of Austria;

(viii) the Kingdom of Denmark;

(ix) the Republic of Finland;

(x) the Kingdom of the Netherlands;

(xi) Switzerland;

(xii) the Federal Republic of Germany;

(xiii) the Republic of Ireland;

(xiv) the Republic of Italy;

(xv) the Kingdom of Spain;

(xvi) the United Mexican States;

(xvii) the Federative Republic of Brazil;

(xviii) the Republic of Argentina;

(xix) the Republic of Venezuela;

(xx) the Kingdom of Belgium; or

(xxi) the Kingdom of Sweden.

(2) The term "qualifying foreign futures contracts" shall mean any contracts for the purchase or sale of a designated foreign government security for future delivery, as "future delivery" is defined in 7 U.S.C. 2, provided such contracts require delivery outside the United States, any of its possessions or territories, and are traded on or through a board of trade, as defined at 7 U.S.C. 2.

(b) Any designated foreign government security shall, for purposes only of the offer, sale or confirmation of sale of qualifying foreign futures contracts, be exempted from all provisions of the Act which by their terms do not apply to an "exempted security" or "exempted securities."

Rule 3a12-9. Exemption of Certain Direct Participation Program Securities From the Arranging Provisions of Sections 7(c) and 11(d)(1)

(a) Direct participation program securities sold on a basis whereby the purchase price is paid to the issuer in one or more mandatory deferred payments shall be deemed to be exempted securities for purposes of the arranging provisions of Sections 7(c) and 11(d)(1) of the Act, provided that:

(1) The securities are registered under the Securities Act of 1933 or are sold or offered exclusively on an intrastate basis in reliance upon Section 3(a)(11) of that Act;

(2) The mandatory deferred payments bear a reasonable relationship to the capital needs and program objectives described in a business development plan disclosed to investors in a registration statement filed with the Commission under the Securities Act of 1933 or, where no registration statement is required to be filed with the Commission, as part of a statement filed with the relevant state securities administrator;

(3) Not less than 50 percent of the purchase price of the direct participation program security is paid by the investor at the time of sale;

(4) The total purchase price of the direct participation program security is due within three years in specified property programs

or two years in non-specified property programs. Such pay-in periods are to be measured from the earlier of the completion of the offering or one year following the effective date of the offering.

(b) For purposes of this Rule:

(1) "Direct participation program" shall mean a program financed through the sale of securities, other than securities that are listed on an exchange, quoted on NASDAQ, or will otherwise be actively traded during the pay-in period as a result of efforts by the issuer, underwriter, or other participants in the initial distribution of such securities, that provides for flow-through tax consequences to its investors; *Provided, however,* that the term "direct participation program" does not include real estate investment trusts, Subchapter S corporate offerings, tax qualified pension and profit sharing plans under Sections 401 and 403(a) of the Internal Revenue Code ("Code"), tax shelter annuities under Section 403(b) of the Code, individual retirement plans under Section 408 of the Code, and any issuer, including a separate account, that is registered under the Investment Company Act of 1940.

(2) "Business development plan" shall mean a specific plan describing the program's anticipated economic development and the amounts of future capital contributions, in the form of mandatory deferred payments, to be required at specified times or upon the occurrence of certain events.

(3) "Specified property program" shall mean a direct participation program in which, at the date of effectiveness, more than 75 percent of the net proceeds from the sale of program securities are committed to specific purchases or expenditures. "Non-specified property program" shall mean any other direct participation program.

Rule 3a12–10. Exemption of Certain Securities Issued by the Resolution Funding Corporation

Securities that are issued by the Resolution Funding Corporation pursuant to section 21B(f) of the Federal Home Loan Bank Act (12 U.S.C. 1421 *et seq.*) are exempt from the operation of all provisions of the Act that by their terms do not apply to any "exempted security" or to "exempted securities."

Rule 3a12–11. Exemption from Sections 8(a), 14(a), 14(b), and 14(c) for Debt Securities Listed on a National Securities Exchange

(a) Debt securities that are listed for trading on a national securities exchange shall be exempt from the restrictions on borrowing of Section 8(a) of the Act (15 U.S.C. 78h(a)).

(b) Debt securities registered pursuant to the provisions of Section 12(b) of the Act (15 U.S.C. 78*l* (b)) shall be exempt from Sections 14(a), 14(b), and 14(c) of the Act (15 U.S.C. 78n(a), (b), and (c)), except that §§ 240.14a–1, 240.14a–2(a), 240.14a–9, 240.14a–13, 240.14b–1, 240.14b–2, 240.14c–1, 240.14c–6 and 240.14c–7 shall continue to apply.

(c) For purposes of this section, debt securities is defined to mean any securities that are not "equity securities" as defined in Section 3(a)(11) of the Act (15 U.S.C. 78c(a)(11)) and § 240.3a11–1 thereunder.

Rule 3a12–12. Exemption from Certain Provisions of Section 16 of the Act for Asset-Backed securities

Asset-backed securities, as defined in § 229.1101 of this chapter, are exempt from section 16 of the Act (15 U.S.C. 78p).

Rule 3a40–1. Designation of Financial Responsibility Rules

The term "financial responsibility rules" for purposes of the Securities Investor Protection Act of 1970 shall include:

(a) Any rule adopted by the Commission pursuant to sections 8, 15(c)(3), 17(a) or 17(e)(1)(A) of the Securities Exchange Act of 1934;

(b) Any rule adopted by the Commission relating to hypothecation or lending of customer securities;

(c) Any rule adopted by any self-regulatory organization relating to capital, margin, recordkeeping, hypothecation or lending requirements; and

(d) Any other rule adopted by the Commission or any self-regulatory organization relating to the protection of funds or securities.

Rule 3a43–1. Customer–Related Government Securities Activities Incidental to Futures–Related Business of a Futures Commission Merchant Registered With the Commodity Futures Trading Commission

(a) A futures commission merchant registered with the Commodity Futures Trading Commission ("CFTC") is not a government securities broker or government securities dealer solely because such futures commission merchant effects transactions in government securities that are defined in paragraph (b) of this rule as incidental to such person's futures-related business.

(b) Provided that the futures commission merchant maintains in a regulated account all funds and securities associated with such government securities transactions (except funds and securities associated with transactions under paragraph (b)(1)(i) of this rule) and does not advertise that it is in the business of effecting transactions in government securities otherwise than in connection with futures or options on futures trading or the investment of margin or excess funds related to such trading or the trading of any other instrument subject to CFTC jurisdiction, the following transactions in government securities are incidental to the futures-related business of such a futures commission merchant:

(1) Transactions as agent for a customer—

(i) To effect delivery pursuant to a futures contract; or

(ii) For risk reduction or arbitrage of existing or contemporaneously created positions in futures or options on futures;

(2) Transactions as agent for a customer for investment of margin and excess funds related to futures or options on futures trading or the trading of other instruments subject to CFTC jurisdiction, provided further that,

(i) Such transactions involve Treasury securities with a maturity of less than 93 days at the time of the transaction.

(ii) Such transactions generate no monetary profit for the futures commission merchant in excess of the costs of executing such transactions, or

(iii) Such transactions are unsolicited, and commissions and other income generated on transactions pursuant to this paragraph (b)(2)(iii) (including transactional fees paid by the futures commission merchant and charged to its customer) do not exceed 2% of such futures commission merchant's total commission revenues;

(3) Exchange of futures for physical transactions as agent for or as principal with a customer; and

(4) Any transaction or transactions that the Commission exempts, either unconditionally or on specified terms and conditions, as incidental to the futures-related business of a specified futures commission merchant, a specified category of futures commission merchants, or futures commission merchants generally.

(c) Definitions. (1) *Customer* means any person for whom the futures commission merchant effects or intends to effect transactions in futures, options on futures, or any other instruments subject to CFTC jurisdiction.

(2) *Regulated account* means a customer segregation account subject to the regulations of the CFTC; provided, however, that, where such regulations do not permit to be maintained in such an account or require to be

maintained in a separate regulated account funds or securities in proprietary accounts or funds or securities used as margin for or excess funds related to futures contracts, options on futures or any other instruments subject to CFTC jurisdiction that trade outside the United States, its territories, or possessions, the term *regulated account* means such separate regulated account or any other account subject to record-keeping regulations of the CFTC.

(3) *Unsolicited transaction* means a transaction that is not effected in a discretionary account or recommended to a customer by the futures commission merchant, an associated person of a futures commission merchant, a business affiliate that is controlled by, controlling, or under common control with the futures commission merchant, or an introducing broker that is guaranteed by the futures commission merchant.

(4) *Futures* and *futures contracts* mean contracts of sale of a commodity for future delivery traded on or subject to the rules of a contract market designated by the CFTC or traded on or subject to the rules of any board of trade located outside the United States, its territories, or possessions.

(5) *Options on futures* means puts or calls on a futures contract traded on or subject to the rules of a contract market designated by the CFTC or traded or subject to the rules of any board of trade located outside the United States, its territories, or possessions.

Rule 3a44-1. Proprietary Government Securities Transactions Incidental to the Futures-Related Business of a CFTC-Regulated Person

(a) A person registered with the Commodity Futures Trading Commission ("CFTC"), a contract market designated by the CFTC, such a contract market's affiliated clearing organization, or any floor trader or such a contract market (hereinafter referred to collectively as a "CFTC-regulated person") is not a government securities dealer solely because such person effects transactions for its own account in government securities that are defined in paragraph (b) of this rule as incidental to such person's futures-related business.

(b) Provided that a CFTC-regulated person does not advertise or otherwise hold itself out as a government securities dealer except as permitted under Rule 3a43-1 the following transactions in government securities for its own account are incidental to the futures-related business of such a CFTC-regulated person:

(1) Transactions to effect delivery of a government security pursuant to a futures contract;

(2) Exchange of futures for physical transactions with (i) a government securities broker or government securities dealer that has registered with the Commission or filed notice pursuant to section 15C(a) of the Act or (ii) a CFTC-regulated person;

(3) Transactions (including repurchase agreements and reverse repurchase agreements) involving segregated customer funds and securities or funds and securities held by a clearing organization with (i) a government securities broker or government securities dealer that has registered with the Commission or filed notice pursuant to section 15C(a) of the Act or (ii) a bank;

(4) Transactions for risk reduction or arbitrage of existing or contemporaneously created positions in futures or options on futures with (i) a government securities broker or government securities dealer that has registered with the Commission or filed notice pursuant to section 15C(a) of the Act or (ii) a CFTC-regulated person;

(5) Repurchase and reverse repurchase agreement transactions between a futures commission merchant acting in a proprietary capacity and another CFTC-regulated person acting in a proprietary capacity and contemporaneous offsetting transactions between such a futures commission merchant and (i) a government securities broker or government securities dealer that has registered with the Commission or filed notice

pursuant to section 15C(a) of the Act, (ii) a bank, or (iii) a CFTC-regulated person acting in a proprietary capacity; and

(6) Any transaction or transactions that the Commission exempts, either unconditionally or on specified terms and conditions, as incidental to the futures related business of a specified CFTC-regulated person, a specified category of CFTC-regulated persons, or CFTC-regulated persons generally.

(c) Definitions. (1) *Segregated customer funds* means funds subject to CFTC segregation requirements.

(2) *Futures* and *futures contracts* mean contracts of sale of a commodity for future delivery traded on or subject to the rules of a contract market designated by the CFTC or traded on or subject to the rules of any board of trade located outside the United States, its territories, or possessions.

(3) *Options on futures* means puts or calls on a futures contract traded on or subject to the rules of a contract market designated by the CFTC or traded on or subject to the rules of any board of trade located outside the United States, its territories, or possessions.

DEFINITIONS

Rule 3a51–1. Definition of Penny Stock

For purposes of section 3(a)(51) of the Act, the term "penny stock" shall mean any equity security other than a security:

(a) That is a reported security, as defined in Rule 11Aa3–1(a) of this chapter;

except that a security that is registered on the American Stock Exchange, Inc. pursuant to the listing criteria of the Emerging Company Marketplace, but that does not otherwise satisfy the requirements of paragraphs (b), (c), or (d) of this rule, shall be a penny stock for purposes of section 15(b)(6) of the Act;

(b) That is issued by an investment company registered under the Investment Company Act of 1940;

(c) That is a put or call option issued by the Options Clearing Corporation;

(d) Except for purposes of section 7(b) of the Securities Act and Rule 419 (17 CFR 230.419), that has a price of five dollars or more.

(1) For purposes of paragraph (d) of this rule:

(i) A security has a price of five dollars or more for a particular transaction if the security is purchased or sold in that transaction at a price of five dollars or more, excluding any broker or dealer commission, commission equivalent, mark-up, or mark-down; and

(ii) Other than in connection with a particular transaction, a security has a price of five dollars or more at a given time if the inside bid quotation is five dollars or more; *provided, however,* that if there is no such inside bid quotation, a security has a price of five dollars or more at a given time if the average of three or more interdealer bid quotations at specified prices displayed at that time in an interdealer quotation system, as defined in Rule 15c2–7(c)(1), by three or more market makers in the security, is five dollars or more.

(iii) The term "inside bid quotation" shall mean the highest bid quotation for the security displayed by a market maker in the security on an automated interdealer quotation system that has the characteristics set forth in Rule 17B(b)(2) of the Act, or such other automated interdealer quotation system designated by the Commission for purposes of this rule at any time in which at least two market makers are contemporaneously displaying on such system bid and offer quotations for the security at specified prices.

(2) If a security is a unit composed of one or more securities, the unit price divided by the

number of shares of the unit that are not warrants, options, rights, or similar securities must be five dollars or more, as determined in accordance with paragraph (d)(1) of this rule, and any share of the unit that is a warrant, option, right, or similar security, or a convertible security, must have an exercise price or conversion price of five dollars or more;

(e) That is registered, or approved for registration upon notice of issuance, on a national securities exchange that makes transaction reports available pursuant to Rule 11Aa3–1 of this chapter, provided that:

(1) Price and volume information with respect to transactions in that security is required to be reported on a current and continuing basis and is made available to vendors of market information pursuant to the rules of the national securities exchange; and

(2) The security is purchased or sold in a transaction that is effected on or through the facilities of the national securities exchange, or that is part of a distribution of the security;

except that a security that satisfies the requirements of this paragraph, but that does not otherwise satisfy the requirements of paragraphs (a), (b), (c), or (d) of this rule, shall be a penny stock for purposes of Section 15(b)(6) of the Act;

(f) That is authorized, or approved for authorization upon notice of issuance, for quotation in the National Association of Securities Dealers' Automated Quotation system (NASDAQ), provided that price and volume information with respect to transactions in that security is required to be reported on a current and continuing basis and is made available to vendors of market information pursuant to the rules of the National Association of Securities Dealers, Inc.;

except that a security that satisfies the requirements of this paragraph, but that does not otherwise satisfy the requirements of paragraphs (a), (b), (c), or (d) of this rule, shall be a penny stock for purposes of section 15(b)(6) of the Act; or

(g) Whose issuer has:

(1) Net tangible assets (*i.e.,* total assets less intangible assets and liabilities) in excess of $2,000,000, if the issuer has been in continuous operation for at least three years, or $5,000,000, if the issuer has been in continuous operation for less than three years; or

(2) Average revenue of at least $6,000,000 for the last three years.

(3) For purposes of paragraph (g) of this section, net tangible assets or average revenues must be demonstrated by financial statements dated less than fifteen months prior to the date of the transaction that the broker or dealer has reviewed and has a reasonable basis for believing are accurate in relation to the date of the transaction, and:

(i) If the issuer is other than a foreign private issuer, are the most recent financial statements for the issuer that have been audited and reported on by an independent public accountant in accordance with the provisions of 17 CFR 210.2–02; or

(ii) If the issuer is a foreign private issuer, are the most recent financial statements for the issuer that have been filed with the Commission or furnished to the Commission pursuant to Rule 240.12g3–2(b); *provided, however,* that if financial statements for the issuer dated less than fifteen months prior to the date of the transaction have not been filed with or furnished to the Commission, financial statements dated within fifteen months prior to the transaction shall be prepared in accordance with generally accepted accounting principles in the country of incorporation, audited in compliance with the requirements of that jurisdiction, and reported on by an accountant duly registered and in good standing in accordance with the regulations of that jurisdiction.

(4) The broker or dealer shall preserve, as part of its records, copies of the financial statements required by paragraph (g)(3) of this rule for the period specified in 17 CFR 240.17a-4(b).

Rule 3a55-1. Method For Determining Market Capitalization and Dollar Value of Average Daily Trading Volume; Application of the Definition of Narrow-Based Security Index

(a) *Market capitalization.* For purposes of Section 3(a)(55)(C)(i)(III)(bb) of the Act (15 U.S.C. 78c(a)(55)(C)(i)(III)(bb)):

(1) On a particular day, a security shall be 1 of 750 securities with the largest market capitalization as of the preceding 6 full calendar months when it is included on a list of such securities designated by the Commission and the CFTC as applicable for that day.

(2) In the event that the Commission and the CFTC have not designated a list under paragraph (a)(1) of this section:

(i) The method to be used to determine market capitalization of a security as of the preceding 6 full calendar months is to sum the values of the market capitalization of such security for each U.S. trading day of the preceding 6 full calendar months, and to divide this sum by the total number of such trading days.

(ii) The 750 securities with the largest market capitalization shall be identified from the universe of all reported securities, as defined in § 240.11Ac1-1, that are common stock or depositary shares.

(b) *Dollar value of ADTV.*

(1) For purposes of Section 3(a)(55)(B) of the Act (15 U.S.C. 78c(a)(55)(B)):

(i)(A) The method to be used to determine the dollar value of ADTV of a security is to sum the dollar value of ADTV of all reported transactions in such security in each jurisdiction as calculated pursuant to paragraphs (b)(1)(ii) and (iii).

(B) The dollar value of ADTV of a security shall include the value of all reported transactions for such security and for any depositary share that represents such security.

(C) The dollar value of ADTV of a depositary share shall include the value of all reported transactions for such depositary share and for the security that is represented by such depositary share.

(ii) For trading in a security in the United States, the method to be used to determine the dollar value of ADTV as of the preceding 6 full calendar months is to sum the value of all reported transactions in such security for each U.S. trading day during the preceding 6 full calendar months, and to divide this sum by the total number of such trading days.

(iii)(A) For trading in a security in a jurisdiction other than the United States, the method to be used to determine the dollar value of ADTV as of the preceding 6 full calendar months is to sum the value in U.S. dollars of all reported transactions in such security in such jurisdiction for each trading day during the preceding 6 full calendar months, and to divide this sum by the total number of trading days in such jurisdiction during the preceding 6 full calendar months.

(B) If the value of reported transactions used in calculating the ADTV of securities under paragraph (b)(1)(iii)(A) is reported in a currency other than U.S. dollars, the total value of each day's transactions in such currency shall be converted into U.S. dollars on the basis of a spot rate of exchange for that day obtained from at least one independent entity that provides or disseminates foreign exchange quotations in the ordinary course of its business.

(iv) The dollar value of ADTV of the lowest weighted 25% of an index is the sum of the dollar value of ADTV of each of the component securities comprising the lowest weighted 25% of such index.

(2) For purposes of Section 3(a)(55)(C)(i)(III)(cc) of the Act (15 U.S.C. 78c(a)(55)(C)(i)(III)(cc)):

(i) On a particular day, a security shall be 1 of 675 securities with the largest dollar value of ADTV as of the preceding 6 full calendar months when it is included on a list of such securities designated by the Commission and the CFTC as applicable for that day.

(ii) In the event that the Commission and the CFTC have not designated a list under paragraph (b)(2) of this section:

(A) The method to be used to determine the dollar value of ADTV of a security as of the preceding 6 full calendar months is to sum the value of all reported transactions in such security in the United States for each U.S. trading day during the preceding 6 full calendar months, and to divide this sum by the total number of such trading days.

(B) The 675 securities with the largest dollar value of ADTV shall be identified from the universe of all reported securities as defined in § 240.11Ac1–1 that are common stock or depositary shares.

(c) *Depositary Shares and Section 12 Registration.* For purposes of Section 3(a)(55)(C) of the Act (15 U.S.C. 78c(a)(55)(C)), the requirement that each component security of an index be registered pursuant to Section 12 of the Act (15 U.S.C. 78*l*) shall be satisfied with respect to any security that is a depositary share if the deposited securities underlying the depositary share are registered pursuant to Section 12 of the Act and the depositary share is registered under the Securities Act of 1933 (15 U.S.C. 77a *et seq.*) on Form F–6 (17 CFR 239.36).

(d) *Definitions.* For purposes of this section:

(1) *CFTC* means Commodity Futures Trading Commission.

(2) *Closing price* of a security means:

(i) If reported transactions in the security have taken place in the United States, the price at which the last transaction in such security took place in the regular trading session of the principal market for the security in the United States.

(ii) If no reported transactions in a security have taken place in the United States, the closing price of such security shall be the closing price of any depositary share representing such security divided by the number of shares represented by such depositary share.

(iii) If no reported transactions in a security or in a depositary share representing such security have taken place in the United States, the closing price of such security shall be the price at which the last transaction in such security took place in the regular trading session of the principal market for the security. If such price is reported in a currency other than U.S. dollars, such price shall be converted into U.S. dollars on the basis of a spot rate of exchange relevant for the time of the transaction obtained from at least one independent entity that provides or disseminates foreign exchange quotations in the ordinary course of its business.

(3) *Depositary share* has the same meaning as in § 240.12b–2.

(4) *Foreign financial regulatory authority* has the same meaning as in Section 3(a)(52) of the Act (15 U.S.C. 78c(a)(52)).

(5) *Lowest weighted 25% of an index.* With respect to any particular day, the lowest weighted component securities comprising, in the aggregate, 25% of an index's weighting for purposes of Section 3(a)(55)(B)(iv) of the Act (15 U.S.C. 78c(a)(55)(B)(iv)) ("lowest weighted 25% of an index") means those securities:

(i) That are the lowest weighted securities when all the securities in such index are ranked from lowest to highest based on the index's weighting methodology; and

(ii) For which the sum of the weight of such securities is equal to, or less than, 25% of the index's total weighting.

(6) *Market capitalization* of a security on a particular day:

(i) If the security is not a depositary share, is the product of:

(A) The closing price of such security on that same day; and

(B) The number of outstanding shares of such security on that same day.

(ii) If the security is a depositary share, is the product of:

(A) The closing price of the depositary share on that same day divided by the number of deposited securities represented by such depositary share; and

(B) The number of outstanding shares of the security represented by the depositary share on that same day.

(7) *Outstanding shares* of a security means the number of outstanding shares of such security as reported on the most recent Form 10–K, Form 10–Q, Form 10–KSB, Form 10–QSB, or Form 20–F (17 CFR 249.310, 249.308a, 249.310b, 249.308b, or 249.220f) filed with the Commission by the issuer of such security, including any change to such number of outstanding shares subsequently reported by the issuer on a Form 8–K (17 CFR 249.308).

(8) *Preceding 6 full calendar months* means, with respect to a particular day, the period of time beginning on the same day of the month 6 months before and ending on the day prior to such day.

(9) *Principal market* for a security means the single securities market with the largest reported trading volume for the security during the preceding 6 full calendar months.

(10) *Reported transaction* means:

(i) With respect to securities transactions in the United States, any transaction for which a transaction report is collected, processed, and made available pursuant to an effective transaction reporting plan, or for which a transaction report, last sale data, or quotation information is disseminated through an automated quotation system as described in Section 3(a)(51)(A)(ii) of the Act (15 U.S.C. 78c(a)(51)(A)(ii)); and

(ii) With respect to securities transactions outside the United States, any transaction that has been reported to a foreign financial regulatory authority in the jurisdiction where such transaction has taken place.

(11) *U.S. trading day* means any day on which a national securities exchange is open for trading.

(12) *Weighting* of a component security of an index means the percentage of such index's value represented, or accounted for, by such component security.

Rule 3a55–2. Indexes Underlying Futures Contracts Trading for Fewer Than 30 Days

(a) An index on which a contract of sale for future delivery is trading on a designated contract market, registered derivatives transaction execution facility, or foreign board of trade is not a narrow-based security index under Section 3(a)(55) of the Act (15 U.S.C. 78c(a)(55)) for the first 30 days of trading, if:

(1) Such index would not have been a narrow-based security index on each trading day of the preceding 6 full calendar months with respect to a date no earlier than 30 days prior to the commencement of trading of such contract;

(2) On each trading day of the preceding 6 full calendar months with respect to a date no earlier than 30 days prior to the commencement of trading such contract:

(i) Such index had more than 9 component securities;

(ii) No component security in such index comprised more than 30 percent of the index's weighting;

(iii) The 5 highest weighted component securities in such index did not comprise, in the aggregate, more than 60 percent of the index's weighting; and

(iv) The dollar value of the trading volume of the lowest weighted 25% of such index was not less than $50 million (or in the case of an index with 15 or more component securities, $30 million); or

(3) On each trading day of the preceding 6 full calendar months, with respect to a date no earlier than 30 days prior to the commencement of trading such contract:

(i) Such index had at least 9 component securities;

(ii) No component security in such index comprised more than 30 percent of the index's weighting; and

(iii) Each component security in such index was:

(A) Registered pursuant to Section 12 of the Act (15 U.S.C. 78) or was a depositary share representing a security registered pursuant to Section 12 of the Act;

(B) 1 of 750 securities with the largest market capitalization that day; and

(C) 1 of 675 securities with the largest dollar value of trading volume that day.

(b) An index that is not a narrow-based security index for the first 30 days of trading pursuant to paragraph (a) of this section, shall become a narrow-based security index if such index has been a narrow-based security index for more than 45 business days over 3 consecutive calendar months.

(c) An index that becomes a narrow-based security index solely because it was a narrow-based security index for more than 45 business days over 3 consecutive calendar months pursuant to paragraph (b) of this section shall not be a narrow-based security index for the following 3 calendar months.

(d) *Definitions.* For purposes of this section:

(1) *Market capitalization* has the same meaning as in § 240.3a55–1(d)(6).

(2) *Dollar value of trading volume* of a security on a particular day is the value in U.S. dollars of all reported transactions in such security on that day. If the value of reported transactions used in calculating dollar value of trading volume is reported in a currency other than U.S. dollars, the total value of each day's transactions shall be converted into U.S. dollars on the basis of a spot rate of exchange for that day obtained from at least one independent entity that provides or disseminates foreign exchange quotations in the ordinary course of its business.

(3) *Lowest weighted 25% of an index* has the same meaning as in § 240.3a55–1(d)(5).

(4) *Preceding 6 full calendar months* has the same meaning as in § 240.3a55–1(d)(8).

(5) *Reported transaction* has the same meaning as in § 240.3a55–1(d)(10).

Rule 3a55–3. Futures Contracts on Security Indexes Trading on or Subject to the Rules of a Foreign Board of Trade

When a contract of sale for future delivery on a security index is traded on or subject to the rules of a foreign board of trade, such index shall not be a narrow-based security index if it would not be a narrow-based security index if a futures contract on such index were traded on a designated contract market or registered derivatives transaction execution facility.

Rule 3b–1. Definition of "Listed"

The term "listed" means admitted to full trading privileges upon application by the issuer or its fiscal agent or, in the case of the securities of a foreign corporation, upon application by a banker engaged in distributing them; and includes securities for which authority to add to the list on official notice of issuance has been granted.

Rule 3b–2. Definition of "Officer"

The term "officer" means a president, vice president, secretary, treasurer or principal financial officer, comptroller or principal accounting officer, and any person routinely performing corresponding functions with respect to any organization whether incorporated or unincorporated.

Rule 3b–4. Definition of "Foreign Government," "Foreign Issuer" and "Foreign Private Issuer"

(a) The term "foreign government" means the government of any foreign country or of any political subdivision of a foreign country.

(b) The term "foreign issuer" means any issuer which is a foreign government, a national of any foreign country or a corporation or other organization incorporated or organized under the laws of any foreign country.

(c) The term "foreign private issuer" means any foreign issuer other than a foreign government except an issuer meeting the following conditions:

(1) More than 50 percent of the issuer's outstanding voting securities are directly or indirectly held of record by residents of the United States; and

(2) Any of the following:

(i) The majority of the executive officers or directors are United States citizens or residents;

(ii) More than 50 percent of the assets of the issuer are located in the United States; or

(iii) The business of the issuer is administered principally in the United States.

Instruction to paragraph (c)(1): To determine the percentage of outstanding voting securities held by U.S. residents:

A. Use the method of calculating record ownership in Rule 12g3–2(a) under the Act (§ 240.12g3–2(a)), except that your inquiry as to the amount of shares represented by accounts of customers resident in the United States may be limited to brokers, dealers, banks and other nominees located in:

(1) The United States,

(2) Your jurisdiction of incorporation, and

(3) The jurisdiction that is the primary trading market for your voting securities, if different than your jurisdiction of incorporation.

B. If, after responsible inquiry, you are unable to obtain information about the amount of shares represented by accounts of customers resident in the United States, you may assume, for purposes of this definition, that the customers are residents of the jurisdiction in which the nominee has its principal place of business.

C. Count shares of voting securities beneficially owned by residents of the United States as reported on reports of beneficial ownership provided to you or filed publicly and based on information otherwise provided to you.

Rule 3b–5. Nonexempt Securities Issued Under Governmental Obligations

(a) Any part of an obligation evidenced by any bond, note, debenture, or other evidence of indebtedness issued *by any governmental unit specified in section 3(a)(12) of the Act* which is payable from payments to be made in respect of property or money which is or will be used, under a lease, sale, or loan arrangement, by or for industrial or commercial enterprise, shall be deemed to be a separate "security" within the meaning of section 3(a)(10) of the Act, issued by the lessee or obligor under the lease, sale or loan arrangement.

(b) An obligation shall not be deemed a separate "security" as defined in paragraph (a) hereof if, (1) the obligation is payable from the general revenues of a governmental unit, specified in Section 3(a)(12) of the Act, having other resources which may be used for payment of the obligation, or (2) the obligation relates to a public project or facility owned and operated by or on behalf of and under the control of a governmental unit specified in such section, or (3) the obligation relates to a facility which is leased to and under the control of an industrial or commercial enterprise but is a part of a public project which, as a whole, is owned by and under the general control of a governmental unit specified in such section, or an instrumentality thereof.

(c) This rule shall apply to transactions of the character described in paragraph (a) only with respect to bonds, notes, debentures or other evidences of indebtedness *sold* after December 31, 1968.

Rule 3b-6. Liability for Certain Statements by Issuers

(a) A statement within the coverage of paragraph (b) of this section which is made by or on behalf of an issuer or by an outside reviewer retained by the issuer shall be deemed not to be a fraudulent statement (as defined in paragraph (d) of this section), unless it is shown that such statement was made or reaffirmed without a reasonable basis or was disclosed other than in good faith.

(b) This rule applies to the following statements:

(1) A forward-looking statement (as defined in paragraph (c) of this section) made in a document filed with the Commission, in Part I of a quarterly report on Form 10-Q and Form 10-QSB, § 249.308a of this chapter, or in an annual report to share-holders meeting the requirements of Rules 14a-3(b) and (c) or 14c-3(a) and (b) under the Securities Exchange Act of 1934, a statement reaffirming such forward-looking statement subsequent to the date the document was filed or the annual report was made publicly available, or a forward-looking statement made prior to the date the document was filed or the date the annual report was made publicly available if such statement is reaffirmed in a filed document, in Part I of a quarterly report on Form 10-Q, or in an annual report made publicly available within a reasonable time after the making of such forward-looking statement; Provided, That

(i) At the time such statements are made or reaffirmed, either the issuer is subject to the reporting requirements of section 13(a) or 15(d) of the Securities Exchange Act of 1934 and has complied with the requirements of Rule 13a-1 or 15d-1 thereunder, if applicable, to file its most recent annual report on Form 10-K and Form 10-KSB or Form 20-F or Form 40-F; or, if the issuer is not subject to the reporting requirements of section 13(a) or 15(d) of the Securities Exchange Act of 1934, the statements are made in a registration statement filed under the Securities Act of 1933 or pursuant to section 12(b) or (g) of the Securities Act of 1934, and

(ii) The statements are not made by or on behalf of an issuer that is an investment company registered under the Investment Company Act of 1940;

(2) Information which is disclosed in a document filed with the Commission, in Part I of a quarterly report on Form 10-Q and Form 10-QSB or in an annual report to shareholders meeting the requirements of Rules 14a-3(b) and (c) or 14c-3(a) and (b) under the Securities Exchange Act of 1934 and which relates to (i) the effects of changing prices on the business enterprise, presented voluntarily or pursuant to Item 303 of Regulation S-K or Regulation S-B or "Management's Discussion and Analysis of Financial Condition and Results of Operations" or Item 5 of Form 20-F, "Operating and Financial Review and Prospects," or Item 302 of Regulation S-K, "Supplementary financial information," or Rule 3-20(c) of Regulation S-X, or (ii) the value of proved oil and gas reserves (such as a standardized measure of discounted future net cash flows relating to proved oil and gas reserves as set forth in paragraphs 30-34 of Statement of Financial Accounting Standards No. 69) pre-

sented voluntarily or pursuant to Item 302 of Regulation S–K.

(c) For the purpose of this rule the term "forward looking statement" shall mean and shall be limited to:

(1) A statement containing a projection of revenues, income (loss), earnings (loss) per share, capital expenditures, dividends, capital structure or other financial items;

(2) A statement of management's plans and objectives for future operations;

(3) A statement of future economic performance contained in management's discussion and analysis of financial condition and results of operations included pursuant to Item 303 of Regulation S–K; or Item 5 of Form 20–F or

(4) Disclosed statements of the assumptions underlying or relating to any of the statements described in (1), (2), or (3) above.

(d) For the purpose of this rule the term "fraudulent statement" shall mean a statement which is an untrue statement of a material fact, a statement false or misleading with respect to any material fact, an omission to state a material fact necessary to make a statement not misleading, or which constitutes the employment of a manipulative, deceptive, or fraudulent device, contrivance, scheme, transaction, act, practice, course of business, or an artifice to defraud, as those terms are used in the Securities Exchange Act of 1934 or the rules or regulations promulgated thereunder.

Rule 3b–7. Definition of "Executive Officer"

The term "executive officer," when used with reference to a registrant, means its president, any vice president of the registrant in charge of a principal business unit, division or function (such as sales, administration, or finance), any other officer who performs a policy making function or any other person who performs similar policy making functions for the registrant. Executive officers of subsidiaries may be deemed executive officers of the registrant if they perform such policy making functions for the registrant.

Rule 3b–8. Definitions of "Qualified OTC Market Maker," "Qualified Third Market Maker" and "Qualified Block Positioner"

For the purposes of Regulation U under the Act (12 CFR 221):

(a) The term "Qualified OTC Market Maker" in an over-the-counter ("OTC") margin security means a dealer in any "OTC Margin Security" [as that term is defined in Section 2(j) of Regulation U (12 CFR 221.2(j))] who (1) is a broker or dealer registered pursuant to Section 15 of the Act, (2) is subject to and is in compliance with Rule 15c3–1, (3) has and maintains minimum net capital, as defined in Rule 15c3–1, of the lesser of (i) $250,000 or (ii) $25,000 plus $5,000 for each security in excess of five with regard to which the broker or dealer is, or is seeking to become a Qualified OTC Market Maker, and (4) except when such activity is unlawful, meets all of the following conditions with respect to such security: (i) he regularly publishes bona fide, competitive bid and offer quotations in a recognized inter-dealer quotation system, (ii) he furnishes bona fide, competitive bid and offer quotations to other brokers and dealers on request, (iii) he is ready, willing and able to effect transactions in reasonable amounts, and at his quoted prices, with other brokers and dealers, and (iv) he has a reasonable average rate of inventory turnover in such security.

(b) The term "Qualified Third Market Maker" means a dealer in any stock registered on a national securities exchange ("exchange") who (1) is a broker or dealer registered pursuant to Section 15 of the Act, (2) is subject to and is in compliance with Rule 15c3–1, (3) has and maintains minimum net capital, as defined in Rule 15c3–1, of the lesser of (i) $500,000 or (ii) $100,000 plus $20,000 for each security in excess of five with regard to which the broker or dealer is, or is seeking to become, a Qualified Third Market Maker, and (4) except when such activity is unlawful, meets all of the following conditions with respect to such security: (i) he furnishes bona fide, competitive bid and offer quotations at all times to other brokers and dealers on request, (ii) he is ready, willing and able to effect transactions for his own account in reasonable amounts, and at his quoted prices with other brokers and dealers, and (iii) he has a reasonable average rate of inventory turnover in such security.

(c) The term "Qualified Block Positioner" means a dealer who (1) is a broker or dealer registered pursuant to Section 15 of the Act, (2) is subject to and in compliance with Rule 15c3–1, (3) has and maintains minimum net capital, as defined in Rule 15c3–1 of $1,000,000 and (4) except when such activity is unlawful, meets all of the following conditions: (i) he engages in the activity of purchasing long or selling short from time to time, from or to a customer (other than a partner or a joint venture or other entity in which a partner, the dealer, or a person associated with such dealer, as defined in Section 3(a)(18) of the Act, participates) a block of stock with a current market value of $200,000 or more in a single transaction, or in several transactions at approximately the same time, from a single source to facilitate a sale or purchase by such customer, (ii) he has determined in the exercise of reasonable diligence that the block could not be sold to or purchased from others on equivalent or better terms, and (iii) he sells the shares comprising the block as rapidly as possible commensurate with the circumstances.

Rule 3b–9. Definition of "Bank" for Purposes of Sections 3(a)(4) and (5) of the Act

The term "bank" as used in the definition of "broker" and "dealer" in Sections 3(a)(4) and (5) of the Act does not include a bank that:

(1) publicly solicits brokerage business for which it receives transaction-related compensation, unless the bank enters into a contractual or other arrangement with a broker-dealer registered under the Act pursuant to which the broker-dealer will offer brokerage services on or off the premises of the bank, provided that:

(i) such broker-dealer is clearly identified as the person performing the brokerage services;

(ii) bank employees perform only clerical and ministerial functions in connection with brokerage transactions unless such employees are qualified as registered representatives pursuant to the requirements of the self-regulatory organizations;

(iii) bank employees do not receive, directly or indirectly, compensation for any brokerage activities unless such employees are qualified as registered representatives pursuant to the requirements of the self-regulatory organizations; and

(iv) such services are provided by the broker-dealer on a basis in which all customers are fully disclosed.

(2) directly or indirectly receives transaction-related compensation for providing brokerage services for trust, managing agency or other accounts to which the bank provides advice, provided, however, that this subsection shall not apply if the bank executes transactions through a registered broker-dealer and:

(i) each account independently chooses the broker-dealer through which execution is effected;

(ii) the bank's personnel do not receive, directly or indirectly, transaction-related compensation or compensation based upon the number of accounts choosing to use the registered broker-dealer; and

(iii) the brokerage services are provided by the broker-dealer on a basis in which all customers are fully disclosed; or

(3) deals in or underwrites securities.

(b) This rule shall not apply to any bank that engages in one or more of the following activities only:

(1) effects transactions in exempted or municipal securities as defined in the Act or in commercial paper, bankers' acceptances or commercial bills;

(2) effects no more than 1,000 transactions each year in securities other than exempted or municipal securities as defined in the Act or in commercial paper, bankers' acceptances or commercial bills;

(3) effects transactions for the investment portfolio of affiliated companies;

(4) effects transactions as part of a program for the investment or reinvestment of bank deposit funds into any no-load open-end investment company registered pursuant to the Investment Company Act of 1940 that attempts to maintain a constant net asset value per share or has an investment policy calling for investment of at least 80% of its assets in debt securities maturing in thirteen months or less;

(5) effects transactions as part of any bonus, profit-sharing, pension, retirement, thrift, savings, incentive, stock purchase, stock ownership, stock appreciation, stock option, dividend reinvestment or similar plan for employees or shareholders of an issuer or its subsidiaries;

(6) effects transactions pursuant to Sections 3(b), 4(2) and 4(6) of the Securities Act of 1933 and the rules and regulations thereunder; or

(7) is subject to Section 15(e) of the Act.

(c) The Commission, upon written request, or upon its own motion, may exempt a bank, either unconditionally or on specific terms and conditions, where the Commission determines that the bank's activities are not within the intended meaning and purpose of this rule.

(d) For purposes of this section, the term "transaction-related compensation" shall mean monetary profit to the bank in excess of cost recovery for providing brokerage execution services.

Rule 3b–11. Definitions Relating to Limited Partnership Roll–Up Transactions for Purposes of Sections 6(b)(9), 14(h) and 15A(b)(12)–(13)

For purposes of Sections 6(b)(9), 14(h) and 15A(b)(12)–(13) of the Act (15 U.S.C. 78f(b)(9), 78n(h) and 78o–3(b)(12)–(13)):

(a) The term *limited partnership roll-up transaction* does not include a transaction involving only entities that are not "finite-life" as defined in Item 901(b)(2) of Regulation S–K (§ 229.901(b)(2) of this chapter).

(b) The term *limited partnership roll-up transaction* does not include a transaction involving only entities registered under the Investment Company Act of 1940 (15 U.S.C. 80a–1 *et seq.*) or any Business Development Company as defined in section 2(a)(48) of that Act (15 U.S.C. 80a–2(a)(48)).

(c) The term *regularly traded* shall be defined as in Item 901(c)(2)(v)(C) of Regulation S–K (§ 229.901(c)(2)(v)(C) of this chapter).

Rule 3b–12. Definition of OTC Derivatives Dealer

The term *OTC derivatives dealer* means any dealer that is affiliated with a registered broker or dealer (other than an OTC derivatives dealer), and whose securities activities:

(a) Are limited to:

(1) Engaging in dealer activities in eligible OTC derivative instruments that are securities;

(2) Issuing and reacquiring securities that are issued by the dealer, including warrants on securities, hybrid securities, and structured notes;

(3) Engaging in cash management securities activities;

(4) Engaging in ancillary portfolio management securities activities; and

(5) Engaging in such other securities activities that the Commission designates by order pursuant to § 240.15a–1(b)(1); and

(b) Consist primarily of the activities described in paragraphs (a)(1), (a)(2), and (a)(3) of this section; and

(c) Do not consist of any other securities activities, including engaging in any transaction in any security that is not an eligible OTC derivative instrument, except as permitted under paragraphs (a)(3), (a)(4), and (a)(5) of this section.

(d) For purposes of this section, the term *hybrid security* means a security that incorporates payment features economically similar to options, forwards, futures, swap agreements, or collars involving currencies, interest or other rates, commodities, securities, indices, quantitative measures, or other financial or economic interests or property of any kind, or any payment or delivery that is dependent on the occurrence or nonoccurrence of any event associated with a potential financial, economic, or commercial consequence (or any combination, permutation, or derivative of such contract or underlying interest).

Rule 3b–13. Definition of Eligible OTC Derivative Instrument

(a) Except as otherwise provided in paragraph (b) of this section, the term *eligible OTC derivative instrument* means any contract, agreement, or transaction that:

(1) Provides, in whole or in part, on a firm or contingent basis, for the purchase or sale of, or is based on the value of, or any interest in, one or more commodities, securities, currencies, interest or other rates, indices, quantitative measures, or other financial or economic interests or property of any kind; or

(2) Involves any payment or delivery that is dependent on the occurrence or nonoccurrence of any event associated with a potential financial, economic, or commercial consequence; or

(3) Involves any combination or permutation of any contract, agreement, or transaction or underlying interest, property, or event described in paragraphs (a)(1) or (a)(2) of this section.

(b) The term *eligible OTC derivative instrument* does not include any contract, agreement, or transaction that:

(1) Provides for the purchase or sale of a security, on a firm basis, unless:

(i) The settlement date for such purchase or sale occurs at least one year following the trade date or, in the case of an eligible forward contract, at least four months following the trade date; or

(ii) The material economic features of the contract, agreement, or transaction consist primarily of features of a type described in paragraph (a) of this section other than the provision for the purchase or sale of a security on a firm basis; or

(2) Provides, in whole or in part, on a firm or contingent basis, for the purchase or sale of, or is based on the value of, or any interest in, any security (or group or index of securities), and is:

(i) Listed on, or traded on or through, a national securities exchange or registered national securities association, or facility or market thereof; or

(ii) Except as otherwise determined by the Commission by order pursuant to § 240.15a–1(b)(2), one of a class of fungible instruments that are standardized as to their material economic terms.

(c) The Commission may issue an order pursuant to § 240.15a–1(b)(3) clarifying whether certain contracts, agreements, or transactions are within the scope of eligible OTC derivative instrument.

(d) For purposes of this section, the term *eligible forward contract* means a forward contract that provides for the purchase or sale of a security other than a government security, provided that, if such contract provides for the purchase or sale of margin stock (as defined in Regulation U of the Regulations of the Board of Governors of the Federal Reserve System, 12 CFR Part 221), such contract either:

(1) Provides for the purchase or sale of such stock by the issuer thereof (or an affiliate that is not a bank or a broker or dealer); or

(2) Provides for the transfer of transaction collateral in an amount that would satisfy the requirements, if any, that would be applicable assuming the OTC derivatives dealer party to such transaction were not eligible for the exemption from Regulation T of the Regulations of the Board of Governors of the Federal Reserve System, 12 CFR part 220, set forth in § 240.36a1–1.

Rule 3b–14. Definition of Cash Management Securities Activities

The term *cash management securities activities* means securities activities that are limited to transactions involving:

(a) Any taking possession of, and any subsequent sale or disposition of, collateral provided by a counterparty, or any acquisition of, and any subsequent sale or disposition of, collateral to be provided to a counterparty, in connection with any securities activities of the dealer permitted under § 240.15a–1 or any non-securities activities of the dealer that involve eligible OTC derivative instruments or other financial instruments;

(b) Cash management, in connection with any securities activities of the dealer permitted under § 240.15a–1 or any non-securities activities of the dealer that involve eligible OTC derivative instruments or other financial instruments; or

(c) Financing of positions of the dealer acquired in connection with any securities activities of the dealer permitted under § 240.15a–1 or any non-securities activities that involve eligible OTC derivative instruments or other financial instrument

Rule 3b–15. Definition of Ancillary Portfolio Management Securities Activities

(a) The term *ancillary portfolio management securities activities* means securities activities that:

(1) Are limited to transactions in connection with:

(i) Dealer activities in eligible OTC derivative instruments;

(ii) The issuance of securities by the dealer; or

(iii) Such other securities activities that the Commission designates by order pursuant to § 240.15a–1(b)(1); and

(2) Are conducted for the purpose of reducing the market or credit risk of the dealer or consist of incidental trading activities for portfolio management purposes; and

(3) Are limited to risk exposures within the market, credit, leverage, and liquidity risk parameters set forth in:

(i) The trading authorizations granted to the associated person (or to the supervisor of such associated person) who executes a particular transaction for, or on behalf of, the dealer; and

(ii) The written guidelines approved by the governing body of the dealer and included in the internal risk management control system for the dealer pursuant to § 240.15c3–4; and

(4) Are conducted solely by one or more associated persons of the dealer who perform substantial duties for, or on behalf of, the dealer in connection with its dealer activities in eligible OTC derivative instruments.

(b) The Commission may issue an order pursuant to § 240.15a–1(b)(4) clarifying whether certain securities activities are within the scope of ancillary portfolio management securities activities.

Rule 3b–16. Definitions of Terms Used in Section 3(a)(1) of the Act

(a) An organization, association, or group of persons shall be considered to constitute, maintain, or provide "a market place or facilities for bringing together purchasers and sellers of securities or for otherwise performing with respect to securities the functions commonly performed by a stock exchange," as those terms are used in section 3(a)(1) of the Act, (15 U.S.C. 78c(a)(1)), if such organization, association, or group of persons:

(1) Brings together the orders for securities of multiple buyers and sellers; and

(2) Uses established, non-discretionary methods (whether by providing a trading facility or by setting rules) under which such orders interact with each other, and the buyers and sellers entering such orders agree to the terms of a trade.

(b) An organization, association, or group of persons shall not be considered to constitute, maintain, or provide "a market place or facilities for bringing together purchasers and sellers of securities or for otherwise performing with respect to securities the functions commonly performed by a stock exchange," solely because such organization, association, or group of persons engages in one or more of the following activities:

(1) Routes orders to a national securities exchange, a market operated by a national securities association, or a broker-dealer for execution; or

(2) Allows persons to enter orders for execution against the bids and offers of a single dealer; and

(i) As an incidental part of these activities, matches orders that are not displayed to any person other than the dealer and its employees; or

(ii) In the course of acting as a market maker registered with a self-regulatory organization, displays the limit orders of such market maker's, or other broker-dealer's, customers; and

(A) Matches customer orders with such displayed limit orders; and

(B) As an incidental part of its market making activities, crosses or matches orders that are not displayed to any person other than the market maker and its employees.

(c) For purposes of this section the term *order* means any firm indication of a willingness to buy or sell a security, as either principal or agent, including any bid or offer quotation, market order, limit order, or other priced order.

(d) For the purposes of this section, the terms *bid* and *offer* shall have the same meaning as under § 240.11Ac1–1.

(e) The Commission may conditionally or unconditionally exempt any organization, association, or group of persons from the definition in paragraph (a) of this section.

Rule 3b–17. Definitions of Terms Used in Section 3(a)(4) of the Act

For purposes of Section 3(a)(4) of the Act (15 U.S.C. 78c(a)(4)):

(a) The term *chiefly compensated* means that the "relationship compensation" received by a bank from a trust or fiduciary account exceeds the "sales compensation" received by the bank from such account during the immediately preceding year, which is either a calendar year or other fiscal year consistently used by the bank for recordkeeping and reporting purposes.

(b) The term *flat or capped per order processing fee equal to not more than the cost incurred by the bank in connection with executing securities transactions for trustee and fiduciary customers* means a fee that is no more than the amount a broker-dealer charged the bank for executing the transaction, plus the costs of any resources of the bank that are exclusively dedicated to transaction execution, comparison, and settlement for trust and fiduciary customers.

(c) The term *indenture trustee* means any trustee for an indenture to which the definition given in Section 303 of the Trust Indenture Act of 1939 (15 U.S.C. 77ccc) applies, and any trustee for an indenture to which the definition in Section 303 of the Trust Indenture Act of 1939 (15 U.S.C. 77ccc) would apply but for an exemption from qualification pursuant to Section 304 of the Trust Indenture Act of 1939 (15 U.S.C. 77ddd).

(d) The term *investment adviser if the bank receives a fee for its investment advice* means a bank that has a relationship with the customer paying the fee in which the bank:

(1) Provides, in return for the fee, continuous and regular investment advice to the customer's account that is based upon the individual needs of the customer; and

(2) Under state law, federal law, contract, or customer agreement owes a duty of loyalty, including an affirmative duty to make full and fair disclosure to the customer of all material facts relating to conflicts.

(e) The term *money market fund* means an open-end management investment company registered under the Investment Company Act of 1940 (15 U.S.C. 80a–1 *et seq.*) that is regulated as a money market fund pursuant to § 270.2a–7 of this chapter.

(f)(1) The term *no-load* in the context of an investment company registered under the Investment Company Act of 1940 (15 U.S.C. 80a–1 *et seq.*) means:

(i) Purchases of the investment company's securities are not subject to a sales load, as that term is defined in Section 2(a)(35) of the Investment Company Act of 1940 (15 U.S.C. 80a–2(a)(35)), or a deferred sales load, as that term is defined in § 270.6c–10 of this chapter; and

(ii) The investment company's total charges against net assets for sales or sales promotion expenses and personal service or the maintenance of shareholder accounts do not exceed 0.25 of 1% of average net assets annually and are disclosed in the money market fund's prospectus.

(2) For purposes of paragraph (f)(1) of this section, charges for the following will not be considered charges for personal service or for the maintenance of shareholder accounts:

(i) Transfer agent and subtransfer agent services for beneficial owners of the investment company shares;

(ii) Aggregating and processing purchase and redemption orders;

(iii) Providing beneficial owners with statements showing their positions in the investment companies;

(iv) Processing dividend payments;

(v) Providing subaccounting services for investment company shares held beneficially;

(vi) Forwarding shareholder communications, such as proxies, shareholder reports, dividend and tax notices, and updating prospectuses to beneficial owners; or

(vii) Receiving, tabulating, and transmitting proxies executed by beneficial owners.

(g)(1) The term *nominal one-time cash fee of a fixed dollar amount* means a payment in either of the following forms that meets the requirements of subparagraph (2):

(i) A payment that does not exceed one hour of the gross cash wages of the unregistered bank employee making a referral; or

(ii) Points in a system or program that covers a range of bank products and non-securities related services where the points count toward a bonus that is cash or non-cash if the points (and their value) awarded for referrals involving securities are not greater than the points (and their value) awarded for activities not involving securities.

(2) Regardless of the form of payment, the payment may not be related to:

(i) The size, value, or completion of any securities transaction;

(ii) The amount of securities-related assets gathered;

(iii) The size or value of any customer's bank or securities account; or

(iv) The customer's financial status.

(h) The term *referral* means a bank employee arranging a first securities-related contact between a registered broker-dealer and a bank customer, but does not include any activity (including any part of the account opening process) related to effecting transactions in securities beyond arranging that first contact.

(i) The term *relationship compensation* means any compensation received by a bank in connection with activities for which the bank relies on an exception under Section 3(a)(4)(B)(ii) of the Act (15 U.S.C. 78c(a)(4)(B)(ii)) that is received directly from a customer or beneficiary, or directly from the assets of the trust or fiduciary account, and consists solely of an administration or annual fee (payable on a monthly, quarterly, or other basis), a percentage of assets under management fee, or a flat or capped per order processing fee equal to not more than the cost incurred by the bank in connection with executing securities transactions for trust and fiduciary accounts, or any combination of such fees.

(j) The term *sales compensation* means any compensation received by a bank in connection with activities for which the bank relies on an exception under Section 3(a)(4)(B)(ii) of the Act (15 U.S.C. 78c(a)(4)(B)(ii)) that:

(1) Is a fee for effecting a transaction in securities that is not a flat or capped per order processing fee equal to not more than the cost incurred by the bank in connection with executing securities transactions for trustee and fiduciary customers;

(2) Is compensation that if paid to a broker or dealer would be payment for order flow, as defined in § 240.10b–10;

(3) Is a finders' fee received in connection with a securities transaction or account, except a fee received pursuant to Section 3(a)(4)(B)(i) of the Act (15 U.S.C. 78c(a)(4)(B)(i));

(4) Is a fee paid for an offering of securities that is not received directly from a customer or beneficiary, or directly from the assets of the trust or fiduciary account;

(5) Is a fee paid pursuant to a Rule 12b–1 plan under the Investment Company Act of 1940 (15 U.S.C. 80a–1 *et seq.*); or

(6) Is a fee paid by an investment company for personal service or the maintenance of shareholder accounts, except a fee that is not part of a Rule 12b–1 plan under the Investment Company Act of 1940 (15 U.S.C. 80a–1 *et seq.*) for:

(i) Transfer agent and subtransfer agent services for beneficial owners of shares in the investment company;

Rule 3b–18. Definitions of Terms Used in Section 3(a)(5) of the Act

For the purposes of section 3(a)(5)(C) of the Act (15 U.S.C. 78c(a)(5)(C)):

(a) The term *affiliate* means any company that controls, is controlled by, or is under common control with another company.

(b) The term *consumer-related receivable* means any obligation incurred by any natural person to pay money arising out of a transaction in which the money, property, insurance, or services (being purchased) are primarily for personal, family, or household purposes.

(c) The term *member* as it relates to the term "syndicate of banks" means a bank that is a participant in a syndicate of banks and together with its affiliates, other than its broker or dealer affiliates, originates no less than 10% of the value of the obligations in a pool of obligations used to back the securities issued through a grantor trust or other separate entity.

(d) The term *obligation* means any note, draft, acceptance, loan, lease, receivable, or other evidence of indebtedness that is not a security issued by a person other than the bank.

(e) The term *originated* means:

(1) Funding an obligation at the time that the obligation is created; or

(2) Initially approving and underwriting the obligation, or initially agreeing to purchase the obligation, provided that:

(i) The obligation conforms to the underwriting standards or is evidenced by the loan documents of the bank or its affiliates, other than its broker or dealer affiliates; and

(ii) The bank or its affiliates, other than its broker or dealer affiliates, fund the obligation in a timely manner, not to exceed six months after the obligation is created.

(f) The term *pool* means more than one obligation or type of obligation grouped together to provide collateral for a securities offering.

(g) The term *predominantly originated* means that no less than 85% of the value of the obligations in any pool were originated by:

(1) The bank or its affiliates, other than its broker or dealer affiliates; or

(2) Banks that are members of a syndicate of banks and affiliates of such banks, other than their broker or dealer affiliates, if the obligations or pool of obligations consist of mortgage obligations or consumer-related receivables.

(3) For this purpose, the bank and its affiliates include any financial institution with which the bank or its affiliates have merged but does not include the purchase of a pool of obligations or the purchase of a line of business.

(h) The term *syndicate of banks* means a group of banks that acts jointly, on a temporary basis, to issue through a grantor trust or other separate entity, securities backed by obligations originated by each of the individual banks or their affiliates, other than their broker or dealer affiliates.

Rule 3b–19. Definition of "issuer" in section 3(a)(8) of the Act in relation to asset-backed securities

The following applies with respect to asset-backed securities under the Act. Terms used in this section have the same meaning as in Item 1101 of Regulation AB (§ 229.1101 of this chapter).

(a) The depositor for the asset-backed securities acting solely in its capacity as depositor to the issuing entity is the "issuer" for purposes of the asset-backed securities of that issuing entity.

(b) The person acting in the capacity as the depositor specified in paragraph (a) of this section is a different "issuer" from that same person acting as a depositor for another issuing entity or for purposes of that person's own securities.

REGISTRATION AND EXEMPTION OF EXCHANGES

Rule 6a–1. Application for Registration as a National Securities Exchange or Exemption from Registration Based on Limited Volume

(a) An application for registration as a national securities exchange, or for exemption from such registration based on limited volume, shall be filed on Form 1 (§ 249.1 of this chapter), in accordance with the instructions contained therein.

(b) Promptly after the discovery that any information filed on Form 1 was inaccurate when filed, the exchange shall file with the Commission an amendment correcting such inaccuracy.

(c) Promptly after the discovery that any information in the statement, any exhibit, or any amendment was inaccurate when filed, the exchange shall file with the Commission an amendment correcting such inaccuracy.

(d) Whenever the number of changes to be reported in an amendment, or the number of amendments filed, are so great that the purpose of clarity will be promoted by the filing of a new complete statement and exhibits, an exchange may, at its election, or shall, upon request of the Commission, file as an amendment a complete new statement together with all exhibits which are prescribed to be filed in connection with Form 1.

Rule 6a–2. Amendments to Application

(a) A national securities exchange, or an exchange exempted from such registration based on limited volume, shall file an amendment to Form 1, (§ 249.1 of this chapter), which shall set forth the nature and effective date of the action taken and shall provide any new information and correct any information rendered inaccurate, on Form 1, (§ 249.1 of this chapter), within 10 days after any action is taken that renders inaccurate, or that causes to be incomplete, any of the following:

(1) Information filed on the Execution Page of Form 1, or amendment thereto; or

(2) Information filed as part of Exhibits C, F, G, H, J, K or M, or any amendments thereto.

(b) On or before June 30 of each year, a national securities exchange, or an exchange exempted from such registration based on limited volume, shall file, as an amendment to Form 1, the following:

(1) Exhibits D and I as of the end of the latest fiscal year of the exchange; and

(2) Exhibits K, M, and N, which shall be up to date as of the latest date practicable within 3 months of the date the amendment is filed.

(c) On or before June 30, 2001 and every 3 years thereafter, a national securities exchange, or an exchange exempted from such registration based on limited volume, shall file, as an amendment to Form 1, complete Exhibits A, B, C and J. The information filed under this paragraph (c) shall be current as of the latest practicable date, but shall, at a minimum, be up to date within 3 months as of the date the amendment is filed.

(d)(1) If an exchange, on an annual or more frequent basis, publishes, or cooperates in the publication of, any of the information required to be filed by paragraphs (b)(2) and (c) of this section, in lieu of filing such information, an exchange may:

(i) Identify the publication in which such information is available, the name, address, and telephone number of the person from whom such publication may be obtained, and the price of such publication; and

(ii) Certify to the accuracy of such information as of its publication date.

(2) If an exchange keeps the information required under paragraphs (b)(2) and (c) of this section up to date and makes it available to the Commission and the public upon request, in lieu of filing such information, an exchange may certify that the information is kept up to date and is available to the Commission and the public upon request.

(3) If the information required to be filed under paragraphs (b)(2) and (c) of this section is available continuously on an Internet web site controlled by an exchange, in lieu of filing such information with the Commission, such exchange may:

(i) Indicate the location of the Internet web site where such information may be found; and

(ii) Certify that the information available at such location is accurate as of its date.

(e) The Commission may exempt a national securities exchange, or an exchange exempted from such registration based on limited volume, from filing the amendment required by this section for any affiliate or subsidiary listed in Exhibit C of the exchange's application for registration, as amended, that either:

(1) Is listed in Exhibit C of the application for registration or notice of registration, as amended, of one or more other national securities exchanges; or

(2) Was an inactive subsidiary throughout the subsidiary's latest fiscal year. Any such exemption may be granted upon terms and conditions the Commission deems necessary or appropriate in the public interest

or for the protection of investors, provided however, that at least one national securities exchange shall be required to file the amendments required by this section for an affiliate or subsidiary described in paragraph (e)(1) of this section.

(f) A national securities exchange registered pursuant to Section 6(g)(1) of the Act (15 U.S.C. 78f(g)(1)) shall be exempt from the requirements of this section.

Rule 6a–3. Supplemental Material to be Filed by Exchanges

(a)(1) A national securities exchange, or an exchange exempted from such registration based on limited volume, shall file with the Commission any material (including notices, circulars, bulletins, lists, and periodicals) issued or made generally available to members of, or participants or subscribers to, the exchange. Such material shall be filed with the Commission within 10 days after issuing or making such material available to members, participants or subscribers.

(2) If the information required to be filed under paragraph (a)(1) of this section is available continuously on an Internet web site controlled by an exchange, in lieu of filing such information with the Commission, such exchange may:

(i) Indicate the location of the Internet web site where such information may be found; and

(ii) Certify that the information available at such location is accurate as of its date.

(b) Within 15 days after the end of each calendar month, a national securities exchange or an exchange exempted from such registration based on limited volume, shall file a report concerning the securities sold on such exchange during the calendar month. Such report shall set forth:

(1) The number of shares of stock sold and the aggregate dollar amount of such stock sold;

(2) The principal amount of bonds sold and the aggregate dollar amount of such bonds sold; and

(3) The number of rights and warrants sold and the aggregate dollar amount of such rights and warrants sold.

(c) A national securities exchange registered pursuant to Section 6(g)(1) of the Act (15 U.S.C. 78f(g)(1)) shall be exempt from the requirements of this section.

Rule 6a–4. Notice of Registration Under Section 6(g) of the Act, Amendment to Such Notice, and Supplemental Materials to be Filed by Exchanges Registered Under Section 6(g) of the Act

(a) *Notice of registration.* (1) An exchange may register as a national securities exchange solely for the purposes of trading security futures products by filing Form 1–N (§ 249.10 of this chapter) (“notice of registration”), in accordance with the instructions contained therein, if:

(i) The exchange is a board of trade, as that term in defined in the Commodity Exchange Act (7 U.S.C. 1a(2)), that:

(A) Has been designated a contract market by the Commodity Futures Trading Commission and such designation is not suspended by order of the Commodity Futures Trading Commission; or

(B) Is registered as a derivative transaction execution facility under Section 5a of the Commodity Exchange Act (7 U.S.C. 7a) and such registration is not suspended by the Commodity Futures Trading Commission; and

(ii) Such exchange does not serve as a market place for transactions in securities other than:

(A) Security futures products; or

(B) Futures on exempted securities or on groups or indexes of securities or options thereon that have been authorized under Section 2(a)(1)(C) of the Commodity Exchange Act (7 U.S.C. 2a).

(2) Promptly after the discovery that any information filed on Form 1–N (§ 249.10 of this chapter) was inaccurate when filed, the exchange shall file with the Commission an amendment correcting such inaccuracy.

(b) *Amendment to notice of registration.* (1) A national securities exchange registered pursuant to Section 6(g)(1) of the Act (15 U.S.C. 78f(g)(1)) ("Security Futures Product Exchange") shall file an amendment to Form 1–N (§ 249.10 of this chapter), which shall set forth the nature and effective date of the action taken and shall provide any new information and correct any information rendered inaccurate, on Form 1–N (§ 249.10 of this chapter), within:

(i) Ten days after any action is taken that renders inaccurate, or that causes to be incomplete, any information filed on the Execution Page of Form 1–N (§ 249.10 of this chapter), or amendment thereto; or

(ii) 30 days after any action is taken that renders inaccurate, or that causes to be incomplete, any information filed as part of Exhibit F to Form 1–N (§ 249.10 of this chapter), or any amendments thereto.

(2) A Security Futures Product Exchange shall maintain records relating to changes in information required in Exhibits C and E to Form 1–N (§ 249.10 of this chapter) which shall be current of as of the latest practicable date, but shall, at a minimum, be up-to-date within 30 days. A Security Futures Product Exchange shall make such records available to the Commission and the public upon request.

(3) On or before June 30, 2002, and by June 30 every year thereafter, a Security Futures Product Exchange shall file, as an amendment to Form 1–N (§ 249.10 of this chapter), Exhibits F, H, and I, which shall be current of as of the latest practicable date, but shall, at a minimum, be up-to-date within three months as of the date the amendment is filed.

(4) On or before June 30, 2004, and by June 30 every three years thereafter, a Security Futures Product Exchange shall file, as an amendment to Form 1–N (§ 249.10 of this chapter), complete Exhibits A, B, C, and E, which shall be current of as of the latest practicable date, but shall, at a minimum, be up-to-date within three months as of the date the amendment is filed.

(5)(i) If a Security Futures Product Exchange, on an annual or more frequent basis, publishes, or cooperates in the publication of, any of the information required to be filed by paragraphs (b)(3) and (b)(4) of this section, in lieu of filing such information, a Security Futures Product Exchange may satisfy this filing requirement by:

(A) Identifying the publication in which such information is available, the name, address, and telephone number of the person from whom such publication may be obtained, and the price of such publication; and

(B) Certifying to the accuracy of such information as of its publication date.

(ii) If a Security Futures Product Exchange keeps the information required under paragraphs (b)(3) and (b)(4) of this section up-to-date and makes it available to the Commission and the public upon request, in lieu of filing such information, a Security Futures Product Exchange may satisfy this filing requirement by certifying that the information is kept up-to-date and is available to the Commission and the public upon request.

(iii) If the information required to be filed under paragraphs (b)(3) and (b)(4) of this section is available continuously on an Internet web site controlled by a Security Futures Product Exchange, in lieu of filing such information with the Commission, such Security Futures Product Exchange may satisfy this filing requirement by:

(A) Indicating the location of the Internet web site where such information may be found; and

(B) Certifying that the information available at such location is accurate as of its date.

(6)(i) The Commission may exempt a Security Futures Product Exchange from filing the amendment required by this section for any affiliate or subsidiary listed in Exhibit C to Form 1–N (§ 249.10 of this chapter), as amended, that either:

(A) Is listed in Exhibit C to Form 1 (§ 249.1 of this chapter) or to Form 1–N (§ 249.10 of this chapter), as amended, of one or more other national securities exchanges; or

(B) Was an inactive affiliate or subsidiary throughout the affiliate's or subsidiary's latest fiscal year.

(ii) Any such exemption may be granted upon terms and conditions the Commission deems necessary or appropriate in the public interest or for the protection of investors, provided however, that at least one national securities exchange shall be required to file the amendments required by this section for an affiliate or subsidiary described in paragraph (b)(6)(i) of this section.

(7) If a Security Futures Product Exchange has filed documents with the Commodity Futures Trading Commission, to the extent that such documents contain information satisfying the Commission's informational requirements, copies of such documents may be filed with the Commission in lieu of the required written notice.

(c) *Supplemental material to be filed by Security Futures Product Exchanges.* (1)(i) A Security Futures Product Exchange shall file with the Commission any material related to the trading of security futures products (including notices, circulars, bulletins, lists, and periodicals) issued or made generally available to members of, participants in, or subscribers to, the exchange. Such material shall be filed with the Commission within ten days after issuing or making such material available to members, participants, or subscribers.

(ii) If the information required to be filed under paragraph (c)(1)(i) of this section is available continuously on an Internet web site controlled by an exchange, in lieu of filing such information with the Commission, such exchange may:

(A) Indicate the location of the Internet web site where such information may be found; and

(B) Certify that the information available at such location is accurate as of its date.

(2) Within 15 days after the end of each calendar month, a Security Futures Product Exchange shall file a report concerning the security futures products traded on such exchange during the previous calendar month. Such a report shall:

(i) For each contract of sale for future delivery of a single security, the number of contracts traded on such exchange during the relevant calendar month and the total number of shares underlying such contracts traded; and

(ii) For each contract of sale for future delivery of a narrow-based security index, the number of contracts traded on such exchange during the relevant calendar month and the total number of shares represented by the index underlying such contracts traded.

Rule 6h–1. Settlement and Regulatory Halt Requirements for Security Futures Products

(a) For the purposes of this section:

(1) *Opening price* means the price at which a security opened for trading, or a price that fairly reflects the price at which a security opened for trading, during the regu-

lar trading session of the national securities exchange or national securities association that lists the security. If the security is not listed on a national securities exchange or a national securities association, then *opening price* shall mean the price at which a security opened for trading, or a price that fairly reflects the price at which a security opened for trading, on the primary market for the security.

(2) *Regular trading session* of a security means the normal hours for business of a national securities exchange or national securities association that lists the security.

(3) *Regulatory halt* means a delay, halt, or suspension in the trading of a security, that is instituted by the national securities exchange or national securities association that lists the security, as a result of:

(i) A determination that there are matters relating to the security or issuer that have not been adequately disclosed to the public, or that there are regulatory problems relating to the security which should be clarified before trading is permitted to continue; or

(ii) The operation of circuit breaker procedures to halt or suspend trading in all equity securities trading on that national securities exchange or national securities association.

(b) *Final settlement prices for security futures products.*

(1) The final settlement price of a cash-settled security futures product must fairly reflect the opening price of the underlying security or securities.

(2) Notwithstanding paragraph (b)(1) of this section, if an opening price for one or more securities underlying a security futures product is not readily available, the final settlement price of the security futures product shall fairly reflect:

(i) The price of the underlying security or securities during the most recent regular trading session for such security or securities; or

(ii) The next available opening price of the underlying security or securities.

(3) Notwithstanding paragraph (b)(1) or (b)(2) of this section, if a clearing agency registered under Section 17A of the Act (15 U.S.C. 78q–1), or exempt from registration pursuant to Section 17A(b)(7) of the Act (15 U.S.C. 78q–1(b)(7)), to which the final settlement price of a security futures product is or would be reported determines, pursuant to its rules, that such final settlement price is not consistent with the protection of investors and the public interest, taking into account such factors as fairness to buyers and sellers of the affected security futures product, the maintenance of a fair and orderly market in such security futures product, and consistency of interpretation and practice, the clearing agency shall have the authority to determine, under its rules, a final settlement price for such security futures product.

(c) *Regulatory trading halts.* The rules of a national securities exchange or national securities association registered pursuant to Section 15A(a) of the Act (15 U.S.C. 78o–3(a)) that lists or trades one or more security futures products must include the following provisions:

(1) Trading of a security futures product based on a single security shall be halted at all times that a regulatory halt has been instituted for the underlying security; and

(2) Trading of a security futures product based on a narrow-based security index shall be halted at all times that a regulatory halt has been instituted for one or more underlying securities that constitute 50 percent or more of the market capitalization of the narrow-based security index.

(d) The Commission may exempt from the requirements of this section, either unconditionally or on specified terms and conditions, any national securities exchange or national securities association, if the Commission determines that such exemption is necessary or appropriate in the public interest and consistent with the protection of investors. An exemption granted pursuant to this paragraph shall not operate as an exemption from any Commodity Futures Trading Commission rules. Any exemption that may be required from such rules must be obtained separately from the Commodity Futures Trading Commission.

HYPOTHECATION OF CUSTOMERS' SECURITIES

Rule 8c-1. Hypothecation of Customers' Securities

(a) *General Provisions.* No member of a national securities exchange, and no broker or dealer who transacts a business in securities through the medium of any such member shall, directly or indirectly, hypothecate or arrange for or permit the continued hypothecation of any securities carried for the account of any customer under circumstances—

(1) that will permit the commingling of securities carried for the account of any such customer with securities carried for the account of any other customer, without first obtaining the written consent of each such customer to such hypothecation;

(2) that will permit such securities to be commingled with securities carried for the account of any person other than a bona fide customer of such member, broker or dealer under a lien for a loan made to such member, broker or dealer; or

(3) that will permit securities carried for the account of customers to be hypothecated, or subjected to any lien or liens or claim or claims of the pledgee or pledgees, for a sum which exceeds the aggregate indebtedness of all customers in respect of securities carried for their accounts; except that this clause shall not be deemed to be violated by reason of an excess arising on any day through the reduction of the aggregate indebtedness of customers on such a day: *Provided,* That funds or securities in an amount sufficient to eliminate such excess paid or placed in transfer to pledgees for the purpose of reducing the sum of the liens or claims to which securities carried for the account of customers are subjected as promptly as practicable after such reduction occurs, but before the lapse of one-half hour after the commencement of banking hours on the next banking day at the place where the largest principal amount of loans of such member, broker or dealer are payable and, in any event, before such member, broker or dealer on such day has obtained or increased any bank loan collateralized by securities carried for the account of customers.

(b) *Definitions.* For the purposes of this rule—

(1) The term *customer* shall not include any general or special partner or any director or officer of such member, broker or dealer, or any participant, as such, in any joint, group or syndicate account with such member, broker or dealer or with any partner, officer or director thereof. The term also shall not include any counterparty who has delivered collateral to an OTC derivatives dealer pursuant to a transaction in an eligible OTC derivative instrument, or pursuant to the OTC derivatives dealer's cash management securities activities or ancillary portfolio management securities activities, and who has received a prominent written notice from the OTC derivatives dealer that:

(i) Except as otherwise agreed in writing by the OTC derivatives dealer and the counterparty, the dealer may repledge or otherwise use the collateral in its business;

(ii) In the event of the OTC derivatives dealer's failure, the counterparty will likely be considered an unsecured creditor of the dealer as to that collateral;

(iii) The Securities Investor Protection Act of 1970 (15 U.S.C. 78aaa through 78lll) does not protect the counterparty; and

(iv) The collateral will not be subject to the requirements of § 240.8c–1, § 240.15c2–1, § 240.15c3–2, or § 240.15c3–3;

(2) the term "securities carried for the account of any customer" shall be deemed to mean:

(i) securities received by or on behalf of such member, broker or dealer for the account of any customer;

(ii) securities sold and appropriated by such member, broker or dealer to a customer, except that if such securities were subject to a lien when appropriated to a customer they shall not be deemed to be "securities carried for the account of any customer" pending their release from such lien as promptly as practicable;

(iii) securities sold, but not appropriated, by such member, broker or dealer to a customer who has made any payment therefor, to the extent that such member, broker or dealer owns and has received delivery of securities of like kind, except that if such securities were subject to a lien when such payment was made they shall not be deemed to be "securities carried for the account of any customer" pending their release from such lien as promptly as practicable;

(3) "aggregate indebtedness" shall not be deemed to be reduced by reason of uncollected items. In computing aggregate indebtedness, related guaranteed and guarantor accounts shall be treated as a single account and considered on a consolidated basis, and balances in accounts carrying both long and short positions shall be adjusted by treating the market value of the securities required to cover such short positions as though such market value were a debit; and

(4) in computing the sum of the liens or claims to which securities carried for the account of customers of a member, broker or dealer are subject, any rehypothecation of such securities by another member, broker or dealer who is subject to this rule or to Rule 15c2–1 shall be disregarded.

(c) *Exemption for Cash Accounts.* The provisions of paragraph (a)(1) hereof shall not apply to any hypothecation of securities carried for the account of a customer in a special cash account within the meaning of section 4(c) of Regulation T of the Board of Governors of the Federal Reserve System: *Provided,* That at or before the completion of the transaction of purchase of such securities for, or of sale of such securities to, such customer, written notice is given or sent to such customer disclosing that such securities are or may be hypothecated under circumstances which will permit the commingling thereof with securities carried for the account of other customers. The term "the completion of the transaction" shall have the meaning given to such term by Rule 15c1–1(b).

(d) *Exemption for Clearinghouse Liens.* The provisions of paragraphs (a)(2), (a)(3), and (f) of this section shall not apply to any lien or claim of the clearing corporation, or similar department or association, of a national securities exchange or a registered national securities association for a loan made and to be repaid on the same calendar day, which is incidental to the clearing of transactions in securities or loans through such corporation, department, or association: *Provided, however,* That for the purpose of paragraph (a)(3) of this section, "aggregate indebtedness of all customers in respect of securities carried for their accounts" shall not include indebtedness in respect of any securities subject to any lien or claim exempted by this paragraph.

(e) *Exemption for Certain Liens on Securities of Noncustomers.* The provisions of paragraph (a)(2) hereof shall not be deemed to prevent such member, broker, or dealer from permitting securities not carried for the account of a customer to be subjected (1) to a lien for a loan made against securities carried for the account of customers, or (2) to a lien for a loan made and to be repaid on the same calendar day. For the purpose of this exemption, a loan shall be deemed to be "made against securities carried for the account of customers" if only securities carried for the account of customers are used to obtain or to increase such loan or as substitutes for other securities carried for the account of customers.

(f) *Notice and Certification Requirements.* No person subject to this section shall hypothecate any security carried for the account of a customer unless, at or prior to the time of each such hypothecation, he gives written notice to the pledge that the security pledged is carried for the account of a customer and that such hypothecation does not contravene any provision of this rule, except that in the case of an omnibus account the member, broker or dealer for whom such account is carried may furnish a signed statement to the person carrying such account that all securities carried therein by such member, broker or dealer will be securities carried for the account of his customers and that the hypothecation thereof by such member, broker or dealer will not contravene any provision of this rule. The provisions of this paragraph shall not apply to any hypothecation of securities under any lien or claim of a pledgee securing a loan made and to be repaid on the same calendar day.

(g) The fact that securities carried for the accounts of customers and securities carried for the accounts of others are represented by one or more certificates in the custody of a clearing corporation or other subsidiary organization of either a national securities exchange or of a registered national securities association, or of a custodian bank, in accordance with a system for the central handling of securities established by a national securities exchange or a registered national securities association, pursuant to which system the hypothecation of such securities is effected by bookkeeping entries without physical delivery of such securities, shall not, in and of itself, result in a commingling of securities prohibited by paragraph (a)(1) or (a)(2) hereof, whenever a participating member, broker or dealer hypothecates securities in accordance with such system: *Provided, however,* That (1) any such custodian of any securities held by or for such system shall agree that it will not for any reason, including the assertion of any claim, right or lien of any kind, refuse or refrain from promptly delivering any such securities (other than securities then hypothecated in accordance with such system) to such clearing corporation or other subsidiary organization or as directed by it, except that nothing in such agreement shall be deemed to require the custodian to deliver any securities in contravention of any notice of levy, seizure or similar notice, or order, or judgment, issued or directed by a governmental agency or court, or officer thereof, having jurisdiction over such custodian, which on its face affects such securities; (2) such systems shall have safeguards in the handling, transfer and delivery of securities and provisions of fidelity bond coverage of the employees and agents of the clearing corporation or other subsidiary organization and for periodic examinations by independent public accountants; and (3) the provisions of this subparagraph (g) shall not be effective with respect to any particular system unless the agreement required by (i) and the safeguards and provisions required by (ii) shall have been deemed adequate by the Commission for the protection of investors, and unless any subsequent amendments to such agreement, safeguards or provisions shall have been deemed adequate by the Commission for the protection of investors.

Rule 9b-1. Options Disclosure Document

(a) *Definitions.* The following definitions shall apply for the purpose of this rule.

(1) "Options market" means a national securities exchange, an automated quotation system of a registered securities association or a foreign securities exchange on which standardized options are traded.

(2) "Options class" means all options contracts covering the same underlying instrument.

(3) "Options disclosure document" means a document, including all amendments and supplements thereto, prepared by one or

more options markets which has been filed with the Commission or distributed in accordance with paragraph (b) of this section. "Definitive options disclosure document" or "document" means an options disclosure document furnished to customers in accordance with paragraph (b) of this section.

(4) "Standardized options" are options contracts trading on a national securities exchange, an automated quotation system of a registered securities association, or a foreign securities exchange which relate to options classes the terms of which are limited to specific expiration dates and exercise prices, or such other securities as the Commission may, by order, designate.

(b)(1) Five preliminary copies of an options disclosure document containing the information specified in paragraph (c) of this rule shall be filed with the Commission by an options market at least 60 days prior to the date definitive copies are furnished to customers, unless the Commission determines otherwise having due regard to the adequacy of the information disclosed and the public interest and protection of investors. Five copies of the definitive options disclosure document shall be filed with the Commission not later than the date the options disclosure document is furnished to customers. Notwithstanding the above, the use of an options disclosure document shall not be permitted unless the options class to which such document relates is the subject of an effective registration statement on Form S–20 under the Securities Act of 1933, or is exempt from registration under the Securities Act of 1933 (15 U.S.C. 77a *et seq.*).

(2)(i) If the information contained in the options disclosure document becomes or will become materially inaccurate or incomplete or there is or will be an omission of material information necessary to make the options disclosure document not misleading, the options market shall amend or supplement its options disclosure document by filing five copies of an amendment or supplement to such options disclosure document with the Commission at least 30 days prior to the date definitive copies are furnished to customers, unless the Commission determines otherwise having due regard to the adequacy of the information disclosed and the public interest and protection of investors. Five copies of the definitive options disclosure document, as amended or supplemented, shall be filed with the Commission not later than the date the amendment or supplement, or the amended options disclosure document, is furnished to customers.

(ii) Notwithstanding paragraph (b)(2)(i) of this section, an options market may distribute an amendment or supplement to an options disclosure document prior to such 30 day period if it determines, in good faith, that such delivery is necessary to ensure timely and accurate disclosure with respect to one or more of the options classes covered by the document. Five copies of any amendment or supplement distributed pursuant to this paragraph shall be filed with the Commission at the time of distribution. In that instance, if the Commission determines, having given due regard to the adequacy of the information disclosed and the public interest and the protection of investors, it may require refiling of the amendment pursuant to paragraph (b)(2)(i) of this section.

(c) *Information required in an options disclosure document.* An options disclosure document shall contain the following information, unless otherwise provided by the Commission, with respect to the options classes covered by the document:

(1) A glossary of terms;

(2) A discussion of the mechanics of exercising the options;

(3) A discussion of the risks of being a holder or writer of the options;

(4) The identification of the market or markets in which the options are traded;

(5) A brief reference to the transaction costs, margin requirements and tax consequences of options trading;

(6) The identification of the issuer of the options;

(7) A general identification of the type of instrument or instruments underlying the options class or classes covered by the document;

(8) If the options are not exempt from registration under the Securities Act of 1933 (15 U.S.C. 77a *et seq.*), the registration of the options on Form S-20 (17 CFR 239.20) and the availability of the prospectus and the information in part II of the registration statement; and

(9) Such other information as the Commission may specify.

(d) *Broker-dealer obligations.* (1) No broker or dealer shall accept an order from a customer to purchase or sell an option contract relating to an options class that is the subject of a definitive options disclosure document, or approve the customer's account for the trading of such option, unless the broker or dealer furnishes or has furnished to the customer a copy of the definitive options disclosure document.

(2) If a definitive options disclosure document relating to an options class is amended or supplemented, each broker and dealer shall promptly send a copy of the definitive amendment or supplement or a copy of the definitive options disclosure document as amended to each customer whose account is approved for trading the options class or classes to which the amendment or supplement relates.

SHORT SALES

Rule 10a-1. Short Sales

(a)(1)(i) No person shall, for his own account or for the account of any other person, effect a short sale of any security registered on, or admitted to unlisted trading privileges on, a national securities exchange, if trades in such security are reported pursuant to an "effective transaction reporting plan" as defined in Rule 11Aa3-1, and information as to such trades is made available in accordance with such plan on a real-time basis to vendors of market transaction information, (A) below the price at which the last sale thereof, regular way, was reported pursuant to an effective transaction reporting plan; or (B) at such price unless such price is above the next preceding different price at which a sale of such security, regular way, was reported pursuant to an effective transaction reporting plan.

(ii) The provisions of paragraph (a)(1)(i) of this rule shall not apply to transactions by any person in NASDAQ securities as defined in Rule 11Aa3-1 except for those NASDAQ securities for which transaction reports are collected, processed, and made available pursuant to the plan originally submitted to the Commission pursuant to Rule 17a-15 (subsequently amended and redesignated as Rule 11Aa3-1) under the Act, which plan was declared effective as of May 17, 1974.

(2) Notwithstanding paragraph (a)(1) of this rule, any exchange, by rule, may require that no person shall, for his own account or the account of any other person, effect a short sale of any such security on that exchange (i) below the price at which the last sale thereof, regular way, was effected on such exchange, or (ii) at such price unless such price is above the next preceding different price at which a sale of such securities, regular way, was effected on such exchange, if that exchange determines that such action is necessary or appropriate in its market in the public interest or for the protection of investors; and, if an exchange adopts such a rule, no person shall, for his own account or for the account of any other person, effect a short sale of any such security on such exchange otherwise than in accordance with such rule, and compliance with any such rule of an exchange shall constitute compliance with this paragraph (a).

(3) In determining the price at which a short sale may be effected after a security goes ex-dividend, ex-right, or ex-any other distribu-

tion, all sale prices prior to the "ex" date may be reduced by the value of such distribution.

(b) No person shall, for his own account or for the account of any other person, effect on a national securities exchange a short sale of any security not covered by paragraph (a) of this rule, (1) below the price at which the last sale thereof, regular way, was effected on such exchange, or (2) at such price unless such price is above the next preceding different price at which a sale of such security, regular way, was effected on such exchange. In determining the price at which a short sale may be effected after a security goes ex-dividend, ex-right, or ex-any other distribution, all sale prices prior to the "ex" date may be reduced by the value of such distribution.

(c) Reserved

(d) Reserved

(e) The provisions of paragraphs (a) and (b) of this rule (and of any exchange rule adopted in accordance with paragraph (a) of this rule) shall not apply to—

(1) Any sale by any person, for an account in which he has an interest, if such person owns the security sold and intends to deliver such security as soon as is possible without undue inconvenience or expense;

(2) Any broker or dealer in respect of a sale, for an account in which he has no interest, pursuant to an order to sell which is marked "long";

(3) Any sale by an odd-lot dealer on an exchange with which it is registered for such security, or any over-the-counter sale by a third market maker to offset odd-lot orders of customers;

(4) Any sale by an odd-lot dealer on an exchange with which it is registered for such security, or any over-the-counter sale by a third market maker to liquidate a long position which is less than a round lot, provided such sale does not change the position of such odd-lot dealer or such market maker by more than the unit of trading;

(5) Any sale of a security covered by paragraph (a) of this rule (except a sale to a stabilizing bid complying with § 242.104 of this Chapter) by a registered specialist or registered exchange market maker for its own account on any exchange with which it is registered for such security, or by a third market maker for its own account over-the-counter,

(i) Effected at a price equal to or above the last sale, regular way, reported for such security pursuant to an effective transaction reporting plan; or

(ii) Effected at a price equal to the most recent offer communicated for the security by such registered specialist, registered exchange market maker or third market maker to an exchange or a national securities association ("association") pursuant to Rule 11Ac1–1, if such offer, when communicated, was equal to or above the last sale, regular way, reported for such security pursuant to an effective transaction reporting plan: *Provided, however,* That any exchange, by rule, may prohibit its registered specialists and registered exchange market makers from availing themselves of the exemption afforded by this paragraph (e)(5) if that exchange determines that such action is necessary or appropriate in its market in the public interest or for the protection of investors;

(6) Any sale of a security covered by paragraph (b) of this rule on a national securities exchange (except a sale to a stabilizing bid complying with § 242.104 of this chapter) effected with the approval of such exchange which is necessary to equalize the price of such security thereon with the current price of such security on another national securities exchange which is the principal exchange market for such security;

(7) Any sale of a security for a special arbitrage account by a person who then owns another security by virtue of which he is, or presently will be, entitled to acquire an equivalent number of securities of the same

class as the securities sold; provided such sale, or the purchase which such sale offsets, is effected for the bona fide purpose of profiting from a current difference between the price of the security sold and the security owned and that such right of acquisition was originally attached to or represented by another security or was issued to all the holders of any such class of securities of the issuer;

(8) Any sale of a security registered on, or admitted to unlisted trading privileges on, a national securities exchange effected for a special international arbitrage account for the bona fide purpose of profiting from a current difference between the price of such security on a securities market not within or subject to the jurisdiction of the United States and on a securities market subject to the jurisdiction of the United States; provided the seller at the time of such sale knows or, by virtue of information currently received, has reasonable grounds to believe that an offer enabling him to cover such sale is then available to him in such foreign securities market and intends to accept such offer immediately;

(9) Reserved.

(10) Any sale by an underwriter, or any member of a syndicate or group participating in the distribution of a security, in connection with an over-allotment of securities, or any lay-off sale by such a person in connection with a distribution of securities through rights or a standby underwriting commitment; or

(11) Any sale of a security covered by paragraph (a) of this rule (except a sale to a stabilizing bid complying with § 242.104 of this chapter by any broker or dealer), for his own account or for the account of any other person, effected at a price equal to the most recent offer communicated by such broker or dealer to an exchange or association pursuant to Rule 11Ac1-1 in an amount less than or equal to the quotation size associated with such offer, if such offer, when communicated, was (i) above the price at which the last sale, regular way, for such security was reported pursuant to an effective transaction reporting plan; or (ii) at such last sale price, if such last sale price is above the next preceding different price at which a sale of such security, regular way, was reported pursuant to an effective transaction reporting plan.

(12) For the purposes of paragraph (e)(8) of this rule, a depositary receipt of a security shall be deemed to be the same security as the security represented by such receipt. For the purposes of paragraphs (e)(3), (4) and (5) of this rule, the term "third market maker" shall mean any broker or dealer who holds itself out as being willing to buy and sell a reported security for its own account on a regular and continuous basis otherwise than on an exchange in amounts of less than block size.

(f) This rule shall not prohibit any transaction or transactions which the Commission, upon written request or upon its own motion, exempts, either unconditionally or on specified terms and conditions.

MANIPULATIVE AND DECEPTIVE DEVICES AND CONTRIVANCES

Rule 10b-1. Prohibition of Use of Manipulative or Deceptive Devices or Contrivances With Respect to Certain Securities Exempted From Registration

The term manipulative or deceptive device or contrivance, as used in section 10(b), is hereby defined to include any act or omission to act with respect to any security exempted from the operation of section 12(a) pursuant to a rule which specifically provides that this rule shall be applicable to such security, if such act or omission to act would have been unlawful under section 9(a), or any rule or regulation heretofore or hereafter prescribed thereunder, if done or omitted to be done with respect to a security registered on a national securities exchange, and the use of any means or instrumentality of interstate commerce or of the mails or of any facility of any national securities exchange to use or employ any such device or contrivance in connection with the purchase or sale of any such security is hereby prohibited.

Rule 10b–3. Employment of Manipulative and Deceptive Devices by Brokers or Dealers

(a) It shall be unlawful for any broker or dealer, directly or indirectly, by the use of any means or instrumentality of interstate commerce, or of the mails, or of any facility of any national securities exchange, to use or employ, in connection with the purchase or sale of any security otherwise than on a national securities exchange, any act, practice, or course of business defined by the Commission to be included within the term "manipulative, deceptive, or other fraudulent device or contrivance," as such term is used in section 15(c)(1) of the Act.

(b) It shall be unlawful for any municipal securities dealer directly or indirectly, by the use of any means or instrumentality of interstate commerce, or of the mails, or of any facility of any national securities exchange, to use or employ, in connection with the purchase or sale of any municipal security, any act, practice, or course of business defined by the Commission to be included within the term "manipulative, deceptive, or other fraudulent device or contrivance," as such term is used in Section 15(c)(1) of the Act.

Rule 10b–5. Employment of Manipulative and Deceptive Devices

It shall be unlawful for any person, directly or indirectly, by the use of any means or instrumentality of interstate commerce, or of the mails, or of any facility of any national securities exchange,

(a) to employ any device, scheme, or artifice to defraud,

(b) to make any untrue statement of a material fact or to omit to state a material fact necessary in order to make the statements made, in the light of the circumstances under which they were made, not misleading, or

(c) to engage in any act, practice, or course of business which operates or would operate as a fraud or deceit upon any person,

in connection with the purchase or sale of any security.

Rule 10b5–1. Trading "on the Basis of" Material Nonpublic Information in Insider Trading Cases

Preliminary Note to § 240.10b5–1: This provision defines when a purchase or sale constitutes trading "on the basis of" material nonpublic information in insider trading cases brought under Section 10(b) of the Act and Rule 10b–5 thereunder. The law of insider trading is otherwise defined by judicial opinions construing Rule 10b–5, and Rule 10b5–1 does not modify the scope of insider trading law in any other respect.

(a) *General.* The "manipulative and deceptive devices" prohibited by Section 10(b) of the Act (15 U.S.C. 78j) and § 240.10b–5 thereunder include, among other things, the purchase or sale of a security of any issuer, on the basis of material nonpublic information about that security or issuer, in breach of a duty of trust or confidence that is owed directly, indirectly, or derivatively, to the issuer of that security or the shareholders of that issuer, or to any other person who is the source of the material nonpublic information.

(b) *Definition of "on the basis of."* Subject to the affirmative defenses in paragraph (c) of this section, a purchase or sale of a security of an issuer is "on the basis of" material nonpublic information about that security or issuer if the person making the purchase or sale was aware of the material nonpublic information when the person made the purchase or sale.

(c) *Affirmative defenses.* (1)(i) Subject to paragraph (c)(1)(ii) of this section, a person's purchase or sale is not "on the basis of" material nonpublic information if the person making the purchase or sale demonstrates that:

(A) Before becoming aware of the information, the person had:

(1) Entered into a binding contract to purchase or sell the security,

(2) Instructed another person to purchase or sell the security for the instructing person's account, or

(3) Adopted a written plan for trading securities;

(B) The contract, instruction, or plan described in paragraph (c)(1)(i)(A) of this Section:

(1) Specified the amount of securities to be purchased or sold and the price at which and the date on which the securities were to be purchased or sold;

(2) Included a written formula or algorithm, or computer program, for determining the amount of securities to be purchased or sold and the price at which and the date on which the securities were to be purchased or sold; or

(3) Did not permit the person to exercise any subsequent influence over how, when, or whether to effect purchases or sales; provided, in addition, that any other person who, pursuant to the contract, instruction, or plan, did exercise such influence must not have been aware of the material nonpublic information when doing so; and

(C) The purchase or sale that occurred was pursuant to the contract, instruction, or plan. A purchase or sale is not "pursuant to a contract, instruction, or plan" if, among other things, the person who entered into the contract, instruction, or plan altered or deviated from the contract, instruction, or plan to purchase or sell securities (whether by changing the amount, price, or timing of the purchase or sale), or entered into or altered a corresponding or hedging transaction or position with respect to those securities.

(ii) Paragraph (c)(1)(i) of this section is applicable only when the contract, instruction, or plan to purchase or sell securities was given or entered into in good faith and not as part of a plan or scheme to evade the prohibitions of this section.

(iii) This paragraph (c)(1)(iii) defines certain terms as used in paragraph (c) of this Section.

(A) *Amount.* "Amount" means either a specified number of shares or other securities or a specified dollar value of securities.

(B) *Price.* "Price" means the market price on a particular date or a limit price, or a particular dollar price.

(C) *Date.* "Date" means, in the case of a market order, the specific day of the year on which the order is to be executed (or as soon thereafter as is practicable under ordinary principles of best execution). "Date" means, in the case of a limit order, a day of the year on which the limit order is in force.

(2) A person other than a natural person also may demonstrate that a purchase or sale of securities is not "on the basis of" material nonpublic information if the person demonstrates that:

(i) The individual making the investment decision on behalf of the person to purchase or sell the securities was not aware of the information; and

(ii) The person had implemented reasonable policies and procedures, taking into consideration the nature of the person's business, to ensure that individuals making investment decisions would not violate the laws prohibiting trading on the basis of material nonpublic information. These policies and procedures may include those that restrict any purchase, sale, and causing any purchase or sale of any security as to which the person has material nonpublic information, or those that prevent such individuals from becoming aware of such information.

Rule 10b5–2. Duties of Trust or Confidence in Misappropriation Insider Trading Cases

Preliminary Note to § 240.10b5–2: This section provides a non-exclusive definition of circumstances in which a person has a duty of trust or confidence for purposes of the "misappropriation" theory of insider trading under Section 10(b) of the Act and Rule 10b–5. The law of insider trading is otherwise defined by judicial opinions construing Rule 10b–5, and Rule 10b5–2 does not modify the scope of insider trading law in any other respect.

(a) *Scope of Rule.* This section shall apply to any violation of Section 10(b) of the Act (15 U.S.C. 78j(b)) and § 240.10b–5 thereunder that is based on the purchase or sale of securities on the basis of, or the communication of, material nonpublic information misappropriated in breach of a duty of trust or confidence.

(b) *Enumerated "duties of trust or confidence."* For purposes of this section, a "duty of trust or confidence" exists in the following circumstances, among others:

(1) Whenever a person agrees to maintain information in confidence;

(2) Whenever the person communicating the material nonpublic information and the person to whom it is communicated have a history, pattern, or practice of sharing confidences, such that the recipient of the information knows or reasonably should know that the person communicating the material nonpublic information expects that the recipient will maintain its confidentiality; or

(3) Whenever a person receives or obtains material nonpublic information from his or her spouse, parent, child, or sibling; *provided,* however, that the person receiving or obtaining the information may demonstrate that no duty of trust or confidence existed with respect to the information, by establishing that he or she neither knew nor reasonably should have known that the person who was the source of the information expected that the person would keep the information confidential, because of the parties' history, pattern, or practice of sharing and maintaining confidences, and because there was no agreement or understanding to maintain the confidentiality of the information.

Rule 10b–9. Prohibited Representations in Connection With Certain Offerings

(a) It shall constitute a "manipulative or deceptive device or contrivance," as used in section 10(b) of the Act, for any person, directly or indirectly, in connection with the offer or sale of any security, to make any representation:

(1) to the effect that the security is being offered or sold on an "all-or-none" basis, unless the security is part of an offering or distribution being made on the condition that all or a specified amount of the consideration paid for such security will be promptly refunded to the purchaser unless (A) all of the securities being offered are sold at a specified price within a specified time, and (B) the total amount due to the seller is received by him by a specified date; or

(2) to the effect that the security is being offered or sold on any other basis whereby all or part of the consideration paid for any such security will be refunded to the purchaser if all or some of the securities are not sold, unless the security is part of an offering or distribution being made on the condition that all or a specified part of the consideration paid for such security will be promptly refunded to the purchaser unless (A) a specified number of units of the security are sold at a specified price within a specified time, and (B) the total amount due to the seller is received by him by a specified date.

(b) This rule shall not apply to any offer or sale of securities as to which the seller has a firm commitment from underwriters others (subject only to customary conditions precedent, including "market outs") for the purchase of all the securities being offered.

Rule 10b–10. Confirmation of Transactions

Preliminary Note. This section requires broker-dealers to disclose specified information in writing to customers at or before completion of a transaction. The requirements under this section that particular information be disclosed is not determinative of a broker-dealer's obligation under the general antifraud provisions of the federal securities laws to disclose additional information to a customer at the time of the customer's investment decision.

(a) *Disclosure Requirement.* It shall be unlawful for any broker or dealer to effect for or with an account of a customer any transaction in, or to induce the purchase or sale by such customer of, any security (other than U.S. Savings Bonds or municipal securities) unless such broker or dealer, at or before completion of such transaction, gives or sends to such customer written notification disclosing:

(1) The date and time of the transaction (or the fact that the time of the transaction will be furnished upon written request to such customer) and the identity, price, and number of shares or units (or principal amount) of such security purchased or sold by such customer; and

(2) Whether the broker or dealer is acting as agent for such customer, as agent for some other person, as agent for both such customer and some other person, or as principal for its own account; and if the broker or dealer is acting as principal, whether it is a market maker in the security (other than by reason of acting as a block positioner); and

(i) If the broker or dealer is acting as agent for such customer, for some other person, or for both such customer and some other person:

(A) The name of the person from whom the security was purchased, or to whom it was sold, for such customer or the fact that the information will be furnished upon written request of such customer; and

(B) The amount of any remuneration received or to be received by the broker from such customer in connection with the transaction unless remuneration paid by such customer is determined pursuant to written agreement with such customer, otherwise than on a transaction basis; and

(C) For a transaction in any subject security as defined in § 240.11Ac1–2 or a security authorized for quotation on an automated interdealer quotation system that has the characteristics set forth in Section 17B of this Act (15 U.S.C. 78q–2), a statement whether payment for order flow is received by the broker or dealer for transactions in such securities and the fact that the source and nature of the compensation received in connection with the particular transaction will be furnished upon written request of the customer provided, however, that brokers or dealers that do not receive payment for order flow in connection with any transaction have no disclosure obligation under this paragraph; and

(D) The source and amount of any other remuneration received or to be received by the broker in connection with the transaction: *Provided, however*, that if, in the case of a purchase, the broker was not participating in a distribution, or in the case of a sale, was not participating in a tender offer, the written notification may state whether any other remuneration has been or will be received and the fact that the source and amount of such other remuneration will be furnished upon written request of such customer; or

(ii) If the broker or dealer is acting as principal for its own account:

(A) In the case where such broker or dealer is not a market maker in an equity security and, if, after having received an order to buy from a customer, the broker or dealer purchased the equity security from another person to offset a contemporaneous sale to such customer or, after having received an order to sell from a customer, the broker or dealer sold the security to another person to offset a contemporaneous purchase from such customer, the difference between the price to the customer and the dealer's contemporaneous purchase (for customer purchases) or sale price (for customer sales); or

(B) In the case of any other transaction in a reported security, or an equity security that is quoted on NASDAQ or traded on a national securities exchange and that is subject to last sale reporting, the reported trade price, the price to the customer in the transaction, and the difference, if any, between the reported trade price and the price to the customer.

(3) Whether any odd-lot differential or equivalent fee has been paid by such customer in connection with the execution of an order for an odd-lot number of shares or units (or principal amount) of a security and the fact that the amount of any such differential or fee will be furnished upon oral or written request: *Provided, however,* that such disclosure need not be made if the differential or fee is included in the remuneration disclosure, or exempted from disclosure, pursuant to paragraph (a)(2)(i)(B) of this section; and

(4) In the case of any transaction in a debt security subject to redemption before maturity, a statement to the effect that such debt security may be redeemed in whole or in part before maturity, that such a redemption could affect the yield represented and the fact that additional information is available upon request; and

(5) In the case of a transaction in a debt security effected exclusively on the basis of a dollar price:

(i) The dollar price at which the transaction was effected, and

(ii) The yield to maturity calculated from the dollar price: *Provided, however,* that this paragraph (a)(5)(ii) shall not apply to a transaction in a debt security that either:

(A) Has a maturity date that may be extended by the issuer thereof, with a variable interest payable thereon; or

(B) Is an asset-backed security, that represents an interest in or is secured by a pool of receivables or other financial assets that are subject continuously to prepayment; and

(6) In the case of a transaction in a debt security effected on the basis of yield:

(i) The yield at which the transaction was effected, including the percentage amount and its characterization (*e.g.,* current yield, yield to maturity, or yield to call) and if effected at yield to call, the type of call, the call date and call price; and

(ii) The dollar price calculated from the yield at which the transaction was effected; and

(iii) If effected on a basis other than yield to maturity and the yield to maturity is lower than the represented yield, the yield to maturity as well as the represented yield: *Provided, however,* that this paragraph (a)(6)(iii) shall not apply to a transaction in a debt security that either:

(A) Has a maturity date that may be extended by the issuer thereof, with a variable interest rate payable thereon; or

(B) Is an asset-backed security, that represents an interest in or is secured by a pool of receivables or other financial assets that are subject continuously to prepayment; and

(7) In the case of a transaction in a debt security that is an asset-backed security, which represents an interest in or is secured by a pool of receivables or other financial assets that are subject continuously to prepayment, a statement indicating that the actual yield of such asset-backed security may vary according to the rate at which the underlying receivables or other financial assets are prepaid and a statement of the fact that information concerning the factors that affect yield (including at a minimum estimated yield, weighted average life, and the prepayment assumptions underlying yield) will be furnished upon written request of such customer; and

(8) In the case of a transaction in a debt security, other than a government security, that the security is unrated by a nationally recognized statistical rating organization, if such is the case; and

(9) That the broker or dealer is not a member of the Securities Investor Protection Corporation (SIPC), or that the broker or dealer clearing or carrying the customer account is not a member of SIPC, if such is the case: *Provided, however,* that this paragraph (a)(9) shall not apply in the case of a transaction in shares of a registered open-end investment company or unit investment trust if:

(i) The customer sends funds or securities directly to, or receives funds or securities directly from, the registered open-end investment company or unit investment trust, its transfer agent, its custodian, or other designated agent, and such person is not an associated person of the broker or dealer required by paragraph (a) of this section to send written notification to the customer; and

(ii) The written notification required by paragraph (a) of this section is sent on behalf of the broker or dealer to the customer by a person described in paragraph (a)(9)(i) of this section.

(b) *Alternative Periodic Reporting.* A broker or dealer may effect transactions for or with the account of a customer without giving or sending to such customer the written notification described in paragraph (a) of this section if:

(1) Such transactions are effected pursuant to a periodic plan or an investment company plan, or effected in shares of any open-end management investment company registered under the Investment Company Act of 1940 that holds itself out as a money market fund and attempts to maintain a stable net asset value per share: *Provided, however,* that no sales load is deducted upon the purchase or redemption of shares in the money market fund; and

(2) Such broker or dealer gives or sends to such customer within five business days after the end of each *quarterly* period, for transactions involving investment company and periodic plans, and after the end of each *monthly* period, for other transactions described in paragraph (b)(1) of this section, a written statement disclosing each purchase or redemption, effected for or with, and each dividend or distribution credited to or reinvested for, the account of such customer during the month; the date of such transaction; the identity, number, and price of any securities purchased or redeemed by such customer in each such transaction; the total number of shares of such securities in such customer's account; any remuneration received or to be received by the broker or dealer in connection therewith; and that any other information required by paragraph (a) of this section will be furnished upon written request: *Provided, however,* that the written statement may be delivered to some other person designated by the customer for distribution to the customer; and

(3) Such customer is provided with prior notification in writing disclosing the intention to send the written information re-

ferred to in paragraph (b)(1) of this section in lieu of an immediate confirmation.

(c) A broker or dealer shall give or send to a customer information requested pursuant to this rule within five business days of receipt of the request; *Provided, however,* That in the case of information pertaining to a transaction effected more than 30 days prior to receipt of the request, the information shall be given or sent to the customer within 15 business days.

(d) Definitions. For the purposes of this section:

(1) "Customer" shall not include a broker or dealer;

(2) "Completion of the transaction" shall have the meaning provided in Rule 15c1–1 under the Act;

(3) "Time of the transaction" means the time of execution, to the extent feasible, of the customer's order;

(4) "Debt security" as used in paragraphs (a)(3), (a)(4), and (a)(5) only, means any security, such as a bond, debenture, note, or any other similar instrument which evidences a liability of the issuer (including any such security that is convertible into stock or a similar security) and fractional or participation interests in one or more of any of the foregoing; *Provided, however,* that securities issued by an investment company registered under the Investment Company Act of 1940 shall not be included in this definition;

(5) "Periodic plan" means any written authorization for a broker acting as agent to purchase or sell for a customer a specific security or securities (other than securities issued by an open end investment company or unit investment trust registered under the Investment Company Act of 1940), in specific amounts (calculated in security units or dollars), at specific time intervals and setting forth the commissions or charges to be paid by the customer in connection therewith (or the manner of calculating them); and

(6) *Investment company plan* means any plan under which securities issued by an open-end investment company or unit investment trust registered under the Investment Company Act of 1940 are purchased by a customer (the payments being made directly to, or made payable to, the registered investment company, or the principal underwriter, custodian, trustee, or other designated agent of the registered investment company), or sold by a customer pursuant to:

(i) An individual retirement or individual pension plan qualified under the Internal Revenue Code; or

(ii) A contractual or systematic agreement under which the customer purchases at the applicable public offering price, or redeems at the applicable redemption price, such securities in specified amounts (calculated in security units or dollars) at specified time intervals and setting forth the commissions or charges to be paid by such customer in connection therewith (or the manner of calculating them); or

(iii) Any other arrangement involving a group of two or more customers and contemplating periodic purchases of such securities by each customer through a person designated by the group; *Provided,* That such arrangement requires the registered investment company or its agent

(A) To give or send to the designated person, at or before the completion of the transaction for the purchase of such securities, a written notification of the receipt of the total amount paid by the group;

(B) To send to anyone in the group who was a customer in the prior quarter and on whose behalf payment has not been received in the current quarter a quarterly written statement reflecting that a payment was not received on his behalf; and

(C) To advise each customer in the group if a payment is not received from the designated person on behalf of the group within 10 days of a date certain specified in the arrangement for delivery of that payment by the designated person and thereafter to send to each such customer the written notification described in paragraph (a) of this section for the next three succeeding payments.

(7) "Reported security" shall have the meaning provided in Rule 11Aa3–1 under the Act.

(8) "Effective transaction reporting plan" shall have the meaning provided in Rule 11Aa3–1 under the Act.

(9) *Payment for order flow* shall mean any monetary payment, service, property, or other benefit that results in remuneration, compensation, or consideration to a broker or dealer from any broker or dealer, national securities exchange, registered securities association, or exchange member in return for the routing of customer orders by such broker or dealer to any broker or dealer, national securities exchange, registered securities association, or exchange member for execution, including but not limited to: research, clearance, custody, products or services; reciprocal agreements for the provision of order flow; adjustment of a broker or dealer's unfavorable trading errors; offers to participate as underwriter in public offerings; stock loans or shared interest accrued thereon; discounts, rebates, or any other reductions of or credits against any fee to, or expense or other financial obligation of, the broker or dealer routing a customer order that exceeds that fee, expense or financial obligation.

(10) *Asset-backed security* means a security that is primarily serviced by the cashflows of a discrete pool of receivables or other financial assets, either fixed or revolving, that by their terms convert into cash within a finite time period plus any rights or other assets designed to assure the servicing or timely distribution of proceeds to the security holders.

(e) *Security Futures Products.* The provisions of paragraphs (a) and (b) of this section shall not apply to a broker or dealer registered pursuant to section 15(b)(11)(A) of the Act (15 U.S.C. 78*o*(b)(11)(A)) to the extent that it effects transactions for customers in security futures products in a futures account (as that term is defined in § 240.15c3–3(a)(15)) and a broker or dealer registered pursuant to section 15(b)(1) of the Act (15 U.S.C. 78*o*(b)(1)) that is also a futures commission merchant registered pursuant to section 4f(a)(1) of the Commodity Exchange Act (7 U.S.C. 6f(a)(1)), to the extent that it effects transactions for customers in security futures products in a futures account (as that term is defined in § 240.15c3–3(a)(15)), *Provided* that:

(1) The broker or dealer that effects any transaction for a customer in security futures products in a futures account gives or sends to the customer no later than the next business day after execution of any futures securities product transaction, written notification disclosing:

(i) The date the transaction was executed, the identity of the single security or narrow-based security index underlying the contract for the security futures product, the number of contracts of such security futures product purchased or sold, the price, and the delivery month;

(ii) The source and amount of any remuneration received or to be received by the broker or dealer in connection with the transaction, including, but not limited to, markups, commissions, costs, fees, and other charges incurred in connection with the transaction, provided, however, that if no remuneration is to be paid for an initiating transaction until the occurrence of the corresponding liquidating transaction, that the broker or dealer may disclose the amount of remuneration only on the confirmation for the liquidating transaction;

(iii) The fact that information about the time of the execution of the transaction, the identity of the other party to the contract, and whether the broker or dealer is acting as agent for such customer, as agent for some other person, as agent for both such customer and some other person, or as principal for its own account, and if the broker or dealer is acting as principal, whether it is engaging in a block transaction or an exchange of security futures products for physical securities, will be available upon written request of the customer; and

(iv) Whether payment for order flow is received by the broker or dealer for such transactions, the amount of this payment and the fact that the source and nature of the compensation received in connection with the particular transaction will be furnished upon written request of the customer; provided, however, that brokers or dealers that do not receive payment for order flow have no disclosure obligation under this paragraph.

(2) *Transitional provision.*

(i) Broker-dealers are not required to comply with paragraph (e)(1)(iii) of this section until June 1, 2003, *Provided* that, if, not withstanding the absence of the disclosure required in that paragraph, the broker-dealer receives a written request from a customer for the information described in paragraph (e)(1)(iii) of this section, the broker-dealer must make the information available to the customer; and

(ii) Broker-dealers are not required to comply with paragraph (e)(1)(iv) of this section until June 1, 2003.

(f) The Commission may exempt any broker or dealer from the requirements of paragraphs (a) and (b) of this section with regard to specific transactions or specific classes of transactions for which the broker or dealer will provide alternative procedures to effect the purposes of this section; any such exemption may be granted subject to compliance with such alternative procedures and upon such other stated terms and conditions as the Commission may impose.

Rule 10b–16. Disclosure of Credit Terms in Margin Transactions

(a) It shall be unlawful for any broker or dealer to extend credit, directly or indirectly, to any customer in connection with any securities transaction unless such broker or dealer has established procedures to assure that each customer

(1) is given or sent at the time of opening the account, a written statement or statements disclosing (i) the conditions under which an interest charge will be imposed; (ii) the annual rate or rates of interest that can be imposed; (iii) the method of computing interest; (iv) if rates of interest are subject to change without prior notice, the specific conditions under which they can be changed; (v) the method of determining the debit balance or balances on which interest is to be charged and whether credit is to be given for credit balances in cash accounts; (vi) what other charges resulting from the extension of credit, if any, will be made and under what conditions; and (vii) the nature of any interest or lien retained by the broker or dealer in the security or other property held as collateral and the conditions under which additional collateral can be required: *Provided, however,* That the requirements of this paragraph (a)(1) will be met in any case where the account is opened by telephone if the information required to be disclosed is orally communicated to the customer at that time and the required written statement or statements are sent to the customer immediately thereafter: *And provided, further,* That in the case of customers to whom credit is already being extended on the effective date of this rule, the written statement or statements required hereunder must be given or sent to said customers within 90 days after the effective date of this rule; and

(2) is given or sent a written statement or statements, at least quarterly, for each account in which credit was extended, disclosing (i) the balance at the beginning of the period; the date, amount and a brief description of each debit and credit entered during such period; the closing balance; and, if interest is charged for a period different from the period covered by the statement, the balance as of the last day of the interest period; (ii) the total interest charge for the period during which interest is charged (or, if interest is charged separately for separate accounts, the total interest charge for each such account), itemized to show the dates on which the interest period began and ended; the annual rate or rates of interest charged and the interest charge for each such different annual rate of interest; and either each different debit balance on which an interest calculation was based or the average debit balance for the interest period, except that if an average debit balance is used, a separate average debit balance must be disclosed for each interest rate applied; and (iii) all other charges resulting from the extension of credit in that account: *Provided, however,* That if the interest charge disclosed on a statement is for a period different from the period covered by the statement, there must be printed on the statement appropriate language to the effect that it should be retained for use in conjunction with the next statement containing the remainder of the required information: *And provided further,* That in the case of "equity funding programs" registered under the Securities Act of 1933, the requirements of this paragraph (a)(2) will be met if the broker or dealer furnishes to the customer, within 1 month after each extension of credit, a written statement or statements containing the information required to be disclosed under this paragraph (a)(2).

(b) It shall be unlawful for any broker or dealer to make any changes in the terms and conditions under which credit charges will be made (as described in the initial statement made under paragraph (a) of this rule), unless the customer shall have been given not less than thirty (30) days written notice of such changes, except that no such prior notice shall be necessary where such changes are required by law: *Provided, however,* That if any change for which prior notice would otherwise be required under this paragraph results in a lower interest charge to the customer than would have been imposed before the change, notice of such change may be given within a reasonable time after the effective date of the change.

Rule 10b-17. Untimely Announcements of Record Dates

(a) It shall constitute a "manipulative or deceptive device or contrivance" as used in section 10(b) of the Act for any issuer of a class of securities publicly traded by the use of any means or instrumentality of interstate commerce or of the mails or of any facility of any national securities exchange to fail to give notice in accordance with paragraph (b) of this section of the following actions relating to such class of securities:

(1) A dividend or other distribution in cash or in kind, except an ordinary interest payment on a debt security, but including a dividend or distribution of any security of the same or another issuer;

(2) A stock split or reverse split; or

(3) A rights or other subscription offering.

(b) Notice shall be deemed to have been given in accordance with this section only if:

(1) Given to the National Association of Securities Dealers, Inc., no later than 10 days prior to the record date involved or, in case of a rights subscription or other offering if such 10 days advance notice is not practical, on or before the record date and in no event later than the effective date of the registration statement to which the offering relates, and such notice includes:

(i) Title of the security to which the declaration relates;

(ii) Date of declaration;

(iii) Date of record for determining holders entitled to receive the dividend or other distribution or to participate in the stock or reverse split;

(iv) Date of payment or distribution or, in the case of a stock or reverse split or rights or other subscription offering, the date of delivery;

(v) For a dividend or other distribution including a stock or reverse split or rights or other subscription offering:

(a) In cash, the amount of cash to be paid or distributed per share, except if exact per share cash distributions cannot be given because of existing conversion rights which may be exercised during the notice period and which may affect the per share cash distribution, then a reasonable approximation of the per share distribution may be provided so long as the actual per share distribution is subsequently provided on the record date.

(b) In the same security, the amount of the security outstanding immediately prior to and immediately following the dividend or distribution and the rate of the dividend or distribution.

(c) In any other security of the same issuer, the amount to be paid or distributed and the rate of the dividend or distribution.

(d) In any security of another issuer, the name of the issuer and title of that security, the amount to be paid or distributed, and the rate of the dividend or distribution and if that security is a right or a warrant, the subscription price.

(e) In any other property (including securities not covered under (b) through (d) of this subdivision) the identity of the property and its value and basis for assigning that value;

(vi) Method of settlement of fractional interests;

(vii) Details of any condition which must be satisfied or Government approval which must be secured to enable payment of distribution; and in

(viii) The case of stock or reverse split in addition to the aforementioned information;

(a) The name and address of the transfer or exchange agent; or

(2) The Commission, upon written request or upon its own motion, exempts the issuer from compliance with subparagraph (1) of this paragraph either unconditionally or on specified terms or conditions, as not constituting a manipulative or deceptive device or contrivance comprehended within the purpose of this section or;

(3) Given in accordance with procedures of the national securities exchange or exchanges upon which a security of such issuer is registered pursuant to section 12 of the Act which contain requirements substantially comparable to those set forth in subparagraph (1) of this paragraph.

(c) The provisions of this rule shall not apply, however, to redeemable securities issued by open-end investment companies registered with the Commission under the Investment Company Act of 1940.

Rule 10b–18. Purchases of Certain Equity Securities by the Issuer and Others

Preliminary Notes to § 240.10b–18

1. Section 240.10b–18 provides an issuer (and its affiliated purchasers) with a "safe harbor" from liability for manipulation under sections 9(a)(2) of the Act and § 240.10b–5 under the Act *solely* by reason of the manner, timing, price, and volume of their repurchases when they repurchase the issuer's common stock in the market in accordance with the section's manner, timing, price, and volume conditions. As a safe harbor, compliance with § 240.10b–18 is voluntary. To come within the safe harbor, however, an issuer's repurchases

must satisfy (on a daily basis) each of the section's four conditions. Failure to meet any one of the four conditions will remove all of the issuer's repurchases from the safe harbor for that day. The safe harbor, moreover, is not available for repurchases that, although made in technical compliance with the section, are part of a plan or scheme to evade the federal securities laws.

2. Regardless of whether the repurchases are effected in accordance with § 240.10b–18, reporting issuers must report their repurchasing activity as required by Item 703 of Regulations S–K and S–B (17 CFR 229.703 and 228.703) and Item 15(e) of Form 20–F (17 CFR 249.220f) (regarding foreign private issuers), and closed-end management investment companies that are registered under the Investment Company Act of 1940 must report their repurchasing activity as required by Item 8 of Form N–CSR (17 CFR 249.331; 17 CFR 274.128).

(a) *Definitions*. Unless otherwise provided, all terms used in this section shall have the same meaning as in the Act. In addition, the following definitions shall apply:

(1) *ADTV* means the average daily trading volume reported for the security during the four calendar weeks preceding the week in which the Rule 10b–18 purchase is to be effected.

(2) *Affiliate* means any person that directly or indirectly controls, is controlled by, or is under common control with, the issuer.

(3) *Affiliated purchaser* means:

(i) A person acting, directly or indirectly, in concert with the issuer for the purpose of acquiring the issuer's securities; or

(ii) An affiliate who, directly or indirectly, controls the issuer's purchases of such securities, whose purchases are controlled by the issuer, or whose purchases are under common control with those of the issuer; *Provided, however*, that "affiliated purchaser" shall not include a broker, dealer, or other person solely by reason of such broker, dealer, or other person effecting Rule 10b–18 purchases on behalf of the issuer or for its account, and shall not include an officer or director of the issuer solely by reason of that officer or director's participation in the decision to authorize Rule 10b–18 purchases by or on behalf of the issuer.

(4) *Agent independent of the issuer* has the meaning contained in § 242.100 of this chapter.

(5) *Block* means a quantity of stock that either:

(i) Has a purchase price of $200,000 or more; or

(ii) Is at least 5,000 shares and has a purchase price of at least $50,000; or

(iii) Is at least 20 round lots of the security and totals 150 percent or more of the trading volume for that security or, in the event that trading volume data are unavailable, is at least 20 round lots of the security and totals at least one-tenth of one percent (.001) of the outstanding shares of the security, exclusive of any shares owned by any affiliate; *Provided, however*, That a block under paragraph (a)(5)(i), (ii), and (iii) shall not include any amount a broker or dealer, acting as principal, has accumulated for the purpose of sale or resale to the issuer or to any affiliated purchaser of the issuer if the issuer or such affiliated purchaser knows or has reason to know that such amount was accumulated for such purpose, nor shall it include any amount that a broker or dealer has sold short to the issuer or to any affiliated purchaser of the issuer if the issuer or such affiliated purchaser knows or has reason to know that the sale was a short sale.

(6) *Consolidated system* means a consolidated transaction or quotation reporting system that collects and publicly disseminates on a current and continuous basis transac-

tion or quotation information in common equity securities pursuant to an effective transaction reporting plan (§ 240.11Aa3–1) or a national market system plan (as defined in § 240.11Aa3–2).

(7) *Market-wide trading suspension* means a market-wide trading halt of 30 minutes or more that is:

(i) Imposed pursuant to the rules of a national securities exchange or a national securities association in response to a market-wide decline during a single trading session; or

(ii) Declared by the Commission pursuant to its authority under section 12(k) of the Act (15 U.S.C. 78*l*(k)).

(8) *Plan* has the meaning contained in § 242.100 of this chapter.

(9) *Principal market* for a security means the single securities market with the largest reported trading volume for the security during the six full calendar months preceding the week in which the Rule 10b–18 purchase is to be effected.

(10) *Public float value* has the meaning contained in § 242.100 of this chapter.

(11) *Purchase price* means the price paid per share as reported, exclusive of any commission paid to a broker acting as agent, or commission equivalent, mark-up, or differential paid to a dealer.

(12) *Riskless principal transaction* means a transaction in which a broker or dealer after having received an order from an issuer to buy its security, buys the security as principal in the market at the same price to satisfy the issuer's buy order. The issuer's buy order must be effected at the same price per-share at which the broker or dealer bought the shares to satisfy the issuer's buy order, exclusive of any explicitly disclosed markup or markdown, commission equivalent, or other fee. In addition, only the first leg of the transaction, when the broker or dealer buys the security in the market as principal, is reported under the rules of a self-regulatory organization or under the Act. For purposes of this section, the broker or dealer must have written policies and procedures in place to assure that, at a minimum, the issuer's buy order was received prior to the offsetting transaction; the offsetting transaction is allocated to a riskless principal account or the issuer's account within 60 seconds of the execution; and the broker or dealer has supervisory systems in place to produce records that enable the broker or dealer to accurately and readily reconstruct, in a time-sequenced manner, all orders effected on a riskless principal basis.

(13) *Rule 10b–18 purchase* means a purchase (or any bid or limit order that would effect such purchase) of an issuer's common stock (or an equivalent interest, including a unit of beneficial interest in a trust or limited partnership or a depository share) by or for the issuer or any affiliated purchaser (including riskless principal transactions). However, it does not include any purchase of such security:

(i) Effected during the applicable restricted period of a distribution that is subject to § 242.102 of this chapter;

(ii) Effected by or for an issuer plan by an agent independent of the issuer;

(iii) Effected as a fractional share purchase (a fractional interest in a security) evidenced by a script certificate, order form, or similar document;

(iv) Effected during the period from the time of public announcement (as defined in § 240.165(f)) of a merger, acquisition, or similar transaction involving a recapitalization, until the earlier of the completion of such transaction or the completion of the vote by target shareholders. This exclusion does not apply to Rule 10b–18 purchases:

(A) Effected during such transaction in which the consideration is solely cash and there is no valuation period; or

(B) Where:

(*1*) The total volume of Rule 10b–18 purchases effected on any single day does not exceed the lesser of 25% of the security's four-week ADTV or the issuer's average daily Rule 10b–18 purchases during the three full calendar months preceding the date of the announcement of such transaction;

(*2*) The issuer's block purchases effected pursuant to paragraph (b)(4) of this section do not exceed the average size and frequency of the issuer's block purchases effected pursuant to paragraph (b)(4) of this section during the three full calendar months preceding the date of the announcement of such transaction; and

(*3*) Such purchases are not otherwise restricted or prohibited;

(v) Effected pursuant to § 240.13e–1;

(vi) Effected pursuant to a tender offer that is subject to § 240.13e–4 or specifically excepted from § 240.13e–4; or

(vii) Effected pursuant to a tender offer that is subject to section 14(d) of the Act (15 U.S. C. 78n(d)) and the rules and regulations thereunder.

(b) *Conditions to be met*. Rule 10b–18 purchases shall not be deemed to have violated the anti-manipulation provisions of sections 9(a)(2) or 10(b) of the Act (15 U.S.C. 78i(a)(2) 78j(b)) or § 240.10b–5 under the Act, solely by reason of the time, price, or amount of the Rule 10b–18 purchases, or the number of brokers or dealers used in connection with such purchases, if the issuer or affiliated purchaser of the issuer effects the Rule 10b–18 purchases according to each of the following conditions:

(1) *One broker or dealer*. Rule 10b–18 purchases must be effected from or through only one broker or dealer on any single day; *Provided, however*, that:

(i) The "one broker or dealer" condition shall not apply to Rule 10b–18 purchases that are not solicited by or on behalf of the issuer or its affiliated purchaser(s);

(ii) Where Rule 10b–18 purchases are effected by or on behalf of more than one affiliated purchaser of the issuer (or the issuer and one or more of its affiliated purchasers) on a single day, the issuer and all affiliated purchasers must use the same broker or dealer; and

(iii) Where Rule 10b–18 purchases are effected on behalf of the issuer by a broker-dealer that is not an electronic communication network (ECN) or other alternative trading system (ATS), that broker-dealer can access ECN or other ATS liquidity in order to execute repurchases on behalf of the issuer (or any affiliated purchaser of the issuer) on that day.

(2) *Time of purchases*. Rule 10b–18 purchases must not be:

(i) The opening (regular way) purchase reported in the consolidated system;

(ii) Effected during the 10 minutes before the scheduled close of the primary trading session in the principal market for the security, and the 10 minutes before the scheduled close of the primary trading session in the market where the purchase is effected, for a security that has an ADTV value of $1 million or more and a public float value of $150 million or more; and

(iii) Effected during the 30 minutes before the scheduled close of the primary trading session in the principal market for the security, and the 30 minutes before the scheduled close of the primary trading session in the market where the purchase is effected, for all other securities;

(iv) However, for purposes of this section, Rule 10b–18 purchases may be effected following the close of the primary trading session until the termination of the period in which last sale prices are reported in the consolidated system so long as such purchases are effected at prices that do not exceed the lower of the closing price of the primary trading session in the principal market for the security and any lower bids or sale prices subsequently reported in the consolidated system, and all of this section's conditions are met. However, for purposes of this section, the issuer may use one broker or dealer to effect Rule 10b–18 purchases during this period that may be different from the broker or dealer that it used during the primary trading session. However, the issuer's Rule 10b–18 purchase may not be the opening transaction of the session following the close of the primary trading session.

(3) *Price of purchases.* Rule 10b–18 purchases must be effected at a purchase price that:

(i) Does not exceed the highest independent bid or the last independent transaction price, whichever is higher, quoted or reported in the consolidated system at the time the Rule 10b–18 purchase is effected;

(ii) For securities for which bids and transaction prices are not quoted or reported in the consolidated system, Rule 10b–18 purchases must be effected at a purchase price that does not exceed the highest independent bid or the last independent transaction price, whichever is higher, displayed and disseminated on any national securities exchange or on any inter-dealer quotation system (as defined in § 240.15c2–11) that displays at least two priced quotations for the security, at the time the Rule 10b–18 purchase is effected; and

(iii) For all other securities, Rule 10b–18 purchases must be effected at a price no higher than the highest independent bid obtained from three independent dealers.

(4) *Volume of purchases.* The total volume of Rule 10b–18 purchases effected by or for the issuer and any affiliated purchasers effected on any single day must not exceed 25 percent of the ADTV for that security; However, once each week, in lieu of purchasing under the 25 percent of ADTV limit for that day, the issuer or an affiliated purchaser of the issuer may effect one block purchase if:

(i) No other Rule 10b–18 purchases are effected that day, and

(ii) The block purchase is not included when calculating a security's four week ADTV under this section.

(c) *Alternative conditions.* The conditions of paragraph (b) of this section shall apply in connection with Rule 10b–18 purchases effected during a trading session following the imposition of a market-wide trading suspension, except:

(1) That the time of purchases condition in paragraph (b)(2) of this section shall not apply, either:

(i) From the reopening of trading until the scheduled close of trading on the day that the market-wide trading suspension is imposed; or

(ii) At the opening of trading on the next trading day until the scheduled close of trading that day, if a market-wide trading suspension was in effect at the close of trading on the preceding day; and

(2) The volume of purchases condition in paragraph (b)(4) of this section is modified so that the amount of Rule 10b–18 purchases must not exceed 100 percent of the ADTV for that security.

(d) *Other purchases.* No presumption shall arise that an issuer or an affiliated purchaser has violated the anti-manipulation provisions of sections 9(a)(2) or 10(b) of the Act (15 U.S.C. 78i(a)(2) or 78j(b)), or § 240.10b–5 under the Act, if the Rule 10b–18 purchases of such issuer or affiliated purchaser do not meet the conditions specified in paragraph (b) or (c) of this section.

10A–1 Notice to the Commission Pursuant to Section 10A of the Act

(a)(1) If any issuer with a reporting obligation under the Act receives a report requiring a notice to the Commission in accordance with section 10A(b)(3) of the Act, 15 U.S.C. 78j–1(b)(3), the issuer shall submit such notice to the Commission's Office of the Chief Accountant within the time period prescribed in that section. The notice may be provided by facsimile, telegraph, personal delivery, or any other means, *provided* it is received by the Office of the Chief Accountant within the required time period.

(2) The notice specified in paragraph (a)(1) of this section shall be in writing and:

(i) Shall identify the issuer (including the issuer's name, address, phone number, and file number assigned to the issuer's filings by the Commission) and the independent accountant (including the independent accountant's name and phone number, and the address of the independent accountant's principal office);

(ii) Shall state the date that the issuer received from the independent accountant the report specified in section 10A(b)(2) of the Act, 15 U.S.C. 78j–1(b)(2);

(iii) Shall provide, at the election of the issuer, either:

(A) A summary of the independent accountant's report, including a description of the act that the independent accountant has identified as a likely illegal act and the possible effect of that act on all affected financial statements of the issuer of those related to the most current three-year period, whichever is shorter; or

(B) A copy of the independent accountant's report; and

(iv) May provide additional information regarding the issuer's views of and response to the independent accountant's report.

(3) Reports of the independent accountant submitted by the issuer to the Commission's Office of the Chief Accountant in accordance with paragraph (a)(2)(iii)(B) of this section shall be deemed to have been made pursuant to section 10A(b)(3) or section 10A(b)(4) of the Act, 15 U.S.C. 78j–1(b)(3) or 78j–1(b)(4), for purposes of the safe harbor provided by section 10A(c) of the Act, 15 U.S.C. 78j–1(c).

(4) Submission of the notice in paragraphs (a)(1) and (a)(2) of this section shall not relieve the issuer from its obligations to comply fully with all other reporting requirements, including, without limitation:

(i) The filing requirements of Form 8–K, § 249.308 of this chapter, and Form N–SAR, § 274.101 of this chapter, regarding a change in the issuer's certifying accountant and

(ii) The disclosure requirements of item 304 of Regulation S–B or item 304 of Regulation S–K, §§ 228.304 or 229.304 of this chapter.

(b)(1) Any independent accountant furnishing to the Commission a copy of a report (or the documentation of any oral report) in accordance with section 10A(b)(3) or section 10A(b)(4) of the Act, 15 U.S.C. 78j–1(b)(3) or 78j–1(b)(4), shall submit that report (or documentation) to the Commission's Office of the Chief Accountant within the time period prescribed by the appropriate section of the Act. The report (or documentation) may be submitted to the Commission's Office of the Chief Accountant by facsimile, telegraph, personal delivery, or any other means, *provided* it is received by the Office of the Chief Accountant within the time period set forth in section 10A(b)(3) or 10A(b)(4) of the Act, 15 U.S.C. 78j–1(b)(3) or 78j–(b)(4), whichever is applicable in the circumstances.

(2) If the report (or documentation) submitted to the Office of the Chief Accountant in accordance with paragraph (b)(1) of this section does not clearly identify both the issuer (including the issuer's name, address, phone number, and file number assigned to the issuer's filings with the Commission) and the independent accountant (including the independent accountant's name and phone number, and the address of the inde-

pendent accountant's principal office), then the independent accountant shall place that information in a prominent attachment to the report (or documentation) and shall submit that attachment to the Office of the Chief Accountant at the same time and in the same manner as the report (or documentation) is submitted to that Office.

(3) Submission of the report (or documentation) by the independent accountant as described in paragraphs (b)(1) and (b)(2) of this section shall not replace, or otherwise satisfy the need for, the newly engaged and former accountants' letters under items 304(a)(2)(D) and 304(a)(3) of Regulation S–K, §§ 229.304(a)(2)(D) and 229.304(a)(3) of this chapter, respectively, and under items 304(a)(2)(D) and 304(a)(3) of Regulation S–B, §§ 228.304(a)(2)(D) and 228.304(a)(3) of this chapter, respectively, and shall not limit, reduce, or affect in any way the independent accountant's obligations to comply fully with all other legal and professional responsibilities, including, without limitation, those under generally accepted auditing standards and the rules or interpretations of the Commission that modify or supplement those auditing standards.

(c) A notice or report submitted to the Office of the Chief Accountant in accordance with paragraphs (a) and (b) of this section shall be deemed to be an investigative record and shall be non-public and exempt from disclosure pursuant to the Freedom of Information Act to the same extent and for the same periods of time that the Commission's investigative records are non-public and exempt from disclosure under, among other applicable provisions, 5 U.S.C. 552(b)(7) and § 200.80(b)(7) of this chapter. Nothing in this paragraph, however, shall relieve, limit, delay, or affect in any way, the obligation of any issuer or any independent accountant to make all public disclosures required by law, by any Commission disclosure item, rule, report, or form, or by any applicable accounting, auditing, or professional standard.

Instruction to Paragraph (c)

Issuers and independent accountants may apply for additional bases for confidential treatment for a notice, report, or part thereof, in accordance with § 200.83 of this chapter. That section indicates, in part, that any person who, pursuant to any requirement of law, submits any information or causes or permits any information to be submitted to the Commission, may request that the Commission afford it confidential treatment by reason of personal privacy or business confidentiality, or for any other reason permitted by Federal law.

10A–2 Auditor Independence

It shall be unlawful for an auditor not to be independent under § 210.2–01(c)(2)(iii)(B), (c)(4), (c)(6), (c)(7), and § 210.2–07.

10A–3. Listing Standards Relating to Audit Committees

(a) Pursuant to section 10A(m) of the Act (15 U.S.C. 78j–1(m)) and section 3 of the Sarbanes–Oxley Act of 2002 (15 U.S.C. 7202):

(1) *National securities exchanges.* The rules of each national securities exchange registered pursuant to section 6 of the Act (15 U.S.C. 78f) must, in accordance with the provisions of this section, prohibit the initial or continued listing of any security of an issuer that is not in compliance with the requirements of any portion of paragraph (b) or (c) of this section.

(2) *National securities associations.* The rules of each national securities association registered pursuant to section 15A of the Act (15 U.S.C. 78o–3) must, in accordance with the provisions of this section, prohibit the initial or continued listing in an automated inter-dealer quotation system of any security of an issuer that is not in compliance with the requirements of any portion of paragraph (b) or (c) of this section.

(3) *Opportunity to cure defects.* The rules required by paragraphs (a)(1) and (a)(2) of this section must provide for appropriate procedures for a listed issuer to have an opportunity to cure any defects that would be the basis for

a prohibition under paragraph (a) of this section, before the imposition of such prohibition. Such rules also may provide that if a member of an audit committee ceases to be independent in accordance with the requirements of this section for reasons outside the member's reasonable control, that person, with notice by the issuer to the applicable national securities exchange or national securities association, may remain an audit committee member of the listed issuer until the earlier of the next annual shareholders meeting of the listed issuer or one year from the occurrence of the event that caused the member to be no longer independent.

(4) *Notification of noncompliance.* The rules required by paragraphs (a)(1) and (a)(2) of this section must include a requirement that a listed issuer must notify the applicable national securities exchange or national securities association promptly after an executive officer of the listed issuer becomes aware of any material noncompliance by the listed issuer with the requirements of this section.

(5) *Implementation.* (i) The rules of each national securities exchange or national securities association meeting the requirements of this section must be operative, and listed issuers must be in compliance with those rules, by the following dates:

(A) July 31, 2005 for foreign private issuers and small business issuers (as defined in § 240.12b–2); and

(B) For all other listed issuers, the earlier of the listed issuer's first annual shareholders meeting after January 15, 2004, or October 31, 2004.

(ii) Each national securities exchange and national securities association must provide to the Commission, no later than July 15, 2003, proposed rules or rule amendments that comply with this section.

(iii) Each national securities exchange and national securities association must have final rules or rule amendments that comply with this section approved by the Commission no later than December 1, 2003.

(b) *Required standards*—(1) *Independence.* (i) Each member of the audit committee must be a member of the board of directors of the listed issuer, and must otherwise be independent; provided that, where a listed issuer is one of two dual holding companies, those companies may designate one audit committee for both companies so long as each member of the audit committee is a member of the board of directors of at least one of such dual holding companies.

(ii) *Independence requirements for non-investment company issuers.* In order to be considered to be independent for purposes of this paragraph (b)(1), a member of an audit committee of a listed issuer that is not an investment company may not, other than in his or her capacity as a member of the audit committee, the board of directors, or any other board committee:

(A) Accept directly or indirectly any consulting, advisory, or other compensatory fee from the issuer or any subsidiary thereof, provided that, unless the rules of the national securities exchange or national securities association provide otherwise, compensatory fees do not include the receipt of fixed amounts of compensation under a retirement plan (including deferred compensation) for prior service with the listed issuer (provided that such compensation is not contingent in any way on continued service); or

(B) Be an affiliated person of the issuer or any subsidiary thereof.

(iii) *Independence requirements for investment company issuers.* In order to be considered to be independent for purposes of this paragraph (b)(1), a member of an audit committee of a listed issuer that is an investment company may not, other than in his or her capacity as a member of the audit committee, the board of directors, or any other board committee:

(A) Accept directly or indirectly any consulting, advisory, or other compensatory fee from the issuer or any subsidiary thereof, provided that, unless the rules of the national securities exchange or national securities association provide otherwise, compensatory fees do not include the receipt of fixed amounts of compensation under a retirement plan (including deferred compensation) for prior service with the listed issuer (provided that such compensation is not contingent in any way on continued service); or

(B) Be an "interested person" of the issuer as defined in section 2(a)(19) of the Investment Company Act of 1940 (15 U.S.C. 80a–2(a)(19)).

(iv) *Exemptions from the independence requirements.*

(A) For an issuer listing securities pursuant to a registration statement under section 12 of the Act (15 U.S.C. 78l), or for an issuer that has a registration statement under the Securities Act of 1933 (15 U.S.C. 77a *et seq.*) covering an initial public offering of securities to be listed by the issuer, where in each case the listed issuer was not, immediately prior to the effective date of such registration statement, required to file reports with the Commission pursuant to section 13(a) or 15(d) of the Act (15 U.S.C. 78m(a) or 78o(d)):

(*1*) All but one of the members of the listed issuer's audit committee may be exempt from the independence requirements of paragraph (b)(1)(ii) of this section for 90 days from the date of effectiveness of such registration statement; and

(*2*) A minority of the members of the listed issuer's audit committee may be exempt from the independence requirements of paragraph (b)(1)(ii) of this section for one year from the date of effectiveness of such registration statement.

(B) An audit committee member that sits on the board of directors of a listed issuer and an affiliate of the listed issuer is exempt from the requirements of paragraph (b)(1)(ii)(B) of this section if the member, except for being a director on each such board of directors, otherwise meets the independence requirements of paragraph (b)(1)(ii) of this section for each such entity, including the receipt of only ordinary-course compensation for serving as a member of the board of directors, audit committee or any other board committee of each such entity.

(C) An employee of a foreign private issuer who is not an executive officer of the foreign private issuer is exempt from the requirements of paragraph (b)(1)(ii) of this section if the employee is elected or named to the board of directors or audit committee of the foreign private issuer pursuant to the issuer's governing law or documents, an employee collective bargaining or similar agreement or other home country legal or listing requirements.

(D) An audit committee member of a foreign private issuer may be exempt from the requirements of paragraph (b)(1)(ii)(B) of this section if that member meets the following requirements:

(*1*) The member is an affiliate of the foreign private issuer or a representative of such an affiliate;

(*2*) The member has only observer status on, and is not a voting member or the chair of, the audit committee; and

(*3*) Neither the member nor the affiliate is an executive officer of the foreign private issuer.

(E) An audit committee member of a foreign private issuer may be exempt from the requirements of paragraph (b)(1)(ii)(B) of this section if that member meets the following requirements:

(*1*) The member is a representative or designee of a foreign government or foreign governmental entity that is an affiliate of the foreign private issuer; and

(*2*) The member is not an executive officer of the foreign private issuer.

(F) In addition to paragraphs (b)(1)(iv)(A) through (E) of this section, the Commission may exempt from the requirements of paragraphs (b)(1)(ii) or (b)(1)(iii) of this section a particular relationship with respect to audit committee members, as the Commission determines appropriate in light of the circumstances.

(2) *Responsibilities relating to registered public accounting firms.* The audit committee of each listed issuer, in its capacity as a committee of the board of directors, must be directly responsible for the appointment, compensation, retention and oversight of the work of any registered public accounting firm engaged (including resolution of disagreements between management and the auditor regarding financial reporting) for the purpose of preparing or issuing an audit report or performing other audit, review or attest services for the listed issuer, and each such registered public accounting firm must report directly to the audit committee.

(3) *Complaints.* Each audit committee must establish procedures for:

(i) The receipt, retention, and treatment of complaints received by the listed issuer regarding accounting, internal accounting controls, or auditing matters; and

(ii) The confidential, anonymous submission by employees of the listed issuer of concerns regarding questionable accounting or auditing matters.

(4) *Authority to engage advisers.* Each audit committee must have the authority to engage independent counsel and other advisers, as it determines necessary to carry out its duties.

(5) *Funding.* Each listed issuer must provide for appropriate funding, as determined by the audit committee, in its capacity as a committee of the board of directors, for payment of:

(i) Compensation to any registered public accounting firm engaged for the purpose of preparing or issuing an audit report or performing other audit, review or attest services for the listed issuer;

(ii) Compensation to any advisers employed by the audit committee under paragraph (b)(4) of this section; and

(iii) Ordinary administrative expenses of the audit committee that are necessary or appropriate in carrying out its duties.

(c) *General exemptions.* (1) At any time when an issuer has a class of securities that is listed on a national securities exchange or national securities association subject to the requirements of this section, the listing of other classes of securities of the listed issuer on a national securities exchange or national securities association is not subject to the requirements of this section.

(2) At any time when an issuer has a class of common equity securities (or similar securities) that is listed on a national securities exchange or national securities association subject to the requirements of this section, the listing of classes of securities of a direct or indirect consolidated subsidiary or an at least 50% beneficially owned subsidiary of the issuer (except classes of equity securities, other than non-convertible, non-participating preferred securities, of such subsidiary) is not subject to the requirements of this section.

(3) The listing of securities of a foreign private issuer is not subject to the requirements of paragraphs (b)(1) through (b)(5) of this section if the foreign private issuer meets the following requirements:

(i) The foreign private issuer has a board of auditors (or similar body), or has statutory auditors, established and selected pursuant to home country legal or listing provisions expressly requiring or permitting such a board or similar body;

(ii) The board or body, or statutory auditors is required under home country legal or listing requirements to be either:

(A) Separate from the board of directors; or

(B) Composed of one or more members of the board of directors and one or more members that are not also members of the board of directors;

(iii) The board or body, or statutory auditors, are not elected by management of such issuer and no executive officer of the foreign private issuer is a member of such board or body, or statutory auditors;

(iv) Home country legal or listing provisions set forth or provide for standards for the independence of such board or body, or statutory auditors, from the foreign private issuer or the management of such issuer;

(v) Such board or body, or statutory auditors, in accordance with any applicable home country legal or listing requirements or the issuer's governing documents, are responsible, to the extent permitted by law, for the appointment, retention and oversight of the work of any registered public accounting firm engaged (including, to the extent permitted by law, the resolution of disagreements between management and the auditor regarding financial reporting) for the purpose of preparing or issuing an audit report or performing other audit, review or attest services for the issuer; and

(vi) The audit committee requirements of paragraphs (b)(3), (b)(4) and (b)(5) of this section apply to such board or body, or statutory auditors, to the extent permitted by law.

(4) The listing of a security futures product cleared by a clearing agency that is registered pursuant to section 17A of the Act (15 U.S.C. 78q–1) or that is exempt from the registration requirements of section 17A pursuant to paragraph (b)(7)(A) of such section is not subject to the requirements of this section.

(5) The listing of a standardized option, as defined in § 240.9b–1(a)(4), issued by a clearing agency that is registered pursuant to section 17A of the Act (15 U.S.C. 78q–1) is not subject to the requirements of this section.

(6) The listing of securities of the following listed issuers are not subject to the requirements of this section:

(i) Asset-Backed Issuers (as defined in § 229.1101 of this chapter);

(ii) Unit investment trusts (as defined in 15 U.S.C. 80a–4(2) of the Investment Company Act of 1940); and

(iii) Foreign governments (as defined in § 240.3b–4(a)).

(7) The listing of securities of a listed issuer is not subject to the requirements of this section if:

(i) The listed issuer, as reflected in the applicable listing application, is organized as a trust or other unincorporated association that does not have a board of directors or persons acting in a similar capacity; and

(ii) The activities of the listed issuer that is described in paragraph (c)(7)(i) of this section are limited to passively owning or holding (as well as administering and distributing amounts in respect of) securities, rights, collateral or other assets on behalf of or for the benefit of the holders of the listed securities.

(d) *Disclosure*. Any listed issuer availing itself of an exemption from the independence standards contained in paragraph (b)(1)(iv) of this section (except paragraph (b)(1)(iv)(B) of this section), the general exemption contained in paragraph (c)(3) of this section or the last sentence of paragraph (a)(3) of this section, must:

(1) Disclose its reliance on the exemption and its assessment of whether, and if so, how, such reliance would materially adversely affect the ability of the audit committee to act independently and to satisfy the other requirements of this section in any proxy or information statement for a meeting of shareholders at which directors are elected that is filed with the Commission pursuant to the requirements of section 14 of the Act (15 U.S.C. 78n); and

(2) Disclose the information specified in paragraph (d)(1) of this section in, or incorporate such information by reference from such proxy or information statement filed with the Commission into, its annual report filed with the Commission pursuant to the

requirements of section 13(a) or 15(d) of the Act (15 U.S.C. 78m(a) or 78o(d)).

(e) *Definitions*. Unless the context otherwise requires, all terms used in this section have the same meaning as in the Act. In addition, unless the context otherwise requires, the following definitions apply for purposes of this section:

(1)(i) The term *affiliate* of, or a person *affiliated* with, a specified person, means a person that directly, or indirectly through one or more intermediaries, controls, or is controlled by, or is under common control with, the person specified.

(ii)(A) A person will be deemed not to be in control of a specified person for purposes of this section if the person:

(*1*) Is not the beneficial owner, directly or indirectly, of more than 10% of any class of voting equity securities of the specified person; and

(*2*) Is not an executive officer of the specified person.

(B) Paragraph (e)(1)(ii)(A) of this section only creates a safe harbor position that a person does not control a specified person. The existence of the safe harbor does not create a presumption in any way that a person exceeding the ownership requirement in paragraph (e)(1)(ii)(A)(*1*) of this section controls or is otherwise an affiliate of a specified person.

(iii) The following will be deemed to be affiliates:

(A) An executive officer of an affiliate;

(B) A director who also is an employee of an affiliate;

(C) A general partner of an affiliate; and

(D) A managing member of an affiliate.

(iv) For purposes of paragraph (e)(1)(i) of this section, dual holding companies will not be deemed to be affiliates of or persons affiliated with each other by virtue of their dual holding company arrangements with each other, including where directors of one dual holding company are also directors of the other dual holding company, or where directors of one or both dual holding companies are also directors of the businesses jointly controlled, directly or indirectly, by the dual holding companies (and, in each case, receive only ordinary-course compensation for serving as a member of the board of directors, audit committee or any other board committee of the dual holding companies or any entity that is jointly controlled, directly or indirectly, by the dual holding companies).

(2) In the case of foreign private issuers with a two-tier board system, the term *board of directors* means the supervisory or non-management board.

(3) In the case of a listed issuer that is a limited partnership or limited liability company where such entity does not have a board of directors or equivalent body, the term *board of directors* means the board of directors of the managing general partner, managing member or equivalent body.

(4) The term *control* (including the terms *controlling, controlled by* and under *common control with*) means the possession, direct or indirect, of the power to direct or cause the direction of the management and policies of a person, whether through the ownership of voting securities, by contract, or otherwise.

(5) The term *dual holding companies* means two foreign private issuers that:

(i) Are organized in different national jurisdictions;

(ii) Collectively own and supervise the management of one or more businesses which are conducted as a single economic enterprise; and

(iii) Do not conduct any business other than collectively owning and supervising such businesses and activities reasonably incidental thereto.

(6) The term *executive officer* has the meaning set forth in § 240.3b–7.

(7) The term *foreign private issuer* has the meaning set forth in § 240.3b–4(c).

(8) The term *indirect* acceptance by a member of an audit committee of any consulting, advisory or other compensatory fee includes acceptance of such a fee by a spouse, a minor child or stepchild or a child or stepchild sharing a home with the member or by an entity in which such member is a partner, member, an officer such as a managing director occupying a comparable position or executive officer, or occupies a similar position (except limited partners, non-managing members and those occupying similar positions who, in each case, have no active role in providing services to the entity) and which provides accounting, consulting, legal, investment banking or financial advisory services to the issuer or any subsidiary of the issuer.

(9) The terms *listed* and *listing* refer to securities listed on a national securities exchange or listed in an automated inter-dealer quotation system of a national securities association or to issuers of such securities.

Instructions to § 240.10A–3

1. The requirements in paragraphs (b)(2) through (b)(5), (c)(3)(v) and (c)(3)(vi) of this section do not conflict with, and do not affect the application of, any requirement or ability under a listed issuer's governing law or documents or other home country legal or listing provisions that requires or permits shareholders to ultimately vote on, approve or ratify such requirements. The requirements instead relate to the assignment of responsibility as between the audit committee and management. In such an instance, however, if the listed issuer provides a recommendation or nomination regarding such responsibilities to shareholders, the audit committee of the listed issuer, or body performing similar functions, must be responsible for making the recommendation or nomination.

2. The requirements in paragraphs (b)(2) through (b)(5), (c)(3)(v), (c)(3)(vi) and Instruction 1 of this section do not conflict with any legal or listing requirement in a listed issuer's home jurisdiction that prohibits the full board of directors from delegating such responsibilities to the listed issuer's audit committee or limits the degree of such delegation. In that case, the audit committee, or body performing similar functions, must be granted such responsibilities, which can include advisory powers, with respect to such matters to the extent permitted by law, including submitting nominations or recommendations to the full board.

3. The requirements in paragraphs (b)(2) through (b)(5), (c)(3)(v) and (c)(3)(vi) of this section do not conflict with any legal or listing requirement in a listed issuer's home jurisdiction that vests such responsibilities with a government entity or tribunal. In that case, the audit committee, or body performing similar functions, must be granted such responsibilities, which can include advisory powers, with respect to such matters to the extent permitted by law.

4. For purposes of this section, the determination of a person's beneficial ownership must be made in accordance with § 240.13d–3.

ADOPTION OF FLOOR TRADING REGULATION (RULE 11a–1)

Rule 11a–1. Regulation of Floor Trading

(a) No member of a national securities exchange, while on the floor of such exchange, shall initiate, directly or indirectly, any transaction in any security admitted to trading on such exchange, for any account in which such member has an interest, or for any such account with respect to which such member has discretion as to the time of execution, the choice of security to be bought or sold, the total amount of any security to be bought or sold, or whether any such transaction shall be one of purchase or sale.

(b) The provisions of paragraph (a) of this rule shall not apply to:

(1) any transaction by a registered specialist in a security in which he is so registered on such exchange;

(2) any transaction for the account of an odd-lot dealer in a security in which he is so registered on such exchange;

(3) any stabilizing transaction effected in compliance with § 242.104 of this chapter to facilitate a distribution of such security in which such member is participating;

(4) any bona fide arbitrage transaction;

(5) any transaction made with the prior approval of a floor official of such exchange to permit such member to contribute to the maintenance of a fair and orderly market in such security, or any purchase or sale to reverse any such transaction;

(6) any transaction to offset a transaction made in error; or

(7) any transaction effected in conformity with a plan designed to eliminate floor trading activities which are not beneficial to the market and which plan has been adopted by an exchange and declared effective by the Commission. For the purpose of this rule, a plan filed with the Commission by a national securities exchange shall not become effective unless the Commission, having due regard for the maintenance of fair and orderly markets, for the public interest, and for the protection of investors, declares the plan to be effective.

(c) For the purpose of this rule the term "on the floor of such exchange" shall include the trading floor; the rooms, lobbies, and other premises immediately adjacent thereto for use of members generally; other rooms, lobbies and premises made available primarily for use by members generally; and the telephone and other facilities in any such place.

(d) Any national securities exchange may apply for an exemption from the provisions of this rule in compliance with the provisions of section 11(c) of the Act.

Rule 11a1–1(T). Transactions Yielding Priority, Parity, and Precedence

(a) A transaction effected on a national securities exchange for the account of a member which meets the requirements of Section 11(a)(1)(G)(i) of the Act shall be deemed, in accordance with the requirements of Section 11(a)(1)(G)(ii), to be not inconsistent with the maintenance of fair and orderly markets and to yield priority, parity, and precedence in execution to orders for the account of persons who are not members or associated with members of the exchange if such transaction is effected in compliance with each of the following requirements:

(1) A member shall disclose that a bid or offer for its account is for its account to any member with whom such bid or offer is placed or to whom it is communicated, and any member through whom that bid or offer is communicated shall disclose to others participating in effecting the order that it is for the account of a member.

(2) Immediately before executing the order, a member (other than the specialist in such security) presenting any order for the account of a member on the exchange shall clearly announce or otherwise indicate to the specialist and to other members then present for the trading in such security on the exchange that he is presenting an order for the account of a member.

(3) Notwithstanding rules of priority, parity, and precedence otherwise applicable, any member presenting for execution a bid or offer for its own account or for the account of another member shall grant priority to any bid or offer at the same price for the account of a person who is not, or is not associated with, a member, irrespective of the size of any such bid or offer or the time when entered.

(b) A member shall be deemed to meet the requirements of section 11(a)(1)(G)(i) of the Act if during its preceding fiscal year more than 50 percent of its gross revenues was derived from one or more of the sources specified in that section. In addition to any revenue which independently meets the requirements of section 11(a)(1)(G)(i), revenue derived from any transaction specified in paragraph (A), (B), or (D) of section 11(a)(1) of the Act or specified in Rule 11a1-4(T) shall be deemed to be revenue derived from one or more of the sources specified in section 11(a)(1)(G)(i). A member may rely on a list of members which are stated to meet the requirements of section 11(a)(1)(G)(i) if such list is prepared, and updated at least annually, by the exchange. In preparing any such list, an exchange may rely on a report which sets forth a statement of gross revenues of a member if covered by a report of independent accountants for such member to the effect that such report has been prepared in accordance with generally accepted accounting principles.

Rule 11a1-2. Transactions for Certain Accounts of Associated Persons of Members

A transaction effected by a member of a national securities exchange for the account of an associated person thereof shall be deemed to be of a kind which is consistent with the purposes of Section 11(a)(1) of the Act, the protection of investors, and the maintenance of fair and orderly markets if the transaction is effected

(a) for the account of and for the benefit of an associated person, if, assuming such transaction were for the account of a member, or

(b) for the account of an associated person but for the benefit of an account carried by such associated person, if, assuming such account were carried on the same basis by a member, the member would have been permitted, under Section 11(a) of the Act and the other rules thereunder, to effect the transaction; *Provided, however*, That a transaction may not be effected by a member for the account of and for the benefit of an associated person under Section 11(a)(1)(G) of the Act and Rule 11a1-1(T) thereunder unless the associated person derived, during its preceding fiscal year, more than 50 percent of its gross revenues from one or more of the sources specified in Section 11(a)(1)(G)(i) of the Act.

Rule 11a1-3(T). Bona Fide Hedge Transactions in Certain Securities

A bona fide hedge transaction effected on a national securities exchange by a member for its own account or an account of an associated person thereof and involving a long or short position in a security entitling the holder to acquire or sell an equity security, and a long or short position in one or more other securities entitling the holder to acquire or sell such equity security, shall be deemed to be of a kind which is consistent with the purposes of section 11(a)(1) of the Act, the protection of investors, and the maintenance of fair and orderly markets.

Rule 11a1-4(T). Bond Transactions on National Securities Exchanges

A transaction in a bond, note, debenture, or other form of indebtedness effected on a national securities exchange by a member for its own account or the account of an associated person thereof shall be deemed to be of a kind which is consistent with the purposes of section 11(a)(1) of the Act, the protection of investors, and the maintenance of fair and orderly markets.

Rule 11a1-5. Transactions by Registered Competitive Market Makers and Registered Equity Market Makers

Any transaction by a New York Stock Exchange registered competitive market maker or an American Stock Exchange registered equity market maker effected in compliance with their respective governing rules shall be deemed to be of a kind which is consistent with the purposes of section 11(a)(1) of the Act, the protection of investors, and the maintenance of fair and orderly markets.

Rule 11a1-6. Transactions for Certain Accounts of OTC Derivatives Dealers

A transaction effected by a member of a national securities exchange for the account of an OTC derivatives dealer that is an associated person of that member shall be deemed to be of a kind that is consistent with the purposes of section 11(a)(1) of the Act (15 U.S.C. 78k(a)(1)), the protection of investors, and the maintenance of fair and orderly markets if, assuming such transaction were for the account of a member, the member would have been permitted, under section 11(a) of the Act and the other rules thereunder (with the exception of § 240.11a1–2), to effect the transaction.

Rule 11a2–2(T). Transactions Effected by Exchange Members Through Other Members

(a) A member of a national securities exchange (the "initiating member") may not effect a transaction on that exchange for its own account, the account of an associated person, or an account with respect to which it or an associated person thereof exercises investment discretion unless:

(1) the transaction is of a kind described in paragraphs A through H of Section 11(a)(1) of the Act and is effected in accordance with applicable rules and regulations thereunder; or

(2) the transaction is effected in compliance with each of the following conditions:

(i) the transaction is executed on the floor, or through use of the facilities, of the exchange by a member (the "executing member") which is not an associated person of the initiating member;

(ii) the order for the transaction is transmitted from off the exchange floor;

(iii) neither the initiating member nor an associated person of the initiating member participates in the execution of the transaction at any time after the order for the transaction has been so transmitted; and

(iv) in the case of a transaction effected for an account with respect to which the initiating member or an associated person thereof exercises investment discretion, neither the initiating member nor any associated person thereof retains any compensation in connection with effecting the transaction; *Provided, however*, That this condition shall not apply to the extent that the person or persons authorized to transact business for the account have expressly provided otherwise by written contract referring to Section 11(a) of the Act and this section executed on or after March 15, 1978, by each of them and by such exchange member or associated person exercising investment discretion.

(b) For purposes of this section, a member "effects" a securities transaction when it performs any function in connection with the processing of that transaction, including, but not limited to, (1) transmission or an order for execution, (2) execution of the order, (3) clearance and settlement of the transaction, and (4) arranging for the performance of any such function.

(c) For purposes of this section, the term "compensation in connection with effecting the transaction" refers to compensation directly or indirectly received or calculated on a transaction-related basis for the performance of any function involved in effecting a securities transaction.

(d) A member, or an associated person of a member, authorized by written contract to retain compensation in connection with effecting transactions pursuant to paragraph (a)(2)(iv) of this section shall furnish at least annually to the person or persons authorized to transact business for the account a statement setting forth the total amount of all compensation retained by the member or any associated person thereof in connection with effecting transactions for that account during the period covered by the statement, which amount shall be exclusive of all amounts paid to others during that period for services rendered in effecting such transactions.

(e) A transaction effected in compliance with the requirements of this section shall be deemed to be of a kind which is consistent with the purposes of Section 11(a)(1) of the Act, the protection of investors, and the maintenance of fair and orderly markets.

(f) The provisions of this section shall not apply to transactions by exchange members to which, by operation of section 11(a)(3) of the Act, section 11(a)(1) of the Act is not effective.

OPTION OF REGULATION ON CONDUCT OF SPECIALISTS

Rule 11b-1. Regulation of Specialists

(a)(1) The rules of a national securities exchange may permit a member of such exchange to register as a specialist and to act as a dealer.

(2) The rules of a national securities exchange permitting a member of such exchange to register as a specialist and to act as a dealer shall include:

(i) Adequate minimum capital requirements in view of the markets for securities on such exchange;

(ii) Requirements, as a condition of a specialist's registration, that a specialist engage in a course of dealings for his own account to assist in the maintenance, so far as practicable, of a fair and orderly market, and that a finding by the exchange of any substantial or continued failure by a specialist to engage in such a course of dealings will result in the suspension or cancellation of such specialist's registration in one or more of the securities in which such specialist is registered;

(iii) Provisions restricting his dealings so far as practicable to those reasonably necessary to permit him to maintain a fair and orderly market or necessary to permit him to act as an odd-lot dealer;

(iv) Provisions stating the responsibilities of a specialist acting as a broker in securities in which he is registered; and

(v) Procedures to provide for the effective and systematic surveillance of the activities of specialists.

(b) If after appropriate notice and opportunity for hearing the Commission finds that a member of a national securities exchange registered with such exchange as a specialist in specified securities has, for any account in which he, his member organization, or any participant therein has any beneficial interest, direct or indirect, effected transactions in such securities which were not part of a course of dealings reasonably necessary to permit such specialist to maintain a fair and orderly market, or to act as an odd-lot dealer, in the securities in which he is registered and were not effected in a manner consistent with the rules adopted by such exchange pursuant to paragraph (a)(2)(iii) of this section, the Commission may by order direct such exchange to cancel, or to suspend for such period as the Commission may determine, such specialist's registration in one or more of the securities in which such specialist is registered: *Provided, however*, If such exchange has itself suspended or canceled such specialist's registration in one or more of the securities in which such specialist is registered, no further sanction shall be imposed pursuant to this paragraph (b) except in a case where the Commission finds substantial or continued misconduct by a specialist: *And provided, further*, That the provisions of this paragraph (b) shall not apply to a member of a national securities exchange exempted pursuant to the provisions of paragraph (d) of this section.

(c) For the purposes of this rule, the term "rules" of an exchange shall mean its constitution, articles of incorporation, by-laws, or rules or instruments corresponding thereto, whatever the name, and its stated policies.

(d) Any national securities exchange may apply for an exemption from the provisions of this rule in compliance with the provisions of section 11(c) of the Act.

EXEMPTION OF CERTAIN SECURITIES FROM SECTION 11(d)(1)

Rule 11d1–1. Exemption of Certain Securities From Section 11(d)(1)

A security shall be exempt from the provisions of section 11(d)(1) with respect to any transaction by a broker and dealer who, directly or indirectly, extends or maintains or arranges for the extension or maintenance of credit on the security to or for a customer if—

(a) The broker and dealer has not sold the security to the customer or bought the security for the customer's account; or

(b) The security is acquired by the customer in exchange with the issuer thereof for an outstanding security of the same issuer on which credit was lawfully maintained for the customer at the time of the exchange; or

(c) The customer is a broker or dealer or bank; or

(d) The security is acquired by the customer through the exercise of a right evidenced by a warrant or certificate expiring within 90 days after issuance, provided such right was originally issued to the customer as a stockholder of the corporation issuing the security upon which credit is to be extended, or as a stockholder of a company distributing such security in order to effectuate the provisions of section 11 of the Public Utility Holding Company Act of 1935. The right shall be deemed to be issued to the customer as a stockholder if he actually owned the stock giving rise to the right when such right accrued, even though such stock was not registered in his name; and in determining such fact the broker and dealer may rely upon a signed statement of the customer which the broker and dealer accepts in good faith; or

(e) Such broker and dealer would otherwise be subject to the prohibition of section 11(d)(1) with respect to 50 percent or less of all the securities of the same class which are outstanding or currently being distributed, and such broker and dealer sold the security to the customer or bought the security for the customer's account on a day when he was not participating in the distribution of any new issue of such security. A broker-dealer shall be deemed to be participating in a distribution of a new issue if (1) he owns, directly or indirectly, any undistributed security of such issue, or (2) he is engaged in any stabilizing activities to facilitate a distribution of such issue, or (3) he is a party to any syndicate agreement under which such stabilizing activities are being or may be undertaken, or (4) he is a party to an executory agreement to purchase or distribute such issue.

Rule 11d1–2. Exemption From Section 11(d)(1) for Certain Investment Company Securities Held by Broker–Dealers as Collateral in Margin Accounts

Any securities issued by a registered open-end investment company or unit investment trust as defined in the Investment Company Act of 1940 shall be exempted from the provisions of Section 11(d)(1) with respect to any transaction by a person who is a broker and a dealer who, directly or indirectly, extends or maintains or arranges for the extension or maintenance of credit on such security, provided such security has been owned by the person to whom credit would be provided for more than 30 days, or purchased by such person pursuant to a plan for the automatic reinvestment of the dividends of such company or trust.

Rule 11d2–1. Exemption From Section 11(d)(2) for Certain Broker–Dealers Effecting Transactions for Customers Security Futures Products in Futures Accounts

A broker or dealer registered pursuant to section 15(b)(1) of the Act (15 U.S.C. 78*o*(b)(1)) that is also a futures commission merchant registered pursuant to section 4f(a)(1) of the Commodity Exchange Act (7 U.S.C. 6f(a)(1)), to the extent that it effects transactions for customers in security futures products in a futures account (as that term is defined in § 240.15c3–3(a)(15)), is exempt from section 11(d)(2) of the Act (15 U.S.C. 78k(d)(2)).

REGISTRATION OF SECURITIES INFORMATION PROCESSORS

Rule 11Aa2–1. Designation of National Market System Securities

The term "national market system security" shall mean any reported security as defined in Rule 11Aa3–1.

Rule 11Aa3–1. Dissemination of Transaction Reports and Last Sale Data With Respect to Transactions in Reported Securities

(a) *Definitions.* For purposes of this section:

(1) The term "transaction report" shall mean a report containing the price and volume associated with a transaction involving the purchase or sale of one or more round lots of a security ("transaction").

(2) The term "transaction reporting plan" shall mean any plan for collecting, processing, making available or disseminating transaction reports with respect to transactions in reported securities filed with the Commission pursuant to, and meeting the requirements of this section.

(3) The term "effective transaction reporting plan" shall mean any transaction reporting plan approved by the Commission pursuant to this section.

(4) The term "reported security" shall mean any security or class of securities for which transaction reports are collected, processed and made available pursuant to an effective transaction reporting plan.

(5) The term "listed equity security" shall mean any equity security listed and registered, or admitted to unlisted trading privileges, on a national securities exchange ("exchange").

(6) The term "NASDAQ security" shall mean any registered equity security for which quotation information is disseminated in the National Association of Securities Dealers Automated Quotation System ("NASDAQ").

(7) The term "transaction reporting association" shall mean any person authorized to implement or administer any transaction reporting plan or behalf of persons acting jointly under paragraph (b) of this section.

(8) The term "interrogation device" shall mean any securities information retrieval system capable of displaying transaction reports or last sale data, upon inquiry, on a current basis on a terminal or other device.

(9) The term "moving ticker" shall mean any continuous real-time moving display of transaction reports or last sale data (other than a market minder) provided on an interrogation or other display device.

(10) The term "market minder" shall mean any service provided by a vendor on an interrogation device or other display which (i) permits real-time monitoring, on a dynamic basis, of transaction reports or last sale data with respect to a particular security, and (ii) displays the most recent transaction report or last sale data with respect to that security until such report or data has been superseded or supplemented by the display of a new transaction report or last sale data reflecting the next reported transaction in that security.

(11) The term "vendor" shall mean any securities information processor engaged in the business of disseminating transaction reports or last sale data with respect to transactions in reported securities to brokers, dealers or investors on a real-time or other current and continuing basis, whether

through an electronic communications network, moving ticker or interrogation device.

(12) The term "last sale data" shall mean any price or volume data associated with a transaction.

(b)(1) Every exchange shall file a transaction reporting plan regarding transactions in listed equity and NASDAQ securities executed through its facilities, and every association shall file a transaction reporting plan regarding transactions in listed equity and NASDAQ securities executed by its members otherwise than on an exchange.

(2) Any transaction reporting plan, or any amendment thereto, filed pursuant to this section shall be filed with the Commission, and considered for approval, in accordance with the procedures set forth in paragraphs (b) and (c) of Rule 11Aa3–2 governing national market system plans. Any such plan, or amendment thereto, shall specify, at a minimum:

(i) The listed equity and NASDAQ securities or classes of such securities for which transaction reports shall be required by the plan;

(ii) Reporting requirements with respect to transactions in listed equity securities and NASDAQ securities, for any broker or dealer subject to the plan;

(iii) The manner of collecting, processing, sequencing, making available and disseminating transaction reports and last sale data reported pursuant to such plan;

(iv) The manner such transaction reports reported pursuant to such plan are to be consolidated with transaction reports from exchanges, associations, and nonmember brokers and dealers reported pursuant to any other effective transaction reporting plan;

(v) The applicable standards and methods which will be utilized to ensure promptness of reporting, and accuracy and completeness of transaction reports;

(vi) Any rules or procedures which may be adopted to ensure that transaction reports or last sale data will not be disseminated in a fraudulent or manipulative manner;

(vii) Specific terms of access to transaction reports made available or disseminated pursuant to the plan; and

(viii) That transaction reports or last sale data made available to any vendor for display on an interrogation device identify the marketplace where each transaction was executed.

(3) No transaction reporting plan filed pursuant to this section, or any amendment to an effective transaction reporting plan, shall become effective unless approved by the Commission or otherwise permitted in accordance with the procedures set forth in Rule 11Aa3–2 governing national market system plans.

(c) *Prohibitions and Reporting Requirements.*

(1) No broker or dealer may execute any transaction in, or induce or attempt to induce the purchase or sale of, any reported security,

(i) On or through the facilities of an exchange unless there is an effective transaction reporting plan with respect to transactions in such security executed on or through such exchange facilities; or

(ii) Otherwise than on an exchange unless there is an effective transaction reporting plan with respect to transactions in such security executed otherwise than on an exchange by such broker or dealer.

(2) No exchange or member thereof shall make available or disseminate, on a current and continuing basis, transaction reports or last sale data with respect to transactions in any reported security executed through the facilities of such exchange except pursuant to an effective transaction reporting plan filed by such exchange (either individually or jointly with other persons).

(3) No association or member thereof shall make available or disseminate, on a current and continuing basis, transaction reports or last sale data with respect to transactions in any reported security executed by a member of such association otherwise than on an exchange except pursuant to an effective transaction reporting plan filed by such association (either individually or jointly with other persons).

(4) Every broker or dealer who is a member of an exchange or association shall promptly transmit to the exchange or association of which it is a member all information required by any effective transaction reporting plan filed by such exchange or association (either individually or jointly with other exchanges and/or associations).

(d) *Retransmission of Transaction Reports or Last Sale Data.* On and after July 5, 1980, notwithstanding any provision of any effective transaction reporting plan, no exchange or association may, either individually or jointly, by rule, stated policy or practice, transaction reporting plan or otherwise, prohibit, condition or otherwise limit, directly or indirectly, the ability of any vendor to retransmit, for display in moving tickers, transaction reports or last sale data made available pursuant to any effective transaction reporting plan; *Provided, however*, That an exchange or association may, by means of an effective transaction reporting plan, condition such retransmission upon appropriate undertakings to ensure that any charges for the distribution of transaction reports or last sale data in moving tickers permitted by paragraph (e) of this section are collected.

(e) *Charges.* Nothing in this section shall preclude any exchange or association, separately or jointly, pursuant to the terms of an effective transaction reporting plan, from imposing reasonable, uniform charges (irrespective of geographic location) for distribution of transaction reports or last sale data.

(f) *Appeals.* The Commission may, in its discretion, entertain appeals in connection with the implementation or operation of any effective transaction reporting plan in accordance with the provisions of paragraph (e) of Rule 11Aa3–2.

(g) *Exemptions.* The Commission may exempt from the provisions of this section, either unconditionally or on specified terms and conditions, any exchange, association, broker, dealer or specified security if the Commission determines that such exemption is consistent with the public interest, the protection of investors and the removal of impediments to, and perfection of the mechanisms of, a national market system.

Rule 11Aa3–2. Filing and Amendment of National Market System Plans

(a) *Definitions.* For purposes of this section,

(1) The term "national market system plan" shall mean any joint self-regulatory organization plan in connection with

(i) The planning, development, operation or regulation of a national market system (or a subsystem thereof) or one or more facilities thereof, or

(ii) The development and implementation of procedures and/or facilities designed to achieve compliance by self-regulatory organizations and their members with any section of this subpart promulgated pursuant to Section 11A of the Act.

(2) The term "effective national market system plan" shall mean any national market system plan approved by the Commission (either temporarily or on a permanent basis) pursuant to this section.

(3) The term "self-regulatory organization" shall mean any national securities exchange ("exchange") or national securities association ("association").

(4) The term "joint self-regulatory organization plan" shall mean a plan as to which two or more self-regulatory organizations, acting jointly, are sponsors.

(5) The term "sponsor," when used in connection with a national market system plan, shall mean any self-regulatory organization which is a signatory to such plan and has agreed to act in accordance with the terms of the plan.

(6) The term "participants," when used in connection with a national market system plan, shall mean any self-regulatory organization which has agreed to act in accordance with the terms of the plan but which is not a signatory of such plan.

(7) The term "plan processor" shall mean any self-regulatory organization or securities information processor acting as an exclusive processor in connection with the development, implementation and/or operation of any facility contemplated by an effective national market system plan.

(8) The term "vendor" shall have the meaning provided in Rule 11Aa3–1.

(b) *Filing of National Market System Plans and Amendments Thereto.*

(1) Any two or more self-regulatory organizations, acting jointly, may file a national market system plan or may propose an amendment to an effective national market system plan ("proposed amendment") by submitting the text of the plan or amendment to the Secretary of the Commission, together with a statement of the purpose of such plan or amendment and, to the extent applicable, the documents and information required by paragraphs (b)(4) and (b)(5) of this section.

(2) The Commission may propose amendments to any effective national market system plan by publishing the text thereof, together with a statement of the purpose of such amendment, in accordance with the provisions of paragraph (c) of this section.

(3) Self-regulatory organizations are authorized to act jointly in (i) planning, developing, and operating any national market subsystem or facility contemplated by a national market system plan, (ii) preparing and filing a national market system plan or any amendment thereto, or (iii) implementing or administering an effective national market system plan.

(4) Every national market system plan filed pursuant to this section, or any amendment thereto, shall be accompanied by (i) copies of all governing or constituent documents relating to any person (other than a self-regulatory organization) authorized to implement or administer such plan on behalf of its sponsors and (ii), to the extent applicable,

(A) A detailed description of the manner in which the plan or amendment, and any facility or procedure contemplated by the plan or amendment, will be implemented;

(B) A listing of all significant phases of development and implementation (including any pilot phase) contemplated by the plan or amendment, together with the projected date of completion of each phase;

(C) An analysis of the impact on competition of implementation of the plan or amendment or of any facility contemplated by the plan or amendment;

(D) A description of any written understandings or agreements between or among plan sponsors or participants relating to interpretations of the plan or conditions for becoming a sponsor or participant in the plan; and

(E) In the case of a proposed amendment, a statement that such amendment has been approved by the sponsors in accordance with the terms of the plan.

(5) Every national market system plan, or any amendment thereto, filed pursuant to this section shall include a description of the manner in which any facility contemplated by the plan or amendment will be operated. Such description shall include, to the extent applicable,

(i) The terms and conditions under which brokers, dealers, and/or self regulatory organizations will be granted or denied access (including specific procedures and standards governing the granting or denial of access);

(ii) The method by which any fees or charges collected on behalf of all of the sponsors and/or participants in connection with access to, or use of, any facility contemplated by the plan or amendment will be determined and imposed (including any provision for distribution of any net proceeds from such fees or charges to the sponsors and/or participants) and the amount of such fees or charges;

(iii) The method by which, and the frequency with which, the performance of any person acting as plan processor with respect to the implementation and/or operation of the plan will be evaluated; and

(iv) The method by which disputes arising in connection with the operation of the plan will be resolved.

(6) In connection with the selection of any person to act as plan processor with respect to any facility contemplated by a national market system plan (including renewal of any contract for any person to so act), the sponsors shall file with the Commission a statement identifying the person selected, describing the material terms under which such person is to serve as plan processor, and indicating the solicitation efforts, if any, for alternative plan processors, the alternatives considered and the reasons for selection of such person.

(7) Any national market system plan (or any amendment thereto) which is intended by the sponsors to satisfy a plan filing requirement contained in any other section of this subpart shall, in addition to compliance with this section, also comply with the requirements of such other section.

(8)(i) A participant in an effective national market system plan shall ensure that a current and complete version of the plan is posted on a plan Web site or on a Web site designated by plan participants within two business days after notification by the Commission of effectiveness of the plan. Each participant in an effective national market system plan shall ensure that such Web site is updated to reflect amendments to such plan within two business days after the plan participants have been notified by the Commission of its approval of a proposed amendment pursuant to paragraph (c) of this section. If the amendment is not effective for a certain period, the plan participants shall clearly indicate the effective date in the relevant text of the plan. Each plan participant also shall provide a link on its own Web site to the Web site with the current version of the plan.

(ii) The plan participants shall ensure that any proposed amendments filed pursuant to paragraph (b) of this section are posted on a plan Web site or a designated Web site no later than two business days after the filing of the proposed amendments with the Commission. The plan participants shall maintain any proposed amendment to the plan on a plan Web site or a designated Web site until the Commission approves the plan amendment and the plan participants update the Web site to reflect such amendment or the plan participants withdraw the proposed amendment. If the plan participants withdraw proposed amendments, the plan participants shall remove such amendments from the plan Web site or designated Web site within two business days of withdrawal. Each plan participant shall provide a link to the Web site with the current version of the plan.

(c) *Effectiveness of National Market System Plans.*

(1) The Commission shall publish notice of the filing of any national market system plan, or any proposed amendment to any effective national market system plan (including any amendment initiated by the Commission), together with the terms of

substance of the filing or a description of the subjects and issues involved, and shall provide interested persons an opportunity to submit written comments. No national market system plan, or any amendment thereto, shall become effective unless approved by the Commission or otherwise permitted in accordance with paragraph (c)(3) of this section.

(2) Within 120 days of the date of publication of notice of filing of a national market system plan or amendment to an effective national market system plan, or within such longer period as the Commission may designate up to 180 days of such date if it finds such longer period to be appropriate and publishes its reasons for so finding or as to which the sponsors consent, the Commission shall approve such plan or amendment, with such changes or subject to such conditions as the Commission may deem necessary or appropriate, if it finds that such plan or amendment is necessary or appropriate in the public interest, for the protection of investors and the maintenance of fair and orderly markets, to remove impediments to, and perfect the mechanisms of, a national market system, or otherwise in furtherance of the purposes of the Act. Approval of a national market system plan, or an amendment to an effective national market system plan (other than an amendment initiated by the Commission), shall be by order. Promulgation of an amendment to an effective national market system plan initiated by the Commission shall be by rule.

(3) A proposed amendment may be put into effect upon filing with the Commission if designated by the sponsors as

(i) Establishing or changing a fee or other charge collected on behalf of all of the sponsors and/or participants in connection with access to, or use of, any facility contemplated by the plan or amendment (including changes in any provision with respect to distribution of any net proceeds from such fees or other charges to the sponsors and/or participants);

(ii) Concerned solely with the administration of the plan, or involving the governing or constituent documents relating to any person (other than a self-regulatory organization) authorized to implement or administer such plan on behalf of its sponsors; or

(iii) Involving solely technical or ministerial matters.

At any time within 60 days of the filing of any such amendment, the Commission may summarily abrogate the amendment and require that such amendment be refiled in accordance with paragraph (b)(1) of this section and reviewed in accordance with paragraph (c)(2) of this section, if it appears to the Commission that such action is necessary or appropriate in the public interest, for the protection of investors, or the maintenance of fair and orderly markets, to remove impediments, to and perfect mechanisms of, a national market system or otherwise in furtherance of the purposes of the Act.

(4) Notwithstanding the provisions of paragraph (c)(1) of this section, a proposed amendment may be put into effect summarily upon publication of notice of such amendment, on a temporary basis not to exceed 120 days, if the Commission finds that such action is necessary or appropriate in the public interest, for the protection of investors or the maintenance of fair and orderly markets, to remove impediments to, and perfect mechanisms of, a national market system or otherwise in furtherance of the purposes of the Act.

(5) Any plan (or amendment thereto) in connection with (i) the planning development, operation or regulation of a national market system (or a subsystem thereof) or one or more facilities thereof, or (ii) the development and implementation of procedures and/or facilities designed to achieve compliance by self-regulatory organizations and/or their members of any section of this subpart promulgated pursuant to section

11A of the Act, approved by the Commission pursuant to section 11A of the Act (or pursuant to any rule or regulation thereunder) prior to the effective date of this section (either temporarily or on a permanent basis) shall be deemed to have been filed and approved pursuant to this section and no additional filing need be made by the sponsors with respect to such plan or amendment; *Provided, however*, That all terms and conditions associated with any such approval (including time limitations) shall continue to be applicable; *and, provided, further*, that any amendment to such plan filed with or approved by the Commission on or after the effective date of this section shall be subject to the provisions of, and considered in accordance with the procedures specified in, this section.

(d) *Compliance With Terms of National Market System Plans.* Each self-regulatory organization shall comply with the terms of any effective national market system plan of which it is a sponsor or a participant. Each self-regulatory organization also shall, absent reasonable justification or excuse, enforce compliance with any such plan by its members and persons associated with its members.

(e) *Appeals.* The Commission may, in its discretion, entertain appeals in connection with the implementation on operation of any effective national market system plan as follows:

(1) Any action taken or failure to act by any person in connection with an effective national market system plan (other than a prohibition or limitation of access reviewable by the Commission pursuant to section 11A(b)(5) or section 19(d) of the Act) shall be subject to review by the Commission, on its own motion or upon application by any person aggrieved thereby (including, but not limited to self-regulatory organizations, brokers, dealers, issuers, and vendors), filed not later than 30 days after notice of such action or failure to act or within such longer period as the Commission may determine.

(2) Application to the Commission for review, or the institution of review by the Commission on its own motion, shall not operate as a stay of any such action unless the Commission determines otherwise, after notice and opportunity for hearing on the question of a stay (which hearing may consist only of affidavits or oral arguments).

(3) In any proceedings for review, if the Commission, after appropriate notice and opportunity for hearing (which hearing may consist solely of consideration of the record of any proceedings conducted in connection with such action or failure to act and an opportunity for the presentation of reasons supporting or opposing such action or failure to act) and upon consideration of such other data, views and arguments as it deems relevant, finds that the action or failure to act is in accordance with the applicable provisions of such plan and that the applicable provisions are, and were, applied in a manner consistent with the public interest, the protection of investors, the maintenance of fair and orderly markets and the removal of impediments to, and perfection of the mechanisms of, a national market system, the Commission, by order, shall dismiss the proceeding. If the Commission does not make any such finding, or if it finds that such action or failure to act imposes any burden on competition not necessary or appropriate in furtherance of the purposes of the Act, the Commission, by order, shall set aside such action and/or require such action with respect to the matter reviewed as the Commission deems necessary or appropriate in the public interest, for the protection of investors, and the maintenance of fair and orderly markets, or to remove impediments to, and perfect the mechanisms of, a national market system.

(f) *Exemptions.* The Commission may exempt from the provisions of this section, either unconditionally or on specified terms and conditions, any self-regulatory organization, member thereof, or specified security, if the Commission determines that such exemption is consistent with the public interest, the protection of investors, the maintenance of fair and orderly markets and the removal of impediments to, and perfection of the mechanisms of, a national market system.

Rule 11Ab2-1. Registration of Securities Information Processors: Form of Application and Amendments

(a) An application for the registration of a securities information processor shall be filed on Form SIP in accordance with the instructions contained therein.

(b) If any information reported in items 1–13 or item 21 of Form SIP or in any amendment thereto, is or becomes inaccurate for any reason, whether before or after the registration has been granted, the securities information processor shall promptly file an amendment on Form SIP correcting such information.

(c) The Commission, upon its own motion or upon application by any securities information processor, may conditionally or unconditionally exempt any securities information processor from any provision of the rules or regulations adopted under Section 11A(b).

(d) Every amendment filed pursuant to this section shall constitute a "report" within the meaning of Sections 17(a), 18(a) and 32(a) of the Act.

Rule 11Ac1-1. Dissemination of Quotations for Reported Securities

(a) *Definitions.* For the purposes of this section:

(1) The term *aggregate quotation size* shall mean the sum of the quotation sizes of all responsible brokers or dealers who have communicated on any exchange bids or offers for a covered security at the same price.

(2) The term *association* shall mean any association of brokers and dealers registered pursuant to Section 15A of the Act (15 U.S.C. 78*o*-3).

(3) The terms *best bid* and *best offer* shall mean the highest priced bid and the lowest priced offer.

(4) The terms *bid* and *offer* shall mean the bid price and the offer price communicated by an exchange member or OTC market maker to any broker or dealer, or to any customer, at which it is willing to buy or sell one or more round lots of a covered security, as either principal or agent, but shall not include indications of interest.

(5) The term *consolidated system* means the consolidated transaction reporting system, including a transaction reporting system operating pursuant to an effective national market system plan.

(6) The term *covered security* shall mean any reported security and any other security for which a transaction report, last sale data or quotation information is disseminated through an automated quotation system as described in Section 3(a)(51)(A)(ii) of the Act (15 U.S.C. 78c(a)(51)(A)(ii)).

(7) The term *effective transaction reporting plan* shall have the meaning provided in § 240.11Aa3-1(a)(3).

(8) The term *electronic communications network,* for the purposes of § 240.11Ac1-1(c)(5), shall mean any electronic system that widely disseminates to third parties orders entered therein by an exchange market maker or OTC market maker, and permits such orders to be executed against in whole or in part; except that the term electronic communications network shall not include:

(i) Any system that crosses multiple orders at one or more specified times at a single price set by the ECN (by algorithm or by any derivative pricing mechanism) and does not allow orders to be crossed or executed against directly by participants outside of such times; or

(ii) Any system operated by, or on behalf of, an OTC market maker or exchange market maker that executes customer orders primarily against the account of such market maker as principal, other than riskless principal.

(9) The term *exchange market maker* shall mean any member of a national securities exchange ("exchange") who is registered as a specialist or market maker pursuant to the rules of such exchange.

(10) The term *exchange-traded security* shall mean any covered security or class of covered securities listed and registered, or admitted to unlisted trading privileges, on an exchange; *provided, however,* That securities not listed on any exchange that are traded pursuant to unlisted trading privileges are excluded.

(11) The term *make available,* when used with respect to bids, offers, quotation sizes and aggregate quotation sizes supplied to quotation vendors by an exchange or association, shall mean to provide circuit connections at the premises of the exchange or association supplying such data, or at a common location determined by mutual agreement of the exchanges and associations, for the delivery of such data to quotation vendors.

(12) The term *odd-lot* shall mean an order for the purchase or sale of a covered security in an amount less than a round lot.

(13) The term *OTC market maker* shall mean any dealer who holds itself out as being willing to buy from and sell to its customers, or otherwise, a covered security for its own account on a regular or continuous basis otherwise than on an exchange in amounts of less than block size.

(14) The term *plan processor* shall have the meaning provided in § 240.11Aa3–2(a)(7).

(15) The term *published aggregate quotation size* shall mean the aggregate quotation size calculated by an exchange and displayed by a quotation vendor on a terminal or other display device at the time an order is presented for execution to a responsible broker or dealer.

(16) The terms *published bid* and *published offer* shall mean the bid or offer of a responsible broker or dealer for a covered security communicated by it to its exchange or association pursuant to this section and displayed by a quotation vendor on a terminal or other display device at the time an order is presented for execution to such responsible broker or dealer.

(17) The term *published quotation size* shall mean the quotation size of a responsible broker or dealer communicated by it to its exchange or association pursuant to this section and displayed by a quotation vendor on a terminal or other display device at the time an order is presented for execution to such responsible broker or dealer.

(18) The term *quotation size,* when used with respect to a responsible broker's or dealer's bid or offer for a covered security, shall mean:

(i) The number of shares (or units of trading) of that covered security which such responsible broker or dealer has specified, for purposes of dissemination to quotation vendors, that it is willing to buy at the bid price or sell at the offer price comprising its bid or offer, as either principal or agent; or

(ii) In the event such responsible broker or dealer has not so specified, a normal unit of trading for that covered security.

(19) The term *quotation vendor* shall mean any securities information processor engaged in the business of disseminating to brokers, dealers or investors on a real-time basis, bids and offers made available pursuant to this section, whether distributed through an electronic communications network or displayed on a terminal or other display device.

(20) The term *reported security* means any security or class of securities for which transaction reports are collected, processed and made available pursuant to an effective transaction reporting plan, or an effective

national market system plan for reporting transactions in listed options.

(21) The term *responsible broker or dealer* shall mean:

(i) When used with respect to bids or offers communicated on an exchange, any member of such exchange who communicates to another member on such exchange, at the location (or locations) designated by such exchange for trading in a covered security, a bid or offer for such covered security, as either principal or agent; *provided, however,* That, in the event two or more members of an exchange have communicated on such exchange bids or offers for a covered security at the same price, each such member shall be considered a "responsible broker or dealer" for that bid or offer, subject to the rules of priority and precedence then in effect on that exchange; and further provided, That for a bid or offer which is transmitted from one member of an exchange to another member who undertakes to represent such bid or offer on such exchange as agent, only the last member who undertakes to represent such bid or offer as agent shall be considered the "responsible broker or dealer" for that bid or offer; and

(ii) When used with respect to bids and offers communicated by a member of an association to another broker or dealer or to a customer otherwise than on an exchange, the member communicating the bid or offer (regardless of whether such bid or offer is for its own account or on behalf of another person).

(22) The term *revised bid or offer* shall mean a market maker's bid or offer which supersedes its published bid or published offer.

(23) The term *revised quotation size* shall mean a market maker's quotation size which supersedes its published quotation size.

(24) The term *specified persons,* when used in connection with any notification required to be provided pursuant to paragraph (b)(3) of this section and any election (or withdrawal thereof) permitted under paragraph (b)(5) of this section, shall mean:

(i) Each quotation vendor;

(ii) Each plan processor; and

(iii) The processor for the Options Price Reporting Authority (in the case of a notification for a subject security which is a class of securities underlying options admitted to trading on any exchange).

(25) The term *subject security* shall mean:

(i) With respect to an exchange:

(A) Any exchange-traded security other than a security for which the executed volume of such exchange, during the most recent calendar quarter, comprised one percent or less of the aggregate trading volume for such security as reported in the consolidated system; and

(B) Any other covered security for which such exchange has in effect an election, pursuant to paragraph (b)(5)(i) of this section, to collect, process, and make available to quotation vendors, bids, offers, quotation sizes, and aggregate quotation sizes communicated on such exchange; and

(ii) With respect to a member of an association:

(A) Any exchange-traded security for which such member acts in the capacity of an OTC market maker unless the executed volume of such member, during the most recent calendar quarter, comprised one percent or less of the aggregate trading volume for such security as reported in the consolidated system; and

(B) Any other covered security for which such member acts in the capacity of an OTC market maker and has in effect an election, pursuant to paragraph (b)(5)(ii) of this section, to communicate to its association bids, offers and quotation sizes for the purpose of making such bids, offers and quotation sizes available to quotation vendors.

(26) The term *customer* means any person that is not a registered broker-dealer.

(27) The term *listed option* means any option traded on a registered national securities exchange or automated facility of a national securities association.

(28) The term *options class* means all of the put option or call option series overlying a security, as defined in Section 3(a)(10) of the Act (15 U.S.C. 78c(a)(10)).

(29) The term *options series* means the contracts in an options class that have the same unit of trade, expiration date, and exercise price, and other terms or conditions.

(30) The term *trading rotation* means, with respect to an options class, the time period on an exchange during which:

(i) Opening, re-opening, or closing transactions in options series in such options class are not yet completed; and

(ii) Continuous trading has not yet commenced or has not yet ended for the day in options series in such options class.

(b) *Dissemination requirements for exchanges and associations.* (1) Every exchange and association shall establish and maintain procedures and mechanisms for collecting bids, offers, quotation sizes and aggregate quotation sizes from responsible brokers or dealers who are members of such exchange or association, processing such bids, offers and sizes, and making such bids, offers and sizes available to quotation vendors, as follows:

(i) Each exchange shall at all times such exchange is open for trading, collect, process and make available to quotation vendors the best bid, the best offer, and aggregate quotation sizes for each subject security listed or admitted to unlisted trading privileges which is communicated on any exchange by any responsible broker or dealer, but shall not include:

(A) Any bid or offer executed immediately after communication and any bid or offer communicated by a responsible broker or dealer other than an exchange market maker which is cancelled or withdrawn if not executed immediately after communication; and

(B) Any bid or offer communicated during a period when trading in that security has been suspended or halted, or prior to the commencement of trading in that security on any trading day, on that exchange.

(ii) Each association shall, at all times that last sale information with respect to reported securities is reported pursuant to an effective transaction reporting plan, collect, process and make available to quotation vendors the best bid, best offer, and quotation sizes communicated otherwise than on an exchange by each member of such association acting in the capacity of an OTC market maker for each subject security and the identity of that member (excluding any bid or offer executed immediately after communication), except during any period when over-the-counter trading in that security has been suspended.

(2) Each exchange shall, with respect to each published bid and published offer representing a bid or offer of a member for a subject security, establish and maintain procedures for ascertaining and disclosing to other members of that exchange, upon presentation of orders sought to be executed by them in reliance upon paragraph (c)(2) of this section, the identity of the responsible broker or dealer who made such bid or offer and the quotation size associated with it.

(3)(i) If, at any time an exchange is open for trading, such exchange determines, pursuant to rules approved by the Securities and Exchange Commission pursuant to section 19(b)(2) of the Act (15 U.S.C. 78s(b)(2)), that the level of trading activities or the existence of unusual market conditions is such that the exchange is incapable of collecting, processing, and making available to quotation vendors the data for a subject security required to be made available pursuant to paragraph (b)(1) of this section in a manner that accurately reflects the current state of the market on such exchange, such exchange shall immediately notify all specified persons of that determination. Upon such notification, responsible brokers or dealers that are members of that exchange shall be relieved of their obligation under paragraphs (c)(2) and (d)(3) of this section and such exchange shall be relieved of its obligations under paragraphs (b)(1) and (2) of this section for that security: *provided, however,* That such exchange will continue, to the maximum extent practicable under the circumstances, to collect, process, and make available to quotation vendors data for that security in accordance with paragraph (b)(1) of this section.

(ii) During any period an exchange, or any responsible broker or dealer that is a member of that exchange, is relieved of any obligation imposed by this section for any subject security by virtue of a notification made pursuant to paragraph (b)(3)(i) of this section, such exchange shall monitor the activity or conditions which formed the basis for such notification and shall immediately renotify all specified persons when that exchange is once again capable of collecting, processing, and making available to quotation vendors the data for that security required to be made available pursuant to paragraph (b)(1) of this section in a manner that accurately reflects the current state of the market on such exchange. Upon such renotification, any exchange or responsible broker or dealer which had been relieved of any obligation imposed by this section as a consequence of the prior notification shall again be subject to such obligation.

(4) Nothing in this section shall preclude any exchange or association from making available to quotation vendors indications of interest or bids and offers for a subject security at any time such exchange or association is not required to do so pursuant to paragraph (b)(1) of this section.

(5)(i) Any exchange may make an election for purposes of paragraph (a)(25)(i)(B) of this section for any covered security, by collecting, processing, and making available bids, offers, quotation sizes, and aggregate quotation sizes in that security; except that for any covered security previously listed or admitted to unlisted trading privileges on only one exchange and not traded by any OTC market maker, such election shall be made by notifying all specified persons, and shall be effective at the opening of trading on the business day following notification.

(ii) Any member of an association acting in the capacity of an OTC market maker may make an election for purposes of paragraph (a)(25)(ii)(B) of this section for any covered security, by communicating to its association bids, offers, and quotation sizes in that security; except that for any other covered security listed or admitted to unlisted trading privileges on only one exchange and not traded by any other OTC market maker, such election shall be made by notifying its association and all specified persons, and shall be effective at the opening of trading on the business day following notification.

(iii) The election of an exchange or member of an association for any covered security pursuant to this paragraph (b)(5) shall cease to be in effect if such exchange or member ceases to make available or communicate bids, offers, and quotation sizes in such security.

(c) *Obligations of responsible brokers and dealers.* (1) Each responsible broker or dealer shall promptly communicate to its exchange or association, pursuant to the procedures established by that exchange or association, its best bids, best offers, and quotation sizes for any subject security.

(2) Subject to the provisions of paragraph (c)(3) of this section, each responsible broker or dealer shall be obligated to execute any order to buy or sell a subject security, other than an odd-lot order, presented to it by another broker or dealer, or any other person belonging to a category of persons with whom such responsible broker or dealer customarily deals, at a price at least as favorable to such buyer or seller as the responsible broker's or dealer's published bid or published offer (exclusive of any commission, commission equivalent or differential customarily charged by such responsible broker or dealer in connection with execution of any such order) in any amount up to its published quotation size.

(3)(i) No responsible broker or dealer shall be obligated to execute a transaction for any subject security as provided in paragraph (c)(2) of this section to purchase or sell that subject security in an amount greater than such revised quotation if:

(A) Prior to the presentation of an order for the purchase or sale of a subject security, a responsible broker or dealer has communicated to its exchange or association, pursuant to paragraph (c)(1) of this section, a revised quotation size; or

(B) At the time an order for the purchase or sale of a subject security is presented, a responsible broker or dealer is in the process of effecting a transaction in such subject security, and immediately after the completion of such transaction, it communicates to its exchange or association a revised quotation size, such responsible broker or dealer shall not be obligated by paragraph (c)(2) of this section to purchase or sell that subject security in an amount greater than such revised quotation size.

(ii) No responsible broker or dealer shall be obligated to execute a transaction for any subject security as provided in paragraph (c)(2) of this section if:

(A) Before the order sought to be executed is presented, such responsible broker or dealer has communicated to its exchange or association pursuant to paragraph (c)(1) of this section, a revised bid or offer; or

(B) At the time the order sought to be executed is presented, such responsible broker or dealer is in the process of effecting a transaction in such subject security, and, immediately after the completion of such transaction, such responsible broker or dealer communicates to its exchange or association pursuant to paragraph (c)(1) of this section, a revised bid or offer; *provided, however*, That such responsible broker or dealer shall nonetheless be obligated to execute any such order in such subject security as provided in paragraph (c)(2) of this section at its revised bid or offer in any amount up to its published quotation size or revised quotation size.

(4) Subject to the provisions of paragraph (b)(4) of this section:

(i) No exchange or OTC market maker may make available, disseminate or otherwise communicate to any quotation vendor, directly or indirectly, for display on a terminal or other display device any bid, offer, quotation size, or aggregate quotation size for any covered security which is not a subject security with respect to such exchange or OTC market maker; and

(ii) No quotation vendor may disseminate or display on a terminal or other display device any bid, offer, quotation size, or aggregate quotation size from any exchange or OTC market maker for any covered security which is not a subject security with respect to such exchange or OTC market maker.

(5)(i) Entry of any priced order for a covered security by an exchange market maker or OTC market maker in that security into an electronic communications network that widely disseminates such order shall be deemed to be:

(A) A bid or offer under this section, to be communicated to the market maker's exchange or association pursuant to paragraph (c) of this section for at least the minimum quotation size that is required by the rules of the market maker's exchange or association if the priced order is for the account of a market maker, or the actual size of the order up to the minimum quotation size required if the priced order is for the account of a customer; and

(B) A communication of a bid or offer to a quotation vendor for display on a display device for purposes of paragraph (c)(4) of this section.

(ii) An exchange market maker or OTC market maker that has entered a priced order for a covered security into an electronic communications network that widely disseminates such order shall be deemed to be in compliance with paragraph (c)(5)(i)(A) of this section if the electronic communications network:

(A)(1) Provides to an exchange or association (or an exclusive processor acting on behalf of one or more exchanges or associations) the prices and sizes of the orders at the highest buy price and the lowest sell price for such security entered in, and widely disseminated by, the electronic communications network by exchange market makers and OTC market makers for the covered security, and such prices and sizes are included in the quotation data made available by the exchange, association, or exclusive processor to quotation vendors pursuant to this section; and

(2) Provides, to any broker or dealer, the ability to effect a transaction with a priced order widely disseminated by the electronic communications network entered therein by an exchange market maker or OTC market maker that is:

(i) Equivalent to the ability of any broker or dealer to effect a transaction with an exchange market maker or OTC market maker pursuant to the rules of the exchange or association to which the electronic communications network supplies such bids and offers; and

(ii) At the price of the highest priced buy order or lowest priced sell order, or better, for the lesser of the cumulative size of such priced orders entered therein by exchange market makers or OTC market makers at such price, or the size of the execution sought by the broker or dealer, for the covered security; or,

(B) Is an alternative trading system that:

(1) Displays orders and provides the ability to effect transactions with such orders under § 242.301(b)(3) of this chapter; and

(2) Otherwise is in compliance with Regulation ATS, § 242.300 through § 242.303 of this chapter.

(d) *Transactions in listed options.*

(1) An exchange or association:

(i) Shall not be required, under paragraph (b) of this section, to collect from responsible brokers or dealers who are members of such exchange or association, or to make available to quotation vendors, the quotation sizes and aggregate quotation sizes for listed options, if such exchange or association establishes by rule and periodically publishes the quotation size for which such responsible brokers or dealers are obligated to execute an order to buy or sell an options series that is a subject security at its published bid or offer under paragraph (c)(2) of this section;

(ii) May establish by rule and periodically publish a quotation size, which shall not be for less than one contract, for which responsible brokers or dealers who are members of such exchange or association are obligated under paragraph (c)(2) of this section to execute an order to buy or sell a listed option for the account of a broker or dealer that is in an amount different from the quotation size for which it is obligated to execute an order for the account of a customer; and

(iii) May establish and maintain procedures and mechanisms for collecting from responsible brokers and dealers who are members of such exchange or association, and making available to quotation vendors, the quotation sizes and aggregate quotation sizes in listed options for which such responsible broker or dealer will be obligated under paragraph (c)(2) of this section to execute an order from a customer to buy or sell a listed option and establish by rule and periodically publish the size, which shall not be less than one contract, for which such responsible brokers or dealers are obligated to execute an order for the account of a broker or dealer.

(2) If, pursuant to paragraph (d)(1) of this section, the rules of an exchange or association do not require its members to communicate to it their quotation sizes for listed options, a responsible broker or dealer that is a member of such exchange or association shall:

(i) Be relieved of its obligations under paragraph (c)(1) of this section to communicate to such exchange or association its quotation sizes for any listed option; and

(ii) Comply with its obligations under paragraph (c)(2) of this section by executing any order to buy or sell a listed option, in an amount up to the size established by such exchange's or association's rules under paragraph (d)(1) of this section.

(3) *Thirty second response.* Each responsible broker or dealer, within thirty seconds of receiving an order to buy or sell a listed option in an amount greater than the quotation size established by an exchange's or association's rules pursuant to paragraph (d)(1) of this section, or its published quotation size must:

(i) Execute the entire order; or

(ii)(A) Execute that portion of the order equal to at least:

(*1*) The quotation size established by an exchange's or association's rules, pursuant to paragraph (d)(1) of this section, to the extent that such exchange or association does not collect and make available to quotation vendors quotation size and aggregate quotation size under paragraph (b) of this section; or

(*2*) Its published quotation size; and

(B) Revise its bid or offer.

(4) Notwithstanding paragraph (d)(3) of this section, no responsible broker or dealer shall be obligated to execute a transaction for any listed option as provided in paragraph (c)(2) of this section if:

(i) Any of the circumstances in paragraph (c)(3) of this section exist; or

(ii) The order for the purchase or sale of a listed option is presented during a trading rotation in that listed option.

(e) *Exemptions.* The Commission may exempt from the provisions of this section, either unconditionally or on specified terms and conditions, any responsible broker or dealer, electronic communications network, exchange, or association if the Commission determines that such exemption is consistent with the public interest, the protection of investors and the removal of impediments to and perfection of the mechanism of a national market system.

Rule 11Ac1–2. Display of Transaction Reports, Last Sale Data and Quotation Information

(a) *Definitions.* For purposes of this section,

(1) The terms "transaction report," "effective transaction reporting plan," "moving ticker," "last sale data," "market minder" and "interrogation device" shall have the meaning provided in Rule 11Aa3–1.

(2) The term "vendor" shall mean any securities information processor engaged in the business of disseminating transaction reports, last sale data or quotation information with respect to subject securities to brokers, dealers or investors on a real-time or other current and continuing basis, whether through an electronic communications network, moving ticker or interrogation device.

(3) The term "NASDAQ" shall mean the electronic inter-dealer quotation system owned and operated by NASDAQ, Inc., a subsidiary of the National Association of Securities Dealers, Inc.

(4) The term "subject security" shall mean

(i) any reported security; and

(ii) any other equity security as to which transaction reports, last sale data or quotation information is disseminated through NASDAQ.

(5) The terms "quotations" and "quotation information" shall mean bids, offers and, where applicable, quotation sizes and aggregate quotation sizes.

(6) The terms "bid" and "offer" shall,

(i) in the case of a reported security have the meaning provided in Rule 11Ac1–1; and

(ii) in the case of any subject security other than a reported security, mean the most recent bid price or offer price of an over-the-counter market maker disseminated through Level 2 or 3 of NASDAQ.

(7) The terms "quotation size," "aggregate quotation size," "third market maker" and "make available" shall have the meaning provided in Rule 11Ac1–1.

(8) The term "consolidated display" shall mean, with respect to a particular reported security,

(i) any display (other than a moving ticker or market minder) of transaction reports for such security from all reporting market centers;

(ii) any display (other than a moving ticker or market minder) of last sale data for such security, or information derived therefrom, based on transaction reports from all reporting market centers; or

(iii) any display of quotation information for that security based on quotations from all reporting market centers.

(9) The term "consolidated price," when used with respect to a particular reported security, shall mean the price of the most recent transaction report for that security reported pursuant to any effective transaction reporting plan.

(10) The term "consolidated volume," when used with respect to a particular reported security, shall mean the volume of the most recent transaction report for that security reported pursuant to any effective transaction reporting plan.

(11) The term "cumulative consolidated volume," when used with respect to a particular reported security, shall mean the cumulative volume of all transaction reports for that security reported pursuant to any effective transaction reporting plan during a particular trading day.

(12) The term "individual market center display" shall mean, with respect to a particular reported security.

(i) any display (other than a moving ticker or market minder) of transaction reports for such security from a particular market center;

(ii) any display (other than a moving ticker or market minder) of last sale data for such security, or information derived therefrom, based on transaction reports from a particular reporting market center; or

(iii) any display of quotation information for that security based on quotations from a particular reporting market center.

(13) The term "over-the-counter market maker" shall mean, with respect to any subject security other than a reported security, any broker or dealer which holds itself out as being willing to buy and sell such security on a regular and continuous basis otherwise than on an exchange in amounts of less than block size.

(14) The term "reporting market center" shall mean,

(i) with respect to a reported security,

(A) any national securities exchange ("exchange") on which, or through whose facilities, transactions in such security are executed and which collects, processes and makes available transaction reports with respect to transactions in such security on a current basis pursuant to Rule 11Aa3–1; and

(B) any person acting in the capacity of a third market maker with respect to such security which reports transactions in such security to a national securities association on a current basis pursuant to Rule 11Aa3–1 and disseminates quotations in such security pursuant to Rule 11Ac1–1; and

(ii) with respect to a subject security other than a reported security, any person acting in the capacity of an over-the-counter market maker who is authorized to disseminate quotations in such security, through NASDAQ, and who makes such quotations available through that system on a regular and continuous basis.

(15) The terms "best bid" and "best offer" shall mean,

(i) with respect to quotations for a reported security, the highest bid or lowest offer for that security made available by any reporting market center pursuant to Rule 11Ac1–1 (excluding any bid or offer made available by an exchange during any period such exchange is relieved of its obligations under paragraphs (b)(1) and (2) of Rule 11Ac1–1 by virtue of subparagraph (b)(3)(i) thereof); *Provided, however,* That in the event two or more reporting market centers make available identical bids or offers for a reported security, the best bid or best offer (as the case may be) shall be computed by ranking all such identical bids or offers (as the case may be) first by size (giving the highest ranking to the bid or offer associated with the largest size), then by time (giving the highest ranking to the bid or offer received first in time); and

(ii) with respect to quotations for a subject security other than a reported security, the highest bid or lowest offer (as the case may be) for such security disseminated by an over-the-counter market maker in Level 2 or 3 of NASDAQ.

(16) The term "quotation montage" shall mean, with respect to a particular subject security, a display on an interrogation device which disseminates simultaneously quotations in that security from all reporting market centers.

(17) The term "representative bid or offer" shall mean any number representing a bid price or an offer price (as the case may be) for a particular subject security which is (i) the mean, median, mode or weighted average of two or more bids or offers of reporting market centers in such security, (ii) calculated with reference to or derived from any such mean, median, mode or weighted average, or (iii) calculated by adding to or subtracting from the bid or offer of any reporting market center in such security any number representing a commission,

commission equivalent, mark-up or differential.

(18) The term "market information," when used with respect to an individual market center display or a consolidated display for a particular reported security, shall mean (i) any transaction reports or last sale data, or information derived therefrom, contained in any such display, (ii) any quotation information contained in any such display, and (iii) any other category of information contained in any such display which relates to the particular reported security involved, including, but not limited to, annual or periodic dividend, ex-dividend date, time of most recent trade and news dissemination.

(19) The term "market linkage system" shall mean any communications and data processing facility which permits orders for the purchase and sale of a subject security to be transmitted from one reporting market center to another such reporting market center.

(20) The term "reported security" shall mean any security or class of securities for which transaction reports are collected, processed and made available pursuant to an effective transaction reporting plan.

(b) *Display Requirements for Transaction Reports and Last Sale Data.*

(1) No vendor shall distribute, publish, display or otherwise provide to brokers and dealers on a real-time or other current and continuing basis, whether through an electronic communications network, moving ticker or interrogation device, transaction reports, last sale data or market information in contravention of the provisions of this section.

(2) On and after the effective date of this section, the following requirements shall be applicable to the display of transaction reports, last sale data or market information with respect to reported securities:

(i) If transaction reports or last sale data with respect to a particular reported security are provided by a vendor on an interrogation device, such vendor shall provide on that device a consolidated display of transaction reports or last sale data for such security which shall include, at a minimum, (A) the consolidated price for such security, (B) the consolidated volume or cumulative consolidated volume for such security, and (C) an identifier indicating the reporting market center associated with such consolidated price and consolidated volume (the "consolidated last sale display").

(ii) The consolidated last sale display shall be accessed by means of retrieval instructions involving a number of key strokes which is fewer than the number of strokes required to access any individual market center display of transaction reports or last sale data provided on that device for such security; *Provided, however*, That, notwithstanding the above requirement, a vendor may provide on that device both the consolidated last sale display and any such individual market center displays made available for such security by means of retrieval instructions involving an equal number of key strokes if the information request or transmit key for the consolidated last sale display is the most prominent.

(iii) Subject to the provisions of subparagraph (b)(2)(ii) of this section, a vendor may provide on an interrogation device an individual market center display of transaction reports or last sale data for a particular reported security for any reporting market center in such security.

(iv) No moving ticker may include an identifier indicating the reporting market center associated with a particular transaction report with respect to a reported security unless such moving ticker includes identifiers for all transaction reports for such security (or an identifiable subset of all such transaction reports) from all reporting market centers in that security in a non-discriminatory manner.

(v) No moving ticker or consolidated last sale display may exclude any transaction report or last sale data based upon the market center in which a transaction has been executed.

(vi) No vendor may provide any category of market information in an individual market center display for a particular subject security unless that category of market information is also provided, on a consolidated basis, as part of the consolidated last sale display for that security; *Provided, however*, That a vendor may delete from such consolidated last sale display up to three categories of information if such deletion is necessary to accommodate the display of any market identifiers required by this section.

(vii) Transaction reports and last sale data from all reporting market centers which are third market makers may be identified in a consolidated last sale display or a moving ticker by a single identifier without identification of the individual third market maker associated with such transaction report or last sale data.

(c) *Display Requirements for Quotation Information.*

(1) No vendor shall distribute, publish, display or otherwise provide to brokers and dealers on a real-time or other current and continuing basis, whether through an electronic communications network, moving ticker or interrogation device, quotation information with respect to subject securities in contravention of the provisions of this section.

(2) On and after the effective date of this section the following requirements shall be applicable to the display of quotation information with respect to subject securities:

(i) If quotation information with respect to a particular subject security is provided by a vendor on an interrogation device, such vendor shall provide on that device a consolidated display of quotation information for such security (the "consolidated quotation display") which shall include, at a minimum,

(A) the best bid and best offer for such security and, in the case of a reported security, (*1*) identifiers indicating the reporting market center making available such best bid and the reporting market center making available such best offer and (*2*) the quotation size or aggregate quotation size associated with such best bid and the quotation size or aggregate quotation size associated with such best offer, or

(B) a quotation montage for that security.

(ii) The consolidated quotation display shall be accessed by means of retrieval instructions involving a number of key strokes which is fewer than the number of strokes required to access any individual market center quotation display provided on that device by such vendors for such security; *Provided, however*, That, notwithstanding the above requirement, a vendor may provide on that device both the consolidated quotation display and any individual market center display of quotation information provided for such security by means of retrieval instructions involving an equal number of key strokes if the information request or transmit key for the consolidated quotation display is the most prominent.

(iii) Subject to the provisions of subparagraph (c)(2)(ii) of this section, a vendor may provide on an interrogation device

(A) an individual market center display of quotation information for a particular subject security for any reporting market center in such security; or

(B) either separately or as the consolidated quotation display, a quotation montage for that security.

(iv) No consolidated quotation display or separate quotation montage provided on an interrogation device may exclude any quotation information based upon the market center making available such information; *Provided, however*, That for purposes of providing the consolidated quotation display or a separate quotation montage for any reported security, quotation information from all reporting market centers which are third market makers may be consolidated to derive at best bid and offer for all such market centers if such interrogation device is capable of displaying, either separately or as part of the consolidated quotation display or separate quotation montage, (A) identifiers indicating the reporting market center making available such best bid and the reporting market center making available such best offer, and (B) the quotation size associated with both such best bid and best offer.

(v) Each individual market center display of quotation information or separate quotation montage for a particular reported security shall include the quotation size or aggregate quotation size associated with each bid or offer disseminated as part of such display or montage.

(vi) No vendor may provide on any interrogation device a representative bid or offer with respect to any subject security.

(d) *Joint Display of Transaction Reports and Quotation Information*. Subject to the provisions of paragraphs (b)(2)(ii) and (c)(2)(ii) of this section regarding the means of access to consolidated last sale displays and consolidated quotation displays, a vendor may combine the consolidated last sale display and the consolidated quotation display for a particular subject security.

(e) *Applicability to Brokers and Dealers*. Subject to the provisions of paragraph (f) of this section, no broker or dealer may operate or maintain any display of transaction reports, last sale data, quotation information or market information which would not be permitted to be provided by a vendor under paragraph (b) or (c) of this section.

(f) *Exchange or Market Linkage System Displays*. The provisions of this section shall not apply to:

(1) the dissemination or display of transactions reports, last sale data, quotation information or market information on the trading floor or through the facilities of an exchange, (2) any display of transaction reports, last sale data, quotation information or market information operated or maintained by a self-regulatory organization for monitoring or surveillance purposes, or (3) any display of transaction reports, last sale data or quotation information in connection with the operation of a market linkage system implemented in accordance with a plan approved by the Commission pursuant to Section 11A(a)(3)(B) of the Act.

(g) *Exemptions*. The Commission may exempt from the provisions of this section, either unconditionally or on specified terms and conditions, any securities information processor, self-regulatory organization, broker, dealer or specified subject security if the Commission determines that such exemption is consistent with the public interest, the protection of investors and the removal of impediments to, and perfection of the mechanisms of, a national market system.

(h) *Effective Date*. The effective date of this section shall be April 5, 1980, except for paragraph c(2)(vi), which shall become effective on July 5, 1980, and paragraphs (b)(2)(ii), (b)(2)(vi) and (c)(2)(i), (ii), (iv), (v) which shall become effective on October 1, 1981.

Rule 11Ac1–3. Customer Account Statements

(a) No broker or dealer acting as agent for a customer may effect any transaction in, induce or attempt to induce the purchase or sale of, or direct orders for purchase or sale of, any subject security as defined in § 240.11Ac1–2 or a security authorized for quotation on an automated inter-dealer quotation system that has the characteristics set forth in section 17B of the Act (15 U.S.C. 78q–2), unless such broker or dealer informs such customer, in writing, upon opening a new account and on an annual basis thereafter, of the following:

(1) The broker's or dealer's policies regarding receipt of payment for order flow as defined in § 240.10b–10(e)(9), from any broker or dealer, national securities exchange, registered securities association, or exchange member to which it routes customers' orders for execution, including a statement as to whether any payment for order flow is received for routing customer orders and a detailed description of the nature of the compensation received; and

(2) The broker's or dealer's policies for determining where to route customer orders that are the subject of payment for order flow as defined in § 240.10b–10(e)(9) absent specific instructions from customers, including a description of the extent to which orders can be executed prices superior to the best bid or best offer as defined in § 240.11Ac1–2.

(b) *Exemptions.* The Commission, upon request or upon its own motion, may exempt by rule or by order, any broker or dealer or any class of brokers or dealers, security or class of securities from the requirements of paragraph (a) of this section with respect to any transaction or class of transactions, either unconditionally or on specified terms and conditions, if the Commission determines that such exemption is consistent with the public interest and the protection of investors.

Rule 11Ac1–4. Display of Customer Limit Orders

(a) *Definitions.* For purposes of this section:

(1) The term *association* shall mean any association of brokers and dealers registered pursuant to Section 15A of the Act (15 U.S.C. 78*o*–3).

(2) The terms *best bid* and *best offer* shall have the meaning provided in § 240.11Ac1–1(a)(3).

(3) The terms *bid* and *offer* shall have the meaning provided in § 240.11Ac1–1(a)(4).

(4) The term *block size* shall mean any order:

(i) Of at least 10,000 shares; or

(ii) For a quantity of stock having a market value of at least $200,000.

(5) The term *covered security* shall mean any "reported security" and any other security for which a transaction report, last sale data or quotation information is disseminated through an automated quotation system as described in section 3(a)(51)(A)(ii) of the Act (15 U.S.C. 78c(a)(51)(A)(ii)).

(6) The term *customer limit order* shall mean an order to buy or sell a covered security at a specified price that is not for the account of either a broker or dealer; *provided, however,* That the term customer limit order shall include an order transmitted by a broker or dealer on behalf of a customer.

(7) The term *electronic communications network* shall have the meaning provided in § 240.11Ac1–1(a)(8).

(8) The term *exchange-traded security* shall have the meaning provided in § 240.11Ac1–1(a)(10).

(9) The term *OTC market maker* shall mean any dealer who holds itself out as being willing to buy from and sell to its customers, or otherwise, a covered security for its own account on a regular or continuous basis otherwise than on a national securities exchange in amounts of less than block size.

(10) The term *reported security* means any security or class of securities for which transaction reports are collected, processed, and made available pursuant to an effective transaction reporting plan.

(b) *Specialists and OTC market makers.* For all covered securities:

(1) Each member of an exchange that is registered by that exchange as a specialist, or is authorized by that exchange to perform functions substantially similar to that of a specialist, shall publish immediately a bid or offer that reflects:

(i) The price and the full size of each customer limit order held by the specialist that is at a price that would improve the bid or offer of such specialist in such security; and

(ii) The full size of each customer limit order held by the specialist that:

(A) Is priced equal to the bid or offer of such specialist for such security;

(B) Is priced equal to the national best bid or offer; and

(C) Represents more than a *de minimis* change in relation to the size associated with the specialist's bid or offer.

(2) Each registered broker or dealer that acts as an OTC market maker shall publish immediately a bid or offer that reflects:

(i) The price and the full size of each customer limit order held by the OTC market maker that is at a price that would improve the bid or offer of such OTC market maker in such security; and

(ii) The full size of each customer limit order held by the OTC market maker that:

(A) Is priced equal to the bid or offer of such OTC market maker for such security;

(B) Is priced equal to the national best bid or offer; and

(C) Represents more than a *de minimis* change in relation to the size associated with the OTC market maker's bid or offer.

(c) *Exceptions.* The requirements in paragraph (b) of this section shall not apply to any customer limit order:

(1) That is executed upon receipt of the order.

(2) That is placed by a customer who expressly requests, either at the time that the order is placed or prior thereto pursuant to an individually negotiated agreement with respect to such customer's orders, that the order not be displayed.

(3) That is an odd-lot order.

(4) That is a block size order, unless a customer placing such order requests that the order be displayed.

(5) That is delivered immediately upon receipt to an exchange or association-sponsored system, or an electronic communications network that complies with the requirements of § 240.11Ac1–1(c)(5)(ii) with respect to that order.

(6) That is delivered immediately upon receipt to another exchange member or OTC market maker that complies with the requirements of this section with respect to that order.

(7) That is an "all or none" order.

(d) *Exemptions.* The Commission may exempt from the provisions of this section, either unconditionally or on specified terms and conditions, any responsible broker or dealer, electronic communications network, exchange, or association if the Commission determines that such exemption is consistent with the public interest, the protection of investors and the removal of impediments to and perfection of the mechanism of a national market system.

Rule 11Ac1–5. Disclosure of Order Execution Information

Preliminary Note: Section 240.11Ac1–5 requires market centers to make available standardized, monthly reports of statistical information concerning their order executions. This information is presented in accordance with uniform standards that are based on broad assumptions about order execution and routing practices. The information will provide a starting point to promote visibility and competition on the part of market centers and broker-dealers, particularly on the factors of execution price and speed. The disclosures required by this section do not encompass all of the factors that may be important to investors in evaluating the order routing services of a broker-dealer. In addition, any particular market center's statistics will encompass varying types of orders routed by different broker-dealers on behalf of customers with a wide range of objectives. Accordingly, the statistical information required by this Section alone does not create a reliable basis to address whether any particular broker-dealer failed to obtain the most favorable terms reasonably available under the circumstances for customer orders.

(a) *Definitions.* For the purposes of this section:

(1) The term *alternative trading system* shall have the meaning provided in § 242.300(c) of this chapter.

(2) The term *average effective spread* shall mean the share-weighted average of effective spreads for order executions calculated, for buy orders, as double the amount of difference between the execution price and the midpoint of the consolidated best bid and offer at the time of order receipt and, for sell orders, as double the amount of difference between the midpoint of the consolidated best bid and offer at the time of order receipt and the execution price.

(3) The term *average realized spread* shall mean the share-weighted average of realized spreads for order executions calculated, for buy orders, as double the amount of difference between the execution price and the midpoint of the consolidated best bid and offer five minutes after the time of order execution and, for sell orders, as double the amount of difference between the midpoint of the consolidated best bid and offer five minutes after the time of order execution and the execution price; provided, however, that the midpoint of the final consolidated best bid and offer disseminated for regular trading hours shall be used to calculate a realized spread if it is disseminated less than five minutes after the time of order execution.

(4) The term *categorized by order size* shall mean dividing orders into separate categories for sizes from 100 to 499 shares, from 500 to 1999 shares, from 2000 to 4999 shares, and 5000 or greater shares.

(5) The term *categorized by order type* shall mean dividing orders into separate categories for market orders, marketable limit orders, inside-the-quote limit orders, at-the-quote limit orders, and near-the-quote limit orders.

(6) The term *categorized by security* shall mean dividing orders into separate categories for each national market system security that is included in a report.

(7) The term *consolidated best bid and offer* shall mean the highest firm bid and the lowest firm offer for a security that is calculated and disseminated on a current and continuous basis pursuant to an effective national market system plan.

(8) The term *covered order* shall mean any market order or any limit order (including immediate-or-cancel orders) received by a market center during regular trading hours at a time when a consolidated best bid and offer is being disseminated, and, if executed, is executed during regular trading hours, but shall exclude any order for which the customer requests special handling for execution, including, but not limited to, orders to be executed at a market opening price or a market closing price, orders submitted with stop prices, orders to be executed only at their full size, orders to be executed on a particular type of tick or bid, orders submitted on a "not held" basis, orders for other than regular settlement, and orders to be executed at prices unrelated to the mar-

ket price of the security at the time of execution.

(9) The term *exchange market maker* shall mean any member of a national securities exchange that is registered as a specialist or market maker pursuant to the rules of such exchange.

(10) The term *executed at the quote* shall mean, for buy orders, execution at a price equal to the consolidated best offer at the time of order receipt and, for sell orders, execution at a price equal to the consolidated best bid at the time of order receipt.

(11) The term *executed outside the quote* shall mean, for buy orders, execution at a price higher than the consolidated best offer at the time of order receipt and, for sell orders, execution at a price lower than the consolidated best bid at the time of order receipt.

(12) The term *executed with price improvement* shall mean, for buy orders, execution at a price lower than the consolidated best offer at the time of order receipt and, for sell orders, execution at a price higher than the consolidated best bid at the time of order receipt.

(13) The terms *inside-the-quote limit order, at-the-quote limit order, and near-the-quote limit order* shall mean non-marketable buy orders with limit prices that are, respectively, higher than, equal to, and lower by $0.10 or less than the consolidated best bid at the time of order receipt, and non-marketable sell orders with limit prices that are, respectively, lower than, equal to, and higher by $0.10 or less than the consolidated best offer at the time of order receipt.

(14) The term *market center* shall mean any exchange market maker, OTC market maker, alternative trading system, national securities exchange, or national securities association.

(15) The term *marketable limit order* shall mean any buy order with a limit price equal to or greater than the consolidated best offer at the time of order receipt, and any sell order with a limit price equal to or less than the consolidated best bid at the time of order receipt.

(16) The term *effective national market system plan* shall have the meaning provided in § 240.11Aa3–2(a)(2).

(17) The term *national market system security* shall have the meaning provided in § 240.11Aa2–1.

(18) The term *OTC market maker* shall mean any dealer that holds itself out as being willing to buy from and sell to its customers, or others, in the United States, a national market system security for its own account on a regular or continuous basis otherwise than on a national securities exchange in amounts of less than block size.

(19) The term *regular trading hours* shall mean the time between 9:30 a.m. and 4:00 p.m. Eastern Time, or such other time as is set forth in the procedures established pursuant to paragraph (c)(2) of this section.

(20) The term *time of order execution* shall mean the time (to the second) that an order was executed at any venue.

(21) The term *time of order receipt* shall mean the time (to the second) that an order was received by a market center for execution.

(b) *Monthly electronic reports by market centers.* (1) Every market center shall make available for each calendar month, in accordance with the procedures established pursuant to paragraph (b)(2) of this section, a report on the covered orders in national market system securities that it received for execution from any person. Such report shall be in electronic form; shall be categorized by security, order type, and order size; and shall include the following columns of information:

(i) For market orders, marketable limit orders, inside-the-quote limit orders, at-the-quote limit orders, and near-the-quote limit orders:

(A) The number of covered orders;

(B) The cumulative number of shares of covered orders;

(C) The cumulative number of shares of covered orders cancelled prior to execution;

(D) The cumulative number of shares of covered orders executed at the receiving market center;

(E) The cumulative number of shares of covered orders executed at any other venue;

(F) The cumulative number of shares of covered orders executed from 0 to 9 seconds after the time of order receipt;

(G) The cumulative number of shares of covered orders executed from 10 to 29 seconds after the time of order receipt;

(H) The cumulative number of shares of covered orders executed from 30 seconds to 59 seconds after the time of order receipt;

(I) The cumulative number of shares of covered orders executed from 60 seconds to 299 seconds after the time of order receipt;

(J) The cumulative number of shares of covered orders executed from 5 minutes to 30 minutes after the time of order receipt; and

(K) The average realized spread for executions of covered orders; and

(ii) For market orders and marketable limit orders:

(A) The average effective spread for executions of covered orders;

(B) The cumulative number of shares of covered orders executed with price improvement;

(C) For shares executed with price improvement, the share-weighted average amount per share that prices were improved;

(D) For shares executed with price improvement, the share-weighted average period from the time of order receipt to the time of order execution;

(E) The cumulative number of shares of covered orders executed at the quote;

(F) For shares executed at the quote, the share-weighted average period from the time of order receipt to the time of order execution;

(G) The cumulative number of shares of covered orders executed outside the quote;

(H) For shares executed outside the quote, the share-weighted average amount per share that prices were outside the quote; and

(I) For shares executed outside the quote, the share-weighted average period from the time of order receipt to the time of order execution.

(2) Every national securities exchange on which national market system securities are traded and national securities association shall act jointly in establishing procedures for market centers to follow in making available to the public the reports required by paragraph (b)(1) of this section in a uniform, readily accessible, and usable electronic form. In the event there is no effective national market system plan establishing such procedures, market centers shall prepare their reports in a consistent, usable, and machine-readable electronic format, and make such reports available for downloading from an Internet web site that is free and readily accessible to the public.

(3) A market center shall make available the report required by paragraph (b)(1) of this section within one month after the end of the month addressed in the report.

(c) *Exemptions.* The Commission may, by order upon application, conditionally or unconditionally exempt any person, security, or transaction, or any class or classes of persons, securities, or transactions, from any provision or provisions of this section, if the Commission determines that such exemption is necessary or appropriate in the public interest, and is consistent with the protection of investors.

Rule 11Ac1–6. Disclosure of Order Routing Information

(a) *Definitions.* For the purposes of this section:

(1) The term *covered security* shall mean:

(i) Any national market system security and any other security for which a transaction report, last sale data or quotation information is disseminated through an automated quotation system as defined in Section 3(a)(51)(A)(ii) of the Act (15 U.S.C. 78c(a)(51)(A)(ii)); and

(ii) Any option contract traded on a national securities exchange for which last sale reports and quotation information are made available pursuant to an effective national market system plan.

(2) The term *customer order* shall mean an order to buy or sell a covered security that is not for the account of a broker or dealer, but shall not include any order for a quantity of a security having a market value of at least $50,000 for a covered security that is an option contract and a market value of at least $200,000 for any other covered security.

(3) The term *directed order* shall mean a customer order that the customer specifically instructed the broker or dealer to route to a particular venue for execution.

(4) The term *make publicly available* shall mean posting on an Internet web site that is free and readily accessible to the public, furnishing a written copy to customers on request without charge, and notifying customers at least annually in writing that a written copy will be furnished on request.

(5) The term *non-directed order* shall mean any customer order other than a directed order.

(6) The term *effective national market system plan* shall have the meaning provided in § 240.11Aa3–2(a)(2).

(7) The term *national market system security* shall have the meaning provided in § 240.11Aa2–1.

(8) The term *payment for order flow* shall have the meaning provided in § 240.10b–10(d)(9).

(9) The term *profit-sharing relationship* shall mean any ownership or other type of affiliation under which the broker or dealer, directly or indirectly, may share in any profits that may be derived from the execution of non-directed orders.

(10) The term *time of the transaction* shall have the meaning provided in § 240.10b–10(d)(3).

(b) *Quarterly report on order routing.* (1) Every broker or dealer shall make publicly available for each calendar quarter a report on its routing of non-directed orders in covered securities during that quarter. For covered securities other than option contracts, such report shall be divided into three separate sections for securities that are listed on the New York Stock Exchange, Inc., securities that are qualified for inclusion in the Nasdaq Stock Market, Inc., and securities that are listed on the American Stock Exchange LLC or any other national securities exchange. Such report also shall include a separate section for covered securities that are option contracts. Each of the four sections in a report shall include the following information:

(i) The percentage of total customer orders for the section that were non-directed orders, and the percentages of total non-directed orders for the section that were market orders, limit orders, and other orders;

(ii) The identity of the ten venues to which the largest number of total non-directed orders for the section were routed for execution and of any venue to which five percent or more of non-directed orders were routed for execution, the percentage of total non-directed orders for the section routed to the venue, and the percentages of total non-directed market orders, total non-directed limit orders, and total non-directed other orders for the section that were routed to the venue; and

(iii) A discussion of the material aspects of the broker's or dealer's relationship with each venue identified pursuant to paragraph (b)(1)(ii) of this section, including a description of any arrangement for payment for order flow and any profit-sharing relationship.

(2) A broker or dealer shall make the report required by paragraph (b)(1) of this section publicly available within one month after the end of the quarter addressed in the report.

(c) *Customer requests for information on order routing*. (1) Every broker or dealer shall, on request of a customer, disclose to its customer the identity of the venue to which the customer's orders were routed for execution in the six months prior to the request, whether the orders were directed orders or non-directed orders, and the time of the transactions, if any, that resulted from such orders.

(2) A broker or dealer shall notify customers in writing at least annually of the availability on request of the information specified in paragraph (c)(1) of this section.

(d) *Exemptions*. The Commission may, by order upon application, conditionally or unconditionally exempt any person, security, or transaction, or any class or classes of persons, securities, or transactions, from any provision or provisions of this section, if the Commission determines that such exemption is necessary or appropriate in the public interest, and is consistent with the protection of investors.

SECURITIES EXEMPTED FROM REGISTRATION

Rule 12a–4. Exemption of Certain Warrants From Section 12(a)

(a) When used in this rule, the following terms shall have the meaning indicated unless the context otherwise requires—

(1) The term "warrant" means any warrant or certificate evidencing a right to subscribe to or otherwise acquire another security, issued or unissued.

(2) The term "beneficiary security" means a security to the holders of which a warrant or right to subscribe to or otherwise acquire another security is granted.

(3) The term "subject security" means a security which is the subject of a warrant or right to subscribe to or otherwise acquire such security.

(4) The term "in the process of admission to dealing," in respect of a specified security means that (i) an application has been filed pursuant to section 12(b) and (c) of the Act for the registration of such security on a national securities exchange; or (ii) the Commission has granted an application made pursuant to section 12(f) of the Act to continue or extend unlisted trading privileges to such security on a national securities exchange; or (iii) written notice has been filed with the Commission by a national securities exchange to the effect that such security has been approved for admission to dealing as a security exempted from the operation of section 12(a) of the Act.

(b) Any issued or unissued warrant granted to the holders of a security admitted to dealing on a national securities exchange shall be exempt from the operation of section 12(a) of the Act to the extent necessary to render lawful the effecting of transactions therein on any national securities exchange (i) on which beneficiary security is admitted to dealing or (ii) on which the subject security is admitted to dealing or is in the process of admission to dealing, subject to the following terms and conditions:

(1) Such warrant by its terms expires within 90 days after the issuance thereof;

(2) A registration statement under the Securities Act of 1933 is in effect as to such

warrant and as to each subject security, or the applicable terms of any exemption from such registration have been met in respect to such warrant and each subject security; and,

(3) Within 5 days after the exchange has taken official action to admit such warrant to dealing, it shall notify the Commission of such action.

(c) Notwithstanding paragraph (b) above, no exemption pursuant to this rule shall be available for transactions in any such warrant on any exchange on which the beneficiary security is admitted to dealing unless—

(1) each subject security is admitted to dealing or is in process of admission to dealing on a national securities exchange, or,

(2) there is available from a registration statement and periodic reports or other data filed by the issuer of the subject security, pursuant to any act administered by the Commission, information substantially equivalent to that available with respect to a security listed and registered on a national securities exchange.

(d) Notwithstanding the foregoing, an unissued warrant shall not be exempt pursuant to this rule unless—

(1) Formal or official announcement has been made by the issuer specifying (i) the terms upon which such warrant and each subject security is to be issued, (ii) the date, if any, as of which the security holders entitled to receive such warrant will be determined, (iii) the approximate date of the issuance of such warrant, and (iv) the approximate date of the issuance of each subject security; and

(2) The members of the exchange are subject to rules which provide that the performance of the contract to purchase and sell an unissued warrant shall be conditioned upon the issuance of such warrant.

(e) The Commission may by order deny or revoke the exemption of a warrant under this rule, if, after appropriate notice and opportunity for hearing to the issuer of such warrant and to the exchange or exchanges on which such warrant is admitted to dealing as an exempted security, it finds that—

(1) Any of the terms or conditions of this rule have not been met with respect to such exemption; or

(2) At any time during the period of such exemption transactions have been effected on any such exchange in such warrant which (i) create or induce a false, misleading or artificial appearance of activity, (ii) unduly or improperly influence the market price, or (iii) make a price which does not reflect the true state of the market; or

(3) Any other facts exist which make such denial or revocation necessary or appropriate in the public interest or for the protection of investors.

(f) If it appears necessary or appropriate in the public interest or for the protection of investors, the Commission may summarily suspend the exemption of such warrant pending the determination by the Commission whether such exemption shall be denied or revoked.

(g) Rule 10b–1 shall be applicable to any warrant exempted by this rule.

Rule 12a–5. Temporary Exemption of Substituted or Additional Securities

(a)(1) Subject to the conditions of subparagraph (a)(2) of this rule, whenever the holders of a security admitted to trading on a national securities exchange (hereinafter called the original security) obtain the right, by operation of law or otherwise, to acquire all or any part of a class of another or substitute security of the same or another issuer, or an additional amount of the original security, then:

(i) all or any part of the class of such other or substituted security shall be temporarily exempted from the operation of section 12(a) to the extent necessary to render lawful transactions therein on an issued or "when-issued" basis on any national securities exchange on which the original, the other or the substituted security is lawfully admitted to trading; and

(ii) the additional amount of the original security shall be temporarily exempted from the operation of section 12(a) to the extent necessary to render lawful transactions therein on a "when-issued" basis on any national securities exchange on which the original security is lawfully admitted to trading.

(2) The exemptions provided by subparagraph (a)(1) shall be available only if the following conditions are met:

(i) a registration statement is in effect under the Securities Act of 1933 to the extent required as to the security which is the subject of such exemption, or the terms of any applicable exemption from registration under such Act have been complied with, if required;

(ii) any stockholder approval necessary to the issuance of the security which is the subject of the exemption, has been obtained; and

(iii) all other necessary official action, other than the filing or recording of charter amendments or other documents with the appropriate state authorities, has been taken to authorize and assure the issuance of the security which is the subject of such exemption.

(b) The exemption provided by this rule shall terminate on the earliest of the following dates:

(1) When registration of the exempt security on the exchange becomes effective;

(2) When the exempt security is granted unlisted trading privileges on the exchange;

(3) The close of business on the 10th day after (i) withdrawal of an application for registration of the exempt security on the exchange; (ii) withdrawal by the exchange of its certification of approval of the exempt security for listing and registration; (iii) withdrawal of an application for admission of the exempt security to unlisted trading privileges on the exchange; or (iv) the sending to the exchange of notice of the entry of an order by the Commission denying an application for admission of the exempt security to unlisted trading privileges on the exchange;

(4) The close of business on the 120th day after the date on which the exempt security was admitted by action of the exchange to trading thereon as a security exempted from the operation of section 12(a) by this rule, unless prior thereto an application for registration of the exempt security or for admission of the exempt security to unlisted trading privileges on the exchange has been filed.

(c) Notwithstanding paragraph (b), the Commission, having due regard for the public interest and the protection of investors, may at any time extend the period of exemption of any security by this rule or may sooner terminate the exemption upon notice to the exchange and to the issuer of the extension or termination thereof.

(d) The exchange shall file with the Commission a notification on Form 26 promptly after taking action to admit any security to trading under this rule: *Provided, however,* That no notification need be filed under this rule concerning the admission or proposed admission to trading of additional amounts of a class of security admitted to trading on such exchange.

(e) Section 240 and 10b–1 shall be applicable to all securities exempted from the operation of section 12(a) by this rule.

Rule 12a–6. Exemption of Securities Underlying Certain Options From Section 12(a)

(a) When used in this Rule, the following terms shall have the meanings indicated unless the context otherwise requires:

(1) The term "option" shall include any put, call, spread, straddle, or other option or privilege of buying a security from or selling a security to another without being bound to do so, but such term shall not include any such option where the writer is: the issuer of the security which may be purchased or sold upon exercise of the option, or is a person that directly, or indirectly, through one or more intermediaries, controls, or is controlled by, or is under common control with such issuer;

(2) The term "underlying security" means a security which relates to or is the subject of an option.

(b) Any underlying security shall be exempt from the operation of Section 12(a) of the Act if all of the following terms and conditions are met:

(1) The related option is duly listed and registered on a national securities exchange;

(2) The only transactions on such exchange with respect to such underlying securities consist of the delivery of and payment for such underlying securities pursuant to the terms of such options relating to the exercise thereof; and

(3) Such underlying security is *(i)* duly listed and registered on another national securities exchange at the time the option is issued; or *(ii)* duly quoted on the National Association of Securities Dealers Automated Quotation System ("NASDAQ") at the time the option is issued.

Rule 12a–7. Exemption of Stock Contained in Standardized Market Baskets From Section 12(a) of the Act

(a) Any component stock of a standardized market basket shall be exempt from the registration requirement of section 12(a) of the Act, solely for the purpose of inclusion in a standardized market basket, provided that all of the following terms and conditions are met:

(1) The standardized market basket has been duly approved by the Commission for listing on a national securities exchange pursuant to the requirements of section 19(b) of the Act; and

(2) The stock is a National Market System security as defined in Rule 11Aa2–1 under the Act and is either:

(i) Listed and registered for trading on a national securities exchange by the issuer or

(ii) Quoted on the National Association of Securities Dealers Automated Quotation System;

(b) When used in this rule, the term standardized market basket means a group of at least 100 stocks purchased or sold in a single execution and at a single trading location with physical delivery and transfer of ownership of each component stock resulting from such execution.

Rule 12a–8. Exemption of Depositary Shares

Depositary shares (as that term is defined in § 240.12b–2) registered on Form F–6 (§ 239.36 of this chapter), but not the underlying deposited securities, shall be exempt from the operation of section 12(a) of the Act (15 U.S.C. 78l(a)).

Rule 12a–9. Exemption of Standardized Options From Section 12(a) of the Act

The provisions of section 12(a) of the Act (15 U.S.C. 78*l*(a)) do not apply in respect of any standardized option, as defined by section 240.9b–1(a)(4), issued by a clearing agency registered under section 17A of the Act (15 U.S.C. 78q–1) and traded on a national securities exchange registered pursuant to section 6(a) of the Act (15 U.S.C. 78f(a)).

REGULATION 12B. REGISTRATION AND REPORTING

ATTENTION ELECTRONIC FILERS

THIS REGULATION SHOULD BE READ IN CONJUNCTION WITH REGULATION S–T (PART 232 OF THIS CHAPTER), WHICH GOVERNS THE PREPARATION AND SUBMISSION OF DOCUMENTS IN ELECTRONIC FORMAT. MANY PROVISIONS RELATING TO THE PREPARATION AND SUBMISSION OF DOCUMENTS IN PAPER FORMAT CONTAINED IN THIS REGULATION ARE SUPERSEDED BY THE PROVISIONS OF REGULATION S–T FOR DOCUMENTS REQUIRED TO BE FILED IN ELECTRONIC FORMAT.

GENERAL

Rule 12b–1. Scope of Regulation

The rules contained in this regulation shall govern all registration statements pursuant to Sections 12(b) and 12(g) of the Act and all reports filed pursuant to Sections 13 and 15(d) of the Act, including all amendments to such statements and reports, except that any provision in a form covering the same subject matter as any such rule shall be controlling.

Rule 12b–2. Definitions

Unless the context otherwise requires, the following terms, when used in the rules contained in this regulation or in Regulation 13A or 15D or in the forms for statements and reports filed pursuant to section 12, 13 or 15(d) of the Act, shall have the respective meanings indicated in this rule:

Accelerated filer. (1) The term "accelerated filer" means an issuer after it first meets the following conditions as of the end of its fiscal year:

(i) The aggregate market value of the voting and non-voting common equity held by non-affiliates of the issuer is $75 million or more;

(ii) The issuer has been subject to the requirements of Section 13(a) or 15(d) of the Act (15 U.S.C. 7m or 78o(d)) for a period of at least twelve calendar months;

(iii) The issuer has filed at least one annual report pursuant to Section 13(a) or 15(d) of the Act; and

(iv) The issuer is not eligible to use Forms 10–KSB and 10–QSB (§ 249.310b and § 249.308b) for its annual and quarterly reports.

Note to paragraph (1): The aggregate market value of the issuer's outstanding voting and non-voting common equity shall be computed by use of the price at which the common equity was last sold, or the average of the bid and asked prices of such common equity, in the principal market for such common equity, as of the last business day of the issuer's most recently completed second fiscal quarter.

(2) *Entering and Exiting Accelerated Filer Status.* (i) The determination for whether a non-accelerated filer becomes an accelerated filer as of the end of the issuer's fiscal year governs the annual report to be filed for that fiscal year, the quarterly and annual reports to be filed for the subsequent fiscal year and all annual and quarterly reports to be filed thereafter while the issuer remains an accelerated filer.

(ii) Once an issuer becomes an accelerated filer, it will remain an accelerated filer unless the issuer becomes eligible to use Forms 10–KSB and 10–QSB for its annual and quarterly reports. In that case, the issuer will not become an accelerated filer again unless it subsequently meets the conditions in paragraph (1) of this definition.

Affiliate. An "affiliate" of, or a person "affiliated" with, a specified person, is a person that directly, or indirectly through one or more intermediaries, controls, or is controlled by, or is under common control with, the person specified.

Amount. The term "amount," when used in regard to securities, means the principal amount if relating to evidences of indebtedness, the number of shares if relating to shares, and the number of units if relating to any other kind of security.

Associate. The term "associate" used to indicate a relationship with any person, means (1) any corporation or organization (other than the registrant or a majority-owned subsidiary of the registrant) of which such person is an officer or partner or is, directly or indirectly, the beneficial owner of 10 percent or more of any class of equity securities, (2) any trust or other estate in which such person has a substantial beneficial interest or as to which such person serves as trustee or in a similar fiduciary capacity, and (3) any relative or spouse of such person, or any relative of such spouse, who has the same home as such person or who is a director or officer of the registrant or any of its parents or subsidiaries.

Certified. The term "certified," when used in regard to financial statements, means examined and reported upon with an opinion expressed by an independent public or certified public accountant.

Charter. The term "charter" includes articles of incorporation, declarations of trust, articles of association or partnership, or any similar instrument, as amended, effecting (either with or without filing with any governmental agency) the organization or creation of an incorporated or unincorporated person.

Common equity. The term "common equity" means any class of common stock or an equivalent interest, including but not limited to a unit of beneficial interests in a trust or a limited partnership interest.

Control. The term "control" (including the terms "controlling," "controlled by" and "under common control with") means the possession, direct or indirect, of the power to direct or cause the direction of the management and policies of a person, whether through the ownership of voting securities, by contract, or otherwise.

Depositary share. The term "depositary share" means a security, evidenced by an American Depositary Receipt, that represents a foreign security or a multiple of or fraction thereof deposited with a depositary.

Employee. The term "employee" does not include a director, trustee, or officer.

Fiscal year. The term "fiscal year" means the annual accounting period or, if no closing date has been adopted, the calendar year ending on December 31.

Majority-owned subsidiary. The term "majority-owned subsidiary" means a subsidiary more than 50 percent of whose outstanding securities representing the right, other than as affected by events of default, to vote for the election of directors, is owned by the subsidiary's parent and/or one or more of the parent's other majority-owned subsidiaries.

Managing underwriter. The term "managing underwriter" includes an underwriter (or underwriters) who, by contract or otherwise, deals with the registrant; organizes the selling effort; receives some benefit directly or indirectly in which all other underwriters similarly situated do not share in proportion to their respective interests in the underwriting; or represents any other underwriters in such matters as maintaining the records of the distribution, arranging the allotments of securities offered or arranging for appropriate stabilization activities, if any.

Material. The term "material," when used to qualify a requirement for the furnishing of information as to any subject, limits the information required to those matters to which there is a substantial likelihood that a reasonable investor would attach importance in determining whether to buy or sell the securities registered.

Parent. A "parent" of a specified person is an affiliate controlling such person directly, or indirectly through one or more intermediaries.

Predecessor. The term "predecessor" means a person the major portion of the business and assets of which another person acquired in a single succession or in a series of related successions in each of which the acquiring person acquiring the major portion of the business and assets of the acquired person.

Previously filed or reported. The terms "previously filed" and "previously reported" mean previously filed with, or reported in, a statement under section 12, a report under section 13 or 15(d), a definitive proxy statement or information statement under section 14 of the Act, or a registration statement under the Securities Act of 1933: *Provided,* That information contained in any such document shall be deemed to have been previously filed with, or reported to, an exchange only if such document is filed with such exchange.

Principal underwriter. The term "principal underwriter" means an underwriter in privity of contract with the issuer of the securities as to which he is underwriter.

Promoter. (1) The term "promoter" includes:

(i) Any person who, acting along or in conjunction with one or more other persons, directly or indirectly takes initiative in founding and organizing the business or enterprise of an issuer; or

(ii) Any person who, in connection with the founding and organizing of the business or enterprise of an issuer, directly or indirectly receives in consideration of services or property, or both services and property, 10 percent or more of any class of securities of the issuer or 10 percent or more of the proceeds from the sale of any class of such securities. However, a person who receives such securities or proceeds either solely as underwriting commissions or solely in consideration of property shall not be deemed a promoter within the meaning of this paragraph if such person does not otherwise take part in founding and organizing the enterprise.

(2) All persons coming within the definition of "promoter" in paragraph (1) of this definition may be referred to as "founders" or "organizers" or by another term provided that such term is reasonably descriptive of those persons' activities with respect to the issuer.

Prospectus. Unless otherwise specified or the context otherwise requires, the term "prospectus" means a prospectus meeting the requirements of section 10(a) of the Securities Act of 1933 as amended.

Registrant. The term "registrant" means an issuer of securities with respect to which a registration statement or report is to be filed.

Registration statement. The term "registration statement" or "statement," when used with reference to registration pursuant to section 12 of the Act, includes both an application for registration of securities on a national securities exchange pursuant to section 12(b) of the Act and a registration statement filed pursuant to section 12(g) of the Act.

Share. The term "share" means a share of stock in a corporation or unit of interest in an unincorporated person.

Significant subsidiary. The term "significant subsidiary" means a subsidiary, including its subsidiaries, which meets any of the following conditions.

(1) The registrant's and its other subsidiaries' investments in and advances to the subsidiary exceed 10 percent of the total assets of the registrant and its subsidiaries consolidated as of the end of the most recently completed fiscal year (for a proposed business combination to be accounted for as a pooling of interests, this condition is also met when the number of common shares exchanged or to be exchanged by the registrant exceeds 10 percent of its total common shares out-

standing at the date the combination is initiated); or

(2) The registrant's and its other subsidiaries' proportionate share of the total assets (after intercompany eliminations) of the subsidiary exceeds 10 percent of the total assets of the registrants and its subsidiaries consolidated as of the end of the most recently completed fiscal year; or

(3) The registrant's and its other subsidiaries' equity in the income from continuing operations before income taxes, extraordinary items and cumulative effect of a change in accounting principle of the subsidiary exceeds 10 percent of such income of the registrant and its subsidiaries consolidated for the most recently completed fiscal year.

Computational note: For purposes of making the prescribed income test the following guidance should be applied:

1. When a loss has been incurred by either the parent and its subsidiaries consolidated or the tested subsidiary, but not both, the equity in the income or loss of the tested subsidiary should be excluded from the income of the registrant and its subsidiaries consolidated for purposes of the computation.

2. If income of the registrant and its subsidiaries consolidated for the most recent fiscal year is at least 10 percent lower than the average of the income for the last five fiscal years, such average income should be substituted for purposes of the computation. Any loss years should be omitted for the purpose of computing average income.

Small Business Issuer. The term "small business issuer" means an entity that meets the following criteria:

1. has revenues of less than $25,000,000;

2. is a U.S. or Canadian issuer;

3. is not an investment company and is not an asset-backed issuer (as defined in § 229.1101 of this chapter); and

4. if a majority owned subsidiary, the parent corporation is also a small business issuer.

Provided however, that an entity is not a small business issuer if it has a public float (the aggregate market value of the issuer's outstanding voting and nonvoting common equity held by non-affiliates) of $25,000,000 or more.

NOTE: The public float of a reporting company shall be computed by use of the price at which the stock was last sold, or the average of the bid and asked prices of such stock, on a date within 60 days prior to the end of its most recent fiscal year. The public float of a company filing an initial registration statement under the Exchange Act shall be determined as of a date within 60 days of the date the registration statement is filed. In the case of an initial public offering of securities, public float shall be computed on the basis of the number of shares outstanding prior to the offering and the estimated public offering price of the securities.

Subsidiary. A "subsidiary" of a specified person is an affiliate controlled by such person directly, or indirectly through one or more intermediaries. (See also "majority-owned subsidiary," "significant subsidiary," and "totally-held subsidiary.")

Succession. The term "succession" means the direct acquisition of the assets comprising a going business, whether by merger, consolidation, purchase, or other direct transfer. The term does not include the acquisition of control of a business unless followed by the direct acquisition of its assets. The term "succeed" and "successor" have meanings correlative to the foregoing.

Totally held subsidiary. The term "totally held subsidiary" means a subsidiary (1) substantially all of whose outstanding securities are owned by its parent and/or the parent's other totally held subsidiaries, and (2) which is not indebted to any person other than its parent and/or the parent's other totally held subsidiaries in an amount which is material in relation to the particular subsidiary, excepting indebtedness incurred in the ordinary course of business which is not overdue and which matures within one year from the date of its creation, whether evidenced by securities or not.

Voting securities. The term "voting securities" means securities the holders of which are presently entitled to vote for the election of directors.

Wholly-owned subsidiary. The term "wholly-owned subsidiary" means a subsidiary substantially all of whose outstanding voting securities are owned by its parent and/or the parent's other wholly-owned subsidiaries.

Rule 12b–3. Title of Securities

Wherever the title of securities is required to be stated there shall be given such information as will indicate the type and general character of the securities, including the following:

(a) In the case of shares, the par or stated value, if any; the rate of dividends, if fixed, and whether cumulative or noncumulative; a brief indication of the preference, if any; and if convertible, a statement to that effect.

(b) In the case of funded debt, the rate of interest; the date of maturity, or if the issue matures serially, a brief indication of the serial maturities, such as "maturing serially from 1950 to 1960"; if the payment of principal or interest is contingent, an appropriate indication of such contingency; a brief indication of the priority of the issue; and if convertible, a statement to that effect.

(c) In the case of any other kind of security, appropriate information of comparable character.

Rule 12b–4. Supplemental Information

The Commission or its staff may, where it is deemed appropriate, request supplemental information concerning the registrant, a registration statement or a periodic or other report under the Act. This information shall not be required to be filed with or deemed part of the registration statement or report. The information shall be returned to the registrant upon request, provided that:

(a) Such request is made at the time such information is furnished to the staff;

(b) The return of such information is consistent with the protection of investors; and

(c) The return of such information is consistent with the provisions of the Freedom of Information Act.

Rule 12b–5. Determination of Affiliates of Banks

In determining whether a person is an "affiliate" or "parent" of a bank or whether a bank is a "subsidiary" or "majority-owned subsidiary" of a person, within the meaning of those terms as defined in Rule 12b–2, voting securities of the bank held by a corporation all of the stock of which is directly owned by the U.S. Government shall not be taken into consideration.

Rule 12b–6. When Securities Are Deemed to Be Registered

A class of securities with respect to which a registration statement has been filed pursuant to section 12 of the Act shall be deemed to be registered for the purposes of sections 13, 14, 15(d) and 16 of the Act and the rules and regulations thereunder only when such statement has become effective as provided in section 12, and securities of said class shall not be subject to sections 13, 14 and 16 of the Act until such statement has become effective as provided in section 12.

FORMAL REQUIREMENTS

Rule 12b–10. Requirements as to Proper Form

Every statement or report shall be on the form prescribed therefor by the Commission, as in effect on the date of filing. Any statement or report shall be deemed to be filed on the proper form unless objection to the form is made by the Commission within 30 days after the date of filing.

Rule 12b–11. Number of Copies—Signatures—Binding

(a) Except as provided in a particular form, three complete copies of each statement or report, including exhibits and all other papers and documents filed as a part thereof, shall be filed with the Commission. At least one complete copy of each statement shall be filed with each exchange on which the securities covered thereby are to be registered. At least one complete copy of each report under section 13 of the Act shall be filed with each exchange on which the registrant has securities registered.

(b) At least one copy of each statement or report filed with the Commission and one copy thereof filed with each exchange shall be manually signed in the manner prescribed by the appropriate form.

(c) Each copy of a statement or report filed with the Commission or with an exchange shall be bound in one or more parts. Copies filed with the Commission shall be bound without stiff covers. The statement or report shall be bound on the left side in such a manner as to leave the reading matter legible.

(d) *Signatures.* Where the Act or the rules, forms, reports or schedules thereunder, including paragraph (b) of this section, require a document filed with or furnished to the Commission to be signed, such document shall be manually signed, or signed using either typed signatures or duplicated or facsimile versions of manual signatures. Where typed, duplicated or facsimile signatures are used, each signatory to the filing shall manually sign a signature page or other document authenticating, acknowledging or otherwise adopting his or her signature that appears in the filing. Such document shall be executed before or at the time the filing is made and shall be retained by the filer for a period of five years. Upon request, the filer shall furnish to the Commission or its staff a copy of any or all documents retained pursuant to this section.

Rule 12b–12. Requirements as to Paper, Printing and Language

(a) Statements and reports shall be filed on good quality, unglazed white paper, no larger than 8½ × 11 inches in size, insofar as practicable. To the extent that the reduction of larger documents would render them illegible, such documents may be filed on paper larger than 8½ × 11 inches in size.

(b) The statement or report and, insofar as practicable, all papers and documents filed as a part thereof, shall be printed, lithographed, mimeographed, or typewritten. However, the statement or report or any portion thereof may be prepared by any similar process which, in the opinion of the Commission, produces copies suitable for a permanent record and microfilming. Irrespective of the process used, all copies of any such material shall be clear, easily readable and suitable for repeated photocopying. Debits in credit categories and credits in debit categories shall be designated so as to be clearly distinguishable as such on photocopies.

(c) The body of all printed statements and reports and all notes to financial statements and other tabular data included therein shall be in roman type at least as large and as legible as 10-point modern type. However, to the extent necessary for convenient presentation, financial statements and other tabular data, including tabular data in notes, may be in roman type at least as large as and as legible as 8-point modern type. All such type shall be leaded at least 2 points.

(d)(1) All Exchange Act filings and submissions must be in the English language, except as otherwise provided by this section. If a filing or submission requires the inclusion of a document that is in a foreign language, a party must submit instead a fair and accurate English translation of the entire foreign language document, except as provided by paragraph (d)(3) of this section.

(2) If a filing or submission subject to review by the Division of Corporation Finance requires the inclusion of a foreign language document as an exhibit or attachment, a party must submit a fair and accurate English translation of the foreign language document if consisting of any of the following, or an amendment of any of the following:

(i) Articles of incorporation, memoranda of association, bylaws, and other comparable documents, whether original or restated;

(ii) Instruments defining the rights of security holders, including indentures qualified or to be qualified under the Trust Indenture Act of 1939;

(iii) Voting agreements, including voting trust agreements;

(iv) Contracts to which directors, officers, promoters, voting trustees or security holders named in a registration statement, report or other document are parties;

(v) Contracts upon which a filer's business is substantially dependent;

(vi) Audited annual and interim consolidated financial information; and

(vii) Any document that is or will be the subject of a confidential treatment request under § 240.24b–2 or § 230.406 of this chapter.

(3)(i) A party may submit an English summary instead of an English translation of a foreign language document as an exhibit or attachment to a filing or submission subject to review by the Division of Corporation Finance, as long as:

(A) The foreign language document does not consist of any of the subject matter enumerated in paragraph (d)(2) of this section; or

(B) The applicable form permits the use of an English summary.

(ii) Any English summary submitted under paragraph (d)(3) of this section must:

(A) Fairly and accurately summarize the terms of each material provision of the foreign language document; and

(B) Fairly and accurately describe the terms that have been omitted or abridged.

(4) When submitting an English summary English translation of a foreign language document under this section, a party must identify the submission as either an English summary or English translation. A party may submit a copy of the unabridged foreign language document when including an English summary or English translation of a foreign language document in a filing or submission. A party must provide a copy of any foreign language document upon the request of Commission staff.

(5) A foreign government or its political subdivision must provide a fair and accurate English translation of its latest annual budget submitted as Exhibit B to Form 18 (§ 249.218 of this chapter) or Exhibit (c) to Form 18–K (§ 249.318 of this chapter) only if one is available. If no English translation is available, a filer must provide a copy of the foreign language version of its latest annual budget as an exhibit.

(6) A Canadian issuer may file an exhibit, attachment or other part of a Form 40–F registration statement or annual report (§ 249.240f of this chapter), Schedule 13E–4F (§ 240.13e–102), Schedule 14D–1F (§ 240.14d–102), or Schedule 14D–9F (§ 240.14d–103), that contains text in both French and English if the issuer included

the French text to comply with the requirements of the Canadian securities administrator or other Canadian authority and, for an electronic filing, if the filing is an HTML document, as defined in Regulation S–T Rule 11 (17 CFR 232.11).

(e) Where a statement or report is distributed to investors through an electronic medium, issuers may satisfy legibility requirements applicable to printed documents, such as paper size and type size and font, by presenting all required information in a format readily communicated to investors.

Rule 12b–13. Preparation of Statement or Report

The statement or report shall contain the numbers and captions of all items of the appropriate form, but the text of the items may be omitted provided the answers thereto are so prepared as to indicate to the reader the coverage of the items without the necessity of his referring to the text of the items or instructions thereto. However, where any item requires information to be given in tabular form, it shall be given in substantially the tabular form specified in the item. All instructions, whether appearing under the items of the form or elsewhere therein, are to be omitted. Unless expressly provided otherwise, if any item is inapplicable or the answer thereto is in the negative, an appropriate statement to that effect shall be made.

Rule 12b–14. Riders; Inserts

Riders shall not be used. If the statement or report is typed on a printed form, and the space provided for the answer to any given item is insufficient, reference shall be made in such space to a full insert page or pages on which the item number and caption and the complete answer are given.

Rule 12b–15. Amendments

All amendments must be filed under cover of the form amended, marked with the letter "A" to designate the document as an amendment, *e.g.*, "10–K/A," and in compliance with pertinent requirements applicable to statements and reports. Amendments filed pursuant to this section must set forth the complete text of each item as amended. Amendments must be numbered sequentially and be filed separately for each statement or report amended. Amendments to a statement may be filed either before or after registration becomes effective. Amendments must be signed on behalf of the registrant by a duly authorized representative of the registrant. An amendment to any report required to include the certifications as specified in § 240.13a–14(a) or § 240.15d–14(a) must include new certifications by each principal executive and principal financial officer of the registrant, and an amendment to any report required to be accompanied by the certifications as specified in § 240.13a–14(b) or § 240.15d–14(b) must be accompanied by new certifications by each principal executive and principal financial officer of the registrant. The requirements of the form being amended will govern the number of copies to be filed in connection with a paper format amendment. Electronic filers satisfy the provisions dictating the number of copies by filing one copy of the amendment in electronic format. An amendment to any report required to include the certifications as specified in § 240.13a–14(d) or § 240.15d–14(d) must include a new certification by an individual specified in § 240.13a–14(e) or § 240.15d—14(e), as applicable. See § 232.309 of this chapter (Rule 309 of Regulation S–T).

GENERAL REQUIREMENTS AS TO CONTENTS

Rule 12b–20. Additional Information

In addition to the information expressly required to be included in a statement or report, there shall be added such further material information, if any, as may be necessary to make the required statements, in the light of the circumstances under which they are made not misleading.

Rule 12b–21. Information Unknown or Not Available

Information required need be given only insofar as it is known or reasonably available to the registrant. If any required information is unknown and not reasonably available to the registrant, either because the obtaining thereof would involve unreasonable effort or expense, or because it rests peculiarly within the knowledge of another person not affiliated with the registrant, the information may be omitted, subject to the following conditions.

(a) The registrant shall give such information on the subject as it possesses or can acquire without unreasonable effort or expense, together with the sources thereof.

(b) The registrant shall include a statement either showing that unreasonable effort or expense would be involved or indicating the absence of any affiliation with the person within whose knowledge the information rests and stating the result of a request made to such person for the information.

Rule 12b–22. Disclaimer of Control

If the existence of control is open to reasonable doubt in any instance, the registrant may disclaim the existence of control and any admission thereof; in such case, however, the registrant shall state the material facts pertinent to the possible existence of control.

Rule 12b–23. Incorporation by Reference

(a) Except for information filed as an exhibit which is covered by Rule 12b–32, information may be incorporated by reference in answer, or partial answer, to any item of a registration statement or report subject to the following provisions:

(1) Financial statements incorporated by reference shall satisfy the requirements of the form or report in which they are incorporated. Financial statements or other financial data required to be given in comparative form for two or more fiscal years or periods shall not be incorporated by reference unless the material incorporated by reference includes the entire period for which the comparative data is given;

(2) Information in any part of the registration statement or report may be incorporated by reference in answer, or partial answer, to any other item of the registration statement or report; and

(3) Copies of any information or financial statement incorporated into a registration statement or report by reference, or copies of the pertinent pages of the document containing such information or statement, shall be filed as an exhibit to the statement or report, except that:

(i) A proxy or information statement incorporated by reference in response to Part III of Form 10–K and Form 10–KSB (17 CFR 249.310 and 249.310b);

(ii) A form of prospectus filed pursuant to 17 CFR 230.424(b) incorporated by reference in response to Item 1 of Form 8–A (17 CFR 249.208a); and

(iii) Information filed on Form 8–K (17 CFR 249.308) need not be filed as an exhibit.

(b) Any incorporation by reference of matter pursuant to this section shall be subject to the provisions of § 228.10(f) and § 229.10(d) of this chapter restricting incorporation by reference of documents which incorporate by reference other information. Material incorporated by reference shall be clearly identified in the reference by page, paragraph, caption or otherwise. Where only certain pages of a document are incorporated by reference and filed as an exhibit, the document from which the material is taken shall be clearly identified in the reference. An express statement that the specified matter is incorporated by reference shall be made at the particular place in the statement or report where the information is required. Matter shall not be incorporated by reference in any case where such incorporation would render the statement or report incomplete, unclear or confusing.

Rule 12b–25. Notification of Inability to Timely File All or Any Required Portion of a Form 10–K, Form 10–KSB, 20–F, 11–K, N–SAR, N–CSR, 10–Q or Form 10–D

(a) If all or any required portion of an annual or transition report on Form 10–K, 10–KSB, 20–F or 11–K (17 CFR 249.310, 249.310b, 249.220f or 249.311), a quarterly or transition report on Form 10–Q or 10–QSB (17 CFR 249.308a or 249.308b), or a distribution report on Form 10-D (17 CFR 249.312) required to be filed pursuant to section 13 or 15(d) of the Act (15 U.S.C. 78m or 78o(d)) and rules thereunder, or if all or any required portion of a semi-annual, annual or transition report on Form N–CSR (17 CFR 249.331; 17 CFR 274.128) or Form N–SAR (17 CFR 249.330; 17 CFR 274.101) required to be filed pursuant to section 13 or 15(d) of the Act or section 30 of the Investment Company Act of 1940 (15 U.S.C. 80a–29) and the rules thereunder, is not filed within the time period prescribed for such report, the registrant, no later than one business day after the due date for such report, shall file a Form 12b–25 (17 CFR 249.322) with the Commission which shall contain disclosure of its inability to file the report timely and the reasons therefor in reasonable detail.

(b) With respect to any report or portion of any report described in paragraph (a) of this section which is not timely filed because the registrant is unable to do so without unreasonable effort or expense, such report shall be deemed to be filed on the prescribed due date for such report if:

(1) The registrant files the Form 12b–25 in compliance with paragraph (a) of this rule and, when applicable, furnishes the exhibit required by paragraph (c) of this rule;

(2) The registrant represents in the Form 12b–25 that:

(i) The reason(s) causing the inability to file timely could not be eliminated by the registrant without unreasonable effort or expense; and

(ii) The subject annual report, semi-annual report or transition report on Form 10–K, 10–KSB, 20–F, 11–K, N–SAR, or N–CSR, or portion thereof, will be filed no later than the fifteenth calendar day following the prescribed due date; or the subject quarterly report or transition report on Form 10–Q or 10–QSB or distribution report on Form 10–D, or portion thereof, will be filed no later than the fifth calendar day following the prescribed due date; and

(3) The report/portion thereof is actually filed within the period specified by paragraph (b)(2)(ii) of this rule.

(c) If paragraph (b) of this rule is applicable and the reason the subject report/portion thereof cannot be filed timely without unreasonable effort or expense relates to the inability of any person, other than the registrant, to furnish any required opinion, report or certification, the Form 12b–25 shall have attached as an exhibit a statement signed by such person stating the specific reasons why such person is unable to furnish the required opinion, report or certification on or before the date such report must be filed.

(d) Notwithstanding paragraph (b) of this rule, a registrant will not be eligible to use any registration statement form under the Securities Act of 1933 the use of which is predicated on timely filed reports until the subject report is actually filed pursuant to paragraph (b)(3) of this rule.

(e) If a Form 12b–25 filed pursuant to paragraph (a) of this rule relates only to a portion of a subject report, the registrant shall:

(1) File the balance of such report and indicate on the cover page thereof which disclosure items are omitted; and

(2) Include, on the upper right corner of the amendment to the report which includes the previously omitted information, the following statement:

The following items were the subject of a Form 12b-25 and are included herein:

(*List Item Numbers*)

(f) The provisions of this rule shall not apply to financial statements to be filed by amendment to a form 10-K and 10-KSB as provided for by paragraph (a) of § 210.3-09 or schedules to be filed by amendment in accordance with General Instruction A to Form 10-K and 10-KSB.

(g) *Electronic filings.* The provisions of this rule shall not apply to reports required to be filed in electronic format if the sole reason the report is not filed within the time period prescribed is that the filer is unable to file the report in electronic format. Filers unable to submit a report in electronic format within the time period prescribed solely due to difficulties with electronic filing should comply with either Rule 201 or 202 of Regulation S-T or apply for an adjustment of filing date pursuant to Rule 13(b) of Regulation S-T.

EXHIBITS

Rule 12b-30. Additional Exhibits

The registrant may file such exhibits as it may desire, in addition to those required by the appropriate form. Such exhibits shall be so marked as to indicate clearly the subject matters to which they refer.

Rule 12b-31. Omission of Substantially Identical Documents

In any case where two or more indentures, contracts, franchises, or other documents required to be filed as exhibits are substantially identical in all material respects except as to the parties thereto, the dates of execution, or other details, the registrant need file a copy of only one of such documents, with a schedule identifying the other documents omitted and setting forth the material details in which such documents differ from the document of which a copy is filed. The Commission may at any time in its discretion require the filing of copies of any document so omitted.

Rule 12b-32. Incorporation of Exhibits by Reference

(a) Any document or part thereof filed with the Commission pursuant to any Act administered by the Commission may, subject to § 228.10(f) and § 229.10(d) of this chapter, be incorporated by reference as an exhibit to any statement or report filed with the Commission by the same or any other person. Any document or part thereof filed with an exchange pursuant to the Act may be incorporated by reference as an exhibit to any statement or report filed with the exchange by the same or any other person.

(b) If any modification has occurred in the text of any document incorporated by reference since the filing thereof, the registrant shall file with the reference a statement containing the text of any such modification and the date thereof.

Rule 12b-33. Annual Reports to Other Federal Agencies

Notwithstanding any rule or other requirement to the contrary, whenever copies of an annual report by a registrant to any other Federal agency are required or permitted to be filed as an exhibit to an application or report filed by such registrant with the Commission or with a securities exchange, only one copy of such annual report need be filed with the Commission and one copy thereof with each such exchange, provided appropriate reference to such copy is made in each copy of the application or report filed with the Commission or with such exchange.

SPECIAL PROVISIONS

Rule 12b-36. Use of Financial Statements Filed Under Other Acts

Where copies of certified financial statements filed under other Acts administered by the Commission are filed with a statement or report, the accountant's certificate shall be manually signed or manually-signed copies of the certificate shall be filed with the financial statements. Where such financial statements are incorporated by reference in a statement or report, the written consent of the accountant to such incorporation by reference shall be filed with the statement or report. Such consent shall be dated and signed manually.

CERTIFICATION BY EXCHANGES AND EFFECTIVENESS OF REGISTRATION

Rule 12d1-1. Registration Effective as to Class or Series

(a) An application filed pursuant to section 12(b) and (c) of the Act for registration of a security on a national securities exchange shall be deemed to apply for registration of the entire class of such security. Registration shall become effective, as provided in section 12(d) of the Act, (1) as to the shares or amounts of such class then issued, and (2) without further application for registration, upon issuance as to additional shares or amounts of such class then or thereafter authorized.

(b) This rule shall apply to classes of securities of which a specified number of shares or amounts was registered or registered upon notice of issuance, and to applications for registration filed, prior to the close of business on January 28, 1954, as well as to classes registered, or applications filed, thereafter.

(c) This rule shall not affect the right of a national securities exchange to require the issuer of a registered security to file documents with or pay fees to the exchange in connection with the modification of such security or the issuance of additional shares or amounts.

(d) If a class of security is issuable in two or more series with different terms, each such series shall be deemed a separate class for the purposes of this regulation.

Rule 12d1-2. Effectiveness of Registration

(a) A request for acceleration of the effective date of registration pursuant to section 12(d) of the Act and Rule 12d1-1 shall be made in writing by either the registrant, the exchange, or both and shall briefly describe the reasons therefor.

(b) A registration statement on Form 8-A (17 CFR 249.208a) for the registration of a class of securities under Section 12(b) of the Act (15 U.S.C. 78l(b)) shall become effective:

(1) If a class of securities is not concurrently being registered under the Securities Act of 1933 ("Securities Act"), upon the later of receipt by the Commission of certification from the national securities exchange or the filing of the Form 8-A with the Commission; or

(2) If a class of securities is concurrently being registered under the Securities Act, upon the later of the filing of the Form 8-A with the Commission, receipt by the Commission of certification from the national securities exchange listed on the Form 8-A or effectiveness of the Securities Act registration statement relating to the class of securities.

(c) A registration statement on Form 8-A (17 CFR 249.208a) for the registration of a class of securities under Section 12(g) of the Act (15 U.S.C. 78l(g)) shall become effective:

(1) If a class of securities is not concurrently being registered under the Securities Act, upon the filing of the Form 8-A with the Commission; or

(2) If class of securities is concurrently being registered under the Securities Act,

upon the later of the filing of the Form 8–A with the Commission or the effectiveness of the Securities Act registration statement relating to the class of securities.

Rule 12d1–3. Requirements as to Certification

(a) Certification that a security has been approved by an exchange for listing and registration pursuant to section 12(d) of the Act and Rule 12d1–1 shall be made by the governing committee or other corresponding authority of the exchange.

(b) The certification shall specify (1) the approval of the exchange for listing and registration; (2) the title of the security so approved; (3) the date of filing with the exchange of the application for registration and of any amendments thereto; and (4) any conditions imposed on such certification. The exchange shall promptly notify the Commission of the partial or complete satisfaction of any such conditions.

(c) The certification may be made by telegram but in such case shall be confirmed in writing. All certifications in writing and all amendments thereto shall be filed with the Commission in duplicate and at least one copy shall be manually signed by the appropriate exchange authority.

Rule 12d1–4. Date of Receipt of Certification by Commission

The date of receipt by the Commission of the certification approving a security for listing and registration shall be the date on which the certification is actually received by the Commission or the date on which the application for registration to which the certification relates is actually received by the Commission, whichever date is later.

Rule 12d1–5. Operation of Certification on Subsequent Amendments

If an amendment to the application for registration of a security is filed with the exchange and with the Commission after the receipt by the Commission of the certification of the exchange approving the security for listing and registration, the certification, unless withdrawn, shall be deemed made with reference to the application as amended.

Rule 12d1–6. Withdrawal of Certification

An exchange may, by notice to the Commission, withdraw its certification prior to the time that the registration to which it relates first becomes effective pursuant to Rule 12d1–1.

SUSPENSION OF TRADING, WITHDRAWAL, AND STRIKING FROM LISTING AND REGISTRATION

Rule 12d2–1. Suspension of Trading

(a) A national securities exchange may suspend from trading a security listed and registered thereon in accordance with its rules. Such exchange shall promptly notify the Commission of any such suspension, the effective date thereof and the reasons therefor.

(b) Any such suspension may be continued until such time as it shall appear to the Commission that such suspension is designed to evade the provisions of section 12(d) and the rules and regulations thereunder relating to the withdrawal and striking of a security from listing and registration. During the continuance of such suspension the exchange shall notify the Commission promptly of any change in the reasons for the suspension. Upon the restoration to trading of any security suspended under this rule, the exchange shall notify the Commission promptly of the effective date thereof.

(c) Suspension of trading shall not terminate the registration of any security.

Rule 12d2–2. Removal From Listing and Registration

(a) A national securities exchange shall file with the Commission an application on Form

25 to strike a security from listing and registration thereon within a reasonable time after the exchange is reliably informed that any of the following conditions exist with respect to such a security:

(1) The entire class of the security has been called for redemption, maturity or retirement; appropriate notice thereof has been given; funds sufficient for the payment of all such securities have been deposited with an agency authorized to make such payments; and such funds have been made available to security holders.

(2) The entire class of the security has been redeemed or paid at maturity or retirement.

(3) The instruments representing the securities comprising the entire class have come to evidence, by operation of law or otherwise, other securities in substitution therefor and represent no other right, except, if such be the fact, the right to receive an immediate cash payment (the right of dissenters to receive the appraisal or fair value of their holdings shall not prevent the application of this provision).

(4) All rights pertaining to the entire class of the security have been extinguished: *Provided, however,* That where such an event occurs as the result of an order of a court or other governmental authority, the order shall be final, all applicable appeal periods shall have expired, and no appeals shall be pending.

EFFECTIVE DATE: Such an application shall be deemed to be granted and shall become effective at the opening of business on such date as the exchange shall specify in said application, but not less than 10 days following the date on which said application is filed with the Commission: *Provided, however,* That in the event removal is being effected under paragraph (a)(3) and the exchange has admitted or intends to admit a successor security to trading under the temporary exemption provided for by Rule 12a–5, such date shall not be earlier than the date on which the successor security is removed from its exempt status.

(b)(1) A national securities exchange may strike a security from listing and registration thereon if (i) trading in such security has been terminated pursuant to a rule of such exchange requiring such termination whenever the security is admitted to trading on another exchange; and (ii) listing and registration of such security has become effective on such other exchange.

(2) A national securities exchange which has stricken a security from listing and registration under the provisions of this paragraph shall send written notice of such action to the Commission within 3 days from the date thereof.

(c) In cases not provided for in paragraph (a) or (b) of this rule, a national securities exchange may file an application to strike a security from listing and registration, in accordance with its rules, on a date specified in the application, which date shall be not less than 10 days after it is filed with the Commission. The Commission will enter an order granting such application on the date specified in the application unless the Commission, by written notice to the exchange, postpones the effective date for a period of not more than 60 days thereafter: *Provided, however,* That the Commission, by written notice to the exchange on or before the effective date, may order a hearing to determine whether the application to strike the security from listing and registration has been made in accordance with the rules of the exchange, or what terms should be imposed by the Commission for the protection of investors.

(d) The issuer of a security listed and registered on a national securities exchange may file an application to withdraw such security from listing and registration on such exchange in accordance with the rules of such exchange. Notice of the filing of such an application shall be published by the Commission in the Federal Register, and such notice shall provide that any interested person may, on or before a date specified, submit to the Commission in writing, all facts bearing upon whether the application to withdraw the security from listing and registration has been made in accordance with the rules of the exchange and what terms should be imposed by the Commission for the protection of investors. An order disposing of the matter will be issued by the Commission on the basis of the application and any other information furnished to the Commission unless prior thereto the Commission orders a hearing on the matter.

(e) An application by an issuer or by a national securities exchange to withdraw or strike a security from listing and registration pursuant to the provisions of paragraph (c) or (d) of this rule shall comply with the following requirements:

(1) The application shall be filed in triplicate, the original of which shall be dated and signed by an authorized official of the exchange, or of the issuer, as the case may be.

(2) If the applicant is the exchange it shall promptly deliver a copy of the application to the issuer and if the applicant is the issuer it shall promptly deliver a copy of the application to the exchange.

(3) The application shall set forth a description of the security involved together with a statement of all material facts relating to the reasons for filing such application for withdrawal or striking from listing and registration.

(4) The application shall set forth the steps taken by the applicant to comply with the rules of the exchange governing the delisting of securities.

(f) If within 30 days after the publication of any rule or regulation which substantially alters or adds to the obligations, or detracts from the rights, of an issuer of a security registered pursuant to application under section 12(b) or (c), or of its officers, directors, or security holders, or of persons soliciting or giving any proxy or consent or authorization with respect to such security, the issuer shall file with the Commission a request that such registration shall expire and shall accompany such request with a written explanation of the reasons why the publication of such rule or regulation leads the issuer to make such request, such registration shall expire immediately upon receipt of such request or immediately before such rule or regulation becomes effective, whichever date is later. The absence of an express reservation, in an application for registration, of the rights herein granted shall not be deemed a waiver thereof.

UNLISTED TRADING

Rule 12f–1. Applications for Permission to Extend Unlisted Trading Privileges

(a) An application to reinstate unlisted trading privileges may be made to the Commission by any national securities exchange for the extension of unlisted trading privileges to any security for which such unlisted trading privileges have been suspended by the Commission, pursuant to section 12(f)(2)(A) of the Act (15 U.S.C. 78*l*(2)(A)). One copy of such application, executed by a duly authorized officer of the exchange, shall be filed and shall set forth.

(1) Name of issuer;

(2) Title of security;

(3) The name of each national securities exchange, if any, on which such security is listed or admitted to unlisted trading privileges; and

(4) Whether transaction information concerning such security is reported in the consolidated transaction reporting system contemplated by Rule 11Aa3–1;

(5) The date of the Commission's suspension of unlisted trading privileges in the security on the exchange;

(6) Any other information which is deemed pertinent to the question of whether the reinstatement of unlisted trading privi-

leges in such security is consistent with the maintenance of fair and orderly markets and the protection of investors; and

(7) that a copy of the instant application has been mailed, or otherwise personally provided, to the issuer of the securities for which unlisted trading privileges are sought and to each exchange listed in item (3) of this section.

Rule 12f–2. Extending Unlisted Trading Privileges to a Security That Is the Subject of an Initial Public Offering

(a) *General provision.* A national securities exchange may extend unlisted trading privileges to a subject security when at least one transaction in the subject security has been effected on the national securities exchange upon which the security is listed and the transaction has been reported pursuant to an effective transaction reporting plan, as defined in § 240.11Aa3–1.

(b) The extension of unlisted trading privileges pursuant to this section shall be subject to all the provisions set forth in Section 12(f) of the Act (15 U.S.C. 78*l*(f)), as amended, and any rule or regulation promulgated thereunder, or which may be promulgated thereunder while the extension is in effect.

(c) *Definitions.* For the purposes of this section:

(1) The term *subject security* shall mean a security that is the subject of an initial public offering, as that term is defined in section 12(f)(1)(G)(i) of the Act (15 U.S.C. 78*l*(f)(1)(G)(i)), and

(2) An *initial public offering commences* at such time as is described in section 12(f)(1)(G)(ii) of the Act (15 U.S.C. 78*l*(f)(1)(G)(ii)).

Rule 12f–3. Termination or Suspension of Unlisted Trading Privileges

(a) The issuer of any security for which unlisted trading privileges on any exchange have been continued or extended, or any broker or dealer who makes or creates a market for such security, or any other person having a bona fide interest in the question of termination or suspension of such unlisted trading privileges, may make application to the Commission for the termination or suspension of such unlisted trading privileges. One duly executed copy of such application shall be filed, and it shall contain the following information;

(1) Name and address of applicant;

(2) A brief statement of the applicant's interest in the question of termination or suspension of such unlisted trading privileges;

(3) Title of security;

(4) Name of issuer;

(5) Amount of such security issued and outstanding (number of shares of stock or principal amount of bonds), stating source of information;

(6) Annual volume of public trading in such security (number of shares of stock or principal amount of bonds) on such exchange for each of the 3 calendar years immediately preceding the date of such application, and monthly volume of trading in such security for each of the 12 calendar months immediately preceding the date of such application;

(7) Price range on such exchange for each of the 12 calendar months immediately preceding the date of such application; and

(8) A brief statement of the information in the applicant's possession, and the sources thereof, with respect to (i) the extent of public trading in such security on such exchange, and (ii) the character of trading in such security on such exchange; and

(9) A brief statement that a copy of the instant application has been mailed, or otherwise personally provided, to the exchange from which the suspension or termination of unlisted trading privileges is sought, and to any other exchange on which such security is listed or traded pursuant to unlisted trading privileges.

(b) Unlisted trading privileges in any security on any national securities exchange may be suspended or terminated by such exchange in accordance with its rules.

Rule 12f-4. Exemption of Securities Admitted to Unlisted Trading Privileges From Sections 13, 14, and 16

(a) Any security for which unlisted trading privileges on any national securities exchange have been continued or extended pursuant to section 12(f) of the Act shall be exempt from section 13 of the Act unless (1) such security or another security of the same issuer is listed and registered on a national securities exchange or registered pursuant to section 12(g) of the Act, or (2) such issuer would be required to file information, documents and reports pursuant to section 15(d) of the Act but for the fact that securities of the issuer are deemed to be "registered on a national securities exchange" within the meaning of section 12(f)(6) of the Act.

(b) Any security for which unlisted trading privileges on any national securities exchange have been continued or extended pursuant to section 12(f) of the Act shall be exempt from section 14 of the Act unless such security is also listed and registered on a national securities exchange or registered pursuant to section 12(g) of the Act.

(c)(1) Any equity security for which unlisted trading privileges on any national securities exchange have been continued or extended pursuant to section 12(f) of the Act shall be exempt from section 16 of the Act unless such security or another equity security of the same issuer is listed and registered on a national securities exchange or registered pursuant to section 12(g) of the Act.

(2) Any equity security for which unlisted trading privileges on any national securities exchange have been continued or extended pursuant to section 12(f) of the Act and which is not listed and registered on any other such exchange or registered pursuant to section 12(g) of the Act shall be exempt from section 16 of the Act insofar as that section would otherwise apply to any person who is directly or indirectly the beneficial owner of more than 10 percent of such security, unless another equity security of the issuer of such unlisted security is so listed or registered and such beneficial owner is a director or officer of such issuer or directly or indirectly the beneficial owner of more than 10 percent of any such listed or registered security.

(d) Any reference in this rule to a security registered pursuant to section 12(g) of the Act shall include, and any reference to a security not so registered shall exclude, any security as to which a registration statement pursuant to such section is at the time required to be effective.

Rule 12f-5. Exchange Rules for Securities to Which Unlisted Trading Privileges Are Extended

A national securities exchange shall not extend unlisted trading privileges to any security unless the national securities exchange has in effect a rule or rules providing for transactions in the class or type of security to which the exchange extends unlisted trading privileges.

EXTENSIONS AND TEMPORARY EXEMPTIONS; DEFINITIONS

Rule 12g-1. Exemption From Section 12(g)

An issuer shall be exempt from the requirement to register any class of equity securities pursuant to section 12(g)(1) if on the last day of its most recent fiscal year the issuer had total assets not exceeding $10,000,000 and, with respect to a foreign private issuer, such securities were not quoted in an automated inter-dealer quotation system.

Rule 12g-2. Securities Deemed to Be Registered Pursuant to Section 12(g)(1) Upon Termination of Exemption Pursuant to Section 12(g)(2)(A) or (B)

Any class of securities which would have been required to be registered pursuant to section 12(g)(1) of the Act except for the fact that it was exempt from such registration by section 12(g)(2)(A) because it was listed and registered on a national securities exchange, or by section 12(g)(2)(B) because it was issued by an investment company registered pursuant to section 8 of the Investment Company Act of 1940, shall upon the termination of the listing and registration of such class or the termination of the registration of such company and without the filing of an additional registration statement be deemed to be registered pursuant to said section 12(g)(1) if at the time of such termination (a) the issuer of such class of securities has elected to be regulated as a business development company pursuant to sections 55 through 65 of the Investment Company Act of 1940 and such election has not been withdrawn, or (b) securities of the class are not exempt from such registration pursuant to section 12 or rules thereunder and all securities of such class are held of record by 300 or more persons.

Rule 12g–3. Registration of Securities of Successor Issuers Under Section 12(b) or 12(g)

(a) Where in connection with a succession by merger, consolidation, exchange of securities, acquisition of assets or otherwise, securities of an issuer that are not already registered pursuant to section 12 of the Act (15 U.S.C. 78l) are issued to the holders of any class of securities of another issuer that is registered pursuant to either section 12(b) or (g) of the Act (15 U.S.C. 78l(b) or (g)), the class of securities so issued shall be deemed to be registered under the same paragraph of section 12 of the Act unless upon consummation of the succession:

(1) Such class is exempt from such registration other than by § 240.12g3–2;

(2) All securities of such class are held of record by less than 300 persons; or

(3) The securities issued in connection with the succession were registered on Form F–8 or Form F–80 (§ 239.38 or § 239.41 of this chapter) and following succession the successor would not be required to register such class of securities under section 12 of the Act (15 U.S.C. 78l) but for this section.

(b) Where in connection with a succession by merger, consolidation, exchange of securities, acquisition of assets or otherwise, securities of an issuer that are not already registered pursuant to section 12 of the Act (15 U.S.C. 78l) are issued to the holders of any class of securities of another issuer that is required to file a registration statement pursuant to either section 12(b) or (g) of the Act (15 U.S.C. 78l(b) or (g)) but has not yet done so, the duty to file such statement shall be deemed to have been assumed by the issuer of the class of securities so issued. The successor issuer shall file a registration statement pursuant to the same paragraph of section 12 of the Act with respect to such class within the period of time the predecessor issuer would have been required to file such a statement unless upon consummation of the succession:

(1) Such class is exempt from such registration other than by § 240.12g3–2;

(2) All securities of such class are held of record by less than 300 persons; or

(3) The securities issued in connection with the succession were registered on Form F–8 or Form F–80 (§ 239.38 or § 239.41 of this chapter) and following the succession the successor would not be required to register such class of securities under section 12 of the Act (15 U.S.C. 78l) but for this section.

(c) Where in connection with a succession by merger, consolidation, exchange of securities, acquisition of assets or otherwise, securities of an issuer that are not already registered pursuant to section 12 of the Act (15 U.S.C. 78l) are issued to the holders of classes of securities of two or more other issuers that are each registered pursuant to section 12 of the Act; the class of securities so issued shall be deemed to be registered under section 12 of the Act unless upon consummation of the succession:

(1) Such class is exempt from such registration other than by § 240.12g3–2;

(2) All securities of such class are held of record by less than 300 persons; or

(3) The securities issued in connection with the succession were registered on Form F–8 or Form F–80 (§ 239.38 or § 239.41 of this chapter) and following succession the successor would not be required to register such class of securities under section 12 of the Act (15 U.S.C. 78l) but for this section.

(d) If the classes of securities issued by two or more predecessor issuers (as described in paragraph (c) of this section) are registered under the same paragraph of section 12 of the Act (15 U.S.C. 78l), the class of securities issued by the successor issuer shall be deemed registered under the same paragraph of section 12 of the Act. If the classes of securities issued by the predecessor issuers are not registered under the same paragraph of section 12 of the Act, the class of securities issued by the successor issuer shall be deemed registered under section 12(g) of the Act (15 U.S.C. 78l(g)).

(e) An issuer that is deemed to have a class of securities registered pursuant to section 12 of the Act (15 U.S.C. 78l) according to paragraph (a), (b), (c) or (d) of this section shall file reports on the same forms and such class of securities shall be subject to the provisions of sections 14 and 16 of the Act (15 U.S.C. 78n and 78p) to the same extent as the predecessor issuers, except as follows:

(1) An issuer that is not a foreign issuer shall not be eligible to file on Form 20–F (§ 249.220f of this chapter) or to use the exemption in § 240.3a12–3.

(2) A foreign private issuer shall be eligible to file on Form 20–F (§ 249.220f of this chapter) and to use the exemption in § 240.3a12–3.

(f) An issuer that is deemed to have a class of securities registered pursuant to section 12 of the Act (15 U.S.C. 78l) according to paragraphs (a), (b), (c) or (d) of this section shall indicate in the Form 8–K (§ 249.308 of this chapter) report filed with the Commission in connection with the succession, pursuant to the requirements of Form 8–K, the paragraph of section 12 of the Act under which the class of securities issued by the successor issuer is deemed registered by operation of paragraphs (a), (b), (c) or (d) of this section. If a successor issuer that is deemed registered under section 12(g) of the Act (15 U.S.C. 78l(g)) by paragraph (d) of this section intends to list a class of securities on a national securities exchange, it must file a registration statement pursuant to section 12(b) of the Act (15 U.S.C. 78l(b)) with respect to that class of securities.

(g) An issuer that is deemed to have a class of securities registered pursuant to section 12 of the Act (15 U.S.C. 78l) according to paragraph (a), (b), (c) or (d) of this section shall file an annual report for each fiscal year beginning on or after the date as of which the succession occurred. Annual reports shall be filed within the period specified in the appropriate form. Each such issuer shall file an annual report for each of its predecessors that had securities registered pursuant to section 12 of the Act (15 U.S.C. 78l) covering the last full fiscal year of the predecessor before the registrant's succession, unless such report has been filed by the predecessor. Such annual report shall contain information that would be required if filed by the predecessor.

Rule 12g3–2. Exemptions for American Depositary Receipts and Certain Foreign Securities

(a) Securities of any class issued by any foreign private issuer shall be exempt from section 12(g) (15 U.S.C. 78*l*(g)) of the Act if the class has fewer than 300 holders resident in the United States. This exemption shall continue until the next fiscal year end at which the issuer has a class of equity securities held by 300 or more persons resident in the United States. For the purpose of determining whether a security is exempt pursuant to this paragraph:

(1) Securities held of record by persons resident in the United States shall be determined as provided in § 240.12g5-1 except that securities held of record by a broker, dealer, bank or nominee for any of them for the accounts of customers resident in the United States shall be counted as held in the United States by the number of separate accounts for which the securities are held. The issuer may rely in good faith on information as to the number of such separate accounts supplied by all owners of the class of its securities which are brokers, dealers, or banks or a nominee for any of them.

(2) Persons in the United States who hold the security only through a Canadian Retirement Account (as that term is defined in rule 237(a)(2) under the Securities Act of 1933 (§ 230.237(a)(2) of this chapter)), shall not be counted as holders resident in the United States.

(b)(1) Securities of any foreign private issuer shall be exempt from Section 12(g) of the Act if the issuer, or a government official or agency of the country of the issuer's domicile or in which it is incorporated or organized,—

(i) Shall furnish to the Commission whatever information in each of the following categories the issuer since the beginning of its last fiscal year (*a*) has made or is required to make public pursuant to the law of the country of its domicile or in which it is incorporated or organized, (*b*) has filed or is required to file with a stock exchange on which its securities are traded and which was made public by such exchange, or (*c*) has distributed or is required to distribute to its security holders;

(ii) Shall furnish to the Commission a list identifying the information referred to in subdivision (i) of this subparagraph and stating when and by whom it is required to be made public, filed with any such exchange or distributed to security holders;

(iii) Shall furnish to the Commission, during each subsequent fiscal year, whatever information is made public as described in (*a*), (*b*) or (*c*) of subdivision (i) of this subparagraph promptly after such information is made or required to be made public as described therein; and

(iv) Shall, promptly after the end of any fiscal year in which any changes shall occur in the kind of information required to be published as referred to in the list furnished under subdivision (ii) of this subparagraph or any subsequent list, furnish to the Commission a revised list reflecting such changes.

(v) Shall furnish to the Commission in connection with the initial submission the following information to the extent known or which can be obtained without unreasonable effort or expense: the number of holders of each class of equity securities resident in the United States, the amount and percentage of each class of outstanding equity securities held by residents in the United States, the circumstances in which such securities were acquired, and the date and circumstances of the most recent public distribution of securities by the issuer or an affiliate thereof.

(2) The information required to be furnished under subdivisions (i) and (ii) of subparagraph (1) of this paragraph shall be furnished on or before the date on which a registration statement under Section 12(g) of the Act would otherwise be required to be filed. Any issuer furnishing information under subparagraph (1)(i) of this paragraph shall notify the Commission that it is furnished pursuant to that paragraph.

(3) The information required to be furnished pursuant to subparagraph (1)(i) and (iii) of this paragraph is information material to an investment decision such as: the financial condition or results of operations; changes in business; acquisitions or dispositions of assets; issuance, redemption or acquisitions of their securities; changes in management or control; the granting of options or the payment of other remuneration to directors or

officers; and transactions with directors, officers or principal security holders.

(4) Only one complete copy of any information or document need be furnished under paragraph (b)(1) of this rule. Such information and documents need not be under cover of any prescribed form and shall not be deemed to be "filed" with the Commission or otherwise subject to the liabilities of section 18 of the Act. Press releases and all other communications or materials distributed directly to securityholders of each class of securities to which the exemption relates shall be in English. English versions or adequate summaries in English may be furnished in lieu of original English translations. No other documents need be furnished unless the issuer has prepared or caused to be prepared English translations, versions, or summaries of them. If no English translations, versions, or summaries have been prepared, a brief description in English of any such documents shall be furnished. Information or documents in a language other than English are not required to be furnished. If practicable, the Commission file number shall appear on the information furnished or in an accompanying letter. Any information or document previously sent to the Commission under cover of Form 40–F or Form 6–K need not be furnished under paragraph (b)(1) of this section.

(5) The furnishing of any information or document under paragraph (b) of this rule shall not constitute an admission for any purpose that the issuer is subject to the Act.

(c) Depositary Shares registered on Form F–6 (§ 239.36 of this chapter), but not the underlying deposited securities, are exempt from section 12(g) of the Act under this paragraph (c).

(d) The exemption provided by paragraph (b) of this rule shall not be available for the following securities:

(1) Securities of a foreign private issuer that has or has had during the prior eighteen months any securities registered under section 12 of the Act or a reporting obligation (suspended or active) under section 15(d) of the Act (other than arising solely by virtue of the use of Form F–7, F–8, F–9, F–10, or F–80);

(2) Securities of a foreign private issuer issued in a transaction (other than a transaction registered on Form F–8, F–9, F–10 or F–80) to acquire by merger, consolidation, exchange of securities, or acquisition of assets, another issuer that had securities registered under section 12 of the Act or a reporting obligation (suspended or active) under section 15(d) of the Act; and

(3) Securities quoted in an "automated inter-dealer quotation system" or securities represented by American Depositary Receipts so quoted unless all the following conditions are met:

(i) Such securities were so quoted on October 5, 1983 and have been continuously traded since;

(ii) The issuer is in compliance with the exemption in paragraph (b) of this rule on October 5, 1983 and has continuously maintained the exemption since; and

(iii) After January 2, 1986, the issuer is organized under the laws of any country except Canada or a political subdivision thereof.

Rule 12g–4. Certification of Termination of Registration Under Section 12(g)

(a) Termination of registration of a class of securities shall take effect in 90 days, or such shorter period as the Commission may determine, after the issuer certifies to the Commission on Form 15 that:

(1) Such class of securities is held of record by: (i) less than 300 persons; or (ii) by less than 500 persons, where the total assets of the issuer have not exceeded $10,000,000 on the last day of each of the issuer's three most recent fiscal years; or

(2) Such class of securities of a foreign private issuer, as defined in Rule 3b–4, is

held of record by: (i) less than 300 persons resident in the United States or (ii) less than 500 persons resident in the United States where the total assets of the issuer have not exceeded $10,000,000 on the last day of each of the issuer's most recent three fiscal years. For purposes of this paragraph, the number of persons resident in the United States shall be determined in accordance with the provisions of Rule 12g3–2(a).

(b) The issuer's duty to file any reports required under section 13(a) shall be suspended immediately upon filing a certification on Form 15, *Provided, however,* That if the certification on Form 15 is subsequently withdrawn or denied, the issuer shall, within 60 days after the date of such withdrawal or denial, file with the Commission all reports which would have been required had the certification on Form 15 not been filed. If the suspension resulted from the issuer's merger into, or consolidation with, another issuer or issuers, the certification shall be filed by the successor issuer.

Rule 12g5–1. Definition of Securities "Held of Record"

(a) For the purpose of determining whether an issuer is subject to the provisions of sections 12(g) and 15(d) of the Act, securities shall be deemed to be "held of record" by each person who is identified as the owner of such securities on records of security holders maintained by or on behalf of the issuer, subject to the following:

(1) In any case where the records of security holders have not been maintained in accordance with accepted practice, any additional person who would be identified as such an owner on such records if they had been maintained in accordance with accepted practice shall be included as a holder of record.

(2) Securities identified as held of record by a corporation, a partnership, a trust whether or not the trustees are named, or other organization shall be included as so held by one person.

(3) Securities identified as held of record by one or more persons as trustees, executors, guardians, custodians or in other fiduciary capacities with respect to a single trust, estate or account shall be included as held of record by one person.

(4) Securities held by two or more persons as co-owners shall be included as held by one person.

(5) Each outstanding unregistered or bearer certificate shall be included as held of record by a separate person, except to the extent that the issuer can establish that, if such securities were registered they would be held of record, under the provisions of this rule, by a lesser number of persons.

(6) Securities registered in substantially similar names where the issuer has reason to believe because of the address or other indications that such names represent the same person, may be included as held of record by one person.

(b) Notwithstanding paragraph (a):

(1) Securities held, to the knowledge of the issuer, subject to a voting trust, deposit agreement or similar arrangement shall be included as held of record by the record holders of the voting trust certificates, certificates of deposit, receipts or similar evidences of interest in such securities: *Provided however,* That the issuer may rely in good faith on such information as is received in response to its request from a nonaffiliated issuer of the certificates or evidences of interest.

(2) Whole or fractional securities issued by a savings and loan association, building and loan association, cooperative bank, homestead association, or similar institution for the sole purpose of qualifying a borrower for membership in the issuer, and which are to be redeemed or repurchased by the issuer when the borrower's loan is terminated,

shall not be included as held of record by any person.

(3) If the issuer knows or has reason to know that the form of holding securities of record is used primarily to circumvent the provisions of section 12(g) or 15(d) of the Act, the beneficial owners of such securities shall be deemed to be the record owners thereof.

Rule 12g5–2. Definition of "Total Assets"

For the purpose of section 12(g)(1) of the Act, the term "total assets" shall mean the total assets as shown on the issuer's balance sheet or the balance sheet of the issuer and its subsidiaries consolidated, whichever is larger, as required to be filed on the form prescribed for registration under this section and prepared in accordance with the pertinent provisions of Regulation S–X. Where the security is a certificate of deposit, voting trust certificate, or certificate or other evidence of interest in a similar trust or agreement, the "total assets" of the issuer of the security held under the trust or agreement shall be deemed to be the "total assets" of the issuer of such certificate or evidence of interest.

Rule 12h–1. Exemptions From Registration Under Section 12(g) of the Act

Issuers shall be exempt from the provisions of section 12(g) of the Act with respect to the following securities:

(a) Any interest or participation in an employee stock bonus, stock purchase, profit sharing, pension, retirement, incentive, thrift, savings or similar plan which is not transferable by the holder except in the event of death or mental incompetency, or any security issued solely to fund such plans;

(b) Any interest or participation in any common trust fund or similar fund maintained by a bank exclusively for the collective investment and reinvestment of monies contributed thereto by the bank in its capacity as a trustee, executor, administrator, or guardian. For purposes of this paragraph (b), the term "common trust fund" shall include a common trust fund which is maintained by a bank which is a member of an affiliated group, as defined in section 1504(a) of the Internal Revenue Code of 1954, and which is maintained exclusively for the investment and reinvestment of monies contributed thereto by one or more bank members of such affiliated group in the capacity of trustee, executor, administrator, or guardian, provided that:

(1) the common trust fund is operated in compliance with the same state and federal regulatory requirements as would apply if the bank maintaining such fund and any other contributing banks were the same entity; and

(2) the rights of persons for whose benefit a contributing bank acts as trustee, executor, administrator or guardian would not be diminished by reason of the maintenance of such common trust fund by another bank member of the affiliated group;

(c) Any class of equity security which would not be outstanding 60 days after a registration statement would be required to be filed with respect thereto;

(d) Any standardized option, as that term is defined in section 240.9b–1(a)(4), that is issued by a clearing agency registered under section 17A of the Act (15 U.S.C. 78q–1) and traded on a national securities exchange registered pursuant to section 6(a) of the Act (15 U.S.C. 78f(a)) or on a national securities association registered pursuant to section 15A(a) of the Act (15 U.S.C. 78o–3(a)); and

(e) Any security futures product that is traded on a national securities exchange registered pursuant to section 6 of the Act (15 U.S.C. 78f) or on a national securities association registered pursuant to section 15A(a) of the Act (15 U.S.C. 78o–3(a)) and cleared by a clearing agency that is registered pursuant to section 17A of the Act (15 U.S.C. 78q–1) or is exempt from registration under section 17A(b)(7) of the Act (15 U.S.C. 78q–1(b)(7)).

Rule 12h–3. Suspension of Duty to File Reports Under Section 15(d)

(a) Subject to paragraphs (c) and (d) of this section, the duty under section 15(d) to file reports required by section 13(a) of the Act with respect to a class of securities specified in paragraph (b) of this section shall be suspended for such class of securities immediately upon filing with the Commission a certification on Form 15 if the issuer of such class has filed all reports required by Section 13(a), without regard to Rule 12b–25, for the shorter of its most recent three fiscal years and the portion of the current year preceding the date of filing Form 15, or the period since the issuer became subject to such reporting obligation. If the certification on Form 15 is subsequently withdrawn or denied, the issuer shall, within 60 days, file with the commission all reports which would have been required if such certification had not been filed.

(b) The classes of securities eligible for the suspension provided in paragraph (a) of this section are:

(1) Any class of securities held of record by: (i) less than 300 persons; or (ii) by less than 500 persons, where the total assets of the issuer have not exceeded $10,000,000 on the last day of each of the issuer's three most recent fiscal years;

(2) Any class of securities of a foreign private issuer, as defined in Rule 3b–4, held of record by: (i) less than 300 persons resident in the United States or (ii) less than 500 persons resident in the United States where the total assets of the issuer have not exceeded $10,000,000 on the last day of each of the issuer's three most recent fiscal years. For purposes of this paragraph, the number of persons resident in the United States shall be determined in accordance with the provisions of Rule 12g3–2(a); and

(3) Any class of securities deregistered pursuant to section 12(d) of the Act if such class would not thereupon be deemed registered under section 12(g) of the Act or the rules thereunder.

(c) This section shall not be available for any class of securities for a fiscal year in which a registration statement relating to that class becomes effective under the Securities Act of 1933, or is required to be updated pursuant to section 10(a)(3) of the Act, and, in the case of paragraphs (b)(1)(ii) and (b)(2)(ii), the two succeeding fiscal years. *Provided, however,* That this paragraph shall not apply to the duty to file reports which arises solely from a registration statement filed by an issuer with no significant assets, for the reorganization of a non-reporting issuer into a one subsidiary holding company in which equity security holders receive the same proportional interest in the holding company as they held in the non-reporting issuer, except for changes resulting from the exercise of dissenting shareholder rights under state law.

(d) The suspension provided by this rule relates only to the reporting obligation under section 15(d) with respect to a class of securities, does not affect any other duties imposed on that class of securities, and shall continue as long as criteria (i) or (ii) in either paragraph (b)(1) or (b)(2) is met on the first day of any subsequent fiscal year. *Provided, however,* That such criteria need not be met if the duty to file reports arises solely from a registration statement filed by an issuer with no significant assets in a reorganization of a non-reporting company into a one subsidiary holding company in which equity security holders receive the same proportional interest in the holding company as they held in the non-reporting issuer except for changes resulting from the exercise of dissenting shareholder rights under state law.

(e) If the suspension provided by this rule is discontinued because a class of securities does not meet the eligibility criteria of paragraph (b) on the first day of an issuer's fiscal year, then the issuer shall resume periodic reporting pursuant to section 15(d) by filing an annual report on Form 10–K for its preceding fiscal year, not later than 120 days after the end of such fiscal year.

Rule 12h–4. Exemption From Duty to File Reports Under Section 15(d)

An issuer shall be exempt from the duty under section 15(d) of the Act to file reports required by section 13(a) of the Act with respect to securities registered under the Securities Act of 1933 on Form F–7, Form F–8 or Form F–80, provided that the issuer is exempt from the obligations of Section 12(g) of the Act pursuant to Rule 12g3–2(b).

Rule 12h–5. Exemption for Subsidiary Issuers of Guaranteed Securities and Subsidiary Guarantors

(a) Any issuer of a guaranteed security, or guarantor of a security, that is permitted to omit financial statements by § 210.3–10 of Regulation S–X of this chapter is exempt from the requirements of Section 13(a) or 15(d) of the Act (15 U.S.C. 78m(a) or 78o(d)).

(b) Any issuer of a guaranteed security, or guarantor of a security, that would be permitted to omit financial statements by § 210.3–10 of Regulation S–X of this chapter, but is required to file financial statements in accordance with the operation of § 210.3–10(g) of Regulation S–X of this chapter, is exempt from the requirements of Section 13(a) or 15(d) of the Act (15 U.S.C. 78m(a) or 78o(d)).

REGULATION 13A. REPORTS OF ISSUERS OF SECURITIES REGISTERED PURSUANT TO SECTION 12

ANNUAL REPORTS

Rule 13a–1. Requirement of Annual Reports

Every issuer having securities registered pursuant to section 12 of the Act (15 U.S.C. 78l) shall file an annual report on the appropriate form authorized or prescribed therefor for each fiscal year after the last full fiscal year for which financial statements were filed in its registration statement. Annual reports shall be filed within the period specified in the appropriate form.

Rule 13a–3. Reporting by Form 40–F Registrant

A registrant that is eligible to use Forms 40–F and 6–K and files reports in accordance therewith shall be deemed to satisfy the requirements of Regulation 13A (Rules 13a–1 through 13a–17 of this chapter).

Rule 13a–10. Transition Reports

(a) Every issuer that changes its fiscal closing date shall file a report covering the resulting transition period between the closing date of its most recent fiscal year end and the opening date of its new fiscal year; *Provided, however,* that an issuer shall file an annual report for any fiscal year that ended before the date on which the issuer determined to change its fiscal year end. In no event shall the transition report cover a period of 12 or more months.

(b) The report pursuant to this rule shall be filed for the transition period not more than the number of days specified in paragraph (j) of this section after either the close of the transition period or the date of the determination to change the fiscal closing date, whichever is later. The report shall be filed on the form appropriate for annual reports of the issuer, shall cover the period from the close of the last fiscal year end and shall indicate clearly the period covered. The financial statements for the transition period filed therewith shall be audited. Financial statements, which may be unaudited, shall be filed for the comparable period of the prior year, or a footnote, which may be unaudited, shall state for the comparable period of the prior year, revenues, gross profits, income taxes, income or loss from continuing operations before extraordinary items and cumulative effect of a change in accounting principles and net income or loss. The effects of any discontinued operations and/or extraordinary items as classified under the provisions of generally accepted accounting principles also shall be shown, if applicable. Per share data based upon such income or loss and net income or loss shall be presented in conformity with applicable accounting standards. Where called for by the time span to be covered, the comparable period financial statements or footnote shall be included in subsequent filings.

(c) If the transition period covers a period of less than six months, in lieu of the report required by paragraph (b) of this rule, a report may be filed for the transition period on Form 10–Q and Form 10–QSB not more than the number of days specified in paragraph (j) of this section after either the close of the transition period or the date of the determination to change the fiscal closing date, whichever is later. The report on Form 10–Q and Form 10–QSB shall cover the period from the close of the last fiscal year end and shall indicate clearly the period covered. The financial statements filed therewith need not be audited but, if they are not audited, the issuer shall file with the first annual report for the newly adopted fiscal year separate audited statements of income and cash flows covering the transition period. The notes to financial statements for the transition period included in such first annual report may be integrated with the notes to financial statements for the full fiscal period. A separate audited balance sheet as of the end of the transition period shall be filed in the annual report only if the audited balance sheet as of the end of the fiscal year prior to the transition period is not filed. Schedules need not be filed in transition reports on Form 10–Q and Form 10–QSB.

(d) Notwithstanding the foregoing in paragraphs (a), (b), and (c) of this rule, if the transition period covers a period of one month or less, the issuer need not file a separate transition report if either:

(1) The first report required to be filed by the issuer for the newly adopted fiscal year after the date of the determination to change the fiscal year end is an annual report, and that report covers the transition period as well as the fiscal year; or

(2)(i) The issuer files with the first annual report for the newly adopted fiscal year separate audited statements of income and cash flows covering the transition period; and

(ii) The first report required to be filed by the issuer for the newly adopted fiscal year after the date of the determination to change the fiscal year end is a quarterly report on Form 10–Q and Form 10–QSB; and

(iii) Information on the transition period is included in the issuer's quarterly report on Form 10–Q and Form 10–QSB for the first quarterly period (except the fourth quarter) of the newly adopted fiscal year that ends after the date of the determination to change the fiscal year. The information covering the transition period required by Part II and Item 2 of Part I may be combined with the information regarding the quarter. However, the financial statements required by Part I, which may be unaudited, shall be furnished separately for the transition period.

(e) Every issuer required to file quarterly reports on Form 10–Q and Form 10–QSB pursuant to Rule 13a–13 of this chapter that changes its fiscal year end shall:

(1) File a quarterly report on Form 10–Q and Form 10–QSB within the time period specified in General Instruction A.1. to that form for any quarterly period (except the fourth quarter) of the old fiscal year that ends before the date on which the issuer determined to change its fiscal year end, except that the issuer need not file such quarterly report if the date on which the quarterly period ends also is the date on which the transition period ends;

(2) File a quarterly report on Form 10–Q and Form 10–QSB within the time specified in General Instruction A.1. to that form for each quarterly period of the old fiscal year within the transition period. In lieu of a quarterly report for any quarter of the old fiscal year within the transition period, the issuer may file a quarterly report on Form 10–Q and Form 10–QSB for any period of three months within the transition period that coincides with a quarter of the newly adopted fiscal year if the quarterly report is filed within the number of days specified in paragraph (j) of this section after the end of such three month period, provided the issuer thereafter continues filing quarterly reports on the basis of the quarters of the newly adopted fiscal year;

(3) Commence filing quarterly reports for the quarters of the new fiscal year no later than the quarterly report for the first quarter of the new fiscal year that ends after the date on which the issuer determined to change the fiscal year end; and

(4) Unless such information is or will be included in the transition report, or the first annual report on Form 10–K and Form 10–KSB for the newly adopted fiscal year, include in the initial quarterly report on Form 10–Q and Form 10–QSB for the newly adopted fiscal year information on any period beginning on the first day subsequent to the period covered by the issuer's final quarterly report on Form 10–Q and Form 10–QSB or annual report on Form 10–K and Form 10–KSB for the old fiscal year. The information covering such period required

by Part II and Item 2 of Part I may be combined with the information regarding the quarter. However, the financial statements required by Part I, which may be unaudited, shall be furnished separately for such period.

Note to paragraphs (c) and (e): If it is not practicable or cannot be cost-justified to furnish in a transition report on Form 10–Q or a quarterly report for the newly adopted fiscal year financial statements for corresponding periods of the prior year where required, financial statements may be furnished for the quarters of the preceding fiscal year that most nearly are comparable if the issuer furnishes an adequate discussion of seasonal and other factors that could affect the comparability of information or trends reflected, an assessment of the comparability of the data, and a representation as to the reason recasting has not been undertaken.

(f) Every successor issuer with securities registered under Section 12 of this Act that has a different fiscal year from that of its predecessor(s) shall file a transition report pursuant to this section, containing the required information about each predecessor, for the transition period, if any, between the close of the fiscal year covered by the last annual report of each predecessor and the date of succession. The report shall be filed for the transition period on the form appropriate for annual reports of the issuer not more than the number of days specified in paragraph (j) of this section after the date of the succession, with financial statements in conformity with the requirements set forth in paragraph (b) of this section. If the transition period covers a period of less than six months, in lieu of a transition report on the form appropriate for the issuer's annual reports, the report may be filed for the transition period on Form 10–Q and Form 10–QSB not more than the number of days specified in paragraph (j) of this section after the date of the succession, with financial statements in conformity with the requirements set forth in paragraph (c) of this rule. Notwithstanding the foregoing, if the transition period covers a period of one month or less, the successor issuer need not file a separate transition report if the information is reported by the successor issuer in conformity with the requirements set forth in paragraph (d) of this rule.

(g)(1) Paragraphs (a) through (f) of this rule shall not apply to foreign private issuers.

(2) Every foreign private issuer that changes its fiscal closing date shall file a report covering the resulting transition period between the closing date of its most recent fiscal year end and the opening date of its new fiscal year. In no event shall a transition report cover a period longer than 12 months.

(3) The report for the transition period shall be filed on Form 20–F responding to all items to which such issuer is required to respond when Form 20–F is used as an annual report. Such report shall be filed within six months after either the close of the transition period or the date on which the issuer made the determination to change the fiscal closing date, whichever is later. The financial statements for the transition period filed therewith shall be audited.

(4) If the transition period covers a period of six or fewer months, in lieu of the report required by paragraph (g)(3) of this rule, a report for the transition period may be filed on Form 20–F responding to Items 5, 8.A.7, 13, 14, and 17 or 18 within three months after either the close of the transition period or the date on which the issuer made the determination to change the fiscal closing date, whichever is later. The financial statements required by either Item 17 or Item 18 shall be furnished for the transition period. Such financial statements may be unaudited and condensed as permitted in Article 10 of Regulation S–X (§ 210.10–01 of this chapter), but if the financial statements are unaudited and condensed, the issuer shall file with the first annual report for the newly adopted fiscal year separate audited statements of income and cash flows covering the transition period.

(5) Notwithstanding the foregoing in paragraphs (g)(2), (g)(3), and (g)(4) of this rule, if the transition period covers a period of one month or less, a foreign private issuer need not file a separate transition report if the first annual report for the newly adopted fiscal year covers the transition period as well as the fiscal year.

(h) The provisions of this rule shall not apply to investment companies required to file reports pursuant to Rule 30b1–1 under the Investment Company Act of 1940.

(i) No filing fee shall be required for a transition report filed pursuant to this rule.

Note 1: In addition to the report or reports required to be filed pursuant to this rule, every issuer, except a foreign private issuer or an investment company required to file reports pursuant to Rule 30b1–1 under the Investment Company Act of 1940, that changes its fiscal closing date is required to file a report on Form 8–K responding to Item 8 thereof within the period specified in General Instruction B.1. to that form.

Note 2: The report or reports to be filed pursuant to this section must include the certification required by § 240.13a–14.

(j)(1) For transition reports to be filed on the form appropriate for annual reports of the issuer, the number of days shall be:

(i) For accelerated filers (as defined in § 240.12b–2):

(A) 90 days for fiscal years ending on or after December 15, 2002 and before December 15, 2003;

(B) 75 days for fiscal years ending on or after December 15, 2003 and before December 15, 2004; and

(C) 60 days for fiscal years ending on or after December 15, 2005; and

(ii) 90 days for all other issuers; and

(2) For transition reports to be filed on Form 10–Q or Form 10–QSB (§ 249.308a or § 249.308b of this chapter), the number of days shall be:

(i) For accelerated filers (as defined in § 240.12b–2):

(A) 45 days for fiscal years ending on or after December 15, 2002 and before December 15, 2004;

(B) 40 days for fiscal years ending on or after December 15, 2004 and before December 15, 2006; and

(C) 35 days for fiscal years ending on or after December 15, 2006; and

(ii) 45 days for all other issuers.

(k)(1) Paragraphs (a) through (g) of this section shall not apply to asset-backed issuers.

(2) Every asset-backed issuer that changes its fiscal closing date shall file a report covering the resulting transition period between the closing date of its most recent fiscal year and the opening date of its new fiscal year. In no event shall a transition report cover a period longer than 12 months.

(3) The report for the transition period shall be filed on Form 10–K (§ 249.310 of this chapter) responding to all items to which such asset-backed issuer is required to respond pursuant to General Instruction J. of Form 10–K. Such report shall be filed within 90 days after the later of either the close of the transition period or the date on which the issuer made the determination to change the fiscal closing date.

(4) Notwithstanding the foregoing in paragraphs (k)(2) and (k)(3) of this section, if the transition period covers a period of one month or less, an asset-backed issuer need not file a separate transition report if the first annual report for the newly adopted fiscal year covers the transition period as well as the fiscal year.

(5) Any obligation of the asset-backed issuer to file distribution reports pursuant to § 240.13a–17 will continue to apply regardless of a change in the asset-backed issuer's fiscal closing date.

Note 1: In addition to the report or reports required to be filed pursuant to this section, every issuer, except a foreign private issuer or an investment company required to file reports pursuant to § 270.30b1–1 of this chapter, that changes its fiscal closing date is required to file a Form 8–K (§ 249.308 of this chapter) report that includes the information required by Item 5.03 of Form 8–K within the period specified in General Instruction B.1. to that form.

Rule 13a–11. Current Reports on Form 8–K

(a) Except as provided in paragraph (b) of this section, every registrant subject to Rule 13a–11 shall file a current report on Form 8–K within the period specified in that form, unless substantially the same information as that required by Form 8–K has been previously reported by the registrant.

(b) This section shall not apply to foreign governments, foreign private issuers required to make reports on Form 6–K (17 CFR 249.306) pursuant to § 240.13a–16, issuers of American Depositary Receipts for securities of any foreign issuer, or investment companies required to file reports pursuant to § 270.30b1–1 of this chapter under the Investment Company Act of 1940, except where such investment companies are required to file notice of a blackout period pursuant to § 245.104 of this chapter.

(c) No failure to file a report on Form 8–K that is required solely pursuant to Item 1.01, 1.02, 2.03, 2.04, 2.05, 2.06 or 4.02(a) or 6.03 of Form 8–K shall be deemed to be a violation of 15 U.S.C. 78j(b) and § 240.10b–5.

Rule 13a–13. Quarterly Reports on Form 10–Q and Form 10–QSB

(a) Except as provided in paragraphs (b) and (c) of this rule, every issuer that has securities registered pursuant to section 12 of the Act and is required to file annual reports pursuant to section 13 of the Act, and has filed or intends to file such reports, on Form 10–K and Form 10–KSB or U5S shall file a quarterly report on Form 10–Q and Form 10–QSB within the period specified in General Instruction A.1. to that form for each of the first three quarters of each fiscal year of the issuer, commencing with the first fiscal quarter following the most recent fiscal year for which full financial statements were included in the registration statement, or, if the registration statement included financial statements for an interim period subsequent to the most recent fiscal year end meeting the requirements of Article 10 of Regulation S–X, for the first fiscal quarter subsequent to the quarter reported upon in the registration statement. The first quarterly report of the issuer shall be filed either within 45 days after the effective date of the registration statement or on or before the date on which such report would have been required to be filed if the issuer had been required to file reports on Form 10–Q and Form 10–QSB as of its last fiscal quarter, whichever is later.

(b) The provisions of this rule shall not apply to the following issuers:

(1) Investment companies required to file reports pursuant to Rule 30b1–1; or

(2) Foreign private issuers required to file reports pursuant to Rule 13a–16; and

(3) Asset-backed issuers required to file reports pursuant to § 240.13a–17.

(c) Part I of the quarterly reports on Form 10–Q or Form 10–QSB need not be filed by:

(1) Mutual life insurance companies; or

(2) Mining companies not in the production stage but engaged primarily in the exploration for the development of mineral deposits other than oil, gas or coal, if all of the following conditions are met:

(i) The registrant has not been in production during the current fiscal year or the two years immediately prior thereto; except that being in production for an aggregate period of not more than eight months over the three-year period shall not be a violation of this condition.

(ii) Receipts from the sale of mineral products or from the operations of mineral producing properties by the registrant and its subsidiaries combined have not exceeded $500,000 in any of the most recent six years and have not aggregated more than $1,500,000 in the most recent six fiscal years.

(d) Notwithstanding the foregoing provisions of this rule, the financial information required by Part I of Form 10-Q and Form 10-QSB shall not be deemed to be "filed" for the purpose of section 18 of the Act or otherwise subject to the liabilities of that section of the Act but shall be subject to all other provisions of the Act.

Rule 13a-14. Certification of Disclosure in Annual and Quarterly Reports

(a) Each report, including transition reports, filed on Form 10-Q, Form 10-QSB, Form 10-K, Form 10-KSB, Form 20-F or Form 40-F (§§ 249.308a, 249.308b, 249.310, 249.310b, 249.220f or 249.240f of this chapter) under section 13(a) of the Act (15 U.S.C. 78m(a)), other than a report filed by an Asset-Backed Issuer (as defined in § 229.1101 of this chapter), must include certifications in the form specified in the applicable exhibit filing requirements of such report and such certifications must be filed as an exhibit to such report. Each principal executive and principal financial officer of the issuer, or persons performing similar functions, at the time of filing of the report must sign a certification.

(b) Each periodic report containing financial statements filed by an issuer pursuant to section 13(a) of the Act (15 U.S.C. 78m(a)) must be accompanied by the certifications required by Section 1350 of Chapter 63 of Title 18 of the United States Code (18 U.S.C. 1350) and such certifications must be furnished as an exhibit to such report as specified in the applicable exhibit requirements for such report. Each principal executive and principal financial officer of the issuer (or equivalent thereof) must sign a certification. This requirement may be satisfied by a single certification signed by an issuer's principal executive and principal financial officers.

(c) A person required to provide a certification specified in paragraph (a), (b) or (d) of this section may not have the certification signed on his or her behalf pursuant to a power of attorney or other form of confirming authority.

(d) Each annual report and transition report filed on Form 10-K (§ 249.310 of this chapter) by an asset-backed issuer under section 13(a) of the Act (15 U.S.C. 78m(a)) must include a certification in the form specified in the applicable exhibit filing requirements of such report and such certification must be filed as an exhibit to such report. Terms used in paragraphs (d) and (e) of this section have the same meaning as in Item 1101 of Regulation AB (§ 229.1101 of this chapter).

(e) With respect to asset-backed issuers, the certification required by paragraph (d) of this section must be signed by either:

(1) The senior officer in charge of securitization of the depositor if the depositor is signing the report; or

(2) The senior officer in charge of the servicing function of the servicer if the servicer is signing the report on behalf of the issuing entity. If multiple servicers are involved in servicing the pool assets, the senior officer in charge of the servicing function of the master servicer (or entity performing the equivalent function) must sign if a representative of the servicer is to sign the report on behalf of the issuing entity.

Rule 13a-15. Controls and Procedures

(a) Every issuer that has a class of securities registered pursuant to section 12 of the Act (15 U.S.C. 78l), other than an Asset-Backed Issuer (as defined in § 229.1101 of this chapter), a small business investment company registered on Form N-5 (§§ 239.24 and 274.5 of this chapter), or a unit investment trust as defined by section 4(2) of the Investment Company Act of 1940 (15 U.S.C. 80a-4(2)), must maintain disclosure controls and procedures (as defined in paragraph (e) of this section) and internal control over financial reporting (as defined in paragraph (f) of this section).

(b) Each such issuer's management must evaluate, with the participation of the issuer's principal executive and principal financial officers, or persons performing similar functions, the effectiveness of the issuer's disclosure controls and procedures, as of the end of each fiscal quarter, except that management must perform this evaluation:

(1) In the case of a foreign private issuer (as defined in § 240.3b–4) as of the end of each fiscal year; and

(2) In the case of an investment company registered under section 8 of the Investment Company Act of 1940 (15 U.S.C. 80a–8), within the 90-day period prior to the filing date of each report requiring certification under § 270.30a–2 of this chapter.

(c) The management of each such issuer, other than an investment company registered under section 8 of the Investment Company Act of 1940, must evaluate, with the participation of the issuer's principal executive and principal financial officers, or persons performing similar functions, the effectiveness, as of the end of each fiscal year, of the issuer's internal control over financial reporting. The framework on which management's evaluation of the issuer's internal control over financial reporting is based must be a suitable, recognized control framework that is established by a body or group that has followed due-process procedures, including the broad distribution of the framework for public comment.

(d) The management of each such issuer, other than an investment company registered under section 8 of the Investment Company Act of 1940, must evaluate, with the participation of the issuer's principal executive and principal financial officers, or persons performing similar functions, any change in the issuer's internal control over financial reporting, that occurred during each of the issuer's fiscal quarters, or fiscal year in the case of a foreign private issuer, that has materially affected, or is reasonably likely to materially affect, the issuer's internal control over financial reporting.

(e) For purposes of this section, the term *disclosure controls and procedures* means controls and other procedures of an issuer that are designed to ensure that information required to be disclosed by the issuer in the reports that it files or submits under the Act (15 U.S.C. 78a *et seq.*) is recorded, processed, summarized and reported, within the time periods specified in the Commission's rules and forms. Disclosure controls and procedures include, without limitation, controls and procedures designed to ensure that information required to be disclosed by an issuer in the reports that it files or submits under the Act is accumulated and communicated to the issuer's management, including its principal executive and principal financial officers, or persons performing similar functions, as appropriate to allow timely decisions regarding required disclosure.

(f) The certification requirements of this section do not apply to XBRL-Related Documents, as defined in § 232.11 of this chapter.

Rule 13a–16. Reports of Foreign Private Issuers on Form 6–K

(a) Every foreign private issuer which is subject to Rule 13a–1 shall make reports on Form 6–K, except that this rule shall not apply to:

(1) Investment companies required to file reports pursuant to Rule 30b1–1; or

(2) issuers of American depositary receipts for securities of any foreign issuer; or

(3) Issuers filing periodic reports on Form 10–K, 10–Q and 8–K; or

(4) Asset-backed issuers, as defined in § 229.1101 of this chapter.

(b) Such reports shall be transmitted promptly after the information required by Form 6–K is made public by the issuer, by the country of its domicile or under the laws of which it was incorporated or organized, or by a foreign securities exchange with which the issuer has filed the information.

(c) Reports furnished pursuant to this rule shall not be deemed to be "filed" for the purpose of section 18 of the Act or otherwise subject to the liabilities of that section.

Rule 13a–17 Reports of Asset-Backed Issuers on Form 10–D (§ 249.312 of this chapter).

Every asset-backed issuer subject to § 240.13a–1 shall make reports on Form 10–D (§ 249.312 of this chapter). Such reports shall be filed within the period specified in Form 10-D.

Rule 13a–18. Compliance with servicing criteria for asset-backed securities.

(a) This section applies to every class of asset-backed securities subject to the reporting requirements of section 13(a) of the Act (15 U.S.C. 78m(a)). Terms used in this section have the same meaning as in Item 1101 of Regulation AB (§ 229.1101 of this chapter).

(b) *Reports on assessments of compliance with servicing criteria for asset-backed securities required.* With regard to a class of asset-backed securities subject to the reporting requirements of section 13(a) of the Act, the annual report on Form 10–K (§ 249.308 of this chapter) for such class must include from each party participating in the servicing function a report regarding its assessment of compliance with the servicing criteria specified in paragraph (d) of Item 1122 of Regulation AB (§ 229.1122(d) of this chapter), as of and for the period ending the end of each fiscal year, with respect to asset-backed securities transactions taken as a whole involving the party participating in the servicing function and that are backed by the same asset type backing the class of asset-backed securities (including the asset-backed securities transaction that is to be the subject of the report on Form 10–K for that fiscal year).

(c) *Attestation reports on assessments of compliance with servicing criteria for asset-backed securities required.* With respect to each report included pursuant to paragraph (b) of this section, the annual report on Form 10–K must also include a report by a registered public accounting firm that attests to, and reports on, the assessment made by the asserting party. The attestation report on assessment of compliance with servicing criteria for asset-backed securities must be made in accordance with standards for attestation engagements issued or adopted by the Public Company Accounting Oversight Board.

Note to § 240.13a–18. If multiple parties are participating in the servicing function, a separate assessment report and attestation report must be included for each party participating in the servicing function. A party participating in the servicing function means any entity (e.g., master servicer, primary servicers, trustees) that is performing activities that address the criteria in paragraph (d) of Item 1122 of Regulation AB (§ 229.1122(d) of this chapter), unless such entity's activities relate only to 5% or less of the pool assets.

Rule 13b2–1. Falsification of Accounting Records

No person shall, directly or indirectly, falsify or cause to be falsified, any book, record or account subject to section 13(b)(2)(A) of the Securities Exchange Act.

Rule 13b2–2. Issuer's Representations in Connection With the Preparation of Required Reports and Documents

(a) No director or officer of an issuer shall, directly or indirectly:

(1) Make or cause to be made a materially false or misleading statement to an accountant in connection with; or

(2) Omit to state, or cause another person to omit to state, any material fact necessary in order to make statements made, in light of the circumstances under which such statements were made, not misleading, to an accountant in connection with:

(i) Any audit, review or examination of the financial statements of the issuer required to be made pursuant to this subpart; or

(ii) The preparation or filing of any document or report required to be filed with the Commission pursuant to this subpart or otherwise.

(b)(1) No officer or director of an issuer, or any other person acting under the direction thereof, shall directly or indirectly take any action to coerce, manipulate, mislead, or fraudulently influence any independent public or certified public accountant engaged in the performance of an audit or review of the financial statements of that issuer that are required to be filed with the Commission pursuant to this subpart or otherwise if that person knew or should have known that such action, if successful, could result in rendering the issuer's financial statements materially misleading.

(2) For purposes of paragraphs (b)(1) and (c)(2) of this section, actions that, "if successful, could result in rendering the issuer's financial statements materially misleading" include, but are not limited to, actions taken at any time with respect to the professional engagement period to coerce, manipulate, mislead, or fraudulently influence an auditor:

(i) To issue or reissue a report on an issuer's financial statements that is not warranted in the circumstances (due to material violations of generally accepted accounting principles, generally accepted auditing standards, or other professional or regulatory standards);

(ii) Not to perform audit, review or other procedures required by generally accepted auditing standards or other professional standards;

(iii) Not to withdraw an issued report; or

(iv) Not to communicate matters to an issuer's audit committee.

(c) In addition, in the case of an investment company registered under section 8 of the Investment Company Act of 1940 (15 U.S.C. 80a–8), or a business development company as defined in section 2(a)(48) of the Investment Company Act of 1940 (15 U.S.C. 80a–2(a)(48)), no officer or director of the company's investment adviser, sponsor, depositor, trustee, or administrator (or, in the case of paragraph (c)(2) of this section, any other person acting under the direction thereof) shall, directly or indirectly:

(1)(i) Make or cause to be made a materially false or misleading statement to an accountant in connection with; or

(ii) Omit to state, or cause another person to omit to state, any material fact necessary in order to make statements made, in light of the circumstances under which such statements were made, not misleading to an accountant in connection with:

(A) Any audit, review, or examination of the financial statements of the investment company required to be made pursuant to this subpart; or

(B) The preparation or filing of any document or report required to be filed with the Commission pursuant to this subpart or otherwise; or

(2) Take any action to coerce, manipulate, mislead, or fraudulently influence any independent public or certified public accountant engaged in the performance of an audit or review of the financial statements of that investment company that are required to be filed with the Commission pursuant to this subpart or otherwise if that person knew or should have known that such action, if successful, could result in rendering the investment company's financial statements materially misleading.

REGULATION 13D–G

ATTENTION ELECTRONIC FILERS

THIS REGULATION SHOULD BE READ IN CONJUNCTION WITH REGULATION S–T (PART 232 OF THIS CHAPTER), WHICH GOVERNS THE PREPARATION AND SUBMISSION OF DOCUMENTS IN ELECTRONIC FORMAT. MANY PROVISIONS RELATING TO THE PREPARATION

AND SUBMISSION OF DOCUMENTS IN PAPER FORMAT CONTAINED IN THIS REGULATION ARE SUPERSEDED BY THE PROVISIONS OF REGULATION S–T FOR DOCUMENTS REQUIRED TO BE FILED IN ELECTRONIC FORMAT.

Rule 13d–1. Filing of Schedule 13D and 13G

(a) Any person who, after acquiring directly or indirectly the beneficial ownership of any equity security of a class which is specified in paragraph (i) of this section, is directly or indirectly the beneficial owner of more than five percent of the class shall, within 10 days after the acquisition, file with the Commission, a statement containing the information required by Schedule 13D (§ 240.13d–101).

(b)(1) A person who would otherwise be obligated under paragraph (a) of this section to file a statement on Schedule 13D (§ 240.13d–101) may, in lieu thereof, file with the Commission, a short-form statement on Schedule 13G (§ 240.13d–102), *Provided,* That:

(i) Such person has acquired such securities in the ordinary course of his business and not with the purpose nor with the effect of changing or influencing the control of the issuer, nor in connection with or as a participant in any transaction having such purpose or effect, including any transaction subject to Rule 13d–3(b); and

(ii) Such person is:

(A) A broker or dealer registered under section 15 of the Act (15 U.S.C. 78o);

(B) A bank as defined in section 3(a)(6) of the Act (15 U.S.C. 78c);

(C) An insurance company as defined in section 3(a)(19) of the Act (15 U.S.C. 78c);

(D) An investment company registered under section 8 of the Investment Company Act of 1940 (15 U.S.C. 80a–8);

(E) Any person registered as an investment adviser under Section 203 of the Investment Advisers Act of 1940 (15 U.S.C. 80b–3) or under the laws of any state;

(F) An employee benefit plan as defined in Section 3(3) of the Employee Retirement Income Security Act of 1974, as amended, 29 U.S.C. 1001 et seq. ("ERISA") that is subject to the provisions of ERISA, or any such plan that is not subject to ERISA that is maintained primarily for the benefit of the employees of a state or local government or instrumentality, or an endowment fund;

(G) A parent holding company or control person, provided the aggregate amount held directly by the parent or control person, and directly and indirectly by their subsidiaries or affiliates that are not persons specified in § 240.13d–1(b)(1)(ii)(A) through (I), does not exceed one percent of the securities of the subject class;

(H) A savings association as defined in Section 3(b) of the Federal Deposit Insurance Act (12 U.S.C. 1813);

(I) A church plan that is excluded from the definition of an investment company under section 3(c)(14) of the Investment Company Act of 1940 (15 U.S.C. 80a–3); and

(J) A group, provided that all the members are persons specified in § 240.13d–1(b)(1)(ii)(A) through (I); and

(iii) Such person has promptly notified any other person (or group within the meaning of Section 13(d)(3) of the Act) on whose behalf it holds, on a discretionary basis, securities exceeding five percent of the class, of any acquisition or transaction on behalf of such other person which might be reportable by the person under Section 13(d) of the Act. This paragraph only requires notice to the account owner of information which the filing person reasonably should be expected to know and which would advise the account owner of an obligation he may have to file a statement pursuant to Section 13(d) of the Act or an amendment thereto.

(2) The Schedule 13G filed pursuant to paragraph (b)(1) of this section shall be filed within 45 days after the end of the calendar year in which the person became obligated under paragraph (b)(1) of this section to report the person's beneficial ownership as of the last day of the calendar year, Provided, That it shall not be necessary to file a Schedule 13G unless the percentage of the class of equity security specified in paragraph (i) of this section beneficially owned as of the end of the calendar year is more than five percent; However, if the person's direct or indirect beneficial ownership exceeds 10 percent of the class of equity securities prior to the end of the calendar year, the initial Schedule 13G shall be filed within 10 days after the end of the first month in which the person's direct or indirect beneficial ownership exceeds 10 percent of the class of equity securities, computed as of the last day of the month.

(c) A person who would otherwise be obligated under paragraph (a) of this section to file a statement on Schedule 13D (§ 240.13d–101) may, in lieu thereof, file with the Commission, within 10 days after an acquisition described in paragraph (a) of this section, a short-form statement on Schedule 13G (§ 240.13d–102). *Provided,* That the person:

(1) Has not acquired the securities with any purpose, or with the effect of, changing or influencing the control of the issuer, or in connection with or as a participant in any transaction having that purpose or effect, including any transaction subject to § 240.13d–3(b);

(2) Is not a person reporting pursuant to paragraph (b)(1) of this section; and

(3) Is not directly or indirectly the beneficial owner of 20 percent or more of the class.

(d) Any person who, as of the end of any calendar year, is or becomes directly or indirectly the beneficial owner of more than five percent of any equity security of a class specified in paragraph (i) of this section and who is not required to file a statement under paragraph (a) of this section by virtue of the exemption provided by Section 13(d)(6)(A) or (B) of the Act (15 U.S.C. 78m(d)(6)(A) or 78m(d)(6)(B)), or because the beneficial ownership was acquired prior to December 22, 1970, or because the person otherwise (except for the exemption provided by Section 13(d)(6)(C) of the Act (15 U.S.C. 78m(d)(6)(C))) is not required to file a statement, shall file with the Commission, within 45 days after the end of the calendar year in which the person became obligated to report under this paragraph (d), a statement containing the information required by Schedule 13G (§ 240.13d–102).

(e)(1) Notwithstanding paragraph (b) and (c) of this section and § 240.13d–2(b), a person that has reported that it is the beneficial owner of more than five percent of a class of equity securities in a statement on Schedule 13G (§ 240.13d–102) pursuant to paragraph (b) or (c) of this section, or is required to report the acquisition but has not yet filed the schedule, shall immediately become subject to §§ 240.13d–1(a) and 240.13d–2(a) and shall file a statement on Schedule 13D (§ 240.13d–101) within 10 days if, and shall remain subject to those requirements for so long as, the person:

(i) Has acquired or holds the securities with a purpose or effect of changing or influencing control of the issuer, or in connection with or as a participant in any transaction having that purpose or effect, including any transaction subject to § 240.13d–3(b); and

(ii) Is at that time the beneficial owner of more than five percent of a class of equity securities described in § 240.13d–1(i).

(2) From the time the person has acquired or holds the securities with a purpose or effect of changing or influencing control of the issuer, or in connection with or as a participant in any transaction having that purpose or effect until the expiration of the tenth day from the date of the filing of the Schedule 13D (§ 240.13d–101) pursuant to this section, that person shall not:

(i) Vote or direct the voting of the securities described therein; or

(ii) Acquire an additional beneficial ownership interest in any equity securities of the issuer of the securities, nor of any person controlling the issuer.

(f)(1) Notwithstanding paragraph (c) of this section and § 240.13d–2(b), persons reporting on Schedule 13G (§ 240.13d–102) pursuant to paragraph (c) of this section shall immediately become subject to §§ 240.13d–1(a) and 240.13d–2(a) and shall remain subject to those requirements for so long as, and shall file a statement on Schedule 13D (§ 240.13d–101) within 10 days of the date on which, the person's beneficial ownership equals or exceeds 20 percent of the class of equity securities.

(2) From the time of the acquisition of 20 percent or more of the class of equity securities until the expiration of the tenth day from the date of the filing of the Schedule 13D (§ 240.13d–101) pursuant to this section, the person shall not:

(i) Vote or direct the voting of the securities described therein, or

(ii) Acquire an additional beneficial ownership interest in any equity securities of the issuer of the securities, nor of any person controlling the issuer.

(g) Any person who has reported an acquisition of securities in a statement on Schedule 13G (§ 240.13d–102) pursuant to paragraph (b) of this section, or has become obligated to report on the Schedule 13G (§ 240.13d–102) but has not yet filed the Schedule, and thereafter ceases to be a person specified in paragraph (b)(1)(ii) of this section or determines that it no longer has acquired or holds the securities in the ordinary course of business shall immediately become subject to § 240.13d–1(a) or § 240.13d–1(c) (if the person satisfies the requirements specified in § 240.13d–1(c)), and §§ 240.13d–2(a), (b) of (d), and shall file, within 10 days thereafter, a statement on Schedule 13D (§ 240.13d–101) or amendment to Schedule 13G, as applicable, if the person is a beneficial owner at that time of more than five percent of the class of equity securities.

(h) Any person who has filed a Schedule 13D (§ 240.13d–101) pursuant to paragraph (e), (f) or (g) of this section may again report its beneficial ownership on Schedule 13G (§ 240.13d–102) pursuant to paragraphs (b) or (c) of this section provided the person qualifies thereunder, as applicable, by filing a Schedule 13G (§ 240.13d–102) once the person determines that the provisions of paragraph (e), (f) or (g) of this section no longer apply.

(i) For the purpose of this regulation, the term "equity security" means any equity security of a class which is registered pursuant to Section 12 of that Act, or any equity security of any insurance company which would have been required to be so registered except for the exemption contained in Section 12(g)(2)(G) of the Act, or any equity security issued by a closed-end investment company registered under the Investment Company Act of 1940; *Provided,* Such term shall not include securities of a class of non-voting securities.

(j) For the purpose of Sections 13(d) and 13(g), any person, in determining the amount of outstanding securities of a class of equity securities, may rely upon information set forth in the issuer's most recent quarterly or annual report, and any current report subsequent thereto, filed with the Commission pursuant to this Act, unless he knows or has reason to believe that the information contained therein is inaccurate.

(k)(1) Whenever two or more persons are required to file a statement containing the information required by Schedule 13D or Schedule 13G with respect to the same securities, only one statement need be filed: *Provided,* That:

(i) Each person on whose behalf the statement is filed is individually eligible to use the Schedule on which the information is filed;

(ii) Each person on whose behalf the statement is filed is responsible for the timely filing of such statement and any amendments thereto, and for the completeness and accuracy of the information concerning such person contained therein; such person is not responsible for the completeness or accuracy of the information concerning the other persons making the filing, unless such person knows or has reason to believe that such information is inaccurate; and

(iii) Such statement identifies all such persons, contains the required information with regard to each such person, indicates that such statement is filed on behalf of all such persons, and includes, as an exhibit, their agreement in writing that such a statement is filed on behalf of each of them.

(2) A group's filing obligation may be satisfied either by a single joint filing or by each of the group's members making an individual filing. If the group's members elect to make their own filings, each such filing should identify all members of the group but the information provided concerning the other persons making the filing need only reflect information which the filing person knows or has reason to know.

Rule 13d–2. Filing of Amendments to Schedules 13D or 13G

(a) If any material change occurs in the facts set forth in the Schedule 13D (§ 240.13d-101) required by § 240.13d–1(a), including, but not limited to, any material increase or decrease in the percentage of the class beneficially owned, the person or persons who were required to file the statement shall promptly file or cause to be filed with the Commission an amendment disclosing that change. An acquisition or disposition of beneficial ownership of securities in an amount equal to one percent or more of the class of securities shall be deemed "material" for purposes of this section; acquisitions or dispositions of less than those amounts may be material, depending upon the facts and circumstances.

(b) Notwithstanding paragraph (a) of this section, and provided that the person filing a Schedule 13G (§ 240.13d–102) pursuant to § 240.13d–1(b) or § 240.13d–1(c) continues to meet the requirements set forth therein, any person who has filed a Schedule 13G (§ 240.13d–102) pursuant to § 240.13d–1(b), § 240.13d–1(c) or § 240.13d–1(d) shall amend the statement within forty-five days after the end of each calendar year if, as of the end of the calendar year, there are any changes in the information reported in the previous filing on that Schedule: Provided, however, That an amendment need not be filed with respect to a change in the percent of class outstanding previously reported if the change results solely from a change in the aggregate number of securities outstanding. Once an amendment has been filed reflecting beneficial ownership of five percent or less of the class of securities, no additional filings are required unless the person thereafter becomes the beneficial owner of more than five percent of the class and is required to file pursuant to § 240.13d–1.

(c) Any person relying on § 240.13d–1(b) that has filed its initial Schedule 13G (§ 240.13d–102) pursuant to that paragraph shall, in addition to filing any amendments pursuant to § 240.13d–2(b), file an amendment on Schedule 13G (§ 240.13d–102) within 10 days after the end of the first month in which the person's direct or indirect beneficial ownership, computed as of the last day of the month, exceeds 10 percent of the class of equity securities. Thereafter, that person shall, in addition to filing any amendments pursuant to § 240.13d–2(b), file an amendment on Schedule 13G (§ 240.13d–102) within 10 days after the end of the first month in which the person's direct or indirect beneficial ownership, computed as of the last day of the month, increases or decreases by more than five percent of the class of equity securities. Once an amendment has been filed reflecting beneficial ownership of five percent or less of the class of securities, no additional filings are required by this paragraph (c).

(d) Any person relying on § 240.13d–1(c) and has filed its initial Schedule 13G (§ 240.13d–102) pursuant to that paragraph shall, in addition to filing any amendments pursuant to § 240.13d–2(b), file an amendment on Schedule 13G (§ 240.13d–102) promptly upon acquiring, directly or indirectly, greater than 10 percent of a class of equity securities specified in § 240.13d–1(d), and thereafter promptly upon increasing or decreasing its beneficial ownership by more than five percent of the class of equity securities. Once an amendment has been filed reflecting beneficial ownership of five percent or less of the class of securities, no additional filings are required by this paragraph (d).

(e) The first electronic amendment to a paper format Schedule 13D (§ 240.13d–101 of this chapter) or Schedule 13G (§ 240.13d–102 of this chapter) shall restate the entire text of the Schedule 13D or 13G, but previously filed paper exhibits to such Schedules are not required to be restated electronically. See Rule 102 of Regulation S–T (§ 232.102 of this chapter) regarding amendments to exhibits previously filed in paper format. Notwithstanding the foregoing, if the sole purpose of filing the first electronic Schedule 13D or 13G amendment is to report a change in beneficial ownership that would terminate the filer's obligation to report, the amendment need not include a restatement of the entire text of the Schedule being amended.

Note to § 240.13d–2: For persons filing a short-form statement pursuant to Rule 13d–1(b) or (c), see also Rules 13d–1(e), (f), and (g).

Rule 13d–3. Determination of Beneficial Owner

(a) For the purposes of section 13(d) and 13(g) of the Act a beneficial owner of a security includes any person who, directly or indirectly, through any contract, arrangement, understanding, relationship, or otherwise has or shares:

(1) *Voting power* which includes the power to vote, or to direct the voting of, such security; and/or,

(2) *Investment power* which includes the power to dispose, or to direct the disposition, of such security.

(b) Any person who, directly or indirectly, creates or uses a trust, proxy, power of attorney, pooling arrangement or any other contract, arrangement, or device with the purpose or effect of divesting such person of beneficial ownership of a security or preventing the vesting of such beneficial ownership as part of a plan or scheme to evade the reporting requirements of section 13(d) or 13(g) of the Act shall be deemed for purposes of such section to be the beneficial owner of such security.

(c) All securities of the same class beneficially owned by a person, regardless of the form which such beneficial ownership takes, shall be aggregated in calculating the number of shares beneficially owned by such person.

(d) Notwithstanding the provisions of paragraphs (a) and (c) of this rule:

(1)(i) A person shall be deemed to be the beneficial owner of a security, subject to the provisions of paragraph (b) of this rule, if that person has the right to acquire beneficial ownership of such security, as defined in Rule 13d–3(a) within sixty days, including but not limited to any right to acquire: (A) through the exercise of any option, warrant or right; (B) through the conversion of a security; (C) pursuant to the power to revoke a trust, discretionary account, or similar arrangement; or (D) pursuant to the automatic termination of a trust, discretionary account or similar arrangement; *Provided, however,* any person who acquires a security or power specified in paragraphs (A), (B) or (C), above, with the purpose or effect of changing or influencing the control of the issuer, or in connection with or as a participant in any transaction having such purpose or effect, immediately upon such acquisition shall be deemed to be the beneficial owner of the securities which may be acquired through the exercise or conversion of such security or power. Any securities not outstanding which are subject to such options, warrants, rights or conversion privileges shall be deemed to be outstanding for the purpose of computing the percentage of outstanding securities of the class owned by such person but shall not be deemed to be outstanding for the purpose of computing the percentage of the class by any other person.

(ii) Paragraph (d)(1)(i) of this section remains applicable for the purpose of determining the obligation to file with respect to the underlying security even though the option, warrant, right or convertible security is of a class of equity security, as defined in § 240.13d–1(i), and may therefore give rise to a separate obligation to file.

(2) A member of a national securities exchange shall not be deemed to be a beneficial owner of securities held directly or indirectly by it on behalf of another person solely because such member is the record holder of such securities and, pursuant to the rules of such exchange, may direct the vote of such securities, without instruction, on other than contested matters or matters that may affect substantially the rights or privileges of the holders of the securities to be voted, but is otherwise precluded by the rules of such exchange from voting without instruction.

(3) A person who in the ordinary course of business is a pledgee of securities under a written pledge agreement shall not be deemed to be the beneficial owner of such pledged securities until the pledgee has taken all formal steps necessary which are required to declare a default and determines that the power to vote or to direct the vote or to dispose or to direct the disposition of such pledged securities will be exercised, provided that:

(i) The pledgee agreement is bona fide and was not entered into with the purpose nor with the effect of changing or influencing the control of the issuer, nor in connection with any transaction having such purpose or effect, including any transaction subject to Rule 13d–3(b);

(ii) The pledgee is a person specified in Rule 13d–1(b)(ii), including persons meeting the conditions set forth in paragraph (G) thereof; and

(iii) The pledgee agreement, prior to default, does not grant to the pledgee:

(A) The power to vote or to direct the vote of the pledged securities; or

(B) The power to dispose or direct the disposition of the pledged securities, other than the grant of such power(s) pursuant to a pledge agreement under which credit is extended subject to Regulation T and in which the pledgee is a broker or dealer registered under section 15 of the Act.

(4) A person engaged in business as an underwriter of securities who acquires securities through his participation in good faith in a firm commitment underwriting registered under the Securities Act of 1933 shall not be deemed to be the beneficial owner of such securities until the expiration of forty days after the date of such acquisition.

Rule 13d–4. Disclaimer of Beneficial Ownership

Any person may expressly declare in any statement filed that the filing of such statement shall not be construed as an admission that such person is, for the purposes of section 13(d) or 13(g) of the Act, the beneficial owner of any securities covered by the statement.

Rule 13d–5. Acquisition of Securities

(a) A person who becomes a beneficial owner of securities shall be deemed to have acquired such securities for purposes of Section 13(d)(1) of the Act, whether such acquisition was through purchase or otherwise. However, executors or administrators of a decedent's estate generally will be presumed not to have acquired beneficial ownership of the securities in the decedent's estate until such time as such executors or administrators are qualified under local law to perform their duties.

(b)(1) When two or more persons agree to act together for the purpose of acquiring, holding, voting or disposing of equity securities of an issuer, the group formed thereby shall be deemed to have acquired beneficial ownership, for purposes of Sections 13(d) and 13(g) of the Act, as of the date of such agreement, of all equity securities of that issuer beneficially owned by any such persons.

(2) Notwithstanding the previous paragraph, a group shall be deemed not to have acquired any equity securities beneficially owned by the other members of the group solely by virtue of their concerted actions relating to the purchase of equity securities directly from an issuer in a transaction not involving a public offering, provided that:

(i) All the members of the group are persons specified in Rule 13d–1(b)(1)(ii);

(ii) The purchase is in the ordinary course of each member's business and not with the purpose nor with the effect of changing or influencing control of the issuer, nor in connection with or as a participant in any transaction having such purpose or effect, including any transaction subject to Rule 13d–3(b);

(iii) There is no agreement among, or between any members of the group to act together with respect to the issuer or its securities except for the purpose of facilitating the specific purchase involved; and

(iv) The only actions among or between any members of the group with respect to the issuer or its securities subsequent to the closing date of the non-public offering are those which are necessary to conclude ministerial matters directly related to the completion of the offer or sale of the securities.

Rule 13d–6. Exemption of Certain Acquisitions

The acquisition of securities of an issuer by a person who, prior to such acquisition, was a beneficial owner of more than five percent of the outstanding securities of the same class as those acquired shall be exempt from section 13(d) of the act, *provided that:*

(a) The acquisition is made pursuant to preemptive subscription rights in an offering made to all holders of securities of the class to which the preemptive subscription rights pertain;

(b) Such person does not acquire additional securities except through the exercise of his pro rata share of the preemptive subscription rights; and

(c) The acquisition is duly reported, if required, pursuant to section 16(a) of the Act and the rules and regulations thereunder.

Rule 13d–7. Dissemination

One copy of the Schedule filed pursuant to §§ 240.13d–1 and 240.13d–2 shall be sent to the issuer of the security at its principal executive office, by registered or certified mail. A copy of Schedules filed pursuant to §§ 240.13d–1(a) and 240.13d–2(a) shall also be sent to each national securities exchange where the security is traded.

Schedule 13D—Information to Be Included in Statements Filed Pursuant to Rule 13d–1(a) and Amendments Thereto Filed Pursuant to Rule 13d–2(a)

SCHEDULE 13D

Under the Securities Exchange Act of 1934

(Amendment No. ______)*

____

(Name of Issuer)

* The remainder of this cover page shall be filled out for a reporting person's initial filing on this form with respect to the subject class of securities, and for any subsequent amendment containing information which would alter disclosures provided in a prior cover page.

The information required on the remainder of this cover page shall not be deemed to be "filed" for the purpose of

(Title of Class of Securities)

(CUSIP Number)

(Name, Address and Telephone Number of Person Authorized to Receive Notices and Communications)

(Date of Event which Requires Filing of this Statement)

If the filing person has previously filed a statement on Schedule 13G to report the acquisition that is the subject of this Schedule 13D, and is filing this schedule because of §§ 240.13d–1(e), 240.13d–1(f) or 240.13d–1(g), check the following box.

Note: Schedules filed in paper format shall include a signed original and five copies of the schedule, including all exhibits. See Rule 13d–7 for other parties to whom copies are to be sent.

CUSIP No.

(1) Names of Reporting Persons. I.R.S. Identification Nos. of Above Persons (Entities Only).		
(2) Check the Appropriate Box if a Member of a Group (See Instructions)		(a) (b)
(3) SEC Use Only		
(4) Source of Funds (See Instructions)		
(5) Check if Disclosure of Legal Proceedings is Required Pursuant to Items 2(d) or 2(e)		
(6) Citizenship or Place of Organization		
Number of Shares Beneficially Owned by Each Reporting Person With	(7) Sole Voting Power	
	(8) Shared Voting Power	
	(9) Sole Dispositive Power	
	(10) Shared Dispositive Power	
(11) Aggregate Amount Beneficially Owned by Each Reporting Person		
(12) Check if the Aggregate Amount in Row (11) Excludes Certain Shares (See Instructions)		
(13) Percent of Class Represented by Amount in Row (11)		
(14) Type of Reporting Person (See Instructions)		

INSTRUCTIONS FOR COVER PAGE

(1) *Names and I.R.S. Identification Numbers of Reporting Persons.* Furnish the full legal name of each person for whom the report is filed—i.e., each person required to sign the schedule itself—including each member of a group. Do not include the name of a person required to be identified in the report but who is not a reporting person. Reporting persons that are entities are also requested to furnish

Section 18 of the Securities Exchange Act of 1934 ("Act") or otherwise subject to the liabilities of that section of the Act but shall be subject to all other provisions of the Act (however, see the Notes).

their I.R.S. identification numbers, although disclosure of such numbers is voluntary, not mandatory (see "Special Instructions for Complying With Schedule 13–D" below).

(2) If any of the shares beneficially owned by a reporting person are held as a member of a group and the membership is expressly affirmed, please check row 2(a). If the reporting person disclaims membership in a group or describes a relationship with other person but does not affirm the existence of a group, please check row 2(b) [unless it is a joint filing pursuant to Rule 13d–1(k)(1) in which case it may not be necessary to check row 2(b)].

(3) The 3rd row is for SEC internal use; please leave blank.

(4) Classify the source of funds or other consideration used or to be used in making the purchases as required to be disclosed pursuant to item 3 of Schedule 13D and insert the appropriate symbol (or symbols if more than one is necessary) in row (4):

Category of Source	**Symbol**
Subject Company (Company whose securities are being acquired)	SC
Bank	BK
Affiliate (of reporting person)	AF
Working Capital (of reporting person)	WC
Personal Funds (of reporting person)	PF
Other	OO

(5) If disclosure of legal proceedings or actions is required pursuant to either items 2(d) or 2(e) of Schedule 13D, row 5 should be checked.

(6) *Citizenship or Place of Organization.* Furnish citizenship if the named reporting person is a natural person. Otherwise, furnish place of organization. (See Item 2 of Schedule 13D).

(7)–(11), (13) *Aggregate Amount Beneficially Owned by Each Reporting Person, etc.* Rows (7) through (11), inclusive, and (13) are to be completed in accordance with the provisions of Item 5 of Schedule 13D. All percentages are to be rounded off to nearest tenth (one place after decimal point).

(12) Check if the aggregate amount reported as beneficially owned in row (11) does not include shares which the reporting person discloses in the report but as to which beneficial ownership is disclaimed pursuant to Rule 13d–4 under the Securities Exchange Act of 1934.

(14) *Type of Reporting Person.* Please classify each "reporting person" according to the following breakdown and place the appropriate symbol (or symbols, i.e., if more than one is applicable, insert all applicable symbols) on the form:

Category	**Symbol**
Broker Dealer	BD
Bank	BK
Insurance Company	IC
Investment Company	IV
Investment Adviser	IA
Employee Benefit Plan or Endowment Fund	EP
Parent Holding Company/Control Person	HC
Savings Association	SA
Church Plan	CP
Corporation	CO
Partnership	PN
Individual	IN
Other	OO

NOTES: Attach as many copies of the second part of the cover page as are needed, one reporting person per page.

Filing persons may, in order to avoid unnecessary duplication, answer items on the schedules (Schedule 13D, 13G or 14D–1) by appropriate cross references to an item or items on the cover page(s). This approach may only be used where the cover page item or items provide all the disclosure required by the schedule item. Moreover, such a use of a cover page item will result in the item becoming a part of the schedule and accordingly being considered as "filed" for purposes of Section 18 of the Securities Exchange Act or otherwise subject to the liabilities of that section of the Act.

Reporting persons may comply with their cover page filing requirements by filing either completed copies of the blank forms available from the Commission, printed or typed facsimiles, or computer printed facsimiles, provided the documents filed have identical formats to the forms prescribed in the Commission's regulations and meet existing Securities Exchange Act rules as to such matters as clarity and size (Securities Exchange Act Rule 12b–12).

SPECIAL INSTRUCTIONS FOR COMPLYING WITH SCHEDULE 13D

Under Sections 13(d) and 23 of the Securities Exchange Act of 1934 and the rules and regulations thereunder, the Commission is authorized to solicit the information required to be supplied by this schedule by certain security holders of certain issuers.

Disclosure of the information specified in this schedule is mandatory, except for I.R.S. identification numbers, disclosure of which is voluntary. The information will be used for the primary purpose of determining and disclosing the holdings of certain beneficial owners of certain equity securities. This statement will be made a matter of public record. Therefore, any information given will be available for inspection by any member of the public.

Because of the public nature of the information, the Commission can utilize it for a variety of purposes, including referral to other governmental authorities or securities self-regulatory organizations for investigatory purposes or in connection with litigation involving the Federal securities laws or other civil, criminal or regulatory statutes or provisions. I.R.S. identification numbers, if furnished, will assist the Commission in identifying security holders and, therefore, in promptly processing statements of beneficial ownership of securities.

Failure to disclose the information requested by this schedule, except for I.R.S. identification numbers, may result in civil or criminal action against the persons involved for violation of the Federal securities laws and rules promulgated thereunder.

GENERAL INSTRUCTIONS

A. The item number and captions of the items shall be included but the text of the items is to be omitted. The answers to the items shall be so prepared as to indicate clearly the coverage of the items without referring to the text of the items. Answer every item. If an item is inapplicable or the answer is in the negative, so state.

B. Information contained in exhibits to the statement may be incorporated by reference in answer or partial answer to any item or sub-item of the statement unless it would render such answer misleading, incomplete, unclear or confusing. Material incorporated by reference shall be clearly identified in the reference by page, paragraph, caption or otherwise. An express statement that the specified matter is incorporated by reference shall be made at the particular place in the statement where the information is required. A copy of any information or a copy of the pertinent pages of a document containing such information which is incorporated by reference shall be submitted with this statement as an exhibit and shall be deemed to be filed with the Commission for all purposes of the Act.

C. If the statement is filed by a general or limited partnership, syndicate, or other group, the information called for by Items 2–6, inclusive, shall be given with respect to (i) each partner of such general partnership; (ii) each partner who is denominated as a general partner or who functions as a general partner of such limited partnership; (iii) each member of such syndicate or group; and (iv) each person controlling such partner or member. If the statement is filed by a corporation or if a person referred to in (i), (ii), (iii) or (iv) of this Instruction is a corporation, the information called for by the above mentioned items shall be given with respect to (a) each executive officer and director of such corporation; (b) each person controlling such corporation; and (c) each executive officer and director of any corporation or other person ultimately in control of such corporation.

Item 1. Security and Issuer

State the title of the class of equity securities to which this statement relates and the name and address of the principal executive offices of the issuer of such securities.

Item 2. Identity and Background

If the person filing this statement or any person enumerated in Instruction C of this statement is a corporation, general partnership, limited partnership, syndicate or other group of persons, state its name, the state or other place of its organization, its principal business, the address of its principal business, the address of its principal office and the information required by (d) and (e) of this Item. If the person filing this statement or any person enumerated in Instruction C is a natural person, provide the information specified in (a) through (f) of this Item with respect to such person(s).

(a) Name;

(b) Residence or business address;

(c) Present principal occupation or employment and the name, principal business and address of any corporation or other organization in which such employment is conducted;

(d) Whether or not, during the last five years, such person has been convicted in a criminal proceeding (excluding traffic violations or similar misdemeanors) and, if so, give the dates, nature of conviction, name and location of court, any penalty imposed, or other disposition of the case;

(e) Whether or not, during the last five years, such person was a party to a civil proceeding of a judicial or administrative body of competent jurisdiction and as a result of such proceeding was or is subject to a judgment, decree or final order enjoining future violations of, or prohibiting or mandating activities subject to, federal or state securities laws or finding any violation with respect to such laws; and, if so, identify and describe such proceedings and summarize the terms of such judgment, decree or final order; and

(f) Citizenship.

Item 3. Source and Amount of Funds or Other Consideration

State the source and the amount of funds or other consideration used or to be used in making the purchases, and if any part of the purchase price is or will be represented by funds or other consideration borrowed or otherwise obtained for the purpose of acquiring, holding, trading or voting the securities, a description of the transaction and the names of the parties thereto. Where material, such information should also be provided with respect to prior acquisitions not previously reported pursuant to this regulation. If the source of all or any part of the funds is a loan made in the ordinary course of business by a bank, as defined in Section 3(a)(6) of the Act, the name of the bank shall not be made available to the public if the person at the time of filing the statement so requests in writing and files such request, naming such bank, with the Secretary of the Commission. If the securities were acquired other than by purchase, describe the method of acquisition.

Item 4. Purpose of Transaction

State the purpose or purposes of the acquisition of securities of the issuer. Describe any plans or proposals which the reporting persons may have which relate to or would result in:

(a) The acquisition by any person of additional securities of the issuer, or the disposition of securities of the issuer;

(b) An extraordinary corporate transaction, such as a merger, reorganization or liquidation, involving the issuer or any of its subsidiaries;

(c) A sale or transfer of a material amount of assets of the issuer or of any of its subsidiaries;

(d) Any change in the present board of directors or management of the issuer, including any plans or proposals to change the number or term of directors or to fill any existing vacancies on the board;

(e) Any material change in the present capitalization or dividend policy of the issuer;

(f) Any other material change in the issuer's business or corporate structure, including but not limited to, if the issuer is a registered closed-end investment company, any plans or proposals to make any changes in its investment policy for which a vote is required by section 13 of the Investment Company Act of 1940;

(g) Changes in the issuer's charter, bylaws or instruments corresponding thereto or other actions which may impede the acquisition of control of the issuer by any person;

(h) Causing a class of securities of the issuer to be delisted from a national securities exchange or to cease to be authorized to be quoted in an inter-dealer quotation system of a registered national securities association;

(i) A class of equity securities of the issuer becoming eligible for termination of registration pursuant to Section 12(g)(4) of the Act; or

(j) Any action similar to any of those enumerated above.

Item 5. Interest in Securities of the Issuer

(a) State the aggregate number and percentage of the class of securities identified pursuant to Item 1 (which may be based on the number of securities outstanding as contained in the most recently available filing with the Commission by the issuer unless the filing person has reason to believe such information is not current) beneficially owned (identifying those shares which there is a right to acquire) by each person named in Item 2. The above mentioned information should also be furnished with respect to persons who, together with any of the persons named in Item 2, comprise a group within the meaning of Section 13(d)(3) of the Act;

(b) For each person named in response to paragraph (a), indicate the number of shares as to which there is sole power to vote or to direct the vote, shared power to vote or to direct the vote, sole power to dispose or to direct the disposition. Provide the applicable information required by Item 2 with respect to each person with whom the power to vote or to direct the vote or to dispose or direct the disposition is shared;

(c) Describe any transactions in the class of securities reported on that were effected during the past sixty days or since the most recent filing on Schedule 13D (§ 240.13d–101), whichever is less, by the persons named in response to paragraph (a).

Instruction. The description of a transaction required by Item 5(c) shall include, but not necessarily be limited to: (1) the identity of the person covered by Item 5(c) who effected the transaction; (2) the date of the transaction; (3) the amount of securities involved; (4) the price per share or unit; and (5) where and how the transaction was effected.

(d) If any other person is known to have the right to receive or the power to direct the receipt of dividends from, or the proceeds from the sale of, such securities, a statement to that effect should be included in response to this time and, if such interest relates to more than five percent of the class, such person should be identified. A listing of the shareholders of an investment company registered under the Investment Company Act of 1940 or the beneficiaries of an employee benefit plan, pension fund or endowment fund is not required.

(e) If applicable, state the date on which the reporting person ceased to be the beneficial owner of more than five percent of the class of securities.

Instruction. For computations regarding securities which represent a right to acquire an underlying security, see Rule 13d–3(d)(1) and the note thereto.

Item 6. Contracts, Arrangements, Understandings or Relationships With Respect to Securities of the Issuer

Describe any contracts, arrangements, understandings or relationships (legal or otherwise) among the persons named in Item 2 and between such persons and any person with respect to any securities of the issuer, including but not limited to transfer or voting of any of the securities, finder's fees, joint ventures, loan or option arrangements, puts or calls, guarantees of profits, division of profits or loss, or the giving or withholding of proxies, naming the persons with whom such contracts, arrangements, understandings or relationships have been entered into. Include such information for any of the securities that are pledged or otherwise subject to a contingency the occurrence of which would give another person voting power or investment power over such securities except that disclosure of standard default and similar provisions contained in loan agreements need not be included.

Item 7. Material to Be Filed as Exhibits

The following shall be filed as exhibits: Copies of written agreements relating to the filing of joint acquisition statements as required by Rule 13d–1(k) (§ 240.13d–1(k)) and copies of all written agreements, contracts, arrangements, understandings, plans, or proposals relating to: (1) The borrowing of funds to finance the acquisition as disclosed in Item 3; (2) the acquisition of issuer control, liquidation, sale of assets, merger, or change in business or corporate structure, or any other matter as disclosed in Item 4; and (3) the transfer or voting of the securities, finder's fees, joint ventures, options, puts, calls, guarantees of loans, guarantees against loss or of profit, or the giving or withholding of any proxy as disclosed in Item 6.

SIGNATURE

After reasonable inquiry and to the best of my knowledge and belief, I certify that the information set forth in this statement is true, complete and correct.

____
(Date)

____
(Signature)

____
(Name/Title)

The original statement shall be signed by each person on whose behalf the statement is filed or his authorized representative. If the statement is signed on behalf of a person by his authorized representative (other than an executive officer or general partner of the filing person), evidence of the representative's authority to sign on behalf of such person shall be filed with the statement, *Provided, however,* That a power of attorney for this purpose which is already on file with the Commission may be incorporated by reference. The name of any title of each person who signs the statement shall be typed or printed beneath his signature.

ATTENTION: Intentional misstatements or omissions of fact constitute Federal criminal violations (See 18 U.S.C. 1001). Rule 13d–102 Schedule 13G Information to be included in statements filed pursuant to Rule 13d–1(b) and amendments thereto filed pursuant to Rule 13d–2(b).

Rule 13e–1. Purchase of Securities by the Issuer During a Third–Party Tender Offer

An issuer that has received notice that it is the subject of a tender offer made under Section 14(d)(1) of the Act (15 U.S.C. 78n), that has commenced under § 240.14d–2 must not purchase any of its equity securities during the tender offer unless the issuer first:

(a) Files a statement with the Commission containing the following information:

(1) The title and number of securities to be purchased;

(2) The names of the persons or classes of persons from whom the issuer will purchase the securities;

(3) The name of any exchange, interdealer quotation system or any other market on or through which the securities will be purchased;

(4) The purpose of the purchase;

(5) Whether the issuer will retire the securities, hold the securities in its treasury, or dispose of the securities. If the issuer intends to dispose of the securities, describe how it intends to do so; and

(6) The source and amount of funds or other consideration to be used to make the purchase. If the issuer borrows any funds or other consideration to make the purchase or enters any agreement for the purpose of acquiring, holding, or trading the securities, describe the transaction and agreement and identify the parties; and

(b) Pays the fee required by § 240.0–11 when it files the initial statement.

(c) This section does not apply to periodic repurchases in connection with an employee benefit plan or other similar plan of the issuer so long as the purchases are made in the ordinary course and not in response to the tender offer.

Instruction to § 240.13e–1: File eight copies if paper filing is permitted.

Rule 13e–3. Going Private Transactions by Certain Issuers or Their Affiliates

(a) *Definitions.* Unless indicated otherwise or the context otherwise requires, all terms used in this section and in Schedule 13E–3 shall have the same meaning as in the Act or elsewhere in the General Rules and Regulations thereunder. In addition, the following definitions apply:

(1) An "affiliate" of an issuer is a person that directly or indirectly through one or more intermediaries controls, is controlled by, or is under common control with such issuer. For the purposes of this section only, a person who is not an affiliate of an issuer at the commencement of such person's tender offer for a class of equity securities of such issuer will not be deemed an affiliate of such issuer prior to the stated termination of such tender offer and any extensions thereof;

(2) The term "purchase" means any acquisition for value including, but not limited to, (i) any acquisition pursuant to the dissolution of an issuer subsequent to the sale or other disposition of substantially all the assets of such issuer to its affiliate, (ii) any acquisition pursuant to a merger, (iii) any acquisition of fractional interests in connection with a reverse stock split, and (iv) any acquisition subject to the control of an issuer or an affiliate of such issuer;

(3) A "Rule 13e–3 transaction" is any transaction or series of transactions involving one or more of the transactions described in paragraph (a)(3)(i) of this section which has either a reasonable likelihood or a purpose of producing, either directly or indirectly, any of the effects described in paragraph (a)(3)(ii) of this section;

(i) The transactions referred to in paragraph (a)(3) of this section are:

(A) A purchase of any equity security by the issuer of such security or by an affiliate of such issuer;

(B) A tender offer for or request or invitation for tenders of any equity security made by the issuer of such class of securities or by an affiliate of such issuer; or

(C) A solicitation subject to Regulation 14A (§§ 240.14a–1 to 240 14b–1) of any proxy, consent or authorization of, or a distribution subject to Regulation 14C (§§ 240.14c–1 to 240.14c–101) of information statements to, any equity security holder by the issuer of the class of securities or by an affiliate of such issuer, in connection with: a merger, consolidation, reclassification, recapitalization, reorganization or similar corporate transaction of an issuer or between an issuer (or its subsidiaries) and its affiliate; a sale of substantially all the assets of an issuer to its affiliate or group of affiliates; or a reverse stock split of any class of equity securities of the issuer involving the purchase of fractional interests.

(ii) The effects referred to in paragraph (a)(3) of this section are:

(A) Causing any class of equity securities of the issuer which is subject to section 12(g) or section 15(d) or the Act to be held of record by less than 300 persons; or

(B) Causing any class of equity securities of the issuer which is either listed on a national securities exchange or authorized to be quoted in an inter-dealer quotation system of a registered national securities association to be neither listed on any national securities exchange nor authorized to be quoted on an inter-dealer quotation system of any registered national securities association.

(4) An "unaffiliated security holder" is any security holder of an equity security subject to a Rule 13e–3 transaction who is not an affiliate of the issuer of such security.

(b) *Application of Section to an Issuer (or an Affiliate of Such Issuer) Subject to Section 12 of the Act.*

(1) It shall be a fraudulent, deceptive or manipulative act or practice, in connection with a Rule 13e–3 transaction, for an issuer which has a class of equity securities registered pursuant to Section 12 of the Act or which is a closed-end investment company registered under the Investment Company Act of 1940, or an affiliate of such issuer, directly or indirectly

(i) To employ any device, scheme or artifice to defraud any person;

(ii) To make any untrue statement of a material fact or to omit to state a material fact necessary in order to make the statements made, in light of the circumstances under which they were made, not misleading; or

(iii) To engage in any act, practice or course of business which operates or would operate as a fraud or deceit upon any person.

(2) As a means reasonably designed to prevent fraudulent, deceptive or manipulative acts or practices in connection with any Rule 13e–3 transaction, it shall be unlawful for an issuer which has a class of equity securities registered pursuant to Section 12 of the Act, or an affiliate of such issuer, to engage, directly or indirectly, in a Rule 13e–3 transaction unless:

(i) Such issuer or affiliate complies with the requirements of paragraphs (d), (e) and (f) of this Section; and

(ii) The Rule 13e–3 transaction is not in violation of paragraph (b)(1) of this section.

(c) *Application of Section to an Issuer (or an Affiliate of Such Issuer) Subject to Section 15(d) of the Act.*

(1) It shall be unlawful as a fraudulent, deceptive or manipulative act or practice for an issuer which is required to file periodic reports pursuant to Section 15(d) of the Act, or an affiliate of such issuer, to engage, directly or indirectly, in a Rule 13e–3 transaction unless such issuer or affiliate complies with the requirements of paragraphs (d), (e) and (f) of this section.

(2) An issuer or affiliate which is subject to paragraph (c)(1) of this section and which is soliciting proxies or distributing information statements in connection with a transaction described in paragraph (a)(3)(i)(A) of this section may elect to use the timing

procedures for conducting a solicitation subject to Regulation 14A (Rules 14a–1 to 14b–1) or a distribution subject to Regulation 14C (Rules 14c–1 to 14c–101) in complying with paragraphs (d), (e) and (f) of this section, *provided,* That if an election is made, such solicitation or distribution is conducted in accordance with the requirements of the respective regulations, including the filing of preliminary copies of soliciting materials or an information statement at the time specified in Regulation 14A or 14C, respectively.

(d) *Material Required to be Filed*. The issuer or affiliate engaging in a Rule 13e–3 transaction must file with the Commission:

(1) A Schedule 13E–3 (§ 240.13e–100), including all exhibits;

(2) An amendment to Schedule 13E–3 reporting promptly any material changes in the information set forth in the schedule previously filed; and

(3) A final amendment to Schedule 13E–3 reporting promptly the results of the Rule 13e–3 transaction.

(e) *Disclosure of Information to Security Holders.*

(1) In addition to disclosing the information required by any other applicable rule or regulation under the federal securities laws, the issuer or affiliate engaging in a § 240.13e–3 transaction must disclose to security holders of the class that is the subject of the transaction, as specified in paragraph (f) of this section, the following:

(i) The information required by Item 1 of Schedule 13E–3 (§ 240.13e–100) (Summary Term Sheet);

(ii) The information required by Items 7, 8 and 9 of Schedule 13E–3, which must be prominently disclosed in a "Special Factors" section in the front of the disclosure document;

(iii) A prominent legend on the outside front cover page that indicates that neither the Securities and Exchange Commission nor any state securities commission has: approved or disapproved of the transaction; passed upon the merits or fairness of the transaction; or passed upon the adequacy or accuracy of the disclosure in the document. The legend also must make it clear that any representation to the contrary is a criminal offense;

(iv) The information concerning appraisal rights required by § 229.1016(f) of this chapter; and

(v) The information required by the remaining items of Schedule 13E–3, except for § 229.1016 of this chapter (exhibits), or a fair and adequate summary of the information.

Instructions to paragraph (e)(1):

1. If the Rule 13e–3 transaction also is subject to Regulation 14A (§§ 240.14a–1 through 240.14b–2) or 14C (§§ 240.14c–1 through 240.14c–101), the registration provisions and rules of the Securities Act of 1933, Regulation 14D or § 240.13e–4, the information required by paragraph (e)(1) of this section must be combined with the proxy statement, information statement, prospectus or tender offer material sent or given to security holders.

2. If the Rule 13e–3 transaction involves a registered securities offering, the legend required by § 229.501(b)(7) of this chapter must be combined with the legend required by paragraph (e)(1)(iii) of this section.

3. The required legend must be written in clear, plain language.

(2) If there is any material change in the information previously disclosed to security holders, the issuer or affiliate must disclose the change promptly to security holders as specified in paragraph (f)(1)(iii) of this section.

(f) *Dissemination of Information to Security Holders.*

(1) If the Rule 13e–3 transaction involves a purchase as described in paragraph (a)(3)(i)(A) of this section or a vote, consent,

authorization, or distribution of information statements as described in paragraph (a)(3)(i)(C) of this section, the issuer or affiliate engaging in the Rule 13e–3 transaction shall:

(i) Provide the information required by paragraph (e) of this section: (A) in accordance with the provisions of any applicable federal or state law, but in no event later than 20 days prior to: any such purchase; any such vote, consent or authorization; or with respect to the distribution of information statements, the meeting date, or if corporate action is to be taken by means of the written authorization or consent of security holders, the earliest date on which corporate action may be taken: *Provided, however,* That if the purchase subject to this section is pursuant to a tender offer excepted from Rule 13e–4 by paragraph (g)(5) of Rule 13e–4, the information required by paragraph (e) of this section shall be disseminated in accordance with paragraph (e) of Rule 13e–4 no later than 10 business days prior to any purchase pursuant to such tender offer, (B) to each person who is a record holder of a class of equity security subject to the Rule 13e–3 transaction as of a date not more than 20 days prior to the date of dissemination of such information.

(ii) If the issuer or affiliate knows that securities of the class of securities subject to the Rule 13e–3 transaction are held of record by a broker, dealer, bank or voting trustee or their nominees, such issuer or affiliate shall (unless Rule 14a–13(a) or 14c–7 is applicable) furnish the number of copies of the information required by paragraph (e) of this section that are requested by such persons (pursuant to inquiries by or on behalf of the issuer or affiliate), instruct such persons to forward such information to the beneficial owners of such securities in a timely manner and undertake to pay the reasonable expenses incurred by such persons in forwarding such information; and

(iii) Promptly disseminate disclosure of material changes to the information required by paragraph (d) of this section in a manner reasonably calculated to inform security holders.

(2) If the Rule 13e–3 transaction is a tender offer or a request or invitation for tenders of equity securities which is subject to Regulation 14D or Rule 13e–4, the tender offer containing the information required by paragraph (e) of this section, and any material change with respect thereto, shall be published, sent or given in accordance with Regulation 14D or Rule 13e–4, respectively, to security holders of the class of securities being sought by the issuer or affiliate.

(g) *Exceptions.* This section shall not apply to:

(1) Any Rule 13e–3 transaction by or on behalf of a person which occurs within one year of the date of termination of a tender offer in which such person was the bidder and became an affiliate of the issuer as a result of such tender offer *provided* that the consideration offered to unaffiliated security holders in such Rule 13e–3 transaction is at least equal to the highest consideration offered during such tender offer and *provided further,* That:

(i) If such tender offer was made for any or all securities of a class of the issuer;

(A) Such tender offer fully disclosed such person's intention to engage in a Rule 13e–3 transaction, the form and effect of such transaction and, to the extent known, the proposed terms thereof; and

(B) Such Rule 13e–3 transaction is substantially similar to that described in such tender offer; or

(ii) If such tender offer was made for less than all the securities of a class of the issuer:

(A) Such tender offer fully disclosed a plan of merger, a plan of liquidation or a similar binding agreement between such person and the issuer with respect to a Rule 13e–3 transaction; and

(B) Such Rule 13e–3 transaction occurs pursuant to the plan of merger, plan of liquidation or similar binding agreement disclosed in the bidder's tender offer.

(2) Any Rule 13e–3 transaction in which the security holders are offered or receive only an equity security *provided,* That:

(i) such equity security has substantially the same rights as the equity security which is the subject of the Rule 13e–3 transaction including, but not limited to, voting, dividends, redemption and liquidation rights except that this requirement shall be deemed to be satisfied if unaffiliated security holders are offered common stock;

(ii) such equity security is registered pursuant to section 12 of the Act or reports are required to be filed by the issuer thereof pursuant to section 15(d) of the Act; and

(iii) if the security which is the subject of the Rule 13e–3 transaction was either listed on a national securities exchange or authorized to be quoted in an inter-dealer quotation system of a registered national securities association, such equity security is either listed on a national securities exchange or authorized to be quoted in an inter-dealer quotation system of a registered national securities association.

(3) Transactions by a holding company registered under the Public Utility Holding Company Act of 1935 in compliance with the provisions of that Act;

(4) Redemptions, calls or similar purchases of an equity security by an issuer pursuant to specific provisions set forth in the instrument(s) creating or governing that class of equity securities; or

(5) Any solicitation by an issuer with respect to a plan of reorganization under Chapter XI of the Bankruptcy Act, as amended, if made after the entry of an order approving such plan pursuant to § 1125(b) of that Act and after, or concurrently with, the transmittal of information concerning such plan as required by § 1125(b) of that Act.

(6) Any tender offer or business combination made in compliance with § 230.802 of this chapter, § 240.13e–4(h)(8) or § 240.14d–1(c).

Schedule 13E–3. Transaction Statement Under Section 13(e) of the Securities Exchange Act of 1934 and Rule 13e–3 Thereunder

Securities and Exchange Commission, Washington, D.C. 20549

Rule 13e–3. Transaction Statement under Section 13(e) of the Securities Exchange Act of 1934 (Amendment No. ___)

____

(Name of the Issuer)

____

(Names of Persons Filing Statement)

____

(Title of Class of Securities)

____

(CUSIP Number of Class of Securities)

____

(Name, Address, and Telephone Numbers of Person Authorized to Receive Notices and Communications on Behalf of the Persons Filing Statement)

This statement is filed in connection with (check the appropriate box):

a. [ ] The filing of solicitation materials or an information statement subject to Regulation 14A (§§ 240.14a–1 through 240.14b–2), Regulation 14C (§§ 240.14c–1 through 240.14c–101) or Rule 13e–3(c) (§ 240.13e–3(c)) under the Securities Exchange Act of 1934 ("the Act").

b. [ ] The filing of a registration statement under the Securities Act of 1933.

c. [ ] A tender offer.

d. [ ] None of the above.

Check the following box if the soliciting materials or information statement referred to in checking box (a) are preliminary copies: [ ]

Check the following box if the filing is a final amendment reporting the results of the transaction [ ]

Calculation of Filing Fee

Transaction Valuation *	Amount of Filing Fee

* Set forth the amount on which the filing fee is calculated and state how it was determined.

[ ] Check the box if any part of the fee is offset as provided by § 240.0–11(a)(2) and identify the filing with which the offsetting fee was previously paid. Identify the previous filing by registration statement number, or the Form or Schedule and the date of its filing.

Amount Previously Paid: ______________

Form or Registration No.: ______________

Filing Party: ______________

Date Filed: ______________

General Instructions:

A. File eight copies of the statement, including all exhibits, with the Commission if paper filing is permitted.

B. This filing must be accompanied by a fee payable to the Commission as required by § 240.0–11(b).

C. If the statement is filed by a general or limited partnership, syndicate or other group, the information called for by Items 3, 5, 6, 10 and 11 must be given with respect to: (i) Each partner of the general partnership; (ii) each partner who is, or functions as, a general partner of the limited partnership; (iii) each member of the syndicate or group; and (iv) each person controlling the partner or member. If the statement is filed by a corporation or if a person referred to in (i), (ii), (iii) or (iv) of this Instruction is a corporation, the information called for by the items specified above must be given with respect to: (a) Each executive officer and director of the corporation; (b) each person controlling the corporation; and (c) each executive officer and director of any corporation or other person ultimately in control of the corporation.

D. Depending on the type of Rule 13e–3 transaction (§ 240.13e–3(a)(3)), this statement must be filed with the Commission:

1. At the same time as filing preliminary or definitive soliciting materials or an information statement under Regulations 14A or 14C of the Act;

2. At the same time as filing a registration statement under the Securities Act of 1933;

3. As soon as practicable on the date a tender offer is first published, sent or given to security holders; or

4. At least 30 days before any purchase of securities of the class of securities subject to the Rule 13e–3 transaction, if the transaction does not involve a solicitation, an information statement, the registration of securities or a tender offer, as described in paragraphs 1, 2 or 3 of this Instruction; and

5. If the Rule 13e–3 transaction involves a series of transactions, the issuer or affiliate must file this statement at the time indicated in paragraphs 1 through 4 of this Instruction for the first transaction and must amend the schedule promptly with respect to each subsequent transaction.

E. If an item is inapplicable or the answer is in the negative, so state. The statement published, sent or given to security holders may omit negative and not applicable responses, except that responses to Items 7, 8 and 9 of this schedule must be provided in full. If the schedule includes any information that is not published, sent or given to security holders, provide that information or specifically incorporate it by reference under the appropriate item number and heading in the schedule. Do not recite the text of disclosure requirements in the schedule or any document published, sent or given to security holders. Indicate clearly the coverage of the requirements without referring to the text of the items.

F. Information contained in exhibits to the statement may be incorporated by reference in answer or partial answer to any item unless it would render the answer misleading, incomplete, unclear or confusing. A copy of any information that is incorporated by reference or a copy of the pertinent pages of a document containing the information must be submitted with this statement as an exhibit, unless it was previously filed with the Commission electronically on EDGAR. If an exhibit contains information responding to more than one item in the schedule, all information in that exhibit may be incorporated by reference once in response to the several items in the schedule for which it provides an answer. Information incorporated by reference is deemed filed with the Commission for all purposes of the Act.

G. If the Rule 13e–3 transaction also involves a transaction subject to Regulation 14A (§§ 240.14a–1 through 240.14b–2) or 14C (§§ 240.14c–1 through 240.14c–101) of the Act, the registration of securities under the Securities Act of 1933 and the General Rules and Regulations of that Act, or a tender offer subject to Regulation 14D (§§ 240.14d–1 through 240.14d–101) or § 240.13e–4, this statement must incorporate by reference the information contained in the proxy, information, registration or tender offer statement in answer to the items of this statement.

H. The information required by the items of this statement is intended to be in addition to any disclosure requirements of any other form or schedule that may be filed with the Commission in connection with the Rule 13e–3 transaction. If those forms or schedules require less information on any topic than this statement, the requirements of this statement control.

I. If the Rule 13e–3 transaction involves a tender offer, then a combined statement on Schedules 13E–3 and TO may be filed with the Commission under cover of Schedule TO (§ 240.14d–100). See Instruction J of Schedule TO (§ 240.14d–100).

J. Amendments disclosing a material change in the information set forth in this statement may omit any information previously disclosed in this statement.

Item 1. Summary Term Sheet

Furnish the information required by Item 1001 of Regulation M–A (§ 229.1001 of this chapter) unless information is disclosed to security holders in a prospectus that meets the requirements of § 230.421(d) of this chapter.

Item 2. Subject Company Information

Furnish the information required by Item 1002 of Regulation M–A (§ 229.1002 of this chapter).

Item 3. Identity and Background of Filing Person

Furnish the information required by Item 1003(a) through (c) of Regulation M-A (§ 229.1003 of this chapter).

Item 4. Terms of the Transaction

Furnish the information required by Item 1004(a) and (c) through (f) of Regulation M–A (§ 229.1004 of this chapter).

Item 5. Past Contacts, Transactions, Negotiations and Agreements

Furnish the information required by Item 1005(a) through (c) and (e) of Regulation M–A (§ 229.1005 of this chapter).

Item 6. Purposes of the Transaction and Plans or Proposals

Furnish the information required by Item 1006(b) and (c)(1) through (8) of Regulation M–A (§ 229.1006 of this chapter).

Instruction to Item 6: In providing the information specified in Item 1006(c) for this item, discuss any activities or transactions that would occur after the Rule 13e–3 transaction.

Item 7. Purposes, Alternatives, Reasons and Effects

Furnish the information required by Item 1013 of Regulation M–A (§ 229.1013 of this chapter).

Item 8. Fairness of the Transaction

Furnish the information required by Item 1014 of Regulation M–A (§ 229.1014 of this chapter).

Item 9. Reports, Opinions, Appraisals and Negotiations

Furnish the information required by Item 1015 of Regulation M–A (§ 229.1015 of this chapter).

Item 10. Source and Amounts of Funds or Other Consideration

Furnish the information required by Item 1007 of Regulation M–A (§ 229.1007 of this chapter).

Item 11. Interest in Securities of the Subject Company

Furnish the information required by Item 1008 of Regulation M–A (§ 229.1008 of this chapter).

Item 12. The Solicitation or Recommendation

Furnish the information required by Item 1012(d) and (e) of Regulation M–A (§ 229.1012 of this chapter).

Item 13. Financial Statements

Furnish the information required by Item 1010(a) through (b) of Regulation M-A (§ 229.1010 of this chapter) for the issuer of the subject class of securities.

Instructions to Item 13:

1. The disclosure materials disseminated to security holders may contain the summarized financial information required by Item 1010(c) of Regulation M–A (§ 229.1010 of this chapter) instead of the financial information required by Item 1010(a) and (b). In that case, the financial information required by Item 1010(a) and (b) of Regulation M–A must be disclosed directly or incorporated by reference in the statement. If summarized financial information is disseminated to security holders, include appropriate instructions on how more complete financial information can be obtained. If the summarized financial information is prepared on the basis of a comprehensive body of accounting principles other than U.S. GAAP, the summarized financial information must be accompanied by a reconciliation as described in Instruction 2.

2. If the financial statements required by this Item are prepared on the basis of a comprehensive body of accounting principles other than U.S. GAAP, provide a reconciliation to U.S. GAAP in accordance with Item 17 of Form 20–F (§ 249.220f of this chapter).

3. The filing person may incorporate by reference financial statements contained in any document filed with the Commission, solely for the purposes of this schedule, if: (a) The financial statements substantially meet the requirements of this Item; (b) an express statement is made that the financial statements are incorporated by reference; (c) the matter incorporated by reference is clearly identified by page, paragraph, caption or otherwise; and (d) if the matter incorporated by reference is not filed with this Schedule, an indication is made where the information may be inspected and copies obtained. Financial statements that are required to be presented in comparative form for two or more fiscal years or periods may not be incorporated by reference unless the material incorporated by reference includes the entire period for which the comparative data is required to be given. See General Instruction F to this Schedule.

Item 14. Persons/Assets, Retained, Employed, Compensated or Used

Furnish the information required by Item 1009 of Regulation M–A (§ 229.1009 of this chapter).

Item 15. Additional Information

Furnish the information required by Item 1011(b) of Regulation M–A (§ 229.1011 of this chapter).

Item 16. Exhibits

File as an exhibit to the Schedule all documents specified in Item 1016(a) through (d), (f) and (g) of Regulation M–A (§ 229.1016 of this chapter).

Signature. After due inquiry and to the best of my knowledge and belief, I certify that the information set forth in this statement is true, complete and correct.

____

(Signature)

____

(Name and title)

____

(Date)

Instruction to Signature: The statement must be signed by the filing person or that person's authorized representative. If the statement is signed on behalf of a person by an authorized representative (other than an executive officer of a corporation or general partner of a partnership), evidence of the representative's authority to sign on behalf of the person must be filed with the statement. The name and any title of each person who signs the statement must be typed or printed beneath the signature. See § 240.12b–11 with respect to signature requirements.

____

(Signature)

____

(Name and Title)

Rule 13e–4. Tender Offers by Issuers

(a) *Definitions.* Unless the context otherwise requires, all terms used in this rule and in Schedule TO shall have the same meaning as in the Act or elsewhere in the General Rules and Regulations thereunder. In addition, the following definitions shall apply:

(1) The term "issuer" means any issuer which has a class of equity security registered pursuant to section 12 of the Act, or which is required to file periodic reports pursuant to section 15(d) of the Act, or which is a closed-end investment company registered under the Investment Company Act of 1940.

(2) The term "issuer tender offer" refers to a tender offer for, or a request or invitation for tenders of, any class of equity security, made by the issuer of such class of equity security or by an affiliate of such issuer.

(3) As used in this rule and in Schedule TO, the term "business day" means any day, other than Saturday, Sunday or a federal holiday, and shall consist of the time period from 12:01 a.m. through 12:00 midnight Eastern Time. In computing any time period under this Rule or Schedule 13E–4, the date of the event that begins the running of such time period shall be included *except that* if such event occurs on other than a business day such period shall begin to run on and shall include the first business day thereafter.

(4) The term *commencement* means 12:01 a.m. on the date that the issuer or affiliate has first published, sent or given the means to tender to security holders. For purposes of this section, the means to tender includes the transmittal form or a statement regarding how the transmittal form may be obtained.

(5) The term "termination" means the date after which securities may not be tendered pursuant to an issuer tender offer.

(6) The term "security holders" means holders of record and beneficial owners of securities of the class of equity security which is the subject of an issuer tender offer.

(7) The term "security position listing" means, with respect to the securities of any issuer held by a registered clearing agency in the name of the clearing agency or its nominee, a list of those participants in the clearing agency on whose behalf the clearing agency holds the issuer's securities and of the participants' respective positions in such securities as of a specified date.

(b) *Filing, Disclosure and Dissemination.* As soon as practicable on the date of commencement of the issuer tender offer, the issuer or affiliate making the issuer tender offer must comply with:

(1) The filing requirements of paragraph (c)(2) of this section;

(2) The disclosure requirements of paragraph (d)(1) of this section; and

(3) The dissemination requirements of paragraph (e) of this section.

(c) *Material Required to Be Filed.* The issuer or affiliate making the issuer tender offer must file with the Commission:

(1) All written communications made by the issuer or affiliate relating to the issuer tender offer, from and including the first public announcement, as soon as practicable on the date of the communication;

(2) A Schedule TO (§ 240.14d–100), including all exhibits;

(3) An amendment to Schedule TO (§ 240.14d–100) reporting promptly any material changes in the information set forth in the schedule previously filed; and

(4) A final amendment to Schedule TO (§ 240.14d–100) reporting promptly the results of the issuer tender offer.

Instructions to § 240.13e–4(c):

1. Pre-commencement communications must be filed under cover of Schedule TO (§ 240.14d–100) and the box on the cover page of the schedule must be marked.

2. Any communications made in connection with an *exchange offer* registered under the Securities Act of 1933 need only be filed under § 230.425 of this chapter and will be deemed filed under this section.

3. Each pre-commencement written communication must include a prominent legend in clear, plain language advising security holders to read the tender offer statement when it is available because it contains important information. The legend also must advise investors that they can get the tender offer statement and other filed documents for free at the Commission's web site and explain which documents are free from the issuer.

4. See §§ 230.135, 230.165 and 230.166 of this chapter for pre-commencement communications made in connection with registered exchange offers.

5. "Public announcement" is any oral or written communication by the issuer, affiliate or any person authorized to act on their behalf that is reasonably designed to, or has the effect of, informing the public or security holders in general about the issuer tender offer.

(d) *Disclosure of Tender Offer Information to Security Holders.*

(1) The issuer or affiliate making the issuer tender offer must disclose, in a manner prescribed by paragraph (e)(1) of this section, the following:

(i) The information required by Item 1 of Schedule TO (§ 240.14d–100) (summary term sheet); and

(ii) The information required by the remaining items of Schedule TO for issuer tender offers, except for Item 12 (exhibits), or a fair and adequate summary of the information.

(2) If there are any material changes in the information previously disclosed to security holders, the issuer or affiliate must disclose the changes promptly to security holders in a manner specified in paragraph (e)(3) of this section.

(3) If the issuer or affiliate disseminates the issuer tender offer by means of summary publication as described in paragraph

(e)(1)(iii) of this section, the summary advertisement must not include a transmittal letter that would permit security holders to tender securities sought in the offer and must disclose at least the following information:

(i) The identity of the issuer or affiliate making the issuer tender offer;

(ii) The information required by § 229.1004(a)(1) and § 229.1006(a) of this chapter;

(iii) Instructions on how security holders can obtain promptly a copy of the statement required by paragraph (d)(1) of this section, at the issuer or affiliate's expense; and

(iv) A statement that the information contained in the statement required by paragraph (d)(1) of this section is incorporated by reference.

(e) *Dissemination of Tender Offers to Security Holders*. An issuer tender offer will be deemed to be published, sent or given to security holders if the issuer or affiliate making the issuer tender offer complies fully with one or more of the methods described in this section.

(1) For issuer tender offers in which the consideration offered consists solely of cash and/or securities exempt from registration under section 3 of the Securities Act of 1933 (15 U.S.C. 77c):

(i) Dissemination of cash issuer tender offers by long-form publication: By making adequate publication of the information required by paragraph (d)(1) of this section in a newspaper or newspapers, on the date of commencement of the issuer tender offer.

(ii) Dissemination of any issuer tender offer by use of stockholder and other lists:

(A) By mailing or otherwise furnishing promptly a statement containing the information required by paragraph (d)(1) of this section to each security holder whose name appears on the most recent stockholder list of the issuer;

(B) By contacting each participant on the most recent security position listing of any clearing agency within the possession or access of the issuer or affiliate making the issuer tender offer, and making inquiry of each participant as to the approximate number of beneficial owners of the securities sought in the offer that are held by the participant;

(C) By furnishing to each participant a sufficient number of copies of the statement required by paragraph (d)(1) of this section for transmittal to the beneficial owners; and

(D) By agreeing to reimburse each participant promptly for its reasonable expenses incurred in forwarding the statement to beneficial owners.

(iii) Dissemination of certain cash issuer tender offers by summary publication:

(A) If the issuer tender offer is not subject to § 240.13e–3, by making adequate publication of a summary advertisement containing the information required by paragraph (d)(3) of this section in a newspaper or newspapers, on the date of commencement of the issuer tender offer; and

(B) By mailing or otherwise furnishing promptly the statement required by paragraph (d)(1) of this section and a transmittal letter to any security holder who requests a copy of the statement or transmittal letter.

Instruction to paragraph (e)(1): For purposes of paragraphs (e)(1)(i) and (e)(1)(iii) of this section, adequate publication of the issuer tender offer may require publication in a newspaper with a national circulation, a newspaper with metropolitan or regional circulation, or a combination of the two, depending upon the facts and circumstances involved.

(2) For tender offers in which the consideration consists solely or partially of securities registered under the Securities Act of 1933, a registration statement containing all of the required information, including pricing information, has been filed and a preliminary prospectus or a prospectus that meets the requirements of Section 10(a) of the Securities Act (15 U.S.C. 77j(a)), including a letter of transmittal, is delivered to security holders. However, for going-private transactions (as defined by § 240.13e–3) and roll-up transactions (as described by Item 901 of Regulation S-K (§ 229.901 of this chapter)), a registration statement registering the securities to be offered must have become effective and only a prospectus that meets the requirements of Section 10(a) of the Securities Act may be delivered to security holders on the date of commencement.

Instructions to paragraph (e)(2):

1. If the prospectus is being delivered by mail, mailing on the date of commencement is sufficient.

2. A preliminary prospectus used under this section may not omit information under § 230.430 or § 230.430A of this chapter.

3. If a preliminary prospectus is used under this section and the issuer must disseminate material changes, the tender offer must remain open for the period specified in paragraph (e)(3) of this section.

4. If a preliminary prospectus is used under this section, tenders may be requested in accordance with § 230.162(a) of this chapter.

(3) If a material change occurs in the information published, sent or given to security holders, the issuer or affiliate must disseminate promptly disclosure of the change in a manner reasonably calculated to inform security holders of the change. In a registered securities offer where the issuer or affiliate disseminates the preliminary prospectus as permitted by paragraph (e)(2) of *this section, the offer must remain* open from the date that material changes to the tender offer materials are disseminated to security holders, as follows:

(i) Five business days for a prospectus supplement containing a material change other than price or share levels;

(ii) Ten business days for a prospectus supplement containing a change in price, the amount of securities sought, the dealer's soliciting fee, or other similarly significant change;

(iii) Ten business days for a prospectus supplement included as part of a post-effective amendment; and

(iv) Twenty business days for a revised prospectus when the initial prospectus was materially deficient.

(f) *Manner of Making Tender Offer.*

(1) The issuer tender offer, unless withdrawn, shall remain open until the expiration of:

(i) at least twenty business days from its commencement; and

(ii) At least ten business days from the date that notice of an increase or decrease in the percentage of the class of securities being sought or the consideration offered or the dealer's soliciting fee to be given is first published, sent or given to security holders. *Provided, however,* That, for purposes of this paragraph, the acceptance for payment by the issuer or affiliate of an additional amount of securities not to exceed two percent of the class of securities that is the subject of the tender offer shall not be deemed to be an increase. For purposes of this paragraph, the percentage of a class of securities shall be calculated in accordance with section 14(d)(3) of the Act.

(2) The issuer or affiliate making the issuer tender offer shall permit securities tendered pursuant to the issuer tender offer to be withdrawn:

(i) At any time during the period such issuer tender offer remains open; and

(ii) If not yet accepted for payment, after the expiration of forty business days from the commencement of the issuer tender offer.

(3) If the issuer or affiliate makes a tender offer for less than all of the outstanding equity securities of a class, and if a greater number of securities is tendered pursuant thereto than the issuer or affiliate is bound or willing to take up and pay for, the securities taken up and paid for shall be taken up and paid for as nearly as may be pro rata, disregarding fractions, according to the number of securities tendered by each security holder during the period such offer remains open; *Provided, however,* That this provision shall not prohibit the issuer or affiliate making the issuer tender offer from:

(i) accepting all securities tendered by persons who own, beneficially or of record, an aggregate of not more than a specified number which is less than one hundred shares of such security and who tender all their securities, before prorating securities tendered by others, or

(ii) accepting by lot securities tendered by security holders who tender all securities held by them and who, when tendering their securities, elect to have either all or none or at least a minimum amount or none accepted, if the issuer or affiliate first accepts all securities tendered by security holders who do not so elect;

(4) In the event the issuer or affiliate making the issuer tender increases the consideration offered after the issuer tender offer has commenced, such issuer or affiliate shall pay such increased consideration to all security holders whose tendered securities are accepted for payment by such issuer or affiliate.

(5) The issuer or affiliate making the tender offer shall either pay the consideration offered, or return the tendered securities, promptly after the termination or withdrawal of the tender offer.

(6) Until the expiration of at least ten business days after the date of termination of the issuer tender offer, neither the issuer nor any affiliate shall make any purchases, otherwise than pursuant to the tender offer, of:

(i) any security which is the subject of the issuer tender offer, or any security of the same class and series, or any right to purchase any such securities; and

(ii) in the case of an issuer tender offer which is an exchange offer, any security being offered pursuant to such exchange offer, or any security of the same class and series, or any right to purchase any such security.

(7) The time periods for the minimum offering periods pursuant to this rule shall be computed on a concurrent as opposed to a consecutive basis.

(8) No issuer or affiliate shall make a tender offer unless:

(i) The tender offer is open to all security holders of the class of securities subject to the tender offer; and

(ii) The consideration paid to any security holder pursuant to the tender offer is the highest consideration paid to any other security holder during such tender offer.

(9) Paragraph (f)(8)(i) of this rule shall not:

(i) Affect dissemination under paragraph (e) of this rule; or

(ii) Prohibit an issuer or affiliate from making a tender offer excluding all security holders in a state where the issuer or affiliate is prohibited from making the tender offer by administrative or judicial action pursuant to a state statute after a good faith effort by the issuer or affiliate to comply with such statute.

(10) Paragraph (f)(8)(ii) of this rule shall not prohibit the offer of more than one type

of consideration in a tender offer, provided that:

(i) Security holders are afforded equal right to elect among each of the types of consideration offered; and

(ii) The highest consideration of each type paid to any security holder is paid to any other security holder receiving that type of consideration.

(11) If the offer and sale of securities constituting consideration offered in an issuer tender offer is prohibited by the appropriate authority of a state after a good faith effort by the issuer or affiliate to register or qualify the offer and sale of such securities in such state:

(i) The issuer or affiliate may offer security holders in such state an alternative form of consideration; and

(ii) Paragraph (f)(10) of this rule shall not operate to require the issuer or affiliate to offer or pay the alternative form of consideration to security holders in any other state.

(12) *Electronic filings.* If the issuer or affiliate is an electronic filer, the minimum offering periods set forth in paragraph (f)(1) of this rule shall be tolled for any period during which it fails to file in electronic format, absent a hardship exemption (§§ 232.201 and 232.202 of this chapter), Schedule TO, the tender offer material specified in Item 9 1016(a)(1) of Regulation M–A, and any amendments thereto. If such documents were filed in paper pursuant to a hardship exemption (see § 232.201 and § 232.202 of this chapter), the minimum offering periods shall be tolled for any period during which a required confirming electronic copy of such Schedule and tender offer material is delinquent.

(g) The requirements of section 13(e)(1) of the Act and Rule 13e–4 and Schedule TO thereunder shall be deemed satisfied with respect to any issuer tender offer, including any exchange offer, where the issuer is incorporated or organized under the laws of Canada or any Canadian province or territory, is a foreign private issuer, and is not an investment company registered or required to be registered under the Investment Company Act of 1940, if less than 40 percent of the class of securities that is the subject of the tender offer is held by U.S. holders, and the tender offer is subject to, and the issuer complies with, the laws, regulations and policies of Canada and/or any of its provinces or territories governing the conduct of the offer (unless the issuer has received an exemption(s) from, and the issuer tender offer does not comply with, requirements that otherwise would be prescribed by this section), *provided that:*

(1) Where the consideration for an issuer tender offer subject to this paragraph consists solely of cash, the entire disclosure document or documents required to be furnished to holders of the class of securities to be acquired shall be filed with the Commission on Schedule 13E–4F and disseminated to shareholders residing in the United States in accordance with such Canadian laws, regulations and policies; or

(2) Where the consideration for an issuer tender offer subject to this paragraph includes securities to be issued pursuant to the offer, any registration statement and/or prospectus relating thereto shall be filed with the Commission along with the Schedule 13E–4F referred to in paragraph (g)(1) of this rule, and shall be disseminated, together with the home jurisdiction document(s) accompanying such Schedule, to shareholders of the issuer residing in the United States in accordance with such Canadian laws, regulations and policies.

NOTE: Notwithstanding the grant of an exemption from one or more of the applicable Canadian regulatory provisions imposing requirements that otherwise would be prescribed by this rule, the issuer tender offer will be eligible to proceed in accordance with the requirements of this rule if the Commission by order determines that the applicable Canadian regulatory provisions are adequate to protect the interest of investors.

(h) This rule shall not apply to:

(1) Calls or redemptions of any security in accordance with the terms and conditions of its governing instruments;

(2) Offers to purchase securities evidenced by a scrip certificate, order form or similar document which represents a fractional interest in a share of stock or similar security;

(3) Offers to purchase securities pursuant to a statutory procedure for the purchase of dissenting security holders' securities;

(4) Any tender offer which is subject to section 14(d) of the Act;

(5) Offers to purchase from security holders who own an aggregate of not more than a specified number of shares that is less than one hundred: *Provided however,* That:

(i) The offer complies with paragraph (f)(8)(i) of this section with respect to security holders who own a number of shares equal to or less than the specified number of shares, except that an issuer can elect to exclude participants in a plan as that term is defined in § 242.100 of this chapter, or to exclude security holders who do not own their shares as of a specified date determined by the issuer; and

(ii) The offer complies with paragraph (f)(8)(ii) of this section or the consideration paid pursuant to the offer is determined on the basis of a uniformly applied formula based on the market price of the subject security;

(6) An issuer tender offer made solely to effect a rescission offer: *Provided, however,* That the offer is registered under the Securities Act of 1933, and the consideration is equal to the price paid by each security holder, plus legal interest if the issuer elects to or is required to pay legal interest;

(7) Offers by closed-end management investment companies to repurchase equity securities pursuant to § 270.23c–3 of this chapter; or

(8) *Cross-border tender offers (Tier I).* Any issuer tender offer (including any exchange offer) where the issuer is a foreign private issuer as defined in § 240.3b–4 if the following conditions are satisfied.

(i) Except in the case of an issuer tender offer which is commenced during the pendency of a tender offer made by a third party in reliance on § 240.14d–1(c), U.S. holders do not hold more than 10 percent of the class of securities sought in the offer (as determined under Instruction 2 to paragraph (h)(8) and paragraph (i) of this section); and

(ii) The issuer or affiliate must permit U.S. holders to participate in the offer on terms at least as favorable as those offered any other holder of the same class of securities that is the subject of the offer; however:

(A) *Registered exchange offers.* If the issuer or affiliate offers securities registered under the Securities Act of 1933 (15 U.S.C. 77a et seq.), the issuer or affiliate need not extend the offer to security holders in those states or jurisdictions that prohibit the offer or sale of the securities after the issuer or affiliate has made a good faith effort to register or qualify the offer and sale of securities in that state or jurisdiction, except that the issuer or affiliate must offer the same cash alternative to security holders in any such state or jurisdiction that it has offered to security holders in any other state or jurisdiction.

(B) *Exempt exchange offers.* If the issuer or affiliate offers securities exempt from registration under § 230.802 of this chapter, the issuer or affiliate need not extend the offer to security holders in those states or jurisdictions that require registration or qualification, except that the issuer or affiliate must offer the same cash alternative to security holders in any such state or jurisdiction that it has offered to security holders in any other state or jurisdiction.

(C) *Cash only consideration*. The issuer or affiliate may offer U.S. holders cash only consideration for the tender of the subject securities, notwithstanding the fact that the issuer or affiliate is offering security holders outside the United States a consideration that consists in whole or in part of securities of the issuer or affiliate, if the issuer or affiliate has a reasonable basis for believing that the amount of cash is substantially equivalent to the value of the consideration offered to non-U.S. holders, and either of the following conditions are satisfied:

(*1*) The offered security is a "margin security" within the meaning of Regulation T (12 CFR 220.2) and the issuer or affiliate undertakes to provide, upon the request of any U.S. holder or the Commission staff, the closing price and daily trading volume of the security on the principal trading market for the security as of the last trading day of each of the six months preceding the announcement of the offer and each of the trading days thereafter; or

(*2*) If the offered security is not a "margin security" within the meaning of Regulation T (12 CFR 220.2), the issuer or affiliate undertakes to provide, upon the request of any U.S. holder or the Commission staff, an opinion of an independent expert stating that the cash consideration offered to U.S. holders is substantially equivalent to the value of the consideration offered security holders outside the United States.

(D) *Disparate tax treatment*. If the issuer or affiliate offers "loan notes" solely to offer sellers tax advantages not available in the United States and these notes are neither listed on any organized securities market nor registered under the Securities Act of 1933 (15 U.S.C. 77a et seq.), the loan notes need not be offered to U.S. holders.

(iii) *Informational documents*.

(A) If the issuer or affiliate publishes or otherwise disseminates an informational document to the holders of the securities in connection with the issuer tender offer (including any exchange offer), the issuer or affiliate must furnish that informational document, including any amendments thereto, in English, to the Commission on Form CB (§ 249.480 of this chapter) by the first business day after publication or dissemination. If the issuer or affiliate is a foreign company, it must also file a Form F–X (§ 239.42 of this chapter) with the Commission at the same time as the submission of Form CB to appoint an agent for service in the United States.

(B) The issuer or affiliate must disseminate any informational document to U.S. holders, including any amendments thereto, in English, on a comparable basis to that provided to security holders in the home jurisdiction.

(C) If the issuer or affiliate disseminates by publication in its home jurisdiction, the issuer or affiliate must publish the information in the United States in a manner reasonably calculated to inform U.S. holders of the offer.

(iv) An investment company registered or required to be registered under the Investment Company Act of 1940 (15 U.S.C. 80a–1 et seq.), other than a registered closed-end investment company, may not use this paragraph (h)(8); or

(9) Any other transaction or transactions, if the Commission, upon written request or upon its own motion, exempts such transaction or transactions, either unconditionally,

or on specified terms and conditions, as not constituting a fraudulent, deceptive or manipulative act or practice comprehended within the purpose of this section.

(i) *Cross-Border Tender Offers (Tier II).* Any issuer tender offer (including any exchange offer) that meets the conditions in paragraph (i)(1) of this section shall be entitled to the exemptive relief specified in paragraph (i)(2) of this section provided that such issuer tender offer complies with all the requirements of this section other than those for which an exemption has been specifically provided in paragraph (i)(2) of this section:

(1) *Conditions.*

(i) The issuer is a foreign private issuer as defined in § 240.3b–4 and is not an investment company registered or required to be registered under the Investment Company Act of 1940 (15 U.S.C. 80a–1 et seq.), other than a registered closed-end investment company; and

(ii) Except in the case of an issuer tender offer which is commenced during the pendency of a tender offer made by a third party in reliance on § 240.14d–1(d), U.S. holders do not hold more than 40 percent of the class of securities sought in the offer (as determined under Instruction 2 to paragraphs (h)(8) and (i) of this section).

(2) *Exemptions.* The issuer tender offer shall comply with all requirements of this section other than the following:

(i) *Equal treatment—loan notes.* If the issuer or affiliate offers loan notes solely to offer sellers tax advantages not available in the United States and these notes are neither listed on any organized securities market nor registered under the Securities Act (15 U.S.C. 77a et seq.), the loan notes need not be offered to U.S. holders, notwithstanding paragraph (f)(8) and (h)(9) of this section.

(ii) *Equal treatment—separate U.S. and foreign offers.* Notwithstanding the provisions of paragraph (f)(8) of this section, an issuer or affiliate conducting an issuer tender offer meeting the conditions of paragraph (i)(1) of this section may separate the offer into two offers: One offer made only to U.S. holders and another offer made only to non-U.S. holders. The offer to U.S. holders must be made on terms at least as favorable as those offered any other holder of the same class of securities that is the subject of the tender offer.

(iii) *Notice of extensions.* Notice of extensions made in accordance with the requirements of the home jurisdiction law or practice will satisfy the requirements of § 240.14e–1(d).

(iv) *Prompt payment.* Payment made in accordance with the requirements of the home jurisdiction law or practice will satisfy the requirements of § 240.14e–1(c).

Instructions to paragraph (h)(8) and (i) of this section:

1. *Home jurisdiction* means both the jurisdiction of the issuer's incorporation, organization or chartering and the principal foreign market where the issuer's securities are listed or quoted.

2. *U.S. holder* means any security holder resident in the United States. To determine the percentage of outstanding securities held by U.S. holders:

i. Calculate the U.S. ownership as of 30 days before the commencement of the issuer tender offer;

ii. Include securities underlying American Depositary Shares convertible or exchangeable into the securities that are the subject of the tender offer when calculating the number of subject securities outstanding, as well as the number held by U.S. holders. Exclude from the calculations other types of securities that are convertible or exchangeable into the securities that are the subject of the tender offer, such as warrants, options and convertible securities. Exclude from those calculations securities held by persons who hold more than 10 percent of the subject securities;

iii. Use the method of calculating record ownership in § 240.12g3–2(a), except that your inquiry as to the amount of securities represented by accounts of customers resident in the United States may be limited to brokers, dealers, banks and other nominees located in the United States, your jurisdiction of incorporation, and the jurisdiction that is the primary trading market for the subject securities, if different than your jurisdiction of incorporation;

iv. If, after reasonable inquiry, you are unable to obtain information about the amount of securities represented by accounts of customers resident in the United States, you may assume, for purposes of this definition, that the customers are residents of the jurisdiction in which the nominee has its principal place of business; and

v. Count securities as beneficially owned by residents of the United States as reported on reports of beneficial ownership that are provided to you or publicly filed and based on information otherwise provided to you.

3. *United States.* United States means the United States of America, its territories and possessions, any State of the United States, and the District of Columbia.

4. The exemptions provided by paragraphs (h)(8) and (i) of this section are not available for any securities transaction or series of transactions that technically complies with paragraph (h)(8) or (i) of this section but are part of a plan or scheme to evade the provisions of this section.

(j)(1) It shall be a fraudulent, deceptive or manipulative act or practice, in connection with an issuer tender offer, for an issuer or an affiliate of such issuer, in connection with an issuer tender offer:

(i) to employ any device, scheme or artifice to defraud any person;

(ii) to make any untrue statement of a material fact or to omit to state a material fact necessary in order to make the statements made, in the light of the circumstances under which they were made, not misleading; or

(iii) to engage in any act, practice or course of business which operates or would operate as a fraud or deceit upon any person.

(2) As a means reasonably designed to prevent fraudulent, deceptive or manipulative acts or practices in connection with any issuer tender offer, it shall be unlawful for an issuer or an affiliate of such issuer to make an issuer tender offer unless:

(i) such issuer or affiliate complies with the requirements of paragraphs (b), (c), (d), (e), and (f) of this rule; and

(ii) the issuer tender offer is not in violation of paragraph (j)(1) of this rule.

Schedule 13E–4F. Tender Offer Statement Pursuant to Section 13(e)(1) of the Securities Exchange Act of 1934 and Rule 13e–4 Thereunder

U.S. SECURITIES AND EXCHANGE COMMISSION

Washington, D.C. 20549

ISSUER TENDER OFFER STATEMENT

(Pursuant to Section 13(e)(1) of the Securities Exchange Act of 1934)

(Amendment No. ______)

____
(Exact number of Issuer as specified in its charter)

____
(Translation of Issuer's Name into English) (if applicable)

____
(Jurisdiction of Issuer's Incorporation or Organization)

____
(Name(s) of Person(s) Filing Statement)

____
(Title of Class of Securities)

____
(CUSIP Number of Class of Securities) (if applicable)

(Name, address (including zip code) and telephone number (including area code) of person authorized to receive notices and communications on behalf of the person(s) filing statement)

(Date tender offer first published, sent or given to securityholders)

Calculation of Filing Fee

Transaction Valuation *	Amount of Filing Fee

* Set forth the amount on which the filing fee is calculated and state how it was determined.

[ ] Check box if any part of the fee is offset as provided by Rule 0–11(a)(2) and identify the filing with which the offsetting fee was previously paid. Identify the previous filing by registration statement number, or the Form or Schedule and the date of its filing.

Amount Previously Paid: ______
Registration No. ______
Filing Party: ______
Form: ______
Date Filed: ______

GENERAL INSTRUCTIONS

I. Eligibility Requirements for Use of Schedule 13E–4F

A. Schedule 13E–4F may be used by any foreign private issuer if: (1) the issuer is incorporated or organized under the laws of Canada or any Canadian province or territory; (2) the issuer is making a cash tender or exchange offer for the issuer's own securities; and (3) less than 40 percent of the class of such issuer's securities outstanding that is the subject of the tender offer is held by U.S. holders. The calculation of securities held by U.S. holders shall be made as of the end of the issuer's last quarter or, if such quarter terminated within 60 days of the filing date, as of the end of the issuer's preceding quarter.

Instructions. 1. For purposes of this Schedule, ''foreign private issuer'' shall be construed in accordance with Rule 405 under the Securities Act.

2. For purposes of this Schedule, the term ''U.S. holder'' shall mean any person whose address appears on the records of the issuer, any voting trustee, any depositary, any share transfer agent or any person acting in a similar capacity on behalf of the issuer as being located in the United States.

3. If this Schedule is filed during the pendency of one or more ongoing cash tender or exchange offers for securities of the class subject to this offer that was commenced or was eligible to be commenced on Schedule 14D–1F and/or Form F–8 or Form F–80, the date for calculation of U.S. ownership for purposes of this Schedule shall be the same as that date used by the initial bidder or issuer.

4. For purposes of this Schedule, the class of subject securities shall not include any securities that may be converted into or are exchangeable for the subject securities.

B. Any issuer using this Schedule must extend the cash tender or exchange offer to U.S. holders of the class of securities subject to the offer upon terms and conditions not less favorable than those extended to any other holder of the same class of such securities, and must comply with the requirements of any Canadian federal, provincial and/or territorial law, regulation or policy relating to the terms and conditions of the offer.

C. This Schedule shall not be used if the issuer is an investment company registered or required to be registered under the Investment Company Act of 1940.

II. Filing Instructions and Fees

A.(1) The issuer must file this Schedule and any amendment to the Schedule (see Part I, Item 1.(b)), including all exhibits and other documents filed as part of the Schedule or amendment, in electronic format via the Commission's Electronic Data Gathering, Analysis, and Retrieval (EDGAR) system in accordance with the EDGAR rules set forth in Regulation S–T (17 CFR Part 232). For assistance with technical questions about EDGAR or to request an access code, call the EDGAR Filer Support Office at (202) 942–8900. For assistance with the EDGAR rules, call the Office of EDGAR and Information Analysis at (202) 942–2940.

(2) If filing the Schedule in paper under a hardship exemption in 17 CFR 232.201 or 232.202 of Regulation S–T, or as otherwise

permitted, the issuer must file with the Commission at its principal office five copies of the complete Schedule and any amendment, including exhibits and all other documents filed as a part of the Schedule or amendment. The issuer must bind, staple or otherwise compile each copy in one or more parts without stiff covers. The issuer must further bind the Schedule or amendment on the side or stitching margin in a manner that leaves the reading matter legible. The issuer must provide three additional copies of the Schedule or amendment without exhibits to the Commission.

B. An electronic filer must provide the signatures required for the Schedule or amendment in accordance with 17 CFR 232.302 of Regulation S–T. An issuer filing in paper must have the original and at least one copy of the Schedule and any amendment signed in accordance with Exchange Act Rule 12b–11(d) (17 CFR 12b–11(d)) by the persons whose signatures are required for this Schedule or amendment. The issuer must also conform the unsigned copies.

C. At the time of filing this Schedule with the Commission, the issuer shall pay to the Commission in accordance with Rule 0–11 of the Exchange Act, a fee in U.S. dollars in the amount prescribed by Section 13(e)(3) of the Exchange Act. See also Rule 0–9 of the Exchange Act.

(1) The value of the securities to be acquired solely for cash shall be the amount of cash to be paid for them, calculated into U.S. dollars.

(2) The value of the securities to be acquired with securities or other non-cash consideration, whether or not in combination with a cash payment for the same securities, shall be based on the market value of the securities to be acquired by the issuer as established in accordance with paragraph (3) of this section.

(3) When the fee is based upon the market value of the securities, such market value shall be established by either the average of the high and low prices reported on the consolidated reporting system (for exchange-traded securities and last sale reported for over-the-counter securities) or the average of the bid and asked price (for other over-the-counter securities) as of a specified date within 5 business days prior to the date of filing the Schedule. If there is no market for the securities to be acquired by the issuer, the value shall be based upon the book value of such securities computed as of the latest practicable date prior to the date of filing of the Schedule, unless the issuer of the securities is in bankruptcy or receivership or has an accumulated capital deficit, in which case one-third of the principal amount, par value or stated value of such securities shall be used.

D. If at any time after the initial payment of the fee the aggregate consideration offered is increased, an additional filing fee based upon such increase shall be paid with the required amended filing.

E. The issuer must file the Schedule or amendment in electronic format in the English language in accordance with 17 CFR 232.306 of Regulation S–T. The issuer may file part of the Schedule or amendment, or exhibit or other attachment to the Schedule or amendment, in both French and English if the issuer included the French text to comply with the requirements of the Canadian securities administrator or other Canadian authority and, for an electronic filing, if the filing is an HTML document, as defined in 17 CFR 232.11 of Regulation S–T. For both an electronic filing and a paper filing, the issuer may provide an English translation or English summary of a foreign language document as an exhibit or other attachment to the Schedule or amendment as permitted by the rules of the applicable Canadian securities administrator.

F. A paper filer must number sequentially the signed original of the Schedule or amendment (in addition to any internal numbering that otherwise may be present) by handwritten, typed, printed or other legible form of notation from the first page through the last page of the Schedule or amendment, including any exhibits or attachments. A paper filer must disclose the total number of pages on the first page of the sequentially numbered Schedule or amendment.

III. Compliance with the Exchange Act

A. Pursuant to Rule 13e–4(g) under the Exchange Act, the issuer shall be deemed to comply with the requirements of Section 13(e)(1) of the Exchange Act and Rule 13e–4 and Schedule 13E–4 thereunder in connection with a cash tender or exchange offer for securities that may be made pursuant to this Schedule, *provided that,* if an exemption has been granted from the requirements of Canadian federal, provincial and/or territorial laws, regulations or policies, and the tender offer does not comply with requirements that otherwise would be prescribed by Rule 13e–4, the issuer (absent an order from the Commission) shall comply with the provisions of Section 13(e)(1) and Rule 13e–4 and Schedule 14E–4 thereunder.

B. Any cash tender or exchange offer made pursuant to this Schedule is not exempt from the antifraud provisions of Section 10(b) of the Exchange Act and Rule 10b–5 thereunder, Section 13(e)(1) of the Exchange Act and Rule 13e–4(b)(1) thereunder, and Section 14(e) of the Exchange Act and Rule 14e–3 thereunder, and this Schedule shall be deemed "filed" for purposes of Section 18 of the Exchange Act.

C. The issuer's attention is directed to Regulation M (§§ 242.100 through 242.105 of this chapter), in the case of an issuer exchange offer, and to Rule 10b–13 under the Exchange Act (§ 240.10b–13), in the case of an issuer cash tender offer or issuer exchange offer. [*See* Exchange Act Release No. 29355 (June 21, 1991) containing an exemption from Rule 10b–13.]

PART I. INFORMATION REQUIRED TO BE SENT TO SHAREHOLDERS

Item 1. Home Jurisdiction Documents

(a) This Schedule shall be accompanied by the entire disclosure document or documents required to be delivered to holders of securities to be acquired by the issuer in the proposed transaction pursuant to the laws, regulations or policies of the Canadian jurisdiction in which the issuer is incorporated or organized, and any other Canadian federal, provincial and/or territorial law, regulation or policy relating to the terms and conditions of the offer. The Schedule need not include any documents incorporated by reference into such disclosure document(s) and not distributed to offerees pursuant to any such law, regulation or policy.

(b) Any amendment made by the issuer to a home jurisdiction document or documents shall be filed with the Commission under cover of this Schedule, which must indicate on the cover page the number of the amendment.

(c) In an exchange offer where securities of the issuer have been or are to be offered or cancelled in the transaction, such securities shall be registered on forms promulgated by the Commission under the Securities Act of 1933 including, where available, the Commission's Form F–8 or F–80 providing for inclusion in that registration statement of the home jurisdiction prospectus.

Item 2. Informational Legends

The following legends, to the extent applicable, shall appear on the outside front cover page of the home jurisdiction document(s) in bold-face roman type at least as high as ten-point modern type and at least two-points leaded:

> This tender offer is made by a foreign issuer for its own securities, and while the offer is subject to disclosure requirements of the country in which the issuer is incorporated or organized, investors should be aware that these requirements are different from those of the United States. Financial

statements included herein, if any, have been prepared in accordance with foreign generally accepted accounting principles and thus may not be comparable to financial statements of United States companies.

The enforcement by investors of civil liabilities under the federal securities laws may be affected adversely by the fact that the issuer is located in a foreign country, and that some or all of its officers and directors are residents of a foreign country.

"Investors should be aware that the issuer or its affiliates, directly or indirectly, may bid for or make purchases of the securities of the issuer subject to the offer, or of its related securities, during the period of the issuer tender offer, as permitted by applicable Canadian laws or provincial laws or regulations."

Note to Item 2. If the home jurisdiction document(s) are delivered through an electronic medium, the issuer may satisfy the legibility requirements for the required legends relating to type size and fonts by presenting the legend in any manner reasonably calculated to draw security holder attention to it.

PART II. INFORMATION NOT REQUIRED TO BE SENT TO SHAREHOLDERS

The exhibits specified below shall be filed as part of the Schedule, but are not required to be sent to shareholders unless so required pursuant to the laws, regulations or policies of Canada and/or any of its provinces or territories. Exhibits shall be lettered or numbered appropriately for convenient reference.

(1) File any reports or information that, in accordance with the requirements of the home jurisdiction(s), must be made publicly available by the issuer in connection with the transaction, but need not be disseminated to shareholders.

(2) File copies of any documents incorporated by reference into the home jurisdiction document(s).

(3) If any name is signed to the Schedule pursuant to power of attorney, manually signed copies of any such power of attorney shall be filed. If the name of any officer signing on behalf of the issuer is signed pursuant to a power of attorney, certified copies of a resolution of the issuer's board of directors authorizing such signature also shall be filed.

PART III. UNDERTAKINGS AND CONSENT TO SERVICE OF PROCESS

1. Undertakings

The Schedule shall set forth the following undertakings of the issue:

(a) The issuer undertakes to make available, in person or by telephone, representatives to respond to inquiries made by the Commission staff, and to furnish promptly, when requested to do so by the Commission staff, information relating to this Schedule or to transactions in said securities.

(b) The issuer also undertakes to disclose in the United States, on the same basis as it is required to make such disclosure pursuant to applicable Canadian federal and/or provincial or territorial laws, regulations or policies, or otherwise discloses, information regarding purchases of the issuer's securities in connection with the cash tender or exchange offer covered by this Schedule. Such information shall be set forth in amendments to this Schedule.

2. Consent to Service of Process

(a) At the time of filing this Schedule, the issuer shall file with the Commission a written irrevocable consent and power of attorney on Form F–X.

(b) Any change to the name or address of a registrant's agent for service shall be communicated promptly to the Commission by amendment to Form F–X referencing the file number of the registrant.

PART IV. SIGNATURES

A. The Schedule shall be signed by each person on whose behalf the Schedule is filed or its authorized representative. If the Schedule is signed on behalf of a person by his authorized representative (other than an executive officer or general partner of the company), evidence of the representative's authority shall be filed with the Schedule.

B. The name of each person who signs the Schedule shall be typed or printed beneath his signature.

C. By signing this Schedule, the person(s) filing the Schedule consents without power of revocation that any administrative subpoena may be served, or any administrative proceeding, civil suit or civil action where the cause of action arises out of or relates to or concerns any offering made or purported to be made in connection with the filing on Schedule 13E–4F or any purchases or sales of any securities in connection therewith, may be commenced against it in any administrative tribunal or in any appropriate court in any place subject to the jurisdiction of any state or of the United States by service of said subpoena or process upon the registrant's designated agent.

After due inquiry and to the best of my knowledge and belief, I certify that the information set forth in this statement is true, complete and correct.

____
(Signature)

____
(Name and Title)

____
(Date)

Rule 13f–1. Reporting by Institutional Investment Managers of Information With Respect to Accounts Over Which They Exercise Investment Discretion

(a)(1) Every institutional investment manager which exercises investment discretion with respect to accounts holding section 13(f) securities, as defined in paragraph (c) of this section, having an aggregate fair market value on the last trading day of any month of any calendar year of at least $100,000,000 shall file a report on Form 13F with the Commission within 45 days after the last day of such calendar year and within 45 days after the last day of each of the first three calendar quarters of the subsequent calendar year.

(2) An amendment to a Form 13F (§ 249.325 of this chapter) report, other than one reporting only holdings that were not previously reported in a public filing for the same period, must set forth the complete text of the Form 13F. Amendments must be numbered sequentially.

(b) For the purposes of this rule, "investment discretion" has the meaning set forth in section 3(a)(35) of the Act. An institutional investment manager shall also be deemed to exercise "investment discretion" with respect to all accounts over which any person under its control exercises investment discretion.

(c) For purposes of this rule "section 13(f) securities" shall mean equity securities of a class described in section 13(d)(1) of the Act that are admitted to trading on a national securities exchange or quoted on the automated quotation system of a registered securities association. In determining what classes of securities are section 13(f) securities, an institutional investment manager may rely on the most recent list of such securities published by the Commission pursuant to section 13(f)(3) of the Act. Only securities of a class on such list shall be counted in determining whether an institutional investment manager must file a report under this rule and only those securities shall be reported in such report. Where a person controls the issuer of a class of equity securities which are "section 13(f) securities" as defined in this rule, those securities shall not be deemed to be "section 13(f) securities" with respect to the controlling person, provided that such person does not otherwise exercise investment discretion with respect to accounts with fair market value of at least

$100,000,000 within the meaning of paragraph (a) of this section.

Form 13F. Information Required of Institutional Investment Managers Pursuant to Section 13(f) of the Securities Exchange Act of 1934 and Rules Thereunder

General Instructions

1. *Rule as to Use of Form 13F.* Institutional investment managers ("Managers") must use Form 13F for reports to the Commission required by Section 13(f) of the Securities Exchange Act of 1934 [15 U.S.C. 78m(f)] ("Exchange Act") and rule 13f–1 [17 CFR 240.13f–1] thereunder. Rule 13f–1(a) provides that every Manager which exercises investment discretion with respect to accounts holding Section 13(f) securities, as defined in rule 13f–1(c), having an aggregate fair market value on the last trading day of any month of any calendar year of at least $100,000,000 shall file a report on Form 13F with the Commission within 45 days after the last day of such calendar year and within 45 days after the last day of each of the first three calendar quarters of the subsequent calendar year.

2. *Rules to Prevent Duplicative Reporting.* If two or more Managers, each of which is required by rule 13f–1 to file a report on Form 13F for the reporting period, exercise investment discretion with respect to the same securities, only one such Manager must include information regarding such securities in its reports on Form 13F.

A Manager having securities over which it exercises investment discretion that are reported by another Manager (or Managers) must identify the Manager(s) reporting on its behalf in the manner described in Special Instruction 6.

A Manager reporting holdings subject to shared investment discretion must identify the other Manager(s) with respect to which the filing is made in the manner described in Special Instruction 8.

3. *Filing of Form 13F.* A Manager must file a Form 13F report with the Commission within 45 days after the end of each calendar year and each of the first three calendar quarters of each calendar year. As required by Section 13(f)(4) of the Exchange Act, a Manager which is a bank, the deposits of which are insured in accordance with the Federal Deposit Insurance Act, must file with the appropriate regulatory agency for the bank a copy of every Form 13F report filed with the Commission pursuant to this subsection by or with respect to such bank. Filers who file Form 13F electronically can satisfy their obligation to file with other regulatory agencies by sending (a) a paper copy of the EDGAR filing (provided the Manager removes or blanks out the confidential access codes); (b) the filing in electronic format, if the regulatory agency with which the filing is being made has made provisions to receive filings in electronic format; or (c) for filers filing in paper format under continuing hardship exemptions, a copy of the Form 13F paper filing.

4. *Official List of Section 13(f) Securities.* The official list of Section 13(f) Securities published by the Commission (the "13F List") lists the securities the holdings of which a Manager is to report on Form 13F. *See* rule 13f–1(c) [17 CFR 240.13f–1(c)]. Form 13F filers may rely on the current 13F List in determining whether they need to report any particular securities holding. Paper copies are available at a reasonable fee from the Securities and Exchange Commission, Public Reference Room, 450 Fifth Street, N.W., Washington, D.C. 20549.

Instructions for Confidential Treatment Requests

Pursuant to Section 13(f)(3) of the Exchange Act [15 U.S.C. 78m(f)(3)], the Commission (1) may prevent or delay public disclosure of information reported on this form in accordance with Section 552 of Title 5 of the United States Code, the Freedom of Information Act [5 U.S.C. 552], and (2) shall not disclose information reported on this form identifying securities held by the account of a natural person or an estate or trust (other than a business trust or investment company). A Manager must submit in accordance with the procedures for requesting confidential treatment any portion of a report which contains information identifying securities held by the account of a natural person or an estate or trust (other than a business trust or investment company).

A Manager should make requests for confidential treatment of information reported on this form in accordance with rule 24b–2 under the Exchange Act [17 CFR 240.24b–2]. Requests relating to the non-disclosure of information identifying the securities held by the account of a natural person or an estate or trust (other than a business trust or investment company) must so state but need not, in complying with paragraph (b)(2)(ii) of rule 24b–2, include an analysis of any applicable exemptions from disclosure under the Commission's rules and regulations adopted under the Freedom of Information Act [17 CFR 200.80].

Paragraph (b) of rule 24b–2 requires a Manager filing confidential information with the Commission to indicate at the appropriate place in the public filing that the confidential portion has been so omitted and filed separately with the Commission. A Manager should comply with this provision by including on the Summary Page, after the Report Summary and prior to the List of Other Included Managers, a statement that confidential information has been omitted from the public Form 13F report and filed separately with the Commission.

A Manager must file in paper, in accordance with rule 101(c)(1)(i) of Regulation S-T [17 CFR 232.101(c)(1)(i)], all requests for and information subject to the request for confidential treatment filed pursuant to Section 13(f)(3) of the Exchange Act. If a Manager requests confidential treatment with respect to information required to be reported on Form 13F, the Manager must file in paper with the Secretary of the Commission an original and four copies of the Form 13F reporting information for which the Manager requests confidential treatment.

A Manager requesting confidential treatment must provide enough factual support for its request to enable the Commission to make an informed judgment as to the merits of the request. The request should address all pertinent factors, including all of the following that are relevant:

1. If confidential treatment is requested as to more than one holding of securities, discuss each holding separately unless the Manager can identify a class or classes of holdings as to which the nature of the factual circumstances and the legal analysis are substantially the same.

2. If a request for confidential treatment is based upon a claim that the subject information is confidential, commercial or financial information, provide the information required by paragraphs 2.a through 2.e of this Instruction except that, if the subject information concerns security holdings that represent open risk arbitrage positions and no previous requests for confidential treatment of those holdings have been made, the Manager need provide only the information required in paragraph 2.f.

a. Describe the investment strategy being followed with respect to the relevant securities holdings, including the extent of any program of acquisition and disposition (note that the term "investment strategy," as used in this instruction, also includes activities such as block positioning).

b. Explain why public disclosure of the securities would, in fact, be likely to reveal the investment strategy; consider this matter in light of the specific reporting requirements of Form 13F (e.g., securities holdings are reported only quarterly and may be aggregated in many cases).

c. Demonstrate that such revelation of an investment strategy would be premature; indicate whether the Manager was engaged in a program of acquisition or disposition of the security both at the end of the quarter and at the time of the filing; and address whether the existence of such a program may otherwise be known to the public.

d. Demonstrate that failure to grant the request for confidential treatment would be likely to cause substantial harm to the Manager's competitive position; show what use competitors could make of the information and how harm to the Manager could ensue.

e. State the period of time for which confidential treatment of the securities holdings is requested. The time period specified may not exceed one (1) year from the date that the Manager is required to file the Form 13F report with the Commission.

f. For securities holdings that represent open risk arbitrage positions, the request must include good faith representations that:

i. The securities holding represents a risk arbitrage position open on the last day of the period for which the Form 13F report is filed; and

ii. The reporting Manager has a reasonable belief as of the period end that it may not close the entire position on or before the date that the Manager is required to file the Form 13F report with the Commission.

If the Manager makes these representations in writing at the time that the Form 13F is filed, the Commission will automatically accord the subject securities holdings confidential treatment for a period of up to one (1) year from the date that the Manager is required to file the Form 13F report with the Commission.

g. At the expiration of the period for which confidential treatment has been granted pursuant to paragraph 2.3 or 2.f of this Instruction (the "Expiration Date"), the Commission, without additional notice to the reporting manager, will make such security holdings public unless a *de novo* request for confidential treatment of the information that meets the requirements of paragraphs 2.a through 2.e of this Instruction is filed with the Commission at least fourteen (14) days in advance of the Expiration Date.

3. If the Commission grants a request for confidential treatment, it may delete details which would identify the Manager and use the information in tabulations required by Section 13(f)(3) absent a separate showing that such use of information could be harmful.

4. Upon the denial by the Commission of a request for confidential treatment, or upon the expiration of the confidential treatment previously granted for a filing, unless a hardship exemption is available, the Manager must submit electronically, within six (6) business days of the expiration or notification of the denial, as applicable, a Form 13F report, or an amendment to its publicly filed Form 13F report, if applicable, listing those holdings as to which the Commission denied confidential treatment or for which confidential treatment has expired. If a Manager files an amendment, the amendment must not be a restatement; the Manager must designate it as an amendment which adds new holdings entries. The Manager must include at the top of the Form 13F Cover Page the following legend to correctly designate the type of filing being made:

THIS FILING LISTS SECURITIES HOLDINGS REPORTED ON THE Form 13F FILED ON (DATE) PURSUANT TO A REQUEST FOR CONFIDENTIAL TREATMENT AND FOR WHICH (THAT REQUEST WAS DENIED/CONFIDENTIAL TREATMENT EXPIRED) ON (DATE).

Special Instructions

1. This form consists of three parts: the Form 13F Cover Page (the "Cover Page"), the Form 13F Summary Page (the "Summary Page"), and the Form 13F Information Table (the "Information Table").

2. When preparing the report, omit all bracketed text. Include brackets used to form check boxes.

The Cover Page

3. The period end date used in the report (and in the EDGAR submission header) is the last day of the calendar year or quarter, as appropriate, even though that date may not be the same as the date used for valuation in accordance with Special Instruction 9.

4. Amendments to a Form 13F report must either restate the Form 13F report in its entirety or include only holdings entries that are being reported in addition to those already reported in a current public Form 13F report for the same period. If the Manager is filing the Form 13F report as an amendment, then, the Manager must check the amendment box on the Cover Page; enter the amendment number; and check the appropriate box to indicate whether the amendment (a) is a restatement or (b) adds new holdings entries. Each amendment must include a complete Cover Page and, if applicable, a Summary Page and Information Table. *See* rule 13f–1(a)(2) [17 CFR 240.13f–1(a)(2)].

5. Present the Cover Page and the Summary Page information in the format and order provided in the form. The Cover Page may include information in addition to the required information, so long as the additional information does not, either by its nature, quantity, or manner of presentation, impede the understanding or presentation of the required information. Place all additional information after the signature of the person signing the report (immediately preceding the Report Type section). Do not include any additional information on the Summary Page or in the Information Table.

6. Designate the Report Type for the Form 13F report by checking the appropriate box in the Report Type section of the Cover Page, and include, where applicable, the List of Other Managers Reporting for this Manager (on the Cover Page), the Summary Page and the Information Table, as follows:

a. If all of the securities with respect to which a Manager has investment discretion are reported by another Manager (or Managers), check the box for Report Type "13F NOTICE," include (on the Cover Page) the List of Other Managers Reporting for this Manager, and omit both the Summary Page and the Information Table.

b. If all of the securities with respect to which a Manager has investment discretion are reported in this report, check the box for Report Type "13F HOLDINGS REPORT," omit from the Cover Page the List of Other Managers Reporting for this Manager, and include both the Summary Page and the Information Table.

c. If only part of the securities with respect to which a Manager has investment discretion is reported by another Manager (or Managers), check the box for Report Type "13F COMBINATION REPORT," include (on the Cover Page) the List of Other Managers Reporting for this Manager, and include both the Summary Page and the Information Table.

Summary Page

7. Include on the Summary Page the Report Summary, containing the Number of Other Included Managers, the Information Table Entry Total and the Information Table Value Total.

a. Enter as the Number of Other Included Managers the total number of other Managers listed in the List of Other Included Managers on the Summary Page, not counting the Manager filing this report. *See* Special Instruction 8. If none, enter the number zero ("0")

b. Enter as the Information Table Entry Total the total number of line entries providing holdings information included in the Information Table.

c. Enter as the Information Table Value Total the aggregate fair market value of all holdings reported in this report, *i.e.*, the total for Column 4 (Fair Market Value) of all line entries in the Information Table. The Manager must express this total as a rounded figure, corresponding to the individual Column 4 entries in the Information Table. *See* Special Instruction 9.

8. Include on the Summary Page the List of Other Included Managers. Use the title, column headings and format provided.

a. If this Form 13F report does not report the holdings of any Manager other than the Manager filing this report, enter the word "NONE" under the title and omit the column headings and list entries.

b. If this Form 13F report reports the holdings of one or more Managers other than the Manager filing this report, enter in the List of Other Included Managers all such Managers together with their respective Form 13F file numbers, if known. (The Form 13F file numbers are assigned to Managers when they file their first Form 13F.) Assign a number to each Manager in the List of Other Included Managers, and present the list in sequential order. The numbers need not be consecutive. The List of Other Managers must include all other Managers identified in Column 7 of the Information Table. Do not include the Manager filing this report.

Information Table

9. In determining fair market value, use the value at the close of trading on the last trading day of the calendar year or quarter, as appropriate. Enter values rounded to the nearest one thousand dollars (with "000" omitted).

10. A Manager may omit holdings otherwise reportable if the Manager holds, on the period end date, fewer than 10,000 shares (or less than $200,000 principal amount in the case of convertible debt securities) and less than $200,000 aggregate fair market value (and option holdings to purchase only such amounts).

11. A Manager must report holdings of options only if the options themselves are Section 13(f) securities. For purposes of the $100,000,000 reporting threshold, the Manager should consider only the value of such options, not the value of the underlying shares. The Manager must give the entries in Columns 1 through 5 and in Columns 7 and 8 of the Information Table, however, in terms of the securities underlying the options, not the options themselves. The Manager must answer Column 6 in terms of the discretion to exercise the option. The Manager must make a separate segregation in respect of securities underlying options for entries for each of the columns, coupled with a designation "PUT" or "CALL" following such segregated entries in Column 5, referring to securities subject respectively to put and call options. A Manager is not required to provide an entry in Column 8 for securities subject to reported call options.

12. Furnish the Information Table using the table title, column headings and format provided. Provide column headings once at the beginning of the Information Table; repetition of column headings on subsequent pages is not required. Present the table in accordance with the column instructions provided in Special Instructions 12.b.i through 12.b.viii. Do not include any additional information in the Information Table. Begin the Information Table on a new page; do not include any portion of the Information Table on either the Cover Page or the Summary Page.

a. In entering information in Columns 4 through 8 of the Information Table, list securities of the same issuer and class with respect to which the Manager exercises sole investment discretion separately from those with respect to which investment discretion is shared. Special Instruction 12.b.vi for Column 6 describes in detail how to report shared investment discretion.

b. Instructions for each column in the Information Table:

i. *Column 1. Name of Issuer.* Enter in Column 1 the name of the issuer for each class of security reported as it appears in the current official list of Section 13(f) Securities published by the Commission in accordance with rule 13f–1(c) (the "13F List"). Reasonable abbreviations are permitted.

ii. *Column 2. Title of Class.* Enter in Column 2 the title of the class of the security reported as it appears in the 13F List. Reasonable abbreviations are permitted.

iii. *Column 3. CUSIP Number.* Enter in Column 3 the nine (9) digit CUSIP number of the security.

iv. *Column 4. Market Value.* Enter in Column 4 the market value of the holding of the particular class of security as prescribed by Special Instruction 9.

v. *Column 5. Amount and Type of Security.* Enter in Column 5 the total number of shares of the class of security or the principal amount of such class. Use the abbreviation "SH" to designate shares and "PRN" to designate principal amount. If the holdings being reported are put or call options, enter the designation "PUT" or "CALL," as appropriate.

vi. *Column 6. Investment Discretion.* Segregate the holdings of securities of a class according to the nature of the investment discretion held by the Manager. Designate investment discretion as "sole" (SOLE); "shared-defined" (DEFINED); or "shared-other" (OTHER), as described below:

(A) *Sole.* Designate as "sole" securities over which the Manager exercised sole investment discretion. Report "sole" securities on one line. Enter the word SOLE in Column 6.

(B) *Shared-Defined.* If investment discretion is shared with controlling and controlled companies (such as bank holding companies and their subsidiaries); investment advisers and investment companies advised by those advisers; or insurance companies and their separate accounts, then designate investment discretion as "shared-defined" (DEFINED).

For each holding of DEFINED securities, segregate the securities into two categories: those securities over which investment discretion is shared with another Manager or Managers on whose behalf this Form 13F report is being filed, and those securities over which investment discretion is shared with any other person, other than a Manager on whose behalf this Form 13F report is being filed.

Enter each of the two segregations of DEFINED securities holdings on a separate line, and enter the designation DEFINED in Column 6. *See* Special Instruction for Column 7.

(C) *Shared-Other.* Designate as "shared-Other" securities (OTHER) those over which investment discretion is shared in a manner other than that described in Special Instruction above.

For each holding of OTHER securities, segregate the securities into two categories: those securities over which investment discretion is shared with another Manager or Managers on whose behalf this Form 13F report is being filed, and those securities over which investment discretion is shared with any other person, other than a Manager on whose behalf this Form 13F report is being filed.

Enter each segregation of OTHER securities holdings on a separate line, and enter the designation "OTHER" in Column 6. *See* Special Instruction for Column 7.

Note: A Manager is deemed to share discretion with respect to all accounts over which any person under its control exercises discretion. A Manager of an institutional account, such as a pension fund or investment company, is not deemed to share discretion with the institution unless the institution actually participated in the investment decision-making.

vii. *Column 7. Other Managers.* Identify each other Manager on whose behalf this Form 13F report is being filed with whom investment discretion is shared as to any reported holding by entering in this column the number assigned to the Manager in the List of Other Included Managers.

Enter this number in Column 7 opposite the segregated entries in Columns 4, 5 and 8 (and the relevant indication of shared discretion set forth in Column 6) as required by the preceding special instruction. Enter no other names or numbers in Column 7.

A Manager must report the conditions of sharing discretion with other Managers consistently for all holdings reported on a single line.

viii. *Column 8. Voting Authority.* Enter the number of shares for which the Manager exercises sole, shared, or no voting authority (none) in this column, as appropriate.

The Commission deems a Manager exercising sole voting authority over specified "routine" matters, and no authority to vote in "non-routine" matters, for purposes of this Form 13F report to have no voting authority. "Non-routine" matters include a contested election of directors, a merger, a sale of substantially all the assets, a change in the articles of incorporation affecting the rights of shareholders, and a change in fundamental investment policy; "routine" matters include selection of an accountant, uncontested election of directors, and approval of an annual report.

If voting authority is shared only in a manner similar to a sharing of investment discretion which would call for a response of "shared-defined" (DEFINED) under Column 6, a Manager should report voting authority as sole under subdivision (a) of Column 8, even though the Manager may be deemed to share investment discretion with that person under Special Instruction 12.-b.vi.

13. Preparation of the electronic filing:

a. No line on the Cover Page or the Summary Page may exceed 80 characters in length. *See* rule 305 of Regulation S-T [17 CFR 232.305].

b. No line in the Form 13F Information Table may exceed 132 characters in length. *See* rule 305 of Regulation S-T [17 CFR 232.305].

c. If the Form 13F Report Type is "13F HOLDINGS REPORT" or "13F COMBINATION REPORT," then place one EDGAR <PAGE> tag at the end of the Cover Page and one <PAGE> tag at the end of the Summary Page. Additional EDGAR <PAGE> tags are not required. Those electing to include additional <PAGE> tags should, for each page containing a <PAGE> tag, include no more than sixty (60) lines per page, including the line on which the <PAGE> tag is placed.

d. In preparing the Form 13F report for electronic filing, a Manager may omit underscoring used in the form to indicate the placement of information that the Manager is to furnish.

e. Use the following EDGAR submission types for the following Form 13F Report Types:

Form 13F report type	EDGAR submission type
13F HOLDINGS REPORT	
Initial Filing	13F-HR
Amendments	13F-HR/A
13F NOTICE	
Initial Filing	13F-NT
Amendments	13F-NT/A
13F COMBINATION REPORT	
Initial Filing	13F-HR
Amendments	13F-HR/A

Paperwork Reduction Act Information

Persons who are to respond to the collection of information contained in this form are not required to respond to the collection of information unless the form displays a currently valid OMB control number.

Section 13(f) of the Exchange Act requires the Commission to adopt rules creating a reporting and disclosure system to collect specific information and to disseminate such information to the public. Rule 13f–1 under the Exchange Act (17 CFR 240.13f–1) requires institutional investment managers who exercise investment discretion over certain accounts of equity securities described in Section 13(d)(1) of the Exchange Act [15 U.S.C. 78m(d)(1)] (generally, exchange traded or NASDAQ-quoted securities) having, in the aggregate, a fair market value of at least $100,000,000 to file quarterly reports with the Commission on Form 13F with respect to the value of those securities over which they have investment discretion.

The purpose of Form 13F is to provide a reporting and disclosure system to collect specific information and to disseminate such information to the public about the holdings of institutional investment managers who exercise investment discretion over certain accounts of equity securities described in Section 13(d)(1) of the Exchange Act [15 U.S.C. 78m(d)(1)] (generally, exchange traded or NASDAQ-quoted securities) having, in the aggregate, a fair market value of at least $100,000,000. We believe that investors will find Form 13F report information useful in tracking institutional investor holdings in their investments and that issuers, too, will find detail as to institutional investor holdings useful because much of their shareholder list may reflect holdings in "street name" rather than beneficial ownership. We believe that mandatory electronic dissemination of this data will help ensure timely and efficient dissemination of this important information. We believe that these reports should have the same degree of availability as other filings with the Commission, and that electronic filing will speed their dissemination in accordance with the intent of Congress.

We estimate that each filer spends an average of 24.7 hours preparing each quarterly report. In addition, we estimate that, each quarter, approximately 50 managers will resubmit information previously filed in paper pursuant to a grant of confidential treatment and that each such manager will spend an additional hour on the resubmission.

Any member of the public may direct to the Commission any comments concerning the accuracy of this burden estimate and any suggestions for reducing this burden.

Responses to the collection of information are mandatory. *See* Section 13(f) of the Exchange Act [15 U.S.C. 78m(f)] and rule 13f–1 [17 CFR 240.13f–1] thereunder.

Section 13(f)(3) of the Exchange Act [15 U.S.C. 78m(f)(3)] authorizes the Commission, as it determines necessary or appropriate in the public interest or for the protection of investors, to delay or prevent public disclosure of any information filed under Section 13(f) upon request. It also prohibits the Commission from disclosing to the public information identifying securities held by the account of a natural person or any estate or trust (other than a business trust or investment company).

This collection of information has been reviewed by OMB in accordance with the clearance requirements of 44 U.S.C. Section 3507.

Form 13F Cover Page

Report for the Calendar Year or Quarter Ended: ____________________

Check here if Amendment []; Amendment Number: ____________________

This Amendment (Check only one.):

☐ is a restatement.

☐ adds new holdings entries.

Institutional Investment Manager Filing this Report:

Name: ____________________

Address: ____________________

____

____

Form 13F File Number: 28-____________

The institutional investment manager filing this report and the person by whom it is signed hereby represent that the person signing the report is authorized to submit it, that all information contained herein is true, correct and complete, and that it is understood that all required items, statements, schedules, lists, and tables, are considered integral parts of this form.

Person Signing this Report on Behalf of Reporting Manager:

Name: ____________

Title: ____________

Phone: ____________

Signature, Place, and Date of Signing:

____

[Signature]

____

[City, State]

____

[Date]

Report Type (Check only one.):

☐ 13F HOLDINGS REPORT. (Check here if all holdings of this reporting manager are reported in this report.)

☐ 13F NOTICE. (Check here if no holdings reported are in this report, and all holdings are reported by other reporting manager(s).)

☐ 13F COMBINATION REPORT. (Check here if a portion of the holdings for this reporting manager are reported in this report and a portion are reported by other reporting manager(s).)

List of Other Managers Reporting for this Manager: [If there are no entries in this list, omit this section.]

Form 13F File Number 28- ____________

Name ____________

[Repeat as necessary.]

Form 13F Summary Page

Report Summary:

Number of Other Included Managers: ____

Form 13F Information Table Entry Total: ____

Form 13F Information Table Value Total: $______ (thousands)

List of Other Included Managers:

Provide a numbered list of the name(s) and Form 13F file number(s) of all institutional investment managers with respect to which this report is filed, other than the manager filing this report. [If there are no entries in this list, state "NONE" and omit the column headings and list entries.]

No. ____________

Form 13F File Number 28- ____________

Name ____________

[Repeat as necessary.]

Form 13F Information Table

Column 1	Column 2	Column 3	Column 4	Column 5			Column 6	Column 7	Column 8		
Name of issuer	Title of class	CUSIP	Value (×$1000)	Shrs or prn amt	SH/PRN	Put/Call	Investment discretion	Other managers	Voting authority Sole	Shared	None

SCHEDULE 13G. Information to Be Included in Statements Filed Pursuant to 13d–1(b), (c) and (d) and Amendments Thereto Filed Pursuant to 13d–2

SCHEDULE 13G

Under the Securities Exchange Act of 1934

(Amendment No._______)*

____
(Name of Issuer)

____
(Title of Class of Securities)

____
(CUSIP Number)

____
(Date of Event Which Requires Filing of this Statement)

Check the appropriate box to designate the rule pursuant to which this Schedule is filed:

[ ] Rule 13d–1(b)

[ ] Rule 13d–1(c)

[ ] Rule 13d–1(d)

Check the following box if a fee is being paid with this statement. (A fee is not required only if the filing person: (1) has a previous statement on file reporting beneficial ownership of more than five percent of the class of securities described in Item 1; and (2) has filed no amendment subsequent thereto reporting beneficial ownership of five percent or less of such class.) (See Rule 13d–7.)

☐

CUSIP No._______

(1) Names of Reporting Persons. I.R.S. Identification Nos. of Above Persons (Entities Only).

(2) Check the Appropriate Box if a Member of a Group (See Instructions)

(a)
(b)

(3) SEC Use Only

(4) Citizenship or Place of Organization

Number of Shares Beneficially Owned by Each Reporting Person With	(5) Sole Voting Power
	(6) Shared Voting Power
	(7) Sole Dispositive Power
	(8) Shared Dispositive Power

(9) Aggregate Amount Beneficially Owned by Each Reporting Person

(10) Check if the Aggregate Amount in Row (9) Excludes Certain Shares (See Instructions)

(11) Percent of Class Represented by Amount in Row (9)

(12) Type of Reporting Person (See Instructions)

INSTRUCTIONS FOR COVER PAGE

(1) *Names and I.R.S. Identification Numbers of Reporting Persons.* Furnish the full legal name of each person for whom the report is filed—i.e., each person required to sign the schedule itself—including each member of a group. Do not include the name of a person required to be identified in the report but who is not a reporting person. Reporting persons that are entities are requested to furnish their I.R.S. identification numbers, although disclosure of such numbers is voluntary, not mandatory (see "SPECIAL INSTRUCTIONS FOR COMPLYING WITH SCHEDULE 13G", below).

(2) If any of the shares beneficially owned by a reporting person are held as a member of a group and that membership is expressly affirmed, please check row 2(a). If the reporting person disclaims membership in a group or describes a relationship with other person but does not affirm the existence of a group, please check row 2(b) [unless it is a joint filing pursu-

* The remainder of this cover page shall be filled out for a reporting person's initial filing on this form with respect to the subject class of securities, and for any subsequent amendment containing information which would alter the disclosures provided in a prior page.

The information required in the remainder of this cover page shall not be deemed to be "filed" for the purpose of Section 18 of the Securities Exchange Act of 1934 ("Act") or otherwise subject to the liabilities of that section of the Act but shall be subject to all other provisions of the Act (however, see Notes).

ant to Rule 13d–1(k)(1) in which case it may not be necessary to check row 2(b)].

(3) The third row is for SEC internal use; please leave blank.

(4) *Citizenship or Place of Organization.* Furnish citizenship if the named reporting person is a natural person. Otherwise, furnish place of organization.

(10) Check if the aggregate amount reported as beneficially owned in row (9) does not include shares as to which beneficial ownership is disclaimed pursuant to Rule 13d–4 under the Securities Exchange Act of 1934.

(5)–(9), (11) *Aggregate Amount Beneficially Owned By Each Reporting Person, etc.* Rows (5) through (9) inclusive, and (11) are to be completed in accordance with the provisions of Item 4 of Schedule 13G. All percentages are to be rounded off to the nearest tenth (one place after decimal point).

(12) *Type of Reporting Person.* Please classify each "reporting person" according to the following breakdown (see Item 3 of Schedule 13G) and place the appropriate symbol on the form:

Category	**Symbol**
Broker Dealer	BD
Bank	BK
Insurance Company	IC
Investment Company	IV
Investment Adviser	IA
Employee Benefit Plan or Endowment Fund	EP
Parent Holding Company/Control Person	HC
Savings Association	SA
Church Plan	CP
Corporation	CO
Partnership	PN
Individual	IN
Other	OO

NOTES: Attach as many copies of the second part of the cover page as are needed, one reporting person per page.

Filing persons may, in order to avoid unnecessary duplication, answer items on the schedules (Schedule 13D, 13G or 14D–1) by appropriate cross references to an item or items on the cover page(s). This approach may only be used where the cover page item or items provide all the disclosure required by the schedule item. Moreover, such a use of a cover page item will result in the item becoming a part of the schedule and accordingly being considered as "filed" for purposes of Section 18 of the Securities Exchange Act or otherwise subject to the liabilities of that section of the Act.

Reporting persons may comply with their cover page filing requirements by filing either completed copies of the blank forms available from the Commission, printed or typed facsimiles, or computer printed facsimiles, provided the documents filed have identical formats to the forms prescribed in the Commission's regulations and meet existing Securities Exchange Act rules as to such matters as clarity and size (Securities Exchange Act Rule 12b–12).

SPECIAL INSTRUCTIONS FOR COMPLYING WITH SCHEDULE 13G

Under Sections 13(d), 13(g) and 23 of the Securities Exchange Act of 1934 and the rules and regulations thereunder, the Commission is authorized to solicit the information required to be supplied by this schedule by certain security holders of certain issuers.

Disclosure of the information specified in this schedule is mandatory, except for I.R.S. identification numbers, disclosure of which is voluntary. The information will be used for the primary purpose of determining and disclosing the holdings of certain beneficial owners of certain equity securities. This statement will be made a matter of public record. Therefore, any information given will be available for inspection by any member of the public.

Because of the public nature of the information, the Commission can use it for a variety of purposes, including referral to other governmental authorities or securities self-regulatory organizations for investigatory purposes or in connection with litigation involving the Federal securities laws or other civil, criminal or regulatory statutes or provisions. I.R.S. identification numbers, if furnished, will assist the Commission in identifying security holders and, therefore, in promptly processing statements of beneficial ownership of securities.

Failure to disclose the information requested by this schedule, except for I.R.S. identification numbers, may result in civil or criminal action against the persons involved for violation of the Federal securities laws and rules promulgated thereunder.

GENERAL INSTRUCTIONS

Instructions. A. Statements filed pursuant to Rule 13d–1(b) containing the information required by this schedule shall be filed not later than February 14 following the calendar year covered by the statement or within the time specified in Rules 13d–1(b)(2) and 13d–2(c). Statements filed pursuant to Rule 13d–1(c) shall be filed within the time specified in Rules 13d–1(c), 13d–2(b) and 13d–2(d). Statements filed pursuant to Rule 13d–1(d) shall be filed not later than February 14 following the calendar year covered by the statement pursuant to Rules 13d–1(d) and 13d–2(b).

B. Information contained in a form which is required to be filed by rules under Section 13(f) [15 USC 78m(f)] for the same calendar year as that covered by a statement on this Schedule may be incorporated by reference in response to any of the items of this Schedule. If such information is incorporated by reference in this Schedule, copies of the relevant pages of such form shall be filed as an exhibit to this Schedule.

C. The item numbers and captions of the items shall be included but the text of the items is to be omitted. The answers to the items shall be so prepared as to indicate clearly the coverage of the items without referring to the text of the items. Answer every item. If an item is inapplicable or the answer is in the negative, so state.

Item 1(a). Name of Issuer

____

Item 1(b). Address of Issuer's Principal Executive Offices

____

Item 2(a). Name of Person Filing

____

Item 2(b). Address of Principal Business Office or, if None, Residence

____

Item 2(c). Citizenship

____

Item 2(d). Title of Class of Securities

____

Item 2(e). CUSIP No.

____

Item 3. If This Statement is Filed Pursuant to §§ 240.13d–1(b) or 240.13d–2(b) or (c), Check Whether the Person Filing is a:

(a) [ ] Broker or dealer registered under section 15 of the Act (15 U.S.C. 78o).

(b) [ ] Bank as defined in section 3(a)(6) of the Act (15 U.S.C. 78c).

(c) [ ] Insurance company as defined in section 3(a)(19) of the Act (15 U.S.C. 78c).

(d) [ ] Investment company registered under section 8 of the Investment Company Act of 1940 (15 U.S.C. 80a–8).

(e) [ ] An investment adviser in accordance with § 240.13d–1(b)(1)(ii)(E);

(f) [ ] An employee benefit plan or endowment fund in accordance with § 240.13d–1(b)(1)(ii)(F);

(g) [ ] A parent holding company or control person in accordance with § 240.13d–1(b)(1)(ii)(G);

(h) [ ] A savings associations as defined in Section 3(b) of the Federal Deposit Insurance Act (12 U.S.C. 1813);

(i) [ ] A church plan that is excluded from the definition of an investment company under section 3(c)(14) of the Investment Company Act of 1940 (15 U.S.C. 80a–3);

(j) [ ] Group, in accordance with § 240.13d–1(b)(1)(ii)(J).

Item 4. Ownership

Provide the following information regarding the aggregate number and percentage of the class of securities of the issuer identified in Item 1.

(a) Amount beneficially owned: ______.

(b) Percent of class: ______.

(c) Number of shares as to which the person has:

(i) Sole power to vote or to direct the vote ______.

(ii) Shared power to vote or to direct the vote ______.

(iii) Sole power to dispose or to direct the disposition of ______.

(iv) Shared power to dispose or to direct the disposition of ______.

Instruction. For computations regarding securities which represent a right to acquire an underlying security see § 240.13d–3(d)(1).

Item 5. Ownership of Five Percent or Less of a Class

If this statement is being filed to report the fact that as of the date hereof the reporting person has ceased to be the beneficial owner of more than five percent of the class of securities, check the following [ ].

Instruction. Dissolution of a group requires a response to this item.

Item 6. Ownership of More Than Five Percent on Behalf of Another Person

If any other person is known to have the right to receive or the power to direct the receipt of dividends from, or the proceeds from the sale of, such securities, a statement to that effect should be included in response to this item and, if such interest relates to more than five percent of the class, such person should be identified. A listing of the shareholders of an investment company registered under the Investment Company Act of 1940 or the beneficiaries of employee benefit plan, pension fund or endowment fund is not required.

Item 7. Identification and Classification of the Subsidiary Which Acquired the Security Being Reported on by the Parent Holding Company or Control Person

If a parent holding company or control person has filed this schedule pursuant to Rule 13d–1(b)(1)(ii)(G), so indicate under Item 3(g) and attach an exhibit stating the identity and the Item 3 classification of the relevant subsidiary. If a parent holding company or control person has filed this schedule pursuant to Rule 13d–1(c) or Rule 13d–1(d), attach an exhibit stating the identification of the relevant subsidiary.

Item 8. Identification and Classification of Members of the Group

If a group has filed this schedule pursuant to § 240.13d–1(b)(1)(ii)(J), so indicate under Item 3(j) and attach an exhibit stating the identity and Item 3 classification of each member of the group. If a group has filed this schedule pursuant to Rule 13d–1(c) or Rule 13d–1(d), attach an exhibit stating the identity of each member of the group.

Item 9. Notice of Dissolution of Group

Notice of dissolution of a group may be furnished as an exhibit stating the date of the dissolution and that all further filings with respect to transactions in the security reported on will be filed, if required, by members of the group, in their individual capacity. See Item 5.

Item 10. Certifications

(a) The following certification shall be included if the statement is filed pursuant to § 240.13d–1(b):

By signing below I certify that, to the best of my knowledge and belief, the securities referred to above were acquired and are held in the ordinary course of business and were not acquired and are not held for the purpose of or with the effect of changing or influencing the control of the issuer of the securities and were not acquired and are not held in connection with or as a participant in any transaction having that purpose or effect.

(b) The following certification shall be included if the statement is filed pursuant to § 240.13d–1(c):

By signing below I certify that, to the best of my knowledge and belief, the securities referred to above were not acquired and are not held for the purpose of or with the effect of changing or influencing the control of the issuer of the securities and were not acquired and are not held in connection with or as a participant in any transaction having that purpose or effect.

* * *

NOTE: Schedules filed in paper format shall include a signed original and five copies of the schedule, including all exhibits. See Rule 13d–7 for other parties for whom copies are to be sent.

ATTENTION: Intentional misstatements or omissions of fact constitute Federal criminal violations (See 18 U.S.C. 1001).

Rule 13k–1. Foreign Bank Exemption from the Insider Lending Prohibition Under Section 13(k).

(a) For the purpose of this section:

(1) *Foreign bank* means an institution:

(i) The home jurisdiction of which is other than the United States;

(ii) That is regulated as a bank in its home jurisdiction; and

(iii) That engages directly in the business of banking.

(2) Home jurisdiction means the country, political subdivision or other place in which a foreign bank is incorporated or organized.

(3) Engages directly in the business of banking means that an institution engages directly in banking activities that are usual for the business of banking in its home jurisdiction.

(4) Affiliate, parent and subsidiary have the same meaning as under 17 CFR 240.12b–2.

(b) An issuer that is a foreign bank or the parent or other affiliate of a foreign bank is exempt from the prohibition of extending, maintaining, arranging for, or renewing credit in the form of a personal loan to or for any of its directors or executive officers under section 13(k) of the Act (15 U.S.C. 78m(k)) with respect to any such loan made by the foreign bank as long as:

(1) Either:

(i) The laws or regulations of the foreign bank's home jurisdiction require the bank to insure its deposits or be subject to a deposit guarantee or protection scheme; or

(ii) The Board of Governors of the Federal Reserve System has determined that the foreign bank or another bank organized in the foreign bank's home jurisdiction is subject to comprehensive supervision or regulation on a consolidated basis by the bank supervisor in its home jurisdiction under 12 CFR 211.24(c); and

(2) The loan by the foreign bank to any of its directors or executive officers or those of its parent or other affiliate:

(i) Is on substantially the same terms as those prevailing at the time for comparable transactions by the foreign bank with other persons who are not executive officers, directors or employees of the foreign bank, its parent or other affiliate; or

(ii) Is pursuant to a benefit or compensation program that is widely available to the employees of the foreign bank, its parent or other affiliate and does not give preference to any of the executive officers or directors of the foreign bank, its parent or other affiliate over any other employees of the foreign bank, its parent or other affiliate; or

(iii) Has received express approval by the bank supervisor in the foreign bank's home jurisdiction.

Notes to paragraph (b):

1. The exemption provided in paragraph (b) of this section applies to a loan by the subsidiary of a foreign bank to a director or executive officer of the foreign bank, its parent or other affiliate as long as the subsidiary is under the supervision or regulation of the bank supervisor in the foreign bank's home jurisdiction, the subsidiary's loan meets the requirements of paragraph (b)(2) of this section, and the foreign bank meets the requirements of paragraph (b)(1) of this section.

2. For the purpose of paragraph (b)(1)(ii) of this section, a foreign bank may rely on a determination by the Board of Governors of the Federal Reserve System that another bank in the foreign bank's home jurisdiction is subject to comprehensive supervision or regulation on a consolidated basis by the bank supervisor under 12 CFR 211.24(c) as long as the foreign bank is under substantially the same banking supervision or regulation as the other bank in their home jurisdiction.(c) As used in paragraph (1) of section 13(k) of the Act (15 U.S.C. 78m(k)(1)), issuer does not include a foreign government, as defined under 17 CFR 230.405, that files a registration statement under the Securities Act of 1933 (15 U.S.C. 77a et seq.) on Schedule B.

REGULATION 14A. SOLICITATION OF PROXIES

ATTENTION ELECTRONIC FILERS

THIS REGULATION SHOULD BE READ IN CONJUNCTION WITH REGULATION S–T (PART 232 OF THIS CHAPTER), WHICH GOVERNS THE PREPARATION AND SUBMISSION OF DOCUMENTS IN ELECTRONIC FORMAT. MANY PROVISIONS RELATING TO THE PREPARATION AND SUBMISSION OF DOCUMENTS IN PAPER FORMAT CONTAINED IN THIS REGULATION ARE SUPERSEDED BY THE PROVISIONS OF REGULATION S–T FOR DOCUMENTS REQUIRED TO BE FILED IN ELECTRONIC FORMAT.

Rule 14a–1. Definitions

Unless the context otherwise requires, all terms used in this regulation have the same meanings as in the Act or elsewhere in the General Rules and Regulations thereunder. In addition, the following definitions apply unless the context otherwise requires:

(a) *Associate.* The term "associate," used to indicate a relationship with any person, means (1) any corporation or organization (other than the registrant or a majority owned subsidiary of the registrant) of which such person is an officer or partner or is, directly or indirectly, the beneficial owner of 10 percent or more of any class of equity securities; (2) any trust or other estate in which such person has a substantial beneficial interest or as to which such person serves as trustee or in a similar fiduciary capacity; and (3) any relative or spouse of such person, or any relative of such spouse, who has the same home as such person or who is a director or officer of the registrant or any of its parents or subsidiaries.

(b) *Employee benefit plan.* For purposes of Rules 14a–13, 14b–1 and 14b–2, the term "employee benefit plan" means any purchase, savings, option, bonus, appreciation, profit sharing, thrift, incentive, pension or similar plan primarily for employees, directors, trustees or officers.

(c) *Entity that exercises fiduciary powers.* The term "entity that exercises fiduciary powers" means any entity that holds securities in nominee name or otherwise on behalf of a beneficial owner but does not include a clearing agency registered pursuant to Section 17A of the Act or a broker or a dealer.

(d) *Exempt employee benefit plan securities.* For purposes of Rules 14a–13, 14b–1 and 14b–2, the term "exempt employee benefit plan securities" means: (1) securities of the registrant held by an employee benefit plan, as defined in paragraph (b) of this rule, where such plan is established by the registrant; or (2) if notice regarding the current solicitation has been given pursuant to Rule 14a–13(a)(1)(ii)(C) or if notice regarding the current request for a list of names, addresses and securities positions of beneficial owners has been given pursuant to Rule 14a–13(b)(3), securities of the registrant held by an employee benefit plan, as defined in paragraph (b) of this rule, where such plan is established by an affiliate of the registrant.

(e) *Last fiscal year.* The term "last fiscal year" of the registrant means the last fiscal year of the registrant ending prior to the date of the meeting for which proxies are to be solicited or, if the solicitation involves written authorizations or consents in lieu of a meeting, the earliest date they may be used to effect corporate action.

(f) *Proxy.* The term "proxy" includes every proxy, consent or authorization within the meaning of section 14(a) of the Act. The consent or authorization may take the form of failure to object or to dissent.

(g) *Proxy statement.* The term "proxy statement" means the statement required by Rule 14a–3(a), whether or not contained in a single document.

(h) *Record date.* The term "record date" means the date as of which the record holders of securities entitled to vote at a meeting or by written consent or authorization shall be determined.

(i) *Record holder*. For purposes of Rules 14a–13, 14b–1 and 14b–2, the term "record holder" means any broker, dealer, voting trustee, bank, association or other entity that exercises fiduciary powers which holds securities of record in nominee name or otherwise or as a participant in a clearing agency registered pursuant to Section 17A of the Act.

(j) *Registrant*. The term "registrant" means the issuer of the securities in respect of which proxies are to be solicited.

(k) *Respondent bank*. For purposes of Rules 14a–13, 14b–1 and 14b–2, the term "respondent bank" means any bank, association or other entity that exercises fiduciary powers which holds securities on behalf of beneficial owners and deposits such securities for safekeeping with another bank, association or other entity that exercises fiduciary powers.

(*l*) *Solicitation*. (1) The terms "solicit" and "solicitation" include:

(i) Any request for a proxy whether or not accompanied by or included in a form of proxy;

(ii) Any request to execute or not to execute, or to revoke, a proxy; or

(iii) The furnishing of a form of proxy or other communication to security holders under circumstances reasonably calculated to result in the procurement, withholding or revocation of a proxy.

(2) The terms do not apply, however, to:

(i) The furnishing of a form of proxy to a security holder upon the unsolicited request of such security holder;

(ii) The performance by the registrant of acts required by Rule 14a–7;

(iii) The performance by any person of ministerial acts on behalf of a person soliciting a proxy; or

(iv) A communication by a security holder who does not otherwise engage in a proxy solicitation (other than a solicitation exempt under Rule 14a–2) stating how the security holder intends to vote and the reasons therefor, provided that the communication:

(A) Is made by means of speeches in public forums, press releases, published or broadcast opinions, statements, or advertisements appearing in a broadcast media, or newspaper, magazine or other bona fide publication disseminated on a regular basis,

(B) Is directed to persons to whom the security holder owes a fiduciary duty in connection with the voting of securities of a registrant held by the security holder, or

(C) Is made in response to unsolicited requests for additional information with respect to a prior communication by the security holder made pursuant to this paragraph (*l*)(2)(iv).

Rule 14a-2. Solicitations to Which Rules 14a-3 to 14a-15 Apply

Sections 240.14a–3 to 240.14a–15, except as specified, apply to every solicitation of a proxy with respect to securities registered pursuant to Section 12 of the Act (15 U.S.C. 78*l*), whether or not trading in such securities has been suspended. To the extent specified below certain of these sections also apply to roll-up transactions that do not involve an entity with securities registered pursuant to Section 12 of the Act.

(a) Rules 14a–3 to 14a–15 do not apply to the following:

(1) Any solicitation by a person in respect to securities carried in his name or in the name of his nominee (otherwise than as voting trustee) or held in his custody, if such person—

(i) Receives no commission or remuneration for such solicitation, directly or indirectly, other than reimbursement of reasonable expenses,

(ii) Furnishes promptly to the person solicited (or such person's household in accordance with § 240.14a-3(e)(1)) a copy of all soliciting material with respect to the same subject matter or meeting received from all persons who shall furnish copies thereof for such purpose and who shall, if requested, defray the reasonable expenses to be incurred in forwarding such material, and

(iii) In addition, does no more than impartially instruct the person solicited to forward a proxy to the person, if any, to whom the person solicited desires to give a proxy, or impartially request from the person solicited instructions as to the authority to be conferred by the proxy and state that a proxy will be given if no instructions are received by a certain date.

(2) Any solicitation by a person in respect of securities of which he is the beneficial owner;

(3) Any solicitation involved in the offer and sale of securities registered under the Securities Act of 1933: *Provided,* That this paragraph shall not apply to securities to be issued in any transaction of the character specified in paragraph (a) of Rule 145 under that Act;

(4) Any solicitation with respect to a plan of reorganization under Chapter 11 of the Bankruptcy Reform Act of 1978, as amended, if made after the entry of an order approving the written disclosure statement concerning a plan of reorganization pursuant to section 1125 of said Act and after, or concurrently with, the transmittal of such disclosure statement as required by section 1125 of said Act;

(5) Any solicitation which is subject to Rule 62 under the Public Utility Holding Company Act of 1935; and

(6) Any solicitation through the medium of a newspaper advertisement which informs security holders of a source from which they may obtain copies of a proxy statement, form of proxy and any other soliciting material and does no more than (i) name the registrant, (ii) state the reason for the advertisement, and (iii) identify the proposal or proposals to be acted upon by security holders.

(b) Rules 14a-3 to 14a-6 (other than 14a-6(g)), 14a-8, and 14a-10 to 14a-15 do not apply to the following:

(1) Any solicitation by or on behalf of any person who does not, at any time during such solicitation, seek directly or indirectly, either on its own or another's behalf, the power to act as proxy for a security holder and does not furnish or otherwise request, or act on behalf of a person who furnishes or requests, a form of revocation, abstention, consent or authorization. *Provided, however,* That the exemption set forth in this paragraph shall not apply to:

(i) The registrant or an affiliate or associate of the registrant (other than an officer or director or any person serving in a similar capacity);

(ii) An officer or director of the registrant or any person serving in a similar capacity engaging in a solicitation financed directly or indirectly by the registrant;

(iii) An officer, director, affiliate or associate of a person that is ineligible to rely on the exemption set forth in this paragraph (other than persons specified in paragraph (b)(1)(i) of this rule), or any person serving in a similar capacity;

(iv) Any nominee for whose election as a director proxies are solicited;

(v) Any person soliciting in opposition to a merger, recapitalization, reorganization, sale of assets or other extraordinary transaction recommended or approved by the board of directors of the registrant who is proposing or intends to propose an alternative transaction to which such person or one of its affiliates is a party;

(vi) Any person who is required to report beneficial ownership of the registrant's equity securities on a Schedule 13D, unless such person has filed a Schedule 13D and has not disclosed pursuant to Item 4 thereto an intent, or reserved the right, to engage in a control transaction, or any contested solicitation for the election of directors;

(vii) Any person who receives compensation from an ineligible person directly related to the solicitation of proxies, other than pursuant to Rule 14a-13;

(viii) Where the registrant is an investment company registered under the Investment Company Act of 1940, an "interested person" of that investment company, as that term is defined in section 2(a)(19) of the Investment Company Act;

(ix) Any person who, because of a substantial interest in the subject matter of the solicitation, is likely to receive a benefit from a successful solicitation that would not be shared pro rata by all other holders of the same class of securities, other than a benefit arising from the person's employment with the registrant; and

(x) Any person acting on behalf of any of the foregoing.

(2) Any solicitation made otherwise than on behalf of the registrant where the total number of persons solicited is not more than ten.

(3) The furnishing of proxy voting advice by any person (the "advisor") to any other person with whom the advisor has a business relationship, if:

(i) The advisor renders financial advice in the ordinary course of his business;

(ii) The advisor discloses to the recipient of the advice any significant relationship with the registrant or any of its affiliates, or a security holder proponent of the matter on which advice is given, as well as any material interest of the advisor in such matter;

(iii) The advisor receives no special commission or remuneration for furnishing the proxy voting advice from any person other than a recipient of the advice and other persons who receive similar advice under this subsection; and

(iv) The proxy voting advice is not furnished on behalf of any person soliciting proxies or on behalf of a participant in an election subject to the provisions of Rule 14a-11; and

(4) Any solicitation in connection with a roll-up transaction as defined in Item 901(c) of Regulation S-K (§ 229.901 of this chapter) in which the holder of a security that is the subject of a proposed roll-up transaction engages in preliminary communications with other holders of securities that are the subject of the same limited partnership roll-up transaction for the purpose of determining whether to solicit proxies, consents, or authorizations in opposition to the proposed limited partnership roll-up transaction; *provided, however,* that:

(i) This exemption shall not apply to a security holder who is an affiliate of the registrant or general partner or sponsor; and

(ii) This exemption shall not apply to a holder of five percent (5%) or more of the outstanding securities of a class that is the subject of the proposed roll-up transaction who engages in the business of buying and selling limited partnership interests in the secondary market unless that holder discloses to the persons to whom the communications are made such ownership interest and any relations of the holder to the parties of the transaction or to the transaction itself, as required by § 240.14a-6(n)(1) and specified in the Notice of Exempt Preliminary Roll-up Communication (§ 240.14a-104). If the communication is oral, this disclosure may be provided to the security holder orally. Whether the communication is written or oral, the notice required by § 240.14a-6(n) and § 240.14a-104 shall be furnished to the Commission.

Rule 14a-3. Information to Be Furnished to Security Holders

(a) No solicitation subject to this regulation shall be made unless each person solicited is concurrently furnished or has previously been furnished with a written proxy statement containing the information specified in Schedule 14A (§ 240.14a-101) or with a written proxy statement included in a registration statement filed under the Securities Act of 1933 on Form S-4 or F-4 (§ 239.25 or § 239.34 of this chapter) or Form N-14 (239.23) and containing the information specified in such Form.

(b) If the solicitation is made on behalf of the registrant, other than an investment company registered under the Investment Company Act of 1940, and relates to an annual (or special meeting in lieu of the annual) meeting of security holders, or written consent in lieu of such meeting, at which directors are to be elected, each proxy statement furnished pursuant to paragraph (a) of this section shall be accompanied or preceded by an annual report to security holders as follows:

Note to Small Business Issuers—A "small business issuer," defined under Rule 12b-2 of the Exchange Act (§ 240.12b-2), shall refer to the disclosure items in Regulation S-B (§ 228.10-702 of this chapter) rather than Regulation S-K (§ 229.10-702 of this chapter). If there is no comparable disclosure item in Regulation S-B, a small business issuer need not provide the information requested. A small business issuer shall provide the information in Item 310(a) of Regulation S-B in lieu of the financial information required by Rule 14a-3(b)(1) (§ 240.14a-3(b)(1)). Small business issuers using the transitional small business issuers disclosure format in the filing of their most recent annual report on Form 10-KSB (§ 249.310b of this chapter) need not provide the information specified below. Rather, those small business issuers shall provide only the financial statements required to be filed in their most recent Form 10-KSB. The inclusion of additional information, including information required of non-transitional small business issuers, in the annual report to security holders will not cause the issuer to be ineligible for the transitional disclosure forms.

(1) The report shall include, for the registrant and its subsidiaries consolidated, audited balance sheets as of the end of each of the two most recent fiscal years and audited statements of income and cash flows for each of the three most recent fiscal years prepared in accordance with Regulation S-X, except that the provisions of Article 3 (other than § 210.3-03(e), 210.3-04 and 210.3-20) and Article 11 shall not apply. Any financial statement schedules or exhibits or separate financial statements which may otherwise be required in filings with the Commission may be omitted. If the financial statements of the registrant and its subsidiaries consolidated in the annual report filed or to be filed with the Commission are not required to be audited, the financial statements required by this paragraph may be unaudited.

Note 1.—If the financial statements for a period prior to the most recently completed fiscal year have been examined by a predecessor accountant, the separate report of the predecessor accountant may be omitted in the report to security holders provided the registrant has obtained from the predecessor accountant a reissued report covering the prior period presented and the successor accountant clearly indicates in the scope paragraph of his report (a) that the financial statements of the prior period were examined by other accountants, (b) the date of their report, (c) the type of opinion expressed by the predecessor accountant, and (d) the substantive reasons therefor, if it was other than unqualified. It should be noted, however, that the separate report of any predecessor accountant is required in filings with the Commission. If, for instance, the financial statements in the annual report to security holders are incorporated by reference in a Form 10–K and Form 10–KSB, the separate report of a predecessor accountant shall be filed in Part II or in Part IV as a financial statement schedule.

Note 2.—For purposes of complying with Rule 14a–3, if the registrant, has changed its fiscal closing date, financial statements covering two years and one period of 9 to 12 months shall be deemed to satisfy the requirements for statements of income and cash flows for the three most recent fiscal years.

(2)(i) Financial statements and notes thereto shall be presented in roman type at least as large and as legible as 10-point modern type. If necessary for convenient presentation, the financial statements may be in roman type as large and as legible as 8-point modern type. All type shall be leaded at least 2-point.

(ii) Where the annual report to security holders is delivered through an electronic medium, issuers may satisfy legibility requirements applicable to printed documents, such as type size and font, by presenting all required information in a format readily communicated to investors.

(3) The report shall contain the supplementary financial information required by Item 302 of Regulation S–K.

(4) The report shall contain information concerning changes in and disagreements with accountants on accounting and financial disclosure required by Item 304 of Regulation S–K.

(5)(i) The report shall contain the selected financial data required by Item 301 of Regulation S–K.

(ii) The report shall contain management's discussion and analysis of financial condition and results of operations required by Item 303 of Regulation S–K or, if applicable, a plan of operation required by Item 303(a) of Regulation S–B.

(iii) The report shall contain the quantitative and qualitative disclosures about market risk required by Item 305 of Regulation S–K (§ 229.305 of this chapter).

(6) The report shall contain a brief description of the business done by the registrant and its subsidiaries during the most recent fiscal year which will, in the opinion of management, indicate the general nature and scope of the business of the registrant and its subsidiaries.

(7) The report shall contain information relating to the registrant's industry segments, classes of similar products or services, foreign and domestic operations and export sales required by paragraphs (b), (c)(1)(i) and (d) of Item 101 of Regulation S–K.

(8) The report shall identify each of the registrant's directors and executive officers, and shall indicate the principal occupation or employment of each such person and the name and principal business of any organization by which such person is employed.

(9) The report shall contain the market price of and dividends on the registrant's common equity and related security holder matters required by Item 201(a), (b) and (c) of Regulation S–K.

(10) The registrant's proxy statement, or the report, shall contain an undertaking in bold face or otherwise reasonably prominent type to provide without charge to each person solicited upon the written request of any

such person, a copy of the registrant's annual report on Form 10–K and Form 10–KSB, including the financial statements and the financial statement schedules, required to be filed with the Commission pursuant to Rule 13a–1 under the Act for the registrant's most recent fiscal year, and shall indicate the name and address (including title or department) of the person to whom such a written request is to be directed. In the discretion of management, a registrant need not undertake to furnish without charge copies of all exhibits to its Form 10–K and Form 10–KSB provided that the copy of the annual report on Form 10–K and Form 10–KSB furnished without charge to requesting security holders is accompanied by a list briefly describing all the exhibits not contained therein and indicating that the registrant will furnish any exhibit upon the payment of a specified reasonable fee which fee shall be limited to the registrant's reasonable expenses in furnishing such exhibit. If the registrant's annual report to security holders complies with all of the disclosure requirements of Form 10–K and Form 10–KSB and is filed with the Commission in satisfaction of its Form 10–K and Form 10–KSB filing requirements, such registrant need not furnish a separate Form 10–K and Form 10–KSB to security holders who receive a copy of such annual report.

NOTE: Pursuant to the undertaking required by paragraph (b)(10) of this rule a registrant shall furnish a copy of its annual report on Form 10–K and Form 10–KSB to a beneficial owner of its securities upon receipt of a written request from such person. Each request must set forth a good faith representation that, as of the record date for the solicitation requiring the furnishing of the annual report to security holders pursuant to paragraph (b) of this rule, the person making the request was a beneficial owner of securities entitled to vote.

(11) Subject to the foregoing requirements, the report may be in any form deemed suitable by management and the information required by paragraphs (b)(5) to (b)(10) of this rule may be presented in an appendix or other separate section of the report, provided that the attention of security holders is called to such presentation.

NOTE: Registrants are encouraged to utilize tables, schedules, charts, and graphic illustrations to present financial information in an understandable manner. Any presentation of financial information must be consistent with the data in the financial statements contained in the report and, if appropriate, should refer to relevant portions of the financial statements and notes thereto.

(12) [Reserved]

(13) Paragraph (b) of this rule shall not apply, however, to solicitations made on behalf of the registrant before the financial statements are available if a solicitation is being made at the same time in opposition to the registrant and if the registrant's proxy statement includes an undertaking in bold face type to furnish such annual report to all persons being solicited at least 20 calendar days before the date of the meeting or, if the solicitation refers to a written consent or authorization in lieu of a meeting, at least 20 calendar days prior to the earliest date on which it may be used to effect corporate action.

(c) Seven copies of the report sent to security holders pursuant to this rule shall be mailed to the Commission, solely for its information, not later than the date on which such report is first sent or given to security holders or the date on which preliminary copies, or definitive copies, if preliminary filing was not required, of solicitation material are filed with the Commission pursuant to Rule 14a–6, whichever date is later. The report is not deemed to be "soliciting material" or to be "filed" with the Commission or subject to this regulation otherwise than as provided in this Rule, or to the liabilities of Section 18 of the Act, except to the extent that the registrant specifically requests that it be treated as a part of the proxy soliciting material or incorporates it in the proxy statement or other filed report by reference.

(d) An annual report to security holders prepared on an integrated basis pursuant to General Instruction H to Form 10–K and Form 10–KSB may also be submitted in satisfaction of this rule. When filed as the annual report on Form 10–K and Form 10–KSB, responses to the Items of that form are subject to section 18 of the Act notwithstanding paragraph (c).

(e)(1)(i) A registrant will be considered to have delivered an annual report or proxy statement to all security holders of record who share an address if:

(A) The registrant delivers one annual report or proxy statement, as applicable, to the shared address;

(B) The registrant addresses the annual report or proxy statement, as applicable, to the security holders as a group (for example, "ABC Fund [or Corporation] Security Holders," "Jane Doe and Household," "The Smith Family"), to each of the security holders individually (for example, "John Doe and Richard Jones") or to the security holders in a form to which each of the security holders has consented in writing;

Note to paragraph (e)(1)(i)(B): Unless the company addresses the annual report or proxy statement to the security holders as a group or to each of the security holders individually, it must obtain, from each security holder to be included in the householded group, a separate affirmative written consent to the specific form of address the company will use.

(C) The security holders consent, in accordance with paragraph (e)(1)(ii) of this section, to delivery of one annual report or proxy statement, as applicable;

(D) With respect to delivery of the proxy statement, the registrant delivers, together with or subsequent to delivery of the proxy statement, a separate proxy card for each security holder at the shared address; and

(E) The registrant includes an undertaking in the proxy statement to deliver promptly upon written or oral request a separate copy of the annual report or proxy statement, as applicable, to a security holder at a shared address to which a single copy of the document was delivered.

(ii) *Consent.* (A) *Affirmative written consent.* Each security holder must affirmatively consent, in writing, to delivery of one annual report or proxy statement, as applicable. A security holder's affirmative written consent will only be considered valid if the security holder has been informed of:

(*1*) The duration of the consent;

(*2*) The specific types of documents to which the consent will apply;

(*3*) The procedures the security holder must follow to revoke consent; and

(*4*) The registrant's obligation to begin sending individual copies to a security holder within thirty days after the security holder revokes consent.

(B) *Implied consent.* The registrant need not obtain affirmative written consent from a security holder for purposes of paragraph (e)(1)(ii)(A) of this section if all of the following conditions are met:

(*1*) The security holder has the same last name as the other security holders at the shared address or the registrant reasonably believes that the security holders are members of the same family;

(*2*) The registrant has sent the security holder a notice at least 60 days before the registrant begins to rely on this section concerning delivery of annual reports and proxy statements to that security holder. The notice must:

(*i*) Be a separate written document;

(*ii*) State that only one annual report or proxy statement, as applicable, will be delivered to the shared address unless the registrant receives contrary instructions;

(*iii*) Include a toll-free telephone number, or be accompanied by a reply form that is pre-addressed with postage provided, that the security holder can use to notify the registrant that the security holder wishes to receive a separate annual report or proxy statement;

(*iv*) State the duration of the consent;

(*v*) Explain how a security holder can revoke consent;

(*vi*) State that the registrant will begin sending individual copies to a security holder within thirty days after the security holder revokes consent; and

(*vii*) Contain the following prominent statement, or similar clear and understandable statement, in bold-face type: "Important Notice Regarding Delivery of Security Holder Documents." This statement also must appear on the envelope in which the notice is delivered. Alternatively, if the notice is delivered separately from other communications to security holders, this statement may appear either on the notice or on the envelope in which the notice is delivered.

Note to paragraph (e)(1)(ii)(B)(2): The notice should be written in plain English. See § 230.421(d)(2) of this chapter for a discussion of plain English principles.

(*3*) The registrant has not received the reply form or other notification indicating that the security holder wishes to continue to receive an individual copy of the annual report or proxy statement, as applicable, within 60 days after the registrant sent the notice; and

(*4*) The registrant delivers the document to a post office box or residential street address.

Note to paragraph (e)(1)(ii)(B)(4): The registrant can assume that a street address is residential unless the registrant has information that indicates the street address is a business.

(iii) *Revocation of consent.* If a security holder, orally or in writing, revokes consent to delivery of one annual report or proxy statement to a shared address, the registrant must begin sending individual copies to that security holder within 30 days after the registrant receives revocation of the security holder's consent.

(iv) *Definition of address.* Unless otherwise indicated, for purposes of this section, address means a street *address,* a post office box number, an electronic mail address, a facsimile telephone number or other similar destination to which paper or electronic documents are delivered, unless otherwise provided in this section. If the registrant has reason to believe that the address is a street address of a multiunit building, the address must include the unit number.

Note to paragraph (e)(1): A person other than the registrant making a proxy solicitation may deliver a single proxy statement to security holders of record or beneficial owners who have separate accounts and share an address if: (a) the registrant or intermediary has followed the procedures in this section; and (b) the registrant or intermediary makes available the shared address information to the person in accordance with § 240.14a–7(a)(2)(i) and (ii).

(2) Notwithstanding paragraphs (a) and (b) of this section, unless state law requires otherwise, a registrant is not required to send an annual report or proxy statement to a security holder if:

(i) An annual report and a proxy statement for two consecutive annual meetings; or

(ii) All, and at least two, payments (if sent by first class mail) of dividends or interest on securities, or dividend reinvestment confirmations, during a twelve month period, have been mailed to such security holder's address and have been returned as undeliverable. If any such security holder delivers or causes to be delivered to the registrant written notice setting forth his then current address for security holder communications purposes, the registrant's obligation to deliver an annual report or a proxy statement under this section is reinstated.

(f) The provisions of paragraph (a) of this rule shall not apply to a communication made by means of speeches in public forums, press releases, published or broadcast opinions, statements, or advertisements appearing in a broadcast media, newspaper, magazine or other bona fide publication disseminated on a regular basis, provided that:

(1) No form of proxy, consent or authorization or means to execute the same is provided to a security holder in connection with the communication; and

(2) At the time the communication is made, a definitive proxy statement is on file with the Commission pursuant to Rule 14a–6(b).

Rule 14a–4. Requirements as to Proxy

(a) The form of proxy (1) shall indicate in boldface type whether or not the proxy is solicited on behalf of the registrant's board of directors or, if provided other than by a majority of the board of directors, shall indicate in bold-face type on whose behalf the solicitation is made; (2) shall provide a specifically designated blank space for dating the proxy card; and (3) shall identify clearly and impartially each separate matter intended to be acted upon, whether or not related to or conditioned on the approval of other matters, and whether proposed by the registrant or by security holders. No reference need be made, however, to proposals as to which discretionary authority is conferred pursuant to paragraph (c) of this rule.

Note to paragraph (a)(3) (electronic filers): Electronic filers shall satisfy the filing requirements of Rule 14a–6(a) or (b) (§ 240.14a–6(a) or (b)) with respect to the form of proxy by filing the form of proxy as an appendix at the end of the proxy statement. Forms of proxy shall not be filed as exhibits or separate documents within an electronic submission.

(b)(1) Means shall be provided in the form of proxy whereby the person solicited is afforded an opportunity to specify by boxes a choice between approval or disapproval of, or abstention with respect to, each separate matter referred to therein as intended to be acted upon, other than elections to office. A proxy may confer discretionary authority with respect to matters as to which a choice is not specified by the security holder provided that the form of proxy states in bold-face type how it is intended to vote the shares represented by the proxy in each such case.

(2) A form of proxy which provides for the election of directors shall set forth the names of persons nominated for election as directors. Such form of proxy shall clearly provide any of the following means for security holders to withhold authority to vote for each nominee:

(i) a box opposite the name of each nominee which may be marked to indicate that authority to vote for such nominee is withheld; or

(ii) an instruction in bold-face type which indicates that the security holder may withhold authority to vote for any nominee by lining through or otherwise striking out the name of any nominee; or

(iii) designated blank spaces in which the shareholder may enter the names of nominees with respect to whom the security holder chooses to withhold authority to vote; or

(iv) any other similar means, provided that clear instructions are furnished indicating how the security holder may withhold authority to vote for any nominee.

Such form of proxy also may provide a means for the security holder to grant authority to vote for the nominees set forth, as a group, provided that there is a similar means for the security holder to withhold authority to vote for such group of nominees. Any such form of proxy which is executed by the security holder in such manner as not to withhold authority to vote for the election of any nominee shall be deemed to grant such authority, provided that the form of proxy so states in bold-face type.

Instructions: 1. Paragraph (2) does not apply in the case of a merger, consolidation or other plan if the election of directors is an integral part of the plan.

2. If applicable state law gives legal effect to votes cast against a nominee, then in lieu of, or in addition to, providing a means for security holders to withhold authority to vote, the registrant should provide a similar means for security holders to vote against each nominee.

(c) A proxy may confer discretionary authority to vote on any of the following matters:

(1) For an annual meeting of shareholders, if the registrant did not have notice of the matter at least 45 days before the date on which the registrant first mailed its proxy materials for the prior year's annual meeting of shareholders (or date specified by an advance notice provision), and a specific statement to that effect is made in the proxy statement or form of proxy. If during the prior year the registrant did not hold an annual meeting, or if the date of the meeting has changed more than 30 days from the prior year, then notice must not have been received a reasonable time before the registrant mails its proxy materials for the current year.

(2) In the case in which the registrant has received timely notice in connection with an annual meeting of shareholders (as determined under paragraph (c)(1) of this section), if the registrant includes, in the proxy statement, advice on the nature of the matter and how the registrant intends to exercise its discretion to vote on each matter. However, even if the registrant includes this information in its proxy statement, it may not exercise discretionary voting authority on a particular proposal if the proponent:

(i) Provides the registrant with a written statement, within the time-frame determined under paragraph (c)(1) of this section, that the proponent intends to deliver a proxy statement and form of proxy to holders of at least the percentage of the company's voting shares required under applicable law to carry the proposal;

(ii) Includes the same statement in its proxy materials filed under § 240.14a–6; and

(iii) Immediately after soliciting the percentage of shareholders required to carry the proposal, provides the registrant with a statement from any solicitor or other person with knowledge that the necessary steps have been taken to deliver a proxy statement and form of proxy to holders of at least the percentage of the company's voting shares required under applicable law to carry the proposal.

(3) For solicitations other than for annual meetings or for solicitations by persons other than the registrant, matters which the persons making the solicitation do not know, a reasonable time before the solicitation, are to be presented at the meeting, if a specific statement to that effect is made in the proxy statement or form of proxy.

(4) Approval of the minutes of the prior meeting if such approval does not amount to ratification of the action taken at that meeting;

(5) The election of any person to any office for which a bona fide nominee is named in the proxy statement and such nominee is unable to serve or for good cause will not serve.

(6) Any proposal omitted from the proxy statement and form of proxy pursuant to Rule 14a–8 or 14a–9 of this chapter.

(7) Matters incident to the conduct of the meeting.

(d) No proxy shall confer authority (1) to vote for the election of any person to any office for which a bona fide nominee is not named in the proxy statement, or (2) to vote at any annual meeting other than the next annual meeting (or any adjournment thereof) to be held after the date on which the proxy statement and form of proxy are first sent or given to security holders. (3) to vote with respect to more than one meeting (and any adjournment thereof) or more than one consent solicitation, or (4) to consent to or authorize any action other than the action proposed to be taken in the proxy statement, or matters referred to in paragraph (c) of this rule. A person shall not be deemed to be a bona fide nominee and he shall not be named as such unless he has consented to being named in the proxy statement and to serve if elected. *Provided, however,* that nothing in this Rule 14a–4 shall prevent any person soliciting in support of nominees who, if elected, would constitute a minority of the board of directors, from seeking authority to vote for nominees named in the registrant's proxy statement, so long as the soliciting party:

(i) Seeks authority to vote in the aggregate for the number of director positions then subject to election;

(ii) Represents that it will vote for all the registrant nominees, other than those registrant nominees specified by the soliciting party;

(iii) Provides the security holder an opportunity to withhold authority with respect to any other registrant nominee by writing the name of that nominee on the form of proxy; and

(iv) States on the form of proxy and in the proxy statement that there is no assurance that the registrant's nominees will serve if elected with any of the soliciting party's nominees.

(e) The proxy statement or form of proxy shall provide, subject to reasonable specified conditions, that the shares represented by the proxy will be voted and that where the person solicited specifies by means of a ballot provided pursuant to paragraph (b) a choice with respect to any matter to be acted upon, the shares will be voted in accordance with the specifications so made.

(f) No person conducting a solicitation subject to this regulation shall deliver a form of proxy, consent or authorization to any security holder unless the security holder concurrently receives, or has previously received, a definitive proxy statement that has been filed with the Commission pursuant to Rule 14a–6(b).

Rule 14a–5. Presentation of Information in Proxy Statement

(a) The information included in the proxy statement shall be clearly presented and the statements made shall be divided into groups according to subject matter and the various groups of statements shall be preceded by appropriate headings. The order of items and sub-items in the schedule need not be followed. Where practicable and appropriate, the information shall be presented in tabular forms. All amounts shall be stated in figures. Information required by more than one applicable item need not be repeated. No statement need be made in response to any item or sub-item which is inapplicable.

(b) Any information required to be included in the proxy statement as to terms of securities or other subject matter which from a standpoint of practical necessity must be determined in the future may be stated in terms of present knowledge and intention. To the extent practicable, the authority to be conferred concerning each such matter shall be confined within limits reasonably related to the need for discretionary authority. Subject to the foregoing, information which is not known to the persons on whose behalf the solicitation is to be made and which it is not reasonably within the power of such persons to ascertain or procure may be omitted, if a brief statement of the circumstances rendering such information unavailable is made.

(c) Any information contained in any other proxy soliciting material which has been furnished to each person solicited in connection with the same meeting or subject matter may be omitted from the proxy statement, if a clear reference is made to the particular document containing such information.

(d)(1) All printed proxy statements shall be in roman type at least as large and as legible as 10-point modern type, except that to the extent necessary for convenient presentation financial statements and other tabular data, but not the notes thereto, may be in roman type at least as large and as legible as 8-point modern type. All such type shall be leaded at least 2 points.

(2) Where a proxy statement is delivered through an electronic medium, issuers may satisfy legibility requirements applicable to printed documents, such as type size and font, by presenting all required information in a format readily communicated to investors.

(e) All proxy statements shall disclose, under an appropriate caption, the following dates:

(1) The deadline for submitting shareholder proposals for inclusion in the registrant's proxy statement and form of proxy for the registrant's next annual meeting, calculated in the manner provided in § 240.14a–8(e)(Question 5); and

(2) The date after which notice of a shareholder proposal submitted outside the processes of § 240.14a–8 is considered untimely, either calculated in the manner provided by § 240.14a–4(c)(1) or as established by the registrant's advance notice provision, if any, authorized by applicable state law.

(f) If the date of the next annual meeting is subsequently advanced or delayed by more than 30 calendar days from the date of the annual meeting to which the proxy statement relates, the registrant shall, in a timely manner, inform shareholders of such change, and the new dates referred to in paragraphs (e)(1) and (e)(2) of this section, by including a notice, under Item 5, in its earliest possible quarterly report on Form 10–Q (§ 249.308a of this chapter) or Form 10–QSB (§ 249.308b of this chapter), or, in the case of investment companies, in a shareholder report under § 270.30d–1 of this chapter under the Investment Company Act of 1940, or, if impracticable, any means reasonably calculated to inform shareholders.

Rule 14a–6. Filing Requirements

(a) *Preliminary proxy statement.* Five preliminary copies of the proxy statement and form of proxy shall be filed with the Commission at least 10 calendar days prior to the date definitive copies of such material are first sent or given to security holders, or such shorter period prior to that date as the Commission may authorize upon a showing of good cause thereunder. A registrant, however, shall not file with the Commission a preliminary proxy statement, form of proxy or other soliciting material to be furnished to security holders concurrently therewith if the solicitation relates to an annual (or special meeting in lieu of the annual) meeting, or for an investment company registered under the Investment Company Act of 1940 (15 U.S.C. 80a-1 *et seq.*) or a business development company, if the solicitation relates to any meeting of security holders at which the only matters to be acted upon are:

(1) The election of directors;

(2) The election, approval or ratification of accountant(s);

(3) A security holder proposal included pursuant to Rule 14a–8 (§ 240.14a–8 of this chapter);

(4) The approval or ratification of a plan as defined in paragraph (a)(7)(ii) of Item 402 of Regulation S–K (§ 229.402(a)(7)(ii) of this chapter) or amendments to such a plan;

(5) With respect to an investment company registered under the Investment Company Act of 1940 or a business development company, a proposal to continue, without change, any advisory or other contract or agreement that previously has been the subject of a proxy solicitation for which proxy material was filed with the Commission pursuant to this section; and/or

(6) With respect to an open-end investment company registered under the Investment Company Act of 1940, a proposal to increase the number of shares authorized to be issued.

This exclusion from filing preliminary proxy material does not apply if the registrant comments upon or refers to a solicitation in opposition in connection with the meeting in its proxy material.

Note 1: The filing of revised material does not recommence the ten day time period unless the revised material contains material revisions or material new proposal(s) that constitute a fundamental change in the proxy material.

Note 2: The official responsible for the preparation of the proxy material should make every effort to verify the accuracy and completeness of the information required by the applicable rules. The preliminary material should be filed with the Commission at the earliest practicable date.

Note 3: *Solicitation in Opposition.* For purposes of the exclusion from filing preliminary proxy material, a "solicitation in opposition" includes: (a) any solicitation opposing a proposal supported by the registrant; and (b) any solicitation supporting a proposal that the registrant does not expressly support, other than a security holder proposal included in the registrant's proxy material pursuant to Rule 14a–8. The inclusion of a security holder proposal in the registrant's proxy material pursuant to Rule 14a–8 does not constitute a "solicitation in opposition," even if the registrant opposes the proposal and/or includes a statement in opposition to the proposal.

Note 4: A registrant that is filing proxy material in preliminary form only because the registrant has commented on or referred to a solicitation in opposition should indicate that fact in a transmittal letter when filing the preliminary material with the Commission.

(b) *Definitive proxy statement and other soliciting material.* Eight definitive copies of the proxy statement, form of proxy and all other soliciting materials, in the same form as the materials sent to security holders, must be filed with the Commission no later than the date they are first sent or given to security holders. Three copies of these materials also must be filed with, or mailed for filing to, each national securities exchange on which the registrant has a class of securities listed and registered.

(c) *Personal solicitation materials.* If part of all of the solicitation involves personal solicitation, then eight copies of all written instructions or other materials that discuss, review or comment on the merits of any matter to be acted on, that are furnished to persons making the actual solicitation for their use directly or indirectly in connection with the solicitation, must be filed with the Commission no later than the date the materials are first sent or given to these persons.

(d) *Release dates.* All preliminary proxy statements and forms of proxy filed pursuant to paragraph (a) of this rule shall be accompanied by a statement of the date on which definitive copies thereof filed pursuant to paragraph (b) of this rule are intended to be released to security holders. All definitive material filed pursuant to paragraph (b) of this rule shall be accompanied by a statement of the date on which copies of such material were released to security holders, or, if not released, the date on which copies thereof are intended to be released. All material filed pursuant to paragraph (c) of this rule shall be accompanied by a statement of the date on which copies thereof were released to the individual who will make the actual solicitation or if not released, the date on which copies thereof are intended to be released.

(e)(1) *Public availability of information.* All copies of preliminary proxy statements and forms of proxy filed pursuant to paragraph (a) of this rule shall be clearly marked "Preliminary Copies," and shall be deemed immediately available for public inspection unless confidential treatment is obtained pursuant to paragraph (e)(2) of this rule.

(2) *Confidential treatment.* If action will be taken on any matter specified in Item 14 of Schedule 14A (§ 240.14a–101), all copies of the preliminary proxy statement and form of proxy filed under paragraph (a) of this section will be for the information of the Commission only and will not be deemed available for public inspection until filed with the Commission in definitive form so long as:

(i) The proxy statement does not relate to a matter or proposal subject to § 240.13e–3 or a roll-up transaction as defined in Item 901(c) of Regulation S–K (§ 229.901(c) of this chapter);

(ii) Neither the parties to the transaction nor any persons authorized to act on their behalf have made any public communications relating to the transaction except for statements where the content is limited to the information specified in § 230.135 of this chapter; and

(iii) The materials are filed in paper and marked "Confidential, For Use of the Commission Only." In all cases, the materials may be disclosed to any department or agency of the United States Government and to the Congress, and the Commission may make any inquiries or investigation into the materials as may be necessary to conduct an adequate review by the Commission.

Instruction to paragraph (e)(2): If communications are made publicly that go beyond the information specified in § 230.135 of this chapter, the preliminary proxy materials must be re-filed promptly with the Commission as public materials.

(f) *Communications not required to be filed.* Copies of replies to inquiries from security holders requesting further information and copies of communications which do no more than request that forms of proxy theretofore solicited be signed and returned need not be filed pursuant to this rule.

(g) *Solicitations subject to Rule 14a–2(b)(1).* (1) Any person who:

(i) Engages in a solicitation pursuant to Rule 14a–2(b)(1), and

(ii) At the commencement of that solicitation owns beneficially securities of the class which is the subject of the solicitation with a market value of over $5 million.

Shall furnish or mail to the Commission, not later than three days after the date the written solicitation is first sent or given to any security holder, five copies of a statement containing the information specified in the Notice of Exempt Solicitation (Rule 14a–103) which statement shall attach as an exhibit all written soliciting materials. Five copies of an amendment to such statement shall be furnished or mailed to the Commission, in connection with dissemination of any additional communications, not later than three days after the date the additional material is first sent or given to any security holder. Three copies of the Notice of Exempt Solicitation and amendments thereto shall, at the same time the materials are furnished or mailed to the Commission, be furnished or mailed to each national securities exchange upon which any class of securities of the registrant is listed and registered.

(2) Notwithstanding paragraph (g)(1) of this rule, no such submission need be made with respect to oral solicitations (other than with respect to scripts used in connection with such oral solicitations), speeches delivered in a public forum, press releases, published or broadcast opinions, statements, and advertisements appearing in a broadcast media, or a newspaper, magazine or other bona fide publication disseminated on a regular basis.

(h) *Revised material.* Where any proxy statement, form of proxy or other material filed pursuant to this rule is amended or revised, two of the copies of such amended or revised material filed pursuant to this rule (or in the case of investment companies registered under the Investment Company Act of 1940, three of such copies) shall be marked to indicate clearly and precisely the changes effected therein. If the amendment or revision alters the text of the material the changes in such text shall be indicated by means of underscoring or in some other appropriate manner.

(i) *Fees.* At the time of filing the proxy solicitation material, the persons upon whose behalf the solicitation is made, other than investment companies registered under the Investment Company Act of 1940 shall pay to the Commission the following applicable fee:

(1) For preliminary proxy material involving acquisitions, mergers, spinoffs, consolidations or proposed sales or other dispositions of substantially all the assets of the company, a fee established in accordance with Rule 0–11 (§ 240.0–11 of this chapter) shall be paid. No refund shall be given.

(2) For all other proxy submissions and submissions made pursuant to § 240.14a–6(g), no fee shall be required.

(j) *Merger proxy materials.*

(1) Any proxy statement, form of proxy or other soliciting material required to be filed by this section that also is either

(i) Included in a registration statement filed under the Securities Act of 1933 on Forms S–4 (§ 239.25 of this chapter), F–4 (§ 239.34 of this chapter) or N–14 (§ 239.23 of this chapter); or

(ii) Filed under § 230.424, § 230.425 or § 230.497 of this chapter is required to be filed only under the Securities Act, and is deemed filed under this section.

(2) Under paragraph (j)(1) of this section, the fee required by paragraph (i) of this section need not be paid.

(k) *Computing time periods.* In computing time periods beginning with the filing date specified in Regulation 14A, the filing date shall be counted as the first day of the time period and midnight of the last day shall constitute the end of the specified time period.

(*l*) *Roll-up transactions.* If a transaction is a roll-up transaction as defined in Item 901(c) of Regulation S–K and is registered (or authorized to be registered) on Form S–4 or Form F–4, the proxy statement of the sponsor or the general partner as defined in Item 901(d) and Item 901(a), respectively, of Regulation S–K must be distributed to security holders no later than the lesser of 60 calendar days prior to the date on which the meeting of security holders is held or action is taken, or the maximum number of days permitted for giving notice under applicable state law.

(m) *Cover page.* Proxy materials filed with the Commission shall include a cover page in the form set forth in Schedule 14A. The cover page required by this paragraph need not be distributed to security holders.

(n) *Solicitations subject to § 240.14a–2(b)(4).* Any person who:

(1) Engages in a solicitation pursuant to § 240.14a–2(b)(4); and

(2) At the commencement of that solicitation both owns five percent (5%) or more of the outstanding securities of a class that is the subject of the proposed roll-up transaction, and engages in the business of buying and selling limited partnership interests in the secondary market, shall furnish or mail to the Commission, not later than three days after the date an oral or written solicitation by that person is first made, sent or provided to any security holder, five copies of a statement containing the information specified in the Notice of Exempt Preliminary Roll-up Communication (§ 240.14a–104). Five copies of any amendment to such statement shall be furnished or mailed to the Commission not later than three days after a communication containing revised material is first made, sent or provided to any security holder.

(o) *Solicitations before furnishing a definitive proxy statement.* Solicitations that are published, sent or given to security holders before they have been furnished a definitive proxy statement must be made in accordance with § 240.14a–12 unless there is an exemption available under § 240.14a–2.

Rule 14a–7. Obligations of Registrants to Provide a List of, or Mail Soliciting Material to, Security Holders

(a) If the registrant has made or intends to make a proxy solicitation in connection with a security holder meeting or action by consent or authorization, upon the written request by any record or beneficial holder of securities of the class entitled to vote at the meeting or to execute a consent or authorization to provide a list of security holders or to mail the requesting security holder's materials, regardless of whether the request references this rule, the registrant shall:

(1) Deliver to the requesting security holder within five business days after receipt of the request:

(i) Notification as to whether the registrant has elected to mail the security holder's soliciting materials or provide a security holder list if the election under paragraph (b) of this rule is to be made by the registrant;

(ii) A statement of the approximate number of record holders and beneficial holders, separated by type of holder and class, owning securities in the same class or classes as holders which have been or are to be solicited on management's behalf, or any more limited group of such holders designated by the security holder if available or retrievable under the registrant's or its transfer agent's security holder data systems; and

(iii) The estimated cost of mailing a proxy statement, form of proxy or other communication to such holders, including to the extent known or reasonably available, the estimated costs of any bank, broker, and similar person through whom the registrant has solicited or intends to solicit beneficial owners in connection with the security holder meeting or action;

(2) Perform the acts set forth in either paragraphs (a)(2)(i) or (a)(2)(ii) of this rule, at the registrant's or requesting security holder's option, as specified in paragraph (b) of this rule:

(i) Mail copies of any proxy statement, form of proxy or other soliciting material furnished by the security holder to the record holders, including banks, brokers, and similar entities, designated by the security holder. A sufficient number of copies must be mailed to the banks, brokers, and similar entities for distribution to all beneficial owners designated by the security holder. If the registrant has received affirmative written or implied consent to deliver a single proxy statement to security holders at a shared address in accordance with the procedures in § 240.14a–3(e)(1), a single copy of the proxy statement furnished by the security holder shall be mailed to that address. The registrant shall mail the security holder material with reasonable promptness after tender of the material to be mailed, envelopes or other containers therefor, postage or payment for postage and other reasonable expenses of effecting such mailing. The registrant shall not be responsible for the content of the material; or

(ii) Deliver the following information to the requesting security holder within five business days of receipt of the request: a reasonably current list of the names, addresses and security positions of the record holders, including banks, brokers and similar entities holding securities in the same class or classes as holders which have been or are to be solicited on management's behalf, or any more limited group of such holders designated by the security holder if available or retrievable under the registrant's or its transfer agent's security holder data systems; the most recent list of names, addresses and security positions of beneficial owners as specified in § 240.14a–13(b), in the possession, or which subsequently comes into the possession, of the registrant; and the names of security holders at a shared address that have consented to delivery of a single copy of proxy materials to a shared address, if the registrant has received written or implied consent in accordance with § 240.14a-3(e)(1). All security holder list information shall be in the form requested by the security holder to the extent that such form is available to the registrant without undue burden or expense. The registrant shall furnish the security holder with updated record holder information on a daily basis or, if not available on a daily basis, at the shortest reasonable intervals, provided, however, the registrant need not provide beneficial or record holder information more current than the record date for the meeting or action.

(b)(1) The requesting security holder shall have the options set forth in paragraph (a)(2) of this section, and the registrant shall have corresponding obligations, if the registrant or general partner or sponsor is soliciting or intends to solicit with respect to:

(i) A proposal that is subject to § 240.13e-3;

(ii) A roll-up transaction as defined in Item 901(c) of Regulation S-K (§ 229.901(c) of this chapter) that involves an entity with securities registered pursuant to Section 12 of the Act (15 U.S.C. 78*l*); or

(iii) A roll-up transaction as defined in Item 901(c) of Regulation S-K (§ 229.901(c) of this chapter) that involves a limited partnership, unless the transaction involves only:

(A) Partnerships whose investors will receive new securities or securities in another entity that are not reported under a transaction reporting plan declared effective before December 17, 1993 by the Commission under Section 11A of the Act (15 U.S.C. 78k-1); or

(B) Partnerships whose investors' securities are reported under a transaction reporting plan declared effective before December 17, 1993 by the Commission under Section 11A of the Act (15 U.S.C. 78k-1).

(2) With respect to all other requests pursuant to this section, the registrant shall have the option to either mail the security holder's material or furnish the security holder list as set forth in this section.

(c) At the time of a list request, the security holder making the request shall:

(1) If holding the registrant's securities through a nominee, provide the registrant with a statement by the nominee or other independent third party, or a copy of a current filing made with the Commission and furnished to the registrant, confirming such holder's beneficial ownership; and

(2) Provide the registrant with an affidavit, declaration, affirmation or other similar document provided for under applicable state law identifying the proposal or other corporate action that will be the subject of the security holder's solicitation or communication and attesting that:

(i) The security holder will not use the list information for any purpose other than to solicit security holders with respect to the same meeting or action by consent or authorization for which the registrant is soliciting or intends to solicit or to communicate with security holders with respect to a solicitation commenced by the registrant; and

(ii) The security holder will not disclose such information to any person other than a beneficial owner for whom the request was made and an employee or agent to the extent necessary to effectuate the communication or solicitation.

(d) The security holder shall not use the information furnished by the registrant pursuant to paragraph (a)(2)(ii) of this rule for any purpose other than to solicit security holders with respect to the same meeting or action by consent or authorization for which the registrant is soliciting or intends to solicit or to communicate with security holders with respect to a solicitation commenced by the registrant; or disclose such information to any person other than an employee, agent, or beneficial owner for whom a request was made to the extent necessary to effectuate the communication or solicitation. The security holder shall return the information provided pursuant to paragraph (a)(2)(ii) of this rule and shall not retain any copies thereof or of any information derived from such information after the termination of the solicitation.

(e) The security holder shall reimburse the reasonable expenses incurred by the registrant in performing the acts requested pursuant to paragraph (a) of this rule.

Notes to Rule 14a–7. 1. Reasonably prompt methods of distribution to security holders may be used instead of mailing. If an alternative distribution method is chosen, the costs of that method should be considered where necessary rather than the costs of mailing.

2. When providing the information required by § 240.14a–7(a)(1)(ii), if the registrant has received affirmative written or implied consent to delivery of a single copy of proxy materials to a shared address in accordance with § 240.14a–3(e)(1), it shall exclude from the number of record holders those to whom it does not have to deliver a separate proxy statement.

Rule 14a–8. Shareholder Proposals

This section addresses when a company must include a shareholder's proposal in its proxy statement and identify the proposal in its form of proxy when the company holds an annual or special meeting of shareholders. In summary, in order to have your shareholder proposal included on a company's proxy card, and included along with any supporting statement in its proxy statement, you must be eligible and follow certain procedures. Under a few specific circumstances, the company is permitted to exclude your proposal, but only after submitting its reasons to the Commission. We structured this section in a question-and-answer format so that it is easier to understand. The references to "you" are to a shareholder seeking to submit the proposal.

(a) *Question 1:* What is a proposal? A shareholder proposal is your recommendation or requirement that the company and/or its board of directors take action, which you intend to present at a meeting of the company's shareholders. Your proposal should state as clearly as possible the course of action that you believe the company should follow. If your proposal is placed on the company's proxy card, the company must also provide in the form of proxy means for shareholders to specify by boxes a choice between approval or disapproval, or abstention. Unless otherwise indicated, the word "proposal" as used in this section refers both to your proposal, and to your corresponding statement in support of your proposal (if any).

(b) *Question 2:* Who is eligible to submit a proposal, and how do I demonstrate to the company that I am eligible? (1) In order to be eligible to submit a proposal, you must have continuously held at least $2,000 in market value, or 1%, of the company's securities entitled to be voted on the proposal at the meeting for at least one year by the date you submit the proposal. You must continue to hold those securities through the date of the meeting.

(2) If you are the registered holder of your securities, which means that your name appears in the company's records as a shareholder, the company can verify your eligibility on its own, although you will still have to provide the company with a written statement that you intend to continue to hold the securities through the date of the meeting of shareholders. However, if like many shareholders you are not a registered holder, the company likely does not know that you are a shareholder, or how many shares you own. In this case, at the time you submit your proposal, you must prove your eligibility to the company in one of two ways:

(i) The first way is to submit to the company a written statement from the "record" holder of your securities (usually a broker or bank) verifying that, at the time you submitted your proposal, you continuously held the securities for at least one year. You must also include your own written statement that you intend to continue to hold the securities through the date of the meeting of shareholders; or

(ii) The second way to prove ownership applies only if you have filed a Schedule 13D (§ 240.13d–101), Schedule 13G (§ 240.13d–102), Form 3 (§ 249.103 of this chapter), Form 4 (§ 249.104 of this chapter) and/or Form 5 (§ 249.105 of this chapter), or amendments to those documents or updated forms, reflecting your ownership of the shares as of or before the date on which the one-year eligibility period begins. If you have filed one of these documents with the SEC, you may demonstrate your eligibility by submitting to the company:

(A) A copy of the schedule and/or form, and any subsequent amendments reporting a change in your ownership level;

(B) Your written statement that you continuously held the required number of shares for the one-year period as of the date of the statement; and

(C) Your written statement that you intend to continue ownership of the shares through the date of the company's annual or special meeting.

(c) *Question 3:* How many proposals may I submit? Each shareholder may submit no more than one proposal to a company for a particular shareholders' meeting.

(d) *Question 4:* How long can my proposal be? The proposal, including any accompanying supporting statement, may not exceed 500 words.

(e) *Question 5:* What is the deadline for submitting a proposal? (1) If you are submitting your proposal for the company's annual meeting, you can in most cases find the deadline in last year's proxy statement. However, if the company did not hold an annual meeting last year, or has changed the date of its meeting for this year more than 30 days from last year's meeting, you can usually find the deadline in one of the company's quarterly reports on Form 10–Q (§ 249.308a of this chapter) or 10–QSB (§ 249.308b of this chapter), or in shareholder reports of investment companies under § 270.30d–1 of this chapter of the Investment Company Act of 1940. In order to avoid controversy, shareholders should submit their proposals by means, including electronic means, that permit them to prove the date of delivery.

(2) The deadline is calculated in the following manner if the proposal is submitted for a regularly scheduled annual meeting. The proposal must be received at the company's principal executive offices not less than 120 calendar days before the date of the company's proxy statement released to shareholders in connection with the previous year's annual meeting. However, if the company did not hold an annual meeting the previous year, or if the date of this year's annual meeting has been changed by more than 30 days from the date of the previous year's meeting, then the deadline is a reasonable time before the company begins to print and mail its proxy materials.

(3) If you are submitting your proposal for a meeting of shareholders other than a regularly scheduled annual meeting, the deadline is a reasonable time before the company begins to print and mail its proxy materials.

(f) *Question 6:* What if I fail to follow one of the eligibility or procedural requirements explained in answers to Questions 1 through 4 of this section? (1) The company may exclude your proposal, but only after it has notified you of the problem, and you have failed adequately to correct it. Within 14 calendar days of receiving your proposal, the company must notify you in writing of any procedural or eligibility deficiencies, as well as of the time frame for your response. Your response must be postmarked, or transmitted electronically, no later than 14 days from the date you received the company's notification. A company need not provide you such notice of a deficiency if the deficiency cannot be remedied, such as if you fail to submit a proposal by the company's properly determined deadline. If the company intends to exclude the proposal, it will later have to make a submission under § 240.14a–8 and provide you with a copy under Question 10 below, § 240.14a–8(j).

(2) If you fail in your promise to hold the required number of securities through the date of the meeting of shareholders, then the company will be permitted to exclude all of your proposals from its proxy materials for any meeting held in the following two calendar years.

(g) *Question 7:* Who has the burden of persuading the Commission or its staff that my proposal can be excluded? Except as otherwise noted, the burden is on the company to demonstrate that it is entitled to exclude a proposal.

(h) *Question 8:* Must I appear personally at the shareholders' meeting to present the proposal? (1) Either you, or your representative who is qualified under state law to present the proposal on your behalf, must attend the meeting to present the proposal. Whether you attend the meeting yourself or send a qualified representative to the meeting in your place, you should make sure that you, or your representative, follow the proper state law procedures for attending the meeting and/or presenting your proposal.

(2) If the company holds its shareholder meeting in whole or in part via electronic media, and the company permits you or your representative to present your proposal via such media, then you may appear through electronic media rather than traveling to the meeting to appear in person.

(3) If you or your qualified representative fail to appear and present the proposal, without good cause, the company will be permitted to exclude all of your proposals from its proxy materials for any meetings held in the following two calendar years.

(i) *Question 9:* If I have complied with the procedural requirements, on what other bases may a company rely to exclude my proposal? (1) Improper under state law: If the proposal is not a proper subject for action by shareholders under the laws of the jurisdiction of the company's organization;

Note to paragraph (i)(1): Depending on the subject matter, some proposals are not considered proper under state law if they would be binding on the company if approved by shareholders. In our experience, most proposals that are cast as recommendations or requests that the board of directors take specified action are proper under state law. Accordingly, we will assume that a proposal drafted as a recommendation or suggestion is proper unless the company demonstrates otherwise.

(2) *Violation of law:* If the proposal would, if implemented, cause the company to violate any state, federal, or foreign law to which it is subject;

Note to paragraph (i)(2): We will not apply this basis for exclusion to permit exclusion of a proposal on grounds that it would violate foreign law if compliance with the foreign law would result in a violation of any state or federal law.

(3) *Violation of proxy rules:* If the proposal or supporting statement is contrary to any of the Commission's proxy rules, including § 240.14a–9, which prohibits materially false or misleading statements in proxy soliciting materials;

(4) *Personal grievance; special interest:* If the proposal relates to the redress of a personal claim or grievance against the company or any other person, or if it is designed to result in a benefit to you, or to further a personal interest, which is not shared by the other shareholders at large;

(5) *Relevance:* If the proposal relates to operations which account for less than 5 percent of the company's total assets at the end of its most recent fiscal year, and for less than 5 percent of its net earnings and gross sales for

its most recent fiscal year, and is not otherwise significantly related to the company's business;

(6) *Absence of power/authority:* If the company would lack the power or authority to implement the proposal;

(7) *Management functions:* If the proposal deals with a matter relating to the company's ordinary business operations;

(8) *Relates to election:* If the proposal relates to an election for membership on the company's board of directors or analogous governing body;

(9) *Conflicts with company's proposal:* If the proposal directly conflicts with one of the company's own proposals to be submitted to shareholders at the same meeting;

Note to paragraph (i)(9): A company's submission to the Commission under this section should specify the points of conflict with the company's proposal.

(10) *Substantially implemented:* If the company has already substantially implemented the proposal;

(11) *Duplication:* If the proposal substantially duplicates another proposal previously submitted to the company by another proponent that will be included in the company's proxy materials for the same meeting;

(12) *Resubmissions:* If the proposal deals with substantially the same subject matter as another proposal or proposals that has or have been previously included in the company's proxy materials within the preceding 5 calendar years, a company may exclude it from its proxy materials for any meeting held within 3 calendar years of the last time it was included if the proposal received:

(i) Less than 3% of the vote if proposed once within the preceding 5 calendar years;

(ii) Less than 6% of the vote on its last submission to shareholders if proposed twice previously within the preceding 5 calendar years; or

(iii) Less than 10% of the vote on its last submission to shareholders if proposed three times or more previously within the preceding 5 calendar years; and

(13) *Specific amount of dividends:* If the proposal relates to specific amounts of cash or stock dividends.

(j) *Question 10:* What procedures must the company follow if it intends to exclude my proposal? (1) If the company intends to exclude a proposal from its proxy materials, it must file its reasons with the Commission no later than 80 calendar days before it files its definitive proxy statement and form of proxy with the Commission. The company must simultaneously provide you with a copy of its submission. The Commission staff may permit the company to make its submission later than 80 days before the company files its definitive proxy statement and form of proxy, if the company demonstrates good cause for missing the deadline.

(2) The company must file six paper copies of the following:

(i) The proposal;

(ii) An explanation of why the company believes that it may exclude the proposal, which should, if possible, refer to the most recent applicable authority, such as prior Division letters issued under the rule; and

(iii) A supporting opinion of counsel when such reasons are based on matters of state or foreign law.

(k) *Question 11:* May I submit my own statement to the Commission responding to the company's arguments?

Yes, you may submit a response, but it is not required. You should try to submit any response to us, with a copy to the company, as soon as possible after the company makes its submission. This way, the Commission staff will have time to consider fully your submission before it issues its response. You should submit six paper copies of your response.

(*l*) *Question 12:* If the company includes my shareholder proposal in its proxy materials, what information about me must it include along with the proposal itself?

(1) The company's proxy statement must include your name and address, as well as the number of the company's voting securities that you hold. However, instead of providing that information, the company may instead include a statement that it will provide the information to shareholders promptly upon receiving an oral or written request.

(2) The company is not responsible for the contents of your proposal or supporting statement.

(m) *Question 13:* What can I do if the company includes in its proxy statement reasons why it believes shareholders should not vote in favor of my proposal, and I disagree with some of its statements?

(1) The company may elect to include in its proxy statement reasons why it believes shareholders should vote against your proposal. The company is allowed to make arguments reflecting its own point of view, just as you may express your own point of view in your proposal's supporting statement.

(2) However, if you believe that the company's opposition to your proposal contains materially false or misleading statements that may violate our anti-fraud rule, § 240.14a–9, you should promptly send to the Commission staff and the company a letter explaining the reasons for your view, along with a copy of the company's statements opposing your proposal. To the extent possible, your letter should include specific factual information demonstrating the inaccuracy of the company's claims. Time permitting, you may wish to try to work out your differences with the company by yourself before contacting the Commission staff.

(3) We require the company to send you a copy of its statements opposing your proposal before it mails its proxy materials, so that you may bring to our attention any materially false or misleading statements, under the following timeframes:

(i) If our no-action response requires that you make revisions to your proposal or supporting statement as a condition to requiring the company to include it in its proxy materials, then the company must provide you with a copy of its opposition statements no later than 5 calendar days after the company receives a copy of your revised proposal; or

(ii) In all other cases, the company must provide you with a copy of its opposition statements no later than 30 calendar days before its files definitive copies of its proxy statement and form of proxy under § 240.14a–6.

Rule 14a–9. False or Misleading Statements

(a) No solicitation subject to this regulation shall be made by means of any proxy statement, form of proxy, notice of meeting or other communication, written or oral, containing any statement which, at the time and in the light of the circumstances under which it is made, is false or misleading with respect to any material fact, or which omits to state any material fact necessary in order to make the statements therein not false or misleading or necessary to correct any statement in any earlier communication with respect to the solicitation of a proxy for the same meeting or subject matter which has become false or misleading.

(b) The fact that a proxy statement, form of proxy or other soliciting material has been filed with or examined by the Commission shall not be deemed a finding by the Commission that such material is accurate or complete or not false or misleading, or that the Commission has passed upon the merits of or approved any statement contained therein or any matter to be acted upon by security holders. No representation contrary to the foregoing shall be made.

NOTE: The following are some examples of what, depending upon particular facts and circumstances, may be misleading within the meaning of this rule.

(a) Predictions as to specific future market values.

(b) Material which directly or indirectly impugns character, integrity or personal reputation, or directly or indirectly makes charges concerning improper, illegal or immoral conduct or associations, without factual foundation.

(c) Failure to so identify a proxy statement, form of proxy and other soliciting material as to clearly distinguish it from the soliciting material of any other person or persons soliciting for the same meeting or subject matter.

(d) Claims made prior to a meeting regarding the results of a solicitation.

Rule 14a-10. Prohibition of Certain Solicitations

No person making a solicitation which is subject to this regulation shall solicit—

(a) Any undated or post-dated proxy; or

(b) Any proxy which provides that it shall be deemed to be dated as of any date subsequent to the date on which it is signed by the security holder.

Rule 14a-12. Solicitation Before Furnishing a Proxy Statement

(a) Notwithstanding the provisions of § 240.14a-3(a), a solicitation may be made before furnishing security holders with a proxy statement meeting the requirements of § 240.14a-3(a) if:

(1) Each written communication includes:

(i) The identity of the participants in the solicitation (as defined in Instruction 3 to Item 4 of Schedule 14A (§ 240.14a-101)) and a description of their direct or indirect interests, by security holdings or otherwise, or a prominent legend in clear, plain language advising security holders where they can obtain that information; and

(ii) A prominent legend in clear, plain language advising security holders to read the proxy statement when it is available because it contains important information. The legend also must explain to investors that they can get the proxy statement, and any other relevant documents, for free at the Commission's web site and describe which documents are available free from the participants; and

(2) A definitive proxy statement meeting the requirements of § 240.14a-3(a) is sent or given to security holders solicited in reliance on this section before or at the same time as the forms of proxy, consent or authorization are furnished to or requested from security holders.

(b) Any soliciting material published, sent or given to security holders in accordance with paragraph (a) of this section must be filed with the Commission no later than the date the material is first published, sent or given to security holders. Three copies of the material must at the same time be filed with, or mailed for filing to, each national securities exchange upon which any class of securities of the registrant is listed and registered. The soliciting material must include a cover page in the form set forth in Schedule 14A (§ 240.14a-101) and the appropriate box on the cover page must be marked. Soliciting material in connection with a registered offering is required to be filed only under § 230.424 or § 230.425 of this chapter, and will be deemed filed under this section.

(c) Solicitations by any person or group of persons for the purpose of opposing a solicitation subject to this regulation by any other person or group of persons with respect to the election or removal of directors at any annual or special meeting of security holders also are subject to the following provisions:

(1) *Application of this rule to annual report.* Notwithstanding the provisions of § 240.14a-3(b) and (c), any portion of the annual report referred to in § 240.14a-3(b) that comments upon or refers to any solici-

tation subject to this rule, or to any participant in the solicitation, other than the solicitation by the management, must be filed with the Commission as proxy material subject to this regulation. This must be filed in electronic format unless an exemption is available under Rules 201 or 202 of Regulation S–T (§ 232.201 or § 232.202 of this chapter).

(2) *Use of reprints or reproductions*. In any solicitation subject to this § 240.14a–12(c), soliciting material that includes, in whole or part, any reprints or reproductions of any previously published material must:

(i) State the name of the author and publication, the date of prior publication, and identify any person who is quoted without being named in the previously published material.

(ii) Except in the case of a public or official document or statement, state whether or not the consent of the author and publication has been obtained to the use of the previously published material as proxy soliciting material.

(iii) If any participant using the previously published material, or anyone on his or her behalf, paid, directly or indirectly, for the preparation or prior publication of the previously published material, or has made or proposes to make any payments or give any other consideration in connection with the publication or republication of the material, state the circumstances.

Instructions to § 240.14a–12:

1. If paper filing is permitted, file eight copies of the soliciting material with the Commission, except that only three copies of the material specified by § 240.14a–12(c)(1) need be filed.

2. Any communications made under this section after the definitive proxy statement is on file but before it is disseminated also must specify that the proxy statement is publicly available and the anticipated date of dissemination.

Rule 14a–13. Obligation of Registrants in Communicating With Beneficial Owners

(a) If the registrant knows that securities of any class entitled to vote at a meeting (or by written consents or authorizations if no meeting is held) with respect to which the registrant intends to solicit proxies, consents or authorizations are held of record by a broker, dealer, voting trustee, bank, association, or other entity that exercises fiduciary powers in nominee name or otherwise, the registrant shall:

(1) By first class mail or other equally prompt means: (i) inquire of each such record holder: (A) whether other persons are the beneficial owners of such securities and if so, the number of copies of the proxy and other soliciting material necessary to supply such material to such beneficial owners; (B) in the case of an annual (or special meeting in lieu of the annual) meeting, or written consents in lieu of such meeting, at which directors are to be elected, the number of copies of the annual report to security holders necessary to supply such report to beneficial owners to whom such reports are to be distributed by such record holder or its nominee and not by the registrant; and (C) if the record holder has an obligation under Rules 14b–1(b)(3) or 14b–2(b)(4)(ii) and (iii) and (3), whether an agent has been designated to act on its behalf in fulfilling such obligation and, if so, the name and address of such agent; and (D) whether it holds the registrant's securities on behalf of any respondent bank and, if so, the name and address of each such respondent bank; and (ii) indicate to each such record holder: (A) whether the registrant, pursuant to paragraph (c) of this rule, intends to distribute the annual report to security holders to beneficial owners of its securities whose names, addresses and securities positions are disclosed pursuant to Rules 14b–1(b)(3) and 14(b)–2(b)(4)(ii) and (iii); (B) the record date; and (C) at the option of the registrant,

any employee benefit plan established by an affiliate of the registrant that holds securities of the registrant that the registrant elects to treat as exempt employee benefit plan securities;

(2) Upon receipt of a record holder's or respondent bank's response indicating, pursuant to Rule 14b–2(b)(1)(i), the names and addresses of its respondent banks, within one business day after the date such response is received, make an inquiry of and give notification to each such respondent bank in the same manner required by paragraph (a)(1) of this rule; *Provided, however,* the inquiry required by paragraphs (a)(1) and (a)(2) of this rule shall not cover beneficial owners of exempt employee benefit plan securities;

(3) Make the inquiry required by paragraph (a)(1) of this section at least 20 business days prior to the record date of the meeting of security holders, or (i) if such inquiry is impracticable 20 business days prior to the record date of a special meeting, as many days before the record date of such meeting as is practicable or, (ii) if consents or authorization are solicited, and such inquiry is impracticable 20 business days before the earliest date on which they may be used to effect corporate action, as many days before that date as is practicable, or (iii) at such later time as the rules of a national securities exchange on which the class of securities in question is listed may permit for good cause shown; *Provided, however*, that if a record holder or respondent bank has informed the registrant that a designated office(s) or department(s) is to receive such inquiries, the inquiry shall be made to such designated office(s) or department(s);

(4) Supply, in a timely manner, each record holder and respondent bank of whom the inquiries required by paragraphs (a)(1) and (a)(2) of this section are made with copies of the proxy, other proxy soliciting material, and/or the annual report to security holders, in such quantities, assembled in such form and at such place(s), as the record holder or respondent bank may reasonably request in order to send such material to each beneficial owner of securities who is to be furnished with such material by the record holder or respondent bank; and

(5) Upon the request of any record holder or respondent bank that is supplied with proxy soliciting material and/or annual reports to security holders pursuant to paragraph (a)(4) of this section, pay its reasonable expenses for completing the mailing of such material to beneficial owners.

NOTE 1: If the registrant's list of security holders indicates that some of its securities are registered in the name of a clearing agency registered pursuant to section 17A of the Act (*e.g.*, "Cede & Co.," nominee for the Depository Trust Company), the registrant shall make appropriate inquiry of the clearing agency and thereafter of the participants in such clearing agency who may hold on behalf of a beneficial owner, or respondent bank and shall comply with the above paragraph with respect to any such participant (see Rule 14a–1(i)).

NOTE 2: The attention of registrants is called to the fact that each broker, dealer, bank, association and other entity that exercises fiduciary powers has an obligation pursuant to Rule 14b–1(b), and Rule 14b–2(b) (except as provided therein with respect to employee benefit plan securities held in nominee name) and, with respect to brokers and dealers, applicable self-regulatory organization requirements to obtain and forward, within the time periods prescribed therein, (a) proxies (or in lieu thereof requests for voting instructions) and proxy soliciting materials to beneficial owners on whose behalf it holds securities, and (b) annual reports to security holders to beneficial owners on whose behalf it holds securities, unless the registrant has notified the record holder or respondent bank that it has assumed responsibility to mail such material to beneficial owners whose names, addresses and securities positions are disclosed pursuant to Rule 14b–1(b)(3) and Rule 14b–2(b)(4)(ii) and (iii).

NOTE 3: The attention of registrants is called to the fact that registrants have an obligation, pursuant to paragraph (d) of this rule, to cause proxies (or in lieu thereof requests for voting instructions), proxy soliciting material and annual reports to security holders to be furnished, in a timely manner, to beneficial owners of exempt employee benefit plan securities.

(b) Any registrant requesting pursuant to Rule 14b–1(b)(3) and Rule 14b–2(b)(4)(ii) and (iii) and (3) a list of names, addresses and securities positions of beneficial owners of its securities who either have consented or have not objected to disclosure of such information shall:

(1) By first class mail or other equally prompt means, inquire of each record holder and each respondent bank identified to the registrant pursuant to Rule 14b–2(b)(4)(i) whether such record holder or respondent bank holds the registrant's securities on behalf of any respondent banks and, if so, the name and address of each such respondent bank;

(2) Request such list to be compiled as of a date no earlier than five business days after the date the registrant's request is received by the record holder or respondent bank; *Provided, however*, that if the record holder or respondent bank has informed the registrant that a designated office(s) or department(s) is to receive such requests, the request shall be made to such designated office(s) or department(s);

(3) Make such request to the following persons that hold the registrant's securities on behalf of beneficial owners: all brokers, dealers, banks, associations and other entities that exercise fiduciary powers; *Provided, however,* such request shall not cover beneficial owners of exempt employee benefit plan securities as defined in Rule 14a–1(d)(1); and, at the option of the registrant, such request may give notice of any employee benefit plan established by an affiliate of the registrant that holds securities of the registrant that the registrant elects to treat as exempt employee benefit plan securities;

(4) Use the information furnished in response to such request exclusively for purposes of corporate communications; and

(5) Upon the request of any record holder or respondent bank to whom such request is made, pay the reasonable expenses, both direct and indirect, of providing beneficial owner information.

NOTE — A registrant will be deemed to have satisfied its obligations under paragraph (b) of this section by requesting consenting and non-objecting beneficial owner lists from a designated agent acting on behalf of the record holder or respondent bank and paying to that designated agent the reasonable expenses of providing the beneficial owner information.

(c) A registrant, at its option, may mail its annual report to security holders to the beneficial owners whose identifying information is provided by record holders and respondent banks, pursuant to Rule 14b–1(c) and Rule 14b–2(e)(2) and (3), provided that such registrant notifies the record holders and respondent banks, at the time it makes the inquiry required by paragraph (a) of this rule, that the registrant will mail the annual report to security holders to the beneficial owners so identified.

(d) If a registrant solicits proxies, consents or authorizations from record holders and respondent banks who hold securities on behalf of beneficial owners, the registrant shall cause proxies (or in lieu thereof requests for voting instructions), proxy soliciting material and annual reports to security holders to be furnished, in a timely manner, to beneficial owners of exempt employee benefit plan securities.

Rule 14a–14. Modified or Superseded Documents

(a) Any statement contained in a document incorporated or deemed to be incorporated by reference shall be deemed to be modified or superseded, for purposes of the proxy statement, to the extent that a statement contained in the proxy statement or in any other subsequently filed document that also is or is deemed to be incorporated by reference modifies or replaces such statement.

(b) The modifying or superseding statement may but need not, state it has modified or superseded a prior statement or include any other information set forth in the document that is not so modified or superseded. The making of a modifying or superseding statement shall not be deemed an admission that the modified or superseded statement, when made, constituted an untrue statement of a material fact, an omission to state a material fact necessary to make a statement not misleading, or the employment of a manipulative, deceptive, or fraudulent device, contrivance, scheme, transaction, act, practice, course of business or artifice to defraud, as those terms are used in the Securities Act of 1933, the Securities Exchange Act of 1934 ("the Act"), the Public Utility Holding Company Act of 1935, the Investment Company Act of 1940, or the rules and regulations thereunder.

(c) Any statement so modified shall not be deemed in its unmodified form to constitute part of the proxy statement for purposes of the Act. Any statement so superseded shall not be deemed to constitute a part of the proxy statement for purposes of the Act.

Rule 14a-15. Differential and Contingent Compensation in Connection With Roll-Up Transactions

(a) It shall be unlawful for any person to receive compensation for soliciting proxies, consents, or authorizations directly from security holders in connection with a roll-up transaction as provided in paragraph (b) of this section, if the compensation is:

(1) Based on whether the solicited proxy, consent, or authorization either approves or disapproves the proposed roll-up transaction; or

(2) Contingent on the approval, disapproval, or completion of the roll-up transaction.

(b) This section is applicable to a roll-up transaction as defined in Item 901(c) of Regulation S-K (§ 229.901(c) of this chapter), except for a transaction involving only:

(1) Finite-life entities that are not limited partnerships;

(2) Partnerships whose investors will receive new securities or securities in another entity that are not reported under a transaction reporting plan declared effective before December 17, 1993 by the Commission under Section 11A of the Act (15 U.S.C. 78k-1); or

(3) Partnerships whose investors' securities are reported under a transaction reporting plan declared effective before December 17, 1993 by the Commission under Section 11A of the Act (15 U.S.C. 78k-1).

SCHEDULE 14A—INFORMATION REQUIRED IN PROXY STATEMENT

Schedule 14A Information

Proxy Statement Pursuant to Section 14(a) of the Securities Exchange Act of 1934 (Amendment No.)

Filed by the Registrant [ ]

Filed by a Party other than the Registrant [ ]

Check the appropriate box:

[ ] Preliminary Proxy Statement

[ ] Confidential, for Use of the Commission Only (as permitted by Rule 14a-6(e)(2))

[ ] Definitive Proxy Statement

[ ] Definitive Additional Materials

[ ] Soliciting Material Under § 240.14a-12

____

(Name of Registrant as Specified In Its Charter)

____

(Name(s) of Person(s) Filing Proxy Statement, if other than the Registrant)

____

Payment of Filing Fee (Check the appropriate box):

[ ] No fee required.

[ ] Fee computed on table below per Exchange Act Rules 14a–6(i)(4) and 0–11

(1) Title of each class of securities to which transaction applies:

____

(2) Aggregate number of securities to which transaction applies:

____

(3) Per unit price or other underlying value of transaction computed pursuant to Exchange Act Rule 0–11 (Set forth the amount on which the filing fee is calculated and state how it was determined):

____

(4) Proposed maximum aggregate value of transaction:

____

(5) Total fee paid:

____

[ ] Fee paid previously with preliminary materials.

[ ] Check box if any part of the fee is offset as provided by Exchange Act Rule 0–11(a)(2) and identify the filing for which the offsetting fee was paid previously. Identify the previous filing by registration statement number, or the Form or Schedule and the date of its filing.

(1) Amount Previously Paid:

____

(2) Form. Schedule or Registration Statement No.:

____

(3) Filing Party:

____

(4) Date Filed:

____

Reg. § 240.14a–101. NOTES: A. Where any item calls for information with respect to any matter to be acted upon and such matter involves other matters with respect to which information is called for by other items of this schedule, the information called for by such other items shall also be given. For example, where a solicitation of security holders is for the purpose of approving the authorization of additional securities which are to be used to acquire another specified company, and the registrants' security holders will not have a separate opportunity to vote upon the transaction, the solicitation to authorize the securities is also a solicitation with respect to the acquisition. Under those facts, information required by Items 11, 13 and 14 shall be furnished.

B. Where any item calls for information with respect to any matter to be acted upon at the meeting, such item need be answered in the registrant's soliciting material only with respect to proposals to be made by or on behalf of the registrant.

C. Except as otherwise specifically provided, where any item calls for information for a specified period in regard to directors, executive officers, officers or other persons holding specified positions or relationships, the information shall be given with regard to any person who held any of the specified positions or relationships at any time during the period. Information need not be included for any portion of the period during which such person did not hold any such position or relationship provided a statement to that effect is made.

D. Information may be incorporated by reference only in the manner and to the extent specifically permitted in the items of this schedule. Where incorporation by reference is used, the following shall apply:

1. Any incorporation by reference of information pursuant to the provisions of this schedule shall be subject to the provisions of § 228.10(f) and § 229.10(d) of this chapter restricting incorporation by reference of documents which incorporate by reference oth-

er information. A registrant incorporating any documents, or portions of documents, shall include a statement on the last page(s) of the proxy statement as to which documents, or portions of documents, are incorporated by reference. Information shall not be incorporated by reference in any case where such incorporation would render the statement incomplete, unclear or confusing.

2. If a document is incorporated by reference but not delivered to security holders, include an undertaking to provide, without charge, to each person to whom a proxy statement is delivered, upon written or oral request of such person and by first class mail or other equally prompt means within one business day of receipt of such request, a copy of any and all of the information that has been incorporated by reference in the proxy statement (not including exhibits to the information that is incorporated by reference unless such exhibits are specifically incorporated by reference into the information that the proxy statement incorporates), and the address (including title or department) and telephone numbers to which such a request is to be directed. This includes information contained in documents filed subsequent to the date on which definitive copies of the proxy statement are sent or given to security holders, up to the date of responding to the request.

3. If a document or portion of a document other than an annual report sent to security holders pursuant to the requirements of Rule 14a–3 with respect to the same meeting or solicitation of consents or authorizations as that to which the proxy statement relates is incorporated by reference in the manner permitted by Item 13(b) or Item 14(e)(1) of this schedule, the proxy statement must be sent to security holders no later than 20 business days prior to the date on which the meeting of such security holders is held or, if no meeting is held, at least 20 business days prior to the date the votes, consents or authorizations may be used to effect the corporate action.

4. *Electronic filings.* If any of the information required by Items 13 or 14 of this Schedule is incorporated by reference from an annual or quarterly report to security holders, such report, or any portion thereof incorporated by reference, shall be filed in electronic format with the proxy statement.

E. In Item 13 of this Schedule, the reference to "meets the requirements of Form S–2" shall refer to a registrant specified in Item 14(a) of this Schedule which meets the requirements for use of Form S–2 and the reference to "meets the requirement of Form S–3" shall refer to a registrant specified in Item 14(a) of this Schedule which meets the following requirements:

(1) the registrant meets the requirements of General Instruction I.A. of Form S–3; and

(2) one of the following is met:

(i) the registrant meets the aggregate market value requirement of General Instruction I.B.1 of Form S–3; or

(ii) action is to be taken as described in Items 11, 12 and 14 of this schedule which concerns non-convertible debt or preferred securities which are "investment grade securities" as defined in General Instruction I.B.2 of Form S–3, except that the time by which the rating must be assigned shall be the date on which definitive copies of the proxy statement are first sent or given to security holders; or

(iii) the registrant is a majority-owned subsidiary and one of the conditions of General Instruction I.C. of Form S–3 is met.

F. *Note to Small Business Issuers.* Registrants and acquirees that meet the definition of "small business issuer" under Rule 12b–2 of the Exchange Act shall refer to the disclosure items in Regulation S–B and not Regulation S–K. If there is no comparable disclosure item in Regulation S–B, small business issuers need not provide the information requested. Small business issuers shall provide the financial information in Item 310 of Regulation S–B in lieu of the financial statements required in Schedule 14A.

G. *Special Note for Small Business Issuers*

(1) Registrants and acquirees which meet the definition of "small business issuer" in Rule 12b–2 of the Exchange Act and filed their latest annual report in accordance with "Information Required in Annual Report of Transitional Small Business Issuers" in Form 10–KSB shall refer to this "Special Note for Small Business Issuers" with respect to the specified items in this Schedule. If paragraph G(2) or G(3), below, does not contain an alternative disclosure instruction, small business issuers should comply with the disclosure item in this schedule, as modified by Instruction F.

(2) Registrants and acquirees that relied upon Alternative 1 in their most recent Form 10–KSB may provide the following information (Question numbers are in reference to Model A of Form 1–A): (a) Questions 37 and 38 instead of Item 6(d); (b) Question 43 instead of Item 7(a); (c) Questions 29–36 and 39 instead of Item 7(b); (d) Questions 40–42 instead of Item 8; (e) Questions 40–42 instead of Item 10; (f) the information required in Part F/S of Form 10–SB instead of the financial statement requirements of Items 13 or 14; (g) Questions 4, 11, and 47–50 instead of Item 13(a)(1)(3); (h) Question 3 instead of the information specified in Items 101 and 102 of Regulation S–B (§ 228.101 and § 228.102 of this chapter); and (i) Questions 4, 11, and 47–50 instead of the information specified in Item 303 of Regulation S–B (§ 228.303 of this chapter).

(3) Registrants and acquirees that relied upon Alternative 2 in their most recent Form 10–KSB may provide the following information ("Model B" refers to Model B of Form 1–A): (a) Item 10 of Model B instead of Item 6(d) of Schedule 14A; (b) Item 8(d) of Model B instead of Item 7(a) of Schedule 14A; (c) Items 8(a)(8)(c) and Item 11 of Model B instead of Item 7(b) of Schedule 14A; (d) Item 9 of Model B instead of Item 8 of Schedule 14A; (e) Item 9 of Model B instead of Item 10 of Schedule 14A; (f) the information required in Part F/S of Form 10–SB instead of the financial statements requirements of Items 13 or 14 of Schedule 14A; (g) Item 6(a)(3)(i) of Model B instead of Item 13(a)(1)(3) of Schedule 14A; (h) Items 6 and 7 of Model B instead of the information specified in Items 101 and 102 of Regulation S–B (§ 228.101 and § 228.102 of this chapter); and (i) Item 6(a)(3)(i) of Model B instead of the information specified in Item 303 of Regulation S–B (§ 228.303 of this chapter).

Item 1. Date, Time and Place Information

(a) State the date, time and place of the meeting of security holders, and the complete mailing address, including ZIP Code, of the principal executive offices of the registrant, unless such information is otherwise disclosed in material furnished to security holders with or preceding the proxy statement. If action is to be taken by written consent, state the date by which consents are to be submitted if state law requires that such a date be specified or if the person soliciting intends to set a date.

(b) On the first page of the proxy statement, as delivered to security holders, state the approximate date on which the proxy statement and form of proxy are first sent or given to security holders.

(c) Furnish the information required to be in the proxy statement by Rule 14a–5(e).

Item 2. Revocability of Proxy

State whether or not the person giving the proxy has the power to revoke it. If the right of revocation before the proxy is exercised is limited or is subject to compliance with any formal procedure, briefly describe such limitation or procedure.

Item 3. Dissenters' Right of Appraisal

Outline briefly the rights of appraisal or similar rights of dissenters with respect to any matter to be acted upon and indicate any statutory procedure required to be followed by dissenting security holders in order to perfect such rights. Where such rights may be exercised only within a limited time after the date of adoption of a proposal, the filing of a charter amendment or other similar act, state whether the persons solicited will be notified of such date.

Instructions. 1. Indicate whether a security holder's failure to vote against a proposal will constitute a waiver of his appraisal or similar rights and whether a vote against a proposal will be deemed to satisfy any notice requirements under State law with respect to appraisal rights. If the State law is unclear, state what position will be taken in regard to these matters.

2. Open-end investment companies registered under the Investment Company Act of 1940 are not required to respond to this item.

Item 4. Persons Making the Solicitation

(a) *Solicitations Not Subject to Rule 14a–12(c).*

(1) If the solicitation is made by the registrant, so state. Give the name of any director of the registrant who has informed the registrant in writing that he intends to oppose any action intended to be taken by the registrant and indicate the action which he intends to oppose.

(2) If the solicitation is made otherwise than by the registrant, so state and give the names of the participants in the solicitation, as defined in paragraphs (a)(iii), (iv), (v) and (vi) of Instruction 3 to this Item.

(3) If the solicitation is to be made otherwise than by the use of the mails, describe the methods to be employed. If the solicitation is to be made by specially engaged employees or paid solicitors, state (i) the material features of any contract or arrangement for such solicitation and identify the parties, and (ii) the cost or anticipated cost thereof.

(4) State the names of the persons by whom the cost of solicitation has been or will be borne, directly or indirectly.

(b) *Solicitations Subject to Rule 14a–12(c).*

(1) State by whom the solicitation is made and describe the methods employed and to be employed to solicit security holders.

(2) If regular employees of the registrant or any other participant in a solicitation have been or are to be employed to solicit security holders, describe the class or classes of employees to be so employed, and the manner and nature of their employment for such purpose.

(3) If specially engaged employees, representatives or other persons have been or are to be employed to solicit security holders, state (i) the material features of any contract or arrangement for such solicitation and the identity of the parties, (ii) the cost or anticipated cost thereof, and (iii) the approximate number of such employees or employees of any other person (naming such other person) who will solicit security holders.

(4) State the total amount estimated to be spent and the total expenditures to date for, in furtherance of, or in connection with the solicitation of security holders.

(5) State by whom the cost of the solicitation will be borne. If such cost is to be borne initially by any person other than the registrant, state whether reimbursement will be sought from the registrant, and, if so, whether the question of such reimbursement will be submitted to a vote of security holders.

(6) If any such solicitation is terminated pursuant to a settlement between the registrant and any other participant in such solicitation, describe the terms of such settlement, including the cost or anticipated cost thereof to the registrant.

Instructions. 1. With respect to solicitations subject to Rule 14a–12(c), costs and expenditures within the meaning of this Item 4 shall include fees for attorneys, accountants, public relations or financial advisers, solicitors, advertising, printing, transportation, litigation and other costs incidental to the solicitation, except that the registrant may exclude the amount of such costs represented by the amount normally expended for a solicitation for an election of directors in the absence of a contest, and costs represented by salaries and wages of regular employees and officers, provided a statement to the effect is included in the proxy statement.

2. The information required pursuant to paragraph (b)(6) of this Item should be included in any amended or revised proxy statement or other soliciting materials relating to the same meeting or subject matter furnished to security holders by the registrant subsequent to the date of settlement.

3. For purposes of this Item 4 and Item 5 of this Schedule 14A:

(a) The terms "participant" and "participant in a solicitation" include the following:

(i) The registrant;

(ii) Any director of the registrant, and any nominee for whose election as a director proxies are solicited;

(iii) Any committee or group which solicits proxies, any member of such committee or group, and any person whether or not named as a member who, acting alone or with one or more other persons, directly or indirectly takes the initiative, or engages, in organizing, directing, or arranging for the financing of any such committee or group;

(iv) Any person who finances or joins with another to finance the solicitation of proxies, except persons who contribute not more than $500 and who are not otherwise participants;

(v) Any person who lends money or furnishes credit or enters into any other arrangements, pursuant to any contract or understanding with a participant, for the purpose of financing or otherwise inducing the purchase, sale, holding or voting of securities of the registrant by any participant or other persons, in support of or in opposition to a participant; except that such terms do not include a bank, broker or dealer who, in the ordinary course of business, lends money or executes orders for the purchase or sale of securities and who is not otherwise a participant; and

(vi) Any person who solicits proxies.

(b) The terms "participant" and "participant in a solicitation" do not include:

(i) Any person or organization retained or employed by a participant to solicit security holders and whose activities are limited to the duties required to be performed in the course of such employment;

(ii) Any person who merely transmits proxy soliciting material or performs other ministerial or clerical duties;

(iii) Any person employed by a participant in the capacity of attorney, accountant, or advertising, public relations or financial adviser, and whose activities are limited to the duties required to be performed in the course of such employment;

(iv) Any person regularly employed as an officer or employee of the registrant or any of its subsidiaries who is not otherwise a participant; or

(v) Any officer or director of, or any person regularly employed by, any other participant, if such officer, director or employee is not otherwise a participant.

Item 5. Interest of Certain Persons in Matters to Be Acted Upon

(a) *Solicitations Not Subject to Rule 14a-12(c).* Describe briefly any substantial interest, direct or indirect, by security holdings or otherwise, of each of the following persons in any matter to be acted upon, other than elections to office:

(1) If the solicitation is made on behalf of the registrant, each person who has been a

director or executive officer of the registrant at any time since the beginning of the last fiscal year.

(2) If the solicitation is made otherwise than on behalf of the registrant, each participant in the solicitation, as defined in paragraphs (a)(iii), (iv), (v), and (vi) of Instruction 3 to Item 4 of this Schedule 14A.

(3) Each nominee for election as a director of the registrant.

(4) Each associate of the foregoing persons.

Instruction. Except in the case of a solicitation subject to this regulation made in opposition to another solicitation subject to this regulation, this sub-item (a) shall not apply to any interest arising from the ownership of securities of the registrant where the security holder receives no extra or special benefit not shared on a pro rata basis by all other holders of the same class.

(b) *Solicitations Subject to Rule 14a–12(c).*

(1) Describe briefly any substantial interest, direct or indirect, by security holdings or otherwise, of each participant as defined in paragraphs (a)(ii), (iii), (iv), (v) and (vi) of Instruction 3 to Item 4 of this Schedule 14A, in any matter to be acted upon at the meeting, and include with respect to each participant the following information, or a fair and accurate summary thereof:

(i) Name and business address of the participant.

(ii) The participant's present principal occupation or employment and the name, principal business and address of any corporation or other organization in which such employment is carried on.

(iii) State whether or not, during the past ten years, the participant has been convicted in a criminal proceeding (excluding traffic violations or similar misdemeanors) and, if so, give dates, nature of conviction, name and location of court, and penalty imposed or other disposition of the case. A negative answer need not be included in the proxy statement or other soliciting material.

(iv) State the amount of each class of securities of the registrant which the participant owns beneficially, directly or indirectly.

(v) State the amount of each class of securities of the registrant which the participant owns of record but not beneficially.

(vi) State with respect to all securities of the registrant purchased or sold within the past two years, the dates on which they were purchased or sold and the amount purchased or sold on each such date.

(vii) If any part of the purchase price or market value of any of the shares specified in paragraph (b)(1)(vi) of this Item is represented by funds borrowed or otherwise obtained for the purpose of acquiring or holding such securities, so state and indicate the amount of the indebtedness as of the latest practicable date. If such funds were borrowed or obtained otherwise than pursuant to a margin account or bank loan in the regular course of business of a bank, broker or dealer, briefly describe the transaction, and state the names of the parties.

(viii) State whether or not the participant is, or was within the past year, a party to any contract, arrangements or understandings with any person with respect to any securities of the registrant, including, but not limited to joint ventures, loan or option arrangements, puts or calls, guarantees against loss or guarantees of profit, division of losses or profits, or the giving or withholding of proxies. If so, name the parties to such contracts, arrangements or understandings and give the details thereof.

(ix) State the amount of securities of the registrant owned beneficially, directly or indirectly, by each of the participant's associates and the name and address of each such associate.

(x) State the amount of each class of securities of any parent or subsidiary of the registrant which the participant owns beneficially, directly or indirectly.

(xi) Furnish for the participant and associates of the participant the information required by Item 404(a) of Regulation S–K.

(xii) State whether or not the participant or any associates of the participant have any arrangement or understanding with any person—

(A) with respect to any future employment by the registrant or its affiliates; or

(B) with respect to any future transactions to which the registrant or any of its affiliates will or may be a party.

If so, describe such arrangement or understanding and state the names of the parties thereto.

(2) With respect to any person, other than a director or executive officer of the registrant acting solely in that capacity, who is a party to an arrangement or understanding pursuant to which a nominee for election as director is proposed to be elected, describe any substantial interest, direct or indirect, by security holdings or otherwise, that such person has in any matter to be acted upon at the meeting, and furnish the information called for by paragraphs (b)(1)(xi) and (xii) of this Item.

Instruction: For purposes of this Item 5, beneficial ownership shall be determined in accordance with Rule 13d–3 under the Act.

Item 6. Voting Securities and Principal Holders Thereof

(a) As to each class of voting securities of the registrant entitled to be voted at the meeting (or by written consents or authorizations if no meeting is held), state the number of shares outstanding and the number of votes to which each class is entitled.

(b) State the record date, if any, with respect to this solicitation. If the right to vote or give consent is not to be determined, in whole or in part, by reference to a record date, indicate the criteria for the determination of security holders entitled to vote or give consent.

(c) If action is to be taken with respect to the election of directors and if the persons solicited have cumulative voting rights: (1) make a statement that they have such rights, (2) briefly describe such rights, (3) state briefly the conditions precedent to the exercise thereof, and (4) if discretionary authority to cumulate votes is solicited, so indicate.

(d) Furnish the information required by Item 403 of Regulation S–K to the extent known by the persons on whose behalf the solicitation is made.

(e) If, to the knowledge of the persons on whose behalf the solicitation is made, a change in control of the registrant has occurred since the beginning of its last fiscal year, state the name of the person(s) who acquired such control, the amount and the source of the consideration used by such person or persons; the basis of the control, the date and a description of the transaction(s) which resulted in the change of control and the percentage of voting securities of the registrant now beneficially owned directly or indirectly by the person(s) who acquired control; and the identity of the person(s) from whom control was assumed. If the source of all or any part of the consideration used is a loan made in the ordinary course of business by a bank as defined by section 3(a)(6) of the Act, the identity of such bank shall be omitted provided a request for confidentiality has been made pursuant to section 13(d)(1)(B) of the Act by the person(s) who acquired control. In lieu thereof, the material shall indicate that the identity of the bank has been so omitted and filed separately with the Commission.

Instructions. 1. State the terms of any loans or pledges obtained by the new control group for the purpose of acquiring control, and the names of the lenders or pledgees.

2. Any arrangements or understandings among members of both the former and new control groups and their associates with respect to election of directors or other matters should be described.

Item 7. Directors and Executive Officers

If action is to be taken with respect to the election of directors, furnish the following information in tabular form to the extent practicable. If, however, the solicitation is made on behalf of persons other than the registrant, the information required need be furnished only as to nominees of the persons making the solicitation.

(a) The information required by instruction 4 to Item 103 of Regulation S–K with respect to directors and executive officers.

(b) The information required by Items 401, 404(a) and (c), and 405 of Regulation S–K.

(c) The information required by Item 404(b) of Regulation S–K (§ 229.404 of this chapter).

(d)(1) State whether or not the issuer has standing audit, nominating and compensation committees of the Board of Directors, or committees performing similar functions. If the registrant has such committees, however designated, identify each committee member, state the number of committee meetings held by each such committee during the last fiscal year and describe briefly the functions performed by such committees. Such disclosure need not be provided to the extent it is duplicative of disclosure provided in accordance with Item 401(i) of Regulation S–K (§ 229.401(i) of this chapter).

(2)(i) If the registrant does not have a standing nominating committee or committee performing similar functions, state the basis for the view of the board of directors that it is appropriate for the registrant not to have such a committee and identify each director who participates in the consideration of director nominees;

(ii) Provide the following information regarding the registrant's director nomination process:

(A) If the nominating committee has a charter, disclose whether a current copy of the charter is available to security holders on the registrant's Web site. If the nominating committee has a charter and a current copy of the charter is available to security holders on the registrant's Web site, provide the registrant's Web site address. If the nominating committee has a charter and a current copy of the charter is not available to security holders on the registrant's Web site, include a copy of the charter as an appendix to the registrant's proxy statement at least once every three fiscal years. If a current copy of the charter is not available to security holders on the registrant's Web site, and is not included as an appendix to the registrant's proxy statement, identify in which of the prior fiscal years the charter was so included in satisfaction of this requirement;

(B) If the nominating committee does not have a charter, state that fact;

(C) If the registrant is a listed issuer (as defined in § 240.10A–3) whose securities are listed on a national securities exchange registered pursuant to section 6(a) of the Act (15 U.S.C. 78f(a)) or in an automated inter-dealer quotation system of a national securities association registered pursuant to section 15A(a) of the Act (15 U.S.C. 78o–3(a)) that has independence requirements for nominating committee members, disclose whether the members of the nominating committee are independent, as independence for nominating committee members is defined in the listing standards applicable to the listed issuer;

(D) If the registrant is not a listed issuer (as defined in § 240.10A–3), disclose whether each of the members of the nominating committee is independent. In determining whether a member is independent, the registrant must use a definition of independence of a national securities exchange registered pursuant to section 6(a) of the Act (15 U.S.C. 78f(a)) or a national securities association registered pursuant to section 15A(a) of the Act (15 U.S.C. 78o–3(a)) that has been approved by the Commission (as that definition may be modified or supplemented), and state which definition it used. Whatever definition the registrant chooses, it must apply that definition consistently to all members of the nominating committee and use the independence standards of the same national securities exchange or national securities association for purposes of nominating committee disclosure under this requirement and audit committee disclosure required under paragraph (d)(3)(iv) of Item 7 of Schedule 14A (§ 240.14a–101);

(E) If the nominating committee has a policy with regard to the consideration of any director candidates recommended by security holders, provide a description of the material elements of that policy, which shall include, but need not be limited to, a statement as to whether the committee will consider director candidates recommended by security holders;

(F) If the nominating committee does not have a policy with regard to the consideration of any director candidates recommended by security holders, state that fact and state the basis for the view of the board of directors that it is appropriate for the registrant not to have such a policy;

(G) If the nominating committee will consider candidates recommended by security holders, describe the procedures to be followed by security holders in submitting such recommendations;

(H) Describe any specific, minimum qualifications that the nominating committee believes must be met by a nominating committee-recommended nominee for a position on the registrant's board of directors, and describe any specific qualities or skills that the nominating committee believes are necessary for one or more of the registrant's directors to possess;

(I) Describe the nominating committee's process for identifying and evaluating nominees for director, including nominees recommended by security holders, and any differences in the manner in which the nominating committee evaluates nominees for director based on whether the nominee is recommended by a security holder;

(J) With regard to each nominee approved by the nominating committee for inclusion on the registrant's proxy card (other than nominees who are executive officers or who are directors standing for re-election), state which one or more of the following categories of persons or entities recommended that nominee: security holder, non-management director, chief executive officer, other executive officer, third-party search firm, or other, specified source. With regard to each such nominee approved by a nominating committee of an investment company, state which one or more of the following additional categories of persons or entities recommended that nominee: security holder, director, chief executive officer, other executive officer, or employee of the investment company's investment adviser, principal underwriter, or any affiliated person of the investment adviser or principal underwriter;

(K) If the registrant pays a fee to any third party or parties to identify or evaluate or assist in identifying or evaluating potential nominees, disclose the function performed by each such third party; and

(L) If the registrant's nominating committee received, by a date not later than the 120th calendar day before the date of the registrant's proxy statement released to security holders in connection with the previous year's annual meeting, a recommended nominee from a security holder that beneficially owned more than 5% of the registrant's voting common stock for at least one year as of the date the recommendation was made, or from a group of security holders that beneficially owned, in the aggregate, more than 5% of the registrant's voting common stock, with each of the securities used to calculate that ownership held for at least one year as of the date the recommendation was made, identify the candidate and the security holder or security holder group that recommended the candidate and disclose whether the nominating committee chose to nominate the candidate, provided, however, that no such identification or disclosure is required without the written consent of both the security holder or security holder group and the candidate to be so identified.

Instructions to paragraph (d)(2)(ii)(L):

1. For purposes of Item 7(d)(2)(ii)(L), the percentage of securities held by a nominating security holder may be determined using information set forth in the registrant's most recent quarterly or annual report, and any current report subsequent thereto, filed with the Commission pursuant to this Act (or, in the case of a registrant that is an investment company registered under the Investment Company Act of 1940, the registrant's most recent report on Form N–CSR (§§ 249.331 and 274.128)), unless the party relying on such report knows or has reason to believe that the information contained therein is inaccurate.

2. For purposes of the registrant's obligation to provide the disclosure specified in Item 7(d)(2)(ii)(L), where the date of the annual meeting has been changed by more than 30 days from the date of the previous year's meeting, the obligation under that Item will arise where the registrant receives the security holder recommendation a reasonable time before the registrant begins to print and mail its proxy materials.

3. For purposes of Item 7(d)(2)(ii)(L), the percentage of securities held by a recommending security holder, as well as the holding period of those securities, may be determined by the registrant if the security holder is the registered holder of the securities. If the security holder is not the registered owner of the securities, he or she can submit one of the following to the registrant to evidence the required ownership percentage and holding period:

A. A written statement from the "record" holder of the securities (usually a broker or bank) verifying that, at the time the security holder made the recommendation, he or she had held the required securities for at least one year; or

B. If the security holder has filed a Schedule 13D (§ 240.13d–101), Schedule 13G (§ 240.13d–102), Form 3 (§ 249.103), Form 4 (§ 249.104), and/or Form 5 (§ 249.105), or amendments to those documents or updated forms, reflecting ownership of the securities as of or before the date of the recommendation, a copy of the schedule and/or form, and any subsequent amendments reporting a change in ownership level, as well as a written statement that the security holder continuously held the securities for the one-year period as of the date of the recommendation.

4. For purposes of the registrant's obligation to provide the disclosure specified in Item 7(d)(2)(ii)(L), the security holder or group must have provided to the registrant, at the time of the recommendation, the written consent of all parties to be identified and, where the security holder or group members are not registered holders, proof that the security holder or group satisfied the required ownership percentage and holding period as of the date of the recommendation.

Instruction to paragraph (d)(2)(ii): For purposes of Item 7(d)(2)(ii), the term "nominating committee" refers not only to nominating committees and committees performing similar functions, but also to groups of directors fulfilling the role of a nominating committee, including the entire board of directors.

(3) If the registrant has an audit committee:

(i) Provide the information required by Item 306 of Regulation S–K (17 CFR 229.306).

(ii) State whether the registrant's Board of Directors has adopted a written charter for the audit committee.

(iii) Include a copy of the written charter, if any, as an appendix to the registrant's proxy statement, unless a copy has been included as an appendix to the registrant's proxy statement within the registrant's past three fiscal years.

(iv)(A) If the registrant is a listed issuer, as defined in § 240.10A–3:

(*1*) Disclose whether the members of the audit committee are independent, as independence for audit committee members is defined in the listing standards applicable to the listed issuer. If the registrant does not have a separately designated audit committee, or committee performing similar functions, the registrant must provide the disclosure with respect to all members of its board of directors.

(*2*) If the listed issuer's board of directors determines, in accordance with the listing standards applicable to the listed issuer, to appoint a director to the audit committee who is not independent (apart from the requirements in § 240.10A–3) because of exceptional or limited or similar circumstances, disclose the nature of the relationship that makes that individual not independent and the reasons for the board of directors' determination.

(B) If the registrant, including a small business issuer, is not a listed issuer, disclose whether the registrant has an audit committee established in accordance with section 3(a)(58)(A) of the Act (15 U.S.C. 78f(a)) and, if so, whether the members of the committee are independent. In determining whether a member is independent, the registrant must use a definition for audit committee member independence of a national securities exchange registered pursuant to section 6(a) of the Act (15 U.S.C. 78o–3(a)) or a national securities association registered pursuant to section 15A(a) of the Act that has been approved by the Commission (as such definition may be modified or supplemented), and state which definition was used.

Whichever definition is chosen must be applied consistently to all members of the audit committee.

(v) The information required by paragraph (d)(3) of this Item shall not be deemed to be "soliciting material," or to be "filed" with the Commission or subject to Regulation 14A or 14C (17 CFR 240.14a–1 et seq. or 240.14c–1 et seq.), other than as provided in this Item, or to the liabilities of section 18 of the Exchange Act (15 U.S.C. 78r), except to the extent that the registrant specifically requests that the information be treated as soliciting material or specifically incorporates it by reference into a document filed under the Securities Act or the Exchange Act. Such information will not be deemed to be incorporated by reference into any filing under the Securities Act or the Exchange Act, except to the extent that the registrant specifically incorporates it by reference.

(vi) The disclosure required by this paragraph (d)(3) need only be provided one time during any fiscal year.

(vii) Investment companies registered under the Investment Company Act of 1940 (15 U.S.C. 80a–1 et seq.), other than closed-end investment companies, need not provide the information required by this paragraph (d)(3).

(e) In lieu of paragraphs (a) through (d)(1) and (d)(2)(ii)(O) of this Item, investment companies registered under the Investment Company Act of 1940 (15 U.S.C. 80a) must furnish the information required by Item 22(b) of this Schedule 14A.

(f) State the total number of meetings of the board of directors (including regularly scheduled and special meetings) which were held during the last full fiscal year. Name each incumbent director who during the last full fiscal year attended fewer than 75 percent of the aggregate of (1) the total number of meetings of the board of directors (held during the period for which he has been a director) and (2) the total number of meetings held by all committees of the board on which he served (during the periods that he served).

(g) If a director has resigned or declined to stand for re-election to the board of directors since the date of the last annual meeting of security holders because of a disagreement with the registrant on any matter relating to the registrant's operations, policies or practices, and if the director has furnished the registrant with a letter describing such disagreement and requesting that the matter be disclosed, the registrant shall state the date of resignation or declination to stand for re-election and summarize the director's description of the disagreement.

If the registrant believes that the description provided by the director is incorrect or incomplete, it may include a brief statement presenting its views of the disagreement.

(h)(1) State whether or not the registrant's board of directors provides a process for security holders to send communications to the board of directors and, if the registrant does not have such a process for security holders to send communications to the board of directors, state the basis for the view of the board of directors that it is appropriate for the registrant not to have such a process;

(2)If the registrant has a process for security holders to send communications to the board of directors:

(i) Describe the manner in which security holders can send communications to the board and, if applicable, to specified individual directors; and

(ii) If all security holder communications are not sent directly to board members, describe the registrant's process for determining which communications will be relayed to board members; and

Instruction to paragraph (h)(2)(ii): For purposes of the disclosure required by this paragraph, a registrant's process for collecting and organizing security holder communications, as well as similar or related activities, need not be disclosed provided that the registrant's process is approved by a majority of the independent directors or, in the case of a registrant that is an investment company, a majority of the directors who are not "interested persons" of the investment company as defined in section 2(a)(19) of the Investment Company Act of 1940 (15 U.S.C. 80a–2(a)(19)).

(3) Describe the registrant's policy, if any, with regard to board members' attendance at annual meetings and state the number of board members who attended the prior year's annual meeting.

Instruction to paragraphs (h)(2) and (h)(3): In lieu of providing the information required by paragraphs (h)(2) and (h)(3) in the proxy statement, the registrant may instead provide the registrant's website address where such information appears.

Instructions to paragraph (h):

1. For purposes of this paragraph, communications from an officer or director of the registrant will not be viewed as "security holder communications." Communications from an employee or agent of the registrant will be viewed as "security holder communications"

for purposes of this paragraph only if those communications are made solely in such employee's or agent's capacity as a security holder.

2. For purposes of this paragraph, security holder proposals submitted pursuant to § 240.14a–8, and communications made in connection with such proposals, will not be viewed as "security holder communications."

Item 8. Compensation of Directors and Executive Officers

Furnish the information required by Item 402 of Regulation S–K if action is to be taken with regard to: (a) the election of directors, (b) any bonus, profit sharing or other compensation plan, contract, or arrangement in which any director, nominee for election as a director, or executive officer of the registrant will participate, (c) any pension or retirement plan in which any such person will participate or (d) the granting or extension to any such person of any options, warrants or rights to purchase any securities, other than warrants or rights issued to security holders as such, on a pro rata basis.

However, if the solicitation is made on behalf of persons other than the registrant, the information required need be furnished only as to nominees of the persons making the solicitation and associates of such nominees. In the case of investment companies registered under the Investment Company Act of 1940 and registrants that have elected to be regulated as business development companies, furnish the information required by Item 22(b)(13) of this Schedule.

Instruction. If an otherwise reportable compensation plan became subject to such requirements because of an acquisition or merger and, within one year of the acquisition or merger, such plan was terminated for purposes of prospective eligibility, the registrant may furnish a description of its obligation to the designated individuals pursuant to the compensation plan. Such description may be furnished in lieu of a description of the compensation plan in the proxy statement.

Item 9. Independent Public Accountants

If the solicitation is made on behalf of the registrant and relates to (1) the annual (or special meeting in lieu of annual) meeting of security holders at which directors are to be elected, or a solicitation of consents or authorizations in lieu of such meeting or (2) the election, approval or ratification of the registrant's accountant, furnish the following information describing the registrant's relationship with its independent public accountant:

(a) The name of the principal accountant selected or being recommended to security holders for election, approval or ratification for the current year. If no accountant has been selected or recommended, so state and briefly describe the reasons therefor.

(b) The name of the principal accountant for the fiscal year most recently completed if different from the accountant selected or recommended for the current year or if no accountant has yet been selected or recommended for the current year.

(c) The proxy statement shall indicate (1) whether or not representatives of the principal accountant for the current year and for the most recently completed fiscal year are expected to be present at the security holders' meeting, (2) whether or not they will have the opportunity to make a statement if they desire to do so and (3) whether or not such representatives are expected to be available to respond to appropriate questions.

(d) If during the registrant's two most recent fiscal years or any subsequent interim period, (1) an independent accountant who was previously engaged as the principal accountant to audit the registrant's financial statements, or an independent accountant on whom the principal accountant expressed reliance in its report regarding a significant subsidiary, has resigned (or indicated it has declined to stand for reelection after the completion of the current audit) or was dismissed, or (2) a new independent accountant has been engaged as either the principal accountant to audit the registrant's financial statements or as an independent accountant on whom the principal accountant has expressed or is expected to express reliance in its report regarding a significant subsidiary, then, notwithstanding any previous disclosure, provide the information required by Item 304(a) of Regulation S–K.

(e)(1) Disclose, under the caption *Audit Fees*, the aggregate fees billed for each of the last two fiscal years for professional services rendered by the principal accountant for the audit of the registrant's annual financial statements and review of financial statements included in the registrant's Form 10–Q (17 CFR 249.308a) or 10–QSB (17 CFR 249.308b) or services that are normally provided by the accountant in connection with statutory and regulatory filings or engagements for those fiscal years.

(2) Disclose, under the caption *Audit–Related Fees*, the aggregate fees billed in each of the last two fiscal years for assurance and related services by the principal accountant that are reasonably related to the performance of the audit or review of the registrant's financial statements and are not reported under paragraph (e)(1) of this section. Registrants shall describe the nature of the services comprising the fees disclosed under this category.

(3) Disclose, under the caption *Tax Fees*, the aggregate fees billed in each of the last two fiscal years for professional services rendered by the principal accountant for tax compliance, tax advice, and tax planning. Registrants shall describe the nature of the services comprising the fees disclosed under this category.

(4) Disclose, under the caption *All Other Fees*, the aggregate fees billed in each of the last two fiscal years for products and services provided by the principal accountant, other than the services reported in paragraphs (e)(1) through (e)(3) of this section. Registrants shall describe the nature of the services comprising the fees disclosed under this category.

(5)(i) Disclose the audit committee's pre-approval policies and procedures described in 17 CFR 210.2–01(c)(7)(i).

(ii) Disclose the percentage of services described in each of paragraphs (e)(2) through (e)(4) of this section that were approved by the audit committee pursuant to 17 CFR 210.2–01(c)(7)(i)(C).

(6) If greater than 50 percent, disclose the percentage of hours expended on the principal accountant's engagement to audit the registrant's financial statements for the most recent fiscal year that were attributed to work performed by persons other than the principal accountant's full-time, permanent employees.

(7) If the registrant is an investment company, disclose the aggregate non-audit fees billed by the registrant's accountant for services rendered to the registrant, and to the registrant's investment adviser (not including any subadviser whose role is primarily portfolio management and is subcontracted with or overseen by another investment adviser), and any entity controlling, controlled by, or under common control with the adviser that provides ongoing services to the registrant for each of the last two fiscal years of the registrant.

(8) If the registrant is an investment company, disclose whether the audit committee of the board of directors has considered whether the provision of non-audit services that were rendered to the registrant's investment adviser (not including any subadviser whose role is primarily portfolio management and is subcontracted with or overseen by another investment adviser), and any entity controlling, controlled by, or under common control with the investment adviser that provides ongoing services to the registrant that

were not pre-approved pursuant to 17 CFR 210.2–01(c)(7)(ii) is compatible with maintaining the principal accountant's independence.

Instruction to Item 9(e).

For purposes of Item 9(e)(2), (3), and (4), registrants that are investment companies must disclose fees billed for services rendered to the registrant and separately, disclose fees required to be approved by the investment company registrant's audit committee pursuant to 17 CFR 210.2–01(c)(7)(ii). Registered investment companies must also disclose the fee percentages as required by item 9(e)(5)(ii) for the registrant and separately, disclose the fee percentages as required by item 9(e)(5)(ii) for the fees required to be approved by the investment company registrant's audit committee pursuant to 17 CFR 210.2–01(c)(7)(ii).

Item 10. Compensation Plans

If action is to be taken with respect to any plan pursuant to which cash or noncash compensation may be paid or distributed, furnish the following information:

(a) *Plans Subject to Security Holder Action.*

(1) Describe briefly the material features of the plan being acted upon, identify each class of persons who will be eligible to participate therein, indicate the approximate number of persons in each such class and state the basis of such participation.

(2)(i) In the tabular format specified below, disclose the benefits or amounts that will be received by or allocated to each of the following under the plan being acted upon, if such benefits or amounts are determinable:

New Plan Benefits

Plan name		
Name and position	Dollar value ($)	Number of units
CEO		
A		
B		
C		
D		
Executive Group		
Non–Executive Director Group		
Non–Executive Officer Employee Group.		

(ii) The table required by paragraph (a)(2)(i) of this Item shall provide information as to the following persons:

(A) Each person (stating name and position) specified in paragraph (a)(3) of Item 402 of Regulation S–K;

Instruction: In the case of investment companies registered under the Investment Company Act of 1940, furnish the information for Compensated Persons as defined in Item 22(b)(13)(i) of this Schedule in lieu of the persons specified in paragraph (a)(3) of Item 402 of Regulation S–K (§ 229.402(a)(3) of this chapter).

(B) All current executive officers as a group;

(C) All current directors who are not executive officers as a group; and

(D) All employees, including all current officers who are not executive officers, as a group.

Instruction to New Plan Benefits Table: Additional columns should be added for each plan with respect to which security holder action is to be taken.

(iii) If the benefits or amounts specified in paragraph (a)(2)(i) of this item are not determinable, state the benefits or amounts which would have been received by or allocated to each of the following for the last completed fiscal year if the plan had been in effect, if such benefits or amounts may be determined, in the table specified in paragraph (a)(2)(i) of this Item:

(A) Each person (stating name and position) specified in paragraph (a)(3) of Item 402 of Regulation S–K;

(B) All current executive officers as a group;

(C) All current directors who are not executive officers as a group; and

(D) All employees, including all current officers who are not executive officers, as a group.

(3) If the plan to be acted upon can be amended, otherwise than by a vote of security holders, to increase the cost thereof to the registrant or to alter the allocation of the benefits as between the persons and groups specified in paragraph (a)(2) of this item, state the nature of the amendments which can be so made.

(b)(1) *Additional information regarding specified plans subject to security holder action.* With respect to any pension or retirement plan submitted for security holder action, state:

(i) The approximate total amount necessary to fund the plan with respect to past services, the period over which such amount is to be paid and the estimated annual payments necessary to pay the total amount over such period; and

(ii) The estimated annual payment to be made with respect to current services. In the case of a pension or retirement plan, information called for by paragraph (a)(2) of this Item may be furnished in the format specified by paragraph (f)(1) of Item 402 of Regulation S–K.

Instruction. In the case of investment companies registered under the Investment Company Act of 1940, refer to instruction 4 in Item 22(b)(13)(i) of this Schedule in lieu of paragraph (f)(1) of Item 402 of Regulation S–K (§ 229.402(f)(1) of this chapter).

(2)(i) With respect to any specific grant of or any plan containing options, warrants or rights submitted for security holder action, state:

(A) The title and amount of securities underlying such options, warrants or rights;

(B) The prices, expiration dates and other material conditions upon which the options, warrants or rights may be exercised;

(C) The consideration received or to be received by the registrant or subsidiary for the granting or extension of the options, warrants or rights;

(D) The market value of the securities underlying the options, warrants, or rights as of the latest practicable date; and

(E) In the case of options, the federal income tax consequences of the issuance and exercise of such options to the recipient and the registrant; and

(ii) State separately the amount of such options received or to be received by the following persons if such benefits or amounts are determinable:

(A) Each person (stating name and position) specified in paragraph (a)(3) of Item 402 of Regulation S–K;

(B) All current executive officers as a group;

(C) All current directors who are not executive officers as a group;

(D) Each nominee for election as a director;

(E) Each associate of any of such directors, executive officers or nominees;

(F) Each other person who received or is to receive 5 percent of such options, warrants or rights; and

(G) All employees, including all current officers who are not executive officers, as a group.

(c) *Information regarding plans and other arrangements not subject to security holder action.* Furnish the information required by Item 201(d) of Regulation S–K (§ 229.201(d) of this chapter).

Instructions to paragraph (c).

1. If action is to be taken as described in paragraph (a) of this Item with respect to the approval of a new compensation plan under which equity securities of the registrant are authorized for issuance, information about the plan shall be disclosed as required under paragraphs (a) and (b) of this Item and shall not be included in the disclosure required by Item

201(d) of Regulation S–K (§ 229.201(d) of this chapter). If action is to be taken as described in paragraph (a) of this Item with respect to the amendment or modification of an existing plan under which equity securities of the registrant are authorized for issuance, the registrant shall include information about securities previously authorized for issuance under the plan (including any outstanding options, warrants and rights previously granted pursuant to the plan and any securities remaining available for future issuance under the plan) in the disclosure required by Item 201(d) of Regulation S–K (§ 229.201(d) of this chapter). Any additional securities that are the subject of the amendments or modification of the existing plan shall be disclosed as required under paragraphs (a) and (b) of this Item and shall not be included in the Item 201(d) disclosure.

Instructions: 1. The term "plan" as used in this Item means any plan as defined in paragraph (a)(7)(ii) of Item 402 of Regulation S–K.

2. If action is to be taken with respect to a material amendment or modification of an existing plan, the item shall be answered with respect to the plan as proposed to be amended or modified and shall indicate any material differences from the existing plan.

3. If the plan to be acted upon is set forth in a written document, three copies thereof shall be filed with the Commission at the time copies of the proxy statement and form of proxy are first filed pursuant to paragraph (a) or (b) of Rule 14a–6. Electronic filers shall file with the Commission a copy of such written plan document in electronic format as an appendix to the proxy statement. It need not be provided to security holders unless it is a part of the proxy statement.

4. Paragraph (b)(2)(ii) does not apply to warrants or rights to be issued to security holders as such on a pro rata basis.

5. The Commission shall be informed, as supplemental information, when the proxy statement is first filed, as to when the options, warrants or rights and the shares called for thereby will be registered under the Securities Act or, if such registration is not contemplated, the section of the Securities Act or rule of the Commission under which exemption from such registration is claimed and the facts relied upon to make the exemption available.

Item 11. Authorization or Issuance of Securities Otherwise Than for Exchange

If action is to be taken with respect to the authorization or issuance of any securities otherwise than for exchange for outstanding securities of the registrant, furnish the following information:

(a) State the title and amount of securities to be authorized or issued.

(b) Furnish the information required by Item 202 of Regulation S–K. If the terms of the securities cannot be stated or estimated with respect to any or all of the securities to be authorized, because no offering thereof is contemplated in the proximate future, and if no further authorization by security holders for the issuance thereof is to be obtained, it should be stated that the terms of the securities to be authorized, including dividend or interest rates, conversion prices, voting rights, redemption prices, maturity dates, and similar matters will be determined by the board of directors. If the securities are additional shares of common stock of a class outstanding, the description may be omitted except for a statement of the preemptive rights, if any. Where the statutory provisions with respect to preemptive rights are so indefinite or complex that they cannot be stated in summarized form, it will suffice to make a statement in the form of an opinion of counsel as to the existence and extent of such rights.

(c) Describe briefly the transaction in which the securities are to be issued including a statement as to (1) the nature and approximate amount of consideration received or to be received by the registrant and (2) the approximate amount devoted to each purpose so far as determinable for which the net proceeds have been or are to be used. If it is impracticable to describe the transaction in which the securities are to be issued, state the reason, indicate the purpose of the authorization of the securities, and state whether further authorization for the issuance of the securities by a vote of security holders will be solicited prior to such issuance.

(d) If the securities are to be issued otherwise than in a public offering for cash, state the reasons for the proposed authorization or issuance and the general effect thereof upon the rights of existing security holders.

(e) Furnish the information required by Item 13(a) of this schedule.

Item 12. Modification or Exchange of Securities

If action is to be taken with respect to the modification of any class of securities of the registrant, or the issuance or authorization for issuance of securities of the registrant in exchange for outstanding securities of the registrant, furnish the following information:

(a) If outstanding securities are to be modified, state the title and amount thereof. If securities are to be issued in exchange for outstanding securities, state the title and amount of securities to be so issued, the title and amount of outstanding securities to be exchanged therefor and the basis of the exchange.

(b) Describe any material differences between the outstanding securities and the modified or new securities in respect of any of the matters concerning which information would be required in the description of the securities in Item 202 of Regulation S–K.

(c) State the reasons for the proposed modification or exchange and the general effect thereof upon the rights of existing security holders.

(d) Furnish a brief statement as to arrears in dividends or as to defaults in principal or interest in respect to the outstanding securities which are to be modified or exchanged and such other information as may be appropriate in the particular case to disclose adequately the nature and effect of the proposed action.

(e) Outline briefly any other material features of the proposed modification or exchange. If the plan of proposed action is set forth in a written document, file copies thereof with the Commission in accordance with Rule 14a–6.

(f) Furnish the information required by Item 13(a) of this Schedule.

Instruction. If the existing security is presently listed and registered on a national securities exchange, state whether the registrant intends to apply for listing and registration of the new or reclassified security on such exchange or any other exchange. If the registrant does not intend to make such application, state the effect of the termination of such listing and registration.

Item 13. Financial and Other Information

(*See* Notes D and E at the beginning of this Schedule.)

(a) Information required. If action is to be taken with respect to any matter specified in Item 11 or 12, furnish the following information:

(1) Financial statements meeting the requirements of Regulation S–X, including financial information required by Rule 3–05 and Article 11 of Regulation S–X with respect to transactions other than that pursuant to which action is to be taken as described in this proxy statement;

(2) Item 302 of Regulation S–K, supplementary financial information;

(3) Item 303 of Regulation S–K, management's discussion and analysis of financial condition and results of operations;

(4) Item 304 of Regulation S–K, changes in and disagreements with accountants on accounting and financial disclosure; and

(5) Item 305 of Regulation S–K, quantitative and qualitative disclosures about market risk; and

(6) A statement as to whether or not representatives of the principal accountants for the current year and for the most recently completed fiscal year:

(i) are expected to be present at the security holders' meeting;

(ii) will have the opportunity to make a statement if they desire to do so; and

(iii) are expected to be available to respond to appropriate questions.

(b) Incorporation by reference. The information required pursuant to paragraph (a) of this Item may be incorporated by reference into the proxy statement as follows:

(1) S–3 registrants. If the registrant meets the requirements of Form S–3 (*see* Note E to this Schedule), it may incorporate by reference to previously-filed documents any of the information required by paragraph (a) of this Item, provided that the requirements of paragraph (c) are met. Where the registrant meets the requirements of Form S–3 and has elected to furnish the required information by incorporation by reference, the registrant may elect to update the information so incorporated by reference to information in subsequently-filed documents.

(2) All registrants. The registrant may incorporate by reference any of the information required by paragraph (a) of this Item, provided that the information is contained in an annual report to security holders or a previously-filed statement or report, such report or statement is delivered to security holders with the proxy statement and the requirements of paragraph (c) are met.

(c) Certain conditions applicable to incorporation by reference. Registrants eligible to incorporate by reference into the proxy statement the information required by paragraph (a) of this Item in the manner specified by paragraphs (b)(1) and (b)(2) may do so only if:

(1) the information is not required to be included in the proxy statement pursuant to the requirement of another Item;

(2) the proxy statement identifies on the last page(s) the information incorporated by reference; and

(3) the material incorporated by reference substantially meets the requirements of this Item or the appropriate portions of this Item.

Instructions to Item 13. 1. Notwithstanding the provisions of this Item, any or all of the information required by paragraph (a) of this Item, not material for the exercise of prudent judgment in regard to the matter to be acted upon may be omitted. In the usual case the information is deemed material to the exercise of prudent judgment where the matter to be acted upon is the authorization or issuance of a material amount of senior securities, but the information is not deemed material where the matter to be acted upon is the authorization or issuance of common stock, otherwise than in an exchange, merger, consolidation, acquisition or similar transaction, the authorization of preferred stock without present intent to issue or the authorization of preferred stock for issuance for cash in an amount constituting fair value.

2. In order to facilitate compliance with Rule 2–02(a) of Regulation S–X, one copy of the definitive proxy statement filed with the Commission shall include a manually signed copy of the accountant's report. If the financial statements are incorporated by reference, a manually signed copy of the accountant's report shall be filed with the definitive proxy statement.

3. Notwithstanding the provisions of Regulation S–X, no schedules other than those prepared in accordance with Rules 12–15, 12–28 and 12–29 (or, for management investment companies, Rules 12–12 through 12–14) of that regulation need be furnished in the proxy statement.

4. Unless registered on a national securities exchange or otherwise required to furnish such information, registered investment companies need not furnish the information required by paragraphs (a)(2) or (3) of this Item.

5. If the registrant submits preliminary proxy material incorporating by reference financial statements required by this Item, the registrant should furnish a draft of the financial statements if the document from which they are incorporated has not been filed with or furnished to the Commission.

6. A registered investment company need not comply with items (a)(2), (a)(3), and (a)(5) of this Item 13.

Item 14. Mergers, Consolidations, Acquisitions and Similar Matters

(See Notes A and D at the beginning of this Schedule.)

Instructions to Item 14:

1. In transactions in which the consideration offered to security holders consists wholly or in part of securities registered under the Securities Act of 1933, furnish the information required by Form S–4 (§ 239.25 of this chapter), Form F–4 (§ 239.34 of this chapter), or Form N–14 (§ 239.23 of this chapter), as applicable, instead of this Item. Only a Form S–4, Form F–4, or Form N–14 must be filed in accordance with § 240.14a–6(j).

2. (a) In transactions in which the consideration offered to security holders consists wholly of cash, the information required by paragraph (c)(1) of this Item for the acquiring company need not be provided unless the information is material to an informed voting decision (e.g., the security holders of the target company are voting and financing is not assured).

(b) Additionally, if only the security holders of the target company are voting:

i. The financial information in paragraphs (b)(8)—(11) of this Item for the acquiring company and the target need not be provided; and

ii. The information in paragraph (c)(2) of this Item for the target company need not be provided.

If, however, the transaction is a going-private transaction (as defined by § 240.13e–3), then the information required by paragraph (c)(2) of this Item must be provided and to the extent that the going-private rules require the information specified in paragraph (b)(8)—(b)(11) of this Item, that information must be provided as well.

3. In transactions in which the consideration offered to security holders consists wholly of securities exempt from registration under the Securities Act of 1933 or a combination of exempt securities and cash, information about the acquiring company required by paragraph (c)(1) of this Item need not be provided if only the security holders of the acquiring company are voting, unless the information is material to an informed voting decision. If only the security holders of the target company are voting, information about the target company in paragraph (c)(2) of this Item need not be provided. However, the information required by paragraph (c)(2) of this Item must be provided if the transaction is a going-private (as defined by § 240.13e–3) or roll-up (as described by Item 901 of Regulation S–K (§ 229.901 of this chapter)) transaction.

4. The information required by paragraphs (b)(8)—(11) and (c) need not be provided if the plan being voted on involves only the acquiring company and one or more of its totally held subsidiaries and does not involve a liquidation or a spin-off.

5. To facilitate compliance with Rule 2–02(a) of Regulation S–X (§ 210.2–02(a) of this chapter) (technical requirements relating to accountants' reports), one copy of the definitive proxy statement filed with the Commission must include a signed copy of the accountant's report. If the financial statements are incorporated by reference, a signed copy of the accountant's report must be filed with the definitive proxy statement. Signatures may be typed if the document is filed electronically on

EDGAR. See Rule 302 of Regulation S–T (§ 232.302 of this chapter).

6. Notwithstanding the provisions of Regulation S–X, no schedules other than those prepared in accordance with § 210.12–15, § 210.12–28 and § 210.12–29 of this chapter (or, for management investment companies, §§ 210.12–12 through 210.12–14 of this chapter) of that regulation need be furnished in the proxy statement.

7. If the preliminary proxy material incorporates by reference financial statements required by this Item, a draft of the financial statements must be furnished to the Commission staff upon request if the document from which they are incorporated has not been filed with or furnished to the Commission.

(a) *Applicability*. If action is to be taken with respect to any of the following transactions, provide the information required by this Item:

(1) A merger or consolidation;

(2) An acquisition of securities of another person;

(3) An acquisition of any other going business or the assets of a going business;

(4) A sale or other transfer of all or any substantial part of assets; or

(5) A liquidation or dissolution.

(b) *Transaction information*. Provide the following information for each of the parties to the transaction unless otherwise specified:

(1) *Summary term sheet*. The information required by Item 1001 of Regulation M–A (§ 229.1001 of this chapter).

(2) *Contact information*. The name, complete mailing address and telephone number of the principal executive offices.

(3) *Business conducted*. A brief description of the general nature of the business conducted.

(4) *Terms of the transaction*. The information required by Item 1004(a)(2) of Regulation M–A (§ 229.1004 of this chapter).

(5) *Regulatory approvals*. A statement as to whether any federal or state regulatory requirements must be complied with or approval must be obtained in connection with the transaction and, if so, the status of the compliance or approval.

(6) *Reports, opinions, appraisals*. If a report, opinion or appraisal materially relating to the transaction has been received from an outside party, and is referred to in the proxy statement, furnish the information required by Item 1015(b) of Regulation M–A (§ 229.1015 of this chapter).

(7) *Past contacts, transactions or negotiations*. The information required by Items 1005(b) and 1011(a)(1) of Regulation M–A (§ 229.1005 of this chapter and § 229.1011 of this chapter), for the parties to the transaction and their affiliates during the periods for which financial statements are presented or incorporated by reference under this Item.

(8) *Selected financial data*. The selected financial data required by Item 301 of Regulation S–K (§ 229.301 of this chapter).

(9) *Pro forma selected financial data*. If material, the information required by Item 301 of Regulation S–K (§ 229.301 of this chapter) for the acquiring company, showing the pro forma effect of the transaction.

(10) *Pro forma information*. In a table designed to facilitate comparison, historical and pro forma per share data of the acquiring company and historical and equivalent pro forma per share data of the target company for the following Items:

(i) Book value per share as of the date financial data is presented pursuant to Item 301 of Regulation S–K (§ 229.301 of this chapter);

(ii) Cash dividends declared per share for the periods for which financial data is presented pursuant to Item 301 of Regulation S–K (§ 229.301 of this chapter); and

(iii) Income (loss) per share from continuing operations for the periods for which financial data is presented pursuant to Item 301 of Regulation S–K (§ 229.301 of this chapter).

Instructions to paragraphs (b)(8), (b)(9) and (b)(10):

1. For a business combination accounted for as a purchase, present the financial information required by paragraphs (b)(9) and (b)(10) only for the most recent fiscal year and interim period. For a business combination accounted for as a pooling, present the financial information required by paragraphs (b)(9) and (b)(10) (except for information with regard to book value) for the most recent three fiscal years and interim period. For purposes of these paragraphs, book value information need only be provided for the most recent balance sheet date.

2. Calculate the equivalent pro forma per share amounts for one share of the company being acquired by multiplying the exchange ratio times each of:

(i) The pro forma income (loss) per share before non-recurring charges or credits directly attributable to the transaction;

(ii) The pro forma book value per share; and

(iii) The pro forma dividends per share of the acquiring company.

3. Unless registered on a national securities exchange or otherwise required to furnish such information, registered investment companies need not furnish the information required by paragraphs (b)(8) and (b)(9) of this Item.

(11) *Financial information*. If material, financial information required by Article 11 of Regulation S–X (§§ 210.10–01 through 229.11–03 of this chapter) with respect to this transaction.

Instructions to paragraph (b)(11):

1. Present any Article 11 information required with respect to transactions other than those being voted upon (where not incorporated by reference) together with the pro forma information relating to the transaction being voted upon. In presenting this information, you must clearly distinguish between the transaction being voted upon and any other transaction.

2. If current pro forma financial information with respect to all other transactions is incorporated by reference, you need only present the pro forma effect of this transaction.

(c) *Information about the parties to the transaction.*

(1) *Acquiring company*. Furnish the information required by Part B (Registrant Information) of Form S–4 (§ 239.25 of this chapter) or Form F–4 (§ 239.34 of this chapter), as applicable, for the acquiring company. However, financial statements need only be presented for the latest two fiscal years and interim periods.

(2) *Acquired company*. Furnish the information required by Part C (Information with Respect to the Company Being Acquired) of Form S–4 (§ 239.25 of this chapter) or Form F–4 (§ 239.34 of this chapter), as applicable.

(d) *Information about parties to the transaction: registered investment companies and business development companies*. If the acquiring company or the acquired company is an investment company registered under the Investment Company Act of 1940 or a business development company as defined by Section 2(a)(48) of the Investment Company Act of 1940, provide the following information for that company instead of the information specified by paragraph (c) of this Item:

(1) Information required by Item 101 of Regulation S–K (§ 229.101 of this chapter), description of business;

(2) Information required by Item 102 of Regulation S–K (§ 229.102 of this chapter), description of property;

(3) Information required by Item 103 of Regulation S–K (§ 229.103 of this chapter), legal proceedings;

(4) Information required by Item 201(a), (b) and (c) of Regulation S–K (§ 229.201(a), (b) and (c) of this chapter), market price of and dividends on the registrant's common equity and related stockholder matters;

(5) Financial statements meeting the requirements of Regulation S–X, including financial information required by Rule 3–05 and Article 11 of Regulation S–X (§ 210.3–05 and § 210.11–01 through § 210.11–03 of this chapter) with respect to transactions other than that as to which action is to be taken as described in this proxy statement;

(6) Information required by Item 301 of Regulation S–K (§ 229.301 of this chapter), selected financial data;

(7) Information required by Item 302 of Regulation S–K (§ 229.302 of this chapter), supplementary financial information;

(8) Information required by Item 303 of Regulation S–K (§ 229.303 of this chapter), management's discussion and analysis of financial condition and results of operations; and

(9) Information required by Item 304 of Regulation S–K (§ 229.304 of this chapter), changes in and disagreements with accountants on accounting and financial disclosure.

Instruction to paragraph (d) of Item 14: Unless registered on a national securities exchange or otherwise required to furnish such information, registered investment companies need not furnish the information required by paragraphs (d)(6), (d)(7) and (d)(8) of this Item.

(e) *Incorporation by reference.*

(1) The information required by paragraph (c) of this section may be incorporated by reference into the proxy statement to the same extent as would be permitted by Form S–4 (§ 239.25 of this chapter) or Form F–4 (§ 239.34 of this chapter), as applicable.

(2) Alternatively, the registrant may incorporate by reference into the proxy statement the information required by paragraph (c) of this Item if it is contained in an annual report sent to security holders in accordance with § 240.14a–3 of this chapter with respect to the same meeting or solicitation of consents or authorizations that the proxy statement relates to and the information substantially meets the disclosure requirements of Item 14 or Item 17 of Form S–4 (§ 239.25 of this chapter) or Form F–4 (§ 239.34 of this chapter), as applicable.

Item 15. Acquisition or Disposition of Property

If action is to be taken with respect to the acquisition or disposition of any property, furnish the following information:

(a) Describe briefly the general character and location of the property.

(b) State the nature and amount of consideration to be paid or received by the registrant or any subsidiary. To the extent practicable, outline briefly the facts bearing upon the question of the fairness of the consideration.

(c) State the name and address of the transferer or transferee, as the case may be and the nature of any material relationship of such person to the registrant or any affiliate of the registrant.

(d) Outline briefly any other material features of the contract or transaction.

Item 16. Restatement of Accounts

If action is to be taken with respect to the restatement of any asset, capital, or surplus account of the registrant, furnish the following information:

(a) State the nature of the restatement and the date as of which it is to be effective.

(b) Outline briefly the reasons for the restatement and for the selection of the particular effective date.

(c) State the name and amount of each account (including any reserve accounts) affected by the restatement and the effect of the restatement thereon. Tabular presentation of the amounts shall be made when appropriate, particularly in the case of recapitalizations.

(d) To the extent practicable, state whether and the extent, if any, to which the restatement will, as of the date thereof, alter the amount available for distribution to the holders of equity securities.

Item 17. Action With Respect to Reports

If action is to be taken with respect to any report of the registrant or of its directors, officers or committees or any minutes of a meeting of its security holders furnish the following information:

(a) State whether or not such action is to constitute approval or disapproval of any of the matters referred to in such reports or minutes.

(b) Identify each of such matters which it is intended will be approved or disapproved, and furnish the information required by the appropriate item or items of this schedule with respect to each such matter.

Item 18. Matters Not Required to Be Submitted

If action is to be taken with respect to any matter which is not required to be submitted to a vote of security holders, state the nature of such matter, the reasons for submitting it to a vote of security holders and what action is intended to be taken by the registrant in the event of a negative vote on the matter by the security holders.

Item 19. Amendment of Charter, Bylaws of Other Documents

If action is to be taken with respect to any amendment of the registrant's charter, bylaws or other documents as to which information is not required above, state briefly the reasons for and the general effect of such amendment.

Instructions. 1. Where the matter to be acted upon is the classification of directors, state whether vacancies which occur during the year may be filled by the board of directors to serve only until the next annual meeting or may be so filled for the remainder of the full term.

2. Attention is directed to the discussion of disclosure regarding anti-takeover and similar proposals in Release No. 34–15230 (October 13, 1978).

Item 20. Other Proposed Action

If action is to be taken on any matter not specifically referred to in this Schedule 14A, describe briefly the substance of each such matter in substantially the same degree of detail as is required by Items 5 to 19, inclusive, of this Schedule, and, with respect to investment companies registered under the Investment Company Act of 1940, Item 22 of this Schedule.

Item 21. Voting Procedures

As to each matter which is to be submitted to a vote of security holders, furnish the following information:

(a) State the vote required for approval or election, other than for the approval of auditors.

(b) Disclose the method by which votes will be counted, including the treatment and effect of abstentions and broker non-votes under applicable state law as well as registrant charter and by-law provisions.

Item 22. Information Required in Investment Company Proxy Statement

(a) *General.*

(1) *Definitions.* Unless the context otherwise requires, terms used in this Item that are defined in § 240.14a–1 (with respect to proxy soliciting material), in § 240.14c–1 (with respect to information statements), and in the Investment Company Act of 1940 shall have the same meanings provided therein and the following terms shall also apply:

(i) *Administrator.* The term "Administrator" shall mean any person who provides significant administrative or business affairs management services to a Fund.

(ii) *Affiliated broker.* The term "Affiliated Broker" shall mean any broker:

(A) That is an affiliated person of the Fund;

(B) That is an affiliated person of such person; or

(C) An affiliated person of which is an affiliated person of the Fund, its investment adviser, principal underwriter, or Administrator.

(iii) *Distribution plan.* The term "Distribution Plan" shall mean a plan adopted pursuant to Rule 12b–1 under the Investment Company Act of 1940 (§ 270.12b–1 of this chapter).

(iv) *Family of Investment Companies.* The term "Family of Investment Companies" shall mean any two or more registered investment companies that:

(A) Share the same investment adviser or principal underwriter; and

(B) Hold themselves out to investors as related companies for purposes of investment and investor services.

(v) *Fund.* The term "Fund" shall mean a Registrant or, where the Registrant is a series company, a separate portfolio of the Registrant.

(vi) *Fund complex.* The term "Fund Complex" shall mean two or more Funds that:

(A) Hold themselves out to investors as related companies for purposes of investment and investor services; or

(B) Have a common investment adviser or have an investment adviser that is an affiliated person of the investment adviser of any of the other Funds.

(vii) *Immediate Family Member.* The term "Immediate Family Member" shall mean a person's spouse; child residing in the person's household (including step and adoptive children); and any dependent of the person, as defined in section 152 of the Internal Revenue Code (26 U.S.C. 152).

(viii) *Officer.* The term "Officer" shall mean the president, vice-president, secretary, treasurer, controller, or any other officer who performs policy-making functions.

(ix) *Parent.* The term "Parent" shall mean the affiliated person of a specified person who controls the specified person directly or indirectly through one or more intermediaries.

(x) *Registrant.* The term "Registrant" shall mean an investment company registered under the Investment Company Act of 1940 (15 U.S.C. 80a) or a business development company as defined by section 2(a)(48) of the Investment Company Act of 1940 (15 U.S.C. 80a–2(a)(48)).

(xi) *Sponsoring Insurance Company.* The term "Sponsoring Insurance Company" of a Fund that is a separate account shall mean the insurance company that establishes and maintains the separate account and that owns the assets of the separate account.

(xii) *Subsidiary.* The term "Subsidiary" shall mean an affiliated person of a specified person who is controlled by the specified person directly, or indirectly through one or more intermediaries.

(3) *General disclosure.* Furnish the following information in the proxy statement of a Fund or Funds:

(i) State the name and address of the Fund's investment adviser, principal underwriter, and Administrator.

(ii) When a Fund proxy statement solicits a vote on proposals affecting more than one Fund or class of securities of a Fund (unless the proposal or proposals are the same and affect all Fund or class shareholders), present a summary of all of the proposals in tabular form on one of the first three pages of the proxy statement and indicate which Fund or class shareholders are solicited with respect to each proposal.

(iii) Unless the proxy statement is accompanied by a copy of the Fund's most recent annual report, state prominently in the proxy statement that the Fund will furnish, without charge, a copy of the annual report and the most recent semi-annual report succeeding the annual report, if any, to a shareholder upon request, providing the name, address, and toll-free telephone number of the person to whom such request shall be directed (or, if no toll-free telephone number is provided, a self-addressed postage paid card for requesting the annual report). The Fund should provide a copy of the annual report and the most recent semi-annual report succeeding the annual report, if any, to the requesting shareholder by first class mail, or other means designed to assure prompt delivery, within three business days of the request.

(iv) If the action to be taken would, directly or indirectly, establish a new fee or expense or increase any existing fee or expense to be paid by the Fund or its shareholders, provide a table showing the current and pro forma fees (with the required examples) using the format prescribed in the appropriate registration statement form under the Investment Company Act of 1940 (for open-end management investment companies, Item 2 of Form N–1A (§ 239.15A); for closed-end management investment companies, Item 3 of Form N–2 (§ 239.14); and for separate accounts that offer variable annuity contracts, Item 3 of Form N–3 (§ 239.17a)).

Instructions. 1. Where approval is sought only for a change in asset breakpoints for a pre-existing fee that would not have increased the fee for the previous year (or have the effect of increasing fees or expenses, but for any other reason would not be reflected in a pro forma fee table), describe the likely effect of the change in lieu of providing pro forma fee information.

2. An action would indirectly establish or increase a fee or expense where, for example, the approval of a new investment advisory contract would result in higher custodial or transfer agency fees.

3. The tables should be prepared in a manner designed to facilitate understanding of the impact of any change in fees or expenses.

4. A Fund that offers its shares exclusively to one or more separate accounts and thus is not required to include a fee table in its prospectus (see Item 2(a)(ii) of Form N–1A (§ 239.15A)) should nonetheless prepare a table showing current and pro forma expenses and disclose that the table does not reflect separate account expenses, including sales load.

(v) If action is to be taken with respect to the election of directors or the approval of an advisory contract, describe any purchases or sales of securities of the investment adviser or its Parents, or Subsidiaries of either, since the beginning of the most recently completed fiscal year by any director or any nominee for election as a director of the Fund.

Instructions. 1. Identify the parties, state the consideration, the terms of payment and describe any arrangement or understanding with respect to the composition of the board of directors of the Fund or of the investment adviser, or with respect to the selection of appointment of any person to any office with either such company.

2. Transactions involving securities in an amount not exceeding one percent of the outstanding securities of any class of the investment adviser or any of its Parents or Subsidiaries may be omitted.

(4) *Electronic filings.* If action is to be taken with respect to any transaction described in Items 11, 12, or 14 of this Schedule 14A and the Fund proxy or information statement is filed electronically, file after the cover page of the proxy statement a Financial Data Schedule in accordance with rule 483 of Regulation C (§ 230.483 of this chapter).

(b) *Election of Directors.* If action is to be taken with respect to the election of directors of a Fund, furnish the following information in the proxy statement in addition to the information (and in the format) required by paragraphs (d)(2) (other than (d)(2)(ii)(D)), (d)(3), (f), (g) and (h).

Instructions to introductory text of paragraph (b). 1. Furnish information with respect to a prospective investment adviser to the extent applicable.

2. If the solicitation is made by or on behalf of a person other than the Fund or an investment adviser of the Fund, provide information only as to nominees of the person making the solicitation.

3. When providing information about directors and nominees for election as directors in response to this Item 22(b), furnish information for directors or nominees who are or would be "interested persons" of the Fund within the meaning of section 2(a)(19) of the Investment Company Act of 1940 (15 U.S.C. 80a–2(a)(19)) separately from the information for directors or nominees who are not or would not be interested persons of the Fund. For example, when furnishing information in a table, you should provide separate tables (or separate sections of a single table) for directors and nominees who are or would be interested persons and for directors or nominees who are not or would not be interested persons. When furnishing information in narrative form, indicate by heading or otherwise the directors or nominees who are or would be interested persons and the directors or nominees who are not or would not be interested persons.

4. No information need be given about any director whose term of office as a director will not continue after the meeting to which the proxy statement relates.

(1) Provide the information required by the following table for each director, nominee for election as director, Officer of the Fund, person chosen to become an Officer of the Fund, and, if the Fund has an advisory board, member of the board. Explain in a footnote to the table any family relationship between the persons listed.

(1)	(2)	(3)	(4)	(5)	(6)
Name, Address, and Age.	Position(s) Held with Fund.	Term of Office and Length of Time Served.	Principal Occupation(s) During Past 5 Years.	Number of Portfolios in Fund Complex Overseen by Director or Nominee for Director.	Other Directorships Held by Director or Nominee for Director

Instructions to paragraph (b)(1). 1. For purposes of this paragraph, the term "family relationship" means any relationship by blood, marriage, or adoption, not more remote than first cousin.

2. No nominee or person chosen to become a director or Officer who has not consented to act as such may be named in response to this Item. In this regard, see Rule 14a–4(d) under the Exchange Act (§ 240.14a–4(d)).

3. If fewer nominees are named than the number fixed by or pursuant to the governing instruments, state the reasons for this procedure and that the proxies cannot be voted for a greater number of persons than the number of nominees named.

4. For each director or nominee for election as director who is or would be an "interested person" of the Fund within the meaning of section 2(a)(19) of the Investment Company Act of 1940 (15 U.S.C. 80a–2(a)(19)), describe, in a footnote or otherwise, the relationship, events, or transactions by reason of which the director or nominee is or would be an interested person.

5. State the principal business of any company listed under column (4) unless the principal business is implicit in its name.

6. Include in column (5) the total number of separate portfolios that a nominee for election as director would oversee if he were elected.

7. Indicate in column (6) directorships not included in column (5) that are held by a director or nominee for election as director in any company with a class of securities registered pursuant to section 12 of the Exchange Act (15 U.S.C. 78*l*), or subject to the requirements of section 15(d) of the Exchange Act (15 U.S.C. 78o(d)), or any company registered as an investment company under the Investment Company Act of 1940, (15 U.S.C. 80a), as amended, and name the companies in which the directorships are held. Where the other directorships include directorships overseeing two or more portfolios in the same Fund Complex, identify the Fund Complex and provide the number of portfolios overseen as a director in the Fund Complex rather than listing each portfolio separately.

(2) For each individual listed in column (1) of the table required by paragraph (b)(1) of this Item, except for any director or nominee for election as director who is not or would not be an "interested person" of the Fund within the meaning of section 2(a)(19) of the Investment Company Act of 1940 (15 U.S.C. 80a–2(a)(19)), describe any positions, including as an officer, employee, director, or general partner, held with affiliated persons or principal underwriters of the Fund.

Instruction to paragraph (b)(2). When an individual holds the same position(s) with two or more registered investment companies that are part of the same Fund Complex, identify the Fund Complex and provide the number of registered investment companies for which the position(s) are held rather than listing each registered investment company separately.

(3) Describe briefly any arrangement or understanding between any director, nominee for election as director, Officer, or person chosen to become an Officer, and any other person(s) (naming the person(s)) pursuant to which he was or is to be selected as a director, nominee, or Officer.

Instruction to paragraph (b)(3). Do not include arrangements or understandings with directors or Officers acting solely in their capacities as such.

(4) Unless disclosed in the table required by paragraph (b)(1) of this Item, describe any positions, including as an officer, employee, director, or general partner, held by any director or nominee for election as director, who is not or would not be an "interested person" of the Fund within the meaning of section 2(a)(19) of the Investment Company Act of 1940 (15 U.S.C. 80a–2(a)(19)), or Immediate Family Member of the director or nominee, during the past five years, with:

(i) The Fund;

(ii) An investment company, or a person that would be an investment company but for the exclusions provided by sections 3(c)(1) and 3(c)(7) of the Investment Company Act of 1940 (15 U.S.C. 80a–3(c)(1) and (c)(7)), having the same investment adviser, principal underwriter, or Sponsoring Insurance Company as the Fund or having an investment adviser, principal underwriter, or Sponsoring Insurance

Company that directly or indirectly controls, is controlled by, or is under common control with an investment adviser, principal underwriter, or Sponsoring Insurance Company of the Fund;

(iii) An investment adviser, principal underwriter, Sponsoring Insurance Company, or affiliated person of the Fund; or

(iv) Any person directly or indirectly controlling, controlled by, or under common control with an investment adviser, principal underwriter, or Sponsoring Insurance Company of the Fund.

Instruction to paragraph (b)(4). When an individual holds the same position(s) with two or more portfolios that are part of the same Fund Complex, identify the Fund Complex and provide the number of portfolios for which the position(s) are held rather than listing each portfolio separately.

(5) For each director or nominee for election as director, state the dollar range of equity securities beneficially owned by the director or nominee as required by the following table:

(i) In the Fund; and

(ii) On an aggregate basis, in any registered investment companies overseen or to be overseen by the director or nominee within the same Family of Investment Companies as the Fund.

(1)	(2)	(3)
Name of Director or Nominee.	Dollar Range of Equity Securities in the Fund.	Aggregate Dollar Range of Equity Securities in All Funds Overseen or to be Overseen by Director or Nominee in Family of Investment Companies

Instructions to paragraph (b)(5). 1. Information should be provided as of the most recent practicable date. Specify the valuation date by footnote or otherwise.

2. Determine "beneficial ownership" in accordance with rule 16a–1(a)(2) under the Exchange Act (§ 240.16a–1(a)(2)).

3. If action is to be taken with respect to more than one Fund, disclose in column (2) the dollar range of equity securities beneficially owned by a director or nominee in each such Fund overseen or to be overseen by the director or nominee.

4. In disclosing the dollar range of equity securities beneficially owned by a director or nominee in columns (2) and (3), use the following ranges: none, $1–$10,000, $10,001–$50,000, $50,001–$100,000, or over $100,000.

(6) For each director or nominee for election as director who is not or would not be an "interested person" of the Fund within the meaning of section 2(a)(19) of the Investment Company Act of 1940 (15 U.S.C. 80a–2(a)(19)), and his Immediate Family Members, furnish the information required by the following table as to each class of securities owned beneficially or of record in:

(i) An investment adviser, principal underwriter, or Sponsoring Insurance Company of the Fund; or

(ii) A person (other than a registered investment company) directly or indirectly controlling, controlled by, or under common control with an investment adviser, principal underwriter, or Sponsoring Insurance Company of the Fund:

(1)	(2)	(3)	(4)	(5)	(6)
Name of Director or Nominee.	Name of Owners and Relationships to Director or Nominee.	Company	Title of Class	Value of Securities ..	Percent of Class

(1)	(2)	(3)	(4)	(5)	(6)

Instructions to paragraph (b)(6). 1. Information should be provided as of the most recent practicable date. Specify the valuation date by footnote or otherwise.

2. An individual is a "beneficial owner" of a security if he is a "beneficial owner" under either rule 13d–3 or rule 16a–1(a)(2) under the Exchange Act (§§ 240.13d–3 or 240.16a–1(a)(2)).

3. Identify the company in which the director, nominee, or Immediate Family Member of the director or nominee owns securities in column (3). When the company is a person directly or indirectly controlling, controlled by, or under common control with an investment adviser, principal underwriter, or Sponsoring Insurance Company, describe the company's relationship with the investment adviser, principal underwriter, or Sponsoring Insurance Company.

4. Provide the information required by columns (5) and (6) on an aggregate basis for each director (or nominee) and his Immediate Family Members.

(7) Unless disclosed in response to paragraph (b)(6) of this Item, describe any direct or indirect interest, the value of which exceeds $60,000, of each director or nominee for election as director who is not or would not be an "interested person" of the Fund within the meaning of section 2(a)(19) of the Investment Company Act of 1940 (15 U.S.C. 80a–2(a)(19)), or Immediate Family Member of the director or nominee, during the past five years, in:

(i) An investment adviser, principal underwriter, or Sponsoring Insurance Company of the Fund; or

(ii) A person (other than a registered investment company) directly or indirectly controlling, controlled by, or under common control with an investment adviser, principal underwriter, or Sponsoring Insurance Company of the Fund.

Instructions to paragraph (b)(7). 1. A director, nominee, or Immediate Family Member has an interest in a company if he is a party to a contract, arrangement, or understanding with respect to any securities of, or interest in, the company.

2. The interest of the director (or nominee) and the interests of his Immediate Family Members should be aggregated in determining whether the value exceeds $60,000.

(8) Describe briefly any material interest, direct or indirect, of any director or nominee for election as director who is not or would not be an "interested person" of the Fund within the meaning of section 2(a)(19) of the Investment Company Act of 1940 (15 U.S.C. 80a–2(a)(19)), or Immediate Family Member of the director or nominee, in any transaction, or series of similar transactions, since the beginning of the last two completed fiscal years of the Fund, or in any currently proposed transaction, or series of similar transactions, in which the amount involved exceeds $60,000 and to which any of the following persons was or is to be a party:

(i) The Fund;

(ii) An Officer of the Fund;

(iii) An investment company, or a person that would be an investment company but for the exclusions provided by sections 3(c)(1) and 3(c)(7) of the Investment Company Act of 1940 (15 U.S.C. 80a–3(c)(1) and (c)(7)), having the same investment adviser, principal underwriter, or Sponsoring Insurance Company as the Fund or having an investment adviser, principal underwriter, or Sponsoring Insurance Company that directly or indirectly controls, is controlled by, or is under common control with an investment adviser, principal underwriter, or Sponsoring Insurance Company of the Fund;

(iv) An Officer of an investment company, or a person that would be an investment company but for the exclusions provided by sections 3(c)(1) and 3(c)(7) of the

Investment Company Act of 1940 (15 U.S.C. 80a–3(c)(1) and (c)(7)), having the same investment adviser, principal underwriter, or Sponsoring Insurance Company as the Fund or having an investment adviser, principal underwriter, or Sponsoring Insurance Company that directly or indirectly controls, is controlled by, or is under common control with an investment adviser, principal underwriter, or Sponsoring Insurance Company of the Fund;

(v) An investment adviser, principal underwriter, or Sponsoring Insurance Company of the Fund;

(vi) An Officer of an investment adviser, principal underwriter, or Sponsoring Insurance Company of the Fund;

(vii) A person directly or indirectly controlling, controlled by, or under common control with an investment adviser, principal underwriter, or Sponsoring Insurance Company of the Fund; or

(viii) An Officer of a person directly or indirectly controlling, controlled by, or under common control with an investment adviser, principal underwriter, or Sponsoring Insurance Company of the Fund.

Instructions to paragraph (b)(8). 1. Include the name of each director, nominee, or Immediate Family Member whose interest in any transaction or series of similar transactions is described and the nature of the circumstances by reason of which the interest is required to be described.

2. State the nature of the interest, the approximate dollar amount involved in the transaction, and, where practicable, the approximate dollar amount of the interest.

3. In computing the amount involved in the transaction or series of similar transactions, include all periodic payments in the case of any lease or other agreement providing for periodic payments.

4. Compute the amount of the interest of any director, nominee, or Immediate Family Member of the director or nominee without regard to the amount of profit or loss involved in the transaction(s).

5. As to any transaction involving the purchase or sale of assets, state the cost of the assets to the purchaser and, if acquired by the seller within two years prior to the transaction, the cost to the seller. Describe the method used in determining the purchase or sale price and the name of the person making the determination.

6. If the proxy statement relates to multiple portfolios of a series Fund with different fiscal years, then, in determining the date that is the beginning of the last two completed fiscal years of the Fund, use the earliest date of any series covered by the proxy statement.

7. Disclose indirect, as well as direct, material interests in transactions. A person who has a position or relationship with, or interest in, a company that engages in a transaction with one of the persons listed in paragraphs (b)(8)(i) through (b)(8)(viii) of this Item may have an indirect interest in the transaction by reason of the position, relationship, or interest. The interest in the transaction, however, will not be deemed "material" within the meaning of paragraph (b)(8) of this Item where the interest of the director, nominee, or Immediate Family Member arises solely from the holding of an equity interest (including a limited partnership interest, but excluding a general partnership interest) or a creditor interest in a company that is a party to the transaction with one of the persons specified in paragraphs (b)(8)(i) through (b)(8)(viii) of this Item, and the transaction is not material to the company.

8. The materiality of any interest is to be determined on the basis of the significance of the information to investors in light of all the circumstances of the particular case. The importance of the interest to the person having the interest, the relationship of the parties to the transaction with each other, and the amount involved in the transaction are among the factors to be considered in determining the significance of the information to investors.

9. No information need be given as to any transaction where the interest of the director, nominee, or Immediate Family Member arises solely from the ownership of securities of a person specified in paragraphs (b)(8)(i) through (b)(8)(viii) of this Item and the director, nominee, or Immediate Family Member receives no extra or special benefit not shared on a pro rata basis by all holders of the class of securities.

10. Transactions include loans, lines of credit, and other indebtedness. For indebtedness, indicate the largest aggregate amount of indebtedness outstanding at any time during the period, the nature of the indebtedness and the transaction in which it was incurred, the amount outstanding as of the latest practicable date, and the rate of interest paid or charged.

11. No information need be given as to any routine, retail transaction. For example, the Fund need not disclose that a director has a credit card, bank or brokerage account, residential mortgage, or insurance policy with a person specified in paragraphs (b)(8)(i) through (b)(8)(viii) of this Item unless the director is accorded special treatment.

(9) Describe briefly any direct or indirect relationship, in which the amount involved exceeds $60,000, of any director or nominee for election as director who is not or would not be an "interested person" of the Fund within the meaning of section 2(a)(19) of the Investment Company Act of 1940 (15 U.S.C. 80a–2(a)(19)), or Immediate Family Member of the director or nominee, that exists, or has existed at any time since the beginning of the last two completed fiscal years of the Fund, or is currently proposed, with any of the persons specified in paragraphs (b)(8)(i) through (b)(8)(viii) of this Item. Relationships include:

(i) Payments for property or services to or from any person specified in paragraphs (b)(8)(i) through (b)(8)(viii) of this Item;

(ii) Provision of legal services to any person specified in paragraphs (b)(8)(i) through (b)(8)(viii) of this Item;

(iii) Provision of investment banking services to any person specified in paragraphs (b)(8)(i) through (b)(8)(viii) of this Item, other than as a participating underwriter in a syndicate; and

(iv) Any consulting or other relationship that is substantially similar in nature and scope to the relationships listed in paragraphs (b)(9)(i) through (b)(9)(iii) of this Item.

Instructions to paragraph (b)(9). 1. Include the name of each director, nominee, or Immediate Family Member whose relationship is described and the nature of the circumstances by reason of which the relationship is required to be described.

2. State the nature of the relationship and the amount of business conducted between the director, nominee, or Immediate Family Member and the person specified in paragraphs (b)(8)(i) through (b)(8)(viii) of this Item as a result of the relationship since the beginning of the last two completed fiscal years of the Fund or proposed to be done during the Fund's current fiscal year.

3. In computing the amount involved in a relationship, include all periodic payments in the case of any agreement providing for periodic payments.

4. If the proxy statement relates to multiple portfolios of a series Fund with different fiscal years, then, in determining the date that is the beginning of the last two completed fiscal years of the Fund, use the earliest date of any series covered by the proxy statement.

5. Disclose indirect, as well as direct, relationships. A person who has a position or relationship with, or interest in, a company that has a relationship with one of the persons listed in paragraphs (b)(8)(i) through (b)(8)(viii) of this Item may have an indirect relationship by reason of the position, relationship, or interest.

6. In determining whether the amount involved in a relationship exceeds $60,000, amounts involved in a relationship of the director (or nominee) should be aggregated with those of his Immediate Family Members.

7. In the case of an indirect interest, identify the company with which a person specified in paragraphs (b)(8)(i) through (b)(8)(viii) of this Item has a relationship; the name of the director, nominee, or Immediate Family Member affiliated with the company and the nature of the affiliation; and the amount of business conducted between the company and the person specified in paragraphs (b)(8)(i) through (b)(8)(viii) of this Item since the beginning of the last two completed fiscal years of the Fund or proposed to be done during the Fund's current fiscal year.

8. In calculating payments for property and services for purposes of paragraph (b)(9)(i) of this Item, the following may be excluded:

A. Payments where the transaction involves the rendering of services as a common contract carrier, or public utility, at rates or charges fixed in conformity with law or governmental authority; or

B. Payments that arise solely from the ownership of securities of a person specified in paragraphs (b)(8)(i) through (b)(8)(viii) of this Item and no extra or special benefit not shared on a pro rata basis by all holders of the class of securities is received.

9. No information need be given as to any routine, retail relationship. For example, the Fund need not disclose that a director has a credit card, bank or brokerage account, residential mortgage, or insurance policy with a person specified in paragraphs (b)(8)(i) through (b)(8)(viii) of this Item unless the director is accorded special treatment.

(10) If an Officer of an investment adviser, principal underwriter, or Sponsoring Insurance Company of the Fund, or an Officer of a person directly or indirectly controlling, controlled by, or under common control with an investment adviser, principal underwriter, or Sponsoring Insurance Company of the Fund, serves, or has served since the beginning of the last two completed fiscal years of the Fund, on the board of directors of a company where a director of the Fund or nominee for election as director who is not or would not be an "interested person" of the Fund within the meaning of section 2(a)(19) of the Investment Company Act of 1940 (15 U.S.C. 80a–2(a)(19)), or Immediate Family Member of the director or nominee, is, or was since the beginning of the last two completed fiscal years of the Fund, an Officer, identify:

(i) The company;

(ii) The individual who serves or has served as a director of the company and the period of service as director;

(iii) The investment adviser, principal underwriter, or Sponsoring Insurance Company or person controlling, controlled by, or under common control with the investment adviser, principal underwriter, or Sponsoring Insurance Company where the individual named in paragraph (b)(10)(ii) of this Item holds or held office and the office held; and

(iv) The director of the Fund, nominee for election as director, or Immediate Family Member who is or was an Officer of the company; the office held; and the period of holding the office.

Instruction to paragraph (b)(10). If the proxy statement relates to multiple portfolios of a series Fund with different fiscal years, then, in determining the date that is the beginning of the last two completed fiscal years of the Fund, use the earliest date of any series covered by the proxy statement.

(11) Provide in tabular form, to the extent practicable, the information required by Items 401(f) and (g), 404(a) and (c), and 405 of Regulation S–K (§§ 229.401(f) and (g), 229.404(a) and (c), and 229.405 of this chapter).

Instruction to paragraph (b)(11). Information provided under paragraph (b)(8) of this Item 22 is deemed to satisfy the requirements of Items 404(a) and (c) of Regulation S–K for information about directors, nominees for election as directors, and Immediate Family Members of directors and nominees, and need not be provided under this paragraph (b)(11).

(12) Describe briefly any material pending legal proceedings, other than ordinary routine litigation incidental to the Fund's business, to which any director or nominee for director or affiliated person of such director or nominee is a party adverse to the Fund or any of its affiliated persons or has a material interest adverse to the Fund or any of its affiliated persons. Include the name of the court where the case is pending, the date instituted, the principal parties, a description of the factual basis alleged to underlie the proceeding, and the relief sought.

(13) For all directors, and for each of the three highest-paid Officers that have aggregate compensation from the Fund for the most recently completed fiscal year in excess of $60,000 ("Compensated Persons"):

(i) Furnish the information required by the following table for the last fiscal year:

COMPENSATION TABLE

(1)	(2)	(3)	(4)	(5)
Name of Person, Position.	Aggregate Compensation From Fund.	Pension or Retirement Benefits Accrued as Part of Fund Expenses.	Estimated Annual Benefits Upon Retirement.	Total Compensation From Fund and Complex Paid to Directors

Instructions to paragraph (b)(13)(i). 1. For column (1), indicate, if necessary, the capacity in which the remuneration is received. For Compensated Persons that are directors of the Fund, compensation is amounts received for service as a director.

2. If the Fund has not completed its first full year since its organization, furnish the information for the current fiscal year, estimating future payments that would be made pursuant to an existing agreement or understanding. Disclose in a footnote to the Compensation Table the period for which the information is furnished.

3. Include in column (2) amounts deferred at the election of the Compensated Person, whether pursuant to a plan established under Section 401(k) of the Internal Revenue Code (26 U.S.C. 401(k)) or otherwise, for the fiscal year in which earned. Disclose in a footnote to the Compensation Table the total amount of deferred compensation (including interest) payable to or accrued for any Compensated Person.

4. Include in columns (3) and (4) all pension or retirement benefits proposed to be paid under any existing plan in the event of retirement at normal retirement date, directly or indirectly, by the Fund or any of its Subsidiaries, or by other companies in the Fund Complex. Omit column (4) where retirement benefits are not determinable.

5. For any defined benefit or actuarial plan under which benefits are determined primarily by final compensation (or average final compensation) and years of service, provide the information required in column (4) in a separate table showing estimated annual benefits payable upon retirement (including amounts attributable to any defined benefit supplementary or excess pension award plans) in specified compensation and years of service classifications. Also provide the estimated credited years of service for each Compensated Person.

6. Include in column (5) only aggregate compensation paid to a director for service on the board and other boards of investment companies in a Fund Complex specifying the number of such other investment companies.

(ii) Describe briefly the material provisions of any pension, retirement, or other plan or any arrangement other than fee arrangements disclosed in paragraph (b)(13)(i) of this Item pursuant to which Compensated Persons are or may be compensated for any services provided, including amounts paid, if any, to the Compensated Person under any such arrangements during the most recently completed fiscal year. Specifically include the criteria used to determine amounts payable under any plan, the length of service or vesting period required by the plan, the retirement age or other event that gives rise to payments under the plan, and whether the payment of benefits is secured or funded by the Fund.

(iii) With respect to each Compensated Person, business development companies must include the information required by Items 402(b)(2)(iv) and 402(c) of Regulation S–K (§§ 229.402(b)(2)(iv) and 229.402(c) of this chapter).

(14) State whether or not the Fund has a separately designated audit committee established in accordance with section 3(a)(58)(A) of the Act (15 U.S.C. 78c(a)(58)(A)). If the entire board of directors is acting as the Fund's audit committee as specified in section 3(a)(58)(B) of the Act (15 U.S.C. 78c(a)(58)(B)), so state. If applicable, provide the disclosure required by § 240.10A–3(d) regarding an exemption from the listing standards for audit committees. Identify the other standing committees of the Fund's board of directors, and provide the following information about each committee, including any separately designated audit committee and any nominating committee:

(i) A concise statement of the functions of the committee;

(ii) The members of the committee and, in the case of a nominating committee, whether or not the members of the committee are "interested parties" of the Fund as defined in section 2(a)(19) of the Investment Company Act of 1940 (15 U.S.C. 80a–2(a)(19)); and

(iii) The number of committee meetings held during the last fiscal year.

Instruction to paragraph (b)(14): For purposes of Item 22(b)(14), the term "nominating committee" refers not only to nominating committees and committees performing similar functions, but also to groups of directors fulfilling the role of a nominating committee, including the entire board of directors.

(c) *Approval of investment advisory contract*. If action is to be taken with respect to an investment advisory contract, include the following information in the proxy statement.

Instruction. Furnish information with respect to a prospective investment adviser to the extent applicable (including the name and address of the prospective investment adviser).

(1) With respect to the existing investment advisory contract:

(i) State the date of the contract and the date on which it was last submitted to a vote of security holders of the Fund, including the purpose of such submission;

(ii) Briefly describe the terms of the contract, including the rate of compensation of the investment adviser;

(iii) State the aggregate amount of the investment adviser's fee and the amount and purpose of any other material payments by the Fund to the investment adviser, or any affiliated person of the investment adviser, during the last fiscal year of the Fund;

(iv) If any person is acting as an investment adviser of the Fund other than pursuant to a written contract that has been approved by the security holders of the company, identify the person and describe the nature of the services and arrangements;

(v) Describe any action taken with respect to the investment advisory contract since the beginning of the Fund's last fiscal year by the board of directors of the Fund (unless described in response to paragraph (c)(1)(vi) of this Item 22); and

(vi) If an investment advisory contract was terminated or not renewed for any reason, state the date of such termination or non-renewal, identify the parties involved, and describe the circumstances of such termination or non-renewal.

(2) State the name, address and principal occupation of the principal executive officer and each director or general partner of the investment adviser.

Instruction. If the investment adviser is a partnership with more than ten general partners, name:

(i) The general partners with the five largest economic interests in the partnership, and, if different, those general partners comprising the management or executive committee of the partnership or exercising similar authority;

(ii) The general partners with significant management responsibilities relating to the fund.

(3) State the names and addresses of all Parents of the investment adviser and show the basis of control of the investment adviser and each Parent by its immediate Parent.

Instructions. 1. If any person named is a corporation, include the percentage of its voting securities owned by its immediate Parent.

2. If any person named is a partnership, name the general partners having the three largest partnership interests (computed by whatever method is appropriate in the particular case).

(4) If the investment adviser is a corporation and if, to the knowledge of the persons making the solicitation or the persons on whose behalf the solicitation is made, any person not named in answer to paragraph (c)(3) of this Item 22 owns, of record or beneficially, ten percent or more of the outstanding voting securities of the investment adviser, indicate that fact and state the name and address of each such person.

(5) Name each officer or director of the Fund who is an officer, employee, director, general partner or shareholder of the investment adviser. As to any officer or director who is not a director or general partner of the investment adviser and who owns securities or has any other material direct or indirect interest in the investment adviser or any other person controlling, controlled by or under common control with the investment adviser, describe the nature of such interest.

(6) Describe briefly and state the approximate amount of, where practicable, any material interest, direct or indirect, of any director of the Fund in any material transactions since the beginning of the most recently completed fiscal year, or in any material proposed transactions, to which the investment adviser of the Fund, any Parent or Subsidiary of the investment adviser (other than another Fund), or any Subsidiary of the Parent of such entities was or is to be a party.

Instructions. 1. Include the name of each person whose interest in any transaction is described and the nature of the relationship by reason of which such interest is required to be described. Where it is not practicable to state the approximate amount of the interest, indicate the approximate amount involved in the transaction.

2. As to any transaction involving the purchase or sale of assets by or to the investment adviser, state the cost of the assets to the purchaser and the cost thereof to the seller if acquired by the seller within two years prior to the transaction.

3. If the interest of any person arises from the position of the person as a partner in a partnership, the proportionate interest of such person in transactions to which the partnership is a party need not be set forth, but state the amount involved in the transaction with the partnership.

4. No information need be given in response to this paragraph (c)(6) of Item 22 with respect to any transaction that is not related to the business or operations of the Fund and

to which neither the Fund nor any of its Parents or Subsidiaries is a party.

(7) Disclose any financial condition of the investment adviser that is reasonably likely to impair the financial ability of the adviser to fulfil its commitment to the fund under the proposed investment advisory contract.

(8) Describe the nature of the action to be taken on the investment advisory contract and the reasons therefor, the terms of the contract to be acted upon, and, if the action is an amendment to, or a replacement of, an investment advisory contract, the material differences between the current and proposed contract.

(9) If a change in the investment advisory fee is sought, state:

(i) The aggregate amount of the investment adviser's fee during the last year;

(ii) The amount that the adviser would have received had the proposed fee been in effect; and

(iii) The difference between the aggregate amounts stated in response to paragraphs (i) and (ii) of this item (c)(9) as a percentage of the amount stated in response to paragraph (i) of this item (c)(9).

(10) If the investment adviser acts as such with respect to any other Fund having a similar investment objective, identify and state the size of such other Fund and the rate of the investment adviser's compensation. Also indicate for any Fund identified whether the investment adviser has waived, reduced, or otherwise agreed to reduce its compensation under any applicable contract.

Instruction. Furnish the information in response to this paragraph (c)(10) of Item 22 in tabular form.

(11) Discuss in reasonable detail the material factors and the conclusions with respect thereto that form the basis for the recommendation of the board of directors that the shareholders approve an investment advisory contract. Include the following in the discussion:

(i) Factors relating to both the board's selection of the investment adviser and approval of the advisory fee and any other amounts to be paid by the Fund under the contract. This would include, but not be limited to, a discussion of the nature, extent, and quality of the services to be provided by the investment adviser; the investment performance of the Fund and the investment adviser; the costs of the services to be provided and profits to be realized by the investment adviser and its affiliates from the relationship with the Fund; the extent to which economies of scale would be realized as the Fund grows; and whether fee levels reflect these economies of scale for the benefit of Fund investors. Also indicate in the discussion whether the board relied upon comparisons of the services to be rendered and the amounts to be paid under the contract with those under other investment advisory contracts, such as contracts of the same and other types of clients (*e.g.*, pension funds and other institutional investors). If the board relied upon such comparisons, describe the comparisons that were relied on and how they assisted the board in determining to recommend that the shareholders approve the advisory contract; and

(ii) If applicable, any benefits derived or to be derived by the investment adviser from the relationship with the Fund such as soft dollar arrangements by which brokers provide research to the Fund or its investment adviser in return for allocating Fund brokerage.

Instructions. 1. Conclusory statements or a list of factors will not be considered sufficient disclosure. Relate the factors to the specific circumstances of the Fund and the investment advisory contract for which approval is sought and state how the board evaluated each factor. For example, it is not sufficient to state that the board considered the amount of the investment advisory fee without stating what the board concluded about the amount of the fee and how that affected its determination to recommend approval of the contract.

2. If any factor enumerated in paragraph (c)(11)(i) of this Item 22 is not relevant to the board's evaluation of the investment advisory contract for which approval is sought, not this and explain the reasons why that factor is not relevant.

(12) Describe any arrangement or understanding made in connection with the proposed investment advisory contract with respect to the composition of the board of directors of the Fund or the investment adviser or with respect to the selection or appointment of any person to any office with either such company.

(13) For the most recently completed fiscal year, state:

(i) The aggregate amount of commissions paid to any Affiliated Broker; and

(ii) The percentage of the Fund's aggregate brokerage commissions paid to any such Affiliated Broker.

Instruction. Identify each Affiliated Broker and the relationships that cause the broker to be an Affiliated Broker.

(14) Disclose the amount of any fees paid by the Fund to the investment adviser, its affiliated persons or any affiliated person of such person during the most recent fiscal year for services provided to the Fund (other than under the investment advisory contract or for brokerage commissions). State whether these services will continue to be provided after the investment advisory contract is approved.

(d) *Approval of distribution plan.* If action is to be taken with respect to a Distribution Plan, include the following information in the proxy statement.

Instruction. Furnish information on a prospective basis to the extent applicable.

(1) Describe the nature of the action to be taken on the Distribution Plan and the reason therefor, the terms of the Distribution Plan to be acted upon, and, if the action is an amendment to, or a replacement of, a Distribution Plan, the material differences between the current and proposed Distribution Plan.

(2) If the Fund has a Distribution Plan in effect:

(i) Provide the date that the Distribution Plan was adopted and the date of the last amendment, if any;

(ii) Disclose the persons to whom payments may be made under the Distribution Plan, the rate of the distribution fee and the purposes for which such fee may be used;

(iii) Disclose the amount of distribution fees paid by the Fund pursuant to the plan during its most recent fiscal year, both in the aggregate and as a percentage of the Fund's average net assets during the period;

(iv) Disclose the name of, and the amount of any payments made under the Distribution Plan by the Fund during its most recent fiscal year to, any person who is an affiliated person of the Fund, its investment adviser, principal underwriter, or Administrator, an affiliated person of such person, or a person that during the most recent fiscal year received 10% or more of the aggregate amount paid under the Distribution Plan by the Fund;

(v) Describe any action taken with respect to the Distribution Plan since the beginning of the Fund's most recent fiscal year by the board of directors of the Fund; and

(vi) If a Distribution Plan was or is to be terminated or not renewed for any reason, state the date or prospective date of such termination or non-renewal, identify the parties involved, and describe the circumstances of such termination or non-renewal.

(3) Describe briefly and state the approximate amount of, where practicable, any ma-

terial interest, direct or indirect, of any director or nominee for election as a director of the Fund in any material transactions since the beginning of the most recently completed fiscal year, or in any material proposed transactions, to which any person identified in response to Item 22(d)(2)(iv) was or is to be a party.

Instructions. 1. Include the name of each person whose interest in any transaction is described and the nature of the relationship by reason of which such interest is required to be described. Where it is not practicable to state the approximate amount of the interest, indicate the approximate amount involved in the transaction.

2. As to any transaction involving the purchase or sale of assets, state the cost of the assets to the purchaser and the cost thereof to the seller if acquired by the seller within two years prior to the transaction.

3. If the interest of any person arises from the position of the person as a partner in a partnership, the proportionate interest of such person in transactions to which the partnership is a party need not be set forth but state the amount involved in the transaction with the partnership.

4. No information need be given in response to this paragraph (d)(3) of Item 22 with respect to any transaction that is not related to the business or operations of the Fund and to which neither the Fund nor any of its Parents or Subsidiaries is a party.

(4) Discuss in reasonable detail the material factors and the conclusions with respect thereto which form the basis for the conclusion of the board of directors that there is a reasonable likelihood that the proposed Distribution Plan (or amendment thereto) will benefit the Fund and its shareholders.

Instruction. Conclusory statements or a list of factors will not be considered sufficient disclosure.

Item 23. Delivery of Documents to Security Holders Sharing an Address

If one annual report or proxy statement is being delivered to two or more security holders who share an address in accordance with § 240.14a–3(e)(1), furnish the following information:

(a) State that only one annual report or proxy statement, as applicable, is being delivered to multiple security holders sharing an address unless the registrant has received contrary instructions from one or more of the security holders;

(b) Undertake to deliver promptly upon written or oral request a separate copy of the annual report or proxy statement, as applicable, to a security holder at a shared address to which a single copy of the documents was delivered and provide instructions as to how a security holder can notify the registrant that the security holder wishes to receive a separate copy of an annual report or proxy statement, as applicable;

(c) Provide the phone number and mailing address to which a security holder can direct a notification to the registrant that the security holder wishes to receive a separate annual report or proxy statement, as applicable, in the future; and

(d) Provide instructions how security holders sharing an address can request delivery of a single copy of annual reports or proxy statements if they are receiving multiple copies of annual reports or proxy statements.

UNIVERSAL BUSINESS CORPORATION

Proxy

270 Universal Center, Horizon, California 91770

This Proxy Is Solicited on Behalf of the Board of Directors.

The undersigned hereby appoints John Red, Mary Blue, and Lee White as Proxies, each with the power to appoint his or her substitute, and hereby authorizes them to represent and to vote, as designated below, all the shares of common stock of Universal Business held on record by the undersigned on October 23, 1980, at the annual meeting of shareholders to be held on December 20, 1980 or any adjournment thereof.

1. ELECTION OF DIRECTORS FOR all nominees listed below (*except as marked to the contrary below*) ☐ WITHHOLD AUTHORITY to vote for all nominees listed below ☐

(INSTRUCTION below) To withhold authority to vote for any individual nominee strike a line through the nominee's name in the list

J. Allen, S. Brown, J. Doe, J. Green, G. Johansen, A. Jones, M. Roe, J. Smith and M. Stanton

2. PROPOSAL TO APPROVE THE APPOINTMENT OF DOLLAR AND CENTS as the independent public accountants of the corporation

☐ FOR ☐ AGAINST ☐ ABSTAIN

3. STOCKHOLDER PROPOSAL RELATING TO FORM AND CONTENT OF POST-MEETING REPORTS:

☐ FOR ☐ AGAINST ☐ ABSTAIN

[C6891]

4. In their discretion the Proxies are authorized to vote upon such other business as may properly come before the meeting

This proxy when properly executed will be voted in the manner directed herein by the undersigned stockholder. If no direction is made, this proxy will be voted for Proposals 1, 2, and 3.

Please sign exactly as name appears below. When shares are held by joint tenants, both should sign. When signing as attorney, as executor, administrator, trustee or guardian, please give full title as such. If a corporation, please sign in full corporate name by President or other authorized officer. If a partnership please sign in partnership name by authorized person.

SAMPLE CARD A

DATED ______________ 1980

____
Signature

PLEASE MARK SIGN DATE AND RETURN THE PROXY CARD PROMPTLY USING THE ENCLOSED ENVELOPE

____
Signature if held jointly

[C6892]

UB UNIVERSAL BUSINESS CORPORATION **Proxy**

270 Universal Center, Horizon, California 91770

This Proxy Is Solicited on Behalf of the Board of Directors.

The undersigned hereby appoints John Red, Mary Blue, and Lee White as Proxies, each with the power to appoint his or her substitute, and hereby authorizes them to represent and to vote, as designated below, all the shares of common stock of Universal Business held on record by the undersigned on October 23, 1980, at the annual meeting of shareholders to be held on December 20, 1980 or any adjournment thereof.

1. ELECTION OF DIRECTORS FOR all nominees listed below (*except as marked to the contrary below*) ☐ WITHHOLD AUTHORITY to vote for all nominees listed below ☐

(INSTRUCTION To withhold authority to vote for any individual nominee write that nominee's name on the space provided below)

J. Allen, S. Brown, J. Doe, J. Green, G. Johansen, A. Jones, M. Roe, J. Smith and M. Stanton

2. PROPOSAL TO APPROVE THE APPOINTMENT OF DOLLAR AND CENTS as the independent public accountants of the corporation

☐ FOR ☐ AGAINST ☐ ABSTAIN

3. STOCKHOLDER PROPOSAL RELATING TO FORM AND CONTENT OF POST-MEETING REPORTS:

☐ FOR ☐ AGAINST ☐ ABSTAIN

[C6894]

4. In their discretion the Proxies are authorized to vote upon such other business as may properly come before the meeting

This proxy when properly executed will be voted in the manner directed herein by the undersigned stockholder. If no direction is made, this proxy will be voted for Proposals 1, 2, and 3.

Please sign exactly as name appears below. When shares are held by joint tenants, both should sign. When signing as attorney, as executor, administrator, trustee or guardian, please give full title as such. If a corporation, please sign in full corporate name by President or other authorized officer. If a partnership please sign in partnership name by authorized person.

SAMPLE CARD B

DATED ______________ 1980

PLEASE MARK SIGN DATE AND RETURN THE PROXY CARD PROMPTLY USING THE ENCLOSED ENVELOPE

Signature

Signature if held jointly

[C6893]

UB UNIVERSAL BUSINESS CORPORATION **Proxy**

270 Universal Center, Horizon, California 91770

This Proxy is Solicited on Behalf of the Board of Directors.

The undersigned hereby appoints John Red, Mary Blue, and Lee White as Proxies, each with the power to appoint his or her substitute, and hereby authorizes them to represent and to vote, as designated below, all the shares of common stock of Universal Business held on record by the undersigned on October 23, 1980, at the annual meeting of shareholders to be held on December 20, 1980 or any adjournment thereof.

1. ELECTION OF DIRECTORS FOR all nominees listed below (*except as marked to the contrary below*) ☐ WITHHOLD AUTHORITY to vote for all nominees listed below ☐

(INSTRUCTION To withhold authority to vote for any individual nominee mark the box next to the nominee's name below)

☐ J. Allen ☐ S. Brown ☐ J. Doe ☐ J. Green ☐ G. Johansen ☐ A. Jones ☐ M. Roe ☐ J. Smith ☐ M. Stanton

2. PROPOSAL TO APPROVE THE APPOINTMENT OF DOLLAR AND CENTS as the independent public accountants of the corporation

☐ FOR ☐ AGAINST ☐ AGAINST

3. STOCKHOLDER PROPOSAL RELATING TO FORM AND CONTENT OF POST-MEETING REPORTS:

☐ FOR ☐ ABSTAIN ☐ ABSTAIN

[C6896]

4. In their discretion the Proxies are authorized to vote upon such other business as may properly come before the meeting.

This proxy when properly executed will be voted in the manner directed herein by the undersigned stockholder. If no direction is made, this proxy will be voted for Proposals 1, 2, and 3.

Please sign exactly as name appears below. When shares are held by joint tenants, both should sign. When signing as attorney, as executor, administrator, trustee or guardian, please give full title as such. If a corporation, please sign in full corporate name by President or other authorized officer. If a partnership please sign in partnership name by authorized person.

SAMPLE CARD C

DATED ______________ 1980

PLEASE MARK SIGN DATE AND RETURN THE PROXY CARD PROMPTLY USING THE ENCLOSED ENVELOPE

Signature

Signature if held jointly

[C6895]

Rule 14a–103. Notice of Exempt Solicitation

U.S. Securities and Exchange Commission
Washington, D.C. 20549

Notice of Exempt Solicitation

1. Name of the Registrant:

____

2. Name of person relying on exemption:

____

3. Address of person relying on the exemption:

____

4. *Written materials.* Attach written material required to be submitted pursuant to Rule 14a–6(g)(1).

Rule 14b–1. Obligation of Registered Brokers and Dealers in Connection With the Prompt Forwarding of Certain Communications to Beneficial Owners

(a) *Definitions.* Unless the context otherwise requires, all terms used in this rule shall have the same meanings as in the Act and, with respect to proxy soliciting material, as in Rule 14a–1 thereunder and, with respect to information statements, as in Rule 14c–1 thereunder. In addition, as used in this rule, the term "registrant" means:

(1) The issuer of a class of securities registered pursuant to Section 12 of the Act; or

(2) An investment company registered under the Investment Company Act of 1940.

(b) *Dissemination and beneficial owner information requirements.* A broker or dealer registered under Section 15 of the Act shall comply with the following requirements for disseminating certain communications to beneficial owners and providing beneficial owner information to registrants.

(1) The broker or dealer shall respond, by first class mail or other equally prompt means, directly to the registrant no later than seven business days after the date it receives an inquiry made in accordance with Rule 14a–13(a) or Rule 14c–7(a) by indicating, by means of a search card or otherwise:

(i) The approximate number of customers of the broker or dealer who are beneficial owners of the registrant's securities that are held of record by the broker, dealer, or its nominee;

(ii) The number of customers of the broker or dealer who are beneficial owners of the registrant's securities who have objected to disclosure of their names, addresses, and securities positions if the registrant has indicated, pursuant to Rule 14a–13(a)(1)(ii)(A) or Rule 14c–7(a)(1)(ii)(A), that it will distribute the annual report to security holders to beneficial owners of its securities whose names, addresses and securities positions are disclosed pursuant to paragraph (b)(3) of this rule; and

(iii) The identity of the designated agent of the broker or dealer, if any, acting on its behalf in fulfilling its obligations under paragraph (b)(3) of this rule; *Provided, however,* that if the broker or dealer has informed the registrant that a designated office(s) or department(s) is to receive such inquiries, receipt for purposes of paragraph (b)(1) of this rule shall mean receipt by such designated office(s) or department(s).

(2) The broker or dealer shall, upon receipt of the proxy, other proxy soliciting material, information statement, and/or annual reports to security holders, forward such materials to its customers who are beneficial owners of the registrant's securities no later than five business days after receipt of the proxy material, information statement or annual reports.

Note to paragraph (b)(2): At the request of a registrant, or on its own initiative so long as the registrant does not object, a broker or dealer may, but is not required to, deliver one annual report, proxy statement or information statement to more than one beneficial owner sharing an address if the requirements set forth in § 240.14a–3(e)(1) (with respect to annual reports and proxy statements) and § 240.14c–3(c) (with respect to annual reports and information statements) applicable to registrants, with the exception of § 240.14a–3(e)(1)(i)(E), are satisfied instead by the broker or dealer.

(3) The broker or dealer shall, through its agent or directly:

(i) Provide the registrant, upon the registrant's request, with the names, addresses, and securities positions, compiled as of a date specified in the registrant's request which is no earlier than five business days after the date the registrant's request is received, of its customers who are beneficial owners of the registrant's securities and who have not objected to disclosure of such information; *Provided, however,* that if the broker or dealer has informed the registrant that a designated office(s) or department(s) is to receive such requests, receipt shall mean receipt by such designated office(s) or department(s); and

(ii) Transmit the data specified in paragraph (b)(3)(i) of this rule to the registrant no later than five business days after the record date or other date specified by the registrant.

NOTE 1.—Where a broker or dealer employs a designated agent to act on its behalf in performing the obligations imposed on the broker or dealer by paragraph (b)(3) of this rule, the five business day time period for determining the date as of which the beneficial owner information is to be compiled is calculated from the date the designated agent receives the registrant's request. In complying with the registrant's request for beneficial owner information under paragraph (b)(3) of this rule, a broker or dealer need only supply the registrant with the names, addresses and securities positions of non-objecting beneficial owners.

NOTE 2.—If a broker or dealer receives a registrant's request less than five business days before the requested compilation date, it must provide a list compiled as of a date that is no more than five business days after receipt and transmit the list within five business days after the compilation date.

(c) *Exceptions to dissemination and beneficial owner information requirements.* A broker or dealer registered under Section 15 of the Act shall be subject to the following with respect to its dissemination and beneficial owner information requirements.

(1) With regard to beneficial owners of exempt employee benefit plan securities, the broker or dealer shall:

(i) Not include information in its response pursuant to paragraph (b)(1) of this rule or forward proxies (or in lieu thereof requests for voting instructions), proxy soliciting material, information statements, or annual reports to security holders pursuant to paragraph (b)(2) of this rule to such beneficial owners; and

(ii) Not include in its response, pursuant to paragraph (b)(3) of this rule, data concerning such beneficial owners.

(2) A broker or dealer need not satisfy:

(i) Its obligations under paragraphs (b)(2) and (b)(3) of this rule if a registrant does not provide assurance of reimbursement of the broker's or dealer's reasonable expenses, both direct and indirect, incurred in connection with performing the obligations imposed by paragraphs (b)(2) and (b)(3) of this rule; or

(ii) Its obligation under paragraph (b)(2) of this rule to forward annual reports to non-objecting beneficial owners identified by the broker or dealer, through its agent or directly, pursuant to paragraph (b)(3) of this rule if the registrant notifies the broker or dealer pursuant to § 240.14a–13(c) or § 240.14c–7(c) that the registrant will mail the annual report to such non-objecting beneficial owners identified by the broker or dealer and delivered in a list to the registrant pursuant to paragraph (b)(3) of this rule.

(3) In its response pursuant to paragraph (b)(1) of this section, a broker or dealer shall not include information about annual reports, proxy statements or information statements that will not be delivered to security holders sharing an address because of the broker or dealer's reliance on the procedures referred to in the Note to paragraph (b)(2) of this section.

Rule 14b–2. Obligation of Banks, Associations and Other Entities That Exercise Fiduciary Powers in Connection With the Prompt Forwarding of Certain Communications to Beneficial Owners

(a) *Definitions.* Unless the context otherwise requires, all terms used in this rule shall have the same meanings as in the Act and, with respect to proxy soliciting material, as in Rule 14a–1 thereunder and, with respect to information statements, as in Rule 14c–1 thereunder. In addition, as used in this rule, the following terms shall apply:

(1) The term "banks" means a bank, association, or other entity that exercises fiduciary powers.

(2) The term "beneficial owner" includes any person who has or shares, pursuant to an instrument, agreement, or otherwise, the power to vote, or to direct the voting of a security.

NOTE 1.—If more than one person shares voting power, the provisions of the instrument creating that voting power shall govern with respect to whether consent to disclosure of beneficial owner information has been given.

NOTE 2.—If more than one person shares voting power or if the instrument creating that voting power provides that such power shall be exercised by different persons depending on the nature of the corporate action involved, all persons entitled to exercise such power shall be deemed beneficial owners; *Provided, however,* that only one such beneficial owner need be designated among the beneficial owners to receive proxies or requests for voting instructions, other proxy soliciting material, information statements, and/or annual reports to security holders, if the person so designated assumes the obligation to disseminate, in a timely manner, such materials to the other beneficial owners.

(3) The term "registrant" means:

(i) The issuer of a class of securities registered pursuant to Section 12 of the Act; or

(ii) An investment company registered under the Investment Company Act of 1940.

(b) *Dissemination and beneficial owner information requirements.* A bank shall comply with the following requirements for disseminating certain communications to beneficial owners and providing beneficial owner information to registrants.

(1) The bank shall:

(i) Respond, by first class mail or other equally prompt means, directly to the registrant, no later than one business day after the date it receives an inquiry made in accordance with Rule 14a–13(a) or Rule 14c–7(a) by indicating the name and address of each of its respondent banks that holds the registrant's securities on behalf of beneficial owners, if any; and

(ii) Respond, by first class mail or other equally prompt means, directly to the registrant no later than seven business days after the date it receives an inquiry made in accordance with Rule 14a–13(a) or Rule 14c–7(a) by indicating, by means of a search card or otherwise:

(A) The approximate number of customers of the bank who are beneficial owners of the registrant's securities that are held of record by the bank or its nominee;

(B) If the registrant has indicated, pursuant to Rule 14a–13(a)(1)(ii)(A) or Rule 14c–7(a)(1)(ii)(A), that it will distribute the annual report to security holders to beneficial owners of its securities whose names, addresses, and securities positions are disclosed pursuant to paragraphs (b)(4)(ii) and (iii) of this rule:

(1) With respect to customer accounts opened on or before December 28, 1986, the number of beneficial owners of the registrant's securities who have affirmatively consented to disclosure of their names, addresses, and securities positions; and

(2) With respect to customer accounts opened after December 28, 1986, the number of beneficial owners of the registrant's securities who have not objected to disclosure of their

names, addresses, and securities positions; and

(C) The identity of its designated agent, if any, acting on its behalf in fulfilling its obligations under paragraphs (b)(4)(ii) and (iii) of this rule; *Provided, however,* that, if the bank or respondent bank has informed the registrant that a designated office(s) or department(s) is to receive such inquiries, receipt for purposes of paragraphs (b)(1)(i) and (ii) of this rule shall mean receipt by such designated office(s) or department(s).

(2) Where proxies are solicited, the bank shall, within five business days after the record date:

(i) Execute an omnibus proxy, including a power of substitution, in favor of its respondent banks and forward such proxy to the registrant; and

(ii) Furnish a notice to each respondent bank in whose favor an omnibus proxy has been executed that it has executed such a proxy, including a power of substitution, in its favor pursuant to paragraph (b)(2)(i) of this rule.

(3) Upon receipt of the proxy, other proxy soliciting material, information statement, and/or annual reports to security holders, the bank shall forward such materials to each beneficial owner on whose behalf it holds securities, no later than five business days after the date it receives such material and, where a proxy is solicited, the bank shall forward, with the other proxy soliciting material and/or the annual report, either:

(i) A properly executed proxy:

(A) indicating the number of securities held for such beneficial owner;

(B) bearing the beneficial owner's account number or other form of identification, together with instructions as to the procedures to vote the securities;

(C) briefly stating which other proxies, if any, are required to permit securities to be voted under the terms of the instrument creating that voting power or applicable state law; and

(D) being accompanied by an envelope addressed to the registrant or its agent, if not provided by the registrant; or

(ii) A request for voting instructions (for which registrant's form of proxy may be used and which shall be voted by the record holder bank or respondent bank in accordance with the instructions received), together with an envelope addressed to the record holder bank or respondent bank.

Note to paragraph (b)(3): At the request of a registrant, or on its own initiative so long as the registrant does not object, a bank may, but is not required to, deliver one annual report, proxy statement or information statement to more than one beneficial owner sharing an address if the requirements set forth in § 240.14a–3(e)(1) (with respect to annual reports and proxy statements) and § 240.14c–3(c) (with respect to annual reports and information statements) applicable to registrants, with the exception of § 240.14a–3(e)(1)(i)(E), are satisfied instead by the bank.

(4) The bank shall:

(i) Respond, by first class mail or other equally prompt means, directly to the registrant no later than one business day after the date it receives an inquiry made in accordance with Rule 14a–13(b)(1) or Rule 14c–7(b)(1) by indicating the name and address of each of its respondent banks that holds the registrant's securities on behalf of beneficial owners, if any;

(ii) Through its agent or directly, provide the registrant, upon the registrant's request, and within the time specified in paragraph (b)(4)(iii) of this rule, with the names, addresses, and securities position, compiled as of a date specified in the registrant's request which is no earlier than five business days after the date the registrant's request is received, of:

(A) With respect to customer accounts opened on or before December 28, 1986, beneficial owners of the registrant's securities on whose behalf it holds securities who have consented affirmatively to disclosure of such information, subject to paragraph (b)(5) of this rule; and

(B) With respect to customer accounts opened after December 28, 1986, beneficial owners of the registrant's securities on whose behalf it holds securities who have not objected to disclosure of such information;

Provided, however, that if the record holder bank or respondent bank has informed the registrant that a designated office(s) or department(s) is to receive such requests, receipt for purposes of paragraphs (b)(4)(i) and (ii) of this rule shall mean receipt by such designated office(s) or department(s); and

(iii) Through its agent or directly, transmit the data specified in paragraph (b)(4)(ii) of this rule to the registrant no later than five business days after the date specified by the registrant.

NOTE 1.—Where a record holder bank or respondent bank employs a designated agent to act on its behalf in performing the obligations imposed on it by paragraphs (b)(4)(ii) and (iii) of this rule, the five business day time period for determining the date as of which the beneficial owner information is to be compiled is calculated from the date the designated agent receives the registrant's request. In complying with the registrant's request for beneficial owner information under paragraph (b)(4)(ii) and (iii) of this rule, a record holder bank or respondent bank need only supply the registrant with the names, addresses and securities positions of affirmatively consenting and non-objecting beneficial owners.

NOTE 2.—If a record holder bank or respondent bank receives a registrant's request less than five business days before the requested compilation date, it must provide a list compiled as of a date that is no more than five business days after receipt and transmit the list within five business days after the compilation date.

(5) For customer accounts opened on or before December 28, 1986, unless the bank has made a good faith effort to obtain affirmative consent to disclosure of beneficial owner information pursuant to paragraph (b)(4)(ii) of this rule, the bank shall provide such information as to beneficial owners who do not object to disclosure of such information. A good faith effort to obtain affirmative consent to disclosure of beneficial owner information shall include, but shall not be limited to, making an inquiry:

(i) Phrased in neutral language, explaining the purpose of the disclosure and the limitations on the registrant's use thereof;

(ii) Either in at least one mailing separate from other account mailings or in repeated mailings; and

(iii) In a mailing that includes a return card, postage paid enclosure.

(c) *Exceptions to dissemination and beneficial owner information requirements.* The bank shall be subject to the following with respect to its dissemination and beneficial owner requirements.

(1) With regard to beneficial owners of exempt employee benefit plan securities, the bank shall not:

(i) Include information in its response pursuant to paragraph (b)(1) of this rule; or forward proxies (or in lieu thereof requests for voting instructions), proxy soliciting material, information statements, or annual reports to security holders pursuant to paragraph (b)(3) of this rule to such beneficial owners; or

(ii) Include in its response pursuant to paragraphs (b)(4) and (b)(5) of this rule data concerning such beneficial owners.

(2) The bank need not satisfy:

(i) Its obligations under paragraphs (b)(2), (b)(3), and (b)(4) of this rule if a registrant does not provide assurance of reimbursement of its reasonable expenses, both direct and indirect, incurred in connection with performing the obligations imposed by paragraphs (b)(2), (b)(3), and (b)(4) of this rule; or

(ii) Its obligation under paragraph (b)(3) of this rule to forward annual reports to consenting and non-objecting beneficial owners identified pursuant to paragraphs (b)(4)(ii) and (iii) of this rule if the registrant notifies the record holder bank or respondent bank, pursuant to Rule 14a–13(c) or Rule 14c–7(c), that the registrant will mail the annual report to beneficial owners whose names, addresses and securities positions are disclosed pursuant to paragraphs (b)(4)(ii) and (iii) of this rule.

(3) For the purposes of determining the fees which may be charged to registrants pursuant to Rule 14a–13(b)(5), Rule 14c–7(a)(5), and paragraph (c)(2) of this rule for performing obligations under paragraphs (b)(2), (b)(3), and (b)(4) of this rule: an amount no greater than that permitted to be charged by brokers or dealers for reimbursement of their reasonable expenses, both direct and indirect, incurred in connection with performing the obligations imposed by paragraphs (b)(2) and (b)(3) of Rule 14b–1, shall be deemed to be reasonable.

(4) In its response pursuant to paragraph (b)(1)(ii)(A) of this section, a bank shall not include information about annual reports, proxy statements or information statements that will not be delivered to security holders sharing an address because of the bank's reliance on the procedures referred to in the Note to paragraph (b)(3) of this section.

REGULATION 14C. DISTRIBUTION OF INFORMATION PURSUANT TO SECTION 14(c)

ATTENTION ELECTRONIC FILERS

THIS REGULATION SHOULD BE READ IN CONJUNCTION WITH REGULATION S–T (PART 232 OF THIS CHAPTER), WHICH GOVERNS THE PREPARATION AND SUBMISSION OF DOCUMENTS IN ELECTRONIC FORMAT. MANY PROVISIONS RELATING TO THE PREPARATION AND SUBMISSION OF DOCUMENTS IN PAPER FORMAT CONTAINED IN THIS REGULATION ARE SUPERSEDED BY THE PROVISIONS OF REGULATION S–T FOR DOCUMENTS REQUIRED TO BE FILED IN ELECTRONIC FORMAT.

Rule 14c–1. Definitions

Unless the context otherwise requires, all terms used in this regulation have the same meanings as in the Act or elsewhere in the general rules and regulations thereunder. In addition, the following definitions apply unless the context otherwise requires:

(a) *Associate.* The term "associate" used to indicate a relationship with any person, means (1) any corporation or organization (other than the registrant or a majority-owned subsidiary of the registrant) of which such person is an officer or partner or is, directly or indirectly, the beneficial owner of 10 percent or more of any class of equity securities, (2) any trust or other estate in which such person has a substantial beneficial interest or as to which such person serves as trustee or in a similar fiduciary capacity, and (3) any relative or spouse of such person, or any relative of such spouse, who has the same home as such person or who is a director or officer of the registrant or any of its parents or subsidiaries.

(b) *Employee benefit plan.* For purposes of Rule 14c–7, the term "employee benefit plan" means any purchase, savings, option, bonus, appreciation, profit sharing, thrift, incentive, pension or similar plan primarily for employees, directors, trustees or officers.

(c) *Entity that exercises fiduciary powers.* The term "entity that exercises fiduciary powers" means any entity that holds securities in nominee name or otherwise on behalf of a beneficial owner but does not include a clearing agency registered pursuant to section 17A of the Act, or a broker or a dealer.

(d) *Exempt employee benefit plan securities.* For purposes of Rule 14c–7, the term "exempt employee benefit plan securities" means: (1) securities of the registrant held by an employee benefit plan, as defined in paragraph (b) of this rule, where such plan is established by the registrant; or (2) if notice regarding the current distribution of information statements has been given pursuant to Rule 14c–7(a)(1)(ii)(C) or if notice regarding the current request for a list of names, addresses and securities positions of beneficial owners has been given pursuant to Rule 14c–7(b)(3), securities of the registrant held by an employee benefit plan, as defined in paragraph (b) of this section, where such plan is established by an affiliate of the registrant.

(e) *Information statement.* The term "information statement" means the statement required by Rule 14c–2, whether or not contained in a single document.

(f) *Last fiscal year.* The term "last fiscal year" of the registrant means the last fiscal year of the registrant ending prior to the date of the meeting with respect to which an information statement is required to be distributed, or if the information statement involves consents or authorizations in lieu of a meeting, the earliest date on which they may be used to effect corporate action.

(g) *Proxy.* The term "proxy" includes every proxy, consent or authorization within the meaning of Section 14(a) of the Act. The consent or authorization may take the form of failure to object or to dissent.

(h) *Record date.* The term "record date" means the date as of which the record holders of securities entitled to vote at a meeting or by written consent or authorization shall be determined.

(i) *Record holder.* For purposes of Rule 14c–7, the term "record holder" means any broker, dealer, voting trustee, bank, association or other entity that exercises fiduciary powers which holds securities of record in nominee name or otherwise or as a participant in a clearing agency registered pursuant to Section 17A of the Act.

(j) *Registrant.* The term "registrant" means:

(1) The issuer of a class of securities registered pursuant to Section 12 of the Act; or

(2) An investment company registered under the Investment Company Act of 1940 that has made a public offering of its securities.

(k) *Respondent bank.* For purposes of Rule 14c–7, the term "respondent bank" means any bank, association or other entity that exercises fiduciary powers which holds securities on behalf of beneficial owners and deposits such securities for safekeeping with another bank, association or other entity that exercises fiduciary powers.

Rule 14c-2. Distribution of Information Statement

(a) In connection with every annual or other meeting of the holders of the class of securities registered pursuant to section 12 of the Act or of a class of securities issued by an investment company registered under the Investment Company Act of 1940 that has made a public offering of securities, including the taking of corporate action by the written authorization or consent of security holders, the registrant shall transmit a written information statement containing the information specified in Schedule 14C (§ 240.14c–101) or written information statements included in registration statements filed under the Securities Act of 1933 on Form S–4 or F–4 (§ 239.25 or § 239.34 of this chapter) or Form N-14 (§ 239.23 of this chapter), and containing the information specified in such form, to every security holder of the class that is entitled to vote or give an authorization or consent in regard to any matter to be acted upon and from whom proxy authorization or consent is not solicited on behalf of the registrant pursuant to Section 14(a) of the Act, *Provided however,* That: (1) in the case of a class of securities in unregistered or bearer form, such statements need to be transmitted only to those security holders whose names are known to the registrant; and (2) no such statements need to be transmitted to a security holder if a registrant would be excused from delivery of an annual report or a proxy statement under Rule 14a-3(e)(2) if such rule were applicable.

(b) The information statement shall be sent or given at least 20 calendar days prior to the meeting date or, in the case of corporate action taken pursuant to the consents or authorizations of security holders, at least 20 calendar days prior to the earliest date on which the corporate action may be taken.

(c) If a transaction is a roll-up transaction as defined in Item 901(c) of Regulation S-K and is registered (or authorized to be registered) on Form S-4 or Form F-4, the information statement must be distributed to security holders no later than the lesser of 60 calendar days prior to the date on which the meeting of security holders is held or action is taken, or the maximum number of days permitted for giving notice under applicable state law.

Rule 14c-3. Annual Report to Be Furnished Security Holders

(a) If the information statement relates to an annual (or special meeting in lieu of the annual) meeting, or written consent in lieu of such meeting, of security holders at which directors of the registrant, other than an investment company registered under the Investment Company Act of 1940, are to be elected, it shall be accompanied or preceded by an annual report to security holders:

(1) The annual report shall contain the information specified in paragraphs (b)(1) through (b)(11) of Rule 14a-3.

(2) [Reserved]

Note to Small Business Issuers—In responding to the disclosure items under paragraph (b) of Rule 14a-3, (§ 240.14a-3 of this chapter) a "small business issuer," defined under Rule 12b-2 of the Exchange Act (§ 240.12b-2), shall refer to the disclosure items in Regulation S-B (§ 228.10—702 of this chapter) rather than Regulation S-K (§ 229.10—702 of this chapter). If there is no comparable disclosure item in Regulation S-B, a small business issuer need not provide the information requested. A small business issuer shall provide the information in Item 310(a) of Regulation S-B in lieu of the financial information required by Rule 14a-3(b)(1) (§ 240.14a3(b)(1)). Small business issuers using the transitional small business issuers disclosure format in the filing of their most recent annual report on Form 10-KSB (§ 249.310b of this chapter) need not provide the information required by paragraph (b) of Rule 14a-3. Rather, those small business issuers shall provide only the financial statements required to be filed in their most recent Form 10-KSB. The inclusion of additional information, including information required of non-transitional small business issuers, in the annual report to security holders will not cause the issuer to be ineligible for the transitional disclosure forms.

(b) Seven copies of the report sent to security holders pursuant to this rule shall be mailed to the Commission, solely for its information, not later than the date on which such report is first sent or given to security holders or the date on which preliminary copies or definitive copies, if preliminary filing was not required, of the information statement are filed with the Commission pursuant to Rule 14c-5, whichever date is later. The report is not deemed to be "filed" with the Commission or subject to this regulation otherwise than as provided in this rule, or to the liabilities of Section 18 of the Act, except to the extent that the registrant specifically requests that it be treated as a part of the information statement or incorporates it in the information statement or other filed report by reference.

(c) A registrant will be considered to have delivered an annual report or information statement to security holders of record who share an address if the requirements set forth in § 240.14a–3(e)(1) are satisfied with respect to the annual report or information statement, as applicable.

Rule 14c–4. Presentation of Information in Information Statement

(a) The information included in the information statement shall be clearly presented and the statements made shall be divided into groups according to subject matter and the various groups of statements shall be preceded by appropriate headings. The order of items and sub-items in the schedule need not be followed. Where practicable and appropriate, the information shall be presented in tabular form. All amounts shall be stated in figures. Information required by more than one applicable item need not be repeated. No statement need be made in response to any item or sub-item which is inapplicable.

(b) Any information required to be included in the information statement as to terms of securities or other subject matter which from a standpoint of practical necessity must be determined in the future may be stated in terms of present knowledge and intention. Subject to the foregoing, information which is not known to the registrant and which it is not reasonably within the power of the registrant to ascertain or procure may be omitted, if a brief statement of the circumstances rendering such information unavailable is made.

(c) All printed information statements shall be in roman type at least as large and as legible as 10-point modern type except that to the extent necessary for convenient presentation, financial statements and other tabular data, but not the notes thereto, may be in roman type at least as large and as legible as 8-point modern type. All such type shall be leaded at least 2 points.

(d) Where an information statement is delivered through an electronic medium, issuers may satisfy legibility requirements applicable to printed documents, such as type size and font, by presenting all required information in a format readily communicated to investors.

Rule 14c–5. Filing Requirements

(a) *Preliminary information statement.* Five preliminary copies of the information statement shall be filed with the Commission at least 10 calendar days prior to the date definitive copies of such statement are first sent or given to security holders, or such shorter period prior to that date as the Commission may authorize upon a showing of good cause therefor. In computing the 10–day period, the filing date of the preliminary copies is to be counted as the first day and the 11th day is the date on which definitive copies of the information statement may be mailed to security holders. A registrant, however, shall not file with the Commission a preliminary information statement if it relates to an annual (or special meeting in lieu of the annual) meeting, of security holders at which the only matters to be acted upon are:

(1) The election of directors;

(2) The election, approval or ratification of accountant(s);

(3) A security holder proposal identified in the registrant's information statement pursuant to Item 4 of Schedule 14C (§ 240.14c–101); and/or

(4) The approval or ratification of a plan as defined in paragraph (a)(7)(ii) of Item 402 of Regulation S–K (§ 229.402(a)(7)(ii) of this chapter) or amendments to such a plan.

This exclusion from filing a preliminary information statement does not apply if the registrant comments upon or refers to a solicitation in opposition in connection with the meeting in its information statement.

NOTE 1.—The filing of revised material does not recommence the ten day time period unless the revised material contains material revisions or material new proposal(s) that constitute a fundamental change in the information statement.

NOTE 2.—The officials responsible for the preparation of the information statement should make every effort to verify the accuracy and completeness of the information required by the applicable rules. The preliminary statement should be filed with the Commission at the earliest practicable date.

NOTE 3.—*Solicitation in Opposition.* For purposes of the exclusion from filing a preliminary information statement, a "solicitation in opposition" includes: (a) any solicitation opposing a proposal supported by the registrant; and (b) any solicitation supporting a proposal that the registrant does not expressly support, other than a security holder proposal identified in the registrant's information statement pursuant to Item 4 of Schedule 14C. The identification of a security holder proposal in the registrant's information statement does not constitute a "solicitation in opposition," even if the registrant opposes the proposal and/or includes a statement in opposition to the proposal.

NOTE 4.—A registrant that is filing an information statement in preliminary form only because the registrant has commented on or referred to an opposing solicitation should indicate that fact in a transmittal letter when filing the preliminary material with the Commission.

(b) *Definitive information statement.* Eight definitive copies of the information statement, in the form in which it is furnished to security holders, must be filed with the Commission no later than the date the information statement is first sent or given to security holders. Three copies of these materials also must be filed with, or mailed for filing to, each national securities exchange on which the registrant has a class of securities listed and registered.

(c) *Release dates.* All preliminary material filed pursuant to paragraph (a) of this rule shall be accompanied by a statement of the date on which copies thereof filed pursuant to paragraph (b) of this rule are intended to be released to security holders. All definitive material filed pursuant to paragraph (b) of this rule shall be accompanied by a statement of the date on which copies of such material have been released to security holders or, if not released, the date on which copies thereof are intended to be released.

(d)(1) *Public availability of information.* All copies of material filed pursuant to paragraph (a) of this rule shall be clearly marked "Preliminary Copies," and shall be deemed immediately available for public inspection unless confidential treatment is obtained pursuant to paragraph (d)(2) of this rule.

(2) *Confidential treatment.* If action will be taken on any matter specified in Item 14 of Schedule 14A (§ 240.14a–101), all copies of the preliminary information statement filed under paragraph (a) of this section will be for the information of the Commission only and will not be deemed available for public inspection until filed with the Commission in definitive form so long as:

(i) The information statement does not relate to a matter or proposal subject to § 240.13e–3 or a roll-up transaction as defined in Item 901(c) of Regulation S–K (§ 229.901(c) of this chapter);

(ii) Neither the parties to the transaction nor any persons authorized to act on their behalf have made any public communications relating to the transaction except for statements where the content is limited to the information specified in § 230.135 of this chapter; and

(iii) The materials are filed in paper and marked "Confidential, For Use of the Commission Only." In all cases, the materials may be disclosed to any department or agency of the United States Government and to the Congress, and the Commission may make any inquiries or investigation into the materials as may be necessary to conduct an adequate review by the Commission.

Instruction to paragraph (d)(2): If communications are made publicly that go beyond the information specified in § 230.135, the materials must be re-filed publicly with the Commission.

(e) *Revised information statements.* Where any information statement filed pursuant to this section is amended or revised, two of the copies of such amended or revised material filed pursuant to this rule shall be marked to indicate clearly and precisely the changes effected therein. If the amendment or revision alters the text of the material, the changes in such text shall be indicated by means of underscoring or in some other appropriate manner.

(f) *Merger material.* Notwithstanding the foregoing provisions of this section, any information statement or other material included in a registration statement filed under the Securities Act of 1933 on Form N–14, S–4, or F–4 shall be deemed filed both for the purposes of that Act and for the purposes of this rule, but separate copies of such material need not be furnished pursuant to this section, nor shall any fee be required under paragraph (a) of this rule. However, any additional material used after the effective date of the registration statement on Form N–14, S–4 or F–4 shall be filed in accordance with this section, unless separate copies of such material are required to be filed as an amendment of such registration statement.

(g) *Fees.* At the time of filing the preliminary information statement regarding an acquisition, merger, spin-off, consolidation or proposed sale or other disposition of substantially all the assets of the company, the registrant shall pay the Commission a fee, no part of which shall be refunded, established in accordance with Rule 0–11.

(h) *Cover page.* Each information statement filed with the Commission shall include a cover page in the form set forth in Schedule 14C. The cover page required by this paragraph need not be distributed to security holders.

Rule 14c–6. False or Misleading Statements

(a) No information statement shall contain any statement which, at the time and in the light of the circumstances under which it is made, is false or misleading with respect to any material fact, or which omits to state any material fact necessary in order to make the statements therein not false or misleading or necessary to correct any statement in any earlier communication with respect to the same meeting or subject matter which has become false or misleading.

(b) The fact that an information statement has been filed with or examined by the Commission shall not be deemed a finding by the Commission that such material is accurate or complete or not false or misleading, or that the Commission has passed upon the merits of or approved any statement contained therein or any matter to be acted upon by security holders. No representation contrary to the foregoing shall be made.

Rule 14c–7. Providing Copies of Material for Certain Beneficial Owners

(a) If the registrant knows that securities of any class entitled to vote at a meeting, or by written authorizations or consents if no meeting is held, are held of record by a broker, dealer, voting trustee, or bank, association, or other entity that exercises fiduciary powers in nominee name or otherwise, the registrant shall:

(1) By first class mail or other equally prompt means: (i) Inquire of each such record holder: (A) Whether other persons are the beneficial owners of such securities and, if so, the number of copies of the information statement necessary to supply such material to such beneficial owners; and (B) in the case of an annual (or special meeting in lieu of the annual) meeting, or written consents in lieu of such meeting, at which directors are to be elected, the number of

copies of the annual report to security holders, necessary to supply such report to such beneficial owners for whom proxy material has not been and is not to be made available and to whom such reports are to be distributed by such record holder or its nominee and not by the registrant; (C) if the record holder or respondent bank has an obligation under Rule 14b-1(b)(3) or Rule 14b-2(b)(4)(ii) and (iii), whether an agent has been designated to act on its behalf in fulfilling such obligation, and, if so, the name and address of such agent; and (D) whether it holds the registrant's securities on behalf of any respondent bank and, if so, the name and address of each such respondent bank; and (ii) indicate to each such record holder: (A) whether the registrant pursuant to paragraph (c) of this rule intends to distribute the annual report to security holders to beneficial owners of its securities whose names, addresses and securities positions are disclosed pursuant to Rule 14b-1(b)(3) and Rule 14b-2(b)(4)(ii) and (iii); (B) the record date; and (C) at the option of the registrant, any employee benefit plan established by an affiliate of the registrant that holds securities of the registrant that the registrant elects to treat as exempt employee benefit plan securities;

(2) Upon receipt of a record holders's or respondent bank's response indicating, pursuant to Rule 14b-2(b)(1)(i), the names and addresses of its respondent banks, within one business day after the date such response is received, make an inquiry of and give notification to each such respondent bank in the same manner required by paragraph (a)(1) of this rule; *Provided, however,* the inquiry required by paragraphs (a)(1) and (a)(2) of this rule shall not cover beneficial owners of exempt employee benefit plan securities.

(3) Make the inquiry required by paragraph (a)(1) of this rule on the earlier of:

(i) At least 20 business days prior to the record date of the meeting of security holders or the record date of written consents in lieu of a meeting; or

(ii) At least 20 business days prior to the date the information statement is required to be sent or given pursuant to Rule 14c-2(b);

Provided, however, That, if a record holder or respondent bank has informed the registrant that a designated office(s) or department(s) is to receive such inquiries, the inquiry shall be made to such designated office(s) or department(s);

(4) Supply, in a timely manner, each record holder and respondent bank of whom the inquiries required by paragraphs (a)(1) and (a)(2) of this rule are made with copies of the information statement and/or the annual report to security holders, in such quantities, assembled in such form and at such places(s), as the record holder or respondent bank may reasonably request in order to send such material to each beneficial owner of securities who is to be furnished with such material by the record holder or respondent bank; and

(5) Upon the request of any record holder or respondent bank that is supplied with information statements and/or annual reports to security holders pursuant to paragraph (a)(3) of this rule, pay its reasonable expenses for completing the mailing of such material to beneficial owners.

NOTE 1.—If the registrant's list of security holders indicates that some of its securities are registered in the name of a clearing agency registered pursuant to section 17A of the Act (*e.g.,* "Cede & Co.," nominee for the Depository Trust Company), the registrant shall make appropriate inquiry of the clearing agency and thereafter of the participants in such a clearing agency who may hold on behalf of a beneficial owner or respondent bank, and shall comply with the above paragraph with respect to any such participant (see Rule 14c-1(h)).

NOTE 2.—The attention of registrants is called to the fact that each broker, dealer, bank, association, and other entity that exercises fiduciary powers has an obligation pursuant to Rule 14b–1 and Rule 14b–2 (except as provided therein with respect to exempt employee benefit plan securities held in nominee name) and with respect to brokers and dealers, applicable self-regulatory organization requirements to obtain and forward, within the time periods prescribed therein, (a) information statements to beneficial owners on whose behalf it holds securities, and (b) annual reports to security holders to beneficial owners on whose behalf it holds securities, unless the registrant has notified the record holder or respondent bank that it has assumed responsibility to mail such material to beneficial owners whose names, addresses and securities positions are disclosed pursuant to Rule 14b–1(b)(3) and Rule 14b–2(b)(4)(ii) and (iii).

NOTE 3.—The attention of registrants is called to the fact that registrants have an obligation, pursuant to paragraph (d) of this rule, to cause information statements and annual reports to security holders to be furnished, in accordance with Rule 14c–2, to beneficial owners of exempt employee benefit plan securities.

(b) Any registrant requesting pursuant to Rule 14b–1(b)(3) and Rule 14b–2(b)(4)(ii) and (iii) a list of names, addresses and securities positions of beneficial owners of its securities who either have consented or have not objected to disclosure of such information shall:

(1) By first class mail or other equally prompt means, inquire of each record holder and each respondent bank identified to the registrant pursuant to Rule 14b–2(e)(1) whether such record holder or respondent bank holds the registrant's securities on behalf of any respondent banks and, if so, the name and address of each such respondent bank;

(2) Request such list be compiled as of a date no earlier than five business days after the date the registrant's request is received by the record holder or respondent bank; *Provided, however,* that if the record holder or respondent bank has informed the registrant that a designated office(s) or department(s) is to receive such requests, the request shall be made to such designated offices(s) or department(s);

(3) Make such request to the following persons that hold the registrant's securities on behalf of beneficial owners: all brokers, dealers, banks, associations and other entities that exercise fiduciary powers; *Provided, however,* such request shall not cover beneficial owners of exempt employee benefit plan securities as defined in Rule 14a–1(d)(1); and, at the option of the registrant, such request may give notice of any employee benefit plan established by an affiliate of the registrant that holds securities of the registrant that the registrant elects to treat as exempt employee benefit plan securities;

(4) Use the information furnished in response to such request exclusively for purposes of corporate communications; and

(5) Upon the request of any record holder or respondent bank to whom such request is made, pay the reasonable expenses, both direct and indirect, of providing beneficial owner information.

NOTE: A registrant will be deemed to have satisfied its obligations under paragraph (b) of this rule by requesting consenting and non-objecting beneficial owner lists from a designated agent acting on behalf of the record holder or respondent bank and paying to that designated agent the reasonable expenses of providing the beneficial owner information.

(c) A registrant, at its option, may send by mail or other equally prompt means, its annual report to security holders to the beneficial owners whose identifying information is provided by record holders and respondent banks, pursuant to § 240.14b–1(b)(3) and § 240.14b–2(b)(4)(ii) and (iii), provided that such registrant notifies the record holders and respondent banks at the time it makes the inquiry required by paragraph (a) of this section that the registrant will send the annual report to security holders to the beneficial owners so identified.

(d) If a registrant furnishes information statements to record holders and respondent banks who hold securities on behalf of beneficial owners, the registrant shall cause information statements and annual reports to security holders to be furnished, in accordance with Rule 14c-2, to beneficial owners of exempt employee benefit plan securities.

REG. 14c-101. SCHEDULE 14C—INFORMATION REQUIRED IN INFORMATION STATEMENT

Schedule 14C Information

Information Statement Pursuant to Section 14(c) of the Securities Exchange Act of 1934 (Amendment No.)

Check the appropriate box:

[ ] Preliminary Information Statement

[ ] Confidential, for Use of the Commission Only (as permitted by Rule 14c-5(d)(2))

[ ] Definitive Information Statement

(Name of Registrant As Specified In Charter)

Payment of Filing Fee (Check the appropriate box):

[ ] No fee required.

[ ] Fee computed on table below per Exchange Act Rules 14c-5(g) and 0-11

(1) Title of each class of securities to which transaction applies:

---

(2) Aggregate number of securities to which transaction applies:

---

(3) Per unit price or other underlying value of transaction computed pursuant to Exchange Act Rule 0-11 (Set forth the amount on which the filing fee is calculated and state how it was determined):

---

(4) Proposed maximum aggregate value of transaction:

---

(5) Total fee paid:

[ ] Fee paid previously with preliminary materials.

[ ] Check box if any part of the fee is offset as provided by Exchange Act Rule 0-11(a)(2) and identify the filing for which the offsetting fee was paid previously. Identify the previous filing by registration statement number, or the Form or Schedule and the date of its filing.

(1) Amount Previously Paid:

---

(2) Form, Schedule or Registration Statement No.:

---

(3) Filing Party:

---

(4) Date Filed:

NOTE: Where any item, other than Item 4, calls for information with respect to any matter to be acted upon at the meeting, or, if no meeting is being held, by written authorization or consent, such item need be answered only with respect to proposals to be made by the registrant. Registrants and acquirees that meet the definition of "small business issuer" under Rule 12b-2 of the Exchange Act shall refer to the disclosure items in Regulation S-B and not Regulation S-K. If there is no comparable disclosure item in Regulation S-B, small business issuers need not provide the information requested. Small business issuers shall provide the financial information in Item 310 of Regulation S-B in lieu of any financial statements required by Item 1 of § 240.14c-101.

Item 1. Information Required by Items of Schedule 14A

Furnish the information called for by all of the items of Schedule 14A (other than Items 1(c), 2, 4 and 5 thereof) which would be applicable to any matter to be acted upon at the meeting if proxies were to be solicited in connection with the meeting. Notes A, C, D and E to Schedule 14A are also applicable to Schedule 14C.

Item 2. Statement That Proxies Are Not Solicited

The following statement shall be set forth on the first page of the information statement in boldface type:

WE ARE NOT ASKING YOU FOR A PROXY AND YOU ARE REQUESTED NOT TO SEND US A PROXY

Item 3. Interest of Certain Persons in or Opposition to Matters to Be Acted Upon

(a) Describe briefly any substantial interest, direct or indirect, by security holdings or otherwise, of each of the following persons in any matter to be acted upon, other than elections to office:

(1) Each person who has been a director or officer of the registrant at any time since the beginning of the last fiscal year.

(2) Each nominee for election as a director of the registrant.

(3) Each associate of the foregoing persons.

(b) Give the name of any director of the registrant who has informed the registrant in writing that he intends to oppose any action to be taken by the registrant at the meeting and indicate the action which he intends to oppose.

Item 4. Proposals by Security Holders

If any security holder entitled to vote at the meeting or by written authorization or consent has submitted to the registrant a reasonable time before the information statement is to be transmitted to security holders a proposal, other than elections to office, which is accompanied by notice of his intention to present the proposal for action at the meeting the registrant shall, if a meeting is held, make a statement to that effect, identify the proposal and indicate the disposition proposed to be made of the proposal by the registrant at the meeting.

Instructions. 1. This item need not be answered as to any proposal submitted with respect to an annual meeting if such proposal is submitted less than 60 days in advance of a day corresponding to the date of mailing a proxy statement or information statement in connection with the last annual meeting of security holders.

2. If the registrant intends to rule a proposal out of order, the Commission shall be so advised 20 calendar days prior to the date the definitive copies of the information statement are filed with the Commission, together with a statement of the reasons why the proposal is not deemed to be a proper subject for action by security holders.

Item 5. Delivery of Documents to Security Holders Sharing an Address

If one annual report or information statement is being delivered to two or more security holders who share an address, furnish the following information in accordance with § 240.14a–3(e)(1):

(a) State that only one annual report or information statement, as applicable, is being delivered to multiple security holders sharing an address unless the registrant has received contrary instructions from one or more of the security holders;

(b) Undertake to deliver promptly upon written or oral request a separate copy of the annual report or information statement, as applicable, to a security holder at a shared address to which a single copy of the documents was delivered and provide instructions as to how a security holder can notify the registrant that the security holder wishes to receive a separate copy of an annual report or information statement, as applicable;

(c) Provide the phone number and mailing address to which a security holder can direct a notification to the registrant that the security holder wishes to receive a separate annual report or proxy statement, as applicable, in the future; and

(d) Provide instructions how security holders sharing an address can request delivery of a single copy of annual reports or information statements if they are receiving multiple copies of annual reports or information statements.

REGULATION 14D

ATTENTION ELECTRONIC FILERS

THIS REGULATION SHOULD BE READ IN CONJUNCTION WITH REGULATIONS S–T (PART 232 OF THIS CHAPTER), WHICH GOVERNS THE PREPARATION AND SUBMISSION OF DOCUMENTS IN ELECTRONIC FORMAT. MANY PROVISIONS RELATING TO THE PREPARATION AND SUBMISSION OF DOCUMENTS IN PAPER FORMAT CONTAINED IN THIS REGULATION ARE SUPERSEDED BY THE PROVISIONS OF REGULATION S–T FOR DOCUMENTS REQUIRED TO BE FILED IN ELECTRONIC FORMAT.

Rule 14d–1. Scope of and Definitions Applicable to Regulations 14D and 14E

(a) *Scope.* Regulation 14D shall apply to any tender offer which is subject to section 14(d)(1) of the Act, including, but not limited to, any tender offer for securities of a class described in that section which is made by an affiliate of the issuer of such class. Regulation 14E shall apply to any tender offer for securities (other than exempted securities) unless otherwise noted therein.

(b) The requirements imposed by sections 14(d)(1) through 14(d)(7) of the Act, Regulation 14D and Schedule TO and 14D–9 thereunder, and Rule 14e–1 of Regulation 14E under the Act, shall be deemed satisfied with respect to any tender offer, including any exchange offer, for the securities of an issuer incorporated or organized under the laws of Canada or any Canadian province or territory, if such issuer is a foreign private issuer and is not an investment company registered or required to be registered under the Investment Company Act of 1940, if less than 40 percent of the class of securities outstanding that is the subject of the tender offer is held by U.S. holders, and the tender offer is subject to, and the bidder complies with, the laws, regulations and policies of Canada and/or any of its provinces or territories governing the conduct of the offer (unless the bidder has received an exemption(s) from, and the tender offer does not comply with, requirements that otherwise would be prescribed by Regulation 14D or 14E), *provided that:*

(1) In the case of tender offers subject to section 14(d)(1) of the Act, where the consideration for a tender offer subject to this rule consists solely of cash, the entire disclosure document or documents required to be furnished to holders of the class of securities to be acquired shall be filed with the Commission on Schedule 14D–1F and disseminated to shareholders of the subject company residing in the United States in accordance with such Canadian laws, regulations and policies; or

(2) Where the consideration for a tender offer subject to this rule includes securities of the bidder to be issued pursuant to the offer, any registration statement and/or prospectus relating thereto shall be filed with the Commission along with the Schedule 14D–1F referred to in paragraph (b)(1) of this rule, and shall be disseminated, together with the home jurisdiction document(s) accompanying such Schedule, to shareholders of the subject company residing in the United States in accordance with such Canadian laws, regulations and policies.

NOTE 1.—For purposes of any tender offer, including any exchange offer, otherwise eligible to proceed in accordance with Rule 14d–1(b) under the Act, the issuer of the subject securities will be presumed to be a foreign private issuer and U.S. holders will be presumed to hold less than 40 percent of such outstanding securities, unless (a) the aggregate trading volume of that class on national securities exchanges in the United States and on NASDAQ exceeded its aggregate trading volume on securities exchanges in Canada and on the Canadian Dealing Network, Inc. ("CDN") over the 12 calendar month period prior to commencement of this offer, or if commenced in response to a prior offer, over the 12 calendar month period prior to the commencement of the initial offer (based on volume figures published by such exchanges and NASDAQ and CDN); (b) the most recent annual report or annual information form filed or submitted by the issuer with securities regulators of Ontario, Quebec, British Columbia or Alberta (or, if the issuer of the subject securities is not a reporting issuer in any of such provinces, with any other Canadian securities regulator) or with the Commission indicates that U.S. holders hold 40 percent or more of the outstanding subject class of securities; or (c) the offeror has actual knowledge that the level of U.S. ownership equals or exceeds 40 percent of such securities.

NOTE 2.—Notwithstanding the grant of an exemption from one or more of the applicable Canadian regulatory provisions imposing requirements that otherwise would be prescribed by Regulation 14D or 14E, the tender offer will be eligible to proceed in accordance with the requirements of this rule if the Commission by order determines that the applicable Canadian regulatory provisions are adequate to protect the interest of investors.

(c) *Tier I.* Any tender offer for the securities of a foreign private issuer as defined in § 240.3b–4 is exempt from the requirements of sections 14(d)(1) through 14(d)(7) of the Act (15 U.S.C. 78n(d)(1) through 78n(d)(7)), Regulation 14D (§ 240.14d–1 through § 240.14d–10) and Schedules TO (§ 240.14d–100) and 14D–9 (§ 240.14d–101) thereunder, and § 240.14e–1 and § 240.14e–2 of Regulation 14E under the Act if the following conditions are satisfied:

(1) *U.S. ownership limitation.* Except in the case of a tender offer which is commenced during the pendency of a tender offer made by a prior bidder in reliance on this paragraph or § 240.13e–4(h)(8), U.S. holders do not hold more than 10 percent of the class of securities sought in the offer (as determined under Instruction 2 to paragraphs (c) and (d) of this section).

(2) *Equal treatment.* The bidder must permit U.S. holders to participate in the offer on terms at least as favorable as those offered any other holder of the same class of securities that is the subject of the tender offer; however:

(i) *Registered exchange offers.* If the bidder offers securities registered under the Securities Act of 1933 (15 U.S.C. 77a et seq.), the bidder need not extend the offer to security holders in those states or jurisdictions that prohibit the offer or sale of the securities after the bidder has made a good faith effort to register or qualify the offer and sale of securities in that state or jurisdiction, except that the bidder must offer the same cash alternative to security holders in any such state or jurisdiction that it has offered to security holders in any other state or jurisdiction.

(ii) *Exempt exchange offers.* If the bidder offers securities exempt from registration under § 230.802 of this chapter, the bidder need not extend the offer to security holders in those states or jurisdictions that require registration or qualification, except that the bidder must offer the same cash alternative to security holders in any such state or jurisdiction that it has offered to security holders in any other state or jurisdiction.

(iii) *Cash only consideration.* The bidder may offer U.S. holders only a cash consideration for the tender of the subject securities, notwithstanding the fact that the bidder is offering security holders outside the United States a consideration that consists in whole or in part of securities of the bidder, so long as the bidder has a reasonable basis for believing that the amount of cash is substantially equivalent to the value of the consideration offered to non-U.S. holders, and either of the following conditions are satisfied:

(A) The offered security is a "margin security" within the meaning of Regulation T (12 CFR 220.2) and the issuer undertakes to provide, upon the request of any U.S. holder or the Commission staff, the closing price and daily trading volume of the security on the principal trading market for the security as of the last trading day of each of the six months preceding the announcement of the offer and each of the trading days thereafter; or

(B) If the offered security is not a "margin security" within the meaning of Regulation T (12 CFR 220.2) the issuer undertakes to provide, upon the request of any U.S. holder or the Commission staff, an opinion of an independent expert stating that the cash consideration offered to U.S. holders is substantially equivalent to the value of the consideration offered security holders outside the United States.

(iv) *Disparate tax treatment*. If the bidder offers loan notes solely to offer sellers tax advantages not available in the United States and these notes are neither listed on any organized securities market nor registered under the Securities Act of 1933 (15 U.S.C. 77a et seq.), the loan notes need not be offered to U.S. holders.

(3) *Informational documents*.

(i) The bidder must disseminate any informational document to U.S. holders, including any amendments thereto, in English, on a comparable basis to that provided to security holders in the home jurisdiction.

(ii) If the bidder disseminates by publication in its home jurisdiction, the bidder must publish the information in the United States in a manner reasonably calculated to inform U.S. holders of the offer.

(iii) In the case of tender offers for securities described in section 14(d)(1) of the Act (15 U.S.C. 78n(d)(1)), if the bidder publishes or otherwise disseminates an informational document to the holders of the securities in connection with the tender offer, the bidder must furnish that informational document, including any amendments thereto, in English, to the Commission on Form CB (§ 249.480 of this chapter) by the first business day after publication or dissemination. If the bidder is a foreign company, it must also file a Form F–X (§ 239.42 of this chapter) with the Commission at the same time as the submission of Form CB to appoint an agent for service in the United States.

(4) *Investment companies*. The issuer of the securities that are the subject of the tender offer is not an investment company registered or required to be registered under the Investment Company Act of 1940 (15 U.S.C. 80a–1 et seq.), other than a registered closed-end investment company.

(d) *Tier II*. A person conducting a tender offer (including any exchange offer) that meets the conditions in paragraph (d)(1) of this section shall be entitled to the exemptive relief specified in paragraph (d)(2) of this section provided that such tender offer complies with all the requirements of this section other than those for which an exemption has been specifically provided in paragraph (d)(2) of this section:

(1) *Conditions*.

(i) The subject company is a foreign private issuer as defined in § 240.3b–4 and is not an investment company registered or required to be registered under the Investment Company Act of 1940 (15 U.S.C. 80a–1 et seq.), other than a registered closed-end investment company;

(ii) Except in the case of a tender offer which is commenced during the pendency of a tender offer made by a prior bidder in reliance on this paragraph or § 240.13e–4(i), U.S. holders do not hold more than 40 percent of the class of securities sought in the offer (as determined under Instruction 2 to paragraphs (c) and (d) of this section); and

(iii) The bidder complies with all applicable U.S. tender offer laws and regulations, other than those for which an exemption has been provided for in paragraph (d)(2) of this section.

(2) *Exemptions.*—

(i) *Equal treatment—loan notes*. If the bidder offers loan notes solely to offer sellers tax advantages not available in the United States and these notes are neither listed on any organized securities market nor registered under the Securities Act of 1933 (15 U.S.C. 77a et seq.), the loan notes need not be offered to U.S. holders, notwithstanding § 240.14d–10.

(ii) *Equal treatment—separate U.S. and foreign offers*. Notwithstanding the provisions of § 240.14d–10, a bidder conducting a tender offer meeting the conditions of paragraph (d)(1) of this section may separate the offer into two offers: one offer made only to U.S. holders and another offer made only to non-U.S. holders. The offer to U.S. holders must be made on terms at least as favorable as those offered any other holder of the same class of securities that is the subject of the tender offers.

(iii) *Notice of extensions*. Notice of extensions made in accordance with the requirements of the home jurisdiction law or practice will satisfy the requirements of § 240.14e–1(d).

(iv) *Prompt payment*. Payment made in accordance with the requirements of the home jurisdiction law or practice will satisfy the requirements of § 240.14e–1(c).

(v) *Subsequent offering period/Withdrawal rights*. A bidder will satisfy the announcement and prompt payment requirements of § 240.14d–11(d), if the bidder announces the results of the tender offer, including the approximate number of securities deposited to date, and pays for tendered securities in accordance with the requirements of the home jurisdiction law or practice and the subsequent offering period commences immediately following such announcement. Notwithstanding section 14(d)(5) of the Act (15 U.S.C. 78n(d)(5)), the bidder need not extend withdrawal rights following the close of the offer and prior to the commencement of the subsequent offering period.

Instructions to paragraphs (c) and (d):

1. *Home jurisdiction* means both the jurisdiction of the subject company's incorporation, organization or chartering and the principal foreign market where the subject company's securities are listed or quoted.

2. *U.S. holder* means any security holder resident in the United States. Except as otherwise provided in Instruction 3 below, to determine the percentage of outstanding securities held by U.S. holders:

i. Calculate the U.S. ownership as of 30 days before the commencement of the tender offer;

ii. Include securities underlying American Depositary Shares convertible or exchangeable into the securities that are the subject of the tender offer when calculating the number of subject securities outstanding, as well as the number held by U.S. holders. Exclude from the calculations other types of securities that are convertible or exchangeable into the securities that are the subject of the tender offer, such as warrants, options and convertible securities. Exclude from those calculations securities held by persons who hold more than 10 percent of the subject securities, or that are held by the bidder;

iii. Use the method of calculating record ownership in Rule 12g3–2(a) under the Act (§ 240.12g3–2(a) of this chapter), except that your inquiry as to the amount of securities represented by accounts of customers resident in the United States may be limited to brokers, dealers, banks and other nominees located in the United States, the subject company's jurisdiction of incorporation or that of each participant in a business combination, and the jurisdiction that is the primary trading market for the subject securities, if different than the subject company's jurisdiction of incorporation;

iv. If, after reasonable inquiry, you are unable to obtain information about the amount of securities represented by accounts of customers resident in the United States, you may assume, for purposes of this definition, that the customers are residents of the jurisdiction in which the nominee has its principal place of business; and

v. Count securities as beneficially owned by residents of the United States as reported on reports of beneficial ownership that are provided to you or publicly filed and based on information otherwise provided to you.

3. In a tender offer by a bidder other than an affiliate of the issuer of the subject securities, the issuer of the subject securities will be presumed to be a foreign private issuer and U.S. holders will be presumed to hold 10 percent or less (40 percent or less in the case of 14d–1(d)) of such outstanding securities, unless:

i. The tender offer is made pursuant to an agreement with the issuer of the subject securities;

ii. The aggregate trading volume of the subject class of securities on all national securities exchanges in the United States, on the Nasdaq market, or on the OTC market, as reported to the NASD, over the 12–calendar-month period ending 30 days before commencement of the offer, exceeds 10 percent (40 percent in the case of 14d–1(d)) of the worldwide aggregate trading volume of that class of securities over the same period;

iii. The most recent annual report or annual information filed or submitted by the issuer with securities regulators of the home jurisdiction or with the Commission indicates that U.S. holders hold more than 10 percent (40 percent in the case of 14d–1(d)) of the outstanding subject class of securities; or

iv. The bidder knows or has reason to know that the level of U.S. ownership exceeds 10 percent (40 percent in the case of 14d–1(d)) of such securities.

4. *United States. United States* means the United States of America, its territories and possessions, any State of the United States, and the District of Columbia.

5. The exemptions provided by paragraphs (c) and (d) of this section are not available for any securities transaction or series of transactions that technically complies with paragraph (c) or (d) of this section but are part of a plan or scheme to evade the provisions of Regulations 14D or 14E.

(e) Notwithstanding paragraph (a) of this section, the requirements imposed by sections 14(d)(1) through 14(d)(7) of the Act [15 U.S.C. 78n(d)(1) through 78n(d)(7)], Regulation 14D promulgated thereunder (§§ 240.14d–1 through 240.14d–10), and §§ 240.14e–1 and 240.14e–2 shall not apply by virtue of the fact that a bidder for the securities of a foreign private issuer, as defined in § 240.3b–4, the subject company of such a tender offer, their representatives, or any other person specified in § 240.14d–9(d), provides any journalist with access to its press conferences held outside of the United States, to meetings with its representatives conducted outside of the United States, or to written press-related materials released outside the United States, at or in which a present or proposed tender offer is discussed, if:

(1) Access is provided to both U.S. and foreign journalists; and

(2) With respect to any written press-related materials released by the bidder or its representatives that discuss a present or proposed tender offer for equity securities registered under Section 12 of the Act [15 U.S.C. 78l], the written press-related materials must state that these written press-related materials are not an extension of a tender offer in the United States for a class of equity securities of the subject company. If the bidder intends to extend the tender offer in the United States at some future time, a statement regarding this intention, and that the procedural and filing requirements of the Williams Act will be satisfied at that time, also must be included in these written press-related materials. No means to tender securities, or coupons that could be returned to indicate interest in the tender offer, may be provided as part of, or attached to, these written press-related materials.

(f) For the purpose of § 240.14d–1(e), a bidder may presume that a target company qualifies as a foreign private issuer if the target company is a foreign issuer and files registration statements or reports on the disclosure forms specifically designated for foreign private issuers, claims the exemption from registration under the Act pursuant to § 240.12g3–2(b), or is not reporting in the United States.

(g) *Definitions.* Unless the context otherwise requires, all terms used in Regulation 14D and Regulation 14E have the same meaning as in the Act and in Rule 12b–2 promulgated thereunder. In addition, for purposes of sections 14(d) and 14(e) of the Act and Regulations 14D and 14E, the following definitions apply:

(1) The term "beneficial owner" shall have the same meaning as that set forth in Rule 13d–3: *Provided, however,* That, except with respect to Rule 14d–3, Rule 14d–9(d) and Item 6 of Schedule 14D–1, the term shall not include a person who does not have or share investment power or who is deemed to be a beneficial owner by virtue of Rule 13d–3(d)(1);

(2) The term "bidder" means any person who makes a tender offer or on whose behalf a tender offer is made: *Provided, however,* That the term does not include an issuer which makes a tender offer for securities of any class of which it is the issuer;

(3) The term "business day" means any day, other than Saturday, Sunday or a federal holiday, and shall consist of the time period from 12:01 a.m. through 12:00 midnight Eastern time. In computing any time period under section 14(d)(5) or section 14(d)(6) of the Act or under Regulation 14D or Regulation 14E, the date of the event which begins the running of such time period shall be included *except that* if such event occurs on other than a business day such period shall begin to run on and shall include the first business day thereafter; and

(4) The term "initial offering period" means the period from the time the offer commences until all minimum time periods, including extensions, required by Regulations 14D (§§ 240.14d–1 through 240.14d–103) and 14E (§§ 240.14e–1 through 240.14e–8) have been satisfied and all conditions to the offer have been satisfied or waived within these time periods.

(5) The term "security holders" means holders of record and beneficial owners of securities which are the subject of a tender offer;

(6) The term "security position listing" means, with respect to securities of any issuer held by a registered clearing agency in the name of the clearing agency or its nominee, a list of those participants in the clearing agency on whose behalf the clearing agency holds the issuer's securities and of the participants' respective positions in such securities as of a specified date.

(7) The term "subject company" means any issuer of securities which are sought by a bidder pursuant to a tender offer;

(8) The term "subsequent offering period" means the period immediately following the initial offering period meeting the conditions specified in § 240.14d–11.

(9) The term "tender offer material" means:

(i) The bidder's formal offer, including all the material terms and conditions of the tender offer and all amendments thereto;

(ii) The related transmittal letter (whereby securities of the subject company which are sought in the tender offer may be transmitted to the bidder or its depositary) and all amendments thereto; and

(iii) Press releases, advertisements, letters and other documents published by the bidder or sent or given by the bidder to security holders which, directly or indirectly, solicit, invite or request tenders of the securities being sought in the tender offer;

(h) *Signatures.* Where the Act or the rules, forms, reports or schedules thereunder require a document filed with or furnished to the Commission to be signed, such document shall be manually signed, or signed using either typed signatures or duplicated or facsimile versions of manual signatures. Where typed, duplicated or facsimile signatures are used, each signatory to the filing shall manually sign a signature page or other document authenticating, acknowledging or otherwise adopting his or her signature that appears in the filing. Such document shall be executed before or at the time the filing is made and shall be retained by the filer for a period of five years. Upon request, the filer shall furnish to the Commission or its staff a copy of any or all documents retained pursuant to this section.

Rule 14d–2. Commencement of a Tender Offer

(a) *Date of commencement.* A bidder will have commenced its tender offer for purposes of section 14(d) of the Act (15 U.S.C. 78n) and the rules under that section at 12:01 a.m. on the date when the bidder has first published, sent or given the means to tender to security holders. For purposes of this section, the means to tender includes the transmittal form or a statement regarding how the transmittal form may be obtained.

(b) *Pre-commencement communications.* A communication by the bidder will not be deemed to constitute commencement of a tender offer if:

(1) It does not include the means for security holders to tender their shares into the offer; and

(2) All written communications relating to the tender offer, from and including the first public announcement, are filed under cover of Schedule TO (§ 240.14d–100) with the Commission no later than the date of the communication. The bidder also must deliver to the subject company and any other bidder for the same class of securities the first communication relating to the transaction that is filed, or required to be filed, with the Commission.

Instructions to paragraph (b)(2):

1. The box on the front of Schedule TO indicating that the filing contains pre-commencement communications must be checked.

2. Any communications made in connection with an exchange offer registered under the Securities Act of 1933 need only be filed under § 230.425 of this chapter and will be deemed filed under this section.

3. Each pre-commencement written communication must include a prominent legend in clear, plain language advising security holders to read the tender offer statement when it is available because it contains important information. The legend also must advise investors that they can get the tender offer statement and other filed documents for free at the Commission's web site and explain which documents are free from the offeror.

4. See §§ 230.135, 230.165 and 230.166 of this chapter for pre-commencement communications made in connection with registered exchange offers.

5. "Public announcement" is any oral or written communication by the bidder, or any person authorized to act on the bidder's behalf, that is reasonably designed to, or has the effect of, informing the public or security holders in general about the tender offer.

(c) *Filing and other obligations triggered by commencement.* As soon as practicable on the date of commencement, a bidder must comply with the filing requirements of § 240.14d–3(a), the dissemination requirements of § 240.14d–4(a) or (b), and the disclosure requirements of § 240.14d–6(a).

Rule 14d–3. Filing and Transmission of Tender Offer Statement

(a) *Filing and Transmittal.* No bidder shall make a tender offer if, after consummation thereof, such bidder would be the beneficial owner of more than 5 percent of the class of the subject company's securities for which the tender offer is made, unless as soon as practicable on the date of the commencement of the tender offer such bidder:

(1) Files with the Commission Delivers a Tender Offer Statement on Schedule TO, including all exhibits thereto;

(2) Delivers a copy of such Schedule TO, including all exhibits thereto:

(i) To the subject company at its principal executive office; and

(ii) To any other bidder, which has filed a Schedule TO with the Commission relating to a tender offer which has not yet terminated for the same class of securities of the subject company, at such bidder's principal executive office or at the address of the person authorized to receive notices and communications (which is disclosed on the cover sheet of such other bidder's Schedule 14D–1);

(3) Gives telephonic notice of the information required by Rule 14d–6(e)(2)(i) and (ii) and mails by means of first class mail a copy of such Schedule TO, including all exhibits thereto:

(i) To each national securities exchange where such class of the subject company's securities is registered and listed for trading (which may be based upon information contained in the subject company's most recent Annual Report on Form 10–K filed with the Commission unless the bidder has reason to believe that such information is not current) which telephonic notice shall be made when practicable prior to the opening of each such exchange; and

(ii) To the National Association of Securities Dealers, Inc. ("NASD") if such class of the subject company's securities is authorized for quotation in the NASDAQ interdealer quotation system.

(b) *Post-Commencement Amendments and Additional Materials.* The bidder making the tender offer must file with the Commission:

(1) An amendment to Schedule TO (§ 240.14d–100) reporting promptly any material changes in the information set forth in the schedule previously filed and including copies of any additional tender offer materials as exhibits; and

(2) A final amendment to Schedule TO (§ 240.14d–100) reporting promptly the results of the tender offer.

Instruction to paragraph (b): A copy of any additional tender offer materials or amendment filed under this section must be sent promptly to the subject company and to any exchange and/or NASD, as required by paragraph (a) of this section, but in no event later than the date the materials are first published, sent or given to security holders.

(c) *Certain Announcements.* Notwithstanding the provisions of paragraph (b) of this rule, if the additional tender offer material or an amendment to Schedule TO discloses only the number of shares deposited to date, and/or announces an extension of the time during which shares may be tendered, then the bidder may file such tender offer material or amendment and send a copy of such tender offer material or amendment to the subject company, any exchange and/or the NASD, as required by paragraph (a) of this rule, promptly after the date such tender offer material is first published or sent or given to security holders.

Rule 14d–4. Dissemination of Tender Offers to Security Holders

As soon as practicable on the date of commencement of a tender offer, the bidder must publish, send or give the disclosure required by § 240.14d–6 to security holders of the class of securities that is the subject of the offer, by complying with all of the requirements of any of the following:

(a) *Cash Tender Offers and Exempt Securities Offers*. For tender offers in which the consideration consists solely of cash and/or securities exempt from registration under section 3 of the Securities Act of 1933 (15 U.S.C. 77c):

(1) *Long-Form Publication.* The bidder makes adequate publication in a newspaper or newspapers of long-form publication of the tender offer.

(2) *Summary Publication.*

(i) If the tender offer is not subject to Rule 13e–3, the bidder makes adequate publication in a newspaper or newspapers of a summary advertisement of the tender offer; and

(ii) Mails by first class mail or otherwise furnishes with reasonable promptness the bidder's tender offer materials to any security holder who requests such tender offer materials pursuant to the summary advertisement or otherwise.

(3) *Use of Stockholder Lists and Security Position Listings*. Any bidder using stockholder lists and security position listings under § 240.14d–5 must comply with paragraph (a)(1) or (2) of this section on or before the date of the bidder's request under § 240.14d–5(a).

Instruction to paragraph (a): Tender offers may be published or sent or given to security holders by other methods, but with respect to summary publication and the use of stockholder lists and security position listings under § 240.14d–5, paragraphs (a)(2) and (a)(3) of this section are exclusive.

(b) *Registered Securities Offers*. For tender offers in which the consideration consists solely or partially of securities registered under the Securities Act of 1933, a registration statement containing all of the required information, including pricing information, has been filed and a preliminary prospectus or a prospectus that meets the requirements of section 10(a) of the Securities Act (15 U.S.C. 77j(a)), including a letter of transmittal, is delivered to security holders. However, for going-private transactions (as defined by § 240.13e–3) and roll-up transactions (as described by Item 901 of Regulation S–K (§ 229.901 of this chapter)), a registration statement registering the securities to be offered must have become effective and only a prospectus that meets the requirements of section 10(a) of the Securities Act may be delivered to security holders on the date of commencement.

Instructions to paragraph (b):

1. If the prospectus is being delivered by mail, mailing on the date of commencement is sufficient.

2. A preliminary prospectus used under this section may not omit information under § 230.430 or § 230.430A of this chapter.

3. If a preliminary prospectus is used under this section and the bidder must disseminate material changes, the tender offer must remain open for the period specified in paragraph (d)(2) of this section.

4. If a preliminary prospectus is used under this section, tenders may be requested in accordance with § 230.162(a) of this chapter.

(c) *Adequate Publication.* Depending on the facts and circumstances involved, adequate publication of a tender offer pursuant to this section may require publication in a newspaper with a national circulation or may only require publication in a newspaper with metropolitan or regional circulation or may require publication in a combination thereof: *Provided, however,* That publication in all editions of a daily newspaper with a national circulation shall be deemed to constitute adequate publication.

(d) *Publication of Changes and Extension of the Offer.*

(1) If a tender offer has been published or sent or given to security holders by one or more of the methods enumerated in paragraph (a) of this section, a material change in the information published, sent or given to security holders shall be promptly disseminated to security holders in a manner reasonably designed to inform security holders of such change; *Provided, however,* That if the bidder has elected pursuant to Rule 14d–5(f)(1) of this section to require the subject company to disseminate amendments disclosing material changes to the tender offer materials pursuant to Rule 14d–5, the bidder shall disseminate material changes in the information published or sent or given to security holders at least pursuant to Rule 14–5.

(2) In a registered securities offer where the bidder disseminates the preliminary prospectus as permitted by paragraph (b) of this section, the offer must remain open from the date that material changes to the tender offer materials are disseminated to security holders, as follows:

(i) Five business days for a prospectus supplement containing a material change other than price or share levels;

(ii) Ten business days for a prospectus supplement containing a change in price, the amount of securities sought, the dealer's soliciting fee, or other similarly significant change;

(iii) Ten business days for a prospectus supplement included as part of a post-effective amendment; and

(iv) Twenty business days for a revised prospectus when the initial prospectus was materially deficient.

Rule 14d–5. Dissemination of Certain Tender Offers by the Use of Stockholder Lists and Security Position Listings

(a) *Obligations of the Subject Company.* Upon receipt by a subject company at its principal executive offices of a bidder's written request, meeting the requirements of paragraph (e) of this rule, the subject company shall comply with the following sub-paragraphs.

(1) The subject company shall notify promptly transfer agents and any other person who will assist the subject company in complying with the requirements of this section of the receipt by the subject company of a request by a bidder pursuant to this section.

(2) The subject company shall promptly ascertain whether the most recently prepared stockholder list, written or otherwise, within the access of the subject company was prepared as of a date earlier than ten business days before the date of the bidder's request and, if so, the subject company shall promptly prepare or cause to be prepared a stockholder list as of the most recent practicable date which shall not be more than ten business days before the date of the bidder's request.

(3) The subject company shall make an election to comply and shall comply with all of the provisions of either paragraph (b) or paragraph (c) of this rule. The subject company's election once made shall not be modified or revoked during the bidder's tender offer and extensions thereof.

(4) No later than the second business day after the date of the bidder's request, the subject company shall orally notify the bid-

der, which notification shall be confirmed in writing, of the subject company's election made pursuant to paragraph (a)(3) of this rule. Such notification shall indicate (i) the approximate number of security holders of the class of securities being sought by the bidder and, (ii) if the subject company elects to comply with paragraph (b) of this rule, appropriate information concerning the location for delivery of the bidder's tender offer materials and the approximate direct costs incidental to the mailing to security holders of the bidder's paragraph (g)(2) of this rule.

(b) *Mailing of Tender Offer Materials by the Subject Company.* A subject company which elects pursuant to paragraph (a)(3) of this rule to comply with the provisions of this paragraph shall perform the acts prescribed by the following subparagraphs.

(1) The subject company shall promptly contact each participant named on the most recent security position listing of any clearing agency within the access of the subject company and make inquiry of each such participant as to the approximate number of beneficial owners of the subject company securities being sought in the tender offer held by each such participant.

(2) No later than the third business day after delivery of the bidder's tender offer materials pursuant to paragraph (g)(1) of this rule, the subject company shall begin to mail or cause to be mailed by means of first class mail a copy of the bidder's tender offer materials to each person whose name appears as a record holder of the class of securities for which the offer is made on the most recent stockholder list referred to in paragraph (a)(2) of this rule. The subject company shall use its best efforts to complete the mailing in a timely manner but in no event shall such mailing be completed in a substantially greater period of time than the subject company would complete a mailing to security holders of its own materials relating to the tender offer.

(3) No later than the third business day after the delivery of the bidder's tender offer materials pursuant to paragraph (g)(1) of this rule, the subject company shall begin to transmit or cause to be transmitted a sufficient number of sets of the bidder's tender offer materials to the participants named on the security position listings described in paragraph (b)(1) of this rule. The subject company shall use its best efforts to complete the transmittal in a timely manner but in no event shall such transmittal be completed in a substantially greater period of time than the subject company would complete a transmittal to such participants pursuant to security position listings of clearing agencies of its own material relating to the tender offer.

(4) The subject company shall promptly give oral notification to the bidder, which notification shall be confirmed in writing, of the commencement of the mailing pursuant to paragraph (b)(2) of this rule and of the transmittal pursuant to paragraph (b)(3) of this rule.

(5) During the tender offer and any extension thereof the subject company shall use reasonable efforts to update the stockholder list and shall mail or cause to be mailed promptly following each update a copy of the bidder's tender offer materials (to the extent sufficient sets of such materials have been furnished by the bidder) to each person who has become a record holder since the later of (i) the date of preparation of the most recent stockholder list referred to in paragraph (a)(2) of this rule or (ii) the last preceding update.

(6) If the bidder has elected pursuant to paragraph (f)(1) of this section to require the subject company to disseminate amendments disclosing material changes to the tender offer materials pursuant to this rule, the subject company, promptly following delivery of each such amendment, shall mail or cause to be mailed a copy of each such amendment to each record holder whose name appears on the shareholder list de-

scribed in paragraphs (a)(2) and (b)(5) of this rule and shall transmit or cause to be transmitted sufficient copies of such amendment to each participant named on security position listings who received sets of the bidder's tender offer materials pursuant to paragraph (b)(3) of this rule.

(7) The subject company shall not include any communication other than the bidder's tender offer materials or amendments thereto in the envelopes or other containers furnished by the bidder.

(8) Promptly following the termination of the tender offer, the subject company shall reimburse the bidder the excess, if any, of the amounts advanced pursuant to paragraph (f)(3)(iii) over the direct costs incidental to compliance by the subject company and its agents in performing the acts required by this section computed in accordance with paragraph (g)(2) of this rule.

(c) *Delivery of Stockholder Lists and Security Position Listings.* A subject company which elects pursuant to paragraph (a)(3) of this rule to comply with the provisions of this paragraph shall perform the acts prescribed by the following subparagraphs.

(1) No later than the third business day after the date of the bidder's request, the subject company must furnish to the bidder at the subject company's principal executive office a copy of the names and addresses of the record holders on the most recent stockholder list referred to in paragraph (a)(2) of this section; the names and addresses of participants identified on the most recent security position listing of any clearing agency that is within the access of the subject company; and the most recent list of names, addresses and security positions of beneficial owners as specified in § 240.14a–13(b), in the possession of the subject company, or that subsequently comes into its possession. All security holder list information must be in the format requested by the bidder to the extent the format is available to the subject company without undue burden or expense.

(2) If the bidder has elected pursuant to paragraph (f)(1) of this rule to require the subject company to disseminate amendments disclosing material changes to the tender offer materials, the subject company shall update the stockholder list by furnishing the bidder with the name and address of each record holder named on the stockholder list, and not previously furnished to the bidder, promptly after such information becomes available to the subject company during the tender offer and any extensions thereof.

(d) *Liability of Subject Company and Others.* Neither the subject company nor any affiliate or agent of the subject company nor any clearing agency shall be:

(1) Deemed to have made a solicitation or recommendation respecting the tender offer within the meaning of section 14(d)(4) based solely upon the compliance or noncompliance by the subject company or any affiliate or agent of the subject company with one or more requirements of this rule;

(2) Liable under any provision of the Federal securities laws to the bidder or to any security holder based solely upon the inaccuracy of the current names or addresses on the stockholder list or security position listing, unless such inaccuracy results from a lack of reasonable care on the part of the subject company or any affiliate or agent of the subject company;

(3) Deemed to be an "underwriter" within the meaning of section (2)(11) of the Securities Act of 1933 for any purpose of that Act or any rule or regulation promulgated thereunder based solely upon the compliance or noncompliance by the subject company or any affiliate or agent of the subject company with one or more of the requirements of this rule;

(4) Liable under any provision of the Federal securities laws for the disclosure in the bidder's tender offer materials, including any amendment thereto, based solely upon

the compliance or noncompliance by the subject company or any affiliate or agent of the subject company with one or more of the requirements of this rule.

(e) *Content of the Bidder's Request.* The bidder's written request referred to in paragraph (a) of this section shall include the following:

(1) The identity of the bidder;

(2) The title of the class of securities which is the subject of the bidder's tender offer;

(3) A statement that the bidder is making a request to the subject company pursuant to paragraph (a) of this rule for the use of the stockholder list and security position listings for the purpose of disseminating a tender offer to security holders;

(4) A statement that the bidder is aware of and will comply with the provisions of paragraph (f) of this rule;

(5) A statement as to whether or not it has elected pursuant to paragraph (f)(1) of this section to disseminate amendments disclosing material changes to the tender offer materials pursuant to this rule; and

(6) The name, address and telephone number of the person whom the subject company shall contact pursuant to paragraph (a)(4) of this rule.

(f) *Obligations of the Bidder.* Any bidder who requests that a subject company comply with the provisions of paragraph (a) of this rule shall comply with the following sub-paragraphs.

(1) The bidder shall make an election whether or not to require the subject company to disseminate amendments disclosing material changes to the tender offer materials pursuant to this rule, which election shall be included in the request referred to in paragraph (a) of this rule and shall not be revocable by the bidder during the tender offer and extensions thereof.

(2) With respect to a tender offer subject to section 14(d)(1) of the Act in which the consideration consists solely of cash and/or securities exempt from registration under section 3 of the Securities Act of 1933, the bidder shall comply with the requirements of Rule 14d–4(a)(3).

(3) If the subject company elects to comply with paragraph (b) of this rule,

(i) The bidder shall promptly deliver the tender offer materials after receipt of the notification from the subject company as provided in paragraph (a)(4) of this rule;

(ii) The bidder shall promptly notify the subject company of any amendment to the bidder's tender offer materials requiring compliance by the subject company with paragraph (b)(6) of this rule and shall promptly deliver such amendment to the subject company pursuant to paragraph (g)(1) of this rule;

(iii) The bidder shall advance to the subject company an amount equal to the approximate cost of conducting mailings to security holders computed in accordance with paragraph (g)(2) of this rule;

(iv) The bidder shall promptly reimburse the subject company for the direct costs incidental to compliance by the subject company and its agents in performing the acts required by this rule computed in accordance with paragraph (g)(2) of this rule which are in excess of the amount advanced pursuant to paragraph (f)(2)(iii) of this rule; and

(v) The bidder shall mail by means of first class mail or otherwise furnish with reasonable promptness the tender offer materials to any security holder who requests such materials.

(4) If the subject company elects to comply with paragraph (c) of this rule,

(i) The bidder shall use the stockholder list and security position listings furnished to the bidder pursuant to paragraph (c) of this rule exclusively in the dissemination of tender offer materials to security holders in connection with the bidder's tender offer and extensions thereof;

(ii) The bidder shall return the stockholder lists and security position listings furnished to the bidder pursuant to paragraph (c) of this rule promptly after the termination of the bidder's tender offer;

(iii) The bidder shall accept, handle and return the stockholder lists and security position listings furnished to the bidder pursuant to paragraph (c) of this section to the subject company on a confidential basis;

(iv) The bidder shall not retain any stockholder list or security position listing furnished by the subject company pursuant to paragraph (c) of this rule, or any copy thereof, nor retain any information derived from any such list or listing or copy thereof after the termination of the bidder's tender offer;

(v) The bidder shall mail by means of first class mail, at its own expense, a copy of its tender offer materials to each person whose identity appears on the stockholder list as furnished and updated by the subject company pursuant to paragraphs (c)(1) and (c)(2) of this rule;

(vi) The bidder shall contact the participants named on the security position listing of any clearing agency, make inquiry of each participant as to the approximate number of sets of tender offer materials required by each such participant, and furnish, at its own expense, sufficient sets of tender offer materials and any amendment thereto to each such participant for subsequent transmission to the beneficial owners of the securities being sought by the bidder;

(vii) The bidder shall mail by means of first class mail or otherwise furnish with reasonable promptness the tender offer materials to any security holder who requests such materials; and

(viii) The bidder shall promptly reimburse the subject company for direct costs incidental to compliance by the subject company and its agents in performing the acts required by this section computed in accordance with paragraph (g)(2) of this rule.

(g) *Delivery of Materials, Computation of Direct Costs.*

(1) Whenever the bidder is required to deliver tender offer materials or amendments to tender offer materials, the bidder shall deliver to the subject company at the location specified by the subject company in its notice given pursuant to paragraph (a)(4) of this rule a number of sets of the materials or of the amendment, as the case may be, at least equal to the approximate number of security holders specified by the subject company in such notice, together with appropriate envelopes or other containers therefor; *Provided, however,* That such delivery shall be deemed not to have been made unless the bidder has complied with paragraph (f)(3)(iii) of this rule at the time the materials or amendments, as the case may be, are delivered.

(2) The approximate direct cost of mailing the bidder's tender offer materials shall be computed by adding (i) the direct cost incidental to the mailing of the subject company's last annual report to shareholders (excluding employee time), less the costs of preparation and printing of the report, and postage, plus (ii) the amount of first class postage required to mail the bidder's tender offer materials. The approximate direct costs incidental to the mailing of the amendments to the bidder's tender offer materials shall be computed by adding (iii) the estimated direct costs of preparing mailing labels, of updating shareholders lists and of third party handling charges plus (iv) the amount of first class postage required to mail the bidder's amendment. Direct costs incidental to the mailing of the bidder's ten-

der offer materials and amendments thereto when finally computed may include all reasonable charges paid by the subject company to third parties for supplies or services, including costs attendant to preparing shareholder lists, mailing labels, handling the bidder's materials, contacting participants named on security position listings and for postage, but shall exclude indirect costs, such as employee time which is devoted to either contesting or supporting the tender offer on behalf of the subject company. The final billing for direct costs shall be accompanied by an appropriate accounting in reasonable detail.

Note to § 240.14d–5. Reasonably prompt methods of distribution to security holders may be used instead of mailing. If alternative methods are chosen, the approximate direct costs of distribution shall be computed by adding the estimated direct costs of preparing the document for distribution through the chosen medium (including updating of shareholder lists) plus the estimated reasonable cost of distribution through that medium. Direct costs incidental to the distribution of tender offer materials and amendments thereto may include all reasonable charges paid by the subject company to third parties for supplies or services, including costs attendant to preparing shareholder lists, handling the bidder's materials, and contacting participants named on security position listings, but shall not include indirect costs, such as employee time which is devoted to either contesting or supporting the tender offer on behalf of the subject company.

Rule 14d–6. Disclosure of Tender Offer Information to Security Holders

(a) *Information Required on Date of Commencement.*—

(1) *Long-Form Publication.* If a tender offer is published, sent or given to security holders on the date of commencement by means of long-form publication under § 240.14d–4(a)(1), the long-form publication must include the information required by paragraph (d)(1) of this section.

(2) *Summary Publication.* If a tender offer is published, sent or given to security holders on the date of commencement by means of summary publication under § 240.14d–4(a)(2):

(i) The summary advertisement must contain at least the information required by paragraph (d)(2) of this section; and

(ii) The tender offer materials furnished by the bidder upon request of any security holder must include the information required by paragraph (d)(1) of this section.

(3) *Use of Stockholder Lists and Security Position Listings.* If a tender offer is published, sent or given to security holders on the date of commencement by the use of stockholder lists and security position listings under § 240.14d–4(a)(3):

(i) The summary advertisement must contain at least the information required by paragraph (d)(2) of this section; and

(ii) The tender offer materials transmitted to security holders pursuant to such lists and security position listings and furnished by the bidder upon the request of any security holder must include the information required by paragraph (d)(1) of this section.

(4) *Other Tender Offers.* If a tender offer is published or sent or given to security holders other than pursuant to § 240.14d–4(a), the tender offer materials that are published or sent or given to security holders on the date of commencement of such offer must include the information required by paragraph (d)(1) of this section.

(b) *Information Required in Other Tender Offer Materials Published After Commencement.* Except for tender offer materials described in paragraphs (a)(2)(ii) and (a)(3)(ii) of this section, additional tender offer materials published, sent or given to security holders after commencement must include:

(1) The identities of the bidder and subject company;

(2) The amount and class of securities being sought;

(3) The type and amount of consideration being offered; and

(4) The scheduled expiration date of the tender offer, whether the tender offer may be extended and, if so, the procedures for extension of the tender offer.

Instruction to paragraph (b): If the additional tender offer materials are summary advertisements, they also must include the information required by paragraphs (d)(2)(v) of this section.

(c) *Material Changes*. A material change in the information published or sent or given to security holders must be promptly disclosed to security holders in additional tender offer materials.

(d) *Information to Be Included.*—

(1) *Tender Offer Materials Other than Summary Publication*. The following information is required by paragraphs (a)(1), (a)(2)(ii), (a)(3)(ii) and (a)(4) of this section:

(i) The information required by Item 1 of Schedule TO (§ 240.14d–100) (Summary Term Sheet); and

(ii) The information required by the remaining items of Schedule TO (§ 240.14d–100) for third-party tender offers, except for Item 12 (exhibits) of Schedule TO (§ 240.14d–100), or a fair and adequate summary of the information.

(2) *Summary Publication*. The following information is required in a summary advertisement under paragraphs (a)(2)(i) and (a)(3)(i) of this section:

(i) The identity of the bidder and the subject company;

(ii) The information required by Item 1004(a)(1) of Regulation M–A (§ 229.1004(a)(1) of this chapter);

(iii) If the tender offer is for less than all of the outstanding securities of a class of equity securities, a statement as to whether the purpose or one of the purposes of the tender offer is to acquire or influence control of the business of the subject company;

(iv) A statement that the information required by paragraph (d)(1) of this section is incorporated by reference into the summary advertisement;

(v) Appropriate instructions as to how security holders may obtain promptly, at the bidder's expense, the bidder's tender offer materials; and

(vi) In a tender offer published or sent or given to security holders by use of stockholder lists and security position listings under § 240.14d–4(a)(3), a statement that a request is being made for such lists and listings. The summary publication also must state that tender offer materials will be mailed to record holders and will be furnished to brokers, banks and similar persons whose name appears or whose nominee appears on the list of security holders or, if applicable, who are listed as participants in a clearing agency's security position listing for subsequent transmittal to beneficial owners of such securities. If the list furnished to the bidder also included beneficial owners pursuant to § 240.14d–5(c)(1) and tender offer materials will be mailed directly to beneficial holders, include a statement to that effect.

(3) *No Transmittal Letter*. Neither the initial summary advertisement nor any subsequent summary advertisement may include a transmittal letter (the letter furnished to security holders for transmission of securities sought in the tender offer) or any amendment to the transmittal letter.

Rule 14d–7. Additional Withdrawal Rights

(a)(1) *Rights.* In addition to the provisions of section 14(d)(5) of the Act, any person who has deposited securities pursuant to a tender offer has the right to withdraw any such securities during the period such offer, request or invitation remains open.

(2) *Exemption during subsequent offering period.* Notwithstanding the provisions of section 14(d)(5) of the Act (15 U.S.C. 78n(d)(5)) and paragraph (a) of this section, the bidder need not offer withdrawal rights during a subsequent offering period.

(b) *Notice of Withdrawal.* Notice of withdrawal pursuant to this section shall be deemed to be timely upon the receipt by the bidder's depositary of a written notice of withdrawal specifying the name(s) of the tendering stockholder(s), the number or amount of the securities to be withdrawn and the name(s) in which the certificate(s) is (are) registered, if different from that of the tendering security holder(s). A bidder may impose other reasonable requirements, including certificate numbers and a signed request for withdrawal accompanied by a signature guarantee, as conditions precedent to the physical release of withdrawn securities.

Rule 14d–8. Exemption From Statutory Pro Rata Requirements

Notwithstanding the pro rata provisions of Section 14(d)(6) of the Act, if any person makes a tender offer or request or invitation for tenders, for less than all of the outstanding equity securities of a class, and if a greater number of securities are deposited pursuant thereto than such person is bound or willing to take up and pay for, the securities taken up and paid for shall be taken up and paid for as nearly as may be pro rata, disregarding fractions, according to the number of securities deposited by each depositor during the period such offer, request or invitation remains open.

Rule 14d–9. Recommendation or Solicitation by the Subject Company and Others

(a) *Pre-Commencement Communications.* A communication by a person described in paragraph (e) of this section with respect to a tender offer will not be deemed to constitute a recommendation or solicitation under this section if:

(1) The tender offer has not commenced under § 240.14d–2; and

(2) The communication is filed under cover of Schedule 14D–9 (§ 240.14d–101) with the Commission no later than the date of the communication.

Instructions to paragraph (a)(2):

1. The box on the front of Schedule 14D–9 (§ 240.14d–101) indicating that the filing contains pre-commencement communications must be checked.

2. Any communications made in connection with an exchange offer registered under the Securities Act of 1933 need only be filed under § 230.425 of this chapter and will be deemed filed under this section.

3. Each pre-commencement written communication must include a prominent legend in clear, plain language advising security holders to read the company's solicitation/recommendation statement when it is available because it contains important information. The legend also must advise investors that they can get the recommendation and other filed documents for free at the Commission's web site and explain which documents are free from the filer.

4. See §§ 230.135, 230.165 and 230.166 of this chapter for pre-commencement communications made in connection with registered exchange offers.

(b) *Post-Commencement Communications.* After commencement by a bidder under § 240.14d–2, no solicitation or recommendation to security holders may be made by any person described in paragraph (e) of this section with respect to a tender offer for such securities unless as soon as practicable on the date such solicitation or recommendation is first published or sent or given to security holders such person complies with the following:

(1) Such person shall file with the Commission a Tender Offer Solicitation/Recommendation Statement on Schedule 14D–9, including all exhibits thereto; and

(2) If such person is either the subject company or an affiliate of the subject company,

(i) Such person shall hand deliver a copy of the Schedule 14D–9 to the bidder at its principal office or at the address of the person authorized to receive notices and communications (which is set forth on the cover sheet of the bidder's Schedule TO filed with the Commission); and

(ii) Such person shall give telephonic notice (which notice to the extent possible shall be given prior to the opening of the market) of the information required by Items 1003(d) and 1012(a) of Regulation M–A and shall mail a copy of the Schedule to each national securities exchange where the class of securities is registered and listed for trading and, if the class is authorized for quotation in the NASDAQ interdealer quotation system, to the National Association of Securities Dealers, Inc. ("NASD").

(3) If such person is neither the subject company nor an affiliate of the subject company.

(i) Such person shall mail a copy of the schedule to the bidder at its principal office or at the address of the person authorized to receive notices and communications (which is set forth on the cover sheet of the bidder's Schedule TO filed with the Commission); and

(ii) Such person shall mail a copy of the Schedule to the subject company at its principal office.

(c) *Amendments.* If any material change occurs in the information set forth in the Schedule 14D–9 required by this rule, the person who filed such Schedule 14D–9 shall:

(1) File with the Commission eight copies of an amendment on Schedule 14D–9 disclosing such change promptly, but not later than the date such material is first published, sent or given to security holders; and

(2) Promptly deliver copies and give notice of the amendment in the same manner as that specified in paragraph (b)(2) or (3) of this rule, whichever is applicable; and

(3) Promptly disclose and disseminate such change in a manner reasonably designed to inform security holders of such change.

(d) *Information Required in Solicitation or Recommendation.* Any solicitation or recommendation to holders of a class of securities referred to in section 14(d)(1) of the Act with respect to a tender offer for such securities shall include the name of the person making such solicitation or recommendation and the information required by Items 1 through 8 of Schedule 14D–9 or a fair and adequate summary thereof: *Provided, however,* That such solicitation or recommendation may omit any of such information previously furnished to security holders of such class of securities by such person with respect to such tender offer.

(e) *Applicability.*

(1) Except as provided in paragraphs (e)(2) and (f) of this rule, this rule shall only apply to the following persons:

(i) The subject company, any director, officer, employee, affiliate or subsidiary of the subject company;

(ii) Any record holder or beneficial owner of any security issued by the subject company, by the bidder, or by any affiliate of either the subject company or the bidder; and

(iii) Any person who makes a solicitation or recommendation to security holders on behalf of any of the foregoing or on behalf of the bidder other than by means of a solicitation or recommendation to security holders which has been filed with the Commission pursuant to this rule or Rule 14d–3.

(2) Notwithstanding paragraph (d)(1) of this section, this section shall not apply to the following persons:

(i) A bidder who has filed a Schedule TO pursuant to Rule 14d–3;

(ii) Attorneys, banks, brokers, fiduciaries or investment advisers who are not participating in a tender offer in more than a ministerial capacity and who furnish information and/or advice regarding such tender offer to their customers or clients on the unsolicited request of such customers or clients or solely pursuant to a contract or a relationship providing for advice to the customer or client to whom the information and/or advice is given.

(iii) Any person specified in paragraph (d)(1) of this section if:

(A) The subject company is the subject of a tender offer conducted under § 240.14d–1(c);

(B) Any person specified in paragraph (e)(1) of this section furnishes to the Commission on Form CB (§ 249.480 of this chapter) the entire informational document it publishes or otherwise disseminates to holders of the class of securities in connection with the tender offer no later than the next business day after publication or dissemination;

(C) Any person specified in paragraph (e)(1) of this section disseminates any informational document to U.S. holders, including any amendments thereto, in English, on a comparable basis to that provided to security holders in the issuer's home jurisdiction; and

(D) Any person specified in paragraph (e)(1) of this section disseminates by publication in its home jurisdiction, such person must publish the information in the United States in a manner reasonably calculated to inform U.S. security holders of the offer.

(f) *Stop-Look-and-Listen Communication.* This rule shall not apply to the subject company with respect to a communication by the subject company to its security holders which only:

(1) Identifies the tender offer by the bidder;

(2) States that such tender offer is under consideration by the subject company's board of directors and/or management;

(3) States that on or before a specified date (which shall be no later than 10 business days from the date of commencement of such tender offer) the subject company will advise such security holders of (i) whether the subject company recommends acceptance or rejection of such tender offer; expresses no opinion and remains neutral toward such tender offer; or is unable to take a position with respect to such tender offer and (ii) the reason(s) for the position taken by the subject company with respect to the tender offer (including the inability to take a position); and

(4) Requests such security holders to defer making determination whether to accept or reject such tender offer until they have been advised of the subject company's position with respect thereto pursuant to paragraph (f)(3) of this rule.

(g) *Statement of Management's Position.* A statement by the subject company's of its position with respect to a tender offer which is required to be published or sent or given to security holders pursuant to Rule 14e–2 shall be deemed to constitute a solicitation or recommendation within the meaning of this section and section 14(d)(4) of the Act.

Rule 14d–10. Equal Treatment of Security Holders

(a) No bidder shall make a tender offer unless:

(1) The tender offer is open to all security holders of the class of securities subject to the tender offer; and

(2) The consideration paid to any security holder pursuant to the tender offer is the

highest consideration paid to any other security holder during such tender offer.

(b) Paragraph (a)(1) of this rule shall not:

(1) Affect dissemination under Rule 14d–4; or

(2) Prohibit a bidder from making a tender offer excluding all security holders in a state where the bidder is prohibited from making the tender offer by administrative or judicial action pursuant to a state statute after a good faith effort by the bidder to comply with such statute.

(c) Paragraph (a)(2) of this rule shall not prohibit the offer of more than one type of consideration in a tender offer, provided that:

(1) Security holders are afforded equal right to elect among each of the types of consideration offered; and

(2) The highest consideration of each type paid to any security holder is paid to any other security holder receiving that type of consideration.

(d) If the offer and sale of securities constituting consideration offered in a tender offer is prohibited by the appropriate authority of a state after a good faith effort by the bidder to register or qualify the offer and sale of such securities in such state:

(1) The bidder may offer security holders in such state an alternative form of consideration; and

(2) Paragraph (c) of this rule shall not operate to require the bidder to offer or pay the alternative form of consideration to security holders in any other state.

(e) This section shall not apply to any tender offer with respect to which the Commission, upon written request or upon its own motion, either unconditionally or on specified terms and conditions, determines that compliance with this rule is not necessary or appropriate in the public interest or for the protection of investors.

Rule 14d–11 Subsequent Offering Period

A bidder may elect to provide a subsequent offering period of three business days to 20 business days during which tenders will be accepted if:

(a) The initial offering period of at least 20 business days has expired;

(b) The offer is for all outstanding securities of the class that is the subject of the tender offer, and if the bidder is offering security holders a choice of different forms of consideration, there is no ceiling on any form of consideration offered;

(c) The bidder immediately accepts and promptly pays for all securities tendered during the initial offering period;

(d) The bidder announces the results of the tender offer, including the approximate number and percentage of securities deposited to date, no later than 9:00 a.m. Eastern time on the next business day after the expiration date of the initial offering period and immediately begins the subsequent offering period;

(e) The bidder immediately accepts and promptly pays for all securities as they are tendered during the subsequent offering period; and

(f) The bidder offers the same form and amount of consideration to security holders in both the initial and the subsequent offering period.

Note § 240.14d–11: No withdrawal rights apply during the subsequent offering period in accordance with § 240.14d–7(a)(2).

Schedule TO. Tender Offer Statement Under Section 14(d)(1) or 13(e)(1) of the Securities Exchange Act of 1934

Securities and Exchange Commission,

Washington, D.C. 20549

Schedule TO

Tender Offer Statement under Section 14(d)(1) or 13(e)(1) of the Securities Exchange Act of 1934
(Amendment No. ______)*

____

(Name of Subject Company (issuer))

____

(Names of Filing Persons (identifying status as offeror, issuer or other person))

____

(Title of Class of Securities)

____

(CUSIP Number of Class of Securities)

(Name, address, and telephone numbers of person authorized to receive notices and communications on behalf of filing persons)

Calculation of Filing Fee

Transaction Valuation *	Amount of Filing Fee

* Set forth the amount on which the filing fee is calculated and state how it was determined.

[ ] Check the box if any part of the fee is offset as provided by Rule 0–11(a)(2) and identify the filing with which the offsetting fee was previously paid. Identify the previous filing by registration statement number, or the Form or Schedule and the date of its filing.

Amount Previously Paid: ______________

Form or Registration No.: ______________

Filing Party: ______________

Date Filed: ______________

[ ] Check the box if the filing relates solely to preliminary communications made before the commencement of a tender offer.

Check the appropriate boxes below to designate any transactions to which the statement relates:

[ ] third-party tender offer subject to Rule 14d–1.

[ ] issuer tender offer subject to Rule 13e–4.

[ ] going-private transaction subject to Rule 13e–3.

[ ] amendment to Schedule 13D under Rule 13d–2.

Check the following box if the filing is a final amendment reporting the results of the tender offer: [ ]

General Instructions:

A. File eight copies of the statement, including all exhibits, with the Commission if paper filing is permitted.

B. This filing must be accompanied by a fee payable to the Commission as required by § 240.0–11.

C. If the statement is filed by a general or limited partnership, syndicate or other group, the information called for by Items 3 and 5–8 for a third-party tender offer and Items 5–8 for an issuer tender offer must be given with respect to: (i) Each partner of the general partnership; (ii) each partner who is, or functions as, a general partner of the limited partnership; (iii) each member of the syndicate or group; and (iv) each person controlling the partner or member. If the statement is filed by a corporation or if a person referred to in (i), (ii), (iii) or (iv) of this Instruction is a corporation, the information called for by the items specified above must be given with respect to: (a) Each executive officer and director of the corporation; (b) each person controlling the corporation; and (c) each executive officer and director of any corporation or other person ultimately in control of the corporation.

D. If the filing contains only preliminary communications made before the commencement of a tender offer, no signature or filing fee is required. The filer need not respond to the items in the schedule. Any pre-commencement communications that are filed under cover of this schedule need not be incorporated by reference into the schedule.

E. If an item is inapplicable or the answer is in the negative, so state. The statement published, sent or given to security holders may omit negative and not applicable responses. If the schedule includes any information that is not published, sent or given to security holders, provide that information or specifically incorporate it by reference under the appropriate item number and heading in the schedule. Do not recite the text of disclosure requirements in the schedule or any document published, sent or given to security holders. Indicate clearly the coverage of the requirements without referring to the text of the items.

F. Information contained in exhibits to the statement may be incorporated by reference in answer or partial answer to any item unless it would render the answer misleading, incomplete, unclear or confusing. A copy of any information that is incorporated by reference or a copy of the pertinent pages of a document containing the information must be submitted with this statement as an exhibit, unless it was previously filed with the Commission electronically on EDGAR. If an exhibit contains information responding to more than one item in the schedule, all information in that exhibit may be incorporated by reference once in response to the several items in the schedule for which it provides an answer. Information incorporated by reference is deemed filed with the Commission for all purposes of the Act.

G. A filing person may amend its previously filed Schedule 13D (§ 240.13d–101) on Schedule TO (§ 240.14d–100) if the appropriate box on the cover page is checked to indicate a combined filing and the information called for by the fourteen disclosure items on the cover page of Schedule 13D (§ 240.13d–101) is provided on the cover page of the combined filing with respect to each filing person.

H. The final amendment required by § 240.14d–3(b)(2) and § 240.13e–4(c)(4) will satisfy the reporting requirements of section 13(d) of the Act with respect to all securities acquired by the offeror in the tender offer.

I. Amendments disclosing a material change in the information set forth in this statement may omit any information previously disclosed in this statement.

J. If the tender offer disclosed on this statement involves a going-private transaction, a combined Schedule TO (§ 240.14d–100) and Schedule 13E–3 (§ 240.13e–100) may be filed with the Commission under cover of Schedule TO. The Rule 13e–3 box on the cover page of the Schedule TO must be checked to indicate a combined filing. All information called for by both schedules must be provided except that Items 1—3, 5, 8 and 9 of Schedule TO may be omitted to the extent those items call for information that duplicates the item requirements in Schedule 13E–3.

K. For purposes of this statement, the following definitions apply:

(1) The term offeror means any person who makes a tender offer or on whose behalf a tender offer is made;

(2) The term issuer tender offer has the same meaning as in Rule 13e–4(a)(2); and

(3) The term third-party tender offer means a tender offer that is not an issuer tender offer.

Special Instructions for Complying With Schedule TO

Under Sections 13(e), 14(d) and 23 of the Act and the rules and regulations of the Act, the Commission is authorized to solicit the information required to be supplied by this schedule.

Disclosure of the information specified in this schedule is mandatory, except for I.R.S. identification numbers, disclosure of which is voluntary. The information will be used for the primary purpose of disclosing tender offer and going-private transactions. This statement will be made a matter of public record. Therefore, any information given will be available for inspection by any member of the public.

Because of the public nature of the information, the Commission can use it for a variety of purposes, including referral to other governmental authorities or securities self-regulatory organizations for investigatory purposes or in connection with litigation involving the Federal securities laws or other civil, criminal or regulatory statutes or provisions. I.R.S. identification numbers, if furnished, will assist the Commission in identifying security holders and, therefore, in promptly processing tender offer and going-private statements.

Failure to disclose the information required by this schedule, except for I.R.S. identification numbers, may result in civil or criminal action against the persons involved for violation of the Federal securities laws and rules.

Item 1. Summary Term Sheet

Furnish the information required by Item 1001 of Regulation M–A (§ 229.1001 of this chapter) unless information is disclosed to security holders in a prospectus that meets the requirements of § 230.421(d) of this chapter.

Item 2. Subject Company Information

Furnish the information required by Item 1002(a) through (c) of Regulation M-A (§ 229.1002 of this chapter).

Item 3. Identity and Background of Filing Person

Furnish the information required by Item 1003(a) through (c) of Regulation M-A (§ 229.1003 of this chapter) for a third-party tender offer and the information required by Item 1003(a) of Regulation M–A (§ 229.1003 of this chapter) for an issuer tender offer.

Item 4. Terms of the Transaction

Furnish the information required by Item 1004(a) of Regulation M–A (§ 229.1004 of this chapter) for a third-party tender offer and the information required by Item 1004(a) through (b) of Regulation M–A (§ 229.1004 of this chapter) for an issuer tender offer.

Item 5. Past Contacts, Transactions, Negotiations and Agreements

Furnish the information required by Item 1005(a) and (b) of Regulation M–A (§ 229.1005 of this chapter) for a third-party tender offer and the information required by Item 1005(e) of Regulation M–A (§ 229.1005) for an issuer tender offer.

Item 6. Purposes of the Transaction and Plans or Proposals

Furnish the information required by Item 1006(a) and (c)(1) through (7) of Regulation M–A (§ 229.1006 of this chapter) for a third-party tender offer and the information required by Item 1006(a) through (c) of Regulation M–A (§ 229.1006 of this chapter) for an issuer tender offer.

Item 7. Source and Amount of Funds or Other Consideration

Furnish the information required by Item 1007(a), (b) and (d) of Regulation M-A (§ 229.1007 of this chapter).

Item 8. Interest in Securities of the Subject Company

Furnish the information required by Item 1008 of Regulation M–A (§ 229.1008 of this chapter).

Item 9. Persons/Assets, Retained, Employed, Compensated or Used

Furnish the information required by Item 1009(a) of Regulation M–A (§ 229.1009 of this chapter).

Item 10. Financial Statements

If material, furnish the information required by Item 1010(a) and (b) of Regulation M–A (§ 229.1010 of this chapter) for the issuer in an issuer tender offer and for the offeror in a third-party tender offer.

Instructions to Item 10:

1. Financial statements must be provided when the offeror's financial condition is material to security holder's decision whether to sell, tender or hold the securities sought. The facts and circumstances of a tender offer, particularly the terms of the tender offer, may influence a determination as to whether finan-

cial statements are material, and thus required to be disclosed.

2. Financial statements are not considered material when: (a) The consideration offered consists solely of cash; (b) the offer is not subject to any financing condition; and either: (c) the offeror is a public reporting company under Section 13(a) or 15(d) of the Act that files reports electronically on EDGAR, or (d) the offer is for all outstanding securities of the subject class. Financial information may be required, however, in a two-tier transaction. See Instruction 5 below.

3. The filing person may incorporate by reference financial statements contained in any document filed with the Commission, solely for the purposes of this schedule, if: (a) The financial statements substantially meet the requirements of this item; (b) an express statement is made that the financial statements are incorporated by reference; (c) the information incorporated by reference is clearly identified by page, paragraph, caption or otherwise; and (d) if the information incorporated by reference is not filed with this schedule, an indication is made where the information may be inspected and copies obtained. Financial statements that are required to be presented in comparative form for two or more fiscal years or periods may not be incorporated by reference unless the material incorporated by reference includes the entire period for which the comparative data is required to be given. See General Instruction F to this schedule.

4. If the offeror in a third-party tender offer is a natural person, and such person's financial information is material, disclose the net worth of the offeror. If the offeror's net worth is derived from material amounts of assets that are not readily marketable or there are material guarantees and contingencies, disclose the nature and approximate amount of the individual's net worth that consists of illiquid assets and the magnitude of any guarantees or contingencies that may negatively affect the natural person's net worth.

5. Pro forma financial information is required in a negotiated third-party cash tender offer when securities are intended to be offered in a subsequent merger or other transaction in which remaining target securities are acquired and the acquisition of the subject company is significant to the offeror under § 210.11–01(b)(1) of this chapter. The offeror must disclose the financial information specified in Item 3(f) and Item 5 of Form S–4 (§ 239.25 of this chapter) in the schedule filed with the Commission, but may furnish only the summary financial information specified in Item 3(d), (e) and (f) of Form S–4 in the disclosure document sent to security holders. If pro forma financial information is required by this instruction, the historical financial statements specified in Item 1010 of Regulation M–A (§ 229.1010 of this chapter) are required for the bidder.

6. The disclosure materials disseminated to security holders may contain the summarized financial information specified by Item 1010(c) of Regulation M–A (§ 229.1010 of this chapter) instead of the financial information required by Item 1010(a) and (b). In that case, the financial information required by Item 1010(a) and (b) of Regulation M–A must be disclosed in the statement. If summarized financial information is disseminated to security holders, include appropriate instructions on how more complete financial information can be obtained. If the summarized financial information is prepared on the basis of a comprehensive body of accounting principles other than U.S. GAAP, the summarized financial information must be accompanied by a reconciliation as described in Instruction 8 of this Item.

7. If the offeror is not subject to the periodic reporting requirements of the Act, the financial statements required by this Item need not be audited if audited financial statements are not available or obtainable without unreasonable cost or expense. Make a statement to that effect and the reasons for their unavailability.

8. If the financial statements required by this Item are prepared on the basis of a comprehensive body of accounting principles other than U.S. GAAP, provide a reconciliation to U.S. GAAP in accordance with Item 17 of Form 20–F (§ 249.220f of this chapter), unless a reconciliation is unavailable or not obtainable without unreasonable cost or expense. At a minimum, however, when financial statements are prepared on a basis other than U.S. GAAP, a narrative description of all material variations in accounting principles, practices and methods used in preparing the non-U.S. GAAP financial statements from those accepted in the U.S. must be presented.

Item 11. Additional Information

Furnish the information required by Item 1011 of Regulation M–A (§ 229.1011 of this chapter).

Item 12. Exhibits

File as an exhibit to the Schedule all documents specified by Item 1016 (a), (b), (d), (g) and (h) of Regulation M–A (§ 229.1016 of this chapter).

Item 13. Information Required by Schedule 13E–3

If the Schedule TO is combined with Schedule 13E–3 (§ 240.13e–100), set forth the information required by Schedule 13E–3 that is not included or covered by the items in Schedule TO.

Signature. After due inquiry and to the best of my knowledge and belief, I certify that the information set forth in this statement is true, complete and correct.

____

(Signature)

____

(Name and title)

____

(Date)

Instruction to Signature: The statement must be signed by the filing person or that person's authorized representative. If the statement is signed on behalf of a person by an authorized representative (other than an executive officer of a corporation or general partner of a partnership), evidence of the representative's authority to sign on behalf of the person must be filed with the statement. The name and any title of each person who signs the statement must be typed or printed beneath the signature. See §§ 240.12b–11 and 240.14d–1(f) with respect to signature requirements.

Schedule 14D–9.

Securities and Exchange Commission,

Washington, D.C. 20549

Schedule 14D–9

Solicitation/Recommendation Statement under Section 14(d)(4) of the Securities Exchange Act of 1934

(Amendment No. __)

____

(Name of Subject Company)

____

(Names of Persons Filing Statement)

____

(Title of Class of Securities)

____

(CUSIP Number of Class of Securities)

____

(Name, address, and telephone numbers of person authorized to receive notices and communications on behalf of the persons filing statement)

[ ] Check the box if the filing relates solely to preliminary communications made before the commencement of a tender offer.

General Instructions:

A. File eight copies of the statement, including all exhibits, with the Commission if paper filing is permitted.

B. If the filing contains only preliminary communications made before the commencement of a tender offer, no signature is required. The filer need not respond to the items in the schedule. Any pre-commencement communications that are filed under cover of this schedule need not be incorporated by reference into the schedule.

C. If an item is inapplicable or the answer is in the negative, so state. The statement published, sent or given to security holders may omit negative and not applicable responses. If the schedule includes any information that is not published, sent or given to security holders, provide that information or specifically incorporate it by reference under the appropriate item number and heading in the schedule. Do not recite the text of disclosure requirements in the schedule or any document published, sent or given to security holders. Indicate clearly the coverage of the requirements without referring to the text of the items.

D. Information contained in exhibits to the statement may be incorporated by reference in answer or partial answer to any item unless it would render the answer misleading, incomplete, unclear or confusing. A copy of any information that is incorporated by reference or a copy of the pertinent pages of a document containing the information must be submitted with this statement as an exhibit, unless it was previously filed with the Commission electronically on EDGAR. If an exhibit contains information responding to more than one item in the schedule, all information in that exhibit may be incorporated by reference once in response to the several items in the schedule for which it provides an answer. Information incorporated by reference is deemed filed with the Commission for all purposes of the Act.

E. Amendments disclosing a material change in the information set forth in this statement may omit any information previously disclosed in this statement.

Item 1. Subject Company Information

Furnish the information required by Item 1002(a) and (b) of Regulation M–A (§ 229.1002 of this chapter).

Item 2. Identity and Background of Filing Person

Furnish the information required by Item 1003(a) and (d) of Regulation M–A (§ 229.1003 of this chapter).

Item 3. Past Contacts, Transactions, Negotiations and Agreements

Furnish the information required by Item 1005(d) of Regulation M–A (§ 229.1005 of this chapter).

Item 4. The Solicitation or Recommendation

Furnish the information required by Item 1012(a) through (c) of Regulation M-A (§ 229.1012 of this chapter).

Item 5. Person/Assets, Retained, Employed, Compensated or Used

Furnish the information required by Item 1009(a) of Regulation M–A (§ 229.1009 of this chapter).

Item 6. Interest in Securities of the Subject Company

Furnish the information required by Item 1008(b) of Regulation M–A (§ 229.1008 of this chapter).

Item 7. Purposes of the Transaction and Plans or Proposals

Furnish the information required by Item 1006(d) of Regulation M–A (§ 229.1006 of this chapter).

Item 8. Additional Information

Furnish the information required by Item 1011(b) of Regulation M–A (§ 229.1011 of this chapter).

Item 9. Exhibits

File as an exhibit to the Schedule all documents specified by Item 1016(a), (e) and (g) of Regulation M–A (§ 229.1016 of this chapter).

Signature. After due inquiry and to the best of my knowledge and belief, I certify that the information set forth in this statement is true, complete and correct.

____

(Signature)

____

(Name and title)

____

(Date)

Instruction to Signature: The statement must be signed by the filing person or that person's authorized representative. If the statement is signed on behalf of a person by an authorized representative (other than an executive officer of a corporation or general partner of a partnership), evidence of the representative's authority to sign on behalf of the person must be filed with the statement. The name and any title of each person who signs the statement must be typed or printed beneath the signature. See § 240.14d–1(f) with respect to signature requirements.

Note: For the scope of and definitions applicable to Regulation 14E, refer to § 240.14d–1.

REGULATION 14E

Rule 14e–1. Unlawful Tender Offer Practices

As a means reasonably designed to prevent fraudulent, deceptive or manipulative acts or practices within the meaning of section 14(e) of the Act, no person who makes a tender offer shall:

(a) Hold such tender offer open for less than twenty business days from the date such tender offer is first published or sent or given to security holders; *provided, however,* that if the tender offer involves a roll-up transaction as defined in Item 901(c) of Regulation S–K and the securities being offered are registered (or authorized to be registered) on Form S–4 or Form F–4, the offer shall not be open for less than sixty calendar days from the date the tender offer is first published or sent to security holders;

(b) Increase or decrease the percentage of the class of securities being sought or the consideration offered or the dealer's soliciting fee to be given in a tender offer unless such tender offer remains open for at least ten business days from the date that notice of such increase or decrease is first published or sent or given to security holders;

Provided, however, That, for purposes of this paragraph, the acceptance for payment by the bidder of an additional amount of securities not to exceed two percent of the class of securities that is the subject of the tender offer shall not be deemed to be an increase. For purposes of this paragraph, the percentage of a class of securities shall be calculated in accordance with section 14(d)(3) of the Act.

(c) Fail to pay the consideration offered or return the securities deposited by or on behalf of security holders promptly after the termination or withdrawal of a tender offer. This paragraph does not prohibit a bidder electing to offer a subsequent offering period under § 240.14d–11 from paying for securities during the subsequent offering period in accordance with that section.

(d) Extend the length of a tender offer without issuing a notice of such extension by press release or other public announcement, which notice shall include disclosure of the approximate number of securities deposited to date and shall be issued no later than the earlier of (i) 9:00 a.m. Eastern time, on the next business day after the scheduled expiration date of the offer or (ii), if the class of securities which is the subject of the tender offer is registered on one or more national securities exchanges, the first opening of any one of such exchanges on the next business day after the scheduled expiration date of the offer.

(e) The periods of time required by paragraphs (a) and (b) of this section shall be tolled for any period during which the bidder has failed to file in electronic format, absent a hardship exemption (§§ 232.201 and 232.202 of this chapter), the Schedule 14D–1 Tender Offer Statement (§ 240.14d–100 of this chapter), any tender offer material specified in paragraph (a) of Item 11 of that Schedule, and any amendments thereto. If such documents were filed in paper pursuant to a hardship exemption (see § 232.201 and § 232.202(d) of this chapter), the minimum offering periods shall be tolled for any period during which a required confirming electronic copy of such Schedule and tender offer material is delinquent.

Rule 14e–2. Position of Subject Company With Respect to a Tender Offer

(a) *Position of Subject Company*. As a means reasonably designed to prevent fraudulent, deceptive or manipulative acts or practices within the meaning of section 14(e) of the Act, the subject company, no later than 10 business days from the date the tender offer is first published or sent or given, shall publish, send or give to security holders a statement disclosing that the subject company:

(1) Recommends acceptance or rejection of the bidder's tender offer;

(2) Expresses no opinion and is remaining neutral toward the bidder's tender offer; or

(3) Is unable to take a position with respect to the bidder's tender offer.

Such statement shall also include the reason(s) for the position (including the inability to take a position) disclosed therein.

(b) *Material Change*. If any material change occurs in the disclosure required by paragraph (a) of this section, the subject company shall promptly publish, send or give a statement disclosing such material charge to security holders.

(c) Any issuer, a class of the securities of which is the subject of a tender offer filed with the Commission on Schedule 14D–1F and conducted in reliance upon and in conformity with Rule 14d–1(b) under the Act, and any director or officer of such issuer where so required by the laws, regulations and policies of Canada and/or any of its provinces or territories, in lieu of the statements called for by paragraph (a) of this rule and Rule 14d–9 under the Act, shall file with the Commission on Schedule 14D–9F the entire disclosure document(s) required to be furnished to holders of securities of the subject issuer by the laws, regulations and policies of Canada and/or any of its provinces or territories governing the conduct of the tender offer, and shall disseminate such document(s) in the United States in accordance with such laws, regulations and policies.

(d) *Exemption for cross-border tender offers*. The subject company shall be exempt from this section with respect to a tender offer conducted under § 240.14d–1(c).

Rule 14e–3. Transactions in Securities on the Basis of Material, Nonpublic Information in the Context of Tender Offers

(a) If any person has taken a substantial step or steps to commence, or has commenced, a tender offer (the "offering person"), it shall constitute a fraudulent, deceptive or manipulative act or practice within the meaning of section 14(e) of the Act for any other person who is in possession of material information relating to such tender offer which information he knows or has reason to know is nonpublic and which he knows or has reason to know has been acquired directly or indirectly from (1) the offering person, (2) the issuer of the securities sought or to be sought by such tender offer, or (3) any officer, director, partner or employee or any other person acting on behalf of the offering person or such issuer, to purchase or sell or cause to be purchased or sold any of such securities or any securities convertible into or exchangeable for any such securities or any option or right to obtain or to dispose of any of the foregoing securities, unless within a reasonable time prior to any purchase or sale such information and its source are publicly disclosed by press release or otherwise.

(b) A person other than a natural person shall not violate paragraph (a) of this rule if such person shows that:

(1) The individual(s) making the investment decision on behalf of such person to purchase or sell any security described in paragraph (a) or to cause any such security to be purchased or sold by or on behalf of others did not know the material, nonpublic information; and

(2) Such person had implemented one or a combination of policies and procedures, reasonable under the circumstances, taking into consideration the nature of the person's business, to ensure that individual(s) making investment decision(s) would not violate paragraph (a), which policies and procedures may include, but are not limited to, (i) those which restrict any purchase, sale and causing any purchase and sale of any such security or (ii) those which prevent such individual(s) from knowing such information.

(c) Notwithstanding anything in paragraph (a) to the contrary, the following transactions shall not be violations of paragraph (a) of this rule:

(1) Purchase(s) of any security described in paragraph (a) by a broker or by another agent on behalf of an offering person; or

(2) Sale(s) by any person of any security described in paragraph (a) to the offering person.

(d)(1) As a means reasonably designed to prevent fraudulent, deceptive or manipulative acts or practices within the meaning of section 14(e) of the Act, it shall be unlawful for any person described in paragraph (d)(2) of this rule to communicate material, nonpublic information relating to a tender offer to any other person under circumstances in which it is reasonably foreseeable that such communication is likely to result in a violation of this section *except* that this paragraph shall not apply to a communication made in good faith.

(i) To the officers, directors, partners or employees of the offering person, to its advisors or to other persons, involved in the planning, financing, preparation or execution of such tender offer;

(ii) To the issuer whose securities are sought or to be sought by such tender offer, to its officers, directors, partners, employees or advisors or to other persons, involved in the planning, financing, preparation or execution of the activities of the issuer with respect to such tender offer; or

(iii) To any person pursuant to a requirement of any statute or rule or regulation promulgated thereunder.

(2) The persons referred to in paragraph (d)(1) of this rule are:

(i) The offering person or its officers, directors, partners, employees or advisors;

(ii) The issuer of the securities sought or to be sought by such tender offer or its officers, directors, partners, employees or advisors;

(iii) Anyone acting on behalf of the persons in paragraph (d)(2)(i) of this rule or the issuer or persons in paragraph (d)(2)(ii) of this rule; and

(iv) Any person in possession of material information relating to a tender offer which information he knows or has reason to know is nonpublic and which he knows or has reason to know has been acquired directly or indirectly from any of the above.

Rule 14e–4. Prohibited Transactions in Connection With Partial Tender Offers

(a) Definitions. For purposes of this rule:

(1) The amount of a person's "net long position" in a subject security shall equal

the excess, if any, of such person's "long position" over such person's "short position." For the purposes of determining the net long position as of the end of the proration period and for tendering concurrently to two or more partial tender offers, securities that have been tendered in accordance with the rule and not withdrawn are deemed to be part of the person's long position.

(i) Such person's "long position," is the amount of subject securities that such person:

(A) or his agent has title to or would have title to but for having lent such securities; or

(B) has purchased, or has entered into an unconditional contract, binding on both parties thereto, to purchase but has not yet received; or

(C) has exercised a standardized call option for; or

(D) has converted, exchanged, or exercised an equivalent security for; or

(E) is entitled to receive upon conversion, exchange, or exercise of an equivalent security.

(ii) Such person's "short position," is the amount of subject securities or subject securities underlying equivalent securities that such person:

(A) has sold, or has entered into an unconditional contract, binding on both parties thereto, to sell; or

(B) has borrowed; or

(C) has written a non-standardized call option, or granted any other right pursuant to which his shares may be tendered by another person; or

(D) is obligated to deliver upon exercise of a standardized option sold on or after the date that a tender offer is first publicly announced or otherwise made known by the bidder to holders of the security to be acquired, if the exercise price of such option is lower than the highest tender offer price or stated amount of the consideration offered for the subject security. For the purpose of this paragraph, if one or more tender offers for the same security are ongoing on such date, the announcement date shall be that of the first announced offer.

(2) The term "equivalent security" means (i) any security (including any option, warrant, or other right to purchase the subject security), issued by the person whose securities are the subject of the offer, that is immediately convertible into, or exchangeable or exercisable for, a subject security, or (ii) any other right or option (other than a standardized call option) that entitles the holder thereto to acquire a subject security, but only if the holder thereof reasonably believes that the maker or writer of the right or option has title to and possession of the subject security and upon exercise will promptly deliver the subject security.

(3) The term "subject security" means a security that is the subject of any tender offer or request or invitation for tenders.

(4) For purposes of this rule, a person shall be deemed to "tender" a security if he (i) delivers a subject security pursuant to an offer, (ii) causes such delivery to be made, (iii) guarantees delivery of a subject security pursuant to a tender offer, (iv) causes a guarantee of such delivery to be given by another person, or (v) uses any other method by which acceptance of a tender offer may be made.

(5) The term "partial tender offer" means a tender offer or request or invitation for tenders for less than all of the outstanding securities subject to the offer in which tenders are accepted either by lot or on a *pro rata* basis for a specified period, or a tender offer for all of the outstanding shares that offers a choice of consideration in which tenders for different forms of consideration may be accepted either by lot or on a *pro rata* basis for a specified period.

(6) The term "standardized call option" means any call option that is traded on an exchange, or for which quotation information is disseminated in an electronic interdealer quotation system of a registered national securities association.

(b) It shall be unlawful for any person acting alone or in concert with others, directly or indirectly, to tender any subject security in a partial tender offer:

(1) For his own account unless at the time of tender, and at the end of the proration period or period during which securities are accepted by lot (including any extensions thereof), he has a net long position equal to or greater than the amount tendered in (i) the subject security and will deliver or cause to be delivered such security for the purpose of tender to the person making the offer within the period specified in the offer; or (ii) an equivalent security and, upon the acceptance of his tender will acquire the subject security by conversion, exchange, or exercise of such equivalent security to the extent required by the terms of the offer, and will deliver or cause to be delivered the subject security so acquired for the purpose of tender to the person making the offer within the period specified in the offer; or

(2) For the account of another person unless the person making the tender (i) possesses the subject security or an equivalent security, or (ii) has a reasonable belief that, upon information furnished by the person on whose behalf the tender is made, such person owns the subject security or an equivalent security and will promptly deliver the subject security or such equivalent security for the purpose of tender to the person making the tender.

(c) This rule shall not prohibit any transaction or transactions which the Commission, upon written request or upon its own motion, exempts, either unconditionally or on specified terms and conditions.

Rule 14e–5. Prohibiting Purchases Outside of a Tender Offer

(a) *Unlawful Activity*. As a means reasonably designed to prevent fraudulent, deceptive or manipulative acts or practices in connection with a tender offer for equity securities, no covered person may directly or indirectly purchase or arrange to purchase any subject securities or any related securities except as part of the tender offer. This prohibition applies from the time of public announcement of the tender offer until the tender offer expires. This prohibition does not apply to any purchases or arrangements to purchase made during the time of any subsequent offering period as provided for in § 240.14d–11 if the consideration paid or to be paid for the purchases or arrangements to purchase is the same in form and amount as the consideration offered in the tender offer.

(b) *Excepted Activity*. The following transactions in subject securities or related securities are not prohibited by paragraph (a) of this section:

(1) *Exercises of Securities*. Transactions by covered persons to convert, exchange, or exercise related securities into subject securities, if the covered person owned the related securities before public announcement;

(2) *Purchases for Plans*. Purchases or arrangements to purchase by or for a plan that are made by an agent independent of the issuer;

(3) *Purchases During Odd-lot Offers*. Purchases or arrangements to purchase if the tender offer is excepted under § 240.13e–4(h)(5);

(4) *Purchases as Intermediary*. Purchases by or through a dealer-manager or its affiliates that are made in the ordinary course of business and made either:

(i) On an agency basis not for a covered person; or

(ii) As principal for its own account if the dealer-manager or its affiliate is not a market maker, and the purchase is made to offset a contemporaneous sale after having received an unsolicited order to buy from a customer who is not a covered person;

(5) *Basket Transactions*. Purchases or arrangements to purchase a basket of securities containing a subject security or a related security if the following conditions are satisfied:

(i) The purchase or arrangement to purchase is made in the ordinary course of business and not to facilitate the tender offer;

(ii) The basket contains 20 or more securities; and

(iii) Covered securities and related securities do not comprise more than 5% of the value of the basket;

(6) *Covering Transactions*. Purchases or arrangements to purchase that are made to satisfy an obligation to deliver a subject security or a related security arising from a short sale or from the exercise of an option by a non-covered person if:

(i) The short sale or option transaction was made in the ordinary course of business and not to facilitate the offer;

(ii) In the case of a short sale, the short sale was entered into before public announcement of the tender offer; and

(iii) In the case of an exercise of an option, the covered person wrote the option before public announcement of the tender offer;

(7) *Purchases Pursuant to Contractual Obligations*. Purchases or arrangements to purchase pursuant to a contract if the following conditions are satisfied:

(i) The contract was entered into before public announcement of the tender offer;

(ii) The contract is unconditional and binding on both parties; and

(iii) The existence of the contract and all material terms including quantity, price and parties are disclosed in the offering materials;

(8) *Purchases or Arrangements to Purchase by an Affiliate of the Dealer-Manager*. Purchases or arrangements to purchase by an affiliate of a dealer-manager if the following conditions are satisfied:

(i) The dealer-manager maintains and enforces written policies and procedures reasonably designed to prevent the flow of information to or from the affiliate that might result in a violation of the federal securities laws and regulations;

(ii) The dealer-manager is registered as a broker or dealer under Section 15(a) of the Act;

(iii) The affiliate has no officers (or persons performing similar functions) or employees (other than clerical, ministerial, or support personnel) in common with the dealer-manager that direct, effect, or recommend transactions in securities; and

(iv) The purchases or arrangements to purchase are not made to facilitate the tender offer;

(9) *Purchases by Connected Exempt Market Makers or Connected Exempt Principal Traders*. Purchases or arrangements to purchase if the following conditions are satisfied:

(i) The issuer of the subject security is a foreign private issuer, as defined in § 240.3b-4(c);

(ii) The tender offer is subject to the United Kingdom's City Code on Takeovers and Mergers;

(iii) The purchase or arrangement to purchase is effected by a connected exempt market maker or a connected exempt principal trader, as those terms are used in the United Kingdom's City Code on Takeovers and Mergers;

(iv) The connected exempt market maker or the connected exempt principal trader complies with the applicable provisions of the United Kingdom's City Code on Takeovers and Mergers; and

(v) The tender offer documents disclose the identity of the connected exempt market maker or the connected exempt principal trader and disclose, or describe how U.S. security holders can obtain, information regarding market making or principal purchases by such market maker or principal trader to the extent that this information is required to be made public in the United Kingdom; and

(10) *Purchases During Cross-Border Tender Offers.* Purchases or arrangements to purchase if the following conditions are satisfied:

(i) The tender offer is excepted under § 240.13e–4(h)(8) or § 240.14d–1(c);

(ii) The offering documents furnished to U.S. holders prominently disclose the possibility of any purchases, or arrangements to purchase, or the intent to make such purchases;

(iii) The offering documents disclose the manner in which any information about any such purchases or arrangements to purchase will be disclosed;

(iv) The offeror discloses information in the United States about any such purchases or arrangements to purchase in a manner comparable to the disclosure made in the home jurisdiction, as defined in § 240.13e–4(i)(3); and

(v) The purchases comply with the applicable tender offer laws and regulations of the home jurisdiction.

(c) *Definitions.* For purposes of this section, the term:

(1) *Affiliate* has the same meaning as in § 240.12b–2;

(2) *Agent independent* of the issuer has the same meaning as in § 242.100(b) of this chapter;

(3) *Covered person means*:

(i) The offeror and its affiliates;

(ii) The offeror's dealer-manager and its affiliates;

(iii) Any advisor to any of the persons specified in paragraph (c)(3)(i) and (ii) of this section, whose compensation is dependent on the completion of the offer; and

(iv) Any person acting, directly or indirectly, in concert with any of the persons specified in this paragraph (c)(3) in connection with any purchase or arrangement to purchase any subject securities or any related securities;

(4) *Plan* has the same meaning as in § 242.100(b) of this chapter;

(5) *Public announcement* is any oral or written communication by the offeror or any person authorized to act on the offeror's behalf that is reasonably designed to, or has the effect of, informing the public or security holders in general about the tender offer;

(6) *Related securities* means securities that are immediately convertible into, exchangeable for, or exercisable for subject securities; and

(7) *Subject securities* has the same meaning as in § 229.1000 of this chapter.

(d) *Exemptive Authority.* Upon written application or upon its own motion, the Commission may grant an exemption from the provisions of this section, either unconditionally or on specified terms or conditions, to any transaction or class of transactions or any security or class of security, or any person or class of persons.

Rule 14e–6. Repurchase Offers by Certain Closed-End Registered Investment Companies

Rules 14e–1 and 14e–2 shall not apply to any offer by a closed-end management investment company to repurchase equity securities of which it is the issuer pursuant to § 270.23c–3 of this chapter.

Rule 14e–7. Unlawful Tender Offer Practices in Connection with Roll–Ups

In order to implement Section 14(h) of the Act (15 U.S.C. 78n(h)):

(a)(1) It shall be unlawful for any person to receive compensation for soliciting tenders directly from security holders in connection with a roll-up transaction as provided in paragraph (a)(2) of this section, if the compensation is:

(i) Based on whether the solicited person participates in the tender offer; or

(ii) Contingent on the success of the tender offer.

(2) Paragraph (a)(1) of this section is applicable to a roll-up transaction as defined in Item 901(c) of Regulation S–K (§ 229.901(c) of this chapter), structured as a tender offer, except for a transaction involving only:

(i) Finite-life entities that are not limited partnerships;

(ii) Partnerships whose investors will receive new securities or securities in another entity that are not reported under a transaction reporting plan declared effective before December 17, 1993 by the Commission under Section 11A of the Act (15 U.S.C. 78k–1); or

(iii) Partnerships whose investors' securities are reported under a transaction reporting plan declared effective before December 17, 1993 by the Commission under Section 11A of the Act (15 U.S.C. 78k–1).

(b)(1) It shall be unlawful for any finite-life entity that is the subject of a roll-up transaction as provided in paragraph (b)(2) of this section to fail to provide a security holder list or mail communications related to a tender offer that is in furtherance of the roll-up transaction, at the option of a requesting security holder, pursuant to the procedures set forth in § 240.14a–7.

(2) Paragraph (b)(1) of this section is applicable to a roll-up transaction as defined in Item 901(c) of Regulation S–K (§ 229.901(c) of this chapter), structured as a tender offer, that involves:

(i) An entity with securities registered pursuant to Section 12 of the Act (15 U.S.C. 78*l*); or

(ii) A limited partnership, unless the transaction involves only:

(A) Partnerships whose investors will receive new securities or securities in another entity that are not reported under a transaction reporting plan declared effective before December 17, 1993 by the Commission under Section 11A of the Act (15 U.S.C. 78k–1); or

(B) Partnerships whose investors' securities are reported under a transaction reporting plan declared effective before December 17, 1993 by the Commission under Section 11A of the Act (15 U.S.C. 78k–1).

Rule 14e–8. Prohibited Conduct in Connection With Pre-Commencement Communications

It is a fraudulent, deceptive or manipulative act or practice within the meaning of section 14(e) of the Act (15 U.S.C. 78n) for any person to publicly announce that the person (or a party on whose behalf the person is acting) plans to make a tender offer that has not yet been commenced, if the person:

(a) Is making the announcement of a potential tender offer without the intention to commence the offer within a reasonable time and complete the offer;

(b) Intends, directly or indirectly, for the announcement to manipulate the market price of the stock of the bidder or subject company; or

(c) Does not have the reasonable belief that the person will have the means to purchase securities to complete the offer.

Rule 14f–1. Change in Majority of Directors

If, pursuant to any arrangement or understanding with the person or persons acquiring securities in a transaction subject to section 13(d) or 14(d) of the Act, any persons are to be elected or designated as directors of the issuer, otherwise than at a meeting of security holders, and the persons so elected or designated will constitute a majority of the directors of the issuer, then, not less than 10 days prior to the date any such person take office as a director, or such shorter period prior to that date as the Commission may authorize upon a showing of good cause therefor, the issuer shall file with the Commission and transmit to all holders of record of securities of the issuer who would be entitled to vote at a meeting for election of directors, information substantially equivalent to the information which would be required by Items 6(a), (d) and (e), 7 and 8 of Schedule 14A of Regulation 14A to be transmitted if such person or persons were nominees for election as directors at a meeting of such security holders.

Eight copies of such information shall be filed with the Commission.

EXEMPTION OF CERTAIN SECURITIES FROM SECTION 15(a)

Rule 15a–1. Securities Activities of OTC Derivatives Dealers

Preliminary Note: OTC derivatives dealers are a special class of broker-dealers that are exempt from certain broker-dealer requirements, including membership in a self-regulatory organization (§ 240.15b9–2), regular broker-dealer margin rules (§ 240.36a1–1), and application of the Securities Investor Protection Act of 1970 (§ 240.36a1–2). OTC derivative dealers are subject to special requirements, including limitations on the scope of their securities activities (§ 240.15a–1), specified internal risk management control systems (§ 240.15c3–4), recordkeeping obligations (§ 240.17a–3(a)(10)), and reporting responsibilities (§ 240.17a–12). They are also subject to alternative net capital treatment (§ 240.15c3–1(a)(5)). This rule 15a–1 uses a number of defined terms in setting forth the securities activities in which an OTC derivatives dealer may engage: "OTC derivatives dealer," "eligible OTC derivative instrument," "cash management securities activities," and "ancillary portfolio management securities activities." These terms are defined under Rules 3b–12 through 3b–15 (§ 240.3b–12 through § 240.3b–15).

(a) The securities activities of an OTC derivatives dealer shall:

(1) Be limited to:

(i) Engaging in dealer activities in eligible OTC derivative instruments that are securities;

(ii) Issuing and reacquiring securities that are issued by the dealer, including warrants on securities, hybrid securities, and structured notes;

(iii) Engaging in cash management securities activities;

(iv) Engaging in ancillary portfolio management securities activities; and

(v) Engaging in such other securities activities that the Commission designates by order pursuant to paragraph (b)(1) of this section; and

(2) Consist primarily of the activities described in paragraphs (a)(1)(i), (a)(1)(ii), and (a)(1)(iii) of this section; and

(3) Not consist of any other securities activities, including engaging in any transaction in any security that is not an eligible OTC derivative instrument, except as permitted under paragraphs (a)(1)(iii), (a)(1)(iv), and (a)(1)(v) of this section.

(b) The Commission, by order, entered upon its own initiative or after considering an application for exemptive relief, may clarify or expand the scope of eligible OTC derivative instruments and the scope of permissible securities activities of an OTC derivatives dealer. Such orders may:

(1) Identify other permissible securities activities;

(2) Determine that a class of fungible instruments that are standardized as to their material economic terms is within the scope of eligible OTC derivative instrument;

(3) Clarify whether certain contracts, agreements, or transactions are within the scope of eligible OTC derivative instrument; or

(4) Clarify whether certain securities activities are within the scope of ancillary portfolio management securities activities.

(c) To the extent an OTC derivatives dealer engages in any securities transaction pursuant to paragraphs (a)(1)(i) through (a)(1)(v) of this section, such transaction shall be effected through a registered broker or dealer (other than an OTC derivatives dealer) that, in the case of any securities transaction pursuant to paragraphs (a)(1)(i), or (a)(1)(iii) through (a)(1)(v) of this section, is an affiliate of the OTC derivatives dealer, except that this paragraph (c) shall not apply if:

(1) The counterparty to the transaction with the OTC derivatives dealer is acting as principal and is:

(i) A registered broker or dealer;

(ii) A bank acting in a dealer capacity, as permitted by U.S. law;

(iii) A foreign broker or dealer; or

(iv) An affiliate of the OTC derivatives dealer; or

(2) The OTC derivatives dealer is engaging in an ancillary portfolio management securities activity, and the transaction is in a foreign security, and a registered broker or dealer, a bank, or a foreign broker or dealer is acting as agent for the OTC derivatives dealer.

(d) To the extent an OTC derivatives dealer induces or attempts to induce any counterparty to enter into any securities transaction pursuant to paragraphs (a)(1)(i) through (a)(1)(v) of this section, any communication or contact with the counterparty concerning the transaction (other than clerical and ministerial activities conducted by an associated person of the OTC derivatives dealer) shall be conducted by one or more registered persons that, in the case of any securities transaction pursuant to paragraphs (a)(1)(i), or (a)(1)(iii) through (a)(1)(v) of this section, is associated with an affiliate of the OTC derivatives dealer, except that this paragraph (d) shall not apply if the counterparty to the transaction with the OTC derivatives dealer is:

(1) A registered broker or dealer;

(2) A bank acting in a dealer capacity, as permitted by U.S. law;

(3) A foreign broker or dealer; or

(4) An affiliate of the OTC derivatives dealer.

(e) For purposes of this section, the term *hybrid security* means a security that incorporates payment features economically similar to options, forwards, futures, swap agreements,or collars involving currencies, interest or other rates, commodities, securities, indices, quantitative measures, or other financial or economic interests or property of any kind, or any payment or delivery that is dependent on the occurrence or nonoccurrence of any event associated with a potential financial, economic, or commercial consequence (or any combination, permutation, or derivative of such contract or underlying interest).

(f) For purposes of this section, the term *affiliate* means any organization (whether incorporated or unincorporated) that directly or indirectly controls, is controlled by, or is under common control with, the OTC derivatives dealer.

(g) For purposes of this section, the term *foreign broker or dealer* means any person not resident in the United States (including any U.S. person engaged in business as a broker or dealer entirely outside the United States, except as otherwise permitted by § 240.15a-6) that is not an office or branch of, or a natural person associated with, a registered broker or dealer, whose securities activities, if conducted in the United States, would be described by the definition of "broker" in section 3(a)(4) of the Act (15 U.S.C. 78c(a)(4)) or "dealer" in section 3(a)(5) of the Act (15 U.S.C. 78c(a)(5)).

(h) For purposes of this section, the term *foreign security* means any security (including a depositary share issued by a United States bank, provided that the depositary share is initially offered and sold outside the United States in accordance with Regulation S (17 CFR 230.901 through 230.904)) issued by a person not organized or incorporated under the laws of the United States, provided the transaction that involves such security is not effected on a national securities exchange or on a market operated by a registered national securities association; or a debt security (including a convertible debt security) issued by an issuer organized or incorporated under the laws of the United States that is initially offered and sold outside the United States in accordance with Regulation S (17 CFR 230.901 through 230.904).

(i) For purposes of this section, the term *registered person* is:

(A) A natural person who is associated with a registered broker or dealer and is registered or approved under the rules of a self-regulatory organization of which such broker or dealer is a member; or

(B) If the counterparty to the transaction with the OTC derivatives dealer is a resident of a jurisdiction other than the United States, a natural person who is not resident in the United States and is associated with a broker or dealer that is registered or licensed by a foreign financial regulatory authority in the jurisdiction in which such counterparty is resident or in which such natural person is located, in accordance with applicable legal requirements, if any.

Rule 15a-2. Exemption of Certain Securities of Cooperative Apartment Houses From Section 15(a)

Shares of a corporation which represents ownership, or entitles the holders thereof to possession and occupancy, of specific apartment units in property owned by such corporations and organized and operated on a cooperative basis are hereby excepted from the operation of section 15(a) of the Act, when such shares are sold by or through a real estate broker licensed under the laws of the political subdivision in which the property is located.

Rule 15a-4. Forty-Five Day Exemption From Registration for Certain Members of National Securities Exchanges

(a) A natural person who is a member of a national securities exchange shall, upon termination of his association with a registered broker-dealer, be exempt, for a period of forty-five days after such termination, from the registration requirement of Section 15(a) of the Act solely for the purpose of continuing to effect transactions on the floor of such exchange if (1) such person has filed with the Commission an application for registration as a broker-dealer and such person complies in all material respects with rules of the Commission applicable to registered brokers and dealers and (2) such exchange has filed with the Commission a statement that it has reviewed such application and that there do not appear to be grounds for its denial.

(b) The exemption from registration provided by this rule shall not be available to any person while there is pending before the Commission any proceeding involving any such person pursuant to Section 15(b)(1)(B) of the Act.

Rule 15a-5. Exemption of Certain Nonbank Lenders

A lender approved under the rules and regulations of the Small Business Administration shall be exempt from the registration requirement of Section 15(a)(1) of the Act if it does not engage in the business of effecting transactions in securities or of buying and selling securities for its own account except in respect of receiving notes evidencing loans to small business concerns and selling the portion of such notes guaranteed by the Small Business Administration through or to a registered broker or dealer or to a bank, a savings institution, an insurance company, or an account over which an investment adviser registered pursuant to the Investment Advisers Act of 1940 exercises investment discretion.

REGISTRATION OF BROKERS AND DEALERS

Rule 15a-6. Exemption of Certain Foreign Brokers or Dealers

(a) A foreign broker or dealer shall be exempt from the registration requirements of sections 15(a)(1) and 15B(a)(1) of the Act to the extent that the foreign broker or dealer:

(1) effects transactions in securities with or for persons that have not been solicited by the foreign broker or dealer; or

(2) furnishes research reports to major U.S. institutional investors, and effects transactions in the securities discussed in the research reports with or for those major U.S. institutional investors, provided that:

(i) the research reports do not recommend the use of the foreign broker or dealer to effect trades in any security;

(ii) the foreign broker or dealer does not initiate contact with those major U.S. institutional investors to follow up on the research reports, and does not otherwise induce or attempt to induce the purchase or sale of any security by those major U.S. institutional investors;

(iii) if the foreign broker or dealer has a relationship with a registered broker or dealer that satisfies the requirements of paragraph (a)(3) of this rule, any transactions with the foreign broker or dealer in securities discussed in the research reports are effected only through that registered broker or dealer, pursuant to the provisions of paragraph (a)(3); and

(iv) the foreign broker or dealer does not provide research to U.S. persons pursuant to any express or implied understanding that those U.S. persons will direct commission income to the foreign broker or dealer; or

(3) induces or attempts to induce the purchase or sale of any security by a U.S. institutional investor or a major U.S. institutional investor, provided that:

(i) the foreign broker or dealer:

(A) effects any resulting transactions with or for the U.S. institutional investor or the major U.S. institutional investor through a registered broker or dealer in the manner described by paragraph (a)(3)(iii) of this rule; and

(B) provides the Commission (upon request or pursuant to agreements reached between any foreign securities authority, including any foreign government, as specified in section 3(a)(50) of the Act, and the Commission or the U.S. Government) with any information or documents within the possession, custody, or control of the foreign broker or dealer, any testimony of foreign associated persons, and any assistance in taking the evidence of other persons, wherever located, that the Commission requests and that relates to transactions under paragraph (a)(3) of this rule, except that if, after the foreign broker or dealer has exercised its best efforts to provide the information, documents, testimony, or assistance, including requesting the appropriate governmental body and, if legally necessary, its customers (with respect to customer information) to permit the foreign broker or dealer to provide the information, documents, testimony, or assistance to the Commission, the foreign broker or dealer is prohibited from providing this information, documents, testimony, or assistance by applicable foreign law or regulations, then this paragraph (a)(3)(i)(B) shall not apply and the foreign broker or dealer will be subject to paragraph (c) of this rule;

(ii) the foreign associated person of the foreign broker or dealer effecting transactions with the U.S. institutional investor or the major U.S. institutional investor:

(A) conducts all securities activities from outside the U.S., except that the foreign associated persons may conduct visits to U.S. institutional investors and major U.S. institutional investors within the United States, provided that:

(*1*) the foreign associated person is accompanied on these visits by an associated person of a registered broker or dealer that accepts responsibility for the foreign associated person's communications with the U.S. institutional investor or the major U.S. institutional investor; and

(*2*) transactions in any securities discussed during the visit by the foreign associated person are effected only through the registered broker or dealer, pursuant to paragraph (a)(3) of this rule; and

(B) is determined by the registered broker or dealer to:

(*1*) not be subject to a statutory disqualification specified in section 3(a)(39) of the Act, or any substantially equivalent foreign

(*i*) expulsion or suspension from membership,

(*ii*) bar or suspension from association,

(*iii*) denial of trading privileges,

(*iv*) order denying, suspending, or revoking registration or barring or suspending association, or

(*v*) finding with respect to causing any such effective foreign suspension, expulsion, or order;

(*2*) not to have been convicted of any foreign offense, enjoined from any foreign act, conduct, or practice, or found to have committed any foreign act substantially equivalent to any of those listed in section 15(b)(4)(B), (C), (D), or (E) of the Act; and

(*3*) not to have been found to have made or caused to be made any false foreign statement or omission substantially equivalent to any of those listed in section 3(a)(39)(E) of the Act; and

(iii) the registered broker or dealer through which the transaction with the U.S. institutional investor or the major U.S. institutional investor is effected:

(A) is responsible for:

(*1*) effecting the transactions conducted under paragraph (a)(3) of this rule, other than negotiating their terms;

(*2*) issuing all required confirmations and statements to the U.S. institutional investor or the major U.S. institutional investor;

(*3*) as between the foreign broker or dealer and the registered broker or dealer, extending or arranging for the extension of any credit to the U.S. institutional investor or the major U.S. institutional investor in connection with the transactions;

(*4*) maintaining required books and records relating to the transactions, including those required by Rules 17a–3 and 17a–4 under the Act;

(*5*) complying with Rule 15c3-1 under the Act with respect to the transactions; and

(*6*) receiving, delivering, and safeguarding funds and securities in connection with the transactions on behalf of the U.S. institutional investor or the major U.S. institutional investor in compliance with Rule 15c3-3 under the Act;

(B) participates through an associated person in all oral communications between the foreign associated person and the U.S. institutional investor, other than a major U.S. institutional investor;

(C) has obtained from the foreign broker or dealer, with respect to each foreign associated person, the types of information specified in Rule 17a-3(a)(12) under the Act, provided that the information required by paragraph (a)(12)(d) of that rule shall include sanctions imposed by foreign securities authorities, exchanges, or associations, including without limitation those described in paragraph (a)(3)(ii)(B) of this rule;

(D) has obtained from the foreign broker or dealer and each foreign associated person written consent to service of process for any civil action brought by or proceeding before the Commission or a self-regulatory organization (as defined in section 3(a)(26) of the Act), providing that process may be served on them by service on the registered broker or dealer in the manner set forth on the registered broker's or dealer's current Form BD; and

(E) maintains a written record of the information and consents required by paragraphs (a)(3)(iii)(C) and (D) of this rule, and all records in connection with trading activities of the U.S. institutional investor or the major U.S. institutional investor involving the foreign broker or dealer conducted under paragraph (a)(3) of this rule, in an office of the registered broker or dealer located in the United States (with respect to nonresident registered brokers or dealers, pursuant to Rule 17a-7(a) under the Act), and makes these records available to the Commission upon request; or

(4) effects transactions in securities with or for, or induces or attempts to induce the purchase or sale of any security by:

(i) a registered broker or dealer, whether the registered broker or dealer is acting as principal for its own account or as agent for others, or a bank acting in a broker or dealer capacity as permitted by U.S. law;

(ii) the African Development Bank, the Asian Development Bank, the Inter-American Development Bank, the International Bank for Reconstruction and Development, the International Monetary Fund, the United Nations, and their agencies, affiliates, and pension funds;

(iii) a foreign person temporarily present in the United States, with whom the foreign broker or dealer had a bona fide, pre-existing relationship before the foreign person entered the United States;

(iv) any agency or branch of a U.S. person permanently located outside the United States, provided that the transactions occur outside the United States; or

(v) U.S. citizens resident outside the United States, provided that the transactions occur outside the United States, and that the foreign broker or dealer does not direct its selling efforts toward identifiable groups of U.S. citizens resident abroad.

(b) When used in this rule,

(1) the term "family of investment companies" shall mean:

(i) except for insurance company separate accounts, any two or more separately registered investment companies under the Investment Company Act of 1940 that share the same investment adviser or principal underwriter and hold themselves out to investors as related companies for purposes of investment and investor services; and

(ii) with respect to insurance company separate accounts, any two or more separately registered separate accounts under the Investment Company Act of 1940 that share the same investment adviser or principal underwriter and function under operational or accounting or control systems that are substantially similar.

(2) the term "foreign associated person" shall mean any natural person domiciled outside the United States who is an associated person, as defined in section 3(a)(18) of the Act, of the foreign broker or dealer, and who participates in the solicitation of a U.S. institutional investor or a major U.S. institutional investor under paragraph (a)(3) of this rule.

(3) the term "foreign broker or dealer" shall mean any non-U.S. resident person (including any U.S. person engaged in business as a broker or dealer entirely outside the United States, except as otherwise permitted by this rule) that is not an office or branch of, or a natural person associated with, a registered broker or dealer, whose securities activities, if conducted in the United States, would be described by the definition of "broker" or "dealer" in sections 3(a)(4) or 3(a)(5) of the Act.

(4) the term "major U.S. institutional investor" shall mean a person that is:

(i) a U.S. institutional investor that has, or has under management, total assets in excess of $100 million; provided, however, that for purposes of determining the total assets of an investment company under this rule, the investment company may include the assets of any family of investment companies of which it is a part; or

(ii) an investment adviser registered with the Commission under section 203 of the Investment Advisers Act of 1940 that has total assets under management in excess of $100 million.

(5) the term "registered broker or dealer" shall mean a person that is registered with the Commission under sections 15(b), 15B(a)(2), or 15C(a)(2) of the Act.

(6) the term "United States" shall mean the United States of America, including the States and any territories and other areas subject to its jurisdiction.

(7) the term "U.S. institutional investor" shall mean a person that is:

(i) an investment company registered with the Commission under section 8 of the Investment Company Act of 1940; or

(ii) a bank, savings and loan association, insurance company, business development company, small business investment company, or employee benefit plan defined in Rule 501(a)(1) of Regulation D under the Securities Act of 1933; a private business development company defined in Rule 501(a)(2); an organization described in section 501(c)(3) of the Internal Revenue Code, as defined in Rule 501(a)(3); or a trust defined in Rule 501(a)(7).

(c) The Commission, by order after notice and opportunity for hearing, may withdraw the exemption provided in paragraph (a)(3) of this rule with respect to the subsequent activities of a foreign broker or dealer or class of foreign brokers or dealers conducted from a foreign country, if the Commission finds that the laws or regulations of that foreign country have prohibited the foreign broker or dealer, or one of a class of foreign brokers or dealers, from providing, in response to a request from the Commission, information or documents within its possession, custody, or control, testimony of foreign associated persons, or assistance in taking the evidence of other persons, wherever located, related to activities exempted by paragraph (a)(3) of this rule.

Rule 15a–7. Exemption From the Definitions of "Broker" or "Dealer" for Banks for Limited Period of Time

(a) A bank is exempt from the definitions of the term "broker" under Section 3(a)(4) of the Act (15 U.S.C. 78c(a)(4)) and the term "dealer" under Section 3(a)(5) of the Act (15 U.S.C. 78c(a)(5)) until October 1, 2001; and

(b) A bank is exempt from the definition of the term "broker" under Section 3(a)(4) of the Act (15 U.S.C. 78c(a)(4)) until January 1, 2002, for activities that meet the conditions of an exception or exemption for banks from the definition of the term "broker" except for those conditions of Section 3(a)(4) of the Act (15 U.S.C. 78c(a)(4)) and the rules thereunder relating to compensation of the bank or its employees.

Rule 15a–8. Exemption for Banks From Section 29 Liability

(a) No contract entered into before January 1, 2003 shall be void or considered voidable by reason of section 29 of the Act (15 U.S.C. 78cc) because any bank that is a party to the contract violated the registration requirements of section 15(a) of the Act (15 U.S.C. 78o(a)) or any applicable provision of the Act (15 U.S.C. 78a *et seq.*) and the rules and regulations thereunder based solely on the bank's status as a broker or dealer when the contract was created.

(b) No contract entered into before March 31, 2005, shall be void or considered voidable by reason of section 29 of the Act (15 U.S.C. 78cc) because any bank that is a party to the contract violated the registration requirements of section 15(a) of the Act (15 U.S.C. 78o(a)) or any applicable provision of the Act (15 U.S.C. 78a *et seq.*) and the rules and regulations thereunder based solely on the bank's status as a dealer when the contract was created.

Rule 15a–9. Exemption From the Definitions of "Broker" and "Dealer" for Savings Associations and Savings Banks

Any savings association or savings bank that has deposits insured by the Federal Deposit Insurance Corporation under the FDIA (12 U.S.C. 1811 *et seq.*), and is not operated for the purpose of evading the provisions of the Act (15 U.S.C. 78a *et seq.*), is exempt from the definitions of the terms "broker" and "dealer" under Sections 3(a)(4) and 3(a)(5) of the Act (15 U.S.C. 78c(a)(4) and 15 U.S.C. 78c(a)(5)), based solely on the savings association's or savings bank's status as a broker or dealer on the same terms and under the same conditions that banks are excepted or exempted, provided that if a savings association or savings bank acts as a municipal securities dealer, it shall be considered a bank municipal securities dealer for purposes of the Act (15 U.S.C. 78a *et seq.*) and the rules thereunder, including the rules of the Municipal Securities Rulemaking Board.

Rule 15a–10. Exemption of Certain Brokers or Dealers With Respect to Security Futures Products

(a) A broker or dealer that is registered by notice with the Commission pursuant to section 15(b)(11)(A) of the Act (15 U.S.C. 78o(b)(11)(A)) and that is not a member of either a national securities exchange registered pursuant to section 6(a) of the Act (15 U.S.C. 78f(a)) or a national securities association registered pursuant to section 15A(a) of the Act (15 U.S.C. 78o–3(a)) will be exempt from the registration requirement of section 15(a)(1) of the Act (15 U.S.C. 78o(a)(1)) solely to act as a broker or a dealer in security futures products.

(b) A broker or dealer that is registered by notice with the Commission pursuant to section 15(b)(11)(A) of the Act (15 U.S.C. 78o(b)(11)(A)) and that is a member of either a national securities exchange registered pursuant to section 6(a) of the Act (15 U.S.C. 78f(a)) or a national securities association registered pursuant to section 15A(a) of the Act (15 U.S.C. 78o–3(a)) will be exempt from the registration requirement of section 15(a)(1) of the Act (15 U.S.C. 78o(a)(1)) solely to act as a broker or a dealer in security futures products, if:

(1) The rules of any such exchange or association of which the broker or dealer is a member provides specifically for a broker or dealer that is registered by notice with the Commission pursuant to section 15(b)(11)(A) of the Act (15 U.S.C. 78o(b)(11)(A)) to become a member of such exchange or association; and

(2) The broker or dealer complies with section 11(a)–(c) of the Act (15 U.S.C. 78k(a)–(c)) with respect to any transactions in security futures products on a national securities exchange registered pursuant to section 6(a) of the Act (15 U.S.C. 78f(a)) of which it is a member, notwithstanding section 15(b)(11)(B)(ii) of the Act (15 U.S.C. 78o(b)(11)(B)(ii)).

Rule 15a–11. Exemption From the Definitions of "Broker" and "Dealer" For Banks Engaging in Securities Lending Transactions

(a) A bank is exempt from the definitions of the terms "broker" and "dealer" under sections 3(a)(4) and 3(a)(5) of the Act (15 U.S.C. 78c(a)(4) and (a)(5)), to the extent that, as a conduit lender, or as an agent, it engages in or effects securities lending transactions, and any securities lending services in connection with such transactions, with or on behalf of a person the bank reasonably believes to be:

(1) A qualified investor as defined in section 3(a)(54)(A) of the Act (15 U.S.C. 78c(a)(54)(A)); or

(2) Any employee benefit plan that owns and invests on a discretionary basis, not less than $25,000,000 in investments.

(b) *Securities lending transaction* means a transaction in which the owner of a security lends the security temporarily to another party pursuant to a written securities lending agreement under which the lender retains the economic interests of an owner of such securities, and has the right to terminate the transaction and to recall the loaned securities on terms agreed by the parties.

(c) *Securities lending services* means:

(1) Selecting and negotiating with a borrower and executing, or directing the execution of the loan with the borrower;

(2) Receiving, delivering, or directing the receipt or delivery of loaned securities;

(3) Receiving, delivering, or directing the receipt or delivery of collateral;

(4) Providing mark-to-market, corporate action, recordkeeping or other services incidental to the administration of the securities lending transaction;

(5) Investing, or directing the investment of, cash collateral; or

(6) Indemnifying the lender of securities with respect to various matters.

(d) For the purposes of this section, the term *conduit lender* means a bank that borrows or loans securities, as principal, for its own account, and contemporaneously loans or borrows the same securities, as principal, for its own account. A bank that qualifies under this definition as a conduit lender at the commencement of a transaction will continue to qualify, notwithstanding whether:

(1) The lending or borrowing transaction terminates and so long as the transaction is replaced within one business day by another lending or borrowing transaction involving the same securities; and

(2) Any substitutions of collateral occur.

Rule 15b1–1. Application for Registration of Brokers or Dealers

(a) An application for registration of a broker or dealer that is filed pursuant to section 15(b) of the Act (15 U.S.C. 78o(b)) shall be filed on Form BD (§ 249.501 of this chapter) in accordance with the instructions to the form. A broker or dealer that is an OTC derivatives dealer shall indicate where appropriate on Form BD that the type o business in which it is engaged is that of acting as an OTC derivatives dealer.

(b) Every application for registration of a broker or dealer that is filed on or after January 25, 1993, shall be filed with the Central Registration Depository operated by the National Association of Securities Dealers, Inc.

(c) An application for registration that is filed with the Central Registration Depository pursuant to this section shall be considered a "report" filed with the Commission for purposes of Sections 15(b), 17(a), 18(a), 32(a) (15 U.S.C. 78o(b), 78q(a), 78r(a), 78ff(a)) and other applicable provisions of the Act.

Rule 15b1-3. Registration of Successor to Registered Broker or Dealer

(a) In the event that a broker or dealer succeeds to and continues the business of a broker or dealer registered pursuant to section 15(b) of the Act, the registration of the predecessor shall be deemed to remain effective as the registration of the successor if the successor, within 30 days after such succession, files an application for registration on Form BD, and the predecessor files a notice of withdrawal from registration on Form BDW; *Provided, however,* That the registration of the predecessor broker or dealer will cease to be effective as the registration of the successor broker or dealer 45 days after the application for registration on Form BD is filed by such successor.

(b) Notwithstanding paragraph (a) of this rule, if a broker or dealer succeeds to and continues the business of a registered predecessor broker or dealer, and the succession is based solely on a change in the predecessor's date or state of incorporation, form of organization, or composition of a partnership, the successor may, within 30 days after the succession, amend the registration of the predecessor broker or dealer on Form BD to reflect these changes. This amendment shall be deemed an application for registration filed by the predecessor and adopted by the successor.

Rule 15b1-4. Registration of Fiduciaries

The registration of a broker or dealer shall be deemed to be the registration of any executor, administrator, guardian, conservator, assignee for the benefit of creditors, receiver, trustee in insolvency or bankruptcy, or other fiduciary, appointed or qualified by order, judgment, or decree of a court of competent jurisdiction to continue the business of such registered broker or dealer: *Provided,* That such fiduciary files with the Commission, within 30 days after entering upon the performance of his duties, a statement setting forth as to such fiduciary substantially the information required by Form BD.

Rule 15b1-5. Consent to Service of Process to Be Furnished by Nonresident Brokers or Dealers and by Nonresident General Partners or Managing Agents of Brokers or Dealers

(a) Each nonresident broker or dealer registered or applying for registration pursuant to section 15(b) of the Securities Exchange Act of 1934, each nonresident general partner of a broker or dealer partnership which is registered or applying for registration, and each nonresident managing agent of any other unincorporated broker or dealer which is registered or applying for registration, shall furnish to the Commission, in a form prescribed by or acceptable to it, a written irrevocable consent and power of attorney which (1) designates the Securities and Exchange Commission as an agent upon whom may be served any process, pleadings, or other papers in any civil suit or action brought in any appropriate court in any place subject to the jurisdiction of the United States, with respect to any cause of action (i) which accrues during the period beginning when such broker or dealer becomes registered pursuant to section 15 of the Securities Exchange Act of 1934 and the rules and regulations thereunder and ending either when such registration is canceled or revoked, or when the Commission receives from such broker or dealer a notice to withdraw from such registration, whichever is earlier, (ii) which arises out of any activity, in any place subject to the jurisdiction of the United States, occurring in connection with the conduct of business of a broker or dealer, and (iii) which is founded, directly or indirectly, upon the provisions of the Securities Act of 1933, the Securities Exchange Act of 1934, the Trust Indenture Act of 1939, the Investment Company Act of 1940, the Investment Advisers Act of 1940, or any rule or regulation under any of said Acts; and (2) stipulates and agrees that any such civil suit or action may be commenced by the service of process upon the Commission and the forwarding of a copy thereof as provided in paragraph (c) of this rule, and that the service as aforesaid of any such process, pleadings, or other papers upon the Commission shall be taken and held in all courts to be as valid and binding as if due personal service thereof had been made.

(b) The required consent and power of attorney shall be furnished to the Commission within the following period of time:

(1) Each nonresident broker or dealer registered at the time this rule becomes effective, and each nonresident general partner or managing agent of an unincorporated broker or dealer registered at the time this rule becomes effective, shall furnish such consent and power of attorney within 60 days after such date;

(2) Each broker or dealer applying for registration after the effective date of this rule shall furnish, at the time of filing such application, all the consents and powers of attorney required to be furnished by such broker or dealer and by each general partner or managing agent thereof: *Provided, however,* That where an application for registration of a broker or dealer is pending at the time this rule becomes effective such consents and powers of attorney shall be furnished within 30 days after this rule becomes effective.

(3) Each broker or dealer registered or applying for registration who or which becomes a nonresident broker or dealer after the effective date of this rule, and each general partner or managing agent, of an unincorporated broker or dealer registered or applying for registration, who becomes a nonresident after the effective date of this rule, shall furnish such consent and power of attorney within 30 days thereafter.

(c) Service of any process, pleadings or other papers on the Commission under this rule shall be made by delivering the requisite number of copies thereof to the Secretary of the Commission or to such other person as the Commission may authorize to act in its behalf. Whenever any process, pleadings or other papers as aforesaid are served upon the Commission, it shall promptly forward a copy thereof by registered or certified mail to the appropriate defendants at their last address of record filed with the Commission. The Commission shall be furnished a sufficient number of copies for such purpose, and one copy for its file.

(d) For purposes of this rule the following definitions shall apply:

(1) The term "broker" shall have the meaning set out in section 3(a)(4) of the Securities Exchange Act of 1934.

(2) The term "dealer" shall have the meaning set out in section 3(a)(5) of the Securities Exchange Act of 1934.

(3) The term "managing agent" shall mean any person, including a trustee, who directs or manages or who participates in the directing or managing of the affairs of any unincorporated organization or association which is not a partnership.

(4) The term "nonresident broker or dealer" shall mean (A) in the case of an individual, one who resides in or has his principal place of business in any place not subject to the jurisdiction of the United States; (B) in the case of a corporation, one incorporated in or having its principal place of business in any place not subject to the jurisdiction of the United States; (C) in the case of a partnership or other unincorporated organization or association, one having its principal place of business in any place not subject to the jurisdiction of the United States.

(5) A general partner or managing agent of a broker or dealer shall be deemed to be a nonresident if he resides in any place not subject to the jurisdiction of the United States.

Rule 15b2-2. Inspection of Newly Registered Brokers and Dealers

(a) *Definition.* For the purpose of this section the term "applicable financial responsibility rules" shall include: (1) any rule adopted by the Commission pursuant to sections 8, 15(c)(3), 17(a), or 17(e)(1)(A) of the Act; (2) any rule adopted by the Commission relating to hypothecation or lending of customer securities; (3) any other rule adopted by the Commission relating to the protection of funds or securities; and (4) any rule adopted by the Secretary of the Treasury pursuant to section 15C(b)(1) of the Act.

(b) Each self-regulatory organization that has responsibility for examining a broker or dealer member (including members that are government securities brokers or government securities dealers registered pursuant to section 15C(a)(1)(A) of the Act) for compliance with applicable financial responsibility rules is authorized and directed to conduct an inspection of the member, within six months of the member's registration with the Commission, to determine whether the member is operating in conformity with applicable financial responsibility rules.

(c) The examining self-regulatory organization is further authorized and directed to conduct an inspection of the member no later than twelve months from the member's registration with the Commission, to determine whether the member is operating in conformity with all other applicable provisions of the Act and rules thereunder.

(d) In each case where the examining self-regulatory organization determines that a broker or dealer member has not commenced actual operations within six months of the member's registration with the Commission, it shall delay the inspection pursuant to this section until the second six month period from the member's registration with the Commission.

(e) No inspection need be conducted as provided for in paragraphs (b) and (c) of this rule if: (1) the member was registered with the Commission prior to April 26, 1982; (2) an inspection of the member has already been conducted by another self-regulatory organization pursuant to this section; (3) an inspection of the member has already been conducted by the Commission pursuant to section 15(b)(2)(C) of the Act; or (4) the member is registered with the Commission pursuant to section 15(b)(11)(A) of the Act (15 U.S.C. 78o(b)(11)(A)).

Rule 15b3-1. Amendments to Application

(a) If the information contained in any application for registration as a broker or dealer, or in any amendment thereto, is or becomes inaccurate for any reason, the broker or dealer shall promptly file with the Central Registration Depository (operated by the National Association of Securities Dealers, Inc.) an amendment on Form BD correcting such information.

(b) Every amendment filed with the Central Registration Depository pursuant to this section shall constitute a "report" filed with the Commission within the meaning of Sections 15(b), 17(a), 18(a), 32(a) (15 U.S.C. 78o(b), 78q(a), 78r(a), 78ff(a)) and other applicable provisions of the Act.

(c) *Temporary re-filing instructions*.

(1) Except as provided in paragraph (c)(3) of this section, every registered broker-dealer shall re-file with the Central Registration Depository, at the time the broker-dealer submits its first amendment on or after August 16, 1999 but, in any event, no later than December 15, 1999, the following information from its current Form BD (17 CFR 249.501):

(i) Question 8 (if answered "Yes," the broker-dealer must also complete relevant items in Section IV of Schedule D);

(ii) Question 9 (if answered "Yes," the broker-dealer must also complete relevant items in Section IV of Schedule D);

(iii) Question 10(a) (if answered "Yes," the broker-dealer must also complete relevant items in Section V of Schedule D);

(iv) Question 10(b) (if answered "Yes," the broker-dealer must also complete relevant items in Section VI of Schedule D);

(v) Question 11 (if any item in Question 11 is answered "Yes," the broker-dealer must also complete the relevant DRP(s)); and

(vi) Schedules A and B.

(2) Every registered broker-dealer, at the time it re-files the information required by paragraph (c)(1) of this section, shall review, and amend as necessary, the information in Form BD that was transferred by the National Association of Securities Dealers to the Central Registration Depository prior to August 16, 1999.

(3) Every registered broker-dealer that has not completed the re-filing requirements provided in paragraphs (c)(1) and (c)(2) of this section, during the period from August 16, 1999 to December 15, 1999, shall submit in paper format to the Central Registration Depository all Schedule E amendments to Form BD. A Schedule E filed pursuant to this paragraph (c) shall not be deemed an "amendment" for purposes of paragraphs (a) and (b) of this section.

(4) The Commission, by order, may exempt any broker or dealer from the filing requirements provided in Form BD (17 CFR 249.501) and paragraphs (c)(1), (c)(2), and (c)(3) of this section under conditions that differ from the filing instructions contained in Form BD and paragraphs (c)(1), (c)(2), and (c)(3) of this section.

Rule 15b5–1. Extension of Registration for Purposes of the Securities Investor Protection Act of 1970 After Cancellation or Revocation

Commission revocation or cancellation of the registration of a broker or dealer pursuant to Section 15(b) of the Act: (i) shall be effective for all purposes, except as hereinafter provided, on the date of the order of revocation or cancellation or, if such order is stayed, on the date the stay is terminated; and (ii) shall be effective six months after the date of the order of revocation or cancellation (or, if such order is stayed, the date the stay is terminated) with respect to a broker's or dealer's registration status as a member within the meaning of Section 3(a)(2) of the Securities Investor Protection Act of 1970 for purposes of the application of Sections 5, 6 and 7 thereof to customer claims arising prior to the date of the order of revocation or cancellation (or, if such order is stayed, the date the stay is terminated).

Rule 15b6–1. Withdrawal From Registration

(a) Notice of withdrawal from registration as a broker or dealer pursuant to Section 15(b) of the Act shall be filed on Form BDW (17 CFR 249.501a) in accordance with the instructions contained therein. Every notice of withdrawal from registration as a broker or dealer shall be filed with the Central Registration Depository (operated by the National Association of Securities Dealers, Inc.) in accordance with applicable filing requirements. Prior to filing a notice of withdrawal from registration on Form BDW (17 CFR 249.501a), a broker or dealer shall amend Form BD (17 CFR 249.501) in accordance with § 240.15b3–1(a) to update any inaccurate information.

(b) A notice of withdrawal from registration filed by a broker or dealer pursuant to Section 15(b) of the Act (15 U.S.C. 78o(b)) shall become effective for all matters (except as provided in this paragraph (b) and in paragraph (c) of this section) on the 60th day after the filing thereof with the Commission, within such longer period of time as to which such broker or dealer consents or which the Commission by order may determine as necessary or appropriate in the public interest or for the protection of investors, or within such shorter period of time as the Commission may determine. If a notice of withdrawal from registration is filed with the Commission at any time subsequent to the date of the issuance of a Commission order instituting proceedings pursuant to Section 15(b) of the Act (15 U.S.C. 78o(b)) to censure, place limitations on the activities, functions or operations of, or suspend or revoke the registration of, such broker or dealer, or if prior to the effective date of the notice of withdrawal pursuant to this paragraph (b), the Commission institutes such a proceeding or a proceeding to impose terms or conditions upon such withdrawal, the notice of withdrawal shall not become effective pursuant to this paragraph (b) except at such time and upon such terms and conditions as the Commission deems necessary or appropriate in the public interest or for the protection of investors.

(c) With respect to a broker's or dealer's registration status as a member within the meaning of Section 3(a)(2) of the Securities Investor Protection Act of 1970 (15 U.S.C. 78ccc(a)(2)) for purposes of the application of Sections 5, 6, and 7 (15 U.S.C. 78eee, 78fff, and 78fff–1) thereof to customer claims arising prior to the effective date of withdrawal pursuant to paragraph (b) of this section, the effective date of a broker's or dealer's withdrawal from registration pursuant to this paragraph (c) shall be six months after the effective date of withdrawal pursuant to paragraph (b) of this section or such shorter period of time as the Commission may determine.

(d) Every notice of withdrawal filed with the Central Registration Depository pursuant to this section shall constitute a "report" filed with the Commission within the meaning of Sections 15(b), 17(a), 18(a), 32(a) (15 U.S.C. 78o(b), 78q(a), 78r(a), 78ff(a)) and other applicable provisions of the Act.

(e) The Commission, by order, may exempt any broker or dealer from the filing requirements provided in Form BDW (17 CFR 249.501a) under conditions that differ from the filing instructions contained in Form BDW.

Rule 15b7–1. Compliance With Qualification Requirements of Self-Regulatory Organizations

No registered broker or dealer shall effect any transaction in, or induce the purchase or sale of, any security unless any natural person associated with such broker or dealer who effects or is involved in effecting such transaction is registered or approved in accordance with the standards of training, experience, competence, and other qualification standards (including but not limited to submitting and maintaining all required forms, paying all required fees, and passing any required examinations) established by the rules of any national securities exchange or national securities association of which such broker or dealer is a member or under the rules of the Municipal Securities Rulemaking Board (if it is subject to the rules of that organization).

Rule 15b9–1. Exemption for Certain Exchange Members

(a) Any broker or dealer required by Section 15(b)(8) of the Act to become a member of a registered national securities association shall be exempt from such requirement if it (1) is a member of a national securities exchange, (2) carries no customer accounts, and (3) has annual gross income derived from purchases and sales of securities otherwise than on a national securities exchange of which it is a member in an amount no greater than $1,000.

(b) The gross income limitation contained in paragraph (a) of this section, shall not apply to income derived from transactions (1) for the dealer's own account with or through another registered broker or dealer or (2) through the Intermarket Trading System.

(c) For purposes of this section, the term "Intermarket Trading System" shall mean the intermarket communications linkage operated jointly by certain self-regulatory organizations pursuant to a plan filed with, and approved by, the Commission pursuant to Rule 11Aa3–2.

Rule 15b9–2. Exemption From SRO Membership for OTC Derivatives Dealers

An OTC derivatives dealer, as defined in § 240.3b–12, shall be exempt from any requirement under section 15(b)(8) of the Act (15 U.S.C. 78o(b)(8)) to become a member of a registered national securities association.

Rule 15b11–1. Registration By Notice of Security Futures Product Broker–Dealers

(a) A broker or dealer may register by notice pursuant to section 15(b)(11)(A) of the Act (15 U.S.C. 78o(b)(11)(A)) if it:

(1) Is registered with the Commodity Futures Trading Commission as a futures commission merchant or an introducing broker, as those terms are defined in the Commodity Exchange Act (7 U.S.C. 1, *et seq.*), respectively;

(2) Is a member of the National Futures Association or another national securities association registered under section 15A(k) of the Act (15 U.S.C. 78o–3(k)); and

(3) Is not required to register as a broker or dealer in connection with transactions in securities other than security futures products.

(b) A broker or dealer registering by notice pursuant to section 15(b)(11)(A) of the Act (15 U.S.C. 78o(b)(11)(A)) must file Form BD–N (17 CFR 249.501b) in accordance with the instructions to the form. A broker or dealer registering by notice pursuant to this section must indicate where appropriate on Form BD–N that it satisfies all of the conditions in paragraph (a) of this section.

(c) If the information contained in any notice of registration filed on Form BD–N (17 CFR 249.501b) pursuant to this section is or becomes inaccurate for any reason, the broker or dealer shall promptly file an amendment on Form BD–N correcting such information.

(d) An application for registration by notice, and any amendments thereto, that are filed on Form BD–N (17 CFR 249.501b) pursuant to this section will be considered a "report" filed with the Commission for purposes of sections 15(b), 17(a), 18(a), 32(a) (15 U.S.C. 78o(b), 78q(a), 78r(a), 78ff(a)) and other applicable provisions of the Act.

RULES RELATING TO OVER–THE–COUNTER MARKETS

Rule 15c1–1. Definitions

As used in any rule adopted pursuant to Section 15(c)(1) of the Act:

(a) The term "customer" shall not include a broker or dealer or a municipal securities dealer; *provided, however,* That the term "customer" shall include a municipal securities dealer (other than a broker or dealer) with respect to transactions in securities other than municipal securities.

(b) The term "the completion of the transaction" means:

(1) In the case of a customer who purchases a security through or from a broker, dealer or municipal securities dealer, except as provided in subparagraph (2) of this paragraph, the time when such customer pays the broker, dealer or municipal securities dealer any part of the purchase price, or, if payment is effected by a bookkeeping entry, the time when such bookkeeping entry is made by the broker, dealer or municipal securities dealer for any part of the purchase price;

(2) In the case of a customer who purchases a security through or from a broker, dealer or municipal securities dealer and who makes payment therefor prior to the time when payment is requested or notification is given that payment is due, the time when such broker, dealer or mu-

nicipal securities dealer delivers the security to or into the account of such customer;

(3) In the case of a customer who sells a security through or to a broker, dealer or municipal securities dealer except as provided in subparagraph (4) of this paragraph, if the security is not in the custody of the broker, dealer or municipal securities dealer at the time of sale, the time when the security is delivered to the broker, dealer or municipal securities dealer, and if the security is in the custody of the broker, dealer or municipal securities dealer at the time of sale, the time when the broker, dealer or municipal securities dealer transfers the security from the account of such customer;

(4) In the case of a customer who sells a security through or to a broker, dealer or municipal securities dealer and who delivers such security to such broker, dealer or municipal securities dealer prior to the time when delivery is requested or notification is given that delivery is due, the time when such broker, dealer or municipal securities dealer makes payment to or into the account of such customer.

Rule 15c1-2. Fraud and Misrepresentation

(a) The term "manipulative, deceptive, or other fraudulent device or contrivance," as used in section 15(c)(1) of the Act, is hereby defined to include any act, practice, or course of business which operates or would operate as a fraud or deceit upon any person.

(b) The term "manipulative, deceptive or other fraudulent device or contrivance," as used in section 15(c)(1) of the Act, is hereby defined to include any untrue statement of a material fact and any omission to state a material fact necessary in order to make the statements made, in the light of the circumstances under which they are made, not misleading, which statement or omission is made with knowledge or reasonable grounds to believe that it is untrue or misleading.

(c) The scope of this rule shall not be limited by any specific definitions of the term "manipulative, deceptive, or other fraudulent device or contrivance" contained in other rules adopted pursuant to section 15(c)(1) of the Act.

Rule 15c1-3. Misrepresentation by Brokers, Dealers and Municipal Securities Dealers as to Registration

The term "manipulative, deceptive, or other fraudulent device or contrivance," as used in Section 15(c)(1) of the Act, is hereby defined to include any representation by a broker or dealer that the registration of a broker or dealer, pursuant to Section 15(b) of the Act, or the registration of a municipal securities dealer pursuant to Section 15B(a) of the Act, or the failure of the Commission to deny or revoke such registration, indicates in any way that the Commission has passed upon or approved the financial standing, business, or conduct of such registered broker, dealer or municipal securities dealer or the merits of any security or any transaction or transactions therein.

Rule 15c1-5. Disclosure of Control

The term "manipulative, deceptive or other fraudulent device or contrivance," as used in Section 15(c)(1) of the Act, is hereby defined to include any act of any broker, dealer or municipal securities dealer controlled by, controlling, or under common control with, the issuer of any security, designed to effect with or for the account of a customer any transaction in, or to induce the purchase or sale by such customer of, such security unless such broker, dealer or municipal securities dealer, before entering into any contract with or for such customer for the purchase or sale of such security, discloses to such customer the existence of such control, and unless such disclosure, if not made in writing, is supplemented by the giving or sending of written disclosure at or before the completion of the transaction.

Rule 15c1–6. Disclosure of Interest in Distributions

The term "manipulative, deceptive, or other fraudulent device or contrivance," as used in Section 15(c)(1) of the Act, is hereby defined to include any act of any broker who is acting for a customer or for both such customer and some other person, or of any dealer or municipal securities dealer who receives or has promise of receiving a fee from a customer for advising such customer with respect to securities, designed to effect with or for the account of such customer any transaction in, or to induce the purchase or sale by such customer of, any security in the primary or secondary distribution of which such broker, dealer or municipal securities dealer is participating or is otherwise financially interested unless such broker, dealer or municipal securities dealer, at or before the completion of each such transaction gives or sends to such customer written notification of the existence of such participation or interest.

Rule 15c1–7. Discretionary Accounts

(a) The term "manipulative, deceptive, or other fraudulent device or contrivance," as used in Section 15(c) of the Act, is hereby defined to include any act of any broker, dealer or municipal securities dealer designed to effect with or for any customer's account in respect to which such broker, dealer or municipal securities dealer or his agent or employee is vested with any discretionary power any transactions of purchase or sale which are excessive in size or frequency in view of the financial resources and character of such account.

(b) The term "manipulative, deceptive, or other fraudulent device or contrivance," as used in Section 15(c)(1) of the Act, is hereby defined to include any act of any broker, dealer or municipal securities dealer designed to effect with or for any customer's account in respect to which such broker, dealer or municipal securities dealer or his agent or employee is vested with any discretionary power any transaction of purchase or sale unless immediately after effecting such transaction such broker, dealer or municipal securities dealer makes a record of such transaction which record includes the name of such customer, the name, amount and price of the security, and the date and time when such transaction took place.

Rule 15c1–8. Sales at the Market

The term "manipulative, deceptive, or other fraudulent device or contrivance," as used in Section 15(c)(1) of the Act, is hereby defined to include any representation made to a customer by a broker, dealer or municipal securities dealer who is participating or otherwise financially interested in the primary or secondary distribution of any security which is not admitted to trading on a national securities exchange that such security is being offered to such customer "at the market" or at a price related to the market price unless such broker, dealer or municipal securities dealer knows or has reasonable grounds to believe that a market for such security exists other than that made, created, or controlled by him, or by any person for whom he is acting or with whom he is associated in such distribution, or by any person controlled by, controlling or under common control with him.

Rule 15c1–9. Use of Pro Forma Balance Sheets

The term "manipulative, deceptive, or other fraudulent device or contrivance," as used in section 15(c)(1) of the Act, is hereby defined to include the use of financial statements purporting to give effect to the receipt and application of any part of the proceeds from the sale or exchange of securities, unless the assumptions upon which each such financial statement is based are clearly set forth as part of the caption to each such statement in type at least as large as that used generally in the body of the statement.

Rule 15c2–1. Hypothecation of Customers' Securities

(a) *General Provisions.* The term "fraudulent, deceptive, or manipulative act or practice," as used in section 15(c)(2) of the Act, is hereby defined to include the direct or indirect hypothecation by a broker or dealer, or his arranging for or permitting, directly, or indirectly, the continued hypothecation of any securities carried for the account of any customer under circumstances—

(1) That will permit the commingling of securities carried for the account of any such customer with securities carried for the account of any other customer, without first obtaining the written consent of each such customer to such hypothecation;

(2) That will permit such securities to be commingled with securities carried for the account of any person other than a bona fide customer of such broker or dealer under a lien for a loan made to such broker or dealer; or

(3) That will permit securities carried for the account of customers to be hypothecated, or subjected to any lien or liens or claim or claims of the pledgee or pledgees, for a sum which exceeds the aggregate indebtedness of all customers in respect of securities carried for their accounts; except that this clause shall not be deemed to be violated by reason of an excess arising on any day through the reduction of the aggregate indebtedness of customers on such day: *Provided,* That funds or securities in an amount sufficient to eliminate such excess are paid or placed in transfer to pledgee for the purpose of reducing the sum of the liens or claims to which securities carried for the account of customers are subject as promptly as practicable after such reduction occurs, but before the lapse of one-half hour after the commencement of banking hours on the next banking day at the place where the largest principal amount of loans of such broker or dealer are payable and, in any event, before such broker or dealer on such day has obtained or increased any bank loan collateralized by securities carried for the account of customers.

(b) *Definitions.* For the purposes of this rule—

(1) The term *customer* shall not include any general or special partner or any director or officer of such broker or dealer, or any participant, as such, in any joint, group or syndicate account with such broker or dealer or with any partner, officer or director thereof. The term also shall not include a counterparty who has delivered collateral to an OTC derivatives dealer pursuant to a transaction in an eligible OTC derivative instrument, or pursuant to the OTC derivatives dealer's cash management securities activities or ancillary portfolio management securities activities, and who has received a prominent written notice from the OTC derivatives dealer that:

(i) Except as otherwise agreed in writing by the OTC derivatives dealer and the counterparty, the dealer may repledge or otherwise use the collateral in its business;

(ii) In the event of the OTC derivatives dealer's failure, the counterparty will likely be considered an unsecured creditor of the dealer as to that collateral;

(iii) The Securities Investor Protection Act of 1970 (15 U.S.C 78aaa through 78lll) does not protect the counterparty; and

(iv) The collateral will not be subject to the requirements of § 240.8c-1, § 240.15c2-1, § 240.15c3-2, or § 240.15c3-3;

(2) The term "securities carried for the account of any customer" shall be deemed to mean:

(i) Securities received by or on behalf of such broker or dealer for the account of any customer;

(ii) Securities sold and appropriated by such broker or dealer to a customer, except that if such securities were subject to a lien when appropriated to a customer they shall not be deemed to be "securities carried for the account of any customer" pending their release from such lien as promptly as practicable;

(iii) Securities sold, but not appropriated, by such broker or dealer to a customer who has made any payment therefor, to the extent that such broker or dealer owns and has received delivery of securities of like kind, except that if such securities were subject to a lien when such payment was made they shall not be deemed to be "securities carried for the account of any customer" pending their release from such lien as promptly as practicable;

(3) "Aggregate indebtedness" shall not be deemed to be reduced by reason of uncollected items. In computing aggregate indebtedness, related guaranteed and guarantor accounts shall be treated as a single account and considered on a consolidated basis, and balances in accounts carrying both long and short positions shall be adjusted by treating the market value of the securities required to cover such short positions as though such market value were a debit; and

(4) In computing the sum of the liens or claims to which securities carried for the account of customers of a broker or dealer are subject, any rehypothecation of such securities by another broker or dealer who is subject to this rule or to Rule 8c–1 shall be disregarded.

(c) *Exemption for Cash Accounts.* The provisions of paragraph (a)(1) hereof shall not apply to any hypothecation of securities carried for the account of a customer in a special cash account within the meaning of section 4(c) of Regulation T of the Board of Governors of the Federal Reserve System: *Provided,* That at or before the completion of the transaction of purchase of such securities for, or of sale of such securities to, such customer, written notice is given or sent to such customer disclosing that such securities are or may be hypothecated under circumstances which will permit the commingling thereof with securities carried for the account of other customers. The term "the completion of the transaction" shall have the meaning given to such term by Rule 15c1–1(b).

(d) *Exemption for Clearing House Liens.* The provisions of paragraphs (a)(2), (a)(3), and (f) of this section shall not apply to any lien or claim of the clearing corporation, or similar department or association, of a national securities exchange or a registered national securities association, for a loan made and to be repaid on the same calendar day, which is incidental to the clearing of transactions in securities or loans through such corporation, department, or association: *Provided, however,* That for the purpose of paragraph (a)(3) of this rule, "aggregate indebtedness of all customers in respect of securities carried for their accounts" shall not include indebtedness in respect of any securities subject to any lien or claim exempted by this paragraph.

(e) *Exemption for Certain Liens on Securities of Noncustomers.* The provisions of paragraph (a)(2) hereof shall not be deemed to prevent such broker or dealer from permitting securities not carried for the account of a customer to be subjected (i) to a lien for a loan made against securities carried for the account of customers, or (ii) to a lien for a loan made and to be repaid on the same calendar day. For the purpose of this exemption, a loan shall be deemed to be "made against securities carried for the account of customers" if only securities carried for the account of customers are used to obtain or to increase such loan or as substitutes for other securities carried for the account of customers.

(f) *Notice and Certification Requirements.* No person subject to this rule shall hypothecate any security carried for the account of a customer unless, at or prior to the time of each such hypothecation, he gives written notice to the pledgee that the security pledged is carried for the account of a customer and that such hypothecation does not contravene any provision of this rule, except that in the case of an omnibus account the broker or dealer for whom such account is carried may furnish a signed statement to the person carrying such account that all securities carried therein by such broker or dealer will be securities carried for the account of his customers and that the hypothecation thereof by such broker or dealer will not contravene any provision of this rule. The provisions of this clause shall not apply to any hypothecation of securities under any lien or claim of a pledgee securing a loan made and to be repaid on the same calendar day.

(g) The fact that securities carried for the accounts of customers and securities carried for the accounts of others are represented by one or more certificates in the custody of a clearing corporation or other subsidiary organization of either a national securities exchange or of a registered national securities association, or of a custodian bank, in accordance with a system for the central handling of securities established by a national securities exchange or a registered national securities association, pursuant to which system the hypothecation of such securities is effected by bookkeeping entries without physical delivery of such securities, shall not, in and of itself, result in a commingling of securities, prohibited by paragraph (*a*)(1) or (*a*)(2) hereof, whenever a participating member, broker or dealer hypothecates securities in accordance with such system: *Provided, however*, That (1) any such custodian of any securities held by or for such system shall agree that it will not for any reason, including the assertion of any claim, right or lien of any kind, refuse or refrain from promptly delivering any such securities (other than securities then hypothecated in accordance with such system) to such clearing corporation or other subsidiary organization or as directed by it, except that nothing in such agreement shall be deemed to require the custodian to deliver any securities in contravention of any notice of levy, seizure or similar notice, or order, or judgment, issued or directed by a governmental agency or court, or officer thereof, having jurisdiction over such custodian, which on its face affects such securities; (2) such systems shall have safeguards in the handling, transfer and delivery of securities and provisions for fidelity bond coverage of the employees and agents of the clearing corporation or other subsidiary organization and for periodic examinations by independent public accountants; and (3) the provisions of this paragraph (g) shall not be effective with respect to any particular system unless the agreement required by (1) and the safeguards and provisions required by (2) shall have been deemed adequate by the Commission for the protection of investors, and unless any subsequent amendments to such agreement, safeguards or provisions shall have been deemed adequate by the Commission for the protection of investors.

Rule 15c2-4. Transmission or Maintenance of Payments Received in Connection With Underwritings

It shall constitute a "fraudulent, deceptive, or manipulative act or practice" as used in Section 15(c)(2) of the Act, for any broker, dealer or municipal securities dealer participating in any distribution of securities, other than a firm-commitment underwriting, to accept any part of the sale price of any security being distributed unless:

(a) The money or other consideration received is promptly transmitted to the persons entitled thereto; or

(b) If the distribution is being made on an "all-or-none" basis, or on any other basis which contemplates that payment is not to be made to the person on whose behalf the distribution is being made until some further event or contingency occurs, (1) the money or other consideration received is promptly deposited in a separate bank account, as agent or trustee for the persons who have the beneficial interests therein, until the appropriate event or contingency has occurred, and then the funds are promptly transmitted or returned to the persons entitled thereto, or (2) all such funds are promptly transmitted to a bank which has agreed in writing to hold all such funds in escrow for the persons who have the beneficial interests therein and to transmit or return such funds directly to the persons entitled thereto when the appropriate event or contingency has occurred.

Rule 15c2–5. Disclosure and Other Requirements When Extending or Arranging Credit in Certain Transactions

(a) It shall constitute a "fraudulent, deceptive, or manipulative act or practice" as used in section 15(c)(2) of the Act for any broker or dealer to offer or sell any security to, or to attempt to induce the purchase of any security by, any person, in connection with which such broker or dealer, directly or indirectly offers to extend any credit to or to arrange any loan for such person, or extends to or participates in arranging any loan for such person, unless such broker or dealer, before any purchase, loan or other related element of the transaction is entered into:

(1) Delivers to such person a written statement setting forth the exact nature and extent of (i) such person's obligations under the particular loan arrangement, including, among other things, the specific charges which such person will incur under such loan in each period during which the loan may continue or be extended, (ii) the risks and disadvantages which such person will incur in the entire transaction, including the loan arrangement, (iii) all commissions, discounts, and other remuneration received and to be received, in connection with the entire transaction including the loan arrangement, by the broker or dealer, by any person controlling, controlled by, or under common control with the broker or dealer, and by any other person participating in the transaction; *Provided, however,* That the broker or dealer shall be deemed to be in compliance with this subparagraph if the customer, before any purchase, loan, or other related element of the transaction is entered into in a manner legally binding upon the customer, receives a statement from the lender, or receives a prospectus or offering circular from the broker or dealer, which statement, prospectus or offering circular contains the information required by this subparagraph; and

(2) Obtains from such person information concerning his financial situation and needs, reasonably determines that the entire transaction, including the loan arrangement, is suitable for such person, and retains in his files a written statement setting forth the basis upon which the broker or dealer made such determination; *Provided, however,* That the written statement referred to in this subparagraph must be made available to the customer on request.

(b) This rule shall not apply to any credit extended or any loan arranged by any broker or dealer subject to the provisions of Regulation T (issued by the Board of Governors of the Federal Reserve System) if such credit is extended or such loan is arranged, in compliance with the requirements of such regulation, only for the purpose of purchasing or carrying the security offered or sold: *Provided, however,* That notwithstanding this paragraph, the provisions of paragraph (a) shall apply in full force with respect to any transaction involving the extension of or arrangement for credit by a broker or dealer (i) in a special insurance premium funding account within the meaning of Section 4(k) of Regulation T or (ii) in compliance with the terms of Rule 3a12–5.

(c) This rule shall not apply to any offer to extend credit or arrange any loan, or to any credit extended or loan arranged, in connection with any offer or sale, or attempt to induce the purchase, of any municipal security.

(d) This section shall not apply to a transaction involving the extension of credit by an OTC derivatives dealer, as defined in § 240.3b–12, if the transaction is exempt from the provisions of Section 7(c) of the Act (15 U.S.C. 78g(c)) pursuant to § 240.36a1–1.

Rule 15c2–7. Identification of Quotations

(a) It shall constitute an attempt to induce the purchase or sale of a security by making a "fictitious quotation" within the meaning of Section 15(c)(2) of the Act, for any broker or dealer to furnish or submit, directly or indirectly, any quotation for a security (other than a municipal security) to an inter-dealer quotation system unless:

(1) The inter-dealer-quotation-system is informed, if such is the case, that the quotation is furnished or submitted

(i) by a correspondent broker or dealer for the account or in behalf of another broker or dealer, and if so, the identity of such other broker or dealer; and/or

(ii) in furtherance of one or more other arrangements (including a joint account, guarantee of profit, guarantee against loss, commission, markup, markdown, indication of interest and accommodation arrangement) between or among brokers or dealers, and if so, the identity of each broker or dealer participating in any such arrangement or arrangements: *Provided, however,* That the provisions of this subparagraph shall not apply if only one of the brokers or dealers participating in any such arrangement or arrangements furnishes or submits a quotation with respect to the security to an inter-dealer-quotation-system.

(2) The inter-dealer-quotation-system to which the quotation is furnished or submitted makes it a general practice to disclose with each published quotation, by appropriate symbol or otherwise, the category or categories (subparagraphs (a)(1)(A) and/or (a)(1)(B)) in furtherance of which the quotation is submitted, and the identities of all other brokers and dealers referred to in subparagraphs (a)(1)(A) and (a)(1)(B) where such information is supplied to the inter-dealer-quotation-system under the provisions of paragraph (a)(1) of this rule.

(b) It shall constitute an attempt to induce the purchase or sale of a security by making a "fictitious quotation," within the meaning of section 15(c)(2) of the Act, for a broker or dealer to enter into any correspondent or other arrangement (including a joint account, guarantee of profit, guarantee against loss, commission, markup, markdown, indication of interest and accommodation arrangement) in furtherance of which two or more brokers or dealers furnish or submit quotations with respect to a particular security unless such broker or dealer informs all brokers or dealers furnishing or submitting such quotations of the existence of such correspondent and other arrangements, and the identity of the parties thereto.

(c) For purposes of this rule:

(1) The term "inter-dealer-quotation-system" shall mean any system of general circulation to brokers and dealers which regularly disseminates quotations of identified brokers or dealers but shall not include a quotation sheet prepared and distributed by a broker or dealer in the regular course of his business and containing only quotations of such broker or dealer.

(2) The term "quotation" shall mean any bid or offer, or any indication of interest (such as OW or BW) in any bid or offer.

(3) The term "correspondent" shall mean a broker or dealer who has a direct line of communication to another broker or dealer located in a different city or geographic area.

Rule 15c2–8. Delivery of Prospectus

(a) It shall constitute a deceptive act or practice, as those terms are used in section 15(c)(2) of the Act, for a broker or dealer to participate in a distribution of securities with respect to which a registration statement has been filed under the Securities Act of 1933 unless he complies with the requirements set forth in paragraphs (b) through (h) of this rule. For the purposes of this rule, a broker or dealer participating in the distribution shall mean any underwriter and any member or proposed member of the selling group.

(b) In connection with an issue of securities, the issuer of which has not previously been required to file reports pursuant to sections

13(a) or 15(d) of the Securities Exchange Act of 1934, unless such issuer has been exempted from the requirement to file reports thereunder pursuant to section 12(h) of the Act, such broker or dealer shall deliver a copy of the preliminary prospectus to any person who is expected to receive a confirmation of sale at least 48 hours prior to the sending of such confirmation. This paragraph (b) does not apply with respect to asset-backed securities (as defined in § 229.1101 of this chapter) that meet the requirements of General Instruction I.B.5 of Form 5-3 (§ 239.13 of this chapter).

(c) Such broker or dealer shall take reasonable steps to furnish to any person who makes written request for a preliminary prospectus between the filing date and a reasonable time prior to the effective date of the registration statement to which such prospectus relates, a copy of the latest preliminary prospectus on file with the Commission. Reasonable steps shall include receiving an undertaking by the managing underwriter or underwriters to send such copy to the address given in the requests.

(d) Such broker or dealer shall take reasonable steps to comply promptly with the written request of any person for a copy of the final prospectus relating to such securities during the period between the effective date of the registration statement and the later of either the termination of such distribution, or the expiration of the applicable 40- or 90-day period under Section 4(3) of the Securities Act of 1933. Reasonable steps shall include receiving an undertaking by the managing underwriter or underwriters to send such copy to the address given in the requests. (The 40-day and 90-day periods referred to above shall be deemed to apply for purposes of this rule irrespective of the provisions of paragraph (b) and (d) of Rule 174 under the Securities Act of 1933.)

(e) Such broker or dealer shall take reasonable steps (1) to make available a copy of the preliminary prospectus relating to such securities to each of his associated persons who is expected, prior to the effective date, to solicit customers' orders for such securities before the making of any such solicitation by such associated persons and (2) to make available to each such associated person a copy of any amended preliminary prospectus promptly after the filing thereof.

(f) Such broker or dealer shall take reasonable steps to make available a copy of the final prospectus relating to such securities to each of his associated persons who is expected, after the effective date, to solicit customers' orders for such securities prior to the making of any such solicitation by such associated persons, unless a preliminary prospectus which is substantially the same as the final prospectus except for matters relating to the price of the stocks, has been so made available.

(g) If the broker or dealer is a managing underwriter of such distribution, he shall take reasonable steps to see to it that all other brokers or dealers participating in such distribution are promptly furnished with sufficient copies, as requested by them, of each preliminary prospectus, each amended preliminary prospectus and the final prospectus to enable them to comply with paragraphs (b), (c), (d), and (e) of this rule.

(h) If the broker or dealer is a managing underwriter of such distribution, he shall take reasonable steps to see that any broker or dealer participating in the distribution or trading in the registered security is furnished reasonable quantities of the final prospectus relating to such securities, as requested by him, in order to enable him to comply with the prospectus delivery requirements of section 5(b)(1) and (2) of the Securities Act of 1933.

(i) This rule shall not require the furnishing of prospectuses in any state where such furnishing would be unlawful under the laws of such state: *Provided, however,* That this provision is not to be construed to relieve a broker or dealer from complying with the requirements of section 5(b)(1) and (2) of the Securities Act of 1933.

(j) For purposes of this section, the term *preliminary prospectus* shall include the term *prospectus subject to completion* as used in 17 CFR 230.434(a), and the term *final prospectus* shall include the term *Section 10(a) prospectus* as used in 17 CFR 230.434(a).

Rule 15c2–11. Initiation or Resumption of Quotations Without Specified Information

Preliminary Note: Brokers and dealers may wish to refer to Securities Exchange Act Release No. 29094 (April 17, 1991), for a discussion of procedures for gathering and reviewing the information required by this rule and the requirement that a broker or dealer have a reasonable basis for believing that the information is accurate and obtained from reliable sources.

(a) As a means reasonably designed to prevent fraudulent, deceptive, or manipulative acts or practices, it shall be unlawful for a broker or dealer to publish any quotation for a security or, directly or indirectly, to submit any such quotation for publication, in any quotation medium (as defined in this section) unless such broker or dealer has in its records the documents and information required by this paragraph (for purposes of this section, "paragraph (a) information"), and, based upon a review of the paragraph (a) information together with any other documents and information required by paragraph (b) of this section, has a reasonable basis under the circumstances for believing that the paragraph (a) information is accurate in all material respects, and that the sources of the paragraph (a) information are reliable. The information required pursuant to this paragraph is:

(1) A copy of the prospectus specified by section 10(a) of the Securities Act of 1933 for an issuer that has filed a registration statement under the Securities Act of 1933, other than a registration statement on Form F–6, which became effective less than 90 calendar days prior to the day on which such broker or dealer publishes or submits the quotation to the quotation medium, Provided That such registration statement has not thereafter been the subject of a stop order which is still in effect when the quotation is published or submitted; or

(2) A copy of the offering circular provided for under Regulation A under the Securities Act of 1933 for an issuer that has filed a notification under Regulation A and was authorized to commence the offering less than 40 calendar days prior to the day on which such broker or dealer publishes or submits the quotation to the quotation medium, Provided That the offering circular provided for under Regulation A has not thereafter become the subject of a suspension order which is still in effect when the quotation is published or submitted; or

(3) A copy of the issuer's most recent annual report filed pursuant to section 13 or 15(d) of the Act or a copy of the annual statement referred to in section 12(g)(2)(G)(i) of the Act, in the case of an issuer required to file reports pursuant to section 13 or 15(d) of the Act or an issuer of a security covered by section 12(g)(2)(B) or (G) of the Act, together with any quarterly and current reports that have been filed under the provisions of the Act by the issuer after such annual report or annual statement; Provided, however, That until such issuer has filed its first annual report pursuant to section 13 or 15(d) of the Act or annual statement referred to in section 12(g)(2)(G)(i) of the Act, the broker or dealer has in its records a copy of the prospectus specified by section 10(a) of the Securities Act of 1933 included in a registration statement filed by the issuer under the Securities Act of 1933, other than a registration statement on Form F–6, that became effective within the prior 16 months, or a copy of any registration statement filed by the issuer under section 12 of the Act that became effective within the prior 16 months, together with any quarterly and current reports filed thereafter under section 13 or 15(d) of the Act; and Provided further, That the broker or dealer has a reasonable basis under the circumstances for believing that the issuer is current in filing annual, quarterly, and current reports filed pursuant to section 13 or 15(d) of the Act, or, in the case of an

insurance company exempted from section 12(g) of the Act by reason of section 12(g)(2)(G) thereof, the annual statement referred to in section 12(g)(2)(G)(i) of the Act; or

(4) The information furnished to the Commission pursuant to § 240.12g3–2(b) since the beginning of the issuer's last fiscal year, in the case of an issuer exempt from section 12(g) of the Act by reason of compliance with the provisions of § 240.12g3–2(b), which information the broker or dealer shall make reasonably available upon request to any person expressing an interest in a proposed transaction in the security with such broker or dealer; or

(5) The following information, which shall be reasonably current in relation to the day the quotation is submitted and which the broker or dealer shall make reasonably available upon request to any person expressing an interest in a proposed transaction in the security with such broker or dealer:

(i) The exact name of the issuer and its predecessor (if any);

(ii) the address of its principal executive offices;

(iii) the state of incorporation, if it is a corporation;

(iv) the exact title and class of the security;

(v) the par or stated value of the security;

(vi) the number of shares or total amount of the securities outstanding as of the end of the issuer's most recent fiscal year;

(vii) the name and address of the transfer agent;

(viii) the nature of the issuer's business;

(ix) the nature of products or services offered;

(x) the nature and extent of the issuer's facilities;

(xi) the name of the chief executive officer and members of the board of directors;

(xii) the issuer's most recent balance sheet and profit and loss and retained earnings statements;

(xiii) similar financial information for such part of the 2 preceding fiscal years as the issuer or its predecessor has been in existence;

(xiv) whether the broker or dealer or any associated person is affiliated, directly or indirectly with the issuer;

(xv) whether the quotation is being published or submitted on behalf of any other broker or dealer, and, if so, the name of such broker or dealer; and

(xvi) whether the quotation is being submitted or published directly or indirectly on behalf of the issuer, or any director, officer or any person, directly or indirectly the beneficial owner of more than 10 percent of the outstanding units or shares of any equity security of the issuer, and, if so, the name of such person, and the basis for any exemption under the federal securities laws for any sales of such securities on behalf of such person.

If such information is made available to others upon request pursuant to this paragraph, such delivery, unless otherwise represented, shall not constitute a representation by such broker or dealer that such information is accurate, but shall constitute a representation by such broker or dealer that the information is reasonably current in relation to the day the quotation is submitted, that the broker or dealer has a reasonable basis under the circumstances for believing the information is accurate in all material respects, and that the information was obtained from sources which the broker or dealer has a reasonable basis for believing are reliable. This paragraph (a)(5) shall not apply to any security of an issuer included in paragraph (a)(3) of this section unless a report or statement of such issuer described in paragraph (a)(3) of this section is not reasonably available to the broker or dealer. A report or statement of an issuer described in paragraph (a)(3) of this section shall be "reasonably available" when such report or statement is filed with the Commission.

(b) With respect to any security the quotation of which is within the provisions of this section, the broker or dealer submitting or publishing such quotation shall have in its records the following documents and information:

(1) A record of the circumstances involved in the submission of publication of such quotation, including the identity of the person or persons for whom the quotation is being submitted or published and any information regarding the transactions provided to the broker or dealer by such person or persons;

(2) A copy of any trading suspension order issued by the Commission pursuant to section 12(k) of the Act respecting any securities of the issuer or its predecessor (if any) during the 12 months preceding the date of the publication or submission of the quotation, or a copy of the public release issued by the Commission announcing such trading suspension order; and

(3) A copy or a written record of any other material information (including adverse information) regarding the issuer which comes to the broker's or dealer's knowledge or possession before the publication or submission of the quotation.

(c) The broker or dealer shall preserve the documents and information required under paragraphs (a) and (b) of this section for a period of not less than three years, the first two years in an easily accessible place.

(d)(1) For any security of an issuer included in paragraph (a)(5) of this section, the broker or dealer submitting the quotation shall furnish to the interdealer quotation system (as defined in paragraph (e)(2) of this section), in such form as such system shall prescribe, at least 3 business days before the quotation is published or submitted, the information regarding the security and the issuer which such broker or dealer is required to maintain pursuant to said paragraph (a)(5) of this section.

(2) For any security of an issuer included in paragraph (a)(3) of this section,

(i) a broker-dealer shall be in compliance with the requirement to obtain current reports filed by the issuer if the broker-dealer obtains all current reports filed with the Commission by the issuer as of a date up to five business days in advance of the earlier of the date of submission of the quotation to the quotation medium and the date of submission of the paragraph (a) information pursuant to Schedule H of the By–Laws of the National Association of Securities Dealers, Inc.; and

(ii) a broker-dealer shall be in compliance with the requirement to obtain the annual, quarterly, and current reports filed by the issuer, if the broker-dealer has made arrangements to receive all such reports when filed by the issuer and it has regularly received reports from the issuer on a timely basis, unless the broker-dealer has a reasonable basis under the circumstances for believing that the issuer has failed to file a required report or has filed a report but has not sent it to the broker-dealer.

(e) For purposes of this section:

(1) "Quotation medium" shall mean any "interdealer quotation system" or any publication or electronic communications network or other device which is used by brokers or dealers to make known to others their interest in transactions in any security, including offers to buy or sell at a stated price or otherwise, or invitations of offers to buy or sell.

(2) "Interdealer quotation system" shall mean any system of general circulation to brokers or dealers which regularly disseminates quotations of identified brokers or dealers.

(3) Except as otherwise specified in this rule, "quotation" shall mean any bid or offer at a specified price with respect to a security, or any indication of interest by a broker or dealer in receiving bids or offers from others for a security, or any indication by a broker or dealer that he wishes to advertise his general interest in buying or selling a particular security.

(4) "Issuer," in the case of quotations for American Depositary Receipts, shall mean the issuer of the deposited shares represented by such American Depositary Receipts.

(f) The provisions of this section shall not apply to:

(1) The publication or submission of a quotation respecting a security admitted to trading on a national securities exchange and which is traded on such an exchange on the same day as, or on the business day next preceding, the day the quotation is published or submitted.

(2) The publication or submission by a broker or dealer, solely on behalf of a customer (other than a person acting as or for a dealer), of a quotation that represents the customer's indication of interest and does not involve the solicitation of the customer's interest; Provided, however, That this paragraph (f)(2) shall not apply to a quotation consisting of both a bid and an offer, each of which is at a specified price, unless the quotation medium specifically identifies the quotation as representing such an unsolicited customer interest.

(3)(i) The publication or submission, in an interdealer quotation system that specifically identifies as such unsolicited customer indications of interest of the kind described in paragraph (f)(2) of this section, of a quotation respecting a security which has been the subject of quotations (exclusive of any identified customer interests) in such a system on each of at least 12 days within the previous 30 calendar days, with no more than 4 business days in succession without a quotation; or

(ii) The publication or submission, in an interdealer quotation system that does not so identify any such unsolicited customer indications of interest, of a quotation respecting a security which has been the subject of both bid and ask quotations in an interdealer quotation system at specified prices on each of at least 12 days within the previous 30 calendar days, with no more than 4 business days in succession without such a two-way quotation;

(iii) A dealer acting in the capacity of market maker, as defined in section 3(a)(38) of the Act, that has published or submitted a quotation respecting a security in an interdealer quotation system and such quotation has qualified for an exception provided in this paragraph (f)(3), may continue to publish or submit quotations for such security in the interdealer quotation system without compliance with this section unless and until such dealer ceases to submit or publish a quotation or ceases to act in the capacity of market maker respecting such security.

(4) The publication or submission of a quotation respecting a municipal security.

(5) The publication or submission of a quotation respecting a security that is authorized for quotation in the NASDAQ system (as defined in § 240.11Ac1–2(a)(3) of this chapter), and such authorization is not suspended, terminated, or prohibited.

(g) The requirement in paragraph (a)(5) of this section that the information with respect to the issuer be "reasonably current" will be presumed to be satisfied, unless the broker or dealer has information to the contrary, if:

(1) The balance sheet is as of a date less than 16 months before the publication or submission of the quotation, the statements of profit and loss and retained earnings are for the 12 months preceding the date of such balance sheet, and if such balance sheet is not as of a date less than 6 months before the publication or submission of the quotation, it shall be accompanied by additional

statements of profit and loss and retained earnings for the period from the date of such balance sheet to a date less than 6 months before the publication or submission of the quotation.

(2) Other information regarding the issuer specified in paragraph (a)(5) of this section is as of a date within 12 months prior to the publication or submission of the quotation.

(h) This rule shall not prohibit any publication or submission of any quotation if the Commission, upon written request or upon its own motion, exempts such quotation either unconditionally or on specified terms and conditions, as not constituting a fraudulent, manipulative or deceptive practice comprehended within the purpose of this rule.

Rule 15c2–12. Municipal Securities Disclosure

Preliminary Note: For a discussion of disclosure obligations relating to municipal securities, issuers, brokers, dealers, and municipal securities dealers should refer to Securities Act Release No. 7049, Securities Exchange Act Release No. 33741, FR–42 (March 9, 1994). For a discussion of the obligations of underwriters to have a reasonable basis for recommending municipal securities, brokers, dealers, and municipal securities dealers should refer to Securities Exchange Act Release No. 26100 (Sept. 22, 1988) and Securities Exchange Act Release No. 26985 (June 28, 1989).

(a) *General.* As a means reasonably designed to prevent fraudulent, deceptive, or manipulative acts or practices, it shall be unlawful for any broker, dealer, or municipal securities dealer (a "Participating Underwriter" when used in connection with an Offering) to act as an underwriter in a primary offering of municipal securities with an aggregate principal amount of $1,000,000 or more (an "Offering") unless the Participating Underwriter complies with the requirements of this section or is exempted from the provisions of this section.

(b) *Requirements.*

(1) Prior to the time the Participating Underwriter bids for, purchases, offers, or sells municipal securities in an Offering, the Participating Underwriter shall obtain and review an official statement that an issuer of such securities deems final as of its date, except for the omission of no more than the following information: the offering price(s), interest rate(s), selling compensation, aggregate principal amount, principal amount per maturity, delivery dates, any other terms or provisions required by an issuer of such securities to be specified in a competitive bid, ratings, other terms of the securities depending on such matters, and the identity of the underwriter(s).

(2) Except in competitively bid offerings, from the time the Participating Underwriter has reached an understanding with an issuer of municipal securities that it will become a Participating Underwriter in an Offering until a final official statement is available, the Participating Underwriter shall send no later than the next business day, by first class mail or other equally prompt means, to any potential customer, on request, a single copy of the most recent preliminary official statement, if any.

(3) The Participating Underwriter shall contract with an issuer of municipal securities or its designated agent to receive, within seven business days after any final agreement to purchase, offer, or sell the municipal securities in an Offering and in sufficient time to accompany any confirmation that requests payment from any customer, copies of a final official statement in sufficient quantity to comply with paragraph (b)(4) of this rule and the rules of the Municipal Securities Rulemaking Board.

(4) From the time the final official statement becomes available until the earlier of (i) ninety days from the end of the underwriting period or (ii) the time when the official statement is available to any person from a nationally recognized municipal securities information repository, but in no case less than twenty five days following the end of the underwriting period, the Participating Underwriter in an Offering shall send no later than the next business day, by first

class mail or other equally prompt means, to any potential customer, on request, a single copy of the final official statement.

(5)(i) A Participating Underwriter shall not purchase or sell municipal securities in connection with an Offering unless the Participating Underwriter has reasonably determined that an issuer of municipal securities, or an obligated person for whom financial or operating data is presented in the final official statement has undertaken, either individually or in combination with other issuers of such municipal securities or obligated persons, in a written agreement or contract for the benefit of holders of such securities, to provide, either directly or indirectly through an indenture trustee or a designated agent:

(A) To each nationally recognized municipal securities information repository and to the appropriate state information depository, if any, annual financial information for each obligated person for whom financial information or operating data is presented in the final official statement, or, for each obligated person meeting the objective criteria specified in the undertaking and used to select the obligated persons for whom financial information or operating data is presented in the final official statement, except that, in the case of pooled obligations, the undertaking shall specify such objective criteria;

(B) If not submitted as part of the annual financial information, then when and if available, to each nationally recognized municipal securities information repository and to the appropriate state information depository, audited financial statements for each obligated person covered by paragraph (b)(5)(i)(A) of this section;

(C) In a timely manner, to each nationally recognized municipal securities information repository or to the Municipal Securities Rulemaking Board, and to the appropriate state information depository, if any, notice of any of the following events with respect to the securities being offered in the Offering, if material:

(*1*) Principal and interest payment delinquencies;

(*2*) Non-payment related defaults;

(*3*) Unscheduled draws on debt service reserves reflecting financial difficulties;

(*4*) Unscheduled draws on credit enhancements reflecting financial difficulties;

(*5*) Substitution of credit or liquidity providers, or their failure to perform;

(*6*) Adverse tax opinions or events affecting the tax-exempt status of the security;

(*7*) Modifications to rights of security holders;

(*8*) Bond calls;

(*9*) Defeasances;

(*10*) Release, substitution, or sale of property securing repayment of the securities;

(*11*) Rating changes; and

(D) In a timely manner, to each nationally recognized municipal securities information repository or to the Municipal Securities Rulemaking Board, and to the appropriate state information depository, if any, notice of a failure of any person specified in paragraph (b)(5)(i)(A) of this section to provide required annual financial information, on or before the date specified in the written agreement or contract.

(ii) The written agreement or contract for the benefit of holders of such securities also shall identify each person for whom annual financial information and notices of material events will be provided, either by name or by the objective criteria used to select such persons, and, for each such person shall:

(A) Specify, in reasonable detail, the type of financial information and operating data to be provided as part of annual financial information;

(B) Specify, in reasonable detail, the accounting principles pursuant to which financial statements will be prepared, and whether the financial statements will be audited; and

(C) Specify the date on which the annual financial information for the preceding fiscal year will be provided, and to whom it will be provided.

(iii) Such written agreement or contract for the benefit of holders of such securities also may provide that the continuing obligation to provide annual financial information and notices of events may be terminated with respect to any obligated person, if and when such obligated person no longer remains an obligated person with respect to such municipal securities.

(c) *Recommendations.* As a means reasonably designed to prevent fraudulent, deceptive, or manipulative acts or practices, it shall be unlawful for any broker, dealer, or municipal securities dealer to recommend the purchase or sale of a municipal security unless such broker, dealer, or municipal securities dealer has procedures in place that provide reasonable assurance that it will receive prompt notice of any event disclosed pursuant to paragraph (b)(5)(i)(C), paragraph (b)(5)(i)(D), and paragraph (d)(2)(ii)(B) of this section with respect to that security.

(d) *Exemptions.* (1) This section shall not apply to a primary offering of municipal securities in authorized denominations of $100,000 or more, if such securities:

(i) Are sold to no more than thirty-five persons each of whom the Participating Underwriter reasonably believes:

(A) Has such knowledge and experience in financial and business matters that it is capable of evaluating the merits and risks of the prospective investment; and

(B) Is not purchasing for more than one account or with a view to distributing the securities; or

(ii) Have a maturity of nine months or less; or

(iii) At the option of the holder thereof may be tendered to an issuer of such securities or its designated agent for redemption or purchase at par value or more at least as frequently as every nine months until maturity, earlier redemption, or purchase by an issuer or its designated agent.

(2) Paragraph (b)(5) of this section shall not apply to an Offering of municipal securities if, at such time as an issuer of such municipal securities delivers the securities to the Participating Underwriters:

(i) No obligated person will be an obligated person with respect to more than $10,000,000 in aggregate amount of outstanding municipal securities, including the offered securities and excluding municipal securities that were offered in a transaction exempt from this section pursuant to paragraph (d)(1) of this section;

(ii) An issuer of municipal securities or obligated person has undertaken, either individually or in combination with other issuers of municipal securities or obligated persons, in a written agreement or contract for the benefit of holders of such municipal securities, to provide:

(A) Upon request to any person or at least annually to the appropriate state information depository, if any, financial information or operating data regarding each obligated person for which financial information or operating data is presented in the final official statement, as specified in the undertaking, which financial information and operating data shall include, at a minimum, that financial information and operating data which is customarily prepared by such obligated person and is publicly available; and

(B) In a timely manner, to each nationally recognized municipal securities information repository or to the Municipal Securities Rulemaking Board, and to the appropriate state information depository, if any, notice of events specified in paragraph (b)(5)(i)(C) of this section with respect to the securities that are the subject of the Offering, if material; and

(iii) the final official statement identifies by name, address, and telephone number the persons from which the foregoing information, data, and notices can be obtained.

(3) The provisions of paragraph (b)(5) of this section, other than paragraph (b)(5)(i)(C) of this section, shall not apply to an Offering of municipal securities, if such municipal securities have a stated maturity of 18 months or less.

(4) The provisions of paragraph (c) of this section shall not apply to municipal securities:

(i) Sold in an Offering to which paragraph (b)(5) of this section did not apply, other than Offerings exempt under paragraph (d)(2)(ii) of this section; or

(ii) Sold in an Offering exempt from this section under paragraph (d)(1) of this section.

(e) *Exemptive Authority.* The Commission, upon written request, or upon its own motion, may exempt any broker, dealer, or municipal securities dealer, whether acting in the capacity of a Participating Underwriter or otherwise, that is a participant in a transaction or class of transactions from any requirement of this section, either unconditionally or on specified terms and conditions, if the Commission determines that such an exemption is consistent with the public interest and the protection of investors.

(f) *Definitions.* For the purposes of this rule—

(1) The term "authorized denominations of $100,000 or more" means municipal securities with a principal amount of $100,000 or more and with restrictions that prevent the sale or transfer of such securities in principal amounts of less than $100,000 other than through a primary offering; except that, for municipal securities with an original issue discount of 10 percent or more, the term means municipal securities with a minimum purchase price of $100,000 or more and with restrictions that prevent the sale or transfer of such securities, in principal amounts that are less than the original principal amount at the time of the primary offering, other than through a primary offering.

(2) The term "end of the underwriting period" means the later of such time as (i) the issuer of municipal securities delivers the securities to the Participating Underwriters or (ii) the Participating Underwriter does not retain, directly or as a member or an underwriting syndicate, an unsold balance of the securities for sale to the public.

(3) The term *final official statement* means a document or set of documents prepared by an issuer of municipal securities or its representatives that is complete as of the date delivered to the Participating Underwriter(s) and that sets forth information concerning the terms of the proposed issue of securities; information, including financial information or operating data, concerning such issuers of municipal securities and those other entities, enterprises, funds, accounts, and other persons material to an evaluation of the Offering; and a description of the undertakings to be provided pursuant to paragraph (b)(5)(i), paragraph (d)(2)(ii), and paragraph (d)(2)(iii) of this section, if applicable, and of any instances in the previous five years in which each person specified pursuant to paragraph (b)(5)(ii) of this section failed to comply, in all material respects, with any previous undertakings in a written contract or agreement specified in paragraph (b)(5)(i) of this section. Financial information or operating data may be set forth in the document or set of documents, or may be included by specific reference to

documents previously provided to each nationally recognized municipal securities information repository, and to a state information depository, if any, or filed with the Commission. If the document is a final official statement, it must be available from the Municipal Securities Rulemaking Board.

(4) The term "issuer of municipal securities" means the governmental issuer specified in section 3(a)(29) of the Act and the issuer of any separate security, including a separate security as defined in Rule 3b–5(a) under the Act.

(5) The term "potential customer" means (i) any person contacted by the Participating Underwriter concerning the purchase of municipal securities that are intended to be offered or have been sold in an Offering, (ii) any person who has expressed an interest to the Participating Underwriter in possibly purchasing such municipal securities, and (iii) any person who has a customer account with the Participating Underwriter.

(6) The term "preliminary official statement" means an official statement prepared by or for an issuer of municipal securities for dissemination to potential customers prior to the availability of the final official statement.

(7) The term "primary offering" means an offering of municipal securities directly or indirectly by or on behalf of an issuer of such securities, including any remarketing of municipal securities (i) that is accompanied by a change in the authorized denomination of such securities from $100,000 or more to less than $100,000, or (ii) that is accompanied by a change in the period during which such securities may be tendered to an issuer of such securities or its designated agent for redemption or purchase from a period of nine months or less to a period of more than nine months.

(8) The term "underwriter" means any person who has purchased from an issuer of municipal securities with a view to, or offers or sells for an issuer of municipal securities in connection with, the offering of any municipal security, or participates or has a direct or indirect participation in any such undertaking, or participates or has a participation in the direct or indirect underwriting of any such undertaking; except, that such term shall not include a person whose interest is limited to a commission, concession, or allowance from an underwriter, broker, dealer, or municipal securities dealer not in excess of the usual and customary distributors' or sellers' commission, concession, or allowance.

(9) The term *annual financial information* means financial information or operating data, provided at least annually, of the type included in the final official statement with respect to an obligated person, or in the case where no financial information or operating data was provided in the final official statement with respect to such obligated person, of the type included in the final official statement with respect to those obligated persons that meet the objective criteria applied to select the persons for which financial information or operating data will be provided on an annual basis. Financial information or operating data may be set forth in the document or set of documents, or may be included by specific reference to documents previously provided to each nationally recognized municipal securities information repository, and to a state information depository, if any, or filed with the Commission. If the document is a final official statement, it must be available from the Municipal Securities Rulemaking Board.

(10) The term *obligated person* means any person, including an issuer of municipal securities, who is either generally or through an enterprise, fund or account of such person committed by contract or other arrangement to support payment of all, or part of the obligations on the municipal securities to be sold in the Offering (other than providers of municipal bond insurance, letters of credit, or other liquidity facilities).

(g) *Transitional Provision.* If on July 28, 1989 a Participating Underwriter was contractually committed to act as underwriter in an Offering of municipal securities originally issued before July 29, 1989, the requirements of paragraphs (b)(3) and (b)(4) shall not apply to the Participating Underwriter in connection with such an Offering. Paragraph (b)(5) of this section shall not apply to a Participating Underwriter that has contractually committed to act as an underwriter in an Offering of municipal securities before July 3, 1995: *except that* paragraph (b)(5)(i)(A) and paragraph (b)(5)(i)(B) shall not apply with respect to fiscal years ending prior to January 1, 1996. Paragraph (c) shall become effective on January 1, 1996. Paragraph (d)(2)(ii) and paragraph (d)(2)(iii) of this section shall not apply to an Offering of municipal securities commencing prior to January 1, 1996.

Rule 15c3-1. Net Capital Requirements for Brokers and Dealers

(a) Every broker or dealer shall at all times have and maintain net capital no less than the greater of the highest minimum requirement applicable to its ratio requirement under paragraph (a)(1) of this rule, or to any of its activities under paragraph (a)(2) of this rule. Each broker or dealer also shall comply with the supplemental requirements of paragraphs (a)(4) and (a)(9) of this rule, to the extent either paragraph is applicable to its activities. In addition, a broker or dealer shall maintain net capital of not less than its own net capital requirement plus the sum of each broker's or dealer's subsidiary or affiliate minimum net capital requirements, which is consolidated pursuant to Appendix C, § 240.15c3-1c. In lieu of applying paragraphs (a)(1) and (a)(2) of this section, an OTC derivatives dealer shall maintain net capital pursuant to paragraph (a)(5) of this section.

Ratio Requirements

Aggregate Indebtedness Standard

(1)(i) No broker or dealer, other than one that elects the provisions of paragraph (a)(1)(ii) of this rule, shall permit its aggregate indebtedness to all other persons to exceed 1500 percent of its net capital (or 800 percent of its net capital for 12 months after commencing business as a broker or dealer).

Alternative Standard

(ii) A broker or dealer may elect not to be subject to the Aggregate Indebtedness Standard of paragraph (a)(1)(i) of this rule. That broker or dealer shall not permit its net capital to be less than the greater of $250,000 or 2 percent of aggregate debit items computed in accordance with the Formula for Determination of Reserve Requirements for Brokers and Dealers (Exhibit A to Rule 15c3-3a). Such broker or dealer shall notify its Examining Authority, in writing, of its election to operate under this paragraph (a)(1)(ii). Once a broker or dealer has notified its Examining Authority, it shall continue to operate under this paragraph unless a change is approved upon application to the Commission. A broker or dealer that elects this standard and is not exempt from Rule 15c3-3 shall:

(A) Make the computation required by § 240.15c3-3(e) and set forth in Exhibit A, Rule 15c3-3a, on a weekly basis and, in lieu of the 1 percent reduction of certain debit items required by Note E(3) in the computation of its Exhibit A requirement, reduce aggregate debit items in such computation by 3 percent;

(B) Include in Items 7 and 8 of Exhibit A, Rule 15c3-3a, the market value of items specified therein more than 7 business days old;

(C) Exclude credit balances in accounts representing amounts payable for securities not yet received from the issuer or its agent which securities are specified in paragraphs (c)(2)(vi)(A) and (E) of this rule and any related debit items from the Exhibit A requirement for 3 business days; and

(D) Deduct from net worth in computing net capital 1 percent of the contract value of all failed to deliver contracts or securities borrowed that were allocated to failed to receive contracts of the same issue and which thereby were excluded from Items 11 or 12 of Exhibit A, Rule 15c3–3a.

Futures Commission Merchants

(iii) No broker or dealer registered as a futures commission merchant shall permit its net capital to be less than the greater of its requirement under paragraph (a)(1)(i) or (ii) of this rule, or 4 percent of the funds required to be segregated pursuant to the Commodity Exchange Act and the regulations thereunder (less the market value of commodity options purchased by option customers on or subject to the rules of a contract market, each such deduction not to exceed the amount of funds in the customer's account).

Minimum Requirements

See Appendix E (§ 240.15c3–1E) for temporary minimum requirements.

Brokers or Dealers That Carry Customer Accounts

(2)(i) A broker or dealer (other than one described in paragraphs (a)(2)(ii) or (a)(8) of this rule) shall maintain net capital of not less than $250,000 if it carries customer or broker or dealer accounts and receives or holds funds or securities for those persons. A broker or dealer shall be deemed to receive funds, or to carry customer or broker or dealer accounts and to receive funds from those persons if, in connection with its activities as a broker or dealer, it receives checks, drafts, or other evidences of indebtedness made payable to itself or persons other than the requisite registered broker or dealer carrying the account of a customer, escrow agent, issuer, underwriter, sponsor, or other distributor of securities. A broker or dealer shall be deemed to hold securities for, or to carry customer or broker or dealer accounts, and hold securities of, those persons if it does not promptly forward or promptly deliver all of the securities of customers or of other brokers or dealers received by the firm in connection with its activities as a broker or dealer. A broker or dealer, without complying with this paragraph (a)(2)(i), may receive securities only if its activities conform with the provisions of paragraphs (a)(2)(iv) or (v) of this rule, and may receive funds only in connection with the activities described in paragraph (a)(2)(v) of this rule.

(ii) A broker or dealer that is exempt from the provisions of Rule 15c3–3 pursuant to paragraph (k)(2)(i) thereof shall maintain net capital of not less than $100,000.

Dealers

(iii) A dealer shall maintain net capital of not less than $100,000. For the purposes of this rule, the term "dealer" includes:

(A) Any broker or dealer that endorses or writes options otherwise than on a registered national securities exchange or a facility of a registered national securities association; and

(B) Any broker or dealer that effects more than ten transactions in any one calendar year for its own investment account. This rule shall not apply to those persons engaging in activities described in paragraphs (a)(2)(v), (a)(2)(vi) or (a)(8) of this rule, or to those persons whose underwriting activities are limited solely to acting as underwriters in best efforts or all or none underwritings in conformity with paragraph (b)(2) of Rule 15c2–4, so long as those persons engage in no other dealer activities.

Brokers or Dealers That Introduce Customer Accounts and Receive Securities

(iv) A broker or dealer shall maintain net capital of not less than $50,000 if it introduces transactions and accounts of customers or other brokers or dealers to another registered broker or dealer that carries such accounts on a fully disclosed basis, and if the broker or dealer receives but does not hold customer or other broker or dealer securities. A broker or dealer operating under this paragraph (a)(2)(iv) of this rule may participate in a firm commitment underwriting without being subject to the provisions of paragraph (a)(2)(iii) of this rule, but may not enter into a commitment for the purchase of shares related to that underwriting.

Brokers or Dealers Engaged in the Sale of Redeemable Shares of Registered Investment Companies and Certain Other Share Accounts

(v) A broker or dealer shall maintain net capital of not less than $25,000 if it acts as a broker or dealer with respect to the purchase, sale and redemption of redeemable shares of registered investment companies or of interests or participations in an insurance company separate account directly from or to the issuer on other than a subscription way basis. A broker or dealer operating under this rule may sell securities for the account of a customer to obtain funds for the immediate reinvestment in redeemable securities of registered investment companies. A broker or dealer operating under this paragraph (a)(2)(v) must promptly transmit all funds and promptly deliver all securities received in connection with its activities as a broker or dealer, and may not otherwise hold funds or securities for, or owe money or securities to, customers.

Other Brokers or Dealers

(vi) A broker or dealer that does not receive, directly or indirectly, or hold funds or securities for, or owe funds or securities to, customers and does not carry accounts of, or for, customers and does not engage in any of the activities described in paragraphs (a)(2)(i) through (v) of this rule shall maintain net capital of not less than $5,000. A broker or dealer operating under this paragraph may engage in the following dealer activities without being subject to the requirements of paragraph (a)(2)(iii) of this rule:

(A) In the case of a buy order, prior to executing such customer's order, it purchases as principal the same number of shares or purchases shares to accumulate the number of shares necessary to complete the order, which shall be cleared through another registered broker or dealer or

(B) In the case of a sell order, prior to executing such customer's order, it sells as principal the same number of shares or a portion thereof, which shall be cleared through another registered broker or dealer.

(3) [Reserved].

Capital Requirements for Market Makers

(4) A broker or dealer engaged in activities as a market maker as defined in paragraph (c)(8) of this rule shall maintain net capital in an amount not less than $2,500 for each security in which it makes a market (unless a security in which it makes a market has a market value of $5 or less, in which event the amount of net capital shall be not less than $1,000 for each such security) based on the average number of such markets made by such broker or dealer during the 30 days immediately preceding the computation date. Under no circumstances shall it have net capital less than that required by the provisions of paragraph (a) of this rule, or be required to maintain net capital of more than $1,000,000 unless required by paragraph (a) of this rule.

(5) In accordance with Appendix F to this section (§ 240.15c3-1f), the Commission may grant an application by an OTC derivatives dealer when calculating net capital to use the market risk standards of Appendix F as to some or all of its positions in lieu of the provisions of paragraph (c)(2)(vi) of this section and the credit risk standards of Ap-

pendix F to its receivables (including counterparty net exposure) arising from transactions in eligible OTC derivative instruments in lieu of the requirements of paragraph (c)(2)(iv) of this section. An OTC derivatives dealer shall at all times maintain tentative net capital of not less than $100 million and net capital of not less than $20 million.

MARKET MAKERS, SPECIALISTS AND CERTAIN OTHER DEALERS

(6)(i) A dealer who meet the conditions of paragraph (a)(6)(ii) of this rule may elect to operate under this paragraph (a)(6) and thereby not apply, except to the extent required by this paragraph (a)(6), the provisions of paragraphs (c)(2)(vi) or Appendix A, Rule 15c3–1a, of this rule to market maker and specialist transactions and, in lieu thereof, apply thereto the provisions of paragraph (a)(6)(iii) of this rule.

(ii) This paragraph (a)(6) shall be available to a dealer who does not effect transactions with other than brokers or dealers, who does not carry customer accounts, who does not effect transactions in unlisted options, and whose market maker or specialist transactions are effected through and carried in a market maker or specialist account cleared by another broker or dealer as provided in paragraph (a)(6)(iv) of this rule.

(iii) A dealer who elects to operate pursuant to this paragraph (a)(6) shall at all times maintain a liquidating equity in respect of securities positions in his market maker or specialist account at least equal to:

(A) An amount equal to 25 percent (5 percent in the case of exempted securities) of the market value of the long positions and 30 percent of the market value of the short positions; provided, however, in the case of long or short positions in options and long or short positions in securities other than options which relate to a bona fide hedged position as defined in paragraph (c)(2)(x)(C) of this rule, such amount shall equal the deductions in respect of such positions specified by paragraph (c)(2)(x)(A)(1)–(9) of this rule.

(B) Such lesser requirement as may be approved by the Commission under specified terms and conditions upon written application of the dealer and the carrying broker or dealer.

(C) For purposes of this paragraph (a)(6)(iii), equity in such specialist or market maker account shall be computed by (1) marking all securities positions long or short in the account to their respective current market values, (2) adding (deducting in the case of a debit balance) the credit balance carried in such specialist or market maker account, and (3) adding (deducting in the case of short positions) the market value of positions long in such account.

(iv) The dealer shall obtain from the broker or dealer carrying the market maker or specialist account a written undertaking which shall be designated "Notice Pursuant to Section Rule 15c3–1(a)(6) of Intention to Carry Specialist or Market Maker Account." Said undertaking shall contain the representations required by this paragraph (a)(6) and shall be filed with the Commission's Washington, D.C. Office, the regional or district office of the Commission for the region or district in which the broker or dealer has its principal place of business and the Designated Examining Authorities of both firms prior to effecting any transactions in said account. The broker or dealer carrying such account:

(A) Shall mark the account to the market not less than daily and shall issue appropriate calls for additional equity which shall be met by noon of the following business day;

(B) Shall notify by telegraph the Commission and the Designated Examining Authorities pursuant to Rule 17a–11, if the market maker or specialist fails to deposit any required equity within the time prescribed in paragraph (a)(6)(iv)(A) above; said telegraphic notice shall be received by the Commission and the Designated Examining Authorities not later than the close of business on the day said call is not met;

(C) Shall not extend further credit in the account if the equity in the account falls below that prescribed in paragraph (a)(6)(iii) above, and

(D) Shall take steps to liquidate promptly existing positions in the account in the event of a failure to meet a call for equity.

(v) No such carrying broker or dealer shall permit the sum of (A) the deductions required by paragraph (c)(2)(x)(A) of this rule in respect of all transactions in market maker accounts guaranteed, endorsed or carried by such broker or dealer pursuant to paragraph (c)(2)(x) of this rule and (B) the equity required by paragraph (iii) of this paragraph (a)(6) in respect of all transactions in the accounts of specialists or market makers in options carried by such broker or dealer pursuant to this paragraph (a)(6) to exceed 1000 percent of such broker's or dealer's net capital as defined in paragraph (c)(2) of this rule for any period exceeding five business days; *Provided,* That solely for purposes of this paragraph (a)(6)(v), deductions or equity required in a specialist or market maker account in respect of positions in fully paid securities (other than options), which do not underlie options listed on the national securities exchange or facility of a national securities association of which the specialist or market maker is a member, need not be recognized. *Provided, further,* That if at any time such sum exceeds 1000 percent of such broker's or dealer's net capital, then the broker or dealer shall immediately transmit telegraphic notice of such event to the principal office of the Commission in Washington, D.C, the regional or district office of the Commission for the region or district in which the broker or dealer maintains its principal place of business, and such broker's or dealer's Designated Examining Authority. *Provided, further,* That if at any time such sum exceeds 1000 percent of such broker's or dealer's net capital, then such broker or dealer shall be subject to the prohibitions against withdrawal of equity capital set forth in paragraph (e) of this rule, and to the prohibitions against reduction, prepayment and repayment of subordination agreements set forth in paragraph (b)(11) of Rule 15c3-1d, as if such broker or dealer's net capital were below the minimum standards specified by each of the aforementioned paragraphs.

ALTERNATIVE NET CAPITAL COMPUTATION FOR BROKER-DEALERS THAT ELECT TO BE SUPERVISED ON A CONSOLIDATED BASIS

(7) In accordance with Appendix E to this section (§ 240.15c3-1e), the Commission may approve, in whole or in part, an application or an amendment to an application by a broker or dealer to calculate net capital using the market risk standards of Appendix E to compute a deduction for market risk on some or all of its positions, instead of the provisions of paragraphs (c)(2)(vi) and (c)(2)(vii) of this section, and using the credit risk standards of Appendix E to compute a deduction for credit risk on certain credit exposures arising from transactions in derivatives instruments, instead of the provisions of paragraph (c)(2)(iv) of this section, subject to any conditions or limitations on the broker or dealer the Commission may require as necessary or appropriate in the public interest or for the protection of investors. A broker or dealer that has been approved to calculate its net capital under Appendix E must:

(i) At all times maintain tentative net capital of not less than $1 billion and net capital of not less than $500 million;

(ii) Provide notice that same day in accordance with § 240.17a-11(g) if the broker's or dealer's tentative net capital is less than $5 billion. The Commission may, upon written application, lower the threshold at which notification is necessary under this paragraph (a)(7)(ii), either unconditionally or on specified terms and conditions, if a broker or dealer satisfies the Commission that notification at the $5 billion threshold is unnecessary because of, among other factors, the special nature of its business, its financial position, its internal risk management system, or its compliance history; and

(iii) Comply with § 240.15c3-4 as though it were an OTC derivatives dealer with respect to all of its business activities, except that paragraphs (c)(5)(xiii), (c)(5)(xiv), (d)(8), and (d)(9) of § 240.15c3-4 shall not apply.

(8) *Municipal Securities Brokers' Brokers*

(i) A municipal securities brokers' broker, as defined in subparagraph (ii) of this paragraph (a)(8), may elect not to be subject to the limitations of paragraph (c)(2)(ix) of this rule provided that such brokers' broker complies with the requirements set out in subparagraphs (iii), (iv) and (v) of this paragraph (a)(8).

(ii) The term municipal securities "brokers' broker" shall mean a municipal securities broker or dealer who acts exclusively as an undisclosed agent in the purchase or sale of municipal securities for a registered broker or dealer or registered municipal securities dealer, who has no "customers" as defined in this rule and who does not have or maintain any municipal securities in its proprietary or other accounts.

(iii) In order to qualify to operate under this paragraph (a)(8), a brokers' broker shall at all times have and maintain net capital of not less than $150,000.

(iv) For purposes of this paragraph (a)(8), a brokers' broker shall deduct from net worth 1% of the contract value of each municipal failed to deliver contract which is outstanding 21 business days or longer. Such deduction shall be increased by any excess of the contract price of the fail to deliver over the market value of the underlying security.

(v) For purposes of this paragraph (a)(8), a brokers' broker may exclude from its aggregate indebtedness computation indebtedness adequately collateralized by municipal securities outstanding for not more than one business day and offset by municipal securities failed to deliver of the same issue and quantity. In no event may a brokers' broker exclude any overnight bank loan attributable to the same municipal securities failed to deliver contract for more than one business day. A brokers' broker need not deduct from net worth the amount by which the market value of securities failed to receive outstanding longer than thirty (30) calendar days exceeds the contract value of those failed to receives as required by Rule 15c3-1(c)(2)(iv)(E).

(9) *Certain Additional Capital Requirements for Brokers or Dealers Engaging in Reverse Repurchase Agreements.* A broker or dealer shall maintain net capital in addition to the amounts required under paragraph (a) of this rule in an amount equal to 10 percent of:

(i) The excess of the market value of United States Treasury Bills, Bonds, and Notes subject to reverse repurchase agreements with any one party over 105 percent of the contract prices (including accrued interest) for reverse repurchase agreements with that party;

(ii) The excess of the market value of securities issued or guaranteed as to principal or interest by an agency of the United States or mortgage related securities as defined in section 3(a)(41) of the Act subject to reverse repurchase agreements with any one party over 110 percent of the contract prices (including accrued interest) for reverse repurchase agreements with that person; and

(iii) The excess of the market value of other securities subject to reverse repurchase agreements with any one party over 120 percent of the contract prices (including accrued interest) for reverse repurchase agreements with that person.

(b) *Exemptions*:

(1) The provisions of this section shall not apply to any specialist:

(i) whose securities business, except for an occasional non-specialist related securities transaction for its own account, is limited to that of acting as an options market maker on a national securities exchange;

(ii) that is a member in good standing and subject to the capital requirements of a national securities exchange;

(iii) that does not transact a business in securities with other than a broker or dealer registered with the Commission under section 15 or section 15C of the Act or a member of a national securities exchange; and

(iv) that is not a clearing member of The Options Clearing Corporation and whose securities transactions are effected through and carried in an account cleared by another broker or dealer registered with the Commission under section 15 of the Act.

(2) A member in good standing of a national securities exchange who acts as a floor broker (and whose activities do not require compliance with other provisions of this rule), may elect to comply, in lieu of the other provisions of this rule, with the following financial responsibility standard: the value of the exchange membership of the member (based on the lesser of the most recent sale price or current bid price for an exchange membership) is not less than $15,000, or an amount equal to the excess of $15,000 over the value of the exchange membership is held by an independent agent in escrow; *Provided,* That the rules of such exchange require that the proceeds from the sale of the exchange membership of the member and the amount held in escrow pursuant to this paragraph shall be subject to the prior claims of the exchange and its clearing corporation and those arising directly from the closing out of contracts entered into on the floor of such exchange.

(3) The Commission may, upon written application, exempt from the provisions of this rule, either unconditionally or on specified terms and conditions, any broker or dealer who satisfies the Commission that, because of the special nature of its business, its financial position, and the safeguards it has established for the protection of customers' funds and securities, it is not necessary in the public interest or for the protection of investors to subject the particular broker or dealer to the provisions of this rule.

(c) *Definitions.* For the purpose of this rule:

AGGREGATE INDEBTEDNESS

(1) The term "aggregate indebtedness" shall be deemed to mean the total money liabilities of a broker or dealer arising in connection with any transaction whatsoever and includes, among other things, money borrowed, money payable against securities loaned and securities "failed to receive," the market value of securities borrowed to the extent to which no equivalent value is paid or credited (other than the market value of margin securities borrowed from customers in accordance with the provisions of Rule 15c3-3 and margin securities borrowed from non-customers), customers' and non-customers' free credit balances, credit balances in customers' and on-customers' accounts having short positions in securities, equities in customers' and non-customers' future commodities accounts and credit balances in customers' and non-customers' commodities accounts, but excluding:

Exclusions from aggregate indebtedness

(i) Indebtedness adequately collateralized by securities which are carried long by the broker or dealer and which have not been sold or by securities which collateralize a secured demand note pursuant to Appendix (D) to this Rule 15c3-1d; indebtedness adequately collateralized by spot commodities which are carried long by the broker or dealer and which have not been sold; or, until October 1, 1976, indebtedness adequately collateralized by municipal securities outstanding for not more than one business day and offset by municipal securities failed to deliver of the same issue and quantity, where such indebtedness is incurred by a broker or dealer effecting transactions solely in municipal securities who is either registered with the Commission or temporarily exempt from such registration pursuant to Rule 15a-1(T) or Rule 15Ba2-3(T);

(ii) Amounts payable against securities loaned, which securities are carried long by the broker or dealer and which have not been sold or which securities collateralize a secured demand note pursuant to Appendix (D);

(iii) Amounts payable against securities failed to receive which securities are carried long by the broker or dealer and which have not been sold or which securities collateralize a secured demand note pursuant to Appendix (D) or amounts payable against securities failed to receive for which the broker or dealer also has a receivable related to securities of the same issue and quantity thereof which are either fails to deliver or securities borrowed by the broker or dealer;

(iv) Credit balances in accounts representing amounts payable for securities or money market instruments not yet received from the issuer or its agent which securities are specified in subdivision (c)(2)(vi)(E) and which amounts are outstanding in such accounts not more than three (3) business days;

(v) Equities in customers' and non-customers' accounts segregated in accordance with the provisions of the Commodity Exchange Act and the rules and regulations thereunder;

(vi) Liability reserves established and maintained for refunds of charges required by Section 27(d) of the Investment Company Act of 1940, but only to the extent of amounts on deposit in a segregated trust account in accordance with Rule 27d-1 under the Investment Company Act of 1940;

(vii) Amounts payable to the extent funds and qualified securities are required to be on deposit and are deposited in a "Special Reserve Bank Account for the Exclusive Benefit of Customers" pursuant to Rule 15c3-3 under the Securities Exchange Act of 1934;

(viii) Fixed liabilities adequately secured by assets acquired for use in the ordinary course of the trade or business of a broker or dealer but no other fixed liabilities secured by assets of the broker or dealer shall be so excluded unless the sole recourse of the creditor for nonpayment of such liability is to such asset;

(ix) Liabilities on open contractual commitments;

(x) Indebtedness subordinated to the claims of creditors pursuant to a satisfactory subordination agreement, as defined in Appendix (D);

(xi) Liabilities which are effectively subordinated to the claims of creditors (but which are not subject to a satisfactory subordination agreement as defined in Appendix (D)) by non-customers of the broker or dealer prior to such subordination, except such subordinations by customers as may be approved by the Examining Authority for such broker or dealer;

(xii) Credit balances in accounts of general partners;

(xiii) Deferred tax liabilities;

(xiv) Eighty-five percent of amounts payable to a registered investment company related to fail to deliver receivables of the same quantity arising out of purchases of shares of those registered investment companies; and

(xv) Eighty-five percent of amounts payable against securities loaned for which the broker or dealer has receivables related to securities of the same class and issue and quantity that are securities borrowed by the broker or dealer.

NET CAPITAL

(2) The term "net capital" shall be deemed to mean the net worth of a broker or dealer, adjusted by:

(i) *Adjustments to net worth related to unrealized profit or loss and deferred tax provisions.* (A) Adding unrealized profits (or deducting unrealized losses) in the accounts of the broker or dealer;

(B)(*1*) In determining net worth, all long and all short positions in listed options shall be marked to their market value and all long and all short securities and commodities positions shall be marked to their market value.

(*2*) In determining net worth, the value attributed to any unlisted option shall be the difference between the option's exercise value and the market value of the underlying security. In the case of an unlisted call, if the market value of the underlying security is less than the exercise value of such call it shall be given no value and in the case of an unlisted put if the market value of the underlying security is more than the exercise value of the unlisted put it shall be given no value.

(C) Adding to net worth the lesser of any deferred income tax liability related to the items in (*1*), (*2*), and (*3*) below, or the sum of (*1*), (*2*) and (*3*) below;

(*1*) The aggregate amount resulting from applying to the amount of the deductions computed in accordance with subparagraph (c)(2)(vi) of this rule and Appendices (A) and (B), the appropriate Federal and State tax rate(s) applicable to any unrealized gain on the asset on which the deduction was computed;

(*2*) Any deferred tax liability related to income accrued which is directly related to an asset otherwise deducted pursuant to this rule;

(*3*) Any deferred tax liability related to unrealized appreciation in value of any asset(s) which has been otherwise deducted from net worth in accordance with the provisions of this rule; and,

(D) Adding, in the case of future income tax benefits arising as a result of unrealized losses, the amount of such benefits not to exceed the amount of income tax liabilities accrued on the books and records of the broker or dealer, but only to the extent such benefits could have been applied to reduce accrued tax liabilities on the date of the capital computation, had the related unrealized losses been realized on that date.

(E) Adding to net worth any actual tax liability related to income accrued which is directly related to an asset otherwise deducted pursuant to this rule.

(ii) *Subordinated Liabilities.* Excluding liabilities of the broker or dealer which are subordinated to the claims of creditors pursuant to a satisfactory subordination agreement, as defined in Appendix (D).

(iii) *Sole Proprietors.* Deducting, in the case of a broker or dealer who is a sole proprietor, the excess of liabilities which have not been incurred in the course of business as a broker or dealer over assets not used in the business.

(iv) *Assets Not Readily Convertible Into Cash.* Deducting fixed assets and assets which cannot be readily converted into cash (less any indebtedness excluded in accordance with subdivision (c)(1)(viii) of this rule) including, among other things:

(A) *Fixed Assets and Prepaid Items.* Real estate; furniture and fixtures; exchange memberships; prepaid rent, insurance and other expenses; goodwill, organization expenses;

(B) *Certain Unsecured and Partly Secured Receivables.* All unsecured advances and loans; deficits in customers' and non-customers' unsecured and partly secured notes; deficits in special omnibus accounts maintained in compliance with the requirements of 12 CFR 220.10 of Regulation T under the Securities Exchange Act of 1934, or similar accounts carried on behalf of another broker or dealer, after application of calls for margin, marks to the market or other required deposits which are outstanding 5 business days or less; deficits in customers' and non-customers' unsecured and partly secured accounts after application of calls for margin, marks to the market or other required deposits that are outstanding 5 business days or less, except deficits in cash accounts as defined in 12 CFR 220.8 of Regulation T under the Securities Exchange Act of 1934 for which not more than one extension respecting a specified securities transaction has been requested and granted, and deducting for securities carried in any of such accounts the percentages specified in paragraphs (c)(2)(vi) of this rule or Appendix A; the market value of stock loaned in excess of the value of any collateral received therefor; receivables arising out of free shipments of securities (other than mutual fund redemptions) in excess of $5,000 per shipment and all free shipments (other than mutual fund redemptions) outstanding more than 7 business days, and mutual fund redemptions outstanding more than 16 business days; any collateral deficiencies in secured demand notes as defined in Appendix D;

(C) Interest receivable, floor brokerage receivable, commissions receivable from other brokers or dealers (other than syndicate profits which shall be treated as required in subparagraph (c)(2)(iv)(E) of this rule), mutual fund concessions receivable and management fees receivable from registered investment companies, all of which receivables are outstanding longer than thirty (30) days from the date they arise; dividends receivable outstanding longer than thirty (30) days from the payable date; good faith deposits arising in connection with a non-municipal securities underwriting, outstanding longer than eleven (11) business days from the settlement of the underwriting with the issuer; receivables due from participation in municipal securities underwriting syndicates and municipal securities joint underwriting accounts which are outstanding longer than sixty (60) days from settlement of the underwriting with the issuer and good faith deposits arising in connection with an underwriting of municipal securities, outstanding longer than sixty (60) days from settlement of the underwriting with the issuer; and receivables due from participation in municipal securities secondary trading joint accounts, which are outstanding longer than sixty (60) days from the date all securities have been delivered by the account manager to the account members;

(D) *Insurance Claims.* Insurance claims which, after seven (7) business days from the date the loss giving rise to the claim is discovered, are not covered by an opinion of outside counsel that the claim is valid and is covered by insurance policies presently in effect; insurance claims which after twenty (20) business days from the date the loss giving rise to the claim is discovered and which are accompanied by an opinion of outside counsel described above, have not been acknowledged in writing by the insurance carrier as due and payable; and insurance claims acknowledged in writing by the carrier as due and payable outstanding longer than twenty (20) business days from the date they are so acknowledged by the carrier; and,

(E) *Other Deductions.* All other unsecured receivables; all assets doubtful of collection less any reserves established therefor; the amount by which the market value of securities failed to receive outstanding longer than thirty (30) calendar days exceeds the contract value of such fails to receive, and the funds on deposit in a "segregated trust account" in accordance with Rule 27d-1 under the Investment Company Act of 1940, but only to the extent that the amount on deposit in such segregated trust account exceeds the amount of liability reserves established and maintained for refunds of charges required by Sections 27(d) and 27(f) of the Investment Company Act of 1940; *Provided,* That any amount deposited in the "Special Reserve Bank Account for the Exclusive Benefit of Customers" established pursuant to Rule 15c3-3 and clearing deposits shall not be so deducted.

(F)(*1*) For purposes of this paragraph:

(*i*) The term "reverse repurchase agreement deficit" shall mean the difference between the contract price for resale of the securities under a reverse repurchase agreement and the market value of those securities (if less than the contract price).

(*ii*) The term "repurchase agreement deficit" shall mean the difference between the market value of securities subject to the repurchase agreement and the contract price for repurchase of the securities (if less than the market value of the securities).

(*iii*) As used in paragraph (F)(*1*), the term "contract price" shall include accrued interest.

(*iv*) Reverse repurchase agreement deficits and the repurchase agreement deficits where the counterparty is the Federal Reserve Bank of New York shall be disregarded.

(*2*)(*i*) In the case of a reverse repurchase agreement, the deduction shall be equal to the reverse repurchase agreement deficit.

(*ii*) In determining the required deductions under subparagraph (F)(*2*)(*i*), the broker or dealer may reduce the reverse repurchase agreement deficit by:

(*A*) Any margin or other deposits held by the broker or dealer on account of the reverse repurchase agreement;

(*B*) Any excess market value of the securities over the contract price for resale of those securities under any other reverse repurchase agreement with the same party;

(*C*) The difference between the contract price for resale and the market value of securities subject to repurchase agreements with the same party (if the market value of those securities is less than the contract price); and

(*D*) Calls for margin, marks to the market, or other required deposits which are outstanding one business day or less.

(*3*)(*i*) In the case of repurchase agreements, the deduction shall be:

(*A*) The excess of the repurchase agreement deficit over 5 percent of the contract price for resale of United States Treasury Bills, Notes and Bonds, 10 percent of the contract price for the resale of securities issued or guaranteed as to principal or interest by an agency of the United States or mortgage related securities as defined in section 3(a)(41) of the Act and 20 percent of the contract price for the resale of other securities and;

(*B*) The excess of the aggregate repurchase agreement deficits with any one party over 25 percent of the broker or dealer's net capital before the application of paragraph (c)(2)(vi) of this rule (less any deduction taken with respect to repurchase agreements with that party under paragraph (c)(2)(iv)(F)(*3*)(*i*)(*A*) of this rule) or, if greater;

(*C*) The excess of the aggregate repurchase agreement deficits over 300 percent of the broker or dealer's net capital before the application of paragraphs (c)(2)(vi) of this rule.

(*ii*) In determining the required deduction under paragraph (F)(*3*)(*i*), the broker or dealer may reduce a repurchase agreement deficit by:

(*A*) Any margin or other deposits held by the broker or dealer on account of a reverse repurchase agreement with the same party to the extent not otherwise used to reduce a reverse repurchase deficit;

(*B*) The difference between the contract price and the market value of securities subject to other repurchase agreements with the same party (if the market value of those securities is less than the contract price) not otherwise used to reduce a reverse repurchase agreement deficit; and

(*C*) Calls for margin, marks to the market, or other required deposits which are outstanding one business day or less to the extent not otherwise used to reduce a reverse repurchase agreement deficit.

(G) *Securities Borrowed.* 1% of the market value of securities borrowed collateralized by an irrevocable letter of credit.

(H) Any receivable from an affiliate of the broker or dealer (not otherwise deducted from net worth) and the market value of any collateral given to an affiliate (not otherwise deducted from net worth) to secure a liability over the amount of the liability of the broker or dealer unless the books and records of the affiliate are made available for examination when requested by the representatives of the Commission or the Examining Authority for the broker or dealer in order to demonstrate the validity of the receivable or payable. The provisions of this subsection shall not apply where the affiliate is a registered broker or dealer, registered government securities broker or dealer or bank as defined in section 3(a)(6) of the Act or insurance company as defined in section 3(a)(19) of the Act or investment company registered under the Investment Company Act of 1940 or federally insured savings and loan association or futures commission merchant registered pursuant to the Commodity Exchange Act.

(v)(A) *Securities Differences.* Deducting the market value of all short securities differences (which shall include securities positions reflected on the securities record which are not susceptible to either count or confirmation) unresolved after discovery in accordance with the following schedule:

Percentage of Market Value of Short Securities Differences	Numbers of Business Days After Discovery
25%	7
50%	14
75%	21
100%	28

(B) Deducting the market value of any long securities differences, where such securities have been sold by the broker or dealer before they are adequately resolved, less any reserves established therefor;

(C) The designated examining authority for a broker or dealer may extend the periods in (A) above for up to 10 business days if it finds that exceptional circumstances warrant an extension.

(vi) *Securities Haircuts.* Deducting the percentages specified in paragraphs (c)(2)(vi) (A) through (M) of this rule (or the deductions prescribed for securities positions set forth in Appendix (A)) of the market value of all securities, money market instruments or options in the proprietary or other accounts of the broker or dealer.

(A)(*1*) *Government Securities.* In the case of a security issued or guaranteed as to principal or interest by the United States or any agency thereof, the applicable percentages of the market value of the net long or short position in each of the categories specified below are:

Category 1

(*i*) Less than 3 months to maturity—0%.

(*ii*) 3 months but less than 6 months to maturity—½ of 1%.

(*iii*) 6 months but less than 9 months to maturity—¾ of 1%.

(*iv*) 9 months but less than 12 months to maturity—1%.

Category 2

(*i*) 1 year but less than 2 years to maturity—1½%.

(*ii*) 2 years but less than 3 years to maturity—2%.

Category 3

(*i*) 3 years but less than 5 years to maturity—3%.

(*ii*) 5 years but less than 10 years to maturity—4%.

Category 4

(*i*) 10 years but less than 15 years to maturity—4½%.

(*ii*) 15 years but less than 20 years to maturity—5%.

(*iii*) 20 years but less than 25 years to maturity—5½%.

(*iv*) 25 years or more to maturity—6%.

Brokers or dealers shall compute a deduction for each category above as follows: Compute the deductions for the net long or short positions in each subcategory above. The deduction for the category shall be the net of the aggregate deductions on the long positions and the aggregate deductions on short positions in each category plus 50% of the lesser of the aggregate deductions on the long or short positions.

(*2*) A broker or dealer may elect to deduct, in lieu of the computation required under paragraph (c)(2)(vi)(A)(*1*) of this rule, the applicable percentages of the market value of the net long or short positions in each of the subcategories specified in paragraph (c)(2)(vi)(A)(*1*) of this rule.

(*3*) In computing deductions under paragraph (c)(2)(vi)(A)(*1*) of this rule, a broker or dealer may elect to exclude the market value of a long or short security from one category and a security from another category, *Provided,* That:

(*i*) Such securities have maturity dates:

(*A*) Between 9 months and 15 months and within 3 months of one another.

(*B*) Between 2 years and 4 years and within 1 year of one another; or

(*C*) Between 8 years and 12 years and within 2 years of one another.

(*ii*) The net market value of the two excluded securities shall remain in the category of the security with the higher market value.

(*4*) In computing deductions under paragraph (c)(2)(vi)(A)(*1*) of this rule, a broker or dealer may include in the categories specified in paragraph (c)(2)(vi)(A)(*1*) of this rule, long or short positions in securities issued by the United States or any agency thereof that are deliverable against long or short positions in futures contracts relating to Government securities, traded on a recognized contract market approved by the Commodity Futures Trading Commission, which are held in the proprietary or other accounts of the broker or dealer. The value of the long or short positions included in the categories shall be determined by the contract value of the futures contract held in the account. The provisions of Appendix B to Rule 15c3-1 will in any event apply to the positions in futures contracts.

(*5*) In the case of a Government securities dealer that reports to the Federal Reserve System, that transacts business directly with the Federal Reserve System, and which maintains at all times a minimum net capital of at least $50,000,000, before application of the deductions provided for in paragraph (c)(2)(vi) of this rule, the deduction for a security issued or guaranteed as to principal or interest by the United States or any agency thereof shall be 75% of the deduction otherwise computed under paragraph (c)(2)(vi)(A) of this rule.

(B)(*1*) *Municipals.* In the case of any municipal security which has a scheduled maturity at date of issue of 731 days or less and which is issued at par value and pays interest at maturity, or which is issued at a discount, and which is not traded flat or in default as to principal or interest, the applicable percentages of the market value on the greater of the long or short position in each of the categories specified below are:

(*i*) Less than 30 days to maturity—0%;

(*ii*) 30 days but less than 91 days to maturity—⅛ of 1%;

(*iii*) 91 days but less than 181 days to maturity—¼ of 1%;

(*iv*) 181 days but less than 271 days to maturity—⅜ of 1%;

(*v*) 271 days but less than 366 days to maturity—½ of 1%;

(*vi*) 366 days but less than 456 days to maturity—¾ of 1%;

(*vii*) 456 days but less than 732 days to maturity—1%.

(*2*) In the case of any municipal security, other than those specified in paragraph (c)(2)(vi)(B)(*1*), which is not traded flat or in default as to principal or interest, the applicable percentages of the market value of the greater of the long or short position in each of the categories specified below are:

(*i*) Less than 1 year to maturity—1%

(*ii*) 1 year but less than 2 years to maturity—2%

(*iii*) 2 years but less than 3½ years to maturity—3%

(*iv*) 3½ years but less than 5 years to maturity—4%

(*v*) 5 years but less than 7 years to maturity—5%

(*vi*) 7 years but less than 10 years to maturity—5½%

(*vii*) 10 years but less than 15 years to maturity—6%

(*viii*) 15 years but less than 20 years to maturity—6½%

(*ix*) 20 years or more to maturity—7%

(C) *Canadian Debt Obligations.* In the case of any security issued or unconditionally guaranteed as to principal and interest by the Government of Canada, the percentages of market value to be deducted shall be the same as in (A) above.

(D)(*1*) In the case of redeemable securities of an investment company registered under the Investment Company Act of 1940, which assets consist of cash or money market instruments and which is generally known as a "money market fund," the deduction shall be 2% of the market value of the greater of the long or short position.

(*2*) In the case of redeemable securities of an investment company registered under the Investment Company Act of 1940, which assets are in the form of cash or securities or money market instruments of any maturity which are described in paragraph (c)(2)(vi)(A) through (C) or (E) of this rule, the deduction shall be 7% of the market value of the greater of the long or short positions.

(*3*) In the case of redeemable securities of an investment company registered under the Investment Company Act of 1940, which assets are in the form of cash or securities or money market instruments which are described in paragraphs (c)(2)(vi)(A) through (C) or (E) and (F) of this rule, the deduction shall be 9% of the market value of the long or short position.

(E) *Commercial Paper, Bankers Acceptances and Certificates of Deposit.* In the case of any short-term promissory note or evidence of indebtedness which has a fixed rate of interest or is sold at a discount, and which has a maturity date at date of issuance not exceeding nine months exclusive of days of grace, or any renewal thereof, the maturity of which is likewise limited and is rated in one of the three highest categories by at least two of the nationally recognized statistical rating organizations (provided that effective January 1, 1977 and until September 1, 1977, this paragraph shall be deemed to require only one such rating), or in the case of any negotiable certificate of deposit or bankers acceptance or similar type of instrument issued or guaranteed by any bank as defined in Section 3(a)(6) of the Securities Exchange Act of 1934, the applicable percentage of the market value of the greater of the long or short position in each of the categories specified below are:

(*1*) Less than 30 days to maturity—0 percent;

(*2*) 30 days but less than 91 days to maturity—⅛ of 1 percent;

(*3*) 91 days but less than 181 days to maturity—¼ of 1 percent;

(*4*) 181 days but less than 271 days to maturity—⅜ of 1 percent;

(*5*) 271 days but less than 1 year to maturity—½ of 1 percent; and

(*6*) With respect to any negotiable certificate of deposit or bankers acceptance or similar type of instrument issued or guaranteed by any bank, as defined above, having 1 year or more to maturity, the deduction shall be on the greater of the long or short position and shall be the same percentage as that prescribed in subdivision (c)(2)(vi)(A) above.

(F)(*1*) *Nonconvertible debt securities.* In the case of nonconvertible debt securities having a fixed interest rate and fixed maturity date and which are not traded flat or in default as to principal or interest and which are rated in one of the four highest rating categories by at least two of the nationally recognized statistical rating organizations, the applicable percentages of the market value of the greater of the long or short position in each of the categories specified below are:

(*i*) Less than 1 year to maturity—2%.

(*ii*) 1 year but less than 2 years to maturity—3%.

(*iii*) 2 years but less than 3 years to maturity—5%.

(*iv*) 3 years but less than 5 years to maturity—6%.

(*v*) 5 years but less than 10 years to maturity—7%.

(*vi*) 10 years but less than 15 years to maturity—7½%.

(*vii*) 15 years but less than 20 years to maturity—8.0%.

(*viii*) 20 years but less than 25 years to maturity—8½%.

(*ix*) 25 years or more to maturity—9.0%.

(*2*) A broker or dealer may elect to exclude from the above categories long or short positions that are hedged with short or long positions in securities issued by the United States or any agency thereof or nonconvertible debt securities having a fixed interest rate and a fixed maturity date and which are not traded flat or in default as to principal or interest and which are rated in one of the four highest rating categories by at least two of the nationally recognized statistical rating organizations if such securities have maturity dates:

(*i*) Less than five years and within 6 months of each other;

(*ii*) Between 5 years and 10 years and within 9 months of each other;

(*iii*) Between 10 years and 15 years and within 2 years of each other; or

(*iv*) 15 years or more and within 10 years of each other.

The broker-dealer shall deduct the amounts specified in subparagraphs (3) and (4) below.

(*3*) With respect to those positions described in subparagraph (2) that include a long or short position in securities issued by the United States or any agency thereof, the broker or dealer shall exclude the hedging short or long United States or agency securities position from the applicable haircut category under paragraph (c)(2)(vi)(A). The broker or dealer shall deduct the percentage of the market value of the hedged long or short position in nonconvertible debt securities as specified in each of the categories below:

(*i*) Less than 5 years to maturity—1½%

(*ii*) 5 years but less than 10 years to maturity—2½%

(*iii*) 10 years but less than 15 years to maturity—2¾%

(*iv*) 15 years or more to maturity—3%

(*4*) With respect to those positions described in paragraph (c)(2)(vi)(F)(2) of this rule that include offsetting long and short positions in nonconvertible debt securities, the broker or dealer shall deduct a percentage of the market value of the hedged long or short position in nonconvertible debt securities as specified in each of the categories below:

(*i*) Less than 5 years to maturity—1¾%

(*ii*) 5 years but less than 10 years to maturity—3%

(*iii*) 10 years but less than 15 years to maturity—3¼%

(*iv*) 15 years or more to maturity—3½%

(*5*) In computing deductions under paragraph (c)(2)(vi)(F)(*3*) of this rule, a broker or dealer may include in the categories specified in paragraph (c)(2)(vi)(F)(*3*) of this rule, long or short positions in securities issued by the United States or any agency thereof that are deliverable against long or short positions in futures contracts relating to Government securities, traded on a recognized contract market approved by the Commodity Futures Trading Commission, which are held in the proprietary or other accounts of the broker or dealer. The value of the long or short positions included in the categories shall be determined by the contract value of the futures contract held in the account.

(*6*) The provisions of Appendix B to Rule 15c3–1 will in any event apply to the positions in futures contracts.

(G) *Convertible Debt Securities.* In the case of a debt security not in default which has a fixed rate of interest and a fixed maturity date and which is convertible into an equity security, the deductions shall be as follows: If the market value is 100 percent or more of the principal amount, the deduction shall be determined as specified in subparagraph (J) below; if the market value is less than the principal amount, the deduction shall be determined as specified in subparagraph (F) above if such securities are rated as required by subparagraph (F) above.

(H) *Preferred Stock.* In the case of cumulative, nonconvertible preferred stock ranking prior to all other classes of stock of the same issuer, which is rated in one of the four highest rating categories by at least two of the nationally recognized statistical rating organizations and which are not in arrears as to dividends, the deduction shall be 10% of the market value of the greater of the long or short position.

(I) *Reserved.*

(J) *All Other Securities.* In the case of all securities or evidences of indebtedness, except those described in Appendix (A) which are not included in any of the percentage categories enumerated in paragraphs (c)(2)(vi)(A) through (H) of this rule or paragraph (c)(2)(vi)(K)(ii) of this rule, the deduction shall be 15 percent of the market value of the greater of the long or short positions and to the extent the market value of the lesser of the long or short positions exceeds 25 percent of the market value of the greater of the long or short positions, the percentage deduction on such excess shall be 15 percent of the market value of such excess. No deduction need be made in the case of:

(1) A security that is convertible into or exchangeable for another security within a period of 90 days, subject to no conditions other than the payment of money, and the other securities into which such security is convertible or for which it is exchangeable, are short in the accounts of such broker or dealer; or

(2) A security that has been called for redemption and that is redeemable within 90 days.

(K) *Securities With a Limited Market.* In the case of securities (other than exempted securities, nonconvertible debt securities, and cumulative nonconvertible preferred stock) which are not: (*1*) traded on a national securities exchange; (*2*) designated as "OTC Margin Stock" pursuant to Regulation T under the Securities Exchange Act of 1934; (*3*) quoted on "NASDAQ"; or (*4*) redeemable shares of investment companies registered under the Investment Company Act of 1940, the deduction shall be as follows:

(*i*) in the case where there are regular quotations in an inter-dealer quotations system for the securities by three or more independent market-makers (exclusive of the computing broker or dealer) and where each such quotation represents a bona fide offer to brokers or dealers to both buy and sell in reasonable quantities at stated prices, or where a ready market as defined in subparagraph (c)(11)(ii) is deemed to exist, the deduction shall be determined in accordance with subparagraph (J) above;

(*ii*) in the case where there are regular quotations in an inter-dealer quotations system for the securities by only one or two independent market-makers (exclusive of the computing broker or dealer) and where each such quotation represents a bona fide offer to brokers or dealers both to buy and sell in reasonable quantities, at stated prices, the deduction on both the long and short position shall be 40 percent.

(L) Where a broker or dealer demonstrates that there is sufficient liquidity for any securities long or short in the proprietary or other accounts of the broker or dealer which are subject to a deduction required by subparagraph (K) above, such deduction, upon a proper showing to the Examining Authority for the broker or dealer, may be appropriately decreased, but in no case shall such deduction be less than that prescribed in subparagraph (J) above.

(M)(*1*) *Undue Concentration.* In the case of money market instruments, or securities of a single class or series of an issuer, including any option written, endorsed or held to purchase or sell securities of such a single class or series of an issuer (other than "exempted securities" and redeemable securities of an investment company registered pursuant to the Investment Company Act of 1940), and securities underwritten (in which case the deduction provided for herein shall be applied after 11 business days), which are long or short in the proprietary or other accounts of a broker or dealer, including securities that are collateral to secured demand notes defined in Appendix (D), and that have a market value of more than 10 percent of the "net capital" of a broker or dealer before the application of paragraph (c)(2)(vi) of this rule or Appendix (A), there shall be an additional deduction from net worth and/or the Collateral Value for securities collateralizing a secured demand note defined in Appendix (D) equal to 50 percent of the percentage deduction otherwise provided by this paragraph (c)(2)(vi) of this rule or Appendix (A), on that portion of the securities position in excess of 10% of the "net capital" of the broker or dealer before the application of paragraph (c)(2)(vi) of this rule and Appendix (A), Rule 15c3–1a. In the case of securities described in paragraph (c)(2)(vi)(J), the additional deduction required by this paragraph (c)(2)(vi)(M) shall be 15 percent.

(*2*) This paragraph (c)(2)(vi)(M) shall apply notwithstanding any long or short position exemption provided for in paragraph (c)(2)(vi)(J) of this rule (except for long or short position exemptions arising out of the first proviso to paragraph (c)(2)(vi)(J)) and the deduction on any such exempted position shall be 15 percent of that portion of the securities position in excess of 10 percent of the broker or dealer's net capital before the application of paragraph (c)(2)(vi) of this rule and Appendix A.

(3) This paragraph (c)(2)(vi)(M) shall be applied to an issue of equity securities only on the market value of such securities in excess of $10,000 or the market value of 500 shares, whichever is greater, or $25,000 in the case of a debt security.

(4) This paragraph (c)(2)(vi)(M) will be applied to an issue of municipal securities having the same security provisions, date of issue, interest rate, day, month and year of maturity only if such securities have a market value in excess of $500,000 in bonds ($5,000,000 in notes) or 10 percent of tentative net capital, whichever is greater, and are held in position longer than 20 business days from the date the securities are received by the syndicate manager from the issuer.

(5) Any specialist that is subject to a deduction required by this paragraph (c)(2)(vi)(M), respecting its specialty stock, that can demonstrate to the satisfaction of the Examining Authority for such broker or dealer that there is sufficient liquidity for such specialist's specialty stock and that such deduction need not be applied in the public interest for the protection of investors, may upon a proper showing to such Examining Authority have such undue concentration deduction appropriately decreased, but in no case shall the deduction prescribed in paragraph (c)(2)(vi)(J) of this rule above be reduced. Each such Examining Authority shall make and preserve for a period of not less than 3 years a record of each application granted pursuant to this paragraph (c)(2)(vi)(M)(5), which shall contain a summary of the justification for the granting of the application.

(N) Any specialist that limits its securities business to that of a specialist (except for an occasional non-specialist related securities transaction for its own account), that does not transact a business in securities with other than a broker or dealer registered with the Commission under section 15 or 15C of the Act or a member of a national securities exchange, and that is not a clearing member of The Options Clearing Corporation need not deduct from net worth in computing net capital those deductions, as to its specialty securities, set forth in paragraph (c)(2)(vi) of this section or Appendix A to this section, except for paragraph (e) of this section limiting withdrawals of equity capital and Appendix D to this section relating to satisfactory subordination agreements. As to a specialist that is solely an options specialist, in paragraph (e) the term "net capital" shall be deemed to mean "net capital before the application of paragraph (c)(2)(vi) of this section or Appendix A to this section" and "excess net capital" shall be deemed to be the amount of net capital before the application of paragraph (c)(2)(vi) of this section or Appendix A to this section in excess of the amount of net capital required under paragraph (a) of this section. In reports filed pursuant to Rule 17a–5 and in making the record required by Rule 17a–3(a)(11) each specialist shall include the deductions that would otherwise have been required by paragraph (c)(2)(vi) of this section or Appendix A to this section in the absence of this paragraph (c)(2)(vi)(N).

(vii) *Non-marketable Securities.* Deducting 100 percent of the carrying value in the case of securities or evidence of indebtedness in the proprietary or other accounts of the broker or dealer, for which there is no ready market, as defined in subparagraph (c)(11) of this rule, and securities, in the proprietary or other accounts of the broker or dealer, which cannot be publicly offered or sold because of statutory, regulatory or contractual arrangements or other restrictions.

(viii) *Open Contractual Commitments.* Deducting, in the case of a broker or dealer that has open contractual commitments (other than those option positions subject to Appendix (A)) the respective deductions as specified in paragraph (c)(2)(vi) of this rule or Appendix (B) from the value (which shall be the market value whenever there is a market) of each net long and each net short position contemplated by any open contractual commitment in the proprietary or other accounts of the broker or dealer.

(A) The deduction for contractual commitments in those securities that are treated in paragraph (c)(2)(vi)(J) of this rule shall be 30 percent unless the class and issue of the securities subject to the open contractual commitment deduction are listed for trading on a national securities exchange or are designated as NASDAQ National Market System Securities.

(B) A broker or dealer that maintains in excess of $250,000 of net capital may add back to net worth up to $150,000 of any deduction computed under this paragraph (c)(2)(viii)(B).

(C) The deduction with respect to any single commitment shall be reduced by the unrealized profit in such commitment, in an amount not greater than the deduction provided for by this paragraph (or increased by the unrealized loss), in such commitment, and in no event shall an unrealized profit on any closed transactions operate to increase net capital.

(ix) Deducting from the contract value of each failed to deliver contract which is outstanding 5 business days or longer (21 business days or longer in the case of municipal securities) the percentages of the market value of the underlying security which would be required by application of the deduction required by paragraph (c)(2)(vi) of this rule. Such deduction, however, shall be increased by any excess of the contract price of the failed to deliver contract over the market value of the underlying security or reduced by any excess of the market value of the underlying security over the contract value of the failed to deliver contract, but not to exceed the amount of such deduction. The designated examining authority for the broker or dealer may, upon application of the broker or dealer, extend for a period up to 5 business days, any period herein specified where it is satisfied that the extension is warranted. The designated examining authority upon expiration of the extension may extend for one additional period of up to 5 business days, any period herein specified when it is satisfied that the extension is warranted.

Brokers or Dealers Carrying Accounts of Listed Option Specialists

(x)(A) With respect to any transaction of a specialist in listed options, who is either not otherwise subject to the provisions of this section or is described in paragraph (c)(2)(vi)(N) of this section, for whose specialist account a broker or dealer acts as a guarantor, endorser, or carrying broker or dealer, such broker or dealer shall adjust its net worth by deducting as of noon of each business day the amounts computed as of the prior business day pursuant to § 240.15c3-1a. The required deductions may be reduced by any liquidating equity that exists in such specialist's market-maker account as of that time and shall be increased to the extent of any liquidating deficit in such account. Noon shall be determined according to the local time where the broker or dealer is headquartered. In no event shall excess equity in the specialist's market-maker account result in an increase of the net capital of any such guarantor, endorser, or carrying broker or dealer.

(B) *Definitions.* *(1)* The term *listed option* shall mean any option traded on a registered national securities exchange or automated facility of a registered national securities association.

(2) For purposes of this section, the equity in an individual specialist's market-maker account shall be computed by:

(i) Marking all securities positions long or short in the account to their respective current market values;

(ii) Adding (deducting in the case of a debit balance) the credit balance carried in such specialist's market-maker account; and

(iii) Adding (deducting in the case of short positions) the market value of positions long in such account.

(C) No guarantor, endorser, or carrying broker or dealer shall permit the sum of the deductions required pursuant to § 240.15c3-1a in respect of all transactions in specialists' market-maker accounts guaranteed, endorsed, or carried by such broker or dealer to exceed 1,000 percent of such broker's or dealer's net capital as defined in § 240.15c3-1(c)(2) for any period exceeding three business days. If at any time such sum exceeds 1,000 percent of such broker's or dealer's net capital, then the broker or dealer shall:

(1) Immediately transmit telegraphic or facsimile notice of such event to the Division of Market Regulation in the headquarters office of the Commission in Washington, D.C., to the district or regional office of the Commission for the district or region in which the broker or dealer maintains its principal place of business, and to its examining authority designated pursuant to Section 17(d) of the Act (15 U.S.C. 78q(d)) ("Designated Examining Authority"); and

(2) Be subject to the prohibitions against withdrawal of equity capital set forth in § 240.15c3-1(e) and to the prohibitions against reduction, prepayment, and repayment of subordination agreements set forth in paragraph (b)(11) of § 240.15c3-1d, as if such broker or dealer's net capital were below the minimum standards specified by each of those paragraphs.

(D) If at any time there is a liquidating deficit in a specialist's market-maker account, then the broker or dealer guaranteeing, endorsing, or carrying listed options transactions in such specialist's market-maker account may not extend any further credit in that account, and shall take steps to liquidate promptly existing positions in the account. This paragraph shall not prevent the broker or dealer from, upon approval by the broker's or dealer's Designated Examining Authority, entering into hedging positions in the specialist's market-maker account. The broker or dealer also shall transmit telegraphic or facsimile notice of the deficit and its amount by the close of business of the following business day to its Designated Examining Authority and the Designated Examining Authority of the specialist, if different from its own.

(E) Upon written application to the Commission by the specialist and the broker or dealer guaranteeing, endorsing, or carrying options transactions in such specialist's market-maker account, the Commission may approve upon specified terms and conditions lesser adjustments to net worth than those specified in § 240.15c3-1a.

Brokers or Dealers Carrying Specialists or Market Makers Accounts

(xi) With respect to a broker or dealer who carries a market maker or specialist account, or with respect to any transaction in options listed on a registered national securities exchange for which a broker or dealer acts as a guarantor or endorser of options written by a specialist in a specialist account, the broker or dealer shall deduct, for each account carried or for each class or series of options guaranteed or endorsed, any deficiency in collateral required by subparagraph (a)(6) of this rule.

(xii) *Deduction From Net Worth for Certain Undermargined Accounts.* Deducting the amount of cash required in each customer's or non-customer's account to meet the maintenance margin requirements of the Examining Authority for the broker or dealer, after application of calls for margin, marks to the market or other required deposits which are outstanding 5 business days or less.

(xiii) *Deduction From Net Worth for Indebtedness Collateralized by Exempted Securities.* Deducting, at the option of the broker or dealer, in lieu of including such amounts in aggregate indebtedness, 4 percent of the amount of any indebtedness secured by exempted securities or municipal securities if such indebtedness would otherwise be includable in aggregate indebtedness.

EXEMPTED SECURITIES

(3) The term "exempted securities" shall mean those securities deemed exempted securities by section 3(a)(12) of the Securities Exchange Act of 1934 and rules thereunder.

CONTRACTUAL COMMITMENTS

(4) The term "contractual commitments" shall include underwriting, when issued, when distributed and delayed delivery contracts, the writing or endorsement of puts and calls and combinations thereof, commitments in foreign currencies, and spot (cash) commodities contracts, but shall not include uncleared regular way purchases and sales of securities and contracts in commodities futures. A series of contracts of purchase or sale of the same security conditioned, if at all, only upon issuance may be treated as an individual commitment.

ADEQUATELY SECURED

(5) Indebtedness shall be deemed to be adequately secured within the meaning of this section when the excess of the market value of the collateral over the amount of the indebtedness is sufficient to make the loan acceptable as a fully secured loan to banks regularly making secured loans to brokers or dealers.

CUSTOMER

(6) The term "customer" shall mean any person from whom, or on whose behalf, a broker or dealer has received, acquired or holds funds or securities for the account of such person, but shall not include a broker or dealer or a registered municipal securities dealer, or a general, special or limited partner or director or officer of the broker or dealer, or any person to the extent that such person has a claim for property or funds which by contract, agreement, or understanding, or by operation of law, is part of the capital of the broker or dealer. *Provided, however,* That the term "customer" shall also include a broker or dealer, but only insofar as such broker or dealer maintains a special omnibus account carried with another broker or dealer in compliance with 12 CFR 220.4(b) of Regulation T under the Securities Exchange Act of 1934.

NON-CUSTOMER

(7) The term "non-customer" means a broker or dealer, registered municipal secu-

rities dealer, general partner, limited partner, officer, director and persons to the extent their claims are subordinated to the claims of creditors of the broker or dealer.

MARKET MAKER

(8) The term "market maker" shall mean a dealer who, with respect to a particular security, (i) regularly publishes bona fide, competitive bid and offer quotations in a recognized interdealer quotation system; or (ii) furnishes bona fide competitive bid and offer quotations on request; and, (iii) is ready, willing and able to effect transactions in reasonable quantities at his quoted prices with other brokers or dealers.

PROMPTLY TRANSMIT AND DELIVER

(9) A broker or dealer is deemed to "promptly transmit" all funds and to "promptly deliver" all securities within the meaning of subparagraphs (a)(2)(i) and (a)(2)(v) of this rule where such transmission or delivery is made no later than noon of the next business day after the receipt of such funds or securities; *Provided, however,* That such prompt transmission or delivery shall not be required to be effected prior to the settlement date for such transactions.

PROMPTLY FORWARD

(10) A broker or dealer is deemed to "promptly forward" funds or securities within the meaning of paragraph (a)(2)(i) of this rule only when such forwarding occurs no later than noon of the next business day following receipt of such funds or securities.

READY MARKET

(11)(i) The term "ready market" shall include a recognized established securities market in which there exists independent bona fide offers to buy and sell so that a price reasonably related to the last sales price or current bona fide competitive bid and offer quotations can be determined for a particular security almost instantaneously and where payment will be received in settlement of a sale at such price within a relatively short time conforming to trade custom.

(ii) A "ready market" shall also be deemed to exist where securities have been accepted as collateral for a loan by a bank as defined in Section 3(a)(6) of the Securities Exchange Act of 1934 and where the broker or dealer demonstrates to its Examining Authority that such securities adequately secure such loans as that term is defined in paragraph (c)(5) of this rule.

EXAMINING AUTHORITY

(12) The term "Examining Authority" of a broker or dealer shall mean for the purposes of Rules 15c3-1 and 15c3-1a-d the national securities exchange or national securities association of which the broker or dealer is a member or, if the broker or dealer is a member of more than one such self-regulatory organization, the organization designated by the Commission as the Examining Authority for such broker or dealer, or if the broker or dealer is not a member of any such self-regulatory organization, the Regional or District Office of the Commission where such broker or dealer has its principal place of business.

ENTITIES THAT HAVE A PRINCIPAL REGULATOR

(13)(i) For purposes of § 240.15c3-1e and § 240.15c3-1g, the term entity that has a principal regulator shall mean a person (other than a natural person) that is not a registered broker or dealer (other than a broker or dealer registered under section 15(b)(11) of the Act (15 U.S.C. 78o(b)(11)), provided that the person is:

(A) An insured depository institution as defined in section 3(c)(2) of the Federal Deposit Insurance Act (12 U.S.C. 1813(c)(2));

(B) Registered as a futures commission merchant or an introducing broker with the Commodity Futures Trading Commission;

(C) Registered with or licensed by a State insurance regulator and issues any insurance, endowment, or annuity policy or contract;

(D) A foreign bank as defined in section 1(b)(7) of the International Banking Act of 1978 (12 U.S.C. 3101(7)) that has its headquarters in a jurisdiction for which any foreign bank has been approved by the Board of Governors of the Federal Reserve System to conduct business pursuant to the standards set forth in 12 CFR 211.24(c), provided such foreign bank represents to the Commission that it is subject to the same supervisory regime as the foreign bank previously approved by the Board of Governors of the Federal Reserve System;

(E) Not primarily in the securities business, and the person is:

(1) A corporation organized under section 25A of the Federal Reserve Act (12 U.S.C. 611 through 633); or

(2) A corporation having an agreement or undertaking with the Board of Governors of the Federal Reserve System under section 25 of the Federal Reserve Act (12 U.S.C. 601 through 604a); or

(F) A person that the Commission finds is another entity that is subject to comprehensive supervision, has in place appropriate arrangements so that information that the person provides to the Commission is sufficiently reliable for the purposes of determining compliance with § 240.15c3–1e and § 240.15c3-1g, and it is appropriate to consider the person to be an entity that has a principal regulator considering all relevant circumstances, including the person's mix of business.

(ii) For purposes of § 240.15c3–1e, § 240.15c3–1g, § 240.17h–1T, and § 240.17h2T, the term ultimate holding company that has a principal regulator shall mean a person (other than a natural person) that:

(A) Is a financial holding company or a company that is treated as a financial holding company under the Bank Holding Company Act of 1956 (12 U.S.C. 1840 et seq.), or

(B) The Commission determines to be an ultimate holding company that has a principal regulator, if that person is subject to consolidated, comprehensive supervision; there are in place appropriate arrangements so that information that the person provides to the Commission is sufficiently reliable for the purposes of determining compliance with § 240.15c3–1e and § 240.15c3–1g; and it is appropriate to consider the person to be an ultimate holding company that has a principal regulator in view of all relevant circumstances, including the person's mix of business.

(14) *Municipal Securities.* The term "municipal securities" shall mean those securities included within the definition of "municipal securities" in section 3(a)(29) of the Securities Exchange of 1934.

(15) The term *tentative net capital* shall mean the net capital of a broker or dealer before deducting the securities haircuts computed pursuant to paragraph (c)(2)(vi) of this section and the charges on inventory computed pursuant to Appendix B to this section (§ 240.15c3–1b). However, for purposes of paragraph (a)(5) of this section, the term *tentative net capital* means the net capital of an OTC derivatives dealer before deducting the charges for market and credit risk as computed pursuant to Appendix F to this section (§ 240.15c3–1f) or paragraph (c)(2)(vi) of this section, if applicable, and increased by the balance sheet value (including counterparty net exposure) resulting from transactions in eligible OTC derivative instruments which would otherwise be deducted by virtue of paragraph (c)(2)(iv) of this section. For purposes of paragraph (a)(7) of this section, the term *tentative net capital* means the net capital of the broker or dealer before deductions for market and credit risk computed pursuant to § 240.15c3–1e or paragraph (c)(2)(vi) of this section, if applicable, and increased by the balance sheet value (including counterparty net exposure) resulting from transactions in

derivative instruments which would otherwise be deducted by virtue of paragraph (c)(2)(iv) of this section. Tentative net capital shall include securities for which there is no ready market, as defined in paragraph (c)(11) of this section, if the use of mathematical models has been approved for purposes of calculating deductions from net capital for those securities pursuant to § 240.15c3-1e.

EQUITY

(d) *Debt-Equity Requirements.* No broker or dealer shall permit the total of outstanding principal amounts of its satisfactory subordination agreements (other than such agreements which qualify under this paragraph (d) as equity capital) to exceed 70 percent of its debt-equity total, as hereinafter defined, for a period in excess of 90 days or for such longer period which the Commission may, upon application of the broker or dealer, grant in the public interest or for the protection of investors. In the case of a corporation, the debt-equity total shall be the sum of its outstanding principal amounts of satisfactory subordination agreements, par or stated value of capital stock, paid in capital in excess of par, retained earnings, unrealized profit and loss or other capital accounts. In the case of a partnership, the debt-equity total shall be the sum of its outstanding principal amounts of satisfactory subordination agreements, capital accounts of partners (exclusive of such partners' securities accounts) subject to the provisions of paragraph (e) of this rule, and unrealized profit and loss. In the case of a sole proprietorship, the debt-equity total shall include the sum of its outstanding principal amounts of satisfactory subordination agreements, capital accounts of the sole proprietorship and unrealized profit and loss. *Provided, however,* That a satisfactory subordination agreement entered into by a partner or stockholder which has an initial term of at least three years and has a remaining term of not less than 12 months shall be considered equity for the purposes of this paragraph (d) if: (1) it does not have any of the provisions for accelerated maturity provided for by subparagraphs (b)(9)(i), (b)(10)(i) or (b)(10)(ii) of Appendix (D) and is maintained as capital subject to the provisions restricting the withdrawal thereof required by paragraph (e) of this rule or (2) the partnership agreement provides that capital contributed pursuant to a satisfactory subordination agreement as defined in Appendix (D) shall in all respects be partnership capital subject to the provisions restricting the withdrawal thereof required by paragraph (e) of this rule.

(e)(1) *Notice Provisions Relating to Limitations on the Withdrawal of Equity Capital.* No equity capital of the broker or dealer or a subsidiary or affiliate consolidated pursuant to Appendix C (Rule 15c3-1c) may be withdrawn by action of a stockholder or a partner or by redemption or repurchase of shares of stock by any of the consolidated entities or through the payment of dividends or any similar distribution, nor may any unsecured advance or loan be made to a stockholder, partner, sole proprietor, employee or affiliate without written notice given in accordance with paragraph (e)(1)(iv) below:

(i) two business days prior to any withdrawals, advances or loans if those withdrawals, advances or loans on a net basis exceed in the aggregate in any 30 calendar day period, 30 percent of the broker or dealer's excess net capital. A broker or dealer, in an emergency situation, may make withdrawals, advances or loans that on a net basis exceed 30 percent of the broker or dealer's excess net capital in any 30 calendar day period without giving the advance notice required by this paragraph, with the prior approval of its Examining Authority. Where a broker or dealer makes a withdrawal with the consent of its Examining Authority, it shall in any event comply with paragraph (e)(1)(ii) hereof; or

(ii) two business days after any withdrawals, advances or loans if those withdrawals, advances or loans on a net basis exceed in the aggregate in any 30 calendar day period,

20 percent of the broker or dealer's excess net capital.

(iii) This paragraph (e)(1) does not apply to:

(A) securities or commodities transactions in the ordinary course of business between a broker or dealer and an affiliate where the broker or dealer makes payment to or on behalf of such affiliate for such transaction and then receives payment from such affiliate for the securities or commodities transaction within two business days from the date of the transaction; or

(B) withdrawals, advances or loans which in the aggregate in any thirty calendar day period, on a net basis, equal $500,000 or less.

(iv) Each required notice shall be effective when received by the Commission in Washington, D.C., the regional or district office of the Commission for the region or district in which the broker or dealer has its principal place of business, the broker or dealer's Examining Authority and the Commodity Futures Trading Commission if such broker or dealer is registered with that Commission.

(2) *Limitations on withdrawal of equity capital.* No equity capital of the broker or dealer or a subsidiary or affiliate consolidated pursuant to Appendix C (Rule 15c3–1e) may be withdrawn by action of a stockholder or a partner or by redemption or repurchase of shares of stock by any of the consolidated entities or through the payment of dividends or any similar distribution, nor may any unsecured advance or loan be made to a stockholder, partner, sole proprietor, employee or affiliate, if after giving effect thereto and to any other such withdrawals, advances or loans and any Payments of Payment Obligations (as defined in Appendix D (Rule 15c3–1d)) under satisfactory subordination agreements which are scheduled to occur within 180 days following such withdrawal, advance or loan if:

(i) the broker or dealer's net capital would be less than 120 percent of the minimum dollar amount required by paragraph (a);

(ii) the broker-dealer is registered as a futures commission merchant, its net capital would be less than 7 percent of the funds required to be segregated pursuant to the Commodity Exchange Act and the regulations thereunder (less the market value of commodity options purchased by option customers on or subject to the rules of a contract market, each such deduction not to exceed the amount of funds in the option customer's account);

(iii) the broker-dealer's net capital would be less than 25 percent of deductions from net worth in computing net capital required by paragraphs (c)(2)(vi), (f) and Appendix A, unless the broker or dealer has the prior approval of the Commission to make such withdrawal;

(iv) the total outstanding principal amounts of satisfactory subordination agreements of the broker or dealer and any subsidiaries or affiliates consolidated pursuant to Appendix C (Rule 15c3–1c) (other than such agreements which qualify as equity under paragraph (d) of this section) would exceed 70% of the debt-equity total as defined in paragraph (d);

(v) the broker or dealer is subject to the aggregate indebtedness limitations of paragraph (a), the aggregate indebtedness of any of the consolidated entities exceeds 1000 percent of its net capital; or

(vi) the broker or dealer is subject to the alternative net capital requirement of paragraph (f), its net capital would be less than 5 percent of aggregate debit items computed in accordance with Rule 15c3–3a.

(3)(i) *Temporary Restrictions on Withdrawal of Net Capital.* The Commission may by order restrict, for a period up to twenty business days, any withdrawal by the broker or dealer of equity capital or unsecured loan or advance to a stockholder, partner, sole proprietor, employee or affiliate if such withdrawal, advance or loan:

(A) when aggregated with all other withdrawals, advances or loans on a net basis during a 30 calendar day period exceeds 30 percent of the broker or dealer's excess net capital; and

(B) the Commission, based on the facts and information available, concludes that the withdrawal, advance or loan may be detrimental to the financial integrity of the broker or dealer, or may unduly jeopardize the broker or dealer's ability to repay its customer claims or other liabilities which may cause a significant impact on the markets or expose the customers or creditors of the broker or dealer to loss without taking into account the application of the Securities Investor Protection Act.

(ii) An order temporarily prohibiting the withdrawal of capital shall be rescinded if the Commission determines that the restriction on capital withdrawal should not remain in effect. The hearing will be held within two business days from the date of the request in writing by the broker or dealer.

(4)(i) *Miscellaneous Provisions.* Excess net capital is that amount in excess of the amount required under paragraph (a). For the purposes of paragraphs (e)(1) and (e)(2), a broker or dealer may use the amount of excess net capital and deductions required under paragraphs (c)(2)(vi), (f) and Appendix A reported in its most recently required filed Form X–17A–5 for the purposes of calculating the effect of a projected withdrawal, advance or loan relative to excess net capital or deductions. The broker or dealer must assure itself that the excess net capital or the deductions reported on the most recently required filed Form X–17A–5 have not materially changed since the time such report was filed.

(ii) The term equity capital includes capital contributions by partners, par or stated value of capital stock, paid-in capital in excess of par, retained earnings or other capital accounts. The term equity capital does not include securities in the securities accounts of partners and balances in limited partners' capital accounts in excess of their stated capital contributions.

(iii) Paragraphs (e)(1) and (e)(2) shall not preclude a broker or dealer from making required tax payments or preclude the payment to partners of reasonable compensation, and such payments shall not be included in the calculation of withdrawals, advances, or loans for purposes of paragraphs (e)(1) and (e)(2).

(iv) For the purpose of this paragraph (e), any transaction between a broker or dealer and a stockholder, partner, sole proprietor, employee or affiliate that results in a diminution of the broker or dealer's net capital shall be deemed to be an advance or loan of net capital.

Rule 15c3–1a. Options (Appendix A to Rule 15c3–1)

(a) *Definitions.* (1) The term *unlisted option* shall mean any option not included in the definition of listed option provided in paragraph (c)(2)(x) of § 240.15c3–1.

(2) The term *option series* refers to listed option contracts of the same type (either a call or a put) and exercise style, covering the same underlying security with the same exercise price, expiration date, and number of underlying units.

(3) The term *related instrument* within an option class or product group refers to futures contracts and options on futures contracts covering the same underlying instrument. In relation to options on foreign currencies a related instrument within an option class also shall include forward contracts on the same underlying currency.

(4) The term *underlying instrument* refers to long and short positions, as appropriate, covering the same foreign currency, the same security, or a security which is exchangeable for or convertible into the underlying security within a period of 90 days. If the exchange or conversion requires the payment of money or

results in a loss upon conversion at the time when the security is deemed an underlying instrument for purposes of this Appendix A, the broker or dealer will deduct from net worth the full amount of the conversion loss. The term underlying instrument shall not be deemed to include securities options, futures contracts, options on futures contracts, qualified stock baskets, or unlisted instruments.

(5) The term *options class* refers to all options contracts covering the same underlying instrument.

(6) The term *product group* refers to two or more option classes, related instruments, underlying instruments, and qualified stock baskets in the same portfolio type (see paragraph (b)(1)(ii) of this section) for which it has been determined that a percentage of offsetting profits may be applied to losses at the same valuation point.

(b) The deduction under this Appendix A to § 240.15c3–1 shall equal the sum of the deductions specified in paragraph (b)(1)(v)(C) or (b)(2) of this section.

Theoretical Pricing Charges

(1)(i) *Definitions.*

(A) The terms *theoretical gains and losses* shall mean the gain and loss in the value of individual option series, the value of underlying instruments, related instruments, and qualified stock baskets within that option's class, at 10 equidistant intervals (valuation points) ranging from an assumed movement (both up and down) in the current market value of the underlying instrument equal to the percentage corresponding to the deductions otherwise required under § 240.15c3–1 for the underlying instrument (see paragraph (a)(1)(iii) of this section). Theoretical gains and losses shall be calculated using a theoretical options pricing model that satisfies the criteria set forth in paragraph (a)(1)(i)(B) of this section.

(B) The term *theoretical options pricing model* shall mean any mathematical model, other than a broker-dealer proprietary model, approved by a Designated Examining Authority. Such Designated Examining Authority shall submit the model to the Commission, together with a description of its methods for approving models. Any such model shall calculate theoretical gains and losses as described in paragraph (a)(1)(i)(A) of this section for all series and issues of equity, index and foreign currency options and related instruments, and shall be made available equally and on the same terms to all registered brokers or dealers. Its procedures shall include the arrangement of the vendor to supply accurate and timely data to each broker-dealer with respect to its services, and the fees for distribution of the services. The data provided to brokers or dealers shall also contain the minimum requirements set forth in paragraph (b)(1)(v)(C) of this section and the product group offsets set forth in paragraph (b)(1)(v)(B) of this section. At a minimum, the model shall consider the following factors in pricing the option:

(*1*) The current spot price of the underlying asset;

(*2*) The exercise price of the option;

(*3*) The remaining time until the option's expiration;

(*4*) The volatility of the underlying asset;

(*5*) Any cash flows associated with ownership of the underlying asset that can reasonably be expected to occur during the remaining life of the option; and

(*6*) The current term structure of interest rates.

(C) The term *major market foreign currency* shall mean the currency of a sovereign nation whose short-term debt is rated in one of the two highest categories by at least two nationally recognized statistical rating organizations and for which there is a substantial inter-bank forward currency market. For purposes of this section, the European Currency Unit (ECU) shall be deemed a major market foreign currency.

(D) The term *qualified stock basket* shall mean a set or basket of stock positions which represents no less than 50% of the capitalization for a high-capitalization or non-high-capitalization diversified market index, or, in the case of a narrow-based index, no less than 95% of the capitalization for such narrow-based index.

(ii) With respect to positions involving listed options in a single specialist's market-maker account, and, separately, with respect to positions involving listed option positions in its proprietary or other account, the broker or dealer shall group long and short positions into the following portfolio types:

(A) Equity options on the same underlying instrument and positions in that underlying instrument;

(B) Options on the same major market foreign currency, positions in that major market foreign currency, and related instruments within those options' classes;

(C) High-capitalization diversified market index options, related instruments within the option's class, and qualified stock baskets in the same index;

(D) Non-high-capitalization diversified index options, related instruments within the index option's class, and qualified stock baskets in the same index; and

(E) Narrow-based index options, related instruments within the index option's class, and qualified stock baskets in the same index.

(iii) Before making the computation, each broker or dealer shall obtain the theoretical gains and losses for each options series and for the related and underlying instruments within those options' class in each specialist's market-maker account guaranteed, endorsed, or carried by a broker or dealer, or in the proprietary or other accounts of that broker or dealer. For each option series, the theoretical options pricing model shall calculate theoretical prices at 10 equidistant valuation points within a range consisting of an increase or a decrease of the following percentages of the daily market price of the underlying instrument:

(A) +(−)15% for equity securities with a ready market, narrow-based indexes, and non-high-capitalization diversified indexes;

(B) +(−)6% for major market foreign currencies;

(C) +(−)20% for all other currencies; and

(D) +(−)10% for high-capitalization diversified indexes.

(iv)(A) As to non-clearing option specialists and market-makers, the percentages of the daily market price of the underlying instrument shall be:

(1) +(−)4½% for major market foreign currencies; and

(2) +6(−)8% for high-capitalization diversified indexes.

(3) +(−)10% for a non-clearing market-maker, or specialist in non-high capitalization diversified index product group.

(B) The provisions of this paragraph (b)(1)(iv) shall expire two years from September 1, 1997, unless otherwise extended by the Commission.

(v)(A) The broker or dealer shall multiply the corresponding theoretical gains and losses at each of the 10 equidistant valuation points by the number of positions held in a particular options series, the related instruments and qualified stock baskets within the option's class, and the positions in the same underlying instrument.

(B) In determining the aggregate profit or loss for each portfolio type, the broker or dealer will be allowed the following offsets in the following order, provided, that in the case of qualified stock baskets, the broker or dealer may elect to net individual stocks between qualified stock baskets and take the appropriate deduction on the remaining, if any, securities:

(1) First, a broker or dealer is allowed the following offsets within an option's class:

(*i*) Between options on the same underlying instrument, positions covering the same underlying instrument, and related instruments within the option's class, 100% of a position's gain shall offset another position's loss at the same valuation point;

(*ii*) Between index options, related instruments within the option's class, and qualified stock baskets on the same index, 95%, or such other amount as designated by the Commission, of gains shall offset losses at the same valuation point;

(*2*) Second, a broker-dealer is allowed the following offsets within an index product group;

(*i*) Among positions involving different high-capitalization diversified index option classes within the same product group, 90% of the gain in a high-capitalization diversified market index option, related instruments, and qualified stock baskets within that index option's class shall offset the loss at the same valuation point in a different high-capitalization diversified market index option, related instruments, and qualified stock baskets within that index option's class;

(*ii*) Among positions involving different non-high-capitalization diversified index option classes within the same product group, 75% of the gain in a non-high-capitalization diversified market index option, related instruments, and qualified stock baskets within that index option's class shall offset the loss at the same valuation point in another non-high-capitalization diversified market index option, related instruments, and qualified stock baskets within that index option's class or product group;

(*iii*) Among positions involving different narrow-based index option classes within the same product group, 90% of the gain in a narrow-based market index option, related instruments, and qualified stock baskets within that index option's class shall offset the loss at the same valuation point in another narrow-based market index option, related instruments, and qualified stock baskets within that index option's class or product group;

(*iv*) No qualified stock basket should offset another qualified stock basket; and

(*3*) Third, a broker-dealer is allowed the following offsets between product groups: Among positions involving different diversified index product groups within the same market group, 50% of the gain in a diversified market index option, a related instrument, or a qualified stock basket within that index option's product group shall offset the loss at the same valuation point in another product group;

(C) For each portfolio type, the total deduction shall be the larger of:

(*1*) The amount for any of the 10 equidistant valuation points representing the largest theoretical loss after applying the offsets provided in paragraph (b)(1)(v)(B) if this section; or

(*2*) A minimum charge equal to 25% times the multiplier for each equity and index option contract and each related instrument within the option's class or product group, or $25 for each option on a major market foreign currency with the minimum charge for futures contracts and options on futures contracts adjusted for contract size differentials, not to exceed market value in the case of long positions in options and options on futures contracts; plus

(*3*) In the case of portfolio types involving index options and related instruments offset by a qualified stock basket, there will be a minimum charge of 5% of the market value of the qualified stock basket for high-capitalization diversified and narrow-based indexes; and

(*4*) In the case of portfolio types involving index options and related instruments offset by a qualified stock basket, there will be a minimum charge of 7½% of the market value of the qualified stock basket for non-high-capitalization diversified indexes.

Alternative Strategy Based Method

(2) A broker or dealer may elect to apply the alternative strategy based method in accordance with the provisions of this paragraph (b)(2).

(i) *Definitions.* (A) The term *intrinsic value* or *in-the-money amount* shall mean the amount by which the exercise value, in the case of a call, is less than the current market value of the underlying instrument, and, in the case of a put, is greater than the current market value of the underlying instrument.

(B) The term *out-of-the-money amount* shall mean the amount by which the exercise value, in the case of a call, is greater than the current market value of the underlying instrument, and, in the case of a put, is less than the current market value of the underlying instrument.

(C) The term *term value* shall mean the current market value of an option contract that is in excess of its intrinsic value.

(ii) Every broker or dealer electing to calculate adjustments to net worth in accordance with the provisions of this paragraph (b)(2) must make the following adjustments to net worth:

(A) Add the time value of a short position in a listed option; and

(B) Deduct the time value of a long position in a listed option, which relates to a position in the same underlying instrument or in a related instrument within the option class or product group as recognized in the strategies enumerated in paragraph (b)(2)(iii)(D) of this section; and

(C) Add the net short market value or deduct the long market value of listed options as recognized in the strategies enumerated in paragraphs (b)(2)(iii)(E)(1) and (2) of this section.

(iii) In computing net capital after the adjustments provided for in paragraph (b)(2)(ii) of this section, every broker or dealer shall deduct the percentages specified in this paragraph (b)(2)(iii) for all listed option positions, positions covering the same underlying instrument and related instruments within the options' class or product group.

Uncovered Calls

(A) Where a broker or dealer is short a call, deducting the percentage required by paragraphs (c)(2)(vi)(A) through (K) of § 240.15c3–1 of the current market value of the underlying instrument for such option reduced by its out-of-the-money amount, to the extent that such reduction does not operate to increase net capital. In no event shall this deduction be less than the greater of $250 for each short call option contract for 100 shares or 50% of the aforementioned percentage.

Uncovered Puts

(B) Where a broker or dealer is short a put, deducting the percentage required by paragraphs (c)(2)(vi)(A) through (K) of § 240.15c3–1 of the current market value of the underlying instrument for such option reduced by its out-of-the-money amount, to the extent that such reduction does not operate to increase net capital. In no event shall the deduction provided by this paragraph be less than the greater of $250 for each short put option contract for 100 shares or 50% of the aforementioned percentage.

Long Positions

(C) Where a broker or dealer is long puts or calls, deducting 50 percent of the market value of the net long put and call positions in the same options series.

Certain Security Positions With Offsetting Options

(D)(1) Where a broker or dealer is long a put for which it has an offsetting long position in the same number of units of the same underlying instrument, deducting the percentage required by paragraphs (c)(2)(vi)(A) through (K) of § 240.15c3–1 of the current market value of the underlying instrument for the long offsetting position, not to exceed the out-of-the-money amount of the option. In no event shall the deduction provided by this paragraph be less than $25 for each option contract for 100 shares, provided that the minimum charge need not exceed the intrinsic value of the option.

(2) Where a broker or dealer is long a call for which it has an offsetting short position in the same number of units of the same underlying instrument, deducting the percentage required by paragraphs (c)(2)(vi)(A) through (K) of § 240.15c3–1 of the current market value of the underlying instrument for the short offsetting position, not to exceed the out-of-the-money amount of the option. In no event shall the deduction provided by this paragraph be less than $25 for each option contract for 100 shares, provided that the minimum charge need not exceed the intrinsic value of the option.

(3) Where a broker or dealer is short a call for which it has an offsetting long position in the same number of units of the same underlying instrument, deducting the percentage required by paragraphs (c)(2)(vi)(A) through (K) of § 240.15c3–1 of the current market value of the underlying instrument for the offsetting long position reduced by the short call's intrinsic value. In no event shall the deduction provided by this paragraph be less than $25 for each option contract for 100 shares.

Certain Spread Positions

(E)(1) Where a broker or dealer is short a listed call and is also long a listed call in the same class of options contracts and the long option expires on the same date as or subsequent to the short option, the deduction, after adjustments required in paragraph (b) of this section, shall be the amount by which the exercise value of the long call exceeds the exercise value of the short call. If the exercise value of the long call is less than or equal to the exercise value of the short call, no deduction is required.

(2) Where a broker or dealer is short a listed put and is also long a listed put in the same class of options contracts and the long option expires on the same date as or subsequent to the short option, the deduction, after the adjustments required in paragraph (b) of this section, shall be the amount by which the exercise value of the short put exceeds the exercise value of the long put. If the exercise value of the long put is equal to or greater than the exercise value of the short put, no deduction is required.

(c) With respect to transactions involving unlisted options, every broker or dealer shall determine the value of unlisted option positions in accordance with the provision of paragraph (c)(2)(i) of § 240.15c3–1, and shall deduct the percentages of all securities positions or unlisted options in the proprietary or other accounts of the broker or dealer specified in this paragraph (c). However, where computing the deduction required for a security position as if the security position had no related unlisted option position and positions in unlisted options as if uncovered would result in a lesser deduction from net worth, the broker or dealer may compute such deductions separately.

Uncovered Calls

(1) Where a broker or dealer is short a call, deducting 15 percent (or such other percentage required by paragraphs (c)(2)(vi)(A) through (K) of § 240.15c3–1) of the current market value of the security underlying such option reduced by any excess of the exercise value of the call over the current market value of the underlying security. In no event shall the deduction provided by this paragraph be less than $250 for each option contract for 100 shares.

Uncovered Puts

(2) Where a broker or dealer is short a put, deducting 15 percent (or such other percentage required by paragraphs (c)(2)(vi)(A) through (K) of § 240.15c3–1) of the current

market value of the security underlying the option reduced by any excess of the market value of the underlying security over the exercise value of the put. In no event shall the deduction provided by this paragraph be less than $250 for each option contract for 100 shares.

Covered Calls

(3) Where a broker or dealer is short a call and long equivalent units of the underlying security, deducting 15 percent (or such other percentage required by paragraphs (c)(2)(vi)(A) through (K) of § 240.15c3–1) of the current market value of the underlying security reduced by any excess of the current market value of the underlying security over the exercise value of the call. No reduction under this paragraph shall have the effect of increasing net capital.

Covered Puts

(4) Where a broker or dealer is short a put and short equivalent units of the underlying security, deducting 15 percent (or such other percentage required by paragraphs (c)(2)(vi)(A) through (K) of § 240.15c3–1) of the current market value of the underlying security reduced by any excess of the exercise value of the put over the market value of the underlying security. No such reduction shall have the effect of increasing net capital.

Conversion Accounts

(5) Where a broker or dealer is long equivalent units of the underlying security, long a put written or endorsed by a broker or dealer and short a call in its proprietary or other accounts, deducting 5 percent (or 50 percent of such other percentage required by paragraphs (c)(2)(vi)(A) through (K) of § 240.15c3–1) of the current market value of the underlying security.

(6) Where a broker or dealer is short equivalent units of the underlying security, long a call written or endorsed by a broker or dealer and short a put in his proprietary or other accounts, deducting 5 percent (or 50 percent of such other percentage required by paragraphs (c)(2)(vi)(A) through (K) of § 240.15c3–1) of the market value of the underlying security.

Long Options

(7) Where a broker or dealer is long a put or call endorsed or written by a broker or dealer, deducting 15 percent (or such other percentage required by paragraphs (c)(2)(vi)(A) through (K) of § 240.15c3–1) of the market value of the underlying security, not to exceed any value attributed to such option in paragraph (c)(2)(i) of § 240.15c3–1.

Rule 15c3–1b. Adjustments to Net Worth and Aggregate Indebtedness for Certain Commodities Transactions (Appendix B to Rule 15c3–1)

(a) Every broker or dealer in computing net capital pursuant to Rule 15c3–1 shall comply with the following:

(1) Where a broker or dealer has an asset or liability which is treated or defined in paragraph (c) of Rule 15c3–1, the inclusion or exclusion of all or part of such asset or liability for the computation of aggregate indebtedness and net capital shall be in accordance with paragraph (c) of Rule 15c3–1 except as specifically provided otherwise in this Appendix B. Where a commodity related asset or liability is specifically treated or defined in 17 CFR 1.17 and is not generally or specifically treated or defined in Rule 15c3–1 or this Appendix B, the inclusion or exclusion of all or part of such asset or liability for the computation of aggregate indebtedness and net capital shall be in accordance with 17 CFR 1.17.

AGGREGATE INDEBTEDNESS

(2) The term "aggregate indebtedness" as defined in paragraph (c)(1) of this section shall exclude with respect to commodity-related transactions:

(i) Indebtedness arising in connection with an advance to a non-proprietary account when such indebtedness is adequately collateralized by spot commodities eligible for delivery on a contract market and when such spot commodities are covered;

(ii) Advances received by the broker or dealer against bill of lading issued in connection with the shipment of commodities sold by the broker or dealer; and

(iii) Equity balances in the accounts of general partners.

NET CAPITAL

(3) In computing net capital as defined in paragraph (c)(2) of this rule, the net worth of a broker or dealer shall be adjusted as follows with respect to commodity-related transactions:

(i) *Unrealized Profit or Loss for Certain Commodities Transactions*.

(A) Unrealized profits shall be added and unrealized losses shall be deducted in the commodities accounts of the broker or dealer, including unrealized profits and losses on fixed price commitments and forward contract; and

(B) The value attributed to any commodity option which is not traded on a contract market shall be the difference between the option's strike price and the market value for the physical or futures contract which is the subject of the option. In the case of a long call commodity option, if the market value for the physical or futures contract which is the subject of the option is less than the strike price of the option, it shall be given no value. In the case of a long put commodity option, if the market value for the physical commodity or futures contract which is the subject of the option is more than the striking price of the option, it shall be given no value.

(ii) Deduct any unsecured commodity futures or option account containing a ledger balance and open trades the combination of which liquidates to a deficit or containing a debit ledger balance only: *Provided, however,* Deficits or debit ledger balances in unsecured customers', noncustomers' and proprietary accounts, which are the subject of calls for margin or other required deposits need not be deducted until the close of business on the business day following the date on which such deficit or debit ledger balance originated.

(iii) Deduct all unsecured receivables, advances and loans except for:

(A) Management fees receivable from commodity pools outstanding no longer than thirty (30) days from the date they are due;

(B) Receivables from foreign clearing organizations;

(C) Receivables from registered futures commission merchants or brokers, resulting from commodity futures or option transactions, except those specifically excluded under paragraph (3)(ii) of this Appendix B. In the case of an introducing broker or an applicant for registration as an introducing broker, include 50 percent of the value of a guarantee or security deposit with a futures commission merchant which carries or intends to carry accounts for the customers of the introducing broker.

(iv) Deduct all inventories (including work in process, finished goods, raw materials and inventories held for resale) except for readily marketable spot commodities; or spot commodities which adequately collateralize indebtedness under paragraph (c)(7) of 17 CFR 1.17.

(v) Guarantee deposits with commodities clearing organizations are not required to be deducted from net worth.

(vi) Stock in commodities clearing organizations to the extent of its margin value is not required to be deducted from net worth.

(vii) Deduct from net worth the amount by which any advances paid by the broker or dealer on cash commodity contracts and used in computing net capital exceeds 95 percent of the market value of the commodities covered by such contracts.

(viii) Do not include equity in the commodity accounts of partners in net worth.

(ix) In the case of all inventory, fixed price commitments and forward contracts, except for inventory and forward contracts in the inter-bank market in those foreign currencies which are purchased or sold for future delivery on or subject to the rules of a contract market and covered by an open futures contract for which there will be no charge, deduct the applicable percentage of the net position specified below:

(A) Inventory which is currently registered as deliverable on a contract market and covered by an open futures contract or by a commodity option on a physical.

No charge

(B) Inventory which is covered by an open futures contract or commodity option.

5% of the market value

(C) Inventory which is not covered.

20% of the market value

(D) Fixed price commitments (open purchases and sales) and forward contracts which are covered by an open futures contract or commodity option.

10% of the market value

(E) Fixed price commitments (open purchases and sales) and forward contracts which are not covered by an open futures contract or commodity option.

20% of the market value

(x) Deduct 4% of the market value of commodity options granted (sold) by option customers on or subject to the rules of a contract market.

(xi) Reserved.

(xii) Deduct for undermargined customer commodity futures accounts the amount of funds required in each such account to meet maintenance margin requirements of the applicable board of trade or, if there are no such maintenance margin requirements, clearing organization margin requirements applicable to such positions, after application of calls for margin, or other required deposits which are outstanding three business days or less. If there are no such maintenance margin requirements or clearing organization margin requirements on such accounts, then deduct the amount of funds required to provide margin equal to the amount necessary after application of calls for margin, or other required deposits outstanding three days or less to restore original margin when the original margin has been depleted by 50 percent or more. *Provided,* To the extent a deficit is deducted from net worth in accordance with paragraph (a)(3)(ii) of this Appendix B, such amount shall not also be deducted under this paragraph (a)(3)(xii). In the event that an owner of a customer account has deposited an asset other than cash to margin, guarantee or secure his account, the value attributable to such asset for purposes of this paragraph shall be the lesser of (A) the value attributable to such asset pursuant to the margin rules of the applicable board of trade, or (B) the market value of such asset after application of the percentage deductions specified in paragraph (a)(3)(ix) of this Appendix B or, where appropriate, specified in paragraph (c)(2)(vi) or (c)(2)(vii) of Rule 15c3-1 of this chapter.

(xiii) Deduct for undermargined noncustomer and omnibus commodity futures accounts the amount of funds required in each such account to meet maintenance margin requirements of the applicable board of trade or, if there are no such maintenance margin requirements, clearing organization margin requirements applicable to such positions, after application of calls for margin, or other required deposits which are outstanding two business days or less. If there are no such maintenance margin requirements or clearing organization margin requirements, then deduct the amount of funds required to provide margin equal to the amount necessary after application of calls for margin, or other required deposits outstanding two days or less to restore original margin when the original margin has been depleted by 50 percent or more. *Provided,* To the extent a deficit is deducted from net worth in accordance with paragraph (a)(3)(ii) of this Appendix B such amount shall not also be deducted under this paragraph (a)(3)(xiii). In the event that an owner of a non-customer or omnibus account has deposited an asset other than cash to margin, guarantee or secure his account, the value attributable to such asset for purposes of this paragraph shall be the lesser of (A) the value attributable to such asset pursuant to the margin rules of the applicable board of trade, or (B) the market value of such asset after application of the percentage deductions specified in paragraph (a)(3)(ix) of this Appendix B or, where appropriate, specified in paragraph (c)(2)(vi) or (c)(2)(vii) of Rule 15c3-1 of this chapter.

(xiv) In the case of open futures contracts and granted (sold) commodity options held in proprietary accounts carried by the broker or dealer which are not covered by a position held by the broker or dealer or which are not the result of a "changer trade" made in accordance with the rules of a contract market, deduct:

(A) For a broker or dealer which is a clearing member of a contract market for the positions on such contract market cleared by such member, the applicable margin requirement of the applicable clearing organization;

(B) For a broker or dealer which is a member of a self-regulatory organization 150% of the applicable maintenance margin requirement of the applicable board of trade or clearing organization, whichever is greater; or

(C) For all other brokers or dealers, 200% of the applicable maintenance margin requirement of the applicable board of trade or clearing organization, whichever is greater; or

(D) For open contracts or granted (sold) commodity options for which there are no applicable maintenance margin requirements, 200% of the applicable initial margin requirement;

Provided, the equity in any such proprietary account shall reduce the deduction required by this paragraph (a)(3)(xiv) if such equity is not otherwise includable in net capital.

(xv) *Options.* In the case of a broker or dealer which is a purchaser of a commodity option which is traded on a contract market the deduction shall be the same safety factor as if the broker or dealer were the grantor of such option in accordance with paragraph (3)(xiv), but in no event shall the safety factor be greater than the market value attributed to such option.

(xvi) In the case of a broker or dealer which is a purchaser of a commodity option not traded on a contract market which has value and such value is used to increase net capital, the deduction is ten percent of the market value of the physical or futures contract which is the subject of such option but in no event more than the value attributed to such option.

(xvii) Deduct 5% of all unsecured receivables includable under paragraph (3)(iii)(C) of this Appendix B used by the broker or dealer in computing "net capital" and which are not receivable from (A) a futures commission merchant registered as such with the Commodity Futures Trading Commission, or (B) a broker or dealer which is registered as such with the Securities and Exchange Commission.

(xviii) A loan or advance or any other form of receivable shall not be considered "secured" for the purposes of paragraph (a)(3) of this Appendix B unless the following conditions exist:

(A) The receivable is secured by readily marketable collateral which is otherwise unencumbered and which can be readily converted into cash: *Provided, however,* That the receivable will be considered secured only to the extent of the market value of such collateral after application of the percentage deductions specified in paragraph (a)(3)(ix) of this Appendix B; and

(B)(*1*) The readily marketable collateral is in the possession or control of the broker or dealer; or

(*2*) The broker or dealer has a legally enforceable, written security agreement, signed by the debtor, and has a perfected security interest in the readily marketable collateral within the meaning of the laws of the State in which the readily marketable collateral is located.

(xix) The term "cover" for purposes of this Appendix B shall mean cover as defined in 17 CFR 1.17(j).

(xx) The term "customer" for purposes of this Appendix B shall mean customer as defined in 17 CFR 1.17(b)(2). The term "non-customer" for purposes of this Appendix B shall mean non-customer as defined in 17 CFR 1.17(b)(4).

Rule 15c3–1c. Consolidated Computations of Net Capital and Aggregate Indebtedness for Certain Subsidiaries and Affiliates (Appendix C to Rule 15c3–1)

(a) *Flow Through Capital Benefits.* Every broker or dealer in computing its net capital and aggregate indebtedness pursuant to Rule 15c3–1 shall, subject to the provisions of paragraphs (b) and (d) of this Appendix, consolidate in a single computation assets and liabilities of any subsidiary or affiliate for which it guarantees, endorses or assumes directly or indirectly the obligations or liabilities. The assets and liabilities of a subsidiary or affiliate whose liabilities and obligations have not been guaranteed, endorsed, or assumed directly or indirectly by the broker or dealer may also be so consolidated if an opinion of counsel is obtained as provided for in paragraph (b) below.

(b) *Required Counsel Opinions.* (1) If the consolidation, provided for in paragraph (a) of this rule, of any such subsidiary or affiliate results in the increase of the broker's or dealer's net capital and/or the decrease of the broker's or dealer's and/or the decrease of the broker's or dealer's minimum net capital requirement paragraph (a) of Rule 15c3–1 and an opinion of counsel described in paragraph (b)(2) of this rule has not been obtained, such benefits shall not be recognized in the broker's or dealer's computation required by this rule.

(2) Except as provided for in paragraph (b)(1) above, consolidation shall be permitted with respect to any subsidiaries or affiliates which are majority owned and controlled by the broker or dealer for which the broker or dealer can demonstrate to the satisfaction of the Commission, through the Examining Authority, by an opinion of counsel that the net asset values, or the portion thereof related to the parent's ownership interest in the subsidiary or affiliate may be caused by the broker or dealer or a trustee appointed pursuant to the Securities Investor Protection Act of 1970 or otherwise, to be distributed to the broker or dealer within 30 calendar days. Such opinion shall also set forth the actions necessary to cause such a distribution to be made, identify the parties having the authority to take such actions, identify and describe the rights of other parties or classes of parties, including

but not limited to customers, general creditors, subordinated lenders, minority shareholders, employees, litigants and governmental or regulatory authorities, who may delay or prevent such a distribution and such other assurances as the Commission or the Examining Authority by rule or interpretation may require. Such opinion shall be current and periodically renewed in connection with the broker's or dealer's annual audit pursuant to Rule 17a–5 under the Securities Exchange Act of 1934 or upon any material change in circumstances.

(c) *Principles of Consolidation.* In preparing a consolidated computation of net capital and/or aggregate indebtedness pursuant to this section, the following minimum and non-exclusive requirements shall be observed:

(1) Consolidated net worth shall be reduced by the estimated amount of any tax reasonably anticipated to be incurred upon distribution of the assets of the subsidiary or affiliate.

(2) Liabilities of a consolidated subsidiary of affiliate which are subordinated to the claims of present and future creditors pursuant to a satisfactory subordination agreement shall not be added to consolidated net worth unless such subordination extends also to the claims of present or future creditors of the parent broker or dealer and all consolidated subsidiaries.

(3) Subordinated liabilities of a consolidated subsidiary or affiliate which are consolidated in accordance with subparagraph (c)(2) above may not be prepaid, repaid or accelerated if any of the entities included in such consolidation would otherwise be unable to comply with the provisions of Appendix (D), Rule 15c3–1d.

(4) Each broker or dealer included within the consolidation shall at all times be in compliance with the net capital requirement to which it is subject.

(d) *Certain Precluded Acts.* No broker or dealer shall guarantee, endorse or assume directly or indirectly any obligation or liability of a subsidiary or affiliate unless the obligation or liability is reflected in the computation of net capital and/or aggregate indebtedness pursuant to Rule 15c3–1 or this Appendix (C), except as provided in paragraph (b)(1) above.

Rule 15c3–1d. Satisfactory Subordination Agreements (Appendix D to Rule 15c3–1)

(a) *Introduction.* (1) This Appendix sets forth minimum and non-exclusive requirements for satisfactory subordination agreements (hereinafter "subordination agreement"). The Examining Authority may require or the broker or dealer may include such other provisions as deemed necessary or appropriate to the extent such provisions do not cause the subordination agreement to fail to meet the minimum requirements of this Appendix (D).

(2) *Certain Definitions.* For purposes of Rule 15c3–1 and this Appendix (D):

(i) A subordination agreement may be either a subordinated loan agreement or a secured demand note agreement.

(ii) The term "subordinated loan agreement" shall mean the agreement or agreements evidencing or governing a subordinated borrowing of cash.

(iii) The term "Collateral Value" of any securities pledged to secure a secured demand note shall mean the market value of such securities after giving effect to the percentage deductions set forth in paragraph (c)(2)(vi) of Rule 15c3–1 except for paragraph (c)(2)(vi)(J). In lieu of the deduction under (c)(2)(vi)(J), the broker or dealer shall reduce the market value of the securities pledged to secure the secured demand note by 30 percent.

(iv) The term "Payment Obligation" shall mean the obligation of a broker or dealer in respect to any subordination agreement (A) to repay cash loaned to the broker or dealer pursuant to a subordinated loan agreement or (B) to return a secured demand note contributed to the broker or dealer or reduce the unpaid principal amount thereof and to return cash or securities pledged as collateral to secure the secured demand note and (C) "Payment" shall mean the performance by a broker or dealer of a Payment Obligation.

(v)(A) The term "secured demand note agreement" shall mean an agreement (including the related secured demand note) evidencing or governing the contribution of a secured demand note to a broker or dealer and the pledge of securities and/or cash with the broker or dealer as collateral to secure payment of such secured demand note. The secured demand note agreement may provide that neither the lender, his heirs, executors, administrators or assigns shall be personally liable on such note and that in the event of default the broker or dealer shall look for payment of such note solely to the collateral then pledged to secure the same.

(B) The secured demand note shall be a promissory note executed by the lender and shall be payable on the demand of the broker or dealer to which it is contributed; *Provided, however,* That the making of such demand may be conditioned upon the occurrence of any of certain events which are acceptable to the Commission and to the Examining Authority for such broker or dealer.

(C) If such note is not paid upon presentment and demand as provided for therein, the broker or dealer shall have the right to liquidate all or any part of the securities then pledged as collateral to secure payment of the same and to apply the net proceeds of such liquidation, together with any cash then included in the collateral, in payment of such note. Subject to the prior rights of the broker or dealer as pledgee, the lender, as defined herein, may retain ownership of the collateral and have the benefit of any increases and bear the risks of any decreases in the value of the collateral and may retain the right to vote securities contained within the collateral and any right to income therefrom or distributions thereon, except the broker or dealer shall have the right to receive and hold as pledgee all dividends payable in securities and all partial and complete liquidating dividends.

(D) Subject to the prior rights of the broker or dealer as pledgee, the lender may have the right to direct the sale of any securities included in the collateral, to direct the purchase of securities with any cash included therein, to withdraw excess collateral or to substitute cash or other securities as collateral, provided that the net proceeds of any such sale and the cash so substituted and the securities so purchased or substituted are held by the broker or dealer, as pledgee, and are included within the collateral to secure payment of the secured demand note, and provided further that no such transaction shall be permitted if, after giving effect thereto, the sum of the amount of any cash, plus the Collateral Value of the securities, then pledged as collateral to secure the secured demand note would be less than the unpaid principal amount of the secured demand note.

(E) Upon payment by the lender, as distinguished from a reduction by the lender which is provided for in subdivision (b)(6)(iii) or reduction by the broker or dealer as provided for in subparagraph (b)(7) of this Appendix (D), of all or any part of the unpaid principal amount of the secured demand note, a broker or dealer shall issue to the lender a subordinated loan agreement in the amount of such payment (or in the case of a broker or dealer that is a partnership credit a capital account of the lender) or issue preferred or common stock of the broker or dealer in the amount of such payment, or any combination of the foregoing, as provided for in the secured demand note agreement.

(F) The term "lender" shall mean the person who lends cash to a broker or dealer pursuant to a subordinated loan agreement and the person who contributes a secured demand note to a broker or dealer pursuant to a secured demand note agreement.

(b) *Minimum Requirements for Subordination Agreements.* (1) Subject to paragraph (a) above, a subordination agreement shall mean a written agreement between the broker or dealer and the lender, which (i) has a minimum term of one year, except for temporary subordination agreements provided for in subparagraph (c)(5) of this Appendix (D), and (ii) is a valid and binding obligation enforceable in accordance with its terms (subject as to enforcement to applicable bankruptcy, insolvency, reorganization, moratorium and other similar laws) against the broker or dealer and the lender and their respective heirs, executors, administrators, successors and assigns.

(2) *Specific Amount.* All subordination agreements shall be for a specific dollar amount which shall not be reduced for the duration of the agreement except by installments as specifically provided for therein and except as otherwise provided in this Appendix (D).

(3) *Effective Subordination.* The subordination agreement shall effectively subordinate any right of the lender to receive any Payment with respect thereto, together with accrued interest or compensation, to the prior payment or provision for payment in full of all claims of all present and future creditors of the broker or dealer arising out of any matter occurring prior to the date on which the related Payment Obligation matures consistent with the provisions of Rule 15c3-1 and Rule 15c3-1d, except for claims which are the subject of subordination agreements which rank on the same priority as or junior to the claim of the lender under such subordination agreements.

(4) *Proceeds of Subordinated Loan Agreements.* The subordinated loan agreement shall provide that the cash proceeds thereof shall be used and dealt with by the broker or dealer as part of its capital and shall be subject to the risks of the business.

(5) *Certain Rights of the Broker or Dealer.* The subordination agreement shall provide that the broker or dealer shall have the right to:

(i) Deposit any cash proceeds of a subordinated loan agreement and any cash pledged as collateral to secure a secured demand note in an account or accounts in its own name in any bank or trust company;

(ii) Pledge, repledge, hypothecate and rehypothecate, any or all of the securities pledged as collateral to secure a secured demand note, without notice, separately or in common with other securities or property for the purpose of securing any indebtedness of the broker or dealer; and

(iii) Lend to itself or others any or all of the securities and cash pledged as collateral to secure a secured demand note.

(6) *Collateral for Secured Demand Notes.* Only cash and securities which are fully paid for and which may be publicly offered or sold without registration under the Securities Act of 1933, and the offer, sale and transfer of which are not otherwise restricted, may be pledged as collateral to secure a secured demand note. The secured demand note agreement shall provide that if at any time the sum of the amount of any cash, plus the Collateral Value of any securities, then pledged as collateral to secure the secured demand note is less than the unpaid principal amount of the secured demand note, the broker or dealer must immediately transmit written notice to that effect to the lender and the Examining Authority for such broker or dealer. The secured demand note agreement shall also require that following such transmittal:

(i) The lender, prior to noon of the business day next succeeding the transmittal of such notice, may pledge as collateral additional cash or securities sufficient, after giving effect to such pledge, to bring the sum of the amount of any cash plus the Collateral Value of any securities, then pledged as collateral to secure the secured demand note, up to an amount not less than the unpaid principal amount of the secured demand note; and

(ii) Unless additional cash or securities are pledged by the lender as provided in (i) above, the broker or dealer at noon on the business day next succeeding the transmittal of notice to the lender must commence sale, for the account of the lender, of such of the securities then pledged as collateral to secure the secured demand note and apply so much of the net proceeds, thereof, together with such of the cash then pledged as collateral to secure the secured demand note as may be necessary to eliminate the unpaid principal amount of the secured demand note; *Provided, however,* That the unpaid principal amount of the secured demand note need not be reduced below the sum of the amount of any remaining cash, plus the Collateral Value of the remaining securities, then pledged as collateral to secure the secured demand note. The broker or dealer may not purchase for its own account any securities subject to such a sale.

(iii) The secured demand note agreement also may provide that, in lieu of the procedures specified in the provisions required by paragraph (b)(6)(ii) of this rule, the lender with the prior written consent of the broker or dealer and the Examining Authority for the broker or dealer may reduce the unpaid principal amount of the secured demand note. After giving effect to such reduction, the aggregate indebtedness of the broker or dealer may not exceed 1000 percent of its net capital or, in the case of a broker or dealer operating pursuant to paragraph (a)(1)(ii) of Rule 15c3–1, net capital may not be less than 5% of aggregate debit items computed in accordance with Rule 15c3–3a, or, if registered as a futures commission merchant, 7% of the funds required to be segregated pursuant to the Commodity Exchange Act and the regulations thereunder (less the market value of commodity options purchased by option customers subject to the rules of a contract market, each such deduction not to exceed the amount of funds in the option customer's account), if greater. No single secured demand note shall be permitted to be reduced by more than 15% of its original principal amount and after such reduction no excess collateral may be withdrawn. No Examining Authority shall consent to a reduction of the principal amount of a secured demand note if, after giving effect to such reduction, net capital would be less than 120% of the minimum dollar amount required by Rule 15c3–1.

Permissive Prepayments

(7) A broker or dealer at its option but not at the option of the lender may, if the subordination agreement so provides, make a Payment of all or any portion of the Payment Obligation thereunder prior to the scheduled maturity date of such Payment Obligation (hereinafter referred to as a "Prepayment"), but in no event may any Prepayment be made before the expiration of one year from the date such subordination agreement became effective. This restriction shall not apply to temporary subordination agreements that comply with the provisions of paragraph (c)(5) of this Appendix D. No Prepayment shall be made, if, after giving effect thereto (and to all Payments of Payment Obligations under any other subordinated agreements then outstanding the maturity or accelerated maturities of which are scheduled to fall due within six months after the date such Prepayment is to occur pursuant to this provision or on or prior to the date on which the Payment Obligation in respect of such Prepayment is scheduled to mature disregarding this provision, whichever date is earlier) without reference to any projected profit or loss of the broker or dealer, either aggregate indebtedness of the broker or dealer would exceed 1000 percent of its net capital or its net capital would be less than 120 percent of the minimum dollar amount required by Rule 15c3–1 or, in the case of a broker or dealer operating pursuant to paragraph (a)(1)(ii) of Rule 15c3–1, its net capital would be less than 5 percent of its aggregate debit items computed in accordance with Rule

15c3-3a, or if registered as a futures commission merchant, 7 percent of the funds required to be segregated pursuant to the Commodity Exchange Act and the regulations thereunder (less the market value of commodity options purchased by option customers subject to the rules of a contract market, each such deduction not to exceed the amount of funds in the option customer's account), if greater, or its net capital would be less than 120 percent of the minimum dollar amount required by paragraph (a)(1)(ii) of Rule 15c3-1. Notwithstanding the above, no Prepayment shall occur without the prior written approval of the Examining Authority for such broker or dealer.

(8) *Suspended Repayment.* (i) The Payment obligation of the broker or dealer in respect of any subordination agreement shall be suspended and shall not mature, if, after giving effect to Payment of such Payment Obligation (and to all Payments of Payment Obligations of such broker or dealer under any other subordination agreement(s) then outstanding that are scheduled to mature on or before such Payment Obligation) either (A) the aggregate indebtedness of the broker or dealer would exceed 1200% of its net capital or, in the case of a broker or dealer operating pursuant to paragraph (a)(1)(ii) of Rule 15c3-1, its net capital would be less than 5% of aggregate debit items computed in accordance with Rule 15c3-3a or, if registered as a futures commission merchant, 6% of the funds required to be segregated pursuant to the Commodity Exchange Act and the regulations thereunder (less the market value of commodity options purchased by option customers on or subject to the rules of a contract market, each such deduction not to exceed the amount of funds in the option customer's account) if greater, or (B) its net capital would be less than 120 percent of the minimum dollar amount required by Rule 15c3-1 including paragraph (a)(1)(ii), if applicable. The subordination agreement may provide that if the Payment Obligation of the broker or dealer thereunder does not mature and is suspended as a result of the requirement of this paragraph (b)(8) for a period of not less than six months, the broker or dealer shall thereupon commence the rapid and orderly liquidation of its business but the right of the lender to receive Payment, together with accrued interest or compensation, shall remain subordinate as required by the provisions of Rule 15c3-1 and Rule 15c3-1d.

(9) *Accelerated Maturity-Obligation to Repay to Remain Subordinate.* (i) Subject to the provisions of subparagraph (b)(8) of this Appendix, a subordination agreement may provide that the lender may, upon prior written notice to the broker or dealer and the Examining Authority given not earlier than six months after the effective date of such subordination agreement, accelerate the date on which the Payment Obligation of the broker or dealer, together with accrued interest or compensation, is scheduled to mature to a date not earlier than six months after the giving of such notice, but the right of the lender to receive Payment, together with accrued interest or compensation, shall remain subordinate as required by the provisions of Rule 15c3-1 and Rule 15c3-1d.

(ii) Notwithstanding the provisions of subparagraph (b)(8) of this Appendix, the Payment Obligation of the broker or dealer with respect to a subordination agreement, together with accrued interest and compensation, shall mature in the event of any receivership, insolvency, liquidation pursuant to the Securities Investor Protection Act of 1970 or otherwise, bankruptcy, assignment for the benefit of creditors, reorganization whether or not pursuant to the bankruptcy laws, or any other marshalling of the assets and liabilities of the broker or dealer but the right of the lender to receive Payment, together with accrued interest or compensation, shall remain subordinate as required by the provisions of Rule 15c3-1 and Rule 15c3-1d.

(10)(i) *Accelerated Maturity of Subordination Agreements on Event of Default and Event of Acceleration—Obligation to Repay to Remain Subordinate.* A subordination agreement may provide that the lender may, upon prior written notice to the broker or dealer and the Examining Authority of the broker or dealer of the occurrence of any Event of Acceleration (as hereinafter defined) given no sooner than six months after the effective date of such subordination agreement, accelerate the date on which the Payment Obligation of the broker or dealer, together with accrued interest or compensation, is scheduled to mature, to the last business day of a calendar month which is not less than six months after notice of acceleration is received by the broker or dealer and the Examining Authority for the broker or dealer. Any subordination agreement containing such Events of Acceleration may also *Provide,* That if upon such accelerated maturity date the Payment Obligation of the broker or dealer is suspended as required by subparagraph (b)(8) of this Appendix (D) and liquidation of the broker or dealer has not commenced on or prior to such accelerated maturity date, then notwithstanding subparagraph (b)(8) of this Appendix the Payment Obligation of the broker or dealer with respect to such subordination agreement shall mature on the day immediately following such accelerated maturity date and in any such event the Payment Obligations of the broker or dealer with respect to all other subordination agreements then outstanding shall also mature at the same time but the rights of the respective lenders to receive Payment, together with accrued interest or compensation, shall remain subordinate as required by the provisions of this Appendix (D). Events of Acceleration which may be included in a subordination agreement complying with this subparagraph (b)(10) shall be limited to:

(A) Failure to pay interest or any installment of principal on a subordination agreement as scheduled;

(B) Failure to pay when due other money obligations of a specified material amount;

(C) Discovery that any material, specified representation or warranty of the broker or dealer which is included in the subordination agreement and on which the subordination agreement was based or continued was inaccurate in a material respect at the time made;

(D) Any specified and clearly measurable event which is included in the subordination agreement and which the lender and the broker or dealer agree (1) is a significant indication that the financial position of the broker or dealer has changed materially and adversely from agreed upon specified norms or (2) could materially and adversely affect the ability of the broker or dealer to conduct its business as conducted on the date the subordination agreement was made; or (3) is a significant change in the senior management of the broker or dealer or in the general business conducted by the broker or dealer from that which obtained on the date the subordination agreement became effective;

(E) Any continued failure to perform agreed covenants included in the subordination agreement relating to the conduct of the business of the broker or dealer or relating to the maintenance and reporting of its financial position; and

(ii) Notwithstanding the provisions of subparagraph (b)(8) of this Appendix, a subordination agreement may, *provide,* That, if liquidation of the business of the broker or dealer has not already commenced, the Payment Obligation of the broker or dealer shall mature, together with accrued interest or compensation, upon the occurrence of an Event of Default (as hereinafter defined). Such agreement may also, *provide,* That, if liquidation of the business of the broker or dealer has not already commenced, the rapid and orderly liquidation of the business of the broker or dealer shall then commence upon the happening of an Event of Default. Any subordination agreement which so provides for maturity of the Payment Obligation upon the occurrence of an Event of Default shall also, *provide,* That the date on which such Event of Default occurs shall, if liquidation of the broker or dealer has not already commenced, be the date on which the Payment Obligations of the broker or dealer with respect to all other subordination agreements then outstanding shall mature but the rights of the respective lenders to receive Payment, together with accrued interest or compensation, shall remain subordinate as required by the provisions of this Appendix (D). Events of Default which may be included in a subordination agreement shall be limited to:

(A) The making of an application by the Securities Investor Protection Corporation for a decree adjudicating that customers of the broker or dealer are in need of protection under the Securities Investor Protection Act of 1970 and the failure of the broker or dealer to obtain the dismissal of such application within 30 days;

(B) The aggregate indebtedness of the broker or dealer exceeding 1500% of its net capital or, in the case of a broker or dealer that has elected to operate under paragraph (a)(1)(ii) of Rule 15c3–1, its net capital computed in accordance therewith is less than 2% of its aggregate debit items computed in accordance with Rule 15c3–3a or, if registered as a futures commission merchant, 4% of the funds required to be segregated pursuant to the Commodity Exchange Act and the regulations thereunder (less the market value of commodity options purchased by option customers on or subject to the rules of a contract market, each such deduction not to exceed the amount of funds in the option customer's account), if greater, throughout a period of 15 consecutive business days, commencing on the day the broker or dealer first determines and notifies the Examining Authority for the broker or dealer, or the Examining Authority or the Commission first determines and notifies the broker or dealer of such fact;

(C) The Commission shall revoke the registration of the broker or dealer;

(D) The Examining Authority shall suspend (and not reinstate within 10 days) or revoke the broker's or dealer's status as a member thereof;

(E) Any receivership, insolvency, liquidation pursuant to the Securities Investor Protection Act of 1970 or otherwise, bankruptcy, assignment for the benefit of creditors, reorganization whether or not pursuant to bankruptcy laws, or any other marshalling of the assets and liabilities of the broker or dealer.

A subordination agreement which contains any of the provisions permitted by this subparagraph (b)(10) shall not contain the provision otherwise permitted by clause (i) of subparagraph (b)(9).

(11) *Brokers and Dealers Carrying the Accounts of Specialists and Market Makers in Listed Options.* A subordination agreement which becomes effective on or after August 1, 1977 in favor of a broker or dealer who guarantees, endorses, carries or clears specialist or market maker transactions in options listed on a national securities exchange or facility of a national securities association shall provide that reduction, prepayment or repayment of the unpaid principal amount thereof, pursuant to those terms of the agreement required or permitted by paragraphs (b)(6)(iii), (b)(7) or (b)(8)(i) of this rule, shall not occur in contravention of paragraphs (a)(6)(v), (a)(7)(iv) or (c)(2)(x)(B)(1) or Rule 15c3–1 insofar as they apply to such broker or dealer.

(c) *Miscellaneous Provisions.*

(1) *Prohibited Cancellation.* The subordination agreement shall not be subject to cancellation by either party; no Payment shall be made with respect thereto and the agreement shall not be terminated, rescinded or modified by mutual consent or otherwise if the effect thereof would be inconsistent with the requirements of Rule 15c3–1 and Rule 15c3–1d.

(2) *Notice of Maturity or Accelerated Maturity.* Every broker or dealer shall immediately notify the Examining Authority for such broker or dealer if, after giving effect to all Payments of Payment Obligations under subordination agreements then outstanding

that are then due or mature within the following six months without reference to any projected profit or loss of the broker or dealer, either the aggregate indebtedness of the broker or dealer would exceed 1200% of its net capital or its net capital would be less than 120% of the minimum dollar amount required by Rule 15c3–1, or, in the case of a broker or dealer who is operating pursuant to paragraph (a)(1)(ii) of Rule 15c3–1, its net capital would be less than 5% of aggregate debit items computed in accordance with Rule 15c3–3a, or, if registered as a futures commission merchant, 6% of the funds required to be segregated pursuant to the Commodity Exchange Act and the regulations thereunder (less the market value of commodity options purchased by option customers on or subject to the rules of a contract market, each such deduction not to exceed the amount of funds in the option customer's account) if greater, or less than 120% of the minimum dollar amount required by paragraph (a)(1)(ii) of Rule 15c3–1.

(3) *Certain Legends.* If all the provisions of a satisfactory subordination agreement do not appear in a single instrument, then the debenture or other evidence of indebtedness shall bear on its face an appropriate legend stating that it is issued subject to the provisions of a satisfactory subordination agreement which shall be adequately referred to and incorporated by reference.

(4) *Legal Title to Securities.* All securities pledged as collateral to secure a secured demand note must be in bearer form, or registered in the name of the broker or dealer or the name of its nominee or custodian.

(5)(i) *Temporary and Revolving Subordination Agreements.* For the purpose of enabling a broker or dealer to participate as an underwriter of securities or other extraordinary activities in compliance with the net capital requirements of Rule 15c3–1, a broker or dealer shall be permitted, on no more than three occasions in any 12 month period, to enter into a subordination agreement on a temporary basis that has a stated term of no more than 45 days from the date such subordination agreement became effective. This temporary relief shall not apply to a broker or dealer if, within the preceding thirty calendar days, it has given notice pursuant to Rule 17a–11, or if immediately prior to entering into such subordination agreement, either:

(A) The aggregate indebtedness of the broker or dealer exceeds 1000% of its net capital or its net capital is less than 120% of the minimum dollar amount required by Rule 15c3–1, or

(B) In the case of a broker or dealer operating pursuant to paragraph (a)(1)(ii) of Rule 15c3–1, its net capital is less than 5% of aggregated debits computed in accordance with Rule 15c3–3a or, if registered as a futures commission merchant, less than 7% of the funds required to be segregated pursuant to the Commodity Exchange Act and the regulations thereunder (less the market value of commodity options purchased by option customers on or subject to the rules of a contract market, each such deduction not to exceed the amount of funds in the option customer's account), if greater, or less than 120% of the minimum dollar amount required by paragraph (a)(1)(ii) of this rule, or

(C) The amount of its then outstanding subordination agreements exceeds the limits specified in paragraph (d) of Rule 15c3–1. Such temporary subordination agreement shall be subject to all other provisions this Appendix D.

(ii) A broker or dealer shall be permitted to enter into a revolving subordinated loan agreement which provides for prepayment within less than one year of all or any portion of the Payment Obligation thereunder at the option of the broker or dealer upon the prior written approval of the Examining Authority for the broker or dealer. The

Examining Authority, however, shall not approve any prepayment if:

(A) After giving effect thereto (and to all Payments of Payment Obligations under any other subordinated agreements then outstanding, the maturity or accelerated maturities of which are scheduled to fall due within six months after the date such prepayment is to occur pursuant to this provision or on or prior to the date on which the Payment Obligation in respect of such prepayment is scheduled to mature disregarding this provision, whichever date is earlier) without reference to any projected profit or loss of the broker or dealer, either aggregate indebtedness of the broker or dealer would exceed 900 percent of its net capital or its net capital would be less than 200 percent of the minimum dollar amount required by Rule 15c3–1 or, in the case of a broker or dealer operating pursuant to paragraph (a)(1)(ii) of Rule 15c3–1, its net capital would be less than 6% of the aggregate debit items computed in accordance with Rule 15c3–3a or, if registered as a futures commission merchant, 10% of the funds required to be segregated pursuant to the Commodity Exchange Act and the regulations thereunder (less the market value of commodity options purchased by option customers on or subject to the rules of a contract market, each such deduction not to exceed the amount of funds in the option customer's account), if greater, or its net capital would be less than 200% of the minimum dollar amount required by paragraph (a)(1)(ii) of this rule or

(B) Pre-tax losses during the latest three-month period equalled more than 15% of current excess net capital. Any subordination agreement entered into pursuant to this subsection (ii) shall be subject to all the other provisions of this Appendix D. Any such subordination agreement shall not be considered equity for purposes of paragraph (d) of Section 15c3–1, despite the length of the initial term of the loan.

(6)(i) *Filing*. Two copies of any proposed subordination agreement (including nonconforming subordination agreements) shall be filed at least 10 days prior to the proposed execution date of the agreement with the Commission's Regional or District Office for the region or district in which the broker or dealer maintains its principal place of business or at such other time as the Regional or District Office for good cause shall accept such filing. Copies of the proposed agreement shall also be filed with the Examining Authority in such quantities and at such time as the Examining Authority may require. The broker or dealer shall also file with said parties a statement setting forth the name and address of the lender, the business relationship of the lender to the broker or dealer, and whether the broker or dealer carried funds or securities for the lender at or about the time the proposed agreement was so filed. All agreements shall be examined by the Commission's Regional or District Office or the Examining Authority with whom such agreement is required to be filed prior to their becoming effective. No proposed agreement shall be a satisfactory subordination agreement for the purposes of this section unless and until the Examining Authority has found the agreement acceptable and such agreement has become effective in the form found acceptable.

(ii) The broker or dealer need not file with the Regional or District Office for the region in which the broker or dealer maintains its principal place of business (if a Regional or District Office is not its Examining Authority) copies of any proposed subordination agreement or the statement described above if the Examining Authority for that broker or dealer has consented to file with the Commission periodic reports (not less than monthly) summarizing for the period, on a firm-by-firm basis, the subordination agreements it has approved for that period. Such reports should include at the minimum, the amount of the loan and its duration, the name of the lender and the business relationship of the lender to the broker or dealer.

(7) *Subordination Agreements in Effect Prior to Adoption.* Any subordination agreement which has been entered into prior to December 20, 1978 and which has been deemed to be satisfactorily subordinated pursuant to Rule 15c3-1 as in effect prior to December 20, 1978, shall continue to be deemed a satisfactory subordination agreement until the maturity of such agreement. *Provided,* That no renewal of an agreement which provides for automatic or optional renewal by the broker or dealer or lender shall be deemed to be a satisfactory subordination agreement unless such renewed agreement meets the requirements of this Appendix within 6 months from December 20, 1978. *Provided, further,* That all subordination agreements must meet the requirements of this Appendix within 5 years of December 20, 1978.

Rule 15c3-1e Deductions for market and credit risk for certain brokers or dealers (Appendix E to 17 CFR 240.15c3-1).

Preliminary Note: Appendices E and G to the net capital rule set forth a program that allows a broker or dealer to use an alternative approach to computing net capital deductions, subject to the conditions described in the Appendices, including supervision of the broker's or dealer's ultimate holding company under the program. The program is designed to reduce the likelihood that financial and operational weakness in the holding company will destabilize the broker or dealer, or the broader financial system. The focus of this supervision of the ultimate holding company is its financial and operational condition and its risk management controls and methodologies.

Application

(a) A broker or dealer may apply to the Commission for authorization to compute deductions for market risk pursuant to this Appendix E in lieu of computing deductions pursuant to §§ 240.15c3-1(c)(2)(vi) and (c)(2)(vii) and to compute deductions for credit risk pursuant to this Appendix E on credit exposures arising from transactions in derivatives instruments (if this Appendix E is used to calculate deductions for market risk on these instruments) in lieu of computing deductions pursuant to § 240.15c3-1(c)(2)(iv):

(1) A broker-dealer shall submit the following information to the Commission with its application:

(i) An executive summary of the information provided to the Commission with its application and an identification of the ultimate holding company of the broker or dealer;

(ii) A comprehensive description of the internal risk management control system of the broker or dealer and how that system satisfies the requirements set forth in § 240.15c3-4;

(iii) A list of the categories of positions that the broker or dealer holds in its proprietary accounts and a brief description of the methods that the broker or dealer will use to calculate deductions for market and credit risk on those categories of positions;

(iv) A description of the mathematical models to be used to price positions and to compute deductions for market risk, including those portions of the deductions attributable to specific risk, if applicable, and deductions for credit risk; a description of the creation, use, and maintenance of the mathematical models; a description of the broker's or dealer's internal risk management controls over those models, including a description of each category of persons who may input data into the models; if a mathematical model incorporates empirical correlations across risk categories, a description of the process for measuring correlations; a description of the backtesting procedures the broker or dealer will use to backtest the mathematical model used to calculate maximum potential exposure; a description of how each mathematical model satisfies the applicable qualitative and quantitative requirements set forth in paragraph (d) of this Appendix E; and a statement describing the extent to which each mathematical model used to compute deductions for market and credit risk will be used as part of the risk analyses and reports presented to senior management;

(v) If the broker or dealer is applying to the Commission for approval to use scenario analysis to calculate deductions for market risk for certain positions, a list of those types of positions, a description of how those deductions will be calculated using scenario analysis, and an explanation of why each scenario analysis is appropriate to calculate deductions for market risk on those types of positions;

(vi) A description of how the broker or dealer will calculate current exposure;

(vii) A description of how the broker or dealer will determine internal credit ratings of counterparties and internal credit risk weights of counterparties, if applicable;

(viii) A written undertaking by the ultimate holding company of the broker or dealer, if it is not an ultimate holding company that has a principal regulator, in a form acceptable to the Commission, signed by a duly authorized person at the ultimate holding company, to the effect that, as a condition of Commission approval of the application of the broker or dealer to compute deductions for market and credit risk pursuant to this Appendix E, the ultimate holding company agrees to:

(A) Comply with all applicable provisions of this Appendix E;

(B) Comply with all applicable provisions of § 240.15c3–1g;

(C) Comply with the provisions of § 240.15c3–4 with respect to an internal risk management control system for the affiliate group as though it were an OTC derivatives dealer with respect to all of its business activities, except that paragraphs (c)(5)(xiii), (c)(5)(xiv), (d)(8), and (d)(9) of § 240.15c3–4 shall not apply;

(D) As part of the internal risk management control system for the affiliate group, establish, document, and maintain procedures for the detection and prevention of money laundering and terrorist financing;

(E) Permit the Commission to examine the books and records of the ultimate holding company and any of its affiliates, if the affiliate is not an entity that has a principal regulator;

(F) If the disclosure to the Commission of any information required as a condition for the broker or dealer to compute deductions for market and credit risk pursuant to this Appendix E could be prohibited by law or otherwise, cooperate with the Commission, to the extent permissible, including by describing any secrecy laws or other impediments that could restrict the ability of material affiliates to provide information on their operations or activities and by discussing the manner in which the ultimate holding company and the broker or dealer propose to provide the Commission with adequate information or assurances of access to information;

(G) Make available to the Commission information about the ultimate holding company or any of its material affiliates that the Commission finds is necessary to evaluate the financial and operational risk within the ultimate holding company and its material affiliates and to evaluate compliance with the conditions of eligibility of the broker or dealer to compute deductions to net capital under the alternative method of this Appendix E;

(H) Make available examination reports of principal regulators for those affiliates of the ultimate holding company that are not subject to Commission examination; and

(I) Acknowledge that, if the ultimate holding company fails to comply in a material manner with any provision of its undertaking, the Commission may, in addition to any other conditions necessary or appropriate in the public interest or for the protection of investors, increase the multiplication factors the ultimate holding company uses to calculate allowances for market and credit risk, as defined in § 240.15c3–1g(a)(2) and (a)(3) or impose any condition with respect to the broker or dealer listed in paragraph (e) of this Appendix E; and

(ix) A written undertaking by the ultimate holding company of the broker or dealer, if the ultimate holding company has a principal regulator, in a form acceptable to the Commission, signed by a duly authorized person at the ultimate holding company, to the effect that, as a condition of Commission approval of the application of the broker or dealer to compute deductions for market and credit risk pursuant to this Appendix E, the ultimate holding company agrees to:

(A) Comply with all applicable provisions of this Appendix E;

(B) Comply with all applicable provisions of § 240.15c3–1g;

(C) Make available to the Commission information about the ultimate holding company that the Commission finds is necessary to evaluate the financial and operational risk within the ultimate holding company and to evaluate compliance with the conditions of eligibility of the broker or dealer to compute net capital under the alternative method of this Appendix E; and

(D) Acknowledge that if the ultimate holding company fails to comply in a material manner with any provision of its undertaking, the Commission may, in addition to any other conditions necessary or appropriate in the public interest or for the protection of investors, impose any condition with respect to the broker or dealer listed in paragraph (e) of this Appendix E;

(2) As a condition of Commission approval, the ultimate holding company of the broker or dealer, if it is not an ultimate holding company that has a principal regulator, shall include the following information with the application:

(i) A narrative description of the business and organization of the ultimate holding company;

(ii) An alphabetical list of the affiliates of the ultimate holding company (referred to as the "affiliate group," which shall include the ultimate holding company), with an identification of the financial regulator, if any, that regulates the affiliate, and a designation of the members of the affiliate group that are material to the ultimate holding company ("material affiliates");

(iii) An organizational chart that identifies the ultimate holding company, the broker or dealer, and the material affiliates;

(iv) Consolidated and consolidating financial statements of the ultimate holding company as of the end of the quarter preceding the filing of the application;

(v) Sample computations for the ultimate holding company of allowable capital and allowances for market risk, credit risk, and operational risk, determined pursuant to § 240.15c3–1g(a)(1)-(a)(4);

(vi) A list of the categories of positions that the affiliate group holds in its proprietary accounts and a brief description of the method that the ultimate holding company proposes to use to calculate allowances for market and credit risk, pursuant to § 240.15c3–1g(a)(2) and (a)(3), on those categories of positions;

(vii) A description of the mathematical models to be used to price positions and to compute the allowance for market risk, including those portions of the allowance attributable to specific risk, if applicable, and the allowance for credit risk; a description of the creation, use, and maintenance of the mathematical models; a description of the ultimate holding company's internal risk management controls over those models, including a description of each category of persons who may input data into the models; if a mathematical model incorporates empirical correlations across risk categories, a description of the process for measuring correlations; a description of the backtesting procedures the ultimate holding company will use to backtest the mathematical model used to calculate maximum potential exposure; a description of how each mathematical model satisfies the applicable qualitative and quantitative requirements set forth in paragraph (d) of this Appendix E; a statement describing the extent to which each mathematical model used to compute allowances for market and credit risk is used as part of the risk analyses and reports presented to senior management; and a description of any positions for which the ultimate holding company proposes to use a method other than VaR to compute an allowance for market risk and a description of how that allowance would be determined;

(viii) A description of how the ultimate holding company will calculate current exposure;

(ix) A description of how the ultimate holding company will determine the credit risk weights of counterparties and internal credit ratings of counterparties, if applicable;

(x) A description of how the ultimate holding company will calculate an allowance for operational risk under § 240.15c3–1g(a)(4);

(xi) For each instance in which a mathematical model used by the broker or dealer to calculate a deduction for market risk or to calculate maximum potential exposure for a particular product or counterparty differs from the mathematical model used by the ultimate holding company to calculate an allowance for market risk or to calculate maximum potential exposure for that same product or counterparty, a description of the difference(s) between the mathematical models;

(xii) A comprehensive description of the risk management control system for the affiliate group that the ultimate holding company has established to manage affiliate group-wide risk, including market, credit, liquidity and funding, legal and compliance, and operational risks, and how that system satisfies the requirements of § 240.15c3–4; and

(xiii) Sample risk reports that are provided to the persons at the ultimate holding company who are responsible for managing group-wide risk and that will be provided to the Commission pursuant to § 240.15c3–1g(b)(1)(i)(H);

(3) As a condition of Commission approval, the ultimate holding company of the broker or dealer, if the ultimate holding company has a principal regulator, shall include the following information with the broker's or dealer's application:

(i) A narrative description of the business and organization of the ultimate holding company;

(ii) An alphabetical list of the affiliates of the ultimate holding company (referred to as the "affiliate group," which shall include the ultimate holding company), with an identification of the financial regulator, if any, that regulates the affiliate, and a designation of those affiliates that are material to the ultimate holding company ("material affiliates");

(iii) An organizational chart that identifies the ultimate holding company, the broker or dealer, and the material affiliates;

(iv) Consolidated and consolidating financial statements of the ultimate holding company as of the end of the quarter preceding the filing of the application;

(v) The most recent capital measurements of the ultimate holding company, as reported to its principal regulator, calculated in accordance with the standards published by the Basel Committee on Banking Supervision, as amended from time to time;

(vi) For each instance in which a mathematical model to be used by the broker or dealer to calculate a deduction for market risk or to calculate maximum potential exposure for a particular product or counterparty differs from the mathematical model used by the ultimate holding company to calculate an allowance for market risk or to calculate maximum potential exposure for that same product or counterparty, a description of the difference(s) between the mathematical models; and

(vii) Sample risk reports that are provided to the persons at the ultimate holding company who are responsible for managing group-wide risk and that will be provided to the Commission under § 240.15c3–1g(b)(1)(i)(H);

(4) The application of the broker or dealer shall be supplemented by other information relating to the internal risk management control system, mathematical models, and financial position of the broker or dealer or the ultimate holding company of the broker or dealer that the Commission may request to complete its review of the application;

(5) The application shall be considered filed when received at the Commission's principal office in Washington, DC. A person who files an application pursuant to this section for which it seeks confidential treatment may clearly mark each page or segregable portion of each page with the words "Confidential Treatment Requested." All information submitted in connection with the application will be accorded confidential treatment, to the extent permitted by law;

(6) If any of the information filed with the Commission as part of the application of the broker or dealer is found to be or becomes inaccurate before the Commission approves the application, the broker or dealer must notify the Commission promptly and provide the Commission with a description of the circumstances in which the information was found to be or has become inaccurate along with updated, accurate information;

(7) The Commission may approve the application or an amendment to the application, in whole or in part, subject to any conditions or limitations the Commission may require, if the Commission finds the approval to be necessary or appropriate in the public interest or for the protection of investors, after determining, among other things, whether the broker or dealer has met the requirements of this Appendix E and is in compliance with other applicable rules promulgated under the Act and by self-regulatory organizations, and whether the ultimate holding company of the broker or dealer is in compliance with the terms of its undertakings, as provided to the Commission;

(8) A broker or dealer shall amend its application to calculate certain deductions for market and credit risk under this Appendix E and submit the amendment to the Commission for approval before it may change materially a mathematical model used to calculate market or credit risk or before it may change materially its internal risk management control system;

(9) As a condition to the broker's or dealer's calculation of deductions for market and credit risk under this Appendix E, an ultimate holding company that does not have a principal regulator shall submit to the Commission, as an amendment to the broker's or dealer's application, any material changes to

a mathematical model or other methods used to calculate allowances for market, credit, and operational risk, and any material changes to the internal risk management control system for the affiliate group. The ultimate holding company must submit these material changes to the Commission before making them;

(10) As a condition for the broker or dealer to compute deductions for market and credit risk under this Appendix E, the broker or dealer agrees that:

(i) It will notify the Commission 45 days before it ceases to compute deductions for market and credit risk under this Appendix E; and

(ii) The Commission may determine by order that the notice will become effective after a shorter or longer period of time if the broker or dealer consents or if the Commission determines that a shorter or longer period of time is necessary or appropriate in the public interest or for the protection of investors; and

(11) Notwithstanding paragraph (a)(10) of this section, the Commission, by order, may revoke a broker's or dealer's exemption that allows it to use the market risk standards of this Appendix E to calculate deductions for market risk, instead of the provisions of § 240.15c3–1(c)(2)(vi) and (c)(2)(vii), and the exemption to use the credit risk standards of this Appendix E to calculate deductions for credit risk on certain credit exposures arising from transactions in derivatives instruments, instead of the provisions of § 240.15c3–1(c)(2)(iv), if the Commission finds that such exemption is no longer necessary or appropriate in the public interest or for the protection of investors. In making its finding, the Commission will consider the compliance history of the broker or dealer related to its use of models, the financial and operational strength of the broker or dealer and its ultimate holding company, the broker's or dealer's compliance with its internal risk management controls, and the ultimate holding company's compliance with its undertakings.

Market Risk

(b) A broker or dealer whose application, including amendments, has been approved under paragraph (a) of this Appendix E shall compute a deduction for market risk in an amount equal to the sum of the following:

(1) For positions for which the Commission has approved the broker's or dealer's use of value-at risk ("VaR") models, the VaR of the positions multiplied by the appropriate multiplication factor determined according to paragraph (d)(1)(iii) of this Appendix E, except that the initial multiplication factor shall be three, unless the Commission determines, based on a review of the broker's or dealer's application or an amendment to the application under paragraph (a) of this Appendix E, including a review of its internal risk management control system and practices and VaR models, that another multiplication factor is appropriate;

(2) For positions for which the VaR model does not incorporate specific risk, a deduction for specific risk to be determined by the Commission based on a review of the broker's or dealer's application or an amendment to the application under paragraph (a) of this Appendix E and the positions involved;

(3) For positions for which the Commission has approved the broker's or dealer's application to use scenario analysis, the greatest loss resulting from a range of adverse movements in relevant risk factors, prices, or spreads designed to represent a negative movement greater than, or equal to, the worst ten-day movement over the four years preceding calculation of the greatest loss, or some multiple of the greatest loss based on the liquidity of the positions subject to scenario analysis. If historical data is insufficient, the deduction shall be the largest loss within a three standard deviation movement in those risk factors, prices, or

spreads over a ten-day period, multiplied by an appropriate liquidity adjustment factor. Irrespective of the deduction otherwise indicated under scenario analysis, the resulting deduction for market risk must be at least $25 per 100 share equivalent contract for equity positions, or one-half of one percent of the face value of the contract for all other types of contracts, even if the scenario analysis indicates a lower amount. A qualifying scenario must include the following:

(i) A set of pricing equations for the positions based on, for example, arbitrage relations, statistical analysis, historic relationships, merger evaluation, or fundamental valuation of an offering of securities;

(ii) Auxiliary relationships mapping risk factors to prices; and

(iii) Data demonstrating the effectiveness of the scenario in capturing market risk, including specific risk; and

(4) For all remaining positions, the deductions specified in §§ 240.15c3–1(c)(2)(vi), (c)(2)(vii), and applicable appendices to § 240.15c3–1.

Credit Risk

(c) A broker or dealer whose application, including amendments, has been approved under paragraph (a) of this Appendix E shall compute a deduction for credit risk on transactions in derivative instruments (if this Appendix E is used to calculate a deduction for market risk on those instruments) in an amount equal to the sum of the following:

(1) A counterparty exposure charge in an amount equal to the sum of the following:

(i) The net replacement value in the account of each counterparty that is insolvent, or in bankruptcy, or that has senior unsecured long-term debt in default; and

(ii) For a counterparty not otherwise described in paragraph (c)(1)(i) of this Appendix E, the credit equivalent amount of the broker's or dealer's exposure to the counterparty, as defined in paragraph (c)(4)(i) of this Appendix E, multiplied by the credit risk weight of the counterparty, as defined in paragraph (c)(4)(vi) of this Appendix E, multiplied by 8%;

(2) A concentration charge by counterparty in an amount equal to the sum of the following:

(i) For each counterparty with a credit risk weight of 20% or less, 5% of the amount of the current exposure to the counterparty in excess of 5% of the tentative net capital of the broker or dealer;

(ii) For each counterparty with a credit risk weight of greater than 20% but less than 50%, 20% of the amount of the current exposure to the counterparty in excess of 5% of the tentative net capital of the broker or dealer; and

(iii) For each counterparty with a credit risk weight of greater than 50%, 50% of the amount of the current exposure to the counterparty in excess of 5% of the tentative net capital of the broker or dealer; and

(3) A portfolio concentration charge of 100% of the amount of the broker's or dealer's aggregate current exposure for all counterparties in excess of 50% of the tentative net capital of the broker or dealer;

(4) Terms.

(i) The credit equivalent amount of the broker's or dealer's exposure to a counterparty is the sum of the broker's or dealer's maximum potential exposure to the counterparty, as defined in paragraph (c)(4)(ii) of this Appendix E, multiplied by the appropriate multiplication factor, and the broker's or dealer's current exposure to the counterparty, as defined in paragraph (c)(4)(iii) of this Appendix E. The broker or dealer must use the multiplication factor determined according to paragraph (d)(1)(v) of this Appendix E, except that the initial multiplication factor shall be one, unless the Commission determines, based on a review of the broker's or dealer's application or an amendment to the application approved under paragraph (a) of this Appendix E, including a review of its internal risk management control system and practices and VaR models, that another multiplication factor is appropriate;

(ii) The maximum potential exposure is the VaR of the counterparty's positions with the broker or dealer, after applying netting agreements with the counterparty meeting the requirements of paragraph (c)(4)(iv) of this Appendix E, taking into account the value of collateral from the counterparty held by the broker or dealer in accordance with paragraph (c)(4)(v) of this Appendix E, and taking into account the current replacement value of the counterparty's positions with the broker or dealer;

(iii) The current exposure of the broker or dealer to a counterparty is the current replacement value of the counterparty's positions with the broker or dealer, after applying netting agreements with the counterparty meeting the requirements of paragraph (c)(4)(iv) of this Appendix E and taking into account the value of collateral from the counterparty held by the broker or dealer in accordance with paragraph (c)(4)(v) of this Appendix E;

(iv) Netting agreements. A broker or dealer may include the effect of a netting agreement that allows the broker or dealer to net gross receivables from and gross payables to a counterparty upon default of the counterparty if:

(A) The netting agreement is legally enforceable in each relevant jurisdiction, including in insolvency proceedings;

(B) The gross receivables and gross payables that are subject to the netting agreement with a counterparty can be determined at any time; and

(C) For internal risk management purposes, the broker-dealer monitors and controls its exposure to the counterparty on a net basis;

(v) Collateral. When calculating maximum potential exposure and current exposure to a counterparty, the fair market value of collateral pledged and held may be taken into account provided:

(A) The collateral is marked to market each day and is subject to a daily margin maintenance requirement;

(B) The collateral is subject to the broker's or dealer's physical possession or control;

(C) The collateral is liquid and transferable;

(D) The collateral may be liquidated promptly by the firm without intervention by any other party;

(E) The collateral agreement is legally enforceable by the broker or dealer against the counterparty and any other parties to the agreement;

(F) The collateral does not consist of securities issued by the counterparty or a party related to the broker or dealer or to the counterparty;

(G) The Commission has approved the broker's or dealer's use of a VaR model to calculate deductions for market risk for the type of collateral in accordance with this Appendix E; and

(H) The collateral is not used in determining the credit rating of the counterparty;

(vi) Credit risk weights of counterparties. A broker or dealer that computes its deductions for credit risk pursuant to this Appendix E shall determine the credit risk weight of a counterparty as follows:

(A) 20% credit risk weight for transactions with counterparties with ratings for senior unsecured long-term debt or commercial paper in one of the two highest rating categories by an NRSRO or equivalent internal rating, if applicable;

(B) 50% credit risk weight for transactions with counterparties with ratings for senior unsecured long-term debt in the third and fourth highest rating categories by an NRSRO or equivalent internal rating, if applicable;

(C) 150% credit risk weight for transactions with counterparties with ratings for senior unsecured long-term debt below the fourth highest rating category by an NRSRO or equivalent internal rating, if applicable;

(D) As part of its initial application or in an amendment, the broker or dealer may request Commission approval to determine credit ratings using internal calculations for counterparties that are not rated by an NRSRO, and the broker or dealer may use these internal credit ratings in lieu of ratings issued by an NRSRO for purposes of determining credit risk weights. Based on the strength of the broker's or dealer's internal credit risk management system, the Commission may approve the application. The broker or dealer must make and keep current a record of the basis for the credit rating for each counterparty;

(E) As part of its initial application or in an amendment, the broker or dealer may request Commission approval to determine credit risk weights based on internal calculations, including internal estimates of the maturity adjustment. Based on the strength of the broker's or dealer's internal credit risk management system, the Commission may approve the application. The broker or dealer must make and keep current a record of the basis for the credit risk weight of each counterparty;

(F) For the portion of a current exposure covered by a written guarantee where that guarantee is an unconditional and irrevocable guarantee of the due and punctual payment and performance of the obligation and the broker or dealer can demand immediate payment from the guarantor after any payment is missed without having to make collection efforts, the broker or dealer may substitute the credit risk weight of the guarantor for the credit risk weight of the counterparty; and

(G) As part of its initial application or in an amendment, the broker or dealer may request Commission approval to reduce deductions for credit risk through the use of credit derivatives.

VaR Models

(d) To be approved, each VaR model must meet the following minimum qualitative and quantitative requirements:

(1) *Qualitative requirements.*

(i) The VaR model used to calculate market or credit risk for a position must be integrated into the daily internal risk management system of the broker or dealer;

(ii) The VaR model must be reviewed both periodically and annually. The periodic review may be conducted by the broker's or dealer's internal audit staff, but the annual review must be conducted by a registered public accounting firm, as that term is defined in section 2(a)(12) of the Sarbanes–Oxley Act of 2002 (15 U.S.C. 7201 et seq.); and

(iii) For purposes of computing market risk, the broker or dealer must determine the appropriate multiplication factor as follows:

(A) Beginning three months after the broker or dealer begins using the VaR model to calculate market risk, the broker or dealer must conduct backtesting of the model by comparing its actual daily net trading profit or loss with the corresponding VaR measure generated by the VaR model, using a 99 percent, one-tailed confidence level with price changes equivalent to a one business-day movement in rates and prices, for each of the past 250 business days, or other period as may be appropriate for the first year of its use;

(B) On the last business day of each quarter, the broker or dealer must identify the number of backtesting exceptions of the VaR model, that is, the number of business days in the past 250 business days, or other period as may be appropriate for the first year of its use, for which the actual net trading loss, if any, exceeds the corresponding VaR measure; and

(C) The broker or dealer must use the multiplication factor indicated in Table 1 of this Appendix E in determining its market risk until it obtains the next quarter's backtesting results;

Table 1.—Multiplication factor based on the number of backtesting exceptions of the VaR model	
Number of exceptions	Multiplication factor
4 or fewer	3.00
5	3.40
6	3.50
7	3.65
8	3.75
9	3.85
10 or more	4.00

(iv) For purposes of incorporating specific risk into a VaR model, a broker or dealer must demonstrate that it has methodologies in place to capture liquidity, event, and default risk adequately for each position. Furthermore, the models used to calculate deductions for specific risk must:

(A) Explain the historical price variation in the portfolio;

(B) Capture concentration (magnitude and changes in composition);

(C) Be robust to an adverse environment; and

(D) Be validated through backtesting; and

(v) For purposes of computing the credit equivalent amount of the broker's or dealer's exposures to a counterparty, the broker or dealer must determine the appropriate multiplication factor as follows:

(A) Beginning three months after it begins using the VaR model to calculate maximum potential exposure, the broker or dealer must conduct backtesting of the model by comparing, for at least 80 counterparties with widely varying types and sizes of positions with the firm, the ten-business day change in its current exposure to the counterparty based on its positions held at the beginning of the ten-business day period with the corresponding ten-business day maximum potential exposure for the counterparty generated by the VaR model;

(B) As of the last business day of each quarter, the broker or dealer must identify the number of backtesting exceptions of the VaR model, that is, the number of ten-business day periods in the past 250 business days, or other period as may be appropriate for the first year of its use, for which the change in current exposure to a counterparty exceeds the corresponding maximum potential exposure; and

(C) The broker or dealer will propose, as part of its application, a schedule of multiplication factors, which must be approved by the Commission based on the number of backtesting exceptions of the VaR model. The broker or dealer must use the multiplication factor indicated in the approved schedule in determining the credit equivalent amount of its exposures to a counterparty until it obtains the next quarter's backtesting results, unless the Commission determines, based on, among other relevant factors, a review of the broker's or dealer's internal risk management control system, including a review of the VaR model, that a different adjustment or other action is appropriate;

(2) *Quantitative requirements*.

(i) For purposes of determining market risk, the VaR model must use a 99 percent, one-tailed confidence level with price changes equivalent to a ten business-day movement in rates and prices;

(ii) For purposes of determining maximum potential exposure, the VaR model must use a 99 percent, one-tailed confidence level with price changes equivalent to a one-year movement in rates and prices; or based on a review of the broker's or dealer's procedures for managing collateral and if the collateral is marked to market daily and the broker or dealer has the ability to call for additional collateral daily, the Commission may approve a time horizon of not less than ten business days;

(iii) The VaR model must use an effective historical observation period of at least one year. The broker or dealer must consider the effects of market stress in its construction of the model. Historical data sets must be updated at least monthly and reassessed whenever market prices or volatilities change significantly; and

(iv) The VaR model must take into account and incorporate all significant, identifiable market risk factors applicable to positions in the accounts of the broker or dealer, including:

(A) Risks arising from the non-linear price characteristics of derivatives and the sensitivity of the market value of those positions to changes in the volatility of the derivatives' underlying rates and prices;

(B) Empirical correlations with and across risk factors or, alternatively, risk factors sufficient to cover all the market risk inherent in the positions in the proprietary or other trading accounts of the broker or dealer, including interest rate risk, equity price risk, foreign exchange risk, and commodity price risk;

(C) Spread risk, where applicable, and segments of the yield curve sufficient to capture differences in volatility and imperfect correlation of rates along the yield curve for securities and derivatives that are sensitive to different interest rates; and

(D) Specific risk for individual positions.

Additional Conditions

(e) As a condition for the broker or dealer to use this Appendix E to calculate certain of its capital charges, the Commission may impose additional conditions on the broker or dealer, which may include, but are not limited to restricting the broker's or dealer's business on a product-specific, category-specific, or general basis; submitting to the Commission a plan to increase the broker's or dealer's net capital or tentative net capital; filing more frequent reports with the Commission; modifying the broker's or dealer's internal risk management control procedures; or computing the broker's or dealer's deductions for market and credit risk in accordance with § 240.15c3-1(c)(2)(vi), (c)(2)(vii), and (c)(2)(iv), as appropriate. If it is not an ultimate holding company that has a principal regulator, the Commission also may require, as a condition of continuation of the exemption, the ultimate holding company of the broker or dealer to file more frequent reports or to modify its group-wide internal risk management control procedures. If the Commission finds it is necessary or appropriate in the public interest or for the protection of investors, the Commission may impose additional conditions on either the broker-dealer, or the ultimate holding company, if it is an ultimate holding company that does not have a principal regulator, if:

(1) The broker or dealer is required by § 240.15c3-1(a)(7)(ii) to provide notice to the Commission that the broker's or dealer's tentative net capital is less than $5 billion;

(2) The broker or dealer or the ultimate holding company of the broker or dealer fails to meet the reporting requirements set forth in § 240.17a-5 or 240.15c3-1g(b), as applicable;

(3) Any event specified in § 240.17a-11 occurs;

(4) There is a material deficiency in the internal risk management control system or in the mathematical models used to price securities or to calculate deductions for market and credit risk or allowances for market and credit risk, as applicable, of the broker or dealer or the ultimate holding company of the broker or dealer;

(5) The ultimate holding company of the broker or dealer fails to comply with its undertakings that the broker or dealer has filed with its application pursuant to paragraph (a)(1)(viii) or (a)(1)(ix) of this Appendix E;

(6) The broker or dealer fails to comply with this Appendix E; or

(7) The Commission finds that imposition of other conditions is necessary or appropriate in the public interest or for the protection of investors.

Rule 15c3–1f. Optional Market and Credit Risk Requirements for OTC Derivatives Dealers (Appendix F to Rule 15c3–1)

Application Requirements

(a) An OTC derivatives dealer may apply to the Commission for authorization to compute capital charges for market and credit risk pursuant to this Appendix F in lieu of computing securities haircuts pursuant to § 240.15c3–1(c)(2)(vi).

(1) An OTC derivatives dealer's application shall contain the following information:

(i) *Executive summary.* An OTC derivatives dealer shall include in its application an Executive Summary of information provided to the Commission.

(ii) *Description of methods for computing market risk charges.* An OTC derivatives dealer shall provide a description of all statistical models used for pricing OTC derivative instruments and for computing value-at-risk ("VAR"), a description of the applicant's controls over those models, and a statement regarding whether the firm has developed its own internal VAR models. If the OTC derivatives dealer's VAR model incorporates empirical correlations across risk categories, the dealer shall describe its process for measuring correlations and describe the qualitative and quantitative aspects of the model which at a minimum must adhere to the criteria set forth in paragraph (e) of this Appendix F. The application shall further state whether the OTC derivatives dealer intends to use an alternative method for computing its market risk charge for equity instruments and, if applicable, a description of how its own theoretical pricing model contains the minimum pricing factors set forth in Appendix A (§ 240.15c3–1a). The application shall also describe any category of securities having no ready market or any category of debt securities which are below investment grade for which the OTC derivatives dealer wishes to use its VAR model to calculate its market risk charge or for which it wishes to use an alternative method for computing this charge and a description of how those charges would be determined.

(iii) *Internal risk management control systems.* An OTC derivatives dealer shall provide a comprehensive description of its internal risk management control systems and how those systems adhere to the requirements set forth in § 240.15c3–4(a) through (d).

(2) The Commission may approve the application after reviewing the application to determine whether the OTC derivatives dealer:

(i) Has adopted internal risk management control systems that meet the requirements set forth in § 240.15c3–4; and

(ii) Has adopted a VAR model that meets the requirements set forth in paragraphs (e)(1) and (e)(2) of this Appendix F.

(3) If the OTC derivatives dealer materially amends its VAR model or internal risk management control systems as described in its application, including any material change in the categories of non-marketable securities that it wishes to include in its VAR model, the dealer shall file an application describing the changes which must be approved by the Commission before the changes may be implemented. After reviewing the application for changes to the dealer's VAR model or internal risk management control systems to determine whether, with the changes, the OTC derivatives dealer's VAR model and internal risk management control systems would meet the requirements set forth in this Appendix F and § 240.15c3–4, the Commission may approve the application.

(4) The applications provided for in this paragraph (a) shall be considered filed when received at the Commission's principal office

in Washington, DC. All applications filed pursuant to this paragraph (a) shall be deemed to be confidential.

Compliance With § 240.15c3-4

(b) An OTC derivatives dealer must be in compliance in all material respects with § 240.15c3-4 regarding its internal risk management control systems in order to be in compliance with § 240.15c3-1.

Market Risk

(c) An OTC derivatives dealer electing to apply this Appendix F shall compute a capital charge for market risk which shall be the aggregate of the charges computed below:

(1) *Value-at-Risk.* An OTC derivatives dealer shall deduct from net worth an amount for market risk for eligible OTC derivative instruments and other positions in its proprietary or other accounts equal to the VAR of these positions obtained from its proprietary VAR model, multiplied by the appropriate multiplication factor in paragraph (e)(1)(iv)(C) of this Appendix F. The OTC derivatives dealer may not elect to calculate its capital charges under this paragraph (c)(1) until its application to use the VAR model has been approved by the Commission.

(2) *Alternative method for equities.* An OTC derivatives dealer may elect to use this alternative method to calculate its market risk for equity instruments, including OTC options, upon approval by the Commission on application by the dealer. Under this alternative method, the deduction for market risk must be the amount computed pursuant to Appendix A to Rule 15c3-1 (§ 240.15c3-1a). In this computation, the OTC derivatives dealer may use its own theoretical pricing model provided that it contains the minimum pricing factors set forth in Appendix A.

(3) *Non-marketable securities.* An OTC derivatives dealer may not use a VAR model to determine a capital charge for any category of securities having no ready market or any category of debt securities which are below investment grade or any derivative instrument based on the value of these categories of securities, unless the Commission has granted, pursuant to paragraph (a)(1) of this Appendix F, its application to use its VAR model for any such category of securities. The dealer in any event may apply, pursuant to paragraph (a)(1) of this Appendix F, for an alternative treatment for any such category of securities, rather than calculate the market risk capital charge for such category of securities under § 240.15c3-1(c)(2)(vi) and (vii).

(4) *Residual positions.* To the extent that a position has not been included in the calculation of the market risk charge in paragraphs (c)(1) through (c)(3) of this section, the market risk charge for the position shall be computed under § 240.15c3-1(c)(2)(vi).

Credit Risk

(d) The capital charge for credit risk arising from an OTC derivatives dealer's transactions in eligible OTC derivative instruments shall be:

(1) The net replacement value in the account of a counterparty (including the effect of legally enforceable netting agreements and the application of liquid collateral) that is insolvent, or in bankruptcy, or that has senior unsecured long-term debt in default;

(2) As to a counterparty not otherwise described in paragraph (d)(1) of this section, the net replacement value in the account of the counterparty (including the effect of legally enforceable netting agreements and the application of liquid collateral) multiplied by 8%, and further multiplied by the counterparty factor. The counterparty factors are:

(i) 20% for counterparties with ratings for senior unsecured long-term debt or commercial paper in the two highest rating categories by a nationally recognized statistical rating organization ("NRSRO");

(ii) 50% for counterparties with ratings for senior unsecured long-term debt in the third and fourth highest ratings categories by an NRSRO; and

(iii) 100% for counterparties with ratings for senior unsecured long-term debt below the four highest rating categories; and

(3) A concentration charge where the net replacement value in the account of any one counterparty (other than a counterparty described in paragraph (d)(1) of this section) exceeds 25% of the OTC derivatives dealer's tentative net capital, calculated as follows:

(i) For counterparties with ratings for senior unsecured long-term debt or commercial paper in the two highest rating categories by an NRSRO, 5% of the amount of the net replacement value in excess of 25% of the OTC derivatives dealer's tentative net capital;

(ii) For counterparties with ratings for senior unsecured long-term debt in the third and fourth highest rating categories by an NRSRO, 20% of the amount of the net replacement value in excess of 25% of the OTC derivatives dealer's tentative net capital; and

(iii) For counterparties with ratings for senior unsecured long-term debt below the four highest rating categories, 50% of the amount of the net replacement value in excess of 25% of the OTC derivatives dealer's tentative net capital.

(4) Counterparties that are not rated by an NRSRO may be rated by the OTC derivatives dealer, or by an affiliated bank or affiliated broker-dealer of the OTC derivatives dealer, upon approval by the Commission on application by the OTC derivatives dealer. After reviewing the application to determine whether the credit rating procedures and rating categories are equivalent to those used by NRSROs and that such ratings are current, the Commission may approve the application. The OTC derivatives dealer must make and keep current a record of the basis for the credit rating for each counterparty. The record must be preserved for a period of not less than three years, the first two years in an easily accessible place.

VAR Models

(e) An OTC derivatives dealer's VAR model must meet the following qualitative and quantitative requirements:

(1) *Qualitative requirements.* An OTC derivatives dealerapplying this Appendix F must have a VAR model that meets the following minimum qualitative requirements:

(i) The OTC derivatives dealer's VAR model must be integrated into the firm's daily risk management process;

(ii) The OTC derivatives dealer must conduct appropriate stress tests of the VAR model, and develop appropriate procedures to follow in response to the results of such tests;

(iii) The OTC derivatives dealer must conduct periodic reviews (which may be performed by internal audit staff) of its VAR model. The OTC derivatives dealer's VAR model also must be subject to annual reviews conducted by independent public accountants; and

(iv) The OTC derivatives dealer must conduct backtesting of the VAR model pursuant to the following procedures:

(A) Beginning one year after the OTC derivatives dealer begins using its VAR model to calculate its net capital, the OTC derivatives dealer must conduct backtesting by comparing each of its most recent 250 business days' actual net trading profit or loss with the corresponding daily VAR measures generated for determining market risk capital charges and calibrated to a one-day holding period and a 99 percent, one-tailed confidence level;

(B) Once each quarter, the OTC derivatives dealer must identify the number of exceptions, that is, the number of business days for which the actual daily net trading loss, if any, exceeded the corresponding daily VAR measure; and

(C) An OTC derivatives dealer must use the multiplication factor indicated in Table 1 of this Appendix F in determining its capital charge for market risk until it obtains the next quarter's backtesting results, unless the Commission determines that a different adjustment or other action is appropriate.

Table 5.—Multiplication Factor Based on Results of Backtesting

Number of exceptions	Multiplication factor
4 or fewer	3.00
5	3.40
6	3.50
7	3.65
8	3.75
9	3.85
10 or more	4.00

(2) *Quantitative requirements.* An OTC derivatives dealer applying this Appendix F must have a VAR model that meets the following minimum quantitative requirements:

(i) The VAR measures must be calculated on a daily basis using a 99 percent, one-tailed confidence level with a price change equivalent to a ten-business day movement in rates and prices;

(ii) The effective historical observation period for VAR measures must be at least one year, and the weighted average time lag of the individual observations cannot be less than six months. Historical data sets must be updated at least every three months and reassessed whenever market prices or volatilities are subject to large changes;

(iii) The VAR measures must include the risks arising from the non-linear price characteristics of options positions and the sensitivity of the market value of the positions to changes in the volatility of the underlying rates or prices. An OTC derivatives dealer must measure the volatility of options positions by different maturities;

(iv) The VAR measures may incorporate empirical correlations within and across risk categories, provided that the OTC derivatives dealer has described its process for measuring correlations in its application to apply this Appendix F and the Commission has approved its application. In the event that the VAR measures do not incorporate empirical correlations across risk categories, the OTC derivatives dealer must add the separate VAR measures for the four major risk categories in paragraph (e)(2)(v) of this Appendix F to determine its aggregate VAR measure; and

(v) The OTC derivatives dealer's VAR model must use risk factors sufficient to measure the market risk inherent in all covered positions. The risk factors must address, at a minimum, the following major risk categories: interest rate risk, equity price risk, foreign exchange rate risk, and commodity price risk. For material exposures in the major currencies and markets, modeling techniques must capture, at a minimum, spread risk and must incorporate enough segments of the yield curve to capture differences in volatility and less-than-perfect correlation of rates along the yield curve. An OTC derivatives dealer must provide the Commission with evidence that the OTC derivatives dealer's VAR model takes account of specific risk in positions, including specific equity risk, if the OTC derivatives dealer intends to utilize its VAR model to compute capital charges for equity price risk.

Rule 15c3–1g Conditions for Ultimate Holding Companies of Certain Brokers or Dealers (Appendix G to 17 CFR 240.15c3–1).

As a condition for a broker or dealer to compute certain of its deductions to capital in accordance with § 240.15c3–1e, pursuant to its undertaking, the ultimate holding company of the broker or dealer shall:

Conditions Regarding Computation of Allowable Capital and Risk Allowances

(a) If it is not an ultimate holding company that has a principal regulator, as that term is defined in § 240.15c3–1(c)(13), calculate allowable capital and allowances for market, credit, and operational risk on a consolidated basis as follows:

(1) *Allowable capital.* The ultimate holding company must compute allowable capital as the sum of:

(i) Common shareholders' equity on the consolidated balance sheet of the holding company less:

(A) Goodwill;

(B) Deferred tax assets, except those permitted for inclusion in Tier 1 capital by the Board of Governors of the Federal Reserve System ("Federal Reserve") (12 CFR 225, Appendix A);

(C) Other intangible assets; and

(D) Other deductions from common stockholders' equity as required by the Federal Reserve in calculating Tier 1 capital (as defined in 12 CFR 225, Appendix A);

(ii) Cumulative and non-cumulative preferred stock, except that the amount of cumulative preferred stock may not exceed 33% of the items included in allowable capital pursuant to paragraph (a)(1)(i) of this Appendix G, excluding cumulative preferred stock, provided that:

(A) The stock does not have a maturity date;

(B) The stock cannot be redeemed at the option of the holder of the instrument;

(C) The stock has no other provisions that will require future redemption of the issue; and

(D) The issuer of the stock can defer or eliminate dividends;

(iii) The sum of the following items on the consolidated balance sheet, to the extent that the sum does not exceed the sum of the items included in allowable capital pursuant to paragraphs (a)(1)(i) and (ii) of this Appendix G:

(A) Cumulative preferred stock in excess of the 33% limit specified in paragraph (a)(1)(ii) of this Appendix G and subject to the conditions of paragraphs (a)(1)(ii)(A) through (D) of this Appendix G;

(B) Subordinated debt if the original weighted average maturity of the subordinated debt is at least five years; each subordinated debt instrument states clearly on its face that repayment of the debt is not protected by any Federal agency or the Securities Investor Protection Corporation; the subordinated debt is unsecured and subordinated in right of payment to all senior indebtedness of the ultimate holding company; and the subordinated debt instrument permits acceleration only in the event of bankruptcy or reorganization of the ultimate holding company under Chapters 7 (liquidation) and 11 (reorganization) of the U.S. Bankruptcy Code; and

(C) As part of the broker's or dealer's application to calculate deductions for market and credit risk under § 240.15c3–1e, an ultimate holding company may request to include, for a period of three years after adoption of this Appendix G, long-term debt that has an original weighted average maturity of at least five years and that cannot be accelerated, except upon the occurrence of certain events as the Commission may approve. As part of a subsequent amendment to the broker's or dealer's application, the broker or dealer may request permission for the ultimate holding company to include long-term debt that meets these criteria in allowable capital for up to an additional two years; and

(iv) Hybrid capital instruments that are permitted for inclusion in Tier 2 capital by the Federal Reserve (as defined in 12 CFR 225, Appendix A);

(2) *Allowance for market risk.* The ultimate holding company shall compute an allowance for market risk for all proprietary positions, including debt instruments, equity instruments, commodity instruments, foreign exchange contracts, and derivative contracts, as the aggregate of the following:

(i) *Value at risk.* The VaR of its positions, multiplied by the appropriate multiplication factor as set forth in § 240.15c3–1e(d). The VaR of the positions must be obtained using approved VaR models meeting the applicable qualitative and quantitative requirements of § 240.15c3–1e(d); and

(ii) *Alternative method.* For positions for which there does not exist adequate historical data to support a VaR model, the ultimate holding company must propose a model that produces a suitable allowance for market risk for those positions;

(3) *Allowance for credit risk.* The ultimate holding company shall compute an allowance for credit risk for certain assets on the consolidated balance sheet and certain off-balance sheet items, including loans and loan commitments, exposures due to derivatives contracts, structured financial products, and other extensions of credit, and credit substitutes as follows:

(i) By multiplying the credit equivalent amount of the ultimate holding company's exposure to the counterparty, as defined in paragraphs (a)(3)(i)(A), (B) and (C) of this Appendix G, by the appropriate credit risk weight, as defined in paragraph (a)(3)(i)(F) of this Appendix G, of the asset, off-balance sheet item, or counterparty, then multiplying that product by 8%, in accordance with the following:

(A) For certain loans and loan commitments, the credit equivalent amount is determined by multiplying the nominal amount of the contract by the following credit conversion factors:

(1) 0% credit conversion factor for loan commitments that:

(i) May be unconditionally cancelled by the lender; or

(ii) May be cancelled by the lender due to credit deterioration of the borrower;

(2) 20% credit conversion factor for:

(i) Loan commitments of less than one year; or

(ii) Short-term self-liquidating trade related contingencies, including letters of credit;

(3) 50% credit conversion factor for loan commitments with an original maturity of greater than one year that contain transaction contingencies, including performance bonds, revolving underwriting facilities, note issuance facilities and bid bonds; and

(4) 100% credit conversion factor for bankers' acceptances, stand-by letters of credit, and forward purchases of assets, and similar direct credit substitutes;

(B) For derivatives contracts and for repurchase agreements, reverse repurchase agreements, stock lending and borrowing, and similar collateralized transactions, the credit equivalent amount is the sum of the ultimate holding company's maximum potential exposure to the counterparty, as defined in paragraph (a)(3)(i)(E) of this Appendix G, multiplied by the appropriate multiplication factor, and the ultimate holding company's current exposure to the counterparty, as defined in paragraph (a)(3)(i)(D) of this Appendix G. The ultimate holding company must use the multiplication factor determined according to § 240.15c3–1e(d)(1)(v), except that the initial multiplication factor shall be one, unless the Commission determines, based on a review of the group-wide internal risk management control system and practices, including a review of the VaR models, that another multiplication factor is appropriate;

(C) The credit equivalent amount for other assets shall be the asset's book value on the ultimate holding company's consolidated balance sheet or other amount as determined according to the standards published by the Basel Committee on Banking Supervision, as amended from time to time;

(D) The current exposure is the current replacement value of a counterparty's positions, after applying netting agreements with that counterparty meeting the requirements of § 240.15c3–1e(c)(4)(iv) and taking into account the value of collateral from the counterparty in accordance with § 240.15c3–1e(c)(4)(v);

(E) The maximum potential exposure is the VaR of the counterparty's positions with the member of the affiliate group, after applying netting agreements with the counterparty meeting the requirements of paragraph (c)(4)(iv) of § 240.15c3–1e, taking into account the value of collateral from the counterparty held by the member of the affiliate in accordance with paragraph (c)(4)(v) of § 240.15c3–1e, and taking into account the current replacement value of the counterparty's positions with the member of the affiliate group, except that for repurchase agreements, reverse repurchase agreements, stock lending and borrowing, and similar collateralized transactions, maximum potential exposure must be calculated using a time horizon of not less than five days;

(F) Credit ratings and credit risk weights shall be determined according to the provisions of paragraphs (c)(4)(vi)(D) and (c)(4)(vi)(E) of § 240.15c3–1e, respectively;

(G) As part of the broker's or dealer's initial application or in an amendment, the ultimate holding company may request Commission approval to reduce allowances for credit risk through the use of credit derivatives;

(H) For the portion of a current exposure covered by a written guarantee, where that guarantee is an unconditional and irrevocable guarantee of the due and punctual payment and performance of the obligation and the ultimate holding company or member of the affiliate group can demand payment after any payment is missed without having to make collection efforts, the ultimate holding company or member of the affiliate group may substitute the credit risk weight of the guarantor for the credit risk weight of the counterparty; or

(ii) As part of the broker's or dealer's initial application or in an amendment to the application, the ultimate holding company may request Commission approval to use a method of calculating credit risk that is consistent with standards published by the Basel Committee on Banking Supervision in International Convergence of Capital Measurement and Capital Standards (July 1988), as amended from time to time; and

(4) Allowance for operational risk. The ultimate holding company shall compute an allowance for operational risk in accordance with the standards published by the Basel Committee on Banking Supervision, as amended from time to time.

Conditions Regarding Reporting Requirements

(b) File reports with the Commission in accordance with the following:

(1) If it is not an ultimate holding company that has a principal regulator, as that term is defined in § 240.15c3–1(c)(13), the ultimate holding company shall file with the Commission:

(i) A report as of the end of each month, filed not later than 30 calendar days after the end of the month. A monthly report need not be filed for a month-end that coincides with a fiscal quarter-end. The monthly report shall include:

(A) A consolidated balance sheet and income statement (including notes to the financial statements) for the ultimate holding company and statements of allowable capital and allowances for market, credit, and operational risk computed pursuant to paragraph (a) of this Appendix G, except that the consolidated balance sheet and income statement for the first month of the fiscal year may be filed at a later time to which the Commission agrees (when reviewing the affiliated broker's or dealer's application under § 240.15c3–1e(a)).

(B) A graph reflecting, for each business line, the daily intra-month VaR;

(C) Consolidated credit risk information, including aggregate current exposure and current exposures (including commitments) listed by counterparty for the 15 largest exposures;

(D) The 10 largest commitments listed by counterparty;

(E) Maximum potential exposure listed by counterparty for the 15 largest exposures;

(F) The aggregate maximum potential exposure;

(G) A summary report reflecting the geographic distribution of the ultimate holding company's exposures on a consolidated basis for each of the top ten countries to which it is exposed (by residence of the main operating group of the counterparty); and

(H) Certain regular risk reports provided to the persons responsible for managing group-wide risk as the Commission may request from time to time;

(ii) A quarterly report as of the end of each fiscal quarter, filed not later than 35 calendar days after the end of the quarter. The quarterly report shall include, in addition to the information contained in the monthly report as required by paragraph (b)(1)(i) of this Appendix G, the following:

(A) Consolidating balance sheets and income statements for the ultimate holding company. The consolidating balance sheet must provide information regarding each material affiliate of the ultimate holding company in a separate column, but may aggregate information regarding members of the affiliate group that are not material affiliates into one column;

(B) The results of backtesting of all internal models used to compute allowable capital and allowances for market and credit risk indicating, for each model, the number of backtesting exceptions;

(C) A description of all material pending legal or arbitration proceedings, involving either the ultimate holding company or any of its affiliates, that are required to be disclosed by the ultimate holding company under generally accepted accounting principles;

(D) The aggregate amount of unsecured borrowings and lines of credit, segregated into categories, scheduled to mature within twelve months from the most recent fiscal quarter as to each material affiliate; and

(E) For a quarter-end that coincides with the ultimate holding company's fiscal year-end, the ultimate holding company need not include consolidated and consolidating balance sheets and income statements in its quarterly reports. The consolidating balance sheet and income statement for the quarter-end that coincides with the fiscal year-end may be filed at a later time to which the Commission agrees (when reviewing the affiliated broker's or dealer's application under § 240.15c3–1e(a));

(iii) An annual audited report as of the end of the ultimate holding company's fiscal year, filed not later than 65 calendar days after the end of the fiscal year. The annual report shall include:

(A) Consolidated financial statements for the ultimate holding company audited by a registered public accounting firm, as that term is defined in section 2(a)(12) of the Sarbanes–Oxley Act of 2002 (15 U.S.C. 7201 et seq.). The audit shall be made in accordance with the rules promulgated by the Public Company Accounting Oversight Board. The audited financial statements must include a supporting schedule containing statements of allowable capital and allowances for market, credit, and operational risk computed pursuant to paragraph (a) of this Appendix G; and

(B) A supplemental report entitled "Accountant's Report on Internal Risk Management Control System" prepared by a registered public accounting firm, as that term is defined in section 2(a)(12) of the Sarbanes–Oxley Act of 2002 (15 U.S.C. 7201 et seq.), indicating the results of the registered public accounting firm's review of the ultimate holding company's compliance with § 240.15c3–4. The procedures are to be performed and the report is to be prepared in accordance with procedures agreed upon by the ultimate holding company and the registered public accounting firm conducting the review. The agreed-upon procedures are to be performed and the report is to be prepared in accordance with rules promulgated by the Public Company Accounting Oversight Board. The ultimate holding company must file, before commencement of the initial review, the procedures agreed upon by the ultimate holding company and the registered public accounting firm with the Division of Market Regulation, Office of Financial Responsibility, at Commission's principal office in Washington, DC. Before commencement of each subsequent review, the ultimate holding company must notify the Commission of any changes in the procedures;

(iv) An organizational chart, as of the ultimate holding company's fiscal year-end, concurrently with its quarterly report for the quarter-end that coincides with its fiscal year-end. The ultimate holding company must provide quarterly updates of the organizational chart if a material change in the information provided to the Commission has occurred;

(2) If the ultimate holding company is an entity that has a principal regulator, as that term is defined in § 240.15c3–1(c)(13), the ultimate holding company must file with the Commission:

(i) A quarterly report as of the end of each fiscal quarter, filed not later than 35 calendar days after the end of the quarter, or a later time to which the Commission may agree upon application. The quarterly report shall include:

(A) Consolidated (including notes to the financial statements) and consolidating balance sheets and income statements for the ultimate holding company;

(B) Its most recent capital measurements computed in accordance with the standards published by the Basel Committee on Banking Supervision, as amended from time to time, as reported to its principal regulator;

(C) Certain regular risk reports provided to the persons responsible for managing group-wide risk as the Commission may request from time to time; and

(D) For a quarter-end that coincides with the ultimate holding company's fiscal year-end, the ultimate holding company need not include consolidated and consolidating balance sheets and income statements in its quarterly reports. The consolidating balance sheet and income statement for the quarter-end that coincides with the fiscal year-end may be filed at a later time to which the Commission agrees (when reviewing the affiliated broker's or dealer's application under § 240.15c3–1e(a)).

(ii) An annual audited report as of the end of the ultimate holding company's fiscal year, filed with the Commission when required to be filed by any regulator;

(3) The reports that the ultimate holding company must file in accordance with paragraph (b) of this Appendix G will be considered filed when two copies are received at the Commission's principal office in Washington, DC. A person who files reports pursuant to this section for which he or she seeks confidential treatment may clearly mark each page or segregable portion of each page with the words "Confidential Treatment Requested." The copies shall be addressed to the Division of Market Regulation, Risk Assessment Group; and

(4) The reports that the ultimate holding company must file with the Commission in accordance with paragraph (b) of this Ap-

pendix G will be accorded confidential treatment to the extent permitted by law.

Conditions Regarding Records To Be Made

(c) If it is not an ultimate holding company that has a principal regulator, make and keep current the following records:

(1) A record of the results of funding and liquidity stress tests that the ultimate holding company has conducted in response to the following events at least once each quarter and a record of the contingency plan to respond to each of these events:

(i) A credit rating downgrade of the ultimate holding company;

(ii) An inability of the ultimate holding company to access capital markets for unsecured short-term funding;

(iii) An inability of the ultimate holding company to access liquid assets in regulated entities across international borders when the events described in paragraphs (c)(1)(i) or (ii) of this Appendix G occur; and

(iv) An inability of the ultimate holding company to access credit or assets held at a particular institution when the events described in paragraphs (c)(1)(i) or (ii) of this Appendix G occur;

(2) A record of the basis for the determination of credit risk weights for each counterparty;

(3) A record of the basis for the determination of internal credit ratings for each counterparty; and

(4) A record of the calculations of allowable capital and allowances for market, credit and operational risk computed currently at least once per month on a consolidated basis.

Conditions Regarding Preservation of Records

(d)(1) Must preserve the following information, documents, and reports for a period of not less than three years in an easily accessible place using any media acceptable under § 240.17a–4(f):

(i) The documents created in accordance with paragraph (c) of this Appendix G;

(ii) Any application or documents filed with the Commission pursuant to § 240.15c3–1e and this Appendix G and any written responses received from the Commission;

(iii) All reports and notices filed with the Commission pursuant to § 240.15c3–1e and this Appendix G; and

(iv) If the ultimate holding company does not have a principal regulator, all written policies and procedures concerning the group-wide internal risk management control system established pursuant to § 240.15c3–1e(a)(1)(viii)(C); and

(2) The ultimate holding company may maintain the records referred to in paragraph (d)(1) of this Appendix G either at the ultimate holding company, at an affiliate, or at a records storage facility, provided that the records are located within the United States. If the records are maintained by an entity other than the ultimate holding company, the ultimate holding company shall obtain and file with the Commission a written undertaking by the entity maintaining the records, in a form acceptable to the Commission, signed by a duly authorized person at the entity maintaining the records, to the effect that the records will be treated as if the ultimate holding company were maintaining the records pursuant to this section and that the entity maintaining the records will permit examination of such records at any time or from time to time during business hours by representatives or designees of the Commission and will promptly furnish the Commission or its designee a true, legible, complete, and current paper copy of any or all or any part of such records. The election to operate pursuant to the provisions of this paragraph shall not relieve the ultimate holding company that is

required to maintain and preserve such records from any of its reporting or recordkeeping responsibilities under this section.

Conditions Regarding Notification

(e) The ultimate holding company of a broker or dealer that computes certain of its capital charges in accordance with § 240.15c3–1e shall:

(1) Send notice promptly (but within 24 hours) after the occurrence of the following events:

(i) The early warning indications of low capital as the Commission may agree;

(ii) The ultimate holding company files a Form 8–K (17 CFR 249.308) with the Commission; and

(iii) A material affiliate declares bankruptcy or otherwise becomes insolvent; and

(2) If it is not an ultimate holding company that has a principal regulator, as defined in § 240.15c3–1(c)(13), send notice promptly (but within 24 hours) after the occurrence of the following events:

(i) The ultimate holding company becomes aware that an NRSRO has determined to reduce materially its assessment of the creditworthiness of a material affiliate or the credit rating(s) assigned to one or more outstanding short or long-term obligations of a material affiliate;

(ii) The ultimate holding company becomes aware that any financial regulatory agency or self-regulatory organization has taken significant enforcement or regulatory action against a material affiliate; and

(iii) The occurrence of any backtesting exception under § 240.15c3–1e(d)(1)(iii) or (iv) that would require that the ultimate holding company use a higher multiplication factor in the calculation of its allowances for market or credit risk;

(3) Every notice given or transmitted by paragraph (e) of this Appendix G will be given or transmitted to the Division of Market Regulation, Office of Financial Responsibility, at the principal office of the Commission in Washington, DC. A person who files notification pursuant to this section for which he or she seeks confidential treatment may clearly mark each page or segregable portion of each page with the words "Confidential Treatment Request." For the purposes of this Appendix G, "notice" shall be given or transmitted by telegraphic notice or facsimile transmission. The notice described by paragraph (e)(2) of this Appendix G may be transmitted by overnight delivery. Notices filed pursuant to this paragraph will be accorded confidential treatment to the extent permitted by law; and

(4) Upon the written request of the ultimate holding company, or upon its own motion, the Commission may grant an extension of time or an exemption from any of the requirements of this paragraph (e) either unconditionally or on specified terms and conditions as are necessary or appropriate in the public interest or for the protection of investors.

Rule 15c3-2. Customers' Free Credit Balances

No broker or dealer shall use any funds arising out of any free credit balance carried for the account of any customer in connection with the operation of the business of such broker or dealer unless such broker or dealer has established adequate procedures pursuant to which each customer for whom a free credit balance is carried will be given or sent, together with or as a part of the customer's statement of account, whenever sent but not less frequently than once every 3 months, a written statement informing such customer of the amount due to the customer by such broker or dealer on the date of such statement, and containing a written notice that (i) such funds are not segregated and may be used in the operation of the business of such broker or dealer, and (ii) such funds are payable on the demand of the customer: *Provided, however,*

That this rule shall not apply to a broker or dealer which is also a banking institution supervised and examined by state or Federal authority having supervision over banks. For the purpose of this rule the term "customer" shall mean every person other than a broker or dealer.

Rule 15c3-3. Customer Protection—Reserves and Custody of Securities

(a) *Definitions.* For the purpose of this section:

(1) The term *customer* shall mean any person from whom or on whose behalf a broker or dealer has received or acquired or holds funds or securities for the account of that person. The term shall not include a broker or dealer, a municipal securities dealer, or a government securities broker or government securities dealer. The term shall, however, include another broker or dealer to the extent that broker or dealer maintains an omnibus account for the account of customers with the broker or dealer in compliance with Regulation T (12 CFR 220.1 through 220.19). The term shall not include a general partner or director or principal officer of the broker or dealer or any other person to the extent that person has a claim for property or funds which by contract, agreement or understanding, or by operation of law, is part of the capital of the broker or dealer or is subordinated to the claims of creditors of the broker or dealer. In addition, the term shall not include a person to the extent that the person has a claim for security futures products held in a futures account, or any security futures product and any futures product held in a "proprietary account" as defined by the Commodity Futures Trading Commission in § 1.3(y) of this chapter. The term also shall not include a counterparty who has delivered collateral to an OTC derivatives dealer pursuant to a transaction in an eligible OTC derivative instrument, or pursuant to the OTC derivatives dealer's cash management securities activities or ancillary portfolio management securities activities, and who has received a prominent written notice from the OTC derivatives dealer that:

(i) Except as otherwise agreed in writing by the OTC derivatives dealer and the counterparty, the dealer may repledge or otherwise use the collateral in its business;

(ii) In the event of the OTC derivatives dealer's failure, the counterparty will likely be considered an unsecured creditor of the dealer as to that collateral;

(iii) The Securities Investor Protection Act of 1970 (15 U.S.C. 78aaa *et seq.*) does not protect the counterparty; and

(iv) The collateral will not be subject to the requirements of § 240.8c-1, § 240.15c2-1, § 240.15c3-2, or § 240.15c3-3.

(2) The term "securities carried for the account of a customer" (hereinafter also "customer securities") shall mean:

(i) Securities received by or on behalf of a broker or dealer for the account of any customer and securities carried long by a broker or dealer for the account of any customer; and

(ii) Securities sold to, or bought for, a customer by a broker or dealer.

(3) The term "fully paid securities" shall include all securities carried for the account of a customer in a special cash account as defined in Regulation T promulgated by the Board of Governors of the Federal Reserve System, as well as margin equity securities within the meaning of Regulation T which are carried for the account of a customer in a general account or any special account under Regulation T during any period when section 8 of Regulation T specifies that margin equity securities shall have no loan value in a general account or special convertible debt security account, and all such margin equity securities in such account if they are fully paid: *Provided, however,* That the term "fully paid securities" shall not apply to any

securities which are purchased in transactions for which the customer has not made full payment.

(4) The term "margin securities" shall mean those securities carried for the account of a customer in a general account as defined in Regulation T, as well as securities carried in any special account (such general or special accounts hereinafter referred to as "margin accounts") other than the securities referred to in subparagraph (3) of this paragraph.

(5) The term "excess margin securities" shall mean those securities referred to in subparagraph (4) of this paragraph carried for the account of a customer having a market value in excess of 140 percent of the total of the debit balances in the customer's account or accounts encompassed by subparagraph (a)(4) of this paragraph which the broker or dealer identifies as not constituting margin securities.

(6) The term "qualified security" shall mean a security issued by the United States or a security in respect of which the principal and interest are guaranteed by the United States.

(7) The term "bank" shall mean a bank as defined in section 3(a)(6) of the Act and shall also mean any building and loan, savings and loan or similar banking institution subject to supervision by a Federal banking authority. With respect to a broker or dealer who maintains his principal place of business in the Dominion of Canada, the term "bank" shall also mean a Canadian bank subject to supervision by an authority of the Dominion of Canada.

(8) The term "free credit balances" shall mean liabilities of a broker or dealer to customers which are subject to immediate cash payment to customers on demand, whether resulting from sales of securities, dividends, interest, deposits or otherwise, excluding, however, funds in commodity accounts which are segregated in accordance with the Commodity Exchange Act or in a similar manner.

(9) The term "other credit balances" shall mean cash liabilities of a broker or dealer to customers other than free credit balances and funds in commodities accounts segregated as aforesaid.

(10) The term "funds carried for the account of any customer" (hereinafter also "customer funds") shall mean all free credit and other credit balances carried for the account of the customer.

(11) The term "principal officer" shall mean the president, executive vice president, treasurer, secretary or any other person performing a similar function with the broker or dealer.

(12) The term "household members and other persons related to principals" includes husbands or wives, children, sons-in-law or daughters-in-law and any household relative to whose support a principal contributes directly or indirectly. For purposes of this paragraph (a)(12), a principal shall be deemed to be a director, general partner, or principal officer of the broker or dealer.

(13) The term "affiliated person" includes any person who directly or indirectly controls a broker or dealer or any person who is directly or indirectly controlled by or under common control with the broker or dealer. Ownership of 10% or more of the common stock of the relevant entity will be deemed prima facie control of that entity for purposes of this paragraph.

(14) The term *securities account* shall mean an account that is maintained in accordance with the requirements of section 15(c)(3) of the Act (15 U.S.C. 78*o*(c)(3)) and § 240.15c3-3.

(15) The term *futures account* (also referred to as "commodity account") shall mean an account that is maintained in accordance with the segregation requirements of section 4d of the Commodity Exchange Act (7 U.S.C. 6d) and the rules thereunder.

(b) *Physical Possession or Control of Securities.* (1) A broker or dealer shall promptly obtain and shall thereafter maintain the physical possession or control of all fully paid securities and excess margin securities carried by a broker or dealer for the account of customers.

(2) A broker or dealer shall not be deemed to be in violation of the provisions of subparagraph (1) of this paragraph regarding physical possession or control of customers' securities if, solely as the result of normal business operations, temporary lags occur between the time when a security is required to be in the possession or control of the broker or dealer and the time that it is placed in his physical possession or under his control, provided that the broker or dealer takes timely steps in good faith to establish prompt physical possession or control. The burden of proof shall be on the broker or dealer to establish that the failure to obtain physical possession or control of securities carried for the account of customers as required by subparagraph (1) of this paragraph is merely temporary and solely the result of normal business operations including same day receipt and redelivery (turnaround), and to establish that he has taken timely steps in good faith to place them in his physical possession or control.

(3) A broker or dealer shall not be deemed to be in violation of the provisions of paragraph (b)(1) of this rule regarding physical possession or control of fully-paid or excess margin securities borrowed from any person, *Provided,* That the broker or dealer and the lender, at or before the time of the loan, enter into a written agreement that, at a minimum;

(i) Sets forth in a separate schedule or schedules the basis of compensation for any loan and generally the rights and liabilities of the parties as to the borrowed securities;

(ii) Provides that the lender will be given a schedule of the securities actually borrowed at the time of the borrowing of the securities;

(iii) Specifies that the broker or dealer:

(A) Must provide to the lender, upon the execution of the agreement or by the close of the business day of the loan if the loan occurs subsequent to the execution of the agreement, collateral, which fully secures the loan of securities, consisting exclusively of cash or United States Treasury bills and Treasury notes or an irrevocable letter of credit issued by a bank as defined in section 3(a)(6)(A)–(C) (15 U.S.C. 78c(a)(6)(A)–(C)) of the Act or such other collateral as the Commission designates as permissible by order as necessary or appropriate in the public interest and consistent with the protection of investors after giving consideration to the collateral's liquidity, volatility, market depth and location, and the issuer's creditworthiness; and

(B) Must mark the loan to the market not less than daily and, in the event that the market value of all the outstanding securities loaned at the close of trading at the end of the business day exceeds 100 percent of the collateral then held by the lender, the borrowing broker or dealer must provide additional collateral of the type described in paragraph (b)(3)(iii)(A) of this section to the lender by the close of the next business day as necessary to equal, together with the collateral then held by the lender, not less than 100 percent of the market value of the securities loaned; and

(iv) Contains a prominent notice that the provisions of the Securities Investor Protection Act of 1970 may not protect the lender with respect to the securities loan transaction and that, therefore, the collateral delivered to the lender may constitute the only source of satisfaction of the broker's or dealer's obligation in the event the broker or dealer fails to return the securities.

(4)(i) Notwithstanding paragraph (K)(2)(i) of this rule, a broker or dealer that retains custody of securities that are the subject of a repurchase agreement between the broker or dealer and a counterparty shall:

(A) Obtain the repurchase agreement in writing;

(B) Confirm in writing the specific securities that are the subject of a repurchase transaction pursuant to such agreement at the end of the trading day on which the transaction is initiated and at the end of any other day during which other securities are substituted if the substitution results in a change to issuer, maturity date par amount or coupon rate as specified in the previous confirmation;

(C) Advise the counterparty in the repurchase agreement that the Securities Investor Protection Corporation has taken the position that the provisions of the Securities Investor Protection Act of 1970 do not protect the counterparty with respect to the repurchase agreement;

(D) Maintain possession or control of securities that are the subject of the agreement.

(ii) For purposes of this paragraph (b)(4), securities are in the broker's or dealer's control only if they are in the control of the broker or dealer within the meaning of Rule 15c3–3(c)(1), (c)(3), (c)(5) or (c)(6) of this title.

(iii) A broker or dealer shall not be in violation of the requirement to maintain possession or control pursuant to paragraph (b)(4)(i)(D) during the trading day if:

(A) in the written repurchase agreement, the counterparty grants the broker or dealer the right to substitute other securities for those subject to the agreement; and

(B) the provision in the written repurchase agreement governing the right, if any, to substitute is immediately preceded by the following disclosure statement, which must be prominently displayed:

"REQUIRED DISCLOSURE"

"The [seller] is not permitted to substitute other securities for those subject to this agreement and therefore must keep the [buyer's] securities segregated at all times, unless in this agreement the [buyer grants the [seller]] the right to substitute other securities. If the buyer grants the right to substitute, this means that the [buyer's] securities will likely be commingled with the [seller's] own securities during the trading day. The [buyer] is advised that, during any trading day that the [buyer's] securities are commingled with the [seller's] securities, they will be subject to liens granted by the [seller] to its clearing bank and may be used by the [seller] for deliveries on other securities transactions. Whenever the securities are commingled, the [seller's] ability to resegregate substitute securities for the [buyer] will be subject to the [seller's] ability to satisfy the clearing lien or to obtain substitute securities."

(iv) A confirmation issued in accordance with paragraph (b)(4)(i)(B) of this rule shall specify the issuer, maturity date, coupon rate, par amount and market value of the security and shall further identify a CUSIP or mortgage-backed security pool number, as appropriate, except that a CUSIP or a pool number is not required on the confirmation if it is identified in internal records of the broker or dealer that designate the specific security of the counterparty. For purposes of this paragraph (b)(4)(iv), the market value of any security that is the subject of the repurchase transaction shall be the most recently available bid price plus accrued interest, obtained by any reasonable and consistent methodology.

(v) This paragraph (b)(4) shall not apply to a repurchase agreement between the broker or dealer and another broker or dealer (including a government securities broker or dealer), a registered municipal securities dealer, or a general partner or director or principal officer of the broker or dealer or any person to the extent that his claim is explicitly subordinated to the claims of creditors of the broker or dealer.

(c) *Control of Securities.* Securities under the control of a broker or dealer shall be deemed to be securities which:

(1) Are represented by one or more certificates in the custody or control of a clearing corporation or other subsidiary organization of either national securities exchanges or of a registered national securities association, or of a custodian bank in accordance with a system for the central handling of securities complying with the provisions of Rule 8c-1(g) and Rule 15c2-1(g), the delivery of which certificates to the broker or dealer does not require the payment of money or value, and if the books or records of the broker or dealer identify the customers entitled to receive specified numbers or units of the securities so held for such customers collectively; or

(2) Are carried for the account of any customer by a broker or dealer and are carried in a special omnibus account in the name of such broker or dealer with another broker or dealer in compliance with the requirements of section 4(b) of Regulation T under the Act, such securities being deemed to be under the control of such broker or dealer to the extent that he has instructed such carrying broker or dealer to maintain physical possession or control of them free of any charge, lien, or claim of any kind in favor of such carrying broker or dealer or any persons claiming through such carrying broker or dealer; or

(3) Are the subject of bona fide items of transfer; provided that securities shall be deemed not to be the subject of bona fide items of transfer if, within 40 calendar days after they have been transmitted for transfer by the broker or dealer to the issuer or its transfer agent, new certificates conforming to the instructions of the broker or dealer have not been received by him, he has not received a written statement by the issuer or its transfer agent acknowledging the transfer instructions and the possession of the securities or he has not obtained a revalidation of a window ticket from a transfer agent with respect to the certificate delivered for transfer; or

(4) Are in the custody of a foreign depository, foreign clearing agency or foreign custodian bank which the Commission upon application from a broker or dealer or upon its own motion shall designate as a satisfactory control location for securities; or

(5) Are in the custody or control of a bank as defined in section 3(a)(6) of the Act, the delivery of which securities to the broker or dealer does not require the payment of money or value and the bank having acknowledged in writing that the securities in its custody or control are not subject to any right, charge, security interest, lien or claim of any kind in favor of a bank or any person claiming through the bank; or

(6)(i) Are held in or are in transit between offices of the broker or dealer; or (ii) are held by a corporate subsidiary if the broker or dealer owns and exercises a majority of the voting rights of all of the voting securities of such subsidiary, assumes or guarantees all of the subsidiary's obligations and liabilities, operates the subsidiary as a branch office of the broker or dealer, and assumes full responsibility for compliance by the subsidiary and all of its associated persons with the provisions of the federal securities laws as well as for all of the other acts of the subsidiary and such associated persons; or

(7) Are held in such other locations as the Commission shall upon application from a broker or dealer find and designate to be adequate for the protection of customer securities.

(d) *Requirement to Reduce Securities to Possession or Control.* Not later than the next business day, a broker or dealer, as of the close of the preceding business day, shall determine from his books or records the quantity of fully paid securities and excess margin securities in his possession or control and the quantity of fully paid securities and excess margin securities not in his possession or control. In making this daily determination inactive margin accounts (accounts having no activity by reason of purchase or sale of securities, receipt or delivery of cash or securities or similar type events) may be computed not less than once weekly. If such books or records indicate, as of such close of the business day, that such broker or dealer has not obtained physical possession or control of all fully paid and excess margin securities as required by this section and there are securities of the same issue and class in any of the following noncontrol locations:

(1) Securities subject to a lien securing moneys borrowed by the broker or dealer or securities loaned to another broker or dealer, then the broker or dealer shall, not later than the business day following the day on which such determination is made, issue instructions for the release of such securities from the lien or return of such loaned securities and shall obtain physical possession or control of such securities within 2 business days following the date of issuance of the instructions in the case of securities subject to lien securing borrowed moneys and within 5 business days following the date of issuance of instructions in the case of securities loaned; or

(2) Securities included on his books or records as failed to receive more than 30 calendar days, then the broker or dealer shall, not later than the business day following the day on which such determination is made, take prompt steps to obtain physical possession or control of securities so failed to receive through a buy-in procedure or otherwise; or

(3) Securities receivable by the broker or dealer as a security dividend receivable, stock split or similar distribution for more than 45 calendar days, then the broker or dealer shall, not later than the business day following the day on which such determination is made, take prompt steps to obtain physical possession or control of securities so receivable through a buy-in procedure or otherwise.

(4) A broker or dealer which is subject to the requirements of Rule 15c3–3 with respect to physical possession or control of fully paid and excess margin securities shall prepare and maintain a current and detailed description of the procedures which it utilizes to comply with the possession or control requirements set forth in this section. The records required herein shall be made available upon request to the Commission and to the designated examining authority for such broker or dealer.

(e) *Special Reserve Bank Account for the Exclusive Benefit of Customers.* (1) Every broker or dealer shall maintain with a bank or banks at all times when deposits are required of hereinafter specified a "Special Reserve Bank Account for the Exclusive Benefit of Customers" (hereinafter referred to as the "Reserve Bank Account"), and it shall be separate from any other bank account of the broker or dealer. Such broker or dealer shall at all times maintain in such Reserve Bank Account, through deposits made therein, cash and/or qualified securities in amounts computed in accordance with the formula set forth in Rule 15c3–3a.

(2) It shall be unlawful for any broker or dealer to accept or use any of the amounts under items comprising Total Credits under the formula referred to in subparagraph (1) of this paragraph except for the specified purposes indicated under items comprising Total Debits under the formula, and, to the extent Total Credits exceed Total Debits, the net amount thereof shall be maintained in the Reserve Bank Account pursuant to subparagraph (e)(1) of this paragraph.

(3) Computations necessary to determine the amount required to be deposited as specified in subparagraph (1) of this paragraph shall be made weekly, as of the close of the last business day of the week and the deposit so computed shall be made no later than 1 hour after the opening of banking business on the second following business day; *Provided, however,* a broker or dealer which has aggregate indebtedness not exceeding 800 percent of net

capital (as defined in Rule 15c3–1) or in the capital rules of a national securities exchange of which it is a member and exempt from Rule 15c3–1 by paragraph (b)(2) of this rule and which carries aggregate customer funds (as defined in paragraph (a)(10) of this rule), as computed at the last required computation pursuant to this rule, not exceeding $1 million, may in the alternative make the computation monthly, as of the close of the last business day of the month, and, in such event, shall deposit not less than 105 percent of the amount so computed no later than 1 hour after the opening of banking business on the second following business day.

If a broker or dealer, computing on a monthly basis, has, at the time of any required computation, aggregate indebtedness in excess of 800 percent of net capital, such broker or dealer shall thereafter compute weekly as aforesaid until four successive weekly computations are made, none of which were made at a time when his aggregate indebtedness exceeded 800 percent of his net capital.

Computations in addition to the computations required in this subparagraph (3), may be made as of the close of any other business day, and the deposits so computed shall be made no later than 1 hour after the opening of banking business on the second following business day.

The broker or dealer shall make and maintain a record of each such computation made pursuant to this subparagraph (3) or otherwise and preserve each such record in accordance with Rule 17a–4.

(f) *Notification of Banks.* A broker or dealer required to maintain the Reserve Bank Account prescribed by this section or who maintains a Special Account referred to in paragraph (k) of this rule shall obtain and preserve in accordance with Rule 17a–4 a written notification from each bank in which he has his Reserve Bank Account or Special Account that the bank was informed that all cash and/or qualified securities deposited therein are being held by the bank for the exclusive benefit of customers of the broker or dealer in accordance with the regulations of the Commission, and are being kept separate from any other accounts maintained by the broker or dealer with the bank, and the broker or dealer shall have a written contract with the bank which provides that the cash and/or qualified securities shall at no time be used directly or indirectly as security for a loan to the broker or dealer by the bank and, shall be subject to no right, charge, security interest, lien or claim of any kind in favor of the bank or any person claiming through the bank.

(g) *Withdrawals From the Reserve Bank Account.* A broker or dealer may make withdrawals from his Reserve Bank Account if and to the extent that at the time of the withdrawal the amount remaining in the Reserve Bank Account is not less than the amount then required by paragraph (e) of this rule. A bank may presume that any request for withdrawal from a Reserve Bank Account is in conformity and compliance with this paragraph (g). On any business day on which a withdrawal is made, the broker or dealer shall make a record of the computation on the basis of which he makes such withdrawal, and he shall preserve such computation in accordance with Rule 17a–4.

(h) *Buy-In of Short Security Differences.* A broker or dealer shall within 45 calendar days after the date of the examination, count, verification and comparison of securities pursuant to Rule 17a–13 or otherwise or to the annual report of financial condition in accordance with Rule 17a–5 or 17a–12, buy-in all short security differences which are not resolved during the 45-day period.

(i) *Notification in the Event of Failure to Make a Required Deposit.* If a broker or dealer shall fail to make in his reserve bank account or special account a deposit, as required by this rule, the broker or dealer shall by telegram immediately notify the Commission and the regulatory authority for the broker or dealer, which examines such broker or dealer as to financial responsibility and shall promptly thereafter confirm such notification in writing.

(j) [*Reserved*]

(k) *Exemptions.* (1) The provisions of this rule shall not be applicable to a broker or dealer meeting all of the following conditions:

(i) His dealer transactions (as principal for his own account) are limited to the purchase, sale, and redemption of redeemable securities of registered investment companies or of interests or participations in an insurance company separate account, whether or not registered as an investment company; except that a broker or dealer transacting business as a sole proprietor may also effect occasional transactions in other securities for his own account with or through another registered broker or dealer;

(ii) His transactions as broker (agent) are limited to: (*a*) The sale and redemption of redeemable securities of registered investment companies or of interests or participations in an insurance company separate account, whether or not registered as an investment company; (*b*) the solicitation of share accounts for savings and loan associations insured by an instrumentality of the United States; and (*c*) the sale of securities for the account of a customer to obtain funds for immediate reinvestment in redeemable securities of registered investment companies; and

(iii) He promptly transmits all funds and delivers all securities received in connection with his activities as a broker or dealer, and does not otherwise hold funds or securities for, or owe money or securities to, customers.

(iv) Notwithstanding the foregoing, this section shall not apply to any insurance company which is a registered broker-dealer, and which otherwise meets all of the conditions in subdivisions (i), (ii), and (iii) of this subparagraph, solely by reason of its participation in transactions that are a part of the business of insurance, including the purchasing, selling, or holding of securities for or on behalf of such company's general and separate accounts.

(2) The provisions of this rule shall not be applicable to a broker or dealer:

(i) Who carries no margin accounts, promptly transmits all customer funds and delivers all securities received in connection with his activities as a broker or dealer, does not otherwise hold funds or securities for, or owe money or securities to, customers and effectuates all financial transactions between the broker or dealer and his customers through one or more bank accounts, each to be designated as "Special Account for the Exclusive Benefit of Customers of (name of the broker or dealer)"; or

(ii) Who, as an introducing broker or dealer, clears all transactions with and for customers on a fully disclosed basis with a clearing broker or dealer, and who promptly transmits all customer funds and securities to the clearing broker or dealer which carries all of the accounts of such customers and maintains and preserves such books and records pertaining thereto pursuant to the requirements of Rule 17a–3 and Rule 17a–4, as are customarily made and kept by a clearing broker or dealer.

(3) Upon written application by a broker or dealer, the Commission may exempt such broker or dealer from the provisions of this section, either unconditionally or on specified terms and conditions, if the Commission finds that the broker or dealer has established safeguards for the protection of funds and securities of customers comparable with those provided for by this section and that it is not necessary in the public interest or for the protection of investors to subject the particular broker or dealer to the provisions of this rule.

(*l*) *Delivery of Securities.* Nothing stated in this rule shall be construed as affecting the absolute right of a customer of a broker or dealer to receive in the course of normal business operations following demand made on the broker or dealer, the physical delivery of certificates for:

(1) Fully paid securities to which he is entitled and,

(2) Margin securities upon full payment by such customer to the broker or dealer of his indebtedness to the broker or dealer; and, subject to the right of the broker or dealer under section 7(b) of regulation T to retain collateral for his own protection beyond the requirements of regulation T, excess margin securities not reasonably required to collateralize such customer's indebtedness to the broker or dealer.

(m) *Completion of Sell Orders on Behalf of Customers.* If a broker or dealer executes a sell order of a customer (other than an order to execute a sale of securities which the seller does not own) and if for any reason whatever the broker or dealer has not obtained possession of the securities from the customer within 10 business days after the settlement date, the broker or dealer shall immediately thereafter close the transaction with the customer by purchasing securities of like kind and quantity: *Provided, however,* The term "customer" for the purpose of this paragraph (m) shall not include a broker or dealer who maintains a special omnibus account with another broker or dealer in compliance with section 4(b) of regulation T.

[Paragraph (m) is suspended with respect to exempted securities by virtue of SEC Exchange Act Release No. 10093 (Apr. 10, 1973).]

(n) *Extensions of Time.* If an appropriate committee of a registered national securities exchange or a registered national securities association is satisfied that a broker or dealer is acting in good faith in making the application and that exceptional circumstances warrant such action, such committee, on application of the broker or dealer, may extend any period specified in paragraphs (d)(2) and (3), paragraph (h) and paragraph (m) of this section, relating to the requirement that such broker or dealer take action within a designated period of time to buy-in in a security, for one or more limited periods commensurate with the circumstances. Each such committee shall make and preserve for a period of not less than 3 years a record of each extension granted pursuant to this paragraph (n) which shall contain a summary of the justification for the granting of the extension.

(*o*) *Security futures products.*—(1) *Where security futures products shall be held.* A broker or dealer registered with the Commission pursuant to section 15(b)(1) of the Act (15 U.S.C. 78*o*(b)(1)) that is also a futures commission merchant registered with the Commodity Futures Trading Commission pursuant to section 4f(a)(1) of the Commodity Exchange Act (7 U.S.C. 6f(a)(1)):

(i) Shall hold a customer's security futures products in either a securities account or a futures account; and

(ii) Shall establish written policies or procedures for determining whether customer security futures products will be placed in a securities account or a futures account and, if applicable, the process by which a customer may elect the type or types of account in which security futures products will be held (including the procedure to be followed if a customer fails to make an election of account type).

(2) *Disclosure and record requirements.*—(i) Except as provided in paragraph (*o*)(2)(ii), before a broker or dealer registered with the Commission pursuant to section 15(b)(1) of the Act (15 U.S.C. 78*o*(b)(1)) accepts the first order for a security futures product from or on behalf of a customer, the broker or dealer shall furnish the customer with a disclosure document containing the following information:

(A) A description of the protections provided by the requirements set forth under this section and the Securities Investor Protection Act of 1970 (15 U.S.C. 78aaa *et seq.*) applicable to a securities account;

(B) A description of the protections provided by the requirements set forth under section 4d of the Commodity Exchange

Act (7 U.S.C. 6d) applicable to a futures account;

(C) A statement indicating whether the customer's security futures products will be held in a securities account or a futures account, or whether the firm permits customers to make or change an election of account type; and

(D) A statement that, with respect to holding the customer's security futures products in a securities account or a futures account, the alternative regulatory scheme is not available to the customer with relation to that account.

(ii) Where a customer account containing an open security futures product position is transferred to a broker or dealer registered with the Commission pursuant to section 15(b)(1) of the Act (15 U.S.C. 78o(b)(1)), that broker or dealer may instead provide the statements described in paragraphs (*o*)(2)(i)(C) and (*o*)(2)(i)(D) of this section no later than ten business days after the date the account is received.

(3) *Changes in account type.* A broker or dealer registered with the Commission pursuant to section 15(b)(1) of the Act (15 U.S.C. 78*o*(b)(1)) that is also a futures commission merchant registered pursuant to section 4f(a)(1) of the Commodity Exchange Act (7 U.S.C. 6f(a)(1)) may change the type of account in which a customer's security futures products will be held; *provided* that:

(i) The broker or dealer creates a record of each change in account type, including the name of the customer, the account number, the date the broker or dealer received the customer's request to change the account type, if applicable, and the date the change in account type became effective; and

(ii) The broker or dealer, at least ten days before the customer's account type is changed:

(A) Notifies the customer in writing of the date that the change will become effective; and

(B) Provides the customer with the disclosures described in paragraph (*o*)(2)(i) of this section.

Rule 15c3–3a. Exhibit A—Formula for Determination of Reserve Requirements of Brokers and Dealers Under Rule 15c3–3

	Credits		**Debits**
1.	Free credit balances and other credit balances in customers' security accounts. (See Note A)	$XXX	
2.	Monies borrowed collateralized by securities carried for the account of customers. (See Note B)	XXX	
3.	Monies payable against customers' securities loaned. (See Note C)	XXX	
4.	Customers' securities failed to receive. (See Note D)	XXX	
5.	Credit balances in firm accounts which are attributable to principal sales to customers.	XXX	
6.	Market value of stock dividends, stock splits and similar distributions receivable outstanding over 30 calendar days.	XXX	
7.	Market value of short security count differences over 30 calendar days old.	XXX	
8.	Market value of short securities and credits (not to be offset by longs or by debits) in all suspense accounts over 30 calendar days.	XXX	
9.	Market value of securities which are in transfer in excess of 40 calendar days and have not been confirmed to be in transfer by the transfer agent or the issuer during the 40 days.	XXX	
10.	Debit balances in customers' cash and margin		

Credits		Debits
	accounts excluding unsecured accounts and accounts doubtful of collection. (See Note E)	XXX
11.	Securities borrowed to effectuate short sales by customers and securities borrowed to make delivery on customers' securities failed to deliver.	XXX
12.	Failed to deliver of customers' securities not older than 30 calendar days.	XXX
13.	Margin required and on deposit with the Options Clearing Corporation for all option contracts written or purchased in customer accounts. (See Note F)	XXX
		Total Credits / Total Debits
14.	Margin related to security futures products written, purchased or sold in customer accounts required and on deposit with a clearing agency registered with the Commission under section 17A of the Act (15 U.S.C. 17A) or a derivatives clearing organization registered with the Commodity Futures Trading Commission under section 5b of the Commodity Exchange Act (7 U.S.C. 7a–1). (See Note G)	XXX
	Total Credits	
	Total Debits	
15.	Excess of total credits (sum of items 1–9) over total debits (sum of items 10–14) required to be on deposit in the "Reserve Bank Account" (§ 240.15c3–3(e)). If the computation is made monthly as permitted by this section, the deposit shall be not less than 105 percent of the excess of total credits over total debits.	XXX

NOTE A: Item 1 shall include all outstanding drafts payable to customers which have been applied against free credit balances or other credit balances and shall also include checks drawn in excess of a bank balance per the records of the broker or dealer.

NOTE B: Item 2 shall include the amount of options-related or security futures product-related Letters of Credit obtained by a member of a registered clearing agency or a derivatives clearing organization which are collateralized by customers' securities, to the extent of the member's margin requirement at the registered clearing agency or derivatives clearing organization.

NOTE C: Item 3 shall include in addition to monies payable against customers' securities loaned the amount by which the market value of securities loaned exceeds the collateral value received from the lending of such securities.

NOTE D: Item 4 shall include in addition to customers' securities failed to receive the amount by which the market value of securities failed to receive and outstanding more than thirty (30) calendar days exceeds their contract value.

NOTE E: (1) Debit balances in margin accounts shall be reduced by the amount by which a specific security (other than an exempted security) which is collateral for margin accounts exceeds in aggregate value 15 percent of the aggregate value of all securities which collateralize all margin accounts receivable; *provided, however,* the required reduction shall not be in excess of the amount of the debit balance required to be excluded because of this concentration rule. A specified security is deemed to be collateral for a margin account only to the extent it represents in value not more than 140 percent of the customer debit balance in a margin account.

(2) Debit balances in special omnibus accounts, maintained in compliance with the requirements of Section 4(b) of Regulation T

under the Act (12 CFR 220.4(b)) or similar accounts carried on behalf of another broker or dealer, shall be reduced by any deficits in such accounts (or if a credit, such credit shall be increased) less any calls for margin, marks to the market, or other required deposits which are outstanding 5 business days or less.

(3) Debit balances in customers' cash and margin accounts included in the formula under item 10 shall be reduced by an amount equal to 1 percent of their aggregate value.

(4) Debit balances in cash and margin accounts of household members and other persons related to principals of a broker or dealer and debit balances in cash and margin accounts of affiliated persons of a broker or dealer shall be excluded from the Reserve Formula, unless the broker or dealer can demonstrate that such debit balances are directly related to credit items in the formula.

(5) Debit balances in margin accounts (other than omnibus accounts) shall be reduced by the amount by which any single customer's debit balance exceeds 25% (to the extent such amount is greater than $50,000) of the broker-dealer's tentative net capital (*i.e.*, net capital prior to securities haircuts) unless the broker or dealer can demonstrate that the debit balance is directly related to credit items in the Reserve Formula. Related accounts (*e.g.*, the separate accounts of an individual, accounts under common control or subject to cross guarantees) shall be deemed to be a single customer's accounts for purposes of this provision.

If the registered national securities exchange or the registered national securities association having responsibility for examining the broker or dealer ("designated examining authority") is satisfied, after taking into account the circumstances of the concentrated account including the quality, diversity, and marketability of the collateral securing the debit balances of margin accounts subject to this provision, that the concentration of debit balances is appropriate, then such designated examining authority may grant a partial or plenary exception from this provision. The debit balance may be included in the Reserve Formula computation for five business days from the day the request is made.

(6) Debit balances of joint accounts, custodian accounts, participation in hedge funds or limited partnerships or similar type accounts or arrangements of a person who would be excluded from the definition of customer ("non-customer") with persons includible in the definition of customer shall be included in the Reserve Formula in the following manner: if the percentage ownership of the non-customer is less than 5 percent then the entire debit balance shall be included in the formula; if such percentage ownership is between 5 percent and 50 percent then the portion of the debit balance attributable to the non-customer shall be excluded from the formula unless the broker or dealer can demonstrate that the debit balances is directly related to credit items in the formula; if such percentage ownership is greater than 50 percent, then the entire debit balance shall be excluded from the formula unless the broker or dealer can demonstrate that the debit balance is directly related to credit items in the formula.

NOTE F: Item 13 shall include the amount of margin required and on deposit with Options Clearing Corporation to the extent such margin is represented by cash, proprietary qualified securities, and letters of credit collateralized by customers' securities.

NOTE G: (a) Item 14 shall include the amount of margin required and on deposit with a clearing agency registered with the Commission under section 17A of the Act (15 U.S.C. 78q–1) or a derivatives clearing organization registered with the Commodity Futures Trading Commission under section 5b of the Commodity Exchange Act (7 U.S.C. 7a–1) for customer accounts to the extent that the margin is represented by cash, proprietary qualified securities, and letters of credit collateralized by customers' securities.

(b) Item 14 shall apply only if the broker or dealer has the margin related to security futures products on deposit with:

(1) A registered clearing agency or derivatives clearing organization that:

(i) Maintains the highest investment-grade rating from a nationally recognized statistical rating organization; or

(ii) Maintains security deposits from clearing members in connection with regulated options or futures transactions and assessment power over member firms that equal a combined total of at least $2 billion, at least $500 million of which must be in the form of security deposits. For purposes of this Note G, the term "security deposits" refers to a general fund, other than margin deposits or their equivalent, that consists of cash or securities held by a registered clearing agency or derivative clearing organization; or

(iii) Maintains at least $3 billion in margin deposits; or

(iv) Does not meet the requirements of paragraphs (b)(1)(i) through (b)(1)(iii) of this Note G, if the Commission has determined, upon a written request for exemption by or for the benefit of the broker or dealer, that the broker or dealer may utilize such a registered clearing agency or derivatives clearing organization. The Commission may, in its sole discretion, grant such an exemption subject to such conditions as are appropriate under the circumstances, if the Commission determines that such conditional or unconditional exemption is necessary or appropriate in the public interest, and is consistent with the protection of investors; and

(2) A registered clearing agency or derivatives clearing organization that, if it holds funds or securities deposited as margin for security futures products in a bank, as defined in section 3(a)(6) of the Act (15 U.S.C. 78c(a)(6)), obtains and preserves written notification from the bank at which it holds such funds and securities or at which such funds and securities are held on its behalf. The written notification shall state that all funds and/or securities deposited with the bank as margin (including customer security futures products margin), or held by the bank and pledged to such registered clearing agency or derivatives clearing agency as margin, are being held by the bank for the exclusive benefit of clearing members of the registered clearing agency or derivatives clearing organization (subject to the interest of such registered clearing agency or derivatives clearing organization therein), and are being kept separate from any other accounts maintained by the registered clearing agency or derivatives clearing organization with the bank. The written notification also shall provide that such funds and/or securities shall at no time be used directly or indirectly as security for a loan to the registered clearing agency or derivatives clearing organization by the bank, and shall be subject to no right, charge, security interest, lien, or claim of any kind in favor of the bank or any person claiming through the bank. This provision, however, shall not prohibit a registered clearing agency or derivatives clearing organization from pledging customer funds or securities as collateral to a bank for any purpose that the rules of the Commission or the registered clearing agency or derivatives clearing organization otherwise permit; and

(3) A registered clearing agency or derivatives clearing organization that establishes, documents, and maintains:

(i) Safeguards in the handling, transfer, and delivery of cash and securities;

(ii) Fidelity bond coverage for its employees and agents who handle customer funds or securities. In the case of agents of a registered clearing agency or derivatives clearing organization, the agent may provide the fidelity bond coverage; and

(iii) Provisions for periodic examination by independent public accountants; and

(4) A derivatives clearing organization that, if it is not otherwise registered with the Commission, has provided the Commission with a written undertaking, in a form acceptable to the Commission, executed by a duly authorized person at the derivatives clearing organization, to the effect that, with respect to the clearance and settlement of the customer security futures products of the broker-dealer, the derivatives clearing organization will permit the Commission to examine the books and records of the derivatives clearing organization for compliance with the requirements set forth in § 240.15c3–3a, Note G. (b)(1) through (3).

(c) Item 14 shall apply only if a broker or dealer determines, at least annually, that the registered clearing agency or derivatives clearing organization with which the broker or dealer has on deposit margin related to securities future products meets the conditions of this Note G.

Rule 15c3–4. Internal Risk Management Control Systems for OTC Derivatives Dealers

(a) An OTC derivatives dealer shall establish, document, and maintain a system of internal risk management controls to assist it in managing the risks associated with its business activities, including market, credit, leverage, liquidity, legal, and operational risks.

(b) An OTC derivatives dealer shall consider the following when adopting its internal control system guidelines, policies, and procedures:

(1) The ownership and governance structure of the OTC derivatives dealer;

(2) The composition of the governing body of the OTC derivatives dealer;

(3) The management philosophy of the OTC derivatives dealer;

(4) The scope and nature of established risk management guidelines;

(5) The scope and nature of the permissible OTC derivatives activities;

(6) The sophistication and experience of relevant trading, risk management, and internal audit personnel;

(7) The sophistication and functionality of information and reporting systems; and

(8) The scope and frequency of monitoring, reporting, and auditing activities.

(c) An OTC derivatives dealer's internal risk management control system shall include the following elements:

(1) A risk control unit that reports directly to senior management and is independent from business trading units;

(2) Separation of duties between personnel responsible for entering into a transaction and those responsible for recording the transaction in the books and records of the OTC derivatives dealer;

(3) Periodic reviews (which may be performed by internal audit staff) and annual reviews (which must be conducted by independent certified public accountants) of the OTC derivatives dealer's risk management systems;

(4) Definitions of risk, risk monitoring, and risk management; and

(5) Written guidelines, approved by the OTC derivatives dealer's governing body, that include and discuss the following:

(i) The OTC derivatives dealer's consideration of the elements in paragraph (b) of this section;

(ii) The scope, and the procedures for determining the scope, of authorized activities or any nonquantitative limitation on the scope of authorized activities;

(iii) Quantitative guidelines for managing the OTC derivatives dealer's overall risk exposure;

(iv) The type, scope, and frequency of reporting by management on risk exposures;

(v) The procedures for and the timing of the governing body's periodic review of the risk monitoring and risk management written guidelines, systems, and processes;

(vi) The process for monitoring risk independent of the business or trading units whose activities create the risks being monitored;

(vii) The performance of the risk management function by persons independent from or senior to the business or trading units whose activities create the risks;

(viii) The authority and resources of the groups or persons performing the risk monitoring and risk management functions;

(ix) The appropriate response by management when internal risk management guidelines have been exceeded;

(x) The procedures to monitor and address the risk that an OTC derivatives transaction contract will be unenforceable;

(xi) The procedures requiring the documentation of the principal terms of OTC derivatives transactions and other relevant information regarding such transactions;

(xii) The procedures authorizing specified employees to commit the OTC derivatives dealer to particular types of transactions;

(xiii) The procedures to prevent the OTC derivatives dealer from engaging in any securities transaction that is not permitted under § 240.15a–1; and

(xiv) The procedures to prevent the OTC derivatives dealer from improperly relying on the exceptions to § 240.15a–1(c) and § 240.15a–1(d), including the procedures to determine whether a counterparty is acting in the capacity of principal or agent.

(d) Management must periodically review, in accordance with written procedures, the OTC derivatives dealer's business activities for consistency with risk management guidelines including that:

(1) Risks arising from the OTC derivatives dealer's OTC derivatives activities are consistent with prescribed guidelines;

(2) Risk exposure guidelines for each business unit are appropriate for the business unit;

(3) The data necessary to conduct the risk monitoring and risk management function as well as the valuation process over the OTC derivatives dealer's portfolio of products is accessible on a timely basis and information systems are available to capture, monitor, analyze, and report relevant data;

(4) Procedures are in place to enable management to take action when internal risk management guidelines have been exceeded;

(5) Procedures are in place to monitor and address the risk that an OTC derivatives transaction contract will be unenforceable;

(6) Procedures are in place to identify and address any deficiencies in the operating systems and to contain the extent of losses arising from unidentified deficiencies;

(7) Procedures are in place to authorize specified employees to commit the OTC derivatives dealer to particular types of transactions, to specify any quantitative limits on such authority, and to provide for the oversight of their exercise of such authority;

(8) Procedures are in place to prevent the OTC derivatives dealer from engaging in any securities transaction that is not permitted under § 240.15a–1;

(9) Procedures are in place to prevent the OTC derivatives dealer from improperly relying on the exceptions to § 240.15a–1(c) and § 240.15a–1(d), including procedures to determine whether a counterparty is acting in the capacity of principal or agent;

(10) Procedures are in place to provide for adequate documentation of the principal terms of OTC derivatives transactions and other relevant information regarding such transactions;

(11) Personnel resources with appropriate expertise are committed to implementing the risk monitoring and risk management systems and processes; and

(12) Procedures are in place for the periodic internal and external review of the risk monitoring and risk management functions.

Rule 15c6-1. Settlement Cycle

(a) Except as provided in paragraphs (b), (c) and (d) of this section, a broker or dealer shall not effect or enter into a contract for the purchase or sale of a security (other than an exempted security, government security, municipal security, commercial paper, bankers' acceptances, or commercial bills) that provides for payment of funds and delivery of securities later than the third business day after the date of the contract unless otherwise expressly agreed to by the parties at the time of the transaction.

(b) Paragraphs (a) and (c) of this section shall not apply to contracts:

(1) For the purchase or sale of limited partnership interests that are not listed on an exchange or for which quotations are not disseminated through an automated quotation system of a registered securities association;

(2) For the purchase or sale of securities that the Commission may from time to time, taking into account then existing market practices, exempt by order from the requirements of paragraph (a) of this section, either unconditionally or on specified terms and conditions, if the Commission determines that such exemption is consistent with the public interest and the protection of investors.

(c) Paragraph (a) of this section shall not apply to contracts for the sale for cash of securities that are priced after 4:30 p.m. Eastern time on the date such securities are priced and that are sold by an issuer to an underwriter pursuant to a firm commitment underwritten offering registered under the Securities Act of 1933 or sold to an initial purchaser by a broker-dealer participating in such offering provided that a broker or dealer shall not effect or enter into a contract for the purchase or sale of such securities that provides for payment of funds and delivery of securities later than the fourth business day after the date of the contract unless otherwise expressly agreed to by the parties at the time of the transaction.

(d) For purposes of paragraphs (a) and (c) of this section, the parties to a contract shall be deemed to have expressly agreed to an alternate date for payment of funds and delivery of securities at the time of the transaction for a contract for the sale for cash of securities pursuant to a firm commitment offering if the managing underwriter and the issuer have agreed to such date for all securities sold pursuant to such offering and the parties to the contract have not expressly agreed to another date for payment of funds and delivery of securities at the time of the transaction.

REGULATION 15D—REPORTS OF REGISTRANTS UNDER THE SECURITIES ACT OF 1933

ANNUAL REPORTS

Rule 15d-1. Requirements of Annual Reports

Every registrant under the Securities Act of 1933 shall file an annual report, on the appropriate form authorized or prescribed therefor, for the fiscal year in which the registration statement under the Securities Act of 1933 became effective and for each fiscal year thereafter, unless the registrant is exempt from such filing by section 15(d) of the Act or rules thereunder. Annual reports shall be filed within the period specified in the appropriate report form.

Rule 15d-2. Special Financial Report

(a) If the registration statement under the Securities Act of 1933 did not contain certified financial statements for the registrant's last full fiscal year (or for the life of the registrant if less than a full fiscal year) preceding the fiscal year in which the registration statement became effective, the registrant shall, within 90 days after the effective date of the registration statement, file a special report furnishing certified financial statements for such last full fiscal year or other period, as the case may be, meeting the requirements of the form appropriate for annual reports of the registrant. If the registrant is a foreign private issuer as defined in Rule 405 of this chapter, then the special financial report shall be filed on the appropriate form for annual reports of the registrant and shall be filed by the later of 90 days after the date on which the registration statement became effective, or six months following the end of the registrant's latest full fiscal year.

(b) The report shall be filed under cover of the facing sheet of the form appropriate for annual reports of the registrant, shall indicate on the facing sheet that it contains only financial statements for the fiscal year in question, and shall be signed in accordance with the requirements of the annual report form.

Rule 15d-3. Reports for Depositary Shares Registered on Form F-6

Annual and other reports are not required with respect to Depositary Shares registered on Form F-6 (§ 230.36 of this chapter). The exemption in this section does not apply to any deposited securities registered on any other form under the Securities Act of 1933.

Rule 15d-4. Reporting by Form 40-F Registrants

A registrant that is eligible to use Forms 40-F and 6-K and files reports in accordance therewith shall be deemed to satisfy the requirements of Regulation 15D.

Rule 15d-5. Reporting by Successor Issuers

(a) Where in connection with a succession by merger, consolidation, exchange of securities, acquisition of assets or otherwise, securities of any issuer that is not required to file reports pursuant to section 15(d) (15 U.S.C. 78o(d)) of the Act are issued to the holders of any class of securities of another issuer that is required to file such reports, the duty to file reports pursuant to such section shall be deemed to have been assumed by the issuer of the class of securities so issued. The successor issuer shall, after the consummation of the succession, file reports in accordance with section 15(d) of the Act (15 U.S.C. 78o(d)) and the rules and regulations thereunder, unless that issuer is exempt from filing such reports or the duty to file such reports is suspended under section 15(d) of the Act (15 U.S.C. 78o(d)).

(b) An issuer that is deemed to be a successor issuer according to paragraph (a) of this rule shall file reports on the same forms as the predecessor issuer except as follows:

(1) An issuer that is not a foreign issuer shall not be eligible to file on Form 20-F.

(2) A foreign private issuer shall be eligible to file on Form 20-F.

(c) The provisions of paragraph (a) of this rule shall not apply to an issuer of securities in connection with a succession that was registered on Form F-8 or Form F-10 or Form F-80.

Rule 15d-6. Suspension of Duty to File Reports

If the duty of an issuer to file reports pursuant to section 15(d) of the Act as to any fiscal year is suspended as provided in section 15(d) of the Act, such issuer shall, within 30 days after the beginning of the first fiscal year, file a notice on Form 15 informing the Commission of such suspension unless Form 15 has already been filed pursuant to Rule 12h-3. If the suspension resulted from the issuer's merger into, or consolidation with, another issuer or issuers, the notice shall be filed by the successor issuer.

OTHER REPORTS

Rule 15d-10. Transition Reports

(a) Every issuer that changes its fiscal closing date shall file a report covering the resulting transition period between the closing date of its most recent fiscal year and the opening date of its new fiscal year; *Provided, however,* that an issuer shall file an annual report for any fiscal year that ended before the date on which the issuer determined to change its fiscal year end. In no event shall the transition report cover a period of 12 or more months.

(b) The report pursuant to this section shall be filed for the transition period not more than the number of days specified in paragraph (j) of this section after either the close of the transition period or the date of the determination to change the fiscal closing date, whichever is later. The report shall be filed on the form appropriate for annual reports of the issuer, shall cover the period from the close of the last fiscal year end and shall indicate clearly the period covered. The financial statements for the transition period filed therewith shall be audited. Financial statements, which may be unaudited, shall be filed for the comparable period of the prior year, or a footnote, which may be unaudited, shall state for the comparable period of the prior year, revenues, gross profits, income taxes, income or loss from continuing operations before extraordinary items and cumulative effect of a change in accounting principles and net income or loss. The effects of any discontinued operations and/or extraordinary items as classified under the provisions of generally accepted accounting principles also shall be shown, if applicable. Per share data based upon such income or loss and net income or loss shall be presented in conformity with applicable accounting standards. Where called for by the time span to be covered, the comparable period financial statements or footnote shall be included in subsequent filings.

(c) If the transition period covers a period of less than six months, in lieu of the report required by paragraph (b) of this rule, a report may be filed for the transition period on Form 10–Q and Form 10–QSB not more than the number of days specified in paragraph (j) of this section after either the close of the transition period or the date of the determination to change the fiscal closing date, whichever is later. The report of Form 10–Q and Form 10–QSB shall cover the period from the close of the last fiscal year end and shall indicate clearly the period covered. The financial statements filed therewith need not be audited but, if they are not audited, the issuer shall file with the first annual report for the newly adopted fiscal year separate audited statements of income and cash flows covering the transition period. The notes to financial statements for the transition period included in such first annual report may be integrated with the notes to financial statements for the full fiscal period. A separate audited balance sheet as of the end of the transition period shall be filed in the annual report only if the audited balance sheet as of the end of the fiscal year prior to the transition period is not filed. Schedules need not be filed in transition reports on Form 10–Q and Form 10–QSB.

(d) Notwithstanding the foregoing in paragraphs (a), (b), and (c) of this rule, if the transition period covers a period of one month or less, the issuer need not file a separate transition report if either:

(1) the first report required to be filed by the issuer for the newly adopted fiscal year after the date of the determination to change the fiscal year end is an annual report, and that report covers the transition period as well as the fiscal year; or

(2)(i) the issuer files with the first annual report for the newly adopted fiscal year separate audited statements of income and cash flows covering the transition period; and

(ii) the first report required to be filed by the issuer for the newly adopted fiscal year after the date of the determination to change the fiscal year end is a quarterly report on Form 10–Q and Form 10–QSB; and

(iii) information on the transition period is included in the issuer's quarterly report on Form 10–Q and Form 10–QSB for the first quarterly period (except the fourth quarter) of the newly adopted fiscal year that ends after the date of the determination to change the fiscal year. The information covering the transition period required by Part II and Item 2 of Part I may be combined with the information regarding the quarter. However, the financial statements required by Part I, which may be unaudited, shall be furnished separately for the transition period.

(e) Every issuer required to file quarterly reports on Form 10–Q and Form 10–QSB pursuant to Rule 15d-13 of this chapter that changes its fiscal year end shall:

(1) File a quarterly report on Form 10–Q and Form 10–QSB within the time period specified in General Instruction A.1. to that form for any quarterly period (except the fourth quarter) of the old fiscal year that ends before the date on which the issuer determined to change its fiscal year end, except that the issuer need not file such quarterly report if the date on which the quarterly period ends also is the date on which the transition period ends;

(2) File a quarterly report on Form 10–Q and Form 10–QSB within the time specified in General Instruction A.1. to that form for each quarterly period of the old fiscal year within the transition period. In lieu of a quarterly report for any quarter of the old fiscal year within the transition period, the issuer may file a quarterly report on Form 10–Q and Form 10–QSB for any period of three months within the transition period that coincides with a quarter of the newly adopted fiscal year if the quarterly report is filed within the number of days specified in paragraph (j) of this section after the end of such three month period, provided the issuer thereafter continues filing quarterly reports on the basis of the quarters of the newly adopted fiscal year;

(3) Commence filing quarterly reports for the quarters of the new fiscal year no later than the quarterly report for the first quarter of the new fiscal year that ends after the date on which the issuer determined to change the fiscal year end; and

(4) Unless such information is or will be included in the transition report, or the first annual report on Form 10–K and Form 10–KSB include in the initial quarterly report on Form 10–Q and Form 10–QSB for the newly adopted fiscal year information on any period beginning on the first day subsequent to the period covered by the issuer's final quarterly report on Form 10–Q and Form 10–QSB or annual report on Form 10–K and Form 10–KSB for the old fiscal year. The information covering such period required by Part II and Item 2 of Part I may be combined with the information regarding the quarter. However, the financial statements required by Part I, which may be unaudited, shall be furnished separately for such period.

Note to paragraphs (c) and (e): If it is not practicable or cannot be cost-justified to furnish in a transition report on Form 10–Q and Form 10–QSB or a quarterly report for the newly adopted fiscal year financial statements for corresponding periods of the prior year where required, financial statements may be furnished for the quarters of the preceding fiscal year that most nearly are comparable if the issuer furnishes an adequate discussion of seasonal and other factors that could affect the comparability of information or trends reflected, an assessment of the comparability of the data, and a representation as to the reason recasting has not been undertaken.

(f) Every successor issuer that has a different fiscal year from that of its predecessor(s) shall file a transition report pursuant to this rule, containing the required information about each predecessor, for the transition period, if any, between the close of the fiscal year covered by the last annual report of each predecessor and the date of succession. The report shall be filed for the transition period on the form appropriate for annual reports of the issuer not more than the number of days specified in paragraph (j) of this section after the date of the succession, with financial statements in conformity with the requirements set forth in paragraph (b) of this rule. If the transition period covers a period of less than six months, in lieu of a transition report on the form appropriate for the issuer's annual reports, the report may be filed for the transition period on Form 10–Q and Form 10–QSB not more than the number of days specified in paragraph (j) of this section after the date of the succession, with financial statements in conformity with the requirements set forth in paragraph (c) of this rule. Notwithstanding the foregoing, if the transition period covers a period of one month or less, the successor issuer need not file a separate transition report if the information is reported by the successor issuer in conformity with the requirements set forth in paragraph (d) of this rule.

(g)(1) Paragraphs (a) through (f) of this rule shall not apply to foreign private issuers.

(2) Every foreign private issuer that changes its fiscal closing date shall file a report covering the resulting transition period between the closing date of its most recent year and the opening date of its new fiscal year. In no event shall a transition report cover a period longer than 12 months.

(3) The report for the transition period shall be filed on Form 20–F responding to all items to which such issuer is required to respond when Form 20–F is used as an annual report. Such report shall be filed within six months after either the close of the transition period or the date on which the issuer made the determination to change the fiscal closing date, whichever is later. The financial statements for the transition period filed therewith shall be audited.

(4) If the transition period covers a period of six or fewer months, in lieu of the report required by paragraph (g)(3) of this rule, a report for the transition period may be filed on Form 20–F responding to Items 5, 8.A.7., 13, 14, and 17 or 18 within three months after either the close of the transition period or the date on which the issuer made the determination to change the fiscal closing date, whichever is later. The financial statements required by either Item 17 or Item 18 shall be furnished for the transition period. Such financial statements may be unaudited and condensed as permitted in Article 10 of Regulation S–X (§ 210.10–01 of this chapter), but if the financial statements are unaudited and condensed, the issuer shall file with the first annual report for the newly adopted fiscal year separate audited statements of income and cash flows covering the transition period.

(5) Notwithstanding the foregoing in paragraphs (g)(2), (g)(3), and (g)(4) of this rule, if the transition period covers a period of one month or less, a foreign private issuer need not file a separate transition report if the first annual report for the newly adopted fiscal year covers the transition period as well as the fiscal year.

(h) The provisions of this rule shall not apply to investment companies required to file reports pursuant to Rule 30b1–1 under the Investment Company Act of 1940.

(i) No filing fee shall be required for a transition report filed pursuant to this rule.

Note 1:—In addition to the report or reports required to be filed pursuant to this rule, every issuer, except a foreign private issuer or an investment company required to file reports pursuant to Rule 30b1–1 under the Investment Company Act of 1940, that changes its fiscal closing date is required to file a report on Form 8–K responding to Item 8 thereof within the period specified in General Instruction B.1. to that form.

Note 2: The report or reports to be filed pursuant to this section must include the certification required by § 240.15d–14.

(j)(1) For transition reports to be filed on the form appropriate for annual reports of the issuer, the number of days shall be:

(i) For accelerated filers (as defined in § 240.12b–2):

(A) 90 days for fiscal years ending on or after December 15, 2002 and before December 15, 2003;

(B) 75 days for fiscal years ending on or after December 15, 2003 and before December 15, 2005; and

(C) 60 days for fiscal years ending on or after December 15, 2005; and

(ii) 90 days for all other issuers; and

(2) For transition reports to be filed on Form 10–Q or Form 10–QSB (§ 249.308a or § 249.308b of this chapter), the number of days shall be:

(i) For accelerated filers (as defined in § 240.12b–2):

(A) 45 days for fiscal years ending on or after December 15, 2002 and before December 15, 2004;

(B) 40 days for fiscal years ending on or after December 15, 2004 and before December 15, 2006; and

(C) 35 days for fiscal years ending on or after December 15, 2006; and

(ii) 45 days for all other issuers.

(k)(1) Paragraphs (a) through (g) of this section shall not apply to asset-backed issuers.

(2) Every asset-backed issuer that changes its fiscal closing date shall file a report covering the resulting transition period between the closing date of its most recent fiscal year and the opening date of its new fiscal year. In no event shall a transition report cover a period longer than 12 months.

(3) The report for the transition period shall be filed on Form 10–K (§ 249.310 of this chapter) responding to all items to which such asset-backed issuer is required to respond pursuant to General Instruction J. of Form 10-K. Such report shall be filed within 90 days after the later of either the close of the transition period or the date on which the issuer made the determination to change the fiscal closing date.

(4) Notwithstanding the foregoing in paragraphs (k)(2) and (k)(3) of this section, if the transition period covers a period of one month or less, an asset-backed issuer need not file a separate transition report if the first annual report for the newly adopted fiscal year covers the transition period as well as the fiscal year.

(5) Any obligation of the asset-backed issuer to file distribution reports pursuant to § 240.15d–17 will continue to apply regardless of a change in the asset-backed issuer's fiscal closing date.

Note 1: In addition to the report or reports required to be filed pursuant to this section, every issuer, except a foreign private issuer or an investment company required to file reports pursuant to § 270.30b1–1 of this chapter, that changes its fiscal closing date is required to file a Form 8–K (§ 249.308 of this chapter) report that includes the information required by Item 5.03 of Form 8–K within the period specified in General Instruction B.1. to that form.

Rule 15d–11. Current Reports on Form 8–K

(a) Except as provided in paragraph (b) of this section, every registrant subject to Rule 15d–1 shall file a current report on Form 8–K within the period specified in that form unless substantially the same information as that required by Form 8–K has been previously reported by the registrant.

(b) This section shall not apply to foreign governments, foreign private issuers required to make reports on Form 6–K (17 CFR 249.306) pursuant to § 240.15d–16, issuers of American Depositary Receipts for securities of any foreign issuer, or investment companies required to file periodic reports pursuant to § 270.30b1–1 of this chapter under the Investment Company Act of 1940, except where such investment companies are required to file notice of a blackout period pursuant to § 245.104 of this chapter.

(c) No failure to file a report on Form 8–K that is required solely pursuant to Item 1.01, 1.02, 2.03, 2.04, 2.05, 2.06 or 4.02(a) or 6.03 of

Form 8–K shall be deemed to be a violation of 15 U.S.C. 78j(b) and § 240.10b–5.

Rule 15d–13. Quarterly Reports on Form 10–Q and Form 10–QSB

(a) Except as provided in paragraphs (b) and (c) of this rule, every issuer that has securities registered pursuant to the Securities Act of 1933 and is required to file annual reports pursuant to section 15(d) of the Securities Exchange Act of 1934 on Form 10–K and Form 10–KSB or U5S shall file a quarterly report on Form 10–Q and Form 10–QSB within the period specified in General Instruction A.1. to that form for each of the first three quarters of each fiscal year of the issuer, commencing with the first fiscal quarter following the most recent fiscal year for which full financial statements were included in the registration statement, or, if the registration statement included financial statements for an interim period subsequent to the most recent fiscal year end meeting the requirements of Article 10 of Regulation S–X, for the first fiscal quarter subsequent to the quarter reported upon in the registration statement. The first quarterly report of the issuer shall be filed either within 45 days after the effective date of the registration statement or on or before the date on which such report would have been required to be filed if the issuer had been required to file reports on Form 10–Q and Form 10–QSB as of its last fiscal quarter, whichever is later.

(b) The provisions of this rule shall not apply to the following issuers:

(1) Investment companies required to file reports pursuant to Rule 30b1–1; or

(2) Foreign private issuers required to file reports pursuant to Rule 15d–16.

(c) Part I of the quarterly reports on Form 10–Q or Form 10–QSB need not be filed by:

(1) Mutual life insurance companies; or

(2) Mining companies not in the production stage but engaged primarily in the exploration for the development of mineral deposits other than oil, gas or coal, if all of the following conditions are met:

(i) The registrant has not been in production during the current fiscal year or the two years immediately prior thereto; except that being in production for an aggregate period of not more than eight months over the three-year period shall not be a violation of this condition.

(ii) Receipts from the sale of mineral products or from the operations of mineral producing properties by the registrant and its subsidiaries combined have not exceeded $500,000 in any of the most recent six years and have not aggregated more than $1,500,000 in the most recent six fiscal years; and

Asset-backed issuers required to file reports pursuant to § 240.15d–17.

(d) Notwithstanding the foregoing provisions of this rule, the financial information required by Part I of Form 10–Q and Form 10–QSB shall not be deemed to be "filed" for the purpose of section 18 of the Act or otherwise subject to the liabilities of that section of the Act but shall be subject to all other provisions of the Act.

(e) Notwithstanding the foregoing provisions of this rule, the financial information required by Part I of Form 10–Q and Form 10–QSB, or financial information submitted in lieu thereof pursuant to paragraph (d) of this rule, shall not be deemed to be "filed" for the purpose of section 18 of the Act or otherwise subject to the liabilities of that section of the Act but shall be subject to all other provisions of the Act.

Rule 15d–14. Certification of Disclosure in Annual and Quarterly Reports

(a) Each report, including transition reports, filed on Form 10–Q, Form 10–QSB, Form 10–K, Form 10–KSB, Form 20–F or Form 40–F (§§ 249.308a, 249.308b, 249.310, 249.310b, 249.220f or 249.240f of this chapter) under section 15(d) of the Act (15 U.S.C. 78o(d)), other than a report filed by an Asset–

Backed Issuer (as defined in § 229.1101 of this chapter), must include certifications in the form specified in the applicable exhibit filing requirements of such report and such certifications must be filed as an exhibit to such report. Each principal executive and principal financial officer of the issuer, or persons performing similar functions, at the time of filing of the report must sign a certification.

(b) Each periodic report containing financial statements filed by an issuer pursuant to section 15(d) of the Act (15 U.S.C. 78o(d)) must be accompanied by the certifications required by Section 1350 of Chapter 63 of Title 18 of the United States Code (18 U.S.C. 1350) and such certifications must be furnished as an exhibit to such report as specified in the applicable exhibit requirements for such report. Each principal executive and principal financial officer of the issuer (or equivalent thereof) must sign a certification. This requirement may be satisfied by a single certification signed by an issuer's principal executive and principal financial officers.

(c) A person required to provide a certification specified in paragraph (a), (b) or (d) of this section may not have the certification signed on his or her behalf pursuant to a power of attorney or other form of confirming authority.

(d) Each annual report and transition report filed on Form 10–K (§ 249.310 of this chapter) by an asset-backed issuer under section 15(d) of the Act (15 U.S.C. 78o(d)) must include a certification in the form specified in the applicable exhibit filing requirements of such report and such certification must be filed as an exhibit to such report. Terms used in paragraphs (d) and (e) of this section have the same meaning as in Item 1101 of Regulation AB (§ 229.1101 of this chapter).

(e) With respect to asset-backed issuers, the certification required by paragraph (d) of this section must be signed by either:

(1) The senior officer in charge of securitization of the depositor if the depositor is signing the report; or

(2) The senior officer in charge of the servicing function of the servicer if the servicer is signing the report on behalf of the issuing entity. If multiple servicers are involved in servicing the pool assets, the senior officer in charge of the servicing function of the master servicer (or entity performing the equivalent function) must sign if a representative of the servicer is to sign the report on behalf of the issuing entity.

(f) The certification requirements of this section do not apply to XBRL-Related Documents, as defined in § 232.11 of this chapter.

Rule 15d-15. Controls and Procedures

(a) Every issuer that files reports under section 15(d) of the Act (15 U.S.C. 78o(d)), other than an Asset-Backed Issuer (as defined in § 229.1101), a small business investment company registered on Form N–5 (§§ 239.24 and 274.5 of this chapter), or a unit investment trust as defined in section 4(2) of the Investment Company Act of 1940 (15 U.S.C. 80a–4(2)), must maintain disclosure controls and procedures (as defined in paragraph (e) of this section) and internal control over financial reporting (as defined in paragraph (f) of this section).

(b) Each such issuer's management must evaluate, with the participation of the issuer's principal executive and principal financial officers, or persons performing similar functions, the effectiveness of the issuer's disclosure controls and procedures, as of the end of each fiscal quarter, except that management must perform this evaluation:

(1) In the case of a foreign private issuer (as defined in § 240.3b–4) as of the end of each fiscal year; and

(2) In the case of an investment company registered under section 8 of the Investment Company Act of 1940 (15 U.S.C. 80a–8), within the 90-day period prior to the filing date of each report requiring certification under § 270.30a–2 of this chapter.

(c) The management of each such issuer, other than an investment company registered under section 8 of the Investment Company Act of 1940, must evaluate, with the participation of the issuer's principal executive and principal financial officers, or persons performing similar functions, the effectiveness, as of the end of each fiscal year, of the issuer's internal control over financial reporting. The framework on which management's evaluation of the issuer's internal control over financial reporting is based must be a suitable, recognized control framework that is established by a body or group that has followed due-process procedures, including the broad distribution of the framework for public comment.

(d) The management of each such issuer, other than an investment company registered under section 8 of the Investment Company Act of 1940, must evaluate, with the participation of the issuer's principal executive and principal financial officers, or persons performing similar functions, any change in the issuer's internal control over financial reporting, that occurred during each of the issuer's fiscal quarters, or fiscal year in the case of a foreign private issuer, that has materially affected, or is reasonably likely to materially affect, the issuer's internal control over financial reporting.

(e) For purposes of this section, the term disclosure controls and procedures means controls and other procedures of an issuer that are designed to ensure that information required to be disclosed by the issuer in the reports that it files or submits under the Act (15 U.S.C. 78a *et seq.*) is recorded, processed, summarized and reported, within the time periods specified in the Commission's rules and forms. Disclosure controls and procedures include, without limitation, controls and procedures designed to ensure that information required to be disclosed by an issuer in the reports that it files or submits under the Act is accumulated and communicated to the issuer's management, including its principal executive and principal financial officers, or persons performing similar functions, as appropriate to allow timely decisions regarding required disclosure.

(f) The term *internal control over financial reporting* is defined as a process designed by, or under the supervision of, the issuer's principal executive and principal financial officers, or persons performing similar functions, and effected by the issuer's board of directors, management and other personnel, to provide reasonable assurance regarding the reliability of financial reporting and the preparation of financial statements for external purposes in accordance with generally accepted accounting principles and includes those policies and procedures that:

(1) Pertain to the maintenance of records that in reasonable detail accurately and fairly reflect the transactions and dispositions of the assets of the issuer;

(2) Provide reasonable assurance that transactions are recorded as necessary to permit preparation of financial statements in accordance with generally accepted accounting principles, and that receipts and expenditures of the issuer are being made only in accordance with authorizations of management and directors of the issuer; and

(3) Provide reasonable assurance regarding prevention or timely detection of unauthorized acquisition, use or disposition of the issuer's assets that could have a material effect on the financial statements.

Rule 15d–16. Reports of Foreign Private Issuers on Form 6–K

(a) Every foreign private issuer which is subject to Rule 15d–1 shall make reports on Form 6–K, except that this rule shall not apply to:

(1) Investment companies required to file reports pursuant to Rule 30b1–1; or

(2) Issuers of American depositary receipts for securities of any foreign issuer; and

(3) Asset-backed issuers, as defined in § 229.1101 of this chapter.

(b) Such reports shall be transmitted promptly after the information required by Form 6–K is made public by the issuer, by the country of its domicile or under the laws of which it was incorporated or organized or by a foreign securities exchange with which the issuer has filed the information.

(c) Reports furnished pursuant to this rule shall not be deemed to be "filed" for the purpose of section 18 of the Act or otherwise subject to the liabilities of that section.

Rule 15d–17. Reports of Asset-backed Issuers on Form 10–D (§ 249.312 of this chapter).

Every asset-backed issuer subject to § 240.15d–1 shall make reports on Form 10–D (§ 249.312 of this chapter). Such reports shall be filed within the period specified in Form 10–D.

Rule 15d–18. Compliance with Servicing Criteria for Asset-backed Securities.

(a) This section applies to every class of asset-backed securities subject to the reporting requirements of section 15(d) of the Act (15 U.S.C. 78o(d)). Terms used in this section have the same meaning as in Item 1101 of Regulation AB (§ 229.1101 of this chapter).

(b) Reports on assessments of compliance with servicing criteria for asset-backed securities required. With regard to a class of asset-backed securities subject to the reporting requirements of section 15(d) of the Act, the annual report on Form 10–K (§ 249.308 of this chapter) for such class must include from each party participating in the servicing function a report regarding its assessment of compliance with the servicing criteria specified in paragraph (d) of Item 1122 of Regulation AB (§ 229.1122(d) of this chapter), as of and for the period ending the end of each fiscal year, with respect to asset-backed securities transactions taken as a whole involving the party participating in the servicing function and that are backed by the same asset type backing the class of asset-backed securities (including the asset-backed securities transaction that is to be the subject of the report on Form 10–K for that fiscal year).

(c) Attestation reports on assessments of compliance with servicing criteria for asset-backed securities required. With respect to each report included pursuant to paragraph (b) of this section, the annual report on Form 10–K must also include a report by a registered public accounting firm that attests to, and reports on, the assessment made by the asserting party. The attestation report on assessment of compliance with servicing criteria for asset-backed securities must be made in accordance with standards for attestation engagements issued or adopted by the Public Company Accounting Oversight Board.

Note to § 240.15d–18. If multiple parties are participating in the servicing function, a separate assessment report and attestation report must be included for each party participating in the servicing function. A party participating in the servicing function means any entity (e.g., master servicer, primary servicers, trustees) that is performing activities that address the criteria in paragraph (d) of Item 1122 of Regulation AB (§ 229.1122(d) of this chapter), unless such entity's activities relate only to 5% or less of the pool assets.

EXEMPTION OF CERTAIN ISSUERS FROM SECTION 15(D) OF THE ACT

Rule 15d–21. Reports for Employee Stock Purchase, Savings and Similar Plans

(a) Separate annual and other reports need not be filed pursuant to section 15(d) of the Act with respect to any employee stock purchase, savings or similar plan: *Provided*—

(1) The issuer of the stock or other securities offered to employees through their par-

ticipation in the plan files annual reports on Form 10-K and Form 10-KSB or U5S; and

(2) Such issuer furnishes, as a part of its annual report on such form or as an amendment thereto, the financial statements required by Form 11-K with respect to the plan.

(b) If the procedure permitted by this Rule is followed, the financial statements required by Form 11-K with respect to the plan shall be filed within 120 days after the end of the fiscal year of the plan, either as a part of or as an amendment to the annual report of the issuer for its last fiscal year, *Provided,* that if the fiscal year of the plan ends within 62 days prior to the end of the fiscal year of the issuer, such information, financial statements and exhibits may be furnished as a part of the issuer's next annual report. If a plan subject to the Employee Retirement Income Security Act of 1974 uses the procedure permitted by this Rule, the financial statements required by Form 11-K shall be filed within 180 days after the plan's fiscal year end.

Rule 15d-22. Reporting Regarding Asset-backed Securities under Section 15(d) of the Act.

(a) With respect to an offering of asset-backed securities registered pursuant to § 230.415(a)(1)(x) of this chapter, annual and other reports need not be filed pursuant to section 15(d) of the Act (15 U.S.C. 78o(d)) regarding any class of securities to which such registration statement relates until the first bona fide sale in a takedown of securities under the registration statement.

(b) Regarding any class of asset-backed securities in a takedown off of a registration statement pursuant to § 230.415(a)(1)(x) of this chapter, no annual and other reports need be filed pursuant to section 15(d) of the Act regarding such class of securities as to any fiscal year, other than the fiscal year within which the takedown occurred, if at the beginning of such fiscal year the securities of each class in the takedown are held of record by less than three hundred persons.

(c) Paragraph (a) or (b) of this section does not affect any other reporting obligation applicable with respect to any classes of securities from additional takedowns under the same or different registration statements or any reporting obligation that may be applicable pursuant to section 12 of the Act (15 U.S.C. 78l).

Rule 15d-23. Reporting Regarding Certain Securities Underlying Asset-backed Securities under Section 15(d) of the Act.

(a) Regarding a class of asset-backed securities, if the asset pool for the asset-backed securities includes a pool asset representing an interest in or the right to the payments or cash flows of another asset pool, then no separate annual and other reports need be filed pursuant to section 15(d) of the Act (15 U.S.C. 78o(d)) because of the separate registration of the distribution of the pool asset under the Securities Act (15 U.S.C. 77a et seq.), if the following conditions are met:

(1) Both the issuing entity for the asset-backed securities and the entity that issued the pool asset were established under the direction of the same sponsor and depositor;

(2) The pool asset was created solely to satisfy legal requirements or otherwise facilitate the structuring of the asset-backed securities transaction;

(3) The pool asset is not part of a scheme to avoid the registration or reporting requirements of the Act;

(4) The pool asset is held by the issuing entity and is a part of the asset pool for the asset-backed securities; and

(5) The offering of the asset-backed securities and the offering of the pool asset were both registered under the Securities Act (15 U.S.C. 77a et seq.).

(b) Paragraph (a) of this section does not affect any reporting obligation applicable with respect to the asset-backed securities or any other reporting obligation that may be applicable with respect to the pool asset or any other securities by the issuer of that pool asset pursuant to section 12 or 15(d) of the Act (15 U.S.C. 78l or 78o(d)).

(c) This section does not affect any obligation to provide information regarding the pool asset or the asset pool underlying the pool asset in a filing with respect to the asset-backed securities. See Item 1100(d) of Regulation AB (§ 229.1100(d) of this chapter).

(d) Terms used in this section have the same meaning as in Item 1101 of Regulation AB (§ 229.1101 of this chapter).

PENNY STOCKS

Rule 15g–1. Exemptions for Certain Transactions

The following transactions shall be exempt from Rules 15g–2, 240.15g–3, 15g–4, 240.15g–5, and 15g–6:

(a) Transactions by a broker or dealer:

(1) Whose commissions, commission equivalents, mark-ups, and mark-downs from transactions in penny stocks during each of the immediately preceding three months and during eleven or more of the preceding twelve months, or during the immediately preceding six months, did not exceed five percent of its total commissions, commission equivalents, mark-ups, and mark-downs from transactions in securities during those months; and

(2) Who has not been a market maker in the penny stock that is the subject of the transaction in the immediately preceding twelve months.

Note: Prior to April 28, 1993, commissions, commission equivalents, mark-ups, and mark-downs from transactions in designated securities, as defined in Rule 15c2–6(d)(2) as of April 15, 1992, may be considered to be commissions, commission equivalents, mark-ups, and mark-downs from transactions in penny stocks for purposes of paragraph (a)(1) of this rule.

(b) Transactions in which the customer is an institutional accredited investor, as defined in Rule 501(a) (1), (2), (3), (7), or (8).

(c) Transactions that meet the requirements of Regulation D (17 CFR 230.501–230.508), or transactions with an issuer not involving any public offering pursuant to section 4(2) of the Securities Act of 1933.

(d) Transactions in which the customer is the issuer, or a director, officer, general partner, or direct or indirect beneficial owner of more than five percent of any class of equity security of the issuer, of the penny stock that is the subject of the transaction.

(e) Transactions that are not recommended by the broker or dealer.

(f) Any other transaction or class of transactions or persons or class of persons that, upon prior written request or upon its own motion, the Commission conditionally or unconditionally exempts by order as consistent with the public interest and the protection of investors.

Rule 15g–2. Risk Disclosure Document Relating to the Penny Stock Market

(a) It shall be unlawful for a broker or dealer to effect a transaction in any penny stock for or with the account of a customer unless, prior to effecting such transaction, the broker or dealer has furnished to the customer a document containing the information set forth in Schedule 15G, 17 CFR 240.15g–100, and has obtained from the customer a manually signed and dated written acknowledgment of receipt of the document.

(b) The broker or dealer shall preserve, as part of its records, a copy of the written acknowledgment required by paragraph (a) of this section for the period specified in Rule 17a–4(b) of this chapter.

Rule 15g–3. Broker or Dealer Disclosure of Quotations and Other Information Relating to the Penny Stock Market

(a) *Requirement.* It shall be unlawful for a broker or dealer to effect a transaction in any penny stock with or for the account of a customer unless such broker or dealer discloses to such customer, within the time periods and in the manner required by paragraph (b) of this rule, the following information:

(1) The inside bid quotation and the inside offer quotation for the penny stock.

(2) If paragraph (a)(1) of this rule does not apply because of the absence of an inside bid quotation and an inside offer quotation:

(i) With respect to a transaction effected with or for a customer on a principal basis (other than as provided in paragraph (a)(2)(ii) of this rule):

(A) The dealer shall disclose its offer price for the security:

(1) If during the previous five days the dealer has effected no fewer than three *bona fide* sales to other dealers consistently at its offer price for the security current at the time of those sales, and

(2) If the dealer reasonably believes in good faith at the time of the transaction with the customer that its offer price accurately reflects the price at which it is willing to sell one or more round lots to another dealer. For purposes of paragraph (a)(2)(i)(A) of this rule, "consistently" shall constitute, at a minimum, seventy-five percent of the dealer's *bona fide* inter-dealer sales during the previous five-day period, and, if the dealer has effected only three *bona fide* inter-dealer sales during such period, all three of such sales.

(B) The dealer shall disclose its bid price for the security:

(1) If during the previous five days the dealer has effected no fewer than three *bona fide* purchases from other dealers consistently at its bid price for the security current at the time of those purchases, and

(2) If the dealer reasonably believes in good faith at the time of the transaction with the customer that its bid price accurately reflects the price at which it is willing to buy one or more round lots from another dealer. For purposes of paragraph (a)(2)(i)(B) of this rule, "consistently" shall constitute, at a minimum, seventy-five percent of the dealer's *bona fide* inter-dealer purchases during the previous five-day period, and, if the dealer has effected only three *bona fide* inter-dealer purchases during such period, all three of such purchases.

(C) If the dealer's bid or offer prices to the customer do not satisfy the criteria of paragraphs (a)(2)(i)(A) or (a)(2)(i)(B) of this rule, the dealer shall disclose to the customer:

(1) That it has not effected inter-dealer purchases or sales of the penny stock consistently at its bid or offer price, and

(2) The price at which it last purchased the penny stock from, or sold the penny stock to, respectively, another dealer in a *bona fide* transaction.

(ii) With respect to transactions effected by a broker or dealer with or for the account of the customer:

(A) On an agency basis or

(B) On a basis other than as a market maker in the security, where, after having received an order from the customer to purchase a penny stock, the dealer effects the purchase from another person to offset a contemporaneous sale of the penny stock to such customer, or, after having received an order from the customer to sell the penny stock, the dealer effects the sale to another person to offset a contemporaneous purchase from such customer, the broker or dealer shall disclose the best independent inter-dealer bid and offer prices for the penny stock that the broker or dealer obtains through reasonable diligence. A broker-dealer shall be deemed to have exercised reasonable diligence if it obtains quotations from three market makers in the security (or all known market makers if there are fewer than three).

(3) With respect to bid or offer prices and transaction prices disclosed pursuant to paragraph (a) of this rule, the broker or dealer shall disclose the number of shares to which the bid and offer prices apply.

(b) *Timing.* (1) The information described in paragraph (a) of this rule:

(i) Shall be provided to the customer orally or in writing prior to effecting any transaction with or for the customer for the purchase or sale of such penny stock; and

(ii) Shall be given or sent to the customer in writing, at or prior to the time that any written confirmation of the transaction is given or sent to the customer pursuant to Rule 10b–10 of this chapter.

(2) A broker or dealer, at the time of making the disclosure pursuant to paragraph (b)(1)(i) of this rule, shall make and preserve as part of its records, a record of such disclosure for the period specified in 17 CFR 240.17a–4(b).

(c) *Definitions.* For purposes of this section:

(1) The term *bid price* shall mean the price most recently communicated by the dealer to another broker or dealer at which the dealer is willing to purchase one or more round lots of the penny stock, and shall not include indications of interest.

(2) The term *offer price* shall mean the price most recently communicated by the dealer to another broker or dealer at which the dealer is willing to sell one or more round lots of the penny stock and shall not include indications of interest.

(3) The term *inside bid quotation* for a security shall mean the highest bid quotation for the security displayed by a market maker in the security on a Qualifying Electronic Quotation System, at any time in which at least two market makers are contemporaneously displaying on such system bid and offer quotations for the security at specified prices.

(4) The term *inside offer quotation* for a security shall mean the lowest offer quotation for the security displayed by a market maker in the security on a Qualifying Electronic Quotation System, at any time in which at least two market makers are contemporaneously displaying on such system bid and offer quotations for the security at specified prices.

(5) The term *Qualifying Electronic Quotation System* shall mean an automated inter-dealer quotation system that has the characteristics set forth in section 17B(b)(2) of the Act, or such other automated inter-dealer quotation system designated by the Commission for purposes of this rule.

Rule 15g–4. Disclosure of Compensation to Brokers or Dealers

Preliminary Note: Brokers and dealers may wish to refer to Securities Exchange Act Release No. 30608 (April 20, 1992) for a discussion of the procedures for computing compensation in active and competitive markets, inactive and competitive markets, and dominated and controlled markets.

(a) *Disclosure requirement.* It shall be unlawful for any broker or dealer to effect a transaction in any penny stock for or with the account of a customer unless such broker or dealer discloses to such customer, within the time periods and in the manner required by paragraph (b) of this rule, the aggregate amount of any compensation received by such broker or dealer in connection with such transaction.

(b) *Timing.* (1) The information described in paragraph (a) of this rule:

(i) Shall be provided to the customer orally or in writing prior to effecting any transaction with or for the customer for the purchase or sale of such penny stock; and

(ii) Shall be given or sent to the customer in writing, at or prior to the time that any written confirmation of the transaction is given or sent to the customer pursuant to Rule 10b–10.

(2) A broker or dealer, at the time of making the disclosure pursuant to paragraph (b)(1)(i) of this rule, shall make and preserve as part of the records, a record of each disclosure for the period specified in 17 CFR 240.17a–4(b).

(c) *Definition of compensation.* For purposes of this rule, *compensation* means, with respect to a transaction in a penny stock:

(1) If a broker is acting as agent for a customer, the amount of any remuneration received or to be received by it from such customer in connection with such transaction;

(2) If, after having received a buy order from a customer, a dealer other than a market maker purchased the penny stock as principal from another person to offset a contemporaneous sale to such customer or, after having received a sell order from a customer, sold the penny stock as principal to another person to offset a contemporaneous purchase from such customer, the difference between the price to the customer and such contemporaneous purchase or sale price; or

(3) If the dealer otherwise is acting as principal for its own account, the difference between the price to the customer and the prevailing market price.

(d) *"Active and competitive"* market. For purposes of this rule only, a market may be deemed to be "active and competitive" in determining the prevailing market price with respect to a transaction by a market maker in a penny stock if the aggregate number of transactions effected by such market maker in the penny stock in the five business days preceding such transaction is less than twenty percent of the aggregate number of all transactions in the penny stock reported on a Qualifying Electronic Quotation System (as defined in Rule 15g–3(c)(5)) during such five-day period. No presumption shall arise that a market is not "active and competitive" solely by reason of a market maker not meeting the conditions specified in this paragraph.

Rule 15g–5. Disclosure of Compensation of Associated Persons in Connection With Penny Stock Transactions

(a) *General.* It shall be unlawful for a broker or dealer to effect a transaction in any penny stock for or with the account of a customer unless the broker or dealer discloses to such customer, within the time periods and in the manner required by paragraph (b) of this rule, the aggregate amount of cash compensation that any associated person of the broker or dealer who is a natural person and has communicated with the customer concerning the transaction at or prior to receipt of the customer's transaction order, other than any person whose function is solely clerical or ministerial, has received or will receive from any source in connection with the transaction and that is determined at or prior to the time of the transaction, including separate disclosure, if applicable, of the source and amount of such compensation that is not paid by the broker or dealer.

(b) *Timing.* (1) The information described in paragraph (a) of this rule:

(i) Shall be provided to the customer orally or in writing prior to effecting any transaction with or for the customer for the purchase or sale of such penny stock; and

(ii) Shall be given or sent to the customer in writing at or prior to the time that any written confirmation of the transaction is given or sent to the customer pursuant to Rule 10b–10.

(2) A broker or dealer, at the time of making the disclosure pursuant to paragraph (b)(1)(i) of this rule, shall make and preserve as part of its records, a record of such disclosure for the period specified in Rule 17a–4(b).

(c) *Contingent compensation arrangements.* Where a portion or all of the cash or other compensation that the associated person may receive in connection with the transaction may be determined and paid following the transaction based on aggregate sales volume levels or other contingencies, the written disclosure required by paragraph (b)(1)(ii) of this rule shall state that fact and describe the basis upon which such compensation is determined.

Rule 15g–6. Account Statements for Penny Stock Customers

(a) *Requirement.* It shall be unlawful for any broker or dealer that has effected the sale to any customer, other than in a transaction that is exempt pursuant to Rule 15g–1, of any security that is a penny stock on the last trading day of any calendar month, or any successor of such broker or dealer, to fail to give or send to such customer a written statement containing the information described in paragraphs (c) and (d) of this rule with respect to each such month in which such security is held for the customer's account with the broker or dealer, within ten days following the end of such month.

(b) *Exemptions.* A broker or dealer shall be exempted from the requirement of paragraph (a) of this rule under either of the following circumstances:

(1) If the broker or dealer does not effect any transactions in penny stocks for or with the account of the customer during a period of six consecutive calendar months, then the broker or dealer shall not be required to provide monthly statements for each quarterly period that is immediately subsequent to such six-month period and in which the broker or dealer does not effect any transaction in penny stocks for or with the account of the customer, *provided* that the broker or dealer gives or sends to the customer written statements containing the information described in paragraphs (d) and (e) of this rule on a quarterly basis, within ten days following the end of each such quarterly period.

(2) If, on all but five or fewer trading days of any quarterly period, a security has a price of five dollars or more, the broker or dealer shall not be required to provide a monthly statement covering the security for subsequent quarterly periods, until the end of any such subsequent quarterly period on the last trading day of which the price of the security is less than five dollars.

(c) *Price determinations.* For purposes of paragraphs (a) and (b) of this rule, the price of a security on any trading day shall be determined at the close of business in accordance with the provisions of Rule 3a51–1(d)(1).

(d) *Market and price information.* The statement required by paragraph (a) of this rule shall contain at least the following information with respect to each penny stock covered by paragraph (a) of this rule, as of the last trading day of the period to which the statement relates:

(1) The identity and number of shares or units of each such security held for the customer's account; and

(2) The estimated market value of the security, to the extent that such estimated market value can be determined in accordance with the following provisions:

(i) The highest inside bid quotation for the security on the last trading day of the period to which the statement relates, multiplied by the number of shares or units of the security held for the customer's account; or

(ii) If paragraph (d)(2)(i) of this rule is not applicable because of the absence of an inside bid quotation, and if the broker or dealer furnishing the statement has effected at least ten separate Qualifying Purchases in the security during the last five trading days of the period to which the statement relates, the weighted average price per share paid by the broker or dealer in all Qualifying Purchases effected during such five-day period, multiplied by the number of shares or units of the security held for the customer's account; or

(iii) If neither of paragraphs (d)(2)(i) nor (d)(2)(ii) of this rule is applicable, a statement that there is "no estimated market value" with respect to the security.

(e) *Legend.* In addition to the information required by paragraph (d) of this rule, the written statement required by paragraph (a) of this rule shall include a conspicuous legend that is identified with the penny stocks described in the statement and that contains the following language:

> If this statement contains an estimated value, you should be aware that this value may be based on a limited number of trades or quotes. Therefore, you may not be able to sell these securities at a price equal or near to the value shown. However, the broker-dealer furnishing this statement may not refuse to accept your order to sell these securities. Also, the amount you receive from a sale generally will be reduced by the amount of any commissions or similar charges. If an estimated value is not shown for a security, a value could not be determined because of a lack of information.

(f) *Preservation of records.* Any broker or dealer subject to this rule shall preserve, as part of its records, copies of the written statements required by paragraph (a) of this rule and keep such records for the periods specified in Rule 17a–4(b).

(g) *Definitions.* For purposes of this rule:

(1) The term *Quarterly period* shall mean any period of three consecutive full calendar months.

(2) The *inside bid quotation* for a security shall mean the highest bid quotation for the security displayed by a market maker in the security on a Qualifying Electronic Quotation System, at any time in which at least two market makers are contemporaneously displaying on such system bid and offer quotations for the security at specified prices.

(3) The term *Qualifying Electronic Quotation System* shall mean an automated inter-dealer quotation system that has the characteristics set forth in Rule 17B(b)(2) of the Act, or such other automated inter-dealer quotation system designated by the Commission for purposes of this rule.

(4) The term *Qualifying Purchases* shall mean *bona fide* purchases by a broker or dealer of a penny stock for its own account, each of which involves at least 100 shares, but excluding any block purchase involving more than one percent of the outstanding shares or units of the security.

Rule 15g–8. Sales of Escrowed Securities of Blank Check Companies

As a means reasonably designed to prevent fraudulent, deceptive, or manipulative acts or practices, it shall be unlawful for any person to sell or offer to sell any security that is deposited and held in an escrow or trust account pursuant to Rule 419 under the Securities Act of 1933, or any interest in or related to such security, other than pursuant to a qualified domestic relations order as defined by the Internal Revenue Code of 1986, as amended (26 U.S.C. 1 *et seq.*), or Title I of the Employee Retirement Income Security Act (29 U.S.C. 1001 *et seq.*), or the rules thereunder.

Rule 15g–9. Sales Practice Requirements for Certain Low–Priced Securities

(a) As a means reasonably designed to prevent fraudulent, deceptive, or manipulative acts or practices, it shall be unlawful for a broker or dealer to sell a penny stock to, or to effect the purchase of a penny stock by, any person unless:

(1) the transaction is exempt under paragraph (c) of this rule; or

(2) prior to the transaction:

(i) the broker or dealer has approved the person's account for transactions in penny stocks in accordance with the procedures set forth in paragraph (b) of this rule; and

(ii) the broker or dealer has received from the person a written agreement to the transaction setting forth the identity and quantity of the penny stock to be purchased.

(b) In order to approve a person's account for transactions in penny stocks, the broker or dealer must:

(1) obtain from the person information concerning the person's financial situation, investment experience, and investment objectives;

(2) reasonably determine, based on the information required by paragraph (b)(1) of this rule and any other information known by the broker-dealer, that transactions in penny stocks are suitable for the person, and that the person (or the person's independent adviser in these transactions) has sufficient knowledge and experience in financial matters that the person (or the person's independent adviser in these transactions) reasonably may be expected to be capable of evaluating the risks of transactions in penny stocks;

(3) deliver to the person a written statement:

(i) setting forth the basis on which the broker or dealer made the determination required by paragraph (b)(2) of this rule;

(ii) stating in a highlighted format that it is unlawful for the broker or dealer to effect a transaction in a penny stock subject to the provisions of paragraph (a)(2) of this rule unless the broker or dealer has received, prior to the transaction, a written agreement to the transaction from the person; and

(iii) stating in a highlighted format immediately preceding the customer signature line that:

(A) the broker or dealer is required by this rule to provide the person with the written statement; and

(B) the person should not sign and return the written statement to the broker or dealer if it does not accurately reflect the person's financial situation, investment experience, and investment objectives; and

(4) obtain from the person a manually signed and dated copy of the written statement required by paragraph (b)(3) of this rule.

(c) For purposes of this section, the following transactions shall be exempt:

(1) Transactions that are exempt under Rules 15g–1(a), (b), (d), (e), and (f).

(2) Transactions that meet the requirements of Rule 505 or 506 (including, where applicable, the requirements of Rule 501 through Rule 503, and Rule 507 through Rule 508), or transactions with an issuer not involving any public offering pursuant to section 4(2) of the Securities Act of 1933.

(3) Transactions in which the purchaser is an established customer of the broker or dealer.

(d) For purposes of this section:

(1) The term *penny stock* shall have the same meaning as in Rule 3a51–1.

(2) The term *established customer* shall mean any person for whom the broker or dealer, or a clearing broker on behalf of such broker or dealer, carries an account, and who in such account:

(i) Has effected a securities transaction, or made a deposit of funds or securities, more than one year previously; or

(ii) Has made three purchases of penny stocks that occurred on separate days and involved different issuers.

Schedule 15G—Information to be Included in the Document Distributed Pursuant to Rule 15g–2

Securities and Exchange Commission

Washington, DC 20549

Schedule 15G

Under the Securities Exchange Act of 1934

Instructions to Schedule 15G

A. The information contained in Schedule 15G ("Schedule") must be reproduced in its entirety. No language of the document may be omitted, added to, or altered in any way. No material may be given to a customer that is intended in any way to detract from, rebut, or contradict the Schedule.

B. The document entitled "Important Information on Penny Stocks" must be distributed as the first page of Schedule 15G, and on one page only. The remainder of Schedule 15G, entitled "Further Information," explains the items discussed in the first page in greater detail.

C. The disclosures made through the Schedule are in addition to any other disclosure(s) that are required to be made under the federal securities laws, including without limitation the disclosures required pursuant to the rules adopted under Sections 15(c)(1), 15(c)(2), and 15(g) of the Securities Exchange Act of 1934 respectively.

D. The format and typeface of the document must be reproduced as presented in the Schedule. The document may be reproduced from the Schedule by photographic copying that is clear, complete, and at least satisfies the type-size requirements set forth below for printing. In the alternative, the document may be printed and must meet the following criteria regarding typeface:

1. Words appearing in capital letters in the Schedule must be reproduced in capital letters and printed in bold-face roman type at least as large as ten point modern type and at least two points leaded.

2. Words appearing in lower-case letters must be reproduced in lower-case roman type at least as large as ten point modern type and at least two points leaded.

3. Words that are underlined in the document must be underlined in reproduction and appear in bold-face roman type at least as large as ten-point modern type and at least two points leaded, and meet the criteria for lower-case or capital letters in paragraphs (1) and (2) above, whichever is applicable.

E. Recipients of the document must not be charged any fee for the document.

F. The content of the Schedule is as follows:

Important Information on Penny Stocks

This statement is required by the U.S. Securities and Exchange Commission (SEC) and contains important information on penny stocks. You are urged to read it before making a purchase or sale.

Penny stocks can be very risky.

- Penny stocks are low-priced shares of small companies not traded on an exchange or quoted on NASDAQ. Prices often are not available. Investors in penny stocks often are unable to sell stock back to the dealer that sold them the stock. Thus, you may lose your investment. Be cautious of newly issued penny stock.

- Your sales person is not an impartial advisor but is paid to sell you the stock. Do not rely only on the salesperson, but seek outside advice before you buy any stock. If you have problems with a salesperson, contact the firm's compliance officer or the regulators listed below.

Information you should get.

- *Before you buy penny stock,* federal law requires your salesperson to tell you the *"offer"* and the *"bid"* on the stock, and the *"compensation"* the salesperson and the firm receive for the trade. The firm also must mail a confirmation of these prices to you after the trade.

- You will need this price information to determine what profit, if any, you will have when you sell your stock. The offer price is the wholesale price at which the dealer is willing to sell stock to other dealers. The bid price is the wholesale price at which the dealer is willing to buy the stock from other dealers. In its trade with you, the dealer may add a retail charge to these wholesale prices as compensation (called a "markup" or "markdown").

- The difference between the bid and the offer price is the dealer's *"spread."* A spread that is large compared with the purchase price can make a resale of a stock very costly. To be profitable when you sell, the bid price of your stock must rise above the amount of this spread *and* the compensation charged by both your selling and purchasing dealers. If the dealer has no bid price, you may not be able to sell the stock after you buy it, and may lose your whole investment.

Brokers' duties and customer's rights and remedies.

- If you are a victim of fraud, you may have rights and remedies under state and federal law. You can get the disciplinary history of a salesperson or firm from the NASD at 1–800–289–9990, and additional information from your state securities official, at the North American Securities Administrators Association's central number: (202) 737–0900. You also may contact the SEC with complaints at (202) 272–7440.

Further Information

THE SECURITIES BEING SOLD TO YOU HAVE NOT BEEN APPROVED OR DISAPPROVED BY THE SECURITIES AND EXCHANGE COMMISSION. MOREOVER, THE SECURITIES AND EXCHANGE COMMISSION HAS NOT PASSED UPON THE FAIRNESS OR THE MERITS OF THIS TRANSACTION NOR UPON THE ACCURACY OR ADEQUACY OF THE INFORMATION CONTAINED IN ANY PROSPECTUS OR ANY OTHER INFORMATION PROVIDED BY AN ISSUER OR A BROKER OR DEALER.

Generally, penny stock is a security that:

- Is priced under five dollars;

- Is *not* traded on a national stock exchange or on NASDAQ (the NASD's automated quotation system for actively traded stocks);

- May be listed in the "pink sheets" or the NASD OTC Bulletin Board;

- Is issued by a company that has less than $5 million in net tangible assets and has been in business less than three years, by a company that has under $2 million in net tangible assets and has been in business for at least three years, or by a company that has revenues of $6 million for 3 years.

Use Caution When Investing in Penny Stocks

1. *Do not make a hurried investment decision.* High-pressure sales techniques can be a warning sign of fraud. The salesperson is not an impartial advisor, but is paid for selling stock to you. The salesperson also does not have to watch your investment for you. Thus, you should think over the offer and seek outside advice. Check to see if the information given by the salesperson differs from other information you may have. Also, it is illegal for salespersons to promise that a stock will increase in value or is risk-free, or to guarantee against loss. If you think there is a problem, ask to speak with a compliance official at the firm, and, if necessary, any of the regulators referred to in this statement.

2. *Study the company issuing the stock.* Be wary of companies that have no operating history, few assets, or no defined business purpose. These may be sham or "shell" corporations. Read the prospectus for the company carefully before you invest. Some dealers fraudulently solicit investors' money to buy stock in sham companies, artificially inflate

the stock prices, then cash in their profits before public investors can sell their stock.

3. *Understand the risky nature of these stocks.* You should be aware that you may lose part or all of your investment. Because of large dealer spreads, you will not be able to sell the stock immediately back to the dealer at the same price it sold the stock to you. In some cases, the stock may fall quickly in value. New companies, whose stock is sold in an "initial public offering," often are riskier investments. Try to find out if the shares the salesperson wants to sell you are part of such an offering. Your salesperson must give you a "prospectus" in an initial public offering, but the financial condition shown in the prospectus of new companies can change very quickly.

4. *Know the brokerage firm and the salespeople with whom you are dealing.* Because of the nature of the market for penny stock, you may have to rely solely on the original brokerage firm that sold you the stock for prices and to buy the stock back from you. Ask the National Association of Securities Dealers, Inc. (NASD) or your state securities regulator, which is a member of the North American Securities Administrators Association, Inc. (NASAA), about the licensing and disciplinary record of the brokerage firm and the salesperson contacting you. The telephone numbers of the NASD and NASAA are listed on the first page of this document.

5. *Be cautious if your salesperson leaves the firm.* If the salesperson who sold you the stock leaves his or her firm, the firm may reassign your account to a new salesperson. If you have problems, ask to speak to the firm's branch office manager or a compliance officer. Although the departing salesperson may ask you to transfer your stock to his or her new firm, you do not have to do so. Get information on the new firm. Be wary of requests to sell your securities when the salesperson transfers to a new firm. Also, you have the right to get your stock certificate from your selling firm. You do not have to leave the certificate with that firm or any other firm.

Your Rights

Disclosures to you. Under penalty of federal law, your brokerage firm must tell you the following information at two different times—*before* you agree to buy or sell a penny stock, and after the trade, by *written confirmation:*

• *The bid and offer price quotes for penny stock, and the number of shares to which the quoted prices apply.* The *bid* and *offer* quotes are the wholesale prices at which dealers trade among themselves. These prices give you an idea of the market value of the stock. The dealer must tell you these price quotes if they appear on an automated quotation system approved by the SEC. If not, the dealer must use its own quotes or trade prices. You should calculate the *spread*, the difference between the bid and offer quotes, to help decide if buying the stock is a good investment.

A lack of quotes may mean that the market among dealers is not active. It thus may be difficult to resell the stock. You also should be aware that the actual price charged to you for the stock may differ from the price quoted to you for 100 shares. You should therefore determine, before you agree to a purchase, what the actual sales price (before the *markup*) will be for the exact number of shares you want to buy.

• *The brokerage firm's compensation for the trade.* A *markup* is the amount a dealer adds to the wholesale offer price of the stock and a *markdown* is the amount it subtracts from the wholesale bid price of the stock as *compensation.* A markup/markdown usually serves the same role as a broker's commission on a trade. Most of the firms in the penny stock market will be dealers, not brokers.

• *The compensation received by the brokerage firm's salesperson for the trade.* The brokerage firm must disclose to you, as a total sum, the cash compensation of your salesperson for the trade that is known at the time of the trade. The firm must describe in the written confirmation the nature of any other compensation of your salesperson that is unknown at the time of the trade.

In addition to the items listed above, your brokerage firm must send to you:

• *Monthly account statements. In general, your brokerage firm must send you a monthly statement* that gives an estimate of the value of each penny stock in your account, if there is enough information to make an estimate. If the firm has not bought or sold any penny stocks for your account for six months, it can provide these statements every three months.

• *A Written Statement of Your Financial Situation and Investment Goals.* In general, unless you have had an account with your brokerage firm for more than one year, or you have previously bought three different penny stocks from that firm, your brokerage firm must send you a written statement for you to sign that accurately describes your financial situation, your investment experience, and your investment goals, and that contains a statement of why your firm decided that penny stocks are a suitable investment for you. The firm also must get your written consent to buy the penny stock.

Legal remedies. If penny stocks are sold to you in violation of your rights listed above, or other federal or state securities laws, you may be able to cancel your purchase and get your money back. If the stocks are sold in a fraudulent manner, you may be able to sue the persons and firms that caused the fraud for damages. If you have signed an arbitration agreement, however, you may have to pursue your claim through arbitration. You may wish to contact an attorney. The SEC is not authorized the represent individuals in private litigation.

However, to protect yourself and other investors, you should report any violations of your brokerage firm's duties listed above and other securities laws to the SEC, the NASD, or your state securities administrator at the telephone numbers on the first page of this document. These bodies have the power to stop fraudulent and abusive activity of salespersons and firms engaged in the securities business. Or you can write to the SEC at 450 Fifth St., NW., Washington, DC 20549; the NASD at 1735 K Street, NW., Washington, DC 20006; or NASAA at 555 New Jersey Avenue, NW., Suite 750, Washington, DC 20001. NASAA will give you the telephone number of your state's securities agency. If there is any disciplinary record of a person or a firm, the NASD, NASAA, or your state securities regulator will send you this information if you ask for it.

Market Information

The market for penny stocks. Penny stocks usually are not listed on an exchange or quoted on the NASDAQ system. Instead, they are traded between dealers on the telephone in the "over-the-counter" market. The NASD's OTC Bulletin Board also will contain information on some penny stocks. At times, however, price information for the stocks is not publicly available.

Market domination. In some cases, only one or two dealers, acting as "market makers," may be buying and selling a given stock. You should first ask if a firm is acting as a *broker* (your agent) or as a dealer. A *dealer* buys stock itself to fill your order or already owns the stock. A *market maker* is a dealer who holds itself out as ready to buy and sell stock on a regular basis. If the firm is a market maker, ask how many other market makers are dealing in the stock to see if the firm (or group of firms) dominates the market. When there are only one or two market makers, there is a risk that the dealer or group of dealers may control the market in that stock and set prices that are not based on competitive forces. In recent years, some market makers have created fraudulent markets in certain penny stocks, so that stock prices rose suddenly, but collapsed just as quickly, at a loss to investors.

Mark-ups and mark-downs. The actual price that the customer pays usually includes the mark-up or mark-down. Markups and markdowns are direct profits for the firm and its salespeople, so you should be aware of such amounts to assess the overall value of the trade.

The "spread." The difference between the bid and offer price is the spread. Like a mark-up or mark-down, the spread is another source of profit for the brokerage firm and compensates the firm for the risk of owning the stock. A large spread can make a trade very expensive to an investor. For some penny stocks, the spread between the bid and offer may be a large part of the purchase price of the stock. Where the bid price is much lower than the offer price, the market value of the stock must rise substantially before the stock can be sold at a profit. Moreover, an investor may experience substantial losses if the stock must be sold immediately.

Example: If the bid is $0.04 per share and the offer is $0.10 per share, the spread (difference) is $0.06, which appears to be a small amount. But you would lose $0.06 on every share that you bought for $0.20 if you had to sell that stock immediately to the same firm. If you had invested $5,000 at the $0.10 offer price, the market maker's repurchase price, at $0.04 bid, would be only $2,000; thus you would lose $3,000, or more than half of your investment, if you decided to sell the stock. In addition, you would have to pay compensation (a "mark-up," "mark-down," or commission) to buy and sell the stock.

In addition to the amount of the spread, the price of your stock must rise enough to make up for the compensation that the dealer charged you when it first sold you the stock. Then, when you want to resell the stock, a dealer again will charge compensation, in the form of a markdown. The dealer subtracts the markdown from the price of the stock when it buys the stock from you. Thus, to make a profit, the bid price of your stock must rise above the amount of the original spread, the markup, and the markdown.

Primary offerings. Most penny stocks are sold to the public on an ongoing basis. However, dealers sometimes sell these stocks in initial public offerings. You should pay special attention to stocks of companies that have never been offered to the public before, because the market for these stocks is untested. Because the offering is on a first-time basis, there is generally no market information about the stock to help determine its value. The federal securities laws generally require broker-dealers to give investors a "prospectus," which contains information about the objectives, management, and financial condition of the issuer. In the absence of market information, investors should read the company's prospectus with special care to find out if the stocks are a good investment. However, the prospectus is only a description of the current condition of the company. The outlook of the start-up companies described in a prospectus often is very uncertain.

For more information about penny stocks, contact the Office of Filings, Information, and Consumer Services of the U.S. Securities and Exchange Commission, 450 Fifth Street, NW., Washington, DC 20549, (202) 272-7440.

NATIONAL AND AFFILIATED SECURITIES ASSOCIATIONS

Rule 15Aa-1. Registration of a National or an Affiliated Securities Association

Any application for registration of an association as a national, or as an affiliated securities association shall be made in triplicate on Form X-15AA-1 accompanied by three copies of the exhibits prescribed by the Commission to be filed in connection therewith.

Rule 15Aj-1. Amendments and Supplements to Registration Statements of Securities Associations

Every association applying for registration or registered as a national securities association or as an affiliated securities association shall keep its registration statement up to date in the manner described below:

(a) *Amendments.* Promptly after the discovery of any inaccuracy in the registration statement or in any amendment or supplement thereto the association shall file with the Commission an amendment correcting such inaccuracy.

(b) *Current Supplements.* Promptly after any change which renders no longer accurate any information contained or incorporated in the registration statement or in any amendment or supplement thereto the association shall file with the Commission a current supplement setting forth such change, except that—

(1) Supplements setting forth changes in the information called for in Exhibit C need not be filed until 10 days after the calendar month in which the changes occur, and

(2) No current supplements need be filed with respect to changes in the information called for in Exhibit B.

(3) If changes in the information called for in Items (1) and (2) of Exhibit C are reported in any record which is published at least once a month by the association and promptly filed in triplicate with the Commission, no current supplement need be filed with respect thereto.

(c) *Annual Supplements.* (1) Promptly after March 1 of each year, the association shall file with the Commission an annual consolidated supplement as of such date on Form X–15AJ–2 (§ 249.803) except that:

(i) If the securities association publishes or cooperates in the publication of the information required in Items 6(a) and 6(b) of Form X–15AJ–2 on an annual or more frequent basis, in lieu of filing such an item the securities association may:

(A) Identify the publication in which such information is available, the name, address, and telephone number of the person from whom such publication may be obtained, and the price thereof; and

(B) Certify to the accuracy of such information as of its date.

(ii) Promptly after March 1, 1995, and every three years thereafter each association shall file complete Exhibit A to Form X–15AJ–2. The information contained in this exhibit shall be up to date as of the latest practicable date within 3 months of the date on which these exhibits are filed. If the association publishes or cooperates in the publication of the information required in this exhibit on an annual or more frequent basis, in lieu of filing such exhibit the association may:

(A) Identify the publication in which such information is available, the name, address, and telephone number of the person from whom such publication may be obtained, and the price thereof; and

(B) Certify to the accuracy of such information as of its date. If a securities association keeps the information required in this exhibit up to date and makes it available to the Commission and the public upon request, in lieu of filing such an exhibit a securities association may certify that the information is kept up to date and is available to the Commission and the public upon request.

(2) Promptly after the close of each fiscal year of the association, it shall file with the Commission a supplement setting forth its balance sheet as of the close of such year and its income and expense statement for such year.

(d) *Filing, Dating, etc.* Each amendment or supplement shall be filed in triplicate, at least one of which must be signed and attested, in the same manner as required in the case of the original registration statement, and must conform to the requirements of Form X-15AJ-1, except that the annual consolidated supplement shall be filed on Form X-15AJ-2. All amendments and supplements shall be dated and numbered in order of filing. One amendment or supplement may include any numbers of changes. In addition to the formal filing of amendments and supplements above described, each association shall send to the Commission three copies of any notices, reports, circulars, loose-leaf insertions, riders, new additions, lists, or other records of changes covered by amendments or supplements when, as, and if such records are made available to members of the association.

Rule 15Ba2-1. Application for Registration of Municipal Securities Dealers Which Are Banks or Separately Identifiable Departments or Divisions of Banks

(a) An application for registration, pursuant to Section 15B(a) of the Act, of a municipal securities dealer which is a bank (as defined in section 3(a)(6) of the Act) or a separately identifiable department or division of a bank (as defined by the Municipal Securities Rulemaking Board), shall be filed with the Commission on Form MSD, in accordance with the instructions contained therein.

(b) If the information contained in any application for registration pursuant to paragraph (a) of this rule, or in any amendment to such application, is or becomes inaccurate for any reason, applicant shall promptly file an amendment on Form MSD correcting such information.

(c) Every amendment filed pursuant to this rule shall constitute a "report" within the meaning of sections 17 and 32(a) of the Act.

Rule 15Ba2-2. Application for Registration of Non-bank Municipal Securities Dealers Whose Business Is Exclusively Intrastate

(a) An application for registration, pursuant to section 15B(a) of the Act, of a municipal securities dealer who is not subject to the requirements of Rule 15Ba2-1, that is filed on or after January 25, 1993, shall be filed with the Central Registration Depository (operated by the National Association of Securities Dealers, Inc.) on Form BD in accordance with the instructions contained therein.

(b) Every applicant shall file with its application for registration a statement that such applicant is filing for registration as an intrastate dealer in accordance with the requirements of this rule. Such statement shall be deemed a part of the application for registration.

(c) If the information contained in any application for registration filed pursuant to paragraph (a) of this rule, or in any amendment to such application, is or becomes inaccurate for any reason, the dealer shall promptly file with the Central Registration Depository an amendment on Form BD correcting such information.

(d) Every application or amendment filed with the Central Registration Depository pursuant to this section shall constitute a "report" filed with the Commission within the meaning of Sections 15(b), 15B(c), 17(a), 18(a), 32(a) (15 U.S.C. 78o(b), 78o-4(c), 78q(a), 78r(a), 78ff(a)) and other applicable provisions of the Act.

(e) *Temporary re-filing instructions.*

(1) Except as provided in paragraph (e)(3) of this section, every dealer that is registered in accordance with this section shall re-file with the Central Registration Depository, at the time the dealer submits its first amendment on or after August 16, 1999 but, in any event, no later than December 15, 1999, the following information from its current Form BD:

(i) Question 8 (if answered "Yes," the broker-dealer must also complete relevant items in Section IV of Schedule D);

(ii) Question 9 (if answered "Yes," the broker-dealer must also complete relevant items in Section IV of Schedule D);

(iii) Question 10(a) (if answered "Yes," the broker-dealer must also complete relevant items in Section V of Schedule D);

(iv) Question 10(b) (if answered "Yes," the broker-dealer must also complete relevant items in Section VI of Schedule D);

(v) Question 11 (if any item in Question 11 is answered "Yes," the broker-dealer must also complete the relevant DRP(s)); and

(vi) Schedules A and B.

(2) Every dealer that is registered in accordance with this section, at the time it refiles the information required by paragraph (e)(1) of this section, shall review, and amend as necessary, the information in Form BD that was transferred by the National Association of Securities Dealers to the Central Registration Depository prior to August 16, 1999.

(3) Every dealer that is registered in accordance with this section but that has not completed the re-filing requirements provided in paragraphs (c)(1) and (c)(2) of this section, during the period from August 16, 1999 to December 15, 1999, shall submit in paper format to the Central Registration Depository all Schedule E amendments to Form BD. A Schedule E filed pursuant to this paragraph (e)(3) shall not be deemed an "amendment" for purposes of paragraphs (e)(1) and (e)(2) of this section.

(4) The Commission, by order, may exempt any broker or dealer from the filing requirements provided in Form BD (17 CFR 249.501) and paragraphs (e)(1), (e)(2), and (e)(3) of this section under conditions that differ from the filing instructions contained in Form BD and paragraphs (e)(1), (e)(2), and (e)(3) of this section.

Rule 15Ba2-4. Registration of Successor to Registered Municipal Securities Dealer

(a) In the event that a municipal securities dealer succeeds to and continues the business of a registered municipal securities dealer, the registration of the predecessor shall be deemed to remain effective as the registration of the successor if the successor, within 30 days after such succession, files an application for registration on Form MSD, in the case of a municipal securities dealer that is a bank or a separately identifiable department or division of a bank, or Form BD, in the case of any other municipal securities dealer, and the predecessor files a notice of withdrawal from registration on Form MSDW or Form BDW, as the case may be; *Provided, however,* That the registration of the predecessor dealer will cease to be effective as the registration of the successor dealer 45 days after the application for registration on Form MSD or Form BD is filed by such successor.

(b) Notwithstanding paragraph (a) of this rule, if a municipal securities dealer succeeds to and continues the business of a registered predecessor municipal securities dealer, and the succession is based solely on a change in the predecessor's date or state of incorporation, form of organization, or composition of a partnership, the successor may, within 30 days after the succession, amend the registration of the predecessor dealer on Form MSD, in the case of a predecessor municipal securities dealer that is a bank or a separately identifiable department or division of a bank, or on Form BD, in the case of any other municipal securities dealer, to reflect these changes. This amendment shall be deemed an application for registration filed by the predecessor and adopted by the successor.

Rule 15Ba2-5. Registration of Fiduciaries

The registration of a municipal securities dealer shall be deemed to be the registration of any executor, administrator, guardian, conservator, assignee for the benefit of creditors, receiver, trustee in insolvency or bankruptcy, or other fiduciary, appointed or qualified by order, judgment, or decree of a court of competent jurisdiction to continue the business of such registered municipal securities dealer; provided, that such fiduciary files with the Commission, within 30 days after entering upon the performance of his duties, a statement setting forth as to such fiduciary substantially the information required by Form MSD, if the municipal securities dealer is a bank or a separately identifiable department of a bank, or Form BD, if the municipal securities dealer is other than a bank or a separately identifiable department or division of a bank.

Rule 15Ba2–6. [Reserved.]

Rule 15Bc3–1. Withdrawal From Registration of Municipal Securities Dealers

(a) Notice of withdrawal from registration as a municipal securities dealer pursuant to Section 15B(c) (15 U.S.C. 78o–4(c)) shall be filed on Form MSDW (17 CFR 249.1110), in the case of a municipal securities dealer which is a bank or a separately identifiable department or division of a bank, or Form BDW (17 CFR 249.501a), in the case of any other municipal securities dealer, in accordance with the instructions contained therein. Prior to filing a notice of withdrawal from registration on Form MSDW (17 CFR 249.1110) or Form BDW (17 CFR 249.501a), a municipal securities dealer shall amend Form MSD (17 CFR 249.1100) in accordance with § 240.15Ba2–1(b) or amend Form BD (17 CFR 249.501) in accordance with § 240.15Ba2–2(c) to update any inaccurate information.

(b) Every notice of withdrawal from registration as a municipal securities dealer that is filed on Form BDW (17 CFR 249.501a) shall be filed with the Central Registration Depository (operated by the National Association of Securities Dealers, Inc.) in accordance with applicable filing requirements. Every notice of withdrawal on Form MSDW (17 CFR 249.1110) shall be filed with the Commission.

(c) A notice of withdrawal from registration filed by a municipal securities dealer pursuant to Section 15B(c) (15 U.S.C. 78o–4(c)) shall become effective for all matters on the 60th day after the filing thereof with the Commission, within such longer period of time as to which such municipal securities dealer consents or which the Commission by order may determine as necessary or appropriate in the public interest or for the protection of investors, or within such shorter period of time as the Commission may determine. If a notice of withdrawal from registration is filed with the Commission at any time subsequent to the date of the issuance of a Commission order instituting proceedings pursuant to Section 15B(c) (15 U.S.C. 78o–4(c)) to censure, place limitations on the activities, functions or operations of, or suspend or revoke the registration of, such municipal securities dealer, or if prior to the effective date of the notice of withdrawal pursuant to this paragraph (c), the Commission institutes such a proceeding or a proceeding to impose terms or conditions upon such withdrawal, the notice of withdrawal shall not become effective pursuant to this paragraph (c) except at such time and upon such terms and conditions as the Commission deems necessary or appropriate in the public interest or for the protection of investors.

(d) Every notice of withdrawal filed with the Central Registration Depository pursuant to this section shall constitute a "report" filed with the Commission within the meaning of Sections 15B(c), 17(a), 18(a), 32(a) (15 U.S.C. 78o–4(c), 78q(a), 78r(a), 78ff(a)) and other applicable provisions of the Act.

(e) The Commission, by order, may exempt any broker or dealer from the filing requirements provided in Form BDW (17 CFR 249.501a) under conditions that differ from the filing instructions contained in Form BDW.

Rule 15Bc7-1. Availability of Examination Reports

(a) Upon written request, copies of any report of an examination of a municipal securities dealer made by the Commission or furnished to it by an appropriate regulatory agency pursuant to Section 17(c)(3) of the Act or by a registered securities association pursuant to Section 15B(c)(7)(B) of the Act shall be made available to the Municipal Securities Rulemaking Board (the "Board") by the Commission within thirty days after receiving such report, subject to the following limitations:

(1) The Board shall establish by rule and shall maintain adequate procedures for ensuring the confidentiality of any information made available to it by the Commission pursuant to Section 15B(c)(7)(B) of the Act;

(2) Information made available to the Board shall not identify any municipal securities broker, municipal securities dealer, or associated person that is the subject of a non-public examination report.

(b) If information to be made available to the Board is furnished to the Commission on a separate form prepared by an appropriate regulatory agency other than the Commission or by a registered securities association, that form, rather than a copy of any report of an examination, will be made available to the Board, provided that the conditions set forth in this paragraph are satisfied. Within sixty days of every six month period ending May 31 and November 30, each appropriate regulatory agency or registered securities association making available information on a separate form shall furnish to the Commission two copies of a form containing the information set forth in paragraphs (b)(1) through (b)(8) of this rule. The Commission shall make one copy of the form promptly available to the Board. Copies of any forms furnished pursuant to this paragraph shall not identify any municipal securities broker, municipal securities dealer, or associated person that is the subject of an examination from which information was derived for the form; however, the Commission may obtain for its own use, upon request, the identity of any such examinee or the full examination reports. Furnished forms shall include the following information:

(1) The report period.

(2)(i) With respect to a registered securities association, the number of examinations that formed the basis of the report and, of these examinations, the number that were routine, special, and financial/operational. (ii) With respect to an appropriate regulatory agency that is a bank agency, the number of examinations that formed the basis of the report and, of these examinations, the number that were routine, special, and financial/operational. The number of examinations that formed the basis of the report of bank dealers and the number of examinations of separately identifiable departments or divisions of banks effecting municipal securities transactions.

(3) Indications of the violations of each Board rule found in examinations that formed the basis for the report.

(4) Copies of public notices issued during the report period of any formal actions and non-public information regarding any actions taken on violations of Board rules.

(5) Any comments concerning any questionable practices relating to municipal securities activities, whether or not covered by provisions of the Act and the rules and regulations thereunder, including the rules of the Board.

(6) Descriptions of any significant or recurring customer complaints relating to municipal securities activities received by the appropriate regulatory agency or registered securities association during the report period or by municipal securities dealers during the 12 month period preceding the examination.

(7) Description of any novel issues or interpretations arising under the Board's rules.

(8) Description of any changes to existing Board rules or additional rules that would improve the regulatory scheme for municipal securities professionals or assist in the enforcement of the Board's rules.

(c) Copies of any report of an examination of a municipal securities broker or municipal securities dealer made by the Commission or furnished to it pursuant to Section 15B(c)(7)(B) or Section 17(c)(3) of the Act, or separate forms made available to the Commission pursuant to paragraph (b) of this section, will be maintained in a non-public file.

REGISTRATION OF GOVERNMENT SECURITIES BROKERS AND GOVERNMENT SECURITIES DEALERS

Rule 15Ca1–1. Notice of Government Securities Broker-Dealer Activities

(a) Every government securities broker or government securities dealer that is a broker or dealer registered pursuant to sections 15 or 15B of the Act (other than a financial institution as defined in section 3(a)(46) of the Act) shall file with the Commission written notice on Form BD (§ 249.501 of this chapter) in accordance with the instructions contained therein that it is a government securities broker or government securities dealer. After July 25, 1987, every broker or dealer subject to this paragraph shall file notice that it is a government securities broker or government securities dealer prior to or on the date it begins acting as a government securities broker or government securities dealer.

(b) Every government securities broker or government securities dealer required to file notice under paragraph (a) of this section shall file with the Commission written notice on Form BD in accordance with the instructions contained therein when it ceases to be a government securities broker or government securities dealer. Notice shall be filed within 30 days after the date the broker or dealer has ceased acting as a government securities broker or government securities dealer.

(c) Any notice required pursuant to this section shall be considered filed with the Commission if it is filed with the Central Registration Depository (operated by the National Association of Securities Dealers, Inc.) in accordance with applicable filing requirements.

Rule 15Ca2–1. Application for Registration as a Government Securities Broker or Government Securities Dealer

(a) An application for registration pursuant to section 15C(a)(1)(A) of the Act, of a government securities broker or a government securities dealer that is filed on or after January 25, 1993, shall be filed with the Central Registration Depository (operated by the National Association of Securities Dealers, Inc.) on Form BD in accordance with the instructions contained therein.

(b) Every application or amendment filed pursuant to this rule shall constitute a "report" filed with the Commission within the meaning of Sections 15, 15C, 17(a), 18, 32(a), and other applicable provisions of the Act.

(c) *Temporary Re-Filing Instructions.*

(1) Except as provided in paragraph (c)(3) of this section, every registered government securities broker or government securities dealer shall re-file with the Central Registration Depository, at the time the broker or dealer submits its first amendment on or after August 16, 1999 but, in any event, no later than December 15, 1999, the following information from its current Form BD:

(i) Question 8 (if answered "Yes," the broker-dealer must also complete relevant items in Section IV of Schedule D);

(ii) Question 9 (if answered "Yes," the broker-dealer must also complete relevant items in Section IV of Schedule D);

(iii) Question 10(a) (if answered "Yes," the broker-dealer must also complete relevant items in Section V of Schedule D);

(iv) Question 10(b) (if answered "Yes," the broker-dealer must also complete relevant items in Section VI of Schedule D);

(v) Question 11 (if any item in Question 11 is answered "Yes," the broker-dealer must also complete the relevant DRP(s)); and

(vi) Schedules A and B.

(2) Every registered government securities broker or dealer, at the time it re-files the information required by paragraph (c)(1) of this section, shall review, and amend as necessary, the information in Form BD that was transferred by the National Association of Securities Dealers to the Central Registration Depository prior to August 16, 1999.

(3) Every registered government securities broker or government securities dealer that has not completed the re-filing requirements provided in paragraphs (c)(1) and (c)(2) of this section, during the period from August 16, 1999 to December 15, 1999, shall submit in paper format to the Central Registration Depository all Schedule E amendments to Form BD. A Schedule E filed pursuant to this paragraph (c)(3) shall not be deemed an "amendment" for purposes of paragraphs (c)(1) and (c)(2) of this section.

(4) The Commission, by order, may exempt any broker or dealer from the filing requirements provided in Form BD (17 CFR 249.501) and paragraphs (c)(1), (c)(2), and (c)(3) of this section under conditions that differ from the filing instructions contained in Form BD and paragraphs (c)(1), (c)(2), and (c)(3) of this section.

Rule 15Ca2–2. [Removed and Reserved.]

Rule 15Ca2–3. Registration of Successor to Registered Government Securities Broker or Government Securities Dealer

(a) In the event that a government securities broker or government securities dealer succeeds to and continues the business of a government securities broker or government securities dealer registered pursuant to section 15C(a)(1)(A) of the Act, the registration of the predecessor shall be deemed to remain effective as the registration of the successor if the successor, within 30 days after such succession, files an application for registration on Form BD, and the predecessor files a notice of withdrawal from registration on Form BDW; *Provided, however,* That the registration of the predecessor government securities broker or government securities dealer will cease to be effective as the registration of the successor government securities broker or government securities dealer 45 days after the application for registration on Form BD is filed by such successor.

(b) Notwithstanding paragraph (a) of this rule, if a government securities broker or government securities dealer succeeds to and continues the business of a predecessor government securities broker or government securities dealer that is registered pursuant to section 15C(a)(1)(A) of the Act, and the succession is based solely on a change in the predecessor's date or state of incorporation, form of organization, or composition of a partnership, the successor may, within 30 days after the succession, amend the registration of the predecessor broker or dealer on Form BD of the predecessor to reflect these changes. This amendment shall be deemed an application for registration filed by the predecessor and adopted by the successor.

Rule 15Ca2–4. Registration of Fiduciaries

The registration of a government securities broker or government securities dealer pursuant to section 15C of the Act shall be deemed to be the registration of any executor, administrator, guardian, conservator, assignee for the benefit of creditors, receiver, trustee in insolvency or bankruptcy, or other fiduciary, appointed or qualified by order, judgment, or decree of a court of competent jurisdiction to continue the business of such registered government securities broker or government securities dealer, provided that such fiduciary files with the Commission, no more than 30 days after entering upon the performance of its duties, a statement setting forth as to such fiduciary substantially the information required by Form BD.

Rule 15Ca2-5. Consent to Service of Process to Be Furnished by Non-resident Government Securities Brokers or Government Securities Dealers and by Non-resident General Partners or Managing Agents of Government Securities Brokers or Government Securities Dealers

(a) Each non-resident government securities broker or government securities dealer applying for registration pursuant to section 15C(a)(1)(A) of the Act, each non-resident general partner of a government securities broker or government securities dealer partnership that is applying for such registration, and each non-resident managing agent of any other unincorporated government securities broker or government securities dealer that is applying for registration, shall furnish to the Commission, in a form acceptable to the Commission, a written irrevocable consent and power of attorney that (1) designates the Securities and Exchange Commission as an agent of such government securities broker or government securities dealer upon whom may be served any process, pleadings, or other papers in any civil suit or action brought in any appropriate court in any place subject to the jurisdiction of the United States, with respect to any cause of action (i) that accrues during the period beginning when such government securities broker or government securities dealer becomes registered pursuant to section 15C(a)(1)(A) of the Act and ending either when such registration is cancelled or revoked, or when a notice filed by such government securities broker or government securities dealer to withdraw from such registration becomes effective, whichever is earlier, (ii) that arises out of any activity, in any place subject to the jurisdiction of the United States, occurring in connection with the conduct of the business of such government securities broker or government securities dealer, and (iii) that is founded, directly or indirectly, upon the Securities Act of 1933, the Securities Exchange Act of 1934, the Trust Indenture Act of 1939, the Investment Company Act of 1940, the Investment Advisers Act of 1940, or any rule or regulation under any of those Acts, and (2) stipulates and agrees that any such civil suit or action may be commenced against such government securities broker or government securities dealer by the service of process upon the Commission and the forwarding of a copy thereof as provided in paragraph (c) of this rule and that the service as aforesaid of any such process, pleadings, or other papers upon the Commission shall be taken and held in all courts to be as valid and binding as if due personal service thereof had been made.

(b) Each government securities broker or government securities dealer registered pursuant to section 15C(a)(1)(A) of the Act that becomes a non-resident government securities broker or government securities dealer, and each general partner or managing agent of an unincorporated government securities broker or government securities dealer registered or applying for registration pursuant to section 15C(a)(1)(A) of the Act who becomes a non-resident after such registration or filing of an application for such registration, shall furnish such consent and power of attorney no more than 30 days thereafter.

(c) Service of any process, pleadings or other papers on the Commission under this rule shall be made by delivering the requisite number of copies thereof to the Secretary of the Commission or to such other person as the Commission may authorize to act in its behalf. Whenever any process, pleadings, or other papers as aforesaid are served upon the Commission, it shall promptly forward a copy thereof by registered or certified mail to the appropriate defendants at their last address of record filed with the Commission; but any failure by the Commission to forward such a copy shall have no effect on the validity of the service made upon the Commission. The Commission shall be furnished a sufficient number of copies for such purpose, and one copy for its file.

(d) For purposes of this rule the following definitions shall apply:

(1) The term "managing agent" shall mean any person, including a trustee, who directs or manages or who participates in the directing or managing of the affairs of any unincorporated organization or association that is not a partnership.

(2) The term "non-resident government securities broker or government securities dealer" shall mean (i) in the case of an individual, one who is domiciled in or has his principal place of business in any place not subject to the jurisdiction of the United States, (ii) in the case of a corporation, one incorporated in or having its principal place of business in any place not subject to the jurisdiction of the United States; (iii) in the case of a partnership or other unincorporated organization or association, one having its principal place of business in any place not subject to the jurisdiction of the United States.

(3) A general partner or managing agent of a government securities broker or government securities dealer shall be deemed to be a non-resident if he is domiciled in any place not subject to the jurisdiction of the United States.

Rule 15Cc1–1. Withdrawal From Registration of Government Securities Brokers or Government Securities Dealers

(a) Notice of withdrawal from registration as a government securities broker or government securities dealer pursuant to Section 15C(a)(1)(A) of the Act (15 U.S.C. 78o–5(a)(1)(A)) shall be filed on Form BDW (17 CFR 249.501a) in accordance with the instructions contained therein. Every notice of withdrawal from registration as a government securities broker or dealer shall be filed with the Central Registration Depository (operated by the National Association of Securities Dealers, Inc.) in accordance with applicable filing requirements. Prior to filing a notice of withdrawal from registration on Form BDW (17 CFR 249.501a), a government securities broker or government securities dealer shall amend Form BD (17 CFR 249.501) in accordance with 17 CFR 400.5(a) to update any inaccurate information.

(b) A notice of withdrawal from registration filed by a government securities broker or government securities dealer shall become effective for all matters on the 60th day after the filing thereof with the Commission, within such longer period of time as to which such government securities broker or government securities dealer consents or the Commission by order may determine as necessary or appropriate in the public interest or for the protection of investors, or within such shorter period of time as the Commission may determine. If a notice of withdrawal from registration is filed with the Commission at any time subsequent to the date of the issuance of a Commission order instituting proceedings pursuant to Section 15C(c) (15 U.S.C. 78o–5(c)) to censure, place limitations on the activities, functions or operations of, or suspend or revoke the registration of such government securities broker or government securities dealer, or if prior to the effective date of the notice of withdrawal pursuant to this paragraph (b), the Commission institutes such a proceeding or a proceeding to impose terms or conditions upon such withdrawal, the notice of withdrawal shall not become effective pursuant to this paragraph (b) except at such time and upon such terms and conditions as the Commission deems necessary or appropriate in the public interest or for the protection of investors.

(c) Every notice of withdrawal filed with the Central Registration Depository pursuant to this section shall constitute a "report" filed with the Commission within the meaning of Sections 15(b), 15C(c), 17(a), 18(a), 32(a) (15 U.S.C. 78o(b), 78o–5(c), 78q(a), 78r(a), 78ff(a)) and other applicable provisions of the Act.

(d) The Commission, by order, may exempt any broker or dealer from the filing requirements provided in Form BDW (17 CFR 249.501a) under conditions that differ from the filing instructions contained in Form BDW.

REPORTS OF DIRECTORS, OFFICERS, AND PRINCIPAL SHAREHOLDERS

Rule 16a–1. Definition of Terms

Terms defined in this Rule shall apply solely to Section 16 of the Act and the rules thereunder. These terms shall not be limited to Section 16(a) of the Act but also shall apply to all other subsections under Section 16 of the Act.

(a) The term "beneficial owner" shall have the following applications:

(1) Solely for purposes of determining whether a person is a beneficial owner of more than ten percent of any class of equity securities registered pursuant to Section 12 of the Act, the term "beneficial owner" shall mean any person who is deemed a beneficial owner pursuant to Section 13(d) of the Act and the rules thereunder; *provided, however,* that the following institutions or persons shall not be deemed the beneficial owner of securities of such class held for the benefit of third parties or in customer or fiduciary accounts in the ordinary course of business (or in the case of an employee benefit plan specified in subparagraph (vi) below, of securities of such class allocated to plan participants where participants have voting power) as long as such shares are acquired by such institutions or persons without the purpose or effect of changing or influencing control of the issuer or engaging in any arrangement subject to Rule 13d–3(b):

(i) A broker or dealer registered under section 15 of the Act (15 U.S.C. 78o);

(ii) A bank as defined in section 3(a)(6) of the Act (15 U.S.C. 78c);

(iii) An insurance company as defined in section 3(a)(19) of the Act (15 U.S.C. 78c);

(iv) An investment company registered under section 8 of the Investment Company Act of 1940 (15 U.S.C. 80a–8);

(v) Any person registered as an investment adviser under Section 203 of the Investment Advisers Act of 1940 (15 U.S.C. 80b–3) or under the laws of any state;

(vi) An employee benefit plan as defined in Section 3(3) of the Employee Retirement Income Security Act of 1974, as amended, 29 U.S.C. 1001 et seq. ("ERISA") that is subject to the provisions of ERISA, or any such plan that is not subject to ERISA that is maintained primarily for the benefit of the employees of a state or local government or instrumentality, or an endowment fund;

(vii) A parent holding company or control person, provided the aggregate amount held directly by the parent or control person, and directly and indirectly by their subsidiaries or affiliates that are not persons specified in paragraphs (a)(1)(i) through (ix), does not exceed one percent of the securities of the subject class;

(viii) A savings association as defined in Section 3(b) of the Federal Deposit Insurance Act (12 U.S.C. 1813);

(ix) A church plan that is excluded from the definition of an investment company under section 3(c)(14) of the Investment Company Act of 1940 (15 U.S.C. 80a–3); and

(x) A group, provided that all the members are persons specified in § 240.16a–1(a)(1)(i) through (ix).

(xi) A group, provided that all the members are persons specified in Rule 16a–1(a)(1)(i) through (vii).

Note to paragraph (a). Pursuant to this rule, a person deemed a beneficial owner of more than ten percent of any class of equity securities registered under Section 12 of the

Act would file a Form 3, but the securities holdings disclosed on Form 3, and changes in beneficial ownership reported on subsequent Form 4 or 5, would be determined by the definition of "beneficial owner" in paragraph (a)(2) of this rule.

(2) Other than for purposes of determining whether a person is a beneficial owner of more than ten percent of any class of equity securities registered under Section 12 of the Act, the term "beneficial owner" shall mean any person who, directly or indirectly, through any contract, arrangement, understanding, relationship or otherwise, has or shares a direct or indirect pecuniary interest in the equity securities, subject to the following:

(i) The term "pecuniary interest" in any class of equity securities shall mean the opportunity, directly or indirectly, to profit or share in any profit derived from a transaction in the subject securities.

(ii) The term "indirect pecuniary interest" in any class of equity securities shall include, but not be limited to:

(A) securities held by members of a person's immediate family sharing the same household; *provided, however,* that the presumption of such beneficial ownership may be rebutted; see also Rule 16a–1(a)(4);

(B) a general partner's proportionate interest in the portfolio securities held by a general or limited partnership. The general partner's proportionate interest, as evidenced by the partnership agreement in effect at the time of the transaction and the partnership's most recent financial statements, shall be the greater of:

(*1*) the general partner's share of the partnership's profits, including profits attributed to any limited partnership interests held by the general partner and any other interests in profits that arise from the purchase and sale of the partnership's portfolio securities; or

(*2*) the general partner's share of the partnership capital account, including the share attributable to any limited partnership interest held by the general partner.

(C) a performance-related fee, other than an asset-based fee, received by any broker, dealer, bank, insurance company, investment company, investment adviser, investment manager, trustee or person or entity performing a similar function; *provided, however,* that no pecuniary interest shall be present where:

(*1*) the performance-related fee, regardless of when payable, is calculated based upon net capital gains and/or net capital appreciation generated from the portfolio or from the fiduciary's overall performance over a period of one year or more; and

(*2*) equity securities of the issuer do not account for more than ten percent of the market value of the portfolio. A right to a nonperformance-related fee alone shall not represent a pecuniary interest in the securities;

(D) a person's right to dividends that is separated or separable from the underlying securities. Otherwise, a right to dividends alone shall not represent a pecuniary interest in the securities;

(E) a person's interest in securities held by a trust, as specified in Rule 16a–8(b); and

(F) a person's right to acquire equity securities through the exercise or conversion of any derivative security, whether or not presently exercisable.

(iii) A shareholder shall not be deemed to have a pecuniary interest in the portfolio securities held by a corporation or similar entity in which the person owns securities if the shareholder is not a controlling shareholder of the entity and does not have or share investment control over the entity's portfolio.

(3) Where more than one person subject to Section 16 of the Act is deemed to be a beneficial owner of the same equity securities, all such persons must report as beneficial owners of the securities, either separately or jointly, as provided in § 240.16a–3(j). In such cases, the amount of short-swing profit recoverable shall not be increased above the amount recoverable if there were only one beneficial owner.

(4) Any person filing a statement pursuant to Section 16(a) of the Act may state that the filing shall not be deemed an admission that such person is, for purposes of Section 16 of the Act or otherwise, the beneficial owner of any equity securities covered by the statement.

(5) The following interests are deemed not to confer beneficial ownership for purposes of Section 16 of the Act:

(i) Interests in portfolio securities held by any holding company registered under the Public Utility Holding Company Act of 1935 (15 U.S.C. § 79a *et seq.*);

(ii) Interests in portfolio securities held by any investment company registered under the Investment Company Act of 1940; and

(iii) Interests in securities comprising part of a broad-based, publicly traded market basket or index of stocks, approved for trading by the appropriate federal governmental authority.

(b) The term "call equivalent position" shall mean a derivative security position that increases in value as the value of the underlying equity increases, including, but not limited to, a long convertible security, a long call option, and a short put option position.

(c) The term "derivative securities" shall mean any option, warrant, convertible security, stock appreciation right, or similar right with an exercise or conversion privilege at a price related to an equity security, or similar securities with a value derived from the value of an equity security, but shall not include:

(1) rights of a pledgee of securities to sell the pledged securities;

(2) rights of all holders of a class of securities of an issuer to receive securities pro rata, or obligations to dispose of securities, as a result of a merger, exchange offer, or consolidation involving the issuer of the securities;

(3) rights or obligations to surrender a security, or have a security withheld, upon the receipt or exercise of a derivative security or the receipt or vesting of equity securities, in order to satisfy the exercise price or the tax withholding consequences of receipt, exercise or vesting;

(4) interests in broad-based index options, broad-based index futures, and broad-based publicly traded market baskets of stocks approved for trading by the appropriate federal governmental authority;

(5) interests or rights to participate in employee benefit plans of the issuer;

(6) rights with an exercise or conversion privilege at a price that is not fixed; or

(7) options granted to an underwriter in a registered public offering for the purpose of satisfying over-allotments in such offering.

(d) The term "equity security of such issuer" shall mean any equity security or derivative security relating to an issuer, whether or not issued by that issuer.

(e) The term "immediate family" shall mean any child, stepchild, grandchild, parent, stepparent, grandparent, spouse, sibling, mother-in-law, father-in-law, son-in-law, daughter-in-law, brother-in-law, or sister-in-law, and shall include adoptive relationships.

(f) The term "officer" shall mean an issuer's president, principal financial officer, principal accounting officer (or, if there is no such accounting officer, the controller), any vice-president of the issuer in charge of a principal business unit, division or function (such as sales, administration or finance), any other officer who performs a policy-making function, or any other person who performs similar policy-making functions for the issuer. Officers of the issuer's parent(s) or subsidiaries shall be deemed officers of the issuer if they perform such policy-making functions for the issuer. In addition, when the issuer is a limited partnership, officers or employees of the general partner(s) who perform policy-making functions for the limited partnership are deemed officers of the limited partnership. When the issuer is a trust, officers or employees of the trustee(s) who perform policy-making functions for the trust are deemed officers of the trust.

Note: "Policy-making function" is not intended to include policy-making functions that are not significant. If pursuant to Item 401(b) of Regulation S–K the issuer identifies a person as an "executive officer," it is presumed that the Board of Directors has made that judgment and that the persons so identified are the officers for purposes of Section 16 of the Act, as are such other persons enumerated in this paragraph (f) but not in Item 401(b).

(g) The term "portfolio securities" shall mean all securities owned by an entity, other than securities issued by the entity.

(h) The term "put equivalent position" shall mean a derivative security position that increases in value as the value of the underlying equity decreases, including, but not limited to, a long put option and a short call option position.

Rule 16a–2. Persons and Transactions Subject to Section 16

Any person who is the beneficial owner, directly or indirectly, of more than ten percent of any class of equity securities ("ten percent beneficial owner") registered pursuant to section 12 of the Act (15 U.S.C. 78*l*), any director or officer of the issuer of such securities, and any person specified in section 17(a) of the Public Utility Holding Company Act of 1935 (15 U.S.C. 79q(a)) or section 30(h) of the Investment Company Act of 1940 (15 U.S.C. 80a–29(h)), including any person specified in § 240.16a–8, shall be subject to the provisions of section 16 of the Act (15 U.S.C. 78p).

(a) A transaction(s) carried out by a director or officer in the six months prior to the director or officer becoming subject to Section 16 of the Act shall be subject to Section 16 of the Act and reported on the first required Form 4 only if the transaction(s) occurred within six months of the transaction giving rise to the Form 4 filing obligation and the director or officer became subject to Section 16 of the Act solely as a result of the issuer registering a class of equity securities pursuant to Section 12 of the Act.

(b) A transaction(s) following the cessation of director or officer status shall be subject to Section 16 of the Act only if:

(1) Executed within a period of less than six months of an opposite transaction subject to Section 16(b) of the Act that occurred while that person was a director or officer; and

(2) Not otherwise exempted from Section 16(b) of the Act pursuant to the provisions of this chapter.

Note to Paragraph (b): For purposes of this paragraph, an acquisition and a disposition each shall be an opposite transaction with respect to the other.

(c) The transaction that results in a person becoming a ten percent beneficial owner is not subject to Section 16 of the Act unless the person otherwise is subject to Section 16 of the Act. A ten percent beneficial owner not otherwise subject to Section 16 of the Act must report only those transactions conducted while the beneficial owner of more than ten percent of a class of equity securities of the issuer registered pursuant to Section 12 of the Act.

(d)(1) Transactions by a person or entity shall be exempt from the provisions of Section 16 of the Act for the 12 months following appointment and qualification, to the extent such person or entity is acting as:

(i) Executor or administrator of the estate of a decedent;

(ii) Guardian or member of a committee for an incompetent;

(iii) Receiver, trustee in bankruptcy, assignee for the benefit of creditors, conservator, liquidating agent, or other similar person duly authorized by law to administer the estate or assets of another person; or

(iv) Fiduciary in a similar capacity.

(2) Transactions by such person or entity acting in a capacity specified in paragraph (d)(1) of this section after the period specified in that paragraph shall be subject to Section 16 of the Act only where the estate, trust or other entity is a beneficial owner of more than ten percent of any class of equity security registered pursuant to Section 12 of the Act.

Rule 16a–3. Reporting Transactions and Holdings

(a) Initial statements of beneficial ownership of equity securities required by Section 16(a) of the Act shall be filed on Form 3. Statements of changes in beneficial ownership required by that Section shall be filed on Form 4. Annual statements shall be filed on Form 5. At the election of the reporting person, any transaction required to be reported on Form 5 may be reported on an earlier filed Form 4. All such statements shall be prepared and filed in accordance with the requirements of the applicable form.

(b) A person filing statements pursuant to Section 16(a) of the Act with respect to any class of equity securities registered pursuant to Section 12 of the Act need not file an additional statement on Form 3:

(1) When an additional class of equity securities of the same issuer becomes registered pursuant to Section 12 of the Act; or

(2) When such person assumes a different or an additional relationship to the same issuer (for example, when an officer becomes a director).

(c) Any issuer that has equity securities listed on more than one national securities exchange may designate one exchange as the only exchange with which reports pursuant to Section 16(a) of the Act need be filed. Such designation shall be made in writing and shall be filed with the Commission and with each national securities exchange on which any equity security of the issuer is listed at the time of such election. The reporting person's obligation to file reports with each national securities exchange on which any equity security of the issuer is listed shall be satisfied by filing with the exchange so designated.

(d) Any person required to file a statement with respect to securities of a single issuer under both section 16(a) of the Act (15 U.S.C. 78p(a)) and either section 17(a) of the Public Utility Holding Company Act of 1935 (15 U.S.C. 79q(a)) or section 30(h) of the Investment Company Act of 1940 (15 U.S.C. 80a–29(h)) may file a single statement containing the required information, which will be deemed to be filed under both Acts.

(e) Any person required to file a statement under Section 16(a) of the Act shall, not later than the time the statement is transmitted for filing with the Commission, send or deliver a duplicate to the person designated by the issuer to receive such statements, or, in the absence of such a designation, to the issuer's corporate secretary or person performing equivalent functions.

(f)(1) A Form 5 shall be filed by every person who at any time during the issuer's fiscal year was subject to Section 16 of the Act with respect to such issuer, except as provided in paragraph (2) below. The Form shall be filed within 45 days after the issuer's fiscal year end, and shall disclose the following holdings and transactions not reported previously on Forms 3, 4 or 5:

(i) All transactions during the most recent fiscal year that were exempt from Section 16(b) of the Act, except:

(A) Exercises and conversions of derivative securities exempt under either § 240.16b–3 or § 240.16b–6(b), and any transaction exempt under § 240.16b–3(d), § 240.16b–3(e), or § 240.16b–3(f) (these are required to be reported on Form 4);

(B) Transactions exempt from Section 16(b) of the Act pursuant to § 240.16b–3(c), which shall be exempt from Section 16(a) of the Act; and

(C) Transactions exempt from Section 16(a) of the Act pursuant to another rule;

(ii) Transactions that constituted small acquisitions pursuant to § 240.16a–6(a);

(iii) all holdings and transactions that should have been reported during the most recent fiscal year, but were not; and

(iv) with respect to the first Form 5 requirement for a reporting person, all holdings and transactions that should have been reported in each of the issuer's last two fiscal years but were not, based on the reporting person's reasonable belief in good faith in the completeness and accuracy of the information.

(2) Notwithstanding the above, no Form 5 shall be required where all transactions otherwise required to be reported on the Form 5 have been reported before the due date of the Form 5.

Note: Persons no longer subject to Section 16 of the Act, but who were subject to the Section at any time during the issuer's fiscal year, must file a Form 5 unless paragraph (f)(2) is satisfied. *See also* Rule 16a–2(b) regarding the reporting obligations of persons ceasing to be officers or directors.

(g)(1) A Form 4 must be filed to report: All transactions not exempt from section 16(b) of the Act; All transactions exempt from section 16(b) of the Act pursuant to § 240.16b–3(d), § 240.16b–3(e), or § 240.16b–(f); and all exercises and conversions of derivative securities, regardless of whether exempt from section 16(b) of the Act. Form 4 must be filed before the end of the second business day following the day on which the subject transaction has been executed.

(2) Solely for purposes of section 16(a)(2)(C) of the Act and paragraph (g)(1) of this section, the date on which the executing broker, dealer or plan administrator notifies the reporting person of the execution of the transaction is deemed the date of execution for a transaction where the following conditions are satisfied:

(i) the transaction is pursuant to a contract, instruction or written plan for the purchase or sale of equity securities of the issuer (as defined in § 16a–1(d)) that satisfies the affirmative defense conditions of § 240.10b5–1(c) of this chapter; and

(ii) the reporting person does not select the date of execution.

(3) Solely for purposes of section 16(a)(2)(C) of the Act and paragraph (g)(1) of this section, the date on which the plan administrator notifies the reporting person that the transaction has been executed is deemed the date of execution for a discretionary transaction (as defined in § 16b–3(b)(1)) for which the reporting person does not select the date of execution.

(4) In the case of the transactions described in paragraphs (g)(2) and (g)(3) of this section, if the notification date is later than the third business day following the trade date of the transaction, the date of execution is deemed to be the third business day following the trade date of the transaction.

(5) At the option of the reporting person, transactions that are reportable on Form 5 may be reported on Form 4, so long as the Form 4 is filed no later than the due date of the Form 5 on which the transaction is otherwise required to be reported.

(h) The date of filing with the Commission shall be the date of receipt by the Commission.

(i) *Signatures.* Where Section 16 of the Act, or the rules or forms thereunder, require a document filed with or furnished to the Commission to be signed, such document shall be manually signed, or signed using either typed signatures or duplicated or facsimile versions of manual signatures. Where typed, duplicated or facsimile signatures are used, each signatory to the filing shall manually sign a signature page or other document authenticating, acknowledging or otherwise adopting his or her signature that appears in the filing. Such document shall be executed before or at the time the filing is made and shall be retained by the filer for a period of five years. Upon request, the filer shall furnish to the Commission or its staff a copy of any or all documents retained pursuant to this section.

(j) Where more than one person subject to Section 16 of the Act is deemed to be a beneficial owner of the same equity securities, all such persons must report as beneficial owners of the securities, either separately or jointly. Where persons in a group are deemed to be beneficial owners of equity securities pursuant to § 240.16a–1(a)(1) due to the aggregation of holdings, a single Form 3, 4 or 5 may be filed on behalf of all persons in the group. Joint and group filings must include all required information for each beneficial owner, and such filings must be signed by each beneficial owner, or on behalf of such owner by an authorized person.

(k) Any issuer that maintains a corporate Web site shall post on that Web site by the end of the business day after filing any Form 3, 4, or 5 filed under section 16(a) of the Act as to the equity securities of that issuer. Each such form shall remain accessible on such issuer's Web site for at least a 12-month period. In the case of an issuer that is an investment company and that does not maintain its own Web site, if any of the issuer's investment adviser, sponsor, depositor, trustee, administrator, principal underwriter, or any affiliated person of the investment company maintains a Web site that includes the name of the issuer, the issuer shall comply with the posting requirements by posting the forms on one such Web site.

Rule 16a–4. Derivative Securities

(a) For purposes of Section 16 of the Act, both derivative securities and the underlying securities to which they relate shall be deemed to be the same class of equity securities, *except that* the acquisition or disposition of any derivative security shall be separately reported.

(b) The exercise or conversion of a call equivalent position shall be reported on Form 4 and treated for reporting purposes as:

(1) A purchase of the underlying security; and

(2) A closing of the derivative security position.

(c) The exercise or conversion of a put equivalent position shall be reported on Form 4 and treated for reporting purposes as:

(1) A sale of the underlying security; and

(2) A closing of the derivative security position.

(d) The disposition or closing of a long derivative security position, as a result of cancellation or expiration, shall be exempt from Section 16(a) of the Act if exempt from Section 16(b) of the Act pursuant to § 240.16b–6(d).

Note to § 240.16a–4: A purchase or sale resulting from an exercise or conversion of a derivative security may be exempt from Section 16(b) of the Act pursuant to § 240.16b–3 or § 240.16b–6(b).

Rule 16a–5. Odd–Lot Dealers

Transactions by an odd-lot dealer (a) in odd-lots as reasonably necessary to carry on odd-lot transactions, or (b) in round lots to offset odd-lot transactions previously or simultaneously executed or reasonably anticipated in the usual course of business, shall be exempt from the provisions of Section 16(a) of the Act with respect to participation by such odd-lot dealer in such transaction.

Rule 16a-6. Small Acquisitions

(a) Any acquisition of an equity security or the right to acquire such securities, other than an acquisition from the issuer (including an employee benefit plan sponsored by the issuer), not exceeding $10,000 in market value shall be reported on Form 5, subject to the following conditions:

(1) Such acquisition, when aggregated with other acquisitions of securities of the same class (including securities underlying derivative securities, but excluding acquisitions exempted by rule from Section 16(b) or previously reported on Form 4 or Form 5) within the prior six months, does not exceed a total of $10,000 in market value; and

(2) The person making the acquisition does not within six months thereafter make any disposition, other than by a transaction exempt from Section 16(b) of the Act.

(b) If an acquisition no longer qualifies for the reporting deferral in paragraph (a) of this section, all such acquisitions that have not yet been reported must be reported on Form 4 before the end of the second business day following the day on which the conditions of paragraph (a) of this section are no longer met.

Rule 16a-7. Transactions Effected in Connection With a Distribution

(a) Any purchase and sale, or sale and purchase, of a security that is made in connection with the distribution of a substantial block of securities shall be exempt from the provisions of Section 16(a) of the Act, to the extent specified in this Rule, subject to the following conditions:

(1) The person effecting the transaction is engaged in the business of distributing securities and is participating in good faith, in the ordinary course of such business, in the distribution of such block of securities; and

(2) The security involved in the transaction is:

(i) part of such block of securities and is acquired by the person effecting the transaction, with a view to distribution thereof, from the issuer or other person on whose behalf such securities are being distributed or from a person who is participating in good faith in the distribution of such block of securities; or

(ii) a security purchased in good faith by or for the account of the person effecting the transaction for the purpose of stabilizing the market price of securities of the class being distributed or to cover an over-allotment or other short position created in connection with such distribution.

(b) Each person participating in the transaction must qualify on an individual basis for an exemption pursuant to this section.

Rule 16a-8. Trusts

(a) *Persons Subject to Section 16.* (1) *Trusts.* A trust shall be subject to section 16 of the Act with respect to securities of the issuer if the trust is a beneficial owner, pursuant to § 240.16a-1(a)(1), of more than ten percent of any class of equity securities of the issuer registered pursuant to section 12 of the Act ("ten percent beneficial owner").

(2) *Trustees, Beneficiaries, and Settlors.* In determining whether a trustee, beneficiary, or settlor is a ten percent beneficial owner with respect to the issuer:

(i) such persons shall be deemed the beneficial owner of the issuer's securities held by the trust, to the extent specified by Rule 16a-1(a)(1); and

(ii) settlors shall be deemed the beneficial owner of the issuer's securities held by the trust where they have the power to revoke the trust without the consent of another person.

(b) *Trust Holdings and Transactions.* Holdings and transactions in the issuer's securities held by a trust shall be reported by the trustee on behalf of the trust, if the trust is subject to Section 16 of the Act, except as provided below. Holdings and transactions in the issuer's securities held by a trust (whether or not subject to Section 16 of the Act) may be reportable by other parties as follows:

(1) *Trusts.* The trust need not report holdings and transactions in the issuer's securities held by the trust in an employee benefit plan subject to the Employee Retirement Income Security Act over which no trustee exercises investment control.

(2) *Trustees.* If, as provided by Rule 16a–1(a)(2), a trustee subject to Section 16 of the Act has a pecuniary interest in any holding or transaction in the issuer's securities held by the trust, such holding or transaction shall be attributed to the trustee and shall be reported by the trustee in the trustee's individual capacity, as well as on behalf of the trust. With respect to performance fees and holdings of the trustee's immediate family, trustees shall be deemed to have a pecuniary interest in the trust holdings and transactions in the following circumstances:

(i) a performance fee is received that does not meet the proviso of Rule 16a–1(a)(2)(ii)(C); or

(ii) at least one beneficiary of the trust is a member of the trustee's immediate family. The pecuniary interest of the immediate family member(s) shall be attributed to and reported by the trustee.

(3) *Beneficiaries.* A beneficiary subject to Section 16 of the Act shall have or share reporting obligations with respect to transactions in the issuer's securities held by the trust, if the beneficiary is a beneficial owner of the securities pursuant to Rule 16a–1(a)(2), as follows:

(i) If a beneficiary shares investment control with the trustee with respect to a trust transaction, the transaction shall be attributed to and reported by both the beneficiary and the trust;

(ii) If a beneficiary has investment control with respect to a trust transaction without consultation with the trustee, the transaction shall be attributed to and reported by the beneficiary only; and

(iii) In making a determination as to whether a beneficiary is the beneficial owner of the securities pursuant to Rule 16a–1(a)(2), beneficiaries shall be deemed to have a pecuniary interest in the issuer's securities held by the trust to the extent of their pro rata interest in the trust where the trustee does not exercise exclusive investment control.

Note to Paragraph (b)(3): Transactions and holdings attributed to a trust beneficiary may be reported by the trustee on behalf of the beneficiary, provided that the report is signed by the beneficiary or other authorized person. Where the transactions and holdings are attributed both to the trustee and trust beneficiary, a joint report may be filed in accordance with § 240.16a–3(j).

(4) *Settlors.* If a settlor subject to Section 16 of the Act reserves the right to revoke the trust without the consent of another person, the trust holdings and transactions shall be attributed to and reported by the settlor instead of the trust; *provided, however,* that if the settlor does not exercise or share investment control over the issuer's securities held by the trust, the trust holdings and transactions shall be attributed to and reported by the trust instead of the settlor.

(c) *Remainder interests.* Remainder interests in a trust are deemed not to confer beneficial ownership for purposes of Section 16 of the Act, provided that the persons with the remainder interests have no power, directly or indirectly, to exercise or share investment control over the trust.

(d) A trust, trustee, beneficiary or settlor becoming subject to Section 16(a) of the Act pursuant to this Rule also shall be subject to Sections 16(b) and 16(c) of the Act.

Rule 16a–9. Stock Splits, Stock Dividends, and Pro Rata Rights

The following shall be exempt from Section 16 of the Act:

(a) The increase or decrease in the number of securities held as a result of a stock split or stock dividend applying equally to all securities of a class, including a stock dividend in which equity securities of a different issuer are distributed; and

(b) the acquisition of rights, such as shareholder or preemptive rights, pursuant to a pro rata grant to all holders of the same class of equity securities registered under Section 12 of the Act.

Note: The exercise or sale of a pro rata right shall be reported pursuant to Rule 16a–4 and the exercise shall be eligible for exemption from Section 16(b) of the Act pursuant to Rule 16b–6(b).

Rule 16a–10. Exemptions Under Section 16(a)

Except as provided in Rule 16a–6, any transaction exempted from the requirements of Section 16(a) of the Act, insofar as it is otherwise subject to the provisions of Section 16(b), shall be likewise exempt from Section 16(b) of the Act.

Rule 16a–11. Dividend or Interest Reinvestment Plans

Any acquisition of securities resulting from the reinvestment of dividends or interest on securities of the same issuer shall be exempt from Section 16 of the Act if the acquisition is made pursuant to a plan providing for the regular reinvestment of dividends or interest and the plan provides for broad-based participation, does not discriminate in favor of employees of the issuer, and operates on substantially the same terms for all plan participants.

Rule 16a–12. Domestic Relations Orders

The acquisition or disposition of equity securities pursuant to a domestic relations order, as defined in the Internal Revenue Code or Title I of the Employee Retirement Income Security Act, or the rules thereunder, shall be exempt from Section 16 of the Act.

Rule 16a–13. Change in Form of Beneficial Ownership

A transaction, other than the exercise or conversion of a derivative security or deposit into or withdrawal from a voting trust, that effects only a change in the form of beneficial ownership without changing a person's pecuniary interest in the subject equity securities shall be exempt from Section 16 of the Act.

EXEMPTION OF CERTAIN TRANSACTIONS FROM SECTION 16(b)

Rule 16b–1. Transactions Approved by a Regulatory Authority

(a) Any purchase and sale, or sale and purchase, of a security shall be exempt from Section 16(b) of the Act, if the transaction is effected by an investment company registered under the Investment Company Act of 1940 and both the purchase and sale of such security have been exempted from the provisions of Section 17(a) of the Investment Company Act of 1940, by rule or order of the Commission.

(b) Any purchase and sale, or sale and purchase, of a security shall be exempt from the provisions of Section 16(b) of the Act if:

(1) the person effecting the transaction is either a holding company registered under the Public Utility Holding Company Act of 1935 or a subsidiary thereof; and

(2) both the purchase and the sale of the security have been approved or permitted by the Commission pursuant to the applicable provisions of that Act and the rules and regulations thereunder.

Rule 16b–3. Transactions Between an Issuer and Its Officers or Directors

(a) *General.* A transaction between the issuer (including an employee benefit plan sponsored by the issuer) and an officer or director of the issuer that involves issuer equity securities shall be exempt from Section 16(b) of the Act if the transaction satisfies the applicable conditions set forth in this section.

(b) *Definitions.*

(1) A *Discretionary Transaction* shall mean a transaction pursuant to an employee benefit plan that:

(i) Is at the volition of a plan participant;

(ii) Is not made in connection with the participant's death, disability, retirement or termination of employment;

(iii) Is not required to be made available to a plan participant pursuant to a provision of the Internal Revenue Code; and

(iv) Results in either an intra-plan transfer involving an issuer equity securities fund, or a cash distribution funded by a volitional disposition of an issuer equity security.

(2) An *Excess Benefit Plan* shall mean an employee benefit plan that is operated in conjunction with a Qualified Plan, and provides only the benefits or contributions that would be provided under a Qualified Plan but for any benefit or contribution limitations set forth in the Internal Revenue Code of 1986, or any successor provisions thereof.

(3)(i) A *Non–Employee Director* shall mean a director who:

(A) Is not currently an officer (as defined in § 240.16a–1(f)) of the issuer or a parent or subsidiary of the issuer, or otherwise currently employed by the issuer or a parent or subsidiary of the issuer;

(B) Does not receive compensation, either directly or indirectly, from the issuer or a parent or subsidiary of the issuer, for services rendered as a consultant or in any capacity other than as a director, except for an amount that does not exceed the dollar amount for which disclosure would be required pursuant to § 229.404(a) of this chapter;

(C) Does not possess an interest in any other transaction for which disclosure would be required pursuant to § 229.404(a) of this chapter; and

(D) Is not engaged in a business relationship for which disclosure would be required pursuant to § 229.404(b) of this chapter.

(ii) Notwithstanding paragraph (b)(3)(i) of this section, a *Non–Employee Director* of a closed-end investment company shall mean a director who is not an "interested person" of the issuer, as that term is defined in Section 2(a)(19) of the Investment Company Act of 1940.

(4) A *Qualified Plan* shall mean an employee benefit plan that satisfies the coverage and participation requirements of Sections 410 and 401(a)(26) of the Internal Revenue Code of 1986, or any successor provisions thereof.

(5) A *Stock Purchase Plan* shall mean an employee benefit plan that satisfies the coverage and participation requirements of Sections 423(b)(3) and 423(b)(5), or Section 410, of the Internal Revenue Code of 1986, or any successor provisions thereof.

(c) *Tax-conditioned plans.* Any transaction (other than a Discretionary Transaction) pursuant to a Qualified Plan, an Excess Benefit Plan, or a Stock Purchase Plan shall be exempt without condition.

(d) *Grants, awards and other acquisitions from the issuer.* Any transaction involving a grant, award or other acquisition from the issuer (other than a Discretionary Transaction) shall be exempt if:

(1) The transaction is approved by the board of directors of the issuer, or a committee of the board of directors that is composed solely of two or more Non–Employee Directors;

(2) The transaction is approved or ratified, in compliance with Section 14 of the Act, by either: the affirmative votes of the holders of a majority of the securities of the issuer present, or represented, and entitled to vote at a meeting duly held in accordance with the applicable laws of the state or other jurisdiction in which the issuer is incorporated; or the written consent of the holders of a majority of the securities of the issuer entitled to vote; *provided that* such ratification occurs no later than the date of the next annual meeting of shareholders; or

(3) The issuer equity securities so acquired are held by the officer or director for a period of six months following the date of such acquisition, *provided that* this condition shall be satisfied with respect to a derivative security if at least six months elapse from the date of acquisition of the derivative security to the date of disposition of the derivative security (other than upon exercise or conversion) or its underlying equity security.

(e) *Dispositions to the issuer.* Any transaction involving the disposition to the issuer of issuer equity securities (other than a Discretionary Transaction) shall be exempt, *provided that* the terms of such disposition are approved in advance in the manner prescribed by either paragraph (d)(1) or paragraph (d)(2) of this section.

(f) *Discretionary Transactions.* A Discretionary Transaction shall be exempt only if effected pursuant to an election made at least six months following the date of the most recent election, with respect to any plan of the issuer, that effected a Discretionary Transaction that was:

(1) An acquisition, if the transaction to be exempted would be a disposition; or

(2) A disposition, if the transaction to be exempted would be an acquisition.

Notes to Rule 16b–3

Note (1): The exercise or conversion of a derivative security that does not satisfy the conditions of this section is eligible for exemption from Section 16(b) of the Act to the extent that the conditions of § 240.16b–6(b) are satisfied.

Note (2): Section 16(a) reporting requirements applicable to transactions exempt pursuant to this section are set forth in § 240.16a–3(f) and (g) and § 240.16a–4.

Note (3): The approval conditions of paragraphs (d)(1), (d)(2) and (e) of this section require the approval of each specific transaction, and are not satisfied by approval of a plan in its entirety except for the approval of a plan pursuant to which the terms and conditions of each transaction are fixed in advance, such as a formula plan. Where the terms of a subsequent transaction (such as the exercise price of an option, or the provision of an exercise or tax withholding right) are provided for in a transaction as initially approved pursuant to paragraphs (d)(1), (d)(2) and (e), such subsequent transaction shall not require further specific approval.

Rule 16b–5. Bona Fide Gifts and Inheritance

Both the acquisition and the disposition of equity securities shall be exempt from the operation of Section 16(b) of the Act if they are: (a) bona fide gifts; or (b) transfers of securities by will or the laws of descent and distribution.

Rule 16b–6. Derivative Securities

(a) The establishment of or increase in a call equivalent position or liquidation of or decrease in a put equivalent position shall be deemed a purchase of the underlying security for purposes of Section 16(b) of the Act, and the establishment of or increase in a put equivalent position or liquidation of or decrease in a call equivalent position shall be deemed a sale of the underlying securities for purposes of Section 16(b) of the Act; *provided, however,* that if the increase or decrease occurs as a result of the fixing of the exercise price of a right initially issued without a fixed price, where the date the price is fixed is not known in advance and is outside the control of the recipient, the increase or decrease shall be exempt from Section 16(b) of the Act with respect to any offsetting transaction within the six months prior to the date the price is fixed.

(b) The closing of a derivative security position as a result of its exercise or conversion shall be exempt from the operation of Section 16(b) of the Act, and the acquisition of underlying securities at a fixed exercise price due to the exercise or conversion of a call equivalent position or the disposition of underlying securities at a fixed exercise price due to the exercise of a put equivalent position shall be exempt from the operation of Section 16(b) of the Act; *provided, however,* that the acquisition of underlying securities from the exercise of an out-of-the-money option, warrant, or right shall not be exempt unless the exercise is necessary to comport with the sequential exercise provisions of the Internal Revenue Code (26 U.S.C. § 422A).

Note to Paragraph (b): The exercise or conversion of a derivative security that does not satisfy the conditions of this section is eligible for exemption from Section 16(b) of the Act to the extent that the conditions of § 240.16b–3 are satisfied.

(c) In determining the short-swing profit recoverable pursuant to Section 16(b) of the Act from transactions involving the purchase and sale or sale and purchase of derivative and other securities, the following rules apply:

(1) Short-swing profits in transactions involving the purchase and sale or sale and purchase of derivative securities that have identical characteristics (*e.g.,* purchases and sales of call options of the same strike price and expiration date, or purchases and sales of the same series of convertible debentures) shall be measured by the actual prices paid or received in the short-swing transactions.

(2) Short-swing profits in transactions involving the purchase and sale or sale and purchase of derivative securities having different characteristics but related to the same underlying security (*e.g.,* the purchase of a call option and the sale of a convertible debenture) or derivative securities and underlying securities shall not exceed the difference in price of the underlying security on the date of purchase or sale and the date of sale or purchase. Such profits may be measured by calculating the short-swing profits that would have been realized had the subject transactions involved purchases and sales solely of the derivative security that was purchased or solely of the derivative security that was sold, valued as of the time of the matching purchase or sale, and calculated for the lesser of the number of underlying securities actually purchased or sold.

(d) Upon cancellation or expiration of an option within six months of the writing of the option, any profit derived from writing the option shall be recoverable under Section 16(b) of the Act. The profit shall not exceed the premium received for writing the option. The disposition or closing of a long derivative security position, as a result of cancellation or expiration, shall be exempt from Section 16(b) of the Act where no value is received from the cancellation or expiration.

Rule 16b–7. Mergers, Reclassifications, and Consolidations

(a) The following transactions shall be exempt from the provisions of Section 16(b) of the Act:

(1) The acquisition of a security of a company, pursuant to a merger or consolidation, in exchange for a security of a company which, prior to the merger or consolidation, owned 85 percent or more of either

(i) the equity securities of all other companies involved in the merger or consolidation, or in the case of a consolidation, the resulting company; or

(ii) the combined assets of all the companies involved in the merger or consolidation, computed according to their book values prior to the merger or consolidation as determined by reference to their most recent available financial statements for a 12 month period prior to the merger or consolidation, or such shorter time as the company has been in existence.

(2) The disposition of a security, pursuant to a merger or consolidation, of a company which, prior to the merger or consolidation, owned 85 percent or more of either

(i) the equity securities of all other companies involved in the merger or consolidation or, in the case of a consolidation, the resulting company; or

(ii) the combined assets of all the companies undergoing merger or consolidation, computed according to their book values prior to the merger or consolidation as determined by reference to their most recent available financial statements for a 12 month period prior to the merger or consolidation.

(b) A merger within the meaning of this section shall include the sale or purchase of substantially all the assets of one company by another in exchange for equity securities which are then distributed to the security holders of the company that sold its assets.

(c) Notwithstanding the foregoing, if a person subject to Section 16 of the Act makes any non-exempt purchase of a security in any company involved in the merger or consolidation and any non-exempt sale of a security in any company involved in the merger or consolidation within any period of less than six months during which the merger or consolidation took place, the exemption provided by this Rule shall be unavailable to the extent of such purchase and sale.

Rule 16b–8. Voting Trusts

Any acquisition or disposition of an equity security or certificate representing equity securities involved in the deposit or withdrawal from a voting trust or deposit agreement shall be exempt from Section 16(b) of the Act if substantially all of the assets held under the voting trust or deposit agreement immediately after the deposit or immediately prior to the withdrawal consisted of equity securities of the same class as the security deposited or withdrawn; *provided, however,* that this exemption shall not apply if there is a non-exempt purchase or sale of an equity security of the class deposited within six months (including the date of withdrawal or deposit) of a non-exempt sale or purchase, respectively, of any certificate representing such equity security (other than the actual deposit or withdrawal).

EXEMPTION OF CERTAIN TRANSACTIONS FROM SECTION 16(c)

Rule 16c–1. Brokers

Any transaction shall be exempt from Section 16(c) of the Act to the extent necessary to render lawful the execution by a broker of an order for an account in which the broker has no direct or indirect interest.

Rule 16c–2. Transactions Effected in Connection with a Distribution

Any transaction shall be exempt from Section 16(c) of the Act to the extent necessary to render lawful any sale made by or on behalf of a dealer in connection with a distribution of a substantial block of securities, where the sale is represented by an over-allotment in which the dealer is participating as a member of an underwriting group, or the dealer or a person acting on the dealer's behalf intends in good faith to offset such sale with a security to be acquired by or on behalf of the dealer as a participant in an underwriting, selling, or soliciting-dealer group of which the dealer is a member at the time of the sale, whether or not the security to be acquired is subject to a prior offering to existing security holders or some other class of persons.

Rule 16c–3. Exemption of Sales of Securities to be Acquired

(a) Whenever any person is entitled, incident to ownership of an issued security and without the payment of consideration, to receive another security "when issued" or "when distributed," the sale of the security to be acquired shall be exempt from the operation of Section 16(c) of the Act, *provided that:*

(1) The sale is made subject to the same conditions as those attaching to the right of acquisition;

(2) Such person exercises reasonable diligence to deliver such security to the purchaser promptly after the right of acquisition matures; and

(3) Such person reports the sale on the appropriate form for reporting transactions by persons subject to Section 16(a) of the Act.

(b) This section shall not exempt transactions involving both a sale of the issued security and a sale of a security "when issued" or "when distributed" if the combined transactions result in a sale of more securities than the aggregate of issued securities owned by the seller plus those to be received for the other security "when issued" or "when distributed."

Rule 16c–4. Derivative Securities

Establishing or increasing a put equivalent position shall be exempt from Section 16(c) of the Act, so long as the amount of securities underlying the put equivalent position does not exceed the amount of underlying securities otherwise owned.

ARBITRAGE TRANSACTIONS

Rule 16e–1. Arbitrage Transactions Under Section 16 of the Act

It shall be unlawful for any director or officer of an issuer of an equity security which is registered pursuant to section 12 of the Act to effect any foreign or domestic arbitrage transaction in any equity security of such issuer, whether registered or not, unless he shall include such transaction in the statements required by section 16(a) and shall account to such issuer for the profits arising from such transaction, as provided in section 16(b). The provision of section 16(c) shall not apply to such arbitrage transactions. The provisions of section 16 shall not apply to any bona fide foreign or domestic arbitrage transaction insofar as it is effected by any person other than such director or officer of the issuer of such security.

PRESERVATION OF RECORDS AND REPORTS OF CERTAIN STABILIZING ACTIVITIES

Rule 17a–1. Recordkeeping Rule for National Securities Exchanges, National Securities Associations, Registered Clearing Agencies and the Municipal Securities Rulemaking Board

(a) Every national securities exchange, national securities association, registered clearing agency and the Municipal Securities Rulemaking Board shall keep and preserve at least one copy of all documents, including all correspondence, memoranda, papers, books, notices, accounts, and other such records as shall be made or received by it in the course of its business as such and in the conduct of its self-regulatory activity.

(b) Every national securities exchange, national securities association, registered clearing agency and the Municipal Securities Rulemaking Board shall keep all such documents for a period of not less than five years, the first two years in an early accessible place, subject to the destruction and disposition provisions of Rule 17a–6.

(c) Every national securities exchange, registered securities association, registered clearing agency and the Municipal Securities Rulemaking Board shall, upon request of any representative of the Commission, promptly furnish to the possession of such representative copies of any documents required to be kept and preserved by it pursuant to paragraphs (a) and (b) of this rule.

Rule 17a–2. Recordkeeping Requirements Relating to Stabilizing Activities

(a) *Scope of section.* This section shall apply to any person who effects any purchase of a security subject to § 242.104 of this chapter for the purpose of, or who participates in a syndicate or group that engages in, "stabilizing," as defined in § 242.100 of this chapter, the price of any security; or effects a purchase that is a "syndicate covering transaction," as defined in § 242.100 of this chapter; or imposes a "penalty bid," as defined in § 242.100 of this chapter:

(1) With respect to which a registration statement has been, or is to be, filed pursuant to the Securities Act of 1933 (15 U.S.C. 77a *et seq.*); or

(2) Which is being, or is to be, offered pursuant to an exemption from registration under Regulation A (§§ 230.251 through 230.263 of this chapter) adopted under the Securities Act of 1933 (15 U.S.C. 77a *et seq.*); or

(3) Which is being, or is to be, otherwise offered, if the aggregate offering price of the securities being offered exceeds $5,000,000.

(b) *Definitions.* For purposes of this section, the following definitions shall apply:

(1) The term "manager" shall mean the person stabilizing or effecting syndicate covering transactions or imposing a penalty bid for its sole account or for the account of a syndicate or group in which it is a participant, and who, by contract or otherwise, deals with the issuer, organizes the selling effort, receives some benefit from the underwriting that is not shared by other underwriters, or represents any other underwriters in such matters as maintaining the records of the distribution and arranging for allotments of the securities offered.

(2) The term "exempted security" means an exempted security as defined in Section 3(a)(12) of the Act, including securities issued, or guaranteed both as to principal and interest, by the International Bank for Reconstruction and Development.

(c) *Records relating to stabilizing, syndicate covering transactions, and penalty bids required to be maintained by manager.* Any person subject to this section who acts as a manager and stabilizes or effects syndicate covering transactions or imposes a penalty bid shall:

(1) Promptly record and maintain the following separately retrievable information, for a period of not less than three years, the first two years in an easily accessible place; *Provided, however,* That if the information is in a record required to be made pursuant to § 240.17a–3 or § 240.17a–4, or otherwise preserved, such information need not be maintained in a separate file if the person can sort promptly and retrieve the information as if it had been kept in a separate file as a record made pursuant to, and preserves the information in accordance with the time periods specified in, this paragraph (c)(1):

(i) The name and class of any security stabilized or any security in which syndicate covering transactions have been effected or a penalty bid has been imposed;

(ii) The price, date, and time at which each stabilizing purchase or syndicate covering transaction was effected by the manager or by any participant in the syndicate or group, and whether any penalties were assessed;

(iii) The names and the addresses of the members of the syndicate or group;

(iv) Their respective commitments, or, in the case of a standby or contingent underwriting, the percentage participation of each member of the syndicate or group therein; and

(v) The dates when any penalty bid was in effect.

(3) Promptly notify each of the members of such syndicate or group of the date and time when stabilizing was terminated.

(d) *Notification to manager.* Any person who has a participation in a syndicate account but who is not a manager of such account, and who effects one or more stabilizing purchases or syndicate covering transactions for its sole account or for the account of a syndicate or group, shall within three business days following such purchase notify the manager of the price, date, and time at which such stabilizing purchase or syndicate covering transaction was effected, and shall in addition notify the manager of the date and time when such stabilizing purchase or syndicate covering transaction was terminated. The manager shall maintain such notifications in a separate file, together with the information required by paragraph (c)(1) of this section, for a period of not less than three years, the first two years in an easily accessible place.

Rule 17a–3. Records to Be Made by Certain Exchange Members, Brokers, and Dealers

(a) Every member of a national securities exchange who transacts a business in securities directly with others than members of a national securities exchange, and every broker or dealer who transacts a business in securities through the medium of any such member, and every broker or dealer registered pursuant to section 15 of the Securities Exchange Act of 1934, as amended, shall make and keep current the following books and records relating to its business:

(1) Blotters (or other records of original entry) containing an itemized daily record of all purchases and sales of securities, all receipts and deliveries of securities (including certificate numbers), all receipts and disbursements of cash and all other debits and credits. Such records shall show the account for which each such transaction was effected, the name and amount of securities, the unit and aggregate purchase or sale price (if any), the trade date, and the name or other designation of the person from whom purchased or received or to whom sold or delivered.

(2) Ledgers (or other records) reflecting all assets and liabilities, income and expense and capital accounts.

(3) Ledger accounts (or other records) itemizing separately as to each cash and margin account of every customer and of such member, broker or dealer and partners thereof, all purchases, sales, receipts, and deliveries of securities and commodities for such account and all other debits and credits to such account.

(4) Ledgers (or other records) reflecting the following:

(i) Securities in transfer;

(ii) Dividends and interest received;

(iii) Securities borrowed and securities loaned;

(iv) Moneys borrowed and moneys loaned (together with a record of the collateral therefor and any substitutions in such collateral);

(v) Securities failed to receive and failed to deliver;

(vi) All long and all short securities record differences arising from the examination, count, verification and comparison pursuant to § 240.17a–5, § 240.17a–12, and § 240.17a–13 hereunder (by date of examination, count, verification and comparison showing for each security the number of shares of long or short count differences).

(vii) Repurchase and reverse repurchase agreements;

(5) A securities record or ledger reflecting separately for each security as of the clearance dates all "long" or "short" positions (including securities in safekeeping and securities that are the subjects of repurchase

or reverse repurchase agreements) carried by such member, broker or dealer for its account or for the account of his customers or partners or others and showing the location of all securities long and the offsetting position to all securities short, including long security count differences and short security count differences classified by the date of the physical count and verification in which they were discovered, and in all cases the name or designation of the account in which each position is carried.

(6)(i) A memorandum of each brokerage order, and of any other instruction, given or received for the purchase or sale of securities, whether executed or unexecuted. The memorandum shall show the terms and conditions of the order or instructions and of any modification or cancellation thereof; the account for which entered; the time the order was received; the time of entry; the price at which executed; the identity of each associated person, if any, responsible for the account; the identity of any other person who entered or accepted the order on behalf of the customer or, if a customer entered the order on an electronic system, a notation of that entry; and, to the extent feasible, the time of execution or cancellation. The memorandum need not show the identity of any person, other than the associated person responsible for the account, who may have entered or accepted the order if the order is entered into an electronic system that generates the memorandum and if that system is not capable of receiving an entry of the identity of any person other than the responsible associated person; in that circumstance, the member, broker or dealer shall produce upon request by a representative of a securities regulatory authority a separate record which identifies each other person. An order entered pursuant to the exercise of discretionary authority by the member, broker or dealer, or associated person thereof, shall be so designated. The term *instruction* shall include instructions between partners and employees of a member, broker or dealer. The term *time of entry* shall mean the time when the member, broker or dealer transmits the order or instruction for execution.

(ii) This memorandum need not be made as to a purchase, sale or redemption of a security on a subscription way basis directly from or to the issuer, if the member, broker or dealer maintains a copy of the customer's subscription agreement regarding a purchase, or a copy of any other document required by the issuer regarding a sale or redemption.

(7) A memorandum of each purchase and sale for the account of the member, broker, or dealer showing the price and, to the extent feasible, the time of execution; and, in addition, where the purchase or sale is with a customer other than a broker or dealer, a memorandum of each order received, showing the time of receipt; the terms and conditions of the order and of any modification thereof; the account for which it was entered; the identity of each associated person, if any, responsible for the account; the identity of any other person who entered or accepted the order on behalf of the customer or, if a customer entered the order on an electronic system, a notation of that entry. The memorandum need not show the identity of any person other than the associated person responsible for the account who may have entered the order if the order is entered into an electronic system that generates the memorandum and if that system is not capable of receiving an entry of the identity of any person other than the responsible associated person: in that circumstance, the member, broker or dealer shall produce upon request by a representative of a securities regulatory authority a separate record which identifies each other person. An order with a customer other than a member, broker or dealer entered pursuant to the exercise of discretionary authority by the member, broker or dealer, or associated person thereof, shall be so designated.

(8) Copies of confirmations of all purchases and sales of securities, including all repurchase and reverse repurchase agreements, and copies of notices of all other debits and credits for securities, cash and other items for the account of customers and partners of such member, broker or dealer.

(9) A record in respect of each cash and margin account with such member, broker or dealer indicating (i) the name and address of the beneficial owner of such account, and (ii) except with respect to exempt employee benefit plan securities as defined in Rule 14a–1(d), but only to the extent such securities are held by employee benefit plans established by the issuer of the securities, whether not the beneficial owner of securities registered in the name of such members, brokers or dealers, or a registered clearing agency or its nominee objects to disclosure of his or her identity, address and securities positions to issuers, and (iii) in the case of a margin account, the signature of such owner, *Provided*, That, in the case of a joint account or an account of a corporation, such records are required only in respect of the person or persons authorized to transact business for such account.

(10) A record of all puts, calls, spreads, straddles, and other options in which such member, broker, or dealer has any direct or indirect interest or which such member, broker, or dealer has granted or guaranteed, containing, at least, an identification of the security and the number of units involved. An OTC derivatives dealer shall also keep a record of all eligible OTC derivative instruments as defined in § 240.3b–13 in which the OTC derivatives dealer has any direct or indirect interest or which it has written or guaranteed, containing, at a minimum, an identification of the security or other instrument, the number of units involved, and the identity of the counterparty.

(11) A record of the proof of money balances of all ledger accounts in the form of trial balances, and a record of the computation of aggregate indebtedness and net capital, as of the trial balance date, pursuant to Rule 15c3–1: *Provided, however,* (i) That such computation need not be made by any member, broker or dealer unconditionally exempt form Rule 15c3–1 by subparagraphs (b)(1) or (b)(3), thereof; and (ii) that any member of an exchange whose members are exempt from Rule 15c3–1 by subparagraph (b)(2) thereof shall make a record of the computation of aggregate indebtedness and net capital as of the trial balance date in accordance with the capital rules of at least one of the exchanges therein listed of which it is a member. Such trial balances and computations shall be prepared currently at least once a month.

(12)(i) A questionnaire or application for employment executed by each "associated person" (as defined in paragraph (h)(4) of this section) of the member, broker or dealer, which questionnaire or application shall be approved in writing by an authorized representative of the member, broker or dealer and shall contain at least the following information with respect to the associated person:

(A) The associated person's name, address, social security number, and the starting date of the associated person's employment or other association with the member, broker or dealer;

(B) The associated person's date of birth;

(C) A complete, consecutive statement of all the associated person's business connections for at least the preceding ten years, including whether the employment was part-time or full-time.

(D) A record of any denial of membership or registration, and of any disciplinary action taken, or sanction imposed, upon the associated person by any Federal or State agency, or by any national securities exchange or national securities association, including any finding that the associated person was a cause of any disciplinary action or had violated any law;

(E) A record of any denial, suspension, expulsion or revocation of membership or registration of any member, broker or dealer with which the associated person was associated in any capacity when such action was taken;

(F) A record of any permanent or temporary injunction entered against the associated person or any member, broker or dealer with which the associated person was associated in any capacity at the time such injunction was entered;

(G) A record of any arrest or indictment for any felony, or any misdemeanor pertaining to securities, commodities, banking, insurance or real estate (including, but not limited to, acting as or being associated with a broker-dealer, investment company, investment adviser, futures sponsor, bank, or savings and loan association), fraud, false statements or omissions, wrongful taking of property or bribery, forgery, counterfeiting or extortion, and the disposition of the foregoing.

(H) A record of any other name or names by which the associated person has been known or which the associated person has used, *Provided, however,* that if such associated person has been registered as a registered representative of such member, broker or dealer with, or his employment has been approved by, the National Association of Securities Dealers, Inc., or the American Stock Exchange LLC, the Boston Stock Exchange, Inc., the Chicago Stock Exchange, Inc., the New York Stock Exchange, Inc., the Pacific Exchange, Inc., the Philadelphia Stock Exchange, Inc., the Chicago Board Options Exchange, Inc., the Cincinnati Stock Exchange, Inc. or the International Securities Exchange, then retention of a full, correct, and complete copy of any and all applications for such registration or approval shall be deemed to satisfy the requirements of this subparagraph.

(ii) A record listing every associated person of the member, broker or dealer which shows, for each associated person, every office of the member, broker or dealer where the associated person regularly conducts the business of handling funds or securities or effecting any transactions in, or inducing or attempting to induce the purchase or sale of any security for the member, broker or dealer, and the Central Registration Depository number, if any, and every internal identification number or code assigned to that person by the member, broker or dealer.

(13) Records required to be maintained pursuant to paragraph (d) of Rule 17f–2.

(14) Copies of all Forms X–17F–1A filed pursuant to Rule 17f–1, all agreements between reporting institutions regarding registration or other aspects of Rule 17f–1, and all confirmations or other information received from the Commission or its designee as a result of inquiry.

(15) Records required to be maintained pursuant to paragraph (e) of Rule 17f–2.

(16)(i) The following records regarding any internal broker-dealer system of which such a broker or dealer is the sponsor:

(A) A record of the broker's or dealer's customers that have access to an internal broker-dealer system sponsored by such broker or dealer (identifying any affiliations between such customers and the broker or dealer);

(B) Daily summaries of trading in the internal broker-dealer system, including:

(*1*) Securities for which transactions have been executed through use of such system; and

(*2*) Transaction volume (separately stated for trading occurring during hours when consolidated trade reporting facilities are and are not in operation):

(i) With respect to equity securities, stated in number of trades, number of shares, and total U.S. dollar value;

(ii) With respect to debt securities, stated in total settlement value in U.S. dollars; and

(iii) With respect to other securities, stated in number of trades, number of units of securities, and in dollar value, or other appropriate commonly used measure of value of such securities; and

(C) Time-sequenced records of each transaction effected through the internal broker-dealer system, including date and time executed, price, size, security traded, counterparty identification information, and method of execution (if internal broker-dealer system allows alternative means or locations for execution, such as routing to another market, matching with limit orders, or executing against the quotations of the broker or dealer sponsoring the system).

(ii) For purposes of paragraph (a) of this section, the term:

(A) *Internal broker-dealer system* shall mean any facility, other than a national securities exchange, an exchange exempt from registration based on limited volume, or an alternative trading system as defined in Regulation ATS, §§ 242.300 through 242.303 of this chapter, that provides a mechanism, automated in full or in part, for collecting, receiving, disseminating, or displaying system orders and facilitating agreement to the basic terms of a purchase or sale of a security between a customer and the sponsor, or between two-customers of the sponsor, through use of the internal broker-dealer system or through the broker or dealer sponsor of such system;

(B) *Sponsor* shall mean any broker or dealer that organizes, operates, administers, or otherwise directly controls an internal broker-dealer trading system or, if the operator of the internal broker-dealer system is not a registered broker or dealer, any broker or dealer that, pursuant to contract, affiliation, or other agreement with the system operator, is involved on a regular basis with executing transactions in connection with use of the internal broker-dealer system, other than solely for its own account or as a customer with access to the internal broker-dealer system; and

(C) *System order* means any order or other communication or indication submitted by any customer with access to the internal broker-dealer system for entry into a trading system announcing an interest in purchasing or selling a security. The term "system order" does not include inquiries or indications of interest that are not entered into the internal broker-dealer system.

(17) For each account with a natural person as a customer or owner:

(i)(A) An account record including the customer's or owner's name, tax identification number, address, telephone number, date of birth, employment status (including occupation and whether the customer is an associated person of a member, broker or dealer), annual income, net worth (excluding value of primary residence), and the account's investment objectives. In the case of a joint account, the account record must include personal information for each joint owner who is a natural person; however, financial information for the individual joint owners may be combined. The account record shall indicate whether it has been signed by the associated person responsible for the account, if any, and approved or accepted by a principal of the member, broker or dealer. For accounts in existence on the effective date of this section, the member, broker or dealer must obtain this information within three years of the effective date of the section.

(B) A record indicating that:

(*1*) The member, broker or dealer has furnished to each customer or owner within three years of the effective date of this section, and to each customer or owner who opened an account after the effective date of this section within thirty days of the opening of the account, and thereafter at intervals no greater than thirty-six months, a copy of the account record or an alternate document with all information required by paragraph (a)(17)(i)(A) of this section. The member, broker or dealer may elect to send this notification with the next statement mailed to the customer or owner after the opening of the account. The member, broker or dealer may choose to exclude any tax identification number and date of birth from the account record or alternative document furnished to the customer or owner. The member, broker or dealer shall include with the account record or alternative document provided to each customer or owner an explanation of any terms regarding investment objectives. The account record or alternate document furnished to the customer or owner shall include or be accompanied by prominent statements that the customer or owner should mark any corrections and return the account record or alternate document to the member, broker or dealer, and that the customer or owner should notify the member, broker or dealer of any future changes to information contained in the account record.

(*2*) For each account record updated to reflect a change in the name or address of the customer or owner, the member, broker or dealer furnished a notification of that change to the customer's old address, or to each joint owner, and the associated person, if any, responsible for that account, on or before the 30th day after the date the member, broker or dealer received notice of the change.

(*3*) For each change in the account's investment objectives the member, broker or dealer has furnished to each customer or owner, and the associated person, if any, responsible for that account a copy of the updated customer account record or alternative document with all information required to be furnished by paragraph (a)(17)(i)(B)(*1*) of this section, on or before the 30th day after the date the member, broker or dealer received notice of any change, or, if the account was updated for some reason other than the firm receiving notice of a change, after the date the account record was updated. The member, broker or dealer may elect to send this notification with the next statement scheduled to be mailed to the customer or owner.

(C) For purposes of this paragraph (a)(17), the neglect, refusal, or inability of a customer or owner to provide or update any account record information required under paragraph (a)(17)(i)(A) of this section shall excuse the member, broker or dealer from obtaining that required information.

(D) The account record requirements in paragraph (a)(17)(i)(A) of this section shall only apply to accounts for which the member, broker or dealer is, or has within the past 36 months been, required to make a suitability determination under the federal securities laws or under the requirements of a self-regulatory organization of which it is a member. Additionally, the furnishing requirement in paragraph (a)(17)(i)(B)(*1*) of this section shall not be applicable to an account for which, within the last 36 months, the member, broker or dealer has not been required to make a suitability determination under the federal securities laws or under the requirements of a self-regulatory organization of which it is a member. This paragraph (a)(17)(i)(D) does not relieve a member, broker or dealer from any obligation arising from the rules of a self-regulatory organization of which it is a member regarding the collection of information from a customer or owner.

(ii) If an account is a discretionary account, a record containing the dated signature of each customer or owner granting the authority and the dated signature of each natural person to whom discretionary authority was granted.

(iii) A record for each account indicating that each customer or owner was furnished with a copy of each written agreement entered into on or after the effective date of this paragraph pertaining to that account and that, if requested by the customer or owner, the customer or owner was furnished with a fully executed copy of each agreement.

(18) A record:

(i) As to each associated person of each written customer complaint received by the member, broker or dealer concerning that associated person. The record shall include the complainant's name, address, and account number; the date the complaint was received; the name of any other associated person identified in the complaint; a description of the nature of the complaint; and the disposition of the complaint. Instead of the record, a member, broker or dealer may maintain a copy of each original complaint in a separate file by the associated person named in the complaint along with a record of the disposition of the complaint.

(ii) Indicating that each customer of the member, broker or dealer has been provided with a notice containing the address and telephone number of the department of the member, broker or dealer to which any complaints as to the account may be directed.

(19) A record:

(i) As to each associated person listing each purchase and sale of a security attributable, for compensation purposes, to that associated person. The record shall include the amount of compensation if monetary and a description of the compensation if nonmonetary. In lieu of making this record, a member, broker or dealer may elect to produce the required information promptly upon request of a representative of a securities regulatory authority.

(ii) Of all agreements pertaining to the relationship between each associated person and the member, broker or dealer including a summary of each associated person's compensation arrangement or plan with the member, broker or dealer, including commission and concession schedules and, to the extent that compensation is based on factors other than remuneration per trade, the method by which the compensation is determined.

(20) A record, which need not be separate from the advertisements, sales literature, or communications, documenting that the member, broker or dealer has complied with, or adopted policies and procedures reasonably designed to establish compliance with, applicable federal requirements and rules of a self-regulatory organization of which the member, broker or dealer is a member which require that advertisements, sales literature, or any other communications with the public by a member, broker or dealer or its associated persons be approved by a principal.

(21) A record for each office listing, by name or title, each person at that office who, without delay, can explain the types of records the firm maintains at that office and the information contained in those records.

(22) A record listing each principal of a member, broker or dealer responsible for establishing policies and procedures that are reasonably designed to ensure compliance with any applicable federal requirements or rules of a self-regulatory organization of which the member, broker or dealer is a member that require acceptance or approval of a record by a principal.

(b)(1) This section shall not be deemed to require a member of a national securities exchange, a broker, or dealer who transacts a business in securities through the medium of any such member, or a broker or dealer registered pursuant to section 15 of the Act, to make or keep such records of transactions cleared for such member, broker, or dealer as are customarily made and kept by a clearing broker or dealer pursuant to the requirements of Rule 17a–3 and Rule 17a–4: *Provided,* That the clearing broker or dealer has and maintains net capital of not less than $25,000 and is otherwise in compliance with Rule 15c3–1 or the capital rules of the exchange of which such clearing broker or dealer is a member if the members of such exchange are exempt from Rule 15c3–1 by paragraph (b)(2) thereof.

(2) This section shall not be deemed to require a member of a national securities exchange, a broker, or dealer who transacts a business in securities through the medium of any such member, or a broker or dealer registered pursuant to section 15 of the Act, to make or keep such records of transactions cleared for such member, broker or dealer by a bank as are customarily made and kept by a clearing broker or dealer pursuant to the requirements of Rule 17a–3 and Rule 17a–4: *Provided,* That such member, broker, or dealer obtains from such bank an agreement in writing to the effect that the records made and kept by such bank are the property of the member, broker, or dealer: *And provided further,* That such bank files with the Commission a written undertaking in form acceptable to the Commission and signed by a duly authorized person, that such books and records are available for examination by representatives of the Commission as specified in section 17(a) of the Act, and that it will furnish to the Commission, upon demand, at its principal office in Washington, D.C., or at any regional or district office of the Commission designated in such demand, true, correct, complete, and current copies of any or all of such records. Such undertaking shall include the following provisions:

The undersigned hereby undertakes to maintain and preserve on behalf of [*BD*] the books and records required to be maintained and preserved by [*BD*] pursuant to Rules 17a–3 and 17a–4 under the Securities Exchange Act of 1934 and to permit examination of such books and records at any time or from time to time during business hours by examiners or other representatives of the Securities and Exchange Commission, and to furnish to said Commission at its principal office in Washington, D.C., or at any regional or district office of said Commission specified in a demand made by or on behalf of said Commission for copies of books and records, true, correct, complete, and current copies of any or all, or any part, of such books and records. This undertaking shall be binding upon the undersigned, and the successors and assigns of the undersigned.

Nothing herein contained shall be deemed to relieve such member, broker, or dealer from the responsibility that such books and records be accurately maintained and preserved as specified in Rules 17a–3 and 17a–4.

(c) This rule shall not be deemed to require a member of a national securities exchange, or a broker or dealer registered pursuant to section 15 of the Securities Exchange Act of 1934, as amended, to make or keep such records as are required by paragraph (a) reflecting the sale of United States Tax Savings Notes, United States Defense Savings Stamps, or United States Defense Savings Bonds, Series E, F, and G.

(d) The records specified in paragraph (a) of this rule shall not be required with respect to any cash transaction of $100 or less involving only subscription rights or warrants which by their terms expire within 90 days after the issuance thereof.

(e) For purposes of transactions in municipal securities by municipal securities brokers and municipal securities dealers, compliance with Rule G–8 of the Municipal Securities Rulemaking Board will be deemed to be in compliance with this rule.

(f) *Security futures products.* The provisions of this section shall not apply to security futures product transactions and positions in a futures account (as that term is defined in § 240.15c3–3(a)(15)); *provided,* that the Commodity Futures Trading Commission's recordkeeping rules apply to those transactions and positions.*

(g) Every member, broker or dealer shall make and keep current, as to each office, the books and records described in paragraphs (a)(1), (a)(6), (a)(7), (a)(12), (a)(17), (a)(18)(i), (a)(19), (a)(20), (a)(21), and (a)(22) of this section.

(h) When used in this section:

(1) The term *office* means any location where one or more associated persons regularly conduct the business of handling funds or securities or effecting any transactions in, or inducing or attempting to induce the purchase or sale of, any security.

(2) The term *principal* means any individual registered with a registered national securities association as a principal or branch manager of a member, broker or dealer or any other person who has been delegated supervisory responsibility over associated persons by the member, broker or dealer.

(3) The term *securities regulatory authority* means the Commission, any self-regulatory organization, or any securities commission (or any agency or office performing like functions) of the States.

(4) The term *associated person* means an "associated person of a member" or "associated person of a broker or dealer" as defined in sections 3(a)(21) and 3(a)(18) of the Act (15 U.S.C. 78c(a)(21) and (a)(18)) respectively, but shall not include persons whose functions are solely clerical or ministerial.

Rule 17a–4. Records to Be Preserved by Certain Exchange Members, Brokers, and Dealers

(a) Every member, broker and dealer subject to § 240.17a–3 shall preserve for a period of not less than six years, the first two years in an easily accessible place, all records required to be made pursuant to paragraphs § 240.17a–3(a)(1), (a)(2), (a)(3), (a)(5), (a)(21), (a)(22), and analogous records created pursuant to paragraph § 240.17a–3(f).

(b) Every member, broker and dealer subject to § 240.17a–3 shall preserve for a period of not less than three years, the first two years in an easily accessible place:

(1) All records required to be made pursuant to § 240.17a–3(a)(4), (a)(6), (a)(7), (a)(8), (a)(9), (a)(10), (a)(16), (a)(18), (a)(19), (a)(20), and analogous records created pursuant to § 240.17a–3(f).

(2) All checkbooks, bank statements, canceled checks, and cash reconciliations.

(3) All bills receivable or payable (or copies thereof), paid or unpaid, relating to the business of such member, broker, or dealer, as such.

(4) Originals of all communications received and copies of all communications sent (and any approvals thereof) by the member, broker or dealer (including inter-office memoranda and communications) relating to its business as such, including all communications which are subject to rules of a self-regulatory organization of which the member, broker or dealer is a member regarding communications with the public. As used in this paragraph (b)(4), the term communications includes sales scripts.

(5) All trial balances, computations of aggregate indebtedness and net capital (and working papers in connection therewith), financial statements, branch office reconciliations, and internal audit working papers, relating to the business of such member, broker, or dealer, as such.

(6) All guarantees of accounts and all powers of attorney and other evidence of the granting of any discretionary authority giv-

* As of publication date there are two Rule 17a–3(f) provisions.

en in respect of any account, and copies of resolutions empowering an agent to act on behalf of a corporation.

(7) All written agreements (or copies thereof) entered into by such member, broker, or dealer relating to its business as such, including agreements with respect to any account.

(8) Records which contain the following information in support of amounts included in the report prepared as of the audit date on Form X-17A-5, Part II or Part IIA or Part IIB and in the annual financial statements and schedules required by § 240.17a-5(d) and § 240.17a-12(b):

(i) money balance position, long or short, including description, quantity, price and valuation of each security including contractual commitments in customers' accounts, in cash and fully secured accounts, partly secured accounts, unsecured accounts and in securities accounts payable to customers;

(ii) money balance and position, long or short, including description, quantity, price and valuation of each security including contractual commitments in non-customers' accounts, in cash and fully secured accounts, partly secured and unsecured accounts and in securities accounts payable to non-customers;

(iii) position, long or short, including description, quantity, price and valuation of each security including contractual commitments included in the Computation of Net Capital as commitments, securities owned, securities owned not readily marketable, and other investments owned not readily marketable;

(iv) amount of secured demand note, description of collateral securing such secured demand note including quantity, price and valuation of each security and cash balance securing such secured demand note;

(v) description of futures commodity contracts, contract value on trade date, market value, gain or loss, and liquidating equity or deficit in customers' and non-customers' accounts;

(vi) description of futures commodity contracts, contract value on trade date, market value, gain or loss and liquidating equity or deficit in trading and investment accounts;

(vii) description, money balance, quantity, price and valuation of each spot commodity position or commitments in customers' and non-customers' accounts;

(viii) description, money balance, quantity, price and valuation of each spot commodity position or commitments in trading and investment accounts;

(ix) number of shares, description of security, exercise price, cost and market value of put and call options including short out of the money options having no market or exercise value, showing listed and unlisted put and call options separately;

(x) quantity, price, and valuation of each security underlying the haircut for undue concentration made in the Computation for Net Capital;

(xi) description, quantity, price and valuation of each security and commodity position or contractual commitment, long or short, in each joint account in which the broker or dealer has an interest, including each participant's interest and margin deposit;

(xii) description, settlement date, contract amount, quantity, market price, and valuation for each aged failed to deliver requiring a charge in the Computation of Net Capital pursuant to Rule 15c3-1;

(xiii) detail relating to information for possession or control requirements under Rule 15c3-3 and reported on the schedule in Part II or IIA of Form X-17A-5;

(xiv) detail of all items, not otherwise substantiated which are charged or credited in the Computation of Net Capital pursuant to Rule 15c3–1, such as cash margin deficiencies, deductions related to securities values and undue concentration, aged securities differences and insurance claims receivable; and

(xv) other schedules which are specifically prescribed by the Commission as necessary to support information reported as required by § 240.17a–5 and § 240.17a–12.

(9) The records required to be made pursuant to §§ 240.15c3–3(d)(4) and (*o*).

(10) The records required to be made pursuant to § 240.15c3–4 and the results of the periodic reviews conducted pursuant to § 240.15c3–4(d).

(11) All notices relating to an internal broker-dealer system provided to the customers of the broker or dealer that sponsors such internal broker-dealer system, as defined in paragraph (a)(16)(ii)(A) of § 240.17a–3. Notices, whether written or communicated through the internal broker-dealer trading system or other automated means, shall be preserved under this paragraph (b)(11) if they are provided to all customers with access to an internal broker-dealer system, or to one or more classes of customers. Examples of notices to be preserved under this paragraph (b)(11) include, but are not limited to, notices addressing hours of system operations, system malfunctions, changes to system procedures, maintenance of hardware and software, and instructions pertaining to access to the internal broker-dealer system.

(12) The records required to be made pursuant to § 240.15c3–1e(c)(4)(vi)(D) and (E).

(c) Every member, broker and dealer subject to § 240.17a–3 shall preserve for a period of not less than six years after the closing of any customer's account any account cards or records which relate to the terms and conditions with respect to the opening and maintenance of the account.

(d) Every member, broker and dealer subject to § 240.17a–3 shall preserve during the life of the enterprise and of any successor enterprise all partnership articles or, in the case of a corporation, all articles of incorporation or charter, minute books and stock certificate books (or, in the case of any other form of legal entity, all records such as articles of organization or formation, and minute books used for a purpose similar to those records required for corporations or partnerships), all Forms BD (§ 249.501 of this chapter), all Forms BDW (§ 249.501a of this chapter), all amendments to these forms, all licenses or other documentation showing the registration of the member, broker or dealer with any securities regulatory authority.

(e) Every member, broker and dealer subject to § 240.17a–3 shall maintain and preserve in an easily accessible place:

(1) All records required under paragraph (a)(12) of Rule 17a–3 until at least three years after the associated person's employment and any other connection with the member, broker or dealer has terminated.

(2) All records required under paragraph (a)(13) of Rule 17a–3 until at least three years after the termination of employment or association of those persons required by Rule 17f–2 to be fingerprinted.

(3) All records required pursuant to paragraph (a)(15) of Rule 17a–3 for the life of the enterprise.

(4) All records required pursuant to paragraph (a)(14) of Rule 17a–3 for three years.

(5) All account record information required pursuant to § 240.17a–3(a)(17) until at least six years after the earlier of the date the account was closed or the date on which the information was replaced or updated.

(6) Each report which a securities regulatory authority has requested or required the member, broker or dealer to make and furnish to it pursuant to an order or settlement, and each securities regulatory au-

thority examination report until three years after the date of the report.

(7) Each compliance, supervisory, and procedures manual, including any updates, modifications, and revisions to the manual, describing the policies and practices of the member, broker or dealer with respect to compliance with applicable laws and rules, and supervision of the activities of each natural person associated with the member, broker or dealer until three years after the termination of the use of the manual.

(8) All reports produced to review for unusual activity in customer accounts until eighteen months after the date the report was generated. In lieu of maintaining the reports, a member, broker or dealer may produce promptly the reports upon request by a representative of a securities regulatory authority. If a report was generated in a computer system that has been changed in the most recent eighteen month period in a manner such that the report cannot be reproduced using historical data in the same format as it was originally generated, the report may be produced by using the historical data in the current system, but must be accompanied by a record explaining each system change which affected the reports. If a report is generated in a computer system that has been changed in the most recent eighteen month period in a manner such that the report cannot be reproduced in any format using historical data, the member, broker or dealer shall promptly produce upon request a record of the parameters that were used to generate the report at the time specified by a representative of a securities regulatory authority, including a record of the frequency with which the reports were generated.

(f) The records required to be maintained and preserved pursuant to §§ 240.17a–3 and 240.17a–4 may be immediately produced or reproduced on ''micrographic media'' (as defined in this section) or by means of ''electronic storage media'' (as defined in this section) that meet the conditions set forth in this paragraph and be maintained and preserved for the required time in that form.

(1) For purposes of this section:

(i) The term *micrographic media* means microfilm or microfiche, or any similar medium; and

(ii) The term *electronic storage media* means any digital storage medium or system and, in the case of both paragraphs (f)(1)(i) and (f)(1)(ii) of this section, that meets the applicable conditions set forth in this paragraph (f).

(2) If electronic storage media is used by a member, broker, or dealer, it shall comply with the following requirements:

(i) The member, broker, or dealer must notify its examining authority designated pursuant to Section 17(d) of the Act (15 U.S.C. 78q(d)) prior to employing electronic storage media. If employing any electronic storage media other than optical disk technology (including CD–ROM), the member, broker, or dealer must notify its designated examining authority at least 90 days prior to employing such storage media. In either case, the member, broker, or dealer must provide its own representation or one from the storage medium vendor or other third party with appropriate expertise that the selected storage media meets the conditions set forth in this paragraph (f)(2).

(ii) The electronic storage media must:

(A) Preserve the records exclusively in a non-rewriteable, non-erasable format;

(B) Verify automatically the quality and accuracy of the storage media recording process;

(C) Serialize the original and, if applicable, duplicate units of storage media, and time-date for the required period of retention the information placed on such electronic storage media; and

(D) Have the capacity to readily download indexes and records preserved on the electronic storage media to any medium acceptable under this paragraph (f) as required by the Commission or the self-regulatory organizations of which the member, broker, or dealer is a member.

(3) If a member, broker, or dealer uses micrographic media or electronic storage media, it shall:

(i) At all times have available, for examination by the staffs of the Commission and self-regulatory organizations of which it is a member, facilities for immediate, easily readable projection or production of micrographic media or electronic storage media images and for producing easily readable images.

(ii) Be ready at all times to provide, and immediately provide, any facsimile enlargement which the staffs of the Commission, any self-regulatory organization of which it is a member, or any State securities regulator having jurisdiction over the member, broker or dealer may request.

(iii) Store separately from the original, a duplicate copy of the record stored on any medium acceptable under § 240.17a–4 for the time required.

(iv) Organize and index accurately all information maintained on both original and any duplicate storage media.

(A) At all times, a member, broker, or dealer must be able to have such indexes available for examination by the staffs of the Commission and the self-regulatory organizations of which the broker or dealer is a member.

(B) Each index must be duplicated and the duplicate copies must be stored separately from the original copy of each index.

(C) Original and duplicate indexes must be preserved for the time required for the indexed records.

(v) The member, broker, or dealer must have in place an audit system providing for accountability regarding inputting of records required to be maintained and preserved pursuant to §§ 240.17a–3 and 240.17a–4 to electronic storage media and inputting of any changes made to every original and duplicate record maintained and preserved thereby.

(A) At all times, a member, broker, or dealer must be able to have the results of such audit system available for examination by the staffs of the Commission and the self-regulatory organizations of which the broker or dealer is a member.

(B) The audit results must be preserved for the time required for the audited records.

(vi) The member, broker, or dealer must maintain, keep current, and provide promptly upon request by the staffs of the Commission or the self-regulatory organizations of which the member, broker, or broker-dealer is a member all information necessary to access records and indexes stored on the electronic storage media; or place in escrow and keep current a copy of the physical and logical file format of the electronic storage media, the field format of all different information types written on the electronic storage media and the source code, together with the appropriate documentation and information necessary to access records and indexes.

(vii) For every member, broker, or dealer exclusively using electronic storage media for some or all of its record preservation under this section, at least one third party ("the undersigned"), who has access to and the ability to download information from the member's, broker's, or dealer's electronic storage media to any acceptable medium under this section, shall file with the designated examining authority for the member, broker, or dealer the following undertakings with respect to such records:

The undersigned hereby undertakes to furnish promptly to the U.S. Securities and Exchange Commission ("Commission"), its designees or representatives, any self-regulatory organization of which it is a member, or any State securities regulator having jurisdiction over the member, broker or dealer, upon reasonable request, such information as is deemed necessary by the staffs of the Commission, any self-regulatory organization of which it is a member, or any State securities regulator having jurisdiction over the member, broker or dealer to download information kept on the broker's or dealer's electronic storage media to any medium acceptable under Rule 17a–4.

Furthermore, the undersigned hereby undertakes to take reasonable steps to provide access to information contained on the broker's or dealer's electronic storage media, including, as appropriate, arrangements for the downloading of any record required to be maintained and preserved by the broker or dealer pursuant to Rules 17a–3 and 17a–4 under the Securities Exchange Act of 1934 in a format acceptable to the staffs of the Commission, any self-regulatory organization of which it is a member, or any State securities regulator having jurisdiction over the member, broker or dealer. Such arrangements will provide specifically that in the event of a failure on the part of a broker or dealer to download the record into a readable format and after reasonable notice to the broker or dealer, upon being provided with the appropriate electronic storage medium, the undersigned will undertake to do so, as the staffs of the Commission, any self-regulatory organization of which it is a member, or any State securities regulator having jurisdiction over the member, broker or dealer may request.

(g) If a person who has been subject to Rule 17a–3 ceases to transact a business in securities directly with others than members of a national securities exchange, or ceases to transact a business in securities through the medium of a member of a national securities exchange, or ceases to be registered pursuant to section 15 of the Securities Exchange Act of 1934, as amended, such person shall, for the remainder of the periods of time specified in this rule, continue to preserve the records which he theretofore preserved pursuant to this rule.

(h) For purposes of transactions in municipal securities by municipal securities brokers and municipal securities dealers, compliance with Rule G–9 of the Municipal Securities Rulemaking Board will be deemed to be compliance with this section.

(i) If the records required to be maintained and preserved pursuant to the provisions of Rule 17a–3 and Rule 17a–4 are prepared or maintained by an outside service bureau, depository, bank which does not operate pursuant to Rule 17a–3(b)(2), or other record-keeping service on behalf of the member, broker or dealer required to maintain and preserve such records, such outside entity shall file with the Commission a written undertaking in form acceptable to the Commission, signed by a duly authorized person, to the effect that such records are the property of the member, broker or dealer required to maintain and preserve such records and will be surrendered promptly on request of the member, broker or dealer and including the following provision:

With respect to any books and records maintained or preserved on behalf of [BD], the undersigned hereby undertakes to permit examination of such books and records at any time or from time to time during business hours by representatives or designees of the Securities and Exchange Commission, and to promptly furnish to said Commission or its designee true, correct, complete and current hard copy of any or all or any part of such books and records.

Agreement with an outside entity shall not relieve such member, broker or dealer from the responsibility to prepare and maintain records as specified in this section or in Rule 17a–3.

(j) Every member, broker and dealer subject to this section shall furnish promptly to a representative of the Commission legible, true, complete, and current copies of those records of the member, broker or dealer that are required to be preserved under this section, or any other records of the member, broker or dealer subject to examination under section 17(b) of the Act (15 U.S.C. 78*q*(b)) that are requested by the representative of the Commission.

(k) *Exchanges of futures for physical.*

(1) Except as provided in paragraph (k)(2) of this section, upon request of any designee or representative of the Commission or of any self-regulatory organization of which it is a member, every member, broker or dealer subject to this section shall request and obtain from its customers documentation regarding an exchange of security futures products for physical securities, including documentation of underlying cash transactions and exchanges. Upon receipt of such documentation, the member, broker or dealer shall promptly provide that documentation to the requesting designee or representative.

(2) This paragraph (k) does not apply to an underlying cash transaction(s) or exchange(s) that was effected through a member, broker or dealer registered with the Commission and is of a type required to be recorded pursuant to § 240.17a–3.

(*l*) Records for the most recent two year period required to be made pursuant to § 240.17a–3(g) and paragraphs (b)(4) and (e)(7) of this section which relate to an office shall be maintained at the office to which they relate. If an office is a private residence where only one associated person (or multiple associated persons who reside at that location and are members of the same immediate family) regularly conducts business, and it is not held out to the public as an office nor are funds or securities of any customer of the member, broker or dealer handled there, the member, broker or dealer need not maintain records at that office, but the records must be maintained at another location within the same State as the member, broker or dealer may select. Rather than maintain the records at each office, the member, broker or dealer may choose to produce the records promptly at the request of a representative of a securities regulatory authority at the office to which they relate or at another location agreed to by the representative.

(m) When used in this section:

(1) The term *office* shall have the meaning set forth in § 240.17a–3(h)(1).

(2) The term *principal* shall have the meaning set forth in § 240.17a–3(h)(2).

(3) The term *securities regulatory authority* shall have the meaning set forth in § 240.17a–3(h)(3).

(4) The term *associated person* shall have the meaning set forth in § 240.17a–3(h)(4).

Rule 17a–5. Reports to Be Made by Certain Exchange Members, Brokers, and Dealers

(a) *Filing of Monthly and Quarterly Reports.*

(1) This paragraph (a) shall apply to every broker or dealer registered pursuant to section 15 of the Act.

(2)(i) Every broker or dealer subject to this paragraph (a) who clears transactions or carries customer accounts shall file Part I of Form X–17A–5 within 10 business days after the end of each month.

(ii) Every broker or dealer subject to this paragraph (a) who clears transactions or carries customer accounts shall file Part II of Form X–17A–5 within 17 business days after the end of the calendar quarter and within 17 business days after the date selected for the annual audit of financial statements where said date is other than a calendar quarter. Certain of such brokers or dealers shall file Part IIA in lieu thereof if the nature of their business is limited as described in the instructions to Part II of Form X–17A–5.

(iii) Every broker or dealer who does not clear transactions nor carry customer accounts shall file Part IIA of Form X–17A–5 within 17 business days after the end of each calendar quarter and within 17 business days after the date selected for the annual audit of financial statements where said date is other than the end of the calendar quarter.

(iv) Upon receiving written notice from the Commission or the examining authority designated pursuant to Section 17(d) of the Act, a broker or dealer who receives such notice shall file monthly or at such times as shall be specified, Part II or Part IIA of Form X–17A–5 and such other financial or operational information as shall be required by the Commission or the designated examining authority.

(3) The reports provided for in this paragraph (a) shall be considered filed when received at the Commission's principal office in Washington, D.C. and the regional or district office of the Commission for the region or district in which the broker or dealer has its principal place of business. All reports filed pursuant to this paragraph (a) shall be deemed to be confidential.

(4) The provisions of subparagraphs (2) and (3) of paragraph (a) shall not apply to a member of a national securities exchange or a registered national securities association if said exchange or association maintains records containing the information required by Part I, Part II or Part IIA of Form X–17A–5 as to such member, and transmits to the Commission a copy of the applicable parts of Form X–17A–5 as to such member, pursuant to a plan, procedures and provisions of which have been submitted to and declared effective by the Commission. Any such plan filed by a national securities exchange or a registered national securities association may provide that when a member is also a member of one or more national securities exchanges, or of one or more national securities exchanges and a registered national securities association, the information required to be submitted with respect to any such member may be submitted by only one specified national securities exchange or registered national securities association. For the purposes of this rule, a plan filed with the Commission by a national securities exchange or a registered national securities association shall not become effective unless the Commission, having due regard for the fulfillment of the Commission's duties and responsibilities under the provisions of the Act, declares the plan to be effective. Further, the Commission, in declaring any such plan effective, may impose such terms and conditions relating to the provisions of the plan and the period of its effectiveness as may be deemed necessary or appropriate in the public interest, for the protection of investors, or to carry out the Commission's duties and responsibilities under the Act.

(5) Each broker or dealer that computes certain of its capital charges in accordance with § 240.15c3–1e must file the following additional reports:

(i) Within 17 business days after the end of each month that is not a quarter, as of month-end:

(A) For each product for which the broker or dealer calculates a deduction for market risk other than in accordance with § 240.15c3–1e(b)(1) or (b)(3), the product category and the amount of the deduction for market risk;

(B) A graph reflecting, for each business line, the daily intra-month VaR;

(C) The aggregate value at risk for the broker or dealer;

(D) For each product for which the broker or dealer uses scenario analysis, the product category and the deduction for market risk;

(E) Credit risk information on derivatives exposures, including:

(1) Overall current exposure;

(2) Current exposure (including commitments) listed by counterparty for the 15 largest exposures;

(3) The 10 largest commitments listed by counterparty;

(4) The broker or dealer's maximum potential exposure listed by counterparty for the 15 largest exposures;

(5) The broker or dealer's aggregate maximum potential exposure;

(6) A summary report reflecting the broker or dealer's current and maximum potential exposures by credit rating category; and

(7) A summary report reflecting the broker or dealer's current exposure for each of the top ten countries to which the broker or dealer is exposed (by residence of the main operating group of the counterparty); and

(F) Regular risk reports supplied to the broker's or dealer's senior management in the format described in the application; and

(ii) Within 17 business days after the end of each quarter:

(A) Each of the reports required to be filed in paragraph (a)(5)(i) of this section;

(B) A report identifying the number of business days for which the actual daily net trading loss exceeded the corresponding daily VaR; and

(C) The results of backtesting of all internal models used to compute allowable capital, including VaR and credit risk models, indicating the number of backtesting exceptions.

(6) Upon written application by a broker or dealer to its designated examining authority, the designated examining authority may extend the time for filing the information required by this paragraph (a). The designated examining authority for the broker or dealer shall maintain, in the manner prescribed in Rule 17a–1, a record of each extension granted.

(b) *Report Filed Upon Termination of Membership Interest.*

(1) If a broker or dealer holding any membership interest in a national securities exchange or registered national securities association ceases to be a member in good standing of such exchange or association, such broker or dealer shall, within two business days after such event, file with the Commission Part II or Part IIA of Form X–17A–5 as determined by the standards set forth in paragraphs (a)(2)(ii) and (iii) of this rule as of the date of such event. The report shall be filed at the Commission's principal office in Washington, D.C., and with the regional or district office of the Commission for the region or district in which the broker or dealer has its principal place of business: *Provided, however,* That such report need not be made or filed if the Commission, upon written request or upon its own motion, exempts such broker or dealer, either unconditionally or on specified terms and conditions, from such requirement: *Provided, further,* That the Commission may, upon request of the broker or dealer, grant extensions of time for filing the report specified herein for good cause shown.

(2) Attached to the report required by subparagraph (1) of this paragraph shall be an oath or affirmation that to the best knowledge and belief of the individual making such oath or affirmation the information contained in the report is true and correct. The oath or affirmation shall be made before a person duly authorized to administer such oath or affirmation. If the broker or dealer is a sole proprietorship, the oath or affirmation shall be made by the proprietor; if a partnership, by a general partner; or if a corporation, by the chief executive officer, or

in his absence, by the person authorized to act in his place.

(3) For the purposes of this paragraph (b) "membership interest" shall include the following: full membership, allied membership, associated membership, floor privileges, and any other interest that entitles a broker or dealer to the exercise of any privilege on an exchange or with an association.

(4) For the purposes of this paragraph (b), any broker or dealer shall be deemed to have ceased to be a member in good standing of such exchange or association when he has resigned, withdrawn, or been suspended or expelled from a membership interest in such exchange or association, or has directly or through any associated person sold or entered into an agreement for the sale of a membership interest which would on consummation thereof result in the termination of the broker's or dealer's membership interest in such exchange or association.

(5) Whenever any national securities exchange or registered national securities association takes any action which causes any broker or dealer which is a member of such exchange or association to cease to be a member in good standing of such exchange or association or when such exchange or association learns of any action by such member of any other person which causes such broker or dealer to cease to be a member in good standing of such exchange or association, such exchange or association shall report such action promptly to the Commission, furnishing information as to the circumstances surrounding the event, and shall send a copy of such notification to the broker or dealer and notify such broker or dealer of its responsibilities under this paragraph (b).

(6) One copy of the annual audit report shall be filed at the regional office of the Commission for the region in which the broker or dealer has its principal place of business and the principal office of the designated examining authority for said broker or dealer. Two copies of said report shall be filed at the Commission's principal office in Washington, D.C. Copies thereof shall be provided to all self-regulatory organizations of which said broker or dealer is a member.

(c) *Customer Statements.*

(1) *Who Must Furnish the Statements.* Every broker or dealer shall file with the Commission at its principal office in Washington, D.C., with the regional or district office of the Commission for the region or district in which the broker or dealer has its principal place of business, and with each national securities exchange and registered national securities association of which it is a member, and shall send to its customers the statements prescribed by subparagraphs (2) and (3) of this paragraph (c), except as provided in paragraph (c)(5) of this section or if the activities of such broker or dealer are limited to any one or combination of the following and are conducted in the manner prescribed herein:

(i) As introducing broker or dealer, the forwarding of all the transactions of his customers to a clearing broker or dealer on a fully disclosed basis: *Provided,* That such clearing broker or dealer reflects such transactions on its books and records in accounts it carries in the names of such customers and that the introducing broker or dealer does not hold funds or securities for, or owe funds or securities to, customers other than funds and securities promptly forwarded to the clearing broker or dealer or to customers;

(ii) The prompt forwarding of subscriptions for securities to the issuer, underwriter or other distributor of such securities and of receiving checks, drafts, notes, or other evidences of indebtedness payable solely to the issuer, underwriter or other distributor who delivers the security directly to the subscriber or to a custodian bank, if the broker or dealer does not otherwise hold funds or securities for, or owe money or securities to, customers;

(iii) The sale and redemption of redeemable shares of registered investment companies or the solicitation of share accounts of savings and loan associations in the manner contemplated by the $2,500 minimum net capital requirement of Rule 15c3–1 or the offering to extend any credit to or participate in arranging a loan for a customer to purchase insurance in connection with the sale of redeemable shares of registered investment companies; or

(iv) Conduct which would exempt the broker or dealer from the provisions of Rule 17a–13 by reason of the provisions of paragraph (a) of that rule.

(2) *Audited statements to be furnished.* Audited statements shall be furnished within 105 days after the date of the audited financial statements required by paragraph (d) of this section. The statements may be furnished 30 days after that time limit has expired if the broker or dealer sends them with the next mailing of the broker's or dealer's quarterly customer statements of account. In that case, the broker or dealer must include a statement in that mailing of the amount of the broker's or dealer's net capital and its required net capital in accordance with § 240.15c3–1, as of a fiscal month end that is within the 75-day period immediately preceding the date the statements are sent to customers. The audited statements shall include the following:

(i) A balance sheet with appropriate notes prepared in accordance with generally accepted accounting principles which shall be audited if the financial statements furnished in accordance with paragraph (d) of this rule are required to be certified;

(ii) A footnote containing a statement of the amount of the broker's or dealer's net capital and its required net capital, computed in accordance with Rule 15c3–1. Such statement shall include summary financial statements of subsidiaries consolidated pursuant to Appendix C of Rule 15c3–1, where material, and the effect thereof on the net capital and required net capital of the broker or dealer.

(iii) If in connection with the most recent annual audit report pursuant to Rule 17a–5, the independent accountant commented on any material inadequacies in accordance with paragraphs (g) and (h) of this section, and Rule 17a–11(e), there shall be a statement by the broker or dealer that a copy of such report and comments is currently available for the customer's inspection at the principal office of the Commission in Washington, DC, and the regional or district office of the Commission for the region or district in which the broker or dealer has its principal place of business; and

(iv) A statement indicating that the Statement of Financial Condition of the most recent annual audit report of the broker or dealer pursuant to Rule 17a–5 is available for examination at the principal office of the broker or dealer, and at the regional or district office of the Commission for the region or district in which the broker or dealer has its principal place of business.

(3) *Unaudited Statements to be Furnished.* Unaudited statements dated 6 months from the date of the audited statements required to be furnished by paragraphs (c)(1) and (2) of this section shall be furnished within 65 days after the date of the unaudited statements. The unaudited statements may be furnished 70 days after that time limit has expired if the broker or dealer sends them with the next mailing of the broker's or dealer's quarterly customer statements of account. In that case, the broker or dealer must include a statement in that mailing of the amount of the broker's or dealer's net capital and its required net capital in accordance with § 240.15c3–1, as of a fiscal month end that is within the 75-day period immediately preceding the date the statements are sent to customers. The unaudited statements shall contain the in-

formation specified in paragraphs (c)(2)(i) and (ii) of this section.

(4) *Definition of "Customer"*. For purposes of this paragraph (c), the term "customer" includes any person other than (i) another broker or dealer who is exempted by subparagraph (c)(1), (ii) a general, special or limited partner or director or officer of a broker or dealer, or (iii) any person to the extent that such person has a claim for property or funds which by contract, agreement or understanding, or by operation of law, is part of the capital of the broker or dealer or is subordinated to the claims of creditors of the broker or dealer, for or with whom a broker or dealer has effected a securities transaction in a particular month, which month shall be either the month preceding the balance sheet date or the month following the balance sheet date in which the statement is sent. The term "customer" also includes any person for whom the broker or dealer holds securities for safekeeping or as collateral or for whom the broker or dealer carries a free credit balance in the month in which customers are determined for purposes of this paragraph (c).

(5) *Exemption from Sending Certain Financial Information to Customers.* A broker or dealer is not required to send to its customers the statements prescribed by paragraphs (c)(2) and (c)(3) of this section if the following conditions are met:

(i) The broker or dealer semi-annually sends its customers, at the times it otherwise is required to send its customers the statements prescribed by paragraphs (c)(2) and (c)(3) of this section, a financial disclosure statement that includes:

(A) The amount of the broker's or dealer's net capital and its required net capital in accordance with § 240.15c3–1, as of the date of the statements prescribed by paragraphs (c)(2) and (c)(3) of this section;

(B) To the extent required under paragraph (c)(2)(ii) of this section, a description of the effect on the broker's or dealer's net capital and required net capital of the consolidation of the assets and liabilities of subsidiaries or affiliates consolidated pursuant to Appendix C of §240.15c3–1; and

(C) Any statements otherwise required by paragraphs (c)(2)(iii) and (iv) of this section.

(ii) The financial disclosure statement is given prominence in the materials delivered to customers of the broker or dealer and includes an appropriate caption stating that customers may obtain the statements prescribed by paragraphs (c)(2) and (c)(3) of this section, at no cost, by:

(A) Accessing the broker's or dealer's Web site at the specified Internet Uniform Resource Locator (URL); or

(B) Calling the broker's or dealer's specified toll-free telephone number.

(iii) Not later than 90 days after the date of the audited statements prescribed by paragraph (c)(2) of this section and not later than 75 days after the date of the unaudited statements prescribed by paragraph (c)(3) of this section, the broker or dealer publishes the statements on its Web site, accessible by hyperlinks in either textual or button format, which are separate, prominent links, are clearly visible, and are placed in each of the following locations:

(A) On the broker's or dealer's Web site home page; and

(B) On each page at which a customer can enter or log on to the broker's or dealer's Web site; and

(C) If the Web sites for two or more brokers or dealers can be accessed from the same Home page, on the Home page of the Web site of each broker or dealer.

(iv) The broker or dealer maintains a toll-free telephone number that customers can call to request a copy of the statements prescribed by paragraphs (c)(2) and (c)(3) of this section.

(v) If a customer requests a copy of the statements prescribed by paragraphs (c)(2) and (c)(3) of this section, the broker or dealer sends it promptly at no cost to the customer.

(vi) During the year prior to the date of the statements prescribed by paragraphs (c)(2) and (c)(3) of this section, the broker or dealer was not required by paragraph (e) of § 240.17a–11 to give notice and transmit a report to the Commission.

(d) *Annual Filing of Audited Financial Statements.*

(1)(i) Every broker or dealer registered pursuant to section 15 of the Act shall file annually, on a calendar or fiscal year basis, a report which shall be audited by an independent public accountant. Reports pursuant to this paragraph (d) shall be as of the same fixed or determinable date each year, unless a change is approved in writing by the designated examining authority for the broker or dealer. A copy of such written approval should be sent to the regional or district office of the Commission for the region or district in which the broker or dealer has its principal place of business.

(ii) A broker or dealer succeeding to and continuing the business of another broker or dealer need not file a report under this paragraph as of a date in this fiscal or calendar year in which the succession occurs if the predecessor broker or dealer has filed a report in compliance with this paragraph as of a date in such fiscal or calendar year.

(iii) A broker or dealer which is a member of a national securities exchange and has transacted a business in securities solely with or for other members of a national securities exchange, and has not carried any margin account, credit balance or security for any person who is defined as a "customer" in paragraph (c)(4) of this rule, shall not be required to file a report under this paragraph.

(2) The annual audited report shall contain a Statement of Financial Condition in a format and on a basis which is consistent with the totals reported on the Statement of Financial Condition contained in Form X–17A–5, Part II or Part IIA, a Statement of Income, a Statement of Cash Flow, a Statement of Changes in Stockholders' or Partner's or Sole Proprietor's Equity, and Statement of Changes in Liabilities Subordinated to Claims of General Creditors. Such statements shall be in a format and on a basis which is consistent with such statements as contained in Form X–17A–5, Part II or Part IIA. If the Statement of Financial Condition filed in accordance with instructions to Form X–17A–5, Part II or Part IIA, is not consolidated, a summary of financial data, including the assets, liabilities, and net worth of stockholders' equity, for subsidiaries not consolidated in the Part II or Part IIA Statement of Financial Condition as filed by the broker or dealer should be included in the notes to the consolidated statement of financial condition reported on by the independent public accountant.

(3) Supporting schedules shall include, from Part II or Part IIA of Form X–17A–5, a Computation of Net Capital Under Rule 15c3–1, a Computation for Determination of the Reserve Requirements under Exhibit A of Rule 15c3–3 and Information Relating to the Possession or Control Requirements Under Rule 15c3–3, and shall be filed with said report.

(4) A reconciliation, including appropriate explanations, of the Computation of Net Capital under Rule 15c3–1 and the Computation for Determination of the Reserve Requirements Under Exhibit A of Rule 15c3–3 in the audit report with the broker's or dealer's corresponding unaudited most recent Part II or Part IIA filing shall be filed with said report when material differences exist. If no material differences exist, a statement so indicating shall be filed.

(5) The annual audit report shall be filed not more than sixty (60) days after the date of the financial statements.

(6) One copy of the annual audit report shall be filed at the regional or district office of the Commission for the region or district in which the broker or dealer has its principal place of business and the principal office of the designated examining authority for said broker or dealer. Two copies of said report shall be filed at the Commission's principal office in Washington, D.C. Copies thereof shall be provided to all self-regulatory organizations of which said broker or dealer is a member.

(e) *Nature and Form of Reports.* The financial statements filed pursuant to paragraph (d) of this rule shall be prepared and filed in accordance with the following requirements:

(1)(i) An audit shall be conducted by a public accountant who shall be in fact independent as defined in paragraph (f)(3) herein, and he shall give an opinion covering the statements filed pursuant to paragraph (d): *Provided, however,* That the financial statements filed pursuant to paragraph (d) need not be audited if, since the date of the previous financial statements or report filed pursuant to Rule 15b1–2 or this rule: (A) the securities business of such broker or dealer has been limited to acting as broker (agent) for an issuer in soliciting subscriptions for securities of such issuer, said broker has promptly transmitted to such issuer all funds and promptly delivered to the subscriber all securities received in connection therewith, and said broker has not otherwise held funds or securities for or owed money or securities to customers; or (B) its securities business has been limited to buying and selling evidence of indebtedness secured by mortgage, deed or trust, or other lien upon real estate or leasehold interests, and said broker or dealer has not carried any margin account, credit balance, or security for any securities customer.

(ii) A broker or dealer who files a report which is not covered by an accountant's opinion shall include in the oath or affirmation required by paragraph (e)(2) of this rule a statement of the facts and circumstances relied upon as a basis for exemption from the requirement that financial statements and schedules filed pursuant to paragraph (d) be covered by the opinion of an accountant.

(2) Attached to the report shall be an oath or affirmation that, to the best knowledge and belief of the person making such oath or affirmation, (i) the financial statements and schedules are true and correct and (ii) neither the broker or dealer, nor any partner, officer, or director, as the case may be, has any proprietary interest in any account classified solely as that of a customer. The oath or affirmation shall be made before a person duly authorized to administer such oaths or affirmations. If the broker or dealer is a sole proprietorship, the oath or affirmation shall be made by the proprietor; if a partnership, by a general partner; or if a corporation, by a duly authorized officer.

(3) All of the statements filed pursuant to paragraph (d) shall be public, except that if the Statement of Financial Condition in a format which is consistent with Form X–17A–5, Part II or Part IIA is bound separately from the balance of the annual audited financial statements filed pursuant to subparagraph (d)(1), the balance of the annual audited financial statements shall be deemed confidential, except that they shall be available for official use by any official or employee of the United States or any State, by national securities exchanges and registered national securities associations of which the person filing such report is a member, and by any other person to whom the Commission authorizes disclosure of such information as being in the public interest. Nothing contained in this subparagraph (3) shall be deemed to be in derogation of the rules of any registered national securities association or national securities

exchange which give to customers of a member broker or dealer the right, upon request to such member broker or dealer, to obtain information relative to its financial condition.

(4) The broker or dealer shall file with the report a supplemental report which shall be covered by an opinion of the independent public accountant on the status of the membership of the broker or dealer in the Securities Investor Protection Corporation ("SIPC") if, pursuant to paragraph (e)(1) of this rule, a report of the broker or dealer is required to be covered by an opinion of a certified public accountant or a public accountant who is in fact independent. The supplemental report shall cover the SIPC annual general assessment reconciliation or exclusion from membership forms not previously reported on under this paragraph (4) which were required to be filed on or prior to the date of the report required by paragraph (d) of this rule: *Provided,* That the broker or dealer need not file the supplemental report on the SIPC annual general assessment reconciliation or exclusion from membership form for any period during which the SIPC assessment is a minimum assessment as provided for in Section 4(d)(1)(c) of the Securities Investor Protection Act of 1970, as amended. The supplemental report, an original of which shall be submitted to the regional or district office of the Commission for the region or district in which the broker or dealer has its principal place of business, the Commission's principal office in Washington, the principal office of the designated examining authority for such broker or dealer and the office of SIPC, shall be bound separately, be dated and be signed manually, and shall include the following:

(i) A schedule of assessment payments also showing any overpayments applied and overpayments carried forward including: payment dates, amounts, and name of SIPC collection agent to whom mailed, or

(ii) If exclusion from membership was claimed, a statement that the broker or dealer qualified for exclusion from membership under the Securities Investor Protection Act of 1970, and the date and name of the SIPC collection agent with whom a Certification of Exclusion from Membership (Form SIPC–3) was filed, and

(iii) An accountant's report which shall state that in the accountant's opinion either the assessments were determined fairly in accordance with applicable instructions and forms, or that a claim for exclusion from membership was consistent with income reported. If exceptions are noted, the accountant shall state any corrective action taken or proposed. The accountant's review on which his report is based shall include as a minimum the following procedures:

(A) Comparison of listed assessment payments with respective cash disbursements record entries;

(B) For all or any portion of a fiscal year ending in 1976 and each fiscal year thereafter, comparison of amounts reflected in the annual report required by paragraph (d) of this section, with amounts reported in the Annual General Assessment Reconciliation (Form SIPC–7);

(C) Comparison of adjustments reported in Form SIPC–7 with supporting schedules and working papers supporting adjustments;

(D) Proof of arithmetical accuracy of the calculations reflected in Form SIPC–7 and in the schedules and working papers supporting adjustments; and,

(E) Comparison of the amount of any overpayment applied with the Form SIPC–7 on which it was computed; or,

(F) If exclusion from membership is claimed, the accountant shall review the annual report required by paragraph (d) of this rule for all or any portion of a fiscal year ending in 1976 and each fiscal year thereafter to ascertain that the Certification of Exclusion from Membership (Form SIPC–7) was consistent with the income reported.

(5)(i) For purposes of this section, the term *Year 2000 Problem* shall include problems arising from:

(A) Computer software incorrectly reading the date "01/01/00" as being the year 1900 or another incorrect year;

(B) Computer software incorrectly identifying a date in the Year 1999 or any year thereafter;

(C) Computer software failing to detect that the Year 2000 is a leap year; or

(D) Any other computer software error that is directly or indirectly caused by the problems set forth in paragraph (e)(5)(i)(A), (B), or (C) of this section.

(ii)(A) No later than August 31, 1998, every broker or dealer required to maintain minimum net capital pursuant to § 240.15c3–1(a)(2) of $5,000 or greater as of July 15, 1998, shall file Part I of Form BD-Y2K (§ 249.618 of this chapter) prepared as of July 15, 1998, and no later than April 30, 1999, every broker or dealer required to maintain minimum net capital pursuant to § 240.15c3–1(a)(2) of $5,000 or greater as of March 15, 1999, shall file Part I of Form BD-Y2K prepared as of March 15, 1999.

(B) Every broker or dealer that registers pursuant to section 15 of the Act between July 16, 1998 and December 31, 1998 or between March 16, 1999 and October 1, 1999, and that is required to maintain net capital pursuant to § 240.15c3–1(a)(2) of $5,000 or greater, shall file Part I of Form BD-Y2K (§ 249.18 of this chapter) no later than 30 days after its registration becomes effective. Part I of Form BD-Y2K shall be prepared as of the date its registration became effective.

(iii)(A) No later than August 31, 1998, every broker or dealer with a minimum net capital requirement pursuant to § 240.15c3–1(a)(2) of $100,000 or greater as of July 15, 1998 shall file Part II of Form BD-Y2K (§ 249.618 of this chapter). Part II of Form BD-Y2K shall address each topic in paragraph (e)(5)(iv) of this section as of July 15, 1998.

(B) No later than April 30, 1999, every broker or dealer with a minimum net capital requirement pursuant to § 240.15c3–1(a)(2) of $100,000 or greater as of March 15, 1999 shall file Part II of Form BD-Y2K (§ 249.618 of this chapter). In addition, each broker or dealer subject to paragraph (e)(5)(iii)(A) of this section shall file Part II of Form BD-Y2K pursuant to this paragraph (e)(5)(iii)(B) regardless of its minimum net capital requirement. Part II of Form BD–Y2K shall address each topic in paragraph (e)(5)(iv) of this section as of March 15, 1999.

(C) Every broker or dealer that registers pursuant to section 15 of the Act between July 15, 1998 and December 31, 1998 or between March 16, 1999 and October 1, 1999, and that is required to maintain net capital pursuant to § 240.15c3–1(a)(2) of $100,000 or greater, shall file Part II of Form BD-Y2K (§ 249.18 of this chapter) no later than 30 days after registration becomes effective. Part II of Form BD–Y2K shall address each topic in paragraph (e)(5)(iv) of this section as of the effective date of its registration.

(iv) Part II of Form BD-Y2K (§ 249.618 of this chapter) prepared pursuant to paragraph (e)(5)(iii) of this section shall identify a specific person or persons that are available to discuss the contents of the report and shall include a discussion of the following:

(A) Whether the board of directors (or similar body) of the broker or dealer has approved and funded plans for preparing and testing its computer systems for Year 2000 Problems;

(B) Whether the plans of the broker or dealer exist in writing and address all mission critical computer systems of the broker or dealer wherever located throughout the world;

(C) Whether the broker or dealer has assigned existing employees, hired new employees, or engaged third parties to provide assistance in addressing Year 2000 Problems, and if so, a description of the work that these groups of individuals have performed as of the date of each report;

(D) The current progress of the broker or dealer on each stage of preparation for potential problems caused by Year 2000 Problems. These stages are:

(1) Awareness of potential Year 2000 Problems;

(2) Assessment of what steps the broker or dealer must take to address Year 2000 Problems;

(3) Implementation of the steps needed to address Year 2000 Problems;

(4) Internal testing of software designed to address Year 2000 Problems, including the number and a description of the material exceptions resulting from such testing that are unresolved as of the reporting date;

(5) Point-to-point or industry-wide testing of software designed to address Year 2000 Problems (including testing with other brokers or dealers, other financial institutions, and customers), including the number and a description of the material exceptions resulting from such testing that are unresolved as of the reporting date; and

(6) Implementation of tested software that will address Year 2000 Problems;

(E) Whether the broker or dealer has written contingency plans in the event, that after December 31, 1999, it has problems caused by Year 2000 Problems;

(F) What levels of management of the broker or dealer are responsible for addressing potential problems caused by Year 2000 Problems, including a description of the responsibilities for each level of management regarding the Year 2000 Problems;

(G) Any additional material information concerning its management of Year 2000 Problems that will help the Commission and the designated examining authorities assess the readiness of the broker or dealer for the Year 2000.

(v) The broker or dealer shall file an original and two copies of Form BD-Y2K (§ 249.618 of this chapter) prepared pursuant to paragraph (e)(5) of this section with the Commission's principal office in Washington, D.C. and one copy of Form BD-Y2K with the designated examining authority of the broker or dealer. The reports required by paragraph (e)(5) of this section shall be public.

(vi) No later than April 30, 1999, every broker or dealer required to file Part II of Form BD-Y2K (§ 249.618 of this chapter) pursuant to paragraph (e)(5)(iii)(B) of this section and required to file audited financial statements pursuant to paragraph (d) of this section shall file with its Form BD-Y2K an original and two copies of a report prepared by an independent public accountant regarding the broker's or dealer's process, as of March 15, 1999, for addressing Year 2000 Problems with the Commission's principal office in Washington, DC and one copy of the accountant's report with the designated examining authority of the broker or dealer. The independent public accountant's report shall be prepared in accordance with standards that have been reviewed by the Commission and that have been issued by a national organization that is responsible for promulgating authoritative accounting and auditing standards.

(f)(1) *Qualification of Accountants.* The Commission will not recognize any person as a certified public accountant who is not duly registered in good standing as such under the laws of his place of residence or principal office. The Commission will not recognize any person as a public accountant who is not in good standing and entitled to practice as such under the laws of his place of residence or principal office.

(2) *Designation of Accountant.*

(i) Every broker or dealer which is required by paragraph (d) of this rule to file an annual report of financial statements shall file no later than December 10 of each year a statement with the Commission's principal office in Washington, D.C., the regional or district office of the Commission for the region or district in which its principal place of business is located and the principal office of the designated examining authority for such broker or dealer. Such statement shall indicate the existence of an agreement dated no later than December 1, with an independent public accountant covering a contractual commitment to conduct the broker's or dealer's annual audit during the following calendar year.

(ii) The agreement may be of a continuing nature, providing for successive yearly audits, in which case no further filing is required. If the agreement is for a single audit or if the continuing agreement previously filed has been terminated or amended, a new statement must be filed by the required date.

(iii) The statement shall be headed "Notice pursuant to Rule 17a–5(f)(2)" and shall contain the following information.

(A) name, address, telephone number and registration number of the broker or dealer;

(B) name, address and telephone number of the accounting firm;

(C) the audit date of the broker or dealer for the year covered by the agreement.

(iv) Any broker or dealer which is exempted from the requirement to file an annual audited report of financial statements shall nevertheless file the notice specified herein indicating the data as of which the unaudited report will be prepared.

(v) Notwithstanding the date of filing specified in paragraph (f)(2)(i), every broker or dealer shall file the notice provided for in paragraph (f)(2) within 30 days following the effective date of registration as a broker or dealer.

(3) *Independence of Accountant.* An accountant shall be independent in accordance with the provisions of Rules 2–01(b) and (c) of Regulation S–X.

(4) *Replacement of Accountant.* A broker or dealer shall file a notice which must be received by the Commission's principal office in Washington, D.C., the regional or district office of the Commission for the region or district in which its principal place of business is located, and the principal office of the designated examining authority for such broker or dealer, not more than 15 business days after:

(i) The broker or dealer has notified the accountant whose opinion covered the most recent financial statements filed under paragraph (d) of this rule that his services will not be utilized in future engagements; or

(ii) The broker or dealer has notified an accountant who was engaged to give an opinion covering the financial statements to be filed under paragraph (d) that the engagement has been terminated; or

(iii) An accountant has notified the broker or dealer that he would not continue under an engagement to give an opinion covering the financial statements to be filed under paragraph (d); or

(iv) A new accountant has been engaged to give an opinion covering the financial statements to be filed under paragraph (d) without any notice of termination having been given to or by the previously engaged accountant.

Such notice shall state (A) the date of notification of the termination of the engagement or engagement of the new accountant as applicable and (B) the details of any problems existing during the 24 months (or the period of the engagement if less) preceding such termination or new engagement relating to any matter of accounting principles or practices, financial statement disclosure, auditing scope or procedure, or compliance with applicable rules of the Commission, which problems, if not resolved to the satisfaction of the former accountant, would have caused him to make reference to them in connection with his report on the subject matter of the problems. The problems required to be reported in response to the preceding sentence include both those resolved to the former accountant's satisfaction and those not resolved to the former accountant's satisfaction. Problems contemplated by this rule are those which occur at the decision-making level i.e., between principal financial officers of the broker-dealer and personnel of the accounting firm responsible for rendering its report. The notice shall also state whether the accountant's report on the financial statements for any of the past two years contained an adverse opinion or a disclaimer of opinion or was qualified as to uncertainties, audit scope, or accounting principles, and describe the nature of each such adverse opinion, disclaimer of opinion, or qualification. The broker or dealer shall also request the former accountant to furnish the broker or dealer with a letter addressed to the Commission stating whether he agrees with the statements contained in the notice of the broker or dealer and, if not, stating the respects in which he does not agree. The broker or dealer shall file three copies of the notice and the accountant's letter, one copy of which shall be manually signed by the sole proprietor, or a general partner or a duly authorized corporate officer, as appropriate, and by the accountant, respectively.

(g) *Audit Objectives.*

(1) The audit shall be made in accordance with generally accepted auditing standards and shall include a review of the accounting system, the internal accounting control and procedures for safeguarding securities including appropriate tests thereof for the period since the prior examination date. The audit shall include all procedures necessary under the circumstances to enable the independent public accountant to express an opinion on the statement of financial condition, results of operations, cash flow, and the Computation of Net Capital under § 240.15c3–1, the Computation for Determination of Reserve Requirements for Brokers or Dealers under Exhibit A of § 240.15c3–3, and Information Relating to the Possession or Control Requirements under § 240.15c3–3. The scope of the audit and review of the accounting system, the internal control and procedures for safeguarding securities shall be sufficient to provide reasonable assurance that any material inadequacies existing at the date of the examination in (a) the accounting system; (b) the internal accounting controls; (c) procedures for safeguarding securities; and (d) the practices and procedures whose review is specified in (i), (ii), (iii) and (iv) of this paragraph would be disclosed. Additionally, as specific objectives, the audit shall include reviews of the practices and procedures followed by the client:

(i) In making the periodic computations of aggregate indebtedness and net capital under § 240.17a–3(a)(11) and the reserve required by § 240.15c3–3(e);

(ii) In making the quarterly securities examinations, counts, verifications and comparisons and the recordation of differences required by § 240.17a–13;

(iii) In complying with the requirement for prompt payment for securities of section 4(c) of Regulation T (§ 220.4(c) of chapter II of title–12) of the Board of Governors of the Federal Reserve System; and

(iv) In obtaining and maintaining physical possession or control of all fully paid and excess margin securities of customers as required by § 240.15c3–3. Such review shall include a determination as to the adequacy of the procedures described in the records required to be maintained pursuant to § 240.15c3–3(d)(4).

(2) If the broker or dealer is exempt from § 240.15c3–3, the independent public accountant shall ascertain that the conditions of the exemption were being complied with as of the examination date and that no facts came to his attention to indicate that the exemption had not been complied with during the period since his last examination.

(3) A material inadequacy in the accounting system, internal accounting controls, procedures for safeguarding securities, and practices and procedures referred to in paragraph (g)(1) of this section which is expected to be reported under these audit objectives includes any condition which has contributed substantially to or, if appropriate corrective action is not taken, could reasonably be expected to (i) inhibit a broker or dealer from promptly completing securities transactions or promptly discharging his responsibilities to customers, other broker-dealers or creditors; (ii) result in material financial loss; (iii) result in material misstatements of the broker's or dealer's financial statements; or (iv) result in violations of the Commission's recordkeeping or financial responsibility rules to an extent that could reasonably be expected to result in the conditions described in paragraphs (g)(3)(i), (ii), or (iii) of this section.

(h) *Extent and Timing of Audit Procedures.*

(1) The extent and timing of audit procedures are matters for the independent public accountant to determine on the basis of his review and evaluation of existing internal controls and other audit procedures performed in accordance with generally accepted auditing standards and the audit objectives set forth in paragraph (g) above. In determining the extent of testing, consideration shall be given to the materiality of an area and the possible effect on the financial statements and schedules of a material misstatement in a related account. The performance of auditing procedures involves the proper synchronization of their application and thus comprehends the need to consider simultaneous performance of procedures in certain areas such as, for example, securities counts, transfer verification and customer and broker confirmation in connection with verification of securities positions.

(2) If, during the course of the audit or interim work, the independent public accountant determines that any material inadequacies exist in the accounting system, internal accounting control, procedures for safeguarding securities, or as otherwise defined in paragraph (g)(3) of this section, then the independent public accountant shall call it to the attention of the chief financial officer of the broker or dealer, who shall have a responsibility to inform the Commission and the designated examining authority by telegraphic or facsimile notice within 24 hours thereafter as set forth in Rules 17a–11(e) and (g). The broker or dealer shall also furnish the accountant with a copy of said notice to the Commission by telegram or facsimile within said 24 hour period. If the accountant fails to receive such notice from the broker or dealer within said 24 hour period, or if the accountant disagrees with the statements contained in the notice of the broker or dealer, the accountant shall have a responsibility to inform the Commission and the designated examining authority by report of material inadequacy within 24 hours thereafter as set forth in Rule 17a–11(g). Such report from the accountant shall, if the broker or dealer failed to file a notice, describe any material inadequacies found to exist. If the broker or dealer filed a notice, the accountant shall file a report detailing the aspects, if any, of the broker's or dealer's notice with which the accountant does not agree.

(i) *Accountant's Reports, General Provisions.*

(1) *Technical Requirements.* The accountant's report shall: (i) be dated; (ii) be signed manually; (iii) indicate the city and state where issued; and (iv) identify without detailed enumeration the financial statements and schedules covered by the report.

(2) *Representations as to the Audit.* The accountant's report shall: (i) state whether the audit was made in accordance with generally accepted auditing standards; (ii) state whether the accountant reviewed the procedures followed for safeguarding securities; and (iii) designate any auditing procedures deemed necessary by the accountant under the circumstances of the particular case which have been omitted, and the reason for their omission.

Nothing in this rule shall be construed to imply authority for the omission of any procedure which independent accountants would ordinarily employ in the course of an audit made for the purpose of expressing the opinions required under this rule.

(3) *Opinion to Be Expressed.* The accountant's report shall state clearly the opinion of the accountant: (i) in respect of the financial statements and schedules covered by the report and the accounting principles and practices reflected therein; and (ii) as to the consistency of the application of the accounting principles, or as to any changes in such principles which have a material effect on the financial statements.

(4) *Exceptions.* Any matters to which the accountant takes exception shall be clearly identified, the exception thereto specifically and clearly stated, and, to the extent practicable, the effect of each such exception on the related financial statements given.

(5) *Definitions.* For the purpose of this rule, the terms "audit" (or "examination"), "accountant's report", and "certified" shall have the meanings given in Rule 1–02 of Regulation S–X.

(j) *Accountant's Report on Material Inadequacies.* The broker or dealer shall file concurrently with the annual audit report a supplemental report by the accountant describing any material inadequacies found to exist or found to have existed since the date of the previous audit. The supplemental report shall indicate any corrective action taken or proposed by the broker or dealer in regard thereto. If the audit did not disclose any material inadequacies, the supplemental report shall so state.

(k) *Supplemental Reports.* Each broker or dealer that computes certain of its capital charges in accordance with § 240.15c3-1e shall file concurrently with the annual audit report a supplemental report on management controls, which shall be prepared by a registered public accounting firm (as that term is defined in section 2(a)(12) of the Sarbanes-Oxley Act of 2002 (15 U.S.C. 7201 et seq.)). The supplemental report shall indicate the results of the accountant's review of the internal risk management control system established and documented by the broker or dealer in accordance with § 240.15c3-4. This review shall be conducted in accordance with procedures agreed upon by the broker or dealer and the registered public accounting firm conducting the review. The agreed upon procedures are to be performed and the report is to be prepared in accordance with the rules promulgated by the Public Company Accounting Oversight Board. The purpose of the review is to confirm that the broker or dealer has established, documented, and is in compliance with the internal risk management controls established in accordance with § 240.15c3-4. Before commencement of the review and no later than December 10 of each year, the broker or dealer shall file a statement with the Division of Market Regulation, Office of Financial Responsibility, at the Commission's principal office in Washington, DC that includes:

(1) A description of the agreed-upon procedures agreed to by the broker or dealer and the registered public accounting firm; and

(2) A notice describing changes in those agreed-upon procedures, if any. If there are

no changes, the broker or dealer should so indicate.

(*l*) *Use of Certain Statements Filed With the Securities and Exchange Commission.* At the request of any broker or dealer who is (i) an investment company registered under the Investment Company Act of 1940, or (ii) a sponsor or depositor of such a registered investment company who effects transactions in securities only with, or on behalf of, such registered investment company, the Commission will accept the financial statements filed pursuant to Sections 13 or 15(d) of the Securities Exchange Act of 1934 or Section 30 of the Investment Company Act of 1940 and the rules and regulations promulgated thereunder as a filing pursuant to paragraph (d) of this rule. Such a filing shall be deemed to satisfy the requirements of this rule for any calendar year in which such financial statements are filed, provided that the statements so filed meet the requirements of the other rules under which they are filed with respect to time of filing and content.

(m) *Extensions and Exemptions.*

(1) A broker's or dealer's designated examining authority may extend the period under paragraph (d) of this section for filing annual audit reports. The designated examining authority for the broker or dealer shall maintain, in the manner prescribed in 13.17a–1, a record of each extension granted.

(2) Any "bank" as defined in section 3(a)(6) of the Act (48 Stat. 882; 15 U.S.C. 78c) and any "insurance company" as defined in Section 3(a)(19) of the Act (78 Stat. 565; 15 U.S.C. 78c) registered as a broker or dealer to sell variable contracts but exempt from Rule 15c3–1 shall be exempt from the provisions of this rule.

(3) On written request of any national securities exchange, registered national securities association, broker or dealer, or on its own motion, the Commission may grant an extension of time or an exemption from any of the requirements of this rule either unconditionally or on specified terms and conditions.

(4) The provisions of § 240.17a–5 shall not apply to a broker or dealer registered pursuant to section 15(b)(11)(A) of the Act (15 U.S.C. 78*o*(b)(11)(A)) that is not a member of either a national securities exchange pursuant to section 6(a) of the Act (15 U.S.C. 78f(a)) or a national securities association registered pursuant to section 15A(a) of the Act (15 U.S.C. 78*o*–3(a)).

(n) *Notification of Change of Fiscal Year.*

(1) In the event any broker or dealer finds it necessary to change its fiscal year, it must file, with the Commission's principal office in Washington, DC, the regional or district office of the Commission for the region or district in which the broker or dealer has its principal place of business and the principal office of the designated examining authority for such broker or dealer, a notice of such change.

(2) Such notice shall contain a detailed explanation of the reasons for the change. Any change in the filing period for the audit report must be approved by the designated examining authority pursuant to paragraph (d)(1)(i) of this section.

(*o*) *Filing Requirements.* For purposes of filing requirements as described in Rule 17a–5, such filing shall be deemed to have been accomplished upon receipt at the Commission's principal office in Washington, D.C., with duplicate originals simultaneously filed at the locations prescribed in the particular paragraph of Rule 17a–5 which is applicable.

(p) *Compliance with § 240.17a–12.* An OTC derivatives dealer may comply with § 240.17a–5 by complying with the provisions of § 240.17a–12.

Rule 17a–6. Right of National Securities Exchange, National Securities Association, Registered Clearing Agency or the Municipal Securities Rulemaking Board to Destroy or Dispose of Documents

(a) Any document kept by or on file with a national securities exchange, national securities association, registered clearing agency or the Municipal Securities Rulemaking Board pursuant to the Act or any rule or regulation thereunder may be destroyed or otherwise disposed of by such exchange, association, clearing agency or the Municipal Securities Rulemaking Board at the end of five years or at such earlier date as is specified in a plan for the destruction or disposition of any such documents if such plan has been filed with the Commission by such exchange, association, clearing agency or the Municipal Securities Rulemaking Board and has been declared effective by the Commission.

(b) Such plan may provide that any such document may be transferred to microfilm or other recording medium after such time as specified in the plan and thereafter be maintained and preserved in that form. If a national securities exchange, association, clearing agency or the Municipal Securities Rulemaking Board uses microfilm or other recording medium it shall (1) be ready at all times to provide and immediately provide, easily readable projection of the microfilm or other recording medium and easily readable hard copy thereof, (2) provide indexes permitting the immediate location of any such document on the microfilm or other recording medium, and (3) in the case of microfilm, store a duplicate copy of the microfilm separately from the original microfilm for the time required.

(c) For the purposes of this rule a plan filed with the Commission by a national securities exchange, association, clearing agency or the Municipal Securities Rulemaking Board shall not become effective unless the Commission, having due regard for the public interest and for the protection of investors, declares the plan to be effective. The Commission in its declaration may limit the applications, reports, and documents as to which it shall apply, and may impose any other terms and conditions to the plan and to the period of its effectiveness which it deems necessary or appropriate in the public interest or for the protection of investors.

Rule 17a–7. Records of Nonresident Brokers and Dealers

(a)(1) Except as provided in paragraphs (b) and (c) hereof, each nonresident broker or dealer registered or applying for registration pursuant to section 15 of the Act shall keep, maintain, and preserve, at a place within the United States designated in a notice from him as provided in subparagraph (2) hereof, true, correct, complete and current copies of the books and records which he is required to make, keep current, maintain or preserve pursuant to any provision of any rule or regulation of the Commission adopted under the Act.

(2) Except as provided in paragraphs (b) and (c) hereof, each nonresident broker or dealer subject to this rule shall furnish to the Commission a written notice specifying the address of the place within the United States where the copies of the books and records required to be kept and preserved by him pursuant to subparagraph (1) are located. Each nonresident broker or dealer registered or applying for registration when this rule becomes effective shall file such notice within 30 days after such rule becomes effective. Each nonresident broker or dealer who files an application for registration after this rule becomes effective shall file such notice with such application for registration.

(b) Notwithstanding the provisions of paragraph (a) hereof, a nonresident broker or dealer subject to this rule need not keep or preserve within the United States copies of the books and records referred to in said paragraph (a), if:

(1) Such broker or dealer files with the Commission, at the time or within the period provided by paragraph (a)(2) hereof, a written undertaking in form acceptable to the Commission and signed by a person thereunto duly authorized, to furnish to the Commission, upon demand, at its principal office in Washington, D.C., or at any Regional or District Office of the Commission designated in such demand, true, correct, complete and current copies of any or all of the

books and records which he is required to make, keep current, maintain or preserve pursuant to any provision of any rule or regulation of the Commission adopted under the Act, or any part of such books and records which may be specified in such demand. Such undertaking shall be in substantially the following form:

> The undersigned hereby undertakes to furnish at his own expense to the Securities and Exchange Commission at its principal office in Washington, D.C., or at any Regional Office of said Commission specified in a demand for copies of books and records made by or on behalf of said Commission, true, correct, complete and current copies of any or all, or any part, of the books and records which the undersigned is required to make, keep current or preserve pursuant to any provision of any rule or regulation of the Securities and Exchange Commission under the Securities Exchange Act of 1934. This undertaking shall be suspended during any period when the undersigned is making, keeping current, and preserving copies of all of said books and records at a place within the United States in compliance with rule 17a–7 under the Securities Exchange Act of 1934. This undertaking shall be binding upon the undersigned and the heirs, successors and assigns of the undersigned, and the written irrevocable consents and powers of attorney of the undersigned, its general partners and managing agents filed with the Securities and Exchange Commission shall extend to and cover any action to enforce same; and

(2) Such broker or dealer furnishes to the Commission at his own expense within 14 days after written demand therefor forwarded to him by registered mail at his last address of record filed with the Commission and signed by the Secretary of the Commission or such other person as the Commission may authorize to act in its behalf, true, correct, complete and current copies of any or all books and records which such broker or dealer is required to make, keep current or preserve pursuant to any provision of any rule or regulation of the Commission adopted under the Act, or any part of such books and records which may be specified in said written demand. Such copies shall be furnished to the Commission at its principal office in Washington, D.C. or at any Regional or District Office of the Commission which may be specified in said written demand.

(c) The provisions of this section shall not apply to a broker or dealer registered pursuant to section 15(b)(11)(A) of the Act (15 U.S.C. 78*o*(b)(11)(A)) that is not a member of either a national securities exchange pursuant to section 6(a) of the Act (15 U.S.C. 78f(a)) or a national securities association registered pursuant to section 15A(a) of the Act (15 U.S.C. 78*o*–3(a)).

(d) For purposes of this rule the following definitions shall apply:

(1) The term "broker" shall have the meaning set out in section 3(a)(4) of the Act;

(2) The term "dealer" shall have the meaning set out in section 3(a)(5) of the Act;

(3) The term "nonresident broker or dealer" shall mean (i) in the case of an individual, one who resides in or has his principal place of business in any place not subject to the jurisdiction of the United States; (ii) in the case of a corporation, one incorporated in or having its principal place of business in any place not subject to the jurisdiction of the United States; (iii) in the case of a partnership or other unincorporated organization or association, one having its principal place of business in any place not subject to the jurisdiction of the United States.

Rule 17a–8. Financial Recordkeeping and Reporting of Currency and Foreign Transactions

Every registered broker or dealer who is subject to the requirements of the Currency and Foreign Transactions Reporting Act of

1970 shall comply with the reporting, recordkeeping and record retention requirements of Part 103 of Title 31 of the Code of Federal Regulations. Where Part 103 of Title 31 of the Code of Federal Regulations and Rule 17a–4 of this chapter require the same records or reports to be preserved for different periods of time, such records or reports shall be preserved for the longer period of time.

Rule 17a–10. Report of Revenue and Expenses

(a)(1) Every broker or dealer exempted from the filing requirements of paragraph (a) of Rule 17a–5 shall, not later than 17 business days after the close of each calendar year, file the Facing Page, a Statement of Income (Loss) and balance sheet from Part IIA of Form X–17A–5 and Schedule I of Form X–17A–5 for such calendar year.

(2) Every broker or dealer subject to the filing requirements of paragraph (a) of Rule 17a–5 shall submit Schedule I of Form X–17A–5 with its Form X–17A–5 for the calendar quarter ending December 31 of each year.

(b) The provisions of paragraph (a) of this rule shall not apply to a member of a national securities exchange or a registered national securities association which maintains records containing the information required by Form X–17A–5 as to each of its members, and which transmits to the Commission a copy of the record as to each such member pursuant to a plan, the procedures and provisions of which have been submitted to and declared effective by the Commission. Any such plan filed by a national securities exchange or a registered national securities association may provide that when a member is also a member of one or more national securities exchanges, or of one or more national securities exchanges and a registered national securities association, the information required to be submitted with respect to any such member may be transmitted by only one specified national securities exchange or registered national securities association. For the purpose of this rule, a plan filed with the Commission by a national securities exchange or a registered national securities association shall not become effective unless the Commission, having due regard for the public interest, for the protection of investors, and for the fulfillment of the Commission's functions under the provisions of the Act, declares the plan to be effective. Further, the Commission, in declaring any such plan effective, may impose such terms and conditions relating to the provisions of the plan and the period of its effectiveness as may be deemed necessary or appropriate in the public interest, for the protection of investors, or to carry out the Commission's duties under the Act.

(c) Individual reports filed by, or on behalf of, brokers, dealers or members of national securities exchanges pursuant to this rule are to be considered nonpublic information, except in cases where the Commission determines that it is in the public interest to direct otherwise.

(d) In the event any broker or dealer finds that it cannot file the annual report required by paragraph (a) of this rule within the time specified without undue hardship, it may file with the Commission's principal office in Washington, D.C., prior to the date upon which the report is due, an application for an extension of time to a specified date which shall not be later than 60 days after the close of the calendar year for which the report is to be made. The application shall state the reasons for the requested extension and shall contain an agreement to file the report on or before the specified date.

Rule 17a–11. Notification Provisions for Brokers and Dealers

(a) This section shall apply to every broker or dealer registered with the Commission pursuant to section 15 of the Act.

(b)(1) Every broker or dealer whose net capital declines below the minimum amount required pursuant to Rule 15c3–1 shall give notice of such deficiency that same day in accordance with paragraph (g) of this section.

The notice shall specify the broker or dealer's net capital requirement and its current amount of net capital. If a broker or dealer is informed by its designated examining authority or the Commission that it is, or has been, in violation of Rule 15c3-1 and the broker or dealer has not given notice of the capital deficiency under this Rule 17a-11, the broker or dealer, even if it does not agree that it is, or has been, in violation of Rule 15c3-1, shall give notice of the claimed deficiency, which notice may specify the broker's or dealer's reasons for its disagreement.

(2) In addition to the requirements of paragraph (b)(1) of this section, an OTC derivatives dealer or broker or dealer permitted to compute net capital pursuant to the alternative method of § 240.15c3-1e shall also provide notice if its tentative net capital falls below the minimum amount required pursuant to § 240.15c3-1. The notice shall specify the tentative net capital requirements, and current amount of net capital and tentative net capital, of the OTC derivatives dealer or the broker or dealer permitted to compute net capital pursuant to the alternative method of § 240.15c3-1e.

(c) Every broker or dealer shall send notice promptly (but within 24 hours) after the occurrence of the events specified in paragraphs (c)(1), (c)(2), (c)(3) or (c)(4) of this section in accordance with paragraph (g) of this section:

(1) If a computation made by a broker or dealer subject to the aggregate indebtedness standard of Rule 15c3-1 shows that its aggregate indebtedness is in excess of 1,200 percent of its net capital; or

(2) If a computation made by a broker or dealer, which has elected the alternative standard of Rule 15c3-1, shows that its net capital is less than 5 percent of aggregate debit items computed in accordance with Rule 15c3-3a Exhibit A: Formula for Determination Reserve Requirement of Brokers and Dealers under Rule 15c3-3; or

(3) If a computation made by a broker or dealer pursuant to § 240.15c3-1 shows that its total net capital is less than 120 percent of the broker's or dealer's required minimum net capital, or if a computation made by an OTC derivatives dealer pursuant to § 240.15c3-1 shows that its total tentative net capital is less than 120 percent of the dealer's required minimum tentative net capital.

(4) The occurrence of the fourth and each subsequent backtesting exception under § 240.15c3-1f(e)(1)(iv) during any 250 business day measurement period.

(d) Every broker or dealer who fails to make and keep current the books and records required by Rule 17a-3, shall give notice of this fact that same day in accordance with paragraph (g) of this section, specifying the books and records which have not been made or which are not current. The broker or dealer shall also transmit a report in accordance with paragraph (g) of this section within 48 hours of the notice stating what the broker or dealer has done or is doing to correct the situation.

(e) Whenever any broker or dealer discovers, or is notified by an independent public accountant, pursuant to Rule 17a-5(h)(2) or Rule 17a-12(f)(2) of the existence of any material inadequacy as defined in Rule 17a-5(g) or Rule 17a-12(e)(2), the broker or dealer shall:

(1) Give notice, in accordance with paragraph (g) of this section, of the material inadequacy within 24 hours of such discovery or notification; and

(2) Transmit a report in accordance with paragraph (g) of this section within 48 hours of the notice stating what the broker or dealer has done or is doing to correct the situation.

(f) Every national securities exchange or national securities association that learns that a member broker or dealer has failed to send notice or transmit a report as required by paragraphs (b), (c), (d), or (e) of this section, even after being advised by the securities exchange or the national securities association to send notice or transmit a report, shall immediately give notice of such failure in accordance with paragraph (g) of this section.

(g) Every notice or report required to be given or transmitted by this section shall be given or transmitted to the principal office of the Commission in Washington, D.C., the regional or district office of the Commission for the region or district in which the broker or dealer has its principal place of business, the designated examining authority of which such broker or dealer is a member, and the Commodity Futures Trading Commission if the broker or dealer is registered as a futures commission merchant with such Commission. For the purposes of this section, "notice" shall be given or transmitted by telegraphic notice or facsimile transmission. The report required by paragraphs (d) or (e)(2) of this section may be transmitted by overnight delivery.

(h) Other notice provisions relating to the Commission's financial responsibility or reporting rules are contained in § 240.15c3–1(a)(6)(iv)(B), § 240.15c3–1(a)(6)(v), § 240.15c3–1(a)(7)(ii), § 240.15c3–1(a)(7)(iii), § 240.15c3–1(c)(2)(x)(B)(1), § 240.15c3–1(c)(2)(x)(F)(3), § 240.15c3–1(e), § 240.15c3–1d(c)(2), § 240.15c3–3(i), § 240.17a–5(h)(2) and § 240.17a–12(f)(2).

(i) The provisions of this section shall not apply to a broker or dealer registered pursuant to section 15(b)(11)(A) of the Act (15 U.S.C. 78*o*(b)(11)(A)) that is not a member of either a national securities exchange pursuant to section 6(a) of the Act (15 U.S.C. 78f(a)) or a national securities association registered pursuant to section 15A(a) of the Act (15 U.S.C. 78*o*–3(a)).

Rule 17a–12. Reports to be Made by Certain OTC Derivatives Dealers

(a) *Filing of quarterly reports.* (1) This paragraph (a) shall apply to every OTC derivatives dealer registered pursuant to Section 15 of the Act (15 U.S.C. 78o).

(i) Every OTC derivatives dealer shall file Part IIB of Form X–17A–5 (§ 249.617 of this chapter) within 17 business days after the end of each calendar quarter and within 17 business days after the date selected for the annual audit of financial statements where said date is other than the end of the calendar quarter.

(ii) Upon receiving from the Commission written notice that additional reporting is required, an OTC derivatives dealer shall file monthly, or at such times as shall be specified, Part IIB of Form X–17A–5 (§ 249.617 of this chapter) and such other financial or operational information as shall be required by the Commission.

(2) The reports provided for in this paragraph (a) shall be considered filed when received at the Commission's principal office in Washington, DC. All reports filed pursuant to this paragraph (a) shall be deemed to be confidential.

(3) Upon written application by an OTC derivatives dealer to the Commission, the Commission may extend the time for filing the information required by this paragraph (a). The written application shall be filed with the Commission at its principal office in Washington DC.

(b) *Annual filing of audited financial statements.* (1)(i) Every OTC derivatives dealer registered pursuant to Section 15 of the Act (15 U.S.C. 78o) shall file annually, on a calendar or fiscal year basis, a report which shall be audited by a certified public accountant. Reports filed pursuant to this paragraph (b) shall be as of the same fixed or determinable date each year, unless a change is approved in writing by the Commission.

(ii) An OTC derivatives dealer succeeding to and continuing the business of another OTC derivatives dealer need not file a report under this paragraph (b) as of a date in the fiscal or calendar year in which the succession occurs if the predecessor OTC derivatives dealer has filed a report in compliance with this paragraph (b) as of a date in such fiscal or calendar year.

(2) The annual audit report shall contain a Statement of Financial Condition (in a format and on a basis which is consistent with the total reported on the Statement of Financial Condition contained in Form X–17A–5 (§ 249.617 of this chapter)), Part IIB, a Statement of Income, a Statement of Cash Flows, a Statement of Changes in Stockholders' or Partners' or Sole Proprietor's Equity, and a Statement of Changes in Liabilities Subordinated to Claims of General Creditors. Such statements shall be in a format which is consistent with such statements as contained in Form X–17A–5 (§ 249.617 of this chapter), Part IIB. If the Statement of Financial Condition filed in accordance with instructions to Form X–17A–5 (§ 249.617 of this chapter), Part IIB, is not consolidated, a summary of financial data for subsidiaries not consolidated in the Part IIB Statement of Financial Condition as filed by the OTC derivatives dealer shall be included in the notes to the consolidated statement of financial condition reported on by the certified public accountant. The summary financial data shall include the assets, liabilities, and net worth or stockholders' equity of the unconsolidated subsidiaries.

(3) Supporting schedules shall include, from Part IIB of Form X–17A–5 (§ 249.617 of this chapter), a Computation of Net Capital under § 240.15c3–1.

(4) A reconciliation, including appropriate explanations, of the Computation of Net Capital under § 240.15c3–1 contained in the audit report with the broker's or dealer's corresponding unaudited most recent. Part IIB filing shall be filed with the report when material differences exist. If no material differences exist, a statement so indicating shall be filed.

(5) The annual audit report shall be filed not more than sixty days after the date of the financial statements.

(6) Two copies of the annual audit report shall be filed at the Commission's principal office in Washington, DC.

(c) *Nature and form of reports.* The financial statements filed pursuant to paragraph (b) of this section shall be prepared and filed in accordance with the following requirements:

(1) An audit shall be conducted by a certified public accountant who shall be in fact independent as defined in paragraph (f) of this section, and it shall give an opinion covering the statements filed pursuant to paragraph (b) of this section.

(2) Attached to the report shall be an oath or affirmation that, to the best knowledge and belief of the person making such oath or affirmation, the financial statements and schedules are true and correct and neither the OTC derivatives dealer, nor any partner, officer, or director, as the case may be, has any significant interest in any counterparty or in any account classified solely as that of a counterparty. The oath or affirmation shall be made before a person duly authorized to administer such oaths or affirmations. If the OTC derivatives dealer is a sole proprietorship, the oath or affirmation shall be made by the proprietor; if a partnership, by a general partner; or if a corporation, by a duly authorized officer.

(3) All of the statements filed pursuant to paragraph (b) of this section shall be confidential except that they shall be available for use by any official or employee of the United States or by any other person to whom the Commission authorizes disclosure of such information as being in the public interest.

(d) *Qualification of accountants.* The Commission will not recognize any person as a certified public accountant who is not duly registered and in good standing as such under the laws of the State of his principal office.

(e) *Designation of accountant.* (1) Every OTC derivatives dealer shall file no later than December 10 of each year with the Commission's principal office in Washington, DC a statement indicating the existence of an agreement, dated no later than December 1 of that year, with a certified public accountant covering a contractual commitment to conduct the

OTC derivatives dealer's annual audit during the following calendar year.

(2) If the agreement is of a continuing nature, providing for successive yearly audits, no further filing is required. If the agreement is for a single audit, or if the continuing agreement previously filed has been terminated or amended, a new statement must be filed by the required date.

(3) The statement shall be headed "Notice pursuant to § 240.17a–12(e)" and shall contain the following information:

(i) Name, address, telephone number, and registration number of the OTC derivatives dealer;

(ii) Name, address, and telephone number of the certified public accounting firm; and

(iii) The audit date of the OTC derivatives dealer for the year covered by the agreement.

(4) Notwithstanding the date of filing specified in paragraph (e)(1) of this section, every OTC derivatives dealer shall file the notice provided for in paragraph (e) of this section within 30 days following the effective date of registration as an OTC derivatives dealer.

(f) *Independence of accountant.* A certified public accountant shall be independent in accordance with the provisions of § 210.2–01(b) and (c) of this chapter.

(g) *Replacement of accountant.* (1) An OTC derivatives dealer shall file a notice that must be received by the Commission's principal office in Washington, DC not more than 15 business days after:

(i) The OTC derivatives dealer has notified the certified public accountant whose opinion covered the most recent financial statements filed under paragraph (b) of this section that the certified public accountant's services will not be utilized in future engagements; or

(ii) The OTC derivatives dealer has notified a certified public accountant who was engaged to give an opinion covering the financial statements to be filed under paragraph (b) of this section that the engagement has been terminated; or

(iii) A certified public accountant has notified the OTC derivatives dealer that it will not continue under an engagement or give an opinion covering the financial statements to be filed under paragraph (b) of this section; or

(iv) A new certified public accountant has been engaged to give an opinion covering the financial statements to be filed under paragraph (b) of this section without any notice of termination having been given to or by the previously engaged certified public accountant.

(2) Such notice shall state the date of notification of the termination of the engagement of the former certified public accountant or the engagement of the new certified public accountant, as applicable, and the details of any disagreements existing during the 24 months (or the period of the engagement, if less) preceding such termination or new engagement relating to any matter of accounting principles or practices, financial statement disclosure, auditing scope or procedure, or compliance with applicable rules of the Commission, which disagreements, if not resolved to the satisfaction of the former certified public accountant, would have caused the former certified public accountant to make reference to them in connection with the report on the subject matter of the disagreements. The disagreements required to be reported in response to the preceding sentence include both those resolved to the former certified public accountant's satisfaction and those not resolved to the former certified public accountant's satisfaction. Disagreements contemplated by this section are those that occur at the decision-making level (*i.e.,* between principal financial officers of the OTC derivatives dealer and personnel of the certified public accounting firm responsible for rendering its report). The notice shall also state whether the certified public accountant's report on the financial statements for any of

the past two years contained an adverse opinion or a disclaimer of opinion or was qualified as to uncertainties, audit scope, or accounting principles, and describe the nature of each such adverse opinion, disclaimer of opinion, or qualification. The OTC derivatives dealer shall also request the former certified public accountant to furnish the OTC derivatives dealer with a letter addressed to the Commission stating whether the former certified public accountant agrees with the statements contained in the notice of the OTC derivatives dealer and, if not, stating the respects in which the former certified public accountant does not agree. The OTC derivatives dealer shall file three copies of the notice and the certified public accountant's letter, one copy of which shall be manually signed by the sole proprietor, or a general partner or a duly authorized corporate officer, as appropriate, and by the certified public accountant.

(h) *Audit objectives.* (1) The audit shall be made in accordance with U.S. Generally Accepted Auditing Standards and shall include a review of the accounting system, the internal accounting controls, and procedures for safeguarding securities including appropriate tests thereof for the period since the date of the prior audited financial statements. The audit shall include all procedures necessary under the circumstances to enable the certified public accountant to express an opinion on the statement of financial condition, results of operations, cash flows, and the Computation of Net Capital under § 240.15c3–1. The scope of the audit and review of the accounting system, the internal accounting controls, and procedures for safeguarding securities shall be sufficient to provide reasonable assurance that any material inadequacies existing at the date of the examination in the following are disclosed:

(i) The accounting system;

(ii) The internal accounting controls; and

(iii) The procedures for safeguarding securities.

(2) A material inadequacy in the accounting system, internal accounting controls, procedures for safeguarding securities, and practices and procedures referred to in paragraph (h) (1) of this section that must be reported under these audit objectives includes any condition which has contributed substantially to or, if appropriate corrective action is not taken, could reasonably be expected to:

(i) Inhibit an OTC derivatives dealer from promptly completing securities transactions or promptly discharging its responsibilities to counterparties, other brokers and dealers, or creditors;

(ii) Result in material financial loss;

(iii) Result in material misstatements of the OTC derivatives dealer's financial statements; or

(iv) Result in violations of the Commission's recordkeeping or financial responsibility rules to an extent that could reasonably be expected to result in the conditions described in paragraphs (h)(2)(i), (ii), or (iii) of this section.

(i) *Extent and timing of audit procedures.* (1) The extent and timing of audit procedures are matters for the certified public accountant to determine on the basis of its review and evaluation of existing internal controls and other audit procedures performed in accordance with U.S. Generally Accepted Auditing Standards and the audit objectives set forth in paragraph (h) of this section.

(2) If, during the course of the audit or interim work, the certified public accountant determines that any material inadequacies exist in the accounting system, internal accounting controls, procedures for safeguarding securities, or as otherwise defined in paragraph (h)(2) of this section, then the certified public accountant shall call it to the attention of the chief financial officer of the OTC derivatives dealer, who shall inform the Commission by telegraphic or facsimile notice within 24 hours thereafter as set forth in § 240.17a–11(e) and (g). The OTC derivatives dealer shall also furnish the certified public accountant with a copy of said notice to the Commission by tele-

gram or facsimile within the same 24 hour period. If the certified public accountant fails to receive such notice from the OTC derivatives dealer within that 24 hour period, or if the certified public accountant disagrees with the statements contained in the notice of the OTC derivatives dealer, the certified public accountant shall inform the Commission by report of material inadequacy within 24 hours thereafter as set forth in § 240.17a–11(g). Such report from the certified public accountant shall, if the OTC derivatives dealer failed to file a notice, describe any material inadequacies found to exist. If the OTC derivatives dealer filed a notice, the certified public accountant shall file a report detailing the aspects, if any, of the OTC derivatives dealer's notice with which the certified public accountant does not agree.

(j) *Accountant's report, general provisions.*—(1) *Technical requirements.* The certified public accountant's report shall be dated; be signed manually; indicate the city and state where issued; and identify without detailed enumeration the financial statements and schedules covered by the report.

(2) *Representations as to the audit.* The certified public accountant's report shall state that the audit was made in accordance with U.S. Generally Accepted Auditing Standards; state whether the certified public accountant reviewed the procedures followed for safeguarding securities; and designate any auditing procedures deemed necessary by the certified public accountant under the circumstances of the particular case that have been omitted, and the reason for their omission. Nothing in this section shall be construed to imply authority for the omission of any procedure which certified public accountants would ordinarily employ in the course of an audit made for the purpose of expressing the opinions required under this section.

(3) *Opinion to be expressed.* The certified public accountant's report shall state clearly the opinion of the certified public accountant:

(i) In respect of the financial statements and schedules covered by the report and the accounting principles and practices reflected therein; and

(ii) As to the consistency of the application of the accounting principles, or as to any changes in such principles which have a material effect on the financial statements.

(4) *Exceptions.* Any matters to which the certified public accountant takes exception shall be clearly identified, explained, and, to the extent practicable, the effect of each such exception on the related financial statements shall be provided.

(5) *Definitions.* For the purpose of this section, the terms *audit* (or *examination*), *accountant's report,* and *certified* shall have the meanings given in § 210.1–02 of this chapter.

(k) *Accountant's report on material inadequacies and reportable conditions.* The OTC derivatives dealer shall file concurrently with the annual audit report a supplemental report by the certified public accountant describing any material inadequacies or any matter that would be deemed to be a reportable condition under U.S. Generally Accepted Auditing Standards that are unresolved as of the date of the certified public accountant's report. The report shall also describe any material inadequacies found to have existed since the date of the previous audit. The supplemental report shall indicate any corrective action taken or proposed by the OTC derivatives dealer with regard to any identified material inadequacies or reportable conditions. If the audit did not disclose any material inadequacies or reportable conditions, the supplemental report shall so state.

(*l*) *Accountant's report on management controls.*

(1) The OTC derivatives dealer shall file concurrently with the annual audit report a supplemental report by the certified public accountant indicating the results of the certified public accountant's review of the OTC derivatives dealer's internal risk management control system with respect to the

requirements of § 240.15c3–4. This review shall be conducted in accordance with procedures agreed to by the OTC derivatives dealer and the certified public accountant conducting the review. The purpose of the review is to confirm that the OTC derivatives dealer has established, documented, and maintained an internal risk management control system in accordance with § 240.15c3–4, and is in compliance with that internal risk management control system.

(2) The agreed-upon procedures are to be performed, and the report is to be prepared, in accordance with U.S. Generally Accepted Attestation Standards.

(3) Prior to the commencement of the initial review, every OTC derivatives dealer shall file the procedures to be performed pursuant to paragraph (*l*)(1) of this section with the Commission's principal office in Washington, DC. Prior to the commencement of any subsequent review, every OTC derivatives dealer shall file with the Commission's principal office in Washington, DC a notice of changes to the agreed-upon procedures.

(m) *Accountant's report on inventory pricing and modeling.* (1) The OTC derivatives dealer shall file concurrently with the annual audit report a supplemental report by the certified public accountant indicating the results of the certified public accountant's review of the broker's or dealer's inventory pricing and modeling procedures. This review shall be conducted in accordance with procedures agreed to by the OTC derivatives dealer and by the certified public accountant conducting the review. The purpose of the review is to confirm that the pricing and modeling procedures relied upon by the OTC derivatives dealer conform to the procedures submitted to the Commission as part of its OTC derivatives dealer application, and that the procedures comply with the qualitative and quantitative standards set forth in § 240.15c3–1f.

(2) The agreed-upon procedures are to be performed and the report is to be prepared in accordance with U.S. Generally Accepted Attestation Standards.

(3) Every OTC derivatives dealer shall file prior to the commencement of the initial review, the procedures to be performed pursuant to paragraph (m)(1) of this section with the Commission's principal office in Washington, DC. Prior to the commencement of each subsequent review, every OTC derivatives dealer shall file with the Commission's principal office in Washington, DC notice of changes in the agreed-upon procedures.

(n) *Extensions and exemptions.* Upon the written request of the OTC derivatives dealer, or on its own motion, the Commission may grant an extension of time or an exemption from any of the requirements of this section either unconditionally or on specified terms and conditions.

(*o*) *Notification of change of fiscal year.* (1) In the event any OTC derivatives dealer finds it necessary to change its fiscal year, it must file a notice of such change with the Commission's principal office in Washington, DC.

(2) Such notice shall contain a detailed explanation of the reasons for the change. Any change in the filing period for the audit report must be approved by the Commission.

(p) *Filing requirements.* For purposes of filing requirements as described in § 240.17a–12, these filings shall be deemed to have been accomplished upon receipt at the Commission's principal office in Washington, DC.

Rule 17a–13. Quarterly Security Counts to Be Made by Certain Exchange Members, Brokers and Dealers

(a) This rule shall apply to every member of a national securities exchange who transacts a business in securities directly with or for others than members of a national securities exchange, every broker or dealer (other than a member) who transacts a business in securities through the medium of any member of a national securities exchange, and every broker or dealer registered pursuant to section 15 of the Act; except that a broker or dealer meeting all of the following conditions shall be exempt from the provisions of this section:

(1) His dealer transactions (as principal for his own account) are limited to the purchase, sale, and redemption of redeemable shares of registered investment companies or of interests or participations in an insurance company separate account, whether or not registered as an investment company; except that a broker or dealer transacting business as a sole proprietor may also effect occasional transactions in other securities for his own account with or through another registered broker-dealer;

(2) His transactions as broker (agent) are limited to: (i) The sale and redemption of redeemable securities of registered investment companies or of interests or participations in an insurance company separate account, whether or not registered as an investment company; (ii) the solicitation of share accounts for savings and loan associations insured by an instrumentality of the United States; and (iii) the sale of securities for the account of a customer to obtain funds for immediate reinvestment in redeemable securities of registered investment companies; and

(3) He promptly transmits all funds and delivers all securities received in connection with his activities as a broker or dealer, and does not otherwise hold funds or securities for or owe money or securities to customers.

Notwithstanding the foregoing, this rule shall not apply to any insurance company which is a registered broker-dealer, and which otherwise meets all of the conditions in subparagraphs (1), (2), and (3) of this paragraph solely by reason of its participation in transactions that are a part of the business of insurance, including the purchasing, selling, or holding of securities for or on behalf of such company's general and separate accounts.

(b) Any member, broker, or dealer who is subject to the provisions of this rule shall at least once in each calendar quarter-year:

(1) Physically examine and count all securities held, including securities that are the subjects of repurchase or reverse repurchase agreements;

(2) Account for all securities in transfer, in transit, pledged, loaned, borrowed, deposited, failed to receive, failed to deliver, subject to repurchase or reverse repurchase agreements or otherwise subject to his control or direction but not in his physical possession by examination and comparison of the supporting detail records with the appropriate ledger control accounts;

(3) Verify all securities in transfer, in transit, pledged, loaned, borrowed, deposited, failed to receive, failed to deliver, subject to repurchase or reverse repurchase agreements or otherwise subject to his control or direction but not in his physical possession, where such securities have been in said status for longer than thirty days;

(4) Compare the results of the count and verification with his records; and

(5) Record on the books and records of the member, broker, or dealer all unresolved differences setting forth the security involved and date of comparison in a security count difference account no later than 7 business days after the date of each required quarterly security examination, count, and verification in accordance with the requirements provided in paragraph (c) of this rule. *Provided, however,* That no examination, count, verification, and comparison for the purpose of this section shall be within 2 months of or more than 4 months following a prior examination, count, verification, and comparison made hereunder.

(c) The examination, count, verification, and comparison may be made either as of a date certain or on a cyclical basis covering the entire list of securities. In either case the recordation shall be effected within 7 business days subsequent to the examination, count, verification, and comparison of a particular security. In the event that an examination, count, verification, and comparison is made on a cyclical basis, it shall not extend over more than 1 calendar quarter-year, and no security shall be examined, counted, verified, or compared for the purpose of this rule less than 2 months or more than 4 months after a prior examination, count, verification, and comparison.

(d) The examination, count, verification, and comparison shall be made or supervised by persons whose regular duties do not require them to have direct responsibility for the proper care and protection of the securities or the making or preservation of the subject records.

(e) The provisions of this section shall not apply to a broker or dealer registered pursuant to section 15(b)(11)(A) of the Act (15 U.S.C. 78*o*(b)(11)(A)) that is not a member of either a national securities exchange pursuant to section 6(a) of the Act (15 U.S.C. 78f(a)) or a national securities association registered pursuant to section 15A(a) of the Act (15 U.S.C. 78*o*-3(a)).

(f) The Commission may, upon written request, exempt from the provisions of this section, either unconditionally or on specified terms and conditions, any member, broker, or dealer who satisfies the Commission that it is not necessary in the public interest and for the protection of investors to subject the particular member, broker, or dealer to certain or all of the provisions of this section, because of the special nature of his business, the safeguards he has established for the protection of customers' funds and securities, or such other reason as the Commission deems appropriate.

Rule 17a-19. Form X-17A-19. Report by National Securities Exchanges and Registered National Securities Associations of Changes in the Membership Status of Any of Their Members

Every national securities exchange and every registered national securities association shall file with the Commission at its principal office in Washington, D.C., and with the Securities Investor Protection Corporation such information as is required on Form X-17A-19 within 5 business days of the occurrence of the initiation of the membership of any person or the suspension or termination of the membership of any member. Nothing in this section shall be deemed to relieve a national securities exchange or a registered national securities association of its responsibilities under Rule 17a-5(b)(5) except that, to the extent a national securities exchange or a registered national securities association promptly files a report on Form X-17A-19 including therewith, inter alia, information sufficient to satisfy the requirements of Rule 17a-5(b)(5), it shall not be required to file a report pursuant to Rule 17a-5(b). Upon the occurrence of the events described in this paragraph, every national securities exchange and every registered national securities association shall notify in writing such member of its responsibilities under Rule 17a-5(b).

Rule 17a-22. Supplemental Material of Registered Clearing Agencies

Within ten days after issuing, or making generally available, to its participants or to other entities with whom it has a significant relationship, such as pledgees, transfer agents, or self-regulatory organizations, any material (including, for example, manuals, notices, circulars, bulletins, lists, or periodicals), a registered clearing agency shall file three copies of such material with the Commission. A registered clearing agency for which the Commission is not the appropriate regulatory agency shall at the same time file one copy of such material with its appropriate regulatory agency.

Rule 17a-25. Electronic Submission of Securities Transaction Information By Exchange Members, Brokers, and Dealers

(a) Every member, broker, or dealer subject to § 240.17a-3 shall, upon request, electronically submit to the Commission the securities transaction information as required in this section:

(1) If the transaction was a proprietary transaction effected or caused to be effected by the member, broker, or dealer for any account in which such member, broker, or dealer, or person associated with the member, broker, or dealer, is directly or indirectly interested, such member, broker or dealer shall submit the following information:

(i) Clearing house number, or alpha symbol of the member, broker, or dealer submitting the information;

(ii) Clearing house number(s), or alpha symbol(s) of the member(s), broker(s) or dealer(s) on the opposite side of the transaction;

(iii) Identifying symbol assigned to the security;

(iv) Date transaction was executed;

(v) Number of shares, or quantity of bonds or options contracts, for each specific transaction; whether each transaction was a purchase, sale, or short sale; and, if an options contract, whether open long or short or close long or short;

(vi) Transaction price;

(vii) Account number; and

(viii) The identity of the exchange or other market where the transaction was executed.

(2) If the transaction was effected or caused to be effected by the member, broker, or dealer for any customer account, such member, broker, or dealer shall submit the following information:

(i) Information contained in paragraphs (a)(1)(i) through (a)(1)(viii) of this section;

(ii) Customer name, address(es), branch office number, registered representative number, whether the order was solicited or unsolicited, date account opened, and the customer's tax identification number(s); and

(iii) If the transaction was effected for a customer of another member, broker, or dealer, whether the other member, broker, or dealer was acting as principal or agent on the transaction.

(b) In addition to the information in paragraph (a) of this section, a member, broker, or dealer shall, upon request, electronically submit to the Commission the following securities transaction information for transactions involving entities that trade using multiple accounts:

(1)(i) If part or all of an account's transactions at the reporting member, broker, or dealer have been transferred or otherwise forwarded to one or more accounts at another member, broker, or dealer, an identifier for this type of transaction; and

(ii) If part or all of an account's transactions at the reporting member, broker, or dealer have been transferred or otherwise received from one or more other members, brokers, or dealers, an identifier for this type of transaction.

(2)(i) If part or all of an account's transactions at the reporting member, broker, or dealer have been transferred or otherwise received from another account at the reporting member, broker, or dealer, an identifier for this type of transaction; and

(ii) If part or all of an account's transactions at the reporting member, broker, or dealer have been transferred or otherwise forwarded to one or more other accounts at the reporting member, broker, or dealer, an identifier for this type of transaction.

(3) If an account's transaction was processed by a depository institution, the identifier assigned to the account by the depository institution.

(c) Every member, broker, or dealer shall, upon request, submit to the Commission and, keep current, information containing the full name, title, address, telephone number(s), facsimile number(s); and electronic-mail address(es) for each person designated by the member, broker, or dealer as responsible for processing securities transaction information requests from the Commission.

(d) The member, broker, or dealer should comply with the format for the electronic submission of the securities transaction information described in paragraphs (a) and (b) of this section as specified by the member, broker, or dealer's designated self-regulatory organization under § 240.17d-1, unless otherwise specified by Commission rule.

Rule 17d-1. Examination for Compliance With Applicable Financial Responsibility Rules

(a) Where a member of SIPC is a member of more than one self-regulatory organization, the Commission shall designate by written notice to one of such organizations responsibility for examining such member for compliance with applicable financial responsibility rules. In making such designations the Commission shall take into consideration the regulatory capabilities and procedures of the self-regulatory organizations, availability of staff, convenience of location, unnecessary regulatory duplication, and such other factors as the Commission may consider germane to the protection of investors, the cooperation and coordination among self-regulatory organizations, and the development of a national market system for the clearance and settlement of securities transactions.

(b) Upon designation of responsibility pursuant to paragraph (a), all other self-regulatory organizations of which such person is a member or participant shall be relieved of such responsibility to the extent specified.

(c) After the Commission has acted pursuant to paragraphs (a) and (b), any self-regulatory organization relieved of responsibility with respect to a member may notify customers of, and persons doing business with, such member of the limited nature of its responsibility for such member's compliance with applicable financial responsibility rules.

Rule 17d-2. Program for Allocation of Regulatory Responsibility

(a) Any two or more self-regulatory organizations may file with the Commission within ninety (90) days of the effective date of this rule, and thereafter as changes in designation are necessary or appropriate, a plan for allocating among the self-regulatory organizations the responsibility to receive regulatory reports from persons who are members or participants of more than one of such self-regulatory organizations to examine such persons for compliance, or to enforce compliance by such persons, with specified provisions of the Securities Exchange Act of 1934, the rules and regulations thereunder, and the rules of such self-regulatory organizations, or to carry out other specified regulatory functions with respect to such persons.

(b) Any plan filed hereunder may contain provisions for the allocation among the parties of expenses reasonably incurred by the self-regulatory organization having regulatory responsibilities under the plan.

(c) After appropriate notice and opportunity for comment, the Commission may, by written notice, declare such a plan, or any part of the plan, effective if it finds the plan, or any part thereof, necessary or appropriate in the public interest and for the protection of investors, to foster cooperation and coordination among self-regulatory organizations, or to remove impediments to and foster the development of the national market system and a national system for the clearance and settlement of securities transactions and in conformity with the factors set forth in section 17(d) of the Securities Exchange Act of 1934.

(d) Upon the effectiveness of such a plan or part thereof, any self-regulatory organization which is a party to the plan shall be relieved of responsibility as to any person for whom such responsibility is allocated under the plan to another self-regulatory organization to the extent of such allocation.

(e) Nothing herein shall preclude any self-regulatory organization from entering into more than one plan filed hereunder.

(f) After the Commission has declared a plan or part thereof effective pursuant to paragraph (c) of this rule or acted pursuant to paragraph (g) of this rule, a self-regulatory organization relieved of responsibility may notify customers of, and persons doing business with, such member or participant of the limited nature of its responsibility for such member's or participant's acts, practices, and course of business.

(g) In the event that plans declared effective pursuant to paragraph (c) of this rule do not provide for all members or participants or do not allocate all regulatory responsibilities, the Commission may, after due consideration of the factors enumerated in section 17(d)(1) and notice and opportunity for comment, designate one or more of the self-regulatory organizations responsible for specified regulatory responsibilities with respect to such members or participants.

Rule 17f–1. Requirements for Reporting and Inquiry With Respect to Missing, Lost, Counterfeit or Stolen Securities

(a) *Definitions.* For purposes of this rule:

(1) The term "reporting institution" shall include every national securities exchange, member thereof, registered securities association, broker, dealer, municipal securities dealer, government securities broker, government securities dealer, registered transfer agent, registered clearing agency, participant therein, member of the Federal Reserve System and bank whose deposits are insured by the Federal Deposit Insurance Corporation;

(2) The term "uncertificated security" shall mean a security not represented by an instrument and the transfer of which is registered upon books maintained for that purpose by or on behalf of the issuer;

(3) The term "global certificate securities issue" shall mean a securities issue for which a single master certificate representing the entire issue is registered in the nominee name of a registered clearing agency and for which beneficial owners cannot receive negotiable securities certificates;

(4) The term "customer" shall mean any person with whom the reporting institution has entered into at least one prior securities-related transaction; and

(5) The term "securities-related transaction" shall mean a purchase, sale or pledge of investment securities, or a custodial arrangement for investment securities.

(6) The term "securities certificate" means any physical instrument that represents or purports to represent ownership in a security that was printed by or on behalf of the issuer thereof and shall include any such instrument that is or was:

(i) Printed but not issued;

(ii) Issued and outstanding, including treasury securities;

(iii) Cancelled, which for this purpose means either or both of the procedures set forth in § 240.17Ad–19(a)(1); or

(iv) Counterfeit or reasonably believed to be counterfeit.

(7) The term *issuer* shall include an issuer's:

(i) Transfer agent(s), paying agent(s), tender agent(s), and person(s) providing similar services; and

(ii) Corporate predecessor(s) and successor(s).

(8) The term *missing* shall include any securities certificate that:

(i) Cannot be located or accounted for, but is not believed to be lost or stolen; or

(ii) A transfer agent claims or believes was destroyed in any manner other than by the transfer agent's own certificate destruction procedures as provided in § 240.17Ad–19.

(b) Every reporting institution shall register with the Commission or its designee in accordance with instructions issued by the Commission except:

(1) A member of a national securities exchange who effects securities transactions through the trading facilities of the exchange and has not received or held customer securities within the last six months;

(2) A reporting institution that, within the last six months, limited its securities activities exclusively to uncertificated securities, global securities issues or any securities issue for which neither record nor beneficial owners can obtain a negotiable securities certificate; or

(3) A reporting institution whose business activities, within the last six months, did not involve the handling of securities certificates.

(c) *Reporting Requirements.*

(1) *Stolen Securities.* (i) Every reporting institution shall report to the Commission or its designee, and to a registered transfer agent for the issue, the discovery of the theft or loss of any securities certificates where there is substantial basis for believing that criminal activity was involved. Such report shall be made within one business day of the discovery and, if the certificate numbers of the securities cannot be ascertained at that time, they shall be reported as soon thereafter as possible.

(ii) Every reporting institution shall promptly report to the Federal Bureau of Investigation upon the discovery of the theft or loss of any securities certificate where there is substantial basis for believing that criminal activity was involved.

(2) *Missing or Lost Securities.* Every reporting institution shall report to the Commission or its designee, and to a registered transfer agent for the issue, the discovery of the loss of any securities certificate where criminal actions are not suspected when the securities certificate has been missing or lost for a period of two business days. Such report shall be made within one business day of the end of such period *except* that:

(i) Securities certificates lost, missing, or stolen while in transit to customers, transfer agents, banks, brokers or dealers shall be reported by the delivering institution by the later of two business days after notice of non-receipt or as soon after such notice as the certificate numbers of the securities can be ascertained.

(ii) Where a shipment of retired securities certificates is in transit between any transfer agents, banks, brokers, dealers, or other reporting institutions, with no affiliation existing between such entities, and the delivering institution fails to receive notice of receipt or non-receipt of the certificates, the delivering institution shall act to determine the facts. In the event of non-delivery where the certificates are not recovered by the delivering institution, the delivering institution shall report the certificates as lost, stolen, or missing to the Commission or its designee within a reasonable time under the circumstances but in any event within twenty business days from the date of shipment.

(iii) Securities certificates considered lost or missing as a result of securities counts or verifications required by rule, regulation or otherwise (e.g., dividend record date verification made as a result of firm policy or internal audit function report) shall be reported by the later of ten business days after completion of such securities count or verification or as soon after such count or verification as the certificate numbers of the securities can be ascertained.

(iv) Securities certificates not received during the completion of delivery, deposit or withdrawal shall be reported in the following manner:

(A) Where delivery of securities certificates is through a clearing agency, the delivering institution shall supply to the receiving institution the certificate number of the security within two business days from the date of request from the receiving institution. The receiving institution shall report within one business day of notification of the certificate number;

(B) Where the delivery of securities certificates is in person and where the delivering institution has a receipt, the delivering institution shall supply the receiving institution the certificate numbers of the securities within two business days from the date of request from the receiving institution. The receiving institution shall report within one business day of notification of the certificate number;

(C) Where the delivery of securities certificates is in person and where the delivering institution has no receipt, the delivering institution shall report within two business days of notification of non-receipt by the receiving institution; or

(D) Where delivery of securities certificates is made by mail or via draft, if payment is not received within ten business days, the delivering institution shall confirm with the receiving institution the failure to receive such delivery; if confirmation shows non-receipt, the delivering institution shall report within two business days of such confirmation.

(3) *Counterfeit Securities.* Every reporting institution shall report the discovery of any counterfeit securities certificate to the Commission or its designee, to a registered transfer agent for the issue, and to the Federal Bureau of Investigation within one business day of such discovery.

(4) *Transfer Agent Reporting Obligations.* Every transfer agent shall make the reports required above only if it receives notification of the loss, theft or counterfeiting from a non-reporting institution or if it receives notification other than on a Form X–17F–1A or if the certificate was in its possession at the time of the loss.

(5) *Recovery.* Every reporting institution that originally reported a lost, missing or stolen securities certificate pursuant to this rule shall report recovery of that securities certificate to the Commission or its designee and to a registered transfer agent for the issue within one business day of such recovery or finding. Every reporting institution that originally made a report in which criminality was indicated also shall notify the Federal Bureau of Investigation that the securities certificate has been recovered.

(6) *Information to Be Reported.* All reports made pursuant to this rule shall include, if applicable or available, the following information with respect to each securities certificate:

(i) Issuer;

(ii) Type of security and series;

(iii) Date of issue;

(iv) Maturity date;

(v) Denomination;

(vi) Interest rate;

(vii) Certificate number, including alphabetical prefix or suffix;

(viii) Name in which registered;

(ix) Distinguishing characteristics, if counterfeit;

(x) Date of discovery of loss or recovery;

(xi) CUSIP number;

(xii) Financial Industry Numbering System ("FINS") Number; and

(xiii) Type of loss.

(7) *Forms.* Reporting institutions shall make all reports to the Commission or its designee and to a registered transfer agent for the issue pursuant to this section on Form X–17F–1A. Reporting institutions shall make reports to the Federal Bureau of Investigation pursuant to this Section on Form X–17F–1A, unless the reporting insti-

tution is a member of the Federal Reserve System or a bank whose deposits are insured by the Federal Deposit Insurance Corporation, in which case reports may be made on the form required by the institution's appropriate regulatory agency for reports to the Federal Bureau of Investigation.

(d) *Required Inquiries.* (1) Every reporting institution (except a reporting institution that, acting in its capacity as transfer agent, paying agent, exchange agent or tender agent for an equity issue, or registrar for a bond or other debt issue, compares all transactions against a shareholder or bondholder list and a current list of stop transfers) shall inquire of the Commission or its designee with respect to every securities certificate which comes into its possession or keeping, whether by pledge, transfer or otherwise, to ascertain whether such securities certificate has been reported as missing, lost, counterfeit or stolen, unless:

(i) The securities certificate is received directly from the issuer or issuing agent at issuance;

(ii) The securities certificate is received from another reporting institution or from a Federal Reserve Bank or Branch;

(iii) The securities certificate is received from a customer of the reporting institution; and

(A) is registered in the name of such customer or its nominee; or

(B) was previously sold to such customer, as verified by the internal records of the reporting institution;

(iv) The securities certificate is received as part of a transaction which has an aggregate face value of $10,000 or less in the case of bonds, or market value of $10,000 or less in the case of stocks; or

(v) The securities certificate is received directly from a drop which is affiliated with a reporting institution for the purposes of receiving or delivering certificates on behalf of the reporting institution.

(2) *Form of Inquiry.* Inquiries shall be made in such manner as prescribed by the Commission or its designee.

(3) A reporting institution shall make required inquiries by the end of the fifth business day after a securities certificate comes into its possession or keeping, provided that such inquiries shall be made before the certificate is sold, used as collateral, or sent to another reporting institution.

(e) *Permissive Reports and Inquiries.* Every reporting institution may report to or inquire of the Commission or its designee with respect to any securities certificate not otherwise required by this rule to be the subject of a report or inquiry. The Commission on written request or upon its own motion may permit reports to and inquiries of the system by any other person or entity upon such terms and conditions as it deems appropriate and necessary in the public interest and for the protection of investors.

(f) *Exemptions.* The following types of securities are not subject to paragraphs (c) and (d) of this rule:

(1) Security issues not assigned CUSIP number;

(2) Bond coupons;

(3) Uncertificated securities;

(4) Global securities issues; and

(5) Any securities issue for which neither record nor beneficial owners can obtain a negotiable securities certificate.

(g) Recordkeeping. Every reporting institution shall maintain and preserve in an easily accessible place for three years copies of all Forms X-17F-1A filed pursuant to this section, all agreements between reporting institutions regarding registration or other aspects of this section, and all confirmations or other information received from the Commission or its designee as a result of inquiry.

Rule 17f–2. Fingerprinting of Securities Industry Personnel

(a) *Exemptions from the fingerprinting requirement.* Except as otherwise provided in paragraph (a)(1) or (a)(2) of this rule, every member of a national securities exchange, broker, dealer, registered transfer agent and registered clearing agency shall require that each of its partners, directors, officers and employees be fingerprinted and shall submit, or cause to be submitted, the fingerprints of such persons to the Attorney General of the United States or its designee for identification and appropriate processing.

(1) *Permissive exemptions.* Every member of a national securities exchange, broker, dealer, registered transfer agent and registered clearing agency may claim one or more of the exemptions in paragraph (1)(i), (ii), (iii) or (iv) herein, *Provided*, That all the requirements of paragraph (e) are also satisfied.

(i) *Member of a national securities exchange, broker, dealer or registered clearing agency.* Every person who is a partner, director, officer or employee of a member of a national securities exchange, broker, dealer, or registered clearing agency shall be exempt if that person:

(A) Is not engaged in the sale of securities;

(B) Does not regularly have access to the keeping, handling or processing of (1) securities, (2) moneys, or (3) the original books and records relating to the securities or the monies; and

(C) Does not have direct supervisory responsibility over persons engaged in the activities referred to in paragraphs (a)(1)(i)(A) and (B) above.

(ii) *Registered transfer agents.* Every person who is a partner, director, officer or employee of a registered transfer agent shall be exempt if that person:

(A) Is not engaged in transfer agent functions (as defined in section 3(a)(25) of the Securities Exchange Act of 1934) or activities incidental thereto: or

(B) Meets the conditions in paragraphs (a)(1)(i)(B) and (C) of this rule.

(iii) *Registered broker-dealers engaged in sales of certain securities.* Every partner, director, officer and employee of a registered broker or dealer who satisfies paragraph (a)(1)(i)(B) shall be exempt if that broker or dealer:

(A) Is engaged exclusively in the sale of shares of registered open-end management investment companies, variable contracts, or interests in limited partnerships, unit investment trusts or real estate investment trusts, *Provided* That those securities ordinarily are not evidenced by certificates;

(B) Is current in its continuing obligation under Rules 15b1–1 and 15b3–1(b) to update Item 10 of Form BD to disclose the existence of any statutory disqualification set forth in sections 3(a)(39), 15(b)(4) and 15(b)(6) of the Securities Exchange Act of 1934;

(C) Has insurance or bonding indemnifying it for losses to customers caused by the fraudulent or criminal acts of any of its partners, directors, officers or employees for whom an exemption is being claimed under paragraph (a)(1)(iii); and

(D) Is subject to the jurisdiction of a state insurance department with respect to its sale of variable contracts.

(iv) *Illegible fingerprint cards.* Every person who is a partner, director, officer or employee shall be exempt if that member of a national securities exchange, broker, dealer, registered transfer agent or registered clearing agency, on at least three occasions:

(A) Attempts in good faith to obtain from such person a complete set of fingerprints acceptable to the Attorney

General for its designee for identification and appropriate processing by requiring that person to be fingerprinted, by having that person's fingerprints rolled by a person competent to do so and by submitting the fingerprint cards for the person to the Attorney General of the United States or its designee in accordance with proper procedures;

(B) Has that person's fingerprint cards returned to it by the Attorney General of the United States or its designee without that person's fingerprints having been identified because the fingerprints were illegible; and

(C) Retains the returned fingerprint cards and any other required records in accordance with paragraph (d) of this rule and Rules 17a–3(a)(13), 17a–4(e)(2) and 17Ad–7(e)(1) under the Securities Exchange Act of 1934.

(2) *Other exemptions by application to the Commission.* The Commission, upon specified terms, conditions and periods, may grant exemptions to any class of partners, directors, officers or employees of any member of a national securities exchange, broker, dealer, registered transfer agent or registered clearing agency, if the Commission finds that such action is not inconsistent with the public interest or the protection of investors.

(b) *Fingerprinting pursuant to other law.* Every member of a national securities exchange, broker, dealer, registered transfer agent and registered clearing agency may satisfy the fingerprinting requirement of section 17(f)(2) of the Securities Exchange Act of 1934 as to any partner, director, officer or employee, if:

(1) The person, in connection with his or her present employment with such organization, has been fingerprinted pursuant to any other law, statute, rule or regulation of any state or federal government or agency thereof;

(2) The fingerprint cards for that person are submitted, or are caused to be submitted, to the Attorney General of the United States or its designee for identification and appropriate processing, and the Attorney General or its designee has processed those fingerprint cards; and

(3) The processed fingerprint cards or any substitute records, together with any information received from the Attorney General or its designee, are maintained in accordance with paragraph (d) of this rule.

(c) *Fingerprinting plans of self-regulatory organizations.* The fingerprinting requirement of section 17(f)(2) of the Securities Exchange Act of 1934 may be satisfied by submitting appropriate and complete fingerprint cards to a registered national securities exchange or to a registered national securities association which, pursuant to a plan filed with, and declared effective by, the Commission, forwards such fingerprint cards to the Attorney General of the United States or its designee for identification and appropriate processing. Any plan filed by a registered national securities exchange or a registered national securities association shall not become effective, unless declared effective by the Commission as not inconsistent with the public interest or the protection of investors; and, in declaring any such plan effective, the Commission may impose any terms and conditions relating to the provisions of the plan and the period of its effectiveness as it may deem necessary or appropriate in the public interest, for the protection of investors, or otherwise in furtherance of the purposes of the Securities Exchange Act of 1934.

(d) *Record maintenance.* (1) Every member of a national securities exchange, broker, dealer, registered transfer agent and registered clearing agency shall maintain the processed fingerprint card or any substitute record when such card is not returned after processing, together with any information received from the Attorney General or its designee, for every person required to be fingerprinted under section 17(f)(2) of the Securities Exchange

Act of 1934 and for persons who have complied with this section pursuant to paragraphs (b) or (c) of this rule. Every substitute record shall state the name of the person whose fingerprint card was submitted to the Attorney General of the United States, the name of the member of a national securities exchange, broker, dealer, registered transfer agent or registered clearing agency that submitted the fingerprint card, the name of the person or organization that rolled the fingerprints, the date on which the fingerprints were rolled, and the date the fingerprint card was submitted to the Attorney General of the United States. The processed fingerprint card and every other substitute record containing the information required by this paragraph, together with any information received from the Attorney General of the United States, shall be kept in an easily accessible place at the organization's principal office and shall be made available upon request to the Commission, the appropriate regulatory agency (if not the Commission) or other designated examining authority. The organization's principal office must provide to the regional, branch or satellite office actually employing the person written evidence that the person's fingerprints have been processed by the FBI and must provide to that office a copy of any criminal history record information received from the FBI. All fingerprint cards, records, and information required to be maintained under this paragraph shall be retained for a period of not less than three years after termination of that person's employment or relationship with the organization.

(2) *Record maintenance by designated examining authorities.* The records required to be maintained and preserved by a member of a national securities exchange, broker or dealer pursuant to the requirements of paragraph (d)(1) may be maintained and preserved on behalf of that member, broker or dealer by a self-regulatory organization that is also the designated examining authority for that member, broker or dealer, *Provided*, That the self-regulatory organization has filed in accordance with Rule 17f–2(c) a fingerprinting plan or amendments to an existing plan concerning the storage and maintenance of records and that plan, as amended, has been declared effective by the Commission, and *Provided, further,* That:

(i) Such records are subject at any time, or from time to time, to reasonable periodic, special or other examinations by representatives of the Commission; and

(ii) The self-regulatory organization furnishes to the Commission, upon demand, at either the principal office or at the regional office complete, correct and current hard copies of any and all such records.

(3) *Reproduction of records on microfilm.* The records required to be maintained pursuant to paragraph (d)(1) may be produced or reproduced on microfilm and preserved in that form. If such microfilm substitution for hard copy is made by a member of a national securities exchange, broker, dealer, registered transfer agent or registered clearing agency, or by a self-regulatory organization maintaining and storing records pursuant to paragraph (d)(2), it shall at all times:

(i) Have available for examination by the Commission, the appropriate regulatory agency (if not the Commission) or other designated examining authority, facilities for the immediate, easily readable projection of the microfilm and for the production of easily readable and legible facsimile enlargements;

(ii) File and index the films in such a manner as to permit the immediate location and retrieval of any particular record;

(iii) Be ready to provide, and immediately provide, any facsimile enlargement which the Commission, the appropriate regulatory agency (if not the Commission) or other designated examining authority by their examiners or other representatives may request; and

(iv) For the period for which the microfilm records are required to be maintained, store separately from the original microfilm records a copy of the microfilm records.

(e) *Notice requirement.* Every member of a national securities exchange, broker, dealer, registered transfer agent and registered clearing agency that claims one or more of the exemptions in paragraph (a)(1) of this rule shall make and keep current a statement entitled "Notice Pursuant to Rule 17f–2" containing the information specified in paragraph (e)(1) below.

(1) *Contents of statement.* The Notice required by paragraph (e) of this section shall:

(i) State the name of the organization and state whether it is a member of a national securities exchange, broker, dealer, registered transfer agent, or registered clearing agency;

(ii) Identify by division, department, class, or name and position within the organization all persons who are claimed to have satisfied the fingerprinting requirements of section 17(f)(2) of the Securities Exchange Act of 1934 pursuant to paragraph (b) of this rule;

(iii) Identify by division, department, class, title or position within the organization all persons claimed to be exempt under paragraphs (a)(1)(i)–(iii) of this rule, and identify by name all persons claimed to be exempt under paragraph (a)(1)(iv). Persons identified under this paragraph (e)(1)(iii) shall be exempt from the requirement of section 17(f)(2) of the Securities Exchange Act of 1934 unless notified to the contrary by the Commission;

(iv) Describe, in generic terms, the nature of the duties of the person or classes of persons, and the nature of the functions and operations of the divisions and departments, identified as exempt in paragraph (e)(1)(iii) above; and

(v) Describe the security measures utilized to ensure that only those persons who have been fingerprinted in accordance with the fingerprinting requirement of section 17(f)(2) of the Securities Exchange Act of 1934 or who are exempt under paragraph (a)(1)(iv) of this rule have access to the keeping, handling or processing of securities or monies or the original books and records relating thereto.

(2) *Record maintenance.* A copy of the Notice required to be made and kept current under paragraph (e) of this section shall be kept in an easily accessible place at the organization's principal office and at the office employing the persons for whom exemptions are claimed and shall be made available upon request for inspection by the Commission, appropriate regulatory agency (if not the Commission) or other designated examining authority.

(3) *Exemption from the notice requirement.* A registered transfer agent that performs transfer agent functions only on behalf of itself as an issuer and that receives fewer than 500 items for transfer and fewer than 500 items for processing during any six consecutive months shall be exempt from the Notice requirement of paragraph (e) of this section.

Rule 17h–1T. Risk Assessment Recordkeeping Requirements for Associated Persons of Brokers and Dealers

(a) Requirement to maintain and preserve information. (1) Every broker or dealer registered with the Commission pursuant to section 15 of the Act, and every municipal securities dealer registered pursuant to Section 15B of the Act for which the Commission is the appropriate regulatory agency, unless exempt pursuant to paragraph (d) of this rule, shall maintain and preserve the following information:

(i) An organizational chart which includes the broker or dealer and all its associated persons. Included in the organizational chart shall be a designation of which associated persons are Material Associated Persons as that term is used in paragraph (a)(2) of this rule;

(ii) Written policies, procedures, or systems concerning the broker or dealer's:

(A) Method(s) for monitoring and controlling financial and operational risks to it resulting from the activities of any of its associated persons, other than a natural person;

(B) Financing and capital adequacy, including information regarding sources of funding, together with a narrative discussion by management of the liquidity of the material assets, the structure of debt capital, and sources of alternative funding; and

(C) Trading positions and risks, such as records regarding reporting responsibilities for trading activities, policies relating to restrictions or limitations on trading securities and financial instruments or products, and a description of the types of reviews conducted to monitor existing positions, and limitations or restrictions on trading activities.

(iii) A description of all material pending legal or arbitration proceedings involving a Material Associated Person or the broker or dealer that are required to be disclosed by the ultimate holding company under generally accepted accounting principles on a consolidated basis;

(iv) Consolidated and consolidating balance sheets, prepared in accordance with generally accepted accounting principles, which may be unaudited and which shall include the notes to the financial statements, as of quarter end for the broker or dealer and its ultimate holding company;

(v) Quarterly consolidated and consolidating income statements and consolidated cash flow statements, prepared in accordance with generally accepted accounting principles, which may be unaudited and which shall include the notes to the financial statements, for the broker or dealer and its ultimate holding company;

(vi) The amount as of quarter end, and at month end if greater than quarter end, of the aggregate long and short securities and commodities positions held by each Material Associated Person, including a separate listing of each single unhedged securities or commodities position, other than U.S. government or agency securities, that exceeds the Materiality Threshold at any month end;

(vii) The notional or contractual amounts, and in the case of options, the value of the underlying instruments, as of quarter end, of financial instruments with off-balance sheet risk and financial instruments with concentrations of credit risk (as those terms are used in Statement of Financial Accounting Standards No. 105) where the Material Associated Person operates a trading book, with a separate entry of each commitment where the credit risk (as that term is used in Statement of Financial Accounting Standards No. 105) with respect to a counterparty exceeds the Materiality Threshold at quarter end;

(viii) The aggregate amount as of quarter end, and the amount at month end if greater than quarter end, of all bridge loans and those other material unsecured extensions of credit (not including intra-group receivables) with an initial or remaining maturity of less than one year by each Material Associated Person, together with the allowance for losses for such transactions, including a specific description of any extensions of credit to a single borrower exceeding the Materiality Threshold at any month end;

(ix) The aggregate amount as of quarter end, and the amount at month end if greater than quarter end, of commercial paper, secured and other unsecured borrowing, bank loans, lines of credit, or any other borrowings, and the principal installments of long-term or medium-term debt, scheduled to mature within twelve months from the most recent fiscal quarter for the broker or dealer and each Material Associated Person; and

(x) Data relating to real estate activities, including mortgage loans and investments in real estate, but not including trading positions in whole loans, conducted by each Material Associated Person, including:

(A) Real estate loans and investments by type of property, such as construction and development, residential, commercial and industrial or farmland;

(B) The geographic distribution, as of quarter end, by type of loan or investment where the amount exceeds the Materiality Threshold at quarter end;

(C) The aggregate carrying value of loans which each Material Associated Person deems to be not current as to interest or principal, together with the Material Associated Person's criteria for the determination of which loans are not current, or which are in the process of foreclosure or that have been restructured;

(D) The allowance for losses on loans and on investment real estate by type of loan or investment, and the activity in the allowance for losses account; and

(E) Information about risk concentration in the real estate investment and loan portfolio, including information about risk concentration to a single borrower or location of property if the risk concentration exceeds the Materiality Threshold at quarter end.

(2) The determination of whether an associated person of a broker or dealer is a Material Associated Person shall involve consideration of all aspects of the activities of, and the relationship between, both entities, including without limitation, the following factors:

(i) The legal relationship between the broker or dealer and the associated person;

(ii) The overall financing requirements of the broker or dealer and the associated person, and the degree, if any, to which the broker or dealer and the associated person are financially dependent on each other;

(iii) The degree, if any, to which the broker or dealer or its customers rely on the associated person for operational support or services in connection with the broker's or dealer's business;

(iv) The level of risk present in the activities of the broker's or dealer's associated persons; and

(v) The extent to which the associated person has the authority or the ability to cause a withdrawal of capital from the broker or dealer.

(3) The information, reports and records required by the provisions of this rule shall be maintained and preserved in accordance with the provisions of Rule 17a–4 and shall be kept for a period of not less than three years in an easily accessible place.

(4) For the purposes of this rule and rule 17h–2T, the term "Materiality Threshold" shall mean the greater of:

(i) $100 million; or

(ii) 10 percent of the broker or dealer's tentative net capital based on the most recently filed Form X–17A–5 or 10 percent of the Material Associated Person's tangible net worth, whichever is greater.

(b) *Special provisions with respect to material associated persons subject to the supervision of certain domestic regulators.* A broker or dealer shall be deemed to be in compliance with the recordkeeping requirements of paragraph (a) of this rule with respect to a Material Associated Person if:

(1) Such Material Associated Person is subject to examination by, or the reporting requirements of, a Federal banking agency and the broker or dealer maintains in accordance with the provisions of this rule copies of all reports submitted by such Material Associated Person with the Federal banking agency pursuant to section 5211 of the Revised Statutes, section 9 of the Federal Re-

serve Act, section 7(a) of the Federal Deposit Insurance Act, section 10(b) of the Home Owners' Loan Act, or section 5 of the Bank Holding Company Act of 1956 other than the Form FR 2068; or

(2) If such Material Associated Person is subject to the supervision of an insurance commissioner or other similar official or agency of a state, and the broker or dealer maintains in accordance with the provisions of this rule copies of the Annual and Quarterly Statements with Schedules and Exhibits prepared by the insurance company on forms prescribed by the National Association of Insurance Commissioners; or

(3) In the event an insurance company is not required to prepare Quarterly Statements on forms prescribed by the National Association of Insurance Commissioners, the broker or dealer must maintain and preserve the records required by paragraph (a) of this rule on a quarterly basis; or

(4) In the case of a Material Associated Person that is subject to the supervision of the Commodity Futures Trading Commission, the broker or dealer maintains in accordance with the provisions of this rule copies of the reports filed on Forms 1 FR–FCM or 1 FR–IB by such Material Associated Person with the Commodity Futures Trading Commission.

(c) Special provisions with respect to material associated persons subject to the supervision of a foreign financial regulatory authority. A broker or dealer shall be deemed to be in compliance with the recordkeeping requirements of paragraph (a) of this rule with respect to a Material Associated Person if such broker or dealer maintains in accordance with the provisions of this rule copies of the reports filed by such Material Associated Persons with a Foreign Financial Regulatory Authority. The broker or dealer shall maintain a copy of the original report and a copy translated into the English language. For the purposes of this rule, the term Foreign Financial Regulatory Authority shall have the meaning set forth in section 3(a)(51) of the Act.

(d) *Exemptions.* (1) The provisions of this rule shall not apply to any broker or dealer which is exempt from the provisions of Rule 15c3–3:

(i) Pursuant to paragraph (k)(1) of Rule 15c3–3; or

(ii) Pursuant to paragraph (k)(2) of Rule 15c3–3; or

(iii) If the broker or dealer does not qualify for an exemption from the provisions of Rule 15c3–3 and such broker or dealer does not hold funds or securities for, or owe money or securities to, customers and does not carry the accounts of or for customers; unless

(iv) In the case of paragraphs (d)(1)(ii) or (d)(1)(iii) of this rule, the broker or dealer maintains capital including debt subordinated in accordance with appendix D of Rule 15c3–1 equal to or greater than $20,000,000.

(2) The provisions of this rule shall not apply to any broker or dealer which maintains capital including debt subordinated in accordance with appendix D of Rule 15c3–1 of less than $250,000, even if the broker or dealer hold funds or securities for, or owes money or securities to, customers or carries the accounts of or for customers.

(3) In calculating capital for the purposes of this paragraph, a broker or dealer shall include the equity capital and subordinated debt of any other registered brokers or dealers that are associated with the broker or dealer and are not otherwise exempt from the provisions pursuant to paragraph (d)(1)(i) of this rule.

(4) The provisions of this section shall not apply to a broker or dealer that computes certain of its capital charges in accordance with § 240.15c3–1e if that broker or dealer is affiliated with an ultimate holding company that is not an ultimate holding company that has a principal regulator, as defined in § 240.15c3–1(c)(13).

(5) The Commission may, upon written application by a Reporting Broker or Dealer, exempt from the provisions of this rule, either unconditionally or on specified terms and conditions, any brokers or dealers associated with such Reporting Broker or Dealer. The term "Reporting Broker or Dealer" shall mean, in the case of a broker or dealer that is associated with other registered brokers or dealers, the broker or dealer which maintains the greatest amount of net capital as reported on its most recently fixed Form X–17A–5. In granting exemptions under this rule, the Commission shall consider, among other factors, whether the records and other information required to be maintained pursuant to this rule concerning the Material Associated Persons of the broker or dealer associated with the Reporting Broker or Dealer will be available to the Commission pursuant to Rule 17h–2T.

(4) The provisions of this section shall not apply to a broker or dealer that computes certain of its capital charges in accordance with § 240.15c3–1e if that broker or dealer is affiliated with an ultimate holding company that is not an ultimate holding company that has a principal regulator, as defined in § 240.15c3–1(c)(13).

(5) The provisions of this section shall not apply to a broker or dealer affiliated with a supervised investment bank holding company, as defined in § 240.17i–1(a).

(6) The Commission may, upon written application by a Reporting Broker or Dealer, exempt from the provisions of this section, either unconditionally or on specified terms and conditions, any brokers or dealers associated with such Reporting Broker or Dealer. The term "Reporting Broker or Dealer" shall mean, in the case of a broker or dealer that is associated with other registered brokers or dealers, the broker or dealer which maintains the greatest amount of net capital as reported on its most recently fixed Form X–17A–5. In granting exemptions under this section, the Commission shall consider, among other factors, whether the records and other information required to be maintained pursuant to this section concerning the Material Associated Persons of the broker or dealer associated with the Reporting Broker or Dealer will be available to the Commission pursuant to § 240.17h–2T.

(e) Location of records. A broker or dealer required to maintain records concerning a Material Associated Person pursuant to this rule may maintain those records either at the Material Associated Person or at a records storage facility provided that the records are located within the boundaries of the United States and the records are kept in an easily accessible place, as that term is used in Rule 17a–4. In order to operate pursuant to the provisions of this paragraph, the Material Associated Person or other entity maintaining the records shall file with the Commission a written undertaking in form acceptable to the Commission, signed by a duly authorized person, to the effect that the records will be treated as if the broker or dealer was maintaining the records pursuant to this rule and that the entity maintaining the records undertakes to permit examination of such records at any time or from time to time during business hours by representatives or designees of the Commission and to promptly furnish the Commission or its designee true, correct, complete and current hard copy of any or all or any part of such records. The election to operate pursuant to the provisions of this paragraph shall not relieve the broker or dealer required to maintain and preserve such records from any of its responsibilities under this rule or Rule 17h–2T.

(f) Confidentiality. All information obtained by the Commission pursuant to the provisions of this rule from a broker or dealer concerning a Material Associated Person shall be deemed confidential information for the purposes of section 24(b) of the Act.

(g) Temporary implementation schedule. Every broker or dealer subject to the requirements of this rule shall maintain and preserve the information required by paragraphs (a)(1)(i), (ii), and (iii) of this rule commencing

September 30, 1992. Commencing December 31, 1992, the provisions of this rule shall apply in their entirety.

Rule 17h–2T. Risk Assessment Reporting Requirements for Brokers and Dealers

(a) Reporting requirements of risk assessment information required to be maintained by Rule 17h–1T. (1) Every broker or dealer registered with the Commission pursuant to section 15 of the Act, and every municipal securities dealer registered pursuant to section 15B of the Act for which the Commission is the appropriate regulatory agency, unless exempt pursuant to paragraph (b) of this rule, shall file a Form 17–H within 60 calendar days after the end of each fiscal quarter. The Form 17–H for the fourth fiscal quarter shall be filed within 60 calendar days of the end of the fiscal year. The cumulative year-end financial statements required by Rule 17h–1T may be filed separately within 105 calendar days of the end of the fiscal year.

(2) The reports required to be filed pursuant to paragraph (a)(1) of this rule shall be considered filed when received at the Commission's principal office in Washington, DC.

(3) For the purposes of this rule, the term Material Associated Person shall have the meaning used in Rule 17h–1T.

(b) Exemptions. (1) The provisions of this rule shall not apply to any broker or dealer which is exempt from the provisions of Rule 15c3–3:

(i) Pursuant to paragraph (k)(1) of Rule 15c3–3; or

(ii) Pursuant to paragraph (k)(2) of Rule 15c3–3; or

(iii) If the broker or dealer does not qualify for an exemption from the provisions of Rule 15c3–3 and such broker or dealer does not hold funds or securities for, or owe money or securities to, customers and does not carry the accounts of or for customers; unless

(iv) In the case of paragraphs (b)(1)(ii) or (b)(1)(iii) of this rule, the broker or dealer maintains capital including debt subordinated in accordance with appendix D of Rule 15c3–1 equal to or greater than $20,000,000.

(2) The provisions of this rule shall not apply to any broker or dealer which maintains capital including debt subordinated in accordance with appendix D of Rule 15c3–1 of less than $250,000, even if the broker or dealer hold funds or securities for, or owes money or securities to, customers or carries the accounts of or for customers.

(3) In calculating capital and subordinated debt for the purposes of this rule, a broker or dealer shall include the equity capital and subordinated debt of any other registered brokers or dealers that are associated with the broker or dealer and are not otherwise exempt from the provisions pursuant to paragraph (b)(1)(i) of this rule.

(4) The provisions of this section shall not apply to a broker or dealer that computes certain of its capital charges in accordance with § 240.15c3–1e if that broker or dealer is affiliated with an ultimate holding company that is not an ultimate holding company that has a principal regulator, as defined in § 240.15c3–1(c)(13).

(5) The provisions of this section shall not apply to a broker or dealer affiliated with a supervised investment bank holding company, as defined in § 240.17i–1(a).

(6) The Commission may, upon written application by a Reporting Broker or Dealer, exempt from the provisions of this rule, either unconditionally or on specified terms and conditions, any brokers or dealers associated with the Reporting Broker or Dealer. The term "Reporting Broker or Dealer" shall mean, in the case of a broker or dealer that is associated with other registered brokers or dealers, the broker or dealer which maintains the greatest amount of net capital as reported on its most recently filed Form X–17A–5. In granting exemptions under this rule, the Commission shall consider, among other factors, whether

the records and other information required to be maintained pursuant to Rule 17h–1T concerning the Material Associated Persons of the broker or dealer associated with the Reporting Broker or Dealer will be available to the Commission pursuant to the provisions of this section.

(c) Special provisions with respect to material associated persons subject to the supervision of certain domestic regulators. A broker or dealer shall be deemed to be in compliance with the reporting requirements of paragraph (a) of this rule with respect to a Material Associated Person if:

(1) Such Material Associated Person is subject to examination by or the reporting requirements of a Federal banking agency and the broker or dealer or such Material Associated Person furnishes in accordance with paragraph (a) of this rule copies of reports filed on Form FR Y–9C, Form FR Y–6, Form FR Y–7, and Form FR 2068 by the Material Associated Person with the Federal banking agency pursuant to section 5211 of the Revised Statutes, section 9 of the Federal Reserve Act, section 7(a) of the Federal Deposit Insurance Act, section 10(b) of the Home Owners' Loan Act, or section 5 of the Bank Holding Company Act of 1956; or

(2) If the Material Associated Person is subject to the supervision of an insurance commissioner or other similar official agency of a state; and

(i) In the case of a Material Associated Person organized as a public stock company, the broker or dealer furnishes in accordance with the provisions of this rule copies of the filings made by the insurance company pursuant to sections 13 or 15 of the Act and the Investment Company Act of 1940; or

(ii) In the case of Material Associated Person organized as a mutual insurance company or a non-public stock company, the broker or dealer furnishes in accordance with the provisions of this rule copies of the Annual and Quarterly Statements prepared by the insurance company on forms prescribed by the National Association of Insurance Commissioners. The Annual Statement furnished to the Commission pursuant to this section shall include: The classification (distribution by state) section from the schedule of real estate; distribution by state, the interest overdue (more than three months), in process of foreclosure, and foreclosed properties transferred to real estate during the year sections from the schedule of mortgages; and the quality and maturity distribution of all bonds at statement values and by major types of issues section from the schedule of bonds and stocks. All other Schedules and Exhibits to such Annual and Quarterly Statements shall be maintained at the broker-dealer pursuant to the provisions of Rule 17h–1T but not furnished to the Commission.

(iii) In the event an insurance company organized as a stock or mutual company is not required to prepare Quarterly Statements, the broker or dealer must file with the Commission a Form 17–H in accordance with the provisions of this rule on a quarterly basis.

(3) In the case of a Material Associated Person that is subject to the supervision of the Commodity Futures Trading Commission, the broker or dealer furnishes in accordance with the provisions of this rule copies of the reports filed by the Material Associated Person with the Commodity Futures Trading Commission on Forms 1 FR–FCM or 1 FR–IB.

(4) No broker or dealer shall be required to furnish to the Commission any examination report of any Federal banking agency or any supervisory recommendations or analyses contained therein with respect to a Material Associated Person that is subject to the regulation of a Federal banking agency. All information received by the Commission pursuant to this rule concerning a Material Associated Person that is subject to exami-

nation by or the reporting requirements of a Federal banking agency shall be deemed confidential for the purposes of section 24(b) of the Act.

(5) The furnishing of any information or documents by a broker or dealer pursuant to this rule shall not constitute an admission for any purpose that a Material Associated Person is otherwise subject to the Act. Any documents or information furnished to the Commission by a broker or dealer pursuant to this rule shall not be deemed to be "filed" for the purposes of the liabilities set forth in section 18 of the Act.

(d) Special provisions with respect to material associated persons subject to the supervision of a foreign financial regulatory authority. A broker or dealer shall be deemed to be in compliance with the reporting requirements of this rule with respect to a Material Associated Person if such broker or dealer furnishes in accordance with the provisions of this rule copies of the reports filed by such Material Associated Person with a Foreign Financial Regulatory Authority. The broker or dealer shall file a copy of the original report and a copy translated into the English language. For the purposes of this rule, the term Foreign Financial Regulatory Authority shall have the meaning set forth in section 3(a)(51) of the Act.

(e) Confidentiality. All information obtained by the Commission pursuant to the provisions of this rule from a broker or dealer concerning a Material Associated Person shall be deemed confidential information for the purposes of section 24(b) of the Act.

(f) Temporary implementation schedule. Every broker or dealer subject to the requirements of this rule shall file the information required by Items 1, 2 and 3 of Form 17–H by October 31, 1992. Commencing December 31, 1992, the provisions of this section shall apply in their entirety.

SUPERVISED INVESTMENT BANK HOLDING COMPANY RULES

Preliminary Note: Rules 17i–1 through 17i–8 set forth a program of supervision at the holding company level for supervised investment bank holding companies. This program is designed to reduce the likelihood that financial and operational weakness in a supervised investment bank holding company will destabilize broker or dealer or the broader financial system. The focus of this supervision of the supervised investment bank holding company is its financial and operational condition and its risk management controls and methodologies.

Rule 17i–1. Definitions.

(a) For purposes of §§ 240.17i–1 through 240.17i–8, the terms *investment bank holding company, supervised investment bank holding company, affiliate, bank, bank holding company, company, control, savings association, insured bank, foreign bank, person associated with an investment bank holding company* and *associated person of an investment bank holding company* shall have the same meaning as set forth in section 17(i)(5) of the Act (15 U.S.C. 78q(i)(5)).

(b) For purposes of §§ 240.17i–2 through 240.17i–8, the term *affiliate group* shall include the supervised investment bank holding company and every affiliate of the supervised investment bank holding company.

(c) For purposes of §§ 240.17i–1 through 240.17i–8, the term *material affiliate* shall mean any member of the affiliate group that is material to the supervised investment bank holding company.

Rule 17i–2. Notice of Intention to be Supervised by the Commission as a Supervised Investment Bank Holding Company.

(a) An investment bank holding company that owns or controls a broker or dealer may file with the Commission a written notice of intention to become supervised by the Commission pursuant to section 17(i) of the Act (15 U.S.C. 78q(i)), provided that the investment bank holding company is not:

(1) An affiliate of an insured bank (other than an institution described in paragraph (D), (F), or (G) of section 2(c)(2), or held under section 4(f), of the Bank Holding Company Act of 1956) (12 U.S.C. 1841(c)(2)(D), (F), or (G) and 12 U.S.C. 1843(f)) or a savings association;

(2) A foreign bank, foreign company, or company that is described in section 8(a) of the International Banking Act of 1978 (12 U.S.C. 3106(a)); or

(3) A foreign bank that controls, directly or indirectly, a corporation chartered under section 25A of the Federal Reserve Act (12 U.S.C. 611).

(b) To become supervised as a supervised investment bank holding company an investment bank holding company shall file a notice of intention that includes the following:

(1) A request to become supervised by the Commission as a supervised investment bank holding company;

(2) A statement certifying that the investment bank holding company is not an entity described in section 17(i)(1)(A)(i)-(iii) of the Act (15 U.S.C. 78q(i)(1)(A)(i)-(iii));

(3) Documentation demonstrating that the investment bank holding company owns or controls a broker or dealer that maintains a substantial presence in the securities business as evidenced either by its holding $100 million or more in tentative net capital as calculated pursuant to § 240.15c3-1 or by any other information that the Commission determines is appropriate; and(4) Supplemental information including:

(i) A description of the business and organization of the investment bank holding company;

(ii) An alphabetical list of each member of the affiliate group, with an identification of the financial regulator, if any, by whom the affiliate is regulated, and a designation as to whether the affiliate is a material affiliate;

(iii) An organizational chart that identifies the investment bank holding company, each broker or dealer owned or controlled by the investment bank holding company, and each material affiliate;

(iv) Consolidated and consolidating financial statements of the affiliate group as of the end of the quarter preceding the filing of the notice of intention;

(v) Sample computations for the supervised investment bank holding company of allowable capital and allowances for market risk, credit risk, and operational risk made in accordance with § 240.17i-7(a)-(d);

(vi) A list of the categories of positions that the affiliate group holds in its proprietary accounts and a brief description of the method that the investment bank holding company proposes to use to calculate allowances for market and credit risk on those categories of positions pursuant to § 240.17i-7(b) and (c);

(vii) A description of mathematical models that the investment bank holding company proposes to use to price positions and to compute allowances for market and credit risk (as specified in § 240.17i-7(b) and (c)), including:

(A) A description of the creation, use, and maintenance of the mathematical models;

(B) A description of the internal risk management controls over those models, including a description of each category of persons who may input data into the model;

(C) If the mathematical model incorporates correlations across risk factors, a description of the process used to measure those correlations;

(D) A description of the backtesting procedures the investment bank holding company proposes to use to backtest the models, including a description of the backtest and procedures instituted to respond to test results;

(E) A description of how each mathematical model satisfies the applicable qualitative and quantitative requirements listed in § 240.15c3–1e(d); and

(F) A statement describing the extent to which each mathematical model that it is used to analyze risk and report risk to senior management;

(viii) A description of any positions for which the investment bank holding company proposes to use a method other than Value at Risk to compute an allowance for market risk and a description of how that allowance would be determined;

(ix) A description of how the investment bank holding company proposes to calculate the credit equivalent amount and maximum potential exposure (as defined in §§ 240.17i–7(c)(1)(i) and 240.17i–7(c)(1)(i)(E), respectively);

(x) A description of how the investment bank holding company proposes to calculate credit risk weights and internal credit ratings, if applicable;

(xi) A description of the method the investment bank holding company proposes to use to calculate its allowance for operational risk pursuant to § 240.17i–7(d);

(xii) A comprehensive description of the internal risk management control system the investment bank holding company has established to manage the risks of the affiliate group, including market, credit, leverage, liquidity, legal, and operational risks, and how that system satisfies the requirements of § 240.17i–4;(xiii) Sample risk reports the supervised investment bank holding company regularly provides to the persons responsible for managing risk for the affiliate group that the investment bank holding company proposes to provide to the Commission pursuant to § 240.17i–6(a)(1)(iv);

(xiv) A written undertaking, in a form acceptable to the Commission and signed by a duly authorized person, that provides that if the disclosure of any information with regard to §§ 240.17i–1 through 240.17i–8 would be prohibited by law or otherwise, the supervised investment bank holding company will cooperate with the Commission as needed, including by describing any secrecy laws or other impediments that could restrict the ability of the supervised investment bank holding company or any material affiliate from providing information on its operations or activities and by discussing the manner in which the supervised investment bank holding company proposes to provide the Commission with adequate assurances of access to information; and

(xv) Any other information or documents relating to the investment bank holding company's activities, financial condition, policies, systems for monitoring and controlling financial and operational risks, and transactions and relationships among members of the affiliate group that the Commission may request to complete its review of the notice of intention.

(c) *Amendments to the notice of intention.*

(1) *Prior to a Commission determination.* If any of the information filed with the Commission as part of the notice of intention described in paragraph (b) of this section is found to be or becomes inaccurate before the Commission makes a determination, the investment bank holding company must promptly notify the Commission and provide the Commission with a description of the circumstances in which the information was found to be or has become inaccurate along with updated, accurate information.

(2) *Subsequent to a Commission determination.* A supervised investment bank holding company must amend and resubmit to the Commission its notice of intention, and obtain Commission approval of the amendment, as set forth in paragraph (d)(2)(ii) of this section, before it may make a material change to a mathematical model or other method used to compute allowable capital or allowance for market, credit, or operational

risk, or its internal risk management control systems as described in its notice of intention, as modified from time to time.

(d) *Process for review of notice of intention.*

(1) *When filed.* A notice of intention to be supervised by the Commission as a supervised investment bank holding company and any amendments thereto shall not be complete until the investment bank holding company has filed with the Commission all the documentation and information specified in this section. The notice of intention, and any amendments thereto, shall be considered filed when received at the Office of the Secretary at the Commission's principal office in Washington DC. All notices of intention, amendments thereto, and other information filed in connection with the notice of intention shall be accorded confidential treatment to the extent permitted by law.

(2) *Commission determination.*

(i) An investment bank holding company shall become a supervised investment bank holding company pursuant to section 17(i) of the Act (15 U.S.C. 78q(i)) 45 calendar days after the Commission receives a completed notice of intention to be supervised by the Commission as a supervised investment bank holding company pursuant to paragraph (a) of this section, unless the Commission issues an order determining either that:

(A) The Commission will begin to supervise the investment bank holding company prior to 45 calendar days after the Commission receives the completed notice of intention; or

(B) The Commission will not supervise the investment bank holding company because supervision of the investment bank holding company as a supervised investment bank holding company is not necessary or appropriate in furtherance of the purposes of section 17 of the Act (15 U.S.C. 78q). In addition, the Commission will not consider such supervision necessary or appropriate unless the investment bank holding company demonstrates that it owns or controls a broker or dealer that has a substantial presence in the securities business, which may be demonstrated by a showing that the broker or dealer maintains tentative net capital of $100 million or more.

(ii) The Commission, upon receipt of an amendment to the notice of intention submitted by a supervised investment bank holding company pursuant to paragraph (c)(2) of this section, may approve the amendment after reviewing the amended notice of intention to determine whether the amendment is necessary or appropriate in furtherance of the purposes of section 17 of the Act (15 U.S.C. 78q).

Rule 17i–3. Withdrawal from Supervision by the Commission as a Supervised Investment Bank Holding Company.

(a) A supervised investment bank holding company may withdraw from supervision by the Commission as a supervised investment bank holding company by filing a notice of withdrawal with the Commission. The notice of withdrawal shall include a statement regarding whether the supervised investment bank holding company is in compliance with § 240.17i–2(c).

(b) A notice of withdrawal from supervision as a supervised investment bank holding company shall become effective one year after it is filed with the Commission, unless the Commission issues an order determining that it is necessary or appropriate for the Commission to terminate its supervision of the supervised investment bank holding company within a shorter or longer period to help ensure effective supervision of the material risks to the supervised investment bank holding company and to any associated person of the supervised investment bank holding company that is a broker or dealer, or to prevent evasion of the purposes of section 17 of the Act (15 U.S.C. 78q).

(c) Notwithstanding paragraphs (a) and (b) of this section, the Commission, by order, may discontinue supervision of any supervised investment bank holding company if the Commission finds that:

(1) The supervised investment bank holding company is no longer in existence;

(2) The supervised investment bank holding company has ceased to be an investment bank holding company; or

(3) Continued supervision by the Commission of the supervised investment bank holding company is not necessary or appropriate in furtherance of the purposes of section 17 of the Act (15 U.S.C. 78q).

17i–4. Internal Risk Management Control System Requirements for Supervised Investment Bank Holding Companies.

(a) A supervised investment bank holding company shall comply with § 240.15c3–4 as though it were an OTC derivatives dealer with respect to all of its business activities, except paragraphs (c)(5)(xiii), (c)(5)(xiv), (d)(8), and (d)(9) will not apply; and

(b) As part of its internal risk management control system, a supervised investment bank holding company must establish, document, and maintain procedures for the detection and prevention of money laundering and terrorist financing.

Rule 17i–5 Record Creation, Maintenance, and Access Requirements for Supervised Investment Bank Holding Companies.

(a) A supervised investment bank holding company shall make and keep current the following records:

(1) A record reflecting the results of stress tests, conducted by the supervised investment bank holding company at least once each quarter, of the affiliate group's funding and liquidity with respect to the following events:

(i) A credit rating downgrade of the supervised investment bank holding company;

(ii) An inability of the supervised investment bank holding company to access capital markets for unsecured short-term funding;

(iii) An inability of the supervised investment bank holding company to move liquid assets across international borders when the events described in paragraphs (a)(1)(i) or (ii) of this section occur; and

(iv) An inability of the supervised investment bank holding company to access credit or assets held at a particular institution when the events described in paragraphs (a)(1)(i) or (ii) of this section occur;

(2) The supervised investment bank holding company's contingency plan to respond to the events outlined in paragraphs (a)(1)(i) through (iv) of this section;

(3) A record of the basis for the determination of the credit risk weight and internal credit rating, if applicable, for each counterparty; and

(4) A record of the calculations of allowable capital and allowances for market, credit, and operational risk computed currently at least once each month on a consolidated basis.

(b) Except as provided in paragraph (c) of this section, the supervised investment bank holding company shall preserve for a period of not less than three years in an easily accessible place using any storage media acceptable under § 240.17a–4(f):

(1) The documents created in accordance with paragraph (a) of this section;

(2) All notices of intention, amendments thereto, and other documentation and information filed with the Commission pursuant to § 240.17i–2, and any responses thereto;

(3) All reports and notices filed by the supervised investment bank holding company pursuant to § 240.17i–6;

(4) All notices filed by the supervised investment bank holding company pursuant to § 240.17i–8; and

(5) Records documenting the system of internal risk management controls required to

be established pursuant to § 240.17i–4, including written guidelines, policies, and procedures.

(c) A supervised investment bank holding company may maintain the records specified in paragraph (b) of this section either at the supervised investment bank holding company, at an affiliate, or at a records storage facility, provided that the records are located within the United States. If the records are maintained by an entity other than the supervised investment bank holding company, the supervised investment bank holding company shall file with the Commission a written undertaking in a form acceptable to the Commission from the entity, signed by a duly authorized person at the entity maintaining the records, to the effect that the records will be treated as if the supervised investment bank holding company were maintaining the records pursuant to this section and that the entity maintaining the records undertakes to permit examination of those records at any time or from time to time during business hours by representatives or designees of the Commission and to promptly furnish the Commission or its designee a true, correct, complete and current copy of all or any part of those records in paper, or electronically if the records are stored electronically, as specified by the Commission's representative or designee. The election to store records pursuant to the provisions of this paragraph (c) shall not relieve the supervised investment bank holding company from any of its responsibilities under this section or § 240.17i–6.

(d) All information created pursuant to this section and obtained by the Commission from the supervised investment bank holding company shall be accorded confidential treatment to the extent permitted by law.

Rule 17i–6. Reporting Requirements for Supervised Investment Bank Holding Companies.

(a) *Monthly and quarterly reports*. The supervised investment bank holding company shall file:

(1) A report as of the end of each month, filed not later than 30 calendar days after the end of the month, Except that the monthly report need not be filed for a month-end that coincides with a fiscal quarter-end. The monthly report shall include:

(i) A consolidated balance sheet and income statement (including notes to the financial statements) and statements of allowable capital and allowances for market, credit, and operational risk computed pursuant to § 240.17i–7 for the affiliate group, Except that the consolidated balance sheet and income statement for the first month of the fiscal year may be filed at a time to which the Commission agrees (when making a determination pursuant to § 240.17i–2(d)(2));

(ii) A graph reflecting, for each business line, the daily intra-month Value at Risk;

(iii) Consolidated credit risk information, including:

(A) Aggregate current exposure and current exposures (including commitments) for the 15 largest exposures listed by counterparty;

(B) Aggregate maximum potential exposure and maximum potential exposures for the 15 largest exposures listed by counterparty; and

(C) A summary report reflecting the geographic distribution of the supervised investment bank holding company's exposures, on a consolidated basis, for each of the top ten countries to which it is exposed (by residence of the main operating group of the counterparty); and

(iv) Certain risk reports the supervised investment bank holding company regularly provides to the persons responsible for managing risk for the affiliate group that the Commission may request from time to time.

(2) A report as of the end of each fiscal quarter, filed not later than 35 calendar

days after the end of the quarter, which shall include (except as provided in paragraph (a)(3) below):

(i) The information contained in the monthly report, as set forth in paragraph (1) above;

(ii) A consolidating balance sheet and income statement for the affiliate group, which shall break out information regarding each material affiliate into separate columns, but may consolidate information regarding affiliate group entities that are not material affiliates into one column;

(iii) The results of backtesting of all models used to compute allowable capital and allowances for market and credit risk indicating, for each model, the number of backtesting exceptions;

(iv) A description of all material pending legal or arbitration proceedings involving the supervised investment bank holding company or any member of the affiliate group that are required to be disclosed by the supervised investment bank holding company under generally accepted accounting principles; and

(v) The aggregate amount of unsecured borrowings and lines of credit, segregated into categories, scheduled to mature within twelve months from the most recent fiscal quarter as to each material affiliate.

(3) For a quarter-end that coincides with the supervised investment bank holding company's fiscal year-end, the supervised investment bank holding company need not include in its filing consolidated and consolidating balance sheets and income statements.

(b) *Organizational chart*. The supervised investment holding company shall file, concurrently with its quarterly report for the quarter-end that coincides with the supervised investment bank holding company's fiscal year-end, an organizational chart, as of the investment bank holding company's fiscal year end. Quarterly updates should be provided where a material change in the information provided to the Commission has occurred.

(c) *Additional reports*. Upon receiving notice from the Commission, the supervised investment bank holding company shall file other information as the Commission may request in order to monitor the supervised investment bank holding company's financial or operational condition, risk management system, and transactions and relationships among members of the affiliate group.

(d) *Annual audit report*.

(1) A supervised investment bank holding company shall file an annual audit report as of the end of the supervised investment bank holding company's fiscal year, that includes:

(i) Consolidated financial statements (including notes to the financial statements) for the supervised investment bank holding company. The audited financial statements must include a supporting schedule containing statements of allowable capital and allowances for market, credit and operational risk computed in accordance with § 240.17i–7. The audit must be conducted by a registered public accounting firm (as that term is defined at 15 U.S.C. 7201(a)(12)) in accordance the rules promulgated by the Public Company Accounting Oversight Board; and

(ii) A supplemental report entitled "Accountant's Report on Internal Risk Management Control System" prepared by the registered public accounting firm (as that term is defined at 15 U.S.C. 7201(a)(12)) indicating the results of the accountant's review of the internal risk management control system established and documented by the supervised investment bank holding company in accordance with § 240.17i–4 and utilized by the affiliate group. This review must be conducted by the accountant in accordance with procedures agreed to by the supervised investment bank holding company and the accountant conducting the review. The agreed-upon procedures are to be performed and the report is to be prepared in accordance with the rules promulgated by the Public Company Accounting Oversight Board. The purpose of the review is to confirm that the internal risk management control system complies with the requirements of § 240.17i–4 and that the supervised investment bank holding company and its affiliate group are adhering to the requirements of that internal risk management control system. The supervised investment bank holding company must file, prior to the commencement of the review, the procedures for conducting the audit agreed to by the supervised investment bank holding company and the accountant (pursuant to paragraph (d)(1) of this section). Prior to the commencement of each subsequent review, the supervised investment bank holding company shall file with the Commission a notice of any changes to the agreed-upon procedures.

(2) Annual audit reports prepared pursuant to this paragraph (d) shall be prepared as of the same date as the annual audit of the supervised investment bank holding company's affiliated broker or dealer.

(3) Annual audit reports prepared pursuant to this paragraph (d) shall be filed not later than 65 calendar days after the end of the fiscal year.

(e) *Consolidating Balance Sheet and Income Statement*. The supervised investment bank holding company shall file, concurrently with the annual audit report, an unaudited consolidating balance sheet and income statement, as of the supervised investment bank holding company's fiscal year-end, for the affiliate group.

(f) *Extensions and exemptions*. Upon the written request of the supervised investment bank holding company, or on its own motion, the Commission may conditionally or unconditionally grant or deny an extension of time or an exemption from any of the requirements of paragraphs (a) through (e) of this section to the extent that such exemption or extension of time is necessary or appropriate in the public interest or for the protection of investors.

(g) *When filed*. The reports required to be filed pursuant to this section shall be considered filed when two copies are received at the Commission's principal office in Washington, DC. The copies shall be addressed to the Division of Market Regulation, Office of Financial Responsibility.

(h) *Confidentiality*. All reports and statements filed by the supervised investment bank holding company with the Commission pursuant to this section shall be accorded confidential treatment to the extent permitted by law.

Rule 17i–7. Calculations of Allowable Capital and Risk Allowances or Alternative Capital Assessment.

(a) *Computation of allowable capital*. The supervised investment bank holding company must compute allowable capital on a consolidated basis as the aggregate of the following:

(1) Common shareholders' equity on the consolidated balance sheet of the supervised investment bank holding company less:

(i) Goodwill;

(ii) Deferred tax assets, except those permitted for inclusion in Tier 1 capital by the Board of Governors of the Federal Reserve (12 CFR 225, Appendix A);

(iii) Other intangible assets; and

(iv) Other deductions from common stockholders' equity as required by the Board of Governors of the Federal Reserve in calculating Tier 1 capital (as defined in 12 CFR 225, Appendix A).

(2) Cumulative and non-cumulative preferred stock, except that the amount of cumulative preferred stock may not exceed 33% of the items included in allowable capital pursuant to paragraph (a)(1) of this section, excluding cumulative preferred stock, provided that:

(i) The stock does not have a maturity date;

(ii) The stock cannot be redeemed at the option of the holder of the instrument;

(iii) The stock has no other provisions that will require future redemption of the issue; and

(iv) The issuer of the stock can defer or eliminate dividends; and

(3) The sum of the following items on the consolidated balance sheet, to the extent that sum does not exceed the sum of the items included in allowable capital pursuant to paragraphs (a)(1) and (a)(2) of this section:

(i) Cumulative preferred stock in excess of the 33% limit specified in paragraph (a)(2) and subject to the conditions of paragraphs (a)(2)(i) through (iv) of this section;

(ii) Subordinated debt if the original weighted average maturity of the subordinated debt is at least five years; each subordinated debt instrument states clearly on its face that repayment of the debt is not protected by any Federal agency or the Securities Investor Protection Corporation; the subordinated debt is unsecured and subordinated in right of payment to all senior indebtedness of the holding company; and the subordinated debt instrument permits acceleration only in the event of bankruptcy or reorganization of the holding company under Chapters 7 (liquidation) (11 U.S.C. 7) and 11 (reorganization) (11 U.S.C. 11) of the U.S. Bankruptcy Code; and

(iii) As part of the investment bank holding company's notice of intention, the investment bank holding company may request to include, for a period of three years after the adoption of this Rule (or such other period as the Commission may approve) long-term debt that has an original weighted average maturity of at least five years and that cannot be accelerated, except upon the occurrence of certain events as the Commission may approve. As part of an amendment to the investment bank holding company's notice of intention, the supervised investment bank holding company may request permission to include long-term debt that meets these criteria in allowable capital for an additional two years; and

(4) Hybrid capital instruments that are permitted for inclusion in Tier 2 capital by the Board of Governors of the Federal Reserve (12 CFR 225, Appendix A).

(b) *Allowance for market risk*. The supervised investment bank holding company must compute an allowance for market risk on a consolidated basis for all proprietary positions, including debt instruments, equity instruments, commodity instruments, foreign exchange contracts, and derivative contracts as the aggregate of the following:

(1) *Value at risk*. The Value at Risk measures obtained by applying one or more approved Value at Risk models to each position and multiplying the result by the appropriate multiplication factor. Each Value at Risk model shall meet the applicable qualitative and quantitative requirements set forth in § 240.15c3–1e(d); and

(2) *Alternative method*. For each position for which there is not adequate historical data to support a Value at Risk model, the measure obtained by computing the allowance for market risk using a method described in the supervised investment bank holding company's notice of intention that produces a suitable allowance for market risk for those positions.

(c) *Allowance for credit risk*. The supervised investment bank holding company must compute an allowance for credit risk for certain assets on the consolidated balance sheet and certain off-balance sheet items, including loans and loan commitments, exposures due to derivatives contracts, structured financial products, other extensions of credit, and credit substitutes in as follows:

(1) By multiplying the credit equivalent amount of the supervised investment bank holding company's exposure to the counterparty, as determined according to sub-paragraph (c)(1)(i) below, by the appropriate credit risk weight of the asset or off-balance sheet item or counterparty, as determined according to sub-paragraph (c)(1)(ii) below, then multiplying the product by 8%, in accordance with the following:

(i) *Credit equivalent amount:*

(A) *Certain loans and loan commitments receivable.* The credit equivalent amount for exposures relating to certain loans and loan commitments is determined by multiplying the nominal amount of the contract by the following credit conversion factors:

(1) 0% credit conversion factor for loan commitments that:

(i) May be unconditionally cancelled by the lender; or

(ii) May be cancelled by the lender due to credit deterioration of the borrower;

(2) 20% credit conversion factor for:

(i) Loan commitments of less than one year; or(ii) Short term self-liquidating trade related contingencies, including letters of credit;

(3) 50% credit conversion factor for loan commitments with an original maturity of greater than one year that contain transaction contingencies, including performance bonds, revolving underwriting facilities, note issuance facilities and bid bonds; and

(4) 100% credit conversion factor for loans and bankers' acceptances, stand-by letters of credit, and forward purchases of assets, and similar direct credit substitutes;

(B) *Receivables relating to derivative contracts, repurchase agreements, reverse repurchase agreements, stock loans, stock borrows, and other similar collateralized transactions.* The credit equivalent amount for exposures relating to derivative contracts, repurchase agreements, reverse repurchase agreements, stock loans, stock borrows, and other similar collateralized transactions is the sum of:

(1) The supervised investment bank holding company's current exposure to the counterparty (as defined in paragraph (c)(1)(i)(D) of this section); and

(2) The supervised investment bank holding company's maximum potential exposure to the counterparty (as defined in paragraph (c)(1)(i)(E) of this section) multiplied by the appropriate multiplication factor. The initial multiplication factor shall be one, unless the Commission determines pursuant to § 240.17i–2(d)(2), based on a review of the supervised investment bank holding company's internal risk management control system and practices, including a review of the Value at Risk model used to determine maximum potential exposure, that another multiplication factor is appropriate;

(C) *Credit equivalent amount for other assets.* The credit equivalent amount for other assets shall be the book value of the exposure on the supervised investment bank holding company's consolidated balance sheet or other amount as determined according to the standards published by the Basel Committee on Banking Supervision, as amended from time to time;

(D) The *current exposure* is the current replacement value of a counterparty's positions, after applying the effect of netting agreements with that counterparty meeting the requirements of § 240.15c3–1e(c)(4)(iv) and taking into account the value of collateral from the counterparty in accordance with § 240.15c3–1e(c)(4)(v);

(E) The *maximum potential exposure* is the Value at Risk of the counterparty's positions with the member of the affiliate group, after applying netting agreements with that counterparty meeting the requirements of § 240.15c3–1e(c)(4)(iv) and taking into account the value of collateral from the counterparty in accordance with § 240.15c3–1e(c)(4)(v) obtained using a Value at Risk model that meets the applicable requirements of

§ 240.15c3–1e(d) and the current replacement value of the counterparty's positions with the member of the affiliate group, Except that for repurchase agreements, reverse repurchase agreements, stock lending and borrowing, and similar collateralized transactions, maximum potential exposure shall be calculated using a time horizon of not less than five days;

(ii) *Credit risk weights*.

(A) *General*. The credit risk weights that shall be applied to certain assets and counterparties shall be determined according to standards published by the Basel Committee on Banking Supervision, as modified from time to time;

(B) *Receivables covered by guarantees*. For the portion of a current exposure covered by a written guarantee, where that guarantee is an unconditional and irrevocable guarantee of the due and punctual payment and performance of the obligation and the supervised investment bank holding company or member of the affiliate group can demand payment after any payment is missed without having to make collection efforts, the supervised investment bank holding company or member of the affiliate group may substitute the credit risk weight of the guarantor for the credit risk weight of the counterparty; and

(iii) *Credit derivatives*. Upon a determination by the Commission pursuant to § 240.17i–2(d), the supervised investment bank holding company may use credit derivatives to reduce its allowance for credit risk; or

(2) Upon a determination by the Commission pursuant to § 240.17i–2(d), using a calculation consistent with standards published by the Basel Committee on Banking Supervision in International Convergence of Capital Measurement and Capital Standards (July 1988), as modified from time to time;

(d) *Allowance for operational risk*. A supervised investment bank holding company shall compute an allowance for operational risk on a consolidated basis in accordance with the standards published by the Basel Committee on Banking Supervision, as amended from time to time.

Rule 17i–8. Notification Provisions for Supervised Investment Bank Holding Companies.

(a) A supervised investment bank holding company shall send notice promptly (but within 24 hours), in accordance with paragraph (c) of this section, after the occurrence of the following events:

(1) The occurrence of any backtesting exception, determined in accordance with § 240.15c3–1e(d)(1)(iii) or (iv), that would require that the supervised investment bank holding company use a higher multiplication factor in the calculation of its allowances for market or credit risk;

(2) The early warning indications of low capital as the Commission may agree;

(3) A material affiliate declares bankruptcy or otherwise becomes insolvent;

(4) The supervised investment bank holding company becomes aware that a nationally recognized statistical rating organization has determined to reduce materially its assessment of the creditworthiness of a material affiliate or the credit rating(s) assigned to one or more outstanding short or long-term obligations of an material affiliate;

(5) The supervised investment bank holding company files a Form 8–K (§ 249.308) with the Commission;

(6) The supervised investment bank holding company becomes aware that any financial regulatory agency or self-regulatory organization has taken significant enforcement or regulatory action against a material affiliate; or

(7) The supervised investment bank holding company becomes ineligible to be supervised by the Commission as a supervised investment bank holding company.

(c) Every notice required to be given or transmitted pursuant to this section shall be given or transmitted by telegraphic notice or facsimile transmission to the Division of Market Regulation, Office of Financial Responsibility at the principal office of the Commission in Washington, DC. The notices filed under this section shall be accorded confidential treatment to the extent permitted by law.

(d) Upon the written request of the supervised investment bank holding company, or on its own motion, the Commission may conditionally or unconditionally grant or deny an extension of time or an exemption from any of the requirements of this Rule 17i-8 to the extent that such exemption or extension of time is necessary or appropriate in the public interest or for the protection of investors.

Rule 17Ab2-1. Registration of Clearing Agencies

(a) An application for registration or for exemption from registration as a clearing agency, as defined in Section 3(a)(23) of the Act, or an amendment to any such application shall be filed with the Commission on Form CA-1, in accordance with the instructions thereto.

(b) Any applicant for registration or for exemption from registration as a clearing agency whose application is filed with the Commission on or before November 24, 1975, on and in accordance with the instructions to Form CA-1, with respect to the clearing agency activities described in the application shall, during the period from December 1, 1975 until the Commission grants registration, denies registration or grants an exemption from registration, be exempt from the registration provisions of Section 17A(b) of the Act and the rules and regulations thereunder and, unless the Commission shall otherwise provide by rule or by order, the provisions of the Act and the rules and regulations thereunder which would be applicable to clearing agencies as a result of registration under the Act.

(c)(1) The Commission, upon the request of a clearing agency, may grant registration of the clearing agency in accordance with Sections 17A(b) and 19(a)(1) of the Act but exempt the registrant from one or more of the requirements as to which the Commission is directed to make a determination pursuant to subparagraphs (A)-(1) of Section 17A(b)(3) of the Act, *Provided,* That any such registration shall be effective only for eighteen months from the date the registration is made effective (or such longer period as the Commission may provide by order).

(2) In the case of any clearing agency registered in accordance with subparagraph (1) of this paragraph (c), not later than nine months from the date such registration is made effective the Commission either will grant registration in accordance with Sections 17A(b) and 19(a)(1) of the Act, without exempting the registrant from one or more of the requirements as to which the Commission is directed to make a determination pursuant to subparagraphs (A)-(I) of Section 17A(b)(3) of the Act, or will institute proceedings in accordance with Section 19(a)(1)(B) of the Act to determine whether registration should be denied at the expiration of the registration granted in accordance with paragraph (1) of this paragraph (c).

(d) The filing of an amendment to an application for registration or for exemption from registration as a clearing agency, which registration or exemption has not been granted, or the filing of additional information or documents prior to the granting of registration or an exemption from registration shall extend to ninety days from the date such filing is made (or to such longer period as to which the applicant consents) the period within which the Commission shall grant registration, institute proceedings to determine whether such registration shall be denied, or conditionally or unconditionally exempt registrant from the registration and other provisions of Section 17A of the Act or the rules or regulations thereunder.

(e) If any information reported at items 1-3 of Form CA-1 is or becomes inaccurate, misleading or incomplete for any reason, whether before or after registration or an exemption from registration has been granted, the registrant shall file promptly an amendment on Form CA–1 correcting the inaccurate, misleading or incomplete information.

(f) Every application for registration or for exemption from registration as a clearing agency or amendment to, or additional information or document filed in connection with, any such application shall constitute a "report" or "application" within the meaning of Sections 17, 17A, 19 and 32(a) of the Act.

Rule 17Ac2–1. Application for Registration of Transfer Agents

(a) An application for registration, pursuant to Section 17A(c) of the Act, of a transfer agent for which the Commission is the appropriate regulatory agency, as defined in Section 3(a)(34)(B) of the Act, shall be filed with the Commission on Form TA–1, in accordance with the instructions contained therein and shall become effective on the thirtieth day following the date on which the application is filed, unless the Commission takes affirmative action to accelerate, deny or postpone such registration in accordance with the provisions of Section 17A(c) of the Act.

(b) The filing of any amendment to an application for registration as a transfer agent pursuant to paragraph (a) of this rule, which registration has not become effective, shall postpone the effective date of the registration until the thirtieth day following the date on which the amendment is filed, unless the Commission takes affirmative action to accelerate, deny or postpone the registration in accordance with the provisions of Section 17A(c) of the Act.

(c) If any of the information reported on Form TA–1 or on the SEC Supplement becomes inaccurate, misleading, or incomplete, the registrant shall correct the information by filing an amendment within sixty days following the date on which the information became inaccurate, misleading, or incomplete.

(d) Every registration and amendment filed pursuant to this rule shall constitute a "report" or "application" within the meaning of Sections 17, 17A(c), and 32(a) of the Act.

Rule 17Ac2–2. Annual Reporting Requirement for Registered Transfer Agents

(a) Every transfer agent registered on December 31 must file a report covering the reporting period on Form TA–2 (§ 249b.102 of this chapter) by March 31 following the end of the reporting period. Form TA–2 must be completed in accordance with the instructions contained in the Form.

(1) A registered transfer agent that received fewer than 1,000 items for transfer in the reporting period and that did not maintain master securityholder files for more than 1,000 individual securityholder accounts as of December 31 of the reporting period must complete Questions 1 through 5, 11, and the signature section of Form TA–2.

(2) A named transfer agent that engaged a service company to perform all of its transfer agent functions during the reporting period must complete Questions 1 through 3 and the signature section of Form TA–2.

(3) A named transfer agent that engaged a service company to perform some but not all of its transfer agent functions during the reporting period must complete all of Form TA–2 but should enter zero (0) for those questions that relate to transfer agent functions performed by the service company on behalf of the named transfer agent.

(b) For purposes of this section, the term *reporting period* shall mean the calendar year ending December 31 for which Form TA–2 is being filed. The term *named transfer agent* shall have the same meaning as defined in § 240.17Ad–9(j). The term *service company* shall have the same meaning as defined in § 240.17Ad–9(k).

(c) As a transition measure, transfer agents' next required Form TA–2 filing will be on March 31, 2001, which will cover their activities during calendar Year 2000. This will eliminate the filing for the period ending June 30, 2000, which would have been due on August 31, 2000.

Rule 17Ac3-1. Withdrawal From Registration With the Commission

(a) Notice of withdrawal from registration as a transfer agent with the Commission pursuant to Section 17A(c)(3)(C) of the Act shall be filed on Form TA-W in accordance with the instructions contained thereon.

(b) Except as hereinafter provided, a notice to withdraw from registration filed by a transfer agent pursuant to Section 17A(c)(3)(C) of the Act shall become effective on the sixtieth day after the filing thereof with the Commission or within such shorter period of time as the Commission may determine. If a notice to withdraw from registration is filed with the Commission at any time subsequent to the date of issuance of a Commission order instituting proceedings pursuant to Section 17A(c)(3)(A) of the Act, or if prior to the effective date of the notice of withdrawal the Commission institutes such a proceeding or a proceeding to impose terms and conditions upon such withdrawal, the notice of withdrawal shall not become effective except at such time and upon such terms and conditions as the Commission deems necessary or appropriate in the public interest, for the protection of investors, or in furtherance of the purposes of Section 17A.

(c) Every notice of withdrawal filed pursuant to this rule shall constitute a "report" within the meaning of Sections 17 and 32(a) of the Act.

Rule 17Ad-1. Definitions

As used in this rule and Rules 17Ad-2, 17Ad-3, 17Ad-4, 17Ad-5, 17Ad-6 and 17Ad-7:

(a)(1) The term "item" means:

(i) A certificate or certificates of the same issue of securities covered by one ticket (or, if there is no ticket, presented by one presentor) presented for transfer, or an instruction to a transfer agent which holds securities registered in the name of the presentor to transfer or to make available all or a portion of those securities;

(ii) Each line on a "deposit shipment control list" or a "withdrawal shipment control list" submitted by a registered clearing agency; or

(iii) In the case of an outside registrar, each certificate to be countersigned.

(2) If a "deposit shipment control list" or "withdrawal shipment control list" contains both routine and non-routine transfer instructions, a registered transfer agent shall at its option:

(i) Retain all transfer instructions listed on the shipment control list and treat each line on the shipment control list as a routine item; or

(ii) Return promptly to the registered clearing agency a shipment control list line containing non-routine transfer instructions (together with a copy of the shipment control list, an explanation for the returned instructions and all routine transfer instructions reflected on the same line) and treat each line on the shipment control list that reflects retained transfer instructions as a routine item.

(3) A "deposit shipment control list" means a list of transfer instructions that accompanies certificates to be cancelled and reissued in the nominee name of a registered clearing agency.

(4) A "withdrawal shipment control list" means a list of instructions (either in paper or electronic medium) that:

(i) directs issuance of certificates in the names of persons or entities other than the registered clearing agency; and

(ii) accompanies certificates to be cancelled which are registered in the nominee name of a registered clearing agency, or directs the transfer agent to reduce certificate or position balances maintained by the transfer agent on behalf of a registered clearing agency under that clearing agency's transfer agent custody program.

(b) The term "outside registrar" with respect to a transfer item means a transfer agent which performs only the registrar function for the certificate or certificates presented for transfer and includes the persons performing similar functions with respect to debt issues.

(c) An item is "made available" when

(1) in the case of an item for which the services of an outside registrar are not required, or which has been received from an outside registrar after processing, the transfer agent dispatches or mails the item to, or the item is awaiting pick-up by, the presentor or a person designated by the presentor, or

(2) in the case of an item for which the services of an outside registrar are required, the transfer agent dispatches or mails the item to, or the item is awaiting pick-up by, the outside registrar, or

(3) in the case of an item for which an outside registrar has completed processing, the outside registrar dispatches or mails the item to, or the item is awaiting pick-up by, the presenting transfer agent.

(d) The "transfer" of an item is accomplished when, in accordance with the presentor's instructions, all acts necessary to cancel the certificate or certificates presented for transfer and to issue a new certificate or certificates, including the performance of the registrar function, are completed and the item is made available to the presentor by the transfer agent, or when, in accordance with the presentor's instructions, a transfer agent which holds securities registered in the name of the presentor completes all acts necessary to issue a new certificate or certificates representing all or a portion of those securities and makes available the new certificate or certificates to the presentor or a person designated by the presentor or, with respect to those transfers of record ownership to be accomplished without the physical issuance of certificates, completes registration of change in ownership of all or a portion of those securities.

(e) The "turnaround" of an item is completed when transfer is accomplished or, when an outside registrar is involved, the transfer agent in accordance with the presentor's instructions completes all acts necessary to cancel the certificate or certificates presented for transfer and to issue a new certificate or certificates, and the item is made available to an outside registrar.

(f) The term "process" means the accomplishing by an outside registrar of all acts necessary to perform the registrar function and to make available to the presenting transfer agent the completed certificate or certificates or to advise the presenting transfer agent, orally or in writing, why performance of the registrar function is delayed or may not be completed.

(g) The "receipt" of an item or a written inquiry or request occurs when the item or written inquiry or request arrives at the premises at which the transfer agent performs transfer agent functions, as defined in Section 3(a)(25) of the Act.

(h) A "business day" is any day during which the transfer agent is normally open for business and excludes Saturdays, Sundays and legal holidays or other holidays normally observed by the transfer agent.

(i) An item is "routine" if it does not (1) require requisitioning certificates of an issue for which the transfer agent, under the terms of its agency, does not maintain a supply of certificates; (2) include a certificate as to which the transfer agent has received notice of a stop order, adverse claim or any other restriction on transfer; (3) require any additional certificates, documentation, instructions, assignments, guarantees, endorsements, explanations or opinions of counsel before transfer may be effected; (4) require review of supporting documentation other than assignments, endorsements or stock powers, certified corporate resolutions, signature or other common and ordinary guarantees or appropriate tax or tax waivers; (5) involve a transfer in connection with a reorganization, tender offer, exchange, redemption or liquidation; (6) include a warrant, right or convertible security presented for transfer of record ownership within five business days before any day upon which exercise or conversion privileges lapse or change; (7) include a warrant, right or convertible security presented for exercise or conversion; or (8) include a security of an issue which within the previous 15 business days was offered to the public, pursuant to a registration statement effective under the Securities Act of 1933, in an offering not of a continuing nature.

(j) The term "depository-eligible securities issue" means an issue of securities that is eligible for deposit at any securities depository that is registered with the Commission under the Securities Exchange Act of 1934 as a clearing agency.

Rule 17Ad–2. Turnaround, Processing and Forwarding of Items

(a) Every registered transfer agent (except when acting as an outside registrar) shall turnaround within three business days of receipt at least 90 percent of all routine items received for transfer during a month. For the purposes of this paragraph, items received at or before noon on a business day shall be deemed to have been received at noon on that day, and items received after noon on a business day or received on a day not a business day shall be deemed to have been received at noon on the next business day.

(b) Every registered transfer agent acting as an outside registrar shall process at least 90 percent of all items received during a month (1) by the opening of business on the next business day, in the case of items received at or before noon on a business day, and (2) by noon of the next business day, in the case of items received after noon on a business day. For the purposes of paragraphs (b) and (d) of this rule, "items received" shall not include any item enumerated in Rule 17Ad–1(i)(5), (6), (7) or (8) or any item which is not accompanied by a debit or cancelled certificate. For the purposes of this paragraph, items received on a day not a business day shall be deemed to have been received before noon on the next business day.

(c) Any registered transfer agent which fails to comply with paragraph (a) of this rule with respect to any month shall, within ten business days following the end of such month, file with the Commission and the transfer agent's appropriate regulatory agency, if it is not the Commission, a written notice in accordance with paragraph (h) of this rule. Such notice shall state the number of routine items and the number of non-routine items received for transfer during the month, the number of routine items which the registered transfer agent failed to turnaround in accordance with the requirements of paragraph (a) of this rule, the percentage that such routine items represent of all routine items received during the month, the reasons for such failure, the steps which have been taken, are being taken or will be taken to prevent a future failure and the number of routine items, aged in increments of one business day, which as of the close of business on the last business day of the month have been in its possession for more than four business days and have not been turned around.

(d) Any registered transfer agent which fails to comply with paragraph (b) of this rule with respect to any month shall, within ten business days following the end of such month, file with the Commission and the transfer agent's appropriate regulatory agency, if it is not the Commission, a written notice in accordance with paragraph (h) of this rule. Such notice shall state the number of items received for processing during the month, the number of items which the registered transfer agent failed to process in accordance with the requirements of paragraph (b) of this rule, the percentage that such items represent of all items received during the month, the reasons for such failure and the steps which have been taken, are being taken or will be taken to prevent a future failure, and the number of items which as of the close of business on the last business day of the month have been in the transfer agent's possession for more than the time allowed for processing and have not been processed.

(e)(1) Except as provided in paragraph (e)(2) of this rule, all routine items not turned around within three business days of receipt as required by paragraph (a) of this rule and all items not processed within the periods required by paragraph (b) of this rule shall be turned around promptly, and all non-routine items shall receive diligent and continuous attention and shall be turned around as soon as possible.

(2) A transfer agent that is exempt under Rule 17Ad–4(b) and that has received 30 days notice of depository-eligibility of an issue for which it performs transfer agent functions shall turnaround ninety percent of all routine items received during a month within five business days of receipt. Such transfer agent shall devote diligent and continuous attention to the remaining ten percent of routine items and shall turnaround these items as soon as possible.

(f) A registered transfer agent which receives items at locations other than the premises at which it performs transfer agent functions shall have appropriate procedures to assure, and shall assure, that items are forwarded to such premises promptly.

(g) A registered transfer agent which receives processed items from an outside registrar shall have appropriate procedures to assure, and shall assure, that such items are made available promptly to the presentor.

(h) Any notice required by this section or Rule 17Ad–4 shall be filed as follows:

(1) Any notice required to be filed with the Commission shall be filed in triplicate with the principal office of the Commission in Washington, D.C. 20549 and, in the case of a registered transfer agent for which the Commission is the appropriate regulatory agency, an additional copy shall be filed with the Regional or District Office of the Commission for the region or district in which the registered transfer agent has its principal office for transfer agent activities.

(2) Any notice required to be filed with the Comptroller of the Currency shall be filed with the Office of the Comptroller of the Currency, Administrator of National Banks, Washington, D.C. 20219.

(3) Any notice required to be filed with the Board of Governors of the Federal Reserve System shall be filed with the Board of Governors of the Federal Reserve System, Washington, D.C. 20251 and with the Federal Reserve Bank of the district in which the registered transfer agent's principal banking operations are conducted.

(4) Any notice required to be filed with the Federal Deposit Insurance Corporation shall be filed with the Federal Deposit Insurance Corporation, Washington, D.C. 20429.

Rule 17Ad–3. Limitations on Expansion

(a) Any registered transfer agent which is required to file any notice pursuant to Rule 17Ad–2(c) or (d) for each of three consecutive months shall not, from the fifth business day after the end of the third such month until the end of the next following period of three successive months during which no such notices have been required:

(1) initiate the performance of any transfer agent function or activity for an issue for which the transfer agent does not perform, or is not under agreement to perform, transfer agent functions prior to such fifth business day; and

(2) with respect to an issue for which transfer agent functions are being performed on such fifth business day, initiate for that issue the performance of an addi-

tional transfer agent function or activity which the transfer agent does not perform, or is not under agreement to perform, prior to such fifth business day.

(b) Any registered transfer agent which for each of two consecutive months fails to turnaround at least 75% of all routine items in accordance with the requirements of Rule 17Ad–2(a) or to process at least 75% of all items in accordance with the requirements of Rule 17Ad–2(b) shall be subject to the limitations imposed by paragraph (a) of this section and further shall, within twenty business days after the close of the second such month, send to the chief executive officer of each issuer for which such registered transfer agent acts a copy of the written notice filed pursuant to Rule 17Ad–2(c) or (d) with respect to the second such month.

Rule 17Ad–4. Applicability of Rules 17Ad–2, 17Ad–3 and 17Ad–6(a)(1) Through (7) and (11)

(a) Rules 17Ad–2, 17Ad–3 and 17Ad–6(a)(1) through (7) and (11) shall not apply to interests in limited partnerships, to redeemable securities of investment companies registered under Section 8 of the Investment Company Act of 1940, or to interests in dividend reinvestment programs.

(b)(1) For purposes of this rule, "exempt transfer agent" means a transfer agent that during any six consecutive months shall have received fewer than 500 items for transfer and fewer than 500 items for processing.

(2) Except as provided in paragraph (c) of this rule, an exempt transfer agent that satisfies the requirements of paragraph (b)(3) shall be exempt from the provisions of Rules 17Ad–2(a), (b), (c), (d) and (h), Rule 17Ad–3 and Rules 17Ad–6(a)(2) through (7) and (11).

(3) Within ten business days following the close of the sixth consecutive month described in paragraph (b)(1) of this rule, an exempt transfer agent shall:

(i) If its appropriate regulatory agency is either the Commission or the Office of the Comptroller of the Currency, prepare and maintain in its possession a document certifying that the transfer agent qualifies as exempt under paragraph (b)(1) of this rule; or

(ii) If its appropriate regulatory agency is either the Board of Governors of the Federal Reserve System or the Federal Deposit Insurance Corporation, file with the appropriate regulatory agency a notice certifying that it qualifies as exempt under paragraph (b)(1) of this rule.

(c) Within five business days following the close of each month, every exempt transfer agent shall calculate the number of items which it received during the preceding six months. Whenever any exempt transfer agent no longer qualifies as such under paragraph (b)(1), within ten business days after the end of such month: (1) It shall prepare and maintain in its possession a document so stating, if subject to paragraph (b)(3)(i) of this rule; or (2) It shall file with its appropriate regulatory agency a notice to that effect, if subject to paragraph (b)(3)(ii) of this rule. Thereafter, beginning with the first month following the month in which such document is required to be prepared or such notice is required to be filed, the registered transfer agent no longer shall be exempt under paragraph (b) of this section. Any registered transfer agent which has ceased to be an exempt transfer agent under this paragraph shall not qualify again for exemption until it has conducted its transfer agent operations pursuant to the foregoing rule for six consecutive months following the month in which it was required to prepare the document or prepare and file the notice specified in this paragraph.

Rule 17Ad–5. Written Inquiries and Requests

(a) When any person makes a written inquiry to a registered transfer agent concerning the status of an item presented for transfer during the preceding six months by such person or anyone acting on his behalf, which inquiry identifies the issue, the number of shares (or principal amount of debt securities or number of units if relating to any other kind of security) presented, the approximate date of presentment and the name in which it is registered, the registered transfer agent shall, within five business days following receipt of the inquiry, respond, stating whether the item has been received; if received, whether it has been transferred; if received and not transferred, the reason for the delay and what additional matter, if any, is necessary before transfer may be effected; and, if received and transferred, the date and manner in which the completed item was made available, the addressee and address to which it was made available and the number of any new certificate which was registered and the name in which it was registered. If a new certificate is dispatched or mailed to the presentor within five business days following receipt of an inquiry pertaining to that certificate, no further response to the inquiry shall be required pursuant to this paragraph.

(b) When any broker-dealer requests in writing that a registered transfer agent acknowledge the transfer instructions and the possession of a security presented for transfer by such broker-dealer or revalidate a window ticket with respect to such security and the request identifies the issue, the number of shares (or principal amount of debt securities or number of units if relating to any other kind of security), the approximate date of presentment, the certificate number and the name in which it is registered, every registered transfer agent shall, within five business days following receipt of the request, in writing, confirm or deny possession of the security, and, if the registered transfer agent has possession, (1) acknowledge the transfer instructions or (2) revalidate the window ticket. If a new certificate is dispatched or mailed to the presentor within five business days following receipt of a request pertaining to that certificate, no further response to the inquiry shall be required pursuant to this paragraph.

(c) When any person, or anyone acting under his authority, requests in writing that a transfer agent confirm possession as of a given date of a certificate presented by such person during the 30 days before the date the inquiry is received and the request identifies the issue, the number of shares (or principal amount of debt securities or number of units if relating to any other kind of security), the approximate date of presentment, the certificate number and the name in which the certificate was registered, every registered transfer agent shall, within ten business days following receipt of the request and upon assurance of payment of a reasonable fee if required by such transfer agent, make available a written response to such person, or anyone acting under his authority, confirming or denying possession of such security as of such given date.

(d) When any person requests in writing a transcript of such person's account with respect to a particular issue, either as the account appears currently or as it appeared on a specific date not more than six months prior to the date the registered transfer agent receives the request, every registered transfer agent shall, within twenty business days following receipt of the request and upon assurance of payment of a reasonable fee if required by such transfer agent, make available to such person a transcript, ledger or statement of account in sufficient detail to permit reconstruction of such account as of the date for which the transcript was requested.

(e)(1) *Response to Written Inquiries Concerning Dividend and Interest Payments.* A registered transfer agent shall respond, within ten business days of receipt, to current claims that contain sufficient detail. A registered transfer agent shall respond, within twenty business days of receipt, to aged claims that contain sufficient detail. The response shall indicate in writing that the inquiry has been received, whether the claim requires further research and, if so, a reasonable estimate of how long that research may take. If no further research is required, the response shall indicate whether that claim is being or will be paid and, if not, the reason for not paying the claim. A registered transfer agent shall devote diligent attention to unresolved inquiries and shall resolve all inquiries as soon as possible.

(2) *Misdirected Written Inquiries Concerning Dividend and Interest Payments.* In the event that a transfer agent is not the dividend disbursing or interest paying agent for an issue that is the subject of a claim under this section, but performed those or any transfer agent services for that issue within the preceding three years, the transfer agent shall provide in writing to the inquirer, within ten business days of receipt of the inquiry, the name and address of the current dividend disbursing or interest paying agent. If the transfer agent did not perform those or other transfer agent services for the issue within the preceding three years, the transfer agent must respond to the inquiry and may respond by returning the inquiry with a statement that the transfer agent is not the current dividend disbursing or interest paying agent and that it does not know the name and address of the current dividend disbursing or interest paying agent.

(3) As used in this paragraph:

(i) A "current claim" means a written inquiry concerning non-payment or incorrect payment of dividends or interest, the payment date for which occurred within the preceding six months.

(ii) An "aged claim" means a written inquiry concerning non-payment or incorrect payment of dividends or interest, the payment date for which occurred more than six months before the inquiry.

(iii) "sufficient detail" means a written inquiry or request that identifies: the issue; the name(s) in which the securities are registered; the number of shares (or principal amount of debt securities or number of units for any other kind of security) involved; the approximate record date(s) or payment date(s) relating to the claim; and, with respect to registered broker-dealers, registered clearing agencies, or banks, certificate numbers.

(f) *Telephone Response.*

(1) A transfer agent may satisfy the written response requirements of this section by a telephone response to the inquirer if:

(i) The telephone response resolves that inquiry; and

(ii) The inquirer does not request a written response.

(2) When any person makes a written inquiry or request that would qualify under paragraph (e) of this rule except that it fails to provide sufficient detail as specified in paragraph (e)(3)(iii), a registered transfer agent may telephone the inquirer to obtain the necessary additional detail within the time periods specified in paragraph (e)(1). If the transfer agent does not receive the additional detail within ten business days, the transfer agent immediately shall make a written request for the additional information.

(g)(1) When any person makes a written inquiry or request which would qualify under paragraphs (a), (b), (c) or (d) of this rule except that it fails to provide all of the information specified in those paragraphs, or requests information which refers to a time earlier than the time periods specified in those paragraphs, a registered transfer agent shall confirm promptly receipt of the inquiry or request and respond to it as soon as possible.

(2) When any person makes a written inquiry or request which would qualify under paragraph (e) of this section except that it fails to provide sufficient detail as specified in paragraph (e)(3)(iii), a registered transfer agent must respond to the inquiry within the time periods specified in paragraph (e)(1). A registered transfer agent may respond to such an inquiry in accordance with paragraph (e)(1) as though sufficient detail had been provided, or may return it to the inquirer, requesting the additional necessary details.

Rule 17Ad-6. Recordkeeping

(a) Every registered transfer agent shall make and keep current the following:

(1) a receipt, ticket, schedule, log or other record showing the business day each routine item and each non-routine item is (i) received from the presentor and, if applicable, from the outside registrar and (ii) made available to the presentor and, if applicable, to the outside registrar;

(2) a log, tally, journal, schedule or other record showing for each month:

(i) the number of routine items received;

(ii) the number of routine items received during the month that were turned around within three business days of receipt;

(iii) the number of routine items received during the month that were not turned around within three business days of receipt;

(iv) the number of non-routine items received during the month;

(v) the number of non-routine items received during the month that were turned around;

(vi) the number of routine items that, as of the close of business on the last business day of each month, have been in such registered transfer agent's possession for more than four business days, aged in increments of one business day (beginning on the fifth business day); and

(vii) the number of non-routine items in such registered transfer agent's possession as of the close of business on the last business day of each month;

(3) with respect to items for which the registered transfer agent acts as an outside registrar:

(i) a receipt, ticket, schedule, log or other record showing the date and time:

(A) each item is

(1) received from the presenting transfer agent and

(2) made available to the presenting transfer agent;

(B) each written or oral notice of refusal to perform the registrar function is made available to the presenting transfer agent (and the substance of the notice); and

(ii) a log, tally, journal, schedule or other record showing for each month:

(A) the number of items received;

(B) the number of items processed within the time required by Rule 17Ad–2(b); and

(C) the number of items not processed within the time required by Rule 17Ad–2(b);

(4) a record of calculations demonstrating the registered transfer agent's monitoring of its performance under Rule 17Ad–2(a) and (b);

(5) a copy of any written notice filed pursuant to Rule 17Ad–2;

(6) any written inquiry or request, including those not subject to the requirements of Rule 17Ad–5, concerning an item, showing the date received; a copy of any written response to an inquiry or request, showing the date dispatched or mailed to the presentor; if no response to an inquiry or request was made, the date the certificate involved was made available to the presentor; or, in the case of an inquiry or request under Rule 17Ad–5(a) responded to by telephone, a telephone log or memorandum showing the date and substance of any telephone response to the inquiry;

(7) a log, journal, schedule or other record showing the number of inquiries subject to Rule 17Ad–5(a), (b), (c) and (d) received during each month but not responded to within the required time frames and the number of such inquiries pending as of the

close of business on the last business day of each month;

(8) any document, resolution, contract, appointment or other writing, and any supporting document, concerning the appointment and the termination of such appointment of such registered transfer agent to act in any capacity for any issue on behalf of the issuer, on behalf of itself as the issuer or on behalf of any person who was engaged by the issuer to act on behalf of the issuer;

(9) any record of an active (i.e., unreleased) stop order, notice of adverse claim or any other restriction on transfer;

(10) a copy of any transfer journal and registrar journal prepared by such registered transfer agent; and

(11) any document upon which the transfer agent bases its determination that an item received for transfer was received in connection with a reorganization, tender offer, exchange, redemption, liquidation, conversion or the sale of securities registered pursuant to the Securities Act of 1933 and, accordingly, was not routine under Rule 17Ad–1(i)(5) or (8).

(b) Every registered transfer agent which, under the terms of its agency, maintains security holder records for an issue or which acts as a registrar for an issue shall, with respect to such issue, obtain from the issuer or its transfer agent and retain documentation setting forth the total number of shares or principal amount of debt securities or total number of units if relating to any other kind of security authorized and the total issued and outstanding pursuant to issuer authorization.

(c) Every registered transfer agent which, under the terms of its agency, maintains security holder records for an issue shall, with respect to such issue, retain each cancelled registered bond, debenture, share, warrant or right, other registered evidence of indebtedness, or other certificate of ownership and all accompany documentation, except legal papers returned to the presentor.

Rule 17Ad–7. Record Retention

(a) The records required by Rule 17Ad–6(a)(1), (3)(i), (6) or (11) shall be maintained for a period of not less than two years, the first six months in an easily accessible place.

(b) The records required by Rule 17Ad–6(a)(2), (3)(ii), (4), (5) or (7) shall be maintained for a period of not less than two years, the first year in an easily accessible place.

(c) The records required by Rule 17Ad–6(a)(8), (9) and (10) and (b) shall be maintained in an easily accessible place during the continuance of the transfer agency and shall be maintained for one year after termination of the transfer agency.

(d) The records required by Rule 17Ad–6(c) shall be maintained for a period of not less than six years, the first six months in an easily accessible place.

(e) Every registered transfer agent shall maintain in an easily accessible place:

(1) all records required under Rule 17f–2(d) until at least three years after the termination of employment of those persons required by Rule 17f–2 to be fingerprinted; and

(2) all records required pursuant to Rule 17f–2(e).

(f) Subject to the conditions set forth in this section, the records required to be maintained pursuant to § 240.17Ad–6 may be retained using electronic or micrographic media and may be preserved in those formats for the time required by § 240.17Ad–7. Records stored electronically or micrographically in accordance with this paragraph may serve as a substitute for the hard copy records required to be maintained pursuant to § 240.17Ad–6.

(1) For purposes of this section:

(i) The term *micrographic media* means microfilm or microfiche or any similar medium.

(ii) The term *electronic storage media* means any digital storage medium or system.

(iii) The term *ARA* means your appropriate regulatory agency as that term is defined in 15 U.S.C. 78c(a)(34).

(2) If you as a registered transfer agent use electronic storage media or micrographic media to store your records, you must:

(i) Have available at all times for examination by the staffs of the Commission and of your ARA facilities to project or produce immediately easily readable images of such records;

(ii) Be ready at all times to provide such records that the staffs of the Commission and your ARA or their representatives may request;

(iii) Create an accurate index of such records, store the index with those records, and have the index available at all times for examination by the staffs of the Commission and your ARA;

(iv) Have quality assurance procedures to verify the quality and accuracy of the electronic or micrographic recording process; and

(v) Maintain separately from the originals duplicates of the records and the index that you store on electronic storage media or micrographic media. You may store the duplicates of the indexed records on any medium permitted by this section. You must preserve the duplicate records and index for the same time that is required by this section for the indexed records, and you must have them available at all times for examination by the staffs of the Commission and your ARA.

(3) Any electronic storage media that you use to store your records must:

(i) Ensure the security and integrity of the records by means of manual and automated controls that assure the authenticity and quality of the electronic facsimile, detect attempts to alter or remove the records, and provide means to recover altered, damaged, or lost records resulting from any cause;

(ii) Externally label all removable units of storage media using a unique identifier that allows the manual association of that removable storage unit with its place and order in the recordkeeping system; and

(iii) Uniquely identify files and internally label each file with its unique name, the date and time of file creation, the date and time of last modification or extension, and a file sequence number when the file spans more than one volume.

(4) If you use electronic storage media or micrographic media to store your records, you must establish an audit system that accounts for the inputting of and any changes to every record that is stored on electronic storage media or micrographic media. The results of such audit system must:

(i) Be available at all times for examination by the staffs of the Commission and your ARA; and

(ii) Be preserved for the same time that is required by this section for the underlying records.

(5) If you use electronic storage media or micrographic media to store your records, you must:

(i) Maintain, keep current, and provide promptly upon request by the staffs of the Commission and your ARA all information necessary to access the records and indexes stored on electronic storage media or micrographic media; and

(ii) Place, or have a third party place on your behalf, in escrow with an independent third party and keep current a copy of the physical and logical format of the electronic storage or micrographic media, the field format of all different information types written on the electronic storage media and source code, and the appropriate documentation and information necessary to access records and indexes. The independent escrow agent must file an undertaking signed by a duly authorized person with the Commission and your ARA stating that:

[Name of Third Party] hereby undertakes to furnish promptly upon request to the U.S. Securities and Exchange Commission, its designees, or representatives, upon reasonable request, a current copy of the physical and logical format of the electronic storage or micrographic media, the field format of all different information types written on the electronic storage media and source code, and the appropriate documentation and information necessary to access the records and indexes of [Name of Transfer Agent]'s electronic records management system.

(6)(i) If you use a third party to maintain or preserve some or all of the required records using electronic storage media or micrographic media, such third party shall file a written undertaking signed by a duly authorized person with the Commission and your ARA stating that:

"With respect to any books and records maintained or preserved on behalf of [Name of Transfer Agent], [Name of Third Party] hereby undertakes to permit examination of such books and records at any time or from time to time during business hours by representatives or designees of the U.S. Securities and Exchange Commission, and to promptly furnish to said Commission or its designee true, correct, complete, and current hard copies of any or all or any part of such books and records."

(ii) Agreement with a third party to maintain your records shall not relieve you from the responsibility to prepare and maintain records as specified in this section or in § 240.17Ad–6.

(g) If the records required to be maintained and preserved by a registered transfer agent pursuant to the requirements of Rules 17Ad–6 and 17Ad–7 are maintained and preserved on behalf of the registered transfer agent by an outside service bureau, other recordkeeping service or the issuer, the registered transfer agent shall obtain, from such outside service bureau, other recordkeeping service or the issuer, an agreement, in writing, to the effect that:

(1) such records are subject at any time, or from time to time, to reasonable periodic, special, or other examinations by representatives of the Commission and the appropriate regulatory agency for such registered transfer agent, if it is not the Commission; and

(2) the outside service bureau, recordkeeping service, or issuer will furnish to the Commission and the appropriate regulatory agency, upon demand, at either the principal office or at any regional office, complete, correct and current hard copies of any and all such records.

(h) When a registered transfer agent ceases to perform transfer agent functions for an issue, the responsibility of such transfer agent under Rule 17Ad–7 to retain the records required to be made and keep current under Rule 17Ad–6(a)(1), (6), (9), (10) and (11), (b) and (c) shall end upon the delivery of such records to the successor transfer agent.

(i) The records required by §§ 240.17Ad–17(c) and 240.17Ad–19(c) shall be maintained for a period of not less than three years, the first year in an easily accessible place.

Rule 17Ad–8. Securities Position Listings

(a) For purposes of this section, the term "securities position listing" means, with respect to the securities of any issuer held by a registered clearing agency in the name of the clearing agency or its nominee, a list of those participants in the clearing agency on whose behalf the clearing agency holds the issuer's securities and of the participants' respective positions in such securities as of a specified date.

(b) Upon request, a registered clearing agency shall furnish a securities position listing promptly to each issuer whose securities are held in the name of the clearing agency or its nominee. A registered clearing agency may charge issuers requesting securities position listings a fee designed to recover the reasonable costs of providing the securities position listing to the issuer.

Rule 17Ad–9. Definitions

As used in this section and Rules 17Ad–10, 17Ad–11, 17Ad–12 and 17Ad–13:

(a) "Certificate detail," with respect to certificated securities, includes, at a minimum, all of the following, and with respect to uncertificated securities, includes items (2) through (8):

(1) The certificate number;

(2) The number of shares for equity securities or the principal dollar amount for debt securities;

(3) The securityholder's registration;

(4) The address of the registered securityholder;

(5) The issue date of the security;

(6) The cancellation date of the security;

(7) In the case of redeemable securities of investment companies, an appropriate description of each debit and credit (i.e., designation indicating purchase, redemption, or transfer); and

(8) Any other identifying information about securities and securityholders the transfer agent reasonably deems essential to its recordkeeping system for the efficient and effective research of record differences.

(b) "Master securityholder file" is the official list of individual securityholder accounts. With respect to uncertified securities of companies registered under the Investment Company Act of 1940, the master securityholder file may consist of multiple, but linked, automated files.

(c) A "subsidiary file" is any list or record of accounts, securityholders, or certificates that evidences debits or credits that have not been posted to the master securityholder file.

(d) A "control book" is the record or other document that shows the total number of shares (in the case of equity securities) or the principal dollar amount (in the case of debt securities) authorized and issued by the issuer.

(e) A "credit" is an addition of appropriate certificate detail to the master securityholder file.

(f) A "debit" is a cancellation of appropriate certificate detail from the master securityholder file.

(g) A "record difference" occurs when either (1) The total number of shares or total principal dollar amount of securities in the master securityholder file does not equal the number of shares or principal dollar amount in the control book; or (2) The security transferred or redeemed contains certificate detail different from the certificate detail currently on the master securityholder file, which difference cannot be immediately resolved.

(h) A "recordkeeping transfer agent" is the registered transfer agent that maintains and updates the master securityholder file.

(i) A "co-transfer agent" is the registered transfer agent that transfers securities but does not maintain and update the master securityholder file.

(j) A "named transfer agent" is the registered transfer agent that is engaged by an issuer to perform transfer agent functions for an issue of securities but has engaged a service company to perform some or all of those functions.

(k) A "service company" is the registered transfer agent engaged by a named transfer agent to perform transfer agent functions for that named transfer agent.

(*l*) A "file" includes automated and mutual records.

Rule 17Ad–10. Prompt Posting of Certificate Detail to Master Securityholder Files, Maintenance of Accurate Securityholder Files, Communications Between Co-transfer Agents and Recordkeeping Transfer Agents, Maintenance of Current Control Book, Retention of Certificate Detail and "Buy-in" of Physical Over-Issuance

(a)(1) Every recordkeeping transfer agent shall promptly and accurately post to the master securityholder file debits and credits containing minimum and appropriate certificate detail representing every security transferred, purchased, redeemed or issued; *Provided, however,* that if a security transferred or redeemed contains certificate detail different from that currently posted to the master securityholder file, the credit shall be posted to the master securityholder file and the debit and related certificate detail shall be maintained in a subsidiary file until resolved. The recordkeeping transfer agent shall exercise diligent and continuous attention to resolve the resulting record difference and, once resolved, shall post to the master securityholder file the debit maintained in the subsidiary file. Postings of certificate detail shall remain on the master securityholder file until a debit to a securityholder account is appropriate.

(2) As used in this paragraph, the term "promptly" means the following number of days after issuance, purchase, transfer, or redemption of a security:

(i) With respect to recordkeeping transfer agents (other than transfer agents that perform transfer agent functions with respect to redeemable securities issued by investment companies registered under Section 8 of the Investment Company Act of 1940) that are exempt transfer agents under Rule 17Ad–4(b), 30 calendar days;

(ii) With respect to recordkeeping transfer agents (other than transfer agents that perform transfer agent functions with respect to redeemable securities issued by investment companies registered under Section 8 of the Investment Company Act of 1940) that (A) perform transfer agent functions solely for their own or their affiliated companies' securities issues, and (B) employ batch posting systems, ten business days; and

(iii) With respect to all other recordkeeping transfer agents, five business days;

Provided, however, That all securities transferred, purchased, redeemed or issued prior to record date, but posted subsequent thereto, shall be posted as of the record date.

(3) With respect to posting certificate detail from transfer journals received by the recordkeeping transfer agent from a co-transfer agent, the time frames set forth in paragraph (a)(2) shall commence upon receipt of those journals by the recordkeeping transfer agent.

(b) Every recordkeeping transfer agent shall maintain and keep current an accurate master securityholder file and subsidiary files. If such transfer agent has any record difference, its master securityholder file and subsidiary files must accurately represent all relevant debits and credits until the record difference is resolved. The recordkeeping transfer agent shall exercise diligent and continuous attention to resolve all record differences.

(c)(1) Every co-transfer agent shall dispatch or mail promptly to the recordkeeping transfer agent a record of debits and credits for every security transferred or issued. For the purposes of this paragraph, "promptly" means within two business days following transfer of each security, and, with respect to transfers occurring within five business days of record date, daily.

(2) Within three business days following the end of each month, every co-transfer agent shall mail to the recordkeeping transfer agent

for each issue of securities for which it acts as a co-transfer agent, a report setting forth:

(i) The principal dollar amount of debt securities or the number of shares and related market value of equity securities comprising any buy-in executed by the co-transfer agent during the preceding month pursuant to paragraph (g) of this rule; and

(ii) The reason for the buy-in.

(d) Every co-transfer agent shall respond promptly to all inquiries from the recordkeeping transfer agent regarding records required to be dispatched or mailed by the co-transfer agent pursuant to Rule 17Ad–10(c). For the purposes of this paragraph, "promptly" means within five business days of receipt of an inquiry from a recordkeeping transfer agent.

(e) Every recordkeeping transfer agent shall maintain and keep current an accurate control book for each issue of securities. A change in the control book shall not be made except upon written authorization from a duly authorized agent of the issuer.

(f) Every recordkeeping transfer agent shall retain a record of all certificate detail deleted from the master securityholder file for a period of six years from the date of deletion. In lieu of maintaining a hard copy, a recordkeeping transfer agent may comply with this paragraph by complying with Rule 17Ad–7(f) or Rule 17Ad–7(g).

(g)(1) A registered transfer agent, in the event of any actual physical overissuance that such transfer agent caused and of which it has knowledge, shall, within 60 days of the discovery of such overissuance, buy in securities equal to either the number of shares in the case of equity securities or the principal dollar amount in the case of debt securities. During the 60-day period, the registered transfer agent shall devote diligent attention to resolving the overissuance and recovering the certificates. This paragraph securities equal to the number of shares in the case of equity securities requires a buy-in only by the transfer agent that erroneously issued the certificate(s) giving rise to the physical overissuance, and applies only to those physical overissuances created by transfers or issuances subsequent to September 30, 1983.

(2) If a transfer agent obtains a letter from the party holding the overissued certificates that confirms that the overissued certificate(s) will be returned to the transfer agent not later than thirty days after the expiration of the sixty-day period, the transfer agent need not buy in securities by the sixtieth day. If, however, the certificate(s) are not returned to the transfer agent within the additional thirty-day period, the transfer agent immediately must execute the buy-in in accordance with paragraph (g)(1) of this rule.

(3) If the certificates involved are covered by a surety bond indemnifying the transfer agent for all expenses incurred as a result of actual overissuance, the transfer agent need not buy in the securities. The transfer agent, however, shall devote diligent attention to resolving the overissuance and recovering the certificates.

(4) For purposes of this paragraph, "discovery of the overissuance" occurs when the transfer agent identifies the erroneously issued certificate(s) and the registered securityholder(s).

(h) Subsequent to the effective date of this rule, registered transfer agents that (1) Assume the maintenance and updating of master securityholder files from predecessor transfer agents, (2) Establish a new master securityholder file for a particular issue, or (3) Convert from manual to automated systems, must carry over any existing certificate detail required by this section on the master securityholder file. A recordkeeping transfer agent shall not be required to add certificate detail to the master securityholder file respecting certificates issued prior to the effective date of this section.

Rule 17Ad–11. Reports Regarding Aged Record Differences, Buy-ins and Failure to Post Certificate Detail to Master Securityholder and Subsidiary Files

(a) *Definitions.*

(1) "Issuer capitalization" means the market value of the issuer's authorized and outstanding equity securities or, with respect to a municipal securities issuer, the market value of all debt issues for which the transfer agent performs recordkeeping functions on behalf of that issuer, determined by reference to the control book and current market prices.

(2) An "aged record difference" is a record difference that has existed for more than thirty calendar days.

(b) *Reports to Issuers.*

(1) Within ten business days following the end of each month, every recordkeeping transfer agent shall report the information specified in paragraph (d)(1) of this rule to the persons specified in paragraph (b)(3) of this section, when the aggregate market value of aged record differences in all equity securities issues or debt securities issues maintained on behalf of a particular issuer exceeds the thresholds set forth in the table below.

Issuer Capitalization	Aggregate Market Value of Aged Record Differences Exceed: for EQUITY securities	for DEBT securities
1) $5 million or less	$50,000	$100,000
2) greater than $5 million but less than $50 million	$250,000	$500,000
3) greater than $50 million but less than $150 million	$500,000	$1,000,000
4) greater than $150 million	$1,000,000	$2,000,000

(2) Within ten business days following the end of each month (or within ten days thereafter in the case of a named transfer agent that receives a report from a service company pursuant to paragraph (b)(3)(i)(C)), every recordkeeping transfer agent shall report the information specified in paragraph (d)(2) of this rule to the persons specified in paragraph (b)(3) of this rule, with respect to each issue of securities for which it acts as recordkeeping transfer agent, concerning any securities bought-in pursuant to Rule 17Ad–10(g) or reported as bought-in pursuant to Rule 17Ad–10(c) during the preceding month.

(3) The report shall be sent:

(i) By every recordkeeping transfer agent (other than a recordkeeping transfer agent that performs transfer agent functions solely for its own securities):

(A) To the official performing corporate secretary functions for the issuer of the securities for which the aged record difference exists or for which the buy-in occurred;

(B) With respect to an issue of municipal securities, to the chief financial officer of the issuer of the securities for which the aged record difference exists or for which the buy-in occurred; or

(C) If it acts as a service company, to the named transfer agent; and

(ii) By every named transfer agent that is engaged by an issuer to maintain and update the master securityholder file:

(A) To the official performing corporate secretary functions for the issuer of the securities for which the aged record difference exists or for which the buy-in occurred; or

(B) With respect to an issue of municipal securities, to the chief financial officer of the issuer of the securities for which the aged record difference exists or for which the buy-in occurred.

(c) *Reports to Appropriate Regulatory Agencies.*

(1) Within ten business days following the end of each calendar quarter, every recordkeeping transfer agent shall report the information specified in paragraph (d)(1) of this section to its appropriate regulatory agency in accordance with Rule 17Ad-2(h), when the aggregate market value of aged record differences for all issues for which it performs recordkeeping functions exceeds the thresholds specified below:

(i) $300,000 if it is a recordkeeping transfer agent for 5 or fewer issues;

(ii) $500,000 for 6–24 issues;

(iii) $800,000 for 25–49 issues;

(iv) $1 million for 50–74 issues;

(v) $1.2 million for 75–99 issues;

(vi) $1.4 million for 100–499 issues;

(vii) $1.6 million for 500–999 issues;

(viii) $2.6 million for 1000–1999 issues; and

(ix) An additional $1 million for each additional 1000 issues.

(2) Within ten business days following the end of each calendar quarter, every recordkeeping transfer agent shall report the information specified in paragraph (d)(2) of this section to its appropriate regulatory agency in accordance with Rule 17Ad-2(h), concerning buy-ins of all issues for which it acts as recordkeeping transfer agent, when the aggregate market value of all buy-ins executed pursuant to Rule 17Ad-10(g) during that calendar quarter exceeds $100,000.

(3) When the recordkeeping transfer agent has any debits or credits for securities transferred, purchased, redeemed or issued that are unposted to the master securityholder and/or subsidiary files for more than five business days after debits and credits are required to be posted to the master securityholder file or subsidiary files pursuant to Rule 17Ad-10, it shall immediately report such fact to its appropriate regulatory agency in accordance with Rule 17Ad-2(h) and shall state in that report what steps have been, and are being, taken to correct the situation.

(d) *Content of Reports.*

(1) Each report pursuant to paragraphs (b)(1) and (c)(1) of this rule shall set forth with respect to each issue of securities:

(i) The principal dollar amount and related market value of debt securities or the number of shares and related market value of equity securities comprising the aged record difference (including information concerning aged record differences existing as of the effective date of this section);

(ii) The reasons for the aged record difference; and

(iii) The steps being taken or to be taken to resolve the aged record difference.

(2) Each report pursuant to paragraphs (b)(2) and (c)(2) of this rule shall set forth with respect to each issue of securities:

(i) The principal dollar amount of debt securities and related market value or the number of shares and related market value of equity securities comprising any buy-in executed pursuant to Rule 17Ad-10(g);

(ii) The party that executed the buy-in; and

(iii) The reason for the buy-in.

(e) For purposes of this rule, the market value of an issue shall be determined as of the last business day on which market value information is available during the reporting period.

(f) A copy of any report required under this section shall be retained by the reporting transfer agent for a period of not less than three years, the first year in an easily accessible place.

Rule 17Ad-12. Safeguarding of Funds and Securities

(a) Any registered transfer agent that has custody or possession of any funds or securities related to its transfer agent activities shall assure that: (1) All such securities are held in safekeeping and are handled, in light of all facts and circumstances, in a manner reasonably free from risk of theft, loss or destruction (other than by a transfer agent's certificate destruction procedures pursuant to § 240.17Ad–19) and (2) All such funds are protected, in light of all facts and circumstances, against misuse. In evaluating which particular safeguards and procedures must be employed, the cost of the various safeguards and procedures as well as the nature and degree of potential financial exposure are two relevant factors.

(b) For purposes of this section, the term *securities* shall have the same meaning as the term *securities certificate* as defined in § 240.17f–1(a)(6).

Rule 17Ad–13. Annual Study and Evaluation of Internal Accounting Control

(a) *Accountant's Report.* Every registered transfer agent, except as provided in paragraph (d) of this section, shall file annually with the Commission and the transfer agent's appropriate regulatory agency in accordance with Rule 17Ad–2(h), a report specified in paragraph (a)(1) of this section prepared by an independent accountant concerning the transfer agent's system of internal accounting control and related procedures for the transfer of record ownership and the safeguarding of related securities and funds. That report shall be filed within 90 calendar days of the date of the study and evaluation set forth in paragraph (a)(1).

(1) The accountant's report shall:

(i) State whether the study and evaluation was made in accordance with generally accepted auditing standards using the criteria set forth in paragraph (a)(3) of this rule;

(ii) Describe any material inadequacies found to exist as of the date of the study and evaluation and any corrective action taken, or if no material inadequacy existed, the report shall so state;

(iii) Comment on the current status of any material inadequacy described in the immediately preceding report; and

(iv) Indicate the date of the study and evaluation.

(2) The study and evaluation of the transfer agent's system of internal accounting control for the transfer of record ownership and the safeguarding of related securities and funds shall cover the following:

(i) Transferring securities related to changes of ownership (i.e., cancellation of certificates or other instruments evidencing prior ownership and issuance of certificates or instruments evidencing current ownership);

(ii) Registering changes of ownership on the books and records of the issuer;

(iii) Transferring record ownership as a result of corporate actions (e.g., issuance, retirement, redemption, liquidation, conversion, exchange, tender offer or other types of reorganization);

(iv) Dividend disbursement or interest paying-agent activities;

(v) Administering dividend reinvestment programs; and

(vi) Distributing statements respecting initial offerings of securities.

(3) For purposes of this report, the objectives of a transfer agent's system of internal accounting control for the transfer of record ownership and the safeguarding of related securities and funds should be to provide reasonable, but not absolute, assurance that securities and funds are safeguarded against loss from unauthorized use or disposition and that transfer agent activities are performed promptly and accurately. For purposes of this report, a material inadequacy is a condition for which the independent accountant believes that the prescribed procedures or the degree of compliance with them

do not reduce to a relatively low level the risk that errors or irregularities, in amounts that would have a significant adverse effect on the transfer agent's ability promptly and accurately to transfer record ownership and safeguard related securities and funds, would occur or not be detected within a timely period by employees in the normal course of performing their assigned functions. Occurrence of errors or irregularities more frequently than in isolated instances may be evidence that the system has a material inadequacy. A significant adverse effect on a transfer agent's ability promptly and accurately to transfer record ownership and safeguard related securities and funds could result from any condition or conditions that individually, or taken as a whole, would reasonably be expected to:

(i) Inhibit the transfer agent from promptly and accurately discharging its responsibilities under its contractual agreement with the issuer;

(ii) Result in material financial loss to the transfer agent; or

(iii) Result in a violation of Rules 17Ad–2, 17Ad–10 or 17Ad–12(a).

(b) *Notice of Corrective Action.* If the accountant's report describes any material inadequacy, the transfer agent shall, within sixty calendar days after receipt of the report, notify the Commission and its appropriate regulatory agency in writing regarding the corrective action taken or proposed to be taken.

(c) *Record Retention.* The accountant's report and any documents required by paragraph (b) of this rule shall be maintained by the transfer agent for at least three years, the first year in an easily accessible place.

(d) *Exemptions.* The requirements of Rule 17Ad–13 shall not apply to registered transfer agents that qualify for exemptions pursuant to this paragraph, 17Ad–13(d).

(1) A registered transfer agent shall be exempt if it performs transfer agent functions solely for:

(i) Its own securities;

(ii) Securities issued by a subsidiary in which it owns 51% or more of the subsidiary's capital stock; and

(iii) Securities issued by another corporation that owns 51% or more of the capital stock of the registered transfer agent.

(2) A registered transfer agent shall be exempt if it:

(i) Is an exempt transfer agent pursuant to Rule 17Ad–4(b); and

(ii) In the case of a transfer agent that performs transfer agent functions for redeemable securities issued by companies registered under Section 8 of the Investment Company Act of 1940, maintains master securityholder files consisting of fewer than 1000 shareholder accounts, in the aggregate, for each of such issues for which it performs transfer agent functions.

(3) A registered transfer agent shall be exempt if it is a bank or financial institution subject to regulation by the Board of Governors of the Federal Reserve System, the Office of the Comptroller of the Currency or the Federal Deposit Insurance Corporation, provided that it is not notified to the contrary by its appropriate regulatory agency and provided that a report similar in scope to the requirements of Rule 17Ad–13(a) is prepared for either the bank's board of directors or an audit committee of the board of directors.

Rule 17Ad–14. Tender Agents

(a) *Establishing Book-Entry Depository Accounts.* When securities of a subject company have been declared eligible by one or more qualified registered securities depositories for the services of those depositories at the time a tender or exchange offer is commenced, no registered transfer agent shall act on behalf of the bidder as a depositary, in the case of a tender offer, or an exchange agent, in the case of an exchange offer, in connection with a tender or exchange offer, unless that transfer agent has established, within two business days after commencement of the offer, specially designated accounts. These accounts shall be maintained throughout the duration of the offer, including protection periods, with all qualified registered securities depositories holding the subject company's securities, for purposes of receiving from depository participants securities being tendered to the bidder by book-entry delivery pursuant to transmittal letters and other documentation and for purposes of allowing tender agents to return to depository participants by book-entry movement securities withdrawn from the offer.

(b) *Exclusions.* This rule shall not apply to tender or exchange offers (1) that are made for a class of securities of a subject company that has fewer than (i) 500 security holders of record for that class, or (ii) 500,000 shares of that class outstanding; or (2) that are made exclusively to security holders of fewer than 100 shares of a class of securities.

(c) *Definitions.* For purposes of this rule, (1) the terms "subject company," "business day," "security holders," and "transmittal letter" shall be given the meanings provided in Rule 14d–1(b); (2) unless the context otherwise requires, a tender or exchange offer shall be deemed to have commenced as specified in Rule 14d–2; (3) the term "bidder" shall mean any person who makes a tender or exchange offer or on whose behalf a tender or exchange offer is made; (4) a "qualified registered securities depository" shall mean a registered clearing agency having rules and procedures approved by the Commission pursuant to Section 19 of the Securities Exchange Act of 1934 to enable book-entry delivery of the securities of the subject company to, and return of those securities from, the transfer agent through the facilities of that securities depository; and (5) the term "depositary" refers to that agent of the bidder receiving securities from tendering depository participants and paying those participants for shares tendered. The term "exchange agent" refers to the agent performing like functions in connection with an exchange offer.

(d) *Exemptions.* The Commission may exempt from the provisions of this rule, either unconditionally or on specified terms and conditions, any registered transfer agent, tender or exchange offer, or class of tender or exchange offers, if the Commission determines that an exemption is consistent with the public interest, the protection of investors, the prompt and accurate clearance and settlement of securities transactions, the maintenance of fair and orderly markets, or the removal of impediments to a national clearance and settlement system.

Rule 17Ad–15. Signature Guarantees

(a) Definitions. For purposes of this rule, the following terms shall mean:

(1) "Act" means the Securities Exchange Act of 1934;

(2) "eligible guarantor institution" means:

(i) banks (as that term is defined in Section 3(a) of the Federal Deposit Insurance Act [12 U.S.C. 1813(a)]);

(ii) brokers, dealers, municipal securities dealers, municipal securities brokers, government securities dealers, and government securities brokers, at those terms are defined under the Act;

(iii) credit unions (as that term is defined in Section 19(b)(1)(A) of the Federal Reserve Act [12 U.S.C. 461(b)]);

(iv) national securities exchanges, registered securities associations, clearing agencies, as those terms are used under the Act; and

(v) savings associations (as that term is defined in Section 3(b) of the Federal Deposit Insurance Act [12 U.S.C. 1813(b)]).

(3) "guarantee" means a guarantee of the signature of the person endorsing a certified security, or originating an instruction to

transfer ownership of a security or instructions concerning transfer of securities.

(b) *Acceptance of Signature Guarantees.* A registered transfer agent shall not, directly or indirectly, engage in any activity in connection with a guarantee, including the acceptance or rejection of such guarantee, that results in the inequitable treatment of any eligible guarantor institution or a class of institutions.

(c) *Transfer Agent's Standards and Procedures.* Every registered transfer agent shall establish:

(1) written standards for the acceptance of guarantees of securities transfers from eligible guarantor institutions; and

(2) procedures, including written guidelines where appropriate to ensure that those standards are used in determining whether to accept or reject guarantees from eligible guarantor institutions. Such standards and procedures shall not establish terms and conditions (including those pertaining to financial condition) that, as written or applied, treat different classes of eligible guarantor institutions inequitably, or result in the rejection of a guarantee from an eligible guarantor institution solely because the guarantor institution is of a particular type specified in paragraphs (a)(2)(i)—(a)(2)(iv) of this rule.

(d) *Rejection of Items Presented for Transfer.*

(1) No registered transfer agent shall reject a request for transfer of a certificated or uncertificated security because the certificate, instruction, or documents accompanying the certificate or instruction includes an unacceptable guarantee, unless the transfer agent determines that the guarantor, if it is an eligible guarantor institution, does not satisfy the transfer agent's written standards or procedures.

(2) A registered transfer agent shall notify the guarantor and the presentor of the rejection and the reasons for the rejection within two business days after rejecting a transfer request because of a determination that the guarantor does not satisfy the transfer agent's written standards or procedures. Notification to the presentor may be accomplished by making the rejected item available to the presentor. Notification to the guarantor may be accomplished by telephone, facsimile, or ordinary mail.

(e) *Record Retention.*

(1) Every registered transfer agent shall maintain a copy of the standards and procedures specified in paragraph (c) of this rule in an easily accessible place.

(2) Every registered transfer agent shall make available a copy of the standards and procedures specified in paragraph (c) of this rule to any person requesting a copy of such standards and procedures. The registered transfer agent shall respond within three days of a request for such standards and procedures by sending the requesting party a copy of the requested transfer agent's standards and procedures.

(3) Every registered transfer agent shall maintain, for a period of three years following the date of the rejection, a record of transfers rejected, including the reason for the rejection, who the guarantor was and whether the guarantor failed to meet the transfer agent's guarantee standards.

(f) *Exclusions.* Nothing in this rule shall prohibit a transfer agent from rejecting a request for transfer of a certificated or uncertificated security;

(1) for reasons unrelated to acceptance of the guarantor institution;

(2) because the person acting on behalf of the guarantor institution is not authorized by that institution to act on its behalf, provided that the transfer agent maintains a list of people authorized to act on behalf of that guarantor institution;

(3) because the eligible guarantor institution of a type specified in paragraph (a)(2)(ii) of this rule is neither a member of

a clearing corporation nor maintains net capital of at least $100,000; or

(g) *Signature Guarantee Program.*

(1) A registered transfer agent shall be deemed to comply with paragraph (c) of this rule if its standards and procedures include:

(i) rejecting a request for transfer because the guarantor is neither a member of nor a participant in a signature guarantee program; or

(ii) accepting a guarantee from an eligible guarantor institution who, at the time of issuing the guarantee, is a member of or participant in a signature guarantee program.

(2) Within the first six months after revising its standards and procedures to include a signature guarantee program, the transfer agent shall not reject a request for transfer because the guarantor is neither a member of nor participant in a signature guarantee program, unless the transfer agent has given that guarantor ninety days non-participating or non-member guarantors.

(3) For purposes of paragraph (g) of this rule the term "signature guarantee program," means a program, the terms and conditions of which the transfer agent reasonably determines:

(i) to facilitate the equitable treatment of eligible guarantor institutions; and

(ii) to promote the prompt, accurate and safe transfer of securities by providing:

(A) adequate protection to the transfer agent against risk of financial loss in the event persons have no recourse against the eligible guarantor institution; and

(B) adequate protection to the transfer agent against the issuance of unauthorized guarantees.

Rule 17Ad-16. Notice of Assumption or Termination of Transfer Agent Services

(a) A registered transfer agent that ceases to perform transfer agent services on behalf of an issuer of securities, including a registered transfer agent that ceases to perform transfer agent services on behalf of an issuer of securities because of a merger or acquisition by another transfer agent, shall send written notice of such termination to the appropriate qualified registered securities depository on or before the later of ten calendar days prior to the effective date of such termination or the day the transfer agent is notified of the effective date of such termination. Such notice shall include the full name, address, telephone number, and Financial Industry Number Standard ("FINS") number of the transfer agent ceasing to perform the transfer agent services for the issuer; the issuer's name; the issue or issues handled and their CUSIP number(s); and if known, the name, address, and telephone number of the transfer agent that thereafter will provide transfer services for the issuer. If no successor transfer agent is known, the notice shall include the name and address of a contact person at the issuer.

(b) A registered transfer agent that changes its name or address or that assumes transfer agent services on behalf of an issuer of securities, including a transfer agent that assumes transfer agent services on behalf of an issuer of securities because of a merger or acquisition of another transfer agent, shall send written notice of such to the appropriate qualified registered securities depository on or before the later of ten calendar days prior to the effective date of such change in status or the day the transfer agent is notified of the effective date of such change in status. A notice regarding a change of name or address shall include the full name, address, telephone number, and FINS number of the transfer agent and the location where certificates are received for transfer. A notice regarding the assumption of transfer agent services on behalf of an issuer of securities, including assumption of transfer agent services resulting from the merger or acquisition of another transfer agent, shall include the full name, address, telephone number, and FINS number of the transfer agent assuming the transfer agent services for the issuer; the issuer's name; and the issue or issues handled and their CUSIP number(s).

(c) The notice described in paragraphs (a) and (b) of this section shall be delivered by means of secure communication. For purposes of this section, secure communication shall include telegraph, overnight mail, facsimile, or any other form of secure communication.

(d)(1) The appropriate qualified registered securities depository that receives notice pursuant to paragraphs (a) and (b) of this section shall deliver within 24 hours a copy of such notice to each qualified registered securities depository. A qualified registered securities depository that receives notice pursuant to this section shall deliver a copy of such notice to its own participants within 24 hours.

(2) A qualified registered securities depository may comply with its notice requirements under paragraph (d)(1) of this section by making available the notice of all material information from the notice within 24 hours in a manner set forth in the rules of the qualified registered securities depository.

(3) A qualified registered securities depository shall maintain such notice for a period of not less than two years, the first six months in an easily accessible place. Such notice shall be made available to the Commission or other persons as the Commission may designate by order.

(4) A registered transfer agent that provides notice pursuant to paragraphs (a) and (b) of this section shall maintain such notice for a period of not less than two years, the first six months in an easily accessible place.

(e) For purposes of this section, a *qualified registered securities depository* shall mean a clearing agency registered under Section 17A of the Act (15 U.S.C. 78q–1) that performs clearing agency functions as described in Section 3(a)(23)(A)(i) of the Act (15 U.S.C. 78c(a)(23)(A)(i)) and that has rules and procedures concerning its responsibility for maintaining, updating, and providing appropriate access to the information it receives pursuant to this section.

(f) For purposes of this section, an *appropriate qualified registered securities depository* shall mean the qualified registered securities depository that the Commission so designates by order or, in the absence of such designation, the qualified registered securities depository that is the largest holder of record of all qualified registered securities depositories as of the most recent record date.

Rule 17Ad–17. Transfer Agents' Obligation to Search for Lost Securityholders

(a)(1) Every recordkeeping transfer agent whose master securityholder file includes accounts of lost securityholders shall exercise reasonable care to ascertain the correct addresses of such securityholders. In exercising reasonable care to ascertain for its master securityholder file such lost securityholders' current addresses, each recordkeeping transfer agent shall conduct two data base searches using at least one information data base service. The transfer agent shall search by taxpayer identification number or by name if a search based on taxpayer identification number is not reasonably likely to locate the securityholder. Such data base searches must be conducted without charge to a lost securityholder and with the following frequency:

(i) Between three and twelve months of such securityholder becoming a lost securityholder and

(ii) Between six and twelve months after the transfer agent's first search for such lost securityholder.

(2) A transfer agent may not use a search method or service to establish contact with lost securityholders that results in a charge to

a lost securityholder prior to completing the searches set forth in paragraph (a)(1) of this section.

(3) A transfer agent need not conduct the searches set forth in paragraph (a)(1) of this section for a lost securityholder if:

(i) It has received documentation that such securityholder is decreased or

(ii) The aggregate value of assets listed in the lost securityholder and all securities owned by the lost securityholder as recorded in the transfer agent's master securityholder files, is less than $25; or

(iii) The securityholder is not a natural person.

(b) For purposes of this section:

(1) Information data base service means either:

(i) Any automated data base service that contains addresses from the entire United States geographic area, contains the names of at least 50% of the United States adult population, is indexed by taxpayer identification number or name, and is updated at least four times a year; or

(ii) Any service or combination of services which produces results comparable to those of the service described in paragraph (b)(1)(i) of this section in locating lost securityholders.

(2) Lost securityholder means a securityholder:

(i) To whom an item of correspondence that was sent to the securityholder at the address contained in the transfer agent's master securityholder file has been returned as undeliverable; provided, however, that if such item is re-sent within one month to the lost securityholder, the transfer agent may deem the securityholder to be a lost securityholder as of the day the resent item is returned as undeliverable; and

(ii) For whom the transfer agent has not received information regarding the securityholder's new address.

(c) Every recordkeeping transfer agent shall maintain records to demonstrate compliance with the requirements set forth in this section which shall include written procedures which describe the transfer agent's methodology for complying with this section.

Rule 17Ad–18. Year 2000 Reports to be Made by Certain Transfer Agents

(a) Each registered non-bank transfer agent must file Part I of Form TA-Y2K (§ 249.619 of this chapter) with the Commission describing the transfer agent's preparation for Year 2000 Problems. Part I of Form TA-Y2K shall be filed no later than August 31, 1998, and April 30, 1999. Part I of Form TA-Y2K shall reflect the transfer agent's preparation for the Year 2000 as of July 15, 1998, and March 15, 1999, respectively.

(b) Each registered non-bank transfer agent, except for those transfer agents that qualify for the exemption in paragraph (d) of § 240.17Ad–13, must file with the Commission Part II of Form TA-Y2K (§ 249.619 of this chapter) in addition to Part I of Form TA-Y2K. Part II of Form TA-Y2K report shall address the following topics:

(1) Whether the board of directors (or similar body) of the transfer agent has approved and funded plans for preparing and testing its computer systems for Year 2000 Problems;

(2) Whether the plans of the transfer agent exist in writing and address all mission critical computer systems of the transfer agent wherever located throughout the world;

(3) Whether the transfer agent has assigned existing employees, has hired new employees, or has engaged third parties to provide assistance in addressing Year 2000 Problems; and if so, a description of the work that these groups of individuals have performed as of the date of each report;

(4) The current progress on each stage of preparation for potential problems caused by Year 2000 Problems. These stages are:

(i) Awareness of potential Year 2000 Problems;

(ii) Assessment of what steps the transfer agent must take to address Year 2000 Problems;

(iii) Implementation of the steps needed to address Year 2000 Problems;

(iv) Internal testing of software designed to address Year 2000 Problems, including the number and description of the material exceptions resulting from such testing that are unresolved as of the reporting date;

(v) Point-to point or industry-wide testing of software designed to address Year 2000 Problems (including testing with other transfer agents, other financial institutions, and customers), including the number and description of the material exceptions resulting from such testing that are unresolved as of the reporting date; and

(vi) Implementation of tested software that will address Year 2000 Problems;

(5) Whether the transfer agent has written contingency plans in the event that, after December 31, 1999, it has computer problems caused by Year 2000 Problems; and

(6) What levels of the transfer agent's management are responsible for addressing potential problems caused by Year 2000 Problems, including a description of the responsibilities for each level of management regarding the Year 2000 Problems;

(7) Any additional material information in both reports concerning its management of Year 2000 Problems that could help the Commission assess the transfer agent's readiness for the Year 2000.

(8) Part II of Form TA-Y2K (§ 249.619 of this chapter) shall be filed no later than August 31, 1998, and April 30,999. Part II of Form TA-Y2K shall reflect the transfer agent's preparation for the Year 2000 as of July 15, 1998, and March 15, 1999, respectively.

(c) Any non-bank transfer agent that registers between the adoption of the final rule and December 31, 1999, must file with the Commission Part I of Form TA-Y2K (§ 249.619 of this chapter) no later than 30 days after their registration becomes effective. New transfer agents whose registration with the Commission becomes effective between January 1, 1999, and April 30, 1999, would be required to file the second report due on April 30, 1999.

(d) For purposes of this section, the term Year 2000 Problem shall include problems arising from:

(1) Computer software incorrectly reading the date "01/01/00" as being the year 1900 or another incorrect year;

(2) Computer software incorrectly identifying a date in the Year 1999 or any year thereafter;

(3) Computer software failing to detect that the Year 2000 is a leap year; or

(4) Any other computer software error that is directly or indirectly caused by paragraph (d)(1), (2), or (3) of this section.

(e) For purposes of this section, the term non-bank transfer agent means a transfer agent whose:

(1) Appropriate regulatory agency, as that term is defined by 15 U.S.C. 78(c)(34)(B), is the Securities and Exchange Commission; and

(2) Is not a savings association, as defined by Section 3 of the Federal Deposit Insurance Act, 12 U.S.C. 1813, which is regulated by the Office of Thrift Supervision.

(f) *Nature and form of reports.* No later than April 30, 1999, every nonbank transfer agent required to file Part II of Form TA-Y2K (§ 249.619 of this chapter) pursuant to paragraph (b)(8) of this section shall file with its

Form TA-Y2K an original and two copies of a report prepared by an independent public accountant regarding the nonbank transfer agent's process, as of March 15, 1999, for addressing Year 2000 Problems with the Commission's principal office in Washington, D.C. The independent public accountant's report shall be prepared in accordance with standards that have been reviewed by the Commission and that have been issued by a national organization that is responsible for promulgating authoritative accounting and auditing standards.

Rule 17Ad–19. Requirements for Cancellation, Processing, Storage, Transportation, and Destruction or Other Disposition of Securities Certificates

(a) *Definitions.* For purposes of this section:

(1) The terms *cancelled* or *cancellation* means the process in which a securities certificate:

(i) Is physically marked to clearly indicate that it no longer represents a claim against the issuer; and

(ii) Is voided on the records of the transfer agent.

(2) The term *cancelled certificate facility* means any location where securities certificates are cancelled and thereafter processed, stored, transported, destroyed or otherwise disposed of.

(3) The term *certificate number* means a unique identification or serial number that is assigned and affixed by an issuer or transfer agent to each securities certificate.

(4) The term *controlled access* means the practice of permitting the entry of only authorized personnel to areas where securities certificates are cancelled and thereafter processed, stored, transported, destroyed or otherwise disposed of.

(5) The term *CUSIP number* means the unique identification number that is assigned to each securities issue.

(6) The term *destruction* means the physical ruination of a securities certificate by a transfer agent as part of the certificate destruction procedures that make the reconstruction of the certificate impossible.

(7) The term *otherwise disposed of* means any disposition other than by destruction.

(8) The term *securities certificate* has the same meaning that it has in § 240.17f–1(a)(6).

(b) *Required procedures for the cancellation, storage, transportation, destruction, or other disposition of securities certificates.* Every transfer agent involved in the handling, processing, or storage of securities certificates shall establish and implement written procedures for the cancellation, storage, transportation, destruction, or other disposition of securities certificates. This requirement applies to any agent that the transfer agent uses to perform any of these activities.

(c) *Written procedures.* The written procedures required by paragraph (b) of this section at a minimum shall provide that:

(1) There is controlled access to any cancelled certificate facility;

(2) Each cancelled certificate be marked with the word "CANCELLED" by stamp or perforation on the face of the certificate unless the transfer agent has procedures adopted pursuant to this rule for the destruction of cancelled certificates within three business days of their cancellation;

(3) A record that is indexed and retrievable by CUSIP and certificate number that contains the CUSIP number, certificate number with any prefix or suffix, denomination, registration, issue date, and cancellation date of each cancelled certificate;

(4) A record that is indexed and retrievable by CUSIP and certificate number of each destroyed securities certificate or securities certificate otherwise disposed of, the records must contain for each destroyed or otherwise disposed of certificate the CUSIP number, certificate number with any prefix or

suffix, denomination, registration, issue date, and cancellation date, and additionally for any certificate otherwise disposed of a record of how it was disposed of, the name and address of the party to whom it was disposed, and the date of disposition;

(5) The physical transportation of cancelled certificates be made in a secure manner and that the transfer agent maintain separately a record of the CUSIP number and certificate number of each certificate in transit;

(6) Authorized personnel of the transfer agent or its designee supervise and witness the intentional destruction of any cancelled certificate and retain copies of all records relating to certificates which were destroyed; and

(7) Reports to the Lost and Stolen Securities Program be effected in a timely and complete manner, as provided in § 240.17f–1 of any cancelled certificate that is lost, stolen, missing, or counterfeit.

(d) *Recordkeeping*. Every transfer agent subject to this section shall maintain records that demonstrate compliance with the requirements set forth in this section and that describe the transfer agent's methodology for complying with this section for three years, the first year in an easily accessible place.

(e) *Exemptive authority*. Upon written application or upon its own motion, the Commission may grant an exemption from any of the provisions of this section, either unconditionally or on specific terms and conditions, to any transfer agent or any class of transfer agents and to any securities certificate or any class of securities certificates.

Rule 17Ad–20. Issuer Restrictions or Prohibitions on Ownership by Securities Intermediaries

(a) Except as provided in paragraph (c) of this section, no registered transfer agent shall transfer any equity security registered pursuant to section 12 or any equity security that subjects an issuer to reporting under section 15(d) of the Act (15 U.S.C. 78l or 15 U.S.C. 78o(d)) if such security is subject to any restriction or prohibition on transfer to or from a securities intermediary in its capacity as such.

(b) The term securities intermediary means a clearing agency registered under section 17A of the Act (15 U.S.C. 78q-1) or a person, including a bank, broker, or dealer, that in the ordinary course of its business maintains securities accounts for others in its capacity as such.

(c) The provisions of this section shall not apply to any equity security issued by a partnership as defined in rule 901(b) of Regulation S–K (§ 229.901(b) of this chapter).

Rule 19b–4. Filings With Respect to Proposed Rule Changes by Self-Regulatory Organizations

Preliminary Note: A self-regulatory organization also must refer to Form 19b–4 (17 CFR 249.819) for further requirements with respect to the filing of proposed rule changes.

(a) Filings with respect to proposed rule changes by a self-regulatory organization, except filings with respect to proposed rules changes by self-regulatory organizations submitted pursuant to section 19(b)(7) of the Act (15 U.S.C. 78s(b)(7)), shall be made electronically on Form 19b–4 (17 CFR 249.819).

(b) The term "stated policy, practice, or interpretation" means (1) any material aspect of the operation of the facilities of the self-regulatory organization or (2) any statement made generally available to the membership of, to all participants in, or to persons having or seeking access (including, in the case of national securities exchanges or registered securities associations, through a member) to facilities of, the self-regulatory organization ("specified persons"), or to a group or category of specified persons, that establishes or changes any standard, limit, or guideline with respect to (i) the rights, obligations, or privileges of specified persons or, in the case of national securities exchanges or registered securities associations, persons associated with specified persons, or (ii) the meaning, administration, or enforcement of an existing rule.

(c) A stated policy, practice, or interpretation of the self-regulatory organization shall be deemed to be a proposed rule change unless (1) it is reasonably and fairly implied by an existing rule of the self-regulatory organization or (2) it is concerned solely with the administration of the self-regulatory organization and is not a stated policy, practice, or interpretation with respect to the meaning, administration, or enforcement of an existing rule of the self-regulatory organization.

(d) Regardless of whether it is made generally available, an interpretation of an existing rule of the self-regulatory organization shall be deemed to be a proposed rule change if (1) it is approved or ratified by the governing body of the self-regulatory organization and (2) it is not reasonably and fairly implied by that rule.

(e) For the purposes of this paragraph, *new derivative securities product* means any type of option, warrant, hybrid securities product or any other security, other than a single equity option or a security futures product, whose value is based, in whole or in part, upon the performance of, or interest in, an underlying instrument.

(1) The listing and trading of a new derivative securities product by a self-regulatory organization shall not be deemed a proposed rule change, pursuant to paragraph (c)(1) of this section, if the Commission has approved, pursuant to section 19(b) of the Act (15 U.S.C. 78s(b)), the self-regulatory organization's trading rules, procedures and listing standards for the product class that would include the new derivative securities product and the self-regulatory organization has a surveillance program for the product class.

(2) Recordkeeping and reporting:

(i) Self-regulatory organizations shall retain at their principal place of business a file, available to Commission staff for inspection, of all relevant records and information pertaining to each new derivative securities product traded pursuant to this paragraph (e) for a period of not less than five years, the first two years in an easily accessible place, as prescribed in § 240.17a-1.

(ii) When relying on this paragraph (e), a self-regulatory organization shall submit Form 19b-4(e) (17 CFR 249.820) to the Commission within five business days after commencement of trading a new derivative securities product.

(f) A proposed rule change may take effect upon filing with the Commission pursuant to Section 19(b)(3)(A) of the Act, 15 U.S.C. 78s(b)(3)(A), if properly designated by the self-regulatory organization as:

(1) Constituting a stated policy, practice, or interpretation with respect to the meaning, administration, or enforcement of an existing rule;

(2) Establishing or changing a due, fee, or other charge applicable only to a member;

(3) Concerned solely with the administration of the self-regulatory organization;

(4) Effecting a change in an existing service of a registered clearing agency that:

(i) Does not adversely affect the safeguarding of securities or funds in the custody or control of the clearing agency or for which it is responsible; and

(ii) Does not significantly affect the respective rights or obligations of the clearing agency or persons using the service;

(5) Effecting a change in an existing order-entry or trading system of a self-regulatory organization that:

(i) Does not significantly affect the protection of investors or the public interest;

(ii) Does not impose any significant burden on competition; and

(iii) Does not have the effect of limiting the access to or availability of the system; or

(6) Effecting a change that:

(i) Does not significantly affect the protection of investors or the public interest;

(ii) Does not impose any significant burden on competition; and

(iii) By its terms, does not become operative for 30 days after the date of the filing, or such shorter time as the Commission may designate if consistent with the protection of investors and the public interest; provided that the self-regulatory organization has given the Commission written notice of its intent to file the proposed rule change, along with a brief description and text of the proposed rule change, at least five business days prior to the date of filing of the proposed rule change, or such shorter time as designated by the Commission.

(g) After instituting a proceeding to determine whether a proposed rule change should be disapproved, the Commission will afford the self-regulatory organization and interested persons an opportunity to submit additional written data, views, and arguments and may afford, in the discretion of the Commission, an opportunity to make oral presentations.

(h) Notice of orders issued pursuant to Section 19(b) of the Act will be given by prompt publication thereof, together with a statement of written reasons therefor.

(i) Self-regulatory organizations shall retain at their principal place of business a file, available to interested persons for public inspection and copying, of all findings made pursuant to this section and all correspondence and other communications reduced to writing (including comment letters) to and from such self-regulatory organization concerning any such filing, whether such correspondence and communications are received or prepared before or after the filing of the proposed rule change.

(j) Filings with respect to proposed rule changes by a self-regulatory organization submitted on Form 19b–4 (17 CFR 249.819) electronically shall contain an electronic signature. For the purposes of this section, the term electronic signature means an electronic entry in the form of a magnetic impulse or other form of computer data compilation of any letter or series of letters or characters comprising a name, executed, adopted or authorized as a signature. The signatory to an electronically submitted rule filing shall manually sign a signature page or other document, in the manner prescribed by Form 19b–4, authenticating, acknowledging or otherwise adopting his or her signature that appears in typed form within the electronic filing. Such document shall be executed before or at the time the rule filing is electronically submitted and shall be retained by the filer in accordance with § 240.17a–1.

(k) If the conditions of this section and Form 19b–4 (17 CFR 249.819) are otherwise satisfied, all filings submitted electronically on or before 5:30 p.m. Eastern Standard Time or Eastern Daylight Saving Time, whichever is currently in effect, on a business day, shall be deemed filed on that business day, and all filings submitted after 5:30 p.m. Eastern Standard Time or Eastern Daylight Saving Time, whichever is currently in effect, shall be deemed filed on the next business day.

(*l*) The self-regulatory organization shall post the proposed rule change, and any amendments thereto, on its Web site within two business days after the filing of the proposed rule change, and any amendments thereto, with the Commission. Such proposed rule change and amendments shall be maintained on the self-regulatory organization's Web site until:

(1) In the case of a proposed rule change filed under section 19(b)(2) of the Act (15 U.S.C. 78s(b)(2)), the Commission approves the proposed rule change or the self-regulatory organization withdraws the proposed rule change, or any amendments, or is notified that the proposed rule change is not properly filed; or

(2) In the case of a proposed rule change filed under section 19(b)(3)(A) of the Act (15 U.S.C. 78s(b)(3)(A)), or any amendment thereto, 60 days after the date of filing, unless the self-regulatory organization withdraws the proposed rule change or is notified that the proposed rule change is not properly filed; and

(3) In the case of proposed rule changes approved by the Commission pursuant to section 19(b)(2) of the Act (15 U.S.C. 78s(b)(2)) or noticed by the Commission pursuant to section 19(b)(3)(A) of the Act (15 U.S.C. 78s(b)(3)(A)), the self-regulatory organization updates its rule text as required by paragraph (m) of this section; and

(4) In the case of a proposed rule change, or any amendment thereto, that has been withdrawn or not properly filed, the self-regulatory organization shall remove the proposed rule change, or any amendment, from its Web site within two business days of notification of improper filing or withdrawal by the SRO of the proposed rule change.

(m) Each self-regulatory organization shall post and maintain a current and complete version of its rules on its Web site. The self-regulatory organization shall update its Web site to reflect rule changes within two business days after it has been notified of the Commission's approval of a proposed rule change filed pursuant to section 19(b)(2) of the Act (15 U.S.C. 78s(b)(2)) or of the Commission's notice of a proposed rule change filed pursuant to section 19(b)(3)(A) or section 19(b)(7) of the Act (15 U.S.C. 78s(b)(3)(A) or 15 U.S.C. 78s(b)(7)). If a rule change is not effective for a certain period, the self-regulatory organization shall clearly indicate the effective date in the relevant rule text.

Rule 19b–5. Temporary Exemption From the Filing Requirements of Section 19(b) of the Act

Preliminary Notes

1. The following section provides for a temporary exemption from the rule filing requirement for self-regulatory organizations that file proposed rule changes concerning the operation of a pilot trading system pursuant to section 19(b) of the Act (15 U.S.C. 78s(b), as amended). All other requirements under the Act that are applicable to self-regulatory organizations continue to apply.

2. The disclosures made pursuant to the provisions of this section are in addition to any other applicable disclosure requirements under the federal securities laws.

(a) For purposes of this section, the term *specialist* means any member subject to a requirement of a self-regulatory organization that such member regularly maintain a market in a particular security.

(b) For purposes of this section, the term *trading system* means the rules of a self-regulatory organization that:

(1) Determine how the orders of multiple buyers and sellers are brought together; and

(2) Establish non-discretionary methods under which such orders interact with each other and under which the buyers and sellers entering such orders agree to the terms of trade.

(c) For purposes of this section, the term *pilot trading system* shall mean a trading system operated by a self-regulatory organization that is not substantially similar to any trading system or pilot trading system operated by such self-regulatory organization at any time during the preceding year, and that:

(1)(i) Has been in operation for less than two years;

(ii) Is independent of any other trading system operated by such self-regulatory organization that has been approved by the Commission pursuant to section 19(b) of the Act, (15 U.S.C. 78s(b));

(iii) With respect to each security traded on such pilot trading system, during at least two of the last four consecutive calendar months, has traded no more than 5 percent of the average daily trading volume of such security in the United States; and

(iv) With respect to all securities traded on such pilot trading system, during at least two of the last four consecutive calendar months, has traded no more than 20 percent of the average daily trading volume of all trading systems operated by such self-regulatory organization; or

(2)(i) Has been in operation for less than two years;

(ii) With respect to each security traded on such pilot trading system, during at least two of the last four consecutive calendar months, has traded no more than 1 percent of the average daily trading volume of such security in the United States; and

(iii) With respect to all securities traded on such pilot trading system, during at least two of the last four consecutive calendar months, has traded no more than 20 percent of the average daily trading volume of all trading systems operated by such self-regulatory organization; or

(3)(i) Has been in operation for less than two years; and

(ii)(A) Satisfied the definition of *pilot trading system* under paragraph (c)(1) of this section no more than 60 days ago, and continues to be independent of any other trading system operated by such self-regulatory organization that has been approved by the Commission pursuant to section 19(b) of the Act, (15 U.S.C. 78s(b)); or

(B) Satisfied the definition of *pilot trading system* under paragraph (c)(2) of this section no more than 60 days ago.

(d) A pilot trading system shall be deemed *independent* of any other trading system operated by a self-regulatory organization if:

(1) Such pilot trading system trades securities other than the issues of securities that trade on any other trading system operated by such self-regulatory organization that has been approved by the Commission pursuant to section 19(b) of the Act, (15 U.S.C. 78s(b));

(2) Such pilot trading system does not operate during the same trading hours as any other trading system operated by such self-regulatory organization that has been approved by the Commission pursuant to section 19(b) of the Act, (15 U.S.C. 78s(b)); or

(3) No specialist or market maker on any other trading system operated by such self-regulatory organization that has been approved by the Commission pursuant to section 19(b) of the Act, (15 U.S.C. 78s(b)), is permitted to effect transactions on the pilot trading system in securities in which they are a specialist or market maker.

(e) A self-regulatory organization shall be exempt temporarily from the requirement under section 19(b) of the Act, (15 U.S.C. 78s(b)), to submit on Form 19b–4, 17 CFR 249.819, proposed rule changes for establishing a pilot trading system, if the self-regulatory organization complies with the following requirements:

(1) *Form PILOT*. The self-regulatory organization:

(i) Files Part I of Form PILOT, 17 CFR 249.821, in accordance with the instructions therein, at least 20 days prior to commencing operation of the pilot trading system;

(ii) Files an amendment on Part I of Form PILOT at least 20 days prior to implementing a material change to the operation of the pilot trading system; and

(iii) Files a quarterly report on Part II of Form PILOT within 30 calendar days after the end of each calendar quarter in which the market has operated after the effective date of this section.

(2) *Fair access.*

(i) The self-regulatory organization has in place written rules to ensure that all members of the self-regulatory organization have fair access to the pilot trading system, and that information regarding orders on the pilot trading system is equally available to all members of the self-regulatory organization with access to such pilot trading system.

(ii) Notwithstanding the requirement in paragraph (e)(2)(i) of this section, a specialist on the pilot trading system may have preferred access to information regarding orders that it represents in its capacity as specialist.

(iii) The rules established by a self-regulatory organization pursuant to paragraph (e)(2)(i) of this section will be considered rules governing the pilot trading system for purposes of the temporary exemption under this section.

(3) *Trading rules and procedures and listing standards.*

(i) The self-regulatory organization has in place written trading rules and procedures and listing standards necessary to operate the pilot trading system.

(ii) The rules established by a self-regulatory organization pursuant to paragraph (e)(3)(i) of this section will be considered rules governing the pilot trading system for purposes of the temporary exemption under this section.

(4) *Surveillance.* The self-regulatory organization establishes internal procedures for the effective surveillance of trading activity on the self-regulatory organization's pilot trading system.

(5) *Clearance and settlement.* The self-regulatory organization establishes reasonable clearance and settlement procedures for transactions effected on the self-regulatory organizations pilot trading system.

(6) *Types of securities.* The self-regulatory organization permits to trade on the pilot trading system only securities registered under section 12 of the Act, (15 U.S.C. 78*l*).

(7) *Activities of specialists.*

(i) The self-regulatory organization does not permit any member to be a specialist in a security on the pilot trading system and a specialist in a security on a trading system operated by such self-regulatory organization that has been approved by the Commission pursuant to section 19(b) of the Act, (15 U.S.C. 78s(b)), or on another pilot trading system operated by such self-regulatory organization, if such securities are related securities, except that a member may be a specialist in related securities that the Commission, upon application by the self-regulatory organization, later determines is necessary or appropriate in the public interest and consistent with the protection of investors;

(ii) Notwithstanding paragraph (e)(7)(i) of this section, a self-regulatory organization may permit a member to be a specialist in any security on a pilot trading system, if the pilot trading system is operated during trading hours different from the trading hours of the trading system in which such member is a specialist.

(iii) For purposes of paragraph (e)(7) of this section, the term *related securities* means any two securities in which:

(A) The value of one security is determined, in whole or significant part, by the performance of the other security; or

(B) The value of both securities is determined, in whole or significant part, by the performance of a third security, combination of securities, index, indicator, interest rate or other common factor.

(8) *Examinations, inspections, and investigations.* The self-regulatory organization cooperates with the examination, inspection, or investigation by the Commission of transactions effected on the pilot trading system.

(9) *Recordkeeping.* The self-regulatory organization shall retain at its principal place of business and make available to Commission staff for inspection, all the rules and procedures relating to each pilot trading system operating pursuant to this section for a period of not less than five years, the first two years in an easily accessible place, as prescribed in § 240.17a–1.

(10) *Public availability of pilot trading system rules.* The self-regulatory organization makes publicly available all trading rules and procedures, including those established under paragraphs (e)(2) and (e)(3) of this section.

(11) Every notice or amendment filed pursuant to this paragraph (e) shall constitute a "report" within the meaning of sections 11A, 17(a), 18(a), and 32(a), (15 U.S.C. 78k–1, 78q(a), 78r(a), and 78ff(a)), and any other applicable provisions of the Act. All notices or reports filed pursuant to this paragraph (e) shall be deemed to be confidential until the pilot trading system commences operation.

(f)(1) A self-regulatory organization shall request Commission approval, pursuant to section 19(b)(2) of the Act, (15 U.S.C. 78s(b)(2)), for any rule change relating to the operation of a pilot trading system by submitting Form 19b–4, 17 CFR 249.819, no later than two years after the commencement of operation of such pilot trading system, or shall cease operation of the pilot trading system.

(2) Simultaneous with a request for Commission approval pursuant to section 19(b)(2) of the Act, (15 U.S.C. 78s(b)(2)), a self-regulatory organization may request Commission approval pursuant to section 19(b)(3)(A) of the Act, (15 U.S.C. 78s(b)(3)(A)), for any rule change relating to the operation of a pilot trading system by submitting Form 19b–4, 17 CFR 249.819, effective immediate upon filing, to continue operations of such trading system for a period not to exceed six months.

(g) Notwithstanding paragraph (e) of this section, rule changes with respect to pilot trading systems operated by a self-regulatory organization shall not be exempt from the rule filing requirements of section 19(b)(2) of the Act, (15 U.S.C. 78s(b)(2)), if the Commission determines, after notice to the SRO and opportunity for the SRO to respond, that exemption of such rule changes is not necessary or appropriate in the public interest or consistent with the protection of investors.

Rule 19b–7. Filings With Respect to Proposed Rule Changes Submitted Pursuant to Section 19(b)(7) of the Act

(a) Filings with respect to proposed rule changes required to be submitted pursuant to Section 19(b)(7) of the Act (15 U.S.C. 78s(b)(7)), shall be made on Form 19b–7 (§ 249.822 of this chapter). The Commission will promptly publish a notice of filing of such proposed rule change.

(b) A proposed rule change will not be deemed filed on the date it is received by the Commission unless:

(1) A completed Form 19b–7 (§ 249.822 of this chapter) is submitted; and

(2) In order to elicit meaningful comment, it is accompanied by:

(i) A clear and accurate statement of the basis and purpose of such rule change, including the impact on competition or efficiency, if any; and

(ii) A summary of any written comments (including e-mail) received by the self-regulatory organization on the proposed rule change.

(c) Self-regulatory organizations shall retain at their principle place of business a file, available to interested persons for public inspection and copying, of all filings made pursuant to this section and all correspondence and other communications reduced to writing (including comment letters) to and from such self-regulatory organization concerning such filing, whether such correspondence and communications are received or prepared before or after the filing of the proposed rule change.

Rule 19c–1. Governing Certain Off-Board Agency Transactions by Members of National Securities Exchanges

The rules of each national securities exchange shall provide as follows:

No rule, stated policy or practice of this exchange shall prohibit or condition, or be construed to prohibit or condition or otherwise limit, directly or indirectly, the ability of any member acting as agent to effect any transaction otherwise than on this exchange with another person (except when such member also is acting as agent for such other person in such transaction) in any equity security listed on this exchange or to which unlisted trading privileges on this exchange have been extended.

Rule 19c–3. Governing Off-Board Trading by Members of National Securities Exchanges

The rules of each national securities exchange shall provide as follows:

(a) No rule, stated policy or practice of this exchange shall prohibit or condition, or be construed to prohibit, condition or otherwise limit, directly or indirectly, the ability of any member to effect any transaction otherwise than on this exchange in any reported security listed and registered on this exchange or as to which unlisted trading privileges on this exchange have been extended (other than a put option or call option issued by the Options Clearing Corporation) which is not a covered security.

(b) For purposes of this rule,

(1) The term "Act" shall mean the Securities Exchange Act of 1934, as amended.

(2) The term "exchange" shall mean a national securities exchange registered as such with the Securities and Exchange Commission pursuant to section 6 of the Act.

(3) The term "covered security" shall mean

(i) any equity security or class of equity securities which

(A) was listed and registered on an exchange on April 26, 1979, and

(B) remains listed and registered on at least one exchange continuously thereafter;

(ii) any equity security or class of equity securities which

(A) was traded on one or more exchanges on April 26, 1979, pursuant to unlisted trading privileges permitted by section 12(f)(1)(A) of the Act, and

(B) remains traded on any such exchange pursuant to such unlisted trading privileges continuously thereafter; and

(iii) any equity security or class of equity securities which

(A) is issued in connection with a statutory merger, consolidation or similar plan or reorganization (including a reincorporation or change of domicile) in exchange for an equity security or class of equity securities described in paragraphs (b)(3)(i) or (b)(3)(ii) of this rule,

(B) is listed and registered on an exchange after April 26, 1979, and

(C) remains listed and registered on at least one exchange continuously thereafter.

(4) The term "reported security" shall mean any security or class of securities for which transaction reports are collected, processed and made available pursuant to an effective transaction reporting plan.

(5) The term "transaction report" shall mean a report containing the price and volume associated with a completed transaction involving the purchase or sale of a security.

(6) The term "effective transaction reporting plan" shall mean any plan approved by the Commission pursuant to Rule 11Aa3-1 for collecting, processing and making available transaction reports with respect to transactions in an equity security or class of equity securities.

Rule 19c-4. Governing Certain Listing or Authorization Determinations by National Securities Exchanges and Associations

(a) The rules of each exchange shall provide as follows: No rule, stated policy, practice, or interpretation of this exchange shall permit the listing, or the continuance of the listing, of any common stock or other equity security of a domestic issuer, if the issuer of such security issues any class of security, or takes other corporate action, with the effect of nullifying, restricting or disparately reducing the per share voting rights of holders of an outstanding class or classes of common stock of such issuer registered pursuant to Section 12 of the Act.

(b) The rules of each association shall provide as follows: No rule, stated policy, practice, or interpretation of this association shall permit the authorization for quotation and/or transaction reporting through an automated inter-dealer quotation system ("authorization"), or the continuance of authorization, of any common stock or other equity security of a domestic issuer, if the issuer of such security issues any class of security, or takes other corporate action, with the effect of nullifying, restricting, or disparately reducing the per share voting rights of holders of an outstanding class or classes of common stock of such issuer registered pursuant to Section 12 of the Act.

(c) For the purposes of paragraphs (a) and (b) of this rule, the following shall be presumed to have the effect of nullifying, restricting, or disparately reducing the per share voting rights of an outstanding class or classes of common stock:

(1) corporate action to impose any restriction on the voting power of shares of the common stock of the issuer held by a beneficial or record holder based on the number of shares held by such beneficial or record holder;

(2) corporate action to impose any restriction on the voting power of shares of the common stock of the issuer held by a beneficial or record holder based on the length of time such shares have been held by such beneficial or record holder;

(3) any issuance of securities through an exchange offer by the issuer for shares of an outstanding class of the common stock of the issuer, in which the securities issued have voting rights greater than or less than the per share voting rights of any outstanding class of the common stock of the issuer;

(4) any issuance of securities pursuant to a stock dividend, or any other type of distribution of stock, in which the securities issued have voting rights greater than the per share voting rights of any outstanding class of the common stock of the issuer.

(d) For the purpose of paragraphs (a) and (b) of this rule, the following, standing alone, shall be presumed not to have the effect of nullifying, restricting, or disparately reducing the per share voting rights of holders of an outstanding class or classes of common stock:

(1) the issuance of securities pursuant to an initial registered public offering;

(2) the issuance of any class of securities, through a registered public offering, with voting rights not greater than the per share voting rights of any outstanding class of the common stock of the issuer;

(3) the issuance of any class of securities to effect a bona fide merger or acquisition, with voting rights not greater than the per share voting rights of any outstanding class of the common stock of the issuer;

(4) corporate action taken pursuant to state law requiring a state's domestic corporation to condition the voting rights of a beneficial or record holder of a specified threshold percentage of the corporation's voting stock on the approval of the corporation's independent shareholders.

(e) *Definitions*

The following terms shall have the following meanings for purposes of this section, and the rules of each exchange and association shall include such definitions for the purposes of the prohibition in paragraphs (a) and (b), respectively, of this rule:

(1) The term "Act" shall mean the Securities Exchange Act of 1934, as amended.

(2) The term "common stock" shall include any security of an issuer designated as common stock and any security of an issuer, however designated, which, by statute or by its terms, is a common stock (*e.g.*, a security which entitles the holders thereof to vote generally on matters submitted to the issuer's security holders for a vote).

(3) The term "equity security" shall include any equity security defined as such pursuant to Rule 3a11–1 under the Act.

(4) The term "domestic issuer" shall mean an issuer that is not a "foreign private issuer" as defined in Rule 3b–4 under the Act.

(5) The term "security" shall include any security defined as such pursuant to Section 3(a)(10) of the Act, but shall exclude any class of security having a preference or priority over the issuer's common stock as to dividends, interest payments, redemption or payments in liquidation, if the voting rights of such securities only become effective as a result of specified events, not relating to an acquisition of the common stock of the issuer, which reasonably can be expected to jeopardize the issuer's financial ability to meet its payment obligations to the holders of that class of securities.

(6) The term "exchange" shall mean a national securities exchange, registered as such with the Securities and Exchange Commission pursuant to Section 6 of the Act, which makes transaction reports available pursuant to Rule 11Aa3–1 under the Act; and

(7) The term "association" shall mean a national securities association registered as such with the Securities and Exchange Commission pursuant to Section 15A of the Act.

(f) An exchange or association may adopt a rule, stated policy, practice, or interpretation, subject to the procedures specified by Section 19(b) of the Act, specifying what types of securities issuances and other corporate actions are covered by, or excluded from, the prohibition in paragraphs (a) and (b) of this rule, respectively, if such rule, stated policy, practice, or interpretation is consistent with the protection of investors and the public interest, and otherwise in furtherance of the purposes of the Act and this rule.

Rule 19c–5. Governing the Multiple Listing of Options on National Securities Exchanges

(a) The rules of each national securities exchange that provides a trading market in standardized put or call options shall provide as follows:

(1) On and after January 22, 1990, but not before, no rule, stated policy, practice, or interpretation of this exchange shall prohibit or condition, or be construed to prohibit or condition or otherwise limit, directly or indirectly, the ability of this exchange to list any stock options class first listed on an exchange on or after January 22, 1990, because that options class is listed on another options exchange.

(2) During the period from January 22, 1990, to January 21, 1991, but not before, no rule, stated policy, practice, or interpretation of this exchange shall prohibit or condition, or be construed to prohibit or condition or otherwise limit, directly or indirectly, the ability of this exchange to list up to ten classes of standardized stock options overlying exchange-listed stocks that were listed on another options exchange before January 22, 1990. These ten classes shall be in addition to any option on an exchange-listed stock trading on this exchange that was traded on more than one options exchange before January 22, 1990.

(3) On and after January 21, 1991, but not before, no rule, stated policy, practice, or interpretation of this exchange shall prohibit or condition, or be construed to prohibit or condition or otherwise limit, directly or indirectly, the ability of this exchange to list any stock options class because that options class is listed on another options exchange.

(b) For purposes of paragraph (a)(2) of this rule, if any options class is delisted from an options exchange as a result of a merger of the equity security underlying the option or a failure of the underlying security to satisfy that exchange's options listing standards, then the exchange is permitted to select a replacement option from among those standardized options overlying exchange-listed stocks that were listed on another options exchange before January 22, 1990.

(c) For purposes of this rule, the term "exchange" shall mean a national securities exchange, registered as such with the Commission pursuant to Section 6 of the Securities Exchange Act of 1934, as amended.

(d) For purposes of this rule, the term "standardized option" shall have the same meaning as that term is defined in Rule 9b–1 under the Securities Exchange Act of 1934, as amended.

(e) For purposes of this rule, the term "options class" shall have the same meaning as that term is defined in Rule 9b–1 under the Securities Exchange Act of 1934, as amended.

Rule 19d–1. Notices by Self-Regulatory Organizations of Final Disciplinary Actions, Denials, Bars, or Limitations Respecting Membership, Association, Participation, or Access to Services, and Summary Suspensions

GENERAL

(a) If any self-regulatory organization for which the Commission is the appropriate regulatory agency takes any action described in this rule to which the person affected thereby has consented and such action

(1) conditions or limits membership or participation in, association with a member of, or access to services offered by, such organization or member thereof and

(2) is based upon a statutory disqualification defined in Section 3(a)(39) of the Act, notice thereof shall be filed under Rule 19h–1 and not under this rule.

(b) The notice requirement of Section 19(d)(1) of the Act, concerning an action subject to such section taken by a self-regulatory organization for which the Commission is the appropriate regulatory agency, shall be satisfied by any notice with respect to such action (including a notice filed pursuant to this rule) which contains the information required in the statement supporting the organization's determination required by Section 6(d)(1) or (2), Section 15A(h)(1) or (2), or Section 17A(b)(5)(A) or (B) of the Act, as appropriate.

NOTICE OF FINAL DISCIPLINARY ACTION

(c)(1) Any self-regulatory organization for which the Commission is the appropriate regulatory agency that takes any final disciplinary action with respect to any person shall promptly file a notice thereof with the Commission in accordance with paragraph (d) of this rule. For the purposes of this rule, a "final disciplinary action" shall mean the imposition of any final disciplinary sanction pursuant to Section 6(b)(6), 15A(b)(7), or 17A(b)(3)(G) of the Act or other action of a self-regulatory organization which, after notice and opportunity for hearing, results in any final disposition of charges of:

(i) One or more violations of—

(A) The rules of such organization;

(B) The provisions of the Act or rules thereunder; or

(C) In the case of a municipal securities broker or dealer, the rules of the Municipal Securities Rulemaking Board;

(ii) Acts or practices constituting a statutory disqualification of a type defined in subparagraph (D) or (E) (except prior convictions) of Section 3(a)(39) of the Act; or

(iii) In the case of a proceeding by a national securities exchange or registered securities association based on Sections 6(c)(3)(A)(ii), 6(c)(3)(B)(ii), 15A(g)(3)(A)(ii) or 15A(g)(3)(B)(ii) of the Act, acts or practices inconsistent with just and equitable principles of trade.

Provided, however, That in the case of a disciplinary action in which a national securities exchange imposes a fine not exceeding $1,000 or suspends floor privileges of a clerical employee for not more than five days for violation of any of its regulations concerning personal decorum on a trading floor, the disposition shall not be considered "final" for purposes of this paragraph if the sanctioned person has not sought an adjudication, including a hearing, or otherwise exhausted his administrative remedies at the exchange with respect to the matter. *Provided further,* That this exemption from the notice requirement of this paragraph shall not be available where a decorum sanction is imposed at, or results from, a hearing on the matter.

(2) Any disciplinary action, other than a decorum sanction not deemed "final" under paragraph (c)(1) of this rule, taken by a self-regulatory organization for which the Commission is the appropriate regulatory agency against any person for violation of a rule of the self-regulatory organization which has been designated as a minor rule violation pursuant to a plan or any amendment thereto filed with and declared effective by the Commission under this paragraph, shall not be considered "final" for purposes of paragraph (c)(1) of this rule if the sanction imposed consists of a fine not exceeding $2500 and the sanctioned person has not sought an adjudication, including a hearing, or otherwise exhausted his administrative remedies at the self-regulatory organization with respect to the matter. After appropriate notice of the terms of substance of the filing or a description of the subjects and issues involved and opportunity for interested persons to submit written comment, the Commission may, by order, declare such plan or amendment effective if it finds that such plan or amendment is consistent with the public interest, the protection of investors, or otherwise in the furtherance of the purposes of the Act. The Commission in its order may restrict the categories of violations to be designated as minor rule violations and may impose any other terms or conditions to the plan (including abbreviated reporting of selected minor rule violations) and to the period of its effectiveness which it deems necessary or appropriate in the public interest, for the protection of investors or otherwise in furtherance of the purposes of the Act.

CONTENTS OF NOTICE REQUIRED BY PARAGRAPH (c)(1)

(d) Any notice filed pursuant to paragraph (c)(1) of this section shall consist of the following, as appropriate:

(1) the name of the respondent concerned together with his last known place of residence or business as reflected on the records of the self-regulatory organization and the name of the person, committee, or other organizational unit which brought the charges involved; except that, as to any respondent who has been found not to have violated a provision covered by a charge, identifying information with respect to such person may be deleted insofar as the notice reports the disposition of that charge, unless, prior to the filing of the notice, the respondent requests otherwise;

(2) a statement describing the investigative or other origin of the action;

(3) as charged in the proceeding, the specific provisions of the Act, the rules or regulations thereunder, the rules of the organization, and, in the case of a registered securities association, the rules of the Municipal Securities Rulemaking Board, and, in the event a violation of other statutes or rules constitutes a violation of any rule of the organization, such other statutes or rules; and a statement describing the answer of the respondent to the charges;

(4) a statement setting forth findings of fact with respect to any act or practice which such respondent was charged with having engaged in or omitted; the conclusion of the organization as to whether such respondent is deemed to have violated any provision covered by the charges; and a statement of the organization in support of the resolution of the principal issues raised in the proceedings;

(5) a statement describing any sanction imposed, the reasons therefor, and the date upon which such sanction has or will become effective, together with a finding, if appropriate, as to whether such respondent was a cause of any sanction imposed upon any other person;

(6) such other matters as the organization may deem relevant.

NOTICE OF FINAL DENIAL, BAR, PROHIBITION, TERMINATION OR LIMITATION BASED ON QUALIFICATION OR ADMINISTRATIVE RULES

(e) Any final action of a self-regulatory organization for which the Commission is the appropriate regulatory agency that is taken with respect to any person constituting a denial, bar, prohibition, or limitation of membership, participation or association with a member, or of access to services offered by a self-regulatory organization or a member thereof, and which is based on an alleged failure of any person to:

(1) pass any test or examination required by the rules of the Commission or such organization;

(2) comply with other qualification standards established by rules of the Commission or such organization; or

(3) comply with any administrative requirements of such organization (including failure to pay entry or other dues or fees or to file prescribed forms or reports) not involving charges of violations which may lead to a disciplinary sanction shall not be considered a "disciplinary action" for purposes of paragraph (c) of this rule; but notice thereof shall be promptly filed with the Commission in accordance with paragraph (f) hereof, *Provided, however,* That no disposition of a matter shall be considered "final" pursuant to this paragraph which results merely from a notice of such failure to the person affected, if such person has not sought an adjudication, including a hearing, or otherwise exhausted his administrative remedies within such organization with respect to such a matter.

CONTENTS OF NOTICE REQUIRED BY PARAGRAPH (e)

(f) Any notice filed pursuant to paragraph (e) hereof shall consist of the following, as appropriate:

(1) the name of each person concerned together with his last known place of residence or business as reflected on the records of the organization;

(2) the specific provisions of the Act, the rules or regulations thereunder, the rules of the organization, and, in the case of a registered securities association, the rules of the Municipal Securities Rulemaking Board, upon which the action of the organization was based, and a statement describing the answer of the person concerned;

(3) a statement setting forth findings of fact and conclusions as to each alleged failure of the person to pass any required examination, comply with other qualification standards, or comply with administrative obligations, and a statement of the organization in support of the resolution of the principal issues raised in the proceeding;

(4) the date upon which such action has or will become effective; and

(5) such other matters as the organization may deem relevant.

NOTICE OF FINAL ACTION BASED UPON PRIOR ADJUDICATED STATUTORY DISQUALIFICATIONS

(g) Any self-regulatory organization for which the Commission is the appropriate regulatory agency that takes any final action with respect to any person which:

(1) denies or conditions membership or participation in, or association with a member of, such organization or prohibits or limits access to services offered by such organization or a member thereof; and

(2) is based upon a statutory disqualification of a type defined in subparagraph (A), (B), or (C) of Section 3(a)(39) of the Act or consisting of a prior conviction, as described in subparagraph (E) of said Section 3(a)(39), shall promptly file a notice of such action with the Commission in accordance with paragraph (h) hereof, *Provided, however,* That no disposition of a matter shall be considered "final" pursuant to this paragraph where such person has not sought an adjudication, including a hearing, or otherwise exhausted his administrative remedies within such organization with respect to such a matter.

CONTENTS OF NOTICE REQUIRED BY PARAGRAPH (g)

(h) Any notice filed pursuant to paragraph (g) hereof shall consist of the following, as appropriate:

(1) the name of the person concerned together with his last known place of residence or business as reflected on the records of the organization;

(2) a statement setting forth the principal issues raised, the answer of any person concerned, and a statement of the organization in support of the resolution of the principal issues raised in the proceedings;

(3) any description furnished by or on behalf of the person concerned of the activities engaged in by the person since the adjudication upon which the disqualification is based;

(4) any description furnished by or on behalf of the person concerned of the prospective business or employment in which the person plans to engage and the manner and extent of supervision to be exercised over and by such person;

(5) a copy of the order or decision of the court, the Commission or the self-regulatory organization which adjudicated the matter giving rise to such statutory disqualification;

(6) the nature of the action taken and the date upon which such action is to be made effective; and

(7) such other matters as the organization deems relevant.

NOTICE OF SUMMARY SUSPENSION OF MEMBERSHIP, PARTICIPATION, OR ASSOCIATION, OR SUMMARY LIMITATION OR PROHIBITION OF ACCESS TO SERVICES

(i) If any self-regulatory organization for which the Commission is the appropriate regulatory agency summarily suspends a member, participant, or person associated with a member, or summarily limits or prohibits any person with respect to access to or services offered by the organization or (in the case of a national securities exchange or a registered securities association) a member thereof pursuant to the provisions of Section 6(d)(3), 15A(h)(3) or 17A(b)(5)(C) of the Act, such organization shall, within 24 hours of the effectiveness of such summary suspension, limitation or prohibition notify the Commission of such action, which notice shall contain at least the following information:

(1) the name of the person concerned together with his last known place of residence or business as reflected on the records of the organization;

(2) the date upon which such summary action has or will become effective;

(3) if such summary action is based upon the provisions of Section 6(d)(3)(A), 15A(h)(3)(A), or 17A(b)(5)(C)(i) of the Act, a copy of the relevant order or decision of the self-regulatory organization;

(4) if such summary action is based upon the provisions of Section 6(d)(3)(B) or (C), 15A(h)(3)(B) or (C), or 17A(b)(5)(C)(ii) or (iii) of the Act, a statement describing, as appropriate:

(i) the financial or operating difficulty of the member or participant upon which such organization determined the member or participant could not be permitted to continue to do business with safety to investors, creditors, other members or participants, or the organization;

(ii) the pertinent failure to meet qualification requirements or other prerequisites for access and the basis upon which such organization determined that the person concerned could not be permitted to have access with safety to investors, creditors, other members, or the organization; or

(iii) the default of any delivery of funds or securities to a clearing agency by a participant.

(5) the nature and effective date of the suspension, limitation or prohibition; and

(6) such other matters as the organization deems relevant.

Rule 19d–2. Applications for Stays of Disciplinary Sanctions or Summary Suspensions by a Self-Regulatory Organization

If any self-regulatory organization imposes any final disciplinary sanction as to which a notice is required to be filed with the Commission pursuant to Section 19(d)(1) of the Exchange Act, 15 U.S.C. 78s(d)(1), pursuant to Section 6(b)(6), 15A(b)(7) or 17A(b)(3)(G) of the Act (15 U.S.C. 78f(b)(6), 78*o*–3(b)(7) or 78q–1(b)(3)(G)), or summarily suspends or limits or prohibits access pursuant to Section 6(d)(3), 15A(h)(3) or 17A(b)(5)(C) of the Act (15 U.S.C. 78f(d)(3), 78*o*–3(h)(3) or 78q–1(b)(5)(C)), any person aggrieved thereby for which the Commission is the appropriate regulatory agency may file with the Commission a written motion for a stay of imposition of such action pursuant to Rule 401 of the Commission's Rules of Practice, § 201.401 of this chapter.

Rule 19d–3. Applications for Review of Final Disciplinary Sanctions, Denials of Membership, Participation or Association, or Prohibitions or Limitations of Access to Services Imposed by Self-Regulatory Organizations

Applications to the Commission for review of any final disciplinary sanction, denial or conditioning of membership, participation, bar from association, or prohibition or limitation with respect to access to services offered by a self-regulatory organization or a member thereof by any such organization shall be made pursuant to Rule 420 of the Commission's Rules of Practice, § 201.420 of this chapter.

Rule 19d-4. Notice by the Public Company Accounting Oversight Board of Disapproval of Registration or of Disciplinary Action

(a) *Definitions.*

(1) *Board* means the Public Company Accounting Oversight Board.

(2) *Public accounting firm* shall have the meaning set forth in 15 U.S.C. 7201(a)(11).

(3) *Registered public accounting firm* shall have the meaning set forth in 15 U.S.C. 7201(a)(12).

(4) *Associated person* shall mean a person associated with a registered public accounting firm as defined in 15 U.S.C. 7201(a)(9).

(b)(1) *Notice of disapproval of registration.* If the Board disapproves a completed application for registration by a public accounting firm, the Board shall file a notice of its disapproval with the Commission within 30 days and serve a copy on the public accounting firm.

(2) *Contents of the notice.* The notice required by paragraph (b)(1) of this section shall provide the following information:

(i) The name of the public accounting firm and the public accounting firm's last known address as reflected in the Board's records;

(ii) The basis for the Board's disapproval, and a copy of the Board's written notice of disapproval; and

(iii) Such other information as the Board may deem relevant.

(c)(1) *Notice of disciplinary action.* If the Board imposes any final disciplinary sanction on any registered public accounting firm or any associated person of a registered public accounting firm under 15 U.S.C. 7215(b)(3) or 7215(c), the Board shall file a notice of the disciplinary sanction with the Commission within 30 days and serve a copy on the person sanctioned.

(2) *Contents of the notice.* The notice required by paragraph (c)(1) of this section shall provide the following information:

(i) The name of the registered public accounting firm or the associated person, together with the firm's or the person's last known address as reflected in the Board's records;

(ii) A description of the acts or practices, or omissions to act, upon which the sanction is based;

(iii) A statement of the sanction imposed, the reasons therefor, or a copy of the Board's statement justifying the sanction, and the effective date of such sanction; and

(iv) Such other information as the Board may deem relevant.

Rule 19g2-1. Enforcement of Compliance by National Securities Exchanges and Registered Securities Associations With the Act and Rules and Regulations Thereunder

(a) In enforcing compliance, within the meaning of Section 19(g) of the Act, with the Act and the rules and regulations thereunder by its members and persons associated with its members, a national securities exchange or registered securities association is not required:

(1) To enforce compliance with sections 12 (other than sections 12(j) and 12(k)), 13, 14 (other than section 14(b)), 15(d) and 16 and the rules thereunder except to the extent of any action normally taken with respect to any person which is not a member or a person associated with a member;

(2) To enforce compliance with respect to persons associated with a member, other than securities persons or persons who control a member; and

(3) To conduct examinations as to qualifications of, require filing of periodic reports by, or conduct regular inspections (including examinations of books and records) of, persons associated with a member, other than securities persons whose functions are not solely clerical or ministerial.

(b) For the purpose of this rule:

(1) A "securities person" is a person who is a general partner or officer (or person occupying a similar status or performing similar functions) or employee of a member; *Provided, however,* That a registered broker or dealer which controls, is controlled by, or is under common control with, the member and the general partners and officers (and persons occupying similar status or performing similar functions) and employees of such a registered broker or dealer shall be securities persons if they effect, directly or indirectly, transactions in securities through the member by use of facilities maintained or supervised by such exchange or association; and

(2) "Control" means the power to direct or cause the direction of the management or policies of a company whether through ownership of securities, by contract or otherwise; *Provided, however,* That:

(i) Any person who, directly or indirectly, (A) Has the right to vote 25 percent or more of the voting securities, (B) Is entitled to receive 25 percent or more of the net profits, or (C) Is a director (or person occupying a similar status or performing similar functions) of a company shall be presumed to be a person who controls such company;

(ii) Any person not covered by paragraph (b)(2)(i) of this rule shall be presumed not to be a person who controls such company; and

(iii) Any presumption may be rebutted on an appropriate showing.

Rule 19h-1. Notice by a Self-Regulatory Organization of Proposed Admission to or Continuance in Membership or Participation or Association With a Member of Any Person Subject to a Statutory Disqualification, and Applications to the Commission for Relief Therefrom

(a) *Notice of Admission or Continuance Notwithstanding a Statutory Disqualification.*

(1) Any self-regulatory organization proposing, conditionally or unconditionally, to admit to, or continue any person in, membership or participation or (in the case of a national securities exchange or registered securities association) association with a member, notwithstanding a statutory disqualification, as defined in section 3(a)(39) of the Act, with respect to such person, shall file a notice with the Commission of such proposed admission or continuance. If such disqualified person has not consented to the terms of such proposal, notice of the organization's action shall be filed pursuant to Rule 19d-1 under the Act and not this rule.

(2) With respect to a person associated with a member of a national securities exchange or registered securities association, notices need be filed with the Commission pursuant to this rule only if such person:

(i) Controls such member, is a general partner or officer (or person occupying a similar status or performing similar functions) of such member, is an employee who, on behalf of such member, is engaged in securities advertising, public relations, research, sales, trading, or training or supervision of other employees who engage or propose to engage in such activities, except clerical and ministerial persons engaged in such activities, or is an employee with access to funds, securities or books and records, or

(ii) Is a broker or dealer not registered with the Commission, or controls such (unregistered) broker or dealer or is a general partner or officer (or person occupying a similar status or performing similar functions) of such broker or dealer.

(3) A notice need not be filed with the Commission pursuant to this rule if:

(i) The person subject to the statutory disqualification is already a participant in, a member of, or a person associated with a member of, a self-regulatory organization, and the terms and conditions of the proposed admission by another self-regulatory organization are the same in all material respects as those imposed or not disapproved in connection with such person's prior admission or continuance pursuant to an order of the Commission under paragraph (d) of this rule or other substantially equivalent written communication.

(ii) The self-regulatory organization finds, after reasonable inquiry, that except for the identity of the employer concerned, the terms and conditions of the proposed admission or continuance are the same in all material respects as those imposed or not disapproved in connection with a prior admission or continuance of the person subject to the statutory disqualification pursuant to an order of the Commission under paragraph (d) of this rule or other substantially equivalent written communication and that there is no intervening conduct or other circumstance that would cause the employment to be inconsistent with the public interest or the protection of investors;

(iii) The disqualification consists of (A) an injunction from engaging in any action, conduct, or practice specified in section 15(b)(4)(C) of the Act, which injunction was entered 10 or more years prior to the proposed admission or continuance—*Provided, however,* That in the case of a final or permanent injunction which was preceded by a preliminary injunction against the same person in the same court proceeding, such ten-year period shall begin to run from the date of such preliminary injunction—and/or (B) a finding by the Commission or a self-regulatory organization of a willful violation of the Act, the Securities Act of 1933, the Investment Advisers Act of 1940, the Investment Company Act of 1940, or a rule or regulation under one or more of such Acts and the sanction for such violation is no longer in effect;

(iv) The disqualification previously (A) was a basis for the institution of an administrative proceeding pursuant to a provision of the federal securities laws, and (B) was considered by the Commission in determining a sanction against such person in the proceeding; and the Commission concluded in such proceeding that it would not restrict or limit the future securities activities of such person in the capacity now proposed or, if it imposed any such restrictions or limitations for a specified time period, such time period has elapsed;

(v) The disqualification consists of a court order or judgment of injunction or conviction, and such order or judgment (A) expressly includes a provision that, on the basis of such order or judgment, the Commission will not institute a proceeding against such person pursuant to section 15(b) or 15B of the Act or that the future securities activities of such persons in the capacity now proposed will not be restricted or limited or (B) includes such restrictions or limitations for a specified time period and such time period has elapsed; or

(vi) In the case of a person seeking to become associated with a broker or dealer or municipal securities dealer, the Commission has previously consented to such proposed association pursuant to section 15(b)(6) or 15B(c)(4) of the Act.

In the case of an admission to membership, participation, or association, if an exception provided for in this paragraph (a)(3) is applicable, the self-regulatory organization shall, pursuant to its rules, determine when the admission to membership, participation, or association shall become effective.

(4) If a self-regulatory organization determines to admit to, or continue any person in, membership, participation, or association with a member pursuant to an exception from the notice requirements provided in paragraphs (a)(3)(ii), (iv) or (v) of this rule, such organization shall, within 14 calendar

days of its making of such determination, furnish to the Commission, by letter, a notification setting forth, as appropriate:

(i) The name of the person subject to the statutory disqualification;

(ii) The name of the person's prospective and immediately preceding employers who are (were) brokers or dealers or municipal securities dealers;

(iii) The name of the person's prospective supervisor(s);

(iv) The respective places of such employments as reflected on the records of the self-regulatory organization;

(v) If applicable, the findings of the self-regulatory organization referred to in paragraph (a)(3)(ii) hereof and the nature (including relevant dates) of the previous Commission or court determination referred to in paragraph (a)(3)(iv) or (v) hereof; and

(vi) An identification of any other self-regulatory organization which has indicated its agreement with the terms and conditions of the proposed admission or continuance;

(5) If a notice or notification has been previously filed or furnished pursuant to this rule by a self-regulatory organization, any other such organization need not file or furnish a separate notice or notification pursuant to this rule with respect to the same matter if such other organization agrees with the terms and conditions of the membership, participation or association reflected in the notice or notification so filed or furnished, and such agreement is set forth in the notice or notification.

(6) The notice requirements of sections 6(c)(2), 15A(g)(2), and 17A(b)(4)(A) of the Act concerning an action of a self-regulatory organization subject to one (or more) of such sections and this paragraph (a) shall be satisfied by a notice with respect to such action filed in accordance with paragraph (c) of this rule.

(7) The Commission, by written notice to a self-regulatory organization on or before the thirtieth day after receipt of a notice under this Rule, may direct that such organization not admit to membership, participation, or association with a member any person who is subject to a statutory disqualification for a period not to exceed an additional 60 days beyond the initial 30 day notice period in order that the Commission may extend its consideration of the proposal; *Provided, however,* That during such extended period of consideration, the Commission will not direct the self-regulatory organization to bar the proposed admission to membership, participation or association with a member pursuant to section 6(c)(2), 15A(g)(2), or 17A(b)(4)(A) of the Act, and the Commission will not institute proceedings pursuant to section 15(b) or 15B of the Act on the basis of such disqualification if the self-regulatory organization has permitted the admission to membership, participation or association with a member, on a temporary basis, pending a final Commission determination.

(b) *Preliminary Notifications.* Promptly after receiving an application for admission to, or continuance in, participation or membership in, or association with a member of, a self-regulatory organization which would be required to file with the Commission a notice thereof pursuant to paragraph (a) of this rule if such admission or continuance is ultimately proposed by such organization, the organization shall file with the Commission a notification of such receipt. Such notification shall include, as appropriate:

(1) The date of such receipt;

(2) The names of the person subject to the statutory disqualification and the prospective employer concerned together with their respective last known places of residence or business as reflected on the records of the organization;

(3) The basis for any such disqualification including (if based on a prior adjudication) a copy of the order or decision of the court, the Commission, or the self-regulatory organization which adjudicated the matter giving rise to the disqualification; and

(4) The capacity in which the person concerned is proposed to be employed.

(c) *Contents of Notice of Admission or Continuance.* A notice filed with the Commission pursuant to paragraph (a) hereof shall contain the following, as appropriate:

(1) The name of the person concerned together with his last known place of residence or business as reflected on the records of the self-regulatory organization;

(2) The basis for any such disqualification from membership, participation or association including (if based on a prior adjudication) a copy of the order or decision of the court, the Commission or the self-regulatory organization which adjudicated the matter giving rise to such disqualification;

(3) In the case of an admission, the date upon which it is proposed by the organization that such membership, participation or association shall become effective, which shall be not less than 30 days from the date upon which the Commission receives the notice;

(4) A description by or on behalf of the person concerned of the activities engaged in by the person since the disqualification arose, the prospective business or employment in which the person plans to engage and the manner and extent of supervision to be exercised over and by such person. This description shall be accompanied by a written statement submitted to the self-regulatory organization by the proposed employer setting forth the terms and conditions of such employment and supervision. The description also shall include (i) the qualifications, experience and disciplinary records of the proposed supervisors of the person and their family relationship (if any) to that person; (ii) the findings and results of all examinations conducted, during the two years preceding the filing of the notice, by self-regulatory organizations of the main office of the proposed employer and of the branch office(s) in which the employment will occur to be subject to supervisory controls; (iii) a copy of a completed Form U–4 with respect to the proposed association of such person and a certification by the self-regulatory organization that such person is fully qualified under all applicable requirements to engage in the proposed activities; and (iv) the name and place of employment of any other associated person of the proposed employer who is subject to a statutory disqualification (other than a disqualification specified in paragraph (a)(3)(iii) of this section);

(5) If a hearing on the matter has been held by the organization, a certified record of the hearing together with copies of any exhibits introduced therein;

(6) All written submissions not included in a certified oral hearing record which were considered by the organization in its disposition of the matter;

(7) An identification of any other self-regulatory organization which has indicated its agreement with the terms and conditions of the proposed admission or continuance;

(8) All information furnished in writing to the self-regulatory organization by the staff of the Commission for consideration by the organization in its disposition of the matter or the incorporation by reference of such information, and a statement of the organization's views thereon; and

(9) Such other matters as the organization or person deems relevant.

If the notice contains assertions of material facts not a matter of record before the self-regulatory organization, such facts shall be sworn to by affidavit of the person or organization offering such facts for Commission consideration. The notice may be accompanied by a brief.

(d) *Application to the Commission for Relief From Certain Statutory Disqualifications.* The filing of a notice pursuant to paragraph (a) of this rule shall neither affect nor foreclose any action which the Commission may take with respect to such person pursuant to the provisions of section 15(b), 15B or 19(h) of the Act or any rule thereunder. Accordingly, a notice filed pursuant to paragraph (a) hereof with respect to the membership, participation, or association of any person subject to an "applicable disqualification," as defined in paragraph (f) of this rule, may be accompanied by an application by or on behalf of the person concerned to the Commission for an order declaring, as applicable, that notwithstanding such disqualification, the Commission:

(1) Will not institute proceedings pursuant to section 15(b)(1)(B), 15(b)(4), 15(b)(6), 15B(a)(2), 15B(c)(2), 19(h)(2) or 19(h)(3) of the Act if such person seeks to obtain or continue registration as a broker or dealer or municipal securities dealer or association with a broker or dealer or municipal securities dealer so registered, or membership or participation in a self-regulatory organization;

(2) Will not direct otherwise, as provided in section 6(c)(2), 15A(g)(2), or 17A(b)(4)(A) of the Act; and

(3) Will deem such person qualified pursuant to Rule G–4 of the Municipal Securities Rulemaking Board under the Act.

If a Commission consent is required in order to render a proposed association lawful under section 15(b)(6) or 15B(c)(4) of the Act, an application by or on behalf of the person seeking such consent shall accompany the notice of the proposed association filed pursuant to paragraph (a) hereof.

The Commission may, in its discretion and subject to such terms and conditions as it deems necessary, issue such an order and consent should the Commission determine not to object to the position of the self-regulatory organization set forth in the notice or application; *Provided, however,* That nothing herein shall foreclose the right of any person, at his election, to apply directly to the Commission for such consent, if he makes such application pursuant to the terms of an existing order of the Commission under section 15(b)(6) or 15B(c)(4) of the Act limiting his association with a broker or dealer or municipal securities dealer but explicitly granting him such a right to apply for entry or reentry at a later time.

(e) *Contents of Application to the Commission.* An application to the Commission pursuant to paragraph (d) of this rule shall consist of the following, as appropriate:

(1) The name of the person subject to the disqualification together with his last known place of residence or business as reflected on the records of the self-regulatory organization;

(2) A copy of the order or decision of the court, the Commission or the self-regulatory organization which adjudicated the matter giving rise to such "applicable disqualification";

(3) The nature of the relief sought and the reasons therefor;

(4) A description of the activities engaged in by the person since the disqualification arose;

(5) A description of the prospective business or employment in which the person plans to engage and the manner and extent of supervision to be exercised over and by such person. This description shall be accompanied by a written statement submitted to the self-regulatory organization by the proposed employer setting forth the terms and conditions of such employment and supervision. The description also shall include (i) the qualifications, experience, and disciplinary records of the proposed supervisors of the person and their family relationship (if any) to that person; (ii) the findings and results of all examinations conducted, during the two years preceding the filing of the application, by self-regulatory organizations of the main office of the proposed employer

and of the branch office(s) in which the employment will occur or be subject to supervisory controls; (iii) a copy of a completed Form U–4 with respect to the proposed association of such person and a certification by the self-regulatory organization that such person is fully qualified under all applicable requirements to engage in the proposed activities; and (iv) the name and place of employment of any other associated person of the proposed employer who is subject to a statutory disqualification (other than a disqualification specified in paragraph (a)(3)(iii) of this rule);

(6) If a hearing on the matter has been held by the organization, a certified copy of the hearing record, together with copies of any exhibits introduced therein;

(7) All written submissions not included in a certified oral hearing record which were considered by the organization in its disposition of the matter;

(8) All information furnished in writing to the self-regulatory organization by the staff of the Commission for consideration by the organization in its disposition of the matter or the incorporation by reference of such information, and a statement of the organization's views thereon; and

(9) Such other matters as the organization or person deems relevant.

If the application contains assertions of material facts not a matter of record before the organization, such facts shall be sworn to by affidavit of the person or organization offering such facts for Commission consideration.

(f) *Definitions.* For purposes of this rule:

(1) The term "applicable disqualification" shall mean:

(i) Any effective order of the Commission pursuant to section 15(b)(4) or (6), 15B(c)(2) or (4) or 19(h)(2) or (3) of the Act—

(A) Revoking, suspending or placing limitations on the registration, activities, functions, or operations of a broker or dealer; (B) Suspending, barring, or placing limitations on the association, activities, or functions of an associated person of a broker or dealer;

(B) Suspending, barring, or placing limitations on the association, activities, or functions of an associated person of a broker or dealer;

(C) Suspending or expelling any person from membership or participation in a self-regulatory organization; or

(D) Suspending or barring any person from being associated with a member of a national securities exchange or registered securities association;

(ii) Any conviction or injunction of a type described in section 15(b)(4)(B) or (C) of the Act; or

(iii) A failure under the provisions of Rule G–4 of the Municipal Securities Rulemaking Board under the Act, to meet qualifications standards, and such failure may be remedied by a finding or determination by the Commission pursuant to such rule(s) that the person affected nevertheless meets such standards.

(2) The term "control" shall mean the power to direct or cause the direction of the management or policies of a company whether through ownership of securities, by contract or otherwise; *Provided, however,* That

(i) Any person who, directly or indirectly, (A) has the right to vote 10 percent or more of the voting securities, (B) is entitled to receive 10 percent or more of the net profits, or (C) is a director (or person occupying a similar status or performing similar functions) of a company shall be presumed to be a person who controls such company;

(ii) Any person not covered by paragraph (i) shall be presumed not to be a person who controls such company; and

(iii) Any presumption may be rebutted on an appropriate showing.

(g) Where it deems appropriate to do so, the Commission may determine whether to (1) direct, pursuant to section 6(c)(2), 15A(g)(2) or 17A(b)(4)(A) of the Act, that a proposed admission covered by a notice filed pursuant to paragraph (a) of this rule shall be denied or an order barring a proposed association issued or (2) grant or deny an application filed pursuant to paragraph (d) of this rule on the basis of the notice or application filed by the self-regulatory organization, the person subject to the disqualification, or other applicant (such as the proposed employer) on behalf of such person, without oral hearing. Any request for oral hearing or argument should be submitted with the notice or application.

(h) The Rules of Practice [17 CFR 201] shall apply to proceedings under this rule to the extent that they are not inconsistent with this rule.

INSPECTION AND PUBLICATION OF INFORMATION FILED UNDER THE ACT

Rule 24b–1. Documents to Be Kept Public by Exchanges

Upon action of the Commission granting an exchange's application for registration or exemption, the exchange shall make available to public inspection at its offices during reasonable office hours a copy of the statement and exhibits filed with the Commission (including any amendments thereto) except those portions thereof to the disclosure of which the exchange shall have filed objection pursuant to Rule 24b–2 which objection shall not have been overruled by the Commission pursuant to section 24(b).

Rule 24b–2. Nondisclosure of Information Filed With the Commission and With Any Exchange

Preliminary Note

Confidential treatment requests shall be submitted in paper format only, whether or not the filer is required to submit a filing in electronic format.

(a) Any person filing any registration statement, report, application, statement, correspondence, notice or other document (herein referred to as the material filed) pursuant to the Act may make written objection to the public disclosure of any information contained therein in accordance with the procedure set forth below. The procedure provided in this rule shall be the exclusive means of requesting confidential treatment of information required to be filed under the Act.

(b) The person shall omit from material filed the portion thereof which it desires to keep undisclosed (hereinafter called the confidential portion). In lieu thereof, it shall indicate at the appropriate place in the material filed that the confidential portion has been so omitted and filed separately with the Commission. The person shall file with the copies of the material filed with the Commission:

(1) One copy of the confidential portion, marked "Confidential Treatment," of the material filed with the Commission. The copy shall contain an appropriate identification of the item or other requirement involved and, notwithstanding that the confidential portion does not constitute the whole of the answer, the entire answer thereto; except that in the case where the confidential portion is part of a financial statement or schedule, only the particular financial statement or schedule need be included. The copy of the confidential portion shall be in the same form as the remainder of the material filed;

(2) An application making objection to the disclosure of the confidential portion. Such application shall be on a sheet or sheets separate from the confidential portion, and shall contain (i) an identification of the portion; (ii) a statement of the grounds of objection referring to, and containing an analysis of the applicable exemp-

tion(s) from disclosure under the Commission's rules and regulations adopted under the Freedom of Information Act (17 CFR 200.80), and a justification of the period of time for which confidential treatment is sought; (iii) a written consent to the furnishing of the confidential portion to other government agencies, offices or bodies and to the Congress; and (iv) the name of each exchange, if any, with which the material is filed.

(3) The copy of the confidential portion and the application filed in accordance with this paragraph (b) shall be enclosed in a separate envelope marked "Confidential Treatment" and addressed to The Secretary, Securities and Exchange Commission, Washington, DC 20549.

(c) Pending a determination as to the objection filed the material for which confidential treatment has been applied will not be made available to the public.

(d)(1) If it is determined that the objection should be sustained, a notation to that effect will be made at the appropriate place in the material filed. Such a determination will not preclude reconsideration whenever appropriate, such as upon receipt of any subsequent request under the Freedom of Information Act (5 U.S.C. Section 552) and, if appropriate, revocation of the confidential status of all or a portion of the information in question. Where an initial determination has been made under this rule to sustain objections to disclosure, the Commission will attempt to give the person requesting confidential treatment advance notice, wherever possible, if confidential treatment is revoked.

(2) In any case where an objection to disclosure has been disallowed or where a prior grant of confidential treatment has been revoked, the person who requested such treatment will be so informed by registered or certified mail to the person or his agent for service. Pursuant to § 201.431 of this chapter, persons making objections to disclosure may petition the Commission for review of a determination by the Division disallowing objections or revoking confidential treatment.

(e) The confidential portion shall be made available to the public at the time and according to the conditions specified in subparagraphs (1)–(2) of this paragraph:

(1) Upon the lapse of five days after the dispatch of notice by registered or certified mail of a determination disallowing an objection, if prior to the lapse of such five days the person shall not have communicated to the Secretary of the Commission his intention to seek review by the Commission under § 201.431 of this chapter of the determination made by the Division; or

(2) If such a petition for review shall have been filed under § 201.431 of this chapter, upon final disposition thereof adverse to the petitioner.

(f) If the confidential portion is made available to the public, one copy thereof shall be attached to each copy of the material filed with the Commission and with each exchange.

Rule 24b–3. Information Filed by Issuers and Others Under Sections 12, 13, 14, and 16

(a) Except as otherwise provided in this rule and in Rule 17a–6, each exchange shall keep available to the public, under reasonable regulations as to the manner of inspection, during reasonable office hours, all information regarding a security registered on such exchange which is filed with it pursuant to sections 12, 13, 14, or 16 or any rules or regulations thereunder. This requirement shall not apply to any information to the disclosure of which objection has been filed pursuant to Rule 24b–2, which objection shall not have been overruled by the Commission pursuant to section 24(b). The making of such information available pursuant to this rule shall not be deemed a representation by any exchange as to the accuracy, completeness, or genuineness thereof.

(b) In the case of an application for registration of a security pursuant to section 12 an exchange may delay making available the information contained therein until it has certified to the Commission its approval of such security for listing and registration.

Rule 24c–1. Access to Nonpublic Information

(a) For purposes of this section, the term "nonpublic information" means records, as defined in Section 24(a) of the Act, and other information in the Commission's possession, which are not available for public inspection and copying.

(b) The Commission may, in its discretion and upon a showing that such information is needed, provide nonpublic information in its possession to any of the following persons if the person receiving such nonpublic information provides such assurances of confidentiality as the Commission deems appropriate:

(1) A federal, state, local or foreign government or any political subdivision, authority, agency or instrumentality of such government;

(2) A self-regulatory organization as defined in Section 3(a)(26) of the Act, or any similar organization empowered with self-regulatory responsibilities under the federal securities laws (as defined in Section 3(a)(47) of the Act), the Commodity Exchange Act (7 U.S.C. 1, *et seq.*), or any substantially equivalent foreign statute or regulation;

(3) A foreign financial regulatory authority as defined in Section 3(a)(51) of the Act;

(4) The Securities Investor Protection Corporation or any trustee or counsel for a trustee appointed pursuant to Section 5(b) of the Securities Investor Protection Act of 1970;

(5) A trustee in bankruptcy;

(6) A trustee, receiver, master, special counsel or other person that is appointed by a court of competent jurisdiction or as a result of an agreement between the parties in connection with litigation or an administrative proceeding involving allegations of violations of the securities laws (as defined in Section 3(a)(47) of the Act) or the Commission's Rules of Practice, 17 CFR Part 201, or otherwise, where such trustee, receiver, master, special counsel or other person is specifically designated to perform particular functions with respect to, or as a result of, the litigation or proceeding or in connection with the administration and enforcement by the Commission of the federal securities laws or the Commission's Rules of Practice;

(7) A bar association, state accountancy board or other federal, state, local or foreign licensing or oversight authority, or a professional association or self-regulatory authority to the extent that it performs similar functions; or

(8) A duly authorized agent, employee or representative of any of the above persons.

(c) Nothing contained in this section shall affect:

(1) The Commission's authority or discretion to provide or refuse to provide access to, or copies of, nonpublic information in its possession in accordance with such other authority or discretion as the Commission possesses by statute, rule or regulation; or

(2) The Commission's responsibilities under the Privacy Act of 1974 (5 U.S.C. 552a), or the Right to Financial Privacy Act of 1978 (12 U.S.C. 3401–22) as limited by section 21(h) of the Act.

Rule 31. Section 31 Transaction Fees

(a) *Definitions*. For the purpose of this section, the following definitions shall apply:

(1) *Assessment charge* means the amount owed by a covered SRO for a covered round turn transaction pursuant to section 31(d) of the Act (15 U.S.C. 78ee(d)).

(2) *Billing period* means, for a single calendar year:

(i) January 1 through August 31 ("billing period 1"); or

(ii) September 1 through December 31 ("billing period 2").

(3) *Charge date* means the date on which a covered sale or covered round turn transaction occurs for purposes of determining the liability of a covered SRO pursuant to section 31 of the Act (15 U.S.C. 78ee). The charge date is:

(i) The settlement date, with respect to any covered sale (other than a covered sale resulting from the exercise of an option settled by physical delivery or from the maturation of a security future settled by physical delivery) or covered round turn transaction that a covered SRO is required to report to the Commission based on data that the covered SRO receives from a designated clearing agency;

(ii) The exercise date, with respect to a covered sale resulting from the exercise of an option settled by physical delivery;

(iii) The maturity date, with respect to a covered sale resulting from the maturation of a security future settled by physical delivery; and

(iv) The trade date, with respect to all other covered sales and covered round turn transactions.

(4) *Covered association* means any national securities association by or through any member of which covered sales or covered round turn transactions occur otherwise than on a national securities exchange.

(5) *Covered exchange* means any national securities exchange on which covered sales or covered round turn transactions occur.

(6) *Covered sale* means a sale of a security, other than an exempt sale or a sale of a security future, occurring on a national securities exchange or by or through any member of a national securities association otherwise than on a national securities exchange.

(7) *Covered round turn transaction* means a round turn transaction in a security future, other than a round turn transaction in a future on a narrow-based security index, occurring on a national securities exchange or by or through a member of a national securities association otherwise than on a national securities exchange.

(8) *Covered SRO* means a covered exchange or covered association.

(9) *Designated clearing agency* means a clearing agency registered under section 17A of the Act (15 U.S.C. 78q–1) that clears and settles covered sales or covered round turn transactions.

(10) *Due date* means:

(i) March 15, with respect to the amounts owed by covered SROs under section 31 of the Act (15 U.S.C. 78ee) for covered sales and covered round turn transactions having a charge date in billing period 2; and

(ii) September 30, with respect to the amounts owed by covered SROs under section 31 of the Act (15 U.S.C. 78ee) for covered sales and covered round turn transactions having a charge date in billing period 1.

(11) *Exempt sale* means:

(i) Any sale of a security offered pursuant to an effective registration statement under the Securities Act of 1933 (except a sale of a put or call option issued by the Options Clearing Corporation) or offered in accordance with an exemption from registration afforded by section 3(a) or 3(b) of the Securities Act of 1933 (15 U.S.C. 77c(a) or 77c(b)), or a rule thereunder;

(ii) Any sale of a security by an issuer not involving any public offering within the meaning of section 4(2) of the Securities Act of 1933 (15 U.S.C. 77d(2));

(iii) Any sale of a security pursuant to and in consummation of a tender or exchange offer;

(iv) Any sale of a security upon the exercise of a warrant or right (except a put or call), or upon the conversion of a convertible security;

(v) Any sale of a security that is executed outside the United States and is not reported, or required to be reported, to a transaction reporting association as defined in § 240.11Aa3–1 and any approved plan filed thereunder;

(vi) Any sale of an option on a security index (including both a narrow-based security index and a non-narrow-based security index);

(vii) Any sale of a bond, debenture, or other evidence of indebtedness; and

(viii) Any recognized riskless principal sale.

(12) *Fee rate* means the fee rate applicable to covered sales under section 31(b) or (c) of the Act (15 U.S.C. 78ee(b) or (c)), as adjusted from time to time by the Commission pursuant to section 31(j) of the Act (15 U.S.C. 78ee(j)).

(13) *Narrow-based security index* means the same as in section 3(a)(55)(B) and (C) of the Act (15 U.S.C. 78c(a)(55)(B) and (C)).

(14) *Recognized riskless principal sale* means a sale of a security where all of the following conditions are satisfied:

(i) A broker-dealer receives from a customer an order to buy (sell) a security;

(ii) The broker-dealer engages in two contemporaneous offsetting transactions as principal, one in which the broker-dealer buys (sells) the security from (to) a third party and the other in which the broker-dealer sells (buys) the security to (from) the customer; and

(iii) The Commission, pursuant to section 19(b)(2) of the Act (15 U.S.C. 78s(b)(2)), has approved a proposed rule change submitted by the covered SRO on which the second of the two contemporaneous offsetting transactions occurs that permits that transaction to be reported as riskless.

(15) *Round turn transaction in a security future* means one purchase and one sale of a contract of sale for future delivery.

(16) *Physical delivery exchange-traded option* means a securities option that is listed and registered on a national securities exchange and settled by the physical delivery of the underlying securities.

(17) *Section 31 bill* means the bill sent by the Commission to a covered SRO pursuant to section 31 of the Act (15 U.S.C. 78ee) showing the total amount due from the covered SRO for the billing period, as calculated by the Commission based on the data submitted by the covered SRO in its Form R31 (§ 249.11 of this chapter) submissions for the months of the billing period.

(18) *Trade reporting system* means an automated facility operated by a covered SRO used to collect or compare trade data.

(b) *Reporting of covered sales and covered round turn transactions.*

(1) Each covered SRO shall submit a completed Form R31 (§ 249.11 of this chapter) to the Commission within ten business days after the end of each month.

(2) A covered exchange shall provide on Form R31 the following data on covered sales and covered round turn transactions occurring on that exchange and having a charge date in that month:

(i) The aggregate dollar amount of covered sales that it reported to a designated clearing agency, as reflected in the data provided by the designated clearing agency;

(ii) The aggregate dollar amount of covered sales resulting from the exercise of physical delivery exchange-traded options or from matured security futures, as reflected in the data provided by a designated clearing agency that clears and settles options or security futures;

(iii) The aggregate dollar amount of covered sales that it captured in a trade reporting system but did not report to a designated clearing agency;

(iv) The aggregate dollar amount of covered sales that it neither captured in a trade reporting system nor reported to a designated clearing agency; and

(v) The total number of covered round turn transactions that it reported to a designated clearing agency, as reflected in the data provided by the designated clearing agency.

(3) A covered association shall provide on Form R31 the following data on covered sales and covered round turn transactions occurring by or through any member of such association otherwise than on a national securities exchange and having a charge date in that month:

(i) The aggregate dollar amount of covered sales that it captured in a trade reporting system;

(ii) The aggregate dollar amount of covered sales that it did not capture in a trade reporting system; and

(iii) The total number of covered round turn transactions that it reported to a designated clearing agency, as reflected in the data provided by the designated clearing agency.

(4) *Duties of designated clearing agency.*

(i) A designated clearing agency shall provide a covered SRO, upon request, the data in its possession needed by the covered SRO to complete Part I of Form R31 (§ 249.11 of this chapter).

(ii) If a covered exchange trades physical delivery exchange-traded options or security futures that settle by physical delivery of the underlying securities, the designated clearing agency that clears and settles such transactions shall provide that covered exchange with the data in its possession relating to the covered sales resulting from the exercise of such options or from the matured security futures. If, during a particular month, the designated clearing agency cannot determine the covered exchange on which the options or security futures originally were traded, the designated clearing agency shall assign covered sales resulting from exercises or maturations as follows. To provide Form R31 data to the covered exchange for a particular month, the designated clearing agency shall:

(A) Calculate the aggregate dollar amount of all covered sales in the previous calendar month resulting from exercises and maturations, respectively, occurring on all covered exchanges for which it clears and settles transactions;

(B) Calculate, for the previous calendar month, the aggregate dollar amount of covered sales of physical delivery exchange-traded options occurring on each covered exchange for which it clears and settles transactions, and the aggregate dollar amount of covered sales of physical delivery exchange-traded options occurring on all such exchanges collectively;

(C) Calculate, for the previous calendar month, the total number of covered round turn transactions in security futures that settle by physical delivery that occurred on each covered exchange for which it clears and settles transactions, and the total number of covered round turn transactions in security futures that settle by physical delivery that occurred on all such exchanges collectively;

(D) Determine for the previous calendar month each covered exchange's percentage of the total dollar volume of physical delivery exchange-traded options ("exercise percentage") and each covered exchange's percentage of the total number of covered round turn transactions in security futures that settle by physical delivery ("maturation percentage"); and

(E) In the current month, assign to each covered exchange for which it clears and settles covered sales the exercise percentage of the aggregate dollar amount of covered sales on all covered exchanges resulting from the exercise of physical delivery exchange-traded options and the maturation percentage of all covered sales on all covered exchanges resulting from the maturation of security futures that settle by physical delivery.

(5) A covered SRO shall provide in Part I of Form R31 only the data supplied to it by a designated clearing agency.

(c) *Calculation and billing of section 31 fees.*

(1) The amount due from a covered SRO for a billing period, as reflected in its Section 31 bill, shall be the sum of the monthly amounts due for each month in the billing period.

(2) The monthly amount due from a covered SRO shall equal:

(i) The aggregate dollar amount of its covered sales that have a charge date in that month, times the fee rate; plus

(ii) The total number of its covered round turn transactions that have a charge date in that month, times the assessment charge.

(3) By the due date, each covered SRO shall pay the Commission, either directly or through a designated clearing agency acting as agent, the entire amount due for the billing period, as reflected in its Section 31 bill.

Rule 36a1–1. Exemption from Section 7 for OTC Derivatives Dealers

Preliminary Note

OTC derivatives dealers are a special class of broker-dealers that are exempt from certain broker-dealer requirements, including membership in a self-regulatory organization (§ 240.15b9–2), regular broker-dealer margin rules (§ 240.36a1–1), and application of the Securities Investor Protection Act of 1970 (§ 240.36a1–2). OTC derivative dealers are subject to special requirements, including limitations on the scope of their securities activities (§ 240.15a–1), specified internal risk management control systems (§ 240.15c3–4), recordkeeping obligations (§ 240.17a–3(a)(10)), and reporting responsibilities (§ 240.17a–12). They are also subject to alternative net capital treatment (§ 240.15c3–1(a)(5)).

(a) Except as otherwise provided in paragraph (b) of this section, transactions involving the extension of credit by an OTC derivatives dealer shall be exempt from the provisions of section 7(c) of the Act (15 U.S.C. 78g(c)), provided that the OTC derivatives dealer complies with Section 7(d) of the Act (15 U.S.C. 78g(d)).

(b) The exemption provided under paragraph (a) of this section shall not apply to extensions of credit made directly by a registered broker or dealer (other than an OTC derivatives dealer) in connection with transactions in eligible OTC derivative instruments for which an OTC derivatives dealer acts as counterparty.

Rule 36a1–2. Exemption from SIPA for OTC Derivatives Dealers

Preliminary Note

OTC derivatives dealers are a special class of broker-dealers that are exempt from certain broker-dealer requirements, including membership in a self-regulatory organization (§ 240.15b9–2), regular broker-dealer margin rules (§ 240.36a1–1), and application of the Securities Investor Protection Act of 1970 (§ 240.36a1–2). OTC derivative dealers are subject to special requirements, including limitations on the scope of their securities activities (§ 240.15a–1), specified internal risk management control systems (§ 240.15c3–4), recordkeeping obligations (§ 240.17a–3(a)(10)), and reporting responsibilities (§ 240.17a–12). They are also subject to alternative net capital treatment (§ 240.15c3–1(a)(5)).

OTC derivatives dealers, as defined in § 240.3b–12, shall be exempt from the provisions of the Securities Investor Protection Act of 1970 (15 U.S.C. 78aaa through 78lll).

REGULATION BTR—BLACKOUT TRADING RESTRICTION

(Cite as 17 CFR 245.___)

Sec.

§ 245.100. Definitions

As used in Regulation BTR (§§ 245.100 through 245.104), unless the context otherwise requires:

(a) The term *acquired in connection with service or employment as a director or executive officer*, when applied to a director or executive officer, means that he or she acquired, directly or indirectly, an equity security:

(1) At a time when he or she was a director or executive officer, under a compensatory plan, contract, authorization or arrangement, including, but not limited to, an option, warrants or rights plan, a pension, retirement or deferred compensation plan or a bonus, incentive or profit-sharing plan (whether or not set forth in any formal plan document), including a compensatory plan, contract, authorization or arrangement with a parent, subsidiary or affiliate;

(2) At a time when he or she was a director or executive officer, as a result of any transaction or business relationship described in paragraph (a) or (b) of Item 404 of Regulation S–K (§ 229.404 of this chapter) or, in the case of a foreign private issuer, Item 7.B of Form 20–F (§ 249.220f of this chapter) (but without application of the disclosure thresholds of such provisions), to the extent that he or she has a pecuniary interest (as defined in paragraph (*l*) of this section) in the equity securities;

(3) At a time when he or she was a director or executive officer, as directors' qualifying shares or other securities that he or she must hold to satisfy minimum ownership requirements or guidelines for directors or executive officers;

(4) Prior to becoming, or while, a director or executive officer where the equity security was acquired as a direct or indirect inducement to service or employment as a director or executive officer; or

(5) Prior to becoming, or while, a director or executive officer where the equity security was received as a result of a business combination in respect of an equity security of an entity involved in the business combination that he or she had acquired in connection with service or employment as a director or executive officer of such entity.

(b) Except as provided in § 245.102, the term *blackout period*:

(1) With respect to the equity securities of any issuer (other than a foreign private issuer), means any period of more than three consecutive business days during which the ability to purchase, sell or otherwise acquire or transfer an interest in any equity security of such issuer held in an individual account plan is temporarily suspended by the issuer or by a fiduciary of the plan with respect to not fewer than 50% of the participants or beneficiaries located in the United States and its territories and possessions under all individual account plans (as defined in paragraph (j) of this section) maintained by the issuer that permit participants or beneficiaries to acquire or hold equity securities of the issuer;

(2) With respect to the equity securities of any foreign private issuer (as defined in § 240.3b–4(c) of this chapter), means any period of more than three consecutive business days during which both:

(i) The conditions of paragraph (b)(1) of this section are met; and

(ii)(A) The number of participants and beneficiaries located in the United States and its territories and possessions subject to the temporary suspension exceeds 15% of the total number of employees of the issuer and its consolidated subsidiaries; or

(B) More than 50,000 participants and beneficiaries located in the United States and its territories and possessions are subject to the temporary suspension.

(3) In determining the individual account plans (as defined in paragraph (j) of this section) maintained by an issuer for purposes of this paragraph (b):

(i) The rules under section 414(b), (c), (m) and (*o*) of the Internal Revenue Code (26 U.S.C. 414(b), (c), (m) and (*o*)) are to be applied; and

(ii) An individual account plan that is maintained outside of the United States primarily for the benefit of persons substantially all of whom are nonresident aliens (within the meaning of section 104(b)(4) of the Employee Retirement Income Security Act of 1974 (29 U.S.C. 1003(b)(4))) is not to be considered.

(4) In determining the number of participants and beneficiaries in an individual account plan (as defined in paragraph (j) of this section) maintained by an issuer:

(i) The determination may be made as of any date within the 12-month period preceding the beginning date of the temporary suspension in question; provided that if there has been a significant change in the number of participants or beneficiaries in an individual account plan since the date selected, the determination for such plan must be made as of the most recent practicable date that reflects such change; and

(ii) The determination may be made without regard to overlapping plan participation.

(c)(1) The term *director* has, except as provided in paragraph (c)(2) of this section, the meaning set forth in section 3(a)(7) of the Exchange Act (15 U.S.C. 78c(a)(7)).

(2) In the case of a foreign private issuer (as defined in § 240.3b–4(c) of this chapter), the term *director* means an individual within the definition set forth in section 3(a)(7) of the Exchange Act who is a management employee of the issuer.

(d) The term *derivative security* has the meaning set forth in § 240.16a–1(c) of this chapter.

(e) The term *equity security* has the meaning set forth in section 3(a)(11) of the Exchange Act (15 U.S.C. 78c(a)(11)) and § 240.3a11–1 of this chapter.

(f) The term *equity security of the issuer* means any equity security or derivative security relating to an issuer, whether or not issued by that issuer.

(g) The term *Exchange Act* means the Securities Exchange Act of 1934 (15 U.S.C. 78a *et seq.*).

(h)(1) The term *executive officer* has, except as provided in paragraph (h)(2) of this section, the meaning set forth in § 240.16a–1(f) of this chapter.

(2) In the case of a foreign private issuer (as defined in § 240.3b–4(c) of this chapter), the term *executive officer* means the principal executive officer or officers, the principal financial officer or officers and the principal accounting officer or officers of the issuer.

(i) The term *exempt security* has the meaning set forth in section 3(a)(12) of the Exchange Act (15 U.S.C. 78c(a)(12)).

(j) The term *individual account plan* means a pension plan which provides for an individual account for each participant and for benefits based solely upon the amount contributed to the participant's account, and any income, expenses, gains and losses, and any forfeitures of accounts of other participants which may be allocated to such participant's account, except that such term does not include a one-participant retirement plan (within the meaning of section 101(i)(8)(B) of the Employee Retirement Income Security Act of 1974 (29 U.S.C. 1021(i)(8)(B))), nor does it include a pension plan in which participation is limited to directors of the issuer.

(k) The term *issuer* means an issuer (as defined in section 3(a)(8) of the Exchange Act (15 U.S.C. 78c(a)(8))), the securities of which are registered under section 12 of the Exchange Act (15 U.S.C. 78*l*) or that is required to file reports under section 15(d) of the Exchange Act (15 U.S.C. 78o(d)) or that files or has filed a registration statement that has not yet become effective under the Securities Act of 1933 (15 U.S.C. 77a *et seq.*) and that it has not withdrawn.

(*l*) The term *pecuniary interest* has the meaning set forth in § 240.16a–1(a)(2)(i) of this chapter and the term *indirect pecuniary interest* has the meaning set forth in § 240.16a–1(a)(2)(ii) of this chapter. Section 240.16a–1(a)(2)(iii) of this chapter also shall apply to determine pecuniary interest for purposes of this regulation.

§ 245.101. Prohibition of Insider Trading During Pension Fund Blackout Periods

(a) Except to the extent otherwise provided in paragraph (c) of this section, it is unlawful under section 306(a)(1) of the Sarbanes–Oxley Act of 2002 (15 U.S.C. 7244(a)(1)) for any director or executive officer of an issuer of any equity security (other than an exempt security), directly or indirectly, to purchase, sell or otherwise acquire or transfer any equity security of the issuer (other than an exempt security) during any blackout period with respect to such equity security, if such director or executive officer acquires or previously acquired such equity security in connection with his or her service or employment as a director or executive officer.

(b) For purposes of section 306(a)(1) of the Sarbanes–Oxley Act of 2002, any sale or other transfer of an equity security of the issuer during a blackout period will be treated as a transaction involving an equity security "acquired in connection with service or employment as a director or executive officer" (as defined in § 245.100(a)) to the extent that the director or executive officer has a pecuniary interest (as defined in § 245.100(*l*)) in such equity security, unless the director or executive officer establishes by specific identification of securities that the transaction did not involve an equity security "acquired in connection with service or employment as a director or executive officer." To establish that the equity security was not so acquired, a director or executive officer must identify the source of the equity securities and demonstrate that he or she has utilized the same specific identification for any purpose related to the transaction (such as tax reporting and any applicable disclosure and reporting requirements).

(c) The following transactions are exempt from section 306(a)(1) of the Sarbanes–Oxley Act of 2002:

(1) Any acquisition of equity securities resulting from the reinvestment of dividends in, or interest on, equity securities of the same issuer if the acquisition is made pursuant to a plan providing for the regular reinvestment of dividends or interest and the plan provides for broad-based participation, does not discriminate in favor of employees of the issuer and operates on substantially the same terms for all plan participants;

(2) Any purchase or sale of equity securities of the issuer pursuant to a contract, instruction or written plan entered into by the director or executive officer that satisfies the affirmative defense conditions of § 240.10b5–1(c) of this chapter; provided that the director or executive officer did not enter into or modify the contract, instruction or written plan during the blackout period (as defined in § 245.100(b)) in question, or while aware of the actual or approximate beginning or ending dates of that blackout period (whether or not the director or executive officer received notice of the

blackout period as required by Section 306(a)(6) of the Sarbanes–Oxley Act of 2002 (15 U.S.C. 7244(a)(6)));

(3) Any purchase or sale of equity securities, other than a Discretionary Transaction (as defined in § 240.16b–3(b)(1) of this chapter), pursuant to a Qualified Plan (as defined in § 240.16b–3(b)(4) of this chapter), an Excess Benefit Plan (as defined in § 240.16b–3(b)(2) of this chapter) or a Stock Purchase Plan (as defined in § 240.16b–3(b)(5) of this chapter) (or, in the case of a foreign private issuer, pursuant to an employee benefit plan that either (i) has been approved by the taxing authority of a foreign jurisdiction, or (ii) is eligible for preferential treatment under the tax laws of a foreign jurisdiction because the plan provides for broad-based employee participation); provided that a Discretionary Transaction that meets the conditions of paragraph (c)(2) of this section also shall be exempt;

(4) Any grant or award of an option, stock appreciation right or other equity compensation pursuant to a plan that, by its terms:

(i) Permits directors or executive officers to receive grants or awards; and

(ii) Either:

(A) States the amount and price of securities to be awarded to designated directors and executive officers or categories of directors and executive officers (though not necessarily to others who may participate in the plan) and specifies the timing of awards to directors and executive officers; or

(B) Sets forth a formula that determines the amount, price and timing, using objective criteria (such as earnings of the issuer, value of the securities, years of service, job classification, and compensation levels);

(5) Any exercise, conversion or termination of a derivative security that the director or executive officer did not write or acquire during the blackout period (as defined in § 245.100(b)) in question, or while aware of the actual or approximate beginning or ending dates of that blackout period (whether or not the director or executive officer received notice of the blackout period as required by Section 306(a)(6) of the Sarbanes–Oxley Act of 2002); and either:

(i) The derivative security, by its terms, may be exercised, converted or terminated only on a fixed date, with no discretionary provision for earlier exercise, conversion or termination; or

(ii) The derivative security is exercised, converted or terminated by a counterparty and the director or executive officer does not exercise any influence on the counterparty with respect to whether or when to exercise, convert or terminate the derivative security;

(6) Any acquisition or disposition of equity securities involving a bona fide gift or a transfer by will or the laws of descent and distribution;

(7) Any acquisition or disposition of equity securities pursuant to a domestic relations order, as defined in the Internal Revenue Code or Title I of the Employment Retirement Income Security Act of 1974, or the rules thereunder;

(8) Any sale or other disposition of equity securities compelled by the laws or other requirements of an applicable jurisdiction;

(9) Any acquisition or disposition of equity securities in connection with a merger, acquisition, divestiture or similar transaction occurring by operation of law;

(10) The increase or decrease in the number of equity securities held as a result of a stock split or stock dividend applying equally to all securities of that class, including a stock dividend in which equity securities of a different issuer are distributed; and the acquisition of rights, such as shareholder or pre-emptive rights, pursuant to a pro rata grant to all holders of the same class of equity securities; and

(11) Any acquisition or disposition of an asset-backed security, as defined in § 229.1101 of this chapter.

§ 245.102. Exceptions to Definition of Blackout Period

The term "blackout period," as defined in § 245.100(b), does not include:

(a) A regularly scheduled period in which participants and beneficiaries may not purchase, sell or otherwise acquire or transfer an interest in any equity security of an issuer, if a description of such period, including its frequency and duration and the plan transactions to be suspended or otherwise affected, is:

(1) Incorporated into the individual account plan or included in the documents or instruments under which the plan operates; and

(2) Disclosed to an employee before he or she formally enrolls, or within 30 days following formal enrollment, as a participant under the individual account plan or within 30 days after the adoption of an amendment to the plan. For purposes of this paragraph (a)(2), the disclosure may be provided in any graphic form that is reasonably accessible to the employee; or

(b) Any trading suspension described in § 245.100(b) that is imposed in connection with a corporate merger, acquisition, divestiture or similar transaction involving the plan or plan sponsor, the principal purpose of which is to permit persons affiliated with the acquired or divested entity to become participants or beneficiaries, or to cease to be participants or beneficiaries, in an individual account plan; provided that the persons who become participants or beneficiaries in an individual account plan are not able to participate in the same class of equity securities after the merger, acquisition, divestiture or similar transaction as before the transaction.

§ 245.103. Issuer Right of Recovery; Right of Action by Equity Security Owner

(a) *Recovery of profits.* Section 306(a)(2) of the Sarbanes–Oxley Act of 2002 (15 U.S.C. 7244(a)(2)) provides that any profit realized by a director or executive officer from any purchase, sale or other acquisition or transfer of any equity security of an issuer in violation of section 306(a)(1) of that Act (15 U.S.C. 7244(a)(1)) will inure to and be recoverable by the issuer, regardless of any intention on the part of the director or executive officer in entering into the transaction.

(b) *Actions to recover profit.* Section 306(a)(2) of the Sarbanes–Oxley Act of 2002 provides that an action to recover profit may be instituted at law or in equity in any court of competent jurisdiction by the issuer, or by the owner of any equity security of the issuer in the name and on behalf of the issuer if the issuer fails or refuses to bring such action within 60 days after the date of request, or fails diligently to prosecute the action thereafter, except that no such suit may be brought more than two years after the date on which such profit was realized.

(c) *Measurement of profit.*

(1) In determining the profit recoverable in an action undertaken pursuant to section 306(a)(2) of the Sarbanes–Oxley Act of 2002 from a transaction that involves a purchase, sale or other acquisition or transfer (other than a grant, exercise, conversion or termination of a derivative security) in violation of section 306(a)(1) of that Act of an equity security of an issuer that is registered pursuant to section 12(b) or 12(g) of the Exchange Act (15 U.S.C. 78*l*(b) or (g)) and listed on a national securities exchange or listed in an automated inter-dealer quotation system of a national securities association, profit (including any loss avoided) may be measured by comparing the difference between the amount paid or received for the equity security on the date of the transaction during the blackout period and the average market price of the equity security calculated over the first three trading days after the ending date of the blackout period.

(2) In determining the profit recoverable in an action undertaken pursuant to section 306(a)(2) of the Sarbanes–Oxley Act of 2002 from a transaction that is not described in paragraph (c)(1) of this section, profit (including any loss avoided) may be measured in a manner that is consistent with the objective of identifying the amount of any gain realized or loss avoided by a director or executive officer as a result of a transaction taking place in violation of section 306(a)(1) of that Act during the blackout period as opposed to taking place outside of such blackout period.

(3) The terms of this section do not limit in any respect the authority of the Commission to seek or determine remedies as the result of a transaction taking place in violation of section 306(a)(1) of the Sarbanes–Oxley Act.

§ 245.104. Notice

(a) In any case in which a director or executive officer is subject to section 306(a)(1) of the Sarbanes–Oxley Act of 2002 (15 U.S.C. 7244(a)(1)) in connection with a blackout period (as defined in § 245.100(b)) with respect to any equity security, the issuer of the equity security must timely notify each director or officer and the Commission of the blackout period.

(b) For purposes of this section:

(1) The notice must include:

(i) The reason or reasons for the blackout period;

(ii) A description of the plan transactions to be suspended during, or otherwise affected by, the blackout period;

(iii) A description of the class of equity securities subject to the blackout period;

(iv) The length of the blackout period by reference to:

(A) The actual or expected beginning date and ending date of the blackout period; or

(B) The calendar week during which the blackout period is expected to begin and the calendar week during which the blackout period is expected to end, provided that the notice to directors and executive officers describes how, during such week or weeks, a director or executive officer may obtain, without charge, information as to whether the blackout period has begun or ended; and provided further that the notice to the Commission describes how, during the blackout period and for a period of two years after the ending date of the blackout period, a security holder or other interested person may obtain, without charge, the actual beginning and ending dates of the blackout period.

(C) For purposes of this paragraph (b)(1)(iv), a *calendar week* means a seven-day period beginning on Sunday and ending on Saturday; and

(v) The name, address and telephone number of the person designated by the issuer to respond to inquiries about the blackout period, or, in the absence of such a designation, the issuer's human resources director or person performing equivalent functions.

(2) (i) Notice to an affected director or executive officer will be considered timely if the notice described in paragraph (b)(1) of this section is provided (in graphic form that is reasonably accessible to the recipient):

(A) No later than five business days after the issuer receives the notice required by section 101(i)(2)(E) of the Employment Retirement Income Security Act of 1974 (29 U.S.C. 1021(i)(2)(E)); or

(B) If no such notice is received by the issuer, a date that is at least 15 calendar days before the actual or expected beginning date of the blackout period.

(ii) Notwithstanding paragraph (b)(2)(i) of this section, the requirement to give advance notice will not apply in any case in which the inability to provide advance notice of the blackout period is due to events that were unforeseeable to, or circumstances that were beyond the reasonable control of, the issuer, and the issuer reasonably so determines in writing. Determinations described in the preceding sentence must be dated and signed by an authorized representative of the issuer. In any case in which this exception to the advance notice requirement applies, the issuer must provide the notice described in paragraph (b)(1) of this section, as well as a copy of the written determination, to all affected directors and executive officers as soon as reasonably practicable.

(iii) If there is a subsequent change in the beginning or ending dates of the blackout period as provided in the notice to directors and executive officers under paragraph (b)(2)(i) of this section, an issuer must provide directors and executive officers with an updated notice explaining the reasons for the change in the date or dates and identifying all material changes in the information contained in the prior notice. The updated notice is required to be provided as soon as reasonably practicable, unless such notice in advance of the termination of a blackout period is impracticable.

(3) Notice to the Commission will be considered timely if:

(i) The issuer, except as provided in paragraph (b)(3)(ii) of this section, files a current report on Form 8–K (§ 249.308 of this chapter) within the time prescribed for filing the report under the instructions for the form; or

(ii) In the case of a foreign private issuer (as defined in § 240.3b–4(c) of this chapter), the issuer includes the information set forth in paragraph (b)(1) of this section in the first annual report on Form 20–F (§ 249.220f of this chapter) or 40–F (§ 249.240f of this chapter) required to be filed after the receipt of the notice of a blackout period required by 29 CFR 2520.101–3(c) within the time prescribed for filing the report under the instructions for the form or in an earlier filed report on Form 6–K (§ 249.306).

(iii) If there is a subsequent change in the beginning or ending dates of the blackout period as provided in the notice to the Commission under paragraph (b)(3)(i) of this section, an issuer must file a current report on Form 8–K containing the updated beginning or ending dates of the blackout period, explaining the reasons for the change in the date or dates and identifying all material changes in the information contained in the prior report. The updated notice is required to be provided as soon as reasonably practicable.

REGULATION FD

(Cite as 17 CFR 243.___)

§ 243.100. General Rule Regarding Selective Disclosure

(a) Whenever an issuer, or any person acting on its behalf, discloses any material nonpublic information regarding that issuer or its securities to any person described in paragraph (b)(1) of this section, the issuer shall make public disclosure of that information as provided in § 243.101(e):

(1) Simultaneously, in the case of an intentional disclosure; and

(2) Promptly, in the case of a non-intentional disclosure.

(b)(1) Except as provided in paragraph (b)(2) of this section, paragraph (a) of this section shall apply to a disclosure made to any person outside the issuer:

(i) Who is a broker or dealer, or a person associated with a broker or dealer, as those terms are defined in Section 3(a) of the Securities Exchange Act of 1934 (15 U.S.C. 78c(a));

(ii) Who is an investment adviser, as that term is defined in Section 202(a)(11) of the Investment Advisers Act of 1940 (15 U.S.C. 80b–2(a)(11)); an institutional investment manager, as that term is defined in Section 13(f)(5) of the Securities Exchange Act of 1934 (15 U.S.C. 78m(f)(5)), that filed a report on Form 13F (17 CFR 249.325) with the Commission for the most recent quarter ended prior to the date of the disclosure; or a person associated with either of the foregoing. For purposes of this paragraph, a "person associated with an investment adviser or institutional investment manager" has the meaning set forth in Section 202(a)(17) of the Investment Advisers Act of 1940 (15 U.S.C. 80b–2(a)(17)), assuming for these purposes that an institutional investment manager is an investment adviser;

(iii) Who is an investment company, as defined in Section 3 of the Investment Company Act of 1940 (15 U.S.C. 80a–3), or who would be an investment company but for Section 3(c)(1) (15 U.S.C. 80a–3(c)(1)) or Section 3(c)(7) (15 U.S.C. 80a–3(c)(7)) thereof, or an affiliated person of either of the foregoing. For purposes of this paragraph, "affiliated person" means only those persons described in Section 2(a)(3)(C), (D), (E), and (F) of the Investment Company Act of 1940 (15 U.S.C. 80a–2(a)(3)(C), (D), (E), and (F)), assuming for these purposes that a person who would be an investment company but for Section 3(c)(1) (15 U.S.C. 80a–3(c)(1)) or Section 3(c)(7) (15 U.S.C. 80a–3(c)(7)) of the Investment Company Act of 1940 is an investment company; or

(iv) Who is a holder of the issuer's securities, under circumstances in which it is reasonably foreseeable that the person will purchase or sell the issuer's securities on the basis of the information.

(2) Paragraph (a) of this section shall not apply to a disclosure made:

(i) To a person who owes a duty of trust or confidence to the issuer (such as an attorney, investment banker, or accountant);

(ii) To a person who expressly agrees to maintain the disclosed information in confidence;

(iii) To an entity whose primary business is the issuance of credit ratings, provided the information is disclosed solely for the purpose of developing a credit rating and the entity's ratings are publicly available; or

(iv) In connection with a securities offering registered under the Securities Act, other than an offering of the type described in any of Rule 415(a)(1)(i)–(vi) (§ 230.415(a)(1)(i)–(vi) of this chapter).

§ 243.101. Definitions

This section defines certain terms as used in Regulation FD (§§ 243.100–243.103).

(a) *Intentional.* A selective disclosure of material nonpublic information is ''intentional'' when the person making the disclosure either knows, or is reckless in not knowing, that the information he or she is communicating is both material and nonpublic.

(b) *Issuer.* An ''issuer'' subject to this regulation is one that has a class of securities registered under Section 12 of the Securities Exchange Act of 1934 (15 U.S.C. 78*l*), or is required to file reports under Section 15(d) of the Securities Exchange Act of 1934 (15 U.S.C. 78o(d)), including any closed-end investment company (as defined in Section 5(a)(2) of the Investment Company Act of 1940) (15 U.S.C. 80a–5(a)(2)), but not including any other investment company or any foreign government or foreign private issuer, as those terms are defined in Rule 405 under the Securities Act (§ 230.405 of this chapter).

(c) *Person acting on behalf of an issuer.* ''Person acting on behalf of an issuer'' means any senior official of the issuer (or, in the case of a closed-end investment company, a senior official of the issuer's investment adviser), or any other officer, employee, or agent of an issuer who regularly communicates with any person described in § 243.100(b)(1)(i), (ii), or (iii), or with holders of the issuer's securities. An officer, director, employee, or agent of an issuer who discloses material nonpublic information in breach of a duty of trust or confidence to the issuer shall not be considered to be acting on behalf of the issuer.

(d) *Promptly.* ''Promptly'' means as soon as reasonably practicable (but in no event after the later of 24 hours or the commencement of the next day's trading on the New York Stock Exchange) after a senior official of the issuer (or, in the case of a closed-end investment company, a senior official of the issuer's investment adviser) learns that there has been a non-intentional disclosure by the issuer or person acting on behalf of the issuer of information that the senior official knows, or is reckless in not knowing, is both material and nonpublic.

(e) *Public disclosure.* (1) Except as provided in paragraph (e)(2) of this section, an issuer shall make the ''public disclosure'' of information required by § 243.100(a) by furnishing to or filing with the Commission a Form 8–K (17 CFR 249.308) disclosing that information.

(2) An issuer shall be exempt from the requirement to furnish or file a Form 8–K if it instead disseminates the information through another method (or combination of methods) of disclosure that is reasonably designed to provide broad, non-exclusionary distribution of the information to the public.

(f) *Senior official.* ''Senior official'' means any director, executive officer (as defined in § 240.3b–7 of this chapter), investor relations or public relations officer, or other person with similar functions.

(g) *Securities offering.* For purposes of § 243.100(b)(2)(iv):

(1) *Underwritten offerings.* A securities offering that is underwritten commences when the issuer reaches an understanding with the broker-dealer that is to act as managing underwriter and continues until the later of the end of the period during which a dealer must deliver a prospectus or the sale of the securities (unless the offering is sooner terminated);

(2) *Non-underwritten offerings.* A securities offering that is not underwritten:

(i) If covered by Rule 415(a)(1)(x) (§ 230.415(a)(1)(x) of this chapter), commences when the issuer makes its first bona fide offer in a takedown of securities and continues until the later of the end of the period during which each dealer must deliver a prospectus or the sale of the securities in that takedown (unless the takedown is sooner terminated);

(ii) If a business combination as defined in Rule 165(f)(1) (§ 230.165(f)(1) of this chapter), commences when the first public announcement of the transaction is made and continues until the completion of the vote or the expiration of the tender offer, as applicable (unless the transaction is sooner terminated);

(iii) If an offering other than those specified in paragraphs (a) and (b) of this section, commences when the issuer files a registration statement and continues until the later of the end of the period during which each dealer must deliver a prospectus or the sale of the securities (unless the offering is sooner terminated).

§ 243.102. No Effect on Antifraud Liability

No failure to make a public disclosure required solely by § 243.100 shall be deemed to be a violation of Rule 10b–5 (17 CFR 240.10b–5) under the Securities Exchange Act.

§ 243.103. No Effect on Exchange Act Reporting Status

A failure to make a public disclosure required solely by § 243.100 shall not affect whether:

(a) For purposes of Forms S–2 (17 CFR 239.12), S–3 (17 CFR 239.13) and S–8 (17 CFR 239.16b) under the Securities Act, an issuer is deemed to have filed all the material required to be filed pursuant to Section 13 or 15(d) of the Securities Exchange Act of 1934 (15 U.S.C. 78m or 78o(d)) or, where applicable, has made those filings in a timely manner; or

(b) There is adequate current public information about the issuer for purposes of § 230.144(c) of this chapter (Rule 144(c)).

REGULATIONS M, SHO, ATS, AND AC AND CUSTOMER MARGIN REQUIREMENTS FOR SECURITY FUTURES

Rule 100. Preliminary Note; Definitions

(a) *Preliminary note:* Any transaction or series of transactions, whether or not effected pursuant to the provisions of Regulation M (§§ 242.100–242.105 of this chapter), remain subject to the antifraud and antimanipulation provisions of the securities laws, including, without limitation, Section 17(a) of the Securities Act of 1933 [15 U.S.C. 77q(a)] and Sections 9, 10(b), and 15(c) of the Securities Exchange Act of 1934 [15 U.S.C. 78i, 78j(b), and 78o(c)].

(b) For purposes of Regulation M (§§ 242.100 through 242.105 of this chapter) the following definitions shall apply:

ADTV means the worldwide average daily trading volume during the two full calendar months immediately preceding, or any 60 consecutive calendar days ending within the 10 calendar days preceding, the filing of the registration statement; or, if there is no registration statement or if the distribution involves the sale of securities on a delayed basis pursuant to § 230.415 of this chapter, two full calendar months immediately preceding, or any consecutive 60 calendar days ending within the 10 calendar days preceding, the determination of the offering price.

Affiliated purchaser means:

(1) A person acting, directly or indirectly, in concert with a distribution participant, issuer, or selling security holder in connec-

tion with the acquisition or distribution of any covered security; or

(2) An affiliate, which may be a separately identifiable department or division of a distribution participant, issuer, or selling security holder, that, directly or indirectly, controls the purchases of any covered security by a distribution participant, issuer, or selling security holder, whose purchases are controlled by any such person, or whose purchases are under common control with any such person; or

(3) An affiliate, which may be a separately identifiable department or division of a distribution participant, issuer, or selling security holder, that regularly purchases securities for its own account or for the account of others, or that recommends or exercises investment discretion with respect to the purchase or sale of securities; *Provided, however,* That this paragraph (3) shall not apply to such affiliate if the following conditions are satisfied:

(i) The distribution participant, issuer, or selling security holder:

(A) Maintains and enforces written policies and procedures reasonably designed to prevent the flow of information to or from the affiliate that might result in a violation of §§ 242.101, 242.102, and 242.104; and

(B) Obtains an annual, independent assessment of the operation of such policies and procedures; and

(ii) The affiliate has no officers (or persons performing similar functions) or employees (other than clerical, ministerial, or support personnel) in common with the distribution participant, issuer, or selling security holder that direct, effect, or recommend transactions in securities; and

(iii) The affiliate does not, during the applicable restricted period, act as a market maker (other than as a specialist in compliance with the rules of a national securities exchange), or engage, as a broker or a dealer, in solicited transactions or proprietary trading, in covered securities.

Agent independent of the issuer means a trustee or other person who is independent of the issuer. The agent shall be deemed to be independent of the issuer only if:

(1) The agent is not an affiliate of the issuer; and

(2) Neither the issuer nor any affiliate of the issuer exercises any direct or indirect control or influence over the prices or amounts of the securities to be purchased, the timing of, or the manner in which, the securities are to be purchased, or the selection of a broker or dealer (other than the independent agent itself) through which purchases may be executed; *Provided, however,* That the issuer or its affiliate will not be deemed to have such control or influence solely because it revises not more than once in any three-month period the source of the shares to fund the plan, the basis for determining the amount of its contributions to a plan, or the basis for determining the frequency of its allocations to a plan, or any formula specified in a plan that determines the amount or timing of securities to be purchased by the agent.

Asset-backed security has the meaning contained in § 229.1101 of this chapter.

At-the-market offering means an offering of securities at other than a fixed price.

Business day refers to a 24 hour period determined with reference to the principal market for the securities to be distributed, and that includes a complete trading session for that market.

Completion of participation in a distribution. Securities acquired in the distribution for investment by any person participating in a distribution, or any affiliated purchaser of such person, shall be deemed to be distributed. A person shall be deemed to have completed its participation in a distribution as follows:

(1) An issuer or selling security holder, when the distribution is completed;

(2) An underwriter, when such person's participation has been distributed, including all other securities of the same class that are acquired in connection with the distribution, and any stabilization arrangements and trading restrictions in connection with the distribution have been terminated; *Provided, however,* That an underwriter's participation will not be deemed to have been completed if a syndicate overallotment option is exercised in an amount that exceeds the net syndicate short position at the time of such exercise; and

(3) Any other person participating in the distribution, when such person's participation has been distributed.

Covered security means any security that is the subject of a distribution, or any reference security.

Current exchange rate means the current rate of exchange between two currencies, which is obtained from at least one independent entity that provides or disseminates foreign exchange quotations in the ordinary course of its business.

Distribution means an offering of securities, whether or not subject to registration under the Securities Act, that is distinguished from ordinary trading transactions by the magnitude of the offering and the presence of special selling efforts and selling methods.

Distribution participant means an underwriter, prospective underwriter, broker, dealer, or other person who has agreed to participate or is participating in a distribution.

Electronic communications network has the meaning contained in § 240.11Ac1–1(a)(8) of this chapter.

Employee has the meaning contained in Form S–8 (§ 239.16b of this chapter) relating to employee benefit plans.

Exchange Act means the Securities Exchange Act of 1934 (15 U.S.C. 78a *et seq.*).

Independent bid means a bid by a person who is not a distribution participant, issuer, selling security holder, or affiliated purchaser.

NASD means the National Association of Securities Dealers, Inc. or any of its subsidiaries.

Nasdaq means the Nasdaq system as defined in § 240.11Ac1–2(a)(3) of this chapter.

Nasdaq security means a security that is authorized for quotation on Nasdaq, and such authorization is not suspended, terminated, or prohibited.

Net purchases means the amount by which a passive market maker's purchases exceed its sales.

Offering price means the price at which the security is to be or is being distributed.

Passive market maker means a market maker that effects bids or purchases in accordance with the provisions of § 242.103.

Penalty bid means an arrangement that permits the managing underwriter to reclaim a selling concession from a syndicate member in connection with an offering when the securities originally sold by the syndicate member are purchased in syndicate covering transactions.

Plan means any bonus, profit-sharing, pension, retirement, thrift, savings, incentive, stock purchase, stock option, stock ownership, stock appreciation, dividend reinvestment, or similar plan; or any dividend or interest reinvestment plan or employee benefit plan as defined in § 230.405 of this chapter.

Principal market means the single securities market with the largest aggregate reported trading volume for the class of securities during the 12 full calendar months immediately preceding the filing of the registration statement; or, if there is no registration statement or if the distribution involves the sale of securities on a delayed basis pursuant to § 230.415 of this chapter, during the 12 full calendar months immediately preceding the determination of the offering price. For the purpose of determining the aggregate trading volume in a security, the trading volume of depositary shares representing such security shall be included, and shall be multiplied by the multiple or fraction of the security represented by the depositary share. For purposes of this paragraph, depositary share means a security, evidenced by a depositary receipt, that represents another security, or a multiple or fraction thereof, deposited with a depositary.

Prospective underwriter means a person:

(1) Who has submitted a bid to the issuer or selling security holder, and who knows or is reasonably certain that such bid will be accepted, whether or not the terms and conditions of the underwriting have been agreed upon; or

(2) Who has reached, or is reasonably certain to reach, an understanding with the issuer or selling security holder, or managing underwriter that such person will become an underwriter, whether or not the terms and conditions of the underwriting have been agreed upon.

Public float value shall be determined in the manner set forth on the front page of Form 10–K (§ 249.310 of this chapter), even if the issuer of such securities is not required to file Form 10–K, relating to the aggregate market value of common equity securities held by non-affiliates of the issuer.

Reference period means the two full calendar months immediately preceding the filing of the registration statement or, if there is no registration statement or if the distribution involves the sale of securities on a delayed basis pursuant to § 230.415 of this chapter, the two full calendar months immediately preceding the determination of the offering price.

Reference security means a security into which a security that is the subject of a distribution ("subject security") may be converted, exchanged, or exercised or which, under the terms of the subject security, may in whole or in significant part determine the value of the subject security.

Restricted period means:

(1) For any security with an ADTV value of $100,000 or more of an issuer whose common equity securities have a public float value of $25 million or more, the period beginning on the later of one business day prior to the determination of the offering price or such time that a person becomes a distribution participant, and ending upon such person's completion of participation in the distribution; and

(2) For all other securities, the period beginning on the later of five business days prior to the determination of the offering price or such time that a person becomes a distribution participant, and ending upon such person's completion of participation in the distribution.

(3) In the case of a distribution involving a merger, acquisition, or exchange offer, the period beginning on the day proxy solicitation or offering materials are first disseminated to security holders, and ending upon the completion of the distribution.

Securities Act means the Securities Act of 1933 (15 U.S.C. 77a *et seq.*).

Selling security holder means any person on whose behalf a distribution is made, other than an issuer.

Stabilize or stabilizing means the placing of any bid, or the effecting of any purchase, for the purpose of pegging, fixing, or maintaining the price of a security.

Syndicate covering transaction means the placing of any bid or the effecting of any purchase on behalf of the sole distributor or the underwriting syndicate or group to reduce a short position created in connection with the offering.

30% ADTV limitation means 30 percent of the market maker's ADTV in a covered security during the reference period, as obtained from the NASD.

Underwriter means a person who has agreed with an issuer or selling security holder:

(1) To purchase securities for distribution; or

(2) To distribute securities for or on behalf of such issuer or selling security holder; or

(3) To manage or supervise a distribution of securities for or on behalf of such issuer or selling security holder.

Rule 101. Activities by Distribution Participants

(a) *Unlawful Activity.* In connection with a distribution of securities, it shall be unlawful for a distribution participant or an affiliated purchaser of such person, directly or indirectly, to bid for, purchase, or attempt to induce any person to bid for or purchase, a covered security during the applicable restricted period; *Provided, however,* That if a distribution participant or affiliated purchaser is the issuer or selling security holder of the securities subject to the distribution, such person shall be subject to the provisions of § 242.102, rather than this section.

(b) *Excepted Activity.* The following activities shall not be prohibited by paragraph (a) of this section:

(1) *Research.* The publication or dissemination of any information, opinion, or recommendation, if the conditions of § 230.138 or 230.139 of this chapter are met; or

(2) *Transactions complying with certain other sections.* Transactions complying with § 242.103 or 242.104; or

(3) *Odd-lot transactions.* Transactions in odd-lots; or transactions to offset odd-lots in connection with an odd-lot tender offer conducted pursuant to § 240.13e–4(h)(5) of this chapter; or

(4) *Exercises of securities.* The exercise of any option, warrant, right, or any conversion privilege set forth in the instrument governing a security; or

(5) *Unsolicited transactions.* Unsolicited brokerage transactions; or unsolicited purchases that are not effected from or through a broker or dealer, on a securities exchange, or through an inter-dealer quotation system or electronic communications network; or

(6) *Basket transactions.* (i) Bids or purchases, in the ordinary course of business, in connection with a basket of 20 or more securities in which a covered security does not comprise more than 5% of the value of the basket purchased; or

(ii) Adjustments to such a basket in the ordinary course of business as a result of a change in the composition of a standardized index; or

(7) *De minimis transactions.* Purchases during the restricted period, other than by a passive market maker, that total less than 2% of the ADTV of the security being purchased, or unaccepted bids; *Provided, however,* That the person making such bid or purchase has maintained and enforces written policies and procedures reasonably designed to achieve compliance with the other provisions of this section; or

(8) *Transactions in connection with a distribution.* Transactions among distribution participants in connection with a distribution, and purchases of securities from an issuer or selling security holder in connection with a distribution, that are not effected on a securities exchange, or through an inter-dealer quotation system or electronic communications network; or

(9) *Offers to sell or the solicitation of offers to buy.* Offers to sell or the solicitation of offers to buy the securities being distributed (including securities acquired in stabilizing), or securities offered as principal by the person making such offer or solicitation; or

(10) *Transactions in Rule 144A securities.* Transactions in securities eligible for resale under § 230.144A(d)(3) of this chapter, or any reference security, if the Rule 144A securities are offered or sold in the United States solely to:

(i) Qualified institutional buyers, as defined in § 230.144A(a)(1) of this chapter, or to offerees or purchasers that the seller and any person acting on behalf of the seller reasonably believes are qualified institutional buyers, in transactions exempt from registration under Section 4(2) of the Securities Act (15 U.S.C. 77d(2)) or § 230.144A or 230.501 through 230.508 of this chapter; or

(ii) Persons not deemed to be "U.S. persons" for purposes of § 230.902(*o*)(2) or 230.902(*o*)(7) of this chapter, during a distribution qualifying under paragraph (b)(10)(i) of this section.

(c) *Excepted Securities.* The provisions of this section shall not apply to any of the following securities:

(1) *Actively-traded securities.* Securities that have an ADTV value of at least $1 million and are issued by an issuer whose common equity securities have a public float value of at least $150 million; *Provided, however,* That such securities are not issued by the distribution participant or an affiliate of the distribution participant; or

(2) *Investment grade nonconvertible and asset-backed securities.* Nonconvertible debt securities, nonconvertible preferred securities, and asset-backed securities, that are rated by at least one nationally recognized statistical rating organization, as that term is used in § 240.15c3–1 of this chapter, in one of its generic rating categories that signifies investment grade; or

(3) *Exempted securities.* "Exempted securities" as defined in Section 3(a)(12) of the Exchange Act (15 U.S.C. 78c(a)(12)); or

(4) *Face-amount certificates or securities issued by an open-end management investment company or unit investment trust.* Face-amount certificates issued by a face-amount certificate company, or redeemable securities issued by an open-end management investment company or a unit investment trust. Any terms used in this paragraph (c)(4) that are defined in the Investment Company Act of 1940 (15 U.S.C. 80a–1 *et seq.*) shall have the meanings specified in such Act.

(d) *Exemptive Authority.* Upon written application or upon its own motion, the Commission may grant an exemption from the provisions of this section, either unconditionally or on specified terms and conditions, to any transaction or class of transactions, or to any security or class of securities.

Rule 102. Activities by Issuers and Selling Security Holders During a Distribution

(a) *Unlawful Activity.* In connection with a distribution of securities effected by or on behalf of an issuer or selling security holder, it shall be unlawful for such person, or any affiliated purchaser of such person, directly or indirectly, to bid for, purchase, or attempt to induce any person to bid for or purchase, a covered security during the applicable restricted period; *Except That* if an affiliated purchaser is a distribution participant, such affiliated purchaser may comply with § 242.101, rather than this section.

(b) *Excepted Activity.* The following activities shall not be prohibited by paragraph (a) of this section:

(1) *Odd-lot transactions.* Transactions in odd-lots, or transactions to offset odd-lots in connection with an odd-lot tender offer conducted pursuant to § 240.13e–4(h)(5) of this chapter; or

(2) *Transactions by closed-end investment companies.* (i) Transactions complying with § 270.23c–3 of this chapter; or

(ii) Periodic tender offers of securities, at net asset value, conducted pursuant to § 240.13e–4 of this chapter by a closed-end investment company that engages in a continuous offering of its securities pursuant to § 230.415 of this chapter; *Provided, however,* That such securities are not traded on a securities exchange or through an inter-dealer quotation system or electronic communications network; or

(3) *Redemptions by commodity pools or limited partnerships.* Redemptions by commodity pools or limited partnerships, at a price based on net asset value, which are effected in accordance with the terms and conditions of the instruments governing the securities; *Provided, however,* That such securities are not traded on a securities exchange; or through an inter-dealer quotation system or electronic communications network; or

(4) *Exercises of securities.* The exercise of any option, warrant, right, or any conversion privilege set forth in the instrument governing a security; or

(5) *Offers to sell or the solicitation of offers to buy.* Offers to sell or the solicitation of offers to buy the securities being distributed; or

(6) *Unsolicited purchases.* Unsolicited purchases that are not effected from or through a broker or dealer, on a securities exchange, or through an inter-dealer quotation system or electronic communications network; or

(7) *Transactions in Rule 144A securities.* Transactions in securities eligible for resale under § 230.144A(d)(3) of this chapter, or any reference security, if the Rule 144A securities are offered or sold in the United States solely to:

(i) Qualified institutional buyers, as defined in § 230.144A(a)(1) of this chapter, or to offerees or purchasers that the seller and any person acting on behalf of the seller reasonably believes are qualified institutional buyers, in transactions exempt from registration under Section 4(2) of the Securities Act (15 U.S.C. 77d(2)) or § 230.144A or 230.501 through 230.508 of this chapter; or

(ii) Persons not deemed to be "U.S. persons" for purposes of § 230.902(*o*)(2) or 230.902(*o*)(7) of this chapter, during a distribution qualifying under paragraph (b)(7)(i) of this section.

(c) *Plans.*—(1) Paragraph (a) of this section shall not apply to distributions of securities pursuant to a plan which are made:

(i) Solely to employees or security holders of an issuer or its subsidiaries, or to a trustee or other person acquiring such securities for the accounts of such persons; or

(ii) To persons other than employees or security holders, if bids for or purchases of securities pursuant to the plan are effected solely by an agent independent of the issuer and the securities are from a source other than the issuer or an affiliated purchaser of the issuer.

(2) Bids for or purchases of any security made or effected by or for a plan shall be deemed to be a purchase by the issuer unless the bid is made, or the purchase is effected, by an agent independent of the issuer.

(d) *Excepted Securities.* The provisions of this section shall not apply to any of the following securities:

(1) *Actively-traded reference securities.* Reference securities with an ADTV value of at least $1 million that are issued by an issuer whose common equity securities have a public float value of at least $150 million; *Provided, however,* That such securities are not issued by the issuer, or any affiliate of the issuer, of the security in distribution.

(2) *Investment grade nonconvertible and asset-backed securities.* Nonconvertible debt securities, nonconvertible preferred securities, and asset-backed securities, that are rated by at least one nationally recognized statistical rating organization, as that term is used in § 240.15c3–1 of this chapter, in one of its generic rating categories that signifies investment grade; or

(3) *Exempted securities.* "Exempted securities" as defined in Section 3(a)(12) of the Exchange Act (15 U.S.C. 78c(a)(12)); or

(4) *Face-amount certificates or securities issued by an open-end management invest-*

ment company or unit investment trust. Face-amount certificates issued by a face-amount certificate company, or redeemable securities issued by an open-end management investment company or a unit investment trust. Any terms used in this paragraph (d)(4) that are defined in the Investment Company Act of 1940 (15 U.S.C. 80a–1 *et seq.*) shall have the meanings specified in such Act.

(e) *Exemptive Authority.* Upon written application or upon its own motion, the Commission may grant an exemption from the provisions of this section, either unconditionally or on specified terms and conditions, to any transaction or class of transactions, or to any security or class of securities.

Rule 103. Nasdaq Passive Market Making

(a) *Scope of Section.* This section permits broker-dealers to engage in market making transactions in covered securities that are Nasdaq securities without violating the provisions of § 242.101; *Except That* this section shall not apply to any security for which a stabilizing bid subject to § 242.104 is in effect, or during any at-the-market offering or best efforts offering.

(b) *Conditions to be Met.*

(1) *General limitations.* A passive market maker must effect all transactions in the capacity of a registered market maker on Nasdaq. A passive market maker shall not bid for or purchase a covered security at a price that exceeds the highest independent bid for the covered security at the time of the transaction, except as permitted by paragraph (b)(3) of this section or required by a rule promulgated by the Commission or the NASD governing the handling of customer orders.

(2) *Purchase limitation.* On each day of the restricted period, a passive market maker's net purchases shall not exceed the greater of its 30% ADTV limitation or 200 shares (together, "purchase limitation"); *Provided, however,* That a passive market maker may purchase all of the securities that are part of a single order that, when executed, results in its purchase limitation being equalled or exceeded. If a passive market maker's net purchases equal or exceed its purchase limitation, it shall withdraw promptly its quotations from Nasdaq. If a passive market maker withdraws its quotations pursuant to this paragraph, it may not effect any bid or purchase in the covered security for the remainder of that day, irrespective of any later sales during that day, unless otherwise permitted by § 242.101.

(3) *Requirement to lower the bid.* If all independent bids for a covered security are reduced to a price below the passive market maker's bid, the passive market maker must lower its bid promptly to a level not higher than the then highest independent bid; *Provided, however,* That a passive market maker may continue to bid and effect purchases at its bid at a price exceeding the then highest independent bid until the passive market maker purchases an aggregate amount of the covered security that equals or, through the purchase of all securities that are part of a single order, exceeds the lesser of two times the minimum quotation size for the security, as determined by NASD rules, or the passive market maker's remaining purchasing capacity under paragraph (b)(2) of this section.

(4) *Limitation on displayed size.* At all times, the passive market maker's displayed bid size may not exceed the lesser of the minimum quotation size for the covered security, or the passive market maker's remaining purchasing capacity under paragraph (b)(2) of this section; *Provided, however,* That a passive market maker whose purchasing capacity at any time is between one and 99 shares may display a bid size of 100 shares.

(5) *Identification of a passive market making bid.* The bid displayed by a passive market maker shall be designated as such.

(6) *Notification and reporting to the NASD.* A passive market maker shall notify the NASD in advance of its intention to engage in passive market making, and shall submit to the NASD information regarding passive market making purchases, in such form as the NASD shall prescribe.

(7) *Prospectus disclosure:* The prospectus for any registered offering in which any passive market maker intends to effect transactions in any covered security shall contain the information required in §§ 228.502, 228.508, 229.502, and 229.508 of this chapter.

(c) *Transactions at Prices Resulting from Unlawful Activity.* No transaction shall be made at a price that the passive market maker knows or has reason to know is the result of activity that is fraudulent, manipulative, or deceptive under the securities laws, or any rule or regulation thereunder.

Rule 104. Stabilizing and Other Activities in Connection with an Offering

(a) *Unlawful Activity.* It shall be unlawful for any person, directly or indirectly, to stabilize, to effect any syndicate covering transaction, or to impose a penalty bid, in connection with an offering of any security, in contravention of the provisions of this section. No stabilizing shall be effected at a price that the person stabilizing knows or has reason to know is in contravention of this section, or is the result of activity that is fraudulent, manipulative, or deceptive under the securities laws, or any rule or regulation thereunder.

(b) *Purpose.* Stabilizing is prohibited except for the purpose of preventing or retarding a decline in the market price of a security.

(c) *Priority.* To the extent permitted or required by the market where stabilizing occurs, any person stabilizing shall grant priority to any independent bid at the same price irrespective of the size of such independent bid at the time that it is entered.

(d) *Control of Stabilizing.* No sole distributor or syndicate or group stabilizing the price of a security or any member or members of such syndicate or group shall maintain more than one stabilizing bid in any one market at the same price at the same time.

(e) *At-the-Market Offerings.* Stabilizing is prohibited in an at-the-market offering.

(f) *Stabilizing Levels.—(1) Maximum stabilizing bid.* Notwithstanding the other provisions of this paragraph (f), no stabilizing shall be made at a price higher than the lower of the offering price or the stabilizing bid for the security in the principal market (or, if the principal market is closed, the stabilizing bid in the principal market at its previous close).

(2) *Initiating stabilizing.—*

(i) *Initiating stabilizing when the principal market is open.* After the opening of quotations for the security in the principal market, stabilizing may be initiated in any market at a price no higher than the last independent transaction price for the security in the principal market if the security has traded in the principal market on the day stabilizing is initiated or on the most recent prior day of trading in the principal market and the current asked price in the principal market is equal to or greater than the last independent transaction price. If both conditions of the preceding sentence are not satisfied, stabilizing may be initiated in any market after the opening of quotations in the principal market at a price no higher than the highest current independent bid for the security in the principal market.

(ii) *Initiating stabilizing when the principal market is closed.*

(A) When the principal market for the security is closed, but immediately before the opening of quotations for the security in the market where stabilizing will be initiated, stabilizing may be initiated at a price no higher than the lower of:

(1) The price at which stabilizing could have been initiated in the prin-

cipal market for the security at its previous close; or

(2) The most recent price at which an independent transaction in the security has been effected in any market since the close of the principal market, if the person stabilizing knows or has reason to know of such transaction.

(B) When the principal market for the security is closed, but after the opening of quotations in the market where stabilizing will be initiated, stabilizing may be initiated at a price no higher than the lower of:

(1) The price at which stabilization could have been initiated in the principal market for the security at its previous close; or

(2) The last independent transaction price for the security in that market if the security has traded in that market on the day stabilizing is initiated or on the last preceding business day and the current asked price in that market is equal to or greater than the last independent transaction price. If both conditions of the preceding sentence are not satisfied, under this paragraph (f)(2)(ii)(B)(*2*), stabilizing may be initiated at a price no higher than the highest current independent bid for the security in that market.

(iii) *Initiating stabilizing when there is no market for the security or before the offering price is determined.* If no *bona fide* market for the security being distributed exists at the time stabilizing is initiated, no stabilizing shall be initiated at a price in excess of the offering price. If stabilizing is initiated before the offering price is determined, then stabilizing may be continued after determination of the offering price at the price at which stabilizing then could be initiated.

(3) *Maintaining or carrying over a stabilizing bid.* A stabilizing bid initiated pursuant to paragraph (f)(2) of this section, which has not been discontinued, may be maintained, or carried over into another market, irrespective of changes in the independent bids or transaction prices for the security.

(4) *Increasing or reducing a stabilizing bid.* A stabilizing bid may be increased to a price no higher than the highest current independent bid for the security in the principal market if the principal market is open, or, if the principal market is closed, to a price no higher than the highest independent bid in the principal market at the previous close thereof. A stabilizing bid may be reduced, or carried over into another market at a reduced price, irrespective of changes in the independent bids or transaction prices for the security. If stabilizing is discontinued, it shall not be resumed at a price higher than the price at which stabilizing then could be initiated.

(5) *Initiating, maintaining, or adjusting a stabilizing bid to reflect the current exchange rate.* If a stabilizing bid is expressed in a currency other than the currency of the principal market for the security, such bid may be initiated, maintained, or adjusted to reflect the current exchange rate, consistent with the provisions of this section. If, in initiating, maintaining, or adjusting a stabilizing bid pursuant to this paragraph (f)(5), the bid would be at or below the midpoint between two trading differentials, such stabilizing bid shall be adjusted downward to the lower differential.

(6) *Adjustments to stabilizing bid.* If a security goes ex-dividend, ex-rights, or ex-distribution, the stabilizing bid shall be reduced by an amount equal to the value of the dividend, right, or distribution. If, in reducing a stabilizing bid pursuant to this paragraph (f)(6), the bid would be at or below the midpoint between two trading differentials, such stabilizing bid shall be adjusted downward to the lower differential.

(7) *Stabilizing of components.* When two or more securities are being offered as a unit, the component securities shall not be stabilized at prices the sum of which exceeds the then permissible stabilizing price for the unit.

(8) *Special prices.* Any stabilizing price that otherwise meets the requirements of this section need not be adjusted to reflect special prices available to any group or class of persons (including employees or holders of warrants or rights).

(g) *Offerings with no U.S. Stabilizing Activities*—

(1) Stabilizing to facilitate an offering of a security in the United States shall not be deemed to be in violation of this section if all of the following conditions are satisfied:

(i) No stabilizing is made in the United States;

(ii) Stabilizing outside the United States is made in a jurisdiction with statutory or regulatory provisions governing stabilizing that are comparable to the provisions of this section; and

(iii) No stabilizing is made at a price above the offering price in the United States, except as permitted by paragraph (f)(5) of this section.

(2) For purposes of this paragraph (g), the Commission by rule, regulation, or order may determine whether a foreign statute or regulation is comparable to this section considering, among other things, whether such foreign statute or regulation: specifies appropriate purposes for which stabilizing is permitted; provides for disclosure and control of stabilizing activities; places limitations on stabilizing levels; requires appropriate recordkeeping; provides other protections comparable to the provisions of this section; and whether procedures exist to enable the Commission to obtain information concerning any foreign stabilizing transactions.

(h) *Disclosure and Notification*—(1) Any person displaying or transmitting a bid that such person knows is for the purpose of stabilizing shall provide prior notice to the market on which such stabilizing will be effected, and shall disclose its purpose to the person with whom the bid is entered.

(2) Any person effecting a syndicate covering transaction or imposing a penalty bid shall provide prior notice to the self-regulatory organization with direct authority over the principal market in the United States for the security for which the syndicate covering transaction is effected or the penalty bid is imposed.

(3) Any person subject to this section who sells to, or purchases for the account of, any person any security where the price of such security may be or has been stabilized, shall send to the purchaser at or before the completion of the transaction, a prospectus, offering circular, confirmation, or other document containing a statement similar to that comprising the statement provided for in Item 502(d) of Regulation S–B (§ 228.502(d) of this chapter) or Item 502(d) of Regulation S–K (§ 229.502(d) of this chapter).

(i) *Recordkeeping Requirements.* A person subject to this section shall keep the information and make the notification required by § 240.17a–2 of this chapter.

(j) *Excepted Securities.* The provisions of this section shall not apply to:

(1) *Exempted Securities.* "Exempted securities," as defined in Section 3(a)(12) of the Exchange Act (15 U.S.C. 78c(a)(12)); or

(2) *Transactions of Rule 144A securities.* Transactions in securities eligible for resale under § 230.144A(d)(3) of this chapter, if such securities are offered or sold in the United States solely to:

(i) Qualified institutional buyers, as defined in § 230.144A(a)(1) of this chapter, or to offerees or purchasers that the seller and any person acting on behalf of the seller reasonably believes are qualified institutional buyers, in a transaction exempt from registration under Section 4(2) of the Securities Act (15 U.S.C. 77d(2)) or § 230.144A or 230.501 through 230.508 of this chapter; or

(ii) Persons not deemed to be "U.S. persons" for purposes of § 230.902(*o*)(2) or 230.902(*o*)(7) of this chapter, during a distribution qualifying under paragraph (j)(2)(i) of this section.

(k) *Exemptive Authority.* Upon written application or upon its own motion, the Commission may grant an exemption from the provisions of this section, either unconditionally or on specified terms and conditions, to any transaction or class of transactions, or to any security or class of securities.

Rule 105. Short Selling in Connection with a Public Offering

(a) *Unlawful Activity.* In connection with an offering of securities for cash pursuant to a registration statement or a notification on Form 1–A (§ 239.90 of this chapter) filed under the Securities Act, it shall be unlawful for any person to cover a short sale with offered securities purchased from an underwriter or broker or dealer participating in the offering, if such short sale occurred during the shorter of:

(1) The period beginning five business days before the pricing of the offered securities and ending with such pricing; or

(2) The period beginning with the initial filing of such registration statement or notification on Form 1–A and ending with the pricing.

(b) *Excepted Offerings.* This section shall not apply to offerings that are not conducted on a firm commitment basis.

(c) *Exemptive Authority.* Upon written application or upon its own motion, the Commission may grant an exemption from the provisions of this section, either unconditionally or on specified terms and conditions, to any transaction or class of transactions, or to any security or class of securities by the Commission.

REGULATION SHO—REGULATION OF SHORT SALES

Rule 200. Definition of "Short Sale" and Marking Requirements

(a) The term *short sale* shall mean any sale of a security which the seller does not own or any sale which is consummated by the delivery of a security borrowed by, or for the account of, the seller.

(b) A person shall be deemed to own a security if:

(1) The person or his agent has title to it; or

(2) The person has purchased, or has entered into an unconditional contract, binding on both parties thereto, to purchase it, but has not yet received it; or

(3) The person owns a security convertible into or exchangeable for it and has tendered such security for conversion or exchange; or

(4) The person has an option to purchase or acquire it and has exercised such option; or

(5) The person has rights or warrants to subscribe to it and has exercised such rights or warrants; or

(6) The person holds a security futures contract to purchase it and has received notice that the position will be physically settled and is irrevocably bound to receive the underlying security.

(c) A person shall be deemed to own securities only to the extent that he has a net long position in such securities.

(d) A broker or dealer shall be deemed to own a security, even if it is not net long, if:

(1) The broker or dealer acquired that security while acting in the capacity of a block positioner; and

(2) If and to the extent that the broker or dealer's short position in the security is the subject of offsetting positions created in the course of bona fide arbitrage, risk arbitrage, or bona fide hedge activities.

(e) A broker-dealer shall be deemed to own a security even if it is not net long, if:

(1) The broker-dealer is unwinding index arbitrage position involving a long basket of stock and one or more short index futures traded on a board of trade or one or more standardized options contracts as defined in 17 CFR 240.9b§ 1(a)(4); and

(2) If and to the extent that the broker-dealer's short position in the security is the subject of offsetting positions created and maintained in the course of bona-fide arbitrage, risk arbitrage, or bona fide hedge activities; and

(3) The sale does not occur during a period commencing at the time that the Dow Jones Industrial Average has declined by two percent or more from its closing value on the previous day and terminating upon the establishment of the closing value of the Dow Jones Industrial Average on the next succeeding trading day.

(f) In order to determine its net position, a broker or dealer shall aggregate all of its positions in a security unless it qualifies for independent trading unit aggregation, in which case each independent trading unit shall aggregate all of its positions in a security to determine its net position. Independent trading unit aggregation is available only if:

(1) The broker or dealer has a written plan of organization that identifies each aggregation unit, specifies its trading objective(s), and supports its independent identity;

(2) Each aggregation unit within the firm determines, at the time of each sale, its net position for every security that it trades;

(3) All traders in an aggregation unit pursue only the particular trading objective(s) or strategy(s) of that aggregation unit and do not coordinate that strategy with any other aggregation unit; and

(4) Individual traders are assigned to only one aggregation unit at any time.

(g) A broker or dealer must mark all sell orders of any equity security as "long," "short," or "short exempt."

(1) An order to sell shall be marked "long" only if the seller is deemed to own the security being sold pursuant to paragraphs (a) through (f) of this section and either:

(i) The security to be delivered is in the physical possession or control of the broker or dealer; or

(ii) It is reasonably expected that the security will be in the physical possession or control of the broker or dealer no later than the settlement of the transaction.

(2) A short sale order shall be marked "short exempt" if the seller is relying on an exception from the tick test of 17 CFR 240.10a–1, or any short sale price test of any exchange or national securities association.

(h) Upon written application or upon its own motion, the Commission may grant an exemption from the provisions of this section, either unconditionally or on specified terms and conditions, to any transaction or class of transactions, or to any security or class of securities, or to any person or class of persons.

Rule 201. Price Test [Reserved]

Rule 202T. Temporary Short Sale Rule Suspension

(a) The provisions of 17 CFR 240.10a–1(a) and any short sale price test for any exchange or national securities association shall not apply to short sales in such securities, or during such time periods, as the Commission designates by order as necessary or appropriate in the public interest and consistent with the protection of investors after giving due consideration to the security's liquidity, volatility, market depth and trading market. All other provisions of 17 CFR 240.10a–1, § 242.200, and § 242.203 shall remain in effect.

(b) No self-regulatory organization shall have a rule that is not in conformity with or conflicts with any order issued pursuant to paragraph (a) of this section.

(c) This temporary section will expire on August 6, 2007.

Rule 203. Borrowing and Delivery Requirements

(a) *Long sales.* (1) If a broker or dealer knows or has reasonable grounds to believe that the sale of an equity security was or will be effected pursuant to an order marked "long," such broker or dealer shall not lend or arrange for the loan of any security for delivery to the purchaser's broker after the sale, or fail to deliver a security on the date delivery is due.

(2) The provisions of paragraph (a)(1) of this section shall not apply:

(i) To the loan of any security by a broker or dealer through the medium of a loan to another broker or dealer;

(ii) If the broker or dealer knows, or has been reasonably informed by the seller, that the seller owns the security, and that the seller would deliver the security to the broker or dealer prior to the scheduled settlement of the transaction, but the seller failed to do so; or

(iii) If, prior to any loan or arrangement to loan any security for delivery, or failure to deliver, a national securities exchange, in the case of a sale effected thereon, or a national securities association, in the case of a sale not effected on an exchange, finds:

(A) That such sale resulted from a mistake made in good faith;

(B) That due diligence was used to ascertain that the circumstances specified in § 242.200(g) existed; and

(C) Either that the condition of the market at the time the mistake was discovered was such that undue hardship would result from covering the transaction by a "purchase for cash" or that the mistake was made by the seller's broker and the sale was at a permissible price under any applicable short sale price test.

(b) Short sales.

(1) A broker or dealer may not accept a short sale order in an equity security from another person, or effect a short sale in an equity security for its own account, unless the broker or dealer has:

(i) Borrowed the security, or entered into a bona-fide arrangement to borrow the security; or

(ii) Reasonable grounds to believe that the security can be borrowed so that it can be delivered on the date delivery is due; and

(iii) Documented compliance with this paragraph (b)(1).

(2) The provisions of paragraph (b)(1) of this section shall not apply to:

(i) A broker or dealer that has accepted a short sale order from another registered broker or dealer that is required to comply with paragraph (b)(1) of this section, unless the broker or dealer relying on this exception contractually undertook responsibility for compliance with paragraph (b)(1) of this section;

(ii) Any sale of a security that a person is deemed to own pursuant to § 242.200, provided that the broker or dealer has been reasonably informed that the person intends to deliver such security as soon as all restrictions on delivery have been removed. If the person has not delivered such security within 35 days after the trade date, the broker-dealer that effected the sale must borrow securities or close out the short position by purchasing securities of like kind and quantity;

(iii) Short sales effected by a market maker in connection with bona-fide market making activities in the security for which this exception is claimed; and

(iv) Transactions in security futures.

(3) If a participant of a registered clearing agency has a fail to deliver position at a registered clearing agency in a threshold security for thirteen consecutive settlement days, the participant shall immediately thereafter close out the fail to deliver position by purchasing securities of like kind and quantity:

(i) The provisions of this paragraph (b)(3) shall not apply to the amount of the fail to deliver position that the participant of a registered clearing agency had at a registered clearing agency on the settlement day immediately preceding the day that the security became a threshold security; provided, however, that if the fail to deliver position at the clearing agency is subsequently reduced below the fail to deliver position on the settlement day immediately preceding the day that the security became a threshold security, then the fail to deliver position excepted by this paragraph (b)(3)(i) shall be the lesser amount;

(ii) The provisions of this paragraph (b)(3) shall not apply to the amount of the fail to deliver position in the threshold security that is attributed to short sales by a registered options market maker, if and to the extent that the short sales are effected by the registered options market maker to establish or maintain a hedge on options positions that were created before the security became a threshold security;

(iii) If a participant of a registered clearing agency has a fail to deliver position at a registered clearing agency in a threshold security for thirteen consecutive settlement days, the participant and any broker or dealer for which it clears transactions, including any market maker that would otherwise be entitled to rely on the exception provided in paragraph (b)(2)(iii) of this section, may not accept a short sale order in the threshold security from another person, or effect a short sale in the threshold security for its own account, without borrowing the security or entering into a bona-fide arrangement to borrow the security, until the participant closes out the fail to deliver position by purchasing securities of like kind and quantity;

(iv) If a participant of a registered clearing agency reasonably allocates a portion of a fail to deliver position to another registered broker or dealer for which it clears trades or for which it is responsible for settlement, based on such broker or dealer's short position, then the provisions of this paragraph (b)(3) relating to such fail to deliver position shall apply to the portion of such registered broker or dealer that was allocated the fail to deliver position, and not to the participant; and

(v) A participant of a registered clearing agency shall not be deemed to have fulfilled the requirements of this paragraph (b)(3) where the participant enters into an arrangement with another person to purchase securities as required by this paragraph (b)(3), and the participant knows or has reason to know that the other person will not deliver securities in settlement of the purchase.

(c) *Definitions.*

(1) For purposes of this section, the term market maker has the same meaning as in section 3(a)(38) of the Securities Exchange Act of 1934 ("Exchange Act") (15 U.S.C. 78c(a)(38)).

(2) For purposes of this section, the term participant has the same meaning as in section 3(a)(24) of the Exchange Act (15 U.S.C. 78c(a)(24)).

(3) For purposes of this section, the term registered clearing agency means a clearing agency, as defined in section 3(a)(23)(A) of the Exchange Act (15 U.S.C. 78c(a)(23)(A)),

that is registered with the Commission pursuant to section 17A of the Exchange Act (15 U.S.C. 78q–1).

(4) For purposes of this section, the term security future has the same meaning as in section 3(a)(55) of the Exchange Act (15 U.S.C. 78c(a)(55)).

(5) For purposes of this section, the term settlement day means any business day on which deliveries of securities and payments of money may be made through the facilities of a registered clearing agency.

(6) For purposes of this section, the term threshold security means any equity security of an issuer that is registered pursuant to section 12 of the Exchange Act (15 U.S.C. 78l) or for which the issuer is required to file reports pursuant to section 15(d) of the Exchange Act (15 U.S.C. 78o(d)):

(i) For which there is an aggregate fail to deliver position for five consecutive settlement days at a registered clearing agency of 10,000 shares or more, and that is equal to at least 0.5% of the issue's total shares outstanding;

(ii) Is included on a list disseminated to its members by a self-regulatory organization; and

(iii) *Provided, however,* that a security shall cease to be a threshold security if the aggregate fail to deliver position at a registered clearing agency does not exceed the level specified in paragraph (c)(6)(i) of this section for five consecutive settlement days.

(d) *Exemptive authority*. Upon written application or upon its own motion, the Commission may grant an exemption from the provisions of this section, either unconditionally or on specified terms and conditions, to any transaction or class of transactions, or to any security or class of securities, or to any person or class of persons.

REGULATION ATS—ALTERNATIVE TRADING SYSTEMS

Preliminary Notes

1. An alternative trading system is required to comply with the requirements in this Regulation ATS, unless such alternative trading system:

(a) Is registered as a national securities exchange;

(b) Is exempt from registration as a national securities exchange based on the limited volume of transactions effected on the alternative trading system; or

(c) Trades only government securities and certain other related instruments.

All alternative trading systems must comply with the antifraud, antimanipulation, and other applicable provisions of the federal securities laws.

2. The requirements imposed upon an alternative trading system by Regulation ATS are in addition to any requirements applicable to broker-dealers registered under section 15 of the Act, (15 U.S.C. 78o).

3. An alternative trading system must comply with any applicable state law relating to the offer or sale of securities or the registration or regulation of persons or entities effecting transactions in securities.

4. The disclosures made pursuant to the provisions of this section are in addition to any other disclosure requirements under the federal securities laws.

Rule 300. Definitions

For purposes of this section, the following definitions shall apply:

(a) *Alternative trading system* means any organization, association, person, group of persons, or system:

(1) That constitutes, maintains, or provides a market place or facilities for bringing together purchasers and sellers of securities or for otherwise performing with

respect to securities the functions commonly performed by a stock exchange within the meaning of § 240.3b–16 of this chapter; and

(2) That does not:

(i) Set rules governing the conduct of subscribers other than the conduct of such subscribers' trading on such organization, association, person, group of persons, or system; or

(ii) Discipline subscribers other than by exclusion from trading.

(b) *Subscriber* means any person that has entered into a contractual agreement with an alternative trading system to access such alternative trading system for the purpose of effecting transactions in securities or submitting, disseminating, or displaying orders on such alternative trading system, including a customer, member, user, or participant in an alternative trading system. A subscriber, however, shall not include a national securities exchange or national securities association.

(c) *Affiliate of a subscriber* means any person that, directly or indirectly, controls, is under common control with, or is controlled by, the subscriber, including any employee.

(d) *Debt security* shall mean any security other than an equity security, as defined in § 240.3a11-1 of this chapter, as well as nonparticipatory preferred stock.

(e) *Order* means any firm indication of a willingness to buy or sell a security, as either principal or agent, including any bid or offer quotation, market order, limit order, or other priced order.

(f) *Control* means the power, directly or indirectly, to direct the management or policies of an alternative trading system, whether through ownership of securities, by contract, or otherwise. A person is presumed to *control* an alternative trading system, if that person:

(1) Is a director, general partner, or officer exercising executive responsibility (or having similar status or performing similar functions);

(2) Directly or indirectly has the right to vote 25 percent or more of a class of voting security or has the power to sell or direct the sale of 25 percent or more of a class of voting securities of the alternative trading system; or

(3) In the case of a partnership, has contributed, or has the right to receive upon dissolution, 25 percent or more of the capital of the alternative trading system.

(g) *Covered security* shall have the meaning provided in § 240.11Ac1–1(a)(6) of this chapter, *provided, however*, that a debt or convertible debt security shall not be deemed a covered security for purposes of Regulation ATS.

(h) *Effective transaction reporting plan* shall have the meaning provided in § 240.11Aa3–1(a)(3) of this chapter.

(i) *Exchange market maker* shall have the meaning provided in § 240.11Ac1–1(a)(9) of this chapter.

(j) *OTC market maker* shall have the meaning provided in § 240.11Ac1–1(a)(13) of this chapter.

(k) *Investment grade corporate debt security* shall mean any security that:

(1) Evidences a liability of the issuer of such security;

(2) Has a fixed maturity date that is at least one year following the date of issuance;

(3) Is rated in one of the four highest ratings categories by at least one Nationally Recognized Statistical Ratings Organization; and

(4) Is not an exempted security, as defined in section 3(a)(12) of the Act (15 U.S.C. 78c(a)(12)).

(*l*) *Non-investment grade corporate debt security* shall mean any security that:

(1) Evidences a liability of the issuer of such security;

(2) Has a fixed maturity date that is at least one year following the date of issuance;

(3) Is not rated in one of the four highest ratings categories by at least one Nationally Recognized Statistical Ratings Organization; and

(4) Is not an exempted security, as defined in section 3(a)(12) of the Act (15 U.S.C. 78c(a)(12)).

(m) *Commercial paper* shall mean any note, draft, or bill of exchange which arises out of a current transaction or the proceeds of which have been or are to be used for current transactions, and which has a maturity at the time of issuance of not exceeding nine months, exclusive of days of grace, or any renewal thereof the maturity of which is likewise limited.

Rule 301. Requirements for Alternative Trading Systems

(a) *Scope of section.* An alternative trading system shall comply with the requirements in paragraph (b) of this section, unless such alternative trading system:

(1) Is registered as an exchange under section 6 of the Act, (15 U.S.C. 78f);

(2) Is exempted by the Commission from registration as an exchange based on the limited volume of transactions effected;

(3) Is operated by a national securities association;

(4)(i) Is registered as a broker-dealer under sections 15(b) or 15C of the Act (15 U.S.C. 78o(b), and 78o–5), or is a bank, and

(ii) Limits its securities activities to the following instruments:

(A) Government securities, as defined in section 3(a)(42) of the Act, (15 U.S.C. 78c(a)(42));

(B) Repurchase and reverse repurchase agreements solely involving securities included within paragraph (a)(4)(ii)(A) of this section;

(C) Any put, call, straddle, option, or privilege on a government security, other than a put, call, straddle, option, or privilege that:

(*1*) Is traded on one or more national securities exchanges; or

(*2*) For which quotations are disseminated through an automated quotation system operated by a registered securities association; and

(D) Commercial paper.

(5) Is exempted, conditionally or unconditionally, by Commission order, after application by such alternative trading system, from one or more of the requirements of paragraph (b) of this section. The Commission will grant such exemption only after determining that such an order is consistent with the public interest, the protection of investors, and the removal of impediments to, and perfection of the mechanisms of, a national market system.

(b) *Requirements.* Every alternative trading system subject to this Regulation ATS, pursuant to paragraph (a) of this section, shall comply with the requirements in this paragraph (b).

(1) *Broker-dealer registration.* The alternative trading system shall register as a broker-dealer under section 15 of the Act, (15 U.S.C. 78o).

(2) *Notice.* (i) The alternative trading system shall file an initial operation report on Form ATS, § 249.637 of this chapter, in accordance with the instructions therein, at least 20 days prior to commencing operation as an alternative trading system, or if the alternative trading system is operating as of April 21, 1999, no later than May 11, 1999.

(ii) The alternative trading system shall file an amendment on Form ATS at least 20 calendar days prior to implementing a material change to the operation of the alternative trading system.

(iii) If any information contained in the initial operation report filed under paragraph (b)(2)(i) of this section becomes inaccurate for any reason and has not been previously reported to the Commission as an amendment on Form ATS, the alternative trading system shall file an amendment on Form ATS correcting such information within 30 calendar days after the end of each calendar quarter in which the alternative trading system has operated.

(iv) The alternative trading system shall promptly file an amendment on Form ATS correcting information previously reported on Form ATS after discovery that any information filed under paragraphs (b)(2)(i), (ii) or (iii) of this section was inaccurate when filed.

(v) The alternative trading system shall promptly file a cessation of operations report on Form ATS in accordance with the instructions therein upon ceasing to operate as an alternative trading system.

(vi) Every notice or amendment filed pursuant to this paragraph (b)(2) shall constitute a "report" within the meaning of sections 11A, 17(a), 18(a), and 32(a), (15 U.S.C. 78k–1, 78q(a), 78r(a), and 78ff(a)), and any other applicable provisions of the Act.

(vii) The reports provided for in paragraph (b)(2) of this section shall be considered filed upon receipt by the Division of Market Regulation, Stop 10–2, at the Commission's principal office in Washington, DC. Duplicate originals of the reports provided for in paragraphs (b)(2)(i) through (v) of this section must be filed with surveillance personnel designated as such by any self-regulatory organization that is the designated examining authority for the alternative trading system pursuant to § 240.17d–1 of this chapter simultaneously with filing with the Commission. Duplicates of the reports required by paragraph (b)(9) of this section shall be provided to surveillance personnel of such self-regulatory authority upon request. All reports filed pursuant to this paragraph (b)(2) and paragraph (b)(9) of this section shall be deemed confidential when filed.

(3) *Order display and execution access.* (i) An alternative trading system shall comply with the requirements set forth in paragraph (b)(3)(ii) of this section, with respect to any covered security in which the alternative trading system:

(A) Displays subscriber orders to any person (other than alternative trading system employees); and

(B) During at least 4 of the preceding 6 calendar months, had an average daily trading volume of 5 percent or more of the aggregate average daily share volume for such covered security as reported by an effective transaction reporting plan or disseminated through an automated quotation system as described in section 3(a)(51)(A)(ii) of the Act, (15 U.S.C. 78c(a)(51)(A)(ii)).

(ii) Such alternative trading system shall provide to a national securities exchange or national securities association the prices and sizes of the orders at the highest buy price and the lowest sell price for such covered security, displayed to more than one person in the alternative trading system, for inclusion in the quotation data made available by the exchange or association to quotation vendors pursuant to § 240.11Ac1–1 of this chapter.

(iii) With respect to any order displayed pursuant to paragraph (b)(3)(ii) of this section, an alternative trading system shall provide to any broker-dealer that has access to the national securities exchange or national securities association to which the alternative trading system provides the prices and sizes of displayed orders pursuant to paragraph (b)(3)(ii)(A) of this section, the ability to effect a transaction with such orders that is:

(A) Equivalent to the ability of such broker-dealer to effect a transaction with other orders displayed on the exchange or by the association; and

(B) At the price of the highest priced buy order or lowest priced sell order displayed for the lesser of the cumulative size of such priced orders entered therein at such price, or the size of the execution sought by such broker-dealer.

(4) *Fees.* The alternative trading system shall not charge any fee to broker-dealers that access the alternative trading system through a national securities exchange or national securities association, that is inconsistent with equivalent access to the alternative trading system required by paragraph (b)(3)(iii) of this section. In addition, if the national securities exchange or national securities association to which an alternative trading system provides the prices and sizes of orders under paragraphs (b)(3)(ii) and (b)(3)(iii) of this section establishes rules designed to assure consistency with standards for access to quotations displayed on such national securities exchange, or the market operated by such national securities association, the alternative trading system shall not charge any fee to members that is contrary to, that is not disclosed in the manner required by, or that is inconsistent with any standard of equivalent access established by such rules.

(5) *Fair access.* (i) An alternative trading system shall comply with the requirements in paragraph (b)(5)(ii) of this section, if during at least 4 of the preceding 6 calendar months, such alternative trading system had:

(A) With respect to any covered security, 20 percent or more of the average daily volume in that security reported by an effective transaction reporting plan or disseminated through an automated quotation system as described in section 3(a)(51)(A)(ii) of the Act (15 U.S.C. 78c(a)(51)(A)(ii));

(B) With respect to an equity security that is not a covered security and for which transactions are reported to a self-regulatory organization, 20 percent or more of the average daily volume in that security as calculated by the self-regulatory organization to which such transactions are reported;

(C) With respect to municipal securities, 20 percent or more of the average daily volume traded in the United States;

(D) With respect to investment grade corporate debt, 20 percent or more of the average daily volume traded in the United States;

(E) With respect to non-investment grade corporate debt, 20 percent or more of the average daily volume traded in the United States.

(ii) An alternative trading system shall:

(A) Establish written standards for granting access to trading on its system;

(B) Not unreasonably prohibit or limit any person in respect to access to services offered by such alternative trading system by applying the standards established under paragraph (b)(5)(ii)(A) of this section in an unfair or discriminatory manner; and

(C) Make and keep records of:

(*1*) All grants of access including, for all subscribers, the reasons for granting such access;

(*2*) All denials or limitations of access and reasons, for each applicant, for denying or limiting access.

(D) Report the information required on Form ATS-R, § 249.638 of this chapter, regarding grants, denials, and limitations of access.

(iii) Notwithstanding paragraph (b)(5)(i) of this section, an alternative trading system shall not be required to comply with the requirements in paragraph (b)(5)(ii) of this section, if such alternative trading system:

(A) Matches customer orders for a security with other customer orders;

(B) Such customers' orders are not displayed to any person, other than employees of the alternative trading system; and

(C) Such orders are executed at a price for such security disseminated by an effective transaction reporting plan or through an automated quotation system as described in section 3(a)(51)(A)(ii) of the Act, (15 U.S.C. 78c(a)(51)(A)(ii)), or derived from such prices.

(6) *Capacity, integrity, and security of automated systems.* (i) The alternative trading system shall comply with the requirements in paragraph (b)(6)(ii) of this section, if during at least 4 of the preceding 6 calendar months, such alternative trading system had:

(A) With respect to any covered security, 20 percent or more of the average daily volume reported by the effective transaction reporting plan or disseminated through an automated quotation system as described in Section 3(a)(51)(A)(ii) of the Act, (15 U.S.C. 78c(a)(51)(A)(ii));

(B) With respect to equity securities that are not covered securities and for which transactions are reported to a self-regulatory organization, 20 percent or more of the average daily volume as calculated by the self-regulatory organization to which such transactions are reported;

(C) With respect to municipal securities, 20 percent or more of the average daily volume traded in the United States;

(D) With respect to investment grade corporate debt, 20 percent or more of the average daily volume traded in the United States;

(E) With respect to non-investment grade corporate debt, 20 percent or more of the average daily volume traded in the United States.

(ii) With respect to those systems that support order entry, order routing, order execution, transaction reporting, and trade comparison, the alternative trading system shall:

(A) Establish reasonable current and future capacity estimates;

(B) Conduct periodic capacity stress tests of critical systems to determine such system's ability to process transactions in an accurate, timely, and efficient manner;

(C) Develop and implement reasonable procedures to review and keep current its system development and testing methodology;

(D) Review the vulnerability of its systems and data center computer operations to internal and external threats, physical hazards, and natural disasters;

(E) Establish adequate contingency and disaster recovery plans;

(F) On an annual basis, perform an independent review, in accordance with established audit procedures and standards, of such alternative trading system's controls for ensuring that paragraphs (b)(6)(ii)(A) through (E) of this section are met, and conduct a review by senior management of a report containing the recommendations and conclusions of the independent review; and

(G) Promptly notify the Commission staff of material systems outages and significant systems changes.

(iii) Notwithstanding paragraph (b)(6)(i) of this section, an alternative trading system shall not be required to comply with the requirements in paragraph (b)(6)(ii) of this section, if such alternative trading system:

(A) Matches customer orders for a security with other customer orders;

(B) Such customers' orders are not displayed to any person, other than employees of the alternative trading system; and

(C) Such orders are executed at a price for such security disseminated by an effective transaction reporting plan or through an automated quotation system as described in section 3(a)(51)(A)(ii) of the Act, (15 U.S.C. 78c(a)(51)(A)(ii)), or derived from such prices.

(7) *Examinations, inspections, and investigations.* The alternative trading system shall permit the examination and inspection of its premises, systems, and records, and cooperate with the examination, inspection, or investigation of subscribers, whether such examination is being conducted by the Commission or by a self-regulatory organization of which such subscriber is a member.

(8) *Recordkeeping.* The alternative trading system shall:

(i) Make and keep current the records specified in § 242.302; and

(ii) Preserve the records specified in § 242.303.

(9) *Reporting.* The alternative trading system shall:

(i) File the information required by Form ATS-R (§ 249.638 of this chapter) within 30 calendar days after the end of each calendar quarter in which the market has operated after the effective date of this section; and

(ii) File the information required by Form ATS-R within 10 calendar days after an alternative trading system ceases to operate.

(10) *Procedures to ensure the confidential treatment of trading information.*

(i) The alternative trading system shall establish adequate safeguards and procedures to protect subscribers' confidential trading information. Such safeguards and procedures shall include:

(A) Limiting access to the confidential trading information of subscribers to those employees of the alternative trading system who are operating the system or responsible for its compliance with these or any other applicable rules;

(B) Implementing standards controlling employees of the alternative trading system trading for their own accounts; and

(ii) The alternative trading system shall adopt and implement adequate oversight procedures to ensure that the safeguards and procedures established pursuant to paragraph (b)(10)(i) of this section are followed.

(11) *Name.* The alternative trading system shall not use in its name the word "exchange," or derivations of the word "exchange," such as the term "stock market."

Rule 302. Recordkeeping Requirements for Alternative Trading Systems

To comply with the condition set forth in paragraph (b)(8) of § 242.301, an alternative trading system shall make and keep current the following records:

(a) A record of subscribers to such alternative trading system (identifying any affiliations between the alternative trading system and subscribers to the alternative trading system, including common directors, officers, or owners);

(b) Daily summaries of trading in the alternative trading system including:

(1) Securities for which transactions have been executed;

(2) Transaction volume, expressed with respect to equity securities in:

(i) Number of trades;

(ii) Number of shares traded; and

(iii) Total settlement value in terms of U.S. dollars; and

(3) Transaction volume, expressed with respect to debt securities in:

(i) Number of trades; and

(ii) Total U.S. dollar value; and

(c) Time-sequenced records of order information in the alternative trading system, including:

(1) Date and time (expressed in terms of hours, minutes, and seconds) that the order was received;

(2) Identity of the security;

(3) The number of shares, or principal amount of bonds, to which the order applies;

(4) An identification of the order as related to a program trade or an index arbitrage trade as defined in New York Stock Exchange Rule 80A;

(5) The designation of the order as a buy or sell order;

(6) The designation of the order as a short sale order;

(7) The designation of the order as a market order, limit order, stop order, stop limit order, or other type or order;

(8) Any limit or stop price prescribed by the order;

(9) The date on which the order expires and, if the time in force is less than one day, the time when the order expires;

(10) The time limit during which the order is in force;

(11) Any instructions to modify or cancel the order;

(12) The type of account, *i.e.*, retail, wholesale, employee, proprietary, or any other type of account designated by the alternative trading system, for which the order is submitted;

(13) Date and time (expressed in terms of hours, minutes, and seconds) that the order was executed;

(14) Price at which the order was executed;

(15) Size of the order executed (expressed in number of shares or units or principal amount); and

(16) Identity of the parties to the transaction.

Rule 303. Record Preservation Requirements for Alternative Trading Systems

(a) To comply with the condition set forth in paragraph (b)(9) of § 242.301, an alternative trading system shall preserve the following records:

(1) For a period of not less than three years, the first two years in an easily accessible place, an alternative trading system shall preserve:

(i) All records required to be made pursuant to § 242.302;

(ii) All notices provided by such alternative trading system to subscribers generally, whether written or communicated through automated means, including, but not limited to, notices addressing hours of system operations, system malfunctions, changes to system procedures, maintenance of hardware and software, instructions pertaining to access to the market and denials of, or limitations on, access to the alternative trading system;

(iii) If subject to paragraph (b)(5)(ii) of § 242.301, at least one copy of such alternative trading system's standards for access to trading, all documents relevant to the alternative trading systems decision to grant, deny, or limit access to any person, and all other documents made or received by the alternative trading system in the course of complying with paragraph (b)(5) of § 242.301; and

(iv) At least one copy of all documents made or received by the alternative trading system in the course of complying with paragraph (b)(6) of § 242.301, including all correspondence, memoranda, papers, books, notices, accounts, reports, test scripts, test results, and other similar records.

(2) During the life of the enterprise and of any successor enterprise, an alternative trading system shall preserve:

(i) All partnership articles or, in the case of a corporation, all articles of incorporation or charter, minute books and stock certificate books; and

(ii) Copies of reports filed pursuant to paragraph (b)(2) of § 242.301 of this chapter and records made pursuant to paragraph (b)(5) of § 242.301 of this chapter.

(b) The records required to be maintained and preserved pursuant to paragraph (a) of this section must be produced, reproduced, and maintained in paper form or in any of the forms permitted under § 240.17a–4(f) of this chapter.

(c) Alternative trading systems must comply with any other applicable recordkeeping or reporting requirement in the Act, and the rules and regulations thereunder. If the information in a record required to be made pursuant to this section is preserved in a record made pursuant to § 240.17a–3 or § 240.17a–4 of this chapter, or otherwise preserved by the alternative trading system (whether in summary or some other form), this section shall not require the sponsor to maintain such information in a separate file, provided that the sponsor can promptly sort and retrieve the information as if it had been kept in a separate file as a record made pursuant to this section, and preserves the information in accordance with the time periods specified in paragraph (a) of this section.

(d) The records required to be maintained and preserved pursuant to this section may be prepared or maintained by a service bureau, depository, or other recordkeeping service on behalf of the alternative trading system. An agreement with a service bureau, depository, or other recordkeeping service shall not relieve the alternative trading system from the responsibility to prepare and maintain records as specified in this section. The service bureau, depository, or other recordkeeping service shall file with the Commission a written undertaking in a form acceptable to the Commission, signed by a duly authorized person, to the effect that such records are the property of the alternative trading system required to be maintained and preserved and will be surrendered promptly on request of the alternative trading system, and shall include the following provision: With respect to any books and records maintained or preserved on behalf of (name of alternative trading system), the undersigned hereby undertakes to permit examination of such books and records at any time, or from time to time, during business hours by the staff of the Securities and Exchange Commission, any self-regulatory organization of which the alternative trading system is a member, or any State securities regulator having jurisdiction over the alternative trading system, and to promptly furnish to the Commission, self-regulatory organization of which the alternative trading system is a member, or any State securities regulator having jurisdiction over the alternative trading system a true, correct, complete and current hard copy of any, all, or any part of, such books and records.

(e) Every alternative trading system shall furnish to any representative of the Commission promptly upon request, legible, true, and complete copies of those records that are required to be preserved under this section.

CUSTOMER MARGIN REQUIREMENTS FOR SECURITY FUTURES

Rule 400. Customer Margin Requirements For Security Futures—Authority, Purpose, Interpretation, and Scope

(a) *Authority and purpose.* Sections 242.400 through 242.406 and 17 CFR 41.42 through 41.49 ("this Regulation, §§ 242.400 through 242.406") are issued by the Securities and Exchange Commission ("Commission") jointly with the Commodity Futures Trading Commission ("CFTC"), pursuant to authority delegated by the Board of Governors of the Federal Reserve System under section 7(c)(2)(A) of the Securities Exchange Act of 1934 ("Act") (15 U.S.C. 78g(c)(2)(A)). The principal purpose of this Regulation (§§ 242.400 through 242.406) is to regulate customer margin collected by brokers, dealers, and members of national securities exchanges, including futures commission merchants required to register as brokers or dealers under section 15(b)(11) of the Act (15 U.S.C. 78*o*(b)(11)), relating to security futures.

(b) *Interpretation.* This Regulation (§§ 242.400 through 242.406) shall be jointly interpreted by the Commission and the CFTC, consistent with the criteria set forth in clauses (i) through (iv) of section 7(c)(2)(B) of the Act (15 U.S.C. 78g(c)(2)(B)) and the provisions of Regulation T (12 CFR part 220).

(c) *Scope.* (1) This Regulation (§§ 242.400 through 242.406) does not preclude a self-regulatory authority, under rules that are effective in accordance with section 19(b)(2) of the Act (15 U.S.C. 78s(b)(2)) or section 19(b)(7) of the Act (15 U.S.C. 78s(b)(7)) and, as applicable, section 5c(c) of the Commodity Exchange Act ("CEA") (7 U.S.C. 7a–2(c)), or a security futures intermediary from imposing additional margin requirements on security futures, including higher initial or maintenance margin levels, consistent with this Regulation (§§ 242.400 through 242.406), or from taking appropriate action to preserve its financial integrity.

(2) This Regulation (§§ 242.400 through 242.406) does not apply to:

(i) Financial relations between a customer and a security futures intermediary to the extent that they comply with a portfolio margining system under rules that meet the criteria set forth in section 7(c)(2)(B) of the Act (15 U.S.C. 78g(c)(2)(B)) and that are effective in accordance with section 19(b)(2) of the Act (15 U.S.C. 78s(b)(2)) and, as applicable, section 5c(c) of the CEA (7 U.S.C. 7a–2(c));

(ii) Financial relations between a security futures intermediary and a foreign person involving security futures traded on or subject to the rules of a foreign board of trade;

(iii) Margin requirements that clearing agencies registered under section 17A of the Exchange Act (15 U.S.C. 78q–1) or derivatives clearing organizations registered under section 5b of the CEA (7 U.S.C. 7a–1) impose on their members;

(iv) Financial relations between a security futures intermediary and a person based on a good faith determination by the security futures intermediary that such person is an exempted person; and

(v) Financial relations between a security futures intermediary and, or arranged by a security futures intermediary for, a person relating to trading in security futures by such person for its own account, if such person:

(A) Is a member of a national securities exchange or national securities association registered pursuant to section 15A(a) of the Act (15 U.S.C. 78o–3(a)); and

(B) Is registered with such exchange or such association as a security futures dealer pursuant to rules that are effective in accordance with section 19(b)(2) of the Act (15 U.S.C. 78s(b)(2)) and, as applicable, section 5c(c) of the CEA (7 U.S.C. 7a–2(c)), that:

(*1*) Require such member to be registered as a floor trader or a floor broker with the CFTC under Section 4f(a)(1) of the CEA (7 U.S.C. 6f(a)(1)), or as a dealer with the Commission under section 15(b) of the Act (15 U.S.C. 78o(b));

(*2*) Require such member to maintain records sufficient to prove compliance with this paragraph (c)(2)(v) and the rules of the exchange or association of which it is a member;

(*3*) Require such member to hold itself out as being willing to buy and sell security futures for its own account on a regular or continuous basis; and

(*4*) Provide for disciplinary action, including revocation of such member's registration as a security futures dealer, for such member's failure to comply with this Regulation (§§ 242.400 through 242.406) or the rules of the exchange or association.

(d) *Exemption.* The Commission may exempt, either unconditionally or on specified terms and conditions, financial relations involving any security futures intermediary, customer, position, or transaction, or any class of security futures intermediaries, customers, positions, or transactions, from one or more requirements of this Regulation (§§ 242.400 through 242.406), if the Commission determines that such exemption is necessary or appropriate in the public interest and consistent with the protection of investors. An exemption granted pursuant to this paragraph shall not operate as an exemption from any CFTC rules. Any exemption that may be required from such rules must be obtained separately from the CFTC.

Rule 401. Definitions

(a) For purposes of this Regulation (§§ 242.400 through 242.406) only, the following terms shall have the meanings set forth in this section.

(1) *Applicable margin rules* and *margin rules applicable to an account* mean the rules and regulations applicable to financial relations between a security futures intermediary and a customer with respect to security futures and related positions carried in a securities account or futures account as provided in § 242.402(a) of this Regulation (§§ 242.400 through 242.406).

(2) *Broker* shall have the meaning provided in section 3(a)(4) of the Act (15 U.S.C. 78c(a)(4)).

(3) *Contract multiplier* means the number of units of a narrow-based security index expressed as a dollar amount, in accordance with the terms of the security future contract.

(4) *Current market value* means, on any day:

(i) With respect to a security future:

(A) If the instrument underlying such security future is a stock, the product of the daily settlement price of such security future as shown by any regularly published reporting or quotation service, and the applicable number of shares per contract; or

(B) If the instrument underlying such security future is a narrow-based security index, as defined in section 3(a)(55)(B) of the Act (15 U.S.C. 78c(a)(55)(B)), the product of the daily settlement price of such security future as shown by any regularly published reporting or quotation service, and the applicable contract multiplier.

(ii) With respect to a security other than a security future, the most recent closing sale price of the security, as shown by any regularly published reporting or quotation service. If there is no recent closing sale price, the security futures intermediary may use any reasonable estimate of the market value of the security as of the most recent close of business.

(5) *Customer* excludes an exempted person and includes:

(i) Any person or persons acting jointly:

(A) On whose behalf a security futures intermediary effects a security futures transaction or carries a security futures position; or

(B) Who would be considered a customer of the security futures intermediary according to the ordinary usage of the trade;

(ii) Any partner in a security futures intermediary that is organized as a partnership who would be considered a customer of the security futures intermediary absent the partnership relationship; and

(iii) Any joint venture in which a security futures intermediary participates and which would be considered a customer of the security futures intermediary if the security futures intermediary were not a participant.

(6) *Daily settlement price* means, with respect to a security future, the settlement price of such security future determined at the close of trading each day, under the rules of the applicable exchange, clearing agency, or derivatives clearing organization.

(7) *Dealer* shall have the meaning provided in section 3(a)(5) of the Act (15 U.S.C. 78c(a)(5)).

(8) *Equity* means the equity or margin equity in a securities or futures account, as computed in accordance with the margin rules applicable to the account and subject to adjustment under § 242.404(c), (d) and (e) of this Regulation (§§ 242.400 through 242.406).

(9) *Exempted person* means:

(i) A member of a national securities exchange, a registered broker or dealer, or a registered futures commission merchant, a substantial portion of whose business consists of transactions in securities, commodity futures, or commodity options with persons other than brokers, dealers, futures commission merchants, floor brokers, or floor traders, and includes a person who:

(A) Maintains at least 1000 active accounts on an annual basis for persons other than brokers, dealers, persons associated with a broker or dealer, futures commission merchants, floor brokers, floor traders, and persons affiliated with a futures commission merchant, floor broker, or floor trader that are effecting transactions in securities, commodity futures, or commodity options;

(B) Earns at least $10 million in gross revenues on an annual basis from transactions in securities, commodity futures, or commodity options with persons other than brokers, dealers, persons associated with a broker or dealer, futures commission merchants, floor brokers, floor traders, and persons affiliated with a futures commission merchant, floor broker, or floor trader; or

(C) Earns at least 10 percent of its gross revenues on an annual basis from transactions in securities, commodity futures, or commodity options with persons other than brokers, dealers, persons associated with a broker or dealer, futures commission merchants, floor brokers, floor traders, and persons affiliated with a futures commission merchant, floor broker, or floor trader.

(ii) For purposes of paragraph (a)(9)(i) of this section only, persons affiliated with a futures commission merchant, floor broker, or floor trader means any partner, officer, director, or branch manager of such futures commission merchant, floor broker, or floor trader (or any person occupying a similar status or performing similar functions), any person directly or indirectly controlling, controlled by, or under common control with such futures commission merchant, floor broker, or floor trader, or any employee of such a futures commission merchant, floor broker, or floor trader.

(iii) A member of a national securities exchange, a registered broker or dealer, or a registered futures commission merchant that has been in existence for less than one year may meet the definition of exempted person based on a six-month period.

(10) *Exempted security* shall have the meaning provided in section 3(a)(12) of the Act (15 U.S.C. 78c(a)(12)).

(11) *Floor broker* shall have the meaning provided in Section 1a(16) of the CEA (7 U.S.C. 1a(16)).

(12) *Floor trader* shall have the meaning provided in Section 1a(17) of the CEA (7 U.S.C. 1a(17)).

(13) *Futures account* shall have the meaning provided in § 240.15c3–3(a) of this chapter.

(14) *Futures commission merchant* shall have the meaning provided in Section 1a of the CEA (7 U.S.C. 1a).

(15) *Good faith*, with respect to making a determination or accepting a statement concerning financial relations with a person, means that the security futures intermediary is alert to the circumstances surrounding such financial relations, and if in possession of information that would cause a prudent person not to make the determination or accept the notice or certification without inquiry, investigates and is satisfied that it is correct.

(16) *Listed option* means a put or call option that is:

(i) Issued by a clearing agency that is registered under section 17A of the Act (15 U.S.C. 17q–1) or cleared and guaranteed by a derivatives clearing organization that is registered under Section 5b of the CEA (7 U.S.C. 7a–1); and

(ii) Traded on or subject to the rules of a self-regulatory authority.

(17) *Margin call* means a demand by a security futures intermediary to a customer for a deposit of cash, securities or other assets to satisfy the required margin for security futures or related positions or a special margin requirement.

(18) *Margin deficiency* means the amount by which the required margin in an account is not satisfied by the equity in the account, as computed in accordance with § 242.404 of this Regulation (§§ 242.400 through 242.406).

(19) *Margin equity security* shall have the meaning provided in Regulation T.

(20) *Margin security* shall have the meaning provided in Regulation T.

(21) *Member* shall have the meaning provided in section 3(a)(3) of the Act (15 U.S.C. 78c(a)(3)), and shall include persons registered under section 15(b)(11) of the Act (15 U.S.C. 78*o*(b)(11)) that are permitted to effect transactions on a national securities exchange without the services of another person acting as executing broker.

(22) *Money market mutual fund* means any security issued by an investment company registered under section 8 of the Investment Company Act of 1940 (15 U.S.C. 80a–8) that is considered a money market fund under § 270.2a–7 of this chapter.

(23) *Persons associated with a broker or dealer* shall have the meaning provided in section 3(a)(18) of the Act (15 U.S.C. 78c(a)(18)).

(24) *Regulation T* means Regulation T promulgated by the Board of Governors of the Federal Reserve System, 12 CFR part 220, as amended from time to time.

(25) *Regulation T collateral value*, with respect to a security, means the current market value of the security reduced by the percentage of required margin for a position in the security held in a margin account under Regulation T.

(26) *Related position*, with respect to a security future, means any position in an account that is combined with the security future to create an offsetting position as provided in § 242.403(b)(2) of this Regulation (§§ 242.400 through 242.406).

(27) *Related transaction*, with respect to a position or transaction in a security future, means:

(i) Any transaction that creates, eliminates, increases or reduces an offsetting position involving a security future and a related position, as provided in

§ 242.403(b)(2) of this Regulation (§§ 242.400 through 242.406); or

(ii) Any deposit or withdrawal of margin for the security future or a related position, except as provided in § 242.405(b) of this Regulation (§§ 242.400 through 242.406).

(28) *Securities account* shall have the meaning provided in § 240.15c3–3(a) of this chapter.

(29) *Security futures intermediary* means any creditor as defined in Regulation T with respect to its financial relations with any person involving security futures.

(30) *Self-regulatory authority* means a national securities exchange registered under section 6 of the Act (15 U.S.C. 78f), a national securities association registered under section 15A of the Act (15 U.S.C. 78o–3), a contract market registered under Section 5 of the CEA (7 U.S.C. 7) or Section 5f of the CEA (7 U.S.C. 7b–1), or a derivatives transaction execution facility registered under Section 5a of the CEA (7 U.S.C. 7a).

(31) *Special margin requirement* shall have the meaning provided in § 242.404(e)(1)(ii) of this Regulation (§§ 242.400 through 242.406).

(32) *Variation settlement* means any credit or debit to a customer account, made on a daily or intraday basis, for the purpose of marking to market a security future or any other contract that is:

(i) Issued by a clearing agency that is registered under section 17A of the Act (15 U.S.C. 78q–1) or cleared and guaranteed by a derivatives clearing organization that is registered under Section 5b of the CEA (7 U.S.C. 7a–1); and

(ii) Traded on or subject to the rules of a self-regulatory authority.

(b) Terms used in this Regulation (§§ 242.400 through 242.406) and not otherwise defined in this section shall have the meaning set forth in the margin rules applicable to the account.

(c) Terms used in this Regulation (§§ 242.400 through 242.406) and not otherwise defined in this section or in the margin rules applicable to the account shall have the meaning set forth in the Act and the CEA; if the definitions of a term in the Act and the CEA are inconsistent as applied in particular circumstances, such term shall have the meaning set forth in rules, regulations, or interpretations jointly promulgated by the Commission and the CFTC.

Rule 402. General Provisions

(a) *Applicable margin rules.* Except to the extent inconsistent with this Regulation (§§ 242.400 through 242.406):

(1) A security futures intermediary that carries a security future on behalf of a customer in a securities account shall record and conduct all financial relations with respect to such security future and related positions in accordance with Regulation T and the margin rules of the self-regulatory authorities of which the security futures intermediary is a member.

(2) A security futures intermediary that carries a security future on behalf of a customer in a futures account shall record and conduct all financial relations with respect to such security future and related positions in accordance with the margin rules of the self-regulatory authorities of which the security futures intermediary is a member.

(b) *Separation and consolidation of accounts.*

(1) The requirements for security futures and related positions in one account may not be met by considering items in any other account, except as permitted or required under paragraph (b)(2) of this section or applicable margin rules. If withdrawals of cash, securities or other assets deposited as margin are permitted under this Regulation (§§ 242.400 through 242.406), bookkeeping entries shall be made when such cash, secu-

rities, or assets are used for purposes of meeting requirements in another account.

(2) Notwithstanding paragraph (b)(1) of this section, the security futures intermediary shall consider all futures accounts in which security futures and related positions are held that are within the same regulatory classification or account type and are owned by the same customer to be a single account for purposes of this Regulation (§§ 242.400 through 242.406). The security futures intermediary may combine such accounts with other futures accounts that are within the same regulatory classification or account type and are owned by the same customer for purposes of computing a customer's overall margin requirement, as permitted or required by applicable margin rules.

(c) *Accounts of partners.* If a partner of the security futures intermediary has an account with the security futures intermediary in which security futures or related positions are held, the security futures intermediary shall disregard the partner's financial relations with the firm (as shown in the partner's capital and ordinary drawing accounts) in calculating the margin or equity of any such account.

(d) *Contribution to joint venture.* If an account in which security futures or related positions are held is the account of a joint venture in which the security futures intermediary participates, any interest of the security futures intermediary in the joint account in excess of the interest which the security futures intermediary would have on the basis of its right to share in the profits shall be margined in accordance with this Regulation (§§ 242.400 through 242.406).

(e) *Extensions of credit.* (1) No security futures intermediary may extend or maintain credit to or for any customer for the purpose of evading or circumventing any requirement under this Regulation (§§ 242.400 through 242.406).

(2) A security futures intermediary may arrange for the extension or maintenance of credit to or for any customer by any person, provided that the security futures intermediary does not willfully arrange credit that would constitute a violation of Regulation T, U or X of the Board of Governors of the Federal Reserve System (12 CFR parts 220, 221, and 224) by such person.

(f) *Change in exempted person status.* Once a person ceases to qualify as an exempted person, it shall notify the security futures intermediary of this fact before entering into any new security futures transaction or related transaction that would require additional margin to be deposited under this Regulation (§§ 242.400 through 242.406). Financial relations with respect to any such transactions shall be subject to the provisions of this Regulation (§§ 242.400 through 242.406).

Rule 403. Required Margin

(a) *Applicability.* Each security futures intermediary shall determine the required margin for the security futures and related positions held on behalf of a customer in a securities account or futures account as set forth in this section.

(b) *Required margin.*—(1) *General rule.* The required margin for each long or short position n a security future shall be twenty (20) percent of the current market value of such security future.

(2) *Offsetting positions.* Notwithstanding the margin levels specified in paragraph (b)(1) of this section, a self-regulatory authority may set the required initial or maintenance margin level for an offsetting position involving security futures and related positions at a level lower than the level that would be required under paragraph (b)(1) of this section if such positions were margined separately, pursuant to rules that meet the criteria set forth in section 7(c)(2)(B) of the Act (15 U.S.C. 78g(c)(2)(B)) and are effective in accordance with section 19(b)(2) of the Act (15 U.S.C. 78s(b)(2)) and, as applicable, Section 5c(c) of the CEA (7 U.S.C. 7a–2(c)).

(c) *Procedures for certain margin level adjustments.* An exchange registered under section 6(g) of the Act (15 U.S.C. 78f(g)), or a national securities association registered under section 15A(k) of the Act (15 U.S.C. 78*o*–3(k)), may raise or lower the required margin level for a security future to a level not lower than that specified in this section, in accordance with section 19(b)(7) of the Act (15 U.S.C. 78s(b)(7)).

Rule 404. Type, Form and Use of Margin

(a) *When margin is required.* Margin is required to be deposited whenever the required margin for security futures and related positions in an account is not satisfied by the equity in the account, subject to adjustment under paragraph (c) of this section.

(b) *Acceptable margin deposits.* (1) The required margin may be satisfied by a deposit of cash, margin securities [subject to paragraph (b)(2) of this section], exempted securities, any other asset permitted under Regulation T to satisfy a margin deficiency in a securities margin account, or any combination thereof, each as valued in accordance with paragraph (c) of this section.

(2) Shares of a money market mutual fund may be accepted as a margin deposit for purposes of this Regulation (§§ 242.400 through 242.406), *provided that:*

(i) The customer waives any right to redeem the shares without the consent of the security futures intermediary and instructs the fund or its transfer agent accordingly;

(ii) The security futures intermediary (or clearing agency or derivatives clearing organization with which the shares are deposited as margin) obtains the right to redeem the shares in cash, promptly upon request; and

(iii) The fund agrees to satisfy any conditions necessary or appropriate to ensure that the shares may be redeemed in cash, promptly upon request.

(c) *Adjustments.*

(1) *Futures accounts.* For purposes of this section, the equity in a futures account shall be computed in accordance with the margin rules applicable to the account, subject to the following:

(i) A security future shall have no value;

(ii) Each net long or short position in a listed option on a contract for future delivery shall be valued in accordance with the margin rules applicable to the account;

(iii) Except as permitted in paragraph (e) of this section, each margin equity security shall be valued at an amount no greater than its Regulation T collateral value;

(iv) Each other security shall be valued at an amount no greater than its current market value reduced by the percentage specified for such security in § 240.15c3–1(c)(2)(vi) of this chapter;

(v) Freely convertible foreign currency may be valued at an amount no greater than its daily marked-to-market U.S. dollar equivalent;

(vi) Variation settlement receivable (or payable) by an account at the close of trading on any day shall be treated as a credit (or debit) to the account on that day; and

(vii) Each other acceptable margin deposit or component of equity shall be valued at an amount no greater than its value under Regulation T.

(2) *Securities accounts.* For purposes of this section, the equity in a securities account shall be computed in accordance with the margin rules applicable to the account, subject to the following:

(i) A security future shall have no value;

(ii) Freely convertible foreign currency may be valued at an amount no greater than its daily mark-to-market U.S. dollar equivalent; and

(iii) Variation settlement receivable (or payable) to an account at the close of trading on any day shall be treated as a credit (or debit) by the account on that day.

(d) *Satisfaction restriction.* Any transaction, position or deposit that is used to satisfy the required margin for security futures or related positions under this Regulation (§§ 242.400 through 242.406), including a related position, shall be unavailable to satisfy the required margin for any other position or transaction or any other requirement.

(e) *Alternative collateral valuation for margin equity securities in a futures account.*

(1) Notwithstanding paragraph (c)(1)(iii) of this section, a security futures intermediary need not value a margin equity security at its Regulation T collateral value when determining whether the required margin for the security futures and related positions in a futures account is satisfied, *provided that:*

(i) The margin equity security is valued at an amount no greater than the current market value of the security reduced by the lowest percentage level of margin required for a long position in the security held in a margin account under the rules of a national securities exchange registered pursuant to section 6(a) of the Act (15 U.S.C. 78f(a));

(ii) Additional margin is required to be deposited on any day when the day's security futures transactions and related transactions would create or increase a margin deficiency in the account if the margin equity securities were valued at their Regulation T collateral value, and shall be for the amount of the margin deficiency so created or increased (a "special margin requirement"); and

(iii) Cash, securities, or other assets deposited as margin for the positions in an account are not permitted to be withdrawn from the account at any time that:

(A) Additional cash, securities, or other assets are required to be deposited as margin under this section for a transaction in the account on the same or a previous day; or

(B) The withdrawal, together with other transactions, deposits, and withdrawals on the same day, would create or increase a margin deficiency if the margin equity securities were valued at their Regulation T collateral value.

(2) All security futures transactions and related transactions on any day shall be combined to determine the amount of a special margin requirement. Additional margin deposited to satisfy a special margin requirement shall be valued at an amount no greater than its Regulation T collateral value.

(3) If the alternative collateral valuation method set forth in paragraph (e) of this section is used with respect to an account in which security futures or related positions are carried:

(i) An account that is transferred from one security futures intermediary to another may be treated as if it had been maintained by the transferee from the date of its origin, if the transferee accepts, in good faith, a signed statement of the transferor (or, if that is not practicable, of the customer), that any margin call issued under this Regulation (§§ 242.400 through 242.406) has been satisfied; and

(ii) An account that is transferred from one customer to another as part of a transaction, not undertaken to avoid the requirements of this Regulation (§§ 242.400 through 242.406), may be treated as if it had been maintained for the transferee from the date of its origin, if the security futures intermediary accepts in good faith and keeps with the transferee account a signed statement of the transferor describing the circumstances for the transfer.

(f) *Guarantee of accounts.* No guarantee of a customer's account shall be given any effect for purposes of determining whether the required margin in an account is satisfied, except as permitted under applicable margin rules.

Rule 405. Withdrawal of Margin

(a) *By the customer.* Except as otherwise provided in § 242.404(e)(1)(ii) of this Regulation (§§ 242.400 through 242.406), cash, securities, or other assets deposited as margin for positions in an account may be withdrawn, provided that the equity in the account after such withdrawal is sufficient to satisfy the required margin for the security futures and related positions in the account under this Regulation (§§ 242.400 through 242.406).

(b) *By the security futures intermediary.* Notwithstanding paragraph (a) of this section, the security futures intermediary, in its usual practice, may deduct the following items from an account in which security futures or related positions are held if they are considered in computing the balance of such account:

(1) Variation settlement payable, directly or indirectly, to a clearing agency that is registered under section 17A of the Act (15 U.S.C. 78q–1) or a derivatives clearing organization that is registered under section 5b of the CEA (7 U.S.C. 7a–1);

(2) Interest charged on credit maintained in the account;

(3) Communication or shipping charges with respect to transactions in the account;

(4) Payment of commissions, brokerage, taxes, storage and other charges lawfully accruing in connection with the positions and transactions in the account;

(5) Any service charges that the security futures intermediary may impose; or

(6) Any other withdrawals that are permitted from a securities margin account under Regulation T, to the extent permitted under applicable margin rules.

Rule 406. Undermargined Accounts

(a) *Failure to satisfy margin call.* If any margin call required by this Regulation (§§ 242.400 through 242.406) is not met in full, the security futures intermediary shall take the deduction required with respect to an undermargined account in computing its net capital under Commission or CFTC rules.

(b) *Accounts that liquidate to a deficit.* If at any time there is a liquidating deficit in an account in which security futures are held, the security futures intermediary shall take steps to liquidate positions in the account promptly and in an orderly manner.

(c) *Liquidation of undermargined accounts not required.* Notwithstanding Section 402(a) of this Regulation (§§ 242.400 through 242.406), section 220.4(d) of Regulation T (12 CFR 220.4(d)) respecting liquidation of positions in lieu of deposit shall not apply with respect to security futures carried in a securities account.

REGULATION AC—ANALYST CERTIFICATION

§ 242.500. Definitions

For purposes of Regulation AC (§§ 242.500 through 242.505 of this chapter) the term:

Covered person of a broker or dealer means an associated person of that broker or dealer but does not include:

(1) An associated person:

(i) If the associated person has no officers (or persons performing similar functions) or employees in common with the broker or dealer who can influence the activities of research analysts or the content of research reports; and

(ii) If the broker or dealer maintains and enforces written policies and procedures reasonably designed to prevent the broker or dealer, any controlling persons, officers (or persons performing similar functions), and employees of the broker or dealer from influencing the activities of research analysts and the content of research reports prepared by the associated person.

(2) An associated person who is an investment adviser:

(i) Not registered with the Commission as an investment adviser because of the prohibition of section 203A of the Investment Advisers Act of 1940 (15 U.S.C. 80b–3a); and

(ii) Not registered or required to be registered with the Commission as a broker or dealer.

Note to definition of covered person: An associated person of a broker or dealer who is not a covered person continues to be subject to the federal securities laws, including the anti-fraud provisions of the federal securities laws.

Foreign person means any person who is not a U.S. person.

Foreign security means a security issued by a foreign issuer for which a U.S. market is not the principal trading market.

Public appearance means any participation by a research analyst in a seminar, forum (including an interactive electronic forum), or radio or television or other interview, in which the research analyst makes a specific recommendation or provides information reasonably sufficient upon which to base an investment decision about a security or an issuer.

Registered broker or dealer means a broker or dealer registered or required to register pursuant to section 15 or section 15B of the Securities Exchange Act of 1934 (15 U.S.C. 78o or 78o–4) or a government securities broker or government securities dealer registered or required to register pursuant to section 15C(a)(1)(A) of the Securities Exchange Act of 1934 (15 U.S.C. 78o–5(a)(1)(A)).

Research analyst means any natural person who is primarily responsible for the preparation of the content of a research report.

Research report means a written communication (including an electronic communication) that includes an analysis of a security or an issuer and provides information reasonably sufficient upon which to base an investment decision.

Third party research analyst means:

(1) With respect to a broker or dealer, any research analyst not employed by that broker or dealer or any associated person of that broker or dealer; and

(2) With respect to a covered person of a broker or dealer, any research analyst not employed by that covered person, by the broker or dealer with whom that covered person is associated, or by any other associated person of the broker or dealer with whom that covered person is associated.

United States has the meaning contained in § 230.902(*l*) of this chapter.

U.S. person has the meaning contained in § 230.902(k) of this chapter.

§ 242.501. Certifications In Connection With Research Reports

(a) A broker or dealer or covered person that publishes, circulates, or provides a research report prepared by a research analyst to a U.S. person in the United States shall include in that research report a clear and prominent certification by the research analyst containing the following:

(1) A statement attesting that all of the views expressed in the research report accurately reflect the research analyst's personal views about any and all of the subject securities or issuers; and

(2)(i) A statement attesting that no part of the research analyst's compensation was, is, or will be, directly or indirectly, related to the specific recommendations or views expressed by the research analyst in the research report; or

(ii) A statement:

(A) Attesting that part or all of the research analyst's compensation was, is, or will be, directly or indirectly, related to the specific recommendations or views expressed by the research analyst in the research report;

(B) Identifying the source, amount, and purpose of such compensation; and

(C) Further disclosing that the compensation could influence the recommendations or views expressed in the research report.

(b) A broker or dealer or covered person that publishes, circulates, or provides a research report prepared by a third party research analyst to a U.S. person in the United States shall be exempt from the requirements of this section with respect to such research report if the following conditions are satisfied:

(1) The employer of the third party research analyst has no officers (or persons performing similar functions) or employees in common with the broker or dealer or covered person; and

(2) The broker or dealer (or, with respect to a covered person, the broker or dealer with whom the covered person is associated) maintains and enforces written policies and procedures reasonably designed to prevent the broker or dealer, any controlling persons, officers (or persons performing similar functions), and employees of the broker or dealer from influencing the activities of the third party research analyst and the content of research reports prepared by the third party research analyst.

§ 242.502. Certifications In Connection With Public Appearances

(a) If a broker or dealer publishes, circulates, or provides a research report prepared by a research analyst employed by the broker or dealer or covered person to a U.S. person in the United States, the broker or dealer must make a record within 30 days after any calendar quarter in which the research analyst made a public appearance that contains the following:

(1) A statement by the research analyst attesting that the views expressed by the research analyst in all public appearances during the calendar quarter accurately reflected the research analyst's personal views at that time about any and all of the subject securities or issuers; and

(2) A statement by the research analyst attesting that no part of the research analyst's compensation was, is, or will be, directly or indirectly, related to the specific recommendations or views expressed by the research analyst in such public appearances.

(b) If the broker or dealer does not obtain a statement by the research analyst in accordance with paragraph (a) of this section:

(1) The broker or dealer shall promptly notify in writing its examining authority, designated pursuant to section 17(d) of the Securities Exchange Act of 1934 (15 U.S.C. 78q(d)) and § 240.17d–2 of this chapter, that the research analyst did not provide the certifications specified in paragraph (a) of this section; and

(2) For 120 days following notification pursuant to paragraph (b)(1) of this section, the broker or dealer shall disclose in any research report prepared by the research analyst and published, circulated, or provided to a U.S. person in the United States that the research analyst did not provide the certifications specified in paragraph (a) of this section.

(c) In the case of a research analyst who is employed outside the United States by a foreign person located outside the United States, this section shall only apply to a public appearance while the research analyst is physically present in the United States.

(d) A broker or dealer shall preserve the records specified in paragraphs (a) and (b) of this section in accordance with § 240.17a–4 of this chapter and for a period of not less than 3 years, the first 2 years in an accessible place.

§ 242.503. Certain Foreign Research Reports

A foreign person, located outside the United States and not associated with a registered broker or dealer, who prepares a research report concerning a foreign security and provides it to a U.S. person in the United States in accordance with the provisions of § 240.15a–6(a)(2) of this chapter shall be exempt from the requirements of this regulation.

§ 242.504. Notification to Associated Persons

A broker or dealer shall notify any person with whom that broker or dealer is associated who publishes, circulates, or provides research reports:

(a) Whether the broker or dealer maintains and enforces written policies and procedures reasonably designed to prevent the broker or dealer, any controlling persons, officers (or persons performing similar functions), or employees of the broker or dealer from influencing the activities of research analysts and the content of research reports prepared by the associated person; and

(b) Whether the associated person has any officers (or persons performing similar functions) or employees in common with the broker or dealer who can influence the activities of research analysts or the content of research reports and, if so, the identity of those persons.

§ 242.505. Exclusion For News Media

No provision of this Regulation AC shall apply to any person who:

(a) Is the publisher of any bona fide newspaper, news magazine or business or financial publication of general and regular circulation; and

(b) Is not registered or required to be registered with the Commission as a broker or dealer or investment adviser.

FORMS UNDER THE SECURITIES EXCHANGE ACT OF 1934

UNITED STATES SECURITIES AND EXCHANGE COMMISSION

Washington, D.C. 20549

FORM 3

INITIAL STATEMENT OF BENEFICIAL OWNERSHIP OF SECURITIES

THE COMMISSION IS AUTHORIZED TO SOLICIT THE INFORMATION REQUIRED BY THIS FORM PURSUANT TO SECTIONS 16(a) AND 23(a) OF THE SECURITIES EXCHANGE ACT OF 1934 (15 U.S.C. 78p(a) AND 78w(a)); SECTIONS 17(a) AND 20(a) OF THE PUBLIC UTILITY HOLDING COMPANY ACT OF 1935 (15 U.S.C. 79q(a) AND 79t(a)); AND SECTIONS 30(h) AND 38 OF THE INVESTMENT COMPANY ACT OF 1940 (15 U.S.C. 80a–29(h) AND 80a–37), AND THE RULES AND REGULATIONS THEREUNDER.

DISCLOSURE OF INFORMATION SPECIFIED ON THIS FORM IS MANDATORY, EXCEPT FOR DISCLOSURE OF THE I.R.S. IDENTIFICATION NUMBER OF THE REPORTING PERSON IF SUCH PERSON IS AN ENTITY, WHICH IS VOLUNTARY. IF SUCH NUMBERS ARE FURNISHED, THEY WILL ASSIST THE COMMISSION IN DISTINGUISHING REPORTING PERSONS WITH SIMILAR NAMES AND WILL FACILITATE THE PROMPT PROCESSING OF THE FORM. THE INFORMATION WILL BE USED FOR THE PRIMARY PURPOSE OF DISCLOSING THE HOLDINGS OF DIRECTORS, OFFICERS, AND BENEFICIAL OWNERS OF REGISTERED COMPANIES. INFORMATION DISCLOSED WILL BE A MATTER OF PUBLIC RECORD AND AVAILABLE FOR INSPECTION BY MEMBERS OF THE PUBLIC. THE COMMISSION CAN USE IT IN INVESTIGATIONS OR LITIGATION INVOLVING THE FEDERAL SECURITIES LAWS OR OTHER CIVIL, CRIMINAL, OR REGULATORY STATUTES OR PROVISIONS, AS WELL AS FOR REFERRAL TO OTHER GOVERNMENTAL AUTHORITIES AND SELF–REGULATORY ORGANIZATIONS. FAILURE TO DISCLOSE REQUIRED INFORMATION MAY RESULT IN CIVIL OR CRIMINAL ACTION AGAINST PERSONS INVOLVED FOR VIOLATIONS OF THE FEDERAL SECURITIES LAWS AND RULES.

GENERAL INSTRUCTIONS

1. Who Must File

(a) This Form must be filed by the following persons ("reporting person"):

(i) any director or officer of an issuer with a class of equity securities registered pursuant to Section 12 of the Securities Exchange Act of 1934 ("Exchange Act"); (*Note:* Title is not determinative for purposes of determining "officer" status. *See* Rule 16a–1(f) for the definition of "officer");

(ii) any beneficial owner of greater than 10% of a class of equity securities registered under Section 12 of the Exchange Act, as determined by voting or investment control over the securities pursuant to Rule 16a–1(a)(1) ("ten percent holder");

(iii) any officer or director of a registered holding company pursuant to Section 17 of the Public Utility Holding Company Act of 1935;

(iv) any officer, director, member of an advisory board, investment adviser, affiliated person of an investment adviser, or beneficial owner of more than 10% of any class of outstanding securities (other than short-term paper) of a registered closed-end investment company, under Section 30(f) of the Investment Company Act of 1940; and

(v) any trust, trustee, beneficiary or settlor required to report pursuant to Rule 16a–8.

(b) If a reporting person is not an officer, director, or ten percent holder, the person should check "other" in Item 5 (Relationship of Reporting Person to Issuer) and describe the reason for reporting status in the space provided.

(c) If a person described above does not beneficially own any securities required to be reported (*See* Rule 16a–1 and Instruction 5), the person is required to file this Form and state that no securities are beneficially owned.

2. When Form Must be Filed

(a) This Form must be filed within 10 days after the event by which the person becomes a reporting person (*i.e.*, officer, director, ten percent holder or other person). This Form and any amendment is deemed filed with the Commission or the Exchange on the date it is received by the Commission or the Exchange, respectively. *See*, however, Rule 16a–3(h) regarding delivery to a third party business that guarantees delivery of the filing no later than the specified due date.

(b) A reporting person of an issuer that is registering securities for the first time under Section 12 of the Exchange Act must file this Form no later than the effective date of the registration statement.

(c) A separate Form shall be filed to reflect beneficial ownership of securities of each issuer, except that a single statement shall be filed with respect to the securities of a registered public utility holding company and all of its subsidiary companies.

3. Where Form Must be Filed

(a) File three copies of this Form or any amendment, at least one of which is manually signed, with the Securities and Exchange Commission, 450 5th Street, N.W., Washington, D.C. 20549. (*Note:* Acknowledgment of receipt by the Commission may be obtained by enclosing a self-addressed stamped postcard identifying the Form or amendment filed.)

Alternatively, this Form is permitted to be submitted to the Commission in electronic format at the option of the reporting person pursuant to § 232.101(b)(4) of this chapter.

(b) At the time this Form or any amendment is filed with the Commission, file one copy with each Exchange on which any class of securities of the issuer is registered. If the issuer has designated a single Exchange to receive Section 16 filings, the copy shall be filed with that Exchange only.

(c) Any person required to file this Form or amendment shall, not later than the time the Form or amendment is transmitted for filing with the Commission, send or deliver a copy to the person designated by the issuer to receive the copy or, if no person is so designated, the issuer's corporate secretary (or person performing similar functions) in accordance with Rule 16a–3(e).

4. Class of Securities Reported

(a)(i) Persons reporting pursuant to Section 16(a) of the Exchange Act shall include information as to their beneficial ownership of any class of equity securities of the issuer, even though one or more of such classes may not be registered pursuant to Section 12 of the Act.

(ii) Persons reporting pursuant to Section 17(a) of the Public Utility Holding Company Act of 1935 shall include information as to their beneficial ownership of any class of securities (equity or debt) of the registered holding company and all of its subsidiary companies and specify the name of the parent or subsidiary issuing the securities.

(iii) Persons reporting pursuant to Section 30(f) of the Investment Company Act of 1940 shall include information as to their beneficial ownership of any class of securities (equity or debt) of the registered closed-end investment company (other than "short-term paper" as defined in Section 2(a)(38) of the Investment Company Act).

(b) The title of the security should clearly identify the class, even if the issuer has only one class of securities outstanding; for example, "Common Stock," "Class A Common Stock," "Class B Convertible Preferred Stock," etc.

(c) The amount of securities beneficially owned should state the face amount of debt securities (U.S. Dollars) or the number of equity securities, whichever is appropriate.

5. Holdings Required to be Reported

(a) *General Requirements*

Report holdings of each class of securities of the issuer beneficially owned as of the date of the event requiring the filing of this Form. *See* Instruction 4 as to securities required to be reported.

(b) *Beneficial Ownership Reported (Pecuniary Interest)*

(i) Although for purposes of determining status as a ten percent holder, a person is deemed to beneficially own securities over which that person has voting or investment control (*see* Rule 16a–1(a)(1)), for reporting purposes, a person is deemed to be the beneficial owner of securities if that person has or shares the opportunity, directly or indirectly, to profit or share in any profit derived from a transaction in the securities ("pecuniary interest"). *See* Rule 16a–1(a)(2). *See also* Rule 16a–8 for the application of the beneficial ownership definition to trust holdings and transactions.

(ii) Both direct and indirect beneficial ownership of securities shall be reported. Securities beneficially owned directly are those held in the reporting person's name or in the name of a bank, broker or nominee for the account of the reporting person. In addition, securities held as joint tenants, tenants in common, tenants by the entirety, or as community property are to be reported as held directly. If a person has a pecuniary interest, by reason of any contract understanding or relationship (including a family relationship or arrangement) in securities held in the name of another person, that person is an indirect beneficial owner of those securities. *See* Rule 16a–1(a)(2)(ii) for certain indirect beneficial ownerships.

(iii) Report securities beneficially owned directly on a separate line from those beneficially owned indirectly. Report different forms of indirect ownership on separate lines. The nature of indirect ownership shall be stated as specifically as possible; for example, "By Self as Trustee for X," "By Spouse," "By X Trust," "By Y Corporation," etc.

(iv) In stating the amount of securities owned indirectly through a partnership, corporation, trust, or other entity, report the number of securities representing the reporting person's proportionate interest in securities beneficially owned by that entity. Alternatively, at the option of the reporting person, the entire amount of the entity's interest may be reported. *See* Rule 16a–1(a)(2)(ii)(B) and Rule 16a–1(a)(2)(iii).

(v) Where more than one person beneficially owns the same equity securities, such owners may file Form 3 individually or jointly. Joint and group filings may be made by any designated beneficial owner. Holdings of securities owned separately by any joint or group filer are permitted to be included in the joint filing. Indicate only the name and address of the designated filer in Item 1 of Form 3 and attach a listing of the names and IRS or social security numbers (or addresses in lieu thereof) of each other reporting person. Joint and group filings must include all required information for each beneficial owner, and such filings must be signed by each beneficial owner, or on behalf of such owner by an authorized person. If the space provided for signatures is insufficient, attach a signature page. Submit any attached listing of names or signatures on another Form 3, copy of Form 3 or separate page of 8½ by 11 inch white paper, indicate the number of pages comprising the report (Form plus attachments) at the bottom of each report page (*e.g.*, 1 of 3, 2 of 3, 3 of 3), and include the name of the designated filer and information required by Items 2 and 4 of the Form on the attachment.

(c) *Non-Derivative and Derivative Securities*

(i) Report non-derivative securities beneficially owned in Table I and derivative securities (*e.g.*, puts, calls, options, warrants, convertible securities, or other rights or obligations to buy or sell securities) beneficially owned in Table II. Derivative securities beneficially owned that are both equity securities and convertible or exchangeable for other equity securities (*e.g.*, convertible preferred securities) should be reported only on Table II.

(ii) The title of a derivative security and the title of the equity security underlying the derivative security should be shown separately in the appropriate columns in Table II. The "puts" and "calls" reported in Table II include, in addition to separate puts and calls, any combination of the two, such as spreads and straddles. In reporting an option in Table II, state whether it represents a right to buy, a right to sell, an obligation to buy, or an obligation to sell the equity securities subject to the options.

(iii) Describe in the appropriate columns in Table II characteristics of derivative securities, including title, exercise or conversion price, date exercisable, expiration date, and the title and amount of securities underlying the derivative security.

(iv) Securities constituting components of a unit shall be reported separately on the applicable table (*e.g.*, if a unit has a non-derivative security component and a derivative security component, the non-derivative security component shall be reported in Table I and the derivative security component shall be reported in Table II). The relationship between individual securities comprising the unit shall be indicated in the space provided for explanation of responses.

6. Additional Information

If the space provided in the line items of this Form or space provided for additional comments is insufficient, attach another Form 3, copy of Form 3 or a separate page of 8½ by 11 inch white paper to Form 3, completed as appropriate to include the additional comments. Each attached page must include information required in Items 1, 2 and 4 of the Form. The number of pages comprising the report (Form plus attachments) shall be indicated at the bottom of each report page (*e.g.*, 1 of 3, 2 of 3, 3 of 3). If additional information is not provided in this manner, it will be assumed that no additional information was provided.

7. Signature

(a) If the Form is filed for an individual, it shall be signed by that person or specifically on behalf of the individual by a person authorized to sign for the individual. If signed on behalf of the individual by another person, the authority of such person to sign the Form shall be confirmed to the Commission in writing in an attachment to the Form or as soon as practicable in an amendment by the individual for whom the Form is filed, unless such a confirmation still in effect is on file with the Commission. The confirming statement need only indicate that the reporting person authorizes and designates the named person or persons to file the Form on the reporting person's behalf, and state the duration of the authorization.

(b) If the Form is filed for an corporation, partnership, trust, or other entity, the capacity in which the individual signed shall be set forth (*e.g.*, John Smith, Secretary, on behalf of X Corporation).

FORM 3

U.S. SECURITIES AND EXCHANGE COMMISSION
Washington, D.C. 20549

OMB APPROVAL	
OMB Number:	3235-0104
Expires:	April 30, 1997
Estimated average burden hours per response.	.0.5

INITIAL STATEMENT OF BENEFICIAL OWNERSHIP OF SECURITIES

Filed pursuant to Section 16(a) of the Securities Exchange Act of 1934, Section 17(a) of the Public Utility Holding Company Act of 1935 or Section 30(f) of the Investment Company Act of 1940

1. Name and Address of Reporting Person* (Last) (First) (Middle) (Street) (City) (State) (Zip)	2. Date of Event Requiring Statement (Month/Day/Year)	4. Issuer Name and Ticker or Trading Symbol	6. If Amendment, Date of Original (Month/Day/Year)
* If the Form is filed by more than one Reporting Person, *see* instruction 5(b)(v).	3. I.R.S. Identification Number of Reporting Person, if an entity (Voluntary)	5. Relationship of Reporting Person to Issuer (Check all applicable) ____ Director ____ 10% Owner ____ Officer (give title below) ____ Other (specify below)	7. Individual or Joint/Group Filing (Check applicable line) ____ Form Filed by One Reporting Person ____ Form Filed by More Than One Reporting Person

Table I — Non-Derivative Securities Beneficially Owned

1. Title of Security (Instr. 4)	2. Amount of Securities Beneficially Owned (Instr. 4)	3. Ownership Form: Direct (D) or Indirect (I) (Instr. 5)	4. Nature of Indirect Beneficial Ownership (Instr. 5)

Reminder: Report on a separate line for each class of securities beneficially owned directly or indirectly.
(Print or Type Responses)

(Over)
SEC 1473 (8-92)

FORM 3 (continued) **Table II — Derivative Securities Beneficially Owned (*e.g.*, puts, calls, warrants, options, convertible securities)**

1. Title of Derivative Security (Instr. 4)	2. Date Exercisable and Expiration Date (Month/Day/Year)		3. Title and Amount of Securities Underlying Derivative Security (Instr. 4)		4. Conversion or Exercise Price of Derivative Security	5. Ownership Form of Derivative Security: Direct (D) or Indirect (I) (Instr. 5)	6. Nature of Indirect Beneficial Ownership (Instr. 5)
	Date Exercisable	Expiration Date	Title	Amount or Number of Shares			

Explanation of Responses:

**Intentional misstatements or omissions of facts constitute Federal Criminal Violations.
See 18 U.S.C. 1001 and 15 U.S.C. 78ff(a).

______________________________ **Signature of Reporting Person

______________ Date

Note: File three copies of this Form, one of which must be manually signed. If space provided is insufficient, *See* Instruction 6 for procedure.

Page 2
SEC 1473 (8-92)

UNITED STATES
SECURITIES AND EXCHANGE COMMISSION
Washington, D.C. 20549

FORM 4

STATEMENT OF CHANGES IN BENEFICIAL OWNERSHIP OF SECURITIES

THE COMMISSION IS AUTHORIZED TO SOLICIT THE INFORMATION REQUIRED BY THIS FORM PURSUANT TO SECTIONS 16(a) AND 23(a) OF THE SECURITIES EXCHANGE ACT OF 1934 (15 U.S.C. 78p(a) AND 78w(a)); SECTIONS 17(a) AND 20(a) OF THE PUBLIC UTILITY HOLDING COMPANY ACT OF 1935 (15 U.S.C. 79q(a) AND 79t(a)); AND SECTIONS 30(h) AND 38 OF THE INVESTMENT COMPANY ACT OF 1940 (15 U.S.C. 80a–29(h) AND 80a–37), AND THE RULES AND REGULATIONS THEREUNDER.

DISCLOSURE OF INFORMATION SPECIFIED ON THIS FORM IS MANDATORY, EXCEPT FOR DISCLOSURE OF THE I.R.S. IDENTIFICATION NUMBER OF THE REPORTING PERSON IF SUCH PERSON IS AN ENTITY, WHICH IS VOLUNTARY. IF SUCH NUMBERS ARE FURNISHED, THEY WILL ASSIST THE COMMISSION IN DISTINGUISHING REPORTING PERSONS WITH SIMILAR NAMES AND WILL FACILITATE THE PROMPT PROCESSING OF THE FORM. THE INFORMATION WILL BE USED FOR THE PRIMARY PURPOSE OF DISCLOSING THE TRANSACTIONS AND HOLDINGS OF DIRECTORS, OFFICERS, AND BENEFICIAL OWNERS OF REGISTERED COMPANIES. INFORMATION DISCLOSED WILL BE A MATTER OF PUBLIC RECORD AND AVAILABLE FOR INSPECTION BY MEMBERS OF THE PUBLIC. THE COMMISSION CAN USE IT IN INVESTIGATIONS OR LITIGATION INVOLVING THE FEDERAL SECURITIES LAWS OR OTHER CIVIL, CRIMINAL, OR REGULATORY STATUTES OR PROVISIONS, AS WELL AS FOR REFERRAL TO OTHER GOVERNMENTAL AUTHORITIES AND SELF–REGULATORY ORGANIZATIONS. FAILURE TO DISCLOSE REQUIRED INFORMATION MAY RESULT IN CIVIL OR CRIMINAL ACTION AGAINST PERSONS INVOLVED FOR VIOLATIONS OF THE FEDERAL SECURITIES LAWS AND RULES.

GENERAL INSTRUCTIONS

1. When Form Must be Filed

(a) This Form must be filed on or before the tenth day after the end of the month in which a change in beneficial ownership has occurred (the term "beneficial owner" is defined in Rule 16a–1(a)(2) and discussed in Instruction 4). This Form and any amendment is deemed filed with the Commission or the Exchange on the date it is received by the Commission or Exchange, respectively. *See*, however, Rule 16a–3(h) regarding delivery to a third party business that guarantees delivery of the filing no later than the specified due date.

(b) A reporting person no longer subject to Section 16 of the Securities Exchange Act of 1934 ("Exchange Act") must check the exit box appearing on this Form. However, Forms 4 and 5 obligations may continue to be applicable. *See* Rule 16a–3(f); *see also* Rule 16a–2(b) (transactions after termination of insider status). Form 5 transactions to date may be included on this Form and subsequent Form 5 transactions may be reported on a later Form 4 or Form 5, provided all transactions are reported by the required date.

(c) A separate Form shall be filed to reflect beneficial ownership of securities of each issuer, except that a single statement shall be filed with respect to the securities of a registered public utility holding company and all of its subsidiary companies.

(d) If a reporting person is not an officer, director, or ten percent holder, the person should check "other" in Item 6 (Relationship of Reporting Person to Issuer) and describe the reason for reporting status in the space provided.

2. Where Form Must be Filed

(a) File three copies of this Form or any amendment, at least one of which is manually signed, with the Securities and Exchange Commission, 450 5th Street, N.W., Washington, D.C. 20549. (*Note*: Acknowledgment of receipt by the Commission may be obtained by enclosing a self-addressed stamped postcard identifying the Form or amendment filed.)

Alternatively, this Form is permitted to be submitted to the Commission in electronic format at the option of the reporting person pursuant to § 232.101(b)(4) of this chapter.

(b) At the time this Form or any amendment is filed with the Commission, file one copy with each Exchange on which any class of securities of the issuer is registered. If the issuer has designated a single Exchange to receive Section 16 filings, the copy shall be filed with that Exchange only.

(c) Any person required to file this Form or amendment shall, not later than the time the Form or amendment is transmitted for filing with the Commission, send or deliver a copy to the person designated by the issuer to receive the copy or, if no person is so designated, the issuer's corporate secretary (or person performing similar functions) in accordance with Rule 16a–3(e).

3. Class of Securities Reported

(a)(i) Persons reporting pursuant to Section 16(a) of the Exchange Act shall report each transaction resulting in a change in beneficial ownership of any class of equity securities of the issuer and the beneficial ownership at the end of the month of that class of equity securities, even though one or more of such classes may not be registered pursuant to Section 12 of the Exchange Act.

(ii) Persons reporting pursuant to Section 17(a) of the Public Utility Holding Company Act of 1935 shall report each transaction resulting in a change in beneficial ownership of any class of securities (equity or debt) of the registered holding company and all of its subsidiary companies and the beneficial ownership at the end of the month of that class of securities. Specify the name of the parent or subsidiary issuing the securities.

(iii) Persons reporting pursuant to Section 30(f) of the Investment Company Act of 1940 shall report each transaction resulting in a change in beneficial ownership of any class of securities (equity or debt) of the registered closed-end investment company (other than "short-term paper" as defined in Section 2(a)(38) of the Investment Company Act) and the beneficial ownership at the end of the month of that class of securities.

(b) The title of the security should clearly identify the class, even if the issuer has only one class of securities outstanding; for example, "Common Stock," "Class A Common Stock," "Class B Convertible Preferred Stock," etc.

(c) The amount of securities beneficially owned should state the face amount of debt securities (U.S. Dollars) or the number of equity securities, whichever is appropriate.

4. Transactions and Holdings Required to be Reported

(a) *General Requirements*

(i) Report, in accordance with Rule 16a–3(g), all transactions not exempt from Section 16(b) of the Act and all exercises and conversions of derivative securities, regardless of whether exempt from Section 16(b) of the Act, resulting in a change of beneficial ownership in the issuer's securities. Every transaction shall be reported even though acquisitions and dispositions during the month are equal. Report total beneficial ownership as of the end of the month for each class of securities in which a transaction was reported.

Note: The amount of securities beneficially owned at the end of the month specified in Column 5 of Table I and Column 9 of Table II should reflect those holdings reported or required to be reported by the date of the Form. Transactions and holdings eligible for deferred reporting on Form 5 need not be reflected in the month end total unless the transactions were reported earlier or are included on this Form.

(ii) Each transaction should be reported on a separate line. Transaction codes specified in Item 8 should be used to identify the nature of the transaction resulting in an acquisition or disposition of a security.

Note: Transactions reportable on Form 5 may, at the option of the reporting person, be reported on a Form 4 filed before the due date of the Form 5. (*See* Instruction 8 for the code for voluntarily reported transactions.)

(b) *Beneficial Ownership Reported (Pecuniary Interest)*

(i) Although for purposes of determining status as a ten percent holder, a person is deemed to beneficially own securities over which that person exercises voting or investment control (*see* Rule 16a–1(a)(1)), for reporting transactions and holdings, a person is deemed to be the beneficial owner of securities if that person has the opportunity, directly or indirectly, to profit or share in any profit derived from a transaction in the securities ("pecuniary interest"). *See* Rule 16a–1(a)(2). *See also* Rule 16a–8 for the application of the beneficial ownership definition to trust holdings and transactions.

(ii) Both direct and indirect beneficial ownership of securities shall be reported. Securities beneficially owned directly are those held in the reporting person's name or in the name of a bank, broker or nominee for the account of the reporting person. In addition, securities held as joint tenants, tenants in common, tenants by the entirety, or as community property are to be reported as held directly. If a person has a pecuniary interest, by reason of any contract, understanding or relationship (including a family relationship or arrangement), in securities held in the name of another person, that person is an indirect beneficial owner of the securities. *See* Rule 16a–1(a)(2)(ii) for certain indirect beneficial ownerships.

(iii) Report transactions in securities beneficially owned directly on a separate line from those beneficially owned indirectly. Report different forms of indirect ownership on separate lines. The nature of indirect ownership shall be stated as specifically as possible; for example, "By Self as Trustee for X," "By Spouse," "By X Trust," "By Y Corporation," etc.

(iv) In stating the amount of securities acquired, disposed of, or beneficially owned indirectly through a partnership, corporation, trust, or other entity, report the number of securities representing the reporting person's proportionate interest in transactions conducted by that entity or holdings of that entity. Alternatively, at the option of the reporting person, the entire amount of the entity's interest may be reported. *See* Rule 16a–1(a)(2)(ii)(B) and Rule 16a–1(a)(2)(iii).

(v) Where more than one beneficial owner of the same equity securities must report transactions on Form 4, such owners may file Form 4 individually or jointly. Joint and group filings may be made by any designated beneficial owner. Transactions with respect to securities owned separately by any joint or group filer are permitted to be included in the joint filing. Indicate only the name and address of the designated filer in Item 1 of Form 4 and attach a listing of the names and IRS or social security numbers (or addresses in lieu thereof) of each other reporting person. Joint and group filings must include all required information for each beneficial owner, and such filings must be signed by each beneficial owner, or on behalf of such owner by an authorized person. If the space provided for signatures is insufficient, attach a signature page. Submit any attached listing of names or signatures on another Form 4, copy of Form 4 or separate page of 8½ by 11 inch white paper, indicate the number of pages comprising the report (Form plus attachments) at the bottom of each report page (*e.g.*, 1 of 3, 2 of 3, 3 of 3), and include the name of the designated filer and information required by Items 2 and 4 of the Form on the attachment.

(c) *Non-Derivative and Derivative Securities*

(i) Report acquisitions or dispositions and holdings of non-derivative securities in Table I. Report acquisitions or dispositions and holdings of derivative securities (*e.g.*, puts, calls, options, warrants, convertible securities, or other rights or obligations to buy or sell securities) in Table II. Report the exercise or conversion of a derivative security in Table II (as a disposition of the derivative security) and report in Table I the holdings of the underlying security. Report acquisitions or dispositions and holdings of derivative securities that are both equity securities and convertible or exchangeable for other equity securities (*e.g.*, convertible preferred securities) only in Table II.

(ii) The title of a derivative security and the title of the equity security underlying the derivative security should be shown separately in the appropriate columns in Table II. The "puts" and "calls" reported in Table II include, in addition to separate puts and calls, any combination of the two, such as spreads and straddles. In reporting an option in Table II, state whether it represents a right to buy, a right to sell, an obligation to buy, or an obligation to sell the equity securities subject to the option.

(iii) Describe in the appropriate columns in Table II characteristics of derivative securities, including title, exercise or conversion price, date exercisable, expiration date, and the title and amount of securities underlying the derivative security. If the transaction reported is a purchase or a sale of a derivative security, the purchase or sale price of that derivative security shall be reported in Column 8. If the transaction is the exercise or conversion of a derivative security, leave Column 8 blank and report the exercise or conversion price of the derivative security in Column 2.

(iv) Securities constituting components of a unit shall be reported separately on the applicable table (*e.g.*, if a unit has a non-derivative security component and a derivative security component, the non-derivative security component shall be reported in Table I and the derivative security component shall be reported in Table II). The relationship between individual securities comprising the unit shall be indicated in the space provided for explanation of responses. When securities are purchased or sold as a unit, state the purchase or sale price per unit and other required information regarding the unit securities.

5. Price of Securities

(a) Prices of securities shall be reported in U.S. dollars on a per share basis, not an aggregate basis, except that the aggregate price of debt shall be stated. Amounts reported shall exclude brokerage commissions and other costs of execution.

(b) If consideration other than cash was paid for the security, describe the consideration, including the value of the consideration, in the space provided for explanation of responses.

6. Additional Information

If the space provided in the line items of this Form or space provided for additional comments is insufficient, attach another Form 4, copy of Form 4 or a separate page of 8½ by 11 inch white paper to Form 4, completed as appropriate to include the additional comments. Each attached page must include information required in Items 1, 2 and 4 of the Form. The number of pages comprising the report (Form plus attachments) shall be indicated at the bottom of each report page (*e.g.*, 1 of 3, 2 of 3, 3 of 3). If additional information is not provided in this manner, it will be assumed that no additional information was provided.

7. Signature

(a) If the Form is filed for an individual, it shall be signed by that person or specifically on behalf of the individual by a person authorized to sign for the individual. If signed on behalf of the individual by another person, the authority of such person to sign the Form shall be confirmed to the Commission in writing in an attachment to the Form or as soon as practicable in an amendment by the individual for whom the Form is filed, unless such a confirmation still in effect is on file with the Commission. The confirming statement need only indicate that the reporting person authorizes and designates the named person or persons to file the Form on the reporting person's behalf, and state the duration of the authorization.

(b) If the Form is filed for a corporation, partnership, trust, or other entity, the capacity in which the individual signed shall be set forth (*e.g.*, John Smith, Secretary, on behalf of X Corporation).

8. Transaction Codes

Use the codes listed below to indicate in Table I, Column 3 and Table II, Column 4 the character of the transaction reported. Use the code that most appropriately describes the transaction. If the transaction is not specifically listed, use transaction code "J" and describe the nature of the transaction in the space for explanation of responses. If a transaction is voluntarily reported earlier than required, place "V" in the appropriate column to so indicate; otherwise, the column should be left blank.

If a transaction involves an equity swap or instrument with similar characteristics, use transaction Code "K" in addition to the code(s) that most appropriately describes the transaction, *e.g.*, "S/K" or "P/K."

General Transaction Codes

P—Open market or private purchase of non-derivative or derivative security

S—Open market or private sale of non-derivative or derivative security

V—Transaction voluntarily reported earlier than required

Rule 16b–3 Transaction Codes

A—Grant, award or other acquisition pursuant to Rule 16b–3(d)

D—Disposition to the issuer of issuer equity securities pursuant to Rule 16b–3(e)

F—Payment of exercise price or tax liability by delivering or withholding securities incident to the receipt, exercise, or vesting of a security issued in accordance with Rule 16b–3

I—Discretionary transaction in accordance with Rule 16b–3(f) resulting in acquisition or disposition of issuer securities

M—Exercise or conversion of derivative security exempted pursuant to Rule 16b–3

Derivative Securities Codes (Except for transactions exempted pursuant to Rule 16b–3)

C—Conversion of derivative security

E—Expiration of short derivative position

H—Expiration (or cancellation) of long derivative position with value received

O—Exercise of out-of-the-money derivative security

X—Exercise of in-the-money or at-the-money derivative security

Other Section 16(b) Exempt Transaction and Small Acquisition Codes (Except for Rule 16b–3 codes above)

G—Bona fide gift

L—Small acquisition under Rule 16a–6

W—Acquisition or disposition by will or the laws of descent and distribution

Z—Deposit into or withdrawal from voting trust

Other Transaction Codes

J—Other acquisition or disposition (describe transaction)

K—Transaction in equity swap or instrument with similar characteristics

U—Disposition pursuant to a tender of shares in a change of control transaction

FORM 4

☐ Check this box if no longer subject to Section 16. Form 4 or Form 5 obligations may continue. *See* Instruction 1(b).

U.S. SECURITIES AND EXCHANGE COMMISSION
Washington, D.C. 20549

STATEMENT OF CHANGES IN BENEFICIAL OWNERSHIP

Filed pursuant to Section 16(a) of the Securities Exchange Act of 1934, Section 17(a) of the Public Utility Holding Company Act of 1935 or Section 30(f) of the Investment Company Act of 1940

OMB APPROVAL	
OMB Number:	3235-0287
Expires:	April 30, 1997
Estimated average burden hours per response	0.5

1. Name and Address of Reporting Person*
(Last) (First) (Middle)
(Street)
(City) (State) (Zip)

* If the Form is filed by more than one Reporting Person, *see* instruction 5(b)(v).

2. Issuer Name and Ticker or Trading Symbol

3. I.R.S. Identification Number of Reporting Person, if an entity (Voluntary)

4. Statement for Month/Year

5. If Amendment, Date of Original (Month/Year)

6. If Amendment, Date of Original (Month/Day/Year)

7. Individual or Joint/Group Filing (Check applicable line)
____ Form Filed by One Reporting Person
____ Form Filed by More Than One Reporting Person

Table I — Non-Derivative Securities Acquired, Disposed of, or Beneficially Owned

1. Title of Security (Instr. 3)	2. Transaction Date (Month/Day/Year)	3. Transaction Code (Instr. 8)		4. Securities Acquired (A) or Disposed of (D) (Instr. 3, 4 and 5)			5. Amount of Securities Beneficailly Owned at End of Month (Instr. 3 and 4)	6. Ownership Form: Direct (D) or Indirect (I) (Instr. 4)	7. Nature of Indirect Beneficial Ownership (Instr. 4)
		Code	V	Amount	(A) or (D)	Price			

Reminder: Report on a separate line for each class of securities beneficially owned directly or indirectly.
(Print or Type Responses)

(Over)
SEC 1474 (8/92)

[G5361]

FORM 4 (continued)

Table II — Derivative Securities Acquired, Disposed of, or Beneficially Owned
(*e.g.*, puts, calls, warrants, options, convertible securities)

1. Title of Derivative Security (Instr. 3)	2. Conversion or Exercise Price of Derivative Security	3. Transaction Date (Month/Day/Year)	4. Transaction Code (Instr. 8)		5. Number of Derivative Securities Acquired (A) or Disposed of (D) (Instr. 3, 4, and 5)		6. Date Exercisable and Expiration Date (Month/Day/Year)		7. Title and Amount of Underlying Securities (Instr. 3 and 4)		8. Price of Derivative Security (Instr. 5)	9. Number of Derivative Securities Beneficially Owned at End of Month (Instr. 4)	10. Ownership Form of Derivative Security: Direct (D) or Indirect (I) (Instr. 4)	11. Nature of Indirect Beneficial Ownership (Instr. 4)
			Code	V	(A)	(D)	Date Exercisable	Expiration Date	Title	Amount or Number of Shares				

Explanation of Responses:

**Intentional misstatements or omissions of facts constitute Federal Criminal Violations.
See 18 U.S.C. 1001 and 15 U.S.C. 78ff(a).

**Signature of Reporting Person — Date

Note: File three copies of this Form, one of which must be manually signed.
If space provided is insufficient, *see* Instruction 6 for procedure.

[G5362]

Page 2
SEC 1474 (8/92)

UNITED STATES
SECURITIES AND EXCHANGE COMMISSION
Washington, D.C. 20549

FORM 5

ANNUAL STATEMENT OF BENEFICIAL OWNERSHIP OF SECURITIES

THE COMMISSION IS AUTHORIZED TO SOLICIT THE INFORMATION REQUIRED BY THIS FORM PURSUANT TO SECTIONS 16(a) AND 23(a) OF THE SECURITIES EXCHANGE ACT OF 1934 (15 U.S.C. 78p(a) AND 78w(a)); SECTIONS 17(a) AND 20(a) OF THE PUBLIC UTILITY HOLDING COMPANY ACT OF 1935 (15 U.S.C. 79q(a) AND 79t(a)); AND SECTIONS 30(h) AND 38 OF THE INVESTMENT COMPANY ACT OF 1940 (15 U.S.C. 80a–29(h) AND 80a–37), AND THE RULES AND REGULATIONS THEREUNDER.

DISCLOSURE OF INFORMATION SPECIFIED ON THIS FORM IS MANDATORY, EXCEPT FOR DISCLOSURE OF THE I.R.S. IDENTIFICATION NUMBER OF THE REPORTING PERSON, IF SUCH PERSON IS AN ENTITY, WHICH IS VOLUNTARY. IF SUCH NUMBERS ARE FURNISHED, THEY WILL ASSIST THE COMMISSION IN DISTINGUISHING REPORTING PERSONS WITH SIMILAR NAMES AND WILL FACILITATE THE PROMPT PROCESSING OF THE FORM. THE INFORMATION WILL BE USED FOR THE PRIMARY PURPOSE OF DISCLOSING THE TRANSACTIONS AND HOLDINGS OF DIRECTORS, OFFICERS, AND BENEFICIAL OWNERS OF REGISTERED COMPANIES. INFORMATION DISCLOSED WILL BE A MATTER OF PUBLIC RECORD AND AVAILABLE FOR INSPECTION BY MEMBERS OF THE PUBLIC. THE COMMISSION CAN USE IT IN INVESTIGATIONS OR LITIGATION INVOLVING THE FEDERAL SECURITIES LAWS OR OTHER CIVIL, CRIMINAL, OR REGULATORY STATUTES OR PROVISIONS, AS WELL AS FOR REFERRAL TO OTHER GOVERNMENTAL AUTHORITIES AND SELF–REGULATORY ORGANIZATIONS. FAILURE TO DISCLOSE REQUIRED INFORMATION MAY RESULT IN CIVIL OR CRIMINAL ACTION AGAINST PERSONS INVOLVED FOR VIOLATIONS OF THE FEDERAL SECURITIES LAWS AND RULES.

GENERAL INSTRUCTIONS

1. When Form Must be Filed

(a) This Form must be filed on or before the 45th day after the end of the issuer's fiscal year in accordance with Rule 16a–3(f). This Form and any amendment is deemed filed with the Commission or the Exchange on the date it is received by the Commission or the Exchange, respectively. *See,* however, Rule 16a–3(h) regarding delivery to a third party business that guarantees delivery of the filing no later than the specified due date.

(b) A reporting person no longer subject to Section 16 of the Securities Exchange Act of 1934 ("Exchange Act") must check the exit box appearing on this Form. Transactions and holdings previously reported are not required to be included on this Form. Form 4 or Form 5 obligations may continue to be applicable. *See* Rules 16a–3(f) and 16a–2(b).

(c) A separate Form shall be filed to reflect beneficial ownership of securities of each issuer, except that a single statement shall be filed with respect to the securities of a registered public utility holding company and all of its subsidiary companies.

(d) If a reporting person is not an officer, director, or 10% holder, the person should check "other" in Item 6 (Relationship of Reporting Person to Issuer) and describe the reason for reporting status in the space provided.

2. Where Form Must be Filed

(a) File three copies of this Form or any amendment, at least one of which is manually signed, with the Securities and Exchange Commission, 450 5th Street, N.W., Washington, D.C., 20549. (*Note:* Acknowledgement of receipt by the Commission may be obtained by enclosing a self-addressed stamped postcard identifying the Form or amendment filed.) Alternatively, this Form is permitted to be submitted to the Commission in electronic format at the option of the reporting person pursuant to § 232.101(b)(4) of this chapter.

(b) At the time this Form or any amendment is filed with the Commission, file one copy with each Exchange on which any class of securities of the issuer is registered. If the issuer has designated a single Exchange to receive Section 16 filings, the copy shall be filed with that Exchange only.

(c) Any person required to file this Form or amendment shall, not later than the time the Form or amendment is transmitted for filing with the Commission, send or deliver a copy to the person designated by the issuer to receive the copy or, if no person is so designated, the issuer's corporate secretary (or person performing similar functions) in accordance with Rule 16a–3(e).

3. Class of Securities Reported

(a)(i) Persons reporting pursuant to Section 16(a) of the Exchange Act shall include information as to transactions and holdings required to be reported in any class of equity securities of the issuer and the beneficial ownership at the end of the year of that class of equity securities, even though one or more of such classes may not be registered pursuant to Section 12 of the Exchange Act.

(ii) Persons reporting pursuant to Section 17(a) of the Public Utility Holding Company Act of 1935 shall include transactions and holdings required to be reported in any class of securities (equity or debt) of the registered holding company and any of its subsidiary companies and the beneficial ownership at the end of the issuer's fiscal year of that class of securities. Specify the name of the parent or subsidiary issuing the securities.

(iii) Persons reporting pursuant to Section 30(h) of the Investment Company Act of 1940 shall include transactions and holdings required to be reported in any class of securities (equity or debt) of the registered closed-end investment company (other than "short-term paper" as defined in Section 2(a)(38) of the Act) and the beneficial ownership at the end of the year of that class of securities.

(b) The title of the security should clearly identify the class, even if the issuer has only one class of securities outstanding; for example, "Common Stock," "Class A Common Stock," "Class B Convertible Preferred Stock," etc.

(c) The amount of securities beneficially owned should state the face amount of debt securities (U.S. Dollars) or the number of equity securities, whichever is appropriate.

4. Transactions and Holdings Required to be Reported

(a) *General Requirements*

(i) Pursuant to Rule 16a–3(f), if not previously reported, the following transactions, and total beneficial ownership as of the end of the issuer's fiscal year (or the earlier date applicable to a person ceasing to be an insider during the fiscal year) for any class of securities for which a transaction is reported, shall be reported:

(A) any transaction during the issuer's most recent fiscal year that was exempt from Section 16(b) of the Act, except: (1) any exercise or conversion of derivative securities exempt under either § 240.16b–3 or § 240.16b–6(b) (these are required to be reported on Form 4); (2) any transaction exempt from Section 16(b) of the Act pursuant to Rule 16b–3(c) of this section, which is exempt from Section 16(a) of the Act; and (3) any transaction exempt from Section 16 of the Act pursuant to another Section 16(a) rule;

(B) any small acquisition or series of acquisitions in a six month period during the issuer's fiscal year not exceeding $10,000 in market value (*see* Rule 16a–6); and

(C) any transactions or holdings that should have been reported during the issuer's fiscal year on a Form 3 or Form 4, but were not reported. The first Form 5 filing obligation shall include all holdings and transactions that should have been reported in each of the issuer's last two fiscal years but were not. *See* Instruction 8 for the code to identify delinquent Form 3 holdings or Form 4 transactions reported on this Form 5.

Note: A required Form 3 or Form 4 must be filed within the time specified by the Form. Form 3 holdings or Form 4 transactions reported on Form 5 represent delinquent Form 3 and Form 4 filings.

(ii) Each transaction should be reported on a separate line. Transaction codes specified in Instruction 8 should be used to identify the nature of the transaction resulting in an acquisition or disposition of a security.

(iii) Every transaction shall be reported even though acquisitions and dispositions with respect to a class of securities are equal. Report total beneficial ownership as of the end of the issuer's fiscal year for all classes of securities in which a transaction was reported.

(b) *Beneficial Ownership Reported (Pecuniary Interest)*

(i) Although, for purposes of determining status as a ten percent holder, a person is deemed to beneficially own securities over which that person has voting or investment control (*see* Rule 16a–1(a)(1)), for reporting transactions and holdings, a person is deemed to be the beneficial owner of securities if that person has or shares the opportunity, directly or indirectly, to profit or share in any profit derived from a transaction in the securities ("pecuniary interest"). *See* Rule 16a–1(a)(2). *See also* Rule 16a–8 for the application of the beneficial ownership definition to trust holdings and transactions.

(ii) Both direct and indirect beneficial ownership of securities shall be reported. Securities beneficially owned directly are those held in the reporting person's name or in the name of a bank, broker or nominee for the account of the reporting person. In addition, securities held as joint tenants, tenants in common, tenants by the entirety, or as community property are to be reported as held directly. If a person has a pecuniary interest, by reason of any contract, understanding, or relationship (including a family relationship or arrangement), in securities held in the name of another person, that person is an indirect beneficial owner of the securities. *See* Rule 16a–1(a)(2)(ii) for certain indirect beneficial ownerships.

(iii) Report transactions in securities beneficially owned directly on separate lines from those beneficially owned indirectly. Report different forms of indirect ownership on separate lines. The nature of indirect ownership shall be stated as specifically as possible; for example, "By Self as Trustee for X," "By Spouse," "By X Trust," "By Y Corporation," etc.

(iv) In stating the amount of securities acquired, disposed of, or beneficially owned indirectly through a partnership, corporation, trust, or other entity, report the number of securities representing the reporting person's proportionate interest in transactions conducted by that entity or holdings of that entity. Alternatively, at the option of the reporting person, the entire amount of the entity's interest may be reported. *See* Rule 16a–1(a)(2)(ii)(B) and Rule 16a–1(a)(2)(iii).

(v) Where more than one beneficial owner of the same equity securities must report on Form 5, such owners may file Form 5 individually or jointly. Joint and group filings may be made by any designated beneficial owner. Transactions and holdings with respect to securities owned separately by any joint or group filer are permitted to be included in the joint filing. Indicate only the name and address of the designated filer in Item 1 of Form 5 and attach a listing of the names and IRS or social security numbers (or addresses in lieu thereof) of each other reporting person. Joint and group filings must include all required information for each beneficial owner, and such filings must be signed by each beneficial owner, or on behalf of such owner by an authorized person. If the space provided for signatures is insufficient, attach a signature page. Submit any attached listing of names or signatures on another Form 5, copy of Form 5 or separate page of 8½ by 11 inch white paper, indicate the number of pages comprising the report (Form plus attachments) at the bottom of each report page (*e.g.*, 1 of 3, 2 of 3, 3 of 3), and include the name of the designated filer and information required by Items 2 and 4 of the Form on the attachment.

(c) *Non–Derivative and Derivative Securities*

(i) Report acquisitions or dispositions and holdings of non-derivative securities in Table I. Report acquisitions or dispositions and holdings of derivative securities (*e.g.*, puts, calls, options, warrants, convertible securities, or other rights or obligations to buy or sell securities) in Table II. Report the exercise or conversion of a derivative security in Table II (as a disposition of the derivative security) and report in Table I the holdings of the underlying security. Report acquisitions or dispositions and holdings of derivative securities that are both equity securities and convertible or exchangeable for other equity securities (*e.g.*, convertible preferred securities) only on Table II.

(ii) The title of a derivative security and the title of the equity security underlying the derivative security should be shown separately in the appropriate columns in Table II. The "puts" and "calls" reported in Table II include, in addition to separate puts and calls, any combination of the two, such as spreads and straddles. In reporting an option in Table II, state whether it represents a right to buy, a right to sell, an obligation to buy, or an obligation to sell the equity securities subject to the option.

(iii) Describe in the appropriate columns in Table II characteristics of derivative securities, including title, exercise or conversion price, date exercisable, expiration date, and the title and amount of securities underlying the derivative security. If the transaction reported is a purchase or sale of a derivative security, the purchase or sale price of the derivative security shall be reported in column 8. If the transaction is the exercise or conversion of a derivative security, leave column 8 blank and report the exercise or conversion price of the derivative security in column 2.

(iv) Securities constituting components of a unit shall be reported separately on the applicable table (*e.g.*, if a unit has a non-derivative security component and a derivative security component, the non-derivative security component shall be reported in Table I and the derivative security component shall be reported in Table II). The relationship between individual securities comprising the unit shall be indicated in the space provided for explanation of responses. When securities are purchased or sold as a unit, state the purchase or sale price per unit and other required information regarding the unit securities.

5. Price of Securities

(a) Prices of securities shall be reported in U.S. dollars and on a per share basis, not an aggregate basis, except that the aggregate price of debt shall be stated. Amounts reported shall exclude brokerage commissions and other costs of execution.

(b) If consideration other than cash was paid for the security, describe the consideration, including the value of the consideration in the space provided for explanation of responses.

6. Additional Information

If the space provided in the line items of this Form or space provided for additional comments is insufficient, attach another Form 5, copy of Form 5 or a separate page of 8½ by 11 inch white paper to Form 5, completed as appropriate to include the additional comments. Each attached page must include information required in Items 1, 2 and 4 of the Form. The number of pages comprising the report (Form plus attachments) shall be indicated at the bottom of each report page (*e.g.*, 1 of 3, 2 of 3, 3 of 3). If additional information is not provided in this manner, it will be assumed that no additional information was provided.

7. Signature

(a) If the Form is filed for an individual, it shall be signed by that person or specifically on behalf of the individual by a person authorized to sign for the individual. If signed on behalf of the individual by another person, the authority of such person to sign the Form shall be confirmed to the Commission in writing in an attachment to the Form or as soon as practicable in an amendment by the individual for whom the Form is filed, unless such a confirmation still in effect is on file with the Commission. The confirming statement need only indicate that the reporting person authorizes and designates the named person or persons to file the Form on the reporting person's behalf, and state the duration of the authorization.

(b) If the Form is filed for a corporation, partnership, trust, or other entity, the capacity in which the individual signed shall be set forth (*e.g.*, John Smith, Secretary, on behalf of X Corporation).

8. Transaction Codes

Use the codes listed below to indicate in Table I, Column 3 and Table II, Column 4 the character of the transaction reported. Use the code that most appropriately describes the transaction. If the transaction is not specifically listed, use transaction Code "J" and describe the nature of the transaction in the space for explanation of responses.

If a transaction involves an equity swap or instrument with similar characteristics, use transaction Code "K" in addition to the code(s) that most appropriately describes the transaction, *e.g.*, "S/K" or "P/K."

General Transaction Codes

P—Open market or private purchase of non-derivative or derivative security

S—Open market or private sale of non-derivative or derivative security

Rule 16b–3 Transaction Codes

A—Grant, award or other acquisition pursuant to Rule 16b-3(d)

D—Disposition to the issuer of issuer equity securities pursuant to Rule 16b-3(e)

F—Payment of exercise price or tax liability by delivering or withholding securities incident to the receipt, exercise or vesting of a security issued in accordance with Rule 16b–3

I—Discretionary transaction in accordance with Rule 16b-3(f) resulting in acquisition or disposition of issuer securities

M—Exercise or conversion of derivative security exempted pursuant to Rule 16b–3

Derivative Securities Codes (Except for transactions exempted pursuant to Rule 16b–3)

C—Conversion of derivative security

E—Expiration of short derivative position

H—Expiration (or cancellation) of long derivative position with value received

O—Exercise of out-of-the-money derivative security

X—Exercise of in-the-money or at-the-money derivative security

Other Section 16(b) Exempt Transaction and Small Acquisition Codes (Except for Rule 16b–3 codes above)

G—Bona fide gift

L—Small acquisition under Rule 16a–6

W—Acquisition or disposition by will or the laws of descent and distribution

Z—Deposit into or withdrawal from voting trust

Other Transaction Codes

J—Other acquisition or disposition (describe transaction)

K—Transaction in equity swap or instrument with similar characteristics

U—Disposition pursuant to a tender of shares in a change of control transaction

To indicate that a holding should have been reported previously on Form 3, place a "3" in Table I, column 3 or Table II, column 4, as appropriate. Indicate in the space provided for explanation of responses the event triggering the Form 3 filing obligation. To indicate that a transaction should have been reported previously on Form 4, place a "4" next to the transaction code reported in Table I, column 3 or Table II, column 4 (*e.g.*, an open market purchase of a non-derivative security that should have been reported previously on Form 4 should be designated as "P4"). To indicate that a transaction should have been reported on a previous Form 5, place a "5" in Table I, column 3 or Table II, column 4, as appropriate. In addition, the appropriate box on the front page of the Form should be checked.

Form 3 or Form 4 Holdings or Transactions Not Previously Reported

To indicate that a holding should have been reported previously on Form 3, place a "3" in Table I, column 3 or Table II, column 4, as appropriate. Indicate in the space provided for explanation of responses the event triggering the Form 3 filing obligation. To indicate that a transaction should have been reported previously on Form 4, place a "4" next to the transaction code reported in Table I, column 3 or Table II, column 4 (*e.g.*, an open market purchase of a non-derivative security that should have been reported previously on Form 4 should be designated as "P4"). In addition, the appropriate box on the front page of the Form should be checked.

FORM 5

☐ Check box if no longer subject to Section 16. Form 4 or Form 5 obligations may continue. *See* Instruction 1(b).

☐ Form 3 Holdings Reported

☐ Form 4 Transactions Reported

U.S. SECURITIES AND EXCHANGE COMMISSION
Washington, D.C. 20549

ANNUAL STATEMENT OF CHANGES IN BENEFICIAL OWNERSHIP

Filed pursuant to Section 16(a) of the Securities Exchange Act of 1934, Section 17(a) of the Public Utility Holding Company Act of 1935 or Section 30(h) of the Investment Company Act of 1940

OMB APPROVAL	
OMB Number:	3235-0362
Expires:	April 30, 1997
Estimated average burden hours per response.	1.0

1. Name and Address of Reporting Person* (Last) (First) (Middle) (Street) (City) (State) (Zip) * If the Form is filed by more than one Reporting Person, *see* instruction 5(b)(v).	2. Issuer Name and Ticker or Trading Symbol		6. If Amendment, Date of Original (Month/Day/Year)
	3. I.R.S. Identification Number of Reporting Person, if an entity (Voluntary)	4. Statement for Month/Year 5. If Amendment, Date of Original (Month/Year)	7. Individual or Joint/Group Filing (Check applicable line) ____ Form Filed by One Reporting Person ____ Form Filed by More Than One Reporting Person

Table I — Non-Derivative Securities Acquired, Disposed of, or Beneficially Owned

1. Title of Security (Instr. 3)	2. Transaction Date (Month/Day/Year)	3. Transaction Code (Instr. 8)	4. Securities Acquired (A) or Disposed of (D) (Instr. 3, 4 and 5)			5. Amount of Securities Beneficially Owned at End of Issuer's Fiscal Year (Instr. 3 and 4)	6. Ownership Form: Direct (D) or Indirect (I) (Instr. 4)	7. Nature of Indirect Beneficial Ownership (Instr. 4)
			Amount	(A) or (D)	Price			

Reminder: Report on a separate line for each class of securities beneficially owned directly or indirectly.
(Print or Type Responses)

(Over)
SEC 2270 (3/91)

FORM 5 (continued)

Table II — Derivative Securities Acquired, Disposed of, or Beneficially Owned
***(e.g.*, puts, calls, warrants, options, convertible securities)**

1. Title of Derivative Security (Instr. 3)	2. Conversion or Exercise Price of Derivative Security	3. Transaction Date (Month/Day/Year)	4. Transaction Code (Instr. 8)	5. Number of Derivative Securities Acquired (A) or Disposed of (D) (Instr. 3, 4, and 5)		6. Date Exercisable and Expiration Date (Month/Day/Year)		7. Title and Amount of Underlying Securities (Instr. 3 and 4)		8. Price of Derivative Security (Instr. 5)	9. Number of Derivative Securities Beneficially Owned at End of Year (Instr. 4)	10. Ownership of Derivative Security: Direct (D) or Indirect (I) (Instr. 4)	11. Nature of Indirect Beneficial Ownership (Instr. 4)
				(A)	(D)	Date Exercisable	Expiration Date	Title	Amount or Number of Shares				

Explanation of Responses:

**Intentional misstatements or omissions of facts constitute Federal Criminal Violations.
See 18 U.S.C. 1001 and 15 U.S.C. 78ff(a).

**Signature of Reporting Person

Date

Note: File three copies of this Form, one of which must be manually signed.
If space provided is insufficient, *see* Instruction 6 for procedure.

Page 2
SEC 2270 (3/91)

UNITED STATES
SECURITIES AND EXCHANGE COMMISSION
Washington, D.C. 20549

FORM 8–A

FOR REGISTRATION OF CERTAIN CLASSES OF SECURITIES PURSUANT TO SECTION 12(b) OR (g) OF THE SECURITIES EXCHANGE ACT OF 1934

GENERAL INSTRUCTIONS

A. Rule as to Use of Form 8–A

(a) Subject to paragraph (b) below, this form may be used for registration pursuant to Section 12(b) or (g) of the Securities Exchange Act of 1934 of any class of securities of any issuer which is required to file reports pursuant to Section 13 or 15(d) of that Act or pursuant to an order exempting the exchange on which the issuer has securities listed from registration as a national securities exchange.

(b) If the registrant would be required to file an annual report pursuant to Section 15(d) of the Act for its last fiscal year, except for the fact that the registration statement on this form will become effective before such report is required to be filed, an annual report for such fiscal year shall nevertheless be filed within the period specified in the appropriate annual report form.

(c) If this form is used for the registration of a class of securities under Section 12(b), it shall become effective:

(1) If a class of securities is not concurrently being registered under the Securities Act of 1933 (15 U.S.C. 77a et seq.) ("Securities Act"), upon the later of receipt by the Commission of certification from the national securities exchange listed on this form or the filing of the Form 8–A with the Commission; or

(2) If a class of securities is concurrently being registered under the Securities Act, upon the later of the filing of the Form 8–A with the Commission, receipt by the Commission of certification from the national securities exchange listed on this form or effectiveness of the Securities Act registration statement relating to the class of securities.

(d) If this form is used for the registration of a class of securities under Section 12(g), it shall become effective:

(1) If a class of securities is not concurrently being registered under the Securities Act, upon the filing of the Form 8–A with the Commission; or

(2) If a class of securities is concurrently being registered under the Securities Act, upon the later of the filing of the Form 8–A with the Commission or the effectiveness of the Securities Act registration statement relating to the class of securities.

B. Application of General Rules and Regulations

(a) The General Rules and Regulations under the Act contain certain general requirements which are applicable to registration on any form. These general requirements should be carefully read and observed in the preparation and filing of registration statements on this form.

(b) Particular attention is directed to Regulation 12B which contains general requirements regarding matters such as the kind and size of paper to be used, legibility, information to be given whenever the title of securities is required to be stated, incorporation by reference and the filing of the registration statement. The definitions contained in Rule 12b–2 should be especially noted.

C. Preparation of Registration Statement

This form is not to be used as a blank form to be filled in, but only as a guide in the preparation of the registration statement on paper meeting the requirements of Rule 12b–12. The registration statement shall contain the item numbers and captions, but the text of the items may be omitted. The answers to the items shall be prepared in the manner specified in Rule 12b–13.

D. Signature and Filing of Registration Statement

Eight complete copies of the registration statement, including all papers and documents filed as a part thereof (other than exhibits) shall be filed with the Commission and at least one such copy shall be filed with each exchange on which the securities are to be registered. Exhibits shall be filed with the Commission and with any exchange in accordance with the Instructions as to Exhibits. At least one copy of the registration statement filed with the Commission and one filed with each exchange shall be manually signed. Unsigned copies shall be conformed.

UNITED STATES
SECURITIES AND EXCHANGE COMMISSION

Washington, D.C. 20549

FORM 8–A

FOR REGISTRATION OF CERTAIN CLASSES OF SECURITIES PURSUANT TO SECTION 12(b) OR (g) OF THE SECURITIES EXCHANGE ACT OF 1934

____
(Exact name of registrant as specified in its charter)

____________________ ____________________
(State of incorporation or organization) (I.R.S. Employer Identification No.)

____________________ ____________________
(Address of principal executive offices) (Zip Code)

Securities to be registered pursuant to Section 12(b) of the Act:

Title of each class to be so registered	Name of each exchange on which each class is to be registered

If this form relates to the registration of a class of securities pursuant to Section 12(b) of the Exchange Act and is effective pursuant to General Instruction A.(c), check the following box. [ ]

If this form relates to the registration of a class of securities pursuant to Section 12(g) of the Exchange Act and is effective pursuant to General Instruction A.(d), check the following box. [ ]

Securities Act registration statement file number to which this form relates:

____
(if applicable)

Securities to be registered pursuant to Section 12(g) of the Act:

____
(Title of class)

____
(Title of class)

INFORMATION REQUIRED IN REGISTRATION STATEMENT

Item 1. Description of Registrant's Securities to be Registered

Furnish the information required by Item 202 of Regulation S–K (§ 229.202 of this chapter) or Item 202 of Regulation S–B (§ 228.202 of this chapter), as applicable.

Instruction. If a description of the securities comparable to that required here is contained in any prior filing with the Commission, such description may be incorporated by reference to such other filing in answer to this item. If such description will be included in a form of prospectus subsequently filed by the registrant pursuant to Rule 424(b) under the Securities Act this registration statement shall state that such prospectus shall be deemed to be incorporated by reference into the registration statement. If the securities are to be registered on a national securities exchange and the description has not previously been filed with such exchange, copies of the description shall be filed with copies of the application filed with the exchange.

Item 2. Exhibits

List below all exhibits filed as a part of the registration statement:

Instruction. See the instructions as to exhibits, set forth below.

SIGNATURE

Pursuant to the requirements of Section 12 of the Securities Exchange Act of 1934, the registrant has duly caused this registration statement to be signed on its behalf by the undersigned, thereto duly authorized.

(Registrant)* ____________________

Date ____________________

By ____________________

INSTRUCTIONS AS TO EXHIBITS

If the securities to be registered on this form are to be registered on an exchange on which other securities of the registrant are registered, or are to be registered pursuant to Section 12(g) of this Act, copies of all constituent instruments defining the rights of the holders of each class of such securities, including any contracts or other documents which limit or qualify the rights of such holders, shall be filed as exhibits with each copy of the registration statement filed with the Commission or with an exchange, subject to Rule 12b–32 regarding incorporation of exhibits by reference.

* Print the name and title of the signing officer under his signature.

SECURITIES AND EXCHANGE COMMISSION

Washington, D.C. 20549

FORM 10

GENERAL FORM FOR REGISTRATION OF SECURITIES PURSUANT TO SECTION 12(b) OR (g) OF THE SECURITIES EXCHANGE ACT OF 1934

GENERAL INSTRUCTIONS

A. Rule as to Use of Form 10

Form 10 shall be used for registration pursuant to Section 12(b) or (g) of the Securities Exchange Act of 1934 of classes of securities of issuers for which no other form is prescribed.

B. Application of General Rules and Regulations

(a) The General Rules and Regulations under the Act contain certain general requirements which are applicable to registration on any form. These general requirements should be carefully read and observed in the preparation and filing of registration statements on this form.

(b) Particular attention is directed to Regulation 12B which contains general requirements regarding matters such as the kind and size of paper to be used, the legibility of the registration statement, the information to be given whenever the title of securities is required to be stated, and the filing of the registration statement. The definitions contained in Rule 12b–2 should be especially noted.

C. Preparation of Registration Statement

(a) This form is not to be used as a blank form to be filled in, but only as a guide in the preparation of the registration statement on paper meeting the requirements of Rule 12b–12. The registration statement shall contain the item numbers and captions, but the text of the items may be omitted. The answers to the items shall be prepared in the manner specified in Rule 12b–13.

(b) Unless otherwise stated, the information required shall be given as of a date reasonably close to the date of filing the registration statement.

(c) Attention is directed to Rule 12b–20 which states: "In addition to the information expressly required to be included in a statement or report, there shall be added such further material information, if any, as may be necessary to make the required statements, in light of the circumstances under which they are made, not misleading."

D. Signature and Filing of Registration Statement

Three complete copies of the registration statement, including financial statements, exhibits and all other papers and documents filed as a part thereof, and five additional copies which need not include exhibits, shall be filed with the Commission. At least one complete copy of the registration statement, including financial statements, exhibits and all other papers and documents filed as a part thereof, shall be filed with each exchange on which any class of securities is to be registered. At least one complete copy of the registration statement filed with the Commission and one such copy filed with each exchange shall be manually signed. Copies not manually signed shall bear typed or printed signatures.

E. Omission of Information Regarding Foreign Subsidiaries

Information required by any item or other requirement of this form with respect to any foreign subsidiary may be omitted to the extent that the required disclosure would be detrimental to the registrant. However, financial statements, otherwise required, shall not be omitted pursuant to this instruction. Where information is omitted pursuant to this instruction, a statement shall be made that such information has been omitted and the names of the subsidiaries involved shall be separately furnished to the Commission. The Commission may, in its discretion, call for justification that the required disclosure would be detrimental.

F. Incorporation by Reference

Attention is directed to Rule 12b–23 which provides for the incorporation by reference of information contained in certain documents in answer or partial answer to any item of a registration statement.

SECURITIES AND EXCHANGE COMMISSION

Washington, D.C. 20549

FORM 10

GENERAL FORM FOR REGISTRATION OF SECURITIES

PURSUANT TO SECTION 12(b) OR (g) OF THE SECURITIES EXCHANGE ACT OF 1934

____

(Exact name of registrant as specified in its charter)

____

(State or other jurisdiction of incorporation or organization) (I.R.S. Employer Identification No.)

____

(Address of principal executive offices) (Zip Code)

Registrant's telephone number, including area code ______________

Securities to be registered pursuant to Section 12(b) of the Act:

Title of each class to be so registered	Name of each exchange on which each class is to be registered

Securities to be registered pursuant to Section 12(g) of the Act:

____

(Title of class)

____

(Title of class)

INFORMATION REQUIRED IN REGISTRATION STATEMENT

Item 1. Business

Furnish the information required by Item 101 of Regulation S–K.

Item 2. Financial Information

Furnish the information required by Items 301, 303 and 305 of Regulation S–K.

Item 3. Properties

Furnish the information required by Item 102 of Regulation S–K.

Item 4. Security Ownership of Certain Beneficial Owners and Management

Furnish the information required by Item 403 of Regulation S–K.

Item 5. Directors and Executive Officers

Furnish the information required by Item 401 of Regulation S–K.

Item 6. Executive Compensation

Furnish the information required by Item 402 of Regulation S–K.

Item 7. Certain Relationships and Related Transactions

Furnish the information required by Item 404 of Regulation S–K.

Item 8. Legal Proceedings

Furnish the information required by Item 103 of Regulation S–K.

Item 9. Market Price of and Dividends on the Registrant's Common Equity and Related Stockholder Matters

Furnish the information required by Item 201 of Regulation S–K.

Item 10. Recent Sales of Unregistered Securities

Furnish the information required by Item 701 of Regulation S–K.

Item 11. Description of Registrant's Securities to be Registered

Furnish the information required by Item 202 of Regulation S–K (§ 229.202 of this chapter). If the class of securities to be registered will trade in the form of American Depositary Receipts, furnish Item 202(f) disclosure for such American Depositary Receipts as well.

Item 12. Indemnification of Directors and Officers

Furnish the information required by Item 702 of Regulation S–K.

Item 13. Financial Statements and Supplementary Data

Furnish all financial statements required by Regulation S–X and the supplementary financial information required by Item 302 of Regulation S–K.

Item 14. Changes in and Disagreements With Accountants on Accounting and Financial Disclosure

Furnish the information required by Item 304 of Regulation S–K.

Item 15. Financial Statements and Exhibits

(a) List separately all financial statements filed as part of the registration statement.

(b) Furnish the exhibits required by Item 601 of Regulation S–K.

SIGNATURES

Pursuant to the requirements of Section 12 of the Securities Exchange Act of 1934, the registrant has duly caused this registration statement to be signed on its behalf by the undersigned, thereunto duly authorized.

(Registrant) ______________________

Date ______________________

By (Signature)* ______________________

* Print name and title of the signing officer under his signature.

SECURITIES AND EXCHANGE COMMISSION
Washington, D.C. 20549

FORM 10–SB

GENERAL FORM FOR REGISTRATION OF SECURITIES OF SMALL BUSINESS ISSUERS

Under Section 12(b) or (g) of the Securities Exchange Act of 1934

____
(Name of Small Business Issuer in its charter)

____
(State or other jurisdiction of incorporation or organization) (I.R.S. Employer Identification No.)

____
(Address of principal executive offices) (Zip Code)

Issuer's telephone number, ______________________

Securities to be registered under Section 12(b) of the Act:

Title of each class to be so registered	Name of each exchange on which each class is to be registered

Securities to be registered under Section 12(g) of the Act:

____
(Title of class)

____
(Title of class)

GENERAL INSTRUCTIONS

A. Use of Form 10–SB

1. This Form may be used by a "small business issuer," defined in Rule 12b–2 of the Securities Exchange Act of 1934 (the "Exchange Act"), to register a class of securities under Section 12(b) or (g) of the Exchange Act. For further information as to eligibility to use this form see Item 10(a) of Regulation S–B (17 CFR 228.10 et seq.).

2. If the small business issuer is not organized under the laws of any of the states of or the United States of America, it shall at the time of filing this registration statement, file with the Commission a written irrevocable consent and power of attorney on Form F–X [§ 239.42]. Any change to the name or address of the agent for service of the issuer shall be communicated promptly to the Commission through amendment of the requisite form and referencing the file number of the registration statement.

B. Signature and Filing of Registration Statement

1. File three "complete" copies and five "additional" copies of the registration statement with the Commission and file at least one complete copy with each exchange on which the securities will be registered. A "complete" copy includes financial statements, exhibits and all other papers and documents. An "additional" copy excludes exhibits.

2. Manually sign at least one copy of the report filed with the Commission and each exchange; other copies should have typed or printed signatures.

C. Information to be Incorporated by Reference

Refer to Rule 12b–23 if information will be incorporated by reference from other documents in answer or partial answer to any item of this Form.

INFORMATION REQUIRED IN REGISTRATION STATEMENT

Item 1. Description of Business

Furnish the information required by Item 101 of Regulation S–B.

Item 2. Management's Discussion and Analysis or Plan of Operation

Furnish the information required by Item 303 of Regulation S–B.

Item 3. Description of Property

Furnish the information required by Item 102 of Regulation S–B.

Item 4. Security Ownership of Certain Beneficial Owners and Management

Furnish the information required by Item 403 of Regulation S–B.

Item 5. Directors, Executive Officers, Promoters and Control Persons

Furnish the information required by Item 401 of Regulation S–B.

Item 6. Executive Compensation

Furnish the information required by Item 402 of Regulation S–B.

Item 7. Certain Relationships and Related Transactions

Furnish the information required by Item 404 of Regulation S–B.

Item 8. Legal Proceedings

Furnish the information required by Item 103 of Regulation S–B.

Item 9. Market for Common Equity and Related Stockholder Matters

Furnish the information required by Item 201 of Regulation S–B.

Item 10. Recent Sales of Unregistered Securities

Furnish the information required by Item 701 of Regulation S–B.

Item 11. Description of Securities

Furnish the information required by Item 202 of Regulation S–B.

Item 12. Indemnification of Directors and Officers

Furnish the information required by Item 702 of Regulation S–B.

Item 13. Financial Statements

Furnish the information required by Item 310 of Regulation S–B.

Item 14. Changes In and Disagreements With Accountants on Accounting and Financial Disclosure

Furnish the information required by Item 304 of Regulation S–B.

Item 15. Financial Statements and Exhibits

(a) List separately all financial statements filed as part of the registration statement.

(b) Furnish the exhibits required by Item 601 of Regulation S–B.

SIGNATURES

In accordance with Section 12 of the Securities Exchange Act of 1934, the registrant caused this registration statement to be signed on its behalf by the undersigned, thereunto duly authorized.

____
(Registrant)

Date ______________________________

By ______________________________
(Signature) *

* Print the name and title of each signing officer under his or her signature.

SECURITIES AND EXCHANGE COMMISSION

Washington, D.C. 20549

FORM 10–Q

GENERAL INSTRUCTIONS

A. Rule as to Use of Form 10–Q

1. Form 10–Q shall be used for quarterly reports under Section 13 or 15(d) of the Securities Exchange Act of 1934 (15 U.S.C. 78m or 78o(d)), filed pursuant to Rule 13a–13 (17 CFR 240.13a–13) or Rule 15d–13 (17 CFR 240.15d–13). A quarterly report on this form pursuant to Rule 13a–13 or Rule 15d–13 shall be filed within the following period after the end of each of the first three fiscal quarters of each fiscal year, but no report need be filed for the fourth quarter of any fiscal year:

a. For accelerated filers (as defined in 17 CFR 240.12b–2):

(i) 45 days after the end of the fiscal quarter for fiscal years ending on or after December 15, 2002 and before December 15, 2004;

(ii) 40 days after the end of the fiscal quarter for fiscal years ending on or after December 15, 2004 and before December 15, 2006; and

(iii) 35 days after the end of the fiscal quarter for fiscal years ending on or after December 15, 2006; and

b. 45 days after the end of the fiscal quarter for all other issuers.

2. Form 10–Q also shall be used for transition and quarterly reports under section 13 or 15(d) of the Securities Exchange Act of 1934, filed pursuant to Rule 13a–10 or Rule 15d–10. Such transition or quarterly reports shall be filed in accordance with the requirements set forth in Rule 13a–10 or Rule 15d–10 applicable when the registrant changes its fiscal year end.

B. Application of General Rules and Regulations

1. The General Rules and Regulations under the Act contain certain general requirements which are applicable to reports on any form. These general requirements should be carefully read and observed in the preparation and filing of reports on this form.

2. Particular attention is directed to Regulation 12B which contains general requirements regarding matters such as the kind and size of paper to be used, the legibility of the report, the information to be given whenever the title of securities is required to be stated, and the filing of the report. The definitions contained in Rule 12b–2 should be especially noted. See also Regulations 13A and 15D.

C. Preparation of Report

1. This is not a blank form to be filled in. It is a guide copy to be used in preparing the report in accordance with Rules 12b–11 and 12b–12. The Commission does not furnish blank copies of this form to be filled in for filing.

2. These general instructions are not to be filed with the report. The instructions to the various captions on the form are also to be omitted from the report as filed.

D. Incorporation by Reference

1. If the registrant makes available to its stockholders or otherwise publishes, within the period prescribed for filing the report, a document or statement containing information meeting some or all of the requirements of Part I of this form, the information called for may be incorporated by reference from such published document or statement, in answer or partial answer to any item or items of Part I of this form, provided copies thereof are filed as an exhibit to Part I of the report on this form.

2. Other information may be incorporated by reference in answer or partial answer to any item or items of Part II of this form in accordance with the provisions of Rule 12b–23.

3. If any information required by Part I or Part II is incorporated by reference into an electronic format document from the quarterly report to security holders as provided in General Instruction D, any portion of the quarterly report to security holders incorporated by reference shall be filed as an exhibit in electronic format, as required by Item 601(b)(13) of Regulation S–K.

E. Integrated Reports to Security Holders

Quarterly reports to security holders may be combined with the required information of Form 10–Q and will be suitable for filing with the Commission if the following conditions are satisfied:

1. The combined report contains full and complete answers to all items required by Part I of this form. When responses to a certain item of required disclosure are separated within the combined report, an appropriate cross-reference should be made.

2. If not included in the combined report, the cover page, appropriate responses to Part II, and the required signatures shall be included in the Form 10–Q. Additionally, as appropriate, a cross-reference sheet should be filed indicating the location of information required by the items of the form.

3. If an electronic filer files any portion of a quarterly report to security holders in combination with the required information of Form 10–Q, as provided in this instruction, only such portions filed in satisfaction of the Form 10–Q requirements shall be filed in electronic format.

F. Filed Status of Information Presented

1. Pursuant to Rule 13a–13(d) and Rule 15d–13(d), the information presented in satisfaction of the requirements of Items 1 and 2 of Part I of this form, whether included directly in a report on this form, incorporated therein by reference from a report, document or statement filed as an exhibit to Part I of this form pursuant to Instruction D(1) above, included in an integrated report pursuant to Instruction E above, or contained in a statement regarding computation of per share earnings or a letter regarding a change in accounting principles filed as an exhibit to Part I pursuant to Item 601 of Regulation S–K, except as provided by Instruction F(2) below, shall not be deemed filed for the purpose of Section 18 of the Act or otherwise subject to the liabilities of that section of the Act but shall be subject to the other provisions of the Act.

2. Information presented in satisfaction of the requirements of this form other than those of items 1 and 2 of Part I shall be deemed filed for the purpose of Section 18 of the Act, except that, where information presented in response to Item 1 or 2 of Part I (or as an exhibit thereto) is also used to satisfy Part II requirements through incorporation by reference, only that portion of Part I (or exhibit thereto) consisting of the information required by Part II shall be deemed so filed.

G. Signature and Filing of Report

If the report is filed in paper pursuant to a hardship exemption from electronic filing (see Item 201 *et seq.* of Regulation S–T (17 CFR 232.201 *et seq.*)), three complete copies of the report, including any financial statements, exhibits or other papers or documents filed as a part thereof, and five additional copies which need not include exhibits must be filed with the Commission. At least one complete copy of the report, including any financial statements, exhibits or other papers or documents filed as a part thereof, must be filed with each exchange on which any class of securities of the registrant is registered. At least one complete copy of the report filed with the Commission and one such copy filed with each exchange must be manually signed on the registrant's behalf by a duly authorized officer of the registrant and by the principal financial or chief accounting officer of the registrant. (See Rule 12b–11(d); 17 CFR 240.12b–11(d).) Copies not manually signed must bear typed or printed signatures. In the case where the principal executive officer, principal financial officer or chief accounting officer is also duly authorized to sign on behalf of the registrant, one signature is acceptable provided that the registrant clearly indicates the dual responsibilities of the signatory.

H. Omission of Information by Certain Wholly-Owned Subsidiaries

If, on the date of the filing of its report on Form 10–Q, the registrant meets the conditions specified in paragraph (1) below, then such registrant may omit the information called for in the items specified in paragraph (2) below.

1. Conditions for availability of the relief specified in paragraph (2) below:

a. All of the registrant's equity securities are owned, either directly or indirectly, by a single person which is a reporting company under the Act and which has filed all the material required to be filed pursuant to section 13, 14 or 15(d) thereof, as applicable;

b. During the preceding thirty-six calendar months and any subsequent period of days, there has not been any material default in the payment of principal, interest, a sinking or purchase fund installment, or any other material default not cured within thirty days, with respect to any indebtedness of the registrant or its subsidiaries, and there has not been any material default in the payment of rentals under material long-term leases; and

c. There is prominently set forth, on the cover page of the Form 10–Q, a statement that the registrant meets the conditions set forth in General Instruction H(1)(a) and (b) of Form 10–Q and is therefore filing this Form with the reduced disclosure format.

2. Registrants meeting the conditions specified in paragraph (1) above are entitled to the following relief:

a. Such registrants may omit the information called for by Item 2 of Part I, Management's Discussion and Analysis of Financial Condition and Results of Operations, provided that the registrant includes in the Form 10–Q a management's narrative analysis of the results of operations explaining the reasons for material changes in the amount of revenue and expense items between the most recent fiscal year-to-date period presented and the corresponding year-to-date period in the preceding fiscal year. Explanations of material changes should include, but not be limited to, changes in the various elements which determine revenue and expense levels such as unit sales volume, prices charged and paid, production levels, production cost variances, labor costs and discretionary spending programs. In addition, the analysis should include an explanation of the effect of any changes in accounting principles and practices or method of application that have a material effect on net income as reported.

b. Such registrants may omit the information called for in the following Part II Items: Item 2, Unregistered Sales of Equity Securities and Use of Proceeds; Item 3, Defaults Upon Senior Securities; and Item 4, Submission of Matters to a Vote of Security Holders.

SECURITIES AND EXCHANGE COMMISSION

Washington, D.C. 20549

FORM 10–Q

(Mark One)

[ ] Quarterly report pursuant to section 13 or 15(d) of the Securities Exchange Act of 1934

For the quarterly period ended ______ or

[ ] Transition report pursuant to section 13 or 15(d) of the Securities Exchange Act of 1934

For the Transition period from ______ to ______

Commission file number ______

______

(Exact name of registrant as specified in its charter)

______

(State or other jurisdiction of incorporation or organization) (I.R.S. Employer Identification No.)

______

(Address of principal executive offices) (Zip Code)

______

(Registrant's telephone number, including area code)

______

(Former name, former address and former fiscal year, if changed since last report.)

Indicate by check mark whether the registrant (1) has filed all reports required to be filed by Section 13 or 15(d) of the Securities Exchange Act of 1934 during the preceding 12 months (or for such shorter period that the registrant was required to file such reports), and (2) has been subject to such filing requirements for the past 90 days.

Yes ___. No ___.

APPLICABLE ONLY TO ISSUERS INVOLVED IN BANKRUPTCY PROCEEDINGS DURING THE PRECEDING FIVE YEARS:

Indicate by check mark whether the registrant is an accelerated filer (as defined in Rule 12b–2 or the Exchange Act).

Yes ___. No ___.

APPLICABLE ONLY TO CORPORATE ISSUERS:

Indicate the number of shares outstanding of each of the issuer's classes of common stock, as of the latest practicable date.

PART I—FINANCIAL INFORMATION

Item 1. Financial Statements

Provide the information required by Rule 10–01 of Regulation S–X.

Item 2. Management's Discussion and Analysis of Financial Condition and Results of Operations

Furnish the information required by Item 303 of Regulation S–K.

Item 3. Quantitative and Qualitative Disclosures About Market Risk

Furnish the information required by Item 305 of Regulation S–K (§ 229.305 of this chapter).

Item 4. Controls and Procedures

Furnish the information required by Items 307 of Regulation S–K (17 CFR 229.307) and 308(c) of Regulation S–K (17 CFR 229.308(c)).

PART II—OTHER INFORMATION

Instruction. The report shall contain the item numbers and captions of all applicable items of Part II, but the text of such items may be omitted provided the responses clearly indicate the coverage of the item. Any item which is inapplicable or to which the answer is negative may be omitted and no reference thereto need be made in the report. If substantially the same information has been previously reported by the registrant, an additional report of the information on this form need not be made. The term "previously reported" is defined in Rule 12b–2. A separate response need not be presented in Part II where information called for is already disclosed in the financial information provided in Part I and is incorporated by reference into Part II of the report by means of a statement to that effect in Part II which specifically identifies the incorporated information.

Item 1. Legal Proceedings

Furnish the information required by Item 103 of Regulation S–K. As to such proceedings which have been terminated during the period covered by the report, provide similar information, including the date of termination and a description of the disposition thereof with respect to the registrant and its subsidiaries.

Instruction. A legal proceeding need only be reported in the 10–Q filed for the quarter in which it first became a reportable event and in subsequent quarters in which there have been material developments. Subsequent Form 10–Q filings in the same fiscal year in which a legal proceeding or a material development is reported should reference any previous reports in that year.

Item 2. Unregistered Sales of Equity Securities and Use of Proceeds

(a) Furnish the information required by Item 701 of Regulation S–K (17 CFR 229.701) as to all equity securities of the registrant sold by the registrant during the period covered by the report that were not registered under the Securities Act. If the Item 701 information previously has been included in a Current Report on Form 8–K (17 CFR 249.308), however, it need not be furnished.

(b) If required pursuant to Rule 463 (17 CFR 230.463) of the Securities Act of 1933, furnish the information required by Item 701(f) of Regulation S–K (§ 229.701(f) of this chapter).

Instruction. Working capital restrictions and other limitations upon the payment of dividends are to be reported hereunder.

(c) Furnish the information required by Item 703 of Regulation S–K (§ 229.703 of this chapter) for any repurchase made in the quarter covered by the report. Provide disclosures covering repurchases made on a monthly basis. For example, if the quarter began on January 16 and ended on April 15, the chart would show repurchases for the months from January 16 through February 15, February 16 through March 15, and March 16 through April 15.

Item 3. Defaults Upon Senior Securities

(a) If there has been any material default in the payment of principal, interest, a sinking or purchase fund installment, or any other material default not cured within 30 days, with respect to any indebtedness of the registrant or any of its significant subsidiaries exceeding 5 percent of the total assets of the registrant and its consolidated subsidiaries, identify the indebtedness and state the nature of the default. In the case of such a default in the payment of principal, interest, or a sinking or purchase fund installment, state the amount of the default and the total arrearage on the date of filing this report.

Instruction. This paragraph refers only to events which have become defaults under the governing instruments, i.e., after the expiration of any period of grace and compliance with any notice requirements.

(b) If any material arrearage in the payment of dividends has occurred or if there has been any other material delinquency not cured within 30 days, with respect to any class of preferred stock of the registrant which is registered or which ranks prior to any class of registered securities, or with respect to any class of preferred stock of any significant subsidiary of the registrant, give the title of the class and state the nature of the arrearage or delinquency. In the case of an arrearage in the payment of dividends, state the amount and the total arrearage on the date of filing this report.

Instructions to Item 3.

1. Item 3 need not be answered as to any default or arrearage with respect to any class of securities all of which is held by or for the account of the registrant or its totally held subsidiaries.

2. The information required by Item 3 need not be made if previously disclosed on a report on Form 8–K (17 CFR 249.308).

Item 4. Submission of Matters to a Vote of Security Holders

If any matter has been submitted to a vote of security holders during the period covered by this report, through the solicitation of proxies or otherwise, furnish the following information:

(a) The date of the meeting and whether it was an annual or special meeting.

(b) If the meeting involved the election of directors, the name of each director elected at the meeting and the name of each other director whose term of office as a director continued after the meeting.

(c) A brief description of each matter voted upon at the meeting and state the number of votes cast for, against or withheld, as well as the number of abstentions and broker nonvotes, as to each such matter, including a separate tabulation with respect to each nominee for office.

(d) A description of the terms of any settlement between the registrant and any other participant (as defined in Rule 14a–11 of Regulation 14A under the Act) terminating any solicitation subject to Rule 14a–11, including the cost or anticipated cost to the registrant.

Instructions. 1. If any matter has been submitted to a vote of security holders otherwise than at a meeting of such security holders, corresponding information with respect to such submission shall be furnished. The solicitation of any authorization or consent (other than a proxy to vote at a stockholders' meeting) with respect to any matter shall be deemed a submission of such matter to a vote of security holders within the meaning of this item.

2. Paragraph (a) need be answered only if paragraph (b) or (c) is required to be answered.

3. Paragraph (b) need not be answered if (i) proxies for the meeting were solicited pursuant to Regulation 14 under the Act, (ii) there was no solicitation in opposition to the management's nominees as listed in the proxy statement, and (iii) all of such nominees were elected. If the registrant did not solicit proxies and the board of directors as previously reported to the Commission was re-elected in its entirety, a statement to that effect in answer to paragraph (b) will suffice as an answer thereto.

4. Paragraph (c) must be answered for all matters voted upon at the meeting, including both contested and uncontested elections of directors.

5. If the registrant has furnished to its security holders proxy soliciting material containing the information called for by paragraph (d), the paragraph may be answered by reference to the information contained in such material.

6. If the registrant has published a report containing all of the information called for by this item, the item may be answered by a reference to the information contained in such report.

Item 5. Other Information

(a) The registrant must disclose under this item any information required to be disclosed in a report on Form 8–K during the period covered by this Form 10–Q, but not reported, whether or not otherwise required by this Form 10–Q. If disclosure of such information is made under this term, it need not be repeated in a report on Form 8–K which would otherwise be required to be filed with respect to such information or in a subsequent report on Form 10–Q.

(b) Furnish the information required by Item 401(j) of Regulation S–K (§ 229.401).

Item 6. Exhibits

Furnish the exhibits required by Item 601 of Regulation S–K.

SIGNATURES*

Pursuant to the requirements of the Securities Exchange Act of 1934, the registrant has duly caused this report to be signed on its behalf by the undersigned thereunto duly authorized.

(Registrant) ______________________

Date ______________________ (Signature) ** ______________________

Date ______________________ (Signature) ** ______________________

* See General Instruction G.

** Print name and title of the signing officer under his signature.

SECURITIES AND EXCHANGE COMMISSION
Washington, D.C. 20549

FORM 10–QSB

(Mark One)

[ ] **QUARTERLY REPORT UNDER SECTION 13 OR 15(d) OF THE SECURITIES EXCHANGE ACT OF 1934**

For the quarterly period ended ____________

[ ] **TRANSITION REPORT UNDER SECTION 13 OR 15(d) OF THE EXCHANGE ACT**

For the transition period from ____________ to ____________

Commission file number ____________

____
(Exact name of small business issuer as specified in its charter)

____
(State or other jurisdiction of incorporation or organization) (IRS Employer Identification No.)

____
(Address of principal executive offices)

____
(Issuer's telephone number)

____
(Former name, former address and former fiscal year, if changed since last report)

Check whether the issuer (1) filed all reports required to be filed by Section 13 or 15(d) of the Exchange Act during the past 12 months (or for such shorter period that the registrant was required to file such reports), and (2) has been subject to such filing requirements for the past 90 days. Yes ___ No ___

APPLICABLE ONLY TO ISSUERS INVOLVED IN BANKRUPTCY PROCEEDINGS DURING THE PRECEDING FIVE YEARS

Check whether the registrant filed all documents and reports required to be filed by Section 12, 13 or 15(d) of the Exchange Act after the distribution of securities under a plan confirmed by court. Yes ___ No ___

APPLICABLE ONLY TO CORPORATE ISSUERS

State the number of shares outstanding of each of the issuer's classes of common equity, as of the latest practicable date: ____________

GENERAL INSTRUCTIONS

A. Use of Form 10–QSB

1. A "small business issuer," defined in Rule 12b–2, may use this Form for its transition and quarterly reports under section 13 or 15(d) of the Exchange Act and Rules 13a–13 and 15d–13. For further information as to eligibility to use of this Form see Item 10(a) of Regulation S–B (17 CFR 228.10 *et seq.*). A small business issuer shall file a quarterly report on this form within 45 days after the end of the each of the first three fiscal quarters of each fiscal year. No report need be

filed for the fourth quarter of any fiscal year. Transition reports shall be filed in accordance with the requirements set forth in Rule 13a–10 or Rule 15d–10.

B. Application of General Rules and Regulations

1. The General Rules and Regulations under the Exchange Act, particularly Regulation 12B contain certain general requirements for reports on any form which should be carefully read and observed in the preparation and filing of reports on this Form.

C. Incorporation by Reference

1. If the registrant makes available to its stockholders or otherwise publishes, within the period prescribed for filing the report, a document or statement containing information meeting some or all of the requirements of Part I of this form, the information may be incorporated by reference from such published document or statement, in answer or partial answer to any item or items of Part I of this form provided copies of the document or statement are filed as an exhibit to Part I of the report on this form.

2. Other information may be incorporated by reference in answer or partial answer to any item or items of Part II of this form in accordance with the provisions of Rule 12b–23 of the Exchange Act.

3. If any information required by Part I or Part II is incorporated by reference into an electronic format document from the quarterly report to security holders as provided in General Instruction C, any portion of the quarterly report to security holders incorporated by reference shall be filed as an exhibit in electronic format, as required by Item 601(b)(13) of Regulation S–B.

D. Integrated Reports to Security Holders

Quarterly reports to security holders may be combined with the required information of Form 10–QSB and will be suitable for filing with the Commission if the following conditions are satisfied:

1. The combined report contains full and complete answers to all items required by Part I of this form. When responses to a certain item of required disclosure are separated within the combined report, an appropriate cross-reference should be made.

2. If not included in the combined report, the cover page, appropriate responses to Part II and the required signatures shall be included in the Form 10–QSB. Additionally, as appropriate, a cross-reference sheet should be filed indicating the location of information required by items of the form.

3. If an electronic filer files any portion of a quarterly report to security holders in combination with the required information of Form 10–QSB, as provided in this instruction, only such portions filed in satisfaction of the Form 10–QSB requirements shall be filed in electronic format.

E. Filed Status of Information Presented

1. Under Rules 13a–13(d) and 15d–13(d) of the Exchange Act, the information presented in satisfaction of the requirements of Items 1 and 2 of Part I of this form, whether included directly in a report on this form, incorporated therein by reference from a report, document or statement filed as an exhibit to Part I of this form pursuant to Instruction D(1) above, included in an integrated report pursuant to Instruction D above, or contained in a statement regarding computation of per share earnings or a letter regarding a change in accounting principles filed as an exhibit to Part I under Item 601 of Regulation S–B (§ 228.601 of this chapter) shall not be deemed filed for the purpose of Section 18 of the Exchange Act or otherwise subject to the liabilities of that section of the Act but shall be subject to the other provisions of the Act.

2. Information presented in satisfaction of the requirements of this form other than those of Items 1 and 2 or Part I shall be deemed

filed for the purpose of Section 18 of the Exchange Act; except that, where information presented in response to Item 1 or 2 of Part I (or an exhibit thereto) is also used to satisfy Part II requirements through incorporation by reference, only that portion of Part I (or exhibit thereto) consisting of the information required by Part II shall be deemed so filed.

F. Signature and Filing of Report

1. If the report is filed in paper pursuant to a hardship exemption from electronic filing (see Item 201 *et seq.* of Regulation S–T (17 CFR 232.201 *et seq.*)), file three "complete" copies and five "additional" copies of the report with the Commission and file at least one complete copy with each exchange on which any class of securities of the small business issuer is registered. A "complete" copy includes financial statements, exhibits and all other papers and documents. An "additional" copy excludes exhibits.

2. Manually sign at least one complete copy of the report filed with the Commission and with each exchange; other copies should have typed or printed signatures. (See Rule 12b–11(d) (17 CFR 240.12b–11(d)).) In the case where the principal executive officer, principal financial officer or chief accounting officer is also duly authorized to sign on behalf of the small business issuer, one signature is acceptable provided that the issuer clearly indicates the dual responsibilities of the signatory.

G. Omission of Information by Certain Wholly-Owned Subsidiaries

If, on the date of the filing of its Form 10–QSB, the registrant meets the conditions in paragraph (1) below, then it may omit the information in paragraph (2) below.

1. Conditions for availability of relief specified in paragraph (2) below:

(a) All of the registrant's equity securities are owned, either directly or indirectly, by a single person which is a reporting company and which has filed all the material required to be filed pursuant to section 13, 14 or 15(d) of the Exchange Act.

(b) During the past thirty-six calendar months and any later period, there has not been any material default in the payment of principal, interest, a sinking or purchase fund installment, or any other material default not cured within thirty days, with respect to any indebtedness of the small business issuer, and there has not been any material default in the payment of rentals under material long-term leases; and

(c) There is prominently set forth, on the cover page of the Form 10–QSB, a statement that the registrant meets the conditions set forth in this instruction and is therefore filing this form with the reduced disclosure format.

2. Registrants meeting the conditions in paragraph (1) above are entitled to:

(a) Omit the information called for by Item 303 of Regulation S–B, Management's Discussion and Analysis provided that the issuer includes in the Form 10–QSB a management's narrative analysis of the results of operations explaining the reasons for material changes in the amount of revenue and expense items between the most recent fiscal year-to-date period presented and the corresponding year-to-date period in the preceding fiscal year. Explanations of material changes should include, but not be limited to, changes in the various elements which determine revenue and expense levels such as unit sales volume, prices charged and paid, production levels, production cost variances, labor costs and discretionary spending programs. In addition, the analysis should include an explanation of the effect of any changes in accounting principles and practices or method of application that have a material effect on net income as reported.

(b) Such registrants may omit the information called for by the following Items in Part II: Item 2, 3 and 4.

PART I—FINANCIAL INFORMATION

Item 1. Financial Statements.

Furnish the information required by Item 310(b) of Regulation S–B.

Item 2. Management's Discussion and Analysis or Plan of Operation.

Furnish the information required by Item 303 of Regulation S–B.

Item 3. Controls and Procedures.

Furnish the information required by Item 307 of regulation S–B (§ 228.307 of this chapter).

PART II—OTHER INFORMATION

Instruction to Part II: Any item which is inapplicable or to which the answer is negative may be omitted and no reference thereto need be made in the report. If substantially the same information has been previously reported by the registrant, an additional report of the information on this form need not be made. The term "previously reported" is defined in Rule 12b–2 of the Exchange Act. A separate response need not be presented in Part II where information called for is already disclosed in the financial information in Part I and is incorporated by reference into Part II of the report by means of a statement to that effect in Part II which specifically identifies the incorporated information.

Item 1. Legal Proceedings

Furnish the information required by Item 103 of Regulation S–B. As to proceedings that terminated during the period covered by this report, furnish information similar to that required by Item 103 of Regulation S–B.

Instruction to Item 1: A legal proceeding need only be reported in the Form 10–QSB filed for the quarter in which it first became a reportable event and in subsequent quarters in which there have been material developments. Subsequent Form 10–QSB filings in the same fiscal year in which a legal proceeding or a material development is reported should reference any previous reports in that year.

Item 2. Unregistered Sales of Equity Securities and Use of Proceeds

(a) Furnish the information required by Item 701 of Regulation S–B (17 CFR 228.701) as to all equity securities of the small business issuer sold by the small business issuer during the period covered by the report that were not registered under the Securities Act. If the Item 701 information previously has been included in a Current Report on Form 8–K (17 CFR 249.308), however, it need not be furnished.

(b) Furnish the information required by Item 701 of Regulation S–K (§ 229.701 of this chapter) as to all equity securities of the registrant sold by the registrant during the period covered by the report that were not registered under the Securities Act.

(c) If required pursuant to Rule 463 (17 CFR 230.463) of the Securities Act of 1933, furnish the information required by Item 701(f) of Regulation S–K (§ 229.701(f) of this chapter).

(d) Furnish the information required by Item 703 of Regulation S–B (§ 228.703 of this chapter) for any repurchase made in the quarter covered by the report. Provide disclosures covering repurchases made on a monthly basis. For example, if the quarter began on January 16 and ended on April 15, the chart would show repurchases for the months from January 16 through February 15, February 16 through March 15, and March 16 through April 15.

Instruction to Item 2: 1. Working capital restrictions and other limitations upon the payment of dividends are to be reported.

Item 3. Defaults Upon Senior Securities

(a) If there has been any material default in the payment of principal, interest, a sinking or purchase fund installment, or any other material default not cured within 30 days, with respect to any indebtedness of the small business issuer exceeding 5 percent of the total assets of the issuer identify the indebtedness and state the nature of the default. In the case of such a default in the payment of principal, interest, or a sinking or purchase fund installment, state the amount of the default and the total arrearage on the date of filing this report.

Instruction to Item 3(a): 1. This paragraph refers only to events which have become defaults under the governing instruments, i.e., after the expiration of any period of grace and compliance with any notice requirements.

(b) If any material arrearage in the payment of dividends has occurred or if there has been any other material delinquency not cured within 30 days, with respect to any class of preferred stock of the registrant which is registered or which ranks prior to any class of registered securities, or with respect to any class of preferred stock of any significant subsidiary of the registrant, give the title of the class and state the nature of the arrearage or delinquency. In the case of such a default in the payment of dividends, state the amount and the total arrearage on the date of filing this report.

Instruction to Item 3:

1. Item 3 need not be answered as to any default or arrearage with respect to any class of securities all of which is held by, or for the account of, the registrant or its totally held subsidiaries.

2. The information required by Item 3 need not be made if previously disclosed on a report on Form 8–K (17 CFR 249.308).

Item 4. Submission of Matters to a Vote of Security Holders

If any matter was submitted to a vote of security holders during the period covered by this report, through the solicitation of proxies or otherwise, furnish the following information:

(a) The date of the meeting and whether it was an annual or special meeting.

(b) If the meeting involved the election of directors, the name of each director elected at the meeting and the name of each other director whose term of office as a director continued after the meeting.

(c) A brief description of each matter voted upon at the meeting and state the number of votes cast for, against or withheld, as well as the number of abstentions and broker non-votes, as to each such matter, including a separate tabulation with respect to each nominee for office.

(d) A description of the terms of any settlement between the registrant and any other participant (as defined in Rule 14a–11 of Regulation A under the Exchange Act) terminating any solicitation subject to Rule 14a–11, including the cost or anticipated cost to the registrant.

Instructions to Item 4: 1. If any matter has been submitted to a vote of security holders otherwise than at a meeting of such security holders, corresponding information with respect to such submission should be furnished. The solicitation of any authorization or consent (other than a proxy to vote at a shareholders' meeting) with respect to any matter shall be deemed a submission of such matter to a vote of security holders within the meaning of this item.

2. Paragraph (a) need be answered only if paragraph (b) or (c) is required to be answered.

3. Paragraph (b) need not be answered if (i) proxies for the meeting were solicited pursuant to Regulation 14A under the Exchange Act, (ii) there was no solicitation in opposition to the management's nominees as listed in the proxy statement, and (iii) all of such nominees were elected. If the registrant did not solicit proxies and the board of directors as previously reported to the Committee was re-elected in its entirety, a statement to that effect in answer to paragraph (b) will suffice as an answer thereto.

4. Paragraph (c) must be answered for all matters voted upon at the meeting, including

both contested and uncontested elections of directors.

5. If the registrant has furnished to its security holders proxy soliciting material containing the information called for by paragraph (d), the paragraph may be answered by reference to the information contained in such material.

6. If the registrant has published a report containing all of the information called for by this item, the item may be answered by reference to the information in that report.

Item 5. Other Information

(a) The small business issuer must disclose under this item any information required to be disclosed in a report on Form 8–K during the period covered by this Form 10–QSB, but not reported, whether or not otherwise required by this Form 10–QSB. If disclosure of such information is made under this item, it need not be repeated in a report on Form 8–K which would otherwise be required to be filed with respect to such information or in a subsequent report on Form 10–QSB.

(b) Furnish the information required by Item 401(g) of Regulation S–B (§ 228.401).

Item 6. Exhibits and Reports on Form 8–K

Furnish the exhibits required by Item 601 of Regulation S–B.

SIGNATURES

In accordance with the requirements of the Exchange Act, the registrant caused this report to be signed on its behalf by the undersigned, thereunto duly authorized.

____
(Registrant)

Date ____________________ ____________________
(Signature)*

Date ____________________ ____________________
(Signature)*

* Print the name and title of each signing officer under his signature.

SECURITIES AND EXCHANGE COMMISSION

Washington, D.C. 20549

FORM 10–K

ANNUAL AND TRANSITION REPORTS PURSUANT TO SECTION 13 OR 15(d) OF THE SECURITIES EXCHANGE ACT OF 1934

GENERAL INSTRUCTIONS

A. Rule as to Use of Form 10–K

(1) This Form shall be used for annual reports pursuant to Section 13 or 15(d) of the Securities Exchange Act of 1934 (15 U.S.C. 78m or 78o(d)) (the "Act") for which no other form is prescribed. This Form also shall be used for transition reports filed pursuant to Section 13 or 15(d) of the Act.

(2) Annual reports on this Form shall be filed within the following period:

(a) For accelerated filers (as defined in 17 CFR 240.12b–2):

(i) 90 days after the end of the fiscal year covered by the report for fiscal years ending on or after December 15, 2002 and before December 15, 2003;

(ii) 75 days after the end of the fiscal year covered by the report for fiscal years ending on or after December 15, 2003 and before December 15, 2005; and

(iii) 60 days after the end of the fiscal year covered by the report for fiscal years ending on or after December 15, 2005; and

(b) 90 days after the end of the fiscal year covered by the report for all other registrants.

(3) Transition reports on this Form shall be filed in accordance with the requirements set forth in Rule 13a–10 (17 CFR 240.13a–10) or Rule 15d–10 (17 CFR 240.15d–10) applicable when the registrant changes it fiscal year end.

(4) Notwithstanding paragraphs (2) and (3) of this General Instruction A., all schedules required by Article 12 of Regulation S–X (17 CFR 210.12–01—210.12–29) may, at the option of the registrant, be filed as an amendment to the report not later than 30 days after the applicable due date of the report.

B. Application of General Rules and Regulations

(1) The General Rules and Regulations under the Act contain certain general requirements which are applicable to reports on any form. These general requirements should be carefully read and observed in the preparation and filing of reports on this Form.

(2) Particular attention is directed to Regulation 12B which contains general requirements regarding matters such as the kind and size of paper to be used, the legibility of the report, the information to be given whenever the title of securities is required to be stated, and the filing of the report. The definitions contained in Rule 12b–2 should be especially noted. See also Regulations 13A and 15D.

C. Preparation of Report

(1) This Form is not to be used as a blank form to be filled in, but only as a guide in the preparation of the report on paper meeting the requirements of Rule 12b–12. Except as provided in General Instruction G, the answers to the items shall be prepared in the manner specified in Rule 12b–13.

(2) Except where information is required to be given for the fiscal year or as of a specified date, it shall be given as of the latest practicable date.

(3) Attention is directed to Rule 12b–20, which states: "In addition to the information expressly required to be included in a statement or report, there shall be added such

further material information, if any, as may be necessary to make the required statements, in the light of the circumstances under which they are made, not misleading."

D. Signature and Filing of Report

(1) Three complete copies of the report, including financial statements, financial statement schedules, exhibits, and all other papers and documents filed as a part thereof, and five additional copies which need not include exhibits, shall be filed with the Commission. At least one complete copy of the report, including financial statements, financial statement schedules, exhibits, and all other papers and documents filed as a part thereof, shall be filed with each exchange on which any class of securities of the registrant is registered. At least one complete copy of the report filed with the Commission and one such copy filed with each exchange shall be manually signed. Copies not manually signed shall bear typed or printed signatures.

(2)(a) The report must be signed by the registrant, and on behalf of the registrant by its principal executive officer or officers, its principal financial officer or officers, its controller or principal accounting officer, and by at least the majority of the board of directors or persons performing similar functions. Where the registrant is a limited partnership, the report must be signed by the majority of the board of directors of any corporate general partner who signs the report. (b) The name of each person who signs the report shall be typed or printed beneath his signature. Any person who occupies more than one of the specified positions shall indicate each capacity in which he signs the report. Attention is directed to Rule 12b–11 concerning manual signatures and signatures pursuant to powers of attorney.

(3) Registrants are requested to indicate in a transmittal letter with the Form 10–K whether the financial statements in the report reflect a change from the preceding year in any accounting principles or practices, or in the method of applying any such principles or practices.

E. Disclosure With Respect to Foreign Subsidiaries

Information required by any item or other requirement of this form with respect to any foreign subsidiary may be omitted to the extent that the required disclosure would be detrimental to the registrant. However, financial statements and financial statement schedules, otherwise required, shall not be omitted pursuant to this Instruction. Where information is omitted pursuant to this Instruction, a statement shall be made that such information has been omitted and the names of the subsidiaries involved shall be separately furnished to the Commission. The Commission may, in its discretion, call for justification that the required disclosure would be detrimental.

F. Information as to Employee Stock Purchase, Savings and Similar Plans

Attention is directed to Rule 15d–21 which provides that separate annual and other reports need not be filed pursuant to Section 15(d) of the Act with respect to any employee stock purchase, savings or similar plan if the issuer of the stock or other securities offered to employees pursuant to the plan furnishes to the Commission the information and documents specified in the Rule.

G. Information to Be Incorporated by Reference

(1) Attention is directed to Rule 12b–23 which provides for the incorporation by reference of information contained in certain documents in answer or partial answer to any item of a report.

(2) The information called for by Parts I and II of this Form (Items 1 through 9A or any portion thereof) may, at the registrant's option, be incorporated by reference from the registrant's annual report to security holders furnished to the Commission pursuant to Rule

14a–3(a) or Rule 14c–(a) or from the registrant's annual report to security holders, even if not furnished to the Commission pursuant to Rule 14a–3(b) or Rule 14c–3(a), provided such annual report contains the information required by Rule 14a–3.

NOTE 1. In order to fulfill the requirements of Part I of Form 10–K, the incorporated portion of the annual report to security holders must contain the information required by Items 1–3 of Form 10–K, to the extent applicable.

NOTE 2. If any information required by Part I or Part II is incorporated by reference into an electronic format document from the annual report to security holders as provided in General Instruction G, any portion of the annual report to security holders incorporated by reference shall be filed as an exhibit in electronic format, as required by Item 601(b)(13) of Regulation S–K.

(3) The information required by Part III (Items 10, 11, 12, 13 and 14) may be incorporated by reference from the registrant's definitive proxy statement (filed or required to be filed pursuant to Regulation 14A) or definitive information statement (filed or to be filed pursuant to Regulation 14C) which involves the election of directors, if such definitive proxy statement or information statement is filed with the Commission not later than 120 days after the end of the fiscal year covered by the Form 10–K. However, if such definitive proxy statement or information statement is not filed with the Commission in the 120-day period or is not required to be filed with the Commission by virtue of Rule 3a12–3(b) under the Exchange Act, the Items comprising the Part III information must be filed as part of the Form 10–K, or as an amendment to the Form 10–K, not later than the end of the 120-day period. It should be noted that the information regarding executive officers required by Item 401 of Regulation S–K may be included in Part I of Form 10–K under an appropriate caption. See Instruction 3 to Item 401(b) of Regulation S–K.

(4) No item numbers of captions of items need be contained in the material incorporated by reference into the report. However, the registrant's attention is directed to Rule 12b–23(e) regarding the specific disclosure required in the report concerning information incorporated by reference. When the registrant combines all of the information in Parts I and II of this Form (Items 1 through 9A) by incorporation by reference from the registrant's annual report to security holders and all of the information in Part III of this Form (Items 10 through 14) by incorporating by reference from a definitive proxy statement or information statement involving the election of directors, then, notwithstanding General Instruction C(1), this Form shall consist of the facing or cover page, those sections incorporated from the annual report to security holders, the proxy or information statement, and the information, if any, required by Part IV of this Form, signatures, and a cross reference sheet setting forth the item numbers and captions in Parts I, II and III of this Form and the page and/or pages in the referenced materials where the corresponding information appears.

H. Integrated Reports to Security Holders

Annual reports to security holders may be combined with the required information of Form 10–K and will be suitable for filing with the Commission if the following conditions are satisfied:

(1) The combined report contains full and complete answers to all items required by Form 10–K. When responses to a certain item of required disclosure are separated within the combined report, an appropriate cross-reference should be made. If the information required by Part III of Form 10–K is omitted by virtue of General Instruction G, a definitive proxy or information statement shall be filed.

(2) The cover page and the required signatures are included. As appropriate, a cross-reference sheet should be filed indicat-

ing the location of information required by the items of the Form.

(3) If an electronic filer files any portion of an annual report to security holders in combination with the required information of Form 10–K, as provided in this instruction, only such portions filed in satisfaction of the Form 10–K requirements shall be filed in electronic format.

I. Omission of Information by Certain Wholly-Owned Subsidiaries

If, on the date of the filing of its report on Form 10–K, the registrant meets the conditions specified in paragraph (1) below, then such registrant may furnish the abbreviated narrative disclosure specified in paragraph (2) below.

(1) Conditions for availability of the relief specified in paragraph (2) below.

(a) All of the registrant's equity securities are owned, either directly or indirectly, by a single person which is a reporting company under the Act and which has filed all the material required to be filed pursuant to section 13, 14, or 15(d) thereof, as applicable, and which is named in conjunction with the registrant's description of its business;

(b) During the preceding thirty-six calendar months and any subsequent period of days, there has not been any material default in the payment of principal, interest, a sinking or purchase fund installment, or any other material default not cured within thirty days, with respect to any indebtedness of the registrant or its subsidiaries, and there has not been any material default in the payment of rentals under material long-term leases; and

(c) There is prominently set forth, on the cover page of the Form 10–K, a statement that the registrant meets the conditions set forth in General Instruction (I)(1)(a) and (b) of Form 10–K and is therefore filing this Form with the reduced disclosure format.

(d) The registrant is not an asset-backed issuer, as defined in Item 1101 of Regulation AB (17 CFR 229.1101).

(2) Registrants meeting the conditions specified in paragraph (1) above are entitled to the following relief:

(a) Such registrants may omit the information called for by Item 6, Selected Financial Data, and Item 7, Management's Discussion and Analysis of Financial Condition and Results of Operations provided that the registrant includes in the Form 10–K a management's narrative analysis of the results of operations explaining the reasons for material changes in the amount of revenue and expense items between the most recent fiscal year presented and the fiscal year immediately preceding it. Explanations of material changes should include, but not be limited to, changes in the various elements which determine revenue and expense levels such as unit sales volume, prices charged and paid, production levels, production cost variances, labor costs and discretionary spending programs. In addition, the analysis should include an explanation of the effect of any changes in accounting principles and practices or method of application that have a material effect on net income as reported.

(b) Such registrants may omit the list of subsidiaries exhibit required by Item 601 of Regulation S–K.

(c) Such registrants may omit the information called for by the following otherwise required Items: Item 4, Submission of Matters to a Vote of Security Holders; Item 10, Directors and Executive Officers of the Registrant; Item 11, Management Remuneration; Item 12, Security Ownership of Certain Beneficial Owners and Management; and Item 13, Certain Relationships and Related Transactions.

(d) In response to Item 1, Business, such registrant only need furnish a brief description of the business done by the registrant and its subsidiaries during the most recent fiscal year which will, in the opinion of management, indicate the general nature and scope of the business of the registrant and its subsidiaries, and in response to Item 2, Properties, such registrant only need furnish a brief description of the material properties of the registrant and its subsidiaries to the extent, in the opinion of the management, necessary to an understanding of the business done by the registrant and its subsidiaries.

J. Use of this Form by Asset-Backed Issuers.

The following applies to registrants that are asset-backed issuers. Terms used in this General Instruction J. have the same meaning as in Item 1101 of Regulation AB (17 CFR 229.1101).

(1) *Items that May be Omitted*. Such registrants may omit the information called for by the following otherwise required Items:

(a) Item 1, Business;

(b) Item 2, Properties;

(c) Item 3, Legal Proceedings;

(d) Item 4, Submission of Matters to a Vote of Security Holders;

(e) Item 5, Market for Registrant's Common Equity and Related Stockholder Matters;

(f) Item 6, Selected Financial Data;

(g) Item 7, Management's Discussion and Analysis of Financial Condition and Results of Operations;

(h) Item 7A, Quantitative and Qualitative Disclosures About Market Risk;

(i) Item 8, Financial Statements and Supplementary Data;

(j) Item 9, Changes in and Disagreements With Accountants on Accounting and Financial Disclosure;

(k) Item 9A, Controls and Procedures;

(*l*) If the issuing entity does not have any executive officers or directors, Item 10, Directors and Executive Officers of the Registrant, Item 11, Executive Compensation, Item 12, Security Ownership of Certain Beneficial Owners and Management, and Item 13, Certain Relationships and Related Transactions; and

(m) Item 14, Principal Accountant Fees and Services.

(2) *Substitute Information to be Included*. In addition to the Items that are otherwise required by this Form, the registrant must furnish in the Form 10–K the following information:

(a) Immediately after the name of the issuing entity on the cover page of the Form 10–K, as separate line items, the exact name of the depositor as specified in its charter and the exact name of the sponsor as specified in its charter.

(b) Item 1112(b) of Regulation AB;

(c) Items 1114(b)(2) and 1115(b) of Regulation AB;

(d) Item 1117 of Regulation AB;

(e) Item 1119 of Regulation AB;

(f) Item 1122 of Regulation AB; and

(g) Item 1123 of Regulation AB.

(3) *Signatures*.

The Form 10–K must be signed either:

(a) On behalf of the depositor by the senior officer in charge of securitization of the depositor; or

(b) On behalf of the issuing entity by the senior officer in charge of the servicing function of the servicer. If multiple servicers are involved in servicing the pool assets, the senior officer in charge of the servicing function of the master servicer (or entity performing the equivalent function) must sign if a representative of the servicer is to sign the report on behalf of the issuing entity.

SECURITIES AND EXCHANGE COMMISSION
Washington, D.C. 20549

FORM 10–K

(Mark One)

[ ] Annual report pursuant to section 13 or 15(d) of the Securities Exchange Act of 1934

For the fiscal year ended ______ or

[ ] Transition report pursuant to section 13 or 15(d) of the Securities Exchange Act of 1934

For the transition period from ______ to ______

Commission file number ______

____
(Exact name of registrant as specified in its charter)

____
(State or other jurisdiction of incorporation or organization) (I.R.S. Employer Identification No.)

____
(Address of principal executive offices) (Zip Code)

Registrant's telephone number, including area code ______________

Securities registered pursuant to Section 12(b) of the Act:

Title of each class	Name of each exchange on which registered

Securities registered pursuant to section 12(g) of the Act:

____
(Title of class)

____
(Title of class)

Indicate by check mark whether the registrant (1) has filed all reports required to be filed by Section 13 or 15(d) of the Securities Exchange Act of 1934 during the preceding 12 months (or for such shorter period that the registrant was required to file such reports), and (2) has been subject to such filing requirements for the past 90 days. Yes ___. No ___.

Indicate by check mark if disclosure of delinquent filers pursuant to Item 405 of Regulation S–K is not contained herein, and will not be contained, to the best of registrant's knowledge, in definitive proxy or information statements incorporated by reference in Part III of this Form 10–K or any amendment to this Form 10–K. [ ]

State the aggregate market value of the voting and non-voting common equity held by non-affiliates of the registrant. The aggregate market value shall be computed by reference to the price at which the common equity was sold, or the average bid and asked prices of such common equity, as of a specified date within 60 days prior to the date of filing. (See definition of affiliate in Rule 405, 17 CFR 230.405.)

Indicate by check mark whether the registrant is an accelerated filer (as defined in Rule 12b–2 of the Act). Yes ___. No ___.

State the aggregate market value of the voting and non-voting common equity held by non-affiliates computed by reference to the price at which the common equity was last sold, or the average bid and asked price of such common equity, as of the last business day of the registrant's most recently completed second fiscal quarter.

NOTE: If a determination as to whether a particular person or entity is an affiliate cannot be made without involving unreasonable effort and expense, the aggregate market value of the common stock held by non-affiliates may be calculated on the basis of assumptions reasonable under the circumstances, provided that the assumptions are set forth in this Form.

APPLICABLE ONLY TO REGISTRANTS INVOLVED IN BANKRUPTCY PROCEEDINGS DURING THE PRECEDING FIVE YEARS:

Indicate by check mark whether the registrant has filed all documents and reports required to be filed by Section 12, 13 or 15(d) of the Securities Exchange Act of 1934 subsequent to the distribution of securities under a plan confirmed by a court.

Yes ___. No ___.

(APPLICABLE ONLY TO CORPORATE REGISTRANTS)

Indicate the number of shares outstanding of each of the registrant's classes of common stock, as of the latest practicable date.

DOCUMENTS INCORPORATED BY REFERENCE

List hereunder the following documents if incorporated by reference and the Part of the Form 10–K (e.g., Part I, Part II, etc.) into which the document is incorporated: (1) Any annual report to security holders; (2) Any proxy or information statement; and (3) Any prospectus filed pursuant to Rule 424(b) or (c) under the Securities Act of 1933. The listed documents should be clearly described for identification purposes (e.g., annual report to security holders for fiscal year ended December 24, 1980).

PART I

[See General Instruction G(2)]

Item 1. Business

Furnish the information required by Item 101 of Regulation S–K except that the discussion of the development of the registrant's business need only include developments since the beginning of the fiscal year for which this report is filed.

Item 2. Properties

Furnish the information required by Item 102 of Regulation S–K.

Item 3. Legal Proceedings

(a) Furnish the information required by Item 103 of Regulation S–K.

(b) As to any proceeding that was terminated during the fourth quarter of the fiscal year covered by this report, furnish information similar to that required by Item 103 of Regulation S–K, including the date of termination and a description of the disposition thereof with respect to the registrant and its subsidiaries.

Item 4. Submission of Matters to a Vote of Security Holders

If any matter was submitted during the fourth quarter of the fiscal year covered by this report to a vote of security holders, through the solicitation of proxies or otherwise, furnish the following information:

(a) The date of the meeting and whether it was an annual or special meeting.

(b) If the meeting involved the election of directors, the name of each director elected at the meeting and the name of each other director whose term of office as a director continued after the meeting.

(c) A brief description of each state the number of votes cast for, against or withheld, as well as the number of abstentions and broker nonvotes as to each such matter, including a separate tabulation with respect to each nominee for office.

(d) A description of the terms of any settlement between the registrant and any other participant (as defined in Rule 14a–11 of Regulation 14A under the Act) terminating any solicitation subject to Rule 14a–11, including the cost or anticipated cost to the registrant.

Instructions. 1. If any matter has been submitted to a vote of security holders otherwise than at a meeting of such security holders, corresponding information with respect to such submission shall be furnished. The solicitation of any authorization or consent (other than a proxy to vote at a stockholders' meeting) with respect to any matter shall be deemed a submission of such matter to a vote of security holders within the meaning of this item.

2. Paragraph (a) need be answered only if paragraph (b) or (c) is required to be answered.

3. Paragraph (b) need not be answered if (i) proxies for the meeting were solicited pursuant to Regulation 14A under the Act, (ii) there was no solicitation in opposition to the management's nominees as listed in the proxy statement, and (iii) all of such nominees were elected. If the registrant did not solicit proxies and the board of directors as previously reported to the Commission was re-elected in its entirety, a statement to that effect in answer to paragraph (b) will suffice as an answer thereto.

4. Paragraph (c) must be answered for all matters voted upon at the meeting, including both contested and uncontested elections of directors.

5. If the registrant has furnished to its security holders, proxy soliciting material containing the information called for by paragraph (d), the paragraph may be answered by reference to the information contained in such material.

6. If the registrant has published a report containing all of the information called for by this item, the item may be answered by a reference to the information contained in such report.

PART II

[See General Instruction G(2)]

Item 5. Market for Registrant's Common Equity, Related Stockholder Matters and Issuer Purchases of Equity Securities

(a) Furnish the information required by Item 201 of Regulation S–K (17 CFR 229.201) and Item 701 of Regulation S–K (17 CFR 229.701) as to all equity securities of the registrant sold by the registrant during the period covered by the report that were not registered under the Securities Act. If the Item 701 information previously has been included in a Quarterly Report on Form 10–Q or 10–QSB (17 CFR 249.308a or 249.308b), or in a Current Report on Form 8–K (17 CFR 249.308), it need not be furnished.

(b) If required pursuant to Rule 463 (17 CFR 230.463) of the Securities Act of 1933, furnish the information required by Item 701(f) of Regulation S–K (§ 229.701(f) of this chapter).

(c) Furnish the information required by Item 703 of Regulation S–K (§ 229.703 of this chapter) for any repurchase made in a month within the fourth quarter of the fiscal year covered by the report. Provide disclosures covering repurchases made on a monthly basis. For example, if the fourth quarter began on January 16 and ended on April 15, the chart would show repurchases for the months from January 16 through February 15, February 16 through March 15, and March 16 through April 15.

Item 6. Selected Financial Data

Furnish the information required by Item 301 of Regulation S–K.

Item 7. Management's Discussion and Analysis of Financial Condition and Results of Operation

Furnish the information required by Item 303 of Regulation S–K.

Item 8. Financial Statements and Supplementary Data

Furnish financial statements meeting the requirements of Regulation S–X, except § 210.3–05 and Article 11 thereof, and the supplementary financial information required by Item 302 of Regulation S–K. Financial statements of the registrant and its subsidiaries consolidated (as required by Rule 14a–3(b)) shall be filed under this item. Other financial statements and schedules required under Regulation S–X may be filed as "Financial Statement Schedules" pursuant to Item 13, Exhibits, Financial Statement Schedules, and Reports on Form 8–K, of this Form.

Notwithstanding the above, if the issuer is subject to the reporting provisions of Section 15(d) and such obligation results solely from the issuer having filed a registration statement on Form S–18 which became effective under the Securities Act of 1933 during the last fiscal year, or such obligation applies as to the first or second fiscal year after the registration statement on Form S–18 became effective solely because the issuer had on the first day of the pertinent fiscal year 300 or more record holders of any of its securities to which the Form S–18 related, audited financial statements for the issuer, or for the issuer and its predecessors, may be presented as provided below. The report of the independent accountant shall in all events comply with the requirements of Article 2 of Regulation S–X.

(a) A Form 10–K filed for the fiscal year during which the registrant had a registration statement on Form S–18 become effective may include the following financial statements prepared in accordance with generally accepted accounting principles:

(1) A balance sheet as of the end of each of the two most recent fiscal years; and

(2) Consolidated statements of income, statements of cash flows, and statements of other stockholders' equity for each of the two fiscal years preceding the date of the most recent audited balance sheet being filed.

(b) A Form 10–K filed for the first fiscal year after the registrant had a registration statement on Form S–18 become effective may include financial statements prepared as follows:

(1) Financial statements for the most recent fiscal year prepared in accordance with Regulation S–X, Form and Content of and Requirements for Financial Statements; and

(2) Financial statements previously disclosed in accordance with paragraph (a) for the prior year. These statements do not need to include the compliance items and schedules of Regulation S–X, but should be recast to show the same line items as are set forth for the most recent fiscal year.

(c) A Form 10–K filed for the second fiscal year after the registrant had a registration statement on Form S–18 become effective may include financial statements for the two most recent fiscal years prepared in accordance with Regulation S–X.

Item 9. Changes in and Disagreements With Accountants on Accounting and Financial Disclosure

Furnish the information required by Item 304(b) of Regulation S–K (§ 229.304(b) of this chapter).

Item 9A. Controls and Procedures

Furnish the information required by Items 307 and 308 of Regulation S–K (§ 229.307 and 229.308).

Item 9B. Other Information

The registrant must disclose under this item any information required to be disclosed in a report on Form 8–K during the fourth quarter of the year covered by this Form 10–K, but not reported, whether or not otherwise required by this Form 10–K. If disclosure of such information is made under this item, it need not be repeated in a report on Form 8–K which would otherwise be required to be filed with respect to such information or in a subsequent report on Form 10–K.

Instruction.

With respect to a report on this Form regarding a class of asset-backed securities, the relevant period where disclosure is required is the period since the last required distribution report on Form 10–D (17 CFR 249.312).

PART III

[See General Instruction G(3)]

Item 10. Directors and Executive Officers of the Registrant

Furnish the information required by Items 401, 405 and 406 of Regulation S–K (§§ 229.401, 229.405 and 229.406 of this chapter).

Instruction

Checking the box provided on the cover page of this Form to indicate that Item 405 disclosure of delinquent Form 3, 4, or 5 filers is not contained herein is intended to facilitate Form processing and review. Failure to provide such indication will not create liability for violation of the federal securities laws. The space should be checked only if there is no disclosure in this Form of reporting person delinquencies in response to Item 405 and the registrant, at the time of filing the Form 10–K, has reviewed the information necessary to ascertain, and has determined that, Item 405 disclosure is not expected to be contained in Part III of the Form 10–K or incorporated by reference.

Item 11. Executive Compensation

Furnish the information required by Item 402 Regulation S–K.

Item 12. Security Ownership of Certain Beneficial Owners and Management and Related Stockholder Matters

Furnish the information required by Item 201(d) of Regulation S–K (§ 229.201(d) of this chapter) and by Item 403 of Regulation S–K (§ 229.403 of this chapter).

Item 13. Certain Relationships and Related Transactions

Furnish the information required by Item 404 of Regulation S–K.

Item 14. Principal Accountant Fees and Services

Furnish the information required by Item 9(e) of Schedule 14A (§ 240.14a–101 of this chapter).

(1) Disclose, under the caption *Audit Fees*, the aggregate fees billed for each of the last two fiscal years for professional services rendered by the principal accountant or the audit of the registrant's annual financial statements and review of financial statements included in the registrant's Form 10–Q (17 CFR 249.308a) or 10–QSB (17 CFR 249.308b) or services that are normally provided by the accountant in

connection with statutory and regulatory filings or engagements for those fiscal years.

(2) Disclose, under the caption *Audit–Related Fees*, the aggregate fees billed in each of the last two fiscal years for assurance and related services by the principal accountant that are reasonably related to the performance of the audit or review of the registrant's financial statements and are not reported under Item 9(e)(1) of Schedule 14A. Registrants shall describe the nature of the services comprising the fees disclosed under this category.

(3) Disclose, under the caption *Tax Fees,* the aggregate fees billed in each of the last two fiscal years for professional services rendered by the principal accountant for tax compliance, tax advice, and tax planning. Registrants shall describe the nature of the services comprising the fees disclosed under this category.

(4) Disclose, under the caption *All Other Fees*, the aggregate fees billed in each of the last two fiscal years for products and services provided by the principal accountant, other than the services reported in Items 9(e)(1) through 9(e)(3) of Schedule 14A. Registrants shall describe the nature of the services comprising the fees disclosed under this category.

(5)(i) Disclose the audit committee's pre-approval policies and procedures described in paragraph (c)(7)(i) of Rule 2–01 of Regulation S–X.

(ii) Disclose the percentage of services described in each of Items 9(e)(2) through 9(e)(4) of Schedule 14A that were approved by the audit committee pursuant to paragraph (c)(7)(i)(C) of Rule 2–01 of Regulation S–X.

(6) If greater than 50 percent, disclose the percentage of hours expended on the principal accountant's engagement to audit the registrant's financial statements for the most recent fiscal year that were attributed to work performed by persons other than the principal accountant's full-time, permanent employees.

PART IV

Item 15. Exhibits and Financial Statement Schedules

(a) List the following documents filed as a part of the report:

1. All financial statements;

2. Those financial statement schedules required to be filed by Item 8 of this Form, and by paragraph (d) below.

3. Those exhibits required by Item 601 of Regulation S–K and by paragraph (c) below. Identify in the list each management contract or compensatory plan or arrangement required to be filed as an exhibit to this form pursuant to Item 14(c) of this report.

(b) Registrants shall file, as exhibits to this Form, the exhibits required by Item 601 of Regulation S–K.

(c) Registrants shall file, as financial statement schedules to this Form, the financial statements required by Regulation S–X which are excluded from the annual report to shareholders by Rule 14a–3(b), including (1) separate financial statements of subsidiaries not consolidated and fifty percent or less owned persons; (2) separate financial statements of affiliates whose securities are pledged as collateral and (3) schedules.

Item 16. Principal Accountant Fees and Services

Furnish the information required by Item 9(e) of Schedule 14A (§ 240.14a–101 of this chapter).

(1) Disclose, under the caption *Audit Fees*, the aggregate fees billed for each of the last two fiscal years for professional services rendered by the principal accountant for the audit of the registrant's annual financial statements and review of financial statements included in the registrant's Form 10–Q (17 CFR 249.308a) or 10–QSB (17 CFR 249.308b) or services that are normally provided by the accountant in connection with statutory and regulatory filings or engagements for those fiscal years.

(2) Disclose, under the caption *Audit–Related Fees*, the aggregate fees billed in each of the last two fiscal years for assurance and related services by the principal accountant that are reasonably related to the performance of the audit or review of the registrant's financial statements and are not reported under Item 9(e)(1) of Schedule 14A. Registrants shall describe the nature of the services comprising the fees disclosed under this category.

(3) Disclose, under the caption *Tax Fees,* the aggregate fees billed in each of the last two fiscal years for professional services rendered by the principal accountant for tax compliance, tax advice, and tax planning. Registrants shall describe the nature of the services comprising the fees disclosed under this category.

(4) Disclose, under the caption *All Other Fees*, the aggregate fees billed in each of the last two fiscal years for products and services provided by the principal accountant, other than the services reported in Items 9(e)(1) through 9(e)(3) of Schedule 14A. Registrants shall describe the nature of the services comprising the fees disclosed under this category.

(5)(i) Disclose the audit committee's pre-approval policies and procedures described in paragraph (c)(7)(i) of Rule 2–01 of Regulation S–X.

(ii) Disclose the percentage of services described in each of Items 9(e)(2) through 9(e)(4) of Schedule 14A that were approved by the audit committee pursuant to paragraph (c)(7)(i)(C) of Rule 2–01 of Regulation S–X.

(6) If greater than 50 percent, disclose the percentage of hours expended on the principal accountant's engagement to audit the registrant's financial statements for the most recent fiscal year that were attributed to work performed by persons other than the principal accountant's full-time, permanent employees.

Instruction to Item 16.

A registrant that is an Asset–Backed Issuer (as defined in § 240.13a–14(g) and § 240.15d–14(g) of this chapter) is not required to disclose the information required by this Item.

SIGNATURES

[See General Instruction D]

Pursuant to the requirements of Section 13 or 15(d) of the Securities Exchange Act of 1934, the registrant has duly caused this report to be signed on its behalf by the undersigned, thereunto duly authorized.

(Registrant) ______________________

By (Signature and Title)* ______________

Date ___________________________

Pursuant to the requirements of the Securities Exchange Act of 1934, this report has been signed below by the following persons on behalf of the registrant and in the capacities and on the dates indicated.

By (Signature and Title)

Date ___________________________

By (Signature and Title)

Date ___________________________

* Print the name and title of each signing officer under his signature.

Supplemental Information to be Furnished With Reports Filed Pursuant to Section 15(d) of the Act by Registrants Which Have Not Registered Securities Pursuant to Section 12 of the Act

(a) Except to the extent that the materials enumerated in (1) and/or (2) below are specifically incorporated into this Form by reference (in which case *see* Rule 12b–23(b)), every registrant which files an annual report on this Form pursuant to Section 15(d) of the Act shall furnish to the Commission for its information, at the time of filing its report on this Form, four copies of the following:

(1) Any annual report to security holders covering the registrant's last fiscal year; and

(2) Every proxy statement, form of proxy or other proxy soliciting material sent to more than ten of the registrant's security holders with respect to any annual or other meeting of security holders.

(b) The foregoing material shall not be deemed to be "filed" with the Commission or otherwise subject to the liabilities of Section 18 of the Act, except to the extent that the registrant specifically incorporates it in its annual report on this Form by reference.

(c) If no such annual report or proxy material has been sent to security holders, a statement to that effect shall be included under this caption. If such report or proxy material is to be furnished to security holders subsequent to the filing of the annual report of this Form, the registrant shall so state under this caption and shall furnish copies of such material to the Commission when it is sent to security holders.

SECURITIES AND EXCHANGE COMMISSION
Washington, D.C. 20549

FORM 10–KSB

(Mark One)

[ ] **ANNUAL REPORT UNDER SECTION 13 OR 15(d) OF THE SECURITIES EXCHANGE ACT OF 1934**

For the fiscal year ended __________

[ ] **TRANSITION REPORT UNDER SECTION 13 OR 15(d) OF THE SECURITIES EXCHANGE ACT OF 1943**

For the transition period from ____________ to ____________

Commission file number ____________

____
(Name of small business issuer in its charter)

____________ ____________
(State or other jurisdiction of incorporation or organization) (I.R.S. Employer Identification No.)

____________ ____________
(Address of principal executive offices) (Zip Code)

Issuer's telephone number ____________

Securities registered under Section 12(b) of the Exchange Act:

Title of each class	Name of each exchange on which registered

Securities registered under Section 12(g) of the Exchange Act:

____
(Title of class)

____
(Title of class)

Check whether the issuer (1) filed all reports required to be filed by Section 13 or 15(d) of the Exchange Act during the past 12 months (or for such shorter period that the registrant was required to file such reports), and (2) has been subject to such filing requirements for the past 90 days. Yes ____ No ____

Check if there is no disclosure of delinquent filers in response to Item 405 of Regulation S–B not contained in this form, and no disclosure will be contained, to the best of registrant's knowledge, in definitive proxy or information statements incorporated by reference in Part III of this Form 10–KSB or any amendment to this Form 10–KSB. [ ]

State issuer's revenues for its most recent fiscal year. ____________

State the aggregate market value of the voting and non-voting common equity held by non-affiliates computed by reference to the price at which the common equity was sold, or the average bid and asked price of such common equity, as of a specified date within the past 60 days. (See definition of affiliate in Rule 12b–2 of the Exchange Act.)

Note: If determining whether a person is an affiliate will involve an unreasonable effort and expense, the issuer may calculate the aggregate market value of the common equity held by non-affiliates on the basis of reasonable assumptions, if the assumptions are stated.

(ISSUERS INVOLVED IN BANKRUPTCY PROCEEDING DURING THE PAST FIVE YEARS)

Check whether the issuer has filed all documents and reports required to be filed by Section 12, 13 or 15(d) of the Exchange Act after the distribution of securities under a plan confirmed by a court. Yes ____ No ____

(APPLICABLE ONLY TO CORPORATE REGISTRANTS)

State the number of shares outstanding of each of the issuer's classes of common equity, as of the latest practicable date _______

DOCUMENTS INCORPORATED BY REFERENCE

If the following documents are incorporated by reference, briefly describe them and identify the part of the Form 10–KSB (e.g., Part I, Part II, etc.) into which the document is incorporated: (1) any annual report to security holders; (2) any proxy or information statement; and (3) any prospectus filed pursuant to Rule 424(b) or (c) of the Securities Act of 1933 ("Securities Act"). The list documents should be clearly described for identification purposes (e.g., annual report to security holders for fiscal year ended December 24, 1990).

GENERAL INSTRUCTIONS

A. Use of Form 10–KSB.

This Form may be used by a "small business issuer," defined in Rule 12b–2 of the Exchange Act, for its annual and transitional reports under section 13 or 15(d) of that Act. For further information as to eligibility to use this Form see Item 10(a) of Regulation S–B. Annual reports on this form shall be filed within 90 days after the end of the fiscal year covered by the report. Transition reports shall be filed within the time period specified in Rules 13a–10 or 15d–10 of the Exchange Act.

B. Application of General Rules and Regulations.

The General Rules and Regulations under the Exchange Act; particularly Regulation 12B contain certain general requirements for reports on any form which should be carefully read and observed in the preparation and filing of reports on this Form.

C. Signature and Filing of Report.

1. File three "complete" copies and five "additional" copies of the registration statement with the Commission and file at least one complete copy with each exchange on which the securities will be registered. A "complete" copy includes financial statements, exhibits and all other papers and documents. An "additional" copy excludes exhibits. One of the copies filed with the Commission and each exchange should be manually signed; all other copies should have typed or printed signatures.

2. Who must sign. The small business issuer, its principal executive officer or officers, its principal financial officer, its controller or principal accounting officer and at least a majority of the board of directors or persons performing similar functions. If the small business issuer is a limited partnership, then the general partner and a majority of its board of directors if a corporation must sign the report. Any person who occupies more than one of the specified positions must indicate each capacity in which he or she signs the report. See Rule 12b–11 concerning manual signatures under powers of attorney.

3. Small business issuers are requested to indicate in a transmittal letter with the Form 10–KSB whether the financial statements in the report reflect a change from the preceding year in any accounting principles or practices or in the methods of application of those principles or practices.

D. Information as to Employee Stock Purchase, Savings and Similar Plans.

Separate annual and other reports need not be filed under Section 15(d) of the Exchange Act. For any employee stock purchase, savings or similar plan if the issuer of the securities offered under the plan furnishes to the Commission the information and documents specified in the Rule 15d–21 of the Exchange Act.

E. Information to be Incorporated by Reference.

1. Refer to Rule 12b–23 if information will be incorporated by reference from other documents in answer or partial answer to any item of this Form.

2. The information called for in Parts I and II of this Form, Items 1–9, may be incorporated by reference from:

(a) the registrant's annual report to security holders furnished to the Commission under Rule 14a–3(b) or Rule 14c–3(a) of the Exchange Act; or

(b) the registrant's annual report to shareholders if it contains the information required by Rule 14a–3.

Note to electronic filers: If any information required by Part I or Part II is incorporated by reference from the annual report to security holders as allowed in General Instruction E.2.(a), any portion of the annual report to security holders incorporated by reference shall be filed as an exhibit in electronic format, as required by Item 601(b)(13) of Regulation S–B.

3. The information required by Part III may be incorporated by reference from the registrant's definitive proxy statement (filed or to be filed in accordance with § 240.14a–101, Schedule 14A) or definitive information statement (filed or to be filed pursuant to § 240.14c–101, Schedule 14C) which involves the election of directors, if such definitive proxy or information statement is filed with the Commission not later than 120 days after the end of the fiscal year covered by this Form. If the definitive proxy or information statement is not filed within the 120-day period, the information called for in Part III information must be filed as part of the Form 10–KSB, or as an amendment to the Form 10–KSB, not later than the end of the 120-day period.

4. No item numbers of captions or items need be contained in the material incorporated by reference into the report. However, the registrant's attention is directed to Rule 12b–23(b) of the Exchange Act regarding the specific disclosure required in the report concerning information incorporated by reference. When the registrant combines all of the information in Parts I and II of this Form by incorporation by reference from the registrant's annual report to security holders and all of the information in Part III of this Form by incorporating by reference from a definitive proxy statement or information statement involving the election of directors, then this Form shall consist of the facing or cover page, those sections incorporated from the annual report to security holders, the proxy or information statement, and the information, if any, required by Part IV of this Form, signatures and a cross-reference sheet setting forth the item numbers and captions in Parts I, II and III of this Form and page and/or pages in the referenced materials where the corresponding information appears.

F. Integrated Reports to Security Holders.

Annual reports to security holders may be combined with the required information of this Form and will be suitable for filing with the Commission if the following conditions are satisfied:

1. The combined report contains complete answers to all items required by Form 10–KSB. When responses to a certain item of required disclosure are separated within the combined report, an appropriate cross-reference should be made. If the information required by Part III of Form 10–KSB is omitted by virtue of General Instruction E, a definitive proxy or information statement shall be filed.

2. The cover page and required signatures are included. A cross-reference sheet should be filed indicating the location of information required by items of the Form.

3. If an electronic filer files any portion of an annual report to security holders in combination with the required information of Form 10–KSB, as provided in this instruction, only such portions filed in satisfaction of the Form 10–KSB requirements shall be filed in electronic format.

G. Omission of Information by Certain Wholly–Owned Subsidiaries.

If, on the date of the filing of its report on Form 10–KSB, the registrant meets the conditions specified in paragraph (1) below, then it may furnish the abbreviated narrative disclosure specified in paragraph (2) below.

1. Conditions for availability of relief specified in paragraph (2) below.

(a) All of the registrant's equity securities are owned, either directly or indirectly, by a single person which is a reporting company and which has filed all the material required to be filed under sections 13, 14 or 15(d), as applicable, and which is named in conjunction with the registrant's description of its business;

(b) During the past thirty-six months and any subsequent period of days, there has not been any material default in the payment of principal, interest, a sinking or purchase fund installment, or any other material default not cured within thirty days, with respect to any indebtedness of the registrant or it subsidiaries, and there has not been any material default in the payment of rental under material long-term leases; and

(c) There is prominently set forth on the cover page of the Form 10–KSB, a statement that the registrant meets the conditions set forth in General Instruction G(1)(a) and (b) of Form 10–KSB and therefore is filing this Form with the reduced disclosure format.

2. Registrants meeting the conditions specified in paragraph 1 above are entitled to the following relief:

(a) Such registrants may omit the information called for by Item 303(b), Management's Discussion and Analysis, if required by the Instruction to that Item, provided that the registrant includes in the Form 10–KSB a narrative analysis of the results of operations explaining the reasons for material changes in the amount of revenue and expense items between the most recent fiscal year presented and the fiscal year immediately preceding it. Explanations of material changes should include, but not be limited to, changes in the various elements which determine revenue and expense levels, such as unit sales volume, prices charged and paid, production levels, production cost variances, labor costs and discretionary spending programs. In addition, the analysis should include an explanation of the effect of any changes in accounting principles and practices or method of application that have a material effect on net income as reported.

(b) Such registrants may omit the list of subsidiaries exhibit required by Item 601 of Regulation S–B.

(c) Such registrants may omit the information called for by the following Items: Item 4, Submission of Matters to a Vote of Security Holders; Item 9, Directors and Executive Officers, etc.; Item 10, Executive Compensation; Item 11, Security Ownership of Certain Beneficial Owners, etc.; Item 12,

Certain Relationships and Related Transactions.

PART I

Item 1. Description of Business.

Furnish the information required by Item 101 of Regulation S–B.

Item 2. Description of Property.

Furnish the information required by Item 102 of Regulation S–B.

Item 3. Legal Proceedings.

Furnish the information required by Item 103 of Regulation S–B.

Item 4. Submission of Matters to a Vote of Security Holders.

If any matter was submitted during the fourth quarter of the fiscal year covered by this report to a vote of security holders, through the solicitation of proxies or otherwise, furnish the following information:

(a) The date of the meeting and whether it was an annual or special meeting.

(b) If the meeting involved the election of directors, the name of each director elected at the meeting and the name of each other director whose term of office as a director continued after the meeting.

(c) A brief description of each matter voted upon at the meeting and state the number of votes cast for, against or withheld, as well as the number of abstentions and broker non-votes as to each such matter, including a separate tabulation with respect to each nominee for office.

(d) A description of the terms of any settlement between the registrant and any other participant (as defined in Rule 14a–11 of Regulation A under the Act) terminating any solicitation subject to Rule 14a–11, including the cost or anticipated cost to the registrant.

Instructions to Item 4: 1. If any matter has been submitted to a vote of security holders otherwise than at a meeting of such security holders, corresponding information with respect to such submission should be furnished. The solicitation of any authorization or consent (other than a proxy to vote at a shareholders' meeting) with respect to any matter shall be deemed a submission of such matter to a vote of security holders within the meaning of this item.

2. Paragraph (a) need be answered only if paragraph (b) or (c) is required to be answered.

3. Paragraph (b) need not be answered if (i) proxies for the meeting were solicited pursuant to Regulation 14A under the Act, (ii) there was no solicitation in opposition to the management's nominees as listed in the proxy statement, and (iii) all of such nominees were elected. If the registrant did not solicit proxies and the board of directors as previously reported to the Commission was re-elected in its entirety, a statement to that effect in answer to paragraph (b) will suffice as an answer thereto.

4. Paragraph (c) must be answered for all matters voted upon at the meeting, including both contested and uncontested elections of directors.

5. If the registrant has furnished to its security holders proxy soliciting material containing the information called for by paragraph (d), the paragraph may be answered by reference to the information contained in such material.

6. If the registrant published a report containing all of the information called for by this item, the item may be answered by reference to the information in that report.

PART II

Item 5. Market for Common Equity, Related Stockholder Matters and Small Business Issuer Purchases of Equity Securities.

(a) Furnish the information required by Item 201 of Regulation S–B and Item 701 of Regulation S–B as to all equity securities of the small business issuer sold by the small business issuer during the period covered by the report that were not registered under the Securities Act. If the Item 701 information previously has been included in a Quarterly Report on Form 10–Q or 10–QSB, or on a Current Report on Form 8–K, however, it need not be furnished.

(b) If required pursuant to Rule 463 (17 CFR 230.463) of the Securities Act of 1933, furnish the information required by Item 701(f) of Regulation S–B (§ 228.701(f) of this chapter).

(c) Furnish the information required by Item 703 of Regulation S–B (§ 228.703 of this chapter) for any repurchase made in a month within the fourth quarter of the fiscal year covered by the report. Provide disclosures covering repurchases made on a monthly basis. For example, if the fourth quarter began on January 16 and ended on April 15, the chart would show repurchases for the months from January 16 through February 15, February 16 through March 15, and March 16 through April 15.

Item 6. Management's Discussion and Analysis or Plan of Operation.

Furnish the information required by Item 303 of Regulation S–B.

Item 7. Financial Statements.

Furnish the information required by Item 310(a) of Regulation S–B.

Item 8. Changes In and Disagreements With Accountants on Accounting and Financial Disclosure.

Furnish the information required by Item 304(b) of Regulation S–B.

Item 8A. Control and Procedures.

Furnish the information required by Items 307 of Regulation S–B (17 CFR 228.307) and 308 of Regulation S–B (17 CFR 228.308).

Item 8B. Other Information.

The small business issuer must disclose under this item any information required to be disclosed in a report on Form 8–K during the fourth quarter of the year covered by this Form 10–KSB, but not reported, whether or not otherwise required by this Form 10–KSB. If disclosure of such information is made under this item, it need not be repeated in a report on Form 8–K which would otherwise be required to be filed with respect to such information or in a subsequent report on Form 10–KSB.

PART III

Item 9. Directors and Executive Officers of the Registrant

Furnish the information required by Items 401, 405 and 406 of Regulation S–B (§§ 228.401, 228.405, and 228.406 of this chapter).

Instruction to Item 9: Checking the box provided on the cover page of this Form, to indicate that Item 405 disclosure of delinquent Form 3, 4, or 5 filers is not contained herein, is intended to facilitate Form processing and review. Failure to provide such indication will not create liability for violation of the federal securities laws. The space should be checked only if there is no disclosure in this Form of reporting person delinquencies in response to Item 405 of Regulation S–B (§ 228.405 of this chapter) and the registrant, at the time of filing of the Form 10–KSB, has reviewed the information necessary to ascertain, and has determined that, Item 405 disclosure is not expected to be contained in Part III of the Form 10–KSB or incorporated by reference.

Item 10. Executive Compensation.

Furnish the information required by Item 402 of Regulation S–B.

Item 11. Security Ownership of Certain Beneficial Owners and Management and Related Stockholder Matters.

Furnish the information required by Item 201(d) of Regulation S–B and by Item 403 of Regulation S–B.

Item 12. Certain Relationships and Related Transactions.

Furnish the information required by Item 404 of Regulation S–B.

Item 13. Exhibits.

Furnish the exhibits required by Item 601 of Regulation S–B. Where any financial statement or exhibit is incorporated by reference, the incorporation by reference shall be set forth in the list required by this item. See Exchange Act Rule 12b–23. Identify in the list each management contract or compensatory plan or arrangement required to be filed as an exhibit to this form.

Item 14. Principal Accountant Fees and Services

Furnish the information required by Item 9(e) of Schedule 14A (§ 240.14a–101 of this chapter).

(1) Disclose, under the caption *Audit Fees,* the aggregate fees billed for each of the last two fiscal years for professional services rendered by the principal accountant for the audit of the registrant's annual financial statements and review of financial statements included in the registrant's Form 10–Q (17 CFR 249.308a) or 10–QSB (17 CFR 249.308b) or services that are normally provided by the accountant in connection with statutory and regulatory filings or engagements for those fiscal years.

(2) Disclose, under the caption *Audit–Related Fees,* the aggregate fees billed in each of the last two fiscal years for assurance and related services by the principal accountant that are reasonably related to the performance of the audit or review of the registrant's financial statements and are not reported under Item 9(e)(1) of Schedule 14A. Registrants shall describe the nature of the services comprising the fees disclosed under this category.

(3) Disclose, under the caption *Tax Fees,* the aggregate fees billed in each of the last two fiscal years for professional services rendered by the principal accountant for tax compliance, tax advice, and tax planning. Registrants shall describe the nature of the services comprising the fees disclosed under this category.

(4) Disclose, under the caption *All Other Fees,* the aggregate fees billed in each of the last two fiscal years for products and services provided by the principal accountant, other than the services reported in Items 9(e)(1) through 9(e)(3) of Schedule 14A. Registrants shall describe the nature of the services comprising the fees disclosed under this category.

(5)(i) Disclose the audit committee's pre-approval policies and procedures described in paragraph (c)(7)(i) of Rule 2–01 of Regulation S–X.

(ii) Disclose the percentage of services described in each of Items 9(e)(2) through 9(e)(4) of Schedule 14A that were approved by the audit committee pursuant to paragraph (c)(7)(i)(C) of Rule 2–01 of Regulation S–X.

(6) If greater than 50 percent, disclose the percentage of hours expended on the principal accountant's engagement to audit the registrant's financial statements for the most recent fiscal year that were attributed to work performed by persons other than the principal accountant's full-time, permanent employees.

SIGNATURES

In accordance with Section 13 or 15(d) of the Exchange Act, the registrant caused this report to be signed on its behalf by the undersigned, thereunto duly authorized.

(Registrant) ________________
By (Signature and Title) * ________________
Date ________________

In accordance with the Exchange Act, this report has been signed below by the following persons on behalf of the registrant and in the capacities and on the dates indicated.

By (Signature and Title) * ________________
Date ________________
By (Signature and Title) * ________________
Date ________________

* Print the name and title of each signing officer under his signature.

Supplemental information to be Furnished With Reports Filed Pursuant to Section 15(d) of the Exchange Act By Non-reporting Issuers

(a) Except to the extent that the materials enumerated in (1) and/or (2) below are specifically incorporated into this Form by reference (in which case, see rule 12b–23(b)), every issuer which files an annual report on this Form under Section 15(d) of the Exchange Act shall furnish the Commission for its information, at the time of filing its report on this Form, four copies of the following:

(1) Any annual report to security holders covering the registrant's last fiscal year; and

(2) Every proxy statement, form of proxy or other proxy soliciting material sent to more than ten of the registrant's security holders with respect to any annual or other meeting of security holders.

(b) The Commission will not consider the material to be ''filed'' or subject to the liabilities of Section 18 of the Exchange Act, except if the issuer specifically incorporates it in its annual report on this Form by reference.

(c) If no such annual report or proxy material has been sent to security holders, a statement to that effect shall be included under this caption. If such report or proxy material is to be furnished to security holders subsequent to the filing of the annual report on this Form, the registrant shall so state under this caption and shall furnish copies of such material to the Commission when it is sent to security holders.

SECURITIES AND EXCHANGE COMMISSION
Washington, D.C. 20549

FORM 6–K

REPORT OF FOREIGN ISSUER

Pursuant to Rules 13a–16 and 15d–16 Under the Securities Exchange Act of 1934

GENERAL INSTRUCTIONS

A. Rule as to Use of Form 6–K

This form shall be used by foreign private issuers which are required to furnish reports pursuant to Rule 13a–16 or 15d–16 under the Securities Exchange Act of 1934.

B. Information and Document Required to be Furnished

Subject to General Instruction D herein, an issuer furnishing a report on this form shall furnish whatever information, not required to be furnished on Form 40–F or previously furnished, such issuer (i) makes or is required to make public pursuant to the law of the jurisdiction of its domicile or in which it is incorporated or organized, or (ii) files or is required to file with a stock exchange on which its securities are traded and which was made public by that exchange, or (iii) distributes or is required to distribute to its securityholders.

The information required to be furnished pursuant to (i), (ii) or (iii) above is that which is material with respect to the issuer and its subsidiaries concerning: changes in business; changes in management or control; acquisitions or dispositions of assets; bankruptcy or receivership; changes in registrant's certifying accountants; the financial condition and results of operations; material legal proceedings; changes in securities or in the security for registered securities; defaults upon senior securities; material increases or decreases in the amount outstanding of securities or indebtedness; the results of the submission of matters to a vote of securityholders; transactions with directors, officers or principal securityholders; the granting of options or payment of other compensation to directors or officers; and any other information which the registrant deems of material importance to securityholders.

This report is required to be furnished promptly after the material contained in the report is made public as described above. The information and documents furnished in this report shall not be deemed to be "filed" for the purposes of Section 18 of the Act or otherwise subject to the liabilities of that section.

If a report furnished on this form incorporates by reference any information not previously filed with the Commission, such information must be attached as an exhibit and furnished with the form.

C. Preparation and Filing of Report.

(1) The Form 6–K report shall consist of a cover page, the report or document furnished by the issuer, and a signature page. An issuer must submit the Form 6–K report in electronic format via the Commission's Electronic Data Gathering, Analysis, and Retrieval (EDGAR) system in accordance with the EDGAR rules set forth in Regulation S–T (17 CFR Part 232) except as discussed below. An issuer submitting the Form 6–K in electronic format must provide the signatures required for the Form 6–K report in accordance with Regulation S–T Rule 302 (17 CFR 232.302). For assistance with technical questions about EDGAR or to request an access code, call the EDGAR Filer Support Office at (202) 942–8900. For assistance with the EDGAR rules, call the Office of EDGAR and Information Analysis at (202) 942–2940.

(2) An issuer may submit a Form 6–K in paper under:

- Regulation S–T Rule 101(b)(1) (17 CFR 232.101(b)(1)) if the sole purpose of the Form 6–K is to furnish an annual report to security holders;
- Regulation S–T Rule 101(b)(7) to provide a report or other document that the issuer must furnish and make public under the laws of the jurisdiction in which it is incorporated, domiciled or legally organized (the issuer's "home country"), or under the rules of the home country exchange on which the issuer's securities are traded, as long as the report or other document is not a press release, is not required to be and has not been distributed to the issuer's security holders, and, if discussing a material event, including the disclosure of annual audited or interim consolidated financial results, has already been the subject of a Form 6–K submission or other Commission filing on EDGAR; or
- A hardship exemption provided by Regulation S–T Rule 201 or 202 (17 CFR 232.201 or 232.202).

Note to paragraph (2): An issuer that is or will be incorporating by reference all or part of an annual or other report to security holders, or of any part of a paper Form 6–K, into an electronic filing must file the incorporated portion in electronic format as an exhibit to the filing in accordance with Regulation S–T Rule 303(b) (17 CFR 232.303(b)).

(3) When submitting a Form 6–K in paper under one of the above rules, an issuer must check the appropriate box on the cover page of the Form 6–K. When submitting a Form 6–K in paper under a hardship exemption, an issuer must provide the legend required by Regulation S–T Rule 201(a)(2) or 202(c) (17 CFR 232.201(a)(2) or 232.202(c)) on the cover page of the Form 6–K.

(4) An issuer furnishing the Form 6–K in paper under one of the above rules, or as otherwise permitted by the Commission, must deposit with the Commission eight complete copies of the Form 6–K report. An issuer must also file at least one complete copy of the Form 6–K with each United States stock exchange on which any security of the issuer is listed and registered under Section 12(b) of the Exchange Act. The issuer must have signed at least one of the paper copies deposited with the Commission and one filed with each United States stock exchange in accordance with Exchange Act Rule 12b–11(d) (17 CFR 240.12b–11(d)) when submitting the Form 6–K in paper to the Commission. An issuer submitting the Form 6–K in paper must also conform the unsigned copies. When submitting the Form 6–K in electronic format to the Commission, an issuer may submit a paper copy containing typed signatures to each United States stock exchange in accordance with Regulation S–T Rule 302(c) (17 CFR 232.302(c)).

(5) *XBRL-Related Documents.* XBRL-Related Documents (§ 232.11 of this chapter) can be submitted if listed as exhibit 100.

D. Treatment of Foreign Language Documents.

(1) An issuer must submit the Form 6–K report in electronic format in the English language in accordance with Regulation S–T Rule 306 (17 CFR 232.306) and Exchange Act Rule 12b–12(d) (17 CFR 240.12b–12(d)), as referenced in Regulation S–T Rule 306(a) (17 CFR 232.306(a)), except as otherwise provided by this Form. An issuer submitting the Form 6–K in paper must meet the requirements of Exchange Act Rule 12b–12(d) (17 CFR 240.12b–12(d)). In accordance with, or in addition to, the list of documents specified in Exchange Act Rule 12b–12(d)(2) (17 CFR 240.12b–12(d)(2)), an issuer must provide a full English translation of the following documents furnished under cover of Form 6–K whether submitted electronically or in paper:

- Press releases;
- Communications and other documents distributed directly to security holders for each class of securities to which a reporting

obligation under Exchange Act Section 13(a) or 15(d) pertains, except for offering circulars and prospectuses that relate entirely to securities offerings outside the United States (''foreign offerings''); and

- Documents disclosing annual audited or interim consolidated financial information.

(2) In addition to the documents specified in Exchange Act Rule 12b–12(d)(3) (17 CFR 240.12b–12(d)(3)), an issuer may furnish under cover of Form 6–K, whether submitted electronically or in paper, an English summary instead of a full English translation of a report required to be furnished and made public under the laws of the issuer's home country or the rules of the issuer's home country stock exchange, as long as it is not a press release and is not required to be and has not been distributed to the issuer's security holders. Such a document may include a report disclosing unconsolidated financial information about a parent company.

(3) An issuer is not required to submit under cover of Form 6–K an offering circular or prospectus that pertains solely to a foreign offering, even when an English translation or English summary is available, if the issuer has already submitted a Form 6–K or filed a Form 20–F or other Commission filing on EDGAR that reported material information disclosed in the offering circular or prospectus. If an issuer has not previously disclosed this material information to the Commission, it may submit in electronic format under cover of Form 6–K an English translation or English summary of the portion of the foreign offering circular or prospectus that discusses the new material information.

(4) Any submitted English summary must meet the requirements of Exchange Act Rule 12b–12(d)(3)(ii) (17 CFR 240.12b–12(d)(3)(ii)). An issuer may submit the unabridged foreign language report or other document along with the English summary or English translation as permitted by Regulation S–T Rule 306(b) (17 CFR 232.306(b)) for electronic filings and Exchange Act Rule 12b–12(d)(4) (17 CFR 240.12b–12(d)(4)) for paper filings.

SECURITIES AND EXCHANGE COMMISSION

Washington, D.C. 20549

FORM 6–K

REPORT OF FOREIGN ISSUER

Pursuant to Rule 13a–16 or 15d–16 of the Securities Exchange Act of 1934

For the month of ______________________________, 20___

Commission File Number ______

____
(Translation of registrant's name into English)

____
(Address of principal executive offices)

Indicate by check mark whether the registrant files or will file annual reports under cover of Form 20–F or Form 40–F:

Form 20–F ______ Form 40–F ______

Indicate by check mark if the registrant is submitting the Form 6–K in paper as permitted by Regulation S–T Rule 101(b)(1): ______

Note: Regulation S–T Rule 101(b)(1) only permits the submission in paper of a Form 6–K if submitted solely to provide an attached annual report to security holders.

Indicate by check mark if the registrant is submitting the Form 6–K in paper as permitted by Regulation S–T Rule 101(b)(7): ______

Note: Regulation S–T Rule 101(b)(7) only permits the submission in paper of a Form 6–K if submitted to furnish a report or other document that the registrant foreign private issuer must furnish and make public under the laws of the jurisdiction in which the registrant is incorporated, domiciled or legally organized (the registrant's "home country"), or under the rules of the home country exchange on which the registrant's securities are traded, as long as the report or other document is not a press release, is not required to be and has not been distributed to the registrant's security holders, and, if discussing a material event, has already been the subject of a Form 6–K submission or other Commission filing on EDGAR.

Indicate by check mark whether by furnishing the information contained in this Form, the registrant is also thereby furnishing the information to the Commission pursuant to Rule 12g3–2(b) under the Securities Exchange Act of 1934.

Yes ______ No ______

If "Yes" is marked, indicate below the file number assigned to the registrant in connection with Rule 12g3–2(b): 82–______

SECURITIES AND EXCHANGE COMMISSION
Washington, D.C. 20549

FORM 8–K

CURRENT REPORT

Pursuant to Section 13 or 15(d) of the Securities Exchange Act of 1934

Date of Report (Date of earliest event reported) ______________

____
(Exact name of registrant as specified in its charter)

____
(State or other jurisdiction of incorporation) (Commission File Number) (IRS Employer Identification No.)

____
(Address of principal executive offices) (Zip Code)

Registrant's telephone number, including area code ______________

____
(Former name or former address, if changed since last report.)

Check the appropriate box below if the Form 8–K filing is intended to simultaneously satisfy the filing obligation of the registrant under any of the following provisions (see General Instruction A.2. below):

[ ] Written communications pursuant to Rule 425 under the Securities Act (17 CFR 230.425)

[ ] Soliciting material pursuant to Rule 14a–12 under the Exchange Act (17 CFR 240.14a–12)

[ ] Pre-commencement communications pursuant to Rule 14d–2(b) under the Exchange Act (17 CFR 240.14d–2(b))

GENERAL INSTRUCTIONS

A. Rules as to Use of Form 8–K

1. Form 8–K shall be used for current reports under Section 13 or 15(d) of the Securities Exchange Act of 1934, filed pursuant to Rule 13a–11 or Rule 15d–11 and for reports of nonpublic information required to be disclosed by Regulation FD (§§ 243.100 and 243.101 of this chapter).

2. Form 8–K may be used by a registrant to satisfy its filing obligations pursuant to Rule 425 under the Securities Act, regarding written communications related to business combination transactions, or Rules 14a–12(b) or Rule 14d–2(b) under the Exchange Act, relating to soliciting materials and pre-commencement communications pursuant to tender offers, respectively, provided that the Form 8–K filing satisfies all the substantive requirements of those rules (other than the Rule 425(c) requirement to include certain specified information in any prospectus filed pursuant to such rule). Such filing is also deemed to be filed pursuant to any rule for which the box is checked. A registrant is not required to check the box in connection with Rule 14a–12(b) or Rule 14d–2(b) if the communication is filed pursuant to Rule 425. Communications filed pursuant to Rule 425 are deemed filed under the other applicable sections. See Note 2 to Rule 425, Rule 14a–12(b) and Instruction 2 to Rule 14d–2(b)(2).

B. Events to be Reported and Time for Filing of Reports

1. A report on this form is required to be filed or furnished, as applicable, upon the oc-

currence of any one or more of the events specified in the items in Sections 1–6 and 9 of this form. Unless otherwise specified, a report is to be filed or furnished within four business days after occurrence of the event. If the event occurs on a Saturday, Sunday or holiday on which the Commission is not open for business, then the four business day period shall begin to run on, and include, the first business day thereafter. A registrant either furnishing a report on this form under Item 7.01 (Regulation FD Disclosure) or electing to file a report on this form under Item 8.01 (Other Events) solely to satisfy its obligations under Regulation FD (17 CFR 243.100 and 243.101) must furnish such report or make such filing, as applicable, in accordance with the requirements of Rule 100(a) of Regulation FD (17 CFR 243.100(a)), including the deadline for furnishing or filing such report.

2. The information in a report furnished pursuant to Item 2.02 (Results of Operations and Financial Condition) or Item 7.01 (Regulation FD Disclosure) shall not be deemed to be "filed" for purposes of Section 18 of the Exchange Act or otherwise subject to the liabilities of that section, unless the registrant specifically states that the information is to be considered "filed" under the Exchange Act or incorporates it by reference into a filing under the Securities Act or the Exchange Act. If a report on Form 8–K contains disclosures under Item 2.02 or Item 7.01, whether or not the report contains disclosures regarding other items, all exhibits to such report relating to Item 2.02 or Item 7.01 will be deemed furnished, and not filed, unless the registrant specifies, under Item 9.01 (Financial Statements and Exhibits), which exhibits, or portions of exhibits, are intended to be deemed filed rather than furnished pursuant to this instruction.

3. If the registrant previously has reported substantially the same information as required by this form, the registrant need not make an additional report of the information on this form. To the extent that an item calls for disclosure of developments concerning a previously reported event or transaction, any information required in the new report or amendment about the previously reported event or transaction may be provided by incorporation by reference to the previously filed report. The term previously reported is defined in Rule 12b–2 (17 CFR 240.12b–2).

4. Copies of agreements, amendments or other documents or instruments required to be filed pursuant to Form 8–K are not required to be filed or furnished as exhibits to the Form 8–K unless specifically required to be filed or furnished by the applicable Item. This instruction does not affect the requirement to otherwise file such agreements, amendments or other documents or instruments, including as exhibits to registration statements and periodic reports pursuant to the requirements of Item 601 of Regulation S–K or Item 601 of Regulation S–B, as applicable.

5. When considering current reporting on this form, particularly of other events of material importance pursuant to Item 7.01 (Regulation FD Disclosure) and Item 8.01 (Other Events), registrants should have due regard for the accuracy, completeness and currency of the information in registration statements filed under the Securities Act which incorporate by reference information in reports filed pursuant to the Exchange Act, including reports on this form.

6. A registrant's report under Item 7.01 (Regulation FD Disclosure) or Item 8.01 (Other Events) will not be deemed an admission as to the materiality of any information in the report that is required to be disclosed solely by Regulation FD.

C. Application of General Rules and Regulations

1. The General Rules and Regulations under the Act contain certain general requirements which are applicable to reports on any form. These general requirements should be carefully read and observed in the preparation and filing of reports on this form.

2. Particular attention is directed to Regulation 12B which contains general requirements regarding matters such as the kind and size of paper to be used, the legibility of the report, the information to be given whenever the title of securities is required to be stated, and the filing of the report. The definitions contained in Rule 12b–2 should be especially noted. See also Regulations 13A and 15D.

3. A "small business issuer," defined under Rule 12b–2 of the Exchange Act (§ 240.12b–2 of this chapter), shall refer to the disclosure items in Regulation S–B (17 CFR 228.10 et seq.) and not Regulation S–K. If there is no comparable disclosure item in Regulation S–B, a small business issuer need not provide the information requested. A small business issuer shall provide the information required by Item 310(c) and (d) of Regulation S–B in lieu of the financial information required by Item 7 of this Form.

D. Preparation of Report

This form is not to be used as a blank form to be filled in, but only as a guide in the preparation of the report on paper meeting the requirements of Rule 12b–12. The report shall contain the numbers and captions of all applicable items, but the text of such items may be omitted, provided the answers thereto are prepared in the manner specified in Rule 12b–13. All items that are not required to be answered in a particular report may be omitted and no reference thereto need be made in the report. All instructions should also be omitted.

E. Signature and Filing of Report

Three complete copies of the report, including any financial statements, exhibits or other papers or documents filed as a part thereof, and five additional copies which need not include exhibits, shall be filed with the Commission. At least one complete copy of the report, including any financial statements, exhibits or other papers or documents filed as a part thereof, shall be filed, with each exchange on which any class of securities of the registrant is registered. At least one complete copy of the report filed with the Commission and one such copy filed with each exchange shall be manually signed. Copies not manually signed shall bear typed or printed signatures.

F. Incorporation by Reference

If the registrant makes available to its stockholders or otherwise publishes, within the period prescribed for filing the report, a press release or other document or statement containing information meeting some or all of the requirements of this form, the information called for may be incorporated by reference to such published document or statement, in answer or partial answer to any item or items of this form, provided copies thereof are filed as an exhibit to the report on this form.

G. Use of this Form by Asset–Backed Issuers

The following applies to registrants that are asset-backed issuers. Terms used in this General Instruction G. have the same meaning as in Item 1101 of Regulation AB (17 CFR 229.1101).

1. *Reportable Events That May Be Omitted.*

The registrant need not file a report on this Form upon the occurrence of any one or more of the events specified in the following:

(a) Item 2.01, Completion of Acquisition or Disposition of Assets;

(b) Item 2.02, Results of Operations and Financial Condition;

(c) Item 2.03, Creation of a Direct Financial Obligation or an Obligation under an Off–Balance Sheet Arrangement of a Registrant;

(d) Item 2.05, Costs Associated with Exit or Disposal Activities;

(e) Item 2.06, Material Impairments;

(f) Item 3.01, Notice of Delisting or Failure to Satisfy a Continued Listing Rule or Standard; Transfer of Listing;

(g) Item 3.02, Unregistered Sales of Equity Securities;

(h) Item 4.01, Changes in Registrant's Certifying Accountant;

(i) Item 4.02, Non–Reliance on Previously Issued Financial Statements or a Related Audit Report or Completed Interim Review;

(j) Item 5.01, Changes in Control of Registrant;

(k) Item 5.02, Departure of Directors or Principal Officers; Election of Directors; Appointment of Principal Officers;

(*l*) Item 5.04, Temporary Suspension of Trading Under Registrant's Employee Benefit Plans; and

(m) Item 5.05, Amendments to the Registrant's Code of Ethics, or Waiver of a Provision of the Code of Ethics.

2. *Additional Disclosure for the Form 8–K Cover Page.*

Immediately after the name of the issuing entity on the cover page of the Form 8–K, as separate line items, identify the exact name of the depositor as specified in its charter and the exact name of the sponsor as specified in its charter.

3. *Signatures.*

The Form 8-K must be signed by the depositor. In the alternative, the Form 8–K may be signed on behalf of the issuing entity by a duly authorized representative of the servicer. If multiple servicers are involved in servicing the pool assets, a duly authorized representative of the master servicer (or entity performing the equivalent function) must sign if a representative of the servicer is to sign the report on behalf of the issuing entity.

INFORMATION TO BE INCLUDED IN THE REPORT

Section 1. Registrant's Business and Operations

Item 1.01 Entry into a Material Definitive Agreement.

(a) If the registrant has entered into a material definitive agreement not made in the ordinary course of business of the registrant, or into any amendment of such agreement that is material to the registrant, disclose the following information:

(1) the date on which the agreement was entered into or amended, the identity of the parties to the agreement or amendment and a brief description of any material relationship between the registrant or its affiliates and any of the parties, other than in respect of the material definitive agreement or amendment; and

(2) a brief description of the terms and conditions of the agreement or amendment that are material to the registrant.

(b) For purposes of this Item 1.01, a *material definitive agreement* means an agreement that provides for obligations that are material to and enforceable against the registrant, or rights that are material to the registrant and enforceable by the registrant against one or more other parties to the agreement, in each case whether or not subject to conditions.

Instructions.

1. Any material definitive agreement of the registrant not made in the ordinary course of the registrant's business must be disclosed under this Item 1.01. An agreement is deemed to be not made in the ordinary course of a registrant's business even if the agreement is such as ordinarily accompanies the kind of business conducted by the registrant if it involves the subject matter identified in Item 601(b)(10)(ii)(A)–(D) of Regulation S–K (17 CFR 229.601(b)(10)(ii)(A)–(D)). An agreement involving the subject matter identified in Item 601(b)(10)(iii)(A) or (B) also must be disclosed unless Item 601(b)(10)(iii)(C) would not require the registrant to file a material agreement involving the same subject matter as an exhibit.

2. A registrant must provide disclosure under this Item 1.01 if the registrant succeeds as a party to the agreement or amendment to the

agreement by assumption or assignment (other than in connection with a merger or acquisition or similar transaction).

3. With respect to asset-backed securities, as defined in Item 1101 of Regulation AB (17 CFR 229.1101), disclosure is required under this Item 1.01 regarding the entry into or an amendment to a definitive agreement that is material to the asset-backed securities transaction, even if the registrant is not a party to such agreement (*e.g.*, a servicing agreement with a servicer contemplated by Item 1108(a)(3) of Regulation AB (17 CFR 229.1108(a)(3)).

Item 1.02 Termination of a Material Definitive Agreement.

(a) If a material definitive agreement which was not made in the ordinary course of business of the registrant and to which the registrant is a party is terminated otherwise than by expiration of the agreement on its stated termination date, or as a result of all parties completing their obligations under such agreement, and such termination of the agreement is material to the registrant, disclose the following information:

(1) the date of the termination of the material definitive agreement, the identity of the parties to the agreement and a brief description of any material relationship between the registrant or its affiliates and any of the parties other than in respect of the material definitive agreement;

(2) a brief description of the terms and conditions of the agreement that are material to the registrant;

(3) a brief description of the material circumstances surrounding the termination; and

(4) any material early termination penalties incurred by the registrant.

(b) For purposes of this Item 1.02, the term material definitive agreement shall have the same meaning as set forth in Item 1.01(b).

Instructions.

1. No disclosure is required solely by reason of this Item 1.02 during negotiations or discussions regarding termination of a material definitive agreement unless and until the agreement has been terminated.

2. No disclosure is required solely by reason of this Item 1.02 if the registrant believes in good faith that the material definitive agreement has not been terminated, unless the registrant has received a notice of termination pursuant to the terms of agreement.

3. With respect to asset-backed securities, as defined in Item 1101 of Regulation AB (17 CFR 229.1101), disclosure is required under this Item 1.02 regarding the termination of a definitive agreement that is material to the asset-backed securities transaction (otherwise than by expiration of the agreement on its stated termination date or as a result of all parties completing their obligations under such agreement), even if the registrant is not a party to such agreement (*e.g.*, a servicing agreement with a servicer contemplated by Item 1108(a)(3) of Regulation AB (17 CFR 229.1108(a)(3)).

Item 1.03 Bankruptcy or Receivership.

(a) If a receiver, fiscal agent or similar officer has been appointed for a registrant or its parent, in a proceeding under the U.S. Bankruptcy Code or in any other proceeding under state or federal law in which a court or governmental authority has assumed jurisdiction over substantially all of the assets or business of the registrant or its parent, or if such jurisdiction has been assumed by leaving the existing directors and officers in possession but subject to the supervision and orders of a court or governmental authority, disclose the following information:

(1) the name or other identification of the proceeding;

(2) the identity of the court or governmental authority;

(3) the date that jurisdiction was assumed; and

(4) the identity of the receiver, fiscal agent or similar officer and the date of his or her appointment.

(b) If an order confirming a plan of reorganization, arrangement or liquidation has been entered by a court or governmental authority having supervision or jurisdiction over substantially all of the assets or business of the registrant or its parent, disclose the following;

(1) the identity of the court or governmental authority;

(2) the date that the order confirming the plan was entered by the court or governmental authority;

(3) a summary of the material features of the plan and, pursuant to Item 9.01 (Financial Statements and Exhibits), a copy of the plan as confirmed;

(4) the number of shares or other units of the registrant or its parent issued and outstanding, the number reserved for future issuance in respect of claims and interests filed and allowed under the plan, and the aggregate total of such numbers; and

(5) information as to the assets and liabilities of the registrant or its parent as of the date that the order confirming the plan was entered, or a date as close thereto as practicable.

Instructions.

(1) The information called for in paragraph (b)(5) of this Item 1.03 may be presented in the form in which it was furnished to the court or governmental authority.

(2) With respect to asset-backed securities, disclosure also is required under this Item 1.03 if the depositor (or servicer if the servicer signs the report on Form 10–K (17 CFR 249.310) of the issuing entity) becomes aware of any instances described in paragraph (a)or (b) of this Item with respect to the sponsor, depositor, servicer contemplated by Item 1108(a)(3) of Regulation AB (17 CFR229.1108(a)(3)), trustee, significant obligor, enhancement or support provider contemplated by Items 1114(b) or 1115 of Regulation AB (17 CFR 229.1114(b) or 229.1115) or other material party contemplated by Item 1101(d)(1) of Regulation AB (17 CFR 1101(d)(1)).Terms used in this Instruction 2 have the same meaning as in Item 1101 of Regulation AB (17 CFR 229.1101).

Section 2. Financial Information

Item 2.01 Completion of Acquisition or Disposition of Assets.

If the registrant or any of its majority-owned subsidiaries has completed the acquisition or disposition of a significant amount of assets, otherwise than in the ordinary course of business, disclose the following information:

(a) the date of completion of the transaction;

(b) a brief description of the assets involved;

(c) the identity of the person(s) from whom the assets were acquired or to whom they were sold and the nature of any material relationship, other than in respect of the transaction, between such person(s) and the registrant or any of its affiliates, or any director or officer of the registrant, or any associate of any such director or officer;

(d) the nature and amount of consideration given or received for the assets and, if any material relationship is disclosed pursuant to paragraph (c) of this Item 2.01, the formula or principle followed in determining the amount of such consideration; and

(e) if the transaction being reported is an acquisition and if a material relationship exists between the registrant or any of its affiliates and the source(s) of the funds used in the acquisition, the identity of the source(s) of the funds unless all or any part of the consideration used is a loan made in the ordinary course of business by a bank as defined by Section 3(a)(6) of the Act, in which case the identity of such bank may be omitted provided the registrant:

(1) has made a request for confidentiality pursuant to Section 13(d)(1)(B) of the Act;

and

(2) states in the report that the identity of the bank has been so omitted and filed separately with the Commission.

Instructions.

1. No information need be given as to:

(i) any transaction between any person and any wholly-owned subsidiary of such person;

(ii) any transaction between two or more wholly-owned subsidiaries of any person; or

(iii) the redemption or other acquisition of securities from the public, or the sale or other disposition of securities to the public, by the issuer of such securities or by a wholly-owned subsidiary of that issuer.

2. The term acquisition includes every purchase, acquisition by lease, exchange, merger, consolidation, succession or other acquisition, except that the term does not include the construction or development of property by or for the registrant or its subsidiaries or the acquisition of materials for such purpose. The term disposition includes every sale, disposition by lease, exchange, merger, consolidation, mortgage, assignment or hypothecation of assets, whether for the benefit of creditors or otherwise, abandonment, destruction, or other disposition.

3. The information called for by this Item 2.01 is to be given as to each transaction or series of related transactions of the size indicated. The acquisition or disposition of securities is deemed the indirect acquisition or disposition of the assets represented by such securities if it results in the acquisition or disposition of control of such assets.

4. An acquisition or disposition shall be deemed to involve a significant amount of assets:

(i) if the registrant's and its other subsidiaries' equity in the net book value of such assets or the amount paid or received for the assets upon such acquisition or disposition exceeded 10% of the total assets of the registrant and its consolidated subsidiaries; or

(ii) if it involved a business (see 17 CFR 210.11–01(d)) that is significant (see 17 CFR 210.11–01(b)).

Acquisitions of individually insignificant businesses are not required to be reported pursuant to this Item 2.01 unless they are related businesses (see 17 CFR 210.3–05(a)(3)) and are significant in the aggregate.

5. Attention is directed to the requirements in Item 9.01 (Financial Statements and Exhibits) with respect to the filing of:

(i) financial statements of businesses acquired;

(ii) *pro forma* financial information; and

(iii) copies of the plans of acquisition or disposition as exhibits to the report.

Item 2.02 Results of Operations and Financial Condition.

(a) If a registrant, or any person acting on its behalf, makes any public announcement or release (including any update of an earlier announcement or release) disclosing material non-public information regarding the registrant's results of operations or financial condition for a completed quarterly or annual fiscal period, the registrant shall disclose the date of the announcement or release, briefly identify the announcement or release and include the text of that announcement or release as an exhibit.

(b) A Form 8–K is not required to be furnished to the Commission under this Item 2.02 in the case of disclosure of material non-public information that is disclosed orally, telephonically, by webcast, by broadcast, or by similar means if:

(1) the information is provided as part of a presentation that is complementary to, and initially occurs within 48 hours after, a related, written announcement or release that

has been furnished on Form 8–K pursuant to this Item 2.02 prior to the presentation;

(2) the presentation is broadly accessible to the public by dial-in conference call, by webcast, by broadcast or by similar means;

(3) the financial and other statistical information contained in the presentation is provided on the registrant's website, together with any information that would be required under 17 CFR 244.100; and

(4) the presentation was announced by a widely disseminated press release, that included instructions as to when and how to access the presentation and the location on the registrant's website where the information would be available.

Instructions.

1. The requirements of this Item 2.02 are triggered by the disclosure of material non-public information regarding a completed fiscal year or quarter. Release of additional or updated material non-public information regarding a completed fiscal year or quarter would trigger an additional Item 2.02 requirement.

2. The requirements of paragraph (e)(1)(i) of Item 10 of Regulation S–K (17 CFR 229.10(e)(1)(i)) (or paragraph (h)(1)(i) of Item 10 of Regulation S–B (17 CFR 228.10(h)(1)(i)) in the case of a small business issuer) shall apply to disclosures under this Item 2.02.

3. Issuers that make earnings announcements or other disclosures of material non-public information regarding a completed fiscal year or quarter in an interim or annual report to shareholders are permitted to specify which portion of the report contains the information required to be furnished under this Item 2.02.

4. This Item 2.02 does not apply in the case of a disclosure that is made in a quarterly report filed with the Commission on Form 10–Q (17 CFR 249.308a) (or Form 10–QSB (17 CFR 249.308b)) or an annual report filed with the Commission on Form 10–K (17 CFR 249.310) (or Form 10–KSB (17 CFR 249.310b)).

Item 2.03 Creation of a Direct Financial Obligation or an Obligation under an Off-Balance Sheet Arrangement of a Registrant.

(a) If the registrant becomes obligated on a direct financial obligation that is material to the registrant, disclose the following information:

(1) the date on which the registrant becomes obligated on the direct financial obligation and a brief description of the transaction or agreement creating the obligation;

(2) the amount of the obligation, including the terms of its payment and, if applicable, a brief description of the material terms under which it may be accelerated or increased and the nature of any recourse provisions that would enable the registrant to recover from third parties; and

(3) a brief description of the other terms and conditions of the transaction or agreement that are material to the registrant.

(b) If the registrant becomes directly or contingently liable for an obligation that is material to the registrant arising out of an off-balance sheet arrangement, disclose the following information:

(1) the date on which the registrant becomes directly or contingently liable on the obligation and a brief description of the transaction or agreement creating the arrangement and obligation;

(2) a brief description of the nature and amount of the obligation of the registrant under the arrangement, including the material terms whereby it may become a direct obligation, if applicable, or may be accelerated or increased and the nature of any recourse provisions that would enable the registrant to recover from third parties;

(3) the maximum potential amount of future payments (undiscounted) that the regis-

trant may be required to make, if different; and

(4) a brief description of the other terms and conditions of the obligation or arrangement that are material to the registrant.

(c) For purposes of this Item 2.03, direct financial obligation means any of the following:

(1) a long-term debt obligation, as defined in Item 303(a)(5)(ii)(A) of Regulation S–K (17 CFR 229.303(a)(5)(ii)(A));

(2) a capital lease obligation, as defined in Item 303(a)(5)(ii)(B) of Regulation S–K (17 CFR 229.303(a)(5)(ii)(B));

(3) an operating lease obligation, as defined in Item 303(a)(5)(ii)(C) of Regulation S–K (17 CFR 229.303(a)(5)(ii)(C)); or

(4) a short-term debt obligation that arises other than in the ordinary course of business.

(d) For purposes of this Item 2.03, off-balance sheet arrangement has the meaning set forth in Item 303(a)(4)(ii) of Regulation S–K (17 CFR 229.303(a)(4)(ii)) or Item 303(c)(2) of Regulation S–B (17 CFR 228.303(c)(2)), as applicable.

(e) For purposes of this Item 2.03, short-term debt obligation means a payment obligation under a borrowing arrangement that is scheduled to mature within one year, or, for those registrants that use the operating cycle concept of working capital, within a registrant's operating cycle that is longer than one year, as discussed in Accounting Research Bulletin No. 43, Chapter 3A, Working Capital.

Instructions.

1. A registrant has no obligation to disclose information under this Item 2.03 until the registrant enters into an agreement enforceable against the registrant, whether or not subject to conditions, under which the direct financial obligation will arise or be created or issued. If there is no such agreement, the registrant must provide the disclosure within four business days after the occurrence of the closing or settlement of the transaction or arrangement under which the direct financial obligation arises or is created.

2. A registrant must provide the disclosure required by paragraph (b) of this Item 2.03 whether or not the registrant is also a party to the transaction or agreement creating the contingent obligation arising under the off-balance sheet arrangement. In the event that neither the registrant nor any affiliate of the registrant is also a party to the transaction or agreement creating the contingent obligation arising under the off-balance sheet arrangement in question, the four business day period for reporting the event under this Item 2.03 shall begin on the earlier of (i) the fourth business day after the contingent obligation is created or arises, and (ii) the day on which an executive officer, as defined in 17 CFR 240.3b–7, of the registrant becomes aware of the contingent obligation.

3. In the event that an agreement, transaction or arrangement requiring disclosure under this Item 2.03 comprises a facility, program or similar arrangement that creates or may give rise to direct financial obligations of the registrant in connection with multiple transactions, the registrant shall:

(i) disclose the entering into of the facility, program or similar arrangement if the entering into of the facility is material to the registrant; and

(ii) as direct financial obligations arise or are created under the facility or program, disclose the required information under this Item 2.03 to the extent that the obligations are material to the registrant (including when a series of previously undisclosed individually immaterial obligations become material in the aggregate).

4. For purposes of Item 2.03(b)(3), the maximum amount of future payments shall not be reduced by the effect of any amounts that may possibly be recovered by the registrant under recourse or collateralization provisions in any guarantee agreement, transaction or arrangement.

5. If the obligation required to be disclosed under this Item 2.03 is a security, or a term of a security, that has been or will be sold pursuant to an effective registration statement of the registrant, the registrant is not required to file a Form 8–K pursuant to this Item 2.03, provided that the prospectus relating to that sale contains the information required by this Item 2.03 and is filed within the required time period under Securities Act Rule 424 (§ 230.424 of this chapter).

Item 2.04 Triggering Events That Accelerate or Increase a Direct Financial Obligation or an Obligation under an Off-Balance Sheet Arrangement.

(a) If a triggering event causing the increase or acceleration of a direct financial obligation of the registrant occurs and the consequences of the event, taking into account those described in paragraph (a)(4) of this Item 2.04, are material to the registrant, disclose the following information:

(1) the date of the triggering event and a brief description of the agreement or transaction under which the direct financial obligation was created and is increased or accelerated;

(2) a brief description of the triggering event;

(3) the amount of the direct financial obligation, as increased if applicable, and the terms of payment or acceleration that apply; and

(4) any other material obligations of the registrant that may arise, increase, be accelerated or become direct financial obligations as a result of the triggering event or the increase or acceleration of the direct financial obligation.

(b) If a triggering event occurs causing an obligation of the registrant under an off-balance sheet arrangement to increase or be accelerated, or causing a contingent obligation of the registrant under an off-balance sheet arrangement to become a direct financial obligation of the registrant, and the consequences of the event, taking into account those described in paragraph (b)(4) of this Item 2.04, are material to the registrant, disclose the following information:

(1) the date of the triggering event and a brief description of the off-balance sheet arrangement;

(2) a brief description of the triggering event;

(3) the nature and amount of the obligation, as increased if applicable, and the terms of payment or acceleration that apply; and

(4) any other material obligations of the registrant that may arise, increase, be accelerated or become direct financial obligations as a result of the triggering event or the increase or acceleration of the obligation under the off-balance sheet arrangement or its becoming a direct financial obligation of the registrant.

(c) For purposes of this Item 2.04, the term *direct financial obligation* has the meaning provided in Item 2.03 of this form, but shall also include an obligation arising out of an off-balance sheet arrangement that is accrued under FASB Statement of Financial Accounting Standards No. 5 *Accounting for Contingencies* (SFAS No. 5) as a probable loss contingency.

(d) For purposes of this Item 2.04, the term *off-balance sheet arrangement* has the meaning provided in Item 2.03 of this form.

(e) For purposes of this Item 2.04, a *triggering event* is an event, including an event of default, event of acceleration or similar event, as a result of which a direct financial obligation of the registrant or an obligation of the registrant arising under an off-balance sheet arrangement is increased or becomes accelerated or as a result of which a contingent obligation of the registrant arising out of an off-balance sheet arrangement becomes a direct financial obligation of the registrant.

Instructions.

1. Disclosure is required if a *triggering event* occurs in respect of an obligation of the registrant under an off-balance sheet arrangement and the consequences are material to the registrant, whether or not the registrant is also a party to the transaction or agreement under which the triggering event occurs.

2. No disclosure is required under this Item 2.04 unless and until a triggering event has occurred in accordance with the terms of the relevant agreement, transaction or arrangement, including, if required, the sending to the registrant of notice of the occurrence of a triggering event pursuant to the terms of the agreement, transaction or arrangement and the satisfaction of all conditions to such occurrence, except the passage of time.

3. No disclosure is required solely by reason of this Item 2.04 if the registrant believes in good faith that no triggering event has occurred, unless the registrant has received a notice described in Instruction 2 to this Item 2.04.

4. Where a registrant is subject to an obligation arising out of an off-balance sheet arrangement, whether or not disclosed pursuant to Item 2.03 of this form, if a triggering event occurs as a result of which under that obligation an accrual for a probable loss is required under SFAS No. 5, the obligation arising out of the off-balance sheet arrangement becomes a direct financial obligation as defined in this Item 2.04. In that situation, if the consequences as determined under Item 2.04(b) are material to the registrant, disclosure is required under this Item 2.04.

5. With respect to asset-backed securities, as defined in 17 CFR 229.1101, disclosure also is required under this Item 2.04 if an early amortization, performance trigger or other event, including an event of default, has occurred under the transaction agreements for the asset-backed securities that would materially alter the payment priority or distribution of cash flows regarding the asset-backed securities or the amortization schedule for the asset-backed securities. In providing the disclosure required by this Item, identify the changes to the payment priorities, flow of funds or asset-backed securities as a result. Disclosure is required under this Item whether or not the registrant is a party to the transaction agreement that results in the occurrence identified.

Item 2.05 Costs Associated with Exit or Disposal Activities.

If the registrant's board of directors, a committee of the board of directors or the officer or officers of the registrant authorized to take such action if board action is not required, commits the registrant to an exit or disposal plan, or otherwise disposes of a long-lived asset or terminates employees under a plan of termination described in paragraph 8 of FASB Statement of Financial Accounting Standards No. 146 *Accounting for Costs Associated with Exit or Disposal Activities* (SFAS No. 146), under which material charges will be incurred under generally accepted accounting principles applicable to the registrant, disclose the following information:

(a) the date of the commitment to the course of action and a description of the course of action, including the facts and circumstances leading to the expected action and the expected completion date;

(b) for each major type of cost associated with the course of action (for example, one-time termination benefits, contract termination costs and other associated costs), an estimate of the total amount or range of amounts expected to be incurred in connection with the action;

(c) an estimate of the total amount or range of amounts expected to be incurred in connection with the action; and

(d) the registrant's estimate of the amount or range of amounts of the charge that will result in future cash expenditures, *provided, however*, that if the registrant determines that at the time of filing it is unable in good faith to make a determination of an estimate required by paragraphs (b), (c) or (d) of this Item 2.05, no disclosure of such estimate shall be required; *provided further, however*, that in any such event, the registrant shall file an amended report on Form 8–K under this Item 2.05 within four business days after it makes a determination of such an estimate or range of estimates.

Item 2.06 Material Impairments.

If the registrant's board of directors, a committee of the board of directors or the officer or officers of the registrant authorized to take such action if board action is not required, concludes that a material charge for impairment to one or more of its assets, including, without limitation, impairments of securities or goodwill, is required under generally accepted accounting principles applicable to the registrant, disclose the following information:

(a) the date of the conclusion that a material charge is required and a description of the impaired asset or assets and the facts and circumstances leading to the conclusion that the charge for impairment is required;

(b) the registrant's estimate of the amount or range of amounts of the impairment charge; and

(c) the registrant's estimate of the amount or range of amounts of the impairment charge that will result in future cash expenditures, *provided, however*, that if the registrant determines that at the time of filing it is unable in good faith to make a determination of an estimate required by paragraphs (b) or (c) of this Item 2.06, no disclosure of such estimate shall be required; *provided further, however*, that in any such event, the registrant shall file an amended report on Form 8–K under this Item 2.06 within four business days after it makes a determination of such an estimate or range of estimates.

Instruction.

No filing is required under this Item 2.06 if the conclusion is made in connection with the preparation, review or audit of financial statements required to be included in the next periodic report due to be filed under the Exchange Act, the periodic report is filed on a timely basis and such conclusion is disclosed in the report.

Section 3. Securities and Trading Markets

Item 3.01 Notice of Delisting or Failure to Satisfy a Continued Listing Rule or Standard; Transfer of Listing.

(a) If the registrant has received notice from the national securities exchange or national securities association (or a facility thereof) that maintains the principal listing for any class of the registrant's common equity (as defined in Exchange Act Rule 12b–2 (17 CFR 240.12b–2)) that:

- the registrant or such class of the registrant's securities does not satisfy a rule or standard for continued listing on the exchange or association;

- the exchange has submitted an application under Exchange Act Rule 12d2–2 (17 CFR 240.12d2–2) to the Commission to delist such class of the registrant's securities; or

- the association has taken all necessary steps under its rules to delist the security from its automated inter-dealer quotation system,

the registrant must disclose:

(i) the date that the registrant received the notice;

(ii) the a rule or standard for continued listing on the national securities exchange or national securities association that the registrant fails, or has failed to, satisfy; and

(iii) any action or response that, at the time of filing, the registrant has determined to take in response to the notice.

(b) If the registrant has notified the national securities exchange or national securities association (or a facility thereof) that maintains the principal listing for any class of the registrant's common equity (as defined in Exchange Act Rule 12b–2 (17 CFR 240.12b–2)) that the registrant is aware of any material noncompliance with a rule or standard for continued listing on the exchange or association, the registrant must disclose:

(i) the date that the registrant provided such notice to the exchange or association;

(ii) the rule or standard for continued listing on the exchange or association that the registrant fails, or has failed, to satisfy; and

(iii) any action or response that, at the time of filing, the registrant has determined to take regarding its noncompliance.

(c) If the national securities exchange or national securities association (or a facility thereof) that maintains the principal listing for any class of the registrant's common equity (as defined in Exchange Act Rule 12b–2 (17 CFR 240.12b–2)), in lieu of suspending trading in or delisting such class of the registrant's securities, issues a public reprimand letter or similar communication indicating that the registrant has violated a rule or standard for continued listing on the exchange or association, the registrant must state the date, and summarize the contents of the letter or communication.

(d) If the registrant's board of directors, a committee of the board of directors or the officer or officers of the registrant authorized to take such action if board action is not required, has taken definitive action to cause the listing of a class of its common equity to be withdrawn from the national securities exchange, or terminated from the automated inter-dealer quotation system of a registered national securities association, where such exchange or association maintains the principal listing for such class of securities, including by reason of a transfer of the listing or quotation to another securities exchange or quotation system, describe the action taken and state the date of the action.

Instructions.

1. The registrant is not required to disclose any information required by paragraph (a) of this Item 3.01 where the delisting is a result of one of the following:

- the entire class of the security has been called for redemption, maturity or retirement; appropriate notice thereof has been given; if required by the terms of the securities, funds sufficient for the payment of all such securities have been deposited with an agency authorized to make such payments; and such funds have been made available to security holders;
- the entire class of the security has been redeemed or paid at maturity or retirement;
- the instruments representing the entire class of securities have come to evidence, by operation of law or otherwise, other securities in substitution therefor and represent no other right, except, if true, the right to receive an immediate cash payment (the right of dissenters to receive the appraised or fair value of their holdings shall not prevent the application of this provision); or
- all rights pertaining to the entire class of the security have been extinguished; *provided, however*, that where such an event occurs as the result of an order of a court or other governmental authority, the order shall be final, all applicable appeal periods shall have expired and no appeals shall be pending.

2. A registrant must provide the disclosure required by paragraph (a) or (b) of this Item 3.01, as applicable, regarding any failure to satisfy a rule or standard for continued listing on the national securities exchange or national securities association (or a facility thereof) that maintains the principal listing for any class of the registrant's common equity (as defined in Exchange Act Rule 12b–2 (17 CFR 240.12b–2)) even if the registrant has the benefit of a grace period or similar extension period during which it may cure the deficiency that triggers the disclosure requirement.

3. Notices or other communications subsequent to an initial notice sent to, or by, a registrant under Item 3.01(a), (b) or (c) that continue to indicate that the registrant does

not comply with the same rule or standard for continued listing that was the subject of the initial notice are not required to be filed, but may be filed voluntarily.

4. Registrants whose securities are quoted exclusively (i.e., the securities are not otherwise listed on an exchange or association) on automated inter-dealer quotation systems are not subject to this Item 3.01 and such registrants are thus not required to file a Form 8–K pursuant to this Item 3.01 if the securities are no longer quoted on such quotation system. If a security is listed on an exchange or association and is also quoted on an automated inter-dealer quotation system, the registrant is subject to the disclosure obligations of Item 3.01 if any of the events specified in Item 3.01 occur.

Item 3.02 Unregistered Sales of Equity Securities.

(a) If the registrant sells equity securities in a transaction that is not registered under the Securities Act, furnish the information set forth in paragraphs (a) and (c) through (e) of Item 701 of Regulation S–K or Regulation S–B, as applicable (17 CFR 229.701(a) and (c) through (e) and 228.701(a) and (c) through (e), respectively). For purposes of determining the required filing date for the Form 8–K under this Item 3.02(a), the registrant has no obligation to disclose information under this Item 3.02 until the registrant enters into an agreement enforceable against the registrant, whether or not subject to conditions, under which the equity securities are to be sold. If there is no such agreement, the registrant must provide the disclosure within four business days after the occurrence of the closing or settlement of the transaction or arrangement under which the equity securities are to be sold.

(b) No report need be filed under this Item 3.02 if the equity securities sold, in the aggregate since its last report filed under this Item 3.02 or its last periodic report, whichever is more recent, constitute less than 1% of the number of shares outstanding of the class of equity securities sold. In the case of a small business issuer, no report need be filed if the equity securities sold, in the aggregate since its last report filed under this Item 3.02 or its last periodic report, whichever is more recent, constitute less than 5% of the number of shares outstanding of the class of equity securities sold.

Instructions.

1. For purposes of this Item 3.02, "the number of shares outstanding" refers to the actual number of shares of equity securities of the class outstanding and does not include outstanding securities convertible into or exchangeable for such equity securities.

2. Small business issuer is defined under Item 10(a)(1) of Regulation S–B (17 CFR 228.10(a)(1)).

Item 3.03 Material Modification to Rights of Security Holders.

(a) If the constituent instruments defining the rights of the holders of any class of registered securities of the registrant have been materially modified, disclose the date of the modification, the title of the class of securities involved and briefly describe the general effect of such modification upon the rights of holders of such securities.

(b) If the rights evidenced by any class of registered securities have been materially limited or qualified by the issuance or modification of any other class of securities by the registrant, briefly disclose the date of the issuance or modification, the general effect of the issuance or modification of such other class of securities upon the rights of the holders of the registered securities.

Instruction.

Working capital restrictions and other limitations upon the payment of dividends must be reported pursuant to this Item 3.03.

Section 4. Matters Related to Accountants and Financial Statements

Item 4.01 Changes in Registrant's Certifying Accountant.

(a) If an independent accountant who was previously engaged as the principal accountant to audit the registrant's financial statements, or an independent accountant upon whom the principal accountant expressed reliance in its report regarding a significant subsidiary, resigns (or indicates that it declines to stand for re-appointment after completion of the current audit) or is dismissed, disclose the information required by Item 304(a)(1) of Regulation S–K or Item 304(a)(1) of Regulation S–B, as applicable, including compliance with Item 304(a)(3) of Regulation S–K or Item 304(a)(3) of Regulation S–B (17 CFR 229.304(a)(1) and (a)(3) or 228.304(a)(1) and (a)(3), respectively).

(b) If a new independent accountant has been engaged as either the principal accountant to audit the registrant's financial statements or as an independent accountant on whom the principal accountant is expected to express reliance in its report regarding a significant subsidiary, the registrant must disclose the information required by Item 304(a)(2) of Regulation S–K or Item 304(a)(2) of Regulation S-B, as applicable (17 CFR 229.304(a)(2) or 228.304(a)(2), respectively).

Instruction.

The resignation or dismissal of an independent accountant, or its refusal to stand for re-appointment, is a reportable event separate from the engagement of a new independent accountant. On some occasions, two reports on Form 8–K are required for a single change in accountants, the first on the resignation (or refusal to stand for re-appointment) or dismissal of the former accountant and the second when the new accountant is engaged. Information required in the second Form 8–K in such situations need not be provided to the extent that it has been reported previously in the first Form 8–K.

Item 4.02 Non-Reliance on Previously Issued Financial Statements or a Related Audit Report or Completed Interim Review.

(a) If the registrant's board of directors, a committee of the board of directors or the officer or officers of the registrant authorized to take such action if board action is not required, concludes that any previously issued financial statements, covering one or more years or interim periods for which the registrant is required to provide financial statements under Regulation S–X (17 CFR 210) or Regulation S–B (17 CFR 228), should no longer be relied upon because of an error in such financial statements as addressed in Accounting Principles Board Opinion No. 20, as may be modified, supplemented or succeeded, disclose the following information:

(1) the date of the conclusion regarding the non-reliance and an identification of the financial statements and years or periods covered that should no longer be relied upon;

(2) a brief description of the facts underlying the conclusion to the extent known to the registrant at the time of filing; and

(3) a statement of whether the audit committee, or the board of directors in the absence of an audit committee, or authorized officer or officers, discussed with the registrant's independent accountant the matters disclosed in the filing pursuant to this Item 4.02(a).

(b) If the registrant is advised by, or receives notice from, its independent accountant that disclosure should be made or action should be taken to prevent future reliance on a previously issued audit report or completed interim review related to previously issued financial statements, disclose the following information:

(1) the date on which the registrant was so advised or notified;

(2) identification of the financial statements that should no longer be relied upon;

(3) a brief description of the information provided by the accountant; and

(4) a statement of whether the audit committee, or the board of directors in the absence of an audit committee, or authorized officer or officers, discussed with the independent accountant the matters disclosed in the filing pursuant to this Item 4.02(b).

(c) If the registrant receives advisement or notice from its independent accountant requiring disclosure under paragraph (b) of this Item 4.02, the registrant must:

(1) provide the independent accountant with a copy of the disclosures it is making in response to this Item 4.02 that the independent accountant shall receive no later than the day that the disclosures are filed with the Commission;

(2) request the independent accountant to furnish to the registrant as promptly as possible a letter addressed to the Commission stating whether the independent accountant agrees with the statements made by the registrant in response to this Item 4.02 and, if not, stating the respects in which it does not agree; and

(3) amend the registrant's previously filed Form 8–K by filing the independent accountant's letter as an exhibit to the filed Form 8–K no later than two business days after the registrant's receipt of the letter.

Section 5. Corporate Governance and Management

Item 5.01 Changes in Control of Registrant.

(a) If, to the knowledge of the registrant's board of directors, a committee of the board of directors or authorized officer or officers of the registrant, a change in control of the registrant has occurred, furnish the following information:

(1) the identity of the person(s) who acquired such control;

(2) the date and a description of the transaction(s) which resulted in the change in control;

(3) the basis of the control, including the percentage of voting securities of the registrant now beneficially owned directly or indirectly by the person(s) who acquired control;

(4) the amount of the consideration used by such person(s);

(5) the source(s) of funds used by the person(s), unless all or any part of the consideration used is a loan made in the ordinary course of business by a bank as defined by Section 3(a)(6) of the Act, in which case the identity of such bank may be omitted provided the person who acquired control:

(i) has made a request for confidentiality pursuant to Section 13(d)(1)(B) of the Act; and

(ii) states in the report that the identity of the bank has been so omitted and filed separately with the Commission.

(6) the identity of the person(s) from whom control was assumed; and

(7) any arrangements or understandings among members of both the former and new control groups and their associates with respect to election of directors or other matters.

(b) Furnish the information required by Item 403(c) of Regulation S–K (17 CFR 229.403(c)) or Item 403(c) of Regulation S–B (17 CFR 228.403(c)), as applicable.

Item 5.02 Departure of Directors or Principal Officers; Election of Directors; Appointment of Principal Officers.

(a)(1) If a director has resigned or refuses to stand for re-election to the board of directors since the date of the last annual meeting of shareholders because of a disagreement with the registrant, known to an executive officer of the registrant, as defined in 17 CFR 240.3b–7, on any matter relating to the registrant's operations, policies or practices, or if a director has been removed for cause from the board of directors, disclose the following information:

(i) the date of such resignation, refusal to stand for re-election or removal;

(ii) any positions held by the director on any committee of the board of directors at the time of the director's resignation, refusal to stand for re-election or removal; and

(iii) a brief description of the circumstances representing the disagreement that the registrant believes caused, in whole or in part, the director's resignation, refusal to stand for re-election or removal.

(2) If the director has furnished the registrant with any written correspondence concerning the circumstances surrounding his or her resignation, refusal or removal, the registrant shall file a copy of the document as an exhibit to the report on Form 8–K.

(3) The registrant also must:

(i) provide the director with a copy of the disclosures it is making in response to this Item 5.02 no later than the day the registrant file the disclosures with the Commission;

(ii) provide the director with the opportunity to furnish the registrant as promptly as possible with a letter addressed to the registrant stating whether he or she agrees with the statements made by the registrant in response to this Item 5.02 and, if not, stating the respects in which he or she does not agree; and

(iii) file any letter received by the registrant from the director with the Commission as an exhibit by an amendment to the previously filed Form 8–K within two business days after receipt by the registrant.

(b) If the registrant's principal executive officer, president, principal financial officer, principal accounting officer, principal operating officer or any person performing similar functions retires, resigns or is terminated from that position, or if a director retires, resigns, is removed, or refuses to stand for re-election (except in circumstances described in paragraph (a) of this Item 5.02), disclose the fact that the event has occurred and the date of the event.

(c) If the registrant appoints a new principal executive officer, president, principal financial officer, principal accounting officer, principal operating officer or person performing similar functions, disclose the following information with respect to the newly appointed officer:

(1) the name and position of the newly appointed officer and the date of the appointment;

(2) the information required by Items 401(b), (d), (e) and Item 404(a) of Regulation S–K (17 CFR 229.401(b), (d), (e) and 229.404(a)), or, in the case of a small business issuer, Items 401(a)(4), (a)(5), (c), and Items 404(a) and (b) of Regulation S–B (17 CFR 228.401(a)(4), (a)(5), (c), and 228.404(a) and (b), respectively); and

(3) a brief description of the material terms of any employment agreement between the registrant and that officer.

Instruction to paragraph (c).

If the registrant intends to make a public announcement of the appointment other than by means of a report on Form 8–K, the registrant may delay filing the Form 8–K containing the disclosures required by this Item 5.02(c) until the day on which the registrant otherwise makes public announcement of the appointment of such officer.

(d) If the registrant elects a new director, except by a vote of security holders at an annual meeting or special meeting convened for such purpose, disclose the following information:

(1) the name of the newly elected director and the date of election;

(2) a brief description of any arrangement or understanding between the new director and any other persons, naming such persons, pursuant to which such director was selected as a director;

(3) the committees of the board of directors to which the new director has been, or at the time of this disclosure is expected to be, named; and

(4) the information required by Item 404(a) of Regulation S–K or Item 404(a) of Regulation S–B, as applicable (17 CFR 229.404(a) or 228.404(a), respectively).

Instructions to Item 5.02.

1. The disclosure requirements of this Item 5.02 do not apply to a registrant that is a wholly-owned subsidiary of an issuer with a class of securities registered under Section 12 of the Exchange Act (15 U.S.C. 78l), or that is required to file reports under Section 15(d) of the Exchange Act (15 U.S.C. 78o(d)).

2. To the extent that any information called for in Item 5.02(c)(3) or Item 5.02(d)(3) or Item 5.02(d)(4) is not determined or is unavailable at the time of the required filing, the registrant shall include a statement this effect in the filing and then must file an amendment to its Form 8–K filing under this Item 5.02 containing such information within four business days after the information is determined or becomes available.

Item 5.03 Amendments to Articles of Incorporation or Bylaws; Change in Fiscal Year.

(a) If a registrant with a class of equity securities registered under Section 12 of the Exchange Act (15 U.S.C. 78l) amends its articles of incorporation or bylaws and a proposal for the amendment was not disclosed in a proxy statement or information statement filed by the registrant, disclose the following information:

(1) the effective date of the amendment; and

(2) a description of the provision adopted or changed by amendment and, if applicable, the previous provision.

(b) If the registrant determines to change the fiscal year from that used in its most recent filing with the Commission other than by means of:

(1) a submission to a vote of security holders through the solicitation of proxies or otherwise; or

(2) an amendment to its articles of incorporation or bylaws, disclose the date of such determination, the date of the new fiscal year end and the form (for example, Form 10–K, Form 10–KSB, Form 10–Q or Form 10–QSB) on which the report covering the transition period will be filed.

Instructions to Item 5.03.

(1) Refer to Item 601(b)(3) of Regulation S-K or Regulation S–B (17 CFR 229.601(b)(3) and 228.601(b)(3)), as applicable, regarding the filing of exhibits to this Item 5.03.

(2) With respect to asset-backed securities, as defined in 17 CFR 229.1101, disclosure is required under this Item 5.03 regarding any amendment to the governing documents of the issuing entity, regardless of whether the class of asset-backed securities is reporting under Section 13 or 15(d) of the Exchange Act.

Item 5.04 Temporary Suspension of Trading Under Registrant's Employee Benefit Plans.

(a) No later than the fourth business day after which the registrant receives the notice required by section 101(i)(2)(E) of the Employment Retirement Income Security Act of 1974 (29 U.S.C. 1021(i)(2)(E)), or, if such notice is not received by the registrant, on the same date by which the registrant transmits a timely notice to an affected officer or director within the time period prescribed by Rule 104(b)(2)(i)(B) or 104(b)(2)(ii) of Regulation BTR (17 CFR 245.104(b)(2)(i)(B) or 17 CFR 245.104(b)(2)(ii)), provide the information specified in Rule 104(b) (17 CFR 245.104(b)) and the date the registrant received the notice required by section 101(i)(2)(E) of the Employment Retirement Income Security Act of 1974 (29 U.S.C. 1021(i)(2)(E)), if applicable.

(b) On the same date by which the registrant transmits a timely updated notice to an affected officer or director, as required by the time period under Rule 104(b)(2)(iii) of Regulation BTR (17 CFR 245.104(b)(2)(iii)), provide the information specified in Rule 104(b)(3)(iii) (17 CFR 245.104(b)(2)(iii)).

Item 5.05 Amendments to the Registrant's Code of Ethics, or Waiver of a Provision of the Code of Ethics.

(a) Briefly describe the date and nature of any amendment to a provision of the registrant's code of ethics that applies to the registrant's principal executive officer, principal financial officer, principal accounting officer or controller or persons performing similar functions and that relates to any element of the code of ethics definition enumerated in Item 406(b) of Regulations S–K and S–B (17 CFR 229.406(b) and 228.406(b), respectively).

(b) If the registrant has granted a waiver, including an implicit waiver, from a provision of the code of ethics to an officer or person described in paragraph (a) of this Item 5.05, and the waiver relates to one or more of the elements of the code of ethics definition referred to in paragraph (a) of this Item 5.05, briefly describe the nature of the waiver, the name of the person to whom the waiver was granted, and the date of the waiver.

(c) The registrant does not need to provide any information pursuant to this Item 5.05 if it discloses the required information on its Internet website within four business days following the date of the amendment or waiver and the registrant has disclosed in its most recently filed annual report its Internet address and intention to provide disclosure in this manner. If the registrant elects to disclose the information required by this Item 5.05 through its website, such information must remain available on the website for at least a 12-month period. Following the 12-month period, the registrant must retain the information for a period of not less than five years. Upon request, the registrant must furnish to the Commission or its staff a copy of any or all information retained pursuant to this requirement.

Instructions.

1. The registrant does not need to disclose technical, administrative or other non-substantive amendments to its code of ethics.

2. For purposes of this Item 5.05:

(i) The term *waiver* means the approval by the registrant of a material departure from a provision of the code of ethics; and

(ii) The term *implicit waiver* means the registrant's failure to take action within a reasonable period of time regarding a material departure from a provision of the code of ethics that has been made known to an executive officer, as defined in Rule 3b–7 (17 CFR 240.3b–7) of the registrant.

Section 6-Asset–Backed Securities

The Items in this Section 6 apply only to asset-backed securities. Terms used in this Section 6 have the same meaning as in Item 1101 of Regulation AB (17 CFR 229.1101).

Item 6.01 ABS Informational and Computational Material.

Report under this Item any ABS informational and computational material filed in, or as an exhibit to, this report.

Item 6.02 Change of Servicer or Trustee.

If a servicer contemplated by Item 1108(a)(2) of Regulation AB (17 CFR 229.1108(a)(2)) or a trustee has resigned or has been removed, replaced or substituted, or if a new servicer contemplated by Item 1108(a)(2) of Regulation AB or trustee has been appointed, state the date the event occurred and the circumstances surrounding the change. In addition, provide the disclosure required by Item 1108(d) of Regulation AB (17 CFR 229.1108(c)), as applicable, regarding the servicer or trustee change. If a new servicer contemplated by Item 1108(a)(3) of this Regulation AB or a new trustee has been appointed, provide the information required by Item 1108(b) through (d) of Regulation AB regarding such servicer or Item 1109 of Regulation AB (17 CFR 229.1109) regarding such trustee, as applicable.

Instruction.

To the extent that any information called for by this Item regarding such servicer or trustee is not determined or is unavailable at the time of the required filing, the registrant shall include a statement to this effect in the filing and then must file an amendment to its

Form 8–K filing under this Item 6.02 containing such information within four business days after the information is determined or becomes available.

Item 6.03 Change in Credit Enhancement or Other External Support.

(a) *Loss of existing enhancement or support.* If the depositor (or servicer if the servicer signs the report on Form 10–K (17 CFR 249.310) of the issuing entity) becomes aware that any material enhancement or support specified in Item 1114(a)(1) through (3) of Regulation AB (17 CFR 229.1114(a)(1) through (3)) or Item 1115 of Regulation AB (17 CFR 229.1115) that was previously applicable regarding one or more classes of the asset-backed securities has terminated other than by expiration of the contract on its stated termination date or as a result of all parties completing their obligations under such agreement, then disclose:

(1) the date of the termination of the enhancement;

(2) the identity of the parties to the agreement relating to the enhancement or support;

(3) a brief description of the terms and conditions of the enhancement or support that are material to security holders;

(4) a brief description of the material circumstances surrounding the termination; and

(5) any material early termination penalties paid or to be paid out of the cash flows backing the asset-backed securities.

(b) *Addition of new enhancement or support.* If the depositor (or servicer if the servicer signs the report on Form 10–K (17 CFR 249.310) of the issuing entity) becomes aware that any material enhancement specified in Item 1114(a)(1) through (3) of Regulation AB (17 CFR 229.1114(a)(1) through (3)) or Item 1115 of Regulation AB (17 CFR 229.1115) has been added with respect to one or more classes of the asset-backed securities, then provide the date of addition of the new enhancement or support and the disclosure required by Items 1114 or 1115 of Regulation AB, as applicable, with respect to such new enhancement or support.

(c) *Material change to enhancement or support.* If the depositor (or servicer if the servicer signs the report on Form 10–K (17 CFR 249.310) of the issuing entity) becomes aware that any existing material enhancement or support specified in Item 1114(a)(1) through (3) of Regulation AB or Item 1115 of Regulation AB with respect to one or more classes of the asset-backed securities has been materially amended or modified, disclose:

(1) the date on which the agreement or agreements relating to the enhancement or support was amended or modified;

(2) the identity of the parties to the agreement or agreements relating to the amendment or modification; and

(3) a brief description of the material terms and conditions of the amendment or modification.

Instructions.

1. Disclosure is required under this Item whether or not the registrant is a party to any agreement regarding the enhancement or support if the loss, addition or modification of such enhancement or support materially affects, directly or indirectly, the asset-backed securities, the pool assets or the cash flow underlying the asset-backed securities.

2. To the extent that any information called for by this Item regarding the enhancement or support is not determined or is unavailable at the time of the required filing, the registrant shall include a statement to this effect in the filing and then must file an amendment to its Form 8–K filing under this Item 6.03 containing such information within four business days after the information is determined or becomes available.

3. The instructions to Items 1.01 and 1.02 of this Form apply to this Item.

4. Notwithstanding Items 1.01 and 1.02 of this Form, disclosure regarding changes to material enhancement or support is to be reported under this Item 6.03 in lieu of those Items.

Item 6.04 Failure to Make a Required Distribution.

If a required distribution to holders of the asset-backed securities is not made as of the required distribution date under the transaction documents, and such failure is material, identify the failure and state the nature of the failure to make the timely distribution.

Item 6.05 Securities Act Updating Disclosure.

Regarding an offering of asset-backed securities registered on Form S–3 (17 CFR 239.13), if any material pool characteristic of the actual asset pool at the time of issuance of the asset-backed securities differs by 5% or more (other than as a result of the pool assets converting into cash in accordance with their terms) from the description of the asset pool in the prospectus filed for the offering pursuant to Securities Act Rule 424 (17 CFR 230.424), disclose the information required by Items 1111 and 1112 of Regulation AB (17 CFR 229.1111 and 17 CFR 229.1112) regarding the characteristics of the actual asset pool. If applicable, also provide information required by Items 1108 and 1110 of Regulation AB (17 CFR 229.1108 and 17 CFR 229.1110) regarding any new servicers or originators that would be required to be disclosed under those items regarding the pool assets.

Instruction.

No report is required under this Item if substantially the same information is provided in a post-effective amendment to the Securities Act registration statement or in a subsequent prospectus filed pursuant to Securities Act Rule 424 (17 CFR 230.424).

Section 7. Regulation FD

Item 7.01 Regulation FD Disclosure.

Unless filed under Item 8.01, disclose under this item only information that the registrant elects to disclose through Form 8–K pursuant to Regulation FD (17 CFR 243.100 through 243.103).

Section 8. Other Events

Item 8.01 Other Events.

The registrant may, at its option, disclose under this Item 8.01 any events, with respect to which information is not otherwise called for by this form, that the registrant deems of importance to security holders. The registrant may, at its option, file a report under this Item 8.01 disclosing the nonpublic information required to be disclosed by Regulation FD (17 CFR 243.100 through 243.103).

Section 9. Financial Statements and Exhibits

Item 9.01 Financial Statements and Exhibits.

List below the financial statements, pro forma financial information and exhibits, if any, filed as a part of this report.

(a) *Financial statements of businesses acquired.*

(1) For any business acquisition required to be described in answer to Item 2.01 of this form, financial statements of the business acquired shall be filed for the periods specified in Rule 3–05(b) of Regulation S–X (17 CFR 210.3–05(b)).

(2) The financial statements shall be prepared pursuant to Regulation S–X except that supporting schedules need not be filed. A manually signed accountant's report should be provided pursuant to Rule 2–02 of Regulation S–X (17 CFR 210.2–02).

(3) With regard to the acquisition of one or more real estate properties, the financial statements and any additional information specified by Rule 3–14 of Regulation S–X (17 CFR 210.3–14) shall be filed.

(4) Financial statements required by this item may be filed with the initial report, or

by amendment not later than 71 calendar days after the date that the initial report on Form 8–K must be filed. If the financial statements are not included in the initial report, the registrant should so indicate in the Form 8–K report and state when the required financial statements will be filed. The registrant may, at its option, include unaudited financial statements in the initial report on Form 8–K.

(b) *Pro forma financial information.*

(1) For any transaction required to be described in answer to Item 2.01 of this form, furnish any pro forma financial information that would be required pursuant to Article 11 of Regulation S–X (17 CFR 210).

(2) The provisions of paragraph (a)(4) of this Item 9.01 shall also apply to pro forma financial information relative to the acquired business.

(c) *Exhibits.* The exhibits shall be deemed to be filed or furnished, depending on the relevant item requiring such exhibit, in accordance with the provisions of Item 601 of Regulation S–K (17 CFR 229.601), or Item 601 of Regulation S–B (17 CFR 228.601) and Instruction B.2 to this form.

Instruction.

During the period after a registrant has reported a business combination pursuant to Item 2.01 of this form, until the date on which the financial statements specified by this Item 9.01 must be filed, the registrant will be deemed current for purposes of its reporting obligations under Section 13(a) or 15(d) of the Exchange Act (15 U.S.C. 78m or 78o(d)). With respect to filings under the Securities Act, however, registration statements will not be declared effective and post-effective amendments to registrations statements will not be declared effective unless financial statements meeting the requirements of Rule 3–05 of Regulation S–X (17 CFR 210.3–05) are provided. In addition, offerings should not be made pursuant to effective registration statements, or pursuant to Rules 505 and 506 of Regulation D (17 CFR 230.505 and 230.506) where any purchasers are not accredited investors under Rule 501(a) of that Regulation, until the audited financial statements required by Rule 3–05 of Regulation S–X (17 CFR 210.3–05) are filed; *provided, however*, that the following offerings or sales of securities may proceed notwithstanding that financial statements of the acquired business have not been filed:

(a) offerings or sales of securities upon the conversion of outstanding convertible securities or upon the exercise of outstanding warrants or rights;

(b) dividend or interest reinvestment plans;

(c) employee benefit plans;

(d) transactions involving secondary offerings; or

(e) sales of securities pursuant to Rule 144 (17 CFR 230.144).

SIGNATURES

Pursuant to the requirements of the Securities Exchange Act of 1934, the registrant has duly caused this report to be signed on its behalf by the undersigned hereunto duly authorized.

(Registrant) ____________________

(Signature)* ____________________

Date ____________________

* Print name and title of the signing officer under his signature.

C. INVESTMENT COMPANY ACT OF 1940

15 U.S.C. 80a–1 et seq.

Act	Section 15 U.S.C.	
1	80a–1	Findings and Declaration of Policy
2	80a–2	General Definitions
3	80a–3	Definition of Investment Company
4	80a–4	Classification of Investment Companies
5	80a–5	Subclassification of Management Companies
6	80a–6	Exemptions
7	80a–7	Transactions by Unregistered Investment Companies
8	80a–8	Registration of Investment Companies
9	80a–9	Ineligibility of Certain Affiliated Persons and Underwriters
10	80a–10	Affiliations of Directors
11	80a–11	Offers of Exchange
12	80a–12	Functions and Activities of Investment Companies
13	80a–13	Changes in Investment Policy
14	80a–14	Size of Investment Companies
15	80a–15	Investment Advisory and Underwriting Contracts
16	80a–16	Changes in Board of Directors and Trustees; Provisions Relative to Strict Trusts
17	80a–17	Transactions of Certain Affiliated Persons and Underwriters
18	80a–18	Capital Structure
19	80a–19	Dividends
20	80a–20	Proxies; Voting Trusts; Circular Ownership
21	80a–21	Loans
22	80a–22	Distribution, Redemption, and Repurchase of Redeemable Securities
23	80a–23	Distribution and Repurchase of Securities: Closed-End Companies
24	80a–24	Registration of Securities Under Securities Act of 1933
25	80a–25	Plans of Reorganization
26	80a–26	Unit Investment Trusts
27	80a–27	Periodic Payment Plans
28	80a–28	Face-Amount Certificate Companies
29		[Reserved]
30	80a–30	Periodic and Other Reports; Reports of Affiliated Persons
31	80a–31	Accounts and Records
32	80a–32	Accountants and Auditors
33	80a–33	Filing of Documents With Commission in Civil Actions
34	80a–34	Destruction and Falsification of Reports and Records
35	80a–35	Unlawful Representations and Names
36	80a–36	Breach of Fiduciary Duty
37	80a–37	Larceny and Embezzlement
38	80a–38	Rules, Regulations, and Orders; General Powers of Commission
39	80a–39	Procedure for Issuance of Rules and Regulations
40	80a–40	Procedure for Issuance of Orders
41	80a–41	Hearings by Commission
42	80a–42	Enforcement of Title
43	80a–43	Court Review of Orders
44	80a–44	Jurisdiction of Offenses and Suits
45	80a–45	Information Filed With Commission
46	80a–46	Annual Reports of Commission; Employees of the Commission
47	80a–47	Validity of Contracts
48	80a–48	Liability of Controlling Persons; Preventing Compliance With Title
49	80a–49	Penalties

Section Act	15 U.S.C.	
50	80a–50	Effect on Existing Law
51	80a–51	Separability of Provisions
52	80a–52	Short Title
53	80a–53	Effective Date
54	80a–54	Election to Be Regulated as a Business Development Company
55	80a–55	Functions and Activities of Business Development Companies
56	80a–56	Qualifications of Directors
57	80a–57	Transactions With Certain Affiliates
58	80a–58	Changes in Investment Policy
59	80a–59	Incorporation of Provisions
60	80a–60	Functions and Activities of Business Development Companies
61	80a–61	Capital Structure
62	80a–62	Loans
63	80a–63	Distribution and Repurchase of Securities
64	80a–64	Accounts and Records
65	80a–65	Liability of Controlling Persons; Preventing Compliance With Title

INVESTMENT COMPANY ACT OF 1940

15 U.S.C. 80–1 et seq.

Findings and Declaration of Policy

Section 1. (a) Upon the basis of facts disclosed by the record and reports of the Securities and Exchange Commission made pursuant to section 30 of the Public Utility Holding Company Act of 1935, the facts otherwise disclosed and ascertained, it is hereby found that investment companies are affected with a national public interest in that, among other things—

(1) the securities issued by such companies, which constitute a substantial part of all securities publicly offered, are distributed, purchased, paid for, exchanged, transferred, redeemed, and repurchased by use of the mails and means and instrumentalities of interstate commerce, and in the case of the numerous companies which issue redeemable securities this process of distribution and redemption is continuous;

(2) the principal activities of such companies—investing, reinvesting, and trading in securities—are conducted by use of the mails and means and instrumentalities of interstate commerce, including the facilities of national securities exchanges, and constitute a substantial part of all transactions effected in the securities markets of the Nation;

(3) such companies customarily invest and trade in securities issued by, and may dominate and control or otherwise affect the policies and management of, companies engaged in business in interstate commerce;

(4) such companies are media for the investment in the national economy of a substantial part of the national savings and may have a vital effect upon the flow of such savings into the capital markets; and

(5) the activities of such companies, extending over many States, their use of the instrumentalities of interstate commerce and the wide geographic distribution of their security holders, make difficult, if not impossible, effective State regulation of such companies in the interest of investors.

(b) Upon the basis of facts disclosed by the record and reports of the Securities and Exchange Commission made pursuant to section 30 of the Public Utility Holding Company Act of 1935, and facts otherwise disclosed and ascertained, it is hereby declared that the national public interest and the interest of investors are adversely affected—

(1) when investors purchase, pay for, exchange, receive dividends upon, vote, refrain from voting, sell, or surrender securities issued by investment companies without adequate, accurate, and explicit information, fairly presented, concerning the character of such securities and the circumstances, policies, and financial responsibility of such companies and their management;

(2) when investment companies are organized, operated, managed, or their portfolio securities are selected, in the interest of directors, officers, investment advisers, depositors, or other affiliated persons thereof, in the interest of underwriters, brokers, or dealers, in the interest of special classes of their security holders, or in the interest of other investment companies or persons engaged in other lines of business, rather than in the interest of all classes of such companies' security holders;

(3) when investment companies issue securities containing inequitable or discriminatory provisions, or fail to protect the preferences and privileges of the holders of their outstanding securities;

(4) when the control of investment companies is unduly concentrated through pyra-

miding or inequitable methods of control, or is inequitably distributed, or when investment companies are managed by irresponsible persons;

(5) when investment companies, in keeping their accounts, in maintaining reserves, and in computing their earnings and the asset value of their outstanding securities, employ unsound or misleading methods, or are not subjected to adequate independent scrutiny;

(6) when investment companies are reorganized, become inactive, or change the character of their business, or when the control or management thereof is transferred, without the consent of their security holders;

(7) when investment companies by excessive borrowing and the issuance of excessive amounts of senior securities increase unduly the speculative character of their junior securities; or

(8) when investment companies operate without adequate assets or reserves.

It is hereby declared that the policy and purposes of this title, in accordance with which the provisions of this title shall be interpreted, are to mitigate and, so far as is feasible, to eliminate the conditions enumerated in this section which adversely affect the national public interest and the interest of investors.

General Definitions

Sec. 2. (a) When used in this title, unless the context otherwise requires—

(1) "Advisory board" means a board, whether elected or appointed, which is distinct from the board of directors or board of trustees, of an investment company, and which is composed solely of persons who do not serve such company in any other capacity, whether or not the functions of such board are such as to render its members "directors" within the definition of that term, which board has advisory functions as to investments but has no power to determine that any security or other investment shall be purchased or sold by such company.

(2) "Affiliated company" means a company which is an affiliated person.

(3) "Affiliated person" of another person means (A) any person directly or indirectly owning, controlling, or holding with power to vote, 5 per centum or more of the outstanding voting securities of such other person; (B) any person 5 per centum or more of whose outstanding voting securities are directly or indirectly owned, controlled, or held with power to vote, by such other person; (C) any person directly or indirectly controlling, controlled by, or under common control with, such other person; (D) any officer, director, partner, copartner, or employee of such other person; (E) if such other person is an investment company, any investment adviser thereof or any member of an advisory board thereof; and (F) if such other person is an unincorporated investment company not having a board of directors, the depositor thereof.

(4) "Assignment" includes any direct or indirect transfer of hypothecation of a contract or chose in action by the assignor, or of a controlling block of the assignor's outstanding voting securities by a security holder of the assignor; but does not include an assignment of partnership interests incidental to the death or withdrawal of a minority of the members of the partnership having only a minority interest in the partnership business or to the admission to the partnership of one or more members who, after such admission, shall be only a minority of the members and shall have only a minority interest in the business.

(5) "Bank" means (A) a depository institution (as defined in section 3 of the Federal Deposit Insurance Act) or a branch or agency of a foreign bank (as such terms are defined in section 1(b) of the International Banking Act of 1978), (B) a member bank of the Federal Reserve System, (C) any other banking institution or trust company,

whether incorporated or not, doing business under the laws of any State or the United States, a substantial portion of the business of which consists of receiving deposits or exercising fiduciary powers similar to those permitted to national banks under the authority of the Comptroller of the Currency, and which is supervised and examined by State or Federal authority having supervision over banks, and which is not operated for the purpose of evading the provisions of this title, and (D) a receiver, conservator, or other liquidating agent of any institution or firm included in clauses (A), (B), or (C) of this paragraph.

(6) The term "broker" has the same meaning as given in section 3 of the Securities Exchange Act of 1934, except that such term does not include any person solely by reason of the fact that such person is an underwriter for one or more investment companies.

(7) "Commission" means the Securities and Exchange Commission.

(8) "Company" means a corporation, a partnership, an association, a joint-stock company, a trust, a fund, or any organized group of persons whether incorporated or not; or any receiver, trustee in a case under Title 11 of the United States Code or similar official or any liquidating agent for any of the foregoing, in his capacity as such.

(9) "Control" means the power to exercise a controlling influence over the management or policies of a company, unless such power is solely the result of an official position with such company.

Any person who owns beneficially, either directly or through one or more controlled companies, more than 25 per centum of the voting securities of a company shall be presumed to control such company. Any person who does not so own more than 25 per centum of the voting securities of any company shall be presumed not to control such company. A natural person shall be presumed not to be a controlled person within the meaning of this title. Any such presumption may be rebutted by evidence, but except as hereinafter provided, shall continue until a determination to the contrary made by the Commission by order either on its own motion or on application by an interested person. If an application filed hereunder is not granted or denied by the Commission within sixty days after filing thereof, the determination sought by the application shall be deemed to have been temporarily granted pending final determination of the Commission thereon. The Commission, upon its own motion or upon application, may by order revoke or modify any order issued under this paragraph whenever it shall find that the determination embraced in such original order is no longer consistent with the facts.

(10) "Convicted" includes a verdict, judgment, or plea of guilty, or a finding of guilt on a plea of nolo contendere, if such verdict, judgment, plea, or finding has not been reversed, set aside, or withdrawn, whether or not sentence has been imposed.

(11) The term "dealer" has the same meaning as given in the Securities Exchange Act of 1934, but does not include an insurance company or investment company.

(12) "Director" means any director of a corporation or any person performing similar functions with respect to any organization, whether incorporated or unincorporated, including any natural person who is a member of a board of trustees of a management company created as a common-law trust.

(13) "Employees' securities company" means any investment company or similar issuer all of the outstanding securities of which (other than short-term paper) are beneficially owned (A) by the employees or persons on retainer of a single employer or of two or more employers each of which is an affiliated company of the other, (B) by former employees of such employer or employers, (C) by members of the immediate

family of such employees, persons on retainer, or former employees, (D) by any two or more of the foregoing classes of persons, or (E) by such employer or employers together with any one or more of the foregoing classes of persons.

(14) "Exchange" means any organization, association, or group of persons, whether incorporated or unincorporated, which constitutes, maintains, or provides a market place or facilities for bringing together purchasers and sellers of securities or for otherwise performing with respect to securities the functions commonly performed by a stock exchange as that term is generally understood, and includes the market place and the market facilities maintained by such exchange.

(15) "Face-amount certificate" means any certificate, investment contract, or other security which represents an obligation on the part of its issuer to pay a stated or determinable sum or sums at a fixed or determinable date or dates more than twenty-four months after the date of issuance, in consideration of the payment of periodic installments of a stated or determinable amount (which security shall be known as a face-amount certificate of the "installment type"); or any security which represents a similar obligation on the part of a face-amount certificate company, the consideration for which is the payment of a single lump sum (which security shall be known as a "fully paid" face-amount certificate).

(16) "Government security" means any security issued or guaranteed as to principal or interest by the United States, or by a person controlled or supervised by and acting as an instrumentality of the Government of the United States pursuant to authority granted by the Congress of the United States; or any certificate of deposit for any of the foregoing.

(17) "Insurance company" means a company which is organized as an insurance company, whose primary and predominant business activity is the writing of insurance or the reinsuring of risks underwritten by insurance companies, and which is subject to supervision by the insurance commissioner or a similar official or agency of a State; or any receiver or similar official of any liquidating agent for such a company, in his capacity as such.

(18) "Interstate commerce" means trade, commerce, transportation, or communication among the several States, or between any foreign country and any State, or between any State and any place or ship outside thereof.

(19) "Interested person" of another person means—

(A) when used with respect to an investment company—

(i) any affiliated person of such company,

(ii) any member of the immediate family of any natural person who is an affiliated person of such company,

(iii) any interested person of any investment adviser of or principal underwriter for such company,

(iv) any person or partner or employee of any person who at any time since the beginning of the last two completed fiscal years of such company has acted as legal counsel for such company,

(v) any person or any affiliated person of a person (other than a registered investment company) that, at any time during the 6-month period preceding the date of the determination of whether that person or affiliated person is an interested person, has executed any portfolio transactions for, engaged in any principal transactions with, or distributed shares for—

(I) the investment company;

(II) any other investment company having the same investment adviser as such investment company or holding itself out to investors as a related company for purposes of investment or investor services; or

(III) any account over which the investment company's investment adviser has brokerage placement discretion,

(vi) any person or any affiliated person of a person (other than a registered investment company) that, at any time during the 6-month period preceding the date of the determination of whether that person or affiliated person is an interested person, has loaned money or other property to—

(I) the investment company;

(II) any other investment company having the same investment adviser as such investment company or holding itself out to investors as a related company for purposes of investment or investor services; or

(III) any account for which the investment company's investment adviser has brokerage authority,

(vii) any natural person whom the Commission by order shall have determined to be an interested person by reason of having had, at any time since the beginning of the last two completed fiscal years of such company, a material business or professional relationship with such company or with the principal executive officer of such company or with any other investment company having the same investment adviser or principal underwriter or with the principal executive officer of such other investment company:

Provided, That no person shall be deemed to be an interested person of an investment company solely by reason of (aa) his being a member of its board of directors or advisory board or an owner of its securities, or (bb) his membership in the immediate family of any person specified in clause (aa) of this proviso; and

(B) when used with respect to an investment adviser of or principal underwriter for any investment company—

(i) any affiliated person of such investment adviser or principal underwriter,

(ii) any member of the immediate family of any natural person who is an affiliated person of such investment adviser or principal underwriter,

(iii) any person who knowingly has any direct or indirect beneficial interest in, or who is designated as trustee, executor, or guardian of any legal interest in, any security issued either by such investment adviser or principal underwriter or by a controlling person of such investment adviser or principal underwriter,

(iv) any person or partner or employee of any person who at any time since the beginning of the last two completed fiscal years of such investment company has acted as legal counsel for such investment adviser or principal underwriter,

(v) any person or any affiliated person of a person (other than a registered investment company) that, at any time during the 6-month period preceding the date of the determination of whether that person or affiliated person is an interested person, has executed any portfolio transactions for, engaged in any principal transactions with, or distributed shares for—

(I) the investment company for which the investment adviser or principal underwriter serves as such;

(II) any investment company holding itself out to investors, for purposes of investment or investor services, as a company related to any investment company for which the investment adviser or principal underwriter serves as such; or

(III) any account over which the investment adviser has brokerage placement discretion,

(vi) any person or any affiliated person of a person (other than a registered investment company) that, at any time during the 6-month period preceding the date of the determination of whether that person or affiliated person is an interested person, has loaned money or other property to—

(I) the investment company for which the investment adviser or principal underwriter serves as such;

(II) any investment company holding itself out to investors, for purposes of investment or investor services, as a company related to any investment company for which the investment adviser or principal underwriter serves as such; or

(III) any account over which the investment adviser has borrowing authority,

(vii) any natural person whom the Commission by order shall have determined to be an interested person by reason of having had at any time since the beginning of the last two completed fiscal years of such investment company a material business or professional relationship with such investment adviser or principal underwriter or with the principal executive officer or any controlling person of such investment adviser or principal underwriter.

For the purpose of this paragraph (19), "member of the immediate family" means any parent, spouse of a parent, child, spouse of a child, spouse, brother, or sister, and includes step and adoptive relationships. The Commission may modify or revoke any order issued under clause (vi) of subparagraph (A) or (B) of this paragraph whenever it finds that such order is no longer consistent with the facts. No order issued pursuant to clause (vi) of subparagraph (A) or (B) of this paragraph shall become effective until at least sixty days after the entry thereof, and no such order shall affect the status of any person for the purpose of this title or for any other purpose for any period prior to the effective date of such order.

(20) "Investment adviser" of an investment company means (A) any person (other than a bona fide officer, director, trustee, member of an advisory board, or employee of such company, as such) who pursuant to contract with such company regularly furnishes advice to such company with respect to the desirability of investing in, purchasing or selling securities or other property, or is empowered to determine what securities or other property shall be purchased or sold by such company, and (B) any other person who pursuant to contract with a person described in clause (A) regularly performs substantially all of the duties undertaken by such person described in clause (A); but does not include (i) a person whose advice is furnished solely through uniform publications distributed to subscribers thereto, (ii) a person who furnishes only statistical and other factual information, advice regarding economic factors and trends, or advice as to occasional transactions in specific securities, but without generally furnishing advice or making recommendations regarding the purchase or sale of securities, (iii) a company furnishing such services at cost to one or more investment companies, insurance companies, or other financial institutions, (iv) any person the character and amount of whose compensation for such services must be approved by a court, or (v) such other persons as the Commission may by rules and regulations or order determine not to be within the intent of this definition.

(21) "Investment banker" means any person engaged in the business of underwriting securities issued by other persons, but does not include an investment company, any person who acts as an underwriter in isolat-

ed transactions but not as a part of a regular business, or any person solely by reason of the fact that such person is an underwriter for one or more investment companies.

(22) "Issuer" means every person who issues or proposes to issue any security, or has outstanding any security which it has issued.

(23) "Lend" includes a purchase coupled with an agreement by the vendor to repurchase; "borrow" includes a sale coupled with a similar agreement.

(24) "Majority-owned subsidiary" of a person means a company 50 per centum or more of the outstanding voting securities of which are owned by such person, or by a company which, within the meaning of this paragraph, is a majority-owned subsidiary of such person.

(25) "Means of instrumentality of interstate commerce" includes any facility of a national securities exchange.

(26) "National securities exchange" means an exchange registered under section 6 of the Securities Exchange Act of 1934.

(27) "Periodic payment plan certificate" means (A) any certificate, investment contract, or other security providing for a series of periodic payments by the holder, and representing an undivided interest in certain specified securities or in a unit or fund of securities purchased wholly or partly with the proceeds of such payments, and (B) any security the issuer of which is also issuing securities of the character described in clause (A) and the holder of which has substantially the same rights and privileges as those which holders of securities of the character described in clause (A) have upon completing the periodic payments for which such securities provide.

(28) "Person" means a natural person or a company.

(29) "Principal underwriter" of or for any investment company other than a closed-end company, or of any security issued by such a company, means any underwriter who as principal purchases from such company, or pursuant to contract has the right (whether absolute or conditional) from time to time to purchase from such company, any such security for distribution, or who as agent for such company sells or has the right to sell any such security to a dealer or to the public or both, but does not include a dealer who purchases from such company through a principal underwriter acting as agent for such company. "Principal underwriter" of or for a closed-end company or any issuer which is not an investment company, or of any security issued by such a company or issuer, means any underwriter who, in connection with a primary distribution of securities, (A) is in privity of contract with the issuer or an affiliated person of the issuer; (B) acting alone or in concert with one or more other persons, initiates or directs the formation of an underwriting syndicate; or (C) is allowed a rate of gross commission, spread, or other profit greater than the rate allowed another underwriter participating in the distribution.

(30) "Promoter" of a company or a proposed company means a person who, acting alone or in concert with other persons, is initiating or directing, or has within one year initiated or directed, the organization of such company.

(31) "Prospectus", as used in section 22, means a written prospectus intended to meet the requirements of section 10(a) of the Securities Act of 1933 and currently in use. As used elsewhere, "prospectus" means a prospectus as defined in the Securities Act of 1933.

(32) "Redeemable security" means any security, other than short-term paper, under the terms of which the holder upon its presentation to the issuer or to a person designated by the issuer, is entitled (whether absolutely or only out of surplus) to receive approximately his proportionate share of the

issuer's current net assets, or the cash equivalent thereof.

(33) "Reorganization" means (A) a reorganization under the supervision of a court of competent jurisdiction; (B) a merger or consolidation; (C) a sale of 75 per centum or more in value of the assets of a company; (D) a restatement of the capital of a company, or an exchange of securities issued by a company for any of its own outstanding securities; (E) a voluntary dissolution or liquidation of a company; (F) a recapitalization or other procedure or transaction which has for its purpose the alteration, modification, or elimination of any of the rights, preferences, or privileges of any class of securities issued by a company, as provided in its charter or other instrument creating or defining such rights, preferences, and privileges; (G) an exchange of securities issued by a company for outstanding securities issued by another company or companies, preliminary to and for the purpose of effecting or consummating any of the foregoing; or (H) any exchange of securities by a company which is not an investment company for securities issued by a registered investment company.

(34) "Sale", "sell," "offer to sell", or "offer for sale" includes every contract of sale or disposition of, attempt or offer to dispose of, or solicitation of an offer to buy, a security or interest in a security, for value. Any security given or delivered with, or as a bonus on account of, any purchase of securities or any other thing, shall be conclusively presumed to constitute a part of the subject of such purchase and to have been sold for value.

(35) "Sales load" means the difference between the price of a security to the public and that portion of the proceeds from its sale which is received and invested or held for investment by the issuer (or in the case of a unit investment trust, by the depositor or trustee), less any portion of such difference deducted for trustee's or custodian's fees, insurance premiums, issue taxes, or administrative expenses or fees which are not properly chargeable to sales or promotional activities. In the case of a periodic payment plan certificate, "sales load" includes the sales load on any investment company securities in which the payments made on such certificate are invested, as well as the sales load on the certificate itself.

(36) "Security" means any note, stock, treasury stock, security future, bond, debenture, evidence of indebtedness, certificate of interest or participation in any profit-sharing agreement, collateral-trust certificate, preorganization certificate or subscription, transferable share, investment contract, voting-trust certificate, certificate of deposit for a security, fractional undivided interest in oil, gas, or other mineral rights, any put, call, straddle, option, or privilege on any security (including a certificate of deposit) or on any group or index of securities (including any interest therein or based on the value thereof), or any put, call, straddle, option, or privilege entered into on a national securities exchange relating to foreign currency, or, in general, any interest or instrument commonly known as a "security," or any certificate of interest or participation in, temporary or interim certificate for, guarantee of, or warrant or right to subscribe to or purchase, any of the foregoing.

(37) "Separate account" means an account established and maintained by an insurance company pursuant to the laws of any State or territory of the United States, or of Canada or any province thereof, under which income, gains and losses, whether or not realized, from assets allocated to such account, are, in accordance with the applicable contract, credited to or charged against such account without regard to other income, gains, or losses of the insurance company.

(38) "Short-term paper" means any note, draft, bill of exchange, or banker's acceptance payable on demand or having a maturity at the time of issuance of not exceeding

nine months, exclusive of days of grace, or any renewal thereof payable on demand or having a maturity likewise limited; and such other classes of securities, of a commercial rather than an investment character, as the Commission may designate by rules and regulations.

(39) "State" means any State of the United States, the District of Columbia, Puerto Rico, the Virgin Islands, or any other possession of the United States.

(40) "Underwriter" means any person who has purchased from an issuer with a view to, or sells for an issuer in connection with, the distribution of any security, or participates or has a direct or indirect participation in any such undertaking, or participates or has a participation in the direct or indirect underwriting of any such undertaking; but such term shall not include a person whose interest is limited to a commission from an underwriter or dealer not in excess of the usual and customary distributor's or seller's commission. As used in this paragraph the term "issuer" shall include, in addition to an issuer, any person directly or indirectly controlling or controlled by the issuer, or any person under direct or indirect common control with the issuer. When the distribution of the securities in respect of which any person is an underwriter is completed such person shall cease to be an underwriter in respect of such securities or the issuer thereof.

(41) "Value", with respect to assets of registered investment companies, except as provided in subsection (b) of section 28 of this title, means—

(A) as used in sections 3, 5, and 12 of this title, (i) with respect to securities owned at the end of the last preceding fiscal quarter for which market quotations are readily available, the market value at the end of such quarter; (ii) with respect to other securities and assets owned at the end of the last preceding fiscal quarter, fair value at the end, of such quarter, as determined in good faith by the board of directors; and (iii) with respect to securities and other assets acquired after the end of the last preceding fiscal quarter, the cost thereof; and

(B) as used elsewhere in this title, (i) with respect to securities for which market quotations are readily available, the market value of such securities; and (ii) with respect to other securities and assets, fair value as determined in good faith by the board of directors;

in each case as of such time or times as determined pursuant to this title, and the rules and regulations issued by the Commission hereunder. Notwithstanding the fact that market quotations for securities issued by controlled companies are available, the board of directors may in good faith determine the value of such securities: *Provided,* That the value so determined is not in excess of the higher of market value or asset value of such securities in the case of majority-owned subsidiaries, and is not in excess of market value in the case of other controlled companies.

For purposes of the valuation of those assets of a registered diversified company which are not subject to the limitations provided for in section 5 (b)(1), the Commission may, by rules and regulations or orders, permit any security to be carried at cost, if it shall determine that such procedure is consistent with the general intent and purposes of this title. For purposes of sections 5 and 12, in lieu of values determined as provided in clause (A) above, the Commission shall by rules and regulations permit valuation of securities at cost or other basis in cases where it may be more convenient for such company to make its computations on such basis by reason of the necessity or desirability of complying with the provisions of any United States revenue laws or rules and regulations issued thereunder, or the laws or the rules and regulations issued thereunder of any State in which the securities of such company may be qualified for sale.

The foregoing definition shall not derogate from the authority of the Commission with respect to the reports, information, and documents to be filed with the Commission by any registered company, or with respect to the accounting policies and principles to be followed by any such company, as provided in sections 8, 30, and 31.

(42) "Voting security" means any security presently entitling the owner or holder thereof to vote for the election of directors of a company. A specified percentage of the outstanding voting securities of a company means such amount of its outstanding voting securities as entitles the holder or holders thereof to cast said specified percentage of the aggregate votes which the holders of all the outstanding voting securities of such company are entitled to cast. The vote of a majority of the outstanding voting securities of a company means the vote, at the annual or a special meeting of the security holders of such company duly called, (A) of 67 per centum or more of the voting securities present at such meeting, if the holders of more than 50 per centum of the outstanding voting securities of such company are present or represented by proxy; or (B) of more than 50 per centum of the outstanding voting securities of such company, whichever is the less.

(43) "Wholly-owned subsidiary" of a person means a company 95 per centum or more of the outstanding voting securities of which are owned by such person, or by a company which, within the meaning of this paragraph, is a wholly-owned subsidiary of such person.

(44) "Securities Act of 1933", "Securities Exchange Act of 1934", "Public Utility Holding Company Act of 1935," and "Trust Indenture Act of 1939" means those Acts, respectively, as heretofore or hereafter amended.

(45) "Savings and loan association" means a savings and loan association, building and loan association, cooperative bank, homestead association, or similar institution, which is supervised and examined by State or Federal authority having supervision over any such institution, and a receiver, conservator, or other liquidating agent of any such institution.

(46) "Eligible portfolio company" means any issuer which—

(A) is organized under the laws of, and has its principal place of business in, any State or States;

(B) is neither an investment company as defined in section 3 (other than a small business investment company which is licensed by the Small Business Administration to operate under the Small Business Investment Act of 1958 and which is a wholly-owned subsidiary of the business development company) nor a company which would be an investment company except for the exclusion from the definition of investment company in section 3(c); and

(C) satisfies one of the following:

(i) it does not have any class of securities with respect to which a member of a national securities exchange, broker, or dealer may extend or maintain credit to or for a customer pursuant to rules or regulations adopted by the Board of Governors of the Federal Reserve System under section 7 of the Securities Exchange Act of 1934;

(ii) it is controlled by a business development company, either alone or as part of a group acting together, and such business development company in fact exercises a controlling influence over the management or policies of such eligible portfolio company and, as a result of such control, has an affiliated person who is a director of such eligible portfolio company;

(iii) it has total assets of not more than $4,000,000, and capital and surplus (shareholders' equity less retained earnings) of not less than $2,000,000, except that the Commission may adjust such amounts by rule, regulation, or order to reflect changes in 1 or more generally accepted indices or other indicators for small businesses; or

(iv) it meets such other criteria as the Commission may, by rule, establish as consistent with the public interest, the protection of investors, and the purposes fairly intended by the policy and provisions of this title.

(47) "Making available significant managerial assistance" by a business development company means—

(A) any arrangement whereby a business development company, through its directors, officers, employees, or general partners, offers to provide, and, if accepted, does so provide, significant guidance and counsel concerning the management, operations, or business objectives and policies of a portfolio company;

(B) the exercise by a business development company of a controlling influence over the management or policies of a portfolio company by the business development company acting individually or as part of a group acting together which controls such portfolio company; or

(C) with respect to a small business investment company licensed by the Small Business Administration to operate under the Small Business Investment Act of 1958, the making of loans to a portfolio company.

For purposes of subparagraph (A), the requirement that a business development company make available significant managerial assistance shall be deemed to be satisfied with respect to any particular portfolio company where the business development company purchases securities of such portfolio company in conjunction with one or more other persons acting together, and at least one of the persons in the group makes available significant managerial assistance to such portfolio company, except that such requirement will not be deemed to be satisfied if the business development company, in all cases, makes available significant managerial assistance solely in the manner described in this sentence.

(48) "Business development company" means any closed-end company which—

(A) is organized under the laws of, and has its principal place of business in, any State or States;

(B) is operated for the purpose of making investments in securities described in paragraphs (1) through (3) of section 55(a), and makes available significant managerial assistance with respect to the issuers of such securities, provided that a business development company must make available significant managerial assistance only with respect to the companies which are treated by such business development company as satisfying the 70 per centum of the value of its total assets condition of section 55 provided further that a business development company need not make available significant managerial assistance with respect to any company described in paragraph (46)(C)(iii), or with respect to any other company that meets such criteria as the Commission may by rule, regulation, or order permit, as consistent with the public interest, the protection of investors, and the purposes of this title; and

(C) has elected pursuant to section 54(a) to be subject to the provisions of sections 55 through 65.

(49) "Foreign securities authority" means any foreign government or any governmental body or regulatory organization empowered by a foreign government to administer or enforce its laws as they relate to securities matters.

(50) "Foreign financial regulatory authority" means any (A) foreign securities authority, (B) other governmental body or foreign equivalent of a self-regulatory organization empowered by a foreign government to administer or enforce its laws relating to the regulation of fiduciaries, trusts, commercial lending, insurance, trading in contracts of sale of a commodity for future delivery, or other instruments traded on or subject to the rules of a contract market, board of trade or foreign equivalent, or other financial activities, or (C) membership organization a function of which is to regulate the participation of its members in activities listed above.

(51)(A) "Qualified purchaser" means—

(i) any natural person (including any person who holds a joint, community property, or other similar shared ownership interest in an issuer that is excepted under section 3(c)(7) with that person's qualified purchaser spouse) who owns not less than $5,000,000 in investments, as defined by the Commission;

(ii) any company that owns not less than $5,000,000 in investments and that is owned directly or indirectly by or for 2 or more natural persons who are related as siblings or spouse (including former spouses), or direct lineal descendants by birth or adoption, spouses of such persons, the estates of such persons, or foundations, charitable organizations, or trusts established by or for the benefit of such persons;

(iii) any trust that is not covered by clause (ii) and that was not formed for the specific purpose of acquiring the securities offered, as to which the trustee or other person authorized to make decisions with respect to the trust, and each settlor or other person who has contributed assets to the trust, is a person described in clause (i), (ii), or (iv); or

(iv) any person, acting for its own account or the accounts of other qualified purchasers, who in the aggregate owns and invests on a discretionary basis, not less than $25,000,000 in investments.

(B) The Commission may adopt such rules and regulations applicable to the persons and trusts specified in clauses (i) through (iv) of subparagraph (A) as it determines are necessary or appropriate in the public interest or for the protection of investors.

(C) The term "qualified purchaser" does not include a company that, but for the exceptions provided for in paragraph (1) or (7) of section 3(c), would be an investment company (hereafter in this paragraph referred to as an "excepted investment company"), unless all beneficial owners of its outstanding securities (other than short-term paper), determined in accordance with section 3(c)(1)(A), that acquired such securities on or before April 30, 1996 (hereafter in this paragraph referred to as "pre-amendment beneficial owners"), and all pre-amendment beneficial owners of the outstanding securities (other than short-term paper) of any excepted investment company that, directly or indirectly, owns any outstanding securities of such excepted investment company, have consented to its treatment as a qualified purchaser. Unanimous consent of all trustees, directors, or general partners of a company or trust referred to in clause (ii) or (iii) of subparagraph (A) shall constitute consent for purposes of this subparagraph.

(52) The terms "security future" and "narrow-based security index" have the same meanings as provided in section 3(a)(55) of the Securities Exchange Act of 1934.

(b) No provision in this title shall apply to, or be deemed to include, the United States, a State, or any political subdivision of a State, or any agency, authority, or instrumentality of any one or more of the foregoing, or any corporation which is wholly owned directly or indirectly by any one or more of the foregoing, or any officer, agent, or employee of any of the foregoing acting as such in the course of his official duty, unless such provision makes specific reference thereto.

(c) *Consideration of Promotion of Efficiency, Competition, and Capital Formation.*—Whenever pursuant to this title the Commission is engaged in rulemaking and is required to consider or determine whether an action is consistent with the public interest, the Commission shall also consider, in addition to the protection of investors, whether the action will promote efficiency, competition, and capital formation.

Definition of Investment Company

Sec. 3. (a)(1) When used in this title, "investment company" means any issuer which—

(A) is or holds itself out as being engaged primarily, or proposes to engage primarily, in the business of investing, reinvesting, or trading in securities;

(B) is engaged or proposes to engage in the business of issuing face-amount certificates of the installment type, or has been engaged in such business and has any such certificates outstanding; or

(C) is engaged or proposes to engage in the business of investing, reinvesting, owning, holding, or trading in securities, and owns or proposes to acquire investment securities having a value exceeding 40 per centum of the value of such issuer's total assets (exclusive of Government securities and cash items) on an unconsolidated basis.

(2) As used in this section, "investment securities" includes all securities except (A) Government securities, (B) securities issued by employees' securities companies, and (C) securities issued by majority-owned subsidiaries of the owner which are (i) not investment companies, and (ii) are not relying on the exception from the definition of investment company in paragraph (1) or (7) of subsection (c).

(b) Notwithstanding paragraph (1)(C) of subsection (a), none of the following persons is an investment company within the meaning of this title:

(1) Any issuer primarily engaged, directly or through a wholly-owned subsidiary or subsidiaries, in a business or businesses other than that of investing, reinvesting, owning, holding, or trading in securities.

(2) Any issuer which the Commission, upon application by such issuer, finds and by order declares to be primarily engaged in a business or businesses other than that of investing, reinvesting, owning, holding, or trading in securities either directly or (A) through majority-owned subsidiaries or (B) through controlled companies conducting similar types of businesses. The filing of an application under this paragraph in good faith by an issuer other than a registered investment company shall exempt the applicant for a period of sixty days from all provisions of this title applicable to investment companies as such. For cause shown, the Commission by order may extend such period of exemption for an additional period or periods. Whenever the Commission, upon its own motion or upon application, finds that the circumstances which gave rise to the issuance of an order granting an application under this paragraph no longer exist, the Commission shall by order revoke such order.

(3) Any issuer all the outstanding securities of which (other than short-term paper and directors' qualifying shares) are directly or indirectly owned by a company excepted from the definition of investment company by paragraph (1) or (2) of this subsection.

(c) Notwithstanding subsection (a), none of the following persons is an investment company within the meaning of this title:

(1) Any issuer whose outstanding securities (other than short-term paper) are beneficially owned by not more than one hun-

dred persons and which is not making and does not presently propose to make a public offering of its securities. Such issuer shall be deemed to be an investment company for purposes of the limitations set forth in subparagraphs (A)(i) and (B)(i) of section 12(d)(1) governing the purchase or other acquisition by such issuer of any security issued by any registered investment company and the sale of any security issued by any registered open-end investment company to any such issuer. For purposes of this paragraph:

(A) Beneficial ownership by a company shall be deemed to be beneficial ownership by one person, except that, if the company owns 10 per centum or more of the outstanding voting securities of the issuer, and is, but for the exception provided for in this paragraph or paragraph (7), would be an investment company the beneficial ownership shall be deemed to be that of the holders of such company's outstanding securities (other than short-term paper).

(B) Beneficial ownership by any person who acquires securities or interests in securities of an issuer described in the first sentence of this paragraph shall be deemed to be beneficial ownership by the person from whom such transfer was made, pursuant to such rules and regulations as the Commission shall prescribe as necessary or appropriate in the public interest and consistent with the protection of investors and the purposes fairly intended by the policy and provisions of this title, where the transfer was caused by legal separation, divorce, death, or other involuntary event.

(2)(A) Any person primarily engaged in the business of underwriting and distributing securities issued by other persons, selling securities to customers, and acting as broker, and acting as market intermediary or any one or more of such activities, whose gross income normally is derived principally from such business and related activities.

(B) For purposes of this paragraph—

(i) the term "market intermediary" means any person that regularly holds itself out as being willing contemporaneously to engage in, and that is regularly engaged in, the business of entering into transactions on both sides of the market for a financial contract or one or more such financial contracts; and

(ii) the term "financial contract" means any arrangement that—

(I) takes the form of an individually negotiated contract, agreement, or option to buy, sell, lend, swap, or repurchase, or other similar individually negotiated transaction commonly entered into by participants in the financial markets;

(II) is in respect of securities, commodities, currencies, interest or other rates, other measures of value, or any other financial or economic interest similar in purpose or function to any of the foregoing; and

(III) is entered into in response to a request from a counter party for a quotation, or is otherwise entered into and structured to accommodate the objectives of the counter party to such arrangement.

(3) Any bank or insurance company; any savings and loan association, building and loan association, cooperative bank, homestead association, or similar institution, or any receiver, conservator, liquidator, liquidating agent, or similar official or person thereof or therefor; or any common trust fund or similar fund maintained by a bank exclusively for the collective investment and reinvestment of moneys contributed thereto by the bank in its capacity as a trustee, executor, administrator, or guardian, if—

(A) such fund is employed by the bank solely as an aid to the administration of trusts, estates, or other accounts created and maintained for a fiduciary purpose;

(B) except in connection with the ordinary advertising of the bank's fiduciary services, interests in such fund are not—

(i) advertised; or

(ii) offered for sale to the general public; and

(C) fees and expenses charged by such fund are not in contravention of fiduciary principles established under applicable Federal or State law.

(4) Any person substantially all of whose business is confined to making small loans, industrial banking, or similar businesses.

(5) Any person who is not engaged in the business of issuing redeemable securities, face-amount certificates of the installment type or periodic payment plan certificates, and who is primarily engaged in one or more of the following businesses: (A) Purchasing or otherwise acquiring notes, drafts, acceptances, open accounts receivable, and other obligations representing part or all of the sales price of merchandise, insurance, and services; (B) making loans to manufacturers, wholesalers, and retailers of, and to prospective purchasers of, specified merchandise, insurance, and services; and (C) purchasing or otherwise acquiring mortgages and other liens on and interests in real estate.

(6) Any company primarily engaged, directly or through majority-owned subsidiaries, in one or more of the businesses described in paragraphs (3) (4), and (5), or in one or more of such businesses (from which not less than 25 per centum of such company's gross income during its last fiscal year was derived) together with an additional business or businesses other than investing, reinvesting, owning, holding, or trading in securities.

(7)(A) Any issuer, the outstanding securities of which are owned exclusively by persons who, at the time of acquisition of such securities, are qualified purchasers, and which is not making and does not at that time propose to make a public offering of such securities. Securities that are owned by persons who received the securities from a qualified purchaser as a gift or bequest, or in a case in which the transfer was caused by legal separation, divorce, death, or other involuntary event, shall be deemed to be owned by a qualified purchaser, subject to such rules, regulations, and orders as the Commission may prescribe as necessary or appropriate in the public interest or for the protection of investors.

(B) Notwithstanding subparagraph (A), an issuer is within the exception provided by this paragraph if—

(i) in addition to qualified purchasers, outstanding securities of that issuer are beneficially owned by not more than 100 persons who are not qualified purchasers, if—

(I) such persons acquired any portion of the securities of such issuer on or before September 1, 1996; and

(II) at the time at which such persons initially acquired the securities of such issuer, the issuer was excepted by paragraph (1); and

(ii) prior to availing itself of the exception provided by this paragraph—

(I) such issuer has disclosed to each beneficial owner, as determined under paragraph (1), that future investors will be limited to qualified purchasers, and that ownership in such issuer is no longer limited to not more than 100 persons; and

(II) concurrently with or after such disclosure, such issuer has provided each beneficial owner, as determined under paragraph (1), with a reasonable opportunity to redeem any part or all of their interests in the issuer, notwithstanding any agreement to the contrary between the issuer and such persons, for that person's proportionate share of the issuer's net assets.

(C) Each person that elects to redeem under subparagraph (B)(ii)(II) shall receive an amount in cash equal to that person's proportionate share of the issuer's net assets, unless the issuer elects to provide such person with the option of receiving, and such person agrees to receive, all or a portion of such person's share in assets of the issuer. If the issuer elects to provide such persons with such an opportunity, disclosure concerning such opportunity shall be made in the disclosure required by subparagraph (B)(ii)(I).

(D) An issuer that is excepted under this paragraph shall nonetheless be deemed to be an investment company for purposes of the limitations set forth in subparagraphs (A)(i) and (B)(i) of section 12(d)(1) relating to the purchase or other acquisition by such issuer of any security issued by any registered investment company and the sale of any security issued by any registered open-end investment company to any such issuer.

(E) For purposes of determining compliance with this paragraph and paragraph (1), an issuer that is otherwise excepted under this paragraph and an issuer that is otherwise excepted under paragraph (1) shall not be treated by the Commission as being a single issuer for purposes of determining whether the outstanding securities of the issuer excepted under paragraph (1) are beneficially owned by not more than 100 persons or whether the outstanding securities of the issuer excepted under this paragraph are owned by persons that are not qualified purchasers. Nothing in this subparagraph shall be construed to establish that a person is a bona fide qualified purchaser for purposes of this paragraph or a bona fide beneficial owner for purposes of paragraph (1).

(8) Any company subject to regulation under the Public Utility Holding Company Act of 1935.

(9) Any person substantially all of whose business consists of owning or holding oil, gas, or other mineral royalties or leases, or fractional interests therein, or certificates of interest or participation in or investment contracts relative to such royalties, leases, or fractional interests.

(10)(A) Any company organized and operated exclusively for religious, educational, benevolent, fraternal, charitable, or reformatory purposes—

(i) no part of the net earnings of which inures to the benefit of any private shareholder or individual: or

(ii) which is or maintains a fund described in subparagraph (B).

(B) For the purposes of subparagraph (A)(ii), a fund is described in this subparagraph if such fund is a pooled income fund, collective trust fund, collective investment fund, or similar fund maintained by a charitable organization exclusively for the collective investment and reinvestment of one or more of the following:

(i) assets of the general endowment fund or other funds of one or more charitable organizations;

(ii) assets of a pooled income fund;

(iii) assets contributed to a charitable organization in exchange for the issuance of charitable gift annuities;

(iv) assets of a charitable remainder trust or of any other trust, the remainder interests of which are irrevocably dedicated to any charitable organization;

(v) assets of a charitable lead trust;

(vi) assets of a trust, the remainder interests of which are revocably dedicated to or for the benefit of 1 or more charitable organizations, if the ability to revoke the dedication is limited to circumstances involving—

(I) an adverse change in the financial circumstances of a settlor or an income beneficiary of the trust;

(II) a change in the identity of the charitable organization or organizations having the remainder interest, provided that the new beneficiary is also a charitable organization; or

(III) both the changes described in subclauses (I) and (II);

(vii) assets of a trust not described in clauses (i) through (v), the remainder interests of which are revocably dedicated to a charitable organization, subject to subparagraph (C); or

(viii) such assets as the Commission may prescribe by rule, regulation, or order in accordance with section 6(c).

(C) A fund that contains assets described in clause (vii) of subparagraph (B) shall be excluded from the definition of an investment company for a period of 3 years after the date of enactment of this subparagraph, but only if—

(i) such assets were contributed before the date which is 60 days after the date of enactment of this subparagraph; and

(ii) such assets are commingled in the fund with assets described in one or more of clauses (i) through (vi) and (viii) of subparagraph (B).

(D) For purposes of this paragraph—

(i) a trust or fund is "maintained" by a charitable organization if the organization serves as a trustee or administrator of the trust or fund or has the power to remove the trustees or administrators of the trust or fund and to designate new trustees or administrators;

(ii) the term "pooled income fund" has the same meaning as in section 642(c)(5) of the Internal Revenue Code of 1986;

(iii) the term "charitable organization" means an organization described in paragraphs (1) through (5) of section 170(c) or section 501(c)(3) of the Internal Revenue Code of 1986;

(iv) the term "charitable lead trust" means a trust described in section 170(f)(2)(B), 2055(e)(2)(B), or 2522(c)(2)(B) of the Internal Revenue Code of 1986;

(v) the term "charitable remainder trust" means a charitable remainder annuity trust or a charitable remainder unitrust, as those terms are defined in section 664(d) of the Internal Revenue Code of 1986; and

(vi) the term "charitable gift annuity" means an annuity issued by a charitable organization that is described in section 501(m)(5) of the Internal Revenue Code of 1986.

(11) Any employee's stock bonus, pension, or profit-sharing trust which meets the requirements for qualification under section 401 of the Internal Revenue Code of 1986; or any governmental plan described in section 3(a)(2)(C) of the Securities Act of 1933; or any collective trust fund maintained by a bank consisting solely of assets of such trusts or governmental plans, or both; or any separate account the assets of which are derived solely from (A) contributions under pension or profit-sharing plans which meet the requirements of section 401 of the Internal Revenue Code of 1986 or the requirements for deduction of the employer's contribution under section 404(a)(2) of such Code, (B) contributions under governmental plans in connection with which interests, participations, or securities are exempted from the registration provisions of section 5 of the Securities Act of 1933 by section 3(a)(2)(C) of such Act, and (C) advances made by an insurance company in connection with the operation of such separate account.

(12) Any voting trust the assets of which consist exclusively of securities of a single issuer which is not an investment company.

(13) Any security holders' protective committee or similar issuer having outstanding

and issuing no securities other than certificates of deposit and short-term paper.

(14) Any church plan described in section 414(e) of the Internal Revenue Code of 1986, if, under any such plan, no part of the assets may be used for, or diverted to, purposes other than the exclusive benefit of plan participants or beneficiaries, or any company or account that is—

(A) established by a person that is eligible to establish and maintain such a plan under section 414(e) of the Internal Revenue Code of 1986; and

(B) substantially all of the activities of which consist of—

(i) managing or holding assets contributed to such church plans or other assets which are permitted to be commingled with the assets of church plans under the Internal Revenue Code of 1986; or

(ii) administering or providing benefits pursuant to church plans.

Classification of Investment Companies

Sec. 4. For the purposes of this title, investment companies are divided into three principal classes, defined as follows:

(1) "Face-amount certificate company" means an investment company which is engaged or proposes to engage in the business of issuing face-amount certificates of the installment type, or which has been engaged in such business and has any such certificate outstanding.

(2) "Unit investment trust" means an investment company which (A) is organized under a trust indenture, contract of custodianship or agency, or similar instrument, (B) does not have a board of directors, and (C) issues only redeemable securities, each of which represents an undivided interest in a unit of specified securities; but does not include a voting trust.

(3) "Management company" means any investment company other than a face-amount certificate company or a unit investment trust.

Subclassification of Management Companies

Sec. 5. (a) For the purpose of this title, management companies are divided into open-end and closed-end companies, defined as follows:

(1) "Open-end company" means a management company which is offering for sale or has outstanding any redeemable security of which it is the issuer.

(2) "Closed-end company" means any management company other than an open-end company.

(b) Management companies are further divided into diversified companies and non-diversified companies, defined as follows:

(1) "Diversified company" means a management company which meets the following requirements: At least 75 per centum of the value of its total assets is represented by cash and cash items (including receivables), Government securities, securities of other investment companies, and other securities for the purposes of this calculation limited in respect of any one issuer to an amount not greater in value than 5 per centum of the value of the total assets of such management company and to not more than 10 per centum of the outstanding voting securities of such issuer.

(2) "Non-diversified company" means any management company other than a diversified company.

(c) A registered diversified company which at the time of its qualification as such meets the requirements of paragraph (1) and subsection (b) shall not lose its status as a diversified company because of any subsequent discrepancy between the value of its various investments and the requirements of said paragraph, so long as any such discrepancy existing immediately after its acquisition of any security or other property is neither wholly nor partly the result of such acquisition.

Exemptions

Sec. 6. (a) The following investment companies are exempt from the provisions of this title:

(1) Any company organized or otherwise created under the laws of and having its principal office and place of business in Puerto Rico, the Virgin Islands, or any other possession of the United States; but such exemption shall terminate if any security of which such company is the issuer is offered for sale or sold after the effective date of this title, by such company or an underwriter therefor to a resident of any State other than the State in which such company is organized.

(2) Any company which since the effective date of this title or within five years prior to such date has been reorganized under the supervision of a court of competent jurisdiction, if (A) such company was not an investment company at the commencement of such reorganization proceedings, (B) at the conclusion of such proceedings all outstanding securities of such company were owned by creditors of such company or by persons to whom such securities were issued on account of creditors' claims, and (C) more than 50 per centum of the voting securities of such company, and securities representing more than 50 per centum of the net asset value of such company, are currently owned beneficially by not more than twenty-five persons; but such exemption shall terminate if any security of which such company is the issuer is offered for sale or sold to the public after the conclusion of such proceedings by the issuer or by or through any underwriter. For the purposes of this paragraph, any new company organized as part of the reorganization shall be deemed the same company as its predecessor; and beneficial ownership shall be determined in the manner provided in section 3(c)(1).

(3) Any issuer as to which there is outstanding a writing filed with the Commission by the Federal Savings and Loan Insurance Corporation stating that exemption of such issuer from the provisions of this title is consistent with the public interest and the protection of investors and is necessary or appropriate by reason of the fact that such issuer holds or proposes to acquire any assets or any product of any assets which have been segregated (A) from assets of any company which at the filing of such writing is an insured institution within the meaning of section 401(a) of the National Housing Act, as heretofore or hereafter amended, or (B) as a part of or in connection with any plan for or condition to the insurance of accounts of any company by said corporation or the conversion of any company into a Federal savings and loan association. Any such writing shall expire when canceled by a writing similarly filed or at the expiration of two years after the date of its filing, whichever first occurs; but said corporation may, nevertheless, before, at, or after the expiration of any such writing file another writing or writings with respect to such issuer.

(4) Any company which prior to March 15, 1940, was and now is a wholly-owned subsidiary of a registered face-amount certificate company and was prior to said date and now is organized and operating under the insurance laws of any State and subject to supervision and examination by the insurance commissioner thereof, and which prior to March 15, 1940, was and now is engaged, subject to such laws, in business substantially all of which consists of issuing and selling only to residents of such State and investing the proceeds from, securities providing for or representing participations or interests in tangible assets consisting of mortgages or other liens on real estate or notes or bonds secured thereby or in a fund or deposit of mortgages or other liens on real estate or notes or bonds secured thereby or having outstanding such securities so issued and sold.

(5)(A) Any company that is not engaged in the business of issuing redeemable securities, the operations of which are subject to regulation by the State in which the company is organized under a statute governing entities that provide financial or managerial assistance to enterprises doing business, or proposing to do business, in that State if—

(i) the organizational documents of the company state that the activities of the company are limited to the promotion of economic, business, or industrial development in the State through the provision of financial or managerial assistance to enterprises doing business, or proposing to do business, in that State, and such other activities that are incidental or necessary to carry out that purpose;

(ii) immediately following each sale of the securities of the company by the company or any underwriter for the company, not less than 80 percent of the securities of the company being offered in such sale, on a class-by-class basis, are held by persons who reside or who have a substantial business presence in that State;

(iii) the securities of the company are sold, or proposed to be sold, by the company or by any underwriter for the company, solely to accredited investors, as that term is defined in section 2(a)(15) of the Securities Act of 1933, or to such other persons that the Commission, as necessary or appropriate in the public interest and consistent with the protection of investors, may permit by rule, regulation, or order; and

(iv) the company does not purchase any security issued by an investment company or by any company that would be an investment company except for the exclusions from the definition of the term "investment company" under paragraph (1) or (7) of section 3(c), other than—

(I) any debt security that is rated investment grade by not less than 1 nationally recognized statistical rating organization; or

(II) any security issued by a registered open-end investment company that is required by its investment policies to invest not less than 65 percent of its total assets in securities described in subclause (I) or securities that are determined by such registered open-end investment company to be comparable in quality to securities described in subclause (I).

(B) Notwithstanding the exemption provided by this paragraph, section 9 (and, to the extent necessary to enforce section 9, sections 38 through 51) shall apply to a company described in this paragraph as if the company were an investment company registered under this title.

(C) Any company proposing to rely on the exemption provided by this paragraph shall file with the Commission a notification stating that the company intends to do so, in such form and manner as the Commission may prescribe by rule.

(D) Any company meeting the requirements of this paragraph may rely on the exemption provided by this paragraph upon filing with the Commission the notification required by subparagraph (C), until such time as the Commission determines by order that such reliance is not in the public interest or is not consistent with the protection of investors.

(E) The exemption provided by this paragraph may be subject to such additional terms and conditions as the Commission may by rule, regulation, or order determine are necessary or appropriate in the public interest or for the protection of investors.

(b) Upon application by any employees' security company, the Commission shall by order exempt such company from the provisions of this title and of the rules and regulations hereunder, if and to the extent that such exemption is consistent with the protection of investors. In determining the provisions to which such an order of exemption shall apply, the Commission shall give due weight, among other things, to the form of organization and the capital structure of such company, the persons by whom its voting securities, evidences of indebtedness, and other securities are owned and controlled, the prices at which securities issued by such company are sold and the sales load thereon, the disposition of the proceeds of such sales, the character of the securities in which such proceeds are invested, and any relationship between such company and the issuer of any such security.

(c) The Commission, by rules and regulations upon its own motion, or by order upon application, may conditionally or unconditionally exempt any person, security, or transaction, or any class or classes of persons, securities, or transactions, from any provision or provisions of this title or of any rule or regulation thereunder, if and to the extent that such exemption is necessary or appropriate in the public interest and consistent with the protection of investors and the purposes fairly intended by the policy and provisions of this title.

(d) The Commission, by rules and regulations or order, shall exempt a closed-end investment company from any or all provisions of this title, but subject to such terms and conditions as may be necessary or appropriate in the public interest or for the protection of investors, if—

(1) the aggregate sums received by such company from the sale of all its outstanding securities, plus the aggregate offering price of all securities of which such company is the issuer and which it proposes to offer for sale, do not exceed $10,000,000, or such other amount as the Commission may set by rule, regulation, or order.

(2) no security of which such company is the issuer has been or is proposed to be sold by such company or any underwriter therefor, in connection with a public offering, to any person who is not a resident of the State under the laws of which such company is organized or otherwise created; and

(3) such exemption is not contrary to the public interest or inconsistent with the protection of investors.

(e) If, in connection with any rule, regulation, or order under this section exempting any investment company from any provision of section 7, the Commission deems it necessary or appropriate in the public interest or for the protection of investors that certain specified provisions of this title pertaining to registered investment companies shall be applicable in respect of such company, the provisions so specified shall apply to such company, and to other persons in their transactions and relations with such company, as though such company were a registered investment company.

(f) Any closed-end company which—

(1) elects to be treated as a business development company pursuant to section 54; or

(2) would be excluded from the definition of an investment company by section 3(c)(1), except that it presently proposes to make a public offering of its securities as a business development company, and has notified the Commission, in a form and manner which the Commission may, by rule, prescribe, that it intends in good faith to file, within 90 days, a notification of election to become subject to the provisions of sections 55 through 65,

shall be exempt from sections 1 through 53, except to the extent provided in sections 59 through 65.

Transactions by Unregistered Investment Companies

Sec. 7. (a) No investment company organized or otherwise created under the laws of the United States or of a State and having a board of directors, unless registered under section 8, shall directly or indirectly—

(1) offer for sale, sell, or deliver after sale, by the use of the mails or any means or

instrumentality of interstate commerce, any security or any interest in a security, whether the issuer of such security is such investment company or another person; or offer for sale, sell, or deliver after sale any such security or interest, having reason to believe that such security or interest will be made the subject of a public offering by use of the mails or any means or instrumentality of interstate commerce;

(2) purchase, redeem, retire, or otherwise acquire or attempt to acquire, by use of the mails or any means or instrumentality of interstate commerce, any security or any interest in a security, whether the issuer of such security is such investment company or another person;

(3) control any investment company which does any of the acts enumerated in paragraphs (1) and (2);

(4) engage in any business in interstate commerce; or

(5) control any company which is engaged in any business in interstate commerce.

The provisions of this subsection (a) shall not apply to transactions of an investment company which are merely incidental to its dissolution.

(b) No depositor or trustee of or underwriter for any investment company, organized or otherwise created under the laws of the United States or of a State and not having a board of directors, unless such company is registered under section 8 or exempt under section 6, shall directly or indirectly—

(1) offer for sale, sell, or deliver after sale, by use of the mails or any means or instrumentality of interstate commerce, any security or any interest in a security of which such company is the issuer; or offer for sale, sell, or deliver after sale any such security or interest, having reason to believe that such security or interest will be made the subject of a public offering by use of the mails or any means or instrumentality of interstate commerce;

(2) purchase, redeem, or otherwise acquire or attempt to acquire, by use of the mails or any means or instrumentality of interstate commerce, any security or any interest in a security of which such company is the issuer; or

(3) sell or purchase for the account of such company, by use of the mails or any means or instrumentality of interstate commerce, any security or interest in a security, by whomever issued.

The provisions of this subsection (b) shall not apply to transactions which are merely incidental to the dissolution of an investment company.

(c) No promoter of a proposed investment company, and no underwriter for such a promoter, shall make use of the mails or any means or instrumentality of interstate commerce, directly or indirectly, to offer for sale, sell, or deliver after sale, in connection with a public offering, any preorganization certificate or subscription for such a company.

(d) No investment company, unless organized or otherwise created under the laws of the United States or of a State, and no depositor or trustee of or underwriter for such a company not so organized or created, shall make use of the mails or any means or instrumentality of interstate commerce, directly or indirectly, to offer for sale, sell, or deliver after sale, in connection with a public offering, any security of which such company is the issuer. Notwithstanding the provisions of this subsection and of section 8(a), the Commission is authorized, upon application by an investment company organized or otherwise created under the laws of a foreign country, to issue a conditional or unconditional order permitting such company to register under this title and to make a public offering of its securities by use of the mails and means or instrumentalities of interstate commerce, if the Commission finds that, by reason of special circumstances or arrangements, it is both legally and practically feasible effectively to enforce the provisions of this title against such company and that the issuance of such order is otherwise consistent with the public interest and the protection of investors.

(e) Disclosure by exempt charitable organizations.—Each fund that is excluded from the definition of an investment company under section 3(c)(10)(B) of this Act shall provide, to each donor to such fund, at the time of the donation or within 90 days after the date of enactment of this subsection, whichever is later, written information describing the material terms of the operation of such fund.

Registration of Investment Companies

Sec. 8. (a) Any investment company organized or otherwise created under the laws of the United States or of a State may register for the purposes of this title by filing with the Commission a notification of registration in such form as the Commission shall by rules and regulations prescribe as necessary or appropriate in the public interest or for the protection of investors. An investment company shall be deemed to be registered upon receipt by the Commission of such notification of registration.

(b) Every registered investment company shall file with the Commission, within such reasonable time after registration as the Commission shall fix by rules and regulations, an original and such copies of a registration statement, in such form and containing such of the following information and documents as the Commission shall by rules and regulations prescribe as necessary or appropriate in the public interest or for the protection of investors:

(1) a recital of the policy of the registrant in respect of each of the following types of activities, such recital consisting in each case of a statement whether the registrant reserves freedom of action to engage in activities of such type, and if such freedom of action is reserved, a statement briefly indicating, insofar as is practicable, the extent to which the registrant intends to engage therein: (A) the classification and subclassification, as defined in sections 4 and 5, within which the registrant proposes to operate; (B) borrowing money; (C) the issuance of senior securities; (D) engaging in the business of underwriting securities issued by other persons; (E) concentrating investments in a particular industry or group of industries; (F) the purchase and sale of real estate and commodities, or either of them; (G) making loans to other persons; and (H) portfolio turn-over (including a statement showing the aggregate dollar amount of purchases and sales of portfolio securities, other than Government securities, in each of the last three full fiscal years preceding the filing of such registration statement);

(2) a recital of all investment policies of the registrant, not enumerated in paragraph (1), which are changeable only if authorized by shareholder vote;

(3) a recital of all policies of the registrant, not enumerated in paragraphs (1) and (2), in respect of matters which the registrant deems matters of fundamental policy;

(4) the name and address of each affiliated person of the registrant; the name and principal address of every company, other than the registrant, of which each such person is an officer, director, or partner; a brief statement of the business experience for the preceding five years of each officer and director of the registrant; and

(5) the information and documents which would be required to be filed in order to register under the Securities Act of 1933 and the Securities Exchange Act of 1934 all securities (other than short-term paper) which the registrant has outstanding or proposes to issue.

(c) The Commission shall make provision, by permissive rules and regulations or order, for the filing of the following, or so much of the following as the Commission may designate, in lieu of the information and documents required pursuant to subsection (b):

(1) copies of the most recent registration statement filed by the registrant under the Securities Act of 1933 and currently effec-

tive under such Act, or if the registrant has not filed such a statement, copies of a registration statement filed by the registrant under the Securities Exchange Act of 1934 and currently effective under such Act;

(2) copies of any reports filed by the registrant pursuant to section 13 or 15(d) of the Securities Exchange Act of 1934; and

(3) a report containing reasonably current information regarding the matters included in copies filed pursuant to paragraphs (1) and (2), and such further information regarding matters not included in such copies as the Commission is authorized to require under subsection (b).

(d) If the registrant is a unit investment trust substantially all of the assets of which are securities issued by another registered investment company, the Commission is authorized to prescribe for the registrant, by rules and regulations or order, a registration statement which eliminates inappropriate duplication of information contained in the registration statement filed under this section by such other investment company.

(e) If it appears to the Commission that a registered investment company has failed to file the registration statement required by this section or a report required pursuant to section 30(a) or (b), or has filed such a registration statement or report but omitted therefrom material facts required to be stated therein, or has filed such a registration statement or report in violation of section 34(b), the Commission shall notify such company by registered mail or certified mail of the failure to file such registration statement or report, or of the respects in which such registration statement or report appears to be materially incomplete or misleading, as the case may be, and shall fix a date (in no event earlier than thirty days after the mailing of such notice) prior to which such company may file such registration statement or report or correct the same. If such registration statement or report is not filed or corrected within the time so fixed by the Commission or any extension thereof, the Commission, after appropriate notice and opportunity for hearing, and upon such conditions and with such exemptions as it deems appropriate for the protection of investors, may by order suspend the registration of such company until such statement or report is filed or corrected, or may by order revoke such registration, if the evidence establishes—

(1) that such company has failed to file a registration statement required by this section or a report required pursuant to section 30(a) or (b), or has filed such a registration statement or report but omitted therefrom material facts required to be stated therein, or has filed such a registration statement or report in violation of section 34(b); and

(2) that such suspension or revocation is in the public interest.

(f) Whenever the Commission, on its own motion or upon application, finds that a registered investment company has ceased to be an investment company, it shall so declare by order and upon the taking effect of such order the registration of such company shall cease to be in effect. If necessary for the protection of investors, an order under this subsection may be made upon appropriate conditions. The Commission's denial of any application under this subsection shall be by order.

Ineligibility of Certain Affiliated Persons and Underwriters

Sec. 9. (a) It shall be unlawful for any of the following persons to serve or act in the capacity of employee, officer, director, member of an advisory board, investment adviser, or depositor of any registered investment company, or principal underwriter for any registered open-end company, registered unit investment trust, or registered face-amount certificate company:

(1) any person who within 10 years has been convicted of any felony or misdemeanor involving the purchase or sale of any security or arising out of such person's conduct as an underwriter, broker, dealer, investment adviser, municipal securities

dealer, government securities broker, government securities dealer, bank, transfer agent or entity or person required to be registered under the Commodity Exchange Act, or as an affiliated person, salesman, or employee of any investment company, bank, insurance company, or entity or person required to be registered under the Commodity Exchange Act;

(2) any person who, by reason of any misconduct, is permanently or temporarily enjoined by order, judgment, or decree of any court of competent jurisdiction from acting as an underwriter, broker, dealer, bank, investment adviser, municipal securities dealer, government securities broker, government securities dealer, bank, transfer agent or entity or person required to be registered under the Commodity Exchange Act, or as an affiliated person, salesman, or employee of any investment company, bank, insurance company, or entity or person required to be registered under the Commodity Exchange Act, or from engaging in or continuing any conduct or practice in connection with any such activity or in connection with the purchase or sale of any security; or

(3) a company any affiliated person of which is ineligible, by reason of paragraph (1) or (2), to serve or act in the foregoing capacities.

For the purposes of paragraphs (1), (2), and (3) of this subsection, the term "investment adviser" shall include an investment adviser as defined in title II of this Act.

(b) The Commission may, after notice and opportunity for hearing, by order prohibit, conditionally or unconditionally, either permanently or for such period of time as it in its discretion shall deem appropriate in the public interest, any person from serving or acting as an employee, officer, director, member of an advisory board, investment adviser or depositor of, or principal underwriter for, a registered investment company or affiliated person of such investment adviser, depositor, or principal underwriter, if such person—

(1) has willfully made or caused to be made in any registration statement, application or report filed with the Commission under this title any statement which was at the time and in the light of the circumstances under which it was made false or misleading with respect to any material fact, or has omitted to state in any such registration statement, application, or report any material fact which was required to be stated therein;

(2) has willfully violated any provision of the Securities Act of 1933, or of the Securities Exchange Act of 1934, or of title II of this Act, or of this title, or of the Commodity Exchange Act, or of any rule or regulation under any of such statutes;

(3) has willfully aided, abetted, counseled, commanded, induced, or procured the violation by any other person of the Securities Act of 1933, or of the Securities Exchange Act of 1934, or of title II of this Act, or of this title, or of the Commodity Exchange Act, or of any rule or regulation under any of such statutes;

(4) has been found by a foreign financial regulatory authority to have—

(A) made or caused to be made in any application for registration or report required to be filed with a foreign securities authority, or in any proceeding before a foreign securities authority with respect to registration, any statement that was at the time and in light of the circumstances under which it was made false or misleading with respect to any material fact, or has omitted to state in any application or report to a foreign securities authority any material fact that is required to be stated therein;

(B) violated any foreign statute or regulation regarding transactions in securities or contracts of sale of a commodity for future delivery traded on or subject to the rules of a contract market or any board of trade;

(C) aided, abetted, counseled, commanded, induced, or procured the violation by any other person of any foreign statute or regulation regarding transactions in securities or contracts of sale of a commodity for future delivery traded on or subject to the rules of a contract market or any board of trade;

(5) within 10 years has been convicted by a foreign court of competent jurisdiction of a crime, however denominated by the laws of the relevant foreign government, that is substantially equivalent to an offense set forth in paragraph (1) of subsection (a); or

(6) by reason of any misconduct, is temporarily or permanently enjoined by any foreign court of competent jurisdiction from acting in any of the capacities, set forth in paragraph (2) of subsection (a), or a substantially equivalent foreign capacity, or from engaging in or continuing any conduct or practice in connection with any such activity or in connection with the purchase or sale of any security.

(c) Any person who is ineligible, by reason of subsection (a), to serve or act in the capacities enumerated in that subsection, may file with the Commission an application for an exemption from the provisions of that subsection. The Commission shall by order grant such application, either unconditionally or on an appropriate temporary or other conditional basis, if it is established that the prohibitions of subsection (a), as applied to such person, are unduly or disproportionately severe or that the conduct of such person has been such as not to make it against the public interest or protection of investors to grant such application.

(d) *Money penalties in administrative proceedings.*—

(1) *Authority of Commission.*—In any proceeding instituted pursuant to subsection (b) against any person, the Commission may impose a civil penalty if it finds, on the record after notice and opportunity for hearing, that such person—

(A) has willfully violated any provision of the Securities Act of 1933, the Securities Exchange Act of 1934, the Investment Advisers Act of 1940, or this title, or the rules or regulations thereunder;

(B) has willfully aided, abetted, counseled, commanded, induced, or procured such a violation by any other person; or

(C) has willfully made or caused to be made in any registration statement, application, or report required to be filed with the Commission under this title, any statement which was, at the time and in the light of the circumstances under which it was made false or misleading with respect to any material fact, or has omitted to state in any such registration statement, application, or report any material fact which was required to be stated therein;

and that such penalty is in the public interest.

(2) *Maximum amount of penalty.*—

(A) *First tier.*—The maximum amount of penalty for each act or omission described in paragraph (1) shall be $5,000 for a natural person or $50,000 for any other person.

(B) *Second tier.*—Notwithstanding subparagraph (A), the maximum amount of penalty for each such act or omission shall be $50,000 for a natural person or $250,000 for any other person if the act or omission described in paragraph (1) involved fraud, deceit, manipulation, or deliberate or reckless disregard of a regulatory requirement.

(C) *Third tier.*—Notwithstanding subparagraphs (A) and (B), the maximum amount of penalty for each such act or omission shall be $100,000 for a natural person or $500,000 for any other person if—

(i) the act or omission described in paragraph (1) involved fraud, deceit, manipulation, or deliberate or reckless disregard of a regulatory requirement; and

(ii) such act or omission directly or indirectly resulted in substantial losses or created a significant risk of substantial losses to other persons or resulted in substantial pecuniary gain to the person who committed the act or omission.

(3) *Determination of public interest.*—In considering under this section whether a penalty is in the public interest, the Commission may consider—

(A) whether the act or omission for which such penalty is assessed involved fraud, deceit, manipulation, or deliberate or reckless disregard of a regulatory requirement;

(B) the harm to other persons resulting either directly or indirectly from such act or omission;

(C) the extent to which any person was unjustly enriched, taking into account any restitution made to persons injured by such behavior;

(D) whether such person previously has been found by the Commission, another appropriate regulatory agency, or a self-regulatory organization to have violated the Federal securities laws, State securities laws, or the rules of a self-regulatory organization, has been enjoined by a court of competent jurisdiction from violations of such laws or rules, or has been convicted by a court of competent jurisdiction of violations of such laws or of any felony or misdemeanor described in section 203(e)(2) of the Investment Advisers Act of 1940;

(E) the need to deter such person and other persons from committing such acts or omissions; and

(F) such other matters as justice may require.

(4) *Evidence concerning ability to pay.*—In any proceeding in which the Commission may impose a penalty under this section, a respondent may present evidence of the respondent's ability to pay such penalty. The Commission may, in its discretion, consider such evidence in determining whether such penalty is in the public interest. Such evidence may relate to the extent of such person's ability to continue in business and the collectability of a penalty, taking into account any other claims of the United States or third parties upon such person's assets and the amount of such person's assets.

(e) *Authority to enter an order requiring an accounting and disgorgement.*—In any proceeding in which the Commission may impose a penalty under this section, the Commission may enter an order requiring accounting and disgorgement, including reasonable interest. The Commission is authorized to adopt rules, regulations, and orders concerning payments to investors, rates of interest, periods of accrual, and such other matters as it deems appropriate to implement this subsection.

(f) *Cease-and-desist proceedings.*—

(1) *Authority of the Commission.*—If the Commission finds, after notice and opportunity for hearing, that any person is violating, has violated, or is about to violate any provision of this title, or any rule or regulation thereunder, the Commission may publish its findings and enter an order requiring such person, and any other person that is, was, or would be a cause of the violation, due to an act or omission the person knew or should have known would contribute to such violation, to cease and desist from committing or causing such violation and any future violation of the same provision, rule, or regulation. Such order may, in addition to requiring a person to cease and desist from committing or causing a violation, require such person to comply, or to take steps to effect compliance, with such provision, rule, or regulation, upon such terms and conditions and within such time as the Commission may specify in such order. Any such order may, as the Commission deems appropriate, require future compliance or steps to effect future compliance, either permanently or for such period of time as the Commission may specify, with such provision, rule, or regulation with respect to any security, any issuer, or any other person.

(2) *Hearing.*—The notice instituting proceedings pursuant to paragraph (1) shall fix a hearing date not earlier than 30 days nor later

than 60 days after service of the notice unless an earlier or a later date is set by the Commission with the consent of any respondent so served.

(3) *Temporary order.*—

(A) *In general.*—Whenever the Commission determines that the alleged violation or threatened violation specified in the notice instituting proceedings pursuant to paragraph (1), or the continuation thereof, is likely to result in significant dissipation or conversion of assets, significant harm to investors, or substantial harm to the public interest, including, but not limited to, losses to the Securities Investor Protection Corporation, prior to the completion of the proceeding, the Commission may enter a temporary order requiring the respondent to cease and desist from the violation or threatened violation and to take such action to prevent the violation or threatened violation and to prevent dissipation or conversion of assets, significant harm to investors, or substantial harm to the public interest as the Commission deems appropriate pending completion of such proceedings. Such an order shall be entered only after notice and opportunity for a hearing, unless the Commission, notwithstanding section 40(a) of this title, determines that notice and hearing prior to entry would be impracticable or contrary to the public interest. A temporary order shall become effective upon service upon the respondent and, unless set aside, limited, or suspended by the Commission or a court of competent jurisdiction, shall remain effective and enforceable pending the completion of the proceedings.

(B) *Applicability.*—This paragraph shall apply only to a respondent that acts, or, at the time of the alleged misconduct acted, as a broker, dealer, investment adviser, investment company, municipal securities dealer, government securities broker, government securities dealer, or transfer agent, or is, or was at the time of the alleged misconduct, an associated person of, or a person seeking to become associated with, any of the foregoing.

(4) *Review of temporary orders.*—

(A) *Commission review.*—At any time after the respondent has been served with a temporary cease-and-desist order pursuant to paragraph (3), the respondent may apply to the Commission to have the order set aside, limited, or suspended. If the respondent has been served with a temporary cease-and-desist order entered without a prior Commission hearing, the respondent may, within 10 days after the date on which the order was served, request a hearing on such application and the Commission shall hold a hearing and render a decision on such application at the earliest possible time.

(B) *Judicial review.*—Within—

(i) 10 days after the date the respondent was served with a temporary cease-and-desist order entered with a prior Commission hearing, or

(ii) 10 days after the Commission renders a decision on an application and hearing under subparagraph (A), with respect to any temporary cease-and-desist order entered without a prior Commission hearing.

the respondent may apply to the United States district court for the district in which the respondent resides or has its principal place of business, or for the District of Columbia, for an order setting aside, limiting, or suspending the effectiveness or enforcement of the order, and the court shall have jurisdiction to enter such an order. A respondent served with a temporary cease-and-desist order entered without a prior Commission hearing may not apply to the court except after hearing and decision by the Commission on the respondent's application under subparagraph (A) of this paragraph.

(C) *No automatic stay of temporary order.*—The commencement of proceedings under subparagraph (B) of this paragraph shall not, unless specifically ordered by the court, operate as a stay of the Commission's order.

(D) *Exclusive review.*—Section 43 of this title shall not apply to a temporary order entered pursuant to this section.

(5) *Authority to enter an order requiring an accounting and disgorgement.*—In any cease-and-desist proceeding under subsection (f)(1), the Commission may enter an order requiring accounting and disgorgement, including reasonable interest. The Commission is authorized to adopt rules, regulations, and orders concerning payments to investors, rates of interest, periods of accrual, and such other matters as it deems appropriate to implement this subsection.

(g) For the purposes of this section, the term "investment adviser" includes a corporate or other trustee performing the functions of an investment adviser.

Affiliations of Directors

Sec. 10. (a) No registered investment company shall have a board of directors more than 60 percentum of the members of which are persons who are interested persons of such registered company.

(b) No registered investment company shall—

(1) employ as regular broker any director, officer, or employee of such registered company, or any person of which any such director, officer, or employee is an affiliated person, unless a majority of the board of directors of such registered company shall be persons who are not such brokers or affiliated persons of any of such brokers;

(2) use as a principal underwriter of securities issued by it any director, officer, or employee of such registered company or any person of which any such director, officer, or employee is an interested person, unless a majority of the board of directors of such registered company shall be persons who are not such principal underwriters or interested persons of any of such principal underwriters; or

(3) have as director, officer, or employee any investment banker, or any affiliated person of an investment banker, unless a majority of the board of directors of such registered company shall be persons who are not investment bankers or affiliated persons of any investment banker. For the purposes of this paragraph, a person shall not be deemed an affiliated person of an investment banker solely by reason of the fact that he is an affiliated person of a company of the character described in section 12(d)(3)(A) and (B).

(c) No registered investment company shall have a majority of its board of directors consisting of persons who are officers, directors or employees of any one bank (together with its affiliates and subsidiaries) or any one bank holding company (together with its affiliates and subsidiaries) (as such terms are defined in section 2 of the Bank Holding Company Act of 1956), except that, if on March 15, 1940, any registered investment company had a majority of its directors consisting of persons who are directors, officers, or employees of any one bank, such company may continue to have the same percentage of its board of directors consisting of persons who are directors, officers, or employees of such bank.

(d) Notwithstanding subsections (a) and (b)(2) of this section, a registered investment company may have a board of directors all the members of which, except one, are interested persons of the investment adviser of such company, or are officers or employees of such company, if—

(1) such investment company is an open-end company;

(2) such investment adviser is registered under title II of this Act and is engaged principally in the business of rendering investment supervisory services as defined in title II;

(3) no sales load is charged on securities issued by such investment company;

(4) any premium over net asset value charged by such company upon the issuance of any such security, plus any discount from

net asset value charged on redemption thereof, shall not in the aggregate exceed 2 per centum;

(5) no sales or promotion expenses are incurred by such registered company; but expenses incurred in complying with laws regulating the issue or sale of securities shall not be deemed sales or promotion expenses;

(6) such investment adviser is the only investment adviser to such investment company, and such investment adviser does not receive a management fee exceeding 1 per centum per annum of the value of such company's net assets averaged over the year or taken as of a definite date or dates within the year;

(7) all executive salaries and executive expenses and office rent of such investment company are paid by such investment adviser; and

(8) such investment company has only one class of securities outstanding, each unit of which has equal voting rights with every other unit.

(e) If by reason of the death, disqualification, or bona fide resignation of any director or directors, the requirements of the foregoing provisions of this section or of section 15(f)(1) in respect of directors shall not be met by a registered investment company, the operation of such provisions shall be suspended as to such registered company—

(1) for a period of thirty days if the vacancy or vacancies may be filled by action of the board of directors;

(2) for a period of sixty days if a vote of stockholders is required to fill the vacancy or vacancies; or

(3) for such longer period as the Commission may prescribe, by rules and regulations upon its own motion or by order upon application, as not inconsistent with the protection of investors.

(f) No registered investment company shall knowingly purchase or otherwise acquire, during the existence of any underwriting or selling syndicate, any security (except a security of which such company is the issuer) a principal underwriter of which is an officer, director, member of an advisory board, investment adviser, or employee of such registered company, or is a person (other than a company of the character described in section 12(d)(3)(A) and (B)) of which any such officer, director, member of an advisory board, investment adviser, or employee is an affiliated person, unless in acquiring such security such registered company is itself acting as a principal underwriter for the issuer. The Commission, by rules and regulations upon its own motion or by order upon application, may conditionally or unconditionally exempt any transaction or classes of transactions from any of the provisions of this subsection, if and to the extent that such exemption is consistent with the protection of investors.

(g) In the case of a registered investment company which has an advisory board, such board, as a distinct entity, shall be subject to the same restrictions as to its membership as are imposed upon a board of directors by this section.

(h) In the case of a registered management company which is an unincorporated company not having a board of directors, the provisions of this section shall apply as follows:

(1) the provisions of subsection (a), as modified by subsection (e), shall apply to the board of directors of the depositor of such company;

(2) the provisions of subsections (b) and (c), as modified by subsection (e), shall apply to the board of directors of the depositor and of every investment adviser of such company; and

(3) the provisions of subsection (f) shall apply to purchases and other acquisitions for the account of such company of securities a principal underwriter of which is the depositor or an investment adviser of such compa-

ny, or an affiliated person of such depositor or investment adviser.

Offers of Exchange

Sec. 11. (a) It shall be unlawful for any registered open-end company or any principal underwriter for such a company to make or cause to be made an offer to the holder of a security of such company or of any other open-end investment company to exchange his security for a security in the same or another such company on any basis other than the relative net asset values of the respective securities to be exchanged, unless the terms of the offer have first been submitted to and approved by the Commission or are in accordance with such rules and regulations as the Commission may have prescribed in respect of such offers which are in effect at the time such offer is made. For the purposes of this section, (A) an offer by a principal underwriter means an offer communicated to holders of securities of a class or series but does not include an offer made by such principal underwriter to an individual investor in the course of a retail business conducted by such principal underwriter, and (B) the net asset value means the net asset value which is in effect for the purpose of determining the price at which the securities, or class or series of securities involved, are offered for sale to the public either (1) at the time of the receipt by the offeror of the acceptance of the offer or (2) at such later times as is specified in the offer.

(b) The provisions of this section shall not apply to any offer made pursuant to any plan of reorganization, which is submitted to and requires the approval of the holders of at least a majority of the outstanding shares of the class or series to which the security owned by the offeree belongs.

(c) The provisions of subsection (a) shall be applicable, irrespective of the basis of exchange, (1) to any offer of exchange of any security of a registered open-end company for a security of a registered unit investment trust or registered face-amount certificate company; and (2) to any type of offer of exchange of the securities of registered unit investment trusts or registered face-amount certificate companies for the securities of any other investment company.

Functions and Activities of Investment Companies

Sec. 12. (a) It shall be unlawful for any registered investment company, in contravention of such rules and regulations or orders as the Commission may prescribe as necessary or appropriate in the public interest or for the protection of investors—

(1) to purchase any security on margin except such short-term credits as are necessary for the clearance of transactions;

(2) to participate on a joint or a joint and several basis in any trading account in securities, except in connection with an underwriting in which such registered company is a participant; or

(3) to effect a short sale of any security, except in connection with an underwriting in which such registered company is a participant.

(b) It shall be unlawful for any registered open-end company (other than a company complying with the provisions of section 10(d)) to act as a distributor of securities of which it is the issuer, except through an underwriter, in contravention of such rules and regulations as the Commission may prescribe as necessary or appropriate in the public interest or for the protection of investors.

(c) It shall be unlawful for any registered diversified company to make any commitment as underwriter, if immediately thereafter the amount of its outstanding underwriting commitments, plus the value of its investments in securities of issuers (other than investment companies) of which it owns more than 10 per centum of the outstanding voting securities, exceeds 25 per centum of the value of its total assets.

(d)(1)(A) It shall be unlawful for any registered investment company (the "acquiring company") and any company or companies controlled by such acquiring company to purchase or otherwise acquire any security issued by any other investment company (the "acquired company"), and for any investment company (the "acquiring company") and any company or companies controlled by such acquiring company to purchase or otherwise acquire any security issued by any registered investment company (the "acquired company"), if the acquiring company and any company or companies controlled by it immediately after such purchase or acquisition own in the aggregate—

(i) more than three per centum of the total outstanding voting stock of the acquired company;

(ii) securities issued by the acquired company having an aggregate value in excess of five per centum of the value of the total assets of the acquiring company; or

(iii) securities issued by the acquired company and all other investment companies (other than treasury stock of the acquiring company) having an aggregate value in excess of ten per centum of the value of the total assets of the acquiring company.

(B) It shall be unlawful for any registered open-end investment company (the "acquired company"), any principal underwriter therefor, or any broker or dealer registered under the Securities Exchange Act of 1934, knowingly to sell or otherwise dispose of any security issued by the acquired company to any other investment company (the "acquiring company") or any company or companies controlled by the acquiring company, if immediately after such sale or disposition—

(i) more than three per centum of the total outstanding voting stock of the acquired company is owned by the acquiring company or any company or companies controlled by it; or

(ii) more than ten per centum of the total outstanding voting stock of the acquired company is owned by the acquiring company and other investment companies and companies controlled by them.

(C) It shall be unlawful for any investment company (the "acquiring company") and any company or companies controlled by the acquiring company to purchase or otherwise acquire any security issued by a registered closed-end investment company, if immediately after such purchase or acquisition the acquiring company, other investment companies having the same investment adviser, and companies controlled by such investment companies, own more than ten per centum of the total outstanding voting stock of such closed-end company.

(D) The provisions of this paragraph shall not apply to a security received as a dividend or as a result of an offer of exchange approved pursuant to section 11 or of a plan of reorganization of any company (other than a plan devised for the purpose of evading the foregoing provisions).

(E) The provisions of this paragraph shall not apply to a security (or securities) purchased or acquired by an investment company if—

(i) the depositor of, or principal underwriter for, such investment company is a broker or dealer registered under the Securities Exchange Act of 1934, or a person controlled by such broker or dealer;

(ii) such security is the only investment security held by such investment company (or such securities are the only investment securities held by such investment company, if such investment company is a registered unit investment trust that issues two or more classes or series of securities, each of which provides for the accumulation of shares of a different investment company); and

(iii) the purchase or acquisition is made pursuant to an arrangement with the issuer of, or principal underwriter for the issuer of, the security whereby such investment company is obligated—

(aa) either to seek instructions from its security holders with regard to the voting of all proxies with respect to such security and to vote such proxies only in accordance with such instructions, or to vote the shares held by it in the same proportion as the vote of all other holders of such security, and

(bb) in the event that such investment company is not a registered investment company to refrain from substituting such security unless the Commission shall have approved such substitution in the manner provided in section 26 of this Act.

(F) The provisions of this paragraph shall not apply to securities purchased or otherwise acquired by a registered investment company if—

(i) immediately after such purchase or acquisition not more than three per centum of the total outstanding stock of such issuer is owned by such registered investment company and all affiliated persons of such registered investment company; and

(ii) such registered investment company has not offered or sold after January 1, 1971, and is not proposing to offer or sell any security issued by it through a principal underwriter or otherwise at a public offering price which includes a sales load of more than one and one half per centum.

No issuer of any security purchased or acquired by a registered investment company pursuant to this subparagraph shall be obligated to redeem such security in an amount exceeding 1 per centum of such issuer's total outstanding securities during any period of less than thirty days. Such investment company shall exercise voting rights by proxy or otherwise with respect to any security purchased or acquired pursuant to this subparagraph in the manner prescribed by subparagraph (E) of this subsection.

(G)(i) This paragraph does not apply to securities of a registered open-end investment company or a registered unit investment trust (hereafter in this subparagraph referred to as the "acquired company") purchased or otherwise acquired by a registered open-end investment company or a registered unit investment trust (hereafter in this subparagraph referred to as the "acquiring company") if—

(I) the acquired company and the acquiring company are part of the same group of investment companies;

(II) the securities of the acquired company, securities of other registered open-end investment companies and registered unit investment trusts that are part of the same group of investment companies, Government securities, and short-term paper are the only investments held by the acquiring company;

(III) with respect to—

(aa) securities of the acquired company, the acquiring company does not pay and is not assessed any charges or fees for distribution-related activities, unless the acquiring company does not charge a sales load or other fees or charges for distribution-related activities; or

(bb) securities of the acquiring company, any sales loads and other distribution-related fees charged, when aggregated with any sales load and distribution-related fees paid by the acquiring company with respect to securities of the acquired company, are not excessive under rules adopted pursuant to section 22(b) or section 22(c) by a securities association registered under section 15A of the Securities Exchange Act of 1934, or the Commission;

(IV) the acquired company has a policy that prohibits it from acquiring any securities of registered open-end investment companies or registered unit investment trusts in reliance on this subparagraph or subparagraph (F); and

(V) such acquisition is not in contravention of such rules and regulations as the Commission may from time to time prescribe with respect to acquisitions in accordance with this subparagraph, as necessary and appropriate for the protection of investors.

(ii) For purposes of this subparagraph, the term "group of investment companies" means any 2 or more registered investment companies that hold themselves out to investors as related companies for purposes of investment and investor services.

(H) For the purposes of this paragraph, the value of an investment company's total assets shall be computed as of the time of a purchase or acquisition or as closely thereto as is reasonably possible.

(I) In any action brought to enforce the provisions of this paragraph, the Commission may join as a party the issuer of any security purchased or otherwise acquired in violation of this paragraph, and the court may issue any order with respect to such issuer as may be necessary or appropriate for the enforcement of the provisions of this paragraph.

(2) It shall be unlawful for any registered investment company and any company or companies controlled by such registered investment company to purchase or otherwise acquire any security (except a security received as a dividend or as a result of a plan of reorganization of any company, other than a plan devised for the purpose of evading the provisions of this paragraph) issued by any insurance company of which such registered investment company and any company or companies controlled by such registered company do not, at the time of such purchase or acquisition, own in the aggregate at least 25 per centum of the total outstanding voting stock, if such registered company and any company or companies controlled by it own in the aggregate, or as a result of such purchase or acquisition will own in the aggregate, more than 10 per centum of the total outstanding voting stock of such insurance company.

(3) It shall be unlawful for any registered investment company and any company or companies controlled by such registered investment company to purchase or otherwise acquire any security issued by or any other interest in the business of any person who is a broker, a dealer, is engaged in the business of underwriting, or is either an investment adviser of an investment company or an investment adviser registered under title II of this Act, unless (A) such person is a corporation all of the outstanding securities of which (other than short-term paper, securities representing bank loans, and directors' qualifying shares) are, or after such acquisition will be, owned by one or more registered investment companies; and (B) such person is primarily engaged in the business of underwriting and distributing securities issued by other persons, selling securities to customers, or any one or more of such or related activities, and the gross income of such person normally is derived principally from such business or related activities.

(e) Notwithstanding any provisions of this title, any registered investment company may hereafter purchase or otherwise acquire any security issued by any one corporation engaged or proposing to engage in the business of underwriting, furnishing capital to industry, financing promotional enterprises, purchasing securities of issuers for which no ready market is in existence, and reorganizing companies or similar activities; provided—

(1) That the securities issued by such corporation (other than short-term paper and securities representing bank loans) shall consist solely of one class of common stock and shall have been originally issued or sold for investment to registered investment companies only;

(2) That the aggregate cost of the securities of such corporation purchased by such registered investment company does not exceed 5 per centum of the value of the total assets of such registered company at the time of any purchase or acquisition of such securities; and

(3) That the aggregate paid-in capital and surplus of such corporation does not exceed $100,000,000.

For the purpose of paragraph (1) of section 5(b) any investment in any such corporation shall be deemed to be an investment in an investment company.

(f) Notwithstanding any provisions of this Act, any registered face-amount certificate company may organize not more than two face-amount certificate companies and acquire and own all or any part of the capital stock thereof only if such stock is acquired and held for investment: *Provided,* That the aggregate cost to such registered company of all such stock so acquired shall not exceed six times the amount of the minimum capital stock requirement provided in subdivision (1) of subsection (a) of section 28 for a face-amount company organized on or after March 15, 1940: *And provided further,* That the aggregate cost to such registered company of all such capital stock issued by face-amount certificate companies organized or otherwise created under laws other than the laws of the United States or any State thereof shall not exceed twice the amount of the minimum capital stock requirement provided in subdivision (1) of subsection (a) of section 28 for a company organized on or after March 15, 1940. Nothing contained in this subsection shall be deemed to prevent the sale of any such stock to any other person if the original purchase was made by such registered face-amount certificate company in good faith for investment and not for resale.

(g) Notwithstanding the provisions of this section any registered investment company and any company or companies controlled by such registered company may purchase or otherwise acquire from another investment company or any company or companies controlled by such registered company more than 10 per centum of the total outstanding voting stock of any insurance company owned by any such company or companies, or may acquire the securities of any insurance company if the Commission by order determines that such acquisition is in the public interest because the financial condition of such insurance company will be improved as a result of such acquisition or any plan contemplated as a result thereof. This section shall not be deemed to prohibit the promotion of a new insurance company or the acquisition of the securities of any newly created insurance company by a registered investment company, alone or with other persons. Nothing contained in this section shall in any way affect or derogate from the powers of any insurance commissioner or similar official or agency of the United States or any State, or to affect the right under State law of any insurance company to acquire securities of any other insurance company or insurance companies.

(J) The Commission, by rule or regulation, upon its own motion or by order upon application, may conditionally or unconditionally exempt any person, security, or transaction, or any class or classes of persons, securities, or transactions from any provision of this subsection, if and to the extent that such exemption is consistent with the public interest and the protection of investors.

Changes in Investment Policy

Sec. 13. (a) No registered investment company shall, unless authorized by the vote of a majority of its outstanding voting securities—

(1) change its subclassification as defined in section 5(a)(1) and (2) of this title or its subclassification from a diversified to a nondiversified company;

(2) borrow money, issue senior securities, underwrite securities issued by other persons, purchase or sell real estate or commodities or make loans to other persons, except in each case in accordance with the recitals of policy contained in its registration statement in respect thereto;

(3) deviate from its policy in respect of concentration of investments in any particular industry or group of industries as recited in its registration statement, deviate from any investment policy which is changeable only if authorized by shareholder vote, or deviate from any policy recited in its regis-

tration statement pursuant to section 8(b)(3);

(4) change the nature of its business so as to cease to be an investment company.

(b) In the case of a common-law trust of the character described in section 16(c), either written approval by holders of a majority of the outstanding shares of beneficial interest or the vote of a majority of such outstanding shares cast in person or by proxy at a meeting called for the purpose shall for the purposes of subsection (a) be deemed the equivalent of the vote of a majority of the outstanding voting securities, and the provisions of paragraph (42) of section 2(a) as to a majority shall be applicable to the votes casts at such a meeting.

Size of Investment Companies

Sec. 14. (a) No registered investment company organized after the date of enactment of this title, and no principal underwriter for such a company, shall make a public offering of securities of which such company is the issuer, unless—

(1) such company has a net worth of at least $100,000;

(2) such company has previously made a public offering of its securities, and at the time of such offering had a net worth of at least $100,000; or

(3) provision is made in connection with and as a condition of the registration of such securities under the Securities Act of 1933 which in the opinion of the Commission adequately insures (A) that after the effective date of such registration statement such company will not issue any security or receive any proceeds of any subscription for any security until firm agreements have been made with such company by not more than twenty-five responsible persons to purchase from it securities to be issued by it for an aggregate net amount which plus the then net worth of the company, if any, will equal at least $100,000; (B) that said aggregate net amount will be paid in to such company before any subscriptions for such securities will be accepted from any persons in excess of twenty-five; (C) that arrangements will be made whereby any proceeds so paid in, as well as any sales load, will be refunded to any subscriber on demand without any deduction, in the event that the net proceeds so received by the company do not result in the company having a net worth of at least $100,000 within ninety days after such registration statement becomes effective.

At any time after the occurrence of the event specified in clause (C) of paragraph (3) of this subsection the Commission may issue a stop order suspending the effectiveness of the registration statement of such securities under the Securities Act of 1933 and may suspend or revoke the registration of such company under this title.

(b) The Commission is authorized, at such times as it deems that any substantial further increase in size of investment companies creates any problem involving the protection of investors or the public interest, to make a study and investigation of the effects of size on the investment policy of investment companies and on security markets, on concentration of control of wealth and industry, and on companies in which investment companies are interested, and from time to time to report the results of its studies and investigations and its recommendations to the Congress.

Investment Advisory and Underwriting Contracts

Sec. 15. (a) It shall be unlawful for any person to serve or act as investment adviser of a registered investment company, except pursuant to a written contract, which contract, whether with such registered company or with an investment adviser of such registered company, has been approved by the vote of a majority of the outstanding voting securities of such registered company, and—

(1) precisely describes all compensation to be paid thereunder;

(2) shall continue in effect for a period more than two years from the date of its execution, only so long as such continuance is specifically approved at least annually by the board of directors or by vote of a majority of the outstanding voting securities of such company;

(3) provides, in substance, that it may be terminated at any time, without the payment of any penalty, by the board of directors of such registered company or by vote of a majority of the outstanding voting securities of such company on not more than sixty days' written notice to the investment adviser; and

(4) provides, in substance, for its automatic termination in the event of its assignment.

(b) It shall be unlawful for any principal underwriter for a registered open-end company to offer for sale, sell, or deliver after sale any security of which such company is the issuer, except pursuant to a written contract with such company, which contract—

(1) shall continue in effect for a period more than two years from the date of its execution, only so long as such continuance is specifically approved at least annually by the board of directors or by vote of a majority of the outstanding voting securities of such company; and

(2) provides, in substance, for its automatic termination in the event of its assignment.

(c) In addition to the requirements of subsection (a) and (b) of this section, it shall be unlawful for any registered investment company having a board of directors to enter into, renew, or perform any contract or agreement, written or oral, whereby a person undertakes regularly to serve or act as investment adviser of or principal underwriter for such company unless the terms of such contract or agreement and any renewal thereof have been approved by the vote of a majority of directors, who are not parties to such contract or agreement or interested persons of any such party, cast in person at a meeting called for the purpose of voting on such approval. It shall be the duty of the directors of a registered investment company to request and evaluate, and the duty of an investment adviser to such company to furnish, such information as may reasonably be necessary to evaluate the terms of any contract whereby a person undertakes regularly to serve or act as investment adviser of such company. It shall be unlawful for the directors of a registered investment company, in connection with their evaluation of the terms of any contract whereby a person undertakes regularly to serve or act as investment adviser of such company, to take into account the purchase price or other consideration any person may have paid in connection with a transaction of the type referred to in paragraph (1), (3), or (4) of subsection (f).

(d) In the case of a common-law trust of the character described in section 16(c), either written approval by holders of a majority of the outstanding shares of beneficial interest or the vote of a majority of such outstanding shares cast in person or by proxy at a meeting called for the purpose shall for the purposes of this section be deemed the equivalent of the vote of a majority of the outstanding voting securities, and the provisions of paragraph (42) of section 2(a) as to a majority shall be applicable to the vote cast at such a meeting.

(e) Nothing contained in this section shall be deemed to require or contemplate any action by an advisory board of any registered company or by any of the members of such a board.

(f)(1) An investment adviser, or a corporate trustee performing the functions of an investment adviser, of a registered investment company or an affiliated person of such investment adviser or corporate trustee may receive any amount or benefit in connection with a sale of securities of, or a sale of any other interest in, such investment adviser or corporate trustee which results in an assignment of an investment advisory contract with such company or the change in control of or identity of such corporate trustee, if—

(A) for a period of three years after the time of such action, at least 75 percentum of the members of the board of directors of such registered company or such corporate trustee (or successor thereto, by reorganization or otherwise) are not (i) interested persons of the investment adviser of such company or such corporate trustee, or (ii) interested persons of the predecessor investment adviser or such corporate trustee; and

(B) there is not imposed an unfair burden on such company as a result of such transactions or any express or implied terms, conditions, or understandings applicable thereto.

(2)(A) For the purpose of paragraph (1)(A) of this subsection, interested persons of a corporate trustee shall be determined in accordance with section 2(a)(19)(B): *Provided,* That no person shall be deemed to be an interested person of a corporate trustee solely by reason of (i) his being a member of its board of directors or advisory board or (ii) his membership in the immediate family of any person specified in clause (i) of this subparagraph.

(B) For the purpose of paragraph (1)(B) of this subsection, an unfair burden on a registered investment company includes any arrangement, during the two-year period after the date on which any such transaction occurs, whereby the investment adviser or corporate trustee or predecessor or successor investment advisers or corporate trustee or any interested person of any such adviser or any such corporate trustee receives or is entitled to receive any compensation directly or indirectly (i) from any person in connection with the purchase or sale of securities or other property to, from, or on behalf of such company, other than bona fide ordinary compensation as principal underwriter for such company, or (ii) from such company or its security holders for other than bona fide investment advisory or other services.

(3) If—

(A) an assignment of an investment advisory contract with a registered investment company results in a successor investment adviser to such company, or if there is a change in control of or identity of a corporate trustee of a registered investment company, and such adviser or trustee is then an investment adviser or corporate trustee with respect to other assets substantially greater in amount than the amount of assets of such company, or

(B) as a result of a merger of, or a sale of substantially all the assets by, a registered investment company with or to another registered investment company with assets substantially greater in amount, a transaction occurs which would be subject to paragraph (1)(A) of this subsection,

such discrepancy in size of assets shall be considered by the Commission in determining whether or to what extent an application under section 6(c) for exemption from the provisions of paragraph (1)(A) should be granted.

(4) Paragraph (1)(A) of this subsection shall not apply to a transaction in which a controlling block of outstanding voting securities of an investment adviser to a registered investment company or of a corporate trustee performing the functions of an investment adviser to a registered investment company is—

(A) distributed to the public and in which there is, in fact, no change in the identity of the persons who control such investment adviser or corporate trustee, or

(B) transferred to the investment adviser or the corporate trustee, or an affiliated person or persons of such investment adviser or corporate trustee, or is transferred from the investment adviser or corporate trustee to an affiliated person or persons of the investment adviser or corporate trustee: *Provided,* That (i) each transferee (other than such adviser or trustee) is a natural person and (ii) the transferees (other than such adviser or trustee) owned in the aggregate more than 25 per centum of such voting securities for a period of at least six months prior to such transfer.

Changes in Board of Directors and Trustees; Provisions Relative to Strict Trusts

Sec. 16. (a) No person shall serve as a director of a registered investment company unless elected to that office by the holders of the outstanding voting securities of such company, at an annual or a special meeting duly called for that purpose; except that vacancies occurring between such meetings may be filled in any otherwise legal manner if immediately after filling any such vacancy at least two-thirds of the directors then holding office shall have been elected to such office by the holders of the outstanding voting securities of the company at such an annual or special meeting. In the event that at any time less than a majority of the directors of such company holding office at that time were so elected by the holders of the outstanding voting securities, the board of directors or proper officer of such company shall forthwith cause to be held as promptly as possible and in any event within sixty days a meeting of such holders for the purpose of electing directors to fill any existing vacancies in the board of directors unless the Commission shall by order extend such period. The foregoing provisions of this subsection shall not apply to members of an advisory board.

Nothing herein shall, however, preclude a registered investment company from dividing its directors into classes if its charter, certificate of incorporation, articles of association, by-laws, trust indenture, or other instrument or the law under which it is organized, so provides and prescribes the tenure of office of the several classes: *Provided,* That no class shall be elected for a shorter period than one year or for a longer period than five years and the term of office of at least one class shall expire each year.

(b) Any vacancy on the board of directors of a registered investment company which occurs in connection with compliance with section 15(f)(1)(A) and which must be filled by a person who is not an interested person of either party to a transaction subject to section 15(f)(1)(A) shall be filled only by a person (1) who has been selected and proposed for election by a majority of the directors of such company who are not such interested persons, and (2) who has been elected by the holders of the outstanding voting securities of such company, except that in the case of the death, disqualification, or bona fide resignation of a director selected and elected pursuant to clauses (1) and (2) of this subsection (b), the vacancy created thereby may be filled as provided in subsection (a).

(c) The foregoing provisions of this section shall not apply to a common-law trust existing on the date of enactment of this title under an indenture of trust which does not provide for the election of trustees by the shareholders. No natural person shall serve as trustee of such a trust, which is registered as an investment company, after the holders of record of not less than two-thirds of the outstanding shares of beneficial interest in such trust have declared that he be removed from that office either by declaration in writing filed with the custodian of the securities of the trust or by votes cast in person or by proxy at a meeting called for the purpose. Solicitation of such a declaration shall be deemed a solicitation of a proxy within the meaning of section 20(a).

The trustees of such a trust shall promptly call a meeting of shareholders for the purpose of voting upon the question of removal of any such trustee or trustees when requested in writing so to do by the record holders of not less than 10 per centum of the outstanding shares.

Whenever ten or more shareholders of record who have been such for at least six months preceding the date of application, and who hold in the aggregate either shares having a net asset value of at least $25,000 or at least 1 per centum of the outstanding shares, whichever is less, shall apply to the trustees in writing, stating that they wish to communicate with other shareholders with a view to obtaining signatures to a request for a meeting pursuant to this subsection (c) and accompanied by a form of communication and request which they wish to transmit, the trustees shall within five business days after receipt of such application either—

(1) afford to such applicants access to a list of the names and addresses of all shareholders as recorded on the books of the trust; or

(2) inform such applicants as to the approximate number of shareholders of record, and the approximate cost of mailing to them the proposed communication and form of request.

If the trustees elect to follow the course specified in paragraph (2) of this subsection (b) the trustees, upon the written request of such applicants, accompanied by a tender of the material to be mailed and of the reasonable expenses of mailing, shall, with reasonable promptness, mail such material to all shareholders of record at their addresses as recorded on the books, unless within five business days after such tender the trustees shall mail to such applicants and file with the Commission, together with a copy of the material to be mailed, a written statement signed by at least a majority of the trustees to the effect that in their opinion either such material contains untrue statements of fact or omits to state facts necessary to make the statements contained therein not misleading, or would be in violation of applicable law, and specifying the basis of such opinion.

After opportunity for hearing upon the objections specified in the written statement so filed, the Commission may, and if demanded by the trustees or by such applicants shall, enter an order either sustaining one or more of such objections or refusing to sustain any of them. If the Commission shall enter an order refusing to sustain any of such objections, or if, after the entry of an order sustaining one or more of such objections, the Commission shall find, after notice and opportunity for hearing, that all objections so sustained have been met, and shall enter an order so declaring, the trustees shall mail copies of such material to all shareholders with reasonable promptness after the entry of such order and the renewal of such tender.

Transactions of Certain Affiliated Persons and Underwriters

Sec. 17. (a) It shall be unlawful for any affiliated person or promoter of or principal underwriter for a registered investment company (other than a company of the character described in sections 12(d)(3)(A) and (B)), or any affiliated person of such a person, promoter, or principal underwriter, acting as principal—

(1) knowingly to sell any security or other property to such registered company or to any company controlled by such registered company, unless such sale involves solely (A) securities of which the buyer is the issuer, (B) securities of which the seller is the issuer and which are part of a general offering to the holders of a class of its securities, or (C) securities deposited with the trustee of a unit investment trust or periodic payment plan by the depositor thereof;

(2) knowingly to purchase from such registered company, or from any company controlled by such registered company, any security or other property (except securities of which the seller is the issuer);

(3) to borrow money or other property from such registered company or from any company controlled by such registered company (unless the borrower is controlled by the lender) except as permitted in section 21(b); or

(4) to loan money or other property to such registered company, or to any company controlled by such registered company, in contravention of such rules, regulations, or orders as the Commission may, after consultation with and taking into consideration the views of the Federal banking agencies (as defined in section 3 of the Federal De-

posit Insurance Act), prescribe or issue consistent with the protection of investors.

(b) Notwithstanding subsection (a), any person may file with the Commission an application for an order exempting a proposed transaction of the applicant from one or more provisions of that subsection. The Commission shall grant such application and issue such order of exemption if evidence establishes that—

(1) the terms of the proposed transaction, including the consideration to be paid or received, are reasonable and fair and do not involve overreaching on the part of any person concerned;

(2) the proposed transaction is consistent with the policy of each registered investment company concerned, as recited in its registration statement and reports filed under this title; and

(3) the proposed transaction is consistent with the general purposes of this title.

(c) Notwithstanding subsection (a), a person may, in the ordinary course of business, sell to or purchase from any company merchandise or may enter into a lessor-lessee relationship with any person and furnish the services incident thereto.

(d) It shall be unlawful for any affiliated person of or principal underwriter for a registered investment company (other than a company of the character described in section 12(d)(3)(A) and (B)), or any affiliated person of such a person or principal underwriter, acting as principal to effect any transaction in which such registered company, or a company controlled by such registered company, is a joint or a joint and several participant with such person, principal underwriter, or affiliated person, in contravention of such rules and regulations as the Commission may prescribe for the purpose of limiting or preventing participation by such registered or controlled company on a basis different from or less advantageous than that of such other participant. Nothing contained in this subsection shall be deemed to preclude any affiliated person from acting as manager of any underwriting syndicate or other group in which such registered or controlled company is a participant and receiving compensation therefor.

(e) It shall be unlawful for any affiliated person of a registered investment company, or any affiliated person of such person—

(1) acting as agent, to accept from any source any compensation (other than a regular salary or wages from such registered company) for the purchase or sale of any property to or for such registered company or any controlled company thereof, except in the course of such person's business as an underwriter or broker; or

(2) acting as broker, in connection with the sale of securities to or by such registered company or any controlled company thereof, to receive from any source a commission, fee, or other remuneration for effecting such transaction which exceeds (A) the usual and customary broker's commission if the sale is effected on a securities exchange, or (B) 2 per centum of the sales price if the sale is effected in connection with a secondary distribution of such securities, or (C) 1 per centum of the purchase or sale price of such securities if the sale is otherwise effected unless the Commission shall, by rules and regulations or order in the public interest and consistent with the protection of investors, permit a larger commission.

(f) Custody of securities.—

(1) Every registered management company shall place and maintain its securities and similar investments in the custody of (A) a bank or banks having the qualifications prescribed in paragraph (1) of section 26(a) of this title for the trustees of unit investment trusts; or (B) a company which is a member of a national securities exchange as defined in the Securities Exchange Act of 1934, subject to such rules and regulations as the Commission may from time to time prescribe for the protection of investors; or (C) such registered

company, but only in accordance with such rules and regulations or orders as the Commission may from time to time prescribe for the protection of investors.

(2) Subject to such rules, regulations, and orders as the Commission may adopt as necessary or appropriate for the protection of investors, a registered management company or any such custodian, with the consent of the registered management company for which it acts as custodian, may deposit all or any part of the securities owned by such registered management company in a system for the central handling of securities established by a national securities exchange or national securities association registered with the Commission under the Securities Exchange Act of 1934, or such other person as may be permitted by the Commission, pursuant to which system all securities of any particular class or series of any issues deposited within the system are treated as fungible and may be transferred or pledged by bookkeeping entry without physical delivery of such securities.

(3) Rules, regulations, and orders of the Commission under this subsection, among other things, may make appropriate provision with respect to such matters as the earmarking, segregation, and hypothecation of such securities and investments, and may provide for or require periodic or other inspections by any or all of the following: Independent public accountants, employees and agents of the Commission, and such other persons as the Commission may designate.

(4) No such member which trades in securities for its own account may act as custodian except in accordance with rules and regulations prescribed by the Commission for the protection of investors.

(5) If a registered company maintains its securities and similar investments in the custody of a qualified bank or banks, the cash proceeds from the sale of such securities and similar investments and other cash assets of the company shall likewise be kept in the custody of such a bank or banks, or in accordance with such rules and regulations or orders as the Commission may from time to time prescribe for the protection of investors, except that such a registered company may maintain a checking account in a bank or banks having the qualifications prescribed in paragraph (1) of section 26(a) of this title for the trustee of unit investment trusts with the balance of such account or the aggregate balances of such accounts at no time in excess of the amount of the fidelity bond, maintained pursuant to section 17(g) of this title, covering the officers or employees authorized to draw on such account or accounts.

(6) The Commission may, after consultation with and taking into consideration the views of the Federal banking agencies (as defined in section 3 of the Federal Deposit Insurance Act), adopt rules and regulations, and issue orders, consistent with the protection of investors, prescribing the conditions under which a bank, or an affiliated person of a bank, either of which is an affiliated person, promoter, organizer, or sponsor of, or principal underwriter for, a registered management company may serve as custodian of that registered management company.

(g) The Commission is authorized to require by rules and regulations or orders for the protection of investors that any officer or employee of a registered management investment company who may singly, or jointly with others, have access to securities or funds of any registered company, either directly or through authority to draw upon such funds or to direct generally the disposition of such securities (unless the officer or employee has such access solely through his position as an officer or employee of a bank) be bonded by a reputable fidelity insurance company against larceny and embezzlement in such reasonable minimum amounts as the Commission may prescribe.

(h) After one year from the effective date of this title, neither the charter, certificate of incorporation, articles of association, indenture of trust, nor the by-laws of any registered investment company, nor any other instrument pursuant to which such a company is organized or administered, shall contain any provision which protects or purports to protect any director or officer of such company against any liability to the company or to its security holders to which he would otherwise be subject by reason of willful misfeasance, bad faith, gross negligence or reckless disregard of the duties involved in the conduct of his office.

(i) After one year from the effective date of this title no contract or agreement under which any person undertakes to act as investment adviser of, or principal underwriter for, a registered investment company shall contain any provision which protects or purports to protect such person against any liability to such company or its security holders to which he would otherwise be subject by reason of willful misfeasance, bad faith, or gross negligence, in the performance of his duties, or by reason of his reckless disregard of his obligations and duties under such contract or agreement.

(j) It shall be unlawful for any affiliated person of or principal underwriter for a registered investment company or any affiliated person of an investment adviser of or principal underwriter for a registered investment company, to engage in any act, practice, or course of business in connection with the purchase or sale, directly or indirectly, by such person of any security held or to be acquired by such registered investment company in contravention of such rules and regulations as the Commission may adopt to define, and prescribe means reasonably necessary to prevent, such acts, practices, or courses of business as are fraudulent, deceptive or manipulative. Such rules and regulations may include requirements for the adoption of codes of ethics by registered investment companies and investment advisers of, and principal underwriters for, such investment companies establishing such standards as are reasonably necessary to prevent such acts, practices, or courses of business.

Capital Structure

Sec. 18. (a) It shall be unlawful for any registered closed-end company to issue any class of senior security, or to sell any such security of which it is the issuer, unless—

(1) if such class of senior security represents an indebtedness—

(A) immediately after such issuance or sale, it will have an asset coverage of at least 300 per centum;

(B) provision is made to prohibit the declaration of any dividend (except a dividend payable in stock of the issuer), or the declaration of any other distribution, upon any class of the capital stock of such investment company, or the purchase of any such capital stock, unless, in every such case, such class of senior securities has at the time of the declaration of any such dividend or distribution or at the time of any such purchase an asset coverage of at least 300 per centum after deducting the amount of such dividend, distribution, or purchase price, as the case may be, except that dividends may be declared upon any preferred stock if such senior security representing indebtedness has an asset coverage of at least 200 per centum at the time of declaration thereof after deducting the amount of such dividend; and

(C) provision is made either—

(i) that, if on the last business day of each of twelve consecutive calendar months such class of senior securities shall have an asset coverage of less than 100 per centum, the holders of such securities voting as a class shall be entitled to elect at least a majority of the members of the board of directors of such registered company, such voting right to continue until such class of senior security shall have an asset coverage of 110 per centum or more on the last business day of each of three consecutive calendar months, or

(ii) that, if on the last business day of each of twenty-four consecutive calendar months such class of senior securities shall have an asset coverage of less than 100 per centum, an event of default shall be deemed to have occurred;

(2) if such class of senior security is a stock—

(A) immediately after such issuance or sale it will have an asset coverage of at least 200 per centum;

(B) provision is made to prohibit the declaration of any dividend (except a dividend payable in common stock of the issuer), or the declaration of any other distribution, upon the common stock of such investment company, or the purchase of any such common stock, unless in every such case such class of senior security has at the time of the declaration of any such dividend or distribution or at the time of any such purchase an asset coverage of at least 200 per centum after deducting the amount of such dividend, distribution or purchase price, as the case may be;

(C) provision is made to entitle the holders of such senior securities, voting as a class, to elect at least two directors at all times, and, subject to the prior rights, if any, of the holders of any other class of senior securities outstanding, to elect a majority of the directors if at any time dividends on such class of securities shall be unpaid in an amount equal to two full years' dividends on such securities, and to continue to be so represented until all dividends in arrears shall have been paid or otherwise provided for;

(D) provision is made requiring approval by the vote of a majority of such securities, voting as a class, of any plan of reorganization adversely affecting such securities or of any action requiring a vote of security holders as in section 13(a) provided; and

(E) such class of stock shall have complete priority over any other class as to distribution of assets and payment of dividends, which dividends shall be cumulative.

(b) The asset coverage in respect of a senior security provided for in subsection (a) may be determined on the basis of values calculated as of a time within forty-eight hours (not including Sundays or holidays) next preceding the time of such determination. The time of issue or sale shall, in the case of an offering of such securities to existing stockholders of the issuer, be deemed to be the first date on which such offering is made, and in all other cases shall be deemed to be the time as of which a firm commitment to issue or sell and to take or purchase such securities shall be made.

(c) Notwithstanding the provisions of subsection (a) it shall be unlawful for any registered closed-end investment company to issue or sell any senior security representing indebtedness if immediately thereafter such company will have outstanding more than one class of senior security representing indebtedness, or to issue or sell any senior security which is a stock if immediately thereafter such company will have outstanding more than one class of senior security which is a stock, except that (1) any such class of indebtedness or stock may be issued in one or more series: *Provided,* That no such series shall have a preference or priority over any other series upon the distribution of the assets of such registered closed-end company or in respect of the payment of interest or dividends, and (2) promissory notes or other evidences of indebtedness issued in consideration of any loan, extension, or renewal thereof, made by a bank or other person and privately arranged, and not intended to be publicly distributed, shall not be deemed to be a separate class of senior securities representing indebtedness within the meaning of this subsection (c).

(d) It shall be unlawful for any registered management company to issue any warrant or right to subscribe to or purchase a security of which such company is the issuer, except in the form of warrants or rights to subscribe expiring not later than one hundred and twenty days after their issuance and issued exclusively and ratably to a class or classes of such company's security holders; except that any warrant may be issued in exchange for outstanding warrants in connection with a plan of reorganization.

(e) The provisions of this section 18 shall not apply to any senior securities issued or sold by any registered closed-end company—

(1) for the purpose of refunding through payment, purchase, redemption, retirement, or exchange, any senior security of such registered investment company except that no senior security representing indebtedness shall be so issued or sold for the purpose of refunding any senior security which is a stock; or

(2) pursuant to any plan of reorganization (other than for refunding as referred to in paragraph (i) of this subsection), provided—

(A) that such senior securities are issued or sold for the purpose of substituting or exchanging such senior securities for outstanding senior securities, and if such senior securities represent indebtedness they are issued or sold for the purpose of substituting or exchanging such senior securities for outstanding senior securities representing indebtedness, of any registered investment company which is a party to such plan of reorganization; or

(B) that the total amount of such senior securities so issued or sold pursuant to such plan does not exceed the total amount of senior securities of all the companies which are parties to such plan, and the total amount of senior securities representing indebtedness so issued or sold pursuant to such plan does not exceed the total amount of senior securities representing indebtedness of all such companies, or, alternatively, the total amount of such senior securities so issued or sold pursuant to such plan does not have the effect of increasing the ratio of senior securities representing indebtedness to the securities representing stock or the ratio of senior securities representing stock to securities junior thereto when compared with such ratios as they existed before such reorganization.

(f)(1) It shall be unlawful for any registered open-end company to issue any class of senior security or to sell any senior security of which it is the issuer, except that any such registered company shall be permitted to borrow from any bank: *Provided,* That immediately after any such borrowing there is an asset coverage of at least 300 per centum for all borrowings of such registered company: *And provided further,* That in the event that such asset coverage shall at any time fall below 300 per centum such registered company shall, within three days thereafter (not including Sundays and holidays) or such longer period as the Commission may prescribe by rules and regulations, reduce the amount of its borrowings to an extent that the asset coverage of such borrowings shall be at least 300 per centum.

(2) "Senior security" shall not, in the case of a registered open-end company, include a class or classes or a number of series of preferred or special stock each of which is preferred over all other classes or series in respect of assets specifically allocated to that class or series: *Provided,* That (A) such company has outstanding no class or series of stock which is not so preferred over all other classes or series, or (B) the only other outstanding class of the issuer's stock consists of a common stock upon which no dividend (other than a liquidating dividend) is permitted to be paid and which in the aggregate represents not more than one-half of 1 per centum of the issuer's outstanding voting securities. For the purpose of insuring fair and equitable treatment of the holders of the outstanding voting securities of each class or series of stock of such company, the Commission may by rule, regulation, or order direct that any matter required to be

submitted to the holders of the outstanding voting securities of such company shall not be deemed to have been effectively acted upon unless approved by the holders of such percentage (not exceeding a majority) of the outstanding voting securities of each class or series of stock affected by such matter as shall be prescribed in such rule, regulation, or order.

(g) Unless otherwise provided: "Senior security" means any bond, debenture, note, or similar obligation or instrument constituting a security and evidencing indebtedness, and any stock of a class having priority over any other class as to distribution of assets or payment of dividends; and "senior security representing indebtedness" means any senior security other than stock.

The term "senior security", when used in subparagraphs (B) and (C) of paragraph (1) of subsection (a), shall not include any promissory note or other evidence of indebtedness issued in consideration of any loan, extension, or renewal thereof, made by a bank or other person and privately arranged, and not intended to be publicly distributed; nor shall such term, when used in this section 18, include any such promissory note or other evidence of indebtedness in any case where such a loan is for temporary purposes only and in an amount not exceeding 5 per centum of the value of the total assets of the issuer at the time when the loan is made. A loan shall be presumed to be for temporary purposes if it is repaid within sixty days and is not extended or renewed; otherwise it shall be presumed not to be for temporary purposes. Any such presumption may be rebutted by evidence.

(h) "Asset coverage" of a class of senior security representing an indebtedness of an issuer means the ratio which the value of the total assets of such issuer, less all liabilities and indebtedness not represented by senior securities, bears to the aggregate amount of senior securities representing indebtedness of such issuer. "Asset coverage" of a class of senior security of an issuer which is a stock means the ratio which the value of the total assets of such issuer, less all liabilities and indebtedness not represented by senior securities, bears to the aggregate amount of senior securities representing indebtedness of such issuer plus the aggregate of the involuntary liquidation preference of such class of senior security which is a stock. The involuntary liquidation preference of a class of senior security which is a stock shall be deemed to mean the amount to which such class of senior security would be entitled on involuntary liquidation of the issuer in preference to a security junior to it.

(i) Except as provided in subsection (a) of this section, or as otherwise required by law, every share of stock hereafter issued by a registered management company (except a common-law trust of the character described in section 16(c)) shall be a voting stock and have equal voting rights with every other outstanding voting stock: *Provided,* That this subsection shall not apply to shares issued pursuant to the terms of any warrant or subscription right outstanding on March 15, 1940, or any firm contract entered into before March 15, 1940, to purchase such securities from such company nor to shares issued in accordance with any rules, regulations, or orders which the Commission may make permitting such issue.

(j) Notwithstanding any provision of this title, it shall be unlawful, after the date of enactment of this title, for any registered face-amount certificate company—

(1) to issue, except in accordance with such rules, regulations, or orders as the Commission may prescribe in the public interest or as necessary or appropriate for the protection of investors, any security other than (A) a face-amount certificate; (B) a common stock having a par value and being without preference as to dividends or distributions and having at least equal voting rights with any outstanding security of such company; or (C) short-term payment or promissory notes or other indebtedness issued in consideration of any loan, extension, or renewal thereof, made by a bank or other

person and privately arranged and not intended to be publicly offered;

(2) if such company has outstanding any security, other than such face-amount certificates, common stock, promissory notes, or other evidence of indebtedness, to make any distribution or declare or pay any dividend on any capital security in contravention of such rules and regulations or orders as the Commission may prescribe in the public interest or as necessary or appropriate for the protection of investors or to insure the financial integrity of such company, to prevent the impairment of the company's ability to meet its obligations upon its face-amount certificates; or

(3) to issue any of its securities except for cash or securities including securities of which such company is the issuer.

(k) The provisions of subparagraphs (A) and (B) of paragraph (1) of subsection (a) of this section shall not apply to investment companies operating under the Small Business Investment Act of 1958, and the provisions of paragraph (2) of said subsection shall not apply to such companies so long as such class of senior security shall be held or guaranteed by the Small Business Administration.

Dividends

Sec. 19. (a) It shall be unlawful for any registered investment company to pay any dividend, or to make any distribution in the nature of a dividend payment, wholly or partly from any source other than—

(1) such company's accumulated undistributed net income, determined in accordance with good accounting practice and not including profits or losses realized upon the sale of securities or other properties; or

(2) such company's net income so determined for the current or preceding fiscal year;

unless such payment is accompanied by a written statement which adequately discloses the source or sources of such payment. The Commission may prescribe the form of such statement by rules and regulations in the public interest and for the protection of investors.

(b) It shall be unlawful in contravention of such rules, regulations, or orders as the Commission may prescribe as necessary or appropriate in the public interest or for the protection of investors for any registered investment company to distribute long-term capital gains, as defined in the Internal Revenue Code of 1954, more often than once every twelve months.

Proxies; Voting Trusts; Circular Ownership

Sec. 20. (a) It shall be unlawful for any person, by use of the mails or any means or instrumentality of interstate commerce or otherwise, to solicit or to permit the use of his name to solicit any proxy or consent or authorization in respect of any security of which a registered investment company is the issuer in contravention of such rules and regulations as the Commission may prescribe as necessary or appropriate in the public interest or for the protection of investors.

(b) It shall be unlawful for any registered investment company or affiliated person thereof, any issuer of a voting-trust certificate relating to any security of a registered investment company, or any underwriter of such a certificate, by use of the mails or any means or instrumentality of interstate commerce, or otherwise, to offer for sale, sell, or deliver after sale, in connection with a public offering, any such voting-trust certificate.

(c) No registered investment company shall purchase any voting security if, to the knowledge of such registered company, cross-ownership or circular ownership exists, or after such acquisition will exist, between such registered company and the issuer of such security. Cross-ownership shall be deemed to exist between two companies when each of such companies beneficially owns more than 3 per centum of the outstanding voting securities of the other company. Circular ownership shall be deemed to exist between two companies if such companies are included within a group of three or more companies, each of which—

(1) beneficially owns more than 3 per centum of the outstanding voting securities of one or more other companies of the group; and

(2) has more than 3 per centum of its own outstanding voting securities beneficially owned by another company, or by each of two or more other companies, of the group.

(d) If cross-ownership or circular ownership between a registered investment company and any other company or companies comes into existence upon the purchase by a registered investment company of the securities of another company, it shall be the duty of such registered company, within one year after it first knows of the existence of such cross-ownership or circular ownership, to eliminate the same.

Loans

Sec. 21. It shall be unlawful for any registered management company to lend money or property to any person, directly or indirectly if—

(a) the investment policies of such registered company, as recited in its registration statement and reports filed under this title, do not permit such a loan; or

(b) such person controls or is under common control with such registered company; except that the provisions of this paragraph shall not apply to any loan from a registered company to a company which owns all of the outstanding securities of such registered company, except directors' qualifying shares.

Distribution, Redemption, and Repurchase of Redeemable Securities

Sec. 22. (a) A securities association registered under section 15A of the Securities Exchange Act of 1934 may prescribe, by rules adopted and in effect in accordance with said section and subject to all provisions of said section applicable to the rules of such an association—

(1) a method or methods for computing the minimum price at which a member thereof may purchase from any investment company any redeemable security issued by such company and the maximum price at which a member may sell to such company any redeemable security issued by it or which he may receive for such security upon redemption, so that the price in each case will bear such relation to the current net asset value of such security computed as of such time as the rules may prescribe; and

(2) a minimum period of time which must elapse after the sale or issue of such security before any resale to such company by a member or its redemption upon surrender by a member;

in each case for the purpose of eliminating or reducing so far as reasonably practicable any dilution of the value of other outstanding securities of such company or any other result of such purchase, redemption, or sale which is unfair to holders of such other outstanding securities; and said rules may prohibit the members of the association from purchasing, selling, or surrendering for redemption any such redeemable securities in contravention of said rules.

(b)(1) Such a securities association may also, by rules adopted and in effect in accordance with said section 15A, and notwithstanding the provisions of subsection (b)(6) thereof but subject to all other provisions of said section applicable to the rules of such an association, prohibit its members from purchasing, in connection with a primary distribution of redeemable securities of which any registered investment company is the issuer, any such security from the issuer or from any principal underwriter except at a price equal to the price at which such security is then offered to the public less a commission, discount, or spread which is computed in conformity with a method or methods, and within such limitations as to the relation thereof to said public offering price, as such rules may prescribe in order that the price at which such security is offered or sold to the public shall not include an excessive sales load but shall allow for reasonable compensation for sales personnel, broker-dealers, and underwriters, and for reasonable sales loads to investors. The Commission shall on application or otherwise, if it appears that smaller companies are subject to relatively higher operating costs, make due allowance therefor by granting any such company or class of companies appropriate qualified exemptions from the provisions of this section.

(2) At any time after the expiration of eighteen months from the date of enactment of the Investment Company Amendments Act of 1970 (or, if earlier, after a securities association has adopted for purposes of paragraph (1) any rule respecting excessive sales loads), the Commission may alter or supplement the rules of any securities association as may be necessary to effectuate the purposes of this subsection in the manner provided by section 19(c) of the Securities Exchange Act of 1934.

(3) If any provision of this subsection is in conflict with any provision of any law of the United States in effect on the date this subsection takes effect, the provisions of this subsection shall prevail.

(c) The Commission may make rules and regulations applicable to registered investment companies and to principal underwriters of, and dealers in, the redeemable securities of any registered investment company, whether or not members of any securities association, to the same extent, covering the same subject matter, and for the accomplishment of the same ends as are prescribed in subsection (a) of this section in respect of the rules which may be made by a registered securities association governing its members. Any rules and regulations so made by the Commission, to the extent that they may be inconsistent with the rules of any such association, shall so long as they remain in force supersede the rules of the association and be binding upon its members as well as all other underwriters and dealers to whom they may be applicable.

(d) No registered investment company shall sell any redeemable security issued by it to any person except either to or through a principal underwriter for distribution or at a current public offering price described in the prospectus, and, if such class of security is being currently offered to the public by or through an underwriter, no principal underwriter of such security and no dealer shall sell any such security to any person except a dealer, a principal underwriter, or the issuer, except at a current public offering price described in the prospectus. Nothing in this subsection shall prevent a sale made (i) pursuant to an offer of exchange permitted by section 11 including any offer made pursuant to section 11(b); (ii) pursuant to an offer made solely to all registered holders of the securities, or of a particular class or series of securities issued by the company proportionate to their holdings or proportionate to any cash distribution made to them by the company (subject to appropriate qualifications designed solely to avoid issuance of fractional securities); or (iii) in accordance with rules and regulations of the Commission made pursuant to subsection (b) of section 12.

(e) No registered investment company shall suspend the right of redemption, or postpone the date of payment or satisfaction upon redemption of any redeemable security in accordance with its terms for more than seven days after the tender of such security to the company or its agent designated for that purpose for redemption, except—

(1) for any period (A) during which the New York Stock Exchange is closed other than customary week-end and holiday closings or (B) during which trading on the New York Stock Exchange is restricted;

(2) for any period during which an emergency exists as a result of which (A) disposal by the company of securities owned by it is not reasonably practicable or (B) it is not reasonably practicable for such company

fairly to determine the value of its net assets; or

(3) for such other periods as the Commission may by order permit for the protection of security holders of the company.

The Commission shall by rules and regulations determine the conditions under which (i) trading shall be deemed to be restricted and (ii) an emergency shall be deemed to exist within the meaning of this subsection.

(f) No registered open-end company shall restrict the transferability or negotiability of any security of which it is the issuer except in conformity with the statements with respect thereto contained in its registration statement nor in contravention of such rules and regulations as the Commission may prescribe in the interests of the holders of all of the outstanding securities of such investment company.

(g) No registered open-end company shall issue any of its securities (1) for services; or (2) for property other than cash or securities (including securities of which such registered company is the issuer), except as a dividend or distribution to its security holders or in connection with a reorganization.

Distribution and Repurchase of Securities: Closed-End Companies

Sec. 23. (a) No registered closed-end company shall issue any of its securities (1) for services; or (2) for property other than cash or securities (including securities of which such registered company is the issuer), except as a dividend or distribution to its security holders or in connection with a reorganization.

(b) No registered closed-end company shall sell any common stock of which it is the issuer at a price below the current net asset value of such stock, exclusive of any distributing commission or discount (which net asset value shall be determined as of a time within forty-eight hours, excluding Sundays and holidays, next preceding the time of such determination), except (1) in connection with an offering to the holders of one or more classes of its capital stock; (2) with consent of a majority of its common stockholders; (3) upon conversion of a convertible security in accordance with its terms; (4) upon the exercise of any warrant outstanding on the date of enactment of this Act or issued in accordance with the provisions of section 18(d); or (5) under such other circumstances as the Commission may permit by rules and regulations or orders for the protection of investors.

(c) No registered closed-end company shall purchase any securities of any class of which it is the issuer except—

(1) on a securities exchange or such other open market as the Commission may designate by rules and regulations or orders: *Provided,* That if such securities are stock, such registered company shall, within the preceding six months, have informed stockholders of its intention to purchase stock of such class by letter or report addressed to stockholders of such class; or

(2) pursuant to tenders, after reasonable opportunity to submit tenders given to all holders of securities of the class to be purchased; or

(3) under such other circumstances as the Commission may permit by rules and regulations or orders for the protection of investors in order to insure that such purchases are made in a manner or on a basis which does not unfairly discriminate against any holders of the class or classes of securities to be purchased.

Registration of Securities Under Securities Act of 1933

Sec. 24. (a) In registering under the Securities Act of 1933 any security of which it is the issuer, a registered investment company, in lieu of furnishing a registration statement containing the information and documents specified in schedule A of said Act, may file a registration statement containing the following information and documents:

(1) such copies of the registration statement filed by such company under this title, and of such reports filed by such company pursuant to section 30 or such copies of portions of such registration statement and reports, as the Commission shall designate by rules and regulations; and

(2) such additional information and documents (including a prospectus) as the Commission shall prescribe by rules and regulations as necessary or appropriate in the public interest or for the protection of investors.

(b) It shall be unlawful for any of the following companies, or for any underwriter for such a company, in connection with a public offering of any security of which such company is the issuer, to make use of the mails or any means or instrumentalities of interstate commerce to transmit any advertisement, pamphlet, circular, form letter, or other sales literature addressed to or intended for distribution to prospective investors unless three copies of the full text thereof have been filed with the Commission or are filed with the Commission within ten days thereafter:

(1) any registered open-end company;

(2) any registered unit investment trust; or

(3) any registered face-amount certificate company.

(c) In addition to the powers relative to prospectuses granted the Commission by section 10 of the Securities Act of 1933, the Commission is authorized to require, by rules and regulations or order, that the information contained in any prospectus relating to any periodic payment plan certificate or face-amount certificate registered under the Securities Act of 1933 on or after the effective date of this title be presented in such form and order of items, and such prospectus contain such summaries of any portion of such information, as are necessary or appropriate in the public interest or for the protection of investors.

(d) The exemption provided by paragraph (8) of section 3(a) of the Securities Act of 1933 shall not apply to any security of which an investment company is the issuer. The exemption provided by paragraph (11) of said section 3(a) shall not apply to any security of which a registered investment company is the issuer. The exemption provided by the third clause of section 4(1) now section 4(3) of the Securities Act of 1933, as amended, shall not apply to any transaction in a security issued by a face-amount certificate company or in a redeemable security issued by an open-end management company or unit investment trust, if any other security of the same class is currently being offered or sold by the issuer or by or through an underwriter in a distribution which is not exempted from section 5 of said Act, except to such extent and subject to such terms and conditions as the Commission, having due regard for the public interest and the protection of investors, may prescribe by rules or regulations with respect to any class of persons, securities, or transactions.

(e) For the purposes of section 11 of the Securities Act of 1933, as amended, the effective date of the latest amendment filed shall be deemed the effective date of the registration statement with respect to securities sold after such amendment shall have become effective. For the purposes of section 13 of the Securities Act of 1933, as amended, no such security shall be deemed to have been bona fide offered to the public prior to the effective date of the latest amendment filed pursuant to this subsection. Except to the extent the Commission otherwise provides by rules or regulations as appropriate in the public interest or for the protection of investors, no prospectus relating to a security issued by a face-amount certificate company or a redeemable security issued by an open-end management company or unit investment trust which varies for the purposes of subsection (a)(3) of section 10 of the Securities Act of 1933 from the latest prospectus filed as a part of the registration statement shall be deemed to meet the requirements of said section 10 unless filed as part of an amendment to the registration statement under said Act and such amendment has become effective.

(f) *Registration of Indefinite Amount of Securities.*—

(1) *Registration of securities.*—Upon the effective date of its registration statement, as provided by section 8 of the Securities Act of 1933, a face-amount certificate company, open-end management company, or unit investment trust, shall be deemed to have registered an indefinite amount of securities.

(2) *Payment of registration fees.*—Not later than 90 days after the end of the fiscal year of a company or trust referred to in paragraph (1), the company or trust, as applicable, shall pay a registration fee to the Commission, calculated in the manner specified in section 6(b) of the Securities Act of 1933, based on the aggregate sales price for which its securities (including, for purposes of this paragraph, all securities issued pursuant to a dividend reinvestment plan) were sold pursuant to a registration of an indefinite amount of securities under this subsection during the previous fiscal year of the company or trust, reduced by—

(A) the aggregate redemption or repurchase price of the securities of the company or trust during that year; and

(B) the aggregate redemption or repurchase price of the securities of the company or trust during any prior fiscal year ending not more than 1 year before the date of enactment of the Investment Company Act Amendments of 1996, that were not used previously by the company or trust to reduce fees payable under this section.

(3) *Interest due on late payment.*—A company or trust paying the fee required by this subsection or any portion thereof more than 90 days after the end of the fiscal year of the company or trust shall pay to the Commission interest on unpaid amounts, at the average investment rate for Treasury tax and loan accounts published by the Secretary of the Treasury pursuant to section 3717(a) of title 31, United States Code. The payment of interest pursuant to this paragraph shall not preclude the Commission from bringing an action to enforce the requirements of paragraph (2).

(4) *Rulemaking authority.*—The Commission may adopt rules and regulations to implement this subsection.

(g) *Additional Prospectuses.*—In addition to any prospectus permitted or required by section 10(a) of the Securities Act of 1933, the Commission shall permit, by rules or regulations deemed necessary or appropriate in the public interest or for the protection of investors, the use of a prospectus for purposes of section 5(b)(1) of that Act with respect to securities issued by a registered investment company. Such a prospectus, which may include information the substance of which is not included in the prospectus specified in section 10(a) of the Securities Act of 1933, shall be deemed to be permitted by section 10(b) of that Act.

Plans of Reorganization

Sec. 25. (a) Any person who, by use of the mails or any means or instrumentality of interstate commerce or otherwise, solicits or permits the use of his name to solicit any proxy, consent, authorization, power of attorney, ratification, deposit, or dissent in respect of any plan of reorganization of any registered investment company shall file with, or mail to, the Commission for its information, within twenty-four hours after the commencement of any such solicitation, a copy of such plan and any deposit agreement relating thereto and of any proxy, consent, authorization, power of attorney, ratification, instrument of deposit, or instrument of dissent in respect thereto, if or to the extent that such documents shall not already have been filed with the Commission.

(b) The Commission is authorized, if so requested, prior to any solicitation of security holders with respect to any plan of reorganization, by any registered investment company which is, or any of the securities of which are, the subject of or is a participant in any such plan, or if so requested by the holders of 25 per centum of any class of its outstanding securities, to render an advisory report in respect of the fairness of any such plan and its effect upon any class or classes of security holders. In such event any registered investment company, in respect of which the Commission shall have rendered any such advisory report, shall mail promptly a copy of such advisory report to all its security holders affected by any such plan: *Provided,* That such advisory report shall have been received by it at least forty-eight hours (not including Sundays and holidays) before final action is taken in relation to such plan at any meeting of security holders called to act in relation thereto, or any adjournment of any such meeting, or if no meeting be called, then prior to the final date of acceptance of such plan by security holders. In respect of securities not registered as to ownership, in lieu of mailing a copy of such advisory report, such registered company shall publish promptly a statement of the existence of such advisory report in a newspaper of general circulation in its principal place of business and shall make available copies of such advisory report upon request. Notwithstanding the provision of this section the Commission shall not render such advisory report although so requested by any such investment company or such security holders if the fairness or feasibility of said plan is in issue in any proceeding pending in any court of competent jurisdiction unless such plan is submitted to the Commission for that purpose by such court.

(c) Any district court of the United States in the State of incorporation of a registered investment company, or any such court for the district in which such company maintains its principal place of business, is authorized to enjoin the consummation of any plan of reorganization of such registered investment company upon proceedings instituted by the Commission (which is authorized so to proceed upon behalf of security holders of such registered company, or any class thereof), if such court shall determine that any such plan is not fair and equitable to all security holders.

(d) Nothing contained in this section shall in any way affect or derogate from the powers of the courts of the United States and the Commission with reference to reorganizations contained in Title 11 of the United States Code.

Unit Investment Trusts

Sec. 26. (a) No principal underwriter for or depositor of a registered unit investment trust shall sell, except by surrender to the trustee for redemption, any security of which such trust is the issuer (other than short-term paper), unless the trust indenture, agreement of custodianship, or other instrument pursuant to which such security is issued—

(1) designates one or more trustees or custodians, each of which is a bank, and provides that each such trustee or custodian shall have at all times an aggregate capital, surplus, and undivided profits of a specified minimum amount, which shall not be less than $500,000 (but may also provide, if such trustee or custodian publishes reports of condition at least annually, pursuant to law or to the requirements of its supervising or examining authority, that for the purposes of this paragraph the aggregate capital, surplus, and undivided profits of such trustee or custodian shall be deemed to be its aggregate capital, surplus, and undivided profits as set forth in its most recent report of condition so published);

(2) provides, in substance, (A) that during the life of the trust the trustee or custodian, if not otherwise remunerated, may charge against and collect from the income of the trust, and from the corpus thereof if no income is available, such fees for its services and such reimbursement for its expenses as are provided for in such instrument; (B) that no such charge or collection shall be made except for services theretofore performed or expenses theretofore incurred;

(C) that no payment to the depositor of or a principal underwriter for such trust, or to any affiliated person or agent of such depositor or underwriter, shall be allowed the trustee or custodian as an expense (except that provision may be made for the payment to any such person of a fee), not exceeding such reasonable amount as the Commission may prescribe as compensation for performing bookkeeping and other administrative services, of a character normally performed by the trustee or custodian itself; and (D) that the trustee or custodian shall have possession of all securities and other property in which the funds of the trust are invested, all funds held for such investment, all equalization, redemption, and other special funds of the trust, and all income upon, accretions to, and proceeds of such property and funds, and shall segregate and hold the same in trust (subject only to the charges and collections allowed under clauses (A), (B), and (C) until distribution thereof to the security holders of the trust);

(3) provides, in substance, that the trustee or custodian shall not resign until either (A) the trust has been completely liquidated and the proceeds of the liquidation distributed to the security holders of the trust, or (B) a successor trustee or custodian, having the qualifications prescribed in paragraph (1), has been designated and has accepted such trusteeship or custodianship; and

(4) provides, in substance, (A) that a record will be kept by the depositor or an agent of the depositor of the name and address of, and the shares issued by the trust and held by, every holder of any security issued pursuant to such instrument, insofar as such information is known to the depositor or agent; and (B) that whenever a security is deposited with the trustee in substitution for any security in which such security holder has an undivided interest, the depositor or the agent of the depositor will, within five days after such substitution, either deliver or mail to such security holder a notice of substitution, including an identification of the securities eliminated and the securities substituted, and a specification of the shares of such security holder affected by the substitution.

(b) The Commission may, after consultation with and taking into consideration the views of the Federal banking agencies (as defined in section 3 of the Federal Deposit Insurance Act), adopt rules and regulations, and issue orders, consistent with the protection of investors, prescribing the conditions under which is an affiliated person of a principal underwriter for, or depositor of, a registered unit investment trust, may serve as trustee or custodian under subsection (a)(1).

(c) It shall be unlawful for any depositor or trustee of a registered unit investment trust holding the security of a single issuer to substitute another security for such security unless the Commission shall have approved the substitution. The Commission shall issue an order approving such substitution if the evidence establishes that it is consistent with the protection of investors and the purposes fairly intended by the policy and provisions of this title.

(d) In the event that a trust indenture, agreement of custodianship, or other instrument pursuant to which securities of a registered unit investment trust are issued does not comply with the requirements of subsection (a) of this section, such instrument will be deemed to meet such requirements if a written contract or agreement binding on the parties and embodying such requirements has been executed by the depositor on the one part and the trustee or custodian on the other part, and three copies of such contract of agreement have been filed with the Commission.

(e) Whenever the Commission has reason to believe that a unit investment trust is inactive and that its liquidation is in the interest of the security holders of such trust, the Commission may file a complaint seeking the liquidation of such trust in the district court of the United States in any district wherein any trustee of such trust resides or has its principal place of business. A copy of such complaint shall be served on every trustee of such trust, and notice of the proceeding shall be given such other interested persons in such manner and at such times as the court may direct. If the court determines that such liquidation is in the interest of the security holders of such trust, the court shall order such liquidation and, after payment of necessary expenses, the distribution of the proceeds to the security holders of the trust in such manner and on such terms as may to the court appear equitable.

(f) *Exemption.*—

(1) *In general.*—Subsection (a) does not apply to any registered separate account funding variable insurance contracts, or to the sponsoring insurance company and principal underwriter of such account.

(2) *Limitation on sales.*—It shall be unlawful for any registered separate account funding variable insurance contracts, or for the sponsoring insurance company of such account, to sell any such contract—

(A) unless the fees and charges deducted under the contract, in the aggregate, are reasonable in relation to the services rendered, the expenses expected to be incurred, and the risks assumed by the insurance company, and, beginning on the earlier of August 1, 1997, or the earliest effective date of any registration statement or amendment thereto for such contract following the date of enactment of this subsection, the insurance company so represents in the registration statement for the contract; and

(B) unless the insurance company—

(i) complies with all other applicable provisions of this section, as if it were a trustee or custodian of the registered separate account;

(ii) files with the insurance regulatory authority of the State which is the domiciliary State of the insurance company, an annual statement of its financial condition, which most recent statement indicates that the insurance company has a combined capital and surplus, if a stock company, or an unassigned surplus, if a mutual company, of not less than $1,000,000, or such other amount as the Commission may from time to time prescribe by rule, as necessary or appropriate in the public interest or for the protection of investors; and

(iii) together with its registered separate accounts, is supervised and examined periodically by the insurance authority of such State.

(3) *Fees and charges.*—For purposes of paragraph (2), the fees and charges deducted under the contract shall include all fees and charges imposed for any purpose and in any manner.

(4) *Regulatory authority.*—The Commission may issue such rules and regulations to carry out paragraph (2)(A) as it determines are necessary or appropriate in the public interest or for the protection of investors.

Periodic Payment Plans

Sec. 27. (a) It shall be unlawful for any registered investment company issuing periodic payment plan certificates, or for any depositor of or underwriter for such company, to sell any such certificate, if—

(1) the sales load on such certificate exceeds 9 per centum of the total payments to be made thereon;

(2) more than one-half of any of the first twelve monthly payments thereon, or their equivalent, is deducted for sales load;

(3) the amount of sales load deducted from any one of such first payments exceeds proportionately the amount deducted from any other such payment, or the amount deducted from any subsequent payment exceeds proportionately the amount deducted from any other subsequent payment;

(4) the first payment on such certificate is less than $20, or any subsequent payment is less than $10;

(5) if such registered company is a management company, the proceeds of such certificate or the securities in which such proceeds are invested are subject to management fees (other than fees for administrative services of the character described in clause (C), paragraph (2), of section 26(a)) exceeding such reasonable amount as the Commission may prescribe, whether such fees are payable to such company or to investment advisers thereof; or

(6) if such registered company is a unit investment trust the assets of which are securities issued by a management company, the depositor of or principal underwriter for such trust, or any affiliated person of such depositor or underwriter, is to receive from such management company or any affiliated person thereof any fee or payment on account of payments on such certificate exceeding such reasonable amount as the Commission may prescribe.

(b) If it appears to the Commission, upon application or otherwise, that smaller companies are subjected to relatively higher operating costs and that in order to make due allowance therefor it is necessary or appropriate in the public interest and consistent with the protection of investors that a provision or provisions of paragraph (1), (2), or (3) of subsection (a) relative to sales load be relaxed in the case of certain registered investment companies issuing periodic payment plan certificates, or certain specified classes of such companies, the Commission is authorized by rules and regulations or order to grant any such company or class of companies appropriate qualified exemptions from the provisions of said paragraphs.

(c) It shall be unlawful for any registered investment company issuing periodic payment plan certificates, or for any depositor of or underwriter for such company, to sell any such certificate, unless—

(1) such certificate is a redeemable security; and

(2) the proceeds of all payments on such certificate (except such amounts as are deducted for sales load) are deposited with a trustee or custodian having the qualifications prescribed in paragraph (1) of section 26(a) for the trustee of unit investment trusts, and are held by such trustee or custodian under an indenture or agreement containing, in substance, the provisions required by paragraphs (2) and (3) of section 26(a) for the trust indentures of unit investment trusts.

(d) Notwithstanding subsection (a) of this section, it shall be unlawful for any registered investment company issuing periodic payment plan certificates, or for any depositor of or underwriter for such company, to sell any such certificate unless the certificate provides that the holder thereof may surrender the certificate at any time within the first eighteen months after the issuance of the certificate and receive in payment thereof, in cash, the sum of (1) the value of his account, and (2) an amount, from such underwriter or depositor, equal to that part of the excess paid for sales loading which is over 15 per centum of the gross payments made by the certificate holder. The Commission may make rules and regulations applicable to such underwriters and depositors specifying such reserve requirements as it deems necessary or appropriate in order for such underwriters and depositors to carry out the obligations to refund sales charges required by this subsection.

(e) With respect to any periodic payment plan certificate sold subject to the provisions of subsection (d) of this section, the registered investment company issuing such periodic payment plan certificate, or any depositor of or underwriter for such company, shall in writing (1) inform each certificate holder who has missed three payments or more, within thirty days following the expiration of fifteen months after the issuance of the certificate, or, if any such holder has missed one payment or more after such period of fifteen months but prior to the expiration of eighteen months after the issuance of the certificate, at any time prior to the expiration of such eighteen-month period, of his right to surrender his certificate as specified in subsection (d) of this section, and (2) inform the certificate holder of (A) the value of the holder's account as of the time the written notice was given to such holder, and (B) the amount to which he is entitled as specified in subsection (d) of this section. The Commission may make rules specifying the method, form, and contents of the notice required by this subsection.

(f) With respect to any periodic payment plan (other than a plan under which the amount of sales load deducted from any payment thereon does not exceed 9 per centum of such payment), the custodian bank for such plan shall mail to each certificate holder, within sixty days after the issuance of the certificate, a statement of charges to be deducted from the projected payments on the certificate and a notice of his right of withdrawal as specified in this section. The Commission may make rules specifying the method, form, and contents of the notice required by this subsection. The certificate holder may within forty-five days of the mailing of the notice specified in this subsection surrender his certificate and receive in payment thereof, in cash, the sum of (1) the value of his account, and (2) an amount, from the underwriter or depositor, equal to the difference between the gross payments made and the net amount invested. The Commission may make rules and regulations applicable to underwriters and depositors of companies issuing any such certificate specifying such reserve requirements as it deems necessary or appropriate in order for such underwriters and depositors to carry out the obligations to refund sales charges required by this subsection.

(g) Notwithstanding the provisions of subsections (a) and (d), a registered investment company issuing periodic payment plan certificates may elect, by written notice to the Commission, to be governed by the provisions of subsection (h) rather than the provisions of subsections (a) and (d) of this section.

(h) Upon making the election specified in subsection (g), it shall be unlawful for any such electing registered investment company issuing periodic payment plan certificates, or for any depositor of or underwriter for such company, to sell any such certificate, if—

(1) the sales load on such certificate exceeds 9 per centum of the total payments to be made thereon;

(2) more than 20 per centum of any payment thereon is deducted for sales load, or an average of more than 16 per centum is deducted for sales load from the first forty-eight monthly payments thereon, or their equivalent;

(3) the amount of sales load deducted from any one of the first twelve monthly payments, and thirteenth through twenty-fourth monthly payments, the twenty-fifth through thirty-sixth monthly payments, or the thirty-seventh through forty-eighth monthly payments, or their equivalents, respectively, exceeds proportionately the amount deducted from any other such payment, or the amount deducted from any subsequent payment exceeds proportionately the amount deducted from any other subsequent payment;

(4) the deduction for sales load on the excess of the payment or payments in any month over the minimum monthly payment, or its equivalent, to be made on the certificate exceeds the sales load applicable to payments subsequent to the first forty-eight monthly payments or their equivalent;

(5) the first payment on such certificate is less than $20, or any subsequent payment is less than $10;

(6) if such registered company is a management company, the proceeds of such certificate or the securities in which such proceeds are invested are subject to management fees (other than fees for administrative services of the character described

in clause (C) of paragraph (2) of section 26(a)) exceeding such reasonable amount as the Commission may prescribe, whether such fees are payable to such company or to investment advisers thereof; or

(7) if such registered company is a unit investment trust the assets of which are securities issued by a management company, the depositor of or principal underwriter for such trust, or any affiliated person of such depositor or underwriter, is to receive from such management company or any affiliated person thereof any fee or payment on account of payments on such certificate exceeding such reasonable amount as the Commission may prescribe.

(i)(1) This section does not apply to any registered separate account funding variable insurance contracts, or to the sponsoring insurance company and principal underwriter of such account, except as provided in paragraph (2).

(2) It shall be unlawful for any registered separate account funding variable insurance contracts, or for the sponsoring insurance company of such account, to sell any such contract unless—

(A) such contract is a redeemable security; and

(B) the insurance company complies with section 26(e) and any rules or regulations issued by the Commission under section 26(e).

Face-Amount Certificate Companies

Sec. 28. (a) It shall be unlawful for any registered face-amount certificate company to issue or sell any face-amount certificate, or to collect or accept any payment on any such certificate issued by such company on or after the effective date of this title, unless—

(1) such company, if organized before March 15, 1940, was actively and continuously engaged in selling face-amount certificates on and before that date, and has outstanding capital stock worth upon a fair valuation of assets not less than $50,000; or if organized on or after March 15, 1940, has capital stock in an amount not less than $250,000 which has been bona fide subscribed and paid for in cash; and

(2) such company maintains at all times minimum certificate reserves on all its outstanding face-amount certificates in an aggregate amount calculated and adjusted as follows:

(A) the reserves for each certificate of the installment type shall be based on assumed annual, semi-annual, quarterly, or monthly reserve payments according to the manner in which gross payments for any certificate year are made by the holder, which reserve payments shall be sufficient in amount, as and when accumulated at a rate not to exceed 3½ per centum per annum compounded annually, to provide the minimum maturity or face amount of the certificate when due. Such reserve payments may be graduated according to certificate years so that the reserve payment or payments for the first certificate year shall amount to at least 50 per centum of the required gross annual payment for such year and the reserve payment or payments for each of the second to fifth certificate years inclusive shall amount to at least 93 per centum of each such year's required gross annual payment and for the sixth and each subsequent certificate year the reserve payment or payments shall amount to at least 96 per centum of each such year's required gross annual payment: *Provided*, That such aggregate reserve payments shall amount to at least 93 per centum of the aggregate gross annual payments required to be made by the holder to obtain the maturity of the certificate. The company may at its option take as loading from the gross payment or payments for a certificate year, as and when made by the certificate holder, an amount or amounts equal in the aggregate for such year to not more than the excess, if any, of the gross payment or payments required to be made by the holder for such year, over and above the percentage of the gross annual payment required herein for such year for reserve purposes. Such loading may be taken by the company prior to or after the setting up of the reserve payment or payments for such year and the reserve payment or payments for such year may be graduated and adjusted to correspond with the amount of the gross payment or payments made by the certificate holder for such year less the loading so taken;

(B) if the foregoing minimum percentages of the gross annual payments required under the provisions of such certificate should produce reserve payments larger than are necessary at 3½ per centum per annum compounded annually to provide the minimum maturity or face amount of the certificate when due, the reserve shall be based upon reserve payments accumulated as provided under preceding subparagraph (A) of this paragraph except that in lieu of the 3½ per centum rate specified therein, such rate shall be lowered to the minimum rate, expressed in multiples of one-eighth of 1 per centum, which will accumulate such reserve payments to the maturity value when due;

(C) if the actual annual gross payment to be made by the certificate holder on any certificate issued prior to or after the effective date of this Act is less than the amount of any assumed reserve payment or payments for a certificate year, such company shall maintain as a part of such minimum certificate reserves a deficiency reserve equal to the total present value of future deficiencies in the gross payments, calculated at a rate not to exceed 3½ per centum per annum compounded annually;

(D) for each certificate of the installment type the amount of the reserve shall at any time be at least equal to (1) the then amount of the reserve payments set up under section 28(a)(2)(A) or (B); (2) the accumulations on such reserve payments as computed under subparagraphs (A) or (B) of this paragraph (2); (3) the amount of any deficiency reserve required under subparagraph (C) hereof; and (4) such amount as shall have been credited to the account of each certificate holder in the form of any credit, or any dividend, or any interest in addition to the minimum maturity amount specified in such certificate, plus any accumulations on any amount or amounts so credited, at a rate not exceeding 3½ per centum per annum compounded annually;

(E) for each certificate which is fully paid, including any fully paid obligations resulting from or effected upon the maturity of the previously issued certificate, and for each paid-up certificate issued as provided in subsection (f) of this section prior to maturity, the amount of the reserve shall at any time be at least equal to (1) such amount as and when accumulated at a rate not to exceed 3½ per centum per annum compounded annually, will provide the amount or amounts payable when due and (2) such amount as shall have been credited to the account of each such certificate holder in the form of any credit, or any dividend, or any interest in addition to the minimum maturity amount specified in the certificate, plus any accumulations on any amount or amounts so credited, at a rate not exceeding 3½ per centum per annum compounded annually;

(F) for each certificate of the installment type under which gross payments have been made by or credited to the holder thereof covering a payment period or periods or any part thereof beyond the then current payment period as defined by the terms of such certificate, and for which period or periods no reserve has been set up under subparagraph (A) or (B) hereof, an advance payment reserve shall be set up and maintained in the amount of the present value of any such unapplied advance gross payments, computed at a rate not to exceed 3½ per centum per annum compounded annually;

(G) such appropriate contingency reserves for death and disability benefits and for reinstatement rights on any such certificate providing for such benefits or rights as the Commission shall prescribe by rule, regulation, or order based upon the experience of face-amount companies in relation to such contingencies.

At no time shall the aggregate certificate reserves herein required by subparagraphs (A) to (F), inclusive, be less than the aggregate surrender values and other amounts to which all certificate holders may be then entitled.

For the purpose of this subsection (a), no certificate of the installment type shall be deemed to be outstanding if before a surrender value has been attained the holder thereof has been in continuous default in making his payments thereon for a period of one year.

(b) It shall be unlawful for any registered face-amount certificate company to issue or sell any face-amount certificate, or to collect or accept any payment on any such certificate issued by such company on or after the effective date of this title, unless such company has, in cash or qualified investments, assets having a value not less than the aggregate amount of the capital stock requirement and certificate reserves as computed under the provisions of subsection (a) hereof. As used in this subsection, "qualified investments" means investments of a kind which life-insurance companies are permitted to invest in or hold under the provisions of the Code of the District of Columbia as heretofore or hereafter amended, and such other investments as the Commission shall by rule, regulation, or order authorize as qualified investments. Such investments shall be valued in accordance with the provisions of said Code where such provisions are applicable. Investments to which such provisions do not apply shall be valued in accordance with such rules, regulations, or orders as the Commission shall prescribe for the protection of investors.

(c) The Commission shall by rule, regulation, or order, in the public interest or for the protection of investors, require a registered face-amount certificate company to deposit and maintain, upon such terms and conditions as the Commission shall prescribe and as are appropriate for the protection of investors, with one or more institutions having the qualifications required by paragraph (1) of section 26(a) for a trustee of a unit investment trust, all or any part of the investments maintained by such company as certificate reserve requirements under the provisions of subsection (b) hereof: *Provided, however,* That where qualified investments are maintained on deposit by such company in respect of its liabilities under certificates issued to or held by residents of any State as required by the statute of such State or by any order, regulation, or requirement of such State or any official or agency thereof, the amount so on deposit, but not to exceed the amount of reserves required by subsection (a) hereof for the certificates so issued or held, shall be deducted from the amount of qualified investments that may be required to be deposited hereunder.

Assets which are qualified investments under subsection (b) and which are deposited under or as permitted by this subsection (c), may be used and shall be considered as a part of the assets required to be maintained under the provision of said subsection (b).

(d) It shall be unlawful for any registered face-amount certificate company to issue or sell any face-amount certificate, or to collect or accept any payment on any such certificate issued by such company on or after the effective date of this title, unless such certificate contains a provision or provisions to the effect—

(1) that, in respect of any certificate of the installment type, during the first certificate year the holder of the certificate, upon surrender thereof, shall be entitled to a value payable in cash not less than the reserve payments as specified in subparagraph (A) or (B) of paragraph (2) of subsection (a) and

at the end of such certificate year, a value payable in cash at least equal to 50 per centum of the amount of the gross annual payment required thereby for such year;

(2) that, in respect of any certificate of the installment type, at any time after the expiration of the first certificate year and prior to maturity, the holder of the certificate, upon surrender thereof, shall be entitled to a value payable in cash not less than the then amount of the reserve for such certificate required by numbered items (1) and (2) of subparagraph (D) of paragraph (2) of subsection (a) hereof, less a surrender charge that shall not exceed 2 per centum of the face or maturity amount of the certificate, or 15 per centum of the amount of such reserve, whichever is the lesser, but in no event shall such value be less than 50 per centum of the amount of such reserve. The amount of the surrender value for the end of each certificate year shall be set out in the certificate;

(3) that, in respect of any certificate of the installment type, the holder of the certificate, upon surrender thereof for cash or upon receipt of a paid-up certificate as provided in subsection (f) hereof, shall be entitled to a value payable in cash equal to the then amount of any advance payment reserve under such certificate required by subparagraph (F) of paragraph (2) of subsection (a) hereof in addition to any other amounts due the holder hereunder;

(4) that any time prior to maturity, in respect of any certificate which is fully paid, the holder of the certificate, upon surrender thereof, shall be entitled to a value payable in cash not less than the then amount of the reserve for such certificate required by item (1) of subparagraph (E) of paragraph (2) of subsection (a) hereof, less a surrender charge that shall not exceed 2 per centum of the face or maturity amount of the certificate, or 15 per centum of the amount of such reserve, whichever is the lesser: *Provided, however,* That such surrender charge shall not apply as to any obligations of a fully paid type resulting from the maturity of a previously issued certificate. The amount of the surrender value for the end of each certificate year shall be set out in the certificate;

(5) that in respect of any certificate, the holder of the certificate, upon maturity, upon surrender thereof for cash or upon receipt of a paid-up certificate as provided in subsection (f) hereof, shall be entitled to a value payable in cash equal to the then amount of the reserve, if any, for such certificate required by item (4) of subparagraph (D) of paragraph (2) of subsection (a) hereof or item (2) of subparagraph (E) of paragraph (2) of subsection (a) hereof in addition to any other amounts due the holder hereunder.

The term "certificate year" as used in this section in respect of any certificate of the installment type means a period or periods for which one year's payment or payments as provided by the certificate have been made thereon by the holder and the certificate maintained in force by such payments for the time for which the same have been made, and in respect of any certificate which is fully paid or paid-up means any year ending on the anniversary of the date of issuance of the certificate.

Any certificate may provide for loans or advances by the company to the certificate holder on the security of such certificate upon terms prescribed therein but at an interest rate not exceeding 6 per centum per annum. The amount of the required reserves, deposits, and the surrender values thereof available to the holder may be adjusted to take into account any unpaid balance on such loans or advances and interest thereon, for the purposes of this subsection and subsections (b) and (c) hereof.

Any certificate may provide that the company at its option may, prior to the maturity thereof, defer any payment or payments to the certificate holder to which he may be entitled under this subsection (d), for a period of not more than thirty days: *Provided,* That in the event such option is exercised by the company, interest shall accrue on any payment or payments due to the holder, for the period of such deferment at a rate equal to that used in accumulating the reserves for such certificate: *And provided further,* That the Commission may, by rules and regulations or orders in the public interest or for the protection of investors, make provision for any other deferment upon such terms and conditions as it shall prescribe.

(e) It shall be unlawful for any registered face-amount certificate company to issue or sell any face-amount certificate, or to collect or accept any payment on any such certificate issued by such company on or after the effective date of this title, which certificate makes the holder liable to any legal action or proceeding for any unpaid amount on such certificate.

(f) It shall be unlawful for any registered face-amount certificate company to issue or sell any face-amount certificate, or to collect or accept any payment on any such certificate issued by such company on or after the effective date of this title, (1) unless such face-amount certificate contains a provision or provisions to the effect that the holder shall have an optional right to receive a paid-up certificate in lieu of the then attained cash surrender value provided therein and in the amount of such value plus accumulations thereon at a rate to be specified in the paid-up certificate equal to that used in computing the reserve on the original certificate under subparagraph (A) or (B) of paragraph (2) of subsection (a) of this section, such paid-up certificate to become due and payable at the end of a period equal to the balance of the term of such original certificate before maturity; and during the period prior to maturity such paid-up certificate shall have a cash value upon surrender thereof equal to the then amount of the reserve therefor; and (2) unless such face-amount certificate contains a further provision or provisions to the effect that if the holder be in continuous default in his payments on such certificate for a period of six months without having exercised his option to receive a paid-up certificate, as herein provided, the company at the expiration of such six months shall pay the surrender value in cash if such value is less than $100 or if such value is $100 or more shall issue such paid-up certificate to such holder and such payment or issuance, plus the payment of all other amounts to which he may be then entitled under the original certificate, shall operate to cancel his original certificate: *Provided,* That in lieu of the issuance of a new paid-up certificate the original certificate may be converted into a paid-up certificate with the same effect; and (3) unless, where such certificate provides, in the event of default, for the deferment of payments thereon by the holder or of the due dates of such payments or of the maturity date of the certificate, it shall also provide in effect for the right of reinstatement by the holder of the certificate after default and for an option in the holder, at the time of reinstatement, to make up the payment or payments for the default period next preceding such reinstatement with interest thereon not exceeding 6 per centum per annum, with the same effect as if no such default in making such payments had occurred.

The term "default" as used in this subsection (f) shall, without restricting its usual meaning, include a failure to make a payment or payments as and when provided by the certificate.

(g) The foregoing provisions of this section shall not apply to a face-amount certificate company which on or before the effective date of this Act has discontinued the offering of face-amount certificates to the public and issues face-amount certificates only to the holders of certificates previously issued pursuant to an obligation expressed or implied in such certificates.

(h) It shall be unlawful for any registered face-amount certificate company which does not maintain the minimum certificate reserve on all its outstanding face-amount certificates issued prior to the effective date of this Act, in an aggregate amount calculated and adjusted as provided in section 28, to declare or pay any dividends on the shares of such company for or during any calendar year which shall exceed one-third of the net earnings for the next preceding calendar year or which shall exceed 10 per centum of the aggregate net earnings for the next preceding five calendar years, whichever is the lesser amount, or any dividend which shall have been forbidden by the Commission pursuant to the provision of the next sentence of this paragraph. At least thirty days before such company shall declare, pay, or distribute any dividend, it shall give the Commission written notice of its intention to declare, pay, or distribute the same; and if at any time it shall appear to the Commission that the declaration, payment or distribution of any dividend for or during any calendar year might impair the financial integrity of such company or its ability to meet its liabilities under its outstanding face-amount certificates, it may by order forbid the declaration, distribution, or payment of any such dividend.

(i) The foregoing provisions of this section shall apply to all face-amount certificates issued prior to the effective date of this subsection; to the collection or acceptance of any payment on such certificates; to the issuance of face-amount certificates to the holders of such certificates pursuant to an obligation expressed or implied in such certificates; to the provisions of such certificates; to the minimum certificate reserves and deposits maintained with respect thereto; and to the assets that the issuer of such certificate was and is required to have with respect to such certificates. With respect to all face-amount certificates issued after the effective date of this subsection, the provisions of this section shall apply except as hereinafter provided.

(1) Notwithstanding subparagraph (A) of paragraph (2) of subsection (a), the reserves for each certificate of the installment type shall be based on assumed annual, semiannual, quarterly, or monthly reserve payments according to the manner in which gross payments for any certificate year are made by the holder, which reserve payments shall be sufficient in amount, as and when accumulated at a rate not to exceed 3½ per centum per annum compounded annually, to provide the minimum maturity or face amount of the certificate when due. Such reserve payments may be graduated according to certificate years so that the reserve payment or payments for the first three certificate years shall amount to at least 80 per centum of the required gross annual payment for such years; the reserve payment or payments for the fourth certificate year shall amount to at least 90 per centum of such year's required gross annual payment; the reserve payment or payments for the fifth certificate year shall amount to at least 93 per centum of such year's gross annual payment; and for the sixth and each subsequent certificate year the reserve payment or payments shall amount to at least 96 per centum of each such year's required gross annual payment: *Provided,* That such aggregate reserve payments shall amount to at least 93 per centum of the aggregate gross annual payments required to be made by the holder to obtain the maturity of the certificate. The company may at its option take as loading from the gross payment or payments for a certificate year, as and when made by the certificate holder, an amount or amounts equal in the aggregate for such year to not more than the excess, if any, of the gross payment or payments required to be made by the holder for such year, over and above the percentage of the gross annual payment required herein for such year for reserve purposes. Such loading may be taken by the company prior to or after the setting up of the reserve payment or payments for such year and the reserve payment or payments for such year may be graduated and adjusted to correspond with the amount of the gross payment or payments made by the certificate holder for such year less the loading so taken.

(2) Notwithstanding paragraphs (1) and (2) of subsection (d), (A) in respect of any certificate of the installment type, during

the first certificate year, the holder of the certificate, upon surrender thereof, shall be entitled to a value payable in cash not less than 80 per centum of the amount of the gross payments made on the certificate; and (B) in respect of any certificate of the installment type, at any time after the expiration of the first certificate year and prior to maturity, the holder of the certificate, upon surrender thereof, shall be entitled to a value payable in cash not less than the then amount of the reserve for such certificate required by clauses (1) and (2) of subparagraph (D) of paragraph (2) of subsection (a), less a surrender charge that shall not exceed 2 per centum of the face or maturity amount of the certificate, or 15 per centum of the amount of such reserve, whichever is lesser, but in no event shall such value be less than 80 per centum of the gross payments made on the certificate. The amount of the surrender value for the end of each certificate year shall be set out in the certificate.

Sec. 29. Reserved.

Periodic and Other Reports; Reports of Affiliated Persons

Sec. 30. (a) Every registered investment company shall file annually with with the Commission such information, documents, and reports as investment companies having securities registered on a national securities exchange are required to file annually pursuant to section 13(a) of the Securities Exchange Act of 1934 and the rules and regulations issued thereunder.

(b) Every registered investment company shall file with the Commission—

(1) such information, documents, and reports (other than financial statements), as the Commission may require to keep reasonably current the information and documents contained in the registration statement of such company filed under this title; and

(2) copies of every periodic or interim report or similar communication containing financial statements and transmitted to any class of such company's security holders, such copies to be filed not later than ten days after such transmission.

Any information or documents contained in a report or other communication to security holders filed pursuant to paragraph (2) may be incorporated by reference in any report subsequently or concurrently filed pursuant to paragraph (1).

(c)(1) The Commission shall take such action as it deems necessary or appropriate, consistent with the public interest and the protection of investors, to avoid unnecessary reporting by, and minimize the compliance burdens on, registered investment companies and their affiliated persons in exercising its authority—

(A) under subsection (f); and

(B) under subsection (b)(1), if the Commission requires the filing of information, documents, and reports under that subsection on a basis more frequently than semiannually.

(2) Action taken by the Commission under paragraph (1) shall include considering, and requesting public comment on—

(A) feasible alternatives that minimize the reporting burdens on registered investment companies; and

(B) the utility of such information, documents, and reports to the Commission in relation to the costs to registered investment companies and their affiliated persons of providing such information, documents, and reports.

(d) The Commission shall issue rules and regulations permitting the filing with the Commission, and with any national securities exchange concerned, of copies of periodic reports, or of extracts therefrom, filed by any registered investment company pursuant to subsections (a) and (b), in lieu of any reports and documents required of such company under section 13 or 15(d) of the Securities Exchange Act of 1934.

(e) Every registered investment company shall transmit to its stockholders, at least semiannually, reports containing such of the following information and financial statements or their equivalent, as of a reasonably current date, as the Commission may prescribe by rules and regulations for the protection of investors, which reports shall not be misleading in any material respect in the light of the reports required to be filed pursuant to subsections (a) and (b):

(1) a balance sheet accompanied by a statement of the aggregate value of investments on the date of such balance sheet;

(2) a list showing the amounts and values of securities owned on the date of such balance sheet;

(3) a statement of income, for the period covered by the report, which shall be itemized at least with respect to each category of income and expense representing more than 5 per centum of total income or expense;

(4) a statement of surplus, which shall be itemized at least with respect to each charge or credit to the surplus account which represents more than 5 per centum of the total charges or credits during the period covered by the report;

(5) a statement of the aggregate remuneration paid by the company during the period covered by the report (A) to all directors and to all members of any advisory board for regular compensation; (B) to each director and to each member of an advisory board for special compensation; (C) to all officers; and (D) to each person of whom any officer or director of the company is an affiliated person; and

(6) a statement of the aggregate dollar amount of purchases and sales of investment securities, other than Government securities made during the period covered by the report:

Provided, That if in the judgment of the Commission any item required under this subsection is inapplicable or inappropriate to any specified type or types of investment company, the Commission may by rules and regulations permit in lieu thereof the inclusion of such item of a comparable character as it may deem applicable or appropriate to such type or types of investment company.

(f) The Commission may, by rule, require that semiannual reports containing the information set forth in subsection (e) include such other information as the Commission deems necessary or appropriate in the public interest or for the protection of investors.

(g) *Disclosure to Church Plan Participants.*—A person that maintains a church plan that is excluded from the definition of an investment company solely by reason of section 3(c)(14) shall provide disclosure to plan participants, in writing, and not less frequently than annually, and for new participants joining such a plan after May 31, 1996, as soon as is practicable after joining such plan, that—

(1) the plan, or any company or account maintained to manage or hold plan assets and interests in such plan, company, or account, are not subject to registration, regulation, or reporting under this title, the Securities Act of 1933, the Securities Exchange Act of 1934, or State securities laws; and

(2) plan participants and beneficiaries therefore will not be afforded the protections of those provisions.

(h) *Notice to Commission.*—The Commission may issue rules and regulations to require any person that maintains a church plan that is excluded from the definition of an investment company solely by reason of section 3(c)(14) to file a notice with the Commission containing such information and in such form as the Commission may prescribe as necessary or appropriate in the public interest or consistent with the protection of investors.

(i) Financial statements contained in annual reports required pursuant to subsections (a) and (e), if required by the rules and regulations of the Commission, shall be accompanied by a certificate of independent public accountants. The certificate of such independent public accountants shall be based upon an audit not less in scope or procedures followed than that which independent public accountants would ordinarily make for the purpose of presenting comprehensive and dependable financial statements, and shall contain such information as the Commission may prescribe, by rules and regulations in the public interest or for the protection of investors, as to the nature and scope of the audit and the findings and opinion of the accountants. Each such report shall state that such independent public accountants have verified securities owned, either by actual examination, or by receipt of a certificate from the custodian, as the Commission may prescribe by rules and regulations.

(j) Every person who is directly or indirectly the beneficial owner of more than 10 per centum of any class of outstanding securities (other than short-term paper) of which a registered closed-end company is the issuer or who is an officer, director, member of an advisory board, investment adviser, or affiliated person of an investment adviser of such a company shall in respect of his transactions in any securities of such company (other than short-term paper) be subject to the same duties and liabilities as those imposed by section 16 of the Securities Exchange Act of 1934 upon certain beneficial owners, directors, and officers in respect of their transactions in certain equity securities.

Accounts and Records

Sec. 31. (a) *Maintenance of Records.—*

(1) *In General.*—Each registered investment company, and each underwriter, broker, dealer, or investment adviser that is a majority-owned subsidiary of such a company, shall maintain and preserve such records (as defined in section 3(a)(37) of the Securities Exchange Act of 1934) for such period or periods as the Commission, by rules and regulations, may prescribe as necessary or appropriate in the public interest or for the protection of investors. Each investment adviser that is not a majority-owned subsidiary of, and each depositor of any registered investment company, and each principal underwriter for any registered investment company other than a closed-end company, shall maintain and preserve for such period or periods as the Commission shall prescribe by rules and regulations, such records as are necessary or appropriate to record such person's transactions with such registered company.

(2) *Minimizing compliance burden.*—In exercising its authority under this subsection, the Commission shall take such steps as it deems necessary or appropriate, consistent with the public interest and for the protection of investors, to avoid unnecessary recordkeeping by, and minimize the compliance burden on, persons required to maintain records under this subsection (hereafter in this section referred to as "subject persons"). Such steps shall include considering, and requesting public comment on—

(A) feasible alternatives that minimize the recordkeeping burdens on subject persons;

(B) the necessity of such records in view of the public benefits derived from the independent scrutiny of such records through Commission examination;

(C) the costs associated with maintaining the information that would be required to be reflected in such records; and

(D) the effects that a proposed recordkeeping requirement would have on internal compliance, policies and procedures.

(b) *Examinations of Records.—*

(1) *In general.*—All records required to be maintained and preserved in accordance with subsection (a) shall be subject at any time and from time to time to such reasonable periodic, special, and other examinations by the Commission, or any member or representative thereof, as the Commission may prescribe.

(2) *Availability.*—For purposes of examinations referred to in paragraph (1), any subject person shall make available to the Commission or its representatives any copies or extracts from such records as may be prepared without undue effort, expense, or delay as the Commission or its representatives may reasonably request.

(3) *Commission action.*—The Commission shall exercise its authority under this subsection with due regard for the benefits of internal compliance policies and procedures and the effective implementation and operation thereof.

(c) *Limitations on Disclosure by Commission.*—Notwithstanding any other provision of law, the Commission shall not be compelled to disclose any internal compliance or audit records, or information contained therein, provided to the Commission under this section. Nothing in this subsection shall authorize the Commission to withhold information from the Congress or prevent the Commission from complying with a request for information from any other Federal department or agency requesting the information for purposes within the scope of the jurisdiction of that department or agency, or complying with an order of a court of the United States in an action brought by the United States or the Commission. For purposes of section 552 of title 5, United States Code, this section shall be considered a statute described in subsection (b)(3)(B) of such section 552.

(d) *Definitions.*—For purposes of this section—

(1) the term "internal compliance policies and procedures" means policies and procedures designed by subject persons to promote compliance with the Federal securities laws; and

(2) the term "internal compliance and audit record" means any record prepared by a subject person in accordance with internal compliance policies and procedures.

Regulatory Authority

(e) The Commission may, in the public interest or for the protection of investors, issue rules and regulations providing for a reasonable degree of uniformity in the accounting policies and principles to be followed by registered investment companies in maintaining their accounting records and in preparing financial statements required pursuant to this title.

Exemption Authority

(f) The Commission, upon application made by any registered investment company, may by order exempt a specific transaction or transactions from the provisions of any rule or regulation made pursuant to subsection (e), if the Commission finds that such rule or regulation should not reasonably be applied to such transaction.

Accountants and Auditors

Sec. 32. (a) If shall be unlawful for any registered management company or registered face-amount certificate company to file with the Commission any financial statement signed or certified by an independent public accountant, unless—

(1) such accountant shall have been selected at a meeting held within thirty days before or after the beginning of the fiscal year or before the annual meeting of stockholders in that year by the vote, cast in person, of a majority of those members of the board of directors who are not interested persons of such registered company;

(2) such selection shall have been submitted for ratification or rejection at the next succeeding annual meeting of stockholders if such meeting be held, except that any vacancy occurring between annual meetings, due to the death or resignation of the accountant, may be filled by the vote of a majority of those members of the board of directors who are not interested persons of such registered company, cast in person at a meeting

called for the purpose of voting on such action;

(3) the employment of such accountant shall have been conditioned upon the right of the company by vote of a majority of the outstanding voting securities at any meeting called for the purpose to terminate such employment forthwith without any penalty; and

(4) such certificate or report of such accountant shall be addressed both to the board of directors of such registered company and to the security holders thereof.

If the selection of an accountant has been rejected pursuant to paragraph (2) or his employment terminated pursuant to paragraph (3), the vacancy so occurring may be filled by a vote of a majority of the outstanding voting securities, either at the meeting at which the rejection or termination occurred or, if not so filled, at a subsequent meeting which shall be called for the purpose. In the case of a common-law trust of the character described in section 16(c), no ratification of the employment of such accountant shall be required but such employment may be terminated and such accountant removed by action of the holders of record of a majority of the outstanding shares of beneficial interest in such trust in the same manner as is provided in section 16(c) in respect of the removal of a trustee, and all the provisions therein contained as to the calling of a meeting shall be applicable. In the event of such termination and removal, the vacancy so occurring may be filled by action of the holders of record of a majority of the shares of beneficial interest either at the meeting, if any, at which such termination and removal occurs, or by instruments in writing filed with the custodian, or if not so filed within a reasonable time then at a subsequent meeting which shall be called by the trustees for the purpose. The provisions of paragraph (42) of section 2(a) as to a majority shall be applicable to the vote cast at any meeting of the shareholders of such a trust held pursuant to this subsection.

(b) No registered management company or registered face-amount certificate company shall file with the Commission any financial statement in the preparation of which the controller or other principal accounting officer or employee of such company participated, unless such controller, officer or employee was selected, either by vote of the holders of such company's voting securities at the last annual meeting of such security holders, or by the board of directors of such company.

(c) The Commission is authorized, by rules and regulations or order in the public interest or for the protection of investors, to require accountants and auditors to keep reports, work sheets, and other documents and papers relating to registered investment companies for such period or periods as the Commission may prescribe, and to make the same available for inspection by the Commission or any member or representative thereof.

Filing of Documents With Commission in Civil Actions

Sec. 33. Every registered investment company which is a party and every affiliated person of such company who is a party defendant to any action or claim by a registered investment company or a security holder thereof in a derivative or representative capacity against an officer, director, investment adviser, trustee, or depositor of such company, shall file with the Commission, unless already so filed, (1) a copy of all pleadings, verdicts, or judgments filed with the court or served in connection with such action or claim, (2) a copy of any proposed settlement, compromise, or discontinuance of such action, and (3) a copy of such motions, transcripts, or other documents filed in or issued by the court or served in connection with such action or claim as may be requested in writing by the Commission. If any document referred to in clause (1) or (2)—

(A) is delivered to such company or party defendant, such document shall be filed with the Commission not later than ten days after the receipt thereof; or

(B) is filed in such court or delivered by such company or party defendant, such document shall be filed with the Commission not later than five days after such filing or delivery.

Destruction and Falsification of Reports and Records

Sec. 34. (a) It shall be unlawful for any person, except as permitted by rule, regulation, or order of the Commission, willfully to destroy, mutilate, or alter any account, book, or other document the preservation of which has been required pursuant to section 31(a) or 32(c).

(b) It shall be unlawful for any person to make any untrue statement of a material fact in any registration statement, application, report, account, record, or other document filed or transmitted pursuant to this title or the keeping of which is required pursuant to section 31(a). It shall be unlawful for any person so filing, transmitting, or keeping any such document to omit to state therein any fact necessary in order to prevent the statements made therein, in the light of the circumstances under which they were made, from being materially misleading. For the purposes of this subsection, any part of any such document which is signed or certified by an accountant or auditor in his capacity as such shall be deemed to be made, filed, transmitted, or kept by such accountant or auditor, as well as by the person filing, transmitting, or keeping the complete document.

Unlawful Representations and Names

Sec. 35. (a) *Misrepresentation of Guarantees.*

(1) *In General.*—It shall be unlawful for any person, issuing or selling any security of which a registered investment company is the issuer, to represent or imply in any manner whatsoever that such security or company—

(A) has been guaranteed, sponsored, recommended, or approved by the United States, or any agency, instrumentality or officer of the United States;

(B) has been insured by the Federal Deposit Insurance Corporation; or

(C) is guaranteed by or is otherwise an obligation of any bank or insured depository institution.

(2) *Disclosures.*—Any person issuing or selling the securities of a registered investment company that is advised by, or sold through, a bank shall prominently disclose that an investment in the company is not insured by the Federal Deposit Insurance Corporation or any other government agency. The Commission may, after consultation with and taking into consideration the views of the Federal banking agencies (as defined in section 1813 of Title 12), adopt rules and regulations, and issue orders, consistent with the protection of investors, prescribing the manner in which the disclosure under this paragraph shall be provided.

(3) *Definitions.*—The terms "insured depository institution" and "appropriate Federal banking agency" have the same meanings as given in section 3 of the Federal Deposit Insurance Act.

(b) It shall be unlawful for any person registered under any section of this title to represent or imply in any manner whatsoever that such person has been sponsored, recommended, or approved, or that his abilities or qualifications have in any respect been passed upon by the United States or any agency or officer thereof.

(c) No provision of subsection (a) or (b) shall be construed to prohibit a statement that a person or security is registered under this Act, the Securities Act of 1933, or the Securities Exchange Act of 1934, if such statement is true in fact and if the effect of such registration is not misrepresented.

(d) *Deceptive or Misleading Names.*—It shall be unlawful for any registered investment company to adopt as a part of the name or title of such company, or of any securities of which it is the issuer, any word or words that the Commission finds are materially deceptive or misleading. The Commission is authorized, by rule, regulation, or order, to define such names or titles as are materially deceptive or misleading.

Breach of Fiduciary Duty

Sec. 36. (a) The Commission is authorized to bring an action in the proper district court of the United States, or in the United States court of any territory or other place subject to the jurisdiction of the United States, alleging that a person serving or acting in one or more of the following capacities has engaged within five years of the commencement of the action or is about to engage in any act or practice constituting a breach of fiduciary duty involving personal misconduct in respect of any registered investment company for which such person so serves or acts—

(1) as officer, director, member of any advisory board, investment adviser, or depositor; or

(2) as principal underwriter, if such registered company is an open-end company, unit investment trust, or face-amount certificate company.

If such allegations are established, the court may enjoin such persons from acting in any or all such capacities either permanently or temporarily and award such injunctive or other relief against such person as may be reasonable and appropriate in the circumstances, having due regard to the protection of investors and to the effectuation of the policies declared in section 1(b) of this title.

(b) For the purposes of this subsection, the investment adviser of a registered investment company shall be deemed to have a fiduciary duty with respect to the receipt of compensation for services, or of payments of a material nature, paid by such registered investment company, or by the security holders thereof, to such investment adviser or any affiliated person of such investment adviser. An action may be brought under this subsection by the Commission, or by a security holder of such registered investment company on behalf of such company, against such investment adviser, or any affiliated person of such investment adviser, or any other person enumerated in subsection (a) of this section who has a fiduciary duty concerning such compensation or payments, for breach of fiduciary duty in respect of such compensation or payments paid by such registered investment company or by the security holders thereof to such investment adviser or person. With respect to any such action the following provisions shall apply:

(1) It shall not be necessary to allege or prove that any defendant engaged in personal misconduct, and the plaintiff shall have the burden of proving a breach of fiduciary duty.

(2) In any such action approval by the board of directors of such investment company of such compensation or payments, or of contracts or other arrangements providing for such compensation or payments, and ratification or approval of such compensation or payments, or of contracts or other arrangements providing for such compensation or payments, by the shareholders of such investment company, shall be given such consideration by the court as is deemed appropriate under all the circumstances.

(3) No such action shall be brought or maintained against any person other than the recipient of such compensation or payments, and no damages or other relief shall be granted against any person other than the recipient of such compensation or payments. No award of damages shall be recoverable for any period prior to one year before the action was instituted. Any award of damages against such recipient shall be limited to the actual damages resulting from the breach of fiduciary duty and shall in no event exceed the amount of compensation or payments received from such investment company, or the security holders thereof, by such recipient.

(4) This subsection shall not apply to compensation or payments made in connection with transactions subject to section 17 of this title, or rules, regulations, or orders thereunder, or to sales loads for the acquisition of any security issued by a registered investment company.

(5) Any action pursuant to this subsection may be brought only in an appropriate district court of the United States.

(6) No finding by a court with respect to a breach or fiduciary duty under this subsection shall be made a basis (A) for a finding of a violation of this title for the purposes of sections 9 and 49 of this title, section 15 of the Securities Exchange Act of 1934, or section 203 of title II of this Act, or (B) for an injunction to prohibit any person from serving in any of the capacities enumerated in subsection (a) of this section.

(c) For the purposes of subsections (a) and (b) the term "investment adviser" includes a corporate or other trustee performing the functions of an investment adviser.

Larceny and Embezzlement

Sec. 37. Whoever steals, unlawfully abstracts, unlawfully and willfully converts to his own use or to the use of another, or embezzles any of the moneys, funds, securities, credits, property, or assets of any registered investment company shall be deemed guilty of a crime, and upon conviction thereof shall be subject to the penalties provided in section 49. A judgment of conviction or acquittal on the merits under the laws of any State shall be a bar to any prosecution under this section for the same act or acts.

Rules, Regulations, and Orders; General Powers of Commission

Sec. 38. (a) The Commission shall have authority from time to time to make, issue, amend, and rescind such rules and regulations and such orders as are necessary or appropriate to the exercise of the powers conferred upon the Commission elsewhere in this title, including rules and regulations defining accounting, technical, and trade terms used in this title, and prescribing the form or forms in which information required in registration statements, applications, and reports to the Commission shall be set forth. For the purposes of its rules or regulations the Commission may classify persons, securities, and other matters within its jurisdiction and prescribe different requirements for different classes of persons, securities, or matters.

(b) The Commission, by such rules and regulations or order as it deems necessary or appropriate in the public interest or for the protection of investors, may authorize the filing of any information or documents required to be filed with the Commission under this title, title II of this Act, the Securities Act of 1933, the Securities Exchange Act of 1934, the Public Utility Holding Company Act of 1935, or the Trust Indenture Act of 1939, by incorporating by reference any information or documents theretofore or concurrently filed with the Commission under this title or any of such Acts.

(c) No provision of this title imposing any liability shall apply to any act done or omitted in good faith in conformity with any rule, regulation, or order of the Commission, notwithstanding that such rule, regulation, or order may, after such act or omission, be amended or rescinded or be determined by judicial or other authority to be invalid for any reason.

Procedure for Issuance of Rules and Regulations

Sec. 39. Subject to the provisions of the Federal Register Act and regulations prescribed under the authority thereof, the rules and regulations of the Commission under this title, and amendments thereof, shall be effective upon publication in the manner which the Commission shall prescribe, or upon such later date as may be provided in such rules and regulations.

Procedure for Issuance of Orders

Sec. 40. (a) Orders of the Commission under this title shall be issued only after appropriate notice and opportunity for hearing. Notice to the parties to a proceeding before the Commission shall be given by personal service upon each party or by registered mail or certified mail or confirmed telegraph notice to the party's last known business address. Notice to interested persons, if any, other than parties may be given in the same manner or by publication in the Federal Register.

(b) The Commission may provide, by appropriate rules or regulations, that an application verified under oath may be admissible in evidence in a proceeding before the Commission and that the record in such a proceeding may consist, in whole or in part, of such application.

(c) In any proceeding before the Commission, the Commission, in accordance with such rules and regulations as it may prescribe, shall admit as a party any interested State or State agency, and may admit as a party any representative of interested security holders, or any other person whose participation in the proceeding may be in the public interest or for the protection of investors.

Hearings by Commission

Sec. 41. Hearings may be public and may be held before the Commission, any member or members thereof, or any officer or officers of the Commission designated by it, and appropriate records thereof shall be kept.

Enforcement of Title

Sec. 42. (a) The Commission may make such investigations as it deems necessary to determine whether any person has violated or is about to violate any provision of this title or of any rule, regulation, or order hereunder, or to determine whether any action in any court or any proceeding before the Commission shall be instituted under this title against a particular person or persons, or with respect to a particular transaction or transactions. The Commission shall permit any person to file with it a statement in writing, under oath or otherwise as the Commission shall determine, as to all the facts and circumstances concerning the matter to be investigated.

(b) For the purpose of any investigation or any other proceeding under this title, any member of the Commission, or any officer thereof designated by it, is empowered to administer oaths and affirmations, subpena witnesses, compel their attendance, take evidence, and require the production of any books, papers, correspondence, memoranda, contracts, agreements, or other records which are relevant or material to the inquiry. Such attendance of witnesses and the production of any such records may be required from any place in any State or in any Territory or other place subject to the jurisdiction of the United States at any designated place of hearing.

(c) In case of contumacy by, or refusal to obey a subpena issued to, any person, the Commission may invoke the aid of any court of the United States within the jurisdiction of which such investigation or proceeding is carried on, or where such person resides or carries on business, in requiring the attendance and testimony of witnesses and the production of books, papers, correspondence, memoranda, contracts, agreements, and other records. And such court may issue an order requiring such person to appear before the Commission or member or officer designated by the Commission, there to produce records, if so ordered, or to give testimony touching the matter under investigation or in question; any failure to obey such order of the court may be punished by such court as a contempt thereof. All process in any such case may be served in the judicial district whereof such person is an inhabitant or wherever he may be found. Any person who without just cause shall fail or refuse to attend and testify or to answer any lawful inquiry or to produce books, papers, correspondence, memoranda, contracts, agreements, or other records, if in his or its power so to do, in obedience to the subpena of the Commission, shall be guilty of a misdemeanor, and upon conviction shall be subject to a fine of not more than $1,000 or to imprisonment for a term of not more than one year, or both.

(d) Whenever it shall appear to the Commission that any person has engaged or is about to engage in any act or practice constituting a violation of any provision of this title, or of any rule, regulation, or order hereunder, it may in its discretion bring an action in the proper district court of the United States, or the proper United States court of any Territory or other place subject to the jurisdiction of the United States, to enjoin such acts or practices and to enforce compliance with this title or any rule, regulation, or order hereunder. Upon a showing that such person has engaged or is about to engage in any such act or practice, a permanent or temporary injunction or decree or restraining order shall be granted without bond. In any proceeding under this subsection to enforce compliance with section 7, the court as a court of equity may, to the extent it deems necessary or appropriate, take exclusive jurisdiction and possession of the investment company or companies involved and the books, records, and assets thereof, wherever located; and the court shall have jurisdiction to appoint a trustee, who with the approval of the court shall have power to dispose of any or all of such assets, subject to such terms and conditions as the court may prescribe. The Commission may transmit such evidence as may be available concerning any violation of the provisions of this title, or of any rule, regulation, or order thereunder, to the Attorney General, who, in his discretion, may institute the appropriate criminal proceedings under this title.

(e) *Money penalties in civil actions.—*

(1) *Authority of Commission.*—Whenever it shall appear to the Commission that any person has violated any provision of this title, the rules or regulations thereunder, or a cease-and-desist order entered by the Commission pursuant to section 9(f) of this title, the Commission may bring an action in a United States district court to seek, and the court shall have jurisdiction to impose, upon a proper showing, a civil penalty to be paid by the person who committed such violation.

(2) *Amount of penalty.—*

(A) *First tier.*—The amount of the penalty shall be determined by the court in light of the facts and circumstances. For each violation, the amount of the penalty shall not exceed the greater of (i) $5,000 for a natural person or $50,000 for any other person, or (ii) the gross amount of pecuniary gain to such defendant as a result of the violation.

(B) *Second tier.*—Notwithstanding subparagraph (A), the amount of penalty for each such violation shall not exceed the greater of (i) $50,000 for a natural person or $250,000 for any other person, or (ii) the gross amount of pecuniary gain to such defendant as a result of the violation, if the violation described in paragraph (1) involved fraud, deceit, manipulation, or deliberate or reckless disregard of a regulatory requirement.

(C) *Third tier.*—Notwithstanding subparagraphs (A) and (B), the amount of penalty for each such violation shall not exceed the greater of (i) $100,000 for a natural person or $500,000 for any other person, or (ii) the gross amount of pecuniary gain to such defendant as a result of the violation, if—

(I) the violation described in paragraph (1) involved fraud, deceit, manipulation, or deliberate or reckless disregard of a regulatory requirement; and

(II) such violation directly or indirectly resulted in substantial losses or created a significant risk of substantial losses to other persons.

(3) *Procedures for collection.—*

(A) *Payment of penalty to treasury.*—A penalty imposed under this section shall be payable into the Treasury of the United States, except as otherwise provided in section 308 of the Sarbanes–Oxley Act of 2002.

(B) *Collection of penalties.*—If a person upon whom such a penalty is imposed shall fail to pay such penalty within the time prescribed in the court's order, the Commission may refer the matter to the Attorney General who shall recover such penalty by action in the appropriate United States district court.

(C) *Remedy not exclusive.*—The actions authorized by this subsection may be brought in addition to any other action that the Commission or the Attorney General is entitled to bring.

(D) *Jurisdiction and venue.*—For purposes of section 44 of this title, actions under this paragraph shall be actions to enforce a liability or a duty created by this title.

(4) *Special provisions relating to a violation of a cease-and-desist order.*—In an action to enforce a cease-and-desist order entered by the Commission pursuant to section 9(f), each separate violation of such order shall be a separate offense, except that in the case of a violation through a continuing failure to comply with the order, each day of the failure to comply shall be deemed a separate offense.

Court Review of Orders

Sec. 43. (a) Any person or party aggrieved by an order issued by the Commission under this title may obtain a review of such order in the court of appeals of the United States within any circuit wherein such person resides or has his principal place of business, or in the United States Court of Appeals for the District of Columbia, by filing in such court, within sixty days after the entry of such order, a written petition praying that the order of the Commission be modified or set aside in whole or in part. A copy of such petition shall be forthwith transmitted by the clerk of the court to any member of the Commission, or any officer thereof designated by the Commission for that purpose, and thereupon the Commission shall file in the court the record upon which the order complained of was entered, as provided in section 2112 of title 28, United States Code. Upon the filing of such petition such court shall have jurisdiction, which upon the filing of the record shall be exclusive, to affirm, modify, or set aside such order, in whole or in part. No objection to the order of the Commission shall be considered by the court unless such objection shall have been urged before the Commission or unless there were reasonable grounds for failure so to do. The findings of the Commission as to the facts, if supported by substantial evidence, shall be conclusive. If application is made to the court for leave to adduce additional evidence, and it is shown to the satisfaction of the court that such additional evidence is material and that there were reasonable grounds for failure to adduce such evidence in the proceeding before the Commission, the court may order such additional evidence to be taken before the Commission and to be adduced upon the hearing in such manner and upon such terms and conditions as to the court may seem proper. The Commission may modify its findings as to the facts by reason of the additional evidence so taken, and it shall file with the court such modified or new findings, which, if supported by substantial evidence, shall be conclusive, and its recommendation, if any, for the modification or setting aside of the original order. The judgment and decree of the court affirming, modifying, or setting aside, in whole or in part, any such order of the Commission shall be final, subject to review by the Supreme Court of the United States upon certiorari or certification as provided in section 1254 of title 28, United States Code.

(b) The commencement of proceedings under subsection (a) to review an order of the Commission issued under section 8(e) shall operate as a stay of the Commission's order unless the court otherwise orders. The commencement of proceedings under subsection (a) to review an order of the Commission issued under any provision of this title other than section 8(e) shall not operate as a stay of the Commission's order unless the court specifically so orders.

Jurisdiction of Offenses and Suits

Sec. 44. The district courts of the United States and the United States courts of any

Territory or other place subject to the jurisdiction of the United States shall have jurisdiction of violations of this title or the rules, regulations, or orders thereunder, and, concurrently with State and Territorial courts, of all suits in equity and actions at law brought to enforce any liability or duty created by, or to enjoin any violation of, this title or the rules, regulations, or orders thereunder. Any criminal proceeding may be brought in the district wherein any act or transaction constituting the violation occurred. A criminal proceeding based upon a violation of section 34, or upon a failure to file a report or other document required to be filed under this title, may be brought in the district wherein the defendant is an inhabitant or maintains his principal office or place of business. Any suit or action to enforce any liability or duty created by, or to enjoin any violation of, this title or rules, regulations, or orders thereunder, may be brought in any such district or in the district wherein the defendant is an inhabitant or transacts business, and process in such cases may be served in any district of which the defendant is an inhabitant or transacts business or wherever the defendant may be found. Judgments and decrees so rendered shall be subject to review as provided in sections 1254, 1291, 1292, and 1294 of title 28, United States Code. No costs shall be assessed for or against the Commission in any proceeding under this title brought by or against the Commission in any court. The Commission may intervene as a party in any action or suit to enforce any liability or duty created by, or to enjoin any noncompliance with, section 36(b) of this title at any stage of such action or suit prior to final judgment therein.

Information Filed With Commission

Sec. 45. (a) The information contained in any registration statement, application, report, or other document filed with the Commission pursuant to any provision of this title or of any rule or regulation thereunder (as distinguished from any information or document transmitted to the Commission) shall be made available to the public, unless and except insofar as the Commission, by rules and regulations upon its own motion, or by order upon application, finds that public disclosure is neither necessary nor appropriate in the public interest or for the protection of investors. Except as provided in section 24(c) of the Securities Exchange Act of 1934, it shall be unlawful for any member, officer, or employee of the Commission to use for personal benefit, or to disclose to any person other than an official or employee of the United States or of a State, for official use, or for any such official or employee to use for personal benefit, any information contained in any document so filed or transmitted, if such information is not available to the public.

(b) Photostatic or other copies of information contained in documents filed with the Commission under this title and made available to the public shall be furnished any person at such reasonable charge and under such reasonable limitations as the Commission shall prescribe.

Annual Reports of Commission; Employees of the Commission

Sec. 46. (a) The Commission shall submit annually a report to the Congress covering the work of the Commission for the preceding year and including such information, data, and recommendations for further legislation in connection with the matters covered by this title as it may find advisable.

(b) The provisions of section 4(b) of the Securities Exchange Act of 1934 shall be applicable with respect to the power of the Commission—

(1) to appoint and fix the compensation of such employees as may be necessary for carrying out its functions under this title, and

(2) to lease and allocate such real property as may be necessary for carrying out its functions under this title.

Validity of Contracts

Sec. 47. (a) Any condition, stipulation, or provision binding any person to waive compliance with any provision of this title or with any rule, regulation, or order thereunder shall be void.

(b)(1) A contract that is made, or whose performance involves a violation of this title, or of any rule, regulation, or order thereunder, is unenforceable by either party (or by a nonparty to the contract who acquired a right under the contract with knowledge of the facts by reason of which the making or performance violated or would violate any provision of this title or of any rule, regulation, or order thereunder) unless a court finds that under the circumstances enforcement would produce a more equitable result than nonenforcement and would not be inconsistent with the purposes of this title.

(2) To the extent that a contract described in paragraph (1) has been performed, a court may not deny rescission at the instance of any party unless such court finds that under the circumstances the denial of rescission would produce a more equitable result than its grant and would not be inconsistent with the purposes of this title.

(3) This subsection shall not apply (A) to the lawful portion of a contract to the extent that it may be severed from the unlawful portion of the contract, or (B) to preclude recovery against any person for unjust enrichment.

Liability of Controlling Persons; Preventing Compliance With Title

Sec. 48. (a) It shall be unlawful for any person, directly or indirectly, to cause to be done any act or thing through or by means of any other person which it would be unlawful for such person to do under the provisions of this title or any rule, regulation, or order thereunder.

(b) It shall be unlawful for any person without just cause to hinder, delay, or obstruct the making, filing, or keeping of any information, document, report, record, or account required to be made, filed, or kept under any provision of this title or any rule, regulation, or order thereunder.

Penalties

Sec. 49. Any person who willfully violates any provision of this title or of any rule, regulation, or order hereunder, or any person who willfully in any registration statement, application, report, account, record, or other document filed or transmitted pursuant to this title or the keeping of which is required pursuant to section 31(a) makes any untrue statement of a material fact or omits to state any material fact necessary in order to prevent the statements made therein from being materially misleading in the light of the circumstances under which they were made, shall upon conviction be fined not more than $10,000 or imprisoned not more than five years, or both; but no person shall be convicted under this section for the violation of any rule, regulation, or order if he proves that he had no actual knowledge of such rule, regulation, or order.

Effect on Existing Law

Sec. 50. Except where specific provision is made to the contrary, nothing in this title shall affect (1) the jurisdiction of the Commission under the Securities Act of 1933, the Securities Exchange Act of 1934, the Public Utility Holding Company Act of 1935, the Trust Indenture Act of 1939, or title II of this Act, over any person, security, or transaction, or (2) the rights, obligations, duties, or liabilities of any person under such Acts; nor shall anything in this title affect the jurisdiction of any other commission, board, agency, or officer of the United States or of any State or political subdivision of any State, over any person, security, or transaction, insofar as such jurisdiction does not conflict with any provision of this title or of any rule, regulation, or order hereunder.

Separability of Provisions

Sec. 51. If any provision of this title or any provision incorporated in this title by reference, or the application of any such provision to any person or circumstances, shall be held invalid, the remainder of this title and the application of any such provision to person or circumstances other than those as to which it is held invalid shall not be affected thereby.

Short Title

Sec. 52. This title may be cited as the "Investment Company Act of 1940."

Effective Date

Sec. 53. The effective date of the provisions of this title, so far as the same relate to face-amount certificates or to face-amount certificate companies, is January 1, 1941.

Election to Be Regulated as a Business Development Company

Sec. 54. (a) Any company defined in section 2(a)(48)(A) and (B) may elect to be subject to the provisions of sections 55 through 65 by filing with the Commission a notification of election, if such company—

(1) has a class of its equity securities registered under section 12 of the Securities Exchange Act of 1934; or

(2) has filed a registration statement pursuant to section 12 of the Securities Exchange Act of 1934 for a class of its equity securities.

(b) The Commission may, by rule, prescribe the form and manner in which notification of election under this section shall be given. A business development company shall be deemed to be subject to sections 55 through 65 upon receipt by the Commission of such notification of election.

(c) Whenever the Commission finds, on its own motion or upon application, that a business development company which has filed a notification of election pursuant to subsection (a) of this section has ceased to engage in business, the Commission shall so declare by order revoking such company's election. Any business development company may voluntarily withdraw its election under subsection (a) by filing a notice of withdrawal of election with the Commission, in a form and manner which the Commission may, by rule, prescribe. Such withdrawal shall be effective immediately upon receipt by the Commission.

Functions and Activities of Business Development Companies

Sec. 55. (a) It shall be unlawful for a business development company to acquire any assets (other than those described in paragraphs (1) through (7) of this subsection) unless, at the time the acquisition is made, assets described in paragraphs (1) through (6) below represent at least 70 per centum of the value of its total assets (other than assets described in paragraph (7) below):

(1) securities purchased, in transactions not involving any public offering or in such other transactions as the Commission may, by rule, prescribe if it finds that enforcement of this title and of the Securities Act of 1933 with respect to such transactions is not necessary in the public interest or for the protection of investors by reason of the small amount, or the limited nature of the public offering, involved in such transactions—

(A) from the issuer of such securities, which issuer is an eligible portfolio company, from any person who is, or who within the preceding thirteen months has been, an affiliated person of such eligible portfolio company, or from any other person, subject to such rules and regulations as the Commission may prescribe as necessary or appropriate in the public interest or for the protection of investors; or

(B) from the issuer of such securities, which issuer is described in section 2(a)(46)(A) and (B) but is not an eligible portfolio company because it has issued a class of securities with respect to which a member of a national securities exchange, broker, or dealer may extend or maintain credit to or for a customer pursuant to rules or regulations adopted by the Board of Governors of the Federal Reserve System under section 7 of the Securities Exchange Act of 1934, or from any person who is an officer or employee of such issuer, if—

(i) at the time of the purchase, the business development company owns at least 50 per centum of—

(I) the greatest number of equity securities of such issuer and securities convertible into or exchangeable for such securities; and

(II) the greatest amount of debt securities of such issuer,

held by such business development company at any point in time during the period when such issuer was an eligible portfolio company, except that options, warrants, and similar securities which have by their terms expired and debt securities which have been converted, or repaid or prepaid in the ordinary course of business or incident to a public offering of securities of such issuer, shall not be considered to have been held by such business development company for purposes of this requirement; and

(ii) the business development company is one of the 20 largest holders of record of such issuer's outstanding voting securities;

(2) securities of any eligible portfolio company with respect to which the business development company satisfies the requirements of section 2(a)(46)(C)(ii);

(3) securities purchased in transactions not involving any public offering from an issuer described in sections 2(a)(46)(A) and (B) or from a person who is, or who within the preceding thirteen months has been, an affiliated person of such issuer, or from any person in transactions incident thereto, if such securities were—

(A) issued by an issuer that is, or was immediately prior to the purchase of its securities by the business development company, in bankruptcy proceedings, subject to reorganization under the supervision of a court of competent jurisdiction, or subject to a plan or arrangement resulting from such bankruptcy proceedings or reorganization;

(B) issued by an issuer pursuant to or in consummation of such a plan or arrangement; or

(C) issued by an issuer that, immediately prior to the purchase of such issuer's securities by the business development company, was not in bankruptcy proceedings but was unable to meet its obligations as they came due without material assistance other than conventional lending or financing arrangements;

(4) securities of eligible portfolio companies purchased from any person in transactions not involving any public offering, if there is no ready market for such securities and if immediately prior to such purchase the business development company owns at least 60 per centum of the outstanding equity securities of such issuer (giving effect to all securities presently convertible into or exchangeable for equity securities of such issuer as if such securities were so converted or exchanged);

(5) securities received in exchange for or distributed on or with respect to securities described in paragraphs (1) through (4) of this subsection, or pursuant to the exercise of options, warrants, or rights relating to securities described in such paragraphs;

(6) cash, cash items, Government securities, or high quality debt securities maturing in one year or less from the time of investment in such high quality debt securities; and

(7) office furniture and equipment, interests in real estate and leasehold improvements and facilities maintained to conduct the business operations of the business development company, deferred organization and operating expenses, and other noninvestment assets necessary and appropriate to its operations as a business development company, including notes of indebtedness of directors, officers, employees, and general partners held by a business development company as payment for securities of such company issued in connection with an executive compensation plan described in section 57(j).

(b) For purposes of this section, the value of a business development company's assets shall be determined as of the date of the most recent financial statements filed by such company with the Commission pursuant to section 13 of the Securities Exchange Act of 1934, and shall be determined no less frequently than annually.

Qualifications of Directors

Sec. 56. (a) A majority of a business development company's directors or general partners shall be persons who are not interested persons of such company.

(b) If, by reason of the death, disqualification, or bona fide resignation of any director or general partner, a business development company does not meet the requirements of subsection (a) of this section, or the requirements of section 15(f)(1) of this title with respect to directors, the operation of such provisions shall be suspended for a period of 90 days or for such longer period as the Commission may prescribe, upon its own motion or by order upon application, as not inconsistent with the protection of investors.

Transactions With Certain Affiliates

Sec. 57. (a) It shall be unlawful for any person who is related to a business development company in a manner described in subsection (b) of this section, acting as principal—

(1) knowingly to sell any security or other property to such business development company or to any company controlled by such business development company, unless such sale involves solely (A) securities of which the buyer is the issuer, or (B) the securities of which the seller is the issuer and which are part of a general offering to the holders of a class of its securities;

(2) knowingly to purchase from such business development company or from any company controlled by such business development company, any security or other property (except securities of which the seller is the issuer);

(3) knowingly to borrow money or other property from such business development company or from any company controlled by such business development company (unless the borrower is controlled by the lender), except as permitted in section 21(b) or section 62; or

(4) knowingly to effect any transaction in which such business development company or a company controlled by such business development company is a joint or a joint and several participant with such person in contravention of such rules and regulations as the Commission may prescribe for the purpose of limiting or preventing participation by such business development company or controlled company on a basis less advantageous than that of such person, except that nothing contained in this paragraph shall be deemed to preclude any person from acting as manager of any underwriting syndicate or other group in which such business development company or controlled company is a participant and receiving compensation therefor.

(b) The provisions of subsection (a) of this section shall apply to the following persons:

(1) Any director, officer, employee, or member of an advisory board of a business development company or any person (other than the business development company itself) who is, within the meaning of section

2(a)(3)(C) of this title, an affiliated person of any such person specified in this paragraph.

(2) Any investment adviser or promoter of, general partner in, principal underwriter for, or person directly or indirectly either controlling, controlled by, or under common control with, a business development company (except the business development company itself and any person who, if it were not directly or indirectly controlled by the business development company, would not be directly or indirectly under the control of a person who controls the business development company), or any person who is, within the meaning of section 2(a)(3)(C) or (D), an affiliated person of any such person specified in this paragraph.

(c) Notwithstanding paragraphs (1), (2), and (3) of subsection (a), any person may file with the Commission an application for an order exempting a proposed transaction of the applicant from one or more provisions of such paragraphs. The Commission shall grant such application and issue such order of exemption if evidence establishes that—

(1) the terms of the proposed transaction, including the consideration to be paid or received, are reasonable and fair and do not involve overreaching of the business development company or its shareholders or partners on the part of any person concerned;

(2) the proposed transaction is consistent with the policy of the business development company as recited in the filings made by such company with the Commission under the Securities Act of 1933, its registration statement and reports filed under the Securities Exchange Act of 1934, and its reports to shareholders or partners; and

(3) the proposed transaction is consistent with the general purposes of this title.

(d) It shall be unlawful for any person who is related to a business development company in the manner described in subsection (e) of this section and who is not subject to the prohibitions of subsection (a) of this section, acting as principal—

(1) knowingly to sell any security or other property to such business development company or to any company controlled by such business development company, unless such sale involves solely (A) securities of which the buyer is the issuer, or (B) securities of which the seller is the issuer and which are part of a general offering to the holders of a class of its securities;

(2) knowingly to purchase from such business development company or from any company controlled by such business development company, any security or other property (except securities of which the seller is the issuer);

(3) knowingly to borrow money or other property from such business development company or from any company controlled by such business development company (unless the borrower is controlled by the lender), except as permitted in section 21(b); or

(4) knowingly to effect any transaction in which such business development company or a company controlled by such business development company is a joint or a joint and several participant with such affiliated person in contravention of such rules and regulations as the Commission may prescribe for the purpose of limiting or preventing participation by such business development company or controlled company on a basis less advantageous than that of such affiliated person, except that nothing contained in this paragraph shall be deemed to preclude any person from acting as manager of any underwriting syndicate or other group in which such business development company or controlled company is a participant and receiving compensation therefor.

(e) The provisions of subsection (d) of this section shall apply to the following persons:

(1) Any person (A) who is, within the meaning of section 2(a)(3)(A), an affiliated person of a business development company, (B) who is an executive officer or a director of, or general partner in, any such affiliated

person, or (C) who directly or indirectly either controls, is controlled by, or is under common control with, such affiliated person.

(2) Any person who is an affiliated person of a director, officer, employee, investment adviser, member of an advisory board or promoter of, principal underwriter for, general partner in, or an affiliated person of any person directly or indirectly either controlling or under common control with a business development company (except the business development company itself and any person who, if it were not directly or indirectly controlled by the business development company, would not be directly or indirectly under the control of a person who controls the business development company). For purposes of this subsection, the term "executive officer" means the president, secretary, treasurer, any vice president in charge of a principal business function, and any other person who performs similar policymaking functions.

(f) Notwithstanding subsection (d) of this section, a person described in subsection (e) may engage in a proposed transaction described in subsection (d) if such proposed transaction is approved by the required majority (as defined in subsection (*o*)) of the directors of or general partners in the business development company on the basis that—

(1) the terms thereof, including the consideration to be paid or received, are reasonable and fair to the shareholders or partners of the business development company and do not involve overreaching of such company or its shareholders or partners on the part of any person concerned;

(2) the proposed transaction is consistent with the interests of the shareholders or partners of the business development company and is consistent with the policy of such company as recited in filings made by such company with the Commission under the Securities Act of 1933, its registration statement and reports filed under the Securities Exchange Act of 1934, and its reports to shareholders or partners; and

(3) the directors or general partners record in their minutes and preserve in their records, for such periods as if such records were required to be maintained pursuant to section 31(a), a description of such transaction, their findings, the information or materials upon which their findings were based, and the basis therefor.

(g) Notwithstanding subsection (a) or (d), a person may, in the ordinary course of business, sell to or purchase from any company merchandise or may enter into a lessor-lessee relationship with any person and furnish the services incident thereto.

(h) The directors of or general partners in any business development company shall adopt, and periodically review and update as appropriate, procedures reasonably designed to ensure that reasonable inquiry is made, prior to the consummation of any transaction in which such business development company or a company controlled by such business development company proposes to participate, with respect to the possible involvement in the transaction of persons described in subsections (b) and (e) of this section.

(i) Until the adoption by the Commission of rules or regulations under subsections (a) and (d) of this section, the rules and regulations of the Commission under subsections (a) and (d) of section 17 applicable to registered closed-end investment companies shall be deemed to apply to transactions subject to subsections (a) and (d) of this section. Any rules or regulations adopted by the Commission to implement this section shall be no more restrictive than the rules or regulations adopted by the Commission under subsections (a) and (d) of section 17 that are applicable to all registered closed-end investment companies.

(j) Notwithstanding subsections (a) and (d) of this section, any director, officer, or employee of, or general partner in, a business development company may—

(1) acquire warrants, options, and rights to purchase voting securities of such business development company, and securities issued upon the exercise or conversion thereof, pursuant to an executive compensation plan offered by such company which meets the requirements of section 61(a)(3)(B); and

(2) borrow money from such business development company for the purpose of purchasing securities issued by such company pursuant to an executive compensation plan, if each such loan—

(A) has a term of not more than ten years;

(B) becomes due within a reasonable time, not to exceed sixty days, after the termination of such person's employment or service;

(C) bears interest at no less than the prevailing rate applicable to 90-day United States Treasury bills at the time the loan is made;

(D) at all times is fully collateralized (such collateral may include any securities issued by such business development company); and

(E)(i) in the case of a loan to any officer or employee of such business development company (including any officer or employee who is also a director of such company), is approved by the required majority (as defined in subsection (*o*)) of the directors of or general partners in such company on the basis that the loan is in the best interests of such company and its shareholders or partners; or

(ii) in the case of a loan to any director of such business development company who is not also an officer or employee of such company, or to any general partner in such company, is approved by order of the Commission, upon application, on the basis that the terms of the loan are fair and reasonable and do not involve overreaching of such company or its shareholders or partners.

(k) It shall be unlawful for any person described in subsection (*l*)—

(1) acting as agent, to accept from any source any compensation (other than a regular salary or wages from the business development company) for the purchase or sale of any property to or for such business development company or any controlled company thereof, except in the course of such person's business as an underwriter or broker; or

(2) acting as broker, in connection with the sale of securities to or by the business development company or any controlled company thereof, to receive from any source a commission, fee, or other remuneration for effecting such transaction which exceeds—

(A) the usual and customary broker's commission if the sale is effected on a securities exchange;

(B) 2 per centum of the sales price if the sale is effected in connection with a secondary distribution of such securities; or

(C) 1 per centum of the purchase or sale price of such securities if the sale is otherwise effected,

unless the Commission, by rules and regulations or order in the public interest and consistent with the protection of investors, permits a larger commission.

(*l*) The provisions of subsection (k) of this section shall apply to the following persons:

(1) Any affiliated person of a business development company.

(2)(A) Any person who is, within the meaning of section 2(a)(3)(B), (C), or (D), an affiliated person of any director, officer, employee, or member of an advisory board of the business development company.

(B) Any person who is, within the meaning of section 2(a)(3)(A), (B), (C), or (D), an affiliated person of any investment adviser of, general partner in, or person directly or indirectly either controlling, controlled by, or under common control with, the business development company.

(C) Any person who is, within the meaning of section 2(a)(3)(C), an affiliated person of any person who is an affiliated person of the business development company within the meaning of section 2(a)(3)(A).

(m) For purposes of subsections (a) and (d), a person who is a director, officer, or employee of a party to a transaction and who receives his usual and ordinary fee or salary for usual and customary services as a director, officer, or employee from such party shall not be deemed to have a financial interest or to participate in the transaction solely by reason of his receipt of such fee or salary.

(n)(1) Notwithstanding subsection (a)(4) of this section, a business development company may establish and maintain a profit-sharing plan for its directors, officers, employees, and general partners and such directors, officers, employees and general partners may participate in such profit-sharing plan, if—

(A)(i) in the case of a profit-sharing plan for officers and employees of the business development company (including any officer or employee who is also a director of such company), such profit-sharing plan is approved by the required majority (as defined in subsection (*o*)) of the directors of or general partners in such company on the basis that such plan is reasonable and fair to the shareholders or partners of such company, does not involve overreaching of such company or its shareholders or partners on the part of any person concerned, and is consistent with the interests of the shareholders or partners of such company; or

(ii) in the case of a profit-sharing plan which includes one or more directors of the business development company who are not also officers or employees of such company, or one or more general partners in such company, such profit-sharing plan is approved by order of the Commission, upon application, on the basis that such plan is reasonable and fair to the shareholders or partners of such company, does not involve overreaching of such company or its shareholders or partners on the part of any person concerned, and is consistent with the interests of the shareholders or partners of such company; and

(B) the aggregate amount of benefits which would be paid or accrued under such plan shall not exceed 20 per centum of the business development company's net income after taxes in any fiscal year.

(2) This subsection may not be used where the business development company has outstanding any stock option, warrant, or right issued as part of an executive compensation plan, including a plan pursuant to section 61(a)(3)(B), or has an investment adviser registered or required to be registered under title II of this Act.

(*o*) The term "required majority", when used with respect to the approval of a proposed transaction, plan or arrangement, means both a majority of a business development company's directors or general partners who have no financial interest in such transaction, plan, or arrangement and a majority of such directors or general partners who are not interested persons of such company.

Changes in Investment Policy

Sec. 58. No business development company shall, unless authorized by the vote of a majority of its outstanding voting securities or partnership interests, change the nature of its business so as to cease to be, or to withdraw its election as, a business development company.

Incorporation of Provisions

Sec. 59. Notwithstanding the exemption set forth in section 6(f), sections 1, 2, 3, 4, 5, 6, 9, 10(f), 15(a), (c), and (f), 16(b), 17(f) through (j), 19(a), 20(b), 32(a) and (c), 33 through 47, and 49 through 53 of this title shall apply to a business development company to the same extent as if it were a registered closed-end investment company.

Functions and Activities of Business Development Companies

Sec. 60. Notwithstanding the exemption set forth in section 6(f), section 12 shall apply to a business development company to the same extent as if it were a registered closed-end investment company, except that the Commission shall not prescribe any rule, regulation, or order pursuant to section 12(a)(1) governing the circumstances in which a business development company may borrow from a bank in order to purchase any security.

Capital Structure

Sec. 61. (a) Notwithstanding the exemption set forth in section 6(f), section 18 shall apply to a business development company to the same extent as if it were a registered closed-end investment company, except as follows:

(1) The asset coverage requirements of section 18(a)(1)(A) and (B) applicable to business development companies shall be 200 per centum.

(2) Notwithstanding section 18(c), a business development company may issue more than one class of senior security representing indebtedness.

(A) privately held or guaranteed by the Small Business Administration, or banks, insurance companies, or other institutional investors; and

(B) not intended to be publicly distributed.

(3) Notwithstanding section 18(d)—

(A) a business development company may issue warrants, options, or rights to subscribe or convert to voting securities of such company, accompanied by securities if—

(i) such warrants, options, or rights expire by their terms within ten years;

(ii) such warrants, options, or rights are not separately transferable unless no class of such warrants, options, or rights and the securities accompanying them has been publicly distributed;

(iii) the exercise or conversion price is not less than the current market value at the date of issuance, or if no such market value exists, the current net asset value of such voting securities; and

(iv) the proposal to issue such securities is authorized by the shareholders or partners of such business development company, and such issuance is approved by the required majority (as defined in section 57(*o*)) of the directors of or general partners in such company on the basis that such issuance is in the best interests of such company and its shareholders or partners;

(B) a business development company may issue, to its directors, officers, employees, and general partners, warrants, options, and rights to purchase voting securities of such company pursuant to an executive compensation plan, if—

(i)(I) in the case of warrants, options, or rights issued to any officer or employee of such business development company (including any officer or employee who is also a director of such company), such securities satisfy the conditions in clauses (i), (iii), and (iv) of subparagraph (A); or (II) in the case of warrants, options, or rights issued to any director of such business development company who is not also an officer or employee of such company, or to any general partner in such company, the proposal to issue such securities satisfies the conditions in clauses (i) and (iii) of subparagraph (A), is authorized by the shareholders or partners of such company, and is approved by order of the Commission, upon application, on the basis that the terms of the proposal are fair and reasonable and do not involve overreaching of such company or its shareholders or partners;

(ii) such securities are not transferable except for disposition by gift, will, or intestacy;

(iii) no investment adviser of such business development company receives any compensation described in paragraph (1) of section 205 of title II of this Act, except to the extent permitted by clause (A) or (B) of that section; and

(iv) such business development company does not have a profit-sharing plan described in section 57(n); and

(C) a business development company may issue warrants, options, or rights to subscribe to, convert to, or purchase voting securities not accompanied by securities, if—

(i) such warrants, options, or rights satisfy the conditions in clauses (i) and (iii) of subparagraph (A); and

(ii) the proposal to issue such warrants, options, or rights is authorized by the shareholders or partners of such business development company, and such issuance is approved by the required majority (as defined in section 57(*o*)) of the directors of or general partners in such company on the basis that such issuance is in the best interests of the company and its shareholders or partners.

Notwithstanding this paragraph, the amount of voting securities that would result from the exercise of all outstanding warrants, options, and rights at the time of issuance shall not exceed 25 per centum of the outstanding voting securities of the business development company, except that if the amount of voting securities that would result from the exercise of all outstanding warrants, options, and rights issued to such company's directors, officers, employees, and general partners pursuant to any executive compensation plan meeting the requirements of subparagraph (B) of this paragraph would exceed 15 per centum of the outstanding voting securities of such company, then the total amount of voting securities that would result from the exercise of all outstanding warrants, options, and rights at the time of issuance shall not exceed 20 per centum of the outstanding voting securities of such company.

(4) For purposes of measuring the asset coverage requirements of section 18(a), a senior security created by the guarantee by a business development company of indebtedness issued by another company shall be the amount of the maximum potential liability less the fair market value of the net unencumbered assets (plus the indebtedness which has been guaranteed) available in the borrowing company whose debts have been guaranteed, except that a guarantee issued by a business development company of indebtedness issued by a company which is a wholly-owned subsidiary of the business development company and is licensed as a small business investment company under the Small Business Investment Act of 1958 shall not be deemed to be a senior security of such business development company for purposes of section 18(a) if the amount of the indebtedness at the time of its issuance by the borrowing company is itself taken fully into account as a liability by such business development company, as if it were issued by such business development company, in determining whether such business development company, at that time, satisfies the asset coverage requirements of section 18(a).

(b) A business development company shall comply with the provisions of this section at the time it becomes subject to sections 55 through 65, as if it were issuing a security of each class which it has outstanding at such time.

Loans

Sec. 62. Notwithstanding the exemption set forth in section 6(f), section 21 shall apply to a business development company to the same extent as if it were a registered closed-end investment company, except that nothing in that section shall be deemed to prohibit—

(1) any loan to a director, officer, or employee of, or general partner in, a business development company for the purpose of purchasing securities for such company as part of an executive compensation plan, if such loan meets the requirements of section 57(j); or

(2) any loan to a company controlled by a business development company, which companies could be deemed to be under common control solely because a third person controls such business development company.

Distribution and Repurchase of Securities

Sec. 63. Notwithstanding the exemption set forth in section 6(f), section 23 shall apply to a business development company to the same extent as if it were a registered closed-end investment company, except as follows:

(1) The prohibitions of section 23(a)(2) shall not apply to any company which (A) is a wholly-owned subsidiary of, or directly or indirectly controlled by, a business development company, and (B) immediately after the issuance of any of its securities for property other than cash or securities, will not be an investment company within the meaning of section 3(a).

(2) Notwithstanding the provisions of section 23(b), a business development company may sell any common stock of which it is the issuer at a price below the current net asset value of such stock, and may sell warrants, options, or rights to acquire any such common stock at a price below the current net asset value of such stock, if—

(A) the holders of a majority of such business development company's outstanding voting securities, and the holders of a majority of such company's outstanding voting securities that are not affiliated persons of such company, approved such company's policy and practice of making such sales of securities at the last annual meeting of shareholders or partners within one year immediately prior to any such sale, except that the shareholder approval requirements of this subparagraph shall not apply to the initial public offering by a business development company of its securities;

(B) a required majority (as defined in section 57(*o*)) of the directors of or general partners in such business development company have determined that any such sale would be in the best interests of such company and its shareholders or partners; and

(C) a required majority (as defined in section 57(*o*)) of the directors of or general partners in such business development company, in consultation with the underwriter or underwriters of the offering if it is to be underwritten, have determined in good faith, and as of a time immediately prior to the first solicitation by or on behalf of such company of firm commitments to purchase such securities or immediately prior to the issuance of such securities, that the price at which such securities are to be sold is not less than a price which closely approximates the market value of those securities, less any distributing commission or discount.

(3) A business development company may sell any common stock of which it is the issuer at a price below the current net asset value of such stock upon the exercise of any warrant, option, or right issued in accordance with section 61(a)(3).

Accounts and Records

Sec. 64. (a) Notwithstanding the exemption set forth in section 6(f), section 31 shall apply to a business development company to the same extent as if it were a registered closed-end investment company, except that the reference to the financial statements required to be filed pursuant to section 30 shall be construed to refer to the financial statements required to be filed by such business development company pursuant to section 13 of the Securities Exchange Act of 1934.

(b)(1) In addition to the requirements of subsection (a), a business development company shall file with the Commission and supply annually to its shareholders a written statement, in such form and manner as the Commission may, by rule, prescribe, describing the risk factors involved in an investment in the securities of a business development company due to the nature of such company's investment portfolio and capital structure, and shall supply copies of such statement to any registered broker or dealer upon request.

(2) If the Commission finds it is necessary or appropriate in the public interest and consistent with the protection of investors and the purposes fairly intended by the policy and provisions of this title, the Commission may also require, by rule, any person who, acting as principal or agent, sells a security of a business development company to inform the purchaser of such securities, at or before the time of sale, of the existence of the risk statement prepared by such business development company pursuant to this subsection, and make such risk statement available on request. The Commission, in making such rules and regulations, shall consider, among other matters, whether any such rule or regulation would impose any unreasonable burdens on such brokers or dealers or unreasonably impair the maintenance of fair and orderly markets.

Liability of Controlling Persons; Preventing Compliance With Title

Sec. 65. Notwithstanding the exemption set forth in section 6(f), section 48 shall apply to a business development company to the same extent as if it were a registered closed-end investment company, except that the provisions of section 48(a) shall not be construed to require any company which is not an investment company within the meaning of section 3(a) to comply with the provisions of this title which are applicable to a business development company solely because such company is a wholly-owned subsidiary of, or directly or indirectly controlled by, a business development company.

PART 270—RULES AND REGULATIONS, INVESTMENT COMPANY ACT OF 1940

(Cite as 17 CFR 270.__)

Section

ATTENTION ELECTRONIC FILERS

THIS REGULATION SHOULD BE READ IN CONJUNCTION WITH REGULATIONS S–T (PART 232 OF THIS CHAPTER), WHICH GOVERNS THE PREPARATION AND SUBMISSION OF DOCUMENTS IN ELECTRONIC FORMAT, MANY PROVISIONS RELATING TO THE PREPARATION AND SUBMISSION OF DOCUMENTS IN PAPER FORMAT CONTAINED IN THIS REGULATION ARE SUPERSEDED BY THE PROVISIONS OF REGULATION S–T FOR DOCUMENTS REQUIRED TO BE FILED IN ELECTRONIC FORMAT.

§ 270.0–1 Definition of Terms Used in This Part

(a) As used in the rules and regulations prescribed by the Commission pursuant to the Investment Company Act of 1940, unless the context otherwise requires:

(1) The term "Commission" means the Securities and Exchange Commission.

(2) The term "act" means the Investment Company Act of 1940.

(3) The term "section" refers to a section of the act.

(4) The terms "rule" and "regulations" refer to the rules and regulations adopted by the Commission pursuant to the Act, including the forms for registration and reports and the accompanying instructions thereto.

(5) The term *administrator* means any person who provides significant administrative or business affairs management services to an investment company.

(6)(i) A person is an *independent legal counsel* with respect to the directors who are not interested persons of an investment company ("disinterested directors") if:

(A) A majority of the disinterested directors reasonably determine in the exercise of their judgment (and record the basis for that determination in the minutes of their meeting) that any representation by the person of the company's investment adviser, principal underwriter, administrator ("management organizations"), or any of their control persons, since the beginning of the fund's last two completed fiscal years, is or was sufficiently limited that it is unlikely to adversely affect the professional judgment of the person in providing legal representation to the disinterested directors; and

(B) The disinterested directors have obtained an undertaking from such person to provide them with information necessary to make their determination and to update promptly that information when the person begins to represent, or materially increases his representation of, a management organization or control person.

(ii) The disinterested directors are entitled to rely on the information obtained from the person, unless they know or have reason to believe that the information is materially false or incomplete. The disinterested directors must re-evaluate their determination no less frequently than annually (and record the basis accordingly), except as provided in paragraph (iii) of this section.

(iii) After the disinterested directors obtain information that the person has begun to represent, or has materially increased his representation of, a management organization (or any of its control persons), the person may continue to be an independent legal counsel, for purposes of paragraph (a)(6)(i) of this section, for no longer than three months unless during that period the disinterested directors make a new determination under that paragraph.

(iv) For purposes of paragraphs (a)(6)(i)—(iii) of this section:

(A) The term *person* has the same meaning as in section 2(a)(28) of the Act (15 U.S.C. 80a–2(a)(28)) and, in addition, includes a partner, co-member, or employee of any person; and

(B) The term *control person* means any person (other than an investment company) directly or indirectly controlling, controlled by, or under common control with any of the investment company's management organizations.

(7) Fund governance standards. The board of directors of an investment company ("fund") satisfies the fund governance standards if:

(i) At least seventy-five percent of the directors of the fund are not interested persons of the fund ("disinterested directors") or, if the fund has three directors, all but one are disinterested directors;

(ii) The disinterested directors of the fund select and nominate any other disinterested director of the fund;

(iii) Any person who acts as legal counsel for the disinterested directors of the fund is an independent legal counsel as defined in paragraph (a)(6) of this section;

(iv) A disinterested director serves as chairman of the board of directors of the fund, presides over meetings of the board of directors and has substantially the same responsibilities as would a chairman of a board of directors;

(v) The board of directors evaluates at least once annually the performance of the board of directors and the committees of the board of directors, which evaluation must include a consideration of the effectiveness of the committee structure of the fund board and the number of funds on whose boards each director serves;

(vi) The disinterested directors meet at least once quarterly in a session at which no directors who are interested persons of the fund are present; and

(vii) The disinterested directors have been authorized to hire employees and to retain advisers and experts necessary to carry out their duties.

(b) Unless otherwise specifically provided, the terms used in the rules and regulations in this part shall have the meaning defined in the act. The terms "EDGAR," "EDGAR Filer Manual," "electronic filer," "electronic filing," "electronic format," "electronic submission," "paper format," and "signature" shall have the meanings assigned to such terms in Regulation S–T—General Rules for Electronic Filings (Part 232 of this chapter).

(c) A rule or regulation which defines a term without express reference to the act or to the rules and regulations, or to a portion thereof, defines such terms for all purposes as used both in the act and in the rules and regulations in this part, unless the context otherwise requires.

(d) Unless otherwise specified or the context otherwise requires, the term "prospectus" means a prospectus meeting the requirements of Section 10(a) of the Securities Act of 1933 as amended.

(e) Definition of separate account and conditions for availability of exemption under §§ 270.6c–6, 270.6c–7, 270.6c–8, 270.11a–2, 270.14a–2, 270.15a–3, 270.16a–1, 270.22d–3, 270.22e–1, 270.26a–1, 270.26a–2, 270.27a–2, 270.27a–3, 270.27c–1, and 270.32a–2 of this chapter.

(1) As used in the Rules and Regulations prescribed by the Commission pursuant to the Investment Company Act of 1940, unless otherwise specified or the context otherwise requires, the term "separate account" shall

mean an account established and maintained by an insurance company pursuant to the laws of any state or territory of the United States, or of Canada or any province thereof, under which income, gains and losses, whether or not realized, from assets allocated to such account, are, in accordance with the applicable contract, credited to or charged against such account without regard to other income, gains or losses of the insurance company and the term "variable annuity contract" shall mean any accumulation or annuity contract, any portion thereof, or any unit of interest or participation therein pursuant to which the value of the contract, either prior or subsequent to annuitization, or both, varies according to the investment experience of the separate account in which the contract participates.

(2) As conditions to the availability of exemptive Rules 6c–6, 6c–7, 6c–8, 11a–2, 14a–2, 15a–3, 16a–1, 22c–1, 22d–3, 22e–1, 26a–1, 26a–2, 27a–1, 27a–2, 27a–3, 27c–1, and 32a–2, the separate account shall be legally segregated, the assets of the separate account shall, at the time during the year that adjustments in the reserves are made, have a value at least equal to the reserves and other contract liabilities with respect to such account, and at all other times, shall have a value approximately equal to or in excess of such reserves and liabilities; and that portion of such assets having a value equal to, or approximately equal to, such reserves and contract liabilities shall not be chargeable with liabilities arising out of any other business which the insurance company may conduct.

§ 270.0–2 General Requirements of Papers and Applications

(a) *Filing of Papers.* All papers required to be filed with the Commission pursuant to the Act or the rules and regulations thereunder shall, unless otherwise provided by the rules and regulations in this part, be delivered through the mails or otherwise to the Securities and Exchange Commission, Washington, D.C. 20549. Except as otherwise provided by the rules and regulations, the date on which papers are actually received by the Commission shall be the date of filing thereof. If the last day for the timely filing of such papers falls on a Saturday, Sunday or holiday, such papers may be filed on the first business day following.

(b) *Formal Specifications Respecting Applications.* Every application for an order under any provision of the Act, for which a form with instructions is not specifically prescribed, and every amendment to such application shall be filed in quintuplicate. One copy shall be signed by the applicant but the other four copies may have facsimile or typed signatures. Such applications should be on paper no larger than 8½ × 11 inches in size. To the extent that the reduction of larger documents would render them illegible, such documents may be filed on paper larger than 8½ × 11 inches in size. The left margin should be at least 1½ inches wide and, if the application is bound, it should be bound on the left side. The application must be typed, printed, copied or prepared by any process which, in the opinion of the Commission, produces copies suitable for microfilming. All typewritten or printed matter (including deficits in financial statements) should be set forth in black so as to permit photocopying. Every application for an order under any provision of the Act and every amendment to such application shall be submitted to the Commission in paper only, whether or not the applicant is otherwise required to file in electronic format, unless instructions for electronic filing are included on the form, if any, prescribed for such application.

(c) *Authorizations Respecting Applications.* (1) Every application for an order under any provision of the act, for which a form with instructions is not specifically prescribed and which is executed by a corporation, partnership, or other company and filed with the Commission, shall contain a concise statement of the applicable provisions of the articles of incorporation, bylaws, or similar documents, relating to the right of the person signing and filing such application to take such action on behalf of the applicant, and a statement that all such requirements have been complied with and that the person signing and filing the same is fully authorized to do so. If such authorization is dependent on resolutions of stockholders, directors, or other bodies, such resolutions shall be attached as an exhibit to, or the pertinent provisions thereof shall be quoted in, the application.

(2) If an amendment to any such application shall be filed, such amendment shall contain a similar statement or, in lieu thereof, shall state that the authorization described in the original application is applicable to the individual who signs such amendment and that such authorization still remains in effect.

(3) When any such application or amendment is signed by an agent or attorney, the power of attorney evidencing his authority to sign shall contain similar statements and shall be filed with the Commission.

(d) *Verification of Applications and Statements of Fact.* Every application for an order under any provision of the act, for which a form with instructions is not specifically prescribed and every amendment to such application, and every statement of fact formally filed in support of, or in opposition to, any application or declaration shall be verified by the person executing the same. An instrument executed on behalf of a corporation shall be verified in substantially the following form, but suitable changes may be made in such form for other kinds of companies and for individuals:

State of ______________)
) ss.
County of ____________)

The undersigned being duly sworn deposes and says that he has duly executed the attached ______ dated ______, 19__ for and on behalf of ______________ (Name of Company) that he is the ______________________ (Title of Officer) of such company; and that all action by stockholders, directors, and other bodies necessary to authorize deponent to execute and file such instrument has been taken. Deponent further says that he is familiar with such instrument, and the contents thereof, and that the facts therein set forth are true to the best of his knowledge, information and belief.

____
(Signature)

____
(Type or print name beneath)

Subscribed and sworn to before me a ______ (Title of Officer) this ______ day of ______, 19__.

[Official Seal] ________

My commission expires ________

(e) *Statement of Grounds for Application.* Each application should contain a brief statement of the reasons why the applicant is deemed to be entitled to the action requested with a reference to the provisions of the act and of the rules and regulations under which application is made.

(f) *Name and Address.* Every application shall contain the name and address of each applicant and the name and address of any person to whom any applicant wishes any question regarding the application to be directed.

(g) *Proposed Notice.* A proposed notice of the proceeding initiated by the filing of the application shall accompany each application as an exhibit thereto and, if necessary, shall be modified to reflect any amendments to such application.

(h) The manually signed original (or in the case of duplicate originals, one duplicate original) of all registrations, applications, statements, reports, or other documents filed under the Investment Company Act of 1940, as amended, shall be numbered sequentially (in addition to any internal numbering which otherwise may be present) by handwritten, typed, printed, or other legible form of notation from the facing page of the document through the last page of that document and any exhibits or attachments thereto. Further, the total number of pages contained in a numbered original shall be set forth on the first page of the document.

§ 270.0-3 Amendments to Registration Statements and Reports

Registration statements filed with the Commission pursuant to section 8 and reports filed with the Commission pursuant to section 30 may be amended in the following manner:

(a) Each amendment shall conform to the requirements for the registration statement or report it amends with regard to filing, number of copies filed, size, paper, ink, margins, binding, and similar formal matters.

(b) Each amendment to a particular statement or report shall have a facing sheet as follows:

SECURITIES AND EXCHANGE COMMISSION

Washington, D.C. 20549

Amendment No. ______

to

Form ______

File No. ______

(*Describe the nature of the statement or report*)

Dated ______, 19__

Pursuant to Section ______ of the Investment Company Act of 1940

____

Name of Registrant

____

Address of Principal Office of Registrant

The facing sheet shall contain in addition any other information required on the facing sheet of the form for the statement or report which is being amended. Amendments to a particular statement or report which is being consecutively in the order in which filed with the Commission.

(c) Each amendment shall contain in the manner required in the original statement or report the text of every item to which it relates and shall set out a complete amended answer to each such item. However, amendments to financial statements may contain only the particular statements or schedules in fact amended.

(d) Each amendment shall have a signature sheet containing the form of signature required in the statement or report it amends.

§ 270.0-4 Incorporation by Reference

(a) A registered investment company may, subject to the limitations of § 228.10(f) and § 229.10(d) of this chapter, incorporate by reference as an exhibit, in any registration statement, application or report filed with the Commission, any document or part thereof previously or concurrently filed with the Commission pursuant to any act administered by the Commission. The incorporation may be made whether the matter incorporated was filed by such registered company or any other person. If any modification has occurred in the text of any such document since the filing thereof, the company shall file with the reference a statement containing the text of any such modification and the date thereof. If the number of copies of any document previously or concurrently filed with the Commission is less than the number required to be filed with the registration statement, application or report which incorporates such document, the company shall file therewith as many additional copies of the document as may be necessary to meet the requirements of the registration statement, application or report.

(b) A registered investment company may, subject to the limitations of § 201.24 of this chapter, incorporate by reference, in any registration statement, application or report filed with the Commission any financial statement or part thereof previously or concurrently filed with the Commission pursuant to any act administered by the Commission, if it substantially conforms to the requirements of the form on which such registration statement, application or report is filed. The incorporation may be made whether the matter incorporated was filed by such registered company or any other person. If a certificate of an independent public accountant or accountants is required to accompany a financial statement in any registration statement, application or report, the incorporation by reference of a certificate previously or concurrently filed will not be deemed a compliance with such requirements unless the written consent of the accountant or accountants to such incorporation is filed with the registration statement, application or report.

(c) In each case of incorporation, by reference, the matter incorporated shall be clearly identified in the reference. An express statement shall be made to the effect that the specified matter is incorporated in the registration statement, application, or report at the particular place where the information is required.

(d) Notwithstanding any particular provision permitting incorporation by reference, no registration statement, application or report shall incorporate by reference any exhibit or financial statement which (1) has been withdrawn, or (2) was filed in connection with a registration under the Act, or a registration on a national securities exchange, which has ceased to be effective, or (3) is contained in a registration statement or report subject, at the time of the incorporation by reference, to pending proceedings under section 8(b) or 8(d) of the Securities Act of 1933, section 8(e) of the Act, or to an order entered under any of those Sections, (4) if it is a document that has been filed in paper with respect to an electronic filer under a temporary hardship exemption (§ 232.201 of this chapter) and an electronic format copy has not been submitted.

(e) Notwithstanding any particular provision permitting incorporation by reference, the Commission may refuse to permit such incorporation in any case in which in its judgment such incorporation would render the registration statement application, or report incomplete, unclear, or confusing.

§ 270.0–5 Procedure With Respect to Applications and Other Matters

The procedure herein below set forth will be followed with respect to any proceeding initiated by the filing of an application, or upon the Commission's own motion, pursuant to any section of the Act or any rule or regulation thereunder, unless in the particular case a different procedure is provided:

(a) Notice of the initiation of the proceeding will be published in the Federal Register and will indicate the earliest date upon which an order disposing of the matter may be entered. The notice will also provide that any interested person may, within the period of time specified therein, submit to the Commission in writing any facts bearing upon the desirability of a hearing on the matter and may request that a hearing be held, stating his reasons therefor and the nature of his interest in the matter.

(b) An order disposing of the matter will be issued as of course, following the expiration of the period of time referred to in paragraph (a) of this section, unless the Commission thereafter orders a hearing on the matter.

(c) The Commission will order a hearing on the matter, if it appears that a hearing is necessary or appropriate in the public interest or for the protection of investors, (1) upon the request of an interested person or (2) upon its own motion.

§ 270.0–8 Payment of Fees

All payment of fees shall be made in cash, certified check, or by U.S. postal money order, bank cashier's check, or bank money order payable to the Securities and Exchange Commission, omitting the name or title of any official of the Commission. Payment of fees required by this section shall be made in accordance with the directions set forth in § 202.3a of this chapter.

§ 270.0–9 Liability for Certain Statements by Issuers

(a) A statement within the coverage of paragraph (b) of this section which is made by an issuer shall be deemed not to be a fraudulent statement (as defined in paragraph (c) of this section), unless it is shown that such statement was made without a reasonable basis or was disclosed other than in good faith.

(b) This rule applies to information relating to the effects of changing prices on the business enterprise disclosed in a document transmitted to or filed with the Commission or in an annual report to shareholders meeting the requirements of Rules 14a–3(b) and (c) or 14c–3(a) and (b) under the Securities Exchange Act of 1934.

(c) For the purpose of this rule the term "fraudulent statement" shall mean a statement which is an untrue statement of a material fact, a statement false or misleading with respect to any material fact, an omission to state a material fact necessary to make a statement not misleading, or a fact which is materially misleading in light of the reports required to be filed pursuant to subsections (a) and (b) of section 30 of the Investment Company Act of 1940, as those terms are used in the Investment Company Act of 1940 or the rules or regulations promulgated thereunder.

§ 270.0–10. Small Entities Under the Investment Company Act for Purposes of the Regulatory Flexibility Act

(a) *General.* For purposes of Commission rulemaking in accordance with the provisions of Chapter Six of the Administrative Procedure Act (5 U.S.C. 601 *et seq.*) and unless otherwise defined for purposes of a particular rulemaking, the term *small business* or *small organization* for purposes of the Investment Company Act of 1940 shall mean an investment company that, together with other investment companies in the same group of related investment companies, has net assets of $50 million or less as of the end of its most recent fiscal year. For purposes of this section:

(1) In the case of a management company, the term *group of related investment companies* shall mean two or more management companies (including series thereof) that:

(i) Hold themselves out to investors as related companies for purposes of investment and investor services; and

(ii) Either:

(A) Have a common investment adviser or have investment advisers that are affiliated persons of each other; or

(B) Have a common administrator; and

(2) In the case of a unit investment trust, the term *group of related investment companies* shall mean two or more unit investment trusts (including series thereof) that have a common sponsor.

(b) *Special rule for insurance company separate accounts.* In determining whether an insurance company separate account is a *small business* or *small entity* pursuant to paragraph (a) of this section, the assets of the separate account shall be cumulated with the assets of the general account and all other separate accounts of the insurance company.

(c) *Determination of net assets.* The Commission may calculate its determination of the net assets of a group of related investment companies based on the net assets of each investment company in the group as of the end of such company's fiscal year.

§ 270.0–11 Customer Identification Programs

Each registered open-end company is subject to the requirements of 31 U.S.C. 5318(*l*) and the implementing regulation at 31 CFR 103.131, which requires a customer identification program to be implemented as part of the anti-money laundering program required under subchapter II of chapter 53 of title 31,

United States Code and the implementing regulations issued by the Department of the Treasury at 31 CFR part 103. Where 31 CFR 103.131 and this chapter use different definitions for the same term, the definition in 31 CFR 103.131 shall be used for the purpose of compliance with 31 CFR 103.131. Where 31 CFR 103.131 and this chapter require the same records to be preserved for different periods of time, such records shall be preserved for the longer period of time.

§ 270.2a–1 Valuation of Portfolio Securities in Special Cases

(a) Any investment company whose securities are qualified for sale, or for whose securities application for such qualification has been made, in any State in which the securities owned by such company are required by applicable State law or regulations to be valued at cost or on some other basis different from that prescribed by clause (A) of section 2(a)(41) of the act for the purpose of determining the percentage of its assets invested in any particular type or classification of securities or in the securities of any one issuer, may, in valuing its securities for the purposes of sections 5 and 12 of the act, use the same basis of valuation as that used in complying with such State law or regulations in lieu of the method of valuation prescribed by clause (A) of section 2(a)(41) of the act.

(b) Any open-end company which has heretofore valued its securities at costs for the purpose of qualifying as a "mutual investment company" under the Internal Revenue Code, prior to its amendment by the Revenue Act of 1942, shall henceforth, for the purposes of sections 5 and 12 of the act, value its securities in accordance with the method prescribed in clause (A) of section 2(a)(41) of the act unless such company is permitted under paragraph (a) of this section to use a different method of valuation.

(c) A registered investment company which has adopted for the purposes of sections 5 and 12 of the act a method of valuation permitted by paragraph (a) of this section, shall state in its registration statement filed pursuant to section 8 of the act, or in a report filed pursuant to section 30 of the act, the method of valuation adopted and the facts which justify the adoption of such method. A registered investment company which has adopted for the purposes of sections 5 and 12 of the act a method of valuation permitted by paragraph (a) of this section, unless it shall have adopted such method for the purpose or partly for the purpose of qualifying as a "mutual investment company" under the Internal Revenue Code, shall continue to use that method until it has notified the Commission of its desire to use a different method, and has received from the Commission permission for such change. Such permission may be made effective on a fixed date or within such reasonable time thereafter as may be deemed advisable under the circumstances.

(d) If at any time it appears that the method of valuation adopted by any company pursuant to paragraph (a) of this section is no longer justified by the facts, the Commission may require a change in the method of valuation within a reasonable period of time either to the method prescribed in clause (A) of section 2(a)(41) of the Act or to some other method permitted by paragraph (a) of this section which is justified by the existing facts.

§ 270.2a–2 Effect of Eliminations Upon Valuation of Portfolio Securities

During any fiscal quarter in which elimination of securities from the portfolio of an investment company occur, the securities remaining in the portfolio shall, for the purpose of sections 5 and 12 of the act, be so valued as to give effect to the eliminations in accordance with one of the following methods: (a) Specific certificate, (b) first in—first out, (c) last in—first out, or (d) average value. For these purposes, a single method of elimination shall be used consistently with respect to all portfolio securities. In giving effect to eliminations pursuant to this section values shall be computed in accordance with section 2(a)(41)(A) of the act.

§ 270.2a3-1 Investment Company Limited Partners Not Deemed Affiliated Persons.

Preliminary Note to § 270.2a3-1

This § 270.2a3-1 excepts from the definition of affiliated person in section 2(a)(3) (15 U.S.C. 80a-2(a)(3)) those limited partners of investment companies organized in limited partnership form that are affiliated persons solely because they are partners under section 2(a)(3)(D) (15 U.S.C. 80a-2(a)(3)(D)). Reliance on this § 270.2a3-1 does not except a limited partner that is an affiliated person by virtue of any other provision.

No limited partner of a registered management company or a business development company, organized as a limited partnership and relying on § 270.2a19-2, shall be deemed to be an affiliated person of such company, or any other partner of such company, solely by reason of being a limited partner of such company.

§ 270.2a-4 Definition of "Current Net Asset Value" for Use in Computing Periodically the Current Price of Redeemable Security

(a) The current net asset value of any redeemable security issued by a registered investment company used in computing periodically the current price for the purpose of distribution, redemption, and repurchase means an amount which reflects calculations, whether or not recorded on the books of account, made substantially in accordance with the following, with estimates used where necessary or appropriate:

(1) Portfolio securities with respect to which market quotations are readily available shall be valued at current market value, and other securities and assets shall be valued at fair value as determined in good faith by the board of directors of the registered company.

(2) Changes in holdings of portfolio securities shall be reflected no later than in the first calculation on the first business day following the trade date.

(3) Changes in the number of outstanding shares of the registered company resulting from distributions, redemptions, and repurchases shall be reflected no later than in the first calculation on the first business day following such change.

(4) Expenses, including any investment advisory fees, shall be included to date of calculation. Appropriate provision shall be made for Federal income taxes if required. Investment companies which retain realized capital gains designated as a distribution to shareholders shall comply with paragraph (h) of § 210.6-03 of Regulation S-X.

(5) Dividends receivable shall be included to date of calculation either at ex-dividend dates or record dates, as appropriate.

(6) Interest income and other income shall be included to date of calculation.

(b) The items which would otherwise be required to be reflected by paragraph (a)(4) and (6) of this section need not be so reflected if cumulatively, when netted, they do not amount to as much as one cent per outstanding share.

(c) Notwithstanding the requirements of paragraph (a) of this section, any interim determination of current net asset value between calculations made as of the close of the New York Stock Exchange on the preceding business day and the current business day may be estimated so as to reflect any change in current net asset value since the closing calculation on the preceding business day.

§ 270.2a-6 Certain Transactions Not Deemed Assignments

A transaction which does not result in a change of actual control or management of the investment adviser to, or principal underwriter of, an investment company is not an assignment for purposes of section 15(a)(4) or section 15(b)(2) of the act, respectively.

§ 270.2a–7 Money Market Funds

(a) *Definitions.*

(1) Acquisition (or Acquire) means any purchase or subsequent rollover (but does not include the failure to exercise a Demand Feature).

(2) Amortized Cost Method of valuation means the method of calculating an investment company's net asset value whereby portfolio securities are valued at the fund's Acquisition cost as adjusted for amortization of premium or accretion of discount rather than at their value based on current market factors.

(3) Asset Backed Security means a fixed income security (other than a Government security) issued by a Special Purpose Entity (as defined in this paragraph), substantially all of the assets which consist of Qualifying Assets (as defined in this paragraph). Special Purpose Entity means a trust, corporation, partnership or other entity organized for the sole purpose of issuing securities that entitle their holders to receive payments that depend primarily on the cash flow from Qualifying Assets, but does not include a registered investment company. Qualifying Assets means financial assets, either fixed or revolving, that by their terms convert into cash within a finite time period, plus any rights or other assets designed to assure the servicing or timely distribution of proceeds to security holders.

(4) Business Day means any day, other than Saturday, Sunday, or any customary business holiday.

(5) *Collateralized Fully* means "Collateralized Fully" as defined in § 270.5b–3(c)(1).

(6) Conditional Demand Feature means a Demand Feature that is not an Unconditional Demand Feature. A Conditional Demand Feature is not a Guarantee.

(7) Conduit Security means a security issued by a Municipal Issuer (as defined in this paragraph) involving an arrangement or agreement entered into, directly or indirectly, with a person other than a Municipal Issuer, which arrangement or agreement provides for or secures repayment of the security. Municipal Issuer means a state or territory of the United States (including the District of Columbia), or any political subdivision or public instrumentality of a state or territory of the United States. A Conduit Security does not include a security that is:

(i) Fully and unconditionally guaranteed by a Municipal Issuer; or

(ii) Payable from the general revenues of the Municipal Issuer or other Municipal Issuers (other than those revenues derived from an agreement or arrangement with a person who is not a Municipal Issuer that provides for or secures repayment of the security issued by the Municipal Issuer); or

(iii) Related to a project owned and operated by a Municipal Issuer; or

(iv) Related to a facility leased to and under the control of an industrial or commercial enterprise that is part of a public project which, as a whole, is owned and under the control of a Municipal Issuer.

(8) Demand Feature means:

(i) A feature permitting the holder of a security to sell the security at an exercise price equal to the approximate amortized cost of the security plus accrued interest, if any, at the time of exercise. A Demand Feature must be exercisable either:

(A) At any time on no more than 30 calendar days' notice; or

(B) At specified intervals not exceeding 397 calendar days and upon no more than 30 calendar days' notice; or

(ii) A feature permitting the holder of an Asset Backed Security unconditionally to receive principal and interest within 397 calendar days of making demand.

(9) Demand Feature Issued By A Non-Controlled Person means a Demand Feature issued by:

(i) A person that, directly or indirectly, does not control, and is not controlled by or under common control with the issuer of the security subject to the Demand Feature (control means "control" as defined in section 2(a)(9) of the Act) (15 U.S.C. 80a–2(a)(9)); or

(ii) A sponsor of a Special Purpose Entity with respect to an Asset Backed Security.

(10) Eligible Security means:

(i) A Rated Security with a remaining maturity of 397 calendar days or less that has received a rating from the Requisite NRSROs in one of the two highest short-term rating categories (within which there may be subcategories or gradations indicating relative standing); or

(ii) An Unrated Security that is of comparable quality to a security meeting the requirements for a Rated Security in paragraph (a)(10)(i) of this section, as determined by the money market fund's board of directors; Provided, however, that:

(A) A security that at the time of issuance had a remaining maturity of more than 397 calendar days but that has a remaining maturity of 397 calendar days or less and that is an Unrated Security is not an Eligible Security if the security has received a long-term rating from any NRSRO that is not within the NRSRO's three highest long-term ratings categories (within which there may be sub-categories or gradations indicating relative standing), unless the security has received a long-term rating from the Requisite NRSROs in one of the three highest rating categories:

(B) An Asset Backed Security (other than an Asset Backed Security substantially all of whose Qualifying Assets consist of obligations of one or more Municipal Issuers, as that term is defined in paragraph (a)(7) of this section) shall not be an Eligible Security unless it has received a rating from an NRSRO.

(iii) In addition, in the case of a security that is subject to a Demand Feature or Guarantee:

(A) The Guarantee has received a rating from an NRSRO or the Guarantee is issued by a guarantor that has received a rating from an NRSRO with respect to a class of debt obligations (or any debt obligation within that class) that is comparable in priority and security to the Guarantee, unless:

(*1*) The Guarantee is issued by a person that, directly or indirectly, controls, is controlled by or is under common control with the issuer of the security subject to the Guarantee (other than a sponsor of a Special Purpose Entity with respect to an Asset Backed Security);

(*2*) The security subject to the Guarantee is a repurchase agreement that is Collateralized Fully; or

(*3*) The Guarantee is itself a Government Security; and

(B) The issuer of the Demand Feature or Guarantee, or another institution, has undertaken promptly to notify the holder of the security in the event the Demand Feature or Guarantee is substituted with another Demand Feature or Guarantee (if such substitution is permissible under the terms of the Demand Feature or Guarantee).

(11) Event of Insolvency means "Event of Insolvency" as defined in § 270.5b–3(c)(2).

(12) First Tier Security means any Eligible Security that:

(i) Is a Rated Security that has received a short-term rating from the Requisite NRSROs in the highest short-term rating category for debt obligations (within which there may be sub-categories or gradations indicating relative standing); or

(ii) Is an Unrated Security that is of comparable quality to a security meeting the requirements for a Rated Security in paragraph (a)(12)(i) of this section, as determined by the fund's board of directors; or

(iii) Is a security issued by a registered investment company that is a money market fund; or

(iv) Is a Government Security.

(13) Floating Rate Security means a security the terms of which provide for the adjustment of its interest rate whenever a specified interest rate changes and that at any time until the final maturity of the instrument or the period remaining until the principal amount can be recovered through demand, can reasonably be expected to have a market value that approximates its amortized cost.

(14) Government Security means any "Government security" as defined in section 2(a)(16) of the Act (15 U.S.C. 80a–2(a)(16)).

(15) Guarantee means an unconditional obligation of a person other than the issuer of the security to undertake to pay, upon presentment by the holder of the Guarantee (if required), the principal amount of the underlying security plus accrued interest when due or upon default, or, in the case of an Unconditional Demand Feature, an obligation that entitles the holder to receive upon exercise the approximate amortized cost of the underlying security or securities, plus accrued interest, if any. A Guarantee includes a letter of credit, financial guaranty (bond) insurance, and an Unconditional Demand Feature (other than an Unconditional Demand Feature provided by the issuer of the security).

(16) Guarantee Issued By A Non–Controlled Person means a Guarantee issued by:

(i) A person that, directly or indirectly, does not control, and is not controlled by or under common control with the issuer of the security subject to the Guarantee (control means "control" as defined in section 2(a)(9)) of the Act (15 U.S.C. 80a–2(a)(9)); or

(ii) A sponsor of a Special Purpose Entity with respect to an Asset Backed Security.

(17) NRSRO means any nationally recognized statistical rating organization, as that term is used in paragraphs (c)(2)(vi)(E), (F) and (H) of § 240.15c3–1 of this Chapter, that is not an "affiliated person," as defined in section 2(a)(3)(C) of the Act (15 U.S.C. 80a–2(a)(3)(C)), of the issuer of, or any insurer or provider of credit support for, the security.

(18) Penny–Rounding Method of pricing means the method of computing an investment company's price per share for purposes of distribution, redemption and repurchase whereby the current net asset value per share is rounded to the nearest one percent.

(19) Rated Security means a security that meets the requirements of paragraphs (a)(19)(i) or (ii) of this section, in each case subject to paragraph (a)(19)(iii) of this section:

(i) The security has received a short-term rating from an NRSRO, or has been issued by an issuer that has received a short-term rating from an NRSRO with respect to a class of debt obligations (or any debt obligation within that class) that is comparable in priority and security with the security; or

(ii) The security is subject to a Guarantee that has received a short-term rating from an NRSRO, or a Guarantee issued by a guarantor that has received a short-term rating from an NRSRO with respect to a class of debt obligations (or any debt obligation within that class) that is comparable in priority and security with the Guarantee; but

(iii) A security is not a Rated Security if it is subject to an external credit support agreement (including an arrangement by which the security has become a Refunded Security) that was not in effect when the security was assigned its rating, unless the security has received a short-term rating reflecting the existence of the credit support agreement as provided in paragraph (a)(19)(i) of this section, or the credit support agreement with respect to the security has received a short-term rating as provided in paragraph (a)(19)(ii) of this section.

(20) Refunded Security means "Refunded Security" as defined in § 270.5b–3(c)(4).

(21) Requisite NRSROs means:

(i) Any two NRSROs that have issued a rating with respect to a security or class of debt obligations of an issuer; or

(ii) If only one NRSRO has issued a rating with respect to such security or class of debt obligations of an issuer at the time the fund acquires the security, that NRSRO.

(22) Second Tier Security means any Eligible Security that is not a First Tier Security. Second Tier Conduit Security means any Conduit Security that is an Eligible Security that is not a First Tier Security.

(23) Single State Fund means a Tax Exempt Fund that holds itself out as seeking to maximize the amount of its distributed income that is exempt from the income taxes or other taxes on investments of a particular state and, where applicable, subdivisions thereof.

(24) Tax Exempt Fund means any money market fund that holds itself out as distributing income exempt from regular federal income tax.

(25) Total Assets means, with respect to a money market fund using the Amortized Cost Method, the total amortized cost of its assets and, with respect to any other money market fund, the total market-based value of its assets.

(26) Unconditional Demand Feature means a Demand Feature that by its terms would be readily exercisable in the event of a default in payment of principal or interest on the underlying security or securities.

(27) United States Dollar–Denominated means, with reference to a security, that all principal and interest payments on such security are payable to security holders in United States dollars under all circumstances and that the interest rate of, the principal amount to be repaid, and the timing of payments related to such security do not vary or float with the value of a foreign currency, the rate of interest payable on foreign currency borrowings, or with any other interest rate or index expressed in a currency other than United States dollars.

(28) Unrated Security means a security that is not a Rated Security.

(29) Variable Rate Security means a security the terms of which provide for the adjustment of its interest rate on set dates (such as the last day of a month or calendar quarter) and that, upon each adjustment until the final maturity of the instrument or the period remaining until the principal amount can be recovered through demand, can reasonably be expected to have a market value that approximates its amortized cost.

(b) *Holding Out and Use of Names and Titles.* (1) It shall be an untrue statement of material fact within the meaning of section 34(b) of the Act (15 U.S.C. 80a–33(b)) for a registered investment company, in any registration statement, application, report, account, record, or other document filed or transmitted pursuant to the Act, including any advertisement, pamphlet, circular, form letter, or other sales literature addressed to or intended for distribution to prospective investors that is required to be filed with the Commission by section 24(b) of the Act (15 U.S.C. 80a–24(b)), to hold itself out to investors as a money market fund or the equivalent of a money market fund, unless such registered investment company meets the conditions of paragraphs (c)(2), (c)(3) and (c)(4) of this section.

(2) It shall constitute the use of a materially deceptive or misleading name or title within the meaning of section 35(d) of the Act (15 U.S.C. 80a–34(d)) for a registered investment company to adopt the term "money market" as part of its name or title or the name or title of any redeemable securities of which it is the issuer, or to adopt a name that suggests that it is a money market fund or the equivalent of a money market fund, unless such registered investment company meets the conditions of paragraphs (c)(2), (c)(3), and (c)(4) of this section.

(3) For purposes of this paragraph, a name that suggests that a registered investment company is a money market fund or the equivalent thereof shall include one that uses such terms as "cash," "liquid," "money," "ready assets" or similar terms.

(c) *Share Price Calculations.* The current price per share, for purposes of distribution, redemption and repurchase, of any redeemable security issued by any registered investment company ("money market fund" or "fund"), notwithstanding the requirements of section 2(a)(41) of the Act (15 U.S.C. 80a–2(a)(41)) and of §§ 270.2a–4 and 270.22c–1 thereunder, may be computed by use of the Amortized Cost Method or the Penny–Rounding Method; Provided, however, that:

(1) Board Findings. The board of directors of the money market fund shall determine, in good faith, that it is in the best interests of the fund and its shareholders to maintain a stable net asset value per share or stable price per share, by virtue of either the Amortized Cost Method or the Penny–Rounding Method, and that the money market fund will continue to use such method only so long as the board of directors believes that it fairly reflects the market-based net asset value per share.

(2) Portfolio Maturity. The money market fund shall maintain a dollar-weighted average portfolio maturity appropriate to its objective of maintaining a stable net asset value per share or price per share; Provided, however, that the money market fund will not:

(i) Except as provided in paragraph (c)(2)(ii) of this section, Acquire any instrument with a remaining maturity of greater than 397 calendar days; or

(ii) In the case of a money market fund not using the Amortized Cost Method, Acquire a Government Security with a remaining maturity of greater than 762 calendar days; or

(iii) Maintain a dollar-weighted average portfolio maturity that exceeds ninety days.

(3) Portfolio Quality—(i) General. The money market fund shall limit its portfolio investments to those United States Dollar–Denominated securities that the fund's board of directors determines present minimal credit risks (which determination must be based on factors pertaining to credit quality in addition to any rating assigned to such securities by an NRSRO) and that are at the time of Acquisition Eligible Securities.

(ii) Second Tier Securities. Immediately after the Acquisition of any Second Tier Security:

(A) Taxable Funds. A money market fund that is not a Tax Exempt Fund shall not have invested more than five percent of its Total Assets in securities that are Second Tier Securities; and

(B) Tax Exempt Funds. A money market fund that is a Tax Exempt Fund shall not have invested more than five percent of its Total Assets in Conduit Securities that are Second Tier Conduit Securities.

(iii) Securities Subject to Guarantees. A security that is subject to a Guarantee may be determined to be an Eligible Security or a First Tier Security based solely on whether the Guarantee is an Eligible

Security or First Tier Security, as the case may be.

(iv) Securities Subject to Conditional Demand Features. A security that is subject to a Conditional Demand Feature ("Underlying Security") may be determined to be an Eligible Security or a First Tier Security only if:

(A) The Conditional Demand Feature is an Eligible Security or First Tier Security, as the case may be;

(B) At the time of the Acquisition of the Underlying Security, the money market fund's board of directors has determined that there is minimal risk that the circumstances that would result in the Conditional Demand Feature not being exercisable will occur; and

(1) The conditions limiting exercise either can be monitored readily by the fund, or relate to the taxability, under federal, state or local law, of the interest payments on the security; or

(2) The terms of the Conditional Demand Feature require that the fund will receive notice of the occurrence of the condition and the opportunity to exercise the Demand Feature in accordance with its terms; and

(C) The Underlying Security or any Guarantee of such security (or the debt securities of the issuer of the Underlying Security or Guarantee that are comparable in priority and security with the Underlying Security or Guarantee) has received either a short-term rating or a long-term rating, as the case may be, from the Requisite NRSROs within the NRSROs' two highest short-term or long-term rating categories (within which there may be sub-categories or gradations indicating relative standing) or, if unrated, is determined to be of comparable quality by the money market fund's board of directors to a security that has received a rating from the Requisite NRSROs within the NRSROs' two highest short-term or long-term rating categories, as the case may be.

(4) Portfolio Diversification—(i) Issuer Diversification. The money market fund shall be diversified with respect to issuers of securities Acquired by the fund as provided in paragraphs (c)(4)(i) and (c)(4)(ii) of this section, other than with respect to Government Securities and securities subject to a Guarantee Issued By A Non–Controlled Person.

(A) Taxable and National Funds. Immediately after the Acquisition of any security, a money market fund other than a Single State Fund shall not have invested more than five percent of its Total Assets in securities issued by the issuer of the security; Provided, however, that such a fund may invest up to twenty-five percent of its Total Assets in the First Tier Securities of a single issuer for a period of up to three Business Days after the Acquisition thereof; Provided, further, that the fund may not invest in the securities of more than one issuer in accordance with the foregoing proviso in this paragraph at any time.

(B) Single State Funds. With respect to seventy-five percent of its Total Assets, immediately after the Acquisition of any security, a Single State Fund shall not have invested more than five percent of its Total Assets in securities issued by the issuer of the security; Provided, however, that a Single State Fund shall not invest more than five percent of its Total Assets in securities issued by the issuer of the security unless the securities are First Tier Securities.

(C) Second Tier Securities—(1) Taxable Funds. Immediately after the Acquisition of any Second Tier Security, a money market fund that is not a Tax

Exempt Fund shall not have invested more than the greater of one percent of its Total Assets or one million dollars in securities issued by that issuer that are Second Tier Securities.

(2) Tax Exempt Funds. Immediately after the Acquisition of any Second Tier Conduit Security, a money market fund that is a Tax Exempt Fund shall not have invested more than the greater of one percent of its Total Assets or one million dollars in securities issued by that issuer that are Second Tier Conduit Securities.

(ii) Issuer Diversification Calculations. For purposes of making calculations under paragraph (c)(4)(i) of this section:

(A) Repurchase Agreements. The Acquisition of a repurchase agreement may be deemed to be an Acquisition of the underlying securities, provided the obligation of the seller to repurchase the securities from the money market fund is Collateralized Fully.

(B) Refunded Securities. The Acquisition of a Refunded Security shall be deemed to be an Acquisition of the escrowed Government Securities.

(C) Conduit Securities. A Conduit Security shall be deemed to be issued by the person (other than the Municipal Issuer) ultimately responsible for payments of interest and principal on the security.

(D) Asset Backed Securities—(1) General. An Asset Backed Security Acquired by a fund ("Primary ABS") shall be deemed to be issued by the Special Purpose Entity that issued the Asset Backed Security, Provided, however:

(i) Holdings of Primary ABS. Any person whose obligations constitute ten percent or more of the principal amount of the Qualifying Assets of the Primary ABS ("Ten Percent Obligor") shall be deemed to be an issuer of the portion of the Primary ABS such obligations represent; and

(ii) Holdings of Secondary ABS. If a Ten Percent Obligor of a Primary ABS is itself a Special Purpose Entity issuing Asset Backed Securities ("Secondary ABS"), any Ten Percent Obligor of such Secondary ABS also shall be deemed to be an issuer of the portion of the Primary ABS that such Ten Percent Obligor represents.

(2) Restricted Special Purpose Entities. A Ten Percent Obligor with respect to a Primary or Secondary ABS shall not be deemed to have issued any portion of the assets of a Primary ABS as provided in paragraph (c)(4)(ii)(D)(1) of this section if that Ten Percent Obligor is itself a Special Purpose Entity issuing Asset Backed Securities ("Restricted Special Purpose Entity"), and the securities that it issues (other than securities issued to a company that controls, or is controlled by or under common control with, the Restricted Special Purpose Entity and which is not itself a Special Purpose Entity issuing Asset Backed Securities) are held by only one other Special Purpose Entity.

(3) Demand Features and Guarantees. In the case of a Ten Percent Obligor deemed to be an issuer, the fund shall satisfy the diversification requirements of paragraph (c)(4)(iii) of this section with respect to any Demand Feature or Guarantee to which the Ten Percent Obligor's obligations are subject.

(E) Shares of Other Money Market Funds. A money market fund that Acquires shares issued by another money market fund in an amount that would otherwise be prohibited by paragraph (c)(4)(i) of this section shall nonetheless be deemed in compliance with this section if the board of directors of the Acquiring money market fund reasonably believes that the fund in which it has invested is in compliance with this section.

(iii) Diversification Rules for Demand Features and Guarantees. The money market fund shall be diversified with respect to Demand Features and Guarantees Acquired by the fund as provided in paragraphs (c)(4)(iii) and (c)(4)(iv) of this section, other than with respect to a Demand Feature issued by the same institution that issued the underlying security, or with respect to a Guarantee or Demand Feature that is itself a Government Security.

(A) General. Immediately after the Acquisition of any Demand Feature or Guarantee or security subject to a Demand Feature or Guarantee, a money market fund, with respect to seventy-five percent of its Total Assets, shall not have invested more than ten percent of its Total Assets in securities issued by or subject to Demand Features or Guarantees from the institution that issued the Demand Feature or Guarantee, subject to paragraphs (c)(4)(iii)(B) and (C) of this section.

(B) Second Tier Demand Features or Guarantees. Immediately after the Acquisition of any Demand Feature or Guarantee (or a security after giving effect to the Demand Feature or Guarantee) that is a Second Tier Security, a money market fund shall not have invested more than five percent of its Total Assets in securities issued by or subject to Demand Features or Guarantees from the institution that issued the Demand Feature or Guarantee.

(C) Demand Features or Guarantees Issued by Non–Controlled Persons. Immediately after the Acquisition of any security subject to a Demand Feature or Guarantee, a money market fund shall not have invested more than ten percent of its Total Assets in securities issued by, or subject to Demand Features or Guarantees from the institution that issued the Demand Feature or Guarantee, unless, with respect to any security subject to Demand Features or Guarantees from that institution (other than securities issued by such institution), the Demand Feature or Guarantee is a Demand Feature or Guarantee Issued By A Non–Controlled Person.

(iv) Demand Feature and Guarantee Diversification Calculations—(A) Fractional Demand Features or Guarantees. In the case of a security subject to a Demand Feature or Guarantee from an institution by which the institution guarantees a specified portion of the value of the security, the institution shall be deemed to guarantee the specified portion thereof.

(B) Layered Demand Features or Guarantees. In the case of a security subject to Demand Features or Guarantees from multiple institutions that have not limited the extent of their obligations as described in paragraph (c)(4)(iv)(A) of this section, each institution shall be deemed to have provided the Demand Feature or Guarantee with respect to the entire principal amount of the security.

(v) Diversification Safe Harbor. A money market fund that satisfies the applicable diversification requirements of paragraphs (c)(4) and (c)(5) of this section shall be deemed to have satisfied the diversification requirements of section 5(b)(1) of the Act (15 U.S.C. 80a–5(b)(1)) and the rules adopted thereunder.

(5) Demand Features and Guarantees Not Relied Upon. If the fund's board of directors has determined that the fund is not relying on a Demand Feature or Guarantee to determine the quality (pursuant to paragraph (c)(3) of this section), or maturity (pursuant to paragraph (d) of this section), or liquidity of a portfolio security, and maintains a record of this determination (pursuant to paragraphs (c)(9)(ii) and (c)(10)(vi) of this section), then the fund may disregard such Demand Feature or Guarantee for all purposes of this section.

(6) Downgrades, Defaults and Other Events—(i) Downgrades—(A) General. Upon the occurrence of either of the events specified in paragraphs (c)(6)(i)(A)(1) and (2) of this section with respect to a portfolio security, the board of directors of the money market fund shall reassess promptly whether such security continues to present minimal credit risks and shall cause the fund to take such action as the board of directors determines is in the best interests of the money market fund and its shareholders:

(1) A portfolio security of a money market fund ceases to be a First Tier Security (either because it no longer has the highest rating from the Requisite NRSROs or, in the case of an Unrated Security, the board of directors of the money market fund determines that it is no longer of comparable quality to a First Tier Security); and

(2) The money market fund's investment adviser (or any person to whom the fund's board of directors has delegated portfolio management responsibilities) becomes aware that any Unrated Security or Second Tier Security held by the money market fund has, since the security was Acquired by the fund, been given a rating by any NRSRO below the NRSRO's second highest short-term rating category.

(B) Securities to Be Disposed Of. The reassessments required by paragraph (c)(6)(i)(A) of this section shall not be required if, in accordance with the procedures adopted by the board of directors, the security is disposed of (or matures) within five Business Days of the specified event and, in the case of events specified in paragraph (c)(6)(i)(A)(2) of this section, the board is subsequently notified of the adviser's actions.

(C) Special Rule for Certain Securities Subject to Demand Features. In the event that after giving effect to a rating downgrade, more than five percent of the fund's Total Assets are invested in securities issued by or subject to Demand Features from a single institution that are Second Tier Securities, the fund shall reduce its investment in securities issued by or subject to Demand Features from that institution to no more than five percent of its Total Assets by exercising the Demand Features at the next succeeding exercise date(s), absent a finding by the board of directors that disposal of the portfolio security would not be in the best interests of the money market fund.

(ii) Defaults and Other Events. Upon the occurrence of any of the events specified in paragraphs (c)(6)(ii)(A) through (D) of this section with respect to a portfolio security, the money market fund shall dispose of such security as soon as practicable consistent with achieving an orderly disposition of the security, by sale, exercise of any Demand Feature or otherwise, absent a finding by the board of directors that disposal of the portfolio security would not be in the best interests of the money market fund (which determination may take into account, among other factors, market conditions that could affect the orderly disposition of the portfolio security):

(A) The default with respect to a portfolio security (other than an immaterial default unrelated to the financial condition of the issuer);

(B) A portfolio security ceases to be an Eligible Security;

(C) A portfolio security has been determined to no longer present minimal credit risks; or

(D) An Event of Insolvency occurs with respect to the issuer of a portfolio security or the provider of any Demand Feature or Guarantee.

(iii) Notice to the Commission. In the event of a default with respect to one or more portfolio securities (other than an immaterial default unrelated to the financial condition of the issuer) or an Event of Insolvency with respect to the issuer of the security or any Demand Feature or Guarantee to which it is subject, where immediately before default the securities (or the securities subject to the Demand Feature or Guarantee) accounted for ½ of 1 percent or more of a money market fund's Total Assets, the money market fund shall promptly notify the Commission of such fact and the actions the money market fund intends to take in response to such situation. Notification under this paragraph shall be made telephonically, or by means of a facsimile transmission or electronic mail, followed by letter sent by first class mail, directed to the attention of the Director of the Division of Investment Management.

(iv) Defaults for Purposes of Paragraphs (c)(6)(ii) and (iii). For purposes of paragraphs (c)(6)(ii) and (iii) of this section, an instrument subject to a Demand Feature or Guarantee shall not be deemed to be in default (and an Event of Insolvency with respect to the security shall not be deemed to have occurred) if:

(A) In the case of an instrument subject to a Demand Feature, the Demand Feature has been exercised and the fund has recovered either the principal amount or the amortized cost of the instrument, plus accrued interest; or

(B) The provider of the Guarantee is continuing, without protest, to make payments as due on the instrument.

(7) Required Procedures: Amortized Cost Method. In the case of a money market fund using the Amortized Cost Method:

(i) General. In supervising the money market fund's operations and delegating special responsibilities involving portfolio management to the money market fund's investment adviser, the money market fund's board of directors, as a particular responsibility within the overall duty of care owed to its shareholders, shall establish written procedures reasonably designed, taking into account current market conditions and the money market fund's investment objectives, to stabilize the money market fund's net asset value per share, as computed for the purpose of distribution, redemption and repurchase, at a single value.

(ii) Specific Procedures. Included within the procedures adopted by the board of directors shall be the following:

(A) Shadow Pricing. Written procedures shall provide:

(1) That the extent of deviation, if any, of the current net asset value per share calculated using available market quotations (or an appropriate substitute that reflects current market conditions) from the money market fund's amortized cost price per share, shall be calculated at such intervals as the board of directors determines appropriate and reasonable in light of current market conditions;

(2) For the periodic review by the board of directors of the amount of the deviation as well as the methods used to calculate the deviation; and

(3) For the maintenance of records of the determination of deviation and the board's review thereof.

(B) Prompt Consideration of Deviation. In the event such deviation from the money market fund's amortized cost price per share exceeds ½ of 1 percent, the board of directors shall promptly consider what action, if any, should be initiated by the board of directors.

(C) Material Dilution or Unfair Results. Where the board of directors believes the extent of any deviation from the money market fund's amortized cost price per share may result in material dilution or other unfair results to investors or existing shareholders, it shall cause the fund to take such action as it deems appropriate to eliminate or reduce to the extent reasonably practicable such dilution or unfair results.

(8) Required Procedures: Penny–Rounding Method. In the case of a money market fund using the Penny–Rounding Method, in supervising the money market fund's operations and delegating special responsibilities involving portfolio management to the money market fund's investment adviser, the money market fund's board of directors undertakes, as a particular responsibility within the overall duty of care owed to its shareholders, to assure to the extent reasonably practicable, taking into account current market conditions affecting the money market fund's investment objectives, that the money market fund's price per share as computed for the purpose of distribution, redemption and repurchase, rounded to the nearest one percent, will not deviate from the single price established by the board of directors.

(9) Specific Procedures: Amortized Cost and Penny–Rounding Methods. Included within the procedures adopted by the board of directors for money market funds using either the Amortized Cost or Penny–Rounding Methods shall be the following:

(i) Securities for Which Maturity is Determined by Reference to Demand Features. In the case of a security for which maturity is determined by reference to a Demand Feature, written procedures shall require ongoing review of the security's continued minimal credit risks, and that review must be based on, among other things, financial data for the most recent fiscal year of the issuer of the Demand Feature and, in the case of a security subject to a Conditional Demand Feature, the issuer of the security whose financial condition must be monitored under paragraph (c)(3)(iv) of this section, whether such data is publicly available or provided under the terms of the security's governing documentation.

(ii) Securities Subject to Demand Features or Guarantees. In the case of a security subject to one or more Demand Features or Guarantees that the fund's board of directors has determined that the fund is not relying on to determine the quality (pursuant to paragraph (c)(3) of this section), maturity (pursuant to paragraph (d) of this section) or liquidity of the security subject to the Demand Feature or Guarantee, written procedures shall require periodic evaluation of such determination.

(iii) Adjustable Rate Securities Without Demand Features. In the case of a Variable Rate or Floating Rate Security that is not subject to a Demand Feature and for which maturity is determined pursuant to paragraphs (d)(1), (d)(2) or (d)(4) of this section, written procedures shall require periodic review of whether the interest rate formula, upon readjustment of its interest rate, can reasonably be expected to cause the security to have a market value that approximates its amortized cost value.

(iv) Asset Backed Securities. In the case of an Asset Backed Security, written procedures shall require the fund to periodically determine the number of Ten Percent Obligors (as that term is used in paragraph (c)(4)(ii)(D) of this section) deemed to be the issuers of all or a portion of the Asset Backed Security for purposes of paragraph (c)(4)(ii)(D) of this section; Provided, however, written procedures need not require periodic determinations with respect to any Asset Backed Security that a fund's board of directors has determined, at the time of Acquisition, will not have, or is unlikely to have, Ten Percent Obligors that are deemed to be issuers of all or a portion of that Asset Backed Security for purposes of paragraph (c)(4)(ii)(D) of this section, and maintains a record of this determination.

(10) Record Keeping and Reporting—(i) Written Procedures. For a period of not less than six years following the replacement of such procedures with new procedures (the first two years in an easily accessible place), a written copy of the procedures (and any modifications thereto) described in paragraphs (c)(6) through (c)(9) and (e) of this section shall be maintained and preserved.

(ii) Board Considerations and Actions. For a period of not less than six years (the first two years in an easily accessible place) a written record shall be maintained and preserved of the board of directors' considerations and actions taken in connection with the discharge of its responsibilities, as set forth in this section, to be included in the minutes of the board of directors' meetings.

(iii) Credit Risk Analysis. For a period of not less than three years from the date that the credit risks of a portfolio security were most recently reviewed, a written record of the determination that a portfolio security presents minimal credit risks and the NRSRO ratings (if any) used to determine the status of the security as an Eligible Security, First Tier Security or Second Tier Security shall be maintained and preserved in an easily accessible place.

(iv) Determinations With Respect to Adjustable Rate Securities. For a period of not less than three years from the date when the determination was most recently made, a written record shall be preserved and maintained, in an easily accessible place, of the determination required by paragraph (c)(9)(iii) of this section (that a Variable Rate or Floating Rate Security that is not subject to a Demand Feature and for which maturity is determined pursuant to paragraphs (d)(1), (d)(2) or (d)(4) of this section can reasonably be expected, upon readjustment of its interest rate at all times during the life of the instrument, to have a market value that approximates its amortized cost).

(v) Determinations with Respect to Asset Backed Securities. For a period of not less than three years from the date when the determination was most recently made, a written record shall be preserved and maintained, in an easily accessible place, of the determinations required by paragraph (c)(9)(iv) of this section (the number of Ten Percent Obligors (as that term is used in paragraph (c)(4)(ii)(D) of this section) deemed to be the issuers of all or a portion of the Asset Backed Security for purposes of paragraph (c)(4)(ii)(D) of this section). The written record shall include:

(A) The identities of the Ten Percent Obligors (as that term is used in paragraph (c)(4)(ii)(D) of this section), the percentage of the Qualifying Assets constituted by the securities of each Ten Percent Obligor and the percentage of the fund's Total Assets that are invested in securities of each Ten Percent Obligor; and

(B) Any determination that an Asset Backed Security will not have, or is unlikely to have, Ten Percent Obligors deemed to be issuers of all or a portion of that Asset Backed Security for purposes of paragraph (c)(4)(ii)(D) of this section.

(vi) Evaluations with Respect to Securities Subject to Demand Features or Guarantees. For a period of not less than three years from the date when the evaluation was most recently made, a written record shall be preserved and maintained, in an easily accessible place, of the evaluation required by paragraph (c)(9)(ii) (regarding securities subject to one or more Demand Features or Guarantees) of this section.

(vii) Inspection of Records. The documents preserved pursuant to this paragraph (c)(10) shall be subject to inspection by the Commission in accordance with section 31(b) of the Act (15 U.S.C. 80a–30(b)) as if such documents were records required to be maintained pursuant to rules adopted under section 31(a) of the Act (15 U.S.C. 80a–30(a)). If any action was taken under paragraphs (c)(6)(ii) (with respect to defaulted securities and events of insolvency) or (c)(7)(ii) (with respect to a deviation from the fund's share price of more than ½ of 1 percent) of this section, the money market fund will file an exhibit to the Form N–SAR (17 CFR 274.101) filed for the period in which the action was taken describing with specificity the nature and circumstances of such action. The money market fund will report in an exhibit to such Form any securities it holds on the final day of the reporting period that are not Eligible Securities.

(d) *Maturity of Portfolio Securities.* For purposes of this section, the maturity of a portfolio security shall be deemed to be the period remaining (calculated from the trade date or such other date on which the fund's interest in the security is subject to market action) until the date on which, in accordance with the terms of the security, the principal amount must unconditionally be paid, or in the case of a security called for redemption, the date on which the redemption payment must be made, except as provided in paragraphs (d)(1) through (d)(8) of this section:

(1) Adjustable Rate Government Securities. A Government Security that is a Variable Rate Security where the variable rate of interest is readjusted no less frequently than every 762 calendar days shall be deemed to have a maturity equal to the period remaining until the next readjustment of the interest rate. A Government Security that is a Floating Rate Security shall be deemed to have a remaining maturity of one day.

(2) Short–Term Variable Rate Securities. A Variable Rate Security, the principal amount of which, in accordance with the terms of the security, must unconditionally be paid in 397 calendar days or less shall be deemed to have a maturity equal to the earlier of the period remaining until the next readjustment of the interest rate or the period remaining until the principal amount can be recovered through demand.

(3) Long–Term Variable Rate Securities. A Variable Rate Security, the principal amount of which is scheduled to be paid in more than 397 calendar days, that is subject to a Demand Feature, shall be deemed to have a maturity equal to the longer of the period remaining until the next readjustment of the interest rate or the period remaining until the principal amount can be recovered through demand.

(4) Short–Term Floating Rate Securities. A Floating Rate Security, the principal amount of which, in accordance with the terms of the security, must unconditionally be paid in 397 calendar days or less shall be deemed to have a maturity of one day.

(5) Long–Term Floating Rate Securities. A Floating Rate Security, the principal amount of which is scheduled to be paid in more than 397 calendar days, that is subject to a Demand Feature, shall be deemed to have a maturity equal to the period remaining until the principal amount can be recovered through demand.

(6) Repurchase Agreements. A repurchase agreement shall be deemed to have a maturity equal to the period remaining until the date on which the repurchase of the underlying securities is scheduled to occur, or, where the agreement is subject to demand, the notice period applicable to a demand for the repurchase of the securities.

(7) Portfolio Lending Agreements. A portfolio lending agreement shall be treated as having a maturity equal to the period remaining until the date on which the loaned securities are scheduled to be returned, or where the agreement is subject to demand, the notice period applicable to a

demand for the return of the loaned securities.

(8) Money Market Fund Securities. An investment in a money market fund shall be treated as having a maturity equal to the period of time within which the Acquired money market fund is required to make payment upon redemption, unless the Acquired money market fund has agreed in writing to provide redemption proceeds to the investing money market fund within a shorter time period, in which case the maturity of such investment shall be deemed to be the shorter period.

(e) *Delegation.* The money market fund's board of directors may delegate to the fund's investment adviser or officers the responsibility to make any determination required to be made by the board of directors under this section (other than the determinations required by paragraphs (c)(1) (board findings); (c)(6)(i)(C) (rule for certain securities subject to second tier Demand Features); (c)(6)(ii) (defaults and other events); (c)(7)(i) (general required procedures: Amortized Cost Method); (c)(7)(ii)(A) (shadow pricing), (B) (prompt consideration of deviation), and (C) (material dilution or unfair results); and (c)(8) (required procedures: Penny–Rounding Method) of this section) provided:

(1) Written Guidelines. The Board shall establish and periodically review written guidelines (including guidelines for determining whether securities present minimal credit risks as required in paragraph (c)(3) of this section) and procedures under which the delegate makes such determinations;

(2) Oversight. The Board shall take any measures reasonably necessary (through periodic reviews of fund investments and the delegate's procedures in connection with investment decisions and prompt review of the adviser's actions in the event of the default of a security or Event of Insolvency with respect to the issuer of the security or any Guarantee to which it is subject that requires notification of the Commission under paragraph (c)(6)(iii) of this section) to assure that the guidelines and procedures are being followed.

§ 270.2a19–2 Investment Company General Partners Not Deemed Interested Persons

Preliminary Note to § 270.2a19–2

This § 270.2a19–2 conditionally excepts from the definition of interested person in section 2(a)(19) (15 U.S.C. 80a–2(a)(19)) general partners of investment companies organized in limited partnership form. Compliance with the conditions of this § 270.2a19–2 does not relieve an investment company of any other requirement of this Act, or except a general partner that is an interested person by virtue of any other provision.

(a) *Director General Partners Not Deemed Interested Persons.* A general partner serving as a director of a limited partnership investment company shall not be deemed to be an interested person of such company, or of any investment adviser of, or principal underwriter for, such company, solely by reason of being a partner of the limited partnership investment company, or a copartner in the limited partnership investment company with any investment adviser of, or principal underwriter for, the company, *provided* that the Limited Partnership Agreement contains in substance the following:

(1) Only general partners who are natural persons shall serve as, and perform the functions of, directors of the limited partnership investment company, except that any general partner may act as provided in paragraph (a)(2)(iii) of this section.

(2) A general partner shall not have the authority to act individually on behalf of, or to bind, the Limited Partnership Investment Company, except:

(i) In such person's capacity as investment adviser, principal underwriter, or administrator;

(ii) Within the scope of such person's authority as delegated by the board of directors; or

(iii) In the event that no director of the company remains, to the extent necessary to continue the Limited Partnership Investment Company, for such limited periods as are permitted under the Act to fill director vacancies.

(3) Limited partners shall have all of the rights afforded shareholders under the Act. If a limited partnership interest is transferred in a manner that is effective under the Partnership Agreement, the transferee shall have all of the rights afforded shareholders under the Act.

(4) A general partner shall not withdraw from the Limited Partnership Investment Company or reduce its Federal Tax Status Contribution without giving at least one year's prior written notice to the Limited Partnership Investment Company, if such withdrawal or reduction is likely to cause the company to lose its partnership tax classification. This paragraph (a)(4) shall not apply to an investment adviser general partner if the company terminates its advisory agreement with such general partner.

(b) *Definitions*—(1) "Federal Tax Status Contribution" shall mean the interest (including limited partnership interest) in each material item of partnership income, gain, loss, deduction, or credit, and other contributions, required to be held or made by general partners, pursuant to section 4 of Internal Revenue Service Revenue Procedure 89-12, or any successor provisions thereto.

(2) "Limited Partnership Investment Company" shall mean a registered management company or a business development company that is organized as a limited partnership under state law.

(3) "Partnership Agreement" shall mean the agreement of the partners of the Limited Partnership Investment Company as to the affairs of the limited partnership and the conduct of its business.

§ 270.2a19-3 Certain Investment Company Directors Not Considered Interested Persons Because of Ownership of Index Fund Securities

If a director of a registered investment company ("Fund") owns shares of a registered investment company (including the Fund) with an investment objective to replicate the performance of one or more broad-based securities indices ("Index Fund"), ownership of the Index Fund shares will not cause the director to be considered an "interested person" of the Fund or of the Fund's investment adviser or principal underwriter (as defined by section 2(a)(19)(A)(iii) and (B)(iii) of the Act (15 U.S.C. 80a-2(a)(19)(A)(iii) and (B)(iii))).

§ 270.2a41-1 Valuation of Standby Commitments by Registered Investment Companies

(a) A standby commitment means a right to sell a specified underlying security or securities within a specified period of time and at an exercise price equal to the amortized cost of the underlying security or securities plus accrued interest, if any, at the time of exercise, that may be sold, transferred or assigned only with the underlying security or securities. A standby commitment entitles the holder to receive same day settlement, and will be considered to be from the party to whom the investment company will look for payment of the exercise price. A standby commitment may be assigned a fair value of zero, Provided, That:

(1) The standby commitment is not used to affect the company's valuation of the security or securities underlying the standby commitment; and

(2) Any consideration paid by the company for the standby commitment, whether paid in cash or by paying a premium for the underlying security or securities, is accounted for by the company as unrealized depreciation until the standby commitment is exercised or expires.

§ 270.2a51–1 Definition of Investments For Purposes of Section 2(a)(51) (Definition of "Qualified Purchaser"); Certain Calculations

(a) *Definitions.* As used in this section:

(1) The term Commodity Interests means commodity futures contracts, options on commodity futures contracts, and options on physical commodities traded on or subject to the rules of:

(i) Any contract market designated for trading such transactions under the Commodity Exchange Act and the rules thereunder; or

(ii) Any board of trade or exchange outside the United States, as contemplated in Part 30 of the rules under the Commodity Exchange Act [17 CFR 30.1 through 30.11].

(2) The term Family Company means a company described in paragraph (A)(ii) of section 2(a)(51) of the Act [15 U.S.C. 80a–2(a)(51)].

(3) The term Investment Vehicle means an investment company; a company that would be an investment company but for the exclusions provided by sections 3(c)(1) through 3(c)(9) of the Act [15 U.S.C. 80a–3(c)(1) through 3(c)(9)] or the exemptions provided by §§ 270.3a–6 or 270.3a–7, or a commodity pool.

(4) The term Investments has the meaning set forth in paragraph (b) of this section.

(5) The term Physical Commodity means any physical commodity with respect to which a Commodity Interest is traded on a market specified in paragraph (a)(1) of this section.

(6) The term Prospective Qualified Purchaser means a person seeking to purchase a security of a Section 3(c)(7) Company.

(7) The term Public Company means a company that:

(i) Files reports pursuant to section 13 or 15(d) of the Securities Exchange Act of 1934 [15 U.S.C. 78m or 78o(d)]; or

(ii) Has a class of securities that are listed on a "designated offshore securities market" as such term is defined by Regulation S under the Securities Act of 1933 [17 CFR 230.901 through 230.904].

(8) The term Related Person means a person who is related to a Prospective Qualified Purchaser as a sibling, spouse or former spouse, or is a direct lineal descendant or ancestor by birth or adoption of the Prospective Qualified Purchaser, or is a spouse of such descendant or ancestor, provided that, in the case of a Family Company, a Related Person includes any owner of the Family Company and any person who is a Related Person of such owner.

(9) The term Relying Person means a Section 3(c)(7) Company or a person acting on its behalf.

(10) The term Section 3(c)(7) Company means a company that would be an investment company but for the exclusion provided by section 3(c)(7) of the Act [15 U.S.C. 80a–3(c)(7)].

(b) *Types of Investments.* For purposes of section 2(a)(51) of the Act [15 U.S.C. 80a–2(a)(51)], the term Investments means:

(1) Securities (as defined by section 2(a)(1) of the Securities Act of 1933 [15 U.S.C. 77b(a)(1)]), other than securities of an issuer that controls, is controlled by, or is under common control with the Prospective Qualified Purchaser that owns such securities, unless the issuer of such securities is:

(i) An Investment Vehicle;

(ii) A Public Company; or

(iii) A company with shareholders' equity of not less than $50 million (determined in accordance with generally accepted accounting principles) as reflected on the company's most recent financial statements, provided that such financial statements present the information as of a date within 16 months preceding the date on which the Prospective Qualified Purchaser acquires the securities of a Section 3(c)(7) Company;

(2) Real estate held for investment purposes;

(3) Commodity Interests held for investment purposes;

(4) Physical Commodities held for investment purposes;

(5) To the extent not securities, financial contracts (as such term is defined in section 3(c)(2)(B)(ii) of the Act) [15 U.S.C. 80a-3(c)(2)(B)(ii)] entered into for investment purposes;

(6) In the case of a Prospective Qualified Purchaser that is a Section 3(c)(7) Company, a company that would be an investment company but for the exclusion provided by section 3(c)(1) of the Act [15 U.S.C. 80a-3(c)(1)], or a commodity pool, any amounts payable to such Prospective Qualified Purchaser pursuant to a firm agreement or similar binding commitment pursuant to which a person has agreed to acquire an interest in, or make capital contributions to, the Prospective Qualified Purchaser upon the demand of the Prospective Qualified Purchaser; and

(7) Cash and cash equivalents (including foreign currencies) held for investment purposes. For purposes of this section, cash and cash equivalents include:

(i) Bank deposits, certificates of deposit, bankers acceptances and similar bank instruments held for investment purposes; and

(ii) The net cash surrender value of an insurance policy.

(c) *Investment Purposes.* For purposes of this section:

(1) Real estate shall not be considered to be held for investment purposes by a Prospective Qualified Purchaser if it is used by the Prospective Qualified Purchaser or a Related Person for personal purposes or as a place of business, or in connection with the conduct of the trade or business of the Prospective Qualified Purchaser or a Related Person, provided that real estate owned by a Prospective Qualified Purchaser who is engaged primarily in the business of investing, trading or developing real estate in connection with such business may be deemed to be held for investment purposes. Residential real estate shall not be deemed to be used for personal purposes if deductions with respect to such real estate are not disallowed by section 280A of the Internal Revenue Code [26 U.S.C. 280A].

(2) A Commodity Interest or Physical Commodity owned, or a financial contract entered into, by the Prospective Qualified Purchaser who is engaged primarily in the business of investing, reinvesting, or trading in Commodity Interests, Physical Commodities or financial contracts in connection with such business may be deemed to be held for investment purposes:

(d) *Valuation.* For purposes of determining whether a Prospective Qualified Purchaser is a qualified purchaser, the aggregate amount of investments owned and invested on a discretionary basis by the Prospective Qualified Purchaser shall be the Investments' fair market value on the most recent practicable date or their cost, provided that:

(1) In the case of Commodity Interests, the amount of Investments shall be the value of the initial margin or option premium deposited in connection with such Commodity Interests; and

(2) In each case, there shall be deducted from the amount of Investments owned by the Prospective Qualified Purchaser the amounts specified in paragraphs (e) and (f) of this section, as applicable.

(e) *Deductions.* In determining whether any person is a qualified purchaser there shall be deducted from the amount of such person's Investments the amount of any outstanding indebtedness incurred to acquire or for the purpose of acquiring the Investments owned by such person.

(f) *Deductions: Family Companies:* In determining whether a Family Company is a qualified purchaser, in addition to the amounts specified in paragraph (e) of this section, there shall be deducted from the value of such Family Company's Investments any outstanding indebtedness incurred by an owner of the Family Company to acquire such Investments.

(g) *Special rules for certain Prospective Qualified Purchasers*—(1) Qualified institutional buyers. Any Prospective Qualified Purchaser who is, or who a Relying Person reasonably believes is, a qualified institutional buyer as defined in paragraph (a) of § 230.144A of this chapter, acting for its own account, the account of another qualified institutional buyer, or the account of a qualified purchaser, shall be deemed to be a qualified purchaser provided:

(i) That a dealer described in paragraph (a)(1)(ii) of § 230.144A of this chapter shall own and invest on a discretionary basis at least $25 million in securities of issuers that are not affiliated persons of the dealer; and

(ii) That a plan referred to in paragraph (a)(1)(i)(D) or (a)(1)(i)(E) of § 230.144A of this chapter, or a trust fund referred to in paragraph (a)(1)(i)(F) of § 230.144A of this chapter that holds the assets of such a plan, will not be deemed to be acting for its own account if investment decisions with respect to the plan are made by the beneficiaries of the plan, except with respect to investment decisions made solely by the fiduciary, trustee or sponsor of such plan.

(2) Joint Investments. In determining whether a natural person is a qualified purchaser, there may be included in the amount of such person's Investments any investments held jointly with such person's spouse, or Investments in which such person shares with such person's spouse a community property or similar shared ownership interest. In determining whether spouses who are making a joint investment in a Section 3(c)(7) Company are qualified purchasers, there may be included in the amount of each spouse's Investments any Investments owned by the other spouse (whether or not such Investments are held jointly). In each case, there shall be deducted from the amount of any such Investments the amounts specified in paragraph (e) of this section incurred by each spouse.

(3) Investments by Subsidiaries. For purposes of determining the amount of Investments owned by a company under section 2(a)(51)(A)(iv) of the Act [15 U.S.C. 80a–2(a)(51)(A)(iv)], there may be included Investments owned by majority-owned subsidiaries of the company and Investments owned by a company ("Parent Company") of which the company is a majority-owned subsidiary, or by a majority-owned subsidiary of the company and other majority-owned subsidiaries of the Parent Company.

(4) Certain Retirement Plans and Trusts. In determining whether a natural person is a qualified purchaser, there may be included in the amount of such person's Investments any Investments held in an individual retirement account or similar account the Investments of which are directed by and held for the benefit of such person.

(h) *Reasonable Belief.* The term "qualified purchaser" as used in section 3(c)(7) of the Act [15 U.S.C. 80a–3(c)(7)] means any person that meets the definition of qualified purchaser in section 2(a)(51)(A) of the Act [15 U.S.C. 80a–2(a)(51)(A)] and the rules thereunder, or that a Relying Person reasonably believes meets such definition.

§ 270.2a51–2 Definitions of Beneficial Owner for Certain Purposes Under Sections 2(a)(51) and 3(c)(7) and Determining Indirect Ownership Interests

(a) *Beneficial ownership: General.* Except as set forth in this section, for purposes of sections 2(a)(51)(C) and 3(c)(7)(B)(ii) of the Act [15 U.S.C. 80a–2(a)(51)(C) and –

3(c)(7)(B)(ii)], the beneficial owners of securities of an excepted investment company (as defined in section 2(a)(51)(C) of the Act [15 U.S.C. 80a–2(a)(51)(C)]) shall be determined in accordance with section 3(c)(1) of the Act [15 U.S.C. 80a–3(c)(1)].

(b) *Beneficial ownership: Grandfather provision.* For purposes of section 3(c)(7)(B)(ii) of the Act [15 U.S.C. 80a–3(c)(7)(B)(ii)], securities of an issuer beneficially owned by a company (without giving effect to section 3(c)(1)(A) of the Act [15 U.S.C. 80a–3(c)(1)(A)]) ("owning company") shall be deemed to be beneficially owned by one person unless:

(1) The owning company is an investment company or an excepted investment company;

(2) The owning company, directly or indirectly, controls, is controlled by, or is under common control with, the issuer; and

(3) On October 11, 1996, under section 3(c)(1)(A) of the Act as then in effect, the voting securities of the issuer were deemed to be beneficially owned by the holders of the owning company's outstanding securities (other than short-term paper), in which case, such holders shall be deemed to be beneficial owners of the issuer's outstanding voting securities.

(c) *Beneficial ownership: Consent provision.* For purposes of section 2(a)(51)(C) of the Act [15 U.S.C. 80a–2(a)(51)(C)], securities of an excepted investment company beneficially owned by a company (without giving effect to section 3(c)(1)(A) of the Act [15 U.S.C. 80a–3(c)(1)(A)]) ("owning company") shall be deemed to be beneficially owned by one person unless:

(1) The owning company is an excepted investment company;

(2) The owning company directly or indirectly controls, is controlled by, or is under common control with the excepted investment company or the company with respect to which the excepted investment company is, or will be, a qualified purchaser; and

(3) On April 30, 1996, under section 3(c)(1)(A) of the Act as then in effect, the voting securities of the excepted investment company were deemed to be beneficially owned by the holders of the owning company's outstanding securities (other than short-term paper), in which case the holders of such excepted company's securities shall be deemed to be beneficial owners of the excepted investment company's outstanding voting securities.

(d) *Indirect ownership: Consent provision.* For purposes of section 2(a)(51)(C) of the Act [15 U.S.C. 80a–2(a)(51)(C)], an excepted investment company shall not be deemed to indirectly own the securities of an excepted investment company seeking a consent to be treated as a qualified purchaser ("qualified purchaser company") unless such excepted investment company, directly or indirectly, controls, is controlled by, or is under common control with, the qualified purchaser company or a company with respect to which the qualified purchaser company is or will be a qualified purchaser.

(e) *Required consent: Consent provision.* For purposes of section 2(a)(51)(C) of the Act [15 U.S.C. 80a–2(a)(51)(C)], the consent of the beneficial owners of an excepted investment company ("owning company") that beneficially owns securities of an excepted investment company that is seeking the consents required by section 2(a)(51)(C) ("consent company") shall not be required unless the owning company directly or indirectly controls, is controlled by, or is under common control with the consent company or the company with respect to which the consent company is, or will be, a qualified purchaser.

Notes to § 270.2a51–2:

1. On both April 30, 1996 and October 11, 1996, section 3(c)(1)(A) of the Act as then in effect provided that: (A) Beneficial ownership by a company shall be deemed to be beneficial ownership by one person, ex-

cept that, if the company owns 10 per centum or more of the outstanding voting securities of the issuer, the beneficial ownership shall be deemed to be that of the holders of such company's outstanding securities (other than short-term paper) unless, as of the date of the most recent acquisition by such company of securities of that issuer, the value of all securities owned by such company of all issuers which are or would, but for the exception set forth in this subparagraph, be excluded from the definition of investment company solely by this paragraph, does not exceed 10 per centum of the value of the company's total assets. Such issuer nonetheless is deemed to be an investment company for purposes of section 12(d)(1).

2. Issuers seeking the consent required by section 2(a)(51)(C) of the Act should note that section 2(a)(51)(C) requires an issuer to obtain the consent of the beneficial owners of its securities and the beneficial owners of securities of any "excepted investment company" that directly or indirectly owns the securities of the issuer. Except as set forth in paragraphs (d) (with respect to indirect owners) and (e) (with respect to direct owners) of this section, nothing in this section is designed to limit this consent requirement.

§ 270.2a51-3 Certain Companies as Qualified Purchasers

(a) For purposes of section 2(a)(51)(A)(ii) and (iv) of the Act [15 U.S.C. 80a-2(a)(51)(A)(ii) and (iv)], a company shall not be deemed to be a qualified purchaser if it was formed for the specific purpose of acquiring the securities offered by a company excluded from the definition of investment company by section 3(c)(7) of the Act [15 U.S.C. 80a-3(c)(7)] unless each beneficial owner of the company's securities is a qualified purchaser.

(b) For purposes of section 2(a)(51) of the Act [15 U.S.C. 80a-2(a)(51)], a company may be deemed to be a qualified purchaser if each beneficial owner of the company's securities is a qualified purchaser.

§ 270.3a-1 Certain Prima Facie Investment Companies

Notwithstanding section 3(a)(1)(C) of the Act (15 U.S.C. 80a-3(a)(1)(c)), an issuer will be deemed not to be an investment company under the Act; *Provided,* That:

(a) No more than 45 percent of the value (as defined in section 2(a)(41) of the Act) of such issuer's total assets (exclusive of Government securities and cash items) consists of, and no more than 45 percent of such issuer's net income after taxes (for the last four fiscal quarters combined) is derived from, securities other than:

(1) Government securities;

(2) Securities issued by employees' securities companies;

(3) Securities issued by majority-owned subsidiaries of the issuer (other than subsidiaries relying on the exclusion from the definition of investment company in section 3(b)(3) or section 3(c)(1) of the Act) which are not investment companies; and

(4) Securities issued by companies;

(i) Which are controlled primarily by such issuer;

(ii) Through which such issuer engages in a business other than that of investing, reinvesting, owning, holding or trading in securities; and

(iii) Which are not investment companies;

(b) The issuer is not an investment company as defined in section 3(a)(1)(A) or 3(a)(1)(B) of the Act (15 U.S.C. 80a-3(a)(1)(A) or 80a-3(a)(1)(B)) and is not a special situation investment company; and

(c) The percentages described in paragraph (a) of this section are determined on an unconsolidated basis, except that the issuer shall consolidate its financial statements with the financial statements of any wholly-owned subsidiaries.

§ 270.3a–2 Transient Investment Companies

(a) For purposes of sections 3(a)(1)(A) and 3(a)(1)(C) of the Act (15 U.S.C. 80a–3(a)(1)(A) and 80a–3(a)(1)(C)), an issuer is deemed not to be engaged in the business of investing, reinvesting, owning, holding or trading in securities during a period of time not to exceed one year; *Provided,* That the issuer has a *bona fide* intent to be engaged primarily, as soon as is reasonably possible (in any event by the termination of such period of time), in a business other than that of investing, reinvesting, owning, holding or trading in securities, such intent to be evidenced by:

(1) The issuer's business activities; and

(2) An appropriate resolution of the issuer's board of directors, or by an appropriate action of the person or persons performing similar functions for any issuer not having a board of directors, which resolution or action has been recorded contemporaneously in its minute books or comparable documents.

(b) For purposes of this rule, the period of time described in paragraph (a) shall commence on the earlier of:

(1) The date on which an issuer owns securities and/or cash having a value exceeding 50 percent of the value of such issuer's total assets on either a consolidated or unconsolidated basis; or

(2) The date on which an issuer owns or proposes to acquire investment securities (as defined in section 3(a) of the Act) having a value exceeding 40 per centum of the value of such issuer's total assets (exclusive of Government securities and cash items) on an unconsolidated basis.

(c) No issuer may rely on this section more frequently than once during any three-year period.

§ 270.3a–3 Certain Investment Companies Owned by Companies Which Are Not Investment Companies

Notwithstanding section 3(a)(1)(A) or section 3(a)(1)(C) of the Act (15 U.S.C. 80a–3(a)(1)(A) or 80a–3(a)(1)(C)), an issuer will be deemed not to be an investment company for purposes of the Act; *Provided,* That all of the outstanding securities of the issuer (other than short-term paper, directors' qualifying shares, and debt securities owned by the Small Business Administration) are directly or indirectly owned by a company which satisfies the conditions of § 270.3a–1(a) and which is:

(a) A company that is not an investment company as defined in section 3(a) of the Act;

(b) A company that is an investment company as defined in section 3(a)(1)(C) of the Act (15 U.S.C. 80a–3(a)(1)(C)), but which is excluded from the definition of the term "investment company" by section 3(b)(1) or 3(b)(2) of the Act (15 U.S.C. 80a–3(b)(1) or 80a–3(b)(2)); or

(c) A company that is deemed not to be an investment company for purposes of the Act by rule 3a–1.

§ 270.3a–4 Status of Investment Advisory Programs

Note: This section is a nonexclusive safe harbor from the definition of investment company for programs that provide discretionary investment advisory services to clients. There is no registration requirement under section 5 of the Securities Act of 1933 [15 U.S.C. 77e] with respect to programs that are organized and operated in the manner described in § 270.3a–4. The section is not intended, however, to create any presumption about a program that is not organized and operated in the manner contemplated by the section.

(a) Any program under which discretionary investment advisory services are provided to clients that has the following characteristics will not be deemed to be an investment company within the meaning of the Act [15 U.S.C. 80a, *et seq.*]:

(1) Each client's account in the program is managed on the basis of the client's finan-

cial situation and investment objectives and in accordance with any reasonable restrictions imposed by the client on the management of the account.

(2)(i) At the opening of the account, the sponsor or another person designated by the sponsor obtains information from the client regarding the client's financial situation and investment objectives, and gives the client the opportunity to impose reasonable restrictions on the management of the account;

(ii) At least annually, the sponsor or another person designated by the sponsor contacts the client to determine whether there have been any changes in the client's financial situation or investment objectives, and whether the client wishes to impose any reasonable restrictions on the management of the account or reasonably modify existing restrictions;

(iii) At least quarterly, the sponsor or another person designated by the sponsor notifies the client in writing to contact the sponsor or such other person if there have been any changes in the client's financial situation or investment objectives, or if the client wishes to impose any reasonable restrictions on the management of the client's account or reasonably modify existing restrictions, and provides the client with a means through which such contact may be made; and

(iv) The sponsor and personnel of the manager of the client's account who are knowledgeable about the account and its management are reasonably available to the client for consultation.

(3) Each client has the ability to impose reasonable restrictions on the management of the client's account, including the designation of particular securities or types of securities that should not be purchased for the account, or that should be sold if held in the account; *Provided, however,* that nothing in this section requires that a client have the ability to require that particular securities or types of securities be purchased for the account.

(4) The sponsor or person designated by the sponsor provides each client with a statement, at least quarterly, containing a description of all activity in the client's account during the preceding period, including all transactions made on behalf of the account, all contributions and withdrawals made by the client, all fees and expenses charged to the account, and the value of the account at the beginning and end of the period.

(5) Each client retains, with respect to all securities and funds in the account, to the same extent as if the client held the securities and funds outside the program, the right to:

(i) Withdraw securities or cash;

(ii) Vote securities, or delegate the authority to vote securities to another person;

(iii) Be provided in a timely manner with a written confirmation or other notification of each securities transaction, and all other documents required by law to be provided to security holders; and

(iv) Proceed directly as a security holder against the issuer of any security in the client's account and not be obligated to join any person involved in the operation of the program, or any other client of the program, as a condition precedent to initiating such proceeding.

(b) As used in this section, the term sponsor refers to any person who receives compensation for sponsoring, organizing or administering the program, or for selecting, or providing advice to clients regarding the selection of, persons responsible for managing the client's account in the program. If a program has more than one sponsor, one person shall be designated the principal sponsor, and such person shall be considered the sponsor of the program under this section.

§ 270.3a–5 Exemption for Subsidiaries Organized to Finance the Operations of Domestic or Foreign Companies

(a) A finance subsidiary will not be considered an investment company under section 3(a) of the Act (15 U.S.C. 80a–3(a)) and securities of a finance subsidiary held by the parent company or a company controlled by the parent company will not be considered "investment securities" under section 3(a)(1)(C) of the Act (15 U.S.C. 80a–3(a)(1)(C)); *Provided* That:

(1) Any debt securities of the finance subsidiary issued to or held by the public are unconditionally guaranteed by the parent company as to the payment of principal, interest, and premium, if any (except that the guarantee may be subordinated in right of payment to other debt of the parent company);

(2) Any non-voting preferred stock of the finance subsidiary issued to or held by the public is unconditionally guaranteed by the parent company as to payment of dividends, payment of the liquidation preference in the event of liquidation, and payments to be made under a sinking fund, if a sinking fund is to be provided (except that the guarantee may be subordinated in right of payment to other debt of the parent company);

(3) The parent company's guarantee provides that in the event of a default in payment of principal, interest, premium, dividends, liquidation preference or payments made under a sinking fund on any debt securities or non-voting preferred stock issued by the finance subsidiary, the holders of those securities may institute legal proceedings directly against the parent company (or, in the case of a partnership or joint venture, against the partners or participants in the joint venture) to enforce the guarantee without first proceeding against the finance subsidiary;

(4) Any securities issued by the finance subsidiary which are convertible or exchangeable are convertible or exchangeable only for securities issued by the parent company (and, in the case of a partnership or joint venture, for securities issued by the partners or participants in the joint venture) or for debt securities or non-voting preferred stock issued by the finance subsidiary meeting the applicable requirements of paragraphs (a)(1) through (a)(3);

(5) The finance subsidiary invests in or loans to its parent company or a company controlled by its parent company at least 85% of any cash or cash equivalents raised by the finance subsidiary through an offering of its debts securities or non-voting preferred stock or through other borrowings as soon as practicable, but in no event later than six months after the finance subsidiary's receipt of such cash or cash equivalents;

(6) The finance subsidiary does not invest in, reinvest in, own, hold or trade in securities other than Government securities, securities of its parent company or a company controlled by its parent company (or in the case of a partnership or joint venture, the securities of the partners or participants in the joint venture) or debt securities (including repurchase agreements) which are exempted from the provisions of the Securities Act of 1933 by section 3(a)(3) of that Act; and

(7) Where the parent company is a foreign bank as the term is used in rule 3a–6, the parent company may, in lieu of the guaranty required by paragraph (a)(1) or (a)(2) of this rule, issue, in favor of the holders of the finance subsidiary's debt securities or non-voting preferred stock, as the case may be, an irrevocable letter of credit in an amount sufficient to fund all of the amounts required to be guaranteed by paragraphs (a)(1) and (a)(2) of this rule, *provided,* that:

(i) payment on such letter of credit shall be conditional only upon the presentation of customary documentation, and

(ii) the beneficiary of such letter of credit is not required by either the letter of credit or applicable law to institute proceedings against the finance subsidiary before enforcing its remedies under the letter of credit.

(b) For purposes of this rule,

(1) A "finance subsidiary" shall mean any corporation

(i) All of whose securities other than debts securities or non-voting preferred stock meeting the applicable requirements of paragraphs (a)(1) through (a)(3) or directors' qualifying shares are owned by its parent company or a company controlled by its parent company; and

(ii) The primary purpose of which is to finance the business operations of its parent company or companies controlled by its parent company;

(2) A "parent company" shall mean any corporation, partnership or joint venture

(i) That is not considered an investment company under section 3(a) or that is excepted or exempted by order from the definition of investment company by section 3(b) or by the rules or regulations under section 3(a);

(ii) That is organized or formed under the laws of the United States or of a state or that is a foreign private issuer, or that is a foreign bank or foreign insurance company as those terms are used in Rule 3a-6; and

(iii) In the case of a partnership or joint venture, each partner or participant in the joint venture meets the requirements of paragraphs (b)(2)(i) and (ii).

(3) A "company controlled by the parent company" shall mean any corporation, partnership or joint venture

(i) That is not considered and investment company under section 3(a) or that is excepted or exempted by order from the definition of investment company by section 3(b) or by the rules or regulations under section 3(a);

(ii) That is either organized or formed under the laws of the United States or of a state or that is a foreign private issuer, or that is a foreign bank or foreign insurance company as those terms are used in Rule 3a-6; and

(iii) In the case of a corporation, more than 25 percent of whose outstanding voting securities are beneficially owned directly or indirectly by the parent company; or

(iv) In the case of a partnership or joint venture, each partner or participant in the joint venture meets the requirements of paragraphs (b)(3)(i) and (ii), and the parent company has the power to exercise a controlling influence over the management or policies of the partnership or joint venture.

(4) A "foreign private issuer" shall mean any issuer which is incorporated or organized under the laws of a foreign country, but not a foreign government or political subdivision of a foreign government.

§ 270.3a-6 Foreign Banks and Foreign Insurance Companies

(a) Notwithstanding section 3(a)(1)(A) or section 3(a)(1)(C) of the Act (15 U.S.C. 80a-3(a)(1)(A) or 80a-3(a)(1)(C)), a foreign bank or foreign insurance company shall not be considered an investment company for purposes of the Act.

(b) For purposes of this rule:

(1)(i) *Foreign bank* means a banking institution incorporated or organized under the laws of a country other than the United States, or a political subdivision of a country other than the United States, that is:

(A) Regulated as such by that country's or subdivision's government or any agency thereof;

(B) Engaged substantially in commercial banking activity; and

(C) Not operated for the purpose of evading the provisions of the Act;

(ii) The term *foreign bank* shall also include:

(A) A trust company or loan company that is:

(*1*) Organized or incorporated under the laws of Canada or a political subdivision thereof;

(*2*) Regulated as a trust company or a loan company by that country's or subdivision's government or any agency thereof; and

(*3*) Not operated for the purpose of evading the provisions of the Act; and

(B) A building society that is:

(*1*) Organized under the laws of the United Kingdom or a political subdivision thereof;

(*2*) Regulated as a building society by the country's or subdivision's government or any agency thereof; and

(*3*) Not operated for the purpose of evading the provisions of the Act.

(iii) Nothing in this rule shall be construed to include within the definition of *foreign bank* a common or collective trust or other separate pool of assets organized in the form of a trust or otherwise in which interests are separately offered.

(2) *Engaged substantially in commercial banking activity* means engaged regularly in, and deriving a substantial portion of its business from, extending commercial and other types of credit, and accepting demand and other types of deposits, that are customary for commercial banks in the country in which the head office of the banking institution is located.

(3) *Foreign insurance company* means an insurance company incorporated or organized under the laws of a country other than the United States, or a political subdivision of a country other than the United States, that is:

(i) Regulated as such by that country's or subdivision's government or any agency thereof;

(ii) Engaged primarily and predominantly in:

(A) The writing of insurance agreements of the type specified in section 3(a)(8) of the Securities Act of 1933, except for the substitution of supervision by foreign government insurance regulators for the regulators referred to in that section; or

(B) The reinsurance of risks on such agreements underwritten by insurance companies; and

(iii) Not operated for the purpose of evading the provisions of the Act. Nothing in this rule shall be construed to include within the definition of "foreign insurance company" a separate account or other pool of assets organized in the form of a trust or otherwise in which interests are separately offered.

NOTE: Foreign banks and foreign insurance companies (and certain of their finance subsidiaries and holding companies) relying on rule 3a–6 for exemption from the Act may be required by rule 489 under the Securities Act of 1933 to file Form F–N with the Commission in connection with the filing of a registration statement under the Securities Act of 1933.

§ 270.3a–7 Issuers of Asset-Backed Securities

(a) Notwithstanding section 3(a) of the Act, any issuer who is engaged in the business of purchasing, or otherwise acquiring, and holding eligible assets (and in activities related or incidental thereto), and who does not issue redeemable securities will not be deemed to be an investment company; *Provided that:*

(1) The issuer issues fixed-income securities or other securities which entitle their holders to receive payments that depend primarily on the cash flow from eligible assets;

(2) Securities sold by the issuer or any underwriter thereof are fixed-income securities rated, at the time of initial sale, in one of the four highest categories assigned long-term debt or in an equivalent short-term category (within either of which there may be subcategories or gradations indicating relative standing) by at least one nationally recognized statistical rating organization that is not an affiliated person of the issuer or of any person involved in the organization or operation of the issuer, except that:

(i) Any fixed-income securities may be sold to accredited investors as defined in paragraphs (1), (2), (3), and (7) of Rule 501(a) under the Securities Act of 1933 and any entity in which all of the equity owners come within such paragraphs; and

(ii) Any securities may be sold to qualified institutional buyers as defined in Rule 144A under the Securities Act and to persons (other than any rating organization rating the issuer's securities) involved in the organization or operation of the issuer or an affiliate, as defined in Rule 405 under the Securities Act, of such a person;

Provided, That the issuer or any underwriter thereof effecting such sale exercises reasonable care to ensure that such securities are sold and will be resold to persons specified in paragraphs (a)(2)(i) and (ii) of this section;

(3) The issuer acquires additional eligible assets, or disposes of eligible assets, only if:

(i) The assets are acquired or disposed of in accordance with the terms and conditions set forth in the agreements, indentures, or other instruments pursuant to which the issuer's securities are issued,

(ii) The acquisition or disposition of the assets does not result in a downgrading in the rating of the issuer's outstanding fixed-income securities; and

(iii) The assets are not acquired or disposed of for the primary purpose of recognizing gains or decreasing losses resulting from market value changes; and

(4) If the issuer issues any securities other than securities exempted from the Securities Act by section 3(a)(3) thereof, the issuer:

(i) Appoints a trustee that meets the requirements of section 26(a)(1) of the Act and that is not affiliated, as that term is defined in Rule 405 under the Securities Act, with the issuer or with any person involved in the organization or operation of the issuer, which does not offer or provide credit or credit enhancement to the issuer, and that executes an agreement or instrument concerning the issuer's securities containing provisions to the effect set forth in section 26(a)(3) of the Act;

(ii) Takes reasonable steps to cause the trustee to have a perfected security interest or ownership interest valid against third parties in those eligible assets that principally generate the cash flow needed to pay the fixed-income security holders, provided that such assets otherwise required to be held by the trustee may be released to the extent needed at the time for the operation of the issuer; and

(iii) Takes actions necessary for the cash flows derived from eligible assets for the benefit of the holders of fixed-income securities to be deposited periodically in a segregated account that is maintained or controlled by the trustee consistent with the rating of the outstanding fixed-income securities.

(b) For purposes of this section:

(1) *Eligible assets* means financial assets, either fixed or revolving, that by their terms convert into cash within a finite time period plus any rights or other assets designed to assure the servicing or timely distribution of proceeds to security holders.

(2) *Fixed-income securities* means any securities that entitle the holder to receive:

(i) A stated principal amount; or

(ii) Interest on a principal amount (which may be a notional principal amount) calculated by reference to a fixed rate or to a standard or formula which does not reference any change in the market value or fair value of eligible assets; or

(iii) Interest on a principal amount (which may be a notional principal amount) calculated by reference to auctions among holders and prospective holders, or through remarketing of the security; or

(iv) An amount equal to specified fixed or variable portions of the interest received on the assets held by the issuer; or

(v) Any combination of amounts described in paragraphs (b)(2)(i), (ii), (iii), and (iv) of this section;

Provided, That substantially all of the payments to which the holders of such securities are entitled consist of the foregoing amounts.

§ 230.3a–8. Certain Research and Development Companies

(a) Notwithstanding sections 3(a)(1)(A) and 3(a)(1)(C) of the Act (15 U.S.C. 80a–3(a)(1)(A) and 80a–3(a)(1)(C)), an issuer will be deemed not to be an investment company if:

(1) Its research and development expenses, for the last four fiscal quarters combined, are a substantial percentage of its total expense for the same period;

(2) Its net income derived from investments in securities, for the last four fiscal quarters combined, does not exceed twice the amount of its research and development expenses for the same period;

(3) Its expenses for investment advisory and management activities, investment research and custody, for the last four fiscal quarters, combined, do not exceed five percent of its total expenses for the same period;

(4) Its investments in securities are capital preservation investments, except that:

(i) No more than 10 percent of the issuer's total assets may consist of other investments, or

(ii) No more than 25 percent of the issuer's total assets may consist of other investments, provided that at least 75 percent of such other investments are investments made pursuant to a collaborative research and development arrangement;

(5) It does not hold itself out as being engaged in the business of investing, reinvesting or trading in securities, and it is not a special situation investment company;

(6) It is primarily engaged, directly, through majority-owned subsidiaries, or through companies which it controls primarily, in a business or businesses other than that of investing, reinvesting, owning, holding, or trading in securities, as evidenced by:

(i) The activities of its officers, directors and employees;

(ii) Its public representations of policies;

(iii) Its historical development; and

(iv) An appropriate resolution of its board of directors, which resolution or action has been recorded contemporaneously in its minute books or comparable documents; and

(7) Its board of directors has adopted a written investment policy with respect to the issuer's capital preservation investments.

(b) For purposes of this section:

(1) All assets shall be valued in accordance with section 2(a)(41)(A) of the Act (15 U.S.C. 80a–2(a)(41)(A));

(2) The percentages described in this section are determined on an unconsolidated basis, except that the issuer shall consolidate its financial statements with the financial statements of any wholly-owned subsidiaries;

(3) *Board of directors* means the issuer's board of directors or an appropriate person or persons performing similar functions for any issuer not having a board of directors;

(4) *Capital preservation investment* means an investment that is made to conserve capital and liquidity until the funds are used in the issuer's primary business or businesses;

(5) *Controlled primarily* means controlled within the meaning of section 2(a)(9) of the Act (15 U.S.C. 80a–2(a)(9)) with a degree of control that is greater than that of any other person;

(6) *Investment made pursuant to a collaborative research and development arrangement* means an investment in an investee made pursuant to a business relationship which:

(i) Is designed to achieve narrowly focused goals that are directly related to, and an integral part of, the issue's research and development activities;

(ii) Calls for the issuer to conduct joint research and development activities with the investee or a company controlled primarily by, or which controls primarily, the investee; and

(iii) Is not entered into for the purpose of avoiding regulation under the Act;

(7) *Investments in securities* means all securities other than securities issued by majority-owned subsidiaries and companies controlled primarily by the issuer that conduct similar types of businesses, through which the issuer is engaged primarily in a business other than that of investing, reinvesting, owning, holding, or trading in securities;

(8) *Other investment* means an investment in securities that is not a capital preservation investment; and

(9) *Research and development expenses* means research and development expenses as defined in FASB Statement of Financial Accounting Standards No. 2, Accounting for Research and Development Costs, as currently in effect or as it may be subsequently revised.

§ 270.3c-1 Definition of Beneficial Ownership for Certain Section 3(c)(1) Funds

(a) As used in this section:

(1) The term Covered Company means a company that is an investment company, a Section 3(c)(1) Company or a Section 3(c)(7) Company.

(2) The term Section 3(c)(1) Company means a company that would be an investment company but for the exclusion provided by section 3(c)(1) of the Act [15 U.S.C. 80a–3(c)(1)].

(3) The term Section 3(c)(7) Company means a company that would be an investment company but for the exclusion provided by section 3(c)(7) of the Act [15 U.S.C. 80a–3(c)(7)].

(b) For purposes of section 3(c)(1)(A) of the Act [15 U.S.C. 80a–3(c)(1)(A)], beneficial ownership by a Covered Company owning 10 percent or more of the outstanding voting securities of a Section 3(c)(1) Company shall be deemed to be beneficial ownership by one person, provided that:

(1) On April 1, 1997, the Covered Company owned 10 percent or more of the outstanding voting securities of the Section 3(c)(1) Company or non-voting securities that, on such date and in accordance with the terms of such securities, were convertible into or exchangeable for voting securities that, if converted or exchanged on or after such date, would have constituted 10 percent or more of the outstanding voting securities of the Section 3(c)(1) Company; and

(2) On the date of any acquisition of securities of the Section 3(c)(1) Company by the Covered Company, the value of all securities owned by the Covered Company of all issuers that are Section 3(c)(1) or Section 3(c)(7) Companies does not exceed 10 per-

cent of the value of the Covered Company's total assets.

§ 270.3c–2 Definition of Beneficial Ownership in Small Business Investment Companies

For the purpose of section 3(c)(1) of the Act, beneficial ownership by a company owning 10 per centum or more of the outstanding voting securities of any issuer which is a small business investment company licensed to operate under the Small Business Investment Act of 1958, or which has received from the Small Business Administration notice to proceed to qualify for a license, which notice or license has not been revoked, shall be deemed to be beneficial ownership by one person (a) if and so long as the value of all securities of small business investments companies owned by such company does not exceed 5 percentum of the value of its total assets; or (b) if and so long as such stock of the small business investment company shall be owned by a state development corporation which has been created by or pursuant to an act of the State legislature to promote and assist the growth and development of the economy within such State on a state-wide basis: *Provided,* That such State development corporation is not, or as a result of its investment in the small business investment company (considering such investment as an investment security) would not be, an investment company as defined in section 3 of the Act.

§ 270.3c–3 Definition of Certain Terms Used in Section 3(c)(1) of the Act With Respect to Certain Debt Securities Offered by Small Business Investment Companies

The term "public offering" as used in section 3(c)(1) of the Act shall not be deemed to include the offer and sale by a small business investment company, licensed under the Small Business Investment Act of 1958, of any debt security issued by it which is (a) not convertible into, exchangeable for, or accompanied by any equity security, and (b) guaranteed as to timely payment of principal and interest by the Small Business Administration and backed by the full faith and credit of the United States. The holders of any securities offered and sold as described in this section shall be counted, in the aggregate, as one person for purposes of section 3(c)(1) of the Act.

§ 270.3c–4 Definition of "Common Trust Fund" as Used in Section 3(c)(3) of the Act

The term "common trust fund" as used in section 3(c)(3) of the Act shall include a common trust fund which is maintained by a bank which is a member of an affiliated group, as defined in section 1504(a) of the Internal Revenue Code of 1954, and which is maintained exclusively for the collective investment and reinvestment of monies contributed thereto by one or more bank members of such affiliated group in the capacity of trustee, executor, administrator, or guardian, provided that:

(a) the common trust fund is operated in compliance with the same state and federal regulatory requirements as would apply if the bank maintaining such fund and any other contributing banks were the same entity; and

(b) the rights of persons for whose benefit a contributing bank acts as trustee, executor, administrator, or guardian would not be diminished by reason of the maintenance of such common trust fund by another bank member of the affiliated group.

§ 270.3c–6 Beneficial Ownership by Knowledgeable Employees and Certain Other Persons

(a) As used in this section:

(1) The term Affiliated Management Person means an affiliated person, as such term is defined in section 2(a)(3) of the Act [15 U.S.C. 80a–2(a)(3)], that manages the investment activities of a Covered Company. For purposes of this definition, the term "investment company" as used in section

2(a)(3) of the Act includes a Covered Company.

(2) The term Covered Company means a Section 3(c)(1) Company or a Section 3(c)(7) Company.

(3) The term Executive Officer means the president, any vice president in charge of a principal business unit, division or function (such as sales, administration or finance), any other officer who performs a policy-making function, or any other person who performs similar policy-making functions, for a Covered Company or for an Affiliated Management Person of the Covered Company.

(4) The term Knowledgeable Employee with respect to any Covered Company means any natural person who is:

(i) An Executive Officer, director, trustee, general partner, advisory board member, or person serving in a similar capacity, of the Covered Company or an Affiliated Management Person of the Covered Company; or

(ii) An employee of the Covered Company or an Affiliated Management Person of the Covered Company (other than an employee performing solely clerical, secretarial or administrative functions with regard to such company or its investments) who, in connection with his or her regular functions or duties, participates in the investment activities of such Covered Company, other Covered Companies, or investment companies the investment activities of which are managed by such Affiliated Management Person of the Covered Company; provided that such employee has been performing such functions and duties for or on behalf of the Covered Company or the Affiliated Management Person of the Covered Company, or substantially similar functions or duties for or on behalf of another company for at least 12 months:

(5) The term Section 3(c)(1) Company means a company that would be an investment company but for the exclusion provided by section 3(c)(1) of the Act [15 U.S.C. 80a–3(c)(1)].

(6) The term Section 3(c)(7) Company means a company that would be an investment company but for the exclusion provided by section 3(c)(7) of the Act [15 U.S.C. 80a–3(c)(7)].

(b) For purposes of determining the number of beneficial owners of a Section 3(c)(1) Company, and whether the outstanding securities of a Section 3(c)(7) Company are owned exclusively by qualified purchasers, there shall be excluded securities beneficially owned by:

(1) A person who at the time such securities were acquired was a Knowledgeable Employee of such Company;

(2) A company owned exclusively by Knowledgeable Employees;

(3) Any person who acquires securities originally acquired by a Knowledgeable Employee in accordance with this section, provided that such securities were acquired by such person in accordance with § 270.3c–6.

§ 270.3c–6 Certain Transfers of Interests in Section 3(c)(1) and Section 3(c)(7) Funds

(a) As used in this section:

(1) The term Donee means a person who acquires a security of a Covered Company (or a security or other interest in a company referred to in paragraph (b)(3) of this section) as a gift or bequest or pursuant to an agreement relating to a legal separation or divorce.

(2) The term Section 3(c)(1) Company means a company that would be an investment company but for the exclusion provided by section 3(c)(1) of the Act [15 U.S.C. 80a–3(c)(1)].

(3) The term Section 3(c)(7) Company means a company that would be an investment company but for the exclusion provid-

ed by section 3(c)(7) of the Act [15 U.S.C. 80a–3(c)(7)].

(4) The term Transferee means a Section 3(c)(1) Transferee or a Qualified Purchaser Transferee, in each case as defined in paragraph (b) of this section.

(5) The term Transferor means a Section 3(c)(1) Transferor or a Qualified Purchaser Transferor, in each case as defined in paragraph (b) of this section.

(b) Beneficial ownership by any person ("Section 3(c)(1) Transferee") who acquires securities or interests in securities of a Section 3(c)(1) Company from a person other than the Section 3(c)(1) Company shall be deemed to be beneficial ownership by the person from whom such transfer was made ("Section 3(c)(1) Transferor"), and securities of a Section 3(c)(7) Company that are owned by persons who received the securities from a qualified purchaser other than the Section 3(c)(7) Company ("Qualified Purchaser Transferor") or a person deemed to be a qualified purchaser by this section shall be deemed to be acquired by a qualified purchaser ("Qualified Purchaser Transferee"), provided that the Transferee is:

(1) The estate of the Transferor;

(2) A Donee; or

(3) A company established by the Transferor exclusively for the benefit of (or owned exclusively by) the Transferor and the persons specified in paragraphs (b)(1) and (b)(2) of this section.

§ 270.5b–1 Definition of "Total Assets"

The term "total assets," when used in computing values for the purposes of sections 5 and 12 of the act, shall mean the gross assets of the company with respect to which the computation is made, taken as of the end of the fiscal quarter of the company last preceding the date of computation. This section shall not apply to any company which has adopted either of the alternative methods of valuation permitted by § 270.2a–1.

§ 270.5b–2 Exclusion of Certain Guarantees as Securities of the Guarantor

(a) For the purposes of section 5 of the act, a guarantee of a security shall not be deemed to be a security issued by the guarantor: *Provided,* That the value of all securities issued or guaranteed by the guarantor, and owned by the management company, does not exceed 10 percent of the value of the total assets of such management company.

(b) Notwithstanding paragraph (a) of this section, for the purposes of section 5 of the act, a guarantee by a railroad company of a security issued by a terminal company, warehouse company, switching company, or bridge company, shall not be deemed to be a security issued by such railroad company: *Provided:*

(1) The security is guaranteed jointly or severally by more than one railroad company; and

(2) No one of such guaranteeing railroad companies directly or indirectly controls all of its co-guarantors.

(c) For the purposes of section 5 of the act, a lease or other arrangement whereby a railroad company is or becomes obligated to pay a stipulated annual sum of rental either to another railroad company or to the security holders of such other railroad company shall not be deemed in itself a guarantee.

§ 270.5b–3 Acquisition of Repurchase Agreement or Refunded Security Treated as Acquisition of Underlying Securities

(a) *Repurchase Agreements.* For purposes of sections 5 and 12(d)(3) of the Act (15 U.S.C. 80a–5 and 80a–12(d)(3)), the acquisition of a repurchase agreement may be deemed to be an acquisition of the underlying securities, provided the obligation of the seller to repurchase the securities from the investment company is Collateralized Fully.

(b) *Refunded Securities.* For purposes of section 5 of the Act (15 U.S.C. 80a–5), the acquisition of a Refunded Security is deemed to be an acquisition of the escrowed Government Securities.

(c) *Definitions.* As used in this section:

(1) *Collateralized Fully* in the case of a repurchase agreement means that:

(i) The value of the securities collateralizing the repurchase agreement (reduced by the transaction costs (including loss of interest) that the investment company reasonably could expect to incur if the seller defaults) is, and during the entire term of the repurchase agreement remains, at least equal to the Resale Price provided in the agreement;

(ii) The investment company has perfected its security interest in the collateral;

(iii) The collateral is maintained in an account of the investment company with its custodian or a third party that qualifies as a custodian under the Act;

(iv) The collateral consists entirely of:

(A) Cash items;

(B) Government Securities;

(C) Securities that at the time the repurchase agreement is entered into are rated in the highest rating category by the Requisite NRSROs; or

(D) Unrated Securities that are of comparable quality to securities that are rated in the highest rating category by the Requisite NRSROs, as determined by the investment company's board of directors or its delegate; and

(v) Upon an Event of Insolvency with respect to the seller, the repurchase agreement would qualify under a provision of applicable insolvency law providing an exclusion from any automatic stay of creditors' rights against the seller.

(2) *Event of Insolvency* means, with respect to a person:

(i) An admission of insolvency, the application by the person for the appointment of a trustee, receiver, rehabilitator, or similar officer for all or substantially all of its assets, a general assignment for the benefit of creditors, the filing by the person of a voluntary petition in bankruptcy or application for reorganization or an arrangement with creditors; or

(ii) The institution of similar proceedings by another person which proceedings are not contested by the person; or

(iii) The institution of similar proceedings by a government agency responsible for regulating the activities of the person, whether or not contested by the person.

(3) *Government Security* means any "Government Security" as defined in section 2(a)(16) of the Act (15 U.S.C. 80a–2(a)(16)).

(4) *Refunded Security* means a debt security the principal and interest payments of which are to be paid by Government Securities ("deposited securities") that have been irrevocably placed in an escrow account pursuant to an agreement between the issuer of the debt security and an escrow agent that is not an "affiliated person," as defined in section 2(a)(3)(C) of the Act (15 U.S.C. 80a–2(a)(3)(C)), of the issuer of the debt security, and, in accordance with such escrow agreement, are pledged only to the payment of the debt security and, to the extent that excess proceeds are available after all payments of principal, interest, and applicable premiums on the Refunded Securities, the expenses of the escrow agent and, thereafter, to the issuer or another party; *provided* that:

(i) The deposited securities are not redeemable prior to their final maturity;

(ii) The escrow agreement prohibits the substitution of the deposited securities unless the substituted securities are Government Securities; and

(iii) At the time the deposited securities are placed in the escrow account, or at the time a substitution of the deposited securities is made, an independent certified public accountant has certified to the escrow agent that the deposited securities will satisfy all scheduled payments of principal, interest and applicable premiums on the Refunded Securities; *provided, however*, an independent public accountant need not have provided the certification described in this paragraph (c)(4)(iii) if the security, as a Refunded Security, has received a rating from an NRSRO in the highest category for debt obligations (within which there may be subcategories or gradations indicating relative standing).

(5) *NRSRO* means any nationally recognized statistical rating organization, as that term is used in paragraphs (c)(2)(vi)(E), (F) and (H) of § 240.15c3–1 of this chapter, that is not an "affiliated person," as defined in section 2(a)(3)(C) of the Act (15 U.S.C. 80a–2(a)(3)(C)), of the issuer of, or any insurer or provider of credit support for, the security.

(6) *Requisite NRSROs* means:

(i) Any two NRSROs that have issued a rating with respect to a security or class of debt obligations of an issuer; or

(ii) If only one NRSRO has issued a rating with respect to such security or class of debt obligations of an issuer at the time the investment company acquires the security, that NRSRO.

(7) *Resale Price* means the acquisition price paid to the seller of the securities plus the accrued resale premium on such acquisition price. The accrued resale premium is the amount specified in the repurchase agreement or the daily amortization of the difference between the acquisition price and the resale price specified in the repurchase agreement.

(8) *Unrated Securities* means securities that have not received a rating from the Requisite NRSROs.

§ 270.6b–1 Exemption of Employees' Securities Company Pending Determination of Application

Any employees' securities company while files an application for an order of exemption under section 6(b) of the act (54 Stat. 801; 15 U.S.C. 80a–6) shall be exempt, pending final determination of such application by the Commission, from all provisions of the act applicable to investment companies as such.

§ 270.6c–3 Exemptions for Certain Registered Variable Life Insurance Separate Accounts

A separate account which meets the requirements of paragraph (a) of Rule 6e–2 or paragraph (a) of Rule 6e–3(T) and registers as an investment company under section 8(a) of the Act, and the investment adviser, principal underwriter and depositor of such separate account, shall be exempt for the provisions of the Act specified in paragraph (b) of Rule 6e–2, or paragraph (b) of Rule 6e–3(T), except for sections 7 and 8(a) of the Act, under the same terms and conditions as a separate account claiming exemption under Rule 6e–2 or Rule 6e–2(T).

§ 270.6c–6 Exemption for Certain Registered Separate Accounts and Other Persons

(a) As used in this section,

(1) "Revenue Ruling" shall mean Revenue Ruling 81–225, 1981–41 I.R.B. (October 13, 1981), issued by the Internal Revenue Service on September 25, 1981.

(2) "Existing separate account" shall mean a separate account which is, or is a part of, a unit investment trust registered under the Act, engaged in a continuous offering of its securities on September 25, 1981.

(3) "Existing portfolio company" shall mean a registered open-end management investment company, engaged in a continuous offering of its securities on September 25, 1981, all or part of whose securities were owned by an existing separate account on September 25, 1981.

(4) "New portfolio company" shall mean any registered open-end management investment company the shares of which will be sold to one or more registered separate accounts for the purpose of minimizing the impact of the Revenue Ruling on the contract-owners of an existing separate account, which new portfolio company has the same

(i) investment objectives,

(ii) fundamental policies, and

(iii) voting rights

as the existing portfolio company and has an advisory fee schedule, including expenses assumed by the adviser, that is at least as advantageous to the new portfolio company as was the fee schedule of the existing portfolio company.

(5) "New separate account" shall mean a separate account which

(i) is, or is a part of, a unit investment trust registered under the Act;

(ii) is intended to minimize the impact of the Revenue Ruling on the contract-owners of an existing separate account;

(iii) invests solely in one or more new portfolio companies;

(iv) has the same

(A) sales loads,

(B) depositor, and

(C) custodial arrangements

as the existing separate account; and

(v) has

(A) asset charges,

(B) administrative fees, and

(C) any other fees and charges (not including taxes) that correspond only to fees of the existing separate account and are no greater than those corresponding fees.

(b) Any order of the Commission under the Act, granted to an existing separate account on or before September 25, 1981, shall remain in full force and effect notwithstanding that the existing separate account invests in one or more new portfolio companies in lieu of, or in addition to, investing in one or more existing portfolio companies; *Provided*, That:

(1) No material changes in the facts upon which the order was based have occurred;

(2) All representations, undertakings, and conditions made or agreed to by the existing separate account, and any other person or persons, other than any existing portfolio company, in connection with the issuance of the order are, and continue to be, applicable to the existing separate account and any such other person or persons, unless modified in accordance with this section;

(3) All representations, undertakings, and conditions made or agreed to by the existing portfolio company in connection with the issuance of the order are made or agreed to by the new portfolio company, unless modified in accordance with this section; and

(4) Part II of the Registration Statement under the Securities Act of 1933 of the existing separate account

(i) Indicates that the existing separate account is relying upon paragraph (b) of this section,

(ii) Lists the Investment Company Act release numbers of any orders upon which the existing separate account intends to rely, and

(iii) Contains a representation that the provisions of this paragraph (b) have been complied with.

(c) Any order of the Commission under the Act, granted to an existing separate account on or before September 25, 1981, shall apply with full force and effect to a new separate account and the depositor of and principal underwriter for the new separate account notwithstanding that the new separate account invests in one or more new portfolio companies; *Provided*, That:

(1) No material changes in the facts upon which the order was based have occurred;

(2) All representations, undertakings, and conditions made or agreed to by the depositor, principal underwriter, and any other person or persons other than the existing separate account or any existing portfolio companies, in connection with the issuance of the order are, and continue to be, applicable to such depositor, principal underwriter, and other person or persons, unless modified in accordance with this section;

(3) All representations, undertakings, and conditions made or agreed to by the existing separate account in connection with the issuance of the order are made or agreed to by the new separate account, unless modified in accordance with this section;

(4) All representations, undertakings, and conditions made or agreed to by an existing portfolio company in connection with the issuance of the order are made or agreed to by the new portfolio company, unless modified in accordance with this section; and

(5) Part II of the Registration Statement under the Securities Act of 1933 of the new separate account

(i) indicates that the new separate account is relying upon paragraph (c) of this section,

(ii) lists the Investment Company Act release numbers of any orders upon which the new separate account intends to rely, and

(iii) contains a representation that the provisions of this paragraph (c) have been complied with.

(d) Any affiliated person or depositor of or principal underwriter for a new or existing separate account or any affiliated person of or principal underwriter for a new or existing portfolio company, and any affiliated person of such persons, principal underwriters, or depositor shall be exempt from section 17(d) of the Act [80a–17(d)] and rule 17d–1 thereunder to the extent necessary to permit the organization of one or more new portfolio companies; *Provided,* That, any expenses borne by the existing portfolio company or the new portfolio company in connection with such organization are necessary and appropriate and are allocated in a manner that is fair and reasonable to all of the shareholders of these companies.

(e) Any affiliated person or depositor of or principal underwriter for a new or existing separate account and any affiliated persons of such a person, principal underwriter, or depositor shall be exempt from section 17(d) of the Act and rule 17d–1 thereunder to the extent necessary to permit such person to bear any reasonable expenses arising out of the organization of one or more new portfolio companies or the new separate account.

(f) Any affiliated persons or depositor of or principal underwriter for a new or existing separate account or any affiliated person of or principal underwriter for a new or existing portfolio company, and any affiliated person of such persons, principal underwriters, or depositor shall be exempt from section 17(a) and any existing portfolio company which has made an election pursuant to rule 18f–1 shall be permitted to revoke that election to the extent necessary to permit transactions involving the transfer of assets from the existing portfolio company to a new portfolio company; *Provided,* That:

(1) Such assets are transferred without the imposition of any fees or charges;

(2) The board of directors of the existing portfolio company, including a majority of the directors of the company who are not interested persons of such company, determines that the transfer of assets is fair and reasonable to all shareholders of the company and such determination, and the basis upon which it was made, is recorded in the minute book of the existing portfolio company;

(3) Any securities involved are valued by the existing portfolio company for purposes of the transfer in accordance with its valuation practices for determining net asset value per share; and

(4) With respect to rule 18f–1, the existing separate account requests that the existing portfolio company redeem in kind the shares of the portfolio company held by the separate account.

(g) The new portfolio company shall be exempt from section 2(a)(41) of the Act and rules 2a–4 under the Act to the extent necessary to permit it to use the same method of valuation for the purpose of pricing its shares for sale, redemption, and repurchase, as the existing portfolio company; *Provided,* That:

(1) The existing portfolio company had on September 25, 1981, an order of the Commission exempting it, for the purposes of pricing its shares for sale, redemption, and repurchase, from

(i) Section 2(a)(41) of the Act and rules 2a–4 and 22c–1 under the Act to the extent necessary to permit it to use the amortized cost valuation method or

(ii) Rules 2a–4 and 22c–1 under the Act to the extent necessary to permit it to calculate its net asset value per share to the nearest one cent on share values of $1.00;

(2) All representations, undertakings, and conditions made or agreed to by the existing portfolio company in connection with the order are made or agreed to by the new portfolio company unless modified in accordance with this section; and

(3) Part II of the Registration Statement under the Securities Act of 1933 of the new portfolio company

(i) Indicates that the new portfolio company is relying upon paragraph (g) of this section,

(ii) Lists the Investment Company Act release numbers of any orders upon which the new portfolio company intends to rely, and

(iii) Contains a representation that the provisions of paragraph (g) have been complied with.

(h) The depositor or trustee of an existing separate account shall be exempt from section 26(c) of the Act (15 U.S.C. 80a–26(c)) to the extent necessary to permit the substitution of securities of the new portfolio company for securities of the existing portfolio company; *Provided,* That, within thirty days of such substitution:

(1) The existing separate account notifies all contractowners of the substitution of securities and any determinations of the board of directors of the new portfolio company required by paragraph (d) of this section;

(2) The existing separate account delivers a copy of the prospectus of the new portfolio company to all contractowners; and

(3) The existing separate account, concurrently with the notification referred to in paragraph (h)(1) of this section or the delivery of the prospectus of the new portfolio company referred to in paragraph (h)(2) of this section, whichever is later, offers to those contractowners who would otherwise have surrender rights under their contracts the right, for a period of at least thirty days from the receipt of this offer, to surrender their contracts without the imposition of any withdrawal charge or contingent deferred sales load, and any surrendering contractowner receives the price next determined after the request for surrender is received by the insurance company.

(i) The existing separate account shall be exempt from section 22(d) of the Act to the extent necessary to permit it to comply with paragraph (h) of this section and the principal underwriter for or depositor of the existing separate account shall be exempt from section 26(a)(4)(B) of the Act to the extent necessary to permit them to rely on paragraph (h) of this section.

(j) Notwithstanding section 11 of the Act, the existing separate account or any principal underwriter for the existing separate account may make or cause to be made to the contractowners of the existing separate account an offer to exchange a security funded by an existing portfolio company for a security funded by a new portfolio company without the terms of that offer having first been submitted to and approved by the Commission; *Provided,* That the exchange is to be made on the basis of the relative net asset values of the securities to be exchanged without the imposition of any fees or charges.

(k) Notwithstanding section 11 of the Act, the new separate account or any principal underwriter for the new separate account may make or cause to be made an offer to the contractowners of the existing separate account to exchange their securities for securities of the new separate account without the terms of that offer having first been submitted to and approved by the Commission; *Provided,* That:

(1) The exchange is to be made on the basis of the relative net asset values of the securities to be exchanged without the imposition of any fees or charges; and

(2) If the new separate account imposes a contingent deferred sales load ("sales load") on the securities to be acquired in the exchange

(i) At the time this sales load is imposed, it is calculated as if

(A) The contractowner had been a contractowner of the new separate account from the date on which he became a contractowner of the existing separate account, in the case of a sales load based on the amount of time the contractowner has been invested in the new separate account, and

(B) Amounts attributable to purchase payments made to the existing separate account had been made to the new separate account on the date on which they were made to the existing separate account, in the case of a sales load based on the amount of time purchased payments have been invested in the new separate account, and

(ii) The total sales load imposed does not exceed 9 percent of the sum of the purchase payments made to the new separate account and that portion of purchase payments made to the existing separate account attributable to the securities exchanged.

(*l*) Notwithstanding the foregoing, the provisions of this section will be available to a new separate account or new portfolio company, or to any affiliated person or depositor of or principal underwriter for such a new separate account, to any affiliated person of or principal underwriter for such a new portfolio company, to any affiliated person of such persons, depositor, or principal underwriters, or to any substitution of securities effected in reliance on this section, only if such new separate account or new portfolio company is registered under the Act or such substitution is effected prior to September 21, 1983.

§ 270.6c–7 Exemptions From Certain Provisions of Sections 22(e) and 27 for Registered Separate Accounts Offering Variable Annuity Contracts to Participants in the Texas Optional Retirement Program

A registered separate account, and any depositor of or underwriter for such account, shall be exempt from the provisions of sections 22(e), 27(c)(1), and 27(d) of the Act with respect to any variable annuity contract participating in such account to the extent necessary to permit compliance with the Texas Optional Retirement Program ("Program"), *Provided,* That the separate account, depositor, or underwriter for such account:

(a) Includes appropriate disclosure regarding the restrictions on redemption imposed by the Program in each registration statement, including the prospectus, used in connection with the Program;

(b) Includes appropriate disclosure regarding the restrictions on redemption imposed by the Program in any sales literature used in connection with the offer of annuity contracts to Program participants;

(c) Instructs salespeople who solicit Program participants to purchase annuity contracts specifically to bring the restrictions on redemption imposed by the Program to the attention of potential Program participants;

(d) Obtains from each Program participant who purchases an annuity contract in connection with the Program, prior to or at the time of such purchase, a signed statement acknowledging the restrictions on redemption imposed by the Program; and

(e) Includes in Part II of the separate account's registration statement under the Securities Act of 1933 a representation that this section is being relied upon and that the provisions of paragraphs (a)–(d) of this section have been complied with.

§ 270.6c-8 Exemptions for Registered Separate Accounts to Impose a Deferred Sales Load and to Deduct Certain Administrative Charges

(a) As used in this section "Deferred sales load" shall mean any sales load, including a contingent deferred sales load, that is deducted upon redemption or annuitization of amounts representing all or a portion of a securityholder's interest in a registered separate account.

(b) A registered separate account, and any depositor of or principal underwriter for such account, shall be exempt from the provisions of sections 2(a)(32), 2(a)(35), 22(c), 26(a)(2)(C), 27(c)(1), 27(c)(2), and 27(d) of the Act and rule 22c–1 under the Act to the extent necessary to permit them to impose a deferred sales load on any variable annuity contract participating in such account, *Provided,* That:

(1) The amount of any such sales load imposed, when added to any sales load previously paid on such contract, shall not exceed 9 percent of purchase payments made to date for such contract; and

(2) The terms of any offer to exchange another contract for the contract are in compliance with the requirements of paragraph (d) or (e) of rule 11a–2 under the Act.

(c) A registered separate account, and any depositor of or principal underwriter for such account, shall be exempt from sections 2(a)(32), 22(c), 27(c)(1), and 27(d) of the Act and rule 22c–1 under the Act to the extent necessary to permit them to deduct from the value of any variable annuity contract participating in such account, upon total redemption of the contract prior to the last day of the year, the full annual fee for administrative services that otherwise would have been deducted on that date.

§ 270.6c-10 Exemption for Certain Open-End Management Investment Companies to Impose Deferred Sales Loads

(a) A company and any exempted person shall be exempt from the provisions of sections 2(a)(32), 2(a)(35), and 22(d) of the Act [15 U.S.C. 80a–2(a)(32), 80a–2(a)(35), and 80a–22(d), respectively] and § 270.22c–1 to the extent necessary to permit a deferred sales load to be imposed on shares issued by the company, *Provided,* that:

(1) The amount of the deferred sales load does not exceed a specified percentage of the net asset value or the offering price at the time of purchase;

(2) The terms of the deferred sales load are covered by the provisions of Rule 2830 of the Conduct Rules of the National Association of Securities Dealers, Inc.; and

(3) The same deferred sales load is imposed on all shareholders, except that scheduled variations in or elimination of a deferred sales load may be offered to a particular class of shareholders or transactions, *Provided,* that the conditions in § 270.22d–1 are satisfied. Nothing in this paragraph (a) shall prevent a company from offering to existing shareholders a new scheduled variation that would waive or reduce the amount of a deferred sales load not yet paid.

(b) For purposes of this section:

(1) *Company* means a registered open-end management investment company, other than a registered separate account, and includes a separate series of the company;

(2) *Exempted person* means any principal underwriter of, dealer in, and any other person authorized to consummate transactions in, securities issued by a company; and

(3) *Deferred sales load* means any amount properly chargeable to sales or promotional expenses that is paid by a shareholder after purchase but before or upon redemption.

§ 270.6d-1 Exemption for Certain Closed-End Investment Companies

(a) An application under section 6(d) of the act shall contain the following information:

(1) A brief description of the character of the business and investment policy of the applicant.

(2) The information relied upon by the applicant to satisfy the conditions of paragraphs (1) and (2) of section 6(d) of the act.

(3) The number of holders of each class of the applicant's outstanding securities.

(4) An unconsolidated balance sheet as of a date not earlier than the end of the applicant's first fiscal year, together with a schedule specifying the title, the amount, the book value and, if determinable, the market value of each security in the applicant's portfolio.

(5) An unconsolidated profit and loss statement for the applicant's last fiscal year.

(6) A statement of each provision of the act from which the applicant seeks exemption, together with a statement of the facts by reason of which, in the applicant's opinion, such exemption is not contrary to the public interest or inconsistent with the protection of investors.

(b) There shall be attached to each copy of the application a copy of Form N-8A. The form need not be executed, but it shall be clearly marked on its facing page as an exhibit to the application. The filing of Form N-8A in this manner shall not be construed as the filing of a notification of registration under section 8(a) of the act.

(c) The application may contain any additional information which the applicant desires to submit.

§ 270.6e-2 Exemptions for Certain Variable Life Insurance Separate Accounts

(a) A separate account, and the investment adviser, principal underwriter and depositor of such separate account, shall, except for the exemptions provided in paragraph (b) of this Rule 6e-2, be subject to all provisions of the Act and rules and regulations promulgated thereunder as though such separate account were a registered investment company issuing periodic payment plan certificates if:

(1) Such separate account is established and maintained by a life insurance company pursuant to the insurance laws or code of (i) any state or territory of the United States or the District of Columbia, or (ii) Canada or any province thereof, if it complies to the extent necessary with Rule 7d-1 under the Act;

(2) The assets of the separate account are derived solely from the sale of variable life insurance contracts as defined in paragraph (c)(1) of this Rule 6e-2, and advances made by the life insurance company which established and maintains the separate account ("life insurer") in connection with the operation of such separate account;

(3) The separate account is not used for variable annuity contracts or for funds corresponding to dividend accumulations or other contract liabilities not involving life contingencies;

(4) The income, gains and losses, whether or not realized, from assets allocated to such separate account, are, in accordance with the applicable variable life insurance con-

tract, credited to or charged against such account without regard to other income, gains or losses of the life insurer;

(5) The separate account is legally segregated, and that portion of its assets having a value equal to, or approximately equal to, the reserves and other contract liabilities with respect to such separate account are not chargeable with liabilities arising out of any other business that the life insurer may conduct;

(6) The assets of the separate account have, at each time during the year that adjustments in the reserves are made, a value at least equal to the reserves and other contract liabilities with respect to such separate account, and at all other times, except pursuant to an order of the Commission, have a value approximately equal to or in excess of such reserves and liabilities; and

(7) The investment adviser of the separate account is registered under the Investment Advisers Act of 1940.

(b) If a separate account meets the requirements of paragraph (a) of this section, then such separate account and the other persons described in paragraph (a) of this section shall be exempt from the provisions of the Act as follows:

(1) Section 2(a)(35): *Provided, however,* That the term "sales load," as used in the Act and rules and regulations thereunder, shall have the meaning set forth in paragraph (c)(4) of this Rule.

(2) Section 7.

(3) Section 8 to the extent that:

(i) For purposes of paragraph (a) of section 8, the separate account shall file with the Commission a notification on Form N–6EI–1 which identifies such separate account; and

(ii) For purposes of paragraph (b) of section 8, the separate account shall file with the Commission a form to be designated by the Commission within ninety days after filing the notification on Form N–6EI–1: *Provided, however,* That if the fiscal year of the separate account ends within this ninety day period the form may be filed within ninety days after the end of such fiscal year.

(4) Section 9 to the extent that:

(i) The eligibility restrictions of section 9(a) of the Act shall not be applicable to those persons who are officers, directors and employees of the life insurer or its affiliates who do not participate directly in the management or administration of the separate account or in the sale of variable life insurance contracts funded by such separate account; and

(ii) A life insurer shall be ineligible pursuant to paragraph (3) of section 9(a) of the Act to serve as investment adviser, depositor of or principal underwriter for a variable life insurance separate account only if an affiliated person of such life insurer, ineligible by reason of paragraphs (1) or (2) of section 9(a), participates directly in the management or administration of the separate account or in the sale of variable life insurance contracts funded by such separate account.

(5) Section 13(a) to the extent that:

(i) An insurance regulatory authority may require pursuant to insurance law or regulation that the separate account make (or refrain from making) certain investments which would result in changes in the sub-classification or investment policies of the separate account;

(ii) Changes in the investment policy of the separate account initiated by contractholders or the board of directors of the separate account may be disapproved by the life insurer, provided that such disapproval is reasonable and is based upon a determination by the life insurer in good faith that:

(A) Such change would be contrary to state law; or

(B) Such change would be inconsistent with the investment objectives of the separate account or would result in the purchase of securities for the separate account which vary from the general quality and nature of investments and investment techniques utilized by other separate accounts of the life insurer or of an affiliated life insurance company, which separate accounts have investment objectives similar to the separate account;

(iii) Any action taken in accordance with paragraph (b)(5) (i) or (ii) of this section and the reasons therefor shall be disclosed in the proxy statement for the next meeting of variable life insurance contractholders of the separate account.

(6) Section 14(a): *Provided,* That until the separate account has total assets of at least $100,000 the life insurer shall have (i) a combined capital and surplus, if a stock company, or (ii) an unassigned surplus, if a mutual company, of not less than $1,000,000 as set forth in the balance sheet of such life insurer contained in the registration statement, or any amendment thereto, relating to variable life insurance contracts funded by such separate account filed pursuant to the Securities Act of 1933, as amended.

(7)(i) Section 15(a) to the extent this section requires that the initial written contract pursuant to which the investment adviser serves or acts shall have been approved by the vote of a majority of the outstanding voting securities of the registered company, *provided* that:

(A) Such investment adviser is selected and a written contract is entered into before the effective date of the registration statement under the Securities Act of 1933, as amended, for variable life insurance contracts which are funded by the separate account, and that the terms of the contract are fully disclosed in such registration statement, and

(B) A written contract is submitted to a vote of variable life insurance contractholders at their first meeting after the effective date of the registration statement under the Securities Act of 1933, as amended, on condition that such meeting shall take place within one year after such effective date, unless the time for the holding of such meeting shall be extended by the Commission upon written request for good cause shown;

(ii) Sections 15(a), (b) and (c) to the extent that:

(A) An insurance regulatory authority may disapprove pursuant to insurance law or regulation any contract between the separate account and an investment adviser or principal underwriter;

(B) Changes in the principal underwriter for the separate account initiated by contractholders or the board of directors of the separate account may be disapproved by the life insurer: *Provided,* That such disapproval is reasonable;

(C) Changes in the investment adviser of the separate account initiated by contractholders or the board of directors of the separate account may be disapproved by the life insurer: *Provided,* That such disapproval is reasonable and is based upon a determination by the life insurer in good faith that:

(*1*) The rate of the proposed investment advisory fee will exceed the maximum rate that is permitted to be charged against the assets of the separate account for such services as specified by any variable life insurance contract funded by such separate account; or

(*2*) The proposed investment adviser may be expected to employ investment techniques which vary from the general techniques utilized by the current investment adviser to the separate account, or advise the purchase or sale of securities which would be inconsistent with the investment objectives of the separate account, or which would vary from the quality and nature of investments made by other separate accounts of the life insurer or of an affiliated life insurance company, which separate accounts have investment objectives similar to the separate account;

(D) Any action taken in accordance with paragraph (b)(7)(ii)(A), (B) or (C) of this section and the reasons therefor shall be disclosed in the proxy statement for the next meeting of variable life insurance contractholders of the separate account.

(8) Section 16(a) to the extent that:

(i) Persons serving as directors of the separate account prior to the first meeting of such account's variable life insurance contractholders are exempt from the requirement of section 16(a) of the Act that such persons be elected by the holders of outstanding voting securities of such account at an annual or special meeting called for that purpose, *Provided*, That:

(A) Such persons have been appointed directors of such account by the life insurer before the effective date of the registration statement under the Securities Act of 1933, as amended, for variable life insurance contracts which are funded by the separate account and are identified in such registration statement (or are replacements appointed by the life insurer for any such persons who have become unable to serve as directors), and

(B) An election of directors for such account shall be held at the first meeting of variable life insurance contractholders after the effective date of the registration statement under the Securities Act of 1933, as amended, relating to contracts funded by such account, which meeting shall take place within one year after such effective date, unless the time for holding such meeting shall be extended by the Commission upon written request for good cause shown;

(ii) A member of the board of directors of such separate account may be disapproved or removed by the appropriate insurance regulatory authority if such person is ineligible to serve as a director of the separate account pursuant to insurance law or regulation of the jurisdiction in which the life insurer is domiciled.

(9) Section 17(f) to the extent that the securities and similar investments of the separate account may be maintained in the custody of the life insurer or an insurance company which is an affiliated person of such life insurer: *Provided*, That:

(i) The securities and similar investments allocated to such separate account are clearly identified as to ownership by such account, and such securities and similar investments are maintained in the vault of an insurance company which meets the qualifications set forth in paragraph (b)(9)(ii) of this section, and whose procedures and activities with respect to such safekeeping function are supervised by the insurance regulatory authorities of the jurisdiction in which the securities and similar investments will be held;

(ii) The insurance company maintaining such investments must file with an insurance regulatory authority of a state or territory of the United States or the District of Columbia an annual statement of its financial condition in the form prescribed by the National Association of Insurance Commissioners, must be subject to supervision and inspection by such authority and must be examined periodically as to its financial condition and other affairs by such authority, must hold the securities and similar investments of the separate account in its vault, which vault must be equivalent to that of a bank which is a member of the Federal Reserve

System, and must have a combined capital and surplus, if a stock company, or an unassigned surplus, if a mutual company, of not less than $1,000,000 as set forth in its most recent annual statement filed with such authority;

(iii) Access to such securities and similar investments shall be limited to employees of or agents authorized by the Commission, representatives of insurance regulatory authorities, independent public accountants for the separate account, accountants for the life insurer and to no more than 20 persons authorized pursuant to a resolution of the board of directors of the separate account, which persons shall be directors of the separate account, officers and responsible employees of the life insurer or officers and responsible employees of the affiliated insurance company in whose vault such investments are maintained (if applicable), and access to such securities and similar investments shall be had only by two or more such persons jointly, at least one of whom shall be a director of the separate account or officer of the life insurer;

(iv) The requirement in paragraph (b)(9)(i) of this section that the securities and similar investments of the separate account be maintained in the vault of a qualified insurance company shall not apply to securities deposited with insurance regulatory authorities or deposited in a system for the central handling of securities established by a national securities exchange or national securities association registered with the Commission under the Securities Exchange Act of 1934, as amended, or such person as may be permitted by the Commission, or to securities on loan which are collateralized to the extent of their full market value, or to securities hypothecated, pledged, or placed in escrow for the account of such separate account in connection with a loan or other transaction authorized by specific resolution of the board of directors of the separate account, or to securities in transit in connection with the sale, exchange, redemption, maturity or conversion, the exercise of warrants or rights, assents to changes in terms of the securities, or to other transactions necessary or appropriate in the ordinary course of business relating to the management of securities;

(v) Each person when depositing such securities or similar investments in or withdrawing them from the depository or when ordering their withdrawal and delivery from the custody of the life insurer or affiliated insurance company, shall sign a notation in respect of such deposit, withdrawal or order which shall show (A) the date and time of the deposit, withdrawal or order, (B) the title and amount of the securities or other investments deposited, withdrawn or ordered to be withdrawn, and an identification thereof by certificate numbers or otherwise, (C) the manner of acquisition of the securities or similar investments deposited or the purpose for which they have been withdrawn, or ordered to be withdrawn, and (D) if withdrawn and delivered to another person the name of such person. Such notation shall be transmitted promptly to an officer or director of the separate account or the life insurer designated by the board of directors of the separate account who shall not be a person designated for the purpose of paragraph (b)(9)(iii) of this section. Such notation shall be on serially numbered forms and shall be preserved for at least one year;

(vi) Such securities and similar investments shall be verified by complete examination by an independent public accountant retained by the separate account at least three times during each fiscal year, at least two of which shall be chosen by such accountant without prior notice to such separate account. A certificate of such accountant stating that he has made an examination of such securities and investments and describing the nature and extent of the examination shall be transmitted to the Commission by the accountant promptly after each examination;

(vii) Securities and similar investments of a separate account maintained with a bank or other company whose functions and physical facilities are supervised by federal or state authorities pursuant to any arrangement whereby the directors, officers, employees or agents of the separate account or the life insurer are authorized or permitted to withdraw such investments upon their mere receipt are deemed to be in the custody of the life insurer and shall be exempt from the requirements of section 17(f) so long as the arrangement complies with all provisions of this paragraph (b)(9), except that such securities will be maintained in the vault of a bank or other company rather than the vault of an insurance company.

(10) Section 18(i) to the extent that:

(i) For the purposes of any section of the Act which provides for the vote of securityholders on matters relating to the investment company:

(A) Variable life insurance contractholders shall have one vote for each $100 of cash value funded by the separate account, with fractional votes allocated for amounts less than $100;

(B) The life insurer shall have one vote for each $100 of assets of the separate account not otherwise attributable to contractholders pursuant to paragraph (b)(10)(i)(A) of this section, with fractional votes allocated for amounts less than $100: *Provided,* That after the commencement of sales of variable life insurance contracts funded by the separate account, the life insurer shall cast its votes for and against each matter which may be voted upon by contractholders in the same proportion as the votes cast by contractholders; and

(C) The number of votes to be allocated shall be determined as of a record date not more than 90 days prior to any meeting at which such vote is held: *Provided,* That if a quorum is not present at the meeting, the meeting may be adjourned for up to 60 days without fixing a new record date;

(ii) The requirement of this section that every share of stock issued by a registered management investment company (except a common-law trust of the character described in section 16(b)) shall be a voting stock and have equal voting rights with every other outstanding voting stock shall not be deemed to be violated by actions specifically permitted by any provision of this Rule.

(11) Section 19 to the extent that the provisions of this section shall not be applicable to any dividend or similar distribution paid or payable pursuant to provisions of participating variable life insurance contracts.

(12) Sections 22(d), 22(e), and 27(c)(1) and Rule 22c–1 promulgated under section 22(c) to the extent:

(i) That the amount payable on death and the cash surrender value of each variable life insurance contract shall be determined on each day during which the New York Stock Exchange is open for trading, not less frequently than once daily as of the time of the close of trading on such exchange: *Provided,* That the amount payable on death need not be determined more than once each contract month if such determination does not reduce the participation of the contract in the investment experience of the separate account: *Provided further, however,* That if the net valuation premium for such contract is transferred at least annually, then the amount payable on death need be determined only when such net premium is transferred;

(ii) Necessary for compliance with this Rule 6e–2 or with insurance laws and regulations and established administrative procedures of the life insurer with respect to issuance, transfer and redemption procedures for variable life insurance contracts funded by the separate account including, but not limited to, premium rate structure and premium processing, insurance underwriting standards, and the particular benefit afforded by the contract: *Provided, however,* That any procedure or action shall be reasonable, fair and not discriminatory to the interests of the affected contractholder and to all other holders of contracts of the same class or series funded by the separate account: *And, further provided,* That any such action shall be disclosed in the form required to be filed by the separate account with the Commission pursuant to paragraph (b)(3)(ii) of this Rule 6e–2.

(13) Section 27 to the following extent:

(i) Sections 27(a)(1) and 27(h)(1) to the extent that the sales load, as defined in paragraph (c)(4) of this section, on any variable life insurance contract which is funded by the separate account shall not exceed 9 per centum of the payments to be made thereon during the period equal to the lesser of 20 years or the anticipated life expectancy of the insured named in the contract based on the 1958 Commissioners Standard Ordinary Mortality Table;

(ii) Sections 27(a)(3) and 27(h)(3): *Provided,* That the proportionate amount of sales load deducted from any payment during the contract period shall not exceed the proportionate amount deducted from any prior payment during the contract period except that such amount may exceed the amount deducted from a prior payment if the increase is caused by the grading of cash values into reserves or reductions in the annual cost of insurance;

(iii) Sections 27(c)(2), 26(a)(1) and 26(a)(2): *Provided,* That the life insurer complies, to the extent applicable, with all other provisions of section 26 as if it were a trustee, depositor or custodian for the separate account, and:

(A) Files with the insurance regulatory authority of a state or territory of the United States or of the District of Columbia an annual statement of its financial condition in the form prescribed by the National Association of Insurance Commissioners, which most recent statement indicates that it has a combined capital and surplus, if a stock company, or an unassigned surplus, if a mutual company, of not less than $1,000,000;

(B) Is examined from time to time by the insurance regulatory authority of such state, territory or District of Columbia as to its financial condition and other affairs and is subject to supervision and inspection with respect to its separate account operations; and

(C) Limits the fees for administrative services to amounts that are reasonable in relation to services rendered and expenses incurred. The Commission shall retain jurisdiction regarding the determination of such fees;

(iv) Section 27(c)(1) and section 27(d), to the extent that such sections require that the variable life insurance contract be redeemable or provide for a refund in cash: *Provided,* that such contract provides for election by the contractholder of a cash surrender value or certain nonforfeiture and settlement options which are required or permitted by the insurance law or regulation of the jurisdiction in which the contract is offered: *And further provided,* That unless required by the insurance law or regulation of the jurisdiction in which the contract is offered or unless elected by the contractholder, such contract shall not provide for the automatic imposition of any option, including, but not limited to, an automatic premium loan, which would involve the accrual or payment of an interest or similar charge;

(v) Section 27(d): *Provided,* That the variable life insurance contract gives the holder thereof the right to:

(A) Surrender the contract at any time during the first 24 months after issuance and receive in cash an amount not less than the sum of the present value of his contract which is the cash surrender value next computed after receipt by the life insurer of the request for surrender in proper form, plus, depending upon the period over which such contract has been retained by the contractholder, an amount which is a refund of any excess paid for sales loading prior to surrender: *Provided, however,* That if payments for the contract have not been duly paid on the date the request for surrender is received by the life insurer, and if the sum of the cash surrender value and the amount of any excess sales loading which would otherwise be refundable in cash were applied to provide (without sales loading) a non-forfeiture benefit in accordance with the contract, then the contractholder shall be entitled to receive in cash the present value, next computed after receipt by the life insurer of the request for surrender in proper form, of any non-forfeiture benefit then in force. The amount of sales loading to be refunded shall be equal to that part of the excess paid for sales loading which is over the sum of 30 per centum of payments made for the first contract year plus 10 per centum of the payments made for the second contract year; and

(B) Convert the contract at any time during the first 24 months after issuance so long as payments are duly made to a life insurance policy on the life of the insured which provides for fixed death benefits and cash surrender values pursuant to a plan of insurance specified in the contract issued by the life insurer, or by a life insurance company affiliated with such insurer, which provides for the same initial amount of insurance as the variable life insurance contract and premiums which are based on the same issue, age and risk classification of the insured as the variable life insurance contract, which conversion shall be subject to an equitable adjustment in payments and cash values to reflect variances, if any, in the payments and cash values under the original contract and the new policy: *Provided,* That the method of computing such adjustment shall be filed with the Commission as an exhibit to the form required pursuant to paragraph (b)(3)(ii) of this Rule;

(vi) A depositor or principal underwriter for a variable life insurance contract sold subject to section 27(d) or section 27(f) of the Act, or both, shall be exempt from the requirements of Rule 27d–1 if an insurance company undertakes in writing to guarantee the performance of all obligations of such depositor or principal underwriter under sections 27(d) and 27(f) of the Act to refund charges and such insurance company, depositor and principal underwriter comply with all provisions of Rule 27d–2;

(vii) Section 27(e) and Rule 27e–1 thereunder to the extent that the separate account and the depositor and principal underwriter therefor, when such persons are subject to paragraph (b)(13)(v) of this Rule, are required to provide a notice of right of withdrawal and refund to holders of variable life insurance contracts, if the life insurer or a duly authorized agent provides a notice of withdrawal and refund rights on Form N–27I–1, to the holder of any variable life insurance contract under which a refund may be available, provided that such notice shall be sent by first class mail to the contractholder:

(A) At issuance of the variable life insurance contract, which notice may be sent together with the issued variable life insurance contract and an illustration, in a form appropriate for inclusion in the prospectus for the variable life insurance contract, of gross annual payments, death benefits and cash surrender values applicable to the age, sex and underwriting classification of the insured; and

(B) If the contractholder has failed to make a payment prior to the expiration of the refund right provided by paragraph (b)(13)(v) of this Rule and the contract has not been reinstated within 30 days following the expiration of the grace period provided in the variable life insurance contract for making of any payment due: *Provided, however,* In any event, if a payment is not made when due such notice shall be sent not less than 15 days prior to the expiration of the refund right, which notice may be sent together with a notification that the payment is overdue or an offer to reinstate the contract;

(viii) Section 27(f) and Rule 27f–1: *Provided,* That:

(A) The contractholder may elect to return the contract within 45 days of the date of the execution of the application for insurance or within 10 days after receipt of the issued contract by the contractholder, or within 10 days after mailing of the notice of the right of withdrawal, whichever is later, and receive a refund of all payments made for such contract;

(B) A refund of all payments to redeeming contractholders will not in any way affect the interests in the separate account or the benefits of other variable life insurance contractholders;

(C) Notice of such withdrawal right and a statement of charges on Form N–27I–2 is sent by first class mail to the contractholder, which notice and statement may be accompanied by the variable life insurance contract and an illustration, in a form appropriate for inclusion in the prospectus for the variable life insurance contract, of payments, death benefits and cash surrender values applicable to the age, sex and underwriting classification of the insured;

(D) The contractholder, in conjunction with the notice of withdrawal right referred to in paragraph (b)(13)(viii)(C) of this rule, is provided with a form of request for refund of payments made, which form shall set forth;

(*1*) Instructions as to the manner in which a refund may be obtained including the address to which the request form should be mailed; and

(*2*) Spaces necessary to indicate the date of such request, the contract number and the signature of the contractholder; and

(E) Within 7 days from the receipt of such duly executed timely request for refund, the life insurer will refund in cash to the contractholder the entire amount of payments made on the contract;

(ix) Solely for purposes of paragraphs (b)(13)(v) and (b)(13)(viii) of this Rule, the postmark date on the envelope containing the variable life insurance contract shall determine whether such contract has been submitted for surrender or conversion within the designated period.

(14) Section 32(a)(2): *Provided,* That:

(i) The independent public accountant is selected before the effective date of the registration statement under the Securities Act of 1933, as amended, for variable life insurance contracts which are funded by the separate account, and the identity of such accountant is disclosed in such registration statement, and

(ii) The selection of such accountant is submitted for ratification or rejection to variable life insurance contractholders at their first meeting after the effective date of the registration statement under the Securities Act of 1933, as amended, on condition that such meeting shall take place within one year after such effective date, unless the time for the holding of such meeting shall be extended by the Commission upon written request for good cause shown.

(15) If the separate account is organized as a unit investment trust, all the assets of which consist of the shares of one or more registered management investment companies which offer their shares exclusively to variable life insurance separate accounts of the life insurer or of any affiliated life insurance company:

(i) The eligibility restrictions of section 9(a) of the Act shall not be applicable to those persons who are officers, directors and employees of the life insurer or its affiliates who do not participate directly in the management or administration of any registered management investment company described above;

(ii) The life insurer shall be ineligible pursuant to paragraph (3) of section 9(a) of the Act to serve as investment adviser of or principal underwriter for any registered management investment company described in this paragraph (b)(15) only if an affiliated person of such life insurer, ineligible by reason of paragraphs (1) or (2) of section 9(a), participates in the management or administration of such company;

(iii) The life insurer may vote shares of the registered management investment companies held by the separate account without regard to instructions from contractholders of the separate account if such instructions would require such shares to be voted:

(A) To cause such companies to make (or refrain from making) certain investments which would result in changes in the sub-classification or investment objectives of such companies or to approve or disapprove any contract between such companies and an investment adviser when required to do so by an insurance regulatory authority subject to the provisions of paragraphs (b)(5)(i) and (b)(7)(ii)(A) of this section; or

(B) In favor of changes in investment objectives, investment adviser of or principal underwriter for such companies subject to the provisions of paragraphs (b)(5)(ii) and (b)(7)(ii)(B) and (C) of this section;

(iv) Any action taken in accordance with paragraph (b)(15)(iii)(A) or (B) of this section and the reasons therefor shall be disclosed in the next report to contractholders made pursuant to section 30(e) (15 U.S.C. 80a–29(e)) and § 270.30e–2;

(v) Any registered management investment company established by the insurer and described in this paragraph (b)(15) shall be exempt from Section 14(a) provided that until such company has total assets of at least $100,000 the life insurer shall have at least the minimum net worth prescribed in paragraph (b)(6) above; and

(vi) Any registered management investment company established by the insurer and described in this paragraph (b)(15) shall be exempt from Sections 15(a), 16(a), and 32(a)(2) of the Act, to the extent prescribed by paragraphs (b)(7)(i), (b)(8)(i), and (b)(14), provided that such company complies with the conditions set forth in those paragraphs as if it were a separate account.

(c) When used in this Rule:

(1) "Variable life insurance contract" means a contract of life insurance, subject to regulation under the insurance laws or code of every jurisdiction in which it is offered, funded by a separate account of a life insurer, which contract, so long as payments are duly paid in accordance with its terms, provides for:

(i) A death benefit and cash surrender value which vary to reflect the investment experience of the separate account;

(ii) An initial stated dollar amount of death benefit, and payment of a death benefit guaranteed by the life insurer to be at least equal to such stated amount; and

(iii) Assumption of the mortality and expense risks thereunder by the life insurer for which a charge against the assets of the separate account may be assessed. Such charge shall be disclosed in the prospectus and shall not be less than fifty per centum of the maximum charge for risk assumption as disclosed in the prospectus and as provided for in the contract.

(2) "Incidental insurance benefits" means insurance benefits provided pursuant to the variable life insurance contract, other than the minimum and variable death benefit, which do not vary in amount or duration in accordance with the investment performance of the separate account, and include, but are not limited to, accidental death and dismemberment benefits, disability income benefits, guaranteed insurability options, and family income or fixed benefit term riders.

(3) "Minimum death benefit" is the amount guaranteed by the life insurer to be paid pursuant to a variable life insurance contract in the event of the death of the insured without regard to the investment performance of the separate account funding the variable life insurance contract, if payments are duly made and if there are no outstanding loans, partial withdrawals or partial surrenders, but does not include any incidental insurance benefits.

(4) "Sales load" charged on any payment is the excess of the payment over the sum of the following:

(i) The amount of the cash value for the first contract year, if any, and the amount of the increase in the cash value for each subsequent contract year, that is attributable to payments made and not attributable to investment earnings;

(ii) The cost of insurance for the period for which the payment is made based on the 1958 Commissioners Standard Ordinary Mortality Table and the assumed investment rate specified in the contract;

(iii) A reasonable charge necessary to cover the risk assumed by the life insurer that the variable death benefit will be less than the guaranteed minimum death benefit;

(iv) Any administrative expenses or fees which are reasonable and in amounts not exceeding anticipated administrative expenses and fees not properly chargeable to sales or promotional activities;

(v) A deduction approximately equal to state premium taxes;

(vi) Any additional charge assessed if the insured does not meet standard underwriting requirements;

(vii) Any additional charge assessed specifically for any incidental insurance benefits which do not vary in relation to the performance of the separate account;

(viii) Any additional charge, in the nature of an interest or service charge or administrative fee, assessed when payments are made more frequently than annually;

(ix) For a participating variable life insurance contract, a deduction for dividends to be paid or credited in accordance with the dividend scale in effect on the issue date of the contract assuming a gross annual investment return for the separate account which funds such contract of 4 percent after deduction for any Federal income taxes, which deduction may be determined pursuant to either of the following methods, provided that the same method must be applied with respect to each payment under the contract:

(A) The actuarial level annual equivalent of dividends to be paid or credited over the period described in paragraph (b)(13)(i) of this Rule, based upon the mortality, interest and lapse assumptions used in computing the dividend scale for such contract multiplied by the fraction of the contract year for which the payment is made; or

(B) That portion of the dividend to be paid for the contract year which does not depend on the making of additional payments.

(5) "Assumed investment rate" is the rate of investment return specified in the contract which would be required to be credited to a variable life insurance contract, after deduction of charges for federal income taxes, investment management fees, portfolio transaction expenses and mortality and expense guarantees, to maintain the variable death benefit equal at all times to the amount of death benefit, other than incidental insurance benefits, which would be payable pursuant to the variable life insurance contract if the death benefit did not vary according to the investment experience of the separate account.

(6) "Variable death benefit" is the amount of death benefit, other than incidental insurance benefits, payable under a variable life insurance contract which varies to reflect the investment performance of the separate account, and which would be payable in the absence of the minimum death benefit.

(7) "Payment," as used in paragraphs (b)(13)(i), (b)(13)(ii) and (b)(13)(v)(A) of this Rule and in sections 27(a)(2) and 27(h)(2) solely with respect to variable life insurance contracts, means the gross premium payment made less any portion of such gross premium charged for or attributable to the items specified in paragraphs (c)(4)(vi), (c)(4)(vii) and (c)(4)(viii) of this Rule. "Payment," as used in any other section of the Rule, means the gross premiums paid or payable for the variable life insurance contract.

§ 270.6e-3(T) Temporary Exemptions for Flexible Premium Variable Life Insurance Separate Accounts

(a) A separate account, and its investment adviser, principal underwriter and depositor, shall, except as provided in paragraph (b) of this Rule, comply with all provisions of the Investment Company Act of 1940 and the rules under it that apply to a registered investment company issuing periodic payment play certificates if:

(1) It is a separate account within the meaning of section 2(a)(37) of the Act and is established and maintained by a life insurance company pursuant to the insurance laws or code of (i) any state or territory of the United States or the District of Columbia, or (ii) Canada or any province thereof, if it complies with Rule 7d-1 under the Act (the "life insurer");

(2) The assets of the separate account are derived solely from (i) the sale of flexible premium variable life insurance contracts ("flexible contracts") as defined in paragraph (c)(1) of this Rule, (ii) the sale of scheduled premium variable life insurance contracts ("scheduled contracts") as defined in paragraph (c)(1) of Rule 6e-2 under the Act, (iii) funds corresponding to dividend accumulations with respect to such contracts, and (iv) advances made by the life insurer in connection with the operation of such separate account;

(3) The separate account is not used for variable annuity contracts or other contract liabilities not involving life contingencies;

(4) The separate account is legally segregated, and that part of its assets with a value approximately equal to the reserves and other contract liabilities for such separate account are not chargeable with liabilities arising from any other business of the life insurer;

(5) The value of the assets of the separate account, each time adjustments in the reserves are made, is at least equal to the reserves and other contract liabilities of the separate account, and at all other times approximately equals or exceeds the reserves and liabilities; and

(6) The investment adviser of the separate account is registered under the Investment Advisers Act of 1940.

(b) A separate account that meets the requirements of paragraph (a) of this Rule, and its investment adviser, principal underwriter and depositor shall be exempt with respect to flexible contracts funded by the separate account from the following provisions of the Act:

(1) Section 2(a)(35), *Provided, however,* That the term "sales load," as used in the Act and rules under it, shall have the meaning set forth in paragraph (c)(4) of this Rule. *And provided further,* That in connection with any sales load deducted pursuant to paragraph (d)(1) of this Rule, the separate account and other persons shall be exempt from sections 2(a)(32), 12(b), 22(c), 26(a), 27(c)(1), 27(c)(2), and 27(d), and Rules 12b–1 and 22c–1.

(2) Section 7.

(3) Section 8, to the extent that:

(i) For purposes of paragraph (a) of section 8, the separate account filed with the Commission a notification on Form N–6EI–1 which identifies the separate account; and

(ii) For purposes of paragraph (b) of section 8, the separate account shall file with the Commission the form designated by the Commission within ninety days after filing the notification on Form N–6EI–1, *Provided, however,* That if the fiscal year of the separate account end within this ninety day period, the form may be filed within ninety days after the end of such fiscal year.

(4) Section 9, to the extent that:

(i) The eligibility restrictions of section 9(a) shall not apply to persons who are officers, directors or employees of the life insurer or its affiliates and who do not participate directly in the management or administration of the separate account or in the sale of flexible contracts; and

(ii) A life insurer shall be ineligible under paragraph (3) of section 9(a) to serve as investment adviser, depositor of or principal underwriter for the separate account only if an affiliated person of such life insurer, ineligible by reason of paragraphs (1) or (2) of section 9(a), participates directly in the management or administration of the separate account or in the sale of flexible contracts.

(5) Section 13(a), to the extent that:

(i) An insurance regulatory authority may require pursuant to insurance law or regulation that the separate account make (or refrain from making) certain investments which would result in changes in the sub-classification or investment policies of the separate account;

(ii) Changes in the investment policy of the separate account initiated by its contractholders or board of directors may be disapproved by the life insurer, if the disapproval is reasonable and is based on a good faith determination by the life insurer that:

(A) The change would violate state law; or

(B) The change would not be consistent with the investment objectives of the separate account or would result in the purchase of securities for the separate account which vary from the general quality and nature of investments and investment techniques used by other separate accounts of the life insurer or of an affiliated life insurance company with similar investment objectives;

(iii) Any action described in paragraph (b)(5)(i) or (ii) of this Rule and the reasons for it shall be disclosed in the next communication to contractholders, but in no case, later than twelve months from the date of such action.

(6) Section 14(a), *Provided,* That until the separate account has total assets of at least $100,000, the life insurer shall have (i) a combined capital and surplus, if a stock company, or (ii) an unassigned surplus, if a mutual company, of not less than $1,000,000 as set forth in the balance sheet of such life insurer contained in the registration statement for flexible contracts filed under the Securities Act of 1933.

(7)(i) Section 15(a), to the extent it requires that the initial written contract with the investment adviser shall have been approved by the vote of a majority of the outstanding voting securities of the registered investment company, *Provided,* That:

(A) The investment adviser is selected and a written contract is entered into before the effective date of the 1933 Act registration statement for flexible contracts, and that the terms of the contract are fully disclosed in the registration statement, and

(B) A written contract is submitted to a vote of contractholders at their first meeting and within one year after the effective date of the 1933 Act registration statement, unless the Commission upon written request and for good cause shown extends the time for the holding of such meeting;

(ii) Sections 15(a), (b) and (c), to the extent that:

(A) An insurance regulatory authority may disapprove pursuant to insurance law or regulation any contract between the separate account and an investment adviser or principal underwriter;

(B) Changes in the principal underwriter for the separate account initiated by contractholders or the board of directors of the separate account may be disapproved by the life insurer, *Provided,* That such disapproval is reasonable;

(C) Changes in the investment adviser of the separate account initiated by contractholders or the board of directors of the separate account may be disapproved by the life insurer, *Provided,* That such disapproval is reasonable and is based on a good faith determination by the life insurer that:

(*1*) The proposed investment advisory fee will exceed the maximum rate specified in any flexible contract that may be charged against the assets of the separate account for such services; or

(*2*) The proposed investment adviser may be expected to employ investment techniques which vary from the general techniques used by the current investment adviser to the separate account, or advise the purchase or sale of securities which would not be consistent with the investment objectives of the separate account, or which would vary from the quality and nature of investments made by other separate accounts with similar investment objectives of the life insurer or an affiliated life insurance company;

(D) Any action described in paragraph (b)(7)(ii)(A), (B) or (C) of this Rule and the reasons for it shall be disclosed in the next communication to contractholders, but in no case, later than twelve months from the date of such action.

(8) Section 16(a), to the extent that:

(i) Directors of the separate account serving before the first meeting of the account's contractholders are exempt from the requirement of section 16(a) that they be elected by the holders of outstanding voting securities of the account at an annual or special meeting called for that purpose, *Provided,* That:

(A) Such persons were appointed directors of the account by the life insurer before the effective date of the 1933 Act registration statement for flexible contracts and are identified in the registration statement (or are replacements appointed by the life insurer for any such persons who have become unable to serve as directors), and

(B) An election of directors for the account is held at the first meeting of contractholders and within one year after the effective date of the 1933 Act registration statement for flexible contracts, unless the time for holding the meeting is extended by the Commission upon written request and for good cause shown;

(ii) A member of the board of directors of the separate account may be disapproved or removed by an insurance regulatory authority if the person is not eligible to be a director of the separate account under the law of the life insurer's domicile.

(9) Section 17(f), to the extent that the securities and similar investments of a separate account organized as a management investment company may be maintained in the custody of the life insurer or of an affiliated life insurance company, *Provided,* That:

(i) The securities and similar investments allocated to the separate account are clearly identified as owned by the account, and the securities and similar investments are kept in the vault of an insurance company which meets the qualifications in paragraph (b)(9)(ii) of this Rule, and whose safekeeping function is supervised by the insurance regulatory authorities of the jurisdiction in which the securities and similar investments will be held;

(ii) The insurance company maintaining such investments must file with an insurance regulatory authority of a state or territory of the United States or the District of Columbia an annual statement of its financial condition in the form prescribed by the National Association of Insurance Commissioners, must be subject to supervision and inspection by such authority and must be examined periodically as to its financial condition and other affairs by such authority, must hold the securities and similar investments of the separate account in its vault, which vault must be equivalent to that of a bank which is a member of the Federal Reserve System, and must have a combined capital and surplus, if a stock company, or an unassigned surplus, if a mutual company, of not less than $1,000,000 as set forth in its most recent annual statement filed with such authority;

(iii) Access to such securities and similar investments shall be limited to employees of the Commission, representatives of insurance regulatory authorities, independent public accountants retained by the separate account (or on its behalf by the life insurer), accountants for the life insurer, and to no more than 20 persons authorized by a resolution of the board of directors of the separate account, which persons shall be directors of the separate account, officers and responsible employees of the life insurer or officers and responsible employees of the affiliated life insurance company in whose vault the investments are kept (if applicable), and access to such securities and similar investments shall be had only by two or more such persons jointly, at least one of whom shall be a director of the separate account or officer of the life insurer;

(iv) The requirement in paragraph (b)(9)(i) of this Rule that the securities and similar investments of the separate account be maintained in the vault of a qualified insurance company shall not apply to securities deposited with insurance regulatory authorities or deposited in accordance with any rule under section 17(f), or to securities on loan which are collateralized to the extent of their full market value, or to securities hypothecated, pledged, or placed in escrow for the account of such separate account in connection with a loan or other transaction authorized by specific resolution of the board of directors of the separate account, or to securities in transit in connection with the sale, exchange, redemption, maturity or conversion, the exercise of warrants or rights, assents to changes in terms of the securities, or to other transactions necessary or appropriate in the ordinary course of business relating to the management of securities;

(v) Each person when depositing such securities or similar investments in or withdrawing them from the depository or when ordering their withdrawal and delivery from the custody of the life insurer or affiliated life insurance company, shall sign a notation showing (A) the date and time of the deposit, withdrawal or order, (B) the title and amount of the securities or other investments deposited, withdrawn or ordered to be withdrawn, and an identification thereof by certificate numbers or otherwise, (C) the manner of acquisition of the securities or similar investments deposited or the purpose for which they have been withdrawn, or ordered to be withdrawn, and (D) if withdrawn and delivered to another person, the name of such person. The notation shall be sent promptly to an officer or director of the separate account or the life insurer designated by the board of directors of the separate account who is not himself permitted to have access to the securities or investments under paragraph (b)(9)(iii) of this Rule. The notation shall be on serially numbered forms and shall be kept for at least one year;

(vi) The securities and similar investments shall be verified by complete examination by an independent public accountant retained by the separate account (or on its behalf by the life insurer) at least three times each fiscal year, at least two of which shall be chosen by the accountant without prior notice to the separate account. A certificate of the accountant stating that he has made an examination of such securities and investments and describing the nature and extent of the examination shall be sent to the Commission by the accountant promptly after each examination;

(vii) Securities and similar investments of a separate account maintained with a bank or other company whose functions and physical facilities are supervised by federal or state authorities under any arrangement whereby the directors, officers, employees or agents of the separate account or the life insurer are authorized or permitted to withdraw such investments upon their mere receipt are deemed to be in the custody of the life insurer and shall be exempt from the requirements of Section 17(f) so long as the arrangement complies with all provisions of this paragraph (b)(9), except that such securities will be maintained in the vault of a bank or other company rather than the vault of an insurance company.

(10) Section 18(i), to the extent that:

(i) For the purposes of any section of the Act which provides for the vote of securityholders on matters relating to the investment company:

(A) Flexible contractholders shall have one vote for each $100 of cash value funded by the separate account, with fractional votes allocated for amounts less than $100;

(B) The life insurer shall have one vote for each $100 of assets of the separate account not otherwise attributable to contractholders under paragraph (b)(10)(i)(A) of this Rule, with fractional votes allocated for amounts less than $100, *Provided,* That after the commencement of sales of flexible contracts, the life insurer shall cast its votes for and against each matter which may be voted upon by contractholders in the same proportion as the votes cast by contractholders; and

(C) The number of votes to be allocated shall be determined as of a record date not more than 90 days before any meeting at which such vote is held, *Provided,* That if a quorum is not present at the meeting, the meeting may be adjourned for up to 60 days without fixing a new record date;

(ii) The requirement of this section that every share of stock issued by a registered management investment company (except a common-law trust of the character described in section 16(c)) shall be a voting stock and have equal voting rights with every other outstanding voting stock shall not be deemed to be violated by actions specifically permitted by any provisions of this Rule.

(11) Section 19, to the extent that the provisions of this section shall not apply to any dividend or similar distribution paid or payable under provisions of participating flexible contracts.

(12) Sections 22(c), 22(d), 22(e), and 27(c)(1) and Rule 22c–1 to the extent:

(i) The cash value of each flexible contract shall be computed in accordance with Rule 22c–1(b) under the Act; *Provided, however,* That where actual computation is not necessary for the operation of a particular contract, then the cash value of that contract must only be capable of computation; *And provided further,* That to the extent the calculation of the cash value reflects deductions for the cost of insurance and other insurance benefits or administrative expenses and fees or sales loads, such deductions need only be made at such times as specified in the contract or as necessary for compliance with insurance laws and regulations; and

(ii) The death benefit, unless required by insurance laws and regulations, shall be computed on any day that the investment experience of the separate account would affect the death benefit under the terms of the contract provided that such terms are reasonable, fair, and nondiscriminatory;

(iii) Necessary to comply with this Rule or with insurance laws and regulations and established administrative procedures of the life insurer for issuance, increases in or additions of insurance benefits, transfer and redemption of flexible contracts, including, but not limited to, premium rate structure and premium processing, insurance underwriting standards, and the particular benefit afforded by the contract, *Provided, however,* That any procedure or action shall be reasonable, fair and not discriminatory to the interests of the affected contractholders and to all other holders of contracts of the same class or series funded by the separate account, *And provided further,* That any such action shall be disclosed in the form filed by the separate account with the Commission under paragraph (b)(3)(ii) of this Rule.

(13) Section 27, to the following extent:

(i) Sections 27(a)(1), 27(h)(1), and 27(h)(4), to the extent that sales load, as defined in paragraph (c)(4) of this Rule, deducted does not exceed that permitted by either subparagraph (A) or (B) below:

(A) 9 per centum of the sum of the guideline annual premiums that would be paid during the period equal to the lesser of 20 years or the anticipated life expectancy of the insured named in the contract based on the 1980 Commissioners Standard Ordinary Mortality Table, *Provided,* That this subparagraph (b)(13)(i)(A) shall not prohibit deduction of sales load, in any manner permitted by this Rule, from payments made in excess of the sum of the guideline annual premiums that would be paid during the lesser of 20 years or the anticipated life expectancy of the insured based on the 1980 Commissioners Standard Ordinary Mortality Table; or

(B) 9 per centum of payments made thereon; *Provided,* That the separate account elects by written notice to the Commission to be governed (with respect to each class of flexible contract offered) by either subparagraph (b)(13)(i)(A) or (B); *Provided, however,* That for each class of flexible contract that requires more than four guideline annual premiums within the first two contract periods following issuance of the contract or of an increase in or addition of insurance benefits (within the meaning of paragraph (d)(2)), the separate account must elect to be governed by subparagraph (b)(13)(i)(B).

(ii) Sections 27(a)(3) and 27(h)(3), *Provided,* That the proportionate amount of sales load deducted from any payment shall not exceed the proportionate amount deducted from any prior payment unless an increase is caused by reductions in the annual cost of insurance, or a reduction in the sales load deducted from amounts transferred to a flexible contract from another plan of insurance;

(iii) Sections 27(c)(2), 26(a)(1), and 26(a)(2), to the extent necessary to permit the actions described in paragraphs (A) through (F) of this section, *Provided,* That the life insurer complies with all other applicable provisions of Section 26 as if it were a trustee, depositor or custodian for the separate account; files with the insurance regulatory authority of a state or territory of the United States or of the District of Columbia an annual statement of its financial condition in the form prescribed by the National Association of Insurance Commissioners, which most recent statement indicates that it has a combined capital and surplus, if a stock company, or an unassigned surplus, if a mutual company, of not less than $1,000,000; and is examined from time to time by the insurance regulatory authority of such state, territory or District of Columbia as to its financial condition and other affairs and is subject to supervision and inspection with respect to its separate account operations.

(A) Payment of a fee to the life insurer, or to any affiliated person or agent of the insurer, for bookkeeping or other administrative services provided to the separate account, or for administrative services or expenses incurred in underwriting, issuing, and maintaining flexible contracts, *Provided,* That the fee is not greater than the expenses, without profit:

(*1*) Actually paid by the life insurer for the services provided; and

(*2*) Increased by the value of any services provided directly by the life insurer, as determined in accordance with generally accepted accounting principles consistently applied. The standard set forth in this paragraph shall be applied as follows: if the separate account reserves the right to increase the fee, the fee shall not exceed the cost of the services to be provided for one year; or if the fee is guaranteed not to increase for a specified period of time, the fee shall not exceed the average expected cost of the services to be provided during the period of the guarantee;

(B) The holding of the assets of the separate account by the life insurer without a trust indenture or other such instrument;

(C) When the separate account is organized as a unit investment trust, the holding of the securities of any registered management investment company which offers its shares to the separate account in uncertificated form;

(D) When the separate account is organized as a management investment company, the holding of its assets in any manner permitted by paragraph (b)(9) of this Rule or by section 17(f) or the rules under it;

(E) The deduction of premium or other taxes imposed by any state or other governmental entity, the cost of insurance, charges assessed for incidental insurance benefits or if the insured does not meet standard underwriting requirements, and, if the separate account is organized as a management investment company, an investment advisory fee;

(F) The deduction of a charge for mortality, expense, and any guaranteed death benefit risks assumed by the life insurer under the flexible contracts (collectively, a "risk charge"), *Provided,* That the registration statement under the 1933 Act for flexible contracts includes:

(*1*) A representation that this paragraph is being relied upon;

(*2*) A representation that the level of the risk charge either is:

(*i*) Within the range of industry practice for comparable flexible or scheduled contracts, or

(*ii*) Reasonable in relation to the risks assumed by the life insurer under the contracts;

(*3*) A brief description of the methodology used to support the representation made in response to paragraph (b)(13)(iii)(F)(*2*) of this Rule and an undertaking to keep and make available to the Commission upon request the documents used to support that representation;

(*4*) A representation that either:

(*i*) The proceeds from explicit sales loads will be sufficient to cover the expected costs of distributing the flexible contracts; or

(*ii*)(*A*) The life insurer has concluded that there is a reasonable likelihood that the distribution financing arrangement of the separate account will benefit the separate account and contractholders and will keep and make available to the Commission on request a memorandum setting forth the basis for this representation; and

(*B*) If the separate account is organized as a management investment company, a representation that the account will have a board of directors, a majority of whom are not interested persons of the separate account, formulate and approve any plan under Rule 12b–1 to finance distribution expenses. If the separate account is organized as a unit investment trust, a representation that the account will invest only in management investment companies which have undertaken to have a board of directors, a majority of whom are not interested persons of the company, formulate and approve any plan under Rule 12b–1 to finance distribution expenses.

Notwithstanding the provisions of this paragraph (b)(13)(iii)(F), no risk charge may be deducted in reliance thereupon if the registration statement or amendment thereto which initially sets forth the deduction of such charge or its increase becomes effective by lapse of time pursuant to section 8(a) of the 1933 Act or Rule 485 thereunder. Such charge shall be disclosed in the prospectus and shall not be less than fifty per centum of the maximum charge for risk assumption as disclosed in the prospectus and as provided for in the contract. Any separate account organized under the Act as a management investment company and deducting a risk charge pursuant to this section shall be exempt from section 12(b) and Rule 12b–1 thereunder to the extent that monies derived from the risk charge may be used to finance distribution of the flexible contracts;

(iv) Sections 27(c)(1) and 27(d), and sections 2(a)(32) and 22(c) and Rule 22c–1 thereunder, to the extent that:

(A) Such sections require that the flexible contract be redeemable or provide for a refund in cash, *Provided,* That the contract provides for election by the contractholder of a cash surrender value or certain non-forfeiture and settlement options which are required or permitted by the insurance law or regulation of the jurisdiction in which the contract is offered, *and provided further,* That unless required by the insurance law or regulation of the jurisdiction in which the contract is offered or unless elected by the contractholder, the contract shall not provide for the automatic imposition of any option, including, but not limited to, an automatic premium loan, which would involve the accrual or payment of an interest or similar charge.

(B) Notwithstanding the provisions of paragraph (b)(13)(iv)(A) of this Rule, if the amounts available under the contract to pay the charges due under the contract on any contract processing day are less than such charges due, the contract may provide that the cash surrender value (and any excess paid for sales loading not used to keep the contract in force pursuant to paragraph (b)(13)(iv)(B)(*2*) of this Rule) shall be applied to purchase a non-forfeiture option specified by the life insurer in such contract, *Provided,* That the contract also provides that:

(*1*) Contract processing days occur not less frequently than monthly, and

(*2*) the amount of any excess paid for sales loading (as provided in paragraph (b)(13)(v)(A) of this Rule) shall first be applied to keep the contract in force, *Provided, however,* That if the contractholder subsequently makes a payment, the life insurer may recover such excess loading;

(C) Subject to other provisions of this Rule, sales loads and administrative expenses or fees may be deducted upon redemption.

(v) Section 27(d), *Provided,* That the flexible contract gives the holder thereof the right to:

(A) Surrender the contract at any time during the first 24 months after issuance and receive in cash an amount not less than the sum of the present value of his contract which is the cash surrender value next computed after receipt by the life insurer of the request for surrender in proper form, plus, an amount which is a refund of any excess paid for sales loading prior to or in connection with the surrender. The amount of sales loading to be refunded shall be equal to that part of the sales loading in excess of (1) the sum of 30 per centum of payments in aggregate amount less than or equal to one guideline annual premium, plus 10 per centum of payments in aggregate amount greater than one guideline annual premium but not more than two guideline annual premiums, and (2) 9 per centum of each payment made in excess of two guideline annual premiums;

(B) Convert the contract at any time during the first 24 months after issuance, so long as the contract is in force, to a life insurance policy on the life of the insured under a plan of insurance (other than a plan involving a flexible contract as defined in paragraph (c)(1) of this Rule or a scheduled contract as defined in paragraph (c)(1) of Rule 6e–2) specified in the contract, issued by the life insurer or by an affiliated life insurance company, which provides for *(1)* at the election of the contractholder, either the same death benefit or the same net amount at risk as the flexible contract at the time of conversion and *(2)* premiums (or cost of insurance or other charges, ("charges") if such plan of insurance provides for flexible premiums) which are based on the same issue age and risk classification of the insured as the flexible contract. The conversion shall be subject to an equitable adjustment in payments and cash values to reflect variances, if any, in the payments (or charges), dividends, and cash values under the flexible contract and the new policy. The method of computing such adjustment shall be filed with the Commission as an exhibit to the form required under paragraph (b)(3)(ii) of this Rule;

(vi) A depositor or principal underwriter for a flexible contract sold subject to section 27(d) or section 27(f), or both, shall be exempt from the requirements of Rule 27d–1 if an insurance company undertakes in writing to guarantee the performance of all obligations of such depositor or principal underwriter under sections 27(d) and 27(f) to refund charges, and such insurance company, depositor and principal underwriter comply with all provisions of Rule 27d–2;

(vii) Section 27(e) and Rule 27e–1 thereunder, to the extent that the separate account and the depositor and principal underwriter therefor, when such persons are subject to paragraph (b)(13)(v)(A) of this Rule, are required to provide a notice of right of surrender and refund to holders of flexible contracts, if the life insurer or a duly authorized agent provides a notice of surrender and refund rights on a written document containing information comparable to that required by Form N–27I–1 to the holder of any flexible contract under which a refund may be available, *Provided,* That such notice shall be sent by first class mail or personal delivery to the contractholder:

(A) Upon issuance of the flexible contract, which notice may be sent together with the issued contract and an illustration, in a form appropriate for inclusion in the prospectus for the flexible contract, of guideline annual premiums, death benefits and cash surrender values applicable to the age, sex and underwriting classification of the insured; and

(B) On any contract processing day, prior to the expiration of the surrender and refund right provided in paragraph (b)(13)(v)(A) of this Rule, on which the amounts available under the contract on such day to pay the charges authorized by the contract are less than the amount necessary to keep the contract in force until the next following contract processing day. This notice may be sent together with any notice required by applicable state authority to be sent in these circumstances; *Provided, however,* That the right of surrender and refund provided by paragraph (b)(13)(v)(A) of this Rule shall not expire until not less than 15 days after the mailing or receipt, if personally delivered, of the last notice referred to in this paragraph (b)(13)(vii)(B);

(viii) Section 27(f) and Rule 27f-1 thereunder, *Provided,* That:

(A) The contractholder may elect to return the contract within 45 days of the date of the execution of the application for insurance, or within 10 days after receipt of the issued contract by the contractholder, or within 10 days after mailing or personal delivery of the notice of the right of withdrawal referred to in paragraph (b)(13)(viii)(C) of this Rule, whichever is later, and receive a refund equal to the sum of (*1*) the difference between the payments made, including any contract fees or other charges, and the amounts allocated to the separate account under the contract, (*2*) the value of the amounts allocated to the separate account under the contract on the date the returned contract is received by the insurer or its agent, and (*3*) any contract fees and other changes imposed on the amounts allocated to such separate account, *Provided, however,* That if state law or the contract so require, the redeeming contractholder shall receive a refund of all payments made for such contract;

(B) A refund in accordance with paragraph (b)(13)(viii)(A) of this Rule to redeeming contractholders will not in any way affect the interests in the separate account or the benefits of other flexible or scheduled contractholders;

(C) Notice of such withdrawal right and a statement of contract fees and other charges on a written document containing information comparable to that required by Form N-27I-2 is sent by first class mail or personal delivery to the contractholder, which notice and statement may be accompanied by the flexible contract, and an illustration, in a form appropriate for inclusion in the prospectus for the flexible contract, of guideline annual premiums (or, if the contract is subject to paragraph (b)(13)(i)(B), payments), death benefits and cash surrender values applicable to the age, sex and underwriting classification of the insured;

(D) The contractholder, in conjunction with the notice of withdrawal right referred to in paragraph (b)(13)(viii)(C), is provided with a form of request for refund of the amount computed in accordance with paragraph (b)(13)(viii)(A), which form shall set forth:

(*1*) Instructions as to the manner in which a refund may be obtained, including the address to which the request form should be mailed; and

(*2*) Spaces necessary to indicate the date of such request, the contract number and the signature of the contractholder; and

(E) Within 7 days from the receipt of such duly executed timely request for refund, the life insurer will refund in cash to the contractholder the amount computed in accordance with paragraph (b)(13)(viii)(A) of this Rule; and

(ix) Solely for purposes of paragraphs (b)(13)(v) and (b)(13)(viii) of this Rule, the postmark date on the envelope containing the flexible contract shall determine whether such contract has been submitted for surrender, conversion, or withdrawal within the designated period.

(14) Section 32(a)(2), *Provided,* That:

(i) The independent public accountant is selected before the effective date of the 1933 Act registration statement for flexible contracts, and the identity of the accountant is disclosed in the registration statement, and

(ii) The selection of the accountant is submitted for ratification or rejection to flexible contractholders at their first meeting and within one year after the effective date of the 1933 Act registration statement for flexible contracts, unless the time for holding the meeting is extended by order of the Commission.

(15) If the separate account is organized as a unit investment trust, all the assets of which consist of the shares of one or more registered management investment companies which offer their shares exclusively to separate accounts of the life insurer, or of any affiliated life insurance company, offering either scheduled contracts or flexible contracts, or both; or which also offer their shares to variable annuity separate accounts of the life insurer or of an affiliated life insurance company, or which offer their shares to any such life insurance company in consideration solely for advances made by the life insurer in connection with the operation of the separate account; *Provided,* That: the board of directors of each investment company, constituted with a majority of disinterested directors, will monitor such company for the existence of any material irreconcilable conflict between the interests of variable annuity contractholders and scheduled or flexible contractholders investing in such company; the life insurer agrees that it will be responsible for reporting any potential or existing conflicts to the directors; and if a conflict arises, the life insurer will, at its own cost, remedy such conflict up to and including establishing a new registered management investment company and segregating the assets underlying the variable annuity contracts and the scheduled or flexible contracts; Then:

(i) The eligibility restrictions of section 9(a) shall not apply to those persons who are officers, directors or employees of the life insurer or its affiliates who do not participate directly in the management or administration of any registered management investment company described in this paragraph (b)(15);

(ii) The life insurer shall be ineligible under paragraph (3) of section 9(a) to serve as investment adviser of or principal underwriter for any registered management investment company described in this paragraph (b)(15) only if an affiliated person of such life insurer, ineligible by reason of paragraphs (1) or (2) of section 9(a), participates in the management or administration of such company;

(iii) For purposes of any section of the Act which provides for the vote of securityholders on matters relating to the separate account or the underlying registered investment company, the voting provisions of paragraph (b)(10)(i) and (ii) of this Rule apply, *Provided,* That:

(A) The life insurer may vote shares of the registered management investment companies held by the separate account without regard to instructions from contractholders of the separate account if such instructions would require such shares to be voted:

(*1*) To cause such companies to make (or refrain from making) certain investments which would result in changes in the sub-classification or investment objectives of such companies or to approve or disapprove any contract between such companies and an investment adviser when required to do so by an insurance regulatory authority subject to the provisions of paragraphs (b)(5)(i) and (b)(7)(ii)(A) of this Rule; or

(*2*) In favor of changes in investment objectives, investment adviser of or principal underwriter for such companies subject to the provisions of paragraphs (b)(5)(ii) and (b)(7)(ii)(B) and (C) of this Rule;

(B) Any action taken in accordance with paragraph (b)(15)(iii)(A)(1) or (2) of this section and the reasons therefor shall be disclosed in the next report contractholders made under section 30(e) (15 U.S.C. 80a–29(e)) and § 270.30e–2;

(iv) Any registered management investment company established by the life insurer and described in this paragraph (b)(15) shall be exempt from section 14(a), *Provided,* That until the company has total assets of at least $100,000, the life insurer shall have at least the minimum net worth prescribed in paragraph (b)(6) of this Rule; and

(v) Any registered management investment company established by the life insurer and described in this paragraph (b)(15) shall be exempt from sections 15(a), 16(a), and 32(a)(2), to the extent prescribed by paragraphs (b)(7)(i), (b)(8)(i), and (b)(14) of this Rule, *Provided,* That the company complies with the conditions set forth in those paragraphs as if it were a separate account.

(c) When used in this Rule:

(1) "Flexible premium variable life insurance contract" means a contract of life insurance, subject to regulation under the insurance laws or code of every jurisdiction in which it is offered, funded by a separate account of a life insurer, which contract provides for:

(i) Payments which are not fixed by the life insurer as to both timing and amount: *Provided, however,* That the life insurer may fix the timing and minimum amount of payments for the first two contract periods following issuance of the contract or of an increase in or addition of insurance benefits (within the meaning of paragraph (d)(2)), and may prescribe a reasonable minimum amount for any additional payment;

(ii) A death benefit the amount or duration of which may vary to reflect the investment experience of the separate account;

(iii) A cash value which varies to reflect the investment experience of the separate account; and

(iv) There is a reasonable expectation that subsequent payments will be made.

(2) "Incidental insurance benefits" means insurance benefits provided pursuant to the flexible contract, other than any guaranteed and variable death benefit, which do not have discrete cash values that may vary in amount in accordance with the investment experience of the separate account, and include, but are not limited to, accidental death and dismemberment benefits, disability income benefits, guaranteed insurability options, and family income or fixed benefit term riders.

(3) "Guaranteed death benefit" is any amount guaranteed by the life insurer to be paid pursuant to a flexible contract in the event of the death of the insured without regard to the investment experience of the separate account, if there are no outstanding loans or partial surrenders, but does not include any incidental insurance benefits.

(4) "Sales load" charged during a contract period is the excess of any payments made during the period over the sum of the following:

(i) The amount of the change (whether it is an increase or decrease) in the cash value for the period that is not attributable to net investment earnings or to dividends for a participating flexible contract for the period;

(ii) The cost of insurance for the period based on:

(A) For a flexible contract subject to paragraph (b)(13)(i)(A), the 1980 Commissioners Standard Ordinary Mortality Table and net interest at the annual effective rate specified for purposes of paragraph (c)(8)(i)(B) of this Rule; or

(B) For a flexible contract subject to paragraph (b)(13)(i)(B), either the 1980 Commissioners Standard Ordinary Mortality Table or the 1958 Commissioners Ordinary Mortality Table (whichever relates to rates guaranteed by the contract) and the assumed investment rate specified in the contract, *Provided, however,* That the 1958 Commissioners Ordinary Mortality Table may only be used for those contracts issued before 1990, or such earlier mandatory date for implementation of the 1980 Commissioners Standard Ordinary Mortality Table under the applicable Standard Nonforfeiture Law for life insurance;

(iii) A reasonable charge necessary to cover the risk assumed by the life insurer that the variable death benefit will be less than any guaranteed death benefit;

(iv) Any administrative expenses or fees which are deducted pursuant to paragraph (b)(13)(iii)(A) of this Rule;

(v) A deduction for and approximately equal to state premium taxes;

(vi) Any additional charge assessed if the insured does not meet standard underwriting requirements, including, but not limited to, any additional cost of insurance charge for a contract purchased on a simplified underwriting or guaranteed issue basis;

(vii) Any additional charge assessed specifically for any incidental insurance benefits;

(viii) Any additional charge, the nature of an interest charge, assessed when payments are made more frequently than annually, but only to the extent that such payments are made to fulfill a minimum payment requirement imposed pursuant to paragraph (c)(1)(i) of this Rule;

(ix) Any amounts redeemed by the contractholder or paid out to the beneficiary upon the death of the insured which are not attributable to net investment earnings for the period; and

(x) For a participating flexible contract, a deduction for dividends to be paid or credited in accordance with the dividend scale in effect on the issue date of the contract assuming a net annual investment return for the separate account which funds the contract of 5 per centum. The deduction may be determined by either of the following methods, but the same method must be used for each contract period:

(A) The actuarial level annual equivalent of dividends to be paid or credited over the contract periods described in paragraph (b)(13)(i) of this Rule, based upon the mortality, interest and lapse assumptions used in computing the dividend scale for the contract (and, if the contract is subject to paragraph (b)(13)(i)(A), the assumption that the guideline annual premium will be paid in each contract period) multiplied by the fraction of the contract year represented by the contract period; or

(B) That portion of the dividend to be paid for the contract year which does not depend on the making of payments in addition to those made during the period.

(5) "Contract period" means the period from a contract issue or anniversary date to the earlier of the next following anniversary date (or, if later, the last day of any grace period commencing before such next following anniversary date) or the termination date of the contract.

(6) "Variable death benefit" is the amount of death benefit, other than incidental insurance benefits, payable under a flexible contract which varies to reflect the investment experience of the separate account and which would be payable in the absence of any guaranteed death benefit.

(7) "Payment," as used in paragraphs (b)(13)(i), (b)(13)(ii), and (b)(13)(v)(A) of this Rule and in sections 27(a)(2) and 27(h)(2) solely with respect to flexible contracts, means for a contract period the gross premiums paid less any portion of such gross premiums charged for the items specified in paragraphs (c)(4)(vi), (c)(4)(vii), and (c)(4)(viii) of this Rule. "Payment," as used in any other section of this Rule, means the gross premiums paid or payable for the flexi-

ble contract, *Except,* That "Payment" shall not include any amount deducted by the life insurer to recover excess sales loading previously applied to keep the contract in force pursuant to paragraph (b)(13)(iv)(B)(*2*) of this Rule.

(8)(i) "Guideline annual premium" means the level annual amount that would be payable through the maturity date specified in paragraph (c)(8)(ii)(B) of this Rule for the future benefits under the contract if, subject to the provisions of paragraph (c)(8)(ii) of this Rule:

(A) The payments were fixed by the life insurer as to both timing and amount, and

(B) The payments were based on the 1980 Commissioners Standard Ordinary Mortality Table, net investment earnings at the greater of an annual effective rate of 5 per centum or rate or rates guaranteed at issuance of the flexible contract, the sales load under the contract, and the fees and charges associated with the contract specified in paragraphs (c)(4)(iii), (c)(4)(iv), (c)(4)(v), (c)(4)(vi), (c)(4)(vii), (c)(4)(viii) (for the first two contract periods as permitted by paragraph (c)(1)(i)), and (c)(4)(x) of this Rule.

(ii) In computing the future benefits under the flexible contract for determining the guideline annual premium:

(A) The excess of the amount payable by reason of the death of the insured (determined without regard to any incidental insurance benefits) over the cash value of the contract shall be deemed to be not greater than such excess at the time the contract was issued,

(B) The maturity date shall be the latest maturity date permitted under the contract but not less than 20 years after the date of issue or (if earlier) age 95, and

(C) The amount of any endowment benefit (or sum of endowment benefits) shall be deemed not to exceed the least amount payable by reason of the death of the insured (determined without regard to any incidental insurance benefits) at any time under the contract.

(9) "Cash value" means the amount that would be available in cash upon voluntary termination of a contract by its owner before it becomes payable by death or maturity, without regard to any charges that may be assessed upon such termination and before deduction of any outstanding contract loan.

(10) "Cash surrender value" means the amount available in cash upon voluntary termination of a contract by its owner before it becomes payable by death or maturity, after any charges assessed in connection with the termination have been deducted and before deduction of any outstanding contract loan.

(11) "Net investment earnings" means investment earnings in the separate account after deduction of any asset charges, including but not limited to, such charges for income tax; brokerage and other investment expenses; mortality, expense, and guaranteed death benefit risks; and an investment advisory fee, but not including deductions for sales load. However, "net investment earnings" as used in paragraph (c)(4)(i) of this Rule shall not include any amount deducted pursuant to subparagraphs (ii) through (viii) of paragraph (c)(4).

(12) "Contract processing day" means any day on which charges under the contract are deducted from the separate account.

(d) The following computational rules shall be used in applying this Rule:

(1) Paragraphs (b)(13)(i) and (b)(13)(ii) of this Rule shall be deemed to be satisfied with respect to any flexible contract under which sales load is deducted other than from payments prior to the allocation of net payments to the separate account if:

(i) from issuance of the contract through each contract period, the aggregate amount of sales load deducted is not more than the aggregate amount of sales load that could be deducted under an otherwise identical flexible contract that deducted sales load only from payments prior to their allocation to the separate account; and

(ii)(A) the amount of sales load deducted pursuant to any method permitted under this paragraph (other than asset-based sales loads) does not exceed the proportionate amount of sales load deducted prior thereto pursuant to the same method, unless an increase in such proportionate amount is caused by reductions in the annual cost of insurance, or a reduction in the sales load deducted from amounts transferred to a flexible contract from another plan of insurance; or

(B) for asset-based sales load structures, the percentage of assets taken as sales load does not exceed any of the percentage previously taken pursuant to the same method, unless an increase in such percentage is caused by a reduction in the percentage taken on amounts transferred to a flexible contract from another plan of insurance.

(2)(i) Solely with respect to increases in or additions of insurance benefits requested by a contractholder after issuance of a flexible contract, the contract shall be deemed to satisfy paragraphs (b)(13)(i)(A), (b)(13)(ii), (b)(13)(v), (b)(13)(viii), and (d)(1)(ii) of this Rule, *Provided,* That from issuance of the contract through each contract period the aggregate amount of sales load imposed is not more than the aggregate amount of sales load that would be permissible under the base test contract, as defined in paragraph (d)(2)(iii)(B) of this Rule, and the incremental test contract, as defined in paragraph (d)(2)(iii)(C) of this Rule.

(ii) The following procedures shall be used in applying paragraph (d)(2)(i):

(A) Payments for the actual contract, as defined in paragraph (d)(2)(iii)(A) of this Rule, and the base and incremental test contracts shall, for purposes of demonstrating compliance with the sales load provisions of this Rule, be deemed paid in the following proportionate amounts: level annual payments for the base test contract equal to the guideline annual premium for the contract, commencing upon issuance; level annual payments for the incremental test contract equal to the difference between the guideline annual premium for the actual contract after the increase in or addition of insurance benefits and before such increase or addition, commencing upon such increase or addition; and level annual payments for the actual contract equal to the guideline annual premium for such contract, commencing upon issuance and adjusted for such increase or addition as of the date of such increase or addition, *provided,* That the guideline annual premium used is that defined in paragraph (c)(8);

(B) To the extent that the increases in, or additions of, insurance benefits are funded out of cash value, such cash value shall be proportionately allocated between the base test contract and incremental test contract according to the ratio of their respective guideline annual payments, as described in (d)(2)(ii)(A); and

(C) It is assumed that no redemptions are made under the actual and test contracts.

(D) An incremental test contract may deduct, in any manner permitted by this Rule, not more than 50 per centum of the sales load which would otherwise be permitted under the base test contract, and not be subject to the surrender, conversion, and withdrawal provisions set forth in paragraphs (b)(13)(v)(A) and (B) and (b)(13)(viii) of this Rule, *Provided, however,* That the increased or added benefit will be subject to the surrender, conversion, and withdrawal provisions referenced above if more than such 50 per centum of sales load is assessed.

(iii) For purposes of this paragraph (d)(2):

(A) "Actual contract" shall mean the flexible contract issued to the contractholder, and adjusted for the increase in or addition of insurance benefits, as of the date of the increase or addition;

(B) "Base test contract" shall mean the actual contract had the increase or addition not occurred;

(C) "Incremental test contract" shall mean a flexible contract that, (*1*) is issued on the date of the increase or addition, and (*2*) provides insurance benefits identical to the incremental change in insurance benefits under the actual contract upon such increase or addition; and

(D) Any change in insurance benefits which would occur automatically under a contract, with or without the opportunity for contractholder disapproval, or any change in death benefit operations shall not be considered an "increase in or addition of insurance benefits requested by a contractholder" for purposes of imposing additional sales load.

§ 270.7d–1 Specification of Conditions and Arrangements for Canadian Management Investment Companies Requesting Order Permitting Registration

(a) A management investment company organized under the laws of Canada or any province thereof may obtain an order pursuant to section 7(d) permitting its registration under the act and the public offering of its securities, if otherwise appropriate, upon the filing of an application complying with paragraph (b) of this section. All such applications will be considered by the Commission pursuant to the procedure set forth in § 270.0–5 and other applicable rules. Conditions and arrangements proposed by investment companies organized under the laws of other countries will be considered by the Commission in the light of the special circumstances and local laws involved in each case.

(b) An application filed pursuant to this section shall contain, inter alia, the following undertakings and agreements of the applicant:

(1) Applicant will cause each present and future officer, director, investment adviser, principal underwriter and custodian of the applicant to enter into an agreement, to be filed by applicant with the Commission upon the filing of its registration statement or upon the assumption of such office by such person which will provide, among other things, that each such person agrees (i) to comply with the applicant's Letters Patent (Charter) and By Laws, the act and the rules thereunder, and the undertakings and agreements contained in said application insofar as applicable to such person; (ii) to do nothing inconsistent with the applicant's undertakings and agreements required by this section; (iii) that the undertakings enumerated as subdivisions (i) and (ii) of this subparagraph constitute representations and inducements to the Commission to issue its order in the premises and continue the same in effect, as the case may be; (iv) that each such agreement constitutes a contract between such person and the applicant and its shareholders with the intent that applicant's shareholders shall be beneficiaries of and shall have the status of parties to such agreement so as to enable them to maintain actions at law or in equity within the United States and Canada for any violation thereof. In addition the agreement of each officer and director will contain provisions similar to those contained in subparagraph (6) of this paragraph.

(2) That every agreement and undertaking of the applicant, its officers, directors,

investment adviser, principal underwriter and custodian required by this section (i) constitute inducements to the Commission for the issuance and continuance in effect of, and conditions to, the Commission's order to be entered under this section; (ii) constitute a contract among applicant and applicant's shareholders with the same intent as set forth in subparagraph (1)(iv) of this paragraph; and (iii) failure by the applicant or any of the above enumerated persons to comply with any such agreement and undertaking, unless permitted by the Commission, shall constitute a violation of the order entered under this section.

(3) That the Commission, in its discretion, may revoke its order permitting registration of the applicant and the public offering of its securities if it shall find after notice and opportunity for hearing that there shall have been a violation of such order or the act and may determine whether distribution of applicant's assets is necessary or appropriate in the interests of investors and may so direct.

(4) That applicant will perform every action and thing necessary to cause and assist the custodian of its assets to distribute the same, or the proceeds thereof, if the Commission or a court of competent jurisdiction, shall have so directed by a final order.

(5) That any shareholder of the applicant or the Commission on its own motion or on request of shareholders shall have the right to initiate a proceeding (i) before the Commission for the revocation of the order permitting registration of the applicant or (ii) before a court of competent jurisdiction for the liquidation of applicant and a distribution of its assets to its shareholders and creditors. Such court may enter such order in the event that it shall find, after notice and opportunity for hearing that applicant, its officers, directors, investment adviser, principal underwriter or custodian shall have violated any provision of the act or the Commission's order of registration of the applicant.

A court of competent jurisdiction for the purpose of subparagraphs (4) and (5) of this paragraph means the District Court of the United States of the district in which the assets of the applicant are maintained.

(6) That any shareholder of the applicant shall have the right to bring suit at law or in equity, in any court of the United States or Canada having jurisdiction over applicant, its assets or any of its officers or directors to enforce compliance by applicant, its officers and directors with any provision of applicant's Charter or By Laws, the act and the rules thereunder, or undertakings and agreements required by this section, insofar as applicable to such persons. That such court may appoint a trustee or receiver of the applicant with all powers necessary to implement the purposes of such suit, including the administration of the estate, the collection of corporate property including choses-in-action, and distribution of applicant's assets to its creditors and shareholders. That applicant and its officers and directors waive any objection they may be entitled to raise and any right they may have to object to the power and right of any shareholder of the applicant to bring such suit, reserving, however, their right to maintain that they have complied with the aforesaid provisions, undertakings and agreements, and otherwise to dispute such suit on its merits. Applicant, its officers and directors also agree that any final judgment or decree of any United States court as aforesaid, may be granted full faith and credit by a court of competent jurisdiction of Canada and consent that such Canadian court may enter judgment or decree thereon at the instance of any shareholder, receiver or trustee of the applicant.

(7) Applicant will file, and will cause each of its present or future directors, officers, or investment advisers who is not a resident of the United States to file with the Commission irrevocable designation of the applicant's custodian as an agent in the United

States to accept service of process in any suit, action or proceeding before the Commission or any appropriate court to enforce the provisions of the acts administered by the Commission, or to enforce any right or liability based upon applicant's Charter, By Laws, contracts, or the respective undertakings and agreements of any such person required by this section, or which alleges a liability on the part of any such persons arising out of their service, acts of transactions relating to the applicant.

(8) Applicant's Charter and By Laws, taken together, will contain, so long as applicant is registered under the act in substance the following:

(i) The provisions of the Act as follows: section 2(a): *Provided,* That the term "government securities" defined in section 2(a)(16) may include securities issued or guaranteed by Canada or any instrumentality of the government of Canada; the term "value" defined in section 2(a)(41) may be defined solely for the purposes of sections 5 and 12 in accordance with the provisions of § 270.2a–1 (Rule 2a–1) if the same shall be necessary or desirable to comply with Canadian regulatory or revenue laws or rules or regulations thereunder; the term "bank" defined in section 2(a)(5) shall be defined solely for the purposes of section 9 and 10, as any banking institution; section 4; section 5; section 6(c); section 9; section 10(a), (b), (c), (e), (f) and (g): *Provided,* That the provisions of section 10(d) may be substituted for the provisions of section 10(a) and 10(b)(2) if applicable; section 11; section 12(a), (b), (c), and (d); section 13(a); section 15(a), (b), and (c); section 16(a); sections 17, 18, 19, 20 and 21; section 22(d); section 22(e): *Provided,* That the Toronto Stock Exchange or the Montreal Stock Exchange or both may be included in addition to the New York Stock Exchange; section 22(f); section 22(g); section 23; section 25(a) and (b); section 30(a), (b), (d), (e), and (f); section 31; section 32(a): *Provided,* That provision may be made for the selection and termination of employment of the accountant in compliance with The Companies Act of Canada; section 32(b). Where a provision of the act prohibits or directs action by an investment company, or its directors, officers or employees, the Charter or By Laws shall state that the applicant of its directors, officers or employees shall or shall not act, as the case may be, in conformity with the intent of the statute; where the provision applies to others, such as principal underwriters, investment advisers, controlled companies and affiliated persons, the Charter or By Laws shall also state that the applicant will not permit the prohibited conduct or will obtain the required action. Any of the provisions of sections 11, 12, 15, 18, 22, 23, 30, and 31 may be omitted if not applicable to a company of applicant's classification or sub-classification as defined in section 4 or 5 of the act or if not applicable because the subject matter of such provisions is prohibited by the Charter or By Laws. Other provisions of the act nor specified above may be incorporated in the applicant's Charter or By Laws at its option.

(ii) Any question of interpretation of any term or provision of the Charter or By Laws having a counterpart in or otherwise derived from a term or provision of the act shall be resolved by reference to interpretations, if any, of the corresponding term or provision of the act by the courts of the United States of America or, in the absence of any controlling decision of any such court, by rules, regulations, orders or interpretations of the Commission.

(iii) Applicant will maintain the original or duplicate copies of its books and records at the office of its custodian or other office located within the United States.

(iv) At least a majority of the directors and of the officers of the applicant will be

United States citizens of whom a majority will be resident in the United States.

(v) Except as provided in § 270.17f–5 and § 270.17f–7, applicant will appoint, by contract, a bank, as defined in section 2(a)(5) of the Act (15 U.S.C. 80a–2(a)(5)) and having the qualification described in section 26(a)(1) of the Act (15 U.S.C. 80a–26(a)(1)), to act as trustee of, and maintain in its sole custody in the United States, all of applicant's securities and cash, other than cash necessary to meet applicant's current administrative expenses. The contract will provide, *inter alia*, that the custodian will:

(A) consummate all purchases and sales of securities by applicant, other than purchases and sales on an established securities exchange, through the delivery of securities and receipt of cash, or *vice versa* as the case may be, within the United States, and (B) redeem in the United States such of applicant's shares as shall be surrendered therefor, and (C) distribute applicant's assets, or the proceeds thereof, to applicant's assets, or the proceeds thereof, to applicant's creditors and shareholders, upon service upon the custodian of an order of the Commission or court directing such distribution as provided in paragraphs (b)(3) and (5) of this section.

(vi) Applicant's principal underwriter for the sale of its shares will be a citizen and resident of the United States or a corporation organized under the laws of a state of the United States, and having its principal place of business therein, and if redeemable shares are offered, also a member in good standing of a securities association registered under section 15A of the Securities Exchange Act of 1934.

(vii) Applicant will appoint an accountant, qualified to act as an independent public accountant for the applicant under the act and the rules thereunder, who maintains a permanent office and place of business in the United States.

(viii) Any contract entered into between the applicant and its investment adviser and principal underwriter will contain provisions in compliance with the requirements of sections 15, 17(i) and 31 and the rules thereunder, and require that the investment adviser maintain in the United States its books and records or duplicate copies thereof relating to applicant.

(ix) Applicant's Charter and By Laws will not be changed in any manner inconsistent with this paragraph or the act and the rules thereunder unless authorized by the Commission.

(9) Contracts of the applicant, other than those executed on an established securities exchange which do not involve affiliated persons, will provide that:

(i) Such contracts, irrespective of the place of their execution or performance, will be performed in accordance with the requirements of the act, the Securities Act of 1933, and the Securities Exchange Act of 1934, if the subject matter of such contracts is within the purview of such acts; and

(ii) In effecting the purchase or sale of assets the parties thereto will utilize the United States mails or means of interstate commerce.

(10) Applicant will furnish to the Commission with its registration statement filed under the act a list of persons affiliated with it and with its investment adviser and principal underwriter and will furnish revisions of such list, if any, concurrently with the filing of periodic reports required to be filed under the act.

§ 270.7d–2 Definition of "Public Offering" as Used in Section 7(d) of the Act With Respect to Certain Canadian Tax-Deferred Retirement Savings Accounts

(a) *Definitions*. As used in this section:

(1) *Canadian law* means the federal laws of Canada, the laws of any province or territory of Canada, and the rules or regulations of any federal, provincial, or territorial regulatory authority, or any self-regulatory authority, of Canada.

(2) *Canadian Retirement Account* means a trust or other arrangement, including, but not limited to, a "Registered Retirement Savings Plan" or "Registered Retirement Income Fund" administered under Canadian law, that is managed by the Participant and:

(i) Operated to provide retirement benefits to a Participant; and

(ii) Established in Canada, administered under Canadian law, and qualified for tax-deferred treatment under Canadian law.

(3) *Eligible Security* means a security issued by a Qualified Company that:

(i) Is offered to a Participant, or sold to his or her Canadian Retirement Account, in reliance on this section; and

(ii) May also be purchased by Canadians other than Participants.

(4) *Foreign Government* means the government of any foreign country or of any political subdivision of a foreign country.

(5) *Foreign Issuer* means any issuer that is a Foreign Government, a national of any foreign country or a corporation or other organization incorporated or organized under the laws of any foreign country, except an issuer meeting the following conditions:

(i) More than 50 percent of the outstanding voting securities of the issuer are held of record either directly or through voting trust certificates or depositary receipts by residents of the United States; and

(ii) Any of the following:

(A) The majority of the executive officers or directors are United States citizens or residents;

(B) More than 50 percent of the assets of the issuer are located in the United States; or

(C) The business of the issuer is administered principally in the United States.

(iii) For purposes of this definition, the term *resident,* as applied to security holders, means any person whose address appears on the records of the issuer, the voting trustee, or the depositary as being located in the United States.

(6) *Participant* means a natural person who is a resident of the United States, or is temporarily present in the United States, and who contributes to, or is or will be entitled to receive the income and assets from, a Canadian Retirement Account.

(7) *Qualified Company* means a Foreign Issuer whose securities are qualified for investment on a tax-deferred basis by a Canadian Retirement Account under Canadian law.

(8) *United States* means the United States of America, its territories and possessions, any State of the United States, and the District of Columbia.

(b) *Public Offering.* For purposes of section 7(d) of the Act (15 U.S.C. 80a–7(d)), the term "public offering" does not include the offer to a Participant, or the sale to his or her Canadian Retirement Account, of Eligible Securities issued by a Qualified Company, if the Qualified Company:

(1) Includes in any written offering materials delivered to a Participant, or to his or her Canadian Retirement Account, a prominent statement that the Eligible Security, and the Qualified Company that issued the Eligible Security, are not registered with the U.S. Securities and Exchange Commission, and that the Eligible Security and the Qualified Company are relying on exemptions from registration.

(2) Has not asserted that Canadian law, or the jurisdiction of the courts of Canada,

does not apply in a proceeding involving an Eligible Security.

§ 270.8b–1 Scope of §§ 270.8b–1 to 270.8b–33

The rules contained in §§ 270.8b–1 to 270.8b–33 shall govern all registration statements pursuant to section 8 of the Act (15 U.S.C. 80a–8), including notifications of registration pursuant to section 8(a), and all reports pursuant to section 30(a) or (b) of the Act (15 U.S.C. 80a–29(a) or (b)), including all amendments to such statements and reports, except that any provision in a form covering the same subject matter as any such rule shall be controlling.

§ 270.8b–2 Definitions

Unless the context otherwise requires, the terms in paragraphs (a) through (m) of this section, when used in the rules contained in §§ 270.8b–1 through 270.8b–32, in the rules under section 30(a) or (b) of the Act or in the forms for registration statements and reports pursuant to section 8 or 30(a) or (b) of the Act, shall have the respective meanings indicated in this section. The terms "EDGAR," "EDGAR Filer Manual," "electronic filer," "electronic filing," "electronic format," "electronic submission," "paper format," and "signature" shall have the meanings assigned to such terms in Regulation S–T—General Rules for Electronic Filings (Part 232 of this chapter).

Amount. The term "amount", when used in regard to securities, means the principal amount if relating to evidences of indebtedness, the number of shares if relating to shares, and the number of units if relating to any other kind of security.

Certified. The term "certified", when used in regard to financial statements, means certified by an independent public or independent certified public accountant or accountants.

Charter. The term "charter" includes articles of incorporation, declaration of trust, articles of association or partnership, or any similar instrument, as amended, effecting (either with or without filing with any governmental agency) the organization or creation of an incorporated or unincorporated person.

Employee. The term "employee" does not include a director, trustee, officer or member of the advisory board.

Fiscal year. The term "fiscal year" means the annual accounting period or, if no closing date has been adopted, the calendar year ending on December 31.

Investment income. The term "investment income" means the aggregate of net operating income or loss from real estate and gross income from interest, dividends and all other sources, exclusive of profit or loss on sales of securities or other properties.

Material. The term "material", when used to qualify a requirement for the furnishing of information as to any subject, limits the information required to those matters as to which an average prudent investor ought reasonably to be informed before buying or selling any security of the particular company.

Parent. A "parent" of a specified person is an affiliated person who controls the specified person directly or indirectly through one or more intermediaries.

Previously filed or reported. The terms "previously filed" and "previously reported" mean previously filed with, or reported in, a registration statement filed under section 8 of the act or under the Securities Act of 1933, a report filed under section 30 of the act or section 13 or 15(d) of the Securities Exchange Act of 1934, a definitive proxy statement filed under section 20 of the act or section 14 of the Securities Exchange Act of 1934, or a prospectus filed under the Securities Act of 1933: *Provided,* That information contained in any such document shall be deemed to have been previously filed with, or reported to, an exchange only if such document is filed with such exchange.

Share. The term "share" means a share of stock in a corporation or unit of interest in an unincorporated person.

Significant subsidiary. The term "significant subsidiary" means a subsidiary meeting any one of the following conditions:

(1) The value of the investments in and advances to the subsidiary by its parent and the parent's other subsidiaries, if any exceed 10 percent of the value of the assets of the parent or, if a consolidated balance sheet is filed, the value of the assets of the parent and its consolidated subsidiaries.

(2) The total investment income of the subsidiary or, in the case of a non-investment company subsidiary, the net income exceeds 10 percent of the total investment income of the parent or, if consolidated statements are filed, 10 percent of the total investment income of the parent and its consolidated subsidiaries.

(3) The subsidiary is the parent of one or more subsidiaries and, together with such subsidiaries would, if considered in the aggregate, constitute a significant subsidiary.

Subsidiary. A "subsidiary" of a specified person is an affiliated person who is controlled by the specified person, directly or indirectly, through one or more intermediaries.

Totally-held subsidiary. The term "totally-held subsidiary" means a subsidiary (1) substantially all of whose outstanding securities are owned by its parent and/or the parent's other totally-held subsidiaries, and (2) which is not indebted to any person other than its parent and/or the parent's other totally-held subsidiaries in an amount which is material in relation to the particular subsidiary, excepting indebtedness incurred in the ordinary course of business which is not over-due and which matures within one year from the date of its creation, whether evidenced by securities or not.

§ 270.8b-3 Title of Securities

Wherever the title of securities is required to be stated, there shall be given such information as will indicate the type and general character of the securities, including the following:

(a) In the case of shares, the par or stated value, if any; the rate of dividends, if fixed, and whether cumulative or noncumulative; a brief indication of the preference, if any; and if convertible, a statement to that effect.

(b) In the case of funded debt, the rate of interest; the date of maturity, or if the issue matures serially, a brief indication of the serial maturities, such as "maturing serially from 1950 to 1960"; if the payment of principal or interest is contingent, an appropriate indication of such contingency; a brief indication of the priority of the issue; and if convertible, a statement to that effect.

(c) In the case of any other kind of security, appropriate information of comparable character.

§ 270.8b-4 Interpretation of Requirements

Unless the context clearly shows otherwise:

(a) The forms require information only as to the company filing the registration statement or report.

(b) Whenever any fixed period of time in the past is indicated, such period shall be computed from the date of filing.

(c) Whenever words relate to the future, they have reference solely to present intention.

(d) Any words indicating the holder of a position or office include persons, by whatever titles designated, whose duties are those ordinarily performed by holders of such positions or offices.

§ 270.8b-5 Time of Filing Original Registration Statement

An investment company shall file a registration statement with the Commission on the appropriate form within three months after the filing of notification of registration under section 8(a) of the act, provided that if the fiscal year of the company ends within the three months period, its registration statement may be filed within three months after the end of such fiscal year.

§ 270.8b-10 Requirements as to Proper Form

Every registration statement or report shall be prepared in accordance with the form prescribed therefor by the Commission, as in effect on the date of filing. Any such statement or report shall be deemed to be filed on the proper form unless objection to the form is made by the Commission within thirty days after the date of filing.

§ 270.8b-11 Number of Copies; Signatures; Binding

(a) Three complete copies of each registration statement or report, including exhibits and all other papers and documents filed as a part thereof, shall be filed with the Commission.

(b) In the case of a registration statement filed on Form N-1A (§ 239.15A and § 274.11A of this chapter), Form N-2 (§ 239.14 and § 274.11a-1 of this chapter), Form N-3 (§ 239.17a and § 274.11b of this chapter), Form N-4 (§ 239.17b and § 274.17c of this chapter), or Form N-6 (§ 239.17c and § 274.11d of this chapter), three complete copies of each part of the registration statement (including, if applicable, exhibits and all other papers and documents filed as part of Part C of the registration statement) shall be filed with the Commission.

(c) At least one copy of the registration statement or report shall be manually signed in the manner prescribed by the appropriate form. Unsigned copies shall be conformed. If the signature of any person is affixed pursuant to a power of attorney or other similar authority, a copy of such power of attorney or other authority shall also be filed with the registration statement or report.

(d) Each copy of a registration statement or report filed with the Commission shall be bound in one or more parts, without stiff covers. The bindings shall be made on the left-hand side and in such manner as to leave the reading matter legible.

(e) Duplicated or facsimile versions of manual signatures of persons required to sign any registration statement or report, including all amendments and exhibits to such statements or reports, that are filed or submitted to the Commission under the Act, shall be considered manual signatures for the purposes of the Act and the rules and regulations thereunder; provided that, the original signed document is retained by the filer for a period of five years and, upon request, the filer furnishes to the Commission or the staff the original manually signed document.

§ 270.8b-12 Requirements as to Paper, Printing and Language

(a) Registration statements and reports shall be filed on good quality, unglazed, white paper, no larger than 8½ × 11 inches in size, insofar as practicable. To the extent that the reduction of larger documents would render them illegible, such documents may be filed on paper larger than 8½ by 11 inches in size.

(b) In the case of a registration statement filed on Form N-1A (§ 239.15A and § 274.11A of this chapter), Form N-2 (§ 239.14 and § 274.11a-1 of this chapter), Form N-3 (§ 239.17a and § 274.11b of this chapter), or Form N-4 (§ 239.17b and § 274.11c of this chapter), or Form N-6 (§ 239.17c and § 274.11d of this chapter), Part C of the registration statement shall be filed on good quality, unglazed, white paper, no larger than 8½ by 11 inches in size, insofar as practicable. The prospectus and, if applicable, the Statement of Additional Information, however, may be filed on smaller-sized paper provided that the size of paper used in each document is uniform.

(c) The registration statement or report and, insofar as practicable, all papers and documents filed as a part thereof, shall be printed, lithographed, mimeographed, or typewritten. However, the registration statement or report or any portion thereof may be prepared by any similar process which, in the opinion of the

Commission, produces copies suitable for permanent record. Irrespective of the process used, all copies of any such material shall be clear, easily readable and suitable for repeated photocopying. Debits in credit categories and credits in debit categories shall be designated so as to be clearly distinguishable as such on photocopies.

(d) The body of all printed registration statements and reports and all notes to financial statements and other tabular data included therein shall be in roman type at least as large as 10-point modern type. However, to the extent necessary for convenient presentation, financial statements and other statistical or tabular data, including tabular data in notes, may be set in type at least as large and as legible as 8-point modern type. All types shall be leaded at least 2 points.

(e) Registration statements and reports shall be in the English language. If any exhibit or other paper or document filed with a registration statement or report is in a foreign language, it shall be accompanied by a translation into the English language.

(f) Where a registration statement or report is distributed through an electronic medium, issuers may satisfy legibility requirements applicable to printed documents, such as paper size, type size and font, bold-face type, italics and red ink, by presenting all required information in a format readily communicated to investors, and where indicated, in a manner reasonably calculated to draw investor attention to specific information.

§ 270.8b–13 Preparation of Registration Statement or Report

The registration statement or report shall contain the numbers and captions of all items of the appropriate form, but the text of the items may be omitted provided the answers thereto are so prepared as to indicate to the reader the coverage of the items without the necessity of his referring to the text of the items or instructions thereto. However, where any item requires information to be given in tabular form, it shall be given in substantially the tabular form specified in the item. All instructions, whether appearing under the items of the form or elsewhere therein, are to be omitted from the registration statement or report. Unless expressly provided otherwise, if any item is inapplicable or the answer thereto is in the negative, an appropriate statement to that effect shall be made.

§ 270.8b–14 Riders; Inserts

Riders shall not be used. If the registration statement or report is typed on a printed form, and the space provided for the answer to any given item is insufficient, reference shall be made in such space to a full insert page or pages on which the item number and caption and the complete answer are given.

§ 270.8b–15 Amendments

All amendments shall be filed under cover of the facing sheet of the appropriate form, shall be clearly identified as amendments, and shall comply with all pertinent requirements applicable to registration statements and reports. Amendments shall be filed separately for each separate registration or report amended. Except as permitted under Rule 102(b) of Regulation S–T, any amendment filed under this section shall state the complete text of each item amended. An amendment to any report required to include the certifications as specified in § 270.30a–2(a) must include new certifications by each principal executive and principal financial officer of the registrant, and an amendment to any report required to be accompanied by the certifications as specified in § 240.13a–14(b) or § 240.15d–14(b) and § 270.30a–2(b) must be accompanied by new certifications by each principal executive and principal financial officer to the registrant.

§ 270.8b–16 Amendments to Registration Statements

(a) Every registered management investment company which is required to file a semi-annual report on Form N–SAR, as prescribed by rule 30b1–1 shall amend the registration statement required pursuant to section 8(b) by filing, not more than 120 days after the close of each fiscal year ending on or after the date upon which such registration statement was filed, the appropriate form prescribed for such amendments.

(b) Paragraph (a) of this section shall not apply to a registered closed-end management investment company whose registration statement was filed on Form N–2; provided that the following information is transmitted to shareholders in its annual report to shareholders:

(1) If the company offers a dividend reinvestment plan to shareholders, information about the plan required to be disclosed in the company's prospectus by Item 10.1.e of Form N–2 (§ 274.11a–1);

(2) Any material changes in the company's investment objectives or policies (described in Item 8.2 of Form N–2) that have not been approved by shareholders;

(3) Any changes in the company's charter or by-laws that would delay or prevent a change of control of the company (described in Item 10.1.f of Form N–2) that have not been approved by shareholders;

(4) Any material changes in the principal risk factors associated with investment in the company (described in Item 8.3 of Form N–2); and

(5) Any changes in the persons who are primarily responsible for the day-to-day management of the company's portfolio (described in Item 9.1.c of Form N–2), including any new person's business experience during the past five years and the length of time he or she has been responsible for the management of the portfolio.

(c) In lieu of including a description of the dividend reinvestment plan in its annual report, a company may comply with the disclosure requirement of paragraph (b)(1) of this section concerning a company's dividend reinvestment plan by delivering to each shareholder annually a separate document containing the information about the plan required to be disclosed in the company's prospectus by Item 10.1.e of Form N–2. Any such document shall be deemed to be a record or document subject to the record-keeping requirements of section 31 and the rules adopted thereunder (§ 270.31a–1 *et seq.*).

(d) The changes required to be disclosed by paragraphs (b)(2) through (b)(5) of this section are those that occurred since the later of either the effective date of the company's registration statement relating to its initial offering of securities under the Securities Act of 1933 (or the most recent post-effective amendment thereto) or the close of the period covered by the previously transmitted annual shareholder report.

§ 270.8b–20 Additional Information

In addition to the information expressly required to be included in a registration statement or report, there shall be added such further material information, if any, as may be necessary to make the required statements, in the light of the circumstances under which they are made, not misleading.

§ 270.8b–21 Information Unknown or Not Available

Information required need be given only insofar as it is known or reasonably available to the registrant. If any required information is unknown and not reasonably available to the registrant, either because the obtaining thereof would involve unreasonable effort or expense, or because it rests peculiarly within the knowledge of another person not affiliated with the registrant, the information may be omitted subject to the following conditions:

(a) The registrant shall give such information on the subject as it possesses or can acquire without unreasonable effort or expense, together with the sources thereof.

(b) The registrant shall include a statement either showing that unreasonable effort or expense would be involved or indicating the absence of any affiliation with the person within whose knowledge the information rests and stating the result of a request made to such person for the information.

§ 270.8b–22 Disclaimer of Control

If the existence of control is open to reasonable doubt in any instance, the registrant may disclaim the existence of control and any admission thereof; in such case, however, the registrant shall state the material facts pertinent to the possible existence of control.

§ 270.8b–23 Incorporation by Reference

(a) Any registrant may incorporate by reference, in answer or partial answer to any item of a registration statement or report, any information contained elsewhere in the statement or report or any information contained in any other statement, report or prospectus filed with the Commission under any Act administered by it, so long as a copy of the other statement, report or prospectus is filed with each copy of the registration statement or report in which it is incorporated by reference. In the case of a registration statement, report, or prospectus filed in electronic format, the registrant need not file a copy of the document incorporated by reference if that document also was filed in electronic format. A registrant may incorporate by reference matter contained in an exhibit, however, only to the extent permitted by §§ 270.8b–24 and 270.8b–32.

(b) Any financial statement filed with the Commission pursuant to any act administered by the Commission may be incorporated by reference in a registration statement or report, filed with the Commission by the same or any other person, if it substantially conforms to the requirements of the form on which the statement or report is filed.

(c) Material incorporated by reference shall be clearly identified in the reference. An express statement that the specified matter is incorporated by reference shall be made at the particular place in the registration statement or report where the information is required. Matter shall not be incorporated by reference in any case where such incorporation would render the statement incomplete, unclear or confusing.

§ 270.8b–24 Summaries or Outlines of Documents

Where an item requires a summary or outline of the provisions of any document, only a brief statement shall be made, in succinct and condensed form, as to the most important provisions of the document. In addition to such statement, the summary or outline may incorporate by reference particular items, sections, or paragraphs of any exhibit and may be qualified in its entirety by such reference. Matter contained in an exhibit may be incorporated by reference in answer to an item only to the extent permitted by this section.

§ 270.8b–25 Extension of Time for Furnishing Information

(a) Subject to paragraph (b) of this section, if it is impractical to furnish any required information, document or report at the time it is required to be filed, there may be filed with the Commission as a separate document an application (a) identifying the information, document or report in question, (b) stating why the filing thereof at the time required is impracticable, and (c) requesting an extension of time for filing the information, document or report to a specified date not more than 60 days after the date it would otherwise have to be filed. The application shall be deemed granted unless the Commission, within 10 days after receipt thereof, shall enter an order denying the application. Section 270.0–5 (Rule N–5) shall not apply to such applications.

(b) If it is impracticable to furnish any document or report required to be filed in electronic format at the time it is required to be filed, the electronic filer may file under the temporary hardship provision of rule 201 of Regulation S–T (§ 232.201 of this chapter) or may submit a written application for a continuing hardship exemption, in accordance with Rule 202 of Regulation S–T. Applications for such exemptions shall be considered in accordance with the provisions of those sections and paragraphs (h) and (i) of § 200.30–5 of this chapter.

§ 270.8b–30 Additional Exhibits

A company may file such exhibits as it may desire, in addition to those required by the appropriate form. Such exhibits shall be so marked as to indicate clearly the subject matters to which they refer.

§ 270.8b–31 Omission of Substantially Identical Documents

In any case where two or more indentures, contracts, franchises, or other documents required to be filed as exhibits are substantially identical in all material respects except as to the parties thereto, the dates of execution, or other details, copies of only one of such documents need be filed, with a schedule identifying the other documents omitted and setting forth the material details in which such documents differ from the documents filed. The Commission may at any time in its discretion require the filing of copies of any documents so omitted.

§ 270.8b–32 Incorporation of Exhibits by Reference

(a) Except as provided in paragraph (c) of this section any document or part thereof filed with the Commission pursuant to any Act administered by the Commission may, subject to the limitations of § 228.10(f) and § 229.10(d) of this chapter, be incorporated by reference as an exhibit to any registration statement or report filed with the Commission by the same or any other person.

(b) If any modification has occurred in the text of any document incorporated by reference since the filing thereof, a statement containing the text of such modification and the date thereof shall be filed with the reference.

(c) *Electronic Filings.* A registrant may incorporate by reference into a registration statement or report required to be filed electronically only exhibits that have been filed in electronic format, unless the exhibit has been filed in paper under a hardship exemption (§§ 232.201 or 232.202 of this chapter) and any required confirming copy has been submitted.

§ 270.8b–33 XBRL-Related Documents

A registrant that participates in the voluntary XBRL (eXtensible Business Reporting Language) program may submit, in electronic format as an exhibit to a filing on Form N–CSR (§§ 249.331 and 274.128 of this chapter) or Form N–Q (§§ 249.332 and 274.130 of this chapter) to which they relate, XBRL-Related Documents (§ 232.11 of this chapter). A registrant that submits XBRL-Related Documents as an exhibit to a form must name each XBRL-Related Document "EX–100" as specified in the EDGAR Filer Manual and submit the XBRL-Related Documents in such a manner that will permit the information for each series of an investment company registrant and each contract of an insurance company separate account to be separately identifiable. A registrant may submit such exhibit with, or in an amendment to, the filing to which it relates.

§ 270.8f–1 Deregistration of Certain Registered Investment Companies

A registered investment company that seeks a Commission order declaring that it is no longer an investment company may file an application with the Commission on Form N–8F (17 CFR 274.218) if the investment company:

(a) Has sold substantially all of its assets to another registered investment company or merged into or consolidated with another registered investment company;

(b) Has distributed substantially all of its assets to its shareholders and has completed, or is in the process of, winding up its affairs;

(c) Qualifies for an exclusion from the definition of "investment company" under section 3(c)(1) (15 U.S.C. 80a–3(c)(1)) or section 3(c)(7) (15 U.S.C. 80a–3(c)(7)) of the Act; or

(d) Has become a business development company.

§ 270.10b–1 Definition of Regular Broker or Dealer

The term "regular broker or dealer" of an investment company shall mean:

(a) One of the ten brokers or dealers that received the greatest dollar amount of brokerage commissions by virtue of direct or indirect participation in the company's portfolio transactions during the company's most recent fiscal year;

(b) One of the ten brokers or dealers that engaged as principal in the largest dollar amount of portfolio transactions of the investment company during the company's most recent fiscal year; or

(c) One of the ten brokers or dealers that sold the largest dollar amount of securities of the investment company during the company's most recent fiscal year.

§ 270.10e–1 Death, Disqualification, or Bona Fide Resignation of Directors

If a registered investment company, by reason of the death, disqualification, or bona fide resignation of any director, does not meet any requirement of the Act or any rule or regulation thereunder regarding the composition of the company's board of directors, the operation of the relevant subsection of the Act, rule, or regulation will be suspended as to the company:

(a) For 90 days if the vacancy may be filled by action of the board of directors; or

(b) For 150 days if a vote of stockholders is required to fill the vacancy.

§ 270.10f–1 Conditional Exemption of Certain Underwriting Transactions

Any purchase or other acquisition by a registered management company acting, pursuant to a written agreement, as an underwriter of securities of an issuer which is not an investment company shall be exempt from the provisions of section 10(f) upon the following conditions:

(a) The party to such agreement other than such registered company is a principal underwriter of such securities, which principal underwriter (1) is a person primarily engaged in the business of underwriting and distributing securities issued by other persons, selling securities to customers, or related activities, whose gross income normally is derived principally from such business or related activities, and (2) does not control or is not under common control with such registered company.

(b) No public offering of the securities underwritten by such agreement has been made prior to the execution thereof.

(c) Such securities have been effectively registered pursuant to the Securities Act of 1933 prior to the execution of such agreement.

(d) In regard to any securities underwritten, whether or not purchased, by the registered company pursuant to such agreement, such company shall be allowed a rate of gross commission, spread, concession or other profit not less than the amount allowed to such principal underwriter, exclusive of any amounts received by such principal underwriter as a management fee from other principal underwriters.

(e) Such agreement is authorized by resolution adopted by a vote of not less than a majority of the board of directors of such registered company, none of which majority is an affiliated person of such principal underwriter, of the issuer of the securities underwritten pursuant to such agreement or of any person engaged in a business described in paragraph (a)(1) of this section.

(f) The resolution required in paragraph (e) of this section shall state that it has been adopted pursuant to this section, and shall incorporate the terms of the proposed agreement by attaching a copy thereof as an exhibit or otherwise.

(g) A copy of the resolution required in paragraph (e) of this section, signed by each member of the board of directors of the registered company who voted in favor of its adoption, shall be transmitted to the Commission not later than the fifth day succeeding the date on which such agreement is executed.

§ 270.10f–2 Exercise of Warrants or Rights Received on Portfolio Securities

Any purchase or other acquisition of securities by a registered investment company pursuant to the exercise of warrants or rights to subscribe to or to purchase securities shall be exempt from the provisions of section 10(f) of the act, *Provided,* That the warrants or rights so exercised (a) were offered or issued to such company as a security holder on the same basis as all other holders of the class or classes of securities to whom such warrants or rights were offered or issued, and (b) do not exceed 5 percent of the total amount of such warrants or rights so issued.

§ 270.10f–3 Exemption For the Acquisition of Securities During the Existence of an Underwriting or Selling Syndicate

(a) *Definitions.*—(1) Domestic Issuer means any issuer other than a foreign government, a national of any foreign country, or a corporation or other organization incorporated or organized under the laws of any foreign country.

(2) Eligible Foreign Offering means a public offering of securities, conducted under the laws of a country other than the United States, that meets the following conditions:

(i) The offering is subject to regulation by a "foreign financial regulatory authority," as defined in section 2(a)(50) of the Act [15 U.S.C. 80a–2(a)(50)], in such country;

(ii) The securities are offered at a fixed price to all purchasers in the offering (except for any rights to purchase securities that are required by law to be granted to existing security holders of the issuer);

(iii) Financial statements, prepared and audited in accordance with standards required or permitted by the appropriate foreign financial regulatory authority in such country, for the two years prior to the offering, are made available to the public and prospective purchasers in connection with the offering; and

(iv) If the issuer is a Domestic Issuer, it meets the following conditions:

(A) It has a class of securities registered pursuant to section 12(b) or 12(g) of the Securities Exchange Act of 1934 [15 U.S.C. 78l(b) or 78l(g)] or is required to file reports pursuant to section 15(d) of the Securities Exchange Act of 1934 [15 U.S.C. 78o(d)]; and

(B) It has filed all the material required to be filed pursuant to section 13(a) or 15(d) of the Securities Exchange Act of 1934 [15 U.S.C. 78m(a) or 78o(d)] for a period of at least twelve months immediately preceding the sale of securities made in reliance upon this (or for such shorter period that the issuer was required to file such material).

(3) Eligible Municipal Securities means "municipal securities," as defined in section 3(a)(29) of the Securities Exchange Act of 1934 [15 U.S.C. 78c(a)(29)], that have received an investment grade rating from at least one NRSRO; provided, that if the issuer of the municipal securities, or the entity supplying the revenues or other payments from which the issue is to be paid, has been in continuous operation for less than three years, including the operation of any predecessors, the securities shall have received one of the three highest ratings from an NRSRO.

(4) Eligible Rule 144A Offering means an offering of securities that meets the following conditions:

(i) The securities are offered or sold in transactions exempt from registration under section 4(2) of the Securities Act of 1933 [15 U.S.C. 77d(2)], rule 144A thereunder [§ 230.144A of this chapter], or rules 501–508 thereunder [§§ 230.501–230.508 of this chapter];

(ii) The securities are sold to persons that the seller and any person acting on behalf of the seller reasonably believe to include qualified institutional buyers, as defined in § 230.144A(a)(1) of this chapter; and

(iii) The seller and any person acting on behalf of the seller reasonably believe that the securities are eligible for resale to other qualified institutional buyers pursuant to § 230.144A of this chapter.

(5) NRSRO has the same meaning as that set forth in § 270.2a–7(a)(14).

(6) *Managed portion* of a portfolio of a registered investment company means a discrete portion of a portfolio of a registered investment company for which a subadviser is responsible for providing investment advice, provided that:

(i) The subadviser is not an affiliated person of any investment adviser, promoter, underwriter, officer, director, member of an advisory board, or employee of the registered investment company; and

(ii) The subadviser's advisory contract:

(A) Prohibits it from consulting with any subadviser of the investment company that is a principal underwriter or an affiliated person of a principal underwriter concerning transactions of the investment company in securities or other assets; and

(B) Limits its responsibility in providing advice to providing advice with respect to such portion.

(7) *Series of a series company* means any class or series of a registered investment company that issues two or more classes or series of preferred or special stock, each of which is preferred over all other classes or series with respect to assets specifically allocated to that class or series.

(8) *Subadviser* means an investment adviser as defined in section 2(a)(20)(B) of the Act (15 U.S.C. 80a–2(a)(20)(B)).

(b) *Exemption for purchases by series companies and investment companies with managed portions.* For purposes of this section and section 10(f) of the Act (15 U.S.C. 80a–10(f)), each Series of a Series Company, and each Managed Portion of a registered investment company, is deemed to be a separate investment company. Therefore, a purchase or acquisition of a security by a registered investment company is exempt from the prohibitions of section 10(f) of the Act if section 10(f) of the Act would not prohibit such purchase if each Series and each Managed Portion of the company were a separately registered investment company.

(c) *Conditions.* Any purchase of securities by a registered investment company prohibited by section 10(f) of the Act (15 U.S.C. 80a–10(f)) will be exempt from the provisions of that section if the following conditions are met:

(1) Type of Security. The securities to be purchased are:

(i) Part of an issue registered under the Securities Act of 1933 (15 U.S.C. 77a–aa) that is being offered to the public;

(ii) Part of an issue of government securities, as defined in section 2(a)(16) of the Act (15 U.S.C. 80a–2(a)(16));

(iii) Eligible Municipal Securities;

(iv) Securities sold in an Eligible Foreign Offering; or

(v) Securities sold in an Eligible Rule 144A Offering.

(2) Timing and Price.

(i) The securities are purchased prior to the end of the first day on which any sales are made, at a price that is not more than the price paid by each other purchaser of securities in that offering or in any concurrent offering of the securities (except, in the case of an Eligible Foreign Offering, for any rights to purchase that are required by law to be granted to existing security holders of the issuer); and

(ii) If the securities are offered for subscription upon exercise of rights, the securities shall be purchased on or before the fourth day preceding the day on which the rights offering terminates.

(3) Reasonable Reliance. For purposes of determining compliance with paragraphs (c)(1)(v) and (c)(2)(i) of this section, an investment company may reasonably rely upon written statements made by the issuer or a syndicate manager, or by an underwriter or seller of the securities through which such investment company purchases the securities.

(4) Continuous Operation. If the securities to be purchased are part of an issue registered under the Securities Act of 1933 (15 U.S.C. 77a–aa) that is being offered to the public, are government securities (as defined in section 2(a)(16) of the Act (15 U.S.C. 80a–2(a)(16))), or are purchased pursuant to an Eligible Foreign Offering or an Eligible Rule 144A Offering, the issuer of the securities shall must been in continuous operation for not less than three years, including the operations of any predecessors.

(5) Firm Commitment Underwriting. The securities are offered pursuant to an underwriting or similar agreement under which the underwriters are committed to purchase all of the securities being offered, except those purchased by others pursuant to a rights offering, if the underwriters purchase any of the securities.

(6) Reasonable Commission. The commission, spread or profit received or to be received by the principal underwriters is reasonable and fair compared to the commission, spread or profit received by other such persons in connection with the underwriting of similar securities being sold during a comparable period of time.

(7) Percentage Limit.

(i) Generally. The amount of securities of any class of such issue to be purchased by the investment company, aggregated with purchases by any other investment company advised by the investment company's investment adviser, and any purchases by another account with respect to which the investment adviser has investment discretion if the investment adviser exercised such investment discretion with respect to the purchase, does not exceed the following limits:

(A) If purchased in an offering other than an Eligible Rule 144A Offering, 25 percent of the principal amount of the offering of such class; or

(B) If purchased in an Eligible Rule 144A Offering, 25 percent of the total of:

(*1*) The principal amount of the offering of such class sold by underwriters or members of the selling syndicate to qualified institutional buyers, as defined in § 230.144A(a)(1) of this chapter, plus

(*2*) The principal amount of the offering of such class in any concurrent public offering.

(ii) Exemption from Percentage Limit. The requirement is paragraph (c)(7)(i) of this section applies only if the investment adviser of the investment company is, or is an affiliated person of, a principal underwriter of the security; and

(iii) Separate Aggregation. The requirement in paragraph (c)(7)(i) of this section applies independently with respect to each investment adviser of the investment company that is, or is an affiliated person of, a principal underwriter of the security.

(8) Prohibition of Certain Affiliate Transactions. Such investment company does not purchase the securities being offered directly or indirectly from an officer, director, member of an advisory board, investment adviser or employee of such investment company or from a person of which any such officer, director, member of an advisory board, investment adviser or employee is an affiliated person; provided, that a purchase from a syndicate manager shall not be deemed to be a purchase from a specific underwriter if:

(i) Such underwriter does not benefit directly or indirectly from the transaction; or

(ii) In respect to the purchase of Eligible Municipal Securities, such purchase is not designated as a group sale or otherwise allocated to the account of any person from whom this paragraph prohibits the purchase.

(9) Periodic Reporting. The existence of any transactions effected pursuant to this section shall be reported on the Form N–SAR [§ 274.101 of this chapter] of the investment company and a written record of each such transaction, setting forth from whom the securities were acquired, the identity of the underwriting syndicate's members, the terms of the transaction, and the information or materials upon which the determination described in paragraph (c)(10)(iii) of this section was made shall be attached thereto.

(10) Board Review. The board of directors of the investment company, including a majority of the directors who are not interested persons of the investment company;

(i) Has approved procedures, pursuant to which such purchases may be effected for the company, that are reasonably designed to provide that the purchases comply with all the conditions of this section;

(ii) Approves such changes to the procedures as the board deems necessary; and

(iii) Determines no less frequently than quarterly that all purchases made during the preceding quarter were effected in compliance with such procedures.

(11) *Board Composition.* The board of directors of the investment company satisfies the fund governance standards defined in § 270.0–1(a)(7).

(12) Maintenance of Records. The investment company:

(i) Shall maintain and preserve permanently in an easily accessible place a written copy of the procedures, and any modification thereto, described in paragraphs (c)(10)(i) and (c)(10)(ii) of this section; and

(ii) Shall maintain and preserve for a period not less than six years from the end of the fiscal year in which any transactions occurred, the first two years in an easily accessible place, a written record of each such transaction, setting forth from whom the securities were acquired, the identity of the underwriting syndicate's members, the terms of the transaction, and the information or materials upon which the determination described in paragraph (c)(10)(iii) of this section was made.

§ 270.11a–1 Definition of "Exchange" for Purposes of Section 11 of the Act

(a) For the purposes of section 11 of the Act, the term "exchange" as used therein shall include the issuance of any security by a registered investment company in an amount equal to the proceeds, or any portion of the proceeds, paid or payable—

(1) Upon the repurchase, by or at the instance of such issuer, of an outstanding security the terms of which provide for its termination, retirement or cancellation, or

(2) Upon the termination, retirement or cancellation of an outstanding security of

such issuer in accordance with the terms thereof.

(b) A security shall not be deemed to have been repurchased by or at the instance of the issuer, or terminated, retired or canceled in accordance with the terms of the security if—

(1) The security was redeemed or repurchased at the instance of the holder; or

(2) A security holder's account was closed for failure to make payments as prescribed in the security or instruments pursuant to which the security was issued, and notice of intention to close the account was mailed to the security holder, and he had a reasonable time in which to meet the deficiency; or

(3) Sale of the security was restricted to a specified, limited group of persons and, in accordance with the terms of the security or the instruments pursuant to which the security was issued, upon its being transferred by the holder to a person not a member of the group eligible to purchase the security, the issuer required the surrender of the security and paid the redemption price thereof.

(c) The provisions of paragraph (a) of this section shall not apply if, following the repurchase of an outstanding security by or at the instance of the issuer or the termination, retirement or cancellation of an outstanding security in accordance with the terms thereof—

(1) The proceeds are actually paid to the security holder by or on behalf of the issuer within 7 days, and

(2) No sale and no offer (other than by way of exchange) of any security of the issuer is made by or on behalf of the issuer to the person to whom such proceeds were paid, within 60 days after such payment.

(d) The provisions of paragraph (a) of this section shall not apply to the repurchase, termination, retirement, or cancellation of a security outstanding on the effective date of this section or issued pursuant to a subscription agreement or other plan of acquisition in effect on such date.

§ 270.11a-2 Offers of Exchange by Certain Registered Separate Accounts or Others the Terms of Which Do Not Require Prior Commission Approval

(a) As used in this rule:

(1) "Deferred sales load" shall mean any sales load, including a contingent deferred sales load, that is deducted upon redemption or annuitization of amounts representing all or a portion of a securityholder's interest in a separate account;

(2) "Exchanged security" shall include not only the security or securities (or portion[s] thereof) of a security holder actually exchanged pursuant to an exchange offer but also any security or securities (or portions[s] thereof) of the securityholder previously exchanged for the exchanged security or its predecessors;

(3) "Front-end sales load" shall mean any sales load that is deducted from one or more purchase payments made by a securityholder before they are invested in a separate account; and

(4) "Purchase payments made for the acquired security," as used in paragraphs (c)(2) and (d)(2) of this section, shall not include any purchase payments made for the exchanged security or any appreciation attributable to those purchase payments that are transferred to the offering account in connection with an exchange.

(b) Notwithstanding section 11 of the Act, any registered separate account or any principal underwriter for such an account (collectively, the "offering account") may make or cause to be made an offer to the holder of a security of the offering account, or of any other registered separate account having the same insurance company depositor or sponsor as the offering account or having an insurance company depositor or sponsor that is an affiliate of the offering account's depositor or sponsor, to exchange his security (or portion thereof) (the "exchanged security") for a security (or portion thereof) of the offering account (the "acquired security") without the terms of such exchange offer first having been submitted to and approved by the Commission, as provided below:

(1) If the securities (or portions thereof) involved are variable annuity contracts, then

(i) The exchange must be made on the basis of the relative net asset values of the securities to be exchanged, except that the offering account may deduct at the time of the exchange

(A) An administrative fee which is disclosed in the part of the offering account's registration statement under the Securities Act of 1933 relating to the prospectus, and

(B) Any front-end sales load permitted by paragraph (c) of this section, and

(ii) Any deferred sales load imposed on the acquired security by the offering account shall be calculated in the manner prescribed by paragraph (d) or (e) of this section; or

(2) If the securities (or portions thereof) involved are variable life insurance contracts offered by a separate account registered under the Act as a unit investment trust, then the exchange must be made on the basis of the relative net asset values of the securities to be exchanged, except that the offering account may deduct at the time of the exchange an administrative fee which is disclosed in the part of the offering account's registration statement under the Securities Act of 1933 relating to the prospectus.

(c) If the offering account imposes a front-end sales load on the acquired security, then such sales load

(1) Shall be a percentage that is no greater than the excess of the rate of the front-end sales load otherwise applicable to that security over the rate of any front-end sales load previously paid on the exchanged security.

(2) Shall not exceed 9 percent of the sum of the purchase payments made for the acquired security and the exchanged security.

(d) If the offering account imposes a deferred sales load on the acquired security and the exchanged security also was subject to a deferred sales load, then any deferred sales load imposed on the acquired security

(1) Shall be calculated as if

(i) The holder of the acquired security had been the holder of that security from the date on which he became the holder of the exchanged security and

(ii) Purchase payments made for the exchanged security had been made for the acquired security on the date on which they were made for the exchanged security; and

(2) Shall not exceed 9 percent of the sum of the purchase payments made for the acquired security and the exchanged security.

(e) If the offering account imposes a deferred sales load on the acquired security and the exchanged security also was subject to a deferred sales load, any deferred sales load imposed on the acquired security may not be imposed on purchase payments made for the exchanged security or any appreciation attributable to purchase payments made for the exchanged security that are transferred in connection with the exchange.

(f) Notwithstanding the foregoing, no offer of exchange shall be made in reliance on this section if both a front-end sales load and a deferred sales load are to be imposed on the acquired security or if both such sales loads are imposed on the exchanged security.

§ 270.11a–3 Offers of Exchange by Open–End Investment Companies Other Than Separate Accounts

(a) For purposes of this rule:

(1) "Acquired security" means the security held by a securityholder after completing an exchange pursuant to an exchange offer;

(2) "Administrative fee" means any fee, other than a sales load, deferred sales load or redemption fee, that is

(i) Reasonably intended to cover the costs incurred in processing exchanges of the type for which the fee is charged. *Provided*, That: the offering company will maintain and preserve records of any determination of the costs incurred in connection with exchanges for a period of not less than six years, the first two years in an easily accessible place. The records preserved under this provision shall be subject to inspection by the Commission in accordance with section 31(b) of the Act as if such records were records required to be maintained under rules adopted under section 31(a) of the Act; or

(ii) A nominal fee as defined in paragraph (a)(8) of this rule;

(3) *Deferred sales load* means any amount properly chargeable to sales or promotional expenses that is paid by a shareholder after purchase but before or upon redemption;

(4) "Exchanged security" means

(i) The security actually exchanged pursuant to an exchange offer, and

(ii) Any security previously exchanged for such security or for any of its predecessors;

(5) "Group of investment companies" means any two or more registered open-end investment companies that hold themselves out to investors as related companies for purposes of investment and investor services, and

(i) That have a common investment adviser or principal underwriter, or

(ii) The investment adviser or principal underwriter of one of the companies is an affiliated person as defined in section 2(a)(3) of the Act of the investment adviser or principal underwriter of each of the other companies;

(6) "Offering company" means a registered open-end investment company (other than a registered separate account) or any principal underwriter thereof that makes an offer (an "exchange offer") to the holder of a security of that company, or of another open-end investment company within the same group of investment companies as the offering company, to exchange that security for a security of the offering company;

(7) "Redemption fee" means any fee (other than a sales load, deferred sales load or administrative fee) that is paid to the fund and is reasonably intended to compensate the fund for expenses directly related to the redemption of fund shares; and

(8) "Nominal fee" means a slight or *de minimis* fee.

(b) Notwithstanding section 11(a) of the Act and except as provided in paragraphs (d) and (e) of this rule, in connection with an exchange offer an offering company may cause a securityholder to be charged a sales load on the acquired security, a redemption fee, an administrative fee, or any combination of the foregoing,

Provided, That:

(1) Any administrative fee or scheduled variation thereof is applied uniformly to all securityholders of the class specified;

(2) Any redemption fee charged with respect to the exchanged security or any scheduled variation thereof

(i) Is applied uniformly to all securityholders of the class specified, and

(ii) Does not exceed the redemption fee applicable to a redemption of the exchanged security in the absence of an exchange.

Any scheduled variation of a redemption fee must be reasonably related to the costs to the fund of processing the type of redemptions for which the fee is charged;

(3) No deferred sales load is imposed on the exchanged security at the time of an exchange;

(4) Any sales load charged with respect to the acquired security is a percentage that is no greater than the excess, if any, of the rate of the sales load applicable to that security in the absence of an exchange over the sum of the rates of all sales loads previously paid on the exchanged security,

Provided, That:

(i) The percentage rate of any sales load charged when the acquired security is redeemed, that is solely the result of a deferred sales load imposed on the exchanged security, may be no greater than the excess, if any, of the applicable rate of such sales load, calculated in accordance with paragraph (b)(5) of this rule, over the sum of the rates of all sales loads previously paid on the acquired security, and

(ii) In no event may the sum of the rates of all sales loads imposed prior to and at the time the acquired security is redeemed, including any sales load paid or to be paid with respect to the exchanged security, exceed the maximum sales load rate, calculated in accordance with paragraph (b)(5) of this rule, that would be applicable in the absence of an exchange to the security (exchanged or acquired) with the highest such rate;

(5) Any deferred sales load charged at the time the acquired security is redeemed is calculated as if the holder of the acquired security had held that security from the date on which he became the holder of the exchanged security, *Provided*, That:

(i) The time period during which the acquired security is held need not be included when the amount of the deferred sales load is calculated, if the deferred sales load is

(A) reduced by the amount of any fees collected on the acquired security under the terms of any plan of distribution adopted in accordance with rule 12b–1 under the Act (a "12b–1 plan"), and

(B) solely the result of a sales load imposed on the exchanged security, and no other sales loads, including deferred sales loads, are imposed with respect to the acquired security,

(ii) The time period during which the exchanged security is held need not be included when the amount of the deferred sales load on the acquired security is calculated, if

(A) the deferred sales load is reduced by the amount of any fees previously collected on the exchanged security under the terms of any 12b–1 plan, and

(B) the exchanged security was not subject to any sales load, and

(iii) The holding periods in this subsection may be computed as of the end of the calendar month in which a security was purchased or redeemed;

(6) The prospectus of the offering company discloses

(i) the amount of any administrative or redemption fee imposed on an exchange transaction for its securities, as well as the amount of any administrative or redemption fee imposed on its securityholders to acquire the securities of other investment companies in an exchange transaction, and

(ii) if the offering company reserves the right to change the terms of or terminate an exchange offer, that the exchange offer is subject to termination and its terms are subject to change;

(7) Any sales literature or advertising that mentions the existence of the exchange offer also discloses

(i) the existence of any administrative fee or redemption fee that would be imposed at the time of an exchange; and

(ii) if the offering company reserves the right to change the terms of or terminate the exchange offer, that the exchange offer is subject to termination and its terms are subject to change;

(8) Whenever an exchange offer is to be terminated or its terms are to be amended materially, any holder of a security subject to that offer shall be given prominent notice of the impending termination or amendment at least 60 days prior to the date of termination or the effective date of the amendment,

Provided, That:

(i) No such notice need be given if the only material effect of an amendment is to reduce or eliminate an administrative fee, sales load or redemption fee payable at the time of an exchange, and

(ii) No notice need be given if, under extraordinary circumstances, either

(A) there is a suspension of the redemption of the exchanged security under section 22(e) of the Act and the rules and regulations thereunder, or

(B) the offering company temporarily delays or ceases the sale of the acquired security because it is unable to invest amounts effectively in accordance with applicable investment objectives, policies and restrictions; and

(9) In calculating any sales load charged with respect to the acquired security:

(i) If a securityholder exchanges less than all of his securities, the security upon which the highest sales load rate was previously paid is deemed exchanged first; and

(ii) If the exchanged security was acquired through reinvestment of dividends or capital gains distributions, that security is deemed to have been sold with a sales load rate equal to the sales load rate previously paid on the security on which the dividend was paid or distribution made.

(c) If either no sales load is imposed on the acquired security or the sales load imposed is less than the maximum allowed by paragraph (b)(4) of this rule, the offering company may require the exchanging securityholder to have held the exchanged security for a minimum period of time previously established by the offering company and applied uniformly to all securityholders of the class specified.

(d) Any offering company that has previously made an offer of exchange may continue to impose fees or sales loads permitted by an order under section 11(a) of the Act upon shares purchased before the earlier of (1) One year after the effective date of this section, or (2) When the offer has been brought into compliance with the terms of this rule, and upon shares acquired through reinvestment of dividends or capital gains distributions based on such shares, until such shares are redeemed.

(e) Any offering company that has previously made an offer of exchange cannot rely on this rule to amend such prior offer unless

(1) the offering company's prospectus disclosed, during at least the two year period prior to the amendment of the offer (or, if the fund is less than two years old, at all times the offer has been outstanding) that the terms of the offer were subject to change, or

(2) the only effect of such change is to reduce or eliminate an administrative fee, sales load or redemption fee payable at the time of an exchange.

[The Appendix containing illustrations of the sales load provisions of § 270.11a–3 which appears at 54 F.R. 35187 is omitted.]

§ 270.12b–1 Distribution of Shares by Registered Open-End Management Investment Company

(a)(1) Except as provided in this section, it shall be unlawful for any registered open-end management investment company (other than a company complying with the provisions of section 10(d) of the Act) to act as a distributor of securities of which it is the issuer, except through an underwriter;

(2) For purposes of this section, such a company will be deemed to be acting as a distributor of securities of which it is the issuer, other than through an underwriter, if it engaged directly or indirectly in financing any activity which is primarily intended to result in the sale of shares issued by such company, including, but not necessarily limited to, advertising, compensation of underwriters, dealers, and sales personnel, the printing and mailing of prospectuses to other than current shareholders, and the printing and mailing of sales literature;

(b) A registered, open-end management investment company ("company") may act as a distributor of securities of which it is the issuer, *Provided,* That any payments made by such company in connection with such distribution are made pursuant to a written plan describing all material aspects of the proposed financing of distribution and that all agreements with any person relating to implementation of the plan are in writing, *and further provided,* That:

(1) Such plan has been approved by a vote of at least a majority of the outstanding voting securities of such company, if adopted after any public offering of the company's voting securities or the sale of such securities to persons who are not affiliated persons of the company, affiliated persons of such persons, promoters of the company, or affiliated persons of such promoters;

(2) Such plan, together with any related agreements, has been approved by a vote of the board of directors of such company, and of the directors who are not interested persons of the company and have no direct or indirect financial interest in the operation of the plan or in any agreements related to the plan, cast in person at a meeting called for the purpose of voting on such plan or agreements;

(3) Such plan or agreement provides, in substance:

(i) That it shall continue in effect for a period of more than one year from the date of its execution or adoption only so long as such continuance is specifically approved at least annually in the manner described in paragraph (b)(2);

(ii) That any person authorized to direct the disposition of monies paid or payable by such company pursuant to the plan or any related agreement shall provide to the company's board of directors, and the directors shall review, at least quarterly, a written report of the amounts so expended and the purposes for which such expenditures were made; and

(iii) In the case of a plan, that it may be terminated at any time by vote of a majority of the members of the board of directors of the company who are not interested persons of the company and have no direct or indirect financial interest in the operation of the plan or in any agreements related to the plan or by vote of a majority of the outstanding voting securities of such company;

(iv) In the case of an agreement related to a plan:

(A) That it may be terminated at any time, without the payment of any penalty, by vote of a majority of the members of the board of directors of such company who are not interested persons of the company and have no direct or indirect financial interest in the operation of the plan or in any agreements related to the plan or by vote of a majority of the outstanding voting securities of such company on not more than sixty days' written notice to any other party to the agreement, and

(B) For its automatic termination in the event of its assignment;

(4) Such plan provides that it may not be amended to increase materially the amount to be spent for distribution without shareholder approval and that all material

amendments of the plan must be approved in the manner described in paragraph (b)(2); and

(5) Such plan is implemented and continued in a manner consistent with the provisions of paragraphs (c), (d), and (e) of this section;

(c) A registered open-end management investment company may rely on the provisions of paragraph (b) of this section only if its board of directors satisfies the fund governance standards as defined in § 270.0–1(a)(7);

(d) In considering whether a registered open-end management investment company should implement or continue a plan in reliance on paragraph (b) of this section, the directors of such company shall have a duty to request and evaluate, and any person who is a party to any agreement with such company relating to such plan shall have a duty to furnish, such information as may reasonably be necessary to an informed determination of whether such plan should be implemented or continued; in fulfilling their duties under this paragraph the directors should consider and give appropriate weight to all pertinent factors, and minutes describing the factors considered and the basis for the decision to use company assets for distribution must be made and preserved in accordance with paragraph (f) of this section;

NOTE: For a discussion of factors which may be relevant to a decision to use company assets for distribution, see Investment Company Act Releases Nos. 10862, September 7, 1979, and 11414, October 28, 1980.

(e) A registered open-end management investment company may implement or continue a plan pursuant to paragraph (b) of this section only if the directors who vote to approve such implementation or continuation conclude, in the exercise of reasonable business judgment and in light of their fiduciary duties under state law and under sections 36(a) and (b) [15 U.S.C. 80a–35(a) and (b)] of the Act, that there is a reasonable likelihood that the plan will benefit the company and its shareholders;

(f) A registered open-end management investment company must preserve copies of any plan, agreement or report made pursuant to this section for a period of not less than six years from the date of such plan, agreement or report, the first two years in an easily accessible place;

(g) If a plan covers more than one series or class of shares, the provisions of the plan must be severable for each series or class, and whenever this section provides for any action to be taken with respect to a plan, that action must be taken separately for each series or class affected by the matter. Nothing in this paragraph (g) shall affect the rights of any purchase class under § 270.18f–3(e)(2)(iii); and

(h) Notwithstanding any other provision of this section, a company may not:

(1) Compensate a broker or dealer for any promotion or sale of shares issued by that company by directing to the broker or dealer:

(i) The company's portfolio securities transactions; or

(ii) Any remuneration, including but not limited to any commission, mark-up, mark-down, or other fee (or portion thereof) received or to be received from the company's portfolio transactions effected through any other broker (including a government securities broker) or dealer (including a municipal securities dealer or a government securities dealer); and

(2) Direct its portfolio securities transactions to a broker or dealer that promotes or sells shares issued by the company, unless the company (or its investment adviser):

(i) Is in compliance with the provisions of paragraph (h)(1) of this section with respect to that broker or dealer; and

(ii) Has implemented, and the company's board of directors (including a majority of directors who are not interested persons of the company) has approved, policies and procedures reasonably designed to prevent:

(A) The persons responsible for selecting brokers and dealers to effect the company's portfolio securities transactions from taking into account the brokers' and dealers' promotion or sale of shares issued by the company or any other registered investment company; and

(B) The company, and any investment adviser and principal underwriter of the company, from entering into any agreement (whether oral or written) or other understanding under which the company directs, or is expected to direct, portfolio securities transactions, or any remuneration described in paragraph (h)(1)(ii) of this section, to a broker (including a government securities broker) or dealer (including a municipal securities dealer or a government securities dealer) in consideration for the promotion or sale of shares issued by the company or any other registered investment company.

§ 270.12d2-1 Definition of Insurance Company for Purposes of Sections 12(d)(2) and 12(g) of the Act

For purposes of sections 12(d)(2) and 12(g) of the Act, *insurance company* shall include a foreign insurance company as that term is used in rule 3a-6 under the Act.

§ 270.12d3-1 Exemption of Acquisitions of Securities Issued by Persons Engaged in Securities Related Businesses

(a) Notwithstanding section 12(d)(3) of the Act, a registered investment company, or any company or companies controlled by such registered investment company ("acquiring company") may acquire any security issued by any person, that, in its most recent fiscal year, derived 15 percent or less of its gross revenues from securities related activities unless the acquiring company would control such person after the acquisition.

(b) Notwithstanding section 12(d)(3) of the Act, an acquiring company may acquire any security issued by a person that, in its most recent fiscal year, derived more than 15 percent of its gross revenues from securities related activities, *Provided*, That:

(1) immediately after the acquisition of any equity security, the acquiring company owns not more than five percent of the outstanding securities of that class of the issuer's equity securities;

(2) immediately after the acquisition of any debt security, the acquiring company owns not more than ten percent of the outstanding principal amount of the issuer's debt securities; and

(3) immediately after any such acquisition, the acquiring company has invested not more than five percent of the value of its total assets in the securities of the issuer.

(c) Notwithstanding paragraphs (a) and (b) of this section, this section does not exempt the acquisition of:

(1) A general partnership interest; or

(2) A security issued by the acquiring company's promoter, principal underwriter, or any affiliated person of such promoter, or principal underwriter; or

(3) A security issued by the acquiring company's investment adviser, or an affiliated person of the acquiring company's investment adviser, other than a security issued by a subadviser or an affiliated person of a subadviser of the acquiring company provided that:

(i) *Prohibited relationships.* The subadviser that is (or whose affiliated person is) the issuer is not, and is not an affiliated person of, an investment adviser responsible for providing advice with respect to the portion of the acquiring company that is acquiring the securities, or of any promoter, underwriter, officer, director, member of an advisory board, or employee of the acquiring company;

(ii) *Advisory contract.* The advisory contracts of the Subadviser that is (or whose affiliated person is) the issuer, and any Subadviser that is advising the portion of the acquiring company that is purchasing the securities:

(A) Prohibit them from consulting with each other concerning transactions of the acquiring company in securities or other assets, other than for purposes of complying with the conditions of paragraphs (a) and (b) of this section; and

(B) Limit their responsibility in providing advice to providing advice with respect to a discrete portion of the acquiring company's portfolio.

(d) For purposes of this section:

(1) "Securities related activities" are a person's activities as a broker, a dealer, an underwriter, an investment adviser registered under the Investment Advisers Act of 1940, as amended, or as an investment adviser to a registered investment company.

(2) An issuer's gross revenues from its own securities related activities and from its ratable share of the securities related activities of enterprises of which it owns 20 percent or more of the voting or equity interest should be considered in determining the degree to which an issuer is engaged in securities related activities. Such information may be obtained from the issuer's annual report to shareholders, the issuer's annual reports or registration statement filed with the Commission, or the issuer's chief financial officer.

(3) "Equity security" is as defined in § 240.3a–11 of this chapter.

(4) "Debt security" includes all securities other than equity securities.

(5) Determination of the percentage of an acquiring company's ownership of any class of outstanding equity securities of an issuer shall be made in accordance with the procedures described in the rules under § 240.16 of this chapter.

(6) Where an acquiring company is considering acquiring or has acquired options, warrants, rights, or convertible securities of a securities related business, the determination required by paragraph (b) of this section shall be made as though such options, warrants, rights, or conversion privileges had been exercised.

(7) The following transactions will not be deemed to be an acquisition of securities of a securities related business:

(i) Receipt of stock dividends on securities acquired in compliance with this section;

(ii) Receipt of securities arising from a stock-for-stock split on securities acquired in compliance with this section;

(iii) Exercise of options, warrants, or rights acquired in compliance with this section;

(iv) Conversion of convertible securities acquired in compliance with this section; and

(v) Acquisition of Demand Features or Guarantees, as these terms are defined in § 270.2a–7(a)(8) and § 270.2a–7(a)(15) respectively, provided that, immediately after the acquisition of any Demand Feature or Guarantee, the company will not, with respect to 75 percent of the total value of its assets, have invested more than ten percent of the total value of its assets in securities underlying Demand Features or Guarantees from the same institution. For the purpose of this section, a Demand Feature or Guarantee will be considered to be from the party to whom the company will look for payment of the exercise price.

(8) Any class or series of an investment company that issues two or more classes or series of preferred or special stock, each of which is preferred over all other classes or series with respect to assets specifically allocated to that class or series, shall be treated as if it is a registered investment company.

(9) *Subadviser* means an investment adviser as defined in section 2(a)(20)(B) of the Act (15 U.S.C. 80a–2(a)(20)(B)).

§ 270.13a–1 Exemption for Change of Status by Temporarily Diversified Company

A change of its subclassification by a registered management company from that of a diversified company to that of a nondiversified company shall be exempt from the provisions of section 13(a)(1) of the Act, if such change occurs under the following circumstances:

(a) Such company was a nondiversified company at the time of its registration pursuant to section 8(a) or thereafter legally became a nondiversified company.

(b) After its registration and within 3 years prior to such change, such company became a diversified company.

(c) At the time such company became a diversified company, its registration statement filed pursuant to section 8(b) as supplemented and modified by any amendments and reports theretofore filed, did not state that the registrant proposed to become a diversified company.

§ 270.14a–1 Use of Notification Pursuant to Regulation E Under the Securities Act of 1933

For the purposes of section 14(a)(3) of the Act, registration of securities under the Securities Act of 1933 by a small business investment company operating under the Small Business Investment Act of 1958 shall be deemed to include the filing of a notification under Rule 604 of Regulation E promulgated under said Act if provision is made in connection with such notification which in the opinion of the Commission adequately insures (a) that after the effective date of such notification such company will not issue any security or receive any proceeds of any subscription for any security until firm agreements have been made with such company by not more than twenty-five responsible persons to purchase from it securities to be issued by it for an aggregate net amount which plus the then net worth of the company, if any, will equal at least $100,000; (b) that said aggregate net amount will be paid into such company before any subscriptions for such securities will be accepted from any persons in excess of twenty-five; (c) that arrangements will be made whereby any proceeds so paid in, as well as any sales load, will be refunded to any subscriber on demand without any deduction, in the event that the net proceeds so received by the company do not result in the company having a net worth of at least $100,000 within ninety days after such notification becomes effective.

§ 270.14a–2 Exemption From Section 14(a) of the Act for Certain Registered Separate Accounts and Their Principal Underwriters

(a) A registered separate account, and any principal underwriter for such account, shall be exempt from section 14(a) of the Act with respect to a public offering of variable annuity contracts participating in such account if, at the commencement of such offering, the insurance company establishing and maintaining such separate account shall have (1) a combined capital and surplus, if a stock company, or (2) an unassigned surplus, if a mutual company, of not less than $1,000,000 as set forth in the balance sheet of such insurance company contained in the registration statement or any amendment thereto relating to such contracts filed pursuant to the Securities Act of 1933.

(b) Any registered management investment company which has as a promoter an insurance company meeting the requirements of paragraph (a) of this section and which offers its securities to separate accounts of such insurance company registered under the Act as unit investment trusts ("trust accounts"), and any principal underwriter for such investment company, shall be exempt from section 14(a) with respect to such offering and to the offering of such securities to trust accounts of other insurance companies meeting the requirements of paragraph (a) of this section.

(c) Any registered management investment company exempt from section 14(a) of the Act pursuant to paragraph (b) of this section shall be exempt from sections 15(a), 16(a), and 32(a)(2) of the Act, to the extent prescribed in rules 15a–3, 16a–1, and 32a–2 under the Act, provided that such investment company complies with the conditions set forth in those rules as if it were a separate account.

§ 270.14a–3 Exemption From Section 14(a) for Certain Registered Unit Investment Trusts and Their Principal Underwriters

(a) A registered unit investment trust (hereinafter referred to as the "Trust") engaged exclusively in the business of investing in eligible trust securities, and any principal underwriter for the Trust, shall be exempt from section 14(a) of the Act with respect to a public offering of Trust units; *Provided,* That:

(1) At the commencement of such offering the Trust holds at least $100,000 principal amount of eligible trust securities (or delivery statements relating to contracts for the purchase of any such securities which, together with cash or an irrevocable letter of credit issued by a bank in the amount required for their purchase, are held by the Trust for purchase of the securities);

(2) If, within ninety days from the time that the Trust's registration statement has become effective under the Securities Act of 1933 the net worth of the Trust declines to less than $100,000 or the Trust is terminated, the sponsor for the Trust shall—

(i) refund, on demand and without deduction, all sales charges to any unitholders who purchased Trust units from the sponsor (or from any underwriter or dealer participating in the distribution), and

(ii) liquidate the trust securities held by the Trust and distribute the proceeds thereof to the unitholders of the Trust;

(3) The sponsor instructs the trustee when the eligible trust securities are deposited in the Trust that, in the event that redemptions by the sponsor or any underwriter of units constituting a part of the unsold units results in the Trust having a net worth of less than 40 percent of the principal amount of the eligible trust securities (or delivery statements relating to contracts for the purchase of any such securities which, together with cash or an irrevocable letter of credit issued by a bank in the amount required for their purchase, are held by the Trust for purchase of the securities) initially deposited in the Trust—

(i) the trustee shall terminate the Trust and distribute the assets thereof to the unitholders of the Trust, and

(ii) the sponsor for the Trust shall refund, on demand and without deduction, all sales charges to any unitholder who purchased Trust units from the sponsor or from any underwriter or dealer participating in the distribution.

(b) For the purposes of determining the availability of the exemption provided by the foregoing subsection, the term "eligible trust securities" shall mean:

(1) securities (other than convertible securities) which are issued by a corporation and which have their interest or dividend rate fixed at the time they are issued;

(2) interest bearing obligations issued by a state, or by any agency, instrumentality, authority or political subdivision thereof;

(3) government securities; and

(4) units of a previously issued series of the Trust; *Provided,* That:

(i) the aggregate principal amount of units of existing series so deposited shall not exceed 10% of the aggregate principal amount of the portfolio of the new series;

(ii) the aggregate principal amount of units of any particular existing series so deposited shall not exceed 5% of the aggregate principal amount of the portfolio of the new series;

(iii) no units shall be so deposited which do not substantially meet investment quality criteria at least as high as those applicable to the new series in which such units are deposited;

(iv) the value of the eligible trust securities underlying units of an existing series deposited in a new series shall not, by reason of maturity of such securities according to their terms within ten years following the date of deposit, be reduced sufficiently for such existing series to be voluntarily terminated;

(v) units of existing series so deposited shall constitute units purchased by the sponsor as market maker and not remaining unsold units from the original distribution of such units; and

(vi) the sponsor shall deposit units of existing series in the new series without a sales charge.

§ 270.15a-1 Exemption From Stockholders' Approval of Certain Small Investment Advisory Contracts

An investment adviser of a registered investment company shall be exempt from the requirement of sections 15(a) and 15(e) of the act (54 Stat. 812; 15 U.S.C. 80a-15) that the written contract pursuant to which he acts shall have been approved by the vote of a majority of the outstanding voting securities of such company, if the following conditions are met:

(a) Such investment adviser is not an affiliated person of such company (except as investment adviser) nor of any principal underwriter for such company.

(b) His compensation as investment adviser of such company in any fiscal year of the company during which any such contract is in effect either (1) is not more than $100 or (2) is not more than $2,500 and not more than 1/40 of 1 percent of the value of the company's net assets averaged over the year or taken as of a definite date or dates within the year.

(c) The aggregate compensation of all investment advisers of such company exempted pursuant to this section in any fiscal year of the company either (1) is not more than $200 or (2) is not more than 1/20 of 1 percent of the value of the company's net assets averaged over the year or taken as of a definite date or dates within the year.

§ 270.15a-2 Annual Continuance of Contracts

(a) For purposes of Sections 15(a) and 15(b) of the Act, the continuance of a contract for a period more than two years after the date of its execution shall be deemed to have been specifically approved at least annually by the board of directors or by a vote of a majority of the outstanding voting securities of a registered investment company if such approval occurs:

(1) with respect to the first continuance of a contract, during the 90 days prior to and including the earlier of (i) the date specified in such contract for its termination in the absence of such approval, or (ii) the second anniversary of the date upon which such contract was executed; or

(2) with respect to any subsequent continuance of a contract, during the 90 days prior to and including the first anniversary of the date upon which the most recent previous annual continuance of such contract became effective.

(b) The provisions of paragraph (a) of this section shall not apply to any continuance of a contract which shall have been approved not later than 90 days after the date of adoption of this section, provided that such contract shall expire, by its terms, not later than 17 months from the date of adoption of this section.

Note: This section does not establish the exclusive method of complying with the Act. It provides one procedure by which a registered investment company may comply with the applicable provisions of Sections 15(a) and 15(b) of the Act; it does not preclude any other appropriate procedure. Any annual continuance of a contract approved in accordance with the provisions of paragraphs (a)(1) or (a)(2) of Section 270.15A–2 will constitute a renewal of such contract for the purposes of Section 15(c) of the Act, and therefore such renewal must be approved by the disinterested directors within the times specified in the section for a continuance.

Section 270.15a–2 is adopted pursuant to the authority granted to the Commission in Section 38(a) of the Investment Company Act of 1940. The rule shall become effective October 29, 1976 to afford interested persons sufficient time to become familiar with the rule as adopted.

§ 270.15a–3 Exemption for Initial Period of Investment Adviser of Certain Registered Separate Accounts From Requirement of Security Holder Approval of Investment Advisory Contract

(a) An investment adviser of a registered separate account shall be exempt from the requirement under section 15(a) of the Act that the initial written contract pursuant to which the investment adviser serves or acts shall have been approved by the vote of a majority of the outstanding voting securities of such registered separate account, subject to the following conditions:

(1) Such registered separate account qualifies for exemption from section 14(a) of the Act pursuant to § 270.14a–2, or is exempt therefrom by order of the Commission upon application; and

(2) Such written contract shall be submitted to a vote of variable annuity contract owners at their first meeting after the effective date of the registration statement under the Securities Act of 1933, as amended, relating to variable annuity contracts participating in such account: *Provided,* That such meeting shall take place within 1 year after such effective date, unless the time for the holding of such meeting shall be extended by the Commission upon written request showing good cause therefor.

§ 270.15a–4 Temporary Exemption for Certain Investment Advisers

(a) For purposes of this section:

(1) "Fund" means an investment company, and includes a separate series of the company.

(2) "Interim contract" means a written investment advisory contract:

(i) That has not been approved by a majority of the fund's outstanding voting securities; and

(ii) That has a duration no greater than 150 days following the date on which the previous contract terminates.

(3) "Previous contract" means an investment advisory contract that has been approved by a majority of the fund's outstanding voting securities and has been terminated.

(b) Notwithstanding section 15(a) of the Act (15 U.S.C. 80a–15(a)), a person may act as investment adviser for a fund under an interim contract after the termination of a previous contract as provided in paragraphs (b)(1) or (b)(2) of this section:

(1) In the case of a previous contract terminated by an event described in section 15(a)(3) of the Act (15 U.S.C. 80a–15(a)(3)), by the failure to renew the previous contract, or by an assignment (other than an assignment by an investment adviser or a controlling person of the investment adviser in connection with which assignment the investment adviser or a controlling person directly or indirectly receives money or other benefit):

(i) The compensation to be received under the interim contract is no greater than the compensation the adviser would have received under the previous contract; and

(ii) The fund's board of directors, including a majority of the directors who are not interested persons of the fund, has approved the interim contract within 10 business days after the termination, at a meeting in which directors may participate by any means of communication that allows all directors participating to hear each other simultaneously during the meeting.

(2) In the case of a previous contract terminated by an assignment by an investment adviser or a controlling person of the investment adviser in connection with which assignment the investment adviser or a controlling person directly or indirectly receives money or other benefit:

(i) The compensation to be received under the interim contract is no greater than the compensation the adviser would have received under the previous contract;

(ii) The board of directors, including a majority of the directors who are not interested persons of the fund, has voted in person to approve the interim contract before the previous contract is terminated;

(iii) The board of directors, including a majority of the directors who are not interested persons of the fund, determines that the scope and quality of services to be provided to the fund under the interim contract will be at least equivalent to the scope and quality of services provided under the previous contract;

(iv) The interim contract provides that the fund's board of directors or a majority of the fund's outstanding voting securities may terminate the contract at any time, without the payment of any penalty, on not more than 10 calendar days' written notice to the investment adviser;

(v) The interim contract contains the same terms and conditions as the previous contract, with the exception of its effective and termination dates, provisions governed by paragraphs (b)(2)(i), (b)(2)(iv), and (b)(2)(vi) of this section, and any other differences in terms and conditions that the board of directors, including a majority of the directors who are not interested persons of the fund, finds to be immaterial;

(vi) The interim contract contains the following provisions:

(A) The compensation earned under the contract will be held in an interest-bearing escrow account with the fund's custodian or a bank;

(B) If a majority of the fund's outstanding voting securities approve a contract with the investment adviser by the end of the 150–day period, the amount in the escrow account (including interest earned) will be paid to the investment adviser; and

(C) If a majority of the fund's outstanding voting securities do not approve a contract with the investment adviser, the investment adviser will be paid, out of the escrow account, the lesser of:

(*1*) Any costs incurred in performing the interim contract (plus interest earned on that amount while in escrow); or

(*2*) The total amount in the escrow account (plus interest earned); and

(vii)The board of directors of the investment company satisfies the fund governance standards defined in § 270.0–1(a)(7).

§ 270.16a–1 Exemption for Initial Period of Directors of Certain Registered Accounts From Requirement of Election by Security Holders

(a) Persons serving as the directors of a registered separate account shall, prior to the first meeting of such account's variable annuity contract owners, be exempt from the requirement of section 16(a) of the Act that such persons be elected by the holders of outstanding voting securities of such account at an annual or special meeting called for that purpose, subject to the following conditions:

(1) Such registered separate account qualifies for exemption from section 14(a) of the Act pursuant to § 270.14a–1 or is exempt therefrom by order of the Commission upon application; and

(2) Such persons have been appointed directors of such account by the establishing insurance company; and

(3) An election of directors for such account shall be held at the first meeting of variable annuity contract owners after the effective date of the registration statement under the Securities Act of 1933, as amended, relating to contracts participating in such account: *Provided,* That such meeting shall take place within 1 year after such effective date, unless the time for the holding of such meeting shall be extended by the Commission upon written request showing good cause therefor.

§ 270.17a–1 Exemption of Certain Underwriting Transactions Exempted by § 270.10f–1

Any transaction exempted pursuant to § 270.10f–1 shall be exempt from the provisions of section 17(a)(1) of the act.

§ 270.17a–2 Exemption of Certain Purchase, Sale or Borrowing Transactions

Purchase, sale or borrowing transactions occurring in the usual course of business between affiliated persons of registered investment companies shall be exempt from section 17(a) of the act provided (a) the transactions involve notes, drafts, time payment contracts, bills of exchange, acceptance or other property of a commercial character rather than of an investment character; (b) the buyer or lender is a bank; and (c) the seller or borrower is a bank or is engaged principally in the business of installment financing.

§ 270.17a–3 Exemption of Transactions With Fully Owned Subsidiaries

(a) The following transactions shall be exempt from section 17(a) of the act:

(1) Transactions solely between a registered investment company and one or more of its fully owned subsidiaries or solely between two or more fully owned subsidiaries of such company.

(2) Transactions solely between any subsidiary of a registered investment company and one or more fully owned subsidiaries of such subsidiary or solely between two or more fully owned subsidiaries of such subsidiary.

(b) The term "fully owned subsidiary" as used in this section, means a subsidiary (1) all of whose outstanding securities, other than directors' qualifying shares, are owned by its parent and/or the parent's other fully owned subsidiaries, and (2) which is not indebted to any person other than its parent and/or the parent's other fully owned subsidiaries in an amount which is material in relation to the particular subsidiary, excepting (i) indebtedness incurred in the ordinary course of business which is not overdue and which matures within one year from the date of its creation, whether evidenced by securities or not, and (ii) any other indebtedness to one or more banks or insurance companies.

§ 270.17a–4 Exemption of Transactions Pursuant to Certain Contracts

Transactions pursuant to a contract shall be exempt from section 17(a) of the act if at the time of the making of the contract and for a period of at least six months prior thereto no affiliation or other relationship existed which would operate to make such contract or the subsequent performance thereof subject to the provisions of said section 17(a).

§ 270.17a–5 Pro Rata Distribution Neither "Sale" Nor "Purchase"

When a company makes a pro rata distribution in cash or in kind among its common stockholders without giving any election to any stockholder as to the specific assets which such stockholders shall receive, such distribution shall not be deemed to involve a sale to or a purchase from such distributing company as those terms are used in section 17(a) of the act.

§ 270.17a–6 Exemption for Transactions With Portfolio Affiliates

(a) *Exemption for transactions with portfolio affiliates.* A transaction to which a fund, or a company controlled by a fund, and a portfolio affiliate of the fund are parties is exempt from the provisions of section 17(a) of the Act (15 U.S.C. 80a–17(a)), provided that none of the following persons is a party to the transaction, or has a direct or indirect financial interest in a party to the transaction other than the fund:

(1) An officer, director, employee, investment adviser, member of an advisory board, depositor, promoter of or principal underwriter for the fund;

(2) A person directly or indirectly controlling the fund;

(3) A person directly or indirectly *owning, controlling or holding* with power to vote five percent or more of the outstanding voting securities of the fund;

(4) A person directly or indirectly under common control with the fund, other than:

(i) A portfolio affiliate of the fund; or

(ii) A fund whose sole interest in the transaction or a party to the transaction is an interest in the portfolio affiliate; or

(5) An affiliated person of any of the persons mentioned in paragraphs (a)(1)–(4) of this section, other than the fund or a portfolio affiliate of the fund.

(b) *Definitions.*

(1) *Financial interest.*

(i) The term *financial interest* as used in this section does not include:

(A) Any interest through ownership of securities issued by the fund;

(B) Any interest of a wholly-owned subsidiary of a fund;

(C) Usual and ordinary fees for services as a director;

(D) An interest of a non-executive employee;

(E) An interest of an insurance company arising from a loan or policy made or issued by it in the ordinary course of business to a natural person;

(F) An interest of a bank arising from a loan or account made or maintained by it in the ordinary course of business to or with a natural person, unless it arises from a loan to a person who is an officer, director or executive of a company which is a party to the transaction, or from a loan to a person who directly or indirectly owns, controls, or holds with power to vote, five percent or more of the outstanding voting securities of a company which is a party to the transaction;

(G) An interest acquired in a transaction described in paragraph (d)(3) of § 270.17d–1; or

(H) Any other interest that the board of directors of the fund, including a majority of the directors who are not interested persons of the fund, finds to be not material, provided that the directors record the basis for that finding in the minutes of their meeting.

(ii) A person has a financial interest in any party in which it has a financial interest, in which it had a financial interest within six months prior to the transaction, or in which it will acquire a financial interest pursuant to an arrangement in existence at the time of the transaction.

(2) *Fund* means a registered investment company or separate series of a registered investment company.

(3) *Portfolio affiliate of a fund* means a person that is an affiliated person (or an

affiliated person of an affiliated person) of a fund solely because the fund, a fund under common control with the fund, or both:

(i) Controls such person (or an affiliated person of such person); or

(ii) Owns, controls, or holds with power to vote five percent or more of the outstanding voting securities of such person (or an affiliated person of such person).

§ 270.17a–7 Exemption of Certain Purchase or Sale Transactions Between an Investment Company and Certain Affiliated Persons Thereof

A purchase or sale transaction between registered investment companies or separate series of registered investment companies, which are affiliated persons, or affiliated persons of affiliated persons, of each other, between separate series of a registered investment company, or between a registered investment company or a separate series of a registered investment company and a person which is an affiliated person of such registered investment company (or affiliated person of such person) solely by reason of having a common investment advisor or investment advisers which are affiliated persons of each other, common directors, and/or common officers, is exempt from section 17(a) of the Act; *Provided*, That:

(a) The transaction is a purchase or sale, for no consideration other than cash payment against prompt delivery of a security for which market quotations are readily available;

(b) The transaction is effected at the independent current market price of the security. For purposes of this paragraph the "current market price" shall be:

(1) If the security is a "reported security" as that term is defined in rule 11Aa3–1 under the Securities Exchange Act of 1934, the last sale price with respect to such security reported in the consolidated transaction reporting system ("consolidated system") or the average of the highest current independent bid and lowest current independent offer for such security (reported pursuant to rule 11Ac1–1 under the Securities Exchange Act of 1934) if there are no reported transactions in the consolidated system that day; or

(2) If the security is not a reported security, and the principal market for such security is an exchange, then the last sale on such exchange or the average of the highest current independent bid and lowest current independent offer on such exchange if there are no reported transactions on such exchange that day; or

(3) If the security is not a reported security and is quoted in the NASDAQ System, then the average of the highest current independent bid and lowest current independent offer reported on Level 1 of NASDAQ; or

(4) For all other securities, the average of the highest current independent bid and lowest current independent offer determined on the basis of reasonable inquiry;

(c) The transaction is consistent with the policy of each registered investment company and separate series of a registered investment company participating in the transaction, as recited in its registration statement and reports filed under the Act;

(d) No brokerage commission, fee (except for customary transfer fees), or other remuneration is paid in connection with the transaction;

(e) The board of directors of the investment company, including a majority of the directors who are not interested persons of such investment company, (1) adopts procedures pursuant to which such purchase or sale transactions may be effected for the company, which are reasonably designed to provide that all the conditions of this section in paragraphs (a) through (d) have been complied with, (2) makes and approves such changes as the board deems necessary, and

(3) determines no less frequently than quarterly that all such purchases or sales made during the preceding quarter were effected in compliance with such procedures;

(f)The board of directors of the investment company satisfies the fund governance standards defined in § 270.0–1(a)(7).

(g) The investment company (1) maintains and preserves permanently in an easily accessible place a written copy of the procedures (and any modifications thereto) described in paragraph (e) of this section, and (2) maintains and preserves for a period not less than six years from the end of the fiscal year in which any transactions occurred, the first two years in an easily accessible place, a written record of each such transaction setting forth a description of the security purchased or sold, the identity of the person on the other side of the transaction, the terms of the purchase or sale transaction, and the information or materials upon which the determinations described in paragraph (e)(3) of this section were made.

§ 270.17a-8 Mergers of Affiliated Companies

(a) *Exemption of affiliated mergers.* A Merger of a registered investment company (or a series thereof) and one or more other registered investment companies (or series thereof) or Eligible Unregistered Funds is exempt from sections 17(a)(1) and (2) of the Act (15 U.S.C. 80a–17(a)(1)–(2)) if:

(1) *Surviving company.* The Surviving Company is a registered investment company (or a series thereof).

(2) *Board determinations.* As to any registered investment company (or series thereof) participating in the Merger ("Merging Company"):

(i) The board of directors, including a majority of the directors who are not interested persons of the Merging Company or of any other company or series participating in the Merger, determines that:

(A) Participation in the Merger is in the best interests of the Merging Company; and

(B) The interests of the Merging Company's existing shareholders will not be diluted as a result of the Merger.

Note to paragraph (a)(2)(i): For a discussion of factors that may be relevant to the determinations in paragraph (a)(2)(i) of this section, see Investment Company Act Release No. 25666, July 10, 2002.

(ii) The directors have requested and evaluated such information as may reasonably be necessary to their determinations in paragraph (a)(2)(i) of this section, and have considered and given appropriate weight to all pertinent factors.

(iii) The directors, in making the determination in paragraph (a)(2)(i)(B) of this section, have approved procedures for the valuation of assets to be conveyed by each Eligible Unregistered Fund participating in the Merger. The approved procedures provide for the preparation of a report by an Independent Evaluator, to be considered in assessing the value of any securities (or other assets) for which market quotations are not readily available, that sets forth the fair value of each such asset as of the date of the Merger.

(iv) The determinations required in paragraph (a)(2)(i) of this section and the bases thereof, including the factors considered by the directors pursuant to paragraph (a)(2)(ii) of this section, are recorded fully in the minute books of the Merging Company.

(3) *Shareholder approval.* Participation in the Merger is approved by the vote of a majority of the outstanding voting securities (as provided in section 2(a)(42) of the Act (15 U.S.C. 80a–2(a)(42))) of any Merging Company that is not a Surviving Company, unless—

(i) No policy of the Merging Company that under section 13 of the Act (15 U.S.C.

80a–13) could not be changed without a vote of a majority of its outstanding voting securities, is materially different from a policy of the Surviving Company;

(ii) No advisory contract between the Merging Company and any investment adviser thereof is materially different from an advisory contract between the Surviving Company and any investment adviser thereof, except for the identity of the investment companies as a party to the contract;

(iii) Directors of the Merging Company who are not interested persons of the Merging Company and who were elected by its shareholders, will comprise a majority of the directors of the Surviving Company who are not interested persons of the Surviving Company; and

(iv) Any distribution fees (as a percentage of the fund's average net assets) authorized to be paid by the Surviving Company pursuant to a plan adopted in accordance with § 270.12b–1 are no greater than the distribution fees (as a percentage of the fund's average net assets) authorized to be paid by the Merging Company pursuant to such a plan.

(4) *Board composition.* The board of directors of the Merging Company satisfies the fund governance standards defined in § 270.0–1(a)(7).

(5) *Merger records.* Any Surviving Company preserves written records that describe the Merger and its terms for six years after the Merger (and for the first two years in an easily accessible place).

(b) *Definitions.* For purposes of this section:

(1) *Merger* means the merger, consolidation, or purchase or sale of substantially all of the assets between a registered investment company (or a series thereof) and another company;

(2) *Eligible Unregistered Fund* means:

(i) A collective trust fund, as described in section 3(c)(11) of the Act (15 U.S.C. 80a–3(c)(11));

(ii) A common trust fund or similar fund, as described in section 3(c)(3) of the Act (15 U.S.C. 80a–3(c)(3)); or

(iii) A separate account, as described in section 2(a)(37) of the Act (15 U.S.C. 80a–2(a)(37)), that is neither registered under section 8 of the Act, nor required to be so registered;

(3) *Independent Evaluator means a* person who has expertise in the valuation of securities and other financial assets and who is not an interested person, as defined in section 2(a)(19) of the Act (15 U.S.C. 80a–2(a)(19)), of the Eligible Unregistered Fund or any affiliate thereof except the Merging Company; and

(4) *Surviving Company means a* company in which shareholders of a Merging Company will obtain an interest as a result of a Merger.

§ 270.17a–9 Purchase of Certain Securities from a Money Market Fund by an Affiliate, or an Affiliate of an Affiliate

The purchase of a security that is no longer an Eligible Security (as defined in paragraph (a)(10) of § 270.2a–7) from an open-end investment company holding itself out as a "money market" fund shall be exempt from section 17(a) of the Act [15 U.S.C. 80a–17(a)], provided that:

(a) The purchase price is paid in cash; and

(b) The purchase price is equal to the greater of the amortized cost of the security or its market price (in each case, including accrued interest).

§ 270.17a–10 Exemption for Transactions with Certain Subadvisory Affiliates

(a) *Exemption.* A person that is prohibited by section 17(a) of the Act (15 U.S.C. 80a–17(a)) from entering into a transaction with a fund solely because such person is, or is an affiliated person of, a subadviser of the fund, or a subadviser of a fund that is under common control with the fund, may nonetheless enter into such transaction, if:

(1) *Prohibited Relationship.* The person is not, and is not an affiliated person of, an investment adviser responsible for providing advice with respect to the portion of the fund for which the transaction is entered into, or of any promoter, underwriter, officer, director, member of an advisory board, or employee of the fund.

(2) *Prohibited Conduct.* The advisory contracts of the subadviser that is (or whose affiliated person is) entering into the transaction, and any subadviser that is advising the fund (or portion of the fund) entering into the transaction:

(i) Prohibit them from consulting with each other concerning transactions for the fund in securities or other assets; and

(ii) If both such subadvisers are responsible for providing investment advice to the fund, limit the subadvisers' responsibility in providing advice with respect to a discrete portion of the fund's portfolio.

(b) *Definitions.*

(1) *Fund* means a registered investment company and includes a separate series of a registered investment company.

(2) *Subadviser* means an investment adviser as defined in section 2(a)(20)(B) of the Act (15 U.S.C. 80a–2(a)(20)(B)).

§ 270.17d–1 Applications Regarding Joint Enterprises or Arrangements and Certain Profit-Sharing Plans

(a) No affiliated person of or principal underwriter for any registered investment company (other than a company of the character described in section 12(d)(3)(A) and (B) of the act) and no affiliated person of such a person or principal underwriter, acting as principal, shall participate in, or effect any transaction in connection with, any joint enterprise or other joint arrangement or profit-sharing plan in which any such registered company, or a company controlled by such registered company, is a participant, and which is entered into, adopted or modified subsequent to the effective date of this rule, unless an application regarding such joint enterprise, arrangement or profit-sharing plan has been filed with the Commission and has been granted by an order entered prior to the submission of such plan or modification to security holders for approval, or prior to such adoption or modification if not so submitted, except that the provisions of this rule shall not preclude any affiliated person from acting as manager of any underwriting syndicate or other group in which such registered or controlled company is a participant and receiving compensation therefor.

(b) In passing upon such applications, the Commission will consider whether the participation of such registered or controlled company in such joint enterprise, joint arrangement or profit-sharing plan on the basis proposed is consistent with the provisions, policies and purposes of the act and the extent to which such participation is on a basis different from or less advantageous than that of other participants.

(c) "Joint enterprise or other joint arrangement or profit-sharing plan" as used in this section shall mean any written or oral plan, contract, authorization or arrangement, or any practice or understanding concerning an enterprise or undertaking whereby a registered investment company or a controlled company thereof and any affiliated person of or a principal underwriter for such registered investment company, or any affiliated person of such a person or principal underwriter, have a joint or a joint and several participation, or share in the profits of such enterprise or undertaking, including, but not limited to, any stock option or stock purchase plan, but shall not include an investment advisory contract subject to section 15 of the Act.

(d) Notwithstanding the requirements of paragraph (a) of this section, no application need be filed pursuant to this section with respect to any of the following:

(1) Any profit-sharing, stock option or stock purchase plan provided by any controlled company which is not an investment company for its officers, directors or employees, or the purchase of stock or the granting, modification or exercise of options pursuant to such a plan, *provided*:

(i) No individual participates therein who is either: (*a*) An affiliated person of any investment company which is an affiliated person of such controlled company; or (*b*) an affiliated person of the investment adviser or principal underwriter of such investment company; and

(ii) No participant has been an affiliated person of such investment company, its investment adviser or principal underwriter during the life of the plan and for six months prior to, as the case may be: (*a*) Institution of the profit-sharing plan; (*b*) the purchase of stock pursuant to a stock purchase plan; or (*c*) the granting of any options pursuant to a stock option plan.

(2) Any plan provided by any registered investment company or any controlled company for its officers or employees if such plan has been qualified under section 401 of the Internal Revenue Code of 1954 and all contributions paid under said plan by the employer qualify as deductible under section 404 of said Code.

(3) Any loan or advance of credit to, or acquisition of securities or other property of, a small business concern, or any agreement to do any of the foregoing (''Investments''), made by a bank and a small business investment company (SBIC) licensed under the Small Business Investment Act of 1958, whether such transactions are contemporaneous or separated in time, where the bank is an affiliated person of either (i) the SBIC or (ii) an affiliated person of the SBIC; but reports containing pertinent details as to Investments and transactions relating thereto shall be made at such time, on such forms and by such persons as the Commission may from time to time prescribe.

(4) The issuance by a registered investment company which is licensed by the Small Business Administration pursuant to the Small Business Investment Act of 1958 of stock options which qualify under section 422 of the Internal Revenue Code, as amended, and which conform to § 107.805(b) of Chapter I of Title 13 of the Code of Federal Regulations.

(5) Any joint enterprise or other joint arrangement or profit-sharing plan (''joint enterprise'') in which a registered investment company or a company controlled by such a company, is a participant, and in which a portfolio affiliate (as defined in § 270.17a–6(b)(3)) of such registered investment company is also a participant, provided that:

(i) None of the persons identified in § 270.17a–6(a) is a participant in the joint enterprise, or has a direct or indirect financial interest in a participant in the joint enterprise (other than the registered investment company);

(ii) *Financial interest.*

(A) The term *financial interest* as used in this section does not include:

(*1*) Any interest through ownership of securities issued by the registered investment company;

(*2*) Any interest of a wholly owned subsidiary of the registered investment company;

(*3*) Usual and ordinary fees for services as a director;

(*4*) An interest of a non-executive employee;

(*5*) An interest of an insurance company arising from a loan or policy made or issued by it in the ordinary course of business to a natural person;

(6) An interest of a bank arising from a loan to a person who is an officer, director, or executive of a company which is a participant in the joint transaction or from a loan to a person who directly or indirectly owns, controls, or holds with power to vote, five percent or more of the outstanding voting securities of a company which is a participant in the joint transaction;

(7) An interest acquired in a transaction described in paragraph (d)(3) of this section; or

(8) Any other interest that the board of directors of the investment company, including a majority of the directors who are not interested persons of the investment company, finds to be not material, provided that the directors record the basis for that finding in the minutes of their meeting.

(B) A person has a financial interest in any party in which it has a financial interest, in which it had a financial interest within six months prior to the investment company's participation in the enterprise, or in which it will acquire a financial interest pursuant to an arrangement in existence at the time of the investment company's participation in the enterprise.

(6) The receipt of securities and/or cash by an investment company or a controlled company thereof and an affiliated person of such investment company or an affiliated person of such person pursuant to a plan of reorganization: *Provided,* That no person identified in § 270.17a–6(a)(1) or any company in which such a person has a direct or indirect financial interest (as defined in paragraph (d)(5)(iii) of this section):

(7) Any arrangement regarding liability insurance policies (other than a bond required pursuant to rule 17g–1 under the Act); *Provided,* That

(i) The investment company's participation in the joint liability insurance policy is in the best interests of the investment company;

(ii) The proposed premium for the joint liability insurance policy to be allocated to the investment company, based upon its proportionate share of the sum of the premiums that would have been paid if such insurance coverage were purchased separately by the insured parties, is fair and reasonable to the investment company;

(iii) The joint liability insurance policy does not exclude coverage for bona fide claims made against any director who is not an interested person of the investment company, or against the investment company if it is a codefendant in the claim with the disinterested director, by another person insured under the joint liability insurance policy;

(iv) The board of directors of the investment company, including a majority of the directors who are not interested persons with respect thereto, determine no less frequently than annually that the standards described in paragraphs (i) and (ii) have been satisfied; and

(v) The board of directors of the investment company satisfies the fund governance standards defined in § 270.0–1(a)(7).

(8) An investment adviser's bearing expenses in connection with a merger, consolidation or purchase or sale of substantially all of the assets of a company which involves a registered investment company of which it is an affiliated person.

§ 270.17d–2 Form for Report by Small Business Investment Company and Affiliated Bank

Form N–17D–1 is hereby prescribed as the form for reports required by paragraph (d)(3) of § 270.17d–1.

§ 270.17d–3 Exemption Relating to Certain Joint Enterprises or Arrangements Concerning Payment for Distribution of Shares of a Registered Open-End Management Investment Company

An affiliated person of, or principal underwriter for, a registered open-end management investment company and an affiliated person of such a person or principal underwriter shall be exempt from section 17(d) of the Act and rule 17d–1 thereunder, to the extent necessary to permit any such person or principal underwriter to enter into a written agreement with such company whereby the company will make payments in connection with the distribution of its shares,

Provided, That:

(a) Such agreement is made in compliance with the provisions of § 270.12b–1 of this part; and

(b) No other registered management investment company which is either an affiliated person of such company or an affiliated person of such a person is a party to such agreement.

§ 270.17e–1 Brokerage Transactions on a Securities Exchange

For purposes of section 17(e)(2)(A) of the Act, a commission, fee or other remuneration shall be deemed as not exceeding the usual and customary broker's commission, if:

(a) The commission, fee, or other remuneration received or to be received is reasonable and fair compared to the commission, fee or other remuneration received by other brokers in connection with comparable transactions involving similar securities being purchased or sold on a securities exchange during a comparable period of time;

(b) The board of directors, including a majority of the directors of the investment company who are not interested persons thereof:

(1) Has adopted procedures which are reasonably designed to provide that such commission, fee, or other remuneration is consistent with the standard described in paragraph (a) of this section;

(2) Makes and approves such changes as the board deems necessary; and

(3) Determines no less frequently than quarterly that all transactions effected pursuant to this section during the preceding quarter (other than transactions in which the person acting as broker is a person permitted to enter into a transaction with the investment company by § 270.17a–10) were effected in compliance with such procedures;

(c) The board of directors of the investment company satisfies the fund governance standards defined in § 270.0–1(a)(7); and

(d) The investment company:

(1) Shall maintain and preserve permanently in an easily accessible place a copy of the procedures (and any modification thereto) described in paragraph (b)(1) of this section; and

(2) Shall maintain and preserve for a period not less than six years from the end of the fiscal year in which any transactions occurred, the first two years in an easily accessible place, a record of each such transaction (other than any transaction in which the person acting as broker is a person permitted to enter into a transaction with the investment company by § 270.17a–10) setting forth the amount and source of the commission, fee or other remuneration received or to be received, the identity of the person acting as broker, the terms of the transaction, and the information or materials upon which the findings described in paragraph (b)(3) of this section were made.

§ 270.17f–1 Custody of Securities With Members of National Securities Exchanges

(a) No registered management investment company shall place or maintain any of its securities or similar investments in the custody of a company which is a member of a national securities exchange as defined in the Securities Exchange Act of 1934 (whether or not such company trades in securities for its own account) except pursuant to a written contract which shall have been approved, or if executed before January 1, 1941, shall have been ratified not later than that date, by a majority of the board of directors of such investment company.

(b) The contract shall require, and the securities and investments shall be maintained in accordance with the following:

(1) The securities and similar investments held in such custody shall at all times be individually segregated from the securities and investments of any other person and marked in such manner as to clearly identify them as the property of such registered management company, both upon physical inspection thereof and upon examination of the books of the custodian. The physical segregation and marking of such securities and investments may be accomplished by putting them in separate containers bearing the name of such registered management investment company or by attaching tags or labels to such securities and investments.

(2) The custodian shall have no power or authority to assign, hypothecate, pledge or otherwise to dispose of any such securities and investments, except pursuant to the direction of such registered management company and only for the account of such registered investment company.

(3) Such securities and investments shall be subject to no lien or charge of any kind in favor of the custodian or any persons claiming through the custodian.

(4) Such securities and investment shall be verified by actual examination at the end of each annual and semi-annual fiscal period by an independent public accountant retained by the investment company, and shall be examined by such accountant at least one other time, chosen by the accountant during the fiscal year. A certificate of such accountant stating that an examination of such securities has been made, and describing the nature and extent of the examination, shall be attached to a completed Form N–17f–1 and transmitted to the Commission promptly after each examination.

(5) Such securities and investments shall, at all times, be subject to inspection by the Commission through its employees or agents.

(6) The provisions of subparagraph (1), (2) and (3) of this paragraph shall not apply to securities and similar investment company for or sold to such investment company by the company which is custodian until the securities have been reduced to the physical possession of the custodian and have been paid for by such investment company: *Provided,* That the company which is custodian shall take possession of such securities at the earliest practicable time. Nothing in this subparagraph shall be construed to relieve any company which is a member of a national securities exchange of any obligation under existing law or under the rules of any national securities exchange.

(c) A copy of any contract executed or ratified pursuant to paragraph (a) of this section shall be transmitted to the Commission promptly after execution or ratification unless it has been previously transmitted.

(d) Any contract executed or ratified pursuant to paragraph (a) of this section shall be ratified by the board of directors of the registered management investment company at least annually thereafter.

§ 270.17f–2 Custody of Investments by Registered Management Investment Company

(a) The securities and similar investments of a registered management investment company may be maintained in the custody of such company only in accordance with the provisions of this section. Investments maintained by such a company with a bank or other company whose functions and physical facilities are supervised by Federal or State authority under any arrangement whereunder the directors, officers, employees or agents of such company are authorized or permitted to withdraw such investments upon their mere receipt are deemed to be in the custody of such company and may be so maintained only upon compliance with the provisions of this section.

(b) Except as provided in paragraph (c) of this section, all such securities and similar investments shall be deposited in the safekeeping of, or in a vault or other depository maintained by, a bank or other company whose functions and physical facilities are supervised by Federal or State authority. Investments so deposited shall be physically segregated at all times from those of any other person and shall be withdrawn only in connection with transactions of the character described in paragraph (c) of this section.

(c) The first sentence of paragraph (b) of this section shall not apply to securities on loan which are collateralized to the extent of their full market value, or to securities hypothecated, pledged, or placed in escrow for the account of such investment company in connection with a loan or other transaction authorized by specific resolution of its board of directors, or to securities in transit in connection with the sale, exchange, redemption, maturity or conversion, the exercise of warrants or rights, assents to changes in terms of the securities, or other transactions necessary or appropriate in the ordinary course of business relating to the management of securities.

(d) Except as otherwise provided by law, no person shall be authorized or permitted to have access to the securities and similar investments deposited in accordance with paragraph (b) of this section except pursuant to a resolution of the board of directors of such investment company. Each such resolution shall designate not more than five persons who shall be either officers or responsible employees of such company and shall provide that access to such investments shall be had only by two or more such persons jointly, at least one of whom shall be an officer; except that access to such investments shall be permitted (1) to properly authorized officers and employees of the bank or other company in whose safekeeping the investments are placed and (2) for the purpose of paragraph (f) of this section to the independent public accountant jointly with any two persons so designated or with such officer or employee of such bank or such other company. Such investments shall at all times be subject to inspection by the Commission through its authorized employees or agents accompanied, unless otherwise directed by order of the Commission, by one or more of the persons designated pursuant to this paragraph.

(e) Each person when depositing such securities or similar investments in or withdrawing them from the depository or when ordering their withdrawal and delivery from the safekeeping of the bank or other company, shall sign a notation in respect of such deposit, withdrawal or order which shall show (1) the date and time of the deposit, withdrawal or order, (2) the title and amount of the securities or other investments deposited, withdrawn or ordered to be withdrawn, and an identification thereof by certificate numbers or otherwise, (3) the manner of acquisition of the securities or similar investments deposited or the purpose for which they have been withdrawn, or ordered to be withdrawn, and (4) if withdrawn and delivered to another person the name of such person. Such notation shall be transmitted promptly to an officer or director of the investment company designated by its board of directors who shall not be a person designated for the purpose of paragraph (d) of this section. Such notation shall be on serially numbered forms and shall be preserved for at least one year.

(f) Such securities and similar investments shall be verified by actual examination by an independent public accountant retained by the investment company at least three times during each fiscal year, at least two of which shall be chosen by such accountant without prior notice to such company. A certificate of such accountant, stating that an examination of such securities and investments has been made and describing the nature and extent of the examination shall be attached to a completed Form N–17f–2 and transmitted to the Commission promptly after each examination.

§ 270.17f–3 Free Cash Accounts for Investment Companies With Bank Custodians

No registered investment company having a bank custodian shall hold free cash except, upon resolution of its board of directors, a petty cash account may be maintained in an amount not to exceed $500: *Provided,* That such account is operated under the imprest system and is maintained subject to adequate controls approved by the board of directors over disbursements and reimbursements including, but not limited to fidelity bond coverage of persons having access to such funds.

§ 270.17f–4 Custody of Investment Company Assets With a Securities Depository

(a) *Custody arrangement with a securities depository.* A fund's custodian may place and maintain financial assets, corresponding to the fund's security entitlements, with a securities depository or intermediary custodian, if the custodian:

(1) Is at a minimum obligated to exercise due care in accordance with reasonable commercial standards in discharging its duty as a securities intermediary to obtain and thereafter maintain such financial assets;

(2) Is required to provide, promptly upon request by the fund, such reports as are available concerning the internal accounting controls and financial strength of the custodian; and

(3) Requires any intermediary custodian at a minimum to exercise due care in accordance with reasonable commercial standards in discharging its duty as a securities intermediary to obtain and thereafter maintain financial assets corresponding to the security entitlements of its entitlement holders.

(b) *Direct dealings with securities depository.* A fund may place and maintain financial assets, corresponding to the fund's security entitlements, directly with a securities depository, if:

(1) The fund's contract with the securities depository or the securities depository's written rules for its participants:

(i) Obligate the securities depository at a minimum to exercise due care in accordance with reasonable commercial standards in discharging its duty as a securities intermediary to obtain and thereafter maintain financial assets corresponding to the fund's security entitlements; and

(ii) Requires the securities depository to provide, promptly upon request by the fund, such reports as are available concerning the internal accounting controls and financial strength of the securities depository; and

(2) The fund has implemented internal control systems reasonably designed to prevent unauthorized officer's instructions (by providing at least for the form, content and means of giving, recording and reviewing all officer's instructions).

(c) *Definitions.* For purposes of this section the terms:

(1) *Clearing corporation, financial asset, securities intermediary, and security entitlement* have the same meanings as is attributed to those terms in § 8–102, § 8–103, and §§ 8–501 through 8–511 of the Uniform Commercial Code, 2002 Official Text and Comments, which are incorporated by reference in this section pursuant to 5 U.S.C. 552(a) and 1 CFR part 51. The Director of the Federal Register has approved this incorporation by reference in accordance with 5 U.S.C. 552(a) and 1 CFR part 51. You may obtain a copy of the Uniform Commercial Code from the National Conference of Commissioners on Uniform State Laws, 211 East

Ontario Street, Suite 1300, Chicago, Il 60611. You may inspect a copy at the following addresses: Louis Loss Library, U.S. Securities and Exchange Commission, 450 5th Street, NW., Washington, DC 20549, and Office of the Federal Register, National Archives and Records Administration, 800 North Capitol Street, NW, Suite 700, Washington, DC.

(2) *Custodian* means a bank or other person authorized to hold assets for the fund under section 17(f) of the Act (15 U.S.C. 80a–17(f)) or Commission rules in this chapter, but does not include a fund itself, a foreign custodian whose use is governed by § 270.17f–5 or § 270.17f–7, or a vault, safe deposit box, or other repository for safekeeping maintained by a bank or other company whose functions and physical facilities are supervised by a federal or state authority if the fund maintains its own assets there in accordance with § 270.17f–2.

(3) *Fund* means an investment company registered under the Act and, where the context so requires with respect to a fund that is a unit investment trust or a face-amount certificate company, includes the fund's trustee.

(4) *Intermediary custodian* means any subcustodian that is a securities intermediary and is qualified to act as a custodian.

(5) *Officer's instruction* means a request or direction to a securities depository or its operator, or to a registered transfer agent, in the name of the fund by one or more persons authorized by the fund's board of directors (or by the fund's trustee, if the fund is a unit investment trust or a face-amount certificate company) to give the request or direction.

(6) *Securities depository* means a clearing corporation that is:

(i) Registered with the Commission as a clearing agency under section 17A of the Securities Exchange Act of 1934 (15 U.S.C. 78q–1); or

(ii) A Federal Reserve Bank or other person authorized to operate the federal book entry system described in the regulations of the Department of Treasury codified at 31 CFR 357, Subpart B, or book-entry systems operated pursuant to comparable regulations of other federal agencies.

§ 270.17f–5 Custody of Investment Company Assets Outside the United States

(a) *Definitions.* For purposes of this section:

(1) *Eligible Foreign Custodian* means an entity that is incorporated or organized under the laws of a country other than the United States and that is a Qualified Foreign Bank or a majority-owned direct or indirect subsidiary of a U.S. Bank or bank-holding company.

(2) *Foreign Assets* means any investments (including foreign currencies) for which the primary market is outside the United States, and any cash and cash equivalents that are reasonably necessary to effect the Fund's transactions in those investments.

(3) *Foreign Custody Manager* means a Fund's or a Registered Canadian Fund's board of directors or any person serving as the board's delegate under paragraphs (b) or (d) of this section.

(4) *Fund* means a management investment company registered under the Act (15 U.S.C. 80a) and incorporated or organized under the laws of the United States or of a state.

(5) *Qualified Foreign Bank* means a banking institution or trust company, incorporated or organized under the laws of a country other than the United States, that is regulated as such by the country's government or an agency of the country's government.

(6) *Registered Canadian Fund* means a management investment company incorporated or organized under the laws of Canada and registered under the Act pursuant to the conditions of § 270.7d–1.

(7) *U.S. Bank* means an entity that is:

(i) A banking institution organized under the laws of the United States;

(ii) A member bank of the Federal Reserve System;

(iii) Any other banking institution or trust company organized under the laws of any state or of the United States, whether incorporated or not, doing business under the laws of any state or of the United States, a substantial portion of the business of which consists of receiving deposits or exercising fiduciary powers similar to those permitted to national banks under the authority of the Comptroller of the Currency, and which is supervised and examined by state or federal authority having supervision over banks, and which is not operated for the purpose of evading the provisions of this section; or

(iv) A receiver, conservator, or other liquidating agent of any institution or firm included in paragraphs (a)(7)(i), (ii), or (iii) of this section.

(b) *Delegation.* A Fund's board of directors may delegate to the Fund's investment adviser or officers or to a U.S. Bank or to a Qualified Foreign Bank the responsibilities set forth in paragraphs (c)(1), (c)(2), or (c)(3) of this section, *provided that:*

(1) *Reasonable Reliance.* The board determines that it is reasonable to rely on the delegate to perform the delegated responsibilities;

(2) *Reporting.* The board requires the delegate to provide written reports notifying the board of the placement of Foreign Assets with a particular custodian and of any material change in the Fund's foreign custody arrangements, with the reports to be provided to the board at such times as the board deems reasonable and appropriate based on the circumstances of the Fund's arrangements; and

(3) *Exercise of Care.* The delegate agrees to exercise reasonable care, prudence and diligence such as a person having responsibility for the safekeeping of the Fund's Foreign Assets would exercise, or to adhere to a higher standard of care, in performing the delegated responsibilities.

(c) *Maintaining Assets with an Eligible Foreign Custodian.* A Fund or its Foreign Custody Manager may place and maintain the Fund's Foreign Assets in the care of an Eligible Foreign Custodian, *provided that:*

(1) *General Standard.* The Foreign Custody Manager determines that the Foreign Assets will be subject to reasonable care, based on the standards applicable to custodians in the relevant market, if maintained with the Eligible Foreign Custodian, after considering all factors relevant to the safekeeping of the Foreign Assets, including, without limitation:

(i) The Eligible Foreign Custodian's practices, procedures, and internal controls, including, but not limited to, the physical protections available for certificated securities (if applicable), the method of keeping custodial records, and the security and data protection practices;

(ii) Whether the Eligible Foreign Custodian has the requisite financial strength to provide reasonable care for Foreign Assets;

(iii) The Eligible Foreign Custodian's general reputation and standing; and

(iv) Whether the Fund will have jurisdiction over and be able to enforce judgments against the Eligible Foreign Custodian, such as by virtue of the existence of offices in the United States or consent to service of process in the United States.

(2) *Contract.* The arrangement with the Eligible Foreign Custodian is governed by a written contract that the Foreign Custody Manager has determined will provide reasonable care for Foreign Assets based on the standards specified in paragraph (c)(1) of this section.

(i) The contract must provide:

(A) For indemnification or insurance arrangements (or any combination) that will adequately protect the Fund against the risk of loss of Foreign Assets held in accordance with the contract;

(B) That the Foreign Assets will not be subject to any right, charge, security interest, lien or claim of any kind in favor of the Eligible Foreign Custodian or its creditors, except a claim of payment for their safe custody or administration or, in the case of cash deposits, liens or rights in favor of creditors of the custodian arising under bankruptcy, insolvency, or similar laws;

(C) That beneficial ownership of the Foreign Assets will be freely transferable without the payment of money or value other than for safe custody or administration;

(D) That adequate records will be maintained identifying the Foreign Assets as belonging to the Fund or as being held by a third party for the benefit of the Fund;

(E) That the Fund's independent public accountants will be given access to those records or confirmation of the contents of those records; and

(F) That the Fund will receive periodic reports with respect to the safekeeping of the Foreign Assets, including, but not limited to, notification of any transfer to or from the Fund's account or a third party account containing assets held for the benefit of the Fund.

(ii) The contract may contain, in lieu of any or all of the provisions specified in paragraph (c)(2)(i) of this section, other provisions that the Foreign Custody Manager determines will provide, in their entirety, the same or a greater level of care and protection for the Foreign Assets as the specified provisions, in their entirety.

(3)(i) *Monitoring the Foreign Custody Arrangements.* The Foreign Custody Manager has established a system to monitor the appropriateness of maintaining the Foreign Assets with a particular custodian under paragraph (c)(1) of this section, and to monitor performance of the contract under paragraph (c)(2) of this section.

(ii) If an arrangement with an Eligible Foreign Custodian no longer meets the requirements of this section, the Fund must withdraw the Foreign Assets from the Eligible Foreign Custodian as soon as reasonably practicable.

(d) *Registered Canadian Funds.* Any Registered Canadian Fund may place and maintain its Foreign Assets outside the United States in accordance with the requirements of this section, *provided that:*

(1) The Foreign Assets are placed in the care of an overseas branch of a U.S. Bank that has aggregate capital, surplus, and undivided profits of a specified amount, which must not be less than $500,000; and

(2) The Foreign Custody Manager is the Fund's board of directors, its investment adviser or officers, or a U.S. Bank.

Note to § 270.17f–5: When a Fund's (or its custodian's) custody arrangement with an Eligible Securities Depository (as defined in § 270.17f–7) involves one or more Eligible Foreign Custodians through which assets are maintained with the Eligible Securities Depository, § 270.17f–5 will govern the Fund's (or its custodian's) use of each Eligible Foreign Custodian, while § 270.17f–7 will govern an Eligible Foreign Custodian's use of the Eligible Securities Depository.

§ 270.17f–6 Custody of Investment Company Assets With Futures Commission Merchants and Commodity Clearing Organizations

(a) A Fund may place and maintain cash, securities, and similar investments with a Futures Commission Merchant in amounts necessary to effect the Fund's transactions in Exchange–Traded Futures Contracts and Commodity Options, *Provided that:*

(1) The manner in which the Futures Commission Merchant maintains the Fund's assets shall be governed by a written contract, which provides that:

(i) The Futures Commission Merchant shall comply with the segregation requirements of section 4d(2) of the Commodity Exchange Act (7 U.S.C. 6d(2)) and the rules thereunder (17 CFR Chapter I) or, if applicable, the secured amount requirements of rule 30.7 under the Commodity Exchange Act (17 CFR 30.7);

(ii) The Futures Commission Merchant, as appropriate to the Fund's transactions and in accordance with the Commodity Exchange Act (7 U.S.C. 1 through 25) and the rules and regulations thereunder (including 17 CFR part 30), may place and maintain the Fund's assets to effect the Fund's transactions with another Futures Commission Merchant, a Clearing Organization, a U.S. or Foreign Bank, or a member of a foreign board of trade, and shall obtain an acknowledgement, as required under rules 1.20(a) or 30.7(c) under the Commodity Exchange Act [17 CFR 1.20(a) or 30.7(c)], as applicable, that such assets are held on behalf of the Futures Commission Merchant's customers in accordance with the provisions of the Commodity Exchange Act; and

(iii) The Futures Commission Merchant shall promptly furnish copies of or extracts from the Futures Commission Merchant's records or such other information pertaining to the Fund's assets as the Commission through its employees or agents may request.

(2) Any gains on the Fund's transactions, other than de minimis amounts, may be maintained with the Futures Commission Merchant only until the next business day following receipt.

(3) If the custodial arrangement no longer meets the requirements of this section, the Fund shall withdraw its assets from the Futures Commission Merchant as soon as reasonably practicable.

(b) For purposes of this section:

(1) *Clearing Organization* means a clearing organization as defined in rule 1.3(d) under the Commodity Exchange Act (17 CFR 1.3(d)) and includes a clearing organization for a foreign board of trade.

(2) *Exchange–Traded Futures Contracts and Commodity Options* means commodity futures contracts, options on commodity futures contracts, and options on physical commodities traded on or subject to the rules of:

(i) Any contract market designated for trading such transactions under the Commodity Exchange Act and the rules thereunder; or

(ii) Any board of trade or exchange outside the United States, as contemplated in Part 30 under the Commodity Exchange Act.

(3) *Fund* means an investment company registered under the Act (15 U.S.C. 80a–1 *et seq.*).

(4) *Futures Commission Merchant* means any person that is registered as a futures commission merchant under the Commodity Exchange Act and that is not an affiliated person of the Fund or an affiliated person of such person.

(5) *U.S. or Foreign Bank* means a bank, as defined in section 2(a)(5) of the Act (15 U.S.C. 80a–2(a)(5)), or a banking institution or trust company that is incorporated or organized under the laws of a country other than the United States and that is regulated as such by the country's government or an agency thereof.

§ 270.17f–7 Custody of Investment Company Assets With a Foreign Securities Depository

(a) *Custody arrangement with an eligible securities depository.* A Fund, including a Registered Canadian Fund, may place and maintain its Foreign Assets with an Eligible Securities Depository, *provided that:*

(1) *Risk-limiting safeguards.* The custody arrangement provides reasonable safeguards against the custody risks associated with maintaining assets with the Eligible Securities Depository, including:

(i) *Risk analysis and monitoring.* (A) The fund or its investment adviser has received from the Primary Custodian (or its agent) an analysis of the custody risks associated with maintaining assets with the Eligible Securities Depository; and

(B) The contract between the Fund and the Primary Custodian requires the Primary Custodian (or its agent) to monitor the custody risks associated with maintaining assets with the Eligible Securities Depository on a continuing basis, and promptly notify the Fund or its investment adviser of any material change in these risks.

(ii) *Exercise of care.* The contract between the Fund and the Primary Custodian states that the Primary Custodian will agree to exercise reasonable care, prudence, and diligence in performing the requirements of paragraphs (a)(1)(i)(A) and (B) of this section, or adhere to a higher standard of care.

(2) *Withdrawal of assets from eligible securities depository.* If a custody arrangement with an Eligible Securities Depository no longer meets the requirements of this section, the Fund's Foreign Assets must be withdrawn from the depository as soon as reasonably practicable.

(b) *Definitions.* The terms *Foreign Assets, Fund, Qualified Foreign Bank, Registered Canadian Fund,* and *U.S. Bank* have the same meanings as in § 270.17f–5. In addition:

(1) *Eligible Securities Depository* means a system for the central handling of securities as defined in § 270.17f–4 that:

(i) Acts as or operates a system for the central handling of securities or equivalent book-entries in the country where it is incorporated, or a transnational system for the central handling of securities or equivalent book-entries;

(ii) Is regulated by a foreign financial regulatory authority as defined under section 2(a)(50) of the Act (15 U.S.C. 80a–2(a)(50));

(iii) Holds assets for the custodian that participates in the system on behalf of the Fund under safekeeping conditions no less favorable than the conditions that apply to other participants;

(iv) Maintains records that identify the assets of each participant and segregate the system's own assets from the assets of participants;

(v) Provides periodic reports to its participants with respect to its safekeeping of assets, including notices of transfers to or from any participant's account; and

(vi) Is subject to periodic examination by regulatory authorities or independent accountants.

(2) *Primary Custodian* means a U.S. Bank or Qualified Foreign Bank that contracts directly with a Fund to provide custodial services related to maintaining the Fund's assets outside the United States.

Note to § 270.17f–7: When a Fund's (or its custodian's) custody arrangement with an Eligible Securities Depository involves one or more Eligible Foreign Custodians (as defined in § 270.17f–5) through which assets are maintained with the Eligible Securities Depository, § 270.17f–5 will govern the Fund's (or its custodian's) use of each Eligible Foreign Custodian, while § 270.17f–7 will govern an Eligible Foreign Custodian's use of the Eligible Securities Depository.

§ 270.17g–1 Bonding of Officers and Employees of Registered Management Investment Companies

(a) Each registered management investment company shall provide and maintain a bond which shall be issued by a reputable fidelity insurance company, authorized to do business in the place where the bond is issued, against larceny and embezzlement, covering each officer and employee of the investment company, who may singly, or jointly with others, have access to securities or funds of the investment company, either directly or through authority to draw upon such funds or to direct generally the disposition of such securities, unless the officer or employee has such access solely through its position as an officer or employee of a bank (hereinafter referred to as "covered persons").

(b) The bond may be in the form of (1) an individual bond for each covered person or a schedule or blanket bond covering such persons, (2) a blanket bond which names the registered management investment company as the only insured (hereinafter referred to as "single insured bond") or (3) a bond which names the registered management investment company and one or more other parties as insureds (hereinafter referred to as a "joint insured bond"), such other insured parties being limited to (i) persons engaged in the management or distribution of the shares of the registered investment company, (ii) other registered investment companies which are managed and/or whose shares are distributed by the same persons (or affiliates of such persons), (iii) persons who are engaged in the management and/or distribution of shares of companies included in paragraph (b)(3)(ii) of this section, (iv) affiliated persons of any registered management investment company named in the bond or of any person included in paragraph (b)(3)(i) or (b)(3)(iii) of this section hereinabove who are engaged in the administration of any registered management investment company named as insured in the bond, and (v) any trust, pension, profit-sharing or other benefit plan for officers, directors or employees of persons named in the bond.

(c) A bond of the type described in paragraphs (b)(1) or (b)(2) of this section shall provide that it shall not be cancelled, terminated or modified except after written notice shall have been given by the acting party to the affected party and to the Commission not less than sixty days prior to the effective date of cancellation, termination or modification. A joint insured bond described in paragraph (b)(3) of this section shall provide, that (1) it shall not be cancelled, terminated or modified except after written notice shall have been given by the acting party to the affected party and by the fidelity insurance company to all registered investment companies named as insureds and to the Commission, not less than sixty days prior to the effective date of cancellation, termination, or modification and (2) the fidelity insurance company shall furnish each registered management investment company named as an insured with (i) a copy of the bond and any amendment thereto promptly after the execution thereof, (ii) a copy of each formal filing of a claim under the bond by any other named insured promptly after the receipt thereof, and (iii) notification of the terms of the settlement of each such claim prior to the execution of the settlement.

(d) The bond shall be in such reasonable form and amount as a majority of the board of directors of the registered management investment company who are not "interested persons" of such investment company as defined by section 2(a)(19) of the Act shall approve as often as their fiduciary duties require, but not less than once every twelve months, with due consideration to all relevant factors including, but not limited to, the value of the aggregate assets of the registered management investment company to which any covered person may have access, the type and terms of the arrangements made for the custody and safekeeping of such assets, and the nature of the securities in the company's portfolio: *Provided, however,* That (1) the amount of a single insured bond shall be at least equal to an amount computed in accordance with the following schedule:

Amount of Registered Management Investment Company Gross Assets—at the end of the most recent fiscal quarter prior to date of determination (In Dollars)	Minimum Amount of Bond (In Dollars)
Up to 500,000	50,000.
500,000 to 1,000,000	75,000.
1,000,000 to 2,500,000	100,000.
2,500,000 to 5,000,000	125,000.
5,000,000 to 7,500,000	150,000.
7,500,000 to 10,000,000	175,000.
10,000,000 to 15,000,000	200,000.
15,000,000 to 20,000,000	225,000.
20,000,000 to 25,000,000	250,000.
25,000,000 to 35,000,000	300,000.
35,000,000 to 50,000,000	350,000.
50,000,000 to 75,000,000	400,000.
75,000,000 to 100,000,000	450,000.
100,000,000 to 150,000,000	525,000.
150,000,000 to 250,000,000	600,000.
250,000,000 to 500,000,000	750,000.
500,000,000 to 750,000,000	900,000.
750,000,000 to 1,000,000,000	1,000,000.
1,000,000,000 to 1,500,000,000	1,250,000.
1,500,000,000 to 2,000,000,000	1,500,000.
Over 2,000,000,000	1,500,000 plus 200,000 for each 500,000,000 of gross assets up to a maximum bond of 2,500,000.

(2) A joint insured bond shall be in an amount at least equal to the sum of (i) the total amount of coverage which each registered management investment company named as an insured would have been required to provide and maintain individually pursuant to the schedule hereinabove had each such registered management investment company not been named under a joint insured bond, plus (ii) the amount of each bond which each named insured other than a registered management investment company would have been required to provide and maintain pursuant to federal statutes or regulations had it not been named as an insured under a joint insured bond.

(e) No premium may be paid for any joint insured bond or any amendment thereto unless a majority of the board of directors of each registered management investment company named as an insured therein who are not "interested persons" of such company shall approve the portion of the premium to be paid by such company, taking all relevant factors into consideration including, but not limited to, the number of the other parties named as insured, the nature of the business activities or such other parties, the amount of the joint insured bond, and the amount of the premium for such bond, the ratable allocation of the premium among all parties named as insureds, and the extent to which the share of the premium allocated to the investment company is less than the premium such company would have had to pay if it had provided and maintained a single insured bond.

(f) Each registered management investment company named as an insured in a joint insured bond shall enter into an agreement with all of the other named insureds providing that in the event recovery is received under the bond as a result of a loss sustained by the registered management investment company and one or more other named insureds, the registered management investment company shall receive an equitable and proportionate share of the recovery, but at least equal to the amount which it would have received had it provided and maintained a single insured bond with the minimum coverage required by paragraph (d)(1) of this section.

(g) Each registered management investment company shall:

(1) File with the Commission (i) within 10 days after receipt of an executed bond of the type described in paragraphs (b)(1) or (b)(2) of this section or any amendment thereof, (*a*) a copy of the bond, (*b*) a copy of the resolution of a majority of the board of directors who are not "interested persons" of the registered management investment company approving the form and amount of the bond, and (*c*) a statement as to the period for which premiums have been paid; (ii) within 10 days after receipt of an executed joint insured bond, or any amendment thereof, (*a*) a copy of the bond, (*b*) a copy of the resolution of a majority of the board of directors who are not "interested persons" of the registered management investment company approving the amount, type, form and coverage of the bond and the portion of the premium to be paid by such company, (*c*) a statement showing the amount of the single insured bond which the investment company would have provided and maintained had it not been named as an insured under a joint insured bond, (*d*) a statement as to the period for which premiums have been paid, and (*e*) a copy of each agreement between the investment company and all of the other named insureds entered into pursuant to paragraph (f) of this section, and (iii) a copy of any amendment to the agreement entered into pursuant to paragraph (f) of this section within 10 days, after the execution of such amendment,

(2) File with the Commission, in writing, within five days after the making of any claim under the bond by the investment company, a statement of the nature and amount of the claim.

(3) File with the Commission, within five days of the receipt thereof, a copy of the terms of the settlement of any claim made under the bond by the investment company, and

(4) Notify by registered mail each member of the board of directors of the investment company at his last known residence address of (i) any cancellation, termination or modification of the bond, not less than forty-five days prior to the effective date of the cancellation or termination or modification, (ii) the filing and of the settlement of any claim under the bond by the investment company, at the time the filings required by paragraph (g)(2) and (3) of this section are made with the Commission, and (iii) the filing and of the proposed terms of settlement of any claim under the bond by any other named insured, within five days of the receipt of a notice from the fidelity insurance company.

(h) Each registered management investment company shall designate an officer thereof who shall make the filings and give the notices required by paragraph (g) of this section.

(i) Where the registered management investment company is an unincorporated company managed by a depositor, trustee or investment adviser, the terms "officer" and "employee" shall include for the purposes of this rule, the officers and employees of the depositor, trustee, or investment adviser.

(j) Any joint insured bond provided and maintained by a registered management investment company and one or more other parties shall be a transaction exempt from the provisions of section 17(d) of the Act (15 U.S.C. 80a–17(d)) and the rules thereunder, if:

(1) The terms and provisions of the bond comply with the provisions of this section;

(2) The terms and provisions of any agreement required by paragraph (f) of this section comply with the provisions of that paragraph; and

(3) The board of directors of the investment company satisfies the fund governance standards defined in § 270.0-1(a)(7).

(k) At the next anniversary date of an existing fidelity bond, but not later than one year from the effective date of this rule, arrangements between registered management investment companies and fidelity insurance companies and arrangements between registered management investment companies and other parties named as insureds under joint insured bonds which would not permit compliance with the provisions of this rule shall be modified by the parties so as to effect such compliance.

§ 270.17j-1 Personal Investment Activities of Investment Company Personnel

(a) *Definitions*. For purposes of this section:

(1) *Access Person* means:

(i) Any Advisory Person of a Fund or of a Fund's investment adviser. If an investment adviser's primary business is advising Funds or other advisory clients, all of the investment adviser's directors, officers, and general partners are presumed to be Access Persons of any Fund advised by the investment adviser. All of a Fund's directors, officers, and general partners are presumed to be Access Persons of the Fund.

(A) If an investment adviser is primarily engaged in a business or businesses other than advising Funds or other advisory clients, the term Access Person means any director, officer, general partner or Advisory Person of the investment adviser who, with respect to any Fund, makes any recommendation, participates in the determination of which recommendation will be made, or whose principal function or duties relate to the determination of which recommendation will be made, or who, in connection with his or her duties, obtains any information concerning recommendations on Covered Securities being made by the investment adviser to any Fund.

(B) An investment adviser is "primarily engaged in a business or businesses other than advising Funds or other advisory clients" if, for each of its most recent three fiscal years or for the period of time since its organization, whichever is less, the investment adviser derived, on an unconsolidated basis, more than 50 percent of its total sales and revenues and more than 50 percent of its income (or loss), before income taxes and extraordinary items, from the other business or businesses.

(ii) Any director, officer or general partner of a principal underwriter who, in the ordinary course of business, makes, participates in or obtains information regarding, the purchase or sale of Covered Securities by the Fund for which the principal underwriter acts, or whose functions or duties in the ordinary course of business relate to the making of any recommendation to the Fund regarding the purchase or sale of Covered Securities.

(2) *Advisory Person* of a Fund or of a Fund's investment adviser means:

(i) Any director, officer, general partner or employee of the Fund or investment advisor (or of any company in a control relationship to the Fund or investment advisor) who, in connection with his or her regular functions or duties, makes, participates, in or obtains information regarding, the purchase or sale of Covered Securities by a Fund, or whose functions relate to the making of any recommendations with respect to such purchases or sales; and

(ii) Any natural person in a control relationship to the Fund or investment adviser who obtains information concerning recommendations made to the Fund with regard to the purchase or sale of Covered Securities by the Fund.

(3) *Control* has the same meaning as in section 2(a)(9) of the Act [15 U.S.C. 80a–2(a)(9)].

(4) *Covered Security* means a security as defined in section 2(a)(36) of the Act [15 U.S.C. 80a–2(a)(36)], except that it does not include:

(i) Direct obligations of the Government of the United States;

(ii) Bankers' acceptances, bank certificates of deposit, commercial paper and high quality short-term debt instruments, including repurchase agreements; and

(iii) Shares issued by open-end Funds.

(5) *Fund* means an investment company registered under the Investment Company Act.

(6) An *Initial Public Offering* means an offering of securities registered under the Securities Act of 1933 [15 U.S.C. 77a], the issuer of which, immediately before the registration, was not subject to the reporting requirements of sections 13 or 15(d) of the Securities Exchange Act of 1934 [15 U.S.C. 78m or 78o(d)].

(7) *Investment Personnel* of a Fund or of a Fund's investment adviser means:

(i) Any employee of the Fund or investment adviser (or of any company in a control relationship to the Fund or investment adviser) who, in connection with his or her regular functions or duties, makes or participates in making recommendations regarding the purchase or sale of securities by the Fund.

(ii) Any natural person who controls the Fund or investment adviser and who obtains information concerning recommendations made to the Fund regarding the purchase or sale of securities by the Fund.

(8) *A Limited Offering* means an offering that is exempt from registration under the Securities Act of 1933 pursuant to section 4(2) or section 4(6) [15 U.S.C. 77d(2) or 77d(6)] or pursuant to rule 504, rule 505, or rule 506 [17 CFR 230.504, 230.505, or 230.506] under the Securities Act of 1933.

(9) *Purchase or sale of a Covered Security* includes, among other things, the writing of an option to purchase or sell a Covered Security.

(10) *Security Held or to be Acquired by a Fund* means:

(i) Any Covered Security which, within the most recent 15 days:

(A) Is or has been held by the Fund; or

(B) Is being or has been considered by the Fund or its investment adviser for purchase by the Fund; and

(ii) Any option to purchase or sell and any security convertible into or exchangeable for a Covered Security described in paragraph (a)(10)(i) of this section.

(11) *Automatic Investment Plan* means a program in which regular periodic purchases (or withdrawals) are made automatically in (or from) investment accounts in accordance with a predetermined schedule and allocation. An Automatic Investment Plan includes a dividend reinvestment plan.

(b) *Unlawful Actions*. It is unlawful for any affiliated person of or principal underwriter for a Fund, or any affiliated person of an investment adviser of or principal underwriter for a Fund, in connection with the purchase or sale, directly or indirectly, by the person of a Security Held or to be Acquired by the Fund:

(1) To employ any device, scheme or artifice to defraud the Fund;

(2) To make any untrue statement of a material fact to the Fund or omit to state a material fact necessary in order to make the statements made to the Fund, in light of the circumstances under which they are made, not misleading;

(3) To engage in any act, practice or course of business that operates or would operate as a fraud or deceit on the Fund; or

(4) To engage in any manipulative practice with respect to the Fund.

(c) *Code of Ethics.*

(1) *Adoption and Approval of Code of Ethics.*

(i) Every Fund (other than a money market fund or a Fund that does not invest in Covered Securities) and each investment adviser of and principal underwriter for the Fund, must adopt a written code of ethics containing provisions reasonably necessary to prevent its Access Persons from engaging in any conduct prohibited by paragraph (b) of this section.

(ii) The board of directors of a Fund, including a majority of directors who are not interested persons, must approve the code of ethics of the Fund, the code of ethics of each investment adviser and principal underwriter of the Fund, and any material changes to these codes. The board must base its approval of a code and any material changes to the code on a determination that the code contains provisions reasonably necessary to prevent Access Persons from engaging in any conduct prohibited by paragraph (b) of this section. Before approving a code of a Fund, investment adviser or principal underwriter or any amendment to the code, the board of directors must receive a certification from the Fund, investment adviser or principal underwriter that it has adopted procedures reasonably necessary to prevent Access Persons from violating the Fund's, investment adviser's, or principal underwriter's code of ethics. The Fund's board must approve the code of an investment adviser or principal underwriter before initially retaining the services of the investment adviser or principal underwriter. The Fund's board must approve a material change to a code no later than six months after adoption of the material change.

(iii) If a Fund is a unit investment trust, the Fund's principal underwriter or depositor must approve the Fund's code of ethics, as required by paragraph (c)(1)(ii) of this section. If the Fund has more than one principal underwriter or depositor, the principal underwriters and depositors may designate, in writing, which principal underwriter or depositor must conduct the approval required by paragraph (c)(1)(ii) of this section, if they obtain written consent from the designated principal underwriter or depositor.

(2) *Administration of Code of Ethics.*

(i) The Fund, investment adviser and principal underwriter must use reasonable diligence and institute procedures reasonably necessary to prevent violations of its code of ethics.

(ii) No less frequently than annually, every Fund (other than a unit investment trust) and its investment advisers and principal underwriters must furnish to the Fund's board of directors, and the board of directors must consider, a written report that:

(A) Describes any issues arising under the code of ethics or procedures since the last report to the board of directors, including, but not limited to, information about material violations of the code or procedures and sanctions imposed in response to the material violations; and

(B) Certifies that the Fund, investment adviser or principal underwriter, as applicable, has adopted procedures reasonably necessary to prevent Access Persons from violating the code.

(3) *Exception for Principal Underwriters.* The requirements of paragraphs (c)(1) and (c)(2) of this section do not apply to any principal underwriter unless:

(i) The principal underwriter is an affiliated person of the Fund or of the Fund's investment adviser; or

(ii) An officer, director or general partner of the principal underwriter serves as an officer, director or general partner of the Fund or of the Fund's investment adviser.

(d) *Reporting Requirements of Access Persons.*

(1) *Reports Required.* Unless excepted by paragraph (d)(2) of this section, every Access Person of a Fund (other than a money market fund or a Fund that does not invest in Covered Securities) and every Access Person of an investment adviser of or principal underwriter for the Fund, must report to that Fund, investment adviser or principal underwriter:

(i) *Initial Holdings Reports.* No later than 10 days after the person becomes an Access Person (which information must be current as of a date no more than 45 days prior to the date the person becomes an Access Person):

(A) The title, number of shares and principal amount of each Covered Security in which the Access Person had any direct or indirect beneficial ownership when the person became an Access Person;

(B) The name of any broker, dealer or bank with whom the Access Person maintained an account in which any securities were held for the direct or indirect benefit of the Access Person as of the date the person became an Access Person; and

(C) The date that the report is submitted by the Access Person.

(ii) *Quarterly Transaction Reports.* No later than 30 days after the end of a calendar quarter, the following information:

(A) With respect to any transaction during the quarter in a Covered Security in which the Access Person had any direct or indirect beneficial ownership:

(*1*) The date of the transaction, the title, the interest rate and maturity date (if applicable), the number of shares and the principal amount of each Covered Security involved;

(*2*) The nature of the transaction (i.e., purchase, sale or any other type of acquisition or disposition);

(*3*) The price of the Covered Security at which the transaction was effected;

(*4*) The name of the broker, dealer or bank with or through which the transaction was effected; and

(*5*) The date that the report is submitted by the Access Person.

(B) With respect to any account established by the Access Person in which any securities were held during the quarter for the direct or indirect benefit of the Access Person:

(*1*) The name of the broker, dealer or bank with whom the Access Person established the account;

(*2*) The date the account was established; and

(*3*) The date that the report is submitted by the Access Person.

(iii) *Annual Holdings Reports*. Annually, the following information (which information must be current as of a date no more than 45 days before the report is submitted):

(A) The title, number of shares and principal amount of each Covered Security in which the Access Person had any direct or indirect beneficial ownership;

(B) The name of any broker, dealer or bank with whom the Access Person maintains an account in which any securities are held for the direct or indirect benefit of the Access Person; and

(C) The date that the report is submitted by the Access Person.

(2) *Exceptions from Reporting Requirements.*

(i) A person need not make a report under paragraph (d)(1) of this section with respect to transactions effected for, and Covered Securities held in, any account over which the person has no direct or indirect influence or control.

(ii) A director of a Fund who is not an "interested person" of the Fund within the meaning of section 2(a)(19) of the Act [15 U.S.C. 80a–2(a)(19)], and who would be required to make a report solely by reason of being a Fund director, need not make:

(A) An initial holdings report under paragraph (d)(1)(i) of this section and an annual holdings report under paragraph (d)(1)(iii) of this section; and

(B) A quarterly transaction report under paragraph (d)(1)(ii) of this section, unless the director knew or, in the ordinary course of fulfilling his or her official duties as a Fund director, should have known that during the 15–day period immediately before or after the director's transaction in a Covered Security, the Fund purchased or sold the Covered Security, or the Fund or its investment adviser considered purchasing or selling the Covered Security.

(iii) An Access Person to a Fund's principal underwriter need not make a report to the principal underwriter under paragraph (d)(1) of this section if:

(A) The principal underwriter is not an affiliated person of the Fund (unless the Fund is a unit investment trust) or any investment adviser of the Fund; and

(B) The principal underwriter has no officer, director or general partner who serves as an officer, director or general partner of the Fund or of any investment adviser of the Fund.

(iv) An Access Person to an investment adviser need not make a separate report to the investment adviser under paragraph (d)(1) of this section to the extent the information in the report would duplicate information required to be recorded under §§ 275.204–2(a)(13) of this chapter.

(v) An Access Person need not make a quarterly transaction report under paragraph (d)(1)(ii) of this section if the report would duplicate information contained in broker trade confirmations or account statements received by the Fund, investment adviser or principal underwriter with respect to the Access Person in the time period required by paragraph (d)(1)(ii), if all of the information required by that paragraph is contained in the broker trade confirmations or account statements, or in the records of the Fund, investment adviser or principal underwriter.

(vi) An Access Person need not make a quarterly transaction report under paragraph (d)(1)(ii) of this section with respect to transactions effected pursuant to an Automatic Investment Plan.

(3) *Review of Reports*. Each Fund, investment adviser and principal underwriter to which reports are required to be made by

paragraph (d)(1) of this section must institute procedures by which appropriate management or compliance personnel review these reports.

(4) *Notification of Reporting Obligation*. Each Fund, investment adviser and principal underwriter to which reports are required to be made by paragraph (d)(1) of this section must identify all Access Persons who are required to make these reports and must inform those Access Persons of their reporting obligation.

(5) *Beneficial Ownership*. For purposes of this section, beneficial ownership is interpreted in the same manner as it would be under § 240.16a–1(a)(2) of this chapter in determining whether a person is the beneficial owner of a security for purposes of section 16 of the Securities Exchange Act of 1934 [15 U.S.C. 78p] and the rules and regulations thereunder. Any report required by paragraph (d) of this section may contain a statement that the report will not be construed as an admission that the person making the report has any direct or indirect beneficial ownership in the Covered Security to which the report relates.

(e) *Pre-approval of Investments in IPOs and Limited Offerings*. Investment Personnel of a Fund or its investment adviser must obtain approval from the Fund or the Fund's investment adviser before directly or indirectly acquiring beneficial ownership in any securities in an Initial Public Offering or in a Limited Offering.

(f) *Recordkeeping Requirements*.

(1) Each Fund, investment adviser and principal underwriter that is required to adopt a code of ethics or to which reports are required to be made by Access Persons must, at its principal place of business, maintain records in the manner and to the extent set out in this paragraph (f), and must make these records available to the Commission or any representative of the Commission at any time and from time to time for reasonable periodic, special or other examination:

(A) A copy of each code of ethics for the organization that is in effect, or at any time within the past five years was in effect, must be maintained in an easily accessible place;

(B) A record of any violation of the code of ethics, and of any action taken as a result of the violation, must be maintained in an easily accessible place for at least five years after the end of the fiscal year in which the violation occurs;

(C) A copy of each report made by an Access Person as required by this section, including any information provided in lieu of the reports under paragraph (d)(2)(v) of this section, must be maintained for at least five years after the end of the fiscal year in which the report is made or the information is provided, the first two years in an easily accessible place;

(D) A record of all persons, currently or within the past five years, who are or were required to make reports under paragraph (d) of this section, or who are or were responsible for reviewing these reports, must be maintained in an easily accessible place; and

(E) A copy of each report required by paragraph (c)(2)(ii) of this section must be maintained for at least five years after the end of the fiscal year in which it is made, the first two years in an easily accessible place.

(2) A Fund or investment adviser must maintain a record of any decision, and the reasons supporting the decision, to approve the acquisition by investment personnel of securities under paragraph (e), for at least five years after the end of the fiscal year in which the approval is granted.

§ 270.18c–1 Exemption of Privately Held Indebtedness

The issuance or sale of more than one class of senior securities representing indebtedness by a small business investment company, licensed under the Small Business Investment Act of 1958, shall not be prohibited by section 18(c) so long as such small business investment company does not have outstanding any publicly held indebtedness, and all securities of any such class are (a) privately held by the Small Business Administration, or banks, insurance companies or other institutional investors, (b) not intended to be publicly distributed, and (c) not convertible into, exchangeable for, or accompanied by any option to acquire, any equity security.

§ 270.18c–2 Exemptions of Certain Debentures Issued by Small Business Investment Companies

(a) The issuance or sale of any class of senior security representing indebtedness by a small business investment company licensed under the Small Business Investment Act of 1958 shall not be prohibited by section 18(c) of the Act provided such senior security representing indebtedness is (1) not convertible into, exchangeable for, or accompanied by an option to acquire any equity security; (2) fully guaranteed as to timely payment of all principal and interest by the Small Business Administration and backed by the full faith and credit of the United States; and (3) subordinated to any other debt securities not issued pursuant to this section or, if such security is not so subordinated, that such security, according to its own terms, will not be preferred over any other unsecured debt securities in the payment of principal and interest: *And further provided*, That all other debt securities then outstanding issued by such small business investment company were issued as permitted by § 270.18c–1 or this section.

(b) Any security issued and sold as permitted by paragraph (a) of this section shall be deemed for purposes of § 270.18c–1 to be privately held by the Small Business Administration and for purposes of § 270.18c–1 shall not be deemed to be publicly held outstanding indebtedness.

(c) The issuance or sale of any security as permitted by paragraph (a) of this section shall not be deemed to be a sale to any person other than the Small Business Administration by any small business investment company licensed under the Small Business Investment Company Act of 1958 which is exempt from any provision of the Investment Company Act, if such exemption is conditioned on such company not offering or selling its securities to any person other than the Small Business Administration.

§ 270.18f–1 Exemption From Certain Requirements of Section 18(f)(1) (of the Act) for Registered Open-End Investment Companies Which Have the Right to Redeem in Kind

(a) A registered open-end investment company which has the right to redeem securities of which it is the issuer in assets other than cash may file with the Commission at any time a notification of election on Form N–18F–1 committing itself to pay in cash all requests for redemption by any shareholder of record, limited in amount with respect to each shareholder during any ninety-day period to the lesser of

(1) $250,000 or

(2) 1% of the net asset value of such company at the beginning of such period.

(b) An election pursuant to paragraph (a):

(i) shall be described in either the prospectus or the Statement of Additional Information, at the discretion of the investment company, and

(ii) shall be irrevocable while this rule is in effect unless the Commission by order upon application permits the withdrawal of such notification of election as being appropriate in the public interest and consistent with the protection of investors.

(c) Upon making the election described in paragraph (a), an investment company shall be exempt from the requirements of Section 18(f)(1) of the Act to the extent necessary for such company to effectuate redemptions in the manner set forth in such paragraph.

§ 270.18f–2 Fair and Equitable Treatment for Holders of Each Class or Series of Stock of Series Investment Companies

(a) For purposes of this § 270.18f–2 a series company is a registered open-end investment company which, in accordance with the provisions of section 18(f)(2) of the Act, issues two or more classes or series of preferred or special stock each of which is preferred over all other classes or series in respect of assets specifically allocated to that class or series. Any matter required to be submitted by the provisions of the Act or of applicable State law, or otherwise, to the holders of the outstanding voting securities of a series company shall not be deemed to have been effectively acted upon unless approved by the holders of a majority of the outstanding voting securities of each class or series of stock affected by such matter.

(b) For the purposes of paragraph (a) of this § 270.18f–2, a class or series of stock will be deemed to be affected by such a matter, unless (1) the interests of each class or series in the matter are substantially identical, or (2) the matter does not affect any interest of such class or series.

(c)(1) With respect to the submission of an investment advisory contract to the holders of the outstanding voting securities of a series company for the approval required by section 15(a) of the Act, such matter shall be deemed to be effectively acted upon with respect to any class or series of securities of such company if a majority of the outstanding voting securities of such class or series vote for the approval of such matter, notwithstanding (i) that such matter has not been approved by the holders of a majority of the outstanding voting securities of any other class or series affected by such matter, and (ii) that such matter has not been approved by the vote of a majority of the outstanding voting securities of such company, provided that if such a majority is required by State law or otherwise, such requirement shall apply.

(2) If any class or series of securities of a series company fails to approve an investment advisory contract in the manner required by subparagraph (1) of this paragraph (c), the investment adviser of such company may continue to serve or act in such capacity for the period of time pending such required approval of such contract, of a new contract with the same or different adviser, or other definitive action: *Provided*, That the compensation received by such investment adviser during such period is equal to no more than its actual costs incurred in furnishing investment advisory services to such class or series or the amount it would have received under the advisory contract, whichever is less.

(d) With respect to the submission of a change in investment policy to the holders of the outstanding voting securities of a series company for the approval required by section 13 of the Act, such matter shall be deemed to have been effectively acted upon with respect to any class or series of such company if a majority of the outstanding voting securities of such class or series vote for the approval of such matter, notwithstanding (1) that such matter has not been approved by the holders of a majority of the outstanding voting securities of any other class or series affected by such matter, and (2) that such matter has not been approved by the vote of a majority of the outstanding voting securities of such company: *Provided,* That if such a majority is required by State law or otherwise, such requirement shall apply.

(e) The submission to shareholders of the selection of the independent public accountant of a series company required by section 32(a) (of the Act) shall be exempt from the separate voting requirements of paragraph (a) of this § 270.18f–2.

(f) The submission to shareholders of a contract with a principal underwriter of a series company required by section 15(b) of the Act shall be exempt from the separate voting requirements of paragraph (a) of this § 270.18f–2.

(g) The submission to shareholders of nominees for election as directors required by section 16(a) of the Act shall be exempt from the separate voting requirements of paragraph (a) of this § 270.18f–2.

(h) For the purposes of this § 270.18f–2 a "majority of the outstanding voting securities" of a class or series, (1) when used with respect to a matter required by any provision of the Act to be submitted to the outstanding voting securities of a series company, shall have the same meaning as a "majority of the outstanding voting securities of a company" as defined in section 2(a)(42) of the Act; and (2) when used with respect to any other matter required to be submitted to the outstanding voting securities of a series company, shall mean the lesser of (i) the minimum vote of the outstanding voting securities of a company required by applicable State law or other applicable requirement, or (ii) the minimum vote specified by subparagraph (1) of this paragraph, unless State law requires approval of such matters by a specified percentage of the outstanding voting securities of a particular class or series, in which case, State law shall apply.

§ 270.18f–3 Multiple Class Companies

Notwithstanding sections 18(f)(1) and 18(i) of the Act (15 U.S.C. 80a–18(f)(1) and (i), respectively), a registered open-end management investment company or series or class thereof established in accordance with section 18(f)(2) of the Act (15 U.S.C. 80a–18(f)(2)) whose shares are registered on Form N–1A [§§ 239.15A and 274.11A of this chapter] ("company") may issue more than one class of voting stock, *provided* that:

(a) Each class:

(1)(i) Shall have a different arrangement for shareholder services or the distribution of securities or both, and shall pay all of the expenses of that arrangement;

(ii) May pay a different share of other expenses, not including advisory or custodial fees or other expenses related to the management of the company's assets, if these expenses are actually incurred in a different amount by that class, or if the class receives services of a different kind or to a different degree than other classes; and

(iii) May pay a different advisory fee to the extent that any difference in amount paid is the result of the application of the same performance fee provisions in the advisory contract of the company to the different investment performance of each class;

(2) Shall have exclusive voting rights on any matter submitted to shareholders that relates solely to its arrangement;

(3) Shall have separate voting rights on any matter submitted to shareholders in which the interests of one class differ from the interests of any other class; and

(4) Shall have in all other respects the same rights and obligations as each other class.

(b) Expenses may be waived or reimbursed by the company's adviser, underwriter, or any other provider of services to the company.

(c)(1) Income, realized gains and losses, unrealized appreciation and depreciation, and Fundwide Expenses shall be allocated based on one of the following methods (which method shall be applied on a consistent basis);

(i) To each class based on the net assets of that class in relation to the net assets of the company ("relative net assets");

(ii) To each class based on the Simultaneous Equations Method;

(iii) To each class based on the Settled Shares Method, provided that the company is a Daily Dividend Fund (such a company may allocate income and Fundwide Expenses based on the Settled Shares Method and realized gains and losses and unrealized appreciation and depreciation based on relative net assets);

(iv) To each share without regard to class, provided that the company is a Daily Dividend Fund that maintains the same net asset value per share in each class; that the company has received undertakings from its adviser, underwriter, or any other provider of services to the company, agreeing to waive or reimburse the company for payments to such service provider by one or more classes, as allocated under paragraph (a)(1) of this section, to the extent necessary to assure that all classes of the company maintain the same net asset value per share; and that payments waived or reimbursed under such an undertaking may not be carried forward or recouped at a future date; or

(v) To each class based on any other appropriate method, provided that a majority of the directors of the company, and a majority of the directors who are not interested persons of the company, determine that the method is fair to the shareholders of each class and that the annualized rate of return of each class will generally differ from that of the other classes only by the expense differentials among the classes.

(2) For purposes of this section:

(i) Daily Dividend Fund means any company that has a policy of declaring distributions of net investment income daily, including any money market fund that determines net asset value using the amortized cost method permitted by § 270.2a–7;

(ii) Fundwide Expenses means expenses of the company not allocated to a particular class under paragraph (a)(1) of this section;

(iii) The Settled Shares Method means allocating to each class based on relative net assets, excluding the value of subscriptions receivable; and

(iv) The Simultaneous Equations Method means the simultaneous allocation to each class of each day's income, realized gains and losses, unrealized appreciation and depreciation, and Fundwide Expenses and reallocation to each class of undistributed net investment income, undistributed realized gains or losses, and unrealized appreciation or depreciation, based on the operating results of the company, changes in ownership interests of each class, and expense differentials between the classes, so that the annualized rate of return of each class generally differs from that of the other classes only by the expense differentials among the classes.

(d) Any payments made under paragraph (a) of this section shall be made pursuant to a written plan setting forth the separate arrangement and expense allocation of each class, and any related conversion features or exchange privileges. Before the first issuance of a share of any class in reliance upon this section, and before any material amendment of a plan, a majority of the directors of the company, and a majority of the directors who are not interested persons of the company, shall find that the plan as proposed to be adopted or amended, including the expense allocation, is in the best interests of each class individually and the company as a whole; initial board approval of a plan under this paragraph (d) is not required, however, if the plan does not make any change in the arrangements and expense allocations previously approved by the board under an existing order of exemption. Before any vote on the plan, the directors shall request and evaluate, and any agreement relating to a class arrangement shall require the parties thereto to furnish, such information as may be reasonably necessary to evaluate the plan.

(e)(1) The board of directors of the investment company satisfies the fund governance standards defined in § 270.0–1(a)(7).

(f) Nothing in this section prohibits a company from offering any class with:

(1) An exchange privilege providing that securities of the class may be exchanged for certain securities of another company; or

(2) A conversion feature providing that shares of one class of the company (the "purchase class") will be exchanged automatically for shares of another class of the company (the "target class") after a specified period of time, *provided that:*

(i) The conversion is effected on the basis of the relative net asset values of the two classes without the imposition of any sales load, fee, or other charge;

(ii) The expenses, including payments authorized under a plan adopted pursuant to § 270.12b–1 ("rule 12b–1 plan"), for the target class are not higher than the expenses, including payments authorized under a rule 12b–1 plan, for the purchase class; and

(iii) If the shareholders of the target class approve any increase in expenses allocated to the target class under paragraphs (a)(1)(i) and (a)(1)(ii) of this section, and the purchase class shareholders do not approve the increase, the company will establish a new target class for the purchase class on the same terms as applied to the target class before that increase.

(3) A conversion feature providing that shares of a class in which an investor is no longer eligible to participate may be converted to shares of a class in which that investor is eligible to participate, *provided that:*

(i) The investor is given prior notice of the proposed conversion; and

(ii) The conversion is effected on the basis of the relative net asset values of the two classes without the imposition of any sales load, fee, or other charge.

§ 270.19a–1 Written Statement to Accompany Dividend Payments by Management Companies

(a) Every written statement made pursuant to section 19 by or on behalf of a management company shall be made on a separate paper and shall clearly indicate what portion of the payment per share is made from the following sources:

(1) Net income for the current or preceding fiscal year, or accumulated undistributed net income, or both, not including in either case profits or losses from the sale of securities or other properties.

(2) Accumulated undistributed net profits from the sale of securities or other properties (except that an open-end company may treat as a separate source its net profits from such sales during its current fiscal year).

(3) Paid-in surplus or other capital source. To the extent that a payment is properly designated as being made from a source specified in subparagraph (1) or (2) of this paragraph, it need not be designated as having been made from a source specified in this subparagraph.

(b) If the payment is made in whole or in part from a source specified in paragraph (a)(2) of this section the written statement shall indicate, after giving effect to the part of such payment so specified, the deficit, if any, in the aggregate of (1) accumulated undistributed realized profits less losses on the sale of securities or other properties and (2) the net unrealized appreciation or depreciation of portfolio securities, all as of a date reasonably close to the end of the period as of which the dividend is paid. Any statement made pursuant to the preceding sentence shall specify the amount, if any, of such deficit which represents unrealized depreciation of portfolio securities.

(c) Accumulated undistributed net income and accumulated undistributed net profits from the sale of securities or other properties shall be determined, at the option of the company, either (1) from the date of the organization of the company, (2) from the date of a reorganization, as defined in clause (A) or (B) of section 2(a)(33) of the Act, (3) from the date as of which a write-down of portfolio securities was made in connection with a corporate readjustment, approved by stockholders, of the type known as "quasireorganization," or (4) from January 1, 1925, to the close of the period as of which the dividend is paid, without giving effect to such payment.

(d) For the purpose of this section, open-end companies which upon the sale of their shares allocate to undistributed income or other similar account that portion of the consideration received which represents the approximate per share amount of undistributed net income included in the sales price, and make a corresponding deduction from undistributed net income upon the purchase or redemption of shares need not treat the amounts so allocated as paid-in surplus or other capital source.

(e) For the purpose of this section, the source or sources from which a dividend is paid shall be determined (or reasonably estimated) to the close of the period as of which it is paid without giving effect to such payment. If any such estimate is subsequently ascertained to be inaccurate in a significant amount, a correction thereof shall be made by a written statement pursuant to section 19(a) of the Act or in the first report to stockholders following discovery of the inaccuracy.

(f) Insofar as a written statement made pursuant to section 19(a) of the Act relates to a dividend on preferred stock paid for a period of less than a year, a company may elect to indicate only that portion of the payment which is made from sources specified in paragraph (a)(1) of this section, and need not specify the sources from which the remainder was paid. Every company which in any fiscal year elects to make a statement pursuant to the preceding sentence shall transmit to the holders of such preferred stock, at a date reasonably near the end of the last dividend period in such fiscal year, a statement meeting the requirements of paragraph (a) of this section on an annual basis.

(g) The purpose of this section, in the light of which it shall be construed, is to afford security holders adequate disclosure of the sources from which dividend payments are made. Nothing in this section shall be construed to prohibit the inclusion in any written statement of additional information in explanation of the information required by this section. Nothing in this section shall be construed to permit a dividend payment in violation of any State law or to prevent compliance with any requirement of State law regarding dividends consistent with this rule.

§ 270.19b–1 Frequency of Distribution of Capital Gains

(a) No registered investment company which is a "regulated investment company" as defined in section 851 of the Internal Revenue Code of 1986 ("Code") shall distribute more than one capital gain dividend ("distribution"), as defined in section 852(b)(3)(C) of the Code, with respect to any one taxable year of the company, other than a distribution otherwise permitted by this rule or made pursuant to section 855 of the Code which is supplemental to the prior distribution with respect to the same taxable year of the company and which does not exceed 10% of the aggregate amount distributed for such taxable year.

(b) No registered investment company which is not a "regulated investment company" as defined in section 851 of the Code shall make more than one distribution of long-term capital gains, as defined in the Code, in any one taxable year of the company: *Provided,* That a unit investment trust may distribute capital gain dividends received from a "regulated investment company" within a reasonable time after receipt.

(c) The provisions of this rule shall not apply to a unit investment trust (hereinafter referred to as the "Trust") engaged exclusively in the business of investing in eligible trust securities (as defined in Rule 14a–3(b) under this act); *Provided,* That:

(1) The capital gain distribution is a result of:

(i) an issuer's calling or redeeming an eligible trust debt security held by the Trust,

(ii) the sale of an eligible trust security by the Trust to provide funds for redemption of Trust units when the amount received by the Trust for such sale exceeds the amount required to satisfy the redemption distribution,

(iii) the sale of an eligible trust security to maintain qualification of the Trust as a "regulated investment company" under Section 851 of the Code,

(iv) regular distributions of principal and prepayment of principal on eligible trust securities, or

(v) the sale of an eligible trust security in order to maintain the investment stability of the Trust; and

(2) Capital gains distributions are clearly described as such in a report to the unitholder which accompanies each such distribution.

(d) For purposes of paragraph (c), sales made to maintain the investment stability of the Trust means sales made to prevent deterioration of the value of the eligible trust securities held in the Trust portfolio when one or more of the following factors exist:

(1) A default in the payment of principal or interest on an eligible trust security;

(2) An action involving the issuer of an eligible trust security which adversely affects the ability of such issuer to continue payment of principal or interest on its eligible trust securities; or

(3) A change in market, revenue or credit factors which adversely affects the ability of such issuer to continue payment of principal or interest on its eligible trust securities.

(e) If a registered investment company because of unforeseen circumstances in a particular taxable year proposes to make a distribution which would be prohibited by the provisions of this section, it may file a request with the Commission for authorization to make such a distribution. Such request shall comply with the requirements of § 270.02 of this chapter and shall set forth the pertinent facts and explain the circumstances which the company believes justify such distribution. The request shall be deemed granted unless the Commission within 15 days after receipt thereof shall deny such request as not being necessary or appropriate in the public interest or for the protection of investors and notify the company in writing of such denial.

(f) A registered investment company may make one additional distribution of long-term capital gains, as defined in the Code, with respect to any one taxable year of the company, which distribution is made, in whole or in part, for the purpose of not incurring any tax under section 4982 of the Code. Such additional distribution may be made prior or subsequent to any distribution otherwise permitted by paragraph (a) of this section.

§ 270.20a–1 Solicitation of Proxies, Consents and Authorizations

(a) No person shall solicit or permit the use of his or her name to solicit any proxy, consent, or authorization with respect to any security issued by a registered Fund, except upon compliance with Regulation 14A (§ 240.14a–1 of this chapter), Schedule 14A (§ 240.14a–101 of this chapter), and all other rules and regulations adopted pursuant to Section 14(a) of the Securities Exchange Act of 1934 that would be applicable to such solicitation if it were made in respect of a security registered pursuant to Section 12 of the Securities Exchange Act of 1934.

(b) If the solicitation is made by or on behalf of the management of the investment company, then the investment adviser or any prospective investment adviser and any affiliated person thereof as to whom information is required in the solicitation shall upon request of the investment company promptly transmit to the investment company all information necessary to enable the management of such company to comply with the rules and regulations applicable to such solicitation. If the solicitation is made by any person other than the management of the investment company, on behalf of and with the consent of the investment adviser or prospective investment adviser, then the investment adviser or prospective investment adviser and any affiliated person thereof as to whom information is required in the solicitation shall upon request of the person making the solicitation promptly transmit to such person all information necessary to enable such person to comply with the rules and regulations applicable to the solicitation.

(c) In lieu of the fees specified in Rule 14a–6 of the General Rules and Regulations under the Securities Exchange Act of 1934, at the time of filing the preliminary solicitation material, or, if no preliminary solicitation material is filed, at the time of filing the definitive solicitation material, the person upon whose behalf the solicitation is made shall pay to the Commission a fee of $125, no part of which shall be refunded.

Instruction. Registrants that have made a public offering of securities and that hold security holder votes for which proxies, consents, or authorizations are not being solicited pursuant to the requirements of this rule should refer to Section 14(c) of the Securities Exchange Act of 1934 and the information statement requirements set forth in the rules thereunder.

§ 270.22c–1 Pricing of Redeemable Securities for Distribution, Redemption and Repurchase

(a) No registered investment company issuing any redeemable security, no person designated in such issuer's prospectus as authorized to consummate transactions in any such security, and no principal underwriter of, or dealer in any such security shall sell, redeem, or repurchase any such security except at a price based on the current net asset value of such security which is next computed after receipt of a tender of such security for redemption or of an order to purchase or sell such security; *Provided,* That:

(1) This paragraph shall not prevent a sponsor of a unit investment trust (hereinafter referred to as the "Trust") engaged exclusively in the business of investing in eligible trust securities (as defined in Rule 14a–3(b)) from selling or repurchasing Trust units in a secondary market at a price based on the offering side evaluation of the eligible trust securities in the Trust's portfolio, determined at any time on the last business day of each week, effective for all sales made during the following week, if on the days that such sales or repurchases are made the sponsor receives a letter from a qualified evaluator stating, in its opinion, that:

(i) in the case of repurchases, the current bid price is not higher than the offering side evaluation, computed on the last business day of the previous week; and

(ii) in the case of resales, the offering side evaluation, computed as of the last business day of the previous week, is not more than one-half of one percent ($5.00 on a unit representing $1,000 principal amount of eligible trust securities) greater than the current offering price.

(2) This paragraph shall not prevent any registered investment company from adjusting the price of its redeemable securities sold pursuant to a merger, consolidation or purchase of substantially all of the assets of a company which meets the conditions specified in § 270.17a–8.

(b) For the purposes of this section, (1) the current net asset value of any such security shall be computed no less frequently than once daily, Monday through Friday, at the specific time or times during the day that the board of directors of the investment company sets, in accordance with paragraph (e) of this section, except on (i) days on which changes in the value of the investment company's portfolio securities will not materially affect the current net asset value of the investment company's redeemable securities, (ii) days during which no security is tendered for redemption and no order to purchase or sell such security is received by the investment company; or (iii) customary national business holidays described or listed in the prospectus and local and regional business holidays listed in the prospectus; and (2) a "qualified evaluator" shall mean any evaluator which represents it is in a position to determine, on the basis of an informal evaluation of the eligible trust securities held in the Trust's portfolio, whether—

(i) the current bid price is higher than the offering side evaluation, computed on the last business day of the previous week, and

(ii) the offering side evaluation, computed as of the last business day of the previous week, is more than one-half of one percent ($5.00 on a unit representing $1,000 principal amount of eligible trust securities) greater than the current offering price.

(c) Notwithstanding the provisions above, any registered separate account offering variable annuity contracts, any person designated in such account's prospectus as authorized to consummate transactions in such contracts, and any principal underwriter of or dealer in such contracts shall be permitted to apply the initial purchase payment for any such contract at a price based on the current net asset value of such contract which is next computed:

(1) Not later than two business days after receipt of the order to purchase by the insurance company sponsoring the separate account ("insurer"), if the contract application and other information necessary for processing the order to purchase (collectively, "application") are complete upon receipt; or

(2) Not later than two business days after an application which is incomplete upon receipt by the insurer is made complete, *Provided,* That, if an incomplete application is not made complete within five business days after receipt,

(i) The prospective purchaser shall be informed of the reasons for the delay, and

(ii) The initial purchase payment shall be returned immediately and in full, unless the prospective purchaser specifically consents to the insurer retaining the purchase payment until the application is made complete.

(3) As used in this section:

(i) "Prospective Purchaser" shall mean either an individual contract-owner or an individual participant in a group contract.

(ii) "Initial Purchase Payment" shall refer to the first purchase payment submitted to the insurer by, or on behalf of, a prospective purchaser.

(d) The board of directors shall initially set the time or times during the day that the current net asset value shall be computed, and shall make and approve such changes as the board deems necessary.

§ 270.22d–1 Exemption From Section 22(d) to Permit Sales of Redeemable Securities at Prices Which Reflect Sales Loads Set Pursuant to a Schedule

A registered investment company that is the issuer of redeemable securities, a principal underwriter of such securities or a dealer therein shall be exempt from the provisions of section 22(d) to the extent necessary to permit the sale of such securities at prices that reflect scheduled variations in, or elimination of, the sales load. These price schedules may offer such variations in or elimination of the sales load to particular classes of investors or transactions, *Provided that:*

(a) The company, the principal underwriter and dealers in the company's shares apply an scheduled variation uniformly to all offerees in the class specified;

(b) The company furnishes to existing shareholders and prospective investors adequate information concerning any scheduled variation, as prescribed in applicable registration statement form requirements;

(c) Before making any new sales load variation available to purchasers of the company's shares, the company revises its prospectus and statement of additional information to describe that new variation; and

(d) The company advises existing shareholders of any new sales load variation within one year of the date when that variation is first made available to purchasers of the company's shares.

§ 270.22d-2 Exemption From Section 22(d) for Certain Registered Separate Accounts

A registered separate account, any principal underwriter for such account, any dealer in contracts or units of interest or participations in such contracts issued by such account and any insurance company maintaining such account shall, with respect to any variable annuity contracts, units, or participations therein issued by such account, be exempted from Section 22(d) to the extent necessary to permit the sale of such contracts, units or participations by such persons at prices which reflect variations in the sales load or in any administrative charge or other deductions from the purchase payments; *Provided, however,* that (a) the prospectus discloses as precisely as possible the amount of the variations and the circumstances, if any, in which such variations shall be available or describes the basis of such variations and the manner in which entitlement shall be determined, and (b) any such variations reflect differences in costs or services and are not unfairly discriminatory against any person.

§ 270.22e-1 Exemption From Section 22(e) of the Act During Annuity Payment Period of Variable Annuity Contracts Participating in Certain Registered Separate Accounts

(a) A registered separate account shall during the annuity payment period of variable annuity contracts participating in such account, be exempt from the provisions of section 22(e) of the Act prohibiting the suspension of the right of redemption or postponement of the date of payment or satisfaction upon redemption of any redeemable security, with respect to such contracts under which payments are being made based upon life contingencies.

§ 270.22e-2 Pricing of Redemption in Accordance With Rule 22c-1

An investment company shall not be deemed to have suspended the right of redemption if it prices a redemption request by computing the net asset value of the investment company's redeemable securities in accordance with the provisions of Rule 22c-1.

§ 270.23c-1 Repurchase of Securities by Closed-End Companies

(a) A registered closed-end company may purchase for cash a security of which it is the issuer, subject to the following conditions:

(1) If the security is a stock entitled to cumulative dividends, such dividends are not in arrears.

(2) If the security is a stock not entitled to cumulative dividends, at least 90 percent of the net income of the issuer for the last preceding fiscal year, determined in accordance with good accounting practice and not including profits or losses realized from the sale of securities or other properties was distributed to its shareholders during such fiscal year or within 60 days after the close of such fiscal year.

(3) If the security to be purchased is junior to any class of outstanding security of the issuer representing indebtedness (except notes or other evidences of indebtedness held by a bank or other person, the issuance of which did not involve a public offering) all securities of such class shall have an asset coverage of at least 300 percent immediately after such purchase; and if the security to be purchased is junior to any class of outstanding senior security of the issuer which is a stock, all securities of such class shall have an asset coverage of at least 200 percent immediately after such purchase and shall not be in arrears as to dividends.

(4) The seller of the security is not to the knowledge of the issuer an affiliated person of the issuer.

(5) Payment of the purchase price is accompanied or preceded by a written confirmation of the purchase.

(6) The purchase is made at a price not above the market value, if any, or the asset value of such security, whichever is lower, at the time of such purchase.

(7) The issuer discloses to the seller or, if the seller is acting through a broker, to the seller's broker, either prior to or at the time of purchase the approximate or estimated asset coverage per unit of the security to be purchased.

(8) No brokerage commission is paid by the issuer to any affiliated person of the issuer in connection with the purchase.

(9) The purchase is not made in a manner or on a basis which discriminates unfairly against any holders of the class of securities purchased.

(10) If the security is a stock, the issuer has, within the preceding six months, informed stockholders of its intention to purchase stock of such class by letter or report addressed to all the stockholders of such class.

(11) The issuer files with the Commission, as an exhibit to Form N–CSR (§ 249.331 and § 274.128), a copy of any written solicitation to purchase securities under this section sent or given during the period covered by the report by or on behalf of the issuer to 10 or more persons.

(b) Notwithstanding the conditions of paragraph (a) of this section, a closed-end company may purchase fractional interests in, or fractional rights to receive, any security of which is it the issuer.

(c) This rule does not apply to purchase of securities made pursuant to section 23(c)(1) or (2) of the act. A registered closed-end company may file an application with the Commission for an order under section 23(c)(3) of the act permitting the purchase of any security of which it is the issuer which does not meet the conditions of this rule and which is not to be made pursuant to section 23(c)(1) or (2) of the act.

(d) This rule relates exclusively to the requirements of section 23(c) of the act, and the provisions hereof shall not be construed to authorize any action which contravenes any other applicable law, statutory or otherwise, or the provision of any indenture or other instrument pursuant to which securities of the issuer were issued.

§ 270.23c–2 Call and Redemption of Securities Issued by Registered Closed-End Companies

(a) Notwithstanding the provisions of § 270.23c–1, a registered closed-end investment company may call or redeem any securities of which it is the issuer, in accordance with the terms of such securities or the charter, indenture or other instrument pursuant to which such securities were issued: *Provided*, That, if less than all the outstanding securities of a class or series are to be called or redeemed the call or redemption shall be made by lot, on a pro rata basis, or in such other manner as will not discriminate unfairly against any holder of the securities of such class or series.

(b) A registered closed-end investment company which proposes to call or redeem any securities of which it is the issuer shall file with the Commission notice of its intention to call or redeem such securities at least 30 days prior to the date set for the call or redemption; *Provided, however,* That if notice of the call or the redemption is required to be published in a newspaper or otherwise, notice shall be given to the Commission at least 10 days in advance of the date of publication. Such notice shall be filed in triplicate and shall include (1) the title of the class of securities to be called or redeemed, (2) the date on which the securities are to be called or redeemed, (3) the applicable provisions of the governing instrument pursuant to which the securities are to be called or redeemed and, (4) if less than all the outstanding securities of a class or series are to be called or redeemed, the principal amount or number of shares and the basis upon which the securities to be called or redeemed are to be selected.

§ 270.23c–3 Repurchase Offers by Closed–End Companies

(a) *Definitions.* For purposes of this section:

(1) *Periodic interval* shall mean an interval of three, six, or twelve months.

(2) *Repurchase offer* shall mean an offer pursuant to this section by an investment company to repurchase common stock of which it is the issuer.

(3) *Repurchase offer amount* shall mean the amount of common stock that is the subject of a repurchase offer, expressed as a percentage of such stock outstanding on the repurchase request deadline, that an investment company offers to repurchase in a repurchase offer. The repurchase offer amount shall not be less than five percent nor more than twenty-five percent of the common stock outstanding on a repurchase request deadline. Before each repurchase offer, the repurchase offer amount for that repurchase offer shall be determined by the directors of the company.

(4) *Repurchase payment deadline* with respect to a tender of common stock shall mean the date by which an investment company must pay securities holders for any stock repurchased. A repurchase payment deadline shall occur seven days after the repurchase pricing date applicable to such tender.

(5) *Repurchase pricing date* with respect to a tender of common stock shall mean the date on which an investment company determines the net asset value applicable to the repurchase of the securities. A repurchase pricing date shall occur no later than the fourteenth day after a repurchase request deadline, or the next business day if the fourteenth day is not a business day. In no event shall an investment company determine the net asset value applicable to the repurchase of the stock before the close of business on the repurchase request deadline.

(i) For an investment company making a repurchase offer pursuant to paragraph (b) of this section, the number of days between the repurchase request deadline and the repurchase pricing date for a repurchase offer shall be the maximum number specified by the company pursuant to paragraph (b)(2)(i)(D) of this section.

(ii) For an investment company making a repurchase offer pursuant to paragraph (c) of this section, the repurchase pricing date shall be such date as the company shall disclose to security holders in the notification pursuant to paragraph (b)(4) of this section with respect to such offer.

(iii) For purposes of paragraph (b)(1) of this section, a repurchase pricing date may be a date earlier than the date determined pursuant to paragraph (a)(5)(i) or (ii) of this section if, on or immediately following the repurchase request deadline, it appears that the use of an earlier repurchase pricing date is not likely to result in significant dilution of the net asset value of either stock that is tendered for repurchase or stock that is not tendered.

(6) *Repurchase request* shall mean the tender of common stock in response to a repurchase offer.

(7) *Repurchase request deadline* with respect to a repurchase offer shall mean the date by which an investment company must receive repurchase requests submitted by security holders in response to that offer or withdrawals or modifications of previously submitted repurchase requests. The first repurchase request deadline after the effective date of the registration statement for the common stock that is the subject of a repurchase offer, or after a shareholder vote

adopting the fundamental policy specifying a company's periodic interval, whichever is later, shall occur no later than two periodic intervals thereafter.

(b) *Periodic repurchase offers.* A registered closed-end company or a business development company may repurchase common stock of which it is the issuer from the holders of the stock at periodic intervals, pursuant to repurchase offers made to all holders of the stock, *Provided* that:

(1) The company shall repurchase the stock for cash at the net asset value determined on the repurchase pricing date and shall pay the holders of the stock by the repurchase payment deadline except as provided in paragraph (b)(3) of this section. The company may deduct from the repurchase proceeds only a repurchase fee, not to exceed two percent of the proceeds, that is paid to the company and is reasonably intended to compensate the company for expenses directly related to the repurchase. A company may not condition a repurchase offer upon the tender of any minimum amount of shares.

(2)(i) The company shall repurchase the security pursuant to a fundamental policy, changeable only by a majority vote of the outstanding voting securities of the company, stating:

(A) That the company will make repurchase offers at periodic intervals pursuant to this section, as this section may be amended from time to time;

(B) The periodic intervals between repurchase request deadlines;

(C) The dates of repurchase request deadlines or the means of determining the repurchase request deadlines; and

(D) The maximum number of days between each repurchase request deadline and the next repurchase pricing date.

(ii) The company shall include a statement in its annual report to shareholders of the following:

(A) Its policy under paragraph (b)(2)(i) of this section; and

(B) With respect to repurchase offers by the company during the period covered by the annual report, the number of repurchase offers, the repurchase offer amount and the amount tendered in each repurchase offer, and the extent to which in any repurchase offer the company repurchased stock pursuant to the procedures in paragraph (b)(5) of this section.

(iii) A company shall be deemed to be making repurchase offers pursuant to a policy within paragraph (b)(2)(i) of this section if:

(A) The company makes repurchase offers to its security holders at periodic intervals and, before May 14, 1993, has disclosed in its registration statement its intention to make or consider making such repurchase offers; and

(B) The company's board of directors adopts a policy specifying the matters required by paragraph (b)(2)(i) of this section, and the periodic interval specified therein conforms generally to the frequency of the company's prior repurchase offers.

(3)(i) The company shall not suspend or postpone a repurchase offer except pursuant to a vote of a majority of the directors, including a majority of the directors who are not interested persons of the company, and only:

(A) If the repurchase would cause the company to lose its status as a regulated investment company under Subchapter M of the Internal Revenue Code [26 U.S.C. 851–860];

(B) If the repurchase would cause the stock that is the subject of the offer that is either listed on a national securities exchange or quoted in an inter-dealer quotation system of a national securities association to be neither listed on any national securities exchange nor quoted on any inter-dealer quotation system of a national securities association;

(C) For any period during which the New York Stock Exchange or any other market in which the securities owned by the company are principally traded is closed, other than customary weekend and holiday closings, or during which trading in such market is restricted;

(D) For any period during which an emergency exists as a result of which disposal by the company of securities owned by it is not reasonably practicable, or during which it is not reasonably practicable for the company fairly to determine the value of its net assets; or

(E) For such other periods as the Commission may by order permit for the protection of security holders of the company.

(ii) If a repurchase offer is suspended or postponed, the company shall provide notice to security holders of such suspension or postponement. If the company renews the repurchase offer, the company shall send a new notification to security holders satisfying the requirements of paragraph (b)(4) of this section.

(4)(i) No less than twenty-one and no more than forty-two days before each repurchase request deadline, the company shall send to each holder of record and to each beneficial owner of the stock that is the subject of the repurchase offer a notification providing the following information:

(A) A statement that the company is offering to repurchase its securities from security holders at net asset value;

(B) Any fees applicable to such repurchase;

(C) The repurchase offer amount;

(D) The dates of the repurchase request deadline, repurchase pricing date, and repurchase payment deadline, the risk of fluctuation in net asset value between the repurchase request deadline and the repurchase pricing date, and the possibility that the company may use an earlier repurchase pricing date pursuant to paragraph (a)(5)(iii) of this section;

(E) The procedures for security holders to tender their shares and the right of the security holders to withdraw or modify their tenders until the repurchase request deadline;

(F) The procedures under which the company may repurchase such shares on a pro rata basis pursuant to paragraph (b)(5) of this section;

(G) The circumstances in which the company may suspend or postpone a repurchase offer pursuant to paragraph (b)(3) of this section;

(H) The net asset value of the common stock computed no more than seven days before the date of the notification and the means by which security holders may ascertain the net asset value thereafter; and

(I) The market price, if any, of the common stock on the date on which such net asset value was computed, and the means by which security holders may ascertain the market price thereafter.

(ii) The company shall file three copies of the notification with the Commission within three business days after sending the notification to security holders. Those copies shall be accompanied by copies of Form N–23c–3 (§ 274.221 of this chapter) ("Notification of Repurchase Offer"). The format of the copies shall comply with the requirements for registration statements and reports under § 270.8b–12 of this chapter.

(iii) For purposes of sending a notification to a beneficial owner pursuant to paragraph (b)(4)(i) of this section, where the company knows that shares of common stock that is the subject of a repurchase offer are held of record by a broker, dealer, voting trustee, bank, association or other entity that exercises fiduciary powers in nominee name or otherwise, the company shall follow the procedures for transmitting materials to beneficial owners of securities that are set forth in § 240.14a–13 of this chapter.

(5) If security holders tender more than the repurchase offer amount, the company may repurchase an additional amount of stock not to exceed two percent of the common stock outstanding on the repurchase request deadline. If the company determines not to repurchase more than the repurchase offer amount, or if security holders tender stock in an amount exceeding the repurchase offer amount plus two percent of the common stock outstanding on the repurchase request deadline, the company shall repurchase the shares tendered on a pro rata basis; *Provided, however,* That this provision shall not prohibit the company from:

(i) Accepting all stock tendered by persons who own, beneficially or of record, an aggregate of not more than a specified number which is less than one hundred shares and who tender all of their stock, before prorating stock tendered by others; or

(ii) Accepting by lot stock tendered by security holders who tender all stock held by them and who, when tendering their stock, elect to have either all or none or at least a minimum amount or none accepted, if the company first accepts all stock tendered by security holders who do not so elect.

(6) The company shall permit tenders of stock for repurchase to be withdrawn or modified at any time until the repurchase request deadline but shall not permit tenders to be withdrawn or modified thereafter.

(7)(i) The current net asset value of the company's common stock shall be computed no less frequently than weekly on such day and at such specific time or times during the day that the board of directors of the company shall set.

(ii) The current net asset value of the company's common stock shall be computed daily on the five business days preceding a repurchase request deadline at such specific time or times during the day that the board of directors of the company shall set.

(iii) For purposes of section 23(b), the current net asset value applicable to a sale of common stock by the company shall be the net asset value next determined after receipt of an order to purchase such stock. During any period when the company is offering its common stock, the current net asset value of the common stock shall be computed no less frequently than once daily, Monday through Friday, at the specific time or times during the day that the board of directors of the company shall set, except on:

(A) Days on which changes in the value of the company's portfolio securities will not materially affect the current net asset value of the common stock;

(B) Days during which no order to purchase its common stock is received, other than days when the net asset value would otherwise be computed pursuant to paragraph (b)(7)(i) of this section; or

(C) Customary national, local, and regional business holidays described or listed in the prospectus.

(8) The board of directors of the investment company satisfies the fund governance standards defined in § 270.0–1(a)(7).

(9) Any senior security issued by the company or other indebtedness contracted by the company either shall mature by the next repurchase pricing date or shall provide for the redemption or call of such security or the repayment of such indebtedness by the company by the next repurchase pricing date, either in whole or in part, without penalty or premium, as necessary to permit the company to repurchase securities in such repurchase offer amount as the directors of the company shall determine in compliance with the asset coverage requirements of section 18 or 61, as applicable.

(10)(i) From the time a company sends a notification to shareholders pursuant to paragraph (b)(4) of this section until the repurchase pricing date, a percentage of the company's assets equal to at least 100 percent of the repurchase offer amount shall consist of assets that can be sold or disposed of in the ordinary course of business, at approximately the price at which the company has valued the investment, within a period equal to the period between a repurchase request deadline and the repurchase payment deadline, or of assets that mature by the next repurchase payment deadline.

(ii) In the event that the company's assets fail to comply with the requirements in paragraph (b)(10)(i) of this section, the board of directors shall cause the company to take such action as it deems appropriate to ensure compliance.

(iii) In supervising the company's operations and portfolio management by the investment adviser, the company's board of directors shall adopt written procedures reasonably designed, taking into account current market conditions and the company's investment objectives, to ensure that the company's portfolio assets are sufficiently liquid so that the company can comply with its fundamental policy on repurchases, and comply with the liquidity requirements of paragraph (b)(10)(i) of this section. The board of directors shall review the overall composition of the portfolio and make and approve such changes to the procedures as the board deems necessary.

(11) The company, or any underwriter for the company, shall comply, as if the company were an open-end company, with the provisions of section 24(b) and rules issued thereunder with respect to any advertisement, pamphlet, circular, form letter, or other sales literature addressed to or intended for distribution to prospective investors.

(c) *Discretionary repurchase offers.* A registered closed-end company or a business development company may repurchase common stock of which it is the issuer from the holders of the stock pursuant to a repurchase offer that is not made pursuant to a fundamental policy and that is made to all holders of the stock not earlier than two years after another offer pursuant to this paragraph (c) if the company complies with the requirements of paragraphs (b)(1), (3), (4), (5), (6), (7)(ii), (8), (10)(i), and (10)(ii) of this section.

(d) *Exemption from the definition of redeemable security.* A company that makes repurchase offers pursuant to paragraph (b) or (c) of this section shall not be deemed thereby to be an issuer of redeemable securities within section 2(a)(32).

§ 270.24b–1 Definitions

(a) The term "form letter" as used in section 24(b) of the act includes (1) one of a series of identical sales letters, and (2) any sales letter a substantial portion of which consists of a statement which is in essence identical with similar statements in sales letters sent to 25 or more persons within any period of 90 consecutive days.

(b) The term "distribution" as used in section 24(b) of the act includes the distribution or redistribution to prospective investors of the content of any written sales literature, whether such distribution or redistribution is effected by means of written or oral representations or statements.

(c) The term "rules and regulations" as used in section 24(a) and (c) of the act shall include the forms for registration of securities under the Securities Act of 1933 and the related instructions thereto.

§ 270.24b–2 Filing Copies of Sales Literature

Copies of material filed with the Commission for the sole purpose of complying with section 24(b) of the act either shall be accompanied by a letter of transmittal which makes appropriate references to said section or shall make such appropriate reference on the face of the material. Such material shall be submitted to the Commission in paper only, whether or not the investment company to which the material relates is otherwise required to file in electronic format.

§ 270.24b–3 Sales Literature Deemed Filed

Any advertisement, pamphlet, circular, form letter or other sales literature addressed to or intended for distribution to prospective investors shall be deemed filed with the Commission for purposes of Section 24(b) of the Act upon filing with a national securities association registered under Section 15A of the Securities Exchange Act of 1934 that has adopted rules providing standards for the investment company advertising practices of its members and has established and implemented procedures to review that advertising.

§ 270.24e–1 Filing of Certain Prospectuses as Post-Effective Amendments to Registration Statements Under the Securities Act of 1933

Section 24(e) of the act requires that when a prospectus is revised so that it may be available for use in compliance with section 10(a)(3) of the Securities Act of 1933 for a period extending beyond the time when the previous prospectus would have ceased to be available for such use, such revised prospectus, in order to meet the requirements of section 10 of said act, must be filed as an amendment to the registration statement under said act and such amendment must have become effective prior to the use of the revised prospectus. Except as hereinabove provided, section 24(e) of the act shall not be deemed to govern the times and conditions under which post-effective amendments shall be filed to registration statements under the Securities Act of 1933.

§ 270.24f–2 Registration Under the Securities Act of 1933 of an Indefinite Number of Certain Investment Company Securities

(a) *General.* Any face-amount certificate company, open-end management company or unit investment trust ("issuer") that is deemed to have registered an indefinite amount of securities pursuant to section 24(f) of the Act [15 U.S.C. 80a–24(f)] must, not later than 90 days after the end of any fiscal year during which it has publicly offered such securities, file Form 24F–2 (17 CFR 274.24) with the Commission. Form 24F–2 must be prepared in accordance with the requirements of that Form, and must be accompanied by the payment of a registration fee with respect to the securities sold during the fiscal year in reliance upon registration pursuant to section 24(f) of the Act calculated in the manner specified in section 24(f) of the Act and in the Form. An issuer that pays the registration fee more than 90 days after the end of its fiscal year must pay interest in the manner specified in section 24(f) of the Act and in Form 24F–2.

(b) *Issuer ceasing operations; mergers and other transactions.* For purposes of this section, if an issuer ceases operations, the date the issuer ceases operations will be deemed to be the end of its fiscal year. In the case of a liquidation, merger, or sale of all or substantially all of the assets ("merger") of the issuer, the issuer will be deemed to have ceased operations for purposes of this section on the date the merger is consummated; provided, however, that in the case of a merger of an issuer or a series of an issuer ("Predecessor Issuer") with another issuer or a series of an issuer ("Successor Issuer"), the Predecessor Issuer will not be deemed to have ceased operations and the Successor Issuer will assume the obligations, fees, and redemption credits of the Predecessor Issuer incurred pursuant to section 24(f) of the Act and § 270.24e–2 (as in effect prior to October 11, 1997; see 17 CFR part 240 to end, revised as of April 1, 1997) if the Successor Issuer:

(1) Had no assets or liabilities, other than nominal assets or liabilities, and no operating history immediately prior to the merger;

(2) Acquired substantially all of the assets and assumed substantially all of the liabili-

ties and obligations of the Predecessor Issuer; and

(3) The merger is not designed to result in the Predecessor Issuer merging with, or substantially all of its assets being acquired by, an issuer (or a series of an issuer) that would not meet the conditions of paragraph (b)(1) of this section.

(c) *Counting days.* To determine the date on which Form 24F–2 must be filed with the Commission under paragraph (a) of this section, the first day of the 90–day period is the first calendar day of the fiscal year following the fiscal year for which the Form is to be filed. If the last day of the 90–day period falls on a Saturday, Sunday or federal holiday, the period ends on the first business day thereafter.

Note to paragraph (c): For example, a Form 24F–2 for a fiscal year ending on June 30 must be filed no later than September 28. If September 28 falls on a Saturday or Sunday, the Form must be filed on the following Monday.

§ 270.26a–1 Payment of Administrative Fees to the Depositor or Principal Underwriter of a Unit Investment Trust; Exemptive Relief for Separate Accounts

(a) For purposes of section 26(a)(2)(C) of the Act, payment of a fee to the depositor of or a principal underwriter for a registered unit investment trust, or to any affiliated person or agent of such depositor or underwriter (collectively, "depositor"), for bookkeeping or other administrative services provided to the trust shall be allowed the custodian or trustee ("trustee") as an expense, *Provided,* That such fee is an amount not greater than the expenses, without profit, (1) actually paid by such depositor directly attributable to the services provided and (2) increased by the services provided directly by such depositor, as determined in accordance with generally accepted accounting principles consistently applied.

(b) A registered separate account, and any depositor of or principal underwriter for such account, shall be exempt from the provisions of Sections 26(a) and 27(c)(2) of the Act with respect to any variable annuity contract participating in such account to the extent necessary to permit the deduction of any fee that would be allowed a trustee as an expense as provided in paragraph (a) of this section, *Provided,* That the standard used in paragraph (a) of this section shall be applied as follows: if the separate account reserves the right to increase the fee, the fee shall not be greater than the cost of the services to be provided for one year; if the fee is guaranteed not to increase for a specified period of time, the fee shall not be greater than the average expected cost of the services to be provided during the period of the guarantee.

§ 270.26a–2 Exemptions From Certain Provisions of Sections 26 and 27 for Registered Separate Accounts and Others Regarding Custodianship of and Deduction of Certain Fees and Charges From the Assets of Such Accounts

A registered separate account, and any depositor of or principal underwriter for such account, shall be exempt from the provisions of sections 26(a) and 27(c)(2) of the Act with respect to any variable annuity contract participating in such account to the extent necessary:

(a) To permit the insurance company that sponsors such account to hold the assets of the separate account and to hold such assets not pursuant to a trust indenture or other such instrument;

(b) To permit any separate account registered under the Act as a unit investment trust to hold the securities of any underlying portfolio companies in uncertificated form;

(c) To permit any separate account registered under the Act as a management investment company to hold its assets in any manner permitted by section 17(f) of the Act or any rules thereunder, and

(d) To permit the deduction from the assets of the separate account of amounts for premium taxes imposed by any State or other governmental entity and, if the separate account is registered under the Act as an open-end management investment company, and investment advisory fee.

§ 270.27a-1 Conditions for Compliance With and Exemptions From Certain Provisions of Section 27(a)(1) and Section 27(h)(1) of the Act for Certain Registered Separate Accounts

A registered separate account, and any depositor of or underwriter for such account, shall with respect to any variable annuity contract participating in such account, be deemed to satisfy the requirements of section 27(a)(1) and section 27(h)(1) of the Act if such contract provides for a sales load which will not exceed 9 per centum of the total payments to be made thereon as of a date not later than the end of the 12th year of such payments: *Provided,* That if a contract be issued for any stipulated shorter payment period the sales load under such contract shall not exceed 9 per centum of the total payments thereunder for such period.

§ 270.27a-2 Exemption From Section 27(a)(3) and Section 27(h)(3) of the Act for Certain Registered Separate Accounts

A registered separate account, and any depositor of or underwriter for such account, shall be exempt from paragraph (3) of section 27(a) and paragraph (3) of section 27(h) of the Act: *Provided,* That with respect to any variable annuity contract participating in such account the proportionate amount of sales load deducted from any payment during the contract period shall not exceed the proportionate amount deducted from any prior payment during the contract period.

§ 270.27a-3 Exemption From Section 27(a)(4) and Section 27(h)(5) of the Act for Certain Registered Separate Accounts

A registered separate account, and any depositor of or underwriter for such account, shall be exempt from paragraph (4) of section 27(a) of the Act and paragraph (5) of section 27(h) of the Act as to payments under any variable annuity contract participating in such account which (1) is purchased in connection with a plan which meets the requirements for qualification under section 401 of the Internal Revenue Code of 1954, as amended (Code), or the requirements for deduction of the employer's contributions under section 404(a)(2) of the Code, or (2) meets the requirements of section 403(b) of the Code, but such exemptions shall apply only to contributions or payments within the exclusion allowance for any employee under section 403(b) except as clause (3) hereof applies, or (3) permits no sales load deduction from any payment in excess of 9 per centum of such payment.

§ 270.27c-1 Exemption From Section 27(c)(1) and Section 27(d) of the Act During Annuity Payment Period of Variable Annuity Contracts Participating in Certain Registered Separate Accounts

A registered separate account, and any depositor of or underwriter for such account, shall, during the annuity payment period of variable annuity contracts participating in such account, be exempt from the requirement of paragraph (1) of section 27(c) of the Act that a periodic payment plan certificate be a redeemable security and from section 27(d) of the Act with respect to such contracts under which payments are being made based upon life contingencies.

§ 270.27d-1 Reserve Requirements for Principal Underwriters and Depositors to Carry Out the Obligations to Refund Charges Required by Section 27(d) and Section 27(f) of the Act

(a)(1) Every depositor of or principal underwriter for the issuer of a periodic payment plan certificate sold subject to section 27(d) or section 27(f) of the Act or both, shall deposit and maintain funds in a segregated trust account as a reserve and as security for the purpose of assuring the refund of charges required by sections 27(d) and 27(f) of the Act.

(2) The assets of such trust account may be held as cash or invested only in one or more of (i) government securities as defined in section 2(a)(16) of the Act (except equity securities) or (ii) negotiable certificates of deposit issued by a bank, as defined in section 2(a)(5) of the Act and having capital and surplus of at least $10 million: *Provided*, That no such investment may have a maturity of more than 5 years, no more than 50 percent of the assets may be invested in obligations having a maturity of more than 1 year, and certificates of deposit of a single issuer may not constitute more than 10 percent of the value of the assets in the account.

(3) Any income, gains, or losses from assets allocated to such account, whether or not realized, shall be credited to or charged against such account without regard to other income, gains, or losses of the depositor or principal underwriter.

(4) The assets of such trust account may be withdrawn only as permitted by paragraph (f) of this section and shall in no event be chargeable with liabilities arising out of any aspect of the business of the depositor or principal underwriter other than assuring the ability of the depositor or principal underwriter to refund the amounts required by such sections.

(b) For purposes of this section:

(1) "Excess sales load" on any payment is that portion of the sales load in excess of 15 percent of that payment.

(2) "Monthly payment" shall be the amount of the smallest monthly installment scheduled to be paid during the life of the plan. If payments are required or permitted to be made on a basis less frequently than monthly, an equivalent monthly payment shall be the amount determined by dividing the smallest minimum payment required or permitted in a payment period by the number of months included in such period.

(3) The assets in the segregated trust account shall be valued as follows: (i) With respect to securities for which market quotations are readily available, the market value of such securities; and (ii) with respect to other securities, fair value as determined in good faith by the depositor or principal underwriter.

(c) For every periodic payment plan certificate governed by section 27(d), the depositor or principal underwriter shall deposit into the segregated trust account not less than 45 percent of the excess sales load on each of the first six monthly payments or their equivalent.

(d) For all periodic payment plan certificates governed by section 27(d) which have not been surrendered in accordance with their terms, and for which the depositor or principal underwriter may be liable for the refund of any sales load, the depositor or principal underwriter shall maintain in the segregated trust account an amount equal to not less than 15% of the total refundable sales load on the payments made on those certificates. The depositor or principal underwriter shall also maintain in the segregated trust account such additional amounts as the Commission by order may require for the depositor or principal underwriter to carry out refund obligations pursuant to sections 27(d) and 27(f) of the Act.

(e) For every periodic payment plan certificate governed by section 27(f) of the Act, and for which the depositor or principal underwriter has no obligation to refund any excess sales load pursuant to section 27(d) of the Act, the depositor or principal underwriter shall deposit and maintain during the refund period, at least the following amounts in the segregated trust account:

(1) For certificates that require monthly payments of $100 or less, 20 percent of the difference between the gross payments made and the net amount invested;

(2) For certificates that require monthly payments in excess of $100 and for single payment plan certificates, 30 percent of the

difference between the gross payments made and the net amount invested;

(3) For certificates with respect to which the holder is entitled to receive the greater of the refund provided by section 27(f) (of the Act) or a refund of total payments and upon which a total of at least $1,000 has been paid, 100 percent of the difference between the gross payments made and net amount invested; and

(4) Such additional amounts as the Commission by order may require to carry out the obligation to refund charges pursuant to section 27(f) of the Act.

(f) Assets may be withdrawn from the segregated trust account by each depositor or principal underwriter:

(1) To refund excess sales load to a certificate holder exercising the right of surrender specified in section 27(d) of the Act; or

(2) To refund to a certificate holder exercising the right of withdrawal specified in section 27(f) of the Act the difference between the amount of his gross payments and the net amount invested; or

(3) For any other purpose: *Provided, however,* That such withdrawal shall not reduce the segregated trust account to an amount less than the sum of (i) 130 percent of the amount required to be maintained by paragraph (d) of this section, if any, and (ii) 100 percent of that amount required to be maintained by paragraph (e) of this section, if any.

(g) The minimum amounts required to be maintained by paragraphs (d) and (e) of this section shall be computed at least monthly. Any additional deposits required by paragraphs (d) or (e) of this section shall be made immediately after such computation, and any withdrawals permitted by paragraph (f)(3) of this section may be made only at such time.

(h) Nothing in this section shall be construed to prohibit a depositor or principal underwriter, acting as such for two or more registered investment companies issuing periodic payment plan certificates, from combining in a single segregated trust account the reserves for such companies required by this section.

(i) The refunds required to be made to certificate holders pursuant to sections 27(d) and 27(f) (of the Act) shall be paid in cash not more than 7 days from the date the certificate is received in proper form by the custodian bank or such other paying agent as may be designated under the periodic payment plan.

(j) Each depositor or principal underwriter shall file with the Commission, within the appropriate period of time specified, an Accounting of Segregated Trust Account. Form N–27D–1 (§ 274.127d–1 of this chapter) is hereby prescribed as such accounting form.

§ 270.27d–2 Insurance Company Undertaking in Lieu of Segregated Trust Account

(a) Any depositor of or principal underwriter for the issuer of a periodic payment plan certificate sold subject to section 27(d) or section 27(f) of the Act, or both, shall be exempt from the requirements of § 270.27d–1 if an insurance company (as defined in section 2(a)(17) of the Act) undertakes in writing to guarantee the performance of all obligations of such depositor or principal underwriter to refund charges under sections 27(d) and 27(f) of the Act and paragraph (b) of this section: *Provided, however,* That:

(1) Such insurance company at all times shall have (i) combined capital paid-up, gross paid in and contributed surplus and unassigned surplus, if a stock company, or (ii) unassigned surplus, if a mutual company, at least equal to the larger of (*a*) $1 million or (*b*) 200 percent of the amount of the total refund obligation of the depositor or underwriter pursuant to sections 27(d) and 27(f) (of the Act) less any liability reserve established by such insurance company to meet such obligations; and

(2) Such depositor or underwriter shall file or cause to be filed with the Commission

as an exhibit to the registration statement or any amendment thereto pursuant to the Securities Act of 1933 of the registered investment company issuing periodic payment plan certificates (i) a copy of such written undertaking, and any amendment thereto, (ii) an annual statement certified by a responsible officer of the insurance company indicating that at least on a monthly basis throughout its fiscal year the insurance company has met the requirements of the proviso in subparagraph (1) of this paragraph, and (iii) a Statement of Financial Condition (Balance Sheet) of the insurance company certified by an independent public accountant. Such balance sheet shall be filed at least annually, within 90 days after the close of the insurance company's fiscal year.

(b) The refunds required to be made to certificate holders pursuant to sections 27(d) and 27(f) (of the Act) shall be paid in cash not more than 7 days from the date the certificate is received in proper form by the custodian bank or such other paying agent as may be designated under the periodic payment plan.

§ 270.27e–1 Requirements for Notice to Be Mailed to Certain Purchasers of Periodic Payment Plan Certificates Sold Subject to Section 27(d) of the Act

(a) The notice required by section 27(e) of the Act shall be sent by first class mail and shall be accompanied by a written instruction sheet and a return form to be used in connection with the exercise of the surrender right described in the notice. No other written or graphic material may be included with such notice.

(b) In the event that regular payments throughout the first 18 months of the plan are required less frequently than monthly, such a notice shall be mailed to any certificate holder who has missed any payment or payments equal to or greater in amount than the amount of payments which, if missed, would have required the mailing of a notice if equal monthly payments had been required during such 15- or 18-month periods.

(c) Any payment not made within 31 days after it is due shall be deemed a missed payment whether or not an equivalent payment is made subsequently by the certificate holder.

(d) In the event any such notice is not mailed prior to 15 days before the expiration of the 18th month, the certificate holder shall have 15 days from the date such notice is mailed within which to exercise the right of surrender described therein. Nothing herein contained shall require a second notice to be mailed to any certificate holder who has been mailed a notice within 30 days following 15 months after the issuance of his certificate.

(e) Notwithstanding the requirements of section 27(e) of the Act, no notice need be mailed to a certificate holder if, at the time such notice would be required to be mailed, he would not be entitled to receive any refund of sales loading upon surrender of his certificate.

(f) Form N–27E–1 is hereby prescribed to inform certificate holders of their right to surrender their certificates pursuant to section 27(d) of the Act.

[Form N–27E–1 is omitted.]

§ 270.27f–1 Notice of Right of Withdrawal Required to Be Mailed to Periodic Payment Plan Certificate Holders and Exemption From Section 27(f) for Certain Periodic Payment Plan Certificates

(a) The notice and statement of charges (notice) required by section 27(f) of the Act shall be sent by first-class mail and shall be accompanied by a written instruction sheet and a return form to be used in connection with the exercise of the right of withdrawal described in the notice. Except for a confirmation slip, the plan certificate, and any notice required by applicable State law, no other written or graphic material may be included with such notice.

(b) The notice may be mailed by the issuer, the principal underwriter for, or the depositor of, the issuer or a recordkeeping agent for the issuer if the custodian bank has delegated the mailing of the notice to any of them or the issuer has been permitted to operate without a custodian bank by Commission order.

(c) Solely for purposes of section 27(f) of the Act, the postmark date on the envelope containing the certificate shall determine whether a certificate has been surrendered within the 45-day period.

(d) Form N–27F–1 is hereby prescribed to inform certificate holders, other than holders of plans upon which the amount of sales loan deducted from any payment does not exceed 9 percent of any payment and variable annuity contracts, of their withdrawal right pursuant to section 27(f) of the Act.

[Form N–27F–1 is omitted.]

§ 270.27g–1 Election to Be Governed by Section 27(h)

(a) If any registered investment company which issues or intends to issue a periodic payment plan certificate chooses to be governed by the provisions of section 27(h) (of the Act) rather than the provisions of sections 27(a) and (d) (of the Act), it shall signify such choice by filing with the Commission as an exhibit to its registration statement filed under the Securities Act of 1933 a written Notice of Election to be so governed.

(b) Any registered investment company issuing periodic payment plan certificates which has elected, in accordance with paragraph (a) of this section, to be governed by the provisions of section 27(h) of the Act may thereafter withdraw such election by filing with the Commission, in the manner specified for filing a Notice of Election, a written Notice of Withdrawal of Election: *Provided, however,* That no such withdrawal of election shall be made within 12 months of an election by such company under paragraph (a) of this section and, provided further that such company may not thereafter elect to be governed by the provisions of section 27(h) (of the Act) until an additional 12-month period has elapsed.

§ 270.27h–1 Exemptions From Section 27(h)(4) for Certain Payments

(a) For purposes of this section and section 27(h)(4) of the Act (1) "minimum monthly payment, or its equivalent," shall be the amount of the smallest monthly installment scheduled to be made during the life of the plan; and (2) "quarter" shall be the 3-month period which commences on the date a periodic payment plan is issued and each 3-month period thereafter.

(b) The provisions of section 27(h)(4) (of the Act) shall not apply to:

(1) That portion of the first payment on a periodic payment plan certificate which equals the amount of five minimum monthly payments: *Provided, however,* That the deduction for sales load on any other payments received during the first quarter after the issuance of the certificate may not exceed the sales load applicable to payments subsequent to the first 48 monthly payments or their equivalent;

(2) A payment or payments received in any subsequent quarter which equals the amount of three minimum monthly payments: *Provided, however,* That after an amount equivalent to three minimum monthly payments (not including payments of arrears) is received in any such subsequent quarter the deduction for sales load on any additional payments received in such quarter may not exceed the sales load applicable to payments subsequent to the first 48 monthly payments or their equivalent;

(3) Payments of arrears by a certificate holder who is delinquent in his payments; and

(4) Any payments made on a periodic payment plan certificate out of the proceeds of completion insurance received upon the death of the certificate holder.

§ 270.28b–1 Investment in Loans Partially or Wholly Guaranteed Under the Servicemen's Readjustment Act of 1944, as Amended

(a) The term "qualified investments" as used in section 28(b) of the Investment Company Act of 1940 shall include:

(1) Any loan, any portion of which is guaranteed under Title III of the Servicemen's Readjustment Act of 1944, as amended, and which is secured by a first lien on real estate: *Provided,* The amount of the loan not so guaranteed does not exceed 66⅔ percent of the reasonable value of such real estate as determined by proper appraisal made by an appraiser designated by the Administrator of Veterans' Affairs;

(2) Any secondary loan the full amount of which is guaranteed under section 505(a) of Title III of the above mentioned act and which is secured by a second lien on real estate: *Provided, however,* That any such loan shall be deemed a qualified investment only so long as (i) insurance policies are required to be procured and maintained in an amount sufficient to protect the security against the risks or hazards to which it may be subjected to the extent customary in the locality, and (ii) the loan shall remain guaranteed under Title III of the Servicemen's Readjustment Act of 1944, as amended, to the extent specified in subparagraph (1) or (2) of this paragraph, as the case may be.

(b) Loans made pursuant to this section shall be valued at the original principal amount of the loan less all payments made thereon which have been applied to the reduction of such principal amount.

§ 270.30a-1 Annual Reports for Unit Investment Trusts

Every registered unit investment trust shall file an annual report on Form N-SAR with respect to each calendar year not more than sixty calendar days after the close of each year. A registered unit investment trust that has filed a registration statement with the Commission registering its securities for the first time under the Securities Act of 1933 is relieved of this reporting obligation with respect to any reporting period or portion thereof prior to the date on which that registration statement becomes effective or is withdrawn.

§ 270.30a-2 Certification of Form N-CSR

(a) Each report filed on Form N-CSR (§§ 249.331 and 274.128 of this chapter) or Form N-Q (§§ 249.332 and 274.130 of this chapter) by a registered management investment company must include certifications in the form specified in Item 12(a)(2) of Form N-CSR or Item 3 of Form N-Q, as applicable, and such certifications must be filed as an exhibit to such report. Each principal executive and principal financial officer of the investment company, or persons performing similar functions, at the time of filing of the report must sign a certification.

(b) Each report on Form N-CSR filed by a registered management investment company under Section 13(a) or 15(d) of the Securities Exchange Act of 1934 (15 U.S.C. 78m(a) or 78o(d)) and that contains financial statements must be accompanied by the certifications required by Section 1350 of Chapter 63 of Title 18 of the United States Code (18 U.S.C. 1350) and such certifications must be furnished as an exhibit to such report as specified in Item 12(b) of Form N-CSR. Each principal executive and principal financial officer of the investment company (or equivalent thereof) must sign a certification. This requirement may be satisfied by a single certification signed by an investment company's principal executive and principal financial officers.

(c) A person required to provide a certification specified in paragraph (a) or (b) of this section may not have the certification signed on his or her behalf pursuant to a power of attorney or other form of confirming authority.

(d) The certification requirements of this section do not apply to XBRL-Related Documents, as defined in § 232.11 of this chapter.

§ 270.30a-3 Disclosure Controls and Procedures Related to Preparation of Required Filings

(a) Every registered management investment company, other than a small business investment company registered on Form N-5

(§§ 239.24 and 274.5 of this chapter), must maintain disclosure controls and procedures (as defined in paragraph (c) of this section) and internal control over financial reporting (as defined in paragraph (d) of this section).

(b) Each such registered management investment company's management must evaluate, with the participation of the company's principal executive and principal financial officers, or persons performing similar functions, the effectiveness of the company's disclosure controls and procedures, within the 90-day period prior to the filing date of each report on Form N–CSR (§§ 249.331 and 274.128 of this chapter) and Form N–Q (§§ 249.332 and 274.130 of this chapter).

(c) For purposes of this section, the term *disclosure controls and procedures* means controls and other procedures of a registered management investment company that are designed to ensure that information required to be disclosed by the investment company on Form N–CSR (§§ 249.331 and 274.128 of this chapter) and Form N–Q (§§ 249.332 and 274.130 of this chapter) is recorded, processed, summarized, and reported within the time periods specified in the Commission's rules and forms. Disclosure controls and procedures include, without limitation, controls and procedures designed to ensure that information required to be disclosed by an investment company in the reports that it files or submits on Form N–CSR and Form N–Q is accumulated and communicated to the investment company's management, including its principal executive and principal financial officers, or persons performing similar functions, as appropriate to allow timely decisions regarding required disclosure.

(d) The term *internal control over financial reporting* is defined as a process designed by, or under the supervision of, the registered management investment company's principal executive and principal financial officers, or persons performing similar functions, and effected by the company's board of directors, management, and other personnel, to provide reasonable assurance regarding the reliability of financial reporting and the preparation of financial statements for external purposes in accordance with generally accepted accounting principles and includes those policies and procedures that:

(1) Pertain to the maintenance of records that in reasonable detail accurately and fairly reflect the transactions and dispositions of the assets of the investment company;

(2) Provide reasonable assurance that transactions are recorded as necessary to permit preparation of financial statements in accordance with generally accepted accounting principles, and that receipts and expenditures of the investment company are being made only in accordance with authorizations of management and directors of the investment company; and

(3) Provide reasonable assurance regarding prevention or timely detection of unauthorized acquisition, use, or disposition of the investment company's assets that could have a material effect on the financial statements.

§ 270.30b1–1 Semi-annual Report for Registered Management Investment Companies

Every registered management investment company shall file a semi-annual report on Form N–SAR (§ 274.101 of this chapter) not more than sixty calendar days after the close of each fiscal year and fiscal second quarter. A registered management investment company that has filed a registration statement with the Commission registering its securities for the first time under the Securities Act of 1933 is relieved of this reporting obligation with respect to any reporting period or portion thereof prior to the date on which that registration statement becomes effective or is withdrawn.

§ 270.30b1–2 Semi-Annual Report for Totally-Owned Registered Management Investment Company Subsidiary of Registered Management Investment Company

Notwithstanding the provisions of rules 30a–1 and 30b1–1, a registered investment company that is a totally-owned subsidiary of a registered management investment company need not file a semi-annual report on Form N–SAR if financial information with respect to that subsidiary is reported in the parent's semi-annual report on Form N–SAR.

§ 270.30b1-3 Transition Reports

Every registered management investment company filing reports on Form N–SAR that changes its fiscal year end shall file a report on Form N–SAR not more than 60 calendar days after the later of either the close of the transition period or the date of the determination to change the fiscal year end which report shall not cover a period longer than six months.

§ 270.30b1-4 Report of Proxy Voting Record

Every registered management investment company, other than a small business investment company registered on Form N–5 (§§ 239.24 and 274.5 of this chapter), shall file an annual report on Form N–PX (§ 274.129 of this chapter) not later than August 31 of each year, containing the registrant's proxy voting record for the most recent twelve-month period ended June 30.

§ 270.30b1-5 Quarterly Report

Every registered management investment company, other than a small business investment company registered on Form N–5 (§§ 239.24 and 274.5 of this chapter), shall file a quarterly report on Form N–Q (§ 249.332 and 274.130 of this chapter) not more than 60 days after the close of the first and third quarters of each fiscal year. A registered management investment company that has filed a registration statement with the Commission registering its securities for the first time under the Securities Act of 1933 is relieved of this reporting obligation with respect to any reporting period or portion thereof prior to the date on which that registration statement becomes effective or is withdrawn.

§ 270.30b2-1 Filing of Reports to Stockholders

(a) Every registered management investment company shall file a report on Form N–CSR (§§ 249.331 and 274.128 of this chapter) not later than 10 days after the transmission to stockholders of any report that is required to be transmitted to stockholders under § 270.30e-1.

(b) A registered investment company shall file with the Commission a copy of every periodic or interim report or similar communication containing financial statements that is transmitted by or on behalf of such registered investment company to any class of such company's security holders and that is not required to be filed with the Commission under paragraph (a) of this section. The filing shall be made not later than 10 days after the transmission to security holders.

§ 270.30d-1 Filing of Copies of Reports to Shareholders

A registered management investment company, other than a small business investment company registered on Form N–5 (§§ 239.24 and 274.5 of this chapter), that is required to file annual and quarterly reports pursuant to section 13(a) or 15(d) of the Securities Exchange Act of 1934 (15 U.S.C. 78m(a) or 78o(d)) shall satisfy its requirement to file such reports by the filing, in accordance with the rules and procedures specified therefor, of reports on Form N–CSR (§§ 249.331 and 274.128 of this chapter) and Form N–Q (§§ 249.332 and 274.130 of this chapter). A registered unit investment trust or a small business investment company registered on Form N–5 that is required to file annual and quarterly reports pursuant to section 13(a) or 15(d) of the Securities Exchange Act of 1934 shall satisfy its requirement to file such reports by the filing, in accordance with the rules and procedures specified therefor, of reports on Form N–SAR (§§ 249.330 and 274.101 of this chapter).

§ 270.30e–1 Reports to Stockholders of Management Companies

(a) Every registered management company shall transmit to each stockholder of record, at least semi-annually, a report containing the information required to be included in such reports by the company's registration statement form under the 1940 Act, except that the initial report of a newly registered company shall be made as of a date not later than the close of the fiscal year or half-year occurring on or after the date on which the company's notification of registration under the 1940 Act is filed with the Commission.

(b) If any matter was submitted during the period covered by the shareholder report to a vote of shareholders, through the solicitation of proxies or otherwise, furnish the following information:

(1) The date of the meeting and whether it was an annual or special meeting.

(2) If the meeting involved the election of directors, the name of each director elected at the meeting and the name of each other director whose term of office as a director continued after the meeting.

(3) A brief description of each matter voted upon at the meeting and the number of votes cast for, against or withheld, as well as the number of abstentions and broker non-votes as to each such matter, including a separate tabulation with respect to each matter of nominee for office.

Instruction. The solicitation of any authorization or consent (other than a proxy to vote at a shareholders' meeting) with respect to any matter shall be deemed a submission of such matter to a vote of shareholders within the meaning of this paragraph (b).

(c) Each report shall be transmitted within 60 days after the close of the period for which such report is being made.

(d) An open-end company may transmit a copy of its currently effective prospectus or Statement of Additional Information, or both, under the Securities Act, in place of any report required to be transmitted to shareholders by this section, provided that the prospectus or Statement of Additional Information, or both, include all the information that would otherwise be required to be contained in the report by this section. Such prospectus or Statement of Additional Information, or both, shall be transmitted within 60 days after the close of the period for which the report is being made.

(e) The period of time within which any report prescribed by this rule shall be transmitted may be extended by the Commission upon written request showing good cause therefor. Section 270.0–5 shall not apply to such requests.

(f)(1) A company will be considered to have transmitted a report to shareholders who share an address if:

(i) The company transmits a report to the shared address;

(ii) The company addresses the report to the shareholders as a group (for example, "ABC Fund [or Corporation] Shareholders," "Jane Doe and Household," "The Smith Family") or to each of the shareholders individually (for example, "John Doe and Richard Jones"); and

(iii) The shareholders consent in writing to delivery of one report.

(2) The company need not obtain written consent from a shareholder under paragraph (f)(1)(iii) of this section if all of the following conditions are met:

(i) The shareholder has the same last name as the other shareholders, or the company reasonably believes that the shareholders are members of the same family;

(ii) The company has transmitted a notice to the shareholder at least 60 days before the company begins to rely on this section concerning transmission of reports to that shareholder. The notice must be a separate written statement and:

(A) State that only one report will be delivered to the shared address unless the company receives contrary instructions;

(B) Include a toll-free telephone number or be accompanied by a reply form that is pre-addressed with postage provided, that the shareholder can use to notify the company that he or she wishes to receive a separate report;

(C) State the duration of the consent;

(D) Explain how a shareholder can revoke consent;

(E) State that the company will begin sending individual copies to a shareholder within 30 days after the company receives revocation of the shareholder's consent; and

(F) Contain the following prominent statement, or similar clear and understandable statement, in bold-face type: "Important Notice Regarding Delivery of Shareholder Documents." This statement also must appear on the envelope in which the notice is delivered. Alternatively, if the notice is delivered separately from other communications to investors, this statement may appear either on the notice or on the envelope in which the notice is delivered;

Note to paragraph (f)(2)(ii): The notice should be written in plain English. See § 230.421(d)(2) of this chapter for a discussion of plain English principles.

(iii) The company has not received the reply form or other notification indicating that the shareholder wishes to continue to receive an individual copy of the report, within 60 days after the company sent the notice; and

(iv) The company transmits the report to a post office box or to a residential street address. The company can assume a street address is a residence unless it has information that indicates it is a business.

(3) At least once a year, the company must explain to shareholders who have consented under paragraph (f)(1)(iii) or paragraph (f)(2) of this section how they can revoke their consent. The explanation must be reasonably designed to reach these investors. If a shareholder, orally or in writing, revokes consent to delivery of one report to a shared address, the company must begin sending individual copies to that shareholder within 30 days after the company receives the revocation.

(4) For purposes of this section, *address* means a street address, a post office box number, an electronic mail address, a facsimile telephone number, or other similar destination to which paper or electronic documents are transmitted, unless otherwise provided in this section. If the company has reason to believe that the address is a street address of a multiunit building, the address must include the unit number.

§ 270.30e-2 Reports to Shareholders of Unit Investment Trusts

(a) At least semiannually every registered unit investment trust substantially all the assets of which consist of securities issued by a management company must transmit to each shareholder of record (including record holders of periodic payment plan certificates), a report containing all the applicable information and financial statements or their equivalent, required by § 270.30e-1 to be included in reports of the management company for the same fiscal period. Each of these reports must be transmitted within the period allowed the management company by § 270.30e-1 for transmitting reports to its stockholders.

(b) Any report required by this section will be considered transmitted to a shareholder of record if the unit investment trust satisfies the conditions set forth in § 270.30e-1(f) with respect to that shareholder.

§ 270.30h-1 Applicability of Section 16 of the Exchange Act to Section 30(h)

(a) The filing of any statement prescribed under section 16(a) of the Securities Exchange Act of 1934 (15 U.S.C. 78p(a)) shall satisfy the corresponding requirements of section 30(h) of the Act (15 U.S.C. 80a-29(h)).

(b) The rules under section 16 of the Securities Exchange Act of 1934 (15 U.S.C. 78p) shall apply to any duty, liability or prohibition imposed with respect to a transaction involving any security of a registered closed-end company under section 30(h) of the Act (15 U.S.C. 80a–29(h)).

(c) No statements need be filed pursuant to section 30(h) of the Act (15 U.S.C. 80a–29(h)) by an affiliated person of an investment adviser in his or her capacity as such if such person is solely an employee, other than an officer, of such investment adviser.

§ 270.31a–1 Records to Be Maintained by Registered Investment Companies, Certain Majority-Owned Subsidiaries Thereof, and Other Persons Having Transactions With Registered Investment Companies

(a) Every registered investment company, and every underwriter, broker, dealer, or investment adviser which is a majority-owned subsidiary of such a company, shall maintain and keep current the accounts, books, and other documents relating to its business which constitute the record forming the basis for financial statements required to be filed pursuant to section 30 of the Investment Company Act of 1940 and of the auditor's certificates relating thereto.

(b) Every registered investment company shall maintain and keep current the following books, accounts, and other documents:

(1) Journals (or other records of original entry) containing an itemized daily record in detail of all purchases and sales of securities (including sales and redemptions of its own securities), all receipts and deliveries of securities (including certificate numbers if such detail is not recorded by custodian or transfer agent), all receipts and disbursements of cash and all other debits and credits. Such records shall show for each such transaction the name and quantity of securities, the unit and aggregate purchase or sale price, commission paid, the market on which effected, the trade date, the settlement date, and the name of the person through or from whom purchased or received or to whom sold or delivered. In the case of a money market fund, also identify the provider of any Demand Feature or Guarantee (as defined in § 270.2a–7(a)(8) or § 270.2a–7(a)(15) respectively) and give a brief description of the nature of the Demand Feature or Guarantee (e.g., unconditional demand feature, conditional demand feature, letter of credit, or bond insurance) and, in a subsidiary portfolio investment record, provide the complete legal name and accounting and other information (including sufficient information to calculate coupons, accruals, maturities, puts, and calls) necessary to identify value, and account for each investment.

(2) General and auxiliary ledgers (or other records) reflecting all assets, liability, reserve, capital, income and expense accounts, including:

(i) Separate ledger accounts (or other records) reflecting the following:

(*a*) Securities in transfer; (*b*) Securities in physical possession; (*c*) Securities borrowed and securities loaned; (*d*) Monies borrowed and monies loaned (together with a record of the collateral therefor and substitutions in such collateral); (*e*) Dividends and interest received; (*f*) Dividends receivable and interest accrued.

Instruction. (*a*) and (*b*) of this subdivision shall be stated in terms of securities quantities only; (*c*) and (*d*) of this subdivision shall be stated in dollar amounts and securities quantities as appropriate; (*e*) and (*f*) of this subdivision shall be stated in dollar amounts only.

(ii) Separate ledger accounts (or other records) for each portfolio security, showing (as of trade dates) (*a*) the quantity and unit and aggregate price for each purchase, sale, receipt, and delivery of securities and commodities for such accounts, and (*b*) all other debits and credits for such accounts. Securities positions and money balances in such ledger accounts (or other records) shall be brought forward periodically but not less frequently than at the end of fiscal quarters. Any portfolio security, the salability of which is conditioned, shall be so noted. A memorandum record shall be available setting forth, with respect to each portfolio security account, the amount and declaration ex-dividend, and payment dates of each dividend declared thereon.

(iii) Separate ledger accounts (or other records) for each broker-dealer bank or other person with or through which transactions in portfolio securities are effected, showing each purchase or sale of securities with or through such persons, including details as to the date of the purchase or sale, the quantity and unit and aggregate price of such securities, and the commissions or other compensation paid to such persons. Purchases or sales effected during the same day at the same price may be aggregated.

(iv) Separate ledger accounts (or other records), which may be maintained by a transfer agent or registrar, showing for each shareholder of record of the investment company the number of shares of capital stock of the company held. In respect of share accumulation accounts (arising from periodic investment plans, dividend reinvestment plans, deposit of issued shares by the owner thereof, etc.), details shall be available as to the dates and number of shares of each accumulation, and except with respect to already issued shares deposited by the owner thereof, prices of each such accumulation.

(3) A securities record or ledger reflecting separately for each portfolio security as of trade date all "long" and "short" positions carried by the investment company for its own account and showing the location of all securities long and the off-setting position to all securities short. The record called for by this paragraph shall not be required in circumstances under which all portfolio securities are maintained by a bank or banks or a member or members of a national securities exchange as custodian under a custody agreement or as agent for such custodian.

(4) Corporate charters, certificates of incorporation or trust agreements, and by-laws, and minute books of stockholders' and directors' or trustees' meetings; and minute books of directors' or trustees' committee and advisory board or advisory committee meetings.

(5) A record of each brokerage order given by or in behalf of the investment company for, or in connection with, the purchase or sale of securities, whether executed or unexecuted. Such record shall include the name of the broker, the terms and conditions of the order and of any modification or cancellation thereof, the time of entry or cancellation, the price at which executed, and the time of receipt of report of execution. The record shall indicate the name of the person who placed the order in behalf of the investment company.

(6) A record of all other portfolio purchases or sales showing details comparable to those prescribed in subparagraph (5) of this paragraph.

(7) A record of all puts, calls, spreads, straddles, and other options in which the investment company has any direct or indirect interest or which the investment company has granted or guaranteed; and a record of any contractual commitments to purchase, sell, receive or deliver securities or other property (but not including open orders placed with broker-dealers for the purchase or sale of securities, which may be cancelled by the company on notices without penalty or cost of any kind); containing, at least, an identification of the security, the number of units involved, the option price, the date of maturity, the date of issuance, and the person to whom issued.

(8) A record of the proof of money balances in all ledger accounts (except shareholder accounts), in the form of trial balances. Such trial balances shall be prepared currently at least once a month.

(9) A record for each fiscal quarter, which shall be completed within ten days after the end of such quarter, showing specifically the basis or bases upon which the allocation of orders for the purchase and sale of portfolio securities to named brokers or dealers and the division of brokerage commissions or other compensation on such purchase and sale orders among named persons were made during such quarter. The record shall indicate the consideration given to *(i)* sales of shares of the investment company by brokers or dealers, *(ii)* the supplying of services or benefits by brokers or dealers to the investment company, its investment adviser or principal underwriter or any persons affiliated therewith, and *(iii)* any other considerations other than the technical qualifications of the brokers and dealers as such. The record shall show the nature of the services or benefits made available, and shall describe in detail the application of any general or specific formula or other determinant used in arriving at such allocation of purchase and sale orders and such division of brokerage commissions or other compensation. The record shall also include the identities of the persons responsible for the determination of such allocation and such division of brokerage commissions or other compensation.

(10) A record in the form of an appropriate memorandum identifying the person or persons, committees, or groups authorizing the purchase or sale of portfolio securities. Where an authorization is made by a committee or group, a record shall be kept of the names of its members who participated in the authorization. There shall be retained as part of the record required by this paragraph any memorandum, recommendation, or instruction supporting or authorizing the purchase or sale of portfolio securities. The requirements of this paragraph are applicable to the extent they are not met by compliance with the requirements of subparagraph (4) of this paragraph.

(11) Files of all advisory material received from the investment adviser, any advisory board or advisory committee, or any other persons from whom the investment company accepts investment advice, other than material which is furnished solely through uniform publications distributed generally.

(12) The term "other records" as used in the expressions "journals (or other records of original entry)" and "ledger accounts (or other records)" shall be construed to include, where appropriate, copies of voucher checks, confirmations, or similar documents which reflect the information required by the applicable rule or rules in appropriate sequence and in permanent form, including similar records developed by the use of automatic data processing systems.

(c) Every underwriter, broker, or dealer which is a majority-owned subsidiary of a registered investment company shall maintain in the form prescribed therein such accounts, books and other documents as are required to be maintained by brokers and dealers by rule adopted under section 17 of the Securities Exchange Act of 1934.

(d) Every depositor of any registered investment company, and every principal underwriter for any registered investment company other than a closed-end investment company, shall maintain such accounts, books and other documents as are required to be maintained by brokers and dealers by the rule adopted under section 17 of the Securities Exchange Act of 1934, to the extent such records are necessary or appropriate to record such person's transactions with such registered investment company.

(e) Every investment adviser which is a majority-owned subsidiary of a registered investment company shall maintain in the form prescribed therein such accounts, books and other documents as are required to be maintained by registered investment advisers by rule adopted under section 204 of the Investment Advisers Act of 1940.

(f) Every investment adviser not a majority-owned subsidiary of a registered investment company shall maintain such accounts, books and other documents as are required to be maintained by registered investment advisers by rule adopted under section 204 of the Investment Advisers Act of 1940, to the extent such records are necessary or appropriate to record such person's transactions with such registered investment company.

§ 270.31a–2 Records to Be Preserved by Registered Investment Companies, Certain Majority-Owned Subsidiaries Thereof, and Other Persons Having Transactions With Registered Investment Companies

(a) Every registered investment company shall:

(1) Preserve permanently, the first two years in an easily accessible place, all books and records required to be made pursuant to subparagraphs (1) through (4) of § 270.31a–1(b);

(2) Preserve for a period not less than six years from the end of the fiscal year in which any transactions occurred, the first two years in an easily accessible place, all books and records required to be made pursuant to subparagraphs (5) through (12) or § 270.31a–1(b) and all vouchers, memoranda, correspondence, checkbooks, bank statements, cancelled checks, cash reconciliations, cancelled stock certificates, and all schedules evidencing and supporting each computation of net asset value of the investment company shares, and other documents required to be maintained by § 270.31a–1(a) and not enumerated in § 270.31a–1(b).

(3) Preserve for a period not less than 6 years from the end of the fiscal year last used, the first 2 years in an easily accessible place, any advertisement, pamphlet, circular, form letter or other sales literature addressed to or intended for distribution to prospective investors;

(4) Preserve for a period not less than six years, the first two years in an easily accessible place, any record of the initial determination that a director is not an interested person of the investment company, and each subsequent determination that the director is not an interested person of the investment company. These records must include any questionnaire and any other document used to determine that a director is not an interested person of the company;

(5) Preserve for a period not less than six years, the first two years in an easily accessible place, any materials used by the disinterested directors of an investment company to determine that a person who is acting as legal counsel to those directors is an independent legal counsel; and

(6) Preserve for a period not less than six years, the first two years in an easily accessible place, any documents or other written information considered by the directors of the investment company pursuant to section 15(c) of the Act (15 U.S.C. § 80a–15(c)) in approving the terms or renewal of a contract or agreement between the company and an investment adviser.

(b) Every underwriter, broker, or dealer which is a majority-owned subsidiary of a registered investment company shall preserve for the periods prescribed therein such accounts, books and other documents as are required to be preserved by brokers and dealers by rule adopted under section 17 of the Securities Exchange Act of 1934.

(c) Every depositor of any registered investment company, and every principal underwriter for any registered investment company other than a closed-end company, shall preserve for a period of not less than six years such accounts, books and other documents as are required to be maintained by brokers and dealers by rule adopted under section 17 of the Securities Exchange Act of 1934, to the extent such records are necessary or appropriate to record such person's transactions with such registered investment company.

(d) Every investment adviser which is a majority-owned subsidiary of a registered investment company shall preserve for the periods prescribed therein such accounts, books and other documents as are required to be preserved by investment advisers by rule adopted under section 204 of the Investment Advisers Act of 1940.

(e) Every investment adviser not a majority-owned subsidiary of a registered investment company shall preserve for a period of not less than six years such accounts, books and other documents as are required to be maintained by registered investment advisers by rule adopted under section 204 of the Investment Advisers Act of 1940, to the extent such records are necessary or appropriate to record such person's transactions with such registered investment company.

(f) *Micrographic and electronic storage permitted.*—(1) *General.* The records required to be maintained and preserved under this part may be maintained and preserved for the required time by, or on behalf of, an investment company on:

(i) Micrographic media, including microfilm, microfiche, or any similar medium; or

(ii) Electronic storage media, including any digital storage medium or system that meets the terms of this section.

(2) *General requirements.* The investment company, or person that maintains and preserves records on its behalf, must:

(i) Arrange and index the records in a way that permits easy location, access, and retrieval of any particular record;

(ii) Provide promptly any of the following that the Commission (by its examiners or other representatives) or the directors of the company may request:

(A) A legible, true, and complete copy of the record in the medium and format in which it is stored;

(B) A legible, true, and complete printout of the record; and

(C) Means to access, view, and print the records; and

(iii) Separately store, for the time required for preservation of the original record, a duplicate copy of the record on any medium allowed by this section.

(3) *Special requirements for electronic storage media.* In the case of records on electronic storage media, the investment company, or person that maintains and preserves records on its behalf, must establish and maintain procedures:

(i) To maintain and preserve the records, so as to reasonably safeguard them from loss, alteration, or destruction;

(ii) To limit access to the records to properly authorized personnel, the directors of the investment company, and the Commission (including its examiners and other representatives); and

(iii) To reasonably ensure that any reproduction of a non-electronic original record on electronic storage media is complete, true, and legible when retrieved.

(4) Notwithstanding the provisions of paragraphs (a) through (e) of this section, any record, book or other document may be destroyed in accordance with a plan previously submitted to and approved by the Commission. A plan shall be deemed to have been approved by the Commission if notice to the contrary has not been received within 90 days after submission of the plan to the Commission.

§ 270.31a-3 Records Prepared or Maintained by Other Than Person Required to Maintain and Preserve Them

(a) If the records required to be maintained and preserved pursuant to the provisions of §§ 270.31a-1 and 270.31a-2 are prepared or maintained by others on behalf of the person required to maintain and preserve such records, the person required to maintain and preserve such records shall obtain from such other person an agreement in writing to the effect that such records are the property of the person required to maintain and preserve such records and will be surrendered promptly on request.

(b) In cases where a bank or member of a national securities exchange acts as custodian, transfer agent, or dividend disbursing agent, compliance with this section shall be considered to have been met if such bank or exchange member agrees in writing to make any records relating to such service available upon request and to preserve for the periods prescribed in § 270.31a-2 any such records as are required to be maintained by § 270.31a-1.

§ 270.32a-1 Exemption of Certain Companies From Affiliation Provisions of Section 32(a)

A registered investment company shall be exempt from the provisions of paragraph (1) of section 32(a) of the act, insofar as said paragraph requires that independent public accountants for such company be selected by a majority of certain members of the board of directors, if:

(a) Such company meets the conditions of paragraphs (1) to (8), inclusive, of section 10(d) of the act; and

(b) Such accounts are selected by a majority of all the members of the board of directors.

§ 270.32a-2 Exemption for Initial Period From Vote of Security Holders on Independent Public Accountant for Certain Registered Separate Accounts

(a) A registered separate account shall be exempt from the requirement under paragraph (2) of section 32(a) of the Act that selection of an independent public accountant shall have been submitted for ratification or rejection at the next succeeding annual meeting of security owners, subject to the following conditions:

(1) Such registered separate account qualifies for exemption from section 14(a) of the Act pursuant to § 270.14a-2, or is exempt therefrom by order of the Commission upon application; and

(2) The selection of such accountant shall be submitted for ratification or rejection to variable annuity contract owners at their first meeting after the effective date of the registration statement under the Securities Act of 1933, as amended, relating to contracts participating in such account: *Provided,* That such meeting shall take place within 1 year after such effective date, unless the time for the holding of such meeting shall be extended by the Commission upon written request showing good cause therefor.

§ 270.32a-3 Exemption From Provision of Section 32(a)(1) Regarding the Time Period During Which a Registered Management Investment Company Must Select an Independent Public Accountant

(a) A registered management investment company ("company") organized in a jurisdiction that does not require it to hold regular annual meetings of its stockholders, and which does not hold a regular annual stockholders' meeting in a given fiscal year, shall be exempt in that fiscal year from the requirement of section 32(a)(1) of the Act that the independent public accountant ("accountant") be selected at a board of directors meeting held within 30 days before or after the beginning of the fiscal year or before the annual meeting of stockholders in that year, *provided,* that such company is either:

(1) In a set of investment companies as defined in paragraph (b) of this rule, if not all the members of such set have an identical fiscal year end and if such company selects an accountant at a board of directors meeting held within 90 days before or after the beginning of that fiscal year; or

(2) Not in a set of investment companies, or is in a set, each of whose members has the same fiscal year end, and if such company selects an accountant at a board of directors meeting held within 30 days before or 90 days after the beginning of that fiscal year.

(b) For purposes of this rule, "set of investment companies" means any two or more registered management investment companies that hold themselves out to investors as related companies for purposes of investment and investor services, and

(1) That have a common investment adviser or principal underwriter, or

(2) If the investment adviser or principal underwriter of one of the companies is an affiliated person as defined in section 2(a)(3)(C) of the Act of the investment adviser or principal underwriter of each of the other companies.

§ 270.32a–4 Independent Audit Committees

A registered management investment company or a registered face-amount certificate company is exempt from the requirement of section 32(a)(2) of the Act (15 U.S.C. 80a–32(a)(2)) that the selection of the company's independent public accountant be submitted for ratification or rejection at the next succeeding annual meeting of shareholders, if:

(a) The company's board of directors has established a committee, composed solely of directors who are not interested persons of the company, that has responsibility for overseeing the fund's accounting and auditing processes ("audit committee");

(b) The company's board of directors has adopted a charter for the audit committee setting forth the committee's structure, duties, powers, and methods of operation or set forth such provisions in the fund's charter or bylaws; and

(c) The company maintains and preserves permanently in an easily accessible place a copy of the audit committee's charter and any modification to the charter.

§ 270.34b–1 Sales Literature Deemed to Be Misleading

Any advertisement, pamphlet, circular, form letter, or other sales literature addressed to or intended for distribution to prospective investors that is required to be filed with the Commission by Section 24(b) of the Act ("sales literature") shall have omitted to state a fact necessary in order to make the statements made therein not materially misleading unless the sales literature includes the information specified in paragraphs (a) and (b) of this section.

Note to introductory text of § 270.34b–1: The fact that the sales literature includes the information specified in paragraphs (a) and (b) of this section does not relieve the investment company, underwriter, or dealer of any obligations with respect to the sales literature under the antifraud provisions of the federal securities laws. For guidance about factors to be weighed in determining whether statements, representations, illustrations, and descriptions contained in investment company sales literature are misleading, *see* § 230.156 of this chapter.

(a) Sales literature for a money market fund shall contain the information required by paragraph (b)(4) of § 230.482 of this chapter, presented in the manner required by paragraph (b)(5) of § 230.482 of this chapter.

(b)(1) Except as provided in paragraph (b)(3) of this section:

(i) In any sales literature that contains performance data for an investment company, include the disclosure required by paragraph (b)(3) of § 230.482 of this chapter, presented in the manner required by paragraph (b)(5) of § 230.482 of this chapter.

(ii) In any sales literature for a money market fund:

(A) Accompany any quotation of yield or similar quotation purporting to demonstrate the income earned or distributions made by the money market fund with a quotation of current yield specified by paragraph (e)(1)(i) of § 230.482 of this chapter;

(B) Accompany any quotation of the money market fund's tax equivalent yield or tax equivalent effective yield with a quotation of current yield as specified in § 230.482(e)(1)(iii) of this chapter; and

(C) Accompany any quotation of the money market fund's total return with a quotation of the money market fund's current yield specified in paragraph (e)(1)(i) of § 230.482 of this chapter. Place the quotations of total return and current yield next to each other, in the same size print, and if there is a material difference between the quoted total return and the quoted current yield, include a statement that the yield quotation more closely reflects the current earnings of the money market fund than the total return quotation.

(iii) In any sales literature for an investment company other than a money market fund that contains performance data:

(A) Include the total return information required by paragraph (d)(3) of § 230.482 of this chapter;

(B) Accompany any quotation of performance adjusted to reflect the effect of taxes (not including a quotation of tax equivalent yield or other similar quotation purporting to demonstrate the tax equivalent yield earned or distributions made by the company) with the quotations of total return specified by paragraph (d)(4) of § 230.482 of this chapter;

(C) If the sales literature (other than sales literature for a company that is permitted under § 270.35d-1(a)(4) to use a name suggesting that the company's distributions are exempt from federal income tax or from both federal and state income tax) represents or implies that the company is managed to limit or control the effect of taxes on company performance, include the quotations of total return specified by paragraph (d)(4) of § 230.482 of this chapter;

(D) Accompany any quotation of yield or similar quotation purporting to demonstrate the income earned or distributions made by the company with a quotation of current yield specified by paragraph (d)(1) of § 230.482 of this chapter; and

(E) Accompany any quotation of tax equivalent yield or other similar quotation purporting to demonstrate the tax equivalent yield earned or distributions made by the company with a quotation of tax equivalent yield specified in paragraph (d)(2) and current yield specified by paragraph (d)(1) of § 230.482 of this chapter.

(2) Any performance data included in sales literature under paragraphs (b)(1)(ii) or (iii) of this section must meet the currentness requirements of paragraph (g) of § 230.482 of this chapter.

(3) The requirements specified in paragraph (b)(1) of this section shall not apply to any quarterly, semi-annual, or annual report to shareholders under Section 30 of the Act (15 U.S.C. 80a-29) containing performance data for a period commencing no earlier than the first day of the period covered by the report; nor shall the requirements of paragraphs (d)(3)(ii), (d)(4)(ii), and (g) of § 230.482 of this chapter apply to any such periodic report containing any other performance data.

Note: Sales literature (except that of a money market fund) containing a quotation of yield or tax equivalent yield must also contain the total return information. In the case of sales literature, the currentness provisions apply from the date of distribution and not the date of submission for publication.

§ 270.35d-1 Investment Company Names

(a) For purposes of section 35(d) of the Act (15 U.S.C. 80a-34(d)), a materially deceptive and misleading name of a Fund includes:

(1) *Names suggesting guarantee or approval by the United States government.* A name suggesting that the Fund or the secu-

rities issued by it are guaranteed, sponsored, recommended, or approved by the United States government or any United States government agency or instrumentality, including any name that uses the words "guaranteed" or "insured" or similar terms in conjunction with the words "United States" or "U.S. government."

(2) *Names suggesting investment in certain investments or industries.* A name suggesting that the Fund focuses its investments in a particular type of investment or investments, or in investments in a particular industry or group of industries, unless:

(i) The Fund has adopted a policy to invest, under normal circumstances, at least 80% of the value of its Assets in the particular type of investments, or in investments in the particular industry or industries, suggested by the Fund's name; and

(ii) Either the policy described in paragraph (a)(2)(i) of this section is a fundamental policy under section 8(b)(3) of the Act (15 U.S.C. 80a–8(b)(3)), or the Fund has adopted a policy to provide the Fund's shareholders with at least 60 days prior notice of any change in the policy described in paragraph (a)(2)(i) of this section that meets the requirements of paragraph (c) of this section.

(3) *Names suggesting investment in certain countries or geographic regions.* A name suggesting that the Fund focuses its investments in a particular country or geographic region, unless:

(i) The Fund has adopted a policy to invest, under normal circumstances, at least 80% of the value of its Assets in investments that are tied economically to the particular country or geographic region suggested by its name;

(ii) The Fund discloses in its prospectus the specific criteria used by the Fund to select these investments; and

(iii) Either the policy described in paragraph (a)(3)(i) of this section is a fundamental policy under section 8(b)(3) of the Act (15 U.S.C. 80a–8(b)(3)), or the Fund has adopted a policy to provide the Fund's shareholders with at least 60 days prior notice of any change in the policy described in paragraph (a)(3)(i) of this section that meets the requirements of paragraph (c) of this section.

(4) *Tax-exempt Funds.* A name suggesting that the Fund's distributions are exempt from federal income tax or from both federal and state income tax, unless the Fund has adopted a fundamental policy under section 8(b)(3) of the Act (15 U.S.C. 80–8(b)(3)):

(i) To invest, under normal circumstances, at least 80% of the value of its Assets in investments the income from which is exempt, as applicable, from federal income tax or from both federal and state income tax; or

(ii) To invest, under normal circumstances, its Assets so that at least 80% of the income that it distributes will be exempt, as applicable, from federal income tax or from both federal and state income tax.

(b) The requirements of paragraphs (a)(2) through (a)(4) of this section apply at the time a Fund invests its Assets, except that these requirements shall not apply to any unit investment trust (as defined in section 4(2) of the Act (15 U.S.C. 80a–4(2))) that has made an initial deposit of securities prior to July 31, 2002. If, subsequent to an investment, these requirements are no longer met, the Fund's future investments must be made in a manner that will bring the Fund into compliance with those paragraphs.

(c) A policy to provide a Fund's shareholders with notice of a change in a Fund's investment policy as described in paragraphs (a)(2)(ii) and (a)(3)(iii) of this section must provide that:

(1) The notice will be provided in plain English in a separate written document;

(2) The notice will contain the following prominent statement, or similar clear and understandable statement, in bold-face type: "Important Notice Regarding Change in Investment Policy"; and

(3) The statement contained in paragraph (c)(2) of this section also will appear on the envelope in which the notice is delivered or, if the notice is delivered separately from other communications to investors, that the statement will appear either on the notice or on the envelope in which the notice is delivered.

(d) For purposes of this section:

(1) *Fund* means a registered investment company and any series of the investment company.

(2) *Assets* means net assets, plus the amount of any borrowings for investment purposes.

§ 270.38a-1. Compliance Procedures and Practices of Certain Investment Companies

(a) Each registered investment company and business development company ("fund") must:

(1) *Policies and procedures.* Adopt and implement written policies and procedures reasonably designed to prevent violation of the Federal Securities Laws by the fund, including policies and procedures that provide for the oversight of compliance by each investment adviser, principal underwriter, administrator, and transfer agent of the fund;

(2) *Board approval.* Obtain the approval of the fund's board of directors, including a majority of directors who are not interested persons of the fund, of the fund's policies and procedures and those of each investment adviser, principal underwriter, administrator, and transfer agent of the fund, which approval must be based on a finding by the board that the policies and procedures are reasonably designed to prevent violation of the Federal Securities Laws by the fund, and by each investment adviser, principal underwriter, administrator, and transfer agent of the fund;

(3) *Annual review.* Review, no less frequently than annually, the adequacy of the policies and procedures of the fund and of each investment adviser, principal underwriter, administrator, and transfer agent and the effectiveness of their implementation;

(4) *Chief compliance officer.* Designate one individual responsible for administering the fund's policies and procedures adopted under paragraph (a)(1):

(i) Whose designation and compensation must be approved by the fund's board of directors, including a majority of the directors who are not interested persons of the fund;

(ii) Who may be removed from his or her responsibilities by action of (and only with the approval of) the fund's board of directors, including a majority of the directors who are not interested persons of the fund;

(iii) Who must, no less frequently than annually, provide a written report to the board that, at a minimum, addresses:

(A) The operation of the policies and procedures of the fund and each investment adviser, principal underwriter, administrator, and transfer agent of the fund, any material changes made to those policies and procedures since the date of the last report, and any material changes to the policies and procedures recommended as a result of the annual review conducted pursuant to paragraph (a)(3) of this section; and

(B) Each Material Compliance Matter that occurred since the date of the last report; and

(iv) Who must, no less frequently than annually, meet separately with the fund's independent directors.

(b) *Unit investment trusts*. If the fund is a unit investment trust, the fund's principal underwriter or depositor must approve the fund's policies and procedures and chief compliance officer, must receive all annual reports, and must approve the removal of the chief compliance officer from his or her responsibilities.

(c) *Undue influence prohibited*. No officer, director, or employee of the fund, its investment adviser, or principal underwriter, or any person acting under such person's direction may directly or indirectly take any action to coerce, manipulate, mislead, or fraudulently influence the fund's chief compliance officer in the performance of his or her duties under this rule.

(d) *Recordkeeping*. The fund must maintain:

(1) A copy of the policies and procedures adopted by the fund under paragraph (a)(1) that are in effect, or at any time within the past five years were in effect, in an easily accessible place; and

(2) Copies of materials provided to the board of directors in connection with their approval under paragraph (a)(2) of this rule, and written reports provided to the board of directors pursuant to paragraph (a)(4)(iii) of this rule (or, if the fund is a unit investment trust, to the fund's principal underwriter or depositor, pursuant to paragraph (b) of this rule) for at least five years after the end of the fiscal year in which the documents were provided, the first two years in an easily accessible place; and

(3) Any records documenting the fund's annual review pursuant to paragraph (a)(3) of this rule for at least five years after the end of the fiscal year in which the annual review was conducted, the first two years in an easily accessible place.

(e) *Definitions*. For purposes of this rule:

(1) *Federal Securities Laws* means the Securities Act of 1933 (15 U.S.C. 77a–aa), the Securities Exchange Act of 1934 (15 U.S.C. 78a–mm), the Sarbanes–Oxley Act of 2002 (Pub. L. 107–204, 116 Stat. 745 (2002)), the Investment Company Act of 1940 (15 U.S.C. 80a), the Investment Advisers Act of 1940 (15 U.S.C. 80b), Title V of the Gramm–Leach–Bliley Act (Pub. L. No. 106–102, 113 Stat. 1338 (1999)), any rules adopted by the Commission under any of these statutes, the Bank Secrecy Act (31 U.S.C. 5311–5314; 5316–5332) as it applies to funds, and any rules adopted thereunder by the Commission or the Department of the Treasury.

(2) *A Material Compliance Matter* means any compliance matter about which the fund's board of directors would reasonably need to know to oversee fund compliance, and that involves, without limitation:

(i) A violation of the Federal Securities Laws by the fund, its investment adviser, principal underwriter, administrator or transfer agent (or officers, directors, employees or agents thereof),

(ii) A violation of the policies and procedures of the fund, its investment adviser, principal underwriter, administrator or transfer agent, or

(iii) A weakness in the design or implementation of the policies and procedures of the fund, its investment adviser, principal underwriter, administrator or transfer agent.

§ 270.45a-1 Confidential Treatment of Names and Addresses of Dealers of Registered Investment Company Securities

(a) Exhibits calling for the names and addresses of dealers to or through whom principal underwriters of registered investment companies are currently offering securities and which are required to be furnished with registration statements filed pursuant to section 8(b) of the act, or periodic reports filed pursuant to section 30(a) or section 30(b)(1) of the act, shall be the subject of confidential treatment and shall not be made available to the public, except that the Commission may by order make such exhibits available to the public if, after appropriate notice and opportunity for hearing, it finds that public disclosure of such material is necessary or appropriate in the public interest or for the protection of investors.

(b) The exhibits referred to in paragraph (a) of this section shall be filed in quadruplicate with the Commission at the time the registration statement or periodic report is filed. Such exhibits shall be enclosed in a separate envelope marked "Confidential Treatment" and addressed to the Chairman, Securities and Executive Commission, Washington, D.C. Confidential treatment requests shall be submitted in paper only, whether or not the registrant is required to file in electronic format.

§ 270.57b–1 Exemption for Downstream Affiliates of Business Development Companies

Notwithstanding subsection (b)(2) of section 57 of the Act, the provisions of subsection (a) of that section shall not apply to any person (a) solely because that person is directly or indirectly controlled by a business development company or (b) solely because that person is, within the meaning of section 2(a)(3)(C) or (D) of the Act, an affiliated person of a person described in (a) of this section.

§ 270.60a–1 Exemption for Certain Business Development Companies

Section 12(d)(1)(A) and (C) of the Act shall not apply to the acquisition by a business development company of the outstanding voting securities of a small business investment company licensed to do business under the Small Business Investment Act of 1958 which is operated as a wholly-owned subsidiary of the business development company.

D. INVESTMENT ADVISERS ACT OF 1940

15 U.S.C. § 80b–1 et seq.

Sec. 201. Findings

Upon the basis of facts disclosed by the record and report of the Securities and Exchange Commission made pursuant to section 79z–4 of this title, and facts otherwise disclosed and ascertained, it is found that investment advisers are of national concern, in that, among other things—

(1) their advice, counsel, publications, writings, analyses, and reports are furnished and distributed, and their contracts, subscription agreements, and other arrangements with clients are negotiated and performed, by the use of the mails and means and instrumentalities of interstate commerce;

(2) their advice, counsel, publications, writings, analyses, and reports customarily relate to the purchase and sale of securities traded on national securities exchanges and in interstate over-the-counter markets, securities issued by companies engaged in business in interstate commerce, and securities issued by national banks and member banks of the Federal Reserve System; and

(3) the foregoing transactions occur in such volume as substantially to affect interstate commerce, national securities exchanges, and other securities markets, the national banking system and the national economy.

Sec. 202. Definitions

(a) When used in this title, unless the context otherwise requires, the following definition shall appear:

(1) "Assignment" includes any direct or indirect transfer or hypothecation of an investment advisory contract by the assignor or of a controlling block of the assignor's outstanding voting securities by a security holder of the assignor; but if the investment adviser is a partnership, no assignment of an investment advisory contract shall be deemed to result from the death or withdrawal of a minority of the members of the investment adviser having only a minority interest in the business of the investment adviser, or from the admission to the investment adviser of one or more members who, after such admission, shall be only a minority of the members and shall have only a minority interest in the business.

(2) "Bank" means (A) a banking institution organized under the laws of the United States, (B) a member bank of the Federal Reserve System, (C) any other banking institution or trust company, whether incorporated or not, doing business under the laws of any State or of the United States, a substantial portion of the business of which consists of receiving deposits or exercising fiduciary powers similar to those permitted to national banks under the authority of the Comptroller of the Currency, and which is supervised and examined by State or Federal authority having supervision over banks, and which is not operated for the purpose of evading the provisions of this subchapter, and (D) a receiver, conservator, or other liquidating agent of any institution or firm included in clauses (A), (B), or (C) of this paragraph.

(3) The term "broker" has the same meaning as given in section 3 of the Securities Exchange Act of 1934.

(4) "Commission" means the Securities and Exchange Commission.

(5) "Company" means a corporation, a partnership, an association, a joint-stock company, a trust, or any organized group of persons, whether incorporated or not; or any receiver, trustee in a case under Title 11 of the United States Code, or similar official, or any liquidating agent for any of the foregoing, in his capacity as such.

(6) "Convicted" includes a verdict, judgment, or plea of guilty, or a finding of guilt on a plea of nolo contendere, if such verdict, judgment, plea, or finding has not been reversed, set aside, or withdrawn, whether or not sentence has been imposed.

(7) The term "dealer" has the same meaning as given in section 3 of the Securities Exchange Act of 1934, but does not include an insurance company or investment company.

(8) "Director" means any director of a corporation or any person performing similar functions with respect to any organization, whether incorporated or unincorporated.

(9) "Exchange" means any organization, association, or group of persons, whether incorporated or unincorporated, which constitutes, maintains, or provides a market place or facilities for bringing together purchasers and sellers of securities or for otherwise performing with respect to securities the functions commonly performed by a stock exchange as that term is generally understood, and includes the market place and the market facilities maintained by such exchange.

(10) "Interstate commerce" means trade, commerce, transportation, or communication among the several States, or between any foreign country and any State, or between any State and any place or ship outside thereof.

(11) "Investment adviser" means any person who, for compensation, engages in the business of advising others, either directly or through publications or writings, as to the value of securities or as to the advis-

ability of investing in, purchasing, or selling securities, or who, for compensation and as part of a regular business, issues or promulgates analyses or reports concerning securities; but does not include (A) a bank, or any bank holding company as defined in the Bank Holding Company Act of 1956 which is not an investment company, except that the term "investment adviser" includes any bank or bank holding company to the extent that such bank or bank holding company serves or acts as an investment adviser to a registered investment company, but if, in the case of a bank, such services or actions are performed through a separately identifiable department or division, the department or division, and not the bank itself, shall be deemed to be the investment adviser; (B) any lawyer, accountant, engineer, or teacher whose performance of such services is solely incidental to the practice of his profession; (C) any broker or dealer whose performance of such services is solely incidental to the conduct of his business as a broker or dealer and who receives no special compensation therefor; (D) the publisher of any bona fide newspaper, news magazine or business or financial publication of general and regular circulation; (E) any person whose advice, analyses, or reports relate to no securities other than securities which are direct obligations of or obligations guaranteed as to principal or interest by the United States, or securities issued or guaranteed by corporations in which the United States has a direct or indirect interest which shall have been designated by the Secretary of the Treasury, pursuant to section 3(a)(12) of the Securities Exchange Act of 1934, as exempted securities for the purposes of the Securities Exchange Act of 1934; or (F) such other persons not within the intent of this paragraph, as the Commission may designate by rules and regulations or order.

(12) "Investment company", affiliated person, and "insurance company" have the same meanings as in the Investment Company Act of 1940. "Control" means the power to exercise a controlling influence over the management or policies of a company, unless such power is solely the result of an official position with such company.

(13) "Investment supervisory services" means the giving of continuous advice as to the investment of funds on the basis of the individual needs of each client.

(14) "Means or instrumentality of interstate commerce" includes any facility of a national securities exchange.

(15) "National securities exchange" means an exchange registered under section 6 of the Securities Exchange Act of 1934.

(16) "Person" means a natural person or a company.

(17) The term "person associated with an investment adviser" means any partner, officer, or director of such investment adviser (or any person performing similar functions), or any person directly or indirectly controlling or controlled by such investment adviser, including any employee of such investment adviser, except that for the purposes of section 203 of this title (other than subsection (f) thereof), persons associated with an investment adviser whose functions are clerical or ministerial shall not be included in the meaning of such term. The Commission may by rules and regulations classify, for the purposes of any portion or portions of this title, persons, including employees controlled by an investment adviser.

(18) "Security" means any note, stock, treasury stock, security future, bond, debenture, evidence of indebtedness, certificate of interest or participation in any profit-sharing agreement, collateral-trust certificate, preorganization certificate or subscription, transferable share, investment contract, voting-trust certificate, certificate of deposit for a security, fractional undivided interest in oil, gas, or other mineral rights, any put, call, straddle, option, or privilege on any security (including a certificate of deposit) or on any group or index of securities (includ-

ing any interest therein or based on the value thereof), or any put, call, straddle, option, or privilege entered into on a national securities exchange relating to foreign currency, or, in general, any interest or instrument commonly known as a "security", or any certificate of interest or participation in, temporary or interim certificate for, receipt for, guarantee of, or warrant or right to subscribe to or purchase any of the foregoing.

(19) "State" means any State of the United States, the District of Columbia, Puerto Rico, the Virgin Islands, or any other possession of the United States.

(20) "Underwriter" means any person who has purchased from an issuer with a view to, or sells for an issuer in connection with, the distribution of any security, or participates or has a direct or indirect participation in any such undertaking, or participates or has a participation in the direct or indirect underwriting of any such undertaking; but such term shall not include a person whose interest is limited to a commission from an underwriter or dealer not in excess of the usual and customary distributor's or seller's commission. As used in this paragraph the term "issuer" shall include in addition to an issuer, any person directly or indirectly controlling or controlled by the issuer, or any person under direct or indirect common control with the issuer.

(21) "Securities Act of 1933", "Securities Exchange Act of 1934", "Public Utility Holding Company Act of 1935", and "Trust Indenture Act of 1939", mean those Acts, respectively, as heretofore or hereafter amended.

(22) "Business development company" means any company which is a business development company as defined in sections 2(a)(48) and 55 of title I of this Act and which complies with section 55 of title I of this Act, except that—

(A) the 70 per centum of the value of the total assets condition referred to in sections 2(a)(48) and 55 of title I of this Act shall be 60 per centum for purposes of determining compliance therewith;

(B) such company need not be a closed-end company and need not elect to be subject to the provisions of sections 55 through 65 of title I of this Act; and

(C) the securities which may be purchased pursuant to section 55(a) of title I of this Act may be purchased from any person.

For purposes of this paragraph, all terms in sections 2(a)(48) and 55 of title I of this Act shall have the same meaning set forth in such title as if such company were a registered closed-end investment company, except that the value of the assets of a business development company which is not subject to the provisions of sections 55 through 65 of title I of this Act shall be determined as of the date of the most recent financial statements which it furnished to all holders of its securities, and shall be determined no less frequently than annually.

(23) "Foreign securities authority" means any foreign government, or any governmental body or regulatory organization empowered by a foreign government to administer or enforce its laws as they relate to securities matters.

(24) "Foreign financial regulatory authority" means any (A) foreign securities authority, (B) other governmental body or foreign equivalent of a self-regulatory organization empowered by a foreign government to administer or enforce its laws relating to the regulation of fiduciaries, trusts, commercial lending, insurance, trading in contracts of sale of a commodity for future delivery, or other instruments traded on or subject to the rules of a contract market, board of trade or foreign equivalent, or other financial activities, or (C) membership organization a function of which is to regulate the

participation of the members in activities listed above.

(25) "Supervised person" means any partner, officer, director (or other person occupying a similar status or performing similar functions), or employee of an investment adviser, or other person who provides investment advice on behalf of the investment adviser and is subject to the supervision and control of the investment adviser.

(26) The term "separately identifiable department or division" of a bank means a unit—

(A) that is under the direct supervision of an officer or officers designated by the board of directors of the bank as responsible for the day-to-day conduct of the bank's investment adviser activities for one or more investment companies, including the supervision of all bank employees engaged in the performance of such activities; and

(B) for which all of the records relating to its investment adviser activities are separately maintained in or extractable from such unit's own facilities or the facilities of the bank, and such records are so maintained or otherwise accessible as to permit independent examination and enforcement by the Commission of this Act or the Investment Company Act of 1940 and rules and regulations promulgated under this Act or the Investment Company Act of 1940.

(27) The terms "security future" and "narrow-based security index" have the same meaning as provided in section 3(a)(55) of the Securities Exchange Act of 1934.

(b) No provision in this title shall apply to, or be deemed to include, the United States, a State, or any political subdivision of a State, or any agency, authority, or instrumentality of any one or more of the foregoing, or any corporation which is wholly owned directly or indirectly by any one or more of the foregoing, or any officer, agent, or employee of any of the foregoing acting as such in the course of his official duty, unless such provision makes specific reference thereto.

(c) *Consideration of Promotion of Efficiency, Competition, and Capital Formation.*—Whenever pursuant to this title the Commission is engaged in rulemaking and is required to consider or determine whether an action is necessary or appropriate in the public interest, the Commission shall also consider, in addition to the protection of investors, whether the action will promote efficiency, competition, and capital formation.

Sec. 203. Registration of Investment Advisers

(a) Except as provided in subsection (b) and Section 203A, it shall be unlawful for any investment adviser, unless registered under this section, to make use of the mails or any means or instrumentality of interstate commerce in connection with his or its business as an investment adviser.

(b) The provisions of subsection (a) of this section shall not apply to—

(1) any investment adviser all of whose clients are residents of the State within which such investment adviser maintains his or its principal office and place of business, and who does not furnish advice or issue analyses or reports with respect to securities listed or admitted to unlisted trading privileges on any national securities exchange;

(2) any investment adviser whose only clients are insurance companies;

(3) any investment adviser who during the course of the preceding twelve months has had fewer than fifteen clients and who neither holds himself out generally to the public as an investment adviser nor acts as an investment adviser to any investment company registered under title I of this Act, or a company which has elected to be a business development company pursuant to section 54 of title I of this Act and has not

withdrawn its election. For purposes of determining the number of clients of an investment adviser under this paragraph, no shareholder, partner, or beneficial owner of a business development company, as defined in this title, shall be deemed to be a client of such investment adviser unless such person is a client of such investment adviser separate and apart from his status as a shareholder, partner, or beneficial owner;

(4) any investment adviser that is a charitable organization, as defined in section 3(c)(10)(D) of the Investment Company Act of 1940, or is a trustee, director, officer, employee, or volunteer of such a charitable organization acting within the scope of such person's employment or duties with such organization, whose advice, analyses, or reports are provided only to one or more of the following:

(A) any such charitable organization;

(B) a fund that is excluded from the definition of an investment company under section 3(c)(10)(B) of the Investment Company Act of 1940; or

(C) a trust or other donative instrument described in section 3(c)(10)(B) of the Investment Company Act of 1940, or the trustees, administrators, settlors (or potential settlors), or beneficiaries of any such trust or other instrument;

(5) any plan described in section 414(e) of the Internal Revenue Code of 1986, any person or entity eligible to establish and maintain such a plan under the Internal Revenue Code of 1986, or any trustee, director, officer, or employee of or volunteer for any such plan or person, if such person or entity, acting in such capacity, provides investment advice exclusively to, or with respect to, any plan, person, or entity or any company, account, or fund that is excluded from the definition of an investment company under section 3(c)(14) of the Investment Company Act of 1940; or

(6) any investment adviser that is registered with the Commodity Futures Trading Commission as a commodity trading advisor whose business does not consist primarily of acting as an investment adviser, as defined in section 202(a)(11) of this title, and that does not act as an investment adviser to—

(A) an investment company registered under title I of this Act; or

(B) a company which has elected to be a business development company pursuant to section 54 of title I of this Act and has not withdrawn its election.

(c)(1) An investment adviser, or any person who presently contemplates becoming an investment adviser, may be registered by filing with the Commission an application for registration in such form and containing such of the following information and documents as the Commission, by rule, may prescribe as necessary or appropriate in the public interest or for the protection of investors:

(A) the name and form of organization under which the investment adviser engages or intends to engage in business; the name of the State or other sovereign power under which such investment adviser is organized; the location of his or its principal business office and branch offices, if any; the names and addresses of his or its partners, officers, directors, and persons performing similar functions or, if such an investment adviser be an individual, of such individual; and the number of his or its employees;

(B) the education, the business affiliations for the past ten years, and the present business affiliations of such investment adviser and of his or its partners, officers, directors, and persons performing similar functions and of any controlling person thereof;

(C) the nature of the business of such investment adviser, including the manner of giving advice and rendering analyses or reports;

(D) a balance sheet certified by an independent public accountant and other financial statements (which shall, as the Commission specifies, be certified);

(E) the nature and scope of the authority of such investment adviser with respect to clients' funds and accounts;

(F) the basis or bases upon which such investment adviser is compensated;

(G) whether such investment adviser, or any person associated with such investment adviser, is subject to any disqualification which would be a basis for denial, suspension, or revocation of registration of such investment adviser under the provisions of subsection (e) of this section; and

(H) a statement as to whether the principal business of such investment adviser consists or is to consist of acting as investment adviser and a statement as to whether a substantial part of the business of such investment adviser, consists or is to consist of rendering investment supervisory services.

(2) Within forty-five days of the date of the filing of such application (or within such longer period as to which the applicant consents) the Commission shall—

(A) by order grant such registration; or

(B) institute proceedings to determine whether registration should be denied. Such proceedings shall include notice of the grounds for denial under consideration and opportunity for hearing and shall be concluded within one hundred twenty days of the date of the filing of the application for registration. At the conclusion of such proceedings the Commission, by order, shall grant or deny such registration. The Commission may extend the time for conclusion of such proceedings for up to ninety days if it finds good cause for such extension and publishes its reasons for so finding or for such longer period as to which the applicant consents.

The Commission shall grant such registration if the Commission finds that the requirements of this section are satisfied and that the applicant is not prohibited from registering as an investment adviser under section 203A. The Commission shall deny such registration if it does not make such a finding or if it finds that if the applicant were so registered, its registration would be subject to suspension or revocation under subsection (e) of this section.

(d) Any provision of this title (other than subsection (a) of this section) which prohibits any act, practice, or course of business if the mails or any means or instrumentality of interstate commerce are used in connection therewith shall also prohibit any such act, practice, or course of business by any investment adviser registered pursuant to this section or any person acting on behalf of such an investment adviser, irrespective of any use of the mails or any means or instrumentality of interstate commerce in connection therewith.

(e) The Commission, by order, shall censure, place limitations on the activities, functions, or operations of, suspend for a period not exceeding twelve months, or revoke the registration of any investment adviser if it finds, on the record after notice and opportunity for hearing, that such censure, placing of limitations, suspension, or revocation is in the public interest and that such investment adviser, or any person associated with such investment adviser, whether prior to or subsequent to becoming so associated—

(1) has willfully made or caused to be made in any application for registration or report required to be filed with the Commission under this title, or in any proceeding before the Commission with respect to registration, any statement which was at the time and in the light of the circumstances under which it was made false or misleading with respect to any material fact, or has omitted to state in any such application or report any material fact which is required to be stated therein.

(2) has been convicted within ten years preceding the filing of any application for registration or at any time thereafter of any felony or misdemeanor or of a substantially equivalent crime by a foreign court of com-

petent jurisdiction which the Commission finds—

(A) involves the purchase or sale of any security, the taking of a false oath, the making of a false report, bribery, perjury, burglary, any substantially equivalent activity however denominated by the laws of the relevant foreign government, or conspiracy to commit any such offense;

(B) arises out of the conduct of the business of a broker, dealer, municipal securities dealer, investment adviser, bank, insurance company, government securities broker, government securities dealer, fiduciary, transfer agent, foreign person performing a function substantially equivalent to any of the above, or entity or person required to be registered under the Commodity Exchange Act;

(C) involves the larceny, theft, robbery, extortion, forgery, counterfeiting, fraudulent concealment, embezzlement, fraudulent conversion, or misappropriation of funds or securities or substantially equivalent activity however denominated by the laws of the relevant foreign government; or

(D) involves the violation of section 152, 1341, 1342, or 1343 or chapter 25 or 47 of title 18, United States Code, or a violation of substantially equivalent foreign statute.

(3) has been convicted during the 10–year period preceding the date of filing of any application for registration, or at any time thereafter, of—

(A) any crime that is punishable by imprisonment for 1 or more years, and that is not described in paragraph (2); or

(B) a substantially equivalent crime by a foreign court of competent jurisdiction.

(4) is permanently or temporarily enjoined by order, judgment, or decree of any court of competent jurisdiction, including any foreign court of competent jurisdiction, from acting as an investment adviser, underwriter, broker, dealer, municipal securities dealer, government securities broker, government securities dealer, transfer agent, or entity or person required to be registered under the Commodity Exchange Act or any substantially equivalent statute or regulation, or as an affiliated person or employee of any investment company, bank, insurance company, foreign entity substantially equivalent to any of the above, or entity or person required to be registered under the Commodity Exchange Act or any substantially equivalent statute or regulation, or from engaging in or continuing any conduct or practice in connection with any such activity, or in connection with the purchase or sale of any security.

(5) has willfully violated any provision of the Securities Act of 1933, the Securities Exchange Act of 1934, the Investment Company Act of 1940, this title, the Commodity Exchange Act, or the rules or regulations under any such statutes or any rule of the Municipal Securities Rulemaking Board, or is unable to comply with any such provision.

(6) has willfully aided, abetted, counseled, commanded, induced, or procured the violation by any other person of any provision of the Securities Act of 1933, the Securities Exchange Act of 1934, the Investment Company Act of 1940, this title, the Commodity Exchange Act, the rules or regulations under any of such statutes, or the rules of the Municipal Securities Rulemaking Board, or has failed reasonably to supervise, with a view to preventing violations of the provisions of such statutes, rules, and regulations, another person who commits such a violation, if such other person is subject to his supervision. For the purposes of this paragraph (5) no person shall be deemed to have failed reasonably to supervise any person, if—

(A) there have been established procedures, and a system for applying such procedures, which would reasonably be expected to prevent and detect, insofar as practicable, any such violation by such other person, and

(B) such person has reasonably discharged the duties and obligations incumbent upon him by reason of such procedures and system without reasonable cause to believe that such procedures and system were not being complied with.

(7) is subject to any order of the Commission barring or suspending the right of the person to be associated with an investment adviser;

(8) has been found by a foreign financial regulatory authority to have—

(A) made or caused to be made in any application for registration or report required to be filed with a foreign securities authority, or in any proceeding before a foreign securities authority with respect to registration, any statement that was at the time and in light of the circumstances under which it was made false or misleading with respect to any material fact, or has omitted to state in any application or report to a foreign securities authority any material fact that is required to be stated therein;

(B) violated any foreign statute or regulation regarding transactions in securities or contracts of sale of a commodity for future delivery traded on or subject to the rules of a contract market or any board of trade; or

(C) aided, abetted, counseled, commanded, induced, or procured the violation by any other person of any foreign statute or regulation regarding transactions in securities or contracts of sale of a commodity for future delivery traded on or subject to the rules of a contract market or any board of trade, or has been found, by the foreign financial regulatory authority, to have failed reasonably to supervise, with a view to preventing violations of statutory provisions, and rules and regulations promulgated thereunder, another person who commits such a violation, if such other person is subject to his supervision; or

(9) is subject to any final order of a State securities commission (or any agency or officer performing like functions), State authority that supervises or examines banks, savings associations, or credit unions, State insurance commission (or any agency or office performing like functions), an appropriate Federal banking agency (as defined in section 3 of the Federal Deposit Insurance Act (12 U.S.C. 1813(q))), or the National Credit Union Administration, that—

(A) bars such person from association with an entity regulated by such commission, authority, agency, or officer, or from engaging in the business of securities, insurance, banking, savings association activities, or credit union activities; or

(B) constitutes a final order based on violations of any laws or regulations that prohibit fraudulent, manipulative, or deceptive conduct.

(f) The Commission, by order, shall censure or place limitations on the activities of any person associated, seeking to become associated, or, at the time of the alleged misconduct, associated or seeking to become associated with an investment adviser, or suspend for a period not exceeding twelve months or bar any such person from being associated with an investment adviser, if the Commission finds, on the record after notice and opportunity for hearing, that such censure, placing of limitations, suspension, or bar is in the public interest and that such person has committed or omitted any act or omission enumerated in paragraph (1), (5), (6), (8), or (9) of subsection (e) of this section or has been convicted of any offense specified in paragraph (2) or (3) of subsection (e) within ten years of the commencement of the proceedings under this subsection, or is enjoined from any action, conduct, or practice specified in paragraph (4) of subsection (e). It shall be unlawful for any person as to whom such an order suspending or barring him from being associated with an investment adviser is in effect willfully to become, or to be, associated with an investment adviser without the consent of the Commission, and it shall be unlawful for any investment adviser to permit such a person to become, or remain, a person associated with him without the consent of the Commission, if such investment adviser knew, or in the exercise of reasonable care, should have known, of such order.

(g) Any successor to the business of an investment adviser registered under this section shall be deemed likewise registered hereunder, if within thirty days from its succession to such business it shall file an application for registration under this section, unless and until the Commission, pursuant to subsection (c) or subsection (e) of this section, shall deny registration to or revoke or suspend the registration of such successor.

(h) Any person registered under this section may, upon such terms and conditions as the commission finds necessary in the public interest or for the protection of investors, withdraw from registration by filing a written notice of withdrawal with the Commission. If the Commission finds that any person registered under this section, or who has pending an application for registration filed under this section, is no longer in existence, is not engaged in business as an investment adviser, or is prohibited from registering as an investment adviser under section 203A, the Commission shall by order cancel the registration of such person.

(i) *Money penalties in administrative proceedings.*—

(1) *Authority of commission.*—In any proceeding instituted pursuant to subsection (e) or (f) against any person, the Commission may impose a civil penalty if it finds, on the record after notice and opportunity for hearing, that such person—

(A) has willfully violated any provision of the Securities Act of 1933, the Securities Exchange Act of 1934, the Investment Company Act of 1940, or this title, or the rules or regulations thereunder;

(B) has willfully aided, abetted, counseled, commanded, induced, or procured such a violation by any other person;

(C) has willfully made or caused to be made in any application for registration or report required to be filed with the Commission under this title, or in any proceeding before the Commission with respect to registration, any statement which was, at the time and in the light of the circumstances under which it was made, false or misleading with respect to any material fact, or has omitted to state in any such application or report any material fact which was required to be stated therein; or

(D) has failed reasonably to supervise, within the meaning of subsection (e)(6) of this title, with a view to preventing violations of the provisions of this title and the rules and regulations thereunder, another person who commits such a violation, if such other person is subject to his supervision;

and that such penalty is in the public interest.

(2) *Maximum amount of penalty.*—

(A) *First tier.*—The maximum amount of penalty for each act or omission described in paragraph (1) shall be $5,000 for a natural person or $50,000 for any other person.

(B) *Second tier.*—Notwithstanding subparagraph (A), the maximum amount of penalty for each such act or omission shall be $50,000 for a natural person or $250,000 for any other person if the act or omission described in paragraph (1) involved fraud, deceit, manipulation, or deliberate or reckless disregard of a regulatory requirement.

(C) *Third tier.*—Notwithstanding subparagraphs (A) and (B), the maximum amount of penalty for each such act or omission shall be $100,000 for a natural person or $500,000 for any other person if—

(i) the act or omission described in paragraph (1) involved fraud, deceit, manipulation, or deliberate or reckless disregard of a regulatory requirement; and

(ii) such act or omission directly or indirectly resulted in substantial losses or created a significant risk of substantial losses to other persons or resulted in substantial pecuniary gain to the person who committed the act or omission.

(3) *Determination of public interest.*—In considering under this section whether a penalty is in the public interest, the Commission may consider—

(A) whether the act or omission for which such penalty is assessed involved fraud, deceit, manipulation, or deliberate or reckless disregard of a regulatory requirement;

(B) the harm to other persons resulting either directly or indirectly from such act or omission;

(C) the extent to which any person was unjustly enriched, taking into account any restitution made to persons injured by such behavior;

(D) whether such person previously has been found by the Commission, another appropriate regulatory agency, or a self-regulatory organization to have violated the Federal securities laws, State securities laws, or the rules of a self-regulatory organization, has been enjoined by a court of competent jurisdiction from violations of such laws or rules, or has been convicted by a court of competent jurisdiction of violations of such laws or of any felony or misdemeanor described in section 203(e)(2) of this title;

(E) the need to deter such person and other persons from committing such acts or omissions; and

(F) such other matters as justice may require.

(4) *Evidence concerning ability to pay.*—In any proceeding in which the Commission may impose a penalty under this section, a respondent may present evidence of the respondent's ability to pay such penalty. The Commission may, in its discretion, consider such evidence in determining whether such penalty is in the public interest. Such evidence may relate to the extent of such person's ability to continue in business and the collectability of a penalty, taking into account any other claims of the United States or third parties upon such person's assets and the amount of such person's assets.

(j) *Authority to enter an order requiring an accounting and disgorgement.*—In any proceeding in which the Commission may impose a penalty under this section, the Commission may enter an order requiring accounting and disgorgement, including reasonable interest. The Commission is authorized to adopt rules, regulations, and orders concerning payments to investors, rates of interest, periods of accrual, and such other matters as it deems appropriate to implement this subsection.

(k) *Cease-and-desist proceedings.*—

(1) *Authority of the commission.*—If the Commission finds, after notice and opportunity for hearing, that any person is violating, has violated, or is about to violate any provision of this title, or any rule or regulation thereunder, the Commission may publish its findings and enter an order requiring such person, and any other person that is, was, or would be a cause of the violation, due to an act or omission the person knew or should have known would contribute to such violation, to cease and desist from committing or causing such violation and any future violation of the same provision, rule, or regulation. Such order may, in addition to requiring a person to cease and desist from committing or causing a violation, require such person to comply, or to take steps to effect compliance, with such provision, rule, or regulation, upon such terms and conditions and within such time as the Commission may specify in such order. Any such order may, as the Commission deems appropriate, require future compliance or steps to effect future compliance, either permanently or for such period of time as the Commission may specify, with such provision rule, or regulation with

respect to any security, any issuer, or any other person.

(2) *Hearing.*—The notice instituting proceedings pursuant to paragraph (1) shall fix a hearing date not earlier than 30 days nor later than 60 days after service of the notice unless an earlier or a later date is set by the Commission with the consent of any respondent so served.

(3) *Temporary order.*—

(A) *In general.*—Whenever the Commission determines that the alleged violation or threatened violation specified in the notice instituting proceedings pursuant to paragraph (1), or the continuation thereof, is likely to result in significant dissipation or conversion of assets, significant harm to investors, or substantial harm to the public interest, including, but not limited to, losses to the Securities Investor Protection Corporation, prior to the completion of the proceedings, the Commission may enter a temporary order requiring the respondent to cease and desist from the violation or threatened violation and to take such action to prevent the violation or threatened violation and to prevent dissipation or conversion of assets, significant harm to investors, or substantial harm to the public interest as the Commission deems appropriate pending completion of such proceedings. Such an order shall be entered only after notice and opportunity for a hearing, unless the Commission, notwithstanding section 211(c) of this title, determines that notice and hearing prior to entry would be impracticable to contrary to the public interest. A temporary order shall become effective upon service upon the respondent and, unless set aside, limited, or suspended by the Commission or a court of competent jurisdiction, shall remain effective and enforceable pending the completion of the proceedings.

(B) *Applicability.*—This paragraph shall apply only to a respondent that acts, or, at the time of the alleged misconduct acted, as a broker, dealer, investment adviser, investment company, municipal securities dealer, government securities broker, government securities dealer, or transfer agent, or is, or was at the time of the alleged misconduct, an associated person of, or a person seeking to become associated with, any of the foregoing.

(4) *Review of temporary orders.*—

(A) *Commission review.*—At any time after the respondent has been served with a temporary cease-and-desist order pursuant to paragraph (3), the respondent may apply to the Commission to have the order set aside, limited or suspended. If the respondent has been served with a temporary cease-and-desist order entered without a prior Commission hearing, the respondent may, within 10 days after the date on which the order was served, request a hearing on such application and the Commission shall hold a hearing and render a decision on such application at the earliest possible time.

(B) *Judicial review.*—Within—

(i) 10 days after the date the respondent was served with a temporary cease-and-desist order entered with a prior Commission hearing, or

(ii) 10 days after the Commission renders a decision on an application and hearing under subparagraph (A), with respect to any temporary cease-and-desist order entered without a prior Commission hearing,

the respondent may apply to the United States district court for the district in which the respondent resides or has its principal place of business, or for the District of Columbia, for an order setting aside, limiting, or suspending the effectiveness or enforcement of the order, and the court shall have jurisdiction to enter such an order. A respondent served with a temporary cease-and-desist order entered without a prior Commission hearing may not apply to the court except after hearing and decision by the Commission on the respondent's application under subparagraph (A) of this paragraph.

(C) *No automatic stay of temporary order.*—The commencement of proceedings under subparagraph (B) of this paragraph shall not, unless specifically ordered by the court, operate as a stay of the Commission's order.

(D) *Exclusive review.*—Section 213 of this title shall not apply to a temporary order entered pursuant to this section.

(5) *Authority to enter an order requiring an accounting and disgorgement.*—In any cease-and-desist proceeding under paragraph (1), the Commission may enter an order requiring accounting and disgorgement, including reasonable interest. The Commission is authorized to adopt rules, regulations, and orders concerning payments to investors, rates of interest, periods of accrual, and such other matters as it deems appropriate to implement this subsection.

Sec. 203A. State and Federal Responsibilities

(a) *Advisers Subject to State Authorities.*—

(1) In General.—No investment adviser that is regulated or required to be regulated as an investment adviser in the State in which it maintains its principal office and place of business shall register under section 203, unless the investment adviser—

(A) has assets under management of not less than $25,000,000, or such higher amount as the Commission may, by rule, deem appropriate in accordance with the purposes of this title; or

(B) is an adviser to an investment company registered under title I of this Act.

(2) *Definition.*—For purposes of this subsection, the term assets under management means the securities portfolios with respect to which an investment adviser provides continuous and regular supervisory or management services.

(b) *Advisers Subject to Commission Authority.*—

(1) *In General.*—No law of any State or political subdivision thereof requiring the registration, licensing, or qualification as an investment adviser or supervised person of an investment adviser shall apply to any person—

(A) that is registered under section 203 as an investment adviser, or that is a supervised person of such person, except that a State may license, register, or otherwise qualify any investment adviser representative who has a place of business located within that State; or

(B) that is not registered under section 203 because that person is excepted from the definition of an investment adviser under section 202(a)(11).

(2) *Limitation.*—Nothing in this subsection shall prohibit the securities commission (or any agency or office performing like functions) of any State from investigating and bringing enforcement actions with respect to fraud or deceit against an investment adviser or person associated with an investment adviser.

(c) *Exemptions.*—Notwithstanding subsection (a), the Commission, by rule or regulation upon its own motion, or by order upon application, may permit the registration with the Commission of any person or class of persons to which the application of subsection (a) would be unfair, a burden on interstate commerce, or otherwise inconsistent with the purposes of this section.

(d) *Filing Depositories.*—The Commission may, by rule, require an investment adviser—

(1) to file with the Commission any fee, application, report, or notice required by this title or by the rules issued under this title through any entity designated by the Commission for that purpose; and

(2) to pay the reasonable costs associated with such filing.

(e) *State Assistance.*—Upon request of the securities commissioner (or any agency or officer performing like functions) of any State, the Commission may provide such training, technical assistance, or other reasonable assistance in connection with the regulation of investment advisers by the State.

Sec. 204. Reports by Investment Advisers

Every investment adviser who makes use of the mails or of any means or instrumentality of interstate commerce in connection with his or its business as an investment adviser (other than one specifically exempted from registration pursuant to section 203(b) of this title), shall make and keep for prescribed periods such records (as defined in section 3(a)(37) of the Securities Exchange Act of 1934), furnish such copies thereof and make and disseminate such reports as the Commission, by rule, may prescribe as necessary or appropriate in the public interest or for the protection of investors. All records (as so defined) of such investment advisers are subject at any time, or from time to time, to such reasonable periodic, special, or other examinations by representatives of the Commission as the Commission deems necessary or appropriate in the public interest or for the protection of investors.

Sec. 204A. Prevention of Misuse of Nonpublic Information

Every investment adviser subject to section 204 of this title shall establish, maintain, and enforce written policies and procedures reasonably designed, taking into consideration the nature of such investment adviser's business, to prevent the misuse in violation of this Act or the Securities Exchange Act of 1934, or the rules or regulations thereunder, of material, nonpublic information by such investment adviser or any person associated with such investment adviser. The Commission, as it deems necessary or appropriate in the public interest or for the protection of investors, shall adopt rules or regulations to require specific policies or procedures reasonably designed to prevent misuse in violation of this Act or the Securities Exchange Act of 1934 (or the rules or regulations thereunder) of material, nonpublic information.

Sec. 205. Investment Advisory Contracts

(a) No investment adviser, unless exempt from registration pursuant to section 203(b), shall make use of the mails or any means or instrumentality of interstate commerce, directly or indirectly, to enter into, extend, or renew any investment advisory contract, or in any way to perform any investment advisory contract entered into, extended, or renewed on or after the effective date of this title, if such contract—

(1) provides for compensation to the investment adviser on the basis of a share of capital gains upon or capital appreciation of the funds or any portion of the funds of the client;

(2) fails to provide, in substance, that no assignment of such contract shall be made by the investment adviser without the consent of the other party to the contract; or

(3) fails to provide, in substance, that the investment adviser, if a partnership, will notify the other party to the contract of any change in the membership of such partnership within a reasonable time after such change.

(b) Paragraph (1) of subsection (a) shall not—

(1) be construed to prohibit an investment advisory contract which provides for compensation based upon the total value of a fund averaged over a definite period, or as of definite dates, or taken as of a definite date;

(2) apply to an investment advisory contract with

(A) an investment company registered under title I of this Act, or

(B) any other person (except a trust, governmental plan, collective trust fund, or separate account referred to in section 3(c)(11) of title I of this Act), provided that the contract relates to the investment of assets in excess of $1 million, if the contract provides for compensation based on the asset value of the company or fund under management averaged over a specified period and increasing and decreasing proportionately with the investment performance of the company or fund over a specified period in relation to the investment record of an appropriate index of securities prices or such other measure of investment performance as the Commission by rule, regulation, or order may specify;

(3) apply with respect to any investment advisory contract between an investment adviser and a business development company, as defined in this title, if

(A) the compensation provided for in such contract does not exceed 20 per centum of the realized capital gains upon the funds of the business development company over a specified period or as of definite dates, computed net of all realized capital losses and unrealized capital depreciation, and the condition of section 61(a)(3)(B)(iii) of title I of this Act is satisfied, and

(B) the business development company does not have outstanding any option, warrant, or right issued pursuant to section 61(a)(3)(B) of title I of this Act and does not have a profit-sharing plan described in section 57(n) of title I of this Act;

(4) apply to an investment advisory contract with a company excepted from the definition of an investment company under section 3(c)(7) of title I of this Act; or

(5) apply to an investment advisory contract with a person who is not a resident of the United States.

(c) For purposes of paragraph (2) of subsection (b), the point from which increases and decreases in compensation are measured shall be the fee which is paid or earned when the investment performance of such company or fund is equivalent to that of the index or other measure of performance, and an index of securities prices shall be deemed appropriate unless the Commission by order shall determine otherwise.

(d) As used in paragraphs (2) and (3) of subsection (a), "investment advisory contract" means any contract or agreement whereby a person agrees to act as investment adviser to or to manage any investment or trading account of another person other than an investment company registered under title I of this Act.

(e) The Commission, by rule or regulation, upon its own motion, or by order upon application, may conditionally or unconditionally exempt any person or transaction, or any class or classes of persons or transactions, from subsection (a)(1), if and to the extent that the exemption relates to an investment advisory contract with any person that the Commission determines does not need the protections of subsection (a)(1), on the basis of such factors as financial sophistication, net worth, knowledge of and experience in financial matters, amount of assets under management, relationship with a registered investment adviser, and such other factors as the Commission determines are consistent with this section.

Sec. 206. Prohibited Transactions by Investment Advisers

It shall be unlawful for any investment adviser, by use of the mails or any means or instrumentality of interstate commerce, directly or indirectly—

(1) to employ any device, scheme, or artifice to defraud any client or prospective client;

(2) to engage in any transaction, practice, or course of business which operates as a fraud or deceit upon any client or prospective client;

(3) acting as principal for his own account, knowingly to sell any security to or purchase any security from a client, or acting as broker for a person other than such client, knowingly to effect any sale or purchase of any security for the account of such client, without disclosing to such client in writing before the completion of such trans-

action the capacity in which he is acting and obtaining the consent of the client to such transaction. The prohibitions of this paragraph shall not apply to any transaction with a customer of a broker or dealer if such broker or dealer is not acting as an investment adviser in relation to such transaction;

(4) to engage in any act, practice, or course of business which is fraudulent, deceptive, or manipulative. The Commission shall, for the purposes of this paragraph (4) by rules and regulations define, and prescribe means reasonably designed to prevent, such acts, practices, and courses of business as are fraudulent, deceptive, or manipulative.

Sec. 206A. Exemptions

The Commission, by rules and regulations, upon its own motion, or by order upon application, may conditionally or unconditionally exempt any person or transaction, or any class or classes of persons, or transactions, from any provision or provisions of this title or of any rule or regulation thereunder, if and to the extent that such exemption is necessary or appropriate in the public interest and consistent with the protection of investors and the purposes fairly intended by the policy and provisions of this title.

Sec. 207. Material Misstatements

It shall be unlawful for any person willfully to make any untrue statement of a material fact in any registration application or report filed with the Commission under section 203, or 204 of this title, or willfully to omit to state in any such application or report any material fact which is required to be stated therein.

Sec. 208. General Prohibitions

(a) It shall be unlawful for any person registered under section 203 of this title to represent or imply in any manner whatsoever that such person has been sponsored, recommended, or approved, or that his abilities or qualifications have in any respect been passed upon by the United States or any agency or any officer thereof.

(b) No provision of subsection (a) shall be construed to prohibit a statement that a person is registered under this title or under the Securities Exchange Act of 1934, if such statement is true in fact and if the effect of such registration is not misrepresented.

(c) It shall be unlawful for any person registered under section 203 of this title to represent that he is an investment counsel or to use the name "investment counsel" as descriptive of his business unless (1) his or its principal business consists of acting as investment adviser, and (2) a substantial part of his or its business consists of rendering investment supervisory services.

(d) It shall be unlawful for any person indirectly, or through or by any other person, to do any act or thing which it would be unlawful for such person to do directly under the provisions of this title or any rule or regulation thereunder.

Sec. 209. Enforcement of Title

(a) Whenever it shall appear to the Commission, either upon complaint or otherwise, that the provisions of this title or of any rule or regulation prescribed under the authority thereof, have been or are about to be violated by any person, it may in its discretion require, and in any event shall permit, such person to file with it a statement in writing, under oath or otherwise, as to all the facts and circumstances relevant to such violation, and may otherwise investigate all such facts and circumstances.

(b) For the purposes of any investigation or any proceeding under this title, any member of the Commission or any officer thereof designated by it is empowered to administer oaths and affirmations, subpena witnesses, compel their attendance, take evidence, and require the production of any books, papers, correspondence, memoranda, contracts, agreements, or other records which are relevant or material to the inquiry. Such attendance of witnesses and the production of any such records may be required from any place in any State or in any Territory or other place subject to the jurisdiction of the United States at any designated place of hearing.

(c) In case of contumacy by, or refusal to obey a subpena issued to, any person, the Commission may invoke the aid of any court of the United States within the jurisdiction of which such investigation or proceeding is carried on, or where such person resides or carries on business, in requiring the attendance and testimony of witnesses and the production of books, papers, correspondence, memoranda, contracts, agreements, and other records. And such court may issue an order requiring such person to appear before the Commission or member or officer designated by the Commission, there to produce records, if so ordered, or to give testimony touching the matter under investigation or in question; and any failure to obey such order of the court may be punished by such court as a contempt thereof. All process in any such case may be served in the judicial district whereof such person is an inhabitant or wherever he may be found. Any person who without just cause shall fail or refuse to attend and testify or to answer any lawful inquiry or to produce books, papers, correspondence, memoranda, contracts, agreements, or other records, if in his or its power so to do, in obedience to the subpena of the Commission, shall be guilty of a misdemeanor, and upon conviction shall be subject to a fine of not more than $1,000 or to imprisonment for a term of not more than one year, or both.

(d) Whenever it shall appear to the Commission that any person has engaged, is engaged, or is about to engage in any act or practice constituting a violation of any provision of this title, or of any rule, regulation, or order hereunder, or that any person has aided, abetted, counseled, commanded, induced, or procured, is aiding, abetting, counseling, commanding, inducing, or procuring, or is about to aid, abet, counsel, command, induce, or procure such a violation, it may in its discretion bring an action in the proper district court of the United States, or the proper United States court of any Territory or other place subject to the jurisdiction of the United States, to enjoin such acts or practices and to enforce compliance with this title or any rule, regulation, or order hereunder. Upon a showing that such person has engaged, is engaged, or is about to engage in any such act or practice, or in aiding, abetting, counseling, commanding, inducing, or procuring any such act or practice, a permanent or temporary injunction or decree or restraining order shall be granted without bond. The Commission may transmit such evidence as may be available concerning any violation of the provisions of this subchapter, or of any rule, regulation, or order thereunder, to the Attorney General, who, in his discretion, may institute the appropriate criminal proceedings under this title.

(e) *Money penalties in civil actions.—*

(1) *Authority of commission.*—Whenever it shall appear to the Commission that any person has violated any provision of this title, the rules or regulations thereunder, or a cease-and-desist order entered by the Commission pursuant to section 203(k) of this title, the Commission may bring an action in a United States district court to seek, and the court shall have jurisdiction to impose, upon a proper showing, a civil penalty to be paid by the person who committed such violation.

(2) *Amount of penalty.—*

(A) *First tier.*—The amount of the penalty shall be determined by the court in light of the facts and circumstances. For each violation, the amount of the penalty shall not exceed the greater of (i) $5,000 for a natural person or $50,000 for any other person, or (ii) the gross amount of pecuniary gain to such defendant as a result of the violation.

(B) *Second tier.*—Notwithstanding subparagraph (A), the amount of penalty for each such violation shall not exceed the greater of (i) $50,000 for a natural person or $250,000 for any other person, or (ii) the gross amount of pecuniary gain to such defendant as a result of the violation, if the violation described in paragraph (1) involved fraud, deceit, manipulation, or deliberate or reckless disregard of a regulatory requirement.

(C) *Third tier.*—Notwithstanding subparagraphs (A) and (B), the amount of penalty for each such violation shall not exceed the greater of (i) $100,000 for a natural person or $500,000 for any other person, or (ii) the gross amount of pecuniary gain to such defendant as a result of the violation, if—

(I) the violation described in paragraph (1) involved fraud, deceit, manipulation, or deliberate or reckless disregard of a regulatory requirement; and

(II) such violation directly or indirectly resulted in substantial losses or created a significant risk of substantial losses to other persons.

(3) *Procedures for collection.*—

(A) *Payment of penalty to treasury.*—A penalty imposed under this section shall be payable into the Treasury of the United States, except as otherwise provided in section 308 of the Sarbanes-Oxley Act of 2002.

(B) *Collection of penalties.*—If a person upon whom such a penalty is imposed shall fail to pay such penalty within the time prescribed in the court's order, the Commission may refer the matter to the Attorney General who shall recover such penalty by action in the appropriate United States district court.

(C) *Remedy not exclusive.*—The actions authorized by this subsection may be brought in addition to any other action that the Commission or the Attorney General is entitled to bring.

(D) *Jurisdiction and venue.*—For purposes of section 214 of this title, actions under this paragraph shall be actions to enforce a liability or a duty created by this title.

(4) *Special provisions relating to a violation of a cease-and-desist order.*—In an action to enforce a cease-and-desist order entered by the Commission pursuant to section 203(k), each separate violation of such order shall be a separate offense, except that in the case of a violation through a continuing failure to comply with the order, each day of the failure to comply shall be deemed a separate offense.

Sec. 210. Disclosure of Information by Commission

(a) The information contained in any registration application or report or amendment thereto filed with the Commission pursuant to any provision of this title shall be made available to the public, unless and except insofar as the Commission, by rules and regulations upon its own motion, or by order upon application, finds that public disclosure is neither necessary nor appropriate in the public interest or for the protection of investors. Photostatic or other copies of information contained in documents filed with the Commission under this title and made available to the public shall be furnished to any person at such reasonable charge and under such reasonable limitations as the Commission shall prescribe.

(b) Subject to the provisions of subsections (c) and (d) of section 209 of this title and section 24(c) of the Securities Exchange Act of 1934 the Commission, or any member, officer, or employee thereof, shall not make public the fact that any examination or investigation under this title is being conducted, or the results of or any facts ascertained during any such examination or investigation; and no member, officer, or employee of the Commission shall disclose to any person other than a member, officer, or employee of the Commission any information obtained as a result of any such examination or investigation except with the approval of the Commission. The provisions of this subsection shall not apply—

(1) in the case of any hearing which is public under the provisions of section 212; or

(2) in the case of a resolution or request from either House of Congress.

(c) No provision of this title shall be construed to require, or to authorize the Commission to require any investment adviser engaged in rendering investment supervisory services to disclose the identity, investments, or affairs of any client of such investment adviser, except insofar as such disclosure may be necessary or appropriate in a particular proceeding or investigation having as its object the enforcement of a provision or provisions of this title.

Sec. 210A. Consultation

(a) *Examination Results and Other Information.*

(1) The appropriate Federal banking agency shall provide the Commission upon request the results of any examination, reports, records, or other information to which such agency may have access—

(A) with respect to the investment advisory activities of any—

(i) bank holding company;

(ii) bank; or

(iii) separately identifiable department or division of a bank,

that is registered under section 203 of this title; and

(B) in the case of a bank holding company or bank that has a subsidiary or a separately identifiable department or division registered under that section, with respect to the investment advisory activities of such bank or bank holding company.

(2) The Commission shall provide to the appropriate Federal banking agency upon request the results of any examination, reports, records, or other information with respect to the investment advisory activities of any bank holding company, bank, or separately identifiable department or division of a bank, which is registered under section 203 of this title.

(3) Notwithstanding any other provision of law, the Commission and the appropriate Federal banking agencies shall not be compelled to disclose any information provided under paragraph (1) or (2). Nothing in this paragraph shall authorize the Commission or such agencies to withhold information from Congress, or prevent the Commission or such agencies from complying with a request for information from any other Federal department or agency or any self-regulatory organization requesting the information for purposes within the scope of its jurisdiction, or complying with an order of a court of the United States in an action brought by the United States, the Commission, or such agencies. For purposes of section 552 of Title 5, United States Code, this paragraph shall be considered a statute described in subsection (b)(3)(B) of such section 552.

(b) *Effect on Other Authority.*—Nothing in this section shall limit in any respect the authority of the appropriate Federal banking agency with respect to such bank holding company (or affiliates or subsidiaries thereof), bank, or subsidiary, department, or division or a bank under any other provision of law.

(c) *Definition.*—For purposes of this section, the term ‘‘appropriate Federal banking agency’’ shall have the same meaning as given in section 3 of the Federal Deposit Insurance Act.

Sec. 211. Rules, Regulations, and Orders of Commission

(a) The Commission shall have authority from time to time to make, issue, amend, and rescind such rules and regulations and such orders as are necessary or appropriate to the exercise of the functions and powers conferred upon the Commission elsewhere in this title. For the purposes of its rules or regulations the Commission may classify persons and matters within its jurisdiction and prescribe different requirements for different classes of persons or matters.

(b) Subject to the provisions of chapter 15 of title 44, United States Code, and regulations prescribed under the authority thereof, the rules and regulations of the Commission under this title, and amendments thereof, shall be effective upon publication in the manner which the Commission shall prescribe, or upon such later date as may be provided in such rules and regulations.

(c) Orders of the Commission under this title shall be issued only after appropriate notice and opportunity for hearing. Notice to the parties to a proceeding before the Commission shall be given by personal service upon each party or by registered mail or certified mail or confirmed telegraphic notice to the party's last known business address. Notice to interested persons, if any, other than parties may be given in the same manner or by publication in the Federal Register.

(d) No provision of this title imposing any liability shall apply to any act done or omitted in good faith in conformity with any rule, regulation, or order of the Commission, notwithstanding that such rule, regulation, or order may, after such act or omission, be amended or rescinded or be determined by judicial or other authority to be invalid for any reason.

Sec. 212. Hearings

Hearings may be public and may be held before the Commission, any member or members thereof, or any officer or officers of the Commission designated by it, and appropriate records thereof shall be kept.

Sec. 213. Court Review of Orders

(a) Any person or party aggrieved by an order issued by the Commission under this title may obtain a review of such order in the United States court of appeals within any circuit wherein such person resides or has his principal place of business, or in the United States Court of Appeals for the District of Columbia, by filing in such court, within sixty days after the entry of such order, a written petition praying that the order of the Commission be modified or set aside in whole or in part. A copy of such petition shall be forthwith transmitted by the clerk of the court to any member of the Commission, or any officer thereof designated by the Commission for that purpose, and thereupon the Commission shall file in the court the record upon which the order complained of was entered, as provided in section 2112 of Title 28, United States Code. Upon the filing of such petition such court shall have jurisdiction, which upon the filing of the record shall be exclusive, to affirm, modify, or set aside such order, in whole or in part. No objection to the order of the Commission shall be considered by the court unless such objection shall have been urged before the Commission or unless there were reasonable grounds for failure so to do. The findings of the Commission as to the facts, if supported by substantial evidence, shall be conclusive. If application is made to the court for leave to adduce additional evidence, and it is shown to the satisfaction of the court that such additional evidence is material and that there were reasonable grounds for failure to adduce such evidence in the proceeding before the Commission, the court may order such additional evidence to be taken before the Commission and to be adduced upon the hearing in such manner and upon such terms and conditions as to the court may seem proper. The Commission may modify its findings as to the facts by reason of the additional evidence so taken, and it shall file with the court such modified or new findings, which, if supported by substantial evidence, shall be conclusive, and its recommendation, if any, for the modification or setting aside of the original order. The judgment and decree of the court affirming, modifying, or setting aside, in whole in or in part, any such order of the Commission shall be final, subject to review by the Supreme Court of the United States upon certiorari or certification as provided in section 1254 of title 28, United States Code.

(b) The commencement of proceedings under subsection (a) shall not, unless specifically ordered by the court, operate as a stay of the Commission's order.

Sec. 214. Jurisdiction of Offenses and Suits

The district courts of the United States and the United States courts of any Territory or other place subject to the jurisdiction of the United States shall have jurisdiction of violations of this title or the rules, regulations, or orders thereunder, and, concurrently with State and Territorial courts, of all suits in equity and actions at law brought to enforce any liability or duty created by, or to enjoin any violation of this title or the rules, regulations, or orders thereunder. Any criminal proceeding may be brought in the district wherein any act or transaction constituting the violation occurred. Any suit or action to enforce any liability or duty created by, or to enjoin any violation of this title or rules, regulations, or orders thereunder, may be brought in any such district or in the district wherein the defendant is an inhabitant or transacts business, and process in such cases may be served in any district of which the defendant is an inhabitant or transacts business or wherever the defendant may be found. Judgments and decrees so rendered shall be subject to review as provided in sections 1254, 1291, 1292, and 1294 of title 28, United States Code. No costs shall be assessed for or against the Commission in any proceeding under this title brought by or against the Commission in any court.

Sec. 215. Validity of Contracts

(a) Any condition, stipulation, or provision binding any person to waive compliance with any provision of this title or with any rule, regulation, or order thereunder shall be void.

(b) Every contract made in violation of any provision of this title and every contract heretofore or hereafter made, the performance of which involves the violation of, or the continuance of any relationship or practice in violation of any provision of this title, or any rule, regulation, or order thereunder, shall be void (1) as regards the rights of any person who, in violation of any such provision, rule, regulation, or order, shall have made or engaged in the performance of any such contract, and (2) as regards the rights of any person who, not being a party to such contract, shall have acquired any right thereunder with actual knowledge of the facts by reason of which the making or performance of such contract was in violation of any such provision.

Sec. 216. Annual Reports of Commission

The Commission shall submit annually a report to the Congress covering the work of the Commission for the preceding year and including such information, data, and recommendations for further legislation in connection with the matters covered by this title as it may find advisable.

Sec. 217. Penalties

Any person who willfully violates any provision of this title, or any rule, regulation, or order promulgated by the Commission under authority thereof, shall, upon conviction, be fined not more than $10,000, imprisoned for not more than five years, or both.

Sec. 218. Hiring and Leasing Authority of the Commission

The provisions of section 4(b) of the Securities Exchange Act of 1934 shall be applicable with respect to the power of the Commission—

(1) to appoint and fix the compensation of such other employees as may be necessary for carrying out its functions under this title, and

(2) to lease and allocate such real property as may be necessary for carrying out its functions under this title.

Sec. 219. Separability of Provisions

If any provision of this title or the application of such provision to any person or circumstances shall be held invalid, the remainder of the title and the application of such provision to persons or circumstances other than those as to which it is held invalid shall not be affected thereby.

Sec. 220. Short Title

This title may be cited as the "Investment Advisers Act of 1940".

Sec. 221. Effective Date

This title shall become effective on November 1, 1940.

Sec. 222. State Regulation of Investment Advisers

(a) *Jurisdiction of State Regulators.*—Nothing in this title shall affect the jurisdiction of the securities commissioner (or any agency or officer performing like functions) of any State over any security or any person insofar as it does not conflict with the provisions of this title or the rules and regulations thereunder.

(b) *Dual Compliance Purposes.*—No State may enforce any law or regulation that would require an investment adviser to maintain any books or records in addition to those required under the laws of the State in which it maintains its principal place of business, if the investment adviser—

(1) is registered or licensed as such in the State in which it maintains its principal place of business; and

(2) is in compliance with the applicable books and records requirements of the State in which it maintains its principal place of business.

(c) *Limitation on Capital and Bond Requirements.*—No State may enforce any law or regulation that would require an investment adviser to maintain a higher minimum net capital or to post any bond in addition to any that is required under the laws of the State in which it maintains its principal place of business, if the investment adviser—

(1) is registered or licensed as such in the State in which it maintains its principal place of business; and

(2) is in compliance with the applicable net capital or bonding requirements of the State in which it maintains its principal place of business.

(d) *National De Minimis Standard.*—No law of any State or political subdivision thereof requiring the registration, licensing, or qualification as an investment adviser shall require an investment adviser to register with the securities commissioner of the State (or any agency or officer performing like functions) or to comply with such law (other than any provision thereof prohibiting fraudulent conduct) if the investment adviser—

(1) does not have a place of business located within the State; and

(2) during the preceding 12–month period, has had fewer than 6 clients who are residents of that State.

RULES AND REGULATIONS, INVESTMENT ADVISERS ACT OF 1940

(Cite as 17 CFR § 275.__)

§ 275.0–2 General Procedures for Serving Non-Residents

(a) *General procedures for serving process, pleadings, or other papers on non-resident investment advisers, general partners and managing agents.* Under Forms ADV and ADV–NR [17 CFR 279.1 and 279.4], a person may serve process, pleadings, or other papers on a non-resident investment adviser, or on a non-resident general partner or non-resident managing agent of an investment adviser by serving any or all of its appointed agents:

(1) A person may serve a non-resident investment adviser, non-resident general partner, or non-resident managing agent by furnishing the Commission with one copy of the process, pleadings, or papers, for each named party, and one additional copy for the Commission's records.

(2) If process, pleadings, or other papers are served on the Commission as described in this section, the Secretary of the Commission (Secretary) will promptly forward a copy to each named party by registered or certified mail at that party's last address filed with the Commission.

(3) If the Secretary certifies that the Commission was served with process, pleadings, or other papers pursuant to paragraph (a)(1) of this section and forwarded these documents to a named party pursuant to paragraph (a)(2) of this section, this certification constitutes evidence of service upon that party.

(b) *Definitions.* For purposes of this section:

(1) "Managing Agent" means any person, including a trustee, who directs or manages, or who participates in directing or managing, the affairs of any unincorporated organization or association other than a partnership.

(2) "Non-resident" means:

(i) An individual who resides in any place not subject to the jurisdiction of the United States;

(ii) A corporation that is incorporated in or that has its principal office and place of business in any place not subject to the jurisdiction of the United States; and

(iii) A partnership or other unincorporated organization or association that has its principal office and place of business in any place not subject to the jurisdiction of the United States.

(3) "Principal office and place of business" has the same meaning as in § 275.203A–3(c) of this chapter.

§ 275.0–3 References to Rules and Regulations

The term "rules and regulations" refers to all rules and regulations adopted by the Commission pursuant to the Act, including the forms for registration and reports and the accompanying instructions thereto.

§ 275.0–4 General Requirements of Papers and Applications

(a) *Filings.* (1) All papers required to be filed with the Commission shall, unless otherwise provided by the rules and regulations, be delivered through the mails or otherwise to the Securities and Exchange Commission, Washington, DC 20549. Except as otherwise provided by the rules and regulations, such papers shall be deemed to have been filed with the Commission on the date when they are actually received by it.

(2) All filings required to be made electronically with the Investment Adviser Registration Depository ("IARD") shall, unless otherwise provided by the rules and regulations in this part, be deemed to have been filed with the Commission upon acceptance by the IARD. Filings required to be made through the IARD on a day that the IARD is closed shall be considered timely filed with the Commission if filed with the IARD no later than the following business day.

(3) Filings required to be made through the IARD during the period in December of each year that the IARD is not available for submission of filings shall be considered timely filed with the Commission if filed with the IARD no later than the following January 7.

Note to Paragraph (a)(3): Each year the IARD shuts down to filers for several days during the end of December to process renewals of state notice filings and registrations. During this period, advisers are not able to submit filings through the IARD. Check the Commission's Web site at *http://www.sec.gov/iard* for the dates of the annual IARD shutdown.

(b) *Formal Specifications Respecting Applications.* Every application for an order under any provision of the Act, for which a form with instructions is not specifically prescribed, and every amendment to such application, shall be filed in quintuplicate. One copy shall be signed by the applicant, but the other four copies may have facsimile or typed signatures. Such applications shall be on paper no larger than 8½ × 11 inches in size. To the extent that the reduction of larger documents would render them illegible, those documents may be filed on paper larger than 8½ × 11 inches in size. The left margin should be at least 1½ inches wide and, if the application is bound, it should be bound on the left side. All typewritten or printed matter (including deficits in financial statements) should be set forth in black so as to permit photocopying and microfilming.

(c) *Authorization Respecting Applications.*

(1) Every application for an order under any provision of the Act, for which a form with instructions is not specifically prescribed and which is executed by a corporation, partnership, or other company and filed with the Commission, shall contain a concise statement of the applicable provisions of the articles of incorporation, bylaws, or similar documents, relating to the right of the person signing and filing such application to take such action on behalf of the applicant, and a statement that all such requirements have been complied with and that the person signing and filing the same is fully authorized to do so. If such authorization is dependent on resolutions of stockholders, directors, or other bodies, such resolutions shall be attached as an exhibit to, or the pertinent provisions thereof shall be quoted in, the application.

(2) If an amendment to any such application shall be filed, such amendment shall contain a similar statement or, in lieu thereof, shall state that the authorization described in the original application is applicable to the individual who signs such amendment and that such authorization still remains in effect.

(3) When any such application or amendment is signed by an agent or attorney, the power of attorney evidencing his authority to sign shall contain similar statements and shall be filed with the Commission.

(d) *Verification of Applications and Statements of Fact.* Every application for an order under any provision of the Act, for which a form with instructions is not specifically prescribed and every amendment to such application, and every statement of fact formally filed in support of, or in opposition to, any application or declaration shall be verified by the person executing the same. An instrument executed on behalf of a corporation shall be verified in substantially the following form, but suitable changes may be made in such form for other kinds of companies and for individuals:

State of ____________)
) ss.
County of ____________)

The undersigned being duly sworn deposes and says that he has duly executed the attached ________ dated ________, 19__, for and on behalf of ____________ (Name of company); that he is the ____________ (Title of officer) of such company; and that all action by stockholders, directors, and other bodies necessary to authorize deponent to execute and file such instrument has been taken. Deponent further says that he is familiar with such instrument, and the contents thereof, and that the facts therein set forth are true to the best of his knowledge, information and belief.

____
(Signature)

____
(Type or print name beneath)

Subscribed and sworn to before me a ________ this _____ day of ______, 19__.
(Title of Officer)

[Official Seal] ____________________

My commission expires ____________________

(e) *Statement of Grounds for Application.* Each application should contain a brief statement of the reasons why the applicant is deemed to be entitled to the action requested with a reference to the provisions of the Act and of the rules and regulations under which application is made.

(f) *Name and Address.* Every application shall contain the name and address of each applicant and the name and address of any person to whom any applicant wishes any question regarding the application to be directed.

(g) *Proposed Notice.* A proposed notice of the proceeding initiated by the filing of the application shall accompany each application as an exhibit thereto and, if necessary, shall be modified to reflect any amendments to such application.

(h) *Definition of Application.* For purposes of this rule, an "application" means any application for an order of the Commission under the Act other than an application for registration as an investment adviser.

(i) The manually signed original (or in the case of duplicate originals, one duplicate original) of all registrations, applications, statements, reports, or other documents filed under the Investment Advisers Act of 1940, as amended, shall be numbered sequentially (in addition to any internal numbering which otherwise may be present) by handwritten, typed, printed, or other legible form of notation from the facing page of the document through the last page of that document and any exhibits or attachments thereto. Further, the total number of pages contained in a numbered original shall be set forth on the first page of the document.

§ 275.0-5 Procedure With Respect to Applications and Other Matters

The procedure hereinbelow set forth will be followed with respect to any proceeding initiated by the filing of an application, or upon the Commission's own motion, pursuant to any section of the Act or any rule or regulation thereunder, unless in the particular case a different procedure is provided:

(a) Notice of the initiation of the proceeding will be published in the Federal Register and will indicate the earliest date upon which an order disposing of the matter may be entered. The notice will also provide that any interested person may, within the period of time specified therein, submit to the Commission in writing any facts bearing upon the desirability of a hearing on the matter and may request that a hearing be held, stating his reasons therefor and the nature of his interest in the matter.

(b) An order disposing of the matter will be issued as of course following the expiration of the period of time referred to in paragraph (a), unless the Commission thereafter orders a hearing on the matter.

(c) The Commission will order a hearing on the matter, if it appears that a hearing is necessary or appropriate in the public interest or for the protection of investors, (1) upon the request of any interested person or (2) upon its own motion.

(d) *Definition of Application.* For purposes of this rule, an "application" means any application for an order of the Commission under the Act other than an application for registration as an investment adviser.

§ 275.0–6 Incorporation by Reference in Applications

(a) Any person filing an application may, subject to the limitations of § 228.10(f) and § 229.10(d) of this chapter, incorporate by reference as an exhibit to such application any document or part thereof, including any financial statement or part thereof, previously or concurrently filed with the Commission pursuant to any act administered by the Commission. The incorporation may be made whether the matter incorporated was filed by such applicant or any other person. If any modification has occurred in the text of any such document since the filing thereof, the applicant shall file with the reference a statement containing the text of any such modification and the date thereof. If the number of copies of any document previously or concurrently filed with the Commission is less than the number required to be filed with the application which incorporates such document, the applicant shall file therewith as many additional copies of the document as may be necessary to meet the requirements of the application.

(b) Notwithstanding paragraph (a) of this rule, a certificate of an independent public accountant or accountants previously or concurrently filed may not be incorporated by reference in any application unless the written consent of the accountant or accountants to such incorporation is filed with the application.

(c) In each case of incorporation by reference, the matter incorporated shall be clearly identified in the reference. An express statement shall be made to the effect that the specified matter is incorporated in the application at the particular place where the information is required.

(d) Notwithstanding paragraph (a) of this rule, no application shall incorporate by reference any exhibit or financial statement which (1) has been withdrawn, or (2) was filed under any act administered by the Commission in connection with a registration which has ceased to be effective, or (3) is contained in an application for registration, registration statement, or report subject, at the time of the incorporation by reference, to pending proceedings under Section 8(b) or 8(d) of the Securities Act of 1933, Section 8(e) of the Investment Company Act of 1940, Section 15(b)(4)(A) of the Securities Exchange Act of 1934, Section 203(e)(1) of the Act, or to an order entered under any of those Sections.

(e) Notwithstanding paragraph (a) of this rule, the Commission may refuse to permit incorporation by reference in any case in which in its judgment such incorporation would render an application incomplete, unclear, or confusing.

(f) *Definition of Application.* For purposes of this rule, an "application" means any application for an order of the Commission under the Act other than an application for registration as an investment adviser.

NOTE: Prior to incorporating by reference any document as an exhibit to an application, applicants are advised to review § 228.10(d) and § 229.10(d) of this chapter as in effect at the time the application is filed to determine whether such incorporation by reference would be permissible under that rule.

§ 275.0–7 Small Entities under the Investment Advisers Act for Purposes of the Regulatory Flexibility Act

(a) For purposes of Commission rulemaking in accordance with the provisions of Chapter Six of the Administrative Procedure Act [5 U.S.C. 601] and unless otherwise defined for purposes of a particular rulemaking proceeding, the term of a particular rulemaking proceeding, the term "small business" or "small organization" for purposes of the Investment

Advisers Act of 1940 means an investment adviser that:

(1) Has assets under management, as defined under Section 203A(a)(2) of the Act (15 U.S.C. 80b–3a(a)(2)) and reported on its annual updating amendment to Form ADV [17 CFR 279.1], of less that $25 million, or such higher amount as the Commission may by rule deem appropriate under Section 203A(a)(1)(A) of the Act (15 U.S.C. 80b–3a(a)(1)(A));

(2) Did not have total assets of $5 million or more on the last day of the most recent fiscal year; and

(3) Does not control, is not controlled by, and is not under common control with another investment adviser that has assets under management of $25 million or more (or such higher amount as the Commission may deem appropriate), or any person (other than a natural person) that had total assets of $5 million or more on the last day of the most recent fiscal year.

(b) For purposes of this section:

(1) "Control" means the power, directly or indirectly, to direct the management or policies of a person, whether through ownership of securities, by contract, or otherwise.

(i) A person is presumed to control a corporation if the person:

(A) Directly or indirectly has the right to vote 25 percent or more of a class of the corporation's voting securities; or

(B) Has the power to sell or direct the sale of 25 percent or more of a class of a class of the corporation's voting securities.

(ii) A person is presumed to control a partnership if the person has the right to receive upon dissolution, or has contributed, 25 percent or more of the capital of the partnership.

(iii) A person is presumed to control a limited liability company (LLC) if the person:

(A) Directly or indirectly has the right to vote 25 percent or more of a class of the interests of the LLC;

(B) Has the right to receive upon dissolution, or has contributed 25 percent or more of the capital of the LLC; or

(C) Is an elected manager of the LLC.

(iv) A person is presumed to control a trust if the person is a trustee or managing agent of the trust.

(2) *Total assets* means the total assets as shown on the balance sheet of the investment adviser or other person described above under paragraph (a)(3) of this section, or the balance sheet of the investment adviser or such other person with its subsidiaries consolidated, whichever is larger.

§ 275.202(a)(1)–1 Certain Transactions Not Deemed Assignments

A transaction which does not result in a change of actual control or management of an investment adviser is not an assignment for purposes of section 205(a)(2) of the Act.

§ 275.202(a)(11)T Temporary Rule Regarding Certain Broker-Dealers.

(a) A broker or dealer registered with the Commission under section 15 of the Securities Exchange Act of 1934 (15 U.S.C. 78a) (the "Exchange Act"):

(1) Will not be deemed to be an investment adviser based solely on its receipt of special compensation, provided that:

(i) The broker or dealer does not exercise investment discretion, at that term is defined in section 3(a)(35) of the Exchange Act (15 U.S.C. 78c(a)(35)), over accounts from which it receives special compensation; and

(ii) Any investment advice provided by the broker or dealer with respect to accounts from which it receives special compensation is solely incidental to the brokerage services provided to those accounts; and

(2) Will not be deemed to have received special compensation solely because the broker or dealer charges a commission, mark-up, mark-down or similar fee for brokerage services that is greater than or less than one it charges another customer.

(b) A broker or dealer registered with the Commission under section 15 of the Exchange Act is an investment adviser solely with respect to those accounts for which it provides services or receives compensation that subject the broker or dealer to the Advisers Act.

(c) The temporary section shall expire on April 15, 2005.

§ 275.203–1 Application for Investment Adviser Registration

(a) *Form ADV.* To apply for registration with the Commission as an investment adviser, you must complete and file Form ADV [17 CFR 279.1] by following the instructions in the Form.

(b) *Electronic filing.*

(1) If you apply for registration after January 1, 2001, you must file electronically with the Investment Adviser Registration Depository (IARD), unless you have received a hardship exemption under § 275.203–3.

Note to Paragraph (b)(1): Information on how to file with the IARD is available on the Commission's website at<http://www.sec.gov/iard>.

(2) You are not required to file with the Commission a copy of Part II of Form ADV if you maintain a copy of your Part II (and any brochure you deliver to clients) in your files. The copy maintained in your files in considered filed with the Commission.

Note to Paragraph (b)(2): The Commission has proposed, but not adopted, substantial changes to Part II of Form ADV. Thus, the rules for preparing, delivering, and offering Part II (or a brochure containing at least the information contained in Part II) have not changed. If you are an SEC-registered adviser, however, you no longer have to file Part II with the Commission. Instead, you must keep a copy in your files, and update the information in your Part II whenever it becomes materially inaccurate. If you are a State-registered adviser, State law may continue to require you to file Part II with the appropriate State securities authority on paper, regardless of whether you are filing Part I on paper or through the IARD.

(c) *When filed.* Each Form ADV is considered filed with the Commission upon acceptance by the IARD.

(d) *Filing fees.* You must pay NASD (the operator of the IARD) a filing fee. The Commission has approved the amount of the filing fee. No portion of the filing fee is refundable. Your completed application for registration will not be considered filed with the Commission until you have paid the filing fee.

§ 275.203–2 Withdrawal from Investment Adviser Registration

(a) *Form ADV–W.* You must file Form ADV–W [17 CFR 279.2] to withdraw from investment adviser registration with the Commission (or to withdraw a pending registration application).

(b) *Electronic filing.* Once you have filed your Form ADV [17 CFR 279.1] (or any amendments to Form ADV) electronically with the investment Adviser Registration Depository (IARD), any Form ADV–W you file must be filed with the IARD, unless you have received a hardship exemption under § 275.203–3.

(c) *Effective date—upon filing.* Each Form ADV–W filed under this section is effective upon acceptance by the IARD, provided however that your investment adviser registration will continue for a period of sixty days after acceptance solely for the purpose of commencing a proceeding under section 203(e) of the Act [15 U.S.C. 80b–3(e)].

(d) *Filing fees.* You do not have to pay a fee to file Form ADV–W through the IARD.

(e) *Form ADV–W is a report.* Each Form ADV–W required to be filed under this section is a "report" within the meaning of sections 204 and 207 of the Act [15 U.S.C. 80b–4 and 80b–7].

§ 275.203–3 Hardship Exemptions

This section provides two "hardship exemptions" from the requirement to make Advisers Act filings electronically with the Investment Adviser Registration Depository (IARD).

(a) *Temporary hardship exemption.*

(1) *Eligibility for exemption.* If you are registered with the Commission as an investment adviser and submit electronic filings on the Investment Adviser Registration Depository (IARD) system, but have unanticipated technical difficulties that prevent you from submitting a filing to the IARD system, you may request a temporary hardship exemption from the requirements of this chapter to file electronically.

(2) *Application procedures.* To request a temporary hardship exemption, you must:

(i) File Form ADV–H [17 CFR 279.3] in paper format with NASD no later than one business day after the filing that is the subject of the ADV–H was due; and

(ii) Submit the filing that is the subject of the Form ADV–H in electronic format with the IARD no later than seven business days after the filing was due.

(3) *Effective date—upon filing.* The temporary hardship exemption will be granted when you file a completed Form ADV–H with NASD.

(b) *Continuing hardship exemption.*

(1) *Eligibility for exemption.* If you are a "small business" (as described in paragraph (b)(5) of this section), you may apply for a continuing hardship exemption. The period of the exemption may be no longer than one year after the date on which you apply for the exemption.

(2) *Application procedures.* To apply for a continuing hardship exemption, you must file Form ADV–H with NASD at least ten business days before a filing is due. The Commission will grant or deny your application within ten business days after you file Form ADV–H.

(3) *Effective state—upon approval.* You are not exempt from the electronic filing requirements until and unless the Commission approves your application. If the Commission approves your application, you may submit your filings to NASD in paper format for the period of time for which the exemption is granted.

(4) *Criteria for exemption.* Your application will be granted only if you are able to demonstrate that the electronic filing requirements of this chapter are prohibitively burdensome or expensive.

(5) *Small business.* You are a "small business" for purposes of this section if you are required to answer Item 12 of Form ADV [17 CRF 279.1] and checked "no" to each question in Item 12 that you were required to answer.

Note to Paragraphs (a) and (b): NASD will charge you an additional fee covering its cost to convert to electronic format a filing made in reliance on a continuing hardship exemption.

§ 275.203(b)(3)–1 Definition of "Client" of an Investment Adviser

Preliminary Note to § 275.203(b)(3)–1. This section is a safe harbor and is not intended to specify the exclusive method for determining who may be deemed a single client for purposes of section 203(b)(3) of the Act. Under paragraph (b)(6) of this section, the safe harbor is not available with respect to private funds.

(a) General. You may deem the following to be a single client for purposes of section 203(b)(3) of the Act (15 U.S.C. 80b–3(b)(3)):

(1) A natural person, and:

(i) Any minor child of the natural person;

(ii) Any relative, spouse, or relative of the spouse of the natural person who has the same principal residence;

(iii) All accounts of which the natural person and/or the persons referred to in this paragraph (a)(1) are the only primary beneficiaries; and

(iv) All trusts of which the natural person and/or the persons referred to in this paragraph (a)(1) are the only primary beneficiaries;

(2)(i) A corporation, general partnership, limited partnership, limited liability company, trust (other than a trust referred to in paragraph (a)(1)(iv) of this section), or other legal organization (any of which are referred to hereinafter as a ''legal organization'') to which you provide investment advice based on its investment objectives rather than the individual investment objectives of its shareholders, partners, limited partners, members, or beneficiaries (any of which are referred to hereinafter as an ''owner''); and

(ii) Two or more legal organizations referred to in paragraph (a)(2)(i) of this section that have identical owners.

(b) Special rules. For purposes of this section:

(1) You must count an owner as a client if you provide investment advisory services to the owner separate and apart from the investment advisory services you provide to the legal organization, provided, however, that the determination that an owner is a client will not affect the applicability of this section with regard to any other owner;

(2) You are not required to count an owner as a client solely because you, on behalf of the legal organization, offer, promote, or sell interests in the legal organization to the owner, or report periodically to the owners as a group solely with respect to the performance of or plans for the legal organization's assets or similar matters;

(3) A limited partnership or limited liability company is a client of any general partner, managing member or other person acting as investment adviser to the partnership or limited liability company;

(4) You are not required to count as a client any person for whom you provide investment advisory services without compensation;

(5) If you have your principal office and place of business outside the United States, you are not required to count clients that are not United States residents, but if your principal office and place of business is in the United States, you must count all clients;

(6) You may not rely on paragraph (a)(2)(i) of this section with respect to any private fund as defined in paragraph (d) of this section; and

(7) For purposes of paragraph (b)(5) of this section, a client who is an owner of a private fund is a resident of the place at which the client resides at the time of the client's investment in the fund.

(c) Holding out. If you are relying on this section, you shall not be deemed to be holding yourself out generally to the public as an investment adviser, within the meaning of section 203(b)(3) of the Act (15 U.S.C. 80b–3(b)(3)), solely because you participate in a non-public offering of interests in a limited partnership under the Securities Act of 1933.

(d) Private fund.

(1) A private fund is a company:

(i) That would be an investment company under section 3(a) of the Investment Company Act of 1940 (15 U.S.C. 80a–3(a)) but for the exception provided from that definition by either section 3(c)(1) or section 3(c)(7) of such Act (15 U.S.C. 80a–3(c)(1) or (7));

(ii) That permits its owners to redeem any portion of their ownership interests within two years of the purchase of such interests; and

(iii) Interests in which are or have been offered based on the investment advisory skills, ability or expertise of the investment adviser.

(2) Notwithstanding paragraph (d)(1) of this section, a company is not a private fund if it permits its owners to redeem their ownership interests within two years of the purchase of such interests only in the case of:

(i) Events you find after reasonable inquiry to be extraordinary; and

(ii) Interests acquired through reinvestment of distributed capital gains or income.

(3) Notwithstanding paragraph (d)(1) of this section, a company is not a private fund if it has its principal office and place of business outside the United States, makes a public offering of its securities in a country other than the United States, and is regulated as a public investment company under the laws of the country other than the United States.

§ 275.203(b)(3)–2 Methods for Counting Clients in Certain Private Funds

(a) For purposes of section 203(b)(3) of the Act (15 U.S.C. 80b–3(b)(3)), you must count as clients the shareholders, limited partners, members, or beneficiaries (any of which are referred to hereinafter as an "owner") of a private fund as defined in paragraph (d) of section 275.203(b)(3)–1, unless such owner is your advisory firm or a person described in paragraph (d)(1)(iii) of section 275.205–3.

(b) If you provide investment advisory services to a private fund in which an investment company registered under the Investment Company Act of 1940 (15 U.S.C. 80a–1 to 80a–64) is, directly or indirectly, an owner, you must count the owners of that investment company as clients for purposes of section 203(b)(3) of the Act (15 U.S.C. 80b–3(b)(3)).

(c) If you have your principal office and place of business outside the United States, you may treat a private fund that is organized or incorporated under the laws of a country other than the United States as your client for all purposes under the Act, other than sections 203, 204, 206(1) and 206(2) (15 U.S.C. 80b–3, 80b–4, 80b–6(1) and (2)).

§ 275.203A–1 Eligibility for SEC Registration: Switching to or from SEC Registration

(a) Eligibility for SEC registration.

(1) *Threshold for SEC registration—$30 million of assets under management.* If the State where you maintain your principal office and place of business has enacted an investment adviser statute, you are not required to register with the Commission, unless:

(i) You have assets under management of at least $30,000,000, as reported on your Form ADV [17 CFR 279.1]; or

(ii) You are an investment adviser to an investment company registered under the Investment Company Act of 1940 [15 U.S.C. 80a–1].

(2) *Exemption for Investment Advisers having between $25 and $30 million of assets under management.* If the State where you maintain your principal office and place of business has enacted an investment adviser statute, you may register with the Commission if you have assets under management of at least $25,000,000 but less than $30,000,000, as reported on your Form ADV [17 CFR 279.1]. This paragraph (a)(2) shall not apply if:

(i) You are an investment adviser to an investment company registered under the Investment Company Act of 1940 [15 U.S.C. 80a–1 to 80a–64]; or

(ii) You are eligible for an exemption described in § 275.203A–2 of this chapter.

Note to Paragraphs (a)(1) and (a)(2):

Paragraphs (a)(1) and (a)(2) of this section together make SEC registration optional for certain investment advisers that have between $25 and $30 million of assets under management.

(B) *Switching to or from SEC registration.*

(1) *State-registered advisers—switching to SEC registration.* If you are registered with a State securities authority, you must apply for registration with the Commission within 90 days of filing an annual updating amendment to your Form ADV reporting that you have at least $30 million of assets under management.

(2) *SEC-registered advisers—switching to State registration.* If you are registered with the Commission and file an annual updating amendment to your Form ADV reporting that you no longer have $25 million of assets under management (or are not otherwise eligible for SEC registration), you must file Form ADV–W [17 CFR 279.2] to withdraw your SEC registration within 180 days of your fiscal year end (unless you then have at least $25 million of assets under management or are otherwise eligible for SEC registration). During this period while you are registered with both the Commission and one or more State securities authorities, the Investment Advisers Act of 1940 and applicable State law will apply to your advisory activities.

§ 275.203A–2 Exemptions from Prohibition on SEC Registration

The prohibition of section 203A(a) of the Act [15 U.S.C. 80b–3a(a)] does not apply to:

(a) *Nationally recognized statistical rating organizations.* An investment adviser that is a nationally recognized statistical rating organization, as that term is used in paragraphs (c)(2)(vi)(E), (F), and (H) of § 240.15c3–1 of this chapter.

(b) *Pension Consultants.* (1) An investment adviser that is a "pension consultant," as defined in this section, with respect to assets of plans having an aggregate value of at least $50,000,000.

(2) An investment adviser is a pension consultant, for purposes of paragraph (b) of this section, if the investment adviser provides investment advice to:

(i) Any employee benefit plan described in section 3(3) of the Employee Retirement Income Security Act of 1974 ("ERISA") (29 U.S.C. 1002(3)):

(ii) Any governmental plan described in section 3(32) of ERISA (29 U.S.C. 1002(32)); or

(iii) Any church plan described in section 3(33) of ERISA (29 U.S.C. 1002(33));

(3) In determining the aggregate value of assets of plans, include only that portion of a plan's assets for which the investment adviser provided investment advise (including any advice with respect to the selection of an investment adviser to manage such assets). Determine the aggregate value of assets by cumulating the value of assets of plans with respect to which the investment adviser was last employed or retained by contract to provide investment advice during a 12–month period ended within 90 days of filing Schedule I to Form ADV (17 CFR 279.1).

(c) *Investment advisers controlling, controlled by, or under common control with an investment adviser registered with the Commission.* An investment adviser that controls, is controlled by, or is under common control with, an investment adviser eligible to register and registered with, the Commission ("registered adviser"), provided that the principal office and place of business of the investment adviser is the same as that of the registered adviser. For purposes of this paragraph, control means the power to direct or cause the direction of the management or policies of an investment adviser, whether through ownership of securities, by contract, or otherwise. Any person that directly or indirectly has the right to vote 25 percent or more of the voting securities, or is entitled to 25 percent or more of the profits, of an investment adviser is presumed to control that investment adviser.

(d) *Investment advisers expecting to be eligible for SEC registration within 120 days.* An investment adviser that:

(1) Immediately before it registers with the Commission, is not registered or required to be registered with the Commission or a securities commissioner (or any agency or officer performing like functions) of any State and has a reasonable expectation that it would be eligible to register with the Commission within 120 days after the date the investment adviser's registration with the Commission becomes effective;

(2) Indicates on Schedule D of its Form ADV [17 CFR 279.1] that it will withdraw from registration with the Commission if, on the 120th day after the date the investment adviser's registration with the Commission becomes effective, the investment adviser would be prohibited by section 203A(a) of the Act [15 U.S.C. 80b–3a(a)] from registering with the Commission; and

(3) Notwithstanding § 275.203A–1(b)(2) of this chapter, files a completed Form ADV–W [17 CFR 279.2] withdrawing from registration with the Commission within 120 days after the date the investment adviser's registration with the Commission becomes effective.

(e) *Multi–State investment advisers.* An investment adviser that:

(1) Upon submission of its application for registration with the Commission, is required by the laws of 30 or more States to register as an investment adviser with the securities commissioners (or any agencies or officers performing like functions) in the respective States, and thereafter would, but for this section, be required by the laws of at least 25 States to register as an investment adviser with the securities commissioners (or any agencies or officers performing like functions) in the respective States;

(2) Indicates on Schedule D of its Form ADV that the investment adviser has reviewed the applicable State and federal laws and has concluded that, in the case of an application for registration with the Commission, it is required by the laws of 30 or more States to register as an investment adviser with the State securities authorities in the respective States or, in the case of an amendment to Form ADV, it would be required by the laws of at least 25 States to register as an investment adviser with the State securities authorities in the respective States, within 90 days prior to the date of filing Form ADV;

(3) Undertakes on Schedule D of its Form ADV to withdraw from registration with the Commission if the adviser indicates on an annual updating amendment to Form ADV that the investment adviser would be required by the laws of fewer than 25 States to register as an investment adviser with the securities commissioners (or any agencies or officers performing like functions) in the respective States, and that the investment adviser would be prohibited by section 203A(a) of the Act [15 U.S.C. 80b–3a(a)] from registering with the Commission, by filing a completed Form ADV–W within 180 days of the adviser's fiscal year end (unless the adviser than has at least $25 million of assets under management or is otherwise eligible for SEC registration); and

(4) Maintains in an easily accessible place a record of the States in which the investment adviser has determined it would, but for the exemption, be required to register for a period of not less than five years from the filing of a Form ADV that includes a representation that is based on such record.

(f) *Internet investment advisers.*

(1) An investment adviser that:

(i) Provides investment advice to all of its clients exclusively through an interactive website, except that the investment adviser may provide investment advice to fewer than 15 clients through other means during the preceding twelve months;

(ii) Maintains, in an easily accessible place, for a period of not less than five years from the filing of a Form ADV that includes a representation that the adviser is eligible to register with the Commission under paragraph (f) of this section, a record demonstrating that it provides investment advise to it clients exclusively through an interactive website in accordance with the limits in paragraph (f)(1)(i) of this section; and

(iii) Does not control, is not controlled by, and is not under common control with, another investment adviser that registers with the Commission under paragraph (c) of this section solely in reliance on the adviser registered under paragraph (f) of this section as its *registered adviser*.

(2) For purposes of paragraph (f) of this section, *interactive website* means a website in which computer software-based models or applications provide investment advice to clients based on personal information each client supplies through the website.

(3) An investment adviser may rely on the definition of *client* in § 275.203(b)(3)–1 in determining whether it provides investment advice to fewer than 15 clients under paragraph (f)(1)(i) of this section.

§ 275.203A–3 Definitions

For purposes of section 203A of the Act (15 U.S.C. 80b–3a) and the rules thereunder:

(a)(1) *Investment adviser representative.* "Investment adviser representative" of an investment adviser means a supervised person of the investment adviser:

(i) Who has more than five clients who are natural persons (other than excepted persons described in paragraph (a)(3)(i) of this section); and

(ii) More than ten percent of whose clients are natural persons (other than excepted persons described in paragraph (a)(3)(i) of this section).

(2) Notwithstanding paragraph (a)(1) of this section, a supervised person is not an investment adviser representative if the supervised person:

(i) Does not on a regular basis solicit, meet with, or otherwise communicate with clients of the investment adviser; or

(ii) Provides only impersonal investment advice.

(3) For purposes of this section:

(i) "Excepted person" means a natural person who is a qualified client as described in § 275.205–3(d)(1).

(ii) "Impersonal investment advice" means investment advisory services provided by means of written material or oral statements that do not purport to meet the objectives or needs of specific individuals or accounts.

(4) Supervised persons may rely on the definition of "client" in section 275.203(b)(3)–1, without giving regard to paragraph (b)(6) of that section, to identify clients for purposes of paragraph (a)(1) of this section, except that supervised persons need not count clients that are not residents of the United States.

(b) Place of business. "Place of business" of an investment adviser representative means:

(1) An office at which the investment adviser representative regularly provides investment advisory services, solicits, meets with, or otherwise communicates with clients; and

(2) Any other location that is held out to the general public as a location at which the investment adviser representative provides investment advisory services,

solicits, meets with, or otherwise communicates with clients.

(c) Principal office and place of business. "Principal office and place of business" of an investment adviser means the executive office of the investment adviser from which the officers, partners, or managers of the investment adviser direct, control, and coordinate the activities of the investment adviser.

§ 275.203A-4 Investment Advisers Registered With a State Securities Commission

The Commission shall not assert a violation of section 203 of the Act (15 U.S.C. 80b-3) (or any provision of the Act to which an investment adviser becomes subject upon registration under section 203 of the Act (15 U.S.C. 80b-3)) for the failure of an investment adviser registered with the securities commission (or any agency or office performing like functions) in the State in which it has its principal office and place of business to register with the Commission if the investment adviser reasonably believes that it does not have assets under management of at least $30,000,000 and is therefore not required to register with the Commission.

§ 275.204-1 Amendments to Application for Registration

(a) *When amendment is required.* You must amend your Form ADV [17 CFR 279.1]:

(1) At least annually, within 90 days of the end of your fiscal year; and

(2) More frequently, if required by the instructions to Form ADV.

Note to Paragraph (a): Information on how to file with the Investment Adviser Registration Depository ("IARD") is available on our website at *www.sec.gov/iard.*

(b) *Electronic filing of amendments.*

(1) You must file all amendments to Part 1A of your Form ADV electronically with the IARD, unless you have received a continuing hardship exemption under § 275.203-3.

(2) If you have received a continuing hardship exemption under § 275.203-3, you must, when you are required to amend your Form ADV, file a completed Part 1A of Form ADV on paper with the SEC by mailing it to the NASD.

(c) *Special rule for Part II.* You are not required to file with the Commission a copy of Part II of Form ADV if you maintain a copy of your Part II (and any brochure you deliver to clients) in your files. The copy maintained in your files is considered filed with the Commission.

Note to Paragraph (c): The Commission has proposed, but not adopted, substantial changes to Part II of Form ADV. Thus, the rules for preparing, delivering, and offering Part II (or a brochure containing at least the information contained in Part II) have not changed. If you are an SEC-registered adviser, however, you no longer have to file Part II with the Commission. Instead, you must keep a copy in your files, and update the information in your Part II whenever it becomes materially inaccurate. If you are a State-registered adviser, State law may continue to require you to file Part II with the appropriate State securities authority on paper, regardless of whether you are filing Part I on paper or through the IARD.

(d) *Filing fees.* You must pay the NASD (the operator of the IARD) an initial filing fee when you first electronically file Part 1A of Form ADV. After you pay the initial filing fee, you must pay an annual filing fee each time you file your annual updating amendment. No portion of either fee is refundable. The Commission has approved the filing fees. Your amended Form ADV will not be accepted by NASDR, and thus will not be accepted by NASDR, and thus will not be considered filed with the Commission, until you have paid the filing fee.

(e) *Amendments to Form ADV are reports.* Each amendment required to be filed under this section is a "report" within the meaning of sections 204 and 207 of the Act [15 U.S.C. 80b-4 and 80b-7].

§ 275.204-2 Books and Records to Be Maintained by Investment Advisers

(a) Every investment adviser registered or required to be registered under section 203 of the Act (15 U.S.C. 80b-3) shall make and keep true, accurate and current the following books and records relating to its investment advisory business:

(1) A journal or journals, including cash receipts and disbursements, records, and any other records of original entry forming the basis of entries in any ledger.

(2) General and auxiliary ledgers (or other comparable records) reflecting asset, liability, reserve, capital, income and expense accounts.

(3) A memorandum of each other given by the investment adviser for the purchase or sale of any security, of any instruction received by the investment adviser concerning the purchase, sale, receipt or delivery of a particular security, and of any modification or cancellation of any such order or instruction. Such memoranda shall show the terms and conditions of the order, instruction, modification or cancellation; shall identify the person connected with the investment adviser who recommended the transaction to the client and the person who placed such order; and shall show the account for which entered, the date of entry, and the bank, broker or dealer by or through whom executed where appropriate. Orders entered pursuant to the exercise of discretionary power shall be so designated.

(4) All check books, bank statements, cancelled checks and cash reconciliations of the investment adviser.

(5) All bills or statements (or copies thereof), paid or unpaid, relating to the business of the investment adviser as such.

(6) All trial balances, financial statements, and internal audit working papers relating to the business of such investment adviser.

(7) Originals of all written communications received and copies of all written communications sent by such investment adviser relating to (i) any recommendation made or proposed to be made and any advice given or proposed to be given, (ii) any receipt, disbursement or delivery of funds or securities, or (iii) the placing or execution of any order to purchase or sell any security: *Provided, however,* (*a*) That the investment adviser shall not be required to keep any unsolicited market letters and other similar communications of general public distribution not prepared by or for the investment adviser, and (*b*) that if the investment adviser sends any notice, circular or other advertisement offering any report, analysis, publication or other investment advisory service to more than 10 persons, the investment adviser shall not be required to keep a record of the names and addresses of the persons to whom it was sent; except that if such notice, circular or advertisement is distributed to persons named on any list, the investment adviser shall retain with the copy of such notice, circular or advertisement a memorandum describing the list and the source thereof.

(8) A list or other record of all accounts in which the investment adviser is vested with any discretionary power with respect to the funds, securities or transactions of any client.

(9) All powers of attorney and other evidences of the granting of any discretionary authority by any client to the investment adviser, or copies thereof.

(10) All written agreements (or copies thereof) entered into by the investment adviser with any client or otherwise relating to the business of such investment adviser as such.

(11) A copy of each notice, circular, advertisement, newspaper article, investment letter, bulletin or other communication that

the investment adviser circulates or distributes, directly or indirectly, to 10 or more persons (other than persons connected with such investment adviser), and if such notice, circular, advertisement, newspaper article, investment letter, bulletin, or other communication recommends the purchase or sale of a specific security and does not state the reasons for such recommendation, a memorandum of the investment adviser indicating the reasons therefor.

(12)(i) A copy of the investment adviser's code of ethics adopted and implemented pursuant to § 275.204A–1 that is in effect, or at any time within the past five years was in effect;

(ii) A record of any violation of the code of ethics, and of any action taken as a result of the violation; and

(iii) A record of all written acknowledgments as required by § 275.204A–1(a)(5) for each person who is currently, or within the past five years was, a supervised person of the investment adviser.

(13)(i) A record of each report made by an access person as required by § 275.204A–1(b), including any information provided under paragraph (b)(3)(iii) of that section in lieu of such reports;

(ii) A record of the names of persons who are currently, or within the past five years were, access persons of the investment adviser; and

(iii) A record of any decision, and the reasons supporting the decision, to approve the acquisition of securities by access persons under § 275.204A–1(c), for at least five years after the end of the fiscal year in which the approval is granted.

(14) A copy of each written statement and each amendment or revision thereof, given or sent to any client or prospective client of such investment adviser in accordance with the provisions of Rule 204–3 under the Act, and a record of the dates that each written statement, and each amendment or revision thereof, was given, or offered to be given, to any client or prospective client who subsequently becomes a client.

(15) All written acknowledgements of receipt obtained from clients pursuant to § 275.206(4)–3(a)(2)(iii)(B) of this chapter and copies of the disclosure documents delivered to clients by solicitors pursuant to § 275.206(4)–3 of this chapter.

(16) All accounts, books, internal working papers, and any other records or documents that are necessary to form the basis for or demonstrate the calculation of the performance or rate of return of any or all managed accounts or securities recommendations in any notice, circular, advertisement, newspaper article, investment letter, bulletin or other communication that the investment adviser circulates or distributes, directly or indirectly, to 10 or more persons. (other than persons connected with such investment adviser); provided, however, that, with respect to the performance of managed accounts, the retention of all account statements, if they reflect all debits, credits, and other transactions in a client's account for the period of the statement, and all worksheets necessary to demonstrate the calculation of the performance or rate of return of all managed accounts shall be deemed to satisfy the requirements of this paragraph.

(17)(i) A copy of the investment adviser's policies and procedures formulated pursuant to § 275.206(4)–7(a) of this chapter that are in effect, or at any time within the past five years were in effect, and

(ii) Any records documenting the investment adviser's annual review of those policies and procedures conducted pursuant to § 275.206(4)–7(b) of this chapter.

(b) If an investment adviser subject to paragraph (a) of this section has custody or possession of securities or funds of any client, the records required to be made and kept under paragraph (a) of this section shall include:

(1) A journal or other record showing all purchases, sales, receipts and deliveries of securities (including certificate numbers) for such accounts and all other debits and credits to such accounts.

(2) A separate ledger account for each such client showing all purchases, sales, receipts and deliveries of securities, the date and price of each purchase and sale, and all debits and credits.

(3) Copies of confirmations of all transactions effected by or for the account of any such client.

(4) A record for each security in which any such client has a position, which record shall show the name of each such client having any interest in such security, the amount or interest of each such client, and the location of each such security.

(c)(1) Every investment adviser subject to paragraph (a) of this section who renders any investment supervisory or management service to any client shall, with respect to the portfolio being supervised or managed and to the extent that the information is reasonably available to or obtainable by the investment adviser, make and keep true, accurate and current:

(i) Records showing separately for each such client the securities purchased and sold, and the date, amount and price of each such purchase and sale.

(ii) For each security in which any such client has a current position, information from which the investment adviser can promptly furnish the name of each such client, and the current amount or interest of such client.

(2) Every investment adviser subject to paragraph (a) of this section that exercises voting authority with respect to client securities shall, with respect to those clients, make and retain the following:

(i) Copies of all policies and procedures by §275.206(4)–6.

(ii) A copy of each proxy statement that the investment adviser receives regarding client securities. An investment adviser may satisfy this requirement by relying on a third party to make and retain, on the investment adviser's behalf, a copy of a proxy statement (provided that the adviser has obtained an undertaking from the third party to provide a copy of the proxy statement promptly upon request) or may rely on obtaining a copy of a proxy statement from the Commission's Electronic Data Gathering, Analysis, and Retrieval (EDGAR) system.

(iii) A record of each vote cast by the investment adviser on behalf of a client. An investment adviser may satisfy this requirement by relying on a third party to make and retain, on the investment adviser's behalf, a record of the vote cast (provided that the adviser has obtained an undertaking from the third party to provide a copy of the record promptly upon request).

(iv) A copy of any document created by the adviser that was material to making a decision how to vote proxies on behalf of a client or that memorializes the basis for that decision.

(v) A copy of each written client request for information on how the adviser voted proxies on behalf of the client, and a copy of any written response by the investment adviser to any (written or oral) client request for information on how the adviser voted proxies on behalf of the requesting client.

(d) Any books or records required by this section may be maintained by the investment adviser in such manner that the identity of any client to whom such investment adviser renders investment supervisory services is indicated by numerical or alphabetical code or some similar designation.

(e)(1) All books and records required to be made under the provisions of paragraphs (a) to (c)(1)(i), inclusive, and (c)(2) of this section (except for books and records required to be made under the provisions of paragraphs (a)(11), (a)(12)(i), (a)(12)(iii), (a)(13)(ii), (a)(13)(iii), (a)(16), and (a)(17)(i) of this section), shall be maintained and preserved in an easily accessible place for a period of not less than five years from the end of the fiscal year during which the last entry was made on such record, the first two years in an appropriate office of the investment adviser.

(2) Partnership articles and any amendments thereto, articles of incorporation, charters, minute books, and stock certificate books of the investment adviser and of any predecessor, shall be maintained in the principal office of the investment adviser and preserved until at least three years after termination of the enterprise.

(3)(i) Books and records required to be made under the provisions of paragraphs (a)(11) and (a)(16) of this rule shall be maintained and preserved in an easily accessible place for a period of not less than five years, the first two years in an appropriate office of the investment adviser, from the end of the fiscal year during which the investment adviser last published or otherwise disseminated, directly or indirectly, the notice, circular, advertisement, newspaper article, investment letter, bulletin or other communication.

(ii) *Transition rule.* If you are an investment adviser to a private fund as that term is defined in § 275.203(b)(3)–1, and you were exempt from registration under section 203(b)(3) of the Act (15 U.S.C. 80b–3(b)(3)) prior to February 10, 2005, paragraph (e)(3)(i) of this section does not require you to maintain or preserve books and records that would otherwise be required to be maintained or preserved under the provisions of paragraph (a)(16) of this section to the extent those books and records pertain to the performance or rate of return of such private fund or other account you advise for any period ended prior to February 10, 2005, provided that you were not registered with the Commission as an investment adviser during such period, and provided further that you continue to preserve any books and records in your possession that pertain to the performance or rate of return of such private fund or other account for such period.

(f) An investment adviser subject to paragraph (a) of this section, before ceasing to conduct or discontinuing business as an investment adviser shall arrange for and be responsible for the preservation of the books and records required to be maintained and preserved under this section for the remainder of the period specified in this section, and shall notify the Commission in writing, at its principal office, Washington, D.C., 20549, of the exact address where such books and records will be maintained during such period.

(g) *Micrographic and electronic storage permitted.*—(1) *General.* The records required to be maintained and preserved pursuant to this part may be maintained and preserved for the required time by an investment adviser on:

(i) Micrographic media, including microfilm, microfiche, or any similar medium; or

(ii) Electronic storage media, including any digital storage medium or system that meets the terms of this section.

(2) *General requirements.* The investment adviser must:

(i) Arrange and index the records in a way that permits easy location, access, and retrieval of any particular record;

(ii) Provide promptly any of the following that the Commission (by its examiners or other representatives) may request:

(A) A legible, true, and complete copy of the record in the medium and format in which it is stored;

(B) A legible, true, and complete printout of the record; and

(C) Means to access, view, and print the records; and

(iii) Separately store, for the time required for preservation of the original record, a duplicate copy of the record on any medium allowed by this section.

(3) *Special requirements for electronic storage media.* In the case of records on electronic storage media, the investment adviser must establish and maintain procedures:

(i) To maintain and preserve the records, so as to reasonably safeguard them from loss, alteration, or destruction;

(ii) To limit access to the records to properly authorized personnel and the Commission (including its examiners and other representatives); and

(iii) To reasonably ensure that any reproduction of a non-electronic original record on electronic storage media is complete, true, and legible when retrieved.

(h)(1) Any book or other record made, kept, maintained and preserved in compliance with §§ 240.17a–3 and 240.17a–4 of this chapter under the Securities Exchange Act of 1934, which is substantially the same as the book or other record required to be made, kept, maintained and preserved under this section, shall be deemed to be made, kept, maintained and preserved in compliance with this section.

(2) A record made and kept pursuant to any provision of paragraph (a) of this section, which contains all the information required under any other provision of paragraph (a) of this section, need not be maintained in duplicate in order to meet the requirements of the other provision of paragraph (a) of this section.

(i) As used in this section the term "discretionary power" shall not include discretion as to the price at which or the time when a transaction is or is to be effected, if, before the order is given by the investment adviser, the client has directed or approved the purchase or sale of a definite amount of the particular security.

(j)(1) Except as provided in paragraph (j)(3) hereof, each non-resident investment adviser registered or applying for registration pursuant to Section 203 of the Act shall keep, maintain and preserve, at a place within the United States designated in a notice from him as provided in paragraph (j)(2) of this section true, correct, complete and current copies of books and records which he is required to make, keep current, maintain or preserve pursuant to any provision of any rule or regulation of the Commission adopted under the Act.

(2) Except as provided in paragraph (j)(3) of this section, each nonresident investment adviser subject to this paragraph (j) shall furnish to the Commission a written notice specifying the address of the place within the United States where the copies of the books and records required to be kept and preserved by him pursuant to paragraph (j)(1) hereof are located. Each non-resident investment adviser registered or applying for registration when this paragraph becomes effective shall file such notice within 30 days after such rule becomes effective. Each non-resident investment adviser who files an application for registration after this paragraph becomes effective shall file such notice with such application for registration.

(3) Notwithstanding the provisions of paragraphs (j)(1) and (j)(2) of this section, a nonresident investment adviser need not keep or preserve within the United States copies of the books and records referred to in said paragraphs (j)(1) and (j)(2), if:

(i) Such non-resident investment adviser files with the Commission, at the time or within the period provided by paragraph (j)(2) of this section, a written undertaking, in form acceptable to the Commission and signed by a duly authorized person, to furnish to the Commission, upon demand, at its principal office in Washington, D.C., or at any Regional Office of the Commission designated in such demand, true, correct, complete and current copies of any or all of the books and records which he is required to make, keep current, maintain or preserve pursuant to any provision of any rule or regulation of the Commission adopted under the Act, or any part of such books and records which may be specified in such demand. Such undertaking shall be in substantially the following form:

> The undersigned hereby undertakes to furnish at its own expense to the Securities and Exchange Commission at its principal office in Washington, D.C. or at any Regional Office of said Commission specified in a demand for copies of books and records made by or on behalf of said Commission, true, correct, complete and current copies of any or all, or any part, of the books and records which the undersigned is required to make, keep current or preserve pursuant to any provision of any rule or regulation of the Securities and Exchange Commission under the Investment Advisers Act of 1940. This undertaking shall be suspended during any period when the undersigned is making, keeping current, and preserving copies of all of said books and records at a place within the United States in compliance with Rule 204–2(j) under the Investment Advisers Act of 1940. This undertaking shall be binding upon the undersigned and the heirs, successors and assigns of the undersigned, and the written irrevocable consents and powers of attorney of the undersigned, its general partners and managing agents filed with the Securities and Exchange Commission shall extend to and cover any action to enforce same.

and

(ii) Such non-resident investment adviser furnishes to the Commission, at his own expense 14 days after written demand therefor forwarded to him by registered mail at his last address of record filed with the Commission and signed by the Secretary of the Commission or such person as the Commission may authorize to act in its behalf, true, correct, complete and current copies of any or all books and records which such investment adviser is required to make, keep current or preserve pursuant to any provision of any rule or regulation of the Commission adopted under the Act, or any part of such books and records which may be specified in said written demand. Such copies shall be furnished to the Commission at its principal office in Washington, D.C., or at any Regional Office of the Commission which may be specified in said written demand.

(4) For purposes of this rule the term "non-resident investment adviser" shall have the meaning set out in § 275.0–2(d)(3) under the Act.

(k) Every investment adviser that registers under section 203 of the Act (15 U.S.C. 80b–3) after July 8, 1997 shall be required to preserve in accordance with this section the books and records the investment adviser had been required to maintain by the State in which the investment adviser had its principal office and place of business prior to registering with the Commission.

(*l*) *Records of private funds.* If an investment adviser subject to paragraph (a) of this section advises a private fund (as defined in § 275.203(b)(3)–1), and the adviser or any related person (as defined in Form ADV (17 CFR 279.1)) of the adviser acts as the private fund's general partner, managing member, or in a comparable capacity, the books and records of the private fund are records of the adviser for purposes of section 204 of the Act (15 U.S.C. 80b–4).

§ 275.204–3 Written Disclosure Statements

(a) *General Requirement.* Unless otherwise provided in this rule, an investment adviser, registered or required to be registered pursuant to Section 203 of the Act shall, in accordance with the provisions of this section, furnish each advisory client and prospective advisory client with a written disclosure statement which may be either a copy of Part II of its Form ADV which complies with § 275.204–1(b) under the Act or written document containing at least the information then so required by Part II of Form ADV.

(b) *Delivery.* (1) An investment adviser, except as provided in paragraph (2), shall deliver the statement required by this section to an advisory client or prospective advisory client (i) not less than 48 hours prior to entering into any written or oral investment advisory contract with such client or prospective client, or (ii) at the time of entering into any such contract, if the advisory client has a right to terminate the contract without penalty within five business days after entering into the contract.

(2) Delivery of the statement required by paragraph (1) need not be made in connection with entering into (i) an investment company contract or (ii) a contract for impersonal advisory services.

(c) *Offer to Deliver.* (1) An investment adviser, except as provided in paragraph (2), annually shall, without charge, deliver or offer in writing to deliver upon written request to each of its advisory clients the statement required by this section.

(2) The delivery or offer required by paragraph (1) need not be made to advisory clients receiving advisory services solely pursuant to (i) an investment company contract or (ii) a contract for impersonal advisory services requiring a payment of less than $200;

(3) With respect to an advisory client entering into a contract or receiving advisory services pursuant to a contract for impersonal advisory services which requires a payment of $200 or more, an offer of the type specified in paragraph (1) shall also be made at the time of entering into an advisory contract.

(4) Any statement requested in writing by an advisory client pursuant to an offer required by this paragraph must be mailed or delivered within seven days of the receipt of the request.

(d) *Omission of Inapplicable Information.* If an investment adviser renders substantially different types of investment advisory services to different advisory clients, any information required by Part II of Form ADV may be omitted from the statement furnished to an advisory client or prospective advisory client if such information is applicable only to a type of investment advisory service or fee which is not rendered or charged, or proposed to be rendered or charged, to that client or prospective client.

(e) *Other Disclosures.* Nothing in this rule shall relieve any investment adviser from any obligation pursuant to any provision of the Act or the rules and regulations thereunder or other federal or state law to disclose any information to its advisory clients or prospective advisory clients not specifically required by this rule.

(f) *Sponsors of Wrap Fee Programs.*—(1) An investment adviser, registered or required to be registered pursuant to Section 203 of the Act, that is compensated under a wrap fee program for sponsoring, organizing, or administering the program, or for selecting, or providing advice to clients regarding the selection of, other investment advisers in the program, shall, in lieu of the written disclosure statement required by paragraph (a) of this section and in accordance with the other provisions of this section, furnish each client and prospective client of the wrap fee program with a written disclosure statement containing at least the information required by Schedule H of Form ADV (§ 279.1 of this chapter). Any additional information included in such disclosure statement should be limited to information concerning wrap fee programs sponsored by the investment adviser.

(2) If an investment adviser is required under this paragraph (f) to furnish disclosure statements to clients or prospective clients of more than one wrap fee program, the investment adviser may omit from the disclosure statement furnished to clients and prospective clients of a wrap fee program or programs any information required by Schedule H that is not applicable to clients or prospective clients of that wrap fee program or programs.

(3) An investment adviser need not furnish the written disclosure statement required by

paragraph (f)(1) of this section to clients and prospective clients of a wrap fee program if another investment adviser is required to furnish and does furnish the written disclosure statement to all clients and prospective clients of the wrap fee program.

(4) An investment adviser that is required under this paragraph (f) to furnish a disclosure statement to clients of a wrap fee program shall furnish the disclosure statement to each client of the wrap fee program (including clients that have previously been furnished the brochure required under paragraph (a) of this section) no later than October 1, 1994.

(g) *Definitions.* For the purpose of this rule:

(1) "contract for impersonal advisory services" means any contract relating solely to the provision of investment advisory services (i) by means of written material or oral statements which do not purport to meet the objectives or needs of specific individuals or accounts; (ii) through the issuance of statistical information containing no expression of opinion as to the investment merits of a particular security; or (iii) any combination of the foregoing services.

(2) "entering into," in reference to an investment advisory contract, does not include an extension or renewal without material change of any such contract which is in effect immediately prior to such extension or renewal.

(3) "investment company contract" means a contract with an investment company registered under the Investment Company Act of 1940 which meets the requirements of Section 15(c) of that Act.

(4) *Wrap fee program* means a program under which any client is charged a specified fee or fees not based directly upon transactions in a client's account for investment advisory services (which may include portfolio management or advice concerning the selection of other investment advisers) and execution of client transactions.

§ 275.204A–1 Investment adviser codes of ethics.

(a) Adoption of code of ethics. If you are an investment adviser registered or required to be registered under section 203 of the Act (15 U.S.C. 80b–3), you must establish, maintain and enforce a written code of ethics that, at a minimum, includes:

(1) A standard (or standards) of business conduct that you require of your supervised persons, which standard must reflect your fiduciary obligations and those of your supervised persons;

(2) Provisions requiring your supervised persons to comply with applicable Federal securities laws;

(3) Provisions that require all of your access persons to report, and you to review, their personal securities transactions and holdings periodically as provided below;

(4) Provisions requiring supervised persons to report any violations of your code of ethics promptly to your chief compliance officer or, provided your chief compliance officer also receives reports of all violations, to other persons you designate in your code of ethics; and

(5) Provisions requiring you to provide each of your supervised persons with a copy of your code of ethics and any amendments, and requiring your supervised persons to provide you with a written acknowledgment of their receipt of the code and any amendments.

(b) Reporting requirements.

(1) Holdings reports. The code of ethics must require your access persons to submit to your chief compliance officer or other persons you designate in your code of ethics a report of the access person's current securities holdings that meets the following requirements:

(i) Content of holdings reports. Each holdings report must contain, at a minimum:

(A) The title and type of security, and as applicable the exchange ticker symbol or CUSIP number, number of shares, and principal amount of each reportable security in which the access person has any direct or indirect beneficial ownership;

(B) The name of any broker, dealer or bank with which the access person maintains an account in which any securities are held for the access person's direct or indirect benefit; and

(C) The date the access person submits the report.

(ii) Timing of holdings reports. Your access persons must each submit a holdings report:

(A) No later than 10 days after the person becomes an access person, and the information must be current as of a date no more than 45 days prior to the date the person becomes an access person.

(B) At least once each 12–month period thereafter on a date you select, and the information must be current as of a date no more than 45 days prior to the date the report was submitted.

(2) Transaction reports. The code of ethics must require access persons to submit to your chief compliance officer or other persons you designate in your code of ethics quarterly securities transactions reports that meet the following requirements:

(i) Content of transaction reports. Each transaction report must contain, at a minimum, the following information about each transaction involving a reportable security in which the access person had, or as a result of the transaction acquired, any direct or indirect beneficial ownership:

(A) The date of the transaction, the title, and as applicable the exchange ticker symbol or CUSIP number, interest rate and maturity date, number of shares, and principal amount of each reportable security involved;

(B) The nature of the transaction (i.e., purchase, sale or any other type of acquisition or disposition);

(C) The price of the security at which the transaction was effected;

(D) The name of the broker, dealer or bank with or through which the transaction was effected; and(E) The date the access person submits the report.

(ii) Timing of transaction reports. Each access person must submit a transaction report no later than 30 days after the end of each calendar quarter, which report must cover, at a minimum, all transactions during the quarter.

(3) Exceptions from reporting requirements. Your code of ethics need not require an access person to submit:

(i) Any report with respect to securities held in accounts over which the access person had no direct or indirect influence or control;

(ii) A transaction report with respect to transactions effected pursuant to an automatic investment plan;

(iii) A transaction report if the report would duplicate information contained in broker trade confirmations or account statements that you hold in your records so long as you receive the confirmations or statements no later than 30 days after the end of the applicable calendar quarter.

(c) Pre-approval of certain investments. Your code of ethics must require your access persons to obtain your approval before they directly or indirectly acquire beneficial ownership in any security in an initial public offering or in a limited offering.

(d) Small advisers. If you have only one access person (i.e., yourself), you are not required to submit reports to yourself or to obtain your own approval for investments in any security in an initial public offering or in a limited offering, if you maintain records of all of your holdings and transactions that this section would otherwise require you to report.

(e) Definitions. For the purpose of this section:

(1) Access person means:

(i) Any of your supervised persons:

(A) Who has access to nonpublic information regarding any clients' purchase or sale of securities, or nonpublic information regarding the portfolio holdings of any reportable fund, or

(B) Who is involved in making securities recommendations to clients, or who has access to such recommendations that are nonpublic.

(ii) If providing investment advice is your primary business, all of your directors, officers and partners are presumed to be access persons.

(2) Automatic investment plan means a program in which regular periodic purchases (or withdrawals) are made automatically in (or from) investment accounts in accordance with a predetermined schedule and allocation. An automatic investment plan includes a dividend reinvestment plan.

(3) Beneficial ownership is interpreted in the same manner as it would be under § 240.16a–1(a)(2) of this chapter in determining whether a person has beneficial ownership of a security for purposes of section 16 of the Securities Exchange Act of 1934 (15 U.S.C. 78p) and the rules and regulations thereunder. Any report required by paragraph (b) of this section may contain a statement that the report will not be construed as an admission that the person making the report has any direct or indirect beneficial ownership in the security to which the report relates.

(4) Federal securities laws means the Securities Act of 1933 (15 U.S.C. 77a-aa), the Securities Exchange Act of 1934 (15 U.S.C. 78a-mm), the Sarbanes–Oxley Act of 2002 (Pub.L. 107–204, 116 Stat. 745 (2002)), the Investment Company Act of 1940 (15 U.S.C. 80a), the Investment Advisers Act of 1940 (15 U.S.C. 80b), title V of the Gramm–Leach–Bliley Act (Pub.L. 106–102, 113 Stat. 1338 (1999), any rules adopted by the Commission under any of these statutes, the Bank Secrecy Act (31 U.S.C. 5311–5314; 5316–5332) as it applies to funds and investment advisers, and any rules adopted thereunder by the Commission or the Department of the Treasury.

(5) Fund means an investment company registered under the Investment Company Act.

(6) Initial public offering means an offering of securities registered under the Securities Act of 1933 (15 U.S.C. 77a), the issuer of which, immediately before the registration, was not subject to the reporting requirements of sections 13 or 15(d) of the Securities Exchange Act of 1934 (15 U.S.C. 78m or 78o(d)).

(7) Limited offering means an offering that is exempt from registration under the Securities Act of 1933 pursuant to section 4(2) or section 4(6) (15 U.S.C. 77d(2) or 77d(6)) or pursuant to §§ 230.504, 230.505, or 230.506 of this chapter.

(8) Purchase or sale of a security includes, among other things, the writing of an option to purchase or sell a security.

(9) Reportable fund means:

(i) Any fund for which you serve as an investment adviser as defined in section 2(a)(20) of the Investment Company Act of 1940 (15 U.S.C. 80a-2(a)(20)) (i.e., in most cases you must be approved by the fund's board of directors before you can serve); or

(ii) Any fund whose investment adviser or principal underwriter controls you, is controlled by you, or is under common control with you. For purposes of this section, control has the same meaning as it does in section 2(a)(9) of the Investment Company Act of 1940 (15 U.S.C. 80a–2(a)(9)).

(10) Reportable security means a security as defined in section 202(a)(18) of the Act

(15 U.S.C. 80b–2(a)(18)), except that it does not include:

(i) Direct obligations of the Government of the United States;

(ii) Bankers' acceptances, bank certificates of deposit, commercial paper and high quality short-term debt instruments, including repurchase agreements;

(iii) Shares issued by money market funds;

(iv) Shares issued by open-end funds other than reportable funds; and

(v) Shares issued by unit investment trusts that are invested exclusively in one or more open-end funds, none of which are reportable funds.

§ 275.205–1 Definition of "Investment Performance" of an Investment Company and "Investment Record" of an Appropriate Index of Securities Prices

(a) "Investment performance" of an investment company for any period shall mean the sum of:

(1) The change in its net asset value per share during such period;

(2) The value of its cash distributions per share accumulated to the end of such period; and

(3) The value of capital gains taxes per share paid or payable on undistributed realized long-term capital gains accumulated to the end of such period;

expressed as a percentage of its net asset value per share at the beginning of such period. For this purpose, the value of distributions per share of realized capital gains, of dividends per share paid from investment income and of capital gains taxes per share paid or payable on undistributed realized long-term capital gains shall be treated as reinvested in shares of the investment company at the net asset value per share in effect at the close of business on the record date for the payment of such distributions and dividends and the date on which provision is made for such taxes, after giving effect to such distributions, dividends and taxes.

(b) "Investment record" of an appropriate index of securities prices for any period shall mean the sum of:

(1) The change in the level of the index during such period; and

(2) The value, computed consistently with the index, of cash distributions made by companies whose securities comprise the index accumulated to the end of such period;

expressed as a percentage of the index level at the beginning of such period. For this purpose cash distributions on the securities which comprise the index shall be treated as reinvested in the index at least as frequently as the end of each calendar quarter following the payment of the dividend.

§ 275.205–2 Definition of "Specified Period" Over Which the Asset Value of the Company or Fund Under Management Is Averaged

(a) For purposes of this rule:

(1) "Fulcrum fee" shall mean the fee which is paid or earned when the investment company's performance is equivalent to that of the index or other measure of performance.

(2) "Rolling period" shall mean a period consisting of a specified number of subperiods of definite length in which the most recent subperiod is substituted for the earliest subperiod as time passes.

(b) The specified period over which the asset value of the company or fund under management is averaged shall mean the period over which the investment performance of the company or fund and the investment record of an appropriate index of securities prices or such other measure of investment performance are computed.

(c) Notwithstanding paragraph (b) of this section, the specified period over which the asset value of the company or fund is averaged for the purpose of computing the fulcrum fee may differ from the period over which the asset value is averaged for computing the performance related portion of the fee, only if

(1) The performance related portion of the fee is computed over a rolling period and the total fee is payable at the end of each subperiod of the rolling period; and

(2) The fulcrum fee is computed on the basis of the asset value averaged over the most recent subperiod or subperiods of the rolling period.

§ 275.205–3 Exemption from the Compensation Prohibition of Section 205(a)(1) for Investment Advisers

(a) *General.* The provisions of section 205(a)(1) of the Act (15 U.S.C. 80b–5(a)(1)) will not be deemed to prohibit an investment adviser from entering into, performing, renewing or extending an investment advisory contract that provides for compensation to the investment adviser on the basis of a share of the capital gains upon, or the capital appreciation of, the funds, or any portion of the funds, of a client, *Provided,* That the client entering into the contract subject to this section is a qualified client, as defined in paragraph (d)(1) of this section.

(b) *Identification of the client.* In the case of a private investment company, as defined in paragraph (d)(3) of this section, an investment company registered under the Investment Company Act of 1940, or a business development company, as defined in section 202(a)(22) of the Act (15 U.S.C. 80b–2(a)(22)), each equity owner of any such company (except for the investment adviser entering into the contract and any other equity owners not charged a fee on the basis of a share of capital gains or capital appreciation) will be considered a client for purposes of paragraph (a) of this section.

(c)(1) *Transition rule.* An investment adviser that entered into a contract before August 20, 1998 and satisfied the conditions of this section as in effect on the date that the contract was entered into will be considered to satisfy the conditions of this section; *Provided,* however, that this section will apply with respect to any natural person or company who is not a party to the contract prior to and becomes a party to the contract after August 20, 1998.

(2) Advisers to private funds with nonqualified investors. If you are an investment adviser to a private investment company that is a private fund as that term is defined in § 275.203(b)(3)–1, and you were exempt from registration under section 203(b)(3) of the Act (15 U.S.C. 80b–3(b)(3)) prior to February 10, 2005, paragraph (b) of this section will not apply to the existing account of any equity owner of a private investment company who was an equity owner of that company prior to February 10, 2005.

(3) Advisers to private funds with nonqualified clients. If you are an investment adviser to a private investment company that is a private fund as that term is defined in § 275.203(b)(3)–1, and you were exempt from registration under section 203(b)(3) of the Act (15 U.S.C. 80b–3(b)(3)) prior to February 10, 2005, section 205(a)(1) of the Act (15 U.S.C. 80b–5(a)(1)) will not apply to any investment advisory contract you entered into prior to February 10, 2005, provided, however, that this paragraph will not apply with respect to any contract to which a private investment company is a party, and provided further that section 205(a)(1) of the Act will apply with respect to any natural person or company who is not a party to the contract prior to and becomes a party to the contract on or after February 10, 2005.

(d) *Definitions.* For the purposes of this section:

(1) The term *qualified client* means:

(i) A natural person who or a company that immediately after entering into the contract has at least $750,000 under the management of the investment adviser;

(ii) A natural person who or a company that the investment adviser entering into the contract (and any person acting on his behalf) reasonably believes, immediately prior to entering into the contract, either:

(A) Has a net worth (together, in the case of a natural person, with assets held jointly with a spouse) of more than $1,500,000 at the time the contract is entered into; or

(B) Is a qualified purchaser as defined in section 2(a)(51)(A) of the Investment Company Act of 1940 (15 U.S.C. 80a–2(a)(51)(A)) at the time the contract is entered into; or

(iii) A natural person who immediately prior to entering into the contract is:

(A) An executive officer, director, trustee, general partner, or person serving in a similar capacity, of the investment adviser; or

(B) An employee of the investment adviser (other than an employee performing solely clerical, secretarial or administrative functions with regard to the investment adviser) who, in connection with his or her regular functions or duties, participates in the investment activities of such investment adviser, provided that such employee has been performing such functions and duties for or on behalf of the investment adviser, or substantially similar functions or duties for or on behalf of another company for at least 12 months.

(2) The term *company* has the same meaning as in section 202(a)(5) of the Act (15 U.S.C. 80b–2(a)(5)), but does not include a company that is required to be registered under the Investment Company Act of 1940 but is not registered.

(3) The term *private investment company* means a company that would be defined as an investment company under section 3(a) of the Investment Company Act of 1940 (15 U.S.C. 80a–3(a)) but for the exception provided from that definition by section 3(c)(1) of such Act (15 U.S.C. 80a–3(c)(1)).

(4) The term *executive officer* means the president, any vice president in charge of a principal business unit, division or function (such as sales, administration or finance), any other officer who performs a policy-making function, or any other person who performs similar policy-making functions, for the investment adviser.

§ 275.206(3)–1 Exemption of Investment Advisers Registered as Broker-Dealers in Connection With the Provision of Certain Investment Advisory Services

(a) An investment adviser which is a broker or dealer registered pursuant to Section 15 of the Securities Exchange Act of 1934 shall be exempt from Section 206(3) in connection with any transaction in relation to which such broker or dealer is acting as an investment adviser solely (1) by means of publicly distributed written materials or publicly made oral statements; (2) by means of written materials or oral statements which do not purport to meet the objectives or needs of specific individuals or accounts; (3) through the issuance of statistical information containing no expressions of opinion as to the investment merits of a particular security; or (4) any combination of the foregoing services: *Provided, however,* That such materials and oral statements include a statement that if the purchaser of the advisory communication uses the services of the adviser in connection with a sale or purchase of a security which is a subject of such communication, the adviser may act as principal for its own account or as agent for another person.

(b) For the purpose of this Rule, publicly distributed written materials are those which are distributed to 35 or more persons who pay for such materials, and publicly made oral statements are those made simultaneously to 35 or more persons who pay for access to such statements.

NOTE: The requirement that the investment adviser disclose that it may act as principal or agent for another person in the sale or purchase of a security that is the subject of investment advice does not relieve the investment adviser of any disclosure obligation which, depending upon the nature of the relationship between the investment adviser and the client, may be imposed by subparagraphs (1) or (2) of Section 206 or the other provisions of the federal securities laws.

§ 275.206(3)-2 Agency Cross Transactions for Advisory Clients

(a) An investment adviser, or a person registered as a broker-dealer under section 15 of the Securities Exchange Act of 1934 (15 U.S.C. 78o) and controlling, controlled by, or under common control with an investment adviser, shall be deemed in compliance with the provisions of sections 206(3) of the Act (15 U.S.C. 80b-6(3)) in effecting an agency cross transaction for an advisory client, if:

(1) The advisory client has executed a written consent prospectively authorizing the investment adviser, or any other person relying on this rule, to effect agency cross transactions for such advisory client, provided that such written consent is obtained after full written disclosure that with respect to agency cross transactions the investment adviser or such other person will act as broker for, receive commissions from, and have a potentially conflicting division of loyalties and responsibilities regarding, both parties to such transaction;

(2) The investment adviser, or any other person relying on this rule, sends to each such client a written confirmation at or before the completion of each such transaction, which confirmation includes (i) a statement of the nature of such transaction, (ii) the date such transaction took place, (iii) an offer to furnish upon request, the time when such transaction took place, and (iv) the source and amount of any other remuneration received or to be received by the investment adviser and any other person relying on this rule in connection with the transaction, *Provided, however,* That if, in the case of a purchase, neither the investment adviser nor any other person relying on this rule was participating in a distribution, or in the case of a sale, neither the investment adviser nor any other person relying on this rule was participating in a tender offer, the written confirmation may state whether any other remuneration has been or will be received and that the source and amount of such other remuneration will be furnished upon written request of such customer;

(3) The investment adviser, or any other person relying on this rule, sends to each client, at least annually, and with or as part of any written statement or summary of such account from the investment adviser or such other person, a written disclosure statement identifying the total number of such transactions during the period since the date of the last such statement or summary, and the total amount of all commissions or other remuneration received or to be received by the investment adviser or any other person relying on this rule in connection with such transactions during such period;

(4) Each written disclosure and confirmation required by this rule includes a conspicuous statement that the written consent referred to in paragraph (a)(1) of this section may be revoked at any time by written notice to the investment adviser, or to any other person relying on this rule, from the advisory client; and

(5) No such transaction is effected in which the same investment adviser or an investment adviser and any person controlling, controlled by or under common control with such investment adviser recommended the transaction to both any seller and any purchaser.

(b) For purposes of this rule the term "agency cross transaction for an advisory client" shall mean a transaction in which a person acts as an investment adviser in relation to a transaction in which such investment adviser, or any person controlling, controlled by or under common control with such investment adviser, acts as broker for both such advisory client and for another person on the other side of the transaction.

(c) This rule shall not be construed as relieving in any way the investment adviser or another person relying on this rule from acting in the best interests of the advisory client, including fulfilling the duty with respect to the best price and execution for the particular transaction for the advisory client; nor shall it relieve such person or persons from any disclosure obligation which may be imposed by subparagraphs (1) or (2) of Section 206 of the Act or by other applicable provisions of the federal securities laws.

§ 275.206(4)–1 Advertisements by Investment Advisers

(a) It shall constitute a fraudulent, deceptive, or manipulative act, practice, or course of business within the meaning of section 206(4) of the Act (15 U.S.C. 80b–6(4)) for any investment adviser registered or required to be registered under section 203 of the Act (15 U.S.C. 80b–3), directly or indirectly, to publish, circulate, or distribute any advertisement:

(1) Which refers, directly or indirectly, to any testimonial of any kind concerning the investment adviser or concerning any advice, analysis, report or other service rendered by such investment adviser; or

(2) Which refers, directly or indirectly, to past specific recommendations of such investment adviser which were or would have been profitable to any person: *Provided, however,* That this shall not prohibit an advertisement which sets out or offers to furnish a list of all recommendations made by such investment adviser within the immediately preceding period of not less than one year if such advertisement, and such list if it is furnished separately: (i) State the name of each such security recommended, the late and nature of each such recommendation (e.g., whether to buy, sell or hold), the market price at that time, the price at which the recommendation was to be acted upon, and the market price of each such security as of the most recent practicable date, and (ii) contain the following cautionary legend on the first page thereof in print or type as large as the largest print or type used in the body or text thereof: "it should not be assumed that recommendations made in the future will be profitable or will equal the performance of the securities in this list"; or

(3) Which represents, directly or indirectly, that any graph, chart, formula or other device being offered can in and of itself be used to determine which securities to buy or sell, or when to buy or sell them; or which represents directly or indirectly, that any graph, chart, formula or other device being offered will assist any person in making his own decisions as to which securities to buy, sell, or when to buy or sell them, without prominently disclosing in such advertisement the limitations thereof and the difficulties with respect to its use; or

(4) Which contains any statement to the effect that any report, analysis, or other service will be furnished free or without charge, unless such report, analysis or other service actually is or will be furnished entirely free and without any condition or obligation, directly or indirectly; or

(5) Which contains any untrue statement of a material fact, or which is otherwise false or misleading.

(b) For the purposes of this section the term "advertisement" shall include any notice, circular, letter or other written communication addressed to more than one person, or any notice or other announcement in any publication or by radio or television, which offers (1) any analysis, report, or publication concerning securities, or which is to be used in making any determination as to when to buy or sell any security, or which security to buy or sell, or (2) any graph, chart, formula, or other device to be used in making any determination as to when to buy or sell any security, or which security to buy or sell, or (3) any other investment advisory service with regard to securities.

§ 275.206(4)-2 Custody of Funds or Securities of Clients By Investment Advisers

(a) *Safekeeping required.* If you are an investment adviser registered or required to be registered under section 203 of the Act (15 U.S.C. 80b-3), it is a fraudulent, deceptive, or manipulative act, practice or course of business within the meaning of section 206(4) of the Act (15 U.S.C. 80b-6(4)) for you to have custody of client funds or securities unless—

(1) *Qualified custodian.* A qualified custodian maintains those funds and securities;

(i) In a separate account for each client under that client's name; or

(ii) In accounts that contain only your clients' funds and securities, under your name as agent or trustee for the clients.

(2) *Notice to clients.* If you open an account with a qualified custodian on your client's behalf, either under the client's name or under your name as agent, you notify the client in writing of the qualified custodian's name, address, and the manner in which the funds or securities are maintained, promptly when the account is opened and following any changes to this information.

(3) *Account statements to clients.*—(i) *By qualified custodian.* You have a reasonable basis for believing that the qualified custodian sends an account statement, at least quarterly, to each of your clients for which it maintains funds or securities, identifying the amount of funds and of each security in the account at the end of the period and setting forth all transactions in the account during that period; or

(ii) *By adviser.* (A) You send a quarterly account statement to each of your clients for whom you have custody of funds or securities, identifying the amount of funds and of each security of which you have custody at the end of the period and setting forth all transactions during that period;

(B) An independent public accountant verifies all of those funds and securities by actual examination at least once during each calendar year at a time that is chosen by the accountant without prior notice or announcement to you and that is irregular from year to year, and files a certificate on Form ADV–E [17 CFR 279.8] with the Commission within 30 days after the completion of the examination, stating that it has examined the funds and securities and describing the nature and extent of the examination; and

(C) The independent public accountant, upon finding any material discrepancies during the course of the examination, notifies the Commission within one business day of the finding, by means of a facsimile transmission or electronic mail, followed by first class mail, directed to the attention of the Director of the Office of Compliance Inspections and Examinations; and

(iii) *Special rule for limited partnerships and limited liability companies.* If you are a general partner of a limited partnership (or managing member of a limited liability company, or hold a comparable position for another type of pooled investment vehicle), the account statements required under paragraphs (a)(3)(i) or (a)(3)(ii) of this section must be sent to each limited partner (or member or other beneficial owner).

(4) *Independent representatives.* A client may designate an independent representative to receive, on his behalf, notices and account statements as required under paragraphs (a)(2) and (a)(3) of this section.

(b) *Exceptions.*—(1) *Shares of mutual funds.* With respect to shares of an open-end company as defined in section 5(a)(1) of the Investment Company Act of 1940 (15 U.S.C. 80a-5(a)(1)) ("mutual fund"), you may use the mutual fund's transfer agent in lieu of a qualified custodian for purposes of complying with paragraph (a) of this section;

(2) *Certain privately offered securities.* (i) You are not required to comply with this section with respect to securities that are:

(A) Acquired from the issuer in a transaction or chain of transactions not involving any public offering;

(B) Uncertificated, and ownership thereof is recorded only on books of the issuer or its transfer agent in the name of the client; and

(C) Transferable only with prior consent of the issuer or holders of the outstanding securities of the issuer.

(ii) Notwithstanding paragraph (b)(2)(i) of this section, the provisions of this paragraph (b)(2) are available with respect to securities held for the account of a limited partnership (or limited liability company, or other type of pooled investment vehicle) only if the limited partnership is audited, and the audited financial statements are distributed, as described in paragraph (b)(3) of this section.

(3) *Limited partnerships subject to annual audit.* You are not required to comply with paragraph (a)(3) of this section with respect to the account of a limited partnership (or limited liability company, or another type of pooled investment vehicle) that is subject to audit (as defined in section 2(d) of Article 1 of Regulation S-X (17 CFR 210.1-02(d)) at least annually and distributes its audited financial statements prepared in accordance with generally accepted accounting principles to all limited partners (or members or other beneficial owners) within 120 days of the end of its fiscal year, or in the case of a fund of funds within 180 days of the end of its fiscal year; and

(4) *Registered investment companies.* You are not required to comply with this section (17 CFR 275.206(4)–(2)) (with respect to the account of an investment company registered under the Investment Company Act of 1940 (15 U.S.C. 80a–1 to 80a–64)).

(c) *Definitions.* For the purposes of this section—

(1) *Custody* means holding, directly or indirectly, client funds or securities, or having any authority to obtain possession of them. Custody includes—

(i) Possession of client funds or securities, (but not of checks drawn by clients and made payable to third parties,) unless you receive them inadvertently and you return them to the sender promptly but in any case within three business days of receiving them;

(ii) Any arrangement (including a general power of attorney) under which you are authorized or permitted to withdraw client funds or securities maintained with a custodian upon your instruction to the custodian; and

(iii) Any capacity (such as general partner of a limited partnership, managing member of a limited liability company or a comparable position for another type of pooled investment vehicle, or trustee of a trust) that gives you or your supervised person legal ownership of or access to client funds or securities.

(2) *Independent representative* means a person that—

(i) Acts as agent for an advisory client, including in the case of a pooled investment vehicle, for limited partners of a limited partnership (or members of a limited liability company, or other beneficial owners of another type of pooled investment vehicle) and by law or contract is obliged to act in the best interest of the advisory client or the limited partners (or members, or other beneficial owners);

(ii) Does not control, is not controlled by, and is not under common control with you; and

(iii) Does not have, and has not had within the past two years, a material business relationship with you.

(3) *Qualified custodian* means:

(i) A bank as defined in Section 202(a)(2) of the Advisers Act (15 U.S.C. 80b–2(a)(2)) or a savings association as defined in Section 3(b)(1) of the Federal Deposit Insurance Act [12 U.S.C. 1813(b)(1)] that has deposits insured by the Federal Deposit Insurance Corporation under the Federal Deposit Insurance Act [12 U.S.C. 1811];

(ii) A broker-dealer registered under Section 15(b)(1) of the Securities Exchange Act of 1934 (15 U.S.C. 78o(b)(1)), holding the client assets in customer accounts;

(iii) A futures commission merchant registered under Section 4f(a) of the Commodity Exchange Act [7 U.S.C. 6f(a)], holding the client assets in customer accounts, but only with respect to clients' funds and security futures, or other securities incidental to transactions in contracts for the purchase or sale of a commodity for future delivery and options thereon; and

(iv) A foreign financial institution that customarily holds financial assets for its customers, provided that the foreign financial institution keeps the advisory clients' assets in customer accounts segregated from its proprietary assets.

(4) *Fund of funds* means a limited partnership (or limited liability company, or another type of pooled investment vehicle) that invests 10 percent or more of its total assets in other pooled investment vehicles that are not, and are not advised by, a related person (as defined in Form ADV (17 CFR 279.1)), of the limited partnership, its general partner, or its adviser.

§ 275.206(4)–3 Cash Payments for Client Solicitations

(a) It shall be unlawful for any investment adviser required to be registered pursuant to Section 203 of the Act to pay a cash fee, directly or indirectly, to a solicitor with respect to solicitation activities unless:

(1)(i) the investment adviser is registered under the Act;

(ii) the solicitor is not a person (A) subject to a Commission order issued under Section 203(f) of the Act, or (B) convicted within the previous ten years of any felony or misdemeanor involving conduct described in Section 203(e)(2)(A)–(D) of the Act or (C) who has been found by the Commission to have engaged, or has been convicted of engaging, in any of the conduct specified in paragraphs (1), (5) or (6) of Section 203(e) of the Act, or (D) is subject to an order, judgment or decree described in Section 203(e)(4) or the Act; and

(iii) such cash fee is paid pursuant to a written agreement to which the adviser is a party; and

NOTE: The investment adviser shall retain a copy of each written agreement required by this paragraph as part of the records required to be kept under § 204–2(a)(10) of this chapter.

(2) such cash fee is paid to a solicitor:

(i) with respect to solicitation activities for the provision of impersonal advisory services only; or

(ii) who is (A) a partner, officer, director or employee of such investment advisor or (B) a partner, officer, director or employee of a person which controls, is controlled by, or is under common control with such investment adviser; provided that that status of such solicitor as a partner, officer, director or employee of such investment adviser or other person, and any affiliation between the investment adviser and such other person, is disclosed to the client at the time of the solicitation or referral; or

(iii) other than a solicitor specified in paragraph (a)(2)(i) or (ii) above if all of the following conditions are met:

(A) The written agreement required by paragraph (a)(1)(iii) of this section: (1) describes the solicitation activities to be engaged in by the solicitor on behalf of the investment adviser and the compensation to be received therefore; (2) contains an undertaking by the solicitor to perform his duties under the agreement in a manner consistent with the instructions of the investment adviser and the provisions of the Act and the rules thereunder; (3) requires that the solicitor, at the time of any solicitation activities for which compensation is paid or to be paid by the investment adviser, provide the client with a current copy of the investment adviser's written disclosure statement required by § 275.204–3 of this chapter ("brochure rule") and a separate written disclosure document described in paragraph (b) of this rule.

(B) The investment adviser receives from the client, prior to, or at the time of, entering into any written or oral investment advisory contract with such client, a signed and dated acknowledgement of receipt of the investment adviser's written disclosure statement and the solicitor's written disclosure document.

NOTE: The investment adviser shall retain a copy of each such acknowledgement and solicitor disclosure document as part of the records required to be kept under § 204–2(a)(15) of this chapter.

(C) The investment adviser makes a bona fide effort to ascertain whether the solicitor has complied with the agreement, and has a reasonable basis for believing that the solicitor has so complied.

(b) The separate written disclosure document required to be furnished by the solicitor to the client pursuant to this section shall contain the following information:

(1) The name of the solicitor;

(2) The name of the investment adviser;

(3) The nature of the relationship, including any affiliation, between the solicitor and the investment adviser;

(4) A statement that the solicitor will be compensated for his solicitation services by the investment adviser;

(5) The terms of such compensation arrangement, including a description of the compensation paid or to be paid to the solicitor, and

(6) The amount, if any, for the cost of obtaining his account the client will be charged in addition to the advisory fee, and the differential, if any, among clients with respect to the amount or level of advisory fees charged by the investment adviser if such differential is attributable to the existence of any arrangement pursuant to which the investment adviser has agreed to compensate the solicitor for soliciting clients for, or referring clients to, the investment adviser.

(c) Nothing in this section shall be deemed to relieve any person of any fiduciary or other obligation to which such person may be subject under the law.

(d) For purposes of this section,

(1) "Solicitor" means any person who, directly or indirectly, solicits any client for, or refer any client to, an investment adviser.

(2) "Client" includes any prospective client.

(3) "Impersonal advisory services" means investment advisory services provided solely by means of (i) written materials or oral statements which do not purport to meet the objectives or needs of the specific client, (ii) statistical information containing no expressions of opinions as to the investment merits of particular securities, or (iii) any combination of the foregoing services.

§ 275.206(4)–4 Financial and Disciplinary Information That Investment Advisers Must Disclose to Clients

(a) It shall constitute a fraudulent, deceptive, or manipulative act, practice, or course of business within the meaning of section 206(4) of the Act (15 U.S.C. 80b–6(4)) for any investment adviser registered or required to be registered under section 203 of the Act (15 U.S.C. 80b–3) to fail to disclose to any client or prospective client all material facts with respect to:

(1) A financial condition of the adviser that is reasonably likely to impair the ability of the adviser to meet contractual commitments to clients, if the adviser has discretionary authority (express or implied) or custody over such client's funds or securities, or requires prepayment of advisory fees of more than $500 from such client, 6 months or more in advance; or

(2) A legal or disciplinary event that is material to an evaluation of the adviser's integrity or ability to meet contractual commitments to clients.

(b) It shall constitute a rebuttable presumption that the following legal or disciplinary events involving the adviser or a management person of the adviser (any of the foregoing being referred to hereafter as "person") that were not resolved in the person's favor or subsequently reversed, suspended, or vacated are material within the meaning of paragraph (a)(2) of the rule for a period of 10 years from the time of the event:

(1) A criminal or civil action in a court of competent jurisdiction in which the person—

(i) Was convicted, pleaded guilty or nolo contendere ("no contest") to a felony or misdemeanor, or is the named subject of a pending criminal proceeding (any of the foregoing referred to hereafter as "action"), and such action involved: an investment-related business; fraud, false statements, or omissions; wrongful taking of property; or bribery, forgery, counterfeiting, or extortion;

(ii) Was found to have been involved in a violation of an investment-related statute or regulation; or

(iii) Was the subject of any order, judgment, or decree permanently or temporarily enjoining the person from, or otherwise limiting the person from, engaging in any investment-related activity.

(2) Administrative proceedings before the Securities and Exchange Commission, any other federal regulatory agency or any state agency (any of the foregoing being referred to hereafter as "agency") in which the person—

(i) Was found to have caused an investment-related business to lose its authorization to do business; or

(ii) Was found to have been involved in a violation of an investment-related statute or regulation and was the subject of an order by the agency denying, suspending, or revoking the authorization of the person to act in, or barring or suspending the person's association with, an investment-related business; or otherwise significantly limiting the person's investment-related activities.

(3) Self–Regulatory Organization (SRO) proceedings in which the person—

(i) Was found to have caused an investment-related business to lose its authorization to do business; or

(ii) Was found to have been involved in a violation of the SRO's rules and was the subject of an order by the SRO barring or suspending the person from membership or from association with other members, or expelling the person from membership; fining the person more than $2,500; or otherwise significantly limiting the person's investment-related activities.

(c) The information required to be disclosed by paragraph (a) shall be disclosed to clients promptly, and to prospective clients not less than 48 hours prior to entering into any written or oral investment advisory contract, or no later than the time of entering into such contract if the client has the right to terminate the contract without penalty within five business days after entering into the contract.

(d) For purposes of this rule:

(1) "Management person" means a person with power to exercise, directly or indirectly, a controlling influence over the management or policies of an adviser which is a company or to determine the general investment advice given to clients.

(2) "Found" means determined or ascertained by adjudication or consent in a final SRO proceeding, administrative proceeding, or court action.

(3) "Investment-related" means pertaining to securities, commodities, banking, insurance, or real estate (including, but not limited to, acting as or being associated with a broker-dealer, investment company, investment adviser, government securities broker or dealer, municipal securities dealer, bank, savings and loan association, entity or person required to be registered under the Commodity Exchange Act [7 U.S.C. 1 *et seq.*], or fiduciary).

(4) "Involved" means acting or aiding, abetting, causing, counseling, commanding, inducing, conspiring with or failing reasonably to supervise another in doing an act.

(5) "Self–Regulatory Organization" or "SRO" means any national securities or commodities exchange, registered association, or registered clearing agency.

(e) For purposes of calculating the 10–year period during which events are presumed to be material under paragraph (b), the date of a reportable event shall be the date on which the final order, judgment, or decree was entered, or the date on which any rights of appeal from preliminary orders, judgments, or decrees lapsed.

(f) Compliance with paragraph (b) of this rule shall not relieve any investment adviser from the disclosure obligations of paragraph (a) of the rule; compliance with paragraph (a) of the rule shall not relieve any investment adviser from any other disclosure requirement under the Act, the rules and regulations thereunder, or under any other federal or state law.

NOTE: Registered investment advisers may disclose this information to clients and prospective clients in their "brochure," the written disclosure statement to clients under Rule 204–3; *provided,* that the delivery of the brochure satisfies the timing of disclosure requirements described in paragraph (c) of this rule.

§ 275.206(4)–6 Proxy Voting

If you are an investment adviser registered or required to be registered under section 203 of the Act (15 U.S.C. 80b–3), it is fraudulent, deceptive, or manipulative act, practice or course of business within the meaning of section 206(4) of the Act (15 U.S.C. 80b–6(4)), for you to exercise voting authority with respect to client securities, unless you:

(a) Adopt and implement written policies and procedures that are reasonably designed to ensure that you vote client securities in the best interest of clients, which procedures must include how you address material conflicts that may arise between your interests and those of your clients;

(b) Disclose to clients how they may obtain information from you about how you voted with respect to their securities; and

(c) Describe to clients your proxy voting policies and procedures and, upon request, furnish a copy of the policies and procedures to the requesting client.

§ 275.206(4)–7. Compliance Procedures and Practices

If you are an investment adviser registered or required to be registered under section 203 of the Investment Advisers Act of 1940 (15 U.S.C. 80b–3), it shall be unlawful within the meaning of section 206 of the Act (15 U.S.C. 80b–6) for you to provide investment advice to clients unless you:

(a) *Policies and procedures*. Adopt and implement written policies and procedures reasonably designed to prevent violation, by you and your supervised persons, of the Act and the rules that the Commission has adopted under the Act;

(b) *Annual review*. Review, no less frequently than annually, the adequacy of the policies and procedures established pursuant to this section and the effectiveness of their implementation; and

(c) *Chief compliance officer*. Designate an individual (who is a supervised person) responsible for administering the policies and procedures that you adopt under paragraph (a) of this section

§ 275.222–1 Definitions

For purposes of section 222 (15 U.S.C. 80b–18a) of the Act:

(a) *Place of business*. "Place of business" of an investment adviser means:

(1) An office at which the investment adviser regularly provides investment advisory services, solicits, meets with, or otherwise communicates with clients; and

(2) Any other location that is held out to the general public as a location at which the investment adviser provides investment advisory services, solicits, meets with, or otherwise communicates with clients.

(b) *Principal place of business*. "Principal place of business" of an investment adviser means the executive office of the investment adviser from which the officers, partners, or managers of the investment adviser direct, control, and coordinate the activities of the investment adviser.

§ 275.222–2 Definition of "Client" For Purposes of the National De Minimis Standard

For purposes of section 222(d)(2) of the Act (15 U.S.C. 80b–18a(d)(2)), an investment adviser may rely upon the definition of "client" provided by § 275.203(b)(3)–1 without giving regard to paragraph (b)(6) of that section.

E. SEC RULES OF PRACTICE

(Cite as 17 CFR § ___)

General Rules

Initiation of Proceedings and Prehearing Rules

Rules Regarding Hearings

Appeal to the Commission and Commission Review

Rules Relating to Temporary Orders and Suspensions

Rules Regarding Disgorgement and Penalty Payments

Informal Procedures and Supplementary Information Concerning Adjudicatory Proceedings

Adjustment of Civil Monetary Penalties

§ 201.100 Scope of the Rules of Practice

(a) Unless provided otherwise, these Rules of Practice govern proceedings before the Commission under the statutes that it administers.

(b) These rules do not apply to:

(1) Investigations, except where made specifically applicable by the Rules Relating to Investigations, part 203 of this chapter; or

(2) Actions taken by the duty officer pursuant to delegated authority under 17 CFR 200.43.

(c) The Commission, upon its determination that to do so would serve the interests of justice and not result in prejudice to the parties to the proceeding, may by order direct, in a particular proceeding, that an alternative procedure shall apply or that compliance with an otherwise applicable rule is unnecessary.

§ 201.101 Definitions

(a) For purposes of these Rules of Practice, unless explicitly stated to the contrary:

(1) *Commission* means the United States Securities and Exchange Commission, or a panel of Commissioners constituting a quorum of the Commission, or a single Commissioner acting as duty officer pursuant to 17 CFR 200.43;

(2) *Counsel* means any attorney representing a party or any other person representing a party pursuant to § 201.102(b);

(3) *Disciplinary proceeding* means an action pursuant to § 201.102(e);

(4) *Enforcement proceeding* means an action, initiated by an order instituting proceedings, held for the purpose of determining whether or not a person is about to violate, has violated, has caused a violation of, or has aided or abetted a violation of any statute or rule administered by the Commission, or whether to impose a sanction as defined in Section 551(10) of the Administrative Procedure Act, 5 U.S.C. 551(10);

(5) *Hearing officer* means an administrative law judge, a panel of Commissioners constituting less than a quorum of the Commission, an individual Commissioner, or any other person duly authorized to preside at a hearing;

(6) *Interested division* means a division or an office assigned primary responsibility by the Commission to participate in a particular proceeding;

(7) *Order instituting proceedings* means an order issued by the Commission commencing a proceeding or an order issued by the Commission to hold a hearing;

(8) *Party* means the interested division, any person named as a respondent in an order instituting proceedings, any applicant named in the caption of any order, persons entitled to notice in a stop order proceeding as set forth in § 201.200(a)(2) or any person seeking Commission review of a decision;

(9) *Proceeding* means any agency process initiated:

(i) By an order instituting proceedings; or

(ii) By the filing, pursuant to § 201.410, of a petition for review of an initial decision by a hearing officer; or

(iii) By the filing, pursuant to § 201.420, of an application for review of a self-regulatory organization determination; or

(iv) By the filing, pursuant to § 201.430, of a notice of intention to file a petition for review of a determination made pursuant to delegated authority; or

(v) By the filing, pursuant to § 201.440, of an application for review of a determination by the Public Company Accounting Oversight Board; or

(vi) By the filing, pursuant to § 240.11Aa3–1(f) of this chapter, of an application for review of an action or failure to act in connection with the implementation or operation of any effective transaction reporting plan; or

(vii) By the filing, pursuant to § 240.11Aa3–2(e) of this chapter, of an application for review of an action taken or failure to act in connection with the implementation or operation of any effective national market system plan; or

(viii) By the filing, pursuant to Section 11A(b)(5) of the Securities Exchange Act of 1934, of an application for review of a determination of a registered securities information processor;

(10) *Secretary* means the Secretary of the Commission;

(11) *Temporary sanction* means a temporary cease-and-desist order or a temporary suspension of the registration of a broker, dealer, municipal securities dealer, government securities broker, government securities dealer, or transfer agent pending final determination whether the registration shall be revoked, and

(12) *Board* means the Public Company Accounting Oversight Board.

(b) [Reserved]

§ 201.102 Appearance and Practice Before the Commission

A person shall not be represented before the Commission or a hearing officer except as stated in paragraphs (a) and (b) of this section or as otherwise permitted by the Commission or a hearing officer.

(a) *Representing oneself.* In any proceeding, an individual may appear on his or her own behalf.

(b) *Representing others.* In any proceeding, a person may be represented by an attorney at law admitted to practice before the Supreme Court of the United States or the highest court of any State (as defined in Section 3(a)(16) of the Exchange Act, 15 U.S.C. 78c(a)(16)); a member of a partnership may represent the partnership; a bona fide officer of a corporation, trust or association may represent the corporation, trust or association; and an officer or employee of a state commission or of a department or political subdivision of a state may represent the state commission or the department or political subdivision of the state.

(c) *Former Commission Employees.* Former employees of the Commission must comply with the restrictions on practice contained in the Commission's Conduct Regulation, Subpart M, 17 CFR 200.735.

(d) *Designation of address for service; notice of appearance; power of attorney; withdrawal.* (1) *Representing oneself.* When an individual first makes any filing or otherwise appears on his or her own behalf before the Commission or a hearing officer in a proceeding as defined in § 201.101(a), he or she shall file with the Commission, or otherwise state on the record, and keep current, an address at which any notice or other written communication required to be served upon him or her or furnished to him or her may be sent and a telephone number where he or she may be reached during business hours.

(2) *Representing others.* When a person first makes any filing or otherwise appears in a representative capacity before the Commission or a hearing officer in a proceeding as defined in § 201.101(a), that person shall file with the Commission, and keep current, a written notice stating the name of the proceeding; the representative's name, business address and telephone number; and the name and address of the person or persons represented.

(3) *Power of attorney.* Any individual appearing or practicing before the Commission in

a representative capacity may be required to file a power of attorney with the Commission showing his or her authority to act in such capacity.

(4) *Withdrawal.* Any person seeking to withdraw his or her appearance in a representative capacity shall file a notice of withdrawal with the Commission or the hearing officer. The notice shall state the name, address, and telephone number of the withdrawing representative; the name, address, and telephone number of the person for whom the appearance was made; and the effective date of the withdrawal. If the person seeking to withdraw knows the name, address, and telephone number of the new representative, or knows that the person for whom the appearance was made intends to represent him- or herself, that information shall be included in the notice. The notice must be served on the parties in accordance with § 201.150. The notice shall be filed at least five days before the proposed effective date of the withdrawal.

(e) *Suspension and disbarment.* (1) *Generally.* The Commission may censure a person or deny, temporarily or permanently, the privilege of appearing or practicing before it in any way to any person who is found by the Commission after notice and opportunity for hearing in the matter:

(i) Not to possess the requisite qualifications to represent others; or

(ii) To be lacking in character or integrity or to have engaged in unethical or improper professional conduct; or

(iii) To have willfully violated, or willfully aided and abetted the violation of any provision of the Federal securities laws or the rules and regulations thereunder.

(iv) With respect to persons licensed to practice as accountants, "improper professional conduct" under § 201.102(e)(1)(ii) means:

(A) Intentional or knowing conduct, including reckless conduct, that results in a violation of applicable professional standards; or (B) Either of the following two types of negligent conduct:

(*1*) A single instance of highly unreasonable conduct that results in a violation of applicable professional standards in circumstances in which an accountant knows, or should know, that heightened scrutiny is warranted.

(*2*) Repeated instances of unreasonable conduct, each resulting in a violation of applicable professional standards, that indicate a lack of competence to practice before the Commission.

(2) *Certain professionals and convicted persons.* Any attorney who has been suspended or disbarred by a court of the United States or of any State; or any person whose license to practice as an accountant, engineer, or other professional or expert has been revoked or suspended in any State; or any person who has been convicted of a felony or a misdemeanor involving moral turpitude shall be forthwith suspended from appearing or practicing before the Commission. A disbarment, suspension, revocation or conviction within the meaning of this section shall be deemed to have occurred when the disbarring, suspending, revoking or convicting agency or tribunal enters its judgment or order, including a judgment or order on a plea of nolo contendere, regardless of whether an appeal of such judgment or order is pending or could be taken.

(3) *Temporary suspensions.* An order of temporary suspension shall become effective upon service on the respondent. No order of temporary suspension shall be entered by the Commission pursuant to paragraph (e)(3)(i) of this section more than 90 days after the date on which the final judgment or order entered in a judicial or administrative proceeding described in paragraph (e)(3)(i)(A) or (e)(3)(i)(B) of this section has become effective, whether upon completion of review or appeal procedures or because further review or appeal procedures are no longer available.

(i) The Commission, with due regard to the public interest and without preliminary hearing, may, by order, temporarily suspend from appearing or practicing before it any attorney, accountant, engineer, or other professional or expert who has been by name:

(A) Permanently enjoined by any court of competent jurisdiction, by reason of his or her misconduct in an action brought by the Commission, from violating or aiding and abetting the violation of any provision of the Federal securities laws or of the rules and regulations thereunder; or

(B) Found by any court of competent jurisdiction in an action brought by the Commission to which he or she is a party or found by the Commission in any administrative proceeding to which he or she is a party to have violated (unless the violation was found not to have been willful) or aided and abetted the violation of any provision of the Federal securities laws or of the rules and regulations thereunder.

(ii) Any person temporarily suspended from appearing and practicing before the Commission in accordance with paragraph (e)(3)(i) of this section may, within 30 days after service upon him or her of the order of temporary suspension, petition the Commission to lift the temporary suspension. If no petition has been received by the Commission within 30 days after service of the order, the suspension shall become permanent.

(iii) Within 30 days after the filing of a petition in accordance with paragraph (e)(3)(ii) of this section, the Commission shall either lift the temporary suspension, or set the matter down for hearing at a time and place designated by the Commission, or both, and, after opportunity for hearing, may censure the petitioner or disqualify the petitioner from appearing or practicing before the Commission for a period of time or permanently. In every case in which the temporary suspension has not been lifted, every hearing held and other action taken pursuant to this paragraph (e)(3) shall be expedited in accordance with § 201.500. If the hearing is held before a hearing officer, the time limits set forth in § 201.531 will govern review of the hearing officer's initial decision.

(iv) In any hearing held on a petition filed in accordance with paragraph (e)(3)(ii) of this section, the staff of the Commission shall show either that the petitioner has been enjoined as described in paragraph (e)(3)(i)(A) of this section or that the petitioner has been found to have committed or aided and abetted violations as described in paragraph (e)(3)(i)(B) of this section and that showing, without more, may be the basis for censure or disqualification. Once that showing has been made, the burden shall be upon the petitioner to show cause why he or she should not be censured or temporarily or permanently disqualified from appearing and practicing before the Commission. In any such hearing, the petitioner may not contest any finding made against him or her or fact admitted by him or her in the judicial or administrative proceeding upon which the proceeding under this paragraph (e)(3) is predicated. A person who has consented to the entry of a permanent injunction as described in paragraph (e)(3)(i)(A) of this section without admitting the facts set forth in the complaint shall be presumed for all purposes under this paragraph (e)(3) to have been enjoined by reason of the misconduct alleged in the complaint.

(4) *Filing of prior orders.* Any person appearing or practicing before the Commission who has been the subject of an order, judgment, decree, or finding as set forth in paragraph (e)(3) of this section shall promptly file with the Secretary a copy thereof (together with any related opinion or statement of the agency or tribunal involved). Failure to file any such paper, order, judgment, decree or finding shall not impair the operation of any other provision of this section.

(5) *Reinstatement.* (i) An application for reinstatement of a person permanently suspended or disqualified under paragraph (e)(1) or (e)(3) of this section may be made at any time, and the applicant may, in the Commission's discretion, be afforded a hearing; however, the suspension or disqualification shall continue unless and until the applicant has been reinstated by the Commission for good cause shown.

(ii) Any person suspended under paragraph (e)(2) of this section shall be reinstated by the Commission, upon appropriate application, if all the grounds for application of the provisions of that paragraph are subsequently removed by a reversal of the conviction or termination of the suspension, disbarment, or revocation. An application for reinstatement on any other grounds by any person suspended under paragraph (e)(2) of this section may be filed at any time and the applicant shall be accorded an opportunity for a hearing in the matter; however, such suspension shall continue unless and until the applicant has been reinstated by order of the Commission for good cause shown.

(6) *Other proceedings not precluded.* A proceeding brought under paragraph (e)(1), (e)(2) or (e)(3) of this section shall not preclude another proceeding brought under these same paragraphs.

(7) *Public hearings.* All hearings held under this paragraph (e) shall be public unless otherwise ordered by the Commission on its own motion or after considering the motion of a party.

(f) *Practice defined.* For the purposes of these Rules of Practice, practicing before the Commission shall include, but shall not be limited to:

(1) Transacting any business with the Commission; and

(2) The preparation of any statement, opinion or other paper by any attorney, accountant, engineer or other professional or expert, filed with the Commission in any registration statement, notification, application, report or other document with the consent of such attorney, accountant, engineer or other professional or expert.

§ 201.103 Construction of Rules

(a) The Rules of Practice shall be construed and administered to secure the just, speedy, and inexpensive determination of every proceeding.

(b) In any particular proceeding, to the extent that there is a conflict between these rules and a procedural requirement contained in any statute, or any rule or form adopted thereunder, the latter shall control.

(c) For purposes of these rules:

(1) Any term in the singular includes the plural, and any term in the plural includes the singular, if such use would be appropriate;

(2) Any use of a masculine, feminine, or neuter gender encompasses such other genders as would be appropriate; and

(3) Unless the context requires otherwise, counsel for a party may take any action required or permitted to be taken by such party.

§ 201.104 Business Hours

The Headquarters office of the Commission, at 450 Fifth Street, N.W., Washington, D.C. 20549, is open each day, except Saturdays, Sundays, and Federal legal holidays, from 9 a.m. to 5:30 p.m., Eastern Standard Time or Eastern Daylight Saving Time, whichever is currently in effect in Washington, D.C. Federal legal holidays consist of New Year's Day; Birthday of Martin Luther King, Jr.; Presidents Day; Memorial Day; Independence Day; Labor Day; Columbus Day; Veterans Day; Thanksgiving Day; Christmas Day; and any other day appointed as a holiday in Washington, D.C. by the President or the Congress of the United States.

§ 201.110 Presiding Officer

All proceedings shall be presided over by the Commission or, if the Commission so orders, by a hearing officer. When the Commission designates that the hearing officer shall be an administrative law judge, the Chief Administrative Law Judge shall select, pursuant to 17 CFR 200.30–10, the administrative law judge to preside.

§ 201.111 Hearing Officer: Authority

The hearing officer shall have the authority to do all things necessary and appropriate to discharge his or her duties. No provision of these Rules of Practice shall be construed to limit the powers of the hearing officer provided by the Administrative Procedure Act, 5 U.S.C. 556, 557. The powers of the hearing officer include, but are not limited to, the following:

(a) Administering oaths and affirmations;

(b) Issuing subpoenas authorized by law and revoking, quashing, or modifying any such subpoena;

(c) Receiving relevant evidence and ruling upon the admission of evidence and offers of proof;

(d) Regulating the course of a proceeding and the conduct of the parties and their counsel;

(e) Holding prehearing and other conferences as set forth in § 201.221 and requiring the attendance at any such conference of at least one representative of each party who has authority to negotiate concerning the resolution of issues in controversy;

(f) Recusing himself or herself upon motion made by a party or upon his or her own motion;

(g) Ordering, in his or her discretion, in a proceeding involving more than one respondent, that the interested division indicate, on the record, at least one day prior to the presentation of any evidence, each respondent against whom that evidence will be offered;

(h) Subject to any limitations set forth elsewhere in these Rules of Practice, considering and ruling upon all procedural and other motions, including a motion to correct a manifest error of fact in the initial decision, provided that such a motion to correct is filed within ten days of the initial decision;

(i) Preparing an initial decision as provided in § 201.360;

(j) Upon notice to all parties, reopening any hearing prior to the filing of an initial decision therein, or, if no initial decision is to be filed, prior to the time fixed for the filing of final briefs with the Commission; and

(k) Informing the parties as to the availability of one or more alternative means of dispute resolution, and encouraging the use of such methods.

§ 201.112 Hearing Officer: Disqualification and Withdrawal

(a) *Notice of disqualification.* At any time a hearing officer believes himself or herself to be disqualified from considering a matter, the hearing officer shall issue a notice stating that he or she is withdrawing from the matter and setting forth the reasons therefor.

(b) *Motion for withdrawal.* Any party who has a reasonable, good faith basis to believe that a hearing officer has a personal bias, or is otherwise disqualified from hearing a case, may make a motion to the hearing officer that the hearing officer withdraw. The motion shall be accompanied by an affidavit setting forth in detail the facts alleged to constitute grounds for disqualification. If the hearing officer finds himself or herself not disqualified, he or she shall so rule and shall continue to preside over the proceeding.

§ 201.120 Ex parte Communications

(a) Except to the extent required for the disposition of *ex parte* matters as authorized by law, the person presiding over an evidentiary hearing may not:

(1) Consult a person or party on a fact in issue, unless on notice and opportunity for all parties to participate; or

(2) Be responsible to or subject to the supervision or direction of an employee or agent engaged in the performance of investigative or prosecuting functions for the Commission.

(b) The Commission's code of behavior regarding *ex parte* communications between persons outside the Commission and decisional employees, 17 CFR 200.110 through 200.114, governs other prohibited communications during a proceeding conducted under the Rules of Practice.

§ 201.121 Separation of Functions

Any Commission officer, employee or agent engaged in the performance of investigative or prosecutorial functions for the Commission in a proceeding as defined in § 201.101(a) may not, in that proceeding or one that is factually related, participate or advise in the decision, or in Commission review of the decision pursuant to Section 557 of the Administrative Procedure Act, 5 U.S.C. 557, except as a witness or counsel in the proceeding.

§ 201.140 Commission Orders and Decisions: Signature and Availability

(a) *Signature required.* All orders and decisions of the Commission shall be signed by the Secretary or any other person duly authorized by the Commission.

(b) *Availability for inspection.* Each order and decision shall be available for inspection by the public from the date of entry, unless the order or decision is nonpublic. A nonpublic order or decision shall be available for inspection by any person entitled to inspect it from the date of entry.

(c) *Date of entry of orders.* The date of entry of a Commission order shall be the date the order is signed. Such date shall be reflected in the caption of the order, or if there is no caption, in the order itself.

§ 201.141 Orders and Decisions: Service of Orders Instituting Proceedings and Other Orders and Decisions

(a) *Service of an order instituting proceedings.* (1) *By whom made.* The Secretary, or another duly authorized officer of the Commission, shall serve a copy of an order instituting proceedings on each person named in the order as a party. The Secretary may direct an interested division to assist in making service.

(2) *How made.* (i) *To individuals.* Notice of a proceeding shall be made to an individual by delivering a copy of the order instituting proceedings to the individual or to an agent authorized by appointment or by law to receive such notice. *Delivery* means—handing a copy of the order to the individual; or leaving a copy at the individual's office with a clerk or other person in charge thereof; or leaving a copy at the individual's dwelling house or usual place of abode with some person of suitable age and discretion then residing therein; or sending a copy of the order addressed to the individual by U.S. Postal Service certified, registered or Express Mail and obtaining a confirmation of receipt; or giving confirmed telegraphic notice.

(ii) *To corporations or entities.* Notice of a proceeding shall be made to a person other than a natural person by delivering a copy of the order instituting proceedings to an officer, managing or general agent, or any other agent authorized by appointment or by law to receive such notice, by any method specified in paragraph (a)(2)(i) of this section.

(iii) *Upon persons registered with the Commission.* In addition to any other method of service specified in paragraph (a)(2) of this section, notice may be made to a person currently registered with the Commission as a broker, dealer, municipal securities dealer, government securities broker, government securities dealer, investment adviser, investment company or transfer agent by sending a copy of the order addressed to the most recent business address shown on the person's registration form by

U.S. Postal Service certified, registered or Express Mail and obtaining a confirmation of attempted delivery.

(iv) *Upon persons in a foreign country.* Notice of a proceeding to a person in a foreign country may be made by any method specified in paragraph (a)(2) of this section, or by any other method reasonably calculated to give notice, provided that the method of service used is not prohibited by the law of the foreign country.

(v) *In stop order proceedings.* Notwithstanding any other provision of paragraph (a)(2) of this section, in proceedings pursuant to Section 8 or 10 of the Securities Act of 1933, 15 U.S.C. 77h or 77j, or Sections 305 or 307 of the Trust Indenture Act of 1939, 15 U.S.C. 77eee or 77ggg, notice of the institution of proceedings shall be made by personal service or confirmed telegraphic notice, or a waiver obtain pursuant to paragraph (a)(4) of this section.

(3) *Record of service.* The Secretary shall maintain a record of service on parties (in hard copy or computerized format), identifying the party given notice, the method of service, the date of service, the address to which service was made, and the person who made service. If service is made in person, the certificate of service shall state, if available, the name of the individual to whom the order was given. If service is made by U.S. Postal Service certified or Express Mail, the Secretary shall maintain the confirmation of receipt or of attempted delivery. If service is made to an agent authorized by appointment to receive service, the certificate of service shall be accompanied by evidence of the appointment.

(4) *Waiver of service.* In lieu of service as set forth in paragraph (a)(2) of this section, the party may be provided a copy of the order instituting proceedings by first class mail or other reliable means if a waiver of service is obtained from the party and placed in the record.

(b) *Service of orders or decisions other than an order instituting proceedings.* Written orders or decisions issued by the Commission or by a hearing officer shall be served promptly on each party pursuant to any method of service authorized under paragraph (a) of this section or § 201.150(c)(1)–(3). Such orders or decisions may also be served by facsimile transmission if the party to be served has agreed to accept such service in a writing, signed by the party, and has provided the Commission with information concerning the facsimile machine telephone number and hours of facsimile machine operation. Service of orders or decisions by the Commission, including those entered pursuant to delegated authority, shall be made by the Secretary or, as authorized by the Secretary, by a member of an interested division. Service of orders or decisions issued by a hearing officer shall be made by the Secretary or the hearing officer.

§ 201.150 Service of Papers by Parties

(a) *When required.* In every proceeding as defined in § 201.101(a), each paper, including each notice of appearance, written motion, brief, or other written communication, shall be served upon each party in the proceeding in accordance with the provisions of this section; provided, however, that absent an order to the contrary, no service shall be required for motions which may be heard *ex parte.*

(b) *Upon a person represented by counsel.* Whenever service is required to be made upon a person represented by counsel who has filed a notice of appearance pursuant to § 201.102, service shall be made pursuant to paragraph (c) of this section upon counsel, unless service upon the person represented is ordered by the Commission or the hearing officer.

(c) *How made.* Service shall be made by delivering a copy of the filing. *Delivery* means:

(1) Personal service—handing a copy to the person required to be served; or leaving a copy at the person's office with a clerk or other person in charge thereof, or, if there is no one in charge, leaving it in a conspicuous place therein; or, if the office is closed or

the person to be served has no office, leaving it at the person's dwelling house or usual place of abode with some person of suitable age and discretion then residing therein;

(2) Mailing the papers through the U.S. Postal Service by first class, registered, or certified mail or Express Mail delivery addressed to the person;

(3) Sending the papers through a commercial courier service or express delivery service; or

(4) Transmitting the papers by facsimile transmission where the following conditions are met:

(i) The persons so serving each other have provided the Commission and the parties with notice of the facsimile machine telephone number to be used and the hours of facsimile machine operation;

(ii) The transmission is made at such a time that it is received during the Commission's business hours as defined in § 201.104; and

(iii) The sender of the transmission previously has not been served in accordance with § 201.150 with a written notice from the receipt of the transmission declining service by facsimile transmission.

(d) *When service is complete.* Personal service, service by U.S. Postal Service Express Mail or service by a commercial courier or express delivery service is complete upon delivery. Service by mail is complete upon mailing. Service by facsimile is complete upon confirmation of transmission by delivery of a manually signed receipt.

§ 201.151 Filing of Papers With the Commission: Procedure

(a) *When to file.* All papers required to be served by a party upon any person shall be filed contemporaneously with the Commission. Papers required to be filed with the Commission must be received within the time limit, if any, for such filing. Filing with the Commission may be made by facsimile transmission if the party also contemporaneously transmits to the Commission a non-facsimile original with a manual signature. However, any person filing with the Commission by facsimile transmission will be responsible for assuring that the Commission receives a complete and legible filing within the time limit set for such filing.

(b) *Where to file.* Filing of papers with the Commission shall be made by filing them with the Secretary. When a proceeding is assigned to a hearing officer, a person making a filing with the Secretary shall promptly provide to the hearing officer a copy of any such filing, provided, however, that the hearing officer may direct or permit filings to be made with him or her, in which event the hearing officer shall note thereon the filing date and promptly provide the Secretary with either the original or a copy of any such filings.

(c) *To whom to direct the filing.* Unless otherwise provided, where the Commission has assigned a case to a hearing officer, all motions, objections, applications or other filings made during a proceeding prior to the filing of an initial decision therein, or, if no initial decision is to be filed, prior to the time fixed for the filing of briefs with the Commission, shall be directed to and decided by the hearing officer.

(d) *Certificate of service.* Papers filed with the Commission or a hearing officer shall be accompanied by a certificate stating the name of the person or persons served, the date of service, the method of service and the mailing address or facsimile telephone number to which service was made, if not made in person. If the method of service to any party is different from the method of service to any other party or the method for filing with the Commission, the certificate shall state why a different means of service was used.

§ 201.152 Filing of Papers: Form

(a) *Specifications.* Papers filed in connection with any proceeding as defined in § 201.101(a) shall:

(1) Be on one grade of unglazed white paper measuring 8½ x 11 inches, except that, to the extent that the reduction of larger documents would render them illegible, such documents may be filed on larger paper;

(2) Be typewritten or printed in 12–point or larger typeface or otherwise reproduced by a process that produces permanent and plainly legible copies;

(3) Include at the head of the paper, or on a title page, the name of the Commission, the title of the proceeding, the names of the parties, the subject of the particular paper or pleading, and the file number assigned to the proceeding;

(4) Be paginated with left hand margins at least 1 inch wide, and other margins of at least 1 inch;

(5) Be double-spaced, with single-spaced footnotes and single-spaced indented quotations; and

(6) Be stapled, clipped or otherwise fastened in the upper left corner.

(b) *Signature required.* All papers must be dated and signed as provided in § 201.153.

(c) *Suitability for recordkeeping.* Documents which, in the opinion of the Commission, are not suitable for computer scanning or microfilming may be rejected.

(d) *Number of copies.* An original and three copies of all papers shall be filed.

(e) *Form of briefs.* All briefs containing more than 10 pages shall include a table of contents, an alphabetized table of cases, a table of statutes, and a table of other authorities cited, with references to the pages of the brief wherein they are cited.

(f) *Scandalous or impertinent matter.* Any scandalous or impertinent matter contained in any brief or pleading or in connection with any oral presentation in a proceeding may be stricken on order of the Commission or the hearing officer.

§ 201.153 Filing of Papers: Signature Requirement and Effect

(a) *General requirements.* Following the issuance of an order instituting proceedings, every filing of a party represented by counsel shall be signed by at least one counsel of record in his or her name and shall state that counsel's business address and telephone number. A party who acts as his or her own counsel shall sign his or her individual name and state his or her address and telephone number on every filing.

(b) *Effect of signature.* (1) The signature of a counsel or party shall constitute a certification that:

(i) the person signing the filing has read the filing;

(ii) to the best of his or her knowledge, information, and belief, formed after reasonable inquiry, the filing is well grounded in fact and is warranted by existing law or a good faith argument for the extension, modification, or reversal of existing law; and

(iii) the filing is not made for any improper purpose, such as to harass or to cause unnecessary delay or needless increase in the cost of adjudication.

(2) If a filing is not signed, the hearing officer or the Commission shall strike the filing, unless it is signed promptly after the omission is called to the attention of the person making the filing.

§ 201.154 Motions

(a) *Generally.* Unless made during a hearing or conference, a motion shall be in writing, shall state with particularity the grounds therefor, shall set forth the relief or order sought, and shall be accompanied by a written brief of the points and authorities relied upon. All written motions shall be served in accordance with § 201.150, be filed in accordance with § 201.151, meet the requirements of § 201.152, and be signed in accordance with § 201.153. The Commission or the hearing officer may order that an oral motion be submitted in writing. Unless otherwise ordered by the Commission or the hearing officer, if a motion is properly made to the Commission concerning a proceeding to which a hearing officer is assigned, the proceeding before the hearing officer shall continue pending the determination of the motion by the Commission. No oral argument shall be heard on any motion unless the Commission or the hearing officer otherwise directs.

(b) *Opposing and reply briefs.* Except as provided in § 201.401, briefs in opposition to a motion shall be filed within five days after service of the opposition.

(c) *Length limitation.* A motion, together with the brief in support of the motion, the brief in opposition to the motion, or any reply brief, shall not exceed 15 pages, exclusive of pages containing any table of contents or table of authorities. The page limit shall not apply to any addendum that consists solely of copies of applicable cases, pertinent legislative provisions or rules, or relevant exhibits. Requests for leave to file motions and briefs in excess of 15 pages are disfavored.

§ 201.155 Default; Motion to Set Aside Default

(a) A party to a proceeding may be deemed to be in default and the Commission or the hearing officer may determine the proceeding against that party upon consideration of the record, including the order instituting proceedings, the allegations of which may be deemed to be true, if that party fails:

(1) To appear, in person or through a representative, at a hearing or conference of which that party has been notified;

(2) To answer, to respond to a dispositive motion within the time provided, or otherwise to defend the proceeding; or

(3) To cure a deficient filing within the time specified by the commission or the hearing officer pursuant to § 201.180(b).

(b) A motion to set aside a default shall be made within a reasonable time, state the reasons for the failure to appear or defend, and specify the nature of the proposed defense in the proceeding. In order to prevent injustice and on such conditions as may be appropriate, the hearing officer, at any time prior to the filing of the initial decision, or the Commission, at any time, may for good cause shown set aside a default.

§ 201.160 Time Computation

(a) *Computation.* In computing any period of time prescribed in or allowed by these Rules of Practice or by order of the Commission, the day of the act, event, or default from which the designated period of time begins to run shall not be included. The last day of the period so computed shall be included unless it is a Saturday, Sunday, or Federal legal holiday (as defined in § 201.104), in which event the period runs until the end of the next day that is not a Saturday, Sunday, or Federal legal holiday. Intermediate Saturdays, Sundays, and Federal legal holidays shall be excluded from the computation when the period of time prescribed or allowed is seven days or less, not including any additional time allowed for service by mail in paragraph (b) of this section. If on the day a filing is to be made, weather or other conditions have caused the Secretary's office or other designated filing location to close, the filing deadline shall be extended to the end of the next day that is neither a Saturday, a Sunday, nor a Federal legal holiday.

(b) *Additional time for service by mail.* If service is made by mail, three days shall be added to the prescribed period for response unless an order of the Commission or the hearing officer specifies a date certain for filing. In the event that an order of the Commission or the hearing officer specifies a date certain for filing, no time shall be added for service by mail.

§ 201.161 Extensions of Time, Postponements and Adjournments

(a) *Availability.* Except as otherwise provided by law, the Commission, at any time, or the hearing officer, at any time prior to the filing of his or her initial decision or, if no initial decision is to be filed, at any time prior to the closing of the record, may, for good cause shown, extend or shorten any time limits prescribed by these Rules of Practice for the filing of any papers and may, consistent with paragraph (b) of this section, postpone or adjourn any hearing.

(b) *Considerations in determining whether to extend time limits or grant postponements, adjournments and extensions.* (1) In considering all motions or requests pursuant to paragraph (a) or (b) of this section, the Commission or the hearing officer should adhere to a policy of strongly disfavoring such requests, except in circumstances where the requesting party makes a strong showing that the denial of the request or motion would substantially prejudice their case. In determining whether to grant any requests, the Commission or hearing officer shall consider, in addition to any other relevant factors:

(i) The length of the proceeding to date;

(ii) The number of postponements, adjournments or extensions already granted;

(iii) The stage of the proceedings at the time of the request;

(iv) The impact of the request on the hearing officer's ability to complete the proceeding in the time specified by the Commission; and

(v) Any other such matters as justice may require.

(2) To the extent that the Commission has chosen a timeline under which the hearing would occur beyond the statutory 60-day deadline, this policy of strongly disfavoring requests for postponement will not apply to a request by a respondent to postpone commencement of a cease and desist proceeding hearing beyond the statutory 60-day period.

(c) *Time limit.* (1) Postponements, adjournments or extensions of time for filing papers shall not exceed 21 days unless the Commission or the hearing officer states on the record or sets forth in a written order the reasons why a longer period of time is necessary.

(2) *Stay pending Commission consideration of offers of settlement.* (i) If the Commission staff and one or more respondents in the proceeding file a joint motion notifying the hearing officer that they have agreed in principle to a settlement on all major terms, then the hearing officer shall stay the proceeding as to the settling respondent(s), or in the discretion of the hearing officer as to all respondents, pending completion of Commission consideration of the settlement offer. Any such stay will be contingent upon:

(A) The settling respondent(s) submitting to the Commission staff, within fifteen business days of the stay, a signed offer of settlement in conformance with § 201.240; and

(B) Within twenty business days of receipt of the signed offer, the staff submitting the settlement offer and accompanying recommendation to the Commission for consideration.

(ii) If the parties fail to meet either of these deadlines or if the Commission rejects the offer of settlement, the hearing officer must be promptly notified and, upon notification of the hearing officer, the stay shall lapse and the proceeding will continue. In the circumstance where:

(A) A hearing office has granted a stay because the parties have "agreed in principle to a settlement:"

(B) The agreement in principle does not materialize into a signed settlement offer within 15 business days of the stay; and

(C) The stay lapses, the hearing officer will not be required to grant another stay related to the settlement process until both parties have notified the hearing officer in writing that a signed settlement offer has been prepared, received by the Commission's staff, and will be submitted to the Commission.

(iii) The granting of any stay pursuant to this paragraph (c) shall not affect any deadline set pursuant to § 201.360.

§ 201.180 Sanctions

(a) *Contemptuous conduct.*

(1) *Subject to exclusion or suspension.* Contemptuous conduct by any person before the Commission or a hearing officer during any proceeding, including any conference, shall be grounds for the Commission or the hearing officer to:

(i) Exclude that person from such hearing or conference, or any portion thereof; and/or

(ii) Summarily suspend that person from representing others in the proceeding in which such conduct occurred for the duration, or any portion, of the proceeding.

(2) *Review procedure.* A person excluded from a hearing or conference, or a counsel summarily suspended from practice for the duration or any portion of a proceeding, may seek review of the exclusion or suspension by filing with the Commission, within three days of the exclusion or suspension order, a motion to vacate the order. The Commission shall consider such motion on an expedited basis as provided in § 201.500.

(3) *Adjournment.* Upon motion by a party represented by counsel subject to an order of exclusion or suspension, an adjournment shall be granted to allow the retention of new counsel. In determining the length of an adjournment, the Commission or hearing officer shall consider, in addition to the factors set forth in § 201.161, the availability of co-counsel for the party or of other members of a suspended counsel's firm.

(b) *Deficient filings; leave to cure deficiencies.* The Commission or the hearing officer may reject, in whole or in part, any filing that fails to comply with any requirements of these Rules of Practice or of any order issued in the proceeding in which the filing was made. Any such filings shall not be part of the record. The Commission or the hearing officer may direct a party to cure any deficiencies and to resubmit the filing within a fixed time period.

(c) *Failure to make required filing or to cure deficient filing.* The Commission or the hearing officer may enter a default pursuant to § 201.155, dismiss the case, decide the particular matter at issue against that person, or prohibit the introduction of evidence or exclude testimony concerning that matter if a person fails:

(1) To make a filing required under these Rules of Practice; or

(2) To cure a deficient filing within the time specified by the Commission or the hearing officer pursuant to paragraph (b) of this section.

§ 201.190 Confidential Treatment of Information in Certain Filings

(a) *Application.* An application for confidential treatment pursuant to the provisions of Clause 30 of Schedule A of the Securities Act of 1933, 15 U.S.C. 77aa(30), and Rule 406 thereunder, 17 CFR 230.406; Section 24(b)(2) of the Securities Exchange Act of 1934, 15 U.S.C. 78x(b)(2), and Rule 24b–2 thereunder, 17 CFR 240.24b–2; Section 22(b) of the Public Utility Holding Company Act of 1935, 15 U.S.C. 79v(b), and Rule 104 thereunder, 17 CFR 250.104; Section 45(a) of the Investment Company Act of 1940, 15 U.S.C. 80a–44(a), and Rule 45a–1 thereunder, 17 CFR 270.45a–1; or Section 210(a) of the Investment Advisers Act of 1940, 15 U.S.C. 80b–10(a), shall be filed with the Secretary. The application shall be accompanied by a sealed copy of the materials as to which confidential treatment is sought.

(b) *Procedure for supplying additional information.* The applicant may be required to furnish in writing additional information with respect to the grounds for objection to public disclosure. Failure to supply the information so requested within 14 days from the date of receipt by the applicant of a notice of the information required shall be deemed a waiver of the objection to public disclosure of that portion of the information to which the additional information relates, unless the Commission or the hearing officer shall otherwise order for good cause shown at or before the expiration of such 14–day period.

(c) *Confidentiality of materials pending final decision.* Pending the determination of the application for confidential treatment, transcripts, non-final orders including an initial decision, if any, and other materials in connection with the application shall be placed under seal; shall be for the confidential use only of the hearing officer, the Commission, the applicant, and any other parties and counsel; and shall be made available to the public only in accordance with orders of the Commission.

(d) *Public availability of orders.* Any final order of the Commission denying or sustaining an application for confidential treatment shall be made public. Any prior findings or opinions relating to an application for confidential treatment under this section shall be made public at such time as the material as to which confidentiality was requested is made public.

§ 201.191 Adjudications Not Required to Be Determined on the Record After Notice and Opportunity for Hearing

(a) *Scope of the rule.* This rule applies to every case of adjudication, as defined in 5 U.S.C. 551, pursuant to any statute which the Commission administers, where adjudication is not required to be determined on the record after notice and opportunity for hearing and which the Commission has not chosen to determine on the record after notice and opportunity for hearing.

(b) *Procedure.* In every case of adjudication under paragraph (a) of this section, the Commission shall give prompt notice of any adverse action or final disposition to any person who has requested the Commission to make (or not to make) any such adjudication, and furnish to any such person a written statement of reasons therefor. Additional procedures may be specified in rules relating to specific types of such adjudications. Where any such rule provides for the publication of a Commission order, notice of the action or disposition shall be deemed to be given by such publication.

(c) *Contents of the record.* If the Commission provides notice and opportunity for the submission of written comments by parties to the adjudication or, as the case may be, by other interested persons, written comments received on or before the closing date for comments, unless accorded confidential treatment pursuant to statute or rule of the Commission, become a part of the record of the adjudication. The Commission, in its discretion, may accept and include in the record written comments filed with the Commission after the closing date.

§ 201.192 Rulemaking: Issuance, Amendment and Repeal of Rules of General Application

(a) *By petition.* Any person desiring the issuance, amendment or repeal of a rule of general application may file a petition therefor with the Secretary. Such petition shall include a statement setting forth the text or the substance of any proposed rule or amendment desired or specifying the rule the repeal of which is desired, and stating the nature of his or her interest and his or her reasons for seeking the issuance, amendment or repeal of the rule. The Secretary shall acknowledge, in writing, receipt of the petition and refer it to the appropriate division or office for consideration and recommendation. Such recommendations shall be transmitted with the petition to the Commission for such action as the Commission deems appropriate. The Secretary shall notify the petitioner of the action taken by the Commission.

(b) *Notice of proposed issuance, amendment or repeal of rules.* Except where the Commission finds that notice and public procedure are impracticable, unnecessary, or contrary to the public interest, whenever the Commission proposes to issue, amend, or repeal any rule or regulation of general application other than an interpretive rule; general statement of policy; or rule of agency organization, procedure, or practice; or any matter relating to agency management or personnel or to public property, loans, grants, benefits, or contracts, there shall first be published in the **Federal Register** a notice of the proposed action. Such notice shall include:

(1) A statement of the time, place, and nature of the rulemaking proceeding, with particular reference to the manner in which interested persons shall be afforded the opportunity to participate in such proceeding;

(2) Reference to the authority under which the rule is proposed; and

(3) The terms or substance of the proposed rule or a description of the subjects and issues involved.

§ 201.193 Applications by Barred Individuals for Consent to Associate

Preliminary note

This rule governs applications to the Commission by certain persons, barred by Commission order from association with brokers, dealers, municipal securities dealers, government securities brokers, government securities dealers, investment advisers, investment companies or transfer agents, for consent to become so associated. Applications made pursuant to this section must show that the proposed association would be consistent with the public interest. In addition to the information specifically required by the rule, applications should be supplemented, where appropriate, by written statements of individuals (other than the applicant) who are competent to attest to the applicant's character, employment performance, and other relevant information. Intentional misstatements or omissions of fact may constitute criminal violations of 18 U.S.C. 1001 *et seq.* and other provisions of law.

The nature of the supervision that an applicant will receive or exercise as an associated person with a registered entity is an important matter bearing upon the public interest. In meeting the burden of showing that the proposed association is consistent with the public interest, the application and supporting documentation must demonstrate that the proposed supervision, procedures, or terms and conditions of employment are reasonably designed to prevent a recurrence of the conduct that led to imposition of the bar. As an associated person, the applicant will be limited to association in a specified capacity with a particular registered entity and may also be subject to specific terms and conditions.

Normally, the applicant's burden of demonstrating that the proposed association is consistent with the public interest will be difficult to meet where the applicant is to be supervised by, or is to supervise, another barred individual. In addition, where an applicant wishes to become the sole proprietor of a registered entity and thus is seeking Commission consent notwithstanding an absence of supervision, the applicant's burden will be difficult to meet.

In addition to the factors set forth in paragraph (d) of this section, the Commission will consider the nature of the findings that resulted in the bar when making its determination as to whether the proposed association is consistent with the public interest. In this regard, attention is directed to Rule 5(e) of the Commission's Rules on Informal and Other Procedures, 17 CFR 202.5(e). Among other things, Rule 5(e) sets forth the Commission's policy "not to permit a * * * respondent [in an administrative proceeding] to consent to * * * [an] order that imposes a sanction while denying the allegations in the * * * order for proceedings." Consistent with the rationale underlying that policy, and in order to avoid the appearance that an application made pursuant to this section was granted on the basis of such denial, the Commission will not consider any application that attempts to reargue or collaterally attack the findings that resulted in the Commission's bar order.

(a) *Scope of rule.* Applications for Commission consent to associate, or to change the terms and conditions of association, with a registered broker, dealer, municipal securities dealer, government securities broker, government securities dealer, investment adviser, investment company or transfer agent may be made pursuant to this section where a Commission order bars the individual from association with a registered entity and:

(1) Such barred individual seeks to become associated with an entity that is not a member of a self-regulatory organization; or

(2) The order contains a proviso that application may be made to the Commission after a specified period of time.

(b) *Form of application.* Each application shall be supported by an affidavit, manually signed by the applicant, that addresses the factors set forth in paragraph (d) of this section. One original and three copies of the application shall be filed pursuant to §§ 201.151, 201.152 and 201.153. Each application shall include as exhibits:

(1) A copy of the Commission order imposing the bar:

(2) An undertaking by the applicant to notify immediately the Commission in writing if any information submitted in support of the application becomes materially false or misleading while the application is pending;

(3) The following forms, as appropriate:

(i) A copy of a completed Form U–4, where the applicant's proposed association is with a broker-dealer or municipal securities dealer;

(ii) A copy of a completed Form MSD–4, where the applicant's proposed association is with a bank municipal securities dealer;

(iii) The information required by Form ADV, 17 CFR 279.1, with respect to the applicant, where the applicant's proposed association is with an investment adviser;

(iv) The information required by Form TA–1, 17 CFR 249b.100, with respect to the applicant, where the applicant's proposed association is with a transfer agent; and

(4) A written statement by the proposed employer that describes:

(i) The terms and conditions of employment and supervision to be exercised over such applicant and, where applicable, by such applicant;

(ii) The qualifications, experience, and disciplinary records of the proposed supervisor(s) of the applicant;

(iii) The compliance and disciplinary history, during the two years preceding the filing of the application, of the office in which the applicant will be employed; and

(iv) The names of any other associated persons in the same office who have previously been barred by the Commission, and whether they are to be supervised by the applicant.

(c) *Required showing.* The applicant shall make a showing satisfactory to the Commission that the proposed association would be consistent with the public interest.

(d) *Factors to be addressed.* The affidavit required by paragraph (b) of this section shall address each of the following:

(1) The time period since the imposition of the bar;

(2) Any restitution or similar action taken by the applicant to recompense any person injured by the misconduct that resulted in the bar;

(3) The applicant's compliance with the order imposing the bar;

(4) The applicant's employment during the period subsequent to imposition of the bar;

(5) The capacity or position in which the applicant proposes to be associated;

(6) The manner and extent of supervision to be exercised over such applicant and, where applicable, by such applicant;

(7) Any relevant courses, seminars, examinations or other actions completed by the applicant subsequent to imposition of the bar to prepare for his or her return to the securities business; and

(8) Any other information material to the application.

(e) *Notification to applicant and written statement.* In the event an adverse recommendation is proposed by the staff with respect to an application made pursuant to this section, the applicant shall be so advised and provided with a written statement of the reasons for such recommendation. The applicant shall then have 30 days to submit a written statement in response.

(f) *Concurrent applications.* The Commission will not consider any application submitted pursuant to this section if any other application for consent to associate concerning the same applicant is pending before any self-regulatory organization.

Initiation of Proceedings and Prehearing Rules

§ 201.200 Initiation of Proceedings

(a) *Order instituting proceedings: notice and opportunity for hearing.* (1) *Generally.* Whenever an order instituting proceedings is issued by the Commission, appropriate notice thereof shall be given to each party to the proceeding by the Secretary or another duly designated officer of the Commission. Each party shall be given notice of any hearing within a time reasonable in light of the circumstances, in advance of the hearing; provided, however, no prior notice need be given to a respondent if the Commission has authorized the Division of Enforcement to seek a temporary sanction *ex parte.*

(2) *Stop order proceedings: additional persons entitled to notice.* Any notice of a proceeding relating to the issuance of a stop order suspending the effectiveness of a registration statement pursuant to Section 8(d) of the Securities Act of 1933, 15 U.S.C. 77h(d), shall be sent to or served on the issuer; or, in the case of a foreign government or political subdivision thereof, sent to or served on the underwriter; or, in the case of a foreign or territorial person, sent to or served on its duly authorized representative in the United States named in the registration statement, properly directed in the case of telegraphic notice to the address given in such statement. In addition, if such proceeding is commenced within 90 days after the registration statement has become effective, notice of the proceeding shall be given to the agent for service named on the facing sheet of the registration statement and to each other person designated on the facing sheet of the registration statement as a person to whom copies of communications to such agent are to be sent.

(b) *Content of order.* The order instituting proceedings shall:

(1) State the nature of any hearing;

(2) State the legal authority and jurisdiction under which the hearing is to be held;

(3) Contain a short and plain statement of the matters of fact and law to be considered and determined, unless the order directs an answer pursuant to § 201.220 in which case the order shall set forth the factual and legal basis alleged therefor in such detail as will permit a specific response thereto; and

(4) State the nature of any relief or action sought or taken.

(c) *Time and place of hearing.* The time and place for any hearing shall be fixed with due regard for the public interest and the convenience and necessity of the parties, other participants, or their representatives.

(d) *Amendment to order instituting proceedings.* (1) *By the Commission.* Upon motion by a party, the Commission may, at any time, amend an order instituting proceedings to include new matters of fact or law.

(2) *By the hearing officer.* Upon motion by a party, the hearing officer may, at any time prior to the filing of an initial decision or, if no

initial decision is to be filed, prior to the time fixed for the filing of final briefs with the Commission, amend an order instituting proceedings to include new matters of fact or law that are within the scope of the original order instituting proceedings.

(e) *Publication of notice of public hearings.* Unless otherwise ordered by the Commission, notice of any public hearing shall be given general circulation by release to the public, by publication in the *SEC News Digest* and, where directed, by publication in the **Federal Register**.

§ 201.201 Consolidation and Severance of Proceedings

(a) *Consolidation.* By order of the Commission or a hearing officer, proceedings involving a common question of law or fact may be consolidated for hearing of any or all the matters at issue in such proceedings. The Commission or the hearing officer may make such orders concerning the conduct of such proceedings as it deems appropriate to avoid unnecessary cost or delay. Consolidation shall not prejudice any rights under these Rules of Practice and shall not affect the right of any party to raise issues that could have been raised if consolidation had not occurred. For purposes of this section, no distinction is made between joinder and consolidation of proceedings.

(b) *Severance.* By order of the Commission, any proceeding may be severed with respect to some or all parties. Any motion to sever must be made solely to the Commission and must include a representation that a settlement offer is pending before the Commission or otherwise show good cause.

§ 201.202 Specification of Procedures by Parties in Certain Proceedings

(a) *Motion to specify procedures.* In any proceeding other than an enforcement or disciplinary proceeding, a proceeding to review a determination by a self-regulatory organization pursuant to §§ 201.420 and 201.421, or a proceeding to review a determination of the Board pursuant to §§ 201.440 and 201.441, a party may, at any time up to 20 days prior to the start of a hearing, make a motion to specify the procedures necessary or appropriate for the proceeding with particular reference to:

(1) Whether there should be an initial decision by a hearing officer;

(2) Whether any interested division of the Commission may assist in the preparation of the Commission's decision; and

(3) Whether there should be a 30–day waiting period between the issuance of the Commission's order and the date it is to become effective.

(b) *Objections; effect of failure to object.* Any other party may object to the procedures so specified, and such party may specify such additional procedures as it considers necessary or appropriate. In the absence of such objection or such specification of additional procedures, such other party may be deemed to have waived objection to the specified procedures.

(c) *Approval required.* Any proposal pursuant to paragraph (a) of this section, even if not objected to by any party, shall be subject to the written approval of the hearing officer.

(d) *Procedure upon agreement to waive an initial decision.* If an initial decision is waived pursuant to paragraph (a) of this section, the hearing officer shall notify the Secretary and, unless the Commission directs otherwise within 14 days, no initial decision shall be issued.

§ 201.210 Parties, Limited Participants and Amici Curiae

(a) *Parties in an enforcement or disciplinary proceeding, a proceeding to review a self-regulatory organization determination, or a proceeding to review a Board determination.*

(1) *Generally.* No person shall be granted leave to become a party or non-party participant on a limited basis in an enforcement or disciplinary proceeding, a proceeding to review a determination by a self-regulatory organization pursuant to §§ 201.420 and 201.421, or a

proceeding to review a determination by the Board pursuant to §§ 201.440 and 201.441, except as authorized by paragraph (c) of this section.

(2) *Disgorgement proceedings.* In an enforcement proceeding, a person may state his or her views with respect to a proposed plan of disgorgement or file a proof of claim pursuant to § 201.612.

(b) *Intervention as a party.*

(1) *Generally.* In any proceeding, other than an enforcement proceeding, a disciplinary proceeding, a proceeding to review a self-regulatory determination, or a proceeding to review a Board determination, any person may seek leave to intervene as a party by filing a motion setting forth the person's interest in the proceeding:

(i) In a proceeding under the Public Utility Holding Company Act of 1935, any representative of interested consumers or security holders, or any other person whose participation in the proceeding may be in the public interest or for the protection of investors or consumers, may be admitted as a party upon the filing of a written motion setting forth the person's interest in the proceeding.

(ii) In a proceeding under the Investment Company Act of 1940, any representative of interested security holders, or any other person whose participation in the proceeding may be in the public interest or for the protection of investors, may be admitted as a party upon the filing of a written motion setting forth the person's interest in the proceeding.

(2) *Intervention as of right.* (i) In proceedings under the Public Utility Holding Company Act of 1935, any interested representative, agency, authority or instrumentality of the United States or any interested State, State commission, municipality or other political subdivision of a state shall be admitted as a party to any proceeding upon the filing of a written motion requesting leave to be admitted.

(ii) In proceedings under the Investment Company Act of 1940, any interested State or State agency shall be admitted as a party to any proceeding upon the filing of a written motion requesting leave to be admitted.

(c) *Leave to participate on a limited basis.* In any proceeding, other than an enforcement proceeding, a disciplinary proceeding, a proceeding to review a self-regulatory determination, or a proceeding to review a Board determination, any person may seek leave to participate on a limited basis as a non-party participant as to any matter affecting the person's interests:

(1) *Procedure.* Motions for leave to participate shall be in writing, shall set forth the nature and extent of the movant's interest in the proceeding, and, except where good cause for late filing is shown, shall be filed not later than 20 days prior to the date fixed for the commencement of the hearing. Leave to participate pursuant to this paragraph (c) may include such rights of a party as the hearing officer may deem appropriate. Persons granted leave to participate shall be served in accordance with § 201.150; provided, however, that a party to the proceeding may move that the extent of notice of filings or other papers to be provided to persons granted leave to participate be limited, or may move that the persons granted leave to participate bear the cost of being provided copies of any or all filings or other papers. Persons granted leave to participate shall be bound, except as may be otherwise determined by the hearing officer, by any stipulation between the parties to the proceeding with respect to procedure, including submission of evidence, substitution of exhibits, corrections of the record, the time within which briefs or exceptions may be filed or proposed findings and conclusions may be submitted, the filing of initial decisions, the procedure to be followed in the preparation of decisions and the effective date of the Commission's order in the case. Where the filing of briefs or exceptions or

the submission of proposed findings and conclusions are waived by the parties to the proceedings, a person granted leave to participate pursuant to this paragraph (c) shall not be permitted to file a brief or exceptions or submit proposed findings and conclusions except by leave of the Commission or of the hearing officer.

(2) *Certain persons entitled to leave to participate.* The hearing officer is directed to grant leave to participate under this paragraph (c) to any person to whom it is proposed to issue any security in exchange for one or more bona fide outstanding securities, claims or property interests, or partly in such exchange and partly for cash, where the Commission is authorized to approve the terms and conditions of such issuance and exchange after a hearing upon the fairness of such terms and conditions.

(3) *Leave to participate in certain Commission proceedings by a representative of the United States Department of Justice, a United States Attorney's Office, or a criminal prosecutorial authority of any State or any other political subdivision of a State.* The Commission or the hearing officer may grant leave to participate on a limited basis to an authorized representative of the United States Department of Justice, an authorized representative of a United States Attorney, or an authorized representative of any criminal prosecutorial authority of any State or any other political subdivision of a State for the purpose of requesting a stay during the pendency of a criminal investigation or prosecution arising out of the same or similar facts that are at issue in the pending Commission enforcement or disciplinary proceeding. Upon a showing that such a stay is in the public interest or for the protection of investors, the motion for stay shall be favored. A stay granted under this paragraph (c)(3) may be granted for such a period and upon such conditions as the Commission or the hearing officer deems appropriate.

(d) *Amicus participation.*

(1) *Availability.* An amicus brief may be filed only if:

(i) A motion for leave to file the brief has been granted;

(ii) The brief is accompanied by written consent of all parties;

(iii) The brief is filed at the request of the Commission or the hearing officer; or

(iv) The brief is presented by the United States or an officer or agency thereof, or by a State, Territory or Commonwealth.

(2) *Procedure.* An amicus brief may be filed conditionally with the motion for leave. The motion for leave shall identify the interest of the movant and shall state the reasons why a brief of an amicus curiae is desirable. Except as all parties otherwise consent, any amicus curiae shall file its brief within the time allowed the party whose position the amicus will support, unless the Commission or hearing officer; for cause shown, grants leave for a later filing. In the event that a later filing is allowed, the order granting leave to file shall specify when an opposing party may reply to the brief. A motion of an amicus curiae to participate in oral argument will be granted only for extraordinary reasons.

(e) *Permission to state views.* Any person may make a motion seeking leave to file a memorandum or make an oral statement of his or her views. Any such communication may be included in the record; provided, however, that unless offered and admitted as evidence of the truth of the statements therein made, any assertions of fact submitted pursuant to the provisions of this paragraph (e) will be considered only to the extent that the statements therein made are otherwise supported by the record.

(f) *Modification of participation provisions.* The Commission or the hearing officer may, by order, modify the provisions of this section which would otherwise be applicable, and may impose such terms and conditions on the participation of any person in any proceeding as it may deem necessary or appropriate in the public interest.

§ 201.220 Answer to Allegations

(a) *When required.* In its order instituting proceedings, the Commission may require any party to file an answer to each of the allegations contained therein. Even if not so ordered, any party in any proceeding may elect to file an answer. Any other person granted leave by the Commission or the hearing officer to participate on a limited basis in such proceedings pursuant to § 201.210(c) may be required to file an answer.

(b) *When to file.* Except where a different period is provided by rule or by order, a party required to file an answer as provided in paragraph (a) of this section shall do so within 20 days after service upon the party of the order instituting proceedings. Persons granted leave to participate on a limited basis in the proceeding pursuant to § 201.210(c) may file an answer within a reasonable time, as determined by the Commission or the hearing officer. If the order instituting proceedings is amended, the Commission or the hearing officer may require that an amended answer be filed and, if such an answer is required, shall specify a date for the filing thereof.

(c) *Contents; effect of failure to deny.* Unless otherwise directed by the hearing officer or the Commission, an answer shall specifically admit, deny, or state that the party does not have, and is unable to obtain, sufficient information to admit or deny each allegation in the order instituting proceedings. When a party intends in good faith to deny only a part of an allegation, the party shall specify so much of it as is true and shall deny only the remainder. A statement of a lack of information shall have the effect of a denial. A defense of res judicata, statute of limitations or any other matter constituting an affirmative defense shall be asserted in the answer. Any allegation not denied shall be deemed admitted.

(d) *Motion for more definite statement.* A party may file with an answer a motion for a more definite statement of specified matters of fact or law to be considered or determined. Such motion shall state the respects in which, and the reasons why, each such matter of fact or law should be required to be made more definite. If the motion is granted, the order granting such motion shall set the periods for filing such a statement and any answer thereto.

(e) *Amendments.* A party may amend its answer at any time by written consent of each adverse party or with leave of the Commission or the hearing officer. Leave shall be freely granted when justice so requires.

(f) *Failure to file answer: default.* If a party respondent fails to file an answer required by this section within the time provided, such person may be deemed in default pursuant to § 201.155(a). A party may make a motion to set aside a default pursuant to § 201.155(b).

§ 201.221 Prehearing Conference

(a) *Purposes of conference.* The purposes of a prehearing conference include, but are not limited to:

(1) Expediting the disposition of the proceeding;

(2) Establishing early and continuing control of the proceeding by the hearing officer; and

(3) Improving the quality of the hearing through more thorough preparation.

(b) *Procedure.* On his or her own motion or at the request of a party, the hearing officer may, in his or her discretion, direct counsel or any party to meet for an initial, final or other prehearing conference. Such conferences may be held with or without the hearing officer present as the hearing officer deems appropriate. Where such a conference is held outside the presence of the hearing officer, the hearing officer shall be advised promptly by the parties of any agreements reached. Such conferences also may be held with one or more persons participating by telephone or other remote means.

(c) *Subjects to be discussed.* At a prehearing conference consideration may be given and action taken with respect to any and all of the following:

(1) Simplification and clarification of the issues;

(2) Exchange of witness and exhibit lists and copies of exhibits;

(3) Stipulations, admissions of fact, and stipulations concerning the contents, authenticity, or admissibility into evidence of documents;

(4) Matters of which official notice may be taken;

(5) The schedule for exchanging prehearing motions or briefs, if any;

(6) The method of service for papers other than Commission orders;

(7) Summary disposition of any or all issues;

(8) Settlement of any or all issues;

(9) Determination of hearing dates;

(10) Amendments to the order instituting proceedings or answers thereto;

(11) Production of documents as set forth in § 201.230, and prehearing production of documents in response to subpoenas duces tecum as set forth in § 201.232;

(12) Specification of procedures as set forth in § 201.202; and

(13) Such other matters as may aid in the orderly and expeditious disposition of the proceeding.

(d) *Required prehearing conference.* Except where the emergency nature of a proceeding would make a prehearing conference clearly inappropriate, at least one prehearing conference should be held.

(e) *Prehearing orders.* At or following the conclusion of any conference held pursuant to this section, the hearing officer shall enter a ruling or order which recites the agreements reached and any procedural determinations made by the hearing officer.

(f) *Failure to appear; default.* Any person who is named in an order instituting proceedings as a person against whom findings may be made or sanctions imposed and who fails to appear, in person or through a representative, at a prehearing conference of which he or she has been duly notified may be deemed in default pursuant to § 201.155(a). A party may make a motion to set aside a default pursuant to § 201.155(b).

§ 201.222 Prehearing Submissions

(a) *Submissions generally.* The hearing officer, on his or her own motion, or at the request of a party or other participant, may order any party, including the interested division, to furnish such information as deemed appropriate, including any or all of the following:

(1) An outline or narrative summary of its case or defense;

(2) The legal theories upon which it will rely;

(3) Copies and a list of documents that it intends to introduce at the hearing; and

(4) A list of witnesses who will testify on its behalf, including the witnesses' names, occupations, addresses and a brief summary of their expected testimony.

(b) *Expert witnesses.* Each party who intends to call an expert witness shall submit, in addition to the information required by paragraph (a)(4) of this section, a statement of the expert's qualifications, a listing of other proceedings in which the expert has given expert testimony, and a list of publications authored or co-authored by the expert.

§ 201.230 Enforcement and Disciplinary Proceedings: Availability of Documents for Inspection and Copying

For purposes of this section, the term *documents* shall include writings, drawings, graphs, charts, photographs, recordings and other data compilations, including data stored by computer, from which information can be obtained.

(a) *Documents to be available for inspection and copying.* (1) Unless otherwise provided by this section, or by order of the Commission or the hearing officer, the Division of Enforcement shall make available for inspection and copying by any party documents obtained by the Division prior to the institution of proceedings, in connection with the investigation leading to the Division's recommendation to institute proceedings. Such documents shall include:

(i) Each subpoena issued;

(ii) Every other written request to persons not employed by the Commission to provide documents or to be interviewed;

(iii) The documents turned over in response to any such subpoenas or other written requests;

(iv) All transcripts and transcript exhibits;

(v) Any other documents obtained from persons not employed by the Commission; and

(vi) Any final examination or inspection reports prepared by the Office of Compliance Inspections and Examinations, the Division of Market Regulation, or the Division of Investment Management, if the Division of Enforcement intends either to introduce any such report into evidence or to use any such report to refresh the collection of any witness.

(2) Nothing in this paragraph (a) shall limit the right of the Division to make available any other document, or shall limit the right of a respondent to seek access to or production pursuant to subpoena of any other document, or shall limit the authority of the hearing officer to order the production of any document pursuant to subpoena.

(b) *Documents that may be withheld.*

(1) The Division of Enforcement may withhold a document if:

(i) The document is privileged;

(ii) The document is an internal memorandum, note or writing prepared by a Commission employee, other than an examination or inspection report as specified in paragraph (a)(1)(vi) of this section, or is otherwise attorney work product and will not be offered in evidence;

(iii) The document would disclose the identity of a confidential source; or

(iv) The hearing officer grants leave to withhold a document or category of documents as not relevant to the subject matter of the proceeding or otherwise, for good cause shown.

(2) Nothing in this paragraph (b) authorizes the Division of Enforcement in connection with an enforcement or disciplinary proceeding to withhold, contrary to the doctrine of *Brady v. Maryland,* 373 U.S. 83, 87 (1963) documents that contain material exculpatory evidence.

(c) *Withheld document list.* The hearing officer may require the Division of Enforcement to submit for review a list of documents or categories of documents withheld pursuant to paragraphs (b)(1)(i) through (b)(1)(iv) of this section or to submit any document withheld, and may determine whether any such document should be made available for inspection and copying. When similar documents are withheld pursuant to paragraphs (b)(1)(i) through (b)(1)(iv) of this section, those documents may be identified by category instead of by individual document. The hearing officer retains discretion to determine when an identification by category is insufficient.

(d) *Timing of inspection and copying.* Unless otherwise ordered by the Commission or the hearing officer, the Division of Enforcement shall commence making documents available to a respondent for inspection and copying pursuant to this section no later than 7 days after the service of the order instituting proceedings. In a proceeding in which a temporary cease-and-desist order is sought pursuant to § 201.510 or a temporary suspension of registration is sought pursuant to § 201.520, documents shall be made available no later than the day after service of the decision as to whether to issue a temporary cease-and-desist order or temporary suspension order.

(e) *Place of inspection and copying.* Documents subject to inspection and copying pursuant to this section shall be made available to the respondent for inspection and copying at the Commission office where they are ordinarily maintained, or at such other place as the parties, in writing, may agree. A respondent shall not be given custody of the documents or leave to remove the documents from the Commission's offices pursuant to the requirements of this section other than by written agreement of the Division of Enforcement. Such agreement shall specify the documents subject to the agreement, the date they shall be returned and such other terms or conditions as are appropriate to provide for the safekeeping of the documents.

(f) *Copying costs and procedures.* The respondent may obtain a photocopy of any documents made available for inspection. The respondent shall be responsible for the cost of photocopying. Unless otherwise ordered, charges for copies made by the Division of Enforcement at the request of the respondent will be at the rate charged pursuant to the fee schedule at 17 CFR 200.80e for copies. The respondent shall be given access to the documents at the Commission's offices or such other place as the parties may agree during normal business hours for copying of documents at the respondent's expense.

(g) *Issuance of investigatory subpoenas after institution of proceedings.* The Division of Enforcement shall promptly inform the hearing officer and each party if investigatory subpoenas are issued under the same investigation file number or pursuant to the same order directing private investigation ("formal order") under which the investigation leading to the institution of proceedings was conducted. The hearing officer shall order such steps as necessary and appropriate to assure that the issuance of investigatory subpoenas after the institution of proceedings is not for the purpose of obtaining evidence relevant to the proceedings and that any relevant documents that may be obtained through the use of investigatory subpoenas in a continuing investigation are made available to each respondent for inspection and copying on a timely basis.

(h) *Failure to make documents available—harmless error.* In the event that a document required to be made available to a respondent pursuant to this section is not made available by the Division of Enforcement, no rehearing or redecision of a proceeding already heard or decided shall be required, unless the respondent shall establish that the failure to make the document available was not harmless error.

§ 201.231 Enforcement and Disciplinary Proceedings: Production of Witness Statements

(a) *Availability.* Any respondent in an enforcement or disciplinary proceeding may move that the Division of Enforcement produce for inspection and copying any statement of any person called or to be called as a witness by the Division of Enforcement that pertains, or is expected to pertain, to his or her direct testimony and that would be required to be required to be produced pursuant to the Jencks Act, 18 U.S.C. 3500. For purposes of this section, *statement* shall have the meaning set forth in 18 U.S.C. 3500(e). Such production shall be made at a time and place fixed by the hearing officer and shall be made available to any party, provided, however, that the production shall be made under conditions intended to preserve the items to be inspected or copied.

(b) *Failure to produce—harmless error.* In the event that a statement required to be made available for inspection and copying by a respondent is not turned over by the Division of Enforcement, no rehearing or redecision of a proceeding already heard or decided shall be required unless the respondent establishes that the failure to turn over the statement was not harmless error.

§ 201.232 Subpoenas

(a) *Availability; procedure.* In connection with any hearing ordered by the Commission, a party may request the issuance of subpoenas requiring the attendance and testimony of witnesses at the designated time and place of hearing, and subpoenas requiring the production of documentary or other tangible evidence returnable at any designated time or place. Unless made on the record at a hearing, requests for issuance of a subpoena shall be made in writing and served on each party pursuant to § 201.150. A person whose request for a subpoena has been denied or modified may not request that any other person issue the subpoena.

(1) *Unavailability of hearing officer.* In the event that the hearing officer assigned to a proceeding is unavailable, the party seeking issuance of the subpoena may seek its issuance from the first available of the following persons: the Chief Administrative Law Judge, the law judge most senior in service as a law judge, the duty officer, any other member of the Commission, or any other person designated by the Commission to issue subpoenas. Requests for issuance of a subpoena made to the Commission, or any member thereof, must be submitted to the Secretary, not to an individual Commissioner.

(2) *Signing may be delegated.* A hearing officer may authorize issuance of a subpoena, and may delegate the manual signing of the subpoena to any other person authorized to issue subpoenas.

(b) *Standards for issuance.* Where it appears to the person asked to issue the subpoena that the subpoena sought may be unreasonable, oppressive, excessive in scope, or unduly burdensome, he or she may, in his or her discretion, as a condition precedent to the issuance of the subpoena, require the person seeking the subpoena to show the general relevance and reasonable scope of the testimony or other evidence sought. If after consideration of all the circumstances, the person requested to issue the subpoena determines that the subpoena or any of its terms is unreasonable, oppressive, excessive in scope, or unduly burdensome, he or she may refuse to issue the subpoena, or issue it only upon such conditions as fairness requires. In making the foregoing determination, the person issuing the subpoena may inquire of the other participants whether they will stipulate to the facts sought to be proved.

(c) *Service.* Service shall be made pursuant to the provisions of § 201.150(b) through (d). The provisions of this paragraph (c) shall apply to the issuance of subpoenas for purposes of investigations, as required by 17 CFR 203.8, as well as hearings.

(d) *Tender of fees required.* When a subpoena compelling the attendance of a person at a hearing or deposition is issued at the instance of anyone other than an officer or agency of the United States, service is valid only if the subpoena is accompanied by a tender to the subpoenaed person of the fees for one day's attendance and mileage specified by paragraph (f) of this section.

(e) *Application to quash or modify.*

(1) *Procedure.* Any person to whom a subpoena is directed, or who is an owner, creator or the subject of the documents that are to be produced pursuant to a subpoena, or any party may, prior to the time specified therein for compliance, but in no event more than 15 days after the date of service of such subpoena, request that the subpoena be quashed or modified. Such request shall be made by application filed with the Secretary and served on all parties pursuant to § 201.150. The party on whose behalf the subpoena was issued may, within five days of service of the application, file an opposition to the application. If a hearing officer has been assigned to the proceeding, the application to quash shall be directed to that hearing officer for consideration,

even if the subpoena was issued by another person.

(2) *Standards governing application to quash or modify.* If compliance with the subpoena would be unreasonable, oppressive or unduly burdensome, the hearing officer or the Commission shall quash or modify the subpoena, or may order return of the subpoena only upon specified conditions. These conditions may include but are not limited to a requirement that the party on whose behalf the subpoena was issued shall make reasonable compensation to the person to whom the subpoena was addressed for the cost of copying or transporting evidence to the place for return of the subpoena.

(f) *Witness fees and mileage.* Witnesses summoned before the Commission shall be paid the same fees and mileage that are paid to witnesses in the courts of the United States, and witnesses whose depositions are taken and the persons taking the same shall severally be entitled to the same fees as are paid for like services in the courts of the United States. Witness fees and mileage shall be paid by the party at whose instance the witnesses appear.

§ 201.233 Depositions Upon Oral Examination

(a) *Procedure.* Any party desiring to take the testimony of a witness by deposition shall make a written motion setting forth the reasons why such deposition should be taken including the specific reasons why the party believes the witness will be unable to attend or testify at the hearing; the name and address of the prospective witness; the matters concerning which the prospective witness is expected to be questioned; and the proposed time and place for the taking of the deposition.

(b) *Required finding when ordering a deposition.* In the discretion of the Commission or the hearing officer, an order for deposition may be issued upon a finding that the prospective witness will likely give testimony material to the proceeding; that it is likely the prospective witness, who is then within the United States, will be unable to attend or testify at the hearing because of age, sickness, infirmity, imprisonment, other disability, or absence from the United States, unless it appears that the absence of the witness was procured by the party requesting the deposition; and that the taking of a deposition will serve the interests of justice.

(c) *Contents of order.* An order for deposition shall designate by name a deposition officer. The designated officer may be the hearing officer or any other person authorized to administer oaths by the laws of the United States or of the place where the deposition is to be held. An order for deposition also shall state:

(1) The name of the witness whose deposition is to be taken;

(2) The scope of the testimony to be taken;

(3) The time and place of the deposition;

(4) The manner of recording, preserving and filing the deposition; and

(5) The number of copies, if any, of the deposition and exhibits to be filed upon completion of the deposition.

(d) *Procedure at depositions.* A witness whose testimony is taken by deposition shall be sworn or shall affirm before any questions are put to him or her. Examination and cross-examination of deponents may proceed as permitted at a hearing. The witness being deposed may have counsel present during the deposition.

(e) *Objections to questions or evidence.* Objections to questions or evidence shall be in short form, stating the grounds of objection relied upon. Objections to questions or evidence shall be noted by the deposition officer upon the deposition, but a deposition officer other than the hearing officer shall not have the power to decide on the competency, materiality or relevance of evidence. Failure to object to questions or evidence before the deposition officer shall not be deemed a waiver unless the ground of the objection is one that might have been obviated or removed if presented at that time.

(f) *Filing of depositions.* The questions propounded and all answers or objections shall be recorded or transcribed verbatim, and a transcript prepared by the deposition officer, or under his or her direction. The transcript shall be subscribed by the witness and certified by the deposition officer. The original deposition and exhibits shall be filed with the Secretary. A copy of the deposition shall be available to the deponent and each party for purchase at prescribed rates.

(g) *Payment.* The cost of the transcript shall be paid by the party requesting the deposition.

§ 201.234 Depositions Upon Written Questions

(a) *Availability.* Depositions may be taken and submitted on written questions upon motion of any party. The motion shall include the information specified in § 201.233(a). A decision on the motion shall be governed by the provisions of § 201.233(b).

(b) *Procedure.* Written questions shall be filed with the motion. Within 10 days after service of the motion and written questions, any party may file objections to such written questions and any party may file cross-questions. When a deposition is taken pursuant to this section no persons other than the witness, counsel to the witness, the deposition officer, and, if the deposition officer does not act as reporter, a reporter, shall be present at the examination of the witness. No party shall be present or represented unless otherwise permitted by order. The deposition officer shall propound the questions and cross-questions to the witness in the order submitted.

(c) *Additional requirements.* The order for deposition, filing of the deposition, form of the deposition and use of the deposition in the record shall be governed by paragraphs (c) through (g) of § 201.233, except that no cross-examination shall be made.

§ 201.235 Introducing Prior Sworn Statements of Witnesses Into the Record

(a) At a hearing, any person wishing to introduce a prior, sworn statement of a witness, not a party, otherwise admissible in the proceeding, may make a motion setting forth the reasons therefor. If only part of a statement is offered in evidence, the hearing officer may require that all relevant portions of the statement be introduced. If all of a statement is offered in evidence, the hearing officer may require that portions not relevant to the proceeding be excluded. A motion to introduce a prior sworn statement may be granted if:

(1) The witness is dead;

(2) The witness is out of the United States, unless it appears that the absence of the witness was procured by the party offering the prior sworn statement;

(3) The witness is unable to attend or testify because of age, sickness, infirmity, imprisonment or other disability;

(4) The party offering the prior sworn statement has been unable to procure the attendance of the witness by subpoena; or,

(5) In the discretion of the Commission or the hearing officer, it would be desirable, in the interests of justice, to allow the prior sworn statement to be used. In making this determination, due regard shall be given to the presumption that witnesses will testify orally in an open hearing. If the parties have stipulated to accept a prior sworn statement in lieu of live testimony, consideration shall also be given to the convenience of the parties in avoiding unnecessary expense.

§ 201.240 Settlement

(a) *Availability.* Any person who is notified that a proceeding may or will be instituted against him or her, or any party to a proceeding already instituted, may, at any time, propose in writing an offer of settlement.

(b) *Procedure.* An offer of settlement shall state that it is made pursuant to this section; shall recite or incorporate as a part of the offer the provisions of paragraphs (c)(4) and (5) of this section; shall be signed by the person making the offer, not by counsel; and shall be submitted to the interested division.

(c) *Consideration of offers of settlement.* (1) Offers of settlement shall be considered by the interested division when time, the nature of the proceedings, and the public interest permit.

(2) Where a hearing officer is assigned to a proceeding, the interested division and the party submitting the offer may request that the hearing officer express his or her views regarding the appropriateness of the offer of settlement. A request for the hearing officer to express his or her views on an offer of settlement or otherwise to participate in a settlement conference constitutes a waiver by the persons making the request of any right to claim bias or prejudgment by the hearing officer based on the views expressed.

(3) The interested division shall present the offer of settlement to the Commission with its recommendation, except that, if the division's recommendation is unfavorable, the offer shall not be presented to the Commission unless the person making the offer so requests.

(4) By submitting an offer of settlement, the person making the offer waives, subject to acceptance of the offer:

(i) All hearings pursuant to the statutory provisions under which the proceeding is to be or has been instituted;

(ii) The filing of proposed findings of fact and conclusions of law;

(iii) Proceedings before, and an initial decision by, a hearing officer;

(iv) All post-hearing procedures; and

(v) Judicial review by any court.

(5) By submitting an offer of settlement the person further waives:

(i) Such provisions of the Rules of Practice or other requirements of law as may be construed to prevent any member of the Commission's staff from participating in the preparation of, or advising the Commission as to, any order, opinion, finding of fact, or conclusion of law to be entered pursuant to the offer; and

(ii) Any right to claim bias or prejudgment by the Commission based on the consideration of or discussions concerning settlement of all or any part of the proceeding.

(6) If the Commission rejects the offer of settlement, the person making the offer shall be notified of the Commission's action and the offer of settlement shall be deemed withdrawn. The rejected offer shall not constitute a part of the record in any proceeding against the person making the offer, provided, however, that rejection of an offer of settlement does not affect the continued validity of waivers pursuant to paragraph (c)(5) of this section with respect to any discussions concerning the rejected offer of settlement.

(7) Final acceptance of any offer of settlement will occur only upon the issuance of findings and an order by the Commission.

§ 201.250 Motion for Summary Disposition

(a) After a respondent's answer has been filed and, in an enforcement or a disciplinary proceeding, documents have been made available to that respondent for inspection and copying pursuant to § 201.230, the respondent, or the interested division may make a motion for summary disposition of any or all allegations of the order instituting proceedings with respect to that respondent. If the interested division has not completed presentation of its case in chief, a motion for summary disposition shall be made only with leave of the hearing officer. The facts of the pleadings of the party against whom the motion is made shall be taken as true, except as modified by stipulations or admissions made by that party, by uncontested affidavits, or by facts officially noted pursuant to § 201.323.

(b) The hearing officer shall promptly grant or deny the motion for summary disposition or shall defer decision on the motion. The hearing officer may grant the motion for summary disposition if there is no genuine issue with regard to any material fact and the party making the motion is entitled to a summary disposition as a matter of law. If it appears that a party, for good cause shown, cannot present by affidavit prior to hearing facts essential to justify opposition to the motion, the hearing officer shall deny or defer the motion. A hearing officer's decision to deny leave to file a motion for summary disposition is not subject to interlocutory appeal.

(c) The motion for summary disposition, supporting memorandum of points and authorities, and any declarations, affidavits or attachments shall not exceed 35 pages in length.

Hearings

§ 201.300 Hearings

Hearings for the purpose of taking evidence shall be held only upon order of the Commission. All hearings shall be conducted in a fair, impartial, expeditious and orderly manner.

§ 201.301 Hearings to Be Public

All hearings, except hearings on applications for confidential treatment filed pursuant to § 201.190, hearings held to consider a motion for a protective order pursuant to § 201.322, and hearings on ex parte application for a temporary cease-and-desist order, shall be public unless otherwise ordered by the Commission on its own motion or the motion of a party. No hearing shall be nonpublic where all respondents request that the hearing be made public.

§ 201.302 Record of Hearings

(a) *Recordation.* Unless ordered otherwise by the hearing officer or the Commission, all hearings shall be recorded and a written transcript thereof shall be prepared.

(b) *Availability of a transcript.* Transcripts of public hearings shall be available for purchase at prescribed rates. Transcripts of nonpublic proceedings, and transcripts subject to a protective order pursuant to § 201.322, shall be available for purchase only by parties; provided, however, that any person compelled to submit data or evidence in a hearing may purchase a copy of his or her own testimony.

(c) *Transcript correction.* Prior to the filing of post-hearing briefs or proposed findings and conclusions, or within such earlier time as directed by the Commission or the hearing officer, a party or witness may make a motion to correct the transcript. Proposed corrections of the transcript may be submitted to the hearing officer by stipulation pursuant to § 201.324, or by motion. Upon notice to all parties to the proceeding, the hearing officer may, by order, specify corrections to the transcript.

§ 201.310 Failure to Appear at Hearings: Default

Any person named in an order instituting proceedings as a person against whom findings may be made or sanctions imposed who fails to appear at a hearing of which he or she has been duly notified may be deemed to be in default pursuant to § 201.155(a). A party may make a motion to set aside a default pursuant to § 201.155(b).

§ 201.320 Evidence: Admissibility

The Commission or the hearing officer may receive relevant evidence and shall exclude all evidence that is irrelevant, immaterial or unduly repetitious.

§ 201.321 Evidence: Objections and Offers of Proof

(a) *Objections.* Objections to the admission or exclusion of evidence must be made on the record and shall be in short form, stating the grounds relied upon. Exceptions to any ruling thereon by the hearing officer need not be noted at the time of the ruling. Such exceptions will be deemed waived on appeal to the Commission, however, unless raised:

(1) Pursuant to interlocutory review in accordance with § 201.400;

(2) In a proposed finding or conclusion filed pursuant to § 201.340; or

(3) In a petition for Commission review of an initial decision filed in accordance with § 201.410.

(b) *Offers of proof.* Whenever evidence is excluded from the record, the party offering such evidence may make an offer of proof, which shall be included in the record. Excluded material shall be retained pursuant to § 201.350(b).

§ 201.322 Evidence: Confidential Information, Protective Orders

(a) *Procedure.* In any proceeding as defined in § 201.101(a), a party, any person who is the owner, subject or creator of a document subject to subpoena or which may be introduced as evidence, or any witness who testifies at a hearing may file a motion requesting a protective order to limit from disclosure to other parties or to the public documents or testimony that contain confidential information. The motion should include a general summary or extract of the documents without revealing confidential details. If the movant seeks a protective order against disclosure to other parties as well as the public, copies of the documents shall not be served on other parties. Unless the documents are unavailable, the movant shall file for in camera inspection a sealed copy of the documents as to which the order is sought.

(b) *Basis for issuance.* Documents and testimony introduced in a public hearing are presumed to be public. A motion for a protective order shall be granted only upon a finding that the harm resulting from disclosure would outweigh the benefits of disclosure.

(c) *Requests for additional information supporting confidentiality.* A movant under paragraph (a) of this section may be required to furnish in writing additional information with respect to the grounds for confidentiality. Failure to supply the information so requested within five days from the date of receipt by the movant of a notice of the information required shall be deemed a waiver of the objection to public disclosure of that portion of the documents to which the additional information relates, unless the Commission or the hearing officer shall otherwise order for good cause shown at or before the expiration of such five-day period.

(d) *Confidentiality of documents pending decision.* Pending a determination of a motion under this section, the documents as to which confidential treatment is sought and any other documents that would reveal the confidential information in those documents shall be maintained under seal and shall be disclosed only in accordance with orders of the Commission or the hearing officer. Any order issued in connection with a motion under this section shall be public unless the order would disclose information as to which a protective order has been granted, in which case that portion of the order that would reveal the protected information shall be nonpublic.

§ 201.323 Evidence: Official Notice

Official notice may be taken of any material fact which might be judicially noticed by a district court of the United States, any matter in the public official records of the Commission, or any matter which is peculiarly within the knowledge of the Commission as an expert body. If official notice is requested or taken of a material fact not appearing in the evidence in the record, the parties, upon timely request, shall be afforded an opportunity to establish the contrary.

§ 201.324 Evidence: Stipulations

The parties may, by stipulation, at any stage of the proceeding agree upon any pertinent facts in the proceeding. A stipulation may be received in evidence and, when received, shall be binding on the parties to the stipulation.

§ 201.325 Evidence: Presentation Under Oath or Affirmation

A witness at a hearing for the purpose of taking evidence shall testify under oath or affirmation.

§ 201.326 Evidence: Presentation, Rebuttal and Cross-Examination

In any proceeding in which a hearing is required to be conducted on the record after opportunity for hearing in accord with 5 U.S.C. 556(a), a party is entitled to present its case or defense by oral or documentary evidence, to submit rebuttal evidence, and to conduct such cross-examination as, in the discretion of the Commission or the hearing officer, may be required for a full and true disclosure of the facts. The scope and form of evidence, rebuttal evidence, if any, and cross-examination, if any, in any other proceeding shall be determined by the Commission or the hearing officer in each proceeding.

§ 201.340 Proposed Findings, Conclusions and Supporting Briefs

(a) *Opportunity to file.* Before an initial decision is issued, each party shall have an opportunity, reasonable in light of all the circumstances, to file in writing proposed findings and conclusions together with, or as a part of, its brief.

(b) *Procedure.* Proposed findings of fact must be supported by citations to specific portions of the record. If successive filings are directed, the proposed findings and conclusions of the party assigned to file first shall be set forth in serially numbered paragraphs, and any counter statement of proposed findings and conclusions must, in addition to any other matter, indicate those paragraphs of the proposals already filed as to which there is no dispute. A reply brief may be filed by the party assigned to file first, or, where simultaneous filings are directed, reply briefs may be filed by each party, within the period prescribed therefor by the hearing officer. No further briefs may be filed except with leave of the hearing officer.

(c) *Time for filing.* In any proceeding in which an initial decision is to be issued:

(1) At the end of each hearing, the hearing officer shall, by order, after consultation with the parties, prescribe the period within which proposed findings and conclusions and supporting briefs are to be filed. The party or parties directed to file first shall make its or their initial filing within 30 days of the end of the hearing unless the hearing officer, for good cause shown, permits a different period and sets forth in the order the reasons why the different period is necessary.

(2) The total period within which all such proposed findings and conclusions and supporting briefs and any counter statements of proposed findings and conclusions and reply briefs are to be filed shall be no longer than 90 days after the close of the hearing unless the hearing officer, for good cause shown, permits a different period and sets forth in an order the reasons why the different period is necessary.

§ 201.350 Record in Proceedings Before Hearing Officer; Retention of Documents; Copies

(a) *Contents of the record.* The record shall consist of:

(1) The order instituting proceedings, each notice of hearing and any amendments;

(2) Each application, motion, submission or other paper, and any amendments, motions, objections, and exceptions to or regarding them;

(3) Each stipulation, transcript of testimony and document or other item admitted into evidence;

(4) Each written communication accepted by the hearing officer pursuant to § 201.210;

(5) With respect to a request to disqualify a hearing officer or to allow the hearing officer's withdrawal under § 201.112, each affidavit or transcript of testimony taken and the decision made in connection with the request;

(6) All motions, briefs and other papers filed on interlocutory appeal;

(7) All proposed findings and conclusions;

(8) Each written order issued by the hearing officer or Commission; and

(9) Any other document or item accepted into the record by the hearing officer.

(b) *Retention of documents not admitted.* Any document offered in evidence but excluded, and any document marked for identification but not offered as an exhibit, shall not be considered a part of the record. The Secretary shall retain any such documents until the later of the date upon which a Commission order ending the proceeding becomes final, or the conclusion of any judicial review of the Commission's order.

(c) *Substitution of copies.* A true copy of a document may be substituted for any document in the record or any document retained pursuant to paragraph (b) of this section.

§ 201.351 Transmittal of Documents to Secretary; Record Index; Certification

(a) *Transmittal from hearing officer to Secretary of partial record index.* The hearing officer may, at any time, transmit to the Secretary motions, exhibits or any other original documents filed with or accepted into evidence by the hearing officer, together with a list of such documents.

(b) *Preparation, certification of record index.* Promptly after the close of the hearing, the hearing officer shall transmit to the Secretary an index of the originals of any motions, exhibits or any other documents filed with or accepted into evidence by the hearing officer that have not been previously transmitted to the Secretary, and the Secretary shall prepare a record index. Prior to issuance of an initial decision, or if no initial decision is to be prepared, within 30 days of the close of the hearing, the Secretary shall transmit the record index to the hearing officer and serve a copy of the record index on each party. Any person may file proposed corrections to the record index with the hearing officer within 15 days of service of the record index. The hearing officer shall, by order, direct whether any corrections to the record index shall be made. The Secretary shall make such corrections, if any, and issue a revised record index. If an initial decision is to be issued, the initial decision shall include a certification that the record consists of the items set forth in the record index or revised record index issued by the Secretary.

(c) *Final transmittal of record items to the Secretary.* After the close of the hearing, the hearing officer shall transmit to the Secretary originals of any motions, exhibits or any other documents filed with, or accepted into evidence by, the hearing officer, or any other portions of the record that have not already been transmitted to the Secretary. Prior to service of the initial decision by the Secretary, or if no initial decision is to be issued, within 60 days of the close of the hearing, the Secretary shall inform the hearing officer if any portions of the record are not in the Secretary's custody.

§ 201.360 Initial Decision of Hearing Officer

(a)(1) *When required.* Unless the Commission directs otherwise, the hearing officer shall prepare an initial decision in any proceeding in which the Commission directs a hearing officer to preside at a hearing, provided, however, that an initial decision may be waived by the parties with the consent of the hearing officer pursuant to § 201.202.

(2) *Time period for filing initial decision.* In the order instituting proceedings, the Commission will specify a time period in which the hearing officer's initial decision must be filed with the Secretary. In the Commission's dis-

cretion, after consideration of the nature, complexity, and urgency of the subject matter, and with due regard for the public interest and the protection of investors, this time period will be either 120, 210 or 300 days from the date of service of the order. Under the 300-day timeline, the hearing officer shall issue an order providing that there shall be approximately 4 months from the order instituting the proceeding to the hearing, approximately 2 months for the parties to obtain the transcript and submit briefs, and approximately 4 months after briefing for the hearing officer to issue an initial decision. Under the 210-day timeline, the hearing officer shall issue an order providing that there shall be approximately 2 1/2 months from the order instituting the proceeding to the hearing, approximately 2 months for the parties to review the transcript and submit briefs, and approximately 2 1/2 months after briefing for the hearing officer to issue an initial decision. Under the 120-day timeline, the hearing officer shall issue an order providing that there shall be approximately 1 month from the order instituting the proceeding to the hearing, approximately 2 months for the parties to review the transcript and submit briefs, and approximately 1 month after briefing for the hearing officer to issue an initial decision. These deadlines confer no substantive rights on respondents. If a stay is granted pursuant to § 201.210(c)(3), the time period specified in the order instituting proceedings in which the hearing officer's initial decision must be filed with the Secretary, as well as any other time limits established in orders issued by the hearing officer in the proceeding, shall be automatically tolled during the period while the stay is in effect.

(3) *Motion for extension.* In the event that the hearing officer presiding over the proceeding determines that it will not be possible to issue the initial decision within the specified period of time, the hearing officer should consult with the Chief Administrative Law Judge. Following such consultation, the Chief Administrative Law Judge may determine, in his or her discretion, to submit a motion to the Commission requesting an extension of the time period for filing the initial decision. This motion must be filed no later than 30 days prior to the expiration of the time specified in the order for issuance of an initial decision. The motion will be served upon all parties in the proceeding, who may file with the Commission statements in support of or in opposition to the motion. If the Commission determines that additional time is necessary or appropriate in the public interest, the Commission shall issue an order extending the time period for filing the initial decision.

(b) *Content.* An initial decision shall include: findings and conclusions, and the reasons or basis therefor, as to all the material issues of fact, law or discretion presented on the record and the appropriate order, sanction, relief, or denial thereof. The initial decision shall also state the time period, not to exceed 21 days after service of the decision, except for good cause shown, within which a petition for review of the initial decision may be filed. The reasons for any extension of time shall be stated in the initial decision. The initial decision shall also include a statement that, as provided in paragraph (d) of this section:

(1) The Commission will enter an order of finality as to each party unless a party or an aggrieved person entitled to review timely files a petition for review of the initial decision or a motion to correct a manifest error of fact in the initial decision with the hearing officer, or the Commission determines on its own initiative to review the initial decision; and

(2) If a party or an aggrieved person entitled to review timely files a petition for review or a motion to correct a manifest error of fact in the initial decision with the hearing officer, or if the Commission takes action to review as to a party or an aggrieved person entitled to review, the initial decision shall not become final as to that party or person.

(c) *Filing, service and publication.* The hearing officer shall file the initial decision with the Secretary. The Secretary shall promptly serve the initial decision upon the parties and shall promptly publish notice of the filing thereof in the *SEC News Digest*. Thereafter, the Secretary shall publish the initial decision in the *SEC Docket*; provided, however, that in nonpublic proceedings no notice shall be published unless the Commission otherwise directs.

(d) *Finality*. (1) If a party or an aggrieved person entitled to review timely files a petition for review or a motion to correct a manifest error of fact in the initial decision, or if the Commission on its own initiative orders review of a decision with respect to a party or a person aggrieved who would be entitled to review, the initial decision shall not become final as to that party or person.

(2) If a party or aggrieved person entitled to review fails to file timely a petition for review or a motion to correct a manifest error of fact in the initial decision, and if the Commission does not order review of a decision on its own initiative, the Commission will issue an order that the decision has become final as to that party. The decision becomes final upon issuance of the order. The order of finality shall state the date on which sanctions, if any, take effect. Notice of the order shall be published in the *SEC News Digest* and the SEC website.

Appeal to the Commission and Commission Review

§ 201.400 Interlocutory Review

(a) *Availability*. The Commission may, at any time, on its own motion, direct that any matter be submitted to it for a review. Petitions by parties for interlocutory review are disfavored, and the Commission ordinarily will grant a petition to review a hearing officer ruling prior to its consideration of an initial decision only in extraordinary circumstances. The Commission may decline to consider a ruling certified by a hearing officer pursuant to paragraph (c) of this section or the petition of a party who has been denied certification if it determines that interlocutory review is not warranted or appropriate under the circumstances. This section is the exclusive remedy for review of a hearing officer's ruling prior to Commission consideration of the entire proceeding and is the sole mechanism for appeal of actions delegated pursuant to §§ 200.30–9 and 200.30–10 of this chapter.

(b) *Expedited consideration*. Interlocutory review of a hearing officer's ruling shall be expedited in every way, consistent with the Commission's other responsibilities.

(c) *Certification process*. A ruling submitted to the Commission for interlocutory review must be certified in writing by the hearing officer and shall specify the material relevant to the ruling involved. The hearing officer shall not certify a ruling unless:

(1) His or her ruling would compel testimony of Commission members, officers or employees or the production of documentary evidence in their custody; or

(2) Upon application by a party, within five days of the hearing officer's ruling, the hearing officer is of the opinion that:

(i) The ruling involves a controlling question of law as to which there is substantial ground for difference of opinion; and

(ii) An immediate review of the order may materially advance the completion of the proceeding.

(d) *Proceedings not stayed*. The filing of an application for review or the grant of review shall not stay proceedings before the hearing officer unless he or she, or the Commission, shall so order. The Commission will not consider the motion for a stay unless the motion shall have first been made to the hearing officer.

§ 201.401 Consideration of Stays

(a) *Procedure*. A request for a stay shall be made by written motion, filed pursuant to § 201.154, and served on all parties pursuant to § 201.150. The motion shall state the reasons for the relief requested and the facts relied upon, and, if the facts are subject to dispute, the motion shall be supported by affidavits or other sworn statements or copies thereof. Portions of the record relevant to the relief sought, if available to the movant, shall be filed with the motion. The Commission may issue a stay based on such motion or on its own motion.

(b) *Scope of relief.* The Commission may grant a stay in whole or in part, and may condition relief under this section upon such terms, or upon the implementation of such procedures, as it deems appropriate.

(c) *Stay of a Commission order.* A motion for a stay of a Commission order may be made by any person aggrieved thereby who would be entitled to review in a federal court of appeals. A motion seeking to stay the effectiveness of a Commission order pending judicial review may be made to the Commission at any time during which the Commission retains jurisdiction over the proceeding.

(d) *Stay of an action by a self-regulatory organization.*

(1) *Availability.* A motion for a stay of an action by a self-regulatory organization for which the Commission is the appropriate regulatory agency, for which action review may be sought pursuant to § 201.420, may be made by any person aggrieved thereby at the time an application for review is filed in accordance with § 201.420 or thereafter.

(2) *Summary entry.* A stay may be entered summarily, without notice and opportunity for hearing.

(3) *Expedited consideration.* Where the action complained of has already taken effect and the motion for stay is filed within 10 days of the effectiveness of the action, or where the action complained of, will, by its terms, take effect within five days of the filing of the motion for stay, the consideration of and decision on the motion for a stay shall be expedited in every way, consistent with the Commission's other responsibilities. Where consideration will be expedited, persons opposing the motion for a stay may file a statement in opposition within two days of service of the motion unless the Commission, by written order, shall specify a different period.

(e) *Lifting of stay of action by the Public Company Accounting Oversight Board.* (1) *Availability.* Any person aggrieved by a stay of action by the Board entered in accordance with the 15 U.S.C. 7215(e) for which review has been sought pursuant to § 201.440 or which the Commission has taken up on its motion pursuant to § 201.441 may make a motion to lift the stay. The Commission may, at any time, on its own motion determine whether to lift the automatic stay.

(2) *Summary action.* The Commission may lift a stay summarily, without notice and opportunity for hearing.

(3) *Expedited consideration.* The Commission may expedite consideration of a motion to lift a stay of Board action, consistent with the Commission's other responsibilities. Where consideration is expedited, persons opposing the lifting of the stay may file a statement in opposition within two days of service of the motion requesting lifting of the stay unless the Commission, by written order, shall specify a different period.

§ 201.410 Appeal of Initial Decisions by Hearing Officers

(a) *Petition for review; when available.* In any proceeding in which an initial decision is made by a hearing officer, any party, and any other person who would have been entitled to judicial review of the decision entered therein if the Commission itself had made the decision, may file a petition for review of the decision with the Commission.

(b) *Procedure.* The petition for review of an initial decision shall be filed with the Commission within such time after service of the initial decision as prescribed by the hearing officer pursuant to § 201.360(b) unless a party has filed a motion to correct an initial decision with the hearing officer. If such correction has been sought, a party shall have 21 days from the date of the hearing officer's order resolving the motion to correct to file a petition for review. The petition shall set forth the specific findings and conclusions of the initial decision as to which exception is taken, together with supporting reasons for each exception. Supporting reasons may be stated in summary form. Any exception to an initial decision not stated in the petition for review, or in a previously filed proposed finding made pursuant to § 201.340 may, at the discretion of the Commission, be deemed to have been waived by the petitioner. In the event a petition for review is filed, any other party to the proceeding may file a cross-petition for review within the original time allowed for seeking review or within ten days from the date that the petition for review was filed, whichever is later.

(c) *Financial disclosure statement requirement.* Any person who files a petition for review of an initial decision that asserts that person's inability to pay either disgorgement, interest or a penalty shall file with the opening brief a sworn financial disclosure statement containing the information specified in § 201.630(b).

(d) Reserved.

(e) *Prerequisite to judicial review.* Pursuant to Section 704 of the Administrative Procedure Act, 5 U.S.C. 704, a petition to the Commission for review of an initial decision is a prerequisite to the seeking of judicial review of a final order entered pursuant to such decision.

§ 201.411 Commission Consideration of initial Decisions by Hearing Officers

(a) *Scope of review.* The Commission may affirm, reverse, modify, set aside or remand for further proceedings, in whole or in part, an initial decision by a hearing officer and may make any findings or conclusions that in its judgment are proper and on the basis of the record.

(b) *Standards for granting review pursuant to a petition for review.*

(1) *Mandatory review.* After a petition for review has been filed, the Commission shall review any initial decision that:

(i) Denies any request for action pursuant to Section 8(a) or Section 8(c) of the Securities Act of 1933, 15 U.S.C. 77h(a), (c), or the first sentence of Section 12(d) of the Exchange Act, 15 U.S.C. 78*l* (d);

(ii) Suspends trading in a security pursuant to Section 12(k) of the Exchange Act, 15 U.S.C. 78l(k); or

(iii) Is in a case of adjudication (as defined in 5 U.S.C. 551) not required to be determined on the record after notice and opportunity for hearing (except to the extent there is involved a matter described in 5 U.S.C. 554(a)(1) through (6)).

(2) *Discretionary review.* The Commission may decline to review any other decision. In determining whether to grant review, the Commission shall consider whether the petition for review makes a reasonable showing that:

(i) A prejudicial error was committed in the conduct of the proceeding; or

(ii) The decision embodies:

(A) A finding or conclusion of material fact that is clearly erroneous; or

(B) A conclusion of law that is erroneous; or

(C) An exercise of discretion or decision of law or policy that is important and that the Commission should review.

(c) *Commission review other than pursuant to a petition for review.* The Commission may, on its own initiative, order review of any initial decision, or a portion of any initial decision, within 21 days after the end of the period established for filing a petition for review pursuant to § 201.410(b) or any brief in opposition to a petition for review permitted pursuant to § 201.410(d). A party who does not intend to file a petition for review, and who desires the Commission's determination whether to order review on its own initiative to be made in a shorter time, may make a motion for an expedited decision, accompanied by a written statement that the party waives its right to file a petition for review. The vote of one member of the Commission, conveyed to the Secretary, shall be sufficient to bring a matter before the Commission for review.

(d) *Limitations on matters reviewed.* Review by the Commission of an initial decision shall be limited to the issues specified in the petition for review or the issues, if any, specified in the briefing schedule order issued pursuant to § 201.450(a). On notice to all parties, however, the Commission may, at any time prior to issuance of its decision, raise and determine any other matters that it deems material, with opportunity for oral or written argument thereon by the parties.

(e) *Summary affirmance.* (1) At any time within 21 days after the filing of a petition for review pursuant to § 201.410(b), any party may file a motion in accordance with § 201.154 asking that the Commission summarily affirm an initial decision. Any party may file an opposition and reply to such motion in accordance with § 201.450. Pending determination of the motion for summary affirmance, the Commission, in its discretion, may delay issuance of a briefing schedule order pursuant to § 201.450.

(2) Upon consideration of the motion and any opposition or upon its own initiative, the Commission may summarily affirm an initial decision. The Commission may grant summary affirmance if it finds that no issue raised in the initial decision warrants consideration by the Commission of further oral or written argument. The Commission will decline to grant summary affirmance upon a reasonable showing that a prejudicial error was committed in the conduct of the proceeding or that the decision embodies an exercise of discretion or decision of law or policy that is important and that the Commission should review.

(f) *Failure to obtain a majority.* In the event a majority of participating Commissioners do not agree to a disposition on the merits, the initial decision shall be of no effect, and an order will be issued in accordance with this result.

§ 201.420 Appeal of Determinations by Self–Regulatory Organizations

(a) *Application for review; when available.* An application for review by the Commission may be filed by any person who is aggrieved by a self-regulatory organization determination as to which a notice is required to be filed with the Commission pursuant to Section 19(d)(1) of the Exchange Act, 15 U.S.C. 78s(d)(1). Such determinations include any:

(1) Final disciplinary sanction;

(2) Denial or conditioning of membership or participation;

(3) Prohibition or limitation in respect to access to services offered by that self-regulatory organization or a member thereof; or

(4) Bar from association.

(b) *Procedure.* As required by section 19(d)(1) of the Securities Exchange Act of 1934, 15 U.S.C. 78s(d)(1), and applicant must file an application for review with the Commission within 30 days after the notice of the determination is filed with the Commission and received by the aggrieved person applying for review. The Commission will not extend this 30-day period, absent a showing of extraordinary circumstances. This section is the exclusive remedy for seeking an extension of the 30-day period.

(c) *Application.* An application shall be filed with the Commission pursuant to § 201.151. The applicant shall serve the application on the self-regulatory organization. The application shall identify the determination complained of and set forth in summary form a brief statement of the alleged errors in the determination and supporting reasons therefor. The application shall state an address where the applicant can be served. The application should not exceed two pages in length. If the applicant will be represented by a representative, the application shall be accompanied by the notice of appearance required by § 201.102(d).

(d) *Determination not stayed.* Filing an application for review with the Commission pursuant to paragraph (b) of this section shall not operate as a stay of the complained of determination made by the self-regulatory organization unless the Commission otherwise orders either pursuant to a motion filed in accordance with § 201.401 or on its own motion.

(e) *Certification of the record; service of the index.* Fourteen days after receipt of an application for review or a Commission order for review, the self-regulatory organization shall certify and file with the Commission one copy of the record upon which the action complained of was taken, and shall file with the Commission three copies of an index to such record, and shall serve upon each party one copy of the index.

§ 201.421 Commission Consideration of Determinations by Self-Regulatory Organizations

(a) *Commission review other than pursuant to a petition for review.* The Commission may, on its own initiative, order review of any determination by a self-regulatory organization that could be subject to an application for review pursuant to § 201.420(a) within 40 days after notice thereof was filed with the Commission pursuant to Section 19(d)(1) of the Exchange Act, 15 U.S.C. 78s(d)(1).

(b) *Supplemental briefing.* The Commission may at any time prior to issuance of its decision raise or consider any matter that it deems material, whether or not raised by the parties. Notice to the parties and an opportunity for supplemental briefing with respect to issues not briefed by the parties shall be given where the Commission believes that such briefing would significantly aid the decisional process.

§ 201.430 Appeal of Actions Made Pursuant to Delegated Authority

(a) *Scope of rule.* Any person aggrieved by an action made by authority delegated in §§ 200.30–1 through 200.30–8 or §§ 200.30–11 through 200.30–18 of this chapter may seek review of the action pursuant to paragraph (b) of this section.

(b) *Procedure.*

(1) *Notice of intention to petition for review.* A party or any person aggrieved by an action made pursuant to delegated authority may seek Commission review of the action by filing a written notice of intention to petition for review within five days after actual notice to the party of the action or service of notice of the action pursuant to § 201.141(b), whichever is earlier. The notice shall identify the petitioner and the action complained of, and shall be accompanied by a notice of appearance pursuant to § 201.102(d).

(2) *Petition for review.* Within five days after the filing of a notice of intention to petition for review pursuant to paragraph (b)(1) of this section, the person seeking review shall file a petition for review containing a clear and concise statement of the issues to be reviewed and the reasons why review is appropriate. The petition shall include exceptions to any findings of fact or conclusions of law made, together with supporting reasons for such exceptions based on appropriate citations to such record as may exist. These reasons may be stated in summary form.

(c) *Prerequisite to judicial review.* Pursuant to Section 704 of the Administrative Procedure Act, 5 U.S.C. 704, a petition to the Commission for review of an action made by authority delegated in §§ 200.30–1 through 200.30–18 of this chapter is a prerequisite to the seeking of judicial review of a final order entered pursuant to such an action.

§ 201.431 Commission Consideration of Actions Made Pursuant to Delegated Authority

(a) *Scope of review.* The Commission may affirm, reverse, modify, set aside or remand for further proceedings, in whole or in part, any action made pursuant to authority delegated in §§ 200.30–1 through 200.30–18 of this chapter.

(b) *Standards for granting review pursuant to a petition for review.*

(1) *Mandatory review.* After a petition for review has been filed, the Commission shall review any action that it would be required to review pursuant to § 201.411(b)(1) if the action was made as the initial decision of a hearing officer.

(2) *Discretionary review.* The Commission may decline to review any other action. In determining whether to grant review, the Commission shall consider the factors set forth in § 201.411(b)(2).

(c) *Commission review other than pursuant to a petition for review.* The Commission may, on its own initiative, order review of any action made pursuant to delegated authority at any time, provided, however, that where there are one or more parties to the matter, such review shall not be ordered more than ten days after the action. The vote of one member of the Commission, conveyed to the Secretary, shall be sufficient to bring a matter before the Commission for review.

(d) *Required items in an order for review.* In an order granting a petition for review or directing review on the Commission's own initiative, the Commission shall set forth the time within which any party or other person may file a statement in support of or in opposition to the action made by delegated authority and shall state whether a stay shall be granted, if none is in effect, or shall be continued, if in effect pursuant to paragraph (e) of this section.

(e) *Automatic stay of delegated action.* An action made pursuant to delegated authority shall have immediate effect and be deemed the action of the Commission. Upon filing with the Commission of a notice of intention to petition for review, or upon notice to the Secretary of the vote of a Commissioner that a matter be reviewed, an action made pursuant to delegated authority shall be stayed until the Commission orders otherwise, provided, however, there shall be no automatic stay of an action:

(1) To grant a stay of action by the Commission or a self-regulatory organization as authorized by 17 CFR 200.30–14(g)(5)–(6); or

(2) To commence a subpoena enforcement proceeding as authorized by 17 CFR 200.30–4(a)(10).

(f) *Effectiveness of stay or of Commission decision to modify or reverse a delegated action.* As against any person who shall have acted in reliance upon any action at a delegated level, any stay or any modification or reversal by the Commission of such action shall be effective only from the time such person receives actual notice of such stay, modification or reversal.

§ 201.440 Appeal of Determinations by the Public Company Accounting Oversight Board

(a) *Application for review; when available.* Any person who is aggrieved by a determination of the Board with respect to any final disciplinary sanction, including disapproval of a completed application for registration of a public accounting firm, may file an application for review.

(b) *Procedure.* An aggrieved person may file an application for review with the Commission pursuant to § 201.151 within 30 days after the notice filed by the Board of its determination with the Commission pursuant to § 240.19d–4 of this chapter is received by the aggrieved person applying for review. The applicant shall serve the application on the Board at the same time. The application shall identify the determination complained of, set forth in summary form a brief statement of alleged errors in the determination and supporting reasons therefor, and state an address where the applicant can be served. The notice of appearance required by § 201.102(d) shall accompany the application.

(c) *Stay of determination.* Filing an application for review with the Commission pursuant to paragraph (b) of this section operates as a stay of the Board's determination unless the Commission otherwise orders either pursuant to a motion filed in accordance with § 201.401(e) or upon its own motion.

(d) *Certification of the record; service of the index.* Within fourteen days after receipt of an application for review, the Board shall certify and file with the Commission one copy of the record upon which it took the complained-of action. The Board shall file with the Commission three copies of an index of such record, and shall serve one copy of the index on each party.

§ 201.441 Commission Consideration of Board Determinations

(a) *Commission review other than pursuant to an application for review.* The Commission may, on its own initiative, order review of any final disciplinary sanction, including disapproval of a completed application for registration of a public accounting firm, imposed by the Board that could be subject to an application for review pursuant to § 201.440(a) within 40 days after the Board filed notice thereof pursuant to § 240.19d–4 of this chapter.

(b) *Supplemental briefing.* The Commission may at any time prior to the issuance of its decision raise or consider any matter that it deems material, whether or not raised by the parties. The Commission will give notice to the parties and an opportunity for supplemental briefing with respect to issues not briefed by the parties where the Commission believes that such briefing could significantly aid the decisional process.

§ 201.450 Briefs Filed With the Commission

(a) *Briefing schedule order.* Other than review ordered pursuant to § 201.431, if review of a determination is mandated by statute, rule, or judicial order or the Commission determines to grant review as a matter of discretion, the Commission shall issue a briefing schedule order directing the party or parties to file opening briefs and specifying particular issues, if any, as to which briefing should be limited or directed. Unless otherwise provided, opening briefs shall be filed within 30 days of the date of the briefing schedule order. Opposition briefs shall be filed within 30 days after the date opening briefs are due. Reply briefs shall be filed within 14 days after the date opposition briefs are due. No briefs in addition to those specified in the briefing schedule order may be filed except with leave of the Commission. The briefing schedule order shall be issued:

(1) At the time the Commission orders review on its own initiative pursuant to §§ 201.411 or 201.421, or orders interlocutory review on its own motion pursuant to § 201.400(a); or

(2) Within 21 days, or such longer time as provided by the Commission, after:

(i) The last day permitted for filing a petition for review pursuant to § 201.410(b) or a brief in opposition to a petition for review pursuant to § 201.410(d);

(ii) Receipt by the Commission of an index to the record of a determination of a self-regulatory organization filed pursuant to § 201.420(d);

(iii) Receipt by the Commission of an index to the record of a determination by the Board filed pursuant to § 201.440(d);

(iv) Receipt by the Commission of the mandate of a court of appeals with respect to a judicial remand; or

(v) Certification of a ruling for interlocutory review pursuant to § 201.400(c).

(b) *Contents of briefs.* Briefs shall be confined to the particular matters at issue. Each exception to the findings or conclusions being reviewed shall be stated succinctly. Exceptions shall be supported by citation to the relevant portions of the record, including references to the specific pages relied upon, and by concise argument including citation of such statutes, decisions and other authorities as may be relevant. If the exception relates to the admission or exclusion of evidence, the substance of the evidence admitted or excluded shall be set forth in the brief, in an appendix thereto, or by citation to the record. Reply briefs shall be confined to matters in opposition briefs of other parties.

(c) *Length limitation.* Except with leave of the Commission, opening and opposition briefs shall not exceed 14,000 words and reply briefs shall not exceed 7,000 words, exclusive of pages containing the table of contents, table of authorities, and any addendum that consists solely of copies of applicable cases, pertinent legislative provisions or rules, and exhibits. The number of words shall include pleadings incorporated by reference. Motions to file briefs in excess of these limitations are disfavored.

(d) *Certificate of compliance.* An opening or opposition brief that does not exceed 30 pages in length, exclusive of pages containing the table of contents, table of authorities, and any addendum that consists solely of copies of applicable cases, pertinent legislative provisions, or rules and exhibits, but inclusive of pleadings incorporated by reference, is presumptively considered to contain no more than 14,000 words. A reply brief that does not exceed 15 pages in length, exclusive of pages containing the table of contents, table of authorities, and any addendum that consists solely of copies of applicable cases, pertinent legislative provisions, or rules and exhibits, but inclusive of pleadings incorporated by reference, is presumptively considered to contain no more than 7,000 words. Any brief that exceeds these pages limits must include a certificate by the party's representative, or an unrepresented party, stating that the brief complies with the length limitation set forth in § 201.450(c) and stating the number of words in the brief. The person preparing the certificate may rely on the word count of the word-processing system used to prepare the brief.

§ 201.451 Oral Argument Before the Commission

(a) *Availability.* The Commission, on its own motion or the motion of a party or any other aggrieved person entitled to Commission review, may order oral argument with respect to any matter. Motions for oral argument with respect to whether to affirm all or part of an initial decision by a hearing officer shall be granted unless exceptional circumstances make oral argument impractical or inadvisable. The Commission will consider appeals, motions and other matters properly before it on the basis of the papers filed by the parties without oral argument unless the Commission determines that the presentation of facts and legal arguments in the briefs and record and the decisional process would be significantly aided by oral argument.

(b) *Procedure.* Requests for oral argument shall be made by separate motion accompanying the initial brief on the merits. The Commission shall issue an order as to whether oral argument is to be heard, and if so, the time and place therefor. If oral argument is granted, the time fixed for oral argument shall be changed only by written order of the Commission, for good cause shown. The order shall state at whose request the change is made and the reasons for any such changes. No visual aids may be used at oral argument unless copies have been provided to the Commission and all parties at least five business days before the argument is to be held.

(c) *Time allowed.* Unless the Commission orders otherwise, not more than one half-hour per side will be allowed for oral argument. The Commission may, in its discretion, determine that several persons have a common interest, and that the interests represented will be considered a single side for purposes of allotting time for oral argument. Time will be divided equally among persons on a single side, provided, however, that by mutual agreement they may reallocate their time among themselves. A request for additional time must be made by motion filed reasonably in advance of the date fixed for argument.

(d) *Participation of Commissioners.* A member of the Commission who was not present at the oral argument may participate in the decision of the proceeding, provided that the member has reviewed the transcript of such argument prior to such participation. The decision shall state whether the required review was made.

§ 201.452 Additional Evidence

Upon its own motion or the motion of a party, the Commission may allow the submission of additional evidence. A party may file a motion for leave to adduce additional evidence at any time prior to issuance of a decision by the Commission. Such motion shall show with particularity that such additional evidence is material and that there were reasonable grounds for failure to adduce such evidence previously. The Commission may accept or hear additional evidence, may remand the proceeding to a self-regulatory organization, or may remand or refer the proceeding to a hearing officer for the taking of additional evidence as appropriate.

§ 201.460 Record Before the Commission

The Commission shall determine each matter on the basis of the record.

(a) *Contents of the record.*

(1) In proceedings for final decision before the Commission other than those reviewing a determination by a self-regulatory organization, the record shall consist of:

(i) All items part of the record below in accordance with § 201.350;

(ii) Any petitions for review, cross-petitions or oppositions; and

(iii) All briefs, motions, submissions and other papers filed on appeal or review.

(2) In a proceeding for final decision before the Commission reviewing a determination by a self-regulatory organization, the record shall consist of:

(i) The record certified pursuant to § 201.420(d) by the self-regulatory organization;

(ii) Any application for review; and

(iii) Any submissions, moving papers, and briefs filed on appeal or review.

(3) In a proceeding for final decision before the Commission reviewing a determination of the Board, the record shall consist of:

(i) The record certified pursuant to § 201.440(d) by the Board;

(ii) Any application for review; and

(iii) Any submissions, moving papers, and briefs filed on appeal or review.

(b) *Transmittal of record to Commission.* Within 14 days after the last date set for filing briefs or such later date as the Commission directs, the Secretary shall transmit the record to the Commission.

(c) *Review of documents not admitted.* Any document offered in evidence but excluded by the hearing officer or the Commission and any document marked for identification but not offered as an exhibit shall not be considered a part of the record before the Commission on appeal but shall be transmitted to the Commission by the Secretary if so requested by the Commission. In the event that the Commission does not request the document, the Secretary shall retain the document not admitted into the record until the later of:

(1) The date upon which the Commission's order becomes final, or

(2) The conclusion of any judicial review of that order.

§ 201.470 Reconsideration

(a) *Scope of rule.* A party or any person aggrieved by a determination in a proceeding may file a motion for reconsideration of a final order issued by the Commission.

(b) *Procedure.* A motion for reconsideration shall be filed within 10 days after service of the order complained of, or within such time as the Commission may prescribe upon motion for extension of time filed by the person seeking reconsideration, if the motion is made within the foregoing 10–day period. The motion for reconsideration shall briefly and specifically state the matters of record alleged to have been erroneously decided, the grounds relied upon, and the relief sought. A motion for reconsideration shall conform to the requirements, including page length, provided in § 201.154. No response to a motion for reconsideration shall be filed unless requested by the Commission. Any response so requested shall comply with § 201.154.

§ 201.490 Receipt of Petitions for Judicial Review Pursuant to 28 U.S.C. 2112(a)(1)

The Commission officer and office designated pursuant to 28 U.S.C. 2112(a)(1) to receive copies of petitions for review of Commission orders from the persons instituting review in a court of appeals, are the Secretary and the Office of the Secretary at the Commission's Headquarters. Ten copies of each petition shall be submitted. Each copy shall state on its face that it is being submitted to the Commission pursuant to 28 U.S.C. 2112 by the person or persons who filed the petition in the court of appeals.

Rules Relating to Temporary Orders and Suspensions

§ 201.500 Expedited Consideration of Proceedings

Consistent with the Commission's on the hearing officer's other responsibilities, every hearing shall be held and every decision shall be rendered at the earliest possible time in connection with:

(a) An application for a temporary sanction, as defined in § 201.101(a), or a proceeding to determine whether a temporary sanction should be made permanent;

(b) A motion or application to review an order suspending temporarily the effectiveness of an exemption from registration pursuant to Regulations A, B, E or F under the Securities Act, §§ 230.258, 230.336, 230.610 or 230.656 of this chapter; or,

(c) A motion to or petition to review an order suspending temporarily the privilege of appearing before the Commission under § 201.102(e)(3), or a sanction under § 201.180(a)(1).

§ 201.510 Temporary Cease-and-Desist Orders: Application Process

(a) *Procedure.* A request for entry of a temporary cease-and-desist order shall be made by application filed by the Division of Enforcement. The application shall set forth the statutory provision or rule that each respondent is alleged to have violated; the temporary relief sought against each respondent, including whether the respondent would be required to take action to prevent the dissipation or conversion of assets; and whether the relief is sought *ex parte.*

(b) *Accompanying documents.* The application shall be accompanied by a declaration of facts signed by a person with knowledge of the facts contained therein, a memorandum of points and authorities, a proposed order imposing the temporary relief sought, and, unless relief is sought *ex parte,* a proposed notice of hearing and order to show cause whether the temporary relief should be imposed. If a proceeding for a permanent cease-and-desist order has not already been commenced, a proposed order instituting proceedings to determine whether a permanent cease-and-desist order should be imposed shall also be filed with the application.

(c) *With whom filed.* The application shall be filed with the Secretary or, if the Secretary is unavailable, with the duty officer. In no event shall an application be filed with an administrative law judge.

(d) *Record of proceedings.* Hearings, including *ex parte* presentations made by the Division of Enforcement pursuant to § 201.513, shall be recorded or transcribed pursuant to § 201.302.

§ 201.511. Temporary Cease-and-Desist Orders: Notice; Procedures for Hearing

(a) *Notice: how given.* Notice of an application for a temporary cease-and-desist order shall be made by serving a notice of hearing and order to show cause pursuant to § 201.141(b) or, where timely service of a notice of hearing pursuant to § 201.141(b) is not practicable, by any other means reasonably calculated to give actual notice that a hearing will be held, including telephonic notification of the general subject matter, time, and place of the hearing. If an application is made *ex parte,* pursuant to § 201.513, no notice to a respondent need be given prior to the Commission's consideration of the application.

(b) *Hearing before the Commission.* Except as provided in paragraph (d) of this section, hearings on an application for a temporary cease-and-desist order shall be held before the Commission.

(c) *Presiding officer: designation.* The Chairman shall preside or designate a Commissioner to preside at the hearing. If the Chairman is absent or unavailable at the time of hearing and no other Commissioner has been designated to preside, the duty officer on the day the hearing begins shall preside or designate another Commissioner to preside.

(d) *Procedure at hearing.* (1) The presiding officer shall have all those powers of a hearing officer set forth in § 201.111 and shall rule on the admissibility of evidence and other procedural matters, including, but not limited to whether oral testimony will be heard; the time allowed each party for the submission of evidence or argument; and whether post-hearing submission of briefs, proposed findings of fact and conclusions of law will be permitted and if so, the procedures for submission; provided, however, that the person presiding may consult with other Commissioners participating in the hearing on these or any other question of procedure.

(2) Each Commissioner present at the hearing shall be afforded a reasonable opportunity to ask questions of witnesses, if any, or of counsel.

(3) A party or witness may participate by telephone. Alternative means of remote access, including a video link, shall be permitted in the Commission's discretion. Factors the Commission may consider in determining whether to permit alternative means of remote access include, but are not limited to, whether allowing an alternative means of access will delay the hearing, whether the alternative means is reliable, and whether the party proposing its use has made arrangements to pay for its cost.

(4) After a hearing has begun, the Commission may, on its own motion, or the motion of a party, assign a hearing officer to preside at the taking of oral testimony or other evidence and to certify the record of such testimony or other evidence to the Commission within a fixed period of time. No recommended or initial decision shall be made by such a hearing officer.

§ 201.512 Temporary Cease-and-Desist Orders: Issuance After Notice and Opportunity for Hearing

(a) *Basis for issuance.* A temporary cease-and-desist order shall be issued only if the Commission determines that the alleged violation or threatened violation specified in an order instituting proceedings whether to enter a permanent cease-and-desist order pursuant to Securities Act Section 8A(a), 15 U.S.C. 77h–1(a), Exchange Act Section 21C(a), 15 U.S.C. 78u–3(a), Investment Company Act Section 9(f)(1), 15 U.S.C. 80a–9(f)(1), or Investment Advisers Act Section 203(k)(1), 15 U.S.C. 80b–3(k)(1), or the continuation thereof, is likely to result in significant dissipation or conversion of assets, significant harm to investors, or substantial harm to the public interest, including, but not limited to, losses to the Securities Investor Protection Corporation, prior to the completion of proceedings on the permanent cease-and-desist order.

(b) *Content, scope and form of order.* Every temporary cease-and-desist order granted shall:

(1) Describe the basis for its issuance, including the alleged or threatened violations and the harm that is likely to result without the issuance of an order;

(2) Describe in reasonable detail, and not by reference to the order instituting proceedings or any other document, the act or acts the respondent is to take or refrain from taking; and

(3) Be indorsed with the date and hour of issuance.

(c) *Effective upon service.* A temporary cease-and-desist order is effective upon service upon the respondent.

(d) *Service: how made.* Service of a temporary cease-and-desist order shall be made pursuant to § 201.141(a). The person who serves the order shall promptly file a declaration of service identifying the person served, the method of service, the date of service, the address to which service was made and the person who made service; provided, however, failure to file such a declaration shall have no effect on the validity of the service.

(e) *Commission review.* At any time after the respondent has been served with a temporary cease-and-desist order, the respondent may apply to the Commission to have the order set aside, limited or suspended. The application shall set forth with specificity the facts that support the request.

§ 201.513 Temporary Cease-and-Desist Orders: Issuance Without Prior Notice and Opportunity for Hearing

In addition to the requirements for issuance of a temporary cease-and-desist order set forth in § 201.512, the following requirements shall apply if a temporary cease-and-desist order is to be entered without prior notice and opportunity for hearing:

(a) *Basis for issuance without prior notice and opportunity for hearing.* A temporary cease-and-desist order may be issued without notice and opportunity for hearing only if the Commission determines, from specific facts in the record of the proceeding, that notice and hearing prior to entry of an order would be impracticable or contrary to the public interest.

(b) *Content of the order.* An *ex parte* temporary cease-and-desist order shall state specifically why notice and hearing would have been impracticable or contrary to the public interest.

(c) *Hearing before the Commission.* If a respondent has been served with a temporary cease-and-desist order entered without a prior Commission hearing, the respondent may apply to the Commission to have the order set aside, limited, or suspended, and if the application is made within 10 days after the date on which the order was served, may request a hearing on such application. The Commission shall hold a hearing and render a decision on the respondent's application at the earliest possible time. The hearing shall begin within two days of the filing of the application unless the applicant consents to a longer period or the Commission, by order, for good cause shown, sets a later date. The Commission shall render a decision on the application within five calendar days of its filing, provided, however, that the Commission, by order, for good cause shown, may extend the time within which a decision may be rendered for a single period of five calendar days, or such longer time as consented to by the applicant. If the Commission does not render its decision within 10 days of the respondent's application or such longer time as consented to by the applicant, the temporary order shall be suspended until a decision is rendered.

(d) *Presiding officer, procedure at hearing.* Procedures with respect to the selection of a presiding officer and the conduct of the hearing shall be in accordance with § 201.511.

§ 201.514 Temporary Cease-and-Desist Orders; Judicial Review; Duration

(a) *Availability of judicial review.* Judicial review of a temporary cease-and-desist order shall be available as provided in Section 8A(d)(2) of the Securities Act, 15 U.S.C. 77h–1(d)(2), Section 21C(d)(2) of the Exchange Act, 15 U.S.C. 78u–3(d)(2), Section 9(f)(4)(B) of the Investment Company Act, 15 U.S.C. 80a–9(f)(4)(B), or Section 203(k)(4)(B) of the Investment Advisers Act, 15 U.S.C. 80b–3(k)(4)(B).

(b) *Duration.* Unless set aside, limited, or suspended, either by order of the Commission, a court of competent jurisdiction, or a hearing officer acting pursuant to § 201.531, or by operation of § 201.513, a temporary cease-and-desist order shall remain effective and enforceable until the earlier of:

(1) The completion of the proceedings whether a permanent order shall be entered; or

(2) 180 days, or such longer time as consented to by the respondent, after issuance of a briefing schedule order pursuant to § 201.540(b), if an initial decision whether a permanent order should be entered is appealed.

§ 201.520 Suspension of Registration of Brokers, Dealers, or Other Exchange Act–Registered Entities: Application

(a) *Procedure.* A request for suspension of a registered broker, dealer, municipal securities dealer, government securities broker, government securities dealer, or transfer agent pending a final determination whether the registration shall be revoked shall be made by application filed by the Division of Enforcement. The application shall set forth the statutory provision or rule that each respondent is alleged to have violated and the temporary suspension sought as to each respondent.

(b) *Accompanying documents.* The application shall be accompanied by a declaration of facts signed by a person with knowledge of the facts contained therein, a memorandum of points and authorities, a proposed order imposing the temporary suspension of registration sought, and a proposed notice of hearing and order to show cause whether the temporary suspension of registration should be imposed. If a proceeding to determine whether to revoke the registration permanently has not already been commenced, a proposed order instituting proceedings to determine whether a permanent sanction should be imposed shall also be filed with the application.

(c) *With whom filed.* The application shall be filed with the Secretary or, if the Secretary is unavailable, with the duty officer. In no event shall an application be filed with an administrative law judge.

(d) *Record of hearings.* All hearings shall be recorded or transcribed pursuant to § 201.302.

§ 201.521 Suspension of Registration of Brokers, Dealers, or other Exchange Act–Registered Entities: Notice and Opportunity for Hearing on Application

(a) *How given.* Notice of an application to suspend a registration pursuant to § 201.520 shall be made by serving a notice of hearing and order to show cause pursuant to § 201.141(b) or, where timely service of a notice of hearing pursuant to § 201.141(b) is not practicable, by any other means reasonably calculated to give actual notice that a hearing will be held, including telephonic notification of the general subject matter, time, and place of the hearing.

(b) *Hearing: before whom held.* Except as provided in paragraph (d) of this section, hearings on an application to suspend a registration pursuant to § 201.520 shall be held before the Commission.

(c) *Presiding officer: designation.* The Chairman shall preside or designate a Commissioner to preside at the hearing. If the Chairman is absent or unavailable at the time of hearing and no other Commissioner has been designated to preside, the duty officer on the day the hearing begins shall preside or designate another Commissioner to preside.

(d) *Procedure at hearing.* (1) The presiding officer shall have all those powers of a hearing officer set forth in § 201.111 and shall rule on the admissibility of evidence and other procedural matters, including, but not limited to whether oral testimony will be heard; the time allowed each party for the submission of evidence or argument; and whether post-hearing submission of briefs, proposed findings of fact and conclusions of law will be permitted and if so, the procedures for submission; provided, however, that the person presiding may consult with other Commissioners participating in the hearing on these or any other question of procedure.

(2) Each Commissioner present at the hearing shall be afforded a reasonable opportunity to ask questions of witnesses, if any, or counsel.

(3) A party or witness may participate by telephone. Alternative means of remote access, including a video link, shall be permitted in the Commission's discretion. Factors the Commission may consider in determining whether to permit alternative means of remote access include, but are not limited to, whether allowing an alternative means of access will delay the hearing, whether the alternative means is reliable, and whether the party proposing its use has made arrangements to pay for its cost.

(4) After a hearing has begun, the Commission may, on its own motion or the motion of a party, assign a hearing officer to preside at the taking of oral testimony or other evidence and to certify the record of such testimony or other evidence to the Commission within a fixed period of time. No recommended or initial decision shall be made.

§ 201.522 Suspension of Registration of Brokers, Dealers, or other Exchange Act–Registered Entities: Issuance and Review of Order

(a) *Basis for issuance.* An order suspending a registration, pending final determination as to whether the registration shall be revoked shall be issued only if the Commission finds that the suspension is necessary or appropriate in the public interest or for the protection of investors.

(b) *Content, scope and form of order.* Each order suspending a registration shall:

(1) Describe the basis for its issuance, including the alleged or threatened violations and the harm that is likely to result without the issuance of an order;

(2) Describe in reasonable detail, and not by reference to the order instituting proceedings or any other document, the act or acts the respondent is to take or refrain from taking; and

(3) Be indorsed with the date and hour of issuance.

(c) *Effective upon service.* An order suspending a registration is effective upon service upon the respondent.

(d) *Service: how made.* Service of an order suspending a registration shall be made pursuant to § 201.141(a). The person who serves the order shall promptly file a declaration of service identifying the person served, the method of service, the date of service, the address to which service was made and the person who made service; provided, however, failure to file such a declaration shall have no effect on the validity of the service.

(e) *Commission review.* At any time after the respondent has been served with an order suspending a registration, the respondent may apply to the Commission or the hearing officer to have the order set aside, limited, or suspended. The application shall set forth with specificity the facts that support the request.

§ 201.523 [Reserved]

§ 201.524 Suspension of Registrations: Duration

Unless set aside, limited or suspended by order of the Commission, a court of competent jurisdiction, or a hearing officer acting pursuant to § 201.531, an order suspending a registration shall remain effective and enforceable until the earlier of:

(a) The completion of the proceedings whether the registration shall be permanently revoked; or

(b) 180 days, or such longer time as consented to by the respondent, after issuance of a briefing schedule order pursuant to § 201.540(b), if an initial decision whether the registration shall be permanently revoked is appealed.

§ 201.530 Initial Decision on Permanent Order: Timing for Submitting Proposed Findings and Preparation of Decision

Unless otherwise ordered by the Commission or hearing officer, if a temporary cease-and-desist order or suspension of registration order is in effect, the following time limits shall apply to preparation of an initial decision as to whether such order should be made permanent:

(a) Proposed findings and conclusions and briefs in support thereof shall be filed 30 days after the close of the hearing;

(b) The record in the proceedings shall be served by the Secretary upon the hearing officer three days after the date for the filing of the last brief called for by the hearing officer; and

(c) The initial decision shall be filed with the Secretary at the earliest possible time, but in no event more than 30 days after service of the record, unless the hearing officer, by order, shall extend the time for good cause shown for a period not to exceed 30 days.

§ 201.531 Initial Decision on Permanent Order: Effect on Temporary Order

(a) *Specification of permanent sanction.* If, at the time an initial decision is issued, a temporary sanction is in effect as to any respondent, the initial decision shall specify:

(1) Which terms or conditions of a temporary cease-and-desist order, if any, shall become permanent; and

(2) Whether a temporary suspension of a respondent's registration, if any, shall be made a permanent revocation of registration.

(b) *Modification of temporary order.* If any temporary sanction shall not become permanent under the terms of the initial decision, the hearing officer shall issue a separate order setting aside, limiting or suspending the temporary sanction then in effect in accordance with the terms of the initial decision. The hearing officer shall decline to suspend a term or condition of a temporary cease-and-desist order if it is found that the continued effectiveness of such term or condition is necessary to effectuate any term of the relief ordered in the initial decision, including the payment of disgorgement, interest or penalties. An order modifying temporary sanctions shall be effective 14 days after service. Within one week of service of the order modifying temporary sanctions any party may seek a stay or modification of the order from the Commission pursuant to § 201.401.

§ 201.540 Appeal and Commission Review of Initial Decision Making a Temporary Order Permanent

(a) *Petition for review.* Any person who seeks Commission review of an initial decision as to whether a temporary sanction shall be made permanent shall file a petition for review pursuant to § 201.410, provided, however, that the petition must be filed within 10 days after service of the initial decision.

(b) *Review procedure.* If the Commission determines to grant or order review, it shall issue a briefing schedule order pursuant to

§ 201.450. Unless otherwise ordered by the Commission, opening briefs shall be filed within 21 days of the order granting or ordering review, and opposition briefs shall be filed within 14 days after opening briefs are filed. Reply briefs shall be filed within seven days after opposition briefs are filed. Oral argument, if granted by the Commission, shall be held within 30 days of the issuance of the briefing schedule order.

§ 201.550 Summary Suspensions Pursuant to Exchange Act Section 12(k)(1)(A)

(a) *Petition for termination of suspension.* Any person adversely affected by a suspension pursuant to Section 12(k)(1)(A) of the Exchange Act, 15 U.S.C. 78*l*(k)(1)(A), who desires to show that such suspension is not necessary in the public interest or for the protection of investors may file a sworn petition with the Secretary, requesting that the suspension be terminated. The petition shall set forth the reasons why the petitioner believes that the suspension of trading should not continue and state with particularity the facts upon which the petitioner relies.

(b) *Commission consideration of a petition.* The Commission, in its discretion, may schedule a hearing on the matter, request additional written submissions, or decide the matter on the facts presented in the petition and any other relevant facts known to the Commission. If the petitioner fails to cooperate with, obstructs, or refuses to permit the making of an examination by the Commission, such conduct shall be grounds to deny the petition.

Rules Regarding Disgorgement and Penalty Payments

§ 201.600 Interest on Sums Disgorged

(a) *Interest required.* Prejudgment interest shall be due on any sum required to be paid pursuant to an order of disgorgement. The disgorgement order shall specify each violation that forms the basis for the disgorgement ordered; the date which, for purposes of calculating disgorgement, each such violation was deemed to have occurred; the amount to be disgorged for each such violation; and the total sum to be disgorged. Prejudgment interest shall be due from the first day of the month following each such violation through the last day of the month preceding the month in which payment of disgorgement is made. The order shall state the amount of prejudgment interest owed as of the date of the disgorgement order and that interest shall continue to accrue on all funds owed until they are paid.

(b) *Rate of interest.* Interest on the sum to be disgorged shall be computed at the underpayment rate of interest established under Section 6621(a)(2) of the Internal Revenue Code, 26 U.S.C. 6621(a)(2), and shall be compounded quarterly. The Commission or the hearing officer may, by order, specify a lower rate of prejudgment interest as to any funds which the respondent has placed in an escrow or otherwise guaranteed for payment of disgorgement upon a final determination of the respondent's liability. Escrow and other guarantee arrangements must be approved by the Commission or the hearing officer prior to entry of the disgorgement order.

§ 201.601 Prompt Payment of Disgorgement, Interest and Penalties

(a) *Timing of payments.* Unless otherwise provided, funds due pursuant to an order by the Commission requiring the payment of disgorgement, interest or penalties shall be paid no later than 21 days after service of the order, and funds due pursuant to an order by a hearing officer shall be paid on the first day after the order becomes final pursuant to § 201.360.

(b) *Stays.* A stay of any order requiring the payment of disgorgement, interest or penalties may be sought at any time pursuant to § 201.401.

(c) *Method of making payment.* Payment shall be made by United States postal money order, wire transfer, certified check, bank cashier's check, or bank money order made payable to the Securities and Exchange Commission. The payment shall be mailed or delivered to the office designated by this Commission. Payment shall be accompanied by a letter that identifies the name and number of the case and the name of the respondent making payment. A copy of the letter and the instrument of payment shall be sent to counsel for the Division of Enforcement.

§ 201.630 Inability to Pay Disgorgement, Interest or Penalties

(a) *Generally.* In any proceeding in which an order requiring payment of disgorgement, interest or penalties may be entered, a respondent may present evidence of an inability to pay disgorgement, interest or a penalty. The Commission may, in its discretion, or the hearing officer may, in his or her discretion, consider evidence concerning ability to pay in determining whether disgorgement, interest or a penalty is in the public interest.

(b) *Financial disclosure statement.* Any respondent who asserts an inability to pay disgorgement, interest or penalties may be required to file a sworn financial disclosure statement and to keep the statement current. The financial statement shall show the respondent's assets; liabilities, income or other funds received and expenses or other payments, from the date of the first violation alleged against that respondent in the order instituting proceedings, or such later date as specified by the Commission or a hearing officer, to the date of the order requiring the disclosure statement to be filed. By order, the Commission or the hearing officer may prescribe the use of the Disclosure of Assets and Financial Information Form (*see* Form D–A at § 209.1 of this chapter) or any other form, may specify other time periods for which disclosure is required, and may require such other information as deemed necessary to evaluate a claim of inability to pay.

(c) *Confidentiality.* Any respondent submitting financial information pursuant to this section or § 201.410(c) may make a motion, pursuant to § 201.322, for the issuance of a protective order against disclosure of the information submitted to the public or to any parties other than the Division of Enforcement. Prior to a ruling on the motion, no party receiving information as to which a motion for a protective order has been made may transfer or convey the information to any other person without the prior permission of the Commission or the hearing officer.

(d) *Service required.* Notwithstanding any provision of § 201.322, a copy of the financial disclosure statement shall be served on the Division of Enforcement.

(e) *Failure to file required financial information: sanction.* Any respondent who, after making a claim of inability to pay either disgorgement, interest or a penalty, fails to file a financial disclosure statement when such a filing has been ordered or is required by rule may, in the discretion of the Commission or the hearing officer, be deemed to have waived the claim of inability to pay. No sanction pursuant to §§ 201.155 or 201.180 shall be imposed for a failure to file such a statement.

Informal Procedures and Supplementary Information Concerning Adjudicatory Proceedings

§ 201.900 Informal Procedures and Supplementary Information Concerning Adjudicatory Proceedings

(a) *Guidelines for the timely completion of proceedings.*

(1) Timely resolution of adjudicatory proceedings is one factor in assessing the effectiveness of the adjudicatory program in protecting investors, promoting public confidence in the securities markets and assuring respondents a fair hearing. Establishment of guidelines for the timely completion of key phases of contested administrative proceedings provides a standard for both the Commission and the public to gauge the Commission's adjudicatory program on this criterion. The Com-

mission has directed that, to the extent possible:

(i) A decision by the Commission on review of an interlocutory matter should be completed within 45 days of the date set for filing the final brief on the matter submitted for review.

(ii) A decision by the Commission on a motion to stay a decision that has already taken effect or that will take effect within five days of the filing of the motion, should be issued within five days of the date set for filing of the opposition to the motion for a stay. If the decision complained of has not taken effect, the Commission's decision should be issued within 45 days of the date set for filing of the opposition to the motion for a stay.

(iii) Ordinarily, a decision by the Commission with respect to an appeal from the initial decision of a hearing officer, a review of a determination by a self-regulatory organization, or a remand of a prior Commission decision by a court of appeals should be issued within seven months from the date the petition for review, application for review, or mandate of the court is filed, unless the Commission determines that the matter presents unusual complicating circumstances, in which case a decision by the Commission on the matter may be issued within 11 months from the date the petition for review, application for review, or mandate of the court is filed. The Commission retains discretion to take additional time to dispose of an appeal from the initial decision of a hearing officer, a review of a determination by a self-regulatory organization, or a remand of a prior Commission decision by a court of appeals when the Commission determines that extraordinary facts and circumstances of the matter so require. The deadlines in § 201.900 confer no substantive rights on the parties.

(2) The guidelines in this paragraph (a) do not create a requirement that each portion of a proceeding or the entire proceeding be completed within the periods described. Among other reasons, a proceeding at either the hearing stage or on review by the Commission may require additional time because it is unusually complex or because the record is exceptionally long. In addition, fairness is enhanced if the Commission's deliberative process is not constrained by an inflexible schedule. In some proceedings, deliberation may be delayed by the need to consider more urgent matters, to permit the preparation of dissenting opinions, or for other good cause. The guidelines will be used by the Commission as one of several criteria in monitoring and evaluating its adjudicatory program. The guidelines will be examined periodically, and, if necessary, readjusted in light of changes in the pending caseload and the available level of staff resources.

(b) *Reports to the Commission on pending cases.* The administrative law judges, the Secretary and the General Counsel have each been delegated authority to issue certain orders or adjudicate certain proceedings. *See* 17 CFR 200.30–1, *et seq.* Proceedings are also assigned to the General Counsel for the preparation of a proposed order or opinion which will then be recommended to the Commission for consideration. In order to improve accountability by and to the Commission for management of the docket, the Commission has directed that confidential status reports with respect to all filed adjudicatory proceedings shall be made periodically to the Commission. These reports will be made through the Secretary, with a minimum frequency established by the Commission. In connection with these periodic reports, if a proceeding assigned to an administrative law judge or pending before the Commission has not been concluded within 30 days of the guidelines established in paragraph (a) of this section, the Chief Administrative Law Judge or the General Counsel, respectively, shall specifically apprise the Commission of that fact, and shall describe the procedural posture of the case, project an estimated date for conclusion of the proceeding, and provide such other information as is necessary to enable the Commission to determine whether additional steps are necessary to reach a fair and timely resolution of the matter.

(c) *Publication of information concerning the pending case docket.* Ongoing disclosure of information about the adjudication program caseload increases awareness of the importance of the program, facilitates oversight of the program and promotes confidence in the efficiency and fairness of the program by investors, securities industry participants, self-regulatory organizations and other members of the public. The Commission has directed the Secretary to publish in the *SEC Docket* in the first and seventh months of each fiscal year summary statistical information about the status of pending adjudicatory proceedings and changes in the Commission's caseload over the prior six months. The report will include the number of cases pending before the administrative law judges and the Commission at the beginning and end of the six-month period. The report will also show increases in the caseload arising from new cases being instituted, appealed or remanded to the Commission and decreases in the caseload arising from the disposition of proceedings by issuance of initial decisions, issuance of final decisions issued on appeal of initial decisions, other dispositions of appeals of initial decisions, final decisions on review of self-regulatory organization determinations, other dispositions on review of self-regulatory organization determinations, and decisions with respect to stays or interlocutory motions. For each category of decision, the report shall also show the median age of the cases at the time of the decision and the number of cases decided within the guidelines for the timely completion of adjudicatory proceedings.

Subpart E—Adjustment of Civil Monetary Penalties

§ 201.1003 Adjustment of civil monetary penalties—2005

As required by the Debt Collection Improvement Act of 1996, the maximum amounts of all civil monetary penalties under the Securities Act of 1933, the Securities Exchange Act of 1934, the Investment Company Act of 1940, the Investment Advisers Act of 1940, and certain penalties under the Sarbanes-Oxley Act of 2002 are adjusted for inflation in accordance with Table III to this subpart. The adjustments set forth in Table III apply to violations occurring after February 14, 2005.

TABLE 1 TO SUBPART E.—CIVIL MONETARY PENALTY INFLATION ADJUSTMENTS

U.S. Code Citation	Civil monetary penalty description	Year penalty amount was last set by law	Original statutory maximum penalty amount	Adjusted maximum penalty amount
SECURITIES AND EXCHANGE COMMISSION:				
15 USC 77t(d)	FOR NATURAL PERSON	2001	$6,500	$6,500
	FOR ANY OTHER PERSON	2001	60,000	65,000
	FOR NATURAL PERSON/FRAUD	2001	60,000	65,000
	FOR ANY OTHER PERSON/FRAUD	2001	300,000	325,000
	FOR NATURAL PERSON/SUBSTANTIAL LOSSES OR RISK OF LOSSES TO OTHERS	2001	120,000	130,000
	FOR ANY OTHER PERSON/SUBSTANTIAL LOSSES OR RISK OF LOSSES TO OTHERS	2001	600,000	600,000
15 USC 78ff(b)	EXCHANGE ACT/FAILURE TO FILE INFORMATION DOCUMENTS, REPORTS	1996	110	110
15 USC 78ff (c)(1)(B)	FOREIGN CORRUPT PRACTICES—ANY ISSUER	1996	11,000	11,000
15 USC 78ff (c)(2)(C)	FOREIGN CORRUPT PRACTICES—ANY AGENT OR STOCKHOLDER ACTING ON BEHALF OF ISSUER	1996	11,000	11,000
15 USC 78u–1 (a)(3)	INSIDER TRADING—CONTROLLING PERSONS	2001	1,200,000	1,275,000
15 USC 78u–2	FOR NATURAL PERSON	2001	6,500	6,500
	FOR ANY OTHER PERSON	2001	60,000	65,000
	FOR NATURAL PERSON/FRAUD	2001	60,000	65,000
	FOR ANY OTHER PERSON/FRAUD	2001	300,000	325,000
	FOR NATURAL PERSON/SUBSTANTIAL LOSSES TO OTHERS/GAINS TO SELF	2001	120,000	130,000
	FOR ANY OTHER PERSONS/SUBSTANTIAL LOSSES TO OTHERS/GAIN TO SELF	2001	600,000	650,000
15 USC 78u(d)(3)	FOR NATURAL PERSON	2001	6,500	6,500
	FOR ANY OTHER PERSON	2001	60,000	65,000
	FOR NATURAL PERSON/FRAUD	2001	60,000	65,000
	FOR ANY OTHER PERSON/FRAUD	2001	300,000	325,000
	FOR NATURAL PERSON/SUBSTANTIAL LOSSES OR RISK OF LOSSES TO OTHERS	2001	120,000	130,000
	FOR ANY OTHER PERSON/SUBSTANTIAL LOSSES OR RISK OF LOSSES TO OTHERS	2001	600,000	650,000
15 USC 80a–9(d)	FOR NATURAL PERSON	2001	6,500	6,500
	FOR ANY OTHER PERSON	2001	60,000	65,000
	FOR NATURAL PERSON/FRAUD	2001	60,000	65,000
	FOR ANY OTHER PERSON/FRAUD	2001	300,000	325,000
	FOR NATURAL PERSON/SUBSTANTIAL LOSSES TO OTHERS/GAINS TO SELF	2001	120,000	130,000
	FOR ANY OTHER PERSON/SUBSTANTIAL LOSSES TO OTHERS/GAIN TO SELF	2001	600,000	650,000
15 USC 80a–41(e)	FOR NATURAL PERSON	2001	6,500	6,500
	FOR ANY OTHER PERSON	2001	60,000	65,000
	FOR NATURAL PERSON/FRAUD	2001	60,000	65,000
	FOR ANY OTHER PERSON/FRAUD	2001	300,000	325,000
	FOR NATURAL PERSON/SUBSTANTIAL LOSSES OR RISK OF LOSSES TO OTHERS	2001	120,000	130,000
	FOR ANY OTHER PERSON/SUBSTANTIAL LOSSES OR RISK OF LOSSES TO OTHERS	2001	600,000	650,000
15 USC 80b–3(i)	FOR NATURAL PERSON	2001	6,500	6,500
	FOR ANY OTHER PERSON	2001	60,000	65,000
	FOR NATURAL PERSON/FRAUD	2001	60,000	65,000
	FOR ANY OTHER PERSON/FRAUD	2001	300,000	325,000
	FOR NATURAL PERSON/SUBSTANTIAL LOSSES TO OTHERS/GAIN TO SELF	2001	120,000	130,000
	FOR ANY OTHER PERSON/SUBSTANTIAL LOSSES TO OTHERS/GAIN TO SELF	2001	600,000	650,000

U.S. Code Citation	Civil monetary penalty description	Year penalty amount was last set by law	Original statutory maximum penalty amount	Adjusted maximum penalty amount
15 USC 80b–9(e)	FOR NATURAL PERSON	2001	6,500	6,500
	FOR ANY OTHER PERSON	2001	60,000	65,000
	FOR NATURAL PERSON/FRAUD	2001	60,000	65,000
	FOR ANY OTHER PERSON/FRAUD	2001	300,000	325,000
	FOR NATURAL PERSON/SUBSTANTIAL LOSSES OR RISK OF LOSSES TO OTHERS	2001	120,000	130,000
	FOR ANY OTHER PERSON/SUBSTANTIAL LOSSES OR RISK OF LOSSES TO OTHERS	2002	600,000	650,000
15 USC 7215(c)(4)(D)(i)	FOR NATURAL PERSON	2002	100,000	110,000
	FOR ANY OTHER PERSON	2002	2,000,000	2,100,000
15 USC 7215(c)(4)(D)(ii)	FOR NATURAL PERSON	2002	750,000	800,000
	FOR ANY OTHER PERSON	2002	15,000,000	15,825,000

2. INFORMAL AND OTHER PROCEDURES

Section

---

§ 202.1 General

(a) The statutes administered by the Commission provide generally (1) for the filing with it of certain statements, such as registration statements, periodic and ownership reports, and proxy solicitation material, and for the filing of certain plans of reorganization, applications and declarations seeking Commission approvals; (2) for Commission determination through formal procedures of matters initiated by private parties or by the Commission; (3) for the investigation and examination of persons and records where necessary to carry out the purposes of the statutes and for enforcement of statutory provisions; and (4) for the adoption of rules and regulations where necessary to effectuate the purposes of the statutes.

(b) In addition to the Commission's rules of practice set forth in part 201 of this chapter, the Commission has promulgated rules and regulations pursuant to the several statutes it administers (parts 230, 240, 250, 260, 270 and 275 of this chapter). These parts contain substantive provisions and include as well numerous provisions detailing the procedure for meeting specific standards embodied in the statutes. The Commission's rules and regulations under each of the statutes are available in pamphlet form upon request to the Superintendent of Documents, U.S. Government Printing Office, Washington, DC 20402.

(c) The statutes and the published rules, regulations and forms thereunder prescribe the course and method of formal procedures to be followed in Commission proceedings. These are supplemented where feasible by certain informal procedures designed to aid the public and facilitate the execution of the Commission's functions. There follows a brief description of procedures generally followed by the Commission which have not been formalized in rules.

(d) The informal procedures of the Commission are largely concerned with the rendering of advice and assistance by the Commission's staff to members of the public dealing with the Commission. While opinions expressed by members of the staff do not constitute an official expression of the Commission's views, they represent the views of persons who are continuously working with the provisions of the statute involved. And any statement by the director, associate director, assistant director, chief accountant, chief counsel, or chief financial analyst of a division can be relied upon as representing the views of that division. In certain instances an informal statement of the views of the Commission may be obtained. The staff, upon request or on its own motion, will generally present questions to the Commission which involve matters of substantial importance and where the issues are novel or highly complex, although the granting of a request for an informal statement by the Commission is entirely within its discretion.

§ 202.2 Pre-filing Assistance and Interpretative Advice

The staff of the Commission renders interpretative and advisory assistance to members of the general public, prospective registrants, applicants and declarants. For example, persons having a question regarding the availability of an exemption may secure informal administrative interpretations of the applicable statute or rule as they relate to the particular facts and circumstances presented. Similarly, persons contemplating filings with the Commission may receive advice of a general nature as to the preparation thereof, including information as to the forms to be used and the scope of the items contained in the forms. Inquiries may be directed to an appropriate officer of the Commission's staff. In addition, informal discussions with members of the staff may be arranged whenever feasible, at the Commission's central office or, except in connection with matters under the Public Utility Holding Company Act of 1935 and certain matters under the Investment Company Act of 1940, at one of its regional or district offices.

§ 202.3 Processing of Filings

(a) Registration statements, proxy statements, letters of notification, periodic reports, applications for qualification of indentures, and similar documents filed with the Commission under the Securities Act of 1933 and the Trust Indenture Act of 1939, and certain filings under the Securities Exchange Act of 1934 and the Public Utility Holding Company Act of 1935 are routed to the Division of Corporation Finance, which passes initially on the adequacy of disclosure and recommends the initial action to be taken. If the filing appears to afford inadequate disclosure, as for example through omission of material information or through violation of accepted accounting principles and practices, the usual practice is to bring the deficiency to the attention of the person who filed the document by letter from the Assistant Director assigned supervision over the particular filing, and to afford a reasonable opportunity to discuss the matter and make the necessary corrections. This informal procedure is not generally employed when the deficiencies appear to stem from careless disregard of the statutes and rules or a deliberate attempt to conceal or mislead or where the Commission deems formal proceedings necessary in the public interest. If an electronic filing is not prepared in accordance with the requirements of the current EDGAR Filer Manual, the filing may be suspended and the filer so notified. A similar procedure is followed with respect to filings under the Investment Company Act of 1940 and certain filings relating to investment companies under the Securities Act of 1933, the Securities Exchange Act of 1934, and the Trust Indenture Act of 1939, which are routed to the Division of Investment Management, and filings under the Public Utility Holding

Company Act of 1935 which are also routed to the Division of Investment Management. Reasonable opportunity will be afforded the filer to make the necessary corrections or resubmit the filing as needed. Where it appears that the filing affords adequate disclosure, acceleration of its effectiveness when appropriate normally will be granted. A similar procedure is followed with respect to filings under the Investment Company Act of 1940 and certain filings relating to investment companies under the Securities Act of 1933, the Securities Exchange Act of 1934, and the Trust Indenture Act of 1939, which are routed to the Division of Investment Management, and filings under the Public Utility Holding Company Act of 1935 which are routed to the Division of Corporate Regulation. A similar procedure is also followed in the Commission's Regional Offices with respect to registration statements on Forms SB–1 and SB–2 and related filings under the Trust Indenture Act of 1939.

(b)(1) Applications for registration as brokers, dealers, investment advisers, municipal securities dealers and transfer agents are submitted to the Office of Filings and Information Services where they are examined to determine whether all necessary information has been supplied and whether all required financial statements and other documents have been furnished in proper form. Defective applications may be returned with a request for correction or held until corrected before being accepted as a filing. The files of the Commission and other sources of information are considered to determine whether any person connected with the applicant appears to have engaged in activities which would warrant commencement of proceedings on the question of denial of registration. The staff confers with applicants and makes suggestions in appropriate cases for amendments and supplemental information. Where it appears appropriate in the public interest and where a basis therefore exists, denial proceedings may be instituted. Within forty-five days of the date of the filing of a broker-dealer, investment adviser or municipal securities dealer application (or within such longer period as to which the applicant consents), the Commission shall by order grant registration or institute proceedings to determine whether registration should be denied. An application for registration as a transfer agent shall become effective within 30 days after receipt of the application (or within such shorter period as the Commission may determine). The Office of Filings and Information Services is also responsible for the processing and substantive examination of statements of beneficial ownership of securities and changes in such ownership filed under the Securities Exchange Act of 1934, the Public Utility Holding Company Act of 1935, and the Investment Company Act of 1940, and for the examination of reports filed pursuant to § 230.144 of this chapter.

(2) Applications for registration as national securities exchanges, or exemption from registration as exchanges by reason of such exchanges' limited volume of transactions filed with the Commission are routed to the Division of Market Regulation, which examines these applications to determine whether all necessary information has been supplied and whether all required financial statements and other documents have been furnished in proper form. Defective applications may be returned with a request for correction or held until corrected before being accepted as a filing. The files of the Commission and other sources of information are considered to determine whether any person connected with the applicant appears to have engaged in activities which would warrant commencement of proceedings on the question of denial of registration. The staff confers with applicants and makes suggestions in appropriate cases for amendments and supplemental information. Where it appears appropriate in the public interest and where a basis therefore exists, denial proceedings may be instituted. Within 90 days of the date of publication of a notice of the filing of an application for registration as a national securities exchange, or exemption from registration by reason of such exchanges'

limited volume of transactions (or within such longer period as to which the applicant consents), the Commission shall by order grant registration, or institute proceedings to determine whether registration should be denied as provided in § 240.19(a)(1) of this chapter.

(3) Notice forms for registration as national securities exchanges pursuant to Section 6(g)(1) of the Securities Exchange Act of 1934 (15 U.S.C. 78f(g)(1)) filed with the Commission are routed to the Division of Market Regulation, which examines these notices to determine whether all necessary information has been supplied and whether all other required documents have been furnished in proper form. Defective notices may be returned with a request for correction or held until corrected before being accepted as a filing.

§ 202.3a Instructions for Filing Fees

Payment of filing fees specified by the following rules shall be made according to the directions listed in this part: § 230.111 (17 CFR 230.111), § 240.0–9 (17 CFR 240–0.9), § 260.7a–10 (17 CFR 260.7a–10), and § 270.0–8 (17 CFR 270.0–8). All such fees payable by electronic filers, including those pertaining to documents filed in paper pursuant to a hardship exemption, shall be remitted to the U.S. Treasury designated lockbox depository at the Mellon Bank in Pittsburgh, Pennsylvania, by wire transfer, mail or hand delivery. Fees payable by paper filers may be either remitted to the lockbox depository, or remitted directly to the Commission at 450 Fifth Street N.W., Washington DC 20549. Personal checks cannot be accepted for payment of fees. To ensure proper posting, all filers must include their assigned CIK account numbers on fee payments. If a third party submits a fee payment, the fee payment must specify the account number to which the fee is to be applied. Filing fees paid pursuant to Section 6(b) of the Securities Act of 1933, including fees paid pursuant to Section 24(f) of the Investment Company Act of 1940 (15 U.S.C. 80a–24(f)) or pursuant to Section 307(b) of the Trust Indenture Act of 1939 should be designated as "restricted," except that filing fees paid with respect to registration statements filed pursuant to Rule 462(b) (§ 230.462(b) of this chapter) should be designated as "unrestricted." Specific instructions on the various methods of making fee payments to the lockbox depository are as follows:

(a) *Wire transfer:* Those who wish to wire fee payments may use any bank or wire transfer service to initiate the transaction. All remitters must follow standard Federal Reserve instructions to ensure that fees transferred are received and identifiable. Specific information required for transmission to the Mellon Bank is listed below. Where an item is in **boldface type,** the entry should be made exactly as indicated. Where an item is in *italics,* the filer-specific information should be included.

(1) Receiving Bank's ABA Number (field two): **043000261**

(2) Type Code (field three): **1040**

(3) Name of registrant and name of payor, if different (field nine): **ORG=** *registrant's name/payor's name (if different)*

(4) Receiving Bank's Name (field ten): **MELLONBANK**

(5) Transaction Code (field eleven): **CTR/**

(6) Beneficiary of payment (field twelve): **BNF=SEC/AC–9108739/WRE**

(7) Reference for Beneficiary (field thirteen): **RFB=** *account number to which the fee is to be applied*

(8) Payment Details (field fourteen): To designate funds as restricted: **OBI=R,** Otherwise: **OBI=N.**

(b) *Mail and hand delivery:* Checks and money orders are to be made payable to the Securities and Exchange Commission, omitting the name or title of any official of the Commission. The account number and a notation of "R" (restricted), as applicable, are to be written on the front of the check or money order. Fees transmitted by mail must be addressed to the Securities and Exchange Commission, Post Office Box 360055M, Pittsburgh, Pennsylvania

15252. Fees that are hand delivered must be brought to the Mellon Bank, 27th floor, Three Mellon Bank Center, Fifth Avenue at William Penn Way, Pittsburgh, PA. Hand deliveries will be accepted weekdays from 7:30 a.m. to 4:00 p.m. (eastern time). No deliveries can be made on Federal holidays. All hand deliveries must be in a sealed envelope, with the Commission's lockbox number, 360055M, and the Commission's account number, 9108739, written on the outside. Cash payments must be accompanied by a separate sheet of paper providing the same information specified for checks and money orders.

(c) *Filing fee accounts*: (1) A filing fee account is maintained for each filer who submits a filing requiring a fee on the Commission's EDGAR system or who submits funds to the U.S. Treasury designated depository in anticipation of paying a filing fee. Account statements are regularly prepared and provided to account holders. Account holders must maintain a current account address with the Commission to ensure timely access to these statements.

(2) Funds held in any filing fee account in which there has not been a deposit, withdrawal or other adjustment for more than 180 calendar days will be returned to the account holder, and account statements will not be sent again until a deposit, withdrawal or other adjustment is made with respect to the account. Filers must maintain a current account address to assure the timely return of funds. It may not be possible to return funds from inactive accounts if the Commission is unable to identify a current account address of an account holder after making reasonable efforts to do so.

Note to paragraph (c). A company may update its account and other addresses using two different methods. The preferred and most efficient method is to change them online using the EDGAR filing website. This method ensures data integrity and the most timely update. Alternatively, a company may report a change of addresses on an amended Form ID (17 CFR 239.63; 17 CFR 249.446 and 17 CFR 274.402). Simply changing an address in the text of the cover page of a filing made on the EDGAR system will not be sufficient to update the Commission's account address records.

§ 202.4 Facilitating Administrative Hearings

(a) Applications, declarations, and other requests involving formal Commission action after opportunity for hearing are scrutinized by the appropriate division for conformance with applicable statutory standards and Commission rules and generally the filing party is advised of deficiencies. Prior to passing upon applications and declarations the Commission receives the views of all interested persons at public hearings whenever appropriate; hence, any applicant or declarant seeking Commission approval of proposed transactions by a particular time should file his application or declaration in time to allow for the presentation and consideration of such views.

(b) After the staff has had an opportunity to study an application or declaration, interested persons may informally discuss the problems therein raised to the extent that time and the nature of the case permit (e.g., consideration is usually given to whether the proceeding is contested and if so to the nature of the contest). In such event, the staff will, to the extent feasible, advise as to the nature of the issues raised by the filing, the necessity for any amendments to the documents filed, the type of evidence it believes should be presented at the hearing and, in some instances, the nature, form, and contents of documents to be submitted as formal exhibits. The staff will, in addition, generally advise as to Commission policy in past cases which dealt with the same subject matter as the filing under consideration.

(c) During the course of the hearings, the staff is generally available for informal discussions to reconcile bona fide divergent views not only between itself and other persons interested in the proceedings, but among all interested persons; and, when circumstances permit, an attempt is made to narrow, if possible, the issues to be considered at the formal hearing.

(d) In some instances the Commission in the order accompanying its findings and opinion reserves jurisdiction over certain matters relating to the proceeding, such as payment of fees and expenses, accounting entries, terms and conditions relating to securities to be issued, and other matters. In such cases, upon receipt of satisfactory information and data the Commission considers whether further hearing is required before releasing jurisdiction.

§ 202.5 Enforcement Activities

(a) Where, from complaints received from members of the public, communications from Federal or State agencies, examination of filings made with the Commission, or otherwise, it appears that there may be violation of the acts administered by the Commission or the rules or regulations thereunder, a preliminary investigation is generally made. In such preliminary investigation no process is issued or testimony compelled. The Commission may, in its discretion, make such formal investigations and authorize the use of process as it deems necessary to determine whether any person has violated, is violating, or is about to violate any provision of the federal securities laws or the rules of a self-regulatory organization of which the person is a member or participant. Unless otherwise ordered by the Commission, the investigation or examination is non-public and the reports thereon are for staff and Commission use only.

(b) After investigation or otherwise the Commission may in its discretion take one or more of the following actions: Institution of administrative proceedings looking to the imposition of remedial sanctions, initiation of injunctive proceedings in the courts, and, in the case of a willful violation, reference of the matter to the Department of Justice for criminal prosecution. The Commission may also, on some occasions, refer the matter to, or grant requests for access to its files made by, domestic and foreign governmental authorities or foreign securities authorities, self-regulatory organizations such as stock exchanges or the National Association of Securities Dealers, Inc., and other persons or entities.

(c) Persons who become involved in preliminary or formal investigations may, on their own initiative, submit a written statement to the Commission setting forth their interests and position in regard to the subject matter of the investigation. Upon request, the staff, in its discretion, may advise such persons of the general nature of the investigation, including the indicated violations as they pertain to them, and the amount of time that may be available for preparing and submitting a statement prior to the presentation of a staff recommendation to the Commission for the commencement of an administrative or injunction proceeding. Submissions by interested persons should be forwarded to the appropriate Division Director or Regional Director, or District Administrator with a copy to the staff members conducting the investigation and should be clearly referenced to the specific investigation to which they relate. In the event a recommendation for the commencement of an enforcement proceeding is presented by the staff, any submissions by interested persons will be forwarded to the Commission in conjunction with the staff memorandum.

(d) In instances where the staff has concluded its investigation of a particular matter and has determined that it will not recommend the commencement of an enforcement proceeding against a person, the staff, in its discretion, may advise the party that its formal investigation has been terminated. Such advice if given must in no way be construed as indicating that the party has been exonerated or that no action may ultimately result from the staff's investigation of the particular matter.

(e) The Commission has adopted the policy that in any civil lawsuit brought by it or in any administrative proceeding of an accusatory nature pending before it, it is important to avoid creating, or permitting to be created, an impression that a decree is being entered or a sanction imposed, when the conduct alleged did not, in fact, occur. Accordingly, it hereby announces its policy not to permit a defendant or respondent to consent to a judgment or order that imposes a sanction while denying the allegations in the complaint or order for proceedings. In this regard, the Commission believes that a refusal to admit the allegations is equivalent to a denial, unless the defendant or respondent states that he neither admits nor denies the allegations.

(f) In the course of the Commission's investigations, civil lawsuits, and administrative proceedings, the staff, with appropriate authorization, may discuss with persons involved the disposition of such matters by consent, by settlement, or in some other manner. It is the policy of the Commission, however, that the disposition of any such matter may not, expressly or impliedly, extend to any criminal charges that have been, or may be, brought against any such person or any recommendation with respect thereto. Accordingly, any person involved in an enforcement matter before the Commission who consents, or agrees to consent, to any judgment or order does so solely for the purpose of resolving the claims against him in that investigative, civil, or administrative matter and not for the purpose of resolving any criminal charges that have been, or might be, brought against him. This policy reflects the fact that neither the Commission nor its staff has the authority or responsibility for instituting, conducting, settling, or otherwise disposing of criminal proceedings. That authority and responsibility are vested in the Attorney General and representatives of the Department of Justice.

§ 202.6 Adoption, Revision, and Rescission of Rules and Regulations of General Application

(a) The procedure followed by the Commission in connection with the adoption, revision, and rescission of rules of general application necessarily varies in accordance with the nature of the rule, the extent of public interest therein, and the necessity for speed in its adoption. Rules relating to Commission organization, procedure and management, for example, are generally adopted by the Commission without affording public discussion thereof. On the other hand, in the adoption of substantive rules materially affecting an industry or a segment of the public, such as accounting rules, every feasible effort is made in advance of adoption to receive the views of persons to be affected. In such cases, proposals for the adoption, revision, or rescission of rules are initiated either by the Commission or by members of the public, and to the extent practicable, the practices set forth in paragraph (b) of this section are observed.

(b) After preliminary consideration by the Commission a draft of the proposed rule is published in the FEDERAL REGISTER and mailed to interested persons (e.g., other interested regulatory bodies, principal registrants or persons to be affected, stock exchanges, professional societies and leading authorities on the subject concerned and other persons requesting such draft) for comments. Unless accorded confidential treatment pursuant to statute or rule of the Commission, written comments filed with the Commission on or before the closing date for comments become a part of the public record upon the proposed rule. The Commission, in its discretion, may accept and include in the public record written comments received by the Commission after the closing date.

(c) Following analysis of comments received, the rule may be adopted in the form published or in a revised form in the light of such comments. In some cases, a revised draft is prepared and published and, where appropriate, an oral hearing may be held before final action upon the proposal. Any interested person may appear at the hearing and/or may submit written comment for consideration in accordance with the Commission's notice of the rulemaking procedure to be followed. The rule in the form in which it is adopted by the Commission is publicly released and is published in the FEDERAL REGISTER.

§ 202.7 Submittals

(a) All required statements, reports, applications, etc. must be filed with the principal office of the Commission unless otherwise specified in the Commission's rules, schedules and forms. Reports by exchange members, brokers and dealers required by Rule 17a–5 under the Securities Exchange Act of 1934 must be filed with the appropriate regional official as provided in Rule 255(a) under the Securities Act of 1933, and with the principal office of the Commission and the appropriate regional or district office as provided under Rule 17a–5(a) et seq. under the Securities Exchange Act of 1934.

(b) *Electronic filings.* All documents required to be filed in electronic format with the Commission pursuant to the federal securities laws or the rules and regulations thereunder shall be filed at the principal office in Washington, D.C. via EDGAR by delivery to the Commission of a magnetic tape or diskette, or by direct transmission.

4. RULES RELATING TO INVESTIGATIONS

Section

---

§ 203.1 Application of the Rules of This Part

The rules of this part apply only to investigations conducted by the Commission. They do not apply to adjudicative or rulemaking proceedings.

§ 203.2 Information Obtained in Investigations and Examinations

Information or documents obtained by the Commission in the course of any investigation or examination, unless made a matter of public record, shall be deemed non-public, but the Commission approves the practice whereby officials of the Divisions of Enforcement, Corporation Finance, Market Regulation and Investment Management and the Office of International Affairs at the level of Assistant Director or higher, and officials in Regional or District Offices at the level of Assistant Regional Director or District Administrator or higher, may engage in and may authorize members of the Commission's staff to engage in discussions with persons identified in Rule 24c–1(b) of this chapter concerning information obtained in individual investigations or examinations, including formal investigations conducted pursuant to Commission order.

§ 203.3 Suspension and Disbarment

The provisions of § 201.102(e) of this chapter Rule 102(e) are hereby made specifically applicable to all investigations.

§ 203.4 Applicability of §§ 203.4 Through 203.8

(a) Sections 203.4 through 203.8 shall be applicable to a witness who is sworn in a proceeding pursuant to a Commission order for investigation or examination, such proceeding being hereinafter referred to as a *formal investigative proceeding.*

(b) Formal investigative proceedings may be held before the Commission, before one or more of its members, or before any officer designated by it for the purpose of taking testimony of witnesses and received other evidence. The term *officer conducting the investigation* shall mean any of the foregoing.

§ 203.5 Non-public Formal Investigative Proceedings

Unless otherwise ordered by the Commission, all formal investigative proceedings shall be non-public.

§ 203.6 Transcripts

Transcripts, if any, of formal investigative proceedings shall be recorded solely by the official reporter, or by any other person or means designated by the officer conducting the investigation. A person who has submitted documentary evidence or testimony in a formal investigative proceeding shall be entitled, upon written request, to procure a copy of his documentary evidence or a transcript of his testimony on payment of the appropriate fees: *Provided, however,* That in a non-public formal investigative proceeding the Commission may for good cause deny such request. In any event, any witness, upon proper identification, shall have the right to inspect the official transcripts of the witness' own testimony.

§ 203.7 Rights of Witnesses

(a) Any person who is compelled or requested to furnish documentary evidence or testimony at a formal investigative proceeding shall, upon request, be shown the Commission's order of investigation. Copies of formal orders of investigation shall not be furnished, for their retention, to such persons requesting the same except with the express approval of officials in the Regional or District Offices at the level of Assistant Regional Director or District Administrator or higher, or officials in the Division or Divisions conducting or supervising the investigation at the level of Assistant Director or higher. Such approval shall not be given unless the person granting such approval, in his or her discretion, is satisfied that there exist reasons consistent both with the protection of privacy of persons involved in the investigation and with the unimpeded conduct of the investigation.

(b) Any person compelled to appear, or who appears by request or permission of the Commission, in person at a formal investigative proceeding may be accompanied, represented and advised by counsel, as defined in § 201.101(a) of this chapter (Rule 101(a) of the Commission's Rules of Practice): *Provided, however,* That all witnesses shall be sequestered, and unless permitted in the discretion of the officer conducting the investigation no witness or the counsel accompanying any such witness shall be permitted to be present during the examination of any other witness called in such proceeding.

(c) The right to be accompanied, represented and advised by counsel shall mean the right of a person testifying to have an attorney present with him during any formal investigative proceeding and to have this attorney (1) advise such person before, during and after the conclusion of such examination, (2) question such person briefly at the conclusion of the examination to clarify any of the answers such person has given, and (3) make summary notes during such examination solely for the use of such person.

(d) Unless otherwise ordered by the Commission, in any public formal investigative proceeding, if the record shall contain implications of wrongdoing by any person, such person shall have the right to appear on the record; and in addition to the rights afforded other witnesses hereby, he shall have a reasonable opportunity of cross-examination and production of rebuttal testimony or documentary evidence. *Reasonable* shall mean permitting persons as full an opportunity to assert their position as may be granted consistent with administrative efficiency and with avoidance of undue delay. The determination of reasonableness in each instance shall be made in the discretion of the officer conducting the investigation.

(e) The officer conducting the investigation may report to the Commission any instances where any witness or counsel has been guilty of dilatory, obstructionist or contumacious conduct during the course of an investigation or any other instance of violation of these rules. The Commission will thereupon take such further action as the circumstances may warrant, including suspension or disbarment of counsel from further appearance or practice before it, in accordance with § 201.2(e) of this chapter (Rule 2(e) of the Commission's rules of practice), or exclusion from further participation in the particular investigation.

§ 203.8 Service of Subpoenas

Service of subpoenas issued in formal investigative proceedings shall be effected in the manner prescribed by Rule 232(c) of the Commission's Rules of Practice, § 201.232(c) of this chapter.

F. STANDARDS OF PROFESSIONAL CONDUCT FOR ATTORNEYS APPEARING AND PRACTICING BEFORE THE COMMISSION IN THE REPRESENTATION OF AN ISSUER

(Cite as 17 CFR 205.______)

Sec.

§ 205.1 Purpose and Scope.

This part sets forth minimum standards of professional conduct for attorneys appearing and practicing before the Commission in the representation of an issuer. These standards supplement applicable standards of any jurisdiction where an attorney is admitted or practices and are not intended to limit the ability of any jurisdiction to impose additional obligations on an attorney not inconsistent with the application of this part. Where the standards of a state or other United States jurisdiction where an attorney is admitted or practices conflict with this part, this part shall govern.

§ 205.2 Definitions.

For purposes of this part, the following definitions apply:

(a) *Appearing and practicing* before the Commission:

(1) Means:

(i) Transacting any business with the Commission, including communications in any form;

(ii) Representing an issuer in a Commission administrative proceeding or in connection with any Commission investigation, inquiry, information request, or subpoena;

(iii) Providing advice in respect of the United States securities laws or the Commission's rules or regulations thereunder regarding any document that the attorney has notice will be filed with or submitted to, or incorporated into any document that will be filed with or submitted to, the Commission, including the provision of such advice in the context of preparing, or participating in the preparation of, any such document; or

(iv) Advising an issuer as to whether information or a statement, opinion, or other writing is required under the United States securities laws or the Commission's rules or regulations thereunder to be filed with or submitted to, or incorporated into any document that will be filed with or submitted to, the Commission; but

(2) Does not include an attorney who:

(i) Conducts the activities in paragraphs (a)(1)(i) through (a)(1)(iv) of this section other than in the context of providing legal services to an issuer with whom the attorney has an attorney-client relationship; or

(ii) Is a non-appearing foreign attorney.

(b) *Appropriate response* means a response to an attorney regarding reported evidence of a material violation as a result of which the attorney reasonably believes:

(1) That no material violation, as defined in paragraph (i) of this section, has occurred, is ongoing, or is about to occur;

(2) That the issuer has, as necessary, adopted appropriate remedial measures, including appropriate steps or sanctions to stop any material violations that are ongoing, to prevent any material violation that has yet to occur, and to remedy or otherwise appropriately address any material violation that has already occurred and to minimize the likelihood of its recurrence; or

(3) That the issuer, with the consent of the issuer's board of directors, a committee thereof to whom a report could be made pursuant to § 205.3(b)(3), or a qualified legal compliance committee, has retained or directed an attorney to review the reported evidence of a material violation and either:

(i) Has substantially implemented any remedial recommendations made by such attorney after a reasonable investigation and evaluation of the reported evidence; or

(ii) Has been advised that such attorney may, consistent with his or her professional obligations, assert a colorable defense on behalf of the issuer (or the issuer's officer, director, employee, or agent, as the case may be) in any investigation or judicial or administrative proceeding relating to the reported evidence of a material violation.

(c) *Attorney* means any person who is admitted, licensed, or otherwise qualified to practice law in any jurisdiction, domestic or foreign, or who holds himself or herself out as admitted, licensed, or otherwise qualified to practice law.

(d) *Breach of fiduciary duty* refers to any breach of fiduciary or similar duty to the issuer recognized under an applicable Federal or State statute or at common law, including but not limited to misfeasance, nonfeasance, abdication of duty, abuse of trust, and approval of unlawful transactions.

(e) *Evidence of a material violation* means credible evidence, based upon which it would be unreasonable, under the circumstances, for a prudent and competent attorney not to conclude that it is reasonably likely that a material violation has occurred, is ongoing, or is about to occur.

(f) *Foreign government issuer* means a foreign issuer as defined in 17 CFR 230.405 eligible to register securities on Schedule B of the Securities Act of 1933 (15 U.S.C. 77a *et seq.*, Schedule B).

(g) *In the representation of an issuer means providing legal services as an* attorney for an issuer, regardless of whether the attorney is employed or retained by the issuer.

(h) *Issuer* means an issuer (as defined in section 3 of the Securities Exchange Act of 1934 (15 U.S.C. 78c)), the securities of which are registered under section 12 of that Act (15 U.S.C. 781), or that is required to file reports under section 15(d) of that Act (15 U.S.C. 78o(d)), or that files or has filed a registration statement that has not yet become effective under the Securities Act of 1933 (15 U.S.C. 77a *et seq.*), and that it has not withdrawn, but does not include a foreign government issuer. For purposes of paragraphs (a) and (g) of this section, the term "issuer" includes any person controlled by an issuer, where an attorney provides legal services to such person on behalf of, or at the behest, or for the benefit of the issuer, regardless of whether the attorney is employed or retained by the issuer.

(i) *Material violation* means a material violation of an applicable United States federal or state securities law, a material breach of fiduciary duty arising under United States federal or state law, or a similar material violation of any United States federal or state law.

(j) *Non-appearing foreign attorney* means an attorney:

(1) Who is admitted to practice law in a jurisdiction outside the United States;

(2) Who does not hold himself or herself out as practicing, and does not give legal

advice regarding, United States federal or state securities or other laws (except as provided in paragraph (j)(3)(ii) of this section); and

(3) Who:

(i) Conducts activities that would constitute appearing and practicing before the Commission only incidentally to, and in the ordinary course of, the practice of law in a jurisdiction outside the United States; or

(ii) Is appearing and practicing before the Commission only in consultation with counsel, other than a non-appearing foreign attorney, admitted or licensed to practice in a state or other United States jurisdiction.

(k) *Qualified legal compliance* committee means a committee of an issuer (which also may be an audit or other committee of the issuer) that:

(1) Consists of at least one member of the issuer's audit committee (or, if the issuer has no audit committee, one member from an equivalent committee of independent directors) and two or more members of the issuer's board of directors who are not employed, directly or indirectly, by the issuer and who are not, in the case of a registered investment company, "interested persons" as defined in section 2(a)(19) of the Investment Company Act of 1940 (15 U.S.C. 80a–2(a)(19));

(2) Has adopted written procedures for the confidential receipt, retention, and consideration of any report of evidence of a material violation under § 205.3;

(3) Has been duly established by the issuer's board of directors, with the authority and responsibility:

(i) To inform the issuer's chief legal officer and chief executive officer (or the equivalents thereof) of any report of evidence of a material violation (except in the circumstances described in § 205.3(b)(4));

(ii) To determine whether an investigation is necessary regarding any report of evidence of a material violation by the issuer, its officers, directors, employees or agents and, if it determines an investigation is necessary or appropriate, to:

(A) Notify the audit committee or the full board of directors;

(B) Initiate an investigation, which may be conducted either by the chief legal officer (or the equivalent thereof) or by outside attorneys; and

(C) Retain such additional expert personnel as the committee deems necessary; and

(iii) At the conclusion of any such investigation, to:

(A) Recommend, by majority vote, that the issuer implement an appropriate response to evidence of a material violation; and

(B) Inform the chief legal officer and the chief executive officer (or the equivalents thereof) and the board of directors of the results of any such investigation under this section and the appropriate remedial measures to be adopted; and

(4) Has the authority and responsibility, acting by majority vote, to take all other appropriate action, including the authority to notify the Commission in the event that the issuer fails in any material respect to implement an appropriate response that the qualified legal compliance committee has recommended the issuer to take.

(*l*) *Reasonable* or *reasonably* denotes, with respect to the actions of an attorney, conduct that would not be unreasonable for a prudent and competent attorney.

(m) *Reasonably believes* means that an attorney believes the matter in question and that the circumstances are such that the belief is not unreasonable.

(n) *Report* means to make known to directly, either in person, by telephone, by e-mail, electronically, or in writing.

§ 205.3 Issuer as Client.

(a) *Representing an issuer.* An attorney appearing and practicing before the Commission in the representation of an issuer owes his or her professional and ethical duties to the issuer as an organization. That the attorney may work with and advise the issuer's officers, directors, or employees in the course of representing the issuer does not make such individuals the attorney's clients.

(b) *Duty to report evidence of a material violation.* (1) If an attorney, appearing and practicing before the Commission in the representation of an issuer, becomes aware of evidence of a material violation by the issuer or by any officer, director, employee, or agent of the issuer, the attorney shall report such evidence to the issuer's chief legal officer (or the equivalent thereof) or to both the issuer's chief legal officer and its chief executive officer (or the equivalents thereof) forthwith. By communicating such information to the issuer's officers or directors, an attorney does not reveal client confidences or secrets or privileged or otherwise protected information related to the attorney's representation of an issuer.

(2) The chief legal officer (or the equivalent thereof) shall cause such inquiry into the evidence of a material violation as he or she reasonably believes is appropriate to determine whether the material violation described in the report has occurred, is ongoing, or is about to occur. If the chief legal officer (or the equivalent thereof) determines no material violation has occurred, is ongoing, or is about to occur, he or she shall notify the reporting attorney and advise the reporting attorney of the basis for such determination. Unless the chief legal officer (or the equivalent thereof) reasonably believes that no material violation has occurred, is ongoing, or is about to occur, he or she shall take all reasonable steps to cause the issuer to adopt an appropriate response, and shall advise the reporting attorney thereof. In lieu of causing an inquiry under this paragraph (b), a chief legal officer (or the equivalent thereof) may refer a report of evidence of a material violation to a qualified legal compliance committee under paragraph (c)(2) of this section if the issuer has duly established a qualified legal compliance committee prior to the report of evidence of a material violation.

(3) Unless an attorney who has made a report under paragraph (b)(1) of this section reasonably believes that the chief legal officer or the chief executive officer of the issuer (or the equivalent thereof) has provided an appropriate response within a reasonable time, the attorney shall report the evidence of a material violation to:

(i) The audit committee of the issuer's board of directors;

(ii) Another committee of the issuer's board of directors consisting solely of directors who are not employed, directly or indirectly, by the issuer and are not, in the case of a registered investment company, "interested persons" as defined in section 2(a)(19) of the Investment Company Act of 1940 (15 U.S.C. 80a–2(a)(19)) (if the issuer's board of directors has no audit committee); or

(iii) The issuer's board of directors (if the issuer's board of directors has no committee consisting solely of directors who are not employed, directly or indirectly, by the issuer and are not, in the case of a registered investment company, "interested persons" as defined in section 2(a)(19) of the Investment Company Act of 1940 (15 U.S.C. 80a–2(a)(19))).

(4) If an attorney reasonably believes that it would be futile to report evidence of a material violation to the issuer's chief legal officer and chief executive officer (or the equivalents thereof) under paragraph (b)(1) of this section, the attorney may report such

evidence as provided under paragraph (b)(3) of this section.

(5) An attorney retained or directed by an issuer to investigate evidence of a material violation reported under paragraph (b)(1), (b)(3), or (b)(4) of this section shall be deemed to be appearing and practicing before the Commission. Directing or retaining an attorney to investigate reported evidence of a material violation does not relieve an officer or director of the issuer to whom such evidence has been reported under paragraph (b)(1), (b)(3), or (b)(4) of this section from a duty to respond to the reporting attorney.

(6) An attorney shall not have any obligation to report evidence of a material violation under this paragraph (b) if:

(i) The attorney was retained or directed by the issuer's chief legal officer (or the equivalent thereof) to investigate such evidence of a material violation and:

(A) The attorney reports the results of such investigation to the chief legal officer (or the equivalent thereof); and

(B) Except where the attorney and the chief legal officer (or the equivalent thereof) each reasonably believes that no material violation has occurred, is ongoing, or is about to occur, the chief legal officer (or the equivalent thereof) reports the results of the investigation to the issuer's board of directors, a committee thereof to whom a report could be made pursuant to paragraph (b)(3) of this section, or a qualified legal compliance committee; or

(ii) The attorney was retained or directed by the chief legal officer (or the equivalent thereof) to assert, consistent with his or her professional obligations, a colorable defense on behalf of the issuer (or the issuer's officer, director, employee, or agent, as the case may be) in any investigation or judicial or administrative proceeding relating to such evidence of a material violation, and the chief legal officer (or the equivalent thereof) provides reasonable and timely reports on the progress and outcome of such proceeding to the issuer's board of directors, a committee thereof to whom a report could be made pursuant to paragraph (b)(3) of this section, or a qualified legal compliance committee.

(7) An attorney shall not have any obligation to report evidence of a material violation under this paragraph (b) if such attorney was retained or directed by a qualified legal compliance committee:

(i) To investigate such evidence of a material violation; or

(ii) To assert, consistent with his or her professional obligations, a colorable defense on behalf of the issuer (or the issuer's officer, director, employee, or agent, as the case may be) in any investigation or judicial or administrative proceeding relating to such evidence of a material violation.

(8) An attorney who receives what he or she reasonably believes is an appropriate and timely response to a report he or she has made pursuant to paragraph (b)(1), (b)(3), or (b)(4) of this section need do nothing more under this section with respect to his or her report.

(9) An attorney who does not reasonably believe that the issuer has made an appropriate response within a reasonable time to the report or reports made pursuant to paragraph (b)(1), (b)(3), or (b)(4) of this section shall explain his or her reasons therefor to the chief legal officer (or the equivalent thereof), the chief executive officer (or the equivalent thereof), and directors to whom the attorney reported the evidence of a material violation pursuant to paragraph (b)(1), (b)(3), or (b)(4) of this section.

(10) An attorney formerly employed or retained by an issuer who has reported evidence of a material violation under this part and reasonably believes that he or she has been discharged for so doing may notify the

issuer's board of directors or any committee thereof that he or she believes that he or she has been discharged for reporting evidence of a material violation under this section.

(c) *Alternative reporting procedures for attorneys retained or employed by an issuer that has established a qualified legal compliance committee.* (1) If an attorney, appearing and practicing before the Commission in the representation of an issuer, becomes aware of evidence of a material violation by the issuer or by any officer, director, employee, or agent of the issuer, the attorney may, as an alternative to the reporting requirements of paragraph (b) of this section, report such evidence to a qualified legal compliance committee, if the issuer has previously formed such a committee. An attorney who reports evidence of a material violation to such a qualified legal compliance committee has satisfied his or her obligation to report such evidence and is not required to assess the issuer's response to the reported evidence of a material violation.

(2) A chief legal officer (or the equivalent thereof) may refer a report of evidence of a material violation to a previously established qualified legal compliance committee in lieu of causing an inquiry to be conducted under paragraph (b)(2) of this section. The chief legal officer (or the equivalent thereof) shall inform the reporting attorney that the report has been referred to a qualified legal compliance committee. Thereafter, pursuant to the requirements under § 205.2(k), the qualified legal compliance committee shall be responsible for responding to the evidence of a material violation reported to it under this paragraph (c).

(d) *Issuer confidences.* (1) Any report under this section (or the contemporaneous record thereof) or any response thereto (or the contemporaneous record thereof) may be used by an attorney in connection with any investigation, proceeding, or litigation in which the attorney's compliance with this part is in issue.

(2) An attorney appearing and practicing before the Commission in the representation of an issuer may reveal to the Commission, without the issuer's consent, confidential information related to the representation to the extent the attorney reasonably believes necessary:

(i) To prevent the issuer from committing a material violation that is likely to cause substantial injury to the financial interest or property of the issuer or investors;

(ii) To prevent the issuer, in a Commission investigation or administrative proceeding from committing perjury, proscribed in 18 U.S.C. 1621; suborning perjury, proscribed in 18 U.S.C. 1622; or committing any act proscribed in 18 U.S.C. 1001 that is likely to perpetrate a fraud upon the Commission; or

(iii) To rectify the consequences of a material violation by the issuer that caused, or may cause, substantial injury to the financial interest or property of the issuer or investors in the furtherance of which the attorney's services were used.

§ 205.4 Responsibilities of Supervisory Attorneys.

(a) An attorney supervising or directing another attorney who is appearing and practicing before the Commission in the representation of an issuer is a supervisory attorney. An issuer's chief legal officer (or the equivalent thereof) is a supervisory attorney under this section.

(b) A supervisory attorney shall make reasonable efforts to ensure that a subordinate attorney, as defined in § 205.5(a), that he or she supervises or directs conforms to this part. To the extent a subordinate attorney appears and practices before the Commission in the representation of an issuer, that subordinate attorney's supervisory attorneys also appear and practice before the Commission.

(c) A supervisory attorney is responsible for complying with the reporting requirements in

§ 205.3 when a subordinate attorney has reported to the supervisory attorney evidence of a material violation.

(d) A supervisory attorney who has received a report of evidence of a material violation from a subordinate attorney under § 205.3 may report such evidence to the issuer's qualified legal compliance committee if the issuer has duly formed such a committee.

§ 205.5 Responsibility of a Subordinate Attorneys.

(a) An attorney who appears and practices before the Commission in the representation of an issuer on a matter under the supervision or direction of another attorney (other than under the direct supervision or direction of the issuer's chief legal officer (or the equivalent thereof)) is a subordinate attorney.

(b) A subordinate attorney shall comply with this part notwithstanding that the subordinate attorney acted at the direction of or under the supervision of another person.

(c) A subordinate attorney complies with § 205.3(b) if the subordinate attorney reports to his or her supervising attorney under § 305.3(b) evidence of a material violation of which the subordinate attorney has become aware in appearing and practicing before the Commission.

(d) A subordinate attorney may take the steps permitted or required by § 205.3(b) or (c) if the subordinate attorney reasonably believes that a supervisory attorney to whom he or she has reported evidence of a material violation under § 205.3(b) has failed to comply with § 205.3.

§ 205.6 Sanctions and Discipline.

(a) A violation of this part by any attorney appearing and practicing before the Commission in the representation of an issuer shall subject such attorney to the civil penalties and remedies for a violation of the federal securities laws available to the Commission in an action brought by the Commission thereunder.

(b) An attorney appearing and practicing before the Commission who violates any provision of this part is subject to the disciplinary authority of the Commission, regardless of whether the attorney may also be subject to discipline for the same conduct in a jurisdiction where the attorney is admitted or practices. An administrative disciplinary proceeding initiated by the Commission for violation of this part may result in an attorney being censured, or being temporarily or permanently denied the privilege of appearing or practicing before the Commission.

(c) An attorney who complies in good faith with the provisions of this part shall not be subject to discipline or otherwise liable under inconsistent standards imposed by any state or other United States jurisdiction where the attorney is admitted or practices.

(d) An attorney practicing outside the United States shall not be required to comply with the requirements of this part to the extent that such compliance is prohibited by applicable foreign law.

§ 205.7 No Private Right of Action.

(a) Nothing in this part is intended to, or does, create a private right of action against any attorney, law firm, or issuer based upon compliance or noncompliance with its provisions.

(b) Authority to enforce compliance with this part is vested exclusively in the Commission.

G. PRIVACY OF CONSUMER FINANCIAL INFORMATION (REGULATION S–P)

REGULATION S–P: PRIVACY OF CONSUMER FINANCIAL INFORMATION

(Cite as 17 CFR 248._____)

§ 248.1 Purpose and Scope.

(a) *Purpose.* This part governs the treatment of nonpublic personal information about consumers by the financial institutions listed in paragraph (b) of this section. This part:

(1) Requires a financial institution to provide notice to customers about its privacy policies and practices;

(2) Describes the conditions under which a financial institution may disclose nonpublic personal information about consumers to nonaffiliated third parties; and

(3) Provides a method for consumers to prevent a financial institution from disclosing that information to most nonaffiliated third parties by "opting out" of that disclosure, subject to the exceptions in §§ 248.13, 248.14, and 248.15.

(b) *Scope.* Except with respect to § 248.30(b), this part applies only to nonpublic personal information about individuals who obtain financial products or services primarily for personal, family, or household purposes from the institutions listed below. This part does not apply to information about companies or about individuals who obtain financial products or services primarily for business, commercial, or agricultural purposes. This part applies to brokers, dealers, and investment companies, as well as to investment advisers that are registered with the Commission. It also applies to foreign (non-resident) brokers, dealers, investment companies and investment advisers that are registered with the Commission. These entities are referred to in this part as "you." This part does not apply to foreign (non-resident) brokers, dealers, investment companies and investment advisers that are not registered with the Commission. Nothing in this part modifies, limits, or supersedes the standards governing individually identifiable health information promulgated by the Secretary of Health and Human Services under the authority of sections 262 and 264 of the Health Insurance Portability and Accountability Act of 1996 (42 U.S.C. 1320d–1320d–8).

§ 248.2 Rule of Construction.

(a) The examples in this part and the sample clauses in appendix A of this part provide guidance concerning the rule's application in ordinary circumstances. The facts and circumstances of each individual situation, however, will determine whether compliance with an example or use of a sample clause, to the extent applicable, constitutes compliance with this part.

(b) *Substituted compliance with CFTC financial privacy rules by futures commission merchants and introducing brokers.* Except with respect to § 248.30(b), any futures commission merchant or introducing broker (as those terms are defined in the Commodity Exchange Act (7 U.S.C. 1, *et seq.*)) registered by notice with the Commission for the purpose of conducting business in security futures products pursuant to section 15(b)(11)(A) of the Securities Exchange Act of 1934 (15 U.S.C.78o(b)(11)(A)) that is subject to and in compliance with the financial privacy rules of the Commodity Futures Trading Commission (17 CFR part 160) will be deemed to be in compliance with this part.

§ 248.3 Definitions.

As used in this part, unless the context requires otherwise:

(a) *Affiliate* of a broker, dealer, or investment company, or an investment adviser registered with the Commission means any company that controls, is controlled by, or is under common control with the broker, dealer, or investment company, or investment adviser registered with the Commission. In addition, a broker, dealer, or investment company, or an investment adviser registered with the Commission will be deemed an affiliate of a company for purposes of this part if:

(1) That company is regulated under Title V of the G–L–B Act by the Federal Trade Commission or by a Federal functional regulator other than the Commission; and

(2) Rules adopted by the Federal Trade Commission or another federal functional regulator under Title V of the G–L–B Act treat the broker, dealer, or investment company, or investment adviser registered with the Commission as an affiliate of that company.

(b) *Broker* has the same meaning as in section 3(a)(4) of the Securities Exchange Act of 1934 (15 U.S.C. 78c(a)(4)).

(c)(1) *Clear and conspicuous* means that a notice is reasonably understandable and designed to call attention to the nature and significance of the information in the notice.

(2) *Examples.* (i) *Reasonably understandable.* You make your notice reasonably understandable if you:

(A) Present the information in the notice in clear, concise sentences, paragraphs, and sections;

(B) Use short explanatory sentences or bullet lists whenever possible;

(C) Use definite, concrete, everyday words and active voice whenever possible;

(D) Avoid multiple negatives;

(E) Avoid legal and highly technical business terminology whenever possible; and

(F) Avoid explanations that are imprecise and readily subject to different interpretations.

(ii) *Designed to call attention.* You design your notice to call attention to the nature and significance of the information in it if you:

(A) Use a plain-language heading to call attention to the notice;

(B) Use a typeface and type size that are easy to read;

(C) Provide wide margins and ample line spacing;

(D) Use boldface or italics for key words; and

(E) Use distinctive type size, style, and graphic devices, such as shading or sidebars when you combine your notice with other information.

(iii) *Notices on web sites.* If you provide a notice on a web page, you design your notice to call attention to the nature and significance of the information in it if you use text or visual cues to encourage scrolling down the page if necessary to view the entire notice and ensure that other elements on the web site (such as text, graphics, hyperlinks, or sound) do not distract attention from the notice, and you either:

(A) Place the notice on a screen that consumers frequently access, such as a page on which transactions are conducted; or

(B) Place a link on a screen that consumers frequently access, such as a page on which transactions are conducted, that connects directly to the notice and is labeled appropriately to convey the importance, nature, and relevance of the notice.

(d) *Collect* means to obtain information that you organize or can retrieve by the name of an individual or by identifying number, symbol, or other identifying particular assigned to the individual, irrespective of the source of the underlying information.

(e) *Commission* means the Securities and Exchange Commission.

(f) *Company* means any corporation, limited liability company, business trust, general or limited partnership, association, or similar organization.

(g)(1) *Consumer* means an individual who obtains or has obtained a financial product or service from you that is to be used primarily for personal, family, or household purposes, or that individual's legal representative.

(2) *Examples.* (i) An individual is your consumer if he or she provides nonpublic personal information to you in connection with obtaining or seeking to obtain brokerage services or investment advisory services, whether or not you provide brokerage services to the individual or establish a continuing relationship with the individual.

(ii) An individual is not your consumer if he or she provides you only with his or her name, address, and general areas of investment interest in connection with a request for a prospectus, an investment adviser brochure, or other information about financial products or services.

(iii) An individual is not your consumer if he or she has an account with another broker or dealer (the introducing broker-dealer) that carries securities for the individual in a special omnibus account with you (the clearing broker-dealer) in the name of the introducing broker-dealer, and when you receive only the account numbers and transaction information of the introducing broker-dealer's consumers in order to clear transactions.

(iv) If you are an investment company, an individual is not your consumer when the individual purchases an interest in shares you have issued only through a broker or dealer or investment adviser who is the record owner of those shares.

(v) An individual who is a consumer of another financial institution is not your consumer solely because you act as agent for, or provide processing or other services to, that financial institution.

(vi) An individual is not your consumer solely because he or she has designated you as trustee for a trust.

(vii) An individual is not your consumer solely because he or she is a beneficiary of a trust for which you are a trustee.

(viii) An individual is not your consumer solely because he or she is a participant or a beneficiary of an employee benefit plan that you sponsor or for which you act as a trustee or fiduciary.

(h) *Consumer reporting agency* has the same meaning as in section 603(f) of the Fair Credit Reporting Act (15 U.S.C. 1681a(f)).

(i) *Control* of a company means the power to exercise a controlling influence over the management or policies of a company whether through ownership of securities, by contract, or otherwise. Any person who owns beneficially, either directly or through one or more controlled companies, more than 25 percent of the voting securities of any company is presumed to control the company. Any person who does not own more than 25 percent of the voting securities of any company will be presumed not to control the company. Any presumption regarding control may be rebutted by evidence, but, in the case of an investment company, will continue until the Commission makes a decision to the contrary according to the procedures described in section 2(a)(9) of the Investment Company Act of 1940 (15 U.S.C. 80a–2(a)(9)).

(j) *Customer* means a consumer who has a customer relationship with you.

(k)(1) *Customer relationship* means a continuing relationship between a consumer and you under which you provide one or more financial products or services to the consumer that are to be used primarily for personal, family, or household purposes.

(2) *Examples.* (i) *Continuing relationship.* A consumer has a continuing relationship with you if:

(A) The consumer has a brokerage account with you, or if a consumer's account is transferred to you from another broker-dealer;

(B) The consumer has an investment advisory contract with you (whether written or oral);

(C) The consumer is the record owner of securities you have issued if you are an investment company;

(D) The consumer holds an investment product through you, such as when you act as a custodian for securities or for assets in an Individual Retirement Arrangement;

(E) The consumer purchases a variable annuity from you;

(F) The consumer has an account with an introducing broker or dealer that clears transactions with and for its customers through you on a fully disclosed basis;

(G) You hold securities or other assets as collateral for a loan made to the consumer, even if you did not make the loan or do not effect any transactions on behalf of the consumer; or

(H) You regularly effect or engage in securities transactions with or for a consumer even if you do not hold any assets of the consumer.

(ii) *No continuing relationship.* A consumer does not, however, have a continuing relationship with you if you open an account for the consumer solely for the purpose of liquidating or purchasing securities as an accommodation, *i.e.*, on a one time basis, without the expectation of engaging in other transactions.

(l) *Dealer* has the same meaning as in section 3(a)(5) of the Securities Exchange Act of 1934 (15 U.S.C. 78c(a)(5)).

(m) *Federal functional regulator* means:

(1) The Board of Governors of the Federal Reserve System;

(2) The Office of the Comptroller of the Currency;

(3) The Board of Directors of the Federal Deposit Insurance Corporation;

(4) The Director of the Office of Thrift Supervision;

(5) The National Credit Union Administration Board;

(6) The Securities and Exchange Commission; and

(7) The Commodity Futures Trading Commission.

(n)(1) *Financial institution* means any institution the business of which is engaging in activities that are financial in nature or incidental to such financial activities as described in section 4(k) of the Bank Holding Company Act of 1956 (12 U.S.C. 1843(k)).

(2) *Financial institution* does not include:

(i) The Federal Agricultural Mortgage Corporation or any entity chartered and operating under the Farm Credit Act of 1971 (12 U.S.C. 2001 *et seq.*); or

(ii) Institutions chartered by Congress specifically to engage in securitizations, secondary market sales (including sales of servicing rights), or similar transactions related to a transaction of a consumer, as long as such institutions do not sell or transfer nonpublic personal information to a nonaffiliated third party.

(*o*)(1) *Financial product or service* means any product or service that a financial holding company could offer by engaging in an activity that is financial in nature or incidental to such a financial activity under section 4(k) of the Bank Holding Company Act of 1956 (12 U.S.C. 1843(k)).

(2) *Financial service* includes your evaluation or brokerage of information that you collect in connection with a request or an application from a consumer for a financial product or service.

(p) *G–L–B Act* means the Gramm–Leach–Bliley Act (Pub. L. No. 106–102, 113 Stat. 1338 (1999)).

(q) *Investment adviser* has the same meaning as in section 202(a)(11) of the Investment Advisers Act of 1940 (15 U.S.C. 80b–2(a)(11)).

(r) *Investment company* has the same meaning as in section 3 of the Investment Company Act of 1940 (15 U.S.C. 80a–3), and includes a separate series of the investment company.

(s)(1) *Nonaffiliated third party* means any person except:

(i) Your affiliate; or

(ii) A person employed jointly by you and any company that is not your affiliate (but *nonaffiliated third party* includes the other company that jointly employs the person).

(2) *Nonaffiliated third party* includes any company that is an affiliate solely by virtue

of your or your affiliate's direct or indirect ownership or control of the company in conducting merchant banking or investment banking activities of the type described in section 4(k)(4)(H) or insurance company investment activities of the type described in section 4(k)(4)(I) of the Bank Holding Company Act (12 U.S.C. §§ 1843(k)(4)(H) and (I)).

(t)(1) *Nonpublic personal information* means:

(i) Personally identifiable financial information; and

(ii) Any list, description, or other grouping of consumers (and publicly available information pertaining to them) that is derived using any personally identifiable financial information that is not publicly available information.

(2) *Nonpublic personal information* does not include:

(i) Publicly available information, except as included on a list described in paragraph (t)(1)(ii) of this section or when the publicly available information is disclosed in a manner that indicates the individual is or has been your consumer; or

(ii) Any list, description, or other grouping of consumers (and publicly available information pertaining to them) that is derived without using any personally identifiable financial information that is not publicly available information.

(3) *Examples of lists.* (i) Nonpublic personal information includes any list of individuals' names and street addresses that is derived in whole or in part using personally identifiable financial information that is not publicly available information, such as account numbers.

(ii) Nonpublic personal information does not include any list of individuals' names and addresses that contains only publicly available information, is not derived in whole or in part using personally identifiable financial information that is not publicly available information, and is not disclosed in a manner that indicates that any of the individuals on the list is a consumer of a financial institution.

(u)(1) *Personally identifiable financial information* means any information:

(i) A consumer provides to you to obtain a financial product or service from you;

(ii) About a consumer resulting from any transaction involving a financial product or service between you and a consumer; or

(iii) You otherwise obtain about a consumer in connection with providing a financial product or service to that consumer.

(2) *Examples.* (i) *Information included.* Personally identifiable financial information includes:

(A) Information a consumer provides to you on an application to obtain a loan, credit card, or other financial product or service;

(B) Account balance information, payment history, overdraft history, and credit or debit card purchase information;

(C) The fact that an individual is or has been one of your customers or has obtained a financial product or service from you;

(D) Any information about your consumer if it is disclosed in a manner that indicates that the individual is or has been your consumer;

(E) Any information that a consumer provides to you or that you or your agent otherwise obtain in connection with collecting on a loan or servicing a loan;

(F) Any information you collect through an Internet "cookie" (an information collecting device from a web server); and

(G) Information from a consumer report.

(ii) *Information not included.* Personally identifiable financial information does not include:

(A) A list of names and addresses of customers of an entity that is not a financial institution; or

(B) Information that does not identify a consumer, such as aggregate information or blind data that does not contain personal identifiers such as account numbers, names, or addresses.

(v)(1) *Publicly available information* means any information that you reasonably believe is lawfully made available to the general public from:

(i) Federal, State, or local government records;

(ii) Widely distributed media; or

(iii) Disclosures to the general public that are required to be made by federal, State, or local law.

(2) *Examples.* (i) *Reasonable belief.* (A) You have a reasonable belief that information about your consumer is made available to the general public if you have confirmed, or your consumer has represented to you, that the information is publicly available from a source described in paragraphs (v)(1)(i)–(iii) of this section;

(B) You have a reasonable belief that information about your consumer is made available to the general public if you have taken steps to submit the information, in accordance with your internal procedures and policies and with applicable law, to a keeper of federal, State, or local government records that is required by law to make the information publicly available.

(C) You have a reasonable belief that an individual's telephone number is lawfully made available to the general public if you have located the telephone number in the telephone book or the consumer has informed you that the telephone number is not unlisted.

(D) You do not have a reasonable belief that information about a consumer is publicly available solely because that information would normally be recorded with a keeper of federal, State, or local government records that is required by law to make the information publicly available, if the consumer has the ability in accordance with applicable law to keep that information nonpublic, such as where a consumer may record a deed in the name of a blind trust.

(ii) *Government records.* Publicly available information in government records includes information in government real estate records and security interest filings.

(iii) *Widely distributed media.* Publicly available information from widely distributed media includes information from a telephone book, a television or radio program, a newspaper, or a web site that is available to the general public on an unrestricted basis. A web site is not restricted merely because an Internet service provider or a site operator requires a fee or a password, so long as access is available to the general public.

(w) *You* means:

(1) Any broker or dealer;

(2) Any investment company; and

(3) Any investment adviser registered with the Commission under the Investment Advisers Act of 1940.

Subpart A—Privacy and Opt Out Notices

§ 248.4 Initial Privacy Notice to Consumers Required.

(a) *Initial notice requirement.* You must provide a clear and conspicuous notice that accurately reflects your privacy policies and practices to:

(1) *Customer.* An individual who becomes your customer, not later than when you establish a customer relationship, except as provided in paragraph (e) of this section; and

(2) *Consumer.* A consumer, before you disclose any nonpublic personal information about the consumer to any nonaffiliated third party, if you make such a disclosure other than as authorized by §§ 248.14 and 248.15.

(b) *When initial notice to a consumer is not required.* You are not required to provide an initial notice to a consumer under paragraph (a) of this section if:

(1) You do not disclose any nonpublic personal information about the consumer to any nonaffiliated third party, other than as authorized by §§ 248.14 and 248.15; and

(2) You do not have a customer relationship with the consumer.

(c) *When you establish a customer relationship.* (1) *General rule.* You establish a customer relationship when you and the consumer enter into a continuing relationship.

(2) *Special rule for loans.* You do not have a customer relationship with a consumer if you buy a loan made to the consumer but do not have the servicing rights for that loan.

(3) *Examples of establishing customer relationship.* You establish a customer relationship when the consumer:

(i) Effects a securities transaction with you or opens a brokerage account with you under your procedures;

(ii) Opens a brokerage account with an introducing broker or dealer that clears transactions with and for its customers through you on a fully disclosed basis;

(iii) Enters into an advisory contract with you (whether in writing or orally); or

(iv) Purchases shares you have issued (and the consumer is the record owner of the shares), if you are an investment company.

(d) *Existing customers.* When an existing customer obtains a new financial product or service from you that is to be used primarily for personal, family, or household purposes, you satisfy the initial notice requirements of paragraph (a) of this section as follows:

(1) You may provide a revised privacy notice, under § 248.8, that covers the customer's new financial product or service; or

(2) If the initial, revised, or annual notice that you most recently provided to that customer was accurate with respect to the new financial product or service, you do not need to provide a new privacy notice under paragraph (a) of this section.

(e) *Exceptions to allow subsequent delivery of notice.* (1) You may provide the initial notice required by paragraph (a)(1) of this section within a reasonable time after you establish a customer relationship if:

(i) Establishing the customer relationship is not at the customer's election;

(ii) Providing notice not later than when you establish a customer relationship would substantially delay the customer's transaction and the customer agrees to receive the notice at a later time; or

(iii) A nonaffiliated broker or dealer or investment adviser establishes a customer relationship between you and a consumer without your prior knowledge.

(2) *Examples of exceptions.* (i) *Not at customer's election.* Establishing a customer relationship is not at the customer's election if the customer's account is transferred to you by a trustee selected by the Securities Investor Protection Corporation ("SIPC") and appointed by a United States Court.

(ii) *Substantial delay of customer's transaction.* Providing notice not later than when you establish a customer relationship would substantially delay the customer's transaction when you and the individual agree over the telephone to enter into a customer relationship involving prompt delivery of the financial product or service.

(iii) *No substantial delay of customer's transaction.* Providing notice not later than when you establish a customer relationship would not substantially delay the customer's transaction when the relationship is initiated in person at your office or through other means by which the customer may view the notice, such as on a web site.

(f) *Delivery.* When you are required to deliver an initial privacy notice by this section, you must deliver it according to § 248.9. If you use a short-form initial notice for non-customers according to § 248.6(d), you may deliver your privacy notice according to § 248.6(d)(3).

§ 248.5 Annual Privacy Notice to Customers Required.

(a)(1) *General rule.* You must provide a clear and conspicuous notice to customers that accurately reflects your privacy policies and practices not less than annually during the continuation of the customer relationship. *Annually* means at least once in any period of 12 consecutive months during which that relationship exists. You may define the 12-consecutive-month period, but you must apply it to the customer on a consistent basis.

(2) *Example.* You provide a notice annually if you define the 12-consecutive-month period as a calendar year and provide the annual notice to the customer once in each calendar year following the calendar year in which you provided the initial notice. For example, if a customer opens an account on any day of year 1, you must provide an annual notice to that customer by December 31 of year 2.

(b)(1) *Termination of customer relationship.* You are not required to provide an annual notice to a former customer.

(2) *Examples.* Your customer becomes a former customer when:

(i) The individual's brokerage account is closed;

(ii) The individual's investment advisory contract is terminated;

(iii) You are an investment company and the individual is no longer the record owner of securities you have issued; or

(iv) You are an investment company and your customer has been determined to be a lost securityholder as defined in 17 CFR 240.17a–24(b).

(c) *Special rule for loans.* If you do not have a customer relationship with a consumer under the special provision for loans in § 248.4(c)(2), then you need not provide an annual notice to that consumer under this section.

(d) *Delivery.* When you are required to deliver an annual privacy notice by this section, you must deliver it according to § 248.9.

§ 248.6 Information to be Included in Privacy Notices.

(a) *General rule.* The initial, annual, and revised privacy notices that you provide under §§ 248.4, 248.5, and 248.8 must include each of the following items of information that applies to you or to the consumers to whom you send your privacy notice, in addition to any other information you wish to provide:

(1) The categories of nonpublic personal information that you collect;

(2) The categories of nonpublic personal information that you disclose;

(3) The categories of affiliates and nonaffiliated third parties to whom you disclose nonpublic personal information, other than those parties to whom you disclose information under §§ 248.14 and 248.15;

(4) The categories of nonpublic personal information about your former customers that you disclose and the categories of affiliates and nonaffiliated third parties to whom you disclose nonpublic personal information

about your former customers, other than those parties to whom you disclose information under §§ 248.14 and 248.15;

(5) If you disclose nonpublic personal information to a nonaffiliated third party under § 248.13 (and no other exception applies to that disclosure), a separate statement of the categories of information you disclose and the categories of third parties with whom you have contracted;

(6) An explanation of the consumer's right under § 248.10(a) to opt out of the disclosure of nonpublic personal information to nonaffiliated third parties, including the method(s) by which the consumer may exercise that right at that time;

(7) Any disclosures that you make under section 603(d)(2)(A)(iii) of the Fair Credit Reporting Act (15 U.S.C. 1681a(d)(2)(A)(iii)) (that is, notices regarding the ability to opt out of disclosures of information among affiliates);

(8) Your policies and practices with respect to protecting the confidentiality and security of nonpublic personal information; and

(9) Any disclosure that you make under paragraph (b) of this section.

(b) *Description of nonaffiliated third parties subject to exceptions.* If you disclose nonpublic personal information to third parties as authorized under §§ 248.14 and 248.15, you are not required to list those exceptions in the initial or annual privacy notices required by §§ 248.4 and 248.5. When describing the categories with respect to those parties, you are required to state only that you make disclosures to other nonaffiliated third parties as permitted by law.

(c) *Examples.* (1) *Categories of nonpublic personal information that you collect.* You satisfy the requirement to categorize the nonpublic personal information that you collect if you list the following categories, as applicable:

(i) Information from the consumer;

(ii) Information about the consumer's transactions with you or your affiliates;

(iii) Information about the consumer's transactions with nonaffiliated third parties; and

(iv) Information from a consumer-reporting agency.

(2) *Categories of nonpublic personal information you disclose.* (i) You satisfy the requirement to categorize the nonpublic personal information that you disclose if you list the categories described in paragraph (e)(1) of this section, as applicable, and a few examples to illustrate the types of information in each category.

(ii) If you reserve the right to disclose all of the nonpublic personal information about consumers that you collect, you may simply state that fact without describing the categories or examples of the nonpublic personal information you disclose.

(3) *Categories of affiliates and nonaffiliated third parties to whom you disclose.* You satisfy the requirement to categorize the affiliates and nonaffiliated third parties to whom you disclose nonpublic personal information if you list the following categories, as applicable, and a few examples to illustrate the types of third parties in each category:

(i) Financial service providers;

(ii) Non-financial companies; and

(iii) Others.

(4) *Disclosures under exception for service providers and joint marketers.* If you disclose nonpublic personal information under the exception in § 248.13 to a nonaffiliated third party to market products or services that you offer alone or jointly with another financial institution, you satisfy the disclosure requirement of paragraph (a)(5) of this section if you:

(i) List the categories of nonpublic personal information you disclose, using the same categories and examples you used to meet the requirements of paragraph (a)(2) of this section, as applicable; and

(ii) State whether the third party is:

(A) A service provider that performs marketing services on your behalf or on behalf of you and another financial institution; or

(B) A financial institution with which you have a joint marketing agreement.

(5) *Simplified notices.* If you do not disclose, and do not wish to reserve the right to disclose, nonpublic personal information to affiliates or nonaffiliated third parties except as authorized under §§ 248.14 and 248.15, you may simply state that fact, in addition to the information you must provide under paragraphs (a)(1), (a)(8), (a)(9), and (b) of this section.

(6) *Confidentiality and security.* You describe your policies and practices with respect to protecting the confidentiality and security of nonpublic personal information if you do both of the following:

(i) Describe in general terms who is authorized to have access to the information; and

(ii) State whether you have security practices and procedures in place to ensure the confidentiality of the information in accordance with your policy. You are not required to describe technical information about the safeguards you use.

(d) *Short-form initial notice with opt out notice for non-customers.* (1) You may satisfy the initial notice requirements in §§ 248.4(a)(2), 248.7(b), and 248.7(c) for a consumer who is not a customer by providing a short-form initial notice at the same time as you deliver an opt out notice as required in § 248.7.

(2) A short-form initial notice must:

(i) Be clear and conspicuous;

(ii) State that your privacy notice is available upon request; and

(iii) Explain a reasonable means by which the consumer may obtain the privacy notice.

(3) You must deliver your short-form initial notice according to § 248.9. You are not required to deliver your privacy notice with your short-form initial notice. You instead may simply provide the consumer a reasonable means to obtain your privacy notice. If a consumer who receives your short-form notice requests your privacy notice, you must deliver your privacy notice according to § 248.9.

(4) *Examples of obtaining privacy notice.* You provide a reasonable means by which a consumer may obtain a copy of your privacy notice if you:

(i) Provide a toll-free telephone number that the consumer may call to request the notice; or

(ii) For a consumer who conducts business in person at your office, maintain copies of the notice on hand that you provide to the consumer immediately upon request.

(e) *Future disclosures.* Your notice may include:

(1) Categories of nonpublic personal information that you reserve the right to disclose in the future, but do not currently disclose; and

(2) Categories of affiliates or nonaffiliated third parties to whom you reserve the right in the future to disclose, but to whom you do not currently disclose, nonpublic personal information.

(f) *Sample clauses.* Sample clauses illustrating some of the notice content required by this section are included in Appendix A of this part.

§ 248.7 Form of Opt Out Notice to Consumers; Opt Out Methods.

(a)(1) *Form of opt out notice.* If you are required to provide an opt out notice under § 248.10(a), you must provide a clear and conspicuous notice to each of your consumers that accurately explains the right to opt out under that section. The notice must state:

(i) That you disclose or reserve the right to disclose nonpublic personal information about your consumer to a nonaffiliated third party;

(ii) That the consumer has the right to opt out of that disclosure; and

(iii) A reasonable means by which the consumer may exercise the opt out right.

(2) *Examples.* (i) *Adequate opt out notice.* You provide adequate notice that the consumer can opt out of the disclosure of nonpublic personal information to a nonaffiliated third party if you:

(A) Identify all of the categories of nonpublic personal information that you disclose or reserve the right to disclose, and all of the categories of nonaffiliated third parties to which you disclose the information, as described in § 248.6(a)(2) and (3) and state that the consumer can opt out of the disclosure of that information; and

(B) Identify the financial products or services that the consumer obtains from you, either singly or jointly, to which the opt out direction would apply.

(ii) *Reasonable opt out means.* You provide a reasonable means to exercise an opt out right if you:

(A) Designate check-off boxes in a prominent position on the relevant forms with the opt out notice;

(B) Include a reply form together with the opt out notice;

(C) Provide an electronic means to opt out, such as a form that can be sent via electronic mail or a process at your web site, if the consumer agrees to the electronic delivery of information; or

(D) Provide a toll-free telephone number that consumers may call to opt out.

(iii) *Unreasonable opt out means.* You *do not* provide a reasonable means of opting out if:

(A) The only means of opting out is for the consumer to write his or her own letter to exercise that opt out right; or

(B) The only means of opting out as described in any notice subsequent to the initial notice is to use a check-off box that you provided with the initial notice but did not include with the subsequent notice.

(iv) *Specific opt out means.* You may require each consumer to opt out through a specific means, as long as that means is reasonable for that consumer.

(b) *Same form as initial notice permitted.* You may provide the opt out notice together with or on the same written or electronic form as the initial notice you provide in accordance with § 248.4.

(c) *Initial notice required when opt out notice delivered subsequent to initial notice.* If you provide the opt out notice after the initial notice in accordance with § 248.4, you must also include a copy of the initial notice with the opt out notice in writing or, if the consumer agrees, electronically.

(d) *Joint relationships.* (1) If two or more consumers jointly obtain a financial product or service from you, you may provide a single opt out notice. Your opt out notice must explain how you will treat an opt out direction by a joint consumer.

(2) Any of the joint consumers may exercise the right to opt out. You may either:

(i) Treat an opt out direction by a joint consumer as applying to all of the associated joint consumers; or

(ii) Permit each joint consumer to opt out separately.

(3) If you permit each joint consumer to opt out separately, you must permit one of

the joint consumers to opt out on behalf of all of the joint consumers.

(4) You may not require *all* joint consumers to opt out before you implement *any* opt out direction.

(5) *Example.* If John and Mary have a joint brokerage account with you and arrange for you to send statements to John's address, you may do any of the following, but you must explain in your opt out notice which opt out policy you will follow:

(i) Send a single opt out notice to John's address, but you must accept an opt out direction from either John or Mary;

(ii) Treat an opt out direction by either John or Mary as applying to the entire account. If you do so, and John opts out, you may not require Mary to opt out as well before implementing John's opt out direction; or

(iii) Permit John and Mary to make different opt out directions. If you do so:

(A) You must permit John and Mary to opt out for each other.

(B) If both opt out, you must permit both to notify you in a single response (such as on a form or through a telephone call).

(C) If John opts out and Mary does not, you may only disclose nonpublic personal information about Mary, but not about John and not about John and Mary jointly.

(e) *Time to comply with opt out.* You must comply with a consumer's opt out direction as soon as reasonably practicable after you receive it.

(f) *Continuing right to opt out.* A consumer may exercise the right to opt out at any time.

(g) *Duration of consumer's opt out direction.* (1) A consumer's direction to opt out under this section is effective until the consumer revokes it in writing or, if the consumer agrees, electronically.

(2) When a customer relationship terminates, the customer's opt out direction continues to apply to the nonpublic personal information that you collected during or related to that relationship. If the individual subsequently establishes a new customer relationship with you, the opt out direction that applied to the former relationship does not apply to the new relationship.

(h) *Delivery.* When you are required to deliver an opt out notice by this section, you must deliver it according to § 248.9.

§ 248.8 Revised Privacy Notices.

(a) *General rule.* Except as otherwise authorized in this part, you must not, directly or through any affiliate, disclose any nonpublic personal information about a consumer to a nonaffiliated third party other than as described in the initial notice that you provided to that consumer under § 248.4, unless:

(1) You have provided to the consumer a clear and conspicuous revised notice that accurately describes your policies and practices;

(2) You have provided to the consumer a new opt out notice;

(3) You have given the consumer a reasonable opportunity, before you disclose the information to the nonaffiliated third party, to opt out of the disclosure; and

(4) The consumer does not opt out.

(b) *Examples.* (1) Except as otherwise permitted by §§ 248.13, 248.14, and 248.15, you must provide a revised notice before you:

(i) Disclose a new category of nonpublic personal information to any nonaffiliated third party;

(ii) Disclose nonpublic personal information to a new category of nonaffiliated third party; or

(iii) Disclose nonpublic personal information about a former customer to a nonaffiliated third party, if that former customer has not had the opportunity to exercise an opt out right regarding that disclosure.

(2) A revised notice is not required if you disclose nonpublic personal information to a new nonaffiliated third party that you adequately described in your prior notice.

(c) *Delivery.* When you are required to deliver a revised privacy notice by this section, you must deliver it according to § 248.9.

§ 248.9 Delivering Privacy and Opt Out Notices.

(a) *How to provide notices.* You must provide any privacy notices and opt out notices, including short-form initial notices that this part requires so that each consumer can reasonably be expected to receive actual notice in writing or, if the consumer agrees, electronically.

(b)(1) *Examples of reasonable expectation of actual notice.* You may reasonably expect that a consumer will receive actual notice if you:

(i) Hand-deliver a printed copy of the notice to the consumer;

(ii) Mail a printed copy of the notice to the last known address of the consumer;

(iii) For the consumer who conducts transactions electronically, post the notice on the electronic site and require the consumer to acknowledge receipt of the notice as a necessary step to obtaining a particular financial product or service; or

(iv) For an isolated transaction with the consumer, such as an ATM transaction, post the notice on the ATM screen and require the consumer to acknowledge receipt of the notice as a necessary step to obtaining the particular financial product or service.

(2) *Examples of unreasonable expectation of actual notice.* You may not, however, reasonably expect that a consumer will receive actual notice of your privacy policies and practices if you:

(i) Only post a sign in your branch or office or generally publish advertisements of your privacy policies and practices; or

(ii) Send the notice via electronic mail to a consumer who does not obtain a financial product or service from you electronically.

(c) *Annual notices only.* (1) You may reasonably expect that a customer will receive actual notice of your annual privacy notice if:

(i) The customer uses your web site to access financial products and services electronically and agrees to receive notices at the web site and you post your current privacy notice continuously in a clear and conspicuous manner on the web site; or

(ii) The customer has requested that you refrain from sending any information regarding the customer relationship, and your current privacy notice remains available to the customer upon request.

(2) *Example of reasonable expectation of receipt of annual privacy notice.* You may reasonably expect that consumers who share an address will receive actual notice of your annual privacy notice if you deliver the notice with or in a stockholder or shareholder report under the conditions in 17 CFR 270.30d–1(f) or 17 CFR 270.30d–2(b), or with or in a prospectus under the conditions in 17 CFR 230.154.

(d) *Oral description of notice insufficient.* You may not provide any notice required by this part solely by orally explaining the notice, either in person or over the telephone.

(e) *Retention or accessibility of notices for customers.* (1) For customers only, you must provide the initial notice required by § 248.4(a)(1), the annual notice required by § 248.5(a), and the revised notice required by § 248.8, so that the customer can retain them or obtain them later in writing or, if the customer agrees, electronically.

(2) *Examples of retention or accessibility.* You provide a privacy notice to the customer

so that the customer can retain it or obtain it later if you:

(i) Hand-deliver a printed copy of the notice to the customer;

(ii) Mail a printed copy of the notice to the last known address of the customer; or

(iii) Make your current privacy notice available on a web site (or a link to another web site) for the customer who obtains a financial product or service electronically and agrees to receive the notice at the web site.

(f) *Joint notice with other financial institutions.* You may provide a joint notice from you and one or more of your affiliates or other financial institutions, as identified in the notice, as long as the notice is accurate with respect to you and the other institutions.

(g) *Joint relationships.* If two or more consumers jointly obtain a financial product or service from you, you may satisfy the initial, annual, and revised notice requirements of paragraph (a) of this section by providing one notice to those consumers jointly.

Subpart B—Limits on Disclosures

§ 248.10 Limits on Disclosure of Nonpublic Personal Information to Nonaffiliated Third Parties.

(a)(1) *Conditions for disclosure.* Except as otherwise authorized in this part, you may not, directly or through any affiliate, disclose any nonpublic personal information about a consumer to a nonaffiliated third party unless:

(i) You have provided to the consumer an initial notice as required under § 248.4;

(ii) You have provided to the consumer an opt out notice as required in § 248.7;

(iii) You have given the consumer a reasonable opportunity, before you disclose the information to the nonaffiliated third party, to opt out of the disclosure; and

(iv) The consumer does not opt out.

(2) *Opt out definition.* Opt out means a direction by the consumer that you not disclose nonpublic personal information about that consumer to a nonaffiliated third party, other than as permitted by §§ 248.13, 248.14, and 248.15.

(3) *Examples of reasonable opportunity to opt out.* You provide a consumer with a reasonable opportunity to opt out if:

(i) *By mail.* You mail the notices required in paragraph (a)(1) of this section to the consumer and allow the consumer to opt out by mailing a form, calling a toll-free telephone number, or any other reasonable means within 30 days after the date you mailed the notices.

(ii) *By electronic means.* A customer opens an on-line account with you and agrees to receive the notices required in paragraph (a)(1) of this section electronically, and you allow the customer to opt out by any reasonable means within 30 days after the date that the customer acknowledges receipt of the notices in conjunction with opening the account.

(iii) *Isolated transaction with consumer.* For an isolated transaction, such as the provision of brokerage services to a consumer as an accommodation, you provide the consumer with a reasonable opportunity to opt out if you provide the notices required in paragraph (a)(1) of this section at the time of the transaction and request that the consumer decide, as a necessary part of the transaction, whether to opt out before completing the transaction.

(b) *Application of opt out to all consumers and all nonpublic personal information.* (1) You must comply with this section, regardless of whether you and the consumer have established a customer relationship.

(2) Unless you comply with this section, you may not, directly or through any affiliate, disclose any nonpublic personal information about a consumer that you have

collected, regardless of whether you collected it before or after receiving the direction to opt out from the consumer.

(c) *Partial opt out.* You may allow a consumer to select certain nonpublic personal information or certain nonaffiliated third parties with respect to which the consumer wishes to opt out.

§ 248.11 Limits on Redisclosure and Reuse of Information.

(a)(1) *Information you receive under an exception.* If you receive nonpublic personal information from a nonaffiliated financial institution under an exception in § 248.14 or 248.15, your disclosure and use of that information is limited as follows:

(i) You may disclose the information to the affiliates of the financial institution from which you received the information;

(ii) You may disclose the information to your affiliates, but your affiliates may, in turn, disclose and use the information only to the extent that you may disclose and use the information; and

(iii) You may disclose and use the information pursuant to an exception in §§ 248.14 or 248.15 in the ordinary course of business to carry out the activity covered by the exception under which you received the information.

(2) *Example.* If you receive a customer list from a nonaffiliated financial institution in order to provide account-processing services under the exception in §§ 248.14(a), you may disclose that information under any exception in § 248.14 or 248.15 in the ordinary course of business in order to provide those services. You could also disclose that information in response to a properly authorized subpoena or in the ordinary course of business to your attorneys, accountants, and auditors. You could not disclose that information to a third party for marketing purposes or use that information for your own marketing purposes.

(b)(1) *Information you receive outside of an exception.* If you receive nonpublic personal information from a nonaffiliated financial institution other than under an exception in §§ 248.14 or 248.15, you may disclose the information only:

(i) To the affiliates of the financial institution from which you received the information;

(ii) To your affiliates, but your affiliates may, in turn, disclose the information only to the extent that you can disclose the information; and

(iii) To any other person, if the disclosure would be lawful if made directly to that person by the financial institution from which you received the information.

(2) *Example.* If you obtain a customer list from a nonaffiliated financial institution outside of the exceptions in §§ 248.14 and 248.15:

(i) You may use that list for your own purposes;

(ii) You may disclose that list to another nonaffiliated third party only if the financial institution from which you purchased the list could have lawfully disclosed the list to that third party. That is, you may disclose the list in accordance with the privacy policy of the financial institution from which you received the list, as limited by the opt out direction of each consumer whose nonpublic personal information you intend to disclose, and you may disclose the list in accordance with an exception in §§ 248.14 or 248.15, such as in the ordinary course of business to your attorneys, accountants, or auditors.

(c) *Information you disclose under an exception.* If you disclose nonpublic personal information to a nonaffiliated third party under an exception in §§ 248.14 or 248.15, the third party may disclose and use that information only as follows:

(1) The third party may disclose the information to your affiliates;

(2) The third party may disclose the information to its affiliates, but its affiliates may, in turn, disclose and use the information only to the extent that the third party may disclose and use the information; and

(3) The third party may disclose and use the information pursuant to an exception in §§ 248.14 or 248.15 in the ordinary course of business to carry out the activity covered by the exception under which it received the information.

(d) *Information you disclose outside of an exception.* If you disclose nonpublic personal information to a nonaffiliated third party other than under an exception in §§ 248.14 or 248.15, the third party may disclose the information only:

(1) To your affiliates;

(2) To its affiliates, but its affiliates, in turn, may disclose the information only to the extent the third party can disclose the information; and

(3) To any other person, if the disclosure would be lawful if you made it directly to that person.

§ 248.12 Limits on Sharing Account Number Information for Marketing Purposes.

(a) *General prohibition on disclosure of account numbers.* You must not, directly or through an affiliate, disclose, other than to a consumer reporting agency, an account number or similar form of access number or access code for a consumer's credit card account, deposit account, or transaction account to any nonaffiliated third party for use in telemarketing, direct mail marketing, or other marketing through electronic mail to the consumer.

(b) *Exceptions.* Paragraph (a) of this section does not apply if you disclose an account number or similar form of access number or access code:

(1) To your agent or service provider solely in order to perform marketing for your own products or services, as long as the agent or service provider is not authorized to directly initiate charges to the account; or

(2) To a participant in a private label credit card program or an affinity or similar program where the participants in the program are identified to the customer when the customer enters into the program.

(c) *Example—Account number.* An account number, or similar form of access number or access code, does not include a number or code in an encrypted form, as long as you do not provide the recipient with a means to decode the number or code.

Subpart C—Exceptions

§ 248.13 Exception to Opt Out Requirements for Service Providers and Joint Marketing.

(a) *General rule.* (1) The opt out requirements in §§ 248.7 and 248.10 do not apply when you provide nonpublic personal information to a nonaffiliated third party to perform services for you or functions on your behalf, if you:

(i) Provide the initial notice in accordance with § 248.4; and

(ii) Enter into a contractual agreement with the third party that prohibits the third party from disclosing or using the information other than to carry out the purposes for which you disclosed the information, including use under an exception in §§ 248.14 or 248.15 in the ordinary course of business to carry out those purposes.

(2) *Example.* If you disclose nonpublic personal information under this section to a financial institution with which you perform joint marketing, your contractual agreement with that institution meets the requirements of paragraph (a)(1)(ii) of this section if it prohibits the institution from disclosing

or using the nonpublic personal information except as necessary to carry out the joint marketing or under an exception in §§ 248.14 or 248.15 in the ordinary course of business to carry out that joint marketing.

(b) *Service may include joint marketing.* The services a nonaffiliated third party performs for you under paragraph (a) of this section may include marketing of your own products or services or marketing of financial products or services offered pursuant to joint agreements between you and one or more financial institutions.

(c) *Definition of joint agreement.* For purposes of this section, *joint agreement* means a written contract pursuant to which you and one or more financial institutions jointly offer, endorse, or sponsor a financial product or service.

§ 248.14 Exceptions to Notice and Opt Out Requirements for Processing and Servicing Transactions.

(a) *Exceptions for processing and servicing transactions at consumer's request.* The requirements for initial notice in § 248.4(a)(2), for the opt out in §§ 248.7 and 248.10, and for initial notice in § 248.13 in connection with service providers and joint marketing, do not apply if you disclose nonpublic personal information as necessary to effect, administer, or enforce a transaction that a consumer requests or authorizes, or in connection with:

(1) Processing or servicing a financial product or service that a consumer requests or authorizes;

(2) Maintaining or servicing the consumer's account with you, or with another entity as part of a private label credit card program or other extension of credit on behalf of such entity; or

(3) A proposed or actual securitization, secondary market sale (including sales of servicing rights), or similar transaction related to a transaction of the consumer.

(b) *Necessary to effect, administer, or enforce a transaction* means that the disclosure is:

(1) Required, or is one of the lawful or appropriate methods, to enforce your rights or the rights of other persons engaged in carrying out the financial transaction or providing the product or service; or

(2) Required, or is a usual, appropriate, or acceptable method:

(i) To carry out the transaction or the product or service business of which the transaction is a part, and record, service, or maintain the consumer's account in the ordinary course of providing the financial service or financial product;

(ii) To administer or service benefits or claims relating to the transaction or the product or service business of which it is a part;

(iii) To provide a confirmation, statement, or other record of the transaction, or information on the status or value of the financial service or financial product to the consumer or the consumer's agent or broker;

(iv) To accrue or recognize incentives or bonuses associated with the transaction that are provided by you or any other party;

(v) To underwrite insurance at the consumer's request or for reinsurance purposes, or for any of the following purposes as they relate to a consumer's insurance: Account administration, reporting, investigating, or preventing fraud or material misrepresentation, processing premium payments, processing insurance claims, administering insurance benefits (including utilization review activities), participating in research projects, or as otherwise required or specifically permitted by federal or State law; or

(vi) In connection with:

(A) The authorization, settlement, billing, processing, clearing, transferring, reconciling or collection of amounts charged, debited, or otherwise paid using a debit, credit, or other payment card, check, or account number, or by other payment means;

(B) The transfer of receivables, accounts, or interests therein; or

(C) The audit of debit, credit, or other payment information.

§ 248.15 Other Exceptions to Notice and Opt Out Requirements.

(a) *Exceptions to notice and opt out requirements.* The requirements for initial notice in § 248.4(a)(2), for the opt out in §§ 248.7 and 248.10, and for initial notice in § 248.13 in connection with service providers and joint marketing do not apply when you disclose nonpublic personal information:

(1) With the consent or at the direction of the consumer, provided that the consumer has not revoked the consent or direction;

(2)(i) To protect the confidentiality or security of your records pertaining to the consumer, service, product, or transaction;

(ii) To protect against or prevent actual or potential fraud, unauthorized transactions, claims, or other liability;

(iii) For required institutional risk control or for resolving consumer disputes or inquiries;

(iv) To persons holding a legal or beneficial interest relating to the consumer; or

(v) To persons acting in a fiduciary or representative capacity on behalf of the consumer;

(3) To provide information to insurance rate advisory organizations, guaranty funds or agencies, agencies that are rating you, persons that are assessing your compliance with industry standards, and your attorneys, accountants, and auditors;

(4) To the extent specifically permitted or required under other provisions of law and in accordance with the Right to Financial Privacy Act of 1978 (12 U.S.C. 3401 *et seq.*), to law enforcement agencies (including a federal functional regulator, the Secretary of the Treasury, with respect to 31 U.S.C. Chapter 53, Subchapter II (Records and Reports on Monetary Instruments and Transactions) and 12 U.S.C. Chapter 21 (Financial Recordkeeping), a State insurance authority, with respect to any person domiciled in that insurance authority's State that is engaged in providing insurance, and the Federal Trade Commission), self-regulatory organizations, or for an investigation on a matter related to public safety;

(5)(i) To a consumer reporting agency in accordance with the Fair Credit Reporting Act (15 U.S.C. 1681 *et seq.*), or

(ii) From a consumer report reported by a consumer reporting agency;

(6) In connection with a proposed or actual sale, merger, transfer, or exchange of all or a portion of a business or operating unit if the disclosure of nonpublic personal information concerns solely consumers of such business or unit; or

(7)(i) To comply with federal, State, or local laws, rules and other applicable legal requirements;

(ii) To comply with a properly authorized civil, criminal, or regulatory investigation, or subpoena or summons by federal, State, or local authorities; or

(iii) To respond to judicial process or government regulatory authorities having jurisdiction over you for examination, compliance, or other purposes as authorized by law.

(b) *Examples of consent and revocation of consent.* (1) A consumer may specifically consent to your disclosure to a nonaffiliated mortgage lender of the value of the assets in the consumer's brokerage or investment advisory account so that the lender can evaluate the consumer's application for a mortgage loan.

(2) A consumer may revoke consent by subsequently exercising the right to opt out

of future disclosures of nonpublic personal information as permitted under § 248.7(f).

Subpart D—Relation to Other Laws; Effective Date

§ 248.16 Protection of Fair Credit Reporting Act.

Nothing in this part shall be construed to modify, limit, or supersede the operation of the Fair Credit Reporting Act (15 U.S.C. 1681 *et seq.*), and no inference shall be drawn on the basis of the provisions of this part regarding whether information is transaction or experience information under section 603 of that Act.

§ 248.17 Relation to State Laws.

(a) *In general.* This part shall not be construed as superseding, altering, or affecting any statute, regulation, order, or interpretation in effect in any State, except to the extent that such State statute, regulation, order, or interpretation is inconsistent with the provisions of this part, and then only to the extent of the inconsistency.

(b) *Greater protection under State law.* For purposes of this section, a State statute, regulation, order, or interpretation is not inconsistent with the provisions of this part if the protection such statute, regulation, order, or interpretation affords any consumer is greater than the protection provided under this part, as determined by the Federal Trade Commission, after consultation with the Commission, on the Federal Trade Commission's own motion, or upon the petition of any interested party.

§ 248.18 Effective Date; Transition Rule.

(a) *Effective date.* This part is effective November 13, 2000. In order to provide sufficient time for you to establish policies and systems to comply with the requirements of this part, the compliance date for this part is July 1, 2001.

(b)(1) *Notice requirement for consumers who are your customers on the compliance date.* By July 1, 2001, you must have provided an initial notice, as required by § 248.4, to consumers who are your customers on July 1, 2001.

(2) *Example.* You provide an initial notice to consumers who are your customers on July 1, 2001, if, by that date, you have established a system for providing an initial notice to all new customers and have mailed the initial notice to all your existing customers.

(c) *Two-year grandfathering of service agreements.* Until July 1, 2002, a contract that you have entered into with a nonaffiliated third party to perform services for you or functions on your behalf satisfies the provisions of § 248.13(a)(2), even if the contract does not include a requirement that the third party maintain the confidentiality of nonpublic personal information, as long as you entered into the agreement on or before July 1, 2000.

§§ 248.19–248.29 [Reserved]

§ 248.30 Procedures to Safeguard Customer Records and Information; Disposal of Consumer Report Information.

(a) Every broker, dealer, and investment company, and every investment adviser registered with the Commission must adopt policies and procedures that address administrative, technical, and physical safeguards for the protection of customer records and information. These policies and procedures must be reasonably designed to:

(1) Insure the security and confidentiality of customer records and information;

(2) Protect against any anticipated threats or hazards to the security or integrity of customer records and information; and

(3) Protect against unauthorized access to or use of customer records or information that could result in substantial harm or inconvenience to any customer.

(b) *Disposal of consumer report information and records*—

(1) *Definitions*

(i) *Consumer report* has the same meaning as in section 603(d) of the Fair Credit Reporting Act (15 U.S.C. 1681a(d)).

(ii) *Consumer report information* means any record about an individual, whether in paper, electronic or other form, that is a consumer report or is derived from a consumer report. Consumer report information also means a compilation of such records. Consumer report information does not include information that does not identify individuals, such as aggregate information or blind data.

(iii) *Disposal* means:

(A) The discarding or abandonment of consumer report information; or

(B) The sale, donation, or transfer of any medium, including computer equipment, on which consumer report information is stored.

(iv) *Notice-registered broker-dealers* means a broker or dealer registered by notice with the Commission under section 15(b)(11) of the Securities Exchange Act of 1934 (15 U.S.C. 78o(b)(11)).

(v) *Transfer agent* has the same meaning as in section 3(a)(25) of the Securities Exchange Act of 1934 (15 U.S.C. 78c(a)(25)).

(2) *Proper disposal requirements*—(i) *Standard*. Every broker and dealer other than notice-registered broker-dealers, every investment company, and every investment adviser and transfer agent registered with the Commission, that maintains or otherwise possesses consumer report information for a business purpose must properly dispose of the information by taking reasonable measures to protect against unauthorized access to or use of the information in connection with its disposal.

(ii) *Relation to other laws*. Nothing in this section shall be construed:

(A) To require any broker, dealer, or investment company, or any investment adviser or transfer agent registered with the Commission to maintain or destroy any record pertaining to an individual that is not imposed under other law; or

(B) To alter or affect any requirement imposed under any other provision of law to maintain or destroy any of those records.

H. SARBANES–OXLEY ACT (PUBLIC COMPANY ACCOUNTING REFORM AND CORPORATE RESPONSIBILITY)

(15 U.S.C. § ___)

§ 7201. Definitions.

(a) In general

In this Act, the following definitions shall apply:

(1) Appropriate State regulatory authority

The term "appropriate State regulatory authority" means the State agency or other authority responsible for the licensure or other regulation of the practice of accounting in the State or States having jurisdiction over a registered public accounting firm or associated person thereof, with respect to the matter in question.

(2) Audit

The term "audit" means an examination of the financial statements of any issuer by an independent public accounting firm in accordance with the rules of the Board or the Commission (or, for the period preceding the adoption of applicable rules of the Board under section 7213 of this title, in accordance with then-applicable generally accepted auditing and related standards for such purposes), for the purpose of expressing an opinion on such statements.

(3) Audit committee

The term "audit committee" means—

(A) a committee (or equivalent body) established by and amongst the board of directors of an issuer for the purpose of overseeing the accounting and financial reporting processes of the issuer and audits of the financial statements of the issuer; and

(B) if no such committee exists with respect to an issuer, the entire board of directors of the issuer.

(4) Audit report

The term "audit report" means a document or other record—

(A) prepared following an audit performed for purposes of compliance by an issuer with the requirements of the securities laws; and

(B) in which a public accounting firm either—

(i) sets forth the opinion of that firm regarding a financial statement, report, or other document; or

(ii) asserts that no such opinion can be expressed.

(5) Board

The term "Board" means the Public Company Accounting Oversight Board established under section 7211 of this title.

(6) Commission

The term "Commission" means the Securities and Exchange Commission.

(7) Issuer

The term "issuer" means an issuer (as defined in section 78c of this title), the securities of which are registered under section 78l of this title, or that is required to file reports under section 78o(d) of this title, or that files or has filed a registration statement that has not yet become effective under the Securities Act of 1933 (15 U.S.C. 77a et seq.), and that it has not withdrawn.

(8) Non-audit services

The term "non-audit services" means any professional services provided to an issuer by a registered public accounting firm, other than those provided to an issuer in connection with an audit or a review of the financial statements of an issuer.

(9) Person associated with a public accounting firm

(A) In general

The terms "person associated with a public accounting firm" (or with a "registered public accounting firm") and "associated person of a public accounting firm" (or of a "registered public accounting firm") mean any individual proprietor, partner, shareholder, principal, accountant, or other professional employee of a public accounting firm, or any other independent contractor or entity that, in connection with the preparation or issuance of any audit report—

(i) shares in the profits of, or receives compensation in any other form from, that firm; or

(ii) participates as agent or otherwise on behalf of such accounting firm in any activity of that firm.

(B) Exemption authority

The Board may, by rule, exempt persons engaged only in ministerial tasks from the definition in subparagraph (A), to the extent that the Board determines that any such exemption is consistent with the purposes of this Act, the public interest, or the protection of investors.

(10) Professional standards

The term "professional standards" means—

(A) accounting principles that are—

(i) established by the standard setting body described in section 77s(b) of this title, as amended by this Act, or prescribed by the Commission under section 77s(a) of this title or section 78m(b) of this title; and

(ii) relevant to audit reports for particular issuers, or dealt with in the quality control system of a particular registered public accounting firm; and

(B) auditing standards, standards for attestation engagements, quality control policies and procedures, ethical and competency standards, and independence standards (including rules implementing title II) that the Board or the Commission determines—

(i) relate to the preparation or issuance of audit reports for issuers; and

(ii) are established or adopted by the Board under section 7213(a) of this title, or are promulgated as rules of the Commission.

(11) Public accounting firm

The term "public accounting firm" means—

(A) a proprietorship, partnership, incorporated association, corporation, limited liability company, limited liability partnership, or other legal entity that is engaged in the practice of public accounting or preparing or issuing audit reports; and

(B) to the extent so designated by the rules of the Board, any associated person of any entity described in subparagraph (A).

(12) Registered public accounting firm

The term "registered public accounting firm" means a public accounting firm registered with the Board in accordance with this Act.

(13) Rules of the board

The term "rules of the Board" means the bylaws and rules of the Board (as submitted to, and approved, modified, or amended by the Commission, in accordance with section 7217 of this title), and those stated policies, practices, and interpretations of the Board that the Commission, by rule, may deem to be rules of the Board, as necessary or appropriate in the public interest or for the protection of investors.

(14) Security

The term "security" has the same meaning as in section 78c(a) of this title.

(15) Securities laws

The term "securities laws" means the provisions of law referred to in section 78c(a)(47) of this title, as amended by this Act, and includes the rules, regulations, and orders issued by the Commission thereunder.

(16) State

The term "State" means any State of the United States, the District of Columbia, Puerto Rico, the Virgin Islands, or any other territory or possession of the United States.

§ 7202. Commission Rules and Enforcement

(a) Regulatory action

The Commission shall promulgate such rules and regulations, as may be necessary or appropriate in the public interest or for the protection of investors, and in furtherance of this Act.

(b) Enforcement

(1) In general

A violation by any person of this Act, any rule or regulation of the Commission issued under this Act, or any rule of the Board shall be treated for all purposes in the same manner as a violation of the Securities Exchange Act of 1934 (15 U.S.C.A. §§ 78a et seq.) or the rules and regulations issued thereunder, consistent with the provisions of this Act, and any such person shall be subject to the same penalties, and to the same extent, as for a violation of that Act or such rules or regulations....

(2) to (4) Omitted

(c) Effect on Commission authority

Nothing in this Act or the rules of the Board shall be construed to impair or limit—

(1) the authority of the Commission to regulate the accounting profession, accounting firms, or persons associated with such firms for purposes of enforcement of the securities laws;

(2) the authority of the Commission to set standards for accounting or auditing practices or auditor independence, derived from other provisions of the securities laws or the rules or regulations thereunder, for purposes of the preparation and issuance of any audit report, or otherwise under applicable law; or

(3) the ability of the Commission to take, on the initiative of the Commission, legal, administrative, or disciplinary action against any registered public accounting firm or any associated person thereof.

SUBCHAPTER I—PUBLIC COMPANY ACCOUNTING OVERSIGHT BOARD

§ 7211. Establishment; Administrative Provisions

(a) Establishment of Board

There is established the Public Company Accounting Oversight Board, to oversee the audit of public companies that are subject to the securities laws, and related matters, in order to protect the interests of investors and further the public interest in the preparation of informative, accurate, and independent audit reports for companies the securities of which are sold to, and held by and for, public investors. The Board shall be a body corporate, operate as a nonprofit corporation, and have succession until dissolved by an Act of Congress.

(b) Status

The Board shall not be an agency or establishment of the United States Government, and, except as otherwise provided in this Act, shall be subject to, and have all the powers conferred upon a nonprofit corporation by, the District of Columbia Nonprofit Corporation Act. No member or person employed by, or agent for, the Board shall be deemed to be an officer or employee of or agent for the Federal Government by reason of such service.

(c) Duties of the Board

The Board shall, subject to action by the Commission under section 7217 of this title, and once a determination is made by the Commission under subsection (d) of this section—

(1) register public accounting firms that prepare audit reports for issuers, in accordance with section 7212 of this title;

(2) establish or adopt, or both, by rule, auditing, quality control, ethics, independence, and other standards relating to the preparation of audit reports for issuers, in accordance with section 7213 of this title;

(3) conduct inspections of registered public accounting firms, in accordance with section 7214 of this title and the rules of the Board;

(4) conduct investigations and disciplinary proceedings concerning, and impose appropriate sanctions where justified upon, registered public accounting firms and associated persons of such firms, in accordance with section 7215 of this title;

(5) perform such other duties or functions as the Board (or the Commission, by rule or order) determines are necessary or appropriate to promote high professional standards among, and improve the quality of audit services offered by, registered public accounting firms and associated persons thereof, or otherwise to carry out this Act, in order to protect investors, or to further the public interest;

(6) enforce compliance with this Act, the rules of the Board, professional standards, and the securities laws relating to the preparation and issuance of audit reports and the obligations and liabilities of accountants with respect thereto, by registered public accounting firms and associated persons thereof; and

(7) set the budget and manage the operations of the Board and the staff of the Board.

(d) Commission determination

The members of the Board shall take such action (including hiring of staff, proposal of rules, and adoption of initial and transitional auditing and other professional standards) as may be necessary or appropriate to enable the Commission to determine, not later than 270 days after the date of enactment of this Act, that the Board is so organized and has the capacity to carry out the requirements of this title, and to enforce compliance with this title by registered public accounting firms and associated persons thereof. The Commission shall be responsible, prior to the appointment of the Board, for the planning for the establishment and administrative transition to the Board's operation.

(e) Board membership

(1) Composition

The Board shall have 5 members, appointed from among prominent individuals of integrity and reputation who have a demonstrated commitment to the interests of investors and the public, and an understanding of the responsibilities for and nature of the financial disclosures required of issuers under the securities laws and the obligations of accountants with respect to the preparation and issuance of audit reports with respect to such disclosures.

(2) Limitation

Two members, and only 2 members, of the Board shall be or have been certified public accountants pursuant to the laws of 1 or more States, provided that, if 1 of those 2 members is the chairperson, he or she may not have been a practicing certified public accountant for at least 5 years prior to his or her appointment to the Board.

(3) Full-time independent service

Each member of the Board shall serve on a full-time basis, and may not, concurrent with service on the Board, be employed by any other person or engage in any other professional or business activity. No member of the Board may share in any of the profits of, or receive payments from, a public accounting firm (or any other person, as determined by rule of the Commission), other than fixed continuing payments, subject to such conditions as the Commission may impose, under standard arrangements for the retirement of members of public accounting firms.

(4) Appointment of Board members

(A) Initial Board

Not later than 90 days after the date of enactment of this Act, the Commission, after consultation with the Chairman of the Board of Governors of the Federal Reserve System and the Secretary of the Treasury, shall appoint the chairperson and other initial members of the Board, and shall designate a term of service for each.

(B) Vacancies

A vacancy on the Board shall not affect the powers of the Board, but shall be filled in the same manner as provided for appointments under this section.

(5) Term of service

(A) In general

The term of service of each Board member shall be 5 years, and until a successor is appointed, except that—

(i) the terms of office of the initial Board members (other than the chairperson) shall expire in annual increments, 1 on each of the first 4 anniversaries of the initial date of appointment; and

(ii) any Board member appointed to fill a vacancy occurring before the expiration of the term for which the predecessor was appointed shall be appointed only for the remainder of that term.

(B) Term limitation

No person may serve as a member of the Board, or as chairperson of the Board, for more than 2 terms, whether or not such terms of service are consecutive.

(6) Removal from office

A member of the Board may be removed by the Commission from office, in accordance with section 7217(d)(3), for good cause shown before the expiration of the term of that member.

(f) Powers of the Board

In addition to any authority granted to the Board otherwise in this Act, the Board shall have the power, subject to section 7217 of this title—

(1) to sue and be sued, complain and defend, in its corporate name and through its own counsel, with the approval of the Commission, in any Federal, State, or other court;

(2) to conduct its operations and maintain offices, and to exercise all other rights and powers authorized by this Act, in any State, without regard to any qualification, licensing, or other provision of law in effect in such State (or a political subdivision thereof);

(3) to lease, purchase, accept gifts or donations of or otherwise acquire, improve, use, sell, exchange, or convey, all of or an interest in any property, wherever situated;

(4) to appoint such employees, accountants, attorneys, and other agents as may be necessary or appropriate, and to determine their qualifications, define their duties, and fix their salaries or other compensation (at a level that is comparable to private sector self-regulatory, accounting, technical, supervisory, or other staff or management positions);

(5) to allocate, assess, and collect accounting support fees established pursuant to section 109, for the Board, and other fees and charges imposed under this title; and

(6) to enter into contracts, execute instruments, incur liabilities, and do any and all other acts and things necessary, appropriate, or incidental to the conduct of its operations and the exercise of its obligations, rights, and powers imposed or granted by this title.

(g) Rules of the board

The rules of the Board shall, subject to the approval of the Commission—

(1) provide for the operation and administration of the Board, the exercise of its authority, and the performance of its responsibilities under this Act;

(2) permit, as the Board determines necessary or appropriate, delegation by the Board of any of its functions to an individual member or employee of the Board, or to a division of the Board, including functions with respect to hearing, determining, ordering, certifying, reporting, or otherwise acting as to any matter, except that—

(A) the Board shall retain a discretionary right to review any action pursuant to any such delegated function, upon its own motion;

(B) a person shall be entitled to a review by the Board with respect to any matter so delegated, and the decision of the Board upon such review shall be deemed to be the action of the Board for all purposes (including appeal or review thereof); and

(C) if the right to exercise a review described in subparagraph (A) is declined, or if no such review is sought within the time stated in the rules of the Board, then the action taken by the holder of such delegation shall for all purposes, including appeal or review thereof, be deemed to be the action of the Board;

(3) establish ethics rules and standards of conduct for Board members and staff, including a bar on practice before the Board (and the Commission, with respect to Board-related matters) of 1 year for former members of the Board, and appropriate periods (not to exceed 1 year) for former staff of the Board; and

(4) provide as otherwise required by this Act.

(h) Annual report to the Commission

The Board shall submit an annual report (including its audited financial statements) to the Commission, and the Commission shall transmit a copy of that report to the Committee on Banking, Housing, and Urban Affairs of the Senate, and the Committee on Financial Services of the House of Representatives, not later than 30 days after the date of receipt of that report by the Commission.

§ 7212. Registration with the Board

(a) Mandatory registration

Beginning 180 days after the date of the determination of the Commission under section 7211(d), it shall be unlawful for any person that is not a registered public accounting firm to prepare or issue, or to participate in the preparation or issuance of, any audit report with respect to any issuer.

(b) Applications for registration

(1) Form of application

A public accounting firm shall use such form as the Board may prescribe, by rule, to apply for registration under this section.

(2) Contents of applications

Each public accounting firm shall submit, as part of its application for registration, in such detail as the Board shall specify—

(A) the names of all issuers for which the firm prepared or issued audit reports during the immediately preceding calendar year, and for which the firm expects to prepare or issue audit reports during the current calendar year;

(B) the annual fees received by the firm from each such issuer for audit services, other accounting services, and non-audit services, respectively;

(C) such other current financial information for the most recently completed fiscal year of the firm as the Board may reasonably request;

(D) a statement of the quality control policies of the firm for its accounting and auditing practices;

(E) a list of all accountants associated with the firm who participate in or contribute to the preparation of audit reports, stating the license or certification number of each such person, as well as the State license numbers of the firm itself;

(F) information relating to criminal, civil, or administrative actions or disciplinary proceedings pending against the firm or any associated person of the firm in connection with any audit report;

(G) copies of any periodic or annual disclosure filed by an issuer with the Commission during the immediately preceding calendar year which discloses accounting disagreements between such issuer and the firm in connection with an audit report furnished or prepared by the firm for such issuer; and

(H) such other information as the rules of the Board or the Commission shall specify as necessary or appropriate in the public interest or for the protection of investors.

(3) Consents

Each application for registration under this subsection shall include—

(A) a consent executed by the public accounting firm to cooperation in and compliance with any request for testimony or the production of documents made by the Board in the furtherance of its authority and responsibilities under this title (and an agreement to secure and enforce similar consents from each of the associated persons of the public accounting firm as a condition of their continued employment by or other association with such firm); and

(B) a statement that such firm understands and agrees that cooperation and compliance, as described in the consent required by subparagraph (A), and the securing and enforcement of such consents from its associated persons, in accordance with the rules of the Board, shall be a condition to the continuing effectiveness of the registration of the firm with the Board.

(c) Action on applications

(1) Timing

The Board shall approve a completed application for registration not later than 45 days after the date of receipt of the application, in accordance with the rules of the Board, unless the Board, prior to such date, issues a written notice of disapproval to, or requests more information from, the prospective registrant.

(2) Treatment

A written notice of disapproval of a completed application under paragraph (1) for registration shall be treated as a disciplinary sanction for purposes of sections 7215(d) and 7217(c).

(d) Periodic reports

Each registered public accounting firm shall submit an annual report to the Board, and may be required to report more frequently, as necessary to update the information contained in its application for registration under this section, and to provide to the Board such additional information as the Board or the Commission may specify, in accordance with subsection (b)(2) of this section.

(e) Public availability

Registration applications and annual reports required by this subsection, or such portions of such applications or reports as may be designated under rules of the Board, shall be made available for public inspection, subject to rules of the Board or the Commission, and to applicable laws relating to the confidentiality of proprietary, personal, or other information contained in such applications or reports, provided that, in all events, the Board shall protect from public disclosure information reasonably identified by the subject accounting firm as proprietary information.

(f) Registration and annual fees

The Board shall assess and collect a registration fee and an annual fee from each registered public accounting firm, in amounts that are sufficient to recover the costs of processing and reviewing applications and annual reports.

§ 7213. Auditing, Quality Control, and Independence Standards and Rules

(a) Auditing, quality control, and ethics standards

(1) In general

The Board shall, by rule, establish, including, to the extent it determines appropriate, through adoption of standards proposed by 1 or more professional groups of accountants designated pursuant to paragraph (3)(A) or advisory groups convened pursuant to paragraph (4), and amend or otherwise modify or alter, such auditing and related attestation standards, such quality control standards, and such ethics standards to be used by registered public accounting firms in the preparation and issuance of audit reports, as required by this Act or the rules of the Commission, or as may be necessary or appropriate in the public interest or for the protection of investors.

(2) Rule requirements

In carrying out paragraph (1), the Board—

(A) shall include in the auditing standards that it adopts, requirements that each registered public accounting firm shall—

(i) prepare, and maintain for a period of not less than 7 years, audit work papers, and other information related to any audit report, in sufficient detail to support the conclusions reached in such report;

(ii) provide a concurring or second partner review and approval of such audit report (and other related information), and concurring approval in its issuance, by a qualified person (as prescribed by the Board) associated with the public accounting firm, other than the person in charge of the audit, or by an independent reviewer (as prescribed by the Board); and

(iii) describe in each audit report the scope of the auditor's testing of the internal control structure and procedures of the issuer, required by section 7262(b) of this title, and present (in such report or in a separate report)—

(I) the findings of the auditor from such testing;

(II) an evaluation of whether such internal control structure and procedures—

(aa) include maintenance of records that in reasonable detail accurately and fairly reflect the transactions and dispositions of the assets of the issuer;

(bb) provide reasonable assurance that transactions are recorded as necessary to permit preparation of financial statements in accordance with generally accepted accounting principles, and that receipts and expenditures of the issuer are being made only in accordance with authorizations of management and directors of the issuer; and

(III) a description, at a minimum, of material weaknesses in such internal controls, and of any material noncompliance found on the basis of such testing.

(B) shall include, in the quality control standards that it adopts with respect to the issuance of audit reports, requirements for every registered public accounting firm relating to—

(i) monitoring of professional ethics and independence from issuers on behalf of which the firm issues audit reports;

(ii) consultation within such firm on accounting and auditing questions;

(iii) supervision of audit work;

(iv) hiring, professional development, and advancement of personnel;

(v) the acceptance and continuation of engagements;

(vi) internal inspection; and

(vii) such other requirements as the Board may prescribe, subject to subsection (a)(1) of this section.

(3) Authority to adopt other standards

(A) In general

In carrying out this subsection, the Board—

(i) may adopt as its rules, subject to the terms of section 7217 of this title, any portion of any statement of auditing standards or other professional standards that the Board determines satisfy the requirements of paragraph (1), and that were proposed by 1 or more professional groups of accountants that shall be designated or recognized by the Board, by rule, for such purpose, pursuant to this paragraph or 1 or more advisory groups convened pursuant to paragraph (4); and

(ii) notwithstanding clause (i), shall retain full authority to modify, supplement, revise, or subsequently amend, modify, or repeal, in whole or in part, any portion of any statement described in clause (i).

(B) Initial and transitional standards

The Board shall adopt standards described in subparagraph (A)(i) as initial or transitional standards, to the extent the Board determines necessary, prior to a determination of the Commission under section 7211(d) of this title, and such standards shall be separately approved by the Commission at the time of that determination, without regard to the procedures required by section 7211 of this title that otherwise would apply to the approval of rules of the Board.

(4) Advisory groups

The Board shall convene, or authorize its staff to convene, such expert advisory groups as may be appropriate, which may include practicing accountants and other experts, as well as representatives of other interested groups, subject to such rules as the Board may prescribe to prevent conflicts of interest, to make recommendations concerning the content (including proposed drafts) of auditing, quality control, ethics, independence, or other standards required to be established under this section.

(b) Independence standards and rules

The Board shall establish such rules as may be necessary or appropriate in the public interest or for the protection of investors, to implement, or as authorized under, title II of this Act.

(c) Cooperation with designated professional groups of accountants and advisory groups

(1) In general

The Board shall cooperate on an ongoing basis with professional groups of accountants designated under subsection (a)(3)(A) of this section and advisory groups convened under subsection (a)(4) of this section in the examination of the need for changes in any standards subject to its authority under subsection (a) of this section, recommend issues for inclusion on the agendas of such designated professional groups of accountants or advisory groups, and take such other steps as it deems appropriate to increase the effectiveness of the standard setting process.

(2) Board responses

The Board shall respond in a timely fashion to requests from designated professional groups of accountants and advisory groups referred to in paragraph (1) for any changes in standards over which the Board has authority.

(d) Evaluation of standard setting process

The Board shall include in the annual report required by section 7211(h) of this title the results of its standard setting responsibilities during the period to which the report relates, including a discussion of the work of the Board with any designated professional groups of accountants and advisory groups described in paragraphs (3)(A) and (4) of subsection (a) of this section, and its pending issues agenda for future standard setting projects.

§ 7214. Inspections of Registered Public Accounting Firms

(a) In general

The Board shall conduct a continuing program of inspections to assess the degree of compliance of each registered public accounting firm and associated persons of that firm with this Act, the rules of the Board, the rules of the Commission, or professional standards, in connection with its performance of audits, issuance of audit reports, and related matters involving issuers.

(b) Inspection frequency

(1) In general

Subject to paragraph (2), inspections required by this section shall be conducted—

(A) annually with respect to each registered public accounting firm that regularly provides audit reports for more than 100 issuers; and

(B) not less frequently than once every 3 years with respect to each registered public accounting firm that regularly provides audit reports for 100 or fewer issuers.

(2) Adjustments to schedules

The Board may, by rule, adjust the inspection schedules set under paragraph (1) if the Board finds that different inspection schedules are consistent with the purposes of this Act, the public interest, and the protection of investors. The Board may conduct special inspections at the request of the Commission or upon its own motion.

(c) Procedures

The Board shall, in each inspection under this section, and in accordance with its rules for such inspections—

(1) identify any act or practice or omission to act by the registered public accounting firm, or by any associated person thereof, revealed by such inspection that may be in violation of this Act, the rules of the Board, the rules of the Commission, the firm's own quality control policies, or professional standards;

(2) report any such act, practice, or omission, if appropriate, to the Commission and each appropriate State regulatory authority; and

(3) begin a formal investigation or take disciplinary action, if appropriate, with respect to any such violation, in accordance with this Act and the rules of the Board.

(d) Conduct of inspections

In conducting an inspection of a registered public accounting firm under this section, the Board shall—

(1) inspect and review selected audit and review engagements of the firm (which may include audit engagements that are the subject of ongoing litigation or other controversy between the firm and 1 or more third parties), performed at various offices and by various associated persons of the firm, as selected by the Board;

(2) evaluate the sufficiency of the quality control system of the firm, and the manner of the documentation and communication of that system by the firm; and

(3) perform such other testing of the audit, supervisory, and quality control procedures of the firm as are necessary or appropriate in light of the purpose of the inspection and the responsibilities of the Board.

(e) Record retention

The rules of the Board may require the retention by registered public accounting firms for inspection purposes of records whose retention is not otherwise required by section 7213 of this title or the rules issued thereunder.

(f) Procedures for review

The rules of the Board shall provide a procedure for the review of and response to a draft inspection report by the registered public accounting firm under inspection. The Board shall take such action with respect to such response as it considers appropriate (including revising the draft report or continuing or supplementing its inspection activities before issuing a final report), but the text of any such response, appropriately redacted to protect information reasonably identified by the accounting firm as confidential, shall be attached to and made part of the inspection report.

(g) Report

A written report of the findings of the Board for each inspection under this section, subject to subsection (h), shall be—

(1) transmitted, in appropriate detail, to the Commission and each appropriate State regulatory authority, accompanied by any letter or comments by the Board or the inspector, and any letter of response from the registered public accounting firm; and

(2) made available in appropriate detail to the public (subject to section 7215(b)(5)(A) of this title, and to the protection of such confidential and proprietary information as the Board may determine to be appropriate, or as may be required by law), except that no portions of the inspection report that deal with criticisms of or potential defects in the quality control systems of the firm under inspection shall be made public if those criticisms or defects are addressed by the firm, to the satisfaction of the Board, not later than 12 months after the date of the inspection report.

(h) Interim Commission review

(1) Reviewable matters

A registered public accounting firm may seek review by the Commission, pursuant to such rules as the Commission shall promulgate, if the firm—

(A) has provided the Board with a response, pursuant to rules issued by the Board under subsection (f) of this section, to the substance of particular items in a draft inspection report, and disagrees with the assessments contained in any final report prepared by the Board following such response; or

(B) disagrees with the determination of the Board that criticisms or defects identified in an inspection report have not been addressed to the satisfaction of the Board within 12 months of the date of the inspection report, for purposes of subsection (g)(2) of this section.

(2) Treatment of review

Any decision of the Commission with respect to a review under paragraph (1) shall not be reviewable under section 78y of this title, or deemed to be "final agency action" for purposes of section 704 of Title 5.

(3) Timing

Review under paragraph (1) may be sought during the 30–day period following the date of the event giving rise to the review under subparagraph (A) or (B) of paragraph (1).

§ 7215. Investigations and Disciplinary Proceedings

(a) In general

The Board shall establish, by rule, subject to the requirements of this section, fair procedures for the investigation and disciplining of registered public accounting firms and associated persons of such firms.

(b) Investigations

(1) Authority

In accordance with the rules of the Board, the Board may conduct an investigation of any act or practice, or omission to act, by a registered public accounting firm, any associated person of such firm, or both, that may violate any provision of this Act, the rules of the Board, the provisions of the securities laws relating to the preparation and issuance of audit reports and the obligations and liabilities of accountants with respect thereto, including the rules of the Commission issued under this Act, or professional standards, regardless of how the act, practice, or omission is brought to the attention of the Board.

(2) Testimony and document production

In addition to such other actions as the Board determines to be necessary or appropriate, the rules of the Board may—

(A) require the testimony of the firm or of any person associated with a registered public accounting firm, with respect to any matter that the Board considers relevant or material to an investigation;

(B) require the production of audit work papers and any other document or information in the possession of a registered public accounting firm or any associated person thereof, wherever domiciled, that the Board considers relevant or material to the investigation, and may inspect the books and records of such firm or associated person to verify the accuracy of any documents or information supplied;

(C) request the testimony of, and production of any document in the possession of, any other person, including any client of a registered public accounting firm that the Board considers relevant or material to an investigation under this section, with appropriate notice, subject to the needs of the investigation, as permitted under the rules of the Board; and

(D) provide for procedures to seek issuance by the Commission, in a manner established by the Commission, of a subpoena to require the testimony of, and production of any document in the possession of, any person, including any client of a registered public accounting firm, that the Board considers relevant or material to an investigation under this section.

(3) Noncooperation with investigations

(A) In general

If a registered public accounting firm or any associated person thereof refuses to testify, produce documents, or otherwise cooperate with the Board in connection with an investigation under this section, the Board may—

(i) suspend or bar such person from being associated with a registered public accounting firm, or require the registered public accounting firm to end such association;

(ii) suspend or revoke the registration of the public accounting firm; and

(iii) invoke such other lesser sanctions as the Board considers appropriate, and as specified by rule of the Board.

(B) Procedure

Any action taken by the Board under this paragraph shall be subject to the terms of section 7217(c) of this title.

(4) Coordination and referral of investigations

(A) Coordination

The Board shall notify the Commission of any pending Board investigation involving a potential violation of the securities laws, and thereafter coordinate its work with the work of the Commission's Division of Enforcement, as necessary to protect an ongoing Commission investigation.

(B) Referral

The Board may refer an investigation under this section—

(i) to the Commission;

(ii) to any other Federal functional regulator (as defined in section 6809 of this title), in the case of an investigation that concerns an audit report for an institution that is subject to the jurisdiction of such regulator; and

(iii) at the direction of the Commission, to—

(I) the Attorney General of the United States;

(II) the attorney general of 1 or more States; and

(III) the appropriate State regulatory authority.

(5) Use of documents

(A) Confidentiality

Except as provided in subparagraph (B), all documents and information prepared or received by or specifically for the Board, and deliberations of the Board and its employees and agents, in connection with an inspection under section 7214 of this title or with an investigation under this section, shall be confidential and privileged as an evidentiary matter (and shall not be subject to civil discovery or other legal process) in any proceeding in any Federal or State court or administrative agency, and shall be exempt from disclosure, in the hands of an agency or establishment of the Federal Government, under the Freedom of Information Act (5

U.S.C. 552a), or otherwise, unless and until presented in connection with a public proceeding or released in accordance with subsection (c) of this section.

(B) Availability to Government agencies

Without the loss of its status as confidential and privileged in the hands of the Board, all information referred to in subparagraph (A) may—

(i) be made available to the Commission; and

(ii) in the discretion of the Board, when determined by the Board to be necessary to accomplish the purposes of this Act or to protect investors, be made available to—

(I) the Attorney General of the United States;

(II) the appropriate Federal functional regulator (as defined in section 6809 of this title), other than the Commission, with respect to an audit report for an institution subject to the jurisdiction of such regulator;

(III) State attorneys general in connection with any criminal investigation; and

(IV) any appropriate State regulatory authority, each of which shall maintain such information as confidential and privileged.

(6) Immunity

Any employee of the Board engaged in carrying out an investigation under this Act shall be immune from any civil liability arising out of such investigation in the same manner and to the same extent as an employee of the Federal Government in similar circumstances.

(c) Disciplinary procedures

(1) Notification; recordkeeping

The rules of the Board shall provide that in any proceeding by the Board to determine whether a registered public accounting firm, or an associated person thereof, should be disciplined, the Board shall—

(A) bring specific charges with respect to the firm or associated person;

(B) notify such firm or associated person of, and provide to the firm or associated person an opportunity to defend against, such charges; and

(C) keep a record of the proceedings.

(2) Public hearings

Hearings under this section shall not be public, unless otherwise ordered by the Board for good cause shown, with the consent of the parties to such hearing.

(3) Supporting statement

A determination by the Board to impose a sanction under this subsection shall be supported by a statement setting forth—

(A) each act or practice in which the registered public accounting firm, or associated person, has engaged (or omitted to engage), or that forms a basis for all or a part of such sanction;

(B) the specific provision of this Act, the securities laws, the rules of the Board, or professional standards which the Board determines has been violated; and

(C) the sanction imposed, including a justification for that sanction.

(4) Sanctions

If the Board finds, based on all of the facts and circumstances, that a registered public accounting firm or associated person thereof has engaged in any act or practice, or omitted to act, in violation of this Act, the rules of the Board, the provisions of the securities laws relating to the preparation and issuance of audit reports and the obligations and liabilities of accountants with respect thereto, including the rules of the Commission issued under this Act, or professional standards, the Board may impose such disciplinary or remedial sanctions as it determines appropriate, subject to applicable limitations under paragraph (5), including—

(A) temporary suspension or permanent revocation of registration under this title;

(B) temporary or permanent suspension or bar of a person from further association with any registered public accounting firm;

(C) temporary or permanent limitation on the activities, functions, or operations of such firm or person (other than in connection with required additional professional education or training);

(D) a civil money penalty for each such violation, in an amount equal to—

(i) not more than $100,000 for a natural person or $2,000,000 for any other person; and

(ii) in any case to which paragraph (5) applies, not more than $750,000 for a natural person or $15,000,000 for any other person;

(E) censure;

(F) required additional professional education or training; or

(G) any other appropriate sanction provided for in the rules of the Board.

(5) Intentional or other knowing conduct

The sanctions and penalties described in subparagraphs (A) through (C) and (D)(ii) of paragraph (4) shall only apply to—

(A) intentional or knowing conduct, including reckless conduct, that results in violation of the applicable statutory, regulatory, or professional standard; or

(B) repeated instances of negligent conduct, each resulting in a violation of the applicable statutory, regulatory, or professional standard.

(6) Failure to supervise

(A) In general

The Board may impose sanctions under this section on a registered accounting firm or upon the supervisory personnel of such firm, if the Board finds that—

(i) the firm has failed reasonably to supervise an associated person, either as required by the rules of the Board relating to auditing or quality control standards, or otherwise, with a view to preventing violations of this Act, the rules of the Board, the provisions of the securities laws relating to the preparation and issuance of audit reports and the obligations and liabilities of accountants with respect thereto, including the rules of the Commission under this Act, or professional standards; and

(ii) such associated person commits a violation of this Act, or any of such rules, laws, or standards.

(B) Rule of construction

No associated person of a registered public accounting firm shall be deemed to have failed reasonably to supervise any other person for purposes of subparagraph (A), if—

(i) there have been established in and for that firm procedures, and a system for applying such procedures, that comply with applicable rules of the Board and that would reasonably be expected to prevent and detect any such violation by such associated person; and

(ii) such person has reasonably discharged the duties and obligations incumbent upon that person by reason of such procedures and system, and had no reasonable cause to believe that such procedures and system were not being complied with.

(7) Effect of suspension

(A) Association with a public accounting firm

It shall be unlawful for any person that is suspended or barred from being associated with a registered public accounting firm under this subsection willfully to become or remain associated with any registered public accounting firm, or for any registered public accounting firm that knew, or, in the exercise of reasonable care should have known, of the suspension or bar, to permit such an association, without the consent of the Board or the Commission.

(B) Association with an issuer

It shall be unlawful for any person that is suspended or barred from being associated with an issuer under this subsection willfully to become or remain associated with any issuer in an accountancy or a financial management capacity, and for any issuer that knew, or in the exercise of reasonable care should have known, of such suspension or bar, to permit such an association, without the consent of the Board or the Commission.

(d) Reporting of sanctions

(1) Recipients

If the Board imposes a disciplinary sanction, in accordance with this section, the Board shall report the sanction to—

(A) the Commission;

(B) any appropriate State regulatory authority or any foreign accountancy licensing board with which such firm or person is licensed or certified; and

(C) the public (once any stay on the imposition of such sanction has been lifted).

(2) Contents

The information reported under paragraph (1) shall include—

(A) the name of the sanctioned person;

(B) a description of the sanction and the basis for its imposition; and

(C) such other information as the Board deems appropriate.

(e) Stay of sanctions

(1) In general

Application to the Commission for review, or the institution by the Commission of review, of any disciplinary action of the Board shall operate as a stay of any such disciplinary action, unless and until the Commission orders (summarily or after notice and opportunity for hearing on the question of a stay, which hearing may consist solely of the submission of affidavits or presentation of oral arguments) that no such stay shall continue to operate.

(2) Expedited procedures

The Commission shall establish for appropriate cases an expedited procedure for consideration and determination of the question of the duration of a stay pending review of any disciplinary action of the Board under this subsection.

§ 7216. Foreign Public Accounting Firms

(a) Applicability to certain foreign firms

(1) In general

Any foreign public accounting firm that prepares or furnishes an audit report with respect to any issuer, shall be subject to this Act and the rules of the Board and the Commission issued under this Act, in the same manner and to the same extent as a public accounting firm that is organized and operates under the laws of the United States or any State, except that registration pursuant to section 7212 of this title shall not by itself provide a basis for subjecting such a foreign public accounting firm to the jurisdiction of the Federal or State courts, other than with respect to controversies between such firms and the Board.

(2) Board authority

The Board may, by rule, determine that a foreign public accounting firm (or a class of such firms) that does not issue audit reports nonetheless plays such a substantial role in the preparation and furnishing of such reports for particular issuers, that it is necessary or appropriate, in light of the purposes of this Act and in the public interest or for the protection of investors, that such firm (or class of firms) should be treated as a public accounting firm (or firms) for purposes of registration under, and oversight by the Board in accordance with, this subchapter.

(b) Production of audit workpapers

(1) Consent by foreign firms

If a foreign public accounting firm issues an opinion or otherwise performs material services upon which a registered public accounting firm relies in issuing all or part of any audit report or any opinion contained in an audit report, that foreign public accounting firm shall be deemed to have consented—

(A) to produce its audit workpapers for the Board or the Commission in connection with any investigation by either body with respect to that audit report; and

(B) to be subject to the jurisdiction of the courts of the United States for purposes of enforcement of any request for production of such workpapers.

(2) Consent by domestic firms

A registered public accounting firm that relies upon the opinion of a foreign public accounting firm, as described in paragraph (1), shall be deemed—

(A) to have consented to supplying the audit workpapers of that foreign public accounting firm in response to a request for production by the Board or the Commission; and

(B) to have secured the agreement of that foreign public accounting firm to such production, as a condition of its reliance on the opinion of that foreign public accounting firm.

(c) Exemption authority

The Commission, and the Board, subject to the approval of the Commission, may, by rule, regulation, or order, and as the Commission (or Board) determines necessary or appropriate in the public interest or for the protection of investors, either unconditionally or upon specified terms and conditions exempt any foreign public accounting firm, or any class of such firms, from any provision of this Act or the rules of the Board or the Commission issued under this Act.

(d) Definition

In this section, the term "foreign public accounting firm" means a public accounting firm that is organized and operates under the laws of a foreign government or political subdivision thereof.

§ 7217. Commission Oversight of the Board

(a) General oversight responsibility

The Commission shall have oversight and enforcement authority over the Board, as provided in this Act. The provisions of section 78q(a)(1) (of this title), and of section 78q(b)(1) of this title shall apply to the Board as fully as if the Board were a "registered securities association" for purposes of those sections 78q(a)(1) and 78q(b)(1) of this title.

(b) Rules of the Board

(1) Definition

In this section, the term "proposed rule" means any proposed rule of the Board, and any modification of any such rule.

(2) Prior approval required

No rule of the Board shall become effective without prior approval of the Commission in accordance with this section, other than as provided in section 7213(a)(3)(B) of this title with respect to initial or transitional standards.

(3) Approval criteria

The Commission shall approve a proposed rule, if it finds that the rule is consistent with the requirements of this Act and the securities laws, or is necessary or appropriate in the public interest or for the protection of investors.

(4) Proposed rule procedures

The provisions of paragraphs (1) through (3) of section 78s(b) of this title shall govern the proposed rules of the Board, as fully as if the Board were a "registered securities association" for purposes of that section 78s(b) of this title, except that, for purposes of this paragraph—

(A) the phrase "consistent with the requirements of this title and the rules and regulations thereunder applicable to such organization" in section 78s(b)(2) of this title shall be deemed to read "consistent with the requirements of title I of the Sarbanes–Oxley Act of 2002, and the rules and regulations issued thereunder applicable to such organization, or as necessary or appropriate in the public interest or for the protection of investors"; and

(B) the phrase "otherwise in furtherance of the purposes of this title" in section 78s(b)(3)(C) of this title shall be deemed to read "otherwise in furtherance of the purposes of title I of the Sarbanes–Oxley Act of 2002".

(5) Commission authority to amend rules of the Board

The provisions of section 78s(c) of this title shall govern the abrogation, deletion, or addition to portions of the rules of the Board by the Commission as fully as if the Board were a "registered securities association" for purposes of that section 78s(c) of this title, except that the phrase "to conform its rules to the requirements of this title and the rules and regulations thereunder applicable to such organization, or otherwise in furtherance of the purposes of this title" in section 78s(c) of this title shall, for purposes of this paragraph, be deemed to read "to assure the fair administration of the Public Company Accounting Oversight Board, conform the rules promulgated by that Board to the requirements of title I of the Sarbanes–Oxley Act of 2002, or otherwise further the purposes of that Act, the securities laws, and the rules and regulations thereunder applicable to that Board".

(c) Commission review of disciplinary action taken by the Board

(1) Notice of sanction

The Board shall promptly file notice with the Commission of any final sanction on any registered public accounting firm or on any associated person thereof, in such form and containing such information as the Commission, by rule, may prescribe.

(2) Review of sanctions

The provisions of sections 78s(d)(2) and 78s(e)(1) of this title shall govern the review by the Commission of final disciplinary sanctions imposed by the Board (including sanctions imposed under section 7215(b)(3) of this title for noncooperation in an investigation of the Board), as fully as if the Board were a self-regulatory organization and the Commission were the appropriate regulatory agency for such organization for purposes of those sections 78s(d)(2) and 78s(e)(1) of this title, except that,for purposes of this paragraph—

(A) section 7215(e) of this title (rather than that section 78s(d)(2) of this title) shall govern the extent to which application for, or institution by the Commission on its own motion of, review of any disciplinary action of the Board operates as a stay of such action;

(B) references in that section 78s(e)(1) of this title to "members" of such an organization shall be deemed to be references to registered public accounting firms;

(C) the phrase "consistent with the purposes of this title" in that section 78s(e)(1) of this title shall be deemed to read "consistent with the purposes of this title and title I of the Sarbanes–Oxley Act of 2002";

(D) references to rules of the Municipal Securities Rulemaking Board in that section 78s(e)(1) of this title shall not apply; and

(E) the reference to section 78s(e)(2) of this title shall refer instead to section 7217(c)(3) of this title.

(3) Commission modification authority

The Commission may enhance, modify, cancel, reduce, or require the remission of a sanction imposed by the Board upon a registered public accounting firm or associated person thereof, if the Commission, having due regard for the public interest and the protection of investors, finds, after a proceeding in accordance with this subsection, that the sanction—

(A) is not necessary or appropriate in furtherance of this Act or the securities laws; or

(B) is excessive, oppressive, inadequate, or otherwise not appropriate to the finding or the basis on which the sanction was imposed.

(d) Censure of the Board; other sanctions

(1) Rescission of Board authority

The Commission, by rule, consistent with the public interest, the protection of investors, and the other purposes of this Act and the securities laws, may relieve the Board of any responsibility to enforce compliance with any provision of this Act, the securities laws, the rules of the Board, or professional standards.

(2) Censure of the Board; limitations

The Commission may, by order, as it determines necessary or appropriate in the public interest, for the protection of investors, or otherwise in furtherance of the purposes of this Act or the securities laws, censure or impose limitations upon the activities, functions, and operations of the Board, if the Commission finds, on the record, after notice and opportunity for a hearing, that the Board—

(A) has violated or is unable to comply with any provision of this Act, the rules of the Board, or the securities laws; or

(B) without reasonable justification or excuse, has failed to enforce compliance with any such provision or rule, or any professional standard by a registered public accounting firm or an associated person thereof.

(3) Censure of Board members; removal from office

The Commission may, as necessary or appropriate in the public interest, for the protection of investors, or otherwise in furtherance of the purposes of this Act or the securities laws, remove from office or censure any member of the Board, if the Commission finds, on the record, after notice and opportunity for a hearing, that such member—

(A) has willfully violated any provision of this Act, the rules of the Board, or the securities laws;

(B) has willfully abused the authority of that member; or

(C) without reasonable justification or excuse, has failed to enforce compliance with any such provision or rule, or any professional standard by any registered public accounting firm or any associated person thereof.

§ 7218. Accounting Standards

(a) Omitted

(b) Commission authority

The Commission shall promulgate such rules and regulations to carry out section 77s(b) of this title, as added by this section, as it deems necessary or appropriate in the public interest or for the protection of investors.

(c) No effect on Commission powers

Nothing in this Act, including this section and the amendment made by this section, shall be construed to impair or limit the authority of the Commission to establish accounting principles or standards for purposes of enforcement of the securities laws.

(d) Study and report on adopting principles-based accounting

(1) Study

(A) In general

The Commission shall conduct a study on the adoption by the United States financial reporting system of a principles-based accounting system.

(B) Study topics

The study required by subparagraph (A) shall include an examination of—

(i) the extent to which principles-based accounting and financial reporting exists in the United States;

(ii) the length of time required for change from a rules-based to a principles-based financial reporting system;

(iii) the feasibility of and proposed methods by which a principles-based system may be implemented; and

(iv) a thorough economic analysis of the implementation of a principles-based system.

(2) Report

Not later than 1 year after July 30, 2002, the Commission shall submit a report on the results of the study required by paragraph (1) to the Committee on Banking, Housing, and Urban Affairs of the Senate and the Committee on Financial Services of the House of Representatives.

§ 7219. Funding

(a) In general

The Board, and the standard setting body designated pursuant to section 77s(b) of this title, as amended by section 7218 of this title, shall be funded as provided in this section.

(b) Annual budgets

The Board and the standard setting body referred to in subsection (a) of this section shall each establish a budget for each fiscal year, which shall be reviewed and approved according to their respective internal procedures not less than 1 month prior to the commencement of the fiscal year to which the budget pertains (or at the beginning of the Board's first fiscal year, which may be a short fiscal year). The budget of the Board shall be subject to approval by the Commission. The budget for the first fiscal year of the Board shall be prepared and approved promptly following the appointment of the initial five Board members, to permit action by the Board of the organizational tasks contemplated by section 7211(d) of this title.

(c) Sources and uses of funds

(1) Recoverable budget expenses

The budget of the Board (reduced by any registration or annual fees received under section 7212(e) of this title for the year preceding the year for which the budget is being computed), and all of the budget of the standard setting body referred to in subsection (a) of this section, for each fiscal year of each of those 2 entities, shall be payable from annual accounting support fees, in accordance with subsections (d) and (e) of this section. Accounting support fees and other receipts of the Board and of such standard-setting body shall not be considered public monies of the United States.

(2) Funds generated from the collection of monetary penalties

Subject to the availability in advance in an appropriations Act, and notwithstanding subsection (i) of this section, all funds collected by the Board as a result of the assessment of monetary penalties shall be used to fund a merit scholarship program for undergraduate and graduate students enrolled in accredited degree programs, which program is to be administered by the Board or by an entity or agent identified by the Board.

(d) Annual accounting support fee for the Board

(1) Establishment of fee

The Board shall establish, with the approval of the Commission, a reasonable annual accounting support fee (or a formula for the computation thereof), as may be necessary or appropriate to establish and maintain the Board. Such fee may also cover costs incurred in the Board's first fiscal year (which may be a short fiscal year), or may be levied separately with respect to such short fiscal year.

(2) Assessments

The rules of the Board under paragraph (1) shall provide for the equitable allocation, assessment, and collection by the Board (or an agent appointed by the Board) of the fee established under paragraph (1), among issuers, in accordance with subsection (g) of this section, allowing for differentiation among classes of issuers, as appropriate.

(e) Annual accounting support fee for standard setting body

The annual accounting support fee for the standard setting body referred to in subsection (a) of this section—

(1) shall be allocated in accordance with subsection (g) of this section, and assessed and collected against each issuer, on behalf of the standard setting body, by 1 or more appropriate designated collection agents, as may be necessary or appropriate to pay for the budget and provide for the expenses of that standard setting body, and to provide for an independent, stable source of funding for such body, subject to review by the Commission; and

(2) may differentiate among different classes of issuers.

(f) Limitation on fee

The amount of fees collected under this section for a fiscal year on behalf of the Board or the standards setting body, as the case may be, shall not exceed the recoverable budget expenses of the Board or body, respectively (which may include operating, capital, and accrued items), referred to in subsection (c)(1) of this section.

(g) Allocation of accounting support fees among issuers

Any amount due from issuers (or a particular class of issuers) under this section to fund the budget of the Board or the standard setting body referred to in subsection (a) of this section shall be allocated among and payable to each issuer (or each issuer in a particular class, as applicable) in an amount equal to the total of such amount, multiplied by a fraction—

(1) the numerator of which is the average monthly equity market capitalization of the issuer for the 12–month period immediately preceding the beginning of the fiscal year to which such budget relates; and

(2) the denominator of which is the average monthly equity market capitalization of all such issuers for such 12–month period.

(h) Omitted

(i) Rule of construction

Nothing in this section shall be construed to render either the Board, the standard setting body referred to in subsection (a) of this section, or both, subject to procedures in Congress to authorize or appropriate public funds, or to prevent such organization from utilizing additional sources of revenue for its activities, such as earnings from publication sales, provided that each additional source of revenue shall not jeopardize, in the judgment of the Commission, the actual and perceived independence of such organization.

(j) Start-up expenses of the Board

From the unexpended balances of the appropriations to the Commission for fiscal year 2003, the Secretary of the Treasury is authorized to advance to the Board not to exceed the amount necessary to cover the expenses of the Board during its first fiscal year (which may be a short fiscal year).

SUBCHAPTER II—AUDITOR INDEPENDENCE

§ 7231. Exemption Authority

The Board may, on a case by case basis, exempt any person, issuer, public accounting firm, or transaction from the prohibition on the provision services under section 78j–1(g) of this title, to the extent that such exemption is necessary or appropriate in the public interest and is consistent with the protection of investors, and subject to review by the Commission in the same manner as for rules of the Board under section 7217 of this title.

§ 7232. Study of Mandatory Rotation of Registered Public Accounting Firms

(a) Study and review required

The Comptroller General of the United States shall conduct a study and review of the potential effects of requiring the mandatory rotation of registered public accounting firms.

(b) Report required

Not later than 1 year after July 30, 2002, the Comptroller General shall submit a report to the Committee on Banking, Housing, and Urban Affairs of the Senate and the Committee on Financial Services of the House of Representatives on the results of the study and review required by this section.

(c) Definition

For purposes of this section, the term ''mandatory rotation'' refers to the imposition of a limit on the period of years in which a particular registered public accounting firm may be the auditor of record for a particular issuer.

§ 7233. Commission Authority

(a) Commission regulations

Not later than 180 days after July 30, 2002, the Commission shall issue final regulations to carry out each of subsections (g) through (*l*) of section 78j–1 of this title.

(b) Auditor independence

It shall be unlawful for any registered public accounting firm (or an associated person thereof, as applicable) to prepare or issue any audit report with respect to any issuer, if the firm or associated person engages in any activity with respect to that issuer prohibited by any of subsections (g) through (*l*) of section 78j–1 of this title, or any rule or regulation of the Commission or of the Board issued thereunder.

§ 7234. Considerations by Appropriate State Regulatory Authorities

In supervising nonregistered public accounting firms and their associated persons, appropriate State regulatory authorities should make an independent determination of the proper standards applicable, particularly taking into consideration the size and nature of the business of the accounting firms they supervise and the size and nature of the business of the clients of those firms. The standards applied by the Board under this Act should not be presumed to be applicable for purposes of this section for small and medium sized nonregistered public accounting firms.

SUBCHAPTER III—CORPORATE RESPONSIBILITY

§ 7241. Corporate Responsibility for Financial Reports

(a) Regulations required

The Commission shall, by rule, require, for each company filing periodic reports under section 13(a) or 15(d) of the Securities Exchange Act of 1934 (15 U.S.C. 78m, 78o(d)), that the principal executive officer or officers and the principal financial officer or officers, or persons performing similar functions, certify in each annual or quarterly report filed or submitted under either such section of such Act that—

(1) the signing officer has reviewed the report;

(2) based on the officer's knowledge, the report does not contain any untrue statement of a material fact or omit to state a material fact necessary in order to make the statements made, in light of the circumstances under which such statements were made, not misleading;

(3) based on such officer's knowledge, the financial statements, and other financial in-

formation included in the report, fairly present in all material respects the financial condition and results of operations of the issuer as of, and for, the periods presented in the report;

(4) the signing officers—

(A) are responsible for establishing and maintaining internal controls;

(B) have designed such internal controls to ensure that material information relating to the issuer and its consolidated subsidiaries is made known to such officers by others within those entities, particularly during the period in which the periodic reports are being prepared;

(C) have evaluated the effectiveness of the issuer's internal controls as of a date within 90 days prior to the report; and

(D) have presented in the report their conclusions about the effectiveness of their internal controls based on their evaluation as of that date;

(5) the signing officers have disclosed to the issuer's auditors and the audit committee of the board of directors (or persons fulfilling the equivalent function)—

(A) all significant deficiencies in the design or operation of internal controls which could adversely affect the issuer's ability to record, process, summarize, and report financial data and have identified for the issuer's auditors any material weaknesses in internal controls; and

(B) any fraud, whether or not material, that involves management or other employees who have a significant role in the issuer's internal controls; and

(6) the signing officers have indicated in the report whether or not there were significant changes in internal controls or in other factors that could significantly affect internal controls subsequent to the date of their evaluation, including any corrective actions with regard to significant deficiencies and material weaknesses.

(b) Foreign reincorporations have no effect

Nothing in this section shall be interpreted or applied in any way to allow any issuer to lessen the legal force of the statement required under this section 302, by an issuer having reincorporated or having engaged in any other transaction that resulted in the transfer of the corporate domicile or offices of the issuer from inside the United States to outside of the United States.

(c) Deadline

The rules required by subsection (a) of this section shall be effective not later than 30 days after July 30, 2002.

§ 7242. Improper Influence on Conduct of Audits

(a) Rules to prohibit

It shall be unlawful, in contravention of such rules or regulations as the Commission shall prescribe as necessary and appropriate in the public interest or for the protection of investors, for any officer or director of an issuer, or any other person acting under the direction thereof, to take any action to fraudulently influence, coerce, manipulate, or mislead any independent public or certified accountant engaged in the performance of an audit of the financial statements of that issuer for the purpose of rendering such financial statements materially misleading.

(b) Enforcement

In any civil proceeding, the Commission shall have exclusive authority to enforce this section and any rule or regulation issued under this section.

(c) No preemption of other law

The provisions of subsection (a) of this section shall be in addition to, and shall not supersede or preempt, any other provision of law or any rule or regulation issued thereunder.

(d) Deadline for rulemaking

The Commission shall—

(1) propose the rules or regulations required by this section, not later than 90 days after July 30, 2002; and

(2) issue final rules or regulations required by this section, not later than 270 days after July 30, 2002.

§ 7243. Forfeiture of Certain Bonuses and Profits

(a) Additional compensation prior to noncompliance with Commission financial reporting requirements

If an issuer is required to prepare an accounting restatement due to the material noncompliance of the issuer, as a result of misconduct, with any financial reporting requirement under the securities laws, the chief executive officer and chief financial officer of the issuer shall reimburse the issuer for—

(1) any bonus or other incentive-based or equity-based compensation received by that person from the issuer during the 12–month period following the first public issuance or filing with the Commission (whichever first occurs) of the financial document embodying such financial reporting requirement; and

(2) any profits realized from the sale of securities of the issuer during that 12–month period.

(b) Commission exemption authority

The Commission may exempt any person from the application of subsection (a) of this section, as it deems necessary and appropriate.

§ 7244. Insider Trades During Pension Fund Blackout Periods

(a) Prohibition of insider trading during pension fund blackout periods

(1) In general

Except to the extent otherwise provided by rule of the Commission pursuant to paragraph (3), it shall be unlawful for any director or executive officer of an issuer of any equity security (other than an exempted security), directly or indirectly, to purchase, sell, or otherwise acquire or transfer any equity security of the issuer (other than an exempted security) during any blackout period with respect to such equity security if such director or officer acquires such equity security in connection with his or her service or employment as a director or executive officer.

(2) Remedy

(A) In general

Any profit realized by a director or executive officer referred to in paragraph (1) from any purchase, sale, or other acquisition or transfer in violation of this subsection shall inure to and be recoverable by the issuer, irrespective of any intention on the part of such director or executive officer in entering into the transaction.

(B) Actions to recover profits

An action to recover profits in accordance with this subsection may be instituted at law or in equity in any court of competent jurisdiction by the issuer, or by the owner of any security of the issuer in the name and in behalf of the issuer if the issuer fails or refuses to bring such action within 60 days after the date of request, or fails diligently to prosecute the action thereafter, except that no such suit shall be brought more than 2 years after the date on which such profit was realized.

(3) Rulemaking authorized

The Commission shall, in consultation with the Secretary of Labor, issue rules to clarify the application of this subsection and to prevent evasion thereof. Such rules shall provide for the application of the requirements of paragraph (1) with respect to entities treated as a single employer with respect to an issuer under section 414(b), (c), (m), or (*o*) of Title 26 to the extent necessary to clarify the application of such requirements and to prevent evasion thereof. Such rules may also provide for appropriate exceptions from the requirements of this subsection, including exceptions for purchases pursuant to an automatic dividend reinvestment program or purchases or sales made pursuant to an advance election.

(4) Blackout period

For purposes of this subsection, the term "blackout period", with respect to the equity securities of any issuer—

(A) means any period of more than 3 consecutive business days during which the ability of not fewer than 50 percent of the participants or beneficiaries under all individual account plans maintained by the issuer to purchase, sell, or otherwise acquire or transfer an interest in any equity of such issuer held in such an individual account plan is temporarily suspended by the issuer or by a fiduciary of the plan; and

(B) does not include, under regulations which shall be prescribed by the Commission—

(i) a regularly scheduled period in which the participants and beneficiaries may not purchase, sell, or otherwise acquire or transfer an interest in any equity of such issuer, if such period is—

(I) incorporated into the individual account plan; and

(II) timely disclosed to employees before becoming participants under the individual account plan or as a subsequent amendment to the plan; or

(ii) any suspension described in subparagraph (A) that is imposed solely in connection with persons becoming participants or beneficiaries, or ceasing to be participants or beneficiaries, in an individual account plan by reason of a corporate merger, acquisition, divestiture, or similar transaction involving the plan or plan sponsor.

(5) Individual account plan

For purposes of this subsection, the term "individual account plan" has the meaning provided in section 1002(34) of Title 29, except that such term shall not include a one-participant retirement plan (within the meaning of section 1021(i)(8)(B) of Title 29).

(6) Notice to directors, executive officers, and the Commission

In any case in which a director or executive officer is subject to the requirements of this subsection in connection with a blackout period (as defined in paragraph (4)) with respect to any equity securities, the issuer of such equity securities shall timely notify such director or officer and the Securities and Exchange Commission of such blackout period.

(b) Notice requirements to participants and beneficiaries under ERISA

(1) Omitted

(2) Issuance of initial guidance and model notice

The Secretary of Labor shall issue initial guidance and a model notice pursuant to section 1021(i)(6) of Title 29 not later than January 1, 2003. Not later than 75 days after July 30, 2002, the Secretary shall promulgate interim final rules necessary to carry out the amendments made by this subsection.

(3) Plan amendments

If any amendment made by this subsection requires an amendment to any plan, such plan amendment shall not be required to be made before the first plan year beginning on or after July 30, 2002, if—

(A) during the period after such amendment made by this subsection takes effect and before such first plan year, the plan is operated in good faith compliance with the requirements of such amendment made by this subsection, and

(B) such plan amendment applies retroactively to the period after such amendment made by this subsection takes effect and before such first plan year.

(c) Effective date

The provisions of this section (including the amendments made thereby) shall take effect

180 days after July 30, 2002. Good faith compliance with the requirements of such provisions in advance of the issuance of applicable regulations thereunder shall be treated as compliance with such provisions.

§ 7245. Rules of Professional Responsibility for Attorneys

Not later than 180 days after July 30, 2002, the Commission shall issue rules, in the public interest and for the protection of investors, setting forth minimum standards of professional conduct for attorneys appearing and practicing before the Commission in any way in the representation of issuers, including a rule—

(1) requiring an attorney to report evidence of a material violation of securities law or breach of fiduciary duty or similar violation by the company or any agent thereof, to the chief legal counsel or the chief executive officer of the company (or the equivalent thereof); and

(2) if the counsel or officer does not appropriately respond to the evidence (adopting, as necessary, appropriate remedial measures or sanctions with respect to the violation), requiring the attorney to report the evidence to the audit committee of the board of directors of the issuer or to another committee of the board of directors comprised solely of directors not employed directly or indirectly by the issuer, or to the board of directors.

§ 7246. Fair Funds for Investors

(a) Civil penalties added to disgorgement funds for the relief of victims

If in any judicial or administrative action brought by the Commission under the securities laws (as such term is defined in section 78c(a)(47) of this title) the Commission obtains an order requiring disgorgement against any person for a violation of such laws or the rules or regulations thereunder, or such person agrees in settlement of any such action to such disgorgement, and the Commission also obtains pursuant to such laws a civil penalty against such person, the amount of such civil penalty shall, on the motion or at the direction of the Commission, be added to and become part of the disgorgement fund for the benefit of the victims of such violation.

(b) Acceptance of additional donations

The Commission is authorized to accept, hold, administer, and utilize gifts, bequests and devises of property, both real and personal, to the United States for a disgorgement fund described in subsection (a) of this section. Such gifts, bequests, and devises of money and proceeds from sales of other property received as gifts, bequests, or devises shall be deposited in the disgorgement fund and shall be available for allocation in accordance with subsection (a) of this section.

(c) Study required

(1) Subject of study

The Commission shall review and analyze—

(A) enforcement actions by the Commission over the five years preceding July 30, 2002 that have included proceedings to obtain civil penalties or disgorgements to identify areas where such proceedings may be utilized to efficiently, effectively, and fairly provide restitution for injured investors; and

(B) other methods to more efficiently, effectively, and fairly provide restitution to injured investors, including methods to improve the collection rates for civil penalties and disgorgements.

(2) Report required

The Commission shall report its findings to the Committee on Financial Services of the House of Representatives and the Committee on Banking, Housing, and Urban Affairs of the Senate within 180 days after July 30, 2002, and shall use such findings to revise its rules and regulations as necessary. The report shall include a discussion of regulatory or legislative actions that are recommended or that may be necessary to address concerns identified in the study.

(d) Omitted

(e) Definition

As used in this section, the term "disgorgement fund" means a fund established in any administrative or judicial proceeding described in subsection (a) of this section.

SUBCHAPTER IV—ENHANCED FINANCIAL DISCLOSURES

§ 7261. Disclosures in Periodic Reports

(a) Omitted

(b) Commission rules on pro forma figures

Not later than 180 days after July 30, 2002, the Commission shall issue final rules providing that pro forma financial information included in any periodic or other report filed with the Commission pursuant to the securities laws, or in any public disclosure or press or other release, shall be presented in a manner that—

(1) does not contain an untrue statement of a material fact or omit to state a material fact necessary in order to make the pro forma financial information, in light of the circumstances under which it is presented, not misleading; and

(2) reconciles it with the financial condition and results of operations of the issuer under generally accepted accounting principles.

(c) Study and report on special purpose entities

(1) Study required

The Commission shall, not later than 1 year after the effective date of adoption of off-balance sheet disclosure rules required by section 78m(j) of this title, complete a study of filings by issuers and their disclosures to determine—

(A) the extent of off-balance sheet transactions, including assets, liabilities, leases, losses, and the use of special purpose entities; and

(B) whether generally accepted accounting rules result in financial statements of issuers reflecting the economics of such off-balance sheet transactions to investors in a transparent fashion.

(2) Report and recommendations

Not later than 6 months after the date of completion of the study required by paragraph (1), the Commission shall submit a report to the President, the Committee on Banking, Housing, and Urban Affairs of the Senate, and the Committee on Financial Services of the House of Representatives, setting forth—

(A) the amount or an estimate of the amount of off-balance sheet transactions, including assets, liabilities, leases, and losses of, and the use of special purpose entities by, issuers filing periodic reports pursuant to section 78m or 78*o* of this title;

(B) the extent to which special purpose entities are used to facilitate off-balance sheet transactions;

(C) whether generally accepted accounting principles or the rules of the Commission result in financial statements of issuers reflecting the economics of such transactions to investors in a transparent fashion;

(D) whether generally accepted accounting principles specifically result in the consolidation of special purpose entities sponsored by an issuer in cases in which the issuer has the majority of the risks and rewards of the special purpose entity; and

(E) any recommendations of the Commission for improving the transparency and quality of reporting off-balance sheet transactions in the financial statements and disclosures required to be filed by an issuer with the Commission.

§ 7262. Management Assessment of Internal Controls

(a) Rules required

The Commission shall prescribe rules requiring each annual report required by section 78m(a) or 78*o*(d) of this title to contain an internal control report, which shall—

(1) state the responsibility of management for establishing and maintaining an adequate internal control structure and procedures for financial reporting; and

(2) contain an assessment, as of the end of the most recent fiscal year of the issuer, of the effectiveness of the internal control structure and procedures of the issuer for financial reporting.

(b) Internal control evaluation and reporting

With respect to the internal control assessment required by subsection (a) of this section, each registered public accounting firm that prepares or issues the audit report for the issuer shall attest to, and report on, the assessment made by the management of the issuer. An attestation made under this subsection shall be made in accordance with standards for attestation engagements issued or adopted by the Board. Any such attestation shall not be the subject of a separate engagement.

§ 7263. Exemption

Nothing in section 401, 402, or 404, the amendments made by those sections, or the rules of the Commission under those sections shall apply to any investment company registered under section 80a–8 of this title.

§ 7264. Code of Ethics for Senior Financial Officers

(a) Code of ethics disclosure

The Commission shall issue rules to require each issuer, together with periodic reports required pursuant to section 78m(a) or 78*o*(d) of this title, to disclose whether or not, and if not, the reason therefor, such issuer has adopted a code of ethics for senior financial officers, applicable to its principal financial officer and comptroller or principal accounting officer, or persons performing similar functions.

(b) Changes in codes of ethics

The Commission shall revise its regulations concerning matters requiring prompt disclosure on Form 8–K (or any successor thereto) to require the immediate disclosure, by means of the filing of such form, dissemination by the Internet or by other electronic means, by any issuer of any change in or waiver of the code of ethics for senior financial officers.

(c) Definition

In this section, the term "code of ethics" means such standards as are reasonably necessary to promote—

(1) honest and ethical conduct, including the ethical handling of actual or apparent conflicts of interest between personal and professional relationships;

(2) full, fair, accurate, timely, and understandable disclosure in the periodic reports required to be filed by the issuer; and

(3) compliance with applicable governmental rules and regulations.

(d) Deadline for rulemaking

The Commission shall—

(1) propose rules to implement this section, not later than 90 days after July 30, 2002; and

(2) issue final rules to implement this section, not later than 180 days after July 30, 2002.

§ 7265. Disclosure of Audit Committee Financial Expert

(a) Rules defining "financial expert"

The Commission shall issue rules, as necessary or appropriate in the public interest and consistent with the protection of investors, to require each issuer, together with periodic reports required pursuant to sections 78m(a) and 78*o*(d) of this title, to disclose whether or not, and if not, the reasons therefor, the audit committee of that issuer is comprised of at least 1 member who is a financial expert, as such term is defined by the Commission.

(b) Considerations

In defining the term "financial expert" for purposes of subsection (a) of this section, the Commission shall consider whether a person has, through education and experience as a public accountant or auditor or a principal financial officer, comptroller, or principal accounting officer of an issuer, or from a position involving the performance of similar functions—

(1) an understanding of generally accepted accounting principles and financial statements;

(2) experience in—

(A) the preparation or auditing of financial statements of generally comparable issuers; and

(B) the application of such principles in connection with the accounting for estimates, accruals, and reserves;

(3) experience with internal accounting controls; and

(4) an understanding of audit committee functions.

(c) Deadline for rulemaking

The Commission shall—

(1) propose rules to implement this section, not later than 90 days after July 30, 2002; and

(2) issue final rules to implement this section, not later than 180 days after July 30, 2002.

§ 7266. Enhanced Review of Periodic Disclosures by Issuers

(a) Regular and systematic review

The Commission shall review disclosures made by issuers reporting under section 78m(a) of this title (including reports filed on Form 10–K), and which have a class of securities listed on a national securities exchange or traded on an automated quotation facility of a national securities association, on a regular and systematic basis for the protection of investors. Such review shall include a review of an issuer's financial statement.

(b) Review criteria

For purposes of scheduling the reviews required by subsection (a) of this section, the Commission shall consider, among other factors—

(1) issuers that have issued material restatements of financial results;

(2) issuers that experience significant volatility in their stock price as compared to other issuers;

(3) issuers with the largest market capitalization;

(4) emerging companies with disparities in price to earning ratios;

(5) issuers whose operations significantly affect any material sector of the economy; and

(6) any other factors that the Commission may consider relevant.

(c) Minimum review period

In no event shall an issuer required to file reports under section 78m(a) or 78*o*(d) of this title be reviewed under this section less frequently than once every 3 years.

STATUTE OF LIMITATIONS FOR SECURITIES FRAUD

(28 U.S.C. § 1658(b))

(b) Notwithstanding subsection (a), a private right of action that involves a claim of fraud, deceit, manipulation, or contrivance in contravention of a regulatory requirement concerning the securities laws, as defined in section 3(a)(47) of the Securities Exchange Act of 1934 (15 U.S.C. 78c(a)(47)), may be brought not later than the earlier of—

(1) 2 years after the discovery of the facts constituting the violation; or

(2) 5 years after such violation.

II. RELATED FEDERAL LAWS

COMMODITY EXCHANGE ACT

(7 U.S.C. § 1 et seq.)

(Selected Provisions)

Short Title

Sec. 1. This Act may be cited as the "Commodity Exchange Act."

Definitions

Sec. 1a. DEFINITIONS. As used in this Act:

(1) ALTERNATIVE TRADING SYSTEM.—The term "alternative trading system" means an organization, association, or group of persons that—

(A) is registered as a broker or dealer pursuant to section 15(b) of the Securities Exchange Act of 1934 (except paragraph (11) thereof);

(B) performs the functions commonly performed by an exchange (as defined in section 3(a)(1) of the Securities Exchange Act of 1934);

(C) does not—

(i) set rules governing the conduct of subscribers other than the conduct of such subscribers' trading on the alternative trading system; or

(ii) discipline subscribers other than by exclusion from trading; and

(D) is exempt from the definition of the term "exchange" under such section 3(a)(1) by rule or regulation of the Securities and Exchange Commission on terms that require compliance with regulations of its trading functions.

(2) BOARD OF TRADE. The term "board of trade" means any organized exchange or other trading facility.

(3) COMMISSION. The term "Commission" means the Commodity Futures Trading Commission established under section 2(a)(2).

(4) COMMODITY. The term "commodity" means wheat, cotton, rice, corn, oats, barley, rye, flaxseed, grain sorghums, mill feeds, butter, eggs, Solanum tuberosum (Irish potatoes), wool, wool tops, fats and oils (including lard, tallow, cottonseed oil, peanut oil, soybean oil, and all other fats and oils), cottonseed meal, cottonseed, peanuts, soybeans, soybean meal, livestock, livestock products, and frozen concentrated orange juice, and all other goods and articles, except onions as provided in Public Law 85–839 (7 U.S.C. 13–1), and all services, rights, and interests in which contracts for future delivery are presently or in the future dealt in.

(5) COMMODITY POOL OPERATOR. The term "commodity pool operator" means any person engaged in a business that is of the nature of an investment trust, syndicate, or similar form of enterprise, and who, in connection therewith, solicits, accepts, or receives from others, funds, securities, or property, either directly or through capital contributions, the sale of stock or other forms of securities, or otherwise, for the purpose of trading in any commodity for future delivery on or subject to the rules of any contract market or derivatives transaction execution facility, except that the term does not include such persons not within the intent of the definition of the term as the Commission may specify by rule, regulation, or order.

(6) COMMODITY TRADING ADVISOR.

(A) IN GENERAL. Except as otherwise provided in this paragraph, the term "commodity trading advisor" means any person who—

(i) for compensation or profit, engages in the business of advising others, either directly or through publications, writings, or electronic media, as to the value of or the advisability of trading in—

(I) any contract of sale of a commodity for future delivery made or to be made on or subject to the rules of a contract market or derivatives transaction execution facility;

(II) any commodity option authorized under section 4c; or

(III) any leverage transaction authorized under section 19; or

(ii) for compensation or profit, and as part of a regular business, issues or promulgates analyses or reports concerning any of the activities referred to in clause (i).

(B) EXCLUSIONS. Subject to subparagraph (C), the term "commodity trading advisor" does not include—

(i) any bank or trust company or any person acting as an employee thereof;

(ii) any news reporter, news columnist, or news editor of the print or electronic media, or any lawyer, accountant, or teacher;

(iii) any floor broker or futures commission merchant;

(iv) the publisher or producer of any print or electronic data of general and regular dissemination, including its employees;

(v) the fiduciary of any defined benefit plan that is subject to the Employee Retirement Income Security Act of 1974 (29 U.S.C. 1001 et seq.);

(vi) any contract market; and

(vii) such other persons not within the intent of this paragraph as the Commission may specify by rule, regulation, or order.

(C) INCIDENTAL SERVICES. Subparagraph (B) shall apply only if the furnishing of such services by persons referred to in subparagraph (B) is solely incidental to the conduct of their business or profession.

(D) ADVISORS. The Commission, by rule or regulation, may include within the term "commodity trading advisor", any person advising as to the value of commodities or issuing reports or analyses concerning commodities if the Commission determines that the rule or regulation will effectuate the purposes of this paragraph.

(7) CONTRACT OF SALE. The term "contract of sale" includes sales, agreements of sale, and agreements to sell.

(8) COOPERATIVE ASSOCIATION OF PRODUCERS. The term "cooperative association of producers" means any cooperative association, corporate, or otherwise, not less than 75 percent in good faith owned or controlled, directly or indirectly, by producers of agricultural products and otherwise complying with the Act of February 18, 1922 (42 Stat. 388, chapter 57; 7 U.S.C. 291 and 292), including any organization acting for a group of such associations and owned or controlled by such associations, except that business done for or with the United States, or any agency thereof, shall not be considered either member or nonmember business in determining the compliance of any such association with this Act.

(9) DERIVATIVES CLEARING ORGANIZATION.—

(A) IN GENERAL.—The term "derivatives clearing organization" means a clearinghouse, clearing association, clearing corporation, or similar entity, facility, system, or organization that, with respect to an agreement, contract, or transaction—

(i) enables each party to the agreement, contract, or transaction to substitute, through novation or otherwise, the credit of the derivatives clearing organization for the credit of the parties;

(ii) arranges or provides, on a multilateral basis, for the settlement or netting of obligations resulting from such agreements, contracts, or transactions executed by participants in the derivatives clearing organization; or

(iii) otherwise provides clearing services or arrangements that mutualize or transfer among participants in the derivatives clearing organization the credit risk arising from such agreements, contracts, or transactions executed by the participants.

(B) EXCLUSIONS.—The term "derivatives clearing organization" does not include an entity, facility, system, or organization solely because it arranges or provides for—

(i) settlement, netting, or novation of obligations resulting from agreements, contracts, or transactions, on a bilateral basis and without a central counterparty;

(ii) settlement or netting of cash payments through an interbank payment system; or

(iii) settlement, netting, or novation of obligations resulting from a sale of a commodity in a transaction in the spot market for the commodity.

(10) ELECTRONIC TRADING FACILITY.—The term "electronic trading facility" means a trading facility that—

(A) operates by means of an electronic or telecommunications network; and

(B) maintains an automated audit trail of bids, offers, and the matching of orders or the execution of transactions on the facility.

(11) ELIGIBLE COMMERCIAL ENTITY.—The term "eligible commercial entity" means, with respect to an agreement, contract or transaction in a commodity—

(A) an eligible contract participant described in clause (i), (ii), (v), (vii), (viii), or (ix) of paragraph (12)(A) that, in connection with its business—

(i) has a demonstrable ability, directly or through separate contractual arrangements, to make or take delivery of the underlying commodity;

(ii) incurs risks, in addition to price risk, related to the commodity; or

(iii) is a dealer that regularly provides risk management or hedging services to, or engages in market-making activities with, the foregoing entities involving transactions to purchase or sell the commodity or derivative agreements, contracts, or transactions in the commodity;

(B) an eligible contract participant, other than a natural person or an instrumentality, department, or agency of a State or local governmental entity, that—

(i) regularly enters into transactions to purchase or sell the commodity or derivative agreements, contracts, or transactions in the commodity; and

(ii) either—

(I) in the case of a collective investment vehicle whose participants include persons other than—

(aa) qualified eligible persons, as defined in Commission rule 4.7(a) (17 CFR 4.7(a));

(bb) accredited investors, as defined in Regulation D of the Securities and Exchange Commission under the Securities Act of 1933 (17 CFR 230.501(a)), with total assets of $2,000,000; or

(cc) qualified purchasers, as defined in section 2(a)(51)(A) of the Investment Company Act of 1940;

in each case as in effect on the date of the enactment of the Commodity Futures Modernization Act of 2000, has, or is one of a group of vehicles under common control or management having in the aggregate, $1,000,000,000 in total assets; or

(II) in the case of other persons, has, or is one of a group of persons under common control or management having in the aggregate, $100,000,000 in total assets; or

(C) such other persons as the Commission shall determine appropriate and shall designate by rule, regulation, or order.

(12) ELIGIBLE CONTRACT PARTICIPANT.—The term "eligible contract participant" means—

(A) acting for its own account—

(i) a financial institution;

(ii) an insurance company that is regulated by a State, or that is regulated by a foreign government and is subject to comparable regulation as determined by the Commission, including a regulated subsidiary or affiliate of such an insurance company;

(iii) an investment company subject to regulation under the Investment Company Act of 1940 (15 U.S.C. 80a–1 et seq.) or a foreign person performing a similar role or function subject as such to foreign regulation (regardless of whether each investor in the investment company or the foreign person is itself an eligible contract participant);

(iv) a commodity pool that—

(I) has total assets exceeding $5,000,000; and

(II) is formed and operated by a person subject to regulation under this Act or a foreign person performing a similar role or function subject as such to foreign regulation (regardless of whether each investor in the commodity pool or the foreign person is itself an eligible contract participant);

(v) a corporation, partnership, proprietorship, organization, trust, or other entity—

(I) that has total assets exceeding $10,000,000;

(II) the obligations of which under an agreement, contract, or transaction are guaranteed or otherwise supported by a letter of credit or keepwell, support, or other agreement by an entity described in subclause (I), in clause (i), (ii), (iii), (iv), or (vii), or in subparagraph (C); or

(III) that—

(aa) has a net worth exceeding $1,000,000; and

(bb) enters into an agreement, contract, or transaction in connection with the conduct of the entity's business or to manage the risk associated with an asset or liability owned or incurred or reasonably likely to be owned or incurred by the entity in the conduct of the entity's business;

(vi) an employee benefit plan subject to the Employee Retirement Income Security Act of 1974 (29 U.S.C. 1001 et seq.), a governmental employee benefit plan, or a foreign person performing a similar role or function subject as such to foreign regulation—

(I) that has total assets exceeding $5,000,000; or

(II) the investment decisions of which are made by—

(aa) an investment adviser or commodity trading advisor subject to regulation under the Investment Advisers Act of 1940 (15 U.S.C. 80b–1 et seq.) or this Act;

(bb) a foreign person performing a similar role or function subject as such to foreign regulation;

(cc) a financial institution; or

(dd) an insurance company described in clause (ii), or a regulated subsidiary or affiliate of such an insurance company;

(vii)(I) a governmental entity (including the United States, a State, or a foreign government) or political subdivision of a governmental entity;

(II) a multinational or supranational government entity; or

(III) an instrumentality, agency, or department of an entity described in subclause (I) or (II);

except that such term does not include an entity, instrumentality, agency, or department referred to in subclause (I) or (III) of this clause unless (aa) the entity, instrumentality, agency, or department is a person described in clause (i), (ii), or (iii) of section 1a(11)(A); (bb) the entity, instrumentality, agency, or department owns and invests on a discretionary basis $25,000,000 or more in investments; or (cc) the agreement, contract, or transaction is offered by, and entered into with, an entity that is listed in any of subclauses (I) through (VI) of section 2(c)(2)(B)(ii);

(viii)(I) a broker or dealer subject to regulation under the Securities Exchange Act of 1934 (15 U.S.C. 78a et seq.) or a foreign person performing a similar role or function subject as such to foreign regulation, except that, if the broker or dealer or foreign person is a natural person or proprietorship, the broker or dealer or foreign person shall not be considered to be an eligible contract participant unless the broker or dealer or foreign person also meets the requirements of clause (v) or (xi);

(II) an associated person of a registered broker or dealer concerning the financial or securities activities of which the registered person makes and keeps records under section 15C(b) or 17(h) of the Securities Exchange Act of 1934 (15 U.S.C. 78o–5(b), 78q(h));

(III) an investment bank holding company (as defined in section 17(i) of the Securities Exchange Act of 1934 (15 U.S.C. 78q(i)));

(ix) a futures commission merchant subject to regulation under this Act or a foreign person performing a similar role or function subject as such to foreign regulation, except that, if the futures commission merchant or foreign person is a natural person or proprietorship, the futures commission merchant or foreign person shall not be considered to be an eligible contract participant unless the futures commission merchant or foreign person also meets the requirements of clause (v) or (xi);

(x) a floor broker or floor trader subject to regulation under this Act in connection with any transaction that takes place on or through the facilities of a registered entity or an exempt board of trade, or any affiliate thereof, on which such person regularly trades; or

(xi) an individual who has total assets in an amount in excess of—

(I) $10,000,000; or

(II) $5,000,000 and who enters into the agreement, contract, or transaction in order to manage the risk associated with an asset owned or liability incurred, or reasonably likely to be owned or incurred, by the individual;

(B)(i) a person described in clause (i), (ii), (iv), (v), (viii), (ix), or (x) of subparagraph (A) or in subparagraph (C), acting as broker or performing an equivalent agency function on behalf of another person described in subparagraph (A) or (C); or

(ii) an investment adviser subject to regulation under the Investment Advisers Act of 1940, a commodity trading advisor subject to regulation under this Act, a foreign person performing a similar role or function subject as such to foreign regulation, or a person described in clause (i), (ii), (iv), (v), (viii), (ix), or (x) of subparagraph (A) or in subparagraph (C), in any such case acting as investment manager or fiduciary (but excluding a person acting as broker or performing an equivalent agency function) for another person described in subparagraph (A) or (C) and who is authorized by such person to commit such person to the transaction; or

(C) any other person that the Commission determines to be eligible in light of the financial or other qualifications of the person.

(13) EXCLUDED COMMODITY.—The term "excluded commodity" means—

(i) an interest rate, exchange rate, currency, security, security index, credit risk or measure, debt or equity instrument, index or measure of inflation, or other macroeconomic index or measure;

(ii) any other rate, differential, index, or measure of economic or commercial risk, return, or value that is—

(I) not based in substantial part on the value of a narrow group of commodities not described in clause (i); or

(II) based solely on one or more commodities that have no cash market;

(iii) any economic or commercial index based on prices, rates, values, or levels that are not within the control of any party to the relevant contract, agreement, or transaction; or

(iv) an occurrence, extent of an occurrence, or contingency (other than a change in the price, rate, value, or level of a commodity not described in clause (i)) that is—

(I) beyond the control of the parties to the relevant contract, agreement, or transaction; and

(II) associated with a financial, commercial, or economic consequence.

(14) EXEMPT COMMODITY.—The term "exempt commodity" means a commodity that is not an excluded commodity or an agricultural commodity.

(15) FINANCIAL INSTITUTION.—The term "financial institution" means—

(A) a corporation operating under the fifth undesignated paragraph of section 25 of the Federal Reserve Act (12 U.S.C. 603), commonly known as "an agreement corporation";

(B) a corporation organized under section 25A of the Federal Reserve Act (12 U.S.C. 611 et seq.), commonly known as an "Edge Act corporation";

(C) an institution that is regulated by the Farm Credit Administration;

(D) a Federal credit union or State credit union (as defined in section 101 of the Federal Credit Union Act (12 U.S.C. 1752));

(E) a depository institution (as defined in section 3 of the Federal Deposit Insurance Act (12 U.S.C. 1813));

(F) a foreign bank or a branch or agency of a foreign bank (each as defined in section 1(b) of the International Banking Act of 1978 (12 U.S.C. 3101(b)));

(G) any financial holding company (as defined in section 2 of the Bank Holding Company Act of 1956);

(H) a trust company; or

(I) a similarly regulated subsidiary or affiliate of an entity described in any of subparagraphs (A) through (H).

(16) FLOOR BROKER. The term "floor broker" means any person who, in or surrounding any pit, ring, post, or other place provided by a contract market or derivatives transaction execution facility for the meeting of persons similarly engaged, shall purchase or sell for any other person any commodity for future delivery on or subject to the rules of any contract market or derivatives transaction execution facility.

(17) FLOOR TRADER. The term "floor trader" means any person who, in or surrounding any pit, ring, post, or other place provided by a contract market or derivatives transaction execution facility for the meeting of persons similarly engaged, purchases, or sells solely for such person's own account, any commodity for future delivery on or subject to the rules of any contract market or derivatives transaction execution facility.

(18) FOREIGN FUTURES AUTHORITY. The term "foreign futures authority" means any foreign government, or any department, agency, governmental body, or regulatory organization empowered by a foreign government to administer or enforce a law, rule, or regulation as it relates to a futures or options matter, or any department or agency of a political subdivision of a foreign government empowered to administer or enforce a law, rule, or regulation as it relates to a futures or options matter.

(19) FUTURE DELIVERY. The term "future delivery" does not include any sale of any cash commodity for deferred shipment or delivery.

(20) FUTURES COMMISSION MERCHANT. The term "futures commission merchant" means an individual, association, partnership, corporation, or trust that—

(A) is engaged in soliciting or in accepting orders for the purchase or sale of any commodity for future delivery or on subject to the rules of any contract market or derivatives transaction execution facility; and

(B) in or in connection with such solicitation or acceptance of orders, accepts any money, securities, or property (or extends credit in lieu thereof) to margin, guarantee, or secure any trades or contracts that result or may result therefrom.

(21) HYBRID INSTRUMENT. The term "hybrid instrument" means a security having one or more payments indexed to the value, level, or rate of, or provided for the delivery of, one or more commodities.

(22) INTERSTATE COMMERCE. The term "interstate commerce" means commerce—

(A) between any State, territory, or possession, or the District of Columbia, and any place outside thereof; or

(B) between points within the same state, territory, or possession, or the District of Columbia, but through any place outside thereof, or within any territory or possession, or the District of Columbia.

(23) INTRODUCING BROKER. The term "introducing broker" means any person (except an individual who elects to be and is registered as an associated person of a futures commission merchant) engaged in soliciting or in accepting orders for the purchase or sale of any commodity for future delivery on or subject to the rules of any contract market or derivatives transaction execution facility who does not accept any money, securities, or property (or extend credit in lieu thereof) to margin, guarantee, or secure any trades or contracts that result or may result therefrom.

(24) MEMBER OF A CONTRACT MARKET; MEMBER OF A DERIVATIVES TRANSACTION EXECUTION FACILITY.—The term "member" means, with respect to a registered entity or derivatives transaction execution facility, an individual, association, partnership, corporation, or trust—

(A) owning or holding membership in, or admitted to membership representation on, the registered entity or derivatives transaction execution facility; or

(B) having trading privileges on the registered entity or derivatives transaction execution facility.

(25) NARROW-BASED SECURITY INDEX.—

(A) The term "narrow-based security index" means an index—

(i) that has 9 or fewer component securities;

(ii) in which a component security comprises more than 30 percent of the index's weighting;

(iii) in which the five highest weighted component securities in the aggregate comprise more than 60 percent of the index's weighting; or

(iv) in which the lowest weighted component securities comprising, in the aggregate, 25 percent of the index's weighting have an aggregate dollar value of average daily trading volume of less than $50,000,000 (or in the case of an index with 15 or more component securities, $30,000,000), except that if there are two or more securities with equal weighting that could be included in the calculation of the lowest weighted component securities comprising, in the aggregate, 25 percent of the index's weighting, such securities shall be ranked from lowest to highest dollar value of average daily trading volume and shall be included in the calculation based on their ranking starting with the lowest ranked security.

(B) Notwithstanding subparagraph (A), an index is not a narrow-based security index if—

(i)(I) it has at least 9 component securities;

(II) no component security comprises more than 30 percent of the index's weighting; and

(III) each component security is—

(aa) registered pursuant to section 12 of the Securities Exchange Act of 1934;

(bb) one of 750 securities with the largest market capitalization; and

(cc) one of 675 securities with the largest dollar value of average daily trading volume;

(ii) a board of trade was designated as a contract market by the Commodity Futures Trading Commission with respect to a contract of sale for future delivery on the index, before the date of the enactment of the Commodity Futures Modernization Act of 2000;

(iii)(I) a contract of sale for future delivery on the index traded on a designated contract market or registered derivatives transaction execution facility for at least 30 days as a contract of sale for future delivery on an index that was not a narrow-based security index; and

(II) it has been a narrow-based security index for no more than 45 business days over 3 consecutive calendar months;

(iv) a contract of sale for future delivery on the index is traded on or subject to the rules of a foreign board of trade and meets such requirements as are jointly established by rule or regulation by the Commission and the Securities and Exchange Commission;

(v) no more than 18 months have passed since the date of the enactment of the Commodity Futures Modernization Act of 2000 and—

(I) it is traded on or subject to the rules of a foreign board of trade;

(II) the offer and sale in the United States of a contract of sale for future delivery on the index was authorized before the date of the enactment of the Commodity Futures Modernization Act of 2000; and

(III) the conditions of such authorization continue to be met; or

(vi) a contract of sale for future delivery on the index is traded on or subject to the rules of a board of trade and meets such requirements as are jointly established by rule, regulation, or order by the Commission and the Securities and Exchange Commission.

(C) Within 1 year after the date of the enactment of the Commodity Futures Modernization Act of 2000, the Commission and the Securities and Exchange Commission jointly shall adopt rules or regulations that set forth the requirements under subparagraph (B)(iv).

(D) An index that is a narrow-based security index solely because it was a narrow-based security index for more than 45 business days over 3 consecutive calendar months pursuant to clause (iii) of subparagraph (B) shall not be a narrow-based security index for the 3 following calendar months.

(E) For purposes of subparagraphs (A) and (B)—

(i) the dollar value of average daily trading volume and the market capitalization shall be calculated as of the preceding 6 full calendar months; and

(ii) the Commission and the Securities and Exchange Commission shall, by rule or regulation, jointly specify the method to be used to determine market capitalization and dollar value of average daily trading volume.

(26) OPTION.—The term "option" means an agreement, contract, or transaction that is of the character of, or is commonly known to the trade as, an "option", "privilege",

"indemnity", "bid", "offer", "put", "call", "advance guaranty", or "decline guaranty".

(27) ORGANIZED EXCHANGE.—The term "organized exchange" means a trading facility that—

(A) permits trading—

(i) by or on behalf of a person that is not an eligible contract participant; or

(ii) by persons other than on a principal-to-principal basis; or

(B) has adopted (directly or through another nongovernmental entity) rules that—

(i) govern the conduct of participants, other than rules that govern the submission of orders or execution of transactions on the trading facility; and

(ii) include disciplinary sanctions other than the exclusion of participants from trading.

(28) PERSON. The term "person" imports the plural or singular, and includes individuals, associations, partnerships, corporations, and trusts.

(29) REGISTERED ENTITY.—The term "registered entity" means—

(A) a board of trade designated as a contract market under section 5;

(B) a derivatives transaction execution facility registered under section 5a;

(C) a derivatives clearing organization registered under section 5b; and

(D) a board of trade designated as a contract market under section 5f.

(30) SECURITY.—The term "security" means a security as defined in section 2(a)(1) of the Securities Act of 1933 (15 U.S.C. 77b(a)(1)) or section 3(a)(10) of the Securities Exchange Act of 1934 (15 U.S.C. 78c(a)(10)).

(31) SECURITY FUTURE.—The term "security future" means a contract of sale for future delivery of a single security or of a narrow-based security index, including any interest therein or based on the value thereof, except an exempted security under section 3(a)(12) of the Securities Exchange Act of 1934 as in effect on the date of the enactment of the Futures Trading Act of 1982 (other than any municipal security as defined in section 3(a)(29) of the Securities Exchange Act of 1934 as in effect on the date of the enactment of the Futures Trading Act of 1982). The term "security future" does not include any agreement, contract, or transaction excluded from this Act under section 2(c), 2(d), 2(f), or 2(g) of this Act (as in effect on the date of the enactment of the Commodity Futures Modernization Act of 2000) or title IV of the Commodity Futures Modernization Act of 2000.

(32) SECURITY FUTURES PRODUCT.—The term "security futures product" means a security future or any put, call, straddle, option, or privilege on any security future.

(33) TRADING FACILITY.—

(A) IN GENERAL.—The term "trading facility" means a person or group of persons that constitutes, maintains, or provides a physical or electronic facility or system in which multiple participants have the ability to execute or trade agreements, contracts, or transactions by accepting bids and offers made by other participants that are open to multiple participants in the facility or system.

(B) EXCLUSIONS.—The term "trading facility" does not include—

(i) a person or group of persons solely because the person or group of persons constitutes, maintains, or provides an electronic facility or system that enables participants to negotiate the terms of and enter into bilateral transactions as a result of communications exchanged by the parties and not from interaction of multiple bids and multiple offers within a predetermined, nondiscretionary automated trade matching and execution algorithm;

(ii) a government securities dealer or government securities broker, to the extent that the dealer or broker executes or trades agreements, contracts, or transactions in government securities, or assists persons in communicating about, negotiating, entering into, executing, or trading an agreement, contract, or transaction in government securities (as the terms "government securities dealer", "government securities broker", and "government securities" are defined in section 3(a) of the Securities Exchange Act of 1934 (15 U.S.C. 78c(a))); or

(iii) facilities on which bids and offers, and acceptances of bids and offers effected on the facility, are not binding.

Any person, group of persons, dealer, broker, or facility described in clause (i) or (ii) is excluded from the meaning of the term "trading facility" for the purposes of this Act without any prior specific approval, certification, or other action by the Commission.

(C) SPECIAL RULE.—A person or group of persons that would not otherwise constitute a trading facility shall not be considered to be a trading facility solely as a result of the submission to a derivatives clearing organization of transactions executed on or through the person or group of persons.

Jurisdiction of Commission; Liability of Principal for Act of Agent; Commodity Futures Trading Commission; Transaction in Interstate Commerce

Sec. 2. (a) JURISDICTION OF COMMISSION; COMMODITY FUTURES TRADING COMMISSION.—

(1) JURISDICTION OF COMMISSION.—

(A) IN GENERAL.—

The Commission shall have exclusive jurisdiction, except to the extent otherwise provided in subparagraphs (C) and (D) of this paragraph and subsections (c) through (i) of this section, with respect to accounts, agreements (including any transaction which is of the character of, or is commonly known to the trade as, an "option", "privilege", "indemnity", "bid", "offer", "put", "call", "advance guaranty", or "decline guaranty"), and transactions involving contracts of sale of a commodity for future delivery, traded or executed on a contract market designated or derivatives transaction execution facility registered pursuant to section 5 or 5a or any other board of trade, exchange, or market, and transactions subject to regulation by the Commission pursuant to section 19 of this Act. Except as hereinabove provided, nothing contained in this section shall (I) supersede or limit the jurisdiction at any time conferred on the Securities and Exchange Commission or other regulatory authorities under the laws of the United States or of any State, or (II) restrict the Securities and Exchange Commission and such other authorities from carrying out their duties and responsibilities in accordance with such laws. Nothing in this section shall supersede or limit the jurisdiction conferred on courts of the United States or any State.

(B) LIABILITY OF PRINCIPAL FOR ACT OF AGENT.—The act, omission, or failure of any official, agent, or other person acting for any individual, association, partnership, corporation, or trust within the scope of his employment or office shall be deemed the act, omission, or failure of such individual, association, partnership, corporation, or trust, as well as of such official, agent, or other person.

(C) NOTWITHSTANDING ANY OTHER PROVISION OF LAW.—

(i) This Act shall not apply to and the Commission shall have no jurisdiction to designate a board of trade as a contract market for any transaction whereby any party to such transaction acquires any put, call, or other option on one or more securities (as defined in section 2(1) of the Securities Act of 1933 or section 3(a)(10) of the Securities Exchange Act of 1934 on the date of enactment of the Futures Trading Act of

1982), including any group or index of such securities, or any interest therein or based on the value thereof.

(ii) This Act shall apply to and the Commission shall have exclusive jurisdiction with respect to accounts, agreements (including any transaction which is of the character of, or is commonly known to the trade as, an "option," "privilege," "indemnity," "bid," "offer," "put," "call," "advance guaranty," or "decline guaranty") and transactions involving, and may designate a board of trade as a contract market in, or register a derivatives transaction execution facility that trades or executes, contracts of sale (or options on such contracts) for future delivery of a group or index of securities (or any interest therein or based upon the value thereof): *Provided, however,* That no board of trade shall be designated as a contract market with respect to any such contracts of sale (or options on such contracts) for future delivery, and no derivatives transaction execution facility shall trade or execute such contracts of sale (or options on such contracts) for future delivery, unless the board of trade or the derivatives transaction execution facility, and the applicable contract, meet the following minimum requirements:

(I) Settlement of or delivery on such contract (or option on such contract) shall be effected in cash or by means other than the transfer or receipt of any security, except an exempted security under section 3 of the Securities Act of 1933 or section 3(a)(12) of the Securities Exchange Act of 1934 as in effect on the date of enactment of the Futures Trading Act of 1982 (other than any municipal security, as defined in section 3(a)(29) of the Securities Exchange Act of 1934 on the date of enactment of the Futures Trading Act of 1982);

(II) Trading in such contract (or option on such contract) shall not be readily susceptible to manipulation of the price of such contract (or option on such contract), nor to causing or being used in the manipulation of the price of any underlying security, option on such security or option on a group or index including such securities; and

(III) Such group or index of securities shall not constitute a narrow-based security index.

(iii) If, in its discretion, the Commission determines that a stock index futures contract, notwithstanding its conformance with the requirements in clause (ii) of this subparagraph, can reasonably be used as a surrogate for trading a security (including a security futures product), it may, by order, require such contract and any option thereon be traded and regulated as security futures products as defined in section 3(a)(56) of the Securities Exchange Act of 1934 and section 1a of this Act subject to all rules and regulations applicable to security futures products under this Act and the securities laws as defined in section 3(a)(47) of the Securities Exchange Act of 1934.

(iv) No person shall offer to enter into, enter into, or confirm the execution of any contract of sale (or option on such contract) for future delivery of any security, or interest therein or based on the value thereof, except an exempted security under section 3(a)(12) of the Securities Exchange Act of 1934 as in effect on the date of enactment of the Futures Trading Act of 1982 (other than any municipal security as defined in section 3(a)(29) of the Securities Exchange Act of 1934 on the date of enactment of the Futures Trading Act of 1982), or except as provided in clause (ii) of this subparagraph or subparagraph D, any group or index of such securities or any interest therein or based on the value thereof.

(v)(I) Notwithstanding any other provision of this Act, any contract market in a stock index futures contract (or option thereon) other than a security futures product, or any derivatives transaction execution facility on which such contract or option is traded, shall file with the Board of Governors of the Federal Reserve System any rule establishing or changing the levels of margin (initial and maintenance) for such stock index futures contract (or option thereon) other than security futures products.

(II) The Board may at any time request any contract market or derivatives transaction execution facility to set the margin for any stock index futures contract (or option thereon), other than for any security futures product, at such levels as the Board in its judgment determines are appropriate to preserve the financial integrity of the contract market or derivatives transaction execution facility, or its clearing system, or to prevent systemic risk. If the contract market or derivatives transaction execution facility fails to do so within the time specified by the Board in its request, the Board may direct the contract market or derivatives transaction execution facility to alter or supplement the rules of the contract market or derivatives transaction execution facility as specified in the request.

(III) Subject to such conditions as the Board may determine, the Board may delegate any or all of its authority, relating to margin for any stock index futures contract (or option thereon), other than security futures products, under this clause to the Commission.

(IV) It shall be unlawful for any futures commission merchant to, directly or indirectly, extend or maintain credit to or for, or collect margin from any customer on any security futures product unless such activities comply with the regulations prescribed pursuant to section 7(c)(2)(B) of the Securities Exchange Act of 1934.

(V) Nothing in this clause shall supersede or limit the authority granted to the Commission in section 8a(9) to direct a contract market or registered derivatives transaction execution facility, on finding an emergency to exist, to raise temporary margin levels on any futures contract, or option on the contract covered by this clause, or on any security futures product.

(VI) Any action taken by the Board, or by the Commission acting under the delegation of authority under subclause III, under this clause directing a contract market to alter or supplement a contract market rule shall be subject to review only in the Court of Appeals where the party seeking review resides or has its principal place of business, or in the United States Court of Appeals for the District of Columbia Circuit. The review shall be based on the examination of all information before the Board or the Commission, as the case may be, at the time the determination was made. The court reviewing the action of the Board or the Commission shall not enter a stay or order of mandamus unless the court has determined, after notice and a hearing before a panel of the court, that the agency action complained of was arbitrary, capricious, an abuse of discretion, or otherwise not in accordance with law.

(D)(i) Notwithstanding any other provision of this Act, the Securities and Exchange Commission shall have jurisdiction and authority over security futures as defined in section 3(a)(55) of the Securities Exchange Act of 1934, section 2(a)(16) of the Securities Act of 1933, section 2(a)(52) of the Investment Company Act of 1940, and section 202(a)(27) of the Investment Advisers Act of 1940, options on security futures, and persons effecting transactions in security futures and options thereon, and this Act shall apply to and the Commission shall have jurisdiction with respect to accounts, agreements (including any transaction which is of the character of, or is commonly known to the trade as, an "option", "privilege", "indemnity", "bid", "offer", "put", "call", "advance guaranty", or "decline guaranty"), contracts, and transactions involving, and may designate a board of trade as a contract market in, or register a derivatives transaction execution facility that trades or executes, a security futures product as defined in section 1a of this Act: *Provided, however,* That, except as provided in clause (vi) of this subparagraph, no board of trade shall be designated as a contract market with respect to, or registered as a derivatives transaction execution facility for, any such contracts of sale for future delivery unless the board of trade and the applicable contract meet the following criteria:

(I) Except as otherwise provided in a rule, regulation, or order issued pursuant to clause (v) of this subparagraph, any security underlying the security future, including each component security of a narrow-based security index, is registered pursuant to section 12 of the Securities Exchange Act of 1934.

(II) If the security futures product is not cash settled, the board of trade on which the security futures product is traded has arrangements in place with a clearing agency registered pursuant to section 17A of the Securities Exchange Act of 1934 for the payment and delivery of the securities underlying the security futures product.

(III) Except as otherwise provided in a rule, regulation, or order issued pursuant to clause (v) of this subparagraph, the security future is based upon common stock and such other equity securities as the Commission and the Securities and Exchange Commission jointly determine appropriate.

(IV) The security futures product is cleared by a clearing agency that has in place provisions for linked and coordinated clearing with other clearing agencies that clear security futures products, which permits the security futures product to be purchased on a designated contract market, registered derivatives transaction execution facility, national securities exchange registered under section 6(a) of the Securities Exchange Act of 1934, or national securities association registered pursuant to section 15A(a) of the Securities Exchange Act of 1934 and offset on another designated contract market, registered derivatives transaction execution facility, national securities exchange registered under section 6(a) of the Securities Exchange Act of 1934, or national securities association registered pursuant to section 15A(a) of the Securities Exchange Act of 1934.

(V) Only futures commission merchants, introducing brokers, commodity trading advisors, commodity pool operators or associated persons subject to suitability rules comparable to those of a national securities association registered pursuant to section

15A(a) of the Securities Exchange Act of 1934 solicit, accept any order for, or otherwise deal in any transaction in or in connection with the security futures product.

(VI) The security futures product is subject to a prohibition against dual trading in section 4j of this Act and the rules and regulations thereunder or the provisions of section 11(a) of the Securities Exchange Act of 1934 and the rules and regulations thereunder, except to the extent otherwise permitted under the Securities Exchange Act of 1934 and the rules and regulations thereunder.

(VII) Trading in the security futures product is not readily susceptible to manipulation of the price of such security futures product, nor to causing or being used in the manipulation of the price of any underlying security, option on such security, or option on a group or index including such securities;

(VIII) The board of trade on which the security futures product is traded has procedures in place for coordinated surveillance among such board of trade, any market on which any security underlying the security futures product is traded, and other markets on which any related security is traded to detect manipulation and insider trading, except that, if the board of trade is an alternative trading system, a national securities association registered pursuant to section 15A(a) of the Securities Exchange Act of 1934 or national securities exchange registered pursuant to section 6(a) of the Securities Exchange Act of 1934 of which such alternative trading system is a member has in place such procedures.

(IX) The board of trade on which the security futures product is traded has in place audit trails necessary or appropriate to facilitate the coordinated surveillance required in subclause (VIII), except that, if the board of trade is an alternative trading system, a national securities association registered pursuant to section 15A(a) of the Securities Exchange Act of 1934 or national securities exchange registered pursuant to section 6(a) of the Securities Exchange Act of 1934 of which such alternative trading system is a member has rules to require such audit trails.

(X) The board of trade on which the security futures product is traded has in place procedures to coordinate trading halts between such board of trade and markets on which any security underlying the security futures product is traded and other markets on which any related security is traded, except that, if the board of trade is an alternative trading system, a national securities association registered pursuant to section 15A(a) of the Securities Exchange Act of 1934 or national securities exchange registered pursuant to section 6(a) of the Securities Exchange Act of 1934 of which such alternative trading system is a member has rules to require such coordinated trading halts.

(XI) The margin requirements for a security futures product comply with the regulations prescribed pursuant to section 7(c)(2)(B) of the Securities Exchange Act of 1934, except that nothing in this subclause shall be construed to prevent a board of trade from requiring higher margin levels for a security futures product when it deems such action to be necessary or appropriate.

(ii) It shall be unlawful for any person to offer, to enter into, to execute, to confirm the execution of, or to conduct any office or business anywhere in the United States, its territories or possessions, for the purpose of soliciting, or accepting any order for, or otherwise dealing in, any transaction in, or in connection with, a security futures product unless—

(I) the transaction is conducted on or subject to the rules of a board of trade that—

(aa) has been designated by the Commission as a contract market in such security futures product; or

(bb) is a registered derivatives transaction execution facility for the security futures product that has provided a certification with respect to the security futures product pursuant to clause (vii);

(II) the contract is executed or consummated by, through, or with a member of the contract market or registered derivatives transaction execution facility; and

(III) the security futures product is evidenced by a record in writing which shows the date, the parties to such security futures product and their addresses, the property covered, and its price, and each contract market member or registered derivatives transaction execution facility member shall keep the record for a period of 3 years from the date of the transaction, or for a longer period if the Commission so directs, which record shall at all times be open to the inspection of any duly authorized representative of the Commission.

(iii)(I) Except as provided in subclause (II) but notwithstanding any other provision of this Act, no person shall offer to enter into, enter into, or confirm the execution of any option on a security future.

(II) After 3 years after the date of the enactment of the Commodity Futures Modernization Act of 2000, the Commission and the Securities and Exchange Commission may by order jointly determine to permit trading of options on any security future authorized to be traded under the provisions of this Act and the Securities Exchange Act of 1934.

(iv)(I) All relevant records of a futures commission merchant or introducing broker registered pursuant to section 4f(a)(2), floor broker or floor trader exempt from registration pursuant to section 4f(a)(3), associated person exempt from registration pursuant to section 4k(6), or board of trade designated as a contract market in a security futures product pursuant to section 5f shall be subject to such reasonable periodic or special examinations by representatives of the Commission as the Commission deems necessary or appropriate in the public interest, for the protection of investors, or otherwise in furtherance of the purposes of this Act, and the Commission, before conducting any such examination, shall give notice to the Securities and Exchange Commission of the proposed examination and consult with the Securities and Exchange Commission concerning the feasibility and desirability of coordinating the examination with examinations conducted by the Securities and Exchange Commission in order to avoid unnecessary regulatory duplication or undue regulatory burdens for the registrant or board of trade.

(II) The Commission shall notify the Securities and Exchange Commission of any examination conducted of any futures commission merchant or introducing broker registered pursuant to section 4f(a)(2), floor broker or floor trader exempt from registration pursuant to section 4f(a)(3), associated person exempt from registration pursuant to section 4k(6), or board of trade designated as a contract market in a security futures product pursuant to section 5f, and, upon request, furnish to the Securities and Exchange Commission any examination report and data supplied to or prepared by the Commission in connection with the examination.

(III) Before conducting an examination under subclause (I), the Commission shall use the reports of examinations, unless the information sought is unavailable in the reports, of any futures commission merchant or introducing broker registered pursuant to section 4f(a)(2), floor broker or floor trader exempt from registration pursuant to section 4f(a)(3), associated person exempt from registration pursuant to section 4k(6), or board of trade designated as a contract market in a security futures product pursuant to section 5f that is made by the Securities and Exchange Commission, a national securities association registered pursuant to section 15A(a) of the Securities Exchange Act of 1934 (15 U.S.C. 78o–3(a)), or a national securities exchange registered pursuant to section 6(a) of the Securities Exchange Act of 1934 (15 U.S.C. 78f(a)).

(IV) Any records required under this subsection for a futures commission merchant or introducing broker registered pursuant to section 4f(a)(2), floor broker or floor trader exempt from registration pursuant to section 4f(a)(3), associated person exempt from registration pursuant to section 4k(6), or board of trade designated as a contract market in a security futures product pursuant to section 5f,. shall be limited to records with respect to accounts, agreements, contracts, and transactions involving security futures products.

(v)(I) The Commission and the Securities and Exchange Commission, by rule, regulation, or order, may jointly modify the criteria specified in subclause (I) or (III) of clause (i), including the trading of security futures based on securities other than equity securities, to the extent such modification fosters the development of fair and orderly markets in security futures products, is necessary or appropriate in the public interest, and is consistent with the protection of investors.

(II) The Commission and the Securities and Exchange Commission, by order, may jointly exempt any person from compliance with the criterion specified in clause (i)(IV) to the extent such exemption fosters the development of fair and orderly markets in security futures products, is necessary or appropriate in the public interest, and is consistent with the protection of investors.

(vi)(I) Notwithstanding clauses (i) and (vii), until the compliance date, a board of trade shall not be required to meet the criterion specified in clause (i)(IV).

(II) The Commission and the Securities and Exchange Commission shall jointly publish in the Federal Register a notice of the compliance date no later than 165 days before the compliance date.

(III) For purposes of this clause, the term "compliance date" means the later of—

(aa) 180 days after the end of the first full calendar month period in which the average aggregate comparable share volume for all security futures products based on single equity securities traded on all designated contract markets and registered derivatives transaction execution facilities equals or exceeds 10 percent of the average aggregate comparable share volume of options on single equity securities traded on all national securities exchanges registered pursuant to section 6(a) of the Securities Exchange Act of 1934 and any national securities associations registered pursuant to section 15A(a) of such Act; or

(bb) 2 years after the date on which trading in any security futures product commences under this Act.

(vii) It shall be unlawful for a board of trade to trade or execute a security futures product unless the board of trade has provided the Commission with a certification that the specific security futures product and the board of trade, as applicable, meet the criteria specified in subclauses (I) through (XI) of clause (i), except as otherwise provided in clause (vi).

(E)(i) To the extent necessary or appropriate in the public interest, to promote fair competition, and consistent with promotion of market efficiency, innovation, and expansion of investment opportunities, the protection of investors, and the maintenance of fair and orderly markets, the Commission and the Securities and Exchange Commission shall jointly issue such rules, regulations, or orders as are necessary and appropriate to permit the offer and sale of a security futures product traded on or subject to the rules of a foreign board of trade to United States persons.

(ii) The rules, regulations, or orders adopted under clause (i) shall take into account, as appropriate, the nature and size of the markets that the securities underlying the security futures product reflects.

(F)(i) Nothing in this Act is intended to prohibit a futures commission merchant from carrying security futures products traded on or subject to the rules of a foreign board of trade in the accounts of persons located outside of the United States.

(ii) Nothing in this Act is intended to prohibit any eligible contract participant located in the United States from purchasing or carrying securities futures products traded on or subject to the rules of a foreign board of trade, exchange, or market to the same extent such person may be authorized to purchase or carry other securities traded on a foreign board of trade, exchange, or market so long as any underlying security for such security futures products is traded principally on, by, or through any exchange or market located outside the United States.

(2)(A) There is hereby established, as an independent agency of the United States Government, a Commodity Futures Trading Commission. The Commission shall be composed of five Commissioners who shall be appointed by the President, by and with the advice and consent of the Senate. In nominating persons for appointment, the President shall—

(i) select persons who shall each have demonstrated knowledge in futures trading or its regulation, or the production, merchandising, processing or distribution of one or more of the commodities or other goods and articles, services, rights, and interests covered by this Act; and

(ii) seek to ensure that the demonstrated knowledge of the Commissioners is balanced with respect to such areas.

Not more than three of the members of the Commission shall be members of the same political party. Each Commissioner shall hold office for a term of five years and until his successor is appointed and has qualified, except that he shall not so continue to serve beyond the expiration of the next session of Congress subsequent to the expiration of said fixed term of office, and except (i) any Commissioner appointed to fill a vacancy occurring prior to the expiration of the term for which his predecessor was appointed shall be appointed for the remainder of such term, and (ii) the terms of office of the Commissioners first taking office after the enactment of this paragraph shall expire as designated by the President at the time of nomination, one at the end of one year, one at the end of two years, one at the end of three years, one at the end of four years, and one at the end of five years.

(B) The President shall appoint, by and with the advice and consent of the Senate, a member of the Commission as Chairman, who shall serve as Chairman at the pleasure of the President. An individual may be appointed as Chairman at the same time that person is appointed as a Commissioner. The Chairman shall be the chief administrative officer of the Commission and shall preside at hearings before the Commission. At any time, the President may appoint, by and with the advice and consent of the Senate, a different Chairman, and the Commissioner previously appointed as Chairman may complete that Commissioner's term as a Commissioner.

. . . . .

(b) For the purposes of this Act (but not in any wise limiting the foregoing definition of interstate commerce) a transaction in respect to any article shall be considered to be in interstate commerce if such article is part of that current of commerce usual in the commodity trade whereby commodities and commodity products and byproducts thereof are sent from one State with the expectation that they will end their transit, after purchase, in another, including, in addition to cases within the above general description, all cases where purchase or sale is either for shipment to another State, or for manufacture within the State and the shipment outside the State of the products resulting from such manufacture. Articles normally in such current of commerce shall not be considered out of such commerce through resort being had to any means or device intended to remove transactions in respect thereto from the provisions of this Act. For the purpose of this paragraph the word "State" includes Territory, the District of Columbia, possession of the United States, and foreign nation.

(c) AGREEMENTS, CONTRACTS, AND TRANSACTIONS IN FOREIGN CURRENCY, GOVERNMENT SECURITIES, AND CERTAIN OTHER COMMODITIES.—

(1) IN GENERAL.—Except as provided in paragraph (2), nothing in this Act (other than section 5a (to the extent provided in section 5a(g)), 5b, 5d, or 12(e)(2)(B)) governs or applies to an agreement, contract, or transaction in—

(A) foreign currency;

(B) government securities;

(C) security warrants;

(D) security rights;

(E) resales of installment loan contracts;

(F) repurchase transactions in an excluded commodity; or

(G) mortgages or mortgage purchase commitments.

(2) COMMISSION JURISDICTION.—

(A) AGREEMENTS, CONTRACTS, AND TRANSACTIONS TRADED ON AN ORGANIZED EXCHANGE.—This Act applies to, and the Commission shall have jurisdiction over, an agreement, contract, or transaction described in paragraph (1) that is—

(i) a contract of sale of a commodity for future delivery (or an option on such a contract), or an option on a commodity (other than foreign currency or a security or a group or index of securities), that is executed or traded on an organized exchange; or

(ii) an option on foreign currency executed or traded on an organized exchange that is not a national securities exchange registered pursuant to section 6(a) of the Securities Exchange Act of 1934.

(B) AGREEMENTS, CONTRACTS, AND TRANSACTIONS IN RETAIL FOREIGN CURRENCY.—This Act applies to, and the Commission shall have jurisdiction over, an agreement, contract, or transaction in foreign currency that—

(i) is a contract of sale of a commodity for future delivery (or an option on such a contract) or an option (other than an option executed or traded on a national securities exchange registered pursuant to section 6(a) of the Securities Exchange Act of 1934); and

(ii) is offered to, or entered into with, a person that is not an eligible contract participant, unless the counterparty, or the person offering to be the counterparty, of the person is—

(I) a financial institution;

(II) a broker or dealer registered under section 15(b) or 15C of the Securities Exchange Act of 1934 (15 U.S.C. 78o(b), 78o–5) or a futures commission merchant registered under this Act;

(III) an associated person of a broker or dealer registered under section 15(b) or 15C of the Securities Exchange Act of 1934 (15 U.S.C. 78o(b), 78o–5), or an affiliated person of a futures commission merchant registered under this Act, concerning the financial or securities activities of which the registered person makes and keeps records under section 15C(b) or 17(h) of the Securities Exchange Act of 1934 (15 U.S.C. 78o–5(b), 78q(h)) or section 4f(c)(2)(B) of this Act;

(IV) an insurance company described in section 1a(12)(A)(ii) of this Act, or a regulated subsidiary or affiliate of such an insurance company;

(V) a financial holding company (as defined in section 2 of the Bank Holding Company Act of 1956); or

(VI) an investment bank holding company (as defined in section 17(i) of the Securities Exchange Act of 1934).

(C) Notwithstanding subclauses (II) and (III) of subparagraph (B)(ii), agreements, contracts, or transactions described in subparagraph (B) shall be subject to sections 4b, 4c(b), 6(c) and 6(d) (to the extent that sections 6(c) and 6(d) prohibit manipulation of the market price of any commodity, in interstate commerce, or for future delivery on or subject to the rules of any market), 6c, 6d, and 8(a) if they are entered into by a futures commission merchant or an affiliate of a futures commission merchant that is not also an entity described in subparagraph (B)(ii) of this paragraph.

(d) EXCLUDED DERIVATIVE TRANSACTIONS.—

(1) IN GENERAL.—Nothing in this Act (other than section 5b or 12(e)(2)(B)) governs or applies to an agreement, contract, or transaction in an excluded commodity if—

(A) the agreement, contract, or transaction is entered into only between persons that are eligible contract participants at the time at which the persons enter into the agreement, contract, or transaction; and

(B) the agreement, contract, or transaction is not executed or traded on a trading facility.

(2) ELECTRONIC TRADING FACILITY EXCLUSION.—Nothing in this Act (other than section 5a (to the extent provided in section 5a(g)), 5b, 5d, or 12(e)(2)(B)) governs or applies to an agreement, contract, or transaction in an excluded commodity if—

(A) the agreement, contract, or transaction is entered into on a principal-to-principal basis between parties trading for their own accounts or as described in section 1a(12)(B)(ii);

(B) the agreement, contract, or transaction is entered into only between persons that are eligible contract participants described in subparagraph (A), (B)(ii), or (C) of section 1a(12) at the time at which the persons enter into the agreement, contract, or transaction; and

(C) the agreement, contract, or transaction is executed or traded on an electronic trading facility.

(e) EXCLUDED ELECTRONIC TRADING FACILITIES.—

(1) IN GENERAL.—Nothing in this Act (other than section 12(e)(2)(B)) governs or is applicable to an electronic trading facility that limits transactions authorized to be conducted on its facilities to those satisfying the requirements of section 2(d)(2), 2(g), or 2(h)(3).

(2) EFFECT ON AUTHORITY TO ESTABLISH AND OPERATE.—Nothing in this Act shall prohibit a board of trade designated by the Commission as a contract market or derivatives transaction execution facility, or operating as an exempt board of trade from establishing and operating an electronic trading facility excluded under this Act pursuant to paragraph (1).

(3) EFFECT ON TRANSACTIONS.—No failure by an electronic trading facility to limit transactions as required by paragraph (1) of this subsection or to comply with section 2(h)(5) shall in itself affect the legality, validity, or enforceability of an agreement, contract, or transaction entered into or traded on the electronic trading facility or cause a participant on the system to be in violation of this Act.

(4) SPECIAL RULE.—A person or group of persons that would not otherwise constitute a trading facility shall not be considered to be a trading facility solely as a result of the submission to a derivatives clearing organization of transactions executed on or through the person or group of persons.

(f) EXCLUSION FOR QUALIFYING HYBRID INSTRUMENTS.—

(1) IN GENERAL.—Nothing in this Act (other than section 12(e)(2)(B)) governs or is applicable to a hybrid instrument that is predominantly a security.

(2) PREDOMINANCE.—A hybrid instrument shall be considered to be predominantly a security if—

(A) the issuer of the hybrid instrument receives payment in full of the purchase price of the hybrid instrument, substantially contemporaneously with delivery of the hybrid instrument;

(B) the purchaser or holder of the hybrid instrument is not required to make any payment to the issuer in addition to the purchase price paid under subparagraph (A), whether as margin, settlement payment, or otherwise, during the life of the hybrid instrument or at maturity;

(C) the issuer of the hybrid instrument is not subject by the terms of the instrument to mark-to-market margining requirements; and

(D) the hybrid instrument is not marketed as a contract of sale of a commodity for future delivery (or option on such a contract) subject to this Act.

(3) MARK-TO-MARKET MARGINING REQUIREMENTS.—For the purposes of paragraph (2)(C), mark-to-market margining requirements do not include the obligation of an issuer of a secured debt instrument to increase the amount of collateral held in pledge for the benefit of the purchaser of the secured debt instrument to secure the repayment obligations of the issuer under the secured debt instrument.

(g) EXCLUDED SWAP TRANSACTIONS.—No provision of this Act (other than section 5a (to the extent provided in section 5a(g)), 5b, 5d, or 12(e)(2)) shall apply to or govern any agreement, contract, or transaction in a commodity other than an agricultural commodity if the agreement, contract, or transaction is—

(1) entered into only between persons that are eligible contract participants at the time they enter into the agreement, contract, or transaction;

(2) subject to individual negotiation by the parties; and

(3) not executed or traded on a trading facility. . . .

(h) LEGAL CERTAINTY FOR CERTAIN TRANSACTIONS IN EXEMPT COMMODITIES.—

(1) Except as provided in paragraph (2), nothing in this Act shall apply to a contract, agreement, or transaction in an exempt commodity which—

(A) is entered into solely between persons that are eligible contract participants at the time the persons enter into the agreement, contract, or transaction; and

(B) is not entered into on a trading facility.

(2) An agreement, contract, or transaction described in paragraph (1) of this subsection shall be subject to—

(A) sections 5b and 12(e)(2)(B);

(B) sections 4b, 4o, 6(c), 6(d), 6c, 6d, and 8a, and the regulations of the Commission pursuant to section 4c(b) proscribing fraud in connection with commodity option transactions, to the extent the agreement, contract, or transaction is not between eligible commercial entities (unless one of the entities is an instrumentality, department, or agency of a State or local governmental entity) and would otherwise be subject to such sections and regulations; and

(C) sections 6(c), 6(d), 6c, 6d, 8a, and 9(a)(2), to the extent such sections prohibit manipulation of the market price of any commodity in interstate commerce and the agreement, contract, or transaction would otherwise be subject to such sections.

(3) Except as provided in paragraph (4), nothing in this Act shall apply to an agreement, contract, or transaction in an exempt commodity which is—

(A) entered into on a principal-to-principal basis solely between persons that are eligible commercial entities at the time the persons enter into the agreement, contract, or transaction; and

(B) executed or traded on an electronic trading facility.

(4) An agreement, contract, or transaction described in paragraph (3) of this subsection shall be subject to—

(A) sections 5a (to the extent provided in section 5a(g)), 5b, 5d, and 12(e)(2)(B);

(B) sections 4b and 4o and the regulations of the Commission pursuant to section 4c(b) proscribing fraud in connection with commodity option transactions to the extent the agreement, contract, or transaction would otherwise be subject to such sections and regulations;

(C) sections 6(c) and 9(a)(2), to the extent such sections prohibit manipulation of the market price of any commodity in interstate commerce and to the extent the agreement, contract, or transaction would otherwise be subject to such sections; and

(D) such rules and regulations as the Commission may prescribe if necessary to ensure timely dissemination by the electronic trading facility of price, trading volume, and other trading data to the extent appropriate, if the Commission determines that the electronic trading facility performs a significant price discovery function for transactions in the cash market for the commodity underlying any agreement, contract, or transaction executed or traded on the electronic trading facility.

(5) An electronic trading facility relying on the exemption provided in paragraph (3) shall—

(A) notify the Commission of its intention to operate an electronic trading facility in reliance on the exemption set forth in paragraph (3), which notice shall include—

(i) the name and address of the facility and a person designated to receive communications from the Commission;

(ii) the commodity categories that the facility intends to list or otherwise make available for trading on the facility in reliance on the exemption set forth in paragraph (3);

(iii) certifications that—

(I) no executive officer or member of the governing board of, or any holder of a 10 percent or greater equity interest in, the facility is a person described in any of subparagraphs (A) through (H) of section 8a(2);

(II) the facility will comply with the conditions for exemption under this paragraph; and

(III) the facility will notify the Commission of any material change in the information previously provided by the facility to the Commission pursuant to this paragraph; and

(iv) the identity of any derivatives clearing organization to which the facility transmits or intends to transmit transaction data for the purpose of facilitating the clearance and settlement of transactions conducted on the facility in reliance on the exemption set forth in paragraph (3);

(B)(i)(I) provide the Commission with access to the facility's trading protocols and electronic access to the facility with respect to transactions conducted in reliance on the exemption set forth in paragraph (3); or

(II) provide such reports to the Commission regarding transactions executed on the facility in reliance on the exemption set forth in paragraph (3) as the Commission may from time to time request to enable the Commission to satisfy its obligations under this Act;

(ii) maintain for 5 years, and make available for inspection by the Commission upon request, records of activities related to its business as an electronic trading facility exempt under paragraph (3), including—

(I) information relating to data entry and transaction details sufficient to enable the Commission to reconstruct trading activity on the facility conducted in reliance on the exemption set forth in paragraph (3); and

(II) the name and address of each participant on the facility authorized to enter into transactions in reliance on the exemption set forth in paragraph (3); and

(iii) upon special call by the Commission, provide to the Commission, in a form and manner and within the period specified in the special call, such information related to its business as an electronic trading facility exempt under paragraph (3), including information relating to data entry and transaction details in respect of transactions entered into in reliance on the exemption set forth in paragraph (3), as the Commission may determine appropriate—

(I) to enforce the provisions specified in subparagraphs (B) and (C) of paragraph (4);

(II) to evaluate a systemic market event; or

(III) to obtain information requested by a Federal financial regulatory authority in order to enable the regulator to fulfill its regulatory or supervisory responsibilities;

(C)(i) upon receipt of any subpoena issued by or on behalf of the Commission to any foreign person who the Commission believes is conducting or has conducted transactions in reliance on the exemption set forth in paragraph (3) on or through the electronic trading facility relating to the transactions, promptly notify the foreign person of, and transmit to the foreign person, the subpoena in a manner reasonable under the circumstances, or as specified by the Commission; and

(ii) if the Commission has reason to believe that a person has not timely complied with a subpoena issued by or on behalf of the Commission pursuant to clause (i), and the Commission in writing has directed that a facility relying on the exemption set forth in paragraph (3) deny or limit further transactions by the person, the facility shall deny that person further trading access to the facility or, as applicable, limit that person's access to the facility for liquidation trading only;

(D) comply with the requirements of this paragraph applicable to the facility and require that each participant, as a condition of trading on the facility in reliance on the exemption set forth in paragraph (3), agree to comply with all applicable law;

(E) have a reasonable basis for believing that participants authorized to conduct transactions on the facility in reliance on the exemption set forth in paragraph (3) are eligible commercial entities; and

(F) not represent to any person that the facility is registered with, or designated, recognized, licensed, or approved by the Commission.

(6) A person named in a subpoena referred to in paragraph (5)(C) that believes the person is or may be adversely affected or aggrieved by action taken by the Commission under this section, shall have the opportunity for a prompt hearing after the Commission acts under procedures that the Commission shall establish by rule, regulation, or order.

(i) APPLICATION OF COMMODITY FUTURES LAWS.—

(1) No provision of this Act shall be construed as implying or creating any presumption that—

(A) any agreement, contract, or transaction that is excluded from this Act under section 2(c), 2(d), 2(e), 2(f), or 2(g) of this Act or title IV of the Commodity Futures Modernization Act of 2000, or exempted under section 2(h) or 4(c) of this Act; or

(B) any agreement, contract, or transaction, not otherwise subject to this Act, that is not so excluded or exempted,

is or would otherwise be subject to this Act.

(2) No provision of, or amendment made by, the Commodity Futures Modernization Act of 2000 shall be construed as conferring jurisdiction on the Commission with respect to any such agreement, contract, or transaction, except as expressly provided in section 5a of this Act (to the extent provided in section 5a(g) of this Act), 5b of this Act, or 5d of this Act.

Sec. 5. Findings and Purpose

(a) The transactions subject to this Act are entered into regularly in interstate and international commerce and are affected with a national public interest by providing a means for managing and assuming price risks, discovering prices, or disseminating pricing information through trading in liquid, fair and financially secure trading facilities.

(b) PURPOSE.—It is the purpose of this Act to serve the public interests described in subsection (a) through a system of effective self-regulation of trading facilities, clearing systems, market participants and market professionals under the oversight of the Commission. To foster these public interests, it is further the purpose of this Act to deter and prevent price manipulation or any other disruptions to market integrity; to ensure the financial integrity of all transactions subject to this Act and the avoidance of systemic risk; to protect all market participants from fraudulent or other abusive sales practices and misuses of customer assets; and to promote responsible innovation and fair competition among boards of trade, other markets and market participants.

Sec. 6. Regulation of Futures Trading and Foreign Transactions

(a) Unless exempted by the Commission pursuant to subsection (c), it shall be unlawful for any person to offer to enter into, to enter into, to execute, to confirm the execution of, or to conduct any office or business anywhere in the United States, its territories or possessions, for the purpose of soliciting, or accepting any order for, or otherwise dealing in, any transaction in, or in connection with, a contract for the purchase or sale of a commodity for future delivery (other than a contract which is made on or subject to the rules of a board of trade, exchange, or market located outside the United States, its territories or possessions) unless—

(1) such transaction is conducted on or subject to the rules of a board of trade which has been designated or registered by the Commission as a contract market or derivatives transaction execution facility for such commodity;

(2) such contract is executed or consummated by or through a member of such contract market or derivatives transaction execution facility; and

(3) such contract is evidenced by a record in writing which shows the date, the parties to such contract and their addresses, the property covered and its price, and the terms of delivery: *Provided,* That each contract market member shall keep such record for a period of three years from the date thereof, or for a longer period if the Commission shall so direct, which record shall at all times be open to the inspection of any representative of the Commission or the Department of Justice.

(b) The Commission may adopt rules and regulations proscribing fraud and requiring minimum financial standards, the disclosure of risk, the filing of reports, the keeping of books and records, the safeguarding of customers' funds, and registration with the Commission by any person located in the United States, its territories or possessions, who engages in the offer or sale of any contract of sale of a commodity for future delivery that is made or to be made on or subject to the rules of a board of trade, exchange, or market located outside the United States, its territories or possessions. Such rules and regulations may impose different requirements for such persons depending upon the particular foreign board of trade, exchange, or market involved. No rule or regulation may be adopted by the Commission under this subsection that (1) requires Commission approval of any contract, rule, regulation, or action of any foreign board of trade, exchange, or market, or clearinghouse for such board of trade, exchange, or market, or (2) governs in any way any rule or contract term or action of any foreign board of trade, exchange, or market, or clearinghouse for such board of trade, exchange, or market.

(c)(1) In order to promote responsible economic or financial innovation and fair competition, the Commission by rule, regulation, or order, after notice and opportunity for hearing, may (on its own initiative or on application of any person, including any board of trade designated or registered as a contract market or derivatives transaction execution facility for transactions for future delivery in any commodity under section 5 of this Act) exempt any agreement, contract, or transaction (or class thereof) that is otherwise subject to subsection (a) (including any person or class of persons offering, entering into, rendering advice or rendering other services with respect to, the agreement, contract, or transaction), either unconditionally or on stated terms or conditions or for stated periods and either retroactively or prospectively, or both, from any of the requirements of subsection (a), or from any other provision of this Act (except subparagraphs (C)(ii) and (D) of section 2(a)(1), except that the Commission and the Securities and Exchange Commission may by rule, regulation, or order jointly exclude any agreement, contract, or transaction from section 2(a)(1)(D)), if the Commission determines that the exemption would be consistent with the public interest.

(2) The Commission shall not grant any exemption under paragraph (1) from any of the requirements of subsection (a) unless the Commission determines that—

(A) the requirement should not be applied to the agreement, contract, or transaction for which the exemption is sought and that the exemption would be consistent with the public interest and the purposes of this Act; and

(B) the agreement, contract, or transaction—

(i) will be entered into solely between appropriate persons; and

(ii) will not have a material adverse effect on the ability of the Commission or any contract market or derivatives transaction execution facility to discharge its regulatory or self-regulatory duties under this Act.

(3) For purposes of this subsection, the term "appropriate person" shall be limited to the following persons or classes thereof:

(A) A bank or trust company (acting in an individual or fiduciary capacity).

(B) A savings association.

(C) An insurance company.

(D) An investment company subject to regulation under the Investment Company Act of 1940.

(E) A commodity pool formed or operated by a person subject to regulation under this Act.

(F) A corporation, partnership, proprietorship, organization, trust, or other business entity with a net worth exceeding $1,000,000 or total assets exceeding $5,000,000, or the obligations of which under the agreement, contract or transaction are guaranteed or otherwise supported by a letter of credit or keepwell, support, or other agreement by any such entity or by an entity referred to in subparagraph (A), (B), (C), (H), (I), or (K) of this paragraph.

(G) An employee benefit plan with assets exceeding $1,000,000, or whose investment decisions are made by a bank, trust company, insurance company, investment adviser registered under the Investment Advisers Act of 1940, or a commodity trading advisor subject to regulation under this Act.

(H) Any governmental entity (including the United States, any state, or any foreign government) or political subdivision thereof, or any multinational or supranational entity or any instrumentality, agency, or department of any of the foregoing.

(I) A broker-dealer subject to regulation under the Securities Exchange Act of 1934 acting on its own behalf or on behalf of another appropriate person.

(J) A futures commission merchant, floor broker, or floor trader subject to regulation under this Act acting on its own behalf or on behalf of another appropriate person.

(K) Such other persons that the Commission determines to be appropriate in light of their financial or other qualifications, or the applicability of appropriate regulatory protections.

(4) During the pendency of an application for an order granting an exemption under paragraph (1), the Commission may limit the public availability of any information received from the applicant if the applicant submits a written request to limit disclosure contempo-

raneous with the application, and the Commission determines that—

(A) the information sought to be restricted constitutes a trade secret; or

(B) public disclosure of the information would result in material competitive harm to the applicant.

(5) The Commission may—

(A) promptly following the enactment of this subsection, or upon application by any person, exercise the exemptive authority granted under paragraph (1) with respect to classes of hybrid instruments that are predominantly securities or depository instruments, to the extent that such instruments may be regarded as subject to the provisions of this Act; or

(B) promptly following the enactment of this subsection, or upon application by any person, exercise the exemptive authority granted under paragraph (1) effective as of October 23, 1974, with respect to classes of swap agreements (as defined in section 101 of title 11, United States Code) that are not part of a fungible class of agreements that are standardized as to their material economic terms, to the extent that such agreements may be regarded as subject to the provisions of this Act.

Any exemption pursuant to this paragraph shall be subject to such terms and conditions as the Commission shall determine to be appropriate pursuant to paragraph (1).

(d) The granting of an exemption under this section shall not affect the authority of the Commission under any other provision of this Act to conduct investigations in order to determine compliance with the requirements or conditions of such exemption or to take enforcement action for any violation of any provision of this Act or any rule, regulation or order thereunder caused by the failure to comply with or satisfy such conditions or requirements.

Sec. 6a. Excessive Speculation

(a) Excessive speculation in any commodity under contracts of sale of such commodity for future delivery made on or subject to the rules of contract markets or derivatives transaction execution facilities causing sudden or unreasonable fluctuations or unwarranted changes in the price of such commodity, is an undue and unnecessary burden on interstate commerce in such commodity. For the purpose of diminishing, eliminating, or preventing such burden, the Commission shall, from time to time, after due notice and opportunity for hearing, by rule, regulation, or order, proclaim and fix such limits on the amounts of trading which may be done or positions which may be held by any person under contracts of sale of such commodity for future delivery on or subject to the rules of any contract market or derivatives transaction execution facility as the Commission finds are necessary to diminish, eliminate, or prevent such burden. In determining whether any person has exceeded such limits, the positions held and trading done by any persons directly or indirectly controlled by such person shall be included with the positions held and trading done by such person; and further, such limits upon positions and trading shall apply to positions held by, and trading done by, two or more persons acting pursuant to an expressed or implied agreement or understanding, the same as if the positions were held by, or the trading were done by, a single person. Nothing in this section shall be construed to prohibit the Commission from fixing different trading or position limits for different commodities, markets, futures, or delivery months, or for different number of days remaining until the last day of trading in a contract, or different trading limits for buying and selling operations, or different limits for the purposes of paragraphs (1) and (2) of subsection (b) of this section, or from exempting transactions normally known to the trade as "spreads" or "straddles" or "arbitrage" or from fixing limits applying to such transactions or positions different from limits fixed for other transactions or positions.

The word "arbitrage" in domestic markets shall be defined to mean the same as a "spread" or "straddle". The Commission is authorized to define the term "international arbitrage".

(b) The Commission shall in such rule, regulation, or order, fix a reasonable time (not to exceed ten days) after the promulgation of the rule, regulation, or order; after which, and until such rule, regulation, or order is suspended, modified, or revoked, it shall be unlawful for any person—

(1) directly or indirectly to buy or sell, or agree to buy or sell, under contracts of sale of such commodity for future delivery on or subject to the rules of the contract market or markets or derivatives transaction execution facility or facilities to which the rule, regulation, or order applies, any amount of such commodity during any one business day in excess of any trading limit fixed for one business day by the Commission in such rule, regulation, or order for or with respect to such commodity; or

(2) directly or indirectly to hold or control a net long or a net short position in any commodity for future delivery on or subject to the rules of any contract market or derivatives transaction execution facility in excess of any position limit fixed by the Commission for or with respect to such commodity: *Provided,* That such position limit shall not apply to a position acquired in good faith prior to the effective date of such rule, regulation, or order.

(c) No rule, regulation, or order issued under subsection (a) of this section shall apply to transactions or positions which are shown to be bona fide hedging transactions or positions, as such terms shall be defined by the Commission by rule, regulation, or order consistent with the purposes of this Act. Such terms may be defined to permit producers, purchasers, sellers, middlemen, and users of a commodity or a product derived therefrom to hedge their legitimate anticipated business needs for that period of time into the future for which an appropriate futures contract is open and available on an exchange. To determine the adequacy of this Act and the powers of the Commission acting thereunder to prevent unwarranted price pressures by large hedgers, the Commission shall monitor and analyze the trading activities of the largest hedgers, as determined by the Commission, operating in the cattle, hog, or pork belly markets and shall report its findings and recommendations to the Senate Committee on Agriculture, Nutrition, and Forestry and the House Committee on Agriculture in its annual reports for at least two years following the date of enactment of the Futures Trading Act of 1982.

(d) This section shall apply to a person that is registered as a futures commission merchant, an introducing broker, or a floor broker under authority of this Act only to the extent that transactions made by such person are made on behalf of or for the account or benefit of such person. This section shall not apply to transactions made by, or on behalf of, or at the direction of, the United States, or a duly authorized agency thereof.

(e) Nothing in this section shall prohibit or impair the adoption by any contract market or derivatives transaction execution facility or by any other board of trade licensed, designated or registered by the Commission of any bylaw, rule, regulation, or resolution fixing limits on the amount of trading which may be done or positions which may be held by any person under contracts of sale of any commodity for future delivery traded on or subject to the rules of such contract market or derivatives transaction execution facility, or under options on such contracts or commodities traded on or subject to the rules of such contract market or derivatives transaction execution facility or such board of trade: *Provided,* That if the Commission shall have fixed limits under this section for any contract or under section 6c of this Act for any commodity option, then the limits fixed by the bylaws, rules, regulations, and resolutions adopted by such contract market or derivatives transaction execution facility or such board of trade shall not be higher than the limits fixed by the Commission. It shall be a violation of this Act for any person to violate any bylaw, rule, regulation, or resolution of any contract market or derivatives transaction execution facility other board of trade licensed, designated or registered by the Commission fixing limits on the amount of trading which may be done or positions which may be held by any person under contracts of sale of any commodity for future delivery or under options on such contracts or commodities, if such bylaw, rule, regulation, or resolution has been approved by the Commission: *Provided,* That the provisions of section 13(c) of this Act shall apply only to those who knowingly violate such limits.

Sec. 6b. Fraud, False Reporting, or Deception Prohibited

(a) It shall be unlawful (1) for any member of a registered entity, or for any correspondent, agent, or employee of any member, in or in connection with any order to make, or the making of, any contract of sale of any commodity in interstate commerce, made, or to be made, on or subject to the rules of any registered entity, for or on behalf of any other person, or (2) for any person, in or in connection with any order to make, or the making of, any contract of sale of any commodity for future delivery, made, or to be made, for or on behalf of any other person if such contract for future delivery is or may be used for (A) hedging any transaction in interstate commerce in such commodity or the products or byproducts thereof, or (B) determining the price basis of any transaction in interstate commerce in such commodity, or (C) delivering any such commodity sold, shipped, or received in interstate commerce for the fulfillment thereof—

(i) to cheat or defraud or attempt to cheat or defraud such other person;

(ii) willfully to make or cause to be made to such other person any false report or statement thereof, or willfully to enter or cause to be entered for such person any false record thereof;

(iii) willfully to deceive or attempt to deceive such other person by any means whatsoever in regard to any such order or contract or the disposition or execution of any such order or contract, or in regard to any act of agency performed with respect to such order or contract for such person; or

(iv) to bucket such order, or to fill such order by offset against the order or orders of any other person, or willfully and knowingly and without the prior consent of such person to become the buyer in respect to any selling order of such person, or become the seller in respect to any buying order of such person.

(b) Nothing in this section or any other section of this Act shall be construed to prevent a futures commission merchant or floor broker who shall have in hand, simultaneously, buying and selling orders at the market for different principals for a like quantity of a commodity for future delivery in the same month, from executing such buying and selling orders at the market price: *Provided,* That any such execution shall take place on the floor of the exchange where such orders are to be executed at public outcry across the ring and shall be duly reported, recorded, and cleared in the same manner as other orders executed on such exchange: *And provided further,* That such transactions shall be made in accordance with such rules and regulations as the Commission may promulgate regarding the manner of the execution of such transactions.

(c) Nothing in this section shall apply to any activity that occurs on a board of trade, exchange, or market, or clearinghouse for such board of trade, exchange, or market, located outside the United States, or territories or possessions of the United States, involving any contract of sale of a commodity for future delivery that is made, or to be made, on or subject to the rules of such board of trade, exchange, or market.

Sec. 6c. Prohibited Transactions

(a) IN GENERAL.—

(1) PROHIBITION.—It shall be unlawful for any person to offer to enter into, enter into, or confirm the execution of a transaction described in paragraph (2) involving the purchase or sale of any commodity for future delivery (or any option on such a transaction or option on a commodity) if the transaction is used or may be used to—

(A) hedge any transaction in interstate commerce in the commodity or the product or byproduct of the commodity;

(B) determine the price basis of any such transaction in interstate commerce in the commodity; or

(C) deliver any such commodity sold, shipped, or received in interstate commerce for the execution of the transaction.

(2) TRANSACTION.—A transaction referred to in paragraph (1) is a transaction that—

(A)(i) is, of the character of, or is commonly known to the trade as, a "wash sale" or "accommodation trade"; or

(ii) is a fictitious sale; or

(B) is used to cause any price to be reported, registered, or recorded that is not a true and bona fide price.

Nothing in this section shall be construed to prevent the exchange of futures in connection with cash commodity transactions or of futures for cash commodities, or of transfer trades or office trades if made in accordance with board of trade rules applying to such transactions and such rules shall have been approved by the Commission.

(b) No person shall offer to enter into, enter into, or confirm the execution of, any transaction involving any commodity regulated under this Act which is of the character of, or is commonly known to the trade as, an "option", "privilege", "indemnity", "bid", "offer", "put", "call", "advance guaranty", or "decline guaranty", contrary to any rule, regulation, or order of the Commission prohibiting any such transaction or allowing any such transaction under such terms and conditions as the Commission shall prescribe. Any such order, rule, or regulation may be made only after notice and opportunity for hearing, and the Commission may set different terms and conditions for different markets.

. . .

(f) Nothing in this Act shall be deemed to govern or in any way be applicable to any transaction in an option on foreign currency traded on a national securities exchange.

(g) The Commission shall adopt rules requiring that a contemporaneous written record be made, as practicable, of all orders for execution on the floor or subject to the rules of each contract market or derivatives transaction execution facility placed by a member of the contract market who is present on the floor at the time such order is placed.

Sec. 6d. Dealing by Unregistered Futures Commission Merchants or Introducing Brokers Prohibited; Duties in Handling Customer Receipts; Rules to Avoid Duplicative Regulations

(a) It shall be unlawful for any person to engage as a futures commission merchant or introducing broker in soliciting orders or accepting orders for the purchase or sale of any commodity for future delivery, or involving any contracts of sale of any commodity for future delivery, on or subject to the rules of any contract market or derivatives transaction execution facility unless—

(1) such person shall have registered, under this Act, with the Commission as such futures commission merchant or introducing broker and such registration shall not have expired nor been suspended nor revoked; and

(2) such person shall, if a futures commission merchant, whether a member or nonmember of a contract market or derivatives transaction execution facility, treat and deal

with all money, securities, and property received by such person to margin, guarantee, or secure the trades or contracts of any customer of such person, or accruing to such customer as the result of such trades or contracts, as belonging to such customer. Such money, securities, and property shall be separately accounted for and shall not be commingled with the funds of such commission merchant or be used to margin or guarantee the trades or contracts, or to secure or extend the credit, of any customer or person other than the one for whom the same are held: *Provided, however,* That such money, securities, and property of the customers of such futures commission merchant may, for convenience, be commingled and deposited in the same account or accounts with any bank or trust company or with the clearing house organization of such contract market or derivatives transaction execution facility, and that such share thereof as in the normal course of business shall be necessary to margin, guarantee, secure, transfer, adjust, or settle the contracts or trades of such customers, or resulting market positions, with the clearing-house organization of such contract market or derivatives transaction execution facility or with any member of such contract market, may be withdrawn and applied to such purposes, including the payment of commissions, brokerage, interest, taxes, storage, and other charges, lawfully accruing in connection with such contracts and trades: *Provided, further,* That in accordance with such terms and conditions as the Commission may prescribe by rule, regulation, or order, such money, securities, and property of the customers of such futures commission merchant may be commingled and deposited as provided in this section with any other money, securities, and property received by such futures commission merchant and required by the Commission to be separately accounted for and treated and dealt with as belonging to the customers of such futures commission merchant: *Provided further,* That such money may be invested in obligations of the United States, in general obligations of any State or of any political subdivision thereof, and in obligations fully guaranteed as to principal and interest by the United States, such investments to be made in accordance with such rules and regulations and subject to such conditions as the Commission may prescribe.

(b) It shall be unlawful for any person, including but not limited to any clearing agency of a contract market or derivatives transaction execution facility and any depository, that has received any money, securities, or property for deposit in a separate account as provided in paragraph (2) of this section, to hold, dispose of, or use any such money, securities, or property as belonging to the depositing futures commission merchant or any person other than the customers of such futures commission merchant.

(c) Consistent with this Act, the Commission, in consultation with the Securities and Exchange Commission, shall issue such rules, regulations, or orders as are necessary to avoid duplicative or conflicting regulations applicable to any futures commission merchant registered with the Commission pursuant to section 4f(a) (except paragraph (2) thereof), that is also registered with the Securities and Exchange Commission pursuant to section 15(b) of the Securities Exchange Act (except paragraph (11) thereof), involving the application of—

(1) section 8, section 15(c)(3), and section 17 of the Securities Exchange Act of 1934 and the rules and regulations thereunder related to the treatment of customer funds, securities, or property, maintenance of books and records, financial reporting or other financial responsibility rules (as defined in section 3(a)(40) of the Securities Exchange Act of 1934), involving security futures products; and

(2) similar provisions of this Act and the rules and regulations thereunder involving security futures products.

Sec. 6e. Dealings by Unregistered Floor Trader or Broker Prohibited

It shall be unlawful for any person to act as floor trader in executing purchases and sales, or as floor broker in executing any orders for the purchase or sale, of any commodity for future delivery, or involving any contracts of sale of any commodity for future delivery, on or subject to the rules of any contract market or derivatives transaction execution facility unless such person shall have registered, under this Act, with the Commission as such floor trader or floor broker and such registration shall not have expired nor been suspended nor revoked.

Sec. 6f. Registration and Financial Requirements; Risk Assessment

(a)(1) Any person desiring to register as a futures commission merchant, introducing broker, floor broker, or floor trader hereunder shall be registered upon application to the Commission. The application shall be made in such form and manner as prescribed by the Commission, giving such information and facts as the Commission may deem necessary concerning the business in which the applicant is or will be engaged, including in the case of an application of a futures commission merchant or an introducing broker, the names and addresses of the managers of all branch offices, and the names of such officers and partners, if a partnership, and of such officers, directors, and stockholders, if a corporation, as the Commission may direct. Such person, when registered hereunder, shall likewise continue to report and furnish to the Commission the above-mentioned information and such other information pertaining to such person's business as the Commission may require. Each registration shall expire on December 31 of the year for which issued or at such other time, not less than one year from the date of issuance, as the Commission may by rule, regulation, or order prescribe, and shall be renewed upon application therefor unless the registration has been suspended (and the period of such suspension has not expired) or revoked pursuant to the provisions of this Act.

(2) Notwithstanding paragraph (1), and except as provided in paragraph (3), any broker or dealer that is registered with the Securities and Exchange Commission shall be registered as a futures commission merchant or introducing broker, as applicable, if—

(A) the broker or dealer limits its solicitation of orders, acceptance of orders, or execution of orders, or placing of orders on behalf of others involving any contracts of sale of any commodity for future delivery, on or subject to the rules of any contract market or registered derivatives transaction execution facility to security futures products;

(B) the broker or dealer files written notice with the Commission in such form as the Commission, by rule, may prescribe containing such information as the Commission, by rule, may prescribe as necessary or appropriate in the public interest or for the protection of investors;

(C) the registration of the broker or dealer is not suspended pursuant to an order of the Securities and Exchange Commission; and

(D) the broker or dealer is a member of a national securities association registered pursuant to section 15A(a) of the Securities Exchange Act of 1934.

The registration shall be effective contemporaneously with the submission of notice, in written or electronic form, to the Commission.

(3) A floor broker or floor trader shall be exempt from the registration requirements of section 6e and paragraph (1) of this subsection if—

(A) the floor broker or floor trader is a broker or dealer registered with the Securities and Exchange Commission;

(B) the floor broker or floor trader limits its solicitation of orders, acceptance of orders, or execution of orders, or placing of orders on behalf of others involving any contracts of sale of any commodity for future delivery, on or subject to the rules of any contract market to security futures products; and

(C) the registration of the floor broker or floor trader is not suspended pursuant to an order of the Securities and Exchange Commission.

(4)(A) A broker or dealer that is registered as a futures commission merchant or introducing broker pursuant to paragraph (2), or that is a floor broker or floor trader exempt from registration pursuant to paragraph (3), shall be exempt from the following provisions of this Act and the rules thereunder:

(i) Subsections (b), (d), (e), and (g) of section 6c.

(ii) Sections 6d, 6e, and 6h.

(iii) Subsections (b) and (c) of this section.

(iv) Section 6j.

(v) Section 6k(1).

(vi) Section 6p.

(vii) Section 13a–2.

(viii) Subsections (d) and (g) of section 12.

(ix) Section 20.

(B)(i) Except as provided in clause (ii) of this subparagraph, but notwithstanding any other provision of this Act, the Commission, by rule, regulation, or order, may conditionally or unconditionally exempt any broker or dealer subject to the registration requirement of paragraph (2), or any broker or dealer exempt from registration pursuant to paragraph (3), from any provision of this Act or of any rule or regulation thereunder, to the extent the exemption is necessary or appropriate in the public interest and is consistent with the protection of investors.

(ii) The Commission shall, by rule or regulation, determine the procedures under which an exemptive order under this section shall be granted and may, in its sole discretion, decline to entertain any application for an order of exemption under this section.

(C)(i) A broker or dealer that is registered as a futures commission merchant or introducing broker pursuant to paragraph (2) or an associated person thereof, or that is a floor broker or floor trader exempt from registration pursuant to paragraph (3), shall not be required to become a member of any futures association registered under section 21.

(ii) No futures association registered under section 21 shall limit its members from carrying an account, accepting an order, or transacting business with a broker or dealer that is registered as a futures commission merchant or introducing broker pursuant to paragraph (2) or an associated person thereof, or that is a floor broker or floor trader exempt from registration pursuant to paragraph (3).

(b) Notwithstanding any other provisions of this Act, no person desiring to register as futures commission merchant or as introducing broker shall be so registered unless he meets such minimum financial requirements as the Commission may by regulation prescribe as necessary to insure his meeting his obligations as a registrant, and each person so registered shall at all times continue to meet such prescribed minimum financial requirements: *Provided,* That such minimum financial requirements will be considered met if the applicant for registration or registrant is a member of a contract market or derivatives transaction execution facility and conforms to minimum financial standards and related reporting requirements set by such contract market in its bylaws, rules, regulations, or resolutions and approved by the Commission as adequate to effectuate the purposes of this subsection.

Sec. 6j. Restrictions on Dual Trading in Security Futures Products on Designated Contract Markets and Registered Derivatives Transaction Execution Facilities

(a) The Commission shall issue regulations to prohibit the privilege of dual trading in security futures products on each contract market and registered derivatives transaction execution facility. The regulations issued by the Commission under this section—

(1) shall provide that the prohibition of dual trading thereunder shall take effect upon issuance of the regulations; and

(2) shall provide exceptions, as the Commission determines appropriate, to ensure fairness and orderly trading in security futures product markets, including—

(A) exceptions for spread transactions and the correction of trading errors;

(B) allowance for a customer to designate in writing not less than once annually a named floor broker to execute orders for such customer, notwithstanding the regulations to prohibit the privilege of dual trading required under this section; and

(C) other measures reasonably designed to accommodate unique or special characteristics of individual boards of trade or contract markets, to address emergency or unusual market conditions, or otherwise to further the public interest consistent with the promotion of market efficiency, innovation, and expansion of investment opportunities, the protection of investors, and with the purposes of this section.

(b) As used in this section, the term "dual trading" means the execution of customer orders by a floor broker during the same trading session in which the floor broker executes any trade in the same contract market or registered derivatives transaction execution facility for—

(1) the account of such floor broker;

(2) an account for which such floor broker has trading discretion; or

(3) an account controlled by a person with whom such floor broker has a relationship through membership in a broker association.

(c) As used in this section, the term "broker association" shall include two or more contract market members or registered derivatives transaction execution facility members with floor trading privileges of whom at least one is acting as a floor broker, who—

(1) engage in floor brokerage activity on behalf of the same employer,

(2) have an employer and employee relationship which relates to floor brokerage activity,

(3) share profits and losses associated with their brokerage or trading activity, or

(4) regularly share a deck of orders.

Sec. 6m. Use of Mails or Other Means or Instrumentalities of Interstate Commerce by Commodity Trading Advisors and Commodity Pool Operators; Relation to Other Law

(1) It shall be unlawful for any commodity trading advisor or commodity pool operator, unless registered under this Act, to make use of the mails or any means or instrumentality of interstate commerce in connection with his business as such commodity trading advisor or commodity pool operator: *Provided,* That the provisions of this section shall not apply to any commodity trading advisor who, during the course of the preceding twelve months, has not furnished commodity trading advice to more than fifteen persons and who does not hold himself out generally to the public as a commodity trading advisor. The provisions of this section shall not apply to any commodity trading advisor who is a (1) dealer, processor, broker, or seller in cash market transactions of any commodity specifically set forth in section 2(a) of this Act prior to the enactment of the Commodity Futures Trading Commission Act of 1974 (or products thereof) or (2) nonprofit,

voluntary membership, general farm organization, who provides advice on the sale or purchase of any commodity specifically set forth in section 2(a) of this Act prior to the enactment of the Commodity Futures Trading Commission Act of 1974; if the advice by the person described in clause (1) or (2) of this sentence as a commodity trading advisor is solely incidental to the conduct of that person's business: *Provided,* That such person shall be subject to proceedings under section 14 of this Act.

(2) Nothing in this Act shall relieve any person of any obligation or duty, or affect the availability of any right or remedy available to the Securities and Exchange Commission or any private party arising under the Securities Act of 1933 or the Securities Exchange Act of 1934 governing the issuance, offer, purchase, or sale of securities of a commodity pool, or of persons engaged in transactions with respect to such securities, or reporting by a commodity pool.

(3) Subsection (1) of this section shall not apply to any commodity trading advisor that is registered with the Securities and Exchange Commission as an investment adviser whose business does not consist primarily of acting as a commodity trading advisor, as defined in section 1a(6), and that does not act as a commodity trading advisor to any investment trust, syndicate, or similar form of enterprise that is engaged primarily in trading in any commodity for future delivery on or subject to the rules of any contract market or registered derivatives transaction execution facility.

Sec. 6o. Fraud and Misrepresentation by Commodity Trading Advisors, Commodity Pool Operators, and Associated Persons

(1) It shall be unlawful for a commodity trading advisor, associated person of a commodity trading advisor, commodity pool operator, or associated person of a commodity pool operator by use of the mails or any means or instrumentality of interstate commerce, directly or indirectly—

(A) to employ any device, scheme, or artifice to defraud any client or participant or prospective client or participant; or

(B) to engage in any transaction, practice, or course of business which operates as a fraud or deceit upon any client or participant or prospective client or participant.

(2) It shall be unlawful for any commodity trading advisor, associated person of a commodity trading advisor, commodity pool operator, or associated person of a commodity pool operator registered under this Act to represent or imply in any manner whatsoever that such person has been sponsored, recommended, or approved, or that such person's abilities or qualifications have in any respect been passed upon, by the United States or any agency or officer thereof. This section shall not be construed to prohibit a statement that a person is registered under this Act as a commodity trading advisor, associated person of a commodity trading advisor, commodity pool operator, or associated person of a commodity pool operator, if such statement is true in fact and if the effect of such registration is not misrepresented.

Sec. 7b–1. Designation of Securities Exchanges and Associations as Contract Markets

(a) Any board of trade that is registered with the Securities and Exchange Commission as a national securities exchange, is a national securities association registered pursuant to section 15A(a) of the Securities Exchange Act of 1934, or is an alternative trading system shall be a designated contract market in security futures products if—

(1) such national securities exchange, national securities association, or alternative trading system lists or trades no other contracts of sale for future delivery, except for security futures products;

(2) such national securities exchange, national securities association, or alternative trading system files written notice with the

Commission in such form as the Commission, by rule, may prescribe containing such information as the Commission, by rule, may prescribe as necessary or appropriate in the public interest or for the protection of customers; and

(3) the registration of such national securities exchange, national securities association, or alternative trading system is not suspended pursuant to an order by the Securities and Exchange Commission.

Such designation shall be effective contemporaneously with the submission of notice, in written or electronic form, to the Commission.

(b)(1) A national securities exchange, national securities association, or alternative trading system that is designated as a contract market pursuant to section 5f shall be exempt from the following provisions of this Act and the rules thereunder:

(A) Subsections (c), (e), and (g) of section 6c.

(B) Section 6j.

(C) Section 7.

(D) Section 7a–2.

(E) Section 10a.

(F) Section 12(d).

(G) Section 13(f).

(H) Section 20.

(2) An alternative trading system that is a designated contract market under this section shall be required to be a member of a futures association registered under section 21 and shall be exempt from any provision of this Act that would require such alternative trading system to—

(A) set rules governing the conduct of subscribers other than the conduct of such subscribers' trading on such alternative trading system; or

(B) discipline subscribers other than by exclusion from trading.

(3) To the extent that an alternative trading system is exempt from any provision of this Act pursuant to paragraph (2) of this subsection, the futures association registered under section 21 of which the alternative trading system is a member shall set rules governing the conduct of subscribers to the alternative trading system and discipline the subscribers.

(4)(A) Except as provided in subparagraph (B), but notwithstanding any other provision of this Act, the Commission, by rule, regulation, or order, may conditionally or unconditionally exempt any designated contract market in security futures subject to the designation requirement of this section from any provision of this Act or of any rule or regulation thereunder, to the extent such exemption is necessary or appropriate in the public interest and is consistent with the protection of investors.

(B) The Commission shall, by rule or regulation, determine the procedures under which an exemptive order under this section is granted and may, in its sole discretion, decline to entertain any application for an order of exemption under this section.

(C) An alternative trading system shall not be deemed to be an exchange for any purpose as a result of the designation of such alternative trading system as a contract market under this section.

Sec. 12a. Registration of Commodity Dealers and Associated Persons; Regulation of Contract Markets

The Commission is authorized—

(1) to register futures commission merchants, associated persons of futures commission merchants, introducing brokers, associated persons of introducing brokers, commodity trading advisors, associated persons of commodity trading advisors, commodity pool operators, associated persons of commodity pool operators, floor brokers, and floor traders upon application in accordance with rules and regulations and in the form

and manner to be prescribed by the Commission, which may require the applicant, and such persons associated with the applicant as the Commission may specify, to be fingerprinted and to submit, or cause to be submitted, such fingerprints to the Attorney General for identification and appropriate processing, and in connection therewith to fix and establish from time to time reasonable fees and charges for registrations and renewals thereof: *Provided,* That notwithstanding any provision of this Act, the Commission may grant a temporary license to any applicant for registration with the Commission pursuant to such rules, regulations, or orders as the Commission may adopt, except that the term of any such temporary license shall not exceed six months from the date of its issuance;

(2) upon notice, but without a hearing and pursuant to such rules, regulations, or orders as the Commission may adopt, to refuse to register, to register conditionally, or to suspend or place restrictions upon the registration of, any person and with such a hearing as may be appropriate to revoke the registration of any person—

(A) if a prior registration of such person in any capacity has been suspended (and the period of such suspension has not expired) or has been revoked;

(B) if registration of such person in any capacity has been refused under the provisions of paragraph (3) of this section within five years preceding the filing of the application for registration or at any time thereafter;

(C) if such person is permanently or temporarily enjoined by order, judgment, or decree of any court of competent jurisdiction (except that registration may not be revoked solely on the basis of such temporary order, judgment, or decree), including an order entered pursuant to an agreement of settlement to which the Commission or any Federal or State agency or other governmental body is a party, from (i) acting as a futures commission merchant, introducing broker, floor broker, floor trader, commodity trading advisor, commodity pool operator, associated person of any registrant under this Act, securities broker, securities dealer, municipal securities broker, municipal securities dealer, transfer agent, clearing agency, securities information processor, investment adviser, investment company, or affiliated person or employee of any of the foregoing or (ii) engaging in or continuing any activity where such activity involves embezzlement, theft, extortion, fraud, fraudulent conversion, misappropriation of funds, securities or property, forgery, counterfeiting, false pretenses, bribery, gambling, or any transaction in or advice concerning contracts of sale of a commodity for future delivery, concerning matters subject to Commission regulation under section 4c or 19, or concerning securities.

(D) if such person has been convicted within ten years preceding the filing of the application for registration or any time thereafter of any felony that (i) involves any transactions or advice concerning any contract of sale of a commodity for future delivery, or any activity subject to Commission regulation under section 4c or 19 of this Act, or concerning a security, (ii) arises out of the conduct of the business of a futures commission merchant, introducing broker, floor broker, floor trader, commodity trading advisor, commodity pool operator, associated person of any registrant under this Act, securities broker, securities dealer, municipal securities broker, municipal securities dealer, transfer agent, clearing agency, securities information processor, investment adviser, investment company, or an affiliated person or employee of any of the foregoing, (iii) involves embezzlement, theft, extortion, fraud, fraudulent conversion, misappropriation of funds, securities or property, forgery, counterfeiting, false pretenses, bribery, or gambling, or (iv) involves the violation of section 152, 1001, 1341, 1342, 1343, 1503, 1623, 1961, 1962, 1963, or 2314, or chapter 25, 47, 95, or 96 of title 18, United States Code, or section 7201 or 7206 of the Internal Revenue Code of 1986;

(E) if such person, within ten years preceding the filing of the application or at any time thereafter, has been found in a proceeding brought by the Commission or any Federal or State agency or other governmental body, or by agreement of settlement to which the Commission or any Federal or State agency or other governmental body is a party, (i) to have violated any provision of this Act, the Securities Act of 1933, the Securities Exchange Act of 1934, the Public Utility Holding Company Act of 1935, the Trust Indenture Act of 1939, the Investment Advisers Act of 1940, the Investment Company Act of 1940, the Securities Investors Protection Act of 1970, the Foreign Corrupt Practices Act of 1977, chapter 96 of title 18 of the United States Code, or any similar statute of a State or foreign jurisdiction, or any rule, regulation, or order under any such statutes, or the rules of the Municipal Securities Rulemaking Board where such violation involves embezzlement, theft, extortion, fraud, fraudulent conversion, misappropriation of funds, securities or property, forgery, counterfeiting, false pretenses, bribery, or gambling, or (ii) to have willfully aided, abetted, counseled, commanded, induced, or procured such violation by any other person;

(F) if such person is subject to an outstanding order of the Commission denying privileges on any registered entity to such person, denying, suspending, or revoking such person's membership in any registered entity or registered futures association, or barring or suspending such person from being associated with a registrant under this Act or with a member of a contract market or with a member of a registered futures association;

(G) if, as to any of the matters set forth in this paragraph and paragraph (3), such person willfully made any materially false or misleading statement or omitted to state any material fact in such person's application or any update thereto; or

(H) if refusal, suspension, or revocation of the registration of any principal of such person would be warranted because of a statutory disqualification listed in this paragraph:

Provided, That such person may appeal from a decision to refuse registration, condition registration, suspend, revoke or to place restrictions upon registration made pursuant to the provisions of this paragraph in the manner provided in sections 9 and 15 of this Act; and

Provided further, That for the purposes of paragraphs (2) and (3) of this section, "principal" shall mean, if the person is a partnership, any general partner or, if the person is a corporation, any officer, director, or beneficial owner of at least 10 per centum of the voting shares of the corporation, and any other person that the Commission by rule, regulation, or order determines has the power, directly or indirectly, through agreement or otherwise, to exercise a controlling influence over the activities of such person which are subject to regulation by the Commission;

(3) to refuse to register or to register conditionally any person, if it is found, after opportunity for hearing, that—

(A) such person has been found by the Commission or by any court of competent jurisdiction to have violated, or has consented to findings of a violation of, any provision of this Act, or any rule, regulation, or order thereunder (other than a violation set forth in paragraph (2) of this section), or to have willfully aided, abetted, counseled, commanded, induced, or procured the violation by any other person of any such provision;

(B) such person has been found by any court of competent jurisdiction or by any Federal or State agency or other governmental body, or by agreement of settlement to which any Federal or State agency or other governmental body is a party, (i) to have violated any provision of the Securities Act of 1933, the Securities Exchange Act of 1934, the Public Utility Holding Company Act of 1935, the Trust Indenture Act of 1939, the Investment Advisers Act of 1940, the Investment Company Act of 1940, the Securities Investors Protection Act of 1970, the Foreign Corrupt Practices Act of 1977, or any similar statute of a State or foreign jurisdiction, or any rule, regulation, or order under any such statutes, or the rules of the Municipal Securities Rulemaking Board or (ii) to have willfully aided, abetted, counseled, commanded, induced, or procured such violation by any other person;

(C) such person failed reasonably to supervise another person, who is subject to such person's supervision, with a view to preventing violations of this Act, or of any of the statutes set forth in subparagraph (B) of this paragraph, or of any of the rules, regulations, or orders thereunder, and the person subject to supervision committed such a violation: *Provided,* That no person shall be deemed to have failed reasonably to supervise another person, within the meaning of this subparagraph if (i) there have been established procedures, and a system for applying such procedures, which would reasonably be expected to prevent and detect, insofar as practicable, any such violation by such other person and (ii) such person has reasonably discharged the duties and obligations incumbent upon that person, as supervisor, by reason of such procedures and system, without reasonable cause to believe that such procedures and system were not being complied with;

(D) such person pleaded guilty to or was convicted of a felony other than a felony of the type specified in paragraph (2)(D) of this section, or was convicted of a felony of the type specified in paragraph (2)(D) of this section more than ten years preceding the filing of the application;

(E) such person pleaded guilty to or was convicted of any misdemeanor which (i) involves any transaction or advice concerning any contract of sale of a commodity for future delivery or any activity subject to Commission regulation under section 4c or 19 of this Act or concerning a security, (ii) arises out of the conduct of the business of a futures commission merchant, introducing broker, floor broker, floor trader, commodity trading advisor, commodity pool operator, associated person of any registrant under this Act, securities broker, securities dealer, municipal securities broker, municipal securities dealer, transfer agent, clearing agency, securities information processor, investment adviser, investment company, or an affiliated person or employee of any of the foregoing, (iii) involves embezzlement, theft, extortion, fraud, fraudulent conversion, misappropriation of funds, securities or property, forgery, counterfeiting, false pretenses, bribery, or gambling, (iv) involves the violation of section 152, 1341, 1342, or 1343 or chapter 25, 47, 95, or 96 of title 18, United States Code, or section 7203, 7204, 7205, or 7207 of the Internal Revenue Code of 1986;

(F) such person was debarred by any agency of the United States from contracting with the United States;

(G) such person willfully made any materially false or misleading statement or willfully omitted to state any material fact in such person's application or any update thereto, in any report required to be filed with the Commission by this Act or the regulations thereunder, in any proceeding before the Commission or in any registration disqualification proceeding;

(H) such person has pleaded nolo contendere to criminal charges of felonious conduct, or has been convicted in a State court, in a United States military court, or in a foreign court of conduct which would constitute a felony under Federal law if the offense had been committed under Federal jurisdiction;

(I) in the case of an applicant for registration in any capacity for which there are minimum financial requirements prescribed under this Act or under the rules or regulations of the Commission, such person has not established that such person meets such minimum financial requirements;

(J) such person is subject to an outstanding order denying, suspending, or expelling such person from membership in a registered entity, a registered futures association, any other self-regulatory organization, or any foreign regulatory body that the Commission recognizes as having a comparable regulatory program or barring or suspending such person from being associated with any member or members of such registered entity, association, self-regulatory organization, or foreign regulatory body;

(K) such person has been found by any court of competent jurisdiction or by any Federal or State agency or other governmental body, or by agreement of settlement to which any Federal or State agency or other governmental body is a party, (i) to have violated any statute or any rule, regulation, or order thereunder which involves embezzlement, theft, extortion, fraud, fraudulent conversion, misappropriation of funds, securities or property, forgery, counterfeiting, false pretenses, bribery, or gambling or (ii) to have willfully aided, abetted, counseled, commanded, induced or procured such violation by any other person;

(L) such person has associated with such person* any other person and knows, or in the exercise of reasonable care should know, of facts regarding such other person that are set forth as statutory disqualifications in paragraph (2) of this section, unless such person has notified the Commission of such facts and the Commission has determined that such other person should be registered or temporarily licensed;

(M) there is other good cause; or

(N) any principal, as defined in paragraph (2) of this section, of such person has been or could be refused registration: *Provided,* That pending final determination under this paragraph, registration shall not be granted: *Provided further,* That such person may appeal from a decision to refuse registration or to condition registration made pursuant to this paragraph in the manner provided in sections 9 and 15 of this Act;

(4) in accordance with the procedure provided for in sections 9 and 15 of this Act, to suspend, revoke, or place restrictions upon the registration of any person registered under this Act if cause exists under paragraph (3) of this section which would warrant a refusal of registration of such person, and to suspend or revoke the registration of any futures commission merchant or introducing broker who shall knowingly accept any order for the purchase or sale of any commodity for future delivery on or subject to the rules of any registered entity from any person if such person has been denied trading privileges on any contract market by order of the Commission under sections 9 and 15 of this Act and the period of denial specified in such order shall not have expired: *Provided,* That such person may appeal from a decision to suspend, revoke, or place restrictions upon

* So in original.

registration made pursuant to this paragraph in the manner provided in sections 9 and 15 of this Act;

(5) to make and promulgate such rules and regulations as, in the judgment of the Commission, are reasonably necessary to effectuate any of the provisions or to accomplish any of the purposes of this Act;

(6) to communicate to the proper committee or officer of any registered entity, registered futures association, or self-regulatory organization as defined in section 3(a)(26) of the Securities Exchange Act of 1934, notwithstanding the provisions of section 8 of this Act, the full facts concerning any transaction or market operation, including the names of parties thereto, which in the judgment of the Commission disrupts or tends to disrupt any market or is otherwise harmful or against the best interests of producers, consumers, or investors, or which is necessary or appropriate to effectuate the purposes of this Act: *Provided,* That any information furnished by the Commission under this paragraph shall not be disclosed by such registered entity, registered futures association, or self-regulatory organization except in any self-regulatory action or proceeding;

(7) to alter or supplement the rules of a registered entity insofar as necessary or appropriate by rule or regulation or by order, if after making the appropriate request in writing to a registered entity that such contract market effect on its own behalf specified changes in its rules and practices, and after appropriate notice and opportunity for hearing, the Commission determines that such registered entity has not made the changes so required, and that such changes are necessary or appropriate for the protection of persons producing, handling, processing, or consuming any commodity traded for future delivery on such registered entity, or the product or byproduct thereof, or for the protection of traders or to insure fair dealing in commodities traded for future delivery on such registered entity. Such rules, regulations, or orders may specify changes with respect to such matters as—

(A) terms or conditions in contracts of sale to be executed on or subject to the rules of such registered entity;

(B) the form or manner of execution of purchases and sales for future delivery;

(C) other trading requirements, excepting the setting of levels of margin;

(D) safeguards with respect to the financial responsibility of members;

(E) the manner, method, and place of soliciting business, including the content of such solicitations; and

(F) the form and manner of handling, recording, and accounting for customers' orders, transactions, and accounts;

(8) to make and promulgate such rules and regulations with respect to those persons registered under this Act, who are not members of a registered entity, as in the judgment of the Commission are reasonably necessary to protect the public interest and promote just and equitable principles of trade, including but not limited to the manner, method, and place of soliciting business, including the content of such solicitation;

(9) to direct the registered entity, whenever it has reason to believe that an emergency exists, to take such action as in the Commission's judgment is necessary to maintain or restore orderly trading in or liquidation of any futures contract, including, but not limited to, the setting of temporary emergency margin levels on any futures contract, and the fixing of limits that may apply to a market position acquired in good faith prior to the effective date of the Commission's action. The term "emergency" as used herein shall mean, in addition to threatened or actual market manipulations and corners, any act of the United States or a foreign government affecting a commodity or any other major market disturbance which prevents the market from accurately reflecting the forces of supply and demand

for such commodity. Any action taken by the Commission under this paragraph shall be subject to review only in the United States Court of Appeals for the circuit in which the party seeking review resides or has its principal place of business, or in the United States Court of Appeals for the District of Columbia Circuit. Such review shall be based upon an examination of all the information before the Commission at the time the determination was made. The court reviewing the Commission's action shall not enter a stay or order of mandamus unless it has determined, after notice and hearing before a panel of the court, that the agency action complained of was arbitrary, capricious, an abuse of discretion, or otherwise not in accordance with law. Nothing herein shall be deemed to limit the meaning or interpretation given by a registered entity to the terms "market emergency", "emergency", or equivalent language in its own bylaws, rules, regulations, or resolutions;

(10) to authorize any person to perform any portion of the registration functions under this Act, in accordance with rules, notwithstanding any other provision of law, adopted by such person and submitted to the Commission for approval or, if applicable, for review pursuant to section 21(j) of this Act, and subject to the provisions of this Act applicable to registrations granted by the Commission; and

(11)(A) by written notice served on the person and pursuant to such rules, regulations, and orders as the Commission may adopt, to suspend or modify the registration of any person registered under this Act who is charged (in any information, indictment, or complaint authorized by a United States attorney or an appropriate official of any State) with the commission of or participation in a crime involving a violation of this Act, or a violation of any other provision of Federal or State law that would reflect on the honesty or the fitness of the person to act as a fiduciary (including an offense specified in subparagraph (D) or (E) of paragraph (2)) that is punishable by imprisonment for a term exceeding one year, if the Commission determines that continued registration of the person may pose a threat to the public interest or may threaten to impair public confidence in any market regulated by the Commission.

(B) Prior to the suspension or modification of the registration of a person under this paragraph, the person shall be afforded an opportunity for a hearing at which the Commission shall have the burden of showing that the continued registration of the person does, or is likely to, pose a threat to the public interest or threaten to impair public confidence in any market regulated by the Commission.

(C) Any notice of suspension or modification issued under this paragraph shall remain in effect until such information, indictment, or complaint is disposed of or until terminated by the Commission.

(D) On disposition of such information, indictment, or complaint, the Commission may issue and serve on such person an order pursuant to paragraph (2) or (4) to suspend, restrict, or revoke the registration of such person.

(E) A finding of not guilty or other disposition of the charge shall not preclude the Commission from thereafter instituting any other proceedings under this Act.

(F) A person aggrieved by an order issued under this paragraph may obtain review of such order in the same manner and on the same terms and conditions as are provided in section 6(b).

Sec. 13. Violations Generally; Punishment; Costs of Prosecution

(a) It shall be a felony punishable by a fine of not more than $1,000,000 (or $500,000 in the case of a person who is an individual) or imprisonment for not more than five years, or both, together with the costs of prosecution, for:

(1) Any person registered or required to be registered under this Act, or any employee or agent thereof, to embezzle, steal, purloin, or with criminal intent convert to such person's use or the use of another, any money, securities, or property having a value in excess of $100, which was received by such person or any employee or agent thereof to margin, guarantee, or secure the trades or contracts of any customer or accruing to such customer as a result of such trades or contracts or which otherwise was received from any customer, client, or pool participant in connection with the business of such person. The word "value" as used in this paragraph means face, par, or market value, or cost price, either wholesale or retail, whichever is greater.

(2) Any person to manipulate or attempt to manipulate the price of any commodity in interstate commerce, or for future delivery on or subject to the rules of any registered entity, or to corner or attempt to corner any such commodity or knowingly to deliver or cause to be delivered for transmission through the mails or interstate commerce by telegraph, telephone, wireless, or other means of communication false or misleading or knowingly inaccurate reports concerning crop or market information or conditions that affect or tend to affect the price of any commodity in interstate commerce, or knowingly to violate the provisions of section 6, section 6b, subsections (a) through (e) of subsection 6c, section 6h, section 6o(1), or section 23.

(3) Any person knowingly to make, or cause to be made, any statement in any application, report, or document required to be filed under this Act or any rule or regulation thereunder or any undertaking contained in a registration statement required under this Act, or by any registered entity or registered futures association in connection with an application for membership, or participation therein or to become associated with a member thereof, which statement was false or misleading with respect to any material fact, or knowingly to omit any material fact required to be stated therein or necessary to make the statements therein not misleading.

(4) Any person willfully to falsify, conceal, or cover up by any trick, scheme, or artifice a material fact, make any false, fictitious, or fraudulent statements or representations, or make or use any false writing or document knowing the same to contain any false, fictitious, or fraudulent statement or entry to a registered entity, board of trade, or futures association designated or registered under this Act acting in furtherance of its official duties under this Act.

(5) Any person willfully to violate any other provision of this Act, or any rule or regulation thereunder, the violation of which is made unlawful or the observance of which is required under the terms of this Act, but no person shall be subject to imprisonment under this paragraph for the violation of any rule or regulation if such person proves that he had no knowledge of such rule or regulation.

(b) Any person convicted of a felony under this section shall be suspended from registration under this Act and shall be denied registration or reregistration for five years or such longer period as the Commission may determine, and barred from using, or participating in any manner in, any market regulated by the Commission for five years or such longer period as the Commission shall determine, on such terms and conditions as the Commission may prescribe, unless the Commission determines that the imposition of such suspension, denial of registration or reregistration, or market bar is not required to protect the public interest. The Commission may upon petition later review such disqualification and market bar and for good cause shown reduce the period thereof.

(c) It shall be a felony punishable by a fine of not more than $500,000 or imprisonment for not more than five years, or both, together with the costs of prosecution, for any Commissioner of the Commission or any employee or agent thereof, to participate, directly or indirectly, in any transaction in commodity futures or any transaction of the character of or which is commonly known to the trade as an "option", "privilege", "indemnity", "bid", "offer", "put", "call", "advance guaranty", or "decline guaranty", or any transaction for the delivery of any commodity under a standardized contract commonly known to the trade as a margin account, margin contract, leverage account, or leverage contract, or under any contract, account, arrangement, scheme, or device that the Commission determines serves the same function or functions as such a standardized contract, or is marketed or managed in substantially the same manner as such a standardized contract, or for any such person to participate, directly or indirectly, in any investment transaction in an actual commodity if nonpublic information is used in the investment transaction, if the investment transaction is prohibited by rule or regulation of the Commission, or if the investment transaction is effected by means of any instrument regulated by the Commission. The foregoing prohibitions shall not apply to any transaction or class of transactions that the Commission, by rule or regulation, has determined would not be contrary to the public interest or otherwise inconsistent with the purposes of this subsection.

(d) It shall be a felony punishable by a fine of not more than $500,000 or imprisonment for not more than five years, or both, together with the costs of prosecution—(1) for any Commissioner of the Commission or any employee or agent thereof who, by virtue of his employment or position, acquires information which may affect or tend to affect the price of any commodity futures or commodity and which information has not been made public to impart such information with intent to assist another person, directly or indirectly, to participate in any transaction in commodity futures, any transaction in an actual commodity, or in any transaction of the character of or which is commonly known to the trade as an "option", "privilege", "indemnity", "bid", "offer", "put", "call", "advance guaranty", or "decline guaranty", or in any transaction for the delivery of any commodity under a standardized contract commonly known to the trade as a margin account, margin contract, leverage account, or leverage contract, or under any contract, account, arrangement, scheme, or device that the Commission determines serves the same function or functions as such a standardized contract, or is marketed or managed in substantially the same manner as such a standardized contract; and (2) for any person to acquire such information from any Commissioner of the Commission or any employee or agent thereof and to use such information in any transaction in commodity futures, any transaction in an actual commodity, or in any transaction of the character of or which is commonly known to the trade as an "option", "privilege", "indemnity", "bid", "offer", "put", "call", "advance guaranty", or "decline guaranty", or in any transaction for the delivery of any commodity under a standardized contract commonly known to the trade as a margin account, margin contract, leverage account, or leverage contract, or under any contract, account, arrangement, scheme, or device that the Commission determines serves the same function or functions as such a standardized contract, or is marketed or managed in substantially the same manner as such a standardized contract.

(f) It shall be a felony for any person—

(1) who is an employee, member of the governing board, or member of any committee of a board of trade, registered entity, or registered futures association, in violation of a regulation issued by the Commission, willfully and knowingly to trade for such person's own account, or for or on behalf of any other account, in contracts for future delivery or options thereon on the basis of, or willfully and knowingly to disclose for any

purpose inconsistent with the performance of such person's official duties as an employee or member, any material nonpublic information obtained through special access related to the performance of such duties.

(2) willfully and knowingly to trade for such person's own account, or for or on behalf of any other account, in contracts for future delivery or options thereon on the basis of any material nonpublic information that such person knows was obtained in violation of paragraph (1) from an employee, member of the governing board, or member of any committee of a board of trade, registered entity, or registered futures association.

Such felony shall be punishable by a fine of not more than $500,000, plus the amount of any profits realized from such trading or disclosure made in violation of this subsection, or imprisonment for not more than five years, or both, together with the costs of prosecution.

Sec. 18. Complaints Against Registered Persons

(a)(1) Any person complaining of any violation of any provision of this Act or any rule, regulation, or order issued pursuant to this Act by any person who is registered under this Act may, at any time within two years after the cause of action accrues, apply to the Commission for an order awarding—

(A) actual damages proximately caused by such violation. If an award of actual damages is made against a floor broker in connection with the execution of a customer order, and the futures commission merchant which selected the floor broker for the execution of the customer order is held to be responsible under section 2(a)(1) for the floor broker's violation, such futures commission merchant may be required to satisfy such award; and

(B) in the case of any action arising from a willful and intentional violation in the execution of an order on the floor of a registered entity, punitive or exemplary damages equal to no more than two times the amount of such actual damages. If an award of punitive or exemplary damages is made against a floor broker in connection with the execution of a customer order, and the futures commission merchant which selected the floor broker for the execution of the customer order is held to be responsible under section 2(a)(1) for the floor broker's violation, such futures commission merchant may be required to satisfy such award if the floor broker fails to do so, except that such requirement shall apply to the futures commission merchant only if it willfully and intentionally selected the floor broker with the intent to assist or facilitate the floor broker's violation.

(2)(A) An action may be brought under this subsection by any one or more persons described in this subsection for and in behalf of such person or persons and other persons similarly situated, if the Commission permits such actions pursuant to a final rule issued by the Commission.

(B) Not later than two hundred and seventy days after the date of enactment of this paragraph, the Commission shall propose and publish for public comment such rules as are necessary to carry out subparagraph (A). In developing such rules, the Commission shall consider the potential impact of such actions on resources available to the reparations system established under this Act and the relative merits of bringing such actions in Federal court.

(b) The Commission may promulgate such rules, regulations, and orders as it deems necessary or appropriate for the efficient and expeditious administration of this section. Notwithstanding any other provision of law, such rules, regulations, and orders may prescribe, or otherwise condition, without limitation, the form, filing, and service of pleadings or orders, the nature and scope of discovery, counterclaims, motion practice (including the grounds for dismissal of any claim or counterclaim), hearings (including the waiver thereof, which may relate to the amount in controversy), rights of appeal, if any, and all other matters governing proceedings before the Commission under this section.

(c) In case a complaint is made by a nonresident of the United States, the complainant shall be required, before any formal action is taken on his complaint, to furnish a bond in double the amount of the claim conditioned upon the payment of costs, including a reasonable attorney's fee for the respondent if the respondent shall prevail, and any reparation award that may be issued by the Commission against the complainant on any counterclaim by respondent: *Provided,* That the Commission shall have authority to waive the furnishing of a bond by a complainant who is a resident of a country which permits the filing of a complaint by a resident of the United States without the furnishing of a bond.

(d) If any person against whom an award has been made does not pay the reparation award within the time specified in the Commission's order, the complainant, or any person for whose benefit such order was made, within three years of the date of the order, may file a certified copy of the order of the Commission, in the district court of the United States for the district in which he resides or in which is located the principal place of business of the respondent, for enforcement of such reparation award by appropriate orders. The orders, writs, and processes of such district court may in such case run, be served, and be returnable anywhere in the United States. The petitioner shall not be liable for costs in the district court, nor for costs at any subsequent state of the proceedings, unless they accrue upon his appeal. If the petitioner finally prevails, he shall be allowed a reasonable attorney's fee, to be taxed and collected as a part of the costs of the suit. Subject to the right of appeal under subsection (e) of this section, an order of the Commission awarding reparations shall be final and conclusive.

(e) Any order of the Commission entered hereunder shall be reviewable on petition of any party aggrieved thereby, by the United States Court of Appeals for any circuit in which a hearing was held, or if no hearing was held, any circuit in which the appellee is located under the procedure provided in sections 9 and 15 of this Act. Such appeal shall not be effective unless within 30 days from and after the date of the reparation order the appellant also files with the clerk of the court a bond in double the amount of the reparation awarded against the appellant conditioned upon the payment of the judgment entered by the court, plus interest and costs, including a reasonable attorney's fee for the appellee, if the appellee shall prevail. Such bond shall be in the form of cash, negotiable securities having a market value at least equivalent to the amount of bond prescribed, or the undertaking of a surety company on the approved list of sureties issued by the Treasury Department of the United States. The appellee shall not be liable for costs in said court. If the appellee prevails, he shall be allowed a reasonable attorney's fee to be taxed and collected as a part of his costs.

(f) Unless the party against whom a reparation order has been issued shows to the satisfaction of the Commission within fifteen days from the expiration of the period allowed for compliance with such order that either an appeal as herein authorized has been taken or payment of the full amount of the order (or any agreed settlement thereof) has been made, such party shall be prohibited automatically from trading on all registered entities and, if the party is registered with the Commission, such registration shall be suspended automatically at the expiration of such fifteen-day period until such party shows to the satisfaction of the Commission that payment of such amount with interest thereon to date of payment has been made: *Provided,* That if on appeal the appellee prevails or if the appeal is dismissed, the automatic prohibition against trading and suspension of registration shall become effective at the expiration of thirty days from the date of judgment on the appeal, but if the judgment is stayed by a court of competent jurisdiction, the suspension shall become effective ten days after the expiration of such stay, unless prior thereto the judgment of the court has been satisfied.

(g) Predispute Resolution Agreements for Institutional Customers.—Nothing in this section prohibits a registered futures commission merchant from requiring a customer that is an eligible contract participant, as a condition to the commission merchant's conducting a transaction for the customer, to enter into an agreement waiving the right to file a claim under this section.

Sec. 25. Private Rights of Action

(a)(1) Any person (other than a registered entity or registered futures association) who violates this Act or who willfully aids, abets, counsels, induces, or procures the commission of a violation of this Act shall be liable for actual damages resulting from one or more of the transactions referred to in subparagraphs (A) through (D) of this paragraph and caused by such violation to any other person—

(A) who received trading advice from such person for a fee;

(B) who made through such person any contract of sale of any commodity for future delivery (or option on such contract or any commodity); or who deposited with or paid to such person money, securities, or property (or incurred debt in lieu thereof) in connection with any order to make such contract;

(C) who purchased from or sold to such person or placed through such person an order for the purchase or sale of—

(i) an option subject to section 6c of this Act (other than an option purchased or sold on a registered entity or other board of trade);

(ii) a contract subject to section 23 of this Act; or

(iii) an interest or participation in a commodity pool; or

(D) who purchased or sold a contract referred to in subparagraph (B) hereof if the violation constitutes a manipulation of the price of any such contract or the price of the commodity underlying such contract.

(2) Except as provided in subsection (b), the rights of action authorized by this subsection and by sections 7(d)(13), 7a–1(b)(1)(E), and 21(b)(10) of this Act shall be the exclusive remedies under this Act available to any person who sustains loss as a result of any alleged violation of this Act. Nothing in this subsection shall limit or abridge the rights of the parties to agree in advance of a dispute upon any forum for resolving claims under this section, including arbitration.

(3) In any action arising from a violation in the execution of an order on the floor of a registered entity, the person referred to in paragraph (1) shall be liable for—

(A) actual damages proximately caused by such violation. If an award of actual damages is made against a floor broker in connection with the execution of a customer order, and the futures commission merchant which selected the floor broker for the execution of the customer order is held to be responsible under section 2(a)(1) for the floor broker's violation, such futures commission merchant may be required to satisfy such award; and

(B) where the violation is willful and intentional, punitive or exemplary damages equal to no more than two times the amount of such actual damages. If an award of punitive or exemplary damages is made against a floor broker in connection with the execution of a customer order, and the futures commission merchant which selected the floor broker for the execution of the customer order is held to be responsible under section 2(a)(1) for the floor broker's violation, such futures commission merchant may be required to satisfy such award if the floor broker fails to do so, except that such requirement shall apply to the futures commission merchant only if it willfully and intentionally selected the floor broker with the intent to assist or facilitate the floor broker's violation.

(4) CONTRACT ENFORCEMENT BETWEEN ELIGIBLE COUNTERPARTIES.—No agreement, contract, or transaction between eligible contract participants or persons reasonably believed to be eligible contract participants, and no hybrid instrument sold to any investor, shall be void, voidable, or unenforceable, and no such party shall be entitled to rescind, or recover any payment made with respect to, such an agreement, contract, transaction, or instrument under this section or any other provision of Federal or State law, based solely on the failure of the agreement, contract, transaction, or instrument to comply with the terms or conditions of an exemption or exclusion from any provision of this Act or regulations of the Commission.

(b)(1)(A) A registered entity that fails to enforce any bylaw, rule, regulation, or resolution that it is required to enforce by sections 7 through 7a–2, (B) a licensed board of trade that fails to enforce any bylaw, rule, regulation, or resolution that it is required to enforce by the Commission, or (C) any registered entity that in enforcing any such bylaw, rule, regulation, or resolution violates this Act or any Commission rule, regulation, or order, shall be liable for actual damages sustained by a person who engaged in any transaction on or subject to the rules of such registered entity to the extent of such person's actual losses that resulted from such transaction and were caused by such failure to enforce or enforcement of such bylaws, rules, regulations, or resolutions.

(2) A registered futures association that fails to enforce any bylaw or rule that is required under section 21 of this Act or in enforcing any such bylaw or rule violates this Act or any Commission rule, regulation, or order shall be liable for actual damages sustained by a person that engaged in any transaction specified in subsection (a) of this section to the extent of such person's actual losses that resulted from such transaction and were caused by such failure to enforce or enforcement of such bylaw or rule.

(3) Any individual who, in the capacity as an officer, director, governor, committee member, or employee of a registered entity or a registered futures association willfully aids, abets, counsels, induces, or procures any failure by any such entity to enforce (or any violation of the Act in enforcing) any bylaw, rule, regulation, or resolution referred to in paragraph (1) or (2) of this subsection, shall be liable for actual damages sustained by a person who engaged in any transaction specified in subsection (a) of this section on, or subject to the rules of, such registered entity or, in the case of an officer, director, governor, committee member, or employee of a registered futures association, any transaction specified in subsection (a) of this section, in either case to the extent of such person's actual losses that resulted from such transaction and were caused by such failure or violation.

(4) A person seeking to enforce liability under this section must establish that the registered entity registered futures association, officer, director, governor, committee member, or employee acted in bad faith in failing to take action or in taking such action as was taken, and that such failure or action caused the loss.

(5) The rights of action authorized by this subsection shall be the exclusive remedy under this Act available to any person who sustains a loss as a result of (A) the alleged failure by a registered entity or registered futures association or by any officer, director, governor, committee member, or employee to enforce any bylaw, rule, regulation, or resolution referred to in paragraph (1) or (2) of this subsection or (B) the taking of action in enforcing any bylaw, rule, regulation, or resolution referred to in this subsection that is alleged to have violated this Act, or any Commission rule, regulation, or order.

(c) The United States district courts shall have exclusive jurisdiction of actions brought under this section. Any such action shall be brought not later than two years after the date the cause of action arises. Any action brought under subsection (a) of this section may be brought in any judicial district wherein the defendant is found, resides, or transacts business, or in the judicial district wherein any act or transaction constituting the violation occurs. Process in such action may be served in any judicial district of which the defendant is an inhabitant or wherever the defendant may be found.

GENERAL REGULATIONS UNDER THE COMMODITY EXCHANGE ACT

(17 CFR ___)

PART 34—REGULATION OF HYBRID INSTRUMENTS

Section

§ 34.1 Scope.

The provisions of this part shall apply to any hybrid instrument which may be subject to the Act, and which has been entered into on or after October 23, 1974.

§ 34.2 Definitions.

(a) Hybrid instruments. Hybrid instrument means an equity or debt security or depository instrument as defined in § 34.3(a)(1) with one or more commodity-dependent components that have payment features similar to commodity futures or commodity option contracts or combinations thereof.

(b) Commodity-independent component. Commodity-independent component means the component of a hybrid instrument, the payments of which do not result from indexing to, or calculation by reference to, the price of a commodity.

(c) Commodity-independent value. Commodity-independent value means the present value of the payments attributable to the commodity-independent component calculated as of the time of issuance of the hybrid instrument.

(d) Commodity-dependent component. A commodity-dependent component means a component of a hybrid instrument, the payment of which results from indexing to, or calculation by reference to, the price of a commodity.

(e) Commodity-dependent value. For purposes of application of Rule 34.3(a)(2), a commodity-dependent value means the value of a commodity dependent-component, which when decomposed into an option payout or payouts, is measured by the absolute net value of the put option premia with strike prices less than or equal to the reference price plus the absolute net value of the call option premia with strike prices greater than or equal to the reference price, calculated as of the time of issuance of the hybrid instrument.

(f) Option premium. Option premium means the value of an option on the referenced commodity of the hybrid instrument, and calculated using the same method as that used to determine the issue price of the instrument, or where such premia are not explicitly calculated in determining the issue price of the instrument, the value of such options calculated using a commercially reasonable method appropriate to the instrument being priced.

(g) Reference price. A reference price means a price nearest the current spot or forward price, whichever is used to price instrument, at which a commodity-dependent payment becomes non-zero, or, in the case where two potential reference prices exist, the price that results in the greatest commodity-dependent value.

§ 34.3 Hybrid instrument exemption.

(a) A hybrid instrument is exempt from all provisions of the Act and any person or class of persons offering, entering into, rendering advice or rendering other services with respect to such exempt hybrid instrument is exempt for such activity from all provisions of the Act (except in each case section 2(a)(1)(B)), provided the following terms and conditions are met:

(1) The instrument is:

(i) An equity or debt security within the meaning of section 2(1) of the Securities Act of 1933; or

(ii) A demand deposit, time deposit or transaction account within the meaning of 12 CFR 204.2(b)(1), (c)(1) and (e), respectively, offered by an insured depository institution as defined in section 3 of the Federal Deposit Insurance Act; an insured credit union as defined in section 101 of the Federal Credit Union Act; or a Federal or State branch or agency of a foreign bank as defined in section 1 of the International Banking Act;

(2) The sum of the commodity-dependent values of the commodity-dependent components is less than the commodity-independent value of the commodity-independent component;

(3) Provided that:

(i) An issuer must receive full payment of the hybrid instrument's purchase price, and a purchaser or holder of a hybrid instrument may not be required to make additional out-of-pocket payments to the issuer during the life of the instrument or at maturity; and

(ii) The instrument is not marketed as a futures contract or a commodity option, or, except to the extent necessary to describe the functioning of the instrument or to comply with applicable disclosure requirements, as having the characteristics of a futures contract or a commodity option; and

(iii) The instrument does not provide for settlement in the form of a delivery instrument that is specified as such in the rules of a designed contract market;

(4) The instrument is initially issued or sold subject to applicable federal or state securities or banking laws to persons permitted thereunder to purchase or enter into the hybrid instrument.

BANKRUPTCY REFORM ACT OF 1978

11 U.S.C. ___

(Excerpts)

. . .

§ 364. Obtaining Credit

(a) If the trustee is authorized to operate the business of the debtor under section 721, 1108, 1304, 1203, or 1204 of this title, unless the court orders otherwise, the trustee may obtain unsecured credit and incur unsecured debt in the ordinary course of business allowable under section 503(b)(1) of this title as an administrative expense.

(b) The court, after notice and a hearing, may authorize the trustee to obtain unsecured credit or to incur unsecured debt other than under subsection (a) of this section, allowable under section 503(b)(1) of this title as an administrative expense.

(c) If the trustee is unable to obtain unsecured credit allowable under section 503(b)(1) of this title as an administrative expense, the court, after notice and a hearing, may authorize the obtaining of credit or the incurring of debt—

(1) with priority over any or all administrative expenses of the kind specified in section 503(b) or 507(b) of this title;

(2) secured by a lien on property of the estate that is not otherwise subject to a lien; or

(3) secured by a junior lien on property of the estate that is subject to a lien.

(d)(1) The court, after notice and a hearing, may authorize the obtaining of credit or the incurring of debt secured by a senior or equal lien on property of the estate that is subject to a lien only if—

(A) the trustee is unable to obtain such credit otherwise; and

(B) there is adequate protection of the interest of the holder of the lien on the property of the estate on which such senior or equal lien is proposed to be granted.

(2) In any hearing under this subsection, the trustee has the burden of proof on the issue of adequate protection.

(e) The reversal or modification on appeal of an authorization under this section to obtain credit or incur debt, or of a grant under this section of a priority or a lien, does not affect the validity of any debt so incurred, or any priority or lien so granted, to an entity that extended such credit in good faith, whether or not such entity knew of the pendency of the appeal, unless such authorization and the incurring of such debt, or the granting of such priority or lien, were stayed pending appeal.

(f) Except with respect to an entity that is an underwriter as defined in section 1145(b) of this title, section 5 of the Securities Act of 1933, the Trust Indenture Act of 1939, and any State or local law requiring registration for offer or sale of a security or registration or licensing of an issuer of, underwriter of, or broker or dealer in, a security does not apply to the offer or sale under this section of a security that is not an equity security.

§ 1125. Postpetition Disclosure and Solicitation

(a) In this section—

(1) "adequate information" means information of a kind, and in sufficient detail, as far as is reasonably practicable in light of the nature and history of the debtor and the condition of the debtor's books and records, that would enable a hypothetical reasonable investor typical of holders of claims or interests of the relevant class to make an

informed judgment about the plan, but adequate information need not include such information about any other possible or proposed plan; and

(2) "investor typical of holders of claims or interests of the relevant class" means investor having—

(A) a claim or interest of the relevant class;

(B) such a relationship with the debtor as the holders of other claims or interests of such class generally have; and

(C) such ability to obtain such information from sources other than the disclosure required by this section as holders of claims or interests in such class generally have.

(b) An acceptance or rejection of a plan may not be solicited after the commencement of the case under this title from a holder of a claim or interest with respect to such claim or interest, unless, at the time of or before such solicitation, there is transmitted to such holder the plan or a summary of the plan, and a written disclosure statement approved, after notice and a hearing, by the court as containing adequate information. The court may approve a disclosure statement without a valuation of the debtor or an appraisal of the debtor's assets.

(c) The same disclosure statement shall be transmitted to each holder of a claim or interest of a particular class, but there may be transmitted different disclosure statements, differing in amount, detail, or kind of information, as between classes.

(d) Whether a disclosure statement required under subsection (b) of this section contains adequate information is not governed by any otherwise applicable nonbankruptcy law, rule, or regulation, but an agency or official whose duty is to administer or enforce such a law, rule, or regulation may be heard on the issue of whether a disclosure statement contains adequate information. Such an agency or official may not appeal from, or otherwise seek review of, an order approving a disclosure statement.

(e) A person that solicits acceptance or rejection of a plan, in good faith and in compliance with the applicable provisions of this title, or that participates, in good faith and in compliance with the applicable provisions of this title, in the offer, issuance, sale, or purchase of a security, offered or sold under the plan, of the debtor, of an affiliate participating in a joint plan with the debtor, or of a newly organized successor to the debtor under the plan, is not liable, on account of such solicitation or participation, for violation of any applicable law, rule, or regulation governing solicitation of acceptance or rejection of a plan or the offer, issuance, sale, or purchase of securities.

§ 1145. Exemption From Securities Laws

(a) Except with respect to an entity that is an underwriter as defined in subsection (b) of this section, section 5 of the Securities Act of 1933 and any State or local law requiring registration for offer or sale of a security or registration or licensing of an issuer of, underwriter of, or broker or dealer in, a security does not apply to—

(1) the offer or sale under a plan of a security of the debtor, of an affiliate participating in a joint plan with the debtor, or of a successor to the debtor under the plan—

(A) in exchange for a claim against, an interest in, or a claim for an administrative expense in the case concerning, the debtor or such affiliate; or

(B) principally in such exchange and partly for cash or property;

(2) the offer of a security through any warrant, option, right to subscribe, or conversion privilege that was sold in the manner specified in paragraph (1) of this subsection, or the sale of a security upon the exercise of such a warrant, option, right, or privilege;

(3) the offer or sale, other than under a plan, of a security of an issuer other than the debtor or an affiliate, if—

(A) such security was owned by the debtor on the date of the filing of the petition;

(B) the issuer of such security is—

(i) required to file reports under section 13 or 15(d) of the Securities Exchange Act of 1934; and

(ii) in compliance with the disclosure and reporting provision of such applicable section; and

(C) such offer or sale is of securities that do not exceed—

(i) during the two-year period immediately following the date of the filing of the petition, four percent of the securities of such class outstanding on such date; and

(ii) during any 180-day period following such two-year period, one percent of the securities outstanding at the beginning of such 180-day period; or

(4) a transaction by a stockbroker in a security that is executed after a transaction of a kind specified in paragraph (1) or (2) of this subsection in such security and before the expiration of 40 days after the first date on which such security was bona fide offered to the public by the issuer or by or through an underwriter, if such stockbroker provides, at the time of or before such transaction by such a stockbroker, a disclosure statement approved under section 1125 of this title, and, if the court orders, information supplementing such disclosure statement.

(b)(1) Except as provided in paragraph (2) of this subsection, and except with respect to ordinary trading transactions of an entity that is not an issuer, an entity is an underwriter under section 2(11) of the Securities Act of 1933, if such entity—

(A) purchases a claim against, interest in, or claim for an administrative expense in the case concerning the debtor, if such purchase is with a view to distribution of any security received or to be received in exchange for such a claim or interest;

(B) offers to sell securities offered or sold under the plan for the holders of such securities;

(C) offers to buy securities offered or sold under the plan from the holders of such securities, if such offer to buy is—

(i) with a view to distribution of such securities; and

(ii) under an agreement made in connection with the plan, with the consummation of the plan, or with the offer or sale of securities under the plan; or

(D) is an issuer, as used in such section 2(11), with respect to such securities.

(2) An entity is not an underwriter under section 2(11) of the Securities Act of 1933 or under paragraph (1) of this subsection with respect to an agreement that provides only for—

(A)(i) the matching or combining of fractional interests in securities offered or sold under the plan into whole interests; or

(ii) the purchase or sale of such fractional interests from or to entities receiving such fractional interests under the plan; or

(B) the purchase or sale for such entities of such fractional or whole interests as are necessary to adjust for any remaining fractional interests after such matching.

(3) An entity other than an entity of the kind specified in paragraph (1) of this subsection is not an underwriter under section 2(11) of the Securities Act of 1933 with respect to any securities offered or sold to such entity in the manner specified in subsection (a)(1) of this section.

(c) An offer or sale of securities of the kind and in the manner specified under subsection (a)(1) of this section is deemed to be a public offering.

(d) The Trust Indenture Act of 1939 (15 U.S.C. 77aaa et seq.) does not apply to a note issued under the plan that matures not later than one year after the effective date of the plan.

FOREIGN CORRUPT PRACTICES ACT OF 1977*

15 U.S.C. § 78dd–2

Prohibited Foreign Trade Practices by Domestic Concerns

Sec. 104. (a) *Prohibition.*—It shall be unlawful for any domestic concern, other than an issuer which is subject to section 30A of the Securities Exchange Act of 1934, or for any officer, director, employee, or agent of such domestic concern or any stockholder thereof acting on behalf of such domestic concern, to make use of the mails or any means or instrumentality of interstate commerce corruptly in furtherance of an offer, payment, promise to pay, or authorization of the payment of any money, or offer, gift, promise to give, or authorization of the giving of anything of value to—

(1) any foreign official for purposes of—

(A)(i) influencing any act or decision of such foreign official in his official capacity, (ii) inducing such foreign official to do or omit to do any act in violation of the lawful duty of such official, or (iii) securing any improper advantage; or

(B) inducing such foreign official to use his influence with a foreign government or instrumentality thereof to affect or influence any act or decision of such government or instrumentality.

in order to assist such domestic concern in obtaining or retaining business for or with, or directing business to any person;

(2) any foreign political party or official thereof or any candidate for foreign political office for purposes of—

(A)(i) influencing any act or decision of such party, official, or candidate in its or his official capacity, (ii) inducing such party, official, or candidate to do or omit to do any act in violation of the lawful duty of such party, official, or candidate, or (iii) securing any improper advantage; or

(B) inducing such party, official, or candidate to use its or his influence with a foreign government or instrumentality thereof to affect or influence any act or decision of such government or instrumentality,

in order to assist such domestic concern in obtaining or retaining business for or with, or directing business to, any person; or

(3) any person, while knowing that all or a portion of such money or thing of value will be offered, given, or promised, directly or indirectly, to any foreign official, to any foreign political party or official thereof, or to any candidate for foreign political office, for purposes of—

(A)(i) influencing any act or decision of such foreign official, political party, party official, or candidate in his or its official capacity, (ii) inducing such foreign official, political party, party official, or candidate to do or omit to do any act in violation of the lawful duty of such foreign official, political party, party official, or candidate, or (iii) securing any improper advantage; or

(B) inducing such foreign official, political party, party official, or candidate to use his or its influence with a foreign government or instrumentality thereof to affect or influence any act or decision of such government or instrumentality,

* [Eds.] The Foreign Corrupt Practices Act of 1977 was enacted by P.L. No. 95–213, 91 Stat. 1494 and was amended in 1988 by P.L. 100–418. The statute also amended Sections 13(b)(1) and 13(d)(1) and added Section 30A of the Securities Exchange Act of 1934.

in order to assist such domestic concern in obtaining or retaining business for or with, or directing business to, any person.

(b) *Exception for Routine Governmental Action.*—Subsections (a) and (i) shall not apply to any facilitating or expediting payment to a foreign official, political party, or party official the purpose of which is to expedite or to secure the performance of a routine governmental action by a foreign official, political party, or party official.

(c) *Affirmative Defenses.*—It shall be an affirmative defense to actions under subsection (a) or (i) that—

(1) the payment, gift, offer, or promise of anything of value that was made, was lawful, under the written laws and regulations of the foreign official's, political party's, party official's, or candidate's country; or

(2) the payment, gift, offer, or promise of anything of value that was made, was a reasonable and bona fide expenditure, such as travel and lodging expenses, incurred by or on behalf of a foreign official, party, party official, or candidate and was directly related to—

(A) the promotion, demonstration, or explanation of products or services; or

(B) the execution of performance of a contract with a foreign government or agency thereof.

(d) *Injunctive Relief.*—(1) When it appears to the Attorney General that any domestic concern to which this section applies, or officer, director, employee, agent, or stockholder thereof, is engaged, or about to engage, in any act or practice constituting a violation of subsection (a) or (i) of this section, the Attorney General may, in his discretion, bring a civil action in an appropriate district court of the United States to enjoin such act or practice, and upon a proper showing, a permanent injunction or a temporary restraining order shall be granted without bond.

(2) For the purpose of any civil investigation which, in the opinion of the Attorney General, is necessary and proper to enforce this section, the Attorney General or his designee are empowered to administer oaths and affirmations, subpoena witnesses, take evidence, and require the production of any books, papers, or other documents which the Attorney General deems relevant or material to such investigation. The attendance of witnesses and the production of documentary evidence may be required from any place in the United States, or any territory, possession, or commonwealth of the United States at any designated place of hearing.

(3) In case of contumacy by, or refusal to obey a subpoena issued to, any person, the Attorney General may invoke the aid of any court of the United States within the jurisdiction of which such investigation or proceeding is carried on, or where such person resides or carries on business, in requiring the attendance and testimony of witnesses and the production of books, papers, or other documents. Any such court may issue an order requiring such person to appear before the Attorney General or his designee, there to produce records, if so ordered, or to give testimony touching the matter under investigation. Any failure to obey such order of the court may be punished by such court as a contempt thereof. All process in any such case may be served in the judicial district in which such person resides or may be found. The Attorney General may make such rules relating to civil investigations as may be necessary or appropriate to implement the provisions of this subsection.

(e) *Guidelines by the Attorney General.*—Not later than 6 months after the date of the enactment of the Foreign Corrupt Practices Act Amendments of 1988, the Attorney General, after consultation with the Securities and Exchange Commission, the Secretary of Commerce, the United States Trade Representative, the Secretary of State, and the Secretary of the Treasury, and after obtaining the views of all interested persons through public notice and comment procedures, shall determine to what extent compliance with this section would be enhanced and the business community would be assisted by further clarification of the preceding provisions of this section and may, based on such determination and to the extent necessary and appropriate, issue—

(1) guidelines describing specific types of conduct, associated with common types of export sales arrangements and business contracts, which for purposes of the Department of Justice's present enforcement policy, the Attorney General determines would be in conformance with the preceding provisions of this section; and

(2) general precautionary procedures which domestic concerns may use on a voluntary basis to conform their conduct to the Department of Justice's present enforcement policy regarding the preceding provisions of this section.

The Attorney General shall issue the guidelines and procedures referred to in the preceding sentence in accordance with the provisions of subchapter II of chapter 5 of title 5, United States Code, and those guidelines and procedures shall be subject to the provisions of chapter 7 of that title.

(f) *Opinions of the Attorney General.*—(1) The Attorney General, after consultation with appropriate departments and agencies of the United States and after obtaining the views of all interested persons through public notice and comment procedures, shall establish a procedure to provide responses to specific inquiries by domestic concerns concerning conformance of their conduct with the Department of Justice's present enforcement policy regarding the preceding provisions of this section. The Attorney General shall, within 30 days after receiving such a request, issue an opinion in response to that request. The opinion shall state whether or not certain specified prospective conduct would, for purposes of the Department of Justice's present enforcement policy, violate the preceding provisions of this section. Additional requests for opinions may be filed with the Attorney General regarding other specified prospective conduct that is beyond the scope of conduct specified in previous requests. In any action brought under the applicable provisions of this section, there shall be a rebuttable presumption that conduct, which is specified in a request by a domestic concern and for which the Attorney General has issued an opinion that such conduct is in conformity with the Department of Justice's present enforcement policy, is in compliance with the preceding provisions of this section. Such a presumption may be rebutted by a preponderance of the evidence. In considering the presumption for purposes of this paragraph, a court shall weigh all relevant factors, including but not limited to whether the information submitted to the Attorney General was accurate and complete and whether it was within the scope of the conduct specified in any request received by the Attorney General. The Attorney General shall establish the procedure required by this paragraph in accordance with the provisions of subchapter II of chapter 5 of title 5, United States Code, and that procedure shall be subject to the provisions of chapter 7 of that title.

(2) Any document or other material which is provided to, received by, or prepared in the Department of Justice or any other department or agency of the United States in connection with a request by a domestic concern under the procedure established under paragraph (1), shall be exempt from disclosure under section 552 of title 5, United States Code, and shall not, except with the consent of the domestic concern, be made publicly available, regardless of whether the Attorney General responds to such a request or the domestic concern withdraws such request before receiving a response.

(3) Any domestic concern who has made a request to the Attorney General under paragraph (1) may withdraw such request prior to the time the Attorney General issues an opinion in response to such request. Any request so withdrawn shall have no force or effect.

(4) The Attorney General shall, to the maximum extent practicable, provide timely guid-

ance concerning the Department of Justice's present enforcement policy with respect to the preceding provisions of this section to potential exporters and small businesses that are unable to obtain specialized counsel on issues pertaining to such provisions. Such guidance shall be limited to responses to requests under paragraph (1) concerning conformity of specified prospective conduct with the Department of Justice's present enforcement policy regarding the preceding provisions of this section and general explanations of compliance responsibilities and of potential liabilities under the preceding provisions of this section.

(g) *Penalties.*—(1)(A) Any domestic concern that is not a natural person and that violates subsection (a) or (i) of this section shall be fined not more than $2,000,000.

(B) Any domestic concern that is not a natural person and that violates subsection (a) or (i) of this section shall be subject to a civil penalty of not more than $10,000 imposed in an action brought by the Attorney General.

(2)(A) Any natural person that is an officer, director, employee, or agent of a domestic concern, or stockholder acting on behalf of such domestic concern, who willfully violates subsection (a) or (i) of this section shall be fined not more than $100,000 or imprisoned not more than 5 years, or both.

(B) Any natural person that is an officer, director, employee, or agent of a domestic concern, or stockholder acting on behalf of such domestic concern, who violates subsection (a) or (i) of this section shall be subject to a civil penalty of not more than $10,000 imposed in an action brought by the Attorney General.

(B) Any employee or agent of a domestic concern who is a United States citizen, national, or resident or is otherwise subject to the jurisdiction of the United States (other than an officer, director, or stockholder acting on behalf of such domestic concern), and who willfully violates subsection (a), shall be fined not more than $100,000, or imprisoned not more than 5 years, or both.

(C) Any officer, director, employee, or agent of a domestic concern, or stockholder acting on behalf of such domestic concern, who violates subsection (a) shall be subject to a civil penalty of not more than $10,000 imposed in an action brought by the Attorney General.

(3) Whenever a fine is imposed under paragraph (2) upon any officer, director, employee, agent, or stockholder of a domestic concern, such fine may not be paid, directly or indirectly, by such domestic concern.

(h) *Definitions.*—For purposes of this section:

(1) The term "domestic concern" means—

(A) any individual who is a citizen, national, or resident of the United States; and

(B) any corporation, partnership, association, joint-stock company, business trust, unincorporated organization, or sole proprietorship which has its principal place of business in the United States, or which is organized under the laws of a State of the United States or a territory, possession, or commonwealth of the United States.

(2)(A) The term "foreign official" means any officer or employee of a foreign government or any department, agency, or instrumentality thereof, or of a public international organization, or any person acting in an official capacity for or on behalf of any such government or department, agency, or instrumentality, or for or on behalf of any such public international organization.

(B) For purposes of subparagraph (A), the term "public international organization" means—

(i) an organization that is designated by Executive order pursuant to section 1 of the International Organizations Immunities Act (22 U.S.C. 288); or

(ii) any other international organization that is designated by the President by Executive order for the purposes of this section, effective as of the date of publication of such order in the Federal Register.

(3)(A) A person's state of mind is "knowing" with respect to conduct, a circumstance, or a result if—

(i) such person is aware that such person is engaging in such conduct, that such circumstance exists, or that such result is substantially certain to occur; or

(ii) such person has a firm belief that such circumstance exists or that such result is substantially certain to occur.

(B) when knowledge of the existence of a particular circumstance is required for an offense, such knowledge is established if a person is aware of a high probability of the existence of such circumstance, unless the person actually believes that such circumstance does not exist.

(4)(A) The term "routine governmental action" means only an action which is ordinarily and commonly performed by a foreign official in—

(i) obtaining permits, licenses, or other official documents to qualify a person to do business in a foreign country;

(ii) processing governmental papers, such as visas and work orders;

(iii) providing police protection, mail pick-up and delivery, or scheduling inspections associated with contract performance or inspections related to transit of goods across country;

(iv) providing phone service, power and water supply, loading and unloading cargo, or protecting perishable products or commodities from deterioration; or

(v) actions of a similar nature.

(B) The term "routine governmental action" does not include any decision by a foreign official whether, or on what terms, to award new business to or to continue business with a particular party, or any action taken by a foreign official involved in the decision-making process to encourage a decision to award new business to or continue business with a particular party.

(5) The term "interstate commerce" means trade, commerce, transportation, or communication among the several States, or between any foreign country and any State or between any State and any place or ship outside thereof, and such term includes the intrastate use of—

(A) a telephone or other interstate means of communication, or

(B) any other interstate instrumentality.

(i) *Alternative Jurisdiction.*—

(1) It shall also be unlawful for any United States person to corruptly do any act outside the United States in furtherance of an offer, payment, promise to pay, or authorization of the payment of any money, or offer, gift, promise to give, or authorization of the giving of anything of value to any of the persons or entities set forth in paragraphs (1), (2), and (3) of subsection (a), for the purposes set forth therein, irrespective of whether such United States person makes use of the mails or any means or instrumentality of interstate commerce in furtherance of such offer, gift, payment, promise, or authorization.

(2) As used in this subsection, the term "United States person" means a national of the United States (as defined in section 101 of the Immigration and Nationality Act (8 U.S.C. § 1101)) or any corporation, partnership, association, joint-stock company, business trust, unincorporated organization, or sole proprietorship organized under the laws of the United States or any State, territory, possession, or commonwealth of the United States, or any political subdivision thereof.

Sec. 104A. Prohibited Foreign Trade Practices by Persons Other Than Issuers or Domestic Concerns

(a) *Prohibition.*—It shall be unlawful for any person other than an issuer that is subject to section 30A of the Securities Exchange Act of 1934 or a domestic concern (as defined in section 104 of this Act), or for any officer, director, employee, or agent of such person or any stockholder thereof acting on behalf of such person, while in the territory of the United States, corruptly to make use of the mails or any means or instrumentality of interstate commerce or to do any other act in furtherance of an offer, payment, promise to pay, or authorization of the payment of any money, or offer, gift, promise to give, or authorization of the giving of anything of value to—

(1) any foreign official for purposes of—

(A)(i) influencing any act or decision of such foreign official in his official capacity, (ii) inducing such foreign official to do or omit to do any act in violation of the lawful duty of such official, or (iii) securing any improper advantage; or

(B) inducing such foreign official to use his influence with a foreign government or instrumentality thereof to affect or influence any act or decision of such government or instrumentality,

in order to assist such person in obtaining or retaining business for or with, or directing business to, any person;

(2) any foreign political party or official thereof or any candidate for foreign political office for purposes of—

(A)(i) influencing any act or decision of such party, official, or candidate in its or his official capacity, (ii) inducing such party, official, or candidate to do or omit to do an act in violation of the lawful duty of such party, official, or candidate, or (iii) securing any improper advantage; or

(B) inducing such party, official, or candidate to use its or his influence with a foreign government or instrumentality thereof to affect or influence any act or decision of such government or instrumentality,

in order to assist such person in obtaining or retaining business for or with, or directing business to, any person; or

(3) any person, while knowing that all or a portion of such money or thing of value will be offered, given, or promised, directly or indirectly, to any foreign official, to any foreign political party or official thereof, or to any candidate for foreign political office, for purposes of—

(A)(i) influencing any act or decision of such foreign official, political party, party official, or candidate in his or its official capacity, (ii) inducing such foreign official, political party, party official, or candidate to do or omit to do any act in violation of the lawful duty of such foreign official, political party, party official, or candidate, or (iii) securing any improper advantage; or

(B) inducing such foreign official, political party, party official, or candidate to use his or its influence with a foreign government or instrumentality thereof to affect or influence any act or decision of such government or instrumentality,

in order to assist such person in obtaining or retaining business for or with, or directing business to, any person.

(b) *Exception for Routine Governmental Action.*—Subsection (a) of this section shall not apply to any facilitating or expediting payment to a foreign official, political party, or party official the purpose of which is to expedite or to secure the performance of a routine governmental action by a foreign official, political party, or party official.

(c) *Affirmative Defenses.*—It shall be an affirmative defense to actions under subsection (a) of this section that—

(1) the payment, gift, offer, or promise of anything of value that was made, was lawful under the written laws and regulations of the foreign official's, political party's, party official's, or candidate's country; or

(2) the payment, gift, offer, or promise of anything of value that was made, was a reasonable and bona fide expenditure, such as travel and lodging expenses, incurred by or on behalf of a foreign official, party, party official, or candidate and was directly related to—

(A) the promotion, demonstration, or explanation of products or services; or

(B) the execution or performance of a contract with a foreign government or agency thereof.

(d) *Injunctive Relief.*—

(1) When it appears to the Attorney General that any person to which this section applies, or officer, director, employee, agent, or stockholder thereof, is engaged, or about to engage, in any act or practice constituting a violation of subsection (a) of this section, the Attorney General may, in his discretion, bring a civil action in an appropriate district court of the United States to enjoin such act or practice, and upon a proper showing, a permanent injunction or a temporary restraining order shall be granted without bond.

(2) For the purpose of any civil investigation which, in the opinion of the Attorney General, is necessary and proper to enforce this section, the Attorney General or his designee are empowered to administer oaths and affirmations, subpoena witnesses, take evidence, and require the production of any books, papers, or other documents which the Attorney General deems relevant or material to such investigation. The attendance of witnesses and the production of documentary evidence may be required from any place in the United States, or any territory, possession, or commonwealth of the United States, at any designated place of hearing.

(3) In case of contumacy by, or refusal to obey a subpoena issued to, any person, the Attorney General may invoke the aid of any court of the United States within the jurisdiction of which such investigation or proceeding is carried on, or where such person resides or carries on business, in requiring the attendance and testimony of witnesses and the production of books, papers, or other documents. Any such court may issue an order requiring such person to appear before the Attorney General or his designee, there to produce records, if so ordered, or to give testimony touching the matter under investigation. Any failure to obey such order of the court may be punished by such court as a contempt thereof.

(4) All process in any such case may be served in the judicial district in which such person resides or may be found. The Attorney General may make such rules relating to civil investigations as may be necessary or appropriate to implement the provisions of this subsection.

(e) *Penalties.*—

(1)(A) Any juridical person that violates subsection (a) of this section shall be fined not more than $2,000,000.

(B) Any juridical person that violates subsection (a) of this section shall be subject to a civil penalty of not more than $10,000 imposed in an action brought by the Attorney General.

(2)(A) Any natural person who willfully violates subsection (a) of this section shall be fined not more than $100,000 or imprisoned not more than 5 years, or both.

(B) Any natural person who violates subsection (a) of this section shall be subject to a civil penalty of not more than $10,000 imposed in an action brought by the Attorney General.

(3) Whenever a fine is imposed under paragraph (2) upon any officer, director, employee, agent, or stockholder of a person, such fine may not be paid, directly or indirectly, by such person.

(f) *Definitions.*—For purposes of this section:

(1) The term "person", when referring to an offender, means any natural person other

than a national of the United States (as defined in section 101 of the Immigration and Nationality Act (8 U.S.C. 1101)) or any corporation, partnership, association, joint-stock company, business trust, unincorporated organization, or sole proprietorship organized under the law of a foreign nation or a political subdivision thereof.

(2)(A) The term "foreign official" means any officer or employee of a foreign government or any department, agency, or instrumentality thereof, or of a public international organization, or any person acting in an official capacity for or on behalf of any such government or department, agency, or instrumentality, or for or on behalf of any such public international organization.

(B) For purposes of subparagraph (A), the term "public international organization" means—

(i) an organization that is designated by Executive order pursuant to section 1 of the International Organizations Immunities Act (22 U.S.C. 288); or

(ii) any other international organization that is designated by the President by Executive order for the purposes of this section, effective as of the date of publication of such order in the Federal Register.

(3)(A) A person's state of mind is knowing, with respect to conduct, a circumstance or a result if—

(i) such person is aware that such person is engaging in such conduct, that such circumstance exists, or that such result is substantially certain to occur; or

(ii) such person has a firm belief that such circumstance exists or that such result is substantially certain to occur.

(B) When knowledge of the existence of a particular circumstance is required for an offense, such knowledge is established if a person is aware of a high probability of the existence of such circumstance, unless the person actually believes that such circumstance does not exist.

(4)(A) The term "routine governmental action" means only an action which is ordinarily and commonly performed by a foreign official in—

(i) obtaining permits, licenses, or other official documents to qualify a person to do business in a foreign country;

(ii) processing governmental papers, such as visas and work orders;

(iii) providing police protection, mail pick-up and delivery, or scheduling inspections associated with contract performance or inspections related to transit of goods across country;

(iv) providing phone service, power and water supply, loading and unloading cargo, or protecting perishable products or commodities from deterioration; or

(v) actions of a similar nature.

(B) The term "routine governmental action" does not include any decision by a foreign official whether, or on what terms, to award new business to or to continue business with a particular party, or any action taken by a foreign official involved in the decision-making process to encourage a decision to award new business to or continue business with a particular party.

(5) The term "interstate commerce" means trade, commerce, transportation, or communication among the several States, or between any foreign country and any State or between any State and any place or ship outside thereof, and such term includes the intrastate use of—

(A) a telephone or other interstate means of communication, or

(B) any other interstate instrumentality.

RACKETEER INFLUENCED AND CORRUPT ORGANIZATIONS

18 U.S.C. §§ 1961 et seq.

§ 1961. Definitions

As used in this chapter—

(1) "racketeering activity" means (A) any act or threat involving murder, kidnapping, gambling, arson, robbery, bribery, extortion, dealing in obscene matter, or dealing in a controlled substance or listed chemical (as defined in section 102 of the Controlled Substances Act), which is chargeable under State law and punishable by imprisonment for more than one year; (B) any act which is indictable under any of the following provisions of title 18, United States Code: Section 201 (relating to bribery), section 224 (relating to sports bribery), sections 471, 472, and 473 (relating to counterfeiting), section 659 (relating to theft from interstate shipment) if the act indictable under section 659 is felonious, section 664 (relating to embezzlement from pension and welfare funds), sections 891–894 (relating to extortionate credit transactions), section 1028 (relating to fraud and related activity in connection with identification documents) if the act indictable under section 1028 was committed for the purpose of financial gain, section 1029 (relating to fraud and related activity in connection with access devices), section 1084 (relating to the transmission of gambling information), section 1341 (relating to mail fraud), section 1343 (relating to wire fraud), section 1344 (relating to financial institution fraud), sections 1461–1465 (relating to obscene matter), section 1503 (relating to obstruction of justice), section 1510 (relating to obstruction of criminal investigations), section 1511 (relating to the obstruction of State or local law enforcement), section 1512 (relating to tampering with a witness, victim, or an informant), section 1513 (relating to retaliating against a witness, victim, or an informant), section 1542 (relating to false statement in application and use of passport) if the act indictable under section 1542 was committed for the purpose of financial gain, section 1543 (relating to forgery or false use of passport) if the act indictable under section 1543 was committed for the purpose of financial gain, section 1544 (relating to misuse of passport) if the act indictable under section 1544 was committed for the purpose of financial gain, section 1546 (relating to fraud and misuse of visas, permits, and other documents) if the act indictable under section 1546 was committed for the purpose of financial gain, sections 1581–1591 (relating to peonage and slavery), section 1951 (relating to interference with commerce, robbery, or extortion), section 1952 (relating to racketeering), section 1953 (relating to interstate transportation of wagering paraphernalia), section 1954 (relating to unlawful welfare fund payments), section 1955 (relating to the prohibition of illegal gambling businesses), section 1956 (relating to the laundering of monetary instruments), section 1957 (relating to engaging in monetary transactions in property derived from specified unlawful activity), section 1958 (relating to use of interstate commerce facilities in the commission of murder-for-hire), sections 2251, 2251A, 2252, and 2260 (relating to sexual

exploitation of children), sections 2312 and 2313 (relating to interstate transportation of stolen motor vehicles), sections 2314 and 2315 (relating to interstate transportation of stolen property), section 2318 (relating to trafficking in counterfeit labels for phonorecords, computer programs or computer program documentation or packaging and copies of motion pictures or other audiovisual works), section 2319 (relating to criminal infringement of a copyright), section 2319A (relating to unauthorized fixation of and trafficking in sound recordings and music videos of live musical performances), section 2320 (relating to trafficking in goods or services bearing counterfeit marks), section 2321 (relating to trafficking in certain motor vehicles or motor vehicle parts), sections 2341–2346 (relating to trafficking in contraband cigarettes), sections 2421–24 (relating to white slave traffic), (C) any act which is indictable under title 29, United States Code, section 186 (dealing with restrictions on payments and loans to labor organizations) or section 501(c) (relating to embezzlement from union funds), (D) any offense involving fraud connected with a case under title 11 (except a case under section 157 of this title[1]), fraud in the sale of securities, or the felonious manufacture, importation, receiving, concealment, buying, selling, or otherwise dealing in a controlled substance or listed chemical (as defined in section 102 of the Controlled Substances Act), punishable under any law of the United States, (E) any act which is indictable under the Currency and Foreign Transactions Reporting Act, (F) any act which is indictable under the Immigration and Nationality Act, section 274 (relating to bringing in and harboring certain aliens), section 277 (relating to aiding or assisting certain aliens to enter the United States), or section 278 (relating to importation of alien for immoral purpose) if the act indictable under such section of such Act was committed for the purpose of financial gain, or (G) any act that is indictable under any provision listed in section 2332b(g)(5)(B);

(2) "State" means any State of the United States, the District of Columbia, the Commonwealth of Puerto Rico, any territory or possession of the United States, any political subdivision, or any department, agency, or instrumentality thereof;

(3) "person" includes any individual or entity capable of holding a legal or beneficial interest in property;

(4) "enterprise" includes any individual, partnership, corporation, association, or other legal entity, and any union or group of individuals associated in fact although not a legal entity;

(5) "pattern of racketeering activity" requires at least two acts of racketeering activity, one of which occurred after the effective date of this chapter and the last of which occurred within ten years (excluding any period of imprisonment) after the commission of a prior act of racketeering activity;

(6) "unlawful debt" means a debt (A) incurred or contracted in gambling activity which was in violation of the law of the United States, a State or political subdivision thereof, or which is unenforceable under State or Federal law in whole or in part as to principal or interest because of the laws relating to usury, and (B) which was incurred in connection with the business of gambling in violation of the law of the United States, a State or political subdivision thereof, or the business of lending money or a thing of value at a rate usurious under State or Federal law, where the usurious rate is at least twice the enforceable rate;

(7) "racketeering investigator" means any attorney or investigator so designated by the Attorney General and charged with the duty of enforcing or carrying into effect this chapter;

[1] [Eds.]

(8) "racketeering investigation" means any inquiry conducted by any racketeering investigator for the purpose of ascertaining whether any person has been involved in any violation of this chapter or of any final order, judgment, or decree of any court of the United States, duly entered in any case or proceeding arising under this chapter;

(9) "documentary material" includes any book, paper, document, record, recording, or other material; and

(10) "Attorney General" includes the Attorney General of the United States, the Deputy Attorney General of the United States, the Associate Attorney General of the United States, any Assistant Attorney General of the United States, or any employee of the Department of Justice or any employee of any department or agency of the United States so designated by the Attorney General to carry out the powers conferred on the Attorney General by this chapter. Any department or agency so designated may use in investigations authorized by this chapter either the investigative provisions of this chapter or the investigative power of such department or agency otherwise conferred by law.

§ 1962. Prohibited activities

(a) It shall be unlawful for any person who has received any income derived, directly or indirectly, from a pattern of racketeering activity or through collection of an unlawful debt in which such person has participated as a principal within the meaning of section 2, title 18, United States Code, to use or invest, directly or indirectly, any part of such income, or the proceeds of such income, in acquisition of any interest in, or the establishment or operation of, any enterprise which is engaged in, or the activities of which affect, interstate or foreign commerce. A purchase of securities on the open market for purposes of investment, and without the intention of controlling or participating in the control of the issuer, or of assisting another to do so, shall not be unlawful under this subsection if the securities of the issuer held by the purchaser, the members of his immediate family, and his or their accomplices in any pattern or racketeering activity or the collection of an unlawful debt after such purchase do not amount in the aggregate to one percent of the outstanding securities of any one class, and do not confer, either in law or in fact, the power to elect one or more directors of the issuer.

(b) It shall be unlawful for any person through a pattern of racketeering activity or through collection of an unlawful debt to acquire or maintain, directly or indirectly, any interest in or control of any enterprise which is engaged in, or the activities of which affect, interstate or foreign commerce.

(c) It shall be unlawful for any person employed by or associated with any enterprise engaged in, or the activities of which affect, interstate or foreign commerce, to conduct or participate, directly or indirectly, in the conduct of such enterprise's affairs through a pattern of racketeering activity or collection of unlawful debt.

(d) It shall be unlawful for any person to conspire to violate any of the provisions of subsections (a), (b), or (c) of this section.

§ 1963. Criminal penalties

(a) Whoever violates any provision of section 1962 of this chapter shall be fined under this title or imprisoned not more than 20 years (or for life if the violation is based on a racketeering activity for which the maximum penalty includes life imprisonment), or both, and shall forfeit to the United States, irrespective of any provision of State law—

(1) any interest the person has acquired or maintained in violation of section 1962;

(2) any—

(A) interest in;

(B) security of;

(C) claim against; or

(D) property or contractual right of any kind affording a source of influence over;

any enterprise which the person has established, operated, controlled, conducted, or participated in the conduct of, in violation of section 1962; and

(3) any property constituting, or derived from, any proceeds which the person obtained, directly or indirectly, from racketeering activity or unlawful debt collection in violation of section 1962.

The court, in imposing sentence on such person shall order, in addition to any other sentence imposed pursuant to this section, that the person forfeit to the United States all property described in this subsection. In lieu of a fine otherwise authorized by this section, a defendant who derives profits or other proceeds from an offense may be fined not more than twice the gross profits or other proceeds.

(b) Property subject to criminal forfeiture under this section includes—

(1) real property, including things growing on, affixed to, and found in land; and

(2) tangible and intangible personal property, including rights, privileges, interests, claims and securities.

(c) All right, title, and interest in property described in subsection (a) vests in the United States upon the commission of the act giving rise to forfeiture under this section. Any such property that is subsequently transferred to a person other than the defendant may be the subject of a special verdict of forfeiture and thereafter shall be ordered forfeited to the United States, unless the transferee establishes in a hearing pursuant to subsection (*l*) that he is a bona fide purchaser for value of such property who at the time of purchase was reasonably without cause to believe that the property was subject to forfeiture under this section.

(d)(1) Upon application of the United States, the court may enter a restraining order or injunction, require the execution of a satisfactory performance bond, or take any other action to preserve the availability of property described in subsection (a) for forfeiture under this section—

(A) upon the filing of an indictment or information charging a violation of section 1962 of this chapter and alleging that the property with respect to which the order is sought would, in the event of the conviction, be subject to forfeiture under this section; or

(B) prior to the filing of such an indictment or information, if, after notice to persons appearing to have an interest in the property and opportunity for a hearing, the court determines that—

(i) there is a substantial probability that the United States will prevail on the issue of forfeiture and that failure to enter the order will result in the property being destroyed, removed from the jurisdiction of the court, or otherwise made unavailable for forfeiture; and

(ii) the need to preserve the availability of the property through the entry of the requested order outweighs the hardship on any party against whom the order is to be entered:

Provided, however, That an order entered pursuant to subparagraph (B) shall be effective for not more than ninety days, unless extended by the court for good cause shown or unless an indictment or information described in subparagraph (A) has been filed.

(2) A temporary restraining order under this subsection may be entered upon application of the United States without notice or opportunity for a hearing when an information or indictment has not yet been filed with respect to the property, if the United States demonstrates that there is probable cause to believe that the property with respect to which the order is sought would, in the event of conviction, be subject to forfeiture under this section and that provision of notice will jeopardize the availability of the property for forfeiture. Such a temporary order shall expire not more than ten days after the date on which it is entered, unless extended for good

cause shown or unless the party against whom it is entered consents to an extension for a longer period. A hearing requested concerning an order entered under this paragraph shall be held at the earliest possible time, and prior to the expiration of the temporary order.

(3) The court may receive and consider, at a hearing held pursuant to this subsection, evidence and information that would be inadmissible under the Federal Rules of Evidence.

(e) Upon conviction of a person under this section, the court shall enter a judgment of forfeiture of the property to the United States and shall also authorize the Attorney General to seize all property ordered forfeited upon such terms and conditions as the court shall deem proper. Following the entry of an order declaring the property forfeited, the court may, upon application of the United States, enter such appropriate restraining orders or injunctions, require the execution of satisfactory performance bonds, appoint receivers, conservators, appraisers, accountants, or trustees, or take any other action to protect the interest of the United States in the property ordered forfeited. Any income accruing to, or derived from, an enterprise or an interest in an enterprise which has been ordered forfeited under this section may be used to offset ordinary and necessary expenses to the enterprise which are required by law, or which are necessary to protect the interests of the United States or third parties.

(f) Following the seizure of property ordered forfeited under this section, the Attorney General shall direct the disposition of the property by sale or any other commercially feasible means, making due provision for the rights of any innocent persons. Any property right or interest not exercisable by, or transferable for value to, the United States shall expire and shall not revert to the defendant, nor shall the defendant or any person acting in concert with or on behalf of the defendant be eligible to purchase forfeited property at any sale held by the United States. Upon application of a person, other than the defendant or a person acting in concert with or on behalf of the defendant, the court may restrain or stay the sale or disposition of the property pending the conclusion of any appeal of the criminal case giving rise to the forfeiture, if the applicant demonstrates that proceeding with the sale or disposition of the property will result in irreparable injury, harm or loss to him. Notwithstanding 31 U.S.C. 3302(b), the proceeds of any sale or other disposition of property forfeited under this section and any moneys forfeited shall be used to pay all proper expenses for the forfeiture and the sale, including expenses of seizure, maintenance and custody of the property pending its disposition, advertising and court costs. The Attorney General shall deposit in the Treasury any amounts of such proceeds or moneys remaining after the payment of such expenses.

(g) With respect to property ordered forfeited under this section, the Attorney General is authorized to—

(1) grant petitions for mitigation or remission of forfeiture, restore forfeited property to victims of a violation of this chapter, or take any other action to protect the rights of innocent persons which is in the interest of justice and which is not inconsistent with the provisions of this chapter;

(2) compromise claims arising under this section;

(3) award compensation to persons providing information resulting in a forfeiture under this section;

(4) direct the disposition by the United States of all property ordered forfeited under this section by public sale or any other commercially feasible means, making due provision for the rights of innocent persons; and

(5) take appropriate measures necessary to safeguard and maintain property ordered forfeited under this section pending its disposition.

(h) The Attorney General may promulgate regulations with respect to—

(1) making reasonable efforts to provide notice to persons who may have an interest in property ordered forfeited under this section;

(2) granting petitions for remission or mitigation of forfeiture;

(3) the restitution of property to victims of an offense petitioning for remission or mitigation of forfeiture under this chapter;

(4) the disposition by the United States of forfeited property by public sale or other commercially feasible means;

(5) the maintenance and safekeeping of any property forfeited under this section pending its disposition; and

(6) the compromise of claims arising under this chapter.

Pending the promulgation of such regulations, all provisions of law relating to the disposition of property, or the proceeds from the sale thereof, or the remission or mitigation of forfeitures for violation of the customs laws, and the compromise of claims and the award of compensation to informers in respect of such forfeitures shall apply to forfeitures incurred, or alleged to have been incurred, under the provisions of this section, insofar as applicable and not inconsistent with the provisions hereof. Such duties as are imposed upon the Customs Service or any person with respect to the disposition of property under the customs law shall be performed under this chapter by the Attorney General.

(i) Except as provided in subsection (*l*), no party claiming an interest in property subject to forfeiture under this section may—

(1) intervene in a trial or appeal of a criminal case involving the forfeiture of such property under this section; or

(2) commence an action at law or equity against the United States concerning the validity of his alleged interest in the property subsequent to the filing of an indictment or information alleging that the property is subject to forfeiture under this section.

(j) The district courts of the United States shall have jurisdiction to enter orders as provided in this section without regard to the location of any property which may be subject to forfeiture under this section or which has been ordered forfeited under this section.

(k) In order to facilitate the identification or location of property declared forfeited and to facilitate the disposition of petitions for remission or mitigation of forfeiture, after the entry of an order declaring property forfeited to the United States the court may, upon application of the United States, order that the testimony of any witness relating to the property forfeited be taken by deposition and that any designated book, paper, document, record, recording, or other material not privileged be produced at the same time and place, in the same manner as provided for the taking of depositions under Rule 15 of the Federal Rules of Criminal Procedure.

(*l*)(1) Following the entry of an order of forfeiture under this section, the United States shall publish notice of the order and of its intent to dispose of the property in such manner as the Attorney General may direct. The Government may also, to the extent practicable, provide direct written notice to any person known to have alleged an interest in the property that is the subject of the order of forfeiture as a substitute for published notice as to those persons so notified.

(2) Any person, other than the defendant, asserting a legal interest in property which has been ordered forfeited to the United States pursuant to this section may, within thirty days of the final publication of notice or his receipt of notice under paragraph (1), whichever is earlier, petition the court for a hearing to adjudicate the validity of his alleged interest in the property. The hearing shall be held before the court alone, without a jury.

(3) The petition shall be signed by the petitioner under penalty of perjury and shall set forth the nature and extent of the petitioner's right, title, or interest in the property, the time and circumstances of the petitioner's ac-

quisition of the right, title, or interest in the property, any additional facts supporting the petitioner's claim, and the relief sought.

(4) The hearing on the petition shall, to the extent practicable and consistent with the interests of justice, be held within thirty days of the filing of the petition. The court may consolidate the hearing on the petition with a hearing on any other petition filed by a person other than the defendant under this subsection.

(5) At the hearing, the petitioner may testify and present evidence and witnesses on his own behalf, and cross-examine witnesses who appear at the hearing. The United States may present evidence and witnesses in rebuttal and in defense of its claim to the property and cross-examine witnesses who appear at the hearing. In addition to testimony and evidence presented at the hearing, the court shall consider the relevant portions of the record of the criminal case which resulted in the order of forfeiture.

(6) If, after the hearing, the court determines that the petitioner has established by a preponderance of the evidence that—

(A) the petitioner has a legal right, title, or interest in the property, and such right, title, or interest renders the order of forfeiture invalid in whole or in part because the right, title, or interest was vested in the petitioner rather than the defendant or was superior to any right, title, or interest of the defendant at the time of the commission of the acts which gave rise to the forfeiture of the property under this section; or

(B) the petitioner is a bona fide purchaser for value of the right, title, or interest in the property and was at the time of purchase reasonably without cause to believe that the property was subject to forfeiture under this section;

the court shall amend the order of forfeiture in accordance with its determination.

(7) Following the court's disposition of all petitions filed under this subsection, or if no such petitions are filed following the expiration of the period provided in paragraph (2) for the filing of such petitions, the United States shall have clear title to property that is the subject of the order of forfeiture and may warrant good title to any subsequent purchaser or transferee.

(m) If any of the property described in subsection (a), as a result of any act or omission of the defendant—

(1) cannot be located upon the exercise of due diligence;

(2) has been transferred or sold to, or deposited with, a third party;

(3) has been placed beyond the jurisdiction of the court;

(4) has been substantially diminished in value; or

(5) has been commingled with other property which cannot be divided without difficulty;

the court shall order the forfeiture of any other property of the defendant up to the value of any property described in paragraphs (1) through (5).

§ 1964. Civil remedies

(a) The district courts of the United States shall have jurisdiction to prevent and restrain violations of section 1962 of this chapter by issuing appropriate orders, including, but not limited to: ordering any person to divest himself of any interest, direct or indirect, in any enterprise; imposing reasonable restrictions on the future activities or investments of any person, including, but not limited to, prohibiting any person from engaging in the same type of endeavor as the enterprise engaged in, the activities of which affect interstate or foreign commerce; or ordering dissolution or reorganization of any enterprise, making due provision for the rights of innocent persons.

(b) The Attorney General may institute proceedings under this section. Pending final determination thereof, the court may at any time enter such restraining orders or prohibitions, or take such other actions, including the acceptance of satisfactory performance bonds, as it shall deem proper.

(c) Any person injured in his business or property by reason of a violation of section 1962 of this chapter may sue therefor in any appropriate United States district court and shall recover threefold the damages he sustains and the cost of the suit, including a reasonable attorney's fee, except that no person may rely upon any conduct that would have been actionable as fraud in the purchase or sale of securities to establish a violation of section 1962. The exception contained in the preceding sentence does not apply to an action against any person that is criminally convicted in connection with the fraud, in which case the statute of limitations shall start to run on the date on which the conviction becomes final.

(d) A final judgment or decree rendered in favor of the United States in any criminal proceeding brought by the United States under this chapter shall estop the defendant from denying the essential allegations of the criminal offense in any subsequent civil proceeding brought by the United States.

§ 1965. Venue and process

(a) Any civil action or proceeding under this chapter against any person may be instituted in the district court of the United States for any district in which such person resides, is found, has an agent, or transacts his affairs.

(b) In any action under section 1964 of this chapter in any district court of the United States in which it is shown that the ends of justice require that other parties residing in any other district be brought before the court, the court may cause such parties to be summoned, and process for that purpose may be served in any judicial district of the United States by the marshal thereof.

(c) In any civil or criminal action or proceeding instituted by the United States under this chapter in the district court of the United States for any judicial district, subpenas issued by such court to compel the attendance of witnesses may be served in any other judicial district, except that in any civil action or proceeding no such subpena shall be issued for service upon any individual who resides in another district at a place more than one hundred miles from the place at which such court is held without approval given by a judge of such court upon a showing of good cause.

(d) All other process in any action or proceeding under this chapter may be served on any person in any judicial district in which such person resides, is found, has an agent, or transacts his affairs.

§ 1966. Expedition of actions

In any civil action instituted under this chapter by the United States in any district court of the United States, the Attorney General may file with the clerk of such court a certificate stating that in his opinion the case is of general public importance. A copy of that certificate shall be furnished immediately by such clerk to the chief judge or in his absence to the presiding district judge of the district in which such action is pending. Upon receipt of such copy, such judge shall designate immediately a judge of that district to hear and determine action.

§ 1967. Evidence

In any proceeding ancillary to or in any civil action instituted by the United States under this chapter the proceedings may be open or closed to the public at the discretion of the court after consideration of the rights of affected persons.

§ 1968. Civil investigative demand

(a) Whenever the Attorney General has reason to believe that any person or enterprise may be in possession, custody or control of any documentary materials relevant to a racketeering investigation, he may, prior to the institution of a civil or criminal proceeding thereon, issue in writing, and cause to be served upon such person, a civil investigative demand requiring such person to produce such material for examination.

(b) Each such demand shall—

(1) state the nature of the conduct constituting the alleged racketeering violation which is under investigation and the provision of law applicable thereto;

(2) describe the class or classes of documentary material produced thereunder with such definiteness and certainty as to permit such material to be fairly identified;

(3) state that the demand is returnable forthwith or prescribe a return date which will provide a reasonable period of time within which the material so demanded may be assembled and made available for inspection and copying or reproduction; and

(4) identify the custodian to whom such material shall be made available.

(c) No such demand shall—

(1) contain any requirement which would be held to be unreasonable if contained in a subpena duces tecum issued by a court of the United States in aid of a grand jury investigation of such alleged racketeering violation; or

(2) require the production of any documentary evidence which would be privileged from disclosure if demanded by a subpena duces tecum issued by a court of the United States in aid of a grand jury investigation of such alleged racketeering violation.

(d) Service of any such demand or any petition filed under this section may be made upon a person by—

(1) delivering a duly executed copy thereof to any partner, executive officer, managing agent, or general agent thereof, or to any agent thereof authorized by appointment or by law to receive service of process on behalf of such person, or upon any individual person;

(2) delivering a duly executed copy thereof to the principal office or place of business of the person to be served; or

(3) depositing such copy in the United States mail, by registered or certified mail duly addressed to such person at its principal office or place of business.

(e) A verified return by the individual serving any such demand or petition setting forth the manner of such service shall be prima facie proof of such service. In the case of service by registered or certified mail, such return shall be accompanied by the return post office receipt of delivery of such demand.

(f)(1) The Attorney General shall designate a racketeering investigator to serve as racketeer document custodian, and such additional racketeering investigators as he shall determine from time to time to be necessary to serve as deputies to such officer.

(2) Any person upon whom any demand issued under this section has been duly served shall make such material available for inspection and copying or reproduction to the custodian designated therein at the principal place of business of such person, or at such other place as such custodian and such person thereafter may agree and prescribe in writing or as the court may direct, pursuant to this section on the return date specified in such demand, or on such later date as such custodian may prescribe in writing. Such person may upon written agreement between such person and the custodian substitute for copies of all or any part of such material originals thereof.

(3) The custodian to whom any documentary material is so delivered shall take physical possession thereof, and shall be responsible for the use made thereof and for the return thereof pursuant to this chapter. The custodian may cause the preparation of such copies of such documentary material as may be required for official use under regulations which shall be promulgated by the Attorney General. While in the possession of the custodian, no material so produced shall be available for examination, without the consent of the person who produced

such material, by any individual other than the Attorney General. Under such reasonable terms and conditions as the Attorney General shall prescribe, documentary material while in the possession of the custodian shall be available for examination by the person who produced such material or any duly authorized representatives of such person.

(4) Whenever any attorney has been designated to appear on behalf of the United States before any court or grand jury in any case or proceeding involving any alleged violation of this chapter, the custodian may deliver to such attorney such documentary material in the possession of the custodian as such attorney determines to be required for use in the presentation of such case or proceeding on behalf of the United States. Upon the conclusion of any such case or proceeding, such attorney shall return to the custodian any documentary material so withdrawn which has not passed into the control of such court or grand jury through the introduction thereof into the record of such case or proceeding.

(5) Upon the completion of—

(i) the racketeering investigation for which any documentary material was produced under this chapter, and

(ii) any case or proceeding arising from such investigation, the custodian shall return to the person who produced such material all such material other than copies thereof made by the Attorney General pursuant to this subsection which has not passed into the control of any court or grand jury through the introduction thereof into the record of such case or proceeding.

(6) When any documentary material has been produced by any person under this section for use in any racketeering investigation, and no such case or proceeding arising therefrom has been instituted within a reasonable time after completion of the examination and analysis of all evidence assembled in the course of such investigation, such person shall be entitled, upon written demand made upon the Attorney General, to the return of all documentary material other than copies thereof made pursuant to this subsection so produced by such person.

(7) In the event of the death, disability, or separation from service of the custodian of any documentary material produced under any demand issued under this section or the official relief of such custodian from responsibility for the custody and control of such material, the Attorney General shall promptly—

(i) designate another racketeering investigator to serve as custodian thereof, and

(ii) transmit notice in writing to the person who produced such material as to the identity and address of the successor so designated.

Any successor so designated shall have with regard to such materials all duties and responsibilities imposed by this section upon his predecessor in office with regard thereto, except that he shall not be held responsible for any default or dereliction which occurred before his designation as custodian.

(g) Whenever any person fails to comply with any civil investigative demand duly served upon him under this section or whenever satisfactory copying or reproduction of any such material cannot be done and such person refuses to surrender such material, the Attorney General may file, in the district court of the United States for any judicial district in which such person resides, is found, or transacts business, and serve upon such person a petition for an order of such court for the enforcement of this section, except that if such person transacts business in more than one such district such petition shall be filed in the district in which such person maintains his principal place of business, or in such other district in which such person transacts business as may be agreed upon by the parties to such petition.

(h) Within twenty days after the service of any such demand upon any person, or at any time before the return date specified in the demand, whichever period is shorter, such person may file, in the district court of the United States for the judicial district within which such person resides, is found, or transacts business, and serve upon such custodian a petition for an order of such court modifying or setting aside such demand. The time allowed for compliance with the demand in whole or in part as deemed proper and ordered by the court shall not run during the pendency of such petition in the court. Such petition shall specify each ground upon which the petitioner relies in seeking such relief, and may be based upon any failure of such demand to comply with the provisions of this section or upon any constitutional or other legal right or privilege of such person.

(i) At any time during which any custodian is in custody or control of any documentary material delivered by any person in compliance with any such demand, such person may file, in the district court of the United States for the judicial district within which the office of such custodian is situated, and serve upon such custodian a petition for an order of such court requiring the performance by such custodian of any duty imposed upon him by this section.

(j) Whenever any petition is filed in any district court of the United States under this section, such court shall have jurisdiction to hear and determine the matter so presented, and to enter such order or orders as may be required to carry into effect the provisions of this section.

MAIL AND WIRE FRAUD STATUTES AND OTHER FEDERAL CRIMINAL PROVISIONS

18 U.S.C. ___

§ 1341. Frauds and Swindles

Whoever, having devised or intending to devise any scheme or artifice to defraud, or for obtaining money or property by means of false or fraudulent pretenses, representations, or promises, or to sell, dispose of, loan, exchange, alter, give away, distribute, supply, or furnish or procure for unlawful use any counterfeit or spurious coin, obligation, security, or other article, or anything represented to be or intimated or held out to be such counterfeit or spurious article, for the purpose of executing such scheme or artifice or attempting so to do, places in any post office or authorized depository for mail matter, any matter or thing whatever to be sent or delivered by the Postal Service, or takes or receives therefrom, any such matter or thing, or knowingly causes to be delivered by mail according to the direction thereon, or at the place at which it is directed to be delivered by the person to whom it is addressed, any such matter or thing, shall be fined not more than $1,000 or imprisoned not more than 5 years, or both. If the violation affects a financial institution, such person shall be fined not more than $1,000,000 or imprisoned not more than 30 years, or both.

§ 1343. Fraud by Wire, Radio, or Television

Whoever, having devised or intending to devise any scheme or artifice to defraud, or for obtaining money or property by means of false or fraudulent pretenses, representations, or promises, transmits or causes to be transmitted by means of wire, radio, or television communication in interstate or foreign commerce, any writings, signs, signals, pictures, or sounds for the purpose of executing such scheme or artifice, shall be fined not more than $1,000 or imprisoned not more than 5 years, or both. If the violation affects a financial institution, such person shall be fined not more than $1,000,000 or imprisoned not more than 30 years, or both.

§ 1344. Bank Fraud

Whoever knowingly executes, or attempts to execute, a scheme or artifice—

(1) to defraud a financial institution; or

(2) to obtain any of the moneys, funds, credits, assets, securities, or other property owned by, or under the custody or control of, a financial institution, by means of false or fraudulent pretenses, representations, or promises;

shall be fined not more than $1,000,000 or imprisoned not more than 30 years, or both.

§ 1346. Definition of "Scheme or Artifice to Defraud"

For the purposes of this chapter, the term "scheme or artifice to defraud" includes a scheme or artifice to deprive another of the intangible right of honest services.

§ 1348. Securities Fraud

Whoever knowingly executes, or attempts to execute, a scheme or artifice—

(1) to defraud any person in connection with any security of an issuer with a class of securities registered under section 12 of the Securities Exchange Act of 1934 (15 U.S.C. 78l) or that is required to file reports under section 15(d) of the Securities Exchange Act of 1934 (15 U.S.C. 78o(d)); or

(2) to obtain, by means of false or fraudulent pretenses, representations, or promises, any money or property in connection with the purchase or sale of any security of an

issuer with a class of securities registered under section 12 of the Securities Exchange Act of 1934 (15 U.S.C. 781) or that is required to file reports under section 15(d) of the Securities Exchange Act of 1934 (15 U.S.C. 78o(d));

shall be fined under this title, or imprisoned not more than 25 years, or both.

§ 1349. Attempt and Conspiracy

Any person who attempts or conspires to commit any offense under this chapter shall be subject to the same penalties as those prescribed for the offense, the commission of which was the object of the attempt or conspiracy.

§ 1350. Failure of Corporate Officers to Certify Financial Reports

(a) Certification of Periodic Financial Reports.—Each periodic report containing financial statements filed by an issuer with the Securities Exchange Commission pursuant to section 13(a) or 15(d) of the Securities Exchange Act of 1934 (15 U.S.C. 78m(a) or 78o(d)) shall be accompanied by a written statement by the chief executive officer and chief financial officer (or equivalent thereof) of the issuer.

(b) Content.—The statement required under subsection (a) shall certify that the periodic report containing the financial statements fully complies with the requirements of section 13(a) or 15(d) of the Securities Exchange Act of 1934 (15 U.S.C. 78m or 78o(d)) and that information contained in the periodic report fairly presents, in all material respects, the financial condition and results of operations of the issuer.

(c) Criminal Penalties.—Whoever—

(1) certifies any statement as set forth in subsections (a) and (b) of this section knowing that the periodic report accompanying the statement does not comport with all the requirements set forth in this section shall be fined not more than $1,000,000 or imprisoned not more than 10 years, or both; or

(2) willfully certifies any statement as set forth in subsections (a) and (b) of this section knowing that the periodic report accompanying the statement does not comport with all the requirements set forth in this section shall be fined not more than $5,000,000, or imprisoned not more than 20 years, or both.

§ 1519. Destruction, Alteration, or Falsification of Records in Federal Investigations and Bankruptcy

Whoever knowingly alters, destroys, mutilates, conceals, covers up, falsifies, or makes a false entry in any record, document, or tangible object with the intent to impede, obstruct, or influence the investigation or proper administration of any matter within the jurisdiction of any department or agency of the United States or any case filed under title 11, or in relation to or contemplation of any such matter or case, shall be fined under this title, imprisoned not more than 20 years, or both.

§ 1520. Destruction of Corporate Audit Records

(a)(1) Any accountant who conducts an audit of an issuer of securities to which section 10A(a) of the Securities Exchange Act of 1934 (15 U.S.C. 78j–1(a)) applies, shall maintain all audit or review workpapers for a period of 5 years from the end of the fiscal period in which the audit or review was concluded.

(2) The Securities and Exchange Commission shall promulgate, within 180 days, after adequate notice and an opportunity for comment, such rules and regulations, as are reasonably necessary, relating to the retention of relevant records such as workpapers, documents that form the basis of an audit or review, memoranda, correspondence, communications, other documents, and records (including electronic records) which are created, sent, or received in connection with an audit or review and contain conclusions, opinions, analyses, or financial data relating to such an audit or review, which is conduct-

ed by any accountant who conducts an audit of an issuer of securities to which section 10A(a) of the Securities Exchange Act of 1934 (15 U.S.C. 78j–1(a)) applies. The Commission may, from time to time, amend or supplement the rules and regulations that it is required to promulgate under this section, after adequate notice and an opportunity for comment, in order to ensure that such rules and regulations adequately comport with the purposes of this section.

(b) Whoever knowingly and willfully violates subsection (a)(1), or any rule or regulation promulgated by the Securities and Exchange Commission under subsection (a)(2), shall be fined under this title, imprisoned not more than 10 years, or both.

CIVIL ACTION TO PROTECT AGAINST RETALIATION IN FRAUD CASES

18 U.S.C. § 1514A

§ 1514A. Civil Action to Protect Against Retaliation in Fraud Cases

(a) Whistleblower Protection for Employees of Publicly Traded Companies.—No company with a class of securities registered under section 12 of the Securities Exchange Act of 1934 (15 U.S.C. 78l), or that is required to file reports under section 15(d) of the Securities Exchange Act of 1934 (15 U.S.C. 78o(d)), or any officer, employee, contractor, subcontractor, or agent of such company, may discharge, demote, suspend, threaten, harass, or in any other manner discriminate against an employee in the terms and conditions of employment because of any lawful act done by the employee—

(1) to provide information, cause information to be provided, or otherwise assist in an investigation regarding any conduct which the employee reasonably believes constitutes a violation of section 1341, 1343, 1344, or 1348, any rule or regulation of the Securities and Exchange Commission, or any provision of Federal law relating to fraud against shareholders, when the information or assistance is provided to or the investigation is conducted by—

(A) a Federal regulatory or law enforcement agency;

(B) any Member of Congress or any committee of Congress; or

(C) a person with supervisory authority over the employee (or such other person working for the employer who has the authority to investigate, discover, or terminate misconduct); or

(2) to file, cause to be filed, testify, participate in, or otherwise assist in a proceeding filed or about to be filed (with any knowledge of the employer) relating to an alleged violation of section 1341, 1343, 1344, or 1348, any rule or regulation of the Securities and Exchange Commission, or any provision of Federal law relating to fraud against shareholders.

(b) Enforcement Action.—

(1) In general.—A person who alleges discharge or other discrimination by any person in violation of subsection (a) may seek relief under subsection (c), by—

(A) filing a complaint with the Secretary of Labor; or

(B) if the Secretary has not issued a final decision within 180 days of the filing of the complaint and there is no showing that such delay is due to the bad faith of the claimant, bringing an action at law or equity for de novo review in the appropriate district court of the United States, which shall have jurisdiction over such an action without regard to the amount in controversy.

(2) Procedure.—

(A) In general.—An action under paragraph (1)(A) shall be governed under the rules and procedures set forth in section 42121(b) of title 49, United States Code.

(B) Exception.—Notification made under section 42121(b)(1) of title 49, United States Code, shall be made to the person named in the complaint and to the employer.

(C) Burdens of proof.—An action brought under paragraph (1)(B) shall be governed by the legal burdens of proof set forth in section 42121(b) of title 49, United States Code.

BANK HOLDING COMPANY ACT OF 1956

12 U.S.C. § 1841 et seq.

§ 1843. Interests in Nonbanking Organizations

(a) Ownership or control of voting shares of any company not a bank; engagement in activities other than banking

Except as otherwise provided in this chapter, no bank holding company shall—

(1) after May 9, 1956, acquire direct or indirect ownership or control of any voting shares of any company which is not a bank, or

(2) after two years from the date as of which it becomes a bank holding company, ... retain direct or indirect ownership or control of any voting shares of any company which is not a bank or bank holding company or engage in any activities other than (A) those of banking or of managing or controlling banks and other subsidiaries authorized under this chapter or of furnishing services to or performing services for its subsidiaries, and (B) those permitted under paragraph (8) of subsection (c) of this section subject to all the conditions specified in such paragraph or in any order or regulation issued by the Board under such paragraph....

. . .

(c) Exemptions

The prohibitions in this section shall not ... apply to—

(1) shares of any company engaged or to be engaged solely in one or more of the following activities: (A) holding or operating properties used wholly or substantially by any banking subsidiary of such bank holding company in the operations of such banking subsidiary or acquired for such future use; or (B) conducting a safe deposit business; or (C) furnishing services to or performing services for such bank holding company or its banking subsidiaries; or (D) liquidating assets acquired from such bank holding company or its banking subsidiaries or acquired from any other source prior to May 9, 1956, or the date on which such company became a bank holding company, whichever is later;

(2) shares acquired by a bank holding company or any of its subsidiaries in satisfaction of a debt previously contracted in good faith, but such shares shall be disposed of within a period of two years from the date on which they were acquired, except that the Board is authorized upon application by such bank holding company to extend such period of two years from time to time as to such holding company if, in its judgment, such an extension would not be detrimental to the public interest, and, in the case of a bank holding company which has not disposed of such shares within 5 years after the date on which such shares were acquired, the Board may, upon the application of such company, grant additional exemptions if, in the judgment of the Board, such extension would not be detrimental to the public interest and, either the bank holding company has made a good faith attempt to dispose of such shares during such 5-year period, or the disposal of such shares during such 5-year period would have been detrimental to the company, except that the aggregate duration of such extensions shall not extend beyond 10 years after the date on which such shares were acquired;

(3) shares acquired by such bank holding company from any of its subsidiaries which subsidiary has been requested to dispose of such shares by any Federal or State authority having statutory power to examine such subsidiary, but such bank holding company shall dispose of such shares within a period

of two years from the date on which they were acquired;

(4) shares held or acquired by a bank in good faith in a fiduciary capacity, except where such shares are held under a trust that constitutes a company as defined in section 1841(b) of this title and except as provided in paragraphs (2) and (3) of section 1841(g) of this title;

(5) shares which are of the kinds and amounts eligible for investment by national banking associations under the provisions of section 24 of this title;

(6) shares of any company which do not include more than 5 per centum of the outstanding voting shares of such company;

(7) shares of an investment company which is not a bank holding company and which is not engaged in any business other than investing in securities, which securities do not include more than 5 per centum of the outstanding voting shares of any company;

(8) shares of any company the activities of which had been determined by the Board by regulation or order under this paragraph as of the day before the date of the enactment of the Gramm–Leach–Bliley Act, to be so closely related to banking as to be a proper incident thereto (subject to such terms and conditions contained in such regulation or order, unless modified by the Board);

(k) Engaging in Activities that are Financial in Nature.—

(1) *In general.*—Notwithstanding subsection (a), a financial holding company may engage in any activity, and may acquire and retain the shares of any company engaged in any activity, that the Board, in accordance with paragraph (2), determines (by regulation or order)—

(A) to be financial in nature or incidental to such financial activity; or

(B) is complementary to a financial activity and does not pose a substantial risk to the safety or soundness of depository institutions or the financial system generally.

(2) *Coordination between the Board and the Secretary of the Treasury.*—

(A) Proposals raised before the Board

(i) Consultation.—The Board shall notify the Secretary of the Treasury of, and consult with the Secretary of the Treasury concerning, any request, proposal, or application under this subsection for a determination of whether an activity is financial in nature or incidental to a financial activity.

(ii) Treasury view.—The Board shall not determine that any activity is financial in nature or incidental to a financial activity under this subsection if the Secretary of the Treasury notifies the Board in writing, not later than 30 days after the date of receipt of the notice described in clause (i) (or such longer period as the Board determines to be appropriate under the circumstances) that the Secretary of the Treasury believes that the activity is not financial in nature or incidental to a financial activity or is not otherwise permissible under this section.

(B) Proposals raised by the Treasury.—

(i) Treasury recommendation.—The Secretary of the Treasury may, at any time, recommend in writing that the Board find an activity to be financial in nature or incidental to a financial activity.

(ii) Time period for Board action.—Not later than 30 days after the date of receipt of a written recommendation from the Secretary of the Treasury under clause (i) (or such longer period as the Secretary of the Treasury and the Board determine to be appropriate under the circumstances), the Board shall determine whether to initiate a public rulemaking proposing that the recommended activity be found to be financial in nature or incidental to a financial activity under this subsection, and shall notify the Secretary of the Treasury in writing of the determination of the Board and, if the Board determines not to seek public comment on the proposal, the reasons for that determination.

(3) *Factors to be considered.*—In determining whether an activity is financial in nature or incidental to a financial activity, the Board shall take into account—

(A) the purposes of this chapter and the Gramm–Leach–Bliley Act;

(B) changes or reasonably expected changes in the marketplace in which financial holding companies compete;

(C) changes or reasonably expected changes in the technology for delivering financial services; and

(D) whether such activity is necessary or appropriate to allow a financial holding company and the affiliates of a financial holding company to—

(i) compete effectively with any company seeking to provide financial services in the United States;

(ii) efficiently deliver information and services that are financial in nature through the use of technological means, including any application necessary to protect the security or efficacy of systems for the transmission of data or financial transactions; and

(iii) offer customers any available or emerging technological means for using financial services or for the document imaging of data.

(4) *Activities that are financial in nature.*—For purposes of this subsection, the following activities shall be considered to be financial in nature:

(A) Lending, exchanging, transferring, investing for others, or safeguarding money or securities.

(B) Insuring, guaranteeing, or indemnifying against loss, harm, damage, illness, disability, or death, or providing and issuing annuities, and acting as principal, agent, or broker for purposes of the foregoing, in any State.

(C) Providing financial, investment, or economic advisory services, including advising an investment company (as defined in section 80a–3 of Title 15).

(D) Issuing or selling instruments representing interests in pools of assets permissible for a bank to hold directly.

(E) Underwriting, dealing in, or making a market in securities.

(F) Engaging in any activity that the Board has determined, by order or regulation that is in effect on November 12, 1999, to be so closely related to banking or managing or controlling banks as to be a proper incident thereto (subject to the same terms and conditions contained in such order or regulation, unless modified by the Board).

(G) Engaging, in the United States, in any activity that—

(i) a bank holding company may engage in outside of the United States; and

(ii) the Board has determined, under regulations prescribed or interpretations issued pursuant to subsection (c)(13) (as in effect on the day before November 12, 1999) to be usual in connection with the transaction of banking or other financial operations abroad.

(H) Directly or indirectly acquiring or controlling, whether as principal, on behalf of 1 or more entities (including entities, other than a depository institution or subsidiary of a depository institution, that the bank holding company controls), or otherwise, shares, assets, or ownership interests (including debt or equity securities, partnership interests, trust certificates, or other instruments representing ownership) of a company or other entity, whether or not constituting control of such company or entity, engaged in any activity not authorized pursuant to this section if—

(i) the shares, assets, or ownership interests are not acquired or held by a depository institution or subsidiary of a depository institution;

(ii) such shares, assets, or ownership interests are acquired and held by—

(I) a securities affiliate or an affiliate thereof; or

(II) an affiliate of an insurance company described in subparagraph (I)(ii) that provides investment advice to an insurance company and is registered pursuant to the Investment Advisers Act of 1940 [15 U.S.C.A. § 80b–1 et seq.], or an affiliate of such investment adviser;

as part of a bona fide underwriting or merchant or investment banking activity, including investment activities engaged in for the purpose of appreciation and ultimate resale or disposition of the investment;

(iii) such shares, assets, or ownership interests are held for a period of time to enable the sale or disposition thereof on a reasonable basis consistent with the financial viability of the activities described in clause (ii); and

(iv) during the period such shares, assets, or ownership interests are held, the bank holding company does not routinely manage or operate such company or entity except as may be necessary or required to obtain a reasonable return on investment upon resale or disposition.

(I) Directly or indirectly acquiring or controlling, whether as principal, on behalf of 1 or more entities (including entities, other than a depository institution or subsidiary of a depository institution, that the bank holding company controls) or otherwise, shares, assets, or ownership interests (including debt or equity securities, partnership interests, trust certificates or other instruments representing ownership) of a company or other entity, whether or not constituting control of such company or entity, engaged in any activity not authorized pursuant to this section if—

(i) the shares, assets, or ownership interests are not acquired or held by a depository institution or a subsidiary of a depository institution;

(ii) such shares, assets, or ownership interests are acquired and held by an insurance company that is predominantly engaged in underwriting life, accident and health, or property and casualty insurance (other than credit-related insurance) or providing and issuing annuities;

(iii) such shares, assets, or ownership interests represent an investment made in the ordinary course of business of such insurance company in accordance with relevant State law governing such investments; and

(iv) during the period such shares, assets, or ownership interests are held, the bank holding company does not routinely manage or operate such company except as may be necessary or required to obtain a reasonable return on investment.

(5) *Actions required.*—

(A) In general.—The Board shall, by regulation or order, define, consistent with the purposes of this chapter, the activities described in subparagraph (B) as financial in nature, and the extent to which such activities are financial in nature or incidental to a financial activity.

(B) Activities.—The activities described in this subparagraph are as follows:

(i) Lending, exchanging, transferring, investing for others, or safeguarding financial assets other than money or securities.

(ii) Providing any device or other instrumentality for transferring money or other financial assets.

(iii) Arranging, effecting, or facilitating financial transactions for the account of third parties.

(6) *Required notification.*—

(A) In general.—A financial holding company that acquires any company or commences any activity pursuant to this subsection shall provide written notice to the Board describing the activity commenced or conducted by the company acquired not later than 30 calendar days after commencing the activity or consummating the acquisition, as the case may be.

(B) Approval not required for certain financial activities.—Except as provided in subsection (j) with regard to the acquisition of a savings association, a financial holding company may commence any activity, or acquire any company, pursuant to paragraph (4) or any regulation prescribed or order issued under paragraph (5), without prior approval of the Board.

(7) *Merchant banking activities.*—

(A) Joint regulations.—The Board and the Secretary of the Treasury may issue such regulations implementing paragraph (4)(H), including limitations on transactions between depository institutions and companies controlled pursuant to such paragraph, as the Board and the Secretary jointly deem appropriate to assure compliance with the purposes and prevent evasions of this chapter and the Gramm–Leach-Bliley Act and to protect depository institutions.

(B) Sunset of restrictions on merchant banking activities of financial subsidiaries.—The restrictions contained in paragraph (4)(H) on the ownership and control of shares, assets, or ownership interests by or on behalf of a subsidiary of a depository institution shall not apply to a financial subsidiary (as defined in section 24a of this title) of a bank, if the Board and the Secretary of the Treasury jointly authorize financial subsidiaries of banks to engage in merchant banking activities pursuant to section 122 of the Gramm–Leach–Bliley Act.

(*l*) Conditions for Engaging in Expanded Financial Activities.—

(1) *In general.*—Notwithstanding subsection (k), (n), or (*o*), a bank holding company may not engage in any activity, or directly or indirectly acquire or retain shares of any company engaged in any activity, under subsection (k), (n), or (*o*), other than activities permissible for any bank holding company under subsection (c)(8), unless—

(A) all of the depository institution subsidiaries of the bank holding company are well capitalized;

(B) all of the depository institution subsidiaries of the bank holding company are well managed; and

(C) the bank holding company has filed with the Board—

(i) a declaration that the company elects to be a financial holding company to engage in activities or acquire and retain shares of a company that were not permissible for a bank holding company to engage in or acquire before the enactment of the Gramm–Leach–Bliley Act; and

(ii) a certification that the company meets the requirements of subparagraphs (A) and (B).

(2) *CRA requirement.*—Notwithstanding subsection (k) or (n) of this section, section 24a of this title, or section 1831w(a) of this

title, the appropriate Federal banking agency shall prohibit a financial holding company or any insured depository institution from—

(A) commencing any new activity under subsection (k) or (n) of this section, section 24a of this title, or section 1831w(a) of this title; or

(B) directly or indirectly acquiring control of a company engaged in any activity under subsection (k) or (n) of this section, section 24a of this title, or section 1831w(a) of this title (other than an investment made pursuant to subparagraph (H) or (I) of subsection (k)(4), or section 122 of the Gramm–Leach–Bliley Act, or under section 1831w(a) of this title by reason of such section 122, by an affiliate already engaged in activities under any such provision);

if any insured depository institution subsidiary of such financial holding company, or the insured depository institution or any of its insured depository institution affiliates, has received in its most recent examination under the Community Reinvestment Act of 1977, a rating of less than "satisfactory record of meeting community credit needs".

(3) *Foreign banks.*—For purposes of paragraph (1), the Board shall apply comparable capital and management standards to a foreign bank that operates a branch or agency or owns or controls a commercial lending company in the United States, giving due regard to the principle of national treatment and equality of competitive opportunity.

(m) Provisions Applicable to Financial Holding Companies that Fail to meet Certain Requirements.—

(1) *In general.*—If the Board finds that—

(A) a financial holding company is engaged, directly or indirectly, in any activity under subsection (k), (n), or (*o*), other than activities that are permissible for a bank holding company under subsection (c)(8); and

(B) such financial holding company is not in compliance with the requirements of subsection (*l*)(1);

the Board shall give notice to the financial holding company to that effect, describing the conditions giving rise to the notice.

(2) *Agreement to correct conditions required.*—Not later than 45 days after the date of receipt by a financial holding company of a notice given under paragraph (1) (or such additional period as the Board may permit), the financial holding company shall execute an agreement with the Board to comply with the requirements applicable to a financial holding company under subsection (*l*)(1).

(3) *Board may impose limitations.*—Until the conditions described in a notice to a financial holding company under paragraph (1) are corrected, the Board may impose such limitations on the conduct or activities of that financial holding company or any affiliate of that company as the Board determines to be appropriate under the circumstances and consistent with the purposes of this Act.

(4) *Failure to correct.*—If the conditions described in a notice to a financial holding company under paragraph (1) are not corrected within 180 days after the date of receipt by the financial holding company of a notice under paragraph (1), the Board may require such financial holding company, under such terms and conditions as may be imposed by the Board and subject to such extension of time as may be granted in the discretion of the Board, either—

(A) to divest control of any subsidiary depository institution; or

(B) at the election of the financial holding company instead to cease to engage in any activity conducted by such financial holding company or its subsidiaries (other than a depository institution or a subsidiary of a depository institution) that is not an activity that is permissible for a bank holding company under subsection (c)(8).

(5) *Consultation.*—In taking any action under this subsection, the Board shall consult with all relevant Federal and State regulatory agencies and authorities.

(n) Authority to Retain Limited Nonfinancial Activities and Affiliations.—

(1) *In general.*—Notwithstanding subsection (a), a company that is not a bank holding company or a foreign bank (as defined in section 3101(b)(7) of this title) and becomes a financial holding company after November 12, 1999, may continue to engage in any activity and retain direct or indirect ownership or control of shares of a company engaged in any activity if—

(A) the holding company lawfully was engaged in the activity or held the shares of such company on September 30, 1999;

(B) the holding company is predominantly engaged in financial activities as defined in paragraph (2); and

(C) the company engaged in such activity continues to engage only in the same activities that such company conducted on September 30, 1999, and other activities permissible under this chapter.

(2) *Predominantly financial.*—For purposes of this subsection, a company is predominantly engaged in financial activities if the annual gross revenues derived by the holding company and all subsidiaries of the holding company (excluding revenues derived from subsidiary depository institutions), on a consolidated basis, from engaging in activities that are financial in nature or are incidental to a financial activity under subsection (k) represent at least 85percent of the consolidated annual gross revenues of the company.

(3) *No expansion of grandfathered commercial activities through merger or consolidation.*—A financial holding company that engages in activities or holds shares pursuant to this subsection, or a subsidiary of such financial holding company, may not acquire, in any merger, consolidation, or other type of business combination, assets of any other company that is engaged in any activity that the Board has not determined to be financial in nature or incidental to a financial activity under subsection (k), except this paragraph shall not apply with respect to a company that owns a broadcasting station licensed under title III of the Communications Act of 1934 and the shares of which are under common control with an insurance company since January 1, 1998, unless such company is acquired by, or otherwise becomes an affiliate of, a bank holding company that, at the time such acquisition or affiliation is consummated, is 1 of the 5 largest domestic bank holding companies (as determined on the basis of the consolidated total assets of such companies).

(4) *Continuing revenue limitation on grandfathered commercial activities.*—Notwithstanding any other provision of this subsection, a financial holding company may continue to engage in activities or hold shares in companies pursuant to this subsection only to the extent that the aggregate annual gross revenues derived from all such activities and all such companies does not exceed 15 percent of the consolidated annual gross revenues of the financial holding company (excluding revenues derived from subsidiary depository institutions).

(5) *Cross marketing restrictions applicable to commercial activities.*—

(A) In general.—A depository institution controlled by a financial holding company shall not—

(i) offer or market, directly or through any arrangement, any product or service of a company whose activities are conducted or whose shares are owned or controlled by the financial holding company pursuant to this subsection or subparagraph (H) or (I) of subsection (k)(4); or

(ii) permit any of its products or services to be offered or marketed, directly or through any arrangement, by or through any company described in clause (i).

(B) Rule of construction.—Subparagraph (A) shall not be construed as prohibiting an arrangement between a depository institution and a company owned or controlled pursuant to subsection (k)(4)(I) for the marketing of products or services through statement inserts or Internet websites if—

(i) such arrangement does not violate section 106 of the Bank Holding Company Act Amendments of 1970; and

(ii) the Board determines that the arrangement is in the public interest, does not undermine the separation of banking and commerce, and is consistent with the safety and soundness of depository institutions.

(6) *Transactions with nonfinancial affiliates.*—A depository institution controlled by a financial holding company may not engage in a covered transaction (as defined in section 371c(b)(7) of this title) with any affiliate controlled by the company pursuant to this subsection.

(7) *Sunset of grandfather.*—A financial holding company engaged in any activity, or retaining direct or indirect ownership or control of shares of a company, pursuant to this subsection, shall terminate such activity and divest ownership or control of the shares of such company before the end of the 10–year period beginning on November 12, 1999. The Board may, upon application by a financial holding company, extend such 10–year period by a period not to exceed an additional 5 years if such extension would not be detrimental to the public interest.

(*o*) Regulation of Certain Financial Holding Companies.—Notwithstanding subsection (a), a company that is not a bank holding company or a foreign bank (as defined in section 3101(b)(7) of this title) and becomes a financial holding company after November 12, 1999, may continue to engage in, or directly or indirectly own or control shares of a company engaged in, activities related to the trading, sale, or investment in commodities and underlying physical properties that were not permissible for bank holding companies to conduct in the United States as of September 30, 1997, if—

(1) the holding company, or any subsidiary of the holding company, lawfully was engaged, directly or indirectly, in any of such activities as of September 30, 1997, in the United States;

(2) the attributed aggregate consolidated assets of the company held by the holding company pursuant to this subsection, and not otherwise permitted to be held by a financial holding company, are equal to not more than 5 percent of the total consolidated assets of the bank holding company, except that the Board may increase that percentage by such amounts and under such circumstances as the Board considers appropriate, consistent with the purposes of this Act; and

(3) the holding company does not permit—

(A) any company, the shares of which it owns or controls pursuant to this subsection, to offer or market any product or service of an affiliated depository institution; or

(B) any affiliated depository institution to offer or market any product or service of any company, the shares of which are owned or controlled by such holding company pursuant to this subsection.

GRAMM–LEACH–BLILEY ACT

(Excerpts)

. . .

Sec. 206A. Swap Agreement

(a) In General.—Except as provided in subsection (b), as used in this section, the term "swap agreement" means any agreement, contract, or transaction between eligible contract participants (as defined in section 1a(12) of the Commodity Exchange Act as in effect on the date of enactment of this section), other than a person that is an eligible contract participant under section 1a(12)(C) of the Commodity Exchange Act, the material terms of which (other than price and quantity) are subject to individual negotiation, and that—

(1) is a put, call, cap, floor, collar, or similar option of any kind for the purchase or sale of, or based on the value of, one or more interest or other rates, currencies, commodities, indices, quantitative measures, or other financial or economic interests or property of any kind;

(2) provides for any purchase, sale, payment or delivery (other than a dividend on an equity security) that is dependent on the occurrence, non-occurrence, or the extent of the occurrence of an event or contingency associated with a potential financial, economic, or commercial consequence;

(3) provides on an executory basis for the exchange, on a fixed or contingent basis, of one or more payments based on the value or level of one or more interest or other rates, currencies, commodities, securities, instruments of indebtedness, indices, quantitative measures, or other financial or economic interests or property of any kind, or any interest therein or based on the value thereof, and that transfers, as between parties to the transaction, in whole or in part, the financial risk associated with a future change in any such value or level without also conveying a current or future direct or indirect ownership interest in an asset (including any enterprise or investment pool) or liability that incorporates the financial risk so transferred, including any such agreement, contract, or transaction commonly known as an interest rate swap, including a rate floor, rate cap, rate collar, cross-currency rate swap, basis swap, currency swap, equity index swap, equity swap, debt index swap, debt swap, credit spread, credit default swap, credit swap, weather swap, or commodity swap;

(4) provides for the purchase or sale, on a fixed or contingent basis, of any commodity, currency, instrument, interest, right, service, good, article, or property of any kind; or

(5) is any combination or permutation of, or option on, any agreement, contract, or transaction described in any of paragraphs (1) through (4).

(b) Exclusions.—The term "swap agreement" does not include—

(1) any put, call, straddle, option, or privilege on any security, certificate of deposit, or group or index of securities, including any interest therein based on the value thereof;

(2) any put, call, straddle, option, or privilege entered into on a national securities exchange registered pursuant to section 6(a) of the Securities Exchange Act of 1934 relating to foreign currency;

(3) any agreement, contract, or transaction providing for the purchase or sale of one or more securities on a fixed basis;

(4) any agreement, contract, or transaction providing for the purchase or sale of one or more securities on a contingent basis, unless such agreement, contract, or transac-

tion predicates such purchase or sale on the occurrence of a bona fide contingency that might reasonably be expected to affect or be affected by the creditworthiness of a party other than a party to the agreement, contract, or transaction;

(5) any note, bond, or evidence of indebtedness that is a security as defined in section 2(a)(1) of the Securities Exchange Act of 1933 or section 3(a)(10) of the Securities Exchange Act of 1934; or

(6) any agreement, contract, or transaction that is—

(A) based on a security; and

(B) entered into directly or through an underwriter (as defined in section 2(a) of the Securities Act of 1933) by the issuer of such security for the purposes of raising capital, unless such agreement, contract, or transaction is entered into to manage a risk associated with capital raising.

(c) Rule of Construction Regarding Master Agreements.—As used in this section, the term "swap agreement" shall be construed to include a master agreement that provides for an agreement, contract, or transaction that is a swap agreement pursuant to subsection (a) and (b), together with all supplements to any such master agreement, without regard to whether the master agreement contains an agreement, contract, or transaction that is not a swap agreement pursuant to subsections (a) and (b), except that the master agreement shall be considered to be a swap agreement only with respect to each agreement, contract, or transaction under the master agreement that is a swap agreement pursuant to subsection (a) and (b).

Sec. 206B. Security–Based Swap Agreement

As used in this section, the term "security-based swap agreement" means a swap agreement (as defined in section 206A) of which a material term is based on the price, yield, value, or volatility of any security or any group or index of securities, or any interest therein.

Sec. 206C. Non–Security–Based Swap Agreement

As used in this section, the term "non-security-based swap agreement" means a swap agreement (as defined in section 206A) that is not a security-based swap agreement (as defined in section 206B).

(b) Security Definition.—As used in the amendment made by subsection (a), the term "security" has the meaning as in section 2(a)(1) of the Securities Act of 1933 or section 3(a)(10) of the Securities Exchange Act of 1934.

HART–SCOTT–RODINO ANTITRUST IMPROVEMENTS ACT OF 1976

15 U.S.C. § 18a, Clayton Act § 7A

§ 18a. Premerger Notification and Waiting Period

(a) Filing

Except as exempted pursuant to subsection (c), no person shall acquire, directly or indirectly, any voting securities or assets of any other person, unless both persons (or in the case of a tender offer, the acquiring person) file notification pursuant to rules under subsection (d)(1) and the waiting period described in subsection (b)(1) has expired, if—

(1) the acquiring person, or the person whose voting securities or assets are being acquired, is engaged in commerce or in any activity affecting commerce;

(2) as a result of such acquisition, the acquiring person would hold an aggregate total amount of the voting securities and assets of the acquired person—

(A) in excess of $200,000,000 [adjusted periodically based on percentage changes in the gross national product];

(B)(i) in excess of $50,000,000 (as so adjusted . . .) but not in excess of $200,000,000 (as so adjusted . . .); and

(ii)(I) any voting securities or assets of a person engaged in manufacturing which has annual net sales or total assets of $10,000,000 (as so adjusted . . .) or more are being acquired by any person which has total assets or annual net sales of $100,000,000 (as so adjusted . . .) or more;

(II) any voting securities or assets of a person not engaged in manufacturing which has total assets of $10,000,000 (as so adjusted . . .) or more are being acquired by any person which has total assets or annual net sales of $100,000,000 (as so adjusted . . .) or more; or

(III) any voting securities or assets of a person with annual net sales or total assets of $100,000,000 (as so adjusted . . .) or more are being acquired by any person with total assets or annual net sales of $10,000,000 (as so adjusted . . .) or more.

In the case of a tender offer, the person whose voting securities are sought to be acquired by a person required to file notification under this subsection shall file notification pursuant to rules under subsection (d).

(b) Waiting period; publication; voting securities

(1) The waiting period required under subsection (a) of this section shall—

(A) begin on the date of the receipt by the Federal Trade Commission and the Assistant Attorney General in charge of the Antitrust Division of the Department of Justice (hereinafter referred to in this section as the "Assistant Attorney General") of—

(i) the completed notification required under subsection (a) of this section, or

(ii) if such notification is not completed, the notification to the extent completed and a statement of the reasons for such noncompliance,

from both persons, or, in the case of a tender offer, the acquiring person; and

(B) end on the thirtieth day after the date of such receipt (or in the case of a cash tender offer, the fifteenth day), or on such later date as may be set under subsection (e)(2) or (g)(2) of this section.

(2) The Federal Trade Commission and the Assistant Attorney General may, in individual cases, terminate the waiting period specified in paragraph (1) and allow any person to proceed with any acquisition subject to this section, and promptly shall cause to be published in the Federal Register a notice that neither intends to take any action within such period with respect to such acquisition.

(3) As used in this section—

(A) The term "voting securities" means any securities which at present or upon conversion entitle the owner or holder thereof to vote for the election of directors of the issuer or, with respect to unincorporated issuers, persons exercising similar functions.

(B) The amount or percentage of voting securities or assets of a person which are acquired or held by another person shall be determined by aggregating the amount or percentage of such voting securities or assets held or acquired by such other person and each affiliate thereof.

(c) Exempt transactions

The following classes of transactions are exempt from the requirements of this section—

(1) acquisitions of goods or realty transferred in the ordinary course of business;

(2) acquisitions of bonds, mortgages, deeds of trust, or other obligations which are not voting securities;

(3) acquisitions of voting securities of an issuer at least 50 per centum of the voting securities of which are owned by the acquiring person prior to such acquisition;

(4) transfers to or from a Federal agency or a State or political subdivision thereof;

(5) transactions specifically exempted from the antitrust laws by Federal statute;

(6) transactions specifically exempted from the antitrust laws by Federal statute if approved by a Federal agency, if copies of all information and documentary material filed with such agency are contemporaneously filed with the Federal Trade Commission and the Assistant Attorney General;

(7) transactions which require agency approval under section 10(e) of the Home Owners' Loan Act, section 18(c) of the Federal Deposit Insurance Act (12 U.S.C. 1828(c)), or section 3 of the Bank Holding Company Act of 1956 (12 U.S.C. 1842), except that a portion of a transaction is not exempt under this paragraph if such portion of the transaction (A) is subject to section 4(k) of the Bank Holding Company Act of 1956; and (B) does not require agency approval under section 3 of the Bank Holding Company Act of 1956;

(8) transactions which require agency approval under section 4 of the Bank Holding Company Act of 1956 (12 U.S.C. 1843) or section 5 of the Home Owners' Loan Act of 1933 (12 U.S.C. 1464), if copies of all information and documentary material filed with any such agency are contemporaneously filed with the Federal Trade Commission and the Assistant Attorney General at least 30 days prior to consummation of the proposed transaction, except that a portion of a transaction is not exempt under this paragraph if such portion of the transaction (A) is subject to section 4(k) of the Bank Holding Company Act of 1956; and (B) does not require agency approval under section 4 of the Bank Holding Company Act of 1956;

(9) acquisitions, solely for the purpose of investment, of voting securities, if, as a result of such acquisition, the securities acquired or held do not exceed 10 per centum of the outstanding voting securities of the issuer;

(10) acquisitions of voting securities, if, as a result of such acquisition, the voting securities acquired do not increase, directly or indirectly, the acquiring person's per cen-

tum share of outstanding voting securities of the issuer;

(11) acquisitions, solely for the purpose of investment, by any bank, banking association, trust company, investment company, or insurance company, of (A) voting securities pursuant to a plan of reorganization or dissolution; or (B) assets in the ordinary course of its business; and

(12) such other acquisitions, transfers, or transactions, as may be exempted under subsection (d)(2)(B) of this section.

(d) Commission Rules

The Federal Trade Commission, with the concurrence of the Assistant Attorney General and by rule . . ., consistent with the purposes of this section—

(1) shall require that the notification required under subsection (a) of this section be in such form and contain such documentary material and information relevant to a proposed acquisition as is necessary and appropriate to enable the Federal Trade Commission and the Assistant Attorney General to determine whether such acquisition may, if consummated, violate the antitrust laws; and

(2) may—

(A) define the terms used in this section;

(B) exempt, from the requirements of this section, classes of persons, acquisitions, transfers, or transactions which are not likely to violate the antitrust laws; and

(C) prescribe such other rules as may be necessary and appropriate to carry out the purposes of this section.

(e) Additional information; waiting period extensions

(1)(A) The Federal Trade Commission or the Assistant Attorney General may, prior to the expiration of the 30–day waiting period (or in the case of a cash tender offer, the 15–day waiting period) specified in subsection (b)(1) of this section, require the submission of additional information or documentary material relevant to the proposed acquisition, from a person required to file notification with respect to such acquisition under subsection (a) of this section prior to the expiration of the waiting period specified in subsection (b)(1) of this section, or from any officer, director, partner, agent, or employee of such person.

(B)(i) The Assistant Attorney General and the Federal Trade Commission shall each designate a senior official who does not have direct responsibility for the review of any enforcement recommendation under this section concerning the transaction at issue to hear any petition filed by such person to determine—

(I) whether the request for additional information or documentary material is unreasonably cumulative, unduly burdensome, or duplicative; or

(II) whether the request for additional information or documentary material has been substantially complied with by the petitioning person.

(ii) Internal review procedures for petitions filed pursuant to clause (i) shall include reasonable deadlines for expedited review of such petitions, after reasonable negotiations with investigative staff, in order to avoid undue delay of the merger review process.

(iii) Not later than 90 days after the date of the enactment of This Act, the Assistant Attorney General and the Federal Trade Commission shall conduct an internal review and implement reforms of the merger review process in order to eliminate unnecessary burden, remove costly duplication, and eliminate undue delay, in order to achieve a more effective and more efficient merger review process.

(iv) Not later than 120 days after the date of the enactment of This Act, the Assistant Attorney General and the Federal Trade Commission shall issue or amend their respective industry guidance, regulations, operating manuals, and relevant policy documents, to the extent appropriate, to implement each reform in this subparagraph.

(v) Not later than 180 days after the date of the enactment of This Act, the Assistant Attorney General and the Federal Trade Commission shall each report to Congress—

(I) which reforms each agency has adopted under this subparagraph;

(II) which steps each agency has taken to implement internal reforms under this subparagraph; and

(III) the effects of such reforms.

(2) The Federal Trade Commission or the Assistant Attorney General, in its or his discretion, may extend the 30–day waiting period (or in the case of a cash tender offer, the 15–day waiting period) specified in subsection (b)(1) of this section for an additional period of not more than 30 days (or in the case of a cash tender offer, 10 days) after the date on which the Federal Trade Commission or the Assistant Attorney General, as the case may be, receives from any person to whom a request is made under paragraph (1), or in the case of tender offers, the acquiring person, (A) all the information and documentary material required to be submitted pursuant to such a request, or (B) if such request is not fully complied with, the information and documentary material submitted and a statement of the reasons for such noncompliance. Such additional period may be further extended only by the United States district court, upon an application by the Federal Trade Commission or the Assistant Attorney General pursuant to subsection (g)(2) of this section.

. . .

(g) Civil penalty; compliance; power of court

(1) Any person, or any officer, director, or partner thereof, who fails to comply with any provision of this section shall be liable to the United States for a civil penalty of not more than $10,000 for each day during which such person is in violation of this section. Such penalty may be recovered in a civil action brought by the United States.

(k) If the end of any period of time provided in this section falls on a Saturday, Sunday, or legal public holiday (as defined in section 6103(a) of title 5, United States Code), then such period shall be extended to the end of the next day that is not a Saturday, Sunday, or legal public holiday.

. . .

III. STATE SECURITIES LAWS

UNIFORM SECURITIES ACT (1956)

With 1958 Amendments

An Act [Relating to securities; prohibiting fraudulent practices in relation thereto; requiring the registration of broker-dealers, agents, investment advisers, and securities; and making uniform the law with reference thereto:]

PART I

FRAUDULENT AND OTHER PROHIBITED PRACTICES

Section

PART II

REGISTRATION OF BROKER–DEALERS, AGENTS, AND INVESTMENT ADVISERS

PART III

REGISTRATION OF SECURITIES

PART IV

GENERAL PROVISIONS

PART I

FRAUDULENT AND OTHER PROHIBITED PRACTICES

§ 101. [Sales and Purchases]

It is unlawful for any person, in connection with the offer, sale, or purchase of any security, directly or indirectly

(1) to employ any device, scheme, or artifice to defraud,

(2) to make any untrue statement of a material fact or to omit to state a material fact necessary in order to make the statements made, in the light of the circumstances under which they are made, not misleading, or

(3) to engage in any act, practice, or course of business which operates or would operate as a fraud or deceit upon any person.

§ 102. [Advisory Activities]

(a) It is unlawful for any person who receives any consideration from another person primarily for advising the other person as to the value of securities or their purchase or sale, whether through the issuance of analyses or reports or otherwise,

(1) to employ any device, scheme, or artifice to defraud the other person, or

(2) to engage in any act, practice, or course of business which operates or would operate as a fraud or deceit upon the other person.

(b) It is unlawful for any investment adviser to enter into, extend, or renew any investment advisory contract unless it provides in writing

(1) that the investment adviser shall not be compensated on the basis of a share of capital gains upon or capital appreciation of the funds or any portion of the funds of the client;

(2) that no assignment of the contract may be made by the investment adviser without the consent of the other party to the contract; and

(3) that the investment adviser, if a partnership, shall notify the other party to the contract of any change in the membership of the partnership within a reasonable time after the change.

Clause (1) does not prohibit an investment advisory contract which provides for compensation based upon the total value of a fund averaged over a definite period, or as of definite dates or taken as of a definite date. "Assignment," as used in clause (2), includes any direct or indirect transfer or hypothecation of an investment advisory contract by the assignor or of a controlling block of the assignor's outstanding voting securities by a security holder of the assignor; but, if the investment adviser is a partnership, no assignment of an investment advisory contract is considered to result from the death or withdrawal of a minority of the members of the investment adviser having only a minority interest in the business of the investment adviser, or from the admission to the investment advisor of one or more members who, after admission, will be only a minority of the members and will have only a minority interest in the business.

(c) It is unlawful for any investment adviser to take or have custody of any securities or funds of any client if

(1) the [Administrator] by rule prohibits custody; or

(2) in the absence of rule, the investment adviser fails to notify the [Administrator] that he has or may have custody.

PART II

REGISTRATION OF BROKER-DEALERS, AGENTS, AND INVESTMENT ADVISERS

§ 201. [Registration Requirements]

(a) It is unlawful for any person to transact business in this state as a broker-dealer or agent unless he is registered under this act.

(b) It is unlawful for any broker-dealer or issuer to employ an agent unless the agent is registered. The registration of an agent is not effective during any period when he is not associated with a particular broker-dealer registered under this act or a particular issuer. When an agent begins or terminates a connection with a broker-dealer or issuer, or begins or terminates those activities which make him an agent, the agent as well as the broker-dealer or issuer shall promptly notify the [Administrator].

(c) It is unlawful for any person to transact business in this state as an investment adviser unless (1) he is so registered under this act, (2) he is registered as a broker-dealer without the imposition of a condition under section 204(b)(5), or (3) his only clients in this state are investment companies as defined in the Investment Company Act of 1940 or insurance companies.

(d) Every registration expires one year from its effective date unless renewed. [The [Administrator] may by rule or order prepare an initial schedule for registration renewals so that subsequent renewals of registrations effective on the effective date of this Act may be staggered by calendar months. For this purpose the [Administrator] may by rule reduce the registration fee proportionately.]

§ 202. [Registration Procedure]

(a) A broker-dealer, agent, or investment adviser may obtain an initial or renewal registration by filing with the [Administrator] an application together with a consent to service of process pursuant to section 414(g). The application shall contain whatever information the [Administrator] by rule requires concerning such matters as (1) the applicant's form and place of organization; (2) the applicant's proposed method of doing business; (3) the qualifications and business history of the applicant; in the case of a broker-dealer or investment adviser, the qualifications and business history of any partner, officer, or director, any person occupying a similar status or performing similar functions, or any person directly or indirectly controlling the broker-dealer or investment adviser; and, in the case of an investment adviser, the qualifications and business history of any employee; (4) any injunction or administrative order or conviction of a misdemeanor involving a security or any aspect of the securities business and any conviction of a felony; and (5) the applicant's financial condition and history. The [Administrator] may by rule or order require an applicant for initial registration to publish an announcement of the application in one or more specified newspapers published in this state. If no denial order is in effect and no proceeding is pending under section 204, registration becomes effective at noon of the thirtieth day after an application is filed. The [Administrator] may by rule or order specify an earlier effective date, and [he] may by order defer the effective date until noon of the thirtieth day after the filing of any amendment. Registration of a broker-dealer automatically constitutes registration of any agent who is a partner, officer, or director, or a person occupying a similar status or performing similar functions.

[(b) Every applicant for initial or renewal registration shall pay a filing fee of $______ in the case of a broker-dealer, $______ in the case of an agent, and $______ in the case of an investment adviser. When application is denied or withdrawn, the [Administrator] shall retain $______ of the fee.]

(c) A registered broker-dealer or investment adviser may file an application for registration of a successor, whether or not the successor is then in existence, for the unexpired portion of the year. There shall be no filing fee.

(d) The [Administrator] may by rule require a minimum capital for registered broker-dealers and investment advisers.

(e) The [Administrator] may by rule require registered broker-dealers, agents, and investment advisers to post surety bonds in amounts up to $10,000, and may determine their conditions. Any appropriate deposit of cash or securities shall be accepted in lieu of any bond so required. No bond may be required of any registrant whose net capital, which may be defined by rule, exceeds $25,000. Every bond shall provide for suit thereon by any person who has a cause of action under section 410 and, if the [Administrator] by rule or order requires, by any person who has a cause of action not arising under this act. Every bond shall provide that no suit may be maintained to enforce any liability on the bond unless brought within two years after the sale or other act upon which it is based.

§ 203. [Post–Registration Provisions]

(a) Every registered broker-dealer and investment adviser shall make and keep such accounts, correspondence, memoranda, papers, books, and other records as the [Administrator] by rule prescribes. All records so required shall be preserved for three years unless the [Administrator] by rule prescribes otherwise for particular types of records.

(b) Every registered broker-dealer and investment adviser shall file such financial reports as the [Administrator] by rule prescribes.

(c) If the information contained in any document filed with the [Administrator] is or becomes inaccurate or incomplete in any material respect, the registrant shall promptly file a correcting amendment unless notification of the correction has been given under section 201(b).

(d) All the records referred to in subsection (a) are subject at any time or from time to time to such reasonable periodic, special, or other examinations by representatives of the [Administrator], within or without this state, as the [Administrator] deems necessary or appropriate in the public interest or for the protection of investors. For the purpose of avoiding unnecessary duplication of examinations, the [Administrator], insofar as [he] deems it practicable in administering this subsection, may cooperate with the securities administrators of other states, the Securities and Exchange Commission, and any national securities exchange or national securities association registered under the Securities Exchange Act of 1934.

§ 204. [Denial, Revocation, Suspension, Cancelation, and Withdrawal of Registration]

(a) The [Administrator] may by order deny, suspend, or revoke any registration if [he] finds (1) that the order is in the public interest and (2) that the applicant or registrant or, in the case of a broker-dealer or investment adviser, any partner, officer, or director, any person occupying a similar status or performing similar functions, or any person directly or indirectly controlling the broker-dealer or investment adviser

(A) has filed an application for registration which as of its effective date, or as of any date after filing in the case of an order denying effectiveness, was incomplete in any material respect or contained any statement which was, in light of the circumstances under which it was made, false or misleading with respect to any material fact;

(B) has willfully violated or willfully failed to comply with any provision of this act or a predecessor act or any rule or order under this act or a predecessor act;

(C) has been convicted, within the past ten years, of any misdemeanor involving a security or any aspect of the securities business, or any felony;

(D) is permanently or temporarily enjoined by any court of competent jurisdiction from engaging in or continuing any conduct or practice involving any aspect of the securities business;

(E) is the subject of an order of the [Administrator] denying, suspending, or revoking registration as a broker-dealer, agent, or investment adviser;

(F) is the subject of an order entered within the past five years by the securities administrator of any other state or by the Securities and Exchange Commission denying or revoking registration as a broker-dealer, agent, or investment adviser, or the substantial equivalent of those terms as defined in this act, or is the subject of an order of the Securities and Exchange Commission suspending or expelling him from a national securities exchange or national securities association registered under the Securities Exchange Act of 1934,[1] or is the subject of a United States Post Office fraud order; but (i) the [Administrator] may not institute a revocation or suspension proceeding under clause (F) more than one year from the date of the order relied on, and (ii) [he] may not enter an order under clause (F) on the basis of an order under another state act unless that order was based on facts which would currently constitute a ground for an order under this section;

(G) has engaged in dishonest or unethical practices in the securities business;

(H) is insolvent, either in the sense that his liabilities exceed his assets or in the sense that he cannot meet his obligations as they mature; but the [Administrator] may not enter an order against a broker-dealer or investment adviser under this clause without a finding of insolvency as to the broker-dealer or investment adviser; or

(I) is not qualified on the basis of such factors as training, experience, and knowledge of the securities business, except as otherwise provided in subsection (b).

The [Administrator] may by order deny, suspend, or revoke any registration if [he] finds (1) that the order is in the public interest and (2) that the applicant or registrant

(J) has failed reasonably to supervise his agents if he is a broker-dealer or his employees if he is an investment adviser; or

(K) has failed to pay the proper filing fee; but the [Administrator] may enter only a denial order under this clause, and [he] shall vacate any such order when the deficiency has been corrected.

The [Administrator] may not institute a suspension or revocation proceeding on the basis of a fact or transaction known to [him] when registration became effective unless the proceeding is instituted within the next thirty days.

(b) The following provisions govern the application of section 204(a)(2)(I):

(1) The [Administrator] may not enter an order against a broker-dealer on the basis of the lack of qualification of any person other than (A) the broker-dealer himself if he is an individual or (B) an agent of the broker-dealer.

(2) The [Administrator] may not enter an order against an investment adviser on the basis of the lack of qualification of any person other than (A) the investment adviser himself if he is an individual or (B) any other person who represents the investment

adviser in doing any of the acts which make him an investment adviser.

(3) The [Administrator] may not enter an order solely on the basis of lack of experience if the applicant or registrant is qualified by training or knowledge or both.

(4) The [Administrator] shall consider that an agent who will work under the supervision of a registered broker-dealer need not have the same qualifications as a broker-dealer.

(5) The [Administrator] shall consider that an investment adviser is not necessarily qualified solely on the basis of experience as a broker-dealer or agent. When [he] finds that an applicant for initial or renewal registration as a broker-dealer is not qualified as an investment adviser, [he] may by order condition the applicant's registration as a broker-dealer upon his not transacting business in this state as an investment adviser.

(6) The [Administrator] may by rule provide for an examination, which may be written or oral or both, to be taken by any class of or all applicants, as well as persons who represent or will represent an investment adviser in doing any of the acts which make him an investment adviser.

(c) The [Administrator] may by order summarily postpone or suspend registration pending final determination of any proceeding under this section. Upon the entry of the order, the [Administrator] shall promptly notify the applicant or registrant, as well as the employer or prospective employer if the applicant or registrant is an agent, that it has been entered and of the reasons therefor and that within fifteen days after the receipt of a written request the matter will be set down for hearing. If no hearing is requested and none is ordered by the [Administrator], the order will remain in effect until it is modified or vacated by the [Administrator]. If a hearing is requested or ordered, the [Administrator], after notice of and opportunity for hearing, may modify or vacate the order or extend it until final determination.

(d) If the [Administrator] finds that any registrant or applicant for registration is no longer in existence or has ceased to do business as a broker-dealer, agent, or investment adviser, or is subject to an adjudication of mental incompetence or to the control of a committee, conservator, or guardian, or cannot be located after reasonable search, the [Administrator] may by order cancel the registration or application.

(e) Withdrawal from registration as a broker-dealer, agent, or investment adviser becomes effective thirty days after receipt of an application to withdraw or within such shorter period of time as the [Administrator] may determine, unless a revocation or suspension proceeding is pending when the application is filed or a proceeding to revoke or suspend or to impose conditions upon the withdrawal is instituted within thirty days after the application is filed. If a proceeding is pending or instituted, withdrawal becomes effective at such time and upon such conditions as the [Administrator] by order determines. If no proceeding is pending or instituted and withdrawal automatically becomes effective, the [Administrator] may nevertheless institute a revocation or suspension proceeding under section 204(a)(2)(B) within one year after withdrawal became effective and enter a revocation or suspension order as of the last date on which registration was effective.

(f) No order may be entered under any part of this section except the first sentence of subsection (c) without (1) appropriate prior notice to the applicant or registrant (as well as the employer or prospective employer if the applicant or registrant is an agent), (2) opportunity for hearing, and (3) written findings of fact and conclusions of law.

PART III
REGISTRATION OF SECURITIES

§ 301. [Registration Requirement]

It is unlawful for any person to offer or sell any security in this state unless (1) it is registered under this act or (2) the security or transaction is exempted under section 402.

§ 302. [Registration by Notification]

(a) The following securities may be registered by notification, whether or not they are also eligible for registration by coordination under section 303:

(1) any security whose issuer and any predecessors have been in continuous operation for at least five years if (A) there has been no default during the current fiscal year or within the three preceding fiscal years in the payment of principal, interest, or dividends on any security of the issuer (or any predecessor) with a fixed maturity or a fixed interest or dividend provision, and (B) the issuer and any predecessors during the past three fiscal years have had average net earnings, determined in accordance with generally accepted accounting practices, (i) which are applicable to all securities without a fixed maturity or a fixed interest or dividend provision outstanding at the date the registration statement is filed and equal at least five percent of the amount of such outstanding securities (as measured by the maximum offering price or the market price on a day, selected by the registrant, within thirty days before the date of filing the registration statement, whichever is higher, or book value on a day, selected by the registrant, within ninety days of the date of filing the registration statement to the extent that there is neither a readily determinable market price nor a cash offering price), or (ii) which, if the issuer and any predecessors have not had any security of the type specified in clause (i) outstanding for three full fiscal years, equal at least five percent of the amount (as measured in clause (i)) of all securities which will be outstanding if all the securities being offered or proposed to be offered (whether or not they are proposed to be registered or offered in this state) are issued;

(2) any security (other than a certificate of interest or participation in an oil, gas or mining title or lease or in payments out of production under such a title or lease) registered for nonissuer distribution if (A) any security of the same class has ever been registered under this act or a predecessor act, or (B) the security being registered was originally issued pursuant to an exemption under this act or a predecessor act.

(b) A registration statement under this section shall contain the following information and be accompanied by the following documents in addition to the information specified in section 305(c) and the consent to service of process required by section 414(g):

(1) a statement demonstrating eligibility for registration by notification;

(2) with respect to the issuer and any significant subsidiary: its name, address, and form of organization; the state (or foreign jurisdiction) and the date of its organization; and the general character and location of its business;

(3) with respect to any person on whose behalf any part of the offering is to be made in a non-issuer distribution: his name and address; the amount of securities of the issuer held by him as of the date of the filing of the registration statement; and a statement of his reasons for making the offering;

(4) a description of the security being registered;

(5) the information and documents specified in clauses (8), (10), and (12) of section 304(b); and

(6) in the case of any registration under section 302(a)(2) which does not also satisfy the conditions of section 302(a)(1), a balance sheet of the issuer as of a date within four months prior to the filing of the registration statement, and a summary of earnings for each of the two fiscal years preceding the date of the balance sheet and for any period between the close of the last fiscal year and the date of the balance sheet, or for the period of the issuer's and any predecessors' existence if less than two years.

(c) If no stop order is in effect and no proceeding is pending under section 306, a registration statement under this section automatically becomes effective at [three o'clock Eastern Standard Time] in the afternoon of the second full business day after the filing of the registration statement or the last amendment, or at such earlier time as the [Administrator] determines.

§ 303. [Registration by Coordination]

(a) Any security for which a registration statement has been filed under the Securities Act of 1933 in connection with the same offering may be registered by coordination.

(b) A registration statement under this section shall contain the following information and be accompanied by the following documents in addition to the information specified in section 305(c) and the consent to service of process required by section 414(g):

(1) three copies of the latest form of prospectus filed under the Securities Act of 1933;

(2) if the [Administrator] by rule or otherwise requires, a copy of the articles of incorporation and by-laws (or their substantial equivalents) currently in effect, a copy of any agreements with or among underwriters, a copy of any indenture or other instrument governing the issuance of the security to be registered, and a specimen or copy of the security;

(3) if the [Administrator] requests, any other information, or copies of any other documents, filed under the Securities Act of 1933; and

(4) an undertaking to forward all future amendments to the federal prospectus, other than an amendment which merely delays the effective date of the registration statement, promptly and in any event not later than the first business day after the day they are forwarded to or filed with the Securities and Exchange Commission, whichever first occurs.

(c) A registration statement under this section automatically becomes effective at the moment the federal registration statement becomes effective if all the following conditions are satisfied: (1) no stop order is in effect and no proceeding is pending under section 306; (2) the registration statement has been on file with the [Administrator] for at least ten days; and (3) a statement of the maximum and minimum proposed offering prices and the maximum underwriting discounts and commissions has been on file for two full business days or such shorter period as the [Administrator] permits by rule or otherwise and the offering is made within those limitations. The registrant shall promptly notify the [Administrator] by telephone or telegram of the date and time when the federal registration statement became effective and the content of the price amendment, if any, and shall promptly file a post-effective amendment containing the information and documents in the price amendment. "Price amendment" means the final federal amendment which includes a statement of the offering price, underwriting and selling discounts or commissions, amount of proceeds, conversion rates, call prices, and other matters dependent upon the offering price. Upon failure to receive the required notification and post-effective amendment with respect to the price amendment, the [Administrator] may enter a stop order, without notice or hearing, retroactively denying effectiveness to the registration statement or suspending its effectiveness until compliance with this subsection, if [he] promptly notifies the registrant by telephone or telegram (and promptly confirms by letter or telegram when [he] notifies by telephone) of the issuance of the order. If the registrant proves compliance with the requirements of this subsection as to notice and post-effective amendment, the stop order is void as of the time of its entry. The [Administrator] may by rule or otherwise waive either or both of the conditions specified in clauses (2) and (3). If the federal registration statement becomes effective before all the conditions in this subsection are satisfied and they are not waived, the registration statement automatically becomes effective as soon as all the conditions are satisfied. If the registrant advises the [Administrator] of the date when the federal registration statement is expected to become effective, the [Administrator] shall promptly advise the registrant by telephone or telegram, at the registrant's expense, whether all the conditions are satisfied and whether [he] then contemplates the institution of a proceeding under section 306; but this advice by the [Administrator] does not preclude the institution of such a proceeding at any time.

§ 304. [Registration by Qualification]

(a) Any security may be registered by qualification.

(b) A registration statement under this section shall contain the following information and be accompanied by the following documents in addition to the information specified in section 305(c) and the consent to service of process required by section 414(g):

(1) with respect to the issuer and any significant subsidiary: its name, address, and form of organization; the state or foreign jurisdiction and date of its organization; the general character and location of its business; a description of its physical properties and equipment; and a statement of the general competitive conditions in the industry or business in which it is or will be engaged;

(2) with respect to every director and officer of the issuer, or person occupying a similar status or performing similar functions: his name, address, and principal occupation for the past five years; the amount of securities of the issuer held by him as of a specified date within thirty days of the filing of the registration statement; the amount of the securities covered by the registration statement to which he has indicated his intention to subscribe; and a description of any material interest in any material transaction with the issuer or any significant subsidiary effected within the past three years or proposed to be effected;

(3) with respect to persons covered by clause (2): the remuneration paid during the past twelve months and estimated to be paid during the next twelve months, directly or indirectly, by the issuer (together with all predecessors, parents, subsidiaries, and affiliates) to all those persons in the aggregate;

(4) with respect to any person owning of record, or beneficially if known, ten percent or more of the outstanding shares of any class of equity security of the issuer: the information specified in clause (2) other than his occupation;

(5) with respect to every promoter if the issuer was organized within the past three years: the information specified in clause (2), any amount paid to him within that period or intended to be paid to him, and the consideration for any such payment;

(6) with respect to any person on whose behalf any part of the offering is to be made in a non-issuer distribution: his name and address; the amount of securities of the issuer held by him as of the date of the filing of the registration statement; a description of any material interest in any material transaction with the issuer or any significant subsidiary effected within the past three years or proposed to be effected; and a statement of his reasons for making the offering;

(7) the capitalization and long-term debt (on both a current and a pro forma basis) of the issuer and any significant subsidiary, including a description of each security outstanding or being registered or otherwise offered, and a statement of the amount and kind of consideration (whether in the form of cash, physical assets, services, patents, goodwill, or anything else) for which the issuer or any subsidiary has issued any of its securities within the past two years or is obligated to issue any of its securities;

(8) the kind and amount of securities to be offered; the proposed offering price or the method by which it is to be computed; any variation therefrom at which any proportion of the offering is to be made to any person or class of persons other than the underwriters, with a specification of any such person or class; the basis upon which the offering is to be made if otherwise than for cash; the estimated aggregate underwriting and selling discounts or commissions and finders' fees (including separately cash, securities, contracts, or anything else of value to accrue to the underwriters or finders in connection with the offering) or, if the selling discounts or commissions are variable, the basis of determining them and their maximum and minimum amounts; the estimated amounts of other selling expenses, including legal, engineering, and accounting charges; the name and address of every underwriter and every recipient of a finder's fee; a copy of any underwriting or selling-group agreement pursuant to which the distribution is to be made, or the proposed form of any such agreement whose terms have not yet been determined, and a description of the plan of distribution of any securities which are to be offered otherwise than through an underwriter.

(9) the estimated cash proceeds to be received by the issuer from the offering; the purposes for which the proceeds are to be used by the issuer; the amount to be used for each purpose; the order or priority in which the proceeds will be used for the purposes stated; the amounts of any funds to be raised from other sources to achieve the purposes stated; the sources of any such funds; and, if any part of the proceeds is to be used to acquire any property (including goodwill) otherwise than in the ordinary course of business, the names and addresses of the vendors, the purchase price, the names of any persons who have received commissions in connection with the acquisition, and the amounts of any such commissions and any other expense in connection with the acquisition (including the cost of borrowing money to finance the acquisition);

(10) a description of any stock options or other security options outstanding, or to be created in connection with the offering, together with the amount of any such options held or to be held by every person required to be named in clause (2), (4), (5), (6), or (8) and by any person who holds or will hold ten percent or more in the aggregate of any such options;

(11) the dates of, parties to, and general effect concisely stated of, every management or other material contract made or to be made otherwise than in the ordinary course of business if it is to be performed in whole or in part at or after the filing of the registration statement or was made within the past two years, together with a copy of every such contract; and a description of any pending litigation or proceeding to which the issuer is a party and which materially affects its business or assets (including any such litigation or proceeding known to be contemplated by governmental authorities);

(12) a copy of any prospectus, pamphlet, circular, form letter, advertisement, or other sales literature intended as of the effective date to be used in connection with the offering;

(13) a specimen or copy of the security being registered; a copy of the issuer's articles of incorporation and by-laws, or their substantial equivalents, as currently in effect; and a copy of any indenture or other

instrument covering the security to be registered;

(14) a signed or conformed copy of an opinion of counsel as to the legality of the security being registered (with an English translation if it is in a foreign language), which shall state whether the security when sold will be legally issued, fully paid, and non-assessable, and, if a debt security, a binding obligation of the issuer;

(15) the written consent of any accountant, engineer, appraiser, or other person whose profession gives authority to a statement made by him, if any such person is named as having prepared or certified a report or valuation (other than a public and official document or statement) which is used in connection with the registration statement;

(16) a balance sheet of the issuer as of a date within four months prior to the filing of the registration statement; a profit and loss statement and analysis of surplus for each of the three fiscal years preceding the date of the balance sheet and for any period between the close of the last fiscal year and the date of the balance sheet, or for the period of the issuer's and any predecessors' existence if less than three years; and, if any part of the proceeds of the offering is to be applied to the purchase of any business, the same financial statements which would be required if that business were the registrant; and

(17) such additional information as the [Administrator] requires by rule or order.

(c) A registration statement under this section becomes effective when the [Administrator] so orders.

(d) The [Administrator] may by rule or order require as a condition of registration under this section that a prospectus containing any designated part of the information specified in subsection (b) be sent or given to each person to whom an offer is made before or concurrently with (1) the first written offer made to him (otherwise than by means of a public advertisement) by or for the account of the issuer or any other person on whose behalf the offering is being made, or by any underwriter or broker-dealer who is offering part of an unsold allotment or subscription taken by him as a participant in the distribution, (2) the confirmation of any sale made by or for the account of any such person, (3) payment pursuant to any such sale, or (4) delivery of the security pursuant to any such sale, whichever first occurs.

§ 305. [Provisions Applicable to Registration Generally]

(a) A registration statement may be filed by the issuer, any other person on whose behalf the offering is to be made, or a registered broker-dealer.

[(b) Every person filing a registration statement shall pay a filing fee of ______ percent of the maximum aggregate offering price at which the registered securities are to be offered in this state, but the fee shall in no case be less than $______ or more than $______. When a registration statement is withdrawn before the effective date or a pre-effective stop order is entered under section 306, the [Administrator] shall retain $______ of the fee.]

(c) Every registration statement shall specify (1) the amount of securities to be offered in this state; (2) the states in which a registration statement or similar document in connection with the offering has been or is to be filed; and (3) any adverse order, judgment, or decree entered in connection with the offering by the regulatory authorities in each state or by any court or the Securities and Exchange Commission.

(d) Any document filed under this act or a predecessor act [within five years preceding the filing of a registration statement] may be incorporated by reference in the registration statement to the extent that the document is currently accurate.

(e) The [Administrator] may by rule or otherwise permit the omission of any item of information or document from any registration statement.

(f) In the case of a non-issuer distribution, information may not be required under section 304 or 305(j) unless it is known to the person filing the registration statement or to the persons on whose behalf the distribution is to be made, or can be furnished by them without unreasonable effort or expense.

(g) The [Administrator] may by rule or order require as a condition of registration by qualification or coordination (1) that any security issued within the past three years or to be issued to a promoter for a consideration substantially different from the public offering price, or to any person for a consideration other than cash, be deposited in escrow; and (2) that the proceeds from the sale of the registered security in this state be impounded until the issuer receives a specified amount from the sale of the security either in this state or elsewhere.

(h) The [Administrator] may by rule or order require as a condition of registration that any security registered by qualification or coordination be sold only on a specified form of subscription or sale contract, and that a signed or conformed copy of each contract be filed with the [Administrator] or preserved for any period up to three years specified in the rule or order.

(i) Every registration statement is effective for one year from its effective date, or any longer period during which the security is being offered or distributed in a non-exempted transaction by or for the account of the issuer or other person on whose behalf the offering is being made or by any underwriter or broker-dealer who is still offering part of an unsold allotment or subscription taken by him as a participant in the distribution, except during the time a stop order is in effect under section 306. All outstanding securities of the same class as a registered security are considered to be registered for the purpose of any non-issuer transaction (1) so long as the registration statement is effective and (2) between the thirtieth day after the entry of any stop order suspending or revoking the effectiveness of the registration statement under section 306 (if the registration statement did not relate in whole or in part to a non-issuer distribution) and one year from the effective date of the registration statement. A registration statement may not be withdrawn for one year from its effective date if any securities of the same class are outstanding. A registration statement may be withdrawn otherwise only in the discretion of the [Administrator].

(j) So long as a registration statement is effective, the [Administrator] may by rule or order require the person who filed the registration statement to file reports, not more often than quarterly, to keep reasonably current the information contained in the registration statement and to disclose the progress of the offering.

(k) A registration statement relating to a security issued by a face-amount certificate company or a redeemable security issued by an open-end management company or unit investment trust, as those terms are defined in the Investment Company Act of 1940, may be amended after its effective date so as to increase the securities specified as proposed to be offered. Such an amendment becomes effective when the [Administrator] so orders. Every person filing such an amendment shall pay a filing fee, calculated in the manner specified in subsection (b), with respect to the additional securities proposed to be offered.

§ 306. [Denial, Suspension, and Revocation of Registration]

(a) The [Administrator] may issue a stop order denying effectiveness to, or suspending or revoking the effectiveness of, any registration statement if [he] finds (1) that the order is in the public interest and (2) that

(A) the registration statement as of its effective date or as of any earlier date in the case of an order denying effectiveness, or any amendment under section 305(k) as of its effective date, or any report under section 305(j) is incomplete in any material respect or contains any statement which was, in the light of the circumstances under which it was made, false or misleading with respect to any material fact;

(B) any provision of this act or any rule, order, or condition lawfully imposed under this act has been willfully violated, in connection with the offering, by (i) the person filing the registration statement, (ii) the issuer, any partner, officer, or director of the issuer, any person occupying a similar status or performing similar functions, or any person directly or indirectly controlling or controlled by the issuer, but only if the person filing the registration statement is directly or indirectly controlled by or acting for the issuer, or (iii) any underwriter;

(C) the security registered or sought to be registered is the subject of an administrative stop order or similar order or a permanent or temporary injunction of any court of competent jurisdiction entered under any other federal or state act applicable to the offering; but (i) the [Administrator] may not institute a proceeding against an effective registration statement under clause (C) more than one year from the date of the order or injunction relied on, and (ii) [he] may not enter an order under clause (C) on the basis of an order or injunction entered under any other state act unless that order or injunction was based on facts which would currently constitute a ground for a stop order under this section;

(D) the issuer's enterprise or method of business includes or would include activities which are illegal where performed;

(E) the offering has worked or tended to work a fraud upon purchasers or would so operate;

(F) the offering has been or would be made with unreasonable amounts of underwriters' and sellers' discounts, commissions, or other compensation, or promoters' profits or participation, or unreasonable amounts or kinds of options;

(G) when a security is sought to be registered by notification, it is not eligible for such registration;

(H) when a security is sought to be registered by coordination, there has been a failure to comply with the undertaking required by section 303(b)(4); or

(I) the applicant or registrant has failed to pay the proper filing fee; but the [Administrator] may enter only a denial order under this clause and [he] shall vacate any such order when the deficiency has been corrected.

The [Administrator] may not institute a stop-order proceeding against an effective registration statement on the basis of a fact or transaction known to him when the registration statement became effective unless the proceeding is instituted within the next thirty days.

(b) The [Administrator] may by order summarily postpone or suspend the effectiveness of the registration statement pending final determination of any proceeding under this section. Upon the entry of the order, the [Administrator] shall promptly notify each person specified in subsection (c) that it has been entered and of the reasons therefor and that within fifteen days after the receipt of a written request the matter will be set down for hearing. If no hearing is requested and none is ordered by the [Administrator], the order will remain in effect until it is modified or vacated by the [Administrator]. If a hearing is requested or ordered, the [Administrator], after notice of an opportunity for hearing to each person specified in subsection (c), may modify or vacate the order or extend it until final determination.

(c) No stop order may be entered under any part of this section except the first sentence of subsection (b) without (1) appropriate prior notice to the applicant or registrant, the issuer, and the person on whose behalf the securities are to be or have been offered, (2) opportunity for hearing, and (3) written findings of fact and conclusions of law.

(d) The [Administrator] may vacate or modify a stop order if [he] finds that the conditions which prompted entry have changed or that it is otherwise in the public interest to do so.

PART IV

GENERAL PROVISIONS

§ 401. [Definitions]

When used in this act, unless the context otherwise requires:

(a) "[Administrator]" [substitute any other appropriate term, such as "Commission," "Commissioner," "Secretary," etc.] means the [official or agency designated in section 406(a)].

(b) "Agent" means any individual other than a broker-dealer who represents a broker-dealer or issuer in effecting or attempting to effect purchases or sales of securities. "Agent" does not include an individual who represents an issuer in (1) effecting transactions in a security exempted by clause (1), (2), (3), (10), or (11) of section 402(a), (2) effecting transactions exempted by section 402(b), or (3) effecting transactions with existing employees, partners, or directors of the issuer if no commission or other remuneration is paid or given directly or indirectly for soliciting any person in this state. A partner, officer, or director of a broker-dealer or issuer, or a person occupying a similar status or performing similar functions, is an agent only if he otherwise comes within this definition.

(c) "Broker-dealer" means any person engaged in the business of effecting transactions in securities for the account of others or for his own account. "Broker-dealer" does not include (1) an agent, (2) an issuer, (3) a bank, savings institution, or trust company, or (4) a person who has no place of business in this state if (A) he effects transactions in this state exclusively with or through (i) the issuers of the securities involved in the transactions, (ii) other broker-dealers, or (iii) banks, savings institutions, trust companies, insurance companies, investment companies as defined in the Investment Company Act of 1940,[1] pension or profit-sharing trusts, or other financial institutions or institutional buyers, whether acting for themselves or as trustees, or (B) during any period of twelve consecutive months he does not direct more than fifteen offers to sell or buy into this state in any manner to persons other than those specified in clause (A), whether or not the offeror or any of the offerees is then present in this state.

(d) "Fraud," "deceit," and "defraud" are not limited to common-law deceit.

(e) "Guaranteed" means guaranteed as to payment of principal, interest, or dividends.

(f) "Investment adviser" means any person who, for compensation, engages in the business of advising others, either directly or through publications or writings, as to the value of securities or as to the advisability of investing in, purchasing, or selling securities, or who, for compensation and as a part of a regular business, issues or promulgates analyses or reports concerning securities. "Investment adviser" does not include (1) a bank, savings institution, or trust company; (2) a lawyer, accountant, engineer, or teacher whose performance of these services is solely incidental to the practice of his profession; (3) a broker-dealer whose performance of these services is solely incidental to the conduct of his business as a broker-dealer and who receives no special compensation for them; (4) a publisher of any bona fide newspaper, news magazine, or business or financial publication of general, regular, and paid circulation; (5) a person whose advice, analyses, or reports relate only to securities exempted by section 402(a)(1); (6) a person who has no place of business in this state if (A) his only clients in this state are other investment advisers, broker-dealers, banks, savings institutions, trust companies, insurance companies, investment companies as defined in the Investment Company Act of 1940,[1] pension or profit-sharing trusts, or other financial institutions or institutional buyers, whether acting for themselves or as trustees, or (B) during any period of twelve consecutive months he does not direct business communications into this state in any manner to more than five clients other than those specified in clause (A), whether or not he or any of the persons to whom the communications are directed is then present in this state; or (7) such other persons not within the intent of this paragraph as the [Administrator] may by rule or order designate.

(g) "Issuer" means any person who issues or proposes to issue any security, except that (1) with respect to certificates of deposit, voting-trust certificates, or collateral-trust certificates, or with respect to certificates of interest or shares in an unincorporated investment trust not having a board of directors or persons performing similar functions or of the fixed, restricted management, or unit type, the term "issuer" means the person or persons performing the acts and assuming the duties of depositor or manager pursuant to the provisions of the trust or other agreement or instrument under which the security is issued; and (2) with respect to certificates of interest or participation in oil, gas, or mining titles or leases or in payments out of production under such titles or leases, there is not considered to be any "issuer."

(h) "Non-issuer" means not directly or indirectly for the benefit of the issuer.

(i) "Person" means an individual, a corporation, a partnership, an association, a joint-stock company, a trust where the interests of the beneficiaries are evidenced by a security, an unincorporated organization, a government, or a political subdivision of a government.

(j)(1) "Sale" or "sell" includes every contract of sale of, contract to sell, or disposition of, a security or interest in a security for value.

(2) "Offer" or "offer to sell" includes every attempt or offer to dispose of, or solicitation of an offer to buy, a security or interest in a security for value.

(3) Any security given or delivered with, or as a bonus on account of, any purchase of securities or any other thing is considered to constitute part of the subject of the purchase and to have been offered and sold for value.

(4) A purported gift of assessable stock is considered to involve an offer and sale.

(5) Every sale or offer of a warrant or right to purchase or subscribe to another security of the same or another issuer, as well as every sale or offer of a security which gives the holder a present or future right or privilege to convert into another security of the same or another issuer, is considered to include an offer of the other security.

(6) The terms defined in this subsection do not include (A) any bona fide pledge or loan; (B) any stock dividend, whether the corporation distributing the dividend is the issuer of the stock or not, if nothing of value is given by stockholders for the dividend other than the surrender of a right to a cash or property dividend when each stockholder may elect to take the dividend in cash or property or in stock; (C) any act incident to a class vote by stockholders, pursuant to the certificate of incorporation or the applicable corporation statute, on a merger, consolidation, reclassification of securities, or sale of corporate assets in consideration of the issuance of securities of another corporation; or (D) any act incident to a judicially approved reorganization in which a security is issued in exchange for one or more outstanding securities, claims, or property interests, or partly in such exchange and partly for cash.

(k) "Securities Act of 1933," "Securities Exchange Act of 1934," "Public Utility Holding Company Act of 1935," and "Investment Company Act of 1940" means the federal statutes of those names as amended before or after the effective date of this act.

(*l*) "Security" means any note; stock; treasury stock; bond; debenture; evidence of indebtedness; certificate of interest or participation in any profit-sharing agreement; collateral-trust certificate; preorganization certificate or subscription; transferable share; investment contract; voting-trust certificate; certificate of deposit for a security; certificate of interest or participation in an oil, gas, or mining title or lease or in payments out of production under such a title or lease; or, in general, any interest or instrument commonly known as a "security," or any certificate of interest or participation in, temporary or interim certificate for, receipt for guarantee of, or warrant or right to subscribe to or purchase any of the foregoing. "Security" does not include any insurance or endowment policy or annuity contract under which an insurance company promises to pay [a fixed sum of] money either in a lump sum or periodically for life or for some other specified period.

(m) "State" means any state, territory, or possession of the United States, the District of Columbia, and Puerto Rico.

§ 402. [Exemptions]

(a) The following securities are exempted from sections 301 and 403:

(1) any security (including a revenue obligation) issued or guaranteed by the United States, any state, any political subdivision of a state, or any agency or corporate or other instrumentality of one or more of the foregoing; or any certificate of deposit for any of the foregoing;

(2) any security issued or guaranteed by Canada, any Canadian province, any political subdivision of any such province, any agency or corporate or other instrumentality of one or more of the foregoing, or any other foreign government with which the United States currently maintains diplomatic relations, if the security is recognized as a valid obligation by the issuer or guarantor;

(3) any security issued by and representing an interest in or a debt of, or guaranteed by, any bank organized under the laws of the United States, or any bank, savings institution, or trust company organized and supervised under the laws of any state;

(4) any security issued by and representing an interest in or a debt of, or guaranteed by, any federal savings and loan association, or any building and loan or similar association organized under the laws of any state and authorized to do business in this state;

(5) any security issued by and representing an interest in or a debt of, or guaranteed by, any insurance company organized under the laws of any state and authorized to do business in this state; [but this exemption does not apply to an annuity contract, investment contract, or similar security under which the promised payments are not fixed in dollars but are substantially dependent upon the investment results of a segregated fund or account invested in securities;]

(6) any security issued or guaranteed by any federal credit union or any credit union, industrial loan association, or similar association organized and supervised under the laws of this state;

(7) any security issued or guaranteed by any railroad, other common carrier, public utility, or holding company which is (A) subject to the jurisdiction of the Interstate Commerce Commission; (B) a registered holding company under the Public Utility Holding Company Act of 1935 or a subsidiary of such a company within the meaning of that act; (C) regulated in respect of its rates and charges by a governmental authority of the United States or any state; or (D) regulated in respect of the issuance or guarantee of the security by a governmental authority of the United States, any state, Canada, or any Canadian province;

(8) any security listed or approved for listing upon notice of issuance on the New York Stock Exchange, the American Stock Exchange, or the Midwest Stock Exchange [, or listed on the (insert names of appropriate regional stock exchanges)]; any other secu-

rity of the same issuer which is of senior or substantially equal rank; any security called for by subscription rights or warrants so listed or approved; or any warrant or right to purchase or subscribe to any of the foregoing;

(9) any security issued by any person organized and operated not for private profit but exclusively for religious, educational, benevolent, charitable, fraternal, social, athletic, or reformatory purposes, or as a chamber of commerce or trade or professional association;

(10) any commercial paper which arises out of a current transaction or the proceeds of which have been or are to be used for current transactions, and which evidences an obligation to pay cash within nine months of the date of issuance, exclusive of days of grace, or any renewal of such paper which is likewise limited, or any guarantee of such paper or of any such renewal;

(11) any investment contract issued in connection with an employees' stock purchase, savings, pension, profit-sharing, or similar benefit plan if the [Administrator] is notified in writing thirty days before the inception of the plan or, with respect to plans which are in effect on the effective date of this act, within sixty days thereafter (or within thirty days before they are reopened if they are closed on the effective date of this act);

[(12) insert any desired exemption for cooperatives.]

(b) The following transactions are exempted from sections 301 and 403:

(1) any isolated non-issuer transaction, whether effected through a broker-dealer or not;

(2) any non-issuer distribution of an outstanding security if (A) a recognized securities manual contains the names of the issuer's officers and directors, a balance sheet of the issuer as of a date within eighteen months, and a profit and loss statement for either the fiscal year preceding that date or the most recent year of operations, or (B) the security has a fixed maturity or a fixed interest or dividend provision and there has been no default during the current fiscal year or within the three preceding years, or during the existence of the issuer and any predecessors if less than three years, in the payment of principal, interest, or dividends on the security;

(3) any non-issuer transaction effected by or through a registered broker-dealer pursuant to an unsolicited order or offer to buy; but the [Administrator] may by rule require that the customer acknowledge upon a specified form that the sale was unsolicited, and that a signed copy of each such form be preserved by the broker-dealer for a specified period;

(4) any transaction between the issuer or other person on whose behalf the offering is made and an underwriter, or among underwriters;

(5) any transaction in a bond or other evidence of indebtedness secured by a real or chattel mortgage or deed of trust, or by an agreement for the sale of real estate or chattels, if the entire mortgage, deed of trust, or agreement, together with all the bonds or other evidences of indebtedness secured thereby, is offered and sold as a unit;

(6) any transaction by an executor, administrator, sheriff, marshal, receiver, trustee in bankruptcy, guardian, or conservator;

(7) any transaction executed by a bona fide pledgee without any purpose of evading this act;

(8) any offer or sale to a bank, savings institution, trust company, insurance company, investment company as defined in the Investment Company Act of 1940, pension or profit-sharing trust, or other financial institution or institutional buyer, or to a broker-dealer, whether the purchaser is acting for itself or in some fiduciary capacity;

(9) any transaction pursuant to an offer directed by the offeror to not more than ten persons (other than those designated in paragraph (8)) in this state during any period of twelve consecutive months, whether or not the offeror or any of the offerees is then present in this state, if (A) the seller reasonably believes that all the buyers in this state (other than those designated in paragraph (8)) are purchasing for investment, and (B) no commission or other remuneration is paid or given directly or indirectly for soliciting any prospective buyer in this state (other than those designated in paragraph (8)); but the [Administrator] may by rule or order, as to any security or transaction or any type of security or transaction, withdraw or further condition this exemption, or increase or decrease the number of offerees permitted, or waive the conditions in Clauses (A) and (B) with or without the substitution of a limitation on remuneration;

(10) any offer or sale of a preorganization certificate or subscription if (A) no commission or other remuneration is paid or given directly or indirectly for soliciting any prospective subscriber, (B) the number of subscribers does not exceed ten, and (C) no payment is made by any subscriber;

(11) any transaction pursuant to an offer to existing security holders of the issuer, including persons who at the time of the transaction are holders of convertible securities, non-transferable warrants, or transferable warrants exercisable within not more than ninety days of their issuance, if (A) no commission or other remuneration (other than a standby commission) is paid or given directly or indirectly for soliciting any security holder in this state, or (B) the issuer first files a notice specifying the terms of the offer and the [Administrator] does not by order disallow the exemption within the next five full business days;

(12) any offer (but not a sale) of a security for which registration statements have been filed under both this act and the Securities Act of 1933[3] if no stop order or refusal order is in effect and no public proceeding or examination looking toward such an order is pending under either act.

(c) The [Administrator] may by order deny or revoke any exemption specified in clause (9) or (11) of subsection (a) or in subsection (b) with respect to a specific security or transaction. No such order may be entered without appropriate prior notice to all interested parties, opportunity for hearing, and written findings of fact and conclusions of law, except that the [Administrator] may by order summarily deny or revoke any of the specified exemptions pending final determination of any proceeding under this subsection. Upon the entry of a summary order, the [Administrator] shall promptly notify all interested parties that it has been entered and of the reasons therefor and that within fifteen days of the receipt of a written request the matter will be set down for hearing. If no hearing is requested and none is ordered by the [Administrator], the order will remain in effect until it is modified or vacated by the [Administrator]. If a hearing is requested or ordered, the [Administrator], after notice of and opportunity for hearing to all interested persons, may modify or vacate the order or extend it until final determination. No order under this subsection may operate retroactively. No person may be considered to have violated section 301 or 403 by reason of any offer or sale effected after the entry of an order under this subsection if he sustains the burden of proof that he did not know, and in the exercise of reasonable care could not have known, of the order.

(d) In any proceeding under this act, the burden of proving an exemption or an exception from a definition is upon the person claiming it.

§ 403. [Filing of Sales and Advertising Literature]

The [Administrator] may by rule or order require the filing of any prospectus, pamphlet, circular, form letter, advertisement, or other sales literature or advertising communication addressed or intended for distribution to prospective investors, including clients or prospective clients of an investment adviser unless the security or transaction is exempted by Section 402.

§ 404. [Misleading Filings]

It is unlawful for any person to make or cause to be made, in any document filed with the [Administrator] or in any proceeding under this act, any statement which is, at the time and in the light of the circumstances under which it is made, false or misleading in any material respect.

§ 405. [Unlawful Representations Concerning Registration or Exemption]

(a) Neither (1) the fact that an application for registration under Part II or a registration statement under Part III has been filed nor (2) the fact that a person or security is effectively registered constitutes a finding by the [Administrator] that any document filed under this act is true, complete, and not misleading. Neither any such fact nor the fact that an exemption or exception is available for a security or a transaction means that the [Administrator] has passed in any way upon the merits or qualifications of, or recommended or given approval to, any person, security, or transaction.

(b) It is unlawful to make, or cause to be made, to any prospective purchaser, customer, or client any representation inconsistent with subsection (a).

§ 406. [Administration of Act]

(a) This act shall be administered by the [insert name of local administrative agency and any related provisions on method of selection, salary, term of office, budget, selection and remuneration of personnel, annual reports to the legislature or governor, etc., which are appropriate to the particular state].

(b) It is unlawful for the [Administrator] or any of [his] officers or employees to use for personal benefit any information which is filed with or obtained by the [Administrator] and which is not made public. No provision of this act authorizes the [Administrator] or any of [his] officers or employees to disclose any such information except among themselves or when necessary or appropriate in a proceeding or investigation under this act. No provision of this act either creates or derogates from any privilege which exists at common law or otherwise when documentary or other evidence is sought under a subpoena directed to the [Administrator] or any of his officers or employees.

[(c) Insert a provision, if desired, covering fees for examinations, filings under section 403, and other miscellaneous filings for which no fees are specified elsewhere in this act.]

§ 407. [Investigations and Subpoenas]

(a) The [Administrator] in [his] discretion (1) may make such public or private investigations within or outside of this state as [he] deems necessary to determine whether any person has violated or is about to violate any provision of this act or any rule or order hereunder, or to aid in the enforcement of this act or in the prescribing of rules and forms hereunder, (2) may require or permit any person to file a statement in writing, under oath or otherwise as the [Administrator] determines, as to all the facts and circumstances concerning the matter to be investigated, and (3) may publish information concerning any violation of this act or any rule or order hereunder.

(b) For the purpose of any investigation or proceeding under this act, the [Administrator] or any officer designated by [him] may administer oaths and affirmations, subpoena witnesses, compel their attendance, take evidence, and require the production of any books, papers, correspondence, memoranda, agreements, or other documents or records which the [Administrator] deems relevant or material to the inquiry.

(c) In case of contumacy by, or refusal to obey a subpoena issued to, any person, the [insert name of appropriate court], upon application by the [Administrator], may issue to the person an order requiring him to appear before the [Administrator], or the officer designated by [him], there to produce documentary evidence if so ordered or to give evidence touching the matter under investigation or in question. Failure to obey the order of the court may be punished by the court as a contempt of court.

(d) No person is excused from attending and testifying or from producing any document or record before the [Administrator], or in obedience to the subpoena of the [Administrator] or any officer designated by [him], or in any proceeding instituted by the [Administrator], on the ground that the testimony or evidence (documentary or otherwise) required of him may tend to incriminate him or subject him to a penalty or forfeiture; but no individual may be prosecuted or subjected to any penalty or forfeiture for or on account of any transaction, matter, or thing concerning which he is compelled, after claiming his privilege against self-incrimination, to testify or produce evidence (documentary or otherwise), except that the individual testifying is not exempt from prosecution and punishment for perjury or contempt committed in testifying.

§ 408. [Injunctions]

Whenever it appears to the [Administrator] that any person has engaged or is about to engage in any act or practice constituting a violation of any provision of this act or any rule or order hereunder, [he] may in [his] discretion bring an action in the [insert name of appropriate court] to enjoin the acts or practices and to enforce compliance with this act or any rule or order hereunder. Upon a proper showing a permanent or temporary injunction, restraining order, or writ of mandamus shall be granted and a receiver or conservator may be appointed for the defendant or the defendant's assets. The court may not require the [Administrator] to post a bond.

§ 409. [Criminal Penalties]

(a) Any person who willfully violates any provision of this act except section 404, or who willfully violates any rule or order under this act, or who willfully violates section 404 knowing the statement made to be false or misleading in any material respect, shall upon conviction be fined not more than $5,000 or imprisoned not more than three years, or both; but no person may be imprisoned for the violation of any rule or order if he proves that he had no knowledge of the rule or order. [No indictment or information may be returned under this act more than five years after the alleged violation.]

(b) The [Administrator] may refer such evidence as is available concerning violations of this act or of any rule or order hereunder to the [attorney general or the proper district attorney], who may, with or without such a reference, institute the appropriate criminal proceedings under this act.

(c) Nothing in this act limits the power of the state to punish any person for any conduct which constitutes a crime by statute or at common law.

§ 410. [Civil Liabilities]

(a) Any person who

(1) offers or sells a security in violation of section 201(a), 301, or 405(b), or of any rule or order under section 403 which requires the affirmative approval of sales literature before it is used, or of any condition imposed under section 304(d), 305(g), or 305(h), or

(2) offers or sells a security by means of any untrue statement of a material fact or any omission to state a material fact necessary in order to make the statements made, in the light of the circumstances under which they are made, not misleading (the buyer not knowing of the untruth or omission), and who does not sustain the burden of proof that he did not know, and in the exercise of reasonable care could not have known, of the untruth or omission,

is liable to the person buying the security from him, who may sue either at law or in equity to recover the consideration paid for the security, together with interest at six percent per year from the date of payment, costs, and reasonable attorneys' fees, less the amount of any income received on the security, upon the tender of the security, or for damages if he no longer owns the security.

(b) Every person who directly or indirectly controls a seller liable under subsection (a), every partner, officer, or director of such a seller, every person occupying a similar status or performing similar functions, every employee of such a seller who materially aids in the sale, and every broker-dealer or agent who materially aids in the sale are also liable jointly and severally with and to the same extent as the seller, unless the non-seller who is so liable sustains the burden of proof that he did not know, and in exercise of reasonable care could not have known, of the existence of the facts by reason of which the liability is alleged to exist. There is contribution as in cases of contract among the several persons so liable.

(c) Any tender specified in this section may be made at any time before entry of judgment.

(d) Every cause of action under this statute survives the death of any person who might have been a plaintiff or defendant.

(e) No person may sue under this section more than two years after the contract of sale. No person may sue under this section (1) if the buyer received a written offer, before suit and at a time when he owned the security, to refund the consideration paid together with interest at six percent per year from the date of payment, less the amount of any income received on the security, and he failed to accept the offer within thirty days of its receipt, or (2) if the buyer received such an offer before suit and at a time when he did not own the security, unless he rejected the offer in writing within thirty days of its receipt.

(f) No person who has made or engaged in the performance of any contract in violation of any provision of this act or any rule or order hereunder, or who has acquired any purported right under any such contract with knowledge of the facts by reason of which its making or performance was in violation, may base any suit on the contract.

(g) Any condition, stipulation, or provision binding any person acquiring any security to waive compliance with any provision of this act or any rule or order hereunder is void.

(h) The rights and remedies provided by this act are in addition to any other rights or remedies that may exist at law or in equity, but this act does not create any cause of action not specified in this section or section 202(e).

§ 411. [Judicial Review of Orders]

(a) Any person aggrieved by a final order of the [Administrator] may obtain a review of the order in the [insert name of appropriate court] by filing in court, within sixty days after the entry of the order, a written petition praying that the order be modified or set aside in whole or in part. A copy of the petition shall be forthwith served upon the [Administrator], and thereupon the [Administrator] shall certify and file in court a copy of the filing and evidence upon which the order was entered. When these have been filed, the court has exclusive jurisdiction to affirm, modify, enforce, or set aside the order, in whole or in part. The findings of the [Administrator] as to the facts, if supported by competent, material and substantial evidence, are conclusive. If either party applies to the court for leave to adduce additional material evidence, and shows to the satisfaction of the court that there were reasonable grounds for failure to adduce the evidence in the hearing before the [Administrator], the court may order the additional evidence to be taken before the [Administrator] and to be adduced upon the hearing in such manner and upon such conditions as the court considers proper. The [Administrator] may modify [his] findings and order by reason of the additional evidence and shall file in court the additional evidence together with any modified or new findings or order. [The judgment of the court is final, subject to review by the (insert name of appropriate court).]

(b) The commencement of proceedings under subsection (a) does not, unless specifically ordered by the court, operate as a stay of the [Administrator's] order.

§ 412. [Rules, Forms, Orders, and Hearings]

(a) The [Administrator] may from time to time make, amend, and rescind such rules, forms, and orders as are necessary to carry out the provisions of this act, including rules and forms governing registration statements, applications, and reports, and defining any terms, whether or not used in this act, insofar as the definitions are not inconsistent with the provisions of this act. For the purposes of rules and forms the [Administrator] may classify securities, persons, and matters within [his] jurisdiction, and prescribe different requirements for different classes.

(b) No rule, form, or order may be made, amended, or rescinded unless the [Administrator] finds that the action is necessary or appropriate in the public interest or for the protection of investors and consistent with the purposes fairly intended by the policy and provisions of this act. In prescribing rules and forms the [Administrator] may cooperate with the securities administrators of the other states and the Securities and Exchange Commission with a view to effectuating the policy of this statute to achieve maximum uniformity in the form and content of registration statements, applications, and reports wherever practicable.

(c) The [Administrator] may by rule or order prescribe (1) the form and content of financial statements required under this act, (2) the circumstances under which consolidated financial statements shall be filed, and (3) whether any required financial statements shall be certified by independent or certified public accountants. All financial statements shall be prepared in accordance with generally accepted accounting practices.

(d) All rules and forms of the [Administrator] shall be published.

(e) No provision of this act imposing any liability applies to any act done or omitted in good faith in conformity with any rule, form, or order of the [Administrator], notwithstanding that the rule, form, or order may later be amended or rescinded or be determined by judicial or other authority to be invalid for any reason.

(f) Every hearing in an administrative proceeding shall be public unless the [Administrator] in [his] discretion grants a request joined in by all the respondents that the hearing be conducted privately.

§ 413. [Administrative Files and Opinions]

(a) A document is filed when it is received by the [Administrator].

(b) The [Administrator] shall keep a register of all applications for registration and registration statements which are or have ever been effective under this act and all denial, suspension, or revocation orders which have been entered under this act. The register shall be open for public inspection.

(c) The information contained in or filed with any registration statement, application, or report may be made available to the public under such rules as the [Administrator] prescribes.

(d) Upon request and at such reasonable charges as [he] prescribes, the [Administrator] shall furnish to any person photostatic or other copies (certified under [his] seal of office if requested) of any entry in the register or any document which is a matter of public record. In any proceeding or prosecution under this act, any copy so certified is prima facie evidence of the contents of the entry or document certified.

(e) The [Administrator] in [his] discretion may honor requests from interested persons for interpretative opinions.

§ 414. [Scope of the Act and Service of Process]

(a) Sections 101, 201(a), 301, 405, and 410 apply to persons who sell or offer to sell when (1) an offer to sell is made in this state, or (2) an offer to buy is made and accepted in this state.

(b) Sections 101, 201(a), and 405 apply to persons who buy or offer to buy when (1) an offer to buy is made in this state, or (2) an offer to sell is made and accepted in this state.

(c) For the purpose of this section, an offer to sell or to buy is made in this state, whether or not either party is then present in this state, when the offer (1) originates from this state or (2) is directed by the offeror to this state and received at the place to which it is directed (or at any post office in this state in the case of a mailed offer).

(d) For the purpose of this section, an offer to buy or to sell is accepted in this state when acceptance (1) is communicated to the offeror in this state and (2) has not previously been communicated to the offeror, orally or in writing, outside this state; and acceptance is communicated to the offeror in this state, whether or not either party is then present in this state, when the offeree directs it to the offeror in this state reasonably believing the offeror to be in this state and it is received at the place to which it is directed (or at any post office in this state in the case of a mailed acceptance).

(e) An offer to sell or to buy is not made in this state when (1) the publisher circulates or there is circulated on his behalf in this state any bona fide newspaper or other publication of general, regular, and paid circulation which is not published in this state, or which is published in this state but has had more than two-thirds of its circulation outside this state during the past twelve months, or (2) a radio or television program originating outside this state is received in this state.

(f) Sections 102 and 201(c), as well as section 405 so far as investment advisers are concerned, apply when any act instrumental in effecting prohibited conduct is done in this state, whether or not either party is then present in this state.

(g) Every applicant for registration under this act and every issuer who proposes to offer a security in this state through any person acting on an agency basis in the common-law sense shall file with the [Administrator], in such form as [he] by rule prescribes, an irrevocable consent appointing the [Administrator] or [his] successor in office to be his attorney to receive service of any lawful process in any non-criminal suit, action, or proceeding against him or his successor executor or administrator which arises under this act or any rule or order hereunder after the consent has been filed, with the same force and validity as if served personally on the person filing the consent. A person who has filed such a consent in connection with a previous registration need not file another. Service may be made by leaving a copy of the process in the office of the [Administrator], but it is not effective unless (1) the plaintiff, who may be the [Administrator] in a suit, action, or proceeding instituted by [him], forthwith sends notice of the service and a copy of the process by registered mail to the defendant or respondent at his last address on file with the [Administrator], and (2) the plaintiff's affidavit of compliance with this subsection is filed in the case on or before the return day of the process, if any, or within such further time as the court allows.

(h) When any person, including any nonresident of this state, engages in conduct prohibited or made actionable by this act or any rule or order hereunder, and he has not filed a consent to service of process under subsection (g) and personal jurisdiction over him cannot otherwise be obtained in this state, that conduct shall be considered equivalent to his appointment of the [Administrator] or [his] successor in office to be his attorney to receive service of any lawful process in any non-criminal suit, action, or proceeding against him or his successor executor or administrator which grows out of that conduct and which is brought under this act or any rule or order hereunder, with the same force and validity as if served on him personally. Service may be made by leaving a copy of the process in the office of the [Administrator], and it is not effective unless (1) the plaintiff, who may be the [Administrator] in a suit, action, or proceeding instituted by [him], forthwith sends notice of the service and a copy of the process by registered mail to the defendant or respondent at his last known address or takes other steps which are reasonably calculated to give actual notice, and (2) the plaintiff's affidavit of compliance with this subsection is filed in the case on or before the return day of the process, if any, or within such further time as the court allows.

(i) When process is served under this section, the court, or the [Administrator] in a proceeding before [him], shall order such continuance as may be necessary to afford the defendant or respondent reasonable opportunity to defend.

§ 415. [Statutory Policy]

This act shall be so construed as to effectuate its general purpose to make uniform the law of those states which enact it and to coordinate the interpretation and administration of this act with the related federal regulation.

§ 416. [Short Title]

This act may be cited as the Uniform Securities Act.

§ 417. [Severability of Provisions]

If any provision of this act or the application thereof to any person or circumstance is held invalid, the invalidity shall not affect other provisions or applications of the act which can be given effect without the invalid provision or application, and to this end the provisions of this act are severable.

§ 418. [Repeal and Savings Provisions]

(a) The [identify the existing act or acts] is [are] repealed except as saved in this section.

(b) Prior law exclusively governs all suits, actions, prosecutions, or proceedings which are pending or may be initiated on the basis of facts or circumstances occurring before the effective date of this act, except that no civil suit or action may be maintained to enforce any liability under prior law unless brought within any period of limitation which applied when the cause of action accrued and in any event within two years after the effective date of this act.

(c) All effective registrations under prior law, all administrative orders relating to such registrations, and all conditions imposed upon such registrations remain in effect so long as they would have remained in effect if this act had not been passed. They are considered to have been filed, entered, or imposed under this act, but are governed by prior law.

(d) Prior law applies in respect of any offer or sale made within one year after the effective date of this act pursuant to an offering begun in good faith before its effective date on the basis of an exemption available under prior law.

(e) Judicial review of all administrative orders as to which review proceedings have not been instituted by the effective date of this act are governed by section 411, except that no review proceeding may be instituted unless the petition is filed within any period of limitation which applied to a review proceeding when the order was entered and in any event within sixty days after the effective date of this act.

§ 419. [Time of Taking Effect]

This act shall take effect on [insert date, which should be at least sixty or ninety days after enactment].

UNIFORM SECURITIES ACT (1985) WITH 1988 AMENDMENTS

§ 101. Definitions

As used in this [Act], unless the context otherwise requires:

(1) "[Administrator]" [substitute any other appropriate term, such as "Commission," "Commissioner," "Secretary"] means the [insert name of administrative agency or individual].

(2) "Broker-dealer" means a person engaged in the business of effecting transactions in securities for the account of others or for the person's own account. The term does not include:

(i) a sales representative;

(ii) an issuer, except when effecting transactions other than with respect to its own securities;

(iii) a depository institution; or

(iv) any other person the [Administrator], by rule or order, designates.

(3) "Depository institution" means:

(i) a person that is organized, chartered, or holding an authorization certificate under the laws of a state or of the United States which authorizes the person to receive deposits, including a savings, share, certificate, or deposit account, and which is supervised and examined for the protection of depositors by an official or agency of a state or the United States; and

(ii) a trust company or other institution that is authorized by federal or state law to exercise fiduciary powers of the type a national bank is permitted to exercise under the authority of the Comptroller of the Currency and is supervised and examined by an official or agency of a state or the United States. The term does not include an insurance company or other organization primarily engaged in the insurance business or a Morris Plan bank, industrial loan company, or a similar bank or company unless its deposits are insured by a federal agency.

(4) "Filed" means the actual delivery of a document or application to the [Administrator] or designee of the [Administrator] or to the principal office of the [Administrator].

(5) "Financial or institutional investor" means any of the following, whether acting for itself or others in a fiduciary capacity:

(i) a depository institution;

(ii) an insurance company;

(iii) a separate account of an insurance company;

(iv) an investment company as defined in the Investment Company Act of 1940;

(v) an employee pension, profit-sharing, or benefit plan if the plan has total assets in excess of $5,000,000 or its investment decisions are made by a named fiduciary, as defined in the Employee Retirement Income Security Act of 1974, that is either a broker-dealer registered under the Securities Exchange Act of 1934, an investment adviser registered or exempt from registration under the Investment Advisers Act of 1940, a depository institution, or an insurance company; and

(vi) any other institutional buyer.

(6) "Fraud," "deceit," and "defraud" are not limited to common-law fraud or deceit.

(7) "Investment adviser" means a person who, for compensation, engages in the business of advising others as to the value of securities or as to the advisability of investing in, purchasing, or selling securities or who, for compensation and as a part of a business, issues or promulgates analyses or reports concerning securities. The term does not include:

(i) an employee of an investment adviser;

(ii) a depository institution;

(iii) a lawyer, accountant, engineer, or teacher whose performance of investment advisory services is solely incidental to the practice of the person's profession;

(iv) a broker-dealer whose performance of investment advisory services is solely incidental to the conduct of business as a broker-dealer and who receives no special compensation for the investment advisory services;

(v) a publisher, employee, or columnist of a newspaper, news magazine, or business or financial publication, or an owner, operator, producer, or employee of a cable, radio, or television network, station, or production facility if, in either case, the financial or business news published or disseminated is made available to the general public and the content does not consist of rendering advice on the basis of the specific investment situation of each client;

(vi) a person whose advice, analyses, or reports relate only to securities exempt under paragraph (1) of Section 401(b); and

(vii) any other person the [Administrator], by rule or order, designates.

(8) Except as provided in subparagraph (i), (ii), or (iii), "issuer" means a person who issues or proposes to issue a security, but:

(i) The "issuer" of a collateral trust certificate, voting trust certificate, certificate of deposit for a security, or share in an investment company without a board of directors or persons performing similar functions, is the person performing the acts and assuming the duties of depositor or manager pursuant to the trust or other agreement or instrument under which the security is issued.

(ii) The "issuer" of an equipment trust certificate, including a conditional sales contract or similar security serving the same purpose, is the person to whom the equipment or property is or is to be leased or conditionally sold.

(iii) The "issuer" of a fractional undivided interest in an oil, gas, or other mineral lease or in payments out of production under a lease, right, or royalty is the owner of an interest in the lease or in payments out of production under a lease, right, or royalty, whether whole or fractional, who creates fractional interests for the purpose of sale.

(9) "Nonissuer transaction" means a transaction not directly or indirectly for the benefit of the issuer.

(10) "Person" means an individual, corporation, business trust, estate, trust, partnership, association, joint venture, government, governmental subdivision or agency, or any other legal or commercial entity.

(11) "Price amendment" means the amendment to a registration statement filed under the Securities Act of 1933 or, if no amendment is filed, the prospectus or prospectus supplement filed under the Securities Act of 1933, which includes a statement of the offering price, underwriting and selling discounts or commissions, amount of proceeds, conversion rates, call prices, and other matters dependent upon the offering price.

(12) "Promoter" includes:

(i) a person who, acting alone or in concert with one or more other persons, takes the entrepreneurial initiative in founding or organizing the business or enterprise of an issuer;

(ii) an officer or director owning securities of an issuer or a person who owns, beneficially or of record, ten percent or more of a class of securities of the issuer if the officer, director, or person acquires any of those securities in a transaction within three years before the filing by the issuer of a registration statement under this [Act] and the transaction does not possess the indicia of arms-length bargaining; and

(iii) a member of the immediate family of a person within subparagraph (i) or (ii) if the family member receives securities of the issuer from that person in a transaction within three years before the filing by the issuer of a registration statement under this [Act] and the transaction does not possess the indicia of arms-length bargaining.

(13) "Sale" or "sell" includes every contract of sale, contract to sell, or other disposition, of a security or interest in a security for value. In this context:

(i) "Offer to sell" includes every attempt or offer to dispose of, or solicitation of an offer to purchase, a security or interest in a security for value.

(ii) "Offer to purchase" includes every attempt or offer to obtain, or solicitation of an offer to sell, a security or interest in a security for value, but the term does not include a transaction that is subject to Section 14(d) of the Securities Exchange Act of 1934.

(iii) A security given or delivered with, or as a bonus on account of, a purchase of securities or other item is considered to constitute part of the subject of the purchase and to have been offered and sold for value.

(iv) A gift of assessable stock is deemed to involve an offer and sale.

(v) A sale or offer of a warrant or right to purchase or subscribe to another security of the same or another issuer, or a sale or offer of a security that gives the holder a present or future right or privilege to convert into another security of the same or another issuer, is deemed to include an offer of the other security.

(vi) The terms defined in this paragraph do not include the creation of a security interest or a loan; a stock dividend, whether the corporation distributing the dividend is the issuer of the stock or not, if nothing of value is given by stockholders for the dividend other than the surrender of a right to a cash or property dividend and each stockholder may elect to take the dividend in cash, property, or stock; or an act incident to a judicially approved reorganization in which a security is issued in exchange for one or more outstanding securities, claims, or property interests, or partly in exchange and partly for cash.

(14) "Sales representative" means an individual, other than a broker-dealer, authorized to act and acting for a broker-dealer or issuer in effecting or attempting to effect purchases or sales of securities. A partner, officer, or director of a broker-dealer or issuer, or a person occupying a similar status or performing similar functions, is a sales representative only if the person otherwise comes within the definition.

(15) "Securities Act of 1933," "Securities Exchange Act of 1934," "Public Utility Holding Company Act of 1935," "Investment Company Act of 1940," "Investment Advisers Act of 1940," "Employee Retirement Income Security Act of 1974," "National Housing Act," and "Commodity Exchange Act" means the federal statutes of those names, as amended.

(16) "Security" means: a note; stock; treasury stock; bond; debenture; evidence of indebtedness; certificate of interest or participation in a profit-sharing agreement;

a limited partnership interest; collateral-trust certificate; preorganization certificate or subscription; transferable share; investment contract; voting-trust certificate; certificate of deposit for a security; fractional undivided interest in an oil, gas, or other mineral lease or in payments out of production under a lease, right, or royalty; a put, call, straddle, or option entered into on a national securities exchange relating to foreign currency; a put, call, straddle, or option on a security, certificate of deposit, or group or index of securities, including an interest in or based on the value of any of the foregoing; or, in general, an interest or instrument commonly known as a "security," or a certificate of interest or participation in, temporary or interim certificate for, receipt for, whole or partial guarantee of, or warrant or right to subscribe to or purchase, any of the foregoing. The term does not include:

(i) an insurance or endowment policy or annuity contract under which an insurance company promises to pay a fixed sum of money either in a lump sum or periodically for life or some other specified period; or

(ii) an interest in a contributory or noncontributory pension or welfare plan subject to the Employee Retirement Income Security Act of 1974.

(17) "Self-regulatory organization" means a national securities exchange registered under Section 6 of the Securities Exchange Act of 1934, a national securities association of brokers and dealers registered under Section 15A of the Securities Exchange Act of 1934, a clearing agency registered under Section 17A of the Securities Exchange Act of 1934, the Municipal Securities Rulemaking Board established under Section 15B(b)(1) of the Securities Exchange Act of 1934, or Section 21 of the Commodity Exchange Act.

(18) "State" means a state, commonwealth, territory, or possession of the United States, the District of Columbia, or the Commonwealth of Puerto Rico.

PART II

LICENSING OF BROKER–DEALER, SALES REPRESENTATIVE, AND INVESTMENT ADVISER

§ 201. Licensing of Broker–Dealer and Sales Representative

(a) A person may not transact business in this State as a broker-dealer or sales representative unless licensed or exempt from licensing under this [Act].

(b) A broker-dealer licensed under this [Act] and an issuer may not employ a person as a sales representative in this State unless the sales representative is licensed under this [Act] or is exempt from licensing under this [Act].

(c) A broker-dealer or issuer engaged in offering securities in this State may not employ, directly or indirectly, a person to engage in any activity in this State contrary to a suspension or bar from association with a broker-dealer or investment advisor imposed against that person by the [Administrator]. A broker-dealer or issuer does not violate this subsection unless the broker-dealer or issuer knows or in the exercise of reasonable care should know of the suspension or bar. Upon request from a broker-dealer or issuer and for good cause shown, the [Administrator], by order, may waive the prohibition of this subsection with respect to a person suspended or barred.

§ 202. Exempt Broker–Dealers and Sales Representatives

(a) The following broker-dealers are exempt from the licensing requirements of Section 201:

(1) a broker-dealer who either is registered or, except as provided in subsection (b), is not required to be registered under

the Securities Exchange Act of 1934 and who has no place of business in this State if:

(i) the transactions effected by the broker-dealer in this State are exclusively with the issuer of the securities involved in the transactions, other broker-dealers licensed or exempt under this [Act], or financial or institutional investors;

(ii) the broker-dealer is licensed under the securities act of a state in which the broker-dealer maintains a place of business and the broker-dealer offers and sells in this State to a person who is an existing customer of the broker-dealer and whose principal place of residence is not in this State; or

(iii) the broker-dealer is licensed under the securities law of a state in which the broker-dealer maintains a place of business and the broker-dealer during any 12 consecutive months does not effect transactions with more than [5] persons in this State in addition to transactions with the issuers of the securities involved in the transactions, financial or institutional investors, or broker-dealers, whether or not the offeror or an offeree is then present in this State; and

(2) other broker-dealers the [Administrator] by rule or order exempts.

(b) The exemption provided in subsection (a)(1)(i) is not available to a broker-dealer who deals solely in government securities and is not registered under the Securities Exchange Act of 1934 unless the broker-dealer is subject to supervision as a dealer in government securities by the Federal Reserve Board.

(c) The following sales representatives are exempt from the licensing requirements of Section 201:

(i) a sales representative acting for a broker-dealer exempt under subsection (a);

(ii) a sales representative acting for an issuer in effecting transactions in a security exempted by paragraphs (1) through (4) and (11) through (13) of Section 401(b);

(iii) a sales representative acting for an issuer effecting offers or sales of securities in transactions exempted by Section 402;

(iv) a sales representative acting for an issuer effecting transactions with employees, partners, officers, or directors of the issuer, a parent or a wholly-owned subsidiary of the issuer, if no commission or other similar compensation is paid or given directly or indirectly to the sales representative for soliciting an employee, partner, officer, or director in this State; and

(v) other sales representatives the [Administrator] by rule or order exempts.

§ 203. Licensing of Investment Adviser

(a) A person may not transact business in this State as an investment adviser unless licensed as an investment adviser or exempt from licensing under this [Act].

(b) An investment adviser may not employ, directly or indirectly, a person to engage in any activity in this State contrary to a suspension or bar from association with a broker-dealer or investment adviser imposed against that person by the [Administrator]. An investment adviser does not violate this subsection unless the investment adviser knows or in the exercise of reasonable care should know of the suspension or bar. Upon request from an investment adviser and for good cause shown, the [Administrator], by order, may waive the prohibition of this subsection with respect to a person suspended or barred.

§ 204. Exempt Investment Advisers

The following investment advisers are exempt from the licensing requirements of Section 203:

(1) an investment adviser who is registered or is not required to be registered as an investment adviser under the Investment Advisers Act of 1940 if:

(i) its only clients in this State are other investment advisers, broker-dealers, or financial or institutional investors; (ii) the investment adviser has no place of business in this State and the investment adviser directs business communications in this State to a person who is an existing client of the investment adviser and whose principal place of residence is not in this State; or

(iii) the investment adviser has no place of business in this State and the investment adviser during any 12 consecutive months does not direct business communications in this State to more than [five] present or prospective clients other than those specified in subparagraph (i), whether or not the person or client to whom the communication is directed is present in this State; and

(2) other investment advisers the [Administrator], by rule or order, exempts.

§ 205. Application

(a) An applicant for licensing as a broker-dealer, sales representative, or investment adviser shall file with the [Administrator] an application for licensing and a consent to service of process under Section 708. The application for licensing must contain the information that the [Administrator], by rule, requires.

(b) The requirements of subsection (a) are satisfied by an applicant who has filed and maintains a completed and current registration with the Securities and Exchange Commission or a self-regulatory organization by filing with the [Administrator] notice of the registration in the form and content determined by the [Administrator], by rule, and a consent to service of process under Section 708. The registration information filed with the Securities and Exchange Commission or self-regulatory organization must be available to the [Administrator] through a central registration depository system approved by the [Administrator]. The [Administrator], by order, may require the submission of additional information by an applicant.

§ 206. Licensing Fees

(a) An applicant for licensing shall pay a licensing fee as follows:

(1) broker-dealer [$100] and for each branch office [$50].

(2) sales representative [$25].

(3) investment adviser [$50].

(b) Except in a year in which a licensing fee is paid, a licensed person shall pay an annual fee as follows:

(1) broker-dealer [$75] and for each branch office [$30].

(2) sales representative [$15].

(3) investment adviser [$35].

(c) For purposes of this section, "branch office" means an office of a broker-dealer in this State, other than the principal office in this State of the broker-dealer, from which three or more sales representatives transact business.

(d) If an application is denied or withdrawn or the license is revoked, suspended, or withdrawn, the [Administrator] shall retain the fee paid.

§ 207. Examinations

(a) The [Administrator], by rule or order, may require an examination of:

(1) an applicant for licensing under this Part;

(2) a class of applicants; and

(3) a class of persons who will represent an investment adviser in performing an act that requires licensing as an investment adviser in this State.

(b) An examination may be administered by the [Administrator] or a designee of the [Administrator]. An examination may be oral or written, or both, and may differ for each class of applicants.

(c) The [Administrator], by rule or order, may waive an examination as to a person or class of persons if the [Administrator] determines that an examination is not necessary for the protection of investors.

§ 208. Licensing, General Provisions

(a) Unless a proceeding under Section 212 is instituted or the applicant is notified that the application is incomplete, the license of a broker-dealer, sales representative, or investment adviser becomes effective 30 days after the later of the date an application for licensing is filed and is complete or the date an amendment to an application is filed and is complete, in either case only if all requirements imposed under Section 207 are satisfied. An application is complete when the applicant has furnished information responsive to each applicable item of the application. The [Administrator] by order may authorize an earlier effective date of licensing.

(b) The license of a broker-dealer, sales representative, or investment adviser is effective until terminated by expiration, revocation, or withdrawal.

(c) The license of a sales representative is effective only with respect to transactions effected on behalf of the broker-dealer or issuer for whom the sales representative is licensed.

(d) A person may not act at any one time as a sales representative for more than one broker-dealer or for more than one issuer, unless the broker-dealers or issuers for whom the sales representative acts are affiliated by direct or indirect common control or the [Administrator], by rule or order, authorizes multiple licenses.

(e) If a person licensed as a sales representative terminates association with a broker-dealer or issuer or ceases to be a sales representative, the sales representative and the broker-dealer or issuer on whose behalf the sales representative was acting shall promptly notify the [Administrator].

(f) The [Administrator] by rule may authorize one or more special classifications of licenses as a broker-dealer, sales representative, or investment adviser to be issued to applicants subject to limitations and conditions on the nature of the activities that may be conducted by persons so licensed.

§ 209. Post–Licensing Requirements

(a) The [Administrator] by rule may require that:

(1) a licensed broker-dealer who is not registered under the Securities Exchange Act of 1934 maintain minimum net capital and a prescribed ratio between net capital and aggregate indebtedness, which may vary with type or class of broker-dealer; or

(2) a licensed investment adviser who is not registered under the Investment Advisers Act of 1940 maintain a minimum net worth.

(b) If a licensed broker-dealer or investment adviser knows, or has reasonable cause to know, that a requirement imposed on it under this subsection is not being met, the broker-dealer or investment adviser shall promptly notify the [Administrator] of its current financial condition.

(c) The [Administrator] by rule may require a fidelity bond from a broker-dealer who is not registered under the Securities Exchange Act of 1934.

(d) A licensed broker-dealer or investment adviser shall file with the [Administrator] the financial and other information the [Administrator] by rule or order requires, but:

(1) A licensed broker-dealer required to file financial reports under the Securities Exchange Act of 1934 may satisfy periodic financial report requirements of this subsection by filing with the [Administrator] a copy of the financial reports filed under the Securities Exchange Act of 1934; and

(2) A licensed investment adviser required to file financial reports under the Investment Advisers Act of 1940 may satisfy periodic financial report requirements of this

subsection by filing with the [Administrator] a copy of the financial reports filed under the Investment Advisers Act of 1940.

(e) A licensed broker-dealer, sales representative, or investment adviser shall maintain the records the [Administrator] by rule requires, but compliance with the recordkeeping requirements of the Securities Exchange Act of 1934 by a broker-dealer or the Investment Advisers Act of 1940 by an investment adviser satisfies the requirements of this subsection.

(f) Required records may be maintained in any form of data storage if they are readily accessible to the [Administrator]. Required records must be preserved for [five] years unless the [Administrator] by rule specifies a different period for a particular type or class of records.

(g) If the information contained in a document filed with the [Administrator] as part of the application for licensing or under this section, except information the [Administrator] by rule or order excludes, is or becomes inaccurate or incomplete in a material respect, the licensed person shall promptly file correcting information, unless notification of termination has been given under Section 208(e).

§ 210. Licensing of Successor Firms

(a) A licensed broker-dealer or investment adviser may file an application for licensing of a successor, whether or not the successor is in existence, if the fee the [Administrator] prescribes for the application is submitted with the application.

(b) If a broker-dealer or investment adviser succeeds to and continues the business of a licensed broker-dealer or investment adviser and the successor files an application for licensing within 30 days after the succession, the license of the predecessor remains effective as the license of the successor for 60 days after the succession.

(c) Licensing of each licensed sales representative of the broker-dealer filing an application under subsection (a) or (b) continues without a separate filing or fee upon the licensing of the successor.

§ 211. Power of Inspection

(a) The [Administrator], without notice, may examine in a manner reasonable under the circumstances the records, within or without this State, of a licensed broker-dealer, sales representative, or investment adviser in order to determine compliance with this [Act]. Broker-dealers, sales representatives, and investment advisers shall make their records available to the [Administrator] in legible form.

(b) The [Administrator] may copy records or require a licensed person to copy records and provide the copies to the [Administrator] to the extent and in a manner reasonable under the circumstances.

(c) The [Administrator] may impose a reasonable fee for the expense of conducting an examination under this section.

§ 212. Grounds for Denial, Suspension, or Revocation

(a) The [Administrator] by order may (i) deny, suspend, or revoke a license, (ii) limit the securities activities that an applicant or licensed person may perform in this State, (iii) bar an applicant or licensed person from association with a licensed broker-dealer or investment adviser, or (iv) bar from employment with a licensed broker-dealer or investment adviser a person who is a partner, officer, director, or a person occupying a similar status or performing a similar function for an applicant or licensed person. Subject to Section 213, those actions may be taken only if the [Administrator] finds that the order is in the public interest and that the applicant or licensed person or, in the case of a broker-dealer or investment adviser, a partner, officer, or director, a person occupying a similar status or performing similar functions, or a person directly or indirectly controlling the broker-dealer or investment adviser:

(1) has filed an application for licensing with the [Administrator] which, as of its effective date or any date after filing in the case of an order denying effectiveness, was incomplete in a material respect or contained a statement that was, in light of the circumstances under which it was made, false or misleading with respect to a material fact;

(2) has willfully violated or willfully failed to comply with this [Act], a predecessor act, or a rule or order under this [Act] or a predecessor act;

(3) is the subject of an adjudication or determination, after notice and opportunity for hearing, within the last five years by a securities agency or administrator of another state or a court of competent jurisdiction that the person has willfully violated the Securities Act of 1933, the Securities Exchange Act of 1934, the Investment Advisers Act of 1940, the Investment Company Act of 1940, or the Commodity Exchange Act, or the securities law of any other state but only if the acts constituting the violation of that state's law would constitute a violation of this [Act] had the acts occurred in this State;

(4) within the last ten years, has been convicted of an offense that the [Administrator] finds:

(i) involves the purchase or sale of a security, taking a false oath, making a false report, bribery, perjury, burglary, robbery, or attempt or conspiracy to commit any of those offenses;

(ii) arises out of the conduct of business as a broker-dealer, investment adviser, depository institution, insurance company, or fiduciary; or

(iii) involves the larceny, theft, robbery, extortion, forgery, counterfeiting, fraudulent concealment, embezzlement, fraudulent conversion, or misappropriation of funds or securities or an attempt or conspiracy to commit any of those offenses;

(5) is permanently or temporarily enjoined by a court of competent jurisdiction from acting as an investment adviser, underwriter, broker-dealer, or as an affiliated person or employee of an investment company, depository institution, or insurance company, or from engaging in or continuing conduct or practice in connection with any of the foregoing activities, or in connection with the purchase or sale of a security;

(6) is the subject of an order of the [Administrator] denying, suspending, or revoking the person's license as a broker-dealer, sales representative, or investment adviser;

(7) is the subject of any of the following orders that are currently effective and were issued within the last five years:

(i) an order by the securities agency or administrator of another state or Canadian province or territory, or by the Securities and Exchange Commission, entered after notice and opportunity for hearing, denying, suspending, or revoking the person's license as a broker-dealer, sales representative, or investment adviser, or the substantial equivalent of those terms;

(ii) a suspension or expulsion from membership in or association with a member of a self-regulatory organization;

(iii) a United States Postal Service fraud order;

(iv) a cease and desist order entered after notice and opportunity for hearing by the [Administrator], the securities agency or administrator of another state, or a Canadian province or territory, the Securities and Exchange Commission, or the Commodity Futures Trading Commission; or

(v) an order by the Commodity Futures Trading Commission denying, suspending, or revoking registration under the Commodity Exchange Act;

(8) has engaged in unethical or dishonest practices in the securities business;

(9) is insolvent, either in the sense that liabilities exceed assets or in the sense that

obligations cannot be met as they mature, but the [Administrator] may not enter an order against a broker-dealer or investment adviser under this subsection without a finding of insolvency as to the broker-dealer or investment adviser;

(10) is determined by the [Administrator] in compliance with Section 213 not to be qualified because of the lack of training, experience, and knowledge of the securities business;

(11) has failed reasonably to supervise a sales representative or employee; or

(12) has failed to pay the proper filing fee within 30 days after being notified by the [Administrator] of a deficiency, but the [Administrator] shall vacate an order under this subsection when the deficiency is corrected.

(b) The [Administrator] may not begin a proceeding on the basis of a fact or transaction known to the [Administrator] when the license became effective unless the proceeding is begun within the 90 days after issuance of the license.

(c) If the [Administrator] finds that an applicant or licensed person is no longer in existence, has ceased to do business as a broker-dealer, sales representative, or investment adviser, is adjudicated mentally incompetent or subjected to the control of a committee, conservator, or guardian, or cannot be located after reasonable search, the [Administrator], by order, may deny the application or revoke the license.

§ 213. Denial, Suspension, or Revocation on Grounds of Lack of Qualification

The [Administrator's] determination that an applicant or licensed person lacks qualification under Section 212 is limited by the following provisions:

(1) The [Administrator] may not enter an order against a broker-dealer because of the lack of qualification of (i) a person other than the broker-dealer if the broker-dealer is an individual or (ii) a sales representative of the broker-dealer.

(2) The [Administrator] may not enter an order against an investment adviser because of the lack of qualification of (i) a person other than the investment adviser if the investment adviser is an individual or (ii) any other person who represents the investment adviser in doing an act that makes the person an investment adviser.

(3) The [Administrator] may not enter an order solely because of lack of experience of the applicant or licensed person if the applicant or licensed person is qualified by training or knowledge, or both.

(4) The [Administrator] shall consider that a sales representative who will work under the supervision of a licensed broker-dealer need not have the same qualifications as a broker-dealer.

(5) The [Administrator] shall consider that an investment adviser is not necessarily qualified solely because of experience as a broker-dealer or sales representative.

§ 214. Withdrawal

(a) An application for a license may be withdrawn by the applicant without prejudice before the license becomes effective.

(b) Withdrawal from licensing as a broker-dealer, sales representative, or investment adviser becomes effective 30 days after receipt by the [Administrator] of an application to withdraw or within any shorter period the [Administrator], by order, determines, unless:

(1) a revocation or suspension proceeding is pending when the application is filed;

(2) a proceeding to revoke or suspend or to impose conditions upon the withdrawal is instituted within 30 days after the application is filed; or

(3) additional information is requested by the [Administrator] regarding the withdrawal application.

(c) If a proceeding is pending or instituted under subsection (b), withdrawal becomes effective at the time and upon the conditions the [Administrator] by order determines. If additional information is requested, withdrawal is effective 30 days after the additional information is filed. Although no proceeding is pending or instituted and withdrawal becomes effective, the [Administrator] may institute a proceeding under Section 212 within one year after withdrawal became effective and enter an order as of the last date on which licensing was effective.

§ 215. Custody of Client's Securities and Funds

(a) Unless prohibited by rule or order of the [Administrator], an investment adviser registered under the Investment Advisers Act of 1940 may take or retain custody of securities or funds of a client.

(b) To the extent permitted by rule or order of the [Administrator], an investment adviser exempt from registration under the Investment Advisers Act of 1940, but licensed as an investment adviser under this [Act], may take or retain custody of securities or funds of a client.

PART III

REGISTRATION OF SECURITIES

§ 301. Registration Requirement

A person may not offer to sell or sell a security in this State unless it is registered under this [Act] or the security or transaction is exempt under this [Act].

§ 302. Registration by Filing

(a) Securities for which a registration statement has been filed under the Securities Act of 1933 in connection with the offering of the securities may be registered by filing, whether or not they are also eligible for registration under Section 303 or 304, if:

(1) the issuer is organized under the laws of the United States or a state or, if the issuer is not organized under the laws of the United States or a state, it has appointed a duly authorized agent in the United States for service of process;

(2) the issuer has actively engaged in business operations in the United States for a period of at least 36 consecutive calendar months immediately before the filing of the federal registration statement;

(3) the issuer has registered a class of equity securities under Section 12(b) or 12(g) of the Securities Exchange Act of 1934, which class of securities is held of record by 500 or more persons;

(4) the issuer has:

(i) either a total net worth of $4,000,000 or a total net worth of $2,000,000 and net pretax income from operations before allowances for extraordinary items, for at least two of the three preceding fiscal years;

(ii) not less than 400,000 units of the class of security registered under Section 12 of the Securities Exchange Act of 1934 held by the public, excluding securities held by officers and directors of the issuer, underwriters and persons beneficially owning ten percent or more of that class of security; and

(iii) no outstanding warrants and options held by the underwriters and executive officers and directors of the issuer in an amount exceeding ten percent of the total number of shares to be outstanding after completion of the offering of the securities being registered;

(5) the issuer has been subject to the requirements of Section 12 of the Securities Exchange Act of 1934 and has filed all the material required to be filed under Sections 13 and 14 of that act for at least 36 consecutive calendar months immediately before the

filing of the federal registration statement and the issuer has filed in a timely manner all reports required to be filed during the 12 calendar months next preceding the filing of the federal registration statement;

(6) for at least 30 days during the three months next preceding the offering of the securities registered there have been at least four market makers for the class of equity securities registered under Section 12 of the Securities Exchange Act of 1934;

(7) each of the underwriters participating in the offering of the security and each broker-dealer who will offer the security in this State is a member of or is subject to the rules of fair practice of a national association of securities dealers with respect to the offering and the underwriters have contracted to purchase the securities offered in a principal capacity;

(8) the aggregate commissions or discounts to be received by the underwriters will not exceed ten percent of the aggregate price at which the securities being registered are offered to the public;

(9) neither the issuer nor any of its subsidiaries, since the end of the fiscal year next preceding the filing of the registration statement, have (i) failed to pay a dividend or sinking fund installment on preferred stock, (ii) defaulted on indebtedness for borrowed money, or (iii) defaulted on the rental on one or more long-term leases, which defaults in the aggregate are material to the financial position of the issuer and its subsidiaries, taken as a whole; and

(10) in the case of an equity security, the price at which the security will be offered to the public is not less than five dollars a share.

(b) A registration statement under this section must contain the following information and be accompanied by the following documents in addition to the information specified in Section 305(c) and the consent to service of process required by Section 708:

(1) a statement demonstrating eligibility for registration by filing;

(2) the name, address, and form of organization of the issuer;

(3) with respect to a person on whose behalf a part of the offering is to be made in a nonissuer distribution: name and address; the amount of securities of the issuer held by the person as of the date of the filing of the registration statement; and a statement of the reasons for making the offering;

(4) a description of the security being registered; and

(5) a copy of the latest prospectus filed with the registration statement under and satisfying the requirements of Section 10 of the Securities Act of 1933.

(c) If the information and documents required to be filed by subsection (b) have been on file with the [Administrator] for at least [five] business days or any shorter period the [Administrator] by rule or order allows and the applicable registration fee has been paid before the effectiveness of the federal registration statement, a registration statement under this section automatically becomes effective concurrently with the effectiveness of the federal registration statement. If the federal registration statement becomes effective before the conditions in this subsection are satisfied and they are not waived, the registration statement becomes effective when the conditions are satisfied. The registrant shall promptly notify the [Administrator] by telephone or telegram of the date and time when the federal registration statement became effective and the content of the price amendment, if any, and shall file promptly a post effective amendment containing the information and documents in the price amendment. The [Administrator] shall promptly acknowledge receipt of notification and effectiveness of the registration statement as of the date and time the registration statement became effective with the Securities and Exchange Commission.

§ 303. Registration by Coordination

(a) Securities for which a registration statement has been filed under the Securities Act of 1933 in connection with the offering of the securities may be registered by coordination.

(b) A registration statement under this section must contain the following information and be accompanied by the following documents in addition to the information specified in Section 305(c) and the consent to service of process required by Section 708:

(1) two copies of the latest form of prospectus filed under the Securities Act of 1933;

(2) if the [Administrator] by rule or order requires: a copy of the articles of incorporation and bylaws or their substantial equivalents, currently in effect; a copy of any agreement with or among underwriters; a copy of an indenture or other instrument governing the issuance of the security to be registered; and a specimen, copy, or description of the security;

(3) if the [Administrator] requests, subject to paragraph (2) of Section 703(b), any other information, or copies of any other document, filed under the Securities Act of 1933; and

(4) an undertaking to forward promptly, and not later than the first business day after the day they are forwarded to or filed with the Securities and Exchange Commission, all future amendments to the federal prospectus, other than an amendment that delays the effective date of the registration statement.

(c) A registration statement under this section becomes effective when the federal registration statement becomes effective if all of the following conditions are satisfied:

(1) no stop order is in effect and no proceeding is pending under Section 306;

(2) the registration statement has been on file with the [Administrator] for at least ten days, but if the registration statement is not filed with the [Administrator] within ten days after the initial filing under the Securities Act of 1933, the registration statement has been on file with the [Administrator] for 30 days or any shorter period the [Administrator], by rule or order, specifies; and

(3) a statement of the maximum and minimum proposed offering prices and the maximum underwriting discounts and commissions has been on file for two full business days or any shorter period the [Administrator], by rule or order, specifies and the offering is made within those limitations.

(d) The registrant shall promptly notify the [Administrator] by telephone or telegram of the date and time when the federal registration statement became effective and the content of the price amendment, if any, and shall promptly file a post-effective amendment containing the information and documents in the price amendment.

(e) Upon failure to receive the required notification or post-effective amendment with respect to the price amendment, the [Administrator], without notice or hearing, may enter a stop order retroactively denying effectiveness to the registration statement or suspending its effectiveness until the registrant complies with subsection (d). The [Administrator] shall promptly notify the registrant by telephone or telegram, and promptly confirm by letter or telegram if the [Administrator] notifies by telephone, of the issuance of the order. If the registrant proves compliance with the requirements of subsection (d) as to notice and post-effective amendment, the stop order is void as of its entry.

(f) The [Administrator] by rule or order may waive either or both of the conditions specified in subsection (c)(2) and (3).

(g) If the federal registration statement becomes effective before all of the conditions in subsection (c) are satisfied and they are not waived, the registration statement becomes effective when all the conditions are satisfied. If the registrant advises the [Administrator] of the date when the federal registration statement is expected to become effective, the [Administrator] shall promptly advise the registrant by telephone or telegram, at the registrant's expense, whether all the conditions are satisfied and whether the [Administrator] then contemplates commencing a proceeding under Section 306; but the advice by the [Administrator] does not preclude the institution of a proceeding for a stop order suspending the effectiveness of the registration statement. A stop order issued under this subsection is not retroactive.

(h) The [Administrator] by rule or order may waive or modify the application of a requirement of this section if a provision or an amendment, repeal, or other alteration of the securities registration provisions of the Securities Act of 1933, or the regulations adopted under that act, render the waiver or modification appropriate for further coordination of state and federal registration.

§ 304. Registration by Qualification

(a) A security may be registered by qualification.

(b) A registration statement under this section must contain the following information and be accompanied by the following documents in addition to the information specified in Section 305(c) and the consent to service of process required by Section 708:

(1) with respect to the issuer and any significant subsidiary: its name, address, and form of organization; the state or foreign jurisdiction and date of its organization; the general character and location of its business; a description of its physical property and equipment; and a statement of the general competitive conditions in the industry or business in which it is or will be engaged;

(2) with respect to every director and officer of the issuer, or person occupying a similar status or performing similar functions: name, address, and principal occupation for the last five years; the amount of securities of the issuer held by the person as of a specified date within 30 days before the filing of the registration statement; the amount of the securities covered by the registration statement to which the person has indicated an intention to subscribe; and a description of any material interest in any material transaction with the issuer or a significant subsidiary effected within the last three years or proposed to be effected;

(3) with respect to persons covered by paragraph (2): the compensation paid or given, directly, or indirectly, during the last 12 months and estimated to be paid during the next 12 months, by the issuer, together with all predecessors, parents, subsidiaries, and affiliates, to all those persons in the aggregate;

(4) with respect to a person owning of record, or beneficially if known, ten percent or more of the outstanding shares of a class of equity security of the issuer: the information specified in paragraph (2) other than occupation;

(5) with respect to a promoter, if the issuer was organized within the last three years: the information specified in paragraph (2), the amount paid or intended to be paid to the person within that period and the consideration for the payment;

(6) with respect to a person on whose behalf a part of the offering is to be made in a nonissuer distribution: name and address; the amount of securities of the issuer held by the person as of the date of the filing of the registration statement; a description of any material interest in any material transaction with the issuer, or a significant subsidiary, effected within the last three years or proposed to be effected; and a statement of the reasons for making the offering;

(7) the capitalization and long-term debt, on both a current and a pro forma basis, of the issuer and any significant subsidiary, including a description of each security outstanding or being registered or otherwise offered, and a statement of the amount and kind of consideration, whether in the form

of cash, physical assets, services, patents, goodwill, or anything else, for which the issuer or a subsidiary has issued its securities within the last two years or is obligated to issue its securities;

(8) the kind and amount of securities to be offered; the proposed offering price or the method by which it is to be computed; any variation therefrom at which a proportion of the offering is to be made to a person or class of persons other than the underwriters, with a specification of the person or class; the basis upon which the offering is to be made if other than for cash; the estimated aggregate underwriting and selling discounts or commissions and finders' fees, including separately cash, securities, contracts, or anything else of value to accrue to the underwriters or finders in connection with the offering, or, if the selling discounts or commissions are variable, the basis of determining them and their maximum and minimum amounts; the estimated amounts of other selling expenses, including legal, engineering, and accounting charges; the name and address of every underwriter and every recipient of a finder's fee; a copy of any underwriting or selling-group agreement pursuant to which the distribution is to be made, or the proposed form of the agreement whose terms have not yet been determined; and a description of the plan of distribution of securities that are to be offered other than through an underwriter;

(9) the estimated cash proceeds to be received by the issuer from the offering; the purposes for which the proceeds are to be used by the issuer; the amount to be used for each purpose; the order or priority in which the proceeds will be used for the purposes stated; the amounts of funds to be raised from other sources to achieve the purposes stated; the sources of the funds; and, if part of the proceeds is to be used to acquire property, including goodwill, other than in the ordinary course of business, the names and addresses of the vendors, the purchase price, the names of the persons who have received commissions in connection with the acquisition, and the amounts of commissions and any other expense in connection with the acquisition, including the cost of borrowing money to finance the acquisition;

(10) a description of the stock options or other security options outstanding, or to be created in connection with the offering, and the amount of the options held or to be held by every person required to be named in paragraph (2), (4), (5), (6), or (8) and by a person who holds or will hold ten percent or more in the aggregate of the options;

(11) the dates of, parties to, and general effect concisely stated of, every management or other material contract made or to be made other than in the ordinary course of business, if it is to be performed in whole or in part at or after the filing of the registration statement or was made within the last two years; and a copy of the contract;

(12) a description of any pending litigation or proceedings to which the issuer is a party and that materially affect its business or assets, including any litigation or proceeding known to be contemplated by a governmental authority;

(13) a copy of any prospectus, pamphlet, circular, form letter, advertisement, or other sales literature intended as of the effective date to be used in connection with the offering;

(14) a specimen, copy, or description of the security being registered; a copy of the issuer's articles of incorporation and bylaws, or their substantial equivalents, as currently in effect; and a copy of any indenture or other instrument covering the security to be registered;

(15) a signed or conformed copy of an opinion of counsel as to the legality of the security being registered, with an English translation if it is in a foreign language, which states whether the security when sold will be legally issued, fully paid, and nonas-

sessable, and, if a debt security, a binding obligation of the issuer;

(16) the written consent of an accountant, engineer, appraiser, or other person whose profession gives authority to a statement made by the person, if the person is named as having prepared or certified a report or valuation, other than a public and official document or statement, which is used in connection with the registration statement;

(17) a statement of financial condition of the issuer as of a date within four months preceding the filing of the registration statement; a statement of results of operations and analysis of surplus for each of the three fiscal years preceding the date of the statement of financial condition and for any period between the close of the last fiscal year and the date of the statement of financial condition, or for the period of the issuer's and any predecessors' existence if less than three years; and, if part of the proceeds of the offering is to be applied to the purchase of a business, the same financial statements that would be required if the business were the registrant; and

(18) any additional information the [Administrator] by rule or order specifies.

(c) A registration statement under this section becomes effective 30 calendar days, or any shorter period the [Administrator] by rule or order specifies, after the date the registration statement or the last amendment other than a price amendment is filed, if:

(1) no stop order is in effect and no proceeding is pending under Section 306;

(2) the [Administrator] has not ordered under subsection (d) that effectiveness be delayed; and

(3) the registrant has not requested that effectiveness be delayed.

(d) The [Administrator] may delay effectiveness for a single period of not more than 90 days if the [Administrator] determines the registration statement is not complete in all material respects and promptly notifies the registrant of that determination. The [Administrator] may delay effectiveness for a single period of not more than 30 days if the [Administrator] determines that the delay is necessary, whether or not the [Administrator] previously delayed effectiveness under this subsection.

§ 305. Provisions Applicable to Registration Generally

(a) A registration statement may be filed by the issuer, any other person on whose behalf the offering is to be made, or a broker-dealer licensed under this [Act].

(b) Except as provided in subsection (c), a person filing a registration statement shall pay a fee of [1/20 of one] percent of the maximum aggregate offering price at which the registered securities are to be offered in this State, but not less than [$50] or more than [$500]. If a registration statement is withdrawn before the effective date or a pre-effective stop order is entered under Section 306, the [Administrator] shall retain [$50] of the fee.

(c) An open-end management company, a face-amount certificate company, or a unit investment trust, as defined in the Investment Company Act of 1940, may register an indefinite amount of securities under a registration statement. The registrant, at the time of filing, shall pay a fee of [$100] and within 60 days after the registrant's fiscal year during which its registration statement is effective, pay a fee of [$500] or file a report on a form the [Administrator] by rule adopts, specifying its sale of securities to persons in this State during the fiscal year and pay a fee of [1/20 of one] percent of the aggregate sales price of the securities sold to persons in this State, but the latter fee must not be less than [$50] or more than [$500].

(d) Except as permitted by subsection (c), a registration statement must specify the amount of securities to be offered in this State and the states in which a registration statement or similar document in connection with the offering has been or is to be filed and any adverse order, judgment, or decree entered by a court, the securities agency or administrator in any state, or the Securities and Exchange Commission in connection with the offering.

(e) A document filed under this [Act] or a predecessor act [within five years preceding the filing of a registration statement] may be incorporated by reference in the registration statement if the document is currently accurate.

(f) The [Administrator] by rule or order may permit the omission of an item of information or document from a registration statement.

(g) In the case of a nonissuer offering, the [Administrator] may not require information under subsection (n) or Section 304 unless it is known to the person filing the registration statement or to the person on whose behalf the offering is to be made, or can be furnished by the person without unreasonable effort or expense.

(h) In the case of a registration under Section 303 or 304 by an issuer that has no public market for its shares or no significant earnings from continuing operations during the last five years or any shorter period of its existence, the [Administrator] by rule or order may require as a condition of registration that the following securities be deposited in escrow for not more than [three] years:

(i) a security issued to a promoter within the three years next preceding the offering or to be issued to a promoter for a consideration substantially less than the offering price; and

(ii) a security issued to a promoter for a consideration other than cash, unless the registrant demonstrates that the value of the noncash consideration received in exchange for the security is substantially equal to the offering price for the security.

(i) The [Administrator] by rule or order may determine the conditions of an escrow required under subsection (h), but the [Administrator] may not reject a depositary solely because of its location in another state.

(j) The [Administrator] by rule or order may require as a condition of registration under Section 303 or 304 that the proceeds from the sale of the registered security in this State be impounded until the issuer receives a specified amount from the sale of the security. The [Administrator] by rule or order may determine the conditions of an impoundment required under this subsection, but the [Administrator] may not reject a depositary solely because of its location in another state.

(k) If a security is registered under Section 302 or 303, the prospectus filed under the Securities Act of 1933 must be delivered to each purchaser in accordance with the prospectus delivery requirements of the Securities Act of 1933.

(*l*) If a security is registered under Section 304, an offering document containing information the [Administrator] by rule or order designates must be delivered to each purchaser with or before the earliest of:

(1) the first written offer made to the purchaser by or for the account of the issuer or another person on whose behalf the offering is being made, or by an underwriter or broker-dealer who is offering part of an unsold allotment or subscription taken by it as a participant in the distribution;

(2) confirmation of a sale made by or for the account of a person named in paragraph (1);

(3) payment pursuant to a sale; or

(4) delivery pursuant to a sale.

(m) A registration statement remains effective for one year after its effective date unless the [Administrator] by rule or order extends the period of effectiveness. All outstanding securities of the same class as a registered security are considered to be registered for the purpose of a nonissuer transaction while the registration statement is effective, unless the [Administrator] by rule or order provides otherwise. A registration statement may not be withdrawn after its effective date if any of the securities registered have been sold in this State, unless the [Administrator], by rule or order, provides otherwise. A registration statement is not effective while a stop order is in effect under Section 306(a).

(n) During the period in which an offering is being made pursuant to an effective registration statement, the [Administrator] by rule or order may require the person who filed the registration statement to file reports, not more often than quarterly, to keep reasonably current the information contained in the registration statement and to disclose the progress of the offering.

(*o*) A registration statement filed under Section 302 or 303 may be amended after its effective date to increase the securities specified being offered and sold. The amendment becomes effective upon filing of the amendment and payment of an additional filing fee, calculated in the manner specified in subsection (b) or (c), with respect to the additional securities to be offered and sold. The effectiveness of the amendment relates back to the date of sale of the additional securities being registered.

(p) A registration statement filed under Section 304 may be amended after its effective date to increase the securities specified to be offered and sold, if the public offering price and underwriters' discounts and commissions are not changed from the respective amounts of which the [Administrator] was informed. The amendment becomes effective when the [Administrator] so orders and relates back to the date of sale of the additional securities being registered. A person filing an amendment shall pay an additional filing fee [two] times the initial registration fee, calculated in the manner specified in subsection (b) or (c), with respect to the additional securities to be offered and sold.

§ 306. Denial, Suspension, and Revocation of Registration

(a) The [Administrator] may issue a stop order denying effectiveness to, or suspending or revoking the effectiveness of, a registration statement if the [Administrator] finds that the order is in the public interest and that:

(1) the registration statement as of its effective date or as of the proposed effective date in the case of an order denying effectiveness, an amendment under Section 305(*o*) or (p) as of its effective date, or a report under Section 305(n) is incomplete in a material respect or contains a statement that, in the light of the circumstances under which it was made, was false or misleading with respect to a material fact;

(2) this [Act] or a rule, order, or condition lawfully imposed under this [Act] has been willfully violated, in connection with the offering, by the person filing the registration statement; by the issuer, a partner, officer, or director of the issuer, a person occupying a similar status or performing a similar function, or a person directly or indirectly controlling or controlled by the issuer, but only if the person filing the registration statement is directly or indirectly controlled by or acting for the issuer; or by an underwriter;

(3) the security registered or sought to be registered is the subject of a permanent or temporary injunction of a court of competent jurisdiction or an administrative stop order or similar order entered under any other federal or state law applicable to the offering; but the [Administrator] may not institute a proceeding against an effective registration statement under this paragraph more than one year after the date of the order or injunction relied on, and the [Administrator] may not enter an order under this paragraph on the basis of an order or injunction entered under the securities act of another state unless the order or injunction was based on facts that currently would constitute a ground for a stop order under this section;

(4) the issuer's enterprise or method of business includes or would include activities that are illegal where performed;

(5) the offering has worked or tended to work a fraud upon purchasers or would so operate;

[alternative subparagraph (5): the offering is being made on terms that are unfair, unjust, or inequitable;]

(6) the offering has been or would be made with unreasonable amounts of underwriters' and sellers' discounts, commissions, or other compensation, or promoters' profits or participation, or unreasonable amounts or kinds of options;

(7) a security sought to be registered under Section 302 is not eligible for registration under Section 302;

(8) with respect to a security sought to be registered under Section 303, there has been a failure to comply with the undertaking required by paragraph (4) of Section 303(b); or

(9) the applicant or registrant has failed to pay the proper filing fee; but the [Administrator] may enter only a denial order under this paragraph and shall vacate the order if the deficiency is corrected.

(b) The [Administrator] may not institute a stop-order proceeding:

(1) against an effective registration statement on the basis of a fact or transaction known to the [Administrator] when the registration statement became effective unless the proceeding is begun within 30 days after the registration statement became effective; or

(2) with respect to a registration statement filed under Section 302, on the basis of paragraph (5) or (6) of subsection (a).

(c) The [Administrator] by order under Section 712 may summarily postpone or suspend the effectiveness of a registration statement pending final determination of an administrative proceeding. Upon the entry of the order, the [Administrator] shall promptly notify each person specified in subsection (d) that the order has been entered and of the reasons for the postponement or suspension and that within 15 days after the receipt of a written request from the person the matter will be set down for hearing. If no hearing is requested and none is ordered by the [Administrator], the order remains in effect until it is modified or vacated by the [Administrator]. If a hearing is requested or ordered, the [Administrator], after notice of and opportunity for hearing to each person specified in subsection (d), may modify or vacate the order or extend it until final determination.

(d) A stop order may not be entered under subsection (a) or (b) without (i) appropriate notice to the applicant or registrant, the issuer, and the person on whose behalf the securities are to be or have been offered, (ii) opportunity for hearing, and (iii) written findings of fact and conclusions of law [in accordance with the state administrative procedure act].

(e) The [Administrator] may modify or vacate a stop order entered under this section if the [Administrator] finds that the conditions that prompted entry have changed or that it is otherwise in the public interest.

PART IV

EXEMPTIONS FROM REGISTRATION

§ 401. Exempt Securities

(a) As used in this section:

(1) "Guaranteed" means guaranteed as to payment of all or substantially all of principal and interest or dividends.

(2) "Insured" means insured as to payment of all or substantially all of principal and interest or dividends.

(b) The following securities are exempt from Sections 301 and 405:

(1) a security, including a revenue obligation, issued, insured, or guaranteed by the United States, an agency or corporate or other instrumentality of the United States, an international agency or corporate or other instrumentality of which the United States and one or more foreign governments are members, a state, a political subdivision of a state, or an agency or corporate or other instrumentality of one or more states or their political subdivisions; or a certificate of deposit for any of the foregoing [, but this exemption does not include a security payable solely from revenues to be received from a nongovernmental industrial or commercial enterprise unless the payments are insured or guaranteed by a person whose securities are exempt from registration under paragraph (2), (3), (4), (5), (7), (9), or (13) or the revenues from which the payments are to be made are a direct obligation of such a person];

(2) a security issued, insured, or guaranteed by Canada, a Canadian province or territory, a political subdivision of Canada or a Canadian province or territory, an agency or corporate or other instrumentality of one or more of the foregoing, or any other foreign government or governmental combination or entity with which the United States maintains diplomatic relations, if the security is recognized as a valid obligation by the issuer, insurer, or guarantor;

(3) a security issued by and representing an interest in or a direct obligation of, or guaranteed by, a depository institution if the deposit or share accounts of the depository institution are insured by the Federal Deposit Insurance Corporation, the Federal Savings and Loan Insurance Corporation, the National Credit Union Share Insurance Fund, or a successor to an applicable agency authorized by federal law;

(4) a security issued by and representing an interest in or a direct obligation of, or insured or guaranteed by, an insurance company organized under the laws of any state and authorized to do business in this State;

(5) a security issued or guaranteed by a railroad, other common carrier, public utility, or holding company that is:

(i) subject to the jurisdiction of the Interstate Commerce Commission;

(ii) a registered holding company under the Public Utility Holding Company Act of 1935 or a subsidiary of a registered holding company within the meaning of that act;

(iii) regulated in respect to its rates and charges by a governmental authority of the United States or a state; or

(iv) regulated in respect to the issuance or guarantee of the security by a governmental authority of the United States, a state, Canada, or a Canadian province or territory;

(6) equipment trust certificates in respect to equipment leased or conditionally sold to a person, if securities issued by the person would be exempt under this section;

(7) a security listed or approved for listing upon notice of issuance on the New York Stock Exchange, the American Stock Exchange, or the Midwest Stock Exchange [, or listed on the (insert names of appropriate regional stock exchange)], if, in either case, quotations have been available and public trading has taken place for the class of security listed before the offer or sale of a security in reliance upon this exemption; any other security of the same issuer which is of senior or substantially equal rank; a security called for by subscription right or warrant so listed or approved; or a warrant or right to purchase or subscribe to any of the foregoing;

(8) a security designated or approved for designation upon issuance for inclusion in the national market system by the National Association of Securities Dealers, Inc., if, in either case, quotations have been available and public trading has taken place for the class of security designated before the offer or sale of a security in reliance upon this

exemption; any other security of the same issuer which is of senior or substantially equal rank; a security called for by subscription right or warrant so designated; or a warrant or a right to purchase or subscribe to any of the foregoing;

(9) an option issued by a clearing agency registered under the Securities Exchange Act of 1934, other than an off-exchange futures contract or substantially similar arrangement, if the security, currency, commodity, or other interest underlying the option:

(i) is registered under Section 302, 303, or 304;

(ii) is exempt under this section; or

(iii) is not otherwise required to be registered under this [Act];

(10) a security issued by a person organized and operated not for private profit but exclusively for a religious, educational, benevolent, charitable, fraternal, social, athletic, or reformatory purpose, or as a chamber of commerce or trade or professional association [if at least ten days before a sale of the security the person has filed with the [Administrator] a notice setting forth the material terms of the proposed sale and copies of any sales and advertising literature to be used and the [Administrator] by order does not disallow the exemption within the next five full business days];

(11) a promissory note, draft, bill of exchange, or banker's acceptance that evidences an obligation to pay cash within nine months after the date of issuance, exclusive of days of grace, is issued in denominations of at least $50,000, and receives a rating in one of the three highest rating categories from a nationally recognized statistical rating organization; or a renewal of such an obligation that is likewise limited, or a guarantee of such an obligation or of a renewal;

(12) a security issued in connection with an employees' stock purchase, savings, option, profit-sharing, pension, or similar employees' benefit plan;

(13) a membership or equity interest in, or a retention certificate or like security given in lieu of a cash patronage dividend issued by, a cooperative organized and operated as a nonprofit membership cooperative under the cooperative laws of any state if not traded to the public;

(14) a security issued by an issuer registered as an open-end management investment company or unit investment trust under Section 8 of the Investment Company Act of 1940 if:

(i) the issuer is advised by an investment adviser that is a depository institution exempt from registration under the Investment Adviser Act of 1940 or that is currently registered as an investment adviser, and has been registered, or is affiliated with an adviser that has been registered, as an investment adviser under the Investment Advisers Act of 1940 for at least three years next preceding an offer or sale of a security claimed to be exempt under this paragraph; and the issuer has acted, or is affiliated with an investment adviser that has acted, as investment adviser to one or more registered investment companies or unit investment trusts for at least three years next preceding an offer or sale of a security claimed to be exempt under this paragraph; or

(ii) the issuer has a sponsor that has at all times throughout the three years before an offer or sale of a security claimed to be exempt under this paragraph sponsored one or more registered investment companies or unit investment trusts the aggregate total assets of which have exceeded [$100,000,000].

For the purpose of this paragraph, an investment adviser is affiliated with another investment adviser if it controls, is controlled by, or is under common control with the other investment adviser.

§ 402. Exempt Transactions

The following transactions are exempt from Sections 301 and 405:

(1) an isolated nonissuer transaction, whether or not effected through a broker-dealer;

(2) a nonissuer transaction in an outstanding security if the issuer of the security has a class of securities subject to registration under Section 12 of the Securities Exchange Act of 1934 and has been subject to the reporting requirements of Sections 13 or 15(d) of the Securities Exchange Act of 1934 for not less than 90 days next preceding the transaction; or has filed and maintained with the [Administrator] for not less than 90 days next preceding the transaction information, in such form as the [Administrator] by rule specifies, substantially comparable to the information the issuer would be required to file under Section 12(b) or Section 12(g) of the Securities Exchange Act were the issuer to have a class of its securities registered under Section 12 of the Securities Exchange Act of 1934, and paid a fee with the filing of [$150];

(3) a nonissuer transaction in a security of a class outstanding in the hands of the public for not less than 90 days next preceding the transaction if a nationally recognized securities manual designated by the [Administrator] by rule or order contains:

(i) the names of the issuer's officers and directors;

(ii) a statement of financial condition of the issuer as of a date within the last 18 months; and

(iii) a statement of income or operations (a) for each of the two years next preceding the date of the statement of condition or (b) for the period as of the date of the statement of financial condition if the period of existence is less than two years;

(4) a nonissuer transaction in a security that has a fixed maturity or a fixed interest or dividend provision and there has been no default during the current fiscal year or within the three next preceding years, or during the existence of the issuer, and any predecessors if less than three years, in the payment of principal, interest, or dividends on the security;

(5) a nonissuer transaction effected by or through a registered broker-dealer pursuant to an unsolicited order or offer to purchase;

(6) a transaction between the issuer or other person on whose behalf the offering of a security is made and an underwriter, or a transaction among underwriters;

(7) a transaction in a bond or other evidence of indebtedness secured by a real estate mortgage, deed of trust, personal property security agreement, or by an agreement for the sale of real estate or personal property, if the entire mortgage, deed of trust, or agreement, together with all the bonds or other evidences of indebtedness secured thereby, is offered and sold as a unit;

(8) a transaction by an executor, administrator, sheriff, marshal, receiver, trustee in bankruptcy, guardian, or conservator;

(9) a transaction executed by a bona fide secured party without a purpose of evading this [Act];

(10) an offer to sell or sale of a security to a financial or institutional investor or to a broker-dealer;

(11) a transaction pursuant to an offer to sell securities of an issuer, if the transaction is part of an issue in which there are no more than 25 purchasers in this State, other than those designated in paragraph (10), during any 12 consecutive months; no general solicitation or general advertising is used in connection with the offer to sell or sale of the securities; and no commission or other similar compensation is paid or given, directly or indirectly, to a person, other than a broker-dealer licensed or not required to be licensed under this [Act], for soliciting a prospective purchaser in this State; and either (i) the seller reasonably believes that all

the purchasers in this State, other than those designated in paragraph (10), are purchasing for investment; or (ii) immediately before and immediately after the transaction, the issuer reasonably believes that the securities of the issuer are held by 50 or fewer beneficial owners, other than those designated in paragraph (10), and the transaction is part of an aggregate offering that does not exceed [$500,000] during any 12 consecutive months; but the [Administrator] by rule or order as to a security or transaction or a type of security or transaction, may withdraw or further condition this exemption or waive one or more of the conditions in this paragraph;

(12) an offer to sell or sale of a preorganization certificate or subscription if no commission or other similar compensation is paid or given, directly or indirectly, for soliciting a prospective subscriber; no public advertising or general solicitation is used in connection with the offer to sell or sale; the number of subscribers does not exceed ten; and no payment is made by a subscriber;

(13) an offer to sell or sale of a preorganization certificate or subscription issued in connection with the organization of a depository institution if that organization is under the supervision of an official or agency of a state or of the United States which has and exercises the authority to regulate and supervise the organization of the depositary institution. For purpose of this paragraph, supervision of the organization by an official or agency means that the official or agency by law has authority to require disclosures to prospective investors similar to that required under Section 304, impound proceeds from the sale of a preorganization certificate or subscription until organization of the depositary institution is completed, and require refund to investors if the depositary institution does not obtain a grant of authority from the appropriate official or agency;

(14) a transaction pursuant to an offer to sell to existing security holders of the issuer, including persons who at the time of the transaction are holders of transferable warrants exercisable within not more than 90 days after their issuance, convertible securities, or nontransferable warrants, if:

(i) no commission or other similar compensation other than a standby commission, is paid or given, directly or indirectly, for soliciting a security holder in this State; or

(ii) the issuer first files a notice specifying the terms of the offer to sell and the [Administrator] does not by order disallow the exemption within the next five full business days;

(15) a transaction involving an offer to sell, but not a sale, of a security not exempt from registration under the Securities Act of 1933 if:

(i) a registration or offering statement or similar document as required under the Securities Act of 1933 has been filed, but is not effective;

(ii) a registration statement, if required, has been filed under this [Act], but is not effective; and

(iii) no stop order of which the offeror is aware has been entered by the [Administrator] or the Securities and Exchange Commission, and no examination or public proceeding that may culminate in that kind of order is known by the offeror to be pending;

(16) a transaction involving an offer to sell, but not a sale, of a security exempt from registration under the Securities Act of 1933 if:

(i) a registration statement has been filed under this [Act], but is not effective; and

(ii) no stop order of which the offeror is aware has been entered by the [Administrator] and no examination or public proceeding that may culminate in that kind of order is known by the offeror to be pending; [and]

(17) a transaction involving the distribution of the securities of an issuer to the security holders of another person in connection with a merger, consolidation, exchange of securities, sale of assets, or other reorganization to which the issuer, or its parent or subsidiary, and the other person, or its parent or subsidiary, are parties, if:

(i) the securities to be distributed are registered under the Securities Act of 1933 before the consummation of the transaction; or

(ii) the securities to be distributed are not required to be registered under the Securities Act of 1933, written notice of the transaction and a copy of the materials, if any, by which approval of the transaction will be solicited is given to the [Administrator] at least ten days before the consummation of the transaction and the [Administrator] does not disallow by order the exemption within the next ten days [.] [; and]

[(18)(i) a transaction involving the offer to sell or sale of one or more promissory notes each of which is directly secured by a first lien on a single parcel of real estate, or a transaction involving the offer to sell or sale of participation interests in the notes if the notes and participation interests are originated by a depositary institution and are offered and sold subject to the following conditions:

(A) the minimum aggregate sales price paid by each purchaser may not be less than $250,000;

(B) each purchaser must pay cash either at the time of the sale or within 60 days after the sale; and

(C) each purchaser may buy for that person's own account only;

(ii) a transaction involving the offer to sell or sale of one or more promissory notes directly secured by a first lien on a single parcel of real estate or participation interests in the notes, if the notes and participation interests are originated by a mortgagee approved by the Secretary of Housing and Urban Development under Sections 203 and 211 of the National Housing Act and are offered or sold, subject to the conditions specified in paragraph (i), to a depository institution or insurance company, the Federal Home Loan Mortgage Corporation, the Federal National Mortgage Association, or the Government National Mortgage Association; and

(iii) a transaction between any of the persons described in paragraph (ii) involving a nonassignable contract to buy or sell the securities described in paragraph (i) which contract is to be completed within two years, if:

(A) the seller of the securities pursuant to the contract is one of the parties described in paragraph (i) or (ii) who may originate securities;

(B) the purchaser of securities pursuant to a contract is any other person described in paragraph (ii); and

(C) the conditions described in paragraph (i) are fulfilled.]

§ 403. Additional Exemptions

(a) The [Administrator] by rule may exempt any other security or transaction or class of securities or transactions from Sections 301 and 405.

(b) The [Administrator] by rule may adopt a limited offering transactional exemption that will further the objectives of compatibility with the exemptions from securities registration authorized by the Securities Act of 1933 and uniformity among the states.

§ 404. Revocation of Exemptions

(a) The [Administrator] by order may deny or revoke an exemption specified in paragraph (7), (8), (10), or (12) of Section 401(b) or in Section 402, with respect to a specific security or transaction.

(b) An order issued under this section is not retroactive. A person does not violate Section 301 or 405 by reason of an offer to sell or sale effected after the entry of an order under this section if the person did not know, and in the exercise of reasonable care could not have known, of the order.

§ 405. Filing of Sales and Advertising Literature

The [Administrator] by rule or order may require the filing of a prospectus, pamphlet, circular, form letter, advertisement, or other sales literature or advertising communication addressed or intended for distribution to prospective investors, including clients or prospective clients of an investment adviser, unless the security or transaction is exempt under Section 401 or 402 or the investment adviser is exempt under Section 204.

PART V

FRAUDULENT AND OTHER PROHIBITED PRACTICES

§ 501. Offer, Sale, and Purchase

In connection with an offer to sell, sale, offer to purchase, or purchase, of a security, a person may not, directly or indirectly:

(1) employ a device, scheme, or artifice to defraud;

(2) make an untrue statement of a material fact or omit to state a material fact necessary in order to make the statements made not misleading, in the light of the circumstances under which they are made; or

(3) engage in an act, practice, or course of business that operates or would operate as a fraud or deceit upon a person.

§ 502. Manipulation of Market

(a) Without limiting the general applicability of Section 501, a person may not:

(1) quote a fictitious price with respect to a security;

(2) effect a transaction in a security which involves no change in the beneficial ownership of the security for the purpose of creating a false or misleading appearance of active trading in a security or with respect to the market for the security;

(3) enter an order for the purchase of a security with the knowledge that an order of substantially the same size and at substantially the same time and price for the sale of the security has been, or will be, entered by or for the same, or affiliated, person for the purpose of creating a false or misleading appearance of active trading in a security or with respect to the market for the security;

(4) enter an order for the sale of a security with knowledge that an order of substantially the same size and at substantially the same time and price for the purchase of the security has been, or will be, entered by or for the same, or affiliated, person for the purpose of creating a false or misleading appearance of active trading in a security or with respect to the market for the security; or

(5) employ any other deceptive or fraudulent device, scheme, or artifice to manipulate the market in a security.

(b) A transaction effected in compliance with, or conduct that does not violate, the applicable provisions of the Securities Exchange Act of 1934 and the rules and regulations of the Securities and Exchange Commission thereunder is not a violation of subsection (a).

§ 503. Prohibited Transactions by Investment Advisers

An investment adviser or person who represents an investment adviser in performing an act that requires licensing as an investment adviser under this [Act] may not, directly or indirectly:

(1) employ a device, scheme, or artifice to defraud a client; or

(2) engage in an act, practice, or course of business that operates or would operate as a fraud or deceit upon a client.

§ 504. Misleading Filings

A person may not make or cause to be made, in a document filed with the [Administrator] or in a proceeding under this [Act], a statement that the person knows or has reasonable grounds to know is, at the time and in the light of the circumstances under which it is made, false or misleading in a material respect.

§ 505. Unlawful Representation Concerning Licensing, Registration, or Exemption

(a) Neither the fact that an application for licensing or a registration statement has been filed under this [Act] nor the fact that a person is licensed or a security is registered under this [Act] constitutes a finding by the [Administrator] that a document filed under this [Act] is true, complete, and not misleading. Neither of those facts nor the fact that an exemption or exception is available for a security or a transaction means that the [Administrator] has passed upon the merits or qualifications of, or recommended or given approval to, a person, security, or transaction.

(b) A person may not make, or cause to be made, to a purchaser, customer, or client a representation inconsistent with subsection (a).

PART VI

ENFORCEMENT AND CIVIL LIABILITY

§ 601. Investigation; Subpoena Power

(a) The [Administrator] may make any investigation, within or without this State, the [Administrator] finds necessary to determine whether a person has violated or is about to violate this [Act] or a rule or order of the [Administrator] under this [Act] or to aid in enforcement of this [Act].

(b) Except as provided in Section 703(c), the [Administrator] may publish information concerning a violation of this [Act] or a rule or order of the [Administrator] under this [Act] or concerning types of securities or acts or practices in the offer to sell, sale, offer to purchase, or purchase of types of securities which may operate as a fraud or deceit.

(c) For purposes of an investigation or proceeding under this [Act], the [Administrator] or an officer or employee designated by the [Administrator] by rule or order may administer oaths and affirmations, subpoena witnesses, compel their attendance, take evidence, and require the production, by subpoena or otherwise, of books, papers, correspondence, memoranda, agreements, other documents, and records the [Administrator] considers to be relevant and material to the investigation or proceeding. The [Administrator] may require or permit a person to file a statement, under oath or otherwise as the [Administrator] directs, as to the facts and circumstances concerning the matter to be investigated.

(d) If the activities constituting an alleged violation for which the information is sought would be a violation of this [Act] had the activities occurred in this State, the [Administrator] may issue and apply to enforce subpoenas in this State at the request of a securities agency or administrator of another state.

(e) If a person does not testify or produce the documents required by the [Administrator] or a designated officer or employee pursuant to subpoena, the [Administrator] or designated officer or employee may apply to the court for an order compelling compliance.

(f) A request for an order of compliance may be addressed to:

(1) the [designate court having general trial jurisdiction] Court if the person is subject to service of process in this State; or

(2) a court of another state able to assert jurisdiction over the person refusing to testify or produce, if the person is not subject to service of process in this State.

(g) Not later than the time the [Administrator] requests an order for compliance, the [Administrator] shall either send notice of the request by registered or certified mail, return receipt requested, to the respondent at the last known address or take other steps reasonably calculated to give the respondent actual notice.

§ 602. Enforcement

(a) If the [Administrator] reasonably believes, whether or not based upon an investigation conducted under Section 601, that (i) the sale of a security is subject to registration under this [Act] and the security is being offered or has been offered or sold by the issuer or another person in violation of Section 301 or (ii) a person is acting as a broker-dealer or investment adviser in violation of Section 201 or 203, the [Administrator], in addition to any specific power granted under this [Act] and subject to compliance with the requirements of Section 712, may issue, without a prior hearing, an order against the person engaged in the prohibited activities, directing the person to desist and refrain from further activity until the security is registered or the person is licensed under this [Act]. The cease and desist order must state the section of this [Act] or rule or order of the [Administrator] under this [Act] which the [Administrator] reasonably believes has been or is being violated.

(b) If the [Administrator] reasonably believes, whether or not based upon an investigation conducted under Section 601, that a person has violated this [Act] or a rule or order of the [Administrator] under this [Act], the [Administrator], in addition to any specific power granted under this [Act], after notice and hearing in an administrative proceeding unless the right to notice and hearing is waived by the person against whom the sanction is imposed, may:

(1) issue a cease and desist order against the person;

(2) censure the person, if the person is a licensed broker-dealer, sales representative, or investment adviser;

(3) bar or suspend the person from association with a licensed broker-dealer or investment adviser in this State;

(4) issue an order against an applicant, licensed person, or other person who knowingly violates this [Act] or a rule or order of the [Administrator] under this [Act], imposing a civil penalty up to a maximum of [$2,500] for a single violation or of [$25,000] for multiple violations in a single proceeding or a series of related proceedings; or

(5) initiate one or more applicable actions specified in Section 603.

(c) Imposition of the sanctions under this section is limited as follows:

(1) if the [Administrator] revokes the license of a broker-dealer, sales representative, or investment adviser or bars a person from association with a licensed broker-dealer or investment adviser under this section or Section 212, the imposition of that sanction precludes imposition of the sanction specified in paragraph (4) of subsection (b); and

(2) the imposition by the [Administrator] of one or more sanctions under subsection (b) with respect to a specific violation precludes the [Administrator] from later imposing any other sanctions under paragraphs (1) through (4) of subsection (b) with respect to the violation.

(d) For purposes of determining any sanction to be imposed under paragraphs (1) through (4) of subsection (b), the [Administrator] shall consider, among other factors, the frequency and persistence of the conduct constituting a violation of this [Act] or a rule or order of the [Administrator] under this [Act], the number of persons adversely affected by the conduct, and the resources of the person committing the violation.

§ 603. Power of Court to Grant Relief

(a) Upon a showing by the [Administrator] that a person has violated or is about to violate this [Act] or a rule or order of the [Administrator] under this [Act], the [designate the appropriate court] may grant or impose one or more of the following appropriate legal or equitable remedies:

(1) upon a showing of a violation of this [Act] or a rule or order of the [Administrator] under this [Act]:

(i) a temporary restraining order, permanent or temporary prohibitory or mandatory injunction, or a writ of prohibition or mandamus;

(ii) a civil penalty up to a maximum of [$2,500] for a single violation or of [$25,000] for multiple violations in a single proceeding or a series of related proceedings;

(iii) a declaratory judgment;

(iv) restitution to investors;

(v) the appointment of a receiver or conservator for the defendant or the defendant's assets; and

(vi) other relief the court considers just.

(2) upon a showing that the defendant is about to violate this [Act] or a rule or order of the [Administrator] under this [Act] only:

(i) a temporary restraining order;

(ii) a temporary or permanent injunction; or

(iii) a writ of prohibition or mandamus.

(b) In determining the appropriate relief under subsection (a), the court shall consider enforcement actions taken and sanctions imposed by the [Administrator] under Section 602 in connection with the transactions constituting violations of this [Act] or a rule or order of the [Administrator] under this [Act].

(c) The [Administrator] is not required to post a bond in an action under this section.

(d) Upon a showing by the securities agency or administrator of another state that a person has violated the securities act of that state or a rule or order of the securities agency or administrator of that state, the court, in addition to any other legal or equitable remedies, may impose one or more of the following remedies:

(1) appointment of a receiver, conservator, or ancillary receiver or conservator for the defendant or the defendant's assets located in this State; and

(2) other relief the court considers just.

§ 604. Criminal Penalties

(a) A person who willfully violates a provision of this [Act], except Section 504, or a rule of the [Administrator] under this [Act], or who violates Section 504, knowing the statement made to be false or misleading in any material respect, is guilty of a [insert the language for felony under applicable state law].

(b) A person who willfully violates a stop order or a cease and desist order issued by the [Administrator] under this [Act] is guilty of a [insert the language for misdemeanor under applicable state law].

(c) A person convicted of violating a rule or order under this [Act] may be fined, but may not be imprisoned, if the person proves lack of knowledge of the rule or order.

(d) A criminal prosecution may not be instituted under this section more than [five] years after the alleged violation.

(e) The [Administrator] may refer evidence concerning violations of this [Act] or a rule or order of the [Administrator] under this [Act] to the [Attorney General or District Attorney] who, with or without a reference, may institute appropriate criminal prosecutions under this [Act].

(f) This [Act] does not limit the power of this State to punish a person for conduct constituting a crime under other law.

§ 605. Civil Liability

(a) A person who offers to sell or sells a security in violation of Section 201(a), 301, 305(k), 501(2), or 505(b) or of a condition imposed under Section 305(g), (h), or (i) is liable to one who purchases the security from that person. Upon tender of the security, the purchaser may recover the consideration paid for the security and interest at the legal rate of this State from the date of payment, costs, and reasonable attorney's fees as determined by the court, less the amount of income received on the security. Tender requires only notice of willingness to exchange the security for the amount specified. A purchaser who no longer owns the security may recover damages. Damages are the amount that would be recoverable upon a tender less the value of the security when the purchaser disposed of it, plus interest at the legal rate of this State from the date of disposition of the security, costs, and reasonable attorney's fees determined by the court.

(b) A person who offers or sells a security in violation of Section 501(2) is not liable under subsection (a) if:

(1) the purchaser knew of the untrue statement of a material fact or misleading omission of a statement of a material fact; or

(2) the seller did not know and in the exercise of reasonable care could not have known of the untrue statement or misleading omission.

(c) A person who willfully participates in an act or transaction in violation of Section 502 is liable to a person who purchases or sells a security, other than a security traded on a national securities exchange or quoted on a national automated quotation system administered by a self-regulatory organization, at a price that was affected by the act or transaction for the damages sustained as a result of the act or transaction. Damages are the difference between the price at which the securities were purchased or sold and the market value the securities would have had at the time of the person's purchase or sale in the absence of the act or transaction, plus interest at the legal rate of this State from the date of the act or transaction, costs, and reasonable attorney's fees determined by the court.

(d) A person who directly or indirectly controls another person who is liable under subsection (a) or (c), a partner, officer, or director of the person liable, a person occupying a similar status or performing similar functions, an employee of the person liable if the employee materially aids in the act, omission, or transaction constituting the violation, and a broker-dealer or sales representative who materially aids in the act, omission, or transaction constituting the violation, are also liable jointly and severally with and to the same extent as the other person, but it is a defense that the person did not know, and in the exercise of reasonable care could not have known, of the existence of the facts by which the liability is alleged to exist. With respect to a person who, directly or indirectly, controls another person who is liable under subsection (c), it is also a defense that the controlling person acted in good faith and did not, directly or indirectly, induce the act, omission, or transaction constituting the violation. Contribution among the several persons liable is the same as in cases arising out of breach of contract.

§ 606. Statute of Limitations

A person may not obtain relief under Section 605 unless suit is brought within the earliest of one year after the discovery of the violation, one year after discovery should have been made by the exercise of reasonable care, or three years after the act, omission, or transaction constituting the violation.

§ 607. Offer of Rescission or Settlement

(a) Relief may not be obtained under Section 605(a) if, before suit is commenced, the purchaser:

(1) receives a written offer:

(i) stating the respect in which liability under Section 605 may have arisen and fairly advising the purchaser of the purchaser's rights of rescission;

(ii) if the basis for relief under Section 605(a) is a violation of Section 501(2), including financial and other information necessary to correct all material misstatements or omissions in the information which was required by this [Act] to be furnished to the purchaser as of the time of the sale of the security to the purchaser;

(iii) offering to repurchase the security for cash, payable on delivery of the security, equal to the consideration paid, plus interest at the legal rate of this State from the date of payment, less income received thereon, or, if the purchaser no longer owns the security, offering to pay the purchaser upon acceptance of the offer an amount in cash equal to the damages computed under Section 605(a); and

(iv) stating that the offer may be accepted by the purchaser within 30 days after the date of its receipt by the purchaser or any shorter period, not less than three days, the [Administrator] by order prescribes; and

(2) fails to accept the offer in writing within the period specified under paragraph (1)(iv).

(b) The [Administrator] by rule may prescribe the form in which the information specified in subsection (a) must be contained in an offer made under subsection (a).

(c) An offer under subsection (a) must be delivered to the offeree or sent in a manner which assures actual receipt by the offeree.

(d) If, after acceptance, a rescission offer is not performed in accordance with either its terms or this section, the offeree may obtain relief under Section 605 without regard to this section.

§ 608. Burden of Proof

(a) In a civil action or administrative proceeding under this [Act], a person claiming an exemption or an exception from a definition has the burden of proving the exemption or exception.

(b) In a criminal proceeding, the burden of going forward with evidence of a claim of exemption or exception from a definition is on the person claiming it.

§ 609. Liability; General Provisions

(a) Except as provided in Section 607, a tender required under this [Act] may be made before entry of judgment.

(b) The rights and remedies provided by this [Act] are in addition to any other rights or remedies that exist at law or in equity, but this [Act] does not create any [claim for relief] [cause of action] not specified in this Part.

(c) A [claim for relief] [cause of action] under this [Act] survives the death of a person who might have obtained relief as a plaintiff or defendant.

PART VII
ADMINISTRATION

§ 701. Administration of [Act]

The [Administrator] shall administer this [Act] in accordance with [insert any related provision on method of selection, salary, term of office, budget, selection and compensation of personnel, annual report to the Legislature or Governor, which are appropriate to the particular state].

§ 702. Prohibitions on Use of Information

Neither the [Administrator] nor an employee of the [Administrator] may use for personal gain or benefit information filed with or obtained by the [Administrator] which is not public information. Neither the [Administrator] nor an employee of the [Administrator] may conduct securities dealings based upon information filed with or obtained by the [Administrator], even though public, if there has not been sufficient time for the securities markets to assimilate the information.

§ 703. Public Information; Confidentiality

(a) Except as provided in subsection (b), information and documents filed with or obtained by the [Administrator] are public information and are available for public examination under the [freedom of information or open records laws of this State].

(b) The following information and documents do not constitute public information under subsection (a):

(1) information or documents obtained by the [Administrator] in connection with an investigation under Section 601; and

(2) information or documents filed with the [Administrator] in connection with a registration statement under Part III or a report under Section 209 and constituting trade secrets or commercial or financial information of a person for which that person is entitled to, and has asserted, a claim of confidentiality or privilege authorized by law.

(c) The [Administrator] may disclose:

(1) information obtained in connection with an investigation under Section 601(a) to the extent provided in Section 601(b) subject to the restrictions of subsection (b)(2); and

(2) information obtained in connection with an investigation under Section 601(a), if disclosure is for the purpose of a civil, administrative, or criminal investigation or proceeding by a securities agency, law enforcement agency, or administrator specified in Section 704(a), and the receiving agency or administrator represents in writing that under applicable law protections exist to preserve the integrity, confidentiality, and security of the information.

(d) This [Act] does not create any privilege or diminish any privilege existing at common law, by statute, rule, or otherwise.

§ 704. Cooperation With Other Agencies

(a) To encourage uniform interpretation and administration of this [Act] and effective securities, regulation and enforcement, the [Administrator] may cooperate with the securities agencies or administrators of one or more states, Canadian provinces or territories, or another country, the Securities and Exchange Commission, the Commodity Futures Trading Commission, the Securities Investor Protection Corporation, any self-regulatory organization, any national or international organization of securities officials or agencies, and any governmental law enforcement or regulatory agency.

(b) The cooperation authorized by subsection (a) includes:

(1) establishing a central depository for licensing or registration under this [Act] and for documents or records required or allowed to be maintained under this [Act];

(2) making a joint license or registration examination or investigation;

(3) holding a joint administrative hearing;

(4) filing and prosecuting a joint civil or administrative proceeding;

(5) sharing and exchanging personnel;

(6) sharing and exchanging information and documents subject to the restrictions of [Section 703(b) and (c)] [cite other applicable state law]; and

(7) formulating, in accordance with the [administrative procedure act of this State], rules or proposed rules on matters such as statements of policy, guidelines, and interpretative opinions and releases.

§ 705. Rules, Forms, and Orders

(a) In addition to specific authority otherwise granted by this [Act], the [Administrator]:

(1) shall adopt as a rule a description of the organization of the [Administrator's] office which states the general course and method of its organization and where and how a person may obtain information or make a submission or request;

(2) shall adopt rules of practice setting forth the nature and requirements of all formal and informal procedures available to a person, including a description of all forms and instructions that are to be used by a person dealing with the [Administrator];

(3) may adopt rules, in addition to those otherwise required by this [Act], embodying appropriate standards, principles, and procedural safeguards that the [Administrator] applies in the administration of this [Act]; and

(4) may adopt rules defining any term, whether or not used in this [Act], insofar as the definition is not inconsistent with this [Act].

(b) To keep rules adopted by the [Administrator] in harmony with the regulations adopted by the Securities and Exchange Commission under the federal securities laws and to encourage uniformity with the rules of securities agencies and administrators in other states, the [Administrator], so far as is consistent with this [Act], shall take into consideration the regulations adopted by the Securities and Exchange Commission and the rules of securities agencies and administrators in other states that enact a law comparable to this [Act].

(c) Unless specifically provided in this [Act] to the contrary, a rule or order may not be adopted, amended, or repealed unless the [Administrator] determines that the action is:

(1) in the public interest and appropriate for the protection of investors; and

(2) consistent with the purposes fairly intended by the policy and provisions of this [Act].

(d) The [Administrator] may use his [or her] own experience, technical competence, specialized knowledge, and judgment in the adoption of a rule.

(e) The [Administrator] by rule or order may prescribe:

(1) the form and content of financial statements required under this [Act];

(2) the circumstances under which consolidated financial statements must be filed; and

(3) whether a required financial statement must be certified and by whom. Unless the [Administrator] by rule or order provides otherwise, a financial statement required under this [Act] must be prepared in accordance with generally accepted accounting principles or other accounting principles as are prescribed for the issuer of the financial statement by the Securities and Exchange Commission.

(f) The [Administrator] shall file [in the office of the Secretary of State or other location required by law] and in the [Administrator's] office each rule adopted or amended and all rules existing on the effective date of this [Act] that have not been previously filed. The filing must be done as soon after adoption or amendment of the rule as is practicable. The [Administrator] shall affix to each rule a certification of the time and date of filing and keep a permanent register open to public inspection of all filed rules.

§ 706. Declaratory Orders and Rulings

(a) Any person may petition the [Administrator] for a declaratory order as to the applicability to specified circumstances of a statute, rule, or order under this [Act]. The [Administrator] may issue a declaratory order in response to a petition for that order unless the [Administrator] determines that the petition fails to comply with the [Administrator's] rules or, if the order were issued, would substantially prejudice the rights of a person who would be a necessary party and who does not consent to the determination of the matter by a declaratory order.

(b) The [Administrator], upon application by an interested party, may conduct a hearing and issue a declaratory ruling as to the applicability of this [Act] or a rule or order of the [Administrator] under this [Act] to a person, security, or transaction, or as to the meaning of a term used in this [Act].

§ 707. Good Faith Reliance

No provision of this [Act] imposing liability applies to an act done or omitted in good faith in conformity with:

(1) a rule or order adopted by the [Administrator], notwithstanding that the rule or order is later amended, repealed, or determined by judicial or other authority to be invalid; or

(2) a declaratory order or ruling issued by the [Administrator] under Section 706.

§ 708. Consent to Service of Process

(a) An applicant for licensing or registration under this [Act] or an issuer who proposes to offer a security in this State through an agent shall file with the [Administrator], in the form the [Administrator], by rule, prescribes, an irrevocable consent appointing the [Administrator] the person's agent for service of process in a noncriminal proceeding against the person, a successor, or personal representative, which arises under this [Act] or a rule or order of the [Administrator] under this [Act] after the consent is filed, with the same force and validity as if served personally on the person filing the consent.

(b) A person who has filed a consent complying with subsection (a) in connection with a previous application for licensing or registration need not file an additional consent.

(c) If a person, including a nonresident of this State, engages in conduct prohibited or made actionable by this [Act] or a rule or order of the [Administrator] under this [Act] and the person has not filed a consent to service of process under subsection (a), the engaging in the conduct constitutes the appointment of the [Administrator] as the person's agent for service of process in a noncriminal proceeding against the person, a successor, or personal representative which grows out of the conduct.

(d) A consent to service filed on behalf of an issuer organized or domiciled under the laws of a foreign country whose securities are being offered in this State other than by or through underwriters, must be accompanied by an opinion of counsel stating that a judgment of United States courts will be recognized by the courts of the country in which the issuer is organized or domiciled.

(e) Service under subsection (a) or (c) may be made by leaving a copy of the process in the office of the [Administrator], but it is not effective unless:

(1) the plaintiff, who may be the [Administrator], promptly sends notice of the service and a copy of the process by registered or certified mail, return receipt requested, to the defendant or respondent at the address set forth in the consent to service of process or, if no consent to service of process has been filed, at the last-known address, or takes other steps reasonably calculated to give actual notice; and

(2) the plaintiff files an affidavit of compliance with this subsection in the proceeding on or before the return day of the process, if any, or within such further time as the court, or the [Administrator] in a proceeding before the [Administrator], allows.

(f) Service as provided in subsection (e) may be used in a proceeding before the [Administrator] or by the [Administrator] in a proceeding in which the [Administrator] is the moving party.

(g) If the process is served under subsection (e), the court, or the [Administrator] in a proceeding before the [Administrator], shall order continuances as may be necessary to afford the defendant or respondent reasonable opportunity to defend.

§ 709. Administrative Files and Records

(a) The [Administrator] shall keep one or more registers of:

(1) all applications for licensing and registration under this [Act];

(2) all licenses and registration statements that become effective under this [Act];

(3) all disciplinary and enforcement orders issued and reports of investigation made under this [Act];

(4) all declaratory orders and rulings issued under this [Act]; and

(5) all other orders issued under this [Act].

[(b) The [Administrator] shall maintain records consistent with applicable law.]

[(b) The [Administrator] shall retain:

(1) all licenses and related applications and all registration statements currently effective or that have been effective within the last [five] years;

(2) all licenses and related applications and all registration statements that have been denied, suspended, or revoked within the last [five] years, and the order of suspension, denial, or revocation;

(3) all investigatory files under this [Act] that are open or that have been closed within the last [five] years, and any disciplinary or file-closure order pertaining to the file;

(4) the transcript or record of all administrative hearings held during the last [five] years; and

(5) any other orders of the [Administrator] entered under this [Act].]

(c) All records required to be maintained by subsections (a) and (b) may be maintained in any form of data storage.

(d) Upon request, the [Administrator] shall certify under the seal of office a copy as being a true and correct copy of the records maintained by the office. The [Administrator] by rule may establish reasonable charges for furnishing or certifying copies. In an investigation or proceeding under this [Act], a copy so certified is prima facie evidence of the contents of the records certified.

§ 710. Administrative Proceedings

The [Administrator] may commence an administrative proceeding at any time with respect to a matter within the [Administrator's] jurisdiction. The [Administrator] shall commence an administrative proceeding upon the application of a person, unless:

(1) the [Administrator] lacks jurisdiction over the subject matter;

(2) resolution of the matter requires the [Administrator] to exercise discretion to determine whether or not to issue an order;

(3) a statute vests the [Administrator] with discretion to conduct or not to conduct an administrative proceeding before issuing an order to resolve the matter and, in the exercise of discretion, the [Administrator] determines not to conduct an administrative proceeding;

(4) resolution of the matter does not require the [Administrator] to issue an order that determines the person's legal rights, duties, privileges, immunities, or other legal interests;

(5) the matter is not timely submitted to the [Administrator]; or

(6) the matter is not submitted in a form substantially complying with the rules of the [Administrator].

§ 711. Provisions Applicable to Administrative Proceedings

(a) All actions of the [Administrator] including administrative proceedings, adoption of rules, and issuance of orders are governed by [state administrative procedure act], but:

(1) the issue of a stop order under Section 303(e) is governed by Section 303(e);

(2) the issue of an order pursuant to an emergency administrative proceeding is governed by Section 712; and

(3) the issue of a declaratory order or ruling is governed by Section 706.

(b) All rules and orders issued under this [Act] are subject to judicial review [in accordance with the state administrative procedure act].

§ 712. Emergency Administrative Proceedings

(a) The [Administrator] may use emergency administrative proceedings in a situation involving an immediate danger to the public welfare requiring immediate action.

(b) The [Administrator] may take only such action as is necessary to prevent or avoid the immediate danger to the public welfare that justifies use of emergency administrative proceedings.

(c) The [Administrator] shall issue an order, including a brief statement of findings of fact, conclusions of law, and, if it is an exercise of the agency's discretion, policy reasons for the decision to justify the determination of an immediate danger and the [Administrator's] decision to take the specific action.

(d) The [Administrator] shall give such notice as is practicable to persons who are required to comply with the order. The order is effective when issued.

(e) After issuing an order under this section, the [Administrator] shall proceed as quickly as feasible to complete proceedings that would be required [under the state administrative procedures act] if the matter did not involve an immediate danger.

(f) The record of the [Administrator] consists of the documents regarding the matter that were considered or prepared by the [Administrator]. The [Administrator] shall maintain these documents as the official record.

(g) Unless otherwise required by law, the [Administrator's] record need not constitute the exclusive basis for the [Administrator's] action in emergency administrative proceedings or for judicial review of the action.

(h) An order issued under this section is subject to judicial review [in accordance with the state administrative procedure act].

PART VIII
MISCELLANEOUS PROVISIONS

§ 801. Scope of [Act]

(a) Sections 201, 301, 501, 502, 505, and 605 apply to a person who sells or offers to sell a security if:

(1) an offer to sell is made in this State; or

(2) an offer to purchase is made and accepted in this State.

(b) Sections 201, 501, 502, and 505 apply to a person who purchases or offers to purchase a security if:

(1) an offer to purchase is made in this State; or

(2) an offer to sell is made and accepted in this State.

(c) For the purpose of this section, an offer to sell or to purchase is made in this State, whether or not either person is present in this State, if the offer:

(1) originates in this State; or

(2) is directed by the offeror to a destination in this State and received where it is directed, or at a post office in this State if the offer is mailed.

(d) For the purpose of this section, an offer to purchase or to sell is accepted in this State if acceptance is communicated to the offeror in this State and has not previously been communicated to the offeror, orally or in writing, outside this State. Acceptance is communicated to the offeror in this State, whether or not either person is present in this State, if the offeree directs it to the offeror in this State reasonably believing the offeror is in this State and it is received where it is directed, or at a post office in this State if an acceptance is mailed.

(e) For the purpose of subsections (a) through (d), an offer to sell or to purchase made in a newspaper or other publication of general, regular, and paid circulation is not made in this State if the publication:

(1) is not published in this State; or

(2) is published in this State, but has had more than two-thirds of its circulation outside this State during the last 12 months.

(f) For the purpose of subsection (e), if a publication is published in editions, each edition is a separate publication except for material common to all editions.

(g) For the purpose of subsections (a) through (d), an offer to sell or to purchase made in a radio or television program or other electronic communication received in this State which originates outside this State is not made in this State.

(h) For the purpose of subsection (g), a radio or television program or other electronic communication is considered as having originated in this State if either the broadcast studio or the originating source of transmission is located in this State, unless:

(1) the program or communication is syndicated and distributed from outside this State for redistribution to the general public in this State;

(2) the program or communication is supplied by a radio, television, or other electronic network with the electronic signal originating from outside this State for redistribution to the general public in this State;

(3) the program or communication is an electronic signal that originates outside this State and is captured for redistribution to the general public in this State by a community antenna or cable, radio, cable television, or other electronic system; or

(4) the program or communication consists of an electronic signal that originates in this State, but which is not intended for redistribution to the general public in this State.

§ 802. Contract Provisions

(a) A person subject to this [Act] who makes or engages in the performance of a contract in violation of this [Act] or a rule or order of the [Administrator] under this [Act], or who acquires a right under a contract with knowledge of the facts by which its making or performance is in violation of this [Act], may not obtain relief on the contract.

(b) A provision in a contract entered into or effective in this State, binding a person acquiring a security to waive compliance with this [Act] or a rule or order of the [Administrator] under this [Act] is nonenforceable. A provision in a contract containing (i) an agreement to arbitrate or (ii) a choice of law provision in a contract between persons engaged in the securities business is not a provision waiving compliance with this [Act] and is enforceable in accordance with its terms.

§ 803. Uniformity of Application and Construction

This [Act] shall be applied and construed to effectuate its general purpose to make uniform the law with respect to the subject of this [Act] among states enacting it and to coordinate the interpretation and administration of this [Act] with the related federal laws and regulations.

§ 804. Short Title

This [Act] may be cited as the Uniform Securities Act (1985).

§ 805. Severability Clause

If any provision of this [Act] or its application to any person or circumstances is held invalid, the invalidity does not affect other provisions or applications of this [Act] which can be given effect without the invalid provision or application, and to this end the provisions of the [Act] are severable.

§ 806. Effective Date

This [Act] takes effect on [insert date, which should be at least 60 days after enactment].

§ 807. Repeal and Saving Provisions

(a) The [identify the existing act or acts] is [are] repealed except as saved in this section.

(b) Law repealed by this [Act] exclusively governs a suit, action, prosecution, or proceeding that is pending on the effective date of this [Act] or may be initiated on the basis of facts or circumstances occurring before the effective date of this [Act], but a civil action or proceeding may not be maintained to enforce any liability under law repealed by this [Act] unless brought within the earlier of the period of limitation that applied when the [claim for relief] [cause of action] accrued or two years after the effective date of this [Act].

(c) All effective registrations under law repealed by this [Act], all administrative orders relating to those registrations, and all conditions imposed upon those registrations remain in effect for as long as they would have remained in effect if this [Act] had not been enacted. They are considered to have been filed, issued, or imposed under this [Act], but are governed by the law repealed by this [Act].

(d) A law repealed by this [Act] applies to an offer to sell or sale made within one year after the effective date of this [Act] pursuant to an offering begun in good faith before the effective date of this [Act] on the basis of an exemption available under the repealed law.

(e) Judicial review of all administrative orders as to which review proceedings have not been instituted before the effective date of this [Act] are governed by [state administrative procedure act] but a review proceeding may not be instituted unless the petition for review is filed within the earlier of the period of limitation that applied to a review proceeding when the order was entered or 60 days after the effective date of this [Act].

UNIFORM SECURITIES ACT (2002)

TABLE OF CONTENTS

[ARTICLE] 1
GENERAL PROVISIONS

Section

Section

[ARTICLE] 2
EXEMPTIONS FROM REGISTRATION OF SECURITIES

Section

[ARTICLE] 3
REGISTRATION OF SECURITIES AND NOTICE FILING OF FEDERAL COVERED SECURITIES

Section

[ARTICLE] 4
BROKER-DEALERS, AGENTS, INVESTMENT ADVISERS, INVESTMENT ADVISER REPRESENTATIVE AND FEDERAL COVERED INVESTMENT ADVISERS

Legislative Note

Each state, the District of Columbia, Guam, and Puerto Rico have enacted an administrative procedure act. The procedural provisions of the Act in some instances are intended to augment the state administrative procedure act. In so doing, this Act differs from other uniform acts promulgated by the National Conference of Commissioners on Uniform State Laws (NCCUSL) in that it contains procedural provisions on topics such as administrative rulemaking and adjudication, service of process, judicial review of administrative adjudications, public records, public hearings, and use immunity. Normally a uniform act promulgated by NCCUSL defers to existing state procedural provisions on such matters. This Act reflects a policy decision that these matters should be addressed in this Act to promote uniformity in securities regulation. When a conflict exists between this Act and a state administrative procedure act, this Act is intended to supersede the state administrative procedure act. When, however, a reference is made in this Act to the state administrative procedure act, this Act is intended to follow the state's existing administrative procedure act.

In general in this Act a rule will apply generally and an order will apply to a specific individual, transaction, or matter, although the term order may also apply generally in those states that permit orders of general applicability.

[ARTICLE] 1

GENERAL PROVISIONS

SECTION 101. SHORT TITLE. This [Act] may be cited as the Uniform Securities Act (2002).

SECTION 102. DEFINITIONS. In this [Act], unless the context otherwise requires:

(1) "Administrator" means the [insert title of administrative agency or official].

(2) "Agent" means an individual, other than a broker-dealer, who represents a broker-dealer in effecting or attempting to effect purchases or sales of securities or represents an issuer in effecting or attempting to effect purchases or sales of the issuer's securities. But a partner, officer, or director of a broker-dealer or issuer, or an individual having a similar status or performing similar functions is an agent only if the individual otherwise comes within the term. The term does not include an individual excluded by rule adopted or order issued under this [Act].

(3) "Bank" means:

(A) a banking institution organized under the laws of the United States;

(B) a member bank of the Federal Reserve System;

(C) any other banking institution, whether incorporated or not, doing business under the laws of a State or of the United States, a substantial portion of the business of which consists of receiving deposits or exercising fiduciary powers similar to those permitted to be exercised by national banks under the authority of the Comptroller of the Currency pursuant to Section 1 of Public Law 87–722 (12 U.S.C. Section 92a), and which is supervised and examined by a state or federal agency having supervision over banks, and which is not operated for the purpose of evading this [Act]; and

(D) a receiver, conservator, or other liquidating agent of any institution or firm included in subparagraph (A), (B), or (C).

(4) "Broker-dealer" means a person engaged in the business of effecting transactions in securities for the account of others or for the person's own account. The term does not include:

(A) an agent;

(B) an issuer;

(C) a bank or savings institution if its activities as a broker-dealer are limited to those specified in subsections 3(a)(4)(B)(i) through (vi), (viii) through (x), and (xi) if limited to unsolicited transactions; 3(a)(5)(B); and 3(a)(5)(C) of the Securities Exchange Act of 1934 (15 U.S.C. Sections 78c(a)(4) and (5)) or a bank that satisfies the conditions described in subsection 3(a)(4)(E) of the Securities Exchange Act of 1934 (15 U.S.C. Section 78c(a)(4));

(D) an international banking institution; or

(E) a person excluded by rule adopted or order issued under this [Act].

(5) "Depository institution" means:

(A) a bank; or

(B) a savings institution, trust company, credit union, or similar institution that is organized or chartered under the laws of a State or of the United States, authorized to receive deposits, and supervised and examined by an official or agency of a State or the United States if its deposits or share accounts are insured to the maximum amount authorized by statute by the Federal Deposit Insurance Corporation, the National Credit Union Share Insurance Fund, or a successor authorized by federal law. The term does not include:

(i) an insurance company or other organization primarily engaged in the business of insurance;

(ii) a Morris Plan bank; or

(iii) an industrial loan company.

(6) "Federal covered investment adviser" means a person registered under the Investment Advisers Act of 1940.

(7) "Federal covered security" means a security that is, or upon completion of a transaction will be, a covered security under Section 18(b) of the Securities Act of 1933 (15 U.S.C. Section 77r(b)) or rules or regulations adopted pursuant to that provision.

(8) "Filing" means the receipt under this [Act] of a record by the administrator or a designee of the administrator.

(9) "Fraud," "deceit," and "defraud" are not limited to common law deceit.

(10) "Guaranteed" means guaranteed as to payment of all principal and all interest.

(11) "Institutional investor" means any of the following, whether acting for itself or for others in a fiduciary capacity:

(A) a depository institution or international banking institution;

(B) an insurance company;

(C) a separate account of an insurance company;

(D) an investment company as defined in the Investment Company Act of 1940;

(E) a broker-dealer registered under the Securities Exchange Act of 1934;

(F) an employee pension, profit-sharing, or benefit plan if the plan has total assets in excess of $10,000,000 or its investment decisions are made by a named fiduciary, as defined in the Employee Retirement Income Security Act of 1974, that is a broker-dealer registered under the Securities Exchange Act of 1934, an investment adviser registered or exempt from registration under the Investment Advisers Act of 1940, an investment adviser registered under this [Act], a depository institution, or an insurance company;

(G) a plan established and maintained by a State, a political subdivision of a State, or an agency or instrumentality of a State or a political subdivision of a State for the benefit of its employees, if the plan has total assets in excess of $10,000,000 or its investment decisions are made by a duly designated public official or by a named fiduciary, as defined in the Employee Retirement Income Security Act of 1974, that is a broker-dealer registered under the Securities Exchange Act of 1934, an investment adviser registered or exempt from registration under the Investment Advisers Act of 1940, an investment adviser registered under this [Act], a depository institution, or an insurance company;

(H) a trust, if it has total assets in excess of $10,000,000, its trustee is a depository institution, and its participants are exclusively plans of the types identified in subparagraph (F) or (G), regardless of the size of their assets, except a trust that includes as participants self-directed individual retirement accounts or similar self-directed plans;

(I) an organization described in Section 501(c)(3) of the Internal Revenue Code (26 U.S.C. Section 501(c)(3)), corporation, Massachusetts trust or similar business trust, limited liability company, or partnership, not formed for the specific purpose of acquiring the securities offered, with total assets in excess of $10,000,000;

(J) a small business investment company licensed by the Small Business Administration under Section 301(c) of the Small Business Investment Act of 1958 (15 U.S.C. Section 681(c)) with total assets in excess of $10,000,000;

(K) a private business development company as defined in Section 202(a)(22) of the Investment Advisers Act of 1940 (15 U.S.C. Section 80b–2(a)(22)) with total assets in excess of $10,000,000;

(L) a federal covered investment adviser acting for its own account;

(M) a "qualified institutional buyer" as defined in Rule 144A(a)(1), other than Rule 144A(a)(1)(i)(H), adopted under the Securities Act of 1933 (17 C.F.R. 230.144A);

(N) a "major U.S. institutional investor" as defined in Rule 15a–6(b)(4)(i) adopted under the Securities Exchange Act of 1934 (17 C.F.R. 240.15a–6);

(O) any other person, other than an individual, of institutional character with total assets in excess of $10,000,000 not organized for the specific purpose of evading this [Act]; or

(P) any other person specified by rule adopted or order issued under this [Act].

(12) "Insurance company" means a company organized as an insurance company whose primary business is writing insurance or reinsuring risks underwritten by insurance companies and which is subject to supervision by the insurance commissioner or a similar official or agency of a State.

(13) "Insured" means insured as to payment of all principal and all interest.

(14) "International banking institution" means an international financial institution of which the United States is a member and whose securities are exempt from registration under the Securities Act of 1933.

(15) "Investment adviser" means a person that, for compensation, engages in the business of advising others, either directly or through publications or writings, as to the value of securities or the advisability of investing in, purchasing, or selling securities or that, for compensation and as a part of a regular business, issues or promulgates analyses or reports concerning securities. The term includes a financial planner or other person that, as an integral component of other financially related services, provides investment advice to others for compensation as part of a business or that holds itself out as providing investment advice to others for compensation. The term does not include:

(A) an investment adviser representative;

(B) a lawyer, accountant, engineer, or teacher whose performance of investment advice is solely incidental to the practice of the person's profession;

(C) a broker-dealer or its agents whose performance of investment advice is solely incidental to the conduct of business as a broker-dealer and that does not receive special compensation for the investment advice;

(D) a publisher of a bona fide newspaper, news magazine, or business or financial publication of general and regular circulation;

(E) a federal covered investment adviser;

(F) a bank or savings institution;

(G) any other person that is excluded by the Investment Advisers Act of 1940 from the definition of investment adviser; or

(H) any other person excluded by rule adopted or order issued under this [Act].

(16) "Investment adviser representative" means an individual employed by or associated with an investment adviser or federal covered investment adviser and who makes any recommendations or otherwise gives investment advice regarding securities, manages accounts or portfolios of clients, determines which recommendation or advice regarding securities should be given, provides investment advice or holds herself or himself out as providing investment advice, receives compensation to solicit, offer, or negotiate for the sale of or for selling investment advice, or supervises employees who perform any of the foregoing. The term does not include an individual who:

(A) performs only clerical or ministerial acts;

(B) is an agent whose performance of investment advice is solely incidental to the individual acting as an agent and who does not receive special compensation for investment advisory services;

(C) is employed by or associated with a federal covered investment adviser, unless the individual has a "place of business" in this State as that term is defined by rule adopted under Section 203A of the Investment Advisers Act of 1940 (15 U.S.C. Section 80b–3a) and is

(i) an "investment adviser representative" as that term is defined by rule adopted under Section 203A of the Investment Advisers Act of 1940 (15 U.S.C. Section 80b–3a); or

(ii) not a "supervised person" as that term is defined in Section 202(a)(25) of the Investment Advisers Act of 1940 (15 U.S.C. Section 80b–2(a)(25)); or

(D) is excluded by rule adopted or order issued under this [Act].

(17) "Issuer" means a person that issues or proposes to issue a security, subject to the following:

(A) The issuer of a voting trust certificate, collateral trust certificate, certificate of deposit for a security, or share in an investment company without a board of directors or individuals performing similar functions is the person performing the acts and assuming the duties of depositor or manager pursuant to the trust or other agreement or instrument under which the security is issued.

(B) The issuer of an equipment trust certificate or similar security serving the same purpose is the person by which the property is or will be used or to which the property or equipment is or will be leased or conditionally sold or that is otherwise contractually responsible for assuring payment of the certificate.

(C) The issuer of a fractional undivided interest in an oil, gas, or other mineral lease or in payments out of production under a lease, right, or royalty is the owner of an interest in the lease or in payments out of production under a lease, right, or royalty, whether whole or fractional, that creates fractional interests for the purpose of sale.

(18) "Nonissuer transaction" or "nonissuer distribution" means a transaction or distribution not directly or indirectly for the benefit of the issuer.

(19) "Offer to purchase" includes an attempt or offer to obtain, or solicitation of an offer to sell, a security or interest in a security for value. The term does not include a tender offer that is subject to Section 14(d) of the Securities Exchange Act of 1934 (15 U.S.C. 78n(d)).

(20) "Person" means an individual; corporation; business trust; estate; trust; partnership; limited liability company; association; joint venture; government; governmental subdivision, agency, or instrumentality; public corporation; or any other legal or commercial entity.

(21) "Place of business" of a broker-dealer, an investment adviser, or a federal covered investment adviser means:

(A) an office at which the broker-dealer, investment adviser, or federal covered investment adviser regularly provides brokerage or investment advice or solicits, meets with, or otherwise communicates with customers or clients; or

(B) any other location that is held out to the general public as a location at which the broker-dealer, investment adviser, or federal covered investment adviser provides brokerage or investment advice or solicits, meets with, or otherwise communicates with customers or clients.

(22) "Predecessor act" means the act repealed by Section 702.

(23) "Price amendment" means the amendment to a registration statement filed under the Securities Act of 1933 or, if an amendment is not filed, the prospectus or prospectus supplement filed under the Securities Act of 1933 that includes a statement of the offering price, underwriting and selling discounts or commissions, amount of proceeds, conversion rates, call prices, and other matters dependent upon the offering price.

(24) "Principal place of business" of a broker-dealer or an investment adviser means the executive office of the broker-dealer or investment adviser from which the officers, partners, or managers of the broker-dealer or investment adviser direct, control, and coordinate

the activities of the broker-dealer or investment adviser.

(25) "Record," except in the phrases "of record," "official record," and "public record," means information that is inscribed on a tangible medium or that is stored in an electronic or other medium and is retrievable in perceivable form.

(26) "Sale" includes every contract of sale, contract to sell, or disposition of, a security or interest in a security for value, and "offer to sell" includes every attempt or offer to dispose of, or solicitation of an offer to purchase, a security or interest in a security for value. Both terms include:

(A) a security given or delivered with, or as a bonus on account of, a purchase of securities or any other thing constituting part of the subject of the purchase and having been offered and sold for value;

(B) a gift of assessable stock involving an offer and sale; and

(C) a sale or offer of a warrant or right to purchase or subscribe to another security of the same or another issuer and a sale or offer of a security that gives the holder a present or future right or privilege to convert the security into another security of the same or another issuer, including an offer of the other security.

(27) "Securities and Exchange Commission" means the United States Securities and Exchange Commission.

(28) "Security" means a note; stock; treasury stock; security future; bond; debenture; evidence of indebtedness; certificate of interest or participation in a profit-sharing agreement; collateral trust certificate; preorganization certificate or subscription; transferable share; investment contract; voting trust certificate; certificate of deposit for a security; fractional undivided interest in oil, gas, or other mineral rights; put, call, straddle, option, or privilege on a security, certificate of deposit, or group or index of securities, including an interest therein or based on the value thereof; put, call, straddle, option, or privilege entered into on a national securities exchange relating to foreign currency; or, in general, an interest or instrument commonly known as a "security"; or a certificate of interest or participation in, temporary or interim certificate for, receipt for, guarantee of, or warrant or right to subscribe to or purchase, any of the foregoing. The term:

(A) includes both a certificated and an uncertificated security;

(B) does not include an insurance or endowment policy or annuity contract under which an insurance company promises to pay a fixed [or variable] sum of money either in a lump sum or periodically for life or other specified period;

(C) does not include an interest in a contributory or noncontributory pension or welfare plan subject to the Employee Retirement Income Security Act of 1974;

(D) includes as an "investment contract" an investment in a common enterprise with the expectation of profits to be derived primarily from the efforts of a person other than the investor and a "common enterprise" means an enterprise in which the fortunes of the investor are interwoven with those of either the person offering the investment, a third party, or other investors; and

(E) includes as an "investment contract," among other contracts, an interest in a limited partnership and a limited liability company and an investment in a viatical settlement or similar agreement.

(29) "Self-regulatory organization" means a national securities exchange registered under the Securities Exchange Act of 1934, a national securities association of broker-dealers registered under the Securities Exchange Act of 1934, a clearing agency registered under the Securities Exchange Act of 1934, or the Municipal Securities Rulemaking Board established under the Securities Exchange Act of 1934.

(30) "Sign" means, with present intent to authenticate or adopt a record:

(A) to execute or adopt a tangible symbol; or

(B) to attach or logically associate with the record an electronic symbol, sound, or process.

(31) "State" means a State of the United States, the District of Columbia, Puerto Rico, the United States Virgin Islands, or any territory or insular possession subject to the jurisdiction of the United States.

SECTION 103. REFERENCES TO FEDERAL STATUTES. "Securities Act of 1933" (15 U.S.C. Section 77a et seq.), "Securities Exchange Act of 1934" (15 U.S.C. Section 78a et seq.), "Public Utility Holding Company Act of 1935"(15 U.S.C. Section 79 et seq.), "Investment Company Act of 1940" (15 U.S.C. Section 80a–1 et seq.), "Investment Advisers Act of 1940" (15 U.S.C. Section 80b–1 et seq.), "Employee Retirement Income Security Act of 1974" (29 U.S.C. Section 1001 et seq.), "National Housing Act" (12 U.S.C. Section 1701 et seq.), "Commodity Exchange Act" (7 U.S.C. Section 1 et seq.), "Internal Revenue Code" (26 U.S.C. Section 1 et seq.), "Securities Investor Protection Act of 1970" (15 U.S.C. Section 78aaa et seq.), "Securities Litigation Uniform Standards Act of 1998" (112 Stat. 3227), "Small Business Investment Act of 1958" (15 U.S.C. Section 661 et seq.), and "Electronic Signatures in Global and National Commerce Act" (15 U.S.C. Section 7001 et seq.) mean those statutes and the rules and regulations adopted under those statutes, as in effect on the date of enactment of this [Act] [, or as later amended].

SECTION 104. REFERENCES TO FEDERAL AGENCIES. A reference in this [Act] to an agency or department of the United States is also a reference to a successor agency or department.

SECTION 105. ELECTRONIC RECORDS AND SIGNATURES. This [Act] modifies, limits, and supersedes the federal Electronic Signatures in Global and National Commerce Act, but does not modify, limit, or supersede Section 101(c) of that act (15 U.S.C. Section 7001(c)) or authorize electronic delivery of any of the notices described in Section 103(b) of that act (15 U.S.C. Section 7003(b)). This [Act] authorizes the filing of records and signatures, when specified by provisions of this [Act] or by a rule adopted or order issued under this [Act], in a manner consistent with Section 104(a) of that act (15 U.S.C. Section 7004(a)).

[ARTICLE] 2

EXEMPTIONS FROM REGISTRATION OF SECURITIES

SECTION 201. EXEMPT SECURITIES. The following securities are exempt from the requirements of Sections 301 through 306 and 504:

(1) a security, including a revenue obligation or a separate security as defined in Rule 131 (17 C.F.R. 230.131) adopted under the Securities Act of 1933, issued, insured, or guaranteed by the United States; by a State; by a political subdivision of a State; by a public authority, agency, or instrumentality of one or more States; by a political subdivision of one or more States; or by a person controlled or supervised by and acting as an instrumentality of the United States under authority granted by the Congress; or a certificate of deposit for any of the foregoing;

(2) a security issued, insured, or guaranteed by a foreign government with which the United States maintains diplomatic relations, or any of its political subdivisions, if the security is recognized as a valid obligation by the issuer, insurer, or guarantor;

(3) a security issued by and representing or that will represent an interest in or a direct obligation of, or be guaranteed by:

(A) an international banking institution;

(B) a banking institution organized under the laws of the United States; a member bank of the Federal Reserve System; or a depository institution a substantial portion of the business of which consists or will consist of receiving deposits or share accounts that are insured to the maximum amount authorized by statute by the Federal Deposit Insurance Corporation, the National Credit Union Share Insurance Fund, or a successor authorized by federal law or exercising fiduciary powers that are similar to those permitted for national banks under the authority of the Comptroller of Currency pursuant to Section 1 of Public Law 87–722 (12 U.S.C. Section 92a); or

(C) any other depository institution, unless by rule or order the administrator proceeds under Section 204;

(4) a security issued by and representing an interest in, or a debt of, or insured or guaranteed by, an insurance company authorized to do business in this State;

(5) a security issued or guaranteed by a railroad, other common carrier, public utility, or public utility holding company that is:

(A) regulated in respect to its rates and charges by the United States or a State;

(B) regulated in respect to the issuance or guarantee of the security by the United States, a State, Canada, or a Canadian province or territory; or

(C) a public utility holding company registered under the Public Utility Holding Company Act of 1935 or a subsidiary of such a registered holding company within the meaning of that act;

(6) a federal covered security specified in Section 18(b)(1) of the Securities Act of 1933 (15 U.S.C. Section 77r(b)(1)) or by rule adopted under that provision or a security listed or approved for listing on another securities market specified by rule under this [Act]; a put or a call option contract; a warrant; a subscription right on or with respect to such securities; or an option or similar derivative security on a security or an index of securities or foreign currencies issued by a clearing agency registered under the Securities Exchange Act of 1934 and listed or designated for trading on a national securities exchange, a facility of a national securities exchange, or a facility of a national securities association registered under the Securities Exchange Act of 1934 or an offer or sale, of the underlying security in connection with the offer, sale, or exercise of an option or other security that was exempt when the option or other security was written or issued; or an option or a derivative security designated by the Securities and Exchange Commission under Section 9(b) of the Securities Exchange Act of 1934 (15 U.S.C. Section 78i(b));

(7) a security issued by a person organized and operated exclusively for religious, educational, benevolent, fraternal, charitable, social, athletic, or reformatory purposes, or as a chamber of commerce, and not for pecuniary profit, no part of the net earnings of which inures to the benefit of a private stockholder or other person, or a security of a company that is excluded from the definition of an investment company under Section 3(c)(10)(B) of the Investment Company Act of 1940 (15 U.S.C. Section 80a–3(c)(10)(B)); except that with respect to the offer or sale of a note, bond, debenture, or other evidence of indebtedness issued by such a person, a rule may be adopted under this [Act] limiting the availability of this exemption by classifying securities, persons, and transactions, imposing different requirements for different classes, specifying with respect to paragraph (B) the scope of the exemption and the grounds for denial or suspension, and requiring an issuer:

(A) to file a notice specifying the material terms of the proposed offer or sale and copies of any proposed sales and advertising literature to be used and provide that the exemption becomes effective if the administrator does not disallow the exemption within the period established by the rule;

(B) to file a request for exemption authorization for which a rule under this [Act] may specify the scope of the exemption, the requirement of an offering statement, the filing of sales and advertising literature, the filing of consent to service of process complying with Section 611, and grounds for denial or suspension of the exemption; or

(C) to register under Section 304;

(8) a member's or owner's interest in, or a retention certificate or like security given in lieu of a cash patronage dividend issued by, a cooperative organized and operated as a nonprofit membership cooperative under the cooperative laws of a State, but not a member's or owner's interest, retention certificate, or like security sold to persons other than bona fide members of the cooperative; and

(9) an equipment trust certificate with respect to equipment leased or conditionally sold to a person, if any security issued by the person would be exempt under this section or would be a federal covered security under Section 18(b)(1) of the Securities Act of 1933 (15 U.S.C. Section 77r(b)(1)).

SECTION 202. EXEMPT TRANSACTIONS. The following transactions are exempt from the requirements of Sections 301 through 306 and 504:

(1) an isolated nonissuer transaction, whether effected by or through a broker-dealer or not;

(2) a nonissuer transaction by or through a broker-dealer registered, or exempt from registration under this [Act], and a resale transaction by a sponsor of a unit investment trust registered under the Investment Company Act of 1940, in a security of a class that has been outstanding in the hands of the public for at least 90 days, if, at the date of the transaction:

(A) the issuer of the security is engaged in business, the issuer is not in the organizational stage or in bankruptcy or receivership, and the issuer is not a blank check, blind pool, or shell company that has no specific business plan or purpose or has indicated that its primary business plan is to engage in a merger or combination of the business with, or an acquisition of, an unidentified person;

(B) the security is sold at a price reasonably related to its current market price;

(C) the security does not constitute the whole or part of an unsold allotment to, or a subscription or participation by, the broker-dealer as an underwriter of the security or a redistribution; and

(D) a nationally recognized securities manual or its electronic equivalent designated by rule adopted or order issued under this [Act] or a record filed with the Securities and Exchange Commission that is publicly available contains:

(i) a description of the business and operations of the issuer;

(ii) the names of the issuer's executive officers and the names of the issuer's directors, if any;

(iii) an audited balance sheet of the issuer as of a date within 18 months before the date of the transaction or, in the case of a reorganization or merger when the parties to the reorganization or merger each had an audited balance sheet, a pro forma balance sheet for the combined organization; and

(iv) an audited income statement for each of the issuer's two immediately previous fiscal years or for the period of existence of the issuer, whichever is shorter, or, in the case of a reorganization or merger when each party to the reorganization or merger had audited income statements, a pro forma income statement; or

(E) the issuer of the security has a class of equity securities listed on a national securities exchange registered under the Securities Exchange Act of 1934 or designated for trading on the National Association of Securities Dealers Automated Quotation System, unless the issuer of the security is a unit investment trust registered under the Investment Company Act of 1940; or the issuer of the security, including its predecessors, has been engaged in continuous business for at least three years; or the issuer of the security has total assets of at least $2,000,000 based on an audited balance sheet as of a date within 18 months before the date of the transaction or, in the case of a reorganization or merger when the parties to the reorganization or merger each had the audited balance sheet, a pro forma balance sheet for the combined organization;

(3) a nonissuer transaction by or through a broker-dealer registered or exempt from registration under this [Act] in a security of a foreign issuer that is a margin security defined in regulations or rules adopted by the Board of Governors of the Federal Reserve System;

(4) a nonissuer transaction by or through a broker-dealer registered or exempt from registration under this [Act] in an outstanding security if the guarantor of the security files reports with the Securities and Exchange Commission under the reporting requirements of Section 13 or 15(d) of the Securities Exchange Act of 1934 (15 U.S.C. 78m or 78o(d));

(5) a nonissuer transaction by or through a broker-dealer registered or exempt from registration under this [Act] in a security that:

(A) is rated at the time of the transaction by a nationally recognized statistical rating organization in one of its four highest rating categories; or

(B) has a fixed maturity or a fixed interest or dividend, if:

(i) a default has not occurred during the current fiscal year or within the three previous fiscal years or during the existence of the issuer and any predecessor if less than three fiscal years, in the payment of principal, interest, or dividends on the security; and

(ii) the issuer is engaged in business, is not in the organizational stage or in bankruptcy or receivership, and is not and has not been within the previous 12 months a blank check, blind pool, or shell company that has no specific business plan or purpose or has indicated that its primary business plan is to engage in a merger or combination of the business with, or an acquisition of, an unidentified person;

(6) a nonissuer transaction by or through a broker-dealer registered or exempt from registration under this [Act] effecting an unsolicited order or offer to purchase;

(7) a nonissuer transaction executed by a bona fide pledgee without the purpose of evading this [Act];

(8) a nonissuer transaction by a federal covered investment adviser with investments under management in excess of $100,000,000 acting in the exercise of discretionary authority in a signed record for the account of others;

(9) a transaction in a security, whether or not the security or transaction is otherwise exempt, in exchange for one or more bona fide outstanding securities, claims, or property interests, or partly in such exchange and partly for cash, if the terms and conditions of the issuance and exchange or the delivery and exchange and the fairness of the terms and conditions have been approved by the administrator after a hearing;

(10) a transaction between the issuer or other person on whose behalf the offering is made and an underwriter, or among underwriters;

(11) a transaction in a note, bond, debenture, or other evidence of indebtedness secured by a mortgage or other security agreement if:

(A) the note, bond, debenture, or other evidence of indebtedness is offered and sold with the mortgage or other security agreement as a unit;

(B) a general solicitation or general advertisement of the transaction is not made; and

(C) a commission or other remuneration is not paid or given, directly or indirectly, to a person not registered under this [Act] as a broker-dealer or as an agent;

(12) a transaction by an executor, administrator of an estate, sheriff, marshal, receiver, trustee in bankruptcy, guardian, or conservator;

(13) a sale or offer to sell to:

(A) an institutional investor;

(B) a federal covered investment adviser; or

(C) any other person exempted by rule adopted or order issued under this [Act];

(14) a sale or an offer to sell securities by an issuer, if the transaction is part of a single issue in which:

(A) not more than 25 purchasers are present in this State during any 12 consecutive months, other than those designated in paragraph (13);

(B) a general solicitation or general advertising is not made in connection with the offer to sell or sale of the securities;

(C) a commission or other remuneration is not paid or given, directly or indirectly, to a person other than a broker-dealer registered under this [Act] or an agent registered under this [Act] for soliciting a prospective purchaser in this State; and

(D) the issuer reasonably believes that all the purchasers in this State, other than those designated in paragraph (13), are purchasing for investment;

(15) a transaction under an offer to existing security holders of the issuer, including persons that at the date of the transaction are holders of convertible securities, options, or warrants, if a commission or other remuneration, other than a standby commission, is not paid or given, directly or indirectly, for soliciting a security holder in this State;

(16) an offer to sell, but not a sale, of a security not exempt from registration under the Securities Act of 1933 if:

(A) a registration or offering statement or similar record as required under the Securities Act of 1933 has been filed, but is not effective, or the offer is made in compliance with Rule 165 adopted under the Securities Act of 1933 (17 C.F.R. 230.165); and

(B) a stop order of which the offeror is aware has not been issued against the offeror or by the administrator or the Securities and Exchange Commission, and an audit, inspection, or proceeding that is public and that may culminate in a stop order is not known by the offeror to be pending;

(17) an offer to sell, but not a sale, of a security exempt from registration under the Securities Act of 1933 if:

(A) a registration statement has been filed under this [Act], but is not effective;

(B) a solicitation of interest is provided in a record to offerees in compliance with a rule adopted by the administrator under this [Act]; and

(C) a stop order of which the offeror is aware has not been issued by the administrator under this [Act] and an audit, inspection, or proceeding that may culminate in a stop order is not known by the offeror to be pending;

(18) a transaction involving the distribution of the securities of an issuer to the security holders of another person in connection with a merger, consolidation, exchange of securities, sale of assets, or other reorganization to which the issuer, or its parent or subsidiary and the other person, or its parent or subsidiary, are parties;

(19) a rescission offer, sale, or purchase under Section 510;

(20) an offer or sale of a security to a person not a resident of this State and not present in this State if the offer or sale does not constitute a violation of the laws of the State or foreign jurisdiction in which the offeree or purchaser is present and is not part of an unlawful plan or scheme to evade this [Act];

(21) employees' stock purchase, savings, option, profit-sharing, pension, or similar employees' benefit plan, including any securities, plan interests, and guarantees issued under a compensatory benefit plan or compensation contract, contained in a record, established by the issuer, its parents, its majority-owned subsidiaries, or the majority-owned subsidiaries of

the issuer's parent for the participation of their employees including offers or sales of such securities to:

(A) directors; general partners; trustees, if the issuer is a business trust; officers; consultants; and advisors;

(B) family members who acquire such securities from those persons through gifts or domestic relations orders;

(C) former employees, directors, general partners, trustees, officers, consultants, and advisors if those individuals were employed by or providing services to the issuer when the securities were offered; and

(D) insurance agents who are exclusive insurance agents of the issuer, or the issuer's subsidiaries or parents, or who derive more than 50 percent of their annual income from those organizations;

(22) a transaction involving:

(A) a stock dividend or equivalent equity distribution, whether the corporation or other business organization distributing the dividend or equivalent equity distribution is the issuer or not, if nothing of value is given by stockholders or other equity holders for the dividend or equivalent equity distribution other than the surrender of a right to a cash or property dividend if each stockholder or other equity holder may elect to take the dividend or equivalent equity distribution in cash, property, or stock;

(B) an act incident to a judicially approved reorganization in which a security is issued in exchange for one or more outstanding securities, claims, or property interests, or partly in such exchange and partly for cash; or

(C) the solicitation of tenders of securities by an offeror in a tender offer in compliance with Rule 162 adopted under the Securities Act of 1933 (17 C.F.R. 230.162); or

(23) a nonissuer transaction in an outstanding security by or through a broker-dealer registered or exempt from registration under this [Act], if the issuer is a reporting issuer in a foreign jurisdiction designated by this paragraph or by rule adopted or order issued under this [Act]; has been subject to continuous reporting requirements in the foreign jurisdiction for not less than 180 days before the transaction; and the security is listed on the foreign jurisdiction's securities exchange that has been designated by this paragraph or by rule adopted or order issued under this [Act], or is a security of the same issuer that is of senior or substantially equal rank to the listed security or is a warrant or right to purchase or subscribe to any of the foregoing. For purposes of this paragraph, Canada, together with its provinces and territories, is a designated foreign jurisdiction and The Toronto Stock Exchange, Inc., is a designated securities exchange. After an administrative hearing in compliance with [the state administrative procedure act], the administrator, by rule adopted or order issued under this [Act], may revoke the designation of a securities exchange under this paragraph, if the administrator finds that revocation is necessary or appropriate in the public interest and for the protection of investors.

SECTION 203. ADDITIONAL EXEMPTIONS AND WAIVERS. A rule adopted or order issued under this [Act] may exempt a security, transaction, or offer; a rule under this [Act] may exempt a class of securities, transactions, or offers from any or all of the requirements of Sections 301 through 306 and 504; and an order under this [Act] may waive, in whole or in part, any or all of the conditions for an exemption or offer under Sections 201 and 202.

SECTION 204. DENIAL, SUSPENSION, REVOCATION, CONDITION, OR LIMITATION OF EXEMPTIONS.

(a) [**Enforcement related powers.**] Except with respect to a federal covered security or a transaction involving a federal covered security, an order under this [Act] may deny, suspend application of, condition, limit, or revoke an exemption created under Section 201(3)(C), (7) or (8) or 202 or an exemption or waiver created under Section 203 with respect to a specific security, transaction, or offer. An order under this section may be issued only pursuant to the procedures in Section 306(d) or 604 and only prospectively.

(b) [**Knowledge of order required.**] A person does not violate Section 301, 303 through 306, 504, or 510 by an offer to sell, offer to purchase, sale, or purchase effected after the entry of an order issued under this section if the person did not know, and in the exercise of reasonable care could not have known, of the order.

[ARTICLE] 3
REGISTRATION OF SECURITIES AND NOTICE FILING OF FEDERAL COVERED SECURITIES

SECTION 301. SECURITIES REGISTRATION REQUIREMENT. It is unlawful for a person to offer or sell a security in this State unless:

(1) the security is a federal covered security;

(2) the security, transaction, or offer is exempted from registration under Sections 201 through 203; or

(3) the security is registered under this [Act].

SECTION 302. NOTICE FILING.

(a) [**Required filing of records.**] With respect to a federal covered security, as defined in Section 18(b)(2) of the Securities Act of 1933 (15 U.S.C. Section 77r(b)(2)), that is not otherwise exempt under Sections 201 through 203, a rule adopted or order issued under this [Act] may require the filing of any or all of the following records:

(1) before the initial offer of a federal covered security in this State, all records that are part of a federal registration statement filed with the Securities and Exchange Commission under the Securities Act of 1933 and a consent to service of process complying with Section 611 signed by the issuer and the payment of a fee of $[____];

(2) after the initial offer of the federal covered security in this State, all records that are part of an amendment to a federal registration statement filed with the Securities and Exchange Commission under the Securities Act of 1933; and

(3) to the extent necessary or appropriate to compute fees, a report of the value of the federal covered securities sold or offered to persons present in this State, if the sales data are not included in records filed with the Securities and Exchange Commission and payment of a fee of $[____].

(b) [**Notice filing effectiveness and renewal.**] A notice filing under subsection (a) is effective for one year commencing on the later of the notice filing or the effectiveness of the offering filed with the Securities and Exchange Commission. On or before expiration, the issuer may renew a notice filing by filing a copy of those records filed by the issuer with the Securities and Exchange Commission that are required by rule or order under this [Act] to be filed and by paying a renewal fee of $[____]. A previously filed consent to service of process complying with Section 611 may be incorporated by reference in a renewal. A renewed notice filing becomes effective upon the expiration of the filing being renewed.

(c) [**Notice filings for federal covered securities under Section 18(b)(4)(D).**] With respect to a security that is a federal covered security under Section 18(b)(4)(D) of the Securities Act of 1933(15 U.S.C. Section 77r(b)(4)(D)), a rule under this [Act] may require a notice filing by or on behalf of an issuer to include a copy of Form D, including the Appendix, as promulgated by the Securities and Exchange Commission, and a consent to service of process complying with Section 611 signed by the issuer not later than 15 days after the first sale of the federal covered security in this State and the payment of a fee of $[____]; and the payment of a fee of $[____] for any late filing.

(d) [**Stop orders.**] Except with respect to a federal security under Section 181(b)(1) of the

Securities Act of 1933 (15 U.S.C. Section 77r(b)(1)), if the administrator finds that there is a failure to comply with a notice or fee requirement of this section, the administrator may issue a stop order suspending the offer and sale of a federal covered security in this State. If the deficiency is corrected, the stop order is void as of the time of its issuance and no penalty may be imposed by the administrator.

SECTION 303. SECURITIES REGISTRATION BY COORDINATION.

(a) [**Registration permitted.**] A security for which a registration statement has been filed under the Securities Act of 1933 in connection with the same offering may be registered by coordination under this section.

(b) [**Required records.**] A registration statement and accompanying records under this section must contain or be accompanied by the following records in addition to the information specified in Section 305 and a consent to service of process complying with Section 611:

(1) a copy of the latest form of prospectus filed under the Securities Act of 1933;

(2) a copy of the articles of incorporation and bylaws or their substantial equivalents currently in effect; a copy of any agreement with or among underwriters; a copy of any indenture or other instrument governing the issuance of the security to be registered; and a specimen, copy, or description of the security that is required by rule adopted or order issued under this [Act];

(3) copies of any other information or any other records filed by the issuer under the Securities Act of 1933 requested by the administrator; and

(4) an undertaking to forward each amendment to the federal prospectus, other than an amendment that delays the effective date of the registration statement, promptly after it is filed with the Securities and Exchange Commission.

(c) [**Conditions for effectiveness of registration statement.**] A registration statement under this section becomes effective simultaneously with or subsequent to the federal registration statement when all the following conditions are satisfied:

(1) a stop order under subsection (d) or Section 306 or issued by the Securities and Exchange Commission is not in effect and a proceeding is not pending against the issuer under Section 306; and

(2) the registration statement has been on file for at least 20 days or a shorter period provided by rule adopted or order issued under this [Act].

(d) [**Notice of federal registration statement effectiveness.**] The registrant shall promptly notify the administrator in a record of the date when the federal registration statement becomes effective and the content of any price amendment and shall promptly file a record containing the price amendment. If the notice is not timely received, the administrator may issue a stop order, without prior notice or hearing, retroactively denying effectiveness to the registration statement or suspending its effectiveness until compliance with this section. The administrator shall promptly notify the registrant of an order by telegram, telephone, or electronic means and promptly confirm this notice by a record. If the registrant subsequently complies with the notice requirements of this section, the stop order is void as of the date of its issuance.

(e) [**Effectiveness of registration statement.**] If the federal registration statement becomes effective before each of the conditions in this section is satisfied or is waived by the administrator, the registration statement is automatically effective under this [Act] when all the conditions are satisfied or waived. If the registrant notifies the administrator of the date when the federal registration statement is expected to become effective, the administrator shall promptly notify the registrant by telegram, telephone, or electronic means and promptly confirm this notice by a record, indicating whether all the conditions are satisfied or waived and whether the administrator intends the institution of a proceeding under Section 306. The notice by the administrator does not preclude the institution of such a proceeding.

SECTION 304. SECURITIES REGISTRATION BY QUALIFICATION.

(a) [**Registration permitted.**] A security may be registered by qualification under this section.

(b) [**Required records.**] A registration statement under this section must contain the information or records specified in Section 305, a consent to service of process complying with Section 611, and, if required by rule adopted under this [Act], the following information or records:

(1) with respect to the issuer and any significant subsidiary, its name, address, and form of organization; the State or foreign jurisdiction and date of its organization; the general character and location of its business; a description of its physical properties and equipment; and a statement of the general competitive conditions in the industry or business in which it is or will be engaged;

(2) with respect to each director and officer of the issuer, and other person having a similar status or performing similar functions, the person's name, address, and principal occupation for the previous five years; the amount of securities of the issuer held by the person as of the 30th day before the filing of the registration statement; the amount of the securities covered by the registration statement to which the person has indicated an intention to subscribe; and a description of any material interest of the person in any material transaction with the issuer or a significant subsidiary effected within the previous three years or proposed to be effected;

(3) with respect to persons covered by paragraph (2), the aggregate sum of the remuneration paid to those persons during the previous 12 months and estimated to be paid during the next 12 months, directly or indirectly, by the issuer, and all predecessors, parents, subsidiaries, and affiliates of the issuer;

(4) with respect to a person owning of record or owning beneficially, if known, 10 percent or more of the outstanding shares of any class of equity security of the issuer, the information specified in paragraph (2) other than the person's occupation;

(5) with respect to a promoter, if the issuer was organized within the previous three years, the information or records specified in paragraph (2), any amount paid to the promoter within that period or intended to be paid to the promoter, and the consideration for the payment;

(6) with respect to a person on whose behalf any part of the offering is to be made in a nonissuer distribution, the person's name and address; the amount of securities of the issuer held by the person as of the date of the filing of the registration statement; a description of any material interest of the person in any material transaction with the issuer or any significant subsidiary effected within the previous three years or proposed to be effected; and a statement of the reasons for making the offering;

(7) the capitalization and long term debt, on both a current and pro forma basis, of the issuer and any significant subsidiary, including a description of each security outstanding or being registered or otherwise offered, and a statement of the amount and kind of consideration, whether in the form of cash, physical assets, services, patents, goodwill, or anything else of value, for which the issuer or any subsidiary has issued its securities within the previous two years or is obligated to issue its securities;

(8) the kind and amount of securities to be offered; the proposed offering price or the method by which it is to be computed; any variation at which a proportion of the offering is to be made to a person or class of

persons other than the underwriters, with a specification of the person or class; the basis on which the offering is to be made if otherwise than for cash; the estimated aggregate underwriting and selling discounts or commissions and finders' fees, including separately cash, securities, contracts, or anything else of value to accrue to the underwriters or finders in connection with the offering or, if the selling discounts or commissions are variable, the basis of determining them and their maximum and minimum amounts; the estimated amounts of other selling expenses, including legal, engineering, and accounting charges; the name and address of each underwriter and each recipient of a finder's fee; a copy of any underwriting or selling group agreement under which the distribution is to be made or the proposed form of any such agreement whose terms have not yet been determined; and a description of the plan of distribution of any securities that are to be offered otherwise than through an underwriter;

(9) the estimated monetary proceeds to be received by the issuer from the offering; the purposes for which the proceeds are to be used by the issuer; the estimated amount to be used for each purpose; the order or priority in which the proceeds will be used for the purposes stated; the amounts of any funds to be raised from other sources to achieve the purposes stated; the sources of the funds; and, if a part of the proceeds is to be used to acquire property, including goodwill, otherwise than in the ordinary course of business, the names and addresses of the vendors, the purchase price, the names of any persons that have received commissions in connection with the acquisition, and the amounts of the commissions and other expenses in connection with the acquisition, including the cost of borrowing money to finance the acquisition;

(10) a description of any stock options or other security options outstanding, or to be created in connection with the offering, and the amount of those options held or to be held by each person required to be named in paragraph (2), (4), (5), (6), or (8) and by any person that holds or will hold 10 percent or more in the aggregate of those options;

(11) the dates of, parties to, and general effect concisely stated of each managerial or other material contract made or to be made otherwise than in the ordinary course of business to be performed in whole or in part at or after the filing of the registration statement or that was made within the previous two years, and a copy of the contract;

(12) a description of any pending litigation, action, or proceeding to which the issuer is a party and that materially affects its business or assets, and any litigation, action, or proceeding known to be contemplated by governmental authorities;

(13) a copy of any prospectus, pamphlet, circular, form letter, advertisement, or other sales literature intended as of the effective date to be used in connection with the offering and any solicitation of interest used in compliance with Section 202(17)(B);

(14) a specimen or copy of the security being registered, unless the security is uncertificated; a copy of the issuer's articles of incorporation and bylaws or their substantial equivalents, in effect; and a copy of any indenture or other instrument covering the security to be registered;

(15) a signed or conformed copy of an opinion of counsel concerning the legality of the security being registered, with an English translation if it is in a language other than English, which states whether the security when sold will be validly issued, fully paid, and nonassessable and, if a debt security, a binding obligation of the issuer;

(16) a signed or conformed copy of a consent of any accountant, engineer, appraiser, or other person whose profession gives authority for a statement made by the person, if the person is named as having prepared or certified a report or valuation, other than an official record, that is public, which is used

in connection with the registration statement;

(17) a balance sheet of the issuer as of a date within four months before the filing of the registration statement; a statement of income and a statement of cash flows for each of the three fiscal years preceding the date of the balance sheet and for any period between the close of the immediately previous fiscal year and the date of the balance sheet, or for the period of the issuer's and any predecessor's existence if less than three years; and, if any part of the proceeds of the offering is to be applied to the purchase of a business, the financial statements that would be required if that business were the registrant; and

(18) any additional information or records required by rule adopted or order issued under this [Act].

(c) [**Conditions for effectiveness of registration statement.**] A registration statement under this section becomes effective 30 days, or any shorter period provided by rule adopted or order issued under this [Act], after the date the registration statement or the last amendment other than a price amendment is filed, if:

(1) a stop order is not in effect and a proceeding is not pending under Section 306;

(2) the administrator has not issued an order under Section 306 delaying effectiveness; and

(3) the applicant or registrant has not requested that effectiveness be delayed.

(d) [**Delay of effectiveness of registration statement.**] The administrator may delay effectiveness once for not more than 90 days if the administrator determines the registration statement is not complete in all material respects and promptly notifies the applicant or registrant of that determination. The administrator may also delay effectiveness for a further period of not more than 30 days if the administrator determines that the delay is necessary or appropriate.

(e) [**Prospectus distribution may be required.**] A rule adopted or order issued under this [Act] may require as a condition of registration under this section that a prospectus containing a specified part of the information or record specified in subsection (b) be sent or given to each person to which an offer is made, before or concurrently, with the earliest of:

(1) the first offer made in a record to the person otherwise than by means of a public advertisement, by or for the account of the issuer or another person on whose behalf the offering is being made or by an underwriter or broker-dealer that is offering part of an unsold allotment or subscription taken by the person as a participant in the distribution;

(2) the confirmation of a sale made by or for the account of the person;

(3) payment pursuant to such a sale; or

(4) delivery of the security pursuant to such a sale.

SECTION 305. SECURITIES REGISTRATION FILINGS.

(a) [**Who may file.**] A registration statement may be filed by the issuer, a person on whose behalf the offering is to be made, or a broker-dealer registered under this [Act].

(b) [**Filing fee.**] A person filing a registration statement shall pay a filing fee of $[____]. If a registration statement is withdrawn before the effective date or a pre-effective stop order is issued under Section 306, the administrator shall retain $[____] of the fee.

(c) [**Status of offering.**] A registration statement filed under Section 303 or 304 must specify:

(1) the amount of securities to be offered in this State;

(2) the States in which a registration statement or similar record in connection with the offering has been or is to be filed; and

(3) any adverse order, judgment, or decree issued in connection with the offering by a

State securities regulator, the Securities and Exchange Commission, or a court.

(d) [**Incorporation by reference**.] A record filed under this [Act] or the predecessor act within five years preceding the filing of a registration statement may be incorporated by reference in the registration statement to the extent that the record is currently accurate.

(e) [**Nonissuer distribution**.] In the case of a nonissuer distribution, information or a record may not be required under subsection (i) or Section 304, unless it is known to the person filing the registration statement or to the person on whose behalf the distribution is to be made or unless it can be furnished by those persons without unreasonable effort or expense.

(f) [**Escrow and impoundment**.] A rule adopted or order issued under this [Act] may require as a condition of registration that a security issued within the previous five years or to be issued to a promoter for a consideration substantially less than the public offering price or to a person for a consideration other than cash be deposited in escrow; and that the proceeds from the sale of the registered security in this State be impounded until the issuer receives a specified amount from the sale of the security either in this State or elsewhere. The conditions of any escrow or impoundment required under this subsection may be established by rule adopted or order issued under this [Act], but the administrator may not reject a depository institution solely because of its location in another State.

(g) [**Form of subscription.**] A rule adopted or order issued under this [Act] may require as a condition of registration that a security registered under this [Act] be sold only on a specified form of subscription or sale contract and that a signed or conformed copy of each contract be filed under this [Act] or preserved for a period specified by the rule or order, which may not be longer than five years.

(h) [**Effective period.**] Except while a stop order is in effect under Section 306, a registration statement is effective for one year after its effective date, or for any longer period designated in an order under this [Act] during which the security is being offered or distributed in a nonexempted transaction by or for the account of the issuer or other person on whose behalf the offering is being made or by an underwriter or broker-dealer that is still offering part of an unsold allotment or subscription taken as a participant in the distribution. For the purposes of a nonissuer transaction, all outstanding securities of the same class identified in the registration statement as a security registered under this [Act] are considered to be registered while the registration statement is effective. If any securities of the same class are outstanding, a registration statement may not be withdrawn until one year after its effective date. A registration statement may be withdrawn only with the approval of the administrator.

(i) [**Periodic reports.**] While a registration statement is effective, a rule adopted or order issued under this [Act] may require the person that filed the registration statement to file reports, not more often than quarterly, to keep the information or other record in the registration statement reasonably current and to disclose the progress of the offering.

(j) [**Posteffective amendments**.] A registration statement may be amended after its effective date. The posteffective amendment becomes effective when the administrator so orders. If a posteffective amendment is made to increase the number of securities specified to be offered or sold, the person filing the amendment shall pay a registration fee of $[____]. A posteffective amendment relates back to the date of the offering of the additional securities being registered if, within one year after the date of the sale, the amendment is filed and the additional registration fee is paid.

SECTION 306. DENIAL, SUSPENSION, AND REVOCATION OF SECURITIES REGISTRATION.

(a) [**Stop orders.**] The administrator may issue a stop order denying effectiveness to, or suspending or revoking the effectiveness of, a registration statement if the administrator finds that the order is in the public interest and that:

(1) the registration statement as of its effective date or before the effective date in the case of an order denying effectiveness, an amendment under Section 305(j) as of its effective date, or a report under Section 305(i), is incomplete in a material respect or contains a statement that, in the light of the circumstances under which it was made, was false or misleading with respect to a material fact;

(2) this [Act] or a rule adopted or order issued under this [Act] or a condition imposed under this [Act] has been willfully violated, in connection with the offering, by the person filing the registration statement; by the issuer, a partner, officer, or director of the issuer or a person having a similar status or performing a similar function; a promoter of the issuer; or a person directly or indirectly controlling or controlled by the issuer; but only if the person filing the registration statement is directly or indirectly controlled by or acting for the issuer; or by an underwriter;

(3) the security registered or sought to be registered is the subject of a permanent or temporary injunction of a court of competent jurisdiction or an administrative stop order or similar order issued under any federal, foreign, or state law other than this [Act] applicable to the offering, but the administrator may not institute a proceeding against an effective registration statement under this paragraph more than one year after the date of the order or injunction on which it is based, and the administrator may not issue an order under this paragraph on the basis of an order or injunction issued under the securities act of another State unless the order or injunction was based on conduct that would constitute, as of the date of the order, a ground for a stop order under this section;

(4) the issuer's enterprise or method of business includes or would include activities that are unlawful where performed;

(5) with respect to a security sought to be registered under Section 303, there has been a failure to comply with the undertaking required by Section 303(b)(4);

(6) the applicant or registrant has not paid the filing fee, but the administrator shall void the order if the deficiency is corrected; or

(7) the offering:

(A) will work or tend to work a fraud upon purchasers or would so operate; [or]

(B) has been or would be made with unreasonable amounts of underwriters' and sellers' discounts, commissions, or other compensation, or promoters' profits or participations, or unreasonable amounts or kinds of options[; or

(C) is being made on terms that are unfair, unjust, or inequitable].

(b) [**Enforcement of subsection (a)(7).**] To the extent practicable, the administrator by rule adopted or order issued under this [Act] shall publish standards that provide notice of conduct that violates subsection (a)(7).

(c) [**Institution of stop order.**] The administrator may not institute a stop order proceeding against an effective registration statement on the basis of conduct or a transaction known to the administrator when the registration statement became effective unless the proceeding is instituted within 30 days after the registration statement became effective.

(d) [**Summary process.**] The administrator may summarily revoke, deny, postpone, or suspend the effectiveness of a registration statement pending final determination of an administrative proceeding. Upon the issuance of the order, the administrator shall promptly notify each person specified in subsection (e) that the order has been issued, the reasons for the revocation, denial, postponement, or suspension, and that within 15 days after the receipt of a request in a record from the person the matter will be scheduled for a hearing. If a hearing is not requested and none is ordered by the administrator, within 30 days after the date of service of the order, the order becomes final. If a hearing is requested or ordered, the administrator, after notice of and opportunity for hearing for each person subject to the order, may modify or vacate the order or extend the order until final determination.

(e) [**Procedural requirements for stop order.**] A stop order may not be issued under this section without:

(1) appropriate notice to the applicant or registrant, the issuer, and the person on whose behalf the securities are to be or have been offered;

(2) an opportunity for hearing; and

(3) findings of fact and conclusions of law in a record [in accordance with the state administrative procedure act].

(f) [**Modification or vacation of stop order.**] The administrator may modify or vacate a stop order issued under this section if the administrator finds that the conditions that caused its issuance have changed or that it is necessary or appropriate in the public interest or for the protection of investors.

SECTION 307. WAIVER AND MODIFICATION. The administrator may waive or modify, in whole or in part, any or all of the requirements of Sections 302, 303, and 304(b) or the requirement of any information or record in a registration statement or in a periodic report filed pursuant to Section 305(i).

[ARTICLE] 4
BROKER–DEALERS, AGENTS, INVESTMENT ADVISERS, INVESTMENT ADVISER REPRESENTATIVES, AND FEDERAL COVERED INVESTMENT ADVISERS

SECTION 401. BROKER–DEALER REGISTRATION REQUIREMENT AND EXEMPTIONS.

(a) [**Registration requirement.**] It is unlawful for a person to transact business in this State as a broker-dealer unless the person is registered under this [Act] as a broker-dealer or is exempt from registration as a broker-dealer under subsection (b) or (d).

(b) [**Exemptions from registration.**] The following persons are exempt from the registration requirement of subsection (a):

(1) a broker-dealer without a place of business in this State if its only transactions effected in this State are with:

(A) the issuer of the securities involved in the transactions;

(B) a broker-dealer registered under this [Act] or not required to be registered as a broker-dealer under this [Act];

(C) an institutional investor;

(D) a nonaffiliated federal covered investment adviser with investments under management in excess of $100,000,000 acting for the account of others pursuant to discretionary authority in a signed record;

(E) a bona fide preexisting customer whose principal place of residence is not in this State and the person is registered as a broker-dealer under the Securities Exchange Act of 1934 or not required to be registered under the Securities Exchange Act of 1934 and is registered under the securities act of the State in which the customer maintains a principal place of residence;

(F) a bona fide preexisting customer whose principal place of residence is in this State but was not present in this State when the customer relationship was established, if:

(i) the broker-dealer is registered under the Securities Exchange Act of 1934 or not required to be registered under the Securities Exchange Act of 1934 and is registered under the securities laws of the State in which the customer relationship was established and where the customer had maintained a principal place of residence; and

(ii) within 45 days after the customer's first transaction in this State, the person files an application for registration as a broker-dealer in this State and a further transaction is not effected more than 75 days after the date on which the application is filed, or, if earlier, the date on which the administrator notifies the person that the administrator has denied the application for registration or has stayed the pendency of the application for good cause;

(G) not more than three customers in this State during the previous 12 months, in addition to those customers specified in subparagraphs (A) through (F) and under subparagraph (H), if the broker-dealer is registered under the Securities Exchange Act of 1934 or not required to be registered under the Securities Exchange Act of 1934 and is registered under the securities act of the State in which the broker-dealer has its principal place of business; and

(H) any other person exempted by rule adopted or order issued under this [Act]; and

(2) a person that deals solely in United States government securities and is supervised as a dealer in government securities by the Board of Governors of the Federal Reserve System, the Comptroller of the Currency, the Federal Deposit Insurance Corporation, or the Office of Thrift Supervision.

(c) [**Limits on employment or association.**] It is unlawful for a broker-dealer, or for an issuer engaged in offering, offering to purchase, purchasing, or selling securities in this State, directly or indirectly, to employ or associate with an individual to engage in an activity related to securities transactions in this State if the registration of the individual is suspended or revoked or the individual is barred from employment or association with a broker-dealer, an issuer, an investment adviser, or a federal covered investment adviser by an order of the administrator under this [Act], the Securities and Exchange Commission, or a self-regulatory organization. A broker-dealer or issuer does not violate this subsection if the broker-dealer or issuer did not know and in the exercise of reasonable care could not have known, of the suspension, revocation, or bar. Upon request from a broker-dealer or issuer and for good cause, an order under this [Act] may modify or waive, in whole or in part, the application of the prohibitions of this subsection to the broker-dealer.

(d) [**Foreign transactions.**] A rule adopted or order issued under this [Act] may permit:

(1) a broker-dealer that is registered in Canada or other foreign jurisdiction and that does not have a place of business in this State to effect transactions in securities with or for, or attempt to effect the purchase or sale of any securities by:

(A) an individual from Canada or other foreign jurisdiction who is temporarily present in this State and with whom the broker-dealer had a bona fide customer relationship before the individual entered the United States;

(B) an individual from Canada or other foreign jurisdiction who is present in this State and whose transactions are in a self-directed tax advantaged retirement plan of which the individual is the holder or contributor in that foreign jurisdiction; or

(C) an individual who is present in this State, with whom the broker-dealer customer relationship arose while the individual was temporarily or permanently resident in Canada or the other foreign jurisdiction; and

(2) an agent who represents a broker-dealer that is exempt under this subsection to effect transactions in securities or attempt to effect the purchase or sale of secu-

rities in this State as permitted for a broker-dealer described in paragraph (1).

SECTION 402. AGENT REGISTRATION REQUIREMENT AND EXEMPTIONS.

(a) [**Registration requirement.**] It is unlawful for an individual to transact business in this State as an agent unless the individual is registered under this [Act] as an agent or is exempt from registration as an agent under subsection (b).

(b) [**Exemptions from registration.**] The following individuals are exempt from the registration requirement of subsection (a):

(1) an individual who represents a broker-dealer in effecting transactions in this State limited to those described in Section 15(h)(2) of the Securities Exchange Act of 1934 (15 U.S.C. Section 78(*o*)(2));

(2) an individual who represents a broker-dealer that is exempt under Section 401(b) or (d);

(3) an individual who represents an issuer with respect to an offer or sale of the issuer's own securities or those of the issuer's parent or any of the issuer's subsidiaries, and who is not compensated in connection with the individual's participation by the payment of commissions or other remuneration based, directly or indirectly, on transactions in those securities;

(4) an individual who represents an issuer and who effects transactions in the issuer's securities exempted by Section 202, other than Section 202(11) and (14);

(5) an individual who represents an issuer that effects transactions solely in federal covered securities of the issuer, but an individual who effects transactions in a federal covered security under Section 18(b)(3) or 18(b)(4)(D) of the Securities Act of 1933 (15 U.S.C. Section 77r(b)(3) or 77r(b)(4)(D)) is not exempt if the individual is compensated in connection with the agent's participation by the payment of commissions or other remuneration based, directly or indirectly, on transactions in those securities;

(6) an individual who represents a broker-dealer registered in this State under Section 401(a) or exempt from registration under Section 401(b) in the offer and sale of securities for an account of a nonaffiliated federal covered investment adviser with investments under management in excess of $100,000,000 acting for the account of others pursuant to discretionary authority in a signed record;

(7) an individual who represents an issuer in connection with the purchase of the issuer's own securities;

(8) an individual who represents an issuer and who restricts participation to performing clerical or ministerial acts; or

(9) any other individual exempted by rule adopted or order issued under this [Act].

(c) [**Registration effective only while employed or associated.**] The registration of an agent is effective only while the agent is employed by or associated with a broker-dealer registered under this [Act] or an issuer that is offering, selling, or purchasing its securities in this State.

(d) [**Limit on employment or association.**] It is unlawful for a broker-dealer, or an issuer engaged in offering, selling, or purchasing securities in this State, to employ or associate with an agent who transacts business in this State on behalf of broker-dealers or issuers unless the agent is registered under subsection (a) or exempt from registration under subsection (b).

(e) [**Limit on affiliations.**] An individual may not act as an agent for more than one broker-dealer or one issuer at a time, unless the broker-dealer or the issuer for which the agent acts are affiliated by direct or indirect common control or are authorized by rule or order under this [Act].

SECTION 403. INVESTMENT ADVISER REGISTRATION REQUIREMENT AND EXEMPTIONS.

(a) [**Registration requirement.**] It is unlawful for a person to transact business in this State as an investment adviser unless the person is registered under this [Act] as an investment adviser or is exempt from registration as an investment adviser under subsection (b).

(b) [**Exemptions from registration.**] The following persons are exempt from the registration requirement of subsection (a):

(1) a person without a place of business in this State that is registered under the securities act of the State in which the person has its principal place of business if its only clients in this State are:

(A) federal covered investment advisers, investment advisers registered under this [Act], or broker-dealers registered under this [Act];

(B) institutional investors;

(C) bona fide preexisting clients whose principal places of residence are not in this State if the investment adviser is registered under the securities act of the State in which the clients maintain principal places of residence; or

(D) any other client exempted by rule adopted or order issued under this [Act];

(2) a person without a place of business in this State if the person has had, during the preceding 12 months, not more than five clients that are resident in this State in addition to those specified under paragraph (1); or

(3) any other person exempted by rule adopted or order issued under this [Act].

(c) [**Limits on employment or association.**] It is unlawful for an investment adviser, directly or indirectly, to employ or associate with an individual to engage in an activity related to investment advice in this State if the registration of the individual is suspended or revoked or the individual is barred from employment or association with an investment adviser, federal covered investment adviser, or broker-dealer by an order under this [Act], the Securities and Exchange Commission, or a self-regulatory organization, unless the investment adviser did not know, and in the exercise of reasonable care could not have known, of the suspension, revocation, or bar. Upon request from the investment adviser and for good cause, the administrator, by order, may waive, in whole or in part, the application of the prohibitions of this subsection to the investment adviser.

(d) [**Investment adviser representative registration required.**] It is unlawful for an investment adviser to employ or associate with an individual required to be registered under this [Act] as an investment adviser representative who transacts business in this State on behalf of the investment adviser unless the individual is registered under Section 404(a) or is exempt from registration under Section 404(b).

SECTION 404. INVESTMENT ADVISER REPRESENTATIVE REGISTRATION REQUIREMENT AND EXEMPTIONS.

(a) [**Registration requirement.**] It is unlawful for an individual to transact business in this State as an investment adviser representative unless the individual is registered under this [Act] as an investment adviser representative or is exempt from registration as an investment adviser representative under subsection (b).

(b) [**Exemptions from registration.**] The following individuals are exempt from the registration requirement of subsection (a):

(1) an individual who is employed by or associated with an investment adviser that is exempt from registration under Section 403(b) or a federal covered investment adviser that is excluded from the notice filing requirements of Section 405; and

(2) any other individual exempted by rule adopted or order issued under this [Act].

(c) [**Registration effective only while employed or associated.**] The registration of an investment adviser representative is not effective while the investment adviser representative is not employed by or associated with an investment adviser registered under this [Act] or a federal covered investment adviser that has made or is required to make a notice filing under Section 405.

(d) [**Limit on affiliations.**] An individual may transact business as an investment adviser representative for more than one investment adviser or federal covered investment adviser unless a rule adopted or order issued under this [Act] prohibits or limits an individual from acting as an investment adviser representative for more than one investment adviser or federal covered investment adviser.

(e) [**Limits on employment or association.**] It is unlawful for an individual acting as an investment adviser representative, directly or indirectly, to conduct business in this State on behalf of an investment adviser or a federal covered investment adviser if the registration of the individual as an investment adviser representative is suspended or revoked or the individual is barred from employment or association with an investment adviser or a federal covered investment adviser by an order under this [Act], the Securities and Exchange Commission, or a self-regulatory organization. Upon request from a federal covered investment adviser and for good cause, the administrator, by order issued, may waive, in whole or in part, the application of the requirements of this subsection to the federal covered investment adviser.

(f) [**Referral fees.**] An investment adviser registered under this [Act], a federal covered investment adviser that has filed a notice under Section 405, or a broker-dealer registered under this [Act] is not required to employ or associate with an individual as an investment adviser representative if the only compensation paid to the individual for a referral of investment advisory clients is paid to an investment adviser registered under this [Act], a federal covered investment adviser who has filed a notice under Section 405, or a broker-dealer registered under this [Act] with which the individual is employed or associated as an investment adviser representative.

SECTION 405. FEDERAL COVERED INVESTMENT ADVISER NOTICE FILING REQUIREMENT.

(a) [**Notice filing requirement.**] Except with respect to a federal covered investment adviser described in subsection (b), it is unlawful for a federal covered investment adviser to transact business in this State as a federal covered investment adviser unless the federal covered investment adviser complies with subsection (c).

(b) [**Notice filing requirement not required.**] The following federal covered investment advisers are not required to comply with subsection (c):

(1) a federal covered investment adviser without a place of business in this State if its only clients in this State are:

(A) federal covered investment advisers, investment advisers registered under this [Act], and broker-dealers registered under this [Act];

(B) institutional investors;

(C) bona fide preexisting clients whose principal places of residence are not in this State; or

(D) other clients specified by rule adopted or order issued under this [Act];

(2) a federal covered investment adviser without a place of business in this State if the person has had, during the preceding 12 months, not more than five clients that are resident in this State in addition to those specified under paragraph (1); and

(3) any other person excluded by rule adopted or order issued under this [Act].

(c) [**Notice filing procedure.**] A person acting as a federal covered investment adviser, not excluded under subsection (b), shall file a notice, a consent to service of process complying with Section 611, and such records as have been filed with the Securities and Exchange Commission under the Investment Advisers Act of 1940 required by rule adopted or order issued under this [Act] and pay the fees specified in Section 410(e).

(d) [**Effectiveness of filing.**] The notice under subsection (c) becomes effective upon its filing.

SECTION 406. REGISTRATION BY BROKER–DEALER, AGENT, INVESTMENT ADVISER, AND INVESTMENT ADVISER REPRESENTATIVE.

(a) [**Application for initial registration.**] A person shall register as a broker-dealer, agent, investment adviser, or investment adviser representative by filing an application and a consent to service of process complying with Section 611, and paying the fee specified in Section 410 and any reasonable fees charged by the designee of the administrator for processing the filing. The application must contain:

(1) the information or record required for the filing of a uniform application; and

(2) upon request by the administrator, any other financial or other information or record that the administrator determines is appropriate.

(b) [**Amendment.**] If the information or record contained in an application filed under subsection (a) is or becomes inaccurate or incomplete in a material respect, the registrant shall promptly file a correcting amendment.

(c) [**Effectiveness of registration.**] If an order is not in effect and a proceeding is not pending under Section 412, registration becomes effective at noon on the 45th day after a completed application is filed, unless the registration is denied. A rule adopted or order issued under this [Act] may set an earlier effective date or may defer the effective date until noon on the 45th day after the filing of any amendment completing the application.

(d) [**Registration renewal.**] A registration is effective until midnight on December 31 of the year for which the application for registration is filed. Unless an order is in effect under Section 412, a registration may be automatically renewed each year by filing such records as are required by rule adopted or order issued under this [Act], by paying the fee specified in Section 410, and by paying costs charged by the designee of the administrator for processing the filings.

(e) [**Additional conditions or waivers.**] A rule adopted or order issued under this [Act] may impose such other conditions, not inconsistent with the National Securities Markets Improvement Act of 1996. An order issued under this [Act] may waive, in whole or in part, specific requirements in connection with registration as are in the public interest and for the protection of investors.

SECTION 407. SUCCESSION AND CHANGE IN REGISTRATION OF BROKER–DEALER OR INVESTMENT ADVISER.

(a) [**Succession.**] A broker-dealer or investment adviser may succeed to the current registration of another broker-dealer or investment adviser or a notice filing of a federal covered investment adviser, and a federal covered investment adviser may succeed to the current registration of an investment adviser or notice filing of another federal covered investment adviser, by filing as a successor an application for registration pursuant to Section 401 or 403 or a notice pursuant to Section 405 for the unexpired portion of the current registration or notice filing.

(b) [**Organizational change.**] A broker-dealer or investment adviser that changes its form of organization or State of incorporation or organization may continue its registration by filing an amendment to its registration if the change does not involve a material change in its financial condition or management. The amendment becomes effective when filed or on a date designated by the registrant in its filing. The new organization is a successor to the original registrant for the purposes of this [Act]. If there is a material change in financial condition or management, the broker-dealer or investment adviser shall file a new application for registration. A predecessor registered under this [Act] shall stop conducting its securities business other than winding down transactions and shall file for withdrawal of broker-dealer or investment adviser registration within 45 days after filing its amendment to effect succession.

(c) [**Name change.**] A broker-dealer or investment adviser that changes its name may continue its registration by filing an amendment to its registration. The amendment becomes effective when filed or on a date designated by the registrant.

(d) [**Change of control.**] A change of control of a broker-dealer or investment adviser may be made in accordance with a rule adopted or order issued under this [Act].

SECTION 408. TERMINATION OF EMPLOYMENT OR ASSOCIATION OF AGENT AND INVESTMENT ADVISER REPRESENTATIVE AND TRANSFER OF EMPLOYMENT OR ASSOCIATION.

(a) [**Notice of termination.**] If an agent registered under this [Act] terminates employment by or association with a broker-dealer or issuer, or if an investment adviser representative registered under this [Act] terminates employment by or association with an investment adviser or federal covered investment adviser, or if either registrant terminates activities that require registration as an agent or investment adviser representative, the broker-dealer, issuer, investment adviser, or federal covered investment adviser shall promptly file a notice of termination. If the registrant learns that the broker-dealer, issuer, investment adviser, or federal covered investment adviser has not filed the notice, the registrant may do so.

(b) [**Transfer of employment or association.**] If an agent registered under this [Act] terminates employment by or association with a broker-dealer registered under this [Act] and begins employment by or association with another broker-dealer registered under this [Act]; or if an investment adviser representative registered under this [Act] terminates employment by or association with an investment adviser registered under this [Act] or a federal covered investment adviser that has filed a notice under Section 405 and begins employment by or association with another investment adviser registered under this [Act] or a federal covered investment adviser that has filed a notice under Section 405; then upon the filing by or on behalf of the registrant, within 30 days after the termination, of an application for registration that complies with the requirement of Section 406(a) and payment of the filing fee required under Section 410, the registration of the agent or investment adviser representative is:

(1) immediately effective as of the date of the completed filing, if the agent's Central Registration Depository record or successor record or the investment adviser representative's Investment Adviser Registration Depository record or successor record does not contain a new or amended disciplinary disclosure within the previous 12 months; or

(2) temporarily effective as of the date of the completed filing, if the agent's Central Registration Depository record or successor record or the investment adviser representative's Investment Adviser Registration Depository record or successor record contains a new or amended disciplinary disclosure within the preceding 12 months.

(c) [**Withdrawal of temporary registration.**] The administrator may withdraw a temporary registration if there are or were grounds for discipline as specified in Section 412 and the administrator does so within 30 days after the filing of the application. If the administrator does not withdraw the temporary registration within the 30 day period, registration becomes automatically effective on the 31st day after filing.

(d) [**Power to prevent registration.**] The administrator may prevent the effectiveness of a transfer of an agent or investment adviser representative under subsection (b)(1) or (2) based on the public interest and the protection of investors.

(e) [**Termination of registration or application for registration.**] If the administrator determines that a registrant or applicant for registration is no longer in existence or has ceased to act as a broker-dealer, agent, investment adviser, or investment adviser representative, or is the subject of an adjudication of incapacity or is subject to the control of a committee, conservator, or guardian, or cannot reasonably be located, a rule adopted or order issued under this [Act] may require the registration be canceled or terminated or the application denied. The administrator may reinstate a canceled or terminated registration, with or without hearing, and may make the registration retroactive.

SECTION 409. WITHDRAWAL OF REGISTRATION OF BROKER–DEALER, AGENT, INVESTMENT ADVISER, AND INVESTMENT ADVISER REPRESENTATIVE. Withdrawal of registration by a broker-dealer, agent, investment adviser, or investment adviser representative becomes effective 60 days after the filing of the application to withdraw or within any shorter period as provided by rule adopted or order issued under this [Act] unless a revocation or suspension proceeding is pending when the application is filed. If a proceeding is pending, withdrawal becomes effective when and upon such conditions as required by rule adopted or order issued under this [Act]. The administrator may institute a revocation or suspension proceeding under Section 412 within one year after the withdrawal became effective automatically and issue a revocation or suspension order as of the last date on which registration was effective if a proceeding is not pending.

SECTION 410. FILING FEES.

(a) [**Broker-dealers.**] A person shall pay a fee of $[____] when initially filing an application for registration as a broker-dealer and a fee of $[____] when filing a renewal of registration as a broker-dealer. If the filing results in a denial or withdrawal, the administrator shall retain $[____] of the fee.

(b) [**Agents**.] The fee for an individual is $[____] when filing an application for registration as an agent, a fee of $[____] when filing a renewal of registration as an agent, and a fee of $[____] when filing for a change of registration as an agent. If the filing results in a denial or withdrawal, the administrator shall retain $[____] of the fee.

(c) [**Investment advisers.**] A person shall pay a fee of $[____] when filing an application for registration as an investment adviser and a fee of $[____] when filing a renewal of registration as an investment adviser. If the filing results in a denial or withdrawal, the administrator shall retain $[____] of the fee.

(d) [**Investment adviser representatives.**] The fee for an individual is $[____] when filing an application for registration as an investment adviser representative, a fee of $[____] when filing a renewal of registration as an investment adviser representative, and a fee of $[____] when filing a change of registration as an investment adviser representative. If the filing results in a denial or withdrawal, the administrator shall retain $[____] of the fee.

(e) [**Federal covered investment advisers.**] A federal covered investment adviser required to file a notice under Section 405 shall pay an initial fee of $[____] and an annual notice fee of $[____].

(f) [**Payment.**] A person required to pay a filing or notice fee under this section may transmit the fee through or to a designee as a rule or order provides under this [Act].

[(g) [**Dual agent/investment adviser representative.**] An investment adviser representative who is registered as an agent under Section 402 and who represents a person that is both registered as a broker-dealer under Section 401 and registered as an investment adviser under Section 403 or required as a federal covered investment adviser to make a notice filing under Section 405 is not required to pay an initial or annual registration fee for registration as an investment adviser representative.]

SECTION 411. POSTREGISTRATION REQUIREMENTS.

(a) [**Financial requirements.**] Subject to Section 15(h) of the Securities Exchange Act of 1934 (15 U.S.C. Section 78o(h)) or Section 222 of the Investment Advisers Act of 1940 (15 U.S.C. Section 80b–22), a rule adopted or order issued under this [Act] may establish minimum financial requirements for broker-dealers registered or required to be registered under this [Act] and investment advisers registered or required to be registered under this [Act].

(b) [**Financial reports.**] Subject to Section 15(h) of the Securities Exchange Act of 1934 (15 U.S.C. Section 78o(h)) or Section 222(b) of the Investment Advisers Act of 1940 (15 U.S.C. Section 80b–22), a broker-dealer registered or required to be registered under this [Act] and an investment adviser registered or required to be registered under this [Act] shall file such financial reports as are required by a rule adopted or order issued under this [Act]. If the information contained in a record filed under this subsection is or becomes inaccurate or incomplete in a material respect, the registrant shall promptly file a correcting amendment.

(c) [**Recordkeeping.**] Subject to Section 15(h) of the Securities Exchange Act of 1934 (15 U.S.C. Section 78o(h)) or Section 222 of the Investment Advisers Act of 1940 (15 U.S.C. Section 80b–22):

(1) a broker-dealer registered or required to be registered under this [Act] and an investment adviser registered or required to be registered under this [Act] shall make and maintain the accounts, correspondence, memoranda, papers, books, and other records required by rule adopted or order issued under this [Act];

(2) broker-dealer records required to be maintained under paragraph (1) may be maintained in any form of data storage acceptable under Section 17(a) of the Securities Exchange Act of 1934 (15 U.S.C. Section 78q(a)) if they are readily accessible to the administrator; and

(3) investment adviser records required to be maintained under paragraph (1) may be maintained in any form of data storage required by rule adopted or order issued under this [Act].

(d) [**Audits or inspections.**] The records of a broker-dealer registered or required to be registered under this [Act] and of an investment adviser registered or required to be registered under this [Act] are subject to such reasonable periodic, special, or other audits or inspections by a representative of the administrator, within or without this State, as the administrator considers necessary or appropriate in the public interest and for the protection of investors. An audit or inspection may be made at any time and without prior notice. The administrator may copy, and remove for audit or inspection copies of, all records the administrator reasonably considers necessary or appropriate to conduct the audit or inspection. The administrator may assess a reasonable charge for conducting an audit or inspection under this subsection.

(e) [**Custody and discretionary authority bond or insurance.**] Subject to Section 15(h) of the Securities Exchange Act of 1934 (15 U.S.C. Section 78o(h)) or Section 222 of the Investment Advisers Act of 1940 (15 U.S.C. Section 80b–22), a rule adopted or order issued under this [Act] may require a broker-dealer or investment adviser that has custody of or discretionary authority over funds or securities of a customer or client to obtain insurance or post a bond or other satisfactory form of security in an amount not to exceed $[____]. The administrator may determine the requirements of the insurance, bond, or other satisfactory form of security. Insurance or a bond or other satisfactory form of security may not be required of a broker-dealer registered under this [Act] whose net capital exceeds, or of an investment adviser registered under this [Act] whose minimum financial requirements exceed, the amounts required by rule or order under this [Act]. The insurance, bond, or other satisfactory form of security must permit an action by a person to enforce any liability on the insurance, bond, or other satisfactory form of security if instituted within the time limitations in Section 509(j)(2).

(f) [**Requirements for custody.**] Subject to Section 15(h) of the Securities Exchange Act of 1934 (15 U.S.C. Section 78o(h)) or Section 222 of the Investment Advisers Act of 1940 (15 U.S.C. Section 80b–22), an agent may not have custody of funds or securities of a customer except under the supervision of a broker-dealer and an investment adviser representative may not have custody of funds or securities of a client except under the supervision of an investment adviser or a federal covered investment adviser. A rule adopted or order issued under this [Act] may prohibit, limit, or impose conditions on a broker-dealer regarding custody of funds or securities of a customer and on an investment adviser regarding custody of securities or funds of a client.

(g) [**Investment adviser brochure rule.**] With respect to an investment adviser registered or required to be registered under this [Act], a rule adopted or order issued under this [Act] may require that information or other record be furnished or disseminated to clients or prospective clients in this State as necessary or appropriate in the public interest and for the protection of investors and advisory clients.

(h) [**Continuing education.**] A rule adopted or order issued under this [Act] may require an individual registered under Section 402 or 404 to participate in a continuing education program approved by the Securities and Exchange Commission and administered by a self-regulatory organization or, in the absence of such a program, a rule adopted or order issued under this [Act] may require continuing education for an individual registered under Section 404.

SECTION 412. DENIAL, REVOCATION, SUSPENSION, WITHDRAWAL, RESTRICTION, CONDITION, OR LIMITATION OF REGISTRATION.

(a) [**Disciplinary conditions—applicants.**] If the administrator finds that the order is in the public interest and subsection (d) authorizes the action, an order issued under this [Act] may deny an application, or may condition or limit registration: (1) of an applicant to be a broker-dealer, agent, investment adviser, or investment adviser representative, and (2) if the applicant is a broker-dealer or investment adviser, of any partner, officer, director, person having a similar status or performing similar functions, or person directly or indirectly controlling the broker-dealer or investment adviser.

(b) [**Disciplinary conditions—registrants.**] If the administrator finds that the order is in the public interest and subsection (d) authorizes the action an order issued under this [Act] may revoke, suspend, condition, or limit the registration of a registrant and if the registrant is a broker-dealer or investment adviser, any partner, officer, or director, any person having a similar status or performing similar functions, or any person directly or indirectly controlling the broker-dealer or investment adviser. However, the administrator

(1) may not institute a revocation or suspension proceeding under this subsection based on an order issued by another State that is reported to the administrator or designee later than one year after the date of the order on which it is based; and

(2) under subsection (d)(5)(A) and (B), may not issue an order on the basis of an order under the state securities act of another State unless the other order was based on conduct for which subsection (d) would authorize the action had the conduct occurred in this State.

(c) [**Disciplinary penalties–registrants.**] If the administrator finds that the order is in the public interest and subsection (d)(1) through (6), (8), (9), (10), or (12) and (13) authorizes the action, an order under this [Act] may censure, impose a bar, or impose a civil penalty in an amount not to exceed a maximum of $[____] for a single violation or $[____] for several violations on a registrant and if the registrant is a broker-dealer or investment adviser, any partner, officer, or director, any person having similar functions or any person directly or indirectly controlling the broker-dealer or investment adviser.

(d) [**Grounds for discipline.**] A person may be disciplined under subsections (a) through (c) if the person:

(1) has filed an application for registration in this State under this [Act] or the predecessor act within the previous 10 years, which, as of the effective date of registration or as of any date after filing in the case of an order denying effectiveness, was incomplete in any material respect or contained a statement that, in light of the circumstances under which it was made, was false or misleading with respect to a material fact;

(2) willfully violated or willfully failed to comply with this [Act] or the predecessor act or a rule adopted or order issued under this [Act] or the predecessor act within the previous 10 years;

(3) has been convicted of a felony or within the previous 10 years has been convicted of a misdemeanor involving a security, a commodity future or option contract, or an aspect of a business involving securities, commodities, investments, franchises, insurance, banking, or finance;

(4) is enjoined or restrained by a court of competent jurisdiction in an action instituted by the administrator under this [Act] or the predecessor act, a State, the Securities and Exchange Commission, or the United States from engaging in or continuing an act, practice, or course of business involving an aspect of a business involving securities, commodities, investments, franchises, insurance, banking, or finance;

(5) is the subject of an order, issued after notice and opportunity for hearing by:

(A) the securities, depository institution, insurance, or other financial services regulator of a State or by the Securities and Exchange Commission or other federal agency denying, revoking, barring, or suspending registration as a broker-dealer, agent, investment adviser, federal covered investment adviser, or investment adviser representative;

(B) the securities regulator of a State or by the Securities and Exchange Commission against a broker-dealer, agent, investment adviser, investment adviser representative, or federal covered investment adviser;

(C) the Securities and Exchange Commission or by a self-regulatory organization suspending or expelling the registrant from membership in the self-regulatory organization;

(D) a court adjudicating a United States Postal Service fraud order;

(E) the insurance regulator of a State denying, suspending, or revoking the registration of an insurance agent; or

(F) a depository institution regulator suspending or barring a person from the depository institution business;

(6) is the subject of an adjudication or determination, after notice and opportunity for hearing, by the Securities and Exchange Commission, the Commodity Futures Trading Commission; the Federal Trade Commission; a federal depository institution regulator, or a depository institution, insurance, or other financial services regulator of a State that the person willfully violated the Securities Act of 1933, the Securities Exchange Act of 1934, the Investment Advisers Act of 1940, the Investment Company Act of 1940, or the Commodity Exchange Act, the securities or commodities law of a State, or a federal or state law under which a business involving investments, franchises, insurance, banking, or finance is regulated;

(7) is insolvent, either because the person's liabilities exceed the person's assets or because the person cannot meet the person's obligations as they mature, but the administrator may not enter an order against an applicant or registrant under this paragraph without a finding of insolvency as to the applicant or registrant;

(8) refuses to allow or otherwise impedes the administrator from conducting an audit or inspection under Section 411(d) or refuses access to a registrant's office to conduct an audit or inspection under Section 411(d);

(9) has failed to reasonably supervise an agent, investment adviser representative, or other individual, if the agent, investment adviser representative, or other individual was subject to the person's supervision and committed a violation of this [Act] or the predecessor act or a rule adopted or order issued under this [Act] or the predecessor act within the previous 10 years;

(10) has not paid the proper filing fee within 30 days after having been notified by the administrator of a deficiency, but the administrator shall vacate an order under this paragraph when the deficiency is corrected;

(11) after notice and opportunity for a hearing, has been found within the previous 10 years:

(A) by a court of competent jurisdiction to have willfully violated the laws of a foreign jurisdiction under which the business of securities, commodities, investment, franchises, insurance, banking, or finance is regulated;

(B) to have been the subject of an order of a securities regulator of a foreign jurisdiction denying, revoking, or suspending the right to engage in the business of securities as a broker-dealer, agent, investment adviser, investment adviser representative, or similar person; or

(C) to have been suspended or expelled from membership by or participation in a securities exchange or securities association operating under the securities laws of a foreign jurisdiction;

(12) is the subject of a cease and desist order issued by the Securities and Exchange Commission or issued under the securities, commodities, investment, franchise, banking, finance, or insurance laws of a State;

(13) has engaged in dishonest or unethical practices in the securities, commodities, investment, franchise, banking, finance, or insurance business within the previous 10 years; or

(14) is not qualified on the basis of factors such as training, experience, and knowledge of the securities business. However, in the case of an application by an agent for a broker-dealer that is a member of a self-regulatory organization or by an individual for registration as an investment adviser representative, a denial order may not be based on this paragraph if the individual has successfully completed all examinations required by subsection (e). The administrator may require an applicant for registration under Section 402 or 404 who has not been registered in a State within the two years preceding the filing of an application in this State to successfully complete an examination.

(e) [**Examinations.**] A rule adopted or order issued under this [Act] may require that an examination, including an examination developed or approved by an organization of securities regulators, be successfully completed by a class of individuals or all individuals. An order issued under this [Act] may waive, in whole or in part, an examination as to an individual and a rule adopted under this [Act] may waive, in whole or in part, an examination as to a class of individuals if the administrator determines that the examination is not necessary or appropriate in the public interest and for the protection of investors.

(f) [**Summary process.**] The administrator may suspend or deny an application summarily; restrict, condition, limit, or suspend a registration; or censure, bar, or impose a civil penalty on a registrant before final determination of an administrative proceeding. Upon the issuance of an order, the administrator shall promptly notify each person subject to the order that the order has been issued, the reasons for the action, and that within 15 days after the receipt of a request in a record from the person the matter will be scheduled for a hearing. If a hearing is not requested and none is ordered by the administrator within 30 days after the date of service of the order, the order becomes final by operation of law. If a hearing is requested or ordered, the administrator, after notice of and opportunity for hearing to each person subject to the order, may modify or vacate the order or extend the order until final determination.

(g) [**Procedural requirements.**] An order issued may not be issued under this section, except under subsection (f), without:

(1) appropriate notice to the applicant or registrant;

(2) opportunity for hearing; and

(3) findings of fact and conclusions of law in a record [in accordance with the state administrative procedure act].

(h) [**Control person liability.**] A person that controls, directly or indirectly, a person not in compliance with this section may be disciplined by order of the administrator under subsections (a) through (c) to the same extent as the noncomplying person, unless the controlling person did not know, and in the exercise of reasonable care could not have known, of the existence of conduct that is a ground for discipline under this section.

(i) [**Limit on investigation or proceeding.**] The administrator may not institute a proceeding under subsection(a), (b), or (c) based solely on material facts actually known by the administrator unless an investigation or the proceeding is instituted within one year after the administrator actually acquires knowledge of the material facts.

[ARTICLE] 5

FRAUD AND LIABILITIES

SECTION 501. GENERAL FRAUD. It is unlawful for a person, in connection with the offer, sale, or purchase of a security, directly or indirectly:

(1) to employ a device, scheme, or artifice to defraud;

(2) to make an untrue statement of a material fact or to omit to state a material fact necessary in order to make the statement made, in the light of the circumstances under which it is made, not misleading; or

(3) to engage in an act, practice, or course of business that operates or would operate as a fraud or deceit upon another person.

SECTION 502. PROHIBITED CONDUCT IN PROVIDING INVESTMENT ADVICE.

(a) [**Fraud in providing investment advice.**] It is unlawful for a person that advises others for compensation, either directly or indirectly or through publications or writings, as to the value of securities or the advisability of investing in, purchasing, or selling securities or that, for compensation and as part of a regular business, issues or promulgates analyses or reports relating to securities:

(1) to employ a device, scheme, or artifice to defraud another person; or

(2) to engage in an act, practice, or course of business that operates or would operate as a fraud or deceit upon another person.

(b) [**Rules defining fraud.**] A rule adopted under this [Act] may define an act, practice, or course of business of an investment adviser or an investment adviser representative, other than a supervised person of a federal covered investment adviser, as fraudulent, deceptive, or manipulative, and prescribe means reasonably designed to prevent investment advisers and investment adviser representatives, other than supervised persons of a federal covered investment adviser, from engaging in acts, practices, and courses of business defined as fraudulent, deceptive, or manipulative.

(c) [**Rules specifying contents of advisory contract.**] A rule adopted under this [Act] may specify the contents of an investment advisory contract entered into, extended, or renewed by an investment adviser.

SECTION 503. EVIDENTIARY BURDEN.

(a) [**Civil.**] In a civil action or administrative proceeding under this [Act], a person claiming an exemption, exception, preemption, or exclusion has the burden to prove the applicability of the claim.

(b) [**Criminal.**] In a criminal proceeding under this [Act], a person claiming an exemption, exception, preemption, or exclusion has the burden of going forward with evidence of the claim.

SECTION 504. FILING OF SALES AND ADVERTISING LITERATURE.

(a) [**Filing requirement.**] Except as otherwise provided in subsection (b), a rule adopted or order issued under this [Act] may require the filing of a prospectus, pamphlet, circular, form letter, advertisement, sales literature, or other advertising record relating to a security or investment advice, addressed or intended for distribution to prospective investors, including clients or prospective clients of a person registered or required to be registered as an investment adviser under this [Act].

(b) [**Excluded communications.**] This section does not apply to sales and advertising literature specified in subsection (a) which relates to a federal covered security, a federal covered investment adviser, or a security or transaction exempted by Section 201, 202, or 203 except as required pursuant to Section 201(7).

SECTION 505. MISLEADING FILINGS. It is unlawful for a person to make or cause to be made, in a record that is used in an action or proceeding or filed under this [Act], a statement that, at the time and in the light of the circumstances under which it is made, is false or misleading in a material respect, or, in connection with the statement, to omit to state a material fact necessary to make the statement made, in the light of the circumstances under which it was made, not false or misleading.

SECTION 506. MISREPRESENTATIONS CONCERNING REGISTRATION OR EXEMPTION. The filing of an application for registration, a registration statement, a notice filing under this [Act], the registration of a person, the notice filing by a person, or the registration of a security under this [Act] does not constitute a finding by the administrator that a record filed under this [Act] is true, complete, and not misleading. The filing or registration or the availability of an exemption, exception, preemption, or exclusion for a security or a transaction does not mean that the administrator has passed upon the merits or qualifications of, or recommended or given approval to, a person, security, or transaction. It is unlawful to make, or cause to be made, to a purchaser, customer, client, or prospective customer or client a representation inconsistent with this section.

SECTION 507. QUALIFIED IMMUNITY. A broker-dealer, agent, investment adviser, federal covered investment adviser, or investment adviser representative is not liable to another broker-dealer, agent, investment adviser, federal covered investment adviser, or investment adviser representative for defamation relating to a statement that is contained in a record required by the administrator, or designee of the administrator, the Securities and Exchange Commission, or a self-regulatory organization, unless the person knew, or should have known at the time that the statement was made, that it was false in a material respect or the person acted in reckless disregard of the statement's truth or falsity.

SECTION 508. CRIMINAL PENALTIES.

(a) [**Criminal penalties.**] A person that willfully violates this [Act], or a rule adopted or order issued under this [Act], except Section

504 or the notice filing requirements of Section 302 or 405, or that willfully violates Section 505 knowing the statement made to be false or misleading in a material respect, upon conviction, shall be fined not more than $[____] or imprisoned not more than [____] years, or both. An individual convicted of violating a rule or order under this [Act] may be fined, but may not be imprisoned, if the individual did not have knowledge of the rule or order.

(b) [**Criminal reference not required.**] The [Attorney General or the proper prosecuting attorney] with or without a reference from the administrator, may institute criminal proceedings under this [Act].

(c) [**No limitation on other criminal enforcement**.] This [Act] does not limit the power of this State to punish a person for conduct that constitutes a crime under other laws of this State.

SECTION 509. CIVIL LIABILITY.

(a) [**Securities Litigation Uniform Standards Act.**] Enforcement of civil liability under this section is subject to the Securities Litigation Uniform Standards Act of 1998.

(b) [**Liability of seller to purchaser.**] A person is liable to the purchaser if the person sells a security in violation of Section 301 or, by means of an untrue statement of a material fact or an omission to state a material fact necessary in order to make the statement made, in light of the circumstances under which it is made, not misleading, the purchaser not knowing the untruth or omission and the seller not sustaining the burden of proof that the seller did not know and, in the exercise of reasonable care, could not have known of the untruth or omission. An action under this subsection is governed by the following:

(1) The purchaser may maintain an action to recover the consideration paid for the security, less the amount of any income received on the security, and interest [at the legal rate of interest] from the date of the purchase, costs, and reasonable attorneys' fees determined by the court, upon the tender of the security, or for actual damages as provided in paragraph (3).

(2) The tender referred to in paragraph (1) may be made any time before entry of judgment. Tender requires only notice in a record of ownership of the security and willingness to exchange the security for the amount specified. A purchaser that no longer owns the security may recover actual damages as provided in paragraph (3).

(3) Actual damages in an action arising under this subsection are the amount that would be recoverable upon a tender less the value of the security when the purchaser disposed of it, and interest [at the legal rate of interest] from the date of the purchase, costs, and reasonable attorneys' fees determined by the court.

(c) [**Liability of purchaser to seller.**] A person is liable to the seller if the person buys a security by means of an untrue statement of a material fact or omission to state a material fact necessary in order to make the statement made, in light of the circumstances under which it is made, not misleading, the seller not knowing of the untruth or omission, and the purchaser not sustaining the burden of proof that the purchaser did not know, and in the exercise of reasonable care, could not have known of the untruth or omission. An action under this subsection is governed by the following:

(1) The seller may maintain an action to recover the security, and any income received on the security, costs, and reasonable attorneys' fees determined by the court, upon the tender of the purchase price, or for actual damages as provided in paragraph (3).

(2) The tender referred to in paragraph (1) may be made any time before entry of judgment. Tender requires only notice in a record of the present ability to pay the amount tendered and willingness to take delivery of the security for the amount specified. If the purchaser no longer owns the

security, the seller may recover actual damages as provided in paragraph (3).

(3) Actual damages in an action arising under this subsection are the difference between the price at which the security was sold and the value the security would have had at the time of the sale in the absence of the purchaser's conduct causing liability, and interest [at the legal rate of interest] from the date of the sale of the security, costs, and reasonable attorneys' fees determined by the court.

(d) [**Liability of unregistered broker-dealer and agent.**] A person acting as a broker-dealer or agent that sells or buys a security in violation of Section 401(a), 402(a), or 506 is liable to the customer. The customer, if a purchaser, may maintain an action for recovery of actual damages as specified in subsections (b)(1) through (3), or, if a seller, for a remedy as specified in subsections (c)(1) through (3).

(e) [**Liability of unregistered investment adviser and investment adviser representative.**] A person acting as an investment adviser or investment adviser representative that provides investment advice for compensation in violation of Section 403(a), 404(a), or 506 is liable to the client. The client may maintain an action to recover the consideration paid for the advice, interest [at the legal rate of interest] from the date of payment, costs, and reasonable attorneys' fees determined by the court.

(f) [**Liability for investment advice.**] A person that receives directly or indirectly any consideration for providing investment advice to another person and that employs a device, scheme, or artifice to defraud the other person or engages in an act, practice, or course of business that operates or would operate as a fraud or deceit on the other person, is liable to the other person. An action under this subsection is governed by the following:

(1) The person defrauded may maintain an action to recover the consideration paid for the advice and the amount of any actual damages caused by the fraudulent conduct, interest [at the legal rate of interest] from the date of the fraudulent conduct, costs, and reasonable attorneys' fees determined by the court, less the amount of any income received as a result of the fraudulent conduct.

(2) This subsection does not apply to a broker-dealer or its agents if the investment advice provided is solely incidental to transacting business as a broker-dealer and no special compensation is received for the investment advice.

(g) [**Joint and several liability.**] The following persons are liable jointly and severally with and to the same extent as persons liable under subsections (b) through (f):

(1) a person that directly or indirectly controls a person liable under subsections (b) through (f), unless the controlling person sustains the burden of proof that the person did not know, and in the exercise of reasonable care could not have known, of the existence of conduct by reason of which the liability is alleged to exist;

(2) an individual who is a managing partner, executive officer, or director of a person liable under subsections (b) through (f), including an individual having a similar status or performing similar functions, unless the individual sustains the burden of proof that the individual did not know and, in the exercise of reasonable care could not have known, of the existence of conduct by reason of which the liability is alleged to exist;

(3) an individual who is an employee of or associated with a person liable under subsections (b) through (f) and who materially aids the conduct giving rise to the liability, unless the individual sustains the burden of proof that the individual did not know and, in the exercise of reasonable care could not have known, of the existence of conduct by reason of which the liability is alleged to exist; and

(4) a person that is a broker-dealer, agent, investment adviser, or investment adviser representative that materially aids the conduct giving rise to the liability under subsections (b) through (f), unless the person sustains the burden of proof that the person did not know and, in the exercise of reasonable care could not have known, of the existence of conduct by reason of which liability is alleged to exist.

(h) [**Right of contribution.**] A person liable under this section has a right of contribution as in cases of contract against any other person liable under this section for the same conduct.

(i) [**Survival of cause of action.**] A cause of action under this section survives the death of an individual who might have been a plaintiff or defendant.

(j) [**Statute of limitations.**] A person may not obtain relief:

(1) under subsection (b) for violation of Section 301, or under subsection (d) or (e), unless the action is instituted within one year after the violation occurred; or

(2) under subsection (b), other than for violation of Section 301, or under subsection (c) or (f), unless the action is instituted within the earlier of two years after discovery of the facts constituting the violation or five years after the violation.

(k) [**No enforcement of violative contract.**] A person that has made, or has engaged in the performance of, a contract in violation of this [Act] or a rule adopted or order issued under this [Act], or that has acquired a purported right under the contract with knowledge of conduct by reason of which its making or performance was in violation of this [Act], may not base an action on the contract.

(*l*) [**No contractual waiver.**] A condition, stipulation, or provision binding a person purchasing or selling a security or receiving investment advice to waive compliance with this [Act] or a rule adopted or order issued under this [Act] is void.

(m) [**Survival of other rights or remedies.**] The rights and remedies provided by this [Act] are in addition to any other rights or remedies that may exist, but this [Act] does not create a cause of action not specified in this section or Section 411(e).

SECTION 510. RESCISSION OFFERS. A purchaser, seller, or recipient of investment advice may not maintain an action under Section 509 if:

(1) The purchaser, seller, or recipient of investment advice receives in a record, before the action is instituted:

(A) an offer stating the respect in which liability under Section 509 may have arisen and fairly advising the purchaser, seller, or recipient of investment advice of that person's rights in connection with the offer, and any financial or other information necessary to correct all material misrepresentations or omissions in the information that was required by this [Act] to be furnished to that person at the time of the purchase, sale, or investment advice;

(B) if the basis for relief under this section may have been a violation of Section 509(b), an offer to repurchase the security for cash, payable on delivery of the security, equal to the consideration paid, and interest [at the legal rate of interest] from the date of the purchase, less the amount of any income received on the security, or, if the purchaser no longer owns the security, an offer to pay the purchaser upon acceptance of the offer damages in an amount that would be recoverable upon a tender, less the value of the security when the purchaser disposed of it, and interest [at the legal rate of interest] from the date of the purchase in cash equal to the damages computed in the manner provided in this subsection;

(C) if the basis for relief under this section may have been a violation of Section 509(c), an offer to tender the security, on payment by the seller of an amount equal to the purchase price paid, less income received on the security by the purchaser and interest [at the legal rate of interest] from the date of the sale; or if the purchaser no longer owns the security, an offer to pay the seller upon acceptance of the offer, in cash, damages in the amount of the difference between the price at which the security was purchased and the value the security would have had at the time of the purchase in the absence of the purchaser's conduct that may have caused liability and interest [at the legal rate of interest] from the date of the sale;

(D) if the basis for relief under this section may have been a violation of Section 509(d); and if the customer is a purchaser, an offer to pay as specified in subparagraph (B); or, if the customer is a seller, an offer to tender or to pay as specified in subparagraph (C);

(E) if the basis for relief under this section may have been a violation of Section 509(e), an offer to reimburse in cash the consideration paid for the advice and interest [at the legal rate of interest] from the date of payment; or

(F) if the basis for relief under this section may have been a violation of Section 509(f), an offer to reimburse in cash the consideration paid for the advice, the amount of any actual damages that may have been caused by the conduct, and interest [at the legal rate of interest] from the date of the violation causing the loss;

(2) the offer under paragraph 1 states that it must be accepted by the purchaser, seller, or recipient of investment advice within 30 days after the date of its receipt by the purchaser, seller, or recipient of investment advice or any shorter period, of not less than three days, that the administrator, by order, specifies;

(3) the offeror has the present ability to pay the amount offered or to tender the security under paragraph (1);

(4) the offer under paragraph (1) is delivered to the purchaser, seller, or recipient of investment advice, or sent in a manner that ensures receipt by the purchaser, seller, or recipient of investment advice; and

(5) the purchaser, seller, or recipient of investment advice that accepts the offer under paragraph (1) in a record within the period specified under paragraph (2) is paid in accordance with the terms of the offer.

[ARTICLE] 6
ADMINISTRATION AND JUDICIAL REVIEW

SECTION 601. ADMINISTRATION.

(a) [**Administration.**] The administrator shall administer this [Act] [insert any related provisions on such matters as method of selection, salary, term of office, selection and remuneration of personnel, and annual reports to the legislature or governor that are appropriate to the particular State].

(b) [**Unlawful use of records or information.**] It is unlawful for the administrator or an officer, employee, or designee of the administrator to use for personal benefit or the benefit of others records or other information obtained by or filed with the administrator that are not public under Section 607(b). This [Act] does not authorize the administrator or an officer, employee, or designee of the administrator to disclose the record or information, except in accordance with Section 602, 607(c), or 608.

(c) [**No privilege or exemption created or diminished.**] This [Act] does not create or diminish a privilege or exemption that exists at common law, by statute or rule, or otherwise.

(d) [**Investor education.**] The administrator may develop and implement investor education initiatives to inform the public about investing in securities, with particular emphasis on the prevention and detection of securities fraud. In developing and implementing these initiatives, the administrator may collaborate with public and nonprofit organizations with an interest in investor education. The administrator may accept a grant or donation from a person that is not affiliated with the securities industry or from a nonprofit organization, regardless of whether the organization is affiliated with the securities industry, to develop and implement investor education initiatives. This subsection does not authorize the administrator to require participation or monetary contributions of a registrant in an investor education program.

(e) [**The Securities Investor Education and Training Fund.**] The Securities Investor Education and Training Fund is created to provide funds for the purposes specified in subsection (d). [All monies received by the State by reason of civil penalties pursuant to this [Act] shall be deposited in the Securities Investor Education and Training Fund. The State may insert any other provision concerning appropriations to support this fund as well as procedures for its operations.]

SECTION 602. INVESTIGATIONS AND SUBPOENAS.

(a) [**Authority to investigate.**] The administrator may:

(1) conduct public or private investigations within or outside of this State which the administrator considers necessary or appropriate to determine whether a person has violated, is violating, or is about to violate this [Act] or a rule adopted or order issued under this [Act], or to aid in the enforcement of this [Act] or in the adoption of rules and forms under this [Act];

(2) require or permit a person to testify, file a statement, or produce a record, under oath or otherwise as the administrator determines, as to all the facts and circumstances concerning a matter to be investigated or about which an action or proceeding is to be instituted; and

(3) publish a record concerning an action, proceeding, or an investigation under, or a violation of, this [Act] or a rule adopted or order issued under this [Act] if the administrator determines it is necessary or appropriate in the public interest and for the protection of investors.

(b) [**Administrator powers to investigate.**] For the purpose of an investigation under this [Act], the administrator or its designated officer may administer oaths and affirmations, subpoena witnesses, seek compulsion of attendance, take evidence, require the filing of statements, and require the production of any records that the administrator considers relevant or material to the investigation.

(c) [**Procedure and remedies for noncompliance.**] If a person does not appear or refuses to testify, file a statement, produce records, or otherwise does not obey a subpoena as required by the administrator under this [Act], the administrator [may refer the matter to the Attorney General or the proper attorney, who] may apply to [insert name of the appropriate court] or a court of another State to enforce compliance. The court may:

(1) hold the person in contempt;

(2) order the person to appear before the administrator;

(3) order the person to testify about the matter under investigation or in question;

(4) order the production of records;

(5) grant injunctive relief, including restricting or prohibiting the offer or sale of securities or the providing of investment advice;

(6) impose a civil penalty of not less than $[____] and not greater than $[____] for each violation; and

(7) grant any other necessary or appropriate relief.

(d) [**Application for relief.**] This section does not preclude a person from applying to [insert name of appropriate court] or a court of another State for relief from a request to appear, testify, file a statement, produce records, or obey a subpoena.

(e) [**Use immunity procedure.**] An individual is not excused from attending, testifying, filing a statement, producing a record or other evidence, or obeying a subpoena of the administrator under this [Act] or in an action or proceeding instituted by the administrator under this [Act] on the ground that the required testimony, statement, record, or other evidence, directly or indirectly, may tend to incriminate the individual or subject the individual to a criminal fine, penalty, or forfeiture. If the individual refuses to testify, file a statement, or produce a record or other evidence on the basis of the individual's privilege against self-incrimination, the administrator may apply [to the name of the appropriate court] to compel the testimony, the filing of the statement, the production of the record, or the giving of other evidence. The testimony, record, or other evidence compelled under such an order may not be used, directly or indirectly, against the individual in a criminal case, except in a prosecution for perjury or contempt or otherwise failing to comply with the order.

(f) [**Assistance to securities regulator of another jurisdiction.**] At the request of the securities regulator of another State or a foreign jurisdiction, the administrator may provide assistance if the requesting regulator states that it is conducting an investigation to determine whether a person has violated, is violating, or is about to violate a law or rule of the other State or foreign jurisdiction relating to securities matters that the requesting regulator administers or enforces. The administrator may provide the assistance by using the authority to investigate and the powers conferred by this section as the administrator determines is necessary or appropriate. The assistance may be provided without regard to whether the conduct described in the request would also constitute a violation of this [Act] or other law of this State if occurring in this State. In deciding whether to provide the assistance, the administrator may consider whether the requesting regulator is permitted and has agreed to provide assistance reciprocally within its State or foreign jurisdiction to the administrator on securities matters when requested; whether compliance with the request would violate or prejudice the public policy of this State; and the availability of resources and employees of the administrator to carry out the request for assistance.

SECTION 603. CIVIL ENFORCEMENT.

(a) [**Civil action instituted by administrator.**] If the administrator believes that a person has engaged, is engaging, or is about to engage in an act, practice, or course of business constituting a violation of this [Act] or a rule adopted or order issued under this [Act] or that a person has, is, or is about to engage in an act, practice, or course of business that materially aids a violation of this [Act] or a rule adopted or order issued under this [Act], the administrator may maintain an action in the [insert the name of the court] to enjoin the act, practice, or course of business and to enforce compliance with this [Act] or a rule adopted or order issued under this [Act].

(b) [**Relief available.**] In an action under this section and on a proper showing, the court may:

(1) issue a permanent or temporary injunction, restraining order, or declaratory judgment;

(2) order other appropriate or ancillary relief, which may include:

(A) an asset freeze, accounting, writ of attachment, writ of general or specific execution, and appointment of a receiver or conservator, that may be the administrator, for the defendant or the defendant's assets;

(B) ordering the administrator to take charge and control of a defendant's property, including investment accounts and accounts in a depository institution, rents, and profits; to collect debts; and to acquire and dispose of property;

(C) imposing a civil penalty up to $[____] for a single violation or up to $[____] for more than one violation; an order of rescission, restitution, or disgorgement directed to a person that has engaged in an act, practice, or course of business constituting a violation of this [Act] or the predecessor act or a rule adopted or order issued under this [Act] or the predecessor act; and

(D) ordering the payment of prejudgment and postjudgment interest; or

(3) order such other relief as the court considers appropriate.

(c) [**No bond required.**] The administrator may not be required to post a bond in an action or proceeding under this [Act].

SECTION 604. ADMINISTRATIVE ENFORCEMENT.

(a) [**Issuance of an order or notice.**] If the administrator determines that a person has engaged, is engaging, or is about to engage in an act, practice, or course of business constituting a violation of this [Act] or a rule adopted or order issued under this [Act] or that a person has materially aided, is materially aiding, or is about to materially aid an act, practice, or course of business constituting a violation of this [Act] or a rule adopted or order issued under this [Act], the administrator may:

(1) issue an order directing the person to cease and desist from engaging in the act, practice, or course of business or to take other action necessary or appropriate to comply with this [Act];

(2) issue an order denying, suspending, revoking, or conditioning the exemptions for a broker-dealer under Section 401(b)(1)(D) or (F) or an investment adviser under Section 403(b)(1)(C); or

(3) issue an order under Section 204.

(b) [**Summary process.**] An order under subsection (a) is effective on the date of issuance. Upon issuance of the order, the administrator shall promptly serve each person subject to the order with a copy of the order and a notice that the order has been entered. The order must include a statement whether the administrator will seek a civil penalty or costs of the investigation, a statement of the reasons for the order, and notice that, within 15 days after receipt of a request in a record from the person, the matter will be scheduled for a hearing. If a person subject to the order does not request a hearing and none is ordered by the administrator within 30 days after the date of service of the order, the order, which may include a civil penalty or costs of the investigation if a civil penalty or costs were sought in the statement accompanying the order, becomes final as to that person by operation of law. If a hearing is requested or ordered, the administrator, after notice of and opportunity for hearing to each person subject to the order, may modify or vacate the order or extend it until final determination.

(c) [**Procedure for final order.**] If a hearing is requested or ordered pursuant to subsection (b), a hearing must be held [pursuant to the state administrative procedure act]. A final order may not be issued unless the administrator makes findings of fact and conclusions of law in a record [in accordance with the state administrative procedure act]. The final order may make final, vacate, or modify the order issued under subsection (a).

(d) [**Civil penalty.**] In a final order under subsection (c), the administrator may impose a civil penalty up to $[____] for a single violation or up to $[____] for more than one violation.

(e) [**Costs.**] In a final order, the administrator may charge the actual cost of an investigation or proceeding for a violation of this [Act] or a rule adopted or order issued under this [Act].

(f) [**Filing of certified final order with court; effect of filing.**] If a petition for judicial review of a final order is not filed in accordance with Section 609, the administrator may file a certified copy of the final order with the clerk of a court of competent jurisdiction. The order so filed has the same effect as a judgment of the court and may be recorded, enforced, or satisfied in the same manner as a judgment of the court.

(g) [**Enforcement by court; further civil penalty.**] If a person does not comply with an order under this section, the administrator may petition a court of competent jurisdiction to enforce the order. The court may not require the administrator to post a bond in an action or proceeding under this section. If the court finds, after service and opportunity for hearing, that the person was not in compliance with the order, the court may adjudge the person in civil contempt of the order. The court may impose a further civil penalty against the person for contempt in an amount not less than $[____] but not greater than $[____] for each violation and may grant any other relief the court determines is just and proper in the circumstances.

SECTION 605. RULES, FORMS, ORDERS, INTERPRETATIVE OPINIONS, AND HEARINGS.

(a) [**Issuance and adoption of forms, orders, and rules.**] The administrator may:

(1) issue forms and orders and, after notice and comment, may adopt and amend rules necessary or appropriate to carry out this [Act] and may repeal rules, including rules and forms governing registration statements, applications, notice filings, reports, and other records;

(2) by rule, define terms, whether or not used in this [Act], but those definitions may not be inconsistent with this [Act]; and

(3) by rule, classify securities, persons, and transactions and adopt different requirements for different classes.

(b) [**Findings and cooperation.**] Under this [Act], a rule or form may not be adopted or amended, or an order issued or amended, unless the administrator finds that the rule, form, order, or amendment is necessary or appropriate in the public interest or for the protection of investors and is consistent with the purposes intended by this [Act]. In adopting, amending, and repealing rules and forms, Section 608 applies in order to achieve uniformity among the States and coordination with federal laws in the form and content of registration statements, applications, reports, and other records, including the adoption of uniform rules, forms, and procedures.

(c) [**Financial statements.**] Subject to Section 15(h) of the Securities Exchange Act and Section 222 of the Investment Advisers Act of 1940, the administrator may require that a financial statement filed under this [Act] be prepared in accordance with generally accepted accounting principles in the United States and comply with other requirements specified by rule adopted or order issued under this [Act]. A rule adopted or order issued under this [Act] may establish:

(1) subject to Section 15(h) of the Securities Exchange Act and Section 222 of the Investment Advisors Act of 1940, the form and content of financial statements required under this [Act];

(2) whether unconsolidated financial statements must be filed; and

(3) whether required financial statements must be audited by an independent certified public accountant.

(d) [**Interpretative opinions.**] The administrator may provide interpretative opinions or issue determinations that the administrator will not institute a proceeding or an action under this [Act] against a specified person for engaging in a specified act, practice, or course of business if the determination is consistent with this [Act]. A rule adopted or order issued under this [Act] may establish a reasonable charge for interpretative opinions or determinations that the administrator will not institute an action or a proceeding under this [Act].

(e) [**Effect of compliance.**] A penalty under this [Act] may not be imposed for, and liability does not arise from conduct that is engaged in or omitted in good faith believing it conforms to a rule, form, or order of the administrator under this [Act].

(f) [**Presumption for public hearings.**] A hearing in an administrative proceeding under this [Act] must be conducted in public unless the administrator for good cause consistent with this [Act] determines that the hearing will not be so conducted.

SECTION 606. ADMINISTRATIVE FILES AND OPINIONS.

(a) [**Public register of filings.**] The administrator shall maintain, or designate a person to maintain, a register of applications for registration of securities; registration statements; notice filings; applications for registration of broker-dealers, agents, investment advisers, and investment adviser representatives; notice filings by federal covered investment advisers that are or have been effective under this [Act] or the predecessor act; notices of claims of exemption from registration or notice filing requirements contained in a record; orders issued under this [Act] or the predecessor act; and interpretative opinions or no action determinations issued under this [Act].

(b) [**Public availability.**] The administrator shall make all rules, forms, interpretative opinions, and orders available to the public.

(c) [**Copies of public records.**] The administrator shall furnish a copy of a record that is a public record or a certification that the public record does not exist to a person that so requests. A rule adopted under this [Act] may establish a reasonable charge for furnishing the record or certification. A copy of the record certified or a certificate by the administrator of a record's nonexistence is prima facie evidence of a record or its nonexistence.

SECTION 607. PUBLIC RECORDS; CONFIDENTIALITY.

(a) [**Presumption of public records.**] Except as otherwise provided in subsection (b), records obtained by the administrator or filed under this [Act], including a record contained in or filed with a registration statement, application, notice filing, or report, are public records and are available for public examination.

(b) [**Nonpublic records.**] The following records are not public records and are not available for public examination under subsection (a):

(1) a record obtained by the administrator in connection with an audit or inspection under Section 411(d) or an investigation under Section 602;

(2) a part of a record filed in connection with a registration statement under Sections 301 and 303 through 305 or a record under Section 411(d) that contains trade secrets or confidential information if the person filing the registration statement or report has asserted a claim of confidentiality or privilege that is authorized by law;

(3) a record that is not required to be provided to the administrator or filed under this [Act] and is provided to the administrator only on the condition that the record will not be subject to public examination or disclosure;

(4) a nonpublic record received from a person specified in Section 608(a); [and]

(5) any social security number, residential address, and residential telephone number contained in a record that is filed[; and

(6) a record obtained by the administrator through a designee of the administrator that a rule or order under this [Act] determines has been:

(A) expunged from the administrator's records by the designee; or

(B) determined to be nonpublic or nondisclosable by that designee if the administrator finds the determination to be in the public interest and for the protection of investors].

(c) [**Administrator discretion to disclose.**] If disclosure is for the purpose of a civil, administrative, or criminal investigation, action, or proceeding or to a person specified in Section 608(a), the administrator may disclose a record obtained in connection with an audit or inspection under Section 411(d) or a record obtained in connection with an investigation under Section 602.

SECTION 608. UNIFORMITY AND COOPERATION WITH OTHER AGENCIES.

(a) [**Objective of uniformity.**] The administrator shall, in its discretion, cooperate, coordinate, consult, and, subject to Section 607, share records and information with the securities regulator of another State, Canada, a Canadian province or territory, a foreign jurisdiction, the Securities and Exchange Commission, the United States Department of Justice, the Commodity Futures Trading Commission, the Federal Trade Commission, the Securities Investor Protection Corporation, a self-regulatory organization, a national or international organization of securities regulators, a federal or state banking and insurance regulator, and a governmental law enforcement agency to effectuate greater uniformity in securities matters among the federal government, self-regulatory organizations, States, and foreign governments.

(b) [**Policies to consider.**] In cooperating, coordinating, consulting, and sharing records and information under this section and in acting by rule, order, or waiver under this [Act], the administrator shall, in its discretion, take into consideration in carrying out the public interest the following general policies:

(1) maximizing effectiveness of regulation for the protection of investors;

(2) maximizing uniformity in federal and state regulatory standards; and

(3) minimizing burdens on the business of capital formation, without adversely affecting essentials of investor protection.

(c) [**Subjects for cooperation.**] The cooperation, coordination, consultation, and sharing of records and information authorized by this section includes:

(1) establishing or employing one or more designees as a central depository for registration and notice filings under this [Act] and for records required or allowed to be maintained under this [Act];

(2) developing and maintaining uniform forms;

(3) conducting a joint examination or investigation;

(4) holding a joint administrative hearing;

(5) instituting and prosecuting a joint civil or administrative proceeding;

(6) sharing and exchanging personnel;

(7) coordinating registrations under Sections 301 and 401 through 404 and exemptions under Section 203;

(8) sharing and exchanging records, subject to Section 607;

(9) formulating rules, statements of policy, guidelines, forms, and interpretative opinions and releases;

(10) formulating common systems and procedures;

(11) notifying the public of proposed rules, forms, statements of policy, and guidelines;

(12) attending conferences and other meetings among securities regulators, which may include representatives of governmental and private sector organizations involved in capital formation, deemed necessary or appropriate to promote or achieve uniformity; and

(13) developing and maintaining a uniform exemption from registration for small issuers, and taking other steps to reduce the burden of raising investment capital by small businesses.

SECTION 609. JUDICIAL REVIEW.

(a) [**Judicial review of orders.**] A final order issued by the administrator under this [Act] is subject to judicial review in accordance with [the state administrative procedure act].

[(b) [**Judicial review of rules.**] A rule adopted under this [Act] is subject to judicial review in accordance with [the state administrative procedure act].]

SECTION 610. JURISDICTION.

(a) [**Sales and offers to sell.**] Sections 301, 302, 401(a), 402(a), 403(a), 404(a), 501, 506, 509, and 510 do not apply to a person that sells or offers to sell a security unless the offer to sell or the sale is made in this State or the offer to purchase or the purchase is made and accepted in this State.

(b) [**Purchases and offers to purchase.**] Sections 401(a), 402(a), 403(a), 404(a), 501, 506, 509, and 510 do not apply to a person that purchases or offers to purchase a security unless the offer to purchase or the purchase is made in this State or the offer to sell or the sale is made and accepted in this State.

(c) [**Offers in this State.**] For the purpose of this section, an offer to sell or to purchase a security is made in this State, whether or not either party is then present in this State, if the offer:

(1) originates from within this State; or

(2) is directed by the offeror to a place in this State and received at the place to which it is directed.

(d) [**Acceptances in this State.**] For the purpose of this section, an offer to purchase or to sell is accepted in this State, whether or not either party is then present in this State, if the acceptance:

(1) is communicated to the offeror in this State and the offeree reasonably believes the offeror to be present in this State and the acceptance is received at the place in this State to which it is directed; and

(2) has not previously been communicated to the offeror, orally or in a record, outside this State.

(e) [**Publications, radio, television, or electronic communications.**] An offer to sell or to purchase is not made in this State when a publisher circulates or there is circulated on the publisher's behalf in this State a bona fide newspaper or other publication of general, regular, and paid circulation that is not published in this State, or that is published in this State but has had more than two thirds of its circulation outside this State during the previous 12 months or when a radio or television program or other electronic communication originating outside this State is received in this State. A radio or television program, or other electronic communication is considered as having originated in this State if either the broadcast studio or the originating source of transmission is located in this State, unless:

(1) the program or communication is syndicated and distributed from outside this State for redistribution to the general public in this State;

(2) the program or communication is supplied by a radio, television, or other electronic network with the electronic signal originating from outside this State for redistribution to the general public in this State;

(3) the program or communication is an electronic communication that originates outside this State and is captured for redistribution to the general public in this State by a community antenna or cable, radio, cable television, or other electronic system; or

(4) the program or communication consists of an electronic communication that originates in this State, but which is not intended for distribution to the general public in this State.

(f) [**Investment advice and misrepresentations.**] Sections 403(a), 404(a), 405(a), 502, 505, and 506 apply to a person if the person engages in an act, practice, or course of business instrumental in effecting prohibited or actionable conduct in this State, whether or not either party is then present in this State.

SECTION 611. SERVICE OF PROCESS.

(a) [**Signed consent to service of process.**] A consent to service of process complying with Section 611 required by this [Act] must be signed and filed in the form required by a rule or order under this [Act]. A consent appointing the administrator the person's agent for service of process in a noncriminal action or proceeding against the person, or the person's successor or personal representative under this [Act] or a rule adopted or order issued under this [Act] after the consent is filed, has the same force and validity as if the service were made personally on the person filing the consent. A person that has filed a consent complying with this subsection in connection with a previous application for registration or notice filing need not file an additional consent.

(b) [**Conduct constituting appointment of agent for service.**] If a person, including a nonresident of this State, engages in an act, practice, or course of business prohibited or made actionable by this [Act] or a rule adopted or order issued under this [Act] and the person has not filed a consent to service of process under subsection (a), the act, practice, or course of business constitutes the appointment of the administrator as the person's agent for service of process in a noncriminal action or proceeding against the person or the person's successor or personal representative.

(c) [**Procedure for service of process.**] Service under subsection (a) or (b) may be made by providing a copy of the process to the office of the administrator, but it is not effective unless:

(1) the plaintiff, which may be the administrator, promptly sends notice of the service and a copy of the process, return receipt requested, to the defendant or respondent at the address set forth in the consent to service of process or, if a consent to service of process has not been filed, at the last known address, or takes other reasonable steps to give notice; and

(2) the plaintiff files an affidavit of compliance with this subsection in the action or proceeding on or before the return day of the process, if any, or within the time that the court, or the administrator in a proceeding before the administrator, allows.

(d) [**Service in administrative proceedings or civil actions by administrator.**] Service pursuant to subsection (c) may be used in a proceeding before the administrator or by the administrator in a civil action in which the administrator is the moving party.

(e) [**Opportunity to defend.**] If process is served under subsection (c), the court, or the administrator in a proceeding before the administrator, shall order continuances as are necessary or appropriate to afford the defendant or respondent reasonable opportunity to defend.

SECTION 612. SEVERABILITY CLAUSE. If any provision of this [Act] or its application to any person or circumstances is held invalid, the invalidity does not affect other provisions or applications of this [Act] that can be given effect without the invalid provision or application, and to this end the provisions of this [Act] are severable.

[ARTICLE] 7
TRANSITION

SECTION 701. EFFECTIVE DATE. This [Act] takes effect on [insert date, which should be at least 60 days after enactment].

SECTION 702. REPEALS. The following act is repealed:

[Insert name of former State securities act].

SECTION 703. APPLICATION OF ACT TO EXISTING PROCEEDING AND EXISTING RIGHTS AND DUTIES.

(a) [**Applicability of predecessor act to pending proceedings and existing rights.**] The predecessor act exclusively governs all actions or proceedings that are pending on the effective date of this [Act] or may be instituted on the basis of conduct occurring before the effective date of this [Act], but a civil action may not be maintained to enforce any liability under the predecessor act unless instituted within any period of limitation that applied when the cause of action accrued or within five years after the effective date of this [Act], whichever is earlier.

(b) [**Continued effectiveness under predecessor act.**] All effective registrations under the predecessor act, all administrative orders relating to the registrations, rules, statements of policy, interpretative opinions, declaratory rulings, no action determinations, and conditions imposed on the registrations under the predecessor act remain in effect while they would have remained in effect if this [Act] had not been enacted. They are considered to have been filed, issued, or imposed under this [Act], but are exclusively governed by the predecessor act.

(c) [**Applicability of predecessor act to offers or sales.**] The predecessor act exclusively applies to an offer or sale made within one year after the effective date of this [Act] pursuant to an offering made in good faith before the effective date of this [Act] on the basis of an exemption available under the predecessor act.

NASAA UNIFORM LIMITED OFFERING EXEMPTION

UNIFORM LIMITED OFFERING EXEMPTION

Adopted September 21, 1983

With Amendments Adopted Through April 29, 1989

North American Securities Administrators Association, Inc.

STATUTE

Statute Section. Section ______. The administrator is hereby granted authority to create by rule a limited offering transactional exemption which shall further the objectives of compatibility with federal exemptions and uniformity among the states.

PRELIMINARY NOTES

1. Nothing in this exemption is intended to or should be construed as in any way relieving issuers or persons acting on behalf of issuers from providing disclosure to prospective investors adequate to satisfy the anti-fraud provisions of this state's securities law.

2. In view of the objective of this rule and the purposes and policies underlying this act, the exemption is not available to any issuer with respect to any transaction which, although in technical compliance with this rule, is part of a plan or scheme to evade registration or the conditions or limitations explicitly stated in this rule.

3. Nothing in this rule is intended to relieve registered broker/dealers or agents from the due diligence, suitability, or know your customer standards or any other requirements of law otherwise applicable to such registered persons.

Rule

By authority delegated the administrator in Section ___ of this act to promulgate rules, the following transaction is determined to be exempt from the registration provisions of this act:

1. Any offer or sale of securities offered or sold in compliance with Securities Act of 1933, Regulation D, Rules 230.505 (and/or 230.506)[1], including any offer or sale made exempt by application of Rule 508(a), as made effective in Release No. 33–6389 and as amended in Release Nos. 33–6437; 33–6663, 33–6758, and 33–6825, and which satisfies the following further conditions and limitations:

A. No commission, fee or other remuneration shall be paid or given, directly or indi-

[1] In those states where facts and circumstances permit, it would not be inconsistent with the regulatory objectives of this exemption for a state to elect to accept Rule 506 offerings within the ambit of this exemption. In doing so, however, the state disqualification provisions of this rule and the federal disqualification provisions of Rule 505 should be made applicable.

With inclusion of Rule 506, the major objective of the exemption is not limited to facilitating the capital-raising ability of small business. The removal of the dollar limit makes the exemption available to private placements of all sizes. In large private offerings, the problems associated with determining that all the investors are experienced enough to fully understand the risks of the offering and controlling the manner and scope of the offering so that it does not become a public offering are magnified. Also, and largely because of the removal of the dollar limit, the exemption becomes more attractive to tax shelter investments.

Tax shelter offerings that would be permitted by Rule 506, particularly those with abusively high write-off ratios, involve special facts and circumstances, and enforcement experience shows that they have a greater potential for regulatory concerns and many lack economic substance and fail to contribute to job creation. In recognition of these concerns Rule 506 is not adopted as part of the basic ULOE.

In those states where facts and circumstances permit, it would not be inconsistent with the regulatory objectives of this exemption to further condition the exemption with the following provision:

"In the case of offerings of direct participation programs as defined in Section 34 of Article III of the National Association of Securities Dealers, Inc., Rules of Fair Practice, delivery of a disclosure document containing the information required by Rule 502(b) of Regulation D to individuals covered by Subsections (5), (6) and (7) of Rule 501(a) of Regulation D is required."

rectly, to any person for soliciting any prospective purchaser in this state unless such person is appropriately registered in this state.[2&3]

B. No exemption under this rule shall be available for the securities of any issuer if any of the parties described in Securities Act of 1933, Regulation A, Rule 230.252, section (c), (d), (e) or (f):

1. Has filed a registration statement which is subject of a currently effective registration stop order entered pursuant to any state's securities law within five years prior to the filing of the notice required under this exemption.

2. Has been convicted within five years prior to the filing of the notice required under this exemption of any felony or misdemeanor in connection with the offer, purchase or sale of any security or any felony involving fraud or deceit, including but not limited to forgery, embezzlement, obtaining money under false pretenses, larceny or conspiracy to defraud.

3. Is currently subject to any state administrative enforcement order or judgment entered by that state's securities administrator within five years prior to the filing of the notice required under this exemption or is subject to any state's administrative enforcement order or judgment in which fraud or deceit, including but not limited to making untrue statements of material facts and omitting to state material facts, was found and the order or judgment was entered within five years prior to the filing of the notice required under this exemption.

4. Is subject to any state's administrative enforcement order or judgment which prohibits, denies or revokes the use of any exemption from registration in connection with the offer, purchase or sale of securities.

5. Is currently subject to any order, judgment, or decree of any court of competent jurisdiction temporarily or preliminarily restraining or enjoining, or is subject to any order, judgment or decree of any court of competent jurisdiction, permanently restraining or enjoining, such party from engaging in or continuing any conduct or practice in connection with the purchase or sale of any security or involving the making of any false filing with the state entered within five years prior to the filing of the notice required under this exemption.

6. The prohibitions of paragraphs 1–3 and 5 above shall not apply if the person subject to the disqualification is duly licensed or registered to conduct securities related business in the state in which the administrative order or judgment was entered against such person or if the broker/dealer employing such party is licensed or registered in this state and the Form B–D filed with this state discloses the order, conviction, judgment or decree

[2] In those states where facts and circumstances permit, it would not be inconsistent with the regulatory objectives of this exemption for a state to substitute the following for section 1.A.

a. All persons who offer or sell securities in this state to nonaccredited and/or accredited investors as defined in Securities Act of 1933, Regulation D, Rule 230.501(a)(5)–(6) shall be appropriately registered in accordance with this state's securities law.

It is a defense to a violation of this subsection if the issuer sustains the burden of proof to establish that he or she did not know and in the exercise of reasonable care could not have known that the person who received a commission, fee or other remuneration was not appropriately registered in this state.

[3] In those states where facts and circumstances permit, it would not be inconsistent with the regulatory objectives of this exemption for a state to provide for a system or process to simplify and facilitate the registration of broker/dealers and agents which would not otherwise be required to be registered except for this exemption. Such a system or process should as a minimum, grant jurisdiction as well as the ability to effectively limit and control persons offering and selling securities within the state.

It is a defense to a violation of this subsection if the issuer sustains the burden of proof to establish that he or she did not know and in the exercise of reasonable care could not have known that the person who received a commission, fee or other remuneration was not appropriately registered in this state.

relating to such person. No person disqualified under this subsection may act in a capacity other than that for which the person is licensed or registered.

7. Any disqualification caused by this section is automatically waived if the state securities administrator or agency of the state which created the basis for disqualification determines upon a showing of good cause that it is not necessary under the circumstances that the exemption be denied.

It is a defense to a violation of this subsection if issuer sustains the burden of proof to establish that he or she did not know and in the exercise of reasonable care could not have known that a disqualification under this subsection existed.

C. The issuer shall file with the state administrator a notice on Form D (17CFR239.500):

1. No later than (10 days prior)[4] to the receipt of consideration or the delivery of a subscription agreement by an investor in this state which results from an offer being made in reliance upon this exemption and at such other times and in the form required under Regulation D, Rule 230.503 to be filed with the Securities and Exchange Commission.

2. The notice shall contain an undertaking by the issuer to furnish to the state securities administrator, upon written request, the information furnished by the issuer to offerees, except where the state administrator pursuant to regulation requires that the information be filed at the same time with the filing of the notice.[5]

3. Unless otherwise available, included with or in the initial notice shall be a consent to service of process.

4. Every person filing the initial notice provided for in 1 above shall pay a filing fee of ______.

D. In all sales to nonaccredited investors in this state one of the following conditions must be satisfied or the issuer and any person acting on its behalf shall have reasonable grounds to believe and after making reasonable inquiry shall believe that one of the following conditions is satisfied:

1. The investment is suitable for the purchaser upon the basis of the facts, if any, disclosed by the purchaser as to the purchaser's other security holdings, financial situation and needs. For the purpose of this condition only, it may be presumed that if the investment does not exceed 10% of the investor's net worth, it is suitable.

2. The purchaser either alone or with his/her purchaser representative(s) has such knowledge and experience in financial and business matters that he/she is or they are capable of evaluating the merits and risk of the prospective investment.

3. A failure to comply with a term, condition or requirement of Sections 1.A, [C [6]], and D of this rule will not result in loss of the exemption from the requirements of section [301] of this act for any offer or sale to a particular individual or entity if the person relying on the exemption shows:

A. the failure to comply did not pertain to a term, condition or requirement directly intended to protect that particular individual or entity; and

[4] In those states where facts and circumstances permit, it would not be inconsistent with the regulatory objectives of this exemption for a state to consider a post sale notice patterned after the notice provisions of Regulation D (Rule 230.503).

[5] This latter filing requirement is not intended to provide the basis for a fairness type of review of the offering.

[6] In those states which have adopted a post-sale notice patterned after the notice provisions of Regulation D (Rule 230.503) it would not be inconsistent with the regulatory objectives of this exemption to include the notice filing requirements of section 1.C within the substantial compliance provisions of section 2 or to eliminate the filing as a condition and adopt a rule similar to Rule 230.507.

B. the failure to comply was insignificant with respect to the offering as a whole; and

C. a good faith and reasonable attempt was made to comply with all applicable terms, conditions and requirements of Sections 1.A [C], and D.

4. Where an exemption is established only through reliance upon section 2 of this rule, the failure to comply shall nonetheless be actionable by the [administrator] under section [408] of the Act.[7]

5. Transactions which are exempt under this rule may not be combined with offers and sales exempt under any other rule or section of this act, however, nothing in this limitation shall act as an election. Should for any reason the offer and sale fail to comply with all of the conditions for this exemption, the issuer may claim the availability of any other applicable exemption.

6. The administrator may, by rule or order, increase the number of purchasers or waive any other conditions of this exemption.

7. The exemption authorized by this rule shall be known and may be cited as the "Uniform Limited Offering Exemption."

[7] The cited reference is to the section of the Uniform Securities Act which authorizes the state administrator to bring a civil action to enjoin rule violations. Those states which have authority to bring an administrative enforcement action for rule violations may wish to include a reference to that statutory authority. If the administrator lacks authority to bring enforcement actions based solely on rule violations, he/she may wish to consider a statutory amendment.

†